THE

GENEALOGICAL DICTIONARY OF RHODE ISLAND;

COMPRISING THREE GENERATIONS OF SETTLERS

WHO CAME BEFORE 1690.

(WITH MANY FAMILIES CARRIED TO THE FOURTH GENERATION.)

BY

JOHN OSBORNE AUSTIN.

WITH ADDITIONS AND CORRECTIONS
by JOHN OSBORNE AUSTIN

and ADDITIONS AND CORRECTIONS
by G. ANDREWS MORIARTY

AND A NEW FOREWORD
by ALBERT T. KLYBERG
Librarian, The Rhode Island Historical Society

Baltimore
GENEALOGICAL PUBLISHING CO., INC.
1982

Originally Published
Albany, New York, 1887

Reprinted from a copy loaned to us by
THE RHODE ISLAND HISTORICAL SOCIETY
which contained eight pages of pasted in
ADDITIONS AND CORRECTIONS
by John Osborne Austin

With
ADDITIONS AND CORRECTIONS
by G. Andrews Moriarty
Reprinted with permission from
The American Genealogist
Volumes XIX-XXI, XXIV-XXVIII, XXX, XXXII,
XXXIV-XXXVII, and XXXIX
1943-1963

And With A
FOREWORD by Albert T. Klyberg
Librarian, The Rhode Island Historical Society

Genealogical Publishing Co., Inc.
Baltimore, 1969, 1978, 1982

Library of Congress Catalogue Card Number 68-56072
International Standard Book Number 0-8063-0006-X

Made in the United States of America

To the memory of

James Savage

This work is dedicated

FOREWORD

John Osborne Austin (1849-1918) was born in Providence, Rhode Island, the son of Samuel and Elizabeth Hanson Austin. His ancestry was essentially New England — "beautiful Aquidneck, Nantucket, 'The Cape', Salem and Dover, N. H." Although his formal education did not extend beyond the secondary level (he was graduated from Union Hall School where his father was principal), he traveled widely, was successful in the woolen business, and his writings are convincing evidence of a skilled and tutored mind. Austin's travels included trips to Europe on several occasions, one to the diamond fields of South Africa in 1873, and others to California, the Society Islands and New Zealand. Aside from *The Genealogical Dictionary of Rhode Island* which appeared in 1887, he also authored *The Ancestry of Thirty-three Rhode Islanders* (1889), *The Ancestral Dictionary* (1891), *One Hundred and Sixty Allied Families* (1893), *The Roger Williams Calendar* (1897), *The Journal of William Jefferay, Gentleman* (1899), *More Seven Club Tales* (1900), *Philip and Philippa* (1901), *A Week's Wooing* (1902), *American Authors' Ancestry* (1915), a memorial volume of stories dedicated to his wife (1916), and *Impressions and Reflections of Sixty Years* (1917).

Austin's principal literary contribution was as a genealogist and compiler. As a life-long resident of Providence his major focus in the field of genealogy was Rhode Island, of which the chief example is his *Genealogical Dictionary of Rhode Island.* A member of the Rhode Island Historical Society, he was both a user of and a contributor to its collections of local genealogy. In 1885 the Society passed a resolution at its annual meeting to commend to public notice the forthcoming publication of Austin's *Genealogical Dictionary.* Time has proven their commendation to be well-placed. Today, some eighty years after, it remains a principal, if not the principal, reference tool for Rhode Island. Since it is the Society's own copy of Austin which has been used by the Genealogical Publishing Company, Inc. for reprinting, we are doubly pleased to commend it to public attention again.

It should be noted that certain additions and corrections have been made in the volume. Many of these were made by Austin himself and published in eight supplementary pages. Mr. Clifford P. Monahon, former Librarian and Director of The Rhode Island Historical Society pasted each addition carefully into place. Other notations such as that which appears on page 114 were made from time to time. V.F. on p. 114 refers to a note on the Jennings family contained in the verticle file in our library reading room. The reader should exercise caution in accepting manuscript notations and marginalia, since neither Mr. Austin nor the Society is responsible for them. Finally, additions by Mr. G. Andrews Moriarty which appeared originally in the *American Genealogist* have been reprinted and appear at the end of this reprint edition.

Albert T. Klyberg, *Librarian*
The Rhode Island Historical Society

October, 1968

PREFACE

Any intelligent person is capable of becoming interested in family history. This interest is increasing in this country to such an extent that a great desire is now manifested by many, for a fuller knowledge of their ancestry. Such a knowledge encourages truly democratic ideas, by showing the universal brotherhood of the race.

The material gathered in these pages was drawn from many sources. It is presented to the reader by a clear method, requiring but little explanation; though the plan is a comprehensive one, and the arrangement in some respects original.

There is no attempt made to give a record of persons whose stay was but a temporary one in this colony. The towns annexed to Rhode Island in 1747, and later, are not considered to come strictly within the scope of this work ; yet many families in these towns are included, particularly in Tiverton and Little Compton, which were largely settled from the older part of the colony. In such cases, the towns are reckoned as though always within the bounds of Rhode Island.

It is the hope of the author that this book may prove an incentive to many family genealogies, whereby the records of individuals may be brought down to the present time. To the many persons and associations that have given valuable aid in supplying information, cordial thanks are tendered.

JOHN OSBORNE AUSTIN.

Providence, R. I., 1887.

CONTENTS

INDEX OF FAMILIES.

(The names marked thus * include four generations.)

ABBREVIATIONS

+	after.	m.	married.
(—)	before.	d.	died.
±	about.	ex.	executor.
w.	widow.	div.	divorced.
b.	born.		

1.	2.	3.

ACRES.

JOHN, b. ; d. 1699,
m.
MARGERY, b. ; d. 1699 +

Dorchester, Ms., Newport, New Shoreham, R. I.

1660. He was one of the sixteen purchasers of Block Island, he and his associates paying £400 therefor. His name does not appear with those who had lots, the following year in the first division of lands, but he early came to the island.

1661, Oct. 23, Newport. He, late of Dorchester, Ms., now of Newport, sold 90 acres, in Providence, to William Reape of Newport.

1698, Nov. 12, Will—proved, 1699, Jan. 10. Exx. wife Margery. To her all moveables except legacies. To son-in-law Daniel Tosh and Margery his wife, all right of land in Block Island, Narragansett and Westerly, for life; and then to grandson Acres Tosh. To son-in-law Job Card and Martha his wife and son-in-law Daniel Tosh and Margery his wife confirmation of lands on Block Island, before deeded. To Daniel Tosh a pair of stags. To daughter Margery Tosh an iron pot. To wife Margery all the rest of the personal, and if she leaves any estate at her death, the two daughters are to have it. To wife the feed of three cattle provided by Daniel Tosh. On second thoughts he gives to daughter Margery Tosh all land on Block Island for life.

See: American Genealogist. v. 19, p. 129, ~~221~~

I. MARGERY, b. 1665, May 24. ; d.
m. 1685, Oct. 19,
DANIEL TOSH, b. 1663, Feb. 13. ; d. of William Tosh.

1. Acres, 1687, Apr. 5.
2. Margery, 1689, Apr. 26.
3. Jane, 1691, May 5.
4. Sarah, 1693, Aug. 26.
5. William, 1695, Aug. 26.
6. Elizabeth, 1697, Feb. 19.
7. Martha, 1700, Sep. 8.
8. Mercy, 1703, Jan. 19.

II. MARTHA, b. 1668, Feb. 26. ; d.
m. 1689, Nov.
JOB CARD, b. ; d. of Joseph & Jane ( ) Card.

See: American Genealogist. v. 19, p. 221.
v. 26, p. 228

1. Job, 1690, Sep. 2.
2. Rebecca, 1694, May 4.
3. Martha, 1699, Apr. 6.
4. Margery, 1701, Feb. 19.
5. Jane, 1703, Sep. 18.
6. Sarah, 1705, Aug. 9.

ALDRICH.

JOSEPH[2], (George[1]), b. 1635, Jun. 4. ; d. 1701.
m. 1662, Feb. 26,
PATIENCE OSBORNE, b. ; d. 1705, +
of Osborne.

Braintree, Mass., Providence, R. I.

1682, Nov. 2. His father, by will of this date, gave him his wearing apparel.

1687, Sep. 1. Providence. Taxed 6*d*.

1701, Jun. 26. He made an agreement with his son Joseph, that so long as he and his wife should live together, his said son Joseph should maintain them; giving to them three cows for their use, and ploughing an acre of land if we see cause, during our natural lives; and if either parent died the other was to possess same if need required. Joseph was to maintain his parents in such manner as our condition require, according to best of his ability and our degree. In consideration of this provision, he made over to his son Joseph, the house, house lot, orchard and 20 acres on due performance of agreement; and so long as we, his father and mother live together, half the orchard to be at our disposal for our use and maintenance. The moveables after decease of both parents were to go to son Joseph, except a bed, bedding, warming pan, frying pan, and skillet. Overseers of this agreement (or will) were to be John Hawkins and Peter Place.

1701, Aug. 20. Inventory £18, 3*s*. 9*d*., viz. 3 cows, heifer, calf, 3 swine, warming pan, frying pan, wooden, pewter, and iron ware, table, chairs, spinning wheel, sword, &c.

ALDRICH. 2d column. II. Samuel, had daughters: 5 Mary, 6 Ruth, 7 Abigail. IV. John. He and his brother Samuel were appointed (1725, Apr 20) overseers of will of Joseph Hide, of Providence, R. I., who calls them his brothers-in-law. VI. Mercy, m. Joseph Hide. He d. 1725, Apr. 30. She d. 1725 +. Children, 1. Phebe, 2. Hannah, 3. Patience.

I. JOSEPH, b. 1663, Jul. 14. ; d. 1705, Apr. 24. Providence, R. I.
m.
MARY, b. ; d. 1713 + of

1704, May 1. Will—proved 1705, Jul. 13. Ex. son Joseph. To wife Mary for life all lands and moveable estate, and after death of my loving mother Patience Aldrich, all lands that I had of my father to be also for life to wife. To son Joseph at decease of testator's wife and mother all lands that was my fathers and 10 acres of the other farm in timber land. To youngest son Elias my homestead place. To daughter Sarah Aldrich, £6, paid her by sons when they enjoy the land.

Inventory £26, 4*s*. 11*d*. viz.: 3 cows, 2 heifers, yearling, 16 sheep, 10 lambs, a swine, tailors shears, gun, flax, hemp, swarm of bees, &c.

His will was presented by Samuel Aldrich, brother of deceased Joseph, the executor mentioned in the will being a child and incapable to administer, and town council appointed said Samuel as administrator therefore.

1713, Sep. 15. His widow by reason of insanity being unable to take care of herself, and Overseers of the Poor having committed her to care of John King, who demanded money for her maintenance, the administrator of her husband's estate was ordered to pay £4 to Overseers.

1. Joseph,
2. Elias,
3. Sarah,

II. SAMUEL, b. ; d. 1747, Apr. 2. Providence, Smithfield, R. I.
m.
JANE, b. ; d. 1747 + of

He was a tanner (Samuel Jr., was called in deeds, weaver).

1701, May 6. Freeman.
1706, May. He had leather worth 11*s* 3*d*., taken from him for not training, he being a Quaker.
1712, Mar. 1. He sold John Mowry 8 acres for £2, 15*s*., and Joseph Mowry 10 acres for £3, 10*s*.
1713, Jun. 16. Taxed 16*s*. 2*d*.
1716, Feb. 28. He deeded son James for love, &c., 77 acres.
1716, Oct. 1. His nephew Joseph Aldrich chose him for guardian.
1718, Feb. 27. His son Samuel Aldrich, Jr., in a deposition calls his age about thirty-seven years.
1727, Sep. 9. He deeded son Peter for love, &c., 113 acres adjoining my now dwelling, with a house standing thereon, orchard, &c.
1733, Sep. 14. Smithfield. He deeded son John, for love, &c., homestead on which I dwell, 200 acres, with orchard, &c.
1747, Apr. 20. Administration to widow Jane.
Inventory, carpenter and cooper's tools, linen yarn, pewter, corn, rye, flax, cider, 4 old deer skins, 2 calf skins, walking staff, warming pan, gun, bill of public credit, £184, 6*s*., bible, 3 cows, hog, &c.

1. Samuel, 1681
2. Peter,
3. James,
4. John,

III. EPHRAIM, b. ; d. Providence, Glocester, R. I.
m.
BARBARA, b. ; d. of

1705, Jul. 3. He being discoursed with by town council concerning his mother Patience Aldrich, as to her maintenance (he having her in his care as had been agreed between Ephraim and his brother Joseph) signified to council that he would care for his mother and provide her with meat, drink, clothes, &c., for life. He also agreed to allow her all moveables that were his father's and the use of what was his father's land until his brother Joseph's son who is to inherit it, is of age.

1713, Jun. 16. Taxed 4*s*.
1728, Apr. 17. He and Barbara sold Obadiah Jenckes 51 acres with dwelling house, &c., for £220.
1728, Sep. 28. He bought of Joseph Williams, 118 acres and 102 poles for £118, 15*s*., said land being at Paskhoag on both sides Paskhoag river.
1737, Oct. 8, Glocester. He deeded son Daniel for love, &c., 20 acres, and land where dwelling house stands, north-easterly side of Paskhoag river.

1. Daniel,

IV. JOHN, b. ; d. 1735, Mar. 17. Providence, Scituate, R. I.
m. 1699, Mar. 20,
MARTHA EVANS. b. ; d. 1735 + of Richard & Mary ( ) Evans.

He was a miller.

1682, Nov. 2. He was bequeathed 30*s*., by will of his grandfather George Aldrich "on condition that he live with his grandmother during her life, according to his father's promise."
1701, May 26. Freeman.
1726. Mar. 19. He deeded son David for love, &c., 19 acres, and also 44 acres north-easterly from my corn mill. On same date he deeded 68 acres to son Jonathan.
1727, Jan. 18. He deeded son John, farm, dwelling house, orchard, meadow, &c., all to be his at decease of self and wife, and also ten cows, two heifers, two steers, a bull, six yearlings, a horse, sixty-eight sheep, two swine, cart, plow, chains, &c.
1729, Nov. 29. Will—codicil, 1733, Dec. 21—proved, 1735, Sep. 1. Ex. son Joseph. To wife Martha all household goods, and half the rent of farm that son John liveth upon, which is £7. To son David a small strip of land from my now dwelling house through lands left for a way to go to meeting. To son Aaron all lands both sides of a brook except 10 acres. To son Richard land north of a pond. To son Noah all land near Killingly between old and new line. To son Joseph the other part of rent of farm where son John liveth (viz. £7) as long as wife Martha liveth. In codicil he states that lot given Richard had been sold at his desire and money given him, and also that Joseph having gone away and Richard come in his room, that therefore all rent given Joseph is now to be given Richard. To said Joseph an iron bar, an augur, and sledge. The executorship was refused by son Joseph and widow Martha took administration of the personal estate.
Inventory £64, 11*s*. viz.: wearing apparel, books, pair of spectacles, pewter, worsted comb, cards, 2 linen wheels, warming pan, old table, &c.

1. John,
2. Jonathan,
3. David,
4. Aaron,
5. Richard,
6. Noah,
7. Joseph,

V. SARAH, b. 1677, Oct. 27. ; d.

ALDRICH. 2d column. IV. John. Add daughter (m. Stephen Sheldon).

JOHN, { b.
m. 1650, Oct. 14, { d. 1708, Oct. 30.
ELIZABETH BACON, { b.
{ d.

of Bacon.

Newport, Kings Town, R. I.

He was a Quaker.

1680. Taxed £1. 6*s.* 1*d.*

He died at his son-in-law, Rowland Robinson's house.

Possibly Christopher Allen should be added to his list of children. (He married Elizabeth Seyouche, of Little Compton, in 1687, at Boston; and was of Little Compton, in 1693, of Kings Town, 1703, and died in South Kingstown, 1739, administration on his estate being given to William Robinson. He had at least one son, viz: James, born 1688, June 15.)

See: American Genealogist, Apr., 1954, v. 30, no. 2, p. 121-122.

I. ELIZABETH, { b. 1651, Jul.
m. 1671, Jan. 15, { d. 1714, Mar. 24.
NATHANIEL TOMPKINS, { b.
{ d. 1724, of Tompkins.

1. Elizabeth,
2. Nathaniel, 1676, Dec. 31.
3. Mary, 1677, Sep. 16.
4. Priscilla, 1679, May 24.
5. Samuel, 1681, May. 24.
6. Mercy, 1685, Oct. 20.
7. Sarah,
8. Rebecca,
9. Hannah,

II. MARY, { b. 1653, Feb. 4.
m. { d. 1716, +
ROWLAND ROBINSON, { b. 1654.
{ d. 1716. of Robinson.

1. John, 1680.
2. Rowland, 1682, Jun. 18
3. Joseph,
4. Elizabeth,
5. Mary,
6. Sarah,
7. Mercy,
8. William, 1693, Jan. 26.

III. JOHN, { b. 1654, Nov.
{ d.

IV. MERCY, { b. 1656, Dec.
{ d.

V. PRISCILLA, { b. 1659, Dec.
{ d. 1676, Oct. 24.

VI. SAMUEL, { b. 1661, Apr.
{ d.

ALLEN (JOHN). 1st column. Erase Kings Town. Erase Possibly, &c. Add 1706, Sep. 30. Will—proved 1709, Mar. 16 Ex. son Samuel. He mentions son Samuel, son John Allen's children, (viz: John, Sarah, Elizabeth, Mercy and Mary), son Christopher, daughters Elizabeth Tompkins, Mary Robinson, Mercy Dankin, and granddaughter Mary Tompkins. He gave a legacy to mens' meeting of Friends As his son Samuel was insane the executorship was given to latter's wife Elizabeth.

2d column. VI. Samuel, Newport, R. I., m. Elizabeth Sanford, of Samuel & Sarah (Wodell) Sanford. She b. 1663, Oct. 2, d. 1718, Apr. 4. He was a cordwainer. 1717 ± Will. He mentions wife Elizabeth, daughter Sarah wife of Joseph Peabody, daughter Mary Allen, sons Samuel and Rowland under age. To son John, land in Newport. VII. Christopher, Little Compton, South Kingstown, R. I. He m. 1687, Elizabeth Seyouche, of Little Compton. Children, 1. James, 1688, Jun 15. 1693, Sep. 29. He sold to Joseph Allen, of Dartmouth, 59 acres in Narragansett for £140. 1703-11-14-15-16-20. Kings Town. Deputy. 1714. Captain. 1715. Clerk of Assembly. 1739, Sep 17. Administration to William Robinson. Inventory, £1,823, 7*s.*, 10*d.*, viz: wearing apparel, cane, pair of silver buttons, pair of gold buttons, pocket book and money therein £20, 18*s.*, 11*d.*, 141 sheep, 60 lambs, 2 horses, 5 mares, 15 colts, 2 bulls, 4 oxen, 4 steers, 47 cows, 16 calves, 6 yearlings, bible, law book, 19 silver buttons, bee hive, negroes Moll, Phillis, young Moll, Andrew, Jeffrey, mulatto Jacob, 6 silver spoons, 2 silver porringers, &c, He b. 1664, d. 1739, Sep. 13. His wife, b. 1668, Jul. 7. d. 1737, Mar. 17.

ALLEN (William).

WILLIAM, { b.
m. { d. 1685.
ELIZABETH, { b.
{ d. 1685 +

Portsmouth, (Prudence Island), R. I.

1683, Aug. 21. He and James Greene, Sr., were appointed as messengers to carry a letter from the Rhode Island Assembly to Governor Cranfield, of New Hampshire, at Mr. Richard Smiths' house at Narragansett, and they were to bring answer to Assembly.

1685, Jun. 2. Will—proved 1685, Jun. 29, Exs. wife Elizabeth, eldest son William and eldest daughter, Mary Remington. Overseers, John Albro and Robert Lawton. To eldest son William all lands in Potowomut and all lands and housing in East Greenwich, at age. To second son, Thomas, my now dwelling house in Swanzey, only half thereof to be for wife, Elizabeth, for life, and the stock thereon equally to wife and son Thomas. To sons John and Matthew equally, a share of land in Rehoboth, at age, and to each £20. To daughters Mercy and Sarah Allen £20 each, at eighteen, and a feather bed to each. To wife Elizabeth, household goods and an Indian boy seven years old.

I. MARY, { b.
m. { d. 1710 +
THOMAS REMINGTON, { b.
{ d. 1710. of John & Abigail ( ) Remington.

1. William,
2. Thomas,
3. John,
4. Daniel,
5. Joseph,
6. Stephen,
7. Matthew,
8. Jonathan,
9. Mary,
10. Prudence,

ALLEN (WILLIAM). 2d column. II. William, had children, 1. William, 2. John, 3. Ebenezer. V. Matthew. His wife was daughter of John & Mary ( ) Cook.

II. WILLIAM, { b.
m. { d.
——— { b.
{ d. of

Portsmouth, R. I.

1687, Dec. 13. He was fined 6*s.* 8*d.* for refusing to take oath as grand juryman.

1705. Deputy.

1. John.
2. Son,
3. Son,

III. THOMAS, { b.
m. { d. 1719, Aug. 12.
ANNE BARNES, { b.
{ d. 1719 + of Thomas & Prudence ( ) Barnes.

Swanzey, Mass.

1719, Aug. 10. Will—proved 1719, Sep. 7. Exs. wife Ann, and son Matthew. To wife, a third of real and personal estate in Swanzey. To daughters Elizabeth and Anne £80 each, they having had £20 each already. To daughters Rebecca, Alathsie and Abigail £100 each, at eighteen. To sons Matthew and Thomas, all estate equally, both lands, housing and movables, provided that daughter Elizabeth Hill and other four daughters named Allen, be paid their parts, etc. Inventory, £697, 19*s.*, viz: wearing apparel, £23, money and paper bills, £52, 7*s.*, books £2, arms and ammunition £2, riding beast £8, 4 feather beds, 2 flock beds, 2 pairs of cards, weaving loom, 2 woolen sheets, 2 linen sheets, pair of worsted combs, 3 negro slaves and an Indian maid-servant £164, mare, colt, 5 oxen, 12 cows, 3 heifers, 6 steers, bull, 5 young cattle, 5 calves, 150 sheep and lambs, 17 swine, real estate, £1,800.

1. Elizabeth,
2. Matthew,
3. Thomas, 1706, Oct. 13.
4. Anne,
5. Rebecca,
6. Alathsie,
7. Abigail,

IV. JOHN, { b. 1670, Oct. 26.
m. { d. 1747, Mar. 30
SARAH, { b. 1677, Jun. 14.
{ d. 1747 + of

North Kingstown, R. I.

His wife was born at New Haven.

1747, Apr. 17. Will—proved. Exx. wife Sarah. To wife, all indoor movables, and negroes Simon and Dinah. To three sons, Thomas, William and Jonathan, wearing apparel. To four daughters, Phebe Slocum, Elizabeth Fairbanks, Bathsheba Johnson and Mercy Card, certain money legacies. To son Jonathan, my great bible, etc., and 2 acres of land. To four daughters, the household goods, at wife's death.

1. Thomas,
2. Phebe,
3. Elizabeth,
4. John, 1710, May 15.
5. William, 1710, May 15
6. Jonathan, 1717, Aug. 6.
7. Bathsheba, 1721, Apr. 10.
8. Mercy, 17—, Sep. 4.

V. MATTHEW, { b. 1675, Nov. 20.
m. 1700, May 2, { d.
PHEBE. { b. 1677, Sep. 3.
{ d. of

Portsmouth, Warwick, North Kingstown, R. I.

1709, Feb. 12, Warwick. He and wife Phebe, of Coweset, sold James Andrew, of Providence, several pieces of land at Coweset, for £28.

1737, Sep. 13. He had a certificate from town council of Portsmouth, to town council of North Kingstown, for settlement in latter town.

1. Mercy, 1701, Aug. 17.
2. Phebe, 1704, Apr. 3.
3. Patience, 1708, May 29.
4. Mary, 1710, Apr. 18.

VI. MERCY, { b.
m. 1702. Jan. 1, { d.
JOHN BARNES, { b. 1680, Apr. 9.
{ d. of Thomas & Prudence ( ) Barnes.

1. Ezra, 1703, Mar. 21.
2. John, 1704, Sep. 28.
3. Abial, 1706, Jun. 20.
4. Thomas, 1708, Sep. 18.
5. Anne, 1710, May 7
6. Mercy, 1712, Feb. 26.
7. Phebe, 1713, May 10.
8. Amy, 1716, Jan. 25.
9. William, 1716, May 27.
10. Freelove, 1718, Feb. 23.
11. Benjamin, 1720, Feb. 9.
12. Joseph, 1722, Jan. 30.
13. Hannah, 1725, Jan. 4.
14. Matthew, 1726, Aug. 15.

VII. SARAH, { b.
{ d.

ANDREW.

JOHN, b. d. 1693. (—)
m. (1) ——— b. d.
m. (2) MARY RIDGLY, b. d. 1716 +
of Ridgly.

Kings Town, R. I.

1671, May 20. He gave oath of allegiance.

1672, Jan. 1. He and others bought of Awashuwatt, chief sachem of land called Quohesett, in Narragansett, for a valuable sum, &c., a certain tract in Quohesett, bounded on the east from the house of John Andrew, &c. The sachem's two brothers and three sons, also conveyed their interest.

1676, Aug. He testified at a court martial at Newport, that Awasawim, of Narragansett, laid hands on John Greene, of that place.

1679, Nov. 10. John Mackandrew, alias Andrews, petitioned the Assembly, to remit sentence of General Court of Trials, on account of great infirmity of his body and smallness of his estate. Corporal punishment remitted and £5 of fine.

1683–84. Constable.

1687, Sep. 6. Taxed 4*s.* 8*d.*

I. JOHN, b. d. East Greenwich, R. I.
m. REBECCA, b. d. of

(She m. (2) 1721, Jun. 18, John Nichols).

1693, Aug. 22. He deeded, for love, &c. to his six brothers, viz: William, Charles, James, Thomas, Edmond and Benoni, all interest that I have by my father, deceased, unto 70 acres, which is part of 90 acres at East Greenwich, and if any brother die before twenty-one, his part to go equally to others. The full benefit and improvement of said 70 acres, to be at disposal of mother-in-law, (*i. e.* step-mother) that now is, Mary Andrew, till youngest brother is twenty-one. He agreed to pay to his mother-in-law yearly for life ten bushels of apples.

1698, Apr. 1. Newport. He sold Captain Thomas Fry, of East Greenwich, his interest in a certain tract of land in Narragansett county, near Devil's Foot, bounded partly by land of father, John Andrew, deceased, who had with others, bought lands in 1672, of certain Indians.

1700. East Greenwich. His childrens' birth were recorded here, and his stay at Newport was only a temporary one probably.

1. John, 1693, Jan. 28.
2. Richard, 1694, Sep. 14.
3. Joseph, 1700, Nov. 29.
4. Rachel, 1702, Jul. 12.
5. John, 1704, Aug. 2.

II. WILLIAM, b. 1679, Aug. 23, d. 1762. East Greenwich, R. I.
m. 1700, Sep. 25,
ANNA SEARLE, b. d. of Searle.

1760. His son William Jr. died this year, and administration was given widow Mary.

1762, Jul. 25. Administration to eldest son, John Andrew, of Coventry. Inventory, £503, 1*s.* 6*d.*, viz: wearing apparel, £25, gun, £16, cash, £28, 6*s.* 6*d.*, plate, £2, notes, &c.

1. John, 1702, Mar. 23.
2. Charles, 1705, Apr. 2.
3. Mary, 1708, Jun. 3.
4. William,

(2d WIFE).

III. CHARLES, b. d. 1762, Jan. 13. East Greenwich, R. I.
m.
JUDITH MATTESON, b. 1694, Oct. 16. d. of Henry & Judith ( ) Matteson.

1714. Freeman.

1758, Jun. 25. Will—proved 1762, Jan. 30. Ex. son Edmond. To son Charles 275 acres, north end of my farm in Coventry, an iron bar and £50. To son Jonathan, land in East Greenwich, two blankets, coverlid and £50. To daughter Hannah Andrew, £158 and bed. To daughter Alice Hopkins, £150 and bed. To Thomas Rouse, son of Rebecca Rouse, deceased, 100 acres in Coventry, bed, bible, chest and pewter, at age. To Waite Sweet, daughter of Hannah Matteson, eight ewe sheep, eight lambs, and a heifer, fair with calf, when said Waite is eighteen. To three sons and two daughters, rest of indoor movables. To son Edmond, all my homestead farm, and all outdoor movables. Inventory, £625, 10*s.*, viz: wearing apparel, £75, 10*s.* beds, pewter, eight sheep, 2 cows, 3 old chairs, old woolen wheels, &c.

1. Hannah, 1718, Jul. 25.
2. Thomas, 1720, Dec. 2.
3. James, 1724, Nov. 2.
4. Charles, 1726, Jan. 16.
5. Jonathan, 1729, Jul. 11.
6. Edmond, 1731, Jun. 7.
7. Alice, 1733, Oct. 9.

IV. JAMES, b. d. 1716, Jul. 10. Providence, R. I.
m.
MARTHA JENCKES, b. d. 1719 + of Joseph & Martha (Brown) Jenckes.

(She m. (2) Peleg Cook).

He was a mariner.

1709, Feb 12. He bought of Matthew Allen and wife Phebe, of Cowesct, in Warwick, several parcels of land there for £28.

1716, Jul. 10. Will—proved 1716, Aug. 1. Exx. wife Martha. To her, whole estate, except £3 in money, due from brother, William, which is to go to mother, Mary He desires wife to take best care she is capable of, to tenderly bring up my beloved and only son John.

Inventory, £121, 17*s.* 10*d.*, viz: 2 bibles, sermon book, mariner book, 2 story books, silver dram cup, quadrant, sliding gunter, ink horn, pen-knife, &c.

1719, Oct. 8. His widow Martha, deeded to son John, for love, &c., a half part of 128 acres in Cowesct, and half part of a right in undivided lands there, and said son being in minority, she appoints her brother John Jenckes, of Providence, "Studiant in Physick and Chirurgery," feoffe in trust for said son, &c.

1. John,

V. THOMAS, b. d.

VI. EDWARD, b. d

VII. BENONI, b. d. East Greenwich, R. I.
m.
REBECCA, b. d. of

1. John, 1719, Feb. 2.
2. Elizabeth, 1721, Jan. 27.
3. Eleanor, 1723, May 16.
4. Mary, 1725, Dec. 16.
5. Jonathan, 1727, Feb. 7.
6. Rebecca, 1731, Sep. 10.
7. Johanna, 1733, Jan. 17.
8. Sylvester, 1736, Mar. 24.
9. Ruth, 1736, Mar 24.
10. Benoni, 1739, Mar. 30.

ANDREWS.

EDWARD, b. d.
m
BRIDGET, b. d.

Portsmouth, Warwick, R. I.

1654, Oct. 23. He and wife Bridget, sold Joshua Coggeshall, of Newport, 100 acres, house, &c. at Portsmouth.

1655. Warwick. Freeman.

1655, Jan. 8. He sold Peter Busecot, of Warwick, all housing there, and three lots of 6 acres each, for £20, &c., to be paid as follows: one cow, now at John Coggeshall's, on Rhode Island, to be delivered before May 1st, prized by two indifferent persons; £3 to be paid in good peage at money pay and settled on or before February 14th, and £7 more (the cow and £3 aforesaid, to be settled up by Michaelmas next); also, £10 to be paid in peage Sep. 29th, 1657, and same time 25*s.* for forbearance of last pay-nt. Possession not to be immediate, but pro-ed for.

is assumed that he was father of William[2] and Edward.[2]

I. WILLIAM, b. d. Warwick, R. I.
m. 1680, Oct. 30, [Jas.
ESTHER DEXTER, (w. of b. 1647, Sep. 22. d. 1688 ± Stephen & Sarah (Smith) Arnold.

(She m. (3) Edward Hawkins.)

1. Mary,

II. EDWARD, b. 1649. d. 1699, May, 29. Newport, R. I.

He was buried at Newport.

Thomas Angell. See also: Bowen's THE PROVIDENCE OATH OF ALLEGIANCE, p. 74-5.

 See: American Genealogist, v.21, p.206.

THOMAS, m. ALICE,
b. 1618 ±
d. 1694.
b.
d. 1695.

Salem, Mass. Providence, R. I.

1630, Dec. He came in the ship Lyon, which left Bristol, England, in this month.

1631, Feb. 5. He arrived in Boston, and soon went to Salem.

1636. Providence. He and four others came with Roger Williams, and made settlement earlier than July of this year, having spent the preceding winter at Seekonk.

1637, Aug. 20. (Or a little later). He signed the following compact, having been under age at the time of his arrival with the first settlers: "We, whose names are hereunder, desirous to inhabit in the town of Providence, do promise to subject ourselves in active or passive obedience to all such orders or agreements, as shall be made for public good of the body, in an orderly way, by the major consent of the present inhabitants, masters of families, incorporated together in a town fellowship, and others whom they shall admit unto them, only in civil things." Thirteen persons signed this compact.

1640, Jul. 27. He and thirty-eight others signed an agreement for a form of government.

1652–53. Commissioner.

1655. Juryman.

1655. Constable.

1655. Freeman.

1658, Jan. 27. He sold 5 acres to James Mathewson.

1658–75. Town Clerk.

1665, Feb. 19. He had a lot assigned him in a division of lands.

1676, Aug. 14. He was on a committee that recommended certain conditions under which the Indian captives should be disposed of by the town. They were to be in servitude for terms of years.

1679, Jul. 1. Taxed 5*s.* 7½*d.*

1687, Sep. 1. Taxed 5*s.* 8*d.*, with son James.

1685, May 23. Will—codicil same date, proved 1694, Sep. 18. Exs. wife and son James. Overseers, Nathaniel Waterman and Thomas Olney. To son John, 60 acres in right of first division of lands and 50 acres in second division, with half right of common for feeding cattle, cutting firewood, timber, &c. To son James, my dwelling house next unto the street, with lot where house standeth, another lot adjoining, all my meadows, 20 acres on Weybosset side of water, near Hawkins' Cove, a 6 acre lot, 10 acre lot, half right of Common, and rights in land to be divided. To daughters Anphillis Smith, Mary Arnold, Deborah Sabeere, Alice Whipple and Margery Whipple, each 2*s.* To wife Alice, the dwelling house while widow, and plot of ground adjoining, for a little garden, and the house to be kept in repair by son James, and she to have a cow and the keep of same, by her two sons, another cow being given her by son James, when the first one has become unfit for milk, by age. To her also, 16*s.* paid annually by two sons, till she marry, half being paid by each son, and she to be comfortably maintained by sons, in health and sickness, with suitable attendance, &c., failing to do which, one-third of lands shall be to wife, for her profit, &c. To son John, all cattle, except the cow aforesaid, and all tools and other movables, and all lands undisposed of.

Inventory, £43, 13*s.* 4*d.*, viz: homespun cloth, feather bed, flock bed, cotton and linen sheets, napkins, towels, wearing apparel, 5 chairs, settle, joint form, old table, pewter platters, Dutch blankets, warming pan, 1000 pins, &c.

1694, Oct. 21. Will—proved 1695, Jan. 15. Widow Alice. Ex. son James. To four daughters, Anphillis Smith, Deborah Sabeere, Alice Whipple and Margery Whipple, wearing apparel, &c. To daughter Deborah, two wooden trays, &c., that formerly belonged to my son Hope. To daughter Alice, a trunk and a desk, which my mother gave to me. To son James, £5. To sons John and James, rest of estate equally, except that each daughter was to have so much pewter, as may be a remembrance of me.

Inventory, £46, 5*s.* 2*d.*, (including the 1000 pins).

I. JOHN, m. 1669, Jan. 7. RUTH FIELD,
b. 1646.
d. 1720, Jul. 27.
b.
d. 1727 + of John Field.
Providence, R. I.

1671, May 8. He was fined 20*s.* for not attending Grand Jury.

1676, Aug. 14. He was one of the men "who staid and went not away" in King Philip's War, and so was entitled to a share in the disposition of the Indian captives, whose services were sold for a term of years.

1679, Jul. 1. Taxed 3*s.*

1686. Deputy.

1687, Sep. 1. Taxed 6*s.*

1688. Rateable estate, 2 oxen, 7 cows, 3 two year old cattle, 4 yearlings, bull, 2 horses, 3 hogs, 5 acres planting, 10 acres English pasture, 100 acres in woods.

1704, Jan. 15. He deeded son Thomas, for good affection, &c., 79 acres (except 3 or 4 acres lowland, given John), on both sides Woonasquatucket River, also other land, making in all, 89 acres, together with mansion house, &c.

1704, Jan. 15. He deeded to son John, my mansion house and 58 acres, and a parcel of lowland, both sides of Woonasquatucket River, adjoining the 58 acres.

1705, Apr. 8. He deeded son Daniel, 80 acres, eastern side of Woonasquatucket River, with housing, fences, &c.

1713, Jun. 16. Taxed with son James, 5*s.* 6*d.*

1716, Dec. 14. He calling himself aged about seventy years, testifies that in 1667, he was desired by his uncle, James Asten, to take care of his 60 acre lot.

1720, Sep. 30. Administration to widow Ruth and son Hope. Inventory, £249, 1*s.* 2*d.*, viz: silver money, £11, 9*s.* 8*d.*, 3 spinning wheels, 3 bedsteads, 6 brass kettles, pewter, £3, money scales, warming pan, bible, negro woman, £30, carpenters tools, 5 cows, 4 heifers, ox, bull, steer, calf, 2 hogs, &c.

1. Thomas, 1672, Mar. 25.
2. Mercy, 1675.
3. John.
4. Daniel, 1680, May 2.
5. James, 1684.
6. Hope, 1685, Dec. 12.

II. ANPHILLIS, m. 1663, EDWARD SMITH,
b.
d. 1694 +
b.
d. 1693, Nov. 8. of Christopher & Alice (   ) Smith.

1. Alice, 1664.
2. Edward,
3. Anphillis,
4. Thomas, 1671, Feb. 19.
5. Christopher,
6. Benjamin,
7. Joseph, 1680, Oct. 12.

III. MARY, m. RICHARD ARNOLD,
b.
d. 1695 (—)
b. 1642, Mar. 22.
d. 1710, Apr. 22. of Thomas & Phebe (Parkhurst) Arnold.

1. Richard,
2. John, 1670, Nov. 1.
3. Thomas, 1675, Mar. 24.
4. Mary,

IV. DEBORAH, m. 1668, Nov. 14. STEPHEN SABEERE,
b.
d.
b.
d. of Sabeere.

1. Daniel,
2. John,
3. Alice,

V. ALICE, m. 1669, Jan. 26. ELEAZER WHIPPLE,
b.
d. 1733 +
b. 1646.
d. 1719, Aug. 25. of John & Sarah (   ) Whipple

ANGELL. 2d column. V. Alice. Had also (probably) children. Deborah, 1670, Aug. 1. Hannah, 1695, Mar. 5.

1. Eleazer,
2. Alice, 1675, Jun. 3.
3. James,
4. Margaret,
5. Job,
6. Daniel,
7. Elizabeth,

VI. JAMES, m. 1678, Sep. 3. ABIGAIL DEXTER,
b.
d. 1711, Mar. 3.
b. 1655, Sep. 24.
d. 1711 + of Gregory & Abigail (Fullerton) Dexter.
Providence, R. I.

1676, Aug. 14. His name was in the list of those "who staid and went not away," in King Philip's War.

1679, Jul. 1. Taxed 7½*d.*

1687. Rateable estate, a share of meadow, 7 cows, 2 oxen, bull, 4 two year old cattle, a three year old, sow and horse.

1694–98–99–1704. Deputy.

1711, Mar. 31. Administration to widow Abigail. Inventory, £381, 12*s.* 8*d.*, viz: sword, belt, cane, 3 guns, 2 spinning wheels, 3 pair wool cards, flax, cotton, wool, books, pewter, earthenware, corn, rye, 10 barrels cider, bonds £263, horse, 2 colts, yoke of oxen, 2 cows, &c. The rooms named were, outermost room, easternmost lower bed-room, westernmost lower bed-room, leanto chamber.

1. Abigail, 1679, Feb. 2.
2. Mary, 1680, Mar. 7.
3. James, 1682, Nov. 22.
4. Alice, 1684, Feb 29.
5. Joseph, 1687, Oct. 5.
6. John, 1691, Oct. 4.
7. Deborah, 1695, Apr. 4.
8. Phebe, 1697, Oct. 10.

VII. HOPE, Unmarried.
b.
d. 1685 (—)
Providence, R. I.

VIII. MARGARET, m. JONATHAN WHIPPLE,
b.
d.
b. 1664.
d. 1721, Sep. 8. of John & Sarah (   ) Whipple.

1. Sarah,
2. Margaret,
3. Jonathan, 1692, Feb. 22.
4. Thomas, 1694, Feb. 26.
5. Paratine,
6. Mary,
7. Alice,

ANGELL. 2d column. V. Alice, b. 1649, d 1743, Aug. 13. Children, 1. Eleazer, 2. Alice, 1675, Jun. 3, 3. Margaret, 4. Elizabeth, 1680, 5. Job, 1684, 6. James, 1686, 7. Daniel. VI. James, m. 1678, Sep. 30. His widow, d. 1718 +.

ANTHONY.

JOHN, m. SUSANNA,
b. 1607.
d. 1675, Jul. 28.
b.
d. 1675 (—)

Hempstead, Eng. Portsmouth, R. I.

He was an inn-keeper, as well as having other occupations.

1634, Apr. 16. He came in the ship Hercules, to New England.

1641, Mar. 16. Freeman.

1642, Oct. He sold Richard Tew, of Newport, for good causes, &c., three parcels of land in Newport, east from the Newport Mill, within a tract called the great enclosure, amounting to 50 acres—40 acres given me by town grant; 10 as a servant, at my first coming: also two parcels marsh. Witnesses, Susanna Anthony and Joseph Ladd.

I. JOHN, m. (1) 1669, Nov. 23. FRANCIS WODELL, m. (2) 1694, Jan. 3. SUSANNA ALBRO,
b. 1642.
d. 1715, Oct. 20.
b. 1652, Jul. 6.
d. of William & Mary (   ) Wodell.
b.
d. 1715 + of John & Dorothy (   ) Albro.
Portsmouth, R. I.

1672, Apr. 30. Freeman.

1674. Deputy.

1679, May 5. In testimony relative to a deed that was brought to his house, he called himself aged about thirty-seven years.

1680. Taxed 4*s.* 10*d.*

1688, Apr. 28. He bought of John Potter, of Warwick, and Robert, his son, building, orchard and 28 acres, in Portsmouth, for £60.

1701–3–. He was appointed by Assembly, on the committee for general audit of the Colony's debt.

1709, Dec. 16. His son Joseph, accidently shot himself at Howland's Ferry.

1715, Jul. 26. Will—proved 1715, Oct. 10. Exx. wife Susanna. To her £3, yearly for life, in lieu of

1. John, 1671, Jun. 28.
2. Joseph, 1673, Oct. 28.
3. William, 1676, Jul. 18.
4. Susanna, 1679, Jan. 1.
5. Mary, 1681, Jun. 16.
6. Sarah, 1683, Oct. 1.
7. Elizabeth, 1686, Sep. 14.
8. Alice, 1689, Apr. 26.
9. Samuel, 1691, Oct. 8.
(2d) wife.
10. Albro, 1694, Sep. 25.
11. Sarah, 1697, Aug. 1.
12. John, 1699, Feb. 16.

ANTHONY. 2d column. IV. Joseph. Erase his last child, Abraham. Add a twin sister, Almy, to his daughter, 6, Mary.

1644. Corporal.

1644, Nov. 14. He had land granted at the wading river.

1655. Freeman.

1655, May 25. He was appointed by the Court of Commissioners, to keep a house of entertainment. A convenient sign was to be set out at the most perspicuous place of said house, to give notice to strangers.

1661. Commissioner.

1662, Dec. 29. He had confirmation by Commissioners, of a house and land that he had bought about twenty years before of Robert Potter, deceased. Testimony had before this been given by John Potter, son of Robert, that, in his conscience, he did believe his father sold said house to my uncle, John Anthony, and he engaged, that when he, John Potter, came to full age of twenty-one, he would confirm the sale.

1663, Dec. 3. He bought a house and 3 acres in Portsmouth, of Thomas Clark and Jane, of Newport.

1666, Nov. 7. He sold Daniel Vaughan, of Newport, house and 35 acres, &c., in Portsmouth, for £80.

1666–72. Deputy.

1675, Jul. 28. Will—proved 1675, Aug 21. Ex. son John. Overseers, friends Robert Hodgson and Robert Dennis. To son John, all housing and land in Portsmouth, also, my loom or looms. To daughter Susanna Tripp, fifteen sheep and a cow. To daughter Elizabeth Greene, fifteen sheep and a cow. To all my children, viz: John, Joseph, Abraham, Susanna and Elizbeth, rest of estate, equally.

dower. To daughter Elizabeth Anthony, 5s. she having already had. To son William, 5s. and the housing and land in Portsmouth, that by deed he had already. To daughter Alice Anthony, £10. To son Samuel, 50 acres in Portsmouth, buildings, &c., he paying £3 yearly to my wife and above legacies; and to Samuel also, a silver cup and brass chafing dish. To son William, all movables he has in his house. To sons Albro and John, 6 acres. To son Albro, a great bible and loom. To son John, silver buckles, girdle and dripping pan. To daughter Sarah Anthony, table, drawers and box which I use to put my writings in. To wife Susanna, rest of movable estate.

1. Susanna, 1677, Oct. 31.
2. Mary, 1670, Dec. 9.
3. John, 1673, Jul. 19.
4. Othniel, 1676, Jun. 5.
5. Benjamin, 1678, Feb. 21.
6. Lot, 1684, Dec. 26.

II. { SUSANNA, m. 1665, Sep. 7. JOHN TRIPP, } { b. d. 1716 + b. 1640 ± d. 1719, Nov. 20. } of John & Mary (Paine) Tripp.

1. Peter, 1666, Aug. 25.
2. Elizabeth, 1668, Oct. 17.
3. John, 1671, Feb. 1.
4. Jabez, 1673, Mar. 17.
5. David, 1677, Jun. 24.
6. Thomas, 1682, Nov. 11.
7. John, 1685, Sep. 30.
8. Susanna, 1688, May 24.

III. { ELIZABETH, m. 1665, Aug. 3. JAMES GREENE, } { b. d. 1698 + b. 1626. d. 1698, Apr. 27. } of John & Joan (Tattersall) Greene.

1. John, 1678, Sep. 10.
2. Joseph, 1682, May 19.
3. Susanna, 1684, Oct. 24.
4. Thomas,

IV. { JOSEPH, m. 1676, Apr. 5. MARY WAIT, } { b. d. 1728. b. d. 1713 + } Portsmouth, Tiverton, R. I. of Thomas Wait.

1672, Apr. 30. Freeman.

1692, Mar. 2. Tiverton. He was an inhabitant at organization of town.

1713, Mar. 8. Will—proved 1728, Mar. 19. Ex. son Joseph. To son John, a good horse and maintenance of said horse, £10 yearly, a feather bed and his maintenance. To wife Mary, £12 yearly, chest, bed, use of leanto and privilege in cellar. To son Joseph, all my housing and lands in Tiverton, orchards, &c., and housing and lands in Portsmouth, he paying my son John £10 yearly, and maintaining him and his horse, and paying his mother £10 yearly, and also maintaining my daughter, Susanna Anthony.

Inventory, £1,606, viz: purse and apparel £12, 5s., bible and plate £3, 4s. 8d., stillyards, pewter, beds, land and buildings, £1,500, &c.

1. John, 1672, Nov. 7.
2. Susanna, 1674, Aug. 29.
3. Mary, 1674, Aug. 29.
4. William, 1675, Oct. 31.
5. Susanna, 1677, Oct. 14.
6. Mary, 1680, Jan. 2.
7. Abraham, 1682, Apr. 21.
8. Thomas, 1684, Jun. 30.
9. Alice, 1686, Jan. 22.
10. James, 1686, Jan. 22.
11. Amy, 1688, Jun. 30.
12. Isaac, 1690, Apr. 10.
13. Jacob, 1693, Nov. 15.

V. { ABRAHAM, m. 1671, Dec. 26. ALICE WODELL. } { b. d. 1727, Oct. 10. b. 1650, Feb. 10. d. 1734. } Portsmouth, R. I. of William & Mary (   ) Wodell.

1672, Apr. 30. Freeman.

1703. He took administration on estate of his son, John Anthony, mariner, late master of her Majesty's ship Gosport.

1703-4-5-7-8-9-10-11. Deputy.

1704, Jan. 4. He and three others were given authority to see the laws of the Colony printed.

1709–10. Speaker of House of Deputies.

1727, Jun. 25. Will—proved 1727, Oct. 19. Ex. son William. To wife Alice, for life, use of all the old buildings of now dwelling house (the southerly part), garden, fruit of ten apple trees, keep of a cow, and of a riding beast for life, and use of great andirons. To son Isaac, £200, great coat, riding horse and a third of wearing apparel. To son Jacob, a lot of land in Portsmouth, of 30 acres, called Strawberry Field, and a third of wearing apparel. To daughter Susannah Hicks, £200, and at decease of her mother great iron kettle. To daughter Amy Allen, £100, and what she has had, an oval table and a spice box. To grandson John, son of John, late deceased, £50. To grandson Abraham, son of William, a leathern girdle. To granddaughter Mercy, daughter of Isaac, certain land at decease of wife. To granddaughter Sarah Hicks, a great candle-stick at death of wife. To four grandsons, sons of daughter Mary Sherman, deceased, viz: Abraham, Samson, Peter and Anthony, each £20 at age. To grandson Abraham Allen, a silver spoon. To son William, a third of wearing apparel, and at death of wife, great table, iron, &c. To wife Alice, a horse, cow, feather bed and a quarter of rest of household stuff at her choice. To children Susanna Hicks, Amy Allen and Isaac Anthony, rest of household stuff. To son William, all my dwelling house and rest of lands in Portsmouth, subject to provision for wife, and to her, rest of personal.

Inventory, £336, 2s. 6d., viz: cane, wearing apparel, books £1, feather beds, pewter, carpentry tools, his part of neat cattle £58, horsekind £18, swine £6, spinning wheel, &c.

His widow died at the house of her son William.

ASHLEY.

{ WILLIAM, m. SARAH, } { b. d. 1694, Nov. 24. b. d. 1695 + }

Providence, R. I.

1695, Jan. 15. His inventory was presented by Sarah Ashley, amounting to £12, 4s. 3d., viz: wearing apparel £3, 6s., money 12s., bed, bible, yarn and other lumber 5s., musket, 30 pounds of beef, Indian corn, &c.

ASHLEY. 1st column. The inventory was presented by his only child, Sarah Ashley. 2d column. I. Sarah.

ASHTON. See: American Genealogist, v.21, p.206.

{ JAMES, m. ——— } { b. d. b. d. }

Providence, R. I.

1652–58–59–63. Commissioner.

1655. Freeman.

1662, Feb. 19. He had lot 38, in division of lands.

1663, Oct. 29. He and Joshua Winsor signed a bond, consenting to arbitration on all matters of difference between them, occasioned about a certain lot of land called Matthew Weston's lot.

1665. Deputy.

1679, Jul. 1. Taxed 3s. 1½d.

1687, Sep. 1. Taxed 1s. 1d.

Perhaps James Ashton, of Monmouth, N. J., in 1700, was a son of James, of Providence.

I. { WILLIAM, m. (1) PATIENCE WILLIAMS, m. (2) ELIZABETH BULLOCK, } { b. 1680. d. 1765, Apr. 19. b. d. 1764 (—) b. 1699. d. 1759, Jul. 2. } Providence, R. I. of Daniel & Rebecca (Rhodes) Williams. of John Bullock.

1. Joshua, 1716, Mar.
2. William,
3. Thomas,
4. Rebecca.

He may have been grandson, instead of son of James[1], or he may possibly have been son of William Austin, (the surnames Ashton and Austin being used interchangeably in a limited degree).

1728, Jan. 10. He and wife Patience, for £64, sold Joseph Sheldon a lot measuring 50 by 65 feet.

1764, May 4. Will—proved 1765, May 18. Exs. sons Joshua and William. To son William, my now dwelling house, barn, &c., he supporting his brother Thomas with meat, drink and lodging for life, Thomas not being of a capacity to support himself, and if William neglect or refuse, then half of the estate to be set off for support of Thomas. To daughter Rebecca Sabin, a square table with three drawers. To grandsons John and Jesse, all silver buttons belonging to jacket and breeches of testator. To grandson Stephen, son of William, all my silver coat buttons. To son Joshua Ashton, 5s. in lawful money. To son William, the rest of movables.

He and his second wife were buried in St. John's Church-yard.

James Ashton. See also: Bowen's THE PROVIDENCE OATH OF ALLEGIANCE, p.71-74.

AUDLEY.

{ JOHN, m. MARTHA, } { b. 1641, Jun. d. 1711, Dec. 13. b. 1640, May. d. 1711, Dec. 30. }

Newport, R. I.

1667, May 13. He and others skilled therein, were ordered to repair all arms brought them by order of the Captain or Lieutenant of the Train Band, of Newport.

1672, May 6. His servant having been beaten by an Indian, the latter was fined £11, 20s., and if not paid, to be sold for a slave to Barbadoes.

See: American Genealogist v.19, p.129; v.26, p.229, v.39, p.1.

I. { JOHN, m. (1) LYDIA TILLINGHAST, m. (2) ELIZABETH, } { b. 1666. d. 1738, Jun. 29. b. 1666, Apr. 18. d. 1707, Jun. 30. b. 1684, Jun. d. 1726, Oct. 1. } Newport, R. I. of Pardon & Lydia (Taber) Tillinghast. of

1. John, 1689, Mar.
2. Elisha, 1690, Nov.
3. Martha, 1692.
4. Mary, 1694.
5. Son, 1700, Jul. 8.
6. Lydia, 1702, Jan. 29.
7. Abigail, 1703, Sep. 30.
8. Elizabeth, 1706, Oct.

(2d) wife.

9. Sarah, 1711, Oct.
10. Josiah, 1714, Sep. 12.
11. Jonathan, 1715, Jul.
12. John, 1719, Mar. 12.

1702, Mar. 4 He was a proprietor in common lands.

1716, Jun. 18. He was allowed £3, for services in building the jail.

1724. Deputy.

1728, Mar. 18. He gave deposition concerning Aquidneck Point, in a suit of Jonathan Marsh versus Job Carr. He called himself sixty-two years of age.

1680. Taxed 10*s*.

1685, Aug. 10. He had land laid out at East Greenwich, but never went there to settle.

1698, Jun. 6. He deeded his son Robert, 100 acres in East Greenwich, R. I.

1702, Mar. 4. He was a proprietor in the common lands.

1707, May 28. He was appointed on committee to audit the Colony and General Treasurer's account.

1708, Apr. He and two others were chosen to oversee repairing and finishing the Colony House, for which £100 was appropriated by the Assembly.

He and his wife were buried in Newport Cemetery.

He and both of his wives were buried in Newport Cemetery.

II. ROBERT, { b. { d. East Greenwich, R. I.

1698, Jun. 6. He had a deed of 100 acres in East Greenwich, from his father.

AUDLEY. 1st column, John[2] (John[1]), b. 1642, Feb. 3. Boston. Mass., Newport, R. I. He was a blacksmith. 1685, Mar. 6. He had a legacy of certain land in Roxbury, Mass; from will of his father. 1687, Jul. 17, He and wife Martha, deeded to his Brother Elisha, of Boston tailor, certain land in south part of Boston, devised by father John Odlin, armorer, deceased.

2d column. 1. John, m. (2) Elizabeth Arnold, b 1684, May 19, of Josiah & Sarah (Mills) Arnold,

AUSTIN (WILLIAM).

{ WILLIAM, { b. { d. 1687.
m.
HANNAH, { b. { d.

Providence, R. I.

He was a weaver.

1673. Freeman

1673, Apr. 6. He and Hannah Austin, were witnesses to the marriage of John Lapham and Mary Mann, all being Quakers.

1673–74–75. Deputy.

1674, Jul. 3. He took Moses Lippitt, as an apprentice to learn the trade and occupation of a weaver.

1687. Rateable estate, one house lot.

1687, Sep. 1. Taxed 3*d*., estate of William Austin.

He may possibly have been the father of William Ashton[2] (the surnames Ashton and Austin being used interchangeably in a limited degree).

AYLSWORTH.

{ ARTHUR, { b. 1653. { d. 1726.
m.
MARY BROWN, { b. { d.

of John & Mary (Holmes) Brown.

North Kingstown, R. I.

1679, Jul. 29. Kings Town. He and forty-one others, of Narragansett, signed a petition to the King, praying that he "would put an end to these differences about the government thereof, which hath been so fatal to the prosperity of the place; animosities still arising in people's minds, as they stand affected to this or that government".

1687, Sep. 6. Taxed 3*s*. 5½*d*.

1701. Surveyor of Highways.

1715, Mar. 29. He testified as to certain land, calling himself sixty-two years old, or thereabouts.

1725, Nov. 7. Will — proved 1726. Ex. son Philip. To son Philip, all real estate, and if he die without issue, then to son Chad, and if the latter die, then to heirs of my son Robert. To eldest son Robert, £5. To son Arthur, £3. To son John, £3. To son Chad, bed, &c. To daughters Mary Greene, Elizabeth Dolover, Catherine and Martha, legacies. To son Philip, rest of personal, he paying legacies.

Inventory, beds £71, 1*s*., warming pan, wearing apparel, 2 old books, woolen wheel, carpenters tools, steers, heifers, sheep, lambs, geese, fowls, &c.

1727, Nov. 23. Receipts were given the executor by Peleg Card and Elizabeth, his wife, and John Davis and Martha, his wife, for legacies from father, Arthur Aylsworth's estate.

I. { ROBERT, { b. { d. 1760. Kings Town, Exeter, R. I.
m. 1708, May 20,
ANNA DAVIS, { b. { d. 1761. of Davis.

1700, May 4. He was summoned by Assembly, to answer the charge in court, of being engaged in a riot.

1760, Feb. 25. Administration to widow Anna. Inventory, £572, 7*s*. 3*d*., viz: wearing apparel £16, feather bed, flock bed, warming pan, loom, cash 14*s*., carpenters tools, 2 old books £1, pewter, mare, cow, hog, &c.

1760, May 4. Will—proved 1761, Nov. 10. Widow Anna. Ex. son Ephraim. To son Robert, 5*s*. To son-in-law Jabez Tucker, 5*s*. To grandson Robert Petty, 5*s*. To daughter Amy Rathbone, spectacles and silver bows, worsted combs, &c. To daughter Anna Austin, clasps, &c. To son Ephraim, and daughters Amy and Anna, rest of estate.

Inventory, £199, 12*s*. 6*d*.

1. Robert,
2. Ephraim,
3. Sarah,
4. Mary,
5. Amey,
6. Anna,

II. { ARTHUR, { b. 1685. { d. 1761, Jul. North Kingstown, West Greenwich, R. I.
m.
MARY FRANKLIN, { b. { d. of Franklin.

He was a carpenter, as well as farmer and inn-keeper.

1724, Jun. 22. He bought of William Wanton, 320 acres, being the thirty-first farm in the third or last division, paying therefor £100.

1761, Jul. 4. Will—proved 1761, Aug. 1. Ex. son Jediah. To son Philip, half of land. To son David, the other half of land. To daughter Freelove Tenant, a cow, wearing apparel, &c. To daughter Anstis Calvin, bed, linen wheel, &c. To daughter Barbara Hill, bed, pewter, &c. To grandson John Phillips, 20*s*. To grand daughter Edey Whitman, £4. To son Jediah, 20*s*., and rest of movable estate.

Inventory, £672, viz: pewter, foot wheel, stillyards, warming pan, gun, cow, steer, &c.

1. James,
2. John,
3. Jediah,
4. Philip,
5. David,
6. Freelove,
7. Dimmis, 1725, Jun. 22.
8. Anstis, 1727, Nov. 22.
9. Barbara, 1729, Jun. 13.

III. { JOHN, { b. { d. 1771. North Kingstown, R. I.
m.
DORCAS JONES, { b. { d. of Josiah & Elizabeth ( ) Jones.

1771. Will—proved 1771, May, 15. There has been such havoc made by fire with the record of this will, that little can be gleaned from it.

1. Anthony,
2. Arthur,
3. John,
4. Josiah,
5. Dorcas,
6. Anna,
7. Mary,
8. Phebe,

IV. { PHILIP, { b. 1692. { d. North Kingstown, R. I.
m.
RACHEL GREENE, { b. 1690 May 6. { d. of Daniel & Rebecca (Barrow) Greene.

He lived on his father's homestead.

His five last named children died young.

1. Arthur,
2. Job,
3. Philip,
4. Sarah,
5. Phebe,
6. Martha,
7. Elizabeth,
8. Obadiah,
9. Peleg,
10. Mary,
11. Nancy,
12. Catherine,

V. { CHAD, { b. 1696. { d. 1773, Mar. 23. Scituate, R. I.
m. (1) 1725, Nov. 15.
ELIZABETH MAJOR, { b. { d. of Major.
m. (2)
MARY WOOD, { b. { d. of Wood.

1734. Freeman.

1756, Apr. 23. Will—proved 1773, May 22. Exx. wife Mary. To son Thomas, £15, and what he has had by deed. To daughter Judith Colgrove, 16 acres for life, and then to her son Caleb. To daughter Mary Haines, £50. To daughter Rachel Colgrove, £50. To son Peleg, all real estate and farming tools. To wife and two young daughters, Sarah and Mercy, the residue of personal property

Inventory, £40, 19*s*. 7*d*., viz: a cow, 10 sheep, 2 swine, heifer, 2 calves and household furniture.

1. Thomas, 1726, Aug. 21.
2. Elizabeth, 1728.
3. Judith,
4. Mary,
5. Rachel,
6. Anna,

(2d) wife.

7. Peleg,
8. Sarah,
9. Mercy,

VI. { MARY, { b. { d.
m.
JOHN GREENE, { b. { d. of Benjamin & Humility (Coggeshall) Greene.

AYLSWORTH. 2d column. VI. Mary. Her husband John Greene, d. 1752,

1. Philip,
2. Benjamin,
3. Thomas,
4. Elizabeth,
5. Ruth,
6. William,
7. Josiah,
8. Amos,
9. Jonathan,
10. Caleb,
11. Joseph,
12. Jonathan,

VII. { ELIZABETH, { b. { d.
m. (1)
—— DOLOVER, { b. { d. of Dolover.
m. (2)
PELEG CARD, { b. { d. of Card.

(By 2d husband).

1. Philip,

VIII. Catherine, m. —— Greene, b. d. b. d. of Greene.

IX. Martha, m. John Davis, b. d. 1738. b. d. 1738 + of Davis.

2. William,
3. Mary,
4. Ruth,
5. Phebe,
6. Elizabeth,
7. James,

AYRAULT.

Peter, m. Frances, b. d. 1711, b. 1640. d. 1712, Jan. 3.

Angiers, France, Kings Town, E. Greenwich, R. I. He was a physician.

1686, Nov. 4. An agreement was made between Richard Wharton, of Boston, and certain French Huguenots, for a parcel of land at Narragansett, 100 acres, and a share of meadow being allowed to a family, and about forty-five families taking part in the settlement, which was soon made. 100 acres was set apart for a glebe, and 50 acres for maintenance of a school. There were built about twenty five houses in this settlement.

1390, Feb. 20. The little colony, having come under the government of Rhode Island, the Assembly enacted that they should take the oath of allegiance, which was done, protection being promised.

1692. In this year (according to testimony of Mr. Ayrault, made in 1700), persecutions commenced "by the vulgar sect of they people, who flinging down of our fences, laying open our land to ruin,"&c. He says, "what benefit we expected from our lands for subsistence was destroyed by secretly laying open our fences, by night and day, and what little we had preserved by flying from France, we had laid out under the then improvements, looked so hard upon us to see the cries of our wives and children," &c. The settlement was largely broken up, two families going to Boston and others to New York, according to the narrator, and the Greenwich men who gave the disturbance got our improved land, and soon demolished and pulled down the church; he says: "I being persuaded by many to stay, and having fenced in fifty acres of land, purchased and made very good improvements by a large orchard, garden and vineyard and a good house, was willing to keep my settlement, and bear all outrages committed against me, which further shall be related to, and as many persons in their sickness and extremity would send for me to administer help unto them, which under God's goodness I have been a help to raise many from extreme sickness, yet they have soon forgot labor and rewarded me with endeavoring to root me out of my habitations," &c.

1699. He was one of the founders of Trinity Church, of Newport.

1700, Aug. 7. He made oath to certain declarations before a commission composed of Francis Brinley, Peleg Sanford and Nathaniel Coddington. "That upon the 23d of said July there came unto my house, in said French Town, after sunset, a great number of the town of Greenwich," &c. He was told to go with them to the court, kept on the other side of the river, at house of Pardon Tillinghast. He refused, unless they showed their warrant, but they "laid their hands upon me and dragged me to the river side, and afterwards over said river, and placed me in their court, as they called it." He desired an interpreter, not understanding English, and they told him he should have one on the morrow, and then released him and his son Daniel on Samuel Bennett's word to answer next day, which he did, giving bond to appear at next court. "Let it be considered that I was set upon in my own house at that unseasonable time, with a warrant which they were ashamed to read, or give me a copy of In fine, my wife, an aged woman of sixty years of age, infirm and sick, could not, by all her cries and tears, persuade them to desist, but contrariwise, did strike and fling her on the pavement, where she continued some time for dead, all which I conceive is not only unnatural and inhuman, and against all law and reason, which I submit to a further determination."

1705, May 1. Will—proved 1711, Jun. 4. Ex. son Daniel. To wife Frances, yearly rent of £30, for life. To son Samuel, mariner, at present abroad in the world about his notions and employment, £40. To son Daniel, merchant, of Narragansett, all the rest of estate, money, lands, houses and goods.

Inventory, £118, 19*s.* 11*d.*, (including the estate of Dr. Peter Ayrault, and Frances, his wife), viz: 2 bell metal mortars, gun, old books £1, 3*s.*, sword, cash, silver money £60, old silver plate £6, 11*s.* 3*d.*, old silk petticoat 6*s.*, 2 beds, 3 rugs, 4 dozen napkins, 2 dozen and two coarse napkins, 9 table cloths, 3 towels, 2 fine sheets, 2 blankets, &c.

His widow's tombstone may still be seen in the Updike Cemetery, North Kingstown.

I. Samuel, b. d. 1705 + East Greenwich, R. I.

II. Daniel. m. (1) 1703, May 9, Mary Robineau, m. (2) 1737, Apr. 17, [of Ed. Rebecca Neargrass, (w. b. 1676, Sep. 8. d. 1764, Jun. 25. b. 1684, Jul. 29. d. 1729, Jan. 5. b. 1687. d. 1741, Feb. 5. Kings Town, East Greenwich, Newport, R. I. of —— & Judith ( ) Robineau. of

He was a merchant.

1700, May 4. He was summoned by Assembly to answer the charge in court, of being engaged in a riot.

1712. He sold house and 19 acres in East Greenwich, to David Greene,

1715, May 4. Newport. He, late of East Greenwich, was appellant in an action of debt against Samuel Davis, of Kings Town. The Assembly confirmed two former judgments given by Court of Trials, for the appellee, Davis.

1750, Sep. 4. He and his sons Daniel and Stephen signed a petition with others, to the King, praying that the Assembly might be restrained from making or emitting any more bills of public credit upon loan, without royal permission, the sum on loan already amounting to £390,000, worth at time of issue, £78,111, sterling, but at present only £35,445. Amongst those whose estates were involved in the loan, were numbers of widows and orphans, who were grieviously injured, oppressed and almost ruined.

He and his wife Mary, were buried in Trinity Church-yard. His second wife was buried in Newport Cemetery, as was her first husband.

AYRAULT. 1st. column. Sort for sect, second line after 1692.

1. Mary,	1704, Feb. 16.
2. Peter,	1705, Oct. 4.
3. Daniel,	1707, Nov. 2.
4. Stephen,	1709, Dec. 11.
5. Anthony,	1711, Jan. 15.
6. Elias,	1714, Feb. 13.
7. Judith,	1716, Sep. 8.
8. Frances,	1718, Sep. 23.
9. Samuel,	1720, Mar. 22.
10. Anthony,	
11. Susanna,	1723, Jun. 29.
12. Judith,	1725, Dec. 9.

Henry, b.
m. d.
Ann, b.
d.

Portsmouth, R. I.
1655. Freeman.
1660, Mar. 20. He and wife Ann, sold Thomas Fish, house and land in consideration of fencing of 2 acres, effected by Thomas Fish. Said Henry and Ann to enjoy said house and land for their lives, without rent.
Perhaps Thomas Ayres, of Kings Town, in 1696, was a son of Henry. (The said Thomas had wife Sarah, a daughter b. 1696, Nov. 28, and another daughter, Sarah, b. 1698, May 8).

BABCOCK.

James, b. 1612.
m. (1) d. 1679, Jun. 12.
Sarah, b.
m. (2) d. 1665 ±
Elizabeth, b.
d.

(She m. (2) 1679, Sep. 22, William Johnson.)

Portsmouth, Westerly, R. I.
He was a blacksmith.
1642, Feb. 25. Admitted inhabitant.
1643, Oct. 5. He and another were ordered to look up all the arms in the town. On the same date he had a grant of 10 acres at the first brook.
1650, May 23. He and five others were appointed to mend and make all arms presented to them by any of the town.
1655. Freeman.
1656–58–59. Commissioner.
1657, Dec. 10. He was granted 8 acres.
1664, Mar. 1. Westerly. Upon consideration of his petition the Court requests the Governor and Deputy Governor, to send a letter to the government of Connecticut, to see what they will say by way of answer to such riotous actings as are done and committed by the men of Southertown against the said Babcock, &c.
1665, —— 18. He sold Thomas Fish, for £50, land and dwelling house, barn, orchard, &c., in Portsmouth, his wife Sarah, giving her consent.
1667, May 18. He and others, of Rhode Island, having claimed certain land east of Pawcatuck River, a petition was sent to Connecticut authorities, by Harmon Garret, alias Wequasccoke, Governor of the Pequots, praying "that such men that wear hats and clothes like Englishmen, but have dealt with us like wolves and bears," may be called to account.
1669, May 18. Freeman.
1670, Jun. 18. He was warned by warrant from the Commissioners of Connecticut, to appear before them to make answer for seizure of three Connecticut men, on a warrant issued by Tobias Saunders. He was released on bail.
He gave testimony this year calling his age fifty-eight years, his son James twenty-nine, and his son John twenty-six years.
1676, Mar. 2. He was baptised by Elder William Hiscox, of the Seventh Day Baptist Church.
1679, Sep. 17. Testimony was given before a Court at Westerly, by John and Job Babcock, that James Babcock made the following will, "as he verbally declared before us." To son Job, all smith's tools. To daughter Mary Champlin, a cow. To the eldest daughter of William Champlin, a cow calf. To son Joseph, all housing and lands, at twenty one. To wife Elizabeth, rest of estate for maintenance and bringing up of the three children he had by her, and that his wife Elizabeth be administratrix.
Inventory, £61, 1*s.*, viz: house and land, 20 acres, £30, bellows, anvil, vice and smiths' tools, £5, 2 cows, 2 yearlings and 2 calves, £11, 7 small swine, 2 beds, 3 spinning wheels, pair of cards, 2 chests, churn, cradle, &c.

I. **James**, b. 1641. Westerly, R. I.
m. d. 1698 ±
Jane Brown, b.
d. 1719. of Nicholas Brown.

He was a blacksmith.
1665. He was witness to his father's deed of land in Portsmouth.
1669, May 18. Freeman.
1671, May 17. He, having refused to warn in the inhabitants of Westerly, to attend Court of Justices, held at Westerly, was ordered to be brought before the said court.
1687. Grand Jury.
1694, Nov. 16. His wife Jane, had a legacy of £10 from will of her father.
1699, Jan. 10. Inventory, £97, 8*d.* An agreement was made by the widow Jane and following children: James Babcock, James Lewis, Israel Lewis, George Brown, David Lewis, Roger Larkin, William Babcock. To the widow, 4 cows, 4 steers, calf, 30 sheep, 10 lambs, horse, feather bed, money, £12, warming pan, 20 barrels cider, &c. To son James, heifer, yearling, anvil and other blacksmith tools. To daughter Sarah, 6 ewes, 4 lambs, cow and yearling. To daughter Jane, 5 sheep, half a heifer, bed, &c. To daughter Mary, 3 sheep, cow, &c. To daughter Hannah, a bed, heifer, 3 sheep, &c. To daughter Elizabeth, heifer, bedding, &c.
1699, Aug. 7. His widow was convicted of selling drink by retail contrary to order, and fined 40*s.*, but it was remitted on her petition.
1718, Apr. 30. Will—proved 1719, Feb. 4. Widow Jane. Ex. son James, blacksmith. To daughter Sarah Lewis, 5*s.* To daughter Jane Lewis', eldest daughter Jane, 5*s.* To daughter Elizabeth Lewis' eldest son Elisha, 5*s.* To daughter Mary Brown, a cow. To daughter Hannah Larkin, 5*s.* To grandchildren, William and Peter Babcock, sons of James, two beds. To son James' three sons, rest of household stuff. To son James, all the rest of personal.

1. James,
2. Sarah,
3. Jane,
4. Mary,
5. Hannah,
6. Elizabeth,

II. **John**, b. 1644. Westerly, R. I.
m. d. 1685.
Mary Lawton, b.
d. 1711, Nov. 8. of George & Elizabeth (Hazard) Lawton.
(She m. (2) Erasmus Babbitt.)

Tradition gives his wife as being Mary, daughter of Thomas Lawton, an impossibility, since Thomas Lawton had no such daughter. Other fiction comes with the tradition, but it is assumed to be so far true, that if George Lawton be substituted for Thomas, the tradition may be sustained as to marriage.
1669, May 18. Freeman.
1678, Jun. 12. Conservator of the Peace.
1679, Sep. 17. He took oath of allegiance.
1682–84. Deputy.
1685, Jun. 4. Inventory, £790, 3*s.*, viz: 43 steers, 33 cows, 8 working oxen, 9 three year steers, 9 two year cattle, 21 yearlings, 52 horses, mares and colts, 3 riding horses, old ambling horse, horse called James, 100 sheep, 50 lambs, 76 swine, ox, 2 bulls, 8 beds, silver cup, a dozen pewter platters, a dozen porringers, 2 flagons, warming pan, 3 canoes, 2 steel traps, negro boy, £20, 2 Indian men and an Indian girl, £30, a steer, mare, and four more horses, &c.
1685, Jun. 26. Will, made by Town Council, he having died intestate. Exx. widow Mary. Personal estate divided as follows: To widow, £263. 7*s.* 8*d.* To nine of the children, £57, 2*s.* 4*d.* each at age, viz: to Ann, Mary, John, Job, George, Elihu, Robert, Joseph and Oliver Babcock. The real estate was divided by agreement between James Babcock (son and rightful heir to John, deceased), and his mother, the agreement being ratified by Town Council. To James, half the farm we are now dwelling on, and the new dwelling house, he relinquishing to his mother, all the rest of lands.
1689, Dec. 26. Mrs. Mary Babcock made an agreement with John Fairfield, and wife Anphillis, to maintain them in meat, drink, clothing, &c., they binding themselves to her in all their estate of land and movables, to be entirely hers.
1696, Dec. 28. Mary Babcock, widow, deeded son George, for love, &c., 106 acres.
1699, Mar. 11. James and John Babcock deeded to Oliver, for brotherly love, &c., certain land commodious and convenient to dwelling house, which was formerly our father, John Babcock's, and also land that was formerly our father-in-law (*i. e.* step-father) Erasmus Babbitt's, said land to be Oliver's at decease of our mother, Mary Babbitt.
1698, Apr. 21. The following "orphans" of John Babcock, chose their brother James for guardian, viz: Elihu, Robert, Joseph and Oliver.

1. James,
2. Ann,
3. Mary,
4. John,
5. Job,
6. George,
7. Elihu,
8. Robert,
9. Joseph,
10. Oliver,

III. **Job**, b. Westerly, R. I.
m. d. 1718.
Jane Crandall, b.
d. 1715 (—) of John Crandall.

He was a blacksmith, and was also called miller.
1669, May 18. Freeman.
1679, Sep. 17. He took oath of allegiance.
1680. Constable.
1693, Feb. 15. His wife Jane, had a deed of 100 acres made to her by Samuel Lewis, and Job Babcock husband of said Jane, declared that he had given his wife full power to purchase the land.
1703, May 24. He bought land of the sachem Ninecraft, for £6.
1706, Oct. 31. He deeded son Job, for love, &c., 110 acres.
1715, Mar. 26. Will—proved 1718, Apr. 7. Ex. son John. To son John, my now dwelling house, grist mill, &c. To eldest son Job, 1*s.* To youngest son Benjamin, 1*s.* To daughters Jane Braman, Sarah Hall, Mary Tanner and Elizabeth Braud, 1*s.* each. To daughter Hannah Babcock, a feather bed, pewter and rest of household stuff. To daughter Mercy Babcock, 1*s.* To son John, all that is due after payment of debts and legacies.
Inventory, £8, 2*s.* 5*d.*, viz: feather bed, iron pot, kettle, drinking pot, 2 bottles, lock, 9 yards of cloth, 2¼ pounds linen yarn, &c.

1. Job,
2. John,
3. Benjamin,
4. Jane,
5. Sarah,
6. Mary,
7. Elizabeth,
8. Hannah,
9. Mercy,

IV. **Mary**, b.
m. d. 1747.
William Champlin, b. 1654.
d. 1715, Dec. 1. of Jeffrey Champlin.
(2d Wife.)

1. William,
2. Mary,
3. Ann,

V. **Nathaniel**, b. 1666 ±
d. 1719, Jan. 2.

VI. **Joseph**, b. 1670. Stonington, Conn.
m. (1) 1696, Apr. 13. d.
Dorothy Key, b.
m. (2) 1729, Jan. 1. d. 1727, Dec. 14. of Key.
Hannah Coats, b.
d. of Coats.

1. Elizabeth, 1698, Jan. 29
(2d) wife.
2. Dorothy, 1730, Feb. 2.
3. Abigail, 1731, Apr. 20
4. Joseph, 1733, Oct. 15.
5. John, 1736, Jan. 26.

VII. **Elizabeth**, b.
m. 1706, May 3. d.
Benjamin Sumner, b
d. of Sumner.

RICHARD, b. d.

Newport, R. I.
1668. Freeman.
1669–70–71–72–76. Secretary to Council.
1670–72. Deputy.
1671. Elected General Attorney, but refused the office.
1676, Apr. 11. He was one of the Commissioners appointed "to take care and order the several watches and wards on this island, and appoint the places."
1676, Apr. 20. He had a legacy from the will of Dr. John Clarke, of a concordance and lexicon to it, "written by myself, being the fruit of several years study," (as Mr. Clarke says), also a Hebrew bible and the rest of books.
1677, May 24. He and Peleg Sanford, were chosen Agents to go to England about the intrusion made by Connecticut.

BAILEY (William).

WILLIAM, b. d. 1676 (—)
m.
GRACE PARSONS, b. d. 1677 +

of Hugh & Elizabeth ( ) Parsons.
(She m. (2) Thomas Lawton.)

Newport, R. I.
1655, Jun. 14. He bought of Gabriel Hicks certain land bounded partly by sea, &c.
1656, Mar. 5. He, called William Bailey, Sr., with Gabriel Hicks, sold Joshua Coggeshall, of Portsmouth, 21 acres in Newport.
The evidence is conclusive as to his having sons John and Hugh, and there is ground for belief that Joseph, Edward and Stephen were also his sons.

BAILEY. 2d column. I. John, b. 1653, d. 1736, Jan. 18. His wife, b. 1655, d. 1730, Feb. 13. They were buried in family burial ground, now in Middletown. His daughter Ruth, b 1700, Jan. 27. He had another daughter, viz.: Elizabeth, b. 1698, Jan. 23.

BAILEY (William). 1st column. Add the name of Samuel after Stephen, next to last line.
2d column. VI. Samuel, Newport, R. I., m. Elizabeth Rogers, of Thomas & Sarah ( ) Rogers.

I. JOHN, b. d. 1736. Portsmouth, Newport, R. I.
m.
SUTTON, b. d. of

1. Sarah, 1681, Feb. 27.
2. William, 1684.
3. John,
4. Thomas, 1690.
5. Abigail, 1693.
6. Samuel,
7. Mary,
8. Ruth,

1677, Apr. 20. He leased dwelling house, land and orchard of his step-father, Thomas Lawton, of Portsmouth, and agreed to pay therefor, £10 per year to his mother, Grace Lawton, and £3 per year to Elizabeth Sherman, a married daughter of Thomas Lawton. The agreement was to hold till the death of Grace Lawton, or until she changed her name from Lawton. On same date, John Bailey gave a bond for £80 to Thomas Lawton, the obligation being that he, said John Bailey, should pay £44, in such specie as is mentioned in a will or bond made by Town Council of Portsmouth, for and in behalf of Grace Bailey, widow and relict unto William Bailey, and their children; and John Bailey agrees to fulfill terms of the instrument after the death of his mother, Grace.
1682, Sep. 25. Newport. He, late of Portsmouth, for £140, bought of Thomas Dungan and wife Elizabeth, 50 acres in Newport, and building, garden, &c.
1687, Feb. 14. He and wife Sutton, sold John Briggs, of Portsmouth, for £146, a house and 100 acres in Puncatest.
1691. Freeman.
1733, May 8. Will—proved 1736, Feb. 2. Ex. son Thomas. To grandson William Bailey, eldest son of William, deceased, two eighteen acre lots in Little Compton, with another piece of land there, and a quarter of my neat cattle. To grandson John Bailey, confirmation of land that son William had bequeathed him in will, and another lot of land in Little Compton. To grandson Samuel Bailey, son of William, land in Little Compton. To daughter-in-law Dorothy Bailey, a third of income of above given real estate and of real estate given another grandson, George Bailey—in order to bring up these four grandchildren, each to have as they are of age, the real estate bequeathed them. If Dorothy marries during her sons' minority, her income to cease. To above grandsons, a quarter of all sheep and lambs their father had in his possession at his death—equally, and £100 to be divided to them all, being portion intended for their father. To grandson George Bailey, above named, £100, in bills of public credit, at age, with interest. To son Thomas Bailey, rest of upland, salt marsh, meadows and ledges in Little Compton, with buildings, &c., and a quarter of cattle, sheep and lambs, £100 silver, and £100 bills. To son John, confirmation of part of farm in Newport, lately bought of John Mumford, and other land adjoining now given, making whole farm, and a quarter of cattle, sheep and lambs To son Samuel, half of land in Portsmouth, bought of Thomas Cornell, said son already being seized of other half, and also rest of lands and buildings in Newport, contained in two parcels, one parcel thereof whereon my dwelling house now stands; also £100 in silver @ 8*s*. per oz., a quarter of cattle, sheep and lambs and £620 in bills public credit, in order to pay mortgage, &c. To daughter Mary Reynolds, £5, and what she has had. To daughter Abigail Weeden, £20, she having received a competency. To granddaughter Sarah Walsworth, £200 (£80 in silver and £120 in bills), to be paid within a year after my decease, provided she acquits my executors on account of estate left of my daughter Ruth's, or any other demand whatever, upon my estate, she having already received of me the whole of that estate left her by her father. To grandson Benjamin Bailey, son to my son John Bailey, the sum of £50, silver, at age. To two grandchildren, children of daughter Abigail Weeden, viz: Mary and William Weeden, each £100 in bills, at death of their mother, and interest, meanwhile to their mother, also to them £50 in silver. To two daughters in-law, viz: Martha Simms and Jane Rogers, sum of £5, on condition that they discharge my executor on account of estate left of my daughter Ruth. To each of three sons-in-law, viz: Daniel Sabecre, Jabez Reynolds and William Weeden, 10*s* To my two sons John Bailey and Samuel Bailey, all my looms and weaving tackle, hay fodder, beef, butter, cheese, grain, &c., laid in store for my use and family. To sons Samuel and Thomas all household stuff, equally. To son Thomas Bailey, £420. To daughter-in-law Alice Bailey, in consideration of tender care and regard she takes of me, in my declining years, £100. To son Thomas, rest of personal estate, undisposed of to prevent differences, &c., and any legatee not confirming shall have their part revert to executor, to enable him the better to defend other part of estate against such.

II. JOSEPH, b. d. Newport, R. I.
m.
——— b. d. of

1. Sarah,

1702, Oct. 16. His daughter Sarah's marriage to Samuel Dunn (son of Richard), was recorded at this date.

III. EDWARD, b. d. 1712. Newport, Tiverton, R. I.
m.
FRANCES, b. d. of

1. Edward,
2. Elizabeth,
3. John,
4. Sarah,

1680. Taxed 3*s*. (at Portsmouth).
1681, Mar. 27. He was fined 3*s*. 4*d*., for breach of peace.
1711, Aug. 18. Will. As there were only two witnesses (instead of 3), confirmation was made by legatees by agreement, he having bequeathed son Edward and daughter Sarah Bailey, all estate, real and personal, excepting his interest in Pocasset, which he gave his son John, and Edward and Sarah to allow their mother Frances comfortable maintenance for life. Elizabeth Manchester, wife of George, and daughter of deceased, had as her part, a three year old heifer. (1712, Apr. 7, confirmation by agreement.) See: American Genealogist, v. 19, p. 129.

IV. HUGH, b. d. 1724. Newport, East Greenwich, R. I.
m. (1)
ANNA, b. d. 1721, Feb. 26.
m. (2) 1724, May 30.
ABIGAIL WILLIAMS, b. d. 1724 + of Williams.

1. William, 1696, Apr. 29.
2. Samuel, 1703, Jul. 11.
3. Joseph, 1705, Mar. 2.
4. Hannah, 1708, Jan. 9.
5. Sarah, 1710, Jan. 27.
6. John, 1712 Jan. 6.
7. Jeremiah, 1714, Sep. 21.
8. Anna, 1717, Jan. 21.

His first child was born at Newport, the rest at East Greenwich.
1702. East Greenwich. Freeman.
1724, Aug. 10. Inventory, £155, 7*s*., viz: warming pan, 3 spinning wheels, 5 cows, 2 steers, 2 yearling steers, 3 calves, 2 mares, 1 colt, 43 sheep, 20 lambs, 4 swine, 4 shoats, real estate, £400.
Inventory of William Bailey's land, worth when his father gave it, £50. Inventory of what the widow brought, £30, 15*s*.
1726, Apr. 13. Administration to son Samuel.

V. STEPHEN, b. 1665. d. 1724, Oct. 17. Newport, R. I.
m.
SUSANNA, b. 1673. d. 1723, Apr. 25. of

1. Thomas,
2. Rebecca, 1707.

1724 Jun. 17. He, as guardian of his daughter Rebecca, aged seventeen, brought suit against John Greenman and wife Elizabeth, for defamation.
He and his wife were buried in Newport Cemetery.

BAKER (Thomas). 1st column. He m. Sarah. He was a tailor. 168[illegible], Dec. 24, Newport. He bought of Ralph Paine, of Newport, 25 acres in Providence, for £4. 1639, Feb. 25, Kings Town. He, tailor, and wife Sarah, sold to Joseph Smith, of Providence, for full satisfaction, right of common in Providence, bought of Ralph Paine.

THOMAS, { b. d.
m.
——— { b. d.

Newport, Kings Town, R. I.

1653, Dec. 17. His land is mentioned as adjoining that of George Kenrick, of Newport, in a deed of the latter to William Field, of Providence.

1655. Ordained in this year.

1656. He and William Vaughan and some others left the First Baptist Church and formed a congregation known as the Second Baptist Church, of which he was for a time pastor. The reasons given for this separation are thus stated: "Said persons conceived a prejudice against psalmody, and against the restraints that the liberty of prophesying, was laid under, and also against the doctrine of particular redemption, and against the rite of laying on of hands as a matter of indifference."

1666. Kings Town. He removed thence about this time and gathered a church together, of which he became the first pastor, officiating for many years in that capacity, his successor, Richard Sweet, following in 1710.

I. THOMAS, { b. d. 1743. — North Kingstown, R. I.
m.
MARY, { b. d. 1743 (—) of

1709, May 27. Kings Town. He and five others bought 792 acres of the vacant lands in Narragansett.

1743, Feb. 20. Will—proved. Ex. son Jeremiah. To son Thomas, £50. To son John, 5*s*. To son Abner, £40. To son Josiah, 5*s*. To son Philip, £45. To son Ichabod, £5. To daughters Sarah ——— and Elizabeth Greene, all household goods. To daughter Anne, wife of Stephen Sweet, 5*s*. To son Jeremiah, homestead, buildings, &c.

1. Thomas, 169–, Jan. 7.
2. John, 1699, Sep. 20.
3. Jeremiah, 170–, Jul. 26.
4. Abner, 170–, Mar. 6.
5. Sarah, 170–, Dec. 15.
6. Josiah, 170–, Oct. 11.
7. Joshua, 17—, Feb. 11.
8. Joseph, 17—, Feb. 17.
9. Elizabeth,
10. Ann,
11. Philip,
12. Ruth,
13. Ichabod,

II. BENJAMIN, { b. d. 1726 ± — North Kingstown, R. I.
m. 1705.
MARY H——— { b. d. of

1709, May 27. Kings Town. He and twelve others bought 1824 acres of the vacant lands in Narragansett, near Devil's Foot.

1726 ± Administration to brother Thomas, he having died intestate, leaving children Benjamin and Mercy.

1. Benjamin,
2. Mercy,

III. JAMES, { b. d. — Kings Town, R. I.
m.
PENELOPE WESTCOTT, { b. d. of Amos & Deborah (Stafford) Westcott.

1711, Mar. 13. He gave a receipt, on behalf of his wife, to the town of Warwick, for her part of her mother's estate, returned at death of his wife's brother, Solomon Westcott, who had been supported by the town, he, the said Solomon, being an idiot.

1. Daughter,
2. Daniel,
3. Abel,
4. George,
5. Alice,

BAKER (William).

WILLIAM, { b. d.
m.
MARY, { b. d.

Portsmouth, Warwick, R. I.

1638. He and others were admitted to be inhabitants of the island of Aquidneck, having submitted themselves to the government, that is, or shall be established.

1638, Aug. 23. He had a lot granted him, and was to build at the Spring at farthest, or else his lot was to be disposed of.

1654, Jul. 13. He was one of the witnesses to the deed from Taccomanan to the Warwick purchasers of tract called Potawomut.

1655. Freeman.

1669, Apr. 1. Warwick. He and wife Mary, gave a receipt to Abiah Carpenter, for a yearling heifer.

Descendants of his may have been Mary Baker, who married 1683, Jan., Mark Roberts, and Sarah Baker, who married 1685, Apr. 27, Peter Robertson.

BALCOM.

ALEXANDER, { b. d. 1711, May 4.
m.
JANE HOLBROOK, { b. d. 1711 (—)
of William & Elizabeth ( ) Holbrook.

Portsmouth, Providence, R. I.

He was a mason.

1664, Jan. 31. He is mentioned as now or lately occupying a house in Portsmouth, in a deed of that date, of said house, from Philip Taber to Daniel Wilcox.

1683. Providence. Deputy.

1686, Jul. 14. He bought of Nathan Payne, of Bristol, all his interest in tract of land called Wesquodomsett, twelve miles north of Providence. He subsequently bought other lands in same tract.

1687, Sep. 1. Taxed 2*s*. 3*d*.

1687, Dec. 1. Rateable estate, 2 oxen, 4 cows, mare, 4 acres planting ground.

1702, Nov. 20. Will—proved 1711, Jul. 18. Exs. wife Jane and son John. Overseers, Joseph Jenckes, Jr., and James Brown. To eldest son Alexander, 2*s*., with what he had already had. To Catherine Jenckes, eldest daughter, and Sarah Sheldon, second daughter, each 2*s*. To second son John, my now dwelling house and all my land, situate and being in Providence, after decease of testator and wife. To third son Freegift, 2*s*., and what he had already had. To five younger children, viz: Joseph, Hannah, Samuel, Deborah and Lydia, the rest of estate equally. Administration was taken by son John alone.

Inventory, £35, 4*s*. 7*d*., viz: cattle, sheep, horse, cooper's tools, hammer, trowel, wearing apparel, books, pewter, brassware, &c.

I. ALEXANDER, { b. d. 1728, Jan. 31. — Providence, R. I., Attleboro, Mass.
m.
SARAH WOODCOCK, { b. d. 1728 + of William & Mary ( ) Woodcock.

He was a mason.

1682. He took the oath of allegiance.

1687, Sep. 1. Taxed 1*s*.

1687, Dec. 1. Rateable estate, mare, three year old steer, three year old heifer, and a two year old.

1692. Attleboro.

1701, May 29. He bought of his father-in-law, 20 acres.

1708, Feb. 17. He bought of his mother-in-law, Mary Woodcock, widow, and others, 20 acres, for £3, 20*s*.

1728, Feb. 21. Inventory, £737, 18*s*. 6*d*., viz: real estate £400, paper money, copper money, silver money, silver sleeve buttons, cider mill, yoke of oxen, 5 cows, pair of steers, heifer, 4 two years, 5 yearlings, 20 sheep, mare, indoor utensils, &c.

Administration was given to his widow Sarah.

1. William, 1692, Sep. 3.
2. Catherine, 1694, Feb. 7.
3. Alexander, 1696, Apr. 14.
4. John, 1699, Apr. 29.
5. Baruch, 1702, Jun. 12.
6. Sarah, 1704, Feb. 8.
7. Joseph, 1706, Feb. 23.

II. CATHERINE, { b. d. 1729 +
m.
DANIEL JENCKES, { b. 1663, Apr. 19. d. 1736. of Joseph & Elizabeth ( ) Jenckes.

1. Mary,
2. Elizabeth,
3. Abigail, 1696, Jul. 8.
4. Martha, 1698, Aug. 5.
5. Susanna, 1700, May 24.
6. Daniel, 1702, Mar. 12.
7. Hannah, 1704, Feb. 15.
8. Ruth, 1705, Dec. 9.
9. Joseph, 1709, Mar. 15.

III. SARAH, { b. d.
m.
TIMOTHY SHELDON, { b. 1661, Mar. 29. d. 1744 + of John & Joan (Vincent) Sheldon.

1. Martha, 1687, May 5.
2. Timothy, 1689, Mar. 1.
3. Daniel, 1691, Jan. 29.
4. Mary, 1693, Aug. 1.

IV. JOHN, { b. 1678. d. 1739, Jan. 30. — Providence, Smithfield, R. I.
m.
SARAH BARTLETT, { b. d. 1756, Nov. 19. of Bartlett.

No issue.

1708. Freeman.

1713, Jun. 16 Taxed 12*s*.

1718, Feb. 27. He calls himself aged about forty years, in a deposition at this date.

1735, Aug. 25. Smithfield. Licensed to keep a public house.

1737, Jun. 16. Will—proved 1739, Jan. 31. Ex. Captain Daniel Arnold. To wife Sarah, £30, and half of all other movable estate (except current money, and bills of public credit), and half of lands, westerly end of house, &c., for life. To Captain Daniel Arnold, for love and respect, £30. To negro servant man Toney, £100, and freedom. To brother Joseph Balcom's three sons, viz: Joseph, Samuel and Elijah, 5*s*. each. To cousin (*i. e.* nephew), Alexander Balcom, a fifth of all movables. To cousins Aaron, Noah, Daniel and David Arnold, one-fifth. To cousins Deborah Correy, Martha Comstock, Phebe Comstock, Sarah Balcom and Mary Balcom, one-fifth. To cousins Sarah, John, Deborah and Daniel Hayward, one-fifth. To cousins Elihu, Tabitha, Issbel, Mary and Levi Hix, one-fifth. During life of wife, half the lands to be rented and the income distributed among cousins, viz:

BALCOM. 2d column. IV. John. His wife, b. 1690, Oct. 21, of John & Alice ( ) Bartlett. Add at end of will: The Arnold cousins were children of his niece Martha Jenckes, she having married Daniel Arnold. IX. Deborah. Erase marriage and children.

one-fifth to cousin Alexander Balcom, one-fifth to the four Arnold cousins, one-fifth to brother Joseph Balcom's daughters, one-fifth to children of sister Hannah, and one-fifth to children of sister Lydia. To same cousins (*i. e.* nephews and nieces), rest of movables.

1756, Apr. 27. Will—proved 1756, Nov. 22. Widow Sarah. Exs. brothers Job and Ezra Bartlett. She mentions cousin, Captain Caleb Bartlett, son of my beloved brother, John Bartlett; cousin Alice Cass, wife of John Cass; cousin Jeremiah Inman; cousin Jeremiah Bartlett; cousin Ebenezer Darling, son of my sister Martha, and daughters of sister Martha. She also mentions sister Hannah Staples; cousin Martha Bartlett; cousin Alice Bartlett, daughters of my brother Ezra; cousin Susanna Tillotson, and cousin Richard Bartlett, son of Ezra. To Freelove Herendon, wife of Hezekiah, a legacy. To beloved Elder, Nathaniel Cook, of Cumberland, £30, that my dearly beloved husband, John Balcom, gave me in last will, &c., said money to be used in mending or repairing Baptist meeting house in Smithfield. To brothers Job and Ezra, rest of estate.

Inventory, £1,092, 18*s*. 10*d*.

V. FREEGIFT, b. d. — Providence, Smithfield, R. I.
Unmarried,

1704, Oct. 27. He bought land of Henry Brown.
1708. Freeman.
1718, Oct. 29. The Assembly authorized Town Council to sell his land, he having "for some considerable time been troubled with distraction, and out his head," and not being able to subsist himself.
1722, Jul. 7. The Town Council, of Providence, sold 74 acres for the use of Freegift Balcom.

VI. JOSEPH, b. d. 1733. — Mendon, New Sherborn, Mass.
m.
PHEBE, b. d. 1732 + of

1. Joseph,
2. Samuel,
3. Elijah,
4. Deborah,
5. Martha, 1714, May 21.
6. Phebe,
7. Sarah,
8. Mary,

1717. Mendon.
1732, Mar. 5. Will—proved 1733, May 8. Exs. wife Phebe, and Samuel Read and John Harwood, of Uxbridge. To sons Joseph, Samuel and Elijah, homestead and all real estate lying in Uxbridge and New Sherborn; the eldest son Joseph, having so much more of homestead as shall be thought worth £5. To son Joseph, also, a gun, he paying to his two brothers, 20*s*. apiece. To daughters Deborah, Phebe, Sarah and Mary Balcom, two-thirds of personal estate. To daughter Martha Comstock, 5*s*., and what she had already received. To wife Phebe, a third of personal estate for life, and the improvement of the whole of the real estate, till eldest son arrives at age, provided she remains a widow. To her while widow, which rooms she pleaseth to live in, and the improvement of a third of all real estate.

Inventory, £689, 3*s*., viz: old horse, colt, yoke of oxen, 4 cows, 4 calves, 2 heifers, bull, sheep and lambs, swine, &c.

VII. HANNAH, b. d.
m. 1716, Feb. 22.
EBENEZER HAYWARD, b. d. of Hayward.

1. Sarah,
2. John,
3. Deborah,
4. Daniel,

VIII. SAMUEL, b. d.

IX. DEBORAH, b. d.
m.
—— ARNOLD, b. d. of Arnold.

1. Aaron,
2. Noah,
3. Daniel,
4. David,

X. LYDIA, b. d.
m. 1701, Apr. 14.
DANIEL HIX, b. 1660. d. 1746, Mar. 21. of Hix.

1. Elihu,
2. Tabitha,
3. Isabel,
4. Mary,
5. Levi,

BALCOM. 2d column. X. Lydia m. 1701, Apr. 14, Samuel Hix, b. 1660, d. 1746, Mar. 21. Children, Elihu, Tabitha, Isabel, Mary, Levi. Page 438, Martha Jenckes m. John Arnold (not Daniel Arnold).

BALL. 2d column. VI. Peter. Erase his last child, and last two lines concerning son Edward. VII. John m. (2) 1718, Dec. 2, Sarah Dickens, b. 1696, July 5, of Thomas and Sarah. Children, 3, Catherine, 1719, July 29. 4, Elizabeth, 1720, Aug. 7. 5, Edward, 1727, Mar. 12. 1764, Oct. 9, will-proved, 1769, Apr. 13. Ex. son Edward. He mentions wife Sarah, son Edward, daughters Sarah Dodge, Priscilla Dunn, and Catherine Whaley; and Dunn and Dodge grandchildren. It was his son Edward who kept alive surname of Ball.

BALL.

EDWARD, b. d. 1714.
m.
MARY GEORGE, b. 1645, Sep. 7. d. 1714 +
of Peter & Mary ( ) George.

New Shoreham, R. I.
1678. Freeman.
1702. Deputy Warden.
1704. Sheriff.
1714, Aug. 16. Will—proved 1714, Aug. Exx. wife Mary, and at her death, sons Peter and John. Overseers, Simon Ray and John Sands. To wife Mary, all estate, real and personal, for life. To two sons, Peter and John, whole estate at death of wife (John having old house and land adjoining). To daughter Mary Hall, £5. To daughter Elizabeth Hall, £5. To daughter Jane Dickens, £5. To son Peter, a bed, chair, pewter platter, &c. To granddaughter Patience Hall, 1 cow. To sons Peter and John, land in Shannock (Westerly). To son Edward Ball, £30.

Inventory, 4 cows, 4 heifers, a bull, 3 steers, 2 calves, 20 sheep, 16 lambs, mare, colt, 8 hogs, wearing apparel, 16 cheeses, &c.

See: American Genealogist, v. 19, p. 130.

I. MARY, b. d.
m.
—— HALL, b. d. of Hall.

II. SYBIL, b. d.

See: American Genealogist, v. 19, p. 130

III. ELIZABETH, b. d.
m.
—— HALL, b. d. of Hall.

IV. JANE, b. d.
m.
JOHN DICKENS, b. d. of Nathaniel & Sarah ( ) Dickens.

1. John,

V. EDWARD, b. d.

VI. PETER, b. d. — New Shoreham, R. I.
m. 1716, Jun. 30.
MARY HARRIS, b. d. of Harris.

1. Mercy, 1718, Feb. 2.
2. Thankful, 1721, Oct. 26.
3. Edward, 1726.

1709. Freeman.
1734. Deputy.
1734, Jun. He and four others were appointed by the Assembly, to procure materials for building a pier at Block Island, and making a harbor there.
1735, Aug. He and Captain Simon Ray were appointed to improve the £1,200 allowed to build a pier at Block Island, or repair the old one.

His son Edward, kept alive the surname, with children John, Peter Isaiah, Nathaniel, Edward, Samuel, Elizabeth, Dorcas and Mary.

VII. JOHN, b. 1687, Jun. 10. d.
m. 1710, Sep. 11.
SARAH RATHBONE, b. 1698, Apr. 1. d. of Thomas & Mary (Dickens) Rathbone.

1. Priscilla, 1711, Aug. 9.
2. Sarah, 1714 Aug. 20.

1709. Freeman.

BALLOU (MATURIN). 2d column. 1. John, m. (2) 1679, Jan. 4.

BALLOU (MATURIN).

MATURIN, — b. — d. 1662 ±
m.
HANNAH PIKE, — b. — d. 1714 ±

of Robert & Catherine ( ) Pike.

Providence, R. I.

1646, Jan. 19. He was one of those who had a grant of 25 acres, on certain conditions. (Some of the signers of above agreement did so at a later date than above.)

1658, May 18. Freeman.

1661, Feb. 24. He was granted 6 acres in the Neck, in lieu of 12 acres which he hath yet to take up.

1673, May 6. Hannah Ballou and her father, Robert Pike, had 2 lots laid out together, taking in part of a field that hath been planted by the Indians—situated beyond Loquasquesset, measuring 160 by 120 poles.

1675. His widow's aunt, Justina Patten, (widow of Nathaniel) died in Dorchester, and left a legacy to Hannah Ballou and her children, in money and goods.

1679, Jul. 1. Widow Ballou and her mother taxed together 1*s.* 10½*d.*

1686, Mar. 1. An agreement was made at this date for division of lands, by heirs of Robert Pike and Maturin Ballou. Whereas, it has pleased God to remove Maturin Ballou and Robert Pike, formerly of Providence, each leaving some estate, in housing and lands, and they making no will, nor disposition, &c., and for the preventing of all differences, &c. Those signing were Hannah Ballou, widow of Maturin, and daughter of Robert Pike, John Ballou, eldest son, and James, Peter and Hannah Ballou, the other children of Maturin. The widow Hannah Ballou and her daughter Hannah, had for their share, the house lot which belonged to Robert Pike, and also one belonging to Maturin Ballou, with all the housing on it, and meadow, rights, &c., and three cows, 5 swine, and all household goods, and none of the above estate to be conveyed except with their consent. What estate remained undisposed of, to be to the longest liver, either Hannah the widow, or Hannah the daughter. The sons had portions of land, viz: 60 acres, commonage, &c., to John, and 60 acres, &c., to James, 10 acres, &c., to Peter. Any assistance needed by the widow was to be given equally by 3 sons, John, James and Peter.

1687, Sep. 1. Widow Ballou taxed 6*d.*

1707, Oct. 22. Hannah Ballou, widow, and Hannah Ballou, daughter, deeded a certain right of land to James Ballou.

1712, Jan. 28. Hannah Ballou, widow, deeded certain land to son James.

1712, Mar. 8. His widow Hannah, deeded for love, &c., to sons James and Peter, equally to be divided, all estate, wherever it may be found, of my aunt, Mrs. Patten, formerly of Dorchester, Mass., now deceased. To son James, also, a warehouse lot in Providence.

I. JOHN, — b. — d. 1714 ± — Providence, R. I.
m. (1)
HANNAH LARKIN, — b. — d. — of Edward Larkin.
m. (2)
HANNAH GARRET, — b. — d. — of Garret.

1672, May 1. Freeman.
1676, May 2. He, on his petition, was divorced by act of the Assembly, the Court "finding that from the first of their marriage they lived very discontentedly," &c.
1679, Jul. 1. Taxed 1*s.* 10½*d.*
1684, Oct. 29. Allowed £3 by Assembly, for cure of his wound in late Indian war.
1687, Sep. 1. Taxed 1*s.*
1687. Rateable estate, 64 acres, of which 2 acres was planting land, 2 acres meadow, 4 acres pasture, 3 cows, 2 steers, 2 yearlings, a mare, 5 swine.
1715, Mar. 4. In an indenture of this date, Peter Ballou calls himself "son of John, deceased."

(2d wife.)
1. John, 1683, Aug. 26.
2. Maturin, 1685.
3. Peter, 1689, Aug. 1.
4. Sarah,
5. Hannah,
6. Abigail,

II. JAMES, — b. 1652. — d. 1741 ± — Providence, Smithfield, R. I.
m.
SUSANNAH WHITMAN, — b. 1658, Feb. 28. — d. 1734 ± — of Valentine & Mary ( ) Whitman.

1680, Nov. 15. He gave a receipt to William Stoughton, executor of will of Justina Patten.
1687, Sep. 1. Taxed 3*s.* 2*d.*
1688. Rateable estate, 5 cows, a three years steer, 2 two years, a yearling, 30 acres woodland, 2 acres pasture, 3 acres planting, 2 horses, 1 mare.
1713, Apr. 17. He deeded son James, for love, &c., 60 acres, east side of Pawtucket River, in Wrentham, with right of common and a third of 40 acres in Dedham. On same date, he deeded to son Nathaniel, similar gift, and to son Obadiah, 45 acres in Wrentham.
1723, Nov. 13. He deeded cousin (*i. e.* nephew), Peter Ballou, for love, &c., half of a quarter of a forty foot lot, whereon said Peter's house stands, being laid out in original right of my honored father, Maturin, deceased.
1726, Jul. 27. He deeded son Samuel, all my homestead farm where I now dwell, houses, buildings, &c., and on same date deeded to son Nehemiah, half a right of common, west side of Seven Mile Line, with all the land already laid out there, 200 acres, more or less, being land my said son now dwelleth on.
1734, Apr. 20. Smithfield. He made his will, but it was never probated. Ex. son Samuel. To son Nehemiah, wearing clothes, chest, feather bed, gun, &c. To daughters Susannah Inman and Bathsheba Arnold, a trunk each. To children James, Nathaniel, Obadiah, Susannah and Bathsheba, the goods, &c., in above trunks. To son Samuel, rest of movables.
1741, Apr. 18. He distributed part of his movable estate to children, except Samuel, and took receipts from them.
1744, Jun. 15. He deeded to son Samuel, for love, &c., and in consideration of what said son hath done for me these sixteen years past, in maintenance, &c., and for future maintenance, all movable estate in Smithfield.

1. James, 1684, Nov. 1.
2. Nathaniel, 1687, Apr. 9.
3. Obadiah, 1689, Sep. 6.
4. Samuel, 1692, Jan. 23.
5. Susanna, 1695, Jan. 3.
6. Bathsheba, 1698, Feb. 15.
7. Nehemiah, 1702, Jan. 20.

III. PETER, — b. 1663. — d. 1731, Sep. 1. — Providence, Scituate, R. I.
m.
BARBARA, — b. 1672. — d. 1740. — of

1687, Sep. 1. Taxed 1*s.* 1*d.*
1718, Apr. 7. He sold Daniel Mann, for £250, my dwelling house and lands near adjoining, 82 acres, separated in two pieces by highway.
1718, Apr. 8. He bought of Joseph Dailey, 57½ acres, house, orchard, &c., for £336.
1718, Aug. 25. He testified, calling himself aged about fifty-five years, that his sister Hannah, died in the fore part of Jan., 1712. His wife Barbara, aged about forty-six years, testified that her mother-in-law Hannah Ballou, had no more understanding than a child when her sister-in-law, Hannah Ballou died.
1725, Jul. 2. He sold Joshua Winsor, for £10, certain lands and commons in original right of my honored father, Maturin Ballou.
1731, Aug. 24. Will—proved 1731, Sep. 13. Ex. son Jeremiah. To wife Barbara, feather bed, 3 cows, chest, box, 1 ewe, 1 lamb, 1 pair worsted combs, 2 basins, 2 spoons, 2 trenchers, &c., and use of fire room for life. To son Jeremiah, all lands, buildings, orchards, 1 yoke oxen, 1 mare, 1 cow, 1 calf, 1 feather bed. To granddaughters Phebe and Jerusha King, their mother Phebe King, deceased, already having had estate. To daughter Martha Ballou, 1 cow, 1 feather bed, 1 sheet, 1 mare and two colts. To 4 children Jeremiah Ballou, Barbara Inman, Jemima Sprague and Martha Ballou, all rest of movables equally. Son Jeremiah to provide for wife as maintenance, &c.
Inventory, books 6*s.*, 3 feather beds, flock bed, warming pan, 3 pewter platters, gun, 17 milch cows, 2 yoke oxen, 2 steers, bull, mare, swine, 9 calves, 3 wheels, 2 pair wool cards, &c.
1740, Feb. 15. Will—proved 1740, Mar. 7. Widow Barbara. Ex. son Jeremiah. To daughter Barbara Inman and to Phebe King's 2 daughters, and Jemima Sprague's 3 daughters, and Martha King's 2 daughters, each an equal share of wearing clothes. To son Jeremiah, bed, warming pan, great chair, &c. To Barbara Inman, and my motherless grandchildren, rest, equally.

1. Peter,
2. William,
3. Jeremiah,
4. Barbara,
5. Phebe,
6. Jemima,
7. Martha,

IV. HANNAH, — b. — d. 1712, Jan.
Unmarried.

V. SAMUEL, — b. — d. 1669, Jun. 10.
Unmarried.

1669, Jun. 10. He was drowned at this date, as shown by testimony and Coroner's inquest. Philip Taber, of Providence, aged 64 years, testified that he being in his own house, suddenly heard a noise of holloaing, &c., and went down to the river, which runneth by his house and saw William Wickenden, who told him there was a child drowned, and arriving at the river side, saw a lad lie dead in the bottom of the river, which Wm. Wickenden took out, and Wm. Wickenden's wife came down and taking an apron off the widow Ballou, who came down and stood a pretty way off the child, laid the apron on the lad, &c., and on Taber's asking whose lad it was, Wm. Wickenden made answer it was the widow Ballou's lad. Testimony was also given by Jane Taber, aged 64 years. Verdict of Coroner's inquest "that the lad, the widow Ballou, her son, named Samuel Ballou, going into the river which runneth to the mill in Providence, to wash himself, was by a Providence of God drowned."

BALLOU (ROBERT).

ROBERT, — b. — d. 1668.
m.
SUSANNA, — b. — d. 1668 +

Portsmouth, R. I., Boston, Mass.

1643, Oct. 5. He was granted a lot "he using his trade for the benefit of the town."

1668, Jun. 2. Will—proved 1668, Jur 18. Exx. wife Susanna. Overseers William Brenton, Nicholas Easton, son-in-law George Gardiner, and friend William Vaughan. He calls himself sometime of Rhode Island. To wife Susanna all estate, only to my two daughters 12*d.* apiece, desiring my wife to have a care of my grandchildren, as also of my cousins, William and Henry, and not to be unmindful of them. He did not sign the will, but declared it.
Inventory, £1, 16*s.*, viz: coat, shirt, breeches, shoes, hat, cap, &c.

I. LYDIA, — b. — d. 1722 (—)
m. (1)
GEORGE GARDINER, — b. — d. 1677 ± — of Gardiner.
m. (2) 1678,
WILLIAM HAWKINS, — b. — d. 1723, Jul. 6. — of William & Margaret ( ) Hawkins.

BALLOU (ROBERT). 2d column. 1. Lydia, m. (2) 1678, Jun. 14.

1. Samuel,
2. Joseph,
3. Lydia,
4. Mary,
5. Peregrine,
6. Robert, 1671, May.
7. Jeremiah,
(By 2d husband.)
8. William,
9. Stephen,
10. John,

II. DAUGHTER, — b. — d.

MOSES, b. 1652. d. 1733.
m. (1)
——, b. d.
m. (2) 1692, Mar. 24.
SUSANNA WAIT, b. d. 1758.
of Samuel & Hannah ( ) Wait.

South Kingstown, R. I.

1687, Sep. 6. Kings Town. Taxed 8*s.* 1*d.*

1705, Jul. 7. He and wife Susanna, deeded to his son Moses, 100 acres.

1722, Mar. 17. In a deposition, he calls himself aged seventy years and upwards.

1728, Mar. 29. Will—proved 1733, Dec. 17. Exs. wife Susannah and son Benjamin. To wife while widow, all movables, use of homestead farm and house, and at death what remains of movables to go to wife's daughter. To sons William, Moses, Samuel, Thomas and Joseph, 1*s.* each, they having had their portions. To son Benjamin, 146 acres in Westerly. To son Ezekiel, part of homestead farm, &c., loom, and wearing apparel. To son Daniel, rest of homestead, housing, orchard, &c. To youngest daughter, Ann Barber, a feather bed and £20. To all my married daughters, 5*s.* each, they having had their portions. To heirs of daughter Lydia Mowry, deceased, 5*s.*

Inventory, £452, 19*s.* 7*d.*, viz: horsekind, &c., £13, 2*s.*, neat cattle and sheep £68, swine, geese, linen wheel, 2 woolen wheels, 3 feather beds, warming pan, flock bed, worsted comb, shoemaker's tools, 2 hogsheads cider, bonds £94, books, 8 silver spoons £10, &c.

1755, Sep. 21. Will—proved 1758, Apr. 4 Susannah Barber, widow, of Charlestown. Ex. son Benjamin. To daughter Anne Kenyon, a great bible. To daughter Dinah Wilcox, the heirs of daughter Lydia Mowry, daughter Susannah Perry, widow, and daughters Martha Potter, Ruth Bentley, Mercy Tefft and Ann Kenyon, the rest of estate, equally.

Inventory, £1,351, 10*s*

BARBER. 2d column. V. Samuel. 5, Susanna, 1727, Dec. 19. 6. Edward, 1731, Nov. 17. 7, Moses, 1734, Apr. 10. 8. Samuel, 1737, Jan. 7. 9, Anne, 1739, July 24. 10. Amey, 1742, Nov. 28. 11, Meribah, 1747, Nov. 24.

* Susanna West. In the original record the name is spelled Waist

I. WILLIAM, b. d. 1748. South Kingstown, R. I.
m. (1) 1710, Mar. 22,
MERCY SMITH, b. d. of Smith.
m. (2) 1720, May 1,
SARAH MUMFORD, b. d. 1748 + of Peleg Mumford.

1. Moses,
2. Joseph,
3. Samuel,
4. James,
5. Mercy,
6. Sarah,
7. Elizabeth,
8. Mary,

1712. Kings Town. Freeman.

1744, Nov. 14. Will—proved 1748, May 17. Exs. wife Sarah and son Moses. To wife, her choice of rooms while widow, choice of beds, two cows, riding beast and £20. To son Joseph, £10. To son Samuel, 50 acres, part in South Kingstown and part in Charlestown To son James, 6¼ acres, with saw-mill in South Kingstown, and 10 acres in Charlestown. To daughter Mercy Carpenter, £5, she having had already. To daughter Sarah Barber, a feather bed, £10, and a cow at eighteen, and like legacies to daughters Elizabeth and Mary. To grandson Fenix Carpenter, £5 at age. To son Moses, rest of estate, real and personal.

Inventory, riding beast, bible and other books £3, 5 feather beds, trundle bed, pewter, warming pan, loom, 2 woolen wheels, 3 linen wheels, 6 silver spoons, cane, 2 pair stillyards, 24 sheep, 6 lambs, yoke of oxen, 5 cows and calves, 5 heifers, yearling bull, colt, geese, swine, turkeys, gun, &c.

II. MOSES, b. d. Kings Town, R. I.
m. (1) 1705, May 23,
ELIZABETH ELDRED, b. d. of Thomas & Susannah (Cole) Eldred.
m. (2) 1729, Apr. 9,
MARY LARKIN, b. d. of Larkin.

1. Moses, 1706, Feb. 25.
2. William, 1707, Sep. 4.
3. John, 1709, Apr. 19.
4. Elizabeth, 1711, Mar. 18.
5. Nicholas, 1713, Dec. 23.
6. Bridget, 1716, Jan. 23.

1704, Jan. 19. Constable.
1712. Freeman.
(2d WIFE.)

III. DINAH, b. 1693, Jan. 5. d.
m. 1716, Jun. 4,
EDWARD WILCOX, b. d. of Edward & —— (Hazard) Wilcox.

1. Mary, 1717, Oct. 4.
2. Hannah, 1720, Oct. 29.
3. Lydia, 1725, Apr. 6.
4. Susanna, 1727, Oct. 4.
5. Joseph, 1730, Aug. 27.

IV. LYDIA, b. 1694, Feb, 24. d.
m.
—— MOWRY, b. d. of Mowry.

V. SAMUEL, b. 1695, Nov. 8, d. 1760. Westerly, Richmond, R. I.
m.
ANNE, b. d. 1760 + of

1. Sarah, 1719, Nov. 28.
2. Mary, 1721, Jun. 12.
3. Benjamin, 1723, May 30.
4. Caleb,
5. Edward,
6. Moses,
7. Samuel,
8. Susanna,
9. Anne,
10. Amey,
11. Meribah,

1730. Freeman.

1760, May 27. Will—proved 1760, Jul. 11. Exs. wife Anne and son Caleb. To wife, a third of homestead farm while widow, riding horse, cow and feather bed. To son Benjamin, 5*s.*, he having had. To son Caleb, homestead farm in Richmond, &c., half of saw-mill and all farming and carpenter's tools. To son Edward, 5*s.* To son Moses, certain land. To son Samuel. land in Exeter, and one-eighth of saw-mill and all land in Charlestown. To grandson Daniel Lewis, 5*s.*, in token of love to his mother Sarah, deceased. To daughter Mary Moore, 5*s.* To daughter Susannah Potter, 5*s.* To daughter Anne Austin, 5*s.* To daughter Amey Barber, feather bed. To daughter Meribah Barber, a feather bed at eighteen. To wife Anne, rest of household goods at her disposal, to give to her daughters.

VI. SUSANNAH, b. 1697, Oct. 23. d. 1748 +
m. 1727, Oct. 11,
BENJAMIN PERRY, b. d. 1749. of Edward & Mary (Freeman) Perry.

1. Benjamin, 1729, Nov. 7.
2. Edward, 1731, Mar. 28.
3. Freeman, 1733, Jan. 23.
4. Mary, 1735, Nov. 19.
5. Susanna, 1735, Nov. 19.

VII. THOMAS, b. 1699, Oct. 19. d. 1762. Exeter, R. I.
m.
AVIS, b. d. 1762 + of

1. Martha, 1726, Oct. 9.
2. Dinah, 1729, May 3.
3. Thomas, 1731, Jun. 5.
4. Mary, 1733, Aug. 18.
5. Zebulon, 1736, Jan. 22.

1762, Nov. 9. Administration to widow Avis. Inventory, £538, 13*s.*, viz: 2 bulls, 17 goats, horse, 2 hogs, cooper's tools, testament, &c.

VIII. JOSEPH, b. 1701, Oct. 13. d. 1779. Exeter, R. I.
m. 1724, Feb. 4.
REBECCA POTTER, b. d. of Potter.

1. Nathaniel,
2. Daughter,

1779, Apr. 14. Will—proved 1779, Jun. 7. Ex. grandson Lillibridge Barber. To son Nathaniel and heirs, all lands in Exeter. To grandson Joseph Rathbone, £50, at age. To granddaughter Abigail Wilbour, £100 and like legacy to granddaughter Rebecca Wilcox. To grandson Lillibridge Barber, rest of estate.

IX. MARTHA, b. 1703, Nov. 30. d.
m. 1727, Oct. 3,
THOMAS POTTER, b. d. of Ichabod & Margaret (Helme) Potter.

X. RUTH, b. 1705, Jun. 23. d.
m. 1724, Mar. 4.
GEORGE BENTLEY, b. d. of William & Mary (Eliot) Bentley.

XI. BENJAMIN, b. 1707, Mar. 10. d. Hopkinton, R. I.
m. 1729, Jan. 11,
MARY TEFFT, b. d. of John & Joanna (Sprague) Tefft.

1. Lydia, 1730, Apr. 6.

1761, Apr. 11. He and wife Mary, sold Josiah Barber, 80 acres for £1000.

XII. MERCY, b. 1709, Mar. 13. d.
m
—— TEFFT, b. d. of Tefft.

XIII. EZEKIEL, b. 1710, Mar. 6. d. South Kingstown, R. I.
m. 1736, Nov. 28.
HANNAH WEBSTER, b. d. of Webster.

1734. Freeman.

XIV. ABIGAIL, b. 1713, Jan. 6. d. young.
Unmarried,

XV. DANIEL, b. 1715, Apr. 22. d.

Deliverance Tefft

XVI. ANN, b. 1717, Oct. 8. d.
m.
—— KENYON, b. d. of Kenyon.

BARBER. 2d column. Add another child, viz: Sarah, b. 1682, Mar. 25, d. 1779, Jun. 29, m. 1706, Jun. 24, David Greene, of James & Elizabeth (Anthony) Greene, b. 1677, Jun. 24, d. 1761, Jan. 29. Children, 1. Mary, 1707, Jun. 5. 2. Sarah, 1709, Jan. 20. 3. Elizabeth, 1711, Mar. 25. 4. Susanna, 1713, May 1. 5. Abigail, 1715, Mar. 25. 6. Waite, 1716, Dec. 2. 7. Bathsheba, 1720, Jul. 30. 8. Jonathan, 1722, Aug. 2. 9. Joseph, 1724, May 30. 10. Patience, 1726, Feb. 15.

JAMES,[3] (James[2] James[1]). b. 1623. d. 1702.
m. 1644,
BARBARA DUNGAN, b. 1628 ± d.

of William & Frances (Latham) Dungan.

Harwich, Essex Co., Eng., Newport, R. I.

He embarked with his father, in the same ship with Nicholas Easton, and his father dying on the passage, directed that this son should be in the care of the boy's aunt Christianna, then wife of Thomas Beecher, and subsequently wife of Nicholas Easton. He probably remained with his aunt at Charlestown, Mass., until her marriage with Nicholas Easton, brought her to Newport, in 1639.

1644. Corporal.

1648. Ensign.

1648. Member of General Court of Elections.

1653, May 18. He and another were messengers to demand the statute books of Mr. Coddington.

1655. Freeman.

1655-61-63. Commissioner.

1661. He was a member of the committee to receive contributions to amount of £200, for the agents in England (Roger Williams and John Clarke), who were to obtain charter. The same year he had half of a share allotted at Misquamicut (Westerly), and was appointed one of a committee of Trustees to manage all affairs connected with that purchase. He never settled there.

1663, Jul. 8. Named among those appearing in Royal Charter, granted this year by Charles II.

1663, Oct. 8. He testified about land, calling himself aged about forty years.

1663-64-65-66-71-72-76-77-78. Assistant,

1667-69-70-71-74-76-77-81-83-84-85-86. Deputy.

1670, Jun. 20. He was commissioned, with others in the matter of "an entrance made into our jurisdiction by some of Connecticut, and of their carrying away some of its inhabitants prisoners." Ten days later he was allowed 4*s.* for his "voyage to Narragansett, to the Connecticut commissioners."

1672, Feb. 27. He and John Easton, were arbitrators in a controversy between Stephen Sabeere and Henry Palmer, of Newport.

1674, Sep. 29. He and Caleb Carr, Sr., bought for £60, of Awansuck, squaw sachem of Seaconnet, and her husband Waweeyonit and son Amos, "all our lands lying and being at Seaconnet," &c.

1676, Apr. 4. Voted by Assembly, "that in these troublesome times and straits in this Colony, the Assembly desiring to have the advice and concurrence of the most judicious inhabitants, if it may be had for the good of the whole, do desire at their next sitting, the company and counsel of" sixteen persons, among them James Barker. In the same year he was on a committee to order "watch and ward of the island."

1677. He was on a court to attend to matter of "injurious and illegal acting of some of Connecticut Colony."

1678. Deputy Governor.

1687, Mar. 22. He and his son James, were appointed overseers of John Peabody's will.

1690. He assisted in the ordination of Rev. Richard Dingley, the records of the First Baptist Church stating that it was performed by Mr. Thomas Skinner, of Boston and "James Barker, a ministering brother belonging to this church." A family manuscript calls Mr. Barker "a teaching brother among the Baptists many years."

1696, May 17. He made oath with others, to the inventory of Rev. John Clarke's estate.

I. ELIZABETH, b. d. 1676, Jul. 5.
m. 1666, Nov. 30,
NICHOLAS EASTON, b. 1644, Nov. 12. d. 1677, Feb. 1. of Peter & Ann (Coggeshall) Easton.

Children: 1. Nicholas, 1668, Feb. 24. 2. Elizabeth, 1669, Dec. 6. 3. Freelove, 1671, Mar. 12. 4. Patience, 1675, Apr. 22.

II. JAMES, b. 1648. d. 1722, Dec. — Newport, R. I.
m. 1673,
SARAH JEFFERAY, b. 1656. d. 1736, Feb. of William & Mary (Gould) Jefferay.

Children: 1. James, 1675, Dec. 4. 2. William, 3. Nicholas, 4. Mary, 5. Abigail, 6. Priscilla, 7. Jane, 8. Jeremiah, 1699, Jan. 16.

1667. He enlisted in the troop of horse, formed to protect the island.

His great grandson (James Barker[7]), in a family manuscript already alluded to, calls his ancestor, "a very bold man."

1675. Freeman.

1676, Aug. 24. He was a member of the Court Martial held at Newport, for the trial of certain Indians, charged with being engaged in King Philip's designs.

1678-90-96-1703-5-6-7-8-9-16. Deputy.

1687. Grand Jury. From this date forward he was called Captain.

1695-96-98-99. Assistant.

1702, Feb. 4. He was on a committee of fourteen persons, appointed by the proprietors to attend to division of common lands, and continued a member of the committee till after 1715. He received 18 acres, as his share of lands.

1707, Jan. 23. He with other members of Second Baptist Church, received a deed from their pastor, James Clarke, of the land and church building. Mr. Clarke had bought the land some years before, (1697, Oct. 23), from contributions of the members of his church, taking the deed in his own name, and built the church in the same year that he purchased land. He now, therefore, deeded both land and building to eighteen members of his church. The division of this church from the parent organization occurred in 1656, the reasons therefor being thus stated: "said persons conceived a prejudice against psalmody, and against the restraints that the liberty of prophesying was laid under, and also against the doctrine of particular redemption, and against the rite of laying on of hands as a matter of indifference." (Morgan Edwards gives the names of the separators of the year 1656, as identical with the parties to the deed of 1707, whereas, some of the latter were not born at the earlier date.)

1708. He with others was chosen "to proportion and affix rates of grain and other specie," which were to be received as pay for a tax. They appointed a bushel of corn to be accepted at 2*s*; barley at 1*s.* 8*d*; rye 2*s*, 6*d*; oats 4*d*; wool 9*d*; wheat 3*d*.

III. MARY, b. d. 1723, Sep. 19.
m. (1)
ELISHA SMITH, b. d. 1676 ± of Edward Smith.
m. (2) 1677, Apr. 16,
ISRAEL ARNOLD, b. 1649, Oct. 30. d. 1716, Sep. 15. of Stephen & Sarah (Smith) Arnold.

(By 2d. husband.) 1. Israel, 1678, Jan. 18. 2. Mary, 3. William, 4. Stephen, 5. Elisha, 6. James, 1689. 7. Sarah, 8. Josiah, 9. Joseph, 10. Barbara,

IV. SARAH, b. d.
Unmarried,

V. JOSEPH, b. d. 1725 + — Newport, R. I.
m.
SARAH READ, b. d. of Read.

Children: 1. Joseph, 2. Peter,

1684. Constable.

VI. PETER, b. d. 1725. — Newport, Westerly, R. I.
m. (1) 1692 (—),
FREELOVE BLISS, b. 1672, Nov. 16. d. 1708 + of John & Damaris (Arnold) Bliss.
m. (2) 1712 (—),
SUSANNA SAUNDERS, b. d. 1725 + of Tobias & Mary (Clarke) Saunders.

Children: 1. Penelope, 1698. 2. Freelove, 1698. 3. Peter, 1701. 4. Thomas, 1703, Dec. 31. 5. Hannah,

He belonged to the Seventh Day Baptist Church.

1692. He and his wife Freelove, and her mother, Damaris, were members of the church at Newport.

1712, Feb. 15. He, of Newport, sold to Jeremiah Clarke, 10 acres for £80.

1718. Westerly. He and his wife Susanna, were members of the church.

1725, Dec. 7. Administration to widow Susanna. Bondsmen (for inventory), Edward Bliven and Joseph Barker. Inventory, £902, 5*s.* 2*d.*, viz: wearing apparel £14, 8*s.*, pair of oxen, 4 cows, 3 two year, 4 yearlings, 3 calves, mare, horse, colt, 3 sheep, 3 shoats, cider mill, 2 spinning wheels, warming pan, 2 guns, sword and belt £16, 8*s.*, 3 bibles and other books £1, 15*s.*, old settle, farm and housing £700, &c.

His widow also had bondsmen for her administration of husband's estate, viz; her brothers Edward and Stephen Saunders.

BARKER. 2d column. VI. Peter. His 2d wife was more likely, Susanna Peckham[2] (John[1]). If so, changes should be made in Barker, Peckham, Saunders and Wells pages.

VII. CHRISTIANNA, b. d.
m.
WILLIAM PHILLIPS, b. d. of Michael & Barbara ( ) Phillips.

VIII. WILLIAM, b. 1662. d. 1741, Nov. 3. — Newport, R. I.
m.
ELIZABETH EASTON, b. 1666, Feb. 18. d. 1715, Mar. 24. of Peter & Ann (Coggeshall) Easton.

Children: 1. Ann, 1688, Nov. 29. 2. Elizabeth, 1690, May 24. 3. James, 1692, Jan. 26. 4. Patience, 1694, Apr. 27. 5. Peter, 1696, Jan. 28. 6. Mary, 1698, Jan. 10. 7. William, 1700, Apr. 9. 8. Frances, 1702, Mar. 10. 9. Wait, 1705, Jun. 2. 10. Joshua, 1707, Nov. 10. 11. Abigail, 1707, Nov. 10.

He was a Quaker.

1691. Freeman.

1704-21-22-23-24. Deputy.

BARNES (RICHARD).

RICHARD, b. d. 1687.

Newport, R. I.

1677, Oct. 31. He and forty-seven others were granted 5,000 acres, to be called East Greenwich.

1678, Apr. 30. Freeman.

1682. Solicitor.

1687, Apr. 8. Will—proved 1687, Jun. 22. Ex. friend John Ward. To sister Susanna Loader, £10. To sisters Mary Hyes, Alice Wilkins and Hester, like legacies. To Samuel Bailey, a piece of gold. To William James, £5. To executor, the rest of estate, whether money, sheep, or horsekind.

Inventory, £148, 9*s.*, viz: wearing apparel, £2, saddle, stillyards, rapier, 5 books, pistol, mare, colt, 50 sheep, bond £90, &c.

BARKER. 2d column. II. James, d. 1722, Dec. 1. 1722, Nov. 8. Will—proved 1723, Jan. 7. Ex. son James. To son James, housing and lands whereon I now dwell, 120 acres, bounded westerly on a highway, northerly on land of widow Sarah Tew, &c., southerly on land of brother William Barker, &c; together with houses, orchard, &c., on condition that he confirms by deed of gift to my son Jeremiah, 20 acres where said James dwells, &c. To son William, 500 acres in Narragansett and £100. To daughters Abigail Wright, Jane Lawton and Priscilla Lawton, £50, each. To son Nicholas, £50. To son Jeremiah, 20 acres, negro man Jack and a third of live stock. To granddaughter Sarah Winsor, £10. To son James, two-thirds of live stock. To daughters Abigail, Priscilla and Jane, all plate and pewter. To sons James and Jeremiah, rest of personal. Son James to provide well beloved wife Sarah, his mother, an "honorable, decent and comfortable maintenance." If son Jeremiah, by reason of a long sickness he has had should be weakened in understanding, his brother James to be guardian. Inventory, wearing apparel with plate buttons thereon £22, plate £4, 12*s.*, books, spectacles, razor, &c. Rooms named were new room, out room, leanto out chamber, new chamber, cellar, cheese room. His daughter Mary, was b. 1678, Mar. 13.

VI. Peter. His widow Susanna, d 1733 +. Children by her were 6. Joseph, 7. John, 8. Daughter, 9. Sarah, 10. Barbara, 11. Susanna, 12. Patience His widow m. Peter Wells. 1733, Feb. 1, Susanna Wells, of South Kingstown gave receipt to son in-law (*i. e.* stepson) James Wells, executor of Peter Wells, for £3, due from deceased Peter Wells to "my daughter Sarah Barker." Other receipts showed names of additional children of Peter Barker.

BARNES (THOMAS.) 1st column. His wife was Prudence Albee, daughter of Benjamin Albee.

THOMAS, { b. d. 1706, Jun. 8.
m. (1)
PRUDENCE, { b. d.
m. (2) 1694, Nov. 12, [Clem.
ELIZABETH KING, (w. of { b. d. 1708, Nov. 27.

Swanzey, Mass.

1669. He was in Swanzey as early as this year.

1689, Feb. 7. He was among the proprietors of Rehoboth, named in a list of this date—but not resident there.

1693. Ordained as pastor of Second Baptist Church, and continued in the pastorate till his death.

1705, May 7. Will—proved 1706, Jul. 3 Exs. wife Elizabeth and son Samuel. Overseer, son-in-law Thomas Allen. To wife Elizabeth, the bed, &c., that were hers before marriage, and two cows and two calves, bought for her estate, and pewter, &c, brought into house since she was my wife. To her also, privilege of dwelling in house while his widow, and 20*s.* a year, only wife shall make good the agreement concerning Mary Barnes, according to indentures. (This Mary was daughter of testator's son Thomas.) To eldest son, Thomas, the bed called my bed. To son John, besides 20 acres already given him where his house stands, he gave wearing apparel and shoes. To son Peter, £10. To youngest son, Samuel, rest of estate, as lands, houses, money, goods and cattle, &c., when he is of age, he paying legacies. To daughter Lydia Olney, wife to Thomas Olney, at Providence, £3. To daughter Anne, wife to Thomas Allen, at Swanzey, £6. To daughter Sarah, wife to Benjamin Wight, at Providence, 10*s.*, they having had part. To daughter Elizabeth, wife to John Bullock, at Providence, £7. To youngest daughter, Hannah Barnes, 30*s.*

Inventory, £433, 14*s.* 8*d.*, viz: house and 75 acres, £140, a lot of 60 acres, £60, bible, other books, spectacles, spinning wheel, wool cards, carpenters and joiners tools, cash £6, 6*s.* 6*d.*, 2 deer skins, 1 mare, sheep, neat cattle, swine, &c.

1706, &c. Receipts were given Exs. by John Stone and Hannah, Richard Bowen, of Rehoboth, John Bullock and Elizabeth, of Swanzey, Thomas Allen, of Swanzey, Anne Kay, of Portsmouth, for amount due husband Thomas Kay.

1708, Dec. 27. Inventory, Elizabeth Barnes, widow, £112, 7*s.* 10*d.*, viz: lands, wearing apparel, wax, bayberry, beds, cash, &c. Administration to eldest son, John King, of Providence.

I. LYDIA, { b. d. 1722 +
m. 1687, Jul. 13,
THOMAS OLNEY, { b. 1661, May 4. d. 1718, Mar. 1. of Thomas & Elizabeth (Marsh) Olney.

1. Lydia, 1688, Apr. 30.
2. Phebe, 1689, Oct. 29.
3. Sarah, 1693, Aug. 26.
4. Thomas, 1696, Jan. 18.
5. Elizabeth, 1698, Jan. 29.
6. Anne, 1700, Mar. 26.
7. Mary, 1702, Feb. 25.
8. Obadiah, 1710, Feb. 14.

II. THOMAS, { b. 1670, Nov. 13. d. 1706, Sep. 24. Swanzey, Mass., Providence, R. I.
m. 1697, Mar. 25,
SARAH STONE, { b. d. of Hugh & Abigail (Busecot) Stone.

1. Mary, 1698, Apr. 13.
2. Thomas, 1699, Dec. 8.

1706, Sep. 20. Will—proved 1706. Ex. John Stone. He leaves his son Thomas to the care of John Stone, of Warwick, till of age. His daughter Mary, is bound to Elizabeth Barnes (his step-mother), till of age, and if Elizabeth die before testator's daughter Mary is of age, then Mary is given to care of executor. He wishes his brother-in-law, Thomas Allen and Dr. James Tallman, his careful and kind physician, paid. All rest of estate is given to executor. He died in Swanzey, during temporary residence.

Inventory, £31, 6*s.* 1*d*,

BARNES (THOMAS). 2d column. III. Sarah. Her husband, b. 1674, Jan. 30, d. 1755, Jul. 28, of Samuel and Hannah (Albee) Wight. Children, 1. Benjamin. 2. Jabez. 3. Silvanus. 4. Anne. 5. Sarah. 6. Samuel. IV. Elizabeth. Her husband was son of Richard and Elizabeth (Billington) Bullock.

III. SARAH, { b. 1672, Aug. 27. d.
m.
BENJAMIN WIGHT, { b. d. of Wight.

IV. ELIZABETH, { b. 1675, Feb. 14. d.
m. 1695, Jan. 29,
JOHN BULLOCK, { b. 1664, May 19. d. of Richard & Elizabeth (Ingraham) Bullock.

V. ANNE, { b. d. 1719 +
m.
THOMAS ALLEN, { b. d. 1719, Aug. 12. of William & Elizabeth ( ) Allen.

1. Elizabeth,
2. Matthew,
3. Thomas, 1706, Oct. 13.
4. Anne,
5. Rebecca,
6. Alathsie,
7. Abigail,

VI. JOHN, { b 1680, Apr. 9. d. Providence, R. I.
m. 1702, Jan. 1,
MERCY ALLEN, { b. d. of William & Elizabeth ( ) Allen.

1726, Oct. 15. He bought of Zachariah Eddy and wife Anphillis, 124 acres, for £140.
1728, Apr. 4. He bought of John Church, a quarter of a saw mill, &c., on Chapatset River, for £11.

1. Ezra, 1703, Mar. 21.
2. John, 1704, Sep. 28.
3. Abial, 1706, Jun. 20.
4. Thomas, 1708, Sep. 18.
5. Anne, 1710, May 7.
6. Mercy, 1712, Feb. 26.
7. Phebe, 1713, May 10.
8. Amy, 1716, Jan. 25.
9. William, 1716, May 27.
10. Freelove, 1718, Feb. 23.
11. Benjamin, 1720, Feb. 9.
12. Joseph, 1722, Jan. 30.
13. Hannah, 1725, Jan. 4.
14. Matthew, 1726, Aug. 15.

VII. PETER, { b. 1682, Jun. 1. d. 1757 ± Providence, Smithfield, R. I.
m. 1716, Sep. 29, [Jos.
MARGARET BORDEN, (w. of { b. d. of Jonathan & Margaret (Angell) Whipple.

He was a carpenter.

1708. Freeman.
1715, Mar. 8. He and Benjamin Wight, sold Thomas Angell 198 acres for £250.
1741, Jun. 5. Smithfield. He deeded son Nathan, for love, &c., 91½ acres, part of homestead.
1745, Apr. 17. He deeded son Enoch, for love, &c., half my homestead farm (100 acres in whole).
1750, Apr. 18. He deeded son John, for love, &c., 70 acres adjoining my homestead.
1757, Oct. 15. His son Nathan, of Smithfield, to fulfill desire and request of deceased father, Peter, quit-claimed to brother Enoch, all interest in homestead farm, where Enoch now dwells, with buildings, &c.

1. Nathan, 1718, Aug. 29.
2. Enoch, 1721, Aug 18.
3. Lydia, 1724, Oct. 29.
4. John, 1726, Dec. 31.

VIII. SAMUEL, { b 1685, Mar. 17. d.

IX. HANNAH, { b. 1689, Dec. 21. d.
m.
JOHN STONE, { b. 1675. d. 1759. of Hugh & Abigail (Busecot) Stone.

1. John, 1705.
2. George, 1709.
3. William, 1711.

(2d WIFE, no issue.)

BASTER.

ROGER, { b. d. 1687.
m.
——— { b. d.

Newport, R. I.

1666, May 2. Freeman.

1667, Sep. 26. He had a letter of this date signed A. C., a prisoner in Plymouth Island (England). "There went over to your parts since you did, one Thomas Wilkey and his wife and Sergeant Turner and his, some of which formerly were members of the church of Dartmouth. I have not this long time, by reason of imprisonment heard of them.

1671, Dec. 16. In a letter from Samuel Hubbard, of Newport, to his children at Westerly, he gives some account of the differences between those of the church who held the Seventh Day views and the rest of the congregation. Among those who favored the observance of the Seventh Day, was Roger Baster.

1671, Dec. 23. He and William Hiscox, Stephen Mumford, Samuel Hubbard, sister Mumford, sister Hubbard and sister Rachel Langworthy, &c., entered into a church covenant, as Samuel Hubbard writes.

1678, Jul. 16. He united with others in sending a letter of reproof to Jonathan Rogers, of New London, for carrying a burden on the Sabbath, &c., and in another letter of reproof to Japheth, Indian, for growing cold and vain.

1680. Taxed 2*s.*

It is assumed that Joseph Baster, of Providence, was a son of Roger, also that Sarah Baster (baptised 1674, Mar. 26), was a daughter, and Philip a son.

1687, Apr. 27. Will—presented 1687, Jun. 16.

Inventory, £16, 17*s* 3*d.*

I. JOSEPH, { b. d. 1744 (—). Providence, R. I.
m. 1725, Jul. 6,
DEBORAH INMAN, { b. d. 1762, Dec. 29. of John & Mary (Whitman) Inman.

No issue.

He was a cooper.

1726, Jan. 19. He bought two house lots of Cotton Palmer, for £45, an allusion being made to a covenant entered into before the marriage of said Joseph and Deborah.

On same date, he and wife Deborah, sold two house lots, &c., for £30, to James Dexter.

1744, Apr. 10. Will—proved 1763, Jan. 25. Widow Deborah. Ex. cousin Samuel Bartlett. To all the children of brothers and sisters living at my decease, she gives her estate.

Inventory, £1,847, 13*s.* 7*d.*

II. PHILIP, { b. d.

1692, Jun. 11. He attested to marriage of Sarah Baster.

III. SARAH, { b. 1674 ± d.
m. 1691, Dec. 17,
THOMAS HUNTER, { b. d. 1728, Apr. 25. of Hunter.

BASTER. 1st column. Roger, b. 1631, d. 1687, Apr. 23. Unmarried. He was a blockmaker. Buried in Newport Cemetery. Erase sentence between 1680 and 1687, Apr. 27. Erase 2d and 3d columns.

SAMSON, } b.
m. } d.
DINAH, } b.
} d. 1698, Nov. 16.

of

Jamestown, R. I.

1677, Oct. 31. He and forty-seven others were granted 5,000 acres, to be called East Greenwich.

1680. Taxed 5*s*. 6*d*.

1693, Oct. 24. He bought of Thomas and Abigail Mumford, of Kings Town, for £42, 300 acres, in Pettaconscutt.

1695, Jul. 15. Lieutenant.

1700, Apr. 30, Freeman.

1706–16. Deputy.

1711, Mar. 21. His daughter Dinah, was drowned only three days after her marriage. "The said Dinah Greene, deceased, the 21st of March, 1710–11, and was drowned by the boat upsetting, in going from Newport to Jamestown."

No connection has been traced between Samson Battey and James Battey. The latter, late inhabitant of Hog Island, died 1690, Nov. 17, intestate, and left behind him, wife and children; and she being a weakly woman, for sometime bedridden, and inventory being found inconsiderable, administration was given to John Borden, by the town council of Portsmouth, at the above date.

I. PHEBE, { b. 1687, Jul. 6. | d.
m. 1705, Jan. 3,
WILLIAM THURSTON, { b. 1680. | d. 1717, Jun. 21. of Edward & Susanna (Jefferay) Thurston.

1. Priscilla,
2. Mary,
3. William,

II. JOHN, { b. 1688, Sep. 7. | d. 1767. Warwick, R. I.
m. 1707, Sep. 16,
MARGARET CARR, { b. 1684, Oct. 22. | d. 1765 + of Nicholas & Rebecca (Nicholson) Carr.

1. Samson, 1709, Dec. 18.
2. Nicholas, 1711, May 18.
3. Dinah, 1713, Oct. 12.
4. Rebecca, 1715, Sep. 26.
5. William, 1718, Jan. 20.
6. John, 1720, Mar. 13.
7. Margaret, 1722, Dec. 13.
8. Phebe, 1725, Feb. 20.
9. Caleb, 1729, Jun. 22.

1765, Oct. 31. Will—proved 1767, Apr. 11. Exs. sons John & Caleb. To daughter Dinah Battey, 30 Spanish silver milled dollars, a case of drawers, the best bed, silver porringer and two spoons. To daughter Rebecca Corpe, wife of Thomas Corpe, 30 Spanish milled dollars and a bed. To daughter Phebe Battey, 30 Spanish milled dollars, a bed, spoon, &c. To son William, 100 Spanish milled dollars and a bed. To sons Caleb and John, negro named Newport, and wearing apparel. To grandson Josiah, son of my son Samson, deceased, a silver spoon and small fowling piece, bed, chest, and 30 Spanish milled dollars. To grandson Benjamin, son of son Nicholas, deceased, an English crown. To grandsons Nicholas and Sylvanus, sons of son Nicholas, deceased, 30 Spanish milled dollars each, at age. To wife Margaret, all the rest of household goods, (except great bible), for life, and then to my three daughters, Dinah, Rebecca and Phebe. To wife, best room in house, and use of bed-room, horse, &c., and sons John and Caleb to provide her with necessaries. To son Caleb, the great bible. To daughters Dinah and Phebe, use of great chamber while single. To sons John and Caleb, mansion house and homestead farm in Warwick, and all lands elsewhere, and rest of personal, except books. To son John, Gordian's Geography and Present State of England. The small books, to children equally.

III. DINAH, { b. 1691, May 12. | d. 1711, Mar. 21.
m. 1711, Mar. 15,
FONES GREENE, { b. 1690, Mar. 23. | d. 1758, Jul. 29. of James & Mary (Fones) Greene.

IV. WILLIAM, { b. 1693, Mar. 6. | d. 1749 + Jamestown, R. I.
m.
JANE, { b. | d. of

1. Priscilla, 1712, Apr. 22.
2. Joseph, 1713, Nov. 4.
3. Phebe, 1717, Aug. 31.
4. Rebecca, 1720, Jul. 14.
5. William,

He was ferryman.

1733, Dec. 11. He deeded land, calling himself ferryman.

1717. Freeman.

1719–21. Deputy.

V. CLEMENCE, { b. 1695, Jul. 4. | d.

VI. DAUGHTER, { b. 1698, Oct. 5. | d. 1698, Oct. 5.

BAULSTONE.

WILLIAM, } b. 1600.
m. } d. 1678, Mar. 14.
ELIZABETH, } b. 1597.
} d. 1683, Apr. 15.

of

Boston, Mass., Portsmouth, R. I.

1630, Oct. 19. Freeman.

1630, Nov. 9. He was on a jury for the trial of Walter Palmer, concerning death of Austin Blatcher.

1634, May 14. Sergeant.

1637, Jun. 6. He was licensed to keep a house of entertainment and to sell such claret and white wine as is sent for.

1637, Nov. 2. He was disfranchised, fined £20, and discharged from bearing any public office, for setting his hand to a "seditious libel called a remonstrance or petition." This petition had been signed by himself and others, in the previous March, they affirming that Mr. Wheelwright was innocent, and that the court had condemned the truth of Christ.

1637, Nov. 20. He and others were warned to deliver up all guns, pistols, swords, powder, shot, &c., because "the opinions and revelations of Mr. Wheelwright and Mrs. Hutchinson, have seduced and led into dangerous errors many of the people here in New England"

1638, Mar. 7. Portsmouth. He and eighteen others signed the following compact: "We, whose names are underwritten, do here, solemnly, in the presence of Jehovah, incorporate ourselves into a Bodie Politick, and as he shall help, will submit our persons, lives and estates, unto our Lord Jesus Christ, the King of Kings and Lord of Lords, and to all those perfect and most absolute laws of his, given us in his holy word of truth, to be guided and judged thereby."

1638, May 2. He was fined 20*s*. for selling beer at 2*d*. a quart.

1638, May 13. He was present at a General Meeting, upon public notice.

1638, May 20. He was granted 6 acres. On the same date he was allowed to "erect and set up a house of entertainment for strangers, and also to brew beer and to sell wines or strong waters and such necessary provisions as may be useful in any kind."

1628, Jun. 27. Sergeant of the Train Band.

1640–41. Treasurer for Portsmouth and Newport.

1641–42–43–44–48–57–58–59–60–61–62–63–64–65–66–67–68–69–70–71–72–73. Assistant.

1642. Lieutenant.

1643, Apr. 10. He and another were appointed to go to every inhabitant of Portsmouth and see whether every one of them has powder, and what bullets run.

I. ELIZABETH, { b. | d. 1696 +
m. (1) 1647, Jun. 17,
JOHN COGGESHALL, { b. 1618. | d. 1708, Oct. 1. of John & Mary ( ) Coggeshall.
m. (2) 1655.
THOMAS GOULD, { b. | d. 1693, Aug. 20. of Jeremiah & Priscilla (Grover) Gould.

1. John, 1650, Feb. 12.
2. Elizabeth, 1650, Feb. 12.
3. William, 1654 ±
(By 2d husband, no issue.)

1643-44. Treasurer for Portsmouth.

1644, Aug. 29. He and another were to view the deer that Ousamequin, with ten men were given liberty to kill upon this island, within the town of Portsmouth. The liberty was to kill ten deer, and neither Ousamequin, nor any of his men shall carry any deer or skins off from the island, but at the town of Portsmouth, and to depart from off the island within five days. On the same date, it was ordered that Mr. Baulstone should have £9 a year for John Motts' washing and diet.

1645, Aug. 14. He bought of Thomas Spicer, of New Netherlands, and Michall, his wife, a dwelling house and 8 acres, in Portsmouth, for £18 and last year's rent.

1646, Feb. 4. The wolf catchers were ordered to come to him and Mr. Sanford for their pay. The pay for killing a wolf was £4 from Newport, and 20*s.* from Portsmouth. The town concurred with Newport in an order at this date, for no shooting of deer for two months, that the wolves the more readily come to bait, that they may be catched for the general good of the island.

1654, Oct. 3. His daughter Elizabeth, signed agreement of divorce with first husband.

1654-55-58-59-60-61-62-63. Commissioner.

1655. Freeman.

1659, May 17. He and three others, were appointed to buy land about a place called Nyantecutt, of the sachem Ninecroft.

1664. He was one of the four commissioners appointed to meet the commissioners from Plymouth Colony, to lay out the eastern line.

1667, Aug. 10. He enlisted in a troop of horse.

1677, Mar. 11. Will—proved 1677, Mar. 23. Exs. grandsons John and William Coggeshall. To wife Elizabeth, use of all personal, and use of any room, privilege of fruit in orchard, and to have £12 paid her yearly by grandson John Coggeshall, in consideration of use of my farm, on which he lives (he to pay his grandmother the sum of £5 in money, and rest in a barrel of pork). At death of wife, John is to pay my daughter Elizabeth Gould, said £12. Grandson William Coggeshall (or whoever heirs the lands about this town given him by me), to yearly find and allow my said wife (his grandmother), during her life, pasture and feed for 5 cows, winter and summer, and at her death to continue the pasture and feed for my daughter Elizabeth Gould. To grandson John Coggeshall and male heirs, all my farm in Portsmouth, with buildings, &c. To grandson William Coggeshall and male heirs, lands and meadows in place called Clay Pit lands, &c. If grandson John die without male heirs, his brother William and male heirs to have land, he paying £60 to female heirs of his brother, if there are any. Like privilege for John to inherit from his brother. To grandchild Elizabeth Peck, wife of Thomas, £50. Having had it seriously in mind to give to sons of my brothers in England, in the common fence, yet upon further mature consideration, I not hearing whether any of my kindred are alive, I do therefore give all said land, to 2 grandson's John and William Coggeshall. At death of wife, all personal to be for use of daughter, Gould, and if she be then a widow, the profit of it to be paid her while widow, and if she need it, the profit of a third of the land. To son-in-law Gould, £5.

BEERE.

{ EDWARD, { b.
{ m. { d.
{ —— { b.
{ d.

Dorsetshire, Eng.

I. { JOHN, { b. 1630. Newport, R. I.
{ m. 1664, Sep. 4. { d. 1671, Jul. 29.
{ PATIENCE CLIFTON, { b. 1646, Jul. 2.
{ d. 1692, Oct. 16. of Thomas & Mary ( ) Clifton.

(She m. (2) 1677, May 16, William Allen.)

1. Mary, 1666, Aug. 6.
2. Edward, 1669, Aug. 1.
3. Patience, 1671, Sep. 6.

1671. Freeman.

He died at sea, and the Friends' Records also state that he was the son of Edward Beere, of Dorsetshire.

II. { HENRY, { b. Newport, R. I.
{ m. 1668, Sep. 28, { d. 1691, Jun. 11.
{ PATIENCE SCOTT, { b. 1648.
{ d. 1707 + of Richard & Catherine (Marbury) Scott.

1. Edward,
2. Henry, 1673, Sep. 7.
3. Catherine, 1675, Oct. 22.
4. John, 1678, Dec. 29.
5. Catherine, 1681, Feb. 25.
6. Charles, 1683, Sep. 4.
7. Mary, 1684, Sep. 15

1671. Freeman.

1680. Taxed 13*s.*

1707, Nov. 6. His sons Edward and Henry Beere, mariners, for £250, sold John Beere, all their right in house and lot now or late in occupation of Patience Beere, at decease of our mother Patience, said tenement having been bequeathed by our father Henry, to said mother, for life.

1709, May 4. He and William Wanton, were to be paid £112, 10*s.*, for a quarter of the sloop Endeavour, as voted by the Assembly at this date.

III. { CHARLES, { b. Newport, R. I.
{ d.

1680. Taxed 3*s.*

1688. Licensed.

1688, Sep. 6. He was sued by Joshua Brodbent, for a debt of £20, &c., but plead in defence that he owed nothing.

{ John, { b.
{ d. 1656 +

Warwick, R. I.

1656, Nov. 27. He deeded to Stukeley Westcott, for a maintenance by him, all lands and housing and goods, only reserving power to dispose of £5. A receipt was given him by Stukeley Westcott, for eight head of cattle, nineteen pounds of peage (eight per penny) and a house and land, and agreed to maintain John Bennett, for life, in meat, drink and apparel.

BENNETT (Robert).

{ Robert, { b.
{ d.
m.
{ Rebecca, { b.
{ d.

Newport, R. I.

He was a tailor.

1639. He was in the employ of William Coddington; and was granted 10 acres this year.

1655. Freeman.

BENNETT (Robert). 2d column. IV. Jonathan, m. Anne. She d. 1708 +. 1708, Jul. 5. Will—proved 1708, Sep. 6. Exx. wife Anne. Overseers, Thomas Cornell, and brother Robert Bennett. To first born son John, west half of housing and lands, at age. To son Jonathan, eastern half, and silver tankard at decease of his mother. To daughters Rebecca and Anne Bennett, £30 each, at twenty-one. To wife Anne, rest of personal, and profits of land till eldest son is of age, and her thirds for life. To her also [illegible] windmill on. Inventory, silver spoon, tankard, cup, porringer, &c. 48 oz., at 6s., per oz.; goods in shop, &c.

uel Bennett. See also: Bowen's [illegible] OF ALLEGIANCE, p. 63-65.

I. { Joseph, { b. 1644.
{ d. 1708, May 31.
m.
{ Margaret, { b.
{ d. of

Newport, R. I.

1. Joseph, 1674, Oct. 1.

1668. Freeman.
1679, Oct. 22. Juryman.
1680. Taxed 6s.
1700, May 4. He was appointed High Sheriff by Assembly, during absence of Thomas Mallett.
1702, Mar. 4. He was a proprietor in common lands.
He was buried in Newport Cemetery.

BENNETT (Robert). 2d column. Joseph. He had another child, Mary, who m. John Peckham of Little Compton, R. I., where his widow died after 1723.

II. { Robert, { b. 1650, Mar.
{ d. 1722.
m. (1)
{ Anne Cory, { b.
{ d. of William & Mary (Earle) Cory.
m. (2)
{ Joanna, { b.
{ d. 1726 + of

Newport, Portsmouth, R. I.

1. Caleb,
2. Robert,
3. Joseph,
4. John,
5. Anne,
6. William,
7. Mary,
8. Job,
9. Jonathan,

He was a miller.
1673. Freeman.
1680. Taxed 10s.
1699, May 20. He sold to John Eddy, of Swanzey, 5 acres there, for £8.
1721, Mar. 10. Will—proved 1722, Aug. 13. Ex. son Caleb. Overseers, brother-in-law Thomas Corey, of Tiverton, and son Robert Bennett. To wife Joanna, all estate she brought with her, a cow, garden, fruit of ten apple trees and half dwelling house while widow. To sons Robert, Joseph and John, £5 each. To daughter Anne, wife of John Tallman, 5s. To son William, £10. To daughter Mary, wife of William Fish, £5. To son Job, £10, at age. To son Jonathan, £10, at age. To son Caleb, all housing and lands in Portsmouth, except what is reserved for wife, and that to be also for Caleb, at death of testator's wife, or at her marriage. To son Caleb, windmill and movable estate remaining. If son Caleb die without issue, then to son John.
Inventory, £258, 5s. 1d., viz: wearing apparel, books, money and plate £4, 12s., pewter, walking cane, stillyards, gun, cheese tub, horsekind £18, 10s., neat cattle £13, 10s., swine £4, geese, fowls, loom, &c.
1726, Feb. 16. His widow Joanna, mortgaged to Roger Brailey, of Middleboro, a lot and dwelling house in Portsmouth, for £64.

III. { John, { b. 1652.
{ d.
m.
{ ——— { b.
{ d. of

Newport, R. I.

1 John,

1680. Taxed 5s.
1718. He made a deposition, calling himself aged about sixty-six years.

IV. { Jonathan, { b. 1659.
{ d. 1708, Jul. 11.
m.
{ ——— { b.
{ d. of

Newport, R. I.

1. John.

1689. Taxed 5s.
He was buried in Newport Cemetery.

See: American Genealogist, v. 19, p. 221. v. 24, p. 69., v. [illegible], p. 1

BENNETT (Robert). 2d column. IV. Jonathan had wife, Penelope, and sons. 1. John. 2. Benjamin. 3. William. In 1747 both Benjamin and William died, leaving estate to their brothers and mother Penelope. John and his mother Penelope were living in Durham, N. H., in that year. John had wife Deborah as early as 1719.

BENNETT (Samuel).

{ Samuel, { b.
{ d. 1684, Sep. 4.
m.
{ Anna, { b.
{ d. 1705 +

(She m. (2) Moses Forman.)

Providence, East Greenwich, R. I.

He was a cooper.

1652. General Sergeant,

1652, May 12. He bought of Stukeley Westcott, his house and lot, orchard, meadow, &c.

1655. Freeman.

1656, May 7. He was awarded 24s. for a calf, which Mr. Foote's dogs were proved to have killed (the suit being brought against Henry Fowler, administrator of Henry Foote).

1656, Oct. 27. Sergeant. He was to be paid £20, for his services in that office.

1657. Commissioner.

1660, Oct. 27. He sold certain land to William Carpenter.

1661. Grand Jury.

1666, May 31. He took oath of allegiance

1668-74-78. Deputy.

1678, May 1. East Greenwich. He was granted 100 acres at East Greenwich, by the Assembly; and was to have in the first division of 5,000 acres, if any will relinquish a right, if not, then in the next township of 5,000 acres to be laid out.

1682, Nov. 20. He and wife Anna, confirmed to heirs of Richard Everden, land sold in Everden's lifetime, viz: 34 acres upland and a share of meadow, &c., in Providence, near Solitary Hill.

1684, Aug. 25. Will—proved 1684, Oct. 23. Exx. wife Anna. Overseers, Thomas Olney and John Whipple, Jr. To son Edward, 70 acres at Providence, To son Samuel, 60 acres and meadow.

See: American Genealogist, v. 21, p. 206-207.

I. { Edward, { b.
{ d.

Providence, R. I.

1676, Aug. 14. He was one of the men "who staid and went not away," in King Philip's War, and so was entitled to a share in the disposition of certain Indian captives. The services of these Indians were sold for terms of years.

1686, Nov. 29. He sold Stephen Arnold certain land, which had been owned by father, Samuel Bennett, deceased, for £6, 7s.

II. { Elizabeth, { b.
{ d. 1721 +
m.
{ Edward Inman, { b. 1654.
{ d. 1735, Jun. of Edward Inman.

1. Edward,
2. Samuel,
3. Francis,
4. Benjamin,
5. Joseph,
6. Isaiah,

III. { Samuel, { b.
{ d. 1745, Apr. 15.
m. (1) 1689, Jan. 2
{ Sarah Forman, { b.
{ d. of Forman.
m. (2) 1699, Apr. 25,
{ Desire Berry, { b.
{ d. 1714, Mar. 9. of Berry.
m. (3) 1715,
{ Rachel, { b.
{ d. of

East Greenwich, Coventry, R. I.

1. Samuel, 1690, Sep. 14
2. Sarah, 1693, Jan. 31
3. Hannah, 1697, Apr. 27
4. Elizabeth, 1699, Nov. 19
(2d wife.)
5. Benjamin, 1701, Nov. 7.
6 John, 1703, Oct. 15
7. William, 1706, May 15
8. Priscilla, 1708, Oct. 7.
9. Mary, 1711, Apr. 2.
10. Desire. 1713, Feb. 12

He was a carpenter.
1685. Freeman.
1688. Grand Jury.
1690. Deputy.
1690. Lieutenant.
1703, Feb. 23. He and wife Desire, sold Thomas Fry, for £68, my now dwelling house, orchard, &c., 20 acres.
1715, Dec. 21. He deeded son Samuel, for love, &c., 10 acres. His wife Rachel, joined in deed, calling Samuel, Jr., her son-in-law, (i. e. stepson)

BENNETT (Samuel). 2d column. III. Samuel. His 1st wife was daughter of Moses and Hannah ( ) Forman.

IV. { William, { b. 1673.
{ d. 1753, Jul. 29.
m. 1693 ± [Clement.
{ Rachel Weaver, (w. of { b.
{ d. 1753 (—). of Andrew.

East Greenwich, R. I.

1. William, 1694, Jun. 3.

1690. Freeman.
1709-13. Deputy.

at World's End, Providence. To sons William and Benjamin, certain land at East Greenwich, equally, at age. To wife Anna, homestead land and buildings, at East Greenwich, for her use while widow, and the next day after her marriage, or at her decease, to go to son William. To sons William and Benjamin, all rights of common at East Greenwich, and to them cooper's and carpenter's tools (except a plane to Samuel). To daughter Priscilla, £5 at twenty-one or marriage. To wife, all debts, goods, chattels, &c.

Inventory, £62, 10s., viz: 2 guns, 2 spinning wheels, carpenter's and cooper's tools, churn, 3 cows, 2 yearlings, steer, calf, horse, 8 swine, 5 shoats, &c,

1705, Jun. 19. Anna Foreman and her husband, Moses Foreman, sold Josiah Westcott, land in right of former husband, Samuel Bennett.

1715, Jan. 18. He and wife Rachel, sold David Vaughan, a lot of 11 acres, for £90, reserving ground where honoured father and mother are buried.

1753, Jun. 12. Will—proved 1753, Aug. 25. Ex. grandson Benjamin Bennett. To great-grandson Sweet William Bennett, all my homestead house and lot, where I dwell, only my grandson Benjamin Bennett, is to have the profits during his life, he paying my debts, and if grandson William Bennett's wife Elizabeth survive him, she to have profits while widow. If great-grandson Sweet William Bennett die before he arrives at age, the homestead to go to great-grandson Benjamin (son of Benjamin), and great-grandson Jonathan (son of William). To grandson Benjamin Bennett, all carpenter's tools. To grandson William Bennett, cooper's tools and £5. To granddaughters Alice Weeks, Elizabeth Harris, Ann Greene and Sarah Bennett, each 20s. To each great-grandchild, 5s. To grandson Thomas Bennett, £10. To grandson Benjamin Bennett, rest of estate.

Inventory, £75, 15s. 6d., viz: wearing apparel £12, warming pan, pewter, sun dial, book, debts £10, 1s. 6d., sow, pig, &c.

V. BENJAMIN, b. d. — Portsmouth, (Prudence Island) R. I.

1692, Jul. 26. He (of Prudence Island), sold his brother, William Bennett, of East Greenwich, all my right, by will of father, lately deceased, to one-half of 90 acre farm in East Greenwich.

VI. PRISCILLA, b. d. 1754, Apr. 9. m. 1693, Dec. 21, STUKELEY WESTCOTT, b. 1672, Oct. d. 1750, May 25. of Jeremiah & Eleanor (England) Westcott.

1. Josiah, 1694, Dec. 2.
2. Stukeley, 1698, May 2.
3. Freelove, 1702, Jul. 5.
4. Benjamin, 1709, Dec. 31

BENTLEY.

WILLIAM, b. d. 1720. m. SARAH, b. d. 1720 + of

Kings Town, R. I.

He was a currier.

1679, Jul. 29. He and forty-one others, of Narragansett, sent a petition to the King, praying that "he would put an end to these differences about the government thereof, which hath been so fatal to the prosperity of the place; animosities still arising in people's minds, as they stand affected to this or that government."

1687, Sep. 6. Taxed 4s. 6½ d.

1705, Apr. He had liberty granted by town to set up a house, convenient for the carrying on of his currying trade.

1712, Jan. 20. He and wife Sarah, deeded son James 128 acres.

1714, Jun. 14. He bought of Priscilla Weathers, widow of Thomas, and her son John, 11 acres, for £13.

1715, Mar. 17. He appealed from judgment of Justice Court, in his case against James Updike.

1715, Nov. 1. He deeded to son Thomas, the 11 acres recently bought of widow Weathers and her son.

1718, Aug. 1. His wife testified that Samuel Eldred, father to John, did dwell upon the land where John now dwells, fifty years ago.

1720. Will executed and proved. Exs. wife Sarah and son Benjamin. To eldest son William, 5s., and like amount to sons James and Thomas, and daughter Jane Whitman. To son Benjamin, 8 acres. To wife Sarah, rest of personal.

I. WILLIAM, b. d. 1760. m. (1) 1703, Apr. 21, MARY ELIOT, b. d. of Eliot. m. (2) 1734, Aug. 1, [Israel. BATHSHEBA LEWIS, (w. of b. d. 1760 + of Lewis. — Kings Town, Westerly, Richmond, R. I.

He married his first wife at Stonington, Conn.

1712. Freeman.

1748, Aug. 18. Will—proved 1760, Aug. 12, (by Governor after petition 1760, May). Exx. wife Bathsheba. To eldest son John, 5s., he having had already, and like amount to sons George, Caleb and Ezekiel, eldest daughter Elizabeth Potter, daughters Tabitha Sweet, Ruhama James and Mary James. To wife Bathsheba, all my household goods and movable estate. Executrix to sell homestead and house I now live in, when my son Benjamin Bentley comes to age of fourteen, and divide equally to my five youngest children, viz: William, Thomas, James, Greene and Benjamin Bentley. To wife Bathsheba, all income of whole estate, real and personal, to bring up my five youngest children.

Inventory, £486, 15s., viz: apparel, spinning wheel, linen wheel, cow, 2 sheep, &c.

1. John,
2. George,
3. Caleb,
4. Ezekiel,
5. Elizabeth,
6. Tabitha,
7. Ruhama,
8. Mary,

(2d wife.)

9. William, 1735, May 29.
10. Thomas,
11. James, 1739, Jun. 6.
12. Greene, 1741, Mar. 23.
13. Benjamin, 1744, Jun. 11.

II. JAMES, b. d. m. (1) DOROTHY ALBRO, b. d. of Samuel & Isabel (Lawton) Albro. m. (2) HANNAH ——— b. d. of — Kings Town, R. I.

1712. Freeman.

*1. Hannah, 1703, Mar. 25.

(2d wife.)

2. Daughter, 1718, Dec. 15.

III. THOMAS, b. d. m. 1706, Jun. 6, ELIZABETH CHAMBERLIN, b. d. of Chamberlin. — Kings Town, R. I.

He was a cordwainer.

1712. Freeman.

1718, Mar. He had suit brought against him by Thomas Phillips, for trespass, &c., and answered that he rightfully possesseth in the right of his father, William Bentley.

He may have been identical with Thomas Bentley, of Exeter, who died 1778, and who mentions in his will (dated 1772, Jun. 15, proved 1778, Apr. 15), wife Mary, sons William and Benjamin, and grandson Caleb.

IV. BENJAMIN, b. d. 1744. m. ——— RATHBONE, b. d. of Thomas & Mary (Dickens) Rathbone. — Exeter, R. I.

He was a currier.

1719, Sep. He and his father answered the suit of James and Daniel Updike, in an action for trespass, &c., damage £150.

1725, Feb. 8. He was witness to a deed from Alexander Huling and wife Elizabeth, to Alexander Brown.

1744, Aug. 29. He gave a receipt for his wife's portion of estate of her father.

1750, Apr. 29. His son William married Mary Sweet, daughter of William. At this date, Benjamin Bentley was called of Exeter.

1. William,

V. JANE, b. d. m. 1700, Jan. 6, JOHN WIGHTMAN, b. 1674, Apr. 16. d. 1750. of George & Elizabeth (Updike) Wightman.

1. Alice, 1702, Oct. 16.
2. Sarah, 1704, Jan. 23.
3. John,
4. James,
5. Valentine,
6. Jane,
7. Mary,
8. Deborah,

BERNON.

GABRIEL,[2] (ANDRE,[1]) b. 1644, Apr. 6. d. 1736, Feb. 1. m. (1) 1673, Aug. 23, ESTHER LEROY, b. 1654. d. 1710, Jun. 14. of Leroy. m. (2) 1712, MARY HARRIS, b. d. of Thomas & Elnathan (Tew) Harris.

(She m. (2) 1737, Dec. 3, Nathaniel Brown.)

Rochelle, France, Boston, Mass., Newport, Kings Town, Providence, R. I.

He was a merchant at Rochelle, and early in life engaged in commercial enterprises in Canada, where he resided sometime.

1685. He was thrown into prison, for his crime of Protestantism, and there remained some months.

1686 Amsterdam. He fled thence, on his release from prison.

1687, Feb. London.

1688, Jul. 5. Boston. He arrived at this date in ship Dolphin, from Gravesend. He obtained

I. GABRIEL, b. d. 1706.

Unmarried.

1696, Dec. 29. He wrote to his father, then in England.

1706. The tradition is that he embarked for the West Indies in a vessel which foundered.

II. MARY, b. d. m. ABRAHAM TOURTELLOT, b. d. of Tourtellot.

1. Gabriel, 1694, Sep. 24.
2. Esther, 1696, Jun. 12.
3. Abraham,

III. ESTHER, b. 1677. d. 1746, Oct. 20, m. 1713, May 30, ADAM POWELL, b. 1674. d. 1725, Dec. 24. of Powell.

1. Elizabeth, 1714, Apr. 8.
2. Esther, 1718, May.

IV. SARAH, b. d. m. 1722, Nov. 11, BENJAMIN WHIPPLE, b. 1688, Nov. 11. d. 1788. of Benjamin & Ruth (Mathewson) Whipple.

1. Andrew, 1724, Feb. 3.
2. Benjamin, 1725, Jan. 5.
3. Content, 1727, Aug. 30.
4. Daniel, 1728, Sep. 7.
5. Ephraim, 1729, Nov. 7.
6. Esther, 1731, Mar. 12
7. Mary, 1732, May 28.

a confirmation of a tract at Oxford, Mass., where he subsequently built a grist-mill. The area of the tract was 2,672 acres, which he valued at £1,000. A French settlement existed there for quite a period. While living in Boston, he engaged in the manufacture of rosin, salt, &c.

1693. He went to England and made a contract with the government for supply of naval stores.

1696. He again went to England to further his commercial enterprises.

1697. Newport.

1699, Jun. 1. He and wife Esther and Abraham Tourtellot and wife Mary, and Andrew Faneuil, of Boston, attorney of brother Benjamin Faneuil sold for £110, to Prudence Thompson, wife of Benjamin Thompson, of Roxbury, their mansion house, and 2½ acres in Roxbury (meadow, mowing and orchard).

1699, Sep. 23. He signed a petition for the establishment of an Episcopal church, at Newport (Trinity).

1710, Jun. 14. His first wife died while he was living at Newport, and was buried there, in Newport Cemetery, where the grave stone may still be seen. He moved to Providence after his wife's death, and lived there a short time, marrying his second wife there.

1712. Kings Town. He purchased at about this time, a lot, of Lodowick Updike, at Wickford, and built a wharf, warehouse and sloop.

1714, Mar. 17. He sold John Crawford, of Providence, a warehouse lot there, for £21.

1716, Nov. 2. He having been ordered by Assembly, to sign two acknowledgments, the one for his causelessly charging Capt. John Eldredge, who was by Assembly deemed innocent, and the other for contemptuously and disorderly behaving himself before said Assembly—he accordingly signed two orders, expressing himself as "heartily sorry" for causelessly charging Capt. John Eldred and desiring him "to forgive me my fault in so doing," and also acknowledging his misbehavior before the Assembly.

1718. He was elected one of the vestry of St. Paul's church.

1719. Providence. He moved there this year from Wickford.

1721, Jul. 11. He had his daughter Eve, baptised.

1722. He was instrumental in establishing St. John's church.

1724. He went to England, to urge upon the church authorities there, the needs of the church in Providence.

Several interesting letters have been preserved from him to Rev. James Honeyman, of Newport, and Rev. Mr. McSparrow, of Narragansett, with replies from those gentlemen, &c.

1728, Feb. 16. Will—proved 1736, Feb. 16. Exx. wife Mary. As to goods that former wife Esther left amongst her children, which I had by her, I fully release it to them to agree as they can, and to them he also gives 20*s.* each, viz: Mary Tourtellot, Esther Powell, Sarah Whipple and Jane Coddington. As to rest of estate, that I and my present wife, Mary, are possessed of and entitled to give—disposition was made as follows. To Mary, beloved wife, ⅓ of movables and ⅓ real estate while his widow, and rest to 4 small children, born by present wife, viz: Gabriel, Susannah, Mary and Eve Bernon. To wife, the use of estate to bring up children till of age to receive portions, and the children are committed to her charge, for tuition and bringing up. Negro man Manuel, negro woman Peggy, to be at disposition of wife, as also the negro boy and girl, and the produce of them, if sold, or they themselves, to come into division of estate. One negro child being with daughter Esther Powell, is left to her, and a boy has been given to daughter Sarah and son-in-law Benjamin Whipple.

Inventory, £896, 2*s.* 6*d.*, viz: negro man, woman and 4 children £500, 44 oz. plate and 2 pair of large gold buttons £59, 5 feather beds £120, 1 oval table, 2 tables, 1 small table, tea table, 29 chairs, 2 looking glasses, books, 6 large maps, a silver hilted sword, silver hilted cane, 12 pewter platters and 12 plates, 5 basins and 7 pots of pewter, stillyards, case of glass bottles, 1 horse, 1 cow, 1 calf, 2 swine, 1 warming pan, brass, wearing apparel £40, 10*s.* 6*d.*, lignum vitæ mortar, 1 pair scales with brass weights, &c.

Several interesting memorials of Gabriel Bernon have been preserved by descendants; as carved chairs, a gold rattle, a sword (with date 1414), a psalm book (said by tradition to have been presented to him by a fellow prisoner in France), &c. He was buried beneath St. John's church, and a bronze tablet was placed in that church to his memory.

1736, Jul. 19. The following obituary notice appeared in Boston. "On the first instant, departed this life, at Providence, Mr. Gabriel Bernon, in the 92d year of his age. He was a gentleman by birth and estate, born in Rochelle, in France, and about fifty years ago he left his native country, and the greatest part of his estate; and for the cause of true religion, fled into New England, where he has ever since continued, and behaved himself as a zealous Protestant professor. He was courteous, honest and

V. JANE, m. 1722, Oct. 11, WILLIAM CODDINGTON,
b. 1696, May 15. d. 1752, Jun. 18.
b. 1680, Jul. 15. d. 1755, of Nathaniel & Susannah (Hutchinson) Coddington.

1. Content, 1724, Apr. 12
2. Esther, 1727, Jan. 21.
3. John, 1728, Oct. 23.
4. Jane, 1730, Mar. 29.
5. Francis, 1732, Feb. 2.
6. Anne, 1734, May 30.

(2d. WIFE.)

VI. GABRIEL, Unmarried.
b. d. young.

VII. SUSANNAH, m. 1734, Aug. 23, JOSEPH CRAWFORD,
b. 1716. d. 1802, Feb. 18.
b. 1712. d. 1796, Sep. 29. of William & Sarah (Whipple) Crawford.

1. Sarah, 1734, Sep. 23
2. Joseph, 1736, Oct. 16.
3. Freelove, 1738, Feb. 6.
4. Susannah, 1741, Sep. 19.
5. Mary, 1744, Jan. 1.
6. Candace, 1746, Apr. 28.
7. Esther, 1748, Jul. 20.
8 Lydia, 1751, Apr. 5.
9. Anne, 1759, Jun. 25.

VIII. MARY, m. GIDEON CRAWFORD,
b. 1719, Apr, 1. d. 1789, Oct. 1.
b. 1709, Jan. 29. d. 1795, Sep. 6. of William & Sarah (Whipple) Crawford.

1. Gideon,
2. Mary,
3. John,
4. William,
5. Arthur,
6. Alice,
7. Sarah,
8. Freelove,

IX. EVE, Unmarried.
b. 1721. d. 1776.

ERNON. 1st column. McSparran for McSparrow, fifth line after 1724.

kind, and died in great faith and hope in his Redeemer, and assurance of salvation; and has left a good name among his acquaintances. He evidenced the power of christianity in his great sufferings, by leaving his country and his great estate, that he might worship God according to his conscience. He was decently buried under the Episcopal church at Providence, and a great concourse of people attended his funeral, to whom the Rev. Mr. Brown preached an agreeable and eloquent funeral sermon, from Psalms xxxix: 4."

1775, Aug. 1. Will—proved 1776, Feb. 7. Eve Bernon. Ex. Zachariah Allen. To sister Mary Crawford, wife of Gideon, £30. To niece Freelove, daughter of Mary Crawford, £30. To niece Sarah Cooke, wife of Silas, of Warwick, £30. To Abigail Matthewson, daughter of niece Sarah Cooke, £30. To my friend and kinsman, Zachariah Allen, my lot of land, with dwelling house standing on west side of the main street, in the present occupation of the widow Yeats, on condition that he pay legacies to Mary Crawford, Freelove Crawford, Sarah Cooke and Abigail Matthewson, within one year of testator's decease, but if he refuse, then the above legatees to have it. To Zachariah Allen, a certain mortgage. Negro woman Amey and her son Manny were to be freed, and if by sickness or accident unable to support themselves, then to be maintained by legatees, out of estate given them.

BILLINGS.

SAMUEL, { b. / d.
m. 1658, Jan. 5,
SEABORN TEW, { b. 1640, Jun. 4. / d.
of Richard & Mary (Clarke) Tew.
(She m. (2) Owen Higgins.)

Newport, R. I.

1658, Feb. 23. He bought of Edward Robinson, 8½ acres.

1690, Nov. 25. Amey Ward, widow, and Mary Billings, both of Newport, daughters and co-heirs of Samuel Billings, deceased, of Newport, ratified and confirmed to Henry Tew, a sale that was made by Samuel Billings, deceased, to Richard Tew, deceased, of 1-300 of Conanicut Island.

I. AMEY, { b. 1658, Oct. 20. / d. 1732, Jan. 11.
m. (1)
THOMAS WARD, { b. 1641. / d. 1689, Sep. 25. of John Ward.
m. (2) 1692, Mar. 16,
ARNOLD COLLINS, { b. / d. of Collins.

1. Mary, 1679, Nov. 8.
2. Thomas, 1683, May 20.
3. Richard, 1689, Apr. 15.
(By 2d husband.)
4. Arnold, 1693, Feb. 2.
5. Elizabeth, 1695, Jun. 28.
6. Henry, 1699, Mar. 25.

BILLINGS. 2d column. I. Amey. Her 2d husband d 1735.

II. MARY, { b. 1662, Apr. 5. / d.

BLACKMAR.

JAMES, { b. / d. 1709, Aug. 14.
m.
MARY HAWKINS, { b. / d. 1724, Feb.
of William & Margaret ( ) Hawkins.

Providence, R. I.

1679, Jul. 1. Taxed 1*s.* 3*d.*

1687. Grand Jury.

1687, Sep. Taxed 6*s.*

1688. Rateable estate, 8 cows, 2 oxen, 4 heifers, 1 yearling, 1 horse, 1 mare, 2 colts, 300 acres of land in commons, small quantity of meadow.

1690. Jan. 13. He bought of Thomas Field, his interest in certain lands at Pawtuxet.

1691. Deputy.

1709, Sep. 16. Administration to widow Mary and son John.

Inventory, £127 ± viz: wearing apparel, 2 linen wheels, woolen wheel, pewter, warming pan, gun and sword, corn, hay, 2 oxen, 10 cows, 2 steers, 6 heifers, 2 two years, a horse, 2 swine.

He was buried in the Williams' Burying Ground (now in Roger Williams Park), as was also his widow.

I. JOHN, { b. / d. 1768, Jan. 26. Providence, Glocester, R. I.
m.
JEMIMA, { b. / d. 1769.

1708. Freeman.

1713, Jun. 16. Taxed with his mother, 5*s.*

1714, Jul. 2. He sold Daniel Matthewson, 2 acres near Matthewson's dwelling house, for £3.

1717, Feb. 15. He, as son and heir of James Blackmar, assigned to Richard Knight, a deed of certain land that said James Blackmar had bought of Thomas Field, in 1690.

1722, Dec. 13. He sold Elisha Smith a meadow, for £5, 10*s.*

1760, Nov. 5. Will—proved 1768, May 30. Exs. sons David and Abner who refused, and his widow Jemima, took administration on personal estate. To wife Jemima, 3 acres land, a feather bed, profits of a third of farm and use of all personal estate for life. To grandson James Blackmar, 20*s.* To son Henry, a gun. To son John, £100. To son Nathaniel, lot containing 2 or 3 acres. To sons David and Abner, the rest of homestead, equally. To 3 daughters, Mary Mackintine, Anne Place and Jemima Young, land in Smithfield, and all personal estate at decease of wife.

Inventory, £81, 11*s.* 12*d.*, viz: 3 feather beds, warming pan, silver cup, woolen wheel, money due £24, 15*s.* 4*d.*, cow, heifer, &c.

1769, Aug. 1. Will—proved 1769, Oct. 2. Widow Jemima. Exs. Richard Steere, of Glocester, and Anthony Steere, of Smithfield, who were to sell lands. To granddaughter Jane Blackmar, daughter of son Abner, 15*s.* To granddaughter Jemima Blackmar, daughter of son Nathaniel, 15*s.* To daughters Mary Mackintine, Anne Place and Jemima Young, all the rest of estate, her sons having had full share from their father's estate.

1. James,
2. Henry,
3. John,
4. Theophilus,
5. Nathaniel,
6. David,
7. Abner,
8. Mary,
9. Esther,
10. Anne.
11. Jemima,

II. MARY, { b. / d. 1717, Jul. 1.
m.
THOMAS WILLIAMS, { b. 1672, Feb. 16. / d. 1724, Aug. 27. of Joseph & Lydia (Olney) Williams.

1. Joseph,
2. Thomas,
3. Stephen,
4. John,
5. Abigail,
6. Jonathan,
7. Mary,

III. ELIZABETH, { b. 1682. / d. 1761, Mar.
m.
JAMES WILLIAMS, { b. 1680, Sep. 20. / d. 1757, Jun. 25. of Joseph & Lydia (Olney) Williams.

1. James, 1704, Feb. 20.
2. Anne, 1706, Mar. 17.
3. Sarah, 1707, Dec. 4.
4. Joseph, 1709, Oct. 24.
5. Mary, 1711, Oct. 1.
6. Nathaniel. 1714, Oct. 11.
7. Elizabeth, 1717, Oct. 21.
8. Hannah, 1719, Jun. 22.
9. Lydia, 1724, Oct. 30.
10. Nathan, 1728, Jun. 15.

BLACKSTONE.

WILLIAM, { b. / d. 1675, May 26.
m. 1659, Jul. 4, [John.
SARAH STEPHENSON (w. of { b. / d. 1673, Jun.

Boston, Rehoboth, Mass.

1617 to 1621. He took his degree at Cambridge, Emanuel College.

He was ordained in England, and left there because of a dislike of the Lord Bishop's (neither did he like the Lord Brethren of Boston, as he declared later).

I. JOHN, { b. / d. Rehoboth, Ms., Providence, R. I., Attleboro, Ms., Branford, Ct.
m.
CATHARINE, { b. / d. of

He was a shoemaker.

1675, Jun. 1. A committe was appointed and authorized by the court "to take some present care of the estate of Mr. William Blackstone, deceased, and of his son now left by him, and to see that at the next court, he do propose a man to the court to be his guardian, which in case he do neglect, the court will then see cause to make choice of one for him."

1689, Feb. 7. His name was in the list of those who were proprietors at Rehoboth at this date, but not residents.

1. John, 1700 ±

BLACKSTONE. 2d column. I. John. His son John, b. 1699, Jan. 19. Change last sentence thus—His son John d. 1785, Jan. 3, at Branford, Conn., and was buried in the center of the graveyard. He left two sons and two daughters, and descendants of the name are still (or were recently) living.

1623, Sep. He and William Jefferay were probably of Robert Gorges party, who made settlement this year at Weymouth.

1625. About this time he located on land subsequently included in the limits of Boston.

1628. He gave 12*s.* towards the expense of banishing the notorious Morton, of Merry Mount, who was setting all laws at defiance and scandalizing the rigid virtue of the Puritans.

1629, Apr. 21. William Blackstone, Cler. and William Jefferay, Gent., were authorized to put John Oldham in possession of a grant of land from Mr. Gorges.

1631, May 18. Freeman.

1633, Apr. 1. "It is agreed that William Blackstone shall have fifty acres of ground set off to him near to his house in Boston, to enjoy forever."

1634. Rehoboth. He removed here this or the subsequent year, and was the first permanent white settler. His location was on the banks of the Blackstone (now in the town of Cumberland, R. I.,) and was called by him "Study Hill."

1635, Apr. 7. It was ordered that Nahanton shall give two skins of beaver to Mr. Blackstone, for damage done him in his swine, by setting of traps.

1637. He was thus commented on by Lechford, who visited America this year, and saw him at his home. "One Master Blackstone, a minister, went from Boston, having lived there nine or ten years, because he would not join with the church; he lives near Master Williams, but is far from his opinions."

1666, May 2. He petitioned the Rhode Island Assembly, for relief in reference to molestation from some of Plymouth Colony, in disturbing him in possession of his lands.

1673, Jun. The Rehoboth Records state: "Mrs. Sarah Blackstone, the wife of Mr. William Blackstone, buried about the middle of June, 1673."

1675. May 28. He was buried at this date, as the records state.

1675, May 28. Inventory, £56, 3*s.* 6*d.*, viz: wearing apparel, feather bed, 3 horses, mare, 2 colts, cow, heifer, pewter, great brass kettle, 4 old augurs, hand saw, chisel, warming pan, barrel of a gun, barrel of a pistol, 4 cases of knives, 3 bibles 10*s.*, 6 English books in folio £2, 10., 3 Latin books in folio 15*s.*, 8 biggest books £2, 15 quarto books £1, 17*s.* 6*d.*, 14 small books in quarto 14*s.*, 30 books in large octavo £4, 25 small books £1, 15*s.*, 22 duodecimos £1, 13*s.*, 53 small books without cover 13*s.*, 10 paper books 5*s.*

In the margin of book is written: "This estate was destroyed and carried away with the Indians." The real estate was described, but its value not appraised. The South Neck and land about the house and orchard, amounting to 200 acres, and meadow called Blackstone Meadow.

1679, Jul. 1. Taxed at Providence, William Blackstone's land 1*s.* 3*d.*

1684, Jun. 10. The deposition of John Odlin and three other ancient dwellers in Boston, was given, they testifying that about the year 1634, the then inhabitants of Boston, "did treat and agree with Mr. William Blackstone, for the purchase of his estate and right in any lands within the said neck of land called Boston, and for said purchase agreed that every householder should pay six shillings, which was accordingly collected, none paying less." He reserved 6 acres on Blackstone Point, where his dwelling house stood. The price paid was £30.

It was further testified that "Mr. Blackstone bought a stock of cows with the money he received as above, and removed and dwelt near Providence, where he lived till the day of his death."

1738, Mar. Henry Gardiner, aged ninety-three years, of South Kingstown, deposed that before the Indian war William Blackstone came once a month to preach at Richard Smith's house, being procured by Richard Smith to do so.

1692. Providence. He sold land and removed from his father's location, into Providence this year.

1692, Sep. 10. He let out to John Dailey, for seven years, half of farm bought of David Whipple, and also gave to said Dailey, the right to dwell in my house for said term, in consideration whereof, John Dailey to do half the work on farm during said seven years, both as to clearing of land, fencing, breaking up of land, getting fodder for cattle, &c.; and Dailey to have half the profit of what is raised on said farm for seven years, except my cattle and their produce, only Dailey to have milk of one cow the next summer.

1701. Attleboro. He removed thence this year.

1713. He and his wife were warned out of town.

It is said that his son John married and had children, and died at Branford, 1785, Jan. 3.

BLISS. 2d column. 1. John, d. 1717. His widow d. 1717 + 1717, Feb. 3. Will—proved 1717, Mar. 4. Ex. son Josiah To wife Damaris, all household goods and use for life of land in town. To son Josiah, a lot in Newport. To son George, the rest of lands undisposed of, my windmill, twenty ewe sheep, and a cow. To grandchild Jemima Meacham, £5, at eighteen. To grandchild John Meacham, £5, at age. To grandchild John Jersey, £5, at age.

BLISS.

BLISS. 2d column. 1. John. His widow d. 1720.

GEORGE,[2] (THOMAS,[1]) b. 1591. d. 1667, Aug. 31.
m. ——— b. d.

Lynn, Sandwich, Mass., Newport, R. I.

1635. He came to America with his brother Thomas.

1637. Lynn.

1640, Apr. 16. Sandwich. He had 1¼ acres granted.

1649. Newport.

1650, May 23. He and five others were appointed to mend and make all arms presented to them by the inhabitants of any of the towns.

1655. Freeman.

I. JOHN, b. 1645 ± d. 1715 + Newport, R. I.
m. 1666, Jan. 24,
DAMARIS ARNOLD, b. 1648, Feb. 23. d. 1715 + of Benedict & Damaris (Westcott) Arnold.

1667. Ensign.

1667, May 13. He and three others were directed to go forthwith from house to house throughout Newport, the villages and precincts thereof, to take a precise and exact account of all the arms, ammunition and weapons of war each person is furnished with.

1668, Oct. 29. Freeman.

1671, May 3. His fine of 20*s.*, for not attending court as juryman was remitted, his excuse being "because his wife was near her time of being delivered of a child."

1671, Jun. 7. Juryman.

1679-82-83-95. Deputy.

1680. Taxed £3, 4*s.* 2*d.*

1692. His wife was a member of the Seventh Day Baptist Church.

1696. Major for the Island.

1702, Aug. 10. He had land laid out.

1715, Nov. 29. He and wife Damaris, in consideration of infirmities, &c., deeded 102 acres and dwelling house to son Josiah.

1. Son, 1668, Sep. 29.
2. Damaris, 1670, May 25.
3. Freelove, 1672, Nov. 16.
4. John, 1674, Oct. 22.
5. Henry,
6. Josiah,
7. George,
8. Mercy,

MATTHEW, b. d.
m.
ELEANOR, b. d.

Newport, R. I.

1655. Freeman.

1671, May 8. His wife Eleanor, was bound over to next court, a bond for her appearance being given in sum of £100, by John Peckham, Sr. and Nicholas Cottrell.

1671. Oct. 18. He was indicted for killing several sheep, not his own, but the jury found him not guilty.

1679, Mar. 6. He bought of Henry Brightman, certain land east side of Taunton River, for £45.

I. MARY, b. d. 1715 +
m. (1)
JOHN LAWTON, b. d. 1678 (—). of George & Elizabeth (Hazard) Lawton.
m. (2) 1678, Jun. 3,
GIDEON FREEBORN, b. d. 1720, Feb. 28. of William & Mary ( ) Freeborn.

1. George,
(By 2d husband.)
2. Mary, 1679, Aug. 24.
3. William, 1682, Feb. 3.
4. Gideon, 1684, Apr. 29.
5. Thomas, 1688, Feb. 5.
6. Comfort, 1691.
7. Mercy, 1692.

II. MATTHEW, b. d.

BOOMER. 2d column. II. Matthew. Children, 1, Matthew, 1689, Sep. 29. 2, Lydia, 1690, Dec. 3. 3, Hannah, 1692, Nov. 16. 4, Mary, 1694, Mar. 16. 5, Deborah, 1696, May 1. 6, Caleb, 1698, Mar. 16. 7, Ruth, 1700, May 31, 8. Joshua, 1702, Oct. 8. 9, Mercy.

BOOMER. 2d column. II. Matthew. d. 1744, Freetown, Mass. 1732, Oct. 8. Will—proved 1744, Mar. 20. He mentions wife Hannah, eldest son Matthew, sons Caleb and Joshua, five surviving daughters, Lydia, Mercy Luther, Deborah Mason, Ruth Salisbury, Mary; and children of deceased daughter Hannah Jenckes, &c.

BORDEN.

RICHARD, b. 1601. d. 1671, May 25.
m.
JOAN, b. 1604. d. 1688, Jul. 15.

Portsmouth, R. I.

1638. He was admitted an inhabitant of the island of Aquidneck, having submitted himself to the government that is or shall be established.

1638, May 20. He was allotted 5 acres.

1639, Jan. 2. He and three others were appointed to survey all lands near about, and to bring in a map or plot of said lands.

1640. He was appointed with four others to lay out lands in Portsmouth.

1641, Mar. 16. Freeman.

1653, May 18. He and seven others were appointed a committee for ripening matters that concern Long Island, and in the case concerning the Dutch.

1653–54. Assistant.

1654–55. General Treasurer.

1654–56–57. Commissioner.

1655. Freeman.

1661, Sep. 6. He bought of Shadrach Manton, of Providence, land in Providence, near Newtokonkonut Hill, containing about 60 acres.

1667 ± He was one of the original purchasers of lands in New Jersey, from certain Indians.

1667–70. Deputy.

1671, May 31. Will made by Town Council, on testimony concerning the wishes of deceased. Ex. son Matthew. To widow Joan, the old house and fire room, with leanto and buttery adjoining, and little chamber in new house, and porch chamber joining to it, half the use of great hall, porch room below, cellaring and garret of new house, for life. To her also firewood yearly, use of thirty fruit trees in orchard that she may choose, liberty to keep fowls about the house not exceeding forty, and all household goods at her disposal. She was to have thirty ewe sheep kept for her, with their profit and increase, fifty other sheep kept to halves, three cows kept and their profit, and to have paid her yearly a good, well fed beeve, three well fed swine, ten bushels of wheat, twenty bushels of Indian corn, six bushels of barley malt and four barrels of cider. To son Thomas, all estate in Providence, lands, goods and chattels (except horsekind), he paying his mother Joan yearly, a barrel of pork and firkin of butter. To son Francis, land in New Jersey. To son John, all land about new dwelling house of said John Borden, &c. To son Joseph, £40, within two years of death of his mother. To son Samuel, £40, half in six months after death of father and half in six months after death of mother. To son Benjamin, £40, within four years of death of mother. To daughter Mary Cooke, £5. To daughter Sarah Holmes, £40, within six years after death of mother. To daughter Amey Borden, £100, at age of twenty-one. To granddaughter Amey Cooke, £10, at eighteen. To son Matthew, whole estate after payment of debts and legacies, and if he die without issue, said estate not to remain to any brother older.

Inventory, £1572, 8s. 9d., viz: 200 sheep, 100 lambs, 4 oxen, 9 cows, 4 three years, 5 two years, 7 yearlings, 5 calves, horseflesh at Providence £60, 4 mares on the island £20, horse £7, 10s., 6 colts, horseflesh at New London £8, 30 swine, 11 pigs, negro man and woman £50, 3 negro children £25, turkeys, geese, fowls, Indian corn, rye, wheat, oats, barley, pease, 2 cheese presses, 6 guns, pewter, 2 swords, feather bed, 2 flock beds, hat case, silver bowl £3, cider £2, money £3, peage £8, goods £16, table, form, settle, chairs, warming pan, books 10s., &c.

He was buried in the burying place that Robert Dennis gave Friends in Portsmouth.

1692, Aug. 1. Richard Borden, of Providence, eldest son of Thomas Borden, of Providence, deceased, declared that, whereas, my honored grandfather, Richard Borden, of Portsmouth, being willing to set his house in order and settle

See: American Genealogist, v. 19, p. 130

I. THOMAS, b. d. 1676, Nov. 25. Portsmouth, Providence, R. I.
m. 1664, Jan. 20,
MARY HARRIS, b. d. 1718, Mar. 22. of William & Susanna ( ) Harris.

1. Mary, 1664, Oct.
2. Dinah, 1665, Oct.
3. Richard,
4. William, 1668, Jan. 10.
5. Joseph, 1669, Nov. 25.
6. Mercy, 1672, Nov. 3.
7. Experience, 1675, Jun. 8.
8. Meribah, 1676, Dec. 19.

1655. Freeman.

1665, Feb. 19. Providence. He had lot 44 granted in a division of lands.

1666–70–72. Deputy.

1671, Feb. 15. He had 60 acres laid out.

1675–76. Assistant.

1676, Aug. 24. He was a member of the Court Martial, held at Newport, for the trial of certain Indians, charged with being engaged in King Philip's designs. Several were sentenced to suffer death.

1677, Apr. 23. His will was ratified by Town Council, on the testimony of Walter Newbury and Robert Malins, as to the declaration of his mind and will, he being sick, &c. Exs. father William Harris and brother John Borden. To wife, a third of land for life, and the other two thirds to three sons equally, they having their mother's part at her death. Being asked what he would give his daughters, he said his father, William Harris, had promised to make his daughters' portions as good as he (Thomas), gave his sons, &c. Said Thomas Borden gave to each daughter, £10, at age or marriage. To wife, rest of movable estate to bring up children. He desired that his brother, Joseph Borden, might have his sons Joseph and Mercy, and that his daughter that was at John Borden's, should remain with them till of age. His will was declared at Portsmouth, during a temporary stay there occasioned by the Indian war.

1687, Sep. 1. His widow was taxed 5s. 5d.

1688. Widow Mary's rateable estate, 4 cows, 3 heifers, 2 horses, 2 mares, a swine.

1718, Apr. 28. Administration on widow Mary's estate, to Thomas Harris, at the request of Mr. Richard Borden and Lieutenant Mercy Borden, sons of said Mary. Inventory, £95, 10s. 6d.

II. FRANCIS, b. d. 1703 ± Portsmouth, R. I., Shrewsbury, N. J.
m.
JANE, b. d. 1703 + of

1. Richard,
2. Thomas,
3. Francis,
4. Daughter,

BORDEN. 2d column. II. Francis. Children, 1, Richard, —, Apr. 11. 2, Francis, —, Nov. 1. 3, George, 168–, June 4. 4, Thomas, 1685, Feb. 4.

1655. Freeman.

1678, Sep. 3. Shrewsbury. The court was held at his house.

1688. He sold land to John Lippincott, Sr.

1698. He and wife Jane made application to court with Samuel Leonard, administrator of Francis Jackson, for directions for care of children of Francis Jackson. Two children of Francis Jackson were bound out to Francis Borden and Jane, his wife.

1703, May 4. Will. He mentions wife Jane, eldest son Richard, sons Thomas and Francis and a daughter who married Isaac Hause. He also mentions kinsman Isaac Van Kirk.

III. MARY, b. d. 1691 (—).
m.
JOHN COOK, b. 1631. d. 1691. of Thomas Cook.

1. Mary,
2. Elizabeth, 1653.
3. Sarah,
4. John, 1656.
5. Hannah,
6. Joseph,
7. Martha,
8. Deborah,
9. Thomas,
10. Amey,
11. Samuel,

IV. MATTHEW, b. 1638, May. d. 1708, Jul. 5. Portsmouth, R. I.
m. 1674, Mar. 4,
SARAH CLAYTON, b. 1654. d. 1735, Apr. 19. of Clayton.

1. Mary, 1674, Sep. 20.
2. Matthew, 1676, Aug. 14.
3. Joseph, 1678, Jul. 17.
4. Sarah, 1680, Dec. 29.
5. Ann, 1683, Jan. 5.
6. Thomas, 1685, Apr. 19.
7. Richard, 1687, Oct. 10.
8. Abraham, 1690, Mar. 29.
9. John, 1693, Aug. 29.
10. Benjamin. 1696, Apr. 5.

He was "the first English child born on Rhode Island," as Friends' records declare.

1687. Overseer of the Poor.

1705, Mar. 23. Will—proved 1708, May 21. Exx. wife Sarah. To son Joseph, all my dwelling house and land belonging to it in Portsmouth, he paying my wife Sarah, £20, for life. To wife, use of little chamber with chimney in it, porch chamber, half of great hall, half of cellar, the garret, half of porch, liberty to keep twenty fowls and use of ten apple trees, and son Joseph to keep a horse for her and supply firewood. To son Joseph two oxen, two cows, ten sheep, mare, carts, &c. To son Thomas, half a share in Tiverton £30, silver tankard, mare, ten sheep, two cows, silver spoon and feather bed. To son Richard, land at Cooper's Creek, West Jersey £40, a mare, ten sheep, cow and silver spoon. To son Abraham, land in West Jersey £40, mare, ten sheep, cow and silver spoon. To son John, £140, and silver spoon. To son Benjamin, £140, and silver spoon. To daughter Sarah Hodgson, £30. To daughter Ann Slocum, £30. To granddaughters Sarah and Ann Stodder, each £10. To men's meeting of Friends' on Rhode Island, £5. To wife Sarah, rest of movables.

The Friends' records state that he died at Boston, where he was taken sick of a fever. He was buried in Friends' burial ground at Lynn, Mass.

V. JOHN, b. 1640, Sep. d. 1716, Jun. 4. Portsmouth, R. I.
m. 1670, Dec. 25,
MARY EARLE, b. 1655. d. 1734, Jun. of William & Mary (Walker) Earle.

1. Richard, 1671, Oct. 25.
2. John, 1675.
3. Amey, 1678, May 30.
4. Joseph, 1680, Dec. 3.
5. Thomas, 1682, Dec. 13.
6. Hope, 1685, Mar. 3.
7. Mary,
8. William, 1689, Aug. 15.
9. Benjamin,

See American Genealogist, v. 56, p. 54

1673–80–1700–4–5–8. Deputy.

1679, May 7. His fine for not attending jury remitted, one of his children being very sick.

1684, Jun. 24. He complained to Assembly that he was unjustly molested and arrested for maintaining the rights of this colony against the intrusion of Plymouth colony.

1687. Overseer of the Poor.

1698, Aug. 2. He was permitted to keep the ferry from Rhode Island to Bristol, on equal privilege with Thomas Durfee, for seven years, both being obliged to carry all magistrates, deputies and jurymen ferriage free, and to pay 6s. each, yearly, to general treasury.

1705, Jun. 19. His ferry license was renewed for seven years, together with Abial Tripp.

1716, Feb. 24. Will—proved 1716, Jul. 9. Exx. wife Mary. Overseers son Richard and friend William Anthony. To eldest son Richard, land in Tiverton. To son John, farm at Touisset Neck, Swanzey, half at my decease and half at death or marriage of wife, he paying my daughters, Hope and Mary Borden, £50 each, and to children of daughter Amey Chase, deceased (late wife to Benjamin Chase,

his estate on his children, &c., did make and declare his last will in presence of Daniel Gould, Joseph Nicholson, William Wodell, John Earle, &c., who was called in for that end, and did then order and dispose of his estate to his children, which was approved by Town Council, of Portsmouth, as appeareth under their hands, bearing date 1671, May 31, and I being satisfied by testimony of said four persons, and also of my honored grandmother, wife of said Richard, &c., that it was his real will, &c., and am satisfied, and for £5, paid by my uncles, viz: Matthew and John Borden, of Portsmouth, and Francis Borden, of Shrewsbury, forever quitclaim to uncles Matthew and John, all my interest in lands, &c., in Portsmouth or elsewhere, and to my uncle Francis, all rights in lands in Shrewsbury and elsewhere.

of Tiverton), £15, To grandson Stephen Borden, eldest son of Joseph, deceased, land in Freetown, where son Joseph built a saw mill, said Stephen paying his three brothers, William, George and Joseph, £100 each, as they come of age. To grandson Joseph Borden, a half share at head of Freetown, in Tiverton. To son Thomas Borden, all housing and land in Portsmouth, he keeping for his mother a horse and two cows, giving her two fat swine yearly, allowing her sufficient house room while widow and the keep of half a dozen fowls. To son Thomas, also, rights at Hog Island. To son William, one-half of 1000 acres in Pennsylvania. To son Benjamin, the other half. To daughters Hope and Mary Borden, all lands in Shrewsbury, N. J., and certain lands in Pennsylvania. To wife Mary, movables.

Inventory, wearing apparel, spectacles, feather bed, 2 bibles and several other books, pewter, 5 spinning wheels, three and a quarter years' service of Indian girl £13, cider £1, 4 cows, 2 two years, 2 yearlings, calf, 40 sheep, 20 lambs, 3 swine, some pigs, &c.

1721, Aug. His widow Mary, called herself aged sixty-six years, having been married at sixteen or seventeen, as was stated.

VI. { JOSEPH, { b. 1643, Jul. 3. Portsmouth, R. I., Barbadoes, W. I.
m. { d.
HOPE, { b.
{ d. of

1. Sarah, 1664, Apr. 17.
2. William, 1667, Dec. 31.
3. Hope, 1673, Dec. 26.

VII. { SARAH, { b. 1644, May.
m. { d. 1705 +
JONATHAN HOLMES, { b.
{ d. 1713. of Obadiah & Catharine ( ) Holmes.

1. Obadiah,
2. Jonathan,
3. Samuel,
4. Sarah,
5. Mary,
6. Catharine,
7. Martha. 1675.
8. Lydia,
9. Joseph,

VIII. { SAMUEL, { b. 1645, Jul. Portsmouth, R. I., Westchester, N. Y.
m. 1679, Jun. 1, { d.
ELIZABETH CROSSE, { b.
{ d. of Crosse.

1672, Feb. 10. He sold Lewis Mattox, of Portsmouth, a share of land in Monmouth, N. J.

1674. Freeman.

1679, Jun. 1, Westchester. He was living there at time of his marriage.

IX. { BENJAMIN, { b. 1649, May. Portsmouth, R. I., Burlington Co., N. J.
m. 1670, Sep. 22, { d. 1718 +
ABIGAIL GROVER, { b.
{ d. of James Grover.

1670. Shrewsbury. He was one of those named as having paid for their New Jersey lands. He subsequently held the office of Justice, Commissioner, &c.

1690. He and wife Abigail, in a deed of this date, mention will of James Grover, dated 1685, Dec. 1, wherein he bequeathed mansion house and mill, &c., equally to son James, and sons-in-law Benjamin Borden, Richard Gardner, &c.

1716. Eversham, Burlington Co. He deeded land to son Joseph, of Freehold.

1718. Auchweas, Burlington Co. He deeded son James certain land.

1. Richard, 1672, Jan. 9.
2. Benjamin, 1675, Apr. 6.
3. James, 1677, Sep. 6.
4. Rebecca, 1680, Jun. 8.
5. Safety, 1682, Sep. 6.
6. Amey, 1684, Mar. 4.
7. Joseph, 1687, May 12.
8. Jonathan, 1690, Apr. 14.
9. David, 1692, Mar. 8.
10. Samuel, 1696, Apr. 8.

X. { AMEY, { b. 1654, Feb.
m. 1678, Mar. 27, { d. 1684, Feb. 5.
WILLIAM RICHARDSON, { b.
{ d. of Richardson.

1. William, 1679, Jan. 15.
2. Thomas, 1680, Sep. 10.
3. John, 1683, Feb. 1.

BOSS.

{ EDWARD, { b.
m. { d. 1724, Aug.
SUSANNAH WILKINSON, { b. 1662, Feb.
{ d.

of Lawrence & Susannah (Smith) Wilkinson.

South Kingstown, R. I.

1710, May 17. He and seventeen others bought 7000 acres in Narragansett, of the vacant lands ordered sold by the Assembly.

1724, Sep. 22. Administration on his estate was granted to his son, Edward Boss, of Newport.

Inventory, £1,027, viz: wearing apparel £7, 16s., a pair of oxen £15, 10s., 5 cows £23, 15s., 5 heifers £21, 6 yearlings, 4 calves, 34 cheeses spinning wheel, churn, 4 hogs, negro Abram £60, house and 154 acres £700, 130 acres of land now belonging to Peter Boss, given him by his father, £20.

1725, Jan. 11. The Town Council ordered that Edward Boss, eldest son of deceased, should have the land, he paying proportional sums to brothers and sister.

1725, Sep. Suit was brought by Henry Knowles Jr. and Susannah, his wife, daughter of Edward Boss, deceased, against Edward Boss, of Newport, for £140, due for a fifth of homestead of 154 acres. It was declared that Edward Boss died about Aug., 1724, leaving three sons, Edward the eldest, Jeremiah and Peter, and one daughter, Susannah.

I. { EDWARD, { b. 1685, Jan. 20. Newport, R. I.
m 1709, Apr. 21, { d. 1752, Dec. 25.
PHILLIP CARR, { b. 1688, Dec. 8.
{ d. of Caleb & Phillip (Greene) Carr.

He was a merchant.

1713. Freeman.

1713, Apr. 6. He sold to Rowland Robinson, 284 acres in Narragansett, for £101, 10s.

1727, Mar. He brought suit against Ann Sabeere and Daniel Sabeere, executors of John Sabeere, for £200, for molasses sold.

1. Mary, 1710, Sep. 1.
2. Freelove, 1712, Dec. 5.
3. Abigail, 1715, Feb. 18.
4. Edward, 1716, Nov. 23.
5. Hannah, 1719, Apr. 17.
6. Susanna, 1720, Nov. 2.
7. Joseph, 1722, Jan. 30.
8. Philip, 1725, Sep. 16.
9. Benjamin, 1727, Jul. 23.

II. { SUSANNA, { b. 1687, Jul. 21.
m. 1712, May 8, { d.
HENRY KNOWLES, { b. 1675, Sep. 29.
{ d. 1740, May 1, of William & Alice (Fish) Knowles.

III. { PETER, { b. 1695, Sep. 15. North Kingstown, R. I.
m. 1720, Jan. 28, { d.
AMEY GARDINER, { b.
{ d. of Gardiner.

1722. Kings Town. Freeman.

1726, Sep. 3. North Kingstown. He deposed as to things that Henry Knowles' wife had from Edward Boss's estate, the amount being near £50.

His wife Amey, also deposed to same effect, stating also that her mother-in-law Boss, in her life time had given her daughter, Henry Knowles' wife, a bed, pewter, &c., and that she took some feathers out of another bed to fill said daughter's bed up "because she was going into a difficult family."

1727. Freeman.

He had several other children besides Sarah, but their names are destroyed or illegible on town records.

1. Sarah, 1724, Jul. 5.

IV. { JEREMIAH, { b. Westerly, Richmond, R. I.
m. 1722, Mar. 22, { d. 1774.
MARTHA SPENCER, { b. 1700, Sep. 8.
{ d. 1765 + of Robert & Theodosia (Whaley) Spencer.

1765, Feb. 23. Will—proved 1774, Oct. 18. Ex. son Jonathan. To son Richard, 5s., he having had. To son Edward, 10 acres. To son Joseph, 5s. To son John, 5s. To son Peter, 20 acres. To son Philip, 160 acres in South Kingstown. To grandson Charles Boss, 130 acres in Richmond, at age. To wife Martha, a riding horse, six cows, feather bed, negro girl Judah and best room in house. To daughters Martha Tripp and Hannah Boss, 150 acres. To daughter Hannah, a feather bed. To son Jonathan, my homestead, buildings, &c., and he to have profit of all real estate till all the children are of age. To all children, the rest of personal. Son Jonathan to provide firewood for his mother.

Inventory, £325, 3s. 2½d., viz: wearing apparel £5, 12s, 6d., 4 notes £108, 13s. 7d., money 3s. 6d., bible and other books £1, 4s. 6d., live stock £83, 8s., 2 woolen wheels, negro woman Judah £24, boy Cæsar £11, 5s., linen wheel, warming pan, &c.

1. Richard, 1724, Feb. 26.
2. Edward, 1725, Apr. 20.
3. Susannah, 1728, Feb. 19.
4. Jeremiah, 1729, May 17.
5. Martha, 1731, Feb. 12.
6. Peter, 1732, Sep. 30.
7. Joseph, 1734, Mar. 2.
8. John, 1735, Oct. 14.
9. Hannah, 1737, Oct. 11.
10. Philip,
11. Jonathan,

BOSS. 2d column. 1. Edward, 1752, May 2. Will-proved 1753, Feb. 5. Exs. brothers Jeremiah and Peter. He mentions sons Edward, Joseph and Benjamin, daughters Mary Bowers, Freelove, and Susanna Keeling, and wife—— III. Peter, m. (2) Susanna Stanton. (W. of John.) b. 1716, Dec. 14, d. 1807, Sep. 25, of Theodosius and Rachel (Covey) Lanphere.

BRIGGS (JOHN, OF KINGS TOWN). He d. 1708. He was a Quaker, and meetings were held at his house.

JOHN, { b. / d. 1697 +
m.
FRANCES, { b. / d. 1697 +

Kings Town, R. I.

1671, May 20. Clerk of Military company.

1671, May 20 He took oath of allegiance.

1672, Jan. 1. He and five others bought of Awashuwett, chief sachem of Quohesett, in Narragansett, a tract of land there.

1672, Jan. 11. He bought 57 acres of Richard Smith, for £5.

1673. Freeman.

1687, Sep. 6. Taxed 5s. 8d.

1687. Constable.

1697. He and wife Frances, sold land to William Allen.

It is assumed that Thomas and Daniel were his children, but the evidence is not conclusive.

I. THOMAS, { b. / d. 1736. — Kings Town, East Greenwich, R. I.
m.
MARTHA, { b. / d. — of

1703. East Greenwich. Freeman.
1707, Mar. 19. He and wife Martha, deeded for love, &c., to son-in-law Samuel Gardiner, of East Greenwich, half of 90 acre farm which I now live upon, and the other half at my decease.
1724, Jan. 4. Will—proved 1736, Dec. 25. Exx. wife Martha. To wife, all movables to dispose of, and what she leaves I give to my daughter, Ann Gardiner. To wife also, the income of real estate for life.
Inventory, £151, 5s. 11d., viz: spinning wheel, carpenter's tools, 4 neat cattle, horsekind, sheep, &c.

Children: 1. Ann,

II. DANIEL, { b. / d. 1730. — East Greenwich, R. I.
m.
LYDIA, { b. / d. 1727 (—). — of

1702, Oct. 7. He (of Patience Island), bought of Joseph Wait, of Kings Town, for £40, land in East Greenwich, 90 acres.
1710, Jun. 13. He and wife Lydia, sold Thomas Matteson, 6 acres in East Greenwich, for £10.
1727, Sep. 9. Will—proved 1730, Mar. 28. Ex. son Benjamin. To daughter Hannah Gardiner, wife of Joseph, 40s. To daughter Martha Spencer, wife of Samuel, £10. To daughters Deliverance and Mercy Briggs, each a feather bed and £20, and the indoor movables, equally. To son Benjamin, dwelling house, farm and rest of estate.
Inventory, £523, 19s. 10d., viz: purse and apparel £20, feather bed, warming pan, cane, stillyards, 4 spinning wheels, 2 guns, cider mill, negro boy £54, pair of oxen, 5 cows, 2 mares, 6 geese, 6 fowls, 2 steers, half a yearling heifer, &c.

Children: 1. Benjamin, 2. Hannah, 3. Martha, 1708, Dec. 27. 4. Deliverance, 5. Mercy,

III. JOHN, { b. 1668, Jan. 25. / d. 1747. — North Kingstown, R. I.
m.
SARAH, { b. / d. 1746 + — of

1687, Sep. 6. Kings Town. Taxed 1s.
1712. Freeman.
1746, Apr. 21. Will—proved 1747, Feb. 8. Ex. son Ebenezer. To son John, 5s. To daughter Sarah Smith, 5s. To wife Sarah, household stuff. To daughter Mary Fowler, £5. To daughter Deliverance Briggs, £30. To granddaughter Wait Briggs, a legacy at eighteen. To son Ebenezer, homestead, but privilege to wife in the house while widow.
Inventory, wearing apparel, cow, &c.

Children: 1. John, 2. Ebenezer, 3. Sarah, 4. Mary, 5. Deliverance,

IV. JAMES, { b. 1671, Feb. 12. / d. 1757. — Kings Town, Providence, Cranston, R. I.
m.
SARAH, { b. / d. 1755 (—). — of

1687, Sep. 6. Taxed 1s.
1690. Freeman.
1728, Jun. 15. Providence. He and wife Sarah, deeded youngest son James, for love, &c., part of farm where I now live.
1738, Apr. 25. He and wife Sarah, deeded son-in-law Daniel Colvin and Zipporah, his wife, our daughter, 50 acres, adjoining land we gave our son-in-law, John Blanchard and Sarah, his wife.
1757, Apr. 22. Representations were made to Town Council, of Cranston, by James Briggs, Jr. and Joshua Burlingame, of Cranston, Benjamin Fiske, of Scituate, and Daniel Colvin, of Coventry, that James Briggs, Sr., "is now grown very ancient, decrippled and helpless, and much impaired in his eyesight, understanding and memory." The council appointed his grandson, Moses Briggs, as guardian, and an inventory of his estate was taken, amounting to £613, 2s. (feather bed, &c., £120, linen wheel, 2 silver spoons, &c).
1755, Mar. 20. Will—proved 1757, Aug. 13. Ex. son-in-law, Daniel Colvin. To eldest son John, 1s. To son James, 1s. To seven daughters rest of movables; viz: to Rose Burlingame, Mary Colvin, Anne Burlingame, Susanna Fiske, Elizabeth Abbott, Zipporah Colvin and Frances Colvin. To two granddaughters, Elizabeth Briggs and Sarah Blanchard, an equal part with one of aforesaid daughters.

Children: 1. John, 2. James, 3. Sarah, 4. Rose, 5. Mary, 6. Anne. 7. Susanna, 8. Elizabeth, 9. Zipporah, 10. Frances,

V. FRANCES, { b. 1673, Feb. 26. / d. 1693, Sep. 2.
UNMARRIED,

VI. RICHARD, { b. 1675, Feb. 1. / d. 1733. — Kings Town, East Greenwich, R. I.
m. (1) 1700, Dec. 23,
SUSANNA SPENCER, { b. 1681, Dec. 1. / d. — of John & Susanna ( ) Spencer.
m. (2)
EXPERIENCE, { b. / d. 1733 + — of

1733, Mar. 29. Will—proved 1733, Apr. 28. Ex. son John. To wife Experience, £20, in lieu of her thirds. To son Richard, £5. To son Francis, 8 or 10 acres and £5. To son John, my homestead farm, &c. To son Caleb, 10 acres. To daughter Sarah Aylsworth, £20. To daughter Ann King, £10, five ewe sheep and five lambs. To sons Philip and Daniel, £10 each. To daughters Mary and Alice Briggs, £5 each. To grandsons Richard Briggs, Caleb Tarbox and Richard Matteson, each a heifer improved for them by their respected fathers.
Inventory, £484, viz: cash and wearing apparel £33, 10s., bonds £198, 14s., silver spoon, horse £26, neat cattle £83, &c.

Children:
1. Richard, 1701, Oct. 17.
2. Francis, 1703, Oct. 27.
3. Audrey, 1705, Aug. 10.
4. Susanna. 1707, Dec. 31.
5. John, 1709, Feb. 8.
6. Sarah, 1710, Feb. 27.
7. Caleb, 1713, Feb. 17.
8. Ann, 1715, Oct. 25.
(2d wife.)
9. Mary, 1726, Jan. 27.
10. Philip, 1728, Nov. 7.
11. Daniel, 1730, Mar. 29.
12. Alice, 1732, Feb. 17.

VII. ROBERT, { b. 1678, Nov. 13. / d.

VIII MARY, { b. 1681, Sep. 2, / d.

IX. ANN, { b. 1683, Sep. 2. / d. 1683, Sep. 9.

X. SARAH, { b. 1685, Apr. 12. / d.

BRIGGS (JOHN, OF PORTSMOUTH.)

JOHN, { b. 1609. / d. 1690.
m.
——— { b. / d. 1690 (—)

Portsmouth, R. I.

1638. He was one of those admitted as inhabitants of the island of Aquidneck.

1639, Apr. 30. He and twenty-eight others signed the following compact: "We, whose names are underwritten, do acknowledge ourselves the legal subjects of his Majesty, King Charles, and in his name do hereby bind ourselves into a civil body politicke, unto his laws, according to matters of justice."

I. JOHN, { b. 1642. / d. 1713, Jul. 2. — Portsmouth, Tiverton, R. I.
m.
HANNAH FISHER, { b. / d. 1727 + — of Edward & Judith ( ) Fisher.

1676, Aug. 25, He, aged thirty-five years about, testified as to Low Howland being killed by Indians, and also that Manasses shot at Joseph Russell.
1677, May 24. He and wife Hannah had a deed of 30 acres from her father.
1687, Feb. 14, He bought of John Bailey, of Newport, and Sutton, his wife, 100 acres in Punkansett, Bristol County, Mass., and one-eighth of a share in Little Compton undivided lands, with dwelling house, for £146.
1692, Mar. 2. Tiverton. He was an inhabitant there, at organization of town.
1699, Jul. 18. He deeded youngest son William, of Tiverton, land there.
1703, Jan. 27. He deeded son William, land in or near Little Compton.
1713. Inventory, £39, 13s, 6d., shown by widow Hannah. Wearing apparel £5, pewter, chairs, 2 bedsteads, bed, sheep and lambs £2, neat cattle £11, mare and colt £10, &c.

Children: 1. Edward, 2. John, 3. William, 4. Susanna,

1641, Mar. 16. Freeman.

1643, Oct. 5. He was directed to go to every house to see what arms were defective.

1646, Aug. 24. He bought of John Hall, of Portsmouth, all his house and lot, &c., without molestation, only if I (John Hall), abide upon this land, I am to have the use of the dwelling house for the use of me, or mine, for the space of one year.

1648. Assistant.

1649. Licensed to keep an ordinary.

1654, Aug. 31. Commissioner for uniting the four towns.

1654-55-56-59-61-62-63. Commissioner.

1655. Freeman.

1655, May 25. He was on a committee to build a cage and stocks.

1656. Juryman.

1662, Oct. 6. He bought of John Dunham, Sr. (and Abigail), of Plymouth, a share in Dartmouth, for £42.

1664-65-66-68-69. Deputy.

1673, Feb. 20. He testified (calling himself sixty-four years or thereabouts), in the trial of Thomas Cornell. He had a dream and saw a woman at his bedside, "whereat he was much affrighted and cryed out, in the name of God, what art thou?" The apparition answered, "I am your sister Cornell," and twice said, "see how I was burnt with fire."

1679, Mar. 11. He deeded second son Thomas and wife Mary, for love, &c., one-quarter of a share in Dartmouth (35 acres), and if Thomas die, his wife Mary to enjoy same, if she continues his widow.

1679, Oct. 14. He deeded eldest son John, of Portsmouth, one-half of a share in Dartmouth, and if his wife Hannah survive him, she to enjoy same while widow. If she marry again, then to my grandson John, the second son of my son John, and if he die without issue, then to my son John's next younger son, &c. In case of failure of all, then to go to son John's eldest son Edward, he paying to daughters of son John, £20.

1690, Apr. 19. Will—proved 1690, Nov. 16. Ex. son Enoch. To son Enoch, all and every part of lands and personal estate, goods, chattels, debts and monies, he paying legacies, &c. To eldest son John, son Thomas, son William and daughter Susanna Northway, 1*s.* each, these four children having "long since received their portions and are gone from me." To son Job, three ewes, two wether lambs and two heifers.

1727, Nov. 28. His widow Hannah, being non compos mentis, had guardians appointed for her, viz: Henry Howland and John Russell.

II. THOMAS, { b. } Portsmouth, R. I., Dartmouth, Mass.
m. { d. 1720, Jun. 12.
MARY FISHER, { b.
{ d. 1717 + of Edward & Judith ( ) Fisher.

1667, Aug. 10. He was a member of Capt. Peleg Sanford's horse troop.
1673, May 6. Freeman.
1685, Jun. 2. Dartmouth. Grand Jury.
1717, Dec. 12. Will—proved 1720, Jul. 4. Exs. wife Mary and son John. To wife, half of homestead for life. To son John, rest of homestead, and at death of testator's wife, all the real estate to go to son John. To son Thomas, 5*s.*, he having had his share. To daughter Susanna Wilcox, £10. To daughter Hannah Dyer, £20. To son-in-law John Akin, 5*s.* To son-in-law Henry Howland, 5*s.* To grandson Thomas Briggs, son of John, 2 acres salt marsh. To wife Mary and son John, all the rest, equally.
Inventory, £1,001, 4*s.* 9*d.*, viz: purse and apparel £9, 18*s.* 6*d.*, bible and book 6*s.*, homestead £900, linen wheel, 14 sheep, 5 lambs, 2 oxen, 6 cows, 2 calves, 2 yearlings, 2 steers, half of 3 cattle, a mare, warming pan, &c.

1. Mary, 1671, Aug. 9.
2. Susanna, 1672, Mar. 14.
3. Deborah, 1674, Oct. 16.
4. Hannah, 1676, May 1.
5. John, 1678, Oct. 2.
6. Thomas, 1684, Apr. 27.

III. WILLIAM, { b. 1650. Portsmouth, Little Compton, R. I.
m. 1680, { d. 1716, May 12.
ELIZABETH COOK, { b. 1653.
{ d. 1716 + of John & Mary (Borden) Cook.

1667, Aug. 10. He was a member of Capt. Peleg Sanford's horse troop.
1672, Apr. 30. Freeman.
1716, Apr. 3. Will—proved 1716, Jul. 2. Exs. wife Elizabeth and son Job. Overseers, Robert Dennis, John Woodman and Benjamin Head. To son Job, my now dwelling house and all household stuff and farm I now live on. To son William, land on north side of a certain line, and to son Job, land south side. To son Job, all my stock of cattle, sheep, horses, hogs, money in house where he dwelleth, orchard, &c. To daughter Susanna Dennis, house and land occupied by Thomas Waite. To daughter Deborah Head, £20 and land. To daughter Elizabeth Woodman, £100. To son William, £30, feather bed, table and gun. To wife, £10 per annum, paid by son Job, and her choice of rooms and use of household stuff, and maintenance for her four servants.

1. Susanna, 1681, Apr. 9.
2. John, 1685, Nov. 13.
3. William, 1688, Jan. 11.
4. Elizabeth, 1689, Dec. 27.
5. Thomas, 1693, Sep. 5.
6. Deborah, 1693, Sep. 6.
7. Job, 1696, Aug. 3.

IV. SUSANNA, { b.
m. { d.
——— NORTHWAY, { b.
{ d. of Northway.

BRIGGS (JOHN of PORTSMOUTH.) 2d column. IV. Susanna, b. 1641, d. 1704, Nov. 7.

V. JOB, { b. Portsmouth, Little Compton, R. I.
m. { d. 1733.
ELEANOR, { b.
{ d. 1732 + of

1732, Jan. 7. Will—proved 1733, Apr. 17. Exx. wife Eleanor. To wife, east end of now dwelling house and improvement of all lands where house stands, half movable estate, negro woman Rose, and a feather bed. To eldest son Jeremiah, 5*s.* To Mary Borden, wife of Thomas, £5, besides what she had of her grandmother. To daughter Sarah Durfee, wife of Thomas, £5. To daughter Elizabeth Malum, wife of Mark, £5. To daughter Amy Briggs, feather bed that was her own mother's and £10. To daughter Wait Briggs, feather bed and £5. To son Job, west end of dwelling house and third of homestead. To son John, east end of house after his mother's decease, and one-third of homestead. To son Enoch, one-third homestead. The executrix to sell certain land in Tiverton and one-half movables, to pay debts.
Inventory, £1,051, 13*s.* 7*d.*, viz: apparel £18, 3*s.* 1*d.*, cash £10, pewter, warming pan, pair of worsted combs, sword, spinning wheel, 57 gallons rum, 2 hogsheads cider, bible, testament, psalter, pair of oxen, cow, calf, mare, and homestead and 12 acres £590, 37 acres wild land £130.

1. Jeremiah,
2. Job,
3. John,
4. Enoch,
5. Mary,
6. Sarah,
7. Elizabeth,
8. Amey,
9. Wait,

VI. ENOCH, { b. Portsmouth, R. I.
m. [Daniel. { d. 1734.
HANNAH WILCOX, (w. of { b.
{ d. 1736. of John & Mary (Borden) Cook.

1726, Jun. 2. Will—proved 1734, Apr. 26. Exx. wife Hannah. To wife, while widow, use of all housing and land, and all cattle, horsekind, sheep, swine and personal estate. If she marry again, she to distribute the whole personal estate amongst her three youngest children, viz: Abigail, the wife of John Butts, Sarah Briggs, and Susannah, wife of William Cook. If she do not marry, she is to devise whole produce of real and personal estate to said three youngest daughters. After decease or marriage of wife, the profit of certain land and housing to go to her daughter Abigail Butts, for life, and then to Abigail's daughters Hope and Abigail Moon, or if they have no heirs, to other two daughters of Abigail Butts, viz: Hannah and Constance Butts. The profits of all other land, to go at decease of wife to her daughters, Sarah Briggs and Susanna, wife of William Cook, and heir theirs, or if no heirs, then to daughters of Abigail Butts, and if they have no heirs, then testator gives all his land and housing to brother, Job Briggs. To wife's daughter, Eliphal Brayton, one good cow. To John Moon, grandson of wife, 5*s.*
1734, Jun. 14. Will—proved 1736, Nov. 8. Widow Hannah. To daughter Abigail Butts, sundry household articles. To granddaughter Hannah Wilcox, daughter of son Daniel, lately deceased, a white chest. To daughters Sarah Briggs and Susannah Cook, rest of estate.

1. Abigail,
2. Sarah,
3. Susanna, 1697, Sep. 21.

BRIGHTMAN.

HENRY, { b.
m. { d. 1728.
JOAN, { b.
{ d. 1716 (—).

Portsmouth, Newport, R. I., Freetown, Mass.

1671. Freeman.

1671. Juryman.

1677, Mar. 6. He and wife Joan, sold Matthew Boomer, of Newport, for £45, a half share on east side of Taunton River.

1677, Oct. 31. He and forty-seven others were granted 5,000 acres, to be called East Greenwich. He never went there to settle.

1682-85-90-91. Deputy,

1683, Dec. 31. He bought 23 acres of Daniel Grinnell and wife Mary, for £124.

1687. Constable.

1688. Grand Jury.

1691, Dec. 8. He bought of Nathaniel Howland, south half of a lot in Freetown.

1704, Jun. 20. He and wife Joan, sold George Sisson, 30 acres in Portsmouth, for £280.

1705-6-7-8-9. Newport. Deputy.

1716, Oct. 3. Will — codicil 1728, Feb. 15. — proved 1728, Apr. 9. Exs. three sons William, Thomas and Joseph. To eldest son William, the house he now dwells in and largest silver tankard. To second son Thomas, farm in Dartmouth, house lot in Newport, silver tankard, yoke of oxen, five cows and sixty sheep. To youngest son Joseph, all land in Freetown, silver cup, silver porringer, six silver spoons and my seal ring. To daughter Hester Chandler,

I. HENRY, { b. Portsmouth, R. I.
m. 1694, Aug. { d. 1716 (—).
ELIZABETH LAWTON, { b.
{ d. of Lawton.

No issue.

II. HESTER, { b.
m. { d.
——— CHANDLER, { b.
{ d. of Chandler.

III. WILLIAM, { b. Newport, Portsmouth, R. I.
m. 1708, Jan. 22, { d.
MERCY SPURR, { b.
{ d. of Spurr.

1704. Freeman.
1705, Apr. 16. He, called bachelor, bought 50 acres in Portsmouth, for £350, of John Cory and Elizabeth, his wife.
1721, Aug. 18. Portsmouth. He and wife Mercy, mortgaged 30 acres, for £150.
1733, Apr. 16. He deeded to son William, two lots in Tiverton.

1. Mary, 1710, Jan. 26.
2. Henry, 1711, Nov. 10.
3. William, 1713, Nov. 4.
4. Joseph, 1715, Dec. 11.
5. John, 1718, Mar. 19.
6. Thomas, 1718, Mar. 19.
7. Esther, 1720, May 2.

IV. THOMAS, { b. Dartmouth, Mass.
m. { d.
——— { b.
{ d. of

BRIGHTMAN. 2d column. IV. Thomas. His wife was Penelope.

1735, Nov. 11. He deeded to Henry Brightman, three tracts of land.
1740, Feb. 7. He deeded to son Thomas, 6 acres, being part of homestead, for £36.

1. Henry, 1709, Nov. 4.
2. Mary, 1711, Mar. 15.
3. Esther, 1712, Nov. 7.
4. Sarah, 1715, Nov. 29.
5. Thomas, 1718, Nov. 20.
6. William, 1720, Sep. 20.
7. Joseph,
8. Penelope,
9. Jane, 1730, Apr. 20.

V. SARAH, { b.
m. { d.
HEZEKIAH HOAR, { b. 1678, Nov. 10.
{ d. of Hezekiah & Rebecca ( ) Hoar.

1. Hezekiah,
2. Henry,
3. Rebecca, 1713.
4. Sarah,
5. Mary, 1723.

BRIGHTMAN. 2d column. II. Hester m. John Chandler. VI. Joseph m. Susanna Turner. She d. 1783. 1780, Oct. 19. Will-proved 1783, Nov. 4. Widow Susanna. Ex. son Joseph. She mentions sons Joseph and George, daughter Susanna Tompkins, and grandson James Brightman (alias Pearson).

land in Newport and £50 in cattle or goods. To daughter Sarah Hoar, land I bought of Hezekiah Hoar, in Newport and £50. To sons Thomas and Joseph, all my farm and buildings I bought of Edward Greenman, at Green End, Newport, and my now dwelling house there, and all stock there, to be equally divided to them. To three grandsons, Henry, son of William, Henry, son of Thomas, and Henry, son of Joseph, a lot of land each, in Newport, and to grandson Henry Hoar, a lot of land. To three sons, rest of estate. The will was dated at Newport, but the codicil at Freetown. In the codicil, finding himself more chargeable to son Joseph, by reason of infirmity of age, &c., he gives said Joseph and wife Susanna, bed, &c., not before disposed of.

VI. JOSEPH, b. 1691. d. 1753, Mar. 3.
m.
SUSANNA, b. d. 1751 + of

Freetown, Mass.

1717. Assessor of taxes.

1721. Grand Jury.

1751, Dec. 18. Will—proved 1753, Mar. 28. Exs. sons Joseph and George. To wife Susanna, west end of dwelling house, all indoor movables and income of all real estate while widow To son Joseph, south part of my farm he now dwelleth on, except three square rods for a burying place, &c. To son George, north part of above farm. To son James, my dwelling house, ferry and ferry-boat, my Great Neck of land and other land. To daughter Mary Brightman, £50, great room and bed-room in west end of dwelling house, and privilege in kitchen, while single, and maintenance by my three sons. To daughter Elizabeth Pitts, £20, she having had already. To daughter Susanna Brightman, £50. To Frances Church, £5. To sons Joseph and George, all my stock, and all my farming tools.

1. Henry, 1716, Sep. 19.
2. Joseph, 1718, Apr. 26.
3. George, 1721, Sep. 16.
4. Mary, 1727, Aug. 13.
5. Elizabeth, 1730, Jul. 9.
6. James, 1734, May 22.
7. Susanna, 1736, May 14.

BROOKS.

THOMAS, b. d.
m.
HANNAH, b. d.

Portsmouth, Newport, R. I.

1655. Freeman.

1671, Jan. 30. Newport. He was allowed 15*s*., for five day's service for colony.

1680. Taxed 12*s*. 5*d*.

1687–88. Grand Jury.

1694. He and wife Hannah, deeded land in East Greenwich (their residence being in Newport).

1696, Feb. 22. He bought land in Newport, of Nathaniel and Susanna Coddington.

I. HANNAH, b. 1672, Jul. 6 d.

II. MARY, b. 1674, Jan. 28. d.

BROWN, (BERIAH).

BERIAH, b. d. 1717, Feb.
m. (1) 1685 ±
ABIGAIL PHENIX, b. d.
of Alexander & Abigail (Sewall) Phenix.
m. (2)
ELEANOR, b. d. 1717 +

Kings Town, R. I.

1687, Sep. 6. Taxed 3*s*. 10½*d*.

1703, Jul. 12. He was appointed with others to lay out highways.

1709, May 27. He and five others had 792 acres of vacant lands in Narragansett, allotted to them, by the committee of the Assembly, who were authorized to make sales of same.

1710, Apr. 1. He deeded to son Alexander, certain land in Kings Town, being part of homestead farm.

1717, Feb. 20. He was buried during a snow storm.

1717. Administration to son Alexander.

1717, Mar. 12. His widow Eleanor, gave a receipt to the administrator, and mentions what she had when she married the father of said administrator, and now had received again.

I. ALEXANDER, b. d. 1758.
m. (1)
HONOUR HULING, b. d. of Alexander & Elizabeth (Wightman) Huling.
m. (2)
LYDIA, b. d. 1758 + of

North Kingstown, R. I.

1718, Aug. 30. He was the eldest living son of Beriah Brown, deceased, as testified by Abigail Phenix, widow.

1719, Mar. 26. He exchanged certain land with Elisha Mitchell.

1725, Feb. 8. He bought of Alexander Huling and wife Elizabeth, 50¾ acres for £152.

1758, Aug. 13. Will—proved 1758. He mentions wife Lydia, sons Beriah and Ebenezer, daughters Honour Hopkins, Abigail Phillips, Sarah Dolover and Mary Case, grandchildren Alexander Brown (son of Ebenezer), Alexander Hopkins, Mary and Sarah Phillips, Elisha Case (son of Mitchell), Alexander Arnold, Honour Gardiner, Sarah Wait, &c. He also mentions son-in-law Sanford Case.

1. Honour, ——, Apr. 16.
2. Abigail, 1713, Nov. 15.
3. Beriah, 1715, Jan. 16.
4. Sarah, ——, Jul. 7.
5. Ebenezer, ——, Sep. 20.
6. Ann, ——, Mar. 13.
7. Mary, ——, Jul. 8.

II. CHARLES, b. d. 1751.
m.
ELEANOR, b. d. 1751 + of

North Kingstown, R. I.

1710, Jun. 30. Kings Town. He had a deed from his grandmother, Abigail Phenix, of 130 acres, being homestead farm she had lately bought, and was to be his at her death, she being comfortably supported. She subsequently took a bond from him for £500.

1717, Apr. 16. His grandmother released him from the bond.

1717, Jun. 18. He gave a receipt to his brother Alexander, for £19, 17*s*. 9*d*., in full for his part of father, Beriah Brown's estate, as shown in inventory. The legacy was paid in cattle, sheep and sundry other goods.

1751. Will—proved. He gives to his son John, the same land that the grandmother of testator had deeded him.

1. Alexander,
2. Charles,
3. John,

III. MARY, b. d.
m, 1703, Mar. 18,
JOSEPH CARPENTER, b. d. of Abiah Carpenter.

1. Joseph, 1704, Jan. 7.
2. Abigail, 1705, Oct. 2.
3. Anne, 1705, Oct.
4. Thomas,
5. Martha,

IV. SARAH, b. d.

(2d WIFE, no issue.)

Henry Browne. See also: Bowen's THE PROVIDENCE OATH OF ALLEGIANCE, p.65-67.

BROWN (Henry). See: American Genealogist, v.25, p.249; v.39, p.1

HENRY, m. (1) WAITE WATERMAN, of Richard & Bethiah ( ) Waterman. m. (2) HANNAH MATHEWSON, (w. of James.) of John Field.
{ b. 1625. d. 1703, Feb. 20. } { b. d. } { b. d. 1703 + }

Providence, R. I.

1652–53–54. Commissioner.

1654, Apr. 28. He and Arthur Fenner, were granted a share of meadow at Netuaconkonit Hill.

1655. Freeman.

1656. Constable.

1657, May 14. He was granted a small parcel south side of Ann Harris's lot in the Neck.

1661. Grand Jury.

1664–66–87. Town Treasurer.

1665, Feb. 19. He had lot 61 granted, in a division of lands.

1665–68–71–72–84. Deputy.

1669, Apr. 2. He and wife Waite, sold to Shadrach Manton, 5 acres, dwelling house, &c.

1672–73. Assistant.

1679–80. Town Council.

1680, Apr. 20. In giving testimony, at this date (as to a deed made by John Lippitt, in 1652), he calls himself aged fifty-five years.

1687. Ratable estate, 2 oxen, steer, 2 heifers, mare, colt, 2 swine, 5 acres planting and young orchard, 4 acres old orchard, 4 acres meadow, 30 acres pasture.

1687, Sep. 1. Taxed 8*s*.

1703, Feb. 17. He, having already made his will, commits the ordering of his affairs, &c., to son Richard, giving him power to act for him.

1698, Sep. 22. Will—proved 1703, Mar. 10. Exx. wife Hannah. To son Henry, farm in Providence, with house, &c., near Neutaconkonitt Hill, but if he die without issue, it is to go to son Joseph, and finally to son Richard, if Joseph die without issue. To daughter Phebe Harris, meadow on west side of Moshausick River and 8 acres upland. To son Richard, farm in Loquassuck Woods of about 100 acres. To son Joseph, rights in certain land. To sons Richard and Joseph, land in the Neck, and my homestead, dwelling house, &c., the western part of house to Richard and the eastern part to Joseph, but wife Hannah to have Joseph's part for life, to dwell in. After a few special bequests to Richard and Joseph, all the rest of movables are left to them. To wife's daughter, Lydia Mathewson, a heifer. To son Joseph, two steers, heifer and two calves. To wife, rest of cattle, for her and family while she remains in the house, and at her departure what remains to be for Richard and Joseph.

Inventory, £93, 3*s*., viz: 5 cows, 12 sheep, steer, 2 heifers, sow, 10 shoats, earthern and pewter ware, 4 spoons, 4 chairs, warming pan, &c., besides articles that wife Hannah brought to him, amounting to £8, 1*s*. The rooms mentioned were fire room, leanto bed-room and chamber.

1703, Jul. 28. Widow Hannah gave receipt for movable estate, cattle, &c., to Richard and Joseph Brown, the two sons of late husband, to whom she had committed the office of executor, she being unacquainted with the duties.

I. HENRY, m. DOROTHY, of { b. d. 1727, Nov. 22. } { b. d. } Providence, R. I.

(She m. (2) 1734, Sep. 22, Samuel Swan.)

1687. Ratable estate, cow, heifer, calf, 2 mares, colt, swine, meadow.

1687, Sep. 1. Taxed 2*s*. 6*d*.

1704, Dec. 6. He sold Hope Corp, certain land for £5.

1733, Sep. 3. Administration to son Jeremiah, he being now of age, and widow Dorothy not having sureties. Inventory, £148, 7*s*., viz: yoke of oxen, yoke of steers, cow, heifer, calf, mare, 11 sheep, 4 hogs, 3 shoats, hay, feather bed, warming pan, 14 oz. silver money £10, 10*s*., woolen yarn, &c.

1. Jeremiah,
2. Waite.

II. PHEBE, m. THOMAS HARRIS, of Thomas & Elnathan (Tew) Harris. { b. d. 1723, Aug. 20. } { b. 1665, Oct. 19. d. 1741, Nov. 1. }

1. Wait,	1694, Apr. 21.
2. Phebe,	1698, Dec. 16.
3. John,	1700, Sep. 17.
4. Henry,	1702, Oct. 5.
5. Thomas,	1704, Oct. 21.
6. Charles,	1709.
7. Gideon,	1714, Mar. 15.
8. Lydia,	1715, Jun. 9.

BROWN (HENRY). 2d column. III. Richard. Erase marriage. He m Mary Rhodes, of Malachi & Mary (Carder) Rhodes. IV. Joseph. The surname of his 1st wife's mother was Brown.

III. RICHARD, m. MARY PRAY, of John & Sarah ( ) Pray. { b. 1676 d. 1774, Feb. 20. } { b. d. 1765 (—) } Providence, North Providence, R. I.

He was born at Newport, during King Philip's war.

1708–9–10–11–12. Town Council.

1709–12–23. Deputy.

1765, Oct. 30. Will—proved 1774, May 18. Exs. sons William and Richard. He calls himself of North Providence, but his will was probated at Providence. He also says that he is very aged. To son William, 5*s*. in silver and negro girl Anne, till forty, she then being freed, as also old negro woman Sylvia, who is not to be sold out of the family. His son William, had already received an estate by deed and "on whom another hereditary estate will devolve by my death." To grandson Jesse, son of Richard, 20 acres at Musket's Plain, west of Seven Mile Line, and 60 acres at the Neck in Providence, joining on the east side of old homestead where I dwell. To Richard, also, negro girl Phillis till forty, and then freed, silver cup, feather bed, wearing apparel, carpenter's and cooper's tools. To old negro woman Sylvia, her bed and bedding. To negro girl Sylvia, the younger, an absolute freedom from any service, duty or slavery to any person whatsoever, without her own consent, her said freedom and manumission to commence at my decease. To grandson Dexter Brown, negro boy Peter till forty-five, and then freed. To two sons, residue of real and personal estate, equally.

His son and namesake Richard, lived to even a greater age than his father, and celebrated his one hundredth year by inviting his friends to a dance, at which he played on a violin for their amusement, as is declared.

1. Malachi,	1698, Feb. 1.
2. Mercy,	1703, Dec. 12.
3. William,	1705, Jun. 3.
4. Richard,	1712, Feb. 28.

IV. JOSEPH, m. (1) SARAH PRAY, of John & Sarah ( ) Pray. m. (2) 1728, Jun. 17. ABIJAH WHITMAN, of Valentine & Sarah (Bartlett) Whitman. { b. d. 1742, Jul. 20. } { b. d. } { b. 1708, Jan. 4. d. } Providence, R. I., Attleboro, Mass., Smithfield, R. I.

He bore the title of Captain some years.

1718. Deputy.

1729, Oct. Attleboro. He and others of Attleboro, having prayed they might be annexed to Rhode Island, "supposing themselves to be part thereof," it was voted by Assembly that a committee be empowered at the charge of petitioners, to settle the line between this colony (of Rhode Island), and said province from Pawtucket Falls, north, and that a letter be sent to the General Assembly of that province, moving them to appoint a committee on their part to join with ours, but if they refuse or neglect, then our commissioners to run it themselves, if they see cause, and that the case be sent home to Great Britain in order to be decided, provided petitioners first pay £200 into the hands of persons appointed by this colony to be sent to England with the case, and that two substantial men of the petitioners be bound in sum of £2,000, for sum needed to satisfy whole charge of settling line.

1742, Aug. 12. Administration to Richard Brown, who had whole right by law.

Inventory, pair of oxen, 4 cows, 4 heifers, steer, mare, 4 swine, woolen wheel, gun, bedding, pewter, books, 6 silver spoons, 6½ oz. silver money, &c.

(2d WIFE, no issue.)

1. Abigail,	1704, Oct. 14.
2. Deborah,	1706, Feb. 10.
3. Sarah,	1709, Mar. 19.
4. Anne,	1713, Jan.
5. Stephen,	1715, Mar. 3.
6. Benjamin,	1717, Jan. 28.
7. Mary,	1718, Feb. 12.
8. Martha,	1721, Oct. 23.
9. Amey,	1723, Aug. 21.
10. Joseph,	1727, Feb. 19.
(2d wife.)	
11. Phebe,	1729, Feb. 28.
12. Wait,	1730, Oct. 17.
13. Amey,	1734, Dec. 17.

BROWN (HENRY). 2d column. III. Richard. 1742, Aug. 12. He took administration on estate of Joseph Brown of Smithfield, having whole right by law, ~~so that~~ this may ~~have been an additional son.~~ IV. Joseph, d. 1764, Mar. 13. (not 1742, July 20). He m. (3) Hannah. Children, 14. Abigail, 1752, Mar. 6. 15. Phebe, 1754, Mar. 10. 16. Lillis, 1757, Apr. 2. 17, Abraham, 1760, Mar. 16. He may never have been captain, nor of Attleboro. Erase these lines commencing 1742, Aug. 12. He was last of Glocester, R. I., 1764, Feb. 2. Will-proved 1764. Exs. wife Hannah, and friends Thomas Steere and Benjamin Lapham of Smithfield. He mentions wife Hannah (what she brought, etc.), sons Stephen, Benjamin, and Joseph; daughters Deborah Comstock, Sarah Phillips, Anne Whipple, Martha Farnum, Amey Ballou, Waity Smith, grandson Joseph Whipple, and the rest to Abigail, Phebe, Lillis and Abraham.

This was possible from documents. Is wrong.

BROWN (Nicholas).

NICHOLAS, m. (1) ——— m. (2) FRANCES PARKER, (w. of George.) { b. d. 1694. } { b. d. } { b. d. 1669 + }

Portsmouth, R. I.

1638. He was admitted an inhabitant of the island of Aquidneck.

1639. "Nicholas Browne, doth dismiss himself of the government here."

1639, Apr. 30. He and twenty-eight others signed the following compact: "We, whose names are underwritten, do acknowledge ourselves the legal subjects of his majesty, King Charles, and in his name do hereby bind ourselves into a civil body politicke, unto his laws, according to matters of justice."

1646, Feb. 4. He had 20 acres added to his other 20 acres adjoining it.

1655. Freeman.

1680. Taxed 6*s*. 4*d*.

1694, Nov. 16. Will—proved 1694, Dec. 27. Ex. grandson Tobias. To eldest son Nicholas, 5*s*. To son Abraham, 5*s*. To daughter Jane Babcock, £10. To two granddaughters, Martha and Jane Brown, daughters of son William, deceased, each £10. To grandson Tobias, son of William, all my lands and houses in Rhode Island, and all neat cattle, sheep, horsekind and hogs, carts, plows, corn, hay, pewter, brass, iron, provision, apparel and bedding.

His sons may have gone to New Jersey.

I. NICHOLAS, { b. d. }

II. ABRAHAM, { b. d. }

III. JANE, m. JAMES BABCOCK, of James & Sarah ( ) Babcock. { b. d. 1719. } { b. 1641. d. 1698 ± }

1. James,
2. Sarah,
3. Jane,
4. Mary,
5. Hannah,
6. Elizabeth,

IV. WILLIAM, m. ———, of { b. d. } { b. d. } Portsmouth, R. I.

1680. Taxed 4*s*. 2*d*.

1. Martha,	
2. Jane,	1677.
3. Tobias,	

See American Genealogist, Apr., 1954, v. 30, no. 2, p. 124

BROWN (NICHOLAS). 2d column. I. Nicholas. 1684. He, of New Jersey, testified that he was the deceased Bartholomew West's nearest relation; in a suit when Catherine Brown, sister of Christopher Almy, also testified. Perhaps Catherine was his wife. II. Abraham d. 1714. Mansfield, Burlington County, N. J., 1714, July 10. Will-proved 1714, May 5. Ex. son Abraham. He mentions wife, but not by name, and sons Abraham (b. 1672 ±). Preserved, Nicholas, William, Caleb; daughters Sarah Potter, Elizabeth Alfell; grandson Thomas Potter.

{ THOMAS, { b.
m. { d. 1665 ±
{ ANN, { b.
{ d. 1665 +

Portsmouth, R. I.

1647, Mar. 18. He was one of the witnesses to the will of John Walker.

1647, May 20. Water Bailey.

1655. Freeman.

1655-61-62-63. Commissioner.

1658, Apr. 4. He sold Thomas Lawton 35 acres.

1664. Deputy.

1665, Nov. 6. Ann Brownell, widow and executrix of Thomas Brownell, exchanged certain land with William Brenton, fulfilling a contract made by her husband, previous to his decease.

I. { MARY, { b. 1639.
m. { d. 1739, Jan. 12.
{ ROBERT HAZARD, { b. 1635.
{ d. 1710 + of Thomas & Martha ( ) Hazard.

1. Thomas, 1660.
2. George,
3. Stephen,
4. Martha,
5. Daughter,
6. Robert,
7. Jeremiah, 1675, Mar. 25
8. Mary, 1676.
9. Hannah,

II. { SARAH, { b.
m. 1658, Jun. 1, { d. 1676 Sep. 6.
{ GIDEON FREEBORN, { b.
{ d. 1720, Feb. 28. of William & Mary ( ) Freeborn.

1. Mary, 1664, Feb. 12.
2. Sarah, 1667, Jan. 14.
3. Anne, 1669, Mar. 28.
4. Martha, 1671, Aug. 8.
5. Susanna, 1674, Mar. 24.
6. Patience, 1676, Mar. 4.

III. { MARTHA, { b. 1643, May.
m. (1) { d. 1744, Feb. 15.
JEREMIAH WAIT, { b.
{ d. 1677 (—) of Thomas Wait.
m. (2) { b. 1650.
{ CHARLES DYER, { d. 1709, May 15. of William & Mary ( ) Dyer.

No issue.

IV. { GEORGE, { b. 1646. Portsmouth, R. I.
m. 1673, Dec. 4, { d. 1718, Apr. 20.
{ SUSANNA PEARCE, { b. 1652, Nov. 20.
{ d. 1743, Dec. 24. of Richard & Susanna (Wright) Pearce.

1. Susanna, 1676, Jan. 25.
2. Sarah, 1681, Jun. 14.
3. Mary, 1683, Dec. 8.
4. Martha, 1686, Feb. 18.
5. Thomas, 1688, Jun. 1.
6. Joseph, 1690, Dec. 5.
7. Waite, 1693, Oct. 3.
8. Stephen, 1695, Dec. 3.

1699-1702. Deputy.

1706-7-8-9-10-11. Assistant.

1708, Apr. He was appointed on the committee in regard to vacant lands in Narragansett.

1717, Apr. 17. Will—proved 1718, May 12. Exx. wife Susanna. To son Joseph, all housing and lands where I dwell, except lower room, and that at death of wife. To son Stephen, land in Portsmouth, and all my new house or building thereon, except north end of house reserved for use of my sister, Martha Dyer, and my daughters Susanna and Waite Brownell. To sons Joseph and Stephen, land in Tiverton and Little Compton. To son Joseph, a pair of oxen. To son Stephen, a pair of oxen and two cows. To daughter Susanna Brownell, £50. To daughter Sarah Borden, £30. To daughter Mary, wife of William Hall, £30. To daughter Martha, wife of Samuel Forman, £30. To daughter Waite Brownell, £50, a good feather bed, &c. To sister Martha Dyer, and my daughters Susanna and Waite Brownell, use of north end of new house while unmarried. To wife Susanna, the newest lower room in now dwelling house for life, and the rest of movable estate to be at her disposal, she paying legacies.

Inventory, £961, 5*s.* 10*d.*, viz: wearing apparel, silver money £344, 16*s.* 4*d.*, plate £6, tables, chairs, wheel, loom, weaving gear, cider £1, 10*s.*, carpenter's tools, &c. £7, a horse, sheep £50, 2 oxen, 10 cows, 9 two year old, 5 yearlings, swine, geese, 7 beds, warming pan, &c.

V. { WILLIAM, { b. Portsmouth, Little Compton, R. I., Dartmouth, Mass.
m. { d. 1715.
{ SARAH SMITON, { b.
{ d. 1715 + of William & Sarah ( ) Smiton.

1. Thomas, 1674, May 25.
2. Sarah, 1675, Nov. 25.
3. Martha, 1678, May 24.
4. Anne, 1680, Jun. 4.
5. William, 1682, Aug. 11.
6. Benjamin, 1684, Oct. 20.
7. Robert, 1688, Apr. 11.
8. Mary, 1691, Feb. 13.
9. Smiton, 1691, Feb. 13.
10. George, 1693, Apr. 13.
11. Alice, 1695, Dec. 3.

1677. Freeman.

1683, Jun. 9. Little Compton. Surveyor of Highways.

1684. Constable.

1706, Dec. 4. Dartmouth. He took administration on his son-in-law, Jonathan Tripp's estate, the widow Martha and her second husband, Samuel Hart, refusing.

1714, Nov. 6. Will—proved 1715, Aug. 1. Exx. wife Sarah. Overseers, friend Nathaniel Soule and son Smiton Brownell. To wife, produce of all my land in Little Compton, and all movables for life, except a feather bed to daughter Alice. To son Smiton, all horsekind and cattle, left at wife's decease, and half household stuff. To son George, half household stuff. To son Smiton, all land in Little Compton at wife's decease. To four sons Thomas, William, Benjamin and Robert, 20*s.*, equally. To three daughters Martha, Anne and Mary, 15*s.*, equally.

Inventory, £68, 5*s.*, viz: 10 acres £7, cow, 5 heifers, pair of steers, 3 yearlings, 2 horsekind, 6 swine, 8 geese, 4 beds, warming pan, gun, sword, loom, cheesepress.

VI. { THOMAS, { b. Little Compton, R. I.
m. { d. 1732, May 18.
{ MARY PEARCE, { b. 1654, May 6.
{ d. 1736, May 4. of Richard & Susanna (Wright) Pearce.

1. Thomas, 1679, Feb. 16.
2. John, 1682, Feb. 21.
3. George, 1685, Jan. 19.
4. Jeremiah 1689, Oct. 10.
5. Mary, 1692, Mar. 22.
6. Charles, 1694, Dec. 23.

1730. Will—proved 1732, Jun. 20. Exs. wife Mary and son Thomas. To wife, half of dwelling house and half of orchard, for life, use of all bills and bonds, or £40 per year instead, all my negroes and half of chattels, for life, and use of all household goods. To son Thomas, £10 at decease of wife, and confirmation of deed of gift formerly made, and like legacy to sons John, George and Jeremiah. To son Charles, all farming tools, and half of outdoor stock, £10 and confirmation of deed, he bringing his mother firewood, for life, &c. To granddaughter Mary Carr, £100, two feather beds, trunk, &c., and at death of her grandmother, rest of household goods, but if said granddaughter die before eighteen, then five sons of testator to have.

Inventory, £1,807, 1*s.* 6*d.*, viz: wearing apparel and sword £34. 14*s.* 6*d.*, 5 beds, churn, pair of cards, loom, shoemaker's tools, silver money 14*s.* 8*d.*, English half pence £11, 12*s.* 5*d.* (at 2*d.* apiece), money scales, tankard, bonds £1,052, 12*s.* 1*d.*, mare, pair of oxen, 6 cows, 4 young cattle, 26 sheep, 12 lambs, 3 calves, 23 geese, 11 swine, old negro man and woman £90, hives of bees, &c.

1735, Jun. 9. Will—proved 1736, Nov. 19. Widow Mary. Ex. brother George Pearce. To sons Thomas, George, Jeremiah and Charles, 1*s.* each. To grandson Samuel, son of Charles, a feather bed. To brother George Pearce, a mare, he paying £8 to my son John Brownell. To granddaughter Mary Carr, money, bills and bonds, &c.

Inventory, £175, 12*s.* 4*d.*

VII. { ROBERT, { b. Portsmouth, Little Compton, R. I.
m. { d. 1728, Jul. 22.
{ MARY, { b.
{ d. 1728 + of

1. Thomas, 1687.
2. Anne. 1690, Jan. 27.
3. Benjamin, 1697, Apr. 11.
4. Patience,
5. Margaret,
6. Mary,

1673. Freeman.

1689, Jun. Little Compton. Selectman.

1689, Dec. 25. Ensign.

1690, Mar. 8. He and wife Mary, sold his sister Martha Wait, of Portsmouth, 30 acres in Little Compton, for £20.

1718, Jan. 29. Will—proved 1728, Aug 20. Exx. wife Mary. Overseers, Thomas Brownell, Jr. and Joseph Wilbur, Jr. To son Thomas, land on west side of highway where I live, and 42 acres of other land. To son Benjamin, all housing and land where I live, east of highway, only wife to have one room in the house and income of half the lands, with firewood provided by son Benjamin. To son Benjamin, half of all the stock, he paying legacies. To three daughters Patience, Margaret and Ann, £10 each. To daughter Mary's three children, £5 each. To grandson Wilbur, £5. To wife Mary, the other half of stock, and all household goods for life, and at her death to be divided to daughters.

Inventory, £255, 18*s.* 6*d.*, viz: 2 beds, wearing apparel, broadsword, cheesepress, 18 sheep, 11 lambs, pair of oxen, 2 cows, bull, heifer, 2 calves, colt, young horse, mare, 5 swine, churn, &c.

VIII. { ANN, { b.
m. { d. 1747, Apr. 2.
{ JOSEPH WILBUR, { b.
{ d. 1729, May 4. of William Wilbur.

1. Martha, 1684, Aug. 20.
2. Anne, 1686, May 8.
3. William, 1688, Mar. 25.
4. Joseph, 1689, Dec. 30.
5. John, 1691, Dec. 15.
6. Thomas, 1694, Jan. 14.
7. Mary, 1696, Jan. 4.
8. Benjamin, 1699, Jun. 20.
9. Stephen, 1701, Mar. 22.
10. Abigail, 1703, Aug 21.

BRYER.

JOSEPH, b. 1645. d. 1704, May 31,
m. (1) 1672, Jun. 22,
MARY GOULD, b. 1653, Mar. 2, d. 1691, Jan. 9.
of Daniel & Wait (Coggeshall) Gould.
m. (2) 1692, Feb. 5,
MARY PALMER, b. d.
of Palmer.

Newport, R. I.

His second wife was of Westchester, Pa.

1680. Taxed 18*s*.

1682, Sep. 5. Grand Jury.

He and his first wife were buried in Clifton Burial Ground.

BRYER. 1st column. 1704, will proved. He mentions wife Mary and eldest son Joseph, who is to have the housing in England upon his mother's decease. His 2d wife, b 1670, Mar., d. 1759, Sep. 15. She m. (2) 1705, Christopher Almy. 2d column. I. Elizabeth, d. 1729+. Her husband d. 1729. V. John, d. 1749 (—). He had 4 John.

I. ELIZABETH, b. 1682, Jun. 18. d.
m.
JOSEPH BORDEN, b. 1678, Jul. 17. d. of Matthew & Sarah (Clayton) Borden.
1. Matthew, 2. Thomas, 3. Mary, 4. Sarah, 5. Elizabeth,

(2d WIFE.)

II. MARY, b. 1692, Nov. 8. d.

III. JOSEPH, b. 1694, Sep. 5. d. 1711, Nov. 5.
Unmarried.

IV. MATTHEW, b. 1696, Aug. 23. d.

V. JOHN, b. 1703, Sep. 17. d. Newport, R. I.
m.
ELIZABETH, b. d. of
1725. Freeman.
1. Jonathan, 1724, Oct.
2. Joseph, 1730, Nov. 14.
3. Jonathan, 1732, Dec. 5.

BULGAR. See: American Geneologist, v. 20, p. 181

RICHARD, b. 1608. d. 1679 +
m.
LETTICE, b. d.

Roxbury, Mass., Portsmouth, R. I.

He was a bricklayer.

1631, May 18. Freeman.

1634, Apr. 20. He had his son John baptized.

1637, Nov. 20. He and others, of Roxbury, &c., were ordered to deliver up all guns, pistols, swords, powder, shot, &c., because "the opinions and revelations of Mr. Wheelwright and Mrs. Hutchinson, have seduced and led into dangerous errors many of the people here in New England."

1660–62–63. General Solicitor.

1666, Oct. 11. He sold Thomas Butts, 2 acres for a cow and 10*s* in wampum.

1670, Jan. 28 He and wife Lettice, sold John Simmons 2 acres, for £9.

1679. He was called seventy-one years old.

I. JOHN, b. 1634. d.

BULL (ISAAC).

ISAAC, b. d. 1716.
m. (1)
——— b. d.
m. (2) 1714, Mar. 2,
MARY WALLING, b. d. 1724.
of James Walling.

(She m. (2) 1719, Apr. 18, Joseph Cook.)

Providence, R. I.

He was a carpenter.

1700, Aug. 2. He sold Stephen Sly 110 acres, for £35.

1713, Jun. 16 Taxed 6*s*.

1716, Jan. 5. Will—proved 1716, Apr. 17. Exx. wife Mary. To her, all estate, both real and personal, for life. To son John, 20*s*. To daughters Elizabeth Vaughan, Mary Mowry and Rose Inman, 20*s*. each. To daughter Hannah Bull, after decease of wife, all the rest of estate, but if she have no heirs, then equally to four grandchildren, viz: Isaac Bull, Isaac Vaughan, Uriah Mowry and Aaron Inman. On back side of will, the declaration of Isaac Bull was made—that he was in no ways indebted to his children for any service done for him by them, and that he had made them an offer to look after him during his natural life, and then they should have his estate after him, but they had refused.

Inventory, cash £10, 15*s*. 8*d*., books £2, pewter, carpenter's tools, cordwainer's seat, spinning wheel, gun, hay, corn, oats, grindstone, 2 heifers, 2 yearlings, a swine, 9 sheep, mare, colt, &c.

1725, Jan. 18. Mary Cook, widow and executrix of Isaac Bull, having of late deceased intestate and left committed to her by former husband, Isaac Bull, to her care for his child, therefore it was ordered that James Walling, father of said deceased Mary Cook, take into his possession all estate he can find left by Isaac Bull, for his child, Hannah.

I. JOHN, b. d. Jamestown, R. I.
m.
MARY, b. d. of
1. Isaac, 1708, Jul. 22.
2. John, 1710, Jun. 8.

1707, Jul. 15. He desired liberty to live in town, if he could get a house. His request was granted, if he be no way troublesome to the town.

The births of his children, Isaac and John, were recorded at Jamestown.

II. ELIZABETH, b. d.
m. 1698. Nov. 24,
JOHN VAUGHAN, b. d. of David & Mary ( ) Vaughan.
1. Elizabeth, 1701, Dec. 18.
2. David, 1704, Oct. 25.
3. Isaac, 1707, Mar. 31.
4. George, 1709, Jul. 24.
5. Mary, 1713, Jun. 19.
6. Charity, 1716, Jun. 20.
7. John, 1721, Jul. 8.

III. MARY, b. d.
m. 1701, Nov. 27,
HENRY MOWRY, b. d. 1759, Sep. 23. of Nathaniel & Joanna (Inman) Mowry.
1. Mary, 1702, Sep. 28.
2. Uriah, 1705, Aug. 15.
3. Jonathan, 1708, Jun. 1.
4. Jeremiah, 1711, Apr. 7.
5. Sarah, 1717, Apr. 5.
6. Elisha,
7. Phebe,

IV. ROSE, b. d.
m.
FRANCIS INMAN, b. d. 1776, Feb. 11. of Edward & Elizabeth (Bennett) Inman.
1. Aaron, 1709, Nov. 29.
2. Abiah, 1712, Nov. 4.

(2d WIFE.)

V. HANNAH, b. d.
m.
——— PHILLIPS, b. d. of Phillips.

ROBERT, b. d. 1692,
m. 1655, Nov. 2,
RUTH HUBBARD, b. 1640, Jan. 11. d. 1691 +
of Samuel & Tacy (Cooper) Hubbard.

Newport, Westerly, R. I.

1652, Nov. 19. He was baptized by Joseph Torrey.

1656. Freeman.

1661, Nov. 1. Westerly. He and Tobias Saunders, were arrested by Walter Palmer, constable, and soon after brought before Governor John Endicott, charged with forcible entry and intrusion into the bounds of Southertown, in the Pequot country. He acknowledged he was upon the same land and built a small house there. They were committed to prison, both refusing to find security for appearance at General Court.

1662, May 22. In a letter from Rhode Island to Massachusetts, mention is made of the imprisonment by the latter state of Robert Burdick and Tobias Saunders, for not producing their deeds of Narragansett lands.

1669, May 18. His name was in a list of inhabitants of Westerly.

1671, May 17. He took oath of allegiance.

1675, Jul. He and his family came to Newport on account of the Indian war, returning to Westerly subsequently.

1679, Sep. 17. He took oath of allegiance.

1680-83-85. Deputy.

1683, Sep. 25. Samuel Hubbard, having returned to Newport, from a journey to Rye, &c., detailed some events of the trip. He says: "at Westerly, the first day after the Sabbath, brother Burdick buried a son," and among others there, were grandson John Phillips, and Ruth his wife, and Benjamin Burdick; "a very great burial, above twenty horses."

1691, May 17. He and wife Ruth, sold John Macoone 100 acres, for £10.

1692, Mar. 8. He made an agreement with his son-in-law Joseph Crandall, by which latter was to take care of his father-in-law and find him with suitable meat, drink, washing, lodging and apparel, &c., for life, in consideration of which Joseph Crandall was to have the dwelling house and land adjoining, forever, and until Robert Burdick's death, to have also use of oxen, cart, two cows and eight swine, and then to be returned to be disposed of by will, except the cart and wheels.

1692, Oct. 25. He having died without perfecting his will, an agreement was made by his sons and sons-in-law. What their father had disposed of by legacy to children was to stand, and what remained, to be divided into nine parts. To son-in-law John Phillips, one part. The other eight parts to go to daughters Naomi Rogers and Tacy Maxson, only his wearing apparel to be divided between his sons, Thomas, Benjamin and Samuel. The lands of deceased that are undivided, to go to sons Samuel, Robert and Hubbard Burdick. To son Thomas, two oxen and a hog. To daughter Deborah Crandall, bed, warming pan, &c. To daughter Ruth Phillips, iron pot, a swine, &c. To son Benjamin, heifer, swine and an iron pot. To son Samuel, a heifer and a swine. To son Robert, a cow. To son Hubbard, a cow. To daughter Naomi Rogers, a swine, &c. To daughter Tacy Maxson, a swine.

Inventory, 2 oxen, 2 cows, 2 heifers, 6 swine, mare, wearing apparel, warming pan, pewter, &c.

I. ROBERT, b. d. Westerly, R. I.
m.
DORCAS LEWIS, b. d. of John Lewis.

1711, Oct. 2. He and thirty-three others bought 5,300 acres of the vacant lands in Narragansett, ordered sold by the Assembly.

II. SON, b. d. 1683.

BURDICK. 2d column. III. Hubbard. Children, 1. Hubbard, 1716, Nov. 24. 2. Nathan, 1719, Feb. 19. 3. John, 1721, May 19. 4. Ezekiel.

III. HUBBARD, b. d. 1758. Westerly, Hopkinton, R. I.
m.
HANNAH MAXSON, b. d. 1752 (—). of John & Mary (Moshier) Maxson.

1. Hubbard,
2. Nathan,
3. John,
4. Ezekiel,

1711, Oct. 2. He and thirty-three others, bought 5,300 acres of the vacant lands.

1727. Town Council.

1752, Mar. 19. Will—proved 1758, Apr. 19. Exs. sons Hubbard and Nathan. To son Hubbard, certain land west of farm, south side of highway, &c., great bible, great pot, feather bed and half of farming utensils. To son Nathan, remainder of farm, south side of highway, bed, looking glass and other half of farming utensils. To son John, certain land, a bed and £20, and he to clear the mortgage. To son Ezekiel, 3 acres, a bed and £170, and the mortgage on his land to be cleared by sons Hubbard and Nathan. To grandchildren, 20s. apiece. To son Hubbard, two-fifths of rest of estate and each other son one-fifth.

Inventory, £1,486, viz: chest, money due by notes £425, 13s. 4d., desperate debts £66, 2 beds, loom, warming pan, cow, heifer, yearling, mare, old wheel, 8 sheep, iron goose, &c.

IV. THOMAS, b. d. 1752. Westerly, R. I.
m. (1)
MARTHA, b. d. of
m. (2) 1738, Feb. 9,
PENELOPE RHODES, b. d. 1763. of Rhodes.

BURDICK. 2d column. IV. Thomas, had a son Thomas, who m. 1723, May 1, Abigail Richmond. (At this time Thomas, Sr., lived in Stonington, Ct.). V. Naomi, m. 1678, Mar. 2.

1694, May 19. He and wife Martha, were of Westerly, at this date.

1711, Oct. 2. He and thirty-three others, bought 5,300 acres of the vacant lands.

1752, Jun. 30. Inventory, £621, 13s., shown by widow Penelope, administratrix. Wearing apparel £34, pocket-book and money £1, 3s., flock bed, 3 cows, yearling, pair of oxen, sheep, hogs, mare, &c.

1763, Sep. 1. Inventory, £455, 1s., widow Penelope, shown by administrator Theodoty Vars.

Possibly Penelope was wife of a later Thomas Burdick, instead of this one, in which case this Thomas died before 1752.

BURDICK. 2d column. V. Naomi m. 1678. Mar. 2. Her husband b. 1655, Dec. 3, d. 1697, of James and Elizabeth (Rowland) Rogers. Children, 1. Jonathan. 2. Content. 3, Rachel. 4, Ruth. 5. Elizabeth. 6. Naomi. 7. Catherine.

V. NAOMI, b. d.
m.
JONATHAN ROGERS, b. d. of James Rogers.

1. Content,

VI. RUTH, b. d.
m. 1682 ±
JOHN PHILLIPS, b. d. of Phillips.

VII. BENJAMIN, b. d. 1741. Westerly, R. I.
m. (1)
MARY, b. d. of
m. (2)
JANE SHELLEY, (Widow.) b. d. 1748. of

1. Mary, 1699, Jul. 26.
2. Rachel, 1701, Jul. 5.
3. Peter, 1703, Aug. 5.
4. Benjamin, 1705, Nov. 25.
5. John, 1708, Mar. 24.
6. David, 1710, Feb. 24.
7. William, 1713, Jun. 12.
8. Elisha, 1716, Sep. 22.
(2d wife, no issue.)

1692, Mar. 28. He had 100 acres granted him, south side of great river.

1711, Oct. 2. He and thirty-three others, bought 5,300 acres of the vacant lands.

1716. Deacon of the Seventh Day Baptist Church.

1736, Apr. 25. Will—proved 1741, Apr. 27. Exs. wife Jane and Joseph Maxson, Sr. To wife, one-third income of real estate while widow, and a third movables forever and £5. To son Peter, 5s., he having had. To son Benjamin, 25 acres, but if he do not appear, to go equally to sons John and David. To sons John and David, 5s. each. To sons William and Elisha, rest of lands, equally. To son Elisha, my gun. To daughters Mary Lewis and Rachel Sisson, £5 each. To sons Elisha and William, rest of movables, they paying debts and two mortgages.

Inventory, £157, 8s. 2d., viz: wearing apparel £16, gun, books £1, 16s., mare, 2 cows, heifer, calf, 12 sheep, 2 lambs, sow, 2 shoats, &c.

1748, Oct. 28. Will—proved 1748, Nov. 28. Widow Jane. Ex. son-in-law Joseph Hall. To daughter Sarah Worden, 5s To heirs of daughter Jane Tanner, 5s. To heirs of son Benjamin Shelley, deceased, 5s. To daughter Mary Warren, 5s. To heirs of son Samuel Shelley, 5s. To daughter Susanna Hall, wife of Joseph, rest of estate.

Inventory, £107, 5s. 6d.

VIII. SAMUEL, b. d. 1756. Westerly, R. I.
m.
MARY, b. d. 1752 + of

1. Samuel,
2. Thomas,
3. Edward,
4. Deborah,
5. Tacy,

1711, Oct. 2. He and thirty-three others bought 5,300 acres of the vacant lands.

1752, Sep. 2. Will—proved 1756, Apr. 30. Ex. son Samuel. To son Samuel, carpenter's tools. To son Thomas, land. To son Edward, farming tools. To three sons, wearing apparel, besides what they have had by deeds of gift. To daughter Deborah Champlin, £5, she having had. To daughter Tacy Frink, 20s. To wife Mary, rest of estate.

Inventory, £551, 12s., viz: pair of oxen, cow, 2 two years, 2 swine, warming pan, pewter, &c.

IX. TACY b. d. 1747 +
m.
JOSEPH MAXSON, b. 1672. d. 1750, Sep. of John & Mary (Moshier) Maxson.

1. Joseph, 1692, Mar. 10.
2. John,
3. Tacy,
4. Mary
5. Judith,
6. Ruth,
7. Elizabeth,

X. DEBORAH, b. d.
m.
JOSEPH CRANDALL, b. d. 1737, Sep. 13. of John Crandall.

1. John,
2. Joseph,
3. Daughter,

BURGESS

THOMAS,[2] (Thomas,[1]) b. d. 1687 +
m. (1) 1648, Nov. 8,
ELIZABETH BASSETT, b. d.
of William & Elizabeth ( ) Bassett.
m. (2)
LYDIA GAUNT, b. d. 1684.
of Peter Gaunt.

Sandwich, Mass., Newport, R. I.

1643. His name was in the list of those able to bear arms.

1654. Constable.

1657. He subscribed for the repair of the meeting house and support of the minister.

1659, Oct. 6. He was fined 10s. for refusing to assist George Barlow, marshal of Sandwich.

BURGESS. 2d column. I. Thomas. His 2d wife was widow of Timothy Closson.

(2d WIFE.)

I. THOMAS, b. 1668. d 1743, Jul. 1. Little Compton, R. I.
m. (1)
ESTHER RICHMOND, b. 1669. d. 1706, Nov. 12. of Edward & Abigail (Davis) Richmond.
m. (2) 1707, Oct. 24,
MARTHA CLOSSON, (Wid.) b. 1684, Aug. 20. d. of Joseph & Ann (Brownell) Wilbur.
m. (3)
PATIENCE, b. d. 1743 + of

1. Edward,
2. Deborah,
3. Lydia,
4. Abigail,
5. Esther,
(2d wife.)
6. Joseph, 1708, Aug. 6.
7. John, 1711, Jan. 10.
8. Mary, 1712, Sep. 18.
9. Thomas, 1714, May 25.
10. Martha, 1716, Mar. 28.
11. Jacob, 1717, Nov. 11.
(3d wife.)
12. Mercy, 1722, Feb. 22.
13. Rebecca, 1725, Jun.
14. Martha, 1727, Apr.
15. Nathaniel, 1729, May.

1693, Aug. 1. He sold Major Benjamin Church, of Bristol, a meadow lot of 3 acres in Little Compton, for £7, 10s.

1743, May 10. Will—proved 1743, Aug. 16. Exs. sons Edward and Thomas. To wife Patience, all household goods (with a few exceptions), improvement of my now dwelling house (except great chamber), while widow, improvement of half of the orchard, two cows, riding mare, hive of bees, piece of cloth, twelve bushels of English grain, one hundred and sixty pounds each of pork and beef, twenty pounds wool, ten gallons molasses, and £5 paid yearly, with liberty to keep geese and fowls. To son Edward, a quarter of homestead farm, and house he lives in. To son Joseph, part of my 50

BURGESS. 2d column. I. Thomas. His widow, Patience, d. 1746, Dec.

1660, Jun. 13. He was fined 30*s.* for refusing to assist marshal Barlow, in the execution of his office.

1660, Oct. 2. He was complained of by George Barlow, in an action of defamation, damage being laid at £50. The marshal claimed that Burgess had reported that said Barlow took from Goodman Gaunt, for his fine of £24, seven cows and heifers, two steers, and seven and a half bushels of peas, and that afterwards, one of the cows having died, the said Barlow took another live cow in the stead thereof, because he had not the hide of the dead cow delivered to him. The jury found for plaintiff £3; and defendant was to make an open acknowledgment in the present court or pay £6. The acknowledgment was accordingly made to the satisfaction of the court.

1661, Jun. 10. A divorce was granted to him and wife Elizabeth, and the latter was to have one part in three of his estate, goods and chattels.

1661. Newport. He removed thence about this time.

1667, May 1. Freeman of the colony, he being already freeman of Newport.

1667. Grand Jury.

1671, Jul. 29. He sold a quarter share in Dartmouth, &c., to Thomas Ward, of Newport, for £26, 10*s.*

1673, May 5. He had 44 acres, &c., confirmed to him.

1680. Taxed 18*s.* 1*d.*

1684, Jun. 18. He and wife Lydia, sold Joseph Wilbur, of Portsmouth, 20 acres in Little Compton, for £10, 15*s.* 1687. Grand Jury.

acre lot, and the rest of it to him after three years' use by executors. To son Joseph, also a cow and five yearling ewes. To son John, 20 acre lot and a cow. To son Thomas, rest of homestead and buildings, and wife's part at her death, but if he die without male heir, all said lands to go equally to my two sons, Jacob and Nathaniel, they paying £200 to widow and children of Thomas, if any he leave. To son Jacob, £200, paid by son Edward, and a cow. To son Nathaniel, £200, paid by son Thomas, and my little gun. To son Edward, my desk called father Richmond's desk. To son Thomas, great hand irons. To sons Edward and Thomas, all cattle, sheep and farming tools and a horse. To wife, ten cords of wood, yearly. To daughters Deborah Brownell, Lydia Collins, Abigail Thomas, Hester Wilbur, Mercy Thurston, Rebecca and Martha Burgess, £10 each. To grandson Burgess Thomas, £5. To grandchildren, children of daughter Mary Wood (viz: Thomas, Content, Martha, Abigail, Comfort, Mary and Avis), 10*s.* each. To sons Edward, Joseph and John, wearing apparel.

Inventory, £6,655, 5*s.*, viz: wearing apparel £33, beds, 2 silver spoons, lignum vitæ mortar, books £3, mare, colt, horse, 9 cows, 3 oxen, 3 yearling steers. 3 two years, 3 yearlings, 2 fat oxen, 3 calves, 64 sheep, lambs, 6 swine, 18 geese, homestead farm and orchard £3,500, other land £2,200, &c.

BURLINGAME. 2d column. II. Thomas. His wife Martha, d. 1723. IX. Elizabeth. Her husband Thomas Arnold, d. 1727, Feb. 3.

BURLINGAME.

ROGER, m. MARY, — b. ; d. 1718, Sep. 1. — b. ; d. 1718 ±

Stonington, Conn., Warwick, Providence, R. I.

1654. He is said to have been of Stonington thus early.

1660. Warwick.

1671, Sep. 25. Providence. He and two others were appointed to make a rate and levy an assessment at Mashantatack.

1687, Sep. 1. Taxed 6*s.*

1690. He was elected Deputy from Warwick, but there being much debate in the Assembly, as to the legality of the election, it was ordered that he is not accepted.

1698. Town Council.

1704, Sep 6. He deeded to son Peter, house and 50 acres, subject to the use and profits for Roger and wife for life.

1715, Nov. 28. Will—proved 1718, Sep. 13. Exx. wife Mary, but as she died, the eldest son, John, took administration. Overseers, sons-in-law Thomas Arnold and Amos Stafford, and son Roger Burlingame. To wife Mary, all movables, household goods, cattle and chattels, for life; and then to go to all his daughters and three granddaughters, equally (viz: Roger's daughter Freelove, Mercy's daughter Francis and Alice's daughter Deborah). To son Roger, 50 acres. To grandson John, 50 acres to be laid out. To son Thomas, "the rest of undivided land that was my son Peters," with the proviso "if I and my wife have not occasion to use lands herein given." To three sons John, Thomas and Roger, 20*s.* each.

Inventory, £199, 13*s.* 8*d.*, viz: mare, 3 cows, 3 yearlings, calf, 2 sheep, 2 swine, old sword, wearing apparel, cash, &c,

BURLINGAME. 2d column. VI. Mercy m. Othniel Gorton, b. 1669, Sep. 22, d. 1733, June 13, of John and Margaret (Wheaton) Gorton. Children. 1. Israel. 2. John. 3, Frances, 1707, Mar. 15. 4, Othniel, 1718, Oct. 1, (unless this last was by a later Mercy).

I. JOHN, m. MARY LIPPITT, — b. 1664, Aug. 1. ; d. — b. ; d. of Moses & Mary (Knowles) Lippitt. — Providence, R. I.

1. John,
2. Roger,
3. James,
4. David,
5. Barlingstone 1698, Jun. 25.
6. Benjamin,
7. Elisha,

1687, Sep. 1. Taxed 3*s.*

1712, Dec. 23. He having heired, as eldest brother of Peter, deceased, the latter's deed of gift of their father's homestead, land, dwelling house, &c., which said Peter had received from his father sometime before; it was now agreed by John, that notwithstanding he was entitled to the whole, yet being willing that his brothers, Thomas and Roger, shall share with him, he takes the house and 50 acres to himself and gives the rest equally to them. He provides that if their father and mother need assistance, for their comfortable maintenance, all three brothers to be at equal charge.

1713, Jan. 1. He deeded to eldest son John, for love, &c., all right in lands and housing of my brother Peter, deceased, allowing to my father and mother, Roger and Mary Burlingame, use of house for life, and at their death to return to my said son John.

1719, Mar. 6. His son David, had a legacy from will of his grandmother, Mary Lippitt.

1719, Mar. 18. He sold Samuel Gorton, son of Captain Benjamin Gorton, mansion house and 60 acres in Providence, for £390.

II. THOMAS, m. (1) MARTHA LIPPITT, m. (2) HANNAH WESTCOTT, (w. of Josiah. — b. 1667, Feb. 6. ; d. 1758, Jul. 9. — b. ; d. of Moses & Mary (Knowles) Lippitt. — b. ; d. 1756 + of George & Tabitha (Tefft) Gardiner. — Providence, Cranston, R. I.

1. Thomas, 1688, May 29.
2. Moses,
3. Samuel,
4. Peter,
5. Joshua,
6. Daughter,
7. Mary,
8. Margaret,
9. Sarah,
10. Freelove,
11. Alice,
12. Patience,
13. Stephen,
(2d wife, no issue.)

1687, Sep. 1. Taxed 2*s.*

1715, Sep. 28. He deeded son Moses, 20 acres at Mashantatack, near grantor's dwelling house. He also deeded at sundry times to sons Thomas, Samuel, Peter, Joshua and Stephen.

1726, Aug. 29. He having married the widow of Josiah Westcott, gave bond for his wife's administration on her former husband's estate.

1756, Jun. 5. Will—proved 1758, Oct. 7. Exs. sons Thomas and Peter. To wife Hannah, £6 per year, for life, and £6 per year that her son gave bond for, it being part of her dower of former husband's estate. To sons Thomas and Moses, 5*s.* each. To grandson Samuel Burlingame, 5*s.* To sons Peter and Joshua, 5*s.* each. To granddaughter Freelove Arnold, 5*s.* To grandson John Warner, 5*s.* To daughters Margaret Remington, Sarah Briggs, Freelove Gorton, Alice Westcott and Patience Burlingame, 5*s.* each. To son Stephen, all real and personal estate, after debts and legacies are paid.

Inventory, 2 beds, warming pan, old gun, pewter, cooper's adze, cow, hetchel, stillyards, table, chairs, couch, money scales, &c.

III. MARY, m. 1689, Dec. 19, AMOS STAFFORD, — b. ; d. 1760. — b. 1665, Nov. 8. ; d. 1760. of Samuel & Mercy (Westcott) Stafford.

1. Mary, 1690, Sep. 16.
2. Samuel, 1692, Sep. 24.
3. Mercy. 1694, Sep. 21.
4. Amos, 1702, Apr. 24.
5. Stukeley, 1704, Nov. 7.
6. Patience, 1707, Apr. 21.
7. Freelove, 1709, Oct. 14.

IV. JANE, m. (1) JOHN POTTER, m. (2) 1711, EDWARD POTTER, — b. ; d. — b. 1668, Nov. 21. ; d. 1711. of John & Ruth (Fisher) Potter. — b. 1678, Nov. 25. ; d. of John & Ruth (Fisher) Potter.

1. John, 1692.
2. William,
3. Amey,
4. Mary,
5. Fisher, 1706, Sep. 29.
6. Alice,

V. ALICE, m. ——— — b. ; d. — b. ; d. of

1. Deborah,

VI. MERCY, m. ——— — b. ; d. — b. ; d. of

1. Frances,

VII. ROGER, m. ELEANOR, — b. ; d. — b. ; d. of — Providence, Warwick, Coventry, R. I.

1. Josiah,
2. Jonathan,
3. William,
4. Freelove,
5. Eleanor,

1699, Dec. 16. He brought in a wolf's head and received 10*s.* bounty.

1708, Jun. 4. He and Richard Searle, both of Mashantatack, having been appointed guardians of two daughters of Thomas Ralph, deceased, viz: eldest daughter Alice Searle (wife of Richard), and Eleanor Ralph; proceeded to divide lands.

1722, Jun. He deeded son Josiah, for love, &c., 20 acres at Mashantatack.

1746, May 5. Warwick. He deeded son Jonathan, 11 acres and 80 rods.

1747, Mar. 11. Coventry. He and his son William (and Alice, wife of latter), sold land to James Sweet.

VIII. PETER, Unmarried. — b. ; d. 1712. — Providence, R. I.

IX. ELIZABETH, m. (1) 1706, Dec. 5, THOMAS ARNOLD, m. (2) 1734, Apr. 11, WILLIAM SPENCER, — b 1684, Jan. 9. ; d. 1752, May 5. — b. 1675, Mar. 24. ; d. 1728, Feb. 3. of Richard & Mary (Angell) Arnold. — b. 1672, Jul. 1. ; d. 1748. of John & Susanna (   ) Spencer.

1. Job, 1707, Nov. 16.
2. Jonathan, 1708, Nov. 18.
3. Mary, 1710, Oct. 28.
4. Thomas, 1713, Nov. 4.
5. Elizabeth, 1717,
6. Sarah, 1722, Apr. 10.

X. PATIENCE, m. 1710, Jun. 15, THOMAS OLNEY, — b. 1685. ; d. 1746, Aug. 8. — b. 1686, May 18. ; d. 1752, Jul. 28. of Epenetus & Mary (Whipple) Olney.

1. Lydia, 1711, Jun. 2.
2. Esther, 1714, Jul. 7.

WILLIAM, b. 1637. d. 1729, Dec. 8.
m.
JANE, b. d. 1725 +

Portsmouth, R. I.

1671. Freeman.

1673, Feb. 21. He bought of Henry Lake, of Dartmouth, 2 acres in Portsmouth, for £7.

1680. Taxed 3*s*. 6*d*.

1697, Jun. 14. He bought of William Durfee, and wife Ann, 10 acres, for £50.

1725, Mar. 12. Will—proved 1729, Dec. 8. Ex. son Roger. Overseers, son William Burrington and friend William Anthony. To son William, half of ironware indoor and out and the loom which he frequently weaveth in, he having already received his portion of estate. To son Roger, 41 acres and a house, he maintaining my wife Jane, and his sister Sarah Burrington, with apparel, meat, drink and house room, &c. To son John, 5*s*., he having had. To daughter Alice Brown, wife of Tobias, 5*s*., having already given her. To grandson Joseph Lawton, 5*s*. and same amount each, to granddaughters Sarah and Mary Lawton having already given their mother, my daughter Mary Lawton, considerable. To daughter Sarah Burrington, 5*s*. To daughter Elizabeth Robinson, 5*s*. To grandson William Burrington, son of William, my loom that he commonly weaves in. To son Roger, all the rest of estate.

Inventory, £65, viz: wearing apparel and new cloth provided for apparel, hay £50.

I. WILLIAM, b. d. 1740, Apr. 12. Portsmouth, R. I.
m. (1) 1700, Sep. 10,
SARAH PHETTEPLACE, b. d. 1711, Dec. 8 of Philip Phetteplace.
m. (2) 1727, Apr. 23,
REBECCA FREELOVE, b. d. 1745, Nov. 3. of Morris & Elizabeth (Wilbur) Freelove.

1. Alice, 1701, Jun. 9.
2. William, 1705, Mar. 25.
3. Roger, 1710, May 7.
(2d wife, no issue.)

He was a weaver.

1707. Freeman.

1717, Apr. 17. He bought of John Keese and his mother Ann Keese, for £550, 4*s*., a parcel of land containing 42 acres, 56 rods.

1740, Apr. 12. Will—proved 1740, Apr. 19. Exs. wife and brother Roger. To grandson Robert Burrington, all my housing and land where I now dwell, with rest of my land in Portsmouth, except great chamber and lower room in kitchen, with bed-room in said kitchen, and these also to go to grandson at death or marriage of wife, he paying my wife £100 yearly, for life or while widow. To daughter Alice, wife of Samuel Bailey, £100, paid by grandson Robert, part when he is twenty-one and part later, she having had her part. To granddaughter Mary Burrington, £100. If grandson Robert should die, his part of estate to go to daughter Alice Bailey and granddaughter Mary Burrington, equally. To wife, two feather beds and Indian girl named Ann. To grandson Robert, all living stock and rest of estate, indoors and out, money, bills and bonds.

Inventory, £1,873, 6*s*. 4*d*., viz: wearing apparel £30, 3 oz. silver money £4, 1*s*., money due by bond and two notes £1,085, 12*s*. 6*d*., gun, sword and cartridge box £4, loom, books £1, 10*s*., spinning wheel, wool cards, pewter, cider, swine, horse, 24 neat cattle, 75 sheep, 7 loads and more of hay £60, &c.

1745, Oct. 22. Will—proved 1745, Nov. 11. Widow Rebecca. Ex. kinsman David Anthony. To brother Samuel Freelove, £50, to be delivered into hands of my kinsman, Samuel Forman, of Freetown, for him to hand my brother, for support of said brother and his wife, &c., at discretion of Samuel Forman. To grandchild Robert Burrington, £5. To kinsman David Anthony, and his wife Abigail, £110. To my sister Abigail Burrington, wife to John Burrington, rest of estate, to enable her to support my aged mother, Elizabeth Freelove, for life.

Inventory, £605, 17*s*.

II. ALICE, b. d.
m.
TOBIAS BROWN, b. d. of William Brown.

BURRINGTON. 2d column. II. Alice d. 1734+. Her husband d. 1734. Children, 1, John. 2, William. 3, Nicholas. 4, Robert. 5, Abraham. 6, Sarah. 7. Alice.

III. MARY, b. d. 1711, Nov. 4
m. 1704, May,
JOSEPH LAWTON, b. d. of Daniel & Rebecca ( ) Lawton.

1. Joseph, 1705, Feb. 7.
2. Sarah, 1707, Jun. 20.
3. Mary, 1710, Jun. 10

IV. SARAH, b. d.

V. ELIZABETH, b. d.
m.
—— ROBINSON, b. d. of Robinson.

VI. ROGER, b. d. 1764. Portsmouth, R. I.
m. 1714, Apr. 29,
ELIZABETH SHERIFF, b. 1693, Nov. 16. d. 1759 + of John & Jane (Havens) Sheriff.

1. William, 1717, Nov. 10.
2. Mary, 1721, Apr. 26.
3. Elizabeth, 1724. Aug. 21.
4. Robert, 1726, May 29.
5. William, 1731, Dec. 18.

1724. Freeman.

1759, Sep 23. Will—proved 1764, Apr. 9. Exs. sons Robert and William. To wife Elizabeth, best room and bed, riding horse, cow, money and debts due, while widow. To son Robert, all housing and lands in Tiverton, and stock on said farm and household goods already delivered him. To granddaughter Mary Hambley, £500 at eighteen. To grandson John Hambley, £1,000, at twenty-three years of age To son William, all housing and lands in Portsmouth, and all stock there, he paying legacies, and to him all household goods, except what are given his mother, and rest of personal.

Inventory, £4,951, 6*s*. 11*d*., viz: wearing apparel £207, loom, churn, wheel, cider press, ⅔ of 10 swine and 5 pigs, ⅔ of 70 sheep. ⅔ of 10 cows and 4 yearlings, 3 two year old cattle, 4 geese, 10 goslings, bonds and notes £1,568, 16*s*. 11*d*. &c.

VII. JOHN, b. d. 1756. Portsmouth, R. I.
m. 1720, Sep 14,
ABIGAIL FREELOVE, b. 1690, Mar. 12. d. 1756 + of Morris & Elizabeth (Wilbur) Freelove.

1. Abigail, 1720, Nov. 13.

1719, Dec. 2. He bought 20½ acres, for £205, of Benjamin and Elizabeth Wilbur.

1724. Freeman.

1752, Mar. 30. Will—proved 1756, Dec. 13. Exs. wife Abigail and son-in-law David Anthony. To wife, whole use and improvement of all estate, real and personal, for her support and to pay debts and legacies, and when she dies or marries, my son-in-law David Anthony, and Abigail his wife shall enter to possession for their lives, and when they die, to go to my two grandsons, Burrington Anthony and David Anthony. (The south part of land to go to Burrington Anthony and the rest of lands, buildings and orchard, to go to David Anthony.) To granddaughter Patience Anthony, £100, at age of twenty-one. To granddaughter Elizabeth Anthony, £500, and like amount to granddaughters, Deborah and Rebecca Anthony, all to have at twenty-one years of age.

VIII. ABIGAIL, b. d. 1711, Dec. 4-
Unmarried.

IX. ROBERT, b. d. 1721, Aug. 11.
Unmarried.

BUSECOT.

PETER, b. d. 1692 ±
m.
MARY, b. d. 1692 +

Boston, Mass., Warwick, R. I.

He was a blacksmith.

1636, Sep. 6. He was "censured for drunkenness to be whipped, and to have twenty stripes sharply inflicted, and fined £5, for slighting the Magistrates, or what they could do, saying they could but fine him." His fine was remitted to 20*s*.

1638, Dec. 4 He and Richard Geaves, for quarreling and fighting were referred to the court at Salem. He was for a time at Hartford, Connecticut, ere he came to Rhode Island.

1648, Jun. 5. Warwick. He was recorded as an inhabitant; and had 6 acre house lot granted him the same year.

I. ABIGAIL, b. d. 1723 ±
m.
HUGH STONE, b. 1638. d. 1732. of Stone.

BUSECOT. 2d column. I. Abigail. Children, 9, Mary. 10, Alice.

1. Hugh, 1669.
2. Peter, 1672. Mar. 14.
3. Catharine, 1674, Aug. 22.
4. John, 1675.
5. Sarah,
6. Abigail,
7. Anne, 1682
8. George,

II. PETER, b. d.
Unmarried.

He shot himself accidentally.

III. MARY, b. d. 1696 +
m. 1670, Dec. 15,
PETER SPICER, b. d. 1696. of Spicer.

1. Edward,
2. Samuel,
3. Peter,
4. William,
5. Joseph,
6. Abigail,
7. Ruth,
8. Hannah,
9. Jane,

BUSECOT. 1st column. Erase under date of 1638, the two lines after Salem. 1643, Hartford. He had a trial to make nails with less loss and at as cheap a rate as Thomas Hurlbut. 1647, Sep. 2. Fined 20s. for watch. 1648, Oct. 17. The court (at Hartford) sentenced him to be committed to prison "there to be kept in safe custody till the sermon, and then to stand in the time thereof in the pillory, and after the sermon to be severely whipped." (He had spoken profanely of the members of the church.)

1649, Jan. 18. He sold John Wickes, all his right in a meadow adjacent to Pawtuxet River, for "three quarts of sack, which I have received and am fully satisfied for the same."

1649, Jul. 26. It was ordered that the smith, Peter Busecot, have a lot against Mr. Holliman's lot, and that in case he build upon another man's lot, he shall not forfeit his own for want of building upon it, notwithstanding any further orders to the contrary; "and this to be no precedent," &c.

1651, Mar. 18. Town Sergeant, being chosen in place of John Cook, displaced for misdemeanor.

1651, May 5. Ordered "that the ditch that Peter Busecot made by the side of his lot shall stand, he giving 16 shillings towards the making the highway over the run unto the Neck, by his lot, although some part of the ditch may not be on his own land."

1653, Feb. 7. He was granted a 6 acre lot in some place where it may not be prejudicial, at the discretion of the layers out, which he is to have in full satisfaction for his bill for pay, due him for service due the town.

1655, Jan. 8. He bought of Edward Andrews, all his housing, and three lots of 6 acres each, for £20, &c., to be paid as follows: one cow, now at John Coggeshall's, on Rhode Island, to be delivered before May 1st, prized by two indifferent persons; £3 to be paid in good peage at money pay, and settled on or before February 14th, and £7 more (the cow and the £3 aforesaid, to be settled up by Michaelmas next); also £10, to be paid in peage Sep. 29th, 1657, at money pay, and at same time 25*s*., for forbearance of last payment. Possession not to be immediate, but provided for.

1655. Freeman.

1657. He was sued by Ezekiel Holliman, for debt, by Thomas Bradley, for slander, and by Abigail Sweet, for tresspass and slander, and he brought suit against Thomas Bradley, for both debt and slander.

1659, May 4. He sold Anthony Low, the dwelling house bought of Edward Andrews, as also new shop and 6 acres that house stands on and six other lots adjoining, with commonage, for full satisfaction.

1663, Aug. 5. He and wife Mary, sold a house and lot to Anthony Low.

1681, Jul. 4. He made agreement with Hugh Stone, deeding him 12 acres, but not to be molested in quiet and peaceable possession of his house while he lives, and also to retain for life, orchard on said 12 acres, and privilege of enclosing 3 acres for his use while he lives. His son-in-law to give him a cow already agreed on, and at Peter's death, the house, orchard and all the 12 acres to belong to Hugh Stone. If Peter died within two years, his son-in-law Hugh Stone, was to pay £2, 10*s*. to assignees of said Peter Busecot. Both signed the agreement.

1692. He and wife deeded land.

BUTTS.

BUTTS. 2d column. I. Zaccheus. His widow, Sarah, was probably identical with Sarah Butts who m., 1712, John Cole, of Hugh and Mary (Foxwell) Cole. He d. 1748, Jun. 25. She d. 1748. Both buried at Kickemuit, near Warren, R. I.

THOMAS, b. ; d. 1703.
m.
ELIZABETH, b. ; d. 1702 +

Norfolk, Eng., Portsmouth, Little Compton, R. I.

1662, Nov. 16. Portsmouth. He bought 4 acres of Richard Hart.

1666, Oct. 1. He bought of Richard Bulgar, 2 acres in Portsmouth, for a cow and 10*s*. in wampum.

1668, Nov. 20. He deeded William Earle 7 acres.

1668, Nov. 20. He bought of Ralph Earle, of Dartmouth, a quarter of a purchaser's share of meadow, and an eighth share of upland, &c., in Dartmouth.

1682, Oct. 31. Little Compton. He and James Case, were to be sent for to the next court, to give reason of their being and continuance at Punckateest without liberty first obtained so to do from this government.

1685, Oct. 27. He was granted a division of land in Dartmouth, purchased of Woosamequin and Wamsutta.

1696, Mar. 13. He sold to Edward Gray, of Tiverton, land in Little Compton, for £70.

1702, Dec. 28. Will—proved 1703, Feb. 2. Exx. wife Elizabeth. Overseers, friends Aaron Davis, Jr. and Joseph Wilbur. To eldest son Zaccheus Butts, and his wife Sarah, and my grandchildren Sarah, John, Mary, Abigail and Elizabeth Butts, (all children of said Zaccheus and Sarah), the two and thirtieth part of a purchase right in Dartmouth. To grandson John Butts, son of Zaccheus, 16 acres of woodland in Dartmouth. To son Zaccheus, part of a [illegible]4 acre lot in Little Compton. To son Idido, 30 acres in Little Compton, north side of William Earle's house, and wife Elizabeth and son Moses to build a house sixteen feet square on said 30 acres, and fence in a field and let it out; the rent thereof

See: American Genealogist, v. 19, p. 130.

I. **ZACCHEUS**, b. ; d. 1718 (—). Little Compton, R. I.
m.
SARAH, Cornell, b. ; d. ; of

See: American Genealogist, v. 19, p. 130.

1. Sarah,
2. John,
3. Mary,
4. Abigail,
5. Elizabeth,

1718, Apr. 9. Mary Butts, daughter to Zaccheus Butts, of Little Compton, deceased, sold to Benjamin Chase, of Tiverton, rights in Dartmouth, for £2.

His son John Butts, of Tiverton, m. (1) Susannah Wodell (1712, Dec. 11), and m. (2) Abigail Moon, widow (1724, Jan. 29). He had five children by first wife, and seven by his second wife, the births of all being recorded at Portsmouth, where he moved. Care should be taken not to confound him with his cousin John, son of Moses, who married Alice Wodell (1727, Oct. 26).

II. **IDIDO**, b. ; d.

He moved from Little Compton to Connecticut, by one account, and there married and had a large family of children, as it is said.

III. **MOSES**, b. 1673, Jul. 30; d. 1734, Jun. 9. Little Compton, R. I.
m. Alice Lake, b. ; d. ; of

See: American Genealogist, v. 19, p. 130.

1. Thomas, 1700, Oct. 18.
2. Zaccheus, 1702, Jun 27.
3. Abraham, 1704, Nov. 23.
4. John, 1707, Aug.
5. Anna, 1709, Mar. 28.
6. Elizabeth, 1719, Dec. 5.
7. Hepzibah, 1722, Dec. 19.

IV. **HEPZIBAH**, b. ; d.
m. 1695, Dec. 26,
WILLIAM EARLE, b. ; d. ; of Ralph & Dorcas (Sprague) Earle.

1. Sarah, 1696, Dec. 18.
2. Anna, 1700, Mar. 10.
3. Joseph, 1702, Feb. 9.
4. Thomas, 1704, Jan. 17.
5. Nathaniel, 1705, Jan. 28.
6. Damaris, 1707, Jan. 18.
7. Jonathan, 1712, Jun. 7.

to be for wife and Moses, they being obliged to maintain Idido, during his lameness. If Idido should be restored to his former health, the house and 30 acres to be for him forever, and if he should die without issue, then to return to Moses, my wife Elizabeth having equal share for life. To wife, my now dwelling house, &c., for life, while widow, and then to son Moses. To daughter Hepzibah Earle, at death of wife, a cow, delivered to her for her own use. To granddaughter Sarah Butts, £50 at marriage. To wife Elizabeth, rest of estate, and maid servant Ann Dyer, and Indian woman called Pope.
Inventory, £213, 13*s.* 6*d.*, viz: house and 30 acres £100, 56 acres out land £51, a sixteenth share of land at Dartmouth £9, 2 oxen, 3 cows, 2 yearlings, calf, mare, 7 sheep, 3 swine, wearing apparel £2, 5*s.*, 2 guns, bible, Indian man £4, Indian woman £4, linen wheel, stillyards, &c.

CALVERLY.

{ EDMUND, } b. / d. 1687 +
m.
{ ELIZABETH, } b. / d. 1680 +

Warwick, Newport, R. I.
He was a shoemaker.
1661. He was in Warwick thus early, and brought with him a little memorandum book, still in the clerk's office at that town. It was dated at Ely House, London, 1659, and showed that he had been in the army in England, containing among other things, the roll of soldiers, &c.
1663. Commissioner.
1664. Town Clerk.
1664, Oct. He was suspended from voting in General Assembly, till he should give satisfaction for his charges against Governor Arnold.
1664–65–66–67–68–69–70–71–72–73–79. Deputy.
1669, Oct. 11. He sold 7 acres to John Greene.
1671, Jul. 20. He deeded 50 acres in Mashantatack, for "love and affection to my brother-in-law, Edward Searle, late of Warwick, but now of Mashantatack, as also for love and affection, I have to his wife, Joan Searle, now in Old England, at present." He provided that Edward Searle and his wife should jointly enjoy estate for life, and at death to descend to Edward Searle's younger son Edward, and to John White, son of the said Joan Searle, now in England with his mother. If Joan Searle and her son by 1st husband, refused to accept their part, it was to go at decease of Edward Searle, the elder, to his son Edward, and Ann, the wife of the latter, and their heirs.
1672, Jan. 15. He took Thomas Smith as apprentice, and was to give him at age, two suits of apparel and a set of tools for a shoemaker.
1676. Newport. Captain.
1676, Aug. He was a member of the Court Martial held at Newport, for the trial of certain Indians, charged with being engaged in King Philip's designs. He held the office of Attorney General during this trial.
1677, Oct. 31. He and forty-seven others were granted 5,000 acres, to be called East Greenwich.
1678–79–81. General Solicitor.
1679–82–83–84–85–86. General Sergeant.
1680, Mar. 1. He and wife Elizabeth, sold to Mary Carder, widow of Richard, certain land, for £17.
1681–82. Attorney General.
1682, Oct. 25. He petitioned Assembly, for his charge and attendance, as a keeper on the privateers, late prisoners, sent away for Virginia. The Assembly, on debate, do judge that for his negligence in leaving prison door open, whereby some of the prisoners made an escape, he ought to forfeit the demand, yet considering his poverty, allowed him £5.
1687, Jun. 16. He, late General Sergeant and jailer, was ordered to be allowed 20*s.* for his services.

CARPENTER (ABIAH). 2d column. I. Oliver. The son Oliver, on whose estate he administered 1727, Oct. 4, was perhaps oldest child by an earlier wife than Sarah (as well as some others of his children). He had also by Sarah, 10, Joshua, 1724, Jan. 11, Oliver; 1727, July 24. Erase 6, Oliver and 7, Joshua.

CARPENTER (ABIAH).

{ ABIAH,[3] (Wm.,[2] Wm.[1]) } b. 1643, Apr. 9. / d. 1703 (—).
m.
{ ——— } b. / d.

Rehoboth, Mass., Warwick, R. I.
1652, Oct. 18. His father bought land in Warwick, thus early (of Benedict Arnold), upon which Abiah subsequently settled.
1669, Apr. 1. Warwick. He took a receipt from William Baker, and wife Mary, for a yearling heifer.
1670, Jun. 24. He bought of Edmund Calverly, administrator of Thomas Smith, the house and land that had belonged to latter, for the sum of £40.
1676, Aug. 25. He testified before the Court Martial, which sat at Newport, to try certain Indians charged with being engaged in King Philip's designs. He said that Wenanaquabin, who had

I. { OLIVER, } b. / d. 1727.
m.
{ SARAH, } b. / d. 1727 + of

Warwick, North Kingstown, R. I.

1705, Mar. 18. He deeded brother Joseph, for love, &c., 6 acres, south side of Pawtuxet River, which was my honoured father, Abiah Carpenter's, deceased.
1724, Jul. 27. He deeded son Christopher, of East Greenwich, 180 acres there.
1724, Nov. 23. He deeded son John, of Warwick, 160 acres in East Greenwich.
1727, Oct. 4. North Kingstown. He took administration on estate of his son Oliver, Jr., of East Greenwich.
1727, Nov. 20. Will—proved. Exx. wife Sarah. Overseer, friend Jeremiah Gould. To son ——— £10, he having had considerable estate. To son Solomon, £10. To son Abiah, a legacy at age. To son Thomas, a farm in East Greenwich, where William Sweet dwells. To son Joshua, £200, at age. To youngest son Oliver, £200, at age. To daughter Sarah Carpenter, £150. To daughter ——— £150.

1. John,
2. Christopher,
3. Soloman,
4. Thomas,
5. Abiah,
6. Joshua,
7. Oliver,
8. William, 1701, Jun. 19.
9. Sarah,
10. Hannah, 1708, Oct. 28.

II. { JOSEPH, } b. / d.
m. (1) 1703, Mar. 18,
{ MARY BROWN, } b. / d. of Beriah & Abigail (Phenix) Brown.
m. (2)
{ HANNAH, } b. / d of

Kings Town, East Greenwich, R. I.

1. Joseph, 1704, Jan. 7.
2. Abigail, 1705, Oct. 2.
3. Anne, 1705. Oct. 2.
4. Thomas,
5. Martha,

been living with him, went away from his house sometime in May, 1675, and he did not see him again, nor could hear of him till towards winter. (Wenaquabin had been charged with being at the wounding of John Scott, at Providence).

1678, Oct. 23. He was fined 20s., for not serving on jury.

1682. Deputy.

1687. Grand Jury.

1703, Mar. 18. At the time of his son Joseph's, first marriage, he is mentioned as deceased.

1708, Mar. 16. He exchanged certain land in Warwick, with John Warner, for certain land in Kings Town.

1732, Jan. 16. East Greenwich. He and wife Hannah, for love, &c., deeded to his son Joseph, Jr., 100 acres.

1732, Apr. 29. He and wife Hannah, for love, &c., deeded to his son Thomas, 100 acres.

1740, Mar. 13. His daughter Martha, married John Low, Jr., of Warwick.

III. JOHN, { b. / d. 1753. — East Greenwich, R. I.
m. (1)
——— GRINNELL, { b. / d. — of Matthew Grinnell.
m. (2)
ABIGAIL, { b. / d 1748 + — of

1. Mary,
2. Sarah,
3. Diademe,
4. Dinah,
5. Cornal,
6. Joseph,
(2d wife, no issue.)

1748, Jul. 14. Will—proved 1753, Sep. 10. Exx. wife Abigail. To daughter Mary, a bed, &c., and like legacy to daughters Sarah and Diademe. To daughter Dinah Greene, worsted combs, &c. To wife Abigail, all the goods she brought and movables we have gotten together since marriage, and a cow and mare to be kept for her use, wood provided, with use of house and half profit of farm for life. To sons Cornal and Joseph, all apparel, working tools, oxen, cows, sheep, &c. To son Joseph, 20 acres. To son Cornal, rest of farm.

IV. SOLOMON, { b. 1678. / d. 1750. — South Kingstown, R. I.
m.
ELIZABETH TEFFT, { b. / d. 1750 (—). — of Samuel & Elizabeth (Jenckes) Tefft

1. Elizabeth, 1703, Jan. 4.
2. Solomon, 17—, Feb. 26.
3. Daniel, 1712, Dec. 28.
4. Sarah, 1716, Aug. 24.

1705, May 10. Kings Town. He exchanged lands with Ephraim Bull.

1719, Mar. 20. In a deposition at this date he calls himself aged about forty-one years.

1750, Apr. 30. Will—proved 1750, Oct. 8. Ex. son Daniel. He calls himself ancient. To daughter Elizabeth Braman, £50. To granddaughter Joanna Rogers, £50. To grandson Samuel Carpenter, 20s. at age, his deceased father having had estate. To grandson Joseph Carpenter, £12 at age. To son Daniel, rest of estate.

CARPENTER (WILLIAM).

WILLIAM,[2] (Richard.[1]) { b. / d. 1685, Sep. 7.
m.
ELIZABETH ARNOLD, { b. 1611, Nov. 23. / d. 1683 +
of William & Christian (Peak) Arnold.

Amesbury, Wilts Co., Eng., Providence, R. I.

1637. Providence. He had land granted him.

1638. He was one of the twelve persons to whom Roger Williams deeded land that he had bought of Canonicus and Miantonomi.

1639. He was one of the twelve original members of First Baptist Church.

1640, Jul. 27. He was one of the thirty-nine signers to compact for good government.

1642. He and other Pawtuxet settlers subjected themselves to government of Massachusetts, the separation lasting sixteen years.

1658-60-62-63. Commissioner.

1660. He was on a committee to receive contributions for expenses of agents in England, viz: Roger Williams and John Clarke.

1660, Aug. 2. He deeded to cousin (*i. e.* niece), Joan Sheldon, wife of John Sheldon, 5 acres. He landed one anker of liquor this year.

1661, Feb. 5. He deeded cousin (*i. e.* nephew), William Vincent, 64 acres. He was on a committee to bridge the Pawtuxet, about this time.

1664-65-75-76-79. Deputy.

1665-66-67-68-69-70-71-72. Assistant.

1669. He gave 5s. "for the present." toward expenses of Mr. John Crandall's voyage to Connecticut, and the next year laid down 8s. for the present, to accommodate a committee who were going to Connecticut.

1670, Dec. 8. He deeded land to daughter Priscilla Vincent, and a house and land at Rocky Hill, to son Ephraim.

1671. He was authorized to make assessment on Providence, for arrears of taxes due colony.

1671, Mar. 31. In a confirmatory deed to certain parties, he mentions that it was procured of Indian sachems by himself and his brother Zachariah Rhodes, deceased.

1671, Dec. 14. He deeded sister Fridgswith Vincent, as a free gift, "my dwelling house with what land belongeth to me adjoining to the said house, the which said house is standing in the town of Amesbury, in Wiltshire, and in a street commonly called by the name of Frog Lane, my sister being inhabitant of said town; the which said house did in the original belong to my father, Richard Carpenter, now deceased, but fell to my right, as I was the son and heir unto my aforesaid father," &c.

1673. Town Council.

1675, Feb. 8. "To the town now met the tenth of this instant: I understand that the Town is about the division of the land on the west side of the Seven Mile Line, and I not able to come myself, I thought good to signify unto you what rights, and of whom I bought them, and also to whom I give them; that is to say, for five shares I have the deeds in my hands and are all in the Town Records. That which was Robert Cole's I give to my son Timothy; that which was Roger Mowry's own, I give to my son Silas; that which was Henry Neal's, which I bought of Roger Mowry, I give to my son Benjamin; that which was Robert Colwell's, I bought of Roger Mowry also, and do give it to my daughter

I. JOSEPH, { b. / d. 1683. — Providence, R. I., Oyster Bay, N. Y.
m. (1)
HANNAH CARPENTER, { b. / d. — of William & Abigail (   ) Carpenter.
m. (2)
ANN WICKES, { b. / d. 1692 + — of Francis & Alice (   ) Wickes.

1. Mary,
2. Joseph,
3. William,
4. Nathaniel,
5. Benjamin,
6. John,
7. Daughter,

1659, Apr. 21. The will of William Carpenter, of Rehoboth, proved at this date, gives daughter Hannah certain land at Pawtuxet, a heifer, ewe, bible, "Practice of Piety," &c.

1668. He bought land of the Indians, on Long Island, and moved there about this time.

1673, Jun. 8. Oyster Bay. He exchanged land with brother-in-law, Abiah Carpenter, of Pawtuxet, all my right of lands fell to me by my wife, by will from her father, also other land and £5, to be paid by Michaelmas following.

1674, Sep. 2. He, formerly inhabitant south of Pawtuxet River, in Warwick, sold uncle Stephen Arnold, of Pawtuxet, with approbation and full consent of father William Carpenter, half of all my right of lands and commons, south side of Pawtuxet River, only excepting my dwelling house, lot, &c., and agrees to save him free from any claims of me or now wife Hannah.

1676, May 5. The minutes of New York State Council mention "news being brought from Rhode Island, by Mr. Joseph Carpenter." He reported that the inhabitants were flocking there (unto the island of Rhode Island), from the country and will want provisions, &c

1684, Jul. 9. Administration to widow Ann and son Joseph.

II. LYDIA, { b. / d. 1711, Oct. 1.
m.
BENJAMIN SMITH, { b. 1631 ± / d. 1713, Dec. 23. — of Christopher & Alice (   ) Smith.

1. Benjamin, 1661.
2. Joseph,
3. William, 1664, Dec. 27.
4. Simon,
5. Lydia, 1668.
6 Elizabeth, 1672.

III. EPHRAIM, { b. / d. 1703 ± — Providence, R. I., Oyster Bay, N. Y.
m. (1)
——— { b. / d. 1678 ± — of
m. (2) 1677, Dec. 3,
SUSANNA ENGLAND, { b. / d. 1684. — of William & Elizabeth (   ) England.
m. (3)
LYDIA DICKENSON, { b. 1662, Oct. 5. / d. — of John & Elizabeth (Howland) Dickenson.

1. Ephraim,
2. Susanna,
(2d wife.)
3. Josiah,

1661, Feb. 5. He witnessed a deed from his father to William Vincent.

1670, Dec. 8. He had a deed from his father "of that house, he (Ephraim), now dwelleth in, upon my farm at Rocky Hill.

1671-72. Deputy.

1672, Apr. 2. He was on a committee to go to Narragansett, to take names of the dwellers there and signify to them that the Colony "doth intend such lands shall be improved by peopling the same." (The act was repealed soon after.)

1673, Oct. 29. Fine remitted for not serving on jury, he alleging sickness.

1677, Dec. 3. Oyster Bay. He was married by Thomas Townsend, Justice in the North Riding, of Yorkshire (*i. e.* Oyster Bay.)

1681, Jan. 14. He had land set off to him at North Cove, he having built thereon.

1681-82-83-84-85-86-87. Constable.

1684, Jan. 11. His wife had legacy from will of her step-father, Hugh Parsons.

1685, May 1. He deeded eldest daughter Susannah Carpenter, my homestead and house lot at Rocky Hill, in Providence, 200 acres land there, and third of commons.

1685, May 25. He deeded eldest son Ephraim, lands, meadows, &c., in Providence.

1693, Jul. 1. He and wife Lydia, sold Derrick Albertson, original home lot and other land, reserving right of free egress and regress to burial lot.

1698, Feb. 20. His son Ephraim, Jr., made his will at Pawtuxet, and died two days later. He gave to honored father, now inhabitant of Long Island, all my land, and after bequests to aunt-in-law, Sarah Carpenter (widow of Silas), rest to father.

IV. TIMOTHY, { b. / d. 1726, Aug. 19. — Providence, R. I
m.
HANNAH BURTON, { b. / d. 1726 (—). — of William & Hannah (Wickes) Burton.

1. Ethalannah,
2. Elizabeth,
3. Hannah,
4. Timothy,
5. William,

1687, Sep. 1. Taxed 9s.

1708, Oct. 29. His son William died, and the father took administration on estate.

1724, Dec. 1. Will—proved 1726, Sep. 19. Ex. son Timothy. To him, dwelling house, lands, meadows, &c. at Pawtuxet. To daughter Ethalannah Sweet, 20s. To daughter Elizabeth Williams, £3. To daughter Hannah Arnold, £5. To granddaughter Hannah Carpenter, alias Hannah Arnold, £10. To son Timothy, rest of estate, except 30 acres to grandson Philip Sweet.

Inventory, £185, 13s. 6d., viz: silver money £2, 18s., beds £41, 2s 6d., pewter, gun, carpenter's tools, 14 loads of hay, 2 old horses, 2 hogs, 12 sheep, pair of oxen, 4 cows, 2 heifers, 2 calves, honey bees, &c.

V. WILLIAM, { b. / d. 1676, Jan. 20. — Providence, R. I.
Unmarried.

CARPENTER (WILLIAM). 2d column. III. Ephraim, m. (1) Susannah Harris, of William & Susannah (   ) Harris. Erase her death.

Smith's son Joseph; that which I bought of John Smith, Mason, I give to my son Joseph's son William; and my own I give unto my son William. I do entreat, if the town so please, that this paper may be entered in the Town Records, lest I should fall before I can make another provision." The paper was granted by the town to be recorded, though William Carpenter lived to make a more formal will.

1676, Jan. 20. His house was attacked by about three hundred Indians, and was fired by them, but the flames were extinguished by the defenders. He lost two hundred sheep and fifty cattle, and two of his household were killed.

1676, Apr. 4. It was voted by Assembly "that in these troublesome times and straits in this colony, the Assembly, desiring to have the advice and concurrence of the most judicious inhabitants, if it may be had for the good of the whole, do desire at their next sitting, the company and counsel" (of sixteen persons, among them William Carpenter).

1679, Jul. 1. Taxed £10, 5*s.*, with sons Silas and Benjamin.

1683, Apr. 25. He made a confirmatory deed to the representatives of the thirteen original proprietors of Pawtuxet lands, he being the last survivor and owning three shares, his own thirteenth and two shares that he had purchased.

1679, Feb. 10. Will — codicil 1683, Mar. 15 — proved 1685, Oct. 1. Exs. sons Silas and Benjamin. To eldest son Joseph, 20*s.*, and like amount to daughters Lydia Smith and Priscilla Vincent. To sons Silas, Benjamin, Timothy and Ephraim, land. To grandson Ephraim, eldest son of Ephraim, by his first wife, land, and if he died before twenty-one, then his sister Susanna to have. To grandson William, and grandson Joseph Smith, son of Lydia, certain land, and if Joseph died, Simon to have his share. To daughter Priscilla Vincent, land. To wife Elizabeth, all movable estate, and sons Silas and Benjamin, to take whole care of their mother, "to provide for her in all respects and conditions as a woman ought to be provided for, during her natural life." In codicil, as his son Joseph had died, he gave to grandson Joseph, son of Joseph, legacy intended for his father. As he had heard his son Ephraim was intending to sell, he revoked his legacy and gave to Ephraim, Jr. and Susanna.

Inventory, £22, including 5 night caps, 2 silk neck cloths, &c.

He is supposed to have been killed in an attack on his father's house at Pawtuxet, by the Indians.

VI. PRISCILLA, — b. — d. 1690 +
m. 1670, May 31,
WILLIAM VINCENT, — b. — d. 1695. — of —— & Fridgswith (Carpenter) Vincent.

1. Thomas,
2. Nicholas,
3. William,

VII. BENJAMIN, — b. — d. 1711, Mar. 3. — Providence, R. I.
m.
MARY TILLINGHAST, — b. 1661, Oct. — d. 1711 + — of Pardon & —— (Butterworth) Tillinghast.

1. Benjamin,
2. Joseph,
3. William,

1693-94-96-97-98-99. Town Council.

1708, Mar. 20. He made an agreement with his cousin, Stephen Arnold, as to certain land on Pawtuxet Neck, referring to a deed of exchange between his father and his "uncle Stephen Arnold, father of the said Stephen Arnold."

1711, Apr. 16. Administration to widow Mary. Inventory, £161, 17*s.*, viz: wearing apparel, feather beds, 2 swords, gun, cooper's and carpenter's tools, hay, oats, rye, Indian corn, tobacco, 2 oxen, 6 cows, 5 three year olds, 3 two year, bull, yearling, 2 mares, sheep, swine, cider mill and press, pewter, &c. The rooms named were outward room, bed room, great chamber, leanto chamber.

VIII. SILAS, — b. 1650. — d. 1695, Dec. 25. — Providence, R. I.
m.
SARAH ARNOLD, — b. 1665, Jun. 26. — d. 1701 + — of Stephen & Sarah (Smith) Arnold.

1. Silas,
2. William,
3. Phebe,
4. Sarah,

See American Genealogist V. 36. p. 84 54

1687, Sep. 1. Taxed 13*s.*, together with brother Benjamin.

1695, Dec. 22. Will—proved 1701, Apr. 8. Exs. wife Sarah and father-in-law, Stephen Arnold, and Captain William Hopkins. To eldest son Silas, mansion house, land and meadows at Pawtuxet, east side of Pauchasset River, excepting meadow at Ponagansett. To youngest son William, all my lands in Providence, with aforesaid meadow at Ponagansett. To sons Silas and William, all land west side of Pauchasset River. To daughters Phebe and Sarah Carpenter, £20 each, at eighteen or marriage. To wife Sarah, whole disposal of estate till children come of age, and then she to have one-third of all lands, goods and chattels, and best room in house for life.

Inventory, £131, 19*s.* 6*d.*, viz: 2 oxen, 14 cows, 4 two years, 7 yearlings, 8 calves, 70 sheep, 3 guns, 2 pair stillyards, 3 beds, warming pan, debts due estate £43, 9*s.* 6*d.*, 5 mares, horse, 3 colts, &c.

CARR (CALEB).

CALEB, — b. 1624. — d. 1695, Dec. 17.
m. (1)
MERCY, — b. 1631. — d. 1675, Sep. 21.
m. (2) [John.
SARAH PINNER, (w. of — b. 1651. — d. 1706 +
of Jeremiah & Frances (Latham) Clarke.

Newport, R. I.

1635. He embarked in ship Elizabeth & Ann, at London, aged eleven, and came to America with his older brother Robert.

1654-58-59-60-61-62. Commissioner.

1655. Freeman.

1658, Jun. 22. He bought of William Case, Sr., of Newport, all his interest in Conanicut and Dutch Islands.

1659, Feb. 27. He bought of John West, Sr., of Newport, carpenter, all his interest in Conanicut.

1661, Jul. 13. He bought of Jeremiah Willis, of Newport, 51½ acres in Conanicut.

1661-62. General Treasurer.

1662, Apr. 28. He bought of Henry Bassett, of Newport, all his interest in Conanicut.

1663, Dec. 12. He bought of Henry and Jireh Bull, of Newport, 43 acres in Conanicut Island.

1664-65-67-68-69-70-71-72-74-78-79-90. Deputy.

1670, Oct. 26. He and five others were appointed to make a rate for Conanicut.

1671, Jan. 30. He was allowed £4, for several services done by him and his boat.

1676, Apr. 11. He was one of the commissioners appointed "to take care and order the several watches and wards on this island, and appoint the places."

He this year bought the services of an Indian captive (taken by Providence men), paying twelve bushels of Indian corn therefor.

1679-80-81-82-83-84-85-86-90-91. Assistant.

1687-88. Justice of General Quarter Session and Inferior Court of Common Pleas.

1690, May 7. He and John Holmes, were appointed by Assembly, to agree with carpenters to finish the Town House, forthwith, and to provide boards and nails, and pay for finishing said house out of money and wool in Treasurer's hands.

I. NICHOLAS, — b. 1654, Oct. 22. — d. 1709, Feb. 17. — Jamestown, R. I.
m.
REBECCA NICHOLSON, — b. 1656, Feb. 1. — d. 1703, May 13. — of Joseph & Jane ( ) Nicholson.

1.	Nicholas,	1679, Sep. 19.
2.	Joseph,	1682, Mar. 17.
3.	Benjamin,	1683, Jul. 7.
4.	Margaret,	1684, Oct. 22.
5.	Jane,	1686, Aug. 3.
6.	Caleb,	1688, Mar. 27.
7.	Mercy,	1690, Apr. 20.
8.	Robert,	
9.	Rebecca,	1692, May 12.
10.	Ann,	1694.
11.	Thomas,	1696, Jan. 5.
12.	Benjamin,	1697, Nov. 21.

1679. Freeman.

1680. Ensign.

1680-85-96-99. Deputy.

1687. Overseer of the Poor.

1687. Grand Jury.

1690. Deputy Warden.

1692. Lieutenant.

1693, Apr. 12. His children, Joseph, Nicholas, Jane, Caleb, Robert, Margaret and Thomas, were given legacies from the will of their grandfather, Joseph Nicholson.

1704. Warden.

1709, Jan. 10. Will—proved 1709, Mar. 12. Ex. son Nicholas. To son Nicholas, house and farm, and right in Dutch Island, &c., and if he die without issue, then to my son Thomas, and should latter enjoy it, the part that Thomas is to receive by this will to go to Benjamin. To son Thomas, 70 acres, a pair of oxen, fifty sheep, three cows, a guinea of gold, a silver spoon and a silver cup, at age, and if he die without issue, son Benjamin to have. To son Benjamin, a little house and certain land, ⅜ of Gould Island, £40, a silver spoon, silver beer cup and an Arabian piece of gold, at age. To daughter Margaret Batty, £25, a silver porringer, a silver spoon. To daughter Jane Carr, £50, a feather bed, silver cup, silver spoon, warming pan, &c. To daughter Mercy, £50, feather bed, silver spoon. To daughter Rebecca Carr, £50, feather bed and a silver spoon. To daughter Ann Carr, £50, feather bed and silver spoon.

Inventory, £343, 9*s.* 5*d.*, viz: guinea £1, 10*s.*, 1 piece of gold of outlandish coin 11*s.*, silver money £2, 18*s*, 9*d.*, load stone £1, 10*s.*, olive wood looking glass £1, feather beds, 12 silver spoons £7, 4*s.*, a silver cup £2, 15*s.*, silver cup £2, a two handled silver cup £1, 5*s.*, a very small silver cup and cocoanut shell tipped with silver £1, a silver porringer £2, 10*s.*, silver tankard £14, great warming pan, small warming pan, rapier, 2 guns, pewter, 320 sheep, 10 cows, 5 heifers, 2 oxen, 2 mares, 2 churns, 2 spinning wheels, 6 leather chairs, &c.

II. MERCY, — b. 1656, Apr. 6. — d.

See: American Genealogist, v. 19, p. 130-1

CARR (CALEB). 2d column. III. Caleb His wife may have been daughter of John & Mary (Williams) Sayles, as he named a child Sayles Carr.

III. CALEB, — b. 1657, Aug. 23. — d. 1700, Oct. 10. — Jamestown, R. I.
m.
DEBORAH, — b. — d. 1700 + — of

1.	John,	1681, Jan. 4.
2.	Child,	1682, Sep. 16.
3.	Mercy,	1683, Oct. 7.
4.	Benjamin,	1685, Oct. 31.
5.	Daniel,	1687, Nov. 15.
6.	Peleg,	1690, Mar. 14.
7.	Deborah,	
8.	Robey,	
9.	Rachel,	
10.	Sayles,	1696, Nov. 24.

1684. Deputy.

1700, Jul. 5. Will—proved 1700, Nov. 6. Ex. son John. To son John, all estate, real and personal, except legacies. To wife Deborah, feather bed, great chamber to live in, £10 a year, and her maintenance. To son Benjamin, farm at Coweset, &c., three cows, a breeding mare, forty sheep, a pair of oxen and a breeding sow, at age. If John die without issue, then to his brother Benjamin, and Benjamin's part to go to surviving brothers and sisters. To son Daniel, lands in Warwick, three cows, a pair of oxen, forty sheep, a breeding mare and a breeding sow, at age. To son Peleg, farm at Kings Town, and house on said land that Joseph Austin lives in, and a quarter share of land in Coweset, two cows, thirty sheep, a breeding mare, a pair of oxen and a breeding sow, at age. To son Sayles Carr, land at New Bristol, that I bought of James Burrill, a quarter of undivided lands at Coweset, two cows, thirty sheep, a pair of oxen, a breeding mare, and a breeding sow, and a right in Gould Island, at age. To

See: American Genealogist, V. 19, p. 138.

1695, Jul. 5 He wrote to Governor Fletcher, of New York, in answer to a letter relative to sending the quota of forty-eight men from Rhode Island, to assist in defence of New York, which men were to be sent, or else some other assistance rendered in computation of said forty-eight men.

1695 Governor.

He was drowned.

He and his first wife were buried in the family burial ground.

1694, Mar. 8. Will—proved 1696, Jan. 6. Exs. sons Nicholas and Caleb. To wife Sarah, £40, and three gold rings, she giving one to my daughter Sarah, one to daughter Elizabeth and other to whom she pleaseth. To wife, also, a silver posset, two silver spoons, a milch cow, forty sheep, 1 horse, great looking glass, new great bible, a fifth of beds, pewter and other household stuff, negro woman "Hannah," and use for life of house that son John liveth in, on back side of my dwelling house, while widow, with privilege in yard for wood, use of well, &c., and of lower garden. To son Nicholas, farm in Conanicut, 140 acres, which I formerly leased him for about twenty years, with dwelling house, &c., and right in Dutch Island, and 40 acres on west side of highway, over against my brother Robert Carr, his land in said Conanicut, and a quarter share in Gould Island, and 25 foot in length of land, west side of my warehouse upon my wharf here in Newport, said land 20 foot in breadth, and my great bible, seal ring and little cabinet, he paying my now wife Sarah, yearly, 20*s*. To son Caleb, a farm in Conanicut, with housing he now liveth in, right in Dutch Island, a quarter of land at Gould Island, gold ring I now wear, commonly called, "hand and hand and heart between," and my desk, he paying wife Sarah, while widow, 20*s*. a year. To son John, my dwelling house that I now live in, here in Newport, with all housing, lands and garden (all which lands I bought of Benedict Arnold in his life time), except part reserved for wife. To son John, also, my whole part of Rose Island, and whole of my warehouse standing on my wharf in Newport, my woolen apparel, &c. To son Edward, land at Conanicut (50 ½ and 65 acres), right at Dutch Island, a quarter of my half of Gould Island, my Indian boy "Tom," pair of stillyards, wearing linen, &c. To son Francis, half of my right in a house and land at Newport, and a half share of land at Coweset, a 20*s*. piece of gold, a silver spoon and a fifth of household stuff. To son James, half of above house and land in Newport, right in Misquamicut lands, piece of gold, silver spoon and a fifth of household stuff. To daughter Mercy Paine, and her husband Thomas Paine, land in Newport, and a quarter share in Gould Island, to longest liver, and to Mercy, a silver beer bowl, to be kept in remembrance of me as long as she liveth. To daughter Sarah Carr, certain house and land in Newport, 20*s* gold piece, a fifth of household stuff and £5. To daughter Elizabeth, house and land in Newport, negro boy "Jo," silver spoon, a fifth of household stuff, and £10. To grandson Job Carr, son of Samuel, house where John Davis lives at the sign of the ship, here in Newport, at age. If any of sons Nicholas, Caleb, John, Edward or grandson Job, son of Samuel, die without issue, that part to be divided to whomsoever of five sons survive, they five having all had one mother; and if any of four children by now wife Sarah, die without issue, that part to be divided to survivors, as they had one mother. If wife Sarah, mother of Francis, James, Sarah and Elizabeth see cause, she may take all or any of them; and for their bringing up, shall have estate given them committed to her management till they are of age.

1706, May 1. His widow Sarah, having petitioned for legacy due from her husband's will, it was ordered that said John Carr, shall pay the annual legacy sued for, to his grandmother, Mrs. Sarah Carr, according to the will. (The term grandmother, used in records, should be apparently step-mother.)

daughter Mercy, £50, bed, negro girl "Peg," and a milch cow at eighteen. To daughter Deborah Carr, £50, feather bed, &c., and milch cow at eighteen. To daughter Roby Carr, £50, feather bed, milch cow, &c., at eighteen. To all children, equally, value of a piece of white money and two pieces Arabian gold and a guinea, in token of love to them all. Son John, to bring up his brother and sister to learning without charge.

Inventory, £1,327, 8*d*., viz: house and land at Dutch Island £600. Farm at Bristol £29. Farm at Warwick £60. Farm and house and undivided lands at Coweset £100. Farm and house at Kings Town £50. Land at Gould Island £12, 10*s*. Negro man and woman £50, negro girl £5, feather beds, 6 leather chairs, great chair, pewter, wearing clothes, 2 looms, 200 sheep and lambs, a pair compasses, 4 oxen, 17 cows and steers, a horse, 2 mares, colt, pair oxen and 2 cows at Warwick, a pair of oxen and a cow at Coweset; 6 two year olds, 3 calves and 2 mares on the main, 10 pieces gold (£5) and a guinea, in all £6, 4*s*. To cash paid my brother Nicholas, toward a quarter part of Gould Island £12, 10*s*. To half of shop standing in Newport, now let to Mr. Stephen Mumford, for £3, 5*s*. a year, which shop is between my brother Nicholas Carr and myself—the half value £13.

IV. SAMUEL, b. 1658, Dec. 15. d. 1694 (—) Newport, R. I.
m. ——— b. d. of

1. Job, 1689, Oct. 31.

V. MERCY, b. 1661, Jan. 1. d. 1717.
m. THOMAS PAINE, b. d. 1715. of Paine.

No issue.

VI. JOHN, b. d. 1714. Newport, R. I.
m. WAITE EASTON, b. 1668, Nov. 5. d. 1725, Aug. of Peter & Ann (Coggeshall) Easton.

1. Samuel,
2. Caleb,
3. Ann,
4. John, 1691, Nov. 23.
5. Francis,
6. Patience,

1700, May 4. On petition of himself and Thomas Winterton (the latter of Jamestown), the Assembly granted them the ferry between Newport and Jamestown for seven years, at £5 per year, they carrying officers upon the King's service, and the Post, ferriage free, and maintaining good and suitable boats.

1705. Deputy.

1709, Aug. He was granted privilege of running the ferry for seven years, at £4 per year.

1715, Aug. 26. His estate was settled by his son Samuel, according to his father's wishes. To brother Caleb, a small house, warehouse, wharf, &c. To brother John, my father's mansion house, &c. To brother Francis, tenement in which Alexander Mason dwells. To sister Ann Barker, west half of new house, built by father, half of garden, &c. To sister Patience, other half of said house, &c. To mother, use of all said gifts till children come of age, with certain reservations, and when children are of age they to pay proportional part of £20 per annum to mother. The well to be free to all of brothers and sisters. To mother, all movables, she paying debts. If any child die without issue, property to revert to Samuel and heirs. Bond in sum of £500.

VII. EDWARD, b. 1667. d. 1711, Oct. 14. Jamestown, R. I.
m. 1686, Oct. 6, HANNAH STANTON, b. 1670, Nov. 7. d. 1712 + of John & Mary (Harndel) Stanton.

1. Edward, 1689, Sep. 14.
2. Hannah, 1691, Oct. 13.
3. Mary, 1693, Oct. 26.
4. Mercy, 1696, Feb. 24.
5. Avis, 1698, May 29.
6. Patience, 1701, Feb. 14.
7. James, 1703, Oct. 21.
8 Phebe, 1706, Sep. 6.
9. Sarah, 1708, Dec. 28.

1698. Freeman.

1699–1702–4–5–6–7–9. Deputy.

1699–1702–4–5–6–7–9. Clerk of Assembly.

1701–7. He was appointed on a committee to audit the accounts of colony.

1711, Dec. 22. Will—proved 1712, Jan. 22. Exs. wife Hannah and son Edward. To wife, all household stuff not disposed of, a negro woman, silver beer cup and all silver spoons, all to be at wife's disposal amongst children. To wife, also, liberty to dwell in house while widow, and she to see that children are soberly brought up to learning. To son Edward, north half of farm I now live on, right of land on Gould Island, half right in commons, &c., housing and farming utensils, great table, &c. To son James, south half of farm, with small house on it, half right in commons, right in Dutch Island, great chest, silver spoon, &c., at age. To daughter Hannah Slocum, £5. To daughter Mary Carr, £10, at eighteen, and feather bed, and to daughters Mercy, Avis, Patience, Phebe and Sarah Carr, like legacies at eighteen.

Inventory, £290, 1*s*. 3*d*., viz: feather beds, 2 spoons and 2 cups of silver £4, 7*s*., pewter, pair worsted combs, looms, 15 neat cattle, 4 horsekind, 140 sheep, 4 swine, negro woman £35, &c.

(2d WIFE.)

VIII. FRANCIS. b. d. 1717 (—) Newport, R. I.
m. 1700, Jun. 18, DAMARIS ARNOLD, b. 1684, May 19. d. of Josiah & Sarah (Mills) Arnold.

1. Sarah,

He was a shipwright.

1701. Freeman.

1717. His daughter Sarah, joined with her husband, George Piggott, schoolmaster, in a suit against Stephen Mumford. She is called a minor, though married, and the sole heir of Francis Carr, late of Newport.

IX. JAMES, b. d. Newport, R. I

1701. Freeman.

CARR (CALEB). 2d column. X. Sarah, had also 4, Sarah, 1714. 5. Elizabeth, 1716, Feb. 28. 6. James, 1718, Dec. 31.

X. SARAH, b. 1682. d. 1765, Feb. 8.
m. 1705, Jan. 10, JOHN HAMMETT, b. 1680. d. 1773, Mar. 20. of Hammett.

1. John, 1705, Oct. 10.
2. Mary, 1711, Feb. 14.
3. Thomas, 1712, Apr. 11.

XI. ELIZABETH, b. d.
m. 1701, May 28, JOHN GODFREY, b. d. of John & Sarah ( ) Godfrey.

1. Mary, 1702, Mar. 23.
2. John, 1704, Jan. 31.
3. Caleb, 1706, Jul. 17.
4. Elizabeth, 1709, May 21.

CARR (CALEB). 2d column. VII. Edward. His widow [illegible] 1752. 1748, will-proved 1752 (Newport, R. I.) W[illegible] Hannah. She mentions sons Edward and James, daughters, Hannah Watson, wife of Samuel, of South Kingstown, Mary Chapman, wife of Isaac, of Newport, [illegible] Brown, wife of Samuel, of South Kingstown, Pa[illegible] Westgate, wife of Robert, of Warwick, and Sarah W[illegible]man, wife of Resolved, of Warwick.

CARR (John.)

JOHN, b. / d.

Kings Town, R. I.

1670, Mar. 22. He and an Indian named Quinahunt having broken prison the 26th of December, last past, at night, and got over to Narragansett, where they both gave out threatenings to do mischief to the English thereabout residing, and having been some months past preparing to fight and drawing the Indians into their conspiracy; therefore the Assembly desire the sachems Mosup and Ninecraft to apprehend the said offenders.

1678, Jun. 12. It was ordered by Assembly that all the estate of John Carr shall be liable to answer judgment and sentence of last General Court of Trials held in May last, according to sentence of the court, and the Assembly gives power to any two magistrates to dispose of the body of said Carr to be transported to some other place or country, he serving as a servant till all manner of costs and charge be defrayed by the produce thereof, and to remain in prison for the present.

1686, Jun. 24. Complaint was made to Assembly by James Corse, late servant to John Carr, that he had been dismissed after many years' service without necessary apparel, and the court ordered said Carr to provide said servant one suit of clothes, a shirt, stockings, and shoes, within ten days or else pay £4.

1687, Sep. 6. Taxed 6*s.* 4*d.*

1700 ± Will proved. Overseer Thomas Stanton. He leaves his estate to cousins, apparently, one of them being Ambrose Leach. (Only fragmentary parts of the copy of will are preserved.)

CARR (ROBERT). 2d column. I. Caleb. His widow Phillip, d. 1705 (—). II. Elizabeth, m. (2) Samuel Gardiner, of George & Herodias (Long) Gardiner. He d. 1696, Dec. 8. She d. 1697 +. Children, 1. Elizabeth, 1684. 2. Samuel, 1685, Oct. 28. 3. Martha, 1686, Nov. 16. 4. Patience.

CARR (Robert).

CARR (ROBERT). 2d column. I. Caleb. He was a shipwright. V. Esek. In will change Dosson to Closson.

ROBERT, b. 1614. / d. 1681.
m.
——— b. / d.

Newport, R. I.

He was a tailor.

1635. He embarked in ship Elizabeth and Ann at London, aged twenty-one, bringing with him his younger brother Caleb.

1639, Feb. 21. Portsmouth. Admitted an inhabitant.

1641, Mar. 16. Newport. Freeman.

1655. Freeman.

1670, Jun. 20. His boat was procured by the Sergeant to transport persons that were to go to Narragansett as Commissioners from Rhode Island in regard to the trouble about jurisdiction in Narragansett (between Connecticut and Rhode Island.)

1670, Oct. 26. He and five others were appointed to make a rate for Conanicut Island.

1671, Jan. 30. He was allowed £9, for several public services done by him and his sloop and hands to this day.

1671, Sep. 25. He and others were appointed to make a rate and levy an assessment on Conanicut.

1677, Mar. 16. He deeded two parcels of land for £100, part paid by Nicholas Davis during his life and part by his son Simon Davis since.

1677, Jun. 11. The Assembly met at his house at eight o'clock in the morning.

1678, Nov. 15. He was granted £1, 4*s.* by Assembly for service done by his son Caleb and his sloop, in transporting Magistrates to Narragansett.

1680, Taxed £1, 5*s.* 1½*d.*

1681, Apr. 20. Will—proved 1681, Oct. 4. Exx. wife ——— and sons Caleb and Robert. Overseers, brother Caleb Carr, and Walter Clark. He declares his intention of starting on a voyage to New York and New Jersey. To eldest child Caleb all lands at Jamestown, he paying to testator's wife £10, per annum for life. To John Hicks and his children by daughter Mary, £20. To son Robert dwelling house and wharf at Newport (with liberty to other children to use said wharf and the well), he paying £7 yearly to testator's wife. To son Esek certain land, he paying £3 to testator's wife. To daughter Margaret all the sheep at Jamestown, and proceeds of sale of horseflesh except a colt to son Caleb. To son-in-law James Brown, and children he hath by my daughter Elizabeth, the land he hath built upon, etc.

I. CALEB, b. / d. 1690, — Jamestown, R. I.
m.
PHILLIP GREENE, b. 1658, Oct. 7. / d. 1690 + — of John & Ann (Almy) Greene.
(She m. (2) ——— Dickinson.)

1. Robert, 1678, Jul. 2.
2. Caleb, 1679, Mar. 21.
3. William, 1681, Oct. 16.
4. Robert,
5. Job,
6. Mary,
7. Phillip, 1688, Dec. 8.

1679. Freeman.

1688, Jan. 27. Will—proved 1690, Mar. 3. (Dated at Jamestown and proved at Newport.) Exx. wife Phillip. He mentions wife Phillip, eldest son Caleb, sons William, Robert and Job, daughters Mary Carr and Phillip Carr (not yet eighteen), cousin Nicholas Carr, father Major John Greene and brother-in-law Peter Greene.

1690, Mar. 3. Phillip Carr, widow and executrix of Caleb Carr, of Jamestown, deceased, humbly showeth by petition to Assembly, that there being no Town Council in Jamestown, she cannot there have her husband's will proved, and prays that order be given the Recorder to perfect the matter. The Recorder was ordered (the will having been proved in Council) to place said will in the General Council Book and to grant letters to the executrix.

II. ELIZABETH, b. / d. 1683 +
m.
JAMES BROWN, b. / d. 1683 (—) — of Chad & Elizabeth ( ) Brown.

1. John, 1671.
2. James,
3. Esek, 1679, Mar. 8.

III. MARY, b. / d.
m. (1)
JOHN HICKS, b. / d. — of Hicks.
m. (2)
RALPH EARLE, b. 1660. / d. 1757. — of William & Mary (Walker) Earle.

IV. ROBERT, b. / d. 1704. — Newport, R. I.
m.
ELIZABETH LAWTON, b. / d. 1724. — of George & Elizabeth (Hazard) Lawton.

1. Robert,
2. Abigail,

He was a merchant.

1687. Grand Jury.

1698–99–1700–1–2–3. Assistant.

1699, Aug. 14. He and wife Elizabeth deeded a house and lot to our son George Hicks, for love, &c.

1702, Sep. 17. He was appointed on a Committee to draw up an address to her Majesty, relating to the militia, &c., a demand having been made on Rhode Island by Colonel Dudley, Governor of Massachusetts, for the whole militia of Rhode Island.

1703, Jul. 8. Will—proved 1704, Feb. 5. Exx. wife Elizabeth. Overseer, brother-in-law Robert Lawton. To wife Elizabeth all estate to bring up his children Robert and Abigail till of age, and then Robert to have mansion house at Newport, north side of highway, shop, wharf, warehouse, &c., and seal ring. To daughter Abigail certain land, except what is given George Hicks and a piece of land I gave to set a Church of England on.

1710, Sep. 20. The will of his son Robert (proved 1710, Oct. 2), makes his mother Elizabeth, sole heir.

1722, Mar. 22. Will—proved 1724, July 4. Widow Elizabeth. Exs. Thomas Cornell, George Lawton, and Jonathan Nichols. To grandson James Honeyman, all land and houses and his grandfather's silver hilted sword and seal ring at age, and she also mentions her granddaughter Elizabeth Dunbar, and husband George Dunbar, great-grandson Robert Dunbar, kindred Major James Brown, Esek Brown, wife of Edward Thurston, Job Carr, cooper, the four children of John Hix, ship carpenter, deceased, and the late Mary Hix, now wife of Ralph Earle.

V. ESEK, b. / d. 1744. — Little Compton, R. I.
m.
SUSANNA, b. / d. — of

1. Mary, 1685, Jul. 14.
2. Sarah, 1689, Mar. 19.
3. Elizabeth, 1691, Jul. 29.
4. Esek, 1693, Aug. 23.
5. Anna, 1696, Feb. 28.
6. Martha, 1698, May 29.
7. Susanna, 1700, Sep. 20.
8. Margaret, 1703, Jan. 16.
9. Robert, 1706, Feb. 24.
10. Thankful, 1709, Apr. 27.

1687, Aug. 1. He and wife Susanna sold Robert Carr, of Newport, half an acre there for £20.

1739, May 16. Will—proved 1744, Nov. 12. Ex. son Robert. To son Robert whole estate, real and personal, except the burial place where I have laid my dead, near dwelling house: and he desires that a handsome stone wall be erected about the graves, enclosing quarter of an acre for children and children's children. To children of daughter Mary Brownell, wife of John Brownell, £10. To daughter Sarah Thurston, £5. To daughter Elizabeth, wife of Samuel Wilbur, £5. To daughter Anne, wife of Jonathan Wood, £5. To daughter Susanna, wife of Thomas Wilbur, £3. To children of daughter Margaret Dosson, £60, viz.: £20, each. To daughter Thankful, wife of William Lake, £5. To granddaughter Mary, wife of Nathaniel Potter, 40*s.* To granddaughter Deborah, daughter of son Esek, deceased, £50. at eighteen.

VI. MARGARET, b. / d.

CARR (ROBERT). 2d column. VI. Margaret m. 1670, Richard Hartshorn, of Middletown, N. Y.

THOMAS, m. SARAH, { b. 1636 ± d. 1719 ± } { b. d. 1706 + }

Newport, R. I.

By tradition, he was son of one of the English planting families of Ulster County, Ireland. His father and mother and all his family were destroyed in the Irish massacre (1641, Oct. 23), he, a child being saved by his uncle and carried to his relatives in Gloucestershire. The tradition further says that he sailed for America from Plymouth, England.

1692, May 20. He and Thomas Casey, Jr., were witnesses to a deed from James Sweet of East Greenwich to Thomas Weaver of Newport.

1702, Mar. 4. He had land laid out.

I. THOMAS, m. REBECCA, { b. 1663. d. 1719 (—) } { b. d. 1719 + } of — Newport, R. I.

1. John, 1695.
2. Rebecca, 1698 ±
3. Sarah, 1701.
4. Edmund, 1704.

1692, May 20. He was witness to a deed with Thomas Casey, Sr.

1710, Sep. 5. He (called Thomas Casey Jr.), brought suit against Richard Allen. Judgment was given for defendant.

II. ADAM, m. 1706, Mar. 8. MARY GREENMAN, { b. 1667 ± d. 1765, Apr. } { b. d. 1747 ± } of Edward & Mary ( ) Greenman. — Warwick, Scituate, Coventry, R. I.

1. Thomas, 1706, Nov. 18.
2. Silas, 1708, Oct. 20.
3. Mary, 1710, Sep. 10.
4. Sarah, 1715, Sep. 22.
5. Edward, 1718, Feb. 14.

He was a tailor.

His marriage took place at Newport.

1712, Jul. 31. Warwick. He sold to John Greene, son of James, certain undivided land for £90.

1714, May 4. Freeman.

1719, Jul. 18. He was one of the appraisors of inventory of James Sweet.

1742, Sep. 12. Lieutenant.

1750, Mar. 8. He bought 50 acres in Scituate of son Edward.

1751, Apr. 17. Scituate. He took the oath against bribery and corruption.

1760, Mar. 29. He and son Edward sold to Nathan Brown, of Swanzey, 100 acres in Scituate, and moved to Coventry.

1764, Jul. 10. Will—proved 1765, Apr. 20. Ex. son Edward. He calls himself "far advanced in years." To son Thomas, a French gun. To daughters Mary Weaver and Sarah Whitford, one Spanish milled dollar each. To son Edward the rest of personal estate.

He was buried in his own ground at Scituate.

It is from Thomas[3] (Adam[2], Thomas[1]), through Silas[4], and Wanton[5], that Major General Silas Casey[6], U. S. Army, and his son Colonel Thomas Lincoln Casey[7], U. S. Army, are descended.

III. SAMUEL, m. 1715, Sep. 23. DORCAS ELLIS. { b. 1675 ± d. 1752, Mar. } { b. d. } of Ellis. — Newport, Kings Town, Exeter, R. I.

1. Thomas, 1716 ±
2. Daughter,
3. Daughter,
4. John, 1723 ±
5. Samuel, 1724 ±
6. Gideon, 1726 ±

1713, May 5. Freeman.

1715. Kings Town. Ear mark recorded.

1717. He bought 52 acres of John and Susanna Hyams.

1727. Dec. 30. He sold land.

CASEY. 2d column. III. Samuel. 3d child, Elizabeth, 1720, ±.

1734, Apr. 30. North Kingstown. Freeman.

1737. Justice of the Peace.

1738, Jul. 10. He deeded land to son Thomas.

1740. Grand Jury. He held the offices of Overseer of the Poor, and sealer of flax, &c., at about this time.

1742-43-44-45-46-47. Exeter. Auditor of Town Treasurer's accounts.

1744, Jun. 25. Ear mark recorded.

1744, Jul. 23. He deeded lands to son John.

1745, Apr. 17. He deeded lands to son Samuel Jr.

1745. Moderator of Town Meeting.

1747. Town Council.

1748. Grand Jury.

CASEY. 2d column. III. Samuel. 1717, Oct. 7. He and wife Dorcas, of Newport, and his mother Sarah Davis, sold land to William Phillips. He alludes to honored father, Thomas.

1752, Apr. 8. Administration to son Thomas.

1752, May 7. Inventory £2,803 18*s*. 6*d*., viz: wearing apparel £133, 10*s*., linen wheel, quilting frame, 2 pair cards, warming pan, cheese press, 3 silver spoons, cash £77, 6*s*., books £12, 8*s*. 3 mares horse, 2 colts, 1 pair oxen, 2 pair steers, 14 cows, 10 young cattle, 5 calves, 74 sheep, 29 lambs, 2 sows, 8 pigs, 9 geese, 18 goslings.

CHAMBERLIN.

JOHN, m. (1) 1653, May 19, ANN BROWN, of William Brown. m. (2) CATHERINE CHATHAM, of Chatham. { b. 1626. d. } { b. d. } { b. d. }

Boston, Mass., Newport, R. I.

He was a currier.

1651, He was of Boston thus early.

1660, Jun. 1. He was present at the execution of Mary Dyer, and was drawn to visit those in prison, "and soon tasted of your cruelty and hath been much and long imprisoned by you, and though still you have sorely shot at him yet his bow abides in strength, being enabled to bear all your cruelty and stand a faithful witness for the Lord against you."

1661, Sep. 9. He had been nine times whipped by this date as asserted in Bishop's "New England Judged." The same authority, says that Catharine Chatham, "came from London through many trials and hard travels to Boston and appeared clothed with sackcloth as a sign of the indignation of the Lord coming upon you." She was put into prison, whipped at Dedham, again imprisoned at Boston a long season to pay a fine; "but the Lord otherwise provided for her and disappointed you, for she was took to wife by John Chamberlane and so became an inhabitant of Boston."

1664. Newport.

1666, Apr. The Quaker records give his death at this date, but this could not have been if his daughter Jane was born 1667, Dec.

I. ANN. { b. 1654, Feb. 6. d. }

II. ELIZABETH, { b. 1656, Oct. 25. d. }

III. HENRY, m. ANN, { b. d. 1709 (—) } { b. d. } of — Sandwich, Mass., Shrewsbury, N. J.

1. John.

1680, Mar. 20. He, calling himself eldest son of John Chamberlin, deceased, of Rhode Island, sold Valentine Huddlestone of Newport, all interest in his father's estate in Rhode Island.

His widow Ann is mentioned in records of New Jersey (Freehold), and his son John is spoken of as son of late Henry Chamberlin, in a deed from John to Thomas Layton, in 1709 (Freehold Records.)

IV. WILLIAM, m. ——— { b. d. 1717. } { b. d. } of — Shrewsbury, N. J.

1. Henry.

1680, Mar. 20. He witnessed deed of Henry Chamberlin.

1717, Jul. 8. Administration to John Chamberlin. His son Henry chose John Chamberlin as guardian.

(2d WIFE.)

V. SUSANNA, { b. 1664, Aug. d. }

VI. PELEG, { b. 1666, Aug. d. }

VII. JANE, { b. 1667, Dec. d. }

HOPE,[2] (Richard,[1]) b. 1655, Jan. 30. d. 1698, May 3.
m. ——— b. d.

Braintree, Mass., Westerly, R. I.

1680. Freeman.

1698, May 13. Will—proved 1698, May 19. (The will was verbal but declared by James Cornish and John Maxson to be the will of deceased and administration was given to Susanna Ellis of Stonington, bond being given by her two sons, John and Richard.)

To daughter Elizabeth, a cow. To daughter Hannah, a cow. To that woman my wife (though no wife of mine), 5*s*., adding, "I do protest against her having one penny more of my estate."

To sister Susannah Ellis he gave rest of estate of housing, lands and movables, to be in her care, and that my son shall live with her, she teaching him to be a weaver and when he is of age to have delivered to him the said estate. Sister Ellis to have use of the estate till son is of age and if he die she to have the estate for her and her children, the maids' portions being doubled.

Inventory £59, 6*s*. 6*d*., viz: 5 cows, 4 yearlings, 4 calves, 4 horsekind, 12 sheep, carpenter's tools, books 10*s*., etc.

I. RICHARD, b. 1689, Feb. 20. d.

II. ELIZABETH, b. d.

III. HANNAH, b. d.

CHAPMAN (Ralph). 1st column. Ralph, d. 1711 (—). He had a daughter Mary by 2d wife, and daughter Catharine by 3d wife. 1711, Sep. It appeared by evidence that he had been absent about six years and not heard of, and was by presumption therefore deemed dead. 1701, Nov. 4. Will—proved 1711, Sep. Exx. wife Mary. To son Ralph, 20*s*., having done much for him. To sons John and Isaac, a house lot, each. To son-in-law (*i. e.* stepson) Jeremiah Gould, a lot already sold him—to be laid out. To four daughters Abigail, Mary, Lydia and Catharine Chapman, each a lot. (The lots given children adjoined each other and were each fifty-three feet in breadth). To wife Mary, all houses and lands not mentioned, and she to give what she thinks fit to son Walter, to whom I have not given any part of my estate.

1711, Jun. 27. Will—proved 1711, Sep. 3. Widow Mary. Exs. brother Nathaniel Sheffield and sons Jeremiah and Daniel Gould. She directs that stock and personal estate at Mattapoisett given by late husband be sold. To Isaac Chapman, Abigail Prince, Mary, Catharine and Walter Chapman, children of late husband, £52, divided, and a further amount after debts are paid. To executors, a legacy, and also to sisters Hannah Rodman, Catharine Sheffield and Deliverance Cornell. To grandchildren William and John Chapman, sons of Ralph, each £3. To Sarah, Mary, Catharine and Elizabeth Gould, daughters of son Jeremiah Gould, each £3. To Mary and Ruth Gould, daughters of son Daniel Gould, each £3. To Elizabeth Hix, daughter of my daughter Mary Hix, deceased, £3. Negro Pegg to be set free and certain provision made for her. As to estate real and personal left by husband in Newport; she gives to daughter Catharine Chapman a lot of land, to son Walter, a house and certain land, bed, six chairs, &c., to husband's daughter Mary Chapman, a bed, and to daughter Catharine, the rest of personal estate with certain exceptions. Son Walter to be put to a useful trade, and estate delivered him at age. The debts due to estate of former husband Daniel Gould to go equally to sons Jeremiah and Daniel Gould.

2d column. I. Ralph He was a shipwright. By 1st wife he had a son William, and by 2d wife a son John. 1728, Inventory, £3,135. II. John, d 1710. 1710, Apr. 28. Inventory, £37, 19*s*, 2*d*. Also sundry goods on board the sloop at New York and since returned, 4 firkins nails, 2 cribs of glass, green diamond glass, &c. Administration to widow Patience. V. Abigail. Her husband d. 1719. Children, 1. Abigail.

CHAPMAN (Ralph.)

RALPH,[2] (Ralph.[1]) b. d.
m. (1) MARY, b. d. 1688, May 22.
m. (2) ABIGAIL, b. d. 1694.
m. (3) MARY GOULD, [Daniel. (w. of b. 1661, Jan. 11. d. 1711, Aug. 10.
of Walter & Content (Greenman) Clarke.

Marshfield, Scituate, Mass., Newport, R. I.

He was a shipwright.

1680. Newport. He moved there about this date.

1684. Freeman.

1704, Nov. 4. He deeded to his honored father-in-law, Walter Clarke, and Nathaniel Coddington, merchant, certain land in Newport, with dwelling house, outhouses, garden and orchards; in trust "for the present support of my said wife Mary Chapman, and the child I had by her, my said wife, called Walter Chapman, during her life." Testimony was given by James Cole and William Anthony, that said Chapman came out of his house in Newport, and his wife with him, he did shut the door and did in our presence deliver unto them the house, &c., they (the trustees) taking possession by taking hold of the string of the door, and thus opening the door.

1715. Oct. 20. He and Benjamin Norton, appealed to the Assembly from judgment of Court of Trials, in action of trespass, damage £100, against William Rouse, blacksmith, of Newport. The Assembly confirmed the judgment of Court of Trials, and the appellants desired an appeal from the Assembly to the King and Council, and said Assembly granted the petition, they giving bonds.

He was buried in the Clifton Burial Ground.

I. RALPH, b. 1680, Jan, 7. d. 1728, Feb. 17. Newport, R. I.
m. (1) 1702, Jun. 8, DELIVERANCE SLOCUM, b. 1685, Feb. 10. d. 1711, Aug. 11. of Peleg & Mary (Holder) Slocum.
m. (2) ANN PECKHAM, [Peleg. (w. of b. d. of John & Mary (Sayles) Holmes.

1. John, 1707, Feb.
(2d wife.)
2. Ann, 1721.
3. William, 1727.
4. Peleg,
5. Mary,

He and his first wife were buried in Clifton Burial Ground.

II. JOHN, b. 1682, Aug. 5. d. 1711. Newport, R. I.
m. 1709, Mar. 2, PATIENCE ARNOLD, b. 1684. d. of Oliver & Phebe (Cook) Arnold.

(She m. (2) 1711, Aug. 9, Robert Taylor.)

III. ISAAC, b. 1684, Dec. 19. d. 1765, Feb. 7. Newport, R. I.
m. MARY, b. 1688. d. 1750, Sep. 24. of

1. Isaac, 1715, May 28.
2. James, 1717, Jul. 4.
3. Mary, 1720.
4. John, 1724, Jun. 20.

1708. Freeman.

He and his wife were buried in the Clifton Burial Ground.

CHAPMAN (Ralph). 2d column. Isaac. His wife was Mary Carr, b. 1693, Oct. 26, of Edward and Hannah (Stanton) Carr.

IV. WILLIAM, b. 1687, Mar. 7. d. 1688, May 13.

(2d WIFE.)

V. ABIGAIL, b, 1691, Sep. d. 1715, Oct. 12.
m. ISAAC PRINCE, b. d. of Prince.

VI. LYDIA, b. 1694. d. 1708, Dec.

(3d WIFE.)

VII. WALTER, b. d. 1754. Newport, R. I.

1723. Freeman.

CHAPMAN. (Ralph). 2d column. IX. Catherine m. 1714, Mar. 1, James Sheffield, b. 1694, d. 1762, Apr. 20, of Nathaniel and Mary. Children, 1. Mary, 1716, Sep. 21. 2, Nathaniel, 1718, Feb. 3, Sarah, 1720, June 13. 4, James, 1722, Sep. 20. 5, Rulbe, 1724, Oct. 21. 6, Elizabeth, 1727, Dec. 21. 7, Samuel, 1736, July 15.

CHURCH (Benjamin).

BENJAMIN,[2] (Richard.[1]) b. 1641. d. 1718, Jan. 17.
m. 1667, Dec. 26, ALICE SOUTHWORTH, b. 1647. d. 1719, Mar. 5.
of Constant & Elizabeth (Collier) Southworth.

Duxbury, Mass., Bristol, Little Compton, R. I.

He was a carpenter.

1668–70–72–73–75. Juryman.

1670, May 29. Freeman.

1671, Jun. 5. Constable.

1674, Apr. 10. He drew a lot in Seaconnet lands.

1675. Little Compton. In the preface to his History of the Indian Wars, he says: "In the year 1675, that unhappy and bloody Indian war broke out in Plymouth Colony, where I was then building and beginning a plantation at a place called by the Indians, Sekonit, and since by the English, Little Compton. I was the first Englishman that built upon that Neck, which was full of Indians. My head and hands were full about a new plantation, where nothing was brought to: no preparation of dwelling house, or outhousing or fencing made. Horses and cattle were to be provided, ground to be cleared and broken up, and the uttermost caution to be used to keep myself from offending my Indian neighbours all around me. While I was thus busily employed, and all my time and strength laid out in this laborious undertaking, I received a commission from the government to engage in their

I. THOMAS, b. 1674. d. 1746, Mar. 12. Little Compton, R. I.
m. (1) 1698, Feb. 21, SARAH HAYMAN, b. 1679, Aug. 22. d. of Nathaniel & Elizabeth (Allen) Hayman.
m. (2) 1712, Apr. 16, EDITH WOODMAN, b. 1685, Sep. 7. d. 1718, Jun. 3. of John & Hannah (Timberlake) Woodman.
m. (3) 1719, SARAH, b. 1695. d. 1768, Apr. 22. of

1. Sarah, [illegible], Jan. 15.
2. Elizabeth, 1702. Sep. 9.
3. Thomas, 1704, Aug. 20.
(2d wife.)
4. Elizabeth, 1713, Jan. 10.
5. Hannah, 1714, Sep 23.
6. Priscilla, 1717, Jan. 6.
7. Thomas, 1718, May.
(3d wife.)
8. Thomas, 1720, May 31.
9. Sarah, 1721, May 15.
10. Thomas, 1722, Jul. 13.
11. Benjamin, 1723, Sep. 9.
12. Mary, 1725, Jan. 2.
13. Thomas, 1727, Sep. 1.
14. Benjamin, 1732, Jan. 10.
15. Mercy, 1734, Sep. 18.

He was a carpenter.

1759, Jul. 18. Will—proved 1768, Jun. 7. Widow Sarah. Ex. son Thomas. To grandson Francis Bailey, £100. To grandson Benjamin Church, great bible. To grandson Francis Wilbur, £100. Certain real estate at Hingham, to be sold to pay the £200 above. To daughter Mary Wilbur, black taffeta gown. To daughter Mercy Richmond, snuff colored taffeta gown. To four children, Thomas Church, Sarah Bailey, Mary Wilbur and Mercy Richmond, rest of estate.

Inventory, £14, 7*s*. 9*d*.

II. CONSTANT, b. 1676, May 12. d. 1727, Mar. 9. Freetown, Mass.
m. PATIENCE COOK, b. d. 1727 + of John & Mary ( ) [Cook.

1. Edward, 1716, Jan. 13.
2. Benjamin, 1718, Jan. 6.
3. Mary, 1720, Apr. 13.
4. Martha, 1723, Sep. 20.
5. Constant, 1726, Aug. 12.
6. Nathaniel, 1726, Aug. 12.

He was a captain of militia.

1727, Apr. 3. Inventory, £5,120, of which £661, 5*s*. 9*d*., was personal. Administratrix widow Patience. Housing, barn, cider mill and lands £4,200, purse and apparel £18, 5*s*, books £1, 10*s*., gun, sword, watch £10, negro £90, Indian man £30, 4 oxen, 2 cows, heifer, 3 yearlings, 4 horses, colt, 2 sows, 9 pigs, 9 shoats, turkeys, fowls, wool cards, &c.

III. BENJAMIN, b. 1678. d. young.

CHURCH (Benjamin). 2d column. I. Thomas. Add daughter Alice b. 1706, July 28. 1746, Feb. 20. Will-proved 1746, Apr. 14. Exs. John Hunt, and son Thomas. To wife, Sarah, what she brought and certain provision while widow. To son Thomas, Neck farm, 12 cows and other cattle, 103 sheep, etc., and right (as eldest son of Benjamin,) in land granted Narragansett soldiers. To son Benjamin homestead, etc. He mentions daughters Alice Unis, Elizabeth Lindsey, Hannah Carey, Sarah Bailey Mary and Mercy Church.

defence. And with my commission I received another heart inclining me to put forth my strength in military service. And through the grace of God, I was spirited for that work and direction in it was renewed to me day by day." He closes his address to the reader thus: "And seeing every particle of historical truth is precious, I hope the reader will pass a favourable censure upon an old soldier telling of the many ran-counters he has had and yet is come off alive," &c., adding finally: "I desire prayer, that I may be enabled well to accomplish my spiritual welfare and that I may be more than conqueror through Jesus Christ loving of me." (This was written in his old age, and the book was published in Boston, in 1716).

1675, Dec. 19. He was wounded in the Narragansett Swamp Fight, at which time over a thousand Indians and more than two hundred Englishmen were killed and wounded. There were thirty-five hundred Indians and fifteen hundred colonists engaged in this conflict.

1676, Aug. 12. He organized the party and planned the attack on King Philip, which resulted in the chieftain's death at this date in the swamp near Mount Hope.

1681, Sep. 1. Bristol. He and other proprietors of Mount Hope purchase, met and agreed that the name of the town should be Bristol.

1682–83. Deputy.

1682–83–84–85–86–87–88. Town Council.

1683. Oct. 24. He agreed to make the wolf pits in a month. The town had before this voted to give 40*s.* for two wolf pits, the benefit of said pits, to go to the makers thereof, provided he keep the pits well.

1689, Sep. 6. Major and Commander in Chief of the first expedition against the Indians in the east (Casco, &c).

1690, Sep. 2. Commander of second expedition.

1692, Jul. 25. Commander of third expedition, going to the Penobscot River.

1694. Assessor.

1696, Mar. 23. Moderator of Town Meeting.

1696, Aug. 3. Commander of fourth expedition.

1700, Jan. 18. Tiverton. He deeded son Thomas, for love, &c., certain land, house, &c.

1702, Mar. 27. He deeded son Edward, for love, &c., certain land in Bristol, house, &c.

1704, Mar. 18. Commander of fifth expedition.

1705, Apr. 11. He deeded son Thomas, certain land in Little Compton, ten cows, one hundred sheep, &c.

1705, Jul. 20. He deeded only daughter, Elizabeth Rosbotham, and her husband, Captain Joseph Rosbotham, of Bristol, certain land there.

1705, Nov. 20. Little Compton. He consented to change of roads for public convenience.

1706. Deputy.

1707, Feb. 3. He deeded son Charles, for love, &c., certain land in Little Compton, with buildings, &c.

1707, Apr. 12. He deeded son Constant, for love, &c., mill in Tiverton and land in Freetown, at his death.

1718, Feb. 15. Inventory, sworn to by widow Alice, administratrix. Among the items were, sword and belt £5, cane and gloves 12*s*, wearing apparel £28, 15*s.*, 2 gold rings and 3 pairs of buttons £2, 10*s.*, pair of plate buckles, tankard, cup, porringer, 2 salt cellers and 7 spoons, all in plate, 42 oz. £25, books £2, 2 guns, feather bed, 7 Turkey worked chairs, 16 wooden chairs, churn, pair of stillyards, 2 spinning wheels, pair of cards, silver and gold buttons £2, 2*s.* 6*d.*, cash £2, 16*s.* 6*d.*, Indian corn, oats, rye, 2 barrels cider, 2 horses, mare, 9 cows, 4 heifers, pair of oxen, pair of steers, bull, 7 two year cattle, 10 yearlings, 5 swine, negro man and bedding £60, negro woman £40, servant boy William Heard £10, &c., land in Tiverton, 120½ acres £180

1718, Mar. 6. Agreement of widow Alice and her children, by which the latter gave her authority to sell the Tiverton land, to pay debts and funeral expenses. Signed by Thomas, Constant, Charles and Martha Church, and John and Elizabeth Sampson. (Martha Church was the widow of Edward.)

1736, May 18 Division was made of 500 acres, which had been ordered to be laid out to the heirs of Benjamin Church, deceased, in gore adjoining Rehoboth. (Granted by General Court, 1735, Jun. 13.) The first share, 113 acres, to Charles Church, being the share he had of his brother Thomas. The second share to Charles Church, being his own share. The third share to Charles Church, being share he purchased of Benjamin Church, and George Wanton, and Abigail his wife, heirs of Edward Church, deceased. The fourth share to Elizabeth Sampson, daughter of Benjamin Church. The fifth share to representatives of Constant Church.

IV. EDWARD, b. ; d. 1707. Bristol, R. I.
m.
MARTHA BRENTON, b. 1678. d. 1750, Apr. 14. of William & Hannah (Davis) Brenton.

1. Abigail, 1703, Mar. 4.
2. Benjamin, 1704, Oct. 8.

1703, May 1. It was voted that he "have the privilege of building a pew where room shall present."

1707, Apr. 2. Administration to widow Martha.

His widow was buried in Clifton Burial Ground, at Newport.

V. CHARLES, b. 1682, May 9. d. 1747, Jan. Bristol, R. I.
m. 1708, May 20,
HANNAH PAINE, b. 1685, Apr. 20. d. 1755, Oct. 16. of Nathaniel & Dorothy (   ) Paine.

1. Constant, 1708, Dec. 12.
2. Elizabeth, 1710, Dec. 24.
3. Hannah, 1713, Feb. 20.
4. Nathaniel,
5. Dorothy,
6. Sarah,
7. Mary,

1712, Mar. 24. He and three others were appointed a committee to take down the belfry, or let it stand if it may be with safety to the roof, and to do what shall be needful for making of the roof of the meeting house tight.

He was often appointed on committees, and held various offices—Sheriff, Field Driver, Assessor of Taxes, &c.

1746, Nov. 29. Will—proved 1747, Feb. 24. Exs. three sons-in-law, Thomas Greene, Simon Davis and Samuel Chandler. To wife Hannah, use of house, lot, &c., for life, and certain buildings on Mrs. Elizabeth Vernon's land, which I built for a calash house and to grind chocolate in. To wife, use of other land, and to her a negro woman and boy, best horse, chaise, two best cows, and what household goods she wants, for life. To daughter-in-law Mary Church, widow of eldest son Constant, the use of certain rooms in house where she dwells, till her son Peter, is of age. To grandson Charles, eldest son of Constant, house and land where I dwell, &c., and if he die without issue, then to four grandchildren, viz: Peter and Mary, two of the children of Constant, Hannah, daughter of son Nathaniel, and Charles Davis, son of daughter Hannah. To grandchildren Peter and Mary Church, and Hannah Church, daughter of Nathaniel, certain land. To daughters Elizabeth Greene, wife of Major Thomas Greene, Hannah Davis, wife of Captain Simon Davis, Dorothy Chandler, wife of Samuel, Sarah James, and Mary Chandler, wife of John, certain land to each. To Church of Christ, in Bristol, land for support of gospel in the Presbyterian or Congregational way.

Inventory, £1,153, 3*s.* 6*d.*, viz: wearing apparel £70, decanter, 3 wine glasses, 6 beaker glasses, negro woman and girl £280, small negro girl £40, negroes Rhino, Dido and Rebecca, 4 wheels, 70 oz. 16 pwt. silver £141, 12*s.*, 5 cows, 2 heifers, 76 lbs. pewter, &c.

1755, May 28. Will—proved 1755, Nov. 10. Widow Hannah. Exs. brother-in-law Joseph Russell and son-in-law John Chandler, Jr. To grandson Charles Church, certain land, a horse, two cows and a bed, and if he die, then grandchildren Peter and Mary Church. To children of daughter Elizabeth Greene, viz: Thomas, Nathaniel, Benjamin, Hannah and Mary, certain land. To children of daughter Hannah Davis, deceased, certain land. To daughters Dorothy Chandler, wife of Samuel Chandler, of Woodstock, Sarah James, wife of Leonard James, of Boston, and Mary Chandler, wife of John, Jr., of Worcester, £600 each. To four daughters, a fifth of wearing apparel. To granddaughters Ann Church and Hannah Davis, the other fifth of apparel. To grandson Thomas Greene, Jr., my young mare and a cow. To granddaughter Hannah Church, daughter of Nathaniel, deceased, £300. To grandchildren Peter and Mary Church, the rest of farm, at age. Executors were empowered to sell off my share of real estate, lately improved by my honored mother, madam Dorothy Paine. To granddaughter Hannah Church, rest of estate.

Inventory, £2,439, 8*s.* 4*d.*

VI. ELIZABETH, b. 1684, Mar. 26. d. 1739 +
m. (1)
JOSEPH ROSBOTHAM, b. d. of Rosbotham.
m. (2) 1717, Sep. 11,
JOHN SAMPSON, b. d. 1734. of Sampson.
m. (3) 1739, Jun. 18,
SAMUEL WOODBURY, b. d. of Woodbury.

1. Benjamin, 1701, Dec. 1.
2. Alice, 1704, Aug. 26.
3. Elizabeth, 1708, Sep. 9.
4. Hannah, 1711, Jun. 20.
(By 2d husband.)
5. John, 1719, Jan. 20.
6. Mary, 1719, Jan. 20.
7. John, 1722, May 31.

VII. NATHANIEL, b. 1686, Jul. 1. d. 1687, Feb. 29.

Joseph,[2] (Richard.[1]) — b. 1638. d. 1711, Mar. 5.
m.
Mary Tucker, — b. 1641. d. 1710, Mar. 21.

of John Tucker

Hingham, Mass., Little Compton, R. I.

He was a carpenter.

1679–80. Little Compton. Grand Jury.

1680, Jun. 1. He took oath of fidelity.

1681. Oct. 28. The following order was addressed to him. " Whereas, the court are informed that your neighborhood is destitute of leading men, either to call a meeting or otherwise to act in your public concerns, this court empowers you, the above named Joseph Church, to call your neighborhood at Saconnett, together in convenient time, to make such necessary and wholesome orders as may be for your common good and peace," &c., and choice was to be made and persons sent to said court to serve in the office of constable and as grand jurymen.

1682, Jun. 6. Upon petition of himself and the rest of the proprietors of Saconett, the court granted from this time, a township to be called by name of Little Compton.

1682, Jun. 6. Freeman.

1683–86. Selectman.

1686, Jun. 4. Ensign.

1689, Oct. 2. He was authorized to solemnize marriages.

1689, Dec. 25. He and two others were appointed for the county of Bristol, to settle the charges of the late war.

1690. Deputy.

1690-91. Court associate (county magistrate).

1711, Feb. 15. Will—proved 1711, Mar. 1. Exs. sons Joseph and John. Overseers, friends John Palmer and Thomas Church. He directs that a small farm of 35 acres and dwelling house I now live in, and several other pieces of land, as well as all personal estate, shall be sold to best advantage. To daughters Elizabeth Blackman, Mary Wood, Deborah Gray and Abigail Simmons, enough each to make them equal, with what land they had before. To eldest son Joseph, two shares, and one share each to son John, and daughters Elizabeth, wife of Joseph Blackman, Mary, wife of John Wood, Deborah, wife of Samuel Gray, and Abigail, wife of William Simmons. To Mary Torobono, now living with me, a bed, &c. for her former kindness to my wife and some to myself, provided she continues upon reasonable wages. To Indian boy Amos, half of a 15 acre lot if he serve his time out. Certain sums borrowed of testator are to be put in the inventory and paid, viz: due from Joseph £10, 7*s*. 6*d*., from son John £16, 2*s*., from son-in-law William Simmons £14, 16*s*.

Inventory, £669, 14*s*., viz: wearing apparel £30, 25 acres £175, dwelling house thereon £70, two 24 acre lots £64, two 15 acre lots and three quarters £41, pewter, punch bowl, due from children (as before said), negro man and bed £18, cheese press, 3 pair of old cards, linen wheel, woolen wheel, plate cup 15*s*., silver money £3, 5*s*. 5*d*., mare, 29 sheep, &c.

I. **Joseph,** — b. d. 1715, Dec. 19. — Little Compton, R. I.
m.
Grace Shaw, — b. d. 1737, Mar. 1. — of Anthony & Alice (Stonard) Shaw.

1714, Jan. 11. Will—proved 1716, Jan. 3. Exs. wife Grace and son Nathaniel. Overseers, brother-in-law Israel Shaw and friend Deacon William Pabodie. To wife, a certain room and the household goods, with certain exceptions, a cow, and to be found with meat, corn and firewood, and £10 yearly, while widow, all by son Nathaniel, till son Caleb is of age, and then he to pay half of the £10. At death of wife, the room to go to son the house belongs to, and the household goods then to go to daughters, except a bed. To son Nathaniel, half the lands that I have in three great lots, and one of the houses, barns, &c. The other half of land to son Caleb, with the other house and barn, at age, he paying half of legacies. Son Nathaniel to have his choice of either half. If either Nathaniel or Caleb die without issue, then sons Richard and Israel to have. To son Richard, at twenty-three, £100, and afterwards when he is building a house, to have £50 more. To son Israel, like legacy. To grandson Joseph, £50 at twenty-three. To four daughters, Sarah, Alice, Deborah and Elizabeth, each £50 and a bed when married. To son Nathaniel, benefit of all land, stock, &c, till Caleb is of age, and then half to him. Sons Richard and Israel to be given convenient learning and brought up by executors till fourteen and put out to trade, and grandson Joseph to be put out to a trade if his mother see fit. To sons Nathaniel and Caleb, outlands.

Inventory, homestead £1,800, outlands £280, 42 loads of hay, 3 oxen, 5 steers, 12 cows, 3 heifers, 11 yearlings, 14 calves, 30 sheep, 30 lambs, 3 mares, 2 colts, 12 swine, 2 sows, negro man £50, 2 woolen wheels, 2 linen wheels, 2 pair worsted combs, 2 pair cards, &c.

1732, May 19. Will—proved 1737, Apr. 19. Widow Grace. Exx. daughter Sarah. To sons Nathaniel, Caleb and Richard, 5*s*. each. To grandson Joseph, 5*s*. To granddaughter Grace Church, 5*s*. To son Israel, £10. To daughter Sarah Church, bed, pair of iron dogs, spice mortar, shop, goose house, and all living creatures. To daughter Deborah Briggs, £20. To daughter Elizabeth Palmer, £20. To daughters Sarah, Deborah and Elizabeth, wearing apparel. To daughter Sarah, rest of estate.

Inventory, £222, 18*s*. 5*d*.

1. Joseph, 1689, Jun. 17.
2. Sarah, 1691, Mar. 31.
3. Nathaniel, 1693, Feb. 8.
4. Alice, 1695, Feb. 8.
5. Deborah, 1697, Jan.
6. Elizabeth, 1699, Feb.
7. Caleb, 1701, Oct. 11.
8. Richard, 1703, Nov. 21.
9. Israel, 1707, Apr. 22.

II. **John,** — b. d. 1756, Jan. — Little Compton, R. I.
m.
Rebecca, — b. d. 1748 (—). — of

1748, Dec. 20. Will—proved 1756, Feb. 3. Exs. son Benjamin and Edward. To son Benjamin, northerly part of farm I now live upon and buildings thereon, &c., brass kettle, lignum vitæ mortar, bible, sword, nine plate buttons, shoe buckles, chairs, tables, &c. To son Edward, rest of farm, bed, book called Body of Divinity, silver headed cane, eight plate buttons, loom, &c. To daughter Mary Tisdale, £30, she having had, and like legacy to daughters Elizabeth Crandall and Sarah Crossman. To granddaughter Rebecca Church, a case of drawers. To granddaughter Anstis Church, a foot wheel. To three daughters, household goods. To sons Benjamin and Edward, rest of estate.

Inventory, £325, 2*s*., viz: chest, plate buttons and other plate £5, warming pan, quilting frame, 2 swords, foot wheel, books, carpenter's tools, cow, loom, &c.

1. William, 1694, May 6.
2. John, 1696, Mar. 7.
3. Mary, 1698, Apr.
4. Elizabeth, 1700, Feb. 17.
5. Benjamin, 1702, Jun. 13.
6. Rebecca, 1704, Apr. 12.
7. Edward, 1706, Feb. 22
8. Sarah, 1708, Sep. 13.

III. **Elizabeth,** — b. d.
m.
Joseph Blackman, — b. d. — of Blackman.

CHURCH (Joseph). 2d column. III. Elizabeth, m. 1685, Nov, 12. Joseph Blackman, b. 1661, June 7; d. 1720, of John and Mary (Pond) Blackman.

1. Jonathan,
2. Ichabod, 1692, Mar. 8.
3. Sarah, 1695, Jan. 1.
4. Rebecca, 1696, Jun. 5.
5. Elisha, 1699, Sep. 23.
6. Benjamin, 1701, Nov. 12.
7. Mary, 1704, Feb. 12.
8. Abraham, 1705, Jul. 11.
9. Elizabeth, 1707, Sep. 11

IV. **Mary,** — b. d. 1748, Nov. 11.
m.
John Wood, — b. d. 1740, Feb. 22. — of Wood.

1. John, 1689, Jul. 16.
2. Mary, 1691, Mar. 14.
3. Sarah, 1692, Nov. 6.
4. Deborah, 1694, Mar. 7.
5. Margaret, 1696, Apr. 20.
6. Abigail, 1697, Dec. 6.
7. Elizabeth, 1699, Nov. 6.
8. Hannah, 1701, Oct. 7.
9. Rebecca, 1703, Nov. 4.
10. Joseph, 1705, Dec. 23.
11. Dorothy, 1707, Dec. 12.

V. **Deborah,** — b. d.
m. (1) 1699, Jul. 13,
Samuel Gray, — b. d. 1712, Mar. 23. — of Edward & Dorothy (Lettice) Gray.
m. (2)
Daniel Throope, — b. d. — of Throope.

1. Samuel, 1700, Apr. 16.
2. John, 1701, Apr. 14.
3. Dorothy, 1704, Jan. 14.
4. Joseph, 1706, Jan. 20.
5. Lydia, 1707, Oct. 16.
6. Simeon, 1709, Dec. 15.
7. Ignatius, 1711, Sep. 18.

VI. **Abigail,** — b. d. 1720, Jul. 4.
m.
William Simmons, — b. d. 1765. — of John & Mercy (Pabodie) Simmons.

1. Mercy, 1697, Jul. 1.
2. William, 1699, Sep. 30.
3. Lydia, 1700, Dec. 15.
4. Joseph, 1702, Mar. 4.
5. John, 1704, Aug. 14.
6. Abigail, 1706, Jul. 14.
7. Rebecca, 1708, May 8.
8. Mary, 1709, Oct. 15.
9. Benjamin, 1713, Feb. 2.
10. Ichabod, 1715, Jan. 6.
11. Peleg, 1716, Dec. 21.
12. Sarah, 1718, Aug. 26.

CLARKE (Carew.)

Carew,[4] (Th.,[3] Jno.,[2] Jno.[1]) — b. 1602, Feb. 3. d. 1679, +
m.
Datre, — b. d. 1658, Jul. 13.

Bedfordshire, Eng., Newport, R. I.

His birth was thus recorded by his father, "Carew Clarke, my son, the 3d Feb'y. 1602, being Thursday, about fair day light; baptized the 17th Feb., Wallops Thursday, 3d day of the new moon 1602."

1658, Jul. 13. At the time of his wife's death he was living in Ruffum, Suffolk Co., Eng., as appears from the old family bible.

1676, Apr. 20. He had by terms of his brother John Clarke's will, a life maintenance, with privilege of living in house with the widow of testator, and if he moved from the house, to have £16, per year.

See: American Genealogist, v.19, p.131

CLARKE (JEREMIAH). 1st column. He was of London, England, before coming to Newport. His wife was born in 1609, as shown by baptism. 2d column. III. Jeremiah. His wife was probably daughter of John and Margaret Audley, of Boston.

JEREMIAH, { b.
m. { d. 1652, Jan.
FRANCES DUNGAN, [Wm. (w. of { b. 1611. { d. 1677, Sep.
of Lewis Latham.

(She m. (4) William Vaughan.)

Newport, R. I.

He married in England and brought his wife and his step children to America with him.

1638. He was admitted an inhabitant of island of Aquidneck.

1639, Apr. 28. He and eight others signed the following compact at Portsmouth, preparatory to the settlement of Newport. "It is agreed by us whose hands are underwritten, to propagate a plantation in the midst of the island, or elsewhere, and to engage ourselves to bear equal charge, answerable to our strength and estates in common; and that our determination shall be by major voices of Judge and Elders, the Judge to have a double voice." He signed as Elder, the Judge being William Coddington. He was present at a meeting of the inhabitants this year.

1639. Treasurer, in place of Robert Jeoffreys "till his return from the Dutch."

1639–40. Constable.

1640, Mar. 10. He had land recorded to amount of 116 acres.

He and two others were chosen this year to lay out the remainder of lands at Newport. He attended the General Court of Elections during the year.

1641, Mar. 16. Freeman.

1642. Lieutenant.

1644. Captain.

1644–45–46–47. Treasurer for the town of Newport.

1647–48–49. Treasurer for the four towns of Colony.

1648. Assistant.

1648. President Regent, acting as Governor under this title, pending Governor William Coddington's clearance of certain accusations.

1652, Jan. The Friends' Records thus comment on his death. "Jeremiah Clarke, one of the first English Planters of Rhode Island, he died at Newport in said Island and was buried in the tomb that stands by the street by the water side in Newport, upon the — day of the 11mo., 1651."

1653, May 6. His widow had legacy of 12*d.*, from will of her father Lewis Latham.

1656, Jan. 18. His widow, now wife of Rev. William Vaughan, entered into an agreement with her son Walter Clarke through his guardians John Cranston and James Barker, who are called his brothers-in-law. (James Barker, had married Walter Clarke's half sister Barbara Dungan). By this agreement Walter Clarke was to have the dwelling house where Mrs. Vaughan lived, garden, orchard, and certain lands, which was his inheritance, but his mother was to have possession till September 29th, or until tobacco was cured. The house where Captain John Cranston lived was to be his as appeared by deed. Mrs. Vaughan was to pay all debts, &c., and for that purpose had half of a house which she was to sell, and she also had certain lands, and household goods, &c., for herself and for the children of Jeremiah Clarke other than Walter.

His widow was buried in Newport cemetery, the stone bearing the following inscription. "Here Lyeth ye Body of Mrs. Frances Vaughan, Alius Clarke, ye mother of ye only children of Capt'n Jeremiah Clarke. She died ye 1 week in Sept., 1677, in ye 67th year of her age."

See: American Genealogist, v. 19, p. 131 v. 26, p. 54 and 227

I. WALTER, { b. 1640. Newport, R. I.
m. (1) 1660 ± { d. 1714, May 23.
CONTENT GREENMAN, { b. 1636. { d. 1666, Mar. 27. of John Greenman.
m. (2) 1667, Feb,
HANNAH SCOTT, { b. 1642. { d. 1681, Jul. 24. of Richard & Catharine (Marbury) Scott.
m. (3) 1683, Mar. 6, [Thos.
FREEBORN HART (w. of { b. 1635, Oct. { d. 1710, Jan. 10. of Roger & Mary ( ) Williams.
m. (4) 1711, Aug. 31. [John
SARAH GOULD, (w. of { b. 1664, Oct. { d. 1714, + of Matthew & Mary ( ) Prior.

1. Mary, 1661, Jan. 11.
2. Content.
3. Son.
(2d wife.)
4. Hannah, 1667, Oct. 28.
5. Catharine, 1671, Sep. 6.
6. Frances, 1673, Jan. 17.
7. Jeremiah, 1675, Feb. 21.
8. Deliverance, 1678, Jul. 4.
(3d and 4th wives, no issue.)

1667–70–72–73. Deputy.

1671, Jan. 30. He was allowed £1 for his boat, in transporting of John Easton, Joseph Torrey and Joshua Coggeshall to Providence and bringing them down.

1673–74–75–99. Assistant.

1676–77–86–96–97–98. Governor.

1679–80–81–82–83–84–85–86–1700–1–2–3–4–5–6–7–8–9–10–11–12–13–14. Deputy Governor.

1686, Dec. 22. He and others were apprized by letter from Sir Edmund Andros, of their appointment as members of his Council, and of a meeting to be held at Boston on the 30th instant. He and four other members of the Council from Rhode Island, were present at the first meeting. The members were sworn to allegiance and due administration of Justice.

1690, Feb. 27. He and Walter Newbury read a paper before the Assembly disclaiming the present government, and a governor was chosen instead of Walter Clarke, viz: Henry Bull.

1698, Jun. 11. He deeded Captain James Gould of Newport, mariner, my son-in-law, and Katharine his wife, all that my message and tenement of houses, with the slaughter house and yard in Newport.

1714, Jun. 7. An agreement was made by his heirs, it being declared that in his will of April 14th, made during his sickness, there were several blots, erasures and imperfections. The agreement was signed by Sarah Clarke the widow, Thomas Rodman and Hannah, his wife, Nathaniel Sheffield and Katharine, his wife, George Cornell and Deliverance his wife, and Jeremiah Gould, son of Mary Chapman, deceased. They gave their uncles Latham and Weston Clarke, their father's clothes and four dozen silver buttons. To mother-in-law (*i. e.* stepmother), Sarah Clarke, all estate that she brought her husband, now in being, and a bed, horse, cow, and lot in Newport. To uncle Weston Clarke, our father's seal on which our father's coat of arms is engraven. To Samuel Cranston, Governor, to be equally divided among his children, all personal estate of our late mother-in-law (*i. e.* stepmother) Freeborn Clarke, which she brought. To the widow Sarah, £10 a year for life, and late dwelling house of Walter, well, garden, housing, shops, &c., except the parts confirmed by him to subscribers. The rest of estate was to be divided into five parts, the widow having one of these parts.

1714, Jun. 13. In an agreement of this date, the rest of personal was divided into four parts. To children of deceased sister Mary Chapman, one-quarter. To sisters Hannah Rodman, Katharine Sheffield and Deliverance Cornell, each a quarter. To cousin (*i. e.* nephew) Clarke Rodman, son of Thomas, certain land, housing and shops. To cousin Jeremiah Clarke, son of Weston, certain land. To uncle Latham Clarke, land. To cousin Phillip Harwood, land. To cousin Walter Clarke, son of Weston, rights in New Jersey. To Colonel John Cranston, land. To cousin Jeremiah Clarke, son of Jeremiah, horses in Narragansett. The land that widow has for life to be divided into five parts, viz: to children of Mary Chapman, one-fifth, and a fifth each to sisters Hannah Rodman, Katharine Sheffield, and Deliverance Cornell, and to cousin Phillip Harwood, one-fifth. To uncle James Clarke, £5. To brother Thomas Rodman, £5. To Governor Samuel Cranston, £5. To brother Nathaniel Sheffield, £5. To children of uncle James Clarke and children of aunt Sarah Carr, each 30*s*. To aunt Sarah Carr, £5. To children of uncles Jeremiah, Latham and Weston Clarke, and of our aunt Stanton, each 6*s*. To children of Governor Samuel Cranston, each 6*s*. To brother-in-law (*i. e.* step brother) John Gould, £5. To sisters in-law Wait Gould and Content Gould, each £10. To sister-in law Mary Lawton, silver spoon. To Quakers, £5, for use of poor. For use of poor of Newport, £5. To widow Amy Wood, a fat sheep annually for life. To Clark Rodman, share in town wharf. To Jeremiah Clark, son of Weston, a share in the wharf. To the mansion house our mother lives in another share in wharf, other minor provisions were made in agreement. Administrators appointed were Thomas Rodman, Nathaniel Sheffield and George Cornell.

He was buried in Clifton Burial Ground.

CLARKE (JEREMIAH). 2d column. II. Mary. She had only one child by her 2d husband, viz.: II. Henry, 1688, May 22. VI. James. He probably had also 3 Ann.

II. MARY, { b. 1641.
m. (1) 1658. { d. 1711, Apr. 7.
JOHN CRANSTON, { b. 1626. { d. 1680, Mar. 12. of Cranston.
m. (2)
JOHN STANTON, { b. 1645, Aug. { d. 1713, Oct. 3. of Robert & Avis ( ) Stanton.

1. Samuel, 1659.
2. Caleb,
3. James,
4. Jeremiah,
5. Mary, 1665, Jan. 27.
6. Benjamin,
7. John,
8. Elizabeth, 1671.
9. Peleg,
10. William,
(By 2d husband.)
11. Benjamin, 1684, Mar. 13.
12. Henry, 1688, May 22.

III. JEREMIAH, { b. 1643. Newport, R. I.
m. { d. 1729, Jan. 16.
ANN AUDLEY. { b. { d. 1732, Dec. 15. of Audley.

1. Jeremiah,
2. Frances, 1669, Dec. 15.
3. Henry,
4. James,
5. Samuel,
6. Weston,
7. Mary,
8. Ann, 1675.
9. Sarah,

1666. Freeman.

1696–97–98–99–1700–1–2–3–4–5. Deputy.

1701. Ordained deacon of the Second Baptist Church.

1719, Sep. 17. He deeded son James Clarke, half of lands in Providence, at West Conaug, and in Connecticut for £3, and a further sum of £3 annually during life of Jeremiah and wife Ann. At same date he deeded the other half of above lands to son-in-law Jeremiah Weeden, on same terms. At death of Jeremiah Clarke and his wife, the sum of £17, 10*s*., was to be equally divided among their children by both of persons to whom land was deeded, viz: £17, 10*s*., paid by James Clarke, and £17, 10*s*., paid by Jeremiah Weeden.

IV. LATHAM, { b. 1645. Portsmouth, R. I.
m. (1) { d. 1719, Aug. 1.
HANNAH WILBUR, { b. { d. of Samuel & Hannah (Porter) Wilbur.
m. (2) 1698, Sep. 20, [Walter
ANNE NEWBURY, (w. of { b. 1652, { d. 1732, Feb. 19. of Collins.

1. Latham, 1668.
2. William, 1673, May 27.
3. Abigail, 1674.
4. Elizabeth, 1680.
5. Mary,
6. Ann, 1682.
7. Samuel, 1686.
8. Jeremiah,
9. Amey,

1676, Aug. 24. He was a member of Court Martial, held at Newport for trial of Indians.

1680, Jun. 12. He bought of Henry Greene, late of Acquidneset, now of New Jersey, for £10, 24 acres in Portsmouth for sixteen years certainly, and after that for life of said Henry Greene and wife Sarah, and then Latham Clarke, to deliver possession to true heirs.

1681–82–83–85–90–91–98. Deputy.

1714, Dec. 31. Will—proved 1719, Aug. 10. Ex. son Samuel. To wife Anne £10. To daughter Abigail, wife of Samuel Thurston, £10. To daughter Elizabeth, wife of John Stanton, £10. To daughter Mary, wife of Joseph Fry, £10, and negro girl Peg. To daughter Amey, wife of William Wood, £10, silver tankard and negro boy Isaac. To sons Samuel and William, wearing apparel. To William £10, and negro boy Moses, already having given him all my lands in Kings Town. To son Samuel a year's service of negro Moll, and she then to be free, and to live among my children. To son Samuel, rest of estate, real and personal.

Inventory £187, 18*s*., viz: wearing apparel with plate buttons, cane, pocket knife, razor and tobacco box £20, plate £10, feather bed, couch, 29 chairs, 2 tables, pewter, churns, 2 wheels, negro child and a year's service in Moll £12, 10*s*., pair of oxen, 3 cows, mare, colt, 110 sheep, 4 swine, warming pan, sconce, &c.

CLARKE (JEREMIAH). 2d column. I. Walter. Philip for Phillip, eighth line after 1714, Jun. 13. II. Mary, erase all after her 10th child. She may have had one child, Henry, by her 2d husband. III. Jeremiah, 1728, Jun. 13. Will—codicil, 1729, Jan. 9, proved 1729, Feb. 3. He mentions wife Anne, sons Jeremiah, James, Henry and Weston, daughters Anne Greenman, and Sarah Weeden. He mentions also children of deceased daughter Mary Weeden, viz: Jeremiah, William, Caleb and Francis Weeden, Ann Sanford, Mary ——— and Margaret Weeden; children of deceased daughter Frances Sanford, viz: Samuel, William and John Sanford, Frances Gardner and Sarah Paul; four sons of deceased son Samuel Clarke, viz: John, Audley, Samuel and Daniel Clarke. He mentions son-in-law Jeremiah Weeden. In codicil he alludes to death of daughter Sarah Weeden.

V. WESTON, m. (1) 1668, Dec. 25. MARY EASTON, m. (2) 1691, Nov. 21, REBECCA EASTON, (w. of [Peter

b. 1648, Apr. 5. d. 1728 + — Newport, R. I.
b. 1648, Sep. 25. d. 1690, Nov. 16, of Peter and Ann (Coggeshall) Easton.
b. 1662, Apr. d. 1737, Sep. 16. of Edward & Elizabeth (Mott) Thurston.

1. Mary, 1670, Jan. 11.
2. John, 1672, Sep. 15.
3. Weston, 1674, Feb. 18.
4. Weston, 1677, Apr. 15.
5. Walter,
6. Ann,
7. Jeremiah, 1685, Nov. 29.
8. Patience,
(2d wife.)
9. Jeremiah, 1692, Jul. 27.
10. Mary, 1694, Feb. 8.
11. Elizabeth, 1695, Nov. 5.
12. Weston, 1697, Aug. 25.

1670. Freeman.

1672. Deputy.

1675, May 5. He was authorized by Assembly to keep a common standard gallon of brass exactly according to Winchester corn measure, to be procured from Boston, and weights according to standard of England, and a true beam and scales, two half-hundreds, and a quarter, and a half-quarter, and a seven pound. Every town was ordered to have a sealer of weights and measures. All measures and weights to be tried and sealed by Weston Clarke, and he to have six pence for every measure and weight above a quarter of a hundred, marked by him. The mark to be an anchor.

1676, Aug. 24. He was a member of the Court Martial held for trial of certain Indians.

1676–77–80–81–83–84–85–86. Attorney General.

1681–82–83–84–85. General Treasurer.

1690–91–95–96–97–98–99–1700–1–2–3–4–5–6–7–8–9–10–11–12–13–14. General Recorder.

1698, Aug. 2. He was appointed with others, by Assembly to treat with Connecticut about bounds of colony.

1699, Oct. 25. He was appointed on committee to inspect into transcription of all laws of the Colony and make returns the twenty-first of November, in performance of Earl of Bellamont's request. He was chosen as colony's agent to go to England, to maintain liberties granted in our charter, but he refused to serve.

1703, May 12. He was a member of committee who signed agreement with Connecticut Commissioners in settlement of boundaries between two colonies.

1704, Jan. 4. He was on committee to draw out the colony laws and fit them for the press.

1708, Apr. He was appointed on committee to take census list of freemen of towns, servants, black and white, members of military companies, &c. At same date he was chosen on committee to oversee repairing and finishing the Colony House, £100 being appropriated.

VI. JAMES, m. HOPE POWER,

b. 1649. d. 1736, Dec. 1. — Newport, R. I.
b. 1650. d. 1718, Feb. 27, of Nicholas & Jane (   ) Power.

1. Hope, 1673, Dec. 29.
2. Jonathan, 1681.

1698–1704–5–6–7–8–9–10–11–12–13. Sealer of weights and measures, and packer and guager.

1701. Ordained pastor of Second Baptist Church, and held the office till his death. The ordination was performed by elders John Brown and Pardon Tillinghast, of Providence.

1707, Jan. 23. He deeded to the members of his church certain land that he had bought some years before (1697, Oct. 23), from contributions of members. He had taken the deed in his own name, and built the church in 1697, and now deeded both land and building to the society. Previous to 1697, this church had worshipped in private houses.

1712, Feb. 27. He complained to Assembly that weights and measures of this colony do not agree with neighboring governments, and proposed that there should be measures of brass or copper procured, the which will not be so subject to variation as those of wood which we now have for the standard of this government.

He and his wife were buried in Newport Cemetery.

VII. SARAH, m. (1) JOHN PINNER, m. (2) CALEB CARR,

b. 1651. d. 1706 +
b. d. 1674 (—) of Pinner.
b. 1624. d. 1695, Dec. 17. of Carr.

(By 2d husband.)
1. Francis,
2. James,
3. Sarah, 1682.
4. Elizabeth,

CLARKE (JOHN.)

JOHN,[4] (Thos.[3] Jno.[2] Jno.[1]) m. (1) ELIZABETH HARGES, m. (2) 1671, Feb. 1, JANE FLETCHER, (Wid.) [Nich. m. (3) SARAH DAVIS, (w. of

b. 1609, Oct. 8. d. 1676, Apr. 20.
b. d.
b. d. 1672, Apr. 19.
b. d. 1692 ±

Bedfordshire, Eng., Boston, Mass., Newport, R. I.

No issue (that lived long).

He was a physician, as well as minister.

1637, Nov. 20. Boston. He was disarmed with others, the opinions and revelations of Mr. Wheelwright and Mrs. Hutchinson having led them "into dangerous errors."

1638, Mar. 7. Portsmouth. He and eighteen others signed the following compact: "We, whose names are underwritten, do here solemnly, in the presence of Jehovah, incorporate ourselves into a Bodie Politick, and as he shall help, will submit our persons, lives and estates unto our Lord Jesus Christ, the King of Kings and Lord of Lords, and to all those perfect and most absolute laws of his, given us in his holy word of truth, to be guided and judged thereby."

1639, Jan. 2. He and three others were appointed to survey all the lands near abouts, and bring in a map or plot, &c.

1639, Apr. 28. He and eight others signed the following compact, preparatory to the settlement of Newport. "It is agreed by us, whose hands are underwritten, to propagate a plantation in the midst of the island, or elsewhere, and to engage ourselves to bear equal charge, answerable to our strength and estates in common; and that our determination shall be by major voices of Judge and Elders, the Judge to have a double voice." He signed as Elder, the Judge being William Coddington.

1639, Jun. 5. Newport. He was chosen with three others, to proportion land at Newport, the pay of company which shall lay it forth to be 4*d.* an acre.

1640, Mar. 10. He had 148 acres recorded.

1641, Mar. 17. Freeman.

1644. He was pastor of First Baptist Church, organized this year.

1649–50. Assistant.

1649–50–51. Treasurer of the four towns.

See: American Genealogist, v.19, p.131.

1651, Jul. He and Obadiah Holmes and John Crandall, "being the representatives of the church in Newport, upon the request of William Witter, of Lynn, arrived there, he being a brother in the church, who by reason of his advanced age could not undertake so great a journey." The next day being Sunday, they repaired to Mr. Witter's house to hold religious service, he being about two miles out of town. While Mr. Clarke was preaching, two constables came and apprehended him and his companions, and the next morning they were sent to prison at Boston.

1651, Jul. 31. They were sentenced to pay fines (his being £20), or else be whipped, and to remain in prison till paid, for their meeting at William Witter's about Jul. 21st and then and at other times preaching and blaspheming, &c.

1651, Aug. 31. He wrote from prison to the Honored Court, assembled at Boston, accepting the proffer publicly made the day before of a dispute with the ministers, and therefore, "do desire you would appoint the time when, and the person with whom" the points might be disputed publicly. His fine was paid by friends without his consent. He went to England as agent for the colony, soon after his release from prison.

1655. Freeman.

1663, Nov. 24. The Assembly voted to pay his expenses in procuring the King's Letters Patent for colony. It was further voted: "That in consideration of Mr. John Clarke, aforesaid, his great pains, labour and travail with much faithfulness exercised for above twelve years in behalf of this colony, in England; the thanks of the colony be sent unto him by the Governor and Deputy Governor, and for a gratuity unto him, the Assembly engage that the colony shall pay unto the said John Clarke, or unto his order here in Newport, over and beside what is above engaged, the sum and full value of one hundred pounds sterling, in current pay of the country, also to be paid at or before the twenty-fifth day of December, in the year 1664." After his successful efforts in obtaining the charter, he returned home.

1664-65-66-67-68-70-71. Deputy.

1669-70-71-72. Deputy Governor.

1670, Jun. 29. He and John Greene were chosen agents to go to England, for vindication of our charter before his Majesty, &c., provided Governor Benedict Arnold could not go.

1672, Mar. 5. He was chosen agent to go to England, and manage our appeal to His Majesty, against the violent and illegal intrusions of Connecticut.

1676, Apr. 4. Voted: "That in these troublesome times and straits in this colony, the Assembly desiring to have the advice and concurrence of the most judicious inhabitants, if it may be had for the good of the whole, do desire at their sitting the company and counsel of" (sixteen persons, among whom was John Clarke).

1676, Apr. 20. Will—proved 1676, May 17. Exs. friends William Weeden, Phillip Smith and Richard Bailey. He desired to be buried by his wives Elizabeth and Jane, already deceased. To brother Joseph Clarke, and the children of Joseph by his first wife (except John), to cousin (*i. e.* niece), Fish, wife of Samuel Fish, and her children, and to cousin Mary Saunders, wife of Tobias Saunders, and her children, the produce of sale of lands on Conanicut Island, and in said division brother Joseph and cousins Fish and Mary Saunders to have double share. To each of brother Joseph Clarke's children by his second wife, 1*s*. To cousin John Clarke, son of brother Joseph, by first wife, 6 acres adjoining land of Benedict Arnold. To executors, in trust, 30 acres and dwelling house and a farm of 150 acres, for maintenance of wife Sarah, for life, and she to dwell in house and have improvement of stock. To her, also, two beds and biggest trunk. To daughter-in-law (*i. e.* step-daughter) Sarah Davis, £40 at age. To son-in-law Simon Davis, land. To son-in-law Thomas Davis, £20 at age. To daughter-in-law Mercy Davis, £20 at age. To daughter in-law Hannah Davis, £10. To brother Carew Clarke, his maintenance for life, and he to live in house while my wife keeps house in it, and they can remain in comfort together, and if he move, to have £16 per year. To Katharine Salmon, wife of John, an ewe sheep. To Richard Bailey, a concordance, and lexicon to it, written by myself, being the fruit of several years study, and to him a Hebrew bible and rest of books. To friend Mark Lucar, 50*s*. a year in provisions, for life. At decease of wife, the trustees to distribute and dispose of profits of the farm and marsh for relief of the poor and bringing up of children unto learning (to be a perpetual trust.) The dwelling house and 30 acres to go to cousin John Clarke, at death of testator's wife. If a trustee should die, the others were to choose a third—an understanding person fearing the Lord. To each executor, or trustee, 30*s*. annually forever.

While in England (1652), Mr. Clarke published a book entitled, "Ill news from New England," giving therein an account of the persecutions of his friends in America.

JOSEPH,[4] (Th.[3] Jno.[2] Jno.[1]) b. 1618, Dec. 9. d. 1694, Jun. 1.
m. (1) 1642 ±
——— b. d.
m. (2)
MARGARET, b. d. 1694.

Bedfordshire, Eng., Newport, Westerly, R. I.

1638. Newport. Admitted inhabitant of the island of Aquidneck.

1640. He was present at General Court of elections.

1641, Mar. 17. Freeman.

1644. He was one of the original members of First Baptist Church.

1648. Member of General Court of Trials.

1655. Freeman.

1655–57–58–59. Commissioner.

1658–63–64–65–78–79. Assistant.

1663, Jul. 8. His name appears in charter granted Rhode Island by Charles II.

1668. Westerly. Freeman.

1668–69–70–71–72–90. Deputy.

1669, May 18. His name was in a list of inhabitants.

1677. He was a member of Court of Justices of the Peace, to attend to the matter of injurious and illegal acting of some of Connecticut Colony.

1679. He and thirty-two others, of Westerly, gave oath of allegiance.

1680. Newport. Taxed £1. 13*s*. 3*d*.

1685, Sep. 25. He and wife Margaret, sold Francis Brinley, of Newport, 1–154 part of Conanicut Island (89 acres) and 1–154 part of Dutch Island. (He gave his residence as of Newport, at this time.)

1690. He, with others, was empowered to proportion taxes to respective towns.

He is said to have died at Westerly, though many of his later years appear to have been spent at Newport.

Morgan Edwards states in his History of the Baptists, that Rev. William Peckham married ——— Clarke, niece of Rev. John Clarke. She must have been a daughter of Joseph, as John Clarke's other brothers had no children.

The names of Joseph Clarke's children are learned by the following memorandum, which is appended to the record of will of his brother, Thomas Clarke. "The names of the children of Joseph Clarke, of the town of Newport, that are living this 19th day of December, 1674. Joseph Clarke, William Clarke, Mary Clarke, Sarah Clarke, John Clarke, Susanna Clarke, Joshua Clarke, Thomas Clarke, Cary Clarke, Elizabeth Clarke." The surnames of Mary and Susanna are crossed out, as if they had already married at date of the entry.

See: American Genealogist, v. 19, p. 131. v. 24, p. 69. v. 26, p. 54.

I. JOSEPH, b. 1643, Apr. 2. d. 1727, Jan. 11. Westerly, R. I.
m. (1) 1664, Nov. 16,
BETHIAH HUBBARD, b. 1646, Dec. 19. d. 1707, Apr. 17. of Samuel & Tacy (Cooper) Hubbard.
m. (2) [Thos.
HANNAH PECKHAM, (w. of b. d. 1722 + of William Weeden.

1669–70–71–72–73–74–75–76–77–78–79–80–81–82–83–84–85–86–87–88–89–90–91–92–93–94–95–96–97–98–99–1700. Town Clerk.

1675, Jul. He and his family went to Newport, for fear of the Indian war.

1680. He, having been taken from his house in Westerly, situated two miles east of Pawcatuck River, and thence forced and carried to Hartford, Conn., and fined £10, &c. by authorities of that colony, was therefore reimbursed by Rhode Island Assembly, in sum of £13, 10*s*.

1698–1700–2–4–6–8. Deputy.

1722, Mar. He and wife Hannah, late wife of Thomas Peckham, brought suit against Philip Peckham, for £3 annuity.

1725, Oct 5. Will—proved 1727, Feb. 27. Ex. son Samuel. To daughter Mary Champlin, bed, &c., £5. To daughter Judith Maxson, £5. To daughter Susanna Babcock, £5. To daughter Bethiah Hiscox, 1*s*. His sons, Joseph and John, deceased, already had received their part. To two grandsons, viz: Joseph Clarke's eldest son and John Clarke's eldest son, 12*d*. apiece. To son Thomas Clarke, 1*s*., he having had, and like amounts to sons William and Samuel.

Inventory, £231, 18*s*. 8*d*., viz: bond £69, book accounts, table, yearling horse, 3 working steers, 17¼ acres meadow, other land, &c.

1. Judith, 1667, Oct. 12.
2. Joseph, 1670, Apr. 4.
3. Samuel, 1672, Sep. 29.
4. John, 1675, Aug. 25.
5. Bethiah, 1678, Apr. 11.
6. Mary, 1680, Dec. 27.
7. Susanna, 1683, Aug. 31.
8. Thomas, 1686, Mar. 17.
9. William, 1688, Apr. 21.

II. JOHN, b. d. 1704, Apr. 11. Newport, R. I.

1681, Jul. 23. He, of Newport, was granted 35*s*., by Assembly, for moneys due for service done at Westerly, in the time of his brother Joseph Clarke's imprisonment at Connecticut.

1688. Grand Jury.

III. WILLIAM, b. d. 1683, Sep. 30. Jamestown, R. I.
m.
HANNAH WEEDEN, b. d. 1722 + of William Weeden.

(She m. (2) Thomas Peckham and (3) Joseph Clarke.)

1679, Aug. 1. He petitioned Assembly concerning several Indians, by him and his company taken in time of the war, he then being commander of one of the sloops, in the year 1676. The case was referred to Town Councils of Newport and Portsmouth.

1683, Oct. 19. Administration to widow Hannah. Inventory, 15 head of neat cattle, 60 sheep, 3 horsekind, 10 swine, feather bed, silk grass bed, flock bed, iron, pewter, musket, &c.

1701, Nov. 18. William Clarke, of Jamestown, sold for £140, to uncle John Weeden, certain land in Jamestown and Dutch Island. The deed was signed by William Clarke, Hannah Clarke and Hannah Peckham, and was witnessed by Thomas Peckham, Philip Peckham and William Weeden.

1. William,
2. Thomas, 1682, Feb. 15.
3. Hannah, 1683, Mar. 25.

IV. JOSHUA, b. d. 1702 + Providence, R. I.
m.
ALICE PHILLIPS, b. d. 1702 + of Michael & Barbara ( ) Phillips.

1686, Aug. 17. He had a deed from Edward Inman (for that said Clarke married with the daughter of my now wife, and for the propagation of a neighborhood, &c)., of 66 acres, ten miles north of Providence, near Westquademset.

V. THOMAS, b. d. 1705 +
m.
ELIZABETH, b. d. 1705 +

VI. SUSANNAH, b. d.

VII. MARY, b. d. 1695 +
m.
TOBIAS SAUNDERS, b. d. 1695. of Saunders.

1. John,
2. Edward,
3. Stephen,
4. Benjamin,
5. Susanna,

VIII. SARAH, b. 1663, Jan. 29. d.
m. 1683, Oct. 11,
THOMAS REYNOLDS, b. d. of John Reynolds.

1. Joseph, 1684, Jun. 21.

IX. CAREW, b. d.
m. 1693, Feb. 4,
ANN DYER, b. d. of Samuel & Ann (Hutchinson) Dyer.

CLARKE (JOSEPH.) 2d column. IX. Carew, d. 1760, N. Kingstown. 1755, Apr. 14. Will-proved 1760, July. Exr. grandson Joseph Clarke, (later called Joseph "Jr."). He mentions sons Jonathan, Hutchinson, James, daughters Mary Whitman and Margaret Spencer, grandson William, (son of William, deceased), grandson Cary Dunn, grandsons Cary Spencer and Clark ———, granddaughters Barsheba and Hannah Dunn, grandson Joseph, son of son Elisha, deceased.

1. Carew, 1696, Sep. 20.
2. Ann, 1698, Sep. 8.
3. Joseph, 1699, Oct. 20.
4. Mary, 1700, Aug. 8.
5. Caleb, 1703, May 22.
6. Jonathan, 1705, Aug. 12.
7. William, 1707, Jan. 15.
8. Elisha, 1709, May 6.
9. Samuel, 1711, Oct. 1.
10. Margaret, 1713, Oct. 24.
11. Hutchinson,
12. James,

X. ELIZABETH, b. d.

CLARKE (THOMAS).

THOMAS,[4] (Th.[3] Jno.[2] Jno.[1]) b. 1605. d. 1674, Dec. 2.
m.
JANE, b. d.

Bedfordshire, Eng., Newport, R. I.

1638. He was admitted an inhabitant of the island of Aquidneck.

1641, Mar. 17. Freeman.

1644. He was one of the original members of First Baptist Church.

1655. Freeman.

1663, Dec. 3. He and wife Jane, sold to John Anthony, of Portsmouth, 3 acres and house there.

1674, Jul. 28. Will—proved 1674, Dec. 18. Exs. Obadiah Holmes and John Salmon. To brother Joseph, all lands on this island, housing, &c. To cousin William Clarke, son of brother Joseph, all land at Conanicut Island. To brother Joseph's wife, Margaret, all household stuff. To brother Joseph Clarke's children, except William, the stock on farm which William Clarke enjoys, when his time is out. To brother Joseph Clarke's children, equally, all that is due

See: American Genealogist, v. 19, p. 131

No issue.

from brother John Clarke, for services and tendance when he was gone to England twelve years—looking to and providing for his stock and wintering of them upon my own land; in which time was reared twenty horsekind and about nine score sheep, and 100 acres of land I purchased at Conanicut and a quarter share at Misquamicut and 10 acres at Applegate's Neck upon this island—for which I deserve £20 a year.

CLEMENCE. 1st column. 1670, Oct. 16. He is alluded to in a letter of Roger Williams. "Two Indian children were brought to me by one Thomas Clements, who had his house burnt on the other side of the river. He was in his orchard, and two Indian children came boldly to him the boy being about seven or eight, and the girl (his sister) three or four years old. The boy tells me that a youth, one Mittonan, brought them to the sight of Thomas Clements, and bid them go to that man, and he would give them bread," &c.

CLEMENCE.

THOMAS, b. ; d. 1688.
m.
ELIZABETH, b. ; d. 1721 +

Providence, R. I.

1649, Nov 3. He was granted 25 acres, and all former grants disannulled.

1653, Apr. 20. He endorsed the following document: "*Salus Populi.* The health of the people. An instrument or sovereign Plaister to heal the many fold, present sores in this town or plantation of Providence which do arise about lands, and to prevent the further spreading of them both amongst ourselves and the whole colony: Necessary forthwith to be imposed and applied lest this town should fall into grievous sores, or gangrenes, to the hurt of the whole colony, and thereby this town which was the first in this Bay become the worst." Then follow provisions for several changes in distribution of lands, etc.

1654, Jan. 9. He bought of Wissawyamake, an Indian twenty-three years of age, living at Sekescute near Providence, 8 acres of meadow.

1655. Freeman.

1665. Feb. 19. In a division of lands he drew lot 90.

1665, Jun. 12. He and wife Elizabeth sold John Scott 20 acres.

1666–72. Deputy.

1667. Town Treasurer.

1669, Dec. 15. The Assembly having received information that there is a record in our Town Book entitled "An Instrument or sovereign Plaister," and was endorsed Thomas Clemence, the town having received a copy of the said record and considering the same, the matter therein, do find it to be most destructive to the peace of our plantation and the joint agreements of our town, etc. They therein "do find the said matter to be utterly unwholesome and illegal and do hereby declare the said record to be wholly void," etc.

1676, Aug. 14. He was one of those "who staid and went not away," in King Phillip's War, and so had a share in the disposition of the Indian captives whose services were sold for a term of years.

1679, Jul. 1. Taxed 6*s.* 3*d.*

1681, Feb. 13. He deeded son Richard 60 acres of upland, and meadow, &c., not upon sudden motion but upon deliberate consideration.

1682, Dec. 2. He sold Stephen Arnold for £6, rights in land.

1686, Mar. 29. He had 25½ acres laid out.

1687, Sep. 1. Taxed 5*s.*

1688, May 16. Administration to son Richard by desire of widow Elizabeth.

Inventory, £38, 4*s.*

I. RICHARD, b. ; d. 1723, Oct. 11.
m.
SARAH SMITH, b. ; d. 1725, Oct. 14. of John & Sarah (Whipple) Smith.

The records are apparently in error in giving the birth of either his daughter Sarah or Mary.

1687, Sep. 1. Taxed 5*s.*

1687 Ratable estate: 1 share of meadow, 3 acres tillage, 5 acres pasture, 5 cows, 2 steers, 1 heifer, 2 swine, 2 horses, 1 mare, 1 two year old horse.

1693, Dec. 9. He and wife Sarah had 40 acres laid out in the right of John Smith (miller, deceased), which said 40 acres the said John Smith by will gave to his daughter Sarah. It was situated two miles west of dwelling house of Richard Clemence and a mile north of Neutoconconett Hill.

1716, Feb. 24. He received a deed from John and Josiah Thornton (exrs. to will of John Thornton) of 85 acres which had been their father's, the consideration being £200. This deed was assigned by Richard Clemence (with consent of wife Sarah) for £210, to John and Josiah Thornton again on the 2d of March, following.

1719, May 27. An acknowledgment was taken of his obligation on a bond of £500, given Thomas Olney, the condition being that, whereas Ann Appleby, daughter of Richard, had sold Thomas Olney a 40 foot lot on east side of Town street, as per deed, &c., it was therefore agreed by her father to warrant and defend same, &c., and in default thereof the bond should be paid but otherwise void.

1719, Dec. 19. He sold Captain Richard Waterman, Jr., 30 acres for £80.

1721, Jan. 2. Will—proved 1723, Dec. 9. Ex. son Thomas. To son Thomas all lands, tenements and meadows in Providence both sides of Woonasquatucket river, being all my homestead, also 40 acres on both sides of Hawkins Path at Long Swamp; with exception of privilege allowed to testator's wife. To wife Sarah, two cows, a feather bed, £20, and privilege of dwelling house for life while a widow, and she to have the keep of her cows from her son Thomas, who was further to provide her with bread, corn and firewood, fruit from orchard, &c. To daughter Ann Appleby, two cows. To daughter Sarah Angell and Abigail Thornton, 20*s.*, each. To son Richard, 1*s.* To grandchildren James and Ann Appleby, £10, each when they come of age. To son Thomas all rest of movable estate, he to take care of and provide all things necessary for my ancient mother during the whole term of her natural life.

Inventory £340, 13*s.* 10*d.*, viz: silver money £10, 14*s.* 8*d.*, money scales, 2 warming pans, feather bed, pewter, brass and ironware, corn, oats, wheat, rye, flax, hemp, hay, tobacco, apples, &c., 2 oxen, 13 cows, 1 bull, 3 two year, 4 yearlings, 2 horses, 13 swine, 11 sheep, &c.

1725, Oct. 11. Will—proved 1725, Dec. 6. Widow Sarah Clemence. Ex. brother Wm. Smith. To daughters Sarah Angell and Abigail Thornton, £15 each. To daughter Ann Brown, £10, which sum to be left in executor's hands, the interest on same to be paid Ann until her son James Appleby was of age, and then he to have the £10, or if he died then his sister Ann to have. To son Richard Clemence, £10, and two cows. To three daughters, £20, to be equally divided, only daughter Ann's part to be paid her as her necessity required; and if she died before it was all paid it was to go to her children James and Ann Appleby. The three daughters to have wearing apparel; Sarah Angell having also a feather bed, and apron. To son Thomas rest of estate.

Inventory £161, 4*s.* 4*d.*

1. Sarah, 1688, Nov. 11.
2. Mary, 1689, May 24.
3. Ann, 1690, Dec. 11.
4. Thomas, 1693, Aug. 6.
5. Abigail, 1695, Dec. 4.
6. Richard, 1698, Jul. 19.

II. THOMAS, b. ; d. 1676, Aug. Providence, R. I.
unmarried.

1676, Aug. He was buried this month as town records declare, he and another (buried at about the same time) being called "in the flower of their youth."

III. ELIZABETH, b. 1673, Feb. ; d. 1736 +
m. 1696, Apr. 5.
JAMES MATHEWSON, b. 1666, Aug. 11. ; d. 1737, Jan 7. of James & Hannah (Field) Mathewson.

1. Anne, 1697, Jan. 7.
2. Elizabeth, 1699, Jan. 31.
3. Daniel, 1700, Oct. 6.
4. James, 1702, May 10.
5. Mary,
6. Phillip,
7. Richard,
8. Jeremiah,

IV. CONTENT, b. ; d. 1696, Jun. 30. Providence, R. I.

1696, Oct. 27. Administration to his brother Richard Clemence.

Inventory £50, 15*s.*, viz: 2 oxen, 7 cows, 22 sheep and lambs, horse, 3 calves, 6 swine, cart and wheels, working tools, wearing apparel, fowling piece, &c.

CLIFTON.

THOMAS, b. 1606, ; d. 1681, Jul. 9,
m. 1641,
MARY BUTTERWORTH, b. 1600, ; d. 1687, Jan. 26.
of Butterworth.

Rehoboth, Mass., Newport, R. I.

1641, Jan. 28. Permission was given to James Parker to marry Thomas Clifton and Mary Butterworth.

1641, Jun. 2. Freeman of Massachusetts.

1643. He was at Rehoboth thus early.

1645, Jun. 9. He had a lot in the great plain, in a division of lands to Rehoboth settlers.

1647. Grand Jury.

1753, May 17. Newport. Freeman.

1673–74–75. Deputy.

1678, Jun. 12. A very great hurt having been done to a small child by fast riding; it was enacted by the Assembly that any person presuming to ride a horse at a gallop, &c., in any street between the house that lately John Harndel lived in, and the house where Thomas Clifton lives, shall for the offence pay 5*s.*, fine.

He went to wash himself and was drowned as the Quaker records relate.

He was buried in the Clifton Burial Ground.

I. HOPE, b. ; d. 1681, Jan. 16.
m. 1665, Dec. 30.
CHRISTOPHER HOLDER, b. 1631. ; d. 1688, Jun. 13. of Holder.

1. Christopher 1666, Dec. 23.
2. Hope, 1668, Mar. 25.
3. Patience, 1669, Feb. 12.
4. Patience, 1671, Aug. 16.
5. John, 1672, Aug. 20.
6. Content, 1674, May 22.
7. Ann, 1676, Feb. 29.

II. PATIENCE, b. 1646, Jul. 2. ; d. 1692, Oct. 16.
m. (1) 1664, Sep. 4.
JOHN BEERE, b. 1630. ; d. 1671, Jul. 29. of Edward Beere.
m. (2) 1677, May 16.
WILLIAM ALLEN. b. 1629. ; d. 1718, Mar. 18. of Allen.

1. Mary, 1666, Aug. 6.
2. Edward, 1669, Aug. 1.
3. Patience, 1671, Sep. 6.

See: American Genealogist v.34, p.169

JOHN, b. 1591, d. 1647, Nov. 27.
m.
MARY. b. 1604, d. 1684, Nov. 8.

Essex Co., Eng., Boston, Mass., Newport, R. I.

He was a silk merchant.

1632, Jun. 22. He, with thirty-two others, signed the oath of allegiance, "being about to depart for New England," and sailed within a day or two. He brought with him his wife Mary and children John, Joshua and Ann.

1632, Sep. 16. Boston. He arrived in ship Lyon, Captain Pierce.

1632, Nov. 6. Freeman.

1634, Mar. 4. He gave £5 toward the sea fort.

1634, Apr. 20. He was a member of the First Church, and soon after a deacon.

1634, Sep. 3. He was chosen one of the overseers of powder, shot, &c.

1634. Selectman.

1634–35–36–37. Deputy.

1635, Mar. 4. He and others were authorized to board vessels after twenty-four hours at anchor, take notice of what commodities she has to sell, confer about price, &c.

1635, May 3. He had his daughter Hananiel baptized (and his daughter Bedaiah, 1637, July 30.)

1636, May 25. He was appointed on a committee to make a rate for tax levied upon towns.

1637, Nov. 2. He was deprived of his seat as Deputy for affirming that Mr. Wheelwright is innocent, and that he was persecuted for the truth. At the same date being convicted of disturbing the public peace, he was disfranchised and enjoined not to speak anything to disturb the public peace upon pain of banishment.

1638, Mar. 7. Portsmouth. He and eighteen others signed the following compact. "We whose names are underwritten do here solemnly in the presence of Jehovah, incorporate ourselves into a Bodie Politick, and as he shall help, will submit our persons, lives, and estates unto our Lord Jesus Christ, the King of Kings and Lord of Lords, and to all those perfect and most absolute laws of his given us in his holy word of Truth, to be guided and judged thereby."

1638, May 13. It was ordered that "the meeting house shall be set on the neck of land that goes over to the Maine of the island, where Mr. John Coggeshall and Mr. Sanford shall lay it out."

1638, May 20. He was allotted 6 acres—twenty poles in breadth on the east and ninety-six feet long.

1639, Apr. 28. He and eight others signed the following compact, preparatory to settling at Newport. "It is agreed by us, whose hands are underwritten, to propagate a plantation in the midst of the island, or elsewheres, and to engage ourselves to bear equal charge, answerable to our strength and estates in common; and that our determination shall be by major voices of Judge and Elders, the Judge to have a double voice." He signed as Elder, the Judge being William Coddington.

1640, Mar. 10. Newport. He had 389 acres of land recorded. This year he and two others were appointed to lay out lands in Newport.

1640–41–42–43–44. Assistant.

1644. Corporal.

1647. Moderator.

1647. President of the Colony.

He was buried on his own land.

See: American Genealogist v.19, p.131.

I. JOHN, b. 1618, d. 1708, Oct. 1. Newport, R. I. See: American Genealogist, v.19, p.132.
m. (1) 1647, Jun. 17.
ELIZABETH BAULSTONE, b. ——, d. 1696 + of William & Elizabeth ( ) Baulstone.
m. (2) 1655, Dec. [TON.
PATIENCE THROCKMORTON, b. 1640, d. 1676, Sep. 7. of John Throckmorton.
m. (3).
MARY. b. ——, d. —— of

1. John, 1650, Feb. 12.
2. Elizabeth, 1650, Feb. 12.
3. William, 1654 ±
(2d wife)
4. Freegift, 1657, Mar. 1.
5. James, 1660, Feb. 18.
6. Mary, 1662, Mar. 10.
7. Joseph, 1665, May 31.
8. Rebecca, 1667, Jun. 20.
9. Patience, 1669, Aug. 13.
10. Benjamin, 1672, Jul. 27.
11. Content, 1674, Mar. 28.
12. Content, 1676, May 10.
(3d) wife)
13. Joseph, 1679.
14. Abraham, 1682.
15. Samuel,
16. Elisha,

1651, May 30. He sold Walter Cunigrave a parcel of land "on the east side of the river on which Newport Mill now standeth," &c., containing 160 acres. His mother confirmed the deed.

1653–54. General Treasurer for Portsmouth and Newport.

1654. General Treasurer for Providence and Warwick.

1654, Oct. 3. He and wife Elizabeth signed agreement for divorce.

1654–63. Commissioner.

1655, May 25. Divorce granted by Assembly. (Elizabeth m. (2) Thomas Gould).

1655. Freeman.

1663–64–65–72–74–76–83–84–85–86. Assistant.

1664–65–66–67–68–69–70–71–72. General Treasurer.

1665, Feb. 23. He was empowered to press boats or other things necessary for them appointed to go to Seekonk, as respecting provisions, attendants, &c., out and home for reception and entertainment of the honorable commissioners (in matter of bounds of colony.)

1665–67–68–69–70–71–75–83. Deputy.

1676, Apr. 4. He was on a committee to procure boats for colony's defence for the present. There were to be five boats with five or six men in each. He was also on another committee to take exact account of all inhabitants on the island, English, negroes, and Indians, and make a list thereof, and also to take account of how all persons are provided with corn, guns, powder, shot and lead.

1676, Aug. 24. He was a member of Court Martial held for the trial of Indians.

1676–77–91–92. General Recorder.

1683–84. Major for the Island.

1686–89–90. Deputy Governor.

1708, Jun. 22. Will—proved 1708, Nov. 8. Exs. wife Mary and son Abraham. Overseers, friends Samuel Cranston and Benjamin Newbury. He directs that he be buried without soldiery in arms. To son Freegift, part of farm I now dwell in with buildings, &c., to him and heirs male, he paying certain legacies. To son James, £2. To son Benjamin, another part of farm I dwell in, with buildings, &c., to him and heirs male. To son Joseph, eldest son of my wife Mary, a half of a lot in Newport, with buildings, &c., and £30. To son Abraham, second son of wife Mary, rest of farm I now dwell in, to him and heirs male provided that his mother Mary shall have use of the new dwelling house I built last until her decease, and use of places to keep her horse, cow and poultry, and to lay her wood. To son Samuel, the other half of lot in Newport, abutting the half given Joseph, and £40, but if Samuel should be deceased (being abroad and not knowing where he is), said £40 to go to Joseph and Elisha. To son Elisha, fourth son of wife Mary, a piece of land with buildings, &c., and £40. To Rebecca, wife to John Reynolds, Patience, wife to Samuel Rathbone, and Content, wife to Samuel Norton, each £20, in addition to what I have given them before. To three daughters of Mary Bull, deceased, wife of Ephraim Bull, £5 apiece at age of twenty-one or marriage. To son Benjamin, my seal gold ring. To son Joseph, my buff belt. To son Abraham, my plate buttons and little dram cup. To son Elisha, my silver shoe buckles and shirt buttons. To sons Joseph, Abraham, Samuel and Elisha, all my wearing apparel equally. To son Abraham, all tackling belonging to husbandry, &c., four oxen, four cows, fifty sheep. To son Benjamin, use of cart and oxen to cart firewood, &c. To wife Mary, rest of sheep, neat cattle, horsekind, swine, &c., silver money, plate and household utensils, and what is left at her decease to go to son Benjamin (if he be married and hath a child), and her four sons, viz: Joseph, Abraham, Samuel and Elisha, with four daughters, to say, Mary, wife to Josias Coggeshall, Rebecca, wife to John Reynolds, Patience, wife to Samuel Rathbone, and Content, wife to Samuel Norton. He makes provision that if sons die without issue, certain other sons have, &c. As to certain stock delivered son Freegift, when part of farm was leased him, viz: two hundred sheep, six cows, five calves, and four oxen, all prized at £113, at decease said stock to be divided equally to sons Freegift, Benjamin and Abraham. The burying ground where my mother and father are laid to be fenced, &c. To wife, Indian woman, Jane. To son Abraham, an apprentice. To each overseer a gold ring.

II. JOSHUA, b. 1623, d. 1688, May 1. Newport, Portsmouth, R. I.
m. (1) 1652, Dec. 22.
JOAN WEST, b. 1631, d. 1676, Apr. 24. of —— West.
m. (2) 1677, June 21,
REBECCA RUSSELL. b. ——, d. —— of —— Russell.

1. Mary, 1655, Feb.
2. Joshua, 1656, May.
3. John, 1659, Dec.
4. Josiah, 1662, Nov.
5. Daniel, 1665, Apr.
6. Humility, 1671, Jan.
7. Caleb, 1672, Dec. 17.
8. Isaac,
(2d wife no issue)

1654, Oct. 23. He bought of Edward Andrews and wife Bridget, of Portsmouth, 100 acres there with house, &c. He probably moved to Portsmouth this same year.

1660, Feb. He having embraced Quakerism and being in Plymouth Colony on a visit, he was seized as a Quaker, had his horse taken from him (and sold for £12), and he was put in jail.

1664–66–67–68–70–71–72. Deputy.

1669–70–72–73–74–75–76. Assistant.

1673, May 7. He was appointed on a committee to treat with the Indian Sachems, "and with them seriously to consult and agree of some way to prevent the extreme excess of the Indians' drunkenness." The Sachems to be consulted were Mawsup and Ninecraft of Narragansett, Philip of Mount Hope, Weetamo of Pocasset, and Awashunks of Seaconnet.

1676, Aug. 24. He was a member of the Court Martial held at Newport for the trial of certain Indians charged with being engaged with King Phillip's designs.

His second wife was a Quakeress from London.

1687, Jul. 13. Will—proved 1688, Jul. 5. Ex. son Daniel. Overseers, friends Thomas Townsend and John Coggeshall of Portsmouth. To eldest son Joshua, 120 acres of farm in Newport at southermost end of my farm, with buildings, &c. To second son John, 120 acres of my farm land, with all buildings, part in Portsmouth and part in Newport, adjoining land before given to Joshua, he paying his brother Josias £30, and maintaining half the fence between his land and Joshua's. If John die without issue male, the land to go to my son Josias, he paying to female issue of John, £30. To fourth son Daniel, all the rest of my farm lands with all buildings, orchards, &c., in Portsmouth, adjoining southerly upon land of his brother John, he maintaining half the fence. If Daniel die without issue male, land to go to son Caleb, he paying female issue of Daniel, £20. To fifth son Caleb, at twenty one years of age, £20. To son Isaac, £5, at age. If wife Rebecca, prove with child, 5s. to same at age. To wife, a feather bed, riding mare, cow, twenty ewe sheep, half of pewter, great chest, wearing clothes both woolen and linen, and the still she brought, &c., and £20, and she to have chamber where she lodges, and diet and firewood provided for half a year after testator's decease. To son Daniel, negro man Derrick, and Joseph Johnson, and rest of movable estate, except silver beaker which son Joshua is to have.

Inventory £185, 13s., viz: wearing clothes £10, plate £2, 10s., brass ware, pewter, warming pan, Dutch wheel, negro man, £20, 129 sheep, 21 head neat cattle, 4 horsekind, 15 swine, &c.

III. ANN, b. 1626, d. 1689, Mar. 6. See: American Genealogist, v.19, p.132.
m. 1643, Nov. 15.
PETER EASTON, b. 1622, d. 1694, Feb. 12. of Nicholas Easton.

1. Nicholas, 1644, Nov. 12.
2. John, 1647, Feb. 6.
3. Mary, 1648, Sep. 25.
4. Peter, 1651, Feb. 1.
5. Ann, 1653, Feb. 9.
6. Patience, 1655, Nov. 20.
7. Waite, 1657, Jul. 25.
8. Peter, 1659, Jan. 11.
9. Joshua, 1662, Jul. 30.
10. James, 1664, Jan. 29.
11. Elizabeth, 1666, Feb. 18.
12. Waite. 1668, Nov. 5.
13. James. 1671, Oct. 7.

IV. HANANIEL. b. 1635, d. young.

V. WAIT, b. 1636, Sep. 11, d. 1718, May 9.
m. 1651, Dec. 18.
DANIEL GOULD, b. 1625, d. 1716, Mar. 26. of Jeremiah & Priscilla (Grover) Gould.

1. Mary, 1653, Mar. 2.
2. Thomas, 1655, Feb. 20.
3. Daniel, 1656, Oct. 24.
4. John, 1659, May 4.
5. Priscilla, 1661, Jun. 20.
6. Jeremiah, 1664, May 5.
7. James, 1666, Oct. 13.
8. Jeremiah, 1669, Feb. 2.
9. Content, 1671, Apr. 28.
10. Waite, 1676, May 8.

VI. BEDAIAH. b. 1637, d. young.

JOHN,[2] (Isaac.[1]) — b. — d. 1707.
m. 1651, Dec. 30,
SUSANNA HUTCHINSON, — b. — d. 1713 (—).

of William & Ann (Marbury) Hutchinson.

Sandwich, Kent Co., Eng., Kings Town, R. I.

1634. He came to America with his father and mother (Joan), in the ship Hercules. His father settled at Charlestown, Mass., and from thence the son went later to Boston.

1663. Kings Town. He came to this place earlier than this year, to look after the lands of Edward Hutchinson, his wife's brother.

1667, Apr. 9. He deeded Samuel and Edward Hutchinson, a house in Boston.

1668, May 4. He and other inhabitants of Wickford, petitioned the Connecticut authorities to re-assume their government, or if not, that the petitioners might look for government and protection elsewhere.

1668. Magistrate (under the government of Connecticut).

1670. He was on the jury in case of the murder of Walter House by Thomas Flounders, the jury being called by Connecticut authorities.

1670, Jun. 22. Commissioner. He and three others were appointed to this office by Connecticut, and the inhabitants of Wickford were called upon to yield obedience to them, and not to the Rhode Island officers.

1670, Jul. 15. He, having said before the Rhode Island Governor and Council, that he had not as yet taken an engagement to any office under Connecticut, but did not know how soon he might, and also did own that he did forewarn the Rhode Island Conservators of the Peace from acting in his Majesty's name, &c.; he was committed to the Sergeant, till the next court meeting, and was to find bail for £20, to answer for said contempt. The warning which he gave to the Conservators of the Peace, related to a matter of disputed jurisdiction between the two colonies, in the calling of a jury of inquest in the case of murder of Walter House, of Wickford.

1679, Jul. 29. He and forty-one other inhabitants of Narragansett, petitioned the King, praying that he "would put an end to these differences about the government thereof, which hath been so fatal to the prosperity of the place; animosities still arising in people's minds as they stand affected to this or that government."

1682, Jun. 28. Conservator of the Peace.

He now acted on behalf of the Rhode Island authorities.

1687, Sep. 6. Taxed 11*s*. 9*d*.

1707. Administration to widow Susanna and son William.

1713, Dec. 14. His son William, took receipts from heirs for their full proportion of estate of deceased father and mother, John and Susanna Cole. The receipts were signed by Elisha Cole, Thomas and Susanna Eldred, Thomas and Hannah Place and Elizabeth P——.

COLE (John). 1st column. Change to John[2] (Samuel[1]). Change Sandwich, Kent Co., Eng., to Boston, Mass. Erase sentence 1634, &c.

1666, Dec. 21. He and his eldest son Samuel were mentioned in the will of his father Samuel Cole of Boston.

I. SUSANNA, — b. — d. 1726 (—)
m.
THOMAS ELDRED, — b. 1648, Sep. 8. — d. 1726. — of Samuel & Elizabeth ( ) Eldred.

1. John, 2. Elisha, 3. Susanna, 4. Mary, 5. Bridget, 6. Sarah, 7. Grace, 8. Elizabeth, 9. William, 10. Thomas,

II. SAMUEL, — b. 1656, Mar. 24. — d.

III. MARY, — b. 1658, Oct. 6. — d.

COLE (John). III. Mary, d. 1720±. Unmarried. X. Elizabeth, d. 1744, (—). m. Robert Potter, of Ichabod and Martha (Hazard) Potter. He d. 1745. Children, 1. Barbara, 1688, Feb. 2. 2. Martha, 1699, Aug. 10. 3. Robert, 1702, Jul. 26. 4. Ichabod, 1703, Nov. 30. 5. Susanna, 1705, Feb. 14.

IV. JOHN, — b. 1660, Jan. 23. — d. young.

V. ANN, — b. 1661, Mar. 7. — d. 1704, May 31.
m.
HENRY BULL, — b. — d. 1691 ± — of Jireh Bull.

1. Henry, 1687, Nov. 23.
2. Ephraim, 1690, Jan. 23.
3. Ann, 1690, Jan. 23.

VI. JOHN, — b. 1666, Jan. 17. — d. — Kings Town, R. I.

1687, Sep. 6. Taxed 1*s*. 8½*d*.

VII. HANNAH, — b. 1668, Dec. 17. — d.
m.
THOMAS PLACE, — b. 1663. — d. 1727 — of Enoch & Sarah ( ) Place.

1. Mary, 169–, Jan. 5.
2. Marbury, 169–, May 5.
3. Thomas, 169–, Nov. 2.
4. John, 170–, Apr. 24.
5. Sarah, 170–, May 10.
6. Joseph, 170–, Dec. 22.
7. Samuel, 170–, Sep.
8. Enoch,
9. Ann,

VIII. WILLIAM, — b. 1671, Jul. 13. — d. 1734. — North Kingstown, R. I.
m.
ANN PINDER, — b. — d. — of Jacob Pinder.

1734, Sep. 17. Will—proved. Exs. wife Ann and son John. To wife, half of dwelling house and farm for life, while widow, or £20 a year if she marry again. To son John and his male heirs, house and land. To other four sons, Samuel, Joseph, Benjamin and Wignall, certain land, at age. To daughter Mary Dickenson, a legacy, and to other three daughters, Ann, Hannah and Susanna, a legacy at eighteen. To son John, rest of estate.

1. John, 2. Mary, 3. Samuel, 4. William, 5. Joseph, 6. Benjamin, 7. Wignall, 8. Ann, 9. Hannah, 10. Susanna,

IX. FRANCIS, — b. — d. — Kings Town, R. I.

1687, Sep. 6. Taxed 1*s*.

X. ELIZABETH, — b. — d.
m.
—— P—— — b. — d. — of P——

XI. ELISHA, — b. — d. 1729. — North Kingstown, R. I.
m. 1713.
ELIZABETH DEXTER, — b. 1684. — d. 1756, Oct. 14. — of Dexter.

1. John, 1715.
2. Susanna,
3. Ann, 1718.
4. Elizabeth, 1720.
5. Abigail,
6. Edward,
7. Thomas,

1709-13-15-17-18-25. Deputy.

1718-19-20-21-22-23. Assistant.

1725, Sep. 19. His wife Elizabeth, and children John, Edward, Susanna, Ann, Elizabeth and Abigail, were baptised by Dr. McSparran, of the Episcopal Church.

1726, Jun. 8. He was baptised.

1726, Jun. 14. The Assembly ordered that if he and Stephen Northup, could not agree within three months, so that the mill dam be erected and built up again, so that said mill be caused to grind, then the Town Council, of North Kingstown, were to have valued the yearly income of land and mill, and right of Elisha Cole, in mill, dams, land, &c., and the yearly damage the said Stephen Northup shall sustain by having his land drowned by erecting the dam. The council were then to take the mill, &c., into their custody, paying a certain sum to Cole and Northup yearly, till the latter could agree between themselves to keep the mill going.

He died in London.

1729. Will—proved. Exx. wife Elizabeth. To sons John and Edward, when of age, real estate amounting to 275 acres, including grist mill and saw mill, and house, they paying to each sister, £200. To daughters Susannah, Ann and Elizabeth, £300 each, at age. To wife, rest of estate.

1756, Oct. 16. Dr. McSparran notes that "being wrote to and earnestly entreated to go to Newport for that purpose, I preached a funeral sermon, for, and on account of Elizabeth Cole, widow and relict of the late Elisha Cole, Esq., who died many years ago in London, and buried her in the burying ground in Newport, &c.

COLE (Robert).

ROBERT, — b. — d. 1655.
m.
MARY, — b. — d. 1656 +

(She m. (2) Matthias Harvey.)

Roxbury, Mass., Providence, Warwick, R. I.

1630, Oct. 19. Roxbury, Mass. He requested to be made a freeman.

1631, Aug. 16 Fined 5 marks, for drinking too much aboard ship "Friendship."

1632, May 9. He was appointed on a committee to confer with the court about raising of a public stock.

1633, Apr. 1. He was among those who had gone to Agawam to plant.

He lived for a time at Ipswich and Salem.

1639. Providence. He was one of the twelve original members of First Baptist Church.

1640. He was appointed with three others on a committee on all matters of difference regarding dividing line between Providence and Pawtuxet, and they reported in July, that

COLE (Robert). 1st column. 1638, Oct 8. He was one of the twelve persons to whom Roger Williams deeded land he had bought of Canonicus and Miantonomi.

I. JOHN, — b. — d.
m.
ANN, — b. — d. — of

He may have been identical with that John Cole, whose inventory was taken 1676, Dec. 10, by George Lawton and Robert Hodgson, at Portsmouth, R. I. Amount £43, 2*s*. 5*d*., besides additional inventory including an amount due from the country unto John Cole, for cattle, &c., spent at Mount Hope, July, 1675. (The record of above was made at Plymouth, Mass).

II. ELIZABETH, — b. — d.
m.
JOHN TOWNSEND, — b. — d. 1669. — of John & Elizabeth ( ) Townsend.

1. John, 2. Thomas, 3. Elizabeth, 4. James, 5. Rose, 6. Ann, 7. Sarah, 8. George, 9. Daniel,

III. DELIVERANCE, — b. — d.
m.
RICHARD TOWNSEND, — b. — d. 1671 (—) — of John & Elizabeth ( ) Townsend.

1. Dinah, 2. Leah,

IV. DANIEL, — b. — d. 1692, Nov. 29. — Warwick, R. I., Oyster Bay, N. Y.
m. [Gorton.
MAHERSHALALHASHBAZ — b. — d. — of Samuel & Elizabeth ( ) Gorton.

1. Samuel, 2. Benjamin, 3. Joseph, 4. Susanna,

2d column. I. John, Warwick, R. I., Oyster Bay, N. Y. He had a son Solomon. Erase all the text and add—1683. Jan. 1. His widow being about to marry William Lynes, deeded to her son Solomon, half of her land and estate, she having a life estate in the whole by will of her late husband. IV. Daniel, 1677, Sep. 27. He and his brothers Robert and Nathaniel and two other persons, had confirmation by patent from Governor Andros of lands at Oyster Bay. 1692, Nov 10, Will. VI. Nathaniel. His wife Martha d. 1668, Dec. 17. He m. (2) Deborah. Children, by 1st wife: 1. Nathaniel, 1668, Aug. 24. Children by 2d wife: 2 Caleb. 3. Harvey. 4. Deborah, 1694, Dec. 16. He deeded to sons Caleb and Harvey, land at Duck Pond. (They deeded same to their half brother Nathaniel Jr., 1703, Mar. 29.)

they had seriously and carefully endeavoured to weigh and consider all those differences to bring them to amity and peace. "We have given the fairest and equalest way to produce our peace."

1640, Jul. 27. He and thirty-eight others signed an agreement for a form of government.

1648, Jun. 5. Warwick. He was recorded as an inhabitant.

1653, Jan. 2. He sold Richard Pray, and wife Mary, his house and lot in Providence.

1654, Feb. 27. He and wife Mary, sold Zachariah Rhodes, for £80, dwelling house at Pawtuxet, and certain land.

1655, Oct. 25. Inventory, £501, debts £112, 15*s*.

Administratrix widow Mary Cole. Town Council ordered estate disposed of as follows: To eldest son John, £80 and a mare. To 2d son Daniel, £50, at twenty-one years of age. To 3d son Nathaniel, £40 at age. To 4th son Robert, £40 at age. To daughter Sarah Cole, £40 at marriage or twenty-one The children under age to be under care of mother. If widow died before children came of age, the Town Council to dispose of estate, and if any children died, their part to be distributed. The administratrix was authorized to sell land and give deeds.

His widow, after marrying Matthias Harvey, soon went to Oyster Bay, as did her sons Nathaniel and Daniel, and her daughters who married Townsends.

1656, Apr. 5. His widow Mary, confirmed to son-in-law Richard Townsend, a meadow.

V. { ANN, m. HENRY TOWNSEND, { b. d. { b. d. of John & Elizabeth ( ) Townsend.

VI. { NATHANIEL, m. 1667, Aug. 30, MARTHA WRIGHT, { b. 1640 ± d. { b. d. — Warwick, R. I., Oyster Bay, N. Y. — of Nicholas & Ann ( ) Wright.

VII. { ROBERT, m. 1670, Jan. 1, MERCY WRIGHT, { b. d. 1715, Apr. 16. { b. d. 1708, Oct. 21. — Oyster Bay, N. Y. — of Nicholas & Ann ( ) Wright.

VIII. { SARAH, { b. d.

5. Sarah,
6. Dinah,
7. Mary,
8. Ann,

1. Nathan, 1671, Mar. 18.
2. Tamar, 1673, May 18
3. Dorcas, 1675, May 15.
4. Robert, 1677, Apr. 9.
5. John, 1678, Nov. 15.
6. Charles, 1679, Mar. 4.
7. Freegift, 1682, Jan. 12.
8. Mercy, 1684, Mar. 24.
9. Mary, 1686, Nov. 30.

COLLINS (ARNOLD).

{ ARNOLD, m. (1) SARAH, m. (2) 1692, Mar. 16, AMY WARD, (w. of Thos). { b. d. { b. d. { b. 1658, Oct. 20. d. 1732, Jan. 11.

of Samuel & Seaborn (Tew) Billings.

Newport, R. I.

1690, Mar. 3. It was ordered by the Assembly, that the seal brought in by Mr. Arnold Collins, being the anchor, with the motto Hope, is appointed to be the seal of the colony, he having been employed by the Assembly to make it.

1691, Feb. 15. Richard Hodg died at his house, as the Quaker records state.

1702, Mar. 4. He was one of the proprietors of common lands.

OLLINS (ARNOLD). 1st column. Arnold, d. 1735. 1735, Aug. 4. Will—proved. The name of an heir is obliterated but must have been his son Henry. He mentions daughter Mary, wife of Jeremiah Wilcox, daughter Sarah, wife of Josiah Bliss, daughter Elizabeth Wickham and grandson Arnold Belcher. 2d column. II Sarah, m. (1) —— Belcher, m. (2) Josiah Bliss, of John & Damaris (Arnold) Bliss. Her 2d husband d. 1748. Her children were: 1. Arnold, and by 2d husband: 2. Elizabeth, 3. Henry, 1722. 4. Sarah 5. Amey. 6. William, 1728, Feb. 5. 7. Martha. IV. Elizabeth, m. 1723, Mar. 17. Samuel Wickham, of Samuel & Barbara (Holden) Wickham. He b. 1693, Sep. 2, d. 1753, Feb. 23. Children: 1. Samuel 2. Henry, 1725. 3 Gideon, 1735. 4 Elizabeth, 17[illegible]. 5. Deborah, 1740.

Mary m. to Jeremiah Wilcox by Gov. Samuel Cranston, Dec. 8, 1703.
[illegible] by Mrs. Hazel V. Greenleaf, 1963

I. { SYLVESTER, { b. 1688, Oct. 27. d.

II. { SARAH, { b. 1690, Aug. 13. d.

See American Genealogist, v. 26, p. 222

COLLINS (ARNOLD). 2d column. II. Sarah. Her 1st husband was Benjamin Belcher. He d. 1716. (His will mentions wife and child she is with, besides children, Benjamin, Edward and Phebe, evidently by a former wife. He mentions also brother John Beere, and father, Arnold Collins.)

(2d WIFE.)

III. { ARNOLD, { b. 1693, Feb. 2. d. — Newport, R. I.

1714. Freeman.

IV. { ELIZABETH, { b. 1695, Jun. 28. d.

V. { HENRY, Unmarried. { b. 1699, Mar. 25. d. 1766 ± — Newport, R. I.

He was a merchant.

1729. He was on the committee to erect the building for Seventh Day Baptist Church, of which he was a member.

1742. He was one of the original members of the Newport Artillery Company.

1748, Jun. He deeded a lot for the use of Redwood Library, and the building now in use was erected thereon. He was on the committee that superintended the building of this edifice.

1750, Sep. 4. He and others signed a petition to the King, praying that the Assembly might be restrained from making or emitting any more bills of public credit upon loan, without royal permission, the sum on loan already amounting to £390,000, worth at time of issue £78,111, sterling, but at present only £35,445. Amongst those whose estates were involved in the loan were numbers of widows and orphans, who were grievously injured, oppressed and almost ruined.

1763. He was one of those instrumental in building the Market House (now used for the City Hall). He was one of the proprietors of Long wharf, &c.

He ordered portraits made by Smibert, of not only himself, but of Rev. John Callendar and Bishop Berkeley.

COLLINS (ELIZUR).

{ ELIZUR, m. SARAH WRIGHT, { b. 1622. d. 1683, Sep. 29. { b. d. 1700 ±

of Wright.

(She m. (2) 1685, Jan. 7, John Potter.)

Warwick, R. I.

He was son of that widow Ann Collins, who married John Smith, of Warwick (President of the Colony, 1649), at whose decease in 1663, the widow and her son Elizur Collins, inherited the estate. (She died 1678, Nov. 2, at Warwick.)

1644. Warwick.

1667. He was called aged forty-five, in this year.

1672–73–78. Deputy.

1678, May 20. He, with consent of his mother, Ann Smith, widow, and of his wife Sarah, sold two lots in Warwick Neck, and a town lot to Jonathan Knight.

1683, Oct. 29. The Jury of Grand Inquest, declared, that having made inquiry (1683, Sep. 29), concerning the death of Lieutenant Elizur Collins, casually found dead in his own house, "do absolutely conclude that the said Elizur Collins was actually his own death by hanging himself."

I. { THOMAS, m. (1) 1692, Feb. 17, ABIGAIL HOUSE, m. (2) ANNA, m. (3) MARY, { b. 1664, Oct. 26. d. 1726, Mar. 9. { b. d. of House. { b. d. of { b. d. of — Warwick, R. I.

1726, Mar. 7. Will—proved 1726, Mar. 18. Ex. son Thankful. To wife Mary, half of personal estate, for life, and privilege of bed room, half of great room and cellar, for life, with a third of orchard. To son Elizur, 50*s*. To grandsons William and Thomas, two of the children of son William, deceased, 50*s*. each, at age. To son Thomas, £5. To daughter Sarah Rutenburge, £5. To daughter Ann Collins, £5. To son Samuel Collins, £20 at age. To daughter Abigail Collins, £5 at eighteen. To son Thankful, all the rest and residue of real and personal estate.

Inventory, £146, 15*s*. 8*d*., viz: 1 gun, pewter, woolen and linen wheel, 1 pair oyster rakes, 5 small hogs, 2 mares, 2 horses, 1 colt, 1 pair oxen, 1 heifer, 40 sheep, ½ of 3 yearlings, &c.

1. Elizur, 1693, Nov. 17.
2. William, 1695, Feb. 8.
3. Thomas, 1697, Jan. 31.
4. Sarah, 1698, Oct. 31.
5. Thankful, 1700, Aug. 27.
(2d wife.)
6. Anna, 1707, Jul. 16.
7. Samuel, 1709, May 30.
8. Abigail, 1711, Nov. 20.

II. { ELIZUR, Unmarried. { b. 1666, Jun. 11 d. 1686, Feb. 1. — Warwick, R. I.

1686, Feb. 1. The following verdict was rendered, as to his death: "we, the Grand Inquest, have made diligent inquiry after the death Elizur Collins, who lost his life suddenly, and by all evidences was suddenly accessory to his own death by reason of cutting of a limb, to lower a tree to the ground, and was catched under it, and so by that means died."

III. William, b. 1668, Mar. 8. d.

IV. Ann, b. 1670, Mar. 4. d.

V. Elizabeth, b. 1672, Nov. 1. d. 1724, Sep. 9.
m. 1695, May 9,
Samuel Gorton, b. 1672, Jul. 22. d. 1721, Jun. 5. of John & Margaret (Wheaton) Gorton.

1. Ann, 1696, Feb. 19.
2. Edward, 1698, May 18.
3. Margaret, 1701, May 12.
4. Samuel, 1706, Jan. 2.
5. William,
6. Sarah,
7. Elizabeth,

COLVIN.

John, b. d. 1729,
m. (1)
Dorothy, b. d.
m. (2) 1726, May 30.
Mary Keach. b. d.
of Keach.

Dartmouth, Mass., Providence, R. I.

1705, Aug. 16. He bought 300 acres upland and 7 acres of meadow in Providence, for £110, of Andrew Harris.

1706, Feb. 11. He bought land on north side of Pawtuxet River, at Mashantatack, of John Carder, &c., for £55.

1711, Jun. 23. Providence. He deeded to son John, for love, &c., 30 acres.

1715, Mar. 1. He deeded to son Samuel, for love, &c., 12 acres.

1723, Feb. 20. He and wife Dorothy deeded to son-in-law Peter Roberts and wife Amey, my homestead land where I dwell, and all other real and personal estate.

1727, Jan. 19. He deeded 50 acres with buildings, &c., in Mashantatack, for love, &c., and £150, to daughter Amey and her husband Peter Roberts.

1729, Apr. 4. He bought 20 acres in Mashantatack of Ezekiel Warner, for £46.

He died previous to Nov. 17, of this year.

I. Anna. b. 1679, Mar. 26. d.

II. John, b. 1681, Apr. 19. d. 1764, Jul. 1. Dartmouth, Mass., Providence, Scituate, R. I.
m. (1)
Lydia, b. d. of
m. (2) 1734, Nov. 21.
Mary Dyer, (w. of Chas) b. 1686, Oct. 5. d. of John & Mary (Mann) Lapham.
m. (3)
Margaret, b. d. 1763 + of

His first three children were born in Dartmouth.

1729, Nov. 17. He, called son of John Colvin, deceased, bought 6 acres of Ezekiel Warner for £15.

1735, Jun. 30. He joined in a deed of his wife Mary (widow and executrix of Charles Dyer), to her son John Dyer, of 60 acres, dwelling house, &c., where her husband, said Dyer, had lived.

1735, Jul. 7. He and wife Mary sold to his son Stephen, 13 acres in Mashantatack for £80.

1742, Sep. 27. He deeded an acre and 100 rods, to son Stephen for love, &c.

1745, Sep. 3. Scituate He and his family brought a certificate from Providence.

1757, Apr. 11. He and wife Margaret, sold Jedediah Harris a farm in Cranston.

1763, Sep. 22. Will—proved 1764, Jul. 30. Ex. son Jeremiah. To grandson, Jabez Colvin, a part of homestead. To son Jeremiah, the rest of homestead. To wife Margaret, the use and privilege for life of all goods she brought when she came to live with me, and son Jeremiah to provide her a suitable maintenance for life. To son John's wife, Amey (at decease of wife), a brass kettle. To granddaughter Margaret Colvin, daughter of my son Matthew, deceased, a feather bed, &c. To daughter Lydia Thornton, 30*s*. To daughter, Charity Burlingame, 30*s*. To daughter-in-law Meribah Colvin, wife of son Matthew, 30*s*. To son Jeremiah, rest of estate. To sons Stephen and John nothing because they had already had.

Inventory, £1689, 10*s*. 6*d*., viz: wearing apparel, £153, 5*s*., calf, 2 pairs of steers, 2 cows, mare, 14 old sheep, 8 lambs, 8 goats, a kid, ⅝ of a grindstone, &c.

1. Jonathan, 1704, Jan. 7.
2. Lydia, 1705, Mar. 20.
3. Charity, 1707, Jan. 1.
4. Stephen,
5. John,
6. Hopkins,
7. Matthew,
8. Jeremiah,

III. Stephen, b. 1683, Sep. 24. d.

IV. Abigail, b. 1686, Jul. 28. d.

V. Samuel, b. 1688, Dec. 10. d. 1759, Oct. Providence, Coventry, R. I.
m.
Phebe, b. d. of

1726, Sep. 7. He sold to Peter Roberts, 12 acres for £82.

1754, Oct. 5. Will—proved 1759. Ex. son Samuel. To wife Phebe, privilege of best room, while widow. He gave 5*s*. each to following children, Thomas and Daniel Colvin, Abigail Franklin, Joseph Colvin, Elizabeth Dailey, Sarah Burlingame, Mary Wright, Susannah Colvin, Temperance (or Content) Colvin and Phebe Colvin. To son Richard £54. To son Rufus, £50. To son Samuel all residue of estate real and personal, except the burying place.

Inventory, 2 cows, 5 sheep, hay, £25, &c.

1. Thomas, 1712.
2. Daniel, 1716.
3. Abigail,
4. Joseph,
5. Elizabeth,
6. Sarah,
7. Mary,
8. Susannah,
9. Richard,
10. Content,
11 Phebe,
12. Rufus,
13. Samuel,

VI. Amey, b. 1690, Oct. 31. d. 1743 +
m.
Peter Roberts, b. d. 1743, Aug. 17. of Peter Roberts.

1. Philip,
2. John,
3. Peter,
4. Mary,
5. Sarah,
6. Dorothy,

VII. Deborah. b. 1693, May 28. d.

VIII. James, b. 1695, Nov. 24 d. 1755, Mar. 5 Providence, Coventry, R. I.
m. (1)
———— b. d. of
m. (2)
Anne, b. d. of

1729, Jul. 7. He bought of Randall Holden and wife Rose, 60 or 70 acres in Westquadnaig for £60.

1743, Feb. 2. He was named as one of the executors of Peter Roberts' will, who calls him brother-in-law.

1755, Feb. 24. Will—proved 1755, Mar. 29. Ex. son Josiah. To wife Anne, all indoor movables except a bed and chest. To son Benjamin, 20*s*. To son Caleb, certain land. To son Moses, land where he now dwells. To son Josiah, land near Moses, &c., and all my stock, and out door movables. To son Stephen, 80 acres. To son John, rest of farm where I dwell. To son David, land. To son Henry, £1136, and to be put out to a trade. To daughter Anne, at eighteen, a bed, chest and £322. If any of last wife's children die before arriving of age their portion to go to children of last wife. He provides for a burial place for himself and family.

Inventory, bonds and notes £570, books £4, beds £146, &c.

1. Benjamin,
2. Caleb,
3. Moses,
4. Josiah,
5. Stephen,
6. John,
7. David,
8. Henry,
9. Anne,

COLVIN. 2d column. VIII. James, m. (1) Mary Lippitt, of John & Rebecca (Lippitt) Lippitt.

IX. Josiah, b. 1700, Jun. 6. d.

COLWELL.

ROBERT, b. / d.
m.
MARGARET WHITE, b. / d. 1717 +
of White.

(She m. (2) 1669, Jun. 19, Thomas Walling.)
(She m. (3) 1678, Dec. 25, Daniel Abbott.)

Providence, R. I., Long Island, N. Y.

1654, Apr. 28. He bought a house and house lot of John Fenner, lying betwixt Edward Inman and John Smith.

1660. He had a house lot laid out.

1665, Feb. 19. He had lot 67 assigned him in a division of lands.

1666, May, He took oath of allegiance.

1667, Jul. 2. His petition of May last for freedom of his wife Margaret, was renewed and the court now granted him a divorce from late wife Margaret White, with liberty to contract another marriage.

1670, Dec. 31. He, formerly of Providence, but now of Long Island, sold Richard Pray all rights in Providence, lands divided or undivided.

1678, Jun. 3. There was laid out to Richard Arnold, 5 acres in the right of Robert Colwell.

I. ROBERT, b. 1662, Jan. 9. / d. 1748, Jun.
m.
AMEY DOWNING, b. / d. of Downing.

His children's births were recorded at Bristol, but he may have subsequently moved to Glocester, R. I., where some of his children settled.

1. Margaret, 1699, Jul. 17.
2. Mary, 1700, Nov. 4.
3. Robert, 1702, Jan. 26.
4. Amey, 1703, Jun. 23.
5. Richard, 1705, Mar. 23.
6. Elizabeth, 1706, Sep. 4.
7. John, 1708, Jul. 12.
8. William, 1709, Dec. 23.
9. Sarah, 1711, Jun. 11.
10. Ruth, 1713, Jun. 30.

II. ELIZABETH, b. 1664, Jul. 1. / d.

CONGDON. 2d column. II. Benjamin. Children, 1. Benjamin, 1702, Oct. 20. 2. Francis, 1703, Dec. 6. 3 Joseph, 1705, Feb. 15. 4. John, 1706, Sep. 23. 5. Sarah, 1708, Jun. 26. 6. William, 1711, Nov. 6. 7. James, 1713, May 15. 8. Elizabeth, 1715, Apr. 8. 9. Mary, 1718, Mar. 10. 10. Susannah, 1720, Feb. 7. 11. Stukeley, 1723, Dec. 11. IV. James. His 3d wife was daughter of Robert and Deborah (Peckham) Taylor.

CONGDON.

BENJAMIN, b. 1650 ± / d. 1718, Jun. 19.
m.
ELIZABETH ALBRO, b. / d. 1720, Nov. 15.
of John & Dorothy ( ) Albro.

Portsmouth, Kings Town, R. I.

1671, Sep. 20. He bought of William Brenton, Benedict Arnold, &c., 230 acres in Narragansett, near Pettacomscott, but he did not move thence for some years.

1676, Oct. 18. He was sued by Samuel Reape, for slander, defamation, &c., and the case was left to arbitration.

1677. Freeman.

1677, Apr. 27. He witnessed a deed from George Sisson, of Portsmouth.

1679. He was ordered to move his shop at Newport, to another lot, and if he disobeyed, it was to be pulled down.

1679, Dec. 5. He had a deed of 200 acres, in Narragansett, being part of 7,630 acres laid out by Samuel Wilbur, to Jireh Bull and twenty-four others.

1683, Oct. 20. Kings Town. He, calling himself "late of Portsmouth, planter," sold John Sheldon, 230 acres in Narragansett, near Pettacomscott, for £7, being the land "granted to me by William Brenton, Benedict Arnold," &c.

1687, Sep. 6. Taxed 3*s.* ½*d.*

1710, May 17. He and seventeen others, bought 7,000 acres of the vacant lands in Narragansett, ordered sold by Assembly.

His signature was made to deeds, &c., by mark Z, while his son Benjamin, signed by mark O.

1715, Jul. 2. Will—proved 1718, Dec. 10. Exs. wife Elizabeth and son John. To sons William, John, Benjamin and James, 5*s.* each, they having had their portions. To daughters Elizabeth Wells and Susanna Northup, three cows each, and to grand-daughter Elizabeth Wells, a cow, at decease of wife. To wife, household goods at her disposal, and the farm, orchard and housing, for life. To son John, two cows and a heifer.

Inventory, £38, viz: cows, sheep, 4 silver spoons, wine glasses, earthern and pewter ware, iron pots, skillet, warming pan, napkins, towels, wearing apparel, bed, &c.

He and his wife were buried in the Congdon Burial Ground, at Congdon Hill, near Wickford.

I. WILLIAM, b. / d. 1761. South Kingstown, R. I.
m. (1)
MARY, b. / d. of
m. (2)
MARGARET, b. / d. 1754 + of

1754, Jun. 1. Will—proved 1761, Feb. 9. Ex. son Joseph. To wife Margaret, while widow, the use of three cows, riding horse, two hogs, two feather beds, and also use of largest room, &c., with thirty bushels of corn and ten cords of firewood, yearly. To daughter Margaret Congdon, two feather beds and £150, with house room and keep of horse, while single. To daughter Elizabeth, £100. To daughter Abigail Reynolds, £150 and feather bed. To granddaughter Susanna Congdon, £100 and feather bed at eighteen. To son William, £700, and to each of his children, £20. To wife and three daughters, rest of household goods, and to daughters, rest of money. To wife and daughters, rest of personal estate. To son Joseph, all my lands and estate.

Inventory, £3,443, 10*s.* 11*d.*, viz: wearing apparel £80, 2 woolen wheels, a bay horse, 3 cows, hog, fowls, warming pan, negro man Bristow, &c.

1. Joseph,
2. William, 1698, Jan. 25.
3. Margaret,
4. Elizabeth,
5. Abigail,

II. BENJAMIN, b. / d. 1756. North Kingstown, R. I.
m. 1701, Dec. 1,
FRANCES STAFFORD, b. / d. of Joseph & Sarah (Holden) Stafford.

1712, Feb. 14. He bought of Abel Potter, and his mother Rachel, 57 acres in Mashantatack (Providence), for £200, and the next year bought 3 acres more, for £3.

1713, Feb. 11. He sold his brother, James Congdon, 60 acres and mansion house, at Mashantatack, for £308.

1. Benjamin,
2. William,
3. Stukeley,
4. James,

III. JOHN, b. / d. North Kingstown, R. I.
m.
MARY SMITH, b. / d. of Jeremiah & Mary (Gereardy) Smith.

1710, May 17. Kings Town. He and others bought 2,000 acres of the vacant lands in Narragansett.

1. Jeremiah,
2. Mary,
3. John, 1705.
4. James,

IV. JAMES, b. 1686, Apr. 19. / d. 1757, Sep. 27. Kings Town, Providence, Charlestown, R. I.
m. (1)
MARGARET ELDRED, b. / d. 1728 ± of Samuel & Martha (Knowles) Eldred.
m. (2)
DORCAS WESTCOTT, b / d. 1734 ± of Benjamin & Bethiah (Gardiner) Westcott.
m. (3) 1739, Nov. 15,
MARY HOXSIE, (w. of Jos.) b. 1703, Nov. 23. / d. 1755 + of Robert & Deborah ( ) Taylor.

1706. He was granted ear mark for sheep.

1709. He and three others, bought 430 acres of "vacant lands" ordered sold by Assembly.

1713, Feb. 11. Providence. He bought of his brother, Benjamin Congdon, 60 acres and mansion house, at Mashantatack, for £308.

1714, Oct. 9. He and Richard Searle, bought of John Knowlman, of Warwick, one-quarter of one seventeenth part of Coweset township, in Warwick, for £25.

1718, Dec. 26. He and Richard Searle, bought of Fones Greene, and his mother Mary Greene, widow, for £110, one-fourth of a right in a parcel of land in north-west part of Warwick, called "seven men's farm."

1720. Freeman.

1731-32-33-34. Town Council.

1732. Deputy.

1738, Jun. 6. He sold land in Warwick, for £50, and same year land in South Kingstown, for £900.

1739, Nov. 15. Charlestown. He was married to the widow Mary Hoxsie, at her residence, "that being the usual meeting place in Charlestown," of the Quakers.

1742. He brought in account to court, of his wife's administration on her late husband, Joseph Hoxsie's estate.

1745-55. Moderator of Town meeting.

1745-47-48-49-50. Deputy.

1746-48. Ratemaker.

1747-48. Town Council.

1753, Jan. 13. He deeded son Benjamin, for love, &c., 100 acres, in Providence.

1755, Sep. 11. Will—proved 1757. Exs. sons Benjamin and John. To wife Mary, negro woman Sall, negro girl Phillis, use and improvement of five cows, fifty sheep, three beds and furniture, while widow, and use of negro man Cæsar and Spanish Indian girl Satira, for support of herself and three youngest children, while widow. If she marry, then Cæsar and Satira to go to son Robert, and rest of afore mentioned property to Susanna, Robert and Phebe, equally. To wife, also, riding horse, and to her daughter Susanna, such a horse as her mother may choose for her. To son James, 100 acres in South Kingstown, dwelling house where he lives in Charlestown, with 20 acres and mulatto man Cuff. To son Samuel, bond for £150, I have against him, with accrued interest. To son Benjamin, all my lands and houses in Cranston. To son William, land in South Kingstown and south half of dwelling house in South Kingstown, which my son Joseph lives in. To son John, 40 acres in Charlestown and land in South Kingstown. To son Joseph, north half of house he lives in, and 30 acres. To son Robert, land in Quanaquatogue, Charlestown, subject to claims of his mother for life, and if he die before twenty-one, his brothers James, John and William to have it. To sons William and Joseph, 20 acres in South Kingstown, and to John, William and Joseph, certain land in Charlestown. To

1. James,
2. Penelope,
3. Benjamin,
4. Samuel,
5. William,
6. John,
7. Elizabeth,
8. Martha,
9. Margaret, 1725, Oct. 1.
(2d wife.)
10. Ephraim,
11. Dorcas, 1729, Dec. 14.
12. Joseph, 1733, Apr. 20.
(3d wife.)
13. Robert,
14. Susannah,
15. Phebe,

CONGDON. 2d column. IV. James. His wife Margaret, b. 1683, Feb. 26. Children born by her at following dates: 1. James, 1707, Nov. 27. 2. Penelope, 1709, Oct. 22. 3. Samuel, 1711, Aug. 29. 4. Benjamin, 1712, Aug. 24. 5. John, 1714, Aug. 1. 6. Elizabeth, 1716, June 26. 7. Martha, 1718, Oct. 20. 8. William, 1720, June 9. 9. Margaret, 1725, Oct. 1.

CONGDON. 2d column. I. William, m. (1) 1693, Mar. 3. Mary Brownell, of Robert & Mary ( ) Brownell. She d. 1718 (—). 1718, Jan. 29. In Robert Brownell's will of this date he gives legacies of £5 each to "daughter Mary's three children," she evidently having died. II. Benjamin. 1721, Town Council. 1723, Town Sergeant. 1756, Jan. 15. Will—proved 1756, Oct. 11. To son John, land in Boston Neck where testator now dwells, he paying £500 to my son Benjamin, and £400 to second son Joseph. To nine daughters of son William, deceased, £40. To grandson John Congdon, son of James, deceased, land in Exeter. To grandson Stukeley Congdon, land. To daughters Frances Gardiner and Mary Brown, and to eight children of daughter Mary Brown, certain legacies. To daughter Elizabeth Sweet, for life, certain land. Change list of children. 1 Benjamin 2. Joseph. 3. William. 4. James. 5. John. 6. Frances. 7. Mary. 8. Elizabeth.

daughter Martha, for life, Spanish Indian girl Hannah (and at Martha's decease to her children), also two beds, riding beast, two cows and £100, &c. To daughter Margaret, and her children, Spanish Indian girl Flora; also to her, two beds and all household goods in house where she lives, and two cows. To daughter Dorcas, Spanish Indian girl Grace, for life, and then to her children, and to her, household goods used by her, belonging to me, and horse, two cows, &c. To daughter Susanna, negro girl Lettice, for life, and then to her children, and to her, a bed and £100. To daughter Phebe, £500, at eighteen. To daughter Elizabeth, use for life of Spanish Indian woman Dinah, and then to children, and to her, £100. To daughter Penelope, £50. To son Ephraim, £50. To daughters Elizabeth, Martha and Susanna, use of a room in house given Joseph and William, while said daughters are single, with privilege of dressing victuals in kitchen, and the keep of two cows. To sons Benjamin and John, all the rest of estate, both real and personal, equally.

V. ELIZABETH, { b. / d. 1732 +
m.
JOHN WELLS, { b. 1676, May. / d. 1732. of Peter Wells.

1. John, 2. Benjamin, 3. Mercy, 4. Elizabeth, 5. Daughter, 6. Susanna,

VI. SUSANNA, { b. / d. 1725 +
m.
DAVID NORTHUP, { b. / d. 1725. of Stephen Northup.

1. David, 2. Stephen, 3. Benjamin, 4. Robert,

COOK (JOHN).

JOHN, { b. / d. 1655 ±
m.
MARY, { b. / d. 1682 +

(She m. (2) 1656, Thomas Ralph.)

Warwick, R. I.

1648, Jun. 5. He was received as an inhabitant.

1649. Sergeant.

1652, Jun. 7. He was granted liberty to make a highway between his uncle, Stukeley Westcott, and himself.

1654, Mar. 10. He sold Henry Knowles, dwelling house, &c.

I. JOHN, { b. / d.
m.
PHEBE, { b. / d. of

Warwick, R. I., Connecticut.

1669, Mar. 16. The Warwick authorities gave him the following safe conduct: Whereas, John Cook, the bearer hereof, son of John Cook, deceased, with consent of his father-in-law, Thomas Ralph, of Mashantatack, and own mother, Mary Ralph, wife of Thomas, and other friends relating to the bearer hereof; doth desire to travel abroad towards Long Island, New York, or other parts of the world, in order to seek for some employment, we thought good to desire all persons amongst whom he shall travel, to let him quietly pass without any interruption or molestation.

1684, Oct. 29. His wife Phebe, petitioned the Assembly for a divorce from her husband, John Cook, late of Warwick, who had absented himself for several years, and had not provided maintenance for his wife and children. He was at this time said to be living in the island of New Providence, with another wife. His lands in the colony of Rhode Island were granted for her improvement, till the children came of age.

1690, Jun. 21. He, late of Warwick, now sojourning in Connecticut, sold Jeremiah Smith, of Prudence Island, all right in purchase of Potowamut.

II. ELIZABETH, { b. / d.
m. 1666, Dec. 24,
JOHN HARRADI, { b. / d. of Harradi.

COOPER.

SIMON, { b. / d.
m. 1661, Jan. 20,
MARY TUCKER, { b. / d.

Newport, R. I.

He was a physician.

His wife was called of Shelter Island.

1666, May 2. Freeman.

I. ROBERT, { b. 1664, Oct. 10. / d.

II. JOSEPH, { b. 1667, Feb. 24. / d. 1670, Aug. 8.

III. MARY, { b. 1669, Jul. 20. / d.

IV. SIMON, { b. 1672, Apr. 1. / d.
m. 1695, Jul. 24,
MARTHA PRIOR, { b. 1672, Oct. 15. / d. of Matthew & Mary ( ) Prior.

see American Genealogist, v.35 p.107; v.39, p.2

CORNELL.

THOMAS, { b. / d. 1656 ±
m.
REBECCA, { b. / d. 1673, Feb. 8.

Hertford, Eng., Boston, Mass., Portsmouth, R. I.

1638, Sep. 6. Boston. He was licensed, upon trial, to keep an Inn, in the room of William Baulstone, till next General Court.

1639, Jun. 4. He was fined £30, for several offences, selling wine without license, and beer at 2*d.* a quart.

1639, Jun. 6. He was abated £10 of his fine, and allowed a month to sell off his beer which is upon his hands, and then to cease from keeping entertainment, and the town to provide another.

1641, Feb. 4. Portsmouth. He had a piece of meadow granted, to be fenced at his own cost.

1641, Mar. 16. Freeman.

1641. Constable.

1642–44. Ensign.

1643, Sep. He was for a brief period at New York (Throgg's Neck), but Mr. Winthrop records under this date, that the Indians set upon the English who dwelt under the Dutch, and killed "such of Mr. Throckmorton's and Mr. Cornhill's families, as were at home." He further says of the English settlers: "these people had cast off ordinances and churches," and "for larger accomodation, had subjected themselves to the Dutch, and dwelt scatteringly near a mile asunder. Some that escaped the Indian attack went back to Rhode Island."

1646, Feb. 4. He was granted 100 acres at the

I. THOMAS, { b. / d. 1673, May 23.
m. (1) 1642, Nov. 2.
ELIZABETH FISCOCK, { b. / d. of Fiscock.
m. (2)
SARAH EARLE, { b. / d. 1690 + of Ralph & Joan ( ) Earle.

See: American Genealogist, v.19, p.132

(She m. (2) David Lake.)

Hertford Co., Eng., New York, Portsmouth, R. I.

1. Elizabeth, 1644. 2. Thomas, 1653. 3. Edward, 4. Samuel, 5. Stephen, (2d wife) 6. John, 7. Sarah, 8. Innocent,

1642, Nov. 2. New York. The Dutch records of New Amsterdam, in giving his marriage at this date, call him of Hertford, England, and his wife of Plymouth, England.

He did not go to Rhode Island, till some years after his father removed there.

1644, Jan. 12. He had his daughter Elizabeth baptized.

1655, Mar. 17. Portsmouth. He, called Thomas Cornell, Jr., was chosen with three others to prize land and buildings of John Wood, deceased

1657, Dec. 10. He had a grant of 8 acres.

1663, Aug. 24. He, eldest son of Thomas Cornell, deceased, confirmed a deed his mother had made two years previously to Richard Hart.

1664–70–71–72. Deputy.

1670, May 4. He and three others were appointed to audit the colony's accounts.

1671, Jun. 7. His bill to the Assembly for further encouragement of a troop of horse was referred to next Assembly. At the same date he was desired to be a messenger from this court to carry a letter to the government of Plymouth, and that he be supplied with 20*s.* in silver, toward bearing his charge.

1672, Apr. 2. He was appointed on a committee to go to Narragansett, to take a view of such places there that are fit for plantations, and inquire of the English and Indians who are the owners and who lay claim to such lands and signify that the colony doth intend such lands shall be improved by peopling the same.

1673. His will was ordered by the Assembly to be made by the Town Council, and division of estate made to wife and children of said Thomas Cornell, "lately executed for murdering his mother Mrs. Rebecca Cornell." He having requested by his friends that after his execution his body may be buried by his mother, the request was refused, but yet in favor to the prisoner, the Court consents that if his friends have a desire, they may inter the body in the land lately to him belonging, within twenty feet of the common road.

further side of Wading River (P[illegible]outh).

1646, Jul. 21. He had a grant of a tract of land from the Dutch government of New York, now in Westchester County, N. Y. [illegible] called Cornell's Neck, and there was [illegible] concerning it in 1666, his daughter Sarah Bridges, claiming it from the will of her father said Thomas Cornell.

1653, Aug. 2. He was on a jury in case of Thomas Bradley, who found "that by extremity of heat the said Thomas was overcome, and so perished by himself in the wilderness."

1654. Commissioner.

1655. Freeman.

1657, Dec. 10. Rebecca Cornell was granted 10 acres, in lieu of 10 acres granted her husband.

1659, Aug. 15. Rebecca Cornell deeded to her son and daughter Kent (viz: Thomas Kent), above 10 acres.

1661, Apr. 30. Rebecca Cornell, widow and executrix of Thomas Cornell, sold Richard Hart for £30, two parcels of land containing 8 acres with house, fruit trees, &c.

1663, Oct. 25. She deeded land to son Joshua Cornell, at Dartmouth.

1663, Jul. 27. She deeded to eldest son Thomas Cornell, all her housing, orchard, land and fencing in Portsmouth.

1669. She deeded land to son Samuel, of Dartmouth.

1673, Feb. 8. The Friends' records state "Rebecca Cornell, widow, was killed strangely, at Portsmouth, in her own dwelling house, was twice viewed by the Coroner's Inquest, digged up and buried again by her husband's grave in their own land."

Her son Thomas was charged with her murder, but although the jury's verdict in regard to this affair was, that "he did murder his mother Rebecca, or was aiding or abetting thereto;" yet the evidence in the case would seem to have been in no way conclusive. There was much evidence taken. The son said in his own defence that having discoursed with his mother about an hour and a half he went into the next room and staid three-quarters of an hour. His wife then sent his son Edward to his grandmother to know whether she would have some milk boiled for her supper. The child saw some fire on the floor and came back and fetched the candle. Then Henry Straight, myself and the rest followed in a huddle. Henry Straight saw what he supposed was an Indian, drunk and burnt on the floor, but when Thomas Cornell perceived by the light of the candle who it was, he cried "Oh Lord it is my mother." Her clothes and body were much burned, and the jury found a wound on uppermost part of stomach.

John Briggs testified as to an apparition of a woman that appeared at his bedside in a dream, and he cried out "in the name of God what art thou," the apparition answered "I am your sister Cornell" and thrice said "see how I was burnt with fire."

John Russell, of Dartmouth, testified that George Soule told him (since the decease of Rebecca Cornell), that once coming to the house of Rebecca, in Portsmouth, she told him that in the spring she intended to go and dwell with her son Samuel, but she feared she would be made away with before that. Thomas, Stephen, Edward and John Cornell (sons of Thomas), gave testimony as to their grandmother's death, saying their father was last with her.

Mary Cornell, wife to John, aged twenty-eight years, testified that three or four years past being at her mother-in-law, Rebecca Cornell's, and meeting her on returning from the orchard to the house, she said to deponent that she had been running after pigs and being weak and no help and she being disregarded, she thought to have stabbed a penknife into her heart, that she had in her hand, and then she should be rid of her trouble, but it came to her mind "resist the Devil and he will flee from you" and then she said she was well satisfied. (By one account Thomas Cornell[1] is given two additional children, viz: William[2] and Ann[2]).

See: American Genealogist, v.19, p.132

CORNELL. 2d column. IX Samuel. 1686, Mar. 24. He took oath of fidelity. 1694. Nov. 13. He and others received a confirmatory deed of Dartmouth from William Bradford.

1673, Jul. [illegible] A writing was presented to the Court in Plymouth colony by William Earle, of Dartmouth, which was by some termed the will of Thomas Cornell of Rhode Island, late deceased, in which is mentioned the disposal of some estate in our colony. The court deferred accepting it for the present and appointed William Earle and John Cornell, brother of deceased, to take care of the estate that it be not squandered.

1673, Oct. 29. The court ordered that such part of estate as deceased left in Plymouth colony, should be divided as follows: To widow and three children he had by her one-half. To four eldest children of said Cornell, the other half, which they were to have in land, being sons. The right of widow Sarah, for life, in the lands, was to be paid her out of the personal, if she required it.

Inventory, £77, 19*s.* 6*d.*, of real and personal estate in Dartmouth, viz: 8 mares, 4 geldings, 2 two years, 3 colts, 4 heifers, 4 steers, 5 yearlings, house and land £41, gun, pair of old wheels, scythe, pair of bandoliers, &c.

1679, Jan. 4. Differences having arisen between Thomas Cornell, eldest son of Thomas Cornell, deceased, and David Lake of Nunaquaquit (a neck in New Plymouth), now husband to Sarah, late widow to Thomas Cornell, of Portsmouth, concerning right of dower belonging to said Sarah in estate of late husband, and more especially in farm said Thomas Cornell possesseth, the said differences being in a friendly manner compromised, a full discharge is now given by said Lake, except for a bill of £20.

II. SARAH, b. d.
m. (1) 1643, Sep. 1.
THOMAS WILLETT, b. d. of Willett.
m. (2) 1647, Nov. 3,
CHARLES BRIDGES, b. d. of Bridges.

1. William, 1644.
2. Thomas, 1645.

III. REBECCA, b. d.
m. 1647, Dec. 19.
GEORGE WOOLSEY, b. d. of Woolsey.

IV. ——— b. d.
m.
THOMAS KENT, b. d. of Kent.

1. Sarah,

V. RICHARD, b. d. 1694. Flushing, Rockaway, N. Y.
m.
ELIZABETH, b. d. 1694 + of

1. William,
2. Richard,
3. Thomas,
4. Jacob,
5. John,
6. Daughter,
7. Elizabeth,
8. Sarah,
9. Daughter,
10. Mary,

1666. He was in Flushing as early as this date, but subsequently received a grant at Rockaway. He held the office of Justice of the Peace, at Flushing.

1672, Jun. 21. He, of Cow Bay, N. Y., gave a receipt to Gershom Wodell, of Portsmouth, R. I., for all demands.

1673, Apr. 10. He was appointed by his sisters Sarah Bridges and Rebecca Woolsey, attorney to recover legacies specified by will of deceased mother.

1673, Apr. 20. He transferred his power of attorney to his brother-in-law William Earle, and brother John Cornell.

1693, Nov. 7. Will—proved 1694, Oct. 30. Exs. wife Elizabeth, and sons William and Richard. Overseers, friends, Colonel Thomas Willett, Lieutenant Colonel Thomas Hicks and Captain Daniel Whitehead. To children of John Washburne, deceased, all debts owed them. To son William, certain land at Rockaway after death of wife Elizabeth, and son William also to have dwelling house, orchard, tillage, garden, &c., but Elizabeth to retain these while widow. To son Thomas, certain land. To son Jacob, land. To daughter Elizabeth Lawrence, 10 acres. To daughter Mary Cornell, £100, one-third at eighteen or marriage and two-thirds yearly succeeding. To wife use of all land at Rockaway (except what is given William), the whole command of all my negroes, stock, and utensils of husbandry, except six cows and calves, and a plow share given William, and twelve two year heifers I give to my twelve grandchildren at age; that is to say to the children of my son Richard, my son Washburne, and my son John Lawrence. To daughter Sarah Arnold, two cows. To son William, at death of wife, negroes James and Diana. The lands in Cow Neck and Crab Meadow to be sold to value and divided to all my children. To five sons, undivided lands in Hempstead. To sons Richard, Thomas, Jacob and John, liberty to put horses on heather. To sons Thomas and William, liberty to put swine on beach. To children of deceased John Washburne and Captain Charles Lodwick, money in house.

VI. JOHN, b. d. Dartmouth, Mass., Hempstead, N. Y.
m.
MARY RUSSELL, b. 1645. d. of John & Dorothy ( ) Russell.

1. Richard,
2. Joshua,
3. Mary,
4. John,
5. Caleb,
6. Rebecca,

1673, Jul. 4. Dartmouth. He was one of those appointed by the court to take care of so much of his brother Thomas's estate as was in Dartmouth.

1676. Hempstead. In this year the government of New York sent a vessel eastward to rescue such settlers (driven off by the Indian war) as chose to come to New York and make settlement. In the autumn of this year John Cornell, wife, and five small children, came to the west side of Cow Neck, as shown by records of Hempstead, "having been driven from the east by the Indians." He undertook to build a house, but the Hempstead proprietors considered him an infringer on their rights, and appointed a committee to go and tear his house down. The matter was brought before the court by John Cornell, his brother Richard "being one of the bench." When it became known that John Cornell held a patent from the Governor he was not further molested, and the rioters were fined. His descendants still live on the property.

1689, May 10. Justice of the Peace.

He and his wife were buried on his farm at Sand's Point, part of which is still used for a family burial ground. It is assumed that his wife, who was known to have been Mary Russell, could have been none other than the daughter of John and Dorothy Russell (though the will of John Russell mentions only sons).

VII. JOSHUA, b. d. Dartmouth, Mass.

VIII. ELIZABETH b. d. 1708 +
m. 1661, Jul. 9.
CHRISTOPHER ALMY, b. 1632. d. 1713, Jan. 30. of William & Audry ( ) Almy.

1. Sarah, 1662, Apr. 17.
2. Elizabeth, 1663, Sep. 29.
3. William, 1665, Oct. 27.
4. Ann, 1667, Nov. 29.
5. Christopher, 1669, Dec. 26.
6. Rebecca, 1671, Jan. 26.
7. John, 1673, Apr.
8. Job, 1675, Oct. 10.
9. Child, 1676.

IX. SAMUEL, b. d. Dartmouth, Mass.
m.
DEBORAH, b. d. of

1. Stephen,

CORNELL. 2d column. IX. Samuel. He was perhaps identical with Samuel[3] (Thos.[2] Thos.[1]).

See: American Genealogist, v.19, p.132.

CORP. 2d column. I. John, m. 1711, Oct. 18, Patience Gorton. Perhaps widow of John Gorton,[3] (John,[2] Samuel.[1]) III. Mary, m. 1711, Jan. 23, Samuel Bates.

JOHN, m. DELIVERANCE, — JOHN: b. ; d. 1691, Nov. 1. DELIVERANCE: b. ; d.

(She m. (2) John Gereardy.)

Bristol, R. I.

1689, Nov. 18. He was chosen "Pound keeper and digger of graves, likewise he is chosen sweeper of meeting house, and ringer of the bell, and the Selectmen are to agree with him by the year."

1692, Jan. 18. Voted "that widow Corps shall have three pounds for this year, it being for ringing the bell for Sabbath days and Town meetings, and also for sweeping the meeting house; the year beginning Nov. 18th, 1691."

1702, Mar. 12. Inventory of his real estate was rendered at this date. £95, viz: house and land adjoining, 2 acres, and orchard £45, 10 acre lot £40, commonage £5.

1702, Apr. 13. The lands, having been sold for £95, an agreement was made by his widow, now wife to John Gereardy, of Warwick, R. I., with her oldest son, John Corp, whereby she was to have 35s., for life, for her part, and she to receive now £7, as her due for four years next to come.

I. JOHN, m. PATIENCE, — JOHN: b. 1680; d. 1757. PATIENCE: b. ; d. — of — Warwick, R. I.

1702, Mar. 13. He, eldest son of deceased John Corp, prays that he may dispose of real estate and distribute same, having the leave of his father-in-law (*i. e.* step-father), John Gereardy, and of his mother, Deliverance.

1716. Freeman.

1738, May 23. He, living at this time at Providence, and wife Patience, deeded to son John Corp, of East Greenwich, for £120, a house and 16 acres in Mashantatack.

1757, Sep. 27. Inventory, £529, 15*s.*, set forth by Thomas Corp; wearing apparel £80, cash £44, 7*s.*, pewter, 2 wheels, books £12, warming pan, andirons, 7 cheeses, great chair, pair of scales, small shop £2, 10*s.*, &c.

Children: 1. John, 2. Abner, 3 Mercy, 4. Rebecca, 5. Thomas, 1714, Jul. 21.

II. HOPE, m. —— RHODES, — HOPE: b. 1681, Nov. 8; d. 1765. RHODES: b. ; d. 1762 (—) — of Jeremiah & Madeline (Hawkins) Rhodes. — Providence, Cranston, R. I.

He was the first English child born in Bristol, as the town records declare.

1703, Jan. 16. He bought of Zachariah Jones, of Providence, 25 acres in Mashantatack, for £19, 17*s.*

1714, Feb. 15. He sold Joshua Winsor, a right of common, for £8, 10*s.*

1730, Aug. 22. He deeded son John, for love, &c., 60 acres.

1735, Jun. 7. He deeded son Jeremiah, for love, &c., 8 acres in Pawtuxet, part of homestead.

1736, Feb. 14. He deeded son William, for love, &c., 8 acres, part of homestead.

1736, May 29. He deeded son Joseph, single man, 8 acres. (He afterwards married, and died before his father, as did Jeremiah.)

1762, Dec. 4. Will—proved 1765, Sep. 30. Exx. daughter Phebe Pike. To daughter Phebe, after payment of debts, my dwelling house and all my household goods, an acre of land adjoining, and half my orchard in said acre. To son William, and his two sons born of second wife, £50 each. To son-in-law John King's three sons, £50 each, and to his two daughters, £25 each. To grandson William Corp, 2 acres. To son John, for life, half of rest of farm, and at said son's death, to return to my daughter, Phebe Pike and heirs, to whom the other half is bequeathed, but if son John outlive Phebe, then all estate given her is to go to grandson William Corp.

Inventory, £392, 12*s.*, viz: wearing apparel, 3 feather beds, warming pan, pewter, linen wheel, loom, mare, &c.

Children: 1. John, 2. Jeremiah, 3. William, 4. Joseph, 5. Daughter, 6. Phebe,

III. MARY, — b. 1685, Nov. 2. d.

IV. ELIZABETH, — b. 1688, Mar. 14. d.

V. SARAH, — b. 1690, Nov. 30. d.

CORY.

WILLIAM, m. MARY EARLE, — WILLIAM: b. ; d. 1682. MARY: b. ; d. 1718, Mar. 22.

of Ralph & Joan (   ) Earle.

(She m. (2) 1683 ± Joseph Timberlake.)

Portsmouth, R. I.

He was a house carpenter and miller.

1657, Dec. 10. He had a grant of 8 acres.

1658, May 18. Freeman.

1662, Oct. 28. He let or hired out his now dwelling house, with land fenced, to Peter Folger, of Newport, for five years, the latter agreeing to clear yearly, 2 acres of swamp in farm described, cutting out said 2 acres and sowing three pounds of clear hay seed upon every 2 acres; and Peter Folger also to get out 250 rails by next spring, and at end of term, William Cory to pay worth of fencing.

1669, Dec. 4. He had a deed of a third of a share in Dartmouth, from William Earle

1671, Jan. 7. Juryman.

1676, Apr. 4. He and three others, were appointed to have the care and disposing of one barrel of powder for the town, and the two great guns that now are in the yard of the late deceased Mr. William Brenton, were to be carried to Portsmouth, and placed one on Ferry Neck and one near house of John Borden, the above committee causing said guns to be set on carriages and fitted for service, &c.

1676, Aug. 24. He was a member of the Court Martial, held at Newport, for the trial of certain Indians.

1678–79–80. Deputy.

He held the offices of Lieutenant and Captain, successively.

1681, Jan. 4. Will—proved 1682, Feb. 24. Exx. wife Mary. Overseers, friends William Wodell, John Sanford and George Brownell. To wife, absolutely at her disposal, all lands, &c., with my wind-mill at Portsmouth, and all personal estate, whatsoever and wheresoever, except legacies. To her, for life, use of dwelling house in which I dwell (except two rooms to son William), half the orchard, half the barn and use of half of all the upland and meadows adjoining land belonging to deceased William Hall. To eldest son John, certain land in Portsmouth, with housing, &c., for life, and to such children as he may will it to, but if John have no issue, he may dispose of it to his brothers and sisters

I. JOHN, m. ELIZABETH, — JOHN: b. ; d. 1712. ELIZABETH: b. ; d. 1713 + — of — Portsmouth, Kings Town, R. I.

1679, May 7. On his petition, he was granted by Assembly, land in East Greenwich, out of shares not taken up.

1686. Freeman.

1686, Mar. 22. He, of Portsmouth, had 10 acres of land laid out to him in East Greenwich.

1705, Apr. 4. He bought of Daniel Thurston, and wife Mary, of Newport, 90 acres in East Greenwich, for £40.

1705, Apr. 10. He and wife Elizabeth, sold Jonathan Nichols, of Newport, 12 acres, for £90.

1705, Apr. 16. He and wife Elizabeth, sold to William Brightman, of Newport, 50 acres, for £350.

1707, Oct. 4. He deeded son William, for love, &c., 90 acres, house and meadow, at East Greenwich. (Both he and son were of Portsmouth, at this date.

1707. Kings Town. Deputy.

1712, May 12. Will—proved 1712, Jul. 14. Exx. wife Elizabeth. To wife, certain land and all personal. To son John, house and land, he paying certain legacies. The rest of will illegible or destroyed.

Inventory, wearing apparel, beds, loom, 2 pair of worsted combs, spinning wheel, &c.

1713, Jun. 26. Widow Elizabeth, of Kings Town, sold John Mumford, of Newport, 91 acres in East Greenwich, for £16.

1713, Dec 15. His son Thomas, with consent of mother Elizabeth, put himself apprentice to Christopher Lindsay, of Newport, house carpenter, for the term of four years, eight months and seventeen days.

Children: 1. William, 2. John, 3. Elisha, 4. Joseph, 5. Thomas,

II. WILLIAM, m. MARTHA COOK, — WILLIAM: b. ; d. 1704. MARTHA: b. ; d. 1704 (—) — of John & Mary (Borden) Cook. — Portsmouth, R. I.

1684. Freeman.

1687. Grand Jury.

1695, Jul. 2. He was appointed by Assembly, on committee to propose a method of making a rate.

1695–96. Deputy.

1704, May 14. Will—proved 1704, Jun. 4. Exs. honored mother and my brother-in-law, Joseph Cook. To son Michael, 12 acres, at age, and if he die without issue, to son Thomas. To second son William, all other lands, housing and orchard to me belonging, except 15 acres. To third son Thomas, 5 acres. To son Michael, 10 acres. To daughter Patience Cory, £5, paid by her brother William, a cow and a feather bed. To daughter Mary Cory, a cow. To daughter Amey Cory, a cow, and a bed in room called Margaret's room. To daughter Sarah Cory, £5 and a bed. To four daughters, the rest of movables, when they are eighteen or married.

Children: 1. Michael, 1688, Apr. 21. 2. William, 3. Thomas, 4. Patience, 5. Mary, 6. Amey, 7. Sarah,

III. MERCY, m. (1) CORNELIUS JONES, m. (2) 1704, Nov. 17, CHARLES GONSALES, — MERCY: b. ; d. CORNELIUS JONES: b. ; d. — of — Jones. CHARLES GONSALES: b. ; d. — of — Gonsales.

COREY. 2d column. III. Mercy. Children, 1. Cornelius, 1693, Nov. 1. 2, Ichabod, 1695, Nov. 1, (besides the one by 2d husband).

Children: 1. Charles, 1705, Jun. 15.

of the whole blood. To son William, great lower room of southerly part of dwelling house, which now at this time I inhabit, with the leanto room adjoining, commonly called Margaret's room, half of orchard, profits of half upland and meadow adjoining, and at decease of my wife, his mother, he to have all the rest of lands and house for life, and to his children, if he have any, &c. To third son Thomas, at twenty-one, a half share in Pocasset lands divided and undivided (a share being one-thirtieth part). To fourth son Caleb, at age, a third of a share in Dartmouth, for life, &c. To fifth son Roger, at age, the other half of share in Pocasset land, and if he die without issue, his part to go to his brother Thomas. To eldest daughter Mercy, £10. To second daughter Ann, at eighteen or marriage, £10. To third daughter Mary, £10. To fourth daughter Joan, £10. The children were left to wife's care, to be tenderly brought up and educated.

1682, Jan. 15. His widow took receipt from eldest daughter, Mercy Cory, for legacy, and the year following, took receipt from Robert Bennett, and his wife Ann, daughter of said widow Cory.

1691, Jun. 23. His widow received a writing from Joseph Timberlake, of Little Compton, previous to their marriage. She was to have after marriage, full liberty to improve and dispose of all her former husband's estate, and she gave full power of her estate to Edward Mory and George Brownell, for bringing up of her children, reserving only to myself a mare, four neat cattle, four hogs and four sheep.

1717, Aug. 12. Will — proved 1718, Apr. 14. Widow Mary Timberlake. Ex. son Thomas Cory. To grandson William Cory, son of John, a piece of milled money of value of 5 or 6*s*. To daughter Mercy Gonsales, a piece of money. To son-in-law Charles Gonsales, five cords of wood he owes me. To daughter Sarah Jeffries, an Indian girl's term named Dinah. To grandsons Michael and William Cory, brothers, each a piece of money. To two granddaughters Anne and Mary Bennett, daughters of my daughter Anne Bennett, each a piece of milled gold. To daughter Jane Taylor, use of cupboard and chest, for life, and then to my grandson Samuel Chaplin. To daughter Mary Cook, a quarter of apparel, and like legacy to daughters Jane Taylor and Sarah Jeffries. Whereas, son Thomas Cory, has money I lent him, £29, 9*s*. and £6 remitted him in behalf of my son-in-law Thomas Jeffries, which sums I lent my son-in-law Thomas Jeffries, and £6 I lent my son-in-law Thomas Cook, and £5 I lent my son Roger Cory—these sums are all to be included in rest of movable estate, and the same equally divided with the other quarter of apparel, as follows: to children of daughter Mercy, one-sixth, (with the quarter of apparel,) to daughter Mary Cook, sons Thomas and Roger Cory, and daughters Jane Taylor and Sarah Jeffries, each a sixth.

Inventory, £167, 9*s*. 11*d*.

IV. ANNE, { b. / d.
m.
ROBERT BENNETT, { b. 1650, Mar. / d. 1722. of Robert & Rebecca (   ) Bennett.

1. Caleb,
2. Robert,
3. Joseph,
4. John,
5. Anne,
6. William,
7. Mary,
8. Job,
9. Jonathan,

V. THOMAS, { b. / d. 1738. Tiverton, R. I.
m. (1)
——— { b. / d. of
m. (2) 1732, Feb. 24,
SUSANNA TABER, { b. / d. 1734 + of Taber.

1. William,
2. Thomas,
3. Philip,
4. Patience,
5. Mary,
6. Sarah,

1692, Mar. 2. He was an inhabitant at organization of the town.

1734, Sep. 23. Will—proved 1738, Mar. 21. Exs. sons William & Philip. To eldest son William, half of 120 acres in Pocasset, half of swamp lot and half of 60 acre lot, supposed to have been given him by his grandfather's entail, which I confirm, also other land. To grandson Thomas Cory, son of Thomas, of Dartmouth, deceased, 200 acres and housing, being homestead farm where my son Thomas lived, in Dartmouth, also 40 acres joining my brother-in-law Philip Taber's, all to be his at age. To son Philip, homestead farm where I now live, in Tiverton, 120 acres and housing, two cows, and all young cattle already in his hands, and half the sheep and profit of house and land given grandson John, till said grandson is of age, and Philip to bring John up to learning, till sixteen, and then put him to a trade. To daughter Patience Cory, £250 in household goods, in consideration of what my other two daughters have already had, and of her present weakness, and also Indian boy Sam and Indian girl Dinah, till their time is out. To daughter Mary Durfee, wife of Thomas, £600. To daughter Sarah Brown, wife of Abraham, £600. To daughter Patience Cory, £600. To wife Susanna, £100, and if she happen to have a child or children, he or they to have lands in Tiverton and Dartmouth not given. To son Philip, cart, plow, &c. To all children, rest of personal. To daughter Patience, house room, firewood and keep of cow, &c, till marriage, and riding beast, all kept by son Philip. Inventory, £4,862, 15*s*. 6*d*., viz: house, apparel and books £41, 3*s*. 6*d*., pewter, 6 silver spoons, cheesepress, bonds £2,955, 4*s*. 2*d*., neat cattle £129, horsekind £26, sheep £30, 397 acres wild land in sundry places £1,165, 10*s*.

VI. MARGARET, { b. / d. young.

VII. MARY, { b. / d. 1726 +
m.
THOMAS COOK, { b. / d. 1726. of John & Mary (Borden) Cook.

1. Stephen,
2. Joseph,
3. Chaplin,
4. Deborah,
5. Mary,
6. Amey,

VIII. CALEB, { b. / d. 1704. Dartmouth, Mass
m.
SARAH, { b. / d. 1704 + of

1. Caleb,

1704, Apr. 19. Inventory, £212, 11*s*. 4*d*., shown by widow Sarah, administratrix. House and land £140, wearing clothes, loom, 2 wheels, cards, gun, pewter, money £1, 4*d*., 18 sheep, 6 swine, 6 cows, 4 heifers, steer, 2 yearlings, mare, colt, &c.

IX. ROGER, { b. / d. 1754. Tiverton, Richmond, R. I.
m. (1)
——— { b. / d. of
m. (2) 1718, May 1, [Jno.
REMEMBRANCE DYE, (w.of { b. / d. 1754 + of

1. William,
2. Caleb, 1699, Dec. 25.
3. Roger,
4. Thomas,
5. Patience,
6. Deliverance,

(2d wife.)

7. Samuel, 1720, Feb. 14.
8. Sarah, 1722, May 8.
9. Rosanna, 1723, Oct. 26.
10. John, 1727, Mar. 13.
11. Content,

1722, May 7. Remembrance Cory, administratrix of late husband, John Dye, of Little Compton, rendered account of her disbursements on his estate.

1753, Jan. 6. Will—proved 1754, Jun. 3. Exs. wife Remembrance and son Thomas. To eldest son William, of Tiverton, 5*s*., and all my lands in Tiverton, for life, and then to my daughters Patience, Deliverance, Sarah, Rosanna and Content, the last having a double share, and to live with son William for life. To second son Caleb, of Tiverton, 5*s*., and like amount to third son Roger, and fourth son Thomas, of Tiverton, and fifth son Samuel, of Richmond. To wife Remembrance, all movable estate.

Inventory, £302, 19*s*., viz: wearing apparel £26, 15*s*., pewter, feather bed, 2 old wheels, warming pan, cow, calf, &c., bonds £59, 6*s*. 6*d*.

X. JOAN, { b. / d.
m.
——— TAYLOR, { b. / d. of Taylor.

COTTRELL.

NICHOLAS, { b. / d.
m.
——— { b. / d.

Newport, Westerly, R. I.

1638, May 20. His name was in a list of inhabitants of those admitted since this date.

1655. Freeman.

1661, Mar. 22. He signed certain articles about Misquamicut (Westerly) lands.

1669, May 18. Westerly. Freeman.

1670. Deputy.

1671, May 8. He and another stood bound in sum of £100, for appearance of Eleanor Boomer, wife of Matthew, at next court.

1675, Oct. 27. He and James Thomas, having forfeited their bond, and having petitioned the Assembly, they were to be released, paying 10*s*., apiece, and to bring in the wife of James Thomas, before the Court of Trials in May, 1676, for her to abide the sentence of court.

I. NICHOLAS, { b. / d. 1716. Westerly, R. I.
m.
DOROTHY PENDLETON, { b. / d. 1747 + of James & Hannah (Goodenow) Pendleton.

1. Nicholas,
2. Nathaniel,
3. Samuel,
4. Mary,
5. Dorothy,

He probably had an earlier wife than Dorothy.

1668, Oct. 29. Freeman. He was called at this time Nicholas Cottrell, Jr.

1679, Sep. 17. He took oath of allegiance.

1681, Jun. 8. He bought 200 acres for £30, of Philip Smith and Mary, of Newport, said Philip Smith, being son of Edward, deceased.

1688. Constable.

1696. Deputy.

1709, Jul. 24. Dorothy Cottrell was admitted to the church at Stonington.

1711, Oct. 2. He and thirty-three others bought 5,300 acres of the vacant lands in Narragansett ordered sold by the Assembly.

1716, Jan. 11. Inventory, £114, 8*s*., viz: 2 steers, 6 cows, 2 heifers, 2 two years, 5 yearlings, 4 calves, mare, 2 fat swine, 3 small swine, 33 sheep, money £10, 5*s*., 2 books 4*s*., warming pan, 15 loads of hay, &c. He having died intestate the Town Council appointed his son Nicholas, executor, said Cottrell leaving at his decease five children. To said son Nicholas, possession of land was given, and the movable estate to go to the five children equally.

1747, Apr. 23. His widow, Dorothy, signed a receipt at this date for legacy, from her brother Caleb Pendleton's will.

II. GERSHOM, { b. / d. 1711. Westerly, Kings Town, R. I.
m.
BETHIAH. { b. / d. 1711 + of

1. Stephen,
2. Gershom,
3. Daughter,
4. Mercy,
5. Sarah,
6. Rachel,
7. Elizabeth,
8. Susanna,
9. Judith,
10. Mary,

1679, Sep. 17. He took oath of allegiance.

1693, Feb. 23. He sold a quarter share of land, 100 acres, housing, &c., at Westerly, to William Champlin, for £95.

1711, Dec. 17. Inventory, £28, 15*s*., shown by widow Bethiah and son Stephen, one cow, calf, 3 yearlings, a two year old, 4 swine, 2 mares, colt, 8 sheep, fat hog, pair of cards, 2 wheels, &c.

[CO]TTRELL. 1st column. Nicholas. d. 1680. His 2d wife, Martha, b. 1644, d. 1680+. 1680, Feb., will-proved. He mentions wife, Martha. Children, Jabez, Nicholas, John, Gershom, Eliza, James, Mary, Hannah; grandchildren Hannah Crouse, and Nicholas Osborne. Exr. son Jabez. Sons John and Gershom were at Westerly. Widow Martha, aged 36, testified that she had her part from son-in-law (i. e. step-son) Jabez Cottrell. At time the will was made testator was living at Taunton River. 2d column. II. Gershom. He also had a son John.

COTTRELL. 2d column. I. Nicholas, d. 1715. **Erase his wife's name, death and parentage, and line following. Children, 1. Nicholas, 2. John. 3. Elizabeth. 4. Mary. 5. Dorothy.** He served in the **Narragansett war.** 1715, **Dec. 26, was date of inventory.** Receipts **were given to his son Nicholas, as follows: 1716, Jan. 11, brother John, for land; 1719, Jan. 5, sister Elizabeth (with husband, Samuel Cottrell), £30; 1721, Apr. 4, sister Dorothy (with husband, Edward Larkin), £30; 1723, Apr. 17, sister Mary (with husband, Samuel Cottrell), £30. Erase** lines **commencing 1709, Jul. 24, and 1747, Apr. 23. II. Gershom, m.** 1678, Feb. 13, Bethiah Wilcox.

1719, Aug. 3. Mary Cottrell, daughter to Gershom, deceased, made choice of Job Babcock, to be guardian for her in estate of her brother Gershom, deceased. Personally appeared Thomas Utter, on behalf of his wife, Mercy Crowder, Sarah Money, Rachel, Elizabeth, Susanna, Judith and Mary Cottrell, and all desired that Mr. Job Babcock, might have administration on estate of their brother Gershom, their brother Stephen refusing to administer.

1719, Sep. 14. Administration was now taken by Stephen Cottrell, on his brother Gershom's estate, having consented to act upon consideration.

III. JOHN, { b. ; d. 1721.
m.
ELIZABETH, { b. ; d. — of — Kings Town, R. I.

1. Hannah, 1679.
2. John,
3. Samuel, 1687.
4. Daughter,

1687, Sep. 6. Taxed 3*s*. 7½*d*.

1721. Will—proved. Exs. son John and wife Elizabeth. Overseer, cousin (*i. e.* nephew) Nicholas Cottrell, of Westerly. To wife, Elizabeth, a third of movables. To daughter-in-law Elizabeth ——, a feather bed, mare and chair. To two daughters, rest of movables, viz: to —— and Hannah Cottrell. To son John, other estate.

Inventory, £166, 15*s*.

IV. JABESH, { b. ; d. — Newport, R. I.
m.
ANN PEABODY, { b. ; d. — of John Peabody.

1678, Oct. 23. There was an indictment against him in court.

COVEY.

HOPE, { b. ; d. 1705.
m.
MARY, { b. ; d. 1704 +

Newport, Westerly, R. I.

1680, Apr. 2. He arrived at Newport from Virginia at this date in the company of twenty-five others, five of them being baptized (including himself), as noted in a letter written by Rev. Samuel Hubbard, of Newport, to Isaac Wells, in Jamaica (dated 1681, May 14).

1704, Nov. 8. Will—proved 1705, Feb. 19. Exx. wife Mary. To son James, all lands and housing except what is after mentioned. To wife, all movables till son is of age, and then half to him and the rest to remain to wife, while widow. To daughter Mary Covey, 8*s*. To daughter Rachel Covey, 20*s*. At death of wife what personal remains, to be divided equally to James and Rachel, except a bed and iron pot which wife may give to whoever of the children she will.

Inventory, £68, 14*s*. 6*d*., viz: 10 cattle kind £12, 6*s*., 3 horsekind £4, 10*s*., 11 sheep, 12 swine, 4 beds, warming pan, gun, spinning wheel, cards, 4 barrels cider, wearing clothes £3, carpenter and other tools £3, &c.

I. JAMES, { b. 1687, Mar. 1. ; d. — Westerly, R. I.
m. 1707, Mar. 21,
SARAH LANPHERE, { b. ; d. — of George Lanphere.

1. Sarah, 1708, Jan. 11.
2. Mary, 1709, Sep. 3.
3. Hope, 1712, Sep. 15.
4. James, 1715, Jun. 24.
5. John, 1717, Mar. 16.
6. Joseph, 1719, May 16.
7. Samuel, 1721, Oct. 15.
8. Elisha, 1724, Mar. 7.
9. Elizabeth, 1726, Mar. 2.

II. MARY, { b. ; d.

III. RACHEL, { b. ; d. 1760.
m. 1708, Jan. 22,
THEODOSIUS LANPHERE, { b. ; d. 1749. — of George Lanphere.

1. Theodosius, 1709, Jan. 31.
2. James, 1710, Nov. 22.
3. Joshua, 1712, Nov. 23.
4. Abigail, 1715, Mar. 27.
5. Susanna, 1716, Dec. 14.
6. Nathaniel, 1718, Mar. 22.
7. Mary, 1721, Dec. 14.
8. Samuel, 1723, Dec. 23.
9. Stephen, 1726, Feb. 5.
10. Jabez, 1731, Mar. 25.
11. Joseph, 1736, Sep. 20.

See American Genealogist, v. 20, p. 112. v. 21, p. 207.

COWLAND.

RALPH, { b. ; d. 1679 +
m. (1)
ALICE SHOTTEN, (w. of Samson) { b. ; d. 1666, Aug.
m. (2) 1677, Jun. 25,
JOAN HIDE, { b. ; d. 1679, Nov. 15. — of — Hide.

Portsmouth, R. I.

1640, Aug. 6. Freeman.

1641, Mar. 16. Freeman.

1642. Sargent Senior.

1655. Freeman.

1659, Oct. 13. His wife Alice sympathized with the Quakers, and was apprehended at Boston where she "came to bring linen wherein to wrap the dead bodies of those who were to suffer."

1664, Nov. His wife Alice made her will, giving land to her daughter Rachel Shotten.

CRANDALL.

JOHN, { b. ; d. 1676
m. (1)
——, { b. ; d. 1670, Aug.
m. (2)
HANNAH, { b. ; d. 1678 +

Newport, Westerly, R. I.

He was early associated with the Baptists, at Newport, subsequently becoming the first elder of that denomination at Westerly.

1651, Jul. 21. He, with John Clarke and Obadiah Holmes, "being the representatives of the church in Newport, upon the request of William Witter, of Lynn, arrived there, he being a brother in the church, who by reason of his advanced age, could not undertake so great a journey as to visit the church." While Mr. Clarke was preaching, the constable came into the house and apprehended them, and the next morning they were sent to prison in Boston.

1651, Jul. 31. He was sentenced to pay a fine of £5, or be publicly whipped. He was released from prison upon his promise of appearing at next court.

I. JOHN, { b. ; d. 1704. — Newport, Kings Town, R. I.
m. 1672, Jun. 18,
ELIZABETH GORTON, { b. ; d. 1704 + — of Samuel & Elizabeth (   ) Gorton.

1. John.
2. Peter.
3. Samuel,
4. Elizabeth,
5. Mary,

He was a blacksmith.

1671. Freeman.

1678, May 13. He (calling himself son and heir of John Crandall, of Newport, deceased), for natural love to two beloved brothers, Jeremiah and Eber Crandall, now resident at Newport, and in tuition of their mother, Hannah Crandall, confirmed unto them a certain house, formerly the mansion house of my father, John Crandall, together with 200 acres thereto belonging, lying and being in Westerly, with garden, orchards, &c.

1682, Dec. 12. He sold to George Lawton, Jr., of Freemen's lands, New Plymouth, certain land in Narragansett, for 40*s*.

1704, Jan. 25. Will—proved 1704, Aug. 14. Exx. wife Elizabeth. Overseers, brother Peter Crandall, friend Job Babcock and son-in-law Stephen Wilcox. To son John, 5*s*., he having had already. To son Peter, westernmost part of farm I now dwell on. To son Samuel, rest of land and housing. To daughter Elizabeth Wilcox, 5*s*. To daughter Mary Phillips, 5*s*. To wife Elizabeth, all movables, and whole use of all lands, till sons Peter and Samuel are of age.

Inventory, £62, 9*s*. 6*d*., viz: pair of steers, 3 cows, 3 two years, heifer, calf, 2 horses, 6 swine, pewter, brass, carpenter's tools, beds, warming pan, stillyards, &c.

II. JAMES, { b. ; d. — Westerly, R. I.

1655. Freeman.

1658–59–62–63. Commissioner.

1661, Aug. [illegible] He and eight others signed a letter to [illegible] Commissioners, of R. I., concerning [illegible] land at Westerly, that they and others desired approbation and assistance of Rhode Island, in settling upon.

1661, Sep. 9. He had half a share at Westerly assigned him.

1667. Deputy.

1667, Oct. 17. Westerly. He was complained of in a letter from Connecticut to Rhode Island authorities, for having come on west side of Pawcatuck River and laid out about a mile square of land to his son.

1669, May 14. He and Joseph Torrey, were appointed commissioners to treat with Connecticut, relative to jurisdiction of lands. The sum of 35*s*. was lent to the colony of Rhode Island by individuals, for John Crandall's voyage to Connecticut.

1669, May 18. His name was in the list of inhabitants.

1669, Nov. 18. A letter was sent him by Governor and Assistants of Connecticut, complaining that he and others had appropriated a great parcel of Stonington township, and seeking for satisfaction.

1670, Mar. 11. He and Tobias Saunders, answered on behalf of Westerly, denying any guilt in matter complained of; "but we are very sensible of great wrongs that we have sustained by them for several years." The letter closes: "As for your advice, to agree with those, our neighbors of Stonington and the other gentlemen, we hope that your colony and ours, will, in the first place lovingly agree, and then we question not but there will be an agreement between us and our neighbors of Stonington, and the rest of the gentlemen."

1670, Jun. 19. He, as Conservator of the Peace, of Westerly, wrote a letter a little prior to this date, to the Governor of Rhode Island, informing him of an entrance made into our jurisdiction by some of Connecticut, and of their carrying away some inhabitants prisoners.

1670, Aug. 2. His first wife was buried.

1670, Oct. 3. He deeded son John, of Newport, for love, &c., all my goods, chattels, debts, household utensils and all other personal estate, movable or immovable, quick or dead—putting him in quiet and peaceable possession by payment of 1*s*. in silver, by his son.

1670–71. Deputy (from Westerly.)

1671, Jan. 30. Bills were allowed by Assembly, for hire of a boat to go to Narragansett with Mr. John Crandall, Sr., in the year 1670, and for hire of Sarah Reape's horse, for use of Mr. John Crandall, to go to Hartford.

1671, May 2. He, having been "as is asserted" apprehended and now is in durance, by the Colony of Connecticut, and having desired the advice of the Governor, &c., of Rhode Island, whether to give bond or abide imprisonment, the Assembly advise him to give no bond, and that if he be forced to imprisonment, the colony will bear his charges, and endeavour to justify his actings therein.

1671, May 6. He was allowed 20*s*., to bear his charge to Connecticut.

1675, Jan. 23. In a letter from Ruth Burdick, of Westerly, to her father Samuel Hubbard, of Newport, she says: "Brother Crandall hath the ague and fever still, and have been but little amongst us this winter, sister Crandall is brought to bed with a son, and is in a hopeful way."

He died at Newport, having moved there on account of the Indian war.

1676, Nov. 29. His death is alluded to in a letter from Samuel Hubbard, who also wrote a few years later: "My dear brother, John Crandall, of Squamicut, is dead and his first wife, a sabbath keeper, the first that died in that blessed faith in New England."

His second wife may have been Hannah Gaylord, b. 1647, Jan. 30, daughter of William and Ann (Porter) Gaylord, of Windsor, Conn. (The said Hannah married a Crandall as is shown by the settlement of her brother Hezekiah Gaylord's estate in 1677.)

1679, Sep. 17. He took oath of allegiance.

CRANDALL. 2d column. IV. Sarah, m. (2) Peter Button. (In May, 1689, Ebenezer and John Witter gave receipt to father-in-law, (i. e. step-father) Peter Button and mother Sarah Button, for estate of their father Josiah Witter.) VI. Joseph. Had a 2d wife, Elizabeth, in 1717. VIII. Jeremiah. Births of part of his children. 1. Jeremiah, 1702, June 25. 3. John, 1704, Oct. 1. 5. James, 1706, Sep. 4. 7. Experience, 1709, Dec. 28. 9. Susanna, 1715, Mar. 11. 10. Mary, 1717, May 13. IX. Eber. His son Nathaniel, born 1718, Feb. 28.

III. JANE, b. ; d. 1715 (—).
m.
JOB BABCOCK, b. ; d. 1718. of James & Sarah ( ) Babcock.

1. Job,
2. John,
3. Benjamin,
4. Jane,
5. Sarah,
6. Mary,
7. Elizabeth,
8. Hannah,
9 Mercy,

IV. SARAH, b. ; d.
m.
JOSIAH WITTER, b. ; d. of William & Annis ( ) Witter.

1. John, 1677, Mar. 11.
2. Sarah, 1679, Feb. 7.
3. Hannah, 1681, Mar. 17.

V. PETER, b. ; d. 1734. Westerly, R. I.
m.
MARY, b. ; d. 1734 + of

1. Daughter,
2. Peter,

1679, May 17. He took oath of allegiance.

1681. Freeman.

1692, Mar. 9. He deeded son-in-law George Brown, about 20 acres and house, &c., (that he had bought of Job Babcock), reserving to own use for life, mowing grass and orchard.

1699–1700–1–3–4. Deputy.

1700, Oct. 14. He was chosen Moderator of Town Meeting.

1702, Oct. 23. He was chosen Town Sealer.

1703–8. Justice of the Peace. He was Lieutenant for some years.

1711, Oct. 2. He and thirty-three others, bought 5,300 acres of the vacant lands in Narragansett.

1715, Mar. 14. He sold his brother Joseph, of Kings Town, 30 acres in Westerly.

1734, Jul. 29. Administration to widow Mary. Inventory, £123, 13*s*. 2*d*., viz: silver buttons, buckles, seal, wearing apparel and money £8, 18*s*. 2*d*., beds, spinning wheel, cards, warming pan, gun, mare, cow, 5 swine, 6 hives bees, &c.

VI. JOSEPH, b. ; d. 1737, Sep. 12. Newport, Westerly, Kings Town, Newport, R. I.
m.
DEBORAH BURDICK, b. ; d. of Robert & Ruth (Hubbard) Burdick.

1. John,
2. Joseph,
3 Daughter,

1685, Apr. 11. His wife was baptized by Rev. William Hiscox.

1704, Apr. 20. Westerly. He was chosen Town Councilman, but refused to serve.

1709. He had a daughter baptized (wife of Nathaniel Wells).

1712. Kings Town. He moved thence this year.

1713, Mar. 24. He deeded 100 acres in Westerly, to son John, of that town.

1715, May 8. Newport. He was called to pastorate of Seventh Day Baptist Church, being colleague with William Gibson, till latter's death (1717). The charge was given by Elder Gibson, from 1st Epistle Peter, 5th chapter.

CRANDALL. 2d column. VI. Joseph. Children, 1. John. 2. Joseph. 3. Mary (m. Nathaniel Wells). 4. Deborah (m. 1706, Apr. 13, George Stillman). 5. Tacy (m. 1717, Mar. 3, John Lewis, son of James). 6. Jane (m. 1718, Dec. 8, Cyrus Richmond). IX. Eber. Erase his 3d wife's parentage.

VII. SAMUEL, b. 1663; d. 1736, May 19. Newport, Little Compton, R. I.
m.
SARAH, b. 1666; d. 1758, Aug. 3. of

1. Samuel, 1686, Oct. 30.
2. Mary, 1689, May 17.
3. Jane, 1692, Aug. 23.
4. John, 1695, Jan. 11.
5. Peter, 1697, Oct. 25.
6 Joseph, 1701, Nov. 28.
7. Thomas, 1707, Jul. 27.

(2d WIFE.)

VIII. JEREMIAH, b. ; d. 1718. Newport, Westerly, R. I.
m.
PRISCILLA WARNER, b. ; d. 1750, Feb. 24. of John & Ann (Gorton) Warner.
(She m. (2) Abraham Lockwood.)

1. Jeremiah,
2. Ann,
3. John,
4. Hannah,
5. James,
6. Sarah,
7. Experience,
8. Patience,
9. Susanna,
10. Mary,

1696, Aug. 31. Westerly. He bought 100 acres and housing of John Crandall, Jr., of Kings Town.

1704, May 24. He had ear mark for sheep granted.

1709, Jun. 28. He and twenty-six others bought tract called Shannock Purchase, being part of the vacant lands in Narragansett.

1712, Jul. 18. He and wife Priscilla, gave receipt for legacy of £10, from her father's estate.

1718, Aug. 1. Will—proved 1718, Aug. 28. Ex. brother John Warner, of Warwick. To executor, he gives power to sell real and personal estate. To wife Priscilla, a third of all estate for dower. To eldest son Jeremiah, a double portion of estate. To eldest daughter Ann Crandall and to sons John and James, double portion of rest of estate. To daughters Hannah, Sarah, Experience, Patience, Susanna and Mary Crandall, rest of estate, equally. Authority was given executor to bind all children.

Inventory, £117, 6*s*. 6*d*., viz: 2 oxen, 2 three years steers, 6 cows, 2 heifers, 4 calves, 3 yearlings, 2 mares, 3 colts, sow and pigs, books 15*s*., woolen and linen wheel, &c. The real estate sold for £280.

1725, Dec. 30. His son John died at Warwick, and administration was given John Warner, who gave account of payments as follows: To Priscilla, mother of deceased, £5, 16*s*., and same amount to Hannah Austin, sister of deceased, and to James, Experience, Susannah and Mary Crandall, each a like amount.

1748, Jan. 12. Will—proved 1750, Mar. 17. Widow Priscilla Lockwood, of Providence. Ex. brother Ezekiel Warner. She calls herself late of Warwick, widow of Abraham Lockwood. To daughter Experience Sprague, 40*s*. To grandson Robert Ashton (*i. e.* Austin), 10*s*. To grandson Jeremiah Ashton (*i. e.* Austin), 40*s*. To grandson Jeremiah Sprague, 20*s*. To brother Ezekiel Warner, rest of estate. Inventory £90, 8s. 7d.

IX. EBER, b. 1676; d. 1727. Newport, Westerly, R. I.
m. (1)
———, b. ; d. of
m. (2)
——— LANPHERE, b. ; d. of George Lanphere.
m. (3)
MARY COTTRELL, b. ; d. 1727 + of Nicholas & Dorothy (Pendleton) Cottrell.

(2d wife.)
1. John,
2. Eber,
3. Samuel,
4. Joseph,
(3d wife.)
5. Mary,
6. Nathaniel,
7. Jonathan,
8. Ebenezer,
9. Jeremiah,

1702, Jun. 29. Westerly. Freeman.

1709, Jun. 28. He and twenty-six others bought tract called Shannock Purchase.

1727, Apr. 25. He, with others made agreement concerning a lease of land that their father, George Lanphere, had in part mortgaged.

1727, Aug. 22. Will—proved 1727, Sep, 15. Exs. friend Nicholas Cottrell, of Westerly, and brother Nathaniel Cottrell, of North Kingstown. To wife Mary, equal share of whole estate with all her children, and mine that I had also by my former wife, and wife Mary, to have in addition, her man. To each child, John, Eber, Samuel, Joseph, them former children I had by my second wife, and to my five children that my now wife hath living, Mary, Nathaniel, Jonathan, Ebenezer and Jeremiah, one-tenth of estate, when said children are of age. Executors may sell land and put children out apprentice.

Inventory, £1,376, 5*s*. 6*d*., viz: lands, &c. £850, carpenter's tools, beds, gun, 69 sheep, 30 lambs, 40 swine, 11 calves, 3 heifers, 6 steers, 8 yearlings, 7 cows, 4 oxen, bull, 10 horsekind, mare, &c.

CRANDALL. 2d column. VI. Joseph. His daughter Mary was baptized in 1709, and she was his 3d child. He also had a daughter Jane who m. 1718, Dec. 8, Cyrus Richmond. VII. Samuel. His wife's surname is called Celly upon the records.

John, m. 1658, Mary Clarke,
b. 1626. d. 1680, Mar. 12,
b. 1641. d. 1711, Apr. 7.
of Jeremiah & Frances (Latham) Clarke.
(She m. (2) John Stanton.)

Newport, R. I.

He was a physician.

1644. Drummer of military company of Portsmouth.

1654. Attorney General for Providence and Warwick.

1654–55–56. Attorney General for colony.

1655. Freeman.

1655, May 25. He was on a committee to build a prison at charge of £80; and on same date was on a committee "to ripen against morning some way for suppressing of selling liquors."

1655, Jun. 30. He was on a committee for preventing sale of ammunition to Indians.

1655–56–57–58–60–61–63. Commissioner.

1664, Mar. 1. "Whereas the court have taken notice of the great blessing of God on the good endeavours of Captain John Cranston, of Newport, both in physic and chirurgery, to the great comfort of such as have had occasion to improve his skill and practice," &c., therefore it was unanimously enacted that he should be licensed to administer physic, and practice chirurgery throughout this whole colony, and is by the court styled and recorded Doctor of Physic and Chirurgery.

1664–65–66–67–68. Deputy.

1667, May 13. He and two others were required with all possible speed to mount the great guns upon such carriages as whereby they may be easily conveyed from place to place, for security and defence of place and people.

1668–69–70–71–72. Assistant.

1671, Jan. 30. He was allowed £4, 16*s.* 6*d.*, for his voyage to New York and Seaconck, in the years 1664 and 1665, and for other service done by him.

1672–73–76–77–78. Deputy Governor.

1676, Apr. 11. Major, and chief Captain of all the colony forces, there appearing "absolute necessity for the defence and safety of the colony," &c.

1677–78. Major.

1678, Jun. 29. In a letter of this date written by Samuel Hubbard, of Newport, he mentions that he had a very sore cough last winter and sent for his physician, Major Cranston, who "said he judged none help or hope for sure, but for present refreshment he gave a small vial of spirits which I took and had some sleep, but my cough rather increased."

1678–79–80. Governor.

1680, Jan. 6. He addressed a letter to King Charles II, concerning the "long continued difference between your Majesty's Colony of Connecticut and ourselves, concerning right of jurisdiction," &c. In a postcript he mentions the verdict of the Court of Commissioners in favor of William Harris and partners against the town of Providence, and presents "our proceedings in these affairs, which we would have sent in the ship that William Harris went lately for England in, but William Harris was so secret and private in his voyage that he never came to us to know what he had done by way of return to your Majesty, neither did he let us know of his going."

His gravestone in the cemetery at Newport bears the following inscription. "Here lieth the body of John Cranston, Esq., Govr of the Colony of Rhode Island, etc. He departed this life March 12th, 1680, in the 55th year of his age." The same stone has also the inscription to his son Samuel, both having been directed to be made by the will of the latter. An earlier gravestone, erected to the memory of John Cranston, probably at the time of his death, was discovered in raising the stone with two inscriptions already referred to. This earlier stone bears very nearly the same inscription as the other.

CRANSTON. 2d column. I. Samuel, m. (1) 1680, Nov. Children, 1. John, 1684, Aug. 4. 2. Samuel, 1687, May 11. 3, Thomas, 1692, Aug. 4. 4. Frances, 1694, Nov. 8. 5, Mary, 1697, Jan 6. 6. Hart, 1699, July 26. 7. James, 1701, July 29. X. William d. 1732 (—). In will of James[3] (Samuel,[2] John[1]), 1731, he mentions late uncle William Cranston. It was probably Wm.,[3] (Wm.,[2] John[1]) b. 1692, Dec. 9; d. 1776+, who married Miriam Norton, b. 1695, Dec. 4, and had beside children by her, also following by his 2d wife—8. Mary, 1730, June 14. 9, Amey, 1731, Dec. 17. 10. James, 1733, Sep. 15. 11, Mercy, 1734, Dec. 1. 12, Thomas, 1736, July 3. 13, Miriam, 1738, Jan. 10.

See: American Genoologist, v. 19, p. 133.

CRANSTON. 1st column. 1708, Nov. 1. Will-proved, 1711, Jun. 10. Mary Stanton. She mentions children, Samuel, John and Benjamin Cranston, Elizabeth Brown and Henry Stanton, and certain grandchildren. 2d column. X. William. Possibly he was of the third generation, and a son of Caleb.

I. Samuel, m. (1) Mary Hart, m. (2) 1711, Judith Cranston, (w. of [Caleb
b. 1659, Aug. d. 1727, Apr. 26. Newport, R. I.
b. 1663. d. 1710, Sep. 17, of Thomas & Freeborn (Williams) Hart.
b. d. 1737, May 4, of Simon & Elizabeth ( ) Parrott.

See: American Genealogist, v. 19, p. 133, 222. v. 25, p. 249-250. v. 30, p. 124-125

He was a goldsmith.

1684. Freeman.

1696. Assistant.

1698. Major for the Island.

1698–99–1700–1–2–3–4–5–6–7–8–9–10–11–12–13–14–15–16–17–18–19–20–21–22–23–24–25–26–27. Governor.

1699, May 27. He wrote the Board of Trade in relation to the charge that the Rhode Island government had favored pirates in granting commissions, &c., complaining of false reports made by Esquire Randolph to the Commissioners of His Majesty's Custom, and commending to their Lordships' favor the agent of the colony Jahleel Brenton, late Collector of Customs, who was in England to represent the interests of the colony.

1705, May 7. He was granted £40 by the Assembly, considering the great charge, trouble, &c., he is at for the benefit and good of this, Her Majesty's colony.

1708, Dec. 5. In answer to a letter of inquiry, from the Board of Trade, he states that there arrived 1696, May 30, from the coast of Africa, the brigantine Seaflower, with forty-seven negroes, of which fourteen were disposed of in this colony for betwixt £30 and £35 per head, the rest being transported to Boston, where the owners of vessel lived. In 1700, Aug. 10th and Oct. 19th and 28th, there sailed from this port three vessels directly for coast of Africa, the two former sloops and the latter a ship. These vessels went to Barbadoes from Africa, and there made disposition of their negroes. The whole and only supply of negroes in this colony is from Barbadoes; twenty to thirty a year at £30 to £40 per head when well and sound. There was found but small encouragement for that trade to this colony, our planters having a general dislike for them, by reason of their turbulent and unruly tempers. Planters desiring to purchase are supplied by offspring of those they already have, which increase daily, and the inclination of our people in general is to employ white servants before negroes. In another letter of same date, he says the strength and defence of this colony, consists chiefly (under the Providence of God), in our good look outs, our expeditions by sea and in our militia; the which consists of all males from sixteen to sixty years of age, who are obliged at their own charge to be always provided with a good firelock musket or fusee, a sword, or bayonet, cartridge box with one pound of good powder and four pounds of bullets; who are to be ready upon any alarm to repair to their ensigns at their respective places of rendezvous. A small fort upon an island covers the harbor of Newport, mounted with fifteen pieces of ordnance from six to nine pound ball. As to administration of justice, we have two General Courts of Trials held in March and September. As to trade, the colony never had any immediate or direct trade to or from England, commodities being exported by way of Boston, and £20,000 has for same years past been remitted from the colony to Boston, for English supplies. We have no trade to any place but Curacoa. The inclination of the youth on Rhode Island is mostly to the sea, the land on said island being all taken up and improved in small farms, so that farmers as their families increase are compelled to put the children to trades. Not above two or three vessels were owned in the colony besides those in Newport. Only two or three vessels of Rhode Island were taken in this war, they being light and sharp for running, so that very few of the enemy's privateers in a gale of wind will run or outsail one of our laded vessels. The colony was preparing to print several acts of the Assembly. The freemen numbered 1,015, militia 1,362, white servants 56, black servants 426, total inhabitants, 7,181. Vessels built from 1698 to 1708, were: ships 8, brigantines 11, sloops 84. Sea faring men 140. Vessels owned in 1708, were: 2 brigantines and 27 sloops. Places of trade to and from colony; Jamaica, Barbadoes, Nevis, Antigua, St. Christopher, Mt. Sarratt, Bermuda, Bahamas, Turk's Islands, Tortugas, Maderia, Fayal, Surinam, and Curacoa. Exports, lumber, staves, heading, hoops, beef, pork, butter, cheese, onions, horses, candles, cider, Indian corn, wax and money. Imports, sugar, molasses, salt, ginger, indigo, pimento, rum, wine, pieces of eight, English goods, both woolen and linen, Swedish and Spanish iron.

1720, Jun. 14. He wrote a letter to the Board of Trade in relation to boundaries between Rhode Island and Massachusetts and Connecticut.

1726, Mar. 17. Will—proved 1727, May 1. Exs. wife Judith, son James, and son-in-law Jahleel Brenton. To eldest son John, all estate that came to me by his deceased mother, 80 acres at Jamestown, ¾ acre in Newport, and having advanced £440 in buildings, and walls, &c., and son having had rent of farm in Newport, for 11 years, so that in all £900 had been advanced, he quit-claims to him forever, &c. To son James, house and land in Newport, on Thames street, measuring 70 feet and extending west to salt water, he suffering wife Judith, his mother-in-law (*i. e.* stepmother), to build a warehouse and to land firewood and such goods as are hers or by consignment, she paying an annual rent of a pair of gloves. The two sons of deceased son Samuel, viz: Samuel and Thomas, having had estate bequeathed by their grandfather, Thomas Cornell, he gives them also 700 acres in East Greenwich and £100 each. To son Thomas, absent six years and not heard of, if it please God he be living, 1⅓ shares in Westquadnoid, but if he be dead to go to Thomas's son Peleg, and if he also die, then to eldest son of my son John, and to my son James, and to grandson Samuel, son of Samuel, deceased. Wife Judith, having had a considerable estate at time of marriage, always kept separate and added to by her industry, he now gives her this and also a great bible and £50. To poor people of Newport, £50. To daughter Frances Brenton, £500, besides £300 already given. To son James, £250. To granddaughters Mary Cranston, daughter of John, and Mary and Elizabeth, daughters of Samuel, deceased, each £100, to be at interest till they are 18. To granddaughter Elizabeth Hatch, daughter of daughter Hart, deceased, £250, at 18 or marriage, and if she die to daughters of sons John and James, and daughters of daughter Frances Brenton, wife of Jahleel. To granddaughter Patience Cranston, daughter of son Thomas, £100 at 21 or marriage, and if she die to her brother Peleg. To brother John Cranston, and sister Elizabeth Brown, each £10. To grandchildren living at decease, viz: children of sons John and James and of daughter Frances Brenton, each £5. To daughters-in-law Mary Harwood and Elizabeth Tillinghast, each £5. As to farm at Newport, in possession of son John: "I have found by experience the said farm is not a sufficient estate to maintain a family decently and comfortably," &c., therefore to be sold to pay legacies, &c. To sons John and James and daughter Frances, household goods. To son James, two quart silver tankard, silver hilted sword, clock, and silver tobacco box with his uncle William's name engraved on rim, books, plates, pictures, &c. To son John, small silver tankard, silver tobacco box, marked on the bottom, W. N., silver porringer, two dozen silver jacket buttons, &c. To daughter, Frances Brenton, two silver mugs, pint cup and porringer. To certain grandchildren, silver spoons. To sons John and James, wearing apparel. To executors, £50, "to build a fair tomb over my father's and my own grave," &c., "with a modest inscription cut thereon setting forth our names, &c., that it may be a monument in memory of the Predecessors of the Cranstons in this place to after ages." The rest of personal estate, as a silver gilt communion cup and plate, gold buttons, &c., to son James. To son John, negro Saul. To daughter-in-law Elizabeth Cranston, widow of Samuel, negro Kate. To daughter Frances Brenton, negro Bridget. To granddaughter Elizabeth Hatch, the negro Francisco (in possession of son-in-law Nathaniel Hatch), who had been intended for daughter. Hart Hatch. To son James, negro Tony, and £60 already had to buy a negro girl. To daughter Frances, negro Flora.

His gravestone bears the following inscription: "Here lieth the body of Samuel Cranston, Esq., late Governour of this Colony, aged 68 years, and departed this life April ye 26th, A. D. 1727. He was the son of John Cranston, Esq., who was also Governour here 1680. He was descended from the noble Scottish Lord Cranston and carried in his veins a stream of the ancient Earls of Crawford, Bothwell and Traquair, having for his grandfather James Cranston, Clerk, Chaplain, to King Charles the First. His great grandfather was John Cranston, of Bool, Esq., this last was son to James Cranston, Esq., which James was son of William, Lord Cranston.

Rest happy now, brave patriot, without end
Thy Country's father, and thy Country's friend."

1. Mary,
2. John, 1684, Aug. 4.
3. James,
4. Samuel,
5. Thomas,
6. Frances, 1698.
7. Hart, 1699.
(2d wife no issue).

II. Caleb, m. Judith Parrott,
b. d. Newport, R. I.
b. d. 1737, May 4, of Simon & Elizabeth ( ) Parrott.
(She m. (2) 1711, Samuel Cranston.)

His daughter Elizabeth, married Charles Tillinghast, and Mary married Philip Harwood.

1. John, 1685
2. Elizabeth.
3. Mary,

The Colonel John Cranston, who was born 1685 and died 1760, Nov. 7, must have been son of Caleb, as no brother of the latter could have had a son born thus early (except Samuel, whose son John is otherwise accounted for).

III. JAMES, — b. / d. 1662, Dec. 6.

IV. JEREMIAH, — b. / d. 167–.

He died at the age of fifteen.

V. MARY, — b. 1665, Jan. 27. / d. 1666, Mar. 24.

VI. BENJAMIN, — b. / d. — Newport, R. I.
m.
SARAH GODFREY, — b. / d. — of John & Sarah ( ) Godfrey.

1704. Freeman.
1707. Deputy.

Children: 1. Elizabeth, 1701, Mar. 7. 2. Caleb, 1703, Apr. 3. Sarah, 1705, Apr. 19. 4. Benjamin, 1707, Feb. 27.

VII. JOHN, — b. / d. — Newport, R. I.
m.
ANN NEWBURY, — b. / d. — of Newbury.

1704. Freeman.
1707-9-11-15-16-17-19-20-24. Deputy.
1708, Dec. 5. He was mentioned as captain of a sloop sent in pursuit of a privateer.
1711-16. Speaker of House of Deputies.
1711. He was Colonel in this and other years, but should not be confounded with his nephew John (son of Caleb), who held the same title in later years.
1746. Assistant.

Children: 1. Walter, 2. Benjamin, 3. Elizabeth, 4. Mary, 5. Ann,

VIII. ELIZABETH, — b. 1671. / d. 1736, Jun. 3.
m.
JOHN BROWN, — b. 1671. / d. 1731, Oct. 20, — of James & Elizabeth (Carr) Brown.

Children: 1. John, 1696, Dec. 26. 2. Jeremiah, 3. James, 4. William, 5. Robert, 6. Peleg, 7. Elizabeth,

IX. PELEG, — b. / d.

X. WILLIAM, — b. / d. — Newport, R. I.
m. (1) 1714, Feb. 10,
MIRIAM NORTON, — b. / d. 1728, Feb. 3, — of Norton.
m. (2) 1728, Dec. 14,
MERCY GOULD, — b. 1694, Dec. 13. / d. 1747, May 8, — of Thomas & Elizabeth (Mott) Gould.

Children: 1. Ann, 1715, Dec. 4. 2. Alice, 1717, Sep. 26. 3. Sarah, 1719, Feb. 5. 4. William, 1722, Mar. 19. 5. Elizabeth, 1724, Feb. 7. 6. John, 1726, Jan. 6. 7. Norton, 1727, Dec. 14.

CRAWFORD.

GIDEON,[2] (James.[1]) — b. 1651, Dec. 26. / d. 1707, Oct. 10.
m. 1687, Apr. 13,
FREELOVE FENNER, — b. 1656. / d. 1712, Jun. 1.
of Arthur & Mehitable (Waterman) Fenner.

Lanark, Scotland, Providence, R. I.

His birth was registered at Lanark (as was his father's proclamation of marriage to Anna Weir, 1649, Apr. 27).

He is said to have come from Scotland, in consequence of his relationship to Governor John Cranston (both being by tradition descendants of James Lindsay, 1st Earl of Crawford).

1670. Providence. He arrived in this year.
1687, Sep. 1. Taxed 7*s.* 9*d.*
1688. Ratable estate, shop goods £70, 2 horses, 1 cow, share of 2 colts, 140 acres in the woods.
1688. Constable.
1690-92-94-97-98-99-1701-2-3-4-5-6. Deputy.
1702. Justice of the Peace.
1705. He subscribed £6 toward rebuilding Weybosset Bridge.
1707, Oct. 7. Will—proved 1707, Nov. 5. Exs. wife Freelove and brothers-in-law Thomas and Arthur Fenner, and cousin Richard Waterman, Jr. To wife, ½ of dwelling house, warehouse, &c., for life, and the other ½ to that son whom she may choose to live with her, he to have her ½ also, at her decease. Until the son was 21, she to have the profits of all, and if she chose son William, and he accepted, he was to pay his brother John £100, when 21. The rest of lands, equally, to sons William and John. To daughter Anne Crawford, £50, and to daughter Mary Crawford, £50, when they were 21. To wife, all movable estate, to dispose as she pleased; and the care of children entrusted to her.
Inventory, £1,556, 1*s.* 2*d.*, viz: wearing apparel £20, 7*s.*, silver money £16, 9*s.* 10*d.*, money due by bill and bond £175, 10*s.*, 5 good feather beds £60, 15*s.*, plate £15, 11*s.*, swords, pistols, holsters and other small arms, books £2, 12*s.*, shop goods £355, 9*s.*, sheep £13, 13*s.*, 2 negroes £56, 2 horses £18, cattle £35, 15*s.*, hogs, cheese, butter, hides, tallow, cider £41, 10*s.*, &c.
1712, May 24. Will — proved 1712, Jun. 27.

I. WILLIAM, — b. 1688, Apr. 12. / d. 1720, Aug. 5. — Providence, R. I.
m. 1708, Apr. 22,
SARAH WHIPPLE, — b. 1691, Mar. 29. / d. 1762. — of Joseph & Alice (Smith) Whipple.

1711, May 2. He and Nicholas Power, were appointed to build a bridge at Weybossett.
1711-12-13-17-18-19. Deputy.
1716, Jun. 19. He and two others, having petitioned the Assembly, for liberty to make and dry fish on Starve Goat Island, they were given liberty to use and improve so much of said island, as shall be needful and necessary for their making, drying and securing of fish on said island, during their following the trade of fishery.
1718, Oct. 29. He and two others, were appointed as a committee to view Fort Ann and see what may be proper for fitting and repairing same.
1718. Town Council.
1719-20. Major for the main land.
1720, Aug. 31. Administration on his estate was given his widow Sarah, but she being at present, "something troubled and incomposed in mind," &c., her father, Joseph Whipple, had administration.
Inventory, £3,551, 19*s.* 6*d.*, viz: silver money, spoons and porringer £39, 19*s.* 10*d.*, silver tankard £17, 12*s.* 6*d.*, gold £19, 10*s.*, 5 swords and belt, pistols, 12 pictures, store goods, consisting of 3 hogsheads tobacco, 2½ hogsheads sugar, 14 hogsheads rum, flannel, holland, diaper, scales, stillyards, nails, silk crape, scissors, wax, &c., &c. A negro woman, man and boy £120, Indian girl's time, cider press and mill, 3 horses, 6 oxen, 6 cows, 3 calves, 68 sheep and lambs, a white mare and colt, 3 hogs, hay, &c., sloop "Sarah." Book debts £1000. The rooms, &c. named, were: N. E. chamber, E. chamber, N. W. chamber, W. chamber, garret, meat chamber, old leanto, kitchen cellar, back shop, the Rum Warehouse and Salt Warehouse In the new house, the rooms mentioned, were: N. W. chamber, great chamber, N. chamber, the great room, N. E. room below, and N. W. room and cellar.

Children: 1. Gideon, 1709, Jan. 29. 2. Jeremiah, 1710, Oct. 27. 3. Joseph, 1712. 4. Freelove, 1714, Apr. 12. 5. William, 1715, Dec. 8.

II. ANNE, — b. 1690, May 13. / d.
m. 1711, Nov. 29,
PELEG CARR, — b. 1690, Mar. 14. / d. — of Caleb & Deborah ( ) Carr.

III. JOHN, — b. 1693, Aug. 15. / d. 1719, Mar. 18. — Providence, R. I.
m. 1715, Dec. 20,
AMEY WHIPPLE, — b. 1699, Jun. 16. / d. — of Joseph & Alice (Smith) Whipple.

(She m. (2) 1723, Jun. 26, Robert Gibbs.)
He was called Captain, at his death.
1719, Apr. 20. Administration to his widow Amey. Inventory, £1,614, 2*s.* 15*d.*, silver and gold £149, 8*s.*, brandy, wine, cider, tobacco, ginger, beeswax, silk stockings, knives, calico, cambric, linen, edging laces, holland, swanskin, combs, gloves, shot, lead, starch, indigo, oyster tongs, china, glass and other store goods. Books, 2 canes, sword and belt, pair of pistols, lumber on board sloop "Indian King," &c.
1724, May 4. Inventory of real estate filed, showing £1,665, viz: lot of land, dwelling house, shop, and wharf on west side of Town street £400, Pray's lot £160, lot down town (40 foot) £60. On Weybossett Plain, 20 acres £50. At Stamper's Hill, 2 lots and about 500 acres of other land. Fourteen days later, Amey Gibbs, relict of Capt. John Crawford, brought in account, showing £751, 7*s.* 8*d.*, of personal estate left (after paying debts and widow's thirds), for children.

Children: 1. Anne, 1716, Jul. 17. 2. John, 1718, Sep. 7.

IV. MARY, — b. 1702, Sep. 14. / d.
m. 1724, Oct. 12,
JAMES MITCHELL, — b. / d. 1772, Jan. 17. — of Mitchell.

Children: 1. James, 2. Freelove, 3. Jerusha, 4. Amey, 5. Mary, 6. Anna,

Widow Freelove. Ex. son William. Overseers, brothers Thomas Fenner and Arthur Fenner, and cousin Richard Waterman, Jr. To son William, all my part of sloop Dolphin, it being already registered in his name, and to sons William and John, all my part of sloop building by Nathaniel Brown, of Rehoboth (her 4-8 part of sloop to be rigged out of the estate). To sons William and John, £137 each, in money or merchantable shop goods. To daughter Anne Carr, £100, and to daughter Mary Crawford, £100, when 21. To son John and daughter Mary, a feather bed each, when 21. To daughters Anne and Mary, the rest of household goods. The rest of estate to four children. Daughter Mary to be placed in some situation where she can be brought up by the overseers of the will. Inventory £1382, 12s. 9d.

He and his wife are buried in the North Burial Ground.

A tradition of his descendants, gives him a brother William, who, it is said, came to Providence also, and died there without issue, in 1728.

There is no relationship known to exist between Gideon and Phenix Crawford, of Providence, who married 1717, Feb. 12, Meribah Borden, and died 1755, Nov. 12 aged seventy two years. The birthplace of Phenix Crawford, was at Edinboro, Scotland.

CROSSMAN.

JOHN, b. 1588 ± d. 1688, Jan. 26.

Newport, R. I.

He was a mariner.

1677, Dec. 7. He sold to John Easton and Walter Clarke, of Newport, all rights in Providence, for 40s., for use and benefit of people called Quakers, in Rhode Island, and their successors.

The Quaker records state that he died, aged about one hundred years.

DAILEY.

JOHN, b. d. 1719 +
m.
——— b. d.

Providence, R. I.

1689, Aug. 27. He bought 90 acres of James Phillips.

1690, Jun. 2. He exchanged lands with Ann Pratt.

1703, Apr. 13. He deeded to beloved son Joseph, for divers good causes, 40 acres.

1718, Jan. 30. He, having been in the care of his son-in-law John Rhodes, the latter was to receive from Joseph Dailey, 12s. 6d., and from Morris Brook, 11s. 6d., for keeping their father the last six months.

1719, Oct. 5. His son-in-law John Rhodes, agreed to keep his father-in-law John Dailey, till the twenty-seventh of the month, for £3, 12s., with term already since June 10.

I. JOSEPH, b. d. — Providence, R. I.

1718, Apr. 8. He sold to Peter Ballou, homestead lands, whereon I now dwell, 57½ acres, with house, orchard, &c., for £336.

II. SAMUEL, b. d. — Providence, R. I.

1706, Mar. 9. He sold Zachariah Jones, 40 acres, for £20.

III. ELIZABETH, b. d.
m.
JOHN RHODES, b. d. 1744, Jun. 19. of Jeremiah & Madeline (Hawkins) Rhodes.

IV. ——— b. d.
m.
MORRIS BROOK, b. d. of Brook.

DAILEY. 2d column. Brook for Brook.

DAVIS (AARON).

AARON, b. d. 1713 +
m.
MARY, b. d.

Newport, R. I., Dartmouth, Mass.

He was a mason.

1673, Feb. 25. He sold Peleg Sanford, merchant, a house and 15 acres, &c., for 12½ acres in exchange.

He and wife Mary acknowledged a deed.

1680. Taxed 6s. 10d.

1694, Nov. 13. He was one of the proprietors of Dartmouth, Mass., named in the confirmatory deed of William Bradford.

1698. Dartmouth. Ordained as pastor of the First Baptist Church, succeeding Hugh Moshier, in that office. This church was organized in 1684, and soon embraced persons living in Dartmouth, Tiverton and Little Compton, in its membership.

1707, Apr. 19. He deeded to son Aaron, Jr., of Little Compton, a whole share in Westquadnaig, in Rhode Island.

There seems no reason to doubt that Joshua was his son, and as it is believed that William, Samuel and John, should be added to the list of his children, it is assumed that this was the case.

I. WILLIAM, b. d.
m.
FRANCES, b. d. of — Newport, East Greenwich, R. I.

1. William,
2. Henry,
3. Frances,

1693, Nov. 20. He bought of Ezekiel Hunt, and wife Sarah, of Newport, for £14, 10s., a house and 100 acres in East Greenwich.

1695, Dec 4. East Greenwich. He sold Giles Pearce, 90 acres, for £12.

1715. His son "William Davis, Jr.," was admitted freeman.

1721, Aug. 22. He and Henry Davis, mortgaged 18½ acres, with buildings, for £25, to colony—and Frances, wife of said William, signed as consenting.

1725, Jun. 17. His daughter Frances, married William Case.

II. JOSHUA. b. d. 1736, Jan. 8.
m.
MARY SCOTT, b. 1666, Feb. 1. d. 1734 + of John & Rebecca ( ) Scott. — Newport, East Greenwich, R. I.

1. William,
2. Aaron,
3. John,
4. Rebecca,
5. Katharine,
6. Samuel, 1706.
7. Jeffrey, 1708.

He was a miller.

1694, Aug. 8. He bought of Edward Hopps, and wife Mary, of East Greenwich, certain land, housing and fruit trees there, for £14.

1699, Jul. 3. East Greenwich. Rebecca Whipple assigned all her interest in above deed to daughter Mary Davis, wife of Joshua, and her heirs, said Joshua having benefit for his life.

1712, Mar. 7. He bought of Susannah Smith, of East Greenwich (widow of John Smith, of Newport), and Thomas Smith, her son, for £200, a saw mill, house, &c.

1715, Jan. 20. He and wife Mary, deeded son William, for love, &c., 26 acres.

1725, Aug. 31. He mortgaged his homestead, for £480, 11s., to John Scott, of Newport.

1726, Aug. 30. Captain Sylvanus Scott, declared that the deed of 1694 was by his mother, Rebecca Whipple, put into his hands to keep, upwards of twenty years ago, and that he had it in keeping till about two years ago, and then delivered it to Joshua Davis.

1733, Jan. He deeded son Jeffrey, for love &c., grist mill, &c., and 40 acres.

1734, Jan. 14. He bought of Edward Scott, of Newport, schoolmaster, for £567, houses, buildings and 77 acres, in East Greenwich, and a warrant was given against heirs of John Scott, late of Newport, deceased.

1734, May 27. Will—proved 1736, Jan. 31. Exs. sons Samuel and Jeffrey. To granddaughter Else Davis, daughter of William, 5*s*. To son Aaron, 5*s*. and wearing apparel. To son John, 5*s*. To son Samuel, all right in the forge. To grandson Joshua, son of Aaron, a house lot. To daughter Rebecca Briggs, wife of James Briggs, £10. To daughter Katharine Godfrey, wife of John Godfrey, £10. To granddaughter Mary Paine, £10. To daughters Rebecca and Katharine, the pewter marked with wife's maiden name. To son Jeffrey, a negro boy, he paying £10 to my son Samuel and £9, 15*s*. each, to sons Aaron and John. To wife Mary, whole profit of part of farm I now live on, and of north part of homestead farm, and to her all household stuff, forever, and a milch cow and riding beast to be provided for her by sons Jeffrey and Samuel, each of them paying her £10 per year.

Inventory, £241, 15*s*., viz: purse and wearing apparel £21, stillyards, warming pan, pair of worsted combs, woolen wheel, pewter, looking glass, books £1, iron at forge £6, mare, cow, 6 sheep, 4 lambs, swine, geese, fowls, &c.

III. AARON, b. ; d. 1730, Mar. — Little Compton, R. I.
m.
MARY, b. ; d. 1731, Dec. 19. of

1. Son,
2. Sarah,
3. Abigail, 1697, Mar. 21.
4. Mary, 1699.
5. William, 1707, Jan. 31.
6. Elizabeth, 1709, Aug. 1.

1713. He was one of the appraisers of inventory of John Woodman's estate, and was at this time called Aaron Davis, Jr.

1715, Jan. 7. Will—proved 1730, Apr. 21. Exs. wife Mary and friend Joseph Wanton, of Tiverton. To son William, housing and land at Little Compton, but wife Mary to have it till son is of age, while she remains widow. To daughter Sarah Sheffield, £5. To grandson Aaron Sheffield, £6, at age. To wife, half of household goods and movable estate, and she to have £10 yearly, when son William is of age.

Inventory, wearing apparel, pewter, 2 churns, warming pan, 4 wheels, 2 pair of stillyards, books, plate and paper money £96, 14*s*., silver money £67, negro man, woman and girl £200, 3 swine, pair of oxen, 9 cows, 2 yearling cattle, 23 sheep, 5 horsekind, &c.

IV. SAMUEL, b. ; d. — Kings Town, R. I.
m. 1706.
SARAH ALBRO, b. ; d. of Samuel & Isabel (Lawton) Albro.

He was a cooper.

1714, Mar. 31. Joshua Davis, and wife Mary, testified that Samuel Davis and Daniel Ayrault, came to his house 1708, Apr. 9, and desired him to be a witness to a bill which Samuel Davis gave to Mr. Ayrault, for £7.

1714, Sep. 6. Testimony was given by James Honeyman, that he married Samuel Davis to Sarah Albro, in 1706; and in the same year James Reynolds testified that Samuel Davis married to Mr. Samuel Albro's daughter.

V. JOHN, b. ; d. 1728. — North Kingstown, R. I.
m.
ELIZABETH, b. ; d. 1728 + of

1. John,
2. Mary,

1728. Will—proved. He mentions wife Elizabeth, son John, and daughter Mary Wilcox.

DAVIS (NICHOLAS).

NICHOLAS, b. ; d. 1672, Jul. 24.
m. 1651,
SARAH, b. ; d. 1692 ±

(She m. (2) John Clarke.)

Barnstable, Mass., Newport, R. I.

He was a merchant.

1656, Oct. He and others were brought to trial at Boston. He came into court with his hat on and confessed he had forsaken the ordinances and resorted to the Quakers, and he and the others were banished on pain of death.

1657, Mar. 15. The jury appointed to view the corpse of Simon Davis, late deceased, two years old son of Nicholas Davis; declared that the corpse was taken out of the water in the creek dead, but could not find any violence offered to him that might be cause of death.

1659, Jun. He, having left Barnstable "to reckon with those with whom he traded in Boston and to pay some debts," was apprehended and sent to prison and sentenced by the court to banishment upon pain of death if after the 14th of September following he should be found in jurisdiction of Massachusetts. While he was in court "seeing how slightly they made of the Marshal's cruelty, his wicked and unjust usages of them, destroying their cattle," &c., "the said Nicholas spreading his arms abroad spoke in testimony and zeal that he was a witness for the Lord against their oppression, and would have declared wherein, but they suffered him not to speak, but committed him to prison."

1659, Oct. 6. His house was ordered to be searched for seditious writings, he being a Quaker.

1664, Mar. 1 He brought in ten cases liquor and half a hundred shot.

He was drowned in Newport Harbor, as the Friends' records declare.

1673, Jul. 4. The court in Plymouth colony settled a certain house and land on the widow Sarah, relict of Nicholas Davis, of Rhode Island, sometime of Barnstable, being for her third of his estate if it amount to no more.

1673, Sep. 2. Mrs. Sarah Davis, widow of Nicholas, deceased intestate, complained to the Assembly as to a bond drawn and signed by her to the Town Council of Newport, the condition being that she should pay all her husband's estate in Newport to the creditors. The Assembly declared that the Town Council by law of the colony had full power to order

I. CHILD, b. 1652. ; d.

II. SIMON, b. 1655. ; d. 1657, Mar.

III. SARAH, b. ; d.
m.
JOHN MILES, b. ; d. of Miles.

DAVIS (NICHOLAS). 2d column. III Sarah. Her husband b. 1666, Nov. 19, son of John & Mary ( ) Miles.

IV. SIMON, b. 1660. ; d. 1736, Sep. 11. — Bristol, R. I.
m. 1685, Sep. 24,
ANN LOW, b. ; d. of Anthony & Frances ( ) Low.

1. Nicholas, 1686, Oct. 9.
2. Sarah, 1689, Jun. 15.
3. Ann, 1694, Sep. 23.
4. Hannah, 1696, Jan. 12.
5. Samuel, 1698, Jun. 30.
6. Elizabeth, 1699, Aug 8.
7. Simon, 1701, Oct. 11.
8. Frances, 1703, Sep. 23.

1722, Jun. He and Mercy Osborne, petitioned the Rhode Island Assembly for money due from will of John Clarke, for estate given by said Clarke to his wife, mother of Simon and Mercy. It was voted to give them £100, they executing a full discharge.

1737, Feb. 1. Articles of agreement as to real estate of Simon Davis, late of Bristol, deceased, was made between Nicholas Davis, of Boston, merchant, Simon Davis, of Bristol, mariner, Shubael Norton, of Bristol, mariner, and Sarah, his wife, John Newton of Bristol, mariner, and Ann, his wife, Henry Bragg, of Bristol, merchant, and Elizabeth, his wife and Jonathan Woodbury, of Bristol, attorney on behalf of Francis Throop, of Woodstock, county of Worcester, widow.

V. HANNAH, b. 1661, ; d. 1697, Jul. 17.
m.
WILLIAM BRENTON, b. ; d. 1697, of William & Martha (Burton) Brenton.

1. William,
2. Samuel,
3. Martha,
4. Benjamin, 1686, Dec. 23.
5. Jahleel, 1691, Aug. 15.

VI. THOMAS, b. ; d.

VII. MERCY, b. ; d. 1733, Feb. 16.
m.
JEREMIAH OSBORNE, b. ; d. 1709, of Osborne.

1. Robert, 1684, Aug. 11.
2. Katherine, 1686, Nov. 12.
3. John, 1689, Oct. 31.
4. Jeremiah, 1693, Jul. 25.
5. Margaret, 1695, May 27.
6. Sarah, 1701, May 11.
7. Jeremiah, 1706, Jun. 21.

payment of every person's estate that dyeth intestate, and had power to reform any bond according to reason and law, and power to admeasure and pay widow's dower.

1676, Apr. 20. The will of Dr. John Clarke, of Newport (proved 1676, May 17), gave to wife Sarah, land and dwelling house (in trust of executors) for life. To his daughter-in-law (step-daughter) Sarah Davis, £40, at eighteen. To son-in-law Simon Davis, land. To son-in-law Thomas Davis, £20, at twenty-one. To daughter-in-law Mercy Davis, £20, at eighteen. To daughter-in-law Hannah Davis £10.

1692, Mar. 9. Receipts for legacies from John Clarke's will were given to Philip Smith (the surviving executor) by John Miles and wife Sarah, Jeremiah Osborne and wife Mercy, and Hannah Brenton, her husband William Brenton, being absent. The will had provided that the legacies should be paid at death of testator's wife, and said Sarah Clarke having now deceased the receipts were given.

DENISON.

GEORGE,[3] (Geo.,[2] Wm.,[1]) { b. 1652. d. 1711, Dec. 27.
m.
MERCY GORHAM, { b. 1659, Jan. 20. d. 1725, Sep. 24.
of John & Desire (Howland) Gorham.

Westerly R. I.

1682, Sep. 18. He bought of Anna Stanton, widow, of Stonington, for £24, land to amount of 200 acres given her husband Thomas Stanton, Sr., deceased, by town of Stonington, and by his will given to son Daniel, the latter empowering his mother to sell it.

1683, Nov. 14. He had his son Edward baptized, followed by Joseph, (1683), Mercy (1685), Samuel, (1686), Desire (1688), Elizabeth (1690), Desire (1693), Thankful (1695) and George (1699).

1706, Jun. 3. He and wife Mercy, sold Job Randall of Scituate, certain lands in Westerly, for £80.

1707. Deputy.

1711, Dec. 24. Will—proved 1712, Mar. 10. Exx. wife Mercy. To her all movables. To youngest son George, house and land which I now live on, at his mother's decease, but while she lives she to have improvement and use. To two youngest daughters Desire and Thankful Denison, each £10. To three elder sons, Edward, Joseph, and Samuel, and two elder daughters, Mercy Dunbar and Elizabeth Champlin, nothing, as they had already had.

(The gift to testator's youngest son George was confirmed by the latter's brother Edward.)

I. EDWARD, { b. 1678, d. 1726, Dec. 9. — Westerly, R. I.
m. (1)
MERCY, { b. d. — of
m. (2) 1718, Mar. 2
ANN MINOR, (w. of Sam'l) { b. d. — of John & Phebe (Lay) Denison.

1716. Freeman.

1726, Dec. 26. An inventory of his estate was authorized to be taken as he was "supposed to have been drowned on 9th instant night following."

1727, Jan 30. Administration to son John. Inventory, £1628, 13*s.* 4*d.*, viz: apparel £29, silver tankard £15, gold rings and gold necklace £9, 6*s.*, 6 silver cups, £16, 14*s.*, 12 silver spoons, £15, 3*s.*, quilting frame, spinning wheel, horse and mare £27, Indian man £60, house and lands £570, &c.

1. Edward, 1699.
2. John, 1701.
3. Elisha, 1703.
4. Mary, 1705.
5. Desire, 1707.
6. Abby, 1709.

II. JOSEPH, { b. 1681. d. 1725, Feb. 18. — Stonington, Ct.
m. 1707, Feb. 17,
PRUDENCE MINOR, { b. 1681. d. 1726, May 26, — of Joseph & Mary (Avery) Minor.

1725, Feb. 16. Will—proved 1725, Mar. 23. Exs. wife Prudence and son Joseph. Overseer, brother Joseph Minor. To wife Prudence, £350. To eldest son Joseph, £500. To sons Amos and Nathan, £300 each. To daughters Prudence and Borodel, £100 each. To daughters Joanna, Elizabeth, Thankful and Anne, £80 each. The executors to sell farm I live on when Joseph is of age, and if anything is left at that time over legacies, the amount to be divided in same proportions, only wife to have £50 more than before mentioned. Certain land at Voluntown, &c., to be sold to pay debts. To wife a third of movables within the house suitable for housekeeping, and remainder to six daughters equally.

Inventory, £2,437, 13*s.* 4*d.*, viz: farm and buildings £1,800, wearing apparel £27, 17 three year cattle, 17 two year cattle, 15 cows, 16 yearlings, 6 oxen, 7 horses, 5 colts, 9 swine, 193 sheep, 2 linen wheels, 2 woolen wheels, 220 sheep let out, 24 sheep let out (desperate debt).

1. Joseph, 1707, Sep. 21.
2. Prudence, 1709, Nov. 28.
3 Borodel, 1712, Feb. 14.
4. Amos, 1714, Feb. 18.
5. Nathan, 1716, Feb. 20.
6. Joanna, 1718, Jan. 28.
7. Elizabeth, 1720, Feb. 15.
8. Thankful, 1723, Apr. 27.
9. Anna, 1724, May 3.

III. MERCY, { b. 1683, Mar. 1. d.
m.
MORDECAI DUNBAR, { b. d. — of Dunbar.

1. Thankful, 1712 ±
2. Mary, 1712 ±
3. Elizabeth, 1717 ±

IV. SAMUEL, { b. 1685, d. — Stonington, Saybrook, Ct.
m.
MARY MINOR, (w. of Chris. { b. d. — of Lay.

1716. Saybrook. He moved thence about this time.

1. Sarah, 1710, Jan. 6.
2. Samuel, 1711, Oct. 23.
3. Mercy, 1713.
4. Elizabeth, 1714.
5. Joanna, 1716, Dec. 13.
6. Mary, 1718, Jan. 6.
7. George, 1718, Jan. 6.
8. Christopher 1720.
9. Gideon, 1724.
10. Stephen, 1725, Feb. 6.

V. DESIRE, { b. 1687. d. young.

VI. ELIZABETH, { b. 1689, Feb. 11. d. 1749, Nov. 22.
m. 1705, Dec. 5,
CHRISTOPHER CHAMPLIN { b. 1684, Sep. 26. d. 1734, Oct. 23, — of Christopher Champlin.

1. Christopher 1707, Nov. 30.
2. Joseph, 1709, Aug. 4.
3. Elijah, 1711, Jul. 20.
4. Ann, 1714, Mar. 29.
5. George, 1716, Feb. 15.
6. Elizabeth, 1719, Jan. 10.
7. Thankful, 1721, Mar. 27.
8. Lydia, 1723, Nov. 19.
9. Elijah, 1726, May 23.
10. Jabez, 1728, Aug. 31.
11. Oliver, 1730, May 12.
12. Mary, 1731, Jan. 29.

VII. DESIRE, { b. 1693, d. 1737, Aug. 13.
m. 1712, Feb. 19,
JOHN WILLIAMS, { b. 1692, Oct. d. 1761, Dec. 30, — of John & Martha (Wheeler) Williams.

1. Desire, 1712, Aug. 25.
2. John, 1714, May 11.
3. William, 1716, May 1.
4. Thankful, 1717, Feb. 8.
5 Mercy, 1719, Nov. 7.
6. Thomas, 1721, Sep. 20.
7. Robert, 1723, Mar. 8.
8. George, 1726, Jul. 9.
9. Edward,
10. Deborah,

VIII. THANKFUL, { b. 1695. d.
m. 1713, Dec. 31,
THOMAS STANTON, { b. 1693, Jan. 9. d. — of Robert & Joanna (Gardner) Stanton.

1. Robert, 1716, Nov. 14.
2. Thankful, 1718, Jul. 21.
3. Mary, 1720, May 27.
4. Elizabeth, 1722, Jun. 10.
5. Mercy, 1724, Jun. 14.
6. Prudence, 1726, Apr. 22.
7. Nathan, 1728, Jun. 19.
8. Thomas, 1729, Dec. 17.
9. Anne, 1732, Mar. 22.
10. Desire, 1734, Apr. 22.
11. Hannah, 1736, Sep. 29.

IX. GEORGE, { b. 1698, d. 1737, Jan. 26. — Stonington, Ct.
m. (1) 1721, Sep. 28.
SARAH MINOR, { b. d. 1724, Sep. 27, — of Joseph & Sarah (Tracy) Minor.
m. (2) 1727, May 10,
JOANNA HINCKLEY, { b. d. 1734 + — of Samuel & Martha (Lathrop) Hinckley.

1734, May 1. Will—proved 1738, May 16. Exx. wife Joanna. To wife, profits real and personal while widow, except a bed to son Joseph, which I had by my former wife. To son Joseph, all my farm in Fairfield, after his mother's death or marriage. To daughter Sarah Denison, £100, and half of movables.

Inventory, £401, 3*s.* 10*d.*, viz: wearing apparel £22. 11*s.*, 3 feather beds, large bible, small bible, other books, 7 silver spoons, 6 small silver spoons, silver shoe buckles, piece of gold £1, 6*s.*, cash £40 7*s.* 7*d.*, bond £100, warming pan, hour glass, woolen wheel, linen wheel, carpenter tools.

1. Joseph, 1723, Jan. 26.
2. Sarah, 1724, Sep.
(2d wife.)
3. Elijah, 1728, Jul. 6.
4. George, 1730, Apr. 14.
5. Sarah, 1733, Sep. 7.

DENNIS. 1st column. Parents of Sarah Howland were Henry & Mary (Newland) Howland.

ROBERT, m. 1672, Nov. 19, SARAH HOWLAND, — b. ; d. 1691, Jun. 5. — b. 1645. d. 1712, Oct. 2. of Howland.

Portsmouth, R. I.

1656, Aug. 25. He bought of Job Hawkins, of Boston, and his mother, Jane Hawkins, widow of Richard, 20 acres, in Portsmouth.

1671. Freeman.

1672, Jul. 9. He deeded four rods square of land to Matthew and John Borden, William Wodell and Gideon Freeborn, for a Quaker burying place, "for the love I bear to the truth and the people of God, which are in scorn called Quakers."

1673–84. Deputy.

1676, Mar. 13. He and three others, of Portsmouth, were appointed a committee, to choose their own men as keepers of Indians who were above the age of twelve years (in custody of several inhabitants), that the Indians "should be so secured, as that they may be hindered from doing damage to the inhabitants in this juncture of time," &c. The Indians were to have a sufficient keeper in company with them by day, and to be locked up in the night in a sufficient place of security. Any master offending, was to pay a fine of £5.

1691, May 25. He bought of Jedediah Allen, and Elizabeth, of Shrewsbury, New Jersey, land in Monmouth, New Jersey.

1691, May 11. Will—proved 1691, Jul. 2. Exx. wife Sarah. Overseers, Thomas Cornell and John Anthony. To eldest son Robert, 150 acres, at age, which I bought of my brother-in-law, Jedediah Allen, in county of Monmouth, New Jersey. To son Joseph, at age, all my housing and land where I dwell, he paying my daughter Mary Dennis, £10, within three years, and to my daughter Sarah Dennis, £8, within six years after possession. To son John, a cow, ten sheep and feather bed, at age. To daughter Mary Dennis, my long loom. To wife Sarah, best feather bed, &c., and whole benefit of all movables undisposed of for life, while widow, and benefit of house and land, till son Joseph comes of age, then having a third privilege in house and land, for life, and not to be turned out of doors.

1712, Sep. 26. Will — proved 1712, Oct. 3. Widow Sarah. Exs. son Robert Dennis and son-in-law George Lawton. To son Robert, a cow, ten sheep and feather bed. To son John, a chest, cow, twenty sheep, horse, two yearling cattle, sow, five shoats and 12s. to buy him a bible. To son Joseph, a bed, &c. and 12s. to buy a bible. To daughter Mary Lawton, wife of George, feather bed, &c. and a great bible. To daughter Sarah Fish, widow of Thomas, a feather bed, warming pan, &c. and 12s. to buy a bible. To daughters Mary and Sarah, wearing apparel. To grandchildren Ruth and John Lawton, each 12s. to buy bibles. To all my children, the rest of estate.

I. MARY, m. GEORGE LAWTON, — b. 1673, Sep. 20. d. — b. d. — of John & Mary (Boomer) Lawton.

1. Ruth, 1694, Sep. 20.
2. John,
3. Daughter,
4. Daughter,

II. ROBERT, m. 1700, Jan. 22, SUSANNA BRIGGS, — b. 1677, Nov. 6. d. 1730, Jan. 5. — b. 1681, Apr. 9. d. 1744. — Tiverton, R. I. — of William & Elizabeth (Cook) Briggs.

1. Comfort, 1703, Mar. 12.
2. Anne, 1704, Jul. 3.
3. John, 1706, Jun. 24.
4. Humphrey, 1708, May 12.
5. Tabitha, 1710, Sep. 3.
6. Sarah, 1712, Nov. 2.
7. Lydia, 1716, Feb. 18.
8. Elizabeth, 1719, Feb. 18.
9. Deborah, 1722, Mar. 12.
10. Mary, 1723, Nov. 8.
11. Thomas,

1698. He had ear mark for cattle recorded.

1729, Dec. 29. Will—proved 1730, Feb. 17. Exx. wife Susanna. To her, all land and housing where I live, for life, which was given her by her father, negroes Newport, Quacko, Dinah, £500, all cattle, horsekind, sheep and swine, all other movables, money, all parts of vessels and cargoes, wherever they may be. To son John, house and land, at decease of his mother, £500 and my gun. To son Thomas, certain land and housing leased to James Pettee, and £500, at age. To son-in-law Philip Taylor, and daughter Comfort, his wife, all leather, hides and bark, which was my son Humphrey's, deceased, his possession at his uncle, John Taylor's, in Little Compton (they paying their father, John Taylor, rent due from Humphrey). To Comfort, also, £30. To daughter Anne Dennis, £120 and feather bed. To daughter Tabitha, £100. To daughters Sarah, Elizabeth and Deborah, £100 each, at eighteen. To daughter Lydia, £50, at eighteen. To sons John and Thomas, all lands in Jerseys. If any loss occurs on money out at bond, half to be borne by two sons and other half by daughters.

Inventory, £2,911, 9d., viz: bible and other books £2, money, bills of credit, &c. £111, 4s., silver money £26, 5s., 7 feather beds, stillyards, money scales, silver spoons, 3 guns, sword cane, negro Newport £90, Quacko, like to die, nothing, Dinah £60, neat cattle, horsekind, swine and fowls £14, 4s. 5d., bonds £2,051, 6s. 9d., half of brig, at sea, supposed to be lost, never seen no more, ¼ of a sloop, at sea, to be accounted for when come home.

1743, Jan. 20. Will—proved 1744, May 15. Widow Susanna. Exs. daughters Deborah and Mary. To son John, all homestead in Tiverton, half at death of testator and the other half when all daughters are married. To daughters Tabitha, Lydia, Deborah and Mary, profits of half the farm and house, while unmarried. To daughter Comfort Taylor, £300. To daughter Ann Sanford, £250. To daughter Tabitha Dennis, £300 and feather bed. To daughter Sarah Soule, £200 and negro girl Jenny. To daughters Lydia and Elizabeth Dennis, £200 each. To daughter Deborah Dennis, oval table, &c. To daughter Mary Dennis, negro woman Dinah. To unmarried daughters having residence in house, the service of negro man Newport, while they are unmarried and then to be sold and money equally divided to five daughters, Elizabeth, Sarah, Ann, Deborah and Mary. To daughters Comfort, Ann, Tabitha, Sarah, Lydia, Elizabeth, Deborah and Mary, all outlands in Tiverton. To grandson Robert Dennis, my gun. To daughters Deborah and Mary, rest of personal.

Inventory, £4,863, 9d.

III. SARAH, m. THOMAS FISH, — b. 1679, Oct. 31. d. 1712 + — b. d. 1712 (—). — of Fish.

IV. JOHN, m. ANN BRAYTON, — b. 1682, Aug. 15. d. 1732, Aug. 4. — b. 1683, Jul. 6. d. 1747, Aug. 28. — Portsmouth, Newport, R. I. — of Stephen & Ann (Tallman) Brayton.

1. John,

1709. Freeman.

1718. Deputy.

(1743, Jan. 4. John Dennis, of John and Anne, of Newport, married Lydia Lawton, of John and Abigail, of Portsmouth.)

He and his wife were buried in the burial ground of Robert Dennis, at Portsmouth.

V. JOSEPH, m. 1721, Apr. 20, SARAH DURFEE, — b. 1689, May 25. d. 1759, Oct. 24. — b. 1693, Mar. 1. d. 1759, Apr. 21. — Portsmouth, R. I. — of Thomas & Ann (Freeborn) Durfee.

1. Sarah, 1723, Jul. 1.
2. Sarah, 1725, Apr. 1.
3. Robert, 1727, Sep. 12.
4. Joseph, 1730, Jan. 15
5. Ann, 1731, Dec. 19.
6. Ruth, 1733, Dec. 6.
7. Lydia, 1735, Oct. 12.
8. Freeborn, 1739, Aug. 18.

1710. Freeman.

1720–21–31. Deputy.

1759, Jun. 15. Will—proved 1759, Dec. 10. Ex. son Robert. To son Robert, all housing and lands, wearing apparel, choice of horsekind, two heifers, old breeding sow, all farming and cooper's tools, gun, walking stick, &c. To grandson William Earle, son of my daughter Sarah Earle, £30, at eighteen. To daughter Lydia Fish, a silver cup. To four daughters, Ann Coggeshall, Ruth Cory, Lydia Fish and Freeborn Dennis, rest of household goods and £100 each. To son Joseph's widow, Mercy Dennis, privilege of living in my dwelling house, while widow of my son, and a yearling steer. To daughter Freeborn, privilege of living in house with my son Robert. To son Robert, all my money, debts due, and rest of estate.

Inventory, £3,993, 14s., viz: wearing apparel, £237, pewter, 2 wheels, worsted comb, silver cup and 7 silver spoons £84, books, razor, glass, &c. £4, 10s., 2 cows, 3 young cattle, 2 mares, 4 swine, old sow, 2 heifers, hay £620, cider-mill, &c.

DERBY.

FRANCIS, m. ANN, — b. d. 1663. — b. d.

(She m. (2) John Read.)

Warwick, R. I.

1662, Oct. 1. He bought of John Gereardy, for £4, a right in two shares of meadow.

1663, Apr. 17. He bought of John Sweet, his dwelling house, lot, &c., for £45.

1663, Sep. 4. Will—proved 1663, Oct. 31. Exx. wife Ann. Overseers, Randall Holden and John Greene. To eldest son Francis, dwelling house, and land appertaining, and if he die without issue, then to son Eleazer. To wife Ann, use of land and house, and the rest of estate to be at her disposal to bring up children.

It is assumed that Tristram Derby was his son.

I. FRANCIS, — b. 1660, Jan. 20. d. — Warwick, R. I., Southold, N. Y.

His house was burned by the Indians.

1683. Southold, Long Island. He went thence before this year.

II. ELEAZER, — b. 1662, Mar. 21. d. — Warwick, R. I.

DERBY. 2d column. II. Eleazer, m. Mary 1685. He had moved to Oyster Bay, N. Y., by this date.

1669, Mar. 12. He was apprenticed to Benjamin Barton, with consent of his father-in-law, John Read, and Ann, his wife, own mother of Eleazer.

1686, Feb. 22. He disclaimed any interest in the estate left by his father's will, to his brother Francis.

III. TRISTRAM, m. MARY, — b. d. 1747. — b. d. 1756, Feb. 19. — Providence, Scituate, R. I. — of

1. Tristram,

1715, Dec. 15. He bought of Samuel Fisk, 50 acres, west side of Seven Mile Line, for £30.

1724, Apr. 2. He sold Thomas Scott, 10 acres, for £5.

1725, Jun. 28. He sold to John Stone, 127 acres and other land, for £125.

1747, Aug. 17. Will—proved 1747, Aug. 28. Exx. wife Mary. To her, half of movables. To son Tristram, the other half of movables, but if he never come to New England, then the wife of testator to have that half also.

Inventory, £295, 7s. 9d., viz: plate shirt buttons £1, 15s., purse and apparel £23, 7s, shoe buckles 5s., books and gloves £1, 11s., notes and bonds £160, 9s. 9d., pewter, bed, chest, chair, &c.

1747, Aug. 31. Will—proved 1756, Oct. 6. Widow Mary. Ex. cousin Joshua Angell. To cousin Samuell Angell, a chest. To cousin Mary Angell, the best feather bed, &c. To cousin Avis Angell, a chest and box, &c. To cousins Phebe Evans and Wait Sheldon, two pewter plates each. To cousin Joshua Angell, money, bonds, notes, pewter, &c., and to him, the part of movable estate that was to have been for husband's son Tristram, if he came to New England, or otherwise to be for testatrix.

NATHANIEL, b. d. 1692.
m. (1)
JOAN TYLER, (widow) b. d.
m. (2)
SARAH, b. d. 1723.

(She m. (2) Thomas Brown.)

Providence, Newport, New Shoreham, R. I.

1650, Jul. 27. He sold to Arthur Fenner, 6 acres upland and two spots of meadow. On the same date, he sold Nicholas Power his home lot, lying next to widow Sayles' lot.

1650, Aug. 12. He sold Ralph Earle, of Portsmouth, for full satisfaction, all rights in all my housing, lands, &c., in Providence.

1655. Freeman.

1660. Newport. He probably moved here about this time.

1663, May 26. In a deed of this date, from John Sayles to William Hawkins, he mentions that the land conveyed had formerly belonged to Joan Tyler, afterwards wife to Nathaniel Dickens (and by latter sold to Ralph Earle, who sold it to Sayles).

1671, Jan. 30. He was allowed 4s., for service done for the colony, to be paid out of Thomas Flounder's estate.

1671, May 8. Juryman.

1677. Feb. 28. He sold to certain Hebrews, land now included in the Jewish Cemetery, at Newport.

1680. Taxed 5s.

1690, Oct. 18. Will—proved 1723, Jan. 16. Exx. wife Sarah. To eldest son Thomas, a 60 acre lot and 20 acre lot. To daughter Dorcas Dodge, 20 acres she lives on. The rest of children are left to care of wife Sarah, to whom all other estate is given—land, housing and cattle, and at her death, what is left to go to children unprovided for—and not named in the will.

1705, Jun. 15. Sarah Brown, widow of Nathaniel Dickens, and her two sons, John and Roger Dickens, sold to Thomas Rathbone, for £17, 10s., certain land that Nathaniel Dickens, by will, gave wife Sarah, for life, and at her death to sons John and Roger.

1720, Mar. 7. Will — proved 1723, Jan. 16. Sarah Brown. Exs. husband Thomas Brown and son John Dickens. She mentions the fact that her former husband, Nathaniel Dickens, had given her land on which she dwells, to be at her disposal to children, and that she had possessed land for twenty-eight years. To husband Thomas Brown, she gives for life, half the land where she dwells and half of land in Cow Neck, and at his death, all said land to son John Dickens (who was to have the other half of lands at her death).

The wills of Nathaniel Dickens, and his widow Sarah, were probated on same day. Her second husband, Thomas Brown, died in 1723, a few months after her. (His inventory was taken 1723, May 9.)

See: American Genealogist. v. 19, p. 133.

I. DORCAS, b. 1664. d. 1737, Feb. 18.
m. 1680, Jan. 7,
TRISTRAM DODGE, b. 1647. d. 1733, Aug. 18. of Tristram Dodge.

1. Nathaniel, 1682, Nov. 3.
2. Thomas, 1684, Jan. 23.
3. Ebenezer, 1687, Oct. 21.
4. Hezekiah, 1690, Dec. 25.
5. Dorcas, 1694, May 16.
6. Tristram,
7. Sarah,

II. MARY, b. d.
m. 1685, Apr. 21,
THOMAS RATHBONE, b. 1657. d. 1733, Dec. 26. of John & Margaret ( ) Rathbone.

1. Margaret, 1686, Jan. 17.
2. Mary, 1687, Jan. 24.
3. Patience, 1690, Nov. 14.
4. Constance, 1692, Jan. 17.
5. Thomas, 1695, Jan. 29.
6. Sarah, 1698, Apr. 1.
7. Elizabeth, 1700, Mar. 1.
8. Samuel, 1702, Jul. 1.
9. John, 1705, May 29.
10. Sylvia, 1707, Mar. 1.

III. THOMAS, b. 1668. d. 1718, Sep. 4. New Shoreham, R. I.
m. 1693, Dec. 25,
SARAH, b. 1674. d. 1733, Apr. 24. of

See: American Genealogist, v. 19, p. 134.

1692, Jan. 10. Freeman.

1720. Feb. 9. Administration to widow Sarah. Inventory, £189, 7s., viz: purse and apparel £17, 2 beds, pewter, gun, 300 lbs. cheese, 6 cows, yoke of oxen, bull, 2 yearling, 4 calves, 2 mares, 12 swine, &c.

1733, May 5. Administration on estate of Sarah Dickens, widow of Thomas, was given to her son-in-law, William Tosh. Inventory, £221, 1s.

He and his wife were buried in the town burial ground.

1. Sarah, 1696, Jul. 5.
2. Abigail, 1698, Jan. 19.
3. Mary, 1701, Jul. 5.
4. Thomas, 1703, Aug. 5.
5. Elizabeth, 1705, Mar. 14.
6. William, 1707, May 5.
7. Daniel, 1709, Jun. 10.
8. Michael, 1713, Jul. 9.
9. Anne, 1715, May 7.
10. Dorothy, 1717, Jul. 19.

(2d WIFE.)

IV. JOHN, b. d. New Shoreham, R. I.
m.
JANE BALL, b. d. of Edward & Mary (George) Ball.

See: American Genealogist v. 19, p. 134, 222

1723, Aug. 16. He and wife Joanna, deeded land.

1728, Sep. 1. He deeded son John, for love, &c., 25 acres.

1. John,
Mary

V. ROGER, b. d. New Shoreham, R. I

1709. Freeman.

There was a dau. Mercy
See: American Genealogist
v. 19, p. 134.

DODGE.

TRISTRAM, b. d.
m. ——— b. d.

Newfoundland, New Shoreham, R. I.

He was not one of the original settlers (in 1661), but closely followed them, and early had a grant of land, having come from Newfoundland to teach the art of fishing to the people of New Shoreham, as the records of that town declare.

1664. New Shoreham. Freeman.

1676. Sergeant.

1678. Freeman.

See: American Genealogist
v. 19, p. 134-135.
v. 26, p. 228-9

I. JOHN, b. d. 1729. New Shoreham, R. I.
m.
MARY Enos (Innis) b. d. of

See: American Genealogist. v. 19, p. 135

1729, Jun. 2. Administration to son David. Inventory, £111, viz: 4 oxen, 3 cows, 5 yearlings, 40 sheep, 5 hogs, mare, colt, wearing clothes £5, cash £1, 3s., beds, &c.

1. John, 1680, Jan. 10.
2. Mary, 1682, Apr. 18.
3. John, 1686, Jan. 18.
4. Catharine, 1688, Mar. 17.
5. David, 1691, Dec. 26.
6. Sarah, 1694, Apr. 7.
7. Elizabeth. 1696, Nov. 4.
8. Alexander, 1699, Jun. 15.

II. TRISTRAM, b. 1647. d. 1733, Aug. 18. New Shoreham, R. I.
m. 1680, Jan. 7,
DORCAS DICKENS, b. 1664. d. 1737, Feb. 18. of Nathaniel & Joan ( ) Dickens.

1678. Freeman.

1733, Jul. 30. Will—proved 1735, Jun. 7. Ex. son Nathaniel. To wife Dorcas, house and land on Block Island, for life, and all movables, for life. To son Nathaniel, the land and housing, at death of wife, and to daughters Dorcas Langworthy and Sarah Mitchell, the movables, at wife's death. To sons Thomas, Ebenezer, Hezekiah and Tristram, £10 each, and to daughters Dorcas Langworthy and Sarah Mitchell, £5 each.

He and his wife were buried in the town burial ground.

1. Nathaniel, 1682, Nov. 3.
2. Thomas, 1684, Jan. 23.
3. Ebenezer, 1687, Oct. 21.
4. Hezekiah, 1690, Dec. 25.
5. Dorcas, 1694, May 16.
6. Tristram,
7. Sarah,

III. WILLIAM, b. d. New Shoreham, R. I.
m.
SARAH GEORGE, b. d. of Peter & Mary ( ) George.

See: American Genealogist, v. 19, p. 136.

1. William, 1680, Mar. 8.
2. Elizabeth, 1683, May 1.
3. Mary,
4. Samuel, 1691, Sep. 9.

IV. ISRAEL, b. d New Shoreham, R. I., New London, Conn.

1690. New London.

1720, Oct. 21. He sold for £14, to his brothers, John, Tristram and William, all his interest in housing and lands of their father, Tristram Dodge, late of Block Island, deceased.

V. ANN, b. d. 1723 +
m. 1688, Jan. 10,
JOHN RATHBONE, b. d. 1723. of John & Margaret ( ) Rathbone.

1. Mercy, 1688, Oct. 3.
2. Jonathan, 1691, May 22.
3. John, 1693, Dec. 23.
4. Joshua, 1696, Feb. 19.
5. Benjamin, 1701, Feb. 17.
6. Ann, 1703, Aug. 9.
7. Nathaniel, 1708, Feb. 6.
8. Thomas, 1709, Mar. 2.

DOLOVER.

JOSEPH, b. d. 1731.
m.
RACHEL, b. d. 1731 +

Kings Town, East Greenwich, R. I.

1670. He was on the jury in case of murder of Walter House, the said jury being called by authority of the government of Connecticut.

1679, Jul. 29. He and forty-one other inhabitants of Narragansett sent a petition to the King, praying that he "would put an end to these differences about the government thereof, which hath been so fatal to the prosperity of the place; animosities still arising in people's minds as they stand affected to this or that government."

1687, Sep. 1. Taxed 5*s.* 3½*d.*

1729, Jul. 5. Will—proved 1731, Mar. 27. Exx. wife Rachel. He calls himself very ancient. To son John, 5*s.* To daughter Lydia Parker, 1*s.* To son William, 5*s.* To daughter Mary Huling, 1*s.* To daughter Abigail Niles, 1*s.* To wife all my whole estate, and after both our deaths to grandson William King, son of daughter Abigail, wife of Nathaniel Niles.

Inventory £65, 7*s.* 6*d.*, viz: a cow, 2 shoats, bed, wheel, &c.

I. JOSEPH. b. d. 1709. Kings Town, R. I.

1700, May 4, He was summoned with others, by the Assembly to answer the charge in court of being engaged in a riot.

1709, May 1. Will—proved 1709, Jun. 13. Ex. brother William Dolover. Overseer William Hall. To sister Rebecca Card, wife of Peleg, £20. To sisters Lydia Parker, and Sarah Johnson, wife of Joseph Johnson, of Rhode Island, and Mary Dolover, £20 each. To brother William Dolover, my wood boat, canoe, sails, anchor, and cable. The farm and neck in Warwick to be sold to pay legacies and brother William to have the rest. To overseer, 40*s.*, to buy a ring.

II. JOHN, b. d. East Greenwich, R. I.

1716, Jun. 13. He sold William Hamilton, of East Greenwich, half of 40 acres.

III. REBECCA, b. d.
m.
PELEG CARD, b. d. of Card.

IV. LYDIA, b. d.
m.
—— PARKER, b. d. of Parker.

V. SARAH, b. d. 1731 +
m.
JOSEPH JOHNSON, b. 1677, Oct. 3. d. 1731, of John & Mary ( ) Johnson.

1. Reuben,
2. Stephen,
3. Sarah,
4. Joseph,
5. Gideon,
6. Daniel,
7. Nathaniel.

VI. WILLIAM, b. d. 1709 + Kings Town, R. I.

VII. MARY, b. d.
m.
—— HULING, b. d. of Huling.

VIII. ABIGAIL, b. d.
m. (1)
—— KING, b. d. of King.
m. (2)
NATHANIEL NILES, b. d. of Niles.

DUNGAN. 1st column. His wife was born in 1609, as shown by her baptism.

DUNGAN.

WILLIAM, b. d. 1636.
m.
FRANCES WESTON (widow) b. 1611. d. 1677, Sep.
of Lewis Latham.

(She m. (3) Jeremiah Clarke, (4) William Vaughan.)

London, Middlesex Co., Eng.

He was a perfumer.

His residence was in St. Martin's in the Fields.

He never came to America though his descendants are numerous here. A manuscript account of the Barker family gives some light on his family. "Frances, the wife of Wm. Vaughan died Sept. 1677, in the 67th year of her age. She was daughter of Lewis Latham, she was sometime the wife of Lord Weston, then wife to William Dungan, by whom she had one son and three daughters. Her son Thomas Dungan married and settled in Pennsylvania, and was the first Baptist minister in them parts. Her daughter Barbara married to James Barker, of Rhode Island. After William Dungan died she married Mr. Jeremiah Clarke and came over to New England with her four children above mentioned. She had by her husband Clarke five sons; after he died she married to Mr. Vaughan."

1636, Sep. 13. Will—proved 1636, Oct. 5. Exx. wife Frances. Overseers, Mr. Thomas Gibbon, and Mr. Samuel Smith. To each child £70, viz: to Barbara, William, Frances, and Thomas Dungan; to be paid at full age or marriage of each. If any child die, the survivors to have his or her part. To wife, the government of children's portions and all other my estate during widowhood. If she marry again she to give good security to the overseers for true and sure payment of legacies to children. To wife, all other my estate whatsoever, be it in goods, chattels, leases, ready money, plate or other my substance whatsoever. To overseers 10*s.* apiece to buy them rings.

1656, Jan. 18. His widow being now the wife of Rev. William Vaughan, entered into an agreement with her son, Walter Clarke, through his guardians John Cranston and James Barker, who are called his "brothers-in-law." (John Cranston had married Walter Clarke's own sister, and James Barker had married Walter Clarke's half sister.)

By this agreement Walter Clarke was to have dwelling house where Mrs. Vaughan lived, garden, orchard and certain lands which was his inheritance, but possession to be had by his mother till Sept. 29th, or till tobacco was cured. The house where Captain John Cranston lived

I. BARBARA, b. 1628 ± d.
m. 1644,
JAMES BARKER, b. 1623. d. 1702. of James Barker.

1. Elizabeth,
2. James, 1648.
3. Mary,
4. Sarah,
5. Joseph,
6. Peter,
7. Christianna
8. William, 1662.

II. WILLIAM, b. d.

III. FRANCES, b. 1630 ± d. 1697,
m 1648,
RANDALL HOLDEN, b. 1612. d. 1692, Aug. 23. of Holden.

1. Frances, 1649, Sep. 29.
2. Elizabeth, 1652, Aug.
3. Mary, 1654, Aug.
4. John, 1656, Jan.
5. Sarah, 1658, Feb.
6. Randall, 1660, Apr.
7. Margaret, 1663, Jan.
8. Charles, 1666, Mar. 22.
9. Barbara, 1668, Jul. 2.
10. Susanna, 1670, Dec. 8.
11. Anthony, 1673, Oct. 16.

IV. THOMAS, b. d. 1688. Newport, R. I., Cold Spring, Pa.
m.
ELIZABETH WEAVER, b. d. of Clement & Mary (Freeborn) Weaver.

1. William,
2. Clement,
3. Thomas,
4. Jeremiah,
5. Elizabeth,
6. Mary,
7. John,
8. Rebecca,
9. Sarah.

1656. Freeman.

1671. Juryman.

1677. East Greenwich. He was named with forty-seven others who took grant of 5,000 acres to be called East Greenwich.

1678. Sergeant.

1678-81. Deputy.

1680. Newport. Taxed £1, 2*s.* 6*d.*

1681. Constable.

1682, Jun. 28. He deeded his cousin (*i. e.* nephew) Thomas Weaver, of Newport, 100 acres in East Greenwich, for love, &c.

1682, Sep. 25. He and wife Elizabeth sold John Bailey, late of Portsmouth, 50 acres in Newport, buildings, gardens, &c., for £140.

1684. Cold Spring. He moved there this year and established a Baptist church, of which he was the first pastor. Morgan Edwards gives the following account of him. "In 1684, Thomas Dungan removed from Rhode Island and settled at a place called Cold Spring, Bucks Co., between Bristol and Trenton." After alluding to the breaking up of the church in 1702 (an old grave yard alone marking the site of the church in 1770, when Edwards wrote), he further says of Mr. Dungan, "The Rev. Thomas Dungan, the 1st Baptist minister in the Province, now (1770), exists in a progeny of between 600 and 700." He tells us that the children of Thomas Dungan married as follows:

1. William, m. —— Wing of Rhode Island, and had five children. 2. Clement, no issue. 3. Thomas, m. —— Drake, and had nine children. 4. Jeremiah, m. —— Drake, and had eight children. 5. Elizabeth, m. —— West and had four children. 6. Mary, m. —— Richards, and had three children. 7. John, no issue. 8. Rebecca, m. —— Doyle, and had three children. 9. Sarah, m. —— Kerrel, and had six children.

1686. He baptized and ordained Elias Keach, son of the famous Benjamin Keach of London.

was to be his, as appeared by deed; Mrs. Vaughan was to pay all debts, and for that purpose had half of a house which she was to sell, and she also had certain land, the household goods, &c., for herself and the rest of Jeremiah Clarke's children other than Walter.

William Dungan's widow was buried in Newport Cemetery, the stone bearing the following inscription. "Here Lyeth ye Body of Mrs. Frances Vaughan, Alius Clarke, ye mother of ye only children of Capt'n Jeremiah Clarke. She died, ye 1 week in Sept. 1677 in ye 67th year of her age."

DURFEE. 2d column. VI. Benjamin, b. 1680, d. 1754, Jan. 6. His wife Prudence, b. 1681. Children: 1. James, 1701, Aug. 28. 2. Ann, 1703, Jan. 11. 3. Pope, 1705, Jan. 7. 4. William, 1707, Dec. 5. 5. Benjamin, 1709, Jan. 5. 6. Mary, 1711, Jan. 30. 7. Susannah, 1713, Jan. 28. 8. Martha, 1719, Jul. 15. 9. Thomas, 1721, Nov. 5. VIII. Deliverance, m. 1724, Apr. 23, William Cory, of William & Martha (Cook) Cory. Children: 1. Patience, 1725, Mar. 25. 2. Caleb, 1729, Jul. 13. 3. John, 1731, Sep. 7.

See: American Genealogist, Apr., 1954, v. 30, no. 2, p. 125.

DUNN.

RICHARD, b. ; d. 1690 +
m. ——, b. ; d.

Newport, R. I.

1655. Freeman.

1680. Taxed £1, 12*s.* 2*d.*

1681–1705–7–8–9–11. Deputy.

1702, Jan. 12. He was one of the proprietors in common lands.

DUNN. 2d column. I. Richard, d. 1745+. He had another son, 2, Samuel, b. 1699; d. 1740, Feb., at Jamaica, W. I.; m. 1718, Nov., Ann Clarke, b. 1698, Sep. 8; d. 1746, Nov. 9, of Carew and Ann (Dyer) Clarke. Children, 1, James, 1720, May 1. 2, Richard, 1722, Apr. 21. 3, Samuel, 1724, Feb. 11. 4, Clarke, 1726, Feb. 5, Ann, 1728, May 11. 6, Gideon, 1730, Feb. 26. 7, Cary, 1732, June 11. 8, Bashub, 1734, Apr. 2. 9, Hannah, 1736, Sep. 11. 10, Felix, 1738, Nov. 9. This entry is from an old Bible of Samuel Dunn.[4] (Sam.,[3] Rich.,[2] Rich.,[1]), given by his grandfather Richard Dunn, in 1745. II. Samuel. Erase 2d marriage and children.

I. RICHARD, b. ; d. — Newport, R. I.
m.
HANNAH, b. 1675; d. 1734, Dec. 28. of

1. Son, 1692.

1690. Freeman. (He was called Richard, Jr., at this date.)

He held the title of Captain.

II. SAMUEL, b. ; d. — Newport, R. I.
m. (1) 1702, Oct. 16,
SARAH BAILEY, b. ; d. of Joseph Bailey.
m. (2) 1718, Nov.
ANN CLARKE, b. ; d. of Clarke.

1. Clarke, 1720.
2. Gideon, 1724, Feb. 11.
3. Charles, 1726, Feb. 26.
4. Gideon, 1730, Mar. 26.

III. NATHANIEL, b. 1671; d. 1735, Feb. 28. — New Shoreham, R. I.
m.
ELIZABETH LAWTON, b. 1674, Mar. 12; d. 1741, May 19. of Daniel & Rebecca (   ) Lawton.

1. Richard, 1698.
2. Isaac, 1702.
3. William, 1715.

1717, Feb. 3. He had a suit brought against him by William Dyer, for debt and damage of £80.

He was buried in the town burial ground, as was his wife also.

DURFEE.

THOMAS, b. 1643; d. 1712.
m. (1) ——, b. ; d.
m. (2) DELIVERANCE TRIPP, (w. of Abiel.), b. ; d. 1721.
of William & Mary (   ) Hall.

Portsmouth, R. I.

1664, Oct. His petition for remittance of fine laid upon him at last Court of Trials, for breach of bond, in October last, was denied by Assembly.

1679. He was thirty six years old, at this time.

1680. Taxed 8*s.*

1687–88. Constable.

1689, Jan. 30. He deeded son Thomas, for love, &c., my dwelling house, and land belonging to it, situate in a place called Common Fence, near Pocassett River, 8 acres in extent.

1698, Aug. 2. Upon petition of himself and wife Deliverance, late widow to Abiel Tripp, of Portsmouth, for confirming ferry between Rhode Island and Bristol, upon the heir of said Abiel Tripp, it was enacted by Assembly, that the ferry be stated upon said Thomas Durfee and his wife, till the heir of said Abiel Tripp, come of age, which will be about seven years, and that John Borden, be permitted to keep said ferry on equal privilege with said Durfee, both being obliged to carry all Magistrates, Deputies, Jurymen and all other persons upon his Majesty's service in the colony, and the post, ferriage free, and to pay 6*s.* each, yearly, into the General Treasury, all others being prohibited from using and following the employ without license from the Assembly.

1710, Feb. 4. Will—proved 1712, Jul. 14. Exx. wife Deliverance. To wife, housing and land in Portsmouth, for life, and then to daughters Patience Tallman and Deliverance Durfee, equally. To eldest son Robert, 5*s.*, having already settled certain lands in Freetown upon him. To son Thomas, 5*s.*, he having had already. To son William, 5*s.*, he having had more than £40. To youngest son Benjamin, 50 acres, in Tiverton. To wife Deliverance, a negro called Jack, for life, and at her death, the value of said negro, equally, to two daughters. To grandson Richard, eldest son of Richard, deceased, 5*s.* To grandson Thomas, son of Richard, 60 acres, in Tiverton. To Ann Potter, wife of William Potter, £7. To wife Deliverance and two daughters, rest of lands. To wife, all movable estate.

1718, Apr. 8. Will — proved 1721, Feb. 13. Widow Deliverance. Ex. son Abiel Tripp. To daughter Patience Tallman, two iron pots, an iron kettle, all my cups, handkerchiefs, aprons and shifts, only one to be buried in, and a cedar tub and the rowing boat. To daughter Deliverance Durfee, bed, &c., I now lie on, at my son-in-law Tallman's, and all movables at my son Abiel Tripp's, only what I have given to son Abiel, already.

Inventory, £55, 5*s.*, 6*d.*, viz: purse and apparel £15, 5*s.* 6*d.*, books 10*s.*, the rowing boat and an old axe £1, spinning wheel, warming pan, pewter, looking glass, spice mortar, 11 yards of drugget, sugar box, &c.

I. ROBERT, b. ; d. 1718. — Freetown, Mass.
m.
MARY SANFORD, b. 1664, Mar. 30; d. 1748, Nov. 15. of John & Mary (Gorton) Sanford.

(She m. (2) —— Thomas.)

1. Thomas,
2. John,
3. Benjamin, 1695, Jan. 30.
4. Peleg,
5. Mary,
6. Elizabeth,

1718, May 7. Will—proved 1718, Jun. 2. Exx. wife Mary. To her, all movable estate, and house and land in Freetown, for life. To son Peleg, half of house and land at decease of wife. To daughters Mary and Elizabeth, the other half of house and land at decease of wife. To son Thomas, a house. To children, viz: Thomas, John, Benjamin, Peleg, Mary and Elizabeth, a parcel of land at Pocasset, on the Rhode Island side, equally, to all said children.

II. RICHARD, b. ; d. 1700. — Tiverton, R. I.
m.
ANN ALMY, b. 1667, Nov. 29; d. of Christopher & Elizabeth (Cornell) Almy.

(She m. (2) Benjamin Jefferson.)

1. Richard,
2. Mary,
3. Thomas,
4. Ann,
5. Hope,
6. Amey,

1700, Apr. 10. Inventory, £16, 5*s.*, shown by widow Ann. Wooden and earthern things £1, 6*s.*, glass, pewter, iron and brass £1, 11*s.*, looking glass, linen, beds and bedding £9, clothes £2, 15*s.*, swine 10*s.*, feathers 12*s.*, saddle, pillion, &c.

III. THOMAS, b. ; d. 1729, Feb. 11. — Portsmouth, R. I.
m.
ANN FREEBORN, b. 1669, Mar. 28; d. 1729 (—). of Gideon & Sarah (Brownell) Freeborn.

1. Ann, 1691, Aug. 25.
2. Sarah, 1693, Mar. 1.
3. Freeborn, 1695, Dec. 15.
4. Patience, 1697, Jun. 12.
5. Mary, 1701, Jan. 22.
6. Martha, 1702, Feb. 20.
7. Gideon, 1704, Jan 15.
8. Thomas, 1706, Jun. 6.
9. Susanna,
10. Job,
11. Elizabeth,

1707–9–13. Deputy.

1715, Oct. 13. He and wife Ann, mortgaged certain land, for £350.

1717, Jun. 18. He petitioned Assembly, for a good and sufficient highway, to be laid out to his farm, at Common Fence Point, he having already applied to the committee of town of Portsmouth, but not obtained it. The Assembly ordered the committee to lay out within one month's time, a good, lawful and passable highway, fit for horses and carts to pass and repass.

1720, Oct. 13. He answered the suit of Stephen Brayton, for impounding an ox—saying that said ox was unruly, and broke into his meadow with other cattle.

1728, May 25. He deeded to son Gideon, for love, &c., my farm called Common Fence Farm Point, being the most north-eastern part of Rhode Island, 60 acres.

1728, May 29. He deeded to son Thomas, for love, &c., 14 acres, and two months later, 25 acres.

1729, Feb. 9. Will—proved 1729, Feb. 24. Ex. son Gideon. To son Gideon, four parcels of land, viz: the land where house standeth, called the homestead, where I now dwell, a piece called Spink's ground, a parcel called the Wind Mill Hill land, and another piece called Jennings' land. In consideration of this legacy, Gideon was to give a deed to testator's son Job, of the tract called Common Fence Farm, formerly deeded son Gideon, by his father, and if Gideon failed to give deed within a month of testator's decease, the said four parcels were to be for son Job. When Job is of age and possesses deed of farm, he and my son Thomas, are to come to an equal division of all lands in Common Fence, both aforementioned farm and that which I have given already to Thomas, by two deeds of gift. The house and rest of lands in Common Fence Farm, to be equally shared by sons Thomas and Job. Certain land was to be sold by executor and money equally divided to seven daughters, viz: Ann Estes, Sarah Dennis, Patience, Mary, Martha, Susanna and Elizabeth Durfee. To daughters Mary, Susanna and Elizabeth, a feather bed each, their sisters, Patience and Martha, having already received each a bed. To five unmarried daughters, all pewter, brass, iron pots and rest of household goods undisposed of, and to each, a good cow, and to them while unmarried, the privilege of eastward chamber to live in. To sons Gideon, Thomas and Job, the rest of cattle, horses, sheep and swine, husbandry gear and other movables.

Inventory, £550, 12*s.*, viz: wearing apparel £23, 10*s.*, pocketbook, razor, spectacles, &c. £13, books £1, money scales, his tailor's shears, goose, box iron, heaters, stillyards, spinning wheel, half a pair of worsted combs, negro man and bed £40, poultry £3, 5*s.*, horsekind £53, neat cattle and hay £158, 10*s.*, sheep £62, 10*s.*, swine £11, 10*s.*, &c. The rooms named, were: outward room, bed room, kitchen, bed chamber, outward room chamber, garret and cellar.

His son Job, being under age, choose his uncle, Gideon Freeborn, for guardian, and his daughter Elizabeth, choose her uncle, William Anthony.

IV. WILLIAM, b. ; d. 1727. — Portsmouth, Tiverton, R. I.
m. (1)
ANN, b. ; d. of
m. (2)
MARY, b. ; d. of

1. Samuel,
2. Joseph,
3. David,
4. Abigail,

1697, Jun. 14. He and wife Ann, sold William Burrington, 10 acres, for £50.

1698. Tiverton. He had ear mark for cattle recorded.

1727, Feb. 16. Will—proved 1727, Jun. 24. Exs. sons Samuel and Joseph. To wife Mary, the indoor movables, with certain exceptions, money, two cows, mare, twenty sheep, a swine, six fowls,

It is assumed that Ann Potter, to whom he gave legacy, was his daughter, though he does not directly say so.

DURFEE. 2d column. VI. Benjamin. He had also 10 Samuel, 11. Richard. 1753, Jun. 26. Will-proved, 1754, Feb. 4. He mentions boys, Benjamin, Richard and Thomas, grandson, William Durfee, son of Samuel; grandsons, Joseph Hix, Durfee Hix, and James Durfee; and daughters, Ann Browning, Mary, Susanna and Martha.

negro woman, use of dwelling house, half the orchard and garden spot. To son Samuel, certain land and housing in Tiverton, and land in Dartmouth. To son Joseph, land in Tiverton and Dartmouth. To each son, a negro boy and gun, and to them, all the stock of cattle, &c., and outdoor movables, they paying their sister Abigail, £50 and two good beds. To son David, 5*s.*, he already having had £1,000, in the farm where he lives. To wife, the keep of a horse, &c., by executors, and they to find her with firewood, cut at her door, twenty bushels of corn, two hundred pounds pork and two hundred pounds beef, yearly.

Inventory, £747, 4*s.*, 8*d.*, viz: negro woman and two negro boys £200, plate, silver money &c., £408, 1*s.* 2*d.*, bible, dictionary and other books £1, 8s., 2 guns, cane, 7 feather beds, pewter, cider, 27 geese, fowls, 12 swine, 200 sheep, 80 lambs, 4 oxen, 4 steers, 7 cows, 2 bulls, 2 heifers, 5 yearlings, 8 horsekind, &c.

Real estate, lands and housing £1,700.

V. ANN, m. WILLIAM POTTER, — b. d. b. d. of Nathaniel & Elizabeth (   ) Potter.
1. Nathaniel,
2. William, 1696, Nov. 11.

VI. BENJAMIN, m. PRUDENCE EARLE, — b. d. 1755 ± b. d. 1733, Mar. 12. — Tiverton, Newport, R. I. — of William & Prudence (   ) Earle.
1. Thomas,
2. Daughter,

His wife's death is recorded at Freetown, Mass.

1755, May 14. A division of lands in Freetown, was made at this date: said lands having been given by last will of Benjamin Durfee, late of Newport, deceased, to his son Thomas, and three grandsons. To Thomas Durfee, son of said Benjamin, 138 acres. To grandson William Durfee, 138 acres. To heirs of grandson Joseph Hix, deceased, 220 acres. To grandson James Durfee, 70 acres.

(2d WIFE.)

VII. PATIENCE, m. 1708, Sep. 23, BENJAMIN TALLMAN, — b. d. 1723 ± b. 1684, Jan. 28. d. 1759. — of Peter & Joan (Briggs) Tallman.
1. Benjamin, 1710, Jun. 19.
2. Mary, 1712, Aug. 2.
3. Deliverance, 1715, Feb. 4.
4. William,
5. Patience, 1721, Apr. 6.

VIII. DELIVERANCE, — b. d.

EARLE.

RALPH, m. JOAN, — b. d. 1678. b. d. 1680 +

Portsmouth, R. I.

1638. He and others, were admitted inhabitants of Aquidneck, having submitted themselves to the government, that is or shall be established.

1639, Apr. 30. He and twenty-eight others signed declaration of allegiance. "We, whose names are underwritten, do acknowledge ourselves the legal subjects of his Majesty, King Charles, and in his name, do hereby bind ourselves into a civil body politicke, unto his laws according to matters of justice."

1640, Jan. 7. It was ordered that he and his co-partner, Mr. Wilbur, shall serve the town with good sufficient stuff, viz: well sawn boards at 8*s.* the hundred, and half inch boards at 7*s.*, to be delivered at the pit by the waterside.

1640, Mar. 21. He sold William Baulstone, certain land.

1647. He was chosen to keep an inn, to sell beer and wine, and to entertain strangers.

1649. Treasurer.

1649. Overseer of the Poor.

1651, Jan. 16. He, with three others, was chosen to apportion a tax.

He was again elected Treasurer, this year.

1651, May 21. He deeded Nicholas Hart, of Portsmouth, and Joan, his wife, 8 acres and messuage, for valuable consideration.

1652, Jun. 24. He sold William Arnold, of Providence, land formerly owned by Francis Weston's wife, Margaret, near Pawtuxet Falls.

1654, Apr. 11. He and another, were chosen to oversee the work of the prison, &c.

1655. Freeman.

1655, May 5. Juryman.

1655, May 25. He was appointed by the Court of Commissioners, to keep a house of entertainment. A convenient sign was to be set out at the most perspicuous place, to give notice to strangers.

1658, Dec. 13. He sold William Cadman, 20 acres.

1667, Aug. 10. He joined a troop of horse (afterwards becoming Captain).

At about this time he commenced suit against Richard Lord and James Richards, of Hartford, possessors of land there, claiming that he had purchased the land of Underhill, in 1653, for £20.

1669, Apr. 28. Grand Jury.

1671, Jun. 7. He was appointed with others, to sit as a Special Court, to try "two Indians, now imprisoned upon criminal charge."

1673, Nov. 19. Will — recorded 1678, Jan. 14.

See: American Genealogist, v. 19, p. 165.

I. RALPH, m. 1659 (—) DORCAS SPRAGUE, — b. d. 1716. b. d. — Portsmouth, R. I., Dartmouth, Mass. — of Francis & Lydia (   ) Sprague.
1. John,
2. Ralph,
3. William,
4. Joseph,

1658, May 11. Portsmouth, R. I. Freeman.

1659, Oct. 26. Francis Sprague, of Duxbury, conveyed to his "son-in-law, Ralph Earle, of Rhode Island," &c., ½ share of land at Coakset and Acushena. At about this time Ralph moved to his new lands, and henceforth was of Dartmouth.

1688, Jun. 13. Dartmouth, Mass. He deeded son Ralph, for love, &c., half of westermost island called Elizabeth Island, to be his after my decease.

1689, Oct. 20. He deeded son William, 100 acres in Dartmouth.

1692, Jun. 10. He and wife Dorcas, deeded youngest son Joseph, for love, &c., 200 acres in Dartmouth, and salt marsh, had of father Sprague.

1693, Jul. 24. He deeded son William, for love, &c., ¼ of the island, called by the Indians Pocatahunka, being the westermost island.

1717, Jan. 6. Administration to son John Earle.

II. WILLIAM, m. (1) MARY WALKER, m. (2) PRUDENCE, — b. d. 1715, Jan. 15. b. d. b. d. 1718, Jan. 18. — Portsmouth, R. I., Dartmouth, Mass., Portsmouth, R. I. — of John & Katharine (   ) Walker. — of
1. Mary, 1655.
2. William,
3. Thomas,
4. Ralph, 1660.
5. Caleb,
(2d wife.)
6. John,
7. Prudence,

1654, Apr. 2. He and wife Mary, sold James Sands, their interest in 14 acres, that came by right of late widow Walker; the land having come by marriage of Mary Walker (daughter of widow), to William Earle.

EARLE. 2d column. II. William. His daughter Pruden b. 1681.

1658, May 11. Freeman.

1658. Juryman.

1665, May 1. He and William Cory, were given 1 acre on Briggs' Hill, and ¼ acre near the town pond, to have so long as they maintained a windmill for the town's use. Three years later an exchange was made (between town and Earle and Cory), of 2 acres near the mill for 2 acres elsewhere. (In 1684, the site was called Windmill Hill.)

1667, Dec. 5. His ear mark for cattle was recorded.

1670. Dartmouth, Mass. He probably removed there about this time and staid for a number of years, his interest there being large. He owned 2,000 acres, from his claims in the original division.

1680. Portsmouth. Taxed 8*s.* 6*d.*, with his mother.

1688, Jun. 26. He deeded son Ralph, and Mary, his wife, of Dartmouth, for love, &c., ½ a share of land in Freetown, east side of Taunton River.

1691, May 6. The Assembly met at his house, being removed from Newport, on account of the distemper.

1692, Oct. 6. He deeded son Thomas, of Dartmouth, ¼ share of land there.

1693–1704–1706. Deputy.

1713, Nov. 13. Will—proved 1715, Feb. 8. Ex. son John. Overseers, James Tallman, of Portsmouth, and Benjamin Durfee, of Tiverton. To son William, a brass milkpan, and like gift to sons Thomas, Ralph and John, and daughters Mary Borden, Mary Hix and Prudence Durfee, and to the last a negro girl "Kate," also. To son John, all rest of estate, real and personal, he paying legacies, as follows: To grandson Caleb Earle, 40 acres or £40, at 21. To granddaughter Joan Earle, daughter of Caleb, £10, at 20 years of age. Son John to allow wife comfortable and sufficient maintenance.

The daughter Mary Hix, mentioned in will, was widow of his son Caleb, she having married Joseph Hicks, for her second husband.

III. MARY, m. (1) WILLIAM CORY, m. (2) 1683 ± JOSEPH TIMBERLAKE, — b. d. 1718, Mar. 22. b. d. 1682. b. d. — of Cory. — of Henry & Mary (   ) Timberlake.
1. John,
2. William,
3. Mercy,
4. Anne,
5. Thomas,
6. Margaret,
7. Mary,
8. Caleb,
9. Roger,
10. Joan,
(By 2d husband.)
11. Sarah,

Exx. wife Jone. Overseer, John Tripp, Sr. To wife, all for life, and at her decease, as follows: To eldest son Ralph, and to Ralph, son of son William, all land and housing; said son Ralph having two parts and grandson Ralph, one part. The movable estate to be divided into five parts, of which son Ralph to have two parts, he paying 1*s.* to my son William. The other three parts to three daughters, viz. Mary, the wife of William Cory, Martha, wife of William Wood and Sarah, widow to late deceased, Thomas Cornell.

IV. MARTHA, m. WILLIAM WOOD, — b. d. b. d. 1697. of John Wood.

1. William, 2. George, 3. Josiah, 4. Daniel, 5. John, 6. Joseph, 7. Daughter, 8. Sarah, 9. Margaret, 10. Rebecca,

V. SARAH, m. (1) THOMAS CORNELL, m. (2) DAVID LAKE, — b. d. 1690 + ; b. d. 1673, May 23. of Thomas & Rebecca ( ) Cornell. ; b. d. 1696 + of Lake.

1. John, 2. Sarah, 3. Innocent, (By 2d husband.) 4. Sarah, 1678, May 10. 5. David, 1679, Jun. 2. 6. Jonathan, 1681, Dec. 30. 7. Joel, 1683, Jan. 30. 8. Joseph, 1690, Jun. 15.

EDES.

PHILIP, — b. d. 1682, Mar. 16.

Newport, R. I.

He served as an officer in Cromwell's army.

1671. Freeman.

1673. Juryman.

1679, Jul. 7. Will—Witnesses, John Woodman and William Hiscox. Reference to this will is found in a list of seventeen wills (between 1676 and 1695), that were presented to the court in 1700 by persons interested, the law requiring three witnesses, and these wills having but two.

1680. Taxed £1, 2*s.*

1682, Dec. 20. His death was alluded to in a letter from Samuel Hubbard to Governor Leete. "Your old friend Mr. Philip Eads, a merchant, a precious man, of a holy harmless blameless life and conversation. I judge faithful in what he practices though short in some of Jehovah's requirements, beloved of all sorts of men; his death was much bewailed."

EDMONDS.

ANDREW, m. 1675, Oct. 14, MARY HEARNDEN, — b. 1639. d. 1695. ; b. d. 1696 +

of Benjamin & Elizabeth (White) Hearnden.

Providence, R. I.

1676, Aug. 6. It was voted by Assembly "that Capt'n Andrew Edmonds and his company shall have the one-half of the produce of the Indians, being thirty-five brought in by them." (By an act of Assembly certain Indian men and women able for service were to be sold for nine years.)

1679, Mar. 3. He was granted on account of "his service done in the war time" 4 acres at the place called the narrow passage (now Red Bridge), "he there intending the keeping of a ferry."

1679, Dec. 4. In a deposition he calls himself aged forty or thereabouts.

1687, Jun. 2. Whereas there was some years since by our town of Providence grant made to Andrew Edmonds of a certain quantity of land adjoining to that place of Pawtucket River called the Narrow Passage to the quantity of 4 acres, and Arthur Fenner and Thomas Olney being appointed to bound out same, and they finding it to be very poor and uneven and barren, do allow unto said Andrew Edmunds in lieu of said 4 acres, certain land adjoining his dwelling, that he has already enclosed, and through said land free and sufficient egress and regress is to be at all times for all persons, both for horse and foot, cart and drift to and from the said Narrow Passage, said land being in quantity about 9 acres.

1687, Sep. 1. Taxed 1*s.* 3*d.*

1689, Dec. 25. He was granted 20*s.* per week, by Plymouth colony for his services in the late expedition against the Indians.

1690, Mar. 3. He was granted £6, "for his encouragement for future service," by Assembly, they having received a letter from Captain Arthur Fenner, subscribed by Benjamin Church, signifying that Captain Andrew Edmunds had done very good service in the late Eastern wars, and received £12, being but two-thirds of a captain's pay.

1690, Oct. 31. Mary Edmonds petitioned the Assembly for allowance of £6 in absence of her husband, more than £6 formerly allowed to him, her husband being now gone out in the wars for their Majesties' interest. Ordered to have the £6 paid out of rate of Providence with the greatest expedition as the said rate can be gathered in.

I. MARY, — b. 1676, Oct. 20. d.

II. SARAH, — b. 1678, Feb. 17. d.

EDMONDS. 2d column. II. Sarah m. 1695, Feb. 11, Daniel Hicks, of Daniel and Rebecca (Hanmer) Hicks. He b. 1660; d. 1746, Mar 21. Children. 1, Sarah, 1700, May 30. 2, Joseph, 1702, Oct. 8. 3, Hannah, 1705, Apr. 11. 4, Isaac, 1708, May 11. 5, Benjamin, 1711, Dec. 1.

III. WILLIAM, m. ALICE, — b. 1681, Mar. 7. d. 1725, Dec. 30. ; b. d. 1725 + of — Providence, R. I.

1. James, 2. William, 3. Mary, 4. Phebe, 5. Lydia, 6. Amey, 7. Daughter, 8. Daughter, 9. Daughter.

He was a blacksmith.

1708. Freeman.

1715, Feb. 14. He and wife Alice sold Zachariah Jones, a forty foot lot for £200, situated on west side of highway leading to corn mill, and on east side of river or cove that goes to the mill. The sale included dwelling house, also half of rights in common.

1724. Deputy.

He was called Lieutenant William Edmonds at his death.

1724, Dec. 11. Will—Codicil 1725, Dec. 28, proved 1726, Feb. 7. Exx. wife Alice. To son James, homestead where I dwell, but wife to have whole of back room on north side of house and lands adjoining betwixt highway and Woonasquatucket River with orchard, and also another orchard near my blacksmith shop, all to her for life while his widow, and at her decease or marriage, son James to have. His wife to hold the whole of house and all estate till James is 21, for the support and bringing up of children, and when he is 21 he to provide wood for his mother and keeping of a cow while she is a widow. To son William, lands on both sides of Woonasquatucket River ½ mile west of my dwelling house. To sons James and William, equally my smith shop, and undivided lands. Either son dying before twenty-one the other has his part of estate. To daughter Mary Edmonds, £10, when of age. To each sister of William he is to pay £10, as each is twenty-one (excepting daughter Mary already provided for above.) To wife Alice, feather bed and other household stuff and cow. Rest of estate to seven daughters. The codicil refers to death of son William, and empowers wife to sell certain land, and gives to son James rest of land, only wife Alice is to have use of half of house, barn, land, &c. Inventory £582, 12*s.* 2*d.*, viz: a yoke oxen, 7 cows, a horse, 2 mares, 24 sheep, 8 loads of hay, 4 swine, 150 bushels charcoal, bellows, anvil, &c., 3⅓ oz. silver, 80 lbs. cheese, 18 barrels cider, flax, rye, feathers, wool, beef, butter, &c.

IV. ANDREW, m. (1) MERIBAH FIELD, m. (2) MARY HOBBS, — b. 1683, Jun. 17. d. ; b. d. of Field. ; b. d. of Hobbs. — Providence, R. I.

He kept the ferry at Narrow Passage, for a time after his father's decease.

1707, Oct. 11. He leased his house and land, with use of ferry, situate on north side of Seekonk River alias Pawtucket River, at place called Narrow Passage. The lease was made to John Mason, of Rehoboth, for a term of seven years for £29.

1709, Jun. 1. He sold Thomas Olney 9 acres at Narrow Passage bounded partly by Round Cove, being land formerly granted by town of Providence to honored father Andrew, deceased. Said land, house, meadows, timber, privilege of ferry, &c., was sold for £120, the deed being signed by himself and wife Meribah.

1716, Oct. 31. Petition of Meribah Edmonds, late Meribah Field, for divorce from husband Andrew Edmonds, he having absented himself and lived sometime at Dover, in north-east part of New England, and was there married to Mary Hobbs. Petition granted by Assembly.

b. 1685, Aug. 17

1691, Jun. 24. He was appointed by Assembly Special Constable throughout the main land in this colony.

1695, Jul. 22. Will—proved 1695, Aug. 13. Exx. wife Mary. Overseers, Wm Hopkins, Epenetus Olney, Thomas Olney. To son Andrew all lands in Providence at and about the place called Narrow Passage with privilege of the ferry there, but if he die before he is of age without issue, then sons William and Joseph to have said land, &c., including the house. To wife Mary, profit and income of the house, &c., till son Andrew is of age, and then the house, land and ferry to be relinquished to him, but wife still to have her abode in the house and a third of profits of land and ferry, while she remains a widow. Sons William and Joseph were to have 40s each, paid to them by Andrew, within five years after he was of age, and each daughter was to have 30s. paid her by their brother Andrew. To wife he gave also his wearing apparel and working tools, but they were not to be sold unless required by necessity but that the children may enjoy. All the rest of estate to wife.

1696. His widow was allowed to keep the ferry.

V. JOSEPH, b. ~~1687, Feb. 2.~~ 1686, Aug. 17; d. 1767. Providence, East Greenwich, Warwick, R. I.
m. (1) 1708, Dec. 13.
HANNAH NICHOLS, b. 1684, Mar. 9; d. of Thomas & Mercy (Reynolds) Nichols.
m. (2) 1759, Jun. 7.
ELIZABETH VAUGHAN, b. ; d. 1765 + of Vaughan.

He was a carpenter.

1709, Jun. 2. He and wife Hannah (together with his brother William and wife Alice), sold Thomas Olney (weaver), their interest in certain lands.

1710. East Greenwich. Freeman.

1718. Deputy.

1747-48-58-59. Assistant.

1765, Jun. 9. Will—proved 1767, Jun. 15. Ex. son Andrew. To son Thomas all wearing apparel. To wife Elizabeth, negro named Jeremiah, a good cow, a riding beast, two feather beds, all silver spoons she brought me, and all other things she brought, with use of west end of house and chamber above with bed room adjoining, privilege in cellar and kitchen and half of profits of homestead farm, all to her while widow. If wife refuses this provision in lieu of her dower, then executor to have all. To son Andrew all my homestead farm. To son William, land in Coventry, wife having privilege of getting firewood on premises. To son Andrew, all remaining part of estate both real and personal.

Inventory, £1,271, viz: 6 silver spoons, pewter, warming pan, looking glass, 5 chairs, loom, quilt wheel, bible, 1 yearling bull, 2 cows, a horse, 3 hogs, &c.

VI. Patience b 1687, Feb. 2

1. Thomas, 1709, Oct. 16.
2. Joseph,
3. William,
4. Patience, 1713,
5. Mary, 1714, Jun. 5.
6. Hannah, 1718, Sep. 25,
7. Andrew, 1720, Oct. 23.
(2d wife, no issue)

For corrections see Early Providence Records v. 5, p. 25, 271.

ELDRED.

SAMUEL, b. ; d. 1697 +
m.
ELIZABETH, b. ; d.

Cambridge, Ms., Stonington, Ct., Kings Town, R. I.

1646. He was at Cambridge, thus early.

1659, Oct. 18. It was ordered that Sergeant Eldred should pay Edward Lane, of Boston, for two years rent of farm and stock, at Rumney Marsh (Chelsea).

1668, May 4. Kings Town. He and eighteen others, of Wickford, signed a letter to the General Court, at Hartford, desiring the protection of their government, as promised four years before, for if not, "that so we may look for government and protection elsewhere, being not able to live either in our civil and ecclesiastical matters without government, which both the honor of God and the good of the country now calls upon us to seek after."

1670, Jun. 22. He took constable's oath at Wickford, under appointment of Connecticut, which then and for many years after, disputed the territory with Rhode Island.

He was imprisoned this year, by Rhode Island authorities, for assuming to call a jury on behalf of Connecticut, in a murder case—Thomas Flounders having killed Walter House.

1670, Jul. 13. He wrote from Wickford, to Thomas Stanton, at Stonington: "Mr. Stanton, Sir: This is to inform you how the case stands with the town of Wickford, in respect of Rhode Island. This very day there came down, Mr. Samuel Wilson and Mr. Jireh Bull and Thomas Mumford, with his black staff, and upon this sad accident; and would have panelled the jury, whereupon I told them that they had nothing to do here, to panel a jury; but if they would look upon the corpse, they might, which several of them did. Then they commanded, in his Majesty's name, some to serve, and commanded myself to serve as a juryman upon the inquest, and commanded John Cole and several others, which did refuse. I also warned them to serve in a jury for us, as we were under Connecticut, but they would not, but commanded us not to bury the man till a jury had passed on it, by virtue of their power. So there was mighty commanding in his Majesty's name on both sides, and mighty threatening of carry to jail, insomuch that neither party could get twelve on a side. But at last they commanded all that were on their side to come out and they would panel a jury, if there were but six. Upon that account, the doors were shut where the corpse was, so they called the people to bear witness that they were obstructed in their power, and commanded us in his Majesty's name, not to bury the man, and told us that they would return our answer to their masters. We told them we would return their actings and words to our magistrates. So they commanded all the party to go with them. And so we proceeded and buried the man, and have searched for the murderer, but cannot find him, and therefore, would entreat you to send out after him, and send some this way, for we have never an officer here to grant me one. Sir, I would entreat you be strong and send away word to Connecticut by the first, for we are in greater trouble than ever we were, and like to be in worse, therefore, mind your promises and stand by us. John Cole stood to it and assisted as much as could be, not having taken the oath. Captain Hudson has not been here since, and sir the people will fain be doing, and beg to find that if it be not mended suddenly, it will be bad times here. Not more at present, but remain, yours to serve, Samwill Eldridge."

I. ELIZABETH, b. 1642, Oct. 26; d.

II. SAMUEL, b. 1644, Oct. 26; d. 1720 ± Kings Town, R. I.
m.
MARTHA KNOWLES, b. ; d. 1728. of Henry Knowles.

ELDRED. 2d column. II. Samuel. His daughter Margaret, b. 1683, Feb. 26.

1670, Apr. 16. Juryman in the murder case at Wickford.

1687, Sep. 6. Taxed 4s. ½d.

1688. He had license granted.

1709. He and three others, bought 430 acres of the "vacant lands" in Narragansett, ordered sold by the Assembly.

1714, Dec. 14. His wife had a legacy of £20, from her brother, John Knowles' will. She also had legacies a few years later from her brother, Henry Knowles, and her sister, Mary Lippitt.

1717, Oct. He deeded daughter Penelope, half of a certain tract of land, and to daughter Mary, the other half, calling them wives respectively of Ephraim Gardiner and Robert Brownell.

1721, Aug. 3. Martha Eldred, relict of Samuel, lately deceased, quitclaimed all her interest in above lands, to sons-in-law Robert Brownell and Ephraim Gardiner.

1727, Jan. 24. Will—proved 1728, Oct. 14. Widow Martha. Exs. sons-in-law Ephraim Gardiner and James Congdon. To daughters Penelope Gardiner and Margaret Congdon, equally, £37, in Bills of Public Credit of New England, with interest thereon at eight per cent. To daughter Mary Browning, all my apparel whatsoever. To much esteemed and beloved sons-in-law, Ephraim Gardiner and James Congdon, 9 acres in North Kingstown, that was in times past, part of my son-in-law, Robert Browning's land. To sons-in-law, Ephraim Gardiner and James Congdon, £12, equally divided, said sum being then in hands of Henry Knowles, son of William. (The name of Browning, in the copy of will is in error, but is correctly given in deeds as Brownell.)

1. Penelope,
2. Margaret,
3. Mary,

III. MARY, b. 1646, Jun. 15; d.

IV. THOMAS, b. 1648, Sep. 8; d. 1726. Kings Town, R. I.
m.
SUSANNA COLE, b. ; d. 1726 (—). of John & Susanna (Hutchinson) Cole.

1686. Constable.

1687, Sep. 6. Taxed 10s. ½d.

1692. Lieutenant.

1705, Jul. 12. He with others, appointed to lay out highways.

1726. Administration to eldest son John.

1726, Dec. 22. William Eldred bought certain land for £800, of the other heirs, viz: John Eldred, Elisha Eldred, Jeffrey Champlin, Nicholas Gardiner, Jr., and Mary, his wife, and Bridget Eldred, of North Kingstown, Enoch Kenyon, and Sarah, his wife, of Westerly, Thomas Brownell, and Grace, his wife, of Little Compton, Moses Barber, Jr., and Elizabeth, his wife, of South Kingstown.

1732. The administrator produced receipts from Jeffrey Champlin, Elisha Eldred, Bridget Eldred, Moses Barber, Enoch Kenyon, Nicholas Gardiner and William Eldred, each having having had £10, 13s., of personal estate, small amounts still remaining due to Thomas Brownell, and to John Watson, as guardian of Thomas Eldred.

1. John,
2. Elisha,
3. Susanna,
4. Mary,
5. Bridget,
6. Sarah,
7. Grace,
8. Elizabeth,
9. William,
10. Thomas,

V. JAMES, b. ; d. 1687 (—).

VI. DANIEL, b. ; d. 1726, Aug. 13. Kings Town, R. I., Stonington, Ct., North Kingstown, R. I.
m.
MARY, b. ; d. 1726 + of

1679, Jul. 29. He signed the petition to the King.

1687, Sep. 6. Taxed 2s. 8d.

1702. Captain.

1707, Apr. 6. Stonington. His wife was baptized, and following children: James, Thomas, Freelove, Hannah and Sarah.

1726, Aug. 14. Will—proved. He names wife Mary, sons James, Thomas and Daniel, and daughters Abigail, Mary, Freelove, Hannah and Sarah.

His son Daniel, died in Groton, Conn., and his son James, at Stonington, Conn., and two at least of his daughters married at Stonington (viz: Abigail, m. 1705, Feb. 22, James Miner, and Mary, m. 1709, May 5, John Miner).

1. Abigail, 1688, Aug. 19.
2. Daniel, 1690, Mar. 20.
3. Mary, 1691, Dec. 6.
4. Freelove, 1695, Mar. 25.
5. James, 1696, Dec. 5.
6. Thomas, 1699, Feb. 2.
7. Freelove, 1701, Mar. 29.
8. Hannah, 1703, Mar. 20.
9. Sarah, 1706, Jan. 29.
10. Richard, 1712, Apr. 9.

VII. JOHN, b. ; d. 1724. North Kingstown, R. I.
m.
MARGARET HOLDEN, b. 1663, Jan.; d. 1740. of Randall & Frances (Dungan) Holden.

1679, Jul. 29. He signed the petition to the King.

1687, Sep. 6. Taxed 3s. 5½d.

1688. He had license granted.

1692. Ensign, and subsequently Captain.

1. James,
2. Thomas,
3. Samuel,
4. Robert,
5. Anthony,
6. William,
7. Margaret,
8. Abigail,
9. Barbara,

1670, Jul. 21. Complaint was made, in a letter from Connecticut to Rhode Island authorities, of the seizure of Samuel Eldred and John Cole, the former of whom had been carried to Newport.

1674, Oct 8. He was granted by General Court sitting at Hartford, "the sum of twenty nobles, for his good service in doing and suffering for this colony."

1675, Dec. 13. "The Eldridges, and some other brisk hands," were at Richard Smith's garrison house just before the Narragansett Swamp Fight, as related by Captain Benjamin Church, who says they went on a night adventure with him, surprising and capturing eighteen Indians.

1676, Mar. 7. The council at Hartford, voted that he and John Sweet, "have liberty to transport ten bushels of Indian corn apiece, for their distressed families."

1679, Jul. 29. He and forty-one others, of Narragansett, petitioned the King, praying that he "would put an end to these differences about the government thereof, which hath been so fatal to the prosperity of the place, animosities still arising in people's minds, as they stand affected to this or that government."

1687, Sep. 6. Taxed 3*s.* 4½*d.*

1697, Apr. 13. He deeded to son John, house and 100 acres, with a right on the other side of Pequot Path, and possession was given at this date.

1697. Treasurer.

1699-1700-1-3-4-5-6-7-9-10-11-12-13-15-16. Assistant.

1703. Moderator of Town Meeting. He was on a committee this year, to audit the debt of the colony.

1707-8. Town Council.

1708. His house was the place of meeting for the commissioners on Narragansett vacant lands. He was on a committee this year, to confer with Ninigret, about setting off lands in Narragansett.

1708-9-19. Deputy.

1716, May 2. He and Major Thomas Fry, were granted £20 from the general treasury, to complete the sum of £60, for building a bridge over Reynolds' River, alias Hunt's River, in Narragansett.

This year Gabriel Bernon signed an acknowledgment, and asked forgiveness of Captain John Eldred, and the General Assembly, for causeless slanders, uttered against Captain John Eldred.

1721, Mar. 29. The testimony of Henry Knowles was given, as to the Pequot Path, that it ran to the eastward of the ruins of an old house belonging to old Mr. Eldred, father of the now Captain John Eldred.

1724. Administration by widow Margaret on his estate.

Inventory, £177, 8*s.*

An agreement was made between Margaret Eldred and her children, viz: six sons, James, Thomas, Samuel, Robert, Anthony and William, and three daughters, Margaret Gardiner, wife of William, Abigail and Barbara Eldred. The widow was to have the old end of dwelling house, and a third of homestead farm, except the new house, and that is given son Anthony by deed. To widow, also, all movables, except a mare. To daughter Margaret Gardiner, £20, a feather bed, and silver cup at death of mother. To daughter Abigail, £20, feather bed, mare and new wash leather side saddle. To daughter Barbara, at twenty-one, £20, feather bed and new wash leather side saddle. To six sons, certain portions of land, and Anthony to have the third of homestead farm, at death of widow.

1740. Administration on estate widow Margaret, by son James.

EMERY.

ANTHONY, b. d.
m.
——, b. d.

Portsmouth, R. I.

1643, Mar. 1. The Assembly ordered that if Goodman Emery be still unwilling that Thomas Gorton shall enjoy the 20 acres that was formerly his—then Thomas Gorton was to have another piece of 10 acres, and if Goodman Emery will have the 10 acres, then Thomas Gorton to have the 20 acres.

1671. Juryman.

1671, Oct. 18. He was indicted for digging a well in the King's highway wherein a man was drowned. He was acquitted because the well was filled up.

1704, Apr. 29. The will of his daughter Rebecca's second husband (proved 1704, Aug. 21), names wife Rebecca as executrix. He gave to Rebecca while widow all housing, land and movable estate, and at her decease equally to Patience, Rebecca and Daniel Emery, and my cousin and kinswoman Mary Callender (my brother's daughter by marriage, now known by name of Callender). Daniel Eaton the maker of above will lived in Little Compton.

I. JAMES, b. d. — Portsmouth, R. I., Dedham, Mass.
m.
——, b. d. of

1. Patience, 1681.
2. Rebecca,
3. Daniel,

1700, May 10. Dedham. He, only surviving son of Anthony Emery, late of Portsmouth, deceased, deeded sister Rebecca Eaton, alias Sadler, all interest in lands, estate, goods, and chattels of late Anthony Emery.

The first name of this sister's first husband is learned from a suit brought by Peter Talman (1675, Oct. 20), against Rebecca Sadler, wife of Thomas Sadler, for breach of peace and threatening family.

II. REBECCA, b. d.
m. (1)
THOMAS SADLER, b. d. of Sadler.
m. (2)
DANIEL EATON, b. d. 1704, Jul. 11. of Eaton.

1. Anthony,

ENGLAND.

WILLIAM, b. d.
m.
ELIZABETH, b. 1613. d. 1684 +

(She m. (2) Hugh Parsons).

Portsmouth, R. I.

1644, May 27. He was granted 4 acres.

1684, Jan. 11. The will of Hugh Parsons (proved 1684, Mar. 14), gave to wife Elizabeth's two daughters living on Long Island, viz: Susannah Carpenter and Elizabeth Doty, certain legacies (after disposing of most of his estate to his own kin).

I. WILLIAM, b. 1641, d. 1651. — Taunton, Mass.

1651, Jun. 10. He, being about the age of ten years, servant to Joseph Wilbur of Taunton, went toward evening in a great canoe to get some wood on the other side of the river, and the jury at this date found that he "did fall over the said vessel and so perished in the water."

II. JOSIAH, b. d. — Portsmouth, R. I., Dartmouth, Mass.

1672, Dec. 11. He had 8 acres laid out.

1673, Jan. 1. Dartmouth. He sold Thomas Manchester, Jr., 8 acres in Portsmouth for £13.

1673, Oct. 29. He was one of the appraisers of that part of the inventory of Thomas Cornell that lay in Dartmouth.

III. ELEANOR, b. d. 1686.
m. 1665, Jul. 27.
JEREMIAH WESTCOTT, b. d. 1686. of Stukely Westcott.

1. Jeremiah, 1666, Oct. 7.
2. Eleanor, 1669, Oct. 20
3. Persis, 1670,
4. Stukely, 1672, Oct.
5. Josiah,
6. Samuel,
7. William,
8. Benjamin, 1684, Jul. 4.

IV. SUSANNA, b. d. 1684.
m. 1677, Dec. 3.
EPHRAIM CARPENTER, b. d. 1703 ± of William & Elizabeth (Arnold) Carpenter.

1. Josiah,

V. ELIZABETH, b. d.
m.
—— DOTY, b. d. of Doty.

RICHARD, b. 1646, d. 1727, Sep. 9.
m. 1680, Jun. 10.
PATIENCE ALLEN, b. —, d. 1711, Dec. 4.
of Ralph & Esther (Swift) Allen.

Newport, R. I.

1686. Freeman.

I. MARY, b. —, d. 1705, Oct. 1.
m. 1705,
JOSEPH PECKHAM, b. 1679, Mar. 8, d. 1726, Jan. 14. of John & Sarah ( ) Peckham.

1. Joseph, 1705, Sep. 22.

II. DORCAS, b. 1686, Sep. 29, d. —

EVANS (Richard, of Providence).

EVANS (RICHARD, OF PROVIDENCE). 2d column. II. Richard m. 1708, June 5. Sarah Hawkins, b. 1685, Apr. 15. Children, 1, Sarah, 1709, May 2.

RICHARD, b. —, d. 1727, Jan. 8.
m.
MARY, b. —, d. 1729, Dec. 22.

Rehoboth, Mass., Providence, R. I.

It is believed that he was son of David Evans, merchant of Boston, who died 1663, Jul. 27, leaving widow Mary, and several children.

He gave his occupation as joiner, carpenter and millwright in different deeds.

1680, Feb. 7. His name was in the list of those who were resident proprietors at Rehoboth at this date.

1713, Jun. 16. Providence. Taxed 2*s.* 6*d.*

1718, Jun. 25. He sold Peleg Rhodes, 100 acres for £53.

1718, Jul. 1. He deeded to his son-in-law John Church, now of Providence, formerly of Killingly, for parental affection, &c., 3 tracts of land and ½ a saw mill near Chapatset Falls; about 70 acres in all.

1727, Jan. 6. Will—proved 1727, May 15. Exx. wife Mary. To wife he gives all lands and movable estate and all right in saw mill at Chapachoge, with power to dispose of same and give some part to every one of his children; though he had already disposed to all near what he had to share, viz: to sons Richard and David Evans and daughters Martha Aldrich, Mary Sayer, Elizabeth Church, and Mehitable Plummer. Such part as would have gone to son Richard, he wished his executrix to give to granddaughter Sarah.

Inventory, £98, 3*s.* 6*d.*, viz: 1 horse, ¼ of a saw mill, 3 loads of hay, gun, barrel cider, pewter platter, silver spoon, books, warming pan, &c.

1729. Inventory of widow Mary Evans, estate £52, viz: old gun, joiner's tools, stillyards, pewter, 2½ oz. silver, &c.

EVANS (RICHARD, OF PROVIDENCE). Children b. as follows: 1. Martha, 1679, Jan. 19. 2. Richard, 1681, Aug. 10. 3. David, 1684, Mar. 9. 4. Mary, 1686, Apr. 23. 5. Elizabeth, 1688, Apr. 23. 6. Mehitable, 1692, Jun. 1.

I. RICHARD, b. 1681, Aug. 10, d. 1726, Nov. 28. Providence, R. I.
m.
SARAH HAWKINS, b. —, d. 1727 +. of John & Sarah ( ) Hawkins.

1710, Dec. 29. He and wife Sarah received a deed of 40 acres from John Hawkins, for love, &c.

1713, Jun. 16. Taxed 4*s.*

1727, Mar. 6. Administration on his estate was given his widow Sarah.

Inventory. Real estate included farm on which his dwelling house stood, containing 120 acres £470, also ¼ of common on west side of the seven mile line £10. Personal property £186, 8*s.* 6*d.*, viz: 3 horsekind, 7 cows, 2 steers, 11 sheep, 5 lean swine, 6 barrels of cider, hay, corn, beans, flax, linen cloth, woolen yarn, pork, cheese, gun, warming pan, 2 cow bells, 13 plates of pewter, 6 pewter dishes, old books, purse and wearing apparel £25, 7*s.*

1. Sarah,

II. DAVID, b. —, d. 1754 +. Smithfield, R. I.
m.
ESTHER HAWKINS, b. 1685 Jul. 19, d. —. of Edward & Esther (Arnold) Hawkins.

1713, Jun. 16. Taxed 3*s.*

1728, Nov. 28. He and his mother sold Isaiah Inman 15 acres for £20.

1728, Jun. 15. He and wife Esther sold James Tucker of Warwick, 19 acres for £37, 5*s.*, situated both sides of Chapatset River.

1744, Apr. 14. Smithfield. He deeded son David for love, &c., 19 acres adjoining dwelling house of Joseph Aldrich, of Smithfield.

1754, Dec. 14. He deeded son David, for love, &c., the whole of my homestead farm, whereon I dwell, with buildings, &c.

1. Edward, 1710, Nov. 27.
2. Anne, 1712, Sep. 2.
3. Esther, 1714, Dec. 17.
4. Thankful, 1718, Feb. 17.
5. David, 1721, May 16.
6. Zerviah, 1724, Nov. 17.

III. MARTHA, b. —, d. 1735 +.
m. 1699, Mar. 20,
JOHN ALDRICH, b. —, d. 1735, Mar. 17. of Joseph & Patience (Osborne) Aldrich.

1. John,
2. Jonathan,
3. David,
4. Aaron,
5. Richard,
6. Noah,
7. Joseph,

IV. MARY, b. —, d. —
m.
—— SAYER, b. —, d. —. of Sayer.

V. ELIZABETH, b. —, d. —
m.
JOHN CHURCH, b. —, d. —. of Church.

VI. MEHITABLE, b. —, d. 1742, Jan. 28.
m. (1)
SAMUEL PLUMMER, b. —, d. 1727, Feb. 12. of Plummer.
m. (2)
THOMAS STEERE, b. —, d. 1735, Aug. 27. of John & Hannah (Wickenden) Steere.

1. Joseph,
2. Samuel,
3. Richard,
4. Daughter,
5. Hannah,
(By 2d husband, no issue.)

EVERDEN.

ANTHONY, b. —, d. 1687 (—).
m.
——, b. —, d. —

Providence, R. I.

1666, May. He swore allegiance.

1670. Freeman.

1671, May 8. He was fined 20*s.* for not attending Grand Jury.

1667–72. Town Council.

1667–68–71–72–73. Deputy.

1671, Oct. 18. His warehouse having been broken into by an Indian, the latter was indicted.

1687, Sep. 1. Taxed 8*s.* estate of Anthony Everden.

1712, Dec. 22. Heirs of Anthony Everenden had bounds of lands revised—situated near Benedict Pond.

I. RICHARD. b. —, d. 1682 (—).

EVERDEN. 2d column. I. Richard. Providence, R. I.

1665, Feb. 24. He was witness to a deed from Roger Williams to Richard Arnold.

1668, Jun. He took the oath of allegiance.

1672, Jan. 27. He bought 3 acres on north side of Wanasquatucket River of Edward Smith.

1672, Apr. 30. Freeman.

1682, Nov. 20. His heirs had confirmatory deed from Samuel Bennett and Anne his wife, of East Greenwich, of 34 acres upland and a share of meadow, &c., near Solitary Hill in Providence, which had been sold in Everden's lifetime

II. ELIZABETH, b. —, d. 1698 (—).
m.
JOHN FIELD, b. —, d. 1698. of John Field.

1. John, 1671.
2. Elizabeth, 1673.
3. Richard, 1677.
4. Lydia, 1679.
5. Daniel, 1681.
6. Ruth, 1683.
7. Hannah,

FAIRFIELD.

JOHN, b. —, d. —
m.
ANPHILLIS, b. —, d. —

Newport, Westerly, R. I.

1655. Freeman.

1660. He was one of the orginal purchasers of Westerly.

1661, Mar. 22. He signed certain articles concerning Misquamicut (Westerly) lands.

1669, May 18. Westerly. His name was in a list of inhabitants.

1671, May 17. He took oath of allegiance.

1673. He had a grant of 50 acres from the town of Stonington on the east side of Pawcatuck river.

1679, Sep. 17. He took oath of allegiance.

1687. Overseer of the Poor.

1689, Dec. 26. He deeded to Mary Babcock (widow of John Babcock), all his estate both of land and movables, with consent of his wife, provided said Mary Babock "maintain me and my wife with sufficient meat, drink, clothing, washing and lodging during our lives."

Arthur Fenner. See also: Bowen's THE PROVIDENCE OATH OF ALLEGIANCE, p. 69-71.

 See: American Genealogist, v. 25, p. 250. v. 26, p. 229

ARTHUR,[2] (THOMAS[1].) m. (1) MEHITABLE WATERMAN, of Richard & Bethiah ( ) Waterman. m. (2) 1684, Dec. 16, HOWLONG HARRIS, of William & Susanna ( ) Harris. — b. 1622. d. 1703, Oct. 10. — b. d. 1684 (—). — b. d. 1708, Nov. 19.

Providence, R. I.

He was (by tradition) a lieutenant in Oliver Cromwell's army.

1647, May 15. Thomas Fenner, of Branford, Conn., died at this date, and it seems more than probable that he was father of Arthur, William and John, the two latter owning lands in Connecticut, and making it their home in part—while Arthur lived continuously in Rhode Island, after his removal there. (The inventory of Thomas Fenner amounted to £60, 19s., besides 16 pieces of Dutch money, a boat and its lading and 11 beaver skins, @ 8s. per pound. The inventory showed many articles designed for trading with the Indians.)

1650, Jul. 27. He bought 60 acres of upland and two spots of meadow, of Nathaniel Dickens.

1652, Apr. 27. He bought of John Lippitt, of Warwick, certain lands in Providence.

1653-55-59-60-62-63. Commissioner.

1655. Freeman.

1657-65-66-67-68-72-73-74-75-76-79-80-81-82-83-84-85-86-90. Assistant.

1664, Dec, 27. He was to have the Meere-bank from the corner of his fence round the point unto a little creek or cove, lying next Waskamoquett Point, on condition of his laying down as much land in another place, for town's use, and also to make three stiles, one by his house, another at the hollow and another at aforesaid creek, with liberty to people to pass through on foot, or upon occasion, to land goods upon said land.

1664-70-72-78-79-92-99-1700. Deputy.

1664-73-77-78. Town Council

1665, Feb. 19. He had a lot granted him in a division of lands.

1672-73. Town Treasurer.

1676, Mar. 16. He had relief granted by the following order of the Council, at Hartford, Conn. "Mr. John Fenner had liberty to transport twenty bushels of corn to Rhode Island, for the supply of his brother, Captain Fenner.'

1676, Jun. 19. He was appointed by the Assembly, "Chief Commander of the King's Garrison at Providence; and of all other private garrison or garrisons there (not eclipsing Captain Williams' power in the exercise of the Train Band there, &c)., and have hereby full power and sole command of the soldiers belonging to that garrison," &c.

1676, Aug. 24. He was a member of the Court Martial held at Newport, to try certain Indians.

1676, Oct. 26. He and the rest of the soldiers of the King's garrison at Providence, were discharged from further duty.

1676, Nov. 7. His daughter Sarah was buried.

1677, Oct. 31. The Assembly voted that he should have one barrel of the powder now in the custody of the commissary, William Brinley, in part pay for charge of the King's garrison at Providence, and if lead bullets or shot be in the Colony's store, he was also to have not exceeding one hundred pounds weight.

1680, May 5. He was appointed on a committee to put the laws and acts of the colony into such a method, that they may be put in print.

1683, Sep. 10. He and Major Peleg Sanford, were chosen agents to go to England on Colony affairs in regard to Governor Cranfield, of New Hampshire, and the Commissioners, who had lately been at Kings Town, but would show no commission from the King for holding court.

1687-88. Justice of the General Quarter Session and Inferior Court of Common Pleas.

1687, Sep. 1. He and his wife were taxed 15s. 4d.

1688, Aug. 10. Ratable estate, 300 acres woodland, 20 acres wild pasture, 10 acres English pasture, 3 acres orchard and meadow, 5 acres planting, 2 oxen, 9 cows, 5 three year, 6 two year, 5 yearlings, 4 mares, horse, 10 sheep, 3 swine. He adds: "This is a just account. I pray be not unmindful of the Golden Rule."

1695, Jul. 2. He and two others were chosen by the Assembly, to run the northern line of the colony.

1702, Dec. 25. In a confirmatory deed of this date, he alludes to an agreement made in 1688, he and his brother, John, both being executors of their brother William's will. William had died possessed of lands in Connecticut and Rhode Island, and as John had lands in Connecticut, he took those lands, while Arthur took the Rhode Island lands of their deceased brother, deeds being passed in exchange. In consideration of legacies given to Arthur's daughters,

I. THOMAS, m. (1) ALICE RALPH, of Thomas & Mary ( ) Ralph. m. (2) 1682, Jul. 26, DINAH BORDEN, of Thomas & Mary (Harris) Borden. — b. 1652, Sep. d. 1718, Feb. 27. — b. 1657, Jan. 13. d. 1682 (—). — b. 1664, Oct. d. 1761, Dec. 18. — Providence, R. I.

1. William, 1677, Mar. 11.
(2d wife.)
2. Freelove,
3. Mehitable,
4. Thomas,
5. Richard,
6. Joseph,
7. Mary, 1692.
8. Sarah, 1697.
9. Arthur, 1699, Oct. 17.
10. Eleazer, 1702, Sep. 4.
11. John, 1705, Sep. 17.

1676, Aug. 14. He was one of those "who staid and went not away" in King Philip's war, and so had a share in the disposition of the Indian captives, whose services were sold for a term of years.

1677, Mar. 11. Under this date there is recorded, "a son" as born to Thomas Fenner, and it is assumed that this son was identical with the William Fenner who is mentioned in the will of Thomas Ralph, as his grandson. (Possibly one or two of the children ascribed to the second wife of Thomas Fenner, may have been by his first wife.)

1681. Freeman.

1683-91-95-97-99-1704-5. Deputy.

1687, Sep. 1. Taxed 8s. 2d.

1688. Ratable estate, 2 oxen, 6 cows, 2 three year, 4 two year, 2 mares, 2 colts, 4 swine, 1 share meadow, 4 acres planting, 6 acres pasture and grass land, 287 acres woodland.

1698-99-1700-1-2-3-4-5-6. Town Council.

1701, Sep. 16. He bought of Pardon Tillinghast, house, orchard, &c., which had fallen to latter in default of a payment of £35, from Robert Kilton.

1704. Justice of the Peace.

1707-8-9-10-11-12-13-15-16-17. Assistant.

1711, Dec. 27. He made a written declaration, that he refused to marry Edward Potter to Joan Potter, widow of John, on account of the relationship between Edward and John Potter. (They were brothers, John having fallen from a tree, which caused his death, as the jury of inquest found 1711, Feb. 6.)

1712-13. Major for the Main.

1714, Aug. 24. He sold Thomas and Samuel Kilton, certain land, house, orchard, &c., which he had bought in 1701, of Pardon Tillinghast.

1718, Feb. 19. Will—proved 1718, Mar. 21. Exs. sons Richard and Joseph. To wife Dinah, old part of dwelling house, for life, with sufficient household goods to keep house comfortably, and 2 cows, with keep of same, and such other things as she may need. To daughter Sarah Fenner, £150. To daughters Freelove Westcott, Mehitable Starkweather and Mary Abbott, £5 each, in addition to what they had already had. His poor, helpless child Eleazer, to have sufficient maintenance for life, meat, drink and apparel, washing and lodging and good tending. To son Thomas, 150 acres, and my ½ of dwelling house (which my honoured father gave me by will) for life, and then to go equally to children of said son Thomas. To sons Richard, Joseph, Arthur and John, all rest of estate, lands, reservations and housings, and movable estate, all to them, equally.

Inventory, £433, 19s. 9d., viz: 4 mares, 2 horses, 1 colt, 4 oxen, 1 steer, 1 bull, 15 cows, 13 three year, 10 two year, 9 yearlings, 8 swine, 8 barrels cider, 3 barrels beer, 2 spinning wheels, 5 feather beds, instruments for surveying land £1, 18s., ½ statute book and other books £4, 3s.

He and his second wife were buried in his own family burial ground, on his farm.

II. ARTHUR, m. MARY SMITH, of John & Sarah (Whipple) Smith. — b. d. 1725, Apr. 24. — b. d. 1737, Dec. 13. — Providence, R. I.

1. Arthur,
2. John,
3. Edward,
4. Mary,
5. Mercy,

1687, Sep. 1. Taxed 5s. 4d.

1688. Ratable estate, 3 cows, 1 three year, 3 two year, a yearling, 3 mares, 3 horses, a share of meadow, 2 acres planting, 86 acres woodland, &c., 2 swine.

1699, Nov. 10. He brought in a wolf's head and received 10s. bounty.

1707-10-20. Deputy.

1708, Dec. 31. Having two years before received a deed from his step-mother, Howlong (she calling him son-in-law), of all her household goods, for love, &c.; he now declared by deed, that if at any time she demanded them back, the deed should be considered "waste paper," and she might have use at any time.

1716-17-22-23. Town Council.

1717, May 16. He and wife Mary, confirmed a deed made in 1711, to Ephraim Smith.

1719, Nov. 5. He wrote a letter addressed to his cousin, Richard Brown.

1718-21. Assistant.

1723, Jul. 23. Will—proved 1725, Jul. 3. Exs. sons John and Edward. To wife Mary, all household goods at her disposal, if she remained his widow, but if she married, she ⅓ and ⅔ to children. She to have use of dwelling house, with liberty to pass and repass on my land. To daughters Mary and Mercy Fenner, £100 each. To grandchild Sarah, daughter of son Arthur, deceased, the new dwelling house, wherein her father dwelt, on east side of Neutoconconut Hill, with 4 acres, and 54 acres near said house, at place called Tilers Pond, but if she died before 21, then the property was to go to heirs, male, of testator. To sons John and Edward, all rest of lands and commons, they to pay a certain mortgage, &c. Inventory, £411, 19s. 1d., viz: 8 cows, 1 bull, 2 steers, 4 three year old, 4 two year old, 2 calves, 2 oxen, 22 sheep, 13 lambs, 5 swine, 1 mare, saddle and pillion, corn, rye, hemp, flax, yarn, 4 spinning wheels, 2 guns, cooper's adze, carpenter's adze, augur, chisel, gouge, 3 steel traps, 1 great bible, 1 small bible, 1 testament and other books, &c.

1728, May 20. Will—proved 1738, Mar. 4. Widow Mary. Ex. son Edward. To daughter Mary, wearing apparel and feather bed. To son Edward, and daughters Mary Fenner and Mercy Rutenburg, three cows and twelve sheep. To granddaughter Sarah Fenner, £3. To daughters Mary and Mercy, rest of estate.

Inventory, £116, 2s. 5d.

III. SARAH, Unmarried. — b. d. 1676, Nov.

IV. FREELOVE, m. 1687, Apr. 13, GIDEON CRAWFORD, of James & Anna (Weir) Crawford. — b. 1656. d. 1712, Jun. 1. — b. 1651, Dec. 26. d. 1707, Oct. 10.

1. William, 1688, Apr. 12.
2. Anne, 1690, May 13.
3. John, 1693, Aug. 15.
4. Mary, 1702, Sep. 14.

V. BETHIAH, m. ROBERT KILTON, of Kilton. — b. d. — b. d.

1. Thomas, 1690, Jan. 17
2. Samuel,

VI. PHEBE, m. JOSEPH LATHAM, of Robert & Susanna (Winslow) Latham. — b. d. — b. d.

1. Robert,
2. Sarah,
3. Phebe,

(2d WIFE, no issue.)

FENNER (ARTHUR). 2d column. VII. Samuel, d. 1680 +

Freelove and Bethiah, by their uncle William, their father deeded them 92 acres. (William had left legacies to all the children of Arthur, and also to the children of his brother, John, as was declared.)

1703, Jun. 9. He declared as to lands laid out by him in June, 1675, "a little before the Indian war broke out, when King Philip was in arms against the English."

1703, Aug. 27. Will—proved 1703, Nov. 12. Exs. sons Thomas and Arthur. To wife Howlong, her choice of a cow, and the keep of the cow, and £10 per annum, for life, with any room she may choose, in any of my housing, for life, for her comfortable living, and she to have the household goods at her disposal. To daughters Freelove Crawford and Bethiah Kilton, £10 each, and daughter Phebe Latham, to have 10s., with a further sum of £9 10s., if the executors see fit. To sons Thomas and Arthur, all lands in Providence, whether divided or undivided, to be theirs equally, and they to have all movable estate not disposed of, all cattle and horsekind. The rooms reserved for wife, to belong to the two sons equally, at death of wife.

Inventory, £166, 8s., viz: a yoke of oxen, 5 cows, 6 steers, 4 heifers, 2 yearlings, 6 calves, 2 horses, one of them near or about 30 years old, 29 loads of hay, oats, cheese, butter, pork, 3 bushels malt, 5 barrels beer, 12 barrels cider, 2 barrels peach juice, cider mill and press, 2 spinning wheels, 2 guns and a pistol, 2 pair stillyards, pair of brass scales, money scales, joint rule, hammer, 3 augurs, drawing knife, handsaw, crosscut saw, warming pan, wearing apparel, money in purse 15s., book called The Statute £2, 10s., a great bible £1, 18s., 7 small books, &c.

He was buried on his own land, in what is now the town of Johnston.

FENNER (William). See: American Genealogist, v. 25, p. 250.

WILLIAM,[2] (Thomas[1].) b. ; d. 1680, Aug. 30.

Providence, Newport, R. I.

1658, May 18. Freeman.

1658, Nov. 22. He landed five ankers and a half of strong liquors, and one anker of wine.

1659, May 31. He desired that ten pounds of powder be delivered to his brother Arthur.

1665, Feb. 19. He had lot 56, in a division of lands.

1674, Nov. 10. He, late of Providence, sold John Sheldon about 50 acres, and a 5 acre share of meadow.

(He was probably living at Newport, at this time.)

1680, Oct. 30. Will—(presented to Town Council, of Providence, by his brother, Arthur Fenner, 1681, Jan. 15). Exs. brothers Arthur and John Fenner. He left legacies to the children of his two brothers.

Inventory, £12.

1702, Dec. 25. In a confirmatory deed made by Arthur Fenner, he alludes to an agreement made between himself and his brother John, in 1688, regarding lands that their brother William, had died possessed of. As John had lands in Connecticut, he took what lands William had there, and Arthur took what lands William had in Rhode Island.

FENNER (William). 1680, Aug. 30. Will—proved 1680, Sep. 6 (at Newport). Exs. brothers Arthur and John Fenner. To late sister Lay's two children she left, and to sister Phebe Ward's children, 20s. each. To brother Arthur Fenner's children Samuel and Phebe, £10 apiece, in addition to an equal share in whole estate. To children of brothers Arthur and John Fenner, all estate equally.

FIELD (John). See: American Genealogist, v. 20, p. 181.

JOHN, b. ; d. 1686.
m. ——— b. ; d. 1686 +

Providence, R. I.

1637, Aug. 20. At this date (or a little later) he and twelve others signed the following compact: "We whose names are hereunder, desirous to inhabit in the town of Providence, do promise to subject ourselves in active or passive obedience, to all such orders or agreements as shall be made for public good of the body, in an orderly way, by the major assent of the present inhabitants, masters of families incorporated together into a town fellowship, and such others whom they shall admit unto them, only in civil things."

1640, Jul. 27. He and thirty-eight others signed an agreement for form of government.

1645, Jan. 27. He bought 25 acres and a share of meadow of Ezekiel Holiman.

1655. Freeman.

1659, Oct. 8. Juryman.

1665, Feb. 19. In a division of lots he drew number five.

I. HANNAH, b. ; d. 1703 +
m. (1) JAMES MATHEWSON, b. ; d. 1682. of Mathewson.
m. (2) HENRY BROWN, b. 1625. d. 1703, Feb. 20. of Brown.

1. Ruth,
2. James, 1666, Aug. 11.
3. John,
4. Isabel,
5. Thomas, 1673, Apr. 1.
6. Lydia,
7. Zachariah,
8. Daniel, 1682, Jan. 28.

(By 2d husband, no issue.)

FIELD (John). 1. Hannah. She had 8 Mary, and then 9 Daniel.

II. JOHN, b. ; d. 1698. Providence, R. I., Bridgewater, Mass.
m. ELIZABETH EVERDEN, b. ; d. 1698 (—) of Anthony Everden.

1. John, 1671.
2. Elizabeth, 1673.
3. Richard, 1777.
4. Lydia, 1679.
5. Daniel, 1681.
6. Ruth, 1683.
7. Hannah,

1677. At about this time he moved from Providence to Bridgewater.

1687, Jul. 5. He sold Samuel Comstock of Providence, 2 acres of meadow there for £4, 10s., and his wife Elizabeth conveyed her third also.

1695, May 3. He deeded (for natural love and affection for his deceased brother Zachariah) to four of his brother's children, viz: John, James, Daniel and Joseph, all lands in Providence "which did formerly belong to my honoured father John Field of Providence, deceased"—with certain exceptions of lots previously sold, &c. The land, however, was to be for the use of Sarah Field, widow of Zachariah, during her widowhood or till the boys were 21, at which time they were to have it equally, and they were to provide their mother with a maintenance if she remained a widow after they were of age.

1696, Dec. 28. He deeded John Gurney of Providence, for £20, a tract of land a mile east of Mashwansacut containing 60 acres, and 5 acres of meadow, bounded partly by land "formerly belonging to my

1676. Deputy.

1679, Jul. 1. "Zachary Field and his father" were taxed together.

1686, Mar. 22. His will was exhibited by son Zachariah for probate, but the executrix not appearing, and no witnesses, &c., and the legatees having already proceeded in division, &c., the Town Council refused to probate it. Inventory, £34, 19*s.* 6*d.*

father-in-law, viz: Anthony Everden now deceased." He also sold a half purchase of commonage—all in Providence.

1698, Mar. 8. Administration to eldest son John. Inventory, £167, 19*s.* 8*d.*, viz: 4 oxen £12, 9 cows £18, 3 calves, 3 swine, arms, ammunition, spinning wheel, land £93, 9*s.* 10*d.*

III. DANIEL, { b. / d. 1676, Aug. — Providence, R. I.
Unmarried.

1671, May. He swore allegiance.

1676, Aug. He was buried this month. He and another (buried at about same time) were called "in the flower of their youth."

IV. ZACHARIAH, { b. / d. 1693, Aug. 12. — Providence, R. I.
m.
SARAH THORNTON, { b. / d. 1714, Apr. 16. of John & Sarah ( ) Thornton.
(She m. (2) John Gurney.)

1. Zachariah, 1685, Jan. 30.
2. John,
3. James,
4. Daniel, 1690, Aug. 7.
5. Joseph, 1693.
6. Sarah.

1673. Freeman.

1676, Aug. 14. He was of those "who staid and went not away" in King Philip's war and so had his share in the disposition of the Indian captives whose services were sold for a term of years.

1687, Sep. 1. Taxed 6*s.*

1687. Ratable estate of himself and mother; horse, 2 oxen, 2 cows, 4 heifers, 30 sheep, hog, 8 acres in fence (of which 3 acres is planting land), 8 acres where the house is (of which 1 acre is orchard, 2 acres worn out, and 2 acres planting), 4 acres meadow, a house lot in town, a little orchard and meadow.

1688, Oct. 31. He and wife Sarah deeded land to John Mathewson.

1693, Sep. 12. His widow appeared before Town Council and desired settlement of her husband's estate. She presented inventory and administration was given her and John Thornton.

1695, Aug. 13. Complaint was made by John Thornton and his father John Thornton, Sr., desiring council to take care of children of Zachery Field, that they may be bound out to good places and educated. The council thereupon ordered the mother to look up good places for three eldest boys.

1695, Sep. 17. The widow informed council that she had bound out her sons Zachariah and John to Nathaniel Waterman, and James to Solomon Thornton.

1696, Feb. 4. Her administration was taken away from her and given solely to John Thornton, because she wasted the estate and not so improved it as it ought to be, and had not appeared before council and was "refractory in her actings." On the same date the council ordered that Daniel Field be put out to Nicholas Sheldon till of age.

1714, Mar. 31. Will—proved 1714, Apr. 30, of his widow, who was then wife of John Gurney, and the latter appeared and stated he was present when his deceased wife made her will, and that he consented thereto. Executor was her son Joseph Field. To her son Zachariah she gave 5*s.*, and to sons John, James and Daniel, also 5*s.*, each. To her daughter Sarah, all my brass, pewter and iron vessels, bedding and other utensils for housekeeping. To son Joseph, cattle, sheep and swine and working tools, "they being the product of his care and diligence." Inventory, £61, 15*s.*, viz: 2 cows, 4 heifers, 2 steers, 27 sheep, swine, auger and other tools, wearing apparel, &c.

V. RUTH, { b. / d. 1727 +
m. 1669, Jan. 7.
JOHN ANGELL, { b. 1646. / d. 1720, Jul. 27. of Thomas & Alice ( ) Angell.

1. Thomas, 1672, Mar. 25.
2. Mercy, 1675.
3. John,
4. Daniel, 1680, May 2.
5. James, 1684.
6. Hope, 1685, Dec. 12.

FIELD (THOMAS). see American Genealogist, v.36, p.54.

THOMAS, { b. / d. 1717, Aug. 10.
m.
MARTHA HARRIS, { b. / d. 1717 (—).
of Thomas & Elizabeth ( ) Harris.

Providence, R. I.

He may have been a son of John Field (and it is noticeable that he had grandsons Anthony and Jeremiah Field, as did also John Field, Jr).

1665, Jun. 3. He gave receipt to his aunt, Deborah Field, for legacies which she, as executrix of his uncle, William Field's will, had paid him. The will referred to (dated 1665, May 31), gave to loving cousin (*i. e.* nephew), Thomas Field, now at Providence with me, all that cargo that is now upon sending to the Barbadoes, as also, all my horsekind (with certain exceptions), and four heifers, rights of land at Aquidnesett and Pauchassett, and furs which I have in my house. It was further provided that at death of testator's wife, his nephew Thomas, should have the house and all the lands, &c. (including Saxafrax Neck), thus making him his heir.

1667–70–83–85–92–95–1706. Deputy.

1671, Feb. 20. He had 12 acres laid out.

1673–74. Assistant.

1674. Town Treasurer.

1676, Aug. 14. Town meeting was held "before Thomas Field's house, under a tree, by the water side," to make disposition of Indian captives, whose services were sold for a term of years. He had his share in the sale, as he was one of those "who staid and went not away," in King Philip's war.

1679, Jul. 1. Taxed 1*s.* 9*d.*

1681–82–83–87–88–1702–3–4. Town Council.

1682, Nov. 27. In an agreement about boundary lines between certain parties, allusion is made to Thomas Field, as being nephew and heir to Wm. Field.

1685, Nov. 21. He had lands laid out to him—10¾ acres.

1687. Sep. 1. Taxed 13*s.* 7*d.*

1688. Ratable estate, a bull, 11 cows, 2 oxen, 5 heifers, 3 two year, 8 yearlings, a horse, 6 swine, 6 acres Indian corn and English corn, 2 acres mowing pasture in swamp, 10 acres pasture, 2 shares meadow, 80 acres wild pasture, 300 acres in woods, and rights.

1706, Jul. 23. He and his wife Martha had given to them Margaret Hoggs, the little daughter of

I. THOMAS, { b. 1670, Jan. 3. / d. 1752, Jul. 17. — Providence, R. I.
m. (1)
ABIGAIL DEXTER, { b. / d. of Stephen & Abigail (Whipple) Dexter.
m. (2) 1737, Apr. 28,
ABIGAIL CHAFFEE, { b. / d. 1752 + of Chaffee.

1. Thomas, 1696 ±
2. Stephen,
3. Jeremiah,
4. Nathaniel,
5. Anthony,
6. Joseph,

1725, Jun. 7. He deeded, "for fatherly love and affection, which I have for my eldest son, Thomas Field, Jr.," &c., lot of land where he liveth, in the lands of Pawtuxet, on west side of Pauchasset River, 140 acres and buildings, without limitation.

1730–42. Town Council.

1732, Apr. 5. He deeded son Anthony, for love and good will, certain lands, viz: 5 acres that was my honoured father, Thomas Field's, deceased, also lots of 80 acres and 62 acres, &c.

1737, Apr. 26. He made an agreement with Abigail Chaffee, two days before his marriage, concerning property.

1742. Deputy.

1744, Jan. 18. Will—proved 1752, Dec. 16. Ex. son Jeremiah. To wife Abigail, £40, and all agreements with her to be carried out, she having all estate she brought with her. To son Thomas, £15. To son Jeremiah, 250 acres at Pawtuxet and 150 acres west side Pauchasset River. To son Nathaniel, £4. To son Anthony, 170 acres in Glocester. To son Jeremiah, all movable estate. (Before the will was found, administration was given the widow Abigail, by mistake, but corrected two months later, at above date of will being proved.)

II. MARY, { b. 1673, Jun. 1. / d.

III. AMOS, { b. 1677. / d. young.

FIELD (THOMAS). IV. William, m. Mary Mathewson, of James and Hannah (Field) Mathewson. V. Martha. Erase entirely.

IV. WILLIAM, { b. 1682, Jun. 8. / d. 1729, Nov. 1. — Providence, R. I.
m.
MARY, { b. / d. 1729 + of

1. Martha,
2. Joseph,
3. Nathan,
4. Mary,
5. William
6 Thomas,
7. John, 1712.
8 Charles, 1714, Feb. 6.

1707, Dec. 2. He deeded to brother-in-law Thomas Mathewson, for good-will, &c., 4 acres (confirmed by Thomas Field, father of said William).

1708. Freeman.

1727, Mar. 13. He, of the one part, deeded Nicholas, Richard and Henry Harris, of the other part, for purpose of establishing boundary line, they all choosing Captain William Potter, to make partition between them "of a certain piece of land, being that which was the front of that which was the homestead of our honoured grandfather, Thomas Harris, deceased."

1729, Oct. 16. Will—proved 1729, Dec. 1. Exx. wife Mary. To daughter Martha Brown, 10 sheep and land adjoining James Brown, Jr's. house lot. To son Joseph, lot on Town street. To son Nathan, lot on Town street, &c. To daughter Mary Field, lot on Town street. To sons William and Thomas, all remaining part of homestead land, whereon my dwelling house stands, to them equally, but the whole use and profit to be to wife Mary, till sons are of age, if she does not again marry. If she does marry, she to be quit of it and guardians appointed for the two sons till they are of age. To sons John and Charles, two lots, given me by my honoured mother, Martha, deceased, also other land to them. The lot of land given Martha Brown, to be for her son Gideon, at age, or if he die to his elder brother. To his son Joseph Field he also gave lands at place called Newfield and at the neck, with use to testator's wife, while his widow. To wife, the use of east end of house, called parlor, and privilege in cellar, with liberty of fruit from orchard, but if she again marry, she to have only £30

Elizabeth Hoggs, for them to bring up, instruct and dispose of as their own. (The mother of the child gave her to them.)

1708, Sep. 11. He deeded son William, land situated lying and being in Providence, bounded north by land of Daniel Abbott, south by heirs of Gideon Crawford, east with highway and west with Town street, including dwelling house, &c., half at the signing of deed and half at decease of grantor, reserving a fireroom for use of wife, if she live after me. He further deeded to son William, two parcels of land, one of 30 acres, in place called Waller's Island, in place called Great Swamp, and the other at place called What Cheer, also of 30 acres, with reservation to grantor of privilege of timber, firewood and pasturing at What Cheer, for life. He further deeded him ½ right in lands and meadow, west side of seven mile line and 100 acres east of seven mile line, with other rights, &c., &c. But in case my now wife Martha, mother of said William, should outlive me, then William is to pay her 40*s.* annually, for life.

1709, Dec. 29. He deeded son-in-law John Yates, Jr., for well being and settlement, a lot on west side of Town street, near my dwelling, and three years later deeded him another lot.

1715, May 29. He deeded son Thomas, Jr., for love and affection, &c., all lands and meadows in place called Pumgansett, adjoining land where he now dwelleth, half at signing of deed and other half at decease of grantor (excepting what had before been disposed of to son William), also two other lots of 71 acres and 80 acres, and certain rights.

1717, Nov. 29. Administration to son and heir Thomas, on his estate. Inventory, £54, 2*s.* 4*d.*, viz: a cow that "he brought with him" and 3 cows raised by son Thomas, for his father's use, 2 steers, 2 heifers and 2 calves raised by son Thomas, and 8 sheep and 3 lambs raised by son Thomas, an old bible, warming pan, and old pewter, brass, wearing apparel, &c.

Perhaps his daughter Mary, married John Dexter[3] (Stephen,[2] Gregory.[1])

from estate. She to be provided with firewood by sons Nathan and Joseph, and with meat, drink and clothes by sons William and Thomas. If any son die before arriving at age, the others have his share. All household stuff to wife Mary, for her to give part to daughter Mary. All rest of movable estate after bringing up children, to go to sons. The small children were left in care of wife to bring up.
Inventory, £533, 14*s.* 6*d.*, viz: a pair of oxen, 2 pair steers, a bull, 5 cows, 2 heifers, a bull stag, 4 calves, mare and colt, a horse, 100 sheep, 6 swine, Indian corn, 38 loads of hay, barley, flax, beans, 7 pewter platters, 12 pewter plates, &c., warming pan, old bible, 2 testaments, sundry other small books, tobacco, a sword and belt, pair of pistols, 2 spinning wheels, feathers, flocks, flock bed, 15 chairs, 3 tables, &c.

V. { MARTHA, | b. / d. 1735 +
m.
{ THOMAS MATHEWSON, | b. 1673, Apr. 1. / d. 1735, Oct. 23. | of James & Hannah (Field) Mathewson.

1. Thomas.
2. Amos,

VI. { ELIZABETH, | b. / d.
m. 1709, Jan. 24,
{ JOHN YATES, | b. / d. 1724, Nov. 28. | of John Yates.

1. James, 1710, Jul. 18.
2. John.

FIELD (THOMAS). 1st column. Erase last sentence: "Perhaps," &c.

2d column. II. Mary, d. 1727, Jun., m. John Dexter. He b. 1673, d. 1734, Apr. 22, of Stephen & Abigail (Whipple) Dexter. Children: 1. Naomi, 1698. 2. Mary, 1699. 3. John, 1701. 4. Stephen, 1703. 5. Jeremiah, 1705. 6. Sarah, 1707. 7. Lydia, 1709. 8. William, 1711. 9. Jonathan, 1713. 10. Abigail, 1715.

FIELD (WILLIAM).

{ WILLIAM, | b. / d. 1665.
m.
{ DEBORAH, | b. / d. 1679.

Providence, R. I.

1640, Mar. 20. He bought of Thomas James his dwelling house, field, garden, meadow, land at Sassafras Hill, land at Moshassuck River and all other rights in Providence, for £60.

1640, Jul. 27. He and thirty-eight others signed an agreement for form of government.

1645, Jan. 27. He bought of William Reynolds a share of 6 acres at Foxes Hill and sold it the same day to William Wickenden.

1650–58–59–60–61–62–63–64–65. Assistant.

1655. Freeman.

1656–58–59–60–61–62–63. Commissioner.

1658, Nov. 22. He landed three ankers of liquor.

1659, Mar. 17. He sold Richard Borden of Portsmouth, 80 acres near Nutaconkonitt Hill.

1660, Nov. 27. He bought of John Sanford, Treasurer for Colony of Providence, 60 acres and 12 acre piece.

1665, May 30. Will—proved 1665, Jun. 3. Exx. wife Deborah. To cousin (*i. e.* nephew) Thomas Field, now at Providence with me, all that cargo that is now upon sending to the Barbadoes, as also all my horsekind that I have (saving those which I shall hereafter express), also four heifers, right of land at Aquidnesett, rights above Pauchassett River now in controversy with some men of Warwick, and furs in the house. To servant John Warner, a young mare, being that mare, which goes at Warwick or which lately there went. To wife, two mares, a colt, the rest of the cattle, and rest of goods and movables, as well that which is yet coming from Barbadoes, which is from thence due to me, as the rest which belongeth to me; also my tackling, yokes, and tools. To wife also for life all my home stall or dwelling place that I am at present possessed with, and upland at Saxafrax Neck, and meadow at Pomeconsett. To cousin Thomas Field, the above real estate at death of testator's wife. He desires that his servant John Warner shall serve his time with his now dame.

1666, Jun. 3. His widow took receipt from Thomas Field, for legacy, he calling her his aunt.

No issue.

THOMAS, b. d. 1687.
m.
MARY, b. d. 1699.

Portsmouth, R. I.

1643. He had land granted him.

1655. Freeman.

1660, Mar. 20. He had a deed of house and land from Henry and Ann Ayres, in consideration of fencing 2 acres, but said Henry and Ann were to enjoy said land for their lives without paying rent.

1665. He bought of James Babcock, two parcels of land and dwelling house, barn, and orchard for £50. The same year he sold 4 acres to Thomas Lawton.

1674. Town Council.

1684, May 2. He deeded grandson, Preserved Fish, son of Thomas, deceased, for love, &c., dwelling house and 15 acres where Thomas Fish, Jr., had lived, and said grandson Preserved, to possess it in the year 1700.

1687, Feb. 9. Will—proved 1687, Dec. 13. Exx. wife Mary. To son John, land bought of James Babcock. To son Robert, twenty shillings and like amount to daughters Mehitable, Mary and Alice. To grandson Preserved, son of son Thomas, five shillings. To wife rest of estate.

Inventory, £49, 10*s*.

1697, Sep. 9. Will—Codicil, 1699, Jul. 12—proved 1699. Widow Mary. Ex. son Daniel. To son John, £5. To son Robert, £5, and a cow. To daughter Mehitable Tripp, £5, brass chafing dish, pewter platter, three porringers, chest and pewter plate. To daughter Mary Brayton, £5, table, basin, pewter platter, long cup, and plate. To daughter Alice Knowles, £5, two feather pillows, basin, pewter platters, pewter candlestick, and plate. To daughters Mehitable, Mary and Alice, all wearing apparel both linen and woolen. She mentions grandchildren Preserved and Mehitable, children of son Thomas, deceased; Comfort, Ruth and Thomas, children of son Daniel; Mary, daughter of son John; and Robert, son of son Robert. To daughter Mehitable Tripp, whatever is due her for wool. To son Daniel, all the outward movables. The codicil makes but slight changes.

Inventory, £130, 2*s*.

I. **THOMAS**, b. d. 1684. Portsmouth, R. I.
m. 1668, Dec. 10.
GRIZZEL STRANGE, b. d. of John & Alice ( ) Strange.

1. Alice, 1671, Sep. 15.
2. Grizzel, 1673, Apr. 12.
3. Hope, 1676, Mar. 5.
4. Preserved, 1679, Aug. 12.
5. Mehitable, 1684, Jul. 22.

II. **MEHITABLE**, b. d.
m. 1667, Aug. 6.
JOSEPH TRIPP, b. 1644 ± d. 1718, Nov. 27. of John & Mary (Paine) Tripp.

1. John, 1668, Jul. 6.
2. Thomas, 1670, Mar. 28.
3. Jonathan, 1671, Oct. 5.
4. Peleg, 1673, Nov. 5.
5. Ebenezer, 1675, Dec. 17.
6. James, 1677, Jan. 12.
7. Alice, 1679, Feb. 1.
8. Abiel, 1681, Jan. 8.
9. Mehitable, 1683, Oct. 9.
10. Joseph, 1685, Aug. 24.
11. Jabez, 1687, Nov. 3.
12. Mary, 1689, Aug. 22.
13. Daniel, 1691, Nov. 3.

III **MARY**, b. d. 1747, Apr. 4.
m. 1671, Mar. 18.
FRANCIS BRAYTON, b. d 1718, Jan. 30. of Francis & Mary ( ) Brayton.

1. Mary, 1676, Jan. 1.
2. Thomas, 1681, Jun. 14.
3. Francis, 1684, Mar. 17.
4. David, 1686, Oct. 23.
5. Mehitable, 1693, Jan. 12.
6. Benjamin, 1695, Sep. 8.

IV. **ALICE**, b. d. 1734.
m.
WILLIAM KNOWLES, b. 1645. d. 1727. of Henry Knowles.

1. Henry, 1675, Sep. 29.
2. William,
3. Daniel,
4. Robert,
5. John,
6. Alice,
7. Rose,
8. Martha,
9. Mary,
10. Margaret,

V. **JOHN**, b. d. 1742. Portsmouth, R. I., Dartmouth, Mass.
m.
JOANNA, b. d. 1744, of

1693, Feb. 8. He sold brother Daniel, for £50, land willed by father Thomas.

1737, Apr. 4. Will—proved 1742, Apr. 20. Ex. son Ebenezer. To wife, Joan, £100, household goods, and improvement of cattle and rest of personal. To son Ebenezer, land and ten shillings. To son John, homestead farm, and ten shillings. To daughter Mary Potter, wife of William, £20. To daughter Abigail Case, wife of John, £50. To daughter Mehitable Cornell, wife of William, £20. To daughter Joanna Fisher, wife of John, £50. To daughter Hope Phillips, wife of James, £20. To daughter, Susanna Boyce, wife of Benjamin, £50. To daughter Elizabeth Fish, £80 and best bed. To daughter Sarah Arnold, wife of Anthony, £50. To four grandchildren, viz: Sarah, William, John and Thomas Phillips, children of my daughter, Alice Phillips, deceased, £50, equally divided at age. To grandson Thomas Phillips, all interest in undivided land at Dartmouth. To grandson Joshua Rathbone, son of my daughter Patience Rathbone, deceased, £50. If maintenance for wife be insufficient, she to have further provision made for her.

Inventory, £721, 1*s*. 1*d*., viz: bonds £541, 1*s*. 7*d*., books, pewter, 2 cows, a swine, 4 fowls, spinning wheel, &c.

1744, Apr. 5. Will—proved 1744, Dec. 10. Widow Joanna. Ex. son Ebenezer. To daughter Mary Potter, 10*s*. To grandson John Wickham, 20*s*. To daughter Abigail Case, wife of John, 20*s*. To daughter Joanna Fisher, wife of John Fisher, 20*s*. To son Ebenezer Fish, 10*s*. To daughter Susanna Boyce, wife of Benjamin, 10*s*. To grandson Thomas Phillips, £40, bed, &c. To grandson, John Fisher, 20*s*. To son-in-law James Phillips, little box I keep my writings in. To daughters Mehitable Cornell, wife of William, Hope Phillips, wife of James, and Elizabeth Huddlestone, wife of Seth, rest of estate equally, except farming tools, which were to go to grandson Thomas Phillips.

Inventory, £197, 3*s*.

1. Ebenezer,
2. John,
3. Mary,
4. Abigail,
5. Mehitable,
6. Joanna,
7. Hope,
8. Susanna,
9. Elizabeth,
10. Sarah,
11. Alice,
12. Patience,

VI. **DANIEL**, b. d. 1723, Sep. 16. Portsmouth, R. I.
m. 1682, May 1.
ABIGAIL MUMFORD, b. d. 1717 (—). of Thomas & Sarah (Sherman) Mumford.

1717, Jan. 28. Will—proved 1723, Oct. 14. Exx. daughter Comfort Broadway. To four daughters Comfort Broadway, Sarah, Abigail and Mary Fish, all housing and lands in Portsmouth, they paying to my daughter Ruth Thomas, each £25, within four years. To son Jeremiah, all housing and lands in Kings Town. To children all cattle, horses, sheep, and swine equally. To three youngest daughters Sarah, Abigail, and Mary, rest of movables.

Inventory, £226, 16*s*., viz: wearing apparel, bed, table, 5 chairs, pewter, money scales, cheese, pair of worsted combs, cider, cider mill, neat cattle, £65, mare £5, swine £12, planks, &c.

1. Comfort, 1683, Feb. 7.
2. Thomas, 1685, Jul. 3.
3. Ruth, 1687, Nov. 2.
4. Daniel, 1690, Jul. 11.
5. Sarah, 1694, Jan. 29.
6. Jeremiah, 1698, Sep. 15.
7. Abigail,
8. Mary,

VII. **ROBERT**, b. d. 1730. Portsmouth, R. I.
m. 1686, Sep. 16.
MARY HALL, b. d. 1735, Jun. 8. of Zuriel & Elizabeth (Tripp) Hall.

He was a blacksmith.

1686. Freeman.

1687. He had ear mark for sheep granted.

1694-99-1707-15. Juryman.

1705-6-7-8-9. Pound keeper. He was Lieutenant at time of his death.

1728, Dec. 12. Will—proved 1730. Exs. sons Daniel and David. To son Robert, 5*s*. To son William, land in Tiverton. To daughter Mary Dexter, £10. To daughter Alice Peck, £30, audirons and negro woman Rose at death of parents. To wife Mary, use of south end of house, garden, half the orchard, &c., while widow, and keep of a cow, horse, swine, geese, fowls, &c., with supply of firewood yearly, as also beef, pork and Indian corn (viz: one hundred pounds each of beef and pork and ten bushels of corn yearly). To her as a free gift a horse, cow, and household stuff. To son Daniel, negro boy Jo. To son David, negro boy Tony, "together with all the rest of my smith-working tools whatsoever." To sons Daniel and David equally, rest of personal, and certain land with use of half the house, orchard, &c., and at death of their mother they to have the whole—paying legacies. To son Jonathan, land in Portsmouth. He directs that his burial place be fenced about and cared for and used "for my near relatives."

1735, Apr. 28. Will—proved 1735, Jun. 11. Widow Mary. Exs. sons Daniel and David. To son Robert, great bible, case of bottles and half the old pewter plates with a little table. To daughter Mary Dexter, a dozen pewter plates, great looking glass, half wearing apparel, &c. To son William, a cow, silver cup, red chest, &c. To son Jonathan, a mare, brown chest, great chair, biggest tankard, &c. To daughter Alice Peck, bed, chest, pewter platters, spice mortar, little trundle bed, half wearing apparel, &c. To son Daniel, great chest commonly called "father's chest," silver spoon, called "father's spoon," great porringer, warming pan, linen wheel, great settle, &c. To son David, great cupboard and desk that was his father's, silver spoon "with my name at large thereon," woolen wheel, &c. To granddaughter Mary, daughter of son William, pair of iron dogs, frying pan, box iron and heaters, &c. To two daughters, the rest of estate equally except negro woman's bed and bedding.

Inventory, £160, 3*s*.

1. Robert, 1690, May 17.
2. Mary, 1693, Mar. 1.
3. William, 1695, Jun. 7.
4. Zuriel, 1697, Jul. 10.
5. Isaac, 1699, Dec. 25.
6. Alice, 1702, Jul. 3.
7. Jonathan, 1704, Oct. 27.
8. Daniel, 1707, May 17.
9. David, 1710, Mar. 10.

FISHER.

EDWARD, b. d. 1677.
m.
JUDITH, b. d. 1682 ±

Portsmouth, R. I.

1639, Jul. 1. He had grant of a house lot, next Thomas Wait's.

1644, May 27. He was granted additional land at the upper end of his lot.

1652, Jan. 12. He bought of Henry Lake, of Portsmouth, a dwelling house and 8 acres in Warwick.

1655. Freeman.

1660. Commissioner.

1672–73. Deputy.

1665, Sep. 19. Will—proved 1677, Oct. 5. Exx. now wife Judith. Overseers, William Baulstone and John Briggs, Sr. To wife, whole estate and power to make equal division to my three daughters of what remains at death of said wife, viz: to daughters Ruth Potter, Hannah Briggs and Mary Fisher.

1680. Widow Fisher taxed 5s.

1682, Jan. 6. Receipts were given, for legacies from father-in-law, Edward Fisher's will, by Thomas Briggs, of Dartmouth, husband of Mary, John Potter, of Warwick, husband of Ruth, and John Briggs, of Portsmouth, husband of Hannah.

I. RUTH, b. d.
m. 1664, Jun. 2,
JOHN POTTER, b. 1642 ± d. 1694. of Robert & Isabel ( ) Potter.

1. Robert, 1666, Mar. 5.
2. Fisher, 1667, Jun. 12.
3. John, 1668, Nov. 21.
4. William, 1671, May 23.
5. Samuel, 1672, Jan. 10.
6. Isabel, 1674, Oct. 17.
7. Ruth, 1676, Nov. 29.
8. Edward, 1678, Nov. 25.
9. Content, 1680, Oct. 2.

II. HANNAH, b. d. 1727 +
m.
JOHN BRIGGS, b. 1642. d. 1713, Jul. 2. of John Briggs.

1. Edward,
2. John,
3. William,
4. Susanna,

III. MARY, b. d. 1717 +
m.
THOMAS BRIGGS, b. d. 1720, Jun. 12. of John Briggs.

1. Mary, 1671, Aug. 9.
2. Susanna, 1672, Mar. 14.
3. Deborah, 1674, Oct. 16.
4. Hannah, 1676, May 1.
5. John, 1678, Oct. 2.
6. Thomas, 1684, Apr. 27.

FLOUNDERS.

THOMAS, b. d. 1670.
m.
SARAH, b. d. 1670 +

Kings Town, R. I.

1668, May 4. He, with others of Wickford, petitioned Connecticut authorities for protection of their jurisdiction or that they might look elsewhere for government.

1669, Aug. 27. He complained to Assembly, against Indian named Sawagomet.

1670, Jul. 12. A jury appointed by Connecticut authorities, found that Walter House came to his death by act of Thomas Flounders. Much wrangling occured by the conflict of authority between Rhode Island and Connecticut authorities, both colonies claiming jurisdiction over the territory.

Flounders being examined by the Governor of Rhode Island and the Council, admitted that he struck a blow with a small stick, and that House, holding up his arm, fell backward and hit his head against a rafter, said House being on the threshold and Flounders in the shop.

1670, Oct. 26. He having been lately executed for killing Walter House, and his estate forfeited unto the King; a petition was sent to the Assembly by Edward Greenman and John Greene, of Newport, desiring that the estate should go to his late wife Sarah, after the charge of his execution, &c., had been paid.

The Assembly "commiserating the solitary and poor estate and condition of Sarah, the late wife of the aforenamed Thomas Flounders," &c., for relief and comfort of her and poor infant, granted the petition. The widow for her present relief was to have all bedding and household stuff, a cow and hog, together with the corn.

I. CHILD, b. d.

FONES.

JOHN, b. d. 1703, Dec. 20,
m.
MARGARET, b. d. 1709 +

Newport, Jamestown, King's Town, R. I.

1659, Jun. 19. He, calling himself servant to William Coddington, sold Richard Tew 3-900 part of Conanicut Island for a good ewe and six ewe lambs, or a mare colt.

1672, Jan. 1. He and five others bought of Awashuwett, Chief Sachem of Quohesett in Narragansett, a tract of land there.

1676, Aug. 24. He, with title of Captain, was member of a Court Martial at Newport for trial of Indians, charged with being engaged in King Philip's designs. It was voted that certain ones were guilty and they were sentenced to be shot.

1678, Jun. 12. He and others complained to Assembly, that men of East Greenwich in laying out lands granted them had much intruded on petitioners' land.

1679–80–81. Deputy.

1680. Taxed 14s. 1d.

1682–83. Kings Town. Conservator of the Peace.

1683, Aug. 22. The Assembly met at his house in Narragansett and there received a reply to a

I. JOHN, b. 1663, Sep. d. 1738, Feb. 17. North Kingstown, R. I.
m.
LYDIA SMITH, b. 1668, d. 1741, Jan. 24 of Benjamin & Lydia (Carpenter) Smith.

1687, Sep. 6. Kings Town. Taxed 1s.

1704. Deputy.

1705, Feb. 27. He sold Susanna Smith of Newport, half of a fulling mill that had come to him at decease of his father.

1705, Mar. 10. He and wife Lydia sold Thomas Spencer, 10 acres at East Greenwich.

1709, May 27. He and five others bought 792 acres of vacant lands in Narragansett.

1712, Oct. 14. He and Samuel Fones of Kings Town, Jeremiah Fones of Jamestown, Mary Greene, widow, and Fones Greene, of Warwick, sold David Greene of Jamestown, 13 acres there for £160.

1727, Oct. It was ordered by Assembly that he be given a discharge for the book brought by him and that the book be lodged in the Governor's hands till next session of the Assembly.

1728, Feb. He having petitioned Assembly setting forth that the northern bounds of Pettaquamscutt Purchase are not rightly run and settled by a jury that was empowered by Town Council of North Kingstown for to lay out a highway along said line, whereby great contention is and more is likely to happen to inhabitants on both sides the line if not by this court timely prevented: therefore prays that a committee and surveyor at his charge may be appointed to run same. The Assembly appointed a committee to take a surveyor with them to run the line.

1738, May 16. Will—proved. Exs. daughters Margaret Holmes and Mary Smith. To wife Lydia, the interest of £100 and half of house and farm for life, and then to two daughters Margaret Holmes and Mary Smith. To grandsons Fones Hazard and Fones Smith, legacies. To brother Samuel Fones, land in East Greenwich. To cousin (*i. e.* nephew), John Fones, a legacy.

He and his wife were buried in the Fones Burial Ground, as was his daughter Lydia, who married Job Herrington. His daughter Margaret m. (1) Stephen Hazard.

1. Margaret,
2. Lydia, 1698,
3. Mary,

FONES. 2d column. II. Jeremiah, m. (2) Martha Card (w. of James) daughter of Francis West.

letter sent by them to Gov. Cranfield of New Hampshire, who with others sat at Richard Smith's house at Narragansett. The Assembly prohibited Gov. Cranfield and his associates from holding court in this jurisdiction.

1686, May 28. Justice of the Peace. (Appointed by President and Council then governing New England.)

1686, Jun. 23. Clerk of Court of Commissioners.

1686, Jul. 16. He, with others, signed a petition to the King in regard to the writ of *Quo Warranto*, presenting their full and free submission and resignation of power given in the charter and desiring to be discharged from all levies and contributions which the Assembly would expose them to in sending an agent to England, to which petitioners do not consent.

1687, Jun. 14. Present as one of the Justices at General Quarter Session and Inferior Court of Common Pleas.

1687, Sep. 6. Taxed 18*s*. 8*d*.

1687, Dec. 14. He and two others were empowered to agree with workmen, artists and others for building and erecting in towns of Newport and Kings Town the said two Court Houses.

1691, Mar. 16. He had a legacy from will of Major Richard Smith, of 10*s*. to buy him a ring.

1694, Aug. 5. He bought of John Weeden of Jamestown, certain land there for £10.

1698. Deputy, and Assistant same year.

1700, Apr. 8. His wife gave 12*s*. towards building a Quaker meeting house at Mashapaug.

1700, Aug. 8. He took oath as to his evidence about Dr. Peter Ayrault.

1703. Will—proved. He desired his body should be buried where his two deceased sons, James and Daniel, were laid. To wife use of real and personal estate for life (except legacies). To eldest son John, half of a 300 acre tract and other land. To son Jeremiah 40 acres and dwelling house, and land in Jamestown, silver tobacco box, silver cup, spoons and a third of wearing apparel, &c. To son Samuel, certain land. To grandson Fones Greene, land. Shortly after his death his sons John, Jeremiah and Samuel ratified land to sister Greene of Warwick, and ratified their father's will generally.

1709, Jun. [illegible] His widow is mentioned in giving bounds of certain lands lying near her house.

II. { JEREMIAH, { b. 1665. Kings Town, Jamestown, North Kingstown, R. I.
m. (1) 1694, May 30. { d. 1747.
ELIZBETH, { b.
m. (2) 1710, Nov. 9. { d. 1709, Mar. 2. of
MARTHA CHARD, { b.
{ d. 1747 + of Chard.

1687, Sep. 6. Taxed 1*s*.

1703. Jamestown. Freeman.

1705. Constable.

1727, Dec. 2. Will—proved 1747, Jul. 13. Exx. wife Martha. To son Joseph, homestead farm, orchard, &c., and two silver spoons. To son John, £5. To grandson John Davis, son of daughter Margaret, deceased, great two eared silver ——, at age. To son Daniel, certain land. To two other sons, Samuel and Thomas, land. Another son and granddaughter are mentioned, but names destroyed.

1. James, 1695, Jun.
2. Jeremiah, 1697, Aug.
3. Joseph, 1699, May 11.
4. Daughter, 1701, May 22.
5. Margaret, 1703, Mar. 9.
6. John,

(2d wife.)

7. Mary, 1711, Sep. 20.
8. Daniel, 1713, Mar. 9.
9. Samuel, 1715, Mar. 10.
10. Daughter, 1719, Feb. 23.
11. Thomas,

III. { SAMUEL, { b. 1666. North Kingstown, R. I.
m. (1) { d. 1757, Dec.
ANNE TIBBITTS, { b.
m. (2) { d. 1702 (—) of Henry & Sarah (Stanton) Tibbitts.
MERIBAH, { b.
{ d. of

1687, Sep. 6. Kings Town. Taxed 1*s*.

1700, Apr. 8. He gave £2 toward building Quaker meeting house at Mashapaug.

1704-5-6-7-8-9-10-11-12-13-14-15. Town Clerk.

1708. Justice of the Peace.

1711. Deputy.

1. Ann, 1689, Oct. 16.

(2d wife.)

2. Samuel, 1702, Jul. 4.
3. Sarah, 1703, Jul. 3.
4. Margaret, 1704, Jul. 23.
5. Mary, 1705, Jul. 1.
6. Son, 1706, Dec. 17.
7. Francis, 1710.

IV. { MARY, { b. 1668.
m. 1689, Jan. 29. { d. 1722, Mar. 20.
JAMES GREENE, { b. 1658, Jun. 1.
{ d. 1713, Mar. 2. of James & Deliverance (Potter) Greene.

1. Fones, 1690, Mar. 23.
2. James, 1692, Apr. 2.
3. Mary, 1694, Mar. 16.
4. Daniel, 1696, Apr. 7.
5. Elisha, 1698, Aug. 5.
6. Deliverance 1701, Feb. 12.
7. Mary, 1703, Sep. 25.
8. John, 1706, Feb. 26.
9. Jeremiah, 1708, Dec. 16.
10. Samuel, 1711, Jun. 8.

V. { JAMES, { b. 1670.
{ d. young.

VI. { DANIEL, { b.
{ d. young.

FOSTER.

{ WILLIAM, { b.
m. { d. 1684 +
{ —— { b.
{ d.

Newport, R. I.

1638, Mar. 20. His name appears in a list of inhabitants admitted to Newport after this date.

1639, Nov. 25. Clerk of the Train Band, till another be chosen.

1640, Mar. 10. He had 218 acres recorded.

1641, Mar. 16. Freeman.

1678, Jun. 12. He and others petitioned to the Assembly to be accommodated with lands as the East Greenwich men are.

1680. Taxed £1, 1*s*. 13*d*.

1690, Sep. 29. Will—witnesses, Henry Lilly and Ephraim Turner. A reference to this will is found in a list of seventeen wills (between the dates of 1676 and 1695), that were presented to the Court in 1700 by parties interested, the law requiring three witnesses, and these wills having but two.

Perhaps George Foster, who married Mary Weaver, daughter of Thos[2]. (Clement[1]), was a son of William, or possibly grandson.

Miles Foster, who was a merchant of Newport in 1677, may also have been a son of William Foster.

I. { WILLIAM, { b.
{ d.

GEORGE, b. d. 1677 ±
m. (1)
HERODIAS HICKS, b. d.
of Long.
(She m. (3) John Porter.)
m. (2)
LYDIA BALLOU, b. d. 1722 (—)
of Robert & Susanna ( ) Ballou.
(She m. (2) 1678, Jun. 14, Wm. Hawkins.)

Newport, R. I.

1638. He was admitted an inhabitant of the island of Aquidneck, having submitted himself to the government that is or shall be established.

1640, Mar. 10. He had 58 acres recorded.

1640, Mar. 12. He was present at General Court of Elections.

1641, Mar. 16. Freeman.

1642, Mar. 17. Constable and Senior Sergeant.

1644. Ensign.

1658, May 11. His wife "being the mother of many children," came with her babe at her breast, from Newport to Weymouth, to deliver her religious testimony, for which she was carried to Boston, before Governor John Endicott, who sentenced her to be whipped with ten lashes, as well as her companion, Mary Stanton, who came with her to help bear her child After the whipping with a three fold knotted whip of cords, she was continued for fourteen days longer in prison. The narrator (Bishop's New England Judged), says: "The woman came a very sore journey, and (according to man), hardly accomplishable, through a wilderness of above sixty miles, between Rhode Island and Boston."

"After the savage, inhuman and bloody execution upon her, of your cruelty, aforesaid, kneeled down and prayed the Lord to forgive you."

1660, Jun. 29. He was witness to a deed from Indian called Socho, of a tract of land at Pettaquamscutt.

1662. Commissioner.

1665, May 3. He was before the Assembly upon petition of Horod Long, alias Gardner, his wife. She declared that when her father died (in England), she was sent to London, and was married unknown to her friends, to John Hicks, privately in the under church of Paul's, called St. Faith's Church, she being between thirteen and fourteen years old. She then came to New England with her husband, and lived at Weymouth two and a half years, thence coming to Rhode Island about the year 1640, and there lived ever since till she came to Pettacomscott. Soon after coming to Rhode Island, there happened a difference between her and her husband, John Hicks, and he went away to the Dutch, carrying with him most of her estate, which had been sent her by her mother. (Her mother and brother lost their lives and estate in his Majesty's service she says.) After her desertion by John Hicks, she became wife to George Gardiner, and by him had many children. Testimony as to her marriage to George Gardiner was given by Robert Stanton, who declared that one night at his house both of them did say before him and his wife, that they did take one the other, as man and wife. Horod Gardiner, having lived with her last husband eighteen or twenty years, now desired of Assembly that the estate and labor he had of mine, he may allow it me, and house upon my land I may enjoy without molestation, and that he may allow me my child to bring up, with maintenance for her, and that he be restrained from troubling me more.

1668, Jun. 2. He was made one of the overseers of his father-in-law, Robert Ballou's will.

1673, Oct. 22. Juryman.

1688, Nov. 30. His daughter Mary, gave a receipt for £13, to her father-in-law (*i. e.* stepfather), William Hawkins, of Providence, being balance of legacy of £20, bequeathed by last will of her father, George Gardiner, of Newport, deceased. It is assumed that he had a daughter Dorcas, who became the first wife of John Watson.

Possibly his son Samuel was by his first wife, rather than his second.

Possibly also, Jeremiah was a grandson, rather than son.

The following record, made in an old family bible, 1790, Jul. 11, by William C. Gardiner, is evidently erroneous in many important particulars, but not more so than traditionary statements of families are often found to be.

(Memoranda.)

"Joseph Gardiner, the youngest son of Sir Thomas Gardiner, Knight, came over among the first settlers, and died in Kings county, Rhode Island State, aged 78 years. Born A. D. 1601, died A. D. 1679. Left six sons, viz:

I. BENONI, b. d. 1731 ± Kings Town, R. I.
m.
MARY, b. 1645. d. 1729, Nov. 16. of

1. William, 1671.
2. Nathaniel,
3. Stephen,
4. Isaac, 1687, Jan. 7.
5. Bridget,

1671, May 19. He took oath of allegiance.

1679, Jul. 29. He and forty-one others, of Narragansett, signed a petition to the King, praying that he would "put an end to these differences about the government thereof, which hath been so fatal to the prosperity of the place; animosities still arising in people's minds, as they stand affected to this or that government."

1687, Sep. 6. Taxed 5*s.* 3½*d.*

1705, Sep. 18. He and wife Mary, deeded to son Nathaniel, 100 acres, being west half of farm where Benoni now dwells, and on same day deeded son Stephen, dwelling house, orchard, &c.

1705, Nov. 17. He and Henry, George, William and Nicholas Gardiner, and John Watson, all of Kings Town, and Mary, Tabitha, Joan, Elizabeth and Hannah Gardiner, and Rebecca Watson, their wives, sold John Potter 410 acres (bounded partly by a branch of Point Judith Pond), for £150, said sum to be paid to Thomas Hicks, of Flushing, Long Island.

(This Thomas Hicks, was a son of John Hicks, the first husband of Herodias.)

Neither Tabitha, Joan nor Hannah signed the deed, though the other wives did.

1711, Feb. 16. His son, calling himself "William Gardiner, Jr., son of Benoni," and wife Abigail, with consent of wife's mother, Abigail Remington, relict of John, sold to Henry Gardiner, Sr., all right in farm of wife's father, consisting of 250 acres. (The term William Gardiner, Jr., was used to distinguish him from his uncle of same name, who died this same year.)

1713. He and wife Mary, deeded land to son Isaac.

1727. It is said that in testimony given this year, he calls himself aged ninety years and upwards, but it may well be thought that he did not come so near as his brother Henry, in counting the lapse of time.

1729, Nov. 16. His wife died at her son-in-law, Job Sherman's, at Portsmouth.

1732, Dec. 17. His son William died, aged sixty-one years.

II. HENRY, b. 1645. d. 1744. Kings Town, R. I.
m. (1)
JOAN, b. d. 1715 + of
m. (2) [of John.
ABIGAIL REMINGTON, (w. b. 1656. d. 1744. of Edward & Abigail (Davis) Richmond.

(2d wife.)
1. Henry, 1691, Feb. 25.
2. Ephraim, 1693, Jan. 17.
3. William, 1697, Oct. 27.

1671, May 19. He took oath of allegiance.

1679, Jul. 29. He signed the petition to the King.

1683. Constable.

1687, Sep. 6. Taxed 10*s.* 9*d.*

1688. Grand Jury.

1694, Mar. 27. He was charged by Abigail Remington, with being the father of two children by her, and the court ordered him to indemnify Kings Town for any charge. After the death of his wife, Joan, he certainly recognized Abigail as his wife, and mentioned her as such distinctly in his will.

1703, Jul. 12. He was appointed on a committee to lay out highways.

1715, Nov. 21. He, calling himself Henry Gardiner, Sr., testified as to a highway being stopped twenty-five years before. His wife Joan, also testified.

1738, Mar. He calls himself, aged about ninety-three years, in a deposition as to membership of Church of England in Narragansett.

His wife Abigail, calls herself in eighty-second year.

1732, Oct. 25. Will—proved 1744, May 5. Exs. sons Ephraim and Henry. To wife Abigail, a pacing mare and three of best milch cows, negro wench, six good ewes, bed, and other household stuff sufficient to furnish a room, and all that said wife dies possessed of she may give to my granddaughters. To sons Henry and Ephraim, equally, a farm in Westerly of 200 acres. To grandson Henry, son of William, deceased, 80 or 90 acres in Westerly, at age. To granddaughter Hannah Potter, wife of Thomas, negro Patience. To granddaughter Dorcas Gardiner, daughter of Ephraim, negro Sarah. To son Henry, half my money, lands, horses, hogs, &c., viz: half of all estate not disposed of. To son Ephraim, the other half. (To Henry, a watch, and to Ephraim, a bible also.) To servant Peter, a suit of clothes. To son Ephraim, land in Pettaquamscutt. To sons Henry and Ephraim, rest of estate.

Inventory, £1,016, 1*s.*, viz: wearing apparel £42, 8*s.*, silver money, cane, great bible, books, pewter, stillyards, warming pan, 2 woolen wheels, 2 linen wheels, 5 cows, heifer, 2 oxen, mare, negro Betty and child £120, Patience and child £130, Charity £120, Sarah £130, boy Joseph £70, &c.

1744, Jul. 20. Will—proved 1744, Oct. 8. Widow Abigail. Ex. son Henry. To son Henry, negro Betty, he paying my four grandchildren £40, equally divided. To daughters Martha Sherman and Elizabeth Kenyon, all wearing apparel. To granddaughters Dorcas, daughter of Ephraim, Mary, daughter of Henry, Abigail Worden, daughter of William Gardiner, deceased, and Lydia, daughter to John Gardiner, son to said William, deceased, rest of estate.

Inventory, £266, 6*s.* 6*d.*

GARDINER. 2d column. II. Henry. d. 1744. [illegible]
VI. Dorcas. Her sons John, b. 1676, July 2[illegible]. Samuel, b. [illegible]
1686. XIII. Robert. Erase all except his name. He d.
1690 at Providence, R. I. 1680, Apr. 7. Will proved
1690, Apr. 28. Ex. Father-in-law, (i. e. step-father) William Hawkins. To brother Joseph house in Newport, for life, and then to eldest son, or eldest daughter, under certain conditions, but Joseph to pay his brother Peregrine £13, in accordance with will of testator's father. Also to Joseph rights in Narragansett. To brother Peregrine lands in Providence with certain conditions. To father-in-law, William Hawkins, use and profit of house and lands in Newport for five years, and to him all cattle and other estate.

III. GEORGE, b. d. 1724. Kings Town, R. I.
m.
TABITHA TEFFT, b. 1653. d. 1722 + of John & Mary ( ) Tefft

1. Joseph,
2. Nicholas
3. Samuel,
4. Robert,
5. John,
6. George,
7. Hannah,
8. Tabitha,
9. Joanna,

1671, May 19. He took oath of allegiance.

1673, Nov. 7. He and wife Tabitha, sold Nicholas Gardiner 60 acres.

1679, Jul. 29. He signed the petition to the King.

1687, Sep. 6. Taxed 5*s.* 4½*d.*

1704, Mar. 11. Henry Gardiner, upon whose estate administration was taken at this date by widow ——, is believed to have been a son of George,[2] (or possibly of Benoni).

1709, Jan. 29. He and wife Tabitha, for love to son Nicholas, deeded him 80 acres.

1722, Oct. 29. His wife called her age sixty-nine years, in a deposition made by her as to the age James Wilson would have been if he had lived.

1718. Will—proved 1725, Jan. 18. Ex. son Joseph. To sons Joseph, Nicholas, Samuel, Robert and John, one sheep each, they having had portions. To daughter ——, £20. To daughters Tabitha —— and Joanna ——, each a legacy. To granddaughter Elizabeth Gardiner, daughter of ——, deceased, £15. To wife Tabitha, £45. (The father of granddaughter Elizabeth, it is said, was George,[3] to whom a deed of land had been made by his father, George.[2])

IV. WILLIAM, b. d. 1711. Kings Town, R. I.
m.
ELIZABETH, b. d. 1737. of

1. William,
2. Ann,
3. Elizabeth,
4. Rebecca,
5. Susanna,
6. Dorcas,
7. Tabitha,
8. Rachel

1671, Jan. 21. He (calling himself "son of George Gardiner, of Newport"), bought 200 acres of John Porter, of Pettaquamscutt, and Horod, his wife.

1679, Jul. 29. He signed the petition to the King.

1687, Sep. 6. Taxed 9*s.* 1½*d.*

1688. Constable, and same year on Grand Jury.

1701, May 23. He deeded son and daughter, Joseph and Ann Hull, 204 acres, for love, &c.

1706, Jan. 18. He deeded 20 acres, for love, &c, to son John Gould, and Elizabeth, his wife.

See: American Genealogist, v. 19, p. 222; v. 21, p. 191; v. 34, p. 2

Benoni, died 1781, aged 104, Henry, died 1787, aged 101, Wm., died at sea by pirates, George, lived to see 94 years, Nicholas and Joseph lived also to a great age." &c.

1711, Jan. 18. Will—proved 1711, Mar. 12. Ex. son William. To wife Elizabeth, half of stock of creatures and half of household goods at her disposal (except £40, to be paid daughter Rebecca, at eighteen.) To wife, for life, house, half the orchard and negro man James. To daughter Rebecca, negro girl Zipporah and £40. To daughter Susannah, 50 acres and £20. To daughter Dorcas, negro boy Philip and £35. To daughter Tabitha, £60. To daughter Rachel, land and £60, to be paid by my son-in-law, John Gould, to whom he gave certain land. To daughter Elizabeth, wife of John Gould, £20. To Honour Huling, daughter of Alexander Huling, £5. To son William, all lands remaining, housing and rest of personal estate.

Inventory, £368, 9s. 10d., viz: beds, churn, wearing apparel, hat, gloves, pewter, 4 oxen, 12 cows, 7 three years, 2 two years, 5 horsekind, 142 sheep, 50 lambs, cash £5, negro boy (4 years), girl (2 years) and a negro, 17 years, cart, &c. £93, 18s.

V. { NICHOLAS, * } b. 1654. d. 1712. — Kings Town, R. I.
m.
HANNAH, } b. d. of

1. Nicholas.
2. Ezekiel,
3. George,

1671, May 19. He took oath of allegiance, and same year bought land of John Porter.

1673, Nov. 2. He bought of John and Horod Porter, 100 acres.

1679, Jul. 29. He signed the petition to the King.

1687, Sep. 6. Taxed 15s. 3d.

1701, Mar. 26. He and wife Hannah, for £48, sold John Thomas, of Jamestown, certain land in Kings Town.

1711, Mar. 12. He testified as to certain land, calling his age fifty-seven years or thereabouts.

1712. Administration to son Nicholas.

1714. The administrator declared before Town Council, that his father had died intestate, but that he believed his father intended the estate should be divided equally to himself and two brothers, and he therefore deeded his brother Ezekiel, a farm on the great plain, and to his brother George, 1000 acres, they both possessing when they should arrive at age, and George to pay his brother Nicholas, £40, on coming of age.

VI. { DORCAS, * } b. d.
m.
JOHN WATSON, } b. d. 1728. of Watson.

1. John,
2. Samuel,
3. William,
4. Frances,
5. Ann,
6. Herodias,

VII. { REBECCA, * } b. d.
m.
JOHN WATSON, } b. d. 1728. of Watson.

(2d WIFE)

GARDINER. 2d column. VIII. Samuel. Freetown. Swanzey, Mass. His wife was widow of James Brown and daughter of Robert Carr. He d 1696, Dec. 8. His widow Elizabeth d 1697 (?). Children: 1. Elizabeth, 1684. 2. Samuel, 1685, Oct. 28. 3. Martha 1686, Nov. 16. 4. Patience. 1687, Oct. 31. He bought of George Lawton, 100 acres in Freetown for £250. 1688-90-92. Freetown. Selectman. 1688-90-92, Town Clerk. 1690-92, Deputy. 1693, Dec. 30, Swanzey. He and Ralph Chapman bought land of Ebenezer Brenton for £700 (having already sold his Freetown land). 1696, Selectman. 1697, Feb. 15. Inventory, £1,046, 5s., sworn to by widow Elizabeth IX. Joseph, b. 1669, d. 1726, Aug. 22. He and his wife were buried in Newport Cemetery. Children: 10. William, 1712. 11. Mary, 1718. X. Lydia, d. 1723.

VIII. { SAMUEL, * } b. d. — Newport, R. I.
m.
ELIZABETH, } b. d. of

1. Samuel, 1685, Oct. 28.

IX. { JOSEPH, } b. d. — Newport, R. I.
m. 1693, Nov. 30,
CATHARINE HOLMES, } b. 1673. d. 1758, Oct. 28. of John & Frances (Holden) Holmes.

(She m. (2) Daniel Wightman.)

1. John, 1697, Sep. 17.
2. Robert, 1699, Aug. 16.
3. Frances, 1701, Sep. 7.
4. Joseph, 1703, Apr. 17.
5. George, 1705, Feb. 4.
6. Catharine, 1707, Feb. 1.
7. Lydia, 1709, Mar. 2

He was a cooper.

1691, Jan. 9. He sold 12 acres in Newport, to William Hawkins, of Providence, said land having been owned by George Gardiner, of Newport, father of Joseph and Peregrine Gardiner, as by will appears.

1694, Jun. 21. He and John Stanton, of Newport, sold Joseph Clarke, of Westerly, 200 acres in Narragansett, being part of land formerly in partnership of Robert Stanton, father of John, and George Gardiner, father of Joseph.

1705-10-13-14. Deputy. He held the military title of Lieutenant also.

X. { LYDIA, } b. d.
m. 1689, Apr. 4,
JOSEPH SMITH, } b. d. 1750, Jan. 13. of John & Sarah (Whipple) Smith.

1. Israel, 1690, Jan. 13.
2. Lydia, 1692, May 25.
3. Sarah, 1694, May 24.
4. Joseph, 1695, Dec. 18.
5. Robert, 1698, Mar. 3.
6. Alice, 1700, Jan. 25.
7. William, 1703, Mar. 15.
8. David, 1705, Dec. 10.
9. Jeremiah,

XI. { MARY, # } b. d.

XII. { PEREGRINE, } b. d. — Newport, R. I.

1684, Jun. 11. An agreement was made about his schooling, between his stepfather, William Hawkins, and William Turpin, of Providence, the schoolmaster.

XIII. { ROBERT, * } b. 1671, May. d. 1731, May. — Newport, R. I.

1694, Mar. 18. He was a witness to the will of Caleb Carr.

1699, Sep. 26. Deputy Collector. He answered Lord Bellomont, under oath, several questions relative to his office, and in regard to privateers and pirates.

1713-14-15. Clerk of Assembly.

1713-14-15. Deputy.

1718, Oct. 29. He and two others were appointed on committee to view Fort Ann, and see what may be proper for fitting and repairing same.

He was buried in Trinity Church-yard; the inscription on his tombstone, showing that he was one of the first promoters of the church, and naval officer and collector of the port for many years, &c.

There was a Robert Gardiner, of Providence, who, in his will (dated 1689, Apr. 17), made William Hawkins, Jr., his executor; and the latter presented said will and had administration granted, 1690, Apr. 28. No copy of the will itself is found, however.

XIV. { JEREMIAH, * } b. d. — Newport, R. I.
m.
SARAH, } b. d. of

1. Daughter, 1712, Sep. 23.

* See: American Genealogist, v. 19, p. 222.
# " " " v. 24, p. 69

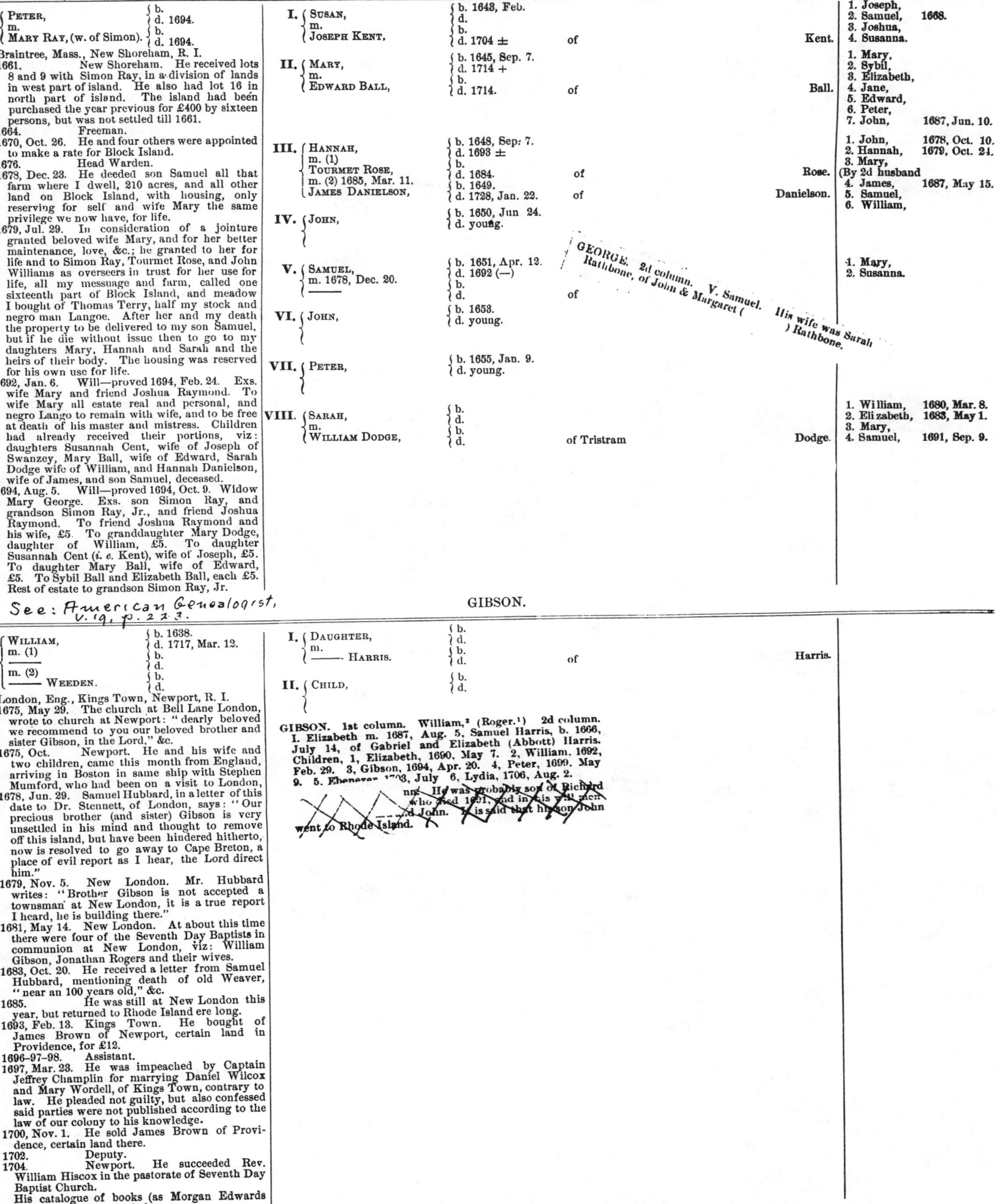

GEORGE.

PETER, b. d. 1694.
m.
MARY RAY, (w. of Simon). b. d. 1694.

Braintree, Mass., New Shoreham, R. I.

1661. New Shoreham. He received lots 8 and 9 with Simon Ray, in a division of lands in west part of island. He also had lot 16 in north part of island. The island had been purchased the year previous for £400 by sixteen persons, but was not settled till 1661.

1664. Freeman.

1670, Oct. 26. He and four others were appointed to make a rate for Block Island.

1676. Head Warden.

1678, Dec. 23. He deeded son Samuel all that farm where I dwell, 210 acres, and all other land on Block Island, with housing, only reserving for self and wife Mary the same privilege we now have, for life.

1679, Jul. 29. In consideration of a jointure granted beloved wife Mary, and for her better maintenance, love, &c.; he granted to her for life and to Simon Ray, Tourmet Rose, and John Williams as overseers in trust for her use for life, all my message and farm, called one sixteenth part of Block Island, and meadow I bought of Thomas Terry, half my stock and negro man Langoe. After her and my death the property to be delivered to my son Samuel, but if he die without issue then to go to my daughters Mary, Hannah and Sarah and the heirs of their body. The housing was reserved for his own use for life.

1692, Jan. 6. Will—proved 1694, Feb. 24. Exs. wife Mary and friend Joshua Raymond. To wife Mary all estate real and personal, and negro Lango to remain with wife, and to be free at death of his master and mistress. Children had already received their portions, viz: daughters Susannah Cent, wife of Joseph of Swanzey, Mary Ball, wife of Edward, Sarah Dodge wife of William, and Hannah Danielson, wife of James, and son Samuel, deceased.

1694, Aug. 5. Will—proved 1694, Oct. 9. Widow Mary George. Exs. son Simon Ray, and grandson Simon Ray, Jr., and friend Joshua Raymond. To friend Joshua Raymond and his wife, £5. To granddaughter Mary Dodge, daughter of William, £5. To daughter Susannah Cent (*i. e.* Kent), wife of Joseph, £5. To daughter Mary Ball, wife of Edward, £5. To Sybil Ball and Elizabeth Ball, each £5. Rest of estate to grandson Simon Ray, Jr.

I. SUSAN, b. 1643, Feb. d.
m.
JOSEPH KENT, b. d. 1704 ± of Kent.
1. Joseph,
2. Samuel, 1668.
3. Joshua,
4. Susanna.

II. MARY, b. 1645, Sep. 7. d. 1714 +
m.
EDWARD BALL, b. d. 1714. of Ball.
1. Mary,
2. Sybil,
3. Elizabeth,
4. Jane,
5. Edward,
6. Peter,
7. John, 1687, Jun. 10.

III. HANNAH, b. 1648, Sep. 7. d. 1693 ±
m. (1)
TOURMET ROSE, b. d. 1684. of Rose.
m. (2) 1685, Mar. 11.
JAMES DANIELSON, b. 1649. d. 1728, Jan. 22. of Danielson.
1. John, 1678, Oct. 10.
2. Hannah, 1679, Oct. 24.
3. Mary,
(By 2d husband
4. James, 1687, May 15.
5. Samuel,
6. William,

IV. JOHN, b. 1650, Jun 24. d. young.

V. SAMUEL, b. 1651, Apr. 12. d. 1692 (—)
m. 1678, Dec. 20.
——— b. d. of
1. Mary,
2. Susanna.

GEORGE. 2d column. V. Samuel. His wife was Sarah Rathbone, of John & Margaret ( ) Rathbone.

VI. JOHN, b. 1653. d. young.

VII. PETER, b. 1655, Jan. 9. d. young.

VIII. SARAH, b. d.
m.
WILLIAM DODGE, b. d. of Tristram Dodge.
1. William, 1680, Mar. 8.
2. Elizabeth, 1683, May 1.
3. Mary,
4. Samuel, 1691, Sep. 9.

See: American Genealogist, v. 19, p. 223.

GIBSON.

WILLIAM, b. 1638. d. 1717, Mar. 12.
m. (1)
——— b. d.
m. (2)
——— WEEDEN. b. d.

London, Eng., Kings Town, Newport, R. I.

1675, May 29. The church at Bell Lane London, wrote to church at Newport: "dearly beloved we recommend to you our beloved brother and sister Gibson, in the Lord," &c.

1675, Oct. Newport. He and his wife and two children, came this month from England, arriving in Boston in same ship with Stephen Mumford, who had been on a visit to London.

1678, Jun. 29. Samuel Hubbard, in a letter of this date to Dr. Stennett, of London, says: "Our precious brother (and sister) Gibson is very unsettled in his mind and thought to remove off this island, but have been hindered hitherto, now is resolved to go away to Cape Breton, a place of evil report as I hear, the Lord direct him."

1679, Nov. 5. New London. Mr. Hubbard writes: "Brother Gibson is not accepted a townsman at New London, it is a true report I heard, he is building there."

1681, May 14. New London. At about this time there were four of the Seventh Day Baptists in communion at New London, viz: William Gibson, Jonathan Rogers and their wives.

1683, Oct. 20. He received a letter from Samuel Hubbard, mentioning death of old Weaver, "near an 100 years old," &c.

1685. He was still at New London this year, but returned to Rhode Island ere long.

1693, Feb. 13. Kings Town. He bought of James Brown of Newport, certain land in Providence, for £12.

1696–97–98. Assistant.

1697, Mar. 23. He was impeached by Captain Jeffrey Champlin for marrying Daniel Wilcox and Mary Wordell, of Kings Town, contrary to law. He pleaded not guilty, but also confessed said parties were not published according to the law of our colony to his knowledge.

1700, Nov. 1. He sold James Brown of Providence, certain land there.

1702. Deputy.

1704. Newport. He succeeded Rev. William Hiscox in the pastorate of Seventh Day Baptist Church.

His catalogue of books (as Morgan Edwards says) showed him a scholar.

I. DAUGHTER, b. d.
m.
——— HARRIS. b. d. of Harris.

II. CHILD, b. d.

GIBSON. 1st column. William,[2] (Roger.[1]) 2d column. I. Elizabeth m. 1687, Aug. 5, Samuel Harris, b. 1666, July 14, of Gabriel and Elizabeth (Abbott) Harris. Children, 1, Elizabeth, 1690, May 7. 2, William, 1692, Feb. 29. 3, Gibson, 1694, Apr. 20. 4, Peter, 1699, May 9. 5. Ebenezer, 1703, July 6, Lydia, 1706, Aug. 2.

~~He was probably son of Richard who died 1691, and in his will mentioned John. It is said that his son John went to Rhode Island.~~

CHRISTOPHER,[2] (Wm.[1]) { b. 1658, Jul. d. 1748, Nov. 22.
m.
DEBORAH PERRY, { b. 1665. d. 1724.

of Edward & Mary (Freeman) Perry.

Sandwich, Dartmouth, Ms., Little Compton, R. I.

1682, Jul. 7. He was fined 10*s.*, "for contemptuously speaking against the dispensers of the word of God." (He was a Quaker.)

1686, Mar. 2. He was fined £7, for resisting Moses Rowley, Jr., constable of Suckaneset, in December last. A little after the court remitted £3 of his fine, he paying 20*s.* to Moses Rowley, for the wound he gave him on his head.

1687, Apr. 9. He had a legacy of a cross-cut saw from the will of his father.

He removed first to Dartmouth, and later in life to Little Compton.

1746, Oct. 5. Will—proved 1748, Dec. 8. Ex. son Enos. To son Christopher, 5*s.* To heirs of daughter Meribah, 25*s.* To daughter Mary Borden, £25. To daughter Deborah Wilbur, 25*s.*, and £200 that her husband, Benjamin Wilbur had of me. To grandson Christopher Borden, certain land at Watuppa Pond, in Tiverton. To grandsons Elijah and Canaan Gifford, wearing apparel. To granddaughters Rachel, Phillis and Dorcas Gifford, all household goods. To son Enos, rest of real and personal.

Inventory, £997, 11*s.* 4*d.*

GIFFORD. 2d column IV. Enos. Children: 1. Deborah, 1725 Apr. 8. 2 Rachel, 1727, Mar. 3. 3. Elijah, 1729, Jul. 22. 4. Canaan, 1731, May 15. 5. Phillis, 1734, May 14, 6. Dorcas, 1736, Aug. 18. 7. Enos, 1740, Mar. 22. 8, Joseph, 1742, Jan 2. VI Christopher. Dartmouth, Mass. Children: 1. William, 1722, Jun. 29 2. Richard, 1725, Dec. 31, 3 Susannah, 1730, Aug. 23. 4. Christopher, 1737, Aug. 8. VIII. John. Possibly his name should be erased.

I. MERIBAH, { b. 1687, Oct. 31. d. 1732, (—).
m. 1708, Jul. 20,
NATHANIEL SOULE, { b. 1684, May 12. d. 1766. of Nathaniel & Rose ( ) Soule.

1. Meribah, 1709, Jun. 10.
2. Jonathan, 1711, Mar. 3.
3. Henry,
4. James,
5. Wesson,

II. CHRISTOPHER, { b. 1689. Sep. 17. d. young.

III. AUDRY, { b. 1689, Sep. 17. d.

IV. ENOS, { b. 1693, Feb. 6. d. 1769, May. Little Compton, R. I.
m.
PHILLIS, { b. d. 1764 + of

1. Elijah, 1729.
2. Canaan, 1731, Jan. 15.
3. Enos, 1734.
4. Joseph,
5. Phillis,
6. Dorcas,
7. Rachel,

1764, Jan. 5. Will—proved 1769, Jun. 6. Ex. son Elijah. To son Elijah, farm in Dartmouth. To son Canaan, southerly part of homestead farm. To sons Elijah and Canaan, a cedar swamp in Dartmouth. To son Enos, the part of home farm on which he now dwells. To son Joseph, rest of homestead farm and 143 Spanish milled dollars. To daughter Phillis Davenport, $1. To daughter Dorcas Manchester, $1. To daughter Rachel Wilbur's children, $1. To wife Phillis, a cow, all money due, side saddle, use of best room in house, keep of cow and of a beast, ten pounds flax, ten pounds wool, twelve bushels corn, one hundred pounds pork, one hundred pounds beef, ten cords of wood and ten bushels apples, yearly, provided by son Canaan. To four sons, all live stock and rest of estate.

Inventory, £3,964, 18*s.*

V. MARY, { b. 1695, Oct. 6. d.
m. 1721, Aug. 14,
THOMAS BORDEN, { b. 1697, Dec. 8. d. 1740, Apr. of Richard & Innocent ( ) Borden.

1. Richard, 1722.
2. Christopher, 1726, Oct. 10.
3. Deborah,
4. Mary,
5. Rebecca,

VI. CHRISTOPHER, { b. 1698, Apr. 15. d.
m. 1721, Jun. 6,
MARY BORDEN, { b. 1701, Jan. 29. d. of Richard & Innocent ( ) Borden.

VII. DEBORAH, { b. 1700, Feb. 2. d.
m. 1724, Nov. 9,
BENJAMIN WILBUR, { b. 1699, Jun. 20. d. of Joseph & Ann (Brownell) Wilbur.

1. Christopher, 1726, Dec. 23.
2. Lydia, 1729, May 3.
3. Judith, 1730, Nov. 23.
4. John, 1733, Jan. 31.
5. Joseph, 1736, Sep. 23.
6. David, 1738.

VIII. JOHN, { b. 1705. d. 1802, Dec. Little Compton, R. I.
m.
———— { b. d. of

1. Ephraim,
2. Judith,
3. Mary, ııı
4. Elizabeth,
5. Lydia,

1798, Dec. 19. Will—proved 1803, Jan. 5. Exs. friend Stephen Brownell and son-in-law Joseph Gifford. To two sons of my son Ephraim, deceased, all land in Little Compton and Westport, except that bought of Jabez Gibbs. To grandson Zebedee Manchester, house and land where he lives. To grandson Ephraim Gifford, son of daughter Judith, deceased, my plate buttons. To grandson John Gibbs, land already deeded him. To three granddaughters, children of daughter Elizabeth Manchester, deceased, £6 each. To granddaughter Mary Taber, child of daughter Mary Reed, £6 and a bed. To Rhoda Manchester, daughter of my daughter Lydia Manchester, deceased, the household stuff that was her mother's and £6. To two granddaughters, Lilla and Judith Gifford, daughters of my daughter Judith Gifford, £6. To granddaughters, rest of estate.

Inventory, $1,266,07.

GODFREY.

JOHN, { b. d. 1702 (—)
m.
SARAH, { b. d. 1702 +

Newport, R. I.

He was a mariner.

1676, Aug. 25. He testified at the Court Martial held at Newport, for the trial of certain Indians, charged with being engaged in King Philip's designs.

1680. Taxed 7*s.*

1684. Freeman.

1689. He was given command of a vessel fitted out from Newport, for pursuit of French privateers that had plundered Block Island.

1693, Oct. 25. A vessel of which he was master, having been seized by a French privateer, a brigantine was sent in pursuit from Newport.

1702, Mar. 4. Widow Godfrey was in the list of proprietors of common lands, at this date.

GODFREY 1st column. His widow d. 1726. 1726 will-proved 1726. Widow Sarah. She mentions son John, daughter Sarah Cranston, son-in-law John Cranston, and Susanna Tayer.

I. JOHN, { b. d. Newport, R. I.
m. 1701, May 28.
ELIZABETH CARR, { b. d. of Caleb & Sarah (Clarke) Carr.

1. Mary, 1702, Mar. 23.
2. John, 1704, Jan. 31.
3. Caleb, 1706, Jul. 17.
4. Elizabeth, 1709, May 21.

II. SARAH, { b. d.
m.
BENJAMIN CRANSTON, { b. d. of John & Mary (Clarke) Cranston.

1. Elizabeth, 1701, Mar. 7.
2. Caleb, 1703, Apr.
3. Sarah, 1705, Apr. 19.
4. Benjamin, 1707, Feb. 27.

III. MARY, { b. d.
m. 1709, Nov.
ISAAC SHERMAN, { b. 1686, Apr. 22. d. 1718 (—) of Benjamin & Hannah (Mowry) Sherman.

1. Benjamin,

IV. PENELOPE, { b. 1685. d. 1761, Mar. 18.
m.
JOHN CRANSTON, { b. 1684, Aug. 4. d. 1745, Oct. 15. of Samuel & Mary (Hart) Cranston.

1. John,
2. Samuel,
3. Thomas,
4. William,
5. James,
6. Jeremiah,
7. Peleg,
8. Caleb,
9. Mary,
10. Hart,
11. Sarah,

From Additions & Corrections supplement: Godfrey. 1st column. He was probably son of Richard Godfrey of Taunton, who died in 1691, and in his will mentions sons Richard and John. It is said that his son John went to Rhode Island.

GOULDING.

ROGER, { b. d. 1702 (—)
m. 1673, Jan. 1.
PENELOPE ARNOLD, { b. 1653, Feb. 10. d. 1702 +

of Benedict & Damaris (Westcott) Arnold.

(She m. (2) ——— Cutler.)

Newport, R. I.

1676, Aug. 11. He and Major Peleg Sanford having discovered the hiding place of King Philip, informed Captain Benjamin Church, and that officer offered the honor of beating up Philip's headquarters to Captain Goulding, who accepted. The result was that the next day King Philip was killed.

1676, Nov. 1. It was ordered by Plymouth Colony, that "whereas Captain Roger Goulding of Rhode Island hath approved himself to be our constant real friend in the late war, and very officious and helpful as occasion hath been, when as our armies and soldiers have been in

GOULDING. 1st column. His widow probably married Thomas Cutler, who had wife Ann in 1699.

See: American Genealogist, v. 19, p. 223

I. DAMARIS, { b. 1676, Mar. 17. d. 1677, Jul. 13.

II. THOMAS, { b. d.

III. GEORGE, { b. 1685, Jul. 30. d. 1742. Newport, R. I.
m. (1) 1707, Aug. 17,
MARY SCOTT, { b. d. of John & Elizabeth (Wanton) Scott.
m. (2)
MARY CRANSTON. (w. of [James. { b. 1704, Feb. 16. d. 1764, of Daniel & Mary (Robineau) Ayrault.

1. Elizabeth, 1713, Jul. 16.
2. Penelope, 1715, May 7.
3. Mary, 1719, Oct. 18.
4. George, 1724, Feb. 28.

1707. Freeman.

1709, Dec. 6. He and wife Mary sold certain land for £70 to John Mumford.

1715, Apr. 11. He and wife Mary sold to Thomas Fry of East Greenwich, 10 acres there for £25.

1716-17-18-19-20-27-28-29-30-31-32-33-34-35-36-37-38-39-40-41-42. Deputy.

1737, Nov. He was appointed by Assembly on committee to examine into circumstances of Fort George, and receive the stores there of Joseph Wanton and deliver same to person appointed by the

those parts and have had necessity of transportation of our men to the said island, and otherwise very ready to do us good, this court doth grant unto the said Captain Roger Goulding one hundred acres of land lying and being upon the north side of Saconett men's line," &c.

1677, May 1. Freeman.

1677, Jul. 13. He and two others complained to Plymouth Colony that they have met with opposition from some persons in their peaceful enjoyment of land granted them, by some threatening speeches. The court replied that they would maintain title against any who molest them in improvement thereof, " but as for words they must bear with them when they meet with them, and pass them over respecting the premises."

1680. Taxed £2, 10*s.* 10*d.*

1685. Deputy.

1685–86–87–90–91. Major for the Island.

1702, Jan. 12. His widow, now Penelope Cutler, was named among the proprietors of common lands as guardian of her son George Goulding.

Governor—also to repair the house at Fort George.

1738, Mar. He deposed that he had heard his mother Penelope declare that her father, Governor Benedict Arnold, was a member of Church of England.

1739, Feb. He was appointed on committee to build the Colony House of brick at Newport where the old one stands. The new one to measure eighty feet by forty and thirty feet stud, and to stand near or quite north and south.

1740, Feb. 26. He was appointed on a committee to procure a good sloop to be built of not exceeding one hundred and fifteen tons, for defence of the colony.

1740, May. He was appointed on committee to provide transports and provisions for purpose of embarking the enlisted men to the general rendezvous for service in war against Spain. The same day he and Jahleel Brenton were appointed to go to Ipswich Court in Massachusetts, to attend trial and give evidence against persons to be tried there for uttering counterfeit bills in imitation of bills of this colony, and he was likewise to attend court in New Hampshire for same purpose.

1740, Sep. He and four other deputies protested against the act of the Assembly for emitting £20,000 in bills of credit, giving five reasons for their protest. They thought the emission of these bills would depreciate the whole paper currency and that a load of debt would be laid on our posterity which they will not be able to bear. Their final reason was thus given: "Because the ruin of this flourishing colony will probably in a great measure be owing to this fatal act, we would have the whole colony and posterity know we have not deserved their imprecations on this occasion, but have endeavoured to preserve and deliver down to posterity the privileges and the property which our ancestors earned with so much hazard, toil and expense." He prayed the Assembly that he might be dismissed from his position as one of the Trustees of the colony and that the same might be put on record.

He was buried in Trinity churchyard.

GRAY.

EDWARD, b. ; d. 1681, Jun.
m. 1651, Jan. 16.
MARY WINSLOW, b. 1630; d. 1663.
of John & Mary (Chilton) Winslow.
m. (2) 1665, Dec. 12.
DOROTHY LETTICE, b. ; d. 1686 +
of Thomas & Ann ( ) Lettice.
(She m. (2) Nathaniel Clarke.)

Plymouth, Mass.

He was a merchant.

1643. He was thus early at Plymouth.

1650, Aug. 7. He was to have a bushel of Indian corn for damage done by the cattle of Edward Doty in his corn.

1655, May 1. He was complained of by Samuel Cuthbert regarding a cow exchanged by Gray for a lot. The court found Cuthbert's complaint in a great measure unjust, Gray having as appeared given Cuthbert leave to make choice of a cow out of his cattle, whereupon the court persuaded Gray to accept three bushels of Indian corn for wintering the cow, and so the difference ended.

1656, Feb. 3. He having had a controversy with Francis Billington about two iron wedges, the court ordered them to be delivered to latter.

1658, Feb. 2. He complained against Joseph Billington for neglecting to pay a small debt due.

1659, Dec. 6. He and another appeared at court to lay claim to a parcel of iron wedges which an Indian had stolen and sold at Taunton, and the court took a course to have the Indian apprehended.

1662, Jun. 3. He was granted a double share of land.

1662, Jun. 10. The house bought by the country of him was to be repaired by order of the court.

1666, Oct. 31. He was awarded 20*s.* from Joseph Billington for hunting his ox with a dog and for wrong done his swine and fence, and he was to have returned to him the scythes used by Billington without Gray's leave.

1667, Mar. 5. His land at Rocky Nook, Plymouth, was to be ranged and have a highway laid out by it.

1668, Jun. 3. He was fined 10*s.* for using reviling speeches to John Bryant on the Lord's day as soon as they came out of the meeting.

1668, Oct. 29. He was to have two barrels of tar, returned him and 8*s.* paid him for proving it was his.

1669, Mar. 2. John Bryant was now fined 10*s.* for using reviling speeches to Edward Gray as soon as they came out of meeting on the Lord's day.

1670, May 29. Freeman.

1670, Jun. 24. He and seven others agreed for two years to pay 8*s.* per small barrel and 12*s.* per great barrel for good merchantable tar delivered at waterside in good casks.

1671, Mar. 8. He was to have paid him 20*s.* from a man for pilfering his tobacco, and the culprit was whipped at the post and ordered to depart the government.

1671. Grand Jury.

1674, Mar. 4. He was granted 100 acres at Titicut.

1676–77–78–79. Deputy.

1677, Jul. 13. He was on committee respecting debts due the colony and to balance accounts between towns concerning late war.

1677, Oct. 3. He was to have, with two others,

I. DESIRE, b. 1651, Nov. 6; d. 1690, Dec. 4.
m. 1672, Jan. 10.
NATH'L SOUTHWORTH, b. 1648; d. 1711, Jan. 14. of Constant & Elizabeth (Collier) Southworth.

1. Constant, 1674, Aug. 12.
2. Mary, 1676, Apr. 3.
3. Ichabod, 1678, Mar.
4. Nathaniel, 1684, May 10
5. Elizabeth,
6. Edward, 1688.

II. MARY, b. 1653, Sep. 18; d.

GRAY. 2d column. ry. Perhaps m. Benjamin Rider. III. Elizabet seth Arnold, of Samuel and Elizabeth. Children dward, 1680, Mar. 20. 2, Penelope, 1682, Apı 3, Desire. 4, Benjamin. 5, James. 6, Elizabeth. ... Sarah m. Samuel Little of Thomas and Anne (Warren) Little. He d. 1707. Children, 1, Thomas. 2, Samuel. 3, Sarah. 4, Edward. VIII. Thomas m. (2) Anna Little, of Ephraim and Mary (Sturtevant) Little.

III. ELIZABETH, b. 1658, Feb. 11; d.

IV. SARAH, b. 1659, Aug. 12; d.

V. JOHN, b. 1661, Oct. 1; d.

(2d WIFE.)

VI. EDWARD, b. 1667, Jan. 31; d. 1726. Tiverton, R. I.
m. (1)
MARY SMITH, b. ; d. of Philip & Mary ( ) Smith.
m. (2)
MARY MANCHESTER, b. ; d. 1729. of William & Mary (Cook) Manchester.

1. Mary, 1691, May 16.
2. Edward, 1693, Jan. 10.
3. Elizabeth, 1695, Jan. 3.
4. Sarah, 1697, Apr. 25.
5. Phebe, 1699, Sep. 6.
6. Philip, 1702, Feb. 11.
7. Thomas, 1704, Feb. 4.
8. Hannah, 1707, Nov. 3.

(2d wife).

9. John, 1712, Aug. 3.
10. Lydia, 1714, May 12.
11. William, 1716, Jul. 17.
12. Samuel, 1718, Aug. 31.

1696, Oct. 7. He bought certain land in Tiverton of Caleb and Lydia Loring of Plymouth for £230.

1722, Dec. 10. Will—proved 1726, Jun. 7. Exs. sons Philip and Thomas. To wife Mary, while widow, the new addition on east side house and use of 6 rows apple trees, and liberty to cut wood, improvement of garden, £100, 6 best cows, 1 mare, negro woman Zilpha and ¼ household stuff. To son Philip, 3 fifty acre lots where I live, buildings, orchard, &c., and other land, he paying my son Thomas £20, and to daughter Hannah, 1 feather bed, &c., to value of £150. To son Thomas, 3 fifty acre lots, &c., he paying my daughter Sarah, legacy with what she has to make her up to £130. To sons Philip and Thomas, jointly, land where my son Edward formerly lived, with buildings, &c., they paying my daughter Elizabeth so much as shall make up what I have given her in life time which appears by book, £150, and also paying bonds which testator obliges himself to pay to daughter-in-law Rebecca Gray, to pay to children of my son Edward, deceased. To son John, 27 acres, &c.. he paying legacy to my daughter Lydia Gray, of £120, good feather bed, &c. To son William under age, 120 acres, &c., and £20, and negro Sambo. To son Samuel, 60 acres and £250 when 21. To sons William and Samuel, land. To daughter Mary, wife of John Bennett, 5*s.*, she having had her part. To daughter Phebe, £150. If either son had by 1st wife die before 21, his part to go to surviving son of 1st wife. If either of sons of last wife die without issue, then part to go to surviving son of last wife. All estate not disposed of to go equally to eight youngest children, viz: Philip, Thomas, John, William, Samuel, Phebe, Hannah and Lydia.

1729, Mar. 19. Inventory, £284, 9*s.* 10*d.* Widow Mary. Administration to brother John Manchester.

VII. SUSANNA, b. 1668, Oct. 15; d.

GRAY. 2d column. VII. Susannah. It is possible that she did not marry John Cole, as noted in Additions and Corrections.

VIII. THOMAS, b. ; d. 1721, Nov. 5. Little Compton, R. I.
m. (1)
ANNA, b. 1673; d. 1706, Oct. 16. of
m. (2)
PHEBE, b. 1666; d. 1746. of

1. Thomas, 1695, May 7.
2. Edward, 1699, Nov. 29
3. Anna, 1702, Jan. 29
4. Rebecca, 1704, Aug. 1.
5. Mary, 1706, Oct. 8.

(2d wife, no issue.)

1704, Nov. 1. He and William Pabodie signed a letter on behalf of the Congregational Church inviting neighboring churches to the ordination of Rev. Richard Billings, which was to take place Nov. 29.

1721, Sep. 21. Will—proved 1721, Nov. 23. Exs. sons Thomas and Edward. To wife Phebe, looking glass, brass kettle, new bible, plate cup, 2 silver spoons, warming pan, 2 feather beds, negro maid "Peg" and ½ household stuff, also great room, bed room, cheese room and cellar in house called "Woodworth house," while widow, and to have 10 cords of wood per year, 10 bushels Indian corn, barley, meat, &c., 2 cows, and keep of same, the new garden and £8, per year. To son Thomas, dwelling house and 50 acre lot, and other land. To son Edward, dwelling house he now liveth in, 50 acres, and other land. To daughter Anna Richmond, mulatto girl "Almy," gold ring, silver spoon and bible. To daughter Rebecca Gray, 2 feather beds, ½ of household stuff, 1 gold ring, 1 silver spoon and £50 and 3 cows. To sons Thomas and Edward, each a feather bed, and son Thomas a cloak, gun, silver spoon, gold ring, negro called "Sarah," mulatto boy "Solomon," and 5 cows. To son Edward, book called Josephus, gold ring, silver spoon, negro called "Will" (letting him have one day a month to himself), mulatto boy called "Jeffrey" and 5 cows. To 3 grandchildren, Barzilla Richmond, Mary Gray and Anstis Gray, 1 cow each. To daughter Rebecca, a good suit of apparel and house room till better provided for. To kinsman Nathaniel Gibbs, son of Warren Gibbs, 3 sheep and 3 lambs. To 2 sons equally, land in Plymouth, Tiverton, &c., and rest of movables.

Inventory, dwelling house and 50 acres £800, dwelling house and 50 acres where Edward lives £800. Other lots of land £1000, £540, £500, £250, &c., 6 working cattle, 19 cows, 6 two year cattle, 14 yearlings, 4 fat oxen, 14 calves, 3 mares, 3 colts, 4 two year horses, 2 yearling mares, 6 score sheep,

GRAY. 2d column. V. John. Plymouth. Mass., m. Joanna Morton. Children: 1. Edward, 1687. 2. Mary. 1688. 3. Ann, 1691. 4. Desire, 1693. 5. Joanna, 1696. 6. Samuel, 1702. 7. Mercy, 1704. VII. Susannah, m. John Cole, of Hugh & Mary (Foxwell) Cole. Children: 1. John. 2. Edward. 3. Thomas. 4. Joseph, 1706. 5. Benjamin, 1708. 6. Elizabeth, 1710. 7. Samuel. 8. Mary. 9. Susanna. VIII. Thomas, m. (2) Phebe Peckham, of John Peckham. XI. Rebecca, m. Ephraim Cole, of James Cole. Children: 1. Ephraim, 1691. 2. Samuel,

1694. 3. Rebecca, 1696. 4. Mary, 1698. 5. Dorothy, 1701. 6. James, 1705. 7. Samuel, 1709.

all the herbage and grass which shall grow on the country's lands at Pocassett and places adjoining for one year, they paying £10 for the privilege.

1678, Jun. 6. He was licensed to sell some small quantities of liquor as he may have occasion, to such as are or may be employed by him in fishing, and such like occasion, for their use and refreshing.

1680, Mar. 5. He and seven others bought Pocasset (Tiverton) lands for £1,100 of Gov. Josiah Winslow. His share was 9–30 of the purchase.

1681, Jul. 7. Administration to widow Dorothy.

1683, Mar. 8. The court allowed his widow £60 out of his estate towards bringing up his three youngest children.

1684, Jul. 1. She was granted £30 for her charges and trouble as administratrix. Guardians were chosen by her children this year as follows: Edward and Hannah chose Captain Nathaniel Thomas. Thomas, Rebecca, Lydia and Samuel, chose Captain Nathaniel Thomas and their mother Dorothy Gray. Anna chose John Walley.

1684, Oct. 28. Mrs. Dorothy Gray consented that her husband's lands should be divided amongst his children before her dower was set off. She brought in her account showing inventory of £1,230, 12*s.* 11*d.*, balanced by debts paid and £657, 15*s.* 10*d.*, divided to widow and children by order of court. Among items of inventory were money, plate, goods and chattels £737, 2*s.* 6*d.*, debts certain, uncertain, and desperate £346, 18*s.* 3*d.* Ketch at sea sold for £40, &c

Among the payments was allowance to widow "for long and great trouble in her said office by making up accounts with many persons both debtor and creditors, at home and at Boston, receiving from and paying of debts to many several persons, and charge to others I employed to write and keep accounts clear: and while I was busied every day about the concerns of the estate in general I was fain to hire a nurse for my younger child, which cost me for about four or five months time three shillings per week and her diet which came to five or six pound; and it is about three years time that I have been thus concerned about the estate in general, with neglect to my own particular concerns, and judge I may well deserve at least fifty pound, whereof the court allows thirty pounds."

1686, Jul. 10. Dorothy Clarke complains against her husband Nathaniel in order to a divorce, and there being such an uncomfortable difference between said Clarke and his wife, fearing lest they should ruin each other in their estate, have mutually agreed to a settlement until the law otherwise determines. The new house is in Nathaniel Clarke's possession as his and his wife's estate, she having liberty to live in part of said house to quantity of half if she pleases. Clarke to have all estate he brought with him, and she to have all estate she brought with her except what each had disposed of. Clarke to have one hogshead of rum in his hands for the finishing of the new house and three barrels of cider for his own drinking or at his dispose. She to deliver him bond given her before marriage and he not to be liable for her debts, nor for administration by her on estate of her late husband Edward Gray. Dorothy not to be charged with Clarke's contracts, &c.

4 score lambs, swine, negro £30, negro woman £30, mulatto boy £50, mulatto boy £45, 2 mulatto girls £50 each, 1 silver cup, 6 silver spoons, malt mill, 2 cheese presses, 4 tables, 15 leather chairs, 15 other chairs, case with 9 bottles, 13 pewter platters, 33 pewter plates, 11 porringers, 7 candlesticks, 1 warming pan, 1 gun, &c.

1723, Jul. 8. Will—proved 1723, Aug. 7, of his son Thomas, mentions honored mother-in-law (*i. e.* stepmother), Phebe Gray, brother Edward, brother-in-law Wm. Richmond and sister Anne, his wife, sister Rebecca, wife of John Pabodie, &c.

1746, May 16 Will—proved 1746, Dec. 15, widow Phebe, aged eighty, late of Little Compton now of Middletown, R. I. Ex. cousin John Taylor, of Middletown. To cousin John Taylor all estate.

IX. SAMUEL, b. ; d. 1712, Mar. 23. Little Compton, R. I.
m. 1699, Jul. 13.
DEBORAH CHURCH, b. ; d. of Joseph & Mary (Tucker) Church.

(She m. (2) Daniel Throope.)

1. Samuel, 1700, Apr. 16.
2. John, 1701, Apr. 14.
3. Dorothy, 1704, Jan. 14.
4. Joseph, 1706, Jan. 20.
5. Lydia, 1707, Oct. 16.
6. Simeon, 1709, Dec. 15.
7. Ignatius, 1711, Sep. 18.

1712, Mar. 20. Will—proved 1712, Apr. 7. Exs. wife Deborah, and brother Thomas Gray. Overseers, friend William Pabodie, Captain John Palmer and brother John Church. To wife Deborah, improvement of whole estate for her and children's maintenance while widow. If she marry to have £100. At marriage or decease of wife, all estate to be divided as follows: To eldest son Samuel, £300 To sons Simeon and Ignatius, £100 each. To daughters Dorothy and Lydia, £100 each. If the estate proves worth more than £800, the residue to go to two youngest sons Simeon and Ignatius.

Inventory, £1,138, 9*s.* 7*d.*, viz: farm and buildings, orchard, &c. £850, outlands £26, feather beds, pewter, 1 pair of worsted combs, 3 pair old cards, 1 woolen wheel, 2 common wheels, 1 churn, 1 cradle, 1 cheese press, 1 warming pan, silver money £12, 4*s.* 7*d.*, 3 mares, 14 cows, 1 heifer, 5 two year old, 3 yearlings, 5 calves, 1 pair oxen, &c.

1713, Jun. 3. Deborah Throope, wife of Daniel Throope, of Bristol, late wife of Samuel Gray, of Little Compton, gave receipt to Thomas Gray.

X. HANNAH, b. ; d.

XI. REBECCA, b. ; d.

XII. LYDIA, b. ; d.
m. 1696, Aug. 7.
CALEB LORING, b. 1674, Jun. 9. ; d. of Thomas & Hannah (Jacob) Loring.

1. Caleb, 1697, Jun. 7.
2. Hannah, 1698, Aug. 7.
3. Ignatius, 1699, Dec. 27
4. Polycarpus, 1702.
5. Caleb, 1704, Oct. 2.
6. Lydia, 1706.
7. Jacob, 1711, May 15.
8. Joseph, 1713, Jul. 25.
9. John, 1715, Nov. 15.
10. Thomas, 1718, Apr. 18.
11. Lydia, 1721, Aug. 23.

XIII. ANNA, b. ; d.

GREENE (JOHN, OF KINGS TOWN).

JOHN, b. ; d. 1695 ±
m.
JOAN, b. ; d. 1682 +

Kings Town, R. I.

1639 ± He came early to Narragansett, living in the family of Richard Smith, as his testimony shows.

1663. He, with others of Wickford, declared themselves in favor of being under jurisdiction of Connecticut, rather than of Rhode Island.

1664, May 11. The Rhode Island authorities sent to his house and took him thence to Newport, where being called soon after before the court to answer for his adhering to government of Connecticut, he answered so as to give offence, but upon asking pardon for that and for adhering to Connecticut, the court passed his offence and he was promised the protection of Rhode Island, as a freeman of that colony.

1671, May 20. He gave oath of allegiance to colony of Rhode Island.

1672, Jan. 1. He and five others bought of Awashuwett, Chief Sachem of Quoheset, in Narragansett, certain land there.

1676, Aug. At a court martial at Newport, Awasawin, of Narragansett, denieth that he laid hands on John Greene, of Narragansett, occasioned about the death of a dumb boy.

I. JOHN, b. 1651, Jun. 6. ; d. 1729, Oct. 6. Kings Town, East Greenwich, Warwick, R. I.
m.
ABIGAIL, b. ; d. 1729 + of

1. James, 1685, Aug. 18.
2. John, 1688, Apr. 9.
3. Jane, 1691, Jan. 30.
4. Uzal, 1694, Jan. 23.
5. Ebenezer,
6. Robert,
7. William,
8. Enfield,
9. Mary,
10. Hannah,

1685. East Greenwich. The births of his three first children were recorded there.

1729, Oct. 2. Will—proved 1729, Oct. 21. Ex. son Robert. He calls himself in seventy-ninth year. To eldest son James, £10. To sons John and Uzal, 5*s.* each, they having had. To son Uzal, 60 acres, where his house stands. To daughter Jane Lee, 40*s.* To daughter Mary Johnson, £6. To daughter Hannah Andrew, £5. To son Ebenezer, all right in Coweset land, east of river where I dwell and a third of saw-mill and a horse of £5 value. To son Robert, half of lands in Coweset, west of river where I dwell and all my housing where I dwell, and other part of saw mill and 300 acres. To son William, the other half of land west of river, but if he prove *non compos mentis*, then Robert to have the land. To daughter Enfield Cook's children, Samuel and Mary, 3*s.* To wife Abigail, £5 for life, a cow, horse, half of household goods, best room in the house, and wood at the door, and keep of horse and cow.

Inventory, £441, 9*s.* 5*d.*, viz: 5 bonds £63, 16*s.* 11*d.*, wearing apparel £9, cash £2, 3s. 7d., beds, pewter, negro man Sambo £20, 10 gallons rum £3, 5*s.*, 10 turkeys, 25 geese and fowls, 2 spinning wheels, gun, anvil, carpenter's tools, 4 oxen, 5 cows, 6 hogs, mare, &c.

II. JAMES, b. 1655. ; d. 1728. North Kingstown, R. I.
m. (1)
ELIZABETH, b. ; d. of
m. (2)
ANN, b. ; d. of

1. John,
2. James,

1679, Jul. 29. He signed the petition to the King.

1687, Sep. 6. Taxed 4*s.* 3*d.*

1699. He sold George Wightman, land bounded south by land of his brother, Edward Greene, the land deeded having been received from grantor's brother Benjamin, who had received it from his brother, John Greene.

1678–79. Conservator of the Peace.

1679, Jul. 21. He made oath "that forty years and more ago, Mr. Richard Smith, that I then lived with, did first begin and make a settlement in the Narragansett, and that by the consent, and with the approbation of the Indian princes and people, and did improve land, mow meadows, several years before Warwick was settled by any Englishmen, and I being present, did see and hear all the Narragansett Princes, being assembled together, give by livery and seizing, some hundreds of acres of land about a mile in length and so down to the sea; this being about thirty years ago, many hundreds of Indians being then present, consenting thereunto."

1679, Jul. 29. He and forty-one others of Narragansett, signed a petition to the King, praying that he "would put an end to these differences about the government thereof, which hath been so fatal to the prosperity of the place; animosities still arising in people's minds, as they stand affected to this or that government."

1682, Mar. 24. He deeded son Daniel, 120 acres bordering on Allen's Harbor, and to son James, 60 acres adjoining, each of said sons to pay 30*s.* annually, as long as their father or mother should live. The land was bounded partly by land of son John.

1692, May 13. He signed as witness to a deed.

He left a will, as shown by allusion in deed of his son Edward.

1700, May 4. He was summoned with others by Assembly, to answer in court, the charge of being guilty of a riot.

1700 ± He and wife Elizabeth, sold land to John Cory.

1721, Mar. 25. In a deposition, he calls himself aged about sixty-six years.

1728, Sep. 10. Will—proved. Exx. wife Ann. To wife, use of all movables, and profits of dwelling house and land adjoining, for life. Son James had already had land given him. To son John, at wife's decease, land and dwelling house.

III. DANIEL, b. ; d. 1730. North Kingstown, R. I.
m. 1689, Jul. 16,
REBECCA BARROW, b. ; d. 1724 + of Barrow.

1. Peleg, 1690, Aug 9.
2. Daniel, 1692, Oct. 8.
3. Jonathan, 1694, Dec 1.
4. Rebecca, 1696, Apr. 12.
5. Rachel, 1698, May 6.
6. Sarah, 1700, Apr. 5.
7 Jonathan, 1705, Jun. 9

1676, Aug. He testified against Awasawin, at a court martial at Newport.

1679, Jul. 29. He signed the petition to the King.

1698. Juryman.

1700, May 4. He was summoned by the Assembly, on charge of being engaged in a riot.

1724. Will—proved 1730, Jun. 9. Ex. son Daniel. He makes provision for wife Rebecca and son Peleg. To son Daniel, my farm and dwelling house. To son Jonathan, £50, bed, &c. To daughter Rebecca, 5*s.* To daughter Rachel, £5. To son Daniel, rest of estate.

Inventory, £107, 11*s.*, viz: cows, sheep, lambs, pigs, spinning wheel, &c.

IV. EDWARD, b. ; d. Kings Town, R. I.
m.
MARY TIBBITTS, b. ; d. of Henry & Sarah (Stanton) Tibbitts.

1. Robert,

1687, Sep. 6. Taxed 3*s.* 10*d.*

1695, Mar. 8. He sold George Vaughan, 10 acres in East Greenwich, for £8, which land fell to me by will of my honored father, lately deceased.

1697, Sep. 4. He sold George Vaughan, 90 acres in East Greenwich, given by father.

1700, May 4. He was summoned with others by Assembly, to answer in court, the charge of being guilty of a riot.

1711, Apr. 6. He sold to Anthony Low, of Warwick, certain land in East Greenwich.

V. BENJAMIN, b. ; d. 1719. Kings Town, East Greenwich, R. I.
m.
HUMILITY COGGESHALL, b. 1671, Jan. ; d. 1719 + of Joshua & Joan (West) Coggeshall.

1. John,
2. Benjamin,
3. Henry,
4. Caleb,
5. Joshua,
6. Mary,
7. Ann,
8. Phebe,
9. Catharine,
10. Sarah,
11. Dinah,
12. Deborah,

It is assumed that his wife Humility, could have been none other than Humility Coggeshall (and the reasons for the supposition are obvious).

1698–1700–1–3. Deputy.

1701. Surveyor of Highways.

1701–3–4. Town Council.

1702. Ratemaker.

1703, Jul. 12. He and others were appointed to lay out highways.

1705, Mar. 26. He sold land, and soon thereafter moved to East Greenwich.

1719, Jan. 7. Will—proved 1719, Mar. 5. Exs. wife Humility and Captain Benjamin Nichols, of Kings Town, and if latter die, then Joshua Coggeshall to succeed him. To wife, all household goods and movables. To son John, farm he lives on. To son Benjamin, half my homestead on north side. To son Henry, other half of homestead. To son Caleb, half my second division farm. To son Joshua, the other half. To five sons, undivided lands and my part of saw-mill, &c., and two eldest sons to be helpful to the other sons in building. If two youngest sons die before coming of age, their part to go to seven daughters. To daughter Mary Spencer, wife of Thomas, 20*s.* To daughter Ann Tennant, wife of Daniel, 20*s.* To daughter Phebe Wells, wife of Thomas, 20*s.* To daughters Katharine, Sarah, Dinah and Deborah Greene, a feather bed each and a good cow (the last three daughters when eighteen or married). To wife, use of homestead if she need it while widow. To Captain Benjamin Nichols, 20*s.*, and if he die same amount to Joshua Coggeshall.

Inventory, £166, 10*s.* 1*d.*, viz: 3 cheese-fats, 2,000 board nails, 4,000 shingle nails, table linen, old books, 3 mares, yoke of oxen, 3 cows, 2 yearlings, 12 swine, 10 geese, 3 spinning wheels, &c.

GREENE (JOHN, OF NEWPORT).

JOHN, b. ; d. 1705 +
m.
MARY JEFFERAY, b. 1642, Mar. 20. ; d. 1705 +
of William & Mary (Gould) Jefferay.

Newport, R. I.

1647, Feb. 20. He bought land of David and Edward Greenman.

1655. Freeman.

1655–56–57–58–60. Commissioner.

1658, May 22. He and Benedict Arnold, bought of Cachanaquant, Chief Sachem of Indians in Narragansett Bay, Goat Island, Coaster's Harbor Island and Dyer's Island, paying therefor £6, 10*s.*

1661, Jan. 24. He sold half a share of land in Conanicut and Dutch Island, to John Sanford.

1671, Jun. 7. Juryman.

1673–78–79. Deputy.

1676. Lieutenant.

1676, Aug. 24. He was a member of the Court Martial held at Newport, for the trial of certain Indians, charged with being engaged in King Philip's designs.

1685, Mar. 14. He (called Lieutenant John Greene, of Newport), having requested the town of East Greenwich, for a town meeting to be called, was admitted a freeman, and having been one of the purchasers there, he was granted 100 acres.

He never settled at East Greenwich probably, but doubtless disposed of his land there, as did so many other Newport owners.

1705, Mar. 17. He and wife Mary, for £32, 8*s.*, sold William Sanford 8 acres.

I. JOHN, b. ; d. 1753. Newport, Middletown, R. I.
m. (1)
SARAH, b. ; d. of
m. (2)
MARY, b. ; d. of

1. John, 1690 ±
2. William,

1722, Feb. 20. He and wife Sarah, sold to Giles Slocum, 30½ acres and 35 rods in Portsmouth, for £460, 16*s.*

1753, Oct. 3. Administration to son John, the widow Mary refusing. - See American Genealogist, v. 21, p. 2

Inventory, £2,166.

GREENE (JOHN, OF NEWPORT). 2d column. I. John m. (2) Sarah Parrott, of John, of Falmouth (now Portland, Maine), 1738. He and wife Sarah deeded her half share in a lot at Falmouth to Phineas Jones, in which it is recited that she was daughter of John Parrott. His son John m. Mary Weeden, of Jeremiah and Mary (Clarke) Weeden. His son William m. Mary Barker, of James and Mary (Cook) Barker.

GREENE (JOHN, OF NEWPORT). 2d column. 1. John. Erase all but item 1722, Feb 20. He d. 1740, at Newport. His wife Sarah d. 1722+. Her full name is said to have been Sarah Peckham. Children, 1. John. 2. Sarah, 1695. 3. Henry. 4. William, 1707. 5. Mary, 1715, Nov. 9. 1716, Sep. 22, he bought 60 acres at Shrewsbury, N. J., of John Colver. 1722, Jun. 15, will-proved, 1740, Aug. 4. Exs., wife Sarah and son John. To son John, the farming utensils &c. on homestead. To son Henry, farm in Shrewsbury, East Jersey. To son William, 5 acres in Portsmouth at age. He mentions also cousins, William Goodberry, Mary Allen, and Ellen Fareort of East Jersey. He made legacies of certain silver marked $_{I}{}^{G}{}_{M}$. Part of his will is illegible. He had a daughter Sarah who married Peleg Rogers. His children William and Mary were buried in Newport cemetery. His son John was called in 1733, "John Greene, Jr., of Greene Inn."

GREENE (JOHN, OF WARWICK) 1st column. Change 1642, Nov., to 1642, Oct. 1.
2d column. I. John. In his will, change Green Hole to Greene Hold. VII. Mary. Her husband d. 1698, Jun. 18.

JOHN,[4] (Rich.[3] Rich.[2] Rob.[1]) b. 1597. d. 1658.
m. (1) 1619, Nov. 4.
JOAN TATTERSALL, b. d.
of Tattersall.
m. (2)
ALICE DANIELS, (widow.) b. d. 1643.
m. (3)
PHILLIP, b. 1601. d. 1688, Mar. 10.

Salisbury, Wilts Co., Eng., Warwick, R. I.

He was probably born at Bowridge Hall, Gillingham, Dorset county, where his father and grandfather resided.

He was a surgeon in Salisbury, and there made his first marriage, at St. Thomas' Church.

1620, Aug. 15. He had his son John baptized, and his other children later, as follows: Peter (1622, Mar. 10), Richard (1623, Mar. 25), James (1626, Jun. 21), Thomas (1628, Jun. 4), Jone (1630, Oct. 3), Mary (1633, May 19).

1635, Apr. 6. He sailed from Southampton, England, in ship James.

1635, Jun. 3. Boston. He arrived at this date with his family; and was afterwards of Salem, for a short period.

1637, Aug. 1. Providence. He (called of New Providence), having spoken against the magistrates contemptuously, stands bound in one hundred marks to appear at the next Quarter Court, by order of the Massachusetts authorities.

1637, Sep. 29. He was fined £20, and to be committed until fine is paid, and enjoined not to come into this jurisdiction (Massachusetts), upon pain of fine or imprisonment at the pleasure of the court, for speaking contemptuously of magistrates.

1638, Mar. 12. A letter from him being received by the court at Massachusetts, wherein the court is charged with usurping the power of Christ over the churches and men's consciences, &c.— he was ordered not to come into that jurisdiction under pain of imprisonment and further censure.

1638, Oct. 8. He was one of the twelve persons to whom Roger Williams deeded land bought of Canonicus and Miantonomi.

1639. He was one of the twelve original members of First Baptist Church.

1642, Nov. He bought land called Occupassuatuxet, of Miantonomi. This land remained in occupation of his heirs until 1782, when it was sold to John Brown, of Providence, and is now occupied by his heirs. ("Spring Green Farm.")

1643, Jan. 12. Warwick. He and ten others bought of Miantonomi, for 144 fathoms of wampum, tract of land called Shawomet (Warwick).

1643, Sep. 12. He, with others of Warwick, was notified to appear at Boston, to hear complaint of Pomham and Socconocco, as to "some unjust and injurious dealing toward them by yourselves." The Warwick men refused to obey the summons, declaring that they were legal subjects of the King of England, and beyond the limits of Massachusetts authority. Soldiers were soon sent, who besieged the settlers in a fortified house. In a parley it was now said "that they held blasphemous errors which they must repent of" or go to Boston for trial, and they were soon carried there, except John Greene, who fortunately escaped. His companions were imprisoned till the next March, and then he and they were banished.

1644. He and Samuel Gorton and Randall Holden, went to England to obtain redress for their wrongs, being obliged to take ship at New York.

1646, Sep. 13. He and Holden returned, successful in their mission, landing in Boston at this date.

1654-55-56-57. Commissioner.

1655. Freeman.

1658, Dec. 28. Will—proved 1659, Jan. 7. Exx. wife Phillip (except in matters in difference between testator and William Arnold, which son John was to attend to). To wife, that part of building now erected, containing large hall and chimney, chamber, garret and little dairy room which butts against the old house, &c., all to her for life, as also half the orchard and swamp, four kine at her choice and two heifers. To son John, neck of land called Ottupashatuxet and meadows belonging thereto, and also a right of land in purchase of Providence. To son Peter, that other house adjoining to aforesaid that was given wife, and at wife's decease, Peter to have hers also, he paying my son John £10, for use of his children. To son Peter, also yoke of steers and half the oxen, he providing wife of testator with thirty loads of wood per year, bringing it in seasonable for her use. To son James, 6 acres and my great lot, with rights at Warwick Neck. To son Thomas, meadow, 6

I. JOHN, b. 1620. d. 1708, Nov. 27. Warwick, R. I.
m.
ANN ALMY, b. 1627. d. 1709, May 17. of William & Audry ( ) Almy.

1651, Feb. 3. He and three others agreed with town to build a mill at our own cost, and to grind the town corn at two quarts in a bushel, the town granting for their encouragement, a lot of land that was formerly Mr. Gorton's.

1652-53-54-55-56-57-58-59-60-61-62-63. Commissioner.

1652-53-54. General Recorder.

1655. Freeman.

1655. General Solicitor.

1657-58-59-60. Attorney General.

1658. Warden

1660, Apr. 30. He was appointed by town "to write to the President and Assistants about the Indians pressing in upon our lands and spoiling our timber, desiring their assistance to suppress their violence."

1660-61-62-63-64-65-66-67-68-69-70-71-72-73-77-78-80-81-82-83-84-85-86-89-90. Assistant.

1664-74-75-77-80. Deputy.

1670, Jun. 29. He and John Clarke were chosen agents to go to England, for vindication of charter before his Majesty, and redeem the same from the injurious violations thereof, by colony of Connecticut.

1671, Jan. 30. He was allowed £10, for his charge and pains in going to the treaty at New London, &c.

1676, Apr. 4. It was voted "that in these troublesome times and straits in this colony, this Assembly, desiring to have the advice and concurrence of the most judicious inhabitants, if it may be had for the good of the whole, do desire at their next sitting, the company and counsel of Mr. Benedict Arnold" and fifteen others, among whom was Captain John Greene.

1679, Jan. 16. His son William made his will (proved 1679, Mar. 12). He left all his estate to wife (Mary), for life, and at her death part to his daughter Mary. He mentions his brothers, Samuel and Peter also.

1679, Feb. 3. He and Randall Holden being in England, were called upon to give information as to Mount Hope; they valued it at £4,000, consisting of 4,000 acres.

1679, Aug. 1. The Assembly ordered £60 paid him and Randall Holden, disbursed by them in England, &c.

1680, May 5. He and two others were empowered by Assembly, to purchase a bell "for the public use of this colony and for giving notice or signifying the several times or sittings of the Assemblys and Courts of Trials and General Councils." The bell was purchased for £3, 10*s*., of Freelove Arnold, daughter of Governor Benedict Arnold.

1683, Sep. 17. He and Randall Holden sent a letter to King Charles II, concerning Governor Cranfield, of New Hampshire, and Commissioners who had lately held court in Kings Town, but who would show no commission from the King.

1683-84-85-86-90-91-96. Major for the Main.

1686, Dec. 22. He was notified by Gov. Andros, of his appointment as a member of his council.

1690, Jan. 30. He, with others, sent a letter of congratulation to William and Mary on their accession to the crown, and informing them that since the deposing of Andros, the former government under the charter had been re-assumed, mentioning also the seizure of Andros in Rhode Island, on his flight from Massachusetts.

1691, Jun. 27. He was voted 10*s*. by the Assembly for his encouragement, for drawing up an address to their Majesties; for drawing up a letter to the Governor of New York, and transcribing it, for writing six commissions, and setting the seals to them for the military officers on the main land.

1690-91-92-93-94-95-96-97-98-99-1700. Deputy Governor.

1706, Dec. 20. Will—proved 1708, Dec. 20. Exs. sons Peter, Job, Richard and Samuel. He calls himself inhabitant of Greene Hole, alias Occupasituxet, in eighty-seventh year, and forasmuch as his wife is in eightieth year of her age and exercised with a lameness in her left side wholly incurable, which, notwithstanding the good help of our children, is like to prove chargeable, "therefore, in case it should please God she should survive me, I ought to have the better care to leave her the better supplied." To her, that part of son Richard's house we now by agreement dwell in during our lives, and use of household goods and provisions, three cows, kept for her by Richard, as also fuel provided by him, and £5 paid her by son Samuel yearly, for life. To son Samuel, the north side of Greene Hole to a certain line, with privilege of fowling, fishing, &c. To son Richard, rest of the Neck, with island near adjoining and housing, barn, orchard, &c., he paying £20 per year to my lame, beloved wife, till her death. To son Peter, all right in undivided lands at Coweset, except 100 acres. To son Job, all right in land belonging to seven purchasers. To daughter Deborah Torrey, £16. To daughter Phillip Dickenson's children, £16, to be improved till they are of age. To daughter Ann Greene, £16. To daughter Catharine Holden, £16. To daughter Audry Spencer, £16. To granddaughter Mary Dyer, £16. To four sons, land undisposed of, and all stock of cow kind and horse kind. He earnestly charges his children to care for his wife, "to manifest their love to me and her, in lending their help unto her, and so I take leave, commending my wife and children to the fear of God, in whose fear I rest, in assured hope of salvation."

Inventory, £167, 9*s*., viz: 15 cows, 2 oxen, 3 steers, 5 horsekind, flagon, tankard, porringer, beaker, candle stick, sconce, chafing dish, brass scales, stillyards, 2 cases bottles, razor, hone, 3 beds, cabinet, desk, 2 guns, pair of pistols, belt, rapier, cane, books £6, silver plate, 2 cups and spoons £8, 5*s*., money £14, table, chairs, &c. Receipts for legacies were given by William and Deborah Torrey, John and Audry Spencer, Edward and Mary Dyer, Charles and Catharine Holden and Ann Greene.

He and his wife were buried on his homestead farm.

1. Deborah,	1649, Aug. 10.
2. John,	1651, Nov. 6.
3. William,	1653, Mar. 1.
4. Peter,	1655, Feb. 7.
5. Job,	1656, Aug. 24.
6. Philip,	1658, Oct. 7.
7. Richard,	1660, Feb. 8.
8. Anne,	1663, Mar. 19.
9. Catharine,	1665, Aug. 15.
10. Audry,	1667, Dec. 27.
11. Samuel,	1671, Jan. 30.

II. PETER, b. 1622. d. 1659. Providence, Warwick, R. I.
m.
MARY GORTON, b. d. 1688 + of Samuel & Elizabeth ( ) Gorton.

No issue.

(She m. (2) 1663, Apr. 17, John Sanford.)

1650. Taxed 1*s*. 8*d*.

1655. Warwick. Freeman.

1658. Commissioner.

1659, May 11. Will—proved 1660, Mar. 1. Exx. wife Mary. Overseers, father Gorton, and brothers John and James Greene. To wife, house and land (given me by late father) for her life, on condition that neither land nor housing be sold from the heir to whom it is to fall at her death. To brother John Greene's son Peter, the housing and land above, and all other land at decease of wife. To brother James Greene, orchard and lot, best jacket and piece of cloth of same to make a pair of breeches. To brother John, best coat, doublet and breeches which was my wedding suit, with the money which my cousin Tripp oweth to me. To brother Thomas, £10 of the money he has with him (£40, 3*s*)., at three blacks a penny, whereof £3, 17*s*. is my mother's, and also my gray cloak and gray serge suit. To Anne Hady, 20*s*. To sister Mary Sweet, 40*s*., which I would have my brother, James Greene, employ for their use. The two draught oxen I have with my brother, John Greene, to make good mine engagement to my mother during her life, and to draw home ten loads of wood per year for my wife, for four years time, if she remain so long unmarried. To wife, whatever is unmentioned. If an heir, male, should be born, then he to have estate in place of cousin (*i. e.* nephew), Peter, and the heir to take possession at death of my mother or wife. If a female heir be born, she to have £60.

III. RICHARD, b. 1623. d. young.

acre lot, &c. To four sons, rights as purchaser of Warwick. To four sons and daughter Mary Sweet, what money can be gotten by law or otherwise from William Arnold, in the case depending betwixt me and him, also my son John hath recovered half of it for his use, according to my former promise. To aforesaid daughter, two kine and a yearling heifer. To grandchild Ann Hade, a heifer and yearling calf to be disposed of by her uncle, James Greene, for her profit, as she shall see best. To son Peter, £20 in peage white and £6 in peage black. To friend Samuel Gorton, 40*s*. To wife Phillip, all undisposed of estate, except a bed and bedstead.

1668, Aug. 27. His widow Phillip, deeded to son-in-law (*i. e.* stepson), John Greene—considering her desolate condition and to free herself of many troubles attending it—my dwelling house, lot and all the rest of estate, household goods, &c., except a cow and some small things already given my granddaughter, Phillip Greene, reserving also wearing apparel. He engaged to provide her with meat, drink, lodging, &c., and £6 per annum, and to transport said pay to Newport at his own cost by Sep. 29th, annually.

IV. JAMES, m. (1) DELIVERANCE POTTER, m. (2) 1665, Aug. 3, ELIZABETH ANTHONY,
b. 1626. d. 1698, Apr. 27. — Warwick, R. I.
b. 1637. d. 1664 ± — of Robert & Isabel ( ) Potter.
b. d. 1698 + — of John & Susanna ( ) Anthony.

1655. Freeman.
1660-61-62-63. Commissioner.
1664-65-66-67-68-69-70-72-73-74-75-85-86-90. Deputy.
1670-71. Assistant.
1683, Aug. 22. He, having been appointed with William Allen, to carry a message from the Rhode Island Assembly to Gov. Cranfield, &c., at Richard Smith's house in Narragansett—reported that upon delivery of the same, " I, the said James Greene, told the said Governor Cranfield, that the letter was sent by the Governor and Assembly of this colony." Governor Cranfield said in answer, "that he knew of no Governor in the King's Province."
1697, Aug. 25. He deeded certain land to eldest son James.
1698, Mar. 22. Will—proved 1698, May 2. Ex. son Jabez. Overseers, brother Major Greene, brother-in-law Benjamin Barton and cousin Thomas Greene. To wife Elizabeth, £80, and privilege to live in west part of house while widow, and a feather bed, horse, side saddle, &c. To son James, half of a farm and great bible, long fowling piece, and £10 divided to his three children. To son Peter, half of a certain piece of land, &c. To son Jabez, house, housing, orchard and land, north of highway. To son David, meadow, upland, weaver's loom, three thousand boards, &c. To son John, 118 acres, other land, bed, wearing clothes and £20, at age. To daughter Sarah Reynolds, £5, and £10 to her children. To daughter Elizabeth Reynolds, £5, and £7 to her children. To daughter Susanna Greene, £35, at eighteen or marriage. To son Jabez, rest of personal and also lands in Potawomut. To each son and daughter and grandchild, a bible.

1. James, 1658, Jun. 1.
2. Mary, 1660, Sep. 28.
3. Elisha, 1663, Mar. 17.
4. Sarah, 1664, Mar. 27.
(2d wife.)
5. Peter, 1666, Aug. 25.
6. Elizabeth, 1668, Oct. 17.
7. John, 1671, Feb. 1.
8. Jabez, 1673, May 17.
9. David, 1677, Jun. 24.
10. Thomas, 1682, Nov. 11.
11. John, 1685, Sep. 30.
12. Susanna, 1688, May 24.

V. THOMAS, m. 1659, Jun. 30, ELIZABETH BARTON,
b. 1628. d. 1717, Jun. 5. — Warwick, R. I.
b. d. 1693, Aug. 20. — of Rufus & Margaret ( ) Barton.

1655. Freeman.
1662. Commissioner.
1667-69-70-71-72-74-78-81-83-84. Deputy.
1678-79-80-84-85. Assistant.
1695, Jul. 2. He was appointed by Assembly, on committee to propose a method of making a rate.
1717, Jan. 25. Will—proved 1717, Jun. 27. Ex. son Richard. To son Benjamin, 100 acres in Coweset. To daughter Welthian Fry, 200 acres in Coweset. To grandson John Greene and granddaughters Elizabeth Gorton, Ann Tillinghast, Phebe Greene and Deborah Greene, 100 acres each, in Coweset. To each grandchild living at decease, a silver spoon of 12*s*. price. To son Richard, rest of lands.
Inventory, £94, 2*s*. 8*d*., viz: wearing apparel, plate, book debts, feather bed, pewter, brass, warming pan, 2 tables, 2 benches, 2 stools, looking-glass, 2 books, &c.

1. Elizabeth, 1660, Jul. 12.
2. Thomas, 1662, Aug. 14.
3. Benjamin, 1666, Jan. 10.
4. Richard, 1667, Mar. 5.
5. Welthian, 1670, Jan. 23.
6. Rufus, 1673, Jan. 6.
7. Nathaniel, 1679, Apr. 10.

VI. JOAN, m. ——— HADE,
b. 1630. d.
b. d. — of Hade.

1. Ann,

VII. MARY, m. JAMES SWEET,
b. 1633. d.
b. 1622. d. 1695 + — of John & Mary ( ) Sweet.

(**2**d and **3**d WIVES, no issue.)

1. Philip, 1655, Jul. 15.
2. James, 1657, May 28.
3. Mary, 1660, Feb. 2.
4. Benoni, 1663, Mar. 28.
5. Valentine, 1665, Feb. 14.
6. Samuel, 1667, Nov. 1.
7. Jeremiah, 1669, Jan. 6.
8. Renewed, 1671, Jul. 16.
9. Sylvester, 1674, Mar. 1.

GRIFFIN.

ROBERT,
b. d.

Newport, R. I.
1655. Freeman.
1655, May 25. He was to be paid the money due him from the colony, out of the first fines taken or rate made, and was to be allowed twelve in the one hundred for his forbearance. On the same date he was one of those appointed by the Court of Commissioners to keep a house of entertainment. A convenient sign was to be set out at the most perspicuous place of said house to give notice to strangers.
1656. Commissioner.
1656, May 23. A debt to him of £6, from the colony was paid.
1659, Aug. 23. He having complained concerning the remainder of £7. 10*s*. that an Indian named Quissuckquoanch owed him, being £5, 10*s*., the court warned said Indian that if he do it not the court will take a speedy course to force him to do right, which will prove troublesome and chargable.
Perhaps Benjamin Griffin, who was one of those who had 5,000 acres granted (1677, Oct. 31), to be called East Greenwich, was a son of Robert. This Benjamin was resident at Newport in 1677.

GUTTREDGE.

ROBERT, m. (1) MARGARET, m. (2) ANNA WILLIAMS, [John. (w. of
b. d. 1692, Dec. 13.
b. 1623. d. 1687, Apr. 5.
b 1650. d. 1723.
of John & Sarah (Palsgrave) Alcock.
New Shoreham, R. I.
1664. Freeman.
1670, Oct. 26. He and four others were appointed to make a rate for Block Island.

(**2**d WIFE.)

I. CATHARINE, m. 1706, Sep. 9. JOHN SANDS,
b. d.
b. 1684. d. 1763, Aug. 15. — of John & Sybil (Ray) Sands.

1. John, 1708, Jan. 1.
2. Robert, 1710, Dec. 26.
3. Edward, 1712, Jan. 17.
4. George,
5. Nathaniel,
6. Joshua,
7. Simon,
8. Gideon,
9. Benjamin,
10. Anna,
11. Sarah,
12. Mary,

See: American Genealogist, v. 19, p. 223.

GUTTREDGE. 1st column. He m. (2) 1689, June 5. 2d column. I. Catherine, b. 1690, June 24; d. 1769, Feb. 10. Children, 4, Mary, 1715. 5, George, 1717. 6, Anna, 1719, Mar. 16. 7, Nathaniel, 1721, Nov. 30. 8, Joshua, 1725, Mar. 22. 9, Simon, 1727, July 12. 10, Gideon, 1729, Oct. 22. 11, Sarah, 1732. 12, Benjamin, 1735, Nov.

1676. Assistant Warden.

1676. Town Clerk.

1687, Apr. 18. He was named executor in trust of will of John Williams of Newport, with the testator's wife Anna (until the testator's son Nathaniel arrived at age). The will was proved in the same year (1687, Oct. 25), and the widow subsequently married Robert Guttredge.

1687. Overseer of the Poor.

1688. Grand Jury.

He came out from Newport in a small boat and stormy weather, and was never heard from; as the town records state.

1692. Inventory, £659, viz: 78 acres and dwelling house, £112, 166 acres £166, also lot of 65 acres, and one of 42 acres, 11 cows, 3 heifers, 2 oxen, 5 steers, a bull, 12 two year cattle, 7 yearlings, 1 horse, 1 mare, 15 swine, 400 sheep, 2 Indian servants, £100, an Indian girl £15, pewter, &c.

See: American Genealogist v. 24, p. 70.

1718, Dec. 12. Will—proved 1723, Jun. 27. Widow Anna. Exs. son John Sands and Robert Westcott. To daughter Arabella Pelham, of Newport, £25. To daughter Elizabeth Paine, £25. All other children had already had their portions. To daughter Elizabeth Paine also a feather bed, &c. The two cows to remain in possession of son Thomas Paine till my grandson Thomas Mecarty is of age, at which time the latter to have a cow. To daughter Mercy Westcott, a feather bed. To grandsons Paulsgrave and John Williams, Joseph Mecarty, and Robert Sands, all rest of estate.

The will was exhibited by Edward Pelham and Anna Bennett, nearest of kin.

Inventory, £116, 8*s*. (Taken 1722, Nov. 21.)

His wife Margaret was buried in the town burial ground.

HALL (Henry).

HENRY, { b. { d. 1705.
m.
———— { b. { d. 1705 +

Newport, Westerly, R. I.

1679, Sep. 17. Westerly. He took oath of allegiance.

1687. Grand Jury.

1691. Deputy.

1705, Sep. 28. Will—Codicil 1705, Sep. 29, proved 1705, Nov. 5. Ex. not named and Town Council appointed his son Edward to that office. To wife, a third of all estate real and personal, at her disposal, and son Edward to take care of her. To son Edward, a third of all land and movables. To all children, a third of estate divided equally. To eldest son Henry, 5*s*. The children all to take care of my wife, their aged mother Codicil gives to son Henry, half of certain tract of land.

Inventory, £204, 4*s*. 2*d*., viz: 15 sheep, 10 lambs, 2 oxen, 10 pigs, 7 swine, 2 mares, 35 loads hay, 1 loom, 2 guns, a cutlass, 5 cows, 2 calves, 6 horses, 4 mares, also 12 mares and horses, 4 colts, a pair of oxen, a bull, 13 steers, 2 heifers, warming pan, &c.

The appointment of his son Edward as executor was asked for by following brothers and brothers-in-law, viz: Henry, James and John Hall, Thomas Stevens and James Adams.

1706. In this and following year receipts were given to executor by brothers and brothers-in-law as follows, viz: Henry, John, and James Hall, Thomas Stevens, James Adams, and Edward Larkin. Oath was also made by John Hall and William Wilkinson, that widow had received her portion.

See: American Genealogist, v. 19, p. 223.

I. HENRY, { b. { d. 1717. — Westerly, R. I.
m.
CONSTANT, { b. { d. 1719. of

1. Henry,
2. Mercy,
3. James,
4. John,
5. Edward,
6. William,
7. Elisha,
8. Susanna,
9. Elizabeth,
10. Lydia,
11. Mary,
12. Martha.

He was a weaver.

1679, Sep. 17. He took oath of allegiance.

1716, Nov. 1. Will—proved 1717, Jul. 22. Exs. friends, John Maxson, Jr., and Joseph Maxson. To wife Constant all movables and whole profit of homestead farm until two youngest daughters Mary and Martha come to age of eighteen, at which time my two sons William and Elisha, shall have my aforesaid farm, and other land, bounded partly by land given son Henry by deed of gift. Wife to continue to have best room in house, and three cows and a riding beast for life, and keep of said cows by two sons, who also are to supply her with firewood and twelve bushels good bread corn yearly. To three sons James, John and Edward, land. To five daughters Susannah Hall, Elizabeth Britten and Lydia, Mary and Martha Hall, 325 acres in Westerly. To son Henry and daughter Mercy Cottrell, 5*s*., each. What is left of movables after wife has brought up children, to go equally to following children, viz: Henry, James, John, Edward, William, Elisha, Susannah, Elizabeth Britten, Lydia, Mary and Martha Hall.

Inventory, £114, 9*s*. 6*d*, viz: 3 oxen, 3 cows, 2 heifers, 3 yearlings, 2 two year old, 2 steers, calves, 4 mares, 4 colts, 19 swine, 2 beds, pewter, 2 spinning wheels, 3 linen wheels, loom, books, 3 guns, &c.

1719, Aug. 4. Administration of Constant Hall's estate by son Henry.

Inventory, £111, 19*s*., 7*d*.

II. EDWARD, { b. { d. 1719. — Westerly, R. I.
m.
MARY, { b. { d. 1719 + of

See: American Genealogist, v. 19, p. 224.

1719, Nov. 4. Administration to widow Mary. Inventory, land £300, 4 oxen, 5 cows, 2 two year, a yearling, 5 calves, a horse, 2 mares, 3 beds, gun, loom, 3 swine, books 12*s*., wheels and cards, &c.

III. JAMES, { b. { d. 1745. — Westerly, R. I.
m.
SARAH BABCOCK, { b. { d. 1734 + of Job & Jane (Crandall) Babcock.

1. Sarah, 1693, Dec. 25.
2. Jane, 1695, Aug. 29.
3. Honor, 1697, Aug. 14.
4. Elizabeth, 1699, Aug. 23.
5. James, 1701, Sep. 17.
6. Joseph, 1703, Jul. 8.
7. Mary, 1705, Nov. 10.
8. Benjamin, 1707, Nov. 19.
9. Amey, 1709, Sep. 26.
10. Jonathan, 1711, Nov. 18.

1734, Apr. 17. Will—proved 1745, Apr. 29. Ex. son Benjamin. To wife Sarah, a third of all estate real and personal for life, use of best room in the house; and two milch cows and a riding beast for ever. To grandson Benjamin Hall, son of James, deceased, 5*s*. To son Joseph, eastward part of homestead, 80 acres. To son Benjamin, rest of homestead, house, &c., 120 acres, he paying my daughter Mary Hall, £10. To daughters Sarah Hall, Honour Hall, Elizabeth Mackson and Mary Hall, all personal equally.

Inventory £394, 18*s*., viz: apparel, £24, 15*s*., pair of compasses, 3 linen wheels, pair of cards, pewter, a yoke of oxen, pair of steers, 3 cows, 2 heifers, 2 yearlings, mare, 18 sheep, 6 lambs, breeding sow, 6 pigs, &c.

IV. JOHN, { b. { d. 1706 + — Westerly, R. I.

See: American Genealogist, v. 19, p. 224.

V. MARY, { b. { d. 1728 +
m.
THOMAS STEVENS, { b. 1678, Dec. 14. { d. 1736. of Henry Stevens.

VI. HONOR, { b. { d.
m.
JAMES ADAMS, { b. { d. of Adams.

1. James, 1698, Jan. 20.
2. John, 1700, May 26.
3. Jonathan, 1702, Sep. 28.
4. Henry, 1704, Sep. 27.
5. Honor, 1706, Jul. 11.
6. Nathaniel, 1709, Mar. 25.
7. Thomas, 1710, Mar. 24.
8. Joseph, 1715, Mar. 4.

VII. ELIZABETH, { b. { d.
m.
EDWARD LARKIN, { b. { d. 1741. of Edward Larkin.

1. Joseph,
2. Edward,
3. John,
4. Samuel,
5. Elizabeth,
6. Penelope.

HALL (William).

William, m. Mary,
b. 1613. d. 1675.
b. d. 1680 +

Portsmouth, R. I.

1638, Aug. 8. He was admitted an inhabitant of Aquidneck.

1644, May 27. Portsmouth. He had a grant of land.

1654, Sep. 3. He sold land to Thomas Manchester.

1654-56-60-63. Commissioner.

1655. Freeman.

1658, Jul. 6. He sold 1-300 of Conanicut and Dutch Islands, to Richard Sisson.

1663. He calls himself aged fifty years or thereabouts, in giving testimony regarding the wishes of John Roome, deceased.

1665-66-67-68-72-73. Deputy.

1666. He and two others were appointed to take area of all highways and driftways not set off.

1672. Town Council.

1673, May 7. He was on a committee to treat with the Indians about drunkenness; "Seriously to consult and agree of some way to prevent the extreme excess of the Indians' drunkenness. The sachems herein intended to be treated withal, are Mawsup and Ninecraft, of the Narragansetts, Philip, of Mount Hope, Weetamo, of Pocasset, Awashunk of Seaconnett; or so many of them as do appear."

1673, Nov. 22. Will — proved 1675, Jan. 31. Exx. his "trusty and well beloved friend and yoke fellow" Mary, with assistance from his sons William and Benjamin, who were to see the will carried out, after her death. To wife, whole estate for life. To son Zuriel, 20 acres at decease of wife, and he to pay his brothers, Benjamin and William, £3. To son Benjamin, homestead, at decease of wife, he paying his sisters, Elizabeth, Rebecca and Deliverance, each £2. To three daughters and son William, the rest of estate, equally.

I. Zuriel, m. Elizabeth Tripp,
b. d. 1691, Sep. 5. Portsmouth, R. I.
b. 1648 ± d. 1701 + of John & Mary (Paine) Tripp.

1688, May 18. His wife had a legacy of £5, a black cloak and a mohair petticoat, from her aunt, Alice Strange's will. (Widow of Lot Strange.)

1691, Sep. 14. Inventory, £84, 5s., shown by widow Elizabeth, administratrix.

1701, Nov. 29. His widow rendered her account, "errors excepted," showing that she had disbursed £63, 11s. Among the charges is one for bringing up her son Benjamin, from his birth till he was seven years old, at £6 per year. She notes charges paid to my two brothers, William and Benjamin Hall. To her three children she had delivered as follows: To Mary, wife of Robert Fish, a heifer; To Joanna, six lambs; To son Zuriel, a cow, horse and 9s. She was ordered to pay over £14 to son Benjamin, and if latter died before twenty-one, his brother and sisters to have it.

1. Mary,
2. Zuriel, 1677.
3. Joanna,
4. Benjamin, 1692, Apr. 13.

II. William, m. 1671, Jan. 26. Alice Tripp,
b. d. 1698. Portsmouth, R. I.
b. 1650 ± d. of John & Mary (Paine) Tripp.

1672, Jun. 17. He bought for £60, dwelling house, orchard and 26 acres in Portsmouth, of Lawrence Gonsales, of Pequemins, county of Albemarle, province of Carolina, tailor, son-in-law to Thomas Kent, of Pequemins, and late of Portsmouth, by marriage with Sarah, eldest daughter of Thomas Kent, power of attorney having been given by father-in-law, said Thomas Kent.

1. William, 1672, Dec. 2.
2. Preserved, 1675, Aug. 29.
3. Abigail, 1677, Dec. 20.
4. Mary, 1679, Sep. 24.
5. John, 1681, Jul. 2.
6. Deliverance, 1683, Jan. 8.
7. Alice, 1685, Jan. 14.
8. Elizabeth, 1687, Oct. 2.
9. Robert, 1690, Feb. 16.

III. Benjamin, m. 1676, Jul. 27. Frances Parker,
b. 1650. d. 1730, Jan. 26. Portsmouth, R. I.
b. d. of George & Frances ( ) Parker.

1678. Freeman.

1680. Taxed with his mother 9s. 3d.

1699-1701-4-5-6-7-13-14. Deputy.

1701-2 Assistant.

1704. Justice of the Peace.

1730, Mar. 9. Administration to son Nathaniel. Inventory, £16, 11s., viz: wearing apparel and cane £6, 5s., feather bed and furniture belonging thereto £10, spectacles and case, glass bottle, staple and roweling needle 6s.

1. Mary, 1678, Apr. 3.
2. William, 1680, Aug. 19.
3. Benjamin, 1682, Jun. 17.
4. George, 1685, Jun. 29.
5. Nathaniel, 1689, Jun. 29.

IV. Elizabeth, m. 1676, Apr. 13. Giles Pearce,
b. d. 1698 +
b. 1651, Jun. 22. d. 1698, Nov. 19. of Richard & Susanna (Wright) Pearce.

1. Jeremiah, 1678, Jan. 22.
2. Susanna, 1679, May 7.
3. Elizabeth, 1682, May 27.
4. John, 1687, Jan. 11.
5. Mary, 1690, Feb. 7.

V. Rebecca,
b. d.

VI. Deliverance, m. (1) 1679, Jan. 30. Abiel Tripp, m. (2) Thomas Durfee,
b. d. 1721.
b. 1653 ± d. 1684, Sep. 10. of John & Mary (Paine) Tripp.
b. 1643. d. 1712. of Durfee.

1. Abiel, 1684, Jun. 22.
(By 2d husband.)
2. Patience,
3. Deliverance,

HALSEY.

George, m. Rebecca,
b. d.
b. 1624. d. 1700, Apr. 22.

Newport, R. I.

1666, May 2. Freeman.

1667, May 13. He and certain others, skilled therein, were to repair all arms brought them by order of the Captain or Lieutenant of the Train Band of Newport.

1680. Taxed 3s.

His wife was buried in Newport Cemetery.

HANNAH.

Robert, m. Mary Wilson,
b. d. 1706.
b. 1663. d. 1737.

of Samuel & —— (Teft) Wilson.
(She m. (2) 1708, Apr. 2, Geo. Webb.)

Kings Town, R. I.

1687, Sep. 6. Taxed 11s. 1d.

1706, Sep. 3. Will—codicil 1706, Sep. 9—proved 1706, Oct. 14. Exx. wife Mary. To son Robert, land where dwelling house stands and 100 acres, &c., but if he die without issue, to go to next heir. To son also, two negro boys, Peter and James, four cows, twenty ewes and all my oxen, &c. To son-in-law Nathaniel Niles, a horse and mare, and to only daughter, Mary Niles, his wife, land, which at decease of Mary and her husband, is to go to her two sons, Nathan and Robert Niles. To granddaughter Mary Niles, a negro girl called Katharine. To wife Mary, all the rest of estate, and 240 acres where house stands to be hers for life, and to her a mulatto girl Freelove, and all movables not given.

Inventory, £378, 12s., viz: 10 horsekind, 6 oxen, 25 cows, 8 two year old, 10 yearlings, 8 calves, 3 swine, negro woman and 5 children £110, 3 feather beds, sword, 2 old guns, 2 spinning wheels, cash £6.

1735. His widow called herself aged seventy-two years, in testimony given this year.

1735, May 19. Will—proved 1737, May 25. Mary Webb, widow of George. Exs. son Robert Hannah and son-in-law Nathaniel Niles. To grandchildren (children of son Robert Hannah, and children of my daughter Mary Niles, wife to Nathaniel), whole estate divided equally.

See: American Geneologist, v. 19, p. 224.

I. Robert, m. (1) Catharine Niles, m. (2) 1730, May 31. Elizabeth Brown,
b. d. 1736. South Kingstown, R. I.
b. 1680, Mar. 13. d. of Nathaniel & Sarah (Sands) Niles.
b. d. of Brown.

1723-24-25-26-27-28-29-30-31-32-33-34-35-36. Town Clerk.

1727-29. Deputy.

1736, Feb. 14. Administration to widow Elizabeth.

Inventory, £1,207, 15s. 9d., viz: apparel £43, 6s., watch £10, silver and gold buttons and shoe buckles £7, 11s., silver spoons £10, 10s., 2 guns, warming pan, quilting frames, cash £6, 18s., bonds and notes £522, 10s. 2d., 4 negroes £225, 2 cows, 1 heifer, 1 mare, old books £4, 9s. 4d.

1. Mary, 1714, Feb. 1.
2. Sarah, 1716, Dec. 10.
3. Tabitha, 1718, Feb. 21.
4. George, 1719, Mar. 26.
5. Catharine, 1721, Jun. 2.
6. Hannah, 1723, Oct. 13.
7. Elizabeth, 1725, Mar. 17.
(2d wife.)
8. Ruth, 1731, Apr. 18.
9. Desire, 1733, Feb. 11.
10. Ann, 1734, Feb. 28.

II. Mary, m. 1699, Jan. 26. Nathaniel Niles,
b. d. 1765 +
b. 1677, Mar. 21. d. 1766. of Nathaniel & Sarah (Sands) Niles.

1. Nathan, 1700, Sep. 12.
2. Robert, 1702, Nov. 9.
3. Mary, 1704, Aug. 10.
4. Jeremiah, 1707, Apr. 7.
5. Sarah, 1711, Jun. 14.
6. Tabitha, 1714, Nov. 14.
7. Silas, 1718, May 26.
8. Paul, 1721, May 16.
9. Silvanus, 1721, May 16.
10. Hannah,
11. Katharine, 1725 Mar. 5.

STEPHEN, b. | d. 1698, Feb. 20.
m.
BRIDGET, b. | d.

Providence, R. I.

He was a blacksmith.

1664, Mar. 28. He had land laid out.

1665, Oct. 27. He had a grant of 25 acres for 10*s.*

1669, Aug. 7. He bought of John and Mary Jones a right of commonage.

1675, May 24. He bought 70 acres of William Hopkins.

1679, Jul. 1. He and son Stephen were taxed together 7*s.* 6*d.*

1682, Aug. 24. He deeded his son John 70 acres, previously bought of William Hopkins.

1687, Sep. 1. Taxed 5*s.*

1687. Ratable estate, 3 acres tillage, 8 acres meadow, 3 acres English pasture, an acre wild pasture, 5 cows, a three year, 2 two years, a horse.

1693, Apr. 10. He and wife Bridget deeded to son Abraham, all homestead estate, not heretofore given, including house, &c., and at their death he to have entire possession, and "to take a special care to see after the estate of his father and mother that they fall not into any strait or wants, but will lawfully and faithfully provide for them such things as they cannot provide for themselves, as may be for their comfort and support in their old age, and as persons of their rank and quality, both in sickness and in health," &c.

1695, Jan. 15. He deeded to son Abraham, 8 acres, specifying that he had not time to sign it in the lifetime of his son, but yet now does so.

1698, Apr. 12. Administration to son John, of Newport. (Israel Harding, of Swanzey became bondsman.)

Inventory, £44, 16*s.* 6*d.*, viz: apparel, beds, iron, brass and pewter, cash 12*s.*, table, chairs, books 3*s.*, meat, butter, 3 cows, 3 heifers, 2 pigs, 2 barrels of cider.

HARDING. 2d column. II. John, b. 1644, d. 1700, May 2. His wife was Sarah Butcher, b. 1652, d. 1716, May 7. She m. (2) Hugh Mosher. Children, 1. Israel. 2. Stephen, 3. Mary. 4. Elizabeth. 5. Amey. 6. Hannah. 1716, May 1, will proved 1716, Jun. 4, widow Sarah Mosher. Ex. friend John Odlin. She mentions son Israel Harding; daughters, Elizabeth Williams, Mary Hookey, Amey Clarke and Hannah Medbury, and son-in-law Stephen Hookey. In this column add VI. Israel. Swanzey Ms. He married Sarah Medbury (w. of John), and had Lydia 1697, Aug. 1.

I. STEPHEN, b. | d. 1680, May 31. — Providence, R. I. — No issue.
m. 1679, Jan. 28.
MERCY WINSOR, b. | d. 1680. of Joshua Winsor.

He was a blacksmith.

1680, Apr. 19. Will—proved 1680, Jun. 25. Ex. brother Abraham. Overseers, Alexander Balcom and Jonathan Sprague. He leaves all his household goods and chattels to his father except so much as shall satisfy my sisters for their tending of me. To brother Abraham, my house, orchard, lands and meadow, &c., as expressed in a deed of gift from father. To brother-in-law Samuel Winsor, my wife's best suit of apparel.

Inventory £68, 13*s.*, viz: dwelling house and 12 acres, 2 cows, 2 yearlings, 2 calves, 6 swine, 2 spinning wheels, &c.

The town records declare that he and his wife "both departed this life in the year 1680."

II. JOHN, b. | d. — Providence, Newport, R. I.
m.
——, b. | d. of

1. Israel,
2. Stephen,

1682, Aug. 24. He had a deed of land from his father, already alluded to.

1684. Newport. Freeman.

1702, Mar. 4. John, Israel and Stephen Harding were proprietors in common lands at Newport.

1715, Jul. 4. Israel Harding of Newport, calling himself son of John, deceased, sold land in Providence to James Brown, of Providence. In another deed in same year Israel sold land in Providence to Jabez Brown, which had been owned by said Israel's honored grandfather Stephen Harding, deceased.

There was a John Hardin, who was the third pastor of Second Baptist Church at Newport. His wife was Sarah Butcher, and his children's names were: Mary, Elizabeth, Amey, Hannah and Israel. He died in 1700, and might be considered identical with the above John, but for the fact that Morgan Edwards (who gives the foregoing account), declares that he came from Kent, in old England, by way of Boston to Newport.

III. ABRAHAM, b. | d. 1694, Nov. 23. — Providence, R. I.
m.
DEBORAH, b. | d. of

(She m. (2) 1695 ± Moses Bartlett.) **HARDING. 2d column. III. Abraham. Daughter Mercy b. 1683.**

1. Israel,
2. Stephen,
3. John,
4. Mercy, 1683
5. Lydia, 1692, Aug. 23.
6. Deborah,
7. Thomas,

He was a blacksmith, and his son Thomas had the same avocation.

1687, Sep. 1. Taxed 4*s.* 2*d.*

1687. Ratable estate 1½ acres pasture, 3½ acres tilled land, 5 acres mowing, 4 cows, heifer, 4 small swine.

1694, Dec 18. Inventory was presented by widow Deborah, who desired administration, but having no bondsman, referred to next meeting, &c.

1696, Mar. 3. The widow having lately changed her condition by marriage with Moses Bartlett, administration was given to her and her now husband on former husband's estate, till next meeting, they to give account and bond.

1698, Apr. 12. Administration on his estate was finally given to Moses Bartlett and wife Deborah, and the children committed to their care.

1711, Jan. 13. Moses Bartlett deeded land to son-in-law (*i. e.* stepson) John Harding. (The next year John sold land to his brother Stephen.)

IV. PRISCILLA, b. | d. 1708 (—)
m.
THOMAS ESTEN, b. 1647, Feb. 17. | d. 1708, Nov. 5. of Thomas & Ann ( ) Esten.

1. Mary.
2. Mercy,

V. SARAH, b. | d. 1731, Aug. 20.
m.
HENRY ESTEN, b. 1651, Jan. 11. | d. 1711, Mar. 23. of Thomas & Ann ( ) Esten.

1. Rebecca, 1695, May 9.
2. Henry, 1697, Aug. 29.
3. Cornelius, 1699, Mar. 9.

HARGILL.

CHRISTOPHER, b. | d. 1709 +
m.
——, b. | d.

Virginia, Newport, R. I.

He was a blacksmith.

1680, Apr. 2. Newport. In a letter from Samuel Hubbard (1681, May 14), of Newport, to Isaac Wells in Jamaica, he says: "A ship came from Virginia, hither 2d day of April, 1680, twenty-six souls, five of them baptized, brother Hargel, a smith, and his wife, brother Henry Key and his wife, Hope Covey."

1682, Jan. 28. Mr. Hubbard, in a letter of this date to John Thornton, of Providence, about the troubles in the church from some who came from Virginia, and also about singing of psalms in public, &c., says: "Brother Christopher Hargill was chief in it, but I think we may see God's hand in it, his declining is made manifest, for he is fallen into his old sin of drunkenness," &c. The church it seems sent for him but he came not and was refused fellowship till he manifested repentance.

1687, Dec. 14. He and Samuel Stapleton were asked in court why they kept not their shops shut on the first day of this instant December, it being a day set apart by his excellency the Governor and Council for thanksgiving and praise. His answer was that his boy opened the shop, and what work his son did was on his own account, and that he was lame or else he did not know but that himself might have wrought.

1709, Mar. 2. In the account of charges paid by executor of Henry Bull, the bill of Christopher Hargill, was 26*s.*

HARGILL. 1st column. His widow Joan d. 1732. 1725, Aug. 31. His widow of Newport, deeded to her grandson, Barnabas Hargill, blacksmith, of Dartmouth, Ms., a lot of land, housing, &c., where she lived, he agreeing to come and maintain her. 1731, Oct. 14, will-proved 1732. widow Joan. She mentions Nathaniel Mumford (son of Captain Richard Mumford), and daughter Mary Dusain, to whom she gave a gold medal inscribed "Remember well and bear in mind—a faithful friend is hard to find."

I. CHRISTOPHER, b. 1696, | d. 1748, Dec. 25. — North Kingstown, R. I.

He was buried in the Casey burial ground.

HARGILL. 1st column. Christopher, b. 1634, Jan. 25, d. 1718, Jun. 25. His wife was Jane. 2d column. I. Barnabas, b. 1671, d. 1690, Oct. 19. II. Caleb, b. 1674, d. 1704, Mar. 7. Children, 1. Christopher, 1696. 2. Barnabas, 1700, +.

John, m. ——— | b. ; d. 1687, Feb. 6. | b. ; d.

Newport, R. I.

1673. Juryman.

1678, Jun. 12. A very great hurt having been done to a small child by fast riding; it was enacted by the Assembly that any person presuming to ride a horse at a gallop, &c., in any street between the house that lately John Harndel lived in, and the house where Thomas Clifton lives, shall for the offence pay 5*s.* fine.

1680. Taxed 4*s.*

1685, Feb. 9. Will—proved 1687. He mentions daughter Mary, wife of John Stanton, and her children Robert (Benjamin?), Mary and Hannah. He also mentions daughter Rebecca, wife of Hugh Mosher.

I. Rebecca, m. **Hugh Mosher**, | b. ; d. | b. 1633. ; d. 1713. of Hugh Mosher.

1. Nicholas, 1666.
2. John, 1668.
3. Joseph, 1670.
4. Mary,
5. James, 1675.
6. Daniel,
7. Rebecca,

II. Mary, | b. 1646. ; d. young.

…ARNDEL. 2d column. III. Mary. Her last child was 7. …enjamin, 1684, Mar. 13.

III. Mary, m. **John Stanton**, | b. 1647, Jul. 6. ; d. 1678 ± | b. 1645, Aug. ; d. 1713, Oct. 3. of Robert & Avis (   ) Stanton.

1. Mary, 1668, Jun. 4.
2. Hannah, 1670, Nov. 7.
3. Patience, 1672, Sep. 10.
4. John, 1674, Apr. 22.
5. Content, 1675, Dec. 20.
6. Robert, 1677, May 4.

HARNDEL. 1st column. 1698, Apr. 22. Will—proved. Exx. daughter Mary Stanton, wife of John. Overseers Robert Hodgson and John Coggeshall. To kinsman Robert Stanton, son to John Stanton, house and 10 acres at age, but if he die without issue then to kinsman Benjamin Stanton, son of John Stanton. To son-in-law John Stanton, a mare, and to kinsman Robert Stanton, a mare To daughter Rebecca, wife of Hugh Mosher, of Portsmouth, a good ewe sheep. To Mary and Hannah Stanton, daughters of John, two good ewe sheep each.

2d column. III Mary. Erase her death, and add to her children: 7. Benjamin, 1684, Mar. 13. 8 Henry, 1688, May 22 (Henry may possibly have been by 2d wife of John Stanton).

HAVENS.

William, m. **Dionis**, | b. ; d. 1683. | b. ; d. 1692 +

Portsmouth, R. I.

1638. He was admitted an inhabitant of the island of Aquidneck, having submitted himself to the government that is or shall be established.

1639, Apr. 30. He and twenty-eight others signed the following compact: "We, whose names are underwritten, do acknowledge ourselves the legal subjects of his Majesty, King Charles, and in his name do hereby bind ourselves into a civil body politicke, unto his laws according to matters of justice."

1644. He had a grant of 4 acres.

1650, May 23. He and five others were appointed to make and mend all arms presented by inhabitants of any of the towns.

1662, Dec. 2. He leased for seven years, to son John, his dwelling house, with all lands belonging thereto, at £5 yearly, payable Mar. 20, in wheat, pease, Indian corn or oats.

1680, Mar. 30. Will—proved 1683, Sep. 25. Exx. wife Dennis. To her, all movables, and dwelling house, lands, orchard, &c. To son John, daughter Sarah Tyler, sons Thomas, Robert, George, daughters Mary Cook, Ruth Card, Dinah Havens, Elizabeth Havens, son William, and daughters Martha, Rebecca and Margaret Havens, 1*s.* each.

I. John, m. **Ann**, | b. ; d. 1687. | b. ; d. 1687 + of   Portsmouth, R. I., Shrewsbury, N. J.

1. William,
2. John,
3. Nicholas,
4. Daniel,
5. Jane,
6. Daughter,
7. Daughter,

1667, Apr. 18. He sold land to Gideon Freeborn.

1668. Monmouth, N. J. He settled at Manasquam.

1686, Aug. His daughter Jane, married John Sheriff, of Portsmouth, R. I.

1687, Mar. 14. Will—proved 1687, Sep. 9. Exs. son William and son-in-law Thomas Wainwight. He mentions sons William, John, Nicholas and Daniel, and sons-in-law George Axtin and Thomas Wainwright.

II. Sarah, m. **John Tyler**, | b. ; d. 1718 + | b. ; d. 1700. of Tyler.

1. Lazarus,
2. Miriam,
3. Tamar,
4. Question,
5. Friendship,

III. Thomas, m. ——— | b. ; d. 1704. | b. ; d. of   Portsmouth, Kings Town, R. I.

1. William,
2. Thomas,
3. Joseph,

1671. Freeman.

1677. Juryman.

1687, Sep. 6. Kings Town. Taxed 10*s.* 11*d.*

1691, Mar. 12. He had 30 sheep in his care belonging to Major Richard Smith, as shown by will of the latter

1704 Administration to eldest son William.

1709, May 27. His sons William, Thomas and Joseph, were concerned in the purchase of a tract of 1,824 acres near Devil's Foot, being part of the vacant lands ordered sold by the Assembly.

IV. Robert, m. **Elizabeth**, | b. ; d. 1712. | b. ; d. 1712 + of   Portsmouth, R. I., Dartmouth, Mass.

1. Robert, 1686.
2. Ruth, 1690, Dec. 14.
3. Elizabeth, 1694, Feb. 1.
4. William, 1698, Jun.
5 George, 1700, Mar. 24.
6. Joseph, 1705, Jun. 9.

1677, Oct. 31. He and forty-seven others were granted 5,000 acres, to be called East Greenwich. He never went there to settle.

1678. Freeman.

1708, Mar. 30. Will—proved 1712, Apr. 7. Exx. wife Elizabeth. To son Robert, all right in lands at Greenwich, and half of land in Dartmouth. To son William, £10 when of age, paid by son Robert. To sons George and Joseph, northerly half of lands in Dartmouth. To daughter Ruth Havens, a young cow. To daughter Elizabeth Havens, a cow from son Joseph, at age. To wife Elizabeth, all other personal, and use of land in Dartmouth, till youngest child is of age.

Inventory, £47, 8*s.* 9*d.*, viz: psalter and other small books, pewter, 2 cows, 2 yearlings, mare, 6 swine, &c., house and land £30.

V. George, m. 1674. **Eleanor Thurston**, | b. ; d. 1702 + | b. 1655 Mar. ; d. 1724 + of Edward & Elizabeth (Mott) Thurston.   Jamestown, R. I., Shelter Island, N. Y.

1. George,
2. Jonathan, 1681, Feb. 2.

(She m. (2) ——— Terry).

HAVENS. 2d column. V. George, b. 1653; d. 1706, Feb. 25. Children, 3. John. 4, William. 5, Ruth. 6. Content. 7, Patience. 8, Desire. 9, Abigail. He was buried in Old Cemetery at New London, Ct. His widow married Thomas Terry of Southold.

1680. Freeman.

1687, Sep. 6. Kings Town. Taxed 5*s.* 3*d.*

1695, Jul. 15. Jamestown. Constable.

1696. He sold farm on Boston Neck for £500.

1701, Nov. 19. Shelter Island. His son George, of Kings Town, in a deed of this date, calls himself son of George, of Shelter Island.

1702, Oct. 26. He (of Shelter Island), sold to Henry Tibbitts, for £80, a farm of 150 acres in Coweset.

1724, Sep. Eleanor Terry, widow, of Newport, formerly widow of George Havens, sued George Tibbitts, son and heir of Henry Tibbitts, for right of dower in lands in South Kingstown, sold by her husband, George Havens, to Henry Tibbitts.

VI. Mary, m. **Thomas Cook**, | b. ; d. | b. ; d. 1670 (—) of Thomas Cook.

1. Thomas,
2. John,
3. George,
4. Stephen,
5. Ebenezer,
6. Phebe, 1665.
7. Martha,

VII. Ruth, m. ——— **Card**, | b. ; d. | b. ; d. of Card.

VIII. Dinah, | b. ; d.

IX. Elizabeth, | b. ; d.

X. William, | b. ; d.

XI. Martha, b. d.

XII. Rebecca, b. d.

XIII. Margaret, b. d.

HAWKINS (Richard).

Richard, b. d. 1656 ±
m.
Jane, b. d. 1656 +

Boston, Mass., Portsmouth, R. I.

1638, Mar. 12. His wife Jane, was given liberty till the beginning of May, and the magistrates (if she did not depart before), to dispose of her: and in the meantime, she is not to meddle in surgery or physic, drinks, plasters or oils, nor to question matters of religion, except with the Elders for satisfaction.

1639, Jul. 1. Portsmouth. He was granted a house lot, to build upon in one year or be forfeited.

1641, Jun. 2. His wife was ordered to depart away from Massachusetts to-morrow morning and not to return again thither upon pain of severe whipping, and her sons were bound in £20 to carry her away according to order.

1644, Dec. 14. He deeded son Job, dwelling house and 30 acres, at decease of said Richard and Jane, father and mother of said Job.

1646, May 2. His wife wrote a letter from Portsmouth.

1655. Freeman.

1656, Dec. 10. His widow Jane, had 8 acres granted her at Portsmouth.

I. James, b. d. 1670. — Boston, Mass.
m.
Mary Mills, b. 1620 ± d. 1671 + of John & Susanna ( ) Mills.

He was a bricklayer.

1651, May 23. He and his brothers, Thomas and Job, petitioned General Court of Massachusetts, for their mother Jane, to live in that jurisdiction.

1669, Jun. 25. Will—proved 1670, Apr. 2. He mentions son James, and daughters Mary, wife of John Kneeland, Ruth, wife of Daniel Fairfield, Damaris, wife of Bartholomew Threeneeles, Elizabeth, wife of Thomas Mercer, and Sarah, wife of John Jenkins.

1671, Apr. 15. His widow Mary, transferred to son James, a legacy from his kinfolk of Rhode Island.

1. Mary,
2. Ruth,
3. Damaris,
4. Elizabeth,
5. Sarah,
6. Susan, 1646, Feb. 13.
7. Peleg, 1648, Mar. 9.
8. James, 1652, Jul. 3.

II. Thomas, b. 1609. d. — Boston, Mass.
m. (1)
Hannah, b. d. 1644, May 27. of
m. (2)
Rebecca, b. d. of

He was a brickburner, as well as baker and innholder.

1655, Apr. 4. His age was called about forty-six years, at this date.

1660. He sold warehouse, wharf, &c., in Boston.

1. Abraham, 1636, Mar. 11.
2. Hannah, 1641, Jan. 20.
3. Job, 1641, Jan. 20.
4. Hope, 1643, Apr. 2.
5. Mary,
(2d wife.)
6. Rebecca, 1745, Jul. 28.
7. Mehitable, 1656, Jan. 27.

III. Job, b. d. — Portsmouth, R. I., Boston, Mass.
m.
Frances, b. d. of

1639. He was granted a house lot, to build on within a year or forfeited.

1639, Apr. 30. He and twenty-eight others signed the following compact: "We, whose names are underwritten, do acknowledge ourselves the legal subjects of his Majesty, King Charles, and in his name do hereby bind ourselves into a civil body politicke, unto his laws according to matters of justice."

1656, Aug. 25. Boston. He sold Robert Dennis, of Portsmouth, 20 acres there (and Jane Hawkins, widow of Richard, waived all her claims to same).

1663, Apr. He sold Edward Fisher, of Portsmouth, 8 acres there.

1. Martha, 1646, Mar. 26.

HAZLETON.

Charles, b. d.
m. (1)
———, b. d.
m. (2) 1693, Aug. 9. [Henry
Hannah Matteson (w. of b. d.
of Hugh & Elizabeth ( ) Parsons.

Kings Town, R. I.

1683, Mar. 20. He, living in Potowomut Neck, sold William Allen of Prudence Island, house and 100 acres.

1684, Oct. 3. He, calling himself Charles Hazleton, Sr., of Kings Town, sold John Wood house and 10 acres in East Greenwich.

1684, Oct. 10. He deeded son Charles land formerly bought of Captain Edward Richmond (then of Newport), reserving to self equal privilege of profits for life, and equal privilege in dwelling house, and at my decease to be to said son Charles, but if wife survive, she to have free egress and regress while widow."

1688. Grand Jury.

I. James, b. d. — Kings Town, R. I.
m. 1678, Apr. 10 [of Robert
Catharine Westcott (w b. d. of

1682, May 3. He and others were warned by Assembly to depart off any lands of Potowomut now in difference (between Kings Town and Warwick), till his Majesty's pleasure be further known, &c.

1683. Constable.

1. Margaret, 1679, Mar. 11.
2. William,

II. Charles, b. d. 1712, Mar. 28. — East Greenwich, R. I.
m. (1) 1688, Mar. 25.
Catharine Westcott, b. 1664, May 16. d. 1692 ± of Robert & Catharine ( ) Westcott.
m. (2)
Elizabeth Whaley, b. d. 1752. of Theophilus & Elizabeth (Mills) Whaley.

1712, Mar. 14. Will—proved 1712, Apr. 12. Exs. wife Elizabeth and son James. To son Charles, 45 acres in north-west corner of farm, he paying to brother Samuel, £5, at age. To son James, all the rest of housing, lands, and orchards, he paying his brother William, £5 at age. If James dies before twenty-one, his part to go to brothers Samuel and William. To wife Elizabeth, rest of estate.

Inventory, £85, 15s., viz: 2 oxen, 2 steers, 3 cows, heifer, yearling, calf, mare, horse, 32 sheep, 17 swine, 2 spinning wheels, 2 guns, cider mill and press, &c.

(2d Wife, no issue.)

1. Charles, 1689, Apr. 11.
(2d wife).
2. James, 1694, Feb. 1.
3. Samuel, 1696, Mar. 25.
4. Catharine, 1697, Oct. 25.
5. Elizabeth, 1699, Oct. 2.
6. William, 1701, Apr. 24.
7. Ann, 1704, Apr. 27.
8. Mary, 1706, Feb. 6.
9. Ellen, 1707, Nov. 15.
10. Martha, 1711, Apr. 10.

HEAD.

Henry, b. d. 1716, Jul. 1.
m.
Elizabeth, b. d. 1748, Jun.

Little Compton, R. I.

1683–84–85–86–89. Deputy.

1686, Feb. He and David Lake were chosen agents for the town to appear at the next court in relation to the non-payment of sum of £15, which the court had ordered that town and adjacent villages to raise for the encouragement of preaching of the gospel, but which said town had refused or neglected to make rates for. The court in March ordered the town to pay £20 for their contempt and neglect, and because they "write rather as equals or neighbours than as delinquents or offenders."

1689, Dec. 25. He was fined 20s. with three others "for their disorderly departure from the General Court."

1690, Jun. 3. Selectman.

1708, Mar. 24. Will—proved 1716, Aug. 20. Exx. wife Elizabeth. To son Jonathan, land and housing where he dwells in Coakset and

I. Jonathan, b. d. 1748. — Little Compton, R. I., Dartmouth, Mass.
m.
Susanna, b. d. 1748 + of

HEAD. 2d column. I. Jonathan m. 1704, Dec. 7, Susanna Wilcox, of Daniel and Elizabeth (Cook) Wilcox.

1742, Dec. 14. Will—proved 1748, Dec. 6. Exs. wife Susanna and friend Samuel Wilbur. To wife, all personal and improvement of real estate while widow. To son Joseph, £5, and at death of wife or at her marriage, all real estate to go to him and his heirs male forever.

Inventory, £3,411, 7s. 6d., viz: homestead farm £2,000, land and mill in Barker's Neck £450, purse and apparel £35, books and spectacles £10, 10s., 2 oxen, 3 cows, 4 young cattle, a horse, 30 sheep, 10 lambs, swine, wheels, carpenter tools, &c.

1. Joseph, 1705, Sep. 1.

II. Henry, b. d. 1755, Mar. 4. — Little Compton, R. I.
m.
Elizabeth, b. d. 1754 + of

1754, Jul. 2. Will—proved 1755, Apr. 1. Ex. son Benjamin. To wife Elizabeth, a room, bed, and a third of income of real estate for life, and after debts and legacies are paid she to have a third of personal forever. To son Benjamin, all real estate and buildings (except the room my wife chooses) and andirons, chest I keep my writings in, farming and carpentering tools, bills, bonds, cattle, horses, swine and apparel. To sons, Henry, Lovet and William, 20s. each. To daughters Abigail Salisbury, Mary Suell, Innocent Salisbury and Elizabeth Jennerson, 20s. each, and to the latter £40, for her doctoring, if so much. To daughter Deborah Paddock, 20s. To daughter Amey Shrieve, 20s. To six daughters, two-thirds of household goods.

Inventory, £1,524, 10s. 8d., viz: apparel £43, 10s., warming pan, cheese press, pair of oxen, 6 cows, heifer, 2 yearlings, 3 mares, horse, swine, 3 geese, a turkey, bond £220, &c.

1. Benjamin,
2. Henry,
3. Lovet,
4. William,
5. Abigail,
6. Mary,
7. Innocent,
8. Elizabeth,
9. Deborah,
10. Amey,

II. Henry m. 1709, June 20, Elizabeth Palmer, b. 1687, Nov. 12, of William and Mary (Richmond) Palmer. Children, 1, Henry, 1709, Nov. 7. 2, Abigail, 1710, Dec. 24. 3, Mary, 1711, Apr. 16. 4, Innocent, 1713, Mar. 13. 5, Lovet, 1714, Sep. 27. 6, Elizabeth, 1716, Mar. 21. 7, Benjamin, 1718, Sep. 17. 8, William, 1721, July 12. 9, Deborah, 1725, Jan. 16. 10, Amey, 1727, May 15.

III. Benjamin. Children, 1, William, 1715, Jan. 13. V. Mary m. William Cuthbert, 1707, Aug. 7. He d. 1747. Children. 1. Henry, 1708, May 14. 2, Alexander, 1710, July 21. 3, Elizabeth, 1712, June 26. 4, Amey, 1719, Oct. 8. 5, Benjamin, 1721, Nov. 22.

certain other lands in Little Compton and two cows. To son Henry, 60 acres where he hath built a house in Little Compton besides what he already had. To son Benjamin, land on easterly side of highway and half the rooms in my dwelling house and all husbandry tools. To wife Elizabeth, land westerly side of highway and the other half of rooms in house for life, and all my stock of neat cattle, horsekind, sheep, hogs, &c., and all household goods. To son Benjamin, at death of wife, the remainder of land and dwelling house, and he to pay my daughters Elizabeth, Mary and Innocent Head, £20 each within three years of wife's decease. To wife, negro man Jeffrey and negro woman Rose. To daughter Elizabeth, a little negro boy called Scipio.

Inventory, £629, 9*s.* 8*d.*, viz: apparel £30, silver money £78, 11*s.*, bills of credit £64, 4*s.* 6*d.*, bonds £186, 12*s.* 2*d.*, 3 feather beds, £30, bible and other books £1, 10*s.*, book called "Dolton's Country Justice" £1, 3 spinning wheels, loom, 3 silver spoons, 4 negroes £40, 32 head neat cattle £100, 5 horsekind £20, cider, corn, hogs £4, sheep £21, lambs, pigs, &c.

1739, Jun. 9. Will—proved 1748, Jul. 11. Widow Elizabeth. Ex. son Henry. She calls herself very aged. To sons Jonathan and Henry, 43 acres. To son Jonathan, 5*s.* To grandson William Head, son of Benjamin, 5*s.* To daughters Elizabeth Wilbur, Mary Cudburth, and Innocent Church, 5*s.*, each. To grandson Lovet Head, and Amey his wife, all my household stuff, and to said granddaughter Amey, a side saddle. To grandson Lovet, also confirmation of a deed already made of ten cows and a bull. To grandson Benjamin Cuthbert, £30. To son Henry, rest of real and personal.

III. { BENJAMIN, { b. / m. 1706, May 3. { d. 1717, Aug. 6. / DEBORAH BRIGGS, { b. 1693, Sep. 6. { d. 1773, Nov. of William & Elizabeth (Cook) Briggs. — Little Compton, R. I.

1. William,

1717, Aug. 3. Will—proved 1719, Mar. Exs. wife Deborah and brother-in-law William Briggs. Overseers, brother Jonathan Head and friend John Peckham. To wife, estate both real and personal while widow and what is yet in my mother's possession in case my mother die during wife's widowhood, that is the improvement of all for her and my child's maintenance. If wife marry again she to have her thirds as law allows, and no more. If she remain a widow till son William is of age, then to son all estate except a room in the house and convenient household stuff, and £20 per annum to wife while widow, paid by son William at age.

Inventory, £535, 9*s.*, viz: land and housing given Benjamin Head, by his father's will £400, apparel £20, 4 silver spoons, bills of credit £56, 13*s.*, 300 pounds new milk cheese £3, 15*s.*, warming pan, pewter, 2 spinning wheels, gun, 2 oxen, 6 cows, 5 two years, 2 yearlings, 15 calves, 4 horsekind, 14 sheep, &c.

IV. { ELIZABETH, { b. / m. 1710, Nov. 2. { d. 1734 + / BENJAMIN WILBUR, { b. { d. 1729. of William Wilbur.

1. Abigail, 1711, Sep. 9.
2. Henry, 1716, Aug. 29.
3. George, 1718, Sep. 23.
4. Joseph,
5. Walter,
6. Barsheba,
7. Elizabeth,
8. Mary,
9. Child,

V. { MARY, { b. / m. 1717, Aug. 7. { d. / WILLIAM CUTHBERT, { b. { d. of Cuthbert.

1. Benjamin,

VI. { INNOCENT, { b. / m. 1717, Aug. 7. { d. / NATHANIEL CHURCH, { b. 1693, Feb. 8. { d. of Joseph & Grace (Shaw) Church.

1. Alice, 1718, Jan. 24.
2. Abigail, 1719, Oct. 8.
3. Benjamin, 1722, Dec. 4.
4. Joseph 1724, Jul. 3.
5. Caleb, 1728, Apr. 28.
6. Deborah, 1729, Aug. 2.
7. Gamaliel, 1732, Feb. 5.
8. Betsey, 1734, Aug. 21.
9. Benjamin, 1737, Feb. 10.

HEARNDEN.

{ BENJAMIN, { b. / m. { d. 1687. / ELIZABETH WHITE, { b. { d. 1701 + of William & Elizabeth ( ) White.

(She m. (2) 1688 ± Richard Pray.)

Providence, R. I.

1662, Oct. 16. He bought of William and Elizabeth White of Boston, for £20, a house and lot of 25 acres in Providence, the money being paid by his wife Elizabeth Hearnden.

1662, Dec. 25. He sold rights in certain lands to Zachariah Rhodes.

1665, Feb. 19. He drew lot 86 in a division of lands.

1669, Jan. 20. His daughter Sarah's intentions of marriage with John Inman, were published, but he took another wife.

1670, May 4. His fine was remitted by Assembly, that had been imposed upon him by General Court of Trials.

1679, Jul. 1. Taxed 1*s.* 3*d.*

1680, Mar. 16. Upon his petition to the Assembly to remit sentence of General Court of Trials against his wife Elizabeth, he pleading his great poverty and the debility of himself and wife, &c., the said fine was absolutely remitted.

1684, May 26. He had 60 acres laid out to him.

1685, Apr. 20. He and wife Elizabeth deeded son Benjamin 60 acres with meadow, &c., he being destitute of a place of settlement.

1686, Mar. 3. He and wife Elizabeth deeded son Joseph, 67 acres, for his well being and settlement, part of the land being ten miles north of Providence.

1687, Feb. 1. Will—presented 1688, Apr. 4. Exx. wife Elizabeth. No further record found.

Inventory, £42, 7*s.* 4*d.* (1687, May 27).

1687, Sep. 1. Estate of deceased Benjamin Hearnden, taxed 4*s.* 2*d.*

1688, Oct. 20. His widow, now the wife of Richard Pray, deeded to her son Isaac Hearnden, the homestead, houses, orchard, &c., given her for life by will of her late husband (dated 1687, Feb. 1, of which she was executrix).

1701, Dec. 13. His widow (now also widow of Richard Pray), for £55 sold Joseph Whipple my dwelling house and 10 acres, being part of it land that formerly belonged to my father one William White, (who is now deceased but was formerly of Providence), and was bought of him by Benjamin Hearnden, and by last will of Benjamin, given me Elizabeth, for life and then to son Isaac, and the latter having deeded same to his mother.

I. { SARAH, { b. / m. 1675, May 15. { d. 1677, Apr. 2. / DAVID WHIPPLE, { b. 1656. { d. 1710, Dec. of John & Sarah ( ) Whipple.

1 David,

II. { ALICE, { b. 1652. / m. 1669, Dec. 25. { d. 1718 + / DANIEL BROWN, { b. { d. 1710, Sep. 29. of Chad & Elizabeth ( ) Brown.

1. Judah,
2. Jabez,
3. Sarah, 1677, Oct. 10.
4. Jeremiah,
5. Hallelujah,
6. Hosannah,
7. Jonathan,
8. Daniel,

III. { MARY, { b. / m. 1675, Oct. 14, { d. 1696 + / ANDREW EDMONDS, { b. 1639. { d. 1695. of Edmonds.

1. Mary, 1676, Oct. 20.
2. Sarah, 1678, Feb. 17.
3. William, 1681, Mar. 7.
4. Andrew, 1683, Jun. 17.
5. Joseph, 1687, Feb. 2.

IV. { BENJAMIN, { b. / m. { d. 1694, Apr. 18. / LYDIA, { b. { d. 1710, Jun. 14. of — Providence, R. I.

1. Benjamin,
2. John,
3. Dorothy,
4. Lydia,
5. Elizabeth,

1671, May. He took oath of allegiance.

1679, Jul. 1. Taxed 11¼*d.*

1681, May 4. He having lately shot at an Indian in the woods, for no other cause as he confessed but for that said Indian would not obey his word and stand at his command, and the Indian though having a gun, having not shot again but went peaceably away, only using some words by way of reproof, blaming him for his violence and cruelty—the Assembly therefore enacted that all his Majesty's subjects are hereby required to behave themselves peaceably towards the Indians in like manner as before the war, &c.

1687, Sep. 1. Taxed 3*s.*

1688. Ratable estate, 2 oxen, 5 cows, heifer, steer, yearling, horse, mare, 5 acres planting land, 5 acres English pasture, an acre of bog meadow, 50 acres unfenced.

1694, Apr. 17. Will—proved 1694, May 30. Exx. wife Lydia. To sons Benjamin and John, all lands and meadows south side of Westquadomscet Brook equally, but use thereof to their mother till they are of age. To wife for life the dwelling house, &c., on north side of river, and at her death to sons. To daughters Dorothy, Lydia and Elizabeth, six sheep at age of twenty-one. To wife Lydia, all movable estate and cattle and she to bring up the children.

Inventory, £29, 2*s.*, viz: 2 oxen, 2 cows, 2 heifers, calf, horse, 11 old sheep, 10 lambs, 3 small swine, 2 guns, axe, carpenter tools, household goods, &c.

1710, Jul. 10. Inventory of estate of widow Lydia, was ordered to be taken by Joseph Williams, Jr., ("he having married one of the daughters") and William Olney.

V. { JOSEPH, { b. / m. { d. 1694, Apr. 19. / SARAH, { b. { d. of — Providence, R. I.

1. Elizabeth, 1675, Jan.
2. Joseph,
3. Ebenezer, 1681, Jun. 21.
4. Job,

1671, May. He took oath of allegiance.

1681, May 25. He apprenticed his daughter Elizabeth to Peter Greene and wife, of Warwick, till eighteen, and states her birth to have been about the middle of January, 1675.

1684, May 26. He had 7 acres laid out.

1687, Sep. 1. Taxed 2*s.*

1688, Apr. 24. He sold William Hearnden 13 acres.

1694, May 30. Administration to widow Sarah, and it was desired that Pardon Tillinghast have the oversight of several young children, and give advice to her.

VI. { WILLIAM, { b. / m. (1) { d. 1727, Aug. 27. / ESTHER, { b. { d. of / m. (2) / DELIVERANCE, { b. { d. 1728. of — Providence, R. I.

1. Thomas, 1687, Mar. 17.
2. Elisha,
3. William,
4. Benjamin,
5. Abigail,
(2d wife).
6. Solomon,
7. Preserved,
8. Esther,
9. Keziah,

He was a shoemaker.

1682 May. He took oath of allegiance.

1687, Sep. 1. Taxed 1*s.* 3*d.*

1713, Jun. 16. Taxed 8*s.* 2*d.*

1724, Apr. 6. He sold Joseph Hearnden, 36 acres with house, &c., for £240.

1727, Jan. 17. Will—proved 1728, Feb. 12. Exx. wife Deliverance. To son Thomas, 2*s.*, and to sons Elisha, William and Benjamin, each 1*s.*, they having had. To son Solomon, 50 acres. To son Preserved, my homestead farm at death of his mother, half at my decease and half at hers. To daughter Abigail Tucker, 1*s.* To daughters Esther, Keziah, Meribah and Martha Hearnden, 40*s.* each. To wife Deliverance, half of homestead for life and all household goods and movables.

Inventory, £170, 14*s.* 2*d.*, viz: bed, &c., yoke of oxen, 3 cows, 2 heifers, calf, horse, corn, rye, oats, tobacco, flax, carpenter tools, warming pan, 2 spinning wheels, pair of cards, &c.

1728, Feb. 12. Administration on his estate was now given to son Preserved, as the executrix had deceased.

10. Meribah,
11. Martha,

VII. { JOHN, { b. / d. 1736 + — Providence, Scituate, R. I.
m. { b. / d. — of
———

1682, May. He took oath of allegiance.

1687, Sep. 1. Taxed 6*s.*

1688. Ratable estate, 2 cows, yearling, horse, mare, 28 acres woodland.

1713, Jun. 16. Taxed 5*s.*

1729, Jun. 8. He deeded eldest son John, for love, &c., 140 acres in Westquadnoid, and on the same date he deeded second son Josiah, 140 acres, and fifth son Stephen, 120 acres.

1731, Aug. 9. He deeded to third son Amos, for love, &c., 150 acres in Westquadnoid.

1736, Jun. 28. Scituate. He deeded son Jonathan, for love, &c., all homestead where I dwell in western part of Scituate, containing 120 acres.

1. John,
2. Josiah,
3. Amos,
4. Jonathan,
5. Stephen,

VIII. { THOMAS, { b. / d. — Providence, R. I.

HEARNDEN. 2d column. VIII. Thomas, d. 1722; m. Hannah. She was given permission from Council to put her children out with consent of brother-in-law William Hearnden, her husband being dead.

1682, May. He took oath of allegiance.

IX. { ISAAC, { b. / d. 1727. — Providence, R. I., Norwich, Ct.
m.
SARAH, { b. / d. 1728 + — of

1689, Feb. 10. He and wife Sarah, deeded to his mother Elizabeth Pray, homestall, house, orchard, &c., having lawful power to dispose of same by deed of gift from mother.

1696, Mar. 31. He sold Samuel Wilkinson, 50 acres and dwelling house, eight miles north of the harbor and near Pawtucket River, for £26.

1724, Jan. 7. Norwich. He sold Robert Currie of Providence, all rights of commonage and undivided land east of Seven Mile Line in Providence, appointed to me by last will of my honored father Benjamin Hearnden, deceased, and again repeated and confirmed, &c., by quit claim made by hand of mother, deceased.

1727, Sep. 3. Will—proved 1728, Aug. 16. Exx. wife Sarah. To her, dwelling house at Norwich and all movables. To eldest son Isaac, at death of his mother, certain land. To son Solomon, rest of lands and meadows at Norwich, he paying certain sums. To son John, 20*s.*, he having had already. To daughter Patience Whaley, £6. To daughters Jemima and Mary Bennett and Prudence Hearnden, £5 each. To granddaughter Eunice Bennett, youngest daughter of Sarah, deceased, 40*s.* at eighteen.

Inventory (taken 1727, Nov. 10), £227, 6*s.* 17*d.*, viz: apparel, books, including doctor's book, psalter, and testament, horse, mare, 3 cows, calf, land and building, £160, &c.

1. Isaac,
2. Solomon,
3. John,
4 Patience,
5. Jemima,
6. Mary,
7. Prudence,
8. Sarah,

HEATH.

{ JOHN, { b. / d. 1712 +
m.
ELIZABETH. { b. 1627, Jul. 13. / d. 1711, Mar. 13.

Portsmouth, East Greenwich, R. I.

1673. Freeman.

1677, Oct. 31. He and forty-seven others were granted 5,000 acres, to be called East Greenwich.

1679–80–82–1703. East Greenwich. Deputy.

1684. Town Clerk.

1687. Overseer of the Poor.

1688. Grand Jury.

1695, Jul. 2. He was appointed on a committee to propose a method for making a rate.

1712, Jan. 5. He deeded mansion house and 10 acres to John Rutenburg, of Warwick, on condition that he should be suffered to dwell in house for life, as also his servant girl Betty, and that house should be kept in repair by John Rutenburg, and £6 per year paid by latter to John Heath. At death of John Heath, Betty to still be allowed to stay in house for life, she paying £2 per year rent to John Rutenburg. On same date, he deeded servant girl Betty, for goodwill and faithful service she hath done me—all personal estate and movables within doors, and all other personal estate, except what was given to mulatto servant Ned—all to be hers at decease of grantor, if she continue faithful. To servant Ned, a pair of oxen, a good bed, all my small tools and half of horse kind after decease, to be given him by Betty, if he continues a faithful servant.

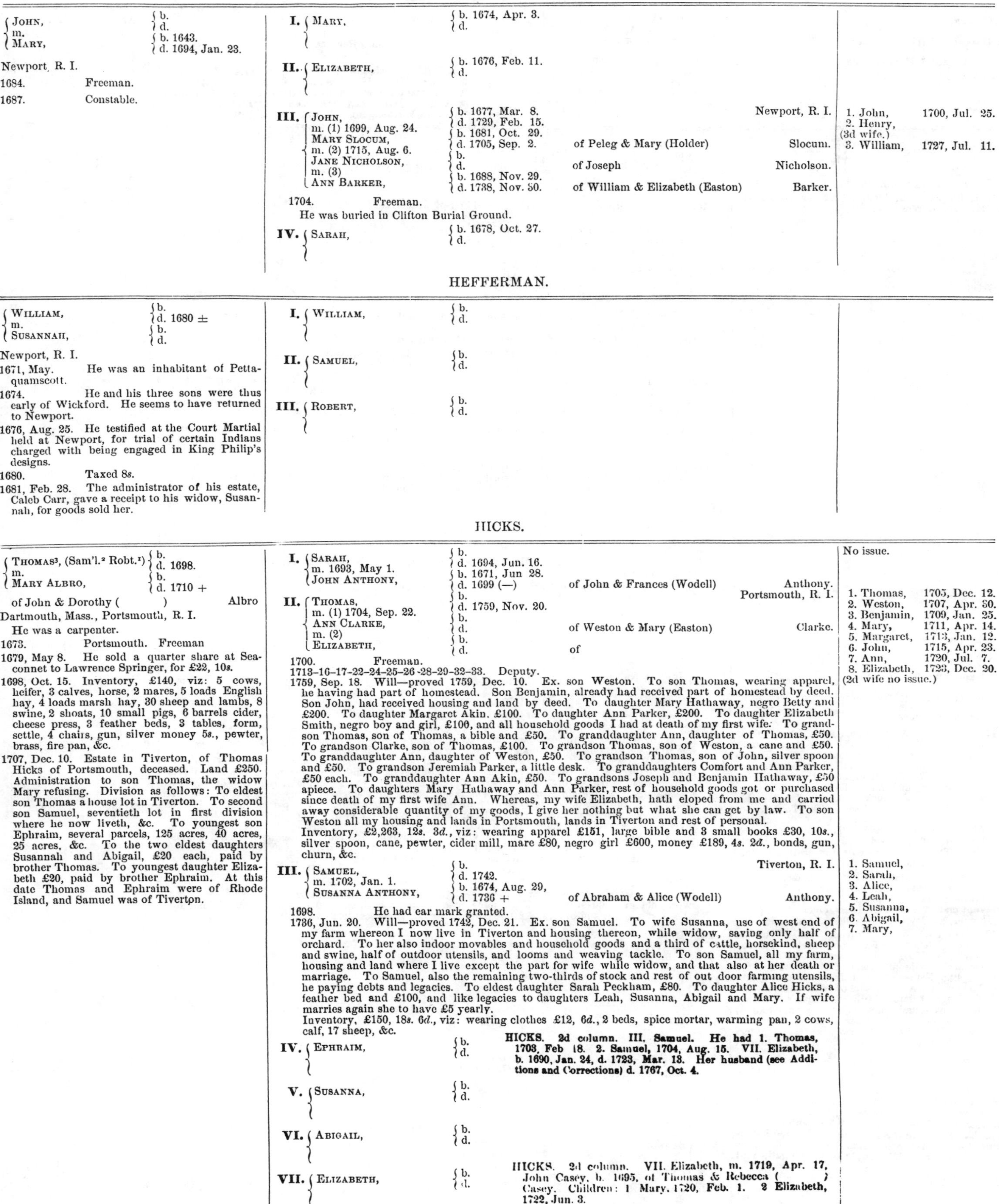

HEDLEY.

JOHN, { b. d.
m.
MARY, { b. 1643. d. 1694, Jan. 23.

Newport, R. I.

1684. Freeman.

1687. Constable.

I. MARY, { b. 1674, Apr. 3. d.

II. ELIZABETH, { b. 1676, Feb. 11. d.

III. JOHN, { b. 1677, Mar. 8. d. 1729, Feb. 15. Newport, R. I.
m. (1) 1699, Aug. 24.
MARY SLOCUM, { b. 1681, Oct. 29. d. 1705, Sep. 2. of Peleg & Mary (Holder) Slocum.
m. (2) 1715, Aug. 6.
JANE NICHOLSON, { b. d. of Joseph Nicholson.
m. (3)
ANN BARKER, { b. 1688, Nov. 29. d. 1738, Nov. 30. of William & Elizabeth (Easton) Barker.

1704. Freeman.
He was buried in Clifton Burial Ground.

1. John, 1700, Jul. 25.
2. Henry,
(3d wife.)
3. William, 1727, Jul. 11.

IV. SARAH, { b. 1678, Oct. 27. d.

HEFFERMAN.

WILLIAM, { b. d. 1680 ±
m.
SUSANNAH, { b. d.

Newport, R. I.

1671, May. He was an inhabitant of Pettaquamscott.

1674. He and his three sons were thus early of Wickford. He seems to have returned to Newport.

1676, Aug. 25. He testified at the Court Martial held at Newport, for trial of certain Indians charged with being engaged in King Philip's designs.

1680. Taxed 8*s*.

1681, Feb. 28. The administrator of his estate, Caleb Carr, gave a receipt to his widow, Susannah, for goods sold her.

I. WILLIAM, { b. d.

II. SAMUEL, { b. d.

III. ROBERT, { b. d.

HICKS.

THOMAS[3], (Sam'l.[2] Robt.[1]) { b. d. 1698.
m.
MARY ALBRO, { b. d. 1710 +

of John & Dorothy ( ) Albro

Dartmouth, Mass., Portsmouth, R. I.

He was a carpenter.

1673. Portsmouth. Freeman

1679, May 8. He sold a quarter share at Seaconnet to Lawrence Springer, for £22, 10*s*.

1698, Oct. 15. Inventory, £140, viz: 5 cows, heifer, 3 calves, horse, 2 mares, 5 loads English hay, 4 loads marsh hay, 30 sheep and lambs, 8 swine, 2 shoats, 10 small pigs, 6 barrels cider, cheese press, 3 feather beds, 3 tables, form, settle, 4 chairs, gun, silver money 5*s*., pewter, brass, fire pan, &c.

1707, Dec. 10. Estate in Tiverton, of Thomas Hicks of Portsmouth, deceased. Land £250. Administration to son Thomas, the widow Mary refusing. Division as follows: To eldest son Thomas a house lot in Tiverton. To second son Samuel, seventieth lot in first division where he now liveth, &c. To youngest son Ephraim, several parcels, 125 acres, 40 acres, 25 acres, &c. To the two eldest daughters Susannah and Abigail, £20 each, paid by brother Thomas. To youngest daughter Elizabeth £20, paid by brother Ephraim. At this date Thomas and Ephraim were of Rhode Island, and Samuel was of Tiverton.

I. SARAH, { b. d. 1694, Jun. 16.
m. 1693, May 1.
JOHN ANTHONY, { b. 1671, Jun 28. d. 1699 (—) of John & Frances (Wodell) Anthony.

No issue.

II. THOMAS, { b. d. 1759, Nov. 20. Portsmouth, R. I.
m. (1) 1704, Sep. 22.
ANN CLARKE, { b. d. of Weston & Mary (Easton) Clarke.
m. (2)
ELIZABETH, { b. d. of

1700. Freeman.

1713-16-17-22-24-25-26-28-29-32-33. Deputy.

1759, Sep. 18. Will—proved 1759, Dec. 10. Ex. son Weston. To son Thomas, wearing apparel, he having had part of homestead. Son Benjamin, already had received part of homestead by deed. Son John, had received housing and land by deed. To daughter Mary Hathaway, negro Betty and £200. To daughter Margaret Akin. £100. To daughter Ann Parker, £200. To daughter Elizabeth Smith, negro boy and girl, £100, and all household goods I had at death of my first wife. To grandson Thomas, son of Thomas, a bible and £50. To granddaughter Ann, daughter of Thomas, £50. To grandson Clarke, son of Thomas, £100. To grandson Thomas, son of Weston, a cane and £50. To granddaughter Ann, daughter of Weston, £50. To grandson Thomas, son of John, silver spoon and £50. To grandson Jeremiah Parker, a little desk. To granddaughters Comfort and Ann Parker, £50 each. To granddaughter Ann Akin, £50. To grandsons Joseph and Benjamin Hathaway, £50 apiece. To daughters Mary Hathaway and Ann Parker, rest of household goods got or purchased since death of my first wife Ann. Whereas, my wife Elizabeth, hath eloped from me and carried away considerable quantity of my goods, I give her nothing but what she can get by law. To son Weston all my housing and lands in Portsmouth, lands in Tiverton and rest of personal.

Inventory, £2,263, 12*s*. 3*d*., viz: wearing apparel £151, large bible and 3 small books £30, 10*s*., silver spoon, cane, pewter, cider mill, mare £80, negro girl £600, money £189, 4*s*. 2*d*., bonds, gun, churn, &c.

1. Thomas, 1705, Dec. 12.
2. Weston, 1707, Apr. 30.
3. Benjamin, 1709, Jan. 25.
4. Mary, 1711, Apr. 14.
5. Margaret, 1713, Jan. 12.
6. John, 1715, Apr. 23.
7. Ann, 1720, Jul. 7.
8. Elizabeth, 1723, Dec. 20.
(2d wife no issue.)

III. SAMUEL, { b. d. 1742. Tiverton, R. I.
m. 1702, Jan. 1.
SUSANNA ANTHONY, { b. 1674, Aug. 29, d. 1736 + of Abraham & Alice (Wodell) Anthony.

1698. He had ear mark granted.

1736, Jun. 20. Will—proved 1742, Dec. 21. Ex. son Samuel. To wife Susanna, use of west end of my farm whereon I now live in Tiverton and housing thereon, while widow, saving only half of orchard. To her also indoor movables and household goods and a third of cattle, horsekind, sheep and swine, half of outdoor utensils, and looms and weaving tackle. To son Samuel, all my farm, housing and land where I live except the part for wife while widow, and that also at her death or marriage. To Samuel, also the remaining two-thirds of stock and rest of out door farming utensils, he paying debts and legacies. To eldest daughter Sarah Peckham, £80. To daughter Alice Hicks, a feather bed and £100, and like legacies to daughters Leah, Susanna, Abigail and Mary. If wife marries again she to have £5 yearly.

Inventory, £150, 18*s*. 6*d*., viz: wearing clothes £12, 6*d*., 2 beds, spice mortar, warming pan, 2 cows, calf, 17 sheep, &c.

1. Samuel,
2. Sarah,
3. Alice,
4. Leah,
5. Susanna,
6. Abigail,
7. Mary,

IV. EPHRAIM, { b. d.

HICKS. 2d column. III. Samuel. He had 1. Thomas, 1703, Feb 18. 2. Samuel, 1704, Aug. 15. VII. Elizabeth, b. 1690, Jan. 24, d. 1723, Mar. 13. Her husband (see Additions and Corrections) d. 1767, Oct. 4.

V. SUSANNA, { b. d.

VI. ABIGAIL, { b. d.

VII. ELIZABETH, { b. d.

HICKS. 2d column. VII. Elizabeth, m. 1719, Apr. 17, John Casey, b. 1695, of Thomas & Rebecca ( ) Casey. Children: 1 Mary, 1720, Feb. 1. 2 Elizabeth, 1722, Jun. 3.

Owen, m. [Samuel. **Seaborn Billings** (w. of
b. d. b. 1640, Jun. 4. d.
of Richard & Mary (Clarke) Tew.
Newport, R. I.

I. (**Richard**, m. —, Apr. 2. **Elizabeth Hiscox**,
b. d. b. d. of William & Rebecca ( ) Hiscox. Newport, R. I.

1701. Freeman.

1. Richard,
2. Anna, 169–, Sep. 6.
3. Ephraim, —, Aug. 24.
4. Henry, —, Apr. 16.
5. Anna, —, Jul. 22.
6. Amey, —, May 29.
7. William, —, Nov. 25.
8. Elizabeth, —, May 4.

HIGGINS. 2d column. I. Richard, d. 1744. His wife's name was Edith. 1743, Dec. 26. Will-proved, 1744, May 7. He mentions son William, deceased son Ephraim's daughter Edith, daughters, Anne Sears, Amey Bissell, Elizabeth Weeden, &c. He was a blacksmith.

HILL

Jonathan, m. **Mary**,
b. d. 1690 (—) b. d.

Warwick, Portsmouth (Prudence Island), R. I.

1661, Jun. 24. The birth of his son Henry was recorded at Warwick.

I. (**Robert**, m. **Mary Pearce**,
b. d. 1711 (—) b. d. of John & Mary ( ) Pearce. Warwick, Portsmouth (Prudence Island), R. I.

(She m. (2) James Sweet.)

1690, Jul. 12. He, calling himself son and heir of Jonathan, deceased, sold Peter Greene 6 acres for £4, 15*s*.

1711, Sep. 17. His widow, now the wife of James Sweet, had a legacy from her mother's will, and at her decease the seven children of Mary, by her former husband Robert Hill, deceased, were to have certain estate.

1. Jonathan,
2. Robert,
3. Daniel,
4. William,
5. John,
6. Susanna,
7. Abigail,

II. (**Jonathan**, m. ——
b. 1657. d. 1731, Sep. 5. b. d. of Portsmouth (Prudence Island), R. I.

1695, Dec. 24. He, calling himself aged about thirty-eight years, deposed as to a conversation between Caleb Carr and son John.

1698, Dec. 24. He and others of Prudence, were parties to a suit.

1703, Jul. 6. He bought of Philip Sweet, quarter of a farm in Coweset, for £50.

1721, Jan. 16. He deeded son Thomas, of Swanzey, for love, &c., 105 acres in Warwick.

1731, Sep. 15. Administration to Jonathan and Caleb Hill. Inventory, £791, 3*s*. 6*d*., viz: wearing apparel, buckles and buttons £30, 5*s*., negro Jane £50, Dinah £50, boy Cuffee £60, child Experience £35, nine years' time of negro Prince £40, 2 spinning wheels, worsted comb, small wheel, 3 pairs of wool cards, 6 cows, 2 steers, bull, 220 sheep, money due from Thomas Hill £40, &c.

Receipts were given the administrators by Daniel Pearce (who married Patience Hill, 1708, Oct.), Thomas Hill, John Allen (who had married Rebecca Hill), Mary Lawton (who married Isaac Lawton, 1705, Dec. 25), Ebenezer Hill and Sarah Hill; all signing as having had their parts of estate.

1748, Dec. 22. His son Caleb's will (proved 1755, Feb. 9), mentions wife Ruth, brothers Thomas, and Ebenezer, sisters Mary Langworthy, Patience Pearce, Sarah Mills, Rebecca Allen, brother Jonathan, deceased, and sons of latter, viz: Barnard, Jonathan and Nathaniel.

1. Jonathan,
2. Caleb,
3. Mary,
4. Patience,
5. Rebecca,
6. Thomas, 1692.
7. Ebenezer,
8. Sarah,

III. (**Henry**, m. **Elizabeth**.
b. 1661, Jun. 24. d. b. d. of Kings Town, East Greenwich, R. I.

1687, Sep. 6. Taxed 1*s*.

1724, Oct. 12. East Greenwich. He and wife Elizabeth, sold to Henry Gardiner, of South Kingstown, 50 acres for £95.

1728, Jun. 23. His daughter Mary married William Nichols.

1. Mary,

HILLIARD.

William, m. **Deborah**,
b. d. 1714, Jan. 24. b. d. 1718, Feb. 15.

Little Compton, R. I.

He was a cooper.

1713, Dec. 15 Will—proved 1714, Feb. 1. Exx. wife Deborah. To wife, use and improvement of all estate, real and personal, for life. To son David, at death of wife, half of all housing and land. To son Jonathan, at death of wife, half of all housing and land. To daughter Deborah, wife of John Paddock, £10. To daughter Esther, wife of Jeremiah Gears, £10. To daughter Mary, wife of John Palmer, £10. To daughter Abigail Hilliard, £15. To daughter Sarah Hilliard, £10 and bed. To wife, rest of movables. The legacies to be paid at death of wife.

Inventory, £866, 3*s*. 2*d*., viz: apparel £18, 7*s*., mare, housing, land and orchard, &c. £600, 2 linen wheels, pair of oxen, 2 steers, 8 cows, 4 yearlings, colt, 16 sheep, 4 swine, Indian servant maid £10, pewter, brass, churn, hour glass, 3 guns, sundry books 10*s*. 9*d*., cheese press, &c.

1717, Jan. 23. Will — proved 1718, Mar. 3. Widow Deborah. Ex. son David. To son David, 2*s*. To son Jonathan, 2*s*. To daughter Deborah, wife of John Paddock, 50*s*. To daughter Esther, wife of Jeremiah Gears, 20*s*. To daughter Abigail, wife of Warren Gibbs, 5*s*. To daughter Sarah Hilliard, a cow and all my iron, pewter, and brass. To four grandchildren, children of my daughter, Mary Palmer, deceased, 10*s*. apiece. To two youngest daughters rest of estate, after debts, &c., viz: to Abigail and Sarah.

Inventory, £100, 16*s*.

HILLIARD. 2d column. I. David. Children, 6, Oliver, 1709. 7, Joseph, 1711. 8, Dorothy, 1713. V. Abigail, Children, 1, Phebe, 1714, Nov. 11. 2, Nathaniel Warren, 1716, Jan. 13. 3, Deborah, 1717, Dec. 19. 4, Thomas, 1721, June 15. 5, Ambrose, 1722, Feb. 25. 6, Jabez, 1725, May 10. 7, John, 1727, May 10. 8, Abigail, 1731, Apr. 23.

I. (**David**, m. (1) 1699, Jul. 13. **Joanna Andros**, m. (2) **Susanna Luther**,
b. d. 1749, Jan. 11. b. d. 1716, Apr. 14. of Andros. b. d. 1777, Apr. 6. of Luther. Little Compton, R. I.

He was called captain at time of his death.

1748, Aug. 1. Will—proved 1749, Feb. 7. Exx. wife Susanna. To wife, my pew in meeting house, negro girl Katie and a third of personal (except a bond due me from son William, for £600, and bond due from son Benoni, for £300, and my farming tools and shop tools), and while widow, the profits of house I now dwell in, except great chamber and of certain land. To son William, £600 bond he gave me for the part of farm he lives on in Stonington, Conn., he paying certain sums. To son Oliver, westerly part of my farm I now dwell on, &c. To four grandchildren (children of deceased son Joseph), £85 to each, at age. To son Benoni, bond of £300, he paying certain sums, &c. To sons Joshua and David, northerly part of my home farm, &c., and remaining part of farm and house which I gave to their mother. To son Joshua, new gun and old sword. To son David, old gun and silver hilted sword. To sons Joshua and David, all farming tools and shop tools. To daughter Deborah Wheaton, £5 (having had). To four grandchildren (children of daughter Priscilla Palmer, deceased), £40 divided at age. To daughter Hannah, wife of John Wilbur, £30. To daughter Abigail Hilliard, a bed which was her sister Mary's, and £100, and great chamber in dwelling house. To Church of Christ, £10. To four youngest children, Joshua, David, Hannah and Abigail, rest of personal.

Inventory, £2,507, 4*s*. 4*d*., viz: apparel £82, 18*s*. 4*d*., 2 canes, shoe buckles, new gun, silver hilted sword, old gun, old sword, desk, warming pan, woolen wheel, cards, 6 new foot wheels, 2 old foot wheels, negro girl and bedding £210, 4 cows, 2 oxen, 3 young cattle, 2 swine, &c.

1. Deborah, 1700, Apr. 4.
2. Lydia, 1702, Oct. 4.
3. William, 1703, Oct. 28.
4. Priscilla, 1705, Nov. 2.
5. John, 1707, Nov. 17.
6 Oliver,
7. Joseph,
8. Benoni, 1716, Mar. 12.

(2d wife.)

9 Mary, 1718, Jun. 23.
10. Joshua, 1719, Oct. 27.
11. Hannah, 1721, Oct. 11.
12. Samuel, 1723, Mar. 19.
13. David, 1726, Sep. 21.
14. Susanna, 1730, Jun. 9.
15. Abigail, 1732, Oct. 11.

II. (**Deborah**, m. 1706, Nov. 11. **John Paddock**,
b. d. b. d of John & Ann (Jones) Paddock.

III. (**Esther**, m. **Jeremiah Gears**,
b. d. b. d. 1721. of George & Sarah (Allyn) Gears.

1. Oliver,
2. Hannah,
3. Esther,
4. Zebulon,
5. Ziporah,
6. Jerusha,

IV. (**Mary**, m. 1705, Dec. 25. **John Palmer**,
b. 1687, Apr. 3. d. 1717, (—). b. 1687, Nov. 24. d. of John & Elizabeth ( ) Palmer.

1. Bridget, 1706, Mar. 17.
2. Amey, 1708, May 24.
3. Deborah, 1710, Jul. 30.
4. John, 1712, Oct. 30.

V. (**Abigail**, m. 1714, Apr. 25. **Warren Gibbs**,
b. 1690, Jul 12. d. b. d. of Gibbs.

VI. (**Sarah**,
b. 1692, Jun. 28. d.

VII. (**Jonathan**, m. **Abigail**,
b. 1696, Nov. 8. d. b. d. 1741, Oct. 5. of Stonington, Conn.

1. David, 1718, Sep. 3.
2. Azariah, 1719, Nov. 30.
3. Joanna, 1722, May 24.
4. Isaac, 1726, Oct. 2.
5. John, 1729, Mar. 12.
6. Ambrose, 1731, Feb. 6.

HILLIARD. 2d column. VII. Jonathan m. Abigail Wilbur b. 1697, Apr. 1, of William & —— (Tallman) Wilbur.

HISCOX.

{ William, { b. 1638,
{ m. { d. 1704, May 24.
{ Rebecca, { b.
{ d.

Newport, R. I.

1671. Freeman.

1671, Jun. 7. Juryman.

1671, Dec. 16. In a letter from Samuel Hubbard of Newport, to his children at Westerly, an account is given of the differences between those who held to the Seventh Day views and the rest of the congregation.

"So it was alleged because some keeping 7th day or sabbath, either they in error or we." Arguments having been used those opposed to the observance "replied fiercely, it was a tumult. J. Torrey stopped them at last."

1671, Dec. 23. Mr. Hubbard writes: "We entered into a church covenant the 23d day Dec. 1671, viz: William Hiscox, Stephen Mumford, Samuel Hubbard, Roger Baster, sister Hubbard, sister Mumford, sister Rachel Langworthy," &c. Mr. Hiscox became pastor of this church, thus formed, and known as the Third or Seventh Day Baptist Church.

1676, Apr. 4. It was voted by Assembly: "That in these troublesome times and straits in this colony, this Assembly desiring to have the advice and concurrence of the most judicious inhabitants, if it may be had for the good of the whole, do desire at their next sitting the company and counsel of," sixteen persons, among whom was William Hiscox.

1680. Taxed 9s.

1680, Feb. 1. He wrote a letter with Samuel Hubbard, to church in Boston, in which they say that William Davol, James Man and Thomas Clarke refused to commune with the church while they walked with it, and that Mr. Holmes hastened their separation by his sermon in 1671.

1683, Oct. 20. In a letter of this date from Samuel Hubbard, of Newport, to William Gibson at New London, he mentions Rebecca Hiscox, who must have been the wife of William.

1702, Mar. 4. He was a proprietor in the common lands.

1703-4. General Treasurer.

He was buried in Newport.

I. { Elizabeth, { b.
{ m. ——, Apr. 2. { d. **HISCOX. 2d column. I. Edith, not Elizabeth.**
{ Richard Higgins, { b.
{ d. of Owen & Seaborn (Tew) Higgins.

1. Richard,
2. Anna, 169–, Sep. 6.
3. Ephraim, ——, Aug. 24.
4. Henry, ——, Apr. 16.
5. Anna, ——, Jul. 22.
6. Amey, ——, May 29.
7. William, ——, Nov. 25.
8. Elizabeth, ——, May 4.

II. { Thomas, { b. 1686. Newport, Westerly, R. I.
{ m. (1) 1703, Oct. 31. { d. 1773, May 20.
{ Bethiah Clarke, { b. 1678, Apr. 11.
{ { d. 1756. of Joseph & Bethiah (Hubbard) Clarke.
{ m. (2)
{ Patience Beebe, { b.
{ d. of Samuel Beebe.

He was a cordwainer.

1706. He united with the church.

1709. Westerly. Freeman.

1712 to 1772. Town Treasurer.

1714-18-20-26-27-34-36-39-40-41. Deputy.

1716. Town Clerk.

1716. Deacon. He also served the church as clerk.

1727. Elder. He was confirmed this year, having been chosen eight years before.

1750. He was called to assist Joseph Maxson in his pastorate.

1. William, 1705, May 31.
2. Ephraim, 1707, Jun. 2.
3. Edith, 1709, Sep. 6.
4. Bethiah,
5. Mary, 1713, Jul. 12.
6. Thomas, 1715, May 7.
7. Joseph, 1717, Apr. 22.
8. Hannah, 1720, Jan. 22.

HOBSON.

{ Henry, { b.
{ m. { d. 1668 (—)
{ Mary, { b.
{ d. 1668 +

Newport, R. I.

1654. Commissioner.

1656, Mar. 17. There being a presentment standing upon a book of records against him, it was ordered by the Court of Commissioners that said presentment should not be prosecuted except by express order from his Highness the Lord Protector.

1658, Mar. 13. He was acquitted of unjust charges but was to pay the officers' fees.

1660, Mar. 7. His servant Philip Pointing, acknowledged in Plymouth Colony Court that he had wronged his master Henry Hobson, of Rhode Island. He was to have had £10 in English goods for his services for a year. He staid twelve weeks and was unfaithful, wronging his master in several particulars. When sent for a cask of liquor he drew it out and disposed of it amongst his consorts, two quarts and upwards, and put water in the cask, and he hid his master's wedges and said he could not find them, and afterwards told Wood that his master said he stole them, which provoked Wood to violently fall out with his master and strike him to the danger of his life. This servant also defamed his master, and raised false reports, &c., saying that he had stolen hogs and a steer; for which he said he was sorry and willing to acknowledge this in public court. The court accordingly found that Henry Hobson was much damnified in his name and estate and he was allowed £4 5s., in his hands of Philip Pointing, as an award, and what had been paid Philip was to go for full satisfaction for service.

1661, Mar. 5. He was to be apprehended by order of the Plymouth Court, who appointed John Brown and Captain Willett to do the service and to take security for his appearance at court to answer for his derision of authorities in counterfeiting the solemnizing of the marriage of Robert Whitcom and Mary Cudworth.

1668, Apr. 21. Mary Hobson, daughter of deceased Henry Hobson, was with consent of her mother Mary, indentured for five years to Latham Clarke, Sr.

I. { Mary, { b.
{ { d.

HOBSON. 2d column I. Mary, d. 1718, (—). m. Thomas Lillibridge, b. 1662, d. 1724. Children, I. Katherine, and doubtless others, though part of the children of Thomas Lillibridge were by his 2d wife, Sarah. II. Henry, d. 1718 ±. 1718 ± will. Ex. Robert Wilcox. "I give and bequeath unto my cousin Robert Wilcox (husband unto my cousin Katharine, the daughter of my sister Mary Lillibridge deceased), my great seal ring, my silver hilted sword, and my silver headed cane." Other items illegible.

ROBERT, b. 1626. d. 1696, May 10.
m. 1665, Aug. 3.
RACHEL SHOTTEN, b. d. 1696 +
of Samson & Alice ( ) Shotten.
New York, Portsmouth, R. I.

1657, Jun. He came to America this month.

1657, Aug. 1. New York. He was beaten and chained for his Quakerism soon after his arrival here and probably did not tarry many years in this jurisdiction.

1667, Oct. 7. Portsmouth. Upon motion of Robert Hodgson, husband of Rachel, only child of Samson Shotten, of Portsmouth, some years since deceased, in regard to lands of Shotten, the Town Council examined and made diligent search and cannot find Shotten made any will, but died intestate, and find Rachel sole heir to deceased, and administration was given Robert Hodgson and wife Rachel therefore.

1673. Freeman.

1676, Apr. 4. He was appointed on a committee to procure boats for colony's defence for the present. There were to be four boats with five or six men to a boat. On the same date it was voted: "that in these troublesome times and straits in this colony, this Assembly desiring to have the advice and concurrence of the most judicious inhabitants, if it may be had for the good of the whole, do desire at their next sitting the company and counsel of" Mr. Benedict Arnold and fifteen others, including Robert Hodgson.

1676, Apr. 11. He was one of the commissioners appointed "to take care and order the several watches and wards on this island and appoint the places."

1683, Aug. 10. He and wife Rachel sold John Anthony two lots of three acres and nine acres respectively, with buildings, &c., for £50.

1686. Deputy.

1696, Apr. 22. Will—proved 1696, May 19. Exx. wife Rachel. Overseers, John Coggeshall and Benjamin Hall. To son Robert, all my land and buildings which came to me from his mother, my said loving wife, except land sold, and two acres given wife. To son Robert, also land in Warwick, purchased from grandfather Samson Shotten, except land sold. To son Robert he further gave all wearing clothes, farming tools, two yearling steers, a silver spoon, and a silver seal, on condition he pay his sister Alice a legacy. To wife, a room while widow, privilege of summer fruit in orchard, ten apple trees and the keep by her son for her use of a cow, ten sheep, and a horse, with £10 paid her yearly by son, and privilege of firewood. To daughter Alice Hodgson, £40. To daughter Mary, land bought of Thomas Wood, in Portsmouth. The two daughters to have use of a chamber while unmarried.

The Friends' Records of Portsmouth, call him an "ancient friend and traveller in God's truth" and state that he died near seventy years of age.

I. MARY, b. 1666, Aug. 6. d.

II. ALICE, b. 1668, Apr. d.

III. ROBERT, b. d. Portsmouth, R. I.
m.
SARAH BORDEN, b. 1680, Dec. 29. d. of Matthew & Sarah (Clayton) Borden,
1. Robert, 1698, Jan. 13.

HOLDEN.

RANDALL, b. 1612. d. 1692, Aug. 23.
m. 1648.
FRANCES DUNGAN, b. 1630 ± d. 1697.
of William & Frances (Latham) Dungan.
Salisbury, Wilts Co., Eng., Warwick, R. I.

1637, Mar. 4. He and Roger Williams were witnesses to deed of Aquidneck, &c., from Canonicus and Miantonomi to William Coddington, &c., for forty fathoms of white beads, and ten coats and twenty hoes to be given by Miantonomi to present inhabitants, who were to remove before winter.

1638, Mar. 7. Portsmouth. One of the nineteen signers of a compact at Portsmouth. "We whose names are underwritten, do here solemnly in the presence of Jehovah, incorporate ourselves into a Bodie Politick, and as he shall help, will submit our persons, lives and estates unto our Lord Jesus Christ, the King of Kings and Lord of Lords, and to all those perfect and most absolute laws of his, given us in his holy word of truth, to be guided and judged thereby."

1638. Marshal. Also elected Corporal.

He had a grant of 5 acres same year.

1641, Mar. 16. Disfranchised with three others and their names cancelled from Roll of Freemen of Newport.

1642, Mar. 17. It was ordered that if he and four others came upon the island armed, they should be disarmed and give surety for good behavior. The same year, he and others desiring to be reunited, "are readily embraced by us."

1643, Jan. 12. Warwick. He and ten others bought of Miantonomi, for 144 fathoms of wampum, tract of land called Shawomet (Warwick).

1643, Sep. 12. He, with others of Warwick, was notified to appear at General Court at Boston,

I. FRANCES, b. 1649, Sep. 29. d. 1679.
m. 1671, Dec. 1.
JOHN HOLMES, b. 1649. d. 1712, Oct. 2. of Obadiah & Catharine ( ) Holmes.
1. John, 1672.
2. Catharine, 1673.

II. ELIZABETH, b. 1652, Aug. d.
m. 1674, Jul. 16.
JOHN RICE, b. 1646. d. 1731, Jan. 6. of Rice.
1. John, 1675.
2. Randall,

III. MARY, b. 1654, Aug. d.
m. 1671, Dec. 1.
JOHN CARDER, b. d. 1700, Oct. 26. of Richard & Mary ( ) Carder.
1. John, 1673, Mar. 6.
2. Mary,
3. William,
4. Richard,
5. Sarah,
6. Joseph.

IV. JOHN, b. 1656, Jan. d. Warwick R. I.

1677, Oct. 31. He and forty-seven others were granted 5,000 acres, to be called East Greenwich.

V. SARAH, b. 1658, Feb. d. 1731.
m.
JOSEPH STAFFORD, b. 1648, Mar. 21. d. 1697 + of Thomas & Elizabeth ( ) Stafford.
1. Stukeley,
2. Joseph,
3. John,
4. Frances,
5. Elizabeth,
6. Mary,
7. Sarah,
8. Margaret,

VI. RANDALL, b. 1660, Apr. d. 1726, Sep. 13. Warwick, R. I.
m. 1687, Jan. 27.
BETHIAH WATERMAN, b. 1664 ± d. 1742, Jul. 23. of Nathaniel & Susanna (Carder) Waterman.
1. John, 1687, Oct. 26.
2. Wait, 1690, Feb. 26.
3. Susanna, 1692, Jan. 21.
4. Randall, 1694, Feb. 2.
5. Wait, 1696, Sep. 2.
6. Mary, 1699, Mar 15.
7. Frances, 1701, Sep. 29.

1696-99-1700-4-14-15-21. Deputy.

1703, May 12. He was a member of commission who signed agreement with Connecticut commissioners in settlement of boundaries between the two colonies.

1705-6-7-8-9-10-11-12-13-15-16-17-18-19-20-21-22-23-24-25. Assistant.

1706. Major for the Main.

1708, Apr. He was appointed on committee on vacant lands at Narragansett.

1714-15. Speaker of House of Deputies.

1718, Nov. 19. Will—proved 1726, Nov. 5. Ex. son Randall. To son John, land at Seven Men's Farm, in Warwick, and two other parcels. To daughter Susannah, £100 in care of wife, for Susan-to hear complaint of two Indian sachems—Pomham and Socconocco, as to "some unjust and injurious dealing toward them by yourselves." The Warwick men declined to obey the summons, declaring that they were legal subjects of the King of England, and beyond the limits of Massachusetts, to whom they would acknowledge no subjection.

Soldiers were soon sent, who besieged the settlers in a fortified house. In a parley it was now said "that they held blasphemous errors which they must repent of" or go to Boston for trial, and they were soon carried thence.

1643, Nov. 3. Having been brought with others before the court, charged with heresy and sedition, they were sentenced to be confined during the pleasure of the court, and should they break jail or preach their heresies or speak against church or state, on conviction they should die. He was sent to the prison at Salem.

1644, Mar. He was released from prison, (but banished both from Massachusetts and Warwick), and same year went to England with Samuel Gorton and John Greene, to obtain redress for their wrongs.

1646, Sep. 13. He and John Greene landed in Boston with a safe conduct through that territory from the Commissioners of Plantations, having obtained the desired vindication of rights of Warwick settlers.

1647, Aug. 8. Town Council. He was frequently Moderator of Town Meetings, and held the office of Town Treasurer, &c.

1647–53–54–55–56–57–58–64–65–76. Assistant.

1648, Aug. 15. In a letter of this date from William Arnold, of Pawtuxet, to the Governor of Massachusetts, some light is thrown upon the differences between the Warwick and Pawtuxet settlers, who were at strife some years. Randall Holden warned Pomham to appear at the court at Plymouth, to answer for some Indians who had been engaged in a brawl with Warwick men, but Pomham answered he "would appeal only to have his cause tried by the court of Massachusetts." The Pawtuxet settlers at this time and for ten years after, were subject to Massachusetts government, and seem to have espoused the cause of Pomham as against the Warwick men.

1651, Feb. 3. He and three others agreed with town to build a mill at their own cost, and to grind the town's corn for two quarts in a bushel, the town granting them a lot for their encouragement.

1652–54–55–57–58–59–60–62–63. Commissioner.

1654, Jul. 13. He and Ezekiel Holliman, on behalf of Warwick inhabitants, bought Potowomet of Indian Sachem Taccomanan, for £15 in wampum peage, "only I am to receive the value of one coat of such cloth as the Indians do now commonly use to wear, annually, as a gratuity, hereafter."

1655. Freeman.

1666–67–69–70–71–72–73–75–80–86. Deputy.

1669, Jun. 24. He, aged fifty-seven or thereabouts, testified about the gift of Dyer's Island to William Dyer.

1671. He was authorized with others to make assessments on towns for arrears of taxes.

1676, Apr. 4. Voted: "That in these troublesome times and straits in this colony, the Assembly, desiring to have the advice and concurrence of the most judicious inhabitants, if it may be had for the good of the whole, do desire at their sitting the company and counsel of" sixteen persons, among whom was Captain Randall Holden.

1679. He was in England this year and wrote a letter with John Greene, about Mount Hope, to the Commissioners of Trade. The expenses of himself and John Greene, amounting to £60, were ordered paid by Assembly.

1681. He sold 750 acres to Stephen Arnold, for £119, 5*s*.

1683. He was appointed on a committee to draft a letter to the King.

1687–88. Justice of Court of Common Pleas.

Perhaps his daughter Frances, had one or two children that are accredited to her husband by his second wife.

nah's use, and at latter's death, to other children of testator. To daughters Wait, Mary and Frances Holden, £100 each and a feather bed, and riding horse also to Wait. To wife, half of rest of real and personal for life, while widow, but if she marry, only £200. To son Randall, other half of real and personal, and at death of wife, her half, he keeping a riding horse for his mother. To him also, a feather bed. If wife married, Randall to have her part then.

Inventory, bonds £549, 15*s*. 9*d*., feather beds, bible and other books £6, 11*s*., 2 great chairs and other chairs, 4 barrels of cider, 3 barrels of beer, 7 small swine and 3 goats in the woods, 2 swine in pen, 135 sheep in woods and 80 lambs, pair of oxen, 10 cows, pair of steers, 3 two year old, 3 yearlings, 4 calves, a bull, 2 horses, 4 mares, 2 colts, 30 fat sheep, gold ring, gun, sword, &c.

1726, Dec. 7. Deed from William Holden, Wait Holden, Thomas Rice, Mary Rice, John Low and Frances Low, to their brother, Randall Holden, of certain land.

1737, Aug. 8. Will—proved 1742, Jul. 31. Widow Bethiah. Exs. sons-in-law William Holden and Thomas Rice. To son John, biggest silver cup, pair of money scales, &c. To son Randall, pair of iron dogs, chest, &c. To daughter Susannah Holden, use of bed for life. To son John, daughter Wait, wife of William Holden, daughter Mary Rice, wife of Thomas, and to three children of Frances Low, deceased (viz: Anthony, Mary and Frances Low), one quarter each of all the rest of estate, both real and personal.

Inventory, £201, 11*s*. 6*d*.

VII. MARGARET, { b. 1663, Jan. / d. 1740.
m.
JOHN ELDRED, { b. / d. 1724. of Samuel & Elizabeth ( ) Eldred.

1. James,
2. Thomas,
3. Samuel,
4. Robert,
5. Anthony,
6. William,
7. Margaret,
8. Abigail,
9. Barbara,

HOLDEN. 2d column. VIII. Charles. His widow, d. 1756.

VIII. CHARLES, { b. 1666, Mar. 22. / d. 1717, Jul. 21. Warwick, R. I.
m.
CATHARINE GREENE, { b. 1665, Aug. 15. / d. of John & Ann (Almy) Greene.

1. Catharine.
2. Charles, 1695, Sep. 24.
3. Frances,
4. Anthony,
5. Ann,
6. William,
7. John,

1702. He gave 3*s*. toward building Quaker meeting house at Mashapaug.

1710–16. Deputy. He bore the title of Lieutenant.

1717, Jul. 12. Will—proved 1717, Aug. 17. Exx. wife Catharine. To her, half of dwelling house, lands, meadows, orchard, &c. To son John, other half of homestead and half of movables, and at death of wife, her part of homestead also, he paying my son William, £10. To son Anthony Holden, 95 acres adjoining homestead, he paying my son Charles, £5. To sons Charles and William, equally, rest of lands and meadows. To daughter Frances Bennett, £5, and like amount to daughters Ann Low and Catharine Rhodes.

Inventory, £187, 12*s*. 8*d*., viz: 2 beds, table cloth, towels, 2 tables, 7 chairs, loom, spinning wheel, linen wheel, gun, pair of scales, plate £8, 6*s*., 2 pair of oxen, 8 cows, 2 two years, 3 yearlings, 4 calves, a bull, 4 horsekind, 4 swine, 13 younger swine, leather in tan vat, cider mill, &c.

IX. BARBARA, { b. 1668, Jul. 2. / d. 1707.
m. 1691, Jun. 4.
SAMUEL WICKHAM, { b. 1664, Jun. 16. / d. 1712 ± of Wickham.

1. Sarah, 1692, Mar. 9.
2. Samuel, 1693, Sep. 2.
3. John, 1695, Jun. 26.
4. Gideon, 1697, Jan. 22
5. Mary, 1698, Jul. 15.
6. Thomas, 1700, Jul. 30
7. Benjamin, 1701, Nov. 17
8. Charles, 1703, Dec. 6.
9. William,
10. Barbara,

X. SUSANNAH, { b. 1670, Dec. 8. / d. 1734, Apr. 11.
m. 1689, Jan. 21.
BENJAMIN GREENE, { b. 1666, Jan. 10. / d. 1757, Feb. 22. of Thomas & Elizabeth (Barton) Greene.

1. Benjamin, 1691, Jun. 10
2 Susannah, 1694, Jul. 16
3. Catharine, 1698, Mar. 31
4. Thomas, 1701, Nov. 30
5. Elizabeth, 1706, Jun. 26
6. Margaret, 1707, Jan. 16

XI. ANTHONY, { b. 1673, Oct. 16. / d.

HOLDER.

CHRISTOPHER, { b. 1631.
m. (1) 1660, Aug. 12. { d. 1688, Jun. 13.
MARY SCOTT, { b.
{ d. 1665, Oct. 17.
of Richard & Catharine (Marbury) Scott.
m. (2) 1665, Dec. 30. { b.
HOPE CLIFTON, { d. 1681, Jan. 16.
of Thomas & Mary ( ) Clifton.

Alverton, Gloucester Co., Eng., Newport, R. I.

1656, Jul. 27. Boston. He arrived this year and soon suffered persecution for his Quaker views.

1657, Aug. 29. He, for speaking a few words "in your meeting after the priest had done, was hauled back by the hair of his head and his mouth violently stopped with a glove and handkerchief thrust thereinto with much fury by one of your church members."

1657, Sep. 23. He was whipped with thirty stripes "as near as the hangman could in one place, measuring his ground and fetching his strokes with great strength and advantage."

1659, Oct. 8. He was visited in prison by Mary Scott and Hope Clifton, who were both apprehended for the offence, as was Mary Dyer in whose company they came.

1659, Nov. 22. He was sentenced to banishment under pain of death if he returned.

He was otherwise persecuted, an ear being cut off, &c.

1673. Newport. Freeman.

1676, Apr. 4. It was voted: "that in these troublesome times and straits in this colony, this Assembly desiring to have the advice and concurrence of the most judicious inhabitants, if it may be had for the good of the whole, do desire at their next sitting the company and counsel of" sixteen persons, among them Christopher Holder.

1680. Taxed £2, 6*s.* 1*d.*

He suffered imprisonment in England several times, having returned thence from England.

1688, Jun. 13. His death is thus recorded: "Christopher Holder, of Puddimore, in the county of Somerset, died at Ircott, in the parish of Almondsbury 13, 4 mo. 1688, and was buried at Hazewell."

I. MARY, { b. 1661, Sep. 16.
{ d. 1737, Sep. 20.
m. 1680 ± { b. 1654, Aug. 17.
PELEG SLOCUM, { d. 1733. of Giles & Joan ( ) Slocum.

1. Mary, 1681, Oct. 29.
2. Deliverance 1683, Feb. 10.
3. Content, 1687, Jul. 3
4. Elizabeth, 1690, Feb. 12.
5. Peleg, 1692, Mar. 24.
6. Giles, 1695, Feb. 21.
7. Holder, 1697, Jun. 14.
8. Giles, 1699.
9. Joseph, 1701, May 13.
10. Sylvester, 1704, Nov. 1.

II. ELIZABETH, { b. 1665, Jan. 4.
{ d.

(2d WIFE.)

III. CHRISTOPHER, { b. 1666, Dec. 23. Winterbourne, Gloucester Co., Eng.
{ d.

He was a clothier.

1692, Jul. 9. He sold to Roger Goulding, 50 acres in Newport, for £100, said land having been owned formerly by Thomas Clifton and since by Christopher Holder, father of grantor.

IV. HOPE, { b. 1668, Mar. 25.
{ d.

V. PATIENCE, { b. 1669, Feb. 12.
{ d.

VI. PATIENCE, { b. 1671, Aug. 16.
{ d.

VII. JOHN, { b. 1672, Aug. 20.
{ d. 1672, Aug. 25.

VIII. CONTENT, { b. 1674, May 22.
{ d. 1676, Aug. 24.

IX. ANN, { b. 1676, Feb. 29.
{ d. 1676, Mar. 21.

HOLDER. 1st column. Change England to Newport, second line after 1680.

HOLLIMAN.

See: American Genealogist, Apr. 1954, v. 30, no. 2, p. 125.

EZEKIEL, { b.
m. (1) { d. 1659, Sep. 17.
SUSANNA OXSTON, { b.
{ d.
of John Oxston.
m. (2) 1638 ± [John { b.
MARY SWEET, (w. of { d. 1681.

Tring, Hertford Co., Eng., Warwick, R. I.

1634. He came to America about this time and for a while was resident of Dedham.

1637. Salem. He had a grant of land in this year.

1638, Mar. 12. Upon appearing before General Court upon summons "because he did not frequent the public assemblies and for seducing many, he was referred by the Court to the ministers for conviction."

1638, Oct. 8. Providence. He was one of the twelve persons to whom Roger Williams deeded land bought of Canonicus and Miantonomi.

1639. He baptized Roger Williams and was thereupon baptized by him, both being among the twelve original members of that church in Providence. He was assistant to Roger Williams in his pastorate. A letter from Rev. Hugh Peters of Salem, in this year to the church at Dorchester, alludes to Mary Holliman and others as having had "the great censure passed upon them in this our church."

1643, Jan. 12. Warwick. He and ten others bought of Miantonomi for 144 fathoms wampum, tract of land called Shawomet (Warwick).

1643. A lot of land that had been granted him at Portsmouth, was now ordered forfeited "by reason there was an order that men should build upon their lots by such a time, which he hath not done."

1645, Jan. 27. He sold to John Field, 25 acres and a share of meadow.

1647. Member of Town Council.

1648. Member of Court of Trial.

1651, Jan. 29. He sold William Harris a right in Pawtuxet, for £20, one part of which to be paid in a cow and steer, Jun. 24th, and rest in good merchantable wampum-peage or cattle, 1653, Sep. 29th. All to be paid unto James Sweet.

1652-53-54-55-56-58-59. Commissioner.

1654, Jul. 13. He and Randall Holden, for themselves and rest of inhabitants of Warwick, bought of Taccommanan for £15, already received by him, and value of one coat of such cloth as the Indians do now commonly use to

I. PRISCILLA, { b.
m. { d. 1652 +
JOHN WARNER, { b. 1615.
{ d. 1654 ± of Warner.

1. John, 1645, Aug. 1.
2. Susanna,
3. Mary,
4. Rachel,

HOLLIMAN. 1st column. Ezekiel,[2] (William,[1]) b. 1586. He was baptized 1587, Jan. 1, at Tring. His father was Church warden.

wear (to be given annually as a gratuity hereafter), a tract of land called Potowomut.

1654, Aug. 1. He and John Greene, Jr., were appointed to view the general laws of the colony and report to next Court of Commissioners what they may find defective or any way jarring, &c.

1655. Freeman.

1656. Magistrate.

1658. Warden.

1658. Nov. 20. He sold to William Carpenter, of Providence, two acres there.

1659, Sep. 27. The Town Council met about ordering his estate, having finished a will. The widow was summoned to appear next morning before the council to hear what was done.

1659, Oct. 5. The widow was again questioned whether she would accept executorship, desiring a speedy answer, having already long waited to the spoiling of some of the estate. She replied accepting the office.

The council besides giving the widow administration on a certain part of his effects, appointed Walter Todd, John Greene and Thomas Olney as guardians for two grandchildren, John and Rachel Warner. To John Warner, all the housing and land in Warwick. To Rachel Warner, all the land in Providence. The guardians were to take charge of certain cattle, &c., for the support of said John and Rachel, and when they were of age to have the stock betwixt them, reserving liberty to council to dispose of part of said stock for Susan Warner or other of the children in England, if need require. To widow Mary Holliman, the rest of stock was given and goods also at her dispose, and use of house and barn, meadow, &c., for life.

Inventory, £183, 6*s*. 6*d*., viz: bible 6*s*., wearing apparel £5, 19*s*., bed, spit, bigger and lesser iron pot, mortar and pestle, peage paid by Mr. Smith £4, horse £11, 2 mares, 2 colts, 6 cows, 2 oxen, 5 two years, 3 yearlings, a sow, hog, 3 little pigs, man servant Jo 9*s*., 2 acres of corn, 40 bushels of corn, &c.

1668, Feb. 22. His widow agreed to surrender to John Warner the house she dwelleth in, &c., on condition that he will allow her the mowing of the grass in the meadow yearly for her use, and liberty to be buried by her husband Mr. Ezekiel Holliman.

1681, Jul. 13. His widow deeded to son-in-law John Gereardy and Renewed his wife, for love, &c., house, lot, orchard, &c.

1681, Jul. 31. Will—proved 1681. Widow Mary. She gives to her son-in-law John 'Gereardy and daughter Renewed his wife, both formerly of Warwick, now of Prudence, all interest in house, lot, meadow and upland in Warwick.

HOLMES (Joshua).

JOSHUA, Sam'l.] b. d. 1694, Apr. 14.
m. 1675, Jun. 15 (w. of
ABIGAIL CHEESEBOROUGH b. d. 1694 +

Westerly, R. I.

1694, May 26. Administration was granted his widow Abigail, his will having been declared a little before his death to witnesses, he not having time before his death to perfect it.

To son-in-law Isaac Thompson, 100 acres near my now dwelling house and his choice of 200 acres of other land in two parcels of 100 acres each. To son Joshua, land on which I dwell, and all the rest of lands, reserving liberty to son-in-law Isaac Thompson, to live in dwelling house five years if he see meet, and the two boys to be helpful to Isaac. To wife Abigail, the whole of movables for life. To son Joshua and son-in-law Isaac Thompson, the cattle at decease of wife, divided equally, only the oxen to be for Joshua.

Inventory, £122, 14*s*. 6*d*., viz: money 9*s*., table, chest, pewter, spinning wheel, cards, bible £2, 14*s*., stillyards, 34 sheep, 28 lambs, 6 horse-kind, 31 swine, 20 head of cattle, &c.

I. MARY, b. d. 1751.
m.
ISAAC THOMPSON, b. d. 1738, of Thompson.

1. Mary, 1697, Jul. 1.
2. Isaac, 1698, Sep. 26.
3. Samuel, 1700, Jul. 29.
4. Abigail, 1701, Jan. 1.
5. Sarah, 1703, Mar. 3.
6. William, 1704, Apr. 10.
7. Nathaniel, 1705, Dec. 31.
8. Anna,
9. Elias, 1708, Nov. 14.
10. Mary, 1710, Mar. 18.
11. Abigail, 1711, Oct. 14.
12. Susanna, 1713, Nov. 25.
13. Joshua, 1714, Aug. 13.
14. Prudence, 1716, Mar. 11.

II. JOSHUA, b. 1678, Aug. 20. d. 1729, Nov. 23. Stonington, Ct.
m. 1698, Nov. 21.
FEAR STURGES, b. d. 1753, Jun. 22. of Sturges.

1. Joshua, 1700, Aug. 14.
2. John, 1702, Jun. 10.
3. Abigail, 1703, Feb. 28.
4. Temperance 1707, Jan. 29.
5. Thankful, 1708, Nov. 12.
6. Thomas, 1711, Jan. 1.
7. Mary, 1713, Mar. 19.
8. Bethiah, 1715, Jul. 29.
9. Marvin, 1717, Nov. 17.

HOLMES (Obadiah).

OBADIAH, b. 1607. d. 1682, Oct. 15.
m.
CATHARINE, b. d. 1682 +

Preston, Lancaster Co., Eng., Newport, R. I.

1639, Dec. 11. Salem. He had two acres granted, being one of the "glassmen," as the manufacturers of glass were called.

1640, May 30. He had his daughter Martha baptized, and later Samuel (1642, Mar. 20), and Obadiah, (1644, Jun. 9).

1641, Dec. The glassmen were to have a loan

I. MARY, b. d. 1690 +
m.
JOHN BROWN, b. 1630. d. 1706 ± of Chad & Elizabeth (   ) Brown.

1. Sarah,
2. John, 1662, Mar. 18.
3. James, 1666.
4. Obadiah,
5. Martha,
6. Mary,
7. Deborah,

II. MARTHA, b. 1640. d. 1682 +

John*

*See: American Geneologist, v. 19, p. 224.

of £30 from the town and were to repay it again "if the works succeed, when they are able." They manufactured the common glass for window frames, &c., and pieces are still occasionally found near the site of their works.

1644, Jun. 31. He drew lot 37 in a division of wood land at Rehoboth.

1645, Jan. 10. His name was in a list of those who had forfeited their lots at Rehoboth for not fencing, or not removing their families.

1646. Rehoboth. He moved here this year, and became a member of Rev. Mr. Newman's church.

1648, Jun. 7. Propounded for freeman.

1649. Grand Jury.

1649, Oct. 29. He entered complaint against Samuel Newman on account of slander, with damages at £100, Newman having said that Holmes took false oath in court. Mr. Newman acknowledged his wrong, saying he could not charge it of his own knowledge, but received information of others.

1650, Jun. 5. He and Joseph Torrey, were bound one for another in the sum of £10, apiece.

1650, Oct. 2. He was presented with others of Rehoboth, by the Grand Jury, for continuing of meeting upon the Lord's Day from house to house, contrary to order of this court.

1650. Newport. He and eight others of Rehoboth, having separated from the church, were baptized, and Mr. Holmes became pastor. He and some others consequently left Rehoboth and came to Newport in this or the subsequent year.

1651, Jul. 21. He, with his neighbors John Crandall and John Clarke, of Newport, were seized at Lynn. They, "being the representatives of the church in Newport, upon the request of William Witter of Lynn, arrived there, he being a brother in the church, who by reason of his advanced age could not undertake so great a journey as to visit the church." While Mr. Clarke was preaching the constable came to Mr. Witter's house and apprehended him, as well as Mr. Holmes and Mr. Crandall, and the next morning they were sent to prison in Boston.

1651, Jul. 31. Sentence was passed: Mr. Holmes was fined £30, Mr. Clarke £20, and Mr. Crandall, £5, and in default of the fine they were to be publicly whipped. Mr. Holmes was kept in prison till September, and then the sentence was executed upon him, viz: thirty stripes. He wrote an account of his sufferings to friends in London shortly after his chastisement. "As the man began to lay the strokes upon my back I said to the people, though my flesh should fail, and my spirit should fail, yet my God would not fail," and he says he prayed unto the Lord not to lay the sin to their charge. "When he had loosed me from the post, having joyfulness in my heart and cheerfulness in my countenance, as the spectators observed, I told the magistrates, you have struck me as with roses: and said moreover although the Lord hath made it easy to me, yet I pray God it may not be laid to your charge." He was advised to make his escape by night, and says: "I departed, and the next day after while I was on my journey, the constables came to search at the house where I lodged, so I escaped their hands and was by the good hand of my Heavenly Father, brought home again to my near relatives, my wife and eight children. The brethren of our town and Providence having taken pains to meet me four miles in the woods where we rejoiced together in the Lord."

1652. Pastor of First Baptist Church, and so continued till his death.

1656. Freeman.

1656–58. Commissioner.

1675. He wrote an account of his life addressed to his children. He alludes to his honored parents as having brought up three sons at the University of Oxford. He had a brother Robert it seems.

1676, Apr. 4. It was voted, "that in these troublesome times and straits in this colony, this Assembly desiring to have the advice and concurrence of the most judicious inhabitants if it may be had for the good of the whole, do desire at their next sitting Mr. Benedict Arnold," Mr. Obadiah Holmes, &c.

1682, Apr. 9. Will—witnesses, Edward Thurston and Weston Clarke. Reference to this will is found in a list of seventeen wills (between 1676 and 1695), that were presented to the court in 1700, by parties interested, the law requiring three witnesses, and these wills having but two.

He was buried in his own field, where a tomb was erected to his memory (in what is now the town of Middletown).

His wife did not long survive him.

III. SAMUEL, b. 1642. d. 1679. Gravesend, N. Y.
m. 1665, Oct. 26.
ALICE STILLWELL, b. 1645. d. of Nicholas & Ann (Van Dyke) Stillwell.

(She m. (2) 1680, William Osborne: (3) 1683, Daniel Lake.)

1679, May 28. Will—proved 1679. The witnesses (John Emmons and John Tilton), declined to swear, being Quakers, and their declaration was finally taken by the Governor, to whom the matter had been referred by the Court.

1. Samuel, 1668, Feb. 12.
2. Ann, 1670, Dec. 20.
3. Joseph, 1672, Mar. 17.
4. Catharine, 1675, Jun. 15.
5. Henry,
6. Mary,

IV. OBADIAH, b. 1644. d. Staten Island, N. Y., Cohansey, N. J.
m.
——— COLE, b. d. of Cole.

1689, Dec. 12. Justice of the Peace.

1690. Cohansey. He was one of the organizers of the Baptist Church.

He was for twelve years a Judge of the Court, in Salem County.

1715, Sep. 8. His son Jonathan[3], died (leaving a son of same name, who married Anna Dominick, of Long Island, and had eight children by her). His son Samuel[3], was drowned when a young man. His daughters married into the Love and Parvine families.

He was a minister at the time of his death, it is stated, though, by another account, he was never regularly ordained, but occasionally preached.

1. Obadiah, 1680.
2. Samuel,
3. Jonathan,
4. Daughter,
5. Daughter,

V. LYDIA, b. d.
m.
JOHN BOWNE, b. d. of William & Ann ( ) Bowne.

1. John, 1664, Apr. 1.
2. Obadiah, 1666, Jul. 18.
3. Deborah, 1668, Jan. 26.
4. Sarah, 1669, Nov. 27.
5. Catharine,

VI. JONATHAN, b. d. 1713. Middletown, N. J., Newport, R. I.
m.
SARAH BORDEN, b. 1644, May, d. 1705 + of Richard & Joan ( ) Borden.

1667, Dec. 30. Middletown, He had lot 9 given him in a division of lands.

1668. Deputy. He was chosen on a committee same year to have a mill built.

1672. Justice. After a few years more residence in New Jersey he returned to Newport.

1684. Newport. Freeman. In same year he sent a power of attorney to Richard Hartshorn to sell lands in Newport.

1690-91-96-98-99-1700-1-2-6-7. Deputy.

1695, July 2. He was appointed on a committee by the Assembly to propose a method of making a rate. He was also appointed with others to run the easterly line of the colony.

1696-97-98-1700-1-2-3. Speaker of the House of Deputies.

1705. Will—proved. 1713, Nov. 2. Ex. son Joseph. Overseers, brother John Holmes, and William Weeden. To wife Sarah, best feather bed, all the plate, and £10 yearly for life. To son Obadiah, the easterly side of the farm in Middletown, in Plain Dealing, East New Jersey, with all the housing, etc., half the salt and fresh meadow, and all the stock I left on said farm. To son Samuel, a house lot in Newport and house upon it and £5. To son Jonathan, the other half of farm in Middletown, half the meadow, a young mare and £5. To sons Obadiah and Jonathan, certain other lands in New Jersey, equally. To daughter Sarah Oulde, £15. To daughter Mary Easton, £15. To two children of daughter Catharine Whiteman £15 equally at eighteen. To daughter Martha Tillinghast, £15. To daughter Lydia Holmes, £20. To son Joseph Holmes, all my farm and housing where I now dwell, and all my rights of land in said Newport, and rest of movables.

1. Obadiah,
2. Jonathan,
3. Samuel,
4. Sarah,
5. Mary,
6. Catharine,
7. Martha, 1675.
8. Lydia,
9. Joseph,

VII. JOHN, b. 1649. d. 1712, Oct. 2. Newport, R. I.
m. (1) 1671, Dec. 1.
FRANCES HOLDEN, b. 1649, Sep. 29. d. 1679. of Randall & Frances (Dungan) Holden.
m. (2) 1680, Oct. 12.
MARY GREENE, (w. of Wm. b. 1652, Jul. 11. d. 1713 + of John & Mary (Williams) Sayles.

Perhaps one or two of the children accredited to his second wife, were by his first.

1669, Aug. 28. He and two others were ordered to assemble the inhabitants of Conanicut Island, to consider what may be most suitable for their defence and preservation against any invasion or insurrection of the Indians.

HOLMES (OBADIAH). VII. John. His widow's will mentions "my five daughters."

1682–1704–5. Deputy.

1690, May 7. He and Caleb Carr were appointed by Assembly to agree with carpenters to finish the Town House forthwith, and to provide boards and nails, they to pay for finishing the house out of money and wool now in Treasurer's hands.

1690-91-92-93-94-95-96-97-98-99-1700-1-2-3-8-9. General Treasurer.

1696. Lieutenant.

1702, May 6. He and Joseph Sheffield were empowered to lease and settle the ferries in the colony, that are not already settled by law.

1708, Apr. He and two others were chosen to oversee the repairing and finishing of the Colony House, for which £100 was appropriated by the Assembly.

1712, Oct. 4. An agreement was signed by his children, he having left his will unfinished. The will mentioned wife Mary, sons John and William, daughters Catharine Gardiner, Frances Carr, Ann Peckham, Deborah Holmes and Phebe Holmes.

1713. Receipts were taken by widow Mary Holmes, and her son William (administrators of personal estate of John Holmes), of John Manchester, and wife Deborah, Joseph Gardiner, and wife Catharine, and Nicholas Carr, and wife Frances.

1. John, 1672.
2. Catharine, 1673.
(2d wife.)
3. William,
4. Mary,
5. Frances,
6. Ann,
7. Susanna,
8. Deborah,
9. Phebe.

VIII. HOPESTILL, b. d.
m.
——— TAYLOR, b. d. of Taylor.

HOLMES. 2d column. IV. Obadiah. 1680, Apr. 17, Sarah Cook, widow of John and his exx.— orders loving son Obadiah Holmes of Staten Island, to sell land at Gravesend. 2d column. VI. Jonathan. His daughter Sarah b. 1665, and in his will changes Sarah Oulde to Sarah Slade.

HOLMES (OBADIAH). 2d column. VII. John. Erase daughter Mary. His widow Mary, d. 1717.

1713, Sep. 21. Will—proved 1717, May 6. Widow Mary. Ex son-in-law Nicholas Carr. To three daughters Mary Dyer, Frances Carr and Ann Peckham, certain legacies.

HOPKINS (THOMAS, OF MASHANTATACK). Instead of his being the father of Joseph and Samuel, possibly the latter were sons of William & Susannah (Goff) Hopkins, of Roxbury, Mass. This William Hopkins, d. 1688, Nov. 8. He had a son Samuel, baptized 1663, Nov. 15, and Joseph, 1657, Mar. 8.

HOOMERY (or HOOMERYHOO) omitted by Austin. See American Genealogist, v. 20, p. 113.

THOMAS, b. d. 1698.
m.
SARAH, b. d. 1699 +

Warwick, Providence, R. I.

1678. Freeman.

1686, Mar. 26. He sold to Edward Searle, Jr., 40 acres in Mashantatack, for £7.

He moved later to the other side of the Pawtuxet River, within the limits of Providence.

1698, Oct. 20. Will—proved 1699, Jan. 13. Exx. wife Sarah. To wife, whole estate, house, lands, goods and chattels.

Inventory, £569, viz: 4 head of cattle £10, horse £3, mare, 8 swine, 3 beds £24, pewter, warming pan, spinning wheel, &c. (The inventory was taken 1698, Dec. 13.)

It is assumed that this Thomas Hopkins, was the father of Samuel, Joseph and Patience, though he mentions no children in his will.

I. SAMUEL, b. d. 1738. South Kingstown, R. I.
m.
SUSANNA, b. d. 1732 + of

1687, Sep. 6. Kings Town. Taxed 2s. 10d.
1697, May 20. He bought 180 acres of John Crandall, Jr.
1707, Sep. 9. He and wife Susanna, sold 9½ acres to John Crowder.
1722, Oct. 16. He and wife Susanna, sold to daughter Susanna Hopkins, 4 acres, for £30.
1732, Mar. 22. Will—proved 1738, Feb. 12. Ex. son Thomas (who had had lands before). To wife Susanna, use of all movables, while widow, and if she marry, what is left to go to my daughter Mary Fowler, who was to have in any event, at death of wife. To grandson Thomas Whaley, 5s., he having had. To grandson Samuel Whaley, 5s.

1. Thomas,
2. Susanna,
3. Mary,
4. Daughter,

II. JOSEPH, b. d. 1735, May 15. Kings Town, East Greenwich, R. I.
m. (1)
PHEBE, b. d. of
m. (2)
MARTHA WHALEY, b. 1680. d. 1773. of Theophilus & Elizabeth (Mills) Whaley.
(She m. (2) Robert Spencer.)

1713. East Greenwich. He moved thence this or previous year.
1735, May 15. Will—proved 1735, Jul. 5. Exs. sons William and Samuel. To wife Martha, best room for life, privilege in orchard, cow, two hogs and keep of same, and all household goods and indoor movables. To son Joseph, 5s. To sons William and Samuel, homestead equally, they paying legacies, &c. To son John, £30. To son Robert, half of outdoor movables, except above, and £30. To son Thomas, £30 at twenty-one. To daughter Phebe Pitcher, a cow. To daughters Hannah and Theodate Hopkins, £25 each, and a good cow to each.

Inventory, £173, 17s. 6d., viz: spinning wheel, wool card, loom, 2 churns, warming pan, table, chairs, pewter, neat cattle £45, 15s., horsekind £10, swine £7, &c.

His widow died at house of her son-in-law, Othniel Gorton.

1. Phebe, 1696, Feb. 8.
2. Joseph, 1698, Apr. 8.
(2d wife.)
3. William,
4. Samuel, 1704, Jan. 6.
5. John, 1712, Apr. 2.
6. Robert, 1713, Jun. 2.
7. Thomas,
8. Hannah,
9. Thedosia, 1718, Apr. 13.
10. Francis,

III. PATIENCE, b. d.
m. 1700, Feb. 2.
JOHN GORTON, b. d. of John & Margaret (Wheaton) Gorton.

1. Patience, 1700, Dec. 12
2. Samuel,
3. Hopkins, 1704, Apr.

HORSWELL.

PETER, b. d. 1733, Jun. 9.
m.
ELIZABETH, b. d. 1733 +

Little Compton, R. I.

1709, Jun. 14. He and Elizabeth were witnesses to will of John Woodman.

1733, Sep. 18. Administration to son John, the widow refusing.

I. SARAH, b. 1693, Jul. d.

II. ELIZABETH, b. 1695, Sep. d.

III. JOHN, b. 1697, Sep. d. 1761, Jul. 24. Little Compton, R. I.
m.
MARY, b. d. 1761 + of

1761, Jun. 1. Will—proved 1761, Aug. 4. Exs. friends Richard Grinnell and Christopher White. To wife Mary, £200 and all household stuff she brought with her when I married her and twenty pounds of wool and privilege of living in house till 25th of March next after my death, and one hundred and twenty pounds of beef, one hundred and twenty pounds of pork, ten bushels Indian corn, all in lieu of dower. To sons Peter and John, 38 acres. To son Peter, house he now lives in and two mares. To son John, black horse. To son Luke, one hundred Spanish dollars, two steers, a cow, ten ewes, a suit of apparel and great coat. To son Benjamin, £300 at twenty-four, and he to be apprenticed. To daughter Betty Wilcox, £100. To sister Judith Horswell, £30. To grandsons, sons of William, deceased, viz: Henry and Francis, £5 apiece at age. To granddaughter Mary Horswell, daughter of John, £5. To granddaughter Hope Head, £5 at eighteen. To son Peter, a swine. To son John, rest of swine and £100. To sons Peter and John, rest of estate.

Inventory, £10,509, 11s. 4d., viz: apparel £446, warming pan, bible and other books £19, 4 oxen, 12 cows, 2 steers, 10 young cattle, 3 calves, 58 sheep, 15 lambs, 3 horsekind, 3 swine, 5 pigs, bonds and notes £2,379, 12s., silver money £4, 18s. 8d., &c.

1. Peter,
2. John,
3. Elizabeth,
4. Daughter,
5. Luke,
6. Benjamin,
7. William,

IV. JUDITH, b. 1699, Sep. 2. d. 1761 +
UNMARRIED,

V. LYDIA, b. 1701, Sep. 3. d.

VI. HANNAH, b. 1706, Apr. 11. d.

VII. PETER, b. 1708. d.

HORSWELL. 2d column. I. Sarah d. 1719, Dec. 18; m. 1716, May 31, John Taylor, b. 1694, Jan. 7; d. 1762, June, of John and Abigail. Children, 1, Elizabeth, 1717, Jan. 5. II. Elizabeth m. 1719, Dec. 24, John Hunt. III. John. His 4th child was Sarah. VI. Hannah m. 1723, Sep. 19, George Rouse, b. 1704, Jan. 9; d. 1775, Oct. 15, of James and Joanna (Miller) Rouse. Children, 1, Elizabeth, 1724, Feb. 23. 2, Mercy, 1727, Jan. 13. 3, Sarah, 1728, Jan. 14. 4, Joanna, 1734, May 31. 5, Lydia, 1736, Apr. 28. 6, Mary, 1738, Mar. 3. 7, Rebecca, 1744, Jan. 17.

HOUSE.

WALTER, b. d. 1670.
m.
MARY, b. d. 1670 +

Kings Town, R. I.

1668, May 4. He, with others of Wickford, petitioned Connecticut authorities, for protection of their jurisdiction, or that they might look elsewhere for government.

1670, Jul. 12. A jury appointed under authority of Connecticut, was called by the constable, Samuel Eldred, and found Walter House to have a hole in the fore part of his head and several other bruises upon his left arm, &c., the injuries having been inflicted by Thomas Flounders. The latter being examined by the Governor and Council of Rhode Island, soon after, admitted that he struck a blow with a small stick, and that House, holding up his arm fell backward and hit his head against a rafter, said House being on the threshold and Flounders in the shop.

Much conflict arose over this case in regard to the jurisdiction of Connecticut and Rhode Island, both colonies claiming authority.

1670, Oct. 13. The summons sent to Narragansett, by Rhode Island Assembly, for witnesses about the murder—were delivered to Mary House, relict of Walter.

Flounders was soon after executed.

HUBBARD.

SAMUEL,[3] (James,[2] Thos[1].) { b. 1610. d. 1689.
m. 1636, Jan. 4.
TACY COOPER, { b. d. 1697 ±
of Cooper.

Mendelsham, Suffolk Co., Eng., Newport, R. I.

He says of himself: "I was born of good parents, my mother brought me up in the fear of the Lord, in Mendelsham, in catechiseing me and hearing choice ministers, &c."

1633, Oct. Salem. He came this month from England.

1634. Watertown, Mass.

1635. He joined the church, "by giving account of my faith," as he says.

1635. Windsor, Conn. He was married there the next year by Mr. Ludlow. (Tacy Cooper had come to Dorchester, 1634, Jun. 9, and moved to Windsor before her marriage.)

1636. Weathersfield, Conn.

1639, May 10. Springfield, Mass. He moved here at this date, and a church was soon gathered; he says there were five men in all, and "my wife soon after added."

1647, May 10. Fairfield. His stay here was short: "God having enlightened both, but mostly my wife, into his holy ordinances of baptizing only of visible believers, and being very zealous for it, she was mostly struck at and answered two terms publicly, where I was also said to be as bad as she, and sore threatened with imprisonment to Hartford jail, if not to renounce it or to remove; that scripture came into our mouths, if they persecute you in one place, flee to another; and so we did 2 day of October, 1648, we went for Rhode Island."

1648, Oct. 12. Newport. They arrived at this date.

1648, Nov. 3. He and his wife were baptized by Rev. John Clarke.

1651, Aug. 7. He was sent by the church to visit the brethren in prison at Boston, viz: John Clarke, Obadiah Holmes and John Crandall.

1652, Oct. "I and my wife had hands laid on us by brother Joseph Torrey."

1655. Freeman.

1657, Oct. 1. "Brother Obadiah Holmes and I went to the Dutch and Gravesend and to Jamaica, and to Flushing and to Cow Bay." They came home Nov. 15th.

1664. He was to be General Solicitor, in case of inability of Lawrence Turner.

1665, Mar. 10. "My wife took up keeping of the Lord's holy seventh day Sabbath."

1665, Apr. "I took it up (our daughter Ruth, 25 Oct., 1666, Rachel, Jan. 15, 1666, Bethiah, Feb., 1666, our son Joseph Clarke, 23 Feb., 1666)."

1668, Apr. 7. I went to Boston to public dispute with those baptized there.

1668, Jul. He wrote his cousin, John Smith, of London, from Boston, where he had been to a disputation: "Through God's great mercy, the Lord have given me in this wilderness, a good, diligent, careful, painful and very loving wife; we, through mercy, live comfortably, praised be God, as co-heirs together of one mind in the Lord, travelling through this wilderness to our heavenly sion, knowing we are pilgrims as our fathers were, and good portion being content therewith. A good house, as with us judged, 25 acres of ground fenced, and four cows which give, one young heifer and three calves, and a very good mare, a trade, a carpenter, a health to follow it, and my wife very diligent and painful, praised be God," &c.

1671, Dec. 16. He wrote to his children at Westerly, about the differences between those favoring the seventh day observance and the rest of the church. Several spoke on both sides. Mr. Hubbard gave his views. Brother Torrey said they required not my faith. Other discussion followed: "They replied fiercely, it was a tumult. J. Torrey stopped them at last."

1671, Dec. 23. "We entered into a church covenant the 23d day December, 1371, viz; William Hiscox, Stephen Mumford, Samuel Hubbard, Roger Baster, sister Hubbard, sister Mumford, Rachel Langworthy," &c.

1675. He says: "I have a testament of

I. NAOMI, { b. 1637, Nov. 18. d. 1637, Nov. 28.

II. NAOMI, { b. 1638, Oct. 19. d. 1643, May 5.

III. RUTH, { b. 1640, Jan. 11. d. 1691 +
m. 1655, Nov. 2.
ROBERT BURDICK, { b. d. 1692. of Burdick.

1. Robert,
2. Son,
3. Hubbard,
4. Thomas,
5. Naomi,
6. Ruth,
7. Benjamin,
8. Samuel,
9. Tacy,
10. Deborah,

HUBBARD. 2d column. IV. Rachel. Her 2d child was James, not Andrew.

IV. RACHEL, { b. 1642, Mar. 10. d.
m. 1658, Nov. 3.
ANDREW LANGWORTHY, { b. d. of Langworthy

1. Samuel,
2. Andrew,

V. SAMUEL, { b. 1644, Mar. 25. d. young.

VI. BETHIAH, { b. 1646, Dec. 19. d. 1707, Apr. 17.
m. 1664, Nov. 16.
JOSEPH CLARKE, { b. 1643, Apr. 2. d. 1727, Jan. 11. of Joseph Clarke.

1. Judith,	1667, Oct. 12.
2. Joseph,	1670, Apr. 4.
3. Samuel,	1672, Sep. 29.
4. John,	1675, Aug. 25.
5. Bethiah,	1678, Apr. 11.
6. Mary,	1680, Dec. 27.
7. Susanna,	1683, Aug. 31.
8. Thomas,	1686, Mar. 17.
9. William,	1688, Apr. 21.

VII. SAMUEL, { b. 1649, Nov. 30. d. 1670, Jan. 20. Newport, R. I.
Unmarried.

my grandfather Cocke's, printed 1549, which he hid in his bedstraw, lest it should be found and burned, in Queen Mary's days."

1675, Nov. 1. He wrote Mr. Henry Reeve, at Jamaica; "Very sudden and strange changes these times afford in this, our age, everywhere, as I hear and now see in N. E. God's hand seems to be stretched out against N. England, by wars by the natives, and many Englishmen fall at present." "This island doth look to ourselves as yet, by mercy not one slain, blessed be God." "My wife and 3 daughters, who are all here by reason of the Indian war, with their 15 children, desire to remember their christian love to you."

1678, Jun. 29. He wrote Dr. Stennett, of London: "From my own house in Mayford, in Newport," &c. He mentions a very sore cough he had last winter, and that he sent for his physician, Major Cranston, who "said he judged none help or hope for sure, but for present refreshment, he gave a small vial of spirits, which I took and had some sleep, but my cough rather increased," &c. "Our Governor died the 19th day of June, 1678, buried 20th day, all this island was invited, many others was there, judged near a thousand people, our brother Hiscox spake there excellently," &c.

1680. Taxed 8*s.* 2*d.*

1686, Dec. 19. He wrote to John Thornton, of Providence: "My old brother who was before me, you and brother Joseph Clarke (only alive) in that ordinance of baptism, I next and my wife in New England, although we stept before you in other ordinances: Oh! let us strive still to be first in the things of God," &c.

1688, May 7. He wrote Richard Brooks, of Boston: "The mesles is not gone here. My daughter Rachel have them and some of her family."

HULING.

JAMES, b. 1635. d. 1687, Mar. 6.
m.
MARGARET, b. 1632. d. 1707, Feb. 16.

Newport, R. I.

1680. Taxed 12*s.*

1684, Nov. 14. Margaret Huling, wife of James Huling, inhabitant of Newport, in Rhode Island, for £80, sold John Huling, of Rhode Island, mariner, a dwelling house and lot on Broad street, New York.

He was buried in Newport Cemetery.

His widow was buried in the Episcopal church yard, at Lewes, Delaware.

I. JOHN, b. 1658 ± d. 1708 + Newport, R. I.
m.
SARAH, b. 1668. d. 1708, Jan. 11. of

HULING. 2d column. I. John. His son b. 1707, Nov. 13.

He was a mariner, and also a merchant.

1680. Taxed £1, 17*s.*

1691, Mar. 21. He received a permit as master of sloop Robert & William.

1704, Jul. 7. He (of Rhode Island, merchant), bought of Thomas Pemberton, a lot sixty feet broad and one hundred feet long, in Lewes, Delaware.

1706, Mar. 24. He sold the above lot to Samuel Davis.

His wife died at Peleg Chamberlain's house, Newport.

Children: 1. Walton,

II. JAMES, b. d.

III. ALEXANDER, b. 1665. d. 1725, Jul. 29. Newport, North Kingstown, R. I.
m.
ELIZABETH WIGHTMAN, b. 1664, Jul. 26. d. 1756. of George & Elizabeth (Updike) Wightman.

He was a carpenter.

1685, Apr. 23. Kings Town. He was witness to an agreement made by the Atherton Company at Narragansett.

1696, May 28. He sold Daniel Eldred, for £105, my now dwelling house and settlement in Narragansett country, with orchard, &c.

1699–1703. Grand Jury.

1700-5-11-12-14-15-16-17-18-19-20-21-22. Ratemaker.

1702, Feb. 18. He was named in a list at Newport, "of those persons that hold and possess lots of land out of the ancient proprietors, and have built large buildings," &c.

1703, Aug. 12. He deeded half an acre for a Baptist meeting house, situated "about 26 rods north-east from my now dwelling house in Kingstown"

1707–8. Deputy.

1720, Dec. 6. He deeded his son James Huling, "westward part of my now dwelling house, which I first builded," with 50 or 60 acres.

1722, Mar. 17. He made a deposition, calling himself fifty-seven years of age.

1725, Feb. 8. He and wife Elizabeth, sold to Alexander Brown, 50¾ acres, for £152.

1725, Jun. 25. Will—proved 1725. Exx. wife Elizabeth. He desires that his senseless daughter, Mary Huling, be maintained out of estate. To wife, whole estate, both real and personal, while widow. To son James, dwelling house I now live in and certain land, sealed gold ring, silver spoon, carpenter's, cooper's and shoemaker's tools, clock, loom, carbine gun, &c. To son Alexander, 50 acres, with other land, silver spoon, fuse gun, sword, walking cane, wearing apparel and silver watch, To daughter Honour Brown, one-quarter of household goods, great silver cup with two handles and silver spoon. To daughter Margaret Havens, one-quarter of household goods and silver tankard, the tankard at her decease going to grandson Alexander Havens. To daughter Elizabeth Nichols, one-quarter of household goods, silver cup and silver spoon. To daughter Catharine Nichols, one-quarter of household goods and two silver spoons. All the above bequests to be in force at death or marriage of wife.

Inventory, £263, 13*s.*

He was buried in the old Baptist yard in North Kingstown.

1756, Jan. 12. Administration on his widow's estate was granted to grandson Alexander Huling, but he refusing, it was given to Thomas Havens.

Children: 1. James, 2. Alexander, 3. Honour, 4. Margaret, 5. Elizabeth, 6. Catharine, 7. Mary,

IV. WALTON, b. d. 1710 ± Newport, R. I., Lewes, Del.
m.
MARTHA, b. d. 1718 + of

He was a mariner.

1693, Mar. 20. He witnessed a deed.

1695. Constable.

1702, Jan. 15. He bought an acre of land of Nathaniel Coddington.

1702, Aug. He had laid out to him, an acre of ground.

1703, Feb. 1. Lewes. He bought two lots of William Clarke.

1704, Oct. 12. He and wife Martha, sold a lot in Newport, to Richard Long.

1704, Nov. 4. He, being master of sloop Unity, six tons burden, bound for Philadelphia, bound himself in sum of £500, to the Governor of New York, to carry no other persons but what shall have a ticket from the Secretary's office of the Province of New York.

1705, Sep. 10. Will—proved 1717, Aug. 3. Exx. wife Martha. To her, one-third of estate, real and personal. To daughters Elizabeth and Esther Huling, and child wife goeth with, rest of estate.

1710, Sep. 3. His widow bought 111 acres in Broad Kiln Creek, Sussex county.

1713, Mar. A suit was decided in his favor against Captain Alexander Huling.

1718, Aug. 8. His widow sold 693 acres in Sussex county.

Children: 1. Elizabeth, 2. Esther,

HULL (JOHN). 2d column. I. Mary. Her husband was son of John and Mary (Clarke) Stanton.

JOHN[3], (Tristram[2], Jos[1].) b. 1654, Mar. d. 1733, Feb. 1.
m. 1684, Oct. 23.
ALICE TEDDEMAN, b. 1659, d. 1734, Dec. 24.

of Edmund Teddeman.

Barnstable, Mass., Jamestown, R. I.

He was a sea captain, and made voyages from Newport to London. He held the religious faith of the Quakers.

He lived in London about two years after his marriage.

1687. He came to Newport this year, and soon settled on Conanicut Island. He brought with him a removal certificate from the Quaker meeting in London (dated 1687, Apr. 27), certifying that he and his wife "had behaved themselves in their lives and conversations as becometh friends of the blessed truth."

1687. Jamestown. He bought 370 acres at north end of the island, and built a house there.

1690, May 6. Freeman.

1695. Town Council, and Assessor.

1695–1704. Town Clerk.

1698–1703–6–7–9. Deputy.

1705, Sep. 8. He was appointed attorney for debts, rents, &c., by his sister, Sarah Allen, of Shrewsbury, N. J., widow and executrix of Joseph Allen, late of Shrewsbury, deceased.

1712. Head Warden.

1715, Feb. 23. He was appointed on a committee to hire out the ferries belonging to this colony.

1733, Jan. 19. Will—proved 1733, Feb. 9. Exs. wife Alice and son John. To son Teddeman, the profit of farm where he dwells in Jamestown, except 100 acres at south end, and that to be his at death of testator's wife. To sons John and Joseph, farm where I dwell, the southerly half to John, and the northerly half to Joseph, with dwelling house, &c., at death of wife. To three sons, all rights in Dutch Island. To son John, negro Ben and writing desk, at death of wife. To son Joseph, gun and all books. To daughter Mary Stanton, £100, she having had. To daughter Alice Borden, £100. To granddaughters Mary and Alice Slocum, £50 each, at eighteen. The rest of land to be sold by executors, and the result, with all movables and rent and profits of land given sons, to be for wife, while widow, and what is left at her death or marriage, not needed for maintenance, to be divided to five children. Executors to take care that my cousin, Mark Ridley, does not suffer or come to want.

Inventory, £629, 10*s*., viz: clock £10, book £1, 10*s*., spinning wheel, pewter, gun, 5 silver spoons, 2 cheese presses, 6 swine, colt, pair of oxen, pair of stags, 9 cows, canoe £3, 180 sheep, 3 two years, 4 yearlings, negro Ben £80, &c.

1733, Sep. 24. Will — proved 1734, Jan. 21. Widow Alice. Ex. son John. To son Teddeman, a clock. To four children, the rest of estate, viz: to John, Joseph, Mary Stanton and Alice Borden.

Inventory, £147, 12*s*. 5*d*.

I. MARY, b. 1685, Sep. 11. d.
m. 1707, May 22.
HENRY STANTON, b. 1688, May 22. d.
of John & Mary (Clarke) Stanton.

1. Mary, 1708, May, 30.
2. Alice, 1709, Oct. 17.
3. Mary, 1712, May 6.
4. Katharine, 1713, Oct. 28.
5. Hannah, 1716, Sep. 25.
6. Henry, 1719, May 22.
7. Joseph, 1724, Mar. 30.

II. CATHARINE, b. 1689, Feb. 23. d. 1717, Apr.
m. 1717, Apr. 18.
THOMAS BORDEN, b. 1682, Dec. 13. d.
of John & Mary (Earle) Borden.

III. TEDDEMAN, b. 1690, Aug. 20. d. Jamestown, R. I.
m. 1711, May 28.
SARAH SANDS, b. 1694, Jan. 30. d.
of Edward & Mary (Williams) Sands.

1. Edward, 1712, Jul. 12.
2. John, 1716, Jun. 22.
3. Robert, 1718, Oct. 9.
4. Mary, 1720, Jul. 28.
5. Sarah, 1728, Jun. 3.

He was a physician.

HULL (JOHN). 2d column. I. Mary. Her husband's mother was Mary Harndel perhaps, instead of Mary Clarke.

1715–17–19–22–23–24–25–26–31–33–39. Deputy.

1717–22–23–24. Clerk of Assembly.

1731. Captain.

1733, Nov. 23. He and wife Sarah, sold 40 acres to Henry Underwood, for £750.

1742. He visited England and is thus described in a letter of introduction from Governor Richard Ward: "Doctor Teddeman Hull, the bearer hereof, being bound for London, in order that you may know the character of the gentleman, I inform you that he is the son of Captain John Hull, late of this colony, under whom Sir Charles Wager was educated, and has the character of an honest man. He has sustained the post of Justice of the Peace, divers years amongst us, and has been several times formerly and latterly a representative from the town of Jamestown. He is of a facetious temper and has a fair estate in lands."

1745, May 1. He and two others were appointed a committee by the Assembly, to view the pier at Block Island, and see if the same be completely finished, and they reported soon after that it was finished.

IV. ALICE, b. 1692, Oct. 22. d.
m. 1715, Jul. 7.
WILLIAM BORDEN, b. 1689, Aug. 15. d.
of John & Mary (Earle) Borden

1. William,

V. JOHN, b. 1695, Jan. 4. d. 1765, Mar. 9. Jamestown, R. I.
m. 1726, Apr. 3.
DAMARIS CARY, b. d. 1765 +
of John & Damaris (Arnold) Cary.

1. Phebe, 1727, Nov. 16.
2. Alice, 1730, May 20.
3. Oliver, 1731, Mar. 16.
4. Hannah, 1733, Jan. 16.
5. Teddeman, 1734, Feb. 1.
6. Joseph, 1736, Feb. 5.
7. Mary, 1739, Feb. 18.
8. Damaris, 1740, Feb. 12.
9. John, 1742, Oct. 21.
10. Freelove, 1744, Oct. 17.
11. Catharine, 1746, Jan. 18.
12. Wager, 1749, Feb. 23.
13. Sarah, 1750, Feb. 7.
14. Abigail, 1750, Feb. 7.

He was a merchant, as well as sea captain.

1720. Freeman.

1748, Aug. He was appointed on a committee to purchase for the colony's use, the two ferry boats and other appurtenances, if the same may be had at a reasonable rate and cheaper than to build new. If a purchase could not be made, then the committee were empowered to build a pier at the west end of highway which runs across Jamestown, and erect a house and purchase two boats, and appoint two persons to tend boats, &c.

1751. Deputy.

1756, Oct. He petitioned Assembly, representing that there is a ferry set up at the Long Wharf, in town of Newport, which hath no mate's boat, and therefore he prays liberty of setting up a ferry on the east side of Jamestown, for transporting of men, women, creatures and everything else, from his wharf in Jamestown, to Newport. The petition was granted on same terms as Thomas Hazard had, for setting up a ferry from the Long Wharf aforesaid.

1759, Nov. 20. Will—codicil 1762, Jul. 30—proved 1765. Exx. wife Damaris. To son Oliver, a farm. To son Teddeman, land at Greenwich, Conn. To sons Joseph and John, the Mount Sorrel Farm. To son John, the Eel Pond Farm. To son Wager, the homestead lands at the ferry. To all his sons, the Dutch Island lands equally divided. The daughters had already been provided with portions during his lifetime. To wife, the profits of estate for life, and she was made residuary legatee.

VI. HANNAH, b. 1697, Mar. 31. d. 1725, Oct. 28.
m. 1721, Apr. 27.
HOLDER SLOCUM, b. 1697, Jun. 14. d. 1758.
of Peleg & Mary (Holder) Slocum.

1. Mary,
2. Alice, 1724, Mar. 19.

VII. JOSEPH, b. 1701, May 6. d. 1773, Oct. 1. Burlington, N. J.
Unmarried.

1723. Freeman.

He held the office of Collector of Customs at New London, Ct., for a time.

He inherited the Teddeman lands, at Burlington, West Jersey.

HULL (JOSEPH). *

JOSEPH[3], (Tristram[2], Jos[1].) b. 1652, Jun. d. 1709 +
m. 1676, Oct.
EXPERIENCE HARPER, b. 1657, Nov. d.

of Robert & Deborah (Perry) Harper.

Barnstable, Mass., Kings Town, R. I.

He was a cooper, trader and preacher.

He sold his Barnstable lands soon after his marriage.

1677, Jul. 23. He had a grant of land at Woods Holl, and soon after purchased other lands near there.

1681, May. The first meeting for worship of the Quakers of Falmouth, was held at his house. He beat the Sheriff soon after this for persecution of him as a Quaker, and was fined £7.

1685, Jul. The court abated his fine for resisting the sheriff.

1695, Jul. 2. Kings Town. He was appointed on a committee by Assembly to propose a method of making a rate.

1696, May 5. Freeman.

1699–1701–2–3. Assistant.

1702. He gave 6*s*. towards building Quaker meeting house at Mashapaug. He was a minister of that denomination.

1703, Oct. 10. He deeded to son John, 75 acres for love, &c.

1706, Oct. 4. Joseph Hull, Tristram Hull, Joseph Hull, Jr., John Hull, Experience Hull and John Hoxsie, sold George Babcock, for

I. TRISTRAM, b. 1677, Oct. 8. d. 1718. Kings Town, Westerly, R. I.
m. 1699, Feb. 9.
ELIZABETH DYER, b. d. 1719.
of Charles & Mary (.) Dyer.

1. Mary,
2. Samuel,
3. Joseph, 1706, Oct. 1.
4. Hannah,
5. Bathsheba,
6. Charles,
7. Stephen,
8. Elizabeth,
9. Sarah,

1696. Constable.

1716, Jul. 1. Will—proved 1718, Jan. 6. Exx. wife Elizabeth. To son Samuel, a tract of land by the seaside with buildings bounded by land of Joseph and John Hull, &c., he paying to his brother Stephen when the latter is of age £100, and if child that wife is with be a son, Samuel to pay him £100 at age. To son Joseph, land at Great Neck, Westerly, 79 acres with buildings. To son Charles, 128 acres in Greenwich. To wife Elizabeth, use of land till son Samuel is of age. To wife the use of all movables to bring up children till daughter Elizabeth is eighteen, except my two Indian servants who are to be hers during their servitude. To daughters Mary, Hannah, Bathsheba and Elizabeth, each a quarter of movable estate at eighteen, and if child wife is with be a daughter, then one-fifth to each.

Inventory, of Tristram Hull, "of Westerly alias Kings Town" £327, 15*s*., viz: wearing clothes, 3 feather beds, 7 chairs, pair of worsted combs, 2 spinning wheels, carpenter tools, gun, pair of stillyards, 16 cows, 18 calves, 2 steers, 4 working cattle, 2 heifers, riding horse, 6 mares, 4 colts, 28 sheep, 8 horsekind, hay £20, 11 swine, &c. The debts were £70. The account of goods was presented by widow Elizabeth Hull and her son-in-law Job Babcock. The widow refused to administer upon the estate by virtue of the will, and administration was given her, she giving bond to pay each child's part at age, and Samuel Dyer, of Newport, offering bond with her, which was accepted.

1719, Jul. 3. Will—proved 1719. Widow Elizabeth. Ex. brother Samuel Dyer, of Newport. To sons Samuel and Joseph, 5*s*. each at age. To daughter Mary Babcock, 5*s*. The executor was empowered to bind out two youngest children under age, and to take out £60, from estate to dispose of to those he binds out children to. The rest of estate to residue of children, viz: to Hannah, Barsheba, Charles, Stephen and Sarah Hull.

II. JOSEPH, b. 1679 ± d. 1748 + Kings Town, Westerly, R. I.
m. (1)
ANN GARDINER, b. d. 1710, Sep. 12.
of William & Elizabeth ( ) Gardiner.
m. (2) 1713, Jan. 1.
SUSANNA GREENE, b. 1688, May 24. d. 1748.
of James & Elizabeth (Anthony) Greene.

1. Ann, 1702, Oct. 26.
2. William, 1705, Jun. 9.
3. Alice, 1708, May 28.
(2d wife).
4. Joseph, 1714, Oct. 4.
5. Susanna, 1716, Apr. 20.
6. Mary, 1719, Feb. 19.
7. Experience 1722, Aug. 25

* American Genealogist, v. 24, no. 4, Oct., 1952, p. 211-212.

£1,000, their interest in 500 acres, being part of land that Joseph Hull bought of Joseph Allen, late of Dartmouth.

1706, Oct. 10. He deeded 100 acres to son Joseph, for love, &c.

1709, Mar 22. He as one of the Trustees for Ninegret, Sachem, for the good service and charge he had been to in propagating the interest of the colony, was allowed £16, 10s., by the Assembly, to be paid out of moneys from sale of vacant lands in Narragansett, or paid in lands, as the committee on vacant lands and Trustees can agree.

The religious meetings of Quakers were held at his residence, described "as a very large wide house."

1709, Jun. 7. Constable.
1714. He bought lands in Westerly.
1724-25-26. Westerly. Town Council.

HULL (JOSEPH). 2d column. III. Mary. Her husband d. 1677, Mar.

III. { MARY, m. JOHN HOXIE, { b. d. HULL (JOSEPH). 2d column. III. Mary m. 1701, John Hoxie 1677; d. 1767. Son Stephen b. 1712, Nov. 28. { b. 1669, Feb. 25. d. 1767. of Lodowick & Mary (Presbury) Hoxie.
1. John,
2 Joseph,
3. Solomon, 1710, Dec.
4. Stephen,
5. Benjamin,

IV. { JOHN, m. 1709, Jul. 11. JEANE CANADA, { b. d. Kings Town, R. I. { b. d. of Canada.

V. { ALICE, m. 1708, Mar. 1 JOHN SEGAR, { b. d. { b. 1684, May 3. d. 1753, Oct. of John Segar.
1. Elizabeth, 1709, Jan. 28.
2. Sarah, 1710, Aug. 17.
3. John, 1712, Nov. 29.
4. Mary, 1715, Feb. 12.
5. Alice, 1717, Jan. 28.
6. Judith, 1719, Mar. 17.
7. Susanna, 1720, Aug. 4.
8. Experience, 1722, Apr. 26.
9. Joseph, 1723, Sep. 6.
10. Hannah, 1725, Feb. 13.
11. Abigail, 1726, May 29.
12. Samuel, 1728, Jan. 25.
13. Elizabeth, 1729, Aug. 27.
14. Barsheba, 1732, Jan. 31

HUNT.

{ BARTHOLOMEW, m. ANN, { b. d. 1687. { b. d. 1687 +

Dover, N. H., Newport, R. I.

1655. Newport. Freeman.

1656, Mar. 17. It was ordered that the town of Newport should pay him for powder and lead that was taken from him. It had been confessed and proved that he had two hundred pounds of powder besides some lead, which an Indian said he bought at Newport.

1687, Feb. 11. Will—proved 1687, Jun. 16. Exx. wife Ann and Major John Albro. To wife, all personal estate, cattle, swine, sheep, household stuff, debts, &c., she paying my four daughters the sum of £4. To sons Bartholomew and Ezekiel, all my housing and land I dwell upon, having given them already by deed of gift, they paying my son John, £30. To wife, use of great room for life, notwithstanding deed of gift to my son Bartholomew, of my mansion house.

Inventory, £36, 9s. (taken 1687, Mar. 5), viz: pewter £4, wearing clothes £3, 10s., warming pan, auger, wool bed, mulatto servant called Gift £12, &c.

I. { BARTHOLOMEW, m. MARTHA, { b. 1654, Dec. 7. d. 1718, Feb. 20. Newport, Tiverton, R. I. { b. d. 1718, Jul. 8. of
1. Adam,
2. John,
3. Edward,
4. William,
5. Ezekiel,
6. Samuel,
7. Joseph,
8. Bartholomew
9. Benjamin,
10. Job,
11. Elizabeth,
12. Ann,
13. Sarah,

1679. Newport. Freeman.

1716, Jan. 9. Will—proved 1718, Apr 7. Exx. wife Martha. To her all my lands and housing and all household goods and all my stock. To son Adam, 1s., he having had. To son John, 1s. To sons Edward, William, Ezekiel, Samuel, Joseph, Bartholomew, Benjamin and Job, each 10s. To daughters Elizabeth, Ann and Sarah, each 10s.

Inventory, £88, 18s. 3d., viz: wearing apparel, feather bed, flock bed, a gun, 23 sheep, 2 pair cards, spinning wheel, 3 cows, 2 heifers, 3 horsekind, 4 swine, 12 geese, 4 turkeys, &c.

II. { ADAM, { b. 1656, Sep. d. young.

III. { NAOMI, m. (1) 1677, Jan. 17. GEORGE LAWTON, m. (2) 1701, Oct. 11. ISAAC LAWTON, { b. 1658, Sep. 15. d. 1721, Jan. 13. { b. d. 1697, Sep. 11. of George & Elizabeth (Hazard) Lawton. { b. 1650, Dec. 11. d. 1732, Jan. 25. of Thomas Lawton.
1. Elizabeth, 1678, Nov. 15.
2. George, 1685, Apr. 30.
3. Robert, 1688, Oct. 14.
4. Job, 1692, Jan. 22.
(By 2d husband, no issue).

IV. { EZEKIEL, m. SARAH, { b. 1663, Mar. 8. d. 1748. Newport, East Greenwich, R. I. { b. d. of
1. Ezekiel,
2. Samuel,
3. Joseph,
4. Bartholomew 1705, Nov. 3.
5. Sarah,
6. Naomi,
7 Ann,
8. Daughter,
9. Bartholomew,

1683, Nov. 5. He bought of William Wilbur, Jr., of Portsmouth, 100 acres in East Greenwich.

1693, Nov. 20. He and Sarah, sold for £14, 10s., to William Davis, of Newport, 100 acres at East Greenwich, with house, &c. He soon after this moved to East Greenwich.

1702, Nov. 8. He bought of Anthony Sadler and wife Mary, of East Greenwich, for £34, house and 10 acres there.

1744, Jan. 5. Will—proved 1748, Nov. 5. Ex. son Joseph. To son Ezekiel, walking stick. To son Samuel, 5s. To son Joseph, gun, &c. To son Bartholomew, homestead at age and to have his brother Joseph for guardian till then (and if Bartholomew die to go to son Joseph's son Joseph). To son Joseph, 25 acres. To grandson Daniel Sweet (son of Daniel), land. To sons Ezekiel, Samuel and Joseph, land in Warwick (two farms there). To son Joseph, farm in North Kingstown. To granddaughter Sarah Hunt (daughter of Joseph), a heifer. To daughter Sarah Freeborn, wife of Thomas, a feather bed. To daughter Naomi Sweet, wife of Daniel, a feather bed. To daughter Ann Hunt, a feather bed. To granddaughter Mary (daughter of late daughter Hunt), a silver spoon, &c. To son Bartholomew, a bed, &c. To son Joseph, rest of out door movables. To daughters Sarah, Naomi and Ann, and granddaughter Mary, indoor movables. To son Joseph, rest of estate.

Inventory, £764, 12s. 4d., viz: a cow, calf, pair of oxen, 14 sheep, mare, 8 swine, 3 heifers, silver spoons, silver cup, silver shirt buttons, cane, gun, pewter, wearing apparel, &c.

V. { JOHN, { b. d.

VI. { DAUGHTER, { b. d.

VII. { DAUGHTER, { b. d.

VIII. { DAUGHTER, { b. d.

IRISH 1st column. His 2d wife, daughter of Constant [Constant?] Southworth

JOHN.[2] (John.[1]) — b. 1645. d. 1717, Feb. 21.
m. (1) 1672.
ELIZABETH, — b. d. 1707, Mar. 8.
m. (2) 1708, May. [Sam'l.
PRISCILLA TALBOT, (w. of — b. d. 1722, Jun. 11.

of Edward & Mary (Pabodie) Southworth.

Duxbury, Mass., Little Compton, R. I.

He was a carpenter.

The family appear to have had their residence in Somersetshire, England, as seen from an indenture of John Irish, the father of above. This indenture was dated 1629, Apr. 20, and recorded in Taunton, Mass. records, 1697, Jul. 12. By the terms thereof, John Irish, of the parish of Clisdon, county of Somerset, laborer, agreed with Timothy Hatherly, of the parish of St. Gloves, in Southwark, county of Surrey, feltmaker, to abide with him five years at Plymouth, New England, having meat, drink and lodging and £5 per year, and at the end of the time, twelve bushels of that country wheat corn, and 25 acres land. John Irish,[1] subsequently went to Duxbury, Mass., where his son John,[2] also lived, prior to coming to Little Compton.

1678, Mar. 5. The court ordered a division of a parcel of land at Saconett, which had belonged to John Irish, deceased, and was by him bequeathed to his two sons, Elias and John, Jr.

1678, Jul. 5. Constable. He was appointed to serve in this office at Saconett, and his liberty and wardship was to extend to Puncateset and places adjacent, and so to Pocassett, and as far as Fall River, and by special order he was to have his oath of office administered by Captain Benjamin Church.

1691, Jan. 7. He and John Woodman, bought of Joseph Wait a piece of salt marsh, for £34.

1715, Nov. 9. Will—proved 1718, Mar. 20. Ex. son David, with assistance of wife. To wife, the part of great lot I live on and half the housing and orchards, while widow, or if she marry, £7 a year. To sons David, Jonathan and John, all right in the sixteenth and seventeenth great lots, &c., and not to be sold except from one to another. To son David, 10 acres without the wood. To son Jedediah, lands in Middleboro, &c. To wife, all interest in my lands at Duxbury, from my father, which I have been so wronged and abused, and imposed about. To four daughters, £20 each, they having already had, viz: Elizabeth, Sarah, Content and Mary. To daughter Joanna, 5s., she having had. If wife should die or leave the farm, the part allotted to her to go to sons Jonathan and John, equally, they paying her £7 yearly. To son John, half of carpenter's tools and a gun. To son David, half of carpenter's tools. To son Jonathan, half of seventeenth lot undisposed of, and to son John, the rest. If daughter-in-law (*i. e.* stepdaughter) Hannah Talbe, live to marry, she to have a cow and ten sheep. To son David, meadow, &c. To wife, the crop in the ground at her disposal for family, and rent of small parcels of land.

Inventory, wearing apparel and jack boots £20, 10s., 3 guns, carbine, warming pan, 3 cheese fats, 2 cheese presses, 30 sheep, 20 lambs, silver spoon, 2 mares, horse, colt, pair of oxen, pair of steers, bull, 16 cows, 2 calves, 2 two years, 7 yearlings, sow, 5 shoats, 2 hives of bees, 8 geese, pair of worsted combs, &c.

1722, Sep. 22. Administration on estate of widow Priscilla Irish, to her son Stephen Talbot. Inventory, £50, 18s. 3*d.*

IX. Mary m. 1715, [Feb 9], William Palmer, b. 1686, Jan. 17, of William [& Mary] (Richmond) Palmer. Children, 1, Jerusha, 1716, [June 1]. 2, Mary, 1719, Feb. 28. 3, William, 1721, [Mar. 7]. 4, David, 1722, Nov, 17. 5, Lawton, 1727, Nov. [24]. 6, Patience, 1730, Jan. 28. 7, Micah, 1732, May 10. [8, Priscilla], 1734, July 5. 9, Content, 1736, Sep. 13. [10 Elizabeth], 1738, Dec. 13.

I. DAVID, — b. 1673. d. 1748.
m.
MARTHA, — b. d. 1760, Feb. 15. of

. 2d column. I. David m. [1699] Jan. 4, Martha Nelson. He d. 1748, Mar. Child[ren, 5,] Jonathan, 1710, Jan. 6. 6, Ruth, 1712, Mar. 5. [7, William], 1714, May 4. 8, Content, 1718, Sep. 3. [III, Jonathan]. Children, 1, Susanna, 1703. 2, Samuel, [1705], 3, Priscilla, 1707. 4, Mary, 1709, May 4. 5, An[na 1713] 6, Jesse. 7, Hannah, 1719. Little Compton, R. I.

1. Elizabeth, 1699, Oct. 17.
2. David, 1703, Jan. 9.
3. Priscilla, 1705, Jan. 18.
4. John, 1708, Jan. 22.
5. William,
6. Ruth,
7. Content,

1746, Jan. 15. Will—proved 1748, Apr. 5. Exx. wife Martha. To wife, use of south-west room in now dwelling house, and entry, part of orchard, keep of a cow, and firewood for life, provided by son John. To son John, all lands and buildings in Little Compton and Tiverton. To son William rights in Pine Islands, lying south of my farm in Rochester, Massachusetts, housing, &c., and 200 acres uplands, and he not to sell same till forty years of age. To him also, a gun, all husbandry tools at Rochester and carpenter's tools, he providing a fat dressed hog of one hundred pounds or more, yearly, for his mother. To son John, 200 acres upland in Rochester, meadow, &c., and certain carpenter tools at Little Compton. To daughters Priscilla Hiller, Ruth Brownell, and Content Gifford, rest of lands in Rochester. To wife Martha, use of half of farm in Rochester for life and half of housing, and the rest of movables.

Inventory, £1,421, 11s., 4*d.*, viz: wearing apparel and cane, 121, 5s., books, spectacles, hone, razor and comb £70, 7s., 2 pair of cards, pair of combs, 2 wheels, warming pan, pewter, mare, 2 cows, 50 sheep, 51 sheep and lambs, notes, &c.

1759, Jun. 20. Will—proved 1760, Apr. 1. Widow Martha. Ex. son-in-law Joseph Gifford, of Dartmouth. To son John, of Little Compton, all farming utensils, and loom. To son William, of Rochester, all my household stuff left at his house, not disposed of. To daughters Priscilla Hiller and Content Gifford, all household goods equally. To grandson Thomas Irish, household things lent him, To sons and daughters, equally, paper money.

Inventory, £2,150, 10s.

II. ELIZABETH, — b. 1674, Feb. d.

IRISH. 2d column. III Jonathan. His wife was Mary Taylor, b. 1682, Oct. 25, of John & Abigail ( ) Taylor. His 5th child was named Ann.

III. JONATHAN, — b. 1678, Jun. 6. d. 1732.
m.
MARY, — b. d. 1732 + of
Little Compton, R. I.

1. Samuel,
2. Jesse,
3. Hannah,
4. Mary,

1732, Aug. 31. Inventory, £1,710, 10s., shown by widow Mary, administratrix. Wearing apparel, £16, pewter, loom, quilting wheel, 4 guns, pistol, yoke of oxen, steer, 4 two year olds, 2 yearlings, 4 cows, 3 calves, 3 horsekind, 7 swine, 3 bonds £344, housing and lands in Little Compton £900, house and land in Tiverton, £120, &c.

1732, Aug. 15. Samuel Irish, son of Jonathan, age of fourteen, chose his mother for guardian, as did Jesse, Hannah and Mary under fourteen.

IV. JOANNA, — b. 1681, Jun. 6. d.
m. 1708, Oct. 11
EDWARD ROBERTSON, — b. d. of Robertson.

1. David,

V. SARAH, — b. 1684, Jan. d. 1739, Oct. 24.
m. 1712, Dec. 4.
WILLIAM SCHREICH, — b. d. of Schreich.

1. Teddeman, 1713, Sep. 4.
2. John, 1716, Feb. 5.
3. William, 1718, Feb. 28.
4. Elizabeth, 1721, Sep. 5.

VI. PRISCILLA, — b. 1686, Apr. 30. d. 1715 (—)
Unmarried.

VII. JEDEDIAH, — b. 1688, Oct. 7. d.
m.
MARY, — b. d. of
Kings Town, Westerly, R. I., Stonington, Ct.

IRISH. 2d column. VII. Jedediah. He had also a son Job; and perhaps George and Jonathan.

1. Jedediah, 1711, Nov. 16.
2. Mary, 1714, Jan. 22.
3. Elizabeth, 1715, Nov. 4.
4. Lydia, 1718, Nov. 6.
5. John, 1720, Jun. 9.
6. Thankful, 1722, Aug 24.
7. Joseph, 1724, Apr. 20.

1716, Feb. 3. He and wife Mary, of Kings Town, took as apprentice for twenty years, David Robertson, son of Joanna Robertson, widow, late of Little Compton.

1722. Ear mark.

1741. Westerly. Freeman.

1754. Stonington.

VIII. CONTENT, — b. 1691, Sep. d.
m. 1715, Jan. 4.
JOSEPH LAWTON, — b. d. of Daniel & Rebecca ( ) Lawton.

1. Rebecca, 1715, Dec. 19.
2. David, 1718, May 21.
3. Priscilla, 1721, Jun. 10.
4. Elizabeth, 1723, Oct. 4.
5. John, 1726, Feb. 28.

IX. MARY, — b. 1695, Apr. 9. d.

X. JOHN, — b. 1699, May 1. d. 1773.
m.
THANKFUL WILBUR, — b. 1700, Jun. 8. d. 1773 + of Samuel & Mary (Potter) Wilbur.
Little Compton, R. I.

1. Edward,
2. Charles, 1723, May 30.
3. Ichabod,
4. Lewis,
5. Mary,
6. Thankful,
7. David,
8. Samuel,

1773, Jan. 30. Will—proved 1773, Aug. 3. Ex. son David. To wife best bed, great bible, half of household stuff, and she to be provided by my sons David and Samuel, with all necessaries of life suitable for such an aged woman, and to be kind and tender of her in her old age, she living with either. To son Edward, sixty Spanish milled dollars. To son Charles, $14. To son Ichabod, $14. To son Lewis, an English crown. To daughters Mary Manchester and Thankful Cook, $7, each. To sons David and Samuel, the rest of estate, real and personal, except that Samuel was to have first the long gun.

Inventory, gun, 2 bibles, other books, silver spoon, 2 sheep, 2 lambs, ox, 3 cows, 3 yearling cattle, 2 calves, horse, 10 swine, &c.

(2d WIFE, no issue.)

X. John m. 1720, May [11, Children], 3, Lydia, 1725, Aug. 9. 4, John, 1727, [Dec. 9]. 5, Levi, 1730, Oct. 20. 6, Mary, 1734. May 16. 7, [Thankful] 1737, June 8. 8, David, 1737, June 8. 9, Ich[abod, 1740] Jan. 6. 10, Lemuel, 1743, Jan. 21. Betwee[n VI. &] VII. place Elizabeth, b. 1687, Aug. 28.

JACQUES

AARON, — b. d. 1711.
m.
HANNAH, — b. d. 1711 +

Kings Town, R. I.

1679, Jul. 29. He and forty-one others of Narragansett, signed a petition to the King, praying that he "would put an end to these differences about the government thereof, which hath been so fatal to the prosperity of the place; animosities still arising in people's minds, as they stand affected to this or that government."

1687, Sep. 6. Taxed 2s. 9*d.*

1709, May 27. He and five others bought 792 acres of the vacant lands in Narragansett.

1711, Apr. 7. Inventory shown by widow Hannah. Spinning wheel, mare, cow, hay, cash, apparel, &c.

I. AARON, — b. 1683, d.
m.
ELIZABETH, — b. d. of
Kings Town, R. I.

1. Hannah,
2. Elisha,
3. Mary,
4. Lydia,

1718. He, called himself thirty-five years old, in a deposition.

II. ELIZABETH, — b. d.
m. 1704, Mar. 8.
RICHARD SWEET, — b. 1676, Feb. 28. d. of Richard & Mehitable (Larkin) Sweet.

III. NATHAN, — b. d. 1722.
m. 1709, Apr. 14.
HANNAH NORRIS, — b. d. of Norris.
Kings Town, R. I.

1722, Oct. 3. Administration to Joseph Mumford. Inventory, £28, 19s.

IV. THOMAS, — b. d. 1744.
m.
HANNAH SPINK, — b. d. 1744 + of Robert Spink.
Kings Town, Exeter, R. I.

1. Thomas,
2. Robert,
3. Samuel,
4. George,
5. Jonathan,

1712. Freeman.

1730, Mar. He and wife Hannah, were parties to a suit against Nicholas Spink, to recover certain lands that had been owned by the father of said Thomas Jacques' wife. 1744, May 31. Will—proved 1744, Dec. 11. Exx. wife Hannah. To wife Hannah, all estate, except 5s. to each of his children, viz: to Thomas, Robert, Samuel, George, Jonathan, Dinah, Elizabeth and Amory. Inventory, £116, 14s., viz: a cow, heifer, mare, &c.		6. Dinah, 7. Elizabeth, 8. Amory,

JAMES (Thomas).

THOMAS, * { b. { d.

Salem, Mass., Providence, R. I.

He is stated to have been a clergyman as well as physician.

1638. He had a grant of land.

1638, Oct. 8. Providence. He was one of the twelve persons to whom Roger Williams deeded land that he had bought of Canonicus and Miantonomi.

1639. He was one of the twelve original members of First Baptist Church.

1640, Mar. 20. He sold to William Field my dwelling house and all my housing in Providence, as also my field, garden, meadow, &c., and land at Sassafrax Hill, land on Moshassuck River and all other rights in Providence, for sum of £60.

1649. He is mentioned in a letter written this year by Roger Williams, who says that he returned from England with a full cargo of goods which were saved though the vessel was wrecked on Rhode Island.

* See: American Geneologist, v. 20, p. 113-114

JAMES (William).

WILLIAM, { b. { d.
m. 1677, Dec. 10.
SUSANNA MARTIN, { b. { d. 1726, Mar. 4.
of Joseph Martin.

(She m. (2) Benjamin Tayer.

Newport, R. I.

1675, May 4. Freeman.

Perhaps he was a son of an earlier William James who was freeman of Newport in 1655.

His widow died at the house of her son John James as the Quaker Records declare.

He and his wife were buried in the Coddington Burial Ground.

I.	JOSEPH,	b. 1680, Feb. 24. d.			
II.	WILLIAM,	b. 1682. d. 1683, May 5.			
III.	SARAH,	b. 1685. d. 1689, Feb. 8.			
IV.	JOHN, m. (1) ANN TAYLOR, m. (2) LYDIA PECKHAM,	b. d. 1766. b. 1686, Sep. d. 1727, Nov. 4. b. 1698, May 8. d. 1778, Jan. 28.	 of John & Abigail ( ) of John & Mary ( )	Newport, R. I. Taylor. Peckham.	1. Martin, 1735, Apr.

See: American Geneologist v. 34, p. 169

JEFFERAY.

WILLIAM[7], (Wm[6]., Thos.[5], Wm[4] Jno[3] Wm[2] Symon[1].) { b. 1591. { d. 1675, Jan. 2.
m. 1640 ±
MARY GOULD. { b. { d. 1675 +
of Jeremiah & Priscilla (Grover) Gould.

Chiddingly, Sussex Co., Eng., Newport, R. I.

He was born at Chiddingly Manor, where his father and more remote ancestors were buried.

1603, Jul. 7. He matriculated as sizar of Caius College, Cambridge.

1606. He took degree of B.A., at graduation.

1610. He took degree of M.A.

1611. His father died this year and the widow moved to London, where her father had been a merchant.

1623, Sep. Weymouth. He and Rev. Wm. Blackstone were probably of Robert Gorges' party who made settlement at this date at Wessaggassett (Weymouth) and they both acted as agents for John Gorges a few years later (1629), being empowered by him to put John Oldham in possession of his afterward contested territory. They were styled at that time "Wm. Blackstone, Cler. and Wm. Jefferay, Gent."

1626. Salem. He was among the first settlers.

1626, Apr. 1. He had legacy from his mother's will, of two houses and bake house and ale house, "with sign of Cordelyon," &c., all anciently known as Flower de Luce, in Southwark.

1628. He and Mr. Burslem gave £2, and Mr. Blackstone, 12s., towards expense of banishing the notorious Morton, of Merry Mount, who was at that time setting all laws at defiance and sadly scandalizing the rigid virtue of the Puritans by his extravagances.

1629, Apr. 21. He is styled "William Jeffries,

See: American Geneologist, v. 19, p. 224.

I.	MARY, m. JOHN GREENE,	b. 1642, Mar. 20. d. b. d.	 of	 Greene.	1. John,
II.	THOMAS,	b. d.			
III.	SUSANNAH, m. EDWARD THURSTON,	b. d. b. 1652, Apr. 1. d. 1690, Dec. 7.	 of Edward & Elizabeth (Mott)	 Thurston.	1. Edward, 1678. 2. William, 1680. 3. Abigail, 1686, Apr. 3. 4. Priscilla, 5. Jonathan,
IV.	PRISCILLA, m. THOMAS CODDINGTON,	b. 1654. d. 1688, Aug. 7. b. 1655, Nov. 5. d. 1694, Mar. 4.	 of William & Ann (Brinley)	 Coddington.	1. William, 1684. 2. Thomas, 1687, Apr. 17.
V.	SARAH, m. 1673. JAMES BARKER,	b. 1656. d. 1736, Feb. b. 1648. d. 1722, Dec.	 of James & Barbara (Dungan)	 Barker.	1. James, 1675, Dec. 4. 2. William, 3. Nicholas, 4. Mary, 5. Abigail, 6. Priscilla, 7. Jane, 8. Jeremiah, 1699, Jan. 16.

JEFFERAY. 2d column. V. Sarah. Her husband d. 1722, Dec. 1.

Gentleman," in a letter of instructions to Salem settlement. He was for a time at Manchester, Mass. (then called for him Jeffreys Creek), at Ipswich, Weymouth, Boston, and even as far eastward as the Isles of Shoals, which he is said to have owned, but used probably only as a fishing stage.

1631, May 18. Freeman.

1634, May. He is called "my very good gossip" by Morton in a letter from the latter, a fact sometimes cited to show they were intimates, but negatived apparently by his subscription for the expulsion of Morton.

1636. He had a legacy of 10*s.*, to buy a ring, by the will of his brother-in-law Hugh Evans, of London.

1641. Weymouth. Commissioner.

1652. Newport. He was on a Committee of four persons who wrote a letter for Newport to towns of Providence and Warwick.

1654, Mar. 27. He sold Lawrence Turner and Tobias Saunders, land at Newport, measuring 67 by 57 rods.

1655. Freeman.

1660, Oct. 16. He was granted 500 acres by General Court of Massachusetts "to be a final issue of all claims by virtue of any grant heretofore made by any Indian whatever." This was in lieu of a grant made to him years before by Indians at Jeffrey's Neck, in Ipswich. He sold the 500 acres to William Hudson.

1661. Commissioner.

1664. Deputy.

1667, May 14. He was appointed on a commission to make a rate for a levy of £150, for the prison, pound and stocks and mounting of great guns.

1674, Dec. 8. Will—proved 1675, Jan. 9. Exx. daughter Mary Greene. Overseers, wife's two brethren John and Daniel Gould, and son-in-law John Greene to assist them. He provides for maintenance of wife Mary. To eldest daughter Mary, wife of John Greene, of Newport, land lying and being in Blackman street near the city of London, of a rent of £18, which was given him by will of his mother Audry, late of Chittingleigh. To son Thomas, houses and tenements in England, except what Mary had. To daughter Sarah, wife of James Barker, £5 in silver, 50*s.* whereof James Barker hath already. To daughters Priscilla and Susanna, 25 acres in Newport. To daughters Priscilla, Mary and Susannah, rest of estate after death of their mother.

He was buried in Newport Cemetery. The inscription on his tombstone is as follows: "Here lyeth interred the body of Wm. Jeffray, Gent., who departed this life on the 2nd day of Jany., 1675, in the 85th year of his age."

"Since every tomb an epitaph can have,
The Muses owe their tribute to this grave.
And to succeeding ages recommend
His worthy name who lived and died their friend;
Being full of days and virtues, love and peace,
God from his troubles gave him a release,
And called him unto the celestial place,
Where happy souls view their Creator's face.

Vivit post funera Virtus."

JENCKES.

JOSEPH,[2] (Joseph.[1]) b. 1632. d. 1717, Jan. 4.
m
ESTHER BALLARD, b. d. 1717 +
of William & Elizabeth ( ) Ballard.

Lynn, Mass., Providence, R. I.

1669, Mar. 25. Warwick. He was granted land on either side of the Pawtuxet, for the employ of his saw-mill, and he, for this favor from the purchasers of Warwick, agreed to let them have boards at 4*s.* 6*d.* the hundred, and all other sawn work to be equivalent to same. The grant included trees of pine, chestnut or oak, within half a mile on each side of the river, that is floatable, the proprietors reserving the right to cut what they need.

1670, Jan. 18. He was foreman of a jury in the case of Thomas Smith, and Ruth, his wife, "who were both drowned in the river of Pawtuxet, the 16th instant at night."

1671, Oct. 10. Providence. He bought 60 acres more or less with right of commonage, of Abel Potter, and wife Rachel, said land belonging formerly to Rachel's grandfather, Ezekiel Holliman, and being situated near Pawtucket Falls. Here he established his forge, saw-mill, &c.

1676. His forge was destroyed by the Indians, in King Philip's War.

1677. Freeman.

1679, Jul. 1. Taxed 12*s.* 6*d.*, including his saw-mill.

1679-80-91. Deputy.

I. JOSEPH, b. 1656. d. 1740, Jun. 15. Providence, R. I.
m. (1)
MARTHA BROWN, b. d. of John & Mary (Holmes) Brown.
m. (2) 1727, Feb. 3. [John.
ALICE DEXTER, (w. of b. 1665. d. 1736, Feb. 19. of John & Sarah (Whipple) Smith.

1. Joseph,
2. Obadiah,
3. Catharine, 1694.
4. Nathaniel,
5. Martha,
6. Lydia,
7. John,
8. Mary,
9. Esther,
(2d wife, no issue.)

1681. Freeman.

1688, Aug. 6. Ratable estate, 3 acres planting land, an acre of orchard, 3 cows, heifer, mare.

1691-98-99-1700-1-2-3-4-5-6-7-8. Deputy.

1698-99-1707-8. Speaker of House of Deputies.

1707-8-9-10-11. Major for the Main.

1708-9-10-11-12. Assistant.

1715-16-17-18-19-20-21-22-23-24-25-26-27. Deputy Governor.

1719, Jun. 8. He deeded his son-in-law, William Turpin, and wife Catharine, 40 acres, for love, &c.

1720, Jul. 7. He was appointed agent in England, on account of the refusal of Connecticut, to stand to and comply with the bounds between the two colonies, as settled by the commissioners of both at Stonington, in the year 1703, and also of the further difference between this colony and the Province of Massachusetts. He was authorized to draw bills of exchange on the General Treasury, for sum of £700, if he shall need or require so much. He to be allowed £60 per year and expenses, and also £60 to furnish himself with necessaries for the voyage. He and the other agent, Richard Partridge, subsequently memorialized the King as to the Connecticut controversy, praying finally that "they may not hereafter be molested, as they have hitherto been to their very great prejudice." His son, Dr. John Jenckes, died in England.

1721, Oct. He exhibited to the Assembly, his account of disbursements of the Colony's money, during his agency, amounting to £300, 18*s.* and it was approved and voted that he "have £30 allowed him as a gratuity out of the General Treasury, for his good service done the colony during his agency."

1726, Jan. 10. He was appointed by Assembly, one of the four commissioners to meet commissioners of Connecticut, to settle line of partition of two colonies.

1727. He wrote a letter on behalf of General Assembly, to King George II, thanking him for continuing unto us the great enjoyment of our ancient charter privileges, great in their nature, but far

1680, May. 5. He and two others were empowered by Assembly to purchase a bell "for the public use of this colony, and for giving notice or signifying the several times or sittings of the Assemblys and Courts of Trials, and General Councils." The bell was purchased for £3, 10*s*. of Freelove Arnold (daughter of Governor Benedict Arnold). Earlier the Assembly had been called together by beat of drum.

1680-81-82-83-84-85-86-89-90-91-95-96-98. Assistant.

1683, Nov. 14. He had land laid out.

1687, Sep. 1. He and his sons, Joseph and Nathaniel, were taxed together 12*s*.

1688, Aug. 6. Ratable estate, 6 acres planting land, 2 acres meadow, 8 acres pasture, 30 acres wild pasture, rights in land, 4 oxen, 7 cows, 2 steers, heifer, yearling, 2 mares, colt, swine, sheep, saw-mill.

1690, Jan. 30. He and five others and the Deputy Governor, wrote a letter to William and Mary, congratulating them on their accession to the throne, and informing them that since the deposition of Sir Edmund Andros, the former government under the charter had been reassumed. They also mentioned the seizure of Andros, in Rhode Island, on his flight from Massachusetts, and his return to that colony, on the demand of Massachusetts.

1695, Jul. 2. He was chosen by the Assembly, to run the eastern line of the colony.

1713, Jun. 16. Taxed 12*s*. 6*d*.

1708, Oct. 21. Will — proved 1717, Feb. 11. Exx. wife Esther (but she declining by reason of age and inability, her son Nathaniel acted at her request, and by appointment of the court). He confirmed deeds already made to sons Joseph, Nathaniel, Ebenezer and William. To sons Nathaniel, Ebenezer and William, other land, and if any further division was made by proprietors of Providence, then the four sons were to share equally. To sons Ebenezer and William, equally, the coal house and his half the forge, at death of himself and wife. To loving wife Esther, all the rest of movable estate, cattle and chattels, for life, and what remains at her death she is to dispose of to children or grandchildren, as she sees fit.

Inventory, £36, 19*s*. 8*d*., viz: wearing apparel, 6 pewter platters, 3 plates, 3 basins, 5 porringers, &c., brass and ironware, old books, money due for cow sold £4, 10*s*., another cow unsold £4, 10*s*., warming pan, smoothing iron, old bible, stillyards, &c.

The family account gives Samuel Miller, as the husband of Joseph Jenckes' daughter Esther. That she married Samuel Millard or Miller (both forms are used) seems certain, but the Rehoboth records are rather confusing in this matter. The record says: Esther Bowen, m. 1682, Jul. 20, Samuel Millard, and had children Esther, b. 1683, Apr. 1, John, b. 1684, Dec. 24, Elizabeth, b. 1686, Oct. 5, Alice, b. 1689, Jul. 3, Margaret, b. 1693, Jul. 12, Samuel, b. 1697, Jun. 30. The record is also given that Hannah Jenckes, of Providence, m. 1701, Jun. 1, Samuel Millard, and had Joseph, b. 1701, Jul. 28. Esther, wife of Samuel Millard, d. 1699, Apr. 11, according to the same record. (The will of Samuel Millard, mentions wife Esther.)

[JE]NCKS. 1st column. Near the end read Esther … (not Hannah) m. Samuel Millard. Samuel Millard [had] two wives named Esther. 2d column. V. Esthe[r] … 1701, June 1, Samuel Millard, b. 1658, Oct. 5; d. … Aug. 31, of John. She d. 1720+. Children. 1. Jo[seph] … 1701, July 28.

greater by being suited to the circumstances of this, your Majesty's colony; or rather in that we, your Majesty's subjects, have had our birth, growth and improvements under the same." He apprizes him of "a regular and beautiful fortification of stone," built at Newport, with a battery where may be mounted sixty guns, &c.

1727-28-29-30-31-32. Governor.

1735, Dec. 22. Will—proved 1736, Apr. 17. Wife Alice. She left her estate to her children, by former husband, John Dexter. Inventory, £201, 2*s*.

1740, Aug. 25. He was "deemed to die intestate by reason of his insanity of mind," and his son Nathaniel, was appointed administrator. Inventory, £124, 1*s*., viz: books £15, 2 cows, flask, tobacco box, wafer box, 2 canes, wearing apparel £84, 13*s*., &c.

He was buried in the North Burial Ground.

1. John,
2. Samuel,
3. Peter,
4. Sarah,
5. Elizabeth,
6. Esther,
7. Mary,
8. Tabitha,
9. Mercy,
10. Susanna,

II. { ELIZABETH, m. SAMUEL TEFFT, } { b. 1658. d. 1740. } { b. 1644. d. 1725. • } of John & Mary ( ) Tefft.

III. { SARAH, m. NATHANIEL BROWN, } { b. d. 1708. } { b. 1661, Jun. 9 d. 1739, Nov. 13. } of John & Lydia (Bucklin) Brown.

1. Esther,	1688, Mar. 25.
2. Nathaniel,	1689, Sep. 24.
3. Nathan,	1691, Sep. 19.
4. John,	1694, Mar. 30.
5. Josiah,	1695, Sep. 18.
6. Sarah,	1698, Feb. 19.
7. Penelope,	1699, May 17.
8. Lydia,	1700, Aug. 11.
9. Mary,	1702, Jan. 18.
10. Keziah,	1704, Mar.
11. Elizabeth,	1706, Jun. 20.

JENCKES. 1st column. Esther Ballard, b. 1633. 2d column. IV. Nathaniel. His wife Hannah, b 1663, Nov. 5, of Jonathan & Hannah (Howland) Bosworth. VI Ebenezer. His wife Mary, b. 1677, Oct. 20, of John & Hannah (Wheaton) Butterworth.

IV. { NATHANIEL, m. 1686, Nov. 4. HANNAH BOSWORTH, } { b. 1662, Jan. 29. d. 1723, Aug. 11. } { b. d. 1723 + } of Bosworth. Providence, R. I.

1. Jonathan,
2. Nathaniel,
3. Hannah,
4. Elizabeth,

1688, Aug. 6. Ratable estate, 2 acres planting land, cow, a two year old, yearling, 2 colts.

1690. Freeman.

1709. Captain, and later held the office of Major.

1709-10-13. Deputy.

1711, May 2. He was appointed by Assembly, with his brother Joseph, to build a bridge at Pawtucket.

1713, Jun. 16. Taxed 14*s*.

1719-20-21-22-23. Town Council.

1721, Apr. 27. Will—codicil 1723, Jul. 31—proved 1723, Oct. 21. Exs. wife Hannah and son Nathaniel. To son Nathaniel, all the homestead, dwelling house, &c., half at death of testator and the other half at death of wife. To Nathaniel also, lands in Attleboro, all right in forge, smith shop, tools, coal house, saw-mill and corn mill, all at Pawtucket, except the saw-mill on east side of the river. The delivery was to be half at testator's death and the other half at death or marriage of wife. To wife Hannah, the use while widow, of half above property. To daughter Elizabeth Jenckes, £50. The rest of personal to go at death of wife, to children and grandchildren. To son Jonathan, £30, paid by his brother Nathaniel, and two children of Jonathan, viz: Jonathan and Mary, who were with their grandfather, the testator, were to have £10 each from Nathaniel, if they staid with said Nathaniel till of age. To daughter Hannah Capron, £5, in case her husband pays £43 which he owes. The codicil reduced the legacy to Jonathan to 10*s*., as he had already received some.

Inventory, £200 ± viz: 4 cows, 2 oxen, 4 two years, 2 yearlings, horse, 26 sheep, 7 swine, bellows, forge, smith tools, vice, anvil, &c., coal, 2 spinning wheels, 4 pair of cards, great bible, other books, &c.

V. { ESTHER, m. SAMUEL MILLARD, } { b. 1664. d. } { b. d. 1720. } of Millard.

VI. { EBENEZER, m. 1695, Mar. 4. MARY BUTTERWORTH, } { b. 1669. d. 1726, Aug. 14. } { b. d. 1726 + } of John & Sarah ( ) Butterworth. Providence, R. I.

1. Sarah,	1695, Dec. 26.
2. Ebenezer,	1699, Sep. 17.
3. Daniel,	1701, Oct. 18.
4. Phebe,	1703, Jan. 16.
5. Rufus,	1704, Dec. 18.
6. Rachel,	1706, Dec. 1.
7. Mary,	1708, Oct. 17.
8. Joseph,	1711, Jun. 25.
9. Mercy,	1712, Aug. 26.
10. Benjamin,	1714, Nov. 3.
11. Freelove,	1717, Sep. 13.
12. Noah,	1717, Sep. 13.
13. Josiah,	1720, Apr. 2.

1719. Ordained pastor of First Baptist Church, and so continued until his death.

1726, Oct. 17. Administration to widow Mary. Inventory, £150, viz: 2 oxen, 5 cows, 3 calves, mare, 9 sheep, weaver's harness, stays and looms, books, &c.

VII. { JOANNA, m. 1692 ± SYLVANUS SCOTT, } { b. 1672. d. 1756, Mar. 12. } { b. 1672, Nov. 10. d. 1742, Jan. 13. } of John & Rebecca ( ) Scott.

1. John,	1694, Sep. 30.
2. Catharine,	1696, Mar. 31.
3. Joseph,	1697, Aug. 15.
4. Rebecca,	1699, Feb. 11.
5. Esther,	1700, Dec. 5.
6. Sylvanus,	1702, Jun. 20.
7. Joanna,	1703, Dec. 11.
8. Charles,	1705, Aug. 23.
9. Sarah,	1707, Jun. 15.
10. Jeremiah,	1709, Mar. 11.
11. Nathaniel,	1711, Apr. 19.

VIII. { ABIGAIL, m. THOMAS WHIPPLE, } { b. d. } { b. d. } of Samuel & Mary (Harris) Whipple.

IX. { WILLIAM, m. (1) PATIENCE SPRAGUE, m. (2) MARY, } { b. 1675. d. 1765, Oct. 2. } { b. d. } { b. d. 1765 + } of Jonathan & Mehitable (Holbrook) Sprague. of . Providence, North Providence, R. I.

1. Joseph,	
2. Susanna,	
3. Mercy,	
4. William,	
5. Patience,	
6. Margaret,	1704.
7. Jonathan,	1707, Jul.
8. John,	1710.
9. Esther,	
10. Mehitable,	

1713, Jun. 16. Taxed 14*s*. 6*d*.

1720, Oct. He, having expended £15 upon Pawtucket bridge, the Assembly, upon his petition, granted piece of land to him north of Blackstone River, in angle of said river, providing that on a survey of the same, if it be worth more than £15 or £16, he to pay overplus to the General Treasury. The surveyors reported 33 acres and 53 poles, worth 10*s*. an acre.

1727-28-29-38. Deputy.

1731, Feb. He was appointed on a committee with six others, to meet the Massachusetts commissioners, to make and finally settle and ascertain the east bounds of this colony.

1731, Oct. He was allowed £100 by Assembly, to build half of a bridge at Pawtucket Falls.

1734-35. Justice of Inferior Court of Common Pleas, for county of Providence, with three others.

1739, Feb. He was appointed by Assembly, to repair the half of great bridge over Pawtucket River (the part built by this colony) and was granted £50 for the purpose. The bridge had been partly carried away by the late great flood of waters.

1739. Smithfield. Deputy.

1740, Dec. 2. He was appointed on a committee to represent and manage the affairs of this colony before the commissioners, to hear and determine the boundaries between Rhode Island and Massachusetts.

1765, Oct. 28. Inventory, £72, 8*s*. 6*d*., presented by Jonathan Jenckes and widow Mary. 2 cows, 2 swine, large bible and 12 other books, warming pan, pewter, silver cup, 4 silver spoons, gun, &c. Jonathan Jenckes appeared before the Town Council, and read the will of his father, and the widow, Mary Jenckes, being present, did not accept of it. Stephen Jenckes, a witness, testified that the deceased was in his right mind.

THOMAS, b. / d. 1674 +
m.
ANN, b. / d. 1684 +

Portsmouth, R. I.

1643. He was received as an inhabitant and gave engagement to the government.

1644, May 27. He and William Hall were granted a lot to be equally divided between them.

1655. Freeman.

1671, Nov. 1. He had received 20*s.* from the Governor, and 2*s.* 9*d.*, from Francis Brayton, for [illegible] service in Assembly's business in Provi[illegible] and Warwick. The Assembly therefore voted to re-imburse said persons.

1674, Jul. 16. He and wife Ann deeded homestead and 16 acres to son Thomas.

1684, Mar. 25. His widow Ann, brought suit against Isaac Lawton.

I. SAMUEL, b. / d. — Portsmouth, R. I.

1655. Freeman.

II. THOMAS, b. / d. 1691. — Portsmouth, R. I.
m.
DOROTHY, b. / d. 1691 + of

Children: 1. Sarah,

1672, Apr. 30. Freeman.

1690, Aug. 5. Will—proved 1691, May 8. Exx. wife Dorothy. Overseers, John Anthony and Elias Williams. To brothers and sisters, 1*s.* each. To wife, all money, goods, &c. The overseers were directed to sell lands and give half the proceeds to wife, and put the other half out to interest for daughter Sarah Jennings' benefit till she be sixteen years old or married. If wife and daughter die, their part to go to brothers and sisters of testator.

III. JOB, b. / d. — Kings Town, R. I.

1687, Sep. 6. Taxed 4*s.*, $2\frac{1}{2}$*d.*

IV. GABRIEL, b. / d. 1711 (—) — Newport, R. I.
m.
SARAH BLAIDS (widow). b. / d. 1713. of

1698, Jan. 11. He deeded wife Sarah, for love, &c., and 1*s.*, all household goods and all other estate real and personal, to be hers at his death.

1711, Jun. 1. Will—proved 1713, Feb. 25. Widow Sarah Jennings. Exs. friend John Bailey, of Rhode Island, and his son William of Seaconnet. To son William Blaids, all estate, house, land, gold, silver, &c.

1714, Sep. Suit was brought by Adam Mott and wife Sarah, termed heir of Gabriel Jennings, against Sarah Hubbard, widow, and Susanna Hamm, widow, for trespass, &c., damage £300. In answer the defendants say that they are tenants to William Blaids, an infant under twenty-one, and that Sarah is not heir to Gabriel, for two brothers of said Jennings, viz: Richard and Joseph, are living, and two sisters, and heirship is in eldest brother now living. Testimony was given that Sarah, the wife of Adam Mott, was daughter of Thomas Jennings, brother of Gabriel.

V. RICHARD, b. / d.

VI. JOSEPH, b. / d.

VII. DAUGHTER, b. / d.

VIII. DAUGHTER, b. / d.

JOHNSON.

JOHN, b. / d. 1702.
m.
MARY, b. / d. 1703 +

Rehoboth, Mass., Westerly, R. I.

It is assumed that John Johnson, of Rehoboth, who had the births of five of his children recorded there, is identical with John Johnson of Westerly, whose will was made there.

1702, May 19. Will—proved 1702, Dec. 8. Ex. son Joseph (at request of widow Mary, 1703, Jan. 5). To son Joseph, land on east side of the common road except half an acre. To son Jonah, land on west side of common road and the above half acre. To wife, for life all improved land, house and movables. To Joseph and Jonah, certain land equally. To son Jonah and daughter Rebecca, all movables equally at wife's death. To son John and daughters Elizabeth and Mary, 1*s.* each.

Inventory, cow, calf, mare, bible and another book 7*s.* &c.

I. JOHN, b. / d. 1733. — Westerly, R. I.
m.
ELIZABETH, b. / d. 1733 + of

1733, Jan. 11. Inventory, £37, 10*s.* 2*d.*, shown by widow Elizabeth. Wearing apparel £5, 18*s.* 6*d.*, gun, cash £1, 5*s.*, silver buttons 4*s.*, &c.

II. MARY, b. / d.

III. ELIZABETH, b. 1673, May 19. / d.

IV. JOSEPH, b. 1677, Oct. 3. / d. 1731. — Westerly, R. I.
m.
SARAH DOLOVER, b. / d. 1731 + of Joseph & Rachel ( ) Dolover.

Children: 1. Reuben, 2. Stephen, 3. Sarah, 4. Joseph, 5. Gideon, 6. Daniel, 7. Nathaniel.

1731, Jun. 19. Will—proved 1731, Jul. 2. Exs. wife Sarah and son Reuben. To son Stephen, two youngest steers. To daughter Sarah, £5. To son Joseph, tools and loom. To son Gideon, £3 at age, and like legacy to sons Daniel and Nathaniel, at age. To wife Sarah and son Reuben, all the rest of movables.

Inventory, £132, 4*s.* 6*d.*, viz: wearing apparel £4, bed, pewter, wooden ware, book 10*s.*, coopers' tools, fishing craft 2*s.*, leather, 2 mares, cattle £50, swine, &c.

V. REBECCA, b. 1679, Nov. 17. / d.

VI. RACHEL, b. 1681, Dec. 23. / d.

VII. JONATHAN, b. 1683, Feb. 20. / d.

VIII. JONAH, b. / d. — Westerly, R. I.
m.
MARY, b. / d. of

Children: 1. John, 1709, Sep. 8.

JONES.

JOHN, b. d. 1684, May 1.
m.
MARY, b. d.

Providence, R. I.

1650, Sep. 2. Taxed 3s. 4d.

1655. Freeman.

1657. Town Sergeant.

1661, Feb. 11. He sold Thomas Olney, Sr., rights in land.

1666, May. He swore allegiance to the King.

1665, Feb. 19. He had lot 34 in a division of lands.

1669, Aug. 17. He and wife Mary sold ½ right of commonage to Stephen Harding, blacksmith.

1679, Jul. 1. Taxed 7½d.

1680, Feb. 16. He sold Joseph Smith (son of John Smith, mason), 4 acres.

1684, May 21. Administration to Joseph Smith (son of John Smith, mason). Inventory, £8, 4s. 1d., viz: bed, &c. £3, 10s., coat and pair of breeches £1, 5s., other wearing apparel, bellows, tongs, table, chest, 3 plates, gloves, mittens, 3 old chairs, firewood, &c.

He may have been father, or at least a relative, of Rowland Jones (taxed in Providence, 1687, Sep. 1, for 1s., and who was of Norwich, Conn., in 1691), and Zacariah Jones (who had wife Madeline, and who bought land in Providence, as early as 1703).

JOY.

THOMAS, b. d.
m.
DOROTHY, b. d. 1676, Aug. 18.

Kings Town, R. I.

1668, May 4. He and others of Wickford, petitioned the General Court at Hartford, asking for the protection of their government.

It is assumed that he was the husband of that widow Dorothy, whose death at Newport is recorded, without clue as to her husband's name.

I. GEORGE, b. d. 1676, Aug. 15. Newport, R. I.

His death and that of his mother were entered in the Quaker records.

KEESE.

JOHN, b. d. 1700, Dec. 10.
m 1682, Sep. 18.
ANN MANTON, b. d. 1728.

of Shadrach & Elizabeth (Smith) Manton.

Portsmouth, R. I.

1675, Apr. 17. He had a deed of 8 acres from Lot Strange, "to thee John Keese and thine."

1688. Constable.

1690, Mar. 3. He bought of Joseph Smith, of Providence, 56½ acres there.

1691. Deputy.

1696, May 4. He bought of Richard Hart and wife Hannah, and Hannah Hart, widow, mother of Richard, two parcels of land containing 8 acres with buildings, &c., for £80.

1700, Dec. 2. Will—proved 1701, Jan. 13. Exx wife Ann. To eldest son William, all land in Providence, twenty ewe sheep in Richard Bennett's custody, a good cow and £5, at age. To son John, 36 acres in Portsmouth, twenty sheep and a cow. To son Shadrach, 16 acres in Portsmouth, meadow in Hog Island, twenty sheep and a cow. To daughter Alice, 40s. and twenty sheep at eighteen or marriage. To daughters Patience and Ann, £10, each. To wife Ann, housing and land where I dwell, half an acre, and all movables.

1726, Oct. 12. His widow Ann, of Newport, sold to Shadrach Keese, of same place, 2 acres in Hog Island, for £26.

1720, May 24. Will — proved 1728, Apr. 2 Widow Ann. Ex. son Shadrach. To son Shadrach, all my housing and lands in Portsmouth where I dwell, he allowing his three sisters Alice, Patience and Anne, to live in said house while unmarried. To son John, 5s. To children Shadrach, Alice, Patience and Ann, all my silver and paper money equally. To daughter Patience, biggest brass kettles, side saddle, pewter pot, and half a mare (the other half she has purchased of me). To daughters Patience and Ann, rest of pewter. To daughter Ann, a riding hood, &c., and a bed. To daughter Patience, wearing apparel. To three daughters rest of estate.

Inventory, £377, 6s. 4d.

I. ALICE, b. 1683, Aug. d.

II. WILLIAM, b. 1685, Oct. 26. d. 1710. Portsmouth, R. I.
Unmarried.

1710, Nov. 12. Will—proved 1710, Dec. 11. Exx. mother Ann. To brothers John and Shadrach, all lands in Providence, equally, they paying to sisters Alice, Patience and Ann, £7 each.

III. PATIENCE, b. 1690, Jun. 27. d.

IV. JOHN, b. 1693, Mar. 14. d. Portsmouth, R. I.

He was a cordwainer.

1717, Apr. 17. He and his mother Ann, for £550, 4s., sold to William Burrington, Jr., 42 acres, 56 rods.

1720, Nov. 7. He confirmed 12 acres to William Burrington.

V. SHADRACH, b. 1695, Oct. 5. d. Portsmouth, Newport, R. I.

1717, Apr. 30. Freeman.

1724, Apr. 1. He sold 58½ acres in Hog Island, for £714, 7s., to Thomas Borden.

1726, Oct. 12. Newport. He sold all his right in Hog Island, 149 acres, to Thomas Borden, for £2,200.

1728, Aug. 13. He sold two parcels of land in Portsmouth, each containing one acre, with a dwelling house on one parcel, for £80 to William Anthony, Jr.

VI. ANN, b. 1698, Oct. 26. d.

MICHAEL, { b. d. 1680.
m.
ISABEL, { b. d.

(She m. (2) 1681, Jun. 4, ——— ———)

Jamestown, R. I.

1669, Aug. 28. He and two others were appointed to execute the order of the council, for the inhabitants of Conanicut Island to assemble and consider what may be most suitable for their defence and preservation against any invasion or insurrection of the Indians.

1677, May 1. Freeman.

1680. Taxed £5, 18*s.* 7½*d.*

KENYON.

JOHN, { b. d.
m.
———, { b. d.

Kings Town, R. I.

The name of this first ancestor is assumed to have been John, and it is also assumed that the three persons mentioned in the next generation were brothers.

I. JOHN, { b. 1657. d. 1732.
m,
———, { b. d. 1732 (—)

Kings Town, Westerly, R. I.

1. John, 1682, Jan.
2. James,
3. Enoch,
4. Joseph,
5. David,
6. Jonathan,

1687, Sep. 6. Taxed 8*s.* 11*d.*

1704, Jul. His son John, Jr., married Elizabeth Remington.

1712, Oct. 16. He deeded to son John, for love, &c., 170 acres where son dwells.

1727, Aug. 28. Westerly. He, calling himself aged seventy years or thereabouts, testified that in the year 1683 or thereabouts, he went to live on the farm that Stephen Northup, of North Kingstown, now lives on, and paid rental to Major Smith, in behalf of Mr. Killum, of Boston, and lived there for eight years, and Stephen Northup went in when I left it.

1728, Mar. 27. His son John, calls himself aged forty-six years last January.

1732, Jun. 12. Will—proved 1732, Jun 26. Ex. son Jonathan. To sons John, James, Enoch, Joseph, and David, £10 each. To son Jonathan, all movable estate, he paying legacies.

Inventory, £189, 8*s.*, viz: wearing apparel £11, 16*s.*, 2 beds, pewter, swine, 4 oxen, 4 cows, 3 calves, 1 steer, 3 yearlings, &c.

II. JAMES, { b. d. 1724.
m.
RUTH, { b. d. 1720 + of

Kings Town, Westerly, R. I.

1. James, 1693, Apr. 17.
2. Thomas,
3. Ebenezer,
4. John,
5. Peter,
6. Sarah,
7. Ruth,

He was a miller.

1687, Sep. 6. Taxed 4*s* 5*d.*

1700, May 2. Ear mark granted for sheep.

1706, Dec. 20. He, calling himself James Kenyon, Sr., with wife Ruth, deeded to George Thomas, of Conanicut, 36 acres, for £25, 10*s.*

1722, Dec. 16. He and wife Ruth, deeded to Jeffery Hazard, 300 acres and housing, for £800.

1720, Mar. 18. Will—proved 1724, May 4. Exs. wife Ruth and son Peter. To wife, all estate, real and personal, for life. To sons James and Thomas, £5 each. To daughter Sarah Crandall, £20. To daughter Ruth Kenyon, £30. All legacies to be paid by sons John and Peter. To son Ebenezer, 10 acres. To sons John and Peter, all the rest of estate, equally, the dwelling house being in John's portion.

Inventory, £335, 13*s.* 6*d.*, viz: 34 sheep, 16 lambs, 2 yearling cattle, 3 cows, 4 oxen, a mare, a swine, beds, warming pan, spinning wheel, &c.

III. ROGER, { b. d.
m. 1683, Oct. 11.
MARY RAY, { b. 1667, May 19. d. 1714, Mar. 1. of Simon & Mary (Thomas) Ray.

New Shoreham, R. I.

1. Roger, 1685, Jan. 25.

See: American Genealogist, v. 19, p. 224.

KILTON.

ROBERT, { b. d.
m.
BETHIAH FENNER, { b. d.

of Arthur & Mehitable (Waterman) Fenner.

Providence, R. I.

He was a bricklayer.

1690. His name was in the list of those who were in Captain Samuel Gallup's company in the expedition against Canada, this year.

1691, Jul. 23. He bought of Richard Smith, of Kings Town, 4 acres in Providence, with buildings, orchard, &c., for £18.

1693, Oct. 2. He, having borrowed £35, for seven years, of Pardon Tillinghast, mortgages his house and land to him, and gives the use of the house for seven years, for the use of the money; and any charges necessary to be laid out for finishing chimney or otherwise, for use or safety of the house are to be repaid by Kilton. It was agreed that Kilton should have use of the land and house for six months after date hereof, if need so require, and that Tillinghast shall have it six months after the seven years be expired.

1695, Oct. 30. The agreement was declared null and void by Pardon Tillinghast, and another one was made.

1701, Sep. 16. He, having failed in making his payment, whereby the house, &c., came into hands of Pardon Tillinghast, and the sum of £35 having been paid by Thomas Fenner, the latter received the property from Pardon Tillinghast.

I. THOMAS, { b. 1690, Jan. 17. d. 1749, May 11.
m. 1716, Sep. 13.
PHEBE DEXTER, { b. 1700, Aug. 4. d. 1766. of John & Alice (Smith) Dexter.

Providence, R. I.

1. Freelove, 1717, Sep. 14.
2. Joseph, 1723, Jun. 2.
3. Thomas, 1725, Sep. 17.
4. William, 1727, Nov. 12.
5. Stephen, 1730, Feb. 16.
6. James,
7. Phebe,

He was a cordwainer.

1714, Aug. 24. He and his brother Samuel, were deeded a house, orchard and certain land by Thomas Fenner. (The same estate that had been mortgaged to Pardon Tillinghast by Robert Kilton.)

1716, Apr. 25. He deeded to brother Samuel, for love and goodwill, and money paid, certain land, being part of that which was our father, Robert Kilton's, and also deeded his brother an equal privilege in the dwelling house, &c.

1720. Freeman.

1749, May 8. Will—proved 1749, Aug. 5. Exx. wife Phebe. To daughter Phebe, £100, at fifteen or marriage. To wife Phebe, all rest of personal estate, which she at her death should distribute among the surviving children. To wife, the use of dwelling house, while his widow, in lieu of dower. To five sons, Joseph, Thomas, William, Stephen and James, all real estate, equally.

Inventory, £1,520, 13*s* 6*d.*, viz: silver tankard and 8 silver spoons £129, money due by bond and note £573, 19*s.* 6*d.*, 4 feather beds, 1 warming pan, 1 gun, 2 spinning wheels, 12 silver buttons, 1 mare, saddle, pillion, &c., 2 cows, 1 calf, 1 swine, cotton and linen yarn, canoe £30, books, &c.

He was buried in the North Burial Ground.

1766, Sep. 5. Will—proved 1766, Nov. 24. Widow Phebe Kilton. Exx. daughter Phebe. To son Stephen, and daughter Phebe Kilton, all real estate, equally. To daughter Phebe, all personal estate.

II. SAMUEL, { b. d. 1740, Dec. 28.
m.
ANNE HARRIS, { b. d. 1740 + of Nicholas & Ann ( ) Harris.

Providence, R. I.

1. John,
2. Sarah,
3. Anne,
4. Mary,

He was a cordwainer.

1718, Apr. 20. He sold Noah Blanding, for £110, land bounded partly by brother Thomas Kilton.

1720. Freeman.

1725, Mar. 2. He sold Uriah Davis land by the salt water, it being a lot I bought of Andrew Harris, whereon my new house stands and my wharf is built, being on the west side of the town, &c.

1741, Jul. 25. Administration to widow Anne.

Inventory, £87, 1*s.*, viz: bible and other books, foot wheel, tow yarn, shoemaker's tools, 2 tables, 8 chairs, pewter, wearing apparel, bedding, churn, &c.

CLEMENT[2], (Clement[1]). b. d. 1694 (—)
m.
ELIZABETH, b. d. 1708, Nov. 27.

(She m. (2) 1694, Nov 12, Thomas Barnes.)

Marshfield, Mass., Providence, R. I.

1682, Jun. 6. Freeman.

1687, May 20. He bought of Ephraim Carpenter, all rights in the lands of Pawtuxet, on west side of Pauchassett River, about 100 acres, being undivided land. He must have moved to Providence very soon after this.

1688. Providence. Ratable estate, 2 oxen, 2 four year steers, cow, 5 heifers, horse.

1708, Dec. 27. Inventory, of Elizabeth Barnes, widow, who died at Swanzey, £112, 7*s.*, 10*d.*, viz: lands, wearing apparel, beds, wax, bayberry, cash, &c. Administration was given on her estate to her eldest son John King, of Providence.

I. JOHN, b. d. 1723, Sep. 18. Providence, R. I.
m. (1)
HANNAH, b. d. of
m. (2)
ELIZABETH, b. d. 1754, Nov. 27. of

1697, Apr. 22. He made an agreement with Thomas Barnes, by which he leased him for two years a dwelling house and 60 acres, and ten neat cattle, cart, plough, &c., for the sum of £6, 10*s.*, per year; reserving for himself the leanto fireroom and room over cellar.

1707, Oct. 29. He appealed to the Assembly from the judgment of a Court of Common Pleas, wherein Joseph Carpenter, of Musketo Cove, Long Island, had received judgment in an action of trespass and ejectment. The verdict of the jury was sustained by the Assembly, and an agreement was made between the parties that Joseph Carpenter should pay John King, for the use of the children of William Vinson, deceased, £20, and King to give possession of house and lands sued for and recovered by verdict.

1711, Nov. 21. He sold his house and 50 acres to John Stone, for £72.

1718, Mar. 11. He sold his brother Thomas King, 12 acres for £4.

1723, Nov. 11. Administration to widow Elizabeth. Inventory, £299, 2*s.*, personal, viz: a yoke of oxen, 6 cows, 2 heifers, 5 calves, 2 mares, 2 colts, 16 swine, 45 sheep, 7 geese, 3 tame turkeys, fowls, 2 hides in the tan vat, apples in orchard which made 25 barrels cider, 20 loads of hay, cider mill, shoemaker's tools, pair of worsted combs, wearing apparel £9, silver money 8*s.* Rooms named were great room, kitchen, bed room, great chamber, leanto chamber, closet and garret. Real estate £1,213, viz: old farm £600, home farm at Soconauset £420, land on the plain £120, other land, £73.

1724, Feb. 10. John King, son of John deceased, represented that land of deceased would be cut up and mangled if it should be divided among all his children according to law of the colony, and that the children's interests would be prejudiced by reason their parts will be so small. It was therefore ordered that all lands after the widow's third, be intrusted to son John, he paying into the council the value of lands and tenements in money or bills of credit, according as lands are appraised, so that the council may on receipt of money pay it to the widow, who has taken administration to bring up the small children.

1738, Mar. 18. Elizabeth King, widow, of Smithfield, sold to her son Josiah, land in Smithfield, for £200. It is assumed that Fearnot, Obadiah, Isaac, Josiah, William and Jemima (all found as adults on the records between 1729 to 1741), were children of John[2], but part of them may have been children of James.[2]

1755, Mar. 3, Administration on estate of widow Elizabeth King, of Cranston, to eldest son John. Inventory, £319, 15*s.*

1. Sarah, 1703, Apr. 1.
2. John, 1705, Mar. 13.
3. Hannah, 1706, Feb. 28.
4. Fearnot,
5. Obadiah,
6. Isaac,
7. Josiah,
8. William,
9. Jemima,
10. Sarah,

II. JAMES, b. d. 1756, Nov. 19. Providence, Glocester, R. I.
m. (1)
——— b. d. of
m. (2) 1734, Oct. 31. [Wm.
PERSIS BROOKS, (w. of b. d. of William Turpin.

1713, Jun. 16. Taxed 7*s.* 3*d.*

1719, Aug. 10. He sold James Thornton, 150 acres for £88.

1721, Sep. 27. He deeded son James, for love, &c., half of 150 acres.

1728, Sep. 24. He deeded son Thomas, for love, &c., 75 acres.

1730, Jan. 17. He deeded son Amos, for love, &c., 198 acres.

1731, Jun. 12. Glocester. He deeded son Clement, 100 acres where I dwell.

1742, Nov. 8. He made up account and gave bond on behalf of his wife Persis, who was administratrix on the personal estate of her former husband, William Brooks, deceased.

1. James,
2. Thomas,
3. Amos,
4. Clement,

III. THOMAS, b. d. 1723, Oct. 10. Providence, R. I.

1719, Jan. 8. He sold Benjamin Wight, a half share of land for £30.

1723, Oct. 1. Will—proved 1723, Nov. 11. Ex. friend William Turpin. He directs that all lands be sold and brother Richard Harris to have refusal £5 cheaper than another will give. To brother John King, chest, wearing apparel and husbandry tools. To nephew Richard Harris, Jr., £10. To friend William Turpin, £5. To brother John King's eldest son and eldest son of brother Ebenezer, the rest of estate.

Inventory, £12, 19*s.*, viz: bible and other small books 12*s.*, apparel £11, 1*s.*, 6*d*,, ink horn, pen knife and paper 2*s.* 6*d.*, chest and old linen, 12*s.*

IV. EBENEZER, b. d. Tiverton, R. I.
m.
HANNAH, b. d. of

1. Mary, 1704, Oct. 21.
2. Benjamin, 1708, Oct. 9.
3. Hannah, 1714, Jun. 15.
4. Ebenezer, 1719, May 23.

V. ——— b. d.
m.
RICHARD HARRIS, b. 1668, Oct. 14. d. 1750. of Thomas & Elnathan (Tew) Harris.

1. Uriah,
2. Richard,
3. Amaziah,
4. Jonathan,
5. David,
6. Preserved,
7. Amity,
8. Dinah,
9. Elnathan,

KNOWLMAN.

JOHN, b. d. 1718.

Warwick, R. I.

1696, Jun. 15. He bought of Henry Reynolds and wife Sarah, certain land in Warwick, for £10.

1706, Mar. 10. He sold 10 acres in Coweset, for £6, to Joseph Matteson.

1708, Aug. 25. He sold to Moses Lippitt, of Warwick, and William Crawford, of Providence, certain land in Warwick for £20.

1714, Oct. 9. He sold to James Congdon and Richard Searle, one-quarter of a seventeenth part of Coweset, for £25.

1716, Jan. 6. He being very aged and not capable of subsisting himself, surrendered all estate real and personal to Town Council, particularly a 50 acre lot (recorded 1718, May 22).

LADD.

JOSEPH, b. d. 1683.
m.
JOANNA, b. d. 1669 +

Portsmouth, R. I.

1642, Oct. He was a witness to a deed from John Anthony to Richard Tew, of land in Newport.

1658, Jan. 11. He bought of William Barker, 10 acres in Portsmouth, with a small dwelling house thereon.

1680. Taxed 1*s.*

1669, Apr. 12. Will—recorded 1683, Jul. 24. Exx. wife Joanna. Overseers, William Wodell and William Hall. To wife, all estate, to bring up children, while widow, but if she marry, the overseers to divide the estate. To son Joseph, at death or marriage of his mother, the house and land, he paying £5 each, to his brothers, William and Daniel. To the two youngest sons, and to daughters Mary and Sarah, the goods and cattle. If eldest son die without issue, the next heir to have.

I. JOSEPH, b. d. Little Compton, R. I.
m.
RACHEL, b. d. of

1. Rachel, 1686, Dec. 17.
2. Daniel, 1687, May 25.
3. William, 1689, May 10.
4. Joseph, 1693, Oct. 16.
5. Mary, 1696, Dec. 29.
6. Benjamin, 1698, Jan. 29.
7. Sarah, 1700, Apr. 5.
8. Jonathan, 1701, Aug 10.
9. Caleb, 1704, Jun. 2.
10. Rebecca, 1706, Sep. 15.

II. WILLIAM, b. d. 1729. Little Compton, R. I.
m. 1696, Feb. 17.
ELIZABETH TOMPKINS, b. d. 1729 + of Nathaniel & Elizabeth (Allen) Tompkins.

1729, Aug. 10. Will—proved 1729, Oct. 21. Exx. wife Elizabeth. To children Joseph, Samuel and Sarah Ladd, Mary Seabury, Priscilla Manchester, Elizabeth Strenil, Katharine, Hannah and Ruth Ladd, each 5*s.* To grandson Nathaniel Ladd, son of William, 15*s.* To wife, rest of estate.

Inventory, £88, 14*s.*, viz: wearing apparel £13, pewter, gun, loom, bible, 2 cows, swine, &c.

1. Sarah, 1696, Mar. 22.
2. William, 1697, Nov. 18.
3. Mary, 1699, Mar. 5.
4. Priscilla, 1700, Jun. 22.
5. Joseph, 1701, Oct. 19.
6. Samuel, 1703, Feb. 26.
7. Elizabeth, 1704, Oct. 12.
8. John, 1706, Jan. 15.
9. Katharine, 1707, Sep. 14.
10. Jeremiah, 1710, Aug. 31.
11. Lydia, 1711, Mar. 1.
12. Hannah, 1712, Aug. 12.
13. Ruth, 1714, Jan. 19.

III. DANIEL, b. d.

IV. MARY, b. d.

V. SARAH, b. d.

LAKE.

DAVID, * b. d. 1696 +
m. [Thos.
SARAH CORNELL, (w. of b. d. 1690 +

of Ralph & Joan ( ) Earle.

Portsmouth, Little Compton, Tiverton, R. I.

1667, Aug. 10. He enlisted in a troop of horse.

1673, Feb. 11. He was a witness to an agreement between the Indian proprietors of Seaconnet.

1676, Nov. 1. He had lands laid out near Seaconnet and Punkatest, and was granted 60 acres, inasmuch as he had "been very useful and serviceable to the country in the late war."

1679, Jan. 4. Differences having arisen between him, of Nunaquaquet, now husband to Sarah, late widow to Thomas Cornell, of Portsmouth, and Thomas Cornell, eldest son of deceased, concerning right of dower of said Sarah, the differences were in a friendly manner compromised.

1681, Jul. 7. He was sued by Benjamin Church and others, for £500, for interrupting them from quiet and peaceable possession of Pocasset lands: "For that said Lake, on or about May, 1680, near to river called Fall River, did interrupt and molest and hinder said complainants from taking or receiving quiet and peaceable possession, said Lake forcibly taking and pulling the turf and twig out of the hands of Joseph Church, attorney to the sellers of the said land, which he had cut to deliver up to said complainants." They further said that Lake pretended title in behalf of himself and others, and said complainants have been kept out of possession and hindered from dividing and settling same with inhabitants, and since which time great waste and spoil of timber had been made. The jury found for plaintiffs for £5, damage and cost of suit.

1683, Mar. 14. He and wife Sarah, for £19, sold Joseph Taber, of Dartmouth, 7 acres there for £19.

1686, Feb. He and Henry Head were chosen agents for the town of Little Compton, to appear at the next court, in relation to the nonpayment of sum of £15, which the court had ordered that town and adjacent villages to raise for the encouragement of preaching of the gospel, but which said town had refused or neglected to make rates for. The court in March, ordered the town to pay £20 for their contempt and neglect and because they "write rather as equals or neighbours, than as delinquents or offenders."

1696, Aug. 29. Tiverton. He bought of Ralph Earle, of Dartmouth, one-eight of a half share (with reservations), for £40.

The relationship between him and Henry Lake, of Portsmouth (who sold a house and 8 acres in Warwick, to Edward Fisher, 1652, Jan. 12), has not been traced.

I. SARAH, * b. 1678, May 10. d.

II. DAVID, ‡ b. 1679, Jun. 2. d. 1767, Aug. 4. Portsmouth, R. I.
m.
MARY WILCOX, b. 1682, Feb. 25. d. 1767 + of Daniel & Hannah (Cook) Wilcox.

1767, Mar. 22. Will—proved 1767, Aug. 10. Ex. friend and neighbour William Hall. To each of my grandchildren, children of my four daughters, deceased, viz: Hannah Cory, Sarah Bennett, Amey Manchester and Elizabeth Sanford, 5*s.* To two daughters, Martha Anthony and Abigail Hart, 5*s.* each. To daughter Mary Wilcox, a clothes press, large chest and heifer. To daughter Ruth Tallman, 5*s.* To daughter Innocent Remington, a frying pan. To son Daniel, a looking glass. To granddaughter Ruth Thomas, daughter of Abigail Hart, and wife of Joseph Thomas, Jr., a bed, two sheep, &c. To wife Mary, use and improvement of all above gifts, for life, and the rest of personal to be at her disposal.

Inventory, £519, viz: bed, looking glass, pewter, woolen wheel, linen wheel, cow £35, &c.

1. Hannah,
2. Sarah,
3. Amy,
4. Elizabeth,
5. Martha,
6. Abigail,
7. Mary,
8. Ruth,
9. Innocent,
10. Daniel,

III. JONATHAN, b. 1681, Dec. 30. d.

IV. JOEL, * b. 1683, Jan. 30. d. 1735. Tiverton, R. I.
m.
SARAH, b. d. 1735 + of

1730, Feb. 18. Will—proved 1735, Oct. 21. Exx. wife Sarah. To wife, use of dwelling house, for life, and all household goods and other movables with some exceptions. To son David, 5*s.* and a table. To son Jonathan, 5*s.* To son Giles, 5*s.* at age. To son Jeremiah, 5*s.*, an iron pot and a kettle, at age. To daughter Hannah, a chest, box iron and 5*s.* To four sons Edward, Joel, Caleb and Joseph, all my lands and housing, &c., equally, at death of wife. To daughter Sarah, all household goods left at death of wife, and 5*s.* paid to her at eighteen.

1. David,
2. Jonathan,
3. Giles,
4. Jeremiah,
5. Hannah,
6. Edward,
7. Joel,
8. Caleb,
9. Joseph,
10. Sarah,

V. JOSEPH, b. 1690, Jun. 15. d.

* See: American Geneologist, V. 19, p. 225, 226.

‡ See: American Geneologist V. 27, p. 220.

see American Genealogist, v.35 p.109

LANGWORTHY.

ANDREW, { b. / d. 1680 +
m. 1658, Nov. 3.
RACHEL HUBBARD, { b. 1642, Mar. 10. / d.

of Samuel & Tacy (Cooper) Hubbard.

Newport, R. I.

1652, Oct. 6. He was baptized by Obadiah Holmes, "at the mill."

1656. Freeman.

1671, Dec. 23. His wife's father writes: "We entered into a church covenant the 23d day December, 1671, viz: William Hiscox, Stephen Mumford, Samuel Hubbard, Roger Baster, sister Hubbard, sister Mumford, Rachel Langworthy," &c.

1674, Sep. 30. His wife was baptized by Rev. William Hiscox, of the Seventh Day Church.

1676, Feb. He joined the Seventh Day Baptist Church.

1680 Taxed 4*s.* 4*d.*

LANGWORTHY. 2d column. II. Andrew. Erase all about him and his children. Insert instead II. James, Newport, R. I. Children, 1. Abigail, 1707, Sep. 20. 2. Mary, 1709, Feb. 27. 3. James, 1711, Apr. 11. 4 Andrew, 1713, Feb. 14. 5. Stephen, 1715, Aug. 6. 6. Jonathan, 1717, Dec. 9. 7. Benjamin, 1720, Sep. 11

I. SAMUEL, { b. / d. 1716 (—)
m.
RACHEL, { b. / d. 1716 (—) of

Newport, Kings Town, R. I.

1711, Oct. 2. Kings Town. He and thirty-three others, bought 5,300 acres of the vacant lands in Narragansett, ordered sold by the Assembly.

1716, Nov. 23. A deposition was made by John Phillips, of Newport, and Ruth, his wife, that Samuel Langworthy was eldest son of Andrew Langworthy, formerly of Newport, and that Samuel died at Pettaquamscutt. Joseph Crandall deposed that Samuel Langworthy, and his wife Rachel, lived in Newport, near Turner's Lane, and died at Pettaquamscutt.

He is assumed to have been the father of Ann (who married Joseph Crandall, 1716, Feb. 15), John (who married Mary Lewis, before 1721), Thomas (who married Content Sanford, 1726, Oct. 11), Joseph (who married Elizabeth Burdick, before 1729), Samuel (who married 1736, Aug. 7, Mary Crandall), Robert (who died young), and Mary. These marriages were at Westerly and Stonington.

By one account three of the above children (viz: Thomas, Robert and Mary), are called children of Robert Langworthy, but search in the public records reveals no Robert Langworthy of so early a date.

1. Ann,
2. John,
3. Thomas, 1704.
4. Joseph,
5. Samuel,
6. Robert,
7. Mary,

II. ANDREW, { b. / d. 1739.
m.
——— { b. / d. of

Newport, R. I.

LANGWORTHY. 2d column. II. Andrew. In 1717 he was living in Little Compton, and sold 100 acres in Westerly to Samuel Langworthy.

He died of small pox at the fort at Newport.

It is assumed that Captain Andrew Langworthy, who died 1776, Apr. 13, aged sixty-three (and who was buried in Newport Cemetery) was his son, and that anothor son was Lawrence.

1. A——— 1707, Sep. 20.
2. Mary, 1709, Feb. 27.
3. Joseph, 1710, May 10.
4. James, 1711, Apr. 11.
5. Andrew, 1713.
6. Lawrence,

LANPHERE.

GEORGE, { b. / d. 1731, Oct. 6.
m.
——— { b. / d.

Westerly, R. 1.

1669, Apr. 18. He bought land of John Clarke.

1671, May 17. He took oath of allegiance to Rhode Island.

1678, Mar. 2. Under this date Samuel Hubbard writes: "Then we went to the waterside at the mill, then brother Hiscox baptized George Lanphear, he came out rejoicing; his wife went into the water, was faint hearted and came back again onbaptized," &c.

1679, Sep. 17. He took oath of allegiance.

1704, Jul. He had 200 acres laid out.

1727, Apr. 25. He being judged incapable of managing his affairs, &c., and his children having by a petition obtained division of our father George Lanphere's estate, the Town Council divided certain land to them or successors. A bond for £1,000 was given, signed as follows: James Covey, Seth Lanphere, Richard Lanphere, Eber Crandall, Theodosius Lanphere, Shadrach Lanphere, James Pendleton, John Lanphere, Mary Button, widow.

I. MARY, { b. / d. 1727 +
m.
PETER BUTTON, { b. / d. 1726. of Button.

LANPHERE. II. Mary. Her daughter Eliphall b. 1694 Dec. 16.

1. Peter, 1688, Jan. 1.
2. Mary, 1689, Oct. 6.
3. Matthias 1692, Jan. 16.
4. Eliphall,
5. Jedediah,
6. Samuel,
7. Cyrus,
8. Joseph,
9. Elizabeth,

II. SHADRACH, { b. / d. 1728, Jan. 29.
m. 1696, Jun. 15.
EXPERIENCE READ. { b. / d. 1732 + of Read.

Stonington, Conn.

(She m. (2) Samuel Lincoln).

1728, Jun. 17. Inventory, £196, 7*s.*, 10*d.*, shown by administrators, Experience and Joseph Lanphere. Wearing apparel, riding mare, gun, sword, 4 books, pair of silver buttons, silver money 18*s.*, beds, linen wheel, cordwainer's tools, 2 sides of sole leather, pair of oxen, 4 cows, 3 heifers, 4 year and vantage, 4 yearlings, 40 sheep, homestead of 16 acres £64, &c.

1732, Feb. 23. Samuel Lincoln and Experience his wife, formerly wife of Shadrach Lanphere, of Stonington, for love to our children Oliver, Ann, Prudence, Experience and Mary Lanphere, of Westerly and Solomon and John Lanphere, of Norwich, Conn., and Hezekiah Lanphere, of Lebanon, Conn., deeded to said eight children 48 acres in Westerly, which former husband Shadrach Lanphere had possessed.

1. Joseph, 1700, Feb. 16.
2. Ann, 1701, Oct. 7.
3. Oliver, 1703, Sep. 3.
4. Prudence, 1706, Aug. 10.
5. Solomon, 1708, Apr. 10.
6. Experience, 1711, Jan.
7. John, 1712, Oct. 15
8. Hezekiah, 1714, Nov. 15.
9. Mary, 1718, Jan. 1.

III. JOHN, { b. / d. 1757.
m.
RUTH, { b. / d. 1730 + of

Westerly, R. I.

1730, Mar. 31. Will—proved 1757, May 30. Ex. son Daniel. To wife Ruth, best feather bed and use of what household goods she needs, and her choice of a room, with maintenance while widow. To son John, 25 acres that I bought of my father George Lanphere. To son Daniel, house I now live in and 46 acres, it being land that my father bought of Mr. John Clarke, by deed bearing date the 18th of April, 1669. To sons Amos and Nathan, rest of land that I had for maintenance of my father George. To daughters Anna Lewis, Ruth Shaw, Experience Satterly, Mary, Patience and Keziah Lanphere, each £5.

Inventory, wearing apparel £30, 10*s.*, foot wheel, woolen wheel, old gun, warming pan, &c.

1. John,
2. Daniel,
3. Amos,
4. Nathan,
5. Anna,
6. Ruth,
7. Experience,
8. Mary,
9. Patience,
10. Keziah,

IV. THEODOSIUS, { b. / d. 1749.
m. 1708, Jan. 22.
RACHEL COVEY, { b. / d. 1760. of Hope & Mary (   ) Covey.

Westerly, R. I.

1738, Feb. 5. Will—proved 1749, Nov. 27. Exx. wife Rachel. To son Theodosius, 40*s.* To rest of children 5*s.* each, viz: To James, Joshua, Abigail Burdick, Susanna Stanton, Nathaniel, Mary, Samuel, Stephen, Jabez and Joseph Lanphere. The younger children to be brought up out of the estate by wife Rachel, and at her death or marriage, all the estate left was to go to children.

Inventory, £125, 11*s.*, 9*d.*, viz: wearing apparel, a cow, books £5, 15*s.*, pewter, &c.

1760, May 26. Widow Rachel's inventory was shown by son Stephen.

1. Theodosius, 1709, Jan. 31.
2. James, 1710, Nov. 22.
3. Joshua, 1712, Nov. 23.
4. Abigail, 1715, Mar. 27.
5. Susanna, 1716, Dec. 14.
6. Nathaniel, 1718, Mar. 22.
7. Mary. 1721, Dec. 14.
8. Samuel, 1723, Dec 23.
9. Stephen, 1726, Feb. 5.
10. Jabez, 1731, Mar. 25.
11. Joseph, 1736, Sep. 20.

V. SETH, { b. / d. 1725 ±
m.
SARAH PENDLETON, { b. 1693 ± / d. 1725 ± of Caleb Pendleton.

Westerly, R. I.

1725, Aug. 30. The following children of Seth Lanphere and wife Sarah, were bound out, viz: Miriam, aged eleven years 10th of October last and Ann aged two years 4th of August, 1725, bound to Joseph Cots, of Stonington, both of them to be learned to read and Miriam to have a heifer at end of service: Aaron Lanphere, bound to William Davis, of Westerly, he being now sixteen years old 10th of May, last, to be learned to read and write and the trade of a cooper and to have £10; Elizabeth Lanphere, bound to John Thompson, of Stonington, being now ten years and twenty days old, and to have two suits of clothes, a cow and a calf; Mary Lanphere, bound to Nehemiah Mason, of Stonington, she being now seven years old the 4th of October last, and to be learned to read and write, to have two suits of clothes, a cow and a calf.

1730, Apr. 27. The Town Council further ordered Elisha Lanphere, child of Seth and Sarah, to be bound out to Samuel Hinckley, of Stonington.

1. Aaron, 1709, May 10.
2. Miriam, 1713, Oct. 10.
3. Elizabeth, 1715, Aug. 10.
4. Mary, 1717, Oct. 4.
5. Ann, 1723, Aug. 4.
6. Elisha,

VI. ——— { b. / d.
m.
EBER CRANDALL, { b. 1676. / d. 1727, of John & Hannah (   ) Crandall.

1. John,
2. Eber,
3. Samuel,
4. Joseph,

VII. SARAH, { b. / d.
m. 1707, Mar. 21.
JAMES COVEY, { b. 1687, Mar 1. / d. of Hope & Mary (   ) Covey.

1. Sarah, 1708, Jan. 11.
2. Mary, 1709, Sep. 3.
3. Hope, 1712, Sep. 15.
4. James, 1715, Jun. 24.
5. John, 1717, Mar. 16.
6. Joseph, 1719, May 16.
7. Samuel, 1721, Oct. 15.
8. Elisha, 1724, Mar. 7.
9. Elizabeth, 1726, Mar. 2.

VIII. ELIZABETH, m. 1710, Jan. 12. JAMES PENDLETON, — b. — d. — b. 1690 ± — d. — of Caleb Pendleton.

1. James, 1710, Nov. 21.
2. Obadiah, 1712, Nov. 1.
3. Christopher 1715, Apr. 12.
4. Elizabeth, 1715, Apr. 12.

IX. RICHARD, m. MARY, — b. — d. — b. — d. — of — Westerly, R. I.

1. Amey, 1715, Jun. 22.
2. Lucy, 1718, Jul. 9.
3. Esther, 1721, Feb. 21.
4. Zerviah, 1724, Oct. 12.
5. Jerusha, 1727, Jan. 25.

LAPHAM.

JOHN, m 1673, Apr. 6. MARY MANN, — b. 1635. d. 1710. — b. d. 1710 + of William & Frances (Hopkins) Mann.

Providence, Newport, R. I., Dartmouth, Mass.

1673. Freeman.

1673. Deputy.

1675. Constable.

1676. His house was burned in the Indian war.

His first child was born at Providence, the next two at Newport, and the rest at Dartmouth.

1679, Jul. 1. Taxed 1*s.* 10½*d.*, John Lapham's land.

1680, May 18. Newport. He testified (calling himself 45 or thereabouts), that about the year 1674, Thomas Suckling and wife, bequeathed to people called Quakers, what estate they should have left at their death, on condition that they should be provided for during their lives, and further testified that the Quakers did supply them, and did board and shingle their house.

1682, Sep. 30. Dartmouth, Mass. At this date his son Thomas' birth is registered on Dartmouth records, and other children subsequently, and he had already moved there probably, though still taxed for land at Providence.

1687. Ratable estate (with Abraham Mann, of Providence), 2 cows, 2 shares of fresh meadow, 12 acres English pasture.

1699, Jan. 6. At a meeting held at John Lapham's house in Dartmouth, Jacob Mott and three others undertook "to build a meeting house for the people of God, in scorn called Quakers; 35 foot long, 30 foot wide and 14 foot stud." John Lapham's contribution was £5. The house was built the same year, and was the first one erected for worship in that town.

1706, Jan. 28 He and wife Mary, had an account given them of what lands they owned in Providence, showing sundry parcels of 102 acres, 80 acres, 28 acres, 20 acres, 4 acres on Fox Hill, 6 acres in Neck, 2 lots in town, &c.

1708, May 25. He and wife Mary, and his son John, and wife Mary, all of Dartmouth, confirmed a deed made by Major William Hopkins, of Providence, to Edward Manton, of same place, declaring that certain lands in Providence, formerly of William Mann, deceased, descended to his two only children, Mary and Abraham, and that Abraham, dying intestate, his sister, Mary Mann, heired of him, and that she married John Lapham and had several children by him, whereby an heir at law may succeed, and as fame doth credibly report that Abraham in his life time, passed away all the above mentioned lands to Major William Hopkins (cousin-german to said Mary Mann), and he having deeded it to Edward Manton, &c.—therefore the confirmation.

1709, Aug. 26. He and wife Mary, of Dartmouth, for love and affection to sons John and Nicholas, deeded to each, a half part of all lands in Providence, divided and undivided, except 4 acres at Fox Hill. On the same date he deeded to daughter Mary Lapham, 4 acres in Providence.

1709, Dec. 5. Will—proved 1710, Apr. 5. Exs. wife Mary and son John. To wife Mary, £20 a year, for life, to be paid her by two sons, John and Nicholas, and a feather bed, young cow, and all household stuff in dwelling house. To daughter Mary Dyer, £80, to be paid her by John and Nicholas, £10 a year by each till paid. To son Nicholas, half of all lands in Dartmouth, he having that part where dwelling house is, with orchard, and to him ½ of weaving looms. To son John, all the rest of housing and lands in Dartmouth, any difference of value between two sons' portion, to be reckoned by two men in the stock of cattle and horses, and so the sons made equal.

1710, Apr. 5. Inventory, £362, 15*s.* 1*d.*, viz: housing and land £250, old horse, 2 oxen, 9 cows, 4 steers, heifer, 2 yearlings, 5 swine, goats running at large, fowls, 3 hives of bees, 4 spinning wheels, 2 looms, feather bed, flock bed, pewter, warming pan, bible, testament and other books, plate £2, 14*s.* 6*d.*, cash £13, 3*s.*, wearing clothes (linen and woolen) £6, 10*s.*, &c.

I. MARY, — b. 1674, Mar. 1. d. 1675, Jul. 10.

LAPHAM. 2d column. II. John, d. 1747, +. He was of Dartmouth that year, and possibly died there.

II. JOHN, m. 1700, Apr. 3. MARY RUSSELL, — b. 1677, Dec. 18. d. 1734 + — b. 1683, Jul. 10. d. — of Joseph & Elizabeth ( ) Russell. — Dartmouth, Mass., Smithfield, R. I.

1. Elizabeth, 1701, Jul. 29.
2. John, 1703, Oct. 2.
3. Thomas, 1705, Dec. 10.
4. Rebecca, 1707, Aug. 5.
5. Joseph,
6. Ruth,
7. Benjamin,
8. Frances,
9. Bathsheba,
10. Joshua, 1722, Mar. 9.
11. Hannah,

1720, Nov. 20. He and brother Nicholas, both of Dartmouth, being equally invested by deed of gift of honored father, John Lapham, deceased, of certain lands in Providence, having already sold part now make division of rest.

1724, Oct. 17. He and his brother Nicholas, both of Dartmouth, sold William Edmonds, of Providence, for £150, land on both sides of Woonasquatucket River, near Edmond's house—44 acres.

1730, Dec. 21. He bought of Daniel and Joanna Jenckes, 150 acres in Providence, with house, &c. for £750.

1732, Nov. 11. He sold Thomas Lapham, of Smithfield, for £100, 50 acres in Smithfield.

1732, Dec. 12. He sold John Lapham, Jr., of Dartmouth, for £400, a certain tract of land in Smithfield, with house, &c.

1733, Sep. 1. He sold John Lapham, Jr., of Smithfield, for £20, 10*s.*, 26 acres in Smithfield.

1733, Sep. 1. He sold Joseph Lapham, of Smithfield, 95 acres in Smithfield, for £75.

1734. Smithfield. Freeman.

His sons all made settlement in Smithfield, R. I., and most of them remained there or in adjoining towns.

III. WILLIAM, Unmarried. — b. 1679, Nov. 29. d. 1702, Aug. 8. — Dartmouth, Mass.

IV. THOMAS, Unmarried. — b. 1682, Sep. 30. d. 1704, May 8. — Dartmouth, Mass.

V. MARY, m. (1) 1709, Aug. 26. CHARLES DYER, m. (2) 1734, Nov. 21. JOHN COLVIN, — b. 1686, Oct. 5. d — b. d. 1727, Jan. 7. — of Charles & Mary ( ) Dyer. — b. 1681, Apr. 19. d. 1764, Jul. 1. — of John & Dorothy ( ) Colvin.

1. Mary,
2. Elizabeth,
3. Charles,
4. Samuel,
5. John,
6. William,
7. Thomas,

VI. NICHOLAS, m. 1726, Dec. 1. MERCY ARNOLD, — b. 1689, Apr. 1. d. 1758. — b. d. 1758 (—) — of John & Mary (Mowry) Arnold. — Dartmouth, Mass.

1. Solomon,
2. Nicholas,
3. Arnold,
4. Abigail,

1745, Jun. 8. He gave a power of attorney to Thomas Lapham, of Smithfield, to sell lands in Providence, Smithfield and Glocester.

1758, Mar. 8. Will—proved 1758, Jul. 11. Ex. son Nicholas. To sons Solomon and Nicholas, homestead farm in Dartmouth, salt marsh, &c., the farm to be so divided that Solomon shall have southerly part with buildings thereon, and Nicholas the northerly part, which formerly belonged to my brother John, together with buildings thereon. To two sons, right in cedar swamp. To son Nicholas, all my right to land in government of Rhode Island, he to take care of my son Arnold Lapham, for life, "he not being likely to be able to get his living." To son Solomon, a cow and heifer and half my sheep, and a feather bed. Farming utensils equally to two sons Solomon and Nicholas. To son Nicholas, all the rest of stock (except a riding beast) and wearing apparel, a gun, two chests and a loom. To daughter Abigail Lapham, £50, to be paid her by Nicholas, and a chest of drawers, a feather bed, warming pan and my riding beast, saddle, &c. To son Nicholas, all the rest within doors and without.

1758, Jun. 17. Inventory, £119, 1*s.* 8*d.*, viz: bible and 3 other books 3*s.* 6*d.*, money £7, 5*s.* 2*d.*, feather beds, pewter, 3 wine glasses, jacket with 12 silver buttons, silver shoe buckles, 2 silver coat buttons, link of silver sleeve buttons, 1 gun, loom, woolen wheel, mare, 5 cows, 3 heifers, 4 calves, steer, yearling, 2 swine, &c.

His son Solomon, moved to Glocester, R. I., and died there (in 1800), where his will was recorded.

LARKIN.

EDWARD, b. d.
m.
———, b. d.

Newport, Westerly, R. I.

1655. Newport. Freeman.

1661, Sep. 9. He had a quarter share of land in the division of Misquamicut (Westerly).

1663. Commissioner.

1669, May 18. Westerly. His name was in the list of inhabitants.

1671, May 17. He took oath of allegiance.

1679, Sep. 17. He took oath of alleigance.

I. MEHITABLE, b. d.
m. 1673, Dec. 15.
RICHARD SWEET, b. d. 1744. of John & Elizabeth ( ) Sweet.

1. Richard, 1676, Feb. 23.
2. Susanna, 1678, Feb. 17.
3. Elizabeth, 1680, Feb. 10.
4. Mary, 1682, Nov. 4.
5. Eleanor, 1687, Jun. 13.

II. HANNAH, b. d.
m.
JOHN BALLOU, b. d. 1714 ± of Maturin & Hannah (Pike) Ballou.

No issue.

III. EDWARD, b. d. 1741. Westerly, R. I.
m. (1)
ELIZABETH HALL, b. d. of Henry Hall.
m. (2)
MARY COTTRELL, b. d. 1743. of Nicholas & Dorothy (Pendleton) Cottrell.

LARKIN. 2d column. III. Edward. Erase mother of his second wife, and say daughter of Nicholas Cottrell.

1701, Dec. 31. He and wife Elizabeth, sold 100 acres to Samuel Lewis.

1705-7-15. Deputy.

1737, Nov. 17. Will—proved 1741, Mar. 30. Exx. wife Mary. To wife, £100, all household goods and improvement of homestead and profits of saw mill and grist mill, for life, to bring up the young children, and then the said homestead to go to son Stephen, but the goods and £100, to be free and clear to wife. To son Stephen, the homestead at death of his mother. To son Nicholas, £100 and 50 acres, at death of wife, and saw and grist mill. To son David, a farm at age. To daughter Elizabeth Babcock, 10 acres where she lives with house and orchard, for life, and then to one of her sons as she sees fit. To daughter Penelope, £30. To daughters Tabitha and Lydia, each £50 at eighteen. To son Nicholas, 10 acres of salt marsh. To son Joseph, 50 acres adjoining land formerly given him. To grandson Joseph, my son Edward's son, 5*s.*, his father having had. To sons John and Samuel, 5*s.*, they having had. To sons John and Samuel, rest of estate.

Inventory, £872, 3*s.*, 5*d.*, viz: wearing apparel, £3, books £6, 5*s.*, 3 beds, pewter, loom, linen wheel, woolen wheel, card, 2 pair of oxen, 3 heifers, bull, 2 steers, 7 cows, yearling, mare, horse, 37 sheep, &c.

1743, Apr. 28. Will—proved 1743, May 30. Widow Mary. Ex. son Nicholas. To son Nicholas, £50. To son Stephen, £50, and bonds against him, if he is not able to pay them. To son David, great bible and the mortgage to be cleared off his land, and a house built sixteen feet square if he live to twenty-one years of age. To daughter Tabitha, a horse. To daughter Lydia, a little bible and £100. To daughters Tabitha and Lydia, all wearing apparel, and a double portion of what is left over the debts. To three sons the rest equally.

1. Joseph,
2. Edward,
3. John,
4. Samuel,
5. Elizabeth,
6. Penelope,
(2d wife).
7. Stephen,
8. Nicholas,
9. David,
10. Tabitha,
11. Lydia,

IV. ROGER, b. d. 1755. Westerly, R. I.
m. (1)
HANNAH BABCOCK, b. d. of James & Jane (Brown) Babcock.
m. (2)
REBECCA TUCKER, (widow), b. d. 1756. of

1706. He and wife Hannah, were witnesses to a deed.

1733. John Larkin, "son of Roger," was freeman. This son must have died before his father.

1755, Jan. 16. Will—proved 1755, Feb. 25. Ex. son Samuel. To wife Rebecca, a third of personal and use of house and land. To daughter Anna Hall, 5*s.*, she having had. To daughter Sarah Lake, 20*s.* To granddaughter Hannah Hall, 5*s.*, her father having had. To son Samuel, the rest of estate.

Inventory, £742, 1*s.*, 9*d.*, viz: 20 sheep, yoke of oxen, 3 cows, heifer, 2 calves, mare, wearing apparel and cloth, £33, 7*s.*, 6*d.*, warming pan, 2 linen wheels, &c.

1755, Apr. 28. His widow Rebecca, became an inhabitant of Richmond, R. I.

1756, Apr. 8. Inventory, estate of widow Rebecca Larkin, of Richmond, £210, 17*s.* Administration to her son Jabez Tucker.

1. John,
2. Samuel,
3. Anna,
4. Sarah,
(2d wife, no issue.)

V. JOHN, b. d. 1705. Westerly, R. I.
m.
REBECCA, b. d. 1705 + of

1705, Jul. 2. Administration to widow Rebecca. The Town Council seeing the estate is small and child to be brought up, gave the widow the personal estate and housing and lands, but the lands only to be hers till the heir is of age. Her husband's brother Edward Larkin, was appointed to oversee and assist the widow.

Inventory, £36, 13*s.*, viz: horse, mare, 2 oxen, 2 stags, 4 cows, 4 yearlings, 2 swine, household stuff, &c.

1. Rebecca, 1701, Oct. 15.

LAWTON (GEORGE).

GEORGE, b. d. 1693, Oct. 5.
m.
ELIZABETH HAZARD, b. d.

of Thomas & Martha ( ) Hazard.

Portsmouth, R. I.

1638. He was admitted an inhabitant to the island of Aquidneck.

1639, Apr. 30. He and twenty-eight others signed the following compact: "We whose names are underwritten do acknowledge ourselves the legal subjects of his Majesty King Charles, and in his name do hereby bind ourselves into a civil body politicke, unto his laws according to matters of justice."

1648, Jan. 25. He had 40 acres granted him "near his brother Thomas."

1648. Member of Court of Trials.

1655, Freeman.

1665-72-75-76-79-80. Deputy.

1671, Aug. 31. A meeting at his house of the Town Council, and Council of War of the two towns, was ordered by Assembly to be held on September 5th, at nine o'clock in the forenoon; "there and then to consider of some ways and means for securing the inhabitants and their estate in these times of imminent danger." Twenty horsemen (ten from each town) completely armed, were to attend at same time and place for the defence of the said Council there sitting, treachery of the Indians being feared.

1672, Mar. 2. He sold Richard Smith, merchant of Newport, 24 acres in Conanicut.

1676, Apr. 4. It was voted by Assembly: "That in these troublesome times and straits in this

I. ISABEL, b. d. 1730, Apr. 1.
m.
SAMUEL ALBRO, b. 1644. d. 1739, Apr. of John & Dorothy ( ) Albro.

1. John,
2. Dorothy,
3. Ruth,
4. Sarah,

II. JOHN, b. d. 1678 (—) Portsmouth, R. I.
m.
MARY BOOMER, b. d. 1715 + of Matthew & Eleanor ( ) Boomer.

(She m. (2) 1678, Jun. 3, Gideon Freeborn.)

1. George,

III. MARY, b. d. 1711, Nov. 8.
m.
JOHN BABCOCK, b. 1644. d. 1685. of James & Sarah ( ) Babcock.

1. James,
2. Ann,
3. Mary,
4. John,
5. Job,
6. George,
7. Elihu,
8. Robert,
9. Joseph,
10. Oliver,

IV. GEORGE, b. d. 1697, Sep. 11. Portsmouth, R. I.
m. 1677, Jan. 17.
NAOMI HUNT, b. 1658, Sep. 15. d. 1721, Jan. 13. of Bartholomew & Ann ( ) Hunt.

(She m. (2) 1701, Oct. 11, Isaac Lawton.)

1697, Sep. 8. Will—proved 1697, Sep. 24. Exx. wife Naomi. To son Job, £600, at eighteen, and to be brought up to learning. To daughter Elizabeth Curtis, £100. To wife, one part of household goods, and one part to son George, and one part to son Robert. To son George, three cows and forty sheep. To sons George and Robert, rest of cattle, sheep, horsekind and hogs, when son George arrives at age of twenty years. To son Robert, the southerly part of farm and half the orchard (100 acres). To son George, rest of farm and other lands in Portsmouth and Narragansett, with housing where I dwell. To wife, great room, little closet, joining little chamber, &c., six foot square in cellar, and garden, all to be hers while widow, and sons George and Robert, to pay her £14 yearly betwixt them while widow, and to keep for her a cow and horse, bringing to her yearly ten cords of wood,

1. Elizabeth, 1678, Nov. 15.
2. George, 1685, Apr. 30.
3. Robert, 1688, Oct. 14.
4. Job, 1692, Jan. 22.

colony, the Assembly desiring to have the advice and concurrence of the most judicious inhabitants, if it may be had for the good of the whole, do desire at their next sitting, the company and counsel of" sixteen persons, among them George Lawton.

1676, May 2. He and John Easton were desired to go to Providence, with all convenient speed, to determine whether garrisons shall be kept there at charge of colony, a petition having been sent to the Assembly from that place concerning their distressed condition in these present times of wars with the Indians.

The messengers were not to exceed the number of three garrisons, with twenty men placed in them at charge of colony, and to continue not above one month's time unless Assembly see cause longer to continue them.

1678, Oct. 30. There was ordered by Assembly to be a meeting held at his house 13th of Jan., next to adjudge and audit all accounts between towns of Newport and Portsmouth, relating to late Indian wars.

1680, May 5. He and two others were empowered by Assembly to purchase a bell "for the public use of this colony, and for giving notice, or signifying the several times or sittings of the Assemblys and Courts of Trial and General Councils." The bell was purchased for £3, 10*s*., of Freelove Arnold, daughter of Governor Benedict Arnold. Earlier than this the Assembly had been called together by beat of drum.

1680-81-82-83-84-85-86-89-90. Assistant.

1688, Jun. 2. He deeded son Robert, for love, &c., all goods, chattels, debts, bills, bonds, movables and immovables.

1690, Jan. 30. He and five other assistants with the Deputy Governor wrote a letter to their Majesties William and Mary, congratulating them on their accession to the crown, and informing them that since the deposition of Governor Andros, the former government under the Charter had been reassumed, and mentioning also the seizure of Andros, in Rhode Island on his flight from confinement in Massachusetts, and his return to Massachusetts on demand of latter colony.

He was buried in his orchard at Portsmouth.

A tradition in the Babcock family gives Mary Lawton, daughter of Thomas, as the wife of John Babcock[2] (James[1]). This could not have been, as Thomas Lawton had no daughter Mary. It is assumed that George Lawton did have a daughter Mary, and she it was who married John Babcock. The names of John Babcock's children seem to sustain the tradition of the family (if George be substituted for Thomas, as father of Mary Lawton.)

two barrels cider, and ten barrels of winter apples. If she marry she must give up house room, and to have £20, per year. To sons George and Robert, carts, plows, &c., equally. To Giffe, £10. To Indian servant Sarah, freedom in five years. To wife Naomi, rest of estate.

Inventory, 200 sheep, 100 lambs, 14 cows, 4 oxen, bull, 3 heifers, 2 steers, 7 yearlings, 6 calves, 2 horses, 2 mares, 2 colts, 11 swine, 2 negro boys £60. Indian girl 25*s*., 7 chairs, 3 tables, looking glass, joint stools, ⅛ brigantine "George" and 150 pounds of lading if she comes home well, but if she doth not come home then nothing, rum and molasses £24, sugar £19, 5*s*., beds, gun, silver plate £30, cash and bills £438, 1*s*., 8*d*., gold spectacles, case and buckles £3, 10*s*., books, 30*s*., wearing apparel, saddle, side saddle, &c.

1699, May 17. His widow took receipt from Holon and Elizabeth Curtis, for legacy.

Portsmouth, R. I.

V. ROBERT, — b. — d. 1706, Jan. 25.
m. 1681, Feb. 16.
MARY WODELL, — b. — d. 1732, Jan. 14. — of Gershom & Mary (Tripp) Wodell.

1. Mary, 1682, Feb. 20.
2. George, 1685, Sep. 1.
3. Elizabeth, 1688, Sep. 12.
4. Robert, 1696, Jan. 5.

1684. Freeman.

1688. Grand Jury. Same year Sealer of weights for Portsmouth.

1690-98-1702. Deputy.

1691, 1702-3. Assistant.

1706, Jan. 8. Will—proved 1706, Feb. 11. Ex. son George. To wife Mary, negro woman, and while widow great room in my dwelling house, cellar, household stuff as much as she wishes and £20. paid her yearly by son George. To daughter Mary Sherman, silver porringer. To daughter Elizabeth Lawton, silver porringer, negro girl Anne and £70, paid half in silver and half in goods at first cost in Boston. To sister Ruth Wodell, negro girl Kate and all my household goods at the Neck, forty sheep, horse and three cows during widowhood. To sons George and Robert Lawton, three negro men and a boy equally. To son Robert, all my lands upon main land (except half share in possession of Gershom Wodell, of Tiverton.) To son George, farm which I bought of his grandfather William Wodell, provided he gives his brother Robert assurance of the land I bought of John Sanford, when he (George) comes of age, also to son George, all my dwelling house, mill, lands, orchards, &c., great silver tankard, great silver basin, little porringer, six spoons and great dram cup, all of silver. To son Robert, a tankard, two basins, porringer, six spoons, three forks and little dram cup, all of silver. To son George, the ring which was my mothers. To son Robert, my seal ring. To sons George and Robert all the rest of my gold and silver and rest of movables.

VI. SUSANNA, — b. — d. 1712, Dec. 9.
m.
THOMAS CORNELL, — b. 1653. — d. 1714, Oct, 11. — of Thomas & Elizabeth (Fiscock) Cornell.

1. Thomas, 1674, Nov. 30.
2. George, 1676.
3. Elizabeth,

VII. RUTH, — b. — d. 1726, Apr. 15.
m. 1681, Feb. 10.
WILLIAM WODELL, — b. 1663. — d. 1699, Jan. 6. — of Gershom & Mary (Tripp) Wodell.

No issue.

VIII. MERCY, — b. — d. 1685 (—)
m. 1682, Jan. 19.
JAMES TRIPP, — b. 1656 ± — d 1730, May 30. — of John & Mary (Paine) Tripp.

No issue.

Portsmouth, R. I.

IX. JOB, — b. — d. 1697, Oct. 8.
Unmarried.

1697, Oct. 6. Will—proved 1697, Nov. 19. Ex. brother Robert. To brother Robert, one sixteenth of brigantine "George" and right in cargo, my negro man "Will," and my horse. To cousin George, son of brother Robert, a negro boy, all money, plate, and gold, great silver headed cane, all my instruments and books and rest of estate unbequeathed. To cousin Robert, son of brother Robert, my little silver headed cane.

X. ELIZABETH, — b. — d. 1724.
m.
ROBERT CARR, — b. — d. 1704. — of Robert Carr.

1. Robert,
2. Abigail,

LAWTON (John).

JOHN, — b. — d.

Newport, R. I.

1638, May 20. His name was in the list of inhabitants admitted since this date.

He may have been a brother of George and Thomas Lawton.

LAWTON (Thomas).

THOMAS, — b. — d. 1681.
m.
——— — b. — d.
m. (2)
GRACE BAILEY, (w. of [Wm. — b. — d. 1677 +
of Hugh and Elizabeth ( ) Parsons.

Portsmouth, R. I.

1639, Apr. 30. He and twenty-eight others signed following compact: "We whose names are underwritten, do acknowledge ourselves the legal subjects of His Majesty King Charles, and in his name do hereby bind ourselves into a civil body politic, unto his laws according to matters of justice."

1653, Aug. 4. He sold William Wodell 60 acres more or less.

1654, Jan. 21. He bought of Henry Knowles, 9 acres, dwelling house, fruit trees, &c., for a valuable consideration.

1655. Freeman.

1655-56-58-61, Commissioner.

1657, Apr. 16. He sold to Thomas Stafford a house, &c., in Warwick.

1660, Jul. 30. He received a deed of lands in Narragansett from Cadganaguant, Chief Sachem, who had "formerly received several kindnesses" from him.

I. ELIZABETH, — b. — d. 1711 +
m. 1657, Jul. 25.
PELEG SHERMAN, — b. 1638. — d. 1719. — of Philip & Sarah (Odding) Sherman.

1. Thomas, 1658, Aug. 8.
2. William, 1659, Oct. 3.
3. Daniel, 1662, Jun. 15.
4. Mary, 1664, Dec. 11.
5. Peleg, 1666, Oct. 8.
6. Ann, 1668, Apr. 30.
7. Elizabeth, 1670, Nov. 25.
8. Samuel, 1672, Jul. 15.
9. Eber, 1674, Oct. 20.
10. John, 1676, Oct. 28.
11. Benjamin, 1677, Jul. 15.
12. Sarah, 1680, Jan. 25.
13. Isabel, 1683, Jun. 3.
14. George, 1687, Dec. 18.

Portsmouth, R. I.

II. DANIEL, — b. — d. 1719, Jun. 28.
m.
REBECCA. — b. — d. 1719 (—) — of

1. Benjamin,
2. Joseph,
3. Thomas, 1666, Mar. 2.
4. Daniel, 1667, Oct. 28.
5. Rebecca, 1669, Feb. 24.
6. Jeremiah, 1670, Dec. 21.
7. Adam, 1672, Jan. 5
8. Elizabeth, 1674, Mar. 12.
9. Mary, 1675, Aug. 31
10. Isaac,
11. Sarah,
12. Jonathan,

1674. Deputy.

1687. Grand Jury.

1719, Feb. 26. Will—proved 1719, Jul. 13. Ex. son Joseph. Overseer, brother Isaac. To son Benjamin, house he now possesses, he paying my grandson Isaac, son of Isaac deceased, £60, at age. To son Joseph, my now dwelling house, &c., with 100 acres, he paying £30 to my daughter Elizabeth, wife of Nathaniel Dunn, £10 to my daughter Mary, wife of James Borden, and £10, to my daughter Sarah, wife of Lawrence Clarke. To son Daniel 5*s*., and like amounts to sons Jeremiah, Adam and Jonathan. To grandson William, son of Thomas, deceased, 5*s*. To son Joseph, rest of movables.

Inventory, £135, 1*s*. 6*d*., viz: bible, warming pan, wearing apparel, plate buttons, cane, silver buttons and plate £12, 6*s*. 8*d*., pewter, money scales, mare, neat cattle £33, sheep and lambs £30, swine £2, &c.

1666. Deputy

1676, Jun. 14. His wife Grace having presented her many grievances to the town often, and to the Assembly several times, for due and sufficient maintenance, she being much neglected in her husband's absence; it was therefore ordered by the Assembly that 6*s*. per week in silver be paid her or her order during her life, or until her said husband Thomas Lawton shall come himself, or maintain her. During his absence or neglect the said sum of 6*s*. per week shall be paid by his agent Daniel Lawton, and an inventory of movable goods in her custody to be taken, which inventory Daniel Lawton shall have. Grace to have the privilege of chamber she is now possessed of, and use of necessary movables, and the rights of her or any of her children now or in future to any estate are not cut off.

1677, Apr. 20. He made an agreement with his stepson John Bailey, whereby Grace, the present wife of Thomas Lawton, should receive £10, per year from John Bailey, and Elizabeth Sherman, daughter of Thomas Lawton, should have £3, per year (40*s*. being in money and other 20*s*. in good sheep's wool at 12*d*. per pound). In consideration of these payments, John Bailey was to have a lease of dwelling house, land and orchard "for term of time my wife Grace Lawton liveth without changing her name by marriage." The term of tenancy not to expire till one year after death or marriage of Grace, the mother of said John Bailey, and for that year the latter was to pay £13. On the same date he sold John Bailey for full satisfaction, all his household goods except a bedstead, chairs, &c.

1674, Jun. 6. Will—proved 1681, Sep. 29. Ex. son Daniel. Overseers, William Wodell and George Sisson. "I do hereby declare that although Grace have not behaved herself towards me as a wife ought to do towards an husband, yet for the manifestation of my care of her, I do hereby give, bequeath unto her all the goods that are yet remaining in my custody of those that were hers when I married her and also one good feather bed and boulster;" also £12, per annum for life in lieu of all right she has. To son Daniel farm now in his possession called "Long Swamp farm," and confirmation of another farm called "Hunting Swamp farm," at expiration of William Wodell's lease of it. To son Isaac a farm at Puncatege and all rights at Martha's Vineyard. To daughter Elizabeth Sherman, wife of Peleg, a quarter of a share in Dartmouth, and a piece of land in Portsmouth. To daughter Elizabeth, also all that my now dwelling house with land about it, and a pasture called "fifty acres." To daughter Ann Slocum, 5*s*. with what she had already received. To daughter Sarah Sisson, £50. To overseers, £5, apiece. To daughters Elizabeth Sherman and Sarah Sisson the rest of real and personal.

III. { Ann, { b. / d.
m. 1669, May 26.
{ Giles Slocum, { b. 1647, Mar. 25. / d. — of Giles & Joan (   ) Slocum.

1. Elizabeth, 1671, Apr. 8.
2. Joanna, 1672, Oct. 9.
3. Ann, 1674, Sep. 15.
4. Mary, 1676, Jan. 30.
5. Sarah, 1679, Mar. 1.
6. Giles, 1680, Dec. 8.
7. John, 1682, Sep. 22.

IV. { Sarah, { b. / d. 1718, Jul. 5.
m. 1667, Aug. 1.
{ George Sisson, { b. 1644. / d. 1718, Sep. 7. — of Richard & Mary (   ) Sisson.

1. Elizabeth, 1669, Aug. 18.
2. Mary, 1670, Oct. 18.
3. Ann, 1672, Dec. 17.
4. Hope, 1674, Dec. 24.
5. Richard, 1676, Sep. 10.
6. Ruth, 1680, May 5.
7. George, 1683, Mar. 23.
8. Abigail, 1685, Mar. 23.
9. Thomas, 1686, Sep. 10.
10. John, 1688, Jun. 26.
11. James, 1690, Jul. 26.

V. { Isaac, { b. 1650, Dec. 11 / d. 1732, Jan. 25. — Portsmouth, R. I.
m. (1).
Mary Sisson, { b. / d. 1674 (—) — of Richard & Mary (   ) Sisson.
m. (2), 1674, Mar. 3.
Elizabeth Tallman, { b. / d. 1701, May 20. — of Peter & Ann (   ) Tallman.
m. (3), 1701, Oct. 11. [Geo.
{ Naomi Lawton, (w. of { b. 1658, Sep. 15. / d. 1721, Jan. 13. — of Bartholomew & Ann (   ) Hunt.

1676. Freeman.

1688. Grand Jury.

1690–91. Assistant.

1696–98–99, 1702–4–5–6–8. Deputy.

1727, Jan. 20. Will—proved 1732, Feb. 14. Ex. son John. To eldest son Isaac, 5*s*., he already having had house and farm he lives on in Portsmouth. To son Thomas, 5*s*. he already having received house and farm in Bristol. To son Job all the house and land he now hath improvement of in Portsmouth, and negro boy Jamme. To five daughters, Sarah Rogers, Anne Almy, Mary Vaughan, Susanna Pearce and Ruth Hall, each 5*s*. they having had already. To five daughters of Elizabeth Smith, deceased, viz: Mary, Elizabeth, Sarah, Phoebe and Hannah, 5*s*. each. To two grandchildren, children of my daughter Isabel Cory, late deceased, viz: Elizabeth and William Cory, each 5*s*. To daughter Ruth Hall, negro girl Phillis. To son John, all my farm whereon I dwell in Portsmouth, with dwelling house, orchard, &c., and all money, silver plate, bonds, household goods, husbandry gear, negro servants, cattle, horses, sheep, &c.

Inventory, £1780, 16*s*., viz: silver money £15, 3*s*., gold ring and 3 pieces of gold £4, wrought plate £67, bonds £886, money scales and weight, stillyards, churn, carpenter's tools, negro man, girl, boy, and child of two months £300, 4 oxen, 11 cows, 5 yearlings, 4 calves, 80 sheep and lambs, horsekind £50, swine £6, &c.

(2d Wife, no issue.)

1. Elizabeth, 1675, Feb. 16.
2. Sarah, 1676, Oct. 25.
3. Ann, 1678, Apr. 25.
4. Isaac, 1681, May 25.
5. Mary, 1683, Apr. 3.
6. Isabel, 1685, Mar. 12.
7. Thomas, 1687, Apr. 25.
8. Susanna, 1689, Apr. 3.
9. Job, 1691, Apr. 28.
10. Ruth, 1694, Apr. 9.
11. John, 1696, Sep. 2.

(1st and 3d wives no issue).

LAY.

{ Edward, { b. 1608. / d. 1692.
m.
{ Martha, { b. / d. 1682 +

Portsmouth, R. I.

1667. Deputy.

1671, Jun. 15. His wife having been attacked by an Indian named John, said Indian was sentenced to death.

1677, Oct. 31. He and forty-seven others were granted 5,000 acres to be called East Greenwich. He never went there to settle.

1679, Aug. 1. He having petitioned the Assembly for liberty to keep an Inn, pleading age and debility of body to hard labor; they recommended the Town council to condescend to his desire. He was called (in the same year) seventy-one years old.

1680, Sep. 7. He was indicted for selling strong drink by retail without license.

1681, Oct. 26. His fine of 40*s*., laid on him by the General Court of Trial, was remitted by Assembly, he pleading age and debility.

1682, Sep. 20. Will—proved 1692, Feb. 11. Exx. wife Martha. Overseers, John Briggs, Caleb Arnold, John Sanford. To wife, all lands and personal estate, more especially because of the great love, affection and tender care found in my said loving wife during time of my sickness. To brother Robert, 1*s*. To brother John's eldest son John, 2*s*. To sons of brothers Robert and John, each 1*s*.

JOHN, b. d. 1690 (—)
m.
——, b. d.

Westerly, R. I.

1661, Mar. 22. He signed certain articles in relation to Misquamicut lands.

1668, Oct. 28. Westerly. Freeman.

1669, May 18. His name was in the list of inhabitants.

1679, Sep. 17. He took oath of allegiance.

There has been no relationship found between him and Robert Lewis, of Newport, who made his will 1682, Apr. 12 (having but two witnesses, though the law required three). Nothing more is learned of this Robert, nor of his will except that it was named in a list of others as deficient in witnesses.

LEWIS. 2d column. V. David b. 1667; d. 1718, Sep. 11. VI. Israel b. 1669; d. 1719, June 28; m. (2) 1718, Mar. 27, Mary Marsh, and had by her 6, Elisha, 1719, Feb. 4.

I. JONATHAN, b. d. 1710. Westerly, R. I., Huntington, N. Y.
m. (1)
JEMIMA WHITEHEAD, b. d. of Whitehead.
m. (2)
DELIVERANCE, b. d. 1708 + of

1679, Sep. 17. He took the oath of allegiance.

1708, Aug. 9. Will—proved 1710, Aug. 11. Exs. Eptemus Platt, Nathaniel Weeks, John Whitman. He mentions wife Deliverance and several children.

1. Sybil, 1685, Oct. 20.
2. Jonathan, 1686, May 5.
3. John, 1688,
4. Richard,
5. Elizabeth,
6. Jemima,
7. Hannah,
8. Sarah,

II. JOHN, b. d. 1735. Westerly, R. I.
m.
ANN, b. d. 1748. of

1688. Grand Jury.

1690, Feb. 6. He sold his brother Daniel, 100 acres, dwelling house, orchard and 4½ acres meadow, which said lands were formerly my father's and given me as may appear, I being the rightful owner since my father's decease.

1701, Nov. 6. He bought of Reuben Wait, of Dartmouth, 50 acres in Westerly, for 40*s*.

1704-9-10. Deputy.

1732, Apr. 14. Will—proved 1735, Apr. 22. Exs. wife Ann and son Joseph. To wife, a third of movables. To children, £5 each, viz: to Joseph, John, William, Mary Dake, Sarah Bemis, Ann Ross, Abigail Slack, Jerusha Lewis. To negro "Will," £10, and his freedom. To all children, rest of estate equally.

Inventory, £413, 11*s*., viz: 2 young oxen, 4 cows, calf, 8 swine, 20 sheep, 11 lambs, horse, mare, silver money £4, 5*s*., &c.

1739, Jul. 25. Will—proved 1748, Feb. 29. Widow Ann. Exx. daughter Jerusha. To each child, 5*s*., viz: to Joseph Lewis, Sarah Bemis, William Lewis, Anna Ross, Abigail Slack and Jerusha Lewis. To grandson William Slack, £10. To the Church of Seventh Day Baptists, in Westerly, £7. To granddaughter Anna Slack, £5. To grandsons Christopher and Joshua Lewis, sons of Jerusha, a pair of steers equally. To daughter Jerusha, rest of estate.

Inventory, £47, 14*s*.

1. Joseph, 1683, Oct. 16.
2. Sarah, 1687, Aug. 17.
3. Mary, 1689, May 4.
4. Ann, 1691, Jan. 6.
5. Abigail, 1693, May 20.
6. John, 1698, Jan. 30.
7. William, 1702, Feb. 1.
8. Jerusha, 1707, Jan. 11.

III. DANIEL, b. d. 1718. Westerly, R. I.
m.
MARY MAXSON, b. d. 1721 + of John & Mary (Mosher) Maxson.

He was a fuller.

1701, Jan. 15. He and wife Mary, deeded land to his brother David.

1704, Jul. 14. He bought 30 acres of Austin Odle.

1711-14. Deputy.

1718, Feb. 1. Will—proved 1718, Feb. 24. Ex. son John. To wife Mary, best room, a third income of land and a third of personal estate. To eldest son John, two-thirds of homestead farm, being the south part, and all the housing, mill and dam. To son Jonathan, remaining part of homestead with housing, &c., at age. To daughters Mary and Dorcas, part of a farm, and to son Daniel, the rest of same farm with housing, &c. To daughter Hannah, £40, at eighteen. To wife and two youngest sons, the rest of estate.

Inventory, cash £6, 3*s*., feather bed, carpenter's tools, 5 cows, 2 heifers, sick cow, pair of cattle, pair of oxen, 35 sheep, lambs, 3 yearling cattle, 5 calves, horse, 3 mares, colt, desperate debts, £80, &c.

1721, Aug. 3. Receipts were given the executor by widow Mary, Robert Burdick and Dorcas, John Langworthy and Mary, Daniel Lewis and Hannah Lewis.

1. John,
2. Jonathan,
3. Mary,
4. Dorcas,
5. Daniel,
6. Hannah,

IV. JAMES, b. d. 1745. Westerly, R. I.
m.
SARAH BABCOCK, b. d. 1740 + of James & Jane (Brown) Babcock.

1740, May 6. Will—proved 1745, Sep. 30. Ex. son James. To son James, a fifth of movables. To wife Sarah, a third of movables for life and then what she leaves to go to son James, and daughters Sarah Enos, Mary Hall and Elizabeth Crandall. To second son John, 5*s*., he having had. To son David, 5*s*. To daughters Sarah Enos, Mary Hall, Elizabeth Crandall and Patience Hall, a fifth each of movables. To grandson Benjamin Lewis, which was son of my daughter Ruth Lewis, £10, taken out before division.

Inventory, £388, 8*s*. 5*d*., viz: wearing apparel £7, pewter, spinning wheel, loom, 4 books, 4 swine, pair of oxen, 4 cows, 3 calves, 23 sheep, heifer, &c.

1. James,
2. Sarah,
3. Mary,
4. Elizabeth,
5. John,
6. David,
7. Patience,
8. Ruth,

V. DAVID, b. d. 1718. Westerly, R. I.
m.
ELIZABETH BABCOCK, b. d. 1718 + of James & Jane (Brown) Babcock.

1701, Jan. 15. He and wife Elizabeth, deeded land to brother Israel.

1718, Nov. 10. His will was offered for probate, but three witnesses declared that when signing he "was not right in his understanding," &c.

1718, Dec. 11. Administration to eldest son Elisha (the widow having refused). Inventory, £329, 15*s*., 11*d*. (sworn to by widow, and son Elisha), viz: 4 beds, wearing apparel, pewter, bible and other books 13*s*., loom, 4 spinning wheels, 10 cows, bull, yoke of oxen, 9 two years, 14 yearlings, 8 calves, 2 horses, 3 mares, 11 colts, 6 swine, sow and pigs, 37½ loads of hay, 8½ loads of oats and straw, 11½ loads of barley and straw, &c.

1719, Jan. 1. The will of his son Elisha (proved 1719, Mar. 2), names eldest brother David, youngest brother Isaac, eldest sister Mary, and youngest sister Prudence. He made his uncle Israel Lewis, executor.

1. Elisha,
2. David,
3. Isaac,
4. Mary,
5. Prudence,

VI. ISRAEL, b. d. 1719. Westerly, R. I.
m.
JANE BABCOCK, b. d. of James & Jane (Brown) Babcock.

1688, Aug. 9. He had a two years heifer given him by will of Tobias Saunders, and was to keep her and her increase till his time was out, and if he proved faithful the cow and increase both to be his, and a gun and sow also.

1719, Oct. 12. Administration to Benjamin Lewis, second son of deceased.

Inventory, £880, 1*s*., 16*d*., viz: 2 wheels, pair of cards, pair of combs, warming pan, 4 oxen, 4 steers, bull, 5 cows, 8 heifers, 7 two years, 7 yearlings, 6 calves, 4 mares, ½ of 2 mares, ½ of a horse, 3 horses, 5 colts, 9 sheep, 4 swine, cheese press, carpenter's tools, shoemaker's tools, &c. Housing and land, £600.

1. Israel, 1695, Jun. 22.
2. Benjamin, 1697, Jun. 8.
3. Jane, 1700, May 21.
4. Ann, 1704, Jul. 13.
5. Nathaniel, 1706, Mar. 23.

VII. SAMUEL, b. d. 1739. Westerly, R. I.
m.
JOANNA, b. d. 1734 + of

1692, Mar. 5. He deeded 100 acres to Jane Babcock, wife of Job, and Job declared he had given his wife full power to purchase the land, disowning any right therein for himself.

1734, Aug. 5. Will—proved 1739, Feb. 1. Ex. friend John Maxson, son of Joseph. To wife Joanna, £5 yearly for life, which I promised to give her for signing a deed of land sold Henry Knowles, and £400 to be laid out of estate for her to have the interest of for comfortable maintenance, &c. To son Samuel, 5*s*., he having had. To son Jonathan, 5*s*. To daughter Joanna Tanner, 5*s*. To daughter

1. Samuel,
2. Jonathan,
3. Joanna,
4. Sarah,

Sarah's son, John Fordice, £100, to lay out in lands by executors. To son Samuel's children, son Jonathan's children and daughter Joanna Tanner's children, the rest of estate at the ages of twenty-one and eighteen, and at decease of wife they to have what is left of household goods and £400.

Inventory, £2,508, 17*s.*, 7*d.*, viz: money and apparel £294, 12*s.*, 1*d.*, bonds, notes, pewter, mare, cow, &c.

VIII. DORCAS, b. d.
m.
ROBERT BURDICK, b. d. of Robert & Ruth (Hubbard) Burdick.

LILLY.

HENRY, b. d.

Newport, R. I.

1668. Freeman.

1676, Aug. 24. Marshal and Crier at a Court Martial held at Newport, for the trial of certain Indians charged with being engaged in King Philip's design. Several of the Indians were sentenced to be executed.

1677, May 2. Keeper of prison.

1677, Oct. 31. He and forty-seven others were granted 5,000 acres to be called East Greenwich.

1680. Taxed £1, 16*s.*

1690, Sep. 29. He was witness to will of William Foster.

LOCKWOOD.

ABRAHAM, b. 1670 ± d. 1747, Jun.
m. (1)
SARAH WESTCOTT, b. 1673. d.
of Amos & Deborah (Stafford) Westcott.
m. (2) [of Jeremiah.
PRISCILLA CRANDALL (w. b. d. 1750, Feb. 24.
of John & Ann (Gorton) Warner.

Warwick, R. I.

1706, Dec. 27. He and wife Sarah, sold John Waterman, for £11, 5*s.*, a right of commonage.

1714, Apr. 27. He bought of Josiah Westcott, for £36, tract of 85 acres in Providence.

1721, Jul. 20. He deeded son Amos, for love, &c., two lots of 6¼ acres.

1728, Jul. 1. He deeded to son Abraham, now of Providence, for love, &c., 85 acres west of Seven Mile Line in Providence.

1746, Nov. 8. Will—proved 1747, Jun. 8. Ex. son Adam. To son Adam, all Warwick land and "New Purchase," also live stock, &c. To son Amos, 20*s.* To daughter Deborah Cole, wife of Nathaniel, £10. To son Abraham, 20*s.* To daughter Sarah Potter, wife of Captain Abel Potter, 20*s.* To wife Priscilla, freedom of house and good maintenance for life.

Inventory, £253, 5*s.*, viz: 3 oxen, 2 cows and calf £112, wearing apparel £3, books, £1, 10*s.*, 4 pewter platters, 3 large plates, 12 small ones, 5 basins, tankard, 2 soup dishes, baker, porringer, 6 spoons, feather bed, &c.

1748, Jan. 12. Will—proved 1750, Mar. 17. Widow Priscilla, of Providence. Ex. brother Ezekiel Warner. To daughter Experience Sprague, 40*s.* To grandson Robert Ashton (*i. e.* Austin), 10*s.* To grandson Jeremiah Ashton (*i. e.* Austin), 40*s.* To grandson Jeremiah Sprague, 20*s.* To brother Ezekiel Warner, rest of estate.

Inventory, £90, 8*s.* 7*d.*

I. ABRAHAM, b. d. 1762 (—)
m.
MARY, b. d. 1766. of
Providence, Scituate, R. I.

1. Abraham,
2. Joseph, 1728, May 14.
3. Jacob,
4. William,
5. Damaris,

1728, Jul. 1. He was of Providence at this date, as seen by deed of his father. The land given him by his father was probably in what afterwards became Scituate.

1734. Scituate. Freeman.

1738, Mar. 14. A receipt was given by Job Randall, of Scituate, to John Clarke, for all debts upon Abraham Lockwood, late of Scituate.

1760, Dec. 22. His son Abraham died (a soldier), administration being given to his brother Joseph.

1762, Aug. 31. Will—proved 1766, Jun. 14. Widow Mary, of Cranston. Exx. daughter Damaris Lockwood. To sons Joseph, Jacob and William, 5*s.*, each. To daughter Damaris, the rest of estate.

II. AMOS, b. 1695 ± d. 1772, Mar. 11.
m. 1725, Dec. 23.
SARAH UTTER, b. 1707, Aug. 1. d. 1781, Jan. 4. of William & Anne (Stone) Utter.
Warwick, R. I.

1. Amos, 1727, Apr. 25.
2. Sarah, 1728, Jan. 26.
3. Ann, 1730, Dec. 28.
4. Benoni, 1733, Nov. 26.
5. Alice, 1735, Oct. 10.
6. Mercy, 1737, Nov. 26.
7. Ruth, 1739 ±
8. Wait, 1742, Sep. 2.
9. Phebe, 1744, Jun. 20.
10. Barbara, 1747, Apr. 24.
11. Abraham, 1748, Dec. 26.
12. Millicent, 1750, Apr. 21.

1723. Freeman. He bought land of Jeremiah Westcott, same year.

1746. He was one of the appraisers on estate of William Utter, Jr.

1749. Deputy. He was called Captain, at this time.

1750, May 22. He had a deed from his father-in-law, for love, &c., of several lots.

1771, Oct. 15. Will—proved 1772, Apr. 11. Ex. son Abraham. To son Abraham, homestead farm and mansion house, subject to life right of wife Sarah, to one-half said house. To wife, a support from son Abraham, with necessaries of life, two milch cows for her use; firewood at door, fifteen bushels of Indian corn, five bushels of rye, one hundred pounds of beef, five score pounds of pork, two barrels cider, two barrels cider beer, with apples, turnips and potatoes as she may have occasion to use, said supplies to be given her yearly. Sons Amos, Benoni and Abraham, had already had land of their father. To daughter, Ruth Battey, table. &c. To daughters Sarah, Anne, Mercy, Ruth and Phebe, 12*s.*, each, and what they had already received. To daughter Alice Healey's five children, 30*s.*, apiece. To daughters Wait, Barbara and Millicent, as much in household goods as sisters had had that are now married, and 12*s.*, apiece. To wife, household goods (except bed and desk) and the money she brought with her, and any household goods not taken up by wife for dower to go to three sons Amos, Benoni and Abraham.

1780, Dec. 16. Will—proved 1781, Mar. 5. Widow Sarah. Ex. son Amos. To sons Amos, Benoni and Abraham, 12*s.* each. To daughter Wait Greene, twelve Spanish milled dollars. To daughter Millicent Lockwood, six silver tablespoons and gold necklace, she paying my daughter Phebe Thomas and granddaughter Sarah Healy, $12 each. To granddaughter Sarah Healy, bed, loom, &c. To son Amos, largest pewter basin. To granddaughter Wait Arnold and grandson Joseph Arnold, 18*s.* each. To seven daughters, rest of estate equally divided, viz: to Sarah Arnold, Mercy Greene, Ruth Batty, Wait Greene, Phebe Thomas, Barbara Brayton and Millicent Lockwood

III. ADAM, b. d.
m. 1734, Dec. 24.
SARAH STRAIGHT, b. d. of Henry Straight.
Warwick, R. I.

1. Ann, 1735, Nov. 17.
2. Sarah, 1737, Jan. 27.
3. Abraham, 1738, Aug. 27.
4. Hannah, 1740, May 30.
5. Adam, 1742, Aug. 12.
6. Deborah, 1745, Sep. 15.
7. Almy, 1747, Feb. 17.
8. Patience, 1749, Mar. 20.
9. Adam, 1752, Jun. 10.
10. Abraham, 1754, Oct. 5.
11. Benajah, 1757, Nov. 20.

LOCKWOOD. 2d column. III. Adam. His wife's mother was Hannah. V. Sarah. Her husband was son of Benjamin and Margaret Potter.

IV. DEBORAH, b. d.
m. 1724, Dec.
NATHANIEL COLE, b. d. of Cole.

1. Sarah, 1726, Mar. 26.
2. Nathaniel, 1728, Sep. 3.
3. Deborah, 1728, Sep. 3.

V. SARAH, b. 1708, Oct. 20. d.
m. 1728, Jun. 16.
ABEL POTTER, b. 1702, Dec. 18. d. of Potter.

1. Phebe, 1728, Sep. 14.
2. Phebe, 1730, Nov. 23.
3. Prudence, 1732, Jun. 27.
4. Margaret, 1735, Feb. 18.
5. Mercy, 1736, May 4.
6. Dinah, 1738, Mar. 2.
7. Abel, 1740, Feb. 17.

(2d WIFE, no issue).

LONG.

PHILIP, b. d. 1726.
m.
HANNAH, b. d. 1726 +

Newport, East Greenwich, R. I.

1677, Oct. 31. He and forty-seven others were granted 5000 acres to be called East Greenwich.

1678, Apr. 30. Freeman.

1680, Mar. 19. East Greenwich. He had 90 acres laid out.

1682, Sep. 15. He exchanged lands with Daniel Vaughan.

1689, Oct. 23. He deeded son Philip, for love, &c., all my 90 acre farm in East Greenwich, only reserving profits of half of said farm for life of self and wife Hannah that now is.

1726, Jun. 11, Administration to widow Hannah. Inventory, £160, 3*s.* 8*d.*, viz: purse £100, apparel £1, 18*s.*, spinning wheel, pewter, 2 cows, 3 sheep, a shoat, 3 geese, &c.

I. PHILIP, b. d. 1713, Feb. 12. East Greenwich, R. I.
m.
SUSANNAH, b. b. 1713 + of

He died intestate, and Town Council made his will, appointing his widow Susannah executrix. To son Ezekiel, when of age, 5*s.* To daughter Elizabeth, £20, at eighteen or marriage, and a like amount to daughters Hannah, Susanna and Mary, at eighteen or marriage. Guardians appointed for children, were Job Babcock and Clement Weaver.

Inventory, £133, 10*s.*, viz: 4 oxen, 9 cows, 3 heifers, 6 yearlings, a calf, 2 mares, 2 horses, 13 swine, 2 spinning wheels, pair of worsted combs, pewter, &c.

1. Ezekiel, 1704, May 9.
2. Elizabeth, 1705, Mar. 10.
3. Hannah, 1707, Nov. 28.
4. Susannah, 1709, Oct. 4.
5. Mary, 1711, Jan. 3.

II. HANNAH, b. d. 1759.
m. 1691, Jan. 1.
CLEMENT WEAVER, b. 1669, Feb. 19. d. 1738, Feb. 19. of Clement Weaver.

1. Clement, 1695, Oct. 27.
2. Alice, 1698, Oct. 22.
3. Jonathan, 1704, Sep.
4. Clement, 1707, Jul. 7.
5. Mary, 1710, Mar. 19.
6. Gideon, 1714, Feb. 22.

LONG. 2d column. III. Abigail, b. 1682, Jun. 20, d. 1774, Apr. 22. She m. Jeremiah Pearce, of Giles and Elizabeth (Hall) Pearce, b. 1678, Jan. 22, d. 1754, Apr. 25. Children, 1. Giles, 1701, Aug. 24. 2. Philip, 1703, Mar. 9. 3. Elizabeth, 1705, Feb. 6. 4. Susannah, 1708, Apr. 8. 5. Jeremiah, 1711, Feb. 18. 6. John, 1713, Mar. 9. 7. William, 1716, Aug. 18. 8. James, 1719, Oct. 30.

LONG. 2d column. IV. Sarah m. Thomas Lan[illegible] of Thomas. He d. 1709, June. Children. 1. Rut[illegible] 1702, Feb. 19. 2, Comfort. 1704. Jan. 1. 3. John. 17[illegible] Oct. 10. 4. Jonathan. 1708, Feb. 20.

LUCAR.

MARK, b. d. 1676, Dec. 26.

Newport, R. I.

1648, Oct. 12. He was one of the twelve members of First Baptist Church in full communion.

1655. Freeman.

He bought land in Monmouth, N. J., but never went there to settle.

1676, Apr. 20. He had a legacy from will of Rev. John Clarke, of 50*s.* a year, in provisions for life.

LYTHERLAND.

WILLIAM, b. 1608. d. 1684 +
m.
MARGARET, b. d.

Boston, Mass., Newport, R. I.

1630. He was thus early at Boston.

1633, Nov. 24. He joined the church. He was afterwards among those who were disarmed for heretical views.

1652. Newport. Town clerk.

1653–54. General Recorder for Portsmouth and Newport.

1654–55–56. General Recorder (for the united colony of four towns).

1655. Freeman.

1684, Jun. 10. He and three others gave their depositions concerning the sale of lands at Boston by William Blackstone. He calls himself aged about seventy-six years, and the declaration of himself and companions was, that they were "ancient dwellers and inhabitants of the Town of Boston in New England from the time of the first planting and settling thereof and continuing so at this day."

From the language used, it would seem probable that he spent his later years at Boston, rather than Newport.

MACOONE.

JOHN, b. d.
m.
———, b. d.

Westerly, R. I.

By one account he came from Aberdeenshire, Scotland; and it is further said that he had two additional sons, viz: Samuel and William, who left Westerly, about 1695 and went to Oyster Bay, N. Y. (Samuel married Martha Cole, and William married Mary Townsend.)

1669, May 18. His name was in a list of inhabitants.

1679, Sep. 17. He took oath of allegiance.

1681. Juryman.

I. ISABEL, b. d. 1753.
m. 1691, Oct. 2.
EDWARD BLIVEN, b. d. 1718. of Bliven.

1. Jane, 1692, May 1.
2. Edward, 1694, Aug. 5.
3. Rachel, 1697, Mar. 19.
4. James, 1702, Oct. 27.
5. John, 1707, Jan. 22.

II. JOHN, b. d. 1733. Westerly, R. I.
m.
ANNE, b. d. 1732 + of

1692, Mar. 28. He was granted 100 acres.

1709, Apr. 7. He had 100 acres granted him.

1724, Apr. 15. He and wife Ann, deeded sons John and Daniel certain land.

1732, Dec. 15. Will—proved 1733, Jun. 29. Exs. two eldest sons John and Daniel. To wife Anne, a third of movables, and a third profits of farm where I dwell, also a feather bed, two cows, a mare, ten sheep, and best room in house, all for life, while widow, and provisions in the house. To eldest son John, a two year old beast, and 10 acres land. To second son Daniel, £5, and a two year old beast and certain land. To daughter Rachel Hall, £5. To daughters Mary Larkin and Abigail Brown, 82 acres equally, and to Mary, a mare, loom, &c., and to Abigail, a mare. To sons William, and Joseph, farm where I dwell (380 acres) equally, except the 10 acres given son John. To sons William and Joseph, also other land and all husbandry tools, and to each of them a three year old heifer, besides cattle they have, &c. To three daughters, Rachel, Mary and Abigail, the rest of movables.

Inventory, £392, 3*s.*, viz: horses, mares, sheep, a pair of oxen, 5 cows, 5 two year old, 5 yearlings, 3 calves, 2 linen wheels, pewter, warming pan, beds, &c.

1. John,
2. Daniel,
3. Rachel,
4. Mary,
5. Abigail,
6. William,
7. Joseph,

MACOONE. 2d column. III. Daniel. His wife was daughter of Enoch and Sarah (   ) Place.

II. DANIEL, m. 1705, Jun. 19. SARAH COOKE, (w. of Geo.) — b. / d. 1746. / b. / d. 1747. of — South Kingstown, R. I.

1. Hannah, 1706, May 18.
2. Abigail, 1707, Dec. 14.
3. Thankful, 1710, Dec. 17.

1706, Feb. 11. He gave bond for £480, to pay the two daughters of his wife by her former husband, £114, 6*s*., each at age, viz: to Sarah and Phebe Cook.

1744, May 22. Will—proved 1746, Nov. 18. Ex. grandson John Steadman. To wife Sarah, for life, certain land, dwelling house, firewood, two feather beds, and other household goods needful (except thirteen silver spoons of which she is to have use for life, and then to granddaughters). To wife also three cows, a riding horse, ten sheep, three hogs and use of negro Peg for life. To son-in-law Thomas Steadman and my daughter Hannah his wife, for life, use of land which son-in-law improves, and at his death to grandson Enoch Steadman. Provision was also made for grandsons James, John, Samuel, Daniel and Thomas Steadman, in lands, &c. To granddaughter Hannah Steadman, a silver porringer. To grandson John Steadman, a silver tankard. To grandson Thomas, certain land and grist-mill at age, and a gun. To daughter Abigail Hazard, if she became a widow, the use of land given Thomas Hazard. To grandson McCoon Williams, at age, land and a saw mill and gun. To son-in-law Thomas Williams and daughter Thankful Williams, improvement for life of certain land. Provision was made for grandsons Joshua, Henry and Thomas Williams. To granddaughter Phebe, daughter of Thankful Williams, £300, a great bible and silver porringer at eighteen. To granddaughter Susannah Hazard, a silver porringer To three eldest granddaughters Hannah, Susannah and Phebe, all my silver spoons. To granddaughters Sarah Steadman, Sarah Hazard and Sarah Williams, at death of wife, all personal estate given wife. The personal estate to be sold and put at interest, and said interest with rent of certain land to be for grandchildren who have no land.

Inventory, £3,778, 16*s*., 6*d*., viz: 5 suits of apparel, horse and bridle £135, 12*s*., silver tankard £60, 3 porringers £91, 10*s*., silver cup £2, 10*s*., 4 pieces of eight, silver buttons, pair of gold buttons £5, 10*s*., book debts £156, 19*s*. 5*d*., bonds, £214, 8*s*. 5*d*., gun, desk, warming pan, hour glass, 2 fat oxen, 8 fat cattle, 4 fat cows, yearling bull, 140 sheep, 60 lambs, 3 yokes of oxen, pair of steers, 12 yearlings, 11 calves, 6 two years, mare, colt, 2 horses, 2 colts, old mare, 7 hogs, a sow, cider mill, cane, half a canoe, books £2, woolen wheel, 2 foot wheels, 11 turkeys, 17 geese, 7 cheese fats, negro man "Will" £40, negro Fisherman £140, Peg £100, Rose £90, Scipio £90, Dinah £90.

1747, Jan. 12. Administration on widow Sarah McCoon's estate to daughter Thankful Williams, widow. Inventory, £22, 17*s*.

MALINS.

ROBERT, m. 1675, Jan. 1. PATIENCE EASTON, — b. 1649. / d. 1679, Aug. 26. / b. 1655, Nov. 20. / d. 1690, Nov. 21.

of Peter & Ann (Coggeshall) Easton.

(She m. (2) 1682, Jun. 7, Thos. Rodman.)

Newport, R. I.

1675. Freeman.

1675, Apr. 23. He bought 400 acres in Pettaquamscut for £30, of William Haviland and wife Hannah, of Flushing, N. Y.

1678 ± Taxed 17*s*.

I. MARY. — b. 1675, Oct. 21. / d.

II. ROBERT, — b. 1677, Jan. 22. / d.

MALLETT.

THOMAS, m. MARY, — b. / d. 1705. / b. / d. 1705 +

Newport, R. I.

He was an Inn keeper.

1699, 1700–1–2. Sheriff.

1703, Jan. 15. He and wife Mary sold to Joseph Fry, a small lot for £10.

1704, Dec. 8. Will—proved 1705, Feb. 5. He mentions wife Mary, son-in-law Jeremiah Wilcox, and wife Mary. To Trinity Church, 40*s*., and to minister, 20*s*. to preach his funeral sermon.

See: American Genealogist, v. 19, p. 226.

I. MARY, m. JEREMIAH WILCOX, — b. / d. / b. / d. of Stephen & Hannah (Hazard) Wilcox.

MANCHESTER.

THOMAS, m. MARGARET WOOD, — b. / d. 1691 + / b. / d. 1693 ±

of John Wood.

Portsmouth, R. I.

1655, Jan. 24. He and wife Margaret sold Thomas Wood, 12 acres.

1655, Mar. 17. In the settlement of John Wood's estate, it was ordered that £8, be paid by John Wood, son of deceased, to his sister Manchester.

1657, Dec. 10. He had a grant of 8 acres.

1658, Jul. 6. He sold Richard Sisson 1-300 of Conanicut and Dutch Islands.

1680. Taxed 4*s*.

1686, Jun. 7. He and wife Margaret testified that they heard and saw Ichabod Sheffield married by William Baulstone (many years before).

1691, Jul. 9. He deeded son John, for divers good causes and considerations, mansion house and all lands in Portsmouth, excepting the piece at the lower end of the ground in possession of son Thomas. One half of said property was to be his at his father's death, and the other half at death of his mother, and said son John was to pay to the grantor's children as follows: To sons Thomas, William and Stephen, 10*s*. apiece, son Job, 20*s*., and daughters Mary

See: American Genealogist, v. 19, p. 226.

I. THOMAS, m. MARY, — b. / d. 1718 + / b. / d. 1718 + of — Portsmouth, R. I.

1 John,

He was a blacksmith.

1667. Juryman.

1673, Jan. 1. He bought 8 acres in Portsmouth for £13, of Josiah England of Dartmouth.

1673. Freeman.

1677, May 2. He was released of a fine for not serving on the jury in October last, he declaring he had not timely notice thereof.

1680. Taxed 5*s*. 6*d*.

1681, Dec. 30. He and wife Mary sold John Pearce, of Portsmouth, a quarter of one-thirtieth share of land at Pocasset.

1686, Mar. 15. He sold 20 acres to William Browning.

1700, May 24. He and wife Mary sold to Gideon Freeborn, 16½ acres, bounded partly by brother John Manchester, with buildings, orchard, &c., for £156.

1718, Jun. 16. He and wife Mary, with his son John and wife Mary, sold 7 acres to Robert Fish, Jr., for £70.

He may have had other sons, as Edward (b. 1698, who married 1720, Feb. 4, Anna Williston), Nathaniel (who married 1716, May 4, Elizabeth Norton), George (who had married before 1712, Apr. 7, Elizabeth, daughter of Edward Bailey), and Thomas (who had wife Mary, and children born from as early a date as 1705), or these may have been sons of Stephen[a] or Job.[a]

and Elizabeth, 10*s.* each. He also deeded to his son John, all and singular my goods, cattle and chattels, implements, necessary debts, bills, bonds, specialties, sums of money, and all other things whatsoever belonging to me at my decease.

II. WILLIAM, b. 1654. d. 1718. Portsmouth, Tiverton, R. I.
m.
MARY COOK, b. d. 1716 + of John and Mary (Borden) Cook.

1. John,
2. William,
3. Mary,
4. Sarah,
5. Deborah,
6. Elizabeth,
7. Margaret,
8. Amey,
9. Susanna,
10. Rebecca,
11. Thomas,

1675. Freeman.

1676, Aug. 25. He testified, calling himself aged twenty-two years or thereabouts, that being at Pocasset, he asked of Peter Norrolt, husband of Weetamoe, who it was that killed Low Howland; his answer was Manasses fetched him out of the water.

1680, Mar. 5. He of Puncatest, and seven others, bought of Gov. Josiah Winslow, &c., lands at Pocasset for £1,100. There were thirty shares in all, of which he had five.

1680, Nov. 24. He and wife Mary, of Puncatest. sold John Cook, Sr., of Portsmouth, a half of thirteen shares in Puncatest, for £60.

1682, Oct. 6. He and Matthew Grinnell sold Thomas Ward, of Newport, a half share at Pocasset for £30.

1692, Mar. 2. Tiverton. He was an inhabitant at the organization of the town.

1712, Jul. 26. He had a deed of 10 acres in Potowomut, from Gideon Freeborn, for love, &c., and the latter calls him kinsman.

1716, Sep. 27. Will—proved 1718, Nov. 3. Ex. son John. To son John, the lands and housing in Tiverton, with certain exceptions, and all household goods and other personal, only wife Mary to have use of half of real estate and movables for life. To son William, certain land. To daughters Mary Gray and Sarah Wilcox, land. To daughter Deborah, land where my son-in-law Samuel Sanford's house now stands. To daughter Elizabeth, £5. To daughter Margaret, £10. To daughter Amey, 40*s.* To daughter Susanna, 40*s.* To daughter Rebecca, £10. To son Thomas, £100, at twenty-two. To son William, grass and herbage of a certain meadow. All legacies to be paid by son John at certain intervals.

Inventory, £1,586, viz: purse and apparel £8, 8*s.*, plate £1, 16*s.*, 3 beds, 2 chests, pewter, pair of oxen, 8 cows, 6 two years, 8 yearlings, 50 sheep and lambs, 9 horsekind, 22 swine, 60 geese, 4 hives of bees, 30 loads of hay, &c., land and housing £1,200.

III. JOHN, b. d. 1708. Portsmouth, R. I.
m.
——— b. d. 1703 (—) of

1. Elizabeth,
2. Mary,
3. Margaret,
4. John,

1677. Freeman.

1678, Jun. 1. He bought of John and William Coggeshall, land in Dartmouth for £7, 10*s.*

1680. Taxed 1*s.*

1693, Jan. 15. He deeded to brother Thomas, land formerly belonging to father Thomas Manchester.

1697, Jun. 3. He sold John Coggeshall 6 acres, for £25.

1703, May 20. Will—proved 1708, Nov. 29. Ex. brother Stephen Manchester. Overseers, brother Thomas Manchester and friend Benjamin Hall. To eldest daughter Elizabeth, a bed, cow, ten sheep, and a chest. To second daughter Mary, a cow, ten sheep, bed, chest and 20*s.* To third daughter Margaret, a bed, chest, cow and ten sheep. To three daughters, rest of movables equally. Brother-in-law Thomas Grinnell, to be guardian to daughter Margaret till sixteen. To son John, all my land and housing in Portsmouth, at age, and till then rent of farm to be divided equally to four children, except 40*s.* per year laid out in making stone walls. Brother-in-law Thomas Grinnell to be guardian to son John, and to receive rents for Margaret and John.

IV. GEORGE, b. d. Portsmouth, R. I.

1680. Freeman.

V. STEPHEN, b. d. 1719 Portsmouth, Tiverton, R. I.
m. (1) 1684, Sep. 13,
ELIZABETH WODELL, b. d. 1697 (—) of Gershom & Mary (Tripp) Wodell.
m. (2)
DAMARIS, b. d. 1719 + of

1. Gershom,
2. Ruth, 1690, May 27.

1684. Freeman.

1685, Jan. 15. He and wife Elizabeth gave receipt for legacy of £10, from will of John Tripp, to his granddaughter Elizabeth Wodell, whom Stephen Manchester had married.

1692, Mar. 2. Tiverton. He was an inhabitant at organization of the town.

1697, Dec. 6. His daughter Ruth had a conditional legacy from will of her uncle William Wodell.

1719, Nov. 5. Inventory, £129, 1*s.* Administration to widow Damaris. Wearing apparel, feather bed, warming pan, pewter, spinning wheel, pair of cards, 6 barrels cider, 3 loads of hay, 2 oxen, 2 cows, house and land £40, swine, gun, &c.

VI. JOB, b. d. 1713. Dartmouth, Mass.
m.
HANNAH, b. d. 1713 + of

1. Stephen, 1689, Apr. 8.

1692, Mar. 2. Tiverton. He was an inhabitant at organization of town. He soon moved to Dartmouth.

1713, Jan. 8. Inventory, £73. Sworn to by widow Hannah. Among items was land £21, table, chairs, 2 beds, gun, 6 swine, pair of oxen, 2 yearlings, 2 calves, &c.

VII. MARY, b. d.

VIII. ELIZABETH, b. d.

MANN (JAMES).

JAMES, b. d.
m.
——— b. d.

Rehoboth, Mass., Newport, R. I.

1650, Oct. 2. His wife and others were presented by Grand Jury for continuing of meeting upon the Lord's day from house to house, contrary to order of this court enacted Jun. 12, 1650.

1653, May 17. Newport. Freeman.

1671. Juryman.

1680. Taxed £1, 2*s.* 3*d.*

1688, Mar. 13. He sold Philip Smith, 40 acres, house, orchard, &c., for £160.

1689, Nov. 13. Will—Executors, Philip Smith and Jonathan Holmes.

1692, Jun. 14. The executors of his will, took a receipt from Arthur Cook, of Philadelphia, attorney for John Parker and Hester his wife, for legacy given testator's cousin John Parker and Hester his wife of £10, and to Hester, his turkey wrought coverlet, and to John, Robert and James, sons of John and Hester, £30, equally divided, and to Hannah, daughter of John and Hester, £5, &c.

See: American Genealogist, v. 3?, p. 2

MANN (THOMAS). 1st column. His 2d wife, b 1656, Nov. 4. She m. (2) 1698, Mar 3, Ebenezer Darling.
2d column. II. Rachel, m. Nehemiah Sheldon, of John & Joan (Vincent) Sheldon. He b. 1672, d. 1754 +. Children, 1. Abraham, 2. Philip, 3. Mary, 4. Rachel, 5. Welthian. VI. Mehitable, d. 1725 ± unmarried. VIII. Daniel, d. 1744, Mar. 31.

THOMAS, b. ; d. 1694, Jul. 18.
m. (1) 1674, Oct. 28.
RACHEL BLISS, b. 1651, Dec. 1. ; d. 1676, Jun.
of Jonathan & Miriam (Harmon) Bliss.
m. (2) 1678, Apr. 9.
MARY WHEATON, b. ; d. 1746 ±
of Robert & Alice (Bowen) Wheaton.
(She m. (2) ——— Darling.)

Rehoboth, Mass., Providence, R. I.

1676, Mar. 26 On this date (Sunday) occurred the memorable conflict in Rehoboth known as "Pierce's Fight," wherein fifty-two English and eleven friendly Indians were killed, while the opposing force of Indians lost one hundred and forty in killed. An idea of this desperate fight may be formed when it is remembered that sixty-three English and twenty friendly Indians fought in a ring back to back, for two hours against overwhelming odds, and with a result of only eleven surviving whites. Rev. Noah Newman, of Rehoboth, in a letter written the day after the battle to Rev. John Cotton, of Plymouth, gives an account of the affair, and says: "Thomas Mann, is just returned with a sore wound." Whether the early death of Thomas Mann (occurring eighteen years after this battle) was owing in any degree to the severe wounds he received in this fight, may be a matter of conjecture.

1682, Mar. 7. He was fined 10*s.* for Sabbath breaking.

1683, Jun. 9. Surveyor of highways.

1689, Feb. 7. His name was in the list of inhabitants of Rehoboth.

1693, Jan. 20. He bought of Ephraim Pierce and wife Hannah, of Rehoboth, for a valuable sum, the housing, barn and farm they have sometime lived on in Providence, with orchard, meadow and commonage. He moved to Providence soon after this purchase.

1694, Jul. 12. Will—proved 1694, Aug. 21. Exx. wife Mary. To wife he gives dwelling house, barn, orchard, &c., until son Thomas is of age and then she to resign half to him. She to have quarter of movable estate, and the improvement of the whole, but if she marries ¾ of said movable estate to go to daughters. To eldest son Thomas, half the homestead when of age or when his mother marries. To son Daniel, land on Palmers River, and "the meadow I had of my father Bliss, upon exchange," and land in Rehoboth, &c. To son John, land in Rehoboth, &c. Any son dying before coming of age, the other sons are to share his estate equally. To daughter Rachel, land in Rehoboth, a cow and £5, which sum was to be paid her by Thomas, when he was of age. To daughter Mary, land and £5, to be paid her by Daniel. To daughter Bethiah, a cow. To daughter Mehitable, land and a cow. To daughter Joanna, a cow and calf bought of Samuel Bartlett. Any daughter dying, the rest were to share her estate. Rest of estate to go to Mary, his wife.

Inventory, £149, 1*s* 6*d.*, viz: a horse, a bull, 2 oxen, 9 cows, 5 heifers, 6 yearlings, 5 calves, sheep and hogs, standing corn, rye, wheat and oats, standing grass, fruit of orchard, pewter, brass and iron ware, woolen and linen yarn, wearing apparel, 2 guns, 13 pistols, 2 holsters, 2 cutlasses and belt, purse £1, 18*s.*, &c.

1699, May 31. His widow had £3, 7*s.*, and a third of movables on settlement of her father's estate.

1716, Oct. 8. His widow (being now Mary Darling), rented to son Thomas Mann, from Jan. 1st, 1715, for five years, all her part of house and land left her by will of husband Thomas Mann, at £5, per year and after that date at £5, 5*s.*, per year for her life. The sum to be paid her as follows: 25*s.* in good pork, 25*s.* Indian corn and rye, and 50*s.* in money.

1731, Nov. 8. Mary Darling, widow, had administration upon estate of her daughter Joanna Mann.

1745, Nov. 4. Mary Darling, widow, of Smithfield, deeded to son John Mann, for £100, all estate, moneys, bills, bonds and household goods.

1753, Nov. 26. Administration on widow Mary Darling's estate was given at Smithfield, to her eldest son Thomas Mann, she having died some years past intestate.

I. CHILD, b. ; d. 1676.

(2d WIFE.)

II. RACHEL, b. 1679, Apr. 15. ; d.

III. MARY, b. 1681, Jan. 11. ; d.
m. 1706, Jan. 12.
EBENEZER SPRAGUE, b. ; d. of John & Elizabeth (Holbrook) Sprague.

1. Mary, 1709, Mar. 1.
2. Ebenezer, 1711, Mar. 1.
3. Daniel, 1713, Mar. 28.
4. Samuel, 1715, Dec. 29.

IV. BETHIAH, b. 1683, Mar. 12. ; d. 1712, Apr. 6.
m. 1699, Nov. 28.
JONATHAN SPRAGUE, b. ; d. 1764, Apr. 22. of Jonathan & Mehitable (Holbrook) Sprague.

1. Jonathan, 1701, Jul. 25.
2. Hezekiah, 1704, Jan. 12.
3. Bethiah, 1707, May 24.
4. Anne, 1709, Mar. 9.
5. Mehitable, 1711, Mar. 24.

V. THOMAS, b. 1685, Jan. 24. ; d. 1754, Oct. 24. Providence, Smithfield, R. I.
m.
MARY WHITING, b. ; d. of Whiting.

1. Thomas, 1713, Jun. 21.
2. Mary, 1715, Aug. 2.
3. Oliver, 1718, Nov 30.
4. Moses, 1720, Feb. 23.
5. John, 1722, May 28.
6. Patience, 1726, Feb. 18.
7. Royal, 1731, Mar. 28.
8. Philip, 1733, May 13.

1710. Mar. 29. He had 10 acres laid out.

1713, Jun. 16. Taxed 9*s.*

1746, May 19. Smithfield. He deeded for £1,000 to John Mann, Jr. (his son) my homestead northwest side Woonsocket Hill, both sides of highway, containing 100 acres.

1754. Administration to son Oliver.

Inventory, £166, 10*s.* 6*d.*, viz: wearing apparel £94, 9*s.*, books £1, old sword, pewter, cooper and carpenter tools, great chair, &c.

1762. His son Royal's estate was administered upon by brother Oliver, the said Royal having gone abroad and not been heard of for about eight years past.

VI. MEHITABLE, b. 1687, Apr. 11. ; d.

VII. JOANNA, b. 1689, Sep. 24. ; d. 1731, Sep. 28.
Unmarried.

VIII. DANIEL, b. 1692, Feb. 16. ; d. 1744. Providence, Glocester, Smithfield, R. I.
m. (1)
———, b. ; d. of
m. (2) 1733, Jan. 11,
JERUSHA MOWRY, b. ; d. 1758 + of Mowry.

1. Bethiah,
2. Andrew,
3. Nathaniel,
4. Daniel,
5. Richard,
6. Anthony,
7. Sarah,
(2d wife.)
8. Susanna, 1736, Jan 15.
9. Abraham,
10. Rhoda,
11. Thomas.

1713, Jun. 16. Taxed 2*s.* 6*d.*

1733, Apr. 30. Glocester. He sold Israel Arnold, homestead of 70 acres, for £415.

1737, Feb. 2. He bought 88 acres and dwelling house in Smithfield, of Jacob Mowry.

1744, May 7. Inventory, £156, 6*s.* 1*d.* Administration to widow Jerusha, though an appeal was taken by Andrew Mann, for himself and brother Daniel (who had chosen him guardian), and by Moses Arnold, guardian of Richard and Anthony Mann, sons of deceased Daniel Mann.

1744, May 10. Nathaniel Mann, of Glocester, for £20, gave receipt to brother Andrew Mann, of Smithfield, for all interest in estate of honored father Daniel, deceased, as viz: his homestead farm in Smithfield, and all other estate real and personal.

1747, May 31. Daniel Mann died (son of deceased Daniel), and by will left all of his estate to brothers Richard and Anthony Mann, and sister Sarah Cruff, wife of Thomas Cruff, Jr. This younger Daniel Mann, lost his life in the war against the Indians, the record says.

1758, Jan. 23. Widow Jerusha Mann, brought in account of charges, among which was £200, for keeping Thomas Mann, son of Daniel, from six months old till seven years; £40, for keeping Rhoda Mann, daughter of Daniel, from two years till four years old; and £20 for keeping Abraham Mann, son of Daniel, from five years till six years old.

IX. JOHN, b. 1695. ; d. 1782, Dec. 17. Providence, Smithfield, R. I.
m. 1720, Jun. 29.
ABIGAIL ARNOLD, b. ; d. 1775 (—) of Eleazer & Eleanor (Smith) Arnold.

1. Abigail, 1720, Dec. 11.
2. Sarah, 1723, Nov. 13.
3. Mary, 1726, Sep. 6.
4. Dorcas, 1731, Jun. 27.
5. John, 1734, Dec. 13

1720, Apr. 23. He bought of his brother Daniel, for £240, his dwelling house in northward part of township and 82 acres in two parcels separated by a highway, also the orchard, &c.

1775, Mar. 6. Will—proved 1783, May 19. Ex. son John. To son John, all real estate in Smithfield and a fifth of all movables, provided he assists my daughter Sarah, as needs may require as long as she lives. To children of daughter Abigail Ballard, deceased, a fifth of movables equally. To daughters Sarah Mann, Mary Lapham and Dorcas Herenden, rest of movables.

Inventory, £7, 1*s.* 6*d.*, viz: wearing apparel £3, 10*s.*, square table, warming pan, iron kettle, trammel, fire shovel, &c. He was buried in the family burying ground on his farm.

MANN (WILLIAM).

WILLIAM, b. ; d. 1650 (—)
m.
FRANCES HOPKINS, b. 1614. ; d. 1700, Feb. 26.
of William & Joanna (Arnold) Hopkins.

Providence, R. I.

1640, Jul. 27. He signed an agreement with thirty-eight others for a form of government.

1641, Nov. 17. He and twelve others complained in a letter to Massachusetts of the "insolent

See: American Genealogist, v. 20, p. 53; p. 227.
v. 27, p. 220-221.

I. ABRAHAM, b. ; d. 1695, Feb. 26.
Unmarried.

1675, Apr. 27. He was allowed to change his 60 acre lot, and pay his change money.

1676, Aug. 14. He was one of those "who staid and went not away" in King Philip's War, and so was allowed a share in the disposition of the Indian captives, whose services were sold for a term of years.

1679, Jul. 1. Taxed 3*s.* 1½*d.* with his mother.

1684, Oct. 29. He was allowed £3, by Assembly for cure of his wound in late Indian war.

and riotous carriages of Samuel Gorton and his company;" and therefore the petitioners desire Massachusetts to "lend us a neighbor-like, helping hand," &c.

1644, Jun. 17. He bought a share of meadow of Robert Morris bounded partly by Spectacle Pond.

1650, Sep. 2. Widow Mann taxed 6*s.* 8*d.*

1651, Jan. 27. His widow, on her complaint to the overseers of her husband's will, was to have relief, or if they neglected they were to forfeit 10*s.*

1664, Apr. 27. His widow was to be visited by a committee, to agree with her about what she oweth the town upon the account of William Burrows, deceased.

1700, Feb. 26. His widow died at Dartmouth, Mass., at her son-in-law John Lapham's.

1685, Oct. 12. He sold to Ephraim Pierce for £5, half a right of commoning in the right of father William, deceased, and by said father's last will, fell to my right, being heir apparent.

1687, Sep. 1. Taxed 2*s.* with estate of John Lapham.

1687. Ratable estate with John Lapham, 2 cows, 2 shares fresh meadow, 12 acres English pasture.

1695, Mar. 19. Administration to John Lapham, of Dartmouth; his wife Mary being next of kin to deceased.

Inventory, £13, 11*s.* 6*d.*, presented by William Hopkins, kinsman of deceased.

II. { MARY, { b. d. 1710 +
m. 1673, Apr. 6.
JOHN LAPHAM, { b. 1635. d. 1710. of Lapham.

1. Mary, 1674, Mar. 1.
2. John, 1677, Dec. 13.
3. William, 1679, Nov. 29.
4. Thomas, 1682, Sep. 30.
5. Mary, 1686, Oct. 5.
6. Nicholas, 1689, Apr. 1.

MARSH.

{ JONATHAN, { b. d. 1704, Jun. 10.
m. (1)
SARAH REAPE, { b. 1664, Apr. 17. d. 1687, Sep. 26.
of William & Sarah ( ) Reape.
m. (2) 1700, Jan. 17.
PHEBE ARNOLD, (w. of Oliver { b. 1665. d. 1732.
of Thomas & Mary (Havens) Cook.
(She m. (3) 1705, Oct. 7, Robert Barker.)

Jamestown, R. I.

1702. Deputy.

1703. He and John Carr, ferrymen, were to carry all Magistrates, Deputies, and members of the General Court over said ferry and charge it to account, that it may be deducted out of what they pay yearly for the ferry.

1704, Jun. 9. Will—proved, 1704, Jul. 3. Exx. wife Phebe. To two sons, William and Jonathan, land in East Jersey, and certain land in Rhode Island, and my silver money, gold, bonds, and book debts. Son William to be overseer for son Jonathan, with advice from mother-in-law (*i. e.* stepmother) Phebe, and William to have a third of improvement of his brother Jonathan's estate for his services. To son William, all household goods and plate that was mine before I married Phebe Arnold, except two silver cups. To son William, also my ferry boat on east side of Jamestown, and negro "Sambo," for seven years, and then freed. To son Jonathan, ferry boat on west side of Jamestown, a negro "Robin," till Jonathan is of age, and then freed, and two silver cups and a silver tankard. To cousin Hester Palmer, daughter of my sister Sarah Palmer, £10. To wife Phebe, all neat cattle, &c. belonging to house in Jamestown, and plate and household stuff not given, a third of real estate and negro "Cuffe," all for life, and then to son Jonathan. To son-in-law (*i. e.* stepson) Oliver Arnold, a horse. To six daughters-in-law, a cow each, and to daughter-in-law, Freelove Arnold, a piece of gold. To wife's kinswoman Abigail Remington, a cow. To son William, wearing apparel. Son Jonathan, to be brought up to learning.

Inventory. £940, 10*s.* 1*d.*, viz: Arabian gold 106 pieces and 2 pistoles, £60, 10*s.*, silver money £28, 11*s.* 4*d.*, bills £336, 11*s.* 10*d.*, 2 silver tankards £20, 2 silver cups £6, silver spoons, wearing apparel, 2 feather beds, ferry boat east side of island £30, ferry boat west side of island £15, negro "Sambo," for seven years yet to come £21, "Robin" £30, "Cuffy" £35.

Inventory of estate received with his wife, £482, 6*s.* 4*d.*, viz: feather beds, warming pan, 6 oxen, 17 cows, 6 two years, 7 yearlings, 7 calves, 860 sheep and lambs, 7 horsekind, 8 swine, negro woman £55, &c.

I. { WILLIAM, { b. d. Newport, R. I., Shrewsbury, N. J.
m.
SARAH, { b. d. of

1707, Mar. 17. He gave a receipt to his mother-in-law (*i. e.* stepmother), Phebe Barker, late wife of Jonathan Marsh.

1709, May 4. He appealed to the Assembly in a case brought against him by Robert Barker, in which the latter had obtained two judgments. He was ordered to make up his accounts relating to estate in his hands, concerning his brother Jonathan.

1709, Oct. 31. He had a deed of gift from his grandmother Sarah Reape, of a house and lot in Newport.

1710, May 2. Freeman.

1715, Apr. 12 Shrewsbury. He was mentioned in the will of his grandmother Sarah Reape, of Shrewsbury, widow of William Reape, of Newport.

II. { JOHN, { b. 1687, Sep. 11. d. 1687, Oct.

(2d WIFE.)

III. { JONATHAN, { b. 1702, Jan. 27. d. 1770, Feb. 18. Newport, R. I.
m. 1728, Oct. 3.
MARY GOULD, { b. 1708, Dec. 20. d. 1786, Jan. 11. of Daniel & Ruth (Sheffield) Gould.

1729, May 6. Freeman.

He was buried in the Clifton Burial Ground.

1. Phebe, 1729, Jun. 16.
2. Daniel, 1731, Oct. 7.
3. Jonathan, 1733, Oct. 17.
4. Mary, 1735, Aug. 24.
5. Gould, 1738, Jul. 12.
6. James, 1740, Sep. 27.
7. Nathaniel, 1742, Jul. 26.
8. William, 1743, Jul. 22.
9. Jeremiah, 1744, Aug. 17.
10. Carr, 1747, Mar.
11. Ruth, 1748.
12. Phebe, 1750.

MARSHALL.

{ EDWARD, { b. d.
m.
MARY, { b. d

Warwick, R. I.

1664, May 5. He and two others having spent five days to bring an Indian to prison from Warwick to Newport, their bill of £3, 2*s.* 6*d.*, was ordered paid.

No relationship is known to exist between him and John Marshall, who was an inhabitant of Aquidneck, in 1639.

I. { EDWARD, { b. 1658, Apr. 10. d.

II. { JOHN, { b. 1660, May 12. d.

III. { THOMAS, { b. 1663, Mar. 1. d. Kings Town, R. I.

1671, May 28. He was apprenticed, with consent of his father and mother, to Rouse Helme, of Kings Town.

1684, Oct. 27. He gave a receipt to Rouse Helme, his apprenticeship being ended.
1687, Sep. 6. Taxed 1*s*.

IV. MARY, b. 1666, Jul. 1. d.

V. CHARLES, b. 1668, Jan. 28. d.

VI. MARTHA, b. 1669, Mar 16. d.

MATHEWSON.

JAMES, b. d. 1682.
m.
HANNAH FIELD, b. d. 1703 +
of John Field.
(She m. (2) Henry Brown.)
Providence, R. I.

1658, Jan. 27. He bought of Thomas Angell, 5 acres on east side of Thomas Clemence's land.

1665, Feb. 19. He had lot 92 in a division of lands.

1668, Feb. 24. He bought of John Brown and wife Mary, 5 acres south-west side of Wanasquatucket River.

1679, Jul. 1. Taxed 5*s*.

1680. Deputy.

1682, Aug. 24. Will—proved 1682, Oct. 17. Exx. wife Hannah. To son James, 120 acres. To son Thomas, 41 acres. To all sons equally my share of land beyond Seven Mile Line. To son Zachariah and the child unborn, if it be a son, my house, and certain land, but if it be a daughter, then all to remain to son Zachariah. To wife all movable goods and cattle at her disposal for daughters.

Inventory, £85, 19*s*., viz: 20 loads of provender, Indian and English corn, household goods, cattle and swine £65, 10*s*., &c.

1687, Sep. 1. His widow was taxed 3*s*. 2*d*.

1698, Sep. 22. Henry Brown, in his will of this date, gave to wife's daughter Lydia Mathewson, a heifer.

1703, Jul. 28. Hannah Brown, widow of Henry, gave receipt for movable estate, cattle, &c., to Richard and Joseph Brown, the two sons of late husband, to whom she had committed the office of executor to which she had been appointed, she being unacquainted with the duties

MATHEWSON. 2d column. V. Thomas. Change wife to Martha Sheldon, b. 1687, May 5, d. 1787, Jul. 25, of Timothy and Sarah (Balcom) Sheldon. VIII. Mary (before IX. Daniel), d. 1729, +, m. William Field, b. 1682, Jun. 8, d. 1729, Nov. 1, of Thomas and Martha (Harris) Field. Children, 1. Martha. 2. Joseph. 3. Nathan. 4. Mary. 5. William. 6. Thomas. 7. John, 1712. 8. Charles, 1714, Feb. 6.

I. RUTH, b. d. 1704 +
m. 1686, Apr. 1.
BENJAMIN WHIPPLE, b. 1654. d. 1704, Mar. 11. of John and Sarah ( ) Whipple.

1. Benjamin, 1688, Nov. 11.
2. Ruth, 1691, May 12.
3. Mary, 1694, Mar. 3.
4. Josiah, 1697, Jul. 29.
5. John, 1700, Feb. 25.
6. Abigail, 1703, Jun. 12.

II. JAMES, b. 1666, Aug. 11. d. 1737, Jan. 7. Providence, Scituate, R. I.
m. 1696, Apr. 5.
ELIZABETH CLEMENCE, b. 1673, Feb. d. 1736 + of Thomas & Elizabeth ( ) Clemence.

1683, May. He brought in a wolf's head.

1687. Ratable estate, pair of oxen, 4 cows, steer, 3 heifers, 6 swine, horse, 3 acres planting land, 4 acres meadow, 9 sheep.

1734, Oct. 2. Scituate. He deeded son James one part of lands and dwelling house, barn, corn mill, and half of saw mill, and to son Philip, one part of lands and half of saw mill.

1736, Dec. 12. Will—proved 1737, Mar. 12. Ex. son Daniel. To son Richard, 110 acres. To son Jeremiah, 40 acres. To son Daniel, 22 acres. To sons Richard and Jeremiah, rest of land. He described certain land given Richard, as in the original right of my honoured father James Mathewson, deceased; and certain land given Jeremiah, was described as in the original right of my honoured grandfather John Field, deceased. To wife Elizabeth, a feather bed, iron pot and kettle, and bell metal skillet. To sons Richard and Jeremiah, a yoke of oxen equally. To son Richard, a steel trap, log chain, &c. To son Daniel, all the rest of movable estate, he taking care of his mother so she shall have all things necessary.

Inventory, £202, 4*s*. 6*d*., viz: yoke of oxen, 3 cows, 2 heifers, feather bed, 2 warming pans, pewter, gun, churn, linen wheel, scales, &c.

1. Anne, 1697, Jan. 7.
2. Elizabeth, 1699, Jan. 31.
3. Daniel, 1700, Oct. 6.
4. James, 1702, May 10.
5. Mary,
6. Philip,
7. Richard,
8. Jeremiah,

III. JOHN, b. d. 1716, Sep. 18. Providence, R. I.
m. 1698, Nov. 17.
DELIVERANCE MALAVERY, b. d. 1716 + of John & Elizabeth ( ) Malavery.

He held the office of Lieutenant.

1716, Oct. 22. Administration to widow Deliverance. Inventory, £353, 3*s*., viz: silver and paper money £78, 4*s*. 7*d*., negro woman £10, 2 guns, 4 oxen, 20 cows, 7 young cattle, mare, swine, small and great, rye, corn, apples, hay, &c.

1. John, 1699, Oct. 6.
2. Lydia, 1701, Jun. 7.
3. Daniel, 1704, Mar. 5.
4. Elizabeth, 1706, Dec. 21.
5. Israel, 1708, Jan. 3.
6. Ann, 1712, Jan. 21.
7. Jemima, 1715, Jul. 10.

IV. ISABEL, b. d. 1719 +
m. 1696, Jun. 9.
JOHN BROWN, b. 1662, Mar. 18. d. 1719, Sep. 19. of John & Mary (Holmes) Brown.

1. John, 1697, Mar. 26.
2. Mary, 1599, Jul. 30.
3. Lydia, 1701, Dec. 21.
4. Isabel, 1705, Apr. 17.
5. Nathan, 1707, Aug. 24.
6. Obadiah, 1710, Aug. 17.

V. THOMAS, b. 1673, Apr. 1. d. 1735, Oct. 23. Providence, Scituate, R. I.
m.
MARTHA FIELD, b. d. 1735 + of Thomas & Martha (Harris) Field.

1707, Dec. 2. He had a deed of 4 acres from William Field, who calls him brother-in-law, and who conveys the land for good will and respect. Thomas Field, father of the said William, confirmed the deed.

1735, Nov. 10. Administration to widow Martha. Inventory, £718, 1*s*. 4*d*., viz: wearing apparel £16, 6*d*., books 12*s*., silver £6, 3*s*. 6*d*., paper money £31, 14*s*. 4*d*., gun, chest, warming pan, 2 pairs still-yards, cider mill, 2 mares, bull, 13 cows, 2 yokes oxen, 8 young cattle, 6 calves, 34 goats, 34 sheep, 6 hogs, 6 shoats, &c.

1. Thomas,
2. Amos,

MATHEWSON. 2d column. V. Thomas. Children... Marth , Deborah, 1714.

VI. LYDIA, b. d.

VII. ZACHARIAH, b. d. 1749, Jan. 5. Providence, R. I.
m. (1)
SARAH, b. d. of
m. (2) 1746, Aug. 4,
JOANNA EDDY, b. d. 1747 + of Eddy.

He was a tanner.

1704, Apr. 5. He had a confirmation of his father's bequest from his brother James.

1704, Jun. 12. He sold Thomas Fenner for £20, half of Round Cove, his wife Sarah releasing dower.

1706, Nov. 16. He took as apprentice Benjamin Taylor, son of John of Newport, and was to teach him to tan leather, &c.

1722, May 30. He and wife Sarah, sold John Hoyle a small piece of land, quarter of a mile south-west of the Great Bridge, over the salt water at the place called Weybosset.

1747, Feb. 15. Will—proved 1749, Jan. 14. Exs. wife Joanna and cousin (*i. e.* nephew) Daniel. To seven daughters, 5*s*. each, viz: to Hannah Gorton, Freelove Nichols, Patience Soule, Sarah Taylor, Amey Carpenter, Mercy Gorton and Abigail Williams. To son Zachariah, Jr., 5*s*. To grandson John Mathewson, son of Nathaniel, 5*s*. To cousin (*i. e.* nephew) Daniel Thornton, son of James, all lands joining east side Woonasquatucket. To wife Joanna, all personal estate in lieu of dower.

Inventory, £44, 2*s*., viz: 4 cows, horse, 3 shoats, canoe, 3 feather beds, gun, pewter, linen and woolen yarn, warming pan, 2 barrels cider, &c.

1. Hannah,
2. Freelove,
3. Patience,
4. Sarah,
5. Amey,
6. Mercy,
7. Abigail,
8. Zachariah,
9. Nathaniel,
(2d wife, no issue.)

VIII. DANIEL, b. 1683, Jan. 28. d. 1751, Jun. 13. Providence, Glocester, R. I.
m. (1) 1704, Feb. 10.
SARAH INMAN, b. d. of John & Mary (Whitman) Inman.
m. (2)
ESTHER, b. d. of
m. (3) 1742, Sep. 26.
CHARITY INMAN, b. d. of Inman.
m. (4) 1747, Jul. 12.
LYDIA MONTAGU, b. d. of Montagu.

1704, Apr. 5. He had his father's bequest ratified to him by James Mathewson, his brother, so that said Daniel, who was unborn when the will was made should not be disinherited, the language of his father's will not having added the word "heirs."

1. Othniel, 1705, Feb. 2.
2. Peregrine, 1707, Sep. 12.
3. Mary, 1710, Nov. 7.
4. Nero, 1713, Jun. 12.
5. Daniel, 1716, Mar. 7.
6. Sylvanus, 1719, Jul. 25.
7. Winchester,
(2d wife.)
8. Hannah, 1733, May 28.
9. Martha, 1736, Jan. 9.
10. John, 1739, Jan. 26.
11. Ruth, 1741, May 15,
(4th wife.)
12. Daniel,
13. Thankful,
14. Lydia,

1718, Jun. 16. Taxed 6*s*.

1750, Jan. 10. Will—proved 1751, Jul. 1. Exx. wife Lydia. Overseers, if wife marries, sons Peregrine and Winchester, till son Daniel is of age. To son Daniel, all homestead at age, except grist mill, and my saw mill. If Daniel die, then to my six daughters, viz: Mary Cooper, Hannah, Martha, Ruth, Thankful and Lydia Mathewson. To son Winchester Mathewson, a quarter of grist mill and saw mill, till Daniel is of age, and then to Daniel, but if he dies then Winchester to have it. To six daughters, other lands. To son Peregrine, land west side of Herring Pond Brook, and privilege to build dam. To son Othniel, a cross cut saw. To wife Lydia, all goods and chattels besides, while widow, for support of herself and family, but if she marries, then only what she brought and £72, and the overseers to use goods for family. Son Daniel to maintain his mother.

Inventory, books, 2 woolen wheels, linen wheel, warming pan, gun, pewter, 2 pairs spectacles, small pieces of silver £1, 5*s*., worsted combs, churn, hogshead cider, &c.

MATTESON.

{ HENRY, { b. 1646.
{ m. { d. 1690 ±
{ HANNAH PARSONS, { b.
{ d.

of Hugh & Elizabeth ( ) Parsons.

(She m. (2) 1693, Aug. 9, Charles Hazleton.)

East Greenwich, R. I.

1678, Jun. 12. He took 100 acres that had been granted John Pearce (the mason), the Assembly permitting the transfer.

1682, Mar. 17. He and wife Hannah, sold David Shippee, all my now dwelling house, &c., 100 acres.

1684, Oct. 27. He testified calling himself thirty-eight years old or thereabout, that at the house of John Spencer, deceased, sometime this last summer, did hear him say that he intended to give unto his son Michael the house and land he the said Spencer lived upon.

1685. Deputy.

1693, Jul. 29. Hannah Matteson sold George Vaughan, for £4, land that her husband Henry Matteson had bought of John Knight, carpenter, measuring 10 acres.

No relationship has been traced between Henry Matteson and Francis Matteson, who in 1657, Jun. 2, was granted accommodation with a house lot among the rest of neighbors at the further end of Ship Cove, in Providence. (It is noticeable that Henry Matteson named a son Francis.)

Mistake in Genealogical Dictionary of Rhode Island Matteson

On page 132, children of Henry and Judith Weaver, Elizabeth, listed as eight child is said not to exist, that Hezekiah is the eighth child and was originally spelled Ezekiah. Arnold vital records of E.Greenwich have shown Elizabeth in place of Hezekiah. Hodges "guessed" that Elizabeth was really Hezekiah. This information is given by Mr. Carleton C. Murdock, 319 Wait Ave., Ithaca, N.Y. Mr. Murdock has a letter from the Town Clerk of East Greenwich and has personally seen the records.

I. { HENRY, { b. East Greenwich, West Greenwich, R. I.
{ m. 1694. { d. 1752, Apr. 18.
{ JUDITH WEAVER, { b.
{ d. 1751 + of Clement Weaver

1694, Apr. 19. He disclaimed any right or title to 10 acres lately sold by my mother Hannah, to George Vaughan.

1701. Deputy.

1751, Jun. 18. Will—proved 1752, Apr. 25. Exs. sons Henry and Jonathan. To wife Judith, movables while widow, and at her death or marriage to granddaughter Roxanna Hall, a great iron kettle. To grandson Peleg Sweet, 10*s*., his mother having had. To my six sons and my daughter Mary Weaver, and heir of my daughter Judith Andrews, deceased, the rest of movables equally.

Inventory, £407, 11*s*. 6*d*., viz: bonds and money £129, 16*s*., wearing apparel, warming pan, cow, calf, heifer, gun, &c.

1. Judith, 1694, Oct. 16.
2. Henry, 1696, Apr. 22.
3. Jonathan, 1701, Jun. 6.
4. Mary, 1704, Feb. 13.
5. John, 1706, Oct. 27.
6. Sarah, 1709, Apr. 13.
7. James, 1712, Mar. 20.
8. Elizabeth, 1714, Dec. 15.
9. Ebenezer, 1718, Mar. 15.
10 Hezekiah,

II. { THOMAS, { b. East Greenwich, R. I.
{ m. 1695, Nov. 14. { d. 1740. Jan. 19.
{ MARTHA SHIPPEE, { b.
{ d. of David & Margaret (Scranton) Shippee.

1717. Deputy.

1740, Jan. 28. Administration to son Thomas. Inventory, £452, 7*s*. 1½*d*., viz: wearing apparel, button mould, 2 pair of wool cards, foot wheel, 3 old cheese fats, 2 spinning wheels, 6½ fowls, 7 turkeys, 4 oxen, 3 cows, steer, 2 calves, mare, colt, 25 sheep, cider mill, hogshead of rum, &c.

1. Deliverance 1696, Aug. 20.
2. Elizabeth, 1700, Oct. 9.
3. Thomas, 1703.
4. Joseph, 1705, Jul. 1.
5. Henry, 1707, Apr. 28.
6. Mercy,

III. { JOSEPH, { b. East Greenwich, R. I.
{ m. (1) { d. 1758.
{ RACHEL, { b.
{ m. (2) { d. of
{ MARTHA, { b.
{ d. 1757 + of

1706, Mar. 10. He bought 10 acres in Coweset, of John Knowlman, for £6.

1757, May 5. Will—proved 1758, Sep. 2. Ex. son William. To wife Martha, profits of homestead while widow, she taking care of my lame daughter Eunice Matteson, till eighteen. To wife, a third of household stuff and at her death to four daughters Alice, Elizabeth, Lois and Eunice. To youngest son Ezekiel, all of farm north side of Mill River, buildings and orchard at death of my wife and lame daughter. To son Jonathan, land. To son Thomas, land. To son John, remaining part of farm and farming tackle. To son William, my riding horse. Son Thomas, gone to army, and if he die his part to go to sons William and Ezekiel, Alice Whitford, Elizabeth and Lois Matteson. To last named three daughters rest of estate.

Inventory, £661, 10*s*., viz: horse, woolen wheel, 2 linen wheels, cow, calf, loom, pair of oxen, hog, &c.

1. Joseph, 1707, Mar. 22.
(2d wife.)
2. Obadiah,
3. Jonathan,
4. William,
5. Alice,
6. Elizabeth,
7. Thomas,
8. John,
9. Ezekiel,
10. Lois,
11. Eunice,

IV. { FRANCIS, { b. 1680, Mar. 15. East Greenwich, Warwick, R. I.
{ m. 1712, May 12. { d. 1750.
{ SARAH NICHOLS, { b.
{ d. of Richard & Phebe ( ) Nichols.

(Perhaps his marriage should have been recorded 1702, instead of 1712, unless he had two wives named Sarah.)

1734. Warwick. Deputy.

1748. His daughter Jane, died unmarried this year, mentioning in her will, her father, some of her brothers, her four sisters and brother-in-law Pasco Whitford, &c.

1750, Mar. 20. Will—proved 1750, Apr. 28. Ex. son Henry. To son John, 86 acres in Coventry. To sons Francis and Henry, my quarter of farm in the Pine Swamp. To sons Thomas and Job, quarter of a farm in Coventry. To son Thomas, the remaining part of farm he lives on, not already given by deed. To son Henry, half of homestead at decease of testator, and the other half a year after death of wife, and son Job to have the benefit of said half of homestead for maintenance of my wife. To sons John, Francis, Thomas and Job, £100 each. To three daughters now living, viz: Sarah Cory, Hannah Whitford and Elizabeth Matteson, £100. To all grandchildren, 5*s*. To daughter Phebe Greene's child that she left, £5, at eighteen. To sons John, Francis, Henry, Thomas and Job and daughters Sarah Cory, Hannah Whitford and Elizabeth Matteson, the rest of movables equally, except my wife's bed, &c. To wife, feather bed, iron pot, kettle, two chairs, and two pewter basins, for life and then to children. To son Henry, all bonds, notes, blacksmith tools, &c. To son Job, plank and board at mill, To sons Thomas and Job, all iron belonging to my saw mill. To son Thomas's son Francis, a lot of land in East Greenwich. To son John's son Francis, a lot in Coventry.

Inventory, £2,530, 3*s*. 9*d*., viz: books £5, purse and apparel £88, 17*s*., bonds and notes £174, 5*s*., cash £7, 2*s*., 2 guns, warming pan, pair of worsted combs, loom, stillyards, foot wheel, punch bowl, saw-mill, iron saws, mare, pair of oxen, 2 cows, heifer, calf, steer, 61 sheep, 2 swine, &c.

1. Sarah, 1703, Apr. 13.
2. John, 1704, Dec. 10.
3. Hannah, 1706, Oct. 10.
4. Francis,
5. Henry,
6. Thomas,
7. Job,
8. Phebe,
9. Elizabeth,
10. Jane,

V. { HANNAH, { b.
{ d.

MATTESON. 2d column. VI. Hezekiah. His wife, b. 1702, Mar. 8.

VI. { HEZEKIAH, { b. East Greenwich, West Greenwich, R. I.
{ m. { d. 1752.
{ MARGARET WESTCOTT, { b.
{ d. 1752 + of Zorobabel & Jane ( ) Westcott.

1720. Freeman.

1752, Apr. 8. Will—proved 1752, Apr. 25. Ex. son Samuel. To son Abraham, land adjoining where he dwells and £10, he having had already. To son Amos, 10. To son Zorobabel, 5*s*. To son Samuel, 26 acres. To daughter Loja Matteson, £50. To daughters Catharine and Ann, £50 each at eighteen. To wife Margaret, best room, a third profit of land not disposed of and a third of movables. To son Samuel, rest of movables, two-thirds of real, and at death of wife the rest of real estate.

Inventory, £728, 4*s*. 8*d*., viz: cash £10, 18*s*. 8*d*., books £1, 5*s*., pair of oxen, riding beast, 18 sheep, 10 goats, 7 swine, two year old mare, loom, foot wheel, 8 other wheels, &c.

1. Abraham,
2. Amos,
3. Zorobabel,
4. Samuel,
5. Loja,
6. Catharine,
7. Ann,

NOEL[2], (Richard[1]). b. d. 1692.
m.
MARY, b. d.

(She m. (2) 1703, Feb. 12, Thomas Coleman.)

New Jersey, Newport, R. I.

He was a merchant.

He was probably born in Stepney Parish, Middlesex County, England, where his father resided for quite a period, if not permanently. He first settled on a tract of 1,972 acres in Burlington County, N. J., a water course still bearing the name of Noel's Run. His father had purchased land (in 1677), of William Penn, &c., trustees of Edward Billynge; a debt from the latter to Mew, of £100, being thus discharged

1686, Apr. 13. Newport. He bought 300 acres called Rocky Farm, for £400, of Nathaniel Coddington and wife Susanna.

1691. Deputy.

1691, Aug. 3. Will—proved 1700, Apr. 4, in England. Exx. wife Mary. Overseers, friends, William Allen, Benjamin Newbury, Peleg Sanford. He declared his intention of going to old England. To wife Mary, while widow, all real and personal estate. If she marry again she was to have out of estate in England £110, and all household stuff. To son Richard, the Rocky farm, mulatto boy "George," and £50, he paying each of his sisters, £5, per annum to help bring them up till of age or married. To him also great bible and silver tankard. To daughter Mary Mew, £100, Indian girl "Jenny," a Spanish silver cup, round silver cup, and silver dram cup with a funnel. To daughter Patience, £100, negro woman "Bess," and six spoons. All land in West Jersey to be sold and proceeds equally divided to wife and three children.

1692, Dec. 22. Testimony was given by Gov. John Easton, &c., that a true copy of above will was presented.

I. RUTH, b. 1682, Dec. 5. d. 1683, Jan. 4.

II. RICHARD, b. 1684, Jan. 1. d. 1721 + Newport, R. I.
m. 1702, Oct. 8.
SARAH COLEMAN, b. 1682. d. 1721, Dec. 10. of Thomas Coleman.

He was a merchant.

1706. Freeman.

1708, May 5. He appealed to the Assembly in a suit of trespass and ejectment against Jahleel Brenton and the appeal was decided in Mew's favor.

1718, May 18. At his house William Allen died.

III. JOHN, b. 1686. d. 1688, Sep. 11.

IV. MARY, b. 1689, Aug. 15. d. 1711, Jul. 22.
m. 1705, Jan. 15.
MICHAEL WANTON, b. 1679, Apr. 9. d. 1741 ± of Edward & Elizabeth ( ) Wanton.

1. Ruth, 1705, Oct. 30.
2. Mary, 1707, Oct. 4.
3. Stephen, 1709, Nov. 18.

V. PATIENCE, b. 1690, Dec. d. 1691, Dec. 27.

MITCHELL.

THOMAS, * b. d.
m.
——— b. d.

New Shoreham, R. I.

1678. Freeman.

1689. Lieutenant.

1689, Jul. 3. Three French privateers landed a force on the island and plundered the inhabitants, killing their cattle, &c. Twice afterward they made descents on the island and Thomas Mitchell and Samuel Niles acted as spies upon their operations on behalf of the party of the inhabitants who had fled to the woods. An account of these depredations was written in later years by Mr. Niles.

No relationship has been traced between him and Elisha Mitchell, of East Greenwich, who died in 1707, and upon whose estate administration was given to son Elisha, the widow Hannah refusing.

*See: American Genealogist, v.19, p.226,227,228 v.36, p.229

I. JOHN, * b. d. New Shoreham, R. I.

MITCHELL. R. I. 2d column. II. Thomas. New Shoreham

1692, Jan. 10. Freeman.

II. THOMAS, b. 1683. d. 1741, Mar. 29.
m.
MARGARET, b. d. 1741 + of

1. Thomas,
2. Margaret,
3. Elizabeth,

1721–23–24–33–35. Deputy.

1723. Lieutenant.

1723, Sep. 28. He and wife Margaret, deeded 20 acres to brother Joseph Mitchell, the land having belonged formerly to the father of said Thomas and Joseph.

1728, Sep. 23. He, calling himself Thomas Mitchell, Sr., of New Shoreham, deeded son Thomas, of Boston, land and messuage that said Thomas, Sr., lives on, consisting of 80 acres, and another lot of 51 acres; for love, &c.

1733. Captain.

1741, Feb. 13. Will—proved 1741, Jun. 4. Exx. wife Margaret. He directed that land in North Kingstown, bought of brother Benjamin, be sold, as also land in New Shoreham, bought of father Thomas Mitchell. To two children Margaret and Elizabeth, house and land equally and farming tackling, &c. To wife Margaret, household goods, &c.

Inventory, £349, viz: beds, pewter, 2 guns, 1 silver hilted sword, books £7, cider mill, negro boy £100, &c.

He was buried in the town burial ground.

III. JOSEPH, * b. d. New Shoreham, R. I.
m. (1) 1703, Jul. 5.
MARY GEORGE, b. d. 1715, Mar. 1. of Samuel George.
m. (2)
DOROTHY DICKENS, b. d. of Dickens.

1. Jonathan, 1704, May 25.
2. John, 1707, Aug. 19.
3. Thomas, 1712, May 30.
4. Mary, 1715, Feb. 5.

1721. Freeman.

IV. GEORGE, b. d. New Shoreham, R. I.
m. 1712, Feb. 27.
SARAH MOTT, b. 1694, Dec. 24. d. of Nathaniel & Sarah (Tosh) Mott.

1. John, 1712, Dec. 8.
2. Rebecca, 1714, Jul. 20.
3. Worden, 1716, Mar. 23.
4. Nathaniel, 1717, Dec. 25.
5. George, 1720, Mar. 5.

1717, Apr. 28. Testimony was given (by John Rathbone, &c.), as to his seizure with two others from a boat, by the crew of a sloop of which Paulsgrave Williams was commander, she being then in the harbor's bay. In a letter written May 31st, by Governor Samuel Cranston to Colonel Shute, he encloses the testimony "that in case the pirate Williams should fall into your Excellency's hands, that the poor men therein mentioned may receive such favour as justice will allow."

1720. Freeman. New Shoreham, R. I.

V. BENJAMIN, b. d.

MOON.

JOHN, b. d. 1723 (—)
m.
SARAH SHERIFF, b. d. 1732, Jun. 24.

of Thomas & Martha ( ) Sheriff.

Newport, R. I.

1680. Taxed 5*s*.

1728, Sep. 25. Will—proved 1732, Jul. 10. Widow Sarah of Portsmouth. Exs. son-in-law Thomas Cory and his wife Sarah. To daughter Sarah Cory, my dwelling house and lot of land for life and then to grandson John Moon, if he be living,

I. JOHN, b. 1685, May 16. d. 1723, Oct. 7. Portsmouth, R. I.
m. 1710, Nov. 30.
ABIGAIL BRIGGS, b. d. of Enoch & Hannah (Cook) Briggs.

1. John, 1711, Aug. 26.
2. Hope, 1712, Dec. 31.
3. Abigail, 1717, May 2.

(She m. (2) 1724, Jan. 29, John Butts.)

1723, Oct. 19. Inventory, £60, 2*s*. 4*d*., shown by his mother Sarah. Wearing apparel, £5, staff, gun, razor, loom, spinning wheel, swine, debts due £28, 14*s*. 11*d*., &c.

II. SARAH, b. d.
m. 1718, Aug. 28.
THOMAS CORY, b. d. of William & Martha (Cook) Cory.

1. Thomas, 1719, Jun. 6.
2. John, 1720, Dec. 8.
3. Caleb, 1730, May 13.

or to his male heirs, but if none, then to my grandson Thomas Cory. To daughter Sarah Cory and her husband Thomas, certain land and at their death to heirs. To grandson John Moon, biggest table. To daughter Abigail Vaughan, best iron kettle and two pewter platters. To daughter Martha Cory, 5*s.* To daughter Elizabeth Moon, 5*s.* To two daughters of son John Moon, Hope and Abigail, 5*s.* each. To daughter Sarah Cory and heirs, rest of estate. Inventory, £30.

He may have been a brother of Robert and Ebenezer Moon, both of whom were living in Newport, in 1676. (An Ebenezer Moon, lived in Kings Town, and had wife Elizabeth and children born from 1706 to later dates.)

III.	ABIGAIL,	b.		
	m.	d.		
	—— VAUGHAN,	b.		
		d.	of	Vaughan.
IV.	MARTHA,	b.		1. William, 1712, Mar. 2.
	m. 1711, May 15.	d.		2. Caleb, 1714, Feb. 1.
	MICHAEL CORY,	b. 1688, Apr. 21.		3. Martha, 1718, Dec. 8.
		d.	of William & Martha (Cook)	Cory.
V.	ELIZABETH,	b.		
		d.		

See: American Genealogist, v. 20, p. 181-182; v. 3[illegible], p. [illegible]

MORRIS.

RICHARD,	b.
	d. 1674 +
m. (1) LEONORA,	b.
	d.
m. (2) Mary,	b.
	d.

Roxbury, Mass., Portsmouth, Newport, R. I.

He and his wife Leonora, were early of the church at Boston.

1630, Nov. 29. Juryman, in the trial of Walter Palmer, concerning death of Austin Batcher.

1631, May 18. Freeman.

1632. Sergeant.

1633, Mar. 4. Ancient (*i. e.* ensign) in Captain Underhill's Company.

1634, Mar. 4. Leftenant.

1634, Sep. 3. He was chosen on committee to lay out works for the fortification on Castle Island, Charlestown and Dorchester.

1634, Sep. 25. He was ordered to train the Company at Roxbury.

1634–35. Deputy.

1636, Mar. 4. He was chosen Lieutenant of the fort at Castle Island, in room of Mr. Gibbons dismissed.

1636, Sep. 8. He was to have £10, yearly from the town of Roxbury, so long as he continued to live at the Castle and doth service to the town of Roxbury.

1637, Nov. 20. He and others were warned to deliver up all guns, pistols, swords, powder, shot, &c., because "the opinions and revelations of Mr. Wheelwright and Mrs. Hutchinson have seduced and led into dangerous errors many of the people here in New England."

1638, Sep. 9. He had leave to depart, having offended in signing the petition or remonstrance and he was ordered to forbear meddling with other people in the matter of opinion lest he be further dealt with, and was advised not to sit down within limits of Massachusetts, &c. The petition referred to (dated 1637, Mar. 15), affirmed that Mr. Wheelwright was innocent and that the court had condemned the truth of Christ.

1638, Sep. 9. He had the promise of his 100 acres ground besides what he had already had.

1639. Dover, N. H. Captain. At Exeter same year.

1641, Mar. 16. Newport. Freeman.

1642. Portsmouth.

1648. Member of General Court of Trials.

1650, May 23. He and five others were ordered to mend and make all arms presented by inhabitants of each town.

1655. Freeman.

1656. Mar. 17. He and two others were sent by warrant for Pomham to come before the court.

1658, Dec. 18. He and wife Mary sold Peter Tallman, 9 acres in Portsmouth, for 35*s.* per acre.

1663, Oct. 19. Newport. He was one of those who engaged to see Newport's share of John Clarke's money paid him.

1664. He was a messenger in the correspondence between Rhode Island and Connecticut.

1665, May 13. His bill for £6, 5*s.*, for his voyage to Connecticut was approved and ordered paid by Assembly.

1667, May 13. He and others skilled therein were ordered by Assembly to repair all arms brought them by the Captain or Lieutenant of Train Band of Newport.

1667, Jul. 2. He was to have £10, paid him, his petition declaring the great charges he hath been at in house room and providing of fuel and candles for the General Courts for many years past; and the Assembly finding that for four or five years past he hath had no satisfaction.

1669–70–72–74. The Assembly still continued to meet at his house.

1672, Nov. 6. Mrs. Morris petioned the Assembly that her grandchild Mary Stokes, standing under sentence to be whipped twice, might have the sentence remitted. It was granted if Mary Stokes pay £5.

HUGH[2], (Hugh.[1]) * b. 1633. d. 1713.
m. (1)
REBECCA HARNDEL, b. d.
of John Harndel.
m. (2)
SARAH, b. d.

Newport, Portsmouth, R. I. Dartmouth, Mass.

1660, Jan. 29. He and five others of Newport, bought certain land at Misquamicut (Westerly), of the Indian sachem Socho, which had been given the latter by Canonicus and Miantonomi, for driving off the Pequots in 1637.

1661, Sep. 9. He had a share at Westerly apportioned him, but did not live there long, if at all.

1663. He called himself about thirty years old, in testimony given this year.

1664. Freeman.

1668, Jul. 8. Portsmouth. He having purchased of Thomas Lawton part of his farm near Hunting Swamp, he obliges himself and heirs to maintain a good fence in the line between himself and Thomas Lawton.

1676, Aug. 24. He was a member of the Court Martial, held at Newport for the trial of certain Indians charged with being engaged in King Philip's designs. Several of them were sentenced to be executed.

1680. Taxed £1, 4s. 1d.

1684. Dartmouth. Ordained as pastor of the First Baptist Church at its organization. (This church soon embraced people living in Dartmouth, Tiverton and Little Compton.)

1691, Nov. 7. He sold to Joseph Braman for 36s. half my share belonging to purchasers of Westquadnoid. (The deed was witnessed by Rebecca Mosher and John Mosher.)

1709, Oct. 12. Will—proved 1713, Dec. 7. Exs. son James, and friend Daniel Sabeere, of Newport. Overseers, friend and kinsman Jeremiah Clarke, and Captain John Stanton, of Newport. To son James, all land in Newport, with house, &c., there, and house and land in Dartmouth, and land in Squamicut (Westerly), Westquadnoid, &c. To grandson Hugh, son of Nicholas, 100 acres, and to other grandsons of surname Mosher, 50 acres each. To wife Sarah, all movables I had with her at marriage. To son James, rest of land. To each grandchild not of my name, 10s. To sons John, Nicholas, Joseph and Daniel, 12d. each. To each daughter, 10s. or 20s., as estate holds out. (He calls himself of Newport at the time of making his will, but before his death had removed to Dartmouth.)

Inventory, £290, 17s. 2d., viz: purse and wearing apparel £8, 8s. 6d., bonds, &c. £133, 14s. 8d., bible and other books £3, dwelling house and land £80, horse, 2 cows, 3 swine, carpenter's tools, pewter, silver plate £5, warming pan, estate brought him by wife £12, 1s. &c.

MOSHER. 1st column. He m. (2) Sarah Harding (w. of John), b. 1652, d. 1716, May 7, dau. of —— Butcher. (For her will see Harding, same sheet.)

I. NICHOLAS, b. 1666. d. 1747, Aug. 14. Dartmouth, Mass., Tiverton, R. I.
m. 1687, Aug. 14.
ELIZABETH, b. d. 1747 + of

1747, Mar. 11. Will—proved 1747, Sep. 7. Ex. son Thomas. To wife Elizabeth, household goods, live stock, money and bonds for life, and at her death, what is left to go as follows: To sons Hugh, Joseph, Thomas and Nicholas, 5s. each. To daughter Mary Allen, a case of drawers. To granddaughter Sarah Pope, a bed. To five daughters and granddaughter Sarah Pope, the rest of estate, bonds and money left at decease of wife, viz: To Mary Allen, Elizabeth Tripp, Mercy Shrieve, Rebecca Wilcox, Margaret Taber, and granddaughter Sarah Pope. (The will was made at Dartmouth, but proved at Tiverton.)

Inventory, £372, 4s. 4d., viz: books £36, pewter, 2 beds, wheels, 2 cows, swine, bonds £150, &c., warming pan, stillyards, &c.

1. Hugh, 1690, Nov. 16.
2. Joseph, 1692, Apr. 7.
3. Mary, 1695, Dec. 16.
4. Elizabeth, 1697, Apr. 16.
5. Thomas, 1699, Feb. 26.
6. Nicholas, 1703, Jan. 17.
7. Mercy, 1705, Jul. 6.
8. Rebecca, 1708, Mar. 20.
9. Ephraim, 1710, Mar. 5.
10. Margaret, 1713, Jan. 17.

II. JOHN, b. 1668. d. 1739, Aug. 1. Dartmouth, Mass.
m. 1692, Mar. 5.
EXPERIENCE KIRBY, b. d. 1745, Mar. 5. of Richard & Patience (Gifford) Kirby.

See: American Genealogist, v.21, p.207. →

1. Robert, 1693, Oct. 12.
2. Hannah, 1697, Nov. 9.
3. Patience, 1698, Mar. 20.
4. Abigail, 1699, Sep. 21.
5. John, 1703, Mar. 12.
6. Hannah, 1712, Mar. 13.
7. Sarah,

III. JOSEPH, b. 1670. d. 1754. Dartmouth, Mass.
m.
LYDIA TABER, b. 1673, Sep. 28. d. 1743 + of Philip & Mary ( ) Taber.

1743, Nov 15. Will—proved 1754, May 7. Exs. sons Philip, Jonathan and James. To wife Lydia, use of all movables while widow, and use of best room in my part of dwelling house, and keep of a cow. To sons Philip and Jonathan, £25, each. To son James, all my homestead and dwelling house, (except room for wife), and husbandry and carpenter's tools. To daughter Ruth Tripp, 40s., and a third of personal at death of mother, and like legacy to daughter Lydia Davol. To children of daughter Rebecca Tripp, deceased, 40s. divided equally, viz: to Hannah, Constant, Rebecca, Daniel, Joseph, Thomas and Charles; and Hannah and Rebecca, to have also the remaining third of personal. To granddaughter Rebecca, daughter of son Benjamin, deceased, £800, at eighteen. To sons Philip, Jonathan and James, certain land.

1. Rebecca, 1695, Dec. 28.
2. Philip, 1697, Dec. 20.
3. Jonathan, 1699, Mar. 13.
4. Joseph, 1701, Jun. 23.
5. James, 1704, Dec. 13.
6. Ruth, 1707, Sep. 17.
7. Benjamin, 1709, Feb. 22.
8. William, 1713, Jul. 29.
9. Lydia,

IV. MARY, b. d. 1748 (—)
m. 1691, May 19.
JOSEPH RATHBONE, b. d. 1749. of John and Margaret ( ) Rathbone.

1. Elizabeth, 1692, Mar. 14.
2. Rebecca, 1694, Mar. 1.
3. Grace, 1695, Jul. 16.
4. Mary, 1697, Mar. 6.
5. Margaret, 1700, Nov. 29.
6. Mercy, 1703, Feb. 14.
7. Hannah, 1706, Mar. 21.
8. Joseph, 1707, Oct. 4.
9. Benjamin, 1710, Feb. 26.
10. Job, 1712, Apr. 1.

MOSHER. 1st column. He was a blacksmith.
2d column. V. James. By one account he had also Mary, 1708. James, 1711.

V. JAMES, b. 1675. d. New Shoreham, R. I., Dartmouth, Mass.
m. (1) 1704, Jul. 9.
CATHARINE TOSH, b. 1672, Jan. 10. d. of William Tosh.
m. (2) 1714, May 22.
MARY DAVOL, b. d. of Jonathan & Hannah (Adley) Davol.

He married his first wife at New Shoreham.

1. Daniel, 1705, Oct. 13.
(2d wife.)
2. William, 1715, Jun. 4.
3. Timothy, 1716, Oct. 27.
4. Jonathan, 1718, May 9.
5. David, 1720, Mar. 29.
6. Jeremiah, 1722, Jun. 16.
7. James,
8. Phebe, 1725,

VI. DANIEL, b. d. 1751. Dartmouth, Mass.
m.
——, b. d. 1751. of

1751, Jul. 22. Will—proved 1751, Sep. 19. Ex. son George. To wife, best bed, half of household goods, cow, and riding beast, for life or widowhood, and she to be provided for by son George with six bushels Indian corn, one hundred pounds good meat, and five cords firewood yearly. To son George, 10 acres salt marsh, half of land where he lives, and a grindstone. To son Roger, half of certain land. To son Benjamin, 10 acres, he paying my son Hugh, 40s. To sons Constant and Ephraim, the rest of lands given Roger and Benjamin. To son Constant, land where he lives, &c. To son Ephraim, land where he formerly lived, &c. To son Daniel, 40s. paid by son George. To daughter Mary Trofford, an iron pot. To three daughters, the rest of personal at death of wife, viz: to Rachel Herenden, Patience Brownell and Mary Trofford.

1. Benjamin, 1706, Apr. 19.
2. Daniel, 1709, Jul. 1.
3. Micah, 1711, Sep. 27.
4. Constant, 1713, Sep. 11.
5. Rachel, 1715, Jun. 14.
6. George, 1717, May 9.
7. Ephraim, 1718, Dec. 8.
8. Roger, 1720, Mar. 30.
9. Hugh, 1722, Mar. 17.
10. Patience, 1724, Jun. 29.
11. Mercy, 1726, Oct. 12.

VII. REBECCA, b. d.

(2d wife, no issue).

MOTT (NATHANIEL).

NATHANIEL, * b. d.
m. 1656. [Peter.
HANNAH SHOOTER (w. of b. d.

Scituate, Braintree, Mass.

1643. He was among those able to bear arms.

1656. Scituate. He married there, and his son Nathaniel was born in that town.

He may have come to New Shoreham, and there died early.

* See: American Genealogist, v. 19, p. 228, 229. v. 34, p. 3.

I. NATHANIEL, * b. 1657, Dec. 28. d. 1717. New Shoreham, R. I.
m. (1) 1682, Nov. 29.
HEPZIBAH WINSLOW, b. d. of Nathaniel & Mary ( ) Winslow.
m (2) 1694, Jan. 23.
SARAH TOSH, b. d. 1717 + of William Tosh.

1683. Freeman.

1695. Town Clerk, and many years thereafter.

1700–10. Deputy.

1710. Lieutenant.

1717, Nov. 14. Will—proved 1717, Dec. 12. Exs. wife Sarah and Captain Simon Ray. To daughter Mary Hancox, £10. To grandchildren William and Hepzibah Hancox, £5, each. To son John, all my lands in Block Island, mortgaged to the colony. To wife Sarah, all other lands, hay, stock, goods, and chattels, while widow, and if she marry, then to son John, at age. To daughters Sarah Mitchell, Lydia Rathbone, Bathsheba, Miriam and Experience Mott, £2, 10s. each, and to sons Edward and Nathaniel Mott, like legacies, all to be paid by son John. To Captain Simon Ray, £2. To son John, other land, and he to bring up his brothers Edward and Nathaniel to read and write.

Inventory, Indian named Harry £20, part of a boat £4, sword, belt, gun, pewter, pair of stillyards, 2 spinning wheels, 2 beds, books, yoke of oxen, 4 cows, 3 heifers, 5 yearlings, 6 calves, 2 mares, colt, 35 sheep, 7 swine, &c.

1. Mary, 1684, Mar. 6.
2. Nathaniel, 1688, Oct. 9.
3. John, 1690, Mar. 25.
(2d wife.)
4. Sarah, 1694, Dec. 24.
5. Lydia, 1697, Mar. 18.
6. John, 1700, Jan. 1.
7. Bathsheba, 1702, Apr. 24.
8. Experience, 1705, Oct. 27.
9. Nathaniel, 1706, Nov. 25.
10. Edward, 1710, Mar. 19.
11. Miriam, 1712, Jul. 20.

II. JOHN, * b. d. New Shoreham, R. I.
m 1683, Oct. 16.
MERCY TOSH, b. d. of William Tosh.

1. Anna, 1684, Jan. 9.
2. Anna, 1685, Jan. 8.
3. Sarah, 1688, Jan. 19.

III. EDWARD, * b. d. 1735. New Shoreham, Westerly, R. I.
m. 1695, Dec. 3. [Wm.
PENELOPE TOSH (w. of b. d. 1735 + of

1700. Constable.

1735, May 26. Administration to widow Penelope. Inventory, £49, 12s. 6d.

Mary,* Lydia*, Samuel*, Elizabeth*, Experience, Ebenezer*.

MUMFORD (STEPHEN). 2d column. I. Stephen. He m., 1st, 1697, Aug. 30, Mary Timberlake, of William and Mary Timberlake.

STEPHEN, b. 1639. d. 1707, Jul.
m.
ANN, b. 1635. d. 1698, Jun. 22.

London, Eng., Newport, R. I.

1664. Newport. He came from London this year (or by some accounts the year after). He joined Mr. Clarke's church though his views favored the observance of the seventh day, and later others came to his way of thinking and left the parent church.

1671. Freeman.

1671, Dec. 23. Samuel Hubbard, of Newport, wrote as follows: "We entered into a church covenant the 23d day of December, 1671, viz: William Hiscox, Stephen Mumford, Samuel Hubbard, Roger Baster, sister Hubbard, sister Mumford, sister Rachel Langworthy," &c.

1675, Mar. 14. He wrote from London: "About the 14th of January, we sailed from Boston and had a comfortable time and fair wind for three weeks, in which time we came to soundings, as they judged near the Isle of Scilly, and then we met with a cross wind that kept us three weeks more, and then we came to anchor in a road between the Isle of Wight and Portsmouth. I took my journey to London in the waggon, where I was received by the brethren with much joy, in some of them who had a great desire to hear of our place and people; some of them talk of coming with me."

1675, Oct. He arrived at Boston on his way back from England, being accompanied by William Gibson and his wife.

1680. Taxed 11*s.* 5*d.*

1687, Nov. 29. He and wife Ann and Robert Ayres and Esther, of one part, and William Phipps, Kt., of Boston, of the other part, made an indenture. At this time he called himself of Jamestown, but it was only a temporary residence probably.

He and his wife were buried in Newport Cemetery.

I. STEPHEN, b. 1666. d. 1731, Jun. 7. Newport, R. I.
m. (1) 1697, Aug.
MARY, b. 1672. d. 1715, Sep. 2. of
m. (2) 1716, Jul. 26.
MARY ROGERS, (w. of Jos.) b. d. of John & Anstis (Gold) Wilkins.

He was a merchant.

1700. He paid a rental of £3, 5*s.*, per year for his shop, which he hired of Nicholas and Caleb Carr.

1702, Feb. 4. He was one of the proprietors of common lands.

1713, Jul. 3. He and wife Mary, sold to James Cole, a lot measuring 45 by 75 feet for £30.

1721, Mar. 22. Agreement as to lands of Samuel Wilkins, of Bristol, deceased, was made by his brethren and sisters, viz: Captain Stephen Mumford and Mary his wife, Captain Benjamin Ellery and Abigail his wife and Mr. Peter Treby and Mehitable, his wife, all of Newport. His second wife had four husbands, viz: ——— Pepper, Richard Jenkins, Joseph Rogers and Stephen Mumford.

He was buried in Newport Cemetery, as was his first wife.

1. Stephen, 1698, Jun. 20.
2. Edward, 1699, Dec. 4.
3. Son, 1701, Dec. 20.
4. Ann, 1704, Nov.
5. John, 1706, Jan.
6. Daughter, 1707, Apr. 18.
7. Son, 1708, Sep. 24.
8. Elizabeth, 1711, Aug. 22.
(2d wife, no issue.)

II. JOHN, b. d. 1749. Newport, Kings Town, Exeter, R. I.
m. 1699, Oct. 20.
PEACE PERRY, b. 1671. d. 1740, Nov. 9. of Edward & Mary (Freeman) Perry.

1703, Oct. 27. He and two others were appointed by Assembly to run the line between Rhode Island and Connecticut, according to agreement of the commissioners of the two colonies.

1707, Oct. 29. He and James Carder were appointed to survey the vacant lands in Narragansett.

1708, Oct. 27. He was appointed on a commission to agree with Ninegret what may be a sufficient competency of land for him and his men to live upon; and to view the state of the country in Narragansett, in order for the settling of a new town.

1708–9. Deputy.

1710, May 17. Kings Town. He bought 8,000 acres of the vacant lands, ordered sold by Assembly.

1716, May. He was appointed on a committee to run and settle the dividing line between Massachusetts and Rhode Island.

1748. His son John died (and mentioned a number of children in his will).

1749, Jan. 21. Will—proved 1749, Mar. 14. Exx. daughter Ann Mumford. To eldest daughter Ann Mumford, all movables, goods, chattels and cattle. To second daughter Peace Borden, £50. To grandson Thomas Hicks, £100 at age. To all my grandchildren, after payment of debts, lands, and money due, equally.

Inventory, £390, 9*s.* 4*d.*, viz: books £5, pewter, compass, cash £3, 18*s.* 4*d.*, silver shoe buckles, 4 hogs, 7 sheep, gun, &c.

1. John, 1699, Aug. 25.
2. Ann, 1701, Apr. 28.
3. Perry, 1704, Mar. 6.
4. Stephen, 1707, Apr. 15.
5. Peace, 1709, Feb. 28.
6. Mary, 1715, Dec. 12.

III. ANN, b. 1673. d. 1699, May.
Unmarried.

MUMFORD (THOMAS).

THOMAS, b. d. 1692 (—)
m.
SARAH SHERMAN, b. 1636. d.
of Philip & Sarah (Odding) Sherman.

Portsmouth, Kings Town, R. I.

1657, Dec. 10. He had a grant of 8 acres.

1658, Jan. 20. He and others purchased a large tract in Pettaquamscut, of certain Indian sachems.

1664, May 5. He was ordered released from prison on giving bonds of £100, to appear when called to speak further to matter concerning Timothy Mather, whom he had accused for speaking words of a very dishonorable nature against his Majesty.

1666, May 14. He wrote a letter dated Newport, to John Hull of Boston (one of his associates in the Pettacomscott Purchase); "My best respects presented to yourself and Mrs. Hull. Sir, my request to you is that you would be pleased to come up to the island, for there is very great necessity of your being here, both concerning our accounts and our deeds." He mentions that other of the partners were desirous of his coming also.

1668, Mar. 15. Kings Town. He and wife Sarah, of Pettacomscott, sold Peleg Sanford, of Newport, 1000 acres upland and meadow in Pettacomscott, for £25.

1670, Jun. 20. Constable. He was ordered by Assembly to seize any persons found exercising jurisdiction in Narragansett in behalf of the colony of Connecticut.

1670, Jun. 21. He was complained of by the commissioners of Connecticut, sitting at Wickford, for assaulting and detaining "two of our men who were inoffensively riding on the King's highway." The letter was addressed to Samuel Wilson, who delivered the men to the Connecticut authorities.

1670, Jun. 29. He was allowed 20*s.* for his attendance upon the Rhode Island Commissioners to New London.

1670, Oct. 26. He and four others were appointed to make a rate for Pettaquamscott.

1683–86. Constable.

1687, Sep. 6. Taxed 7*s.* 11½*d.*

1687–88. Grand Jury.

1690, Oct. 30. He was appointed by Assembly with three others, to make a rate of tax for Kings Town.

He died intestate before Feb. 12, 1692.

I. THOMAS, b. 1656. d. 1726, Apr. South Kingstown, R. I.
m. (1)
ABIGAIL, b. 1670. d. 1707, May 20. of
m. (2) 1708, Nov. 25.
ESTHER TEFFT, b. d. 1726 + of Samuel & Elizabeth (Jenckes) Tefft.

1692, Feb. 12. Kings Town. He deeded 170 acres in Kings Town to sister Abigail Fish, wife of Daniel Fish, of Portsmouth, declaring that his father Thomas Mumford, deceased without having made any will, leaving him heir at law.

1693, Oct. 24. He and wife Abigail sold Samson Battey, of Jamestown, 300 acres in Pettacomscott for £42.

1701. Deputy.

1703. Justice of the Peace.

1707, May 28. His wife having been murdered about two weeks since by a slave belonging to him, and the body of the negro having since been found upon the shore of Little Compton, (he having drowned himself as was believed to prevent being taken alive), it was ordered by Assembly that his head, legs and arms, be cut from his body and hung up in some public place near Newport, and his body to be burnt to ashes, that it may be "something of a terror to others from perpetrating of the like barbarity for the future."

1708, Oct. 22. He deeded son George, 180 acres in Point Judith Neck, being part of my farm which belongeth to my dwelling house.

1708, Nov. 13. He deeded son Thomas certain land already in son's possession, and by him leased out, viz: my former dwelling house lot of 56 acres and buildings, and pasture lot of 200 acres.

1726, Jan. 2. Will—proved 1726, Apr. 11. Exx. wife Esther. To sons Thomas, George, Joseph, Benjamin and Richard, 5*s.* each, and son George to have a negro girl named Morocco. To daughters Sarah, Tabitha and Esther Mumford, each a feather bed. To son John my new house, being my now dwelling house, with 5 acres, and other land. To son William, rest of homestead farm with house thereon, in which William lives, he keeping for my wife Esther a riding beast, two cows and twenty sheep. To wife Esther, rest of movables, and negro slaves, male and female, and at wife's decease, two negro slaves Tobey and Peg, to go to son John; and negro girl Catharine, to go to daughter Sarah Mumford.

Inventory, £634, 14*s.* 7*d*, viz: books £1, 4*s.*, warming pan, gun, pair of stillyards, linen wheel, feather beds, pewter, bond £200, silver weighing 15½ oz., negroes, Tobey £50, Peg £75, Catharine £40, 3 cows, heifer, 2 mares, 2 young horses, colt, 18 sheep, 2 hogs, &c.

He and his first wife were buried in the Mumford Burial Ground.

1. Thomas, 1687, Apr. 1.
2. George, 1689, Jul. 15.
3. Joseph, 1691, Sep. 17.
4. William, 1694, Feb. 18.
5. Benjamin, 1696, Apr. 10.
6. Richard, 1698, Sep. 6.
(2d wife.)
7. John,
8. Sarah,
9. Tabitha,
10. Esther,

II. PELEG, b. 1659. d. 1745. South Kingstown, R. I.
m.
———, b. d. of

1687, Sep. 6. Kings Town. Taxed 3*s.* 1*d.*

1688. Grand Jury.

1713, Aug. 16. He was appointed administrator on estate of Katharine Bull.

1738, Mar. He, calling himself seventy-nine years old, made deposition as to church matters in early times at Narragansett.

1741, Sep. 21. Will—proved 1745, Jul. 8. Ex. kinsman William Mumford. To grandsons Samuel, Peleg and Thomas Mumford, each £20. To granddaughter Abigail Mumford, £10. To granddaughter Content Mumford, 5*s.* To my five children Peleg Mumford, Mary Hanson, Sarah Barber, Elizabeth Foster and Hannah Hopkins, the rest of personal estate. Certain land in South Kingstown consisting of 83 acres to be sold and money equally divided to five children.

1. Peleg,
2. Mary,
3. Sarah,
4. Elizabeth,
5. Hannah,

Inventory, £969, 7s. 3d., viz: silver watch £25, pocket compass, bond £300, silver money and 2 silver buckles £10, money scales, 3 silver spoons, books £2, 10s., gun, feather beds, case and bottles, pewter, linen wheel, warming pan, &c.

III. ABIGAIL, m. 1682, May 1, DANIEL FISH, — b. / d. 1717 (—) ; b. / d. 1723, Sep. 16. of Thomas & Mary ( ) Fish.
1. Comfort, 1683, Feb. 7.
2. Thomas, 1685, Jul. 3.
3. Ruth, 1687, Nov. 2.
4. Daniel, 1690, Jul. 11.
5. Sarah, 1694, Jan. 29.
6. Jeremiah, 1698, Sep. 15.
7. Abigail,
8. Mary,

IV. SARAH, m. BENEDICT ARNOLD, — b. 1668. / d. 1746, Oct. 14. ; b. 1642, Feb. 10. / d. 1727, Jul. 4. of Benedict & Damaris (Westcott) Arnold.
1. Comfort, 1695, May 21.
2. Ann, 1696, Jul. 14.
3. Sarah, 1698, Nov. 3.

NEWBURY (Benjamin).

BENJAMIN, m. LEAH, — b. 1653. / d. 1711, Nov. ; b. 1662. / d. 1740, Feb. 8.

Newport, R. I.

1689, Mar. 18. He asked for administration on estate of his brother-in-law Robert Twin, late of London, deceased. (Inventory, £8, 8s.)

1699–1700. Speaker of the House of Deputies.

1699–1700–4. Deputy.

He and his wife were buried in Clifton Burial Ground.

1711, Dec. 10. Inventory, dial, 9 marmalade glasses, bible and other books, telescope, pair of pistols, 135½ oz. silver, &c. Real estate £917, viz: house, garden, &c. £350, house and land by waterside £400 &c.

I. HUMPHREY, — b. 1684, Oct. 9. / d. young.

II. ANN, m. 1704, Dec. 22. THOMAS RICHARDSON, — b. 1686, Apr. 22. / d. 1728, Apr. 8. ; b. 1680, Sep. 10. / d. 1761, Apr. 28. of William & Amy (Borden) Richardson.

III. LEAH, — b. 1689. / d.

IV. HUMPHREY, — b. 1691, Nov. 25. / d. 1700, Jul. 21.

V. SARAH, m. 1719, May 13. JOSEPH JACOB, — b. 1696, Mar. 1. / d. ; b. / d. of John Jacob.

NEWBURY (Walter).

WALTER, m. 1675, Apr. 13. ANN COLLINS, — b. 1648. / d. 1697, Aug. 6. ; b. 1652. / d. 1732, Feb. 19.

of Collins.

(She m. (2) 1698, Sep. 20, Latham Clarke.)

London, Eng., Newport, R. I.

He was a merchant.

1674, Jul. 9. Newport. He (being called of London, merchant, residing in Newport), bought of William Richardson, mariner, master of ketch "Mayflower," now in the road of New York, a dwelling house in Newport, now in possession of Amey Paine, widow, tenant of William Richardson.

His wife was also of London, as declared by the Friends' records.

1675. Freeman.

1680. Taxed £4, 2s.

1684. Deputy.

1386, Dec. 22. He and others were apprised by letter from Sir Edmund Andros, of their appointment as members of his Council, and that a meeting would be held at Boston, on the 30th instant.

1686–96. Assistant.

1690, Feb. 27. He and Walter Clarke, made their appearance before the Assembly and read a paper disclaiming the government (which had been re-assumed under the charter, after the deposition of Andros), and an assistant was chosen instead of said Newbury.

He was buried in Clifton Burial Ground.

1702, Mar. 24. The Assembly voted that whereas Walter Newbury, of Newport, &c., made his wife Ann, his executrix, and did bequeath to his children, eight in number, £100 apiece, and the remainder real and personal, to his wife Ann; and the executrix having made legal proof that she had disposed of all the personal and yet not fully acquitted debts, and the will having omitted the words, her heirs and assigns, it hath much hindered the advantage of advancing the said real estate, as houses, warehouses, &c., on sale thereof; it was therefore enacted that she have power to make sale of any or all real estate.

I. SANKEY, — b. 1676, Jan. 19. / d. 1676, Aug. 18.

II. SAMUEL, — b. 1677, Mar. 3. / d.

III. SARAH, — b. 1680, Sep. 4. / d. young.

IV. WALTER, m. 1707, Mar. 11. ANNE RODMAN, — b. 1682, Dec. 21. / d. ; b. 1689, Aug. 11. / d. 1715. Newport, R. I., Boston, Mass. of John & Mary ( ) Rodman.

He was a merchant.

1706, Dec. 26. He and Benjamin Newbury, sold William Wanton certain land measuring two hundred feet by forty, with dwellings, warehouse, shops, wharves, &c., for £550.

V. SANKEY, — b. 1684, Jun. 29. / d. 1690, Dec. 16.

VI. ELIZABETH, m. JOHN BORDEN, — b. 1686, Nov. 16. / d. 1737, Mar. 9. ; b. 1693, Aug. 29 / d. 1727, Aug. 16. of Matthew & Sarah (Clayton) Borden.

VII. SARAH, — b. 1686, Nov. 16. / d.

VIII. MARTHA, — b. 1689, Jan. 7. / d. 1689, Aug. 24.

IX. MARY, m. (1) 1709, Sep. 23. JEDEDIAH HOWLAND, m. (2) 1716, Sep. 14. JEREMIAH WILLIAMS, — b. 1691, Feb. / d. ; b. 1685, Aug. 31. / d. 1711, Oct. 5. of Joseph & Rebecca (Hussey) Howland. ; b. / d. of Williams.
1. Joseph, 1710, Oct. 25.

X. SANKEY, — b. / d. Newport, R. I.

1725. Freeman.

XI Ann Mercy m. Col. John Cranston See: American Genealogist, v. 39, p 3.

THOMAS, b. d. 1708 +
m.
HANNAH, b. 1642, Dec, 17. d.

Newport, R. I.

1664. Freeman.

1671, Jun. 7. Juryman.

1677, Oct. 31. He and forty-seven others were granted 5,000 acres to be called East Greenwich.

1679-85-86-90-98. Deputy.

1680. Taxed £1, 9*s.* 7*d.*

1689, Nov. 17. He deeded son John Nichols, of East Greenwich, land there for love, &c.

1703, Nov. 20. He deeded his son John Nichols, of East Greenwich, a parcel of land there for love, &c.

1708, Nov. 5. He deeded son John, for love, &c., land in East Greenwich.

No relationship is known to exist between him and Richard Nichols of East Greenwich (whose widow Phebe made her will 1721, Apr. 5, proved 1727, Mar. 25, in Warwick), or between him and Ruth Nichols, born 1687, Nov. 23 (who married 1704, Oct. 19, Thomas Stoddard, of Little Compton.)

NICHOLS. 2d column. II. Susanna. She probably married Thomas Hazard, b. 1660, d. 1746, of Robert and Mary (Brownell) Hazard. Children, 1. Mary, 1683, Oct. 3. 2. Hannah, 1685, Apr. 14. 3. Sarah, 1687, Jul. 15. 4. Robert, 1689, May 23. 5. Thomas, 1691, May 11. 6. Stephen, 1693, Jun. 13. 7. Jeremiah, 1697, Jun. 5. 8. George, 1699, Jan. 18. 9. Benjamin, 1702, Nov. 2. 10. Jonathan, 1704, Oct. 1.

I. THOMAS, b. 1660, Aug. 6. d. 1745. East Greenwich, R. I.
m.
MERCY REYNOLDS, b. 1664. d. of James & Deborah ( ) Reynolds.

1. Hannah, 1684, Mar. 9.
2. Mercy, 1686, Oct. 26.
3. Deborah, 1688, Feb. 17.
4. Susanna, 1690, May 9.
5. Mary, 1693, Mar. 19.
6. James, 1693, Mar. 19.
7. Elizabeth, 1695, Mar. 16.
8. Frances, 1697, Nov. 29.
9. Comfort, 1701, Mar. 7.
10. Thomas, 1702, Apr. 27.
11. Benjamin, 1703, Jun. 28.

1682. Freeman.

1707-9-11-16-19-21-24-32-36-41. Deputy.

1738, Dec. 27. Will—codicil 1744, Aug. 27—proved 1745, Nov. 30. Ex. grandson Thomas. Overseer, son-in-law Giles Pierce. To son James, negro man and farming tackling. To grandson Thomas, son of Thomas, deceased, my homestead farm where I dwell, &c., he allowing my daughter Frances Pierce, to dwell in a room while she is a widow. If grandson should die, the homestead to go to grandson Thomas, son of James. Son-in-law Joseph Edmonds, of Warwick, to be guardian of grandson Thomas, son of Thomas, and to cause him to be learned to read, write and cipher suitable to his degree. To Joseph Edmonds, profits of farm till Thomas is of age, except £4 a year to be paid daughter Frances Pierce. To grandson Alexander Nichols, 100 acres. To grandson Thomas Nichols, son of James, all the rest of farm where James liveth not already given James, by deed. To grandson Benjamin, son of James, land. To grandson Thomas Edmonds, land. To each grandchild, 1*s.* To daughter-in-law Freelove Nichols, wife of Joseph Nichols, 5*s.* (She was widow of his son Thomas, and had married Joseph Nichols, son of John, for her second husband.) To daughters alive at his decease, all the rest of movables equally. The codicil revokes bequest to son James and gives him £50.

Inventory, £377, viz: purse and wearing apparel £12, warming pan, 2 silver spoons, linen wheel, churn, cider mill, large bible, bond £111, mare, colt, 2 cows, heifer, 2 calves, &c.

II. SUSANNAH, b. 1662, Oct. 15. d.

III. JOHN, b. 1666, Apr. 16. d. 1725. East Greenwich, R. I.
m. (1) 1687, Jun. 8.
HANNAH FORMAN, b. 1665, Jan. 10. d. 1716, Oct. 27. of Forman.
m. (2) 1721, Jun. 18. [John
REBECCA ANDREW, (w. of b. d. 1725 + of

1. John, 1689, Oct. 18.
2. Thomas, 1691, Dec. 13.
3. Hannah, 1694, Feb. 26.
4. Susannah, 1697, Dec. 4.
5. Robert, 1699, Feb. 19.
6. Mary, 1702, Feb. 17.
7. Joseph, 1705, Apr. 1.

1706-17. Deputy.

1725, Sep. 26. Will—proved 1725, Nov. 18. Exs. sons Robert and Joseph. To son John, one-quarter of old farm. To son Thomas, one-quarter of old farm. To son Robert, one-half of old farm. To each of these three sons other land. To son Joseph, land where I dwell, not already given, and houses, &c. To daughter Susanna, wife of Samuel ——, of Warwick, a feather bed, &c., six ewes and £15. To daughter Mary Nichols, two feather beds, six ewes, a cow, horse £25, &c. To wife that now is, Rebecca, £10, a piece of cloth now weaving, besides what I have covenanted for. To children Robert and Mary, privilege to live in west end of house, &c., Robert for three years, and Mary while single.

Inventory, £531, 11*d.*, viz: wearing apparel £19, 13*s.*, 74½ oz. silver £55, 17*s.* 6*d.*, books, spectacles, 2 woolen wheels, linen wheel, pewter, carpenter's tools, 40 sheep, 10 lambs, 4 oxen, 7 cows, 2 three years, 2 two years, 2 yearlings, 2 calves, 4 hogs, &c.

IV. ROBERT, b. 1671, Nov. 22. d. Newport, R. I.
m. 1698, Feb.
MARY CASE, b. d. of Case.

1. Jonathan,

1705, Apr. 24. He and Jonathan Nichols, were witnesses to a deed of Daniel Thurston and wife Mary, of Newport, to John Cory, of Portsmouth (of 90 acres in East Greenwich, for £40).

V. HANNAH, b. 1674, Aug. 7. d. 1723 +
m. 1695, Feb. 22.
WILLIAM ARNOLD, b. 1667, May 31. d. 1723, Sep. 22. of Caleb & Abigail (Wilbur) Arnold.

1. William, 1696, Mar. 18.
2. Josiah, 1698, Feb. 3.
3. Ruth, 1699, Mar. 28.
4. Caleb, 1705, Mar. 14.
5. Hannah, 1708, Jul. 30.
6. Thomas, 1711, Sep. 14.

VI. BENJAMIN, b. 1676, Jan. 28. d. 1736. East Greenwich, North Kingstown, R. I.
m.
MARY, b. d. 1736 (—) of

1. Benjamin, 1698, Aug. 22.
2. Jonathan, 1700, Nov. 27.
3. Ruth, 1703, Mar. 13.
4. Joseph, 1707, Jun. 8.
5. John, 1709, Dec. 20.
6. William, 1712, Mar. 25.
7. Thomas, 1714, Feb. 28.
8. George, 1715, Aug. 25.
9. Ann, 1717, Oct. 16.

1704, Nov. 29. East Greenwich. He sold John Carpenter, for £22, a lot of 50 acres, being part of 80 acres granted honoured father Mr. Thomas Nichols, of Newport, by town of East Greenwich.

1709, May 27. Kings Town. He and twelve others bought 1,824 acres of the vacant lands in Narragansett, situated near Devil's Foot.

1725-26. Deputy. He bore the title of Captain at this time.

1736, Oct. 1. Will—proved. To son ——, certain land. To second son Joseph, a farm in East Greenwich. To third son John, certain land. He mentions also sons William and George, daughter —— (to whom he gives negro Phillis), and then gives son Thomas, rest of estate.

VII. JONATHAN, b. 1681, Jun. 10. d. 1727, Aug. 2. Newport, R. I.
m. 1707, Feb.
ELIZABETH LAWTON, b. 1688, Sep. 12. d. of Robert & Mary (Wodell) Lawton.

1. Mary, 1708, Jan. 8.
2. Hannah, 1709, Sep. 21.
3. Jonathan, 1712, Oct. 24.
4. Robert, 1715, May 20.
5. Elizabeth, 1717, Jul. 15.
6. Sarah, 1719, Jun. 17.
7. Joseph, 1723, May 25
8. Benjamin, 1723, May 25.

1707. Freeman.

1713-14-18 Deputy.

1714-18-19-20-21-22-23-24-25-26-27. Assistant.

1718. Captain.

1721, Jun. 13. He was appointed on committee to rebuild or repair Fort Ann.

1727. Deputy Governor.

VIII. JOSEPH, b. 1684, Apr. 18. d. 1725, May 15. Jamestown, R. I.

1725. Inventory, £9, 19*s.*, viz: cash £1, 1*s.*, horse £2, 10*s.*, wearing apparel £1, bills, £5, 8*s.* (Charges £7, 2*s.*)

IX. ELIZABETH, b. 1688, Jun. 14. d.
m. 1706, Feb. 1.
GIDEON FREEBORN, b. 1684, Apr. 29. d. 1753, Feb. 21. of Gideon & Mary (Boomer) Freeborn.

1. William, 1706, Nov. 19.
2. Gideon, 1708, Oct. 26.
3. Susanna, 1710, Jan. 7.
4. Thomas, 1711, Oct. 11.
5. William, 1713, Mar. 1.
6. Elizabeth, 1714, Jul. 22.
7. Joseph, 1717, Feb. 25.
8. Jonathan, 1719, Mar. 4.
9. Benjamin, 1722, Jan. 9.
10. Hannah, 1726, May 10.

JOSEPH[2], (Edmund[1]). b. d. 1693, Jun.
m.
JANE, b. d. 1691, Apr.

Bootle, Cumberland Co., Eng., Portsmouth, R. I.

His first four children were born at Bootle, Dinah was born at Salem, Benjamin at Barbadoes, Elizabeth at Martinico and Jane at Portsmouth.

He and his wife were among those who earliest joined the Quakers.

1659. Salem.

1660, Jun. 1. On the same day that Mary Dyer was executed, he and his wife were brought before magistrates "to see if the terror thereof could have frighted them, but the power of the Lord in them was above you all, and they feared not you, nor your threats of putting them to death." Before this they had been committed to prison, and banished upon pain of death. They went to Plymouth Colony, being denied to sojourn in Massachusetts, but they could not be admitted, the magistrates telling them "that if they had turned them away at Boston, they would have nothing to do with them," and his wife they threatened to whip, one of them saying "that if she had not been a witch she could not have known that he that was with his son was a priest." "So they passed away in the moving of the Lord to Rhode Island," having been prisoners at Boston, he twenty-four weeks and she eighteen.

1664. He and his wife were "cruelly whipped at Salem, Boston and Dedham," and soon went to Barbadoes.

1669. Portsmouth.

1672, Jun. 17. He, and Thomas Nicholson, and Elizabeth Nicholson, now wife of Nicholas Andrews, children of Edmund Nicholson, of Marblehead, deceased, appointed brother Samuel Nicholson, of Marblehead, attorney to receive of Peleg Sanford, executor of Francis Simpson, of Newport, whatever was bequeathed.

1675, Aug. 20. He sold Arthur Cook, of Ratcliff, County of Middlesex, currier, certain land in Portsmouth.

1678. Freeman.

1685. Deputy.

He died on the ship "Elizabeth," Daniel Gould, Jr., master, coming from Barbadoes, bound for London, as Friends' records declare.

1693, Apr. 12. Will—proved 1693, Sep. 29. Exs. son-in-law Nicholas Carr and daughter Jane Nicolson. Overseers, John Easton and Walter Clarke. The executors were directed to sell house and lands and pay legacies. To son Joseph, £10. To daughter Sarah Ward, wife of John, £30. To daughter Rebecca Carr, wife of Nicholas, £40. To daughter Rachel Peabody, wife of John, £40. To daughter Dinah Burrill, wife of James, £30. To daughter Elizabeth Nicholson, £60. To daughter Jane Nicholson, £100. To granddaughter Jane Nicholson, daughter of Joseph, £5. To grandchildren (children of Nicholas Carr), viz: Joseph Carr, £20, Nicholas Carr, 20s., Jane Carr, £10, Caleb, £10, Robert, £10, Margaret, £5, and Mercy, £5. To grandchildren (children of James Burrill), viz: James, Elizabeth, Dinah and Susanna Burrill, each £5. To grandchildren (children of John Ward), viz: Joseph, 20s. and Elizabeth, 10s. To grandchildren (children of John Peabody), viz: John, 20s., Joseph, £20, and Dorothy, £10. To daughters Elizabeth and Jane Nicholson, rest of estate equally.

1693, Dec. 20. The executors of his estate sold the land, 100 acres, buildings, orchards, &c., for £447, to Joseph Mowry, of Jamestown, R. I.

I. JOSEPH, b. 1650, Nov. 7. d.
m. ——— b. b. of

1. Jane,

II. SARAH, b. 1653, Mar. 1. d. 1705 +
m. JOHN WARD, b. d. 1705. of Ward.

1. Elizabeth,
2. Joseph, 1688, Aug. 18.

III. REBECCA, b. 1656, Feb. 1. d. 1703, May 13.
m. NICHOLAS CARR, b. 1654, Oct. 22. d. 1709, Feb. 17. of Caleb & Mercy ( ) Carr.

1. Nicholas, 1679, Sep. 19.
2. Joseph, 1682, Mar. 7.
3. Benjamin, 1683, Jul. 7.
4. Margaret, 1684, Oct. 22.
5. Jane, 1686, Aug. 3.
6. Caleb, 1688, Mar. 27.
7. Mercy, 1690, Apr. 20.
8. Robert,
9. Rebecca, 1692, May 12.
10. Ann, 1694,
11. Thomas, 1696, Jan. 5.
12. Benjamin, 1697, Nov. 21.

IV. RACHEL, b. 1658, Apr. 22. d. 1711, Nov. 13.
m. JOHN PEABODY, b. d. of John Peabody.

1. John,
2. Joseph,
3. Dorothy,

V. DINAH, b. 1660, Mar. 21. d.
m. JAMES BURRILL, b. d. 1712. of Burrill.

1. Elizabeth, 1685, Sep. 26.
2. James, 1687, Feb. 14.
3. James, 1689, Oct. 2.
4. Dinah, 1691, Feb. 17.
5. Susanna,
6. Hannah, 1694, Jan. 11.
7. Hannah, 1695, Apr. 16.
8. Jane.
9. Francis,

VI. BENJAMIN, b. 1665, Jun. 8. d. 1665, Oct. 8.

VII. ELIZABETH, b. 1667, Jun. 8. d.

VIII. JANE, b. 1669, Sep. 29. d. 1723, Dec. 14.

NILES. 2d column. 1. Samuel m. (1) 1701. May 2[illegible] Elizabeth Thatcher b. 1683, Mar. 7; d. 1716, Feb 10, of Peter and Theodora (Oxenbridge) Thatcher. Children. 1, Elizabeth, 1706, May 16. 2, Sarah, 1708, May 20. 3. Samuel, 1711, May 14. 4, Mary, 1713, May 27. 5. Nathaniel, 1716, Feb. 2. His 2d wife (Ann Coddington) d. 1732, Oct. 25. Children, 6. Elisha, 1718, June 8. 7. Susanna, 1719, July 30. 8, Elisha, 1719, July 30. His 3d marriage was 1737, Dec. 22. This wife b. 1681, Feb. 28. of William and Alice (Bradford) Adams.

NILES.

NATHANIEL[2], (John[1]). b. 1642, Aug. 16. d. 1727, Dec. 22.
m. 1671, Feb. 14.
SARAH SANDS, b. d. 1726 (—)
of James & Sarah (Walker) Sands.

New Shoreham, South Kingstown, R. I

1687. Overseer of the Poor.

1687. Grand Jury.

1710. Kings Town. Freeman.

1726, Apr. 21. Will—proved 1728, Feb. 12. Ex. son Ebenezer. To son Ebenezer, 200 acres and mansion house. To daughter-in-law Mary Niles, a cow. To grandson Nathaniel Niles, son of Samuel, a chest and wearing apparel. To daughter Sarah Helme and granddaughter Sarah Perkins, a chest of drawers divided equally. To daughter Catharine Hannah, a cow. To son Samuel, £350 to be paid by Ebenezer, as agreed in a deed of gift to latter. To son Nathaniel, no legacy, he having had his share by deed of gift. To son Ebenezer, rest of household goods.

Inventory, £5, 16s., 10d., viz: silver cup £2, pewter platter, bedstead, 2 old broken chairs, &c.

He died at Braintree, probably at the house of his son Samuel.

I. SAMUEL, b. 1674, May 1. d. 1762, May 1. New Shoreham, Kings Town, R. I., Braintree, Mass.
m. (1) ELIZABETH THATCHER, b. d. 1716, of Peter Thatcher.
m. (2) 1716, Nov. 22. ANNE CODDINGTON, b. 1677, Dec. 26. d. 1732, of Nathaniel & Susanna (Hutchinson) Coddington.
m. (3) 1737. ELIZABETH WHITING, (w. of Sam'l. b. d. 1762 + of William Adams.

1. Nathaniel,
2. Samuel,
3. Elizabeth,
4. Mary,
(2d wife)
5. Susanna,
6. Elisha.

1689, Jul. 3. Three French privateers landed a force on the island and plundered the inhabitants, killing many of their cattle, &c. They came twice afterward, and though but a lad he was attacked by one of them with a cutlass, as he relates.

1699. He graduated at Harvard College.

1700. He accepted a call to preach at Block Island, and was granted 7 acres in consideration of his settlement.

1702. Kings Town. He preached there some years.

1711, May 23. Braintree. Ordained.

1745. He published "*Tristia Ecclesiarum*, a brief and sorrowful account of the present state of the churches in New England." He wrote, at later periods. "God's Wonder Working Providence for New England, in the reduction of Louisburg, in verse;" "Vindication of Divers Gospel Doctrines. Also a few remarks on Mr. John Bass' Narrative;" "The True Doctrine of Original Sin, in answer to John Taylor of Milton;" History of Indian Wars, &c.

1762, Apr. 29. Will—proved 1762, May 21. Exs. sons Samuel and Elisha. He directs that east part of farm be sold to pay debts, unless sons Samuel or Elisha chose to take it. To wife Elizabeth, £40, and all household goods, &c., remaining, that she brought, to be returned to her, also to her half the value of negro Esther, and the mare she usually rides upon, and she is commended to the care of my children. To her also, a valuable gold ring becoming her character and in "remembrance of me when consuming in the grave." To son Samuel, lands on east of farm where he dwells, my preaching bible, and the gold buttons of shirt collar, great leather chair in my study, and other great chair, negro John, half of cedar swamp, and improvement of certain other land. To son Elisha, my mansion house, homestead and orchard, and half of cedar swamp, and if he have no issue, who arrive to age, then to go to Samuel. To Elisha also, a silver tankard and porringer that was his mother's, a couch, chair, brass kettle, negro "Mingo," and £10, and cow given him by his grandfather Coddington, oval table and the gold buttons at my wrist given me by his own mother. To daughter Elizabeth Hayward, £5, her grandfather, the Rev. Mr. Thatcher, having given her a much larger portion than to his other grandchildren, by his daughter, my first dear wife. To daughter Mary Wales, £27, &c. To grandsons Ebenezer and Elisha, children of daughter Thayer, deceased, certain land at age, and £27, and all the household furniture their grandmother my second wife brought me. To granddaughter Elizabeth Thayer and children of my grandchild Ann Thayer, £27, divided, and half the household stuff. To wife the tea table and appurtenances except what are marked A. C. and such to go to son Elisha. To wife, also a great chair, &c. To son Elisha, large bible, &c. To daughters, some books of divinity. To sons Samuel and Elisha, other books. To son Samuel, a mare, and that which came of her to son Elisha. To two sons rest of estate.

II. NATHANIEL, m. 1699, Jan. 26. MARY HANNAH, — b. 1677, Mar. 21. d. 1766. — b. d. 1765 + of Robert & Mary (Wilson) Hannah. — South Kingstown, R. I.

1. Nathaniel, 1700, Sep. 12.
2. Robert, 1702, Nov. 9.
3. Mary, 1704, Aug. 10.
4. Jeremiah, 1707, Apr. 7.
5. Sarah, 1711, Jun. 14.
6. Tabitha, 1714, Nov. 14.
7. Silas, 1718, May 26.
8. Paul, 1721, May 16.
9. Sylvanus, 1721, May 16.
10. Hannah,
11. Katharine, 1725, Mar. 5.

1709. Kings Town. Justice of the Peace.

1740, Feb. 26. He was appointed by the Assembly to build a watch house at Point Judith. The towns were to have a watch kept in these houses, at their own charge, and to be under regulations of the Council of War.

1765, Sep. 5. Will—proved 1766, Mar. 27. Ex. son Silas. To son Paul, north half of farm, on which I live, and the easterly part of house, with cheese house and improvement of negroes "Andrew" and "Cæsar," and half of farming tools. To son Silas, westerly part of dwelling house, southerly part of farm and small dwelling house on it, negroes "Cuff," "Jabez" and "Peter," half of farming tools, &c. Son Nathan, had already had farm at Groton and 500 acres in this town. To son Jeremiah, a case for clothes, and books, he having had already. To daughter Sarah, negro woman "Zipporah." To daughter Hannah Rodman, negro "Abigail." To daughter Katharine Gardiner, negro "Prue." To wife Mary, negro woman, bed, and a sixth of movables. To five daughters Mary Higgenbotham, Sarah Niles, Tabitha Belton, Hannah Rodman and Katharine Gardiner, each a sixth of movables.

III. KATHARINE, m. ROBERT HANNAH, — b. 1680, Mar. 13. d. — b. d. 1736. of Robert & Mary (Wilson) Hannah

1. Mary, 1714, Feb. 1.
2. Sarah, 1716, Dec. 10,
3. Tabitha, 1718, Feb. 21.
4. George, 1719, Mar. 26.
5. Catharine, 1721, Jun. 2.
6. Hannah, 1723, Oct. 13.
7. Elizabeth, 1725, Mar. 17.

IV. EBENEZER, m. (1) ABIGAIL, m. (2) 1730, Mar. 25. SARAH KENYON. — b. 1683, Dec. 3. d. 1746. — b. d. of — b. d. 1746 + of Kenyon. — Charlestown, R. I.

1. Ebenezer, 1710, Mar. 4.

1746, Aug. 4. Administration to widow Sarah.

Inventory, £707, 8s., viz: wearing apparel £38, 3 silver spoons, sword £14, books £2, 10s., linen wheel, woolen wheel, desk, 25 sheep, 12 lambs, yearling horse, 3 sows, 10 pigs, &c.

V. TABITHA, m. 1708, May 23. ABRAHAM PERKINS, — b. 1685, Jan. 25. d. 1717, Dec. 28. — b d. 1746. of Perkins.

1. Nathaniel, 1711, Jan. 22.
2. Elizabeth, 1713, Mar. 24.
3. Sarah, 1715, Jun. 17.

VI. SARAH, m. 1709, Jul. 21. ROUSE HELME, — b. d. 1748 + — b. d. 1751, May 28. of Rouse & Mary ( ) Helme.

1. James, 1710, May 7.
2. Sands, 1711, Aug. 21.
3. Rouse, 1713, Feb. 11.
4. Nathaniel, 1714, Dec. 17.
5. Benedict, 1717, Feb. 17.
6. Simeon, 1718, Dec. 15.
7. Benedict, 1720, Oct. 3.
8. Silas, 1724, May 20.
9. Sarah, 1727, May 16,
10. Jonathan, 1729, Oct. 14.
11. Oliver, 1731, Jun. 17.
12. Samuel, 1734, Jun 3.

IV. Ebenezer. His 2d wife was daughter of John and Elizabeth (Remington) Kenyon. Children. 4. Sands. 5. Nathan. 6. David. 7, Phebe. 8, (Daughter). 9, (Daughter). [illegible] Hazard.

NILES. 2d column V. Tabitha. She had 4. Tabitha, 1715, Jan. 17. IV, Ebenezer, m. Abigail Hazard, b. [illegible]90, Mar. 19, of George & Penelope (Arnold) Hazard. Children, 1. Ebenezer, 1710, Mar. 4. 2. Penelope. 3. Sarah.

NORTHUP.

STEPHEN, m. —— — b. d. 1687 + — b. d.

Providence, Kings Town, R. I.

1658. Freeman.

1659, Jul. 27. He sold William Carpenter 60 acres at Rocky Hill.

1660. Town Sergeant.

1662, Feb. 8. He sold to William Hawkins all rights between Pawtucket and Pawtuxet rivers.

1665, Feb. 19. He had lot 81 in a division of lands.

1671, May 19. Kings Town. He took oath of allegiance.

1687, Sep. 6. Taxed 5s. ½d.

I. STEPHEN, m. 1684. MARY THOMAS, — b. 1660. d. 1733. — b. d. 1733 + of Thomas. — North Kingstown, R. I.

1. Stephen,
2. Thomas,
3. Henry,
4. Nicholas,
5. Abigail,
6. Mercy,
7. Daughter,
8. Patience, 1705, Jun. 27.

1687, Sep. 6. Kings Town. Taxed 5s. 6d.

1715, Mar. 18. At this date the inventory of his son Stephen was shown by latter's widow Damaris, at Jamestown, where Stephen, Jr. lived.

1715, Aug. 22. He testified as to land at Jamestown, that he had known about thirty-four years before.

1721, Mar. 20. He, calling himself aged about sixty one years, testified that he had known the Pequot Path forty-eight years.

1726, Jun. 14. The Assembly ordered that if he and Elisha Cole could not agree within three months, so that the mill dam be erected and built up again, so that said mill be caused to grind, then the Town Council of North Kingstown were to have valued the yearly income of land and mill, and right of Elisha Cole in mill dam, land, &c., and the yearly damage the said Stephen Northup shall sustain by having his land drowned by erecting the dam. The Council then to take the mill, land, &c., into their custody, erect the dam, and cause the mill to grind, the town paying yearly to Cole and Northup the yearly value of mill, land, dam and river, until such time as Cole and Northup can agree between themselves to keep mill going.

Before this, Stephen Northup had obtained a decree from Assembly against Elisha Cole "to turn the stream or brook between them to his ancient course," whereupon he had pulled the dam down, whereby the mill was rendered useless, and inhabitants of North and South Kingstown are thereby put to very great difficulties to get their bread corn ground, "there being but one grist mill anything near any river commodious for erecting of a grist mill within many miles, which obliges many persons to eat pounded corn," &c.

1733, Jun. 12. Will—proved. Exx. wife Mary (who refused and eldest son took administration). To wife, £200, negro Hagar, household goods, three cows, thirty sheep, and riding beast, and use of dwelling house for life, with orchard, &c. To three sons, Thomas, Henry and Nicholas, certain estate, one-third to each. To daughter Abigail Watson, £50. He also mentions daughters Mercy Allen and Patience Hazard, and grandchildren Elizabeth Eldred, Freelove, Mary and Margaret Watson, Mary Sherman, Stephen, Jonathan and Job Card, Elizabeth and Phebe Allen, and Abigail Gr——.

Inventory, £1,926, negro man £100, 2 women £160, land £1,000 200 sheep, 4 yearlings, 3 two years, 16 cows, warming pan, linen wheel, wearing apparel, &c.

II. HENRY, b. 1663, d. 1740.
m.
MARY, b. , d. 1740 + of

North Kingstown, R. I.

1. Susanna,
2. Mary,
3. Patience,
4. Immanuel, 1699, Jun. 17.

1687, Sep. 6. Kings Town. Taxed 1*s.* 5*d.*

1700, Jun. 5. He contributed 6*s.* toward expense of meeting house, to be set up at or near Mashapaug, for the Quakers.

1709, May 28. He and three others bought 275 acres of the vacant lands in Narragansett.

1727, Aug. 30. He, calling himself sixty-four years or thereabouts, testified as to Stephen Northup's farm.

1740, Oct. 14. Will—proved. Ex. son Immanuel. He mentions wife Mary, daughter Susannah, wife of John Pinder, Mary, wife of Jeffrey Champlin, and Patience, wife of John Congdon, and son Immanuel Northup. After payment of legacies, the rest of estate, real and personal, is left to son Immanuel.

Inventory, cow, calf, 50 sheep, carpenter's tools, wearing apparel, &c.

III. JOSEPH, b. , d. 1726 (—)
m.
HOPESTILL SMITH, b. , d. 1726 + of John & Phillis (Gereardy) Smith.

North Kingstown, R. I.

1. Joseph,
2. ———
3. ———
4. ———
5. ———

1687, Sep. 6. Kings Town. Taxed 3*s.* 11½*d.*

1706, May 1. He and his brother Stephen were defendants in an appeal taken from the Court of Trials by Isaac Royal, plaintiff. The appeal was not sustained by Assembly, and appellant was ordered to pay costs in the Assembly.

1709, Jun. 3. He and eleven others bought the tract known as Swamptown, being part of the vacant lands in Narragansett.

1726. His widow having no bed to lodge on, and there being one in the inventory at £3, she was granted it and the administrator was ordered not to dispose of it. (It is believed that the widow's name was Hopestill, from item below.)

1729, Sep. 1. The will of John Smith, of South Kingstown (proved 1730, Feb. 8), gave to daughter Hopestill Northup, £150, and 200 acres at Coweset, and a bible to each of her five children.

IV. DAVID, b. , d. 1725.
m.
SUSANNA CONGDON, b. , d. 1725 + of Benjamin & Elizabeth (Albro) Congdon.

North Kingstown, R. I.

1. David,
2. Stephen,
3. Benjamin,
4. Robert,

1725. Will—proved. Exx. wife Susanna. To sons David, Stephen, Benjamin and Robert, certain land and cattle, and a feather bed to each. Wife to bring up the younger children.

Inventory, £248, 7*s.*, viz: sheep, lambs, cattle, 5 feather beds, wearing apparel, &c.

OSBORNE.

JEREMIAH, b. , d. 1673.
m.
———, b. , d.

Newport, R. I.

He was a schoolmaster.

1673, Nov. 8. Samuel Hubbard writes at this date: "This week two of Christ church, called Mr. Vahans, departed, to wit, John Turner and Jeremy Osborne, schoolmaster, Lord prepare all."

I. JEREMIAH, b. , d. 1709.
m.
MERCY DAVIS, b. , d. 1733, Feb. 16. of Nicholas & Sarah ( ) Davis.

Bristol, R. I.

1. Robert, 1684, Aug. 11.
2. Katharine, 1686, Nov. 12.
3. John, 1689, Oct. 31.
4. Jeremiah, 1693, Jul. 25.
5. Margaret, 1695, May 27.
6. Sarah, 1701, May 11.
7. Jeremiah, 1706, Jun. 21.

He was an Innholder.

1688, May 20. He agreed to deliver two horses on ship "Newport," Daniel Gould, master, for account of James Greene in Barbadoes.

1696, Oct. 9. He and wife Mercy sold to Nathaniel Byfield of Boston, 22 acres at Poppasquash Neck for £25.

1696, Oct. 11. He bought of Richard Pearce 10 acres for £30.

1708, Jul. Will—proved 1709, Apr. 6. Exx. wife Mercy. To wife, all estate real and personal, for bringing up of her young children; the said real estate being for her life only. At death of wife, a division of real estate to be made, son John having a double portion as law directs, and the rest equally.

Inventory, £412, 3*s.*, viz: warming pan, 2 tankards, 2 cups and porringer of silver £22, 12 barrels cider, 12 gallons rum, 3 cows, 14 sheep, hog, pig, 2 houses and land £255, &c.

PABODIE.

WILLIAM[2], (John[1]). b. 1620, d. 1707, Dec. 13.
m. 1644, Dec. 26.
ELIZABETH ALDEN, b. 1624, d. 1717, May 31.
of John & Priscilla (Mullins) Alden.

Duxbury, Mass., Little Compton, R. I.

1648, Jun. 7. Grand Jury.

1650, Jun. 4. Receiver of the Excise.

1651, Jun. 5. Freeman.

1654–55–56–57–58–59–60–61–62–63–70—71—72—73–74–75–76–77–79–80–81–82. Deputy.

1655, Mar. 6. He was on a jury that found John Walker, guilty of manslaughter "by chance medley."

1657, Jun. 3. He was on a committee to consider what way to take for the accommodation of our honored Governor and magistrates.

1660, May 1. He and another were to lay out a highway "so as it may be the least prejudicial to any," it having been recently stopped up by Henry Howland.

1662, Jun. 10. He and two others were appointed to lay out 230 acres for Captain Standish.

1665, Oct. 3. He and another were to attend to rebuilding bridge over Jones River.

1667, Jul. 27. He was granted "the remainder of that land he paid for, being a parcel of poor silly barren land."

1668–72–73–74–75–80–84. Selectman.

1672, Jul. 1. He received lands for ten years to satisfy a debt of £7, from William and Moses Numaker.

1673, Jun. 3. Coroners Jury.

1677, Jul. 7. He was appointed on a committee to hear complaints and demands of persons to whom the colony was indebted, relating to late war with the natives.

I. JOHN, b. 1645, Oct. 4, d. 1669, Nov. 17.
Unmarried.

Duxbury, Mass.

1669, Nov. 18. The coroner's jury rendered the following verdict, as to his death. "That he riding on the road, his horse carried him underneath the bough of a young tree, and violently forcing his head unto the body thereof, brake his skull, which we do judge was the cause of his death."

II. ELIZABETH, b. 1647, Apr. 24, d.
m. 1666, Nov. 16.
JOHN ROGERS, b. , d. 1732. of John & Frances ( ) Rogers.

1. Hannah, 1668, Nov. 16.
2. John, 1670, Sep. 22.
3. Ruth, 1675, Apr. 18.
4. Sarah, 1677, May 4.
5. Elizabeth,

III. MARY, b. 1648, Aug. 7, d.
m. 1669, Nov. 16.
EDWARD SOUTHWORTH, b. , d. of Constant & Elizabeth (Collier) Southworth.

1. Elizabeth, 1672, Nov.
2. Thomas, 1676.
3. Benjamin, 1680.
4. Constant,
5. John, 1687.
6. Mercy,
7. Priscilla, 1693.

IV. MERCY, b. 1649, Jan. 2, d.
m. 1670 ±
JOHN SIMMONS, b. , d. of Moses & Sarah ( ) Simmons.

1. John, 1671, Feb. 22.
2. William, 1672, Sep. 24.
3. Isaac, 1674, Jan. 28.
4. Martha, 1677, Nov.

V. MARTHA, b. 1650, Feb. 25, d. 1712, Jan. 25.
m. (1) 1677, Apr. 4.
SAMUEL SEABURY, b. 1640, Dec. 10, d. 1681, Aug. 5. of John & Grace ( ) Seabury.
m. (2)
WILLIAM FOBES, b. 1650, d. 1712, Nov. 6. of John & Constant (Mitchell) Fobes.

PABODIE. 2d column. V. Martha. Erase 3d child.

1. Joseph, 1678, Jun. 8.
2. Martha, 1679, Sep. 23.
3. John, 1681.
(By 2d husband.)
4. Elizabeth, 1683.
5. Constant,
6. Mary,
7. Mercy,

VI. PRISCILLA, b. 1653, Jan. 15, d. 1724, Jun. 3.
m. 1677, Dec. 24.
ICHABOD WISWALL, b. 1637, d. 1700, Jul. 23. of Thomas & Elizabeth ( ) Wiswall.

1. Mercy, 1680, Oct. 14.
2. Hannah, 1682, Feb. 22.
3. Perez, 1684, Feb. 5.
4. Percy, 1686, Nov. 22.
5. Priscilla, 1691, Dec. 21.
6. Deborah, 1692.

Paine, John (omitted by Austin) see: American Genealogist, v. 24, p. 70-71.

1680, Jun. 7. He and two others were to bound out Tatamanuckes 1000 acres at Saconnett.
1681, Jul. 7. He was on a committee to proportion rates for taxes.
1681, Oct. 23. He and two others were chosen to run the line betwixt the lands of Saconnett and Punckateeset, to Dartmouth bounds, &c.
1685-86. Little Compton. Selectman.
1686, Mar. 3. He and his partners bought lands at Saconnet Neck, for £75, of Awashunk, Squaw Sachem.
1707, May 13. Will—proved 1708, Feb. 27. Exx. wife Elizabeth and son William. To wife, east end of house at Little Compton and part of the land given formerly to son William, all to be hers while widow; and also to her all household stuff, cattle, bills due and money; but if wife choose to claim her thirds of my land and house at Duxbury (which I sold Samuel Bartlett), and make use of them, then my son William to have the whole of housing and lands at Little Compton, and to pay Samuel Bartlett, 50s., per year during time his mother makes use of her thirds at Duxbury. To son William, after death of his mother, the part of house and land bequeathed her for life. To son William, other land and all my books, tools, &c. To three grandsons, viz: Stephen Southworth, son of daughter Rebecca, deceased, and John and William Pabodie, sons of son William, land at Westquadnaug (west of Providence), part purchased by son-in-law William Fobes of Shubael Painter, and assigned by William Fobes to my son-in-law Ichabod Wiswall. He mentions also son-in-law Edward Southworth. To daughters Mary, Mercy, Martha, Priscilla, Ruth, Sarah, Hannah and Lydia, each 1s., and to heirs of daughters Elizabeth and Rebecca, 1s. To daughter Lydia Grinnell, a set of green curtains, she having already received her part.
Inventory, £407, 14s., viz: 70 acres £315, dwelling house and half a barn £30, mare and colt, a cow and calf, sundry books £6, 2 feather beds, warming pan, churn, cash £2, 10s., &c.
1717, Jun. 17. The "Boston News Letter" of this date thus notices his widow's death. "Little Compton, 31 May. This morning died here Mrs. Elizth Paybody late wife of Mr. William Paybody in the 93d year of her age. She was daughter of John Alden, Esq. and Priscilla his wife, daughter of Mr. Wm. Mullins. This John Alden and Priscilla Mullins were married at Plymouth in New England, where their daughter Elizabeth was born. She was exemplary, virtuous and pious, and her memory is blessed. Her granddaughter Bradford is a grandmother." He and his wife were buried in the Little Compton Cemetery.

VII. SARAH, m. 1681, Nov. 10. JOHN COE,
b. 1656, Aug. 7. d. 1740, Aug. 27. b. 1649, Jun. 30. d. 1728, Dec. 16. of Matthew & Elizabeth (Wakely) Coe.
1. Lydia, 1683, Feb. 26.
2. Sarah, 1686, Feb. 25.
3. Samuel, 1692, Dec. 12.
4. Elizabeth, 1694, Mar. 28.
5. Hannah, 1696, Dec. 29.
6. John, 1699, Feb. 1.
7. Joseph, 1700, Mar. 24.

VIII. RUTH, m. BENJAMIN BARTLETT,
b. 1658, Jun. 27. d. 1740, Aug. 27. b. d. of Benjamin & Sarah (Brewster) Bartlett.
1. Robert, 1679, Dec. 6.
2. Benjamin,
3. Mercy,
4. Priscilla,
5. Deborah,
6. Ruth,
7. Abigail,
8. Rebecca,
9. Sarah,

IX. REBECCA, m. WILLIAM SOUTHWORTH,
b. 1660, Oct. 16. d. 1702, Dec. 3. b. 1659. d. 1719, Jun. 25. of Constant & Elizabeth (Collier) Southworth.
1. Benjamin, 1681, Apr. 18.
2. Joseph, 1683, Feb. 1.
3. Edward, 1684, Nov. 23.
4. Elizabeth, 1686, Sep. 23.
5. Alice, 1688, Jul. 14.
6. Samuel, 1690, Dec. 26.
7. Nathaniel, 1692, Oct. 31.
8. Thomas, 1694, Dec. 13.
9. Stephen, 1696, Mar. 31.

X. HANNAH, m. 1683, Aug. 2. SAMUEL BARTLETT,
b. 1662, Oct. 15. d. b. d. of Benjamin & Sarah (Brewster) Bartlett.
1. Benjamin, 1684, May 4.
2. Joseph, 1686, Apr. 22.
3. Samuel, 1691.
4. Ichabod,
5. Judah,
6. William,

XI. WILLIAM, m. (1) JUDITH, m. (2) ELIZABETH, m. (3) MARY,
b. 1664, Nov. 24. d. 1744, Sep. 17. Little Compton, R. I.
b. 1670. d. 1714, Jul. 26. of
b. 1673 ± d. 1717, Dec. 14. of
b. d. 1743 + of
1. Elizabeth, 1698, Apr. 10.
2. John, 1700, Feb. 7.
3. William, 1702, Feb. 21.
4. Rebecca, 1704, Feb. 29.
5. Priscilla, 1706, Mar. 4.
6. Judith, 1708, Jan. 23.
7. Joseph, 1710, Jul. 26.
8. Mary, 1712, Apr. 4.
(2d wife)
9. Benjamin, 1717, Nov. 25.
(3d wife no issue.)

He was a Deacon.
1743, Aug. 7. Will—proved 1744, Nov. 12. Exs. sons John and William. To wife Mary, a feather bed and household stuff that was hers before marriage; also while widow suitable clothing, house room, meat, drink, washing and lodging, and £5, paid yearly by son William, and £5, by sons John and Joseph. To son John, 120 acres on south side of farm and buildings. To sons William and Joseph, rest of farm, but William's part to be £200 better than Joseph's. To son Benjamin, certain land and all movables in the house that was his mother's. To daughter Elizabeth, wife of Edward Gray, £25. To daughter Rebecca, wife of Joseph Irish, £8. To daughter Priscilla, wife of William Wilcox, £10. The foregoing sums to be paid by son John. To daughter Judith, wife of Benjamin Church, £20. To daughter Mary, wife of Nathaniel Fish, £25. These sums to be paid by son William. To sons John and William, rest of estate.
Inventory, £4,912, viz: homestead farm and buildings, £4,500, other land £100, 2 cows, 3 heifers, colt, mare, old books, 2 combs, money scales, warming pan, wearing apparel £20, churn, cheese tub, &c.
He was buried in the Little Compton Cemetery.

XII. LYDIA, m. DANIEL GRINNELL,
b. 1667, Apr. 3. d. b. d. of Daniel & Mary (Wodell) Grinnell.
Lydia XII. **Add another child Priscilla b. 1680.**
1. Benjamin, 1696, Jan. 12.
2. Peabody,
3. George,
4. Jemima, 1704.
5. Daniel, 1707.

PABODIE. 2d column. XII. Lydia. Erase son Benjamin.

PAINE.

ANTHONY, m. (1) ———, m. (2) 1643. ROSE GRINNELL, (w. of [Matthew.
b. d. 1650. b. d. 1643 (—) b. d. 1673 +
(She m. (3) 1650, James Weeden.)
Portsmouth, R. I.
1638. He was admitted as an inhabitant.
1639, Apr. 30. He and twenty-eight others signed following compact. "We whose names are underwritten, do acknowledge ourselves the legal subjects of His Majesty King Charles, and in his name do hereby bind ourselves into a civil body politic, unto his laws according to matters of justice."
1643, Nov. 10. He entered into an agreement with Rose Grinnell previous to their marriage. She deeded to her three sons Matthew, Thomas and Daniel Grinnell, "two sheeder goats apiece," and to her son Matthew, a cow also. The goats were to abide in the hands of Anthony Paine for three years, and the milk was to be his, but the increase was to belong to her three sons. It was also agreed between Anthony and Rose before their marriage, that upon the death of either, after marriage, the property of the one deceased should go to the children of that person; Rose having four children and Anthony Paine three children.
1649, May 6. Will—proved 1650. Exx. wife Rose. Overseers, Mr. Porter, William Baulstone. "I, Anthony Paine, in my perfect memory, do manifest my mind and last will is to give and bequeath unto my daughter Alice, one cow, she or husband paying unto my daughter Mary Tripp, so much as the cow is judged to be more worth than the heifer; further my mind and will is to give unto my daughter Mary Tripp, one young heifer, and to be made up equal out of the cow, and further my mind and will is to make my wife Rose Paine, my whole and sole executrix, to see my the former covenant, and my last will performed and my debts paid, and Mr. Porter and William Baulstone to see my estate equally divided."
1650, Mar. 18. She was called Rose Weeden in a receipt of this date.
1673, Dec. 17. His widow Rose Weeden of Portsmouth, for £30, and maintenance for life, sold Matthew Grinnell 53 acres.

I. ALICE, m. LOT STRANGE,
b. d. 1690. b. d. 1683, Jul. 30. of Strange.
No issue.

II. MARY, m. (1) JOHN TRIPP, m. (2), 1682, Apr. 4. BENJAMIN ENGELL,
b. d. 1687, Feb. 12. b. 1610. d. 1678. of Tripp. b. d. of Engell.
1. John, 1640 ±
2. Peleg, 1642 ±
3. Joseph, 1644 ±
4. Mary, 1646 ±
5. Elizabeth, 1648 ±
6. Alice, 1650 ±
7. Isabel, 1651 ±
8. Abiel, 1653 ±
9. James, 1656 ±
10. Martha, 1658 ±

III. CHILD,
b. d. young.

(2d WIFE, no issue.)

THOMAS, b. d. 1706, Mar. 25.
m. (1)
CATHARINE, b. d.
m. (2)
——— b. d.

Hingham, Mass., Newport, Westerly, R. I.

1630, Sep. 18. He was on a jury who viewed Austin Bratcher before his burial.

1637. He was at Hingham this year, and again before 1644, having been intermediately at Charlestown, New Haven and Rowley.

1639, Jun. 6. Upon his petition, he was granted a lot at Mr. Roger's plantation.

1640, May 13. He was allowed £12, 15s., for his charge by town of Hingham.

1655. Newport. Freeman.

1664, Mar. 11. He sold his now dwelling house with half an acre of land (originally granted by town to Edward Andrews) bounded westerly by Maidford River, &c., to Richard Tew, together with a marsh near Sachuest River; all for a "certain sum."

1669, May 18. Westerly. His name was in a list of inhabitants at this date.

1671, May 17. He took oath of allegiance.

He was drowned.

I. ELIZABETH, b. d. 1639 ±

II. WILLIAM, b. d. 1639 ±

III. THOMAS, b. d. 1639 ±

IV. THOMAS, b. 1640. d.

V. SHUBAEL, b. d. Westerly, R. I.

1669, May 18. Westerly. His name was in a list of inhabitants.

1670–72. Deputy.

1671, May 17. He was ordered to warn the inhabitants of Westerly to attend a meeting of the Court of Justices. He took oath of allegiance same day.

1679, May 7. His fine of 30s. imposed by Court of Trials for his contempt of authority, was remitted by the Assembly, he declaring himself heartily sorry.

1684, Jul. 24. The case between him and John Williams, was referred to next Assembly, by reason that Shubael Painter is absent, being employed about the country's service.

1688. Constable.

Perhaps he had a son Daniel, as Johanna, wife of Daniel Painter, was admitted to the church at Stonington, 1697, Nov. 28.

PALMER, GEORGE (omitted by Austin) See: American Geneologist v.20, p.53

PALMER.

HENRY, b. d.
m.
——— b. d.

Newport, R. I.

1668. Freeman.

1670, Jul. 13. He was constituted High Constable in a matter of great concernment, viz: the murder of Walter House, at Wickford, and was to repair there and cause the body to be taken up, &c., and to use best endeavors to apprehend the guilty.

1671, Apr. 28. He was granted a license for a public ordinary or victualing house, for entertainment of strangers or others, giving bonds for good order, &c.

1671, May 17. He, as General Constable, was ordered to bring James Babcock, Constable of Westerly, before the court for not warning the inhabitants of Westerly to appear at a meeting.

1672, Feb. 27. The arbitrators, viz: John Easton and James Barker, made the following report as to a quarrel between him and Stephen Sabeere: "We do award that Stephen Sabeere shall acknowledge unto Henry Palmer that he hath done wrong unto him and his wife in saying that his wife is a witch, and would prove her so. We do award that Henry Palmer shall acknowledge unto Stephen Sabeere, that he hath done him wrong in calling of him, the said Stephen, 'French dog, French rogue.'"

1676–77. The General Assembly met at his house.

It is assumed that Joseph and Benjamin were his sons, and possibly William Palmer (of Kings Town in 1687), should be added to the list.

No relationship has been found to exist between him and George Palmer, who was of Warwick in 1655.

I. JOSEPH, b. 1663. d. 1716 + Newport, R. I.

1696, May 5. Freeman.

1716, Mar. He testified, calling himself aged fifty-three years, that his brother Benjamin, who died in Newport, had son Benjamin born in 1695.

II. BENJAMIN, b. d. Newport, R. I.
m.
MARY, b. d. of

1. Benjamin, 1695,

1716, Mar. The testimony of Sarah Coggeshall, wife of Joshua, was given, that she was with Mary Palmer, wife of Benjamin, when she lay in of her son Benjamin, and certainly knows that said Benjamin, son of Mary, was but twenty years old in October, 1715.

PARKER.

GEORGE, b. 1611. d. 1656.
m.
FRANCES, b. d. 1669 +

(She m. (2) Nicholas Brown.)

Portsmouth, R. I.

He was a carpenter.

1634, May 11. He came to America in ship "Elizabeth and Ann," from London, aged twenty-three years.

1638. He was admitted an inhabitant of the island of Aquidneck, having submitted himself to the government that is or shall be established.

1638, Sep. 15. He and seven others were summoned to appear for a riot of drunkenness committed on the 13th. He was ordered to pay 5s., and sit till evening in the stocks.

1641, Mar. 16. Freeman.

1643–44. Sergeant.

1655. Freeman.

1655–56. General Sergeant.

Possibly John Parker[2], though here assumed to be his son, did not bear that relation to George.[1]

I. JOSEPH, b. d. 1685. Shrewsbury, N. J.
m.
——— b. d. of

1. Peter,

1668. Freeman.

1669, Aug. 31. He, calling himself son and heir of George Parker, of Portsmouth, deceased, exchanged 14 acres and dwelling house with Richard Pearce, of Portsmouth, for 20 acres in Portsmouth and £4. He sold on same date 20 acres to John Strange, of Portsmouth, for £34.

1669, Dec. 28. He deeded land to Nicholas Brown, calling himself oldest son of George Parker, and mentioning his mother as Frances Brown.

1676–77–78–79. Justice.

1682. Commissioner to lay out highways.

1683, &c. Member of Legislature.

1685, May. Administration to Jedediah Allen.

1698, Apr. 6. His son Peter, had a legacy from will of John Slocum.

2d column. II. Joseph, d. 1684, Oct 13; m. Margaret. She d. 1684, Jan. 6. Children. 1, Joseph, 1675, June 28. 2, Mary, 1677, Dec. 1. 3, Nathaniel 1679, May 20. 4, Peter, 1681, Sep. 8.

II. MARY, b. d.
m. 1660.
ICHABOD SHEFFIELD, b. 1626. d. 1712, Feb. 4. of Sheffield.

1. Joseph, 1661, Aug. 22.
2. Mary, 1664, Apr. 30.
3. Nathaniel, 1667, Apr. 18.
4. Ichabod, 1670, Mar. 6.
5. Amos, 1673, Jun. 25.

III. PETER, b. d. Portsmouth, R. I., Shrewsbury, N. J.
m.
SARAH COOK, b. d. of Thomas Cook.

1. Penelope,
2. Peter,
3. Sarah,

1664, Oct. Petition of Sarah Parker, for release from husband was postponed to next Assembly.

1667. Shrewsbury. Constable. He held the office many years.

1st column. A George Parker, son of George, was baptized 1613, Mar. 13, in St. John's Church, Margate, Kent county, England.

See: American Genealogist v.20, p.54

1674, Feb. 6. His children Penelope, Peter and Sarah, had each 5s., from the will of their grandfather Thomas Cook, of Portsmouth.
1676. Foreman of Grand Jury.
1680, Jun. 18. He gave receipt to Mary Brown (wife of Jeremiah Brown, and widow and executrix of Thomas Cook), for legacies from his wife's father's estate, which had been made to his wife and children.
1680, Aug. 20. In a letter of this date from John Browne to Governor Andros, he says: "Mr. Peter Parker, is very weak, more like to die than to live."

IV. { MERIBAH, m. 1674 (—) JOHN SLOCUM, } b. d. 1698 + | b. 1645, May 26. d. 1702. of Giles & Joan ( ) Slocum. — No issue.

V. { JOHN, m. ESTHER, } b. d. | b. d. of — Newport, R. I. — 1. John, 2. Robert, 3. James, 4. Hannah,

1655. Freeman.
1677, Oct. 31. He and forty-seven others were granted 5,000 acres to be called East Greenwich.
1680. Taxed 13s.
1688, Feb. 28. He and wife Esther, sold George Sisson, 31 acres for £125, 10s.
1692, Jun. 14. Receipt was given by Arthur Cook, of Philadelphia, as attorney for John Parker and Hester, his wife, to Philip Smith and Jonathan Holmes, executors unto the will of James Mann, of Newport. The said James Mann, had by will (dated 1689, Nov. 13), given cousins John Parker and Hester his wife, £10, and to Hester, his turkey wrought coverlet, and to John, Robert and James, sons of John and Hester, £30 equally divided, and to Hannah, daughter of John and Hester, £5, &c.

VI. { FRANCES, m. 1676, Jul. 27. BENJAMIN HALL, } b. d. | b. 1650. d. 1730, Jan. 26. of William & Mary ( ) Hall. — 1. Mary, 1678, Apr. 3. 2. William, 1680, Aug. 19. 3. Benjamin, 1682, Jun. 17. 4. George, 1685, Jun. 29. 5. Nathaniel, 1689, Jun. 29.

PARROTT.

{ SIMON, m. ELIZABETH, } b. 1634. d. 1718, May 23. | b. 1627. d. 1705, Oct. 20.

Newport, R. I.
1671, May 17. Freeman.
1680. Taxed, £1, 18s. 4½d.
1702, Mar. 4. He was a proprietor in the common lands.

I. { ELIZABETH, m. 1688, Aug. 9. NATHANIEL DYER, } b. d. | b. d. of Samuel & Ann (Hutchinson) Dyer. — 1. Elizabeth, 1689, Sep. 15. 2. Mary, 1691, Dec. 1, 3. Phebe, 169–, Dec. 6. 4. Ann, 1700, Jan. 10.

II. { JUDITH, m. (1) CALEB CRANSTON, m. (2) 1711. SAMUEL CRANSTON, } b. d. 1737, May 4. | b. d. of John & Mary (Clarke) Cranston. | b. 1659, Aug. d. 1727, Apr. 26. of John & Mary (Clarke) Cranston. — 1. John, 1685. 2. Elizabeth, 3. Mary, (By 2d husband, no issue.)

See: American Genealogist v.20, p.54.

PARSONS.

{ HUGH, m. ELIZABETH ENGLAND (w. [of Wm. } b. 1613. d. 1684. | b. 1613. d. 1684 +

Portsmouth, R. I.
1662, Jul. 3. He and wife Elizabeth sold 18 acres to William Wood.
1663. Freeman.
1667, Aug. 10. He enlisted in a troop of horse.
1673, Apr. 11. He and his wife gave testimony concerning the death of Rebecca Cornell, and they called their ages sixty years.
1670, Jul. 20. He declares, that having taken into my custody the estate of my grandchild Hugh Bailey, left and given him by his deceased father William Bailey; he covenants in sum of £100, that at my death and death of present wife, my aforesaid grandson shall be true and absolute owner of all my land I now possess, with buildings, &c.
1672, Apr. 15. If said Hugh die before decease of wife or self, then above mentioned land shall return to my daughter Hannah or her next heir, and to daughter Hannah, to bring up grandson, is given a cow.
1678. Deputy.
1684, Jan. 11. Will—proved 1684, Mar. 14. Exx. wife Elizabeth. Overseers, James Barker, of Newport, William Cadman, George Lawton of Portsmouth. To grandson Hugh Bailey, at decease of wife, my house and land and a third of my stock of movables, but if Hugh Bailey die before he enjoy it, then to his heirs. Wife to bring up grandson and he to be helpful to her. To daughter Hannah Matteson, 1s. To granddaughter Hannah Matteson, 4 ewe sheep. To my wife's two daughters, living on Long Island, viz: Susannah Carpenter and Elizabeth Doty, the rest of estate.

I. { GRACE, m. (1) WILLIAM BAILEY, m. (2) THOMAS LAWTON, } b. d. 1677 + | b. d. of Bailey. | b. d. 1681. of Lawton. — 1. John, 2. Joseph, 3. Edward, 4. Hugh, 5. Stephen, 1665.

II. { HANNAH, m. (1) HENRY MATTESON, m. (2) 1693, Aug. 9. CHARLES HAZLETON, } b. d. | b. 1646. d. 1690 ± of Matteson. | b. d. of Hazleton, — 1. Henry, 2. Thomas, 3. Joseph, 4. Francis, 1680, Mar. 15. 5. Hannah, 6. Hezekiah, (By 2d husband, no issue.)

PEABODY. 1st column. 1687 for 1087.

PARTRIDGE.

{ ALEXANDER, m. —— } b. d. | b. d.

Boston, Mass., Newport, R. I.
1645, Oct. 29. Under this date Governor Winthrop notes as follows: "There came hither to Boston at the same time out of England, one Captain Partridge, who had served the Parliament, but in the ship he broached and zealously maintained divers points of antinomianism and familism, for which he was called before the magistrates," &c. He was requested to sign a renunciation, but refusing, he was ordered out of the jurisdiction; yet the winter being at

hand, and it "being very hard to expose his wife and family to such hardship," some of the magistrates desired a stay of his sentence. "But the major part (by one or two) voting the contrary, he was forced to depart and so went to Rhode Island."

1648. General Sergeant.

1654, May 18. A committee (Edward Smith, Joseph Torrey and James Rogers) was appointed by Assembly to examine and dispose of Captain Partridge's estates, both the reserve and the disposal by William Lytherland and Richard Knight, and their right in what they either have reserved or disposed of "and what the said three shall doe therein shall be authentique."

1655. Freeman.

PATEY.

THOMAS, m. ELIZABETH BEERE (widow. — Thomas: b. ; d. 1695, Aug. — Elizabeth: b. ; d.

Providence, R. I.

1674, Feb. 24. He bought seven acres in the Neck, of Valentine Whitman.

1680, Aug. 23. He bought of John Brown, 14 acres in the Neck, for £14.

1682. He had 3 acres laid out, also 2 acres south-east side of the broad pond.

1685, May 29. He had 1¼ acres laid out in the Neck and a small piece containing some few poles, the said two parcels being allowed him in satisfaction for a footway which goeth through his land in the Neck, where he dwelleth.

1693, May 15. He exchanged lands with Epenetus Olney.

He was drowned.

1695, Sep. 24. Inventory of his estate was presented by his widow Elizabeth and administration on his estate was given to her for the present.

1702, Apr. 14. The widow laid down her administration on husband's estate and it was given her son Benjamin Beere.

1704, Apr. 12. Whereas Thomas Patey had lived sometime in Providence, and bought land and propagated other estates, goods and cattle, but some years since was drowned and no will found, and the widow growing incapable to administer, and therefore her son Benjamin Beere having taken administration, the latter is now by Town Council prohibited from selling land belonging to Thomas Patey's estate.

PATEY. 1st column. His wife was widow of Robert Beere, and daughter of Francis Billington,[2] (John[1]).

PEABODY.

JOHN, b. 1612; d. 1687.
m. (1) ——— b. ; d.
m. (2) 1677 ± MARY ROGERS (w. of James. b. ; d. 1678 +

Newport, R. I.

1678, Jun. 12. A petition having been presented by John Peabody and Mary Peabody late wife to deceased James Rogers, General Sergeant, concerning accounts between colony and deceased, the accounts having been examined by the late General Audit, they found them so imperfect that they could neither allow or disallow the same. It was agreed between petitioners and Assembly, that there is a clear balance of all the aforesaid accounts and a final issue of all differences, &c.,

1680. Taxed £1, 13s.

1687, Mar. 23. Will—proved 1687, Jun. 17. Ex. son John. Overseers, James Barker, Sr., and son James Barker, Jr. He calls himself aged about seventy-five. To son John Peabody, he gave various parcels of land in Newport, all housing there, including a dwelling house and orchard bought of Jonathan Davol, a pair of oxen, and negro boy called Thomas Honeyball, for twelve years term. To six daughters, £24, equally, viz: to Mary Wood, Hannah Reed, Elizabeth Davol, Rebecca Moon, Ann Cottrell and Jane Smith, each having £4. To grandchildren, 10s, apiece. To overseers, 5s. each.

1687, Apr. 18. Inventory, £103, 4s., viz: cash in bag £36, 10s. 10d., wearing apparel, negro Tom Honeyball £18, yoke of oxen, cow, heifer, old mare, sow, 3 shoats, 20 sheep, 18 lambs; also at Dartmouth, 3 cows; half of three two year old cattle, at Little Compton, silver porringer 1s. 6d., small beer cup, pewter tankard, &c.

I. JOHN, b. ; d. ; m. RACHEL NICHOLSON, b. 1658, Apr. 22; d. 1711, Nov. 13; of Joseph & Jane ( ) Nicholson. Newport, R. I.
1. John,
2. Joseph,
3. Dorothy,

II. MARY, b. ; d. ; m. ——— WOOD, b. ; d. ; of Wood.

III. HANNAH, b. ; d. ; m. ——— REED, b. ; d. ; of Reed.

IV. ELIZABETH, b. ; d. ; m. BENJAMIN DAVOL, b. ; d. ; of William Davol.

V. REBECCA, b. ; d. ; m. ——— MOON, b. ; d. ; of Moon.

VI. ANN, b. ; d. ; m. JABESH COTTRELL, b. ; d. ; of Nicholas Cottrell.

VII. JANE, b. ; d. ; m. ——— SMITH, b. ; d. ; of Smith.

JOHN, m. MARY,	b. 1632. d. 1692. b. d. 1711.

Portsmouth (Prudence Island), R. I.

He was a mason.

He was called "John Pearce, mason," to distinguish him from John Pearce[2], (Richard[1]).

1666, Jan. 5. Freeman.

1668, Apr. 14. He bought a house and 38 acres of William Cory

1673, May 7. He called himself aged forty-one years in giving testimony as to death of Rebecca Cornell.

1677, Oct. 31. He and forty-seven others were granted 5,000 acres to be called East Greenwich.

1678, Jan. 12. He was permitted by the Assembly to dispose of his East Greenwich grant of land to Henry Matteson.

1685, Mar. 16. Juryman.

1686, Mar. 5. He was a member of Coroner's jury held at the house of James Sweet, Jr., on Prudence Island.

1691, Feb. 23. He bought of John Greene of Warwick, 420 acres in Natick and a meadow near there.

1691, Aug. 23. He and wife Mary deeded land in Natick to son Daniel, possession to be had at death of said John.

1689, Sep. 23. Will—proved 1692, Apr. 26. Exx. wife Mary. Overseers, John Smith and Jeremiah Smith. To three children, 1s. each, viz: to John Pearce, Jr., Daniel Pearce and Mary Hill, wife of Robert; to John, a cow and my gun, to Daniel, my mulatto boy, to my daughter Mary Hill, negro boy "George." The rest of estate to wife Mary.

1698, Mar. 29. He and others of Prudence Island were parties to a suit.

1711, Sep. 17. Will—proved 1711, Oct. 8. Widow Mary of Prudence Island. Ex. son Daniel. To poor brethren of church in Christ to whom I do belong, in this Island or elsewhere, 40s. The rest of estate except a negro woman to be divided into three equal parts; a third to son John, a third to son Daniel and to daughter Mary Sweet, 5s.; the remaining third (except 5s.) remains in hands of executor, that if at any future time daughter Mary Sweet shall want relief, he shall supply at discretion, and if at her decease any be left undisposed of, to be divided between her seven children whom she had by former husband Robert Hill, viz: Jonathan, Robert, Daniel, William, John, Susannah Havens and Abigail. To son Daniel Pearce, negro woman "Betty," he paying his brother John therefor, £10.

I. JOHN, m. MARTHA BRAYTON,	b. d. 1715 + b. d	Portsmouth (Prudence Island), R. I. of Francis & Mary ( ) Brayton.	1. John, 2. Francis, 3. Preserved,

1692, Jun. 6. Freeman.

1694, 1704. Constable.

1696, Oct. 10. He paid 16s. for 8 acres of land allotted him by the town.

1698. Deputy.

1715, Dec. 5. He deeded to son Preserved, half of a farm in Warwick in part called Natick, that honored father John Pearce, deceased, bought of Major John Greene (half being given me in will of father and half given my brother Daniel).

II. DANIEL, m. (1) ——— m. (2) 1703, Dec. 13. ELIZABETH TUCKER,	b. d. 1731 + b. d. b. d. 1728 +	Portsmouth (Prudence Island), North Kingstown, R. I. of of Tucker.	1. Daniel, 1684, 2. Margaret, 1686, 3. Mary, 1689, 4. John, 1691, (2d wife.) 5. Benoni, 1704, 6. Nathan, 1706, 7. William, 1707,

See: American Genealogist, Jan, 1950, p. 57.

He was a butcher.

1692, Jun. 16. Freeman.

1694-95-97. Constable.

1696, Aug. 19. He was on a committee in regard to the Town Pound.

1698-1701-5-20-21-23-31. Deputy.

1699, Aug. 25. He was on a committee to make a rate.

1700. He bought 760 acres in Narragansett of Benjamin and Jonathan Viall and John Thomas, of Swanzey.

1706, Aug. 20. Juryman.

1707, Sep. 1. Assessor of ratable property.

1708-11. Justice of the Peace.

1708, Oct. His son Daniel was married to Patience Hill, daughter of Jonathan.

1720, Jun. 6. He was furnished with a law book by town of Portsmouth, and was chosen ratemaker.

1721. He and wife Elizabeth deeded to two sons Daniel Pearce, Jr. and John Pearce of Portsmouth, 400 acres in Aquidneset.

1723, Nov. 10. His son Benoni was married to Sarah Rhodes.

1723. North Kingstown. He and wife Elizabeth gave a deed of mortgage for £650, to Colonel Samuel Brown of Salem, on 350 acres, bounded partly by land of Lodowick Updike.

1724. Overseer of the Poor.

1724, Aug. 11. He made a deed of gift to the town of land, for a road from Fones Bridge to the sea, for a driftway for public use.

1724, Oct. 8. His son Nathan was married to Abigail Spink.

1726, Mar. 10. He and wife Elizabeth deeded 200 acres to his son Daniel of Prudence Island.

1726, Mar. 17. He and wife Elizabeth sold their farm of 433 acres in North Kingstown to Daniel and John Pearce of Prudence Island for £3,000.

1728, Jul. His son Daniel Pearce, Jr., and Patience his wife, of Prudence Island, gave bond to the town of North Kingstown to support his father and the latter's wife Elizabeth, and to furnish them the use of a horse.

III. MARY, m. (1) ROBERT HILL, m. (2) JAMES SWEET,	b. d. b. d. 1711 (—) b. 1657, May 28. d. 1725.	of Jonathan & Mary ( ) Hill. of James & Mary (Greene) Sweet.	1. Jonathan, 2. Robert, 3. Daniel, 4. William, 5. John, 6. Susannah, 7. Abigail, (By 2d husband, no issue.)

PEARCE (Richard).

RICHARD, m. SUSANNA WRIGHT,	b. d. 1678. b. d. 1678 (—)

of George Wright.

Portsmouth, R. I.

1654, Feb. 12. He was witness to a deed of land.

1657, Jun. 8. Surveyor of marks of cattle.

1658, May 18. Freeman.

1666, Mar. 16. He bought 2 acres, 7 rods, of Jacob Cole.

1669. He bought 14 acres of Joseph Parker.

1677, Apr. 22. Will—proved 1678, Oct. 28. Ex. son Richard. To son Richard, my now dwelling house, land, orchard, &c., pair of oxen, cart, plough, goods, &c. To sons John, Giles, James, William, George and Jeremiah, each 1s. and to my four daughters, 1s. each.

He calls Richard, his eldest son, but this does not agree with the birth as recorded.

I. MARTHA, m. [DYER. MAHERSHALLAI-HASHBAZ	b. 1645, Sep. 13. d. 1744, Feb. 24. b. d. 1670 (—)	of William & Mary ( ) Dyer.	
II. JOHN, m. MARY TALLMAN,	b. 1647, Sep. 8. d. 1707, Dec. 5. b. d. 1720,	Portsmouth, Tiverton, R. I. of Peter & Ann ( ) Tallman.	1. John, 2. Mary, 3. Susanna, 1672 ± 4. Anne, 1674, Feb. 14 5. Sarah, 6. Elizabeth, 7. Rachel, 8. Alice,

1669, Apr. 28. Freeman.

1681, Dec. 31. He bought of Thomas Manchester, Jr., and wife Mary, land in Pocasset, for £15.

1692, Mar. 2. Tiverton. He was an inhabitant at the organization of the town.

He held the office of ensign.

1707, Dec. 20. Inventory, £519, 3s., sworn to by widow Mary. House and lands £380, gun, cane, 2 bibles and other books, 5 beds, 6 cows, 2 oxen, 2 two years, 3 yearlings, 5 calves, 18 sheep, horsekind, swine, 21 barrels cider, 16 gallons rum, small negro girl £9.

1709, Aug. 3. Agreement between John Pearce, of Tiverton, John Read, Jr., of Freetown, and Mary his wife, Samuel Sherman, of Swanzey, and Sarah his wife, Thomas Cook, Jr., of Tiverton, and Elizabeth his wife, John Cook, son to John Cook, of Tiverton, and Rachel his wife, and Alice Pearce, all children of John Pearce, of Tiverton, deceased, who died intestate. To mother Mary, the first choice of her third of real and personal as law directs. To John Pearce, only son of deceased, the other two-thirds of real and personal, he paying at certain intervals as follows: To Mary Read, £10, Sarah Sherman, £16, Elizabeth Cook, £10, Rachel Cook, £22, Alice Hart, £27, and to children of two sisters who are dead.

1709, Sep. 7. An account by Mary Pearce of what estate her husband had given her children in his lifetime, viz: to Mary Reed, £9, 16s., Susanna Wodell, deceased, £16, Anne Sheffield, deceased, £21, 6s., 6d., Sarah Sherman, £12, 6s. 8d., Elizabeth Cook, £12, 16s, 2d., Rachel Cook, £3, 17s., John Pearce, only son, £1, 16s.

1718, Apr. 5. Will—proved 1720, Jan. 19. Widow Mary. Ex. son-in-law John Read, Jr. To eldest daughter Mary Read, £10, and mulatto girl "Margaret," already deeded. To daughter Alice Pearce, negro "Rose." To son John, 5s. To granddaughter Susannah Wilcox, £5. To granddaughter Susanna Butts, 1s. The negro girl "Experience," to be sold and money divided to five daughters, Mary Reed, Elizabeth Cook, Rachel Cook, Sarah Sherman and Alice Pearce. To daughters Elizabeth Cook, Rachel Cook, Sarah Sherman and Alice Pearce, rest of estate.

Inventory, £141, 11s., 1d.

III. RICHARD, m. EXPERIENCE,	b. 1649, Oct. 3. d. b. d. 1720, Jul. 17.	Portsmouth, Bristol, R. I. of	1. Jonathan, 2. Richard, 3. Abigail, 1690, Oct. 3. 4. Mary, 1693, Aug. 17. 5. Jeremiah, 1695, Aug. 29. 6. Anne, 1699, Feb. 11. 7. Benjamin, 1704, Jan. 11.

1669, Apr. 28. Freeman.

1691, Sep. 7. Bristol. He and wife Experience, sold William Burrington, of Portsmouth, for £48, two parcels of land, 63 acres with buildings, &c.

1696, Oct. 11. He and wife Experience, sold to Jeremiah Osborne, 10 acres for £30.
It is assumed that Jonathan Pearce, of Bristol (who had children by wife Elizabeth, from 1703), was a son of Richard².

IV. GILES, m. 1676, Apr. 13. ELIZABETH HALL,
b. 1651, Jul. 22. d. 1698, Nov. 19. — Portsmouth, East Greenwich, R. I.
b. d. 1698 + — of William & Mary ( ) Hall.

1. Jeremiah, 1678, Jan. 22.
2. Susanna, 1679, May 7.
3. Elizabeth, 1682, May 27.
4. John, 1687, Jan. 11.
5. Mary, 1690, Feb. 7.

1673, May 6. Freeman.
1673. Ear mark recorded.
1677, Oct. 31. He and forty-seven others were granted 5,000 acres to be called East Greenwich.
1690. East Greenwich. Deputy.
1690. Moderator of Town meeting. Member of Town Council same year.
1698, Nov 15. Will—proved 1698, Dec. 7. Exx. wife Elizabeth. To her while widow, the occupation and profit of house and land and orchard belonging thereto, till son John is of age, he then having half of profits, and the whole at wife's death. To eldest son Jeremiah, a house, 90 acres, &c., a pair of oxen, and three cows. To son John, all lands in East Greenwich undisposed of, a pair of oxen, and three cows, at age. To eldest daughter Susanna Pearce, a feather bed, £30, two cows, and a heifer, and after decease of wife to have negro girl "Frances." To daughter Elizabeth Pearce, a feather bed, £30, two cows, and a heifer. To daughter Mary Pearce, at eighteen, a feather bed, two cows and a heifer. To wife rest of personal.
Inventory, £167, 4*s*., viz: 4 oxen, 7 cows, heifer, 4 calves, 18 sheep, 8 lambs, horse, mare, 4 spinning wheels, 2 guns, carpenter's tools, negro girl, &c.

V. SUSANNA, m. 1673, Dec. 4. GEORGE BROWNELL,
b. 1652, Nov. 20. d. 1743, Dec. 24.
b. 1646. d. 1718, Apr. 20. — of Thomas & Ann ( ) Brownell.

1. Susanna, 1676, Jan. 25.
2. Sarah, 1681, Jun. 14.
3. Mary, 1683, Dec. 8.
4. Martha, 1686, Feb. 18.
5. Thomas, 1688, Jun. 1.
6. Joseph, 1690, Dec. 5.
7. Waite, 1693, Oct. 3.
8. Stephen, 1695, Dec. 3.

VI. MARY, m. THOMAS BROWNELL,
b. 1654, May 6. d. 1736, May 4.
b. d. 1732, May 18. — of Thomas & Ann ( ) Brownell.

1. Thomas, 1679, Feb. 16.
2. John, 1682, Feb. 21.
3. George, 1685, Jan. 19.
4. Jeremiah, 1689, Oct. 10.
5. Mary, 1692, Mar. 22.
6. Charles, 1694, Dec. 23.

VII. JEREMIAH, b. 1656, Nov. 17. d.

VIII. JAMES, b. 1658, Dec. 6. d.

IX. DAUGHTER, b. 1661, Jul. 7. d

X. GEORGE, m. (1) 1687, Apr. 7. ALICE HART, m. (2) 1721, Mar. 22. TEMPERANCE KIRBY,
b. 1662, Jul. 10. d. 1752, Aug. 30. — Little Compton, R. I.
b. 1664, Mar. 8. d. 1718, Mar. 11. — of Richard & Hannah ( ) Hart.
b. 1670, May 5. d. 1761, Feb. 5. — of Richard & Patience (Gifford) Kirby.

1. Susanna, 1688, Aug. 21.
2. James, 1691, Sep. 4.
3. Samuel, 1695, Feb. 3.
4. George, 1697, Mar. 2.
5. Mary, 1700, May 16.
(2d wife, no issue.)

1696, Jul. 4. He and wife Alice, sold his brother-in-law Richard Hart, of Portsmouth, 100 acres, buildings, &c., for £108.
1752, Jun. 26. Will—proved 1752. Exs. sons James and George. To wife Temperance, £100, and all household goods in house that she brought when I married her, and a good cow. To son James, £30. To son George, certain land and husbandry tools. To grandson George Thurston, £72. To daughter Mary Simmons, £60. To three children James and George Pearce, and Mary Simmons, the rest of household goods. To sons James and George, confirmation of deeds already made of most of my real estate. To these two sons rest of estate.
Inventory, £945, 11*s*., viz: wearing apparel, £90, bed, pewter, 3 wheels, cattle kind £150, sheep £7, cash and bonds £321, 19*s*. mill and press £5, geese, books £1, cheese, &c.

XI. WILLIAM, b. 1664, Dec. 22. d.

Weaver - See p. 12
Weaver genealogy by Lucius Weaver.
II Elmer²

PECKHAM.

JOHN, m. (1) MARY CLARKE, of ... m. (2) ELEANOR,
b. d. 1681 +
b. d. 1648 (—) — Clarke.
b. d.
Newport R. I.

1638, May 20. His name appears in a list of those who were admitted inhabitants of Newport after this date.
1640. His bounds were established: "a parcel of land containing 32 acres more or less, lying south-easterly upon Hambrook Mill, the east end thereof butting upon Stony River, bounded on the south with land of John Layton, on the north by Thomas Clarke's land, on the west by the way that goes to Sachem's Meadow," &c.
1641, Mar. 16. Freeman.
1648. He was one of the ten male members in full communion, of the First Baptist Church. The same year Eleanor Peckham was baptized.
1651, May 30. In a deed of this date from Joshua Coggeshall and mother Mary Coggeshall, to Walter Conigrave, the land is described as bounded "on land granted to Mary Clarke, now deceased, sometime the wife of John Peck-

See: American Genealogist v. 20. p. 84. (64) v. 24, p. 72.

I. JOHN, m. SARAH,
b. 1645 ± d. 1712 ± — Newport, R. I.
b. d. — of

1. Elizabeth, 1668, Sep. 17
2. John, 1673, Jun. 9.
3. Mary, 1674, Sep. 30.
4. Reuben, 1676, Feb. 3.
5. Peleg, 1677, Dec. 11.
6. Joseph, 1679, Mar. 8.
7. Sarah, 1680, Sep. 5.
8. Timothy, 1681, Aug. 5.
9. Benjamin, 1684, Jun. 9.
10. Isaac, 1688, Apr. 11.
11. Sarah, 1690, Jun. 26.

1668, Oct. 29. Freeman.
1670. The Assembly voted to allow £1, to "John Peckham, Jr., for the hire of his horse to go to Hartford with Mr. Torrey, and for Mr. Crandall's horse."
1671, Jun. 7. Juryman in case of two Indians imprisoned on criminal charges.
1677, Oct. 31. He and forty-seven others were granted a plantation of 5,000 acres to be called East Greenwich.
1677, Sep. 15. He sold Caleb Carr of Newport, 1-450 share of Conanicut Island (10 acres), and rights in township and Dutch Island for £7.
1680. Taxed 13*s*. 4*d*.
1688, Mar. 18. He bought 30 acres in Little Compton, of his brother James, for £14.
His son John moved to Little Compton, and Benjamin went to South Kingstown.

II. WILLIAM, m. (1) ——— CLARKE, m. (2) PHEBE WEEDEN,
b. 1647 ± d. 1734, Jun. 2. — Newport, R. I.
b. d. — of Joseph Clarke.
b. 1660 ± d. 1745. — of William Weeden.

1. William, 1675, Aug. 30.
(2d wife.)
2. Samuel,
3. Mary,
4. Phebe,
5. Deborah,

1684. Juryman.
1696-98. Deputy. In a little memorandum book he writes: "This is my book, it cost two shillings, I pray you look. Sept. the ninth, 1698."
1702, Jul. 13. He was granted a share of 18 acres, in a division of proprietors' lands.
1708, Mar. 3. He and others on behalf of the church, sold John Vaughan, for £18, "a house at Green End which was their meeting house."

ham." (The grant referred to was made previous to 1644.) Mary Clarke was perhaps the sister of Rev. John Clarke, as he had a sister of that name born 1607.

1655. Freeman.

His residence was in that part of Newport which afterwards became Middletown, and a stone marked I P (on land owned by William F. Peckham) is supposed to mark his grave.

1680. Taxed £1, 7*s.* 3*d.*

1681, Jan. 6. Will—witnesses John Clarke and Henry Tew. A reference to this will is found in a list of seventeen wills (between the dates of 1676 and 1695), that were presented to the Court in 1700, by parties interested, the law requiring three witnesses, and these wills having but two.

PECKHAM, 2d column. V. Clement, d. 1712. His widow Lydia d. 1712+. He was a weaver. 1712, Feb. 19. Will-proved 1712, Apr. 7. Ex. son Job. To wife Lydia, dwelling house, land, &c., while widow, and a cow, horse, feather bed, wool bed, &c. To son Job all right in Tiverton lands, rest of horses, cattle, &c., and a loom. VII. Sarah. She may have married John Greene, d. 1740, of John and Mary (Jefferay) Greene. Children, 1. John. 2. Sarah, 1695. 3. Henry. 4. William, 1707. 5. Mary, 1715, Nov. 9. If this is correct it may have been Sarah Peckham 3 (John 2, John 1), who married William Weeden.

1711, Nov. 15. Ordained as pastor of the First Baptist Church, by Samuel Luther of Swanzey, minister, and Samuel Bullock of Swanzey, deacon.
1726, Apr. 24. He with others signed a letter which was sent Rev. Joseph Crandall's church (Seventh Day Baptist) regarding some doctrinal differences.
1726, May 19. He ordained Rev. John Comer, as assistant pastor.
1730, Mar. 3. Mr. Comer notes in his diary: "This day I went to visit Elder Peckcom, who discoursed to my satisfaction about ye trouble and ye things of God."
1731, Oct. 13. Rev. John Callender was ordained as colleague, in place of Mr. Comer.
1734, Jul. 3. Will—proved. To son William, certain land. To son Samuel, my now dwelling house and land in Newport, bounded east by John Greene's land, south by the highway, &c. He mentions daughters Mary Thomas, Phebe Tripp and Deborah Clarke. His wife Phebe was to be supported by his sons William and Samuel.
1734, Sep. 24. Will—proved 1745. Widow Phebe, of Middletown. Exxs. daughters Mary Barker, Phebe Weeden and Deborah Clarke. To granddaughter Phebe, daughter of son Samuel, a silver spoon. To granddaughter Phebe Barker, little brass kettle and silver spoon. To granddaughter Deborah Barker, a silver spoon. To three daughters Mary Barker, Phebe Weeden and Deborah Clarke, all the rest of estate, half thereof to Deborah, and the other half to Mary and Phebe equally. Inventory, £165, 16*s.*

III. STEPHEN, { b. ; d. 1724, Apr. 23. — Newport, R. I., Dartmouth, Mass.
m. 1682 ±
MARY, { b. ; d. 1724 + — of

1. Stephen, 1683, Feb. 23.
2. Samuel, 1685, Aug. 17.
3. Eleanor, 1686, Jan. 12.
4. William, 1688, Oct. 27.
5. Mary, 1690, Aug. 17.
6. Hannah, 1691, Jan. 28.
7. John, 1697, Jan. 15.
8. Deborah, 1699, Jun. 18.
9. Joseph, 1701, Feb. 2.
10. Jean, 1703, Jan. 23.
11. Isaiah, 1705, Sep. 14.

1677, Oct. 31. He was among those to whom was granted 5,000 acres to be called East Greenwich.
1686, Mar. 24. Dartmouth. He took oath of fidelity.
1694, Nov. 13. He was one of those who had a confirmatory deed of Dartmouth from William Bradford.
1722, Dec. 1. Will—proved 1724, May 19. Exx. wife Mary. To her improvement of all lands and movable estate, while widow. To son Stephen, northerly part of homestead farm with housing. To son Samuel, middle part of homestead. To son William southerly part of homestead. To son John, the westerly end of homestead. To son Joseph, land and meadows at Coxet. To son Josiah, land. To five daughters Eleanor, Mary, Hannah, Deborah and Jean, all movables.
Inventory, £1,807, 5*s.*, viz: homestead £1,500, consisting of 255 acres, other lands, a mare, 2 pair of oxen, 8 cows, 4 heifers, 3 steers, 5 calves, ½ of a bull, 2 yearlings, 36 sheep, 12 swine, 3 turkeys, 2 ganders, 4 geese, 33 goslings, 15 fowls, 3 pigeons, hive of bees, carpenter's tools, feather beds, linen wheel, mouse trap, pewter, pair of worsted combs, cider mill, &c.

IV. THOMAS, { b. ; d. 1709. — Newport, R. I.
m. (1)
———, { b. ; d. — of
m. (2)
HANNAH CLARKE [Wm. (w. of { b. ; d. 1722 + — of William Weeden.
(She m. (3) Joseph Clarke.)

1. Thomas,
2. Philip,
3. Sarah,
(2d wife.)
4. Daniel,
5. James,

1677, Oct. 31. He was among those to whom was granted 5,000 acres to be called East Greenwich.
1680. Taxed 17*s.* 3*d.*
1702, Mar. 4. He was one of the proprietors in common lands.
1708. Deputy.
1708, May 21. Will—codicil 1708, Nov. 16.—proved 1709, Feb. 27. Ex. son Philip. To son Thomas, 1*s.*, he having already had. To daughter Sarah Underwood, £5. To son Daniel, a yoke and £30, at age. To son James, a square barrel gun, dwelling house and land adjoining. To sons Daniel and James, carpenter's tools. To son Philip, rest of land and housing. To wife, all my cash, and £3, yearly, with use of mare, cow and household goods. To said wife Hannah, the use of land and house given James. At death of wife all household goods, cow, mare, &c., to go to sons Daniel and James.
1709, Mar. 7. Daniel and James Peckham, sons of Thomas, chose their mother Hannah, as guardian.
1722, Mar. Joseph Clarke of Westerly, and Hannah his wife, late wife of Thomas Peckham, brought suit against Philip Peckham, for £3, annuity.
His son Daniel went to Westerly.

V. CLEMENT, { b. ; d. 1706 + — Newport, R. I.
m.
———, { b. ; d. — of

1. Job,

1702, Mar. 4. He was one of the proprietors in common lands.

VI. JAMES, { b. ; 1712, Feb. 26. — Newport, R. I.

1712, Mar. 10. An inventory of his Newport estate was shown, and his eldest surviving brother William Peckham, and Joseph Peckham, nephew to deceased, desired that administration might be granted to Thomas Peckham and William Weeden, Jr., both of Newport.
1712, Mar. 21. Inventory of the part of his real estate in Little Compton, £644, 9*s.* 6d., was shown by administrators William Peckham of Newport and Captain Thomas Gray of Little Compton. Included in the list was a lot of 100 acres, valued at £499, and several other pieces of land.
A power of attorney was given William and Philip Peckham and John Taylor, to sell real estate of deceased, signed by following as legal representatives: Eleanor Peckham, John Spooner, Rebecca Spooner, Isaac Peckham, Deborah Taylor, Thomas Gray, Phebe Gray, Peter Taylor, Elizabeth Taylor, Thomas Peckham, Stephen Peckham, Peter Barker, Susanna Barker, William Weeden, Sarah Weeden, John Underwood, Sarah Underwood, John Peckham, Daniel Peckham, Timothy Peckham.
In a sale made shortly after, Job Peckham's right was excepted,

VII. SARAH, { b. ; d.
m.
WILLIAM WEEDEN, { b. ; d. 1722 + — of William Weeden.

PECKHAM. 2d column. VII. Sarah, had 1. Mary. IX. Deborah. Her son John, b. 1694, not 1684.

VIII. REBECCA, { b. ; d.
m.
JOHN SPOONER, { b. ; d. 1734 + — of William & Elizabeth (Partridge) Spooner.

1. William, 1680, May 11.
2. Jonathan, 1681, Aug. 28.
3. Elizabeth, 1683, Jun. 19.
4. Eleanor, 1685, Feb. 1.
5. Phebe, 1687, May 11.
6. Nathan, 1689, Sep. 21.
7. Rebecca, 1691, Oct. 8.
8. Deborah, 1694, Aug. 10.
9. Barnabas, 1699, Feb. 6.

PECKHAM. 2d column. IX. Deborah. Erase children and give the right ones from Taylor page.

IX. DEBORAH, { b. ; d.
m.
ROBERT TAYLOR, { b. 1653, Oct. ; d. 1707, Jun. 12. — of Robert & Mary (Hodges) Taylor.

1. Mary, 1682, Oct. 25.
2. Anna, 1686, Sep.
3. Margaret, 1688, Jul.
4. Lydia, 1691, Apr.
5. John, 1684, Jan. 7.
6. Robert, 1695, Dec.
7. Philip, 1697, May 13.

X. PHEBE, { b. 1666. ; d. 1746.
m.
THOMAS GRAY, { b. ; d. 1721, Nov. 5. — of Edward & Dorothy (Lettice) Gray.

No issue.

XI. ELIZABETH, { b. ; d. 1714, May 24.
m.
PETER TAYLOR, { b. 1661, Jul. ; d. 1736. — of Robert & Mary (Hodges) Taylor.

1. Peter, 1697, Oct. 20.
2. Elizabeth, 1701, Jan. 4.
3. Mary, 1703, Dec. 20.

EDWARD[2], (Herbert[1]). b. d. 1730, Sep. 20.
m. 1682, Apr. 18.
FREELOVE ARNOLD, b. 1661, Jul. 20. d. 1711, Sep. 8.

of Benedict & Damaris (Westcott) Arnold.
Newport, R. I.

He was a shipwright.

1684. Freeman.

1688. Grand Jury.

1702, Mar. 4. He was a proprietor in the common lands.

1707. Deputy.

1711, Aug. 25. He and wife Freelove, deeded to daughter Elizabeth Goodson, wife of John, certain land.

1710, Jan. 7. Will—of wife Freelove (with consent of husband), proved 1732, May 3, against protest of son Edward. To son Edward, farm in Neck, called Lemmington. To son Thomas, certain land, wharf, warehouse, &c., and my stone windmill. To daughter Elizabeth, certain land, she maintaining the fence between her land and sister Penelope. To daughter Penelope, my now dwelling house, &c. To cousin Freelove, daughter of brother Oliver Arnold, a legacy.

1718, Mar. 25. He was presented for leaving his cellar open to the street, and summoned to appear.

1726. He quit claimed to son Thomas, on condition of annual payment of £30, all right and title present and future to all homestead, &c., in Newport, viz: mansion house, wharf, warehouse, shops, barn, windmill, &c.

See: American Genealogist, v.20, p. 64-65.

I. EDWARD, b. d. 1741. Newport, R. I.
m. 1718, Mar. 14.
ARABELLA WILLIAMS, b. d. of John & Ann (Alcock) Williams.

1. Hermione, 1718, Dec. 3.
2. Elizabeth, 1721, Oct. 20.
3. Penelope, 1724, May 23.

(She m. (2) 1741, Sep. 24, John Holman.)

1710, Sep. 5. He and his brother Thomas, were indicted for a seditious tumult and bound over in sum of £20 to next court.

1713, Oct. 24. Edward Pelham, Jr., and Thomas Pelham, of Newport, and Abigail, wife of said Thomas, sold for £1,000, land which was property of Herbert Pelham, father of said Captain Edward Pelham.

1717, May 15. He gave his man Harry his freedom.

1731, May. He brought suit against Peter Coggeshall and others for trespass and witholding land, with five shops and warehouse; said estate having been bequeathed by Benedict Arnold, to his daughter Freelove, who married 1682, Apr. 18, Captain Edward Pelham, father of plaintiff, and she having died 1711, Sep. 8, still possessed of land which by law of England, descends to plaintiff. In answer the defendant submitted will of Freelove Pelham, also deed of Edward Pelham, 1711, Aug. 25, of his courtesy in the estate to daughter Elizabeth Goodson. After much litigation it would appear that the plaintiff won his case.

1741, May 21. Will—proved 1741. To daughter Hermione, wife of John Bannister, he gave (after other bequests) 8 acres " with an old stone wind mill thereon standing."

His daughter Penelope, married subsequent to her father's death, Joseph Cowley (1741, Nov. 15).

II. THOMAS, b. d. 1727 (—) Newport, R. I.
m. 1713 (—)
ABIGAIL, b. d. 1727 + of

1. John.

He was a merchant.

1718. Mar. He was sued by Nathaniel Dyer, for £17, 5*s.*, 7*d.*, being for sundry parcels of butchers meat.

1720, Oct. He having a decree in the Court of Trials in his favor against Jahleel Brenton, the latter appealed therefrom to the Assembly.

1723, Nov. 4. He gave a receipt for £79, 1*s.* 3*d.*, for certain land sold.

172–. Will—He mentions wife Abigail, son John, not twenty-one, and sister Penelope Pelham. He speaks of lands in province of Massachusetts.

1727, Mar. 21. His widow and executrix Abigail, leased the upper mill field, and lower mill field, 12 acres in all.

III. ELIZABETH, b. d.
m. (1) 1711, Jun. 26.
JOHN GOODSON, b. d. of Goodson.
m. (2) 1719, Nov. 11.
PETER COGGESHALL, b. d. of Coggeshall.

VI. PENELOPE, b. d.

PELHAM. 2d column. VI. Penelope, should be IV.

PENDLETON. - See: American Genealogist, v.20, p. 65. v.21, p. 208

JAMES[2], (Bryan[1]). b. d. 1709, Nov. 29.
m. (1)
MARY, b. d. 1655, Nov. 7.
m. (2) 1656, Apr. 29.
HANNAH GOODENOW, b. d. 1709 +

of Edmund & Ann ( ) Goodenow.
Portsmouth, N. H., Westerly, R. I.

1674. Stonington.

1675, Apr. 18. He had his daughter Sarah baptized, and other children as follows: Eleanor (1679 Jul. 20), Dorothy (1686, Oct. 3).

1679, Sep. 17. Westerly. He took oath of allegiance.

1686, May 28. Justice of the Peace.

1687–88. Justice of Inferior Court of Common Pleas.

1703, Jan. 26. Agreement of surviving children of James Pendleton: They having a gift of land given us by our grandfather Brian Pendleton, to be divided amongst us after our father's decease, as by deed bearing date 1674, Aug. 31; and our brother Caleb, having built upon said land, we mutually agree for ourselves, with full consent of father James Pendleton, that our brother Caleb shall have his part of land (given us by grandfather Brian Pendleton) where he now is. Signed by Joseph Pendleton, Edmond Pendleton, Eleanor Pendleton, Dorothy Pendleton, Eleazer and Ann Brown, Patience Pendleton, Mary Pendleton. (The last two were probably wives respectively of Joseph and Edmond.)

1703, Feb. 9. Will—proved 1709, Dec. 21. Exx. wife Hannah, and son Caleb. Overseers, Rev. James Noyes, Stonington, and Captain James Babcock, Westerly. To son Joseph, part of neck of land on east side Pawcatuck River already deeded. To son Edmond, part of aforesaid neck already deeded him. To wife Hannah, for life, the other part of neck, and at her decease to son Caleb, and at Caleb's death, to said Caleb's eldest son. The farm and land where I dwell, given me by honored father Major Brian Pendleton, to go according to entail to children. Sons by present wife Hannah, viz: Joseph, Edmond and Caleb, to decide by lot which of them shall have now dwelling house, according to deed of gift of my father, and such one shall pay to my daughters Ann, Eleanor and Dorothy, a certain proportion, &c. To wife Hannah, half of dwelling house for life, and all cattle, and to her remaining

PENDLETON. 1st column. His 2d wife, b. 1639, Nov. 28, d 1726 +.

I. JAMES, b. 1650, Nov. 1. d. young.

PENDLETON. 2d column. II. Mary, m. (1) —— Cross, m. (2) 1685, May 25, Nicholas Mowry.

PENDLETON. 2d column. II. Mary m. (1) —— Britton; m. (2) Joseph Cross; m. (3) 1685, May 25, Nicholas Mowry — one child, viz., William Britton.

II. MARY, b. d.

III. HANNAH, b. d.

2d column. III. Hannah, m. 1697, Jan. 13, John Bush. V. Joseph, d. 1706, Sep. 18. His 2d wife was daughter of William and Rebecca (Avery) Potts. She m., 2d, Samuel Rogers. VI. Edmond. His 5th child was Dorothy. 1751 May 31. Receipts were given by Hannah Britton (not Button), widow of James Britton, of Dighton, Ms., Mary Pendleton, Oliver and Rebecca Steward, and John and Dorothy Jemison, VIII. Caleb. His wife was Elizabeth. His will should read to grandsons Caleb and Joshua Wilcox (not Babcock). X. Eleanor. She d. 1713, (—). Her husband d. 1713. Children, 1. Sarah, 1710, ±. XI. Dorothy. Change her husband's death to 1727, and erase all the children.

(2d WIFE.)

IV. BRYAN, b. 1659, Sep. 27. d. young.

V. JOSEPH, b. 1661, Dec. 29. d. 1706, Sep. Westerly, R. I.
m. (1) 1696, Jul. 8.
DEBORAH MINER, b. d. 1697, Sep. 8. of Ephraim & Hannah (Avery) Miner.
m. (2) 1700, Dec. 11.
PATIENCE POTTS, b. d. 1706 + of William Potts.

1. Deborah, 1697, Aug. 29.
(2d wife.)
2. Joseph, 1702, Mar. 3.
3. William, 1704, Mar. 23.
4. Joshua, 1706, Feb. 22.

1679, Sep. 17. He took oath of allegiance.

1702–3–5. Town Clerk.

1706, Sep. 17. Will—proved 1706, Oct. 10. Exx. wife Patience. Overseers, Captain James and Captain John Babcock. To wife Patience, a third of income of whole estate for life, and to bring up children, she having benefit of all estates (lands and movables) till they are of age. To eldest son Joseph, dwelling house and half homestead farm, and other half to son William, when they are of age. To youngest son Joshua, all other lands. To daughter Deborah, a mare in a month, and £30, at age, and son Joseph to pay her £10, within two years of his coming to his estate, and son William also to pay her £10, in same manner. To children, rest of estate equally.

Inventory, £155, 17*s.*, viz: 3 beds, 12 chairs, pewter, 2 wheels, gun, 2 oxen, 10 cows, 6 yearlings, 3 steers, a bull, 7 calves, 23 sheep, 9 geese, &c.

1706, Sep. 20. He was buried.

VI. EDMOND, b. 1664, Jun. 24. d. 1750. Westerly, R. I.
m.
MARY, b. d. of

1. Edmond,
2. Hannah, 1700 ±
3. Mary, 1702 ±
4. Rebecca,
5. Daughter,

1700. Jul. 28. He and his wife were admitted to the church at Stonington, and on same date his daughter Hannah was baptized (and Mary, 1702, Sep. 6).

1750, Apr. 30. Administration to son Edmond. Inventory, £1,375, 16*s*, viz: wearing apparel £19, 10*s.*, 2 old books 12*s.*, wheel, pewter, 5 geese, 8 swine, 4 cows, ox, 2 two years, yearling, note £40, &c. Receipts were given by Hannah Button, Mary Pendleton and Rececca Steward, daughters of deceased, and by John Jenneson.

part of household goods. To son Caleb, at death of wife, my husbandry tools. To wife's three daughters aforesaid, the household goods and stock at death of wife. To my two daughters Mary and Hannah, had by former wife, £5, each (testator's father Brian having given them considerable in town of Wells, Maine, and two-thirds of his household goods as in his will appears). Wife directed to give unto her daughters Eleanor and Dorothy, enough to make them equal with daughter Ann Brown, who after her marriage had cattle and household goods. By codicil he gave land to daughter Eleanor Pendleton, and whereas son Caleb's eldest son James was to have had at death of Caleb, this is revoked and Caleb's second son Caleb to have, and if he die, then third son Brian; and if son Caleb die without male issue living, then Caleb's second daughter Elizabeth to have, and if she die to next daughter, &c.

Inventory, £105, 16s. 2d., viz: a bed, 6 silver spoons, 2 silver cups, 4 pewter platters, several books £3, table linen, 2 guns, 2 oxen, 9 cows, 9 two year old, 7 yearlings, 7 calves, 39 sheep, horse, mare, sow, 2 shoats, &c.

1711, Apr. 11. An agreement of his children was made as to division of lands derived from their grandfather Bryan Pendleton, signed by the widow Hannah and Edmond and Caleb Pendleton, Eleazer Brown, William Walker and Nicholas Cottrell and their wives.

(His daughter Dorothy may not have been the mother of all the children of Nicholas Cottrell.)

VII. { Ann, m. 1693, Oct. 18. Eleazer Brown,
{ b. 1667, Nov. 12. d.
{ b. 1670, Aug. 4. d. 1734, Nov. 30. of Thomas & Mary (Newhall) Brown.

1. Jonathan, 1694, Jul. 12.
2. James, 1696, Jun. 1.
3. Eleazer, 1698, May 4.
4. Anna, 1700, Feb. 1.
5. Ebenezer, 1702, Jan. 28.
6. Mary, 1703, Nov. 28.
7. Hannah, 1705, Dec. 12.
8. Patience, 1707, Dec. 28.
9. Abigail, 1712, Feb. 3.
10. Ruth, 1714, Jun. 30.

VIII. { Caleb, m. ———
{ b. 1669, Aug. 8. d. 1746. **d. 1746, Mar. 19.** Westerly, R. I. **VIII. Caleb**
{ b. d. 1745 (—) of

1. James, 1690 ±
2. Sarah, 1693 ±
3. Hannah, 1695 ±
4. Caleb, 1697 ±
5. Elizabeth, 1699 ±
6. Brian, 1701 ±
7. Ann, 1703 ±
8. Read,
9. Susanna,
10. Ruth,

1693, Jul. 23. He had his son James baptized, and other children, as follows: Sarah (1693, Jul. 23), Hannah (1695, Jul. 7), Caleb (1697, Jun. 6), Elizabeth (1699, Jun. 25), Brian (1701, Jun. 15), Ann (1703, Aug. 22).

1745, Mar. 10. Will—proved 1746, Mar. 31. Ex. son-in-law Benoni Smith. To son James, 10s. To son Brian, 10s., both these sons having had already. To daughter Sarah Lanphere, £3. To daughter Anna Babcock, wife of Samuel, £5, she having more because testator was sick in her house. To daughters Elizabeth Brown, Susanna Wilcox, Ruth Smith and Read Saunders, 10s. each. To son-in-law Stephen Wilcox, money he owed me and gun he had. To sister Dorothy Cottrell, £3. To Thomas Hiscox, a teacher of gospel, £3. To grandson Benajah Pendleton, son of Caleb, 40s. To granddaughter Elizabeth Babcock, my biggest trunk. To granddaughter Hannah Smith, my cow and least trunk. To granddaughter Mary Saunders, bed and furniture. To grandson Nathaniel Babcock, £5. To grandsons Caleb and Joshua Babcock, five steel traps. To grandson William Smith, my gun. To granddaughter Anne Babcock, a silver spoon. To granddaughter Elizabeth Smith, a silver spoon. To son-in-law Benoni Smith, my wearing apparel and rest of estate.

Inventory, £147, 4s., viz: wearing apparel £42, 4s., silver buttons and buckles 11s., silver headed cane £1, steel traps £6, gun £10, cow £10, boat £33, money £28, 10s., &c.

IX. { Sarah,
{ b. d. young.

X. { Eleanor, m. William Walker,
{ b. d.
{ b. d. of Walker.

XI. { Dorothy, m. Nicholas Cottrell,
{ b d. 1747 +
{ b. d. 1716. of Nicholas Cottrell.

1. Nicholas,
2. Nathaniel,
3. Samuel,
4. Mary,
5. Dorothy,

PERRY.

{ Samuel[2], (Edward[1]). m. 1690, May 9. Mary Tucker,
{ b. 1664. d. 1716, Jul. 2.
{ b. 1668, Aug. 16. d. 1716 +

of Henry & Martha (   ) Tucker.

Sandwich, Mass., Newport, Kings Town, R. I.

1701. Kings Town. Freeman.

1709, Sep. 28 He bought 236 acres of the vacant lands in Narragansett, ordered sold by the Assembly.

1716, Jun. 16. Will—proved 1716, Jul. 16. Exx. wife Mary. Overseers, Jacob Mott, of Portsmouth, and John Tucker, of Dartmouth. (He dated the will while temporarily at Newport.) To wife Mary, all movables, two negro men Abraham and Dominic, with other servants, and thirds of estate as law directs for life, and at her decease the negro Abraham to go to eldest son James, and negro Domine to second son Edward. To eldest son James, homestead and mill with 146 acres and 170 acres also, bought of Benedict Arnold To second son Edward, 500 acres in Westerly. To third son Samuel, land in Lewis' Neck, 130 acres, and another piece of 50 acres. To fourth son Simeon 200 acres To youngest son Benjamin, 100 acres and other land. Other land to amount of several hundred acres given sons as they shall arrive at age, and until then to remain with their mother. To wife great room and half cellar for life.

Inventory, £730, 16s. 7d., viz: wearing apparel, 5 feather beds, flock bed, 3 beds for servants, 6 working cattle, 15 cows, 6 yearlings, a steer, bull, 6 calves, horse, 5 two year horses, yearling, 3 colts, 6 mares, pewter, carpenter's tools, a dozen silver spoons, 3 looms, 2 men slaves £130, cooper's tools, warming pan, &c.

The Friends' records say that he died at Samuel Holmes', at Newport, aged fifty-two years.

PERRY. 1st column. His widow d. 1725, +.
2d column. V. Benjamin He had a son Benjamin, and, perhaps three daughters.

PERRY. 2d column. 1. James. His wife Alice's father was James not John. III. Samuel. His wife d. 1756, Jun. 27. Additional births of children: 6. Edward, 1730, Jun. 15. 7. John, 1732, May 15. 8. Alice, 1734, Feb. 25. 9. Stephen, 1736, Jan. 6. 10. Sarah, 1738, Feb. 16. 11. Ruth, 1740, Jun. 17. 12. Susanna, 1742, Mar. 25. 13. Meribah, 1744, Aug. 18.

I. { James, m. (1) 1718, Nov. 11. Alice Easton, m. (2) 1733, Nov. 15. Anna Bennett,
{ b. d. 1774. South Kingstown, R. I.
{ b. 1695, Nov. 4. d. 1732, Feb. 7. of John & Miriam (Allen) Easton.
{ b. d. of Jonathan & Anne (   ) Bennett.

1. Mary, 1719, Oct. 25.
2. James, 1728, Oct. 27.
(2d wife)
3. Alice, 1736, Jul. 20.
4. Jonathan, 1738, Sep. 2.
5. Samuel, 1740, Feb. 24.

1744. Deputy.

1766, Oct. 3. Will—proved 1774, Sep. 21. Exx. wife Anna. To son James, 200 acres of homestead farm with a dwelling house and two mills thereon, also 170 acres of other land, the use of mustee servant Job, for eight years and then freed, and a copper kettle used for dyeing cloth. To son Jonathan, rest of homestead farm with a dwelling house, &c., a farm in Charlestown, 200 acres more in South Kingstown, and other land, use of negro Jacob, for six years, and Henry, for twenty years, who were then to be free. To him also servant Sarah and her two children and boy Daniel. To son Samuel, 372 acres, called Green Hill Farm, also 100 acres in Charlestown, with dwelling house, 200 acres more in South Kingstown, servant Peter for ten years, George for twenty years, servant Hannah, and child Mary. To grandson James, son of James, 200 acres in Charlestown, at age. To son-in-law Sylvester Robinson, mustee servant John till forty years of age and then free. To grandchildren John Potter, Jr., Mary Hazard, wife of Enoch, and William Potter, £150, in Bills of Public Credit equal to Spanish milled dollars at 6s., each. To daughter Alice Robinson, £150. To three sons James, Jonathan and Samuel, cattle and horses, except a cow and riding horse, and to them all farming and carpenter's tools. To wife Anna, riding horse, cow, three servants, all household goods, and ten bushels corn annually and residue of estate.

II. { Edward.
{ b. d.

III. { Samuel, m. 1718, Nov. 3. Susannah Hazard,
{ b. 1695, d. 1775, Dec. 21. Westerly, Charlestown, R. I.
{ b. 1699, Apr. 28. d. 1756, of Stephen & Elizabeth (Helme) Hazard.

1. Elizabeth, 1719, Nov. 3.
2. Mary, 1721, Jun. 10.
3. Samuel, 1723, Apr. 19.
4. Simeon, 1726, Mar. 31.
5. Hannah, 1728, Apr. 13.
6. Edward,
7. John,
8. Stephen,
9. Sarah,
10. Ruth,
11. Susanna,
12. Meribah,

1723, Apr. 30. Freeman.
1727. Town Council.
1739-40-41-42-46. Charlestown. Deputy.
1740, Sep. He and Governor Richard Ward were appointed Trustees to the Sachem Ninegret.
1744, May. He was appointed on a committee with Deputy Governor Joseph Whipple and four others, to determine what is ratable estate, and prepare a bill for same and present it to next session of Assembly.

1767, Nov. 6. Will—proved 1776, Jan. 1. Ex. son Simeon. To son Simeon part of homestead farm 153¼ acres, &c To son Edward, 130 acres of homestead. To son John, 112½ acres of homestead and apparel. To three sons Simeon, Edward and John, two hill lots, 300 acres. To son Stephen, farm in Hopkinton, 150 acres, and iron works, saw mill, fulling mill and smith tools, utensils for dyeing, shearing and pressing cloth, and negro boy Absalom. To daughters Elizabeth Babcock, Mary Dodge, Hannah Clarke, Sarah Babcock, Ruth Perry, Susanna Babcock and Meribah Perry, each a ninth of negroes, cattle, sheep, horses and household goods. To granddaughter Mary Perry, a ninth ten years after testator's decease. To granddaughter Alice Soule, a ninth at eighteen. To daughters, Ruth and Meribah Perry, use of three lower rooms in east part of my now dwelling house for five years, and said four sons to keep for each of them a cow and riding beast, and these two daughters to have use of old garden.

Inventory, £206, 19s. 4½d., viz: apparel, £12, desk, woolen wheel, walking staff, bible, churn, mare, &c.

IV. { Simeon,
{ b. d.

V. { Benjamin, m. 1729, Jul. 10. Elizabeth Hazard,
{ b. 1701 ± d. South Kingstown, R. I.
{ b. d. of Stephen & Elizabeth (Helme) Hazard.

1735, May 6. Freeman.

He should not be confounded with his uncle Benjamin, who married 1727, Oct. 11, Susannah Barber, and who was the ancestor of Commodore Oliver Hazard Perry.

PERRY. 2d column. V. Benjamin d. 1772. Children, 1. Benjamin. 2, Martha. 3, Hannah. 4, Dorcas. 5, Susannah. 6, Elizabeth. 7, Sarah. 8, Alice, 1772. Will-proved 1772, Dec. 11. He mentions wife Elizabeth, son Benjamin, and daughters Martha Babcock, Hannah Hazard, Dorcas Potter, Susannah, Elizabeth, Sarah, and Alice. To son Benjamin 100 acres, homestead farm.

ALEXANDER, b. d. 1687 (—)
m. b. d.
——
m. (2)
ABIGAIL SEWALL, b. 1650, Aug. 14. d. 1718 +
of Thomas Sewall.

New York, Kings Town, R. I.

1643. He was thus early at New Amsterdam (New York).

1651, Oct. 8. He had his son Jacob, baptized in the Dutch Church.

1652. Kings Town.

1663, Jul. 3. He and others of Narragansett desired to be under the protection of Connecticut.

1668, May 4. He and others of Wickford petitioned Connecticut authorities for protection of their jurisdiction, or that they might look elsewhere for government.

1679, Jul. 29. He and forty-one others of Narragansett signed a petition to the King praying that he "would put an end to these differences about the government thereof which hath been so fatal to the prosperity of the place; animosities still arising in peoples minds as they stand affected to this or that government."

1680. Taxed 1*s*. 6*d*.

1683. His daughter was married this year according to testimony of Henry Gardiner, given in 1738, who declares that fifty-five years ago Mr. Spear, a minister of the Church of England, preached at Richard Smith's house for a year and used to preach at Jireh Bull's, and "married Beriah Brown to his wife."

1687, Sep. 6. Widow Phenix, taxed 2*s*. ½*d*.

1698. At about this time his widow Abigail was allowed a certain sum by the town for care of her father Thomas Sewall, in his sickness.

1709, Jun. 3. His widow bought 163 acres with John Hyams, of the vacant lands in Narragansett, ordered sold by the Assembly.

1710, Jun. 30. His widow deeded to her grandson Charles Brown, 130 acres, whereupon a complaint was made to Town Council that she had conveyed her estate away and might become chargable to town, and she took a bond from her grandson (which she released in 1717).

1715, Mar. 25. His widow in testimony at this date, calls herself aged about sixty-five years.

1718, Aug. 30. His widow testified that Alexander Brown, was the eldest son living of Beriah Brown, deceased.

It is certain that Abigail was his child by second wife, and it seems probable that Alexander, was also by her.

The late Stephen Whitney Phenix, compiled a chart of this family, from which part of the foregoing is an abstract.

I. JACOB, b. 1651. d. 1727 + New York.
m. 1686, Jun. 4. [Wm.
ANNA BUCK, (w. of b. d. of Tielman & Magdalena ( ) Van Vleeck.

1. John,
2. Alexander,
3. Alexander,
4. Jacob,

1685, Nov. 2. He bought land near what is now Athens, N. Y.

1686, Jan. 11. He bought a house on the north side of Beaver street, where he lived until his death.

1686, Jun. 2. Member of the Dutch Church.

1687, Jan. 12. He had his son John, baptized in the Dutch Church at New York, and other children as follows: Alexander (1689, May 5); Alexander (1690, Dec. 5); Jacob (1694, Nov. 4).

1698. Freeman.

(2d WIFE).

II. ABIGAIL, b. d.
m. 1685 ±
BERIAH BROWN, b. d. 1717, Feb. of Brown.

1. Alexander,
2. Charles,
3. Mary,
4. Sarah,

III. ALEXANDER, b. d.
m. 1704, Oct. 29. [Isaac.
HESTER MONTAIGNE (w. of b. d. of Van Vorst.

1. Maria,
2. Hester,
3. Alexander,
4. Cornelia,
5. Hester,
6. Alexander,

At the time of his marriage he was called of New Albany.

1705, Apr. 18. He had his daughter Maria, baptized in the Dutch Church, at New York, and other children as follows: Hester (1707, Jun. 1); Alexander (1709, Apr. 3); Cornelia (1711, Sep. 9); Hester (1714, Jun. 13); Alexander (1716, Apr. 22).

PHETTEPLACE.

PHILIP, b. d. 1687 +
m. b. d.
——

Portsmouth, R. I.

The records of Portsmouth give but scanty items referring to him, but there seems no reason to doubt that he was the first ancestor of those bearing the name in Rhode Island.

1681, Jul. 30. He signed as witness to will of Philip Sherman.

1687, Mar. 22. He testified as witness to will of Philip Sherman.

I. SARAH, b. d. 1711, Dec. 8.
m. 1700, Sep. 10.
WILLIAM BURRINGTON, b. d. 1740, Apr. 12. of William & Jane ( ) Burrington.

1. Alice, 1701, Jun. 9.
2. William, 1705, Mar. 25.
3. Roger, 1710, May 7.

II. WALTER, b. d. 1753, Dec. 29. Providence, Glocester, R. I.
m. 1709, Aug. 4.
JOANNA MOWRY, b. d. 1750 (—) of Nathaniel & Joanna (Inman) Mowry.

1. Jonathan,
2. Job,
3. Philip,
4. Benjamin,
5. Sarah,
6. Mercy,
7. Mary,

1711, Mar. 22. He bought of John and Nicholas Lapham, of Dartmouth, 20 acres in Providence, for £8.

1713, Feb. 4. He bought of Malachi Rhodes, of Warwick, 30 acres in Providence, for £9.

1713, Jan. 16. Taxed 3*s*.

1714, Jan. 11. He sold John Mowry, Jr., 16 acres for £6, 8*s*.

1715, Sep. 12. He and wife Joanna, had a deed from her father Nathaniel Mowry, of a parcel of meadow for their use till their son Job was of age and then to said Job and his heirs.

1719, May 2. He sold Henry Mowry, 59 acres in north-west part of town near Westquadomset, being land where I dwell, with house, &c., for £100.

1731-36-45-46. Glocester. Deputy.

1746, Sep. 29. He and three other deputies dissented from the vote of Assembly for additional works at Fort George, giving several reasons for such dissent. They thought the Colony was not in condition to be at such an expense (£2,120), as was proposed, and the fort already was sufficient to withstand an attack of private men of war, while the works proposed would not be strong enough for a defence against the fleet of any sovereign prince. They deemed it wiser to keep the money in hands of Treasurer, till it be known in what place and manner we shall be attacked by the enemy.

1750, Jan. 9. Will—proved 1754, Jan. 15. Ex. son Jonathan. To son Job, land south-easterly from latter's dwelling house, and my mare. To son Philip, wearing apparel. To son Benjamin, small piece of land. The burial place to be forever reserved where late wife is buried. To son Jonathan, rest of land, house, barn, &c., he paying legacies. To daughter Sarah Eddy, £100. To daughter Mercy Phetteplace, £110, and £50 yearly for ten years. To son Jonathan, all money, bills, bonds and notes. To son-in-law Samuel Phetteplace, a piece of home-made cloth. To daughter Mary, my colt. To sons and daughters except Jonathan, rest of personal.

III. PHILIP, b. d. 1752. Kings Town, Providence, West Greenwich, R. I.
m.
ANN, b. d. of

1703. He gave 6*s*., toward building a Quaker meeting house to be set up at or near Mashapaug "which is to be a free house for the worship of the Lord God of Heaven and earth (that is) for all true worshippers who worship him in spirit and in truth."

1704, Jun. 9. He was a witness to will of Jonathan Marsh, of Jamestown.

1712, Mar. 25. Kings Town. He (of Narragansett) bought of Ebenezer Staples and wife Huldah, of Mendon, 50 acres in Providence, for £20.

1713, Feb. 4. Providence. He bought of Malachi Rhodes, of Warwick, 30 acres in Providence, for £9.

1713, Mar. 20. He sold John Mowry, Jr., 16 acres for £4.

1730, Jan. 1. He sold Benjamin Hearnden, son of Benjamin, deceased, 30 acres for £1.

1752, Apr. 13. Will—proved. Exx. wife Ann. To wife, all lands while widow. To son-in-law John Partelow, the lands at death of wife. To daughters-in-law Mary and Lucy Partelow, all personal estate.

Inventory, £185, 6s., viz: house and furniture £35, wearing apparel £9, 10s., 2 cross cut saws £15, pewter, iron and woodware, beds, 4,000 shingles £20, 1,000 feet boards £15, &c.

IV. SAMUEL, b. ; d. 1762 + — Portsmouth, R. I.
m. 1713, Nov. 3.
ABIGAIL HAMMOND, b. ; d. 1762 + — of Hammond.

1. Sarah, 1714, Nov. 9.
2. Jonathan, 1716, Jul. 28.
3. Abigail, 1720, May 17.
4. Rachel, 1723, Jul. 12.
5. John, 1726, Feb. 17.
6. George, 1728, May 2.
7. Samuel, 1730, Jun. 10.
8. Benjamin, 1732, May 25.
9. Rebecca, 1734, Oct. 5.

He was a fellmonger, and also calls himself skinner.

1722, May 1. Freeman.

1739, Sep. 24. He sold to John Wing, 10 acres at a place called Great Field, for £300.

1762, Oct. 23. He and wife Abigail, sold to Jonathan Phetteplace, for £600, a gore of 8 rods with house and shop in Portsmouth.

Perhaps he moved to Newport, where his son Jonathan was living in 1767, and sold in that year (1767, Jul. 27), the same gore and shop that he had received by deed from his father.

PHILLIPS.

MICHAEL, b. ; d. 1689 (—)
m.
BARBARA, b. ; d. 1706 +

(She m. (2) Edward Inman.)

Newport, R. I.

1668. Freeman.

1686, Aug. 17. His widow's husband, Edward Inman, deeded her daughter's husband Joshua Clarke, 66 acres ten miles north of Providence, for good respect, &c.

1689, May 22. His widow joined with her second husband Edward Inman, in a deed of gift of certain land situated on Pawtucket River (ten miles north of Providence) to her sons John, James and Richard Phillips.

1706, Aug. 26. His widow, who was now the widow also of her second husband Edward Inman, declined administration on latter's estate.

Possibly he had another son, viz: Thomas Phillips of Newport, who had wife Mercy, and a daughter Elizabeth born 1685, Dec. 5.

No relationship is known to exist between Michael Phillips and Samuel, who died 1736, Mar. 30, in his eighty-first year, and was buried in the Episcopal Cemetery at North Kingstown.

I. JOHN, b. ; d. — Newport, R. I.
m.
REBECCA, b. ; d. — of

1. Barbara, 1687, Mar. 15.
2. John,
3. Michael,
4. Benjamin,
5. William,
6. Samuel,

1696. Freeman.

1730, Mar. 25. The names of his children are learned from an indenture of this date, wherein Michael Phillips of North Kingstown, was given power of attorney to dispose of lands in Warwick, which had belonged to his brother John Phillips of Newport, glover, deceased. The heirs signing were Ruth Phillips, widow of John, Isaac Peckham, Benjamin Phillips, weaver, William Phillips, house carpenter, and Samuel Phillips, all of Newport.

II. WILLIAM, b. ; d. — Newport, R. I.
m.
CHRISTIANA BARKER, b. ; d. — of James & Barbara (Dungan) Barker.

1696. Freeman.

III. JAMES, b. ; d. 1746, Dec. 12. — Providence, Smithfield, R. I.
m. (1)
MARY MOWRY, b. ; d. — of John & Mary ( ) Mowry.
m. (2) 1728, Nov. 25.
ELIZABETH FOSTER, b. ; d. 1747 + — of Foster.

1. Michael,
2. John,
3. Jeremiah,
4. Joshua,
5. Samuel,
6. Mary,
7. Phebe,
8. Elizabeth,
(2d wife.)
9. Charles,

1688, Aug. His name was in a list of one hundred and seventy-two persons over the age of sixteen and taxable.

1713, Jun. 16. Taxed 8s.

1721, Sep. 8. His son John died, administration being given to brother Michael.

1733, Sep. 7. Smithfield. He deeded son Jeremiah 30 acres given by father-in-law John Mowry, deceased, and bounded partly by land that belonged to father-in-law (*i. e.* stepfather) Edward Inman, deceased.

1743, Aug. 19. He deeded son Joshua, for love, &c., quarter of land where my house stands.

1747, Jan. 17. Administration was refused by widow Elizabeth, and then given to Michael Phillips, eldest son of deceased.

Inventory, bills of credit £188, pewter, 2 old wheels, 2 old swords and daggers, 8 fowls, 2 small swine, calf, mare, &c.

1748, Aug. 15. The administrator presented receipts of his brothers and sisters to the Town Council. The receipts were from Mary Stafford, Samuel Phillips, Joshua Phillips, Jeremiah Phillips, John Ballou, Jr., Phebe Thornton, wife of Thomas Thornton, and from the widow Elizabeth, for herself and her son Charles Phillips. The widow calls Michael her son-in-law (*i. e.* stepson).

IV. RICHARD, b. 1667. ; d. 1747, Dec. 13. — Providence, Smithfield, R. I.
m.
SARAH MOWRY, b. ; d. — of Nathaniel & Joanna (Inman) Mowry.

1. John,
2. William,
3. Richard,
4. Mercy,
5. Ruth,

1688, Aug. His name was in the list of taxable persons.

1703, Jan. 23. He bought of John Sayles his dwelling house, barn, &c., at Mashapauge, with his lands there, for £100.

1713, Jun. 16. Taxed 16s.

1717, Jun. 1. He testified as to certain land, calling himself aged about fifty years.

1727, Apr. 8. He and wife Sarah deeded to son John, south half of homestead farm with dwelling house, &c., and on same date to son William, the north half of homestead with dwelling house, orchard, &c.

1747, Jun. 3. Will—proved 1748, Mar. 21. Ex. son John. To son John, all estate.

Inventory, £100, ± viz: bed, warming pan, pewter, wearing apparel, 2 tables, 3 chairs, &c.

V. JOSEPH, b. ; d. 1719, Sep. 3. — Providence, R. I.
m.
ELIZABETH MALAVERY, b. ; d. 1719 + — of John & Elizabeth ( ) Malavery.

1. John,
2. Joseph,
3. David,
4. Daniel,
5. Elizabeth,
6. Phebe,
7. Jeremiah,

1688, Aug. His name was in the list of taxable persons.

1713, Jun. 16. Taxed 6s.

1719, Aug. 21. Will—proved 1719, Oct. 5. Exx. wife Elizabeth. To her, all housing and lands where I dwell, for life. To son Joseph, cow and what he had from land of deceased brother John. To son David, 3 acres and a cow. To son Daniel, a cow. To daughters Elizabeth and Phebe, a cow each. To son Jeremiah, after wife's decease, house, &c.

Inventory, £105, 5s, viz: warming pan, sword, belt, gun, pewter, feathers, flax, spinning wheel, mare, yearling colt, 5 cows, 2 yearlings, 2 calves, &c.

VI. ALICE, b. ; d. 1702 +
m.
JOSHUA CLARKE, b. ; d. 1702 + — of Joseph Clarke.

PIERCE. 2d column. VI. Michael, m. (1) Judith. Children, 1. Ephraim, 1712, Nov. 9. 2. Wheeler, 1714, Jul. 11; m. (2) 1719, Oct. 15, Mary Wood. Children, 3. Sarah, 1720, Sep. 13. 4. Mary, 1721, Oct. 26. 5. Phebe, 1723, Feb. 16. 6. Elizabeth, 1725, Apr. 7. 7. Michael, 1728, Sep. 25. 8. Freelove, 1730, Feb. 5. 9. Bethiah. VII. John, of Swanzey, Mass., d. 1750. 1738, Jun. 28. Will—proved 1750, Nov. 6. He mentions wife Patience, sons Miall, John, Jonathan, Clother, Samuel, daughters Ruth Cornell, Jael Chase, Mary Norton.

EPHRAIM[2] (Michael[1]), b. d. 1719, Sep. 14.
m.
HANNAH HOLBROOK, b. d. 1719 +
of John & Elizabeth ( ) Holbrook.

Rehoboth, Mass., Providence, Warwick, R. I.

1677, Mar. 9. Providence. He bought of Valentine and Mary Whitman, 60 acres for £15.

1685, Oct. 12. He bought of Abraham Mann, for £5, a half right of commoning in right of Abraham's father William Mann, deceased, which fell to Abraham by last will of his father.

1688. Constable.

1691, Oct. 12. He and his wife having had a difference, he gave notice to all persons not to buy or sell or have any trading with her, upon their peril. He had sometime before been "over persuaded" to sign an instrument concerning the ordering of his estate wherein it is by some conceded that the power of disposition of the estate lies in my said wife.

1693, Jan. 20. Rehoboth. He and wife Hannah, sold Thomas Mann, the housing, barn, and farm they had sometime lived on in Providence, with orchard, meadow, &c.

1698, Feb. 1. Swanzey. He and wife Hannah, sold Simon Davis, of Bristol, 16 acres for £24, 3s.

1718, Jul. 18. Will—proved 1719, Sep. 28. Ex. son Azrikim. To wife Hannah, £50, a feather bed, best room in dwelling house, garden, nine apple trees, an acre of land, clear profit of a cow, a sufficiency of firewood, and half profits of household goods. To son Ephraim, £20 and a cow, having already given him sufficient. To son Michael, £30, a cow and half of apparel. To daughters Rachel Peet, Hannah Martin and Experience Wheaton, £30, each. To son John, a cow and half wearing apparel. To grandchild Ruth Pierce, great iron skillet. To son Azrikim, rest of lands, tenements, goods and chattels.

Inventory, £198, 5s., viz: wearing apparel £6, 6 chairs, 2 tables, 2 books 12s., pair of oxen, pair of steers, 5 cows, 2 heifers, yearling bull, mare, 18 small cheeses, negro woman and child £50, bond from Samuel Wheaton £20, &c.

I. AZRIKIM, b. 1672, Jan. 4, d. Rehoboth, Mass.
m. (1) 1696, Dec. 31.
SARAH HAYWARD, b. 1676, Mar. 2. d. 1712, Aug. 12. of William & Sarah ( ) Hayward.
m. (2) 1713, May 29.
ELIZABETH ESTEN, b. 1683, Apr. 8. d. 1718, Aug. 18 of Henry & Elizabeth (Manton) Esten.

Children: 1. Azrikim, 1697, Dec. 3. 2. Samuel, 3. Benjamin, 4. Sarah, 1707, Oct. 2. (2d wife.) 5. Joseph, 1714, Apr. 7. 6. Hopestill, 1716, Aug. 14. 7. Elizabeth, 1716, Aug. 14. 8. Tabitha, 1717, Aug. 27.

II. EPHRAIM, b. d.

III. RACHEL, b. d.
m.
——— PEET, b. d. of Peet.

III. Rachel b. 1676; d. 1756, Nov. 12; m. Samuel Peck, b. 1672, Oct. 11; d. 1736, June 9, of Joseph. Children, 1, Hannah, 1697, July 21. 2, Elizabeth, 1700, June 5. 3, Benjamin, 1702, May 26. 4, Rachel, 1704, Sep. 12. 5, Samuel, 1706, Dec. 2. 6, Abiezer, 1714, Apr. 21.

IV. HANNAH, b. d.
m.
——— MARTIN, b. d. of Martin.

IV. Hannah m. John Martin, of John. Children, 1, John, 1703, May 14. 2, Mary, 1705, Jan. 7. 3, Thomas, 1707, Aug. 18

V. EXPERIENCE, b. d.
m.
——— WHEATON, b. d. of Wheaton.

V. Experience m. 1709, Oct. 24, Samuel Wheaton, b. 1683, July 21, of Samuel and Elizabeth (Wood) Wheaton. Children, 1, Elizabeth, 1710, Oct. 30. 2, Samuel, 1714, Nov. 8. 3, Sarah, 1716, Aug. 19. 4, Samuel, 1718, Dec. 31. 5, Levi, 1722, June 25.

See: American Genealogist, v 36, p. 56

VI. MICHAEL, b. 1698, Apr. 24. d. 1764.
m.
MARY, b. d. 1748 + of

VI. Michael m. (1) 1711, Nov. 26, Joanna Rounds. His 2d wife (Mary Wood) was daughter of John and Bethia (Mason) Wood.

Children: 1. Michael, 2. Mary, 3. Phebe, 4. Elizabeth, 5. Freelove, 6. Bethiah,

1748, Aug. 22. Will—proved 1764, Jan. 3. Ex. son Michael. To wife Mary, a third of real and personal while widow. To daughters Mary Manchester, Phebe, Elizabeth, Freelove and Bethiah Pierce, £30, each, and a cow each, to all but Mary, the unmarried daughters having privilege to dwell in house. To son Michael, the homestead farm and stock of farming tools.

Inventory, £130, 3s. 1½d., viz: wearing apparel, linen hand wheel, foot wheel, woolen wheel, 2 churns, pewter, 5 loads of hay, 20 sheep, 2 cows, heifer, pigs, yearling steer, silver sleeve button, and buckles, &c.

VII. JOHN, b. d.

2d column. I. Azrikim. His 1st wife's mother was Sarah Butterworth. II. Ephraim b. 1674±; d. 1772, Glocester, R. I.; m. Mary Low, of John and Mary (Rhodes) Low. Children, 1, Mial, 1693, Apr. 24. 2, Mary, 1697, Nov. 16. 3, David, 1701, July 26. 4, Elizabeth, 1703, May 30. 5, Ruth, 1708. 6, Ephraim, 1769, Apr. 29. Will-proved 1772, May 15. Exs. James Brown of Swanzey, and Barnet Eddy of Providence. He mentions daughters Elizabeth Eddy, widow, of Providence; and Ruth Brown, wife of James, of Swanzey; son Ephraim and Mary his wife; granddaughters Mary Thomas and Desire Pierce.

PIERCE. 1st column. His wife's mother was Sarah (not Elizabeth). He had a daughter Elizabeth b. 1678; d. 1679.

PIKE.

ROBERT, b. d. 1674 ±
m.
CATHARINE, b. d. 1679 +

Providence, R. I.

1645. He was of Providence thus early.

1646, Jan. 19. He was one of those who had a grant of 25 acres on certain conditions. (Some of those who signed above agreement did so at a later date than 1646.)

1654, Mar. 19. He had 5 acres laid out of low lands on south side of West River to make meadow, bounded on the west end with a black oak marked on four sides and on the east end by the grape vine.

1655, Nov. 3. Our neighbor Pike having divers times applied himself with complaints to town for relief in this his sad condition of his wife's distraction—the Town Treasurer was authorized to pay him 50s. and upon his further want or complaint, to amount of £10 or more promised him by town.

1658, May 18. Freeman.

1662, Mar. 7. He was given leave to exchange his meadow lying by the West River, for land in the Neck.

1665, Feb. 19. He had lot 52 in a division of lands.

1673, May 6. Robert Pike and his daughter Hannah Ballou, had two lots laid out together, taking in part of a field that hath been planted by the Indians, situated beyond Loquasqusset measuring 160 by 120 poles.

1675. His widow had a legacy from will of her late husband's sister Justina Patten, widow of Nathaniel, of Dorchester.

1679, Jul. 1. Widow Ballou and her mother were taxed together 1s. 10½d.

1686, Mar. 1. An agreement was made for division of lands by heirs of Robert Pike and Maturin Ballou, both deceased, they having left some estate in housing and lands and having left no will. The agreement was signed by Hannah Ballou, widow of Maturin and daughter of Robert Pike, John Ballou, eldest son, and James, Peter and Hannah Ballou, the other children of Maturin.

I. HANNAH, b. d. 1714 ±
m.
MATURIN BALLOU, b. d. 1662 ± of Ballou.

Children: 1. John, 2. James, 1652. 3. Peter, 1663. 4. Hannah, 5. Samuel,

PINDER.

JACOB, b. d.
m.
———, b. d.

Newport, Kings Town, R. I.

1680. Taxed 3s.

1687, Sep. 6. Kings Town. Taxed 2s. 2d.

I. JOHN, b. d. Kings Town, R. I.
m.
SUSANNA NORTHUP, b. d. of Henry & Mary ( ) Northup.

1719, Aug. 27. He testified that his honoured father Jacob Pinder and John Thomas, hired a farm of James and Daniel Updike.

II. ANN, b. d.
m.
WILLIAM COLE, b. 1671, Jul. 13. d. 1734. of John & Susanna (Hutchinson) Cole.

Children: 1. John, 2. Mary, 3. Samuel, 4. William, 5. Joseph, 6. Benjamin, 7. Wignall, 8. Ann, 9. Hannah, 10. Susannah,

ENOCH, b. 1631.
m. 1657, Nov. 5. d. 1695.
SARAH, b.
d. 1695 +

Dorchester, Mass., Kings Town, R. I.

1657, Nov. 5. Dorchester. He was married there.

1663, Jul. 3. Kings Town. He and others of Narragansett, desired to be under protection of Connecticut.

1664, May 5. He was ordered released from prison on giving bonds for £100, to appear and speak further to matter concerning Timothy Mather, whom he accused of speaking words of a very dishonorable nature against his majesty.

1671, May 19. He took oath of allegiance to Rhode Island.

1687, Sep. 6. Taxed 10*s.* 4*d.*

1688. Grand Jury.

1693, Oct. 1. Under this date Daniel Gould records in his Journal: "I went over the water in a canoe, with old Place to Canonicut."

1695, May 31. Will—proved 1695, Sep. 11. Exx. wife Sarah. Overseers, Thomas Mumford and Josiah Arnold. He calls himself aged sixty-four years. To wife Sarah, whole estate, real and personal, for life, for support in old age. To youngest son Joseph, at decease of wife, my dwelling house and 100 acres, about half a mile west of Sugar House Hill, and he then to be executor. If Joseph die without issue, the said house and land to go to the eldest of the male heirs of the Places of my issue. All movables in wife's possession at her death to go equally to sons and daughters, viz: Enoch, Peter, Thomas and Joseph Place and Sarah Cook.

Inventory, £17, 19*s.*, viz: cow, heifer, 2 yearlings, calf, 4 sheep, 2 or 3 lambs, pewter, iron, &c.

PLACE. 2d column. IV. Joseph. His wife was Joanna Place, of John and Sarah. 1703, Jan. 21. Deed of this date at Boston, shows that Joanna, daughter of John and Sarah Place of Boston, married Joseph Place of Kings Town, R. I. (This John Place was son of Peter of Boston, who came in ship Freelove in 1635, aged 20).

I. ENOCH, b. Kings Town, R. I.
m. d. 1708.
MARY SWEET, b. 1660, Feb. 2.
d. 1746. of James & Mary (Greene) Sweet.

(She m. (2) 1707, May 23, Samuel Wickham.)

1687, Sep. 6. Taxed 3*s.* 1*d.*

1695, Mar. 19. He and wife Mary sold for £65, to Jonathan Knight of Warwick, all rights in Mashantatack.

1702. Will—proved 1703, Dec. 13. Exx. wife Mary. To cousin Mercy Westcott, a cow. To wife Mary and daughter Mary, rest of estate.

After the death of Samuel Wickham, the widow having the inventory of her first husband inventoried with her second husband's estate, notwithstanding last will of Enoch Place gave half his real and personal estate to his daughter Mary, it was ordered by Town Council that a guardian be appointed for the orphan, that no wrong may be done her.

1738, Jun. 17. Will—proved 1746, Jan. 15. Widow Mary Wickham, South Kingstown. Ex. son-in-law George Hazard. To daughter Mary Hazard, whole profit and income of all my estate real and personal for life (except legacies), and at her death to grandson Benjamin Hazard one half the farm given me by my husband Enoch Place's will, being in North Kingstown. To said grandson, also other land in North Kingstown, purchased of my brother Samuel Sweet, deceased, another lot of 40 acres, and a silver spoon. To grandson Simeon Hazard, 40 acres in North Kingstown, which I purchased of my son-in-law (*i. e.* stepson) Samuel Wickham of Newport, also a silver spoon. To grandson George Place Hazard, £100, at age, and a silver cup. To grandson Enoch Hazard, £100, at age and a silver spoon. To granddaughter Mary Hazard, £140, at age, a feather bed, silver porringer, two silver spoons, pewter platter, &c. To granddaughter Susannah Hazard, £120, at age, a feather bed, two silver spoons, silver cup, &c. To daughter Mary Hazard, rest of estate.

Inventory, £622, 13*s.*

1. Mary, 1697, Oct. 16.

II. PETER, b. Providence, Glocester, R. I.
m. (1) 1685, Dec. 24. d. 1735, Jul. 6.
SARAH STEERE, b.
d. of John & Hannah (Wickenden) Steere.
m. (2) [ow. b.
MARY BOWDITCH, (wid- d. 1740, May 25. of

He was a cooper.

1682, Mar. 13. He desired a grant from the town of 40 feet square, above high water mark, by the water side, adjoining land of his master Thomas Harris.

1687, Sep. 1. Taxed 2*s.*

1713, May 17. He deeded son Joseph, for love, &c., half of farm where I dwell.

1713, Jun. 16. Taxed 16*s.* 6*d.*

1714, May 15. He deeded son Nathan for love, &c., 74½ acres.

He was pastor of the Baptist Church of Smithfield for some years, that organization including at first much territory outside of that town.

1733, Aug. 27. Will—codicil, 1734, Aug. 19.—proved 1735. Ex. son-in-law Thomas Shippee of Smithfield. To grandson Peter, son of Joseph, 29 acres. To son Joseph, certain land. The homestead to be sold and proceeds divided equally to children, except son Nathan, who was to have half as much as others, because he had already had part of his portion. The movable estate to be divided equally to children, except Nathan, who was to have half as much as others. The codicil mentions that he had lately married, and to wife Mary he gives all estate she brought and best room for life while widow, and she to be provided for by executor.

Inventory, £847, 19*s.* 9*d.*, personal property, viz: books, hour glass, cooper's tools, 2 pair of cards, pewter, churn, bonds £650, 13*s.* 3*d.*, 4 cows, 2 calves, 5 sheep, 2 swine, &c. Real estate £500.

1740, May 25 Will—proved 1740, May 31. Widow Mary Place of Smithfield. Ex. John Winsor. She mentions sons Joseph and Moses Bowditch, daughters Mary Davis, Mercy Phillips, Patience Aswine, Hope Walling, Catharine Latham, and granddaughter Mary Bowditch.

1. Sarah, 1686, Nov. 12.
2. Nathan, 1688, Nov. 4.
3. Joseph, 1691, May 18.
4. Hannah, 1693, Aug. 6.
5. Aminette, 1695, Sep. 16.
6. Dinah, 1697, Feb. 10.
7. Ruth, 1700, Oct. 7.
8. Penelope, 1706, Jun. 27.

III. THOMAS, b. 1663 North Kingstown, R. I
m. d. 1727.
HANNAH COLE, b.
d. of John & Susanna (Hutchinson) Cole.

1709, May 28. Kings Town. He and three others bought 275 acres of the vacant lands in Narragansett.

1727, Aug. 30. North Kingstown. He, calling himself sixty-four years old or thereabouts, testified as to land of Stephen Northup.

1727, Nov. 20. Will—proved. Exs. wife Hannah and son Thomas. To wife, all household goods. To son Thomas, my dwelling house, land, &c. To son Enoch, 88 acres. To son Samuel, land. To daughter Marbury Stafford, £5. To daughter Ann Place, a cow, mare, and £3. To three sons, rest of estate real and personal, they taking care of my wife Hannah.

1. Mary, 169–, Jan. 5.
2. Marbury, 169–, May 5.
3. Thomas, 169–, Nov. 2.
4. John, 170–, Apr. 24.
5. Sarah, 170–, May 10.
6. Joseph, 170–, Dec. 22.
7. Samuel, 170–, Sep.
8. Enoch,
9. Ann,

IV. JOSEPH, b. Kings Town, R. I.
m. 1698, Nov. 9. d.
JOANNA, b.
d. of

1687, Sep. 6. Taxed 1*s.*

1. Son, 1700, Jan. 9.
2. Enoch, 1701, Apr. 12.
3. Daughter, 1706,
4. Hannah, 1709, Sep.
5. Peter, 1714, Jul.

V. SARAH, b.
m. (1) d. 1747.
GEORGE COOK, b.
d. 1704. of Cook.
m. (2) 1705, Jun. 19. b.
DANIEL MACOONE, d. 1746. of John Macoone.

1. Sarah,
2. Phebe,

(By 2d husband.)

3. Hannah, 1706, May 18.
4. Abigail, 1707, Dec. 14.
5. Thankful, 1710, Dec. 17.

POCOCKE.

JOHN, b.
m. 1677 ± d.
MARY ALMY, (w. of John.) b.
d.

of James & Mary ( ) Cole.

Newport, R. I.

1677, Jun. 28. Mary Pococke, formerly wife of John Almy, acknowledged a deed that she and her former husband had made in 1675.

1680. Taxed 12*s.*

1682-83-84-85-90-98-99-1700-1-2. Attorney General.

1684. General Solicitor.

POMEROY.

ORPHEUS, b.
m. d. 1683.
MARY, b.
d. 1683 +

Portsmouth, R. I.

1683, Mar. 13. Will—proved 1683, Jul. 10. Exx. wife Mary. To her, all real and personal except legacy. To Nicholas Whitford of Portsmouth, loom, &c.

John, m. (1) [ow. **Margaret Odding**, (wid- m. (2) [vorcee of George. **Herodias Gardiner**, (di- { b. d. 1674 + { b. d. { b. d. of Long. Boston, Mass., Portsmouth, Kings Town, R. I.	**I.** **Hannah**, m. **Samuel Wilbur**, { b. d. 1722, Apr. 6. { b. d. 1679 ± of Samuel & Ann ( ) Wilbur.	1. **Abigail**, 2. **Hannah**, 3. **John**, 4. **Elizabeth**, 1665, 5. **Mary**, 6. **Rebecca**,

1633, Nov. 5. Freeman.

He and his wife Margaret were members of the church.

He was first at Roxbury but soon went to Boston.

1637, Nov. 20. He and others were ordered to deliver up all guns, pistols, swords, powder, shot, &c., because "the opinions and revelations of Mr. Wheelwright and Mrs. Hutchinson have seduced and led into dangerous errors many of the people here in New England."

1638, Mar, 7. Portsmouth. He and eighteen others signed the following compact: "We, whose names are underwritten, do here solemnly in the presence of Jehovah, incorporate ourselves into a Bodie Politicke, and as he shall help will submit our persons, lives and estates, unto our Lord Jesus Christ, the King of Kings and Lord of Lords, and to all those perfect and most absolute laws of his, given us in his holy word of truth, to be guided and judged thereby."

1638, Mar. 12. He having had license to depart from Massachusetts, that government summoned him and others to appear, if they had not gone before, at the next court to answer such things as shall be objected.

1638, May 13. He was present at a general meeting, upon public notice.

1639, Jun. 2. He and three others were ordered to survey all lands near about and to bring in a map or plot of said lands.

1640–41–42–43–44–50–64. Assistant.

1655. Freeman.

1657, Jan. 20. He and others bought of certain Indian Sachems, a large tract called the Pettaquamscott Purchase.

1658–59–60–61. Commissioner.

1665, May 3. Kings Town. His wife Margaret petitioned the Assembly complaining that her said husband did not give her suitable care, and that he is gone from her, leaving her in such a necessitous state, that unavoidably she is brought to a near dependence upon her children for her daily support, to her very great grief of heart. She desired suitable provision for her support out of his estate. The court being satisfied that the complaints are true, and having a deep sense upon their hearts of this sad condition which this poor ancient matron is by this means reduced into—enacted that all estate real and personal of John Porter in this jurisdiction is secured, &c., until he hath settled a competent estate upon his aged wife.

1665, Jun. 27. He was released from the restraint he was put under as to disposal of his estate, he having settled on his wife for life, such an estate as doth fully satisfy her.

1670, Oct. 26. He and four others were given full power to make a rate for Pettaquamscutt.

1671, Jan. 1. He and wife Horod deeded William Gardiner, son of George Gardiner of Newport, 200 acres in Narragansett, bounded westerly by Henry Gardiner.

1671, May 19. He took oath of allegiance.

1671, Sep. 26. He and wife Horod sold 240 acres in Portsmouth, for £400, to Richard Smith.

1671, Dec. 27. He and wife Horod deeded a sixteenth interest in 1000 acres (laid out to purchasers of Narragansett land), to Nicholas Gardiner.

1674, May 11. He had a suit brought against him by Richard Smith, and the jury found for plaintiff in the sum of £23, 5*s*.

His first wife's daughter Sarah Odding (by her her former husband), married Philip Sherman.

POTTER (George).

George, m. ——— { b. d. { b. d. (She m. (2) Nicholas Niles.) Portsmouth, R. I.	**I.** Abel, m. 1669, Nov. 16. Rachel Warner, { b. d. 1692. { b. d. 1724, Nov. 8. of John & Priscilla (Holliman) Warner. Portsmouth, Providence, Warwick, R. I.	1. George, 2. John, 3. Mary, 4. Abel, 5. Benjamin, 6. Stephen, 7. Ichabod, 8. Job,

1638. He was admitted an inhabitant of island of Aquidneck.

1639, Apr. 30. He and twenty-eight others signed the following compact: "We whose names are underwritten do acknowledge ourselves the legal subjects of his Majesty King Charles, and in his name do hereby bind ourselves into a civil body politicke, unto his laws according to matters of Justice."

1646, Feb. 4. Whereas Nicholas Niles, father-in-law (*i. e.* stepfather) of Abel Potter, hath bound him the said Abel Potter with Mr. William Baulstone, for the term of eighteen years, with the consent of the said Abel; for the better security of Mr. Baulstone, the town consenteth herein and approveth thereof.

1664, Sep. 5. He and Nathaniel Potter confirmed a deed of 8 acres, that was once in their fathers' possession, said deed having been made by Samuel Wilbur to John Tripp, shaft carpenter, 1663, May 7. (By "fathers' possession," the respective father of each was meant.)

1667, May 3. Dartmouth, Mass. He bought of John Read, for £36, a right in Mashantatack.

1671, Oct. 10. Providence. He and wife Rachel of Mashantatack, sold 60 acres and commoning, situated near Pawtuxet Falls, to Joseph Jenckes, said land belonging formerly to Rachel's grandfather Ezekiel Holliman.

1677, May 1. Freeman.

1682, Oct. 6. He sold to Roger Burlingame half of a meadow, for £2.

1687, Sep. 1. Taxed 4*s.*

1692, Jan. 14. Will—proved 1692, Mar. 9. Exx. wife Rachel. To eldest son George, 60 acres where he has made preparation for building, also a meadow adjoining, a heifer, iron pot already promised, and use of oxen and cart to do his work at such times as they may be conveniently spared, for three years, with liberty in orchard for his family's use, and to make and have three barrels of cider for seven years, he paying to daughter Mary, at eighteen years of age, £5. To wife Rachel, all the rest of lands, housing, orchard, &c., she dividing it amongst my children, according to her discretion, provided always that all my children have part thereof, excepting George and Stephen. To youngest son Stephen, at death of wife, all the homestead house, orchard, &c., being 50 acres of land, he paying to sister Mary, £5, within two years after possession. Sons Abel and Benjamin to pay their sister Mary, £5, within two years after they come of age.

1724, Nov. 6. Will—proved 1724, Nov. 23. Widow Rachel, of Providence. Exs. two youngest sons Ichabod and Job Potter. To eldest son John, 5*s.*, and like amount to sons Abel, Benjamin and Stephen. To daughter Mary Stone, a bed, warming pan, and iron pot. To sons Ichabod and Job, all right and interest in lands at Mashantatack. To son Ichabod, a chest and iron trammel. To son Job, iron trammel and fire tongs.

Inventory, £14, 19*s.*

POTTER (Robert).

ROBERT, b. ; d. 1655.
m. (1)
ISABEL, b. ; d. 1643.
m. (2)
SARAH, b. ; d. 1686.

(She m. (2) 1657, Feb. 19, John Sanford.)

Lynn, Roxbury, Mass., Warwick, R. I.

1630. Lynn.

1631, Sep. 3. Freeman.

1634. Roxbury.

1637, May 3. He had his daughter Deliverance baptized.

1638, Mar. 12. He appeared before the General Court, and was given liberty till next court, being bound in sum of £20, to then appear, and referred in the meanwhile to the church of Roxbury.

1638, May 2. He appearing before court, was enjoined to again appear at next session unless he be with his family removed out of the plantation before.

1638, Jun. He again appeared before court.

1638. Portsmouth. He was admitted an inhabitant of the island of Aquidneck.

1639, Apr. 30. At this date he and twenty-eight others signed the following compact: "We whose names are underwritten do acknowledge ourselves the legal subjects of his Majesty King Charles, and in his name do hereby bind ourselves into a civil body politicke, unto his laws according to matters of justice."

1642. He sold his house and land in Portsmouth, to his brother-in-law John Anthony.

1642, Jan. 12. Warwick. He and ten others bought of Miantonomi for 144 fathoms of wampum, tract of land called Shawomett (Warwick).

1643, Sep. 3. He, with others of Warwick, was notified to appear at General Court, at Boston, to hear complaint of two Indian sachems, Pomham and Socconocco, as to "some unjust and injurious dealing toward them by yourselves." The Warwick men declined to obey the summons, declaring that they were legal subjects of the King of England and beyond the limits of Massachusetts territory, to whom they would acknowledge no subjection. Soldiers were soon sent who besieged the settlers in a fortified house. In a parley it was now said, "that they held blasphemous errors which they must repent of" or go to Boston for trial, and they were soon carried thence. At the time of the capture of the Warwick men, their wives and children were forced to betake themselves to the woods and suffered hardships that resulted in the death of three women at least, one of these being the wife of Robert Potter.

1643, Nov. 3. Having been brought with others before the court, charged with heresy and sedition, they were sentenced to be confined during the pleasure of the court, and should they break jail or preach their heresies or speak against church or state, on conviction they should die. He was sent to the prison at Rowley.

1644, Mar. He was released from prison but banished from both Massachusetts and Warwick.

1649. He was licensed to keep an inn.

1651. Commissioner.

1655, May 25. He was appointed by the Court of Commissioners to keep a house of entertainment. A convenient sign was to be set out at the most perspicuous place of said house to give notice to strangers.

1656, May 14. Inventory, £42, 10*s.*, in cattle and movable goods, besides housing and land. It was ordered that John Potter, son of Robert Potter, late deceased, be maintained in apparel

I. ELIZABETH, b. ; d.
m.
RICHARD HARCUTT, b. ; d. 1696 ± of Harcutt.

1. Daniel,
2. Isabel,
3. Elizabeth,
4. Mary,
5. Meribah,
6. Mercy,
7. Dorothy,
8. Sarah,
9. Benjamin,

II. DELIVERANCE, b. 1637. ; d. 1664 ±
m. [illegible]
JAMES GREENE, b. 1626. ; d. 1698, Apr. 27. of John & Joan (Tattersall) Greene.

1. James, 1658, Jun. 1.
2. Mary, 1660, Sep. 28.
3. Elisha, 1663, Mar. 17.
4. Sarah, 1664, Mar. 27.

III. ISABEL, b. ; d. 1724, Aug. 26.
m. (1)
——— MOSS, b. ; d. of Moss.
m. (2) 1701 ±
WILLIAM BURTON, b. ; d. 1714, Feb. 20. of Burton.

No issue.

IV. JOHN, b. 1642 ± ; d. 1694. Warwick, R. I.
m. (1) 1664, Jun. 2.
RUTH FISHER, b. ; d. of Edward & Judith ( ) Fisher.
m. (2) 1685, Jan. 7
SARAH COLLINS, (w. of Eleazer. b. ; d. 1700 + of Wright.

1. Robert, 1666, Mar. 5.
2. Fisher, 1667, Jun. 12.
3. John, 1668, Nov. 21.
4 William, 1671, May 23.
5. Samuel, 1672, Jan. 10.
6. Isabel, 1674, Oct. 17.
7. Ruth, 1676, Nov. 29.
8. Edward, 1678, Nov. 25.
9. Content, 1680, Oct. 2.
(2d wife, no issue.)

1660, Feb. 6. He testified that in his conscience he did believe his father sold a certain house, &c., in Portsmouth, to my uncle John Anthony, and engages that when he comes to full age of twenty-one years he will confirm said sale.

1667–71–72–80–83. Deputy.

1676, Aug. 24. He was a member of the Court Martial held at Newport, for the trial of certain Indians charged with being engaged in King Philip's designs.

1679, May 7. On his petition he was granted by Assembly, 36*s.*, due him for service some years since, being constable, in securing and sending Indians to Newport.

1685–86. Assistant.

1687, Jun. 15. The petition of Sarah Potter, of Warwick, to court, was referred to Justices of the Peace, of Providence, Warwick and Rochester (*i. e.* Kings Town).

1687, Oct. 10. He deeded to eldest son Robert, 200 acres for love, &c.

1688, Apr. 28. He and his son Robert sold John Anthony, of Portsmouth, buildings, orchard and 28 acres in Portsmouth, for £60.

1692, Oct. 6. He deeded to sons Fisher and John, 100 acres each.

1693, Feb. 14. He deeded to son Samuel, 80 acres.

1694, Apr. 10. His son Robert, after premising that his father John, lately died intestate, now deems it incumbent as eldest son to dispose of estate left undisposed of by father. To two youngest brothers Edward and Content, he deeds a third of certain land, the other two-thirds having already been deeded to brother Samuel.

1700, May. Sarah Potter, gave 2*s.* 6*d.*, toward building Quaker meeting house at Mashapaug.

four years. Estate indebted £29, 12s., and other uncertain debts not yet brought in. Engaged to wife of Captain Lawton, for £20, borrowed of Captain Lawton in his life time in the year 1646, which is not yet paid, with use annexed for ten years time.

1656, Jun. 11. The Town Council found not enough estate to discharge debts without sale of land, and ordered Mr Holden and Mr. Holliman to sell the house and land and give a just account. The council gives to Sarah Potter, wife of late deceased Robert, the household goods, cattle and hogs to dispose of. Whereas, Sarah Potter, wife of Robert, late deceased intestate, without administration from council seized upon house and turned out the tenant set in by them, and also sold and disposed of goods and received some debts, wherefore the council consider she is engaged as administratrix.

1658, Aug. 26. The Council met concerning debts of Mr. Robert Potter's estate. Mr. Throckmorton was allowed to hold remainder of his goods provided he send for it, being evident they were not sold, but left to be sold by him. Ordered that James Greene, for what moneys he hath or may disburse upon John Potter for clothing of him, shall either have so much time in the house and land, or so much rent as it shall be let for. He was also allowed to sell a parcel of land belonging to house of Mr. Robert Potter, deceased, situated on other side of the street.

1660, Feb. 6. Testimony was given by John Tripp, Sr., of Portsmouth, that he heard his uncle Robert Potter say he had sold certain land to John Anthony.

1662, Dec. 22. Testimony of John Briggs, of Portsmouth, that he heard Robert Potter say a little before his death (at the house of Robert Potter, at Warwick, in company of John Tripp), that he had sold his brother his house and land in Portsmouth.

1662, Dec. 29. On the above testimony, and the agreement of Robert Potter's son John to confirm when he came of age, the commissioners confirmed house and land to John Anthony, the property having been sold by Robert Potter to John Anthony, about twenty years since.

1686, Mar. 16. Will—proved 1686, May 4. Widow Sarah Sanford, of Boston. Exs. William and John Mason, Jr. To daughters of brother Robert Sanford and sister Mary Turner, £10, divided equally. To the children of John Potter, Elizabeth Potter and Deliverance Potter, £10 equally divided. To executors rest of estate.

PRATT.

JOHN, b. d.
m.
ANN, b. d.

Kings Town, R. I.

1671, May 20. He took oath of allegiance to Rhode Island (as did also Samuel Pratt, who may have been a brother).

I.	DELIVERANCE,	b. 1664, Nov. 13. d.
II.	MARY,	b. 1666. d.
III.	EBENEZER,	b. 1669, Aug. 31. d.
IV.	PHINEAS,	b. 1671, Apr. d.
V.	JOSHUA,	b 1673, Jan. 10. d.
VI.	JEREMY,	b. 1674, Oct. 18. d.
VII.	MERCY,	b. 1676, Dec. 23. d.

RANDALL (JOHN).

JOHN, b d. 1685.
m.
ELIŻABETH, b. d. 1685 +

Newport, Westerly, R. I.

He and his wife were at Newport a short time as appears.

37. Westerly. He was there thus early.

667, May 6. He and others of Rhode Island having claimed certain land east of Pawcatuck River, a petition was sent to Connecticut

I. JOHN, b. 1666. d. Stonington, Conn.
m. (1)
ABIGAIL, b. d. 1705, Dec. of
m. (2) 1706, Nov. 25.
MARY BALDWIN, b. 1675, Feb. 24. d. of John & Deborah (Palmer) Baldwin.

1695, Sep. 1. His wife Abigail was admitted to the church at Stonington.

1720, Aug. 16. He, calling himself aged fifty-four years, testified concerning the head of Pawcatuck river, having as he says lived for the greatest part of his time, on or near the banks of said river.

1. Elizabeth,	1696, Jul. 4.
2. Mary,	1698, Dec. 16.
3. John,	1701, Dec. 2.
4. Dorothy,	1703, Dec. 7.
5. Abigail,	1705, Dec. 4.
(2d wife.)	
6. Sarah,	1707, Nov. 10.
7. Nathan,	1709, Jul. 7.
8. Ichabod,	1711, Oct. 21.
9. Sarah,	1714, Mar. 12.
10. Joseph,	1715, Jun. 2.
11. Benjamin,	1715, Jun. 2.
12. Rebecca,	1717, Jul. 31.
13. Joseph,	1720, Jul. 17.

authorities by Harmon Garret, *alias* Wequascooke, Governor of the Pequots, praying "that such men that wear hats and clothes like Englishmen, but have dealt with us like wolves and bears," may be called to account.

1669, May 18. His name was in a list of inhabitants.

1669–70. Deputy.

1670. He bought a lot of land on the Pawcatuck River.

1671, May 8. Fined 20*s.* for not attending jury.

1671, May 17. He took oath of allegiance.

1678, Mar. 1. He and his wife signed a letter with four others of the Westerly church, addressed to the Newport church: "We your brethren and sisters assembled together at the house of Tobias Sanders, wisheth you all grace, mercy and peace in our Lord Jesus Christ, and that both you and we may stand firm ever and stable in the faith and order of the gospel," &c., with much further exhortation and excellent advice—"to resist the wiles of the devil," &c.

1679, Sep. 17. He took the oath of allegiance.

1685. His widow petitioned to be allowed to improve the lands of deceased husband.

II. STEPHEN, b. 1668 ±, d. — Stonington, Conn.
m. 1697, Dec 24.
ABIGAIL SABIN, b. 1678, Aug. 16, d. — of Joseph & Waitstill ( ) Sabin.

1711, Oct. 2. He and thirty-three others bought 5,300 acres of the vacant lands in Narragansett ordered sold by the Assembly.

1. Abigail, 1698, Dec. 10.
2. Samuel, 1701, May 19.
3. Stephen, 1705, Mar. 13.
4. Jonathan, 1708, Mar. 7.
5. Elizabeth, 1709, Sep. 25.
6. Phebe, 1712, Sep. 18.
7. William, 1716, Feb. 26.
8. David, 1719, May 4.

III. MATTHEW, b. 1671, d. 1736. Stonington, Conn.
m.
ELEANOR, b. —, d. 1735 + of —— & Elizabeth

1694, Jun. 2. He had his daughter Eleanor baptized, followed by Mercy (1696, May 16), and Mary (1700, Apr. 21).

1720, Aug. 16. He, calling himself aged forty-nine years, testified to the same effect as his brother John.

1722, May 5. His wife had a legacy from the will of Nicholas Utter of Stonington, of £10, he calling her daughter-in-law (*i. e.* stepdaughter.)

1735, Dec. 19. Will—proved 1736, Mar. 29. Exs sons Matthew and Benjamin. To wife, a third of personal, a mare, choice of livestock, best room in house, a third of cellar, a third of back leanto, and a third profit real estate, while widow. To sons Matthew and Benjamin, lands in Stonington (except house and 50 acres where William Steward dwells), divided in a certain way, and to them utensils, carts, plows, &c., equally. To five daughters Eleanor, Mercy, Patience, Thankful and Elizabeth, the rest of personal and above house and 50 acres.

Inventory, £2,600, viz: wearing apparel, beds, 4 sows, 2 barrows, 2 boars, 3 shoats, 2 yoke of oxen, 5 cows, 5 heifers, bull, yearling, 4 mares, 2 colts, 33 sheep, 21 geese, 4 turkeys, &c.

1. Eleanor, 1694 ±
2. Mercy, 1696 ±
3. Mary, 1700 ±
4. Matthew,
5. Benjamin,
6. Patience,
7. Thankful,
8. Elizabeth,

IV. PETER, b. —, d. — Stonington, Preston, Conn.
m. (1) 1706, Nov. 27.
ELIZABETH POLLEY, b. —, d. — of Polley.
m. (2) 1719, Sep.
PHEBE BENJAMIN, b. —, d. — of Benjamin.

1719. Preston. He went thence about this time and the births of his children by his second wife, were there recorded.

1. Prudence, 1709, Apr. 10.
2. Peter, 1711, Dec. 2.
3. Peter, 1713, May 31.
(2d wife.)
4. Elizabeth, 1720, Jun 20.
5. Greenfield, 1722, Oct. 8.
6. Samuel, 1726, Apr. 13.

RANDALL (WILLIAM).

RANDALL (WILLIAM). 2d column. I. William, b. 1675, Sep 11. His wife, b. 1676, d. 1753, Sep. 12. His son Jonathan, b. 1706, and Henry, 1709.

WILLIAM[2], (William[1]), b 1647, Dec., d. 1712, Apr. 11.
m.
REBECCA FOWLER, b. —, d. 1730, Mar. 23. of Henry Fowler.

Scituate, Mass., Providence, R. I.

He was a miller.

1674. Nov. Providence. He took up a stray horse branded on the fore shoulder with F, a small star in the forehead and all four feet white, and he made proclamation thereof.

1684, Nov. 1. He had a deed of a 60 acre lot, and a 20 acre lot and three shares of meadow, &c., from Henry Fowler.

1687, Sep. 1. Taxed 5*s.* 11*d.*

1688. Ratable estate, 5 cows, 2 three years, a two year, 2 horses, 5 acres planting, 10 acres meadow, 80 acres wood-land.

1701. Deputy.

1702, Mar. 2. He deeded to eldest son William, for love, &c., two shares of meadow which I bought of my father-in-law Henry Fowler, said land being situated at south end of Antashantuck Neck, adjoining Hawkins Hole.

1702, Oct. 24. He freed his negro Peter Palmer, in consideration of good and faithful service, &c., and he was "to be his own man at his own disposing."

1705, Mar 9. He mortgaged half of an 80 acre tract, with house thereon in which he lived, the mill standing on said half tract, and another piece of land of 85 acres; for the amount of £94, 8*s.*, to his brother Job Randall, of Scituate, Mass.

1708, Jun. 17. He "being now aged and decrepit and weak of body and therefore become incapable to carry on my affairs for a livlihood," deeded to son William, for a comfortable maintenance during life, the mansion house, grist mill, outhousing, cellar, and all lands adjoining, and other lands in Providence so far west as the Seven Mile Line. The profits of cattle, increase of stock of all sorts of neat kind, sheep, swine, &c., to be for son William, from year to year, except what his father should see cause to put away; always provided that whereas the housing lieth under some engagement to my brother Job, and Mr. Gideon Crawford, now deceased, and Joseph Whipple, the said son William shall cast clear those engagements, and provide at all times a comfortable place of abode for his father, taking care of him for life.

1712, May 2. Administration to son William. Inventory, £17, 9*s.*, viz: gun, 9½ sheep, 5½ lambs, purse and wearing apparel £3, 5*s.*, and a pair of jack-boots.

1730, Aug. 3. Rebecca Randall, widow; administration to son William. Inventory, £125, viz: wearing apparel and silver money 3*s.*, 3*d.*, paper bills of credit £12, 3*s.*, 1*d.*, due on bond £19, 9*s.*, due on account £5, lace, mohair, silk, feather bed, pewter, spectacles, new sash, 2 spinning wheels, 3 cards, deers' leather, &c

I. WILLIAM, b. —, d. 1742, Jul. 8. Providence, R. I.
m.
ABIAL, b. —, d. 1740 + of

He was a miller.

1699, Apr. 5. He brought in a wolf's head and received 10*s.* bounty.

1703, Jan. 1. He bought of Joseph Latham 3¾ acres for £3.

1715, Dec. 7. He paid the mortgage to his uncle Job (contracted ten years previously by his father).

1724, Mar. 14. He deeded son William, for love, &c., 30 acres, to son Joseph, 35 acres, and in April of same year to son John, 20½ acres.

1728, Oct. 30. He deeded son Job, 23 acres with buildings, &c., for love, &c.

1729, Aug. 16. He deeded son Jonathan, 40 acres, for love, &c.

1733, Oct. 26. He deeded son Henry, west end of dwelling house where I now dwell, called the new house, half my grist mill, and half of all my homestead where I dwell on westerly side of Pauchasset River.

1737, Jan. 11. He deeded to youngest son Jeremiah, for love, &c., 25 acres.

1740, Apr. 19. Will—proved 1742, Aug. 30. Ex. son Henry. To wife Abial all household goods for life and to dispose of to daughters. To son William, £5. To son Joseph, £3. To son John, £5. To son Jonathan, 5*s.* To son Job, 5*s.* To son Henry, 5*s.* To son Jeremiah, 5*s.*, and 16 poles of land adjoining the water running in the trench of my mill, which I reserved in a deed given my son Henry, it being reserved for a tan yard. To daughter Abial Joy, £10. To daughter Mary Colwell, my third part of a small saw mill and £10. To daughter Hannah Briggs, £10. To daughter Rebecca Randall, £10.

Inventory, £180, 3*s.*, 6*d.*, viz: wearing apparel £28, 10*s.*, bond £25, notes £16, horse, cow, wheel, wool cards, hetchel, feather beds, pewter, warming pan, &c.

His daughter Rebecca, married Thomas Collins, in the same year her father died. His sons William, Joseph, and John, married respectively Mercy, Lydia, and Martha Williams, daughters of Joseph and Lydia (Hearnden) Williams.

1. William,
2. Joseph,
3. John,
4. Abial,
5. Jonathan,
6. Job,
7. Mary,
8. Henry,
9. Jeremiah,
10. Hannah,
11. Rebecca,

II. HENRY, b. —, d. — Providence, R. I.

1708. Freeman.

III. JONATHAN, b. —, d. 1724, Oct. 7. Providence, R. I.
m. 1712,
BETHIAH HOWARD, b. —, d. — of John & Sarah (Latham) Howard.

(She m. (2) John Hays.)

He was a physician.

1724, Nov. 26. Inventory, £30 ±, viz: horse, mare, colt, cow, vials, mortar, &c., "after his father-in-law Mr. John Howard, of Bridgewater, had carried away the most part of said Randall's goods in the night with a cart."

As the widow absented herself and refused administration, it was given to William Harris, a principal creditor.

1. John,
2. Joseph,

IV. JOSEPH, b. 1684, d. 1760, Mar. 30. Providence, R. I.
m. 1716, Jul. 26.
AMEY ESTEN, b. 1685, Jun. 1, d. 1764, Feb. 8. of Henry & Elizabeth (Manton) Esten.

He was a shipwright.

1717, Nov. 4. He and wife Amey, for £18, 10*s.*, sold Captain William Crawford, half of 12¾ acres (the other half being in hands of Cornelius and Henry Esten), being land that was given by Shadrach Manton, deceased, to his grandchildren, daughters of Mr. Henry Esten, deceased.

1721, May 5. He sold to William Page half of a warehouse lot on the west side of the Town street, for £9, said lot being 20 feet broad and extending to salt water.

1748, May 16. Will—proved 1760, May 29. Ex. son Peter. To wife Amey, all personal estate including household goods, cattle, &c., and a third of profits of homestead farm for life. To son Henry, £5. To daughter Amey Randall, £600, and privilege of living in house while single. To son Peter, all real estate, he paying legacy to Amey.

He and his wife were buried in North Burial Ground.

1. Amey, 1717, May 27.
2. Joseph, 1718, Aug. 25.
3. Henry, 1720, Mar. 2.
4. Peter, 1723, Jun. 12.

V. MARY, b. —, d. —
m. 1712, Jun. 24.
ZACHARIAH RHODES, b. 1687, Nov. 5, d. 1740, Jun. 10. of John & Wait (Waterman) Rhodes.

1. William, 1712, Nov. 18.
2. Mercy, 1714, Apr. 11.
3. Rebecca, 1716, Jun. 29.
4. Mary, 1720.

JOHN, * | b. | d. 1702.
m.
MARGARET, | b. | d. 1702 +

New Shoreham, R. I.

1661, Apr. He came to Block Island with the first settlers, being one of the sixteen purchasers of the island. He, with Edward Vorse, received lot 4 in north part of the island and lot 10 in south-east part of island. The island had been purchased the year before for £400 of John Endicott, Richard Bellingham, Daniel Dennison and William Hawthorne (who had received a grant of it from Massachusetts two years before).

1664, May 1. Freeman.

1676. Surveyor of highways.

1679, Sep. 21. He and wife Margaret, deeded son John, for love, &c., all our message and mansion house at Block Island and if John, Jr., died without issue, then estate to revert to other heirs of John, Sr.

1680. Taxed 11*s*.

1681-82-83-84. Deputy.

1683, Dec. 28. He and wife Margaret, deeded land to Sarah George, wife of Samuel George.

1686, Jul. 16. He signed with others a petition to the King in regard to the writ of *Quo Warranto*, presenting their full and free submission and resignation of power given in the charter, and desiring to be discharged from all levies and contributions which the Assembly would expose them to in sending an agent to England, to which the petitioners do not consent.

1688. Grand Jury.

1702, Feb. 12. Will—proved 1702, Oct. 6. Exx. wife Margaret. To son Samuel, a table and cupboard. To wife Margaret, all other movables (viz: chattels, household goods, sheep, cattle, horsekind, &c.), and to her the income of the Newport house for life. At her death the Newport house to go to grandson John, son of John, and grandson John, son of William (the latter having east side of house). To wife, certain land, and 40*s*. to be paid her yearly, while widow, by sons John, William, Joseph and Samuel, each paying that amount. To wife also was given negro man for life, and then to son Thomas, for three years, at end of which time to be free. At death of wife, household goods to go to three daughters, Sarah, Margaret and Elizabeth, and five sons to have at that time all cattle, &c., equally.

Inventory, £86, 11*s*., 8*d*., viz: 6 three year cattle, 2 working cattle, 2 cows, a yearling, 50 sheep, 20 lambs. At the Newport house: beds, pewter, plate £15, 18*s*., wearing apparel, bible, gun, &c.

* See: American Genealogist, v.20, p.55-56.

I. THOMAS, * | b. 1657. | d. 1733, Dec. 26. | New Shoreham, R. I.
m. 1685, Apr. 21.
MARY DICKENS, | b. | d. | of Nathaniel & Joan ( ) Dickens.

1696, May 5. Freeman.

1700-3-4-5-11-17-30-31. Deputy.

1702, May 6. He was appointed on a committee to audit the General Treasurer's accounts and all other Colony debts.

1702. Lieutenant.

1728, Mar. 20. He and wife Mary, sold land to Simon Ray.

1730. Captain.

1733, Nov. 16. Will—proved 1734, Jun. 10. Exx. wife Mary, and brother Samuel. To wife all real estate for life and personal at her disposal. To son John, at death of wife, all homestead farm and some land bought of father Dickens and a negro boy. To son Thomas, the farm he already had deed of, &c., and a negro girl. To son Samuel, a house and lot of 18 acres, another lot of 36 acres and a negro girl.

Inventory, 4 oxen, 9 cows, 6 two year cattle, 8 calves, 180 sheep, 30 lambs, horse, mare, 7 swine, 25 loads of hay, pair of stillyards, warming pan, silver tankard, silver cup, negro named Mingo £60, negro woman £80, negro boy £80, 2 negro wenches £200, &c.

1744, Aug. 29. Receipts were given to Samuel Rathbone by sons and sons-in-law of Thomas Rathbone, deceased, as follows, viz: John Rathbone (son), John Rathbone (son-in-law), Thomas Rathbone, Samuel Rathbone, Benjamin Bentley, Samuel Eldred.

He was buried in the Town Burial Ground.

1. Margaret, 1686, Jan. 17.
2. Mary, 1687, Jan. 24.
3. Patience, 1690, Nov. 14.
4. Constance, 1692, Jan. 17.
5. Thomas, 1695, Jan. 29.
6. Sarah, 1698, Apr. 1.
7. Elizabeth, 1700, Mar. 1.
8. Samuel, 1702, Jul. 1.
9. John, 1705, May 29.
10. Sylvia, 1707, Mar. 16.

II. JOHN, * | b. | d. 1723. | New Shoreham, R. I.
m. 1688, Jan. 10.
ANN DODGE, | b. | d. 1723 + | of Tristram Dodge.

1696, May 5. Freeman.

1717, Apr. 28. He testified in relation to the seizure of three men (from a boat that he was in) by a pirate sloop, of which Paulsgrave Williams was commander, then in the harbor's bay. The men taken were George Mitchell, William Tosh and Dr. James Sweet. Governor Cranston wrote Colonel Shute in regard to the matter, "that in case the pirate Williams should fall into your excellency's hands that the poor men therein mentioned may receive such favor as justice will allow."

1720, Mar. 8. Will—proved 1723, Mar. 9. Exx. wife Anne. To wife whole profits of all housing and lands on Block Island for life, and all personal forever. To eldest son Jonathan, having already had £100, he gives nothing. To daughter Mercy, nothing, she having had portion at marriage. To son John, all housing and land on Block Island, he paying legacies. To son Joshua, £50. To son Benjamin, £50, at 21. To sons Nathaniel and Thomas, each £50 at age. To daughter Anne, £30 at death of wife.

Inventory, £149, 7*s*., 10*d*., viz: 2 mares, a colt, 2 oxen, 6 cows, 2 heifers, 2 two year cattle, 4 yearlings, 5 sheep, pewter, bible and four other books, carpenter's tools, &c.

1. Mercy, 1688, Oct. 3.
2. Jonathan, 1691, May 22.
3. John, 1693, Dec. 23.
4. Joshua, 1696, Feb. 19.
5. Benjamin, 1701, Feb. 17.
6. Ann, 1703, Aug. 9.
7. Nathaniel, 1708, Feb. 6.
8. Thomas, 1709, Mar. 2.

III. WILLIAM, | b. | d. 1727. | New Shoreham, Westerly, R. I.
m. 1680, Dec 18.
SARAH, | b. | d. | of

1688. Constable.

1696, May 5. Freeman.

1727, Sep. 18. Will—proved 1727, Oct. 30. Exs. sons John, of North Kingstown, and Jonathan, of Johnstown, Ct. To son John, house and land where I dwell (90 acres) and a mare, he paying £240 as follows: To testator's daughter Anna Dodge, £50, and to daughter Mercy Rathbone, £50, and the rest of sum (viz: £140) to be laid up in bank for relief of children and grandchildren at discretion of executors. To son Ebenezer, two yearlings, cattle and all the sheep. To son Jonathan, two or three acres of meadow. To grandson William (son of John), a gun. To four sons William, John, Jonathan and Ebenezer, husbandry tools. To eldest son William, 5*s*., he having had already. To son Jonathan, a warming pan. To daughter Mercy Rathbone, 2 beds. To granddaughter Mercy Rathbone, 1 bed, &c. To son Ebenezer, pottage pot, &c. To daughters Anna Dodge, Dorcas West and Mercy Rathbone, rest of movables. To son Ebenezer, negro woman Jenny.

Inventory, £503, 13*s*., 6*d*., viz: clothing of himself and wife £28, 5 beds, house and lands £280, 4 steers, 4 cows, 4 two year cattle, 5 yearlings, 17 swine, 23 sheep, 2 mares, a colt, 6 tame geese, pewter, warming pan, spinning wheel, worsted combs, money £1, 12*s*., 6*d*., &c.

1. William, 1681, Nov. 12.
2. Cera, 1682, Dec. 8.
3. John, 1684, Jan. 9.
4. Thomas, 1686, Jan. 21.
5. Jonathan, 1688, Nov. 25.
6. Elizabeth, 1691, May 30.
7. Ann, 1693, Jul. 9.
8. Dorcas, 1695, Jan. 14.
9. Ebenezer, 1696, Jan. 28.
10. Mercy, 1699, Jul. 5.
11. Eleanor, 1701, Aug. 1.

IV. JOSEPH, | b. | d. 1749. | New Shoreham, Kings Town, Exeter, R. I.
m. 1691, May 19.
MARY MOSHER, | b. | d. 1748 (—) | of Hugh & Rebecca (Harndel) Mosher.

1696. Freeman.

1709, Sep. 28. Kings Town. He bought 100 acres of the vacant lands ordered sold by the Assembly.

1748, Dec. 26. Will—proved 1749, Aug. 8. Ex. son Joseph. To son Joseph, dwelling house and 59 acres and farming tools and one-half household goods. To son Benjamin, all wearing apparel, he having had his part of estate. To heirs of deceased son Job, 10*s*. To heirs of deceased daughter Grace Gates, 10*s*. To heirs of deceased daughter Rebecca Harris, 10*s*. To granddaughter Abigail Gates, bed I lie on, &c. To daughter Hannah Eldred, 10*s*. To four daughters, Elizabeth Rathbone, Mary Gardiner, Margaret Green and Mercy Rathbone, half household goods.

1. Elizabeth, 1692, Mar. 14.
2. Rebecca, 1694, Mar. 1.
3. Grace, 1695, Jul. 16.
4. Mary, 1697, Mar. 6.
5. Margaret, 1700, Nov. 29.
6. Mercy, 1703, Feb. 14.
7. Hannah, 1706, Mar. 21.
8. Joseph, 1707, Oct. 4.
9. Benjamin, 1710, Feb. 26.
10. Job, 1712, Apr. 1.

V. SAMUEL, | b. 1672, Aug. 3. | d. 1757, Jan. 24. | New Shoreham, R. I.
m. 1692, Nov. 3.
PATIENCE COGGESHALL, | b. 1669, Aug. 13. | d. 1747, Aug. 3. | of John & Patience (Throckmorton) Coggeshall.

1749, Jan. 4. He deeded son Samuel, for love, &c., house and certain land, farming tackling, and carpentering tools and certain household goods. On same date he received a lease from his son of the message where the father dwelt, at rental of 1 mark a year for life.

1752, Mar. 28. Will—proved 1757. Jan. 1. Ex. son Samuel. To eldest son Thomas, £10, he having already had by deed of gift his portion. To second son Samuel, nothing, he having had already. To third son James, £10, he having already had. To fourth son Abraham, nothing, having already had. To four daughters Patience Dodge, Mary Gould, Wait Dickens and Rebecca Rider £25 each. To daughters Patience and Wait, bedding. To grandchildren Coggeshall Rathbone, Mary Rathbone and Catharine Rathbone (children of son Abraham), each £20 at age. To grandson Walter Rathbone, my old mare. To grandson Samuel Rathbone (son of Samuel), young mare. To grandson Elijah Rathbone, a gun. All cattle, sheep, &c., to be sold to pay legacies.

Inventory, £196, 10*s*., 8*d*., viz: 3 cows, 10 sheep, 2 calves, a yearling steer, 7 geese, pewter, 2 cases and bottles, &c.

He was buried in the Town Burial Ground, as was his wife also.

1. Thomas, 1693, May 3.
2. Patience, 1697, Aug. 21.
3. Mary, 1700, Sep. 11.
4. Wait, 1702, Dec. 30.
5. Samuel, 1705, Apr. 16.
6. James, 1707, Apr. 10.
7. Abraham, 1709, Nov. 23.
8. Rebecca, 1713, Jan. 9.

VI. SARAH, | b. | d.
m. 1678, Dec. 20.
SAMUEL GEORGE, | b. 1651, Apr. 12. | d. 1692 (—) | of Peter & Mary ( ) George.

1. Mary.
2. Susanna,

VII. MARGARET, | b. | d.

VIII. ELIZABETH, | b. | d.

SIMON[2], (Simon[1]). ✱ b. 1636. d. 1737, Mar. 17.
m. (1)
MARY THOMAS, b. d.
of Nathaniel Thomas.
m. (2)
ELIZABETH, b. d.

Braintree, Mass., New Shoreham, R. I.

1660, Aug. 27. He was present at a meeting at the house of Dr. John Alcock, of Roxbury, Mass., to confer about the settlement of Block Island, and he agreed to pay a sixteenth of the purchase money for said island, and his part of expense of removing families there. He with certain others built a shallop for the convenience of transporting families to the island. The price paid for the island was £400, by sixteen individuals.

1661, Apr. New Shoreham. He came hither this month with the first settlers. In the division of lands he received lot 17 in the north part of the island, and in company with Peter George, he had also lots 8 and 9 in the northwest part of the island.

1664. Freeman.

1676. Deputy Warden.

1682, Nov. 13. He bought of Nathaniel Thomas of Marshfield, land in Pocasset, for £100.

1687–88. Justice of General Quarter Sessions and Inferior Court of Common Pleas.

1689, Jul. 3. Three French privateers landed a force of men and plundered the inhabitants, remaining some time on the island. They demanded money of Mr. Ray, and on his informing them that he had none at his command, struck him on the head with a rail, so that it was feared by his wife they had killed him.

1690, Oct. 18. He and Elizabeth Ray witnessed the will of Nathaniel Dickens.

1700. Head Warden (in this and other years).

1704, Sep. He addressed the Town Council in a communication as follows: "Whereas Penewess, the late Sachem, being dead, to whom the land reserved for him belonged, and now belongeth to his countrymen, whereof Ninecraft being willing for to assist them in the putting of the land to rent so as to be at a certainty of receiving rent yearly for it; I pray you let there be no bar nor hindrance towards that proceeding," &c.

He was blind during the latter part of his life.

He was buried in the Town Burying Ground. His epitaph sets forth that he was one of the chief magistrates, and that he frequently instructed in the more important concerns of our holy religion, &c.

✱ See: American Genealogist v. 20, p. 56-57.
‡ v. 27, p. 221

I. SYBIL, b. 1665, Mar. 19. d. 1733, Dec. 23.
m.
JOHN SANDS, b. 1652. d. 1712, Mar. 15. of James & Sarah (Walker) Sands.

1. John, 1686,
2. Nathaniel, 1687,
3. Edward, 1691,
4. George, 1694,
5. Mary, 1697,
6. Catharine, 1700,
7. Dorothy, 1703,
8. Abigail, 1708,

II. MARY, ✱ ‡ b. 1667, May 19. d. 1714, Mar. 1.
m. 1683, Oct. 11.
ROGER KENYON, b. d. of John Kenyon.

1. Roger, 1685, Jan. 25.

III. DOROTHY, ✱ ‡ b. 1669, Oct. 16. d.
m.
SAMUEL SANDS, b. d. 1716. of James & Sarah (Walker) Sands.

1. Sybil,
2. Mercy,
3. Ann,
4. Sarah,
5. Mary,
6 Samuel,

IV. SIMON, ✱ b. 1672, Apr. 9. d. 1755, Mar. 19. New Shoreham, R. I.
m. (1) 1695, Jan. 17.
JUDITH MAINWARING, b. 1676. d. 1706, Feb. 17. of Oliver & Hannah (Raymond) Mainwaring.
m. (2)
DEBORAH GREENE, b. d. 1755 + of Job & Phebe (Sayles) Greene.

1. Simon, 1697, Jan. 26.
2. Gideon, 1698, Nov. 17.
3. Nathaniel, 1700, Jan. 8.
4. Mary, 1702, Dec. 21.
(2d wife.)
5. Judith, 1726, Oct. 4.
6. Anna, 1728, Sep. 27.
7. Catharine, 1731, Jul. 10.
8. Phebe, 1733, Sep. 10.

1692, Jan. 10. Freeman.

1705. Captain.

1705-8-9-10-11-13-14-15-20-21-22-23-25-29-30-31-34-35-36-37-41. Deputy.

1717, Mar. His son Simon died at New Providence.

1723, Jun. 18. The Assembly ordered that £123, be paid to him for the use of New Shoreham to assist them in rebuilding their pier, the work to be done in two years time.

1726, May 26. He freed three negroes, who he says had been brought up with him from their infancy, said freedom to take effect on death of both Simon and his wife.

1734, Jun. He and four others were appointed a committee by the Assembly to procure materials for building a pier at Block Island, and making a harbor there.

1735, Aug. He and Peter Ball were appointed to improve the £1,200, allowed to build a pier at Block Island, or to repair the old one.

1737, Oct. 11. Will—proved 1755, Mar. 31. Exx. wife Deborah. To grandson Simon Ray, at twenty-three years of age, the lands, tenements, housing, &c., that were my father's, he paying my grandson Simon Thomas, £500. If grandson Simon should die, then daughters Judith, Ann, Catharine and Phebe, were to have the estate. To grandson Simon Ray, also twenty cows, all with calves by their side, or fair with calf, a bull, five yearlings, five two years, and fifty sheep; and if he die, then four daughters of testator to have the stock. To grandson Simon Ray, all books, guns, and a sword. To grandson Simon Thomas, £500, one-half at fourteen and the other half at age. To kinsman Silas Clapp, £100. To four daughters all the rest of estate. To wife Deborah, use of all lands, stock, &c., till grandson Simon Ray is twenty-three, she paying him £50, at age and £50, at twenty-three.

Inventory, £7,468, 1s. 5d., viz: mare, 2 colts, 2 cows, 2 calves, 10 sheep, gun, churn, 2 woolen wheels, silver tankard, porringer, spoons, &c., weighing 60 oz. £275, 8s. 4d., tankard £128, porringer £36, 3 dozen and eleven silver jacket buttons £21, 10s. 10d., books £40, pair of worsted combs, bond due from Godfrey Malbone, and other bonds, viz: 2 for £900, 1 for £280, 10s., &c.

The widow requested that her son-in law Samuel Ward might administer on estate, she refusing the executorship. Her request was joined in by John Littlefield, who married Phebe, and by Judith Hubbard and Catharine Ray, two other daughters. The four daughters of Simon Ray by his last wife, married as follows: Judith to Thomas Hubbard of Boston, Anna to Samuel Ward, Catharine to William Greene and Phebe to John Littlefield. (Two of these husbands became governors of the state, viz: Samuel Ward and William Greene.)

He was buried in the Town Burial Ground. His epitaph describes him as filling the most important offices with honor to himself and advantage to his country, and declares that he was a lover of learning, justice and benevolence, ever attentive to the interests of this island, &c.

(2d WIFE, no issue.)

RAY. 2d column. IV. Simon, m. (2) 1725, Nov. 22. His 2d wife, b. 1690, Feb. 28, d. 1763, Dec. 11, at Warwick, R. I. 1762, Jan. 14. Will—proved 1764, Mar. 12. She mentions daughter Judith Hubbard, father Job Greene, deceased, daughters Ann Ward and Catharine Greene, grandchildren Simon Ray Littlefield, William, Catharine, Phebe and Ann Littlefield, son-in-law William Greene, Jr.

REAPE (SAMUEL).

SAMUEL, b. d.
m. 1667, Jan. 11. [Zachariah.
JOANNA RHODES (w. of b. 1617, Feb. 27. d. 1692 +
of William & Christian (Peak) Arnold.

Providence, Newport, R. I.

1672. Deputy.

1674, Sep. 2. He owned half of a corn mill at Pawtuxet Falls, and the other half having been sold by Joseph Carpenter to his uncle Stephen Arnold, some trouble arose. Silas Carpenter went with some corn to grind, having an order from Stephen Arnold on Samuel Reape, but the latter refused in a rage, and Silas had to carry the corn to Providence to get it ground. To all of which Silas deposed.

1676, Oct. 18. Newport. He sued Benjamin Congdon for slander, defamation, &c., and the case was left to arbitration.

1680, Sep. 7. He was sued by Thomas Eldred, who recovered £5, 13s.

No issue.

REAPE (WILLIAM.)

WILLIAM, b. 1628. d. 1670, Aug. 6.
m.
SARAH, b. d. 1716 ±

Newport, R. I.

He was a merchant, and as he held the religious faith of the Quakers, he traveled quite extensively, both in his business calling and accompanying the Quaker preachers sometimes.

I. ———, b. d.
m.
WILLIAM BRINLEY, b. d. 1704. of Francis & Hannah (Carr) Brinley.

1. William,

II. SARAH, b. 1664, Apr. 17. d. 1687, Sep. 26.
m.
JONATHAN MARSH, b. d. 1704, Jun. 10. of Marsh.

1. William,
2. John, 1687, Sep. 11.

1661, Feb. 5. He and Peter Pierson, having been apprehended at a Quaker meeting in Sandwich, were brought before the court at Plymouth, and "after some speech betwixt the court and them, and some menacing speeches and proud carriages and expressions uttered by the said William Reape," &c., the law of the Colony was read to them and they were required to depart on the morrow, which they did, taking journey towards Rhode Island.

1662. He was arrested with other Quakers on Long Island.

1665. He was active in promoting the settlement at Monmouth, New Jersey.

1666, May 2. Freeman.

1667. Deputy.

1667, Aug. 10. He enlisted in a troop of horse.

1667–68. Assistant.

1670, Jul. 5. He was a member of the Court held at Monmouth, N. J., at this date.

1671, Jan. 30. His widow was allowed £1, for hire of her horse for the use of Mr. John Crandall, to go to Hartford on public business.

1671, May 8. His widow brought suit against her husband's brother Samuel, for a difference of £1,000 between them, and the matter was left to arbitration.

1702, Mar. 4. Widow Reape was one of the proprietors in the common lands at Newport.

1709, Oct. 31. His widow Sarah, of Shrewsbury, N. J., for love, &c., to grandson William Marsh, son of daughter Sarah Marsh, deceased, of Newport, deeded him a house and lot in Newport.

1715, Apr. 12. Will—Codicil 1716, Jan. 7. Widow Sarah, of Shrewsbury. Exs. William Lawrence and Richard Hartshorne. She gives her plantation, &c., to son William, in case he comes to his senses. She mentions grandsons William Marsh and William Brindley, giving to the latter a house and lot bought of the town of Newport. The executors were given power to sell her house and land in Weymouth, in old England, county of Dorsetshire. To kinswoman Mary Ware, formerly wife of Edward Williams, 20*s.* and two sheep apiece for her children. To Edith Brier, widow of Nathaniel Brier, and to her children Joseph, Elizabeth and Mary Brier, certain legacies, to be paid out of proceeds of sale of housing in old England. (These legatees lived in Weymouth.) To grandson William Brindley and his three sons Francis, William and Thomas, legacies were given. To Quaker meeting of Shrewsbury, 40*s.* She names granddaughters Sarah Marsh, and Elizabeth Brindley. She also gives a legacy to William Brindley's youngest son named Reape Brindley, and to Sarah Brindley she gives a gold ring and silver spoon. She desires her grandsons William Brindley and William Marsh to aid executors in seeing her son William Reape, cared for.

William Reape was buried in the Clifton Burial Ground, at Newport.

III. { WILLIAM, { b. 1667, Dec. 31. / d. 1715 + — Newport, R. I., Shrewsbury, N. J.

1692. Monmouth, N. J. Juryman. He is mentioned in deeds (sometimes with his mother quite frequently in New Jersey records, but perhaps did not take up a permanent residence there.

REMINGTON.

{ JOHN, { b. / d. 1709 +
m.
{ ABIGAIL, { b. / d.

Haverhill, Mass., Jamestown, Warwick, R. I.

His children Daniel and Hannah were born at Haverhill.

1669, Aug. 28. Jamestown. He and two others were ordered to assemble inhabitants of Conanicut Island, to consider what may be most suitable for their defence and preservation against any invasion or insurrection of the Indians.

1677, Oct. 31. He and forty-seven others were granted 5000 acres, to be called East Greenwich.

1680. Taxed 6*s.* 8*d.*, "John Remington and sons"

1709, Aug. 13. Warwick. Whereas by deed of gift dated 1695, May 24, he had given son Thomas Remington of Warwick, all my right which I had at Haverhill, Mass., and said deed being damnified through disaster, so that it is scarce legible, and being willing gift should stand, therefore for love, &c., he deeds son Thomas said right in Haverhill, viz: a house, and town lot containing 4 acres, also two orchards and 40 acres called Fishing River.

I. { JOHN, { b. / d. 1688. — Newport, Kings Town, R. I.
m. 1679 ±
{ ABIGAIL RICHMOND, { b. 1656. / d. 1744. — of Edward & Abigail (Davis) Richmond.

1. Abigail, 1681,
2. Martha,
3. Elizabeth,
4. Hannah,

(She m. (2) Henry Gardiner.)

1678, Apr. 30. Freeman.

1687, Sep. 6. Kings Town. Taxed 7*s.* 6½*d.*

1688, Dec. 12. Administration to widow Abigail. Inventory, £46, 17*s.* 9*d.*

1701, Nov. 19. Martha Remington, daughter of John, deceased, with consent of her mother Abigail Remington, united with George Havens, Jr., and wife in a deed of rights in 220 acres to Henry Gardiner, for £100.

1701, Dec. 29. Elizabeth and Hannah Remington, daughters of deceased John, with consent of their mother Abigail, sold Henry Gardiner rights for £100.

1711, Feb. 16. William Gardiner, Jr., son of Benoni and wife Abigail, with consent of wife's mother Abigail Remington, relict of John, sold to Henry Gardiner, Sr., all right in farm of wife's father, 250 acres.

1718, Nov. 25. John Kenyon and Elizabeth his wife, formerly Elizabeth Remington, sold to Henry Gardiner, certain land, for £45.

1718, Dec. 13. Eber Sherman and wife Martha also sold land to Henry Gardiner.

1738. His widow Abigail Gardiner deposed that her father Edward Richmond, deceased, was a member of the Church of England. She calls herself in eighty-second year.

1744, Jul. 20. Will—proved 1744, Oct. 8. Widow Abigail Gardiner, South Kingstown. Ex. son Henry Gardiner. To son Henry, negro Betty, he paying four grandchildren £40, equally divided. To daughters Martha Sherman and Elizabeth Kenyon, all wearing apparel. To grandchildren Dorcas, daughter of Ephraim Gardiner, Mary, daughter of Henry, Abigail Worden, daughter of William, deceased, and Lydia, daughter to John Gardiner, son to said William, deceased, the rest of estate.

Inventory, £266, 6*s.* 6*d.*

II. { JOSEPH, { b. / d. — Jamestown, R. I.
m.
{ ———, { b. / d. — of

1. John, 1680, Apr. 12.

1682, Sep. 5. Juryman.

III. DANIEL, m. —— { b. 1661, Oct. 18. d. } { b. d. } of — Jamestown, R. I.

1. Abigail, 1686, Mar. 26.

1697, Sep. 10. His daughter Abigail had a legacy of £10, from will of Oliver Arnold, who calls her his wife Phebe's kinswoman, Abigail Remington, daughter of Daniel Remington of Jamestown.

IV. HANNAH, { b. 1664, Jul. 3. d. }

V. STEPHEN, m. PENELOPE, { b. d. 1738. } { b. 1666. d. 1740 + } of — Jamestown, R. I.

1. Mary, 1686, Sep. 20.
2. Sarah, 1688, Aug. 29.
3. Gershom, 1690, Dec. 3.
4. Phebe, 1693, May 29.
5. Stephen, 1696, Mar. 29.
6. Alice, 1698, Nov. 28.
7. Hannah, 1701, Mar. 10.
8. Penelope,

1688. Grand Jury.

1695, Jul. 15. Elected Ensign. Subsequently he was Captain.

1708, Oct. 27. An appeal against him was made to Assembly by Jahleel Brenton (executor of will of William Brenton, deceased), for withholding from said Brenton 256 acres in Jamestown. The appellant was given leave to redeem the mortgage of above said lands.

1738, Mar. 2. Administration to widow Penelope. Inventory, £416, 9*s.* 5*d.*, viz: feather bed, pewter, scales, bonds £313, 12*s.*, 10 sheep, 3 swine, 2 cows, &c.

1740, Mar. 19. His widow, calling herself aged about seventy-four years, affirmed that her husband Stephen Remington and his brother Joseph, in the year 1687, took a lease of Colonel Peleg Sanford, of 400 acres in Jamestown for seven years, and at the expiration thereof her husband took another lease of 256 acres (part of the 400), and held the same till Sanford's death, after which he leased of executors of Peleg Sanford, till his son William Sanford was of age, and at death of the latter, leased of Grizzel his widow, as guardian of William Sanford's heirs. After marriage of Grizzel, to Nathaniel Cotton, the lease was from Nathaniel and Grizzel, as guardians, till the estate of William Sanford was divided amongst his heirs, after which Gershom Remington, son of the affirmant, took a lease from Thomas Hutchinson, who married one of the daughters of William Sanford. The 256 acres whereon the affirmant's son Gershom Remington now lives, has been held by said Joseph, Stephen and Gershom Remington, from the year 1687 till present time, and is the same land of which Ebenezer and Benjamin Brenton each claim one-seventh part.

VI. THOMAS, m. MARY ALLEN, { b. d. 1710. } { b. d. 1710 + } of William & Elizabeth ( ) Allen. — Portsmouth (Prudence Island), Warwick, R. I.

1. William,
2. Thomas,
3. John,
4. Daniel,
5. Joseph,
6. Stephen,
7. Matthew,
8. Jonathan,
9. Mary,
10. Prudence,

His father-in-law was of Prudence Island, and he lived there some time.

1704. Warwick. Freeman.

1710, May 20. Will—proved 1710, Sep. 26. Exs. wife Mary and son William. To wife, all household stuff and movables within doors, she giving to each of my daughters at eighteen or marriage, a feather bed, viz: to daughters Mary and Prudence. To son John, 40 acres out of south-west corner of farm provided he pay his brother Thomas £10, within two years after John is twenty-one. To son Thomas, half remainder of farm (across north end) provided he pay each of my sons at twenty-one the sum of £11, viz: to Daniel, Joseph, Stephen, Matthew and Jonathan, as each arrives at that age, and to pay daughters Mary and Prudence, each £7, 10*s.* To wife Mary and son William, rest of estate. Executors were given power to bind children apprentices to good trades.

Inventory, £113, 7*s* 10*d.*, viz: yoke of oxen, 2 pair of steers, 8 cows, 2 yearlings, bull, 4 horses, 49 sheep, 13 lambs, 2 sows, a yearling swine, 3 beds, pair of cards, pair of stillyards, pewter, &c.

RICE.

JOHN, m. 1674, Jul. 16. **ELIZABETH HOLDEN.** { b. 1646. d. 1731, Jan. 6. } { b. 1652, Aug. d. }

of Randall & Frances (Dungan) Holden.

Warwick, R. I.

He was "born in old England and came with Mr. Calverly," the Warwick records declare. (Edmund Calverly was in Warwick as early as 1661.)

1675. Freeman.

1687. Grand Jury.

1710. Deputy.

I. JOHN, m. 1695, Jul. 25. ELNATHAN WHIPPLE, { b. 1675. d. 1755, Jan. 9. } { b. 1675, Jan. 2. d. 1753 + } of John & Mary (Olney) Whipple. — Warwick, R. I.

1. John, 1696, Apr. 6.
2. Elizabeth, 1698, May 8.
3. Thomas, 1700, Apr. 26.
4. Mary, 1702, Sep. 22.
5. Nathan, 1704, Jan. 20.
6. Barbara, 1706, Apr. 24.
7. William, 1708, Mar. 25.
8. Mary, 1710, Jan. 24.
9. Lydia, 1711, Dec. 30.
10. Randall, 1714, May 22.
11. Elnathan, 1716, Aug. 4.

1696. Freeman.

1705–14–15–16–18–19–21–22–27. Deputy.

1721. Captain.

1729, Feb. He and Benjamin Greene were authorized by the Assembly to draw £30, from the General Treasury towards rebuilding the Pawtuxet Bridge.

1753, Aug. 17. Will—proved 1755, Feb. 10. Ex. son Randall. To grandson Thomas, son of John, deceased, 35 acres adjoining land where he lives, he paying grandson John, son of William, £100, at decease of my wife, and also paying £100, to my son Nathan, and Thomas to also pay his brother Henry, £100. In case of death of grandson John, the £100 to be paid his brother James. To son Thomas, all my lands in forks of Pawtuxet River, two other lots of land and £25. To son Nathan, a meadow share and two small lots near the fulling mill. To five daughters Elizabeth Spencer, Barbara Langford, Mary Gorton, Lydia Sweet and Elnathan Hill, each £80. To wife, all indoor movables, negro called Moll, one-quarter income of estate and benefit of dwelling house for life. To three sons Thomas, Nathan and Randall, all wearing apparel. To son Randall, negro boy Rufus, he paying grandson James, £100, at age. To son Nathan, £100 at decease of wife and liberty to plant 2 acres in common field for life Executor of will to provide wife with firewood. To son Randall, all homestead both sides the way, and all other lands, stock and movables. To three sons, equally the bonds and money.

Inventory, £3361, 16*s.* 2*d.*, viz: bonds £1047, 9*s.* 6*d.*, books £15, notes £273, 11*s.* 8*d.*, sword and belt, spinning wheel, 8 silver spoons, warming pan, 5 candle sticks, cheese tub, 7 cows, 2 heifers, 2 yearlings, 2 calves, pair of oxen, 60 sheep, 6 swine, 2 mares, 1 yearling mare, negro boy £250, negro girl £200, &c.

II. RANDALL, m. ELIZABETH, { b. d. 1742 ± } { b. d. 1745 + } of — Warwick, R. I.

1. Randall,
2. Richard,
3. Isaac,
4. John,
5. George,

1731, Nov. 15. He deeded son Randall, for love, &c., 50 acres.

1733, Aug. 4. He deeded son Richard, for love, &c., 70 acres.

1737, Mar. 2. He and wife Elizabeth sold Nathan Rice of East Greenwich, 128 acres and 68 rods, for £380, 8*s.*

1742, Aug. 30. Account of disbursements from his estate was given by the administrator Randall Rice of Coventry, who showed that he had paid out of the estate of his father Randall Rice, late of Warwick, deceased, the sum of £203, 4*s.* 8*d.*

1745, Nov. 2. His son John Rice of Coventry, in his will of this date, mentions his mother Elizabeth and brothers George (deceased), Richard, &c.

WILLIAM, b. d. 1684 +
m. (1)
ANN, b. 1625. d. 1669, May.
m. (2) 1670, Aug. 30.
DELIVERANCE SCOTT, b. d. 1676, Feb. 10.
of Richard & Catharine (Marbury) Scott.
m. (3) 1678, Mar. 27.
AMEY BORDEN, b. 1654, Feb. d. 1684, Feb. 5.
of Richard & Joan ( ) Borden.

Newport, R. I., Flushing, N. Y.

He was a shipmaster.

His first wife died at the house of Thomas Cornell, Portsmouth, as Friends' records state. She was buried 1669, May 5.

His second wife died on board the ship lying at anchor before New York. She was buried at Gravesend.

1638. He was admitted an inhabitant of the island of Aquidneck.

1639, Apr. 30. Portsmouth. He and twenty-eight others signed the following compact: "We whose names are underwritten do acknowledge ourselves the legal subjects of his Majesty King Charles, and in his name do hereby bind ourselves into a civil body politicke, unto his laws according to matters of justice."

1655. Freeman.

By one account another generation intervenes, and it was William, Jr., who married in 1670 and 1678, if that account be correct.

(3d WIFE.)

I. WILLIAM, b. 1679, Jan. 15. d.

II. THOMAS, b. 1680, Sep. 10. d. 1761, Apr. 28.
m. (1) 1704, Dec. 22.
ANNE NEWBURY, b. 1686, Apr. 22. d. 1728, Apr. 8. of Benjamin & Leah ( ) Newbury.
m. (2) 1729, Aug. 14
MARY WANTON, b. 1700, Jun. 10. d. 1777, Apr. 21. of Joseph & Sarah (Freeborn) Wanton.

1729, Oct. 10. He, as Clerk of Quarterly Meeting of Friends held at Portsmouth at this date, signed a petition to the Assembly, protesting against the unjust laws of the Colony, by which fines were laid on their houses, stripped of necessaries, &c.; being great sufferers "for our conscientiously refusing to bear arms or appear in the training field."

(2d wife.)
1. Amey, 1730.
2. Sarah, 1733, Mar. 31.
3. Anne, 1735, Jul. 3.
4. William, 1736, Feb. 10.
5. Thomas, 1739, Apr. 24.
6. Elizabeth, 1741, May 19.

III. JOHN, b. 1683, Feb. 1. d. 1706, Sep. 26.
m. 1704, Feb. 20.
ANN RODMAN, b. 1686, Nov. 16. d. 1714, Jun. 25. of Thomas & Patience (Easton) Rodman.

He died at Antigua.

1. Joseph, 1707, Mar. 9.

RICHMOND.

EDWARD[2] (John[1]). * b. 1632. d. 1696.
m. (1)
ABIGAIL DAVIS, b. d.
of Davis.
m. (2)
AMEY BULL, b. d.
of Henry & Elizabeth ( ) Bull.

Newport, Little Compton, R. I.

1657, May 20. The petition of Abigail Davis daughter-in-law (*i. e.* stepdaughter), of John Cowdall, having been read by a committee of the Assembly, it was shown that her marriage with Richard Ussell, was for fear of being forced to it by her father and mother, and later in the same year the said marriage was declared an unlawful one by the Assembly. She was thus enabled to marry Edward Richmond, whom she had declared in her petition to be her choice.

1661, Sep. 9. He had a share in Misquamicut (Westerly) lands appointed to him.

1663, Dec. 14. He had a legacy of 40 acres, and wearing apparel, from the will of his father John Richmond, of Taunton.

1667-69-70-72. General Solicitor.

1676, Aug. 6. It was voted by the Assembly "that Lieutenant Edward Richmond, with his company, shall be allowed and have the one-half of the produce of the seven Indians they brought in." By an act of the Assembly certain Indian men and women able for service, were to be sold for nine years.

1676, Aug. 23. He was clerk of a court martial that was held for the trial of four Indians, who according to the sentence of the court were executed.

1677, Jun. 11. He and three others were appointed to go to such persons in Newport as they see cause, to know who will advance money for the Colony's use in sending the agents to England.

1677, Oct. 31. He and forty-seven others were granted 5,000 acres to be called East Greenwich.

1677-78-79-80. Attorney General.

1678-79. Deputy.

1680. Taxed 14*s*.

1683, Jun. 6. Little Compton. He took oath of fidelity.

1683-84-85-89-90. Selectman

1686. Deputy.

1686, Jun. 4. Lieutenant. On the same date he was fined £5, for furnishing an Indian with some rum or strong liquor.

1690, May 20. Captain.

1691, Aug. 7. He and his children were mentioned in the will of his sister Sarah Stoughton, wife of Nicholas.

1692, Feb. 2. He bought of Daniel Wilcox, the twenty-seventh lot in Little Compton for £50.

1692, Feb. 16. He sold to "my father-in-law" Henry Bull, of Newport, being grandfather to my two youngest children, 120 acres in Little Compton, for £80, for the use and behoof of

* See: American Genealogist, v. 20, p. 57.

I. EDWARD, b. d.
m.
SARAH, b. 1667. d. 1743, Feb. 14. of

Little Compton, R. I.

His wife was buried in Newport Cemetery.

1. Abigail, 1684.
2. Edward, 1689, Dec. 3.
3. Anna, 1693, Jan. 22.
4. Elizabeth, 1694.
5. Benjamin, 1696, Jan. 10.
6. Amey, 1697, Nov. 22.
7. Mary, 1700, Mar. 15.
8. Esther, 1703, Feb. 3.
9. Abigail, 1704, Nov. 25.
10. Elizabeth, 1707, Nov. 15.

RICHMOND. 2d column. II. John. His daughter Elizabeth b. 1715, Aug. 23.

II. JOHN, b. d. 1738 +
m.
ELIZABETH, b. d. of

Kings Town, Westerly, R. I.

1. Cyrus,
2. Abigail,
3. Sarah,
4. Stephen, 1704, Oct. 3.
5. Anne, 1706, Nov. 1.
6. Elizabeth.

1710, Feb. 28. He sold to George Havens of Groton, Ct., my dwelling house and 200 acres in Kings Town for £400.

1711, Oct. 2. Westerly. He and thirty-three others bought 5,300 acres in Narragansett of the vacant lands.

1716, Jan. 12. He sold certain land.

1716. Freeman.

1722, May 5. He was appointed one of the executors of Nicholas Utter's will, and was given a legacy of £5.

1727, Nov. 4. He and wife Elizabeth, sold 60 acres in Hunting Swamp Farm, in Portsmouth, for £1,300 to William Wood and John Allen, of Newport.

1729-33. Deputy.

1738, Aug. 29. He as Justice of the Peace, married Thomas Burdick to Penelope Rhodes.

III. ABIGAIL, b. 1656. d. 1744.
m. (1) 1679 ±
JOHN REMINGTON, b. d. 1688. of John & Abigail ( ) Remington.
m. (2)
HENRY GARDINER, b. 1645. d. 1744. of George & Herodias (Long) Gardiner.

1. Abigail, 1681.
2. Martha
3. Elizabeth,
4. Hannah,
(By 2d husband.)
5. Henry, 1691, Feb. 25.
6. Ephraim, 1693, Jan. 17.
7. William, 1697, Oct. 27.

IV. MARY, b. d.
m.
WILLIAM PALMER, b. d. of Palmer.

1. William, 1686, Jan. 17.
2. Elizabeth, 1687, Nov. 12.
3. Joseph, 1689, Jun. 19.
4. Susanna, 1692, Oct. 24.
5. John, 1694, Nov. 13.
6. Thomas, 1697, Jan. 7.
7. Mary, 1699, Jan. 10.
8. Benjamin, 1700, Nov. 3.
9. Abigail, 1702, Apr. 5.
10. Patience, 1704, Feb. 19.
11. Sylvester, 1706, May 2.
12. Peleg, 1708, Mar. 8.

RICHMOND. 2d column. II. John, d. 1740. Children, 7. Rebecca, 8. Esther, 9. Content, 10. Priscilla.

1740, Feb. 24. Will—proved 1740, Jul. 28. Ex. son Stephen. To wife Elizabeth, for life, bed, linen, chests, six best chairs, pewter, profits of orchard, riding beast, two cows, &c. To son Cyrus, of Stonington, half of wearing apparel. To son Stephen, the other half. To daughter Rebecca Worden, a brass kettle, bed, &c. To daughters Sarah Lawton, Esther Tracy, of Preston, Ct., Ann Hoxsie, and Content Davis, household utensils, &c. To granddaughter Ruth Reynolds, daughter of my daughter Priscilla, two pewter plates, and to grandsons Richmond Reynolds and Joseph Reynolds, 5*s*. each at age. To daughter Abigail Burdick's five children, Simeon, Abigail, Edmond, Jonathan and Elizabeth, 5*s*., each. To daughter Elizabeth Hull's three children, Sarah, Tristram and Hannah, 5*s*., each. The executor was impowered to sell farm and all stock.

Inventory, £395, 2*s*., 11*d*., viz: wearing apparel £38, 17*s*., 6*d*., 12 plate buttons £3, 8*s*., sundry reading books £4, 5*s*., spectacles, seal, wax, and studs 9*s*., 2 warming pans, 11 chairs, 1 great chair, 4 pewter platters, 4 porringers, 13 plates, 16 wooden trenchers, mare, 2½ hives of bees, 2 ewes, 3 lambs, case of bottles, cards, wool wheel, old lancet, &c.

V. ELIZABETH, b. 1666, Dec. 6. d. 1717, Feb. 9.
m.
JOHN PALMER, b. 1665, May 18. d. 1752, Oct. 13. of Palmer.

1. John, 1687, Nov. 24.
2. Sarah, 1689, Sep. 29.
3. Elizabeth, 1691, Nov. 17.
4. Edward, 1693, Aug. 29.
5. Job, 1695, Sep. 17.
6. Aaron, 1697, Dec. 19.
7. Anna, 1699, Mar. 24.
8. Isaac, 1701, Jan. 14.
9. William, 1703, Mar. 18.
10. Esther, 1706, Aug. 31.
11. Henry, 1709, Oct. 11.

VI. ESTHER, b. 1669. d. 1706, Nov. 12.
m.
THOMAS BURGESS, b. 1668. d. 1743, Jul. 1. of Thomas & Lydia (Gaunt) Burgess.

1. Edward,
2. Deborah,
3. Lydia,
4. Abigail,
5. Esther,

my two youngest children Henry and Ann, with housing, garden, &c., reserving to self and wife Amey, the whole profits for life.

1696, Dec. 8. Inventory, £326, 6s., sworn to by the administrator Edward Richmond, eldest son of deceased. 2 oxen, 6 cows, 4 heifers, 2 yearlings, 5 calves, 2 mares, 3 colts, 2 horses, sheep, 2 fat swine, 8 lean swine, 18 loads of hay, pewter, cheese press, warming pan, arms, stillyards, sundry pieces of land, &c.

1696, Dec. 20. His estate was divided among his children as follows: To eldest son Edward, land £36, 3s., 4d., movables £27, 16s., 6d. To John Richmond, in his own right and right of sister Abigail Remington, land £36, 3s., 4d., movables £27, 16s., 6d. To William Palmer, land £18, 1s., 8d., movables, £13, 3s., 3d., and a like amount each to John Palmer, Sylvester Richmond, Sarah Richmond and Thomas Burge.

He was a member of the Church of England, according to the testimony of his daughter Abigail Gardiner, who deposed to that effect in 1738, calling herself in her eighty-second year.

VII. SYLVESTER, b. 1672. d. 1754, Nov. 20. Little Compton, R. I., Dartmouth, Mass.
m. (1) ELIZABETH ROGERS, b. d. 1724, Oct. 23. of John & Elizabeth (Pabodie) Rogers.
m. (2) 1728, Jan. DEBORAH LORING, b. d. 1770, Oct. 18. of Loring.

1. William, 1694, Oct. 10.
2. Elizabeth, 1696, May 10.
3. Sylvester, 1698, Jun. 30.
4. Peleg, 1700, Oct. 25.
5. Perez, 1702, Oct. 5.
6. Ichabod, 1704, Feb. 27.
7. Ruth, 1705, Mar. 7.
8. Hannah, 1709, Jul. 9.
9. Sarah, 1711, Oct. 31.
10. Mary, 1713, Nov. 29.
11. Rogers, 1716, May 25.
(2d wife, no issue.)

1701, May 29. He bought of John Rogers, of Boston, merchant, a tract of land in Little Compton, for £83; the grantor calling him son-in-law.

1704, Feb. 8. He bought 40 acres in Little Compton, for £60, of William Earle.

1727, Feb. 7. He made a covenant with Deborah Loring and Caleb Loring, previous to marriage to said Deborah.

He held the title of Colonel. He was one of the original members of First Congregational Church.

1752, Dec. 29. Will—proved 1754, Dec. 3. Ex. son Peleg. To wife Deborah, £18, 6s., 8d., riding chaise, easy chair and silver tankard, for her use, and what things she brought at marriage agreeable to covenant between self and wife and Caleb Loring, before marriage, dated 1727, Feb. 7. To wife also maintenance by testator's son Perez out of estate I shall give him. To son William, all lands joining his homestead in Little Compton, he paying my grandson Gamaliel Richmond, son of Peleg, £13, 6s., 8d., and to my granddaughter Mary Paine, who was daughter of my daughter Sarah deceased, £13, 6s., 8d. To son Sylvester, 30 acres in Dartmouth and £205, 13s., 4d., paid him by my son Perez. To son Peleg, 200 Spanish milled dollars, half of it in live stock. To son Ichabod, £33, 6s., 8d., and 3 acres in Little Compton and use of room in west end of my dwelling house and a bed. To son Rogers, £200, half in stock. To daughter Elizabeth, £40, and silver tankard at death of wife, and if Elizabeth die before wife, then the tankard to go to grandson and granddaughter Fisher, children of said Elizabeth. To daughter Ruth, £40 and two silver spoons. To daughter Mary, £20. To granddaughter Mary Paine, £5. To grandson Sylvester, son of Sylvester, my silver hilted sword. To grandson Joshua, son of Perez, a brace of pistols and holsters. To grandson Sylvester, son of William, three halberts and a fire lock gun. To grandson Richmond Loring, son of my daughter Mary, £20. To negroes Nat and Kate, their freedom. To daughter Elizabeth, £6, a feather bed, and other household stuff. To daughters Ruth and Mary, a bed and £6, each. To son Perez, my now dwelling house and homestead farm, and the rest of real and personal estate, he supporting my aged wife and giving to his brothers Peleg and Ichabod, a suit of apparel, each.

VIII. SARAH, b. d.

(2d WIFE.)

IX. HENRY, b. d.

IX. Henry, d. 1714, Sep. 30, Boston, Mass.; m. Jemima Smith, of John. No issue.

X. ANN, b. d.
m. 1704, Apr. 6. HENRY TEW, b. 1681 ± d. 1732, of Henry & Dorcas ( ) Tew.

1. Henry, 1705, Jan. 23
2. Amey, 1707, May 18.
3. Ann, 1709, Nov. 2.
4. Elizabeth, 1711, May 13
5. Edward, 1712, Aug. 8.
6. Amey, 1714, Jun. 1.
7. James, 1715, Sep. 2.
8. Edward, 1717, Sep. 4.
9. Dorcas, 1719, Sep. 21.

ROBERTS (PETER).

PETER, b. d. 1706 +
m. ——— b. d.

Providence, R. I.

1687, Sep. 1. Taxed 6s.

1706, Nov. 30. He deeded his son William for love, &c., all real estate, lands, tenements, movables, utensils, &c., only reserving my bed, bedstead and chest, and privilege of egress and regress to house.

I. WILLIAM, b. d. 1726, Feb. 25. Providence, R. I.
m. AMEY, b. d. 1726 + of

1. William,
2. Jane,
3. David,
4. Thomas,
5. Peter,

1718, Jun. 2. He bought of Joshua Turner (son of Joshua, deceased), a sixteenth of a right of land, for £24.

1726, Apr. 11. Administration to widow Amey. Inventory, £306, 13s. 10d., viz: bonds £117, 17s. 4d., books £1, feather bed, flock bed, 7 chairs, 2 tables, 2 linen wheels, woolen wheel, pewter, old gun, 2 barrels of cider, corn, beans, mare, 35 sheep, pair of oxen, 6 cows, 2 yearlings, sow and 5 shoats, hay, &c.

1739, May 26. Widow's account of administration showed £107, personal left. To Amey the widow, a third. To William Roberts, Jane Fenner, David, Thomas and Peter, the rest. The eldest, William, having £22, 5s. 4d, and others, £11, 2s. 8½d., each.

1740, Apr. 16. His son William took receipt from brother David, for a deed to him of 29 acres, a third part of deceased father William Roberts' real estate. At same date William took receipt from Daniel Fenner and Jane his wife, for 14½ acres.

II. PETER, b. d. 1743, Aug. 17. Providence, R. I.
m. AMEY COLVIN, b. 1690, Oct. 31. d. 1743 + of John & Dorothy ( ) Colvin.

1. Philip,
2. John,
3. Peter,
4. Mary,
5. Sarah,
6. Dorothy,

1723, Feb. 23. He and wife Amey sold Richard Knight, for £35, a parcel of land, being a sixteenth right.

1727, Jan. 19. He and wife Amey had a deed of 50 acres in Mashantatack, for love, &c., and £150 paid by them to John Colvin, who calls them daughter and son-in-law.

1743, Feb. 2. Will—proved 1743, Sep. 19. Exs. son Philip and brother-in-law James Colvin. To wife Amey, all indoor movables, 2 cows, a mare and ten sheep, and son Philip to provide keep for the animals and furnish her with twelve bushels of Indian corn yearly, while she is widow of testator. To her also, the best room in the house and a bed room for life while widow. To son Philip, the homestead farm to him and heirs to third generation. To son John, all right of land in Warwick, in part called Nachick, to continue to third generation. To son Peter, £200, at age, to be paid him half by Philip and half by John. To daughters Mary, Sarah and Dorothy Roberts, £30, each, Mary to receive her legacy within a year, and her sisters at eighteen or marriage. Son Philip was to have profits of his brother John's land in Warwick, till John came of age.

Inventory, £965, 8s. 3d, viz: books £1, 3s., bible, plate, buttons, buckles, cup and other silver £4, 1s. 6d., 6 feather beds, £164, 15s., 2 flock beds £22, 15s., 2 linen wheels, woolen wheel, loom, gun, woolen and linen yarns, 469 lbs. new milk cheese, corn, oats, rye, flax, a bull, bull stag, 9 cows, 2 heifers, 2 yearlings, 7 calves, mare, 31 sheep, 2 pair steers, 6 swine, 6 shoats, stack of bees, 24 loads of hay, &c.

THOMAS, b. d. 1676, Apr.
m. b. d.

Providence, R. I.

By one account his wife was a sister of William Harris.

1650, Sep. 2. Taxed 13s. 4d.

1656, Jan. 28. He was granted a share of meadow to be laid out in the swamp by William Field's wolf trap.

1656–61. Commissioner.

1665, Feb. 19. He had lot 89 in a division of land.

1670–72. Deputy.

He died at Newport.

1679, Jul. 1. "Thomas Roberts' land" was taxed 5s. 1½d. at Providence.

No relationship has been traced between him and Peter Roberts of Providence, or Mark Roberts of Warwick (who married 1683, Jan. 1, Mary Baker).

1679, Dec. 5. Administration on estate of Thomas Roberts was given to Captain Richard Smith of Narragansett, in behalf of Christopher Roberts of Arlingham, County of Gloucester. The said Christopher Roberts was nephew and heir of Thomas Roberts.

ROBERTS (THOMAS). 1st column. 1676, July, William and Thomas Harris asked administration of Town Council of Newport on estate of widow of Thomas Roberts, they being the only brothers of deceased. She had died shortly after her husband, who had no child by her.

ROBINSON.

ROBINSON. 2d column. I. John. His wife b. 1683, Oct. 3, of Thomas and Susanna Hazard. (Not of Robert.)

ROWLAND, b. 1654. d. 1716.
m.
MARY ALLEN, b. 1653, Feb. 4. d. 1716 +
of John & Elizabeth (Bacon) Allen.

Long Bluff, Cumberland Co., Eng., Kings Town, R. I.

1675. He came to America this year.

1684, Nov. 28. Newport. He bought of Benjamin Church, for £45, a lot at Saconnet, and 40 acres at Tymsumbe.

1705. Kings Town. Deputy.

1709, Sep. 27. He bought 3,000 acres of the vacant lands ordered sold by the Assembly.

1713, Jan. 26. Will—proved 1716, Jul 16. Exs. wife Mary and son William. To wife, 80 acres and house in which William Dunkin lives, and grist mill, for life. To son William, all housing and 300 acres in Boston Neck, and 300 acres in Westerly. To daughter Elizabeth Browne, £40. To daughter Mary Mumford, £40. To daughter Sarah Barton, £40. To daughter Mercy Robinson, £100. To four grandchildren, daughters of son John deceased, 10s., each. To wife and son William, all movables, they paying legacies. To son William, at decease of his mother, all housing, mills and lands that was hers for life.

Inventory, £2,166, viz: 473 sheep, 300 lambs, bull, 15 oxen, 22 steers and heifers, 56 cows, 28 two years, 26 yearlings, 30 calves, 12 horses, 26 mares, 16 colts, 53 swine (said stock being kept at several farms), 9 negroes £375, wearing apparel, feather beds, 2 spinning wheels, pewter, money £64, 15s., 8 silver spoons £5, 12s., 3 guns, churn, 140 cheeses, desk, great bible and other books £2, 16s., joiner's tools, bonds and book debts, £216, 16s., &c.

He and his wife were buried in the Quaker Burial Ground, two miles south-east of Tower Hill Village.

I. JOHN, b. 1680. d. 1712, Apr. 6. Newport, R. I.
m. 1704, Oct. 19.
MARY HAZARD. b. 1676. d. 1722. of Robert & Mary (Brownell) Hazard.
1. Mary, 1705, Sep. 30.
2. Sarah, 1707, Jan. 22.
3. Ruth, 1709, Mar. 12.
4. Susanna, 1712, Feb. 9.

He was buried in Clifton Burial Ground. The inscription on tombstone calls him thirty-two years old.

II. ROWLAND, b. 1682, Jun. 18. d. 1693.

III. JOSEPH, b. d. young.

ROBINSON. IV. Elizabeth. Her husband was probably son of Jeremiah and Mary ( ) Brown.

See American Genealogist, v. 28, no. 4, Oct., 1952, p. 212.

IV. ELIZABETH, b. d. 1752 +
m. 1707, Nov. 2
WILLIAM BROWN, b. 1676. d. 1753. of Brown.
1. John, 1708, Aug. 6.
2. Mary, 1710, Jun. 4.
3. Thomas, 1711, Aug. 23.
4. Elizabeth, 1713, Feb. 28.
5. Ruth, 1715, Sep. 25.
6. Robert, 1718, Jul. 26.
7. George, 1721, Sep. 30.

V. MARY, b. d.
m. 1709, Aug. 7.
GEORGE MUMFORD, b. 1689, Jul. 15. d. 1745. of Thomas & Abigail ( ) Mumford.
1. Mercy, 1710, Nov. 15.
2. Abigail, 1713, Apr. 7.

VI. SARAH, b d. 1760.
m. 1705, Jan. 4.
RUFUS BARTON, b. 1673. d. 1752. of Benjamin & Susannah (Gorton) Barton.
1. Rufus,
2. Rowland,
3. Margaret,
4. Sarah,
5. William,

VII. MERCY, b. d. 1762.
m. 1714, Oct. 28.
JOHN POTTER, b. 1695, May 20. d. 1739. of John & Sarah (Wilson) Potter.
1. John, 1716.
2. Christopher 1717.
3. Christopher 1719.
4. Mary, 1721.
5. William, 1723, Jan. 21.
6. Samuel, 1725, Jan. 20.
7. Mercy, 1727, Aug. 15.
8. Sarah, 1730, Aug. 11.

ROBINSON. 2d column. VII. Mercy. Her husband d. 1739, Apr. 11. Add full date of birth of part of the children. 1. John, 1715, Jan. 3. 2. Christopher, 1717, Nov. 5. 3. Christopher, 1719, Nov. 8. 4. Mary, 1721, May 24.

VIII. WILLIAM, b. 1693, Jan. 26. d. 1751, Sep. 19. South Kingstown, R. I.
m. (1) 1718 ±
MARTHA POTTER, b. 1692, Dec. 20. d. 1725, Nov. of John & Sarah (Wilson) Potter.
m. (2) 1727, Mar. 2. [Caleb
ABIGAIL HAZARD, (w. of b. 1700. d. 1772, May 22. of William & Abigail (Remington) Gardiner.
1. Rowland, 1719, Oct. 8.
2. John, 1721, Jul. 23.
3. Marah, 1723, Jan. 27.
4. Elizabeth, 1724, Jun. 16.
5. Martha, 1725, Nov. 11.
(2d wife.)
6. Christopher 1727, Dec. 31.
7. William, 1729, Aug. 1.
8. Thomas, 1731, Jan. 25.
9. Abigail, 1732, Dec. 19.
10. Sylvester, 1735, Jan. 23.
11. Mary, 1736, Oct. 8.
12. James, 1738, Dec. 31.
13 John, 1743, Jan. 13.

1724-25-26-27-28-34-35-36-41-42. Deputy.

1735-36-41-42. Speaker of House of Deputies.

1742, Nov. He was appointed by the Assembly on a committee with four others, to see if there was a necessity of dividing the "woods part" of Newport, from the more compact part. The petitioners had set forth that the compact part consisted chiefly of merchants and tradesmen, while the woods part consisted of farmers, and it was deemed that affairs could be managed with greater regularity, order and justice by making two towns. (That part of Newport called the woods, was set off under the name of Middletown the next year.)

1745-46-47-48. Deputy Governor.

1747, Jan. 15. Will—proved 1751, Oct. 14. Exx. wife Abigail. To wife, £1000, negro Old Pete, girl Roco, woman Lydia, two feather beds, and my clock. To son Rowland, all my farm in Boston Neck, which he now liveth on. To son Christopher, house and 160 acres in South Kingstown. To son William, farm of 200 acres in South Kingstown and negro young Peter. To son Thomas, 80 acres in South Kingstown, other land and negro boy Jo. To sons Christopher and Thomas, equally, 117 acres in South Kingstown. To sons Sylvester and James, equally, a farm of 360 acres at Point Judith. To son John, 168 acres in South Kingstown. To son Sylvester, negro boy Jack and £100, at age. To son James, negro named James and £100 at age. To daughter Elizabeth Hazard, £700 and a feather bed. To daughter Martha Clarke, £700, and a feather bed. To daughter Abigail, £1,200, at nineteen, and negro Isabel and a feather bed. To daughter Mary, £1,200, at nineteen, negro Nane and two feather beds. To daughters Elizabeth, Martha, Abigail and Mary, my four silver porringers marked with first two letters of my name. To wife, use of all land, except that given Rowland, till sons come of age, with liberty for her to cut firewood from any lands for life for her own burning, she making no waste.

Inventory, £21,573, 5s., 5d., viz: wearing apparel £130, cash £176, 2s., bonds and notes £5,255, 11s., 3d., pair of gold buttons, pair of shin buckles, and a band buckle £12, 29 cows, 17 oxen, 8 heifers, 18 two years, 26 yearlings, 28 calves, 30 horsekind, 17 store pigs, 18 fat shoats, 16 shoats, 4 sows, 195 lambs, cider mill and press £20, negroes—Old Sue nothing, Old Mingo nothing, Jeffrey, £350, Lucy £280, Phillis £200, Peter Knowles £100, girls Sue and Cynthia and boy Simon £300, Old Pete £175, Lydia £300, Roco £320, Young Pete £500, Jo £400, Jack £450, Jemmy £250, Samuel £450, Isabel £300, Nanna £250, corn in crib £650, 2 old wheels, parts of 2 old linen wheels, table linen £22, clock £145, pair of worsted combs, silver in buffet in great room £374, 8*s.*, books and desk £5, pocket book and cash £113, 6*s.*, 6*d.*, English and marsh hay £850, barley stack £20, cheese fats, cheeses, &c. The rooms were cheese room, milk room, kitchen, store bedroom, great room, great room bedroom, store closet, dining room, north-east bedroom, great chamber, dining room bedroom, dining room chamber, dining room chamber bedroom, cellar.

1770, May 12. Will—proved 1772, Sep. 14. Widow Abigail. Exs. sons Sylvester and John Robinson. To three sons William, Robert and Caleb Hazard, one hundred and twenty Spanish milled dollars divided. To son Christopher Robinson, a silver tankard, silver porringers and $30. To sons William, and Thomas Robinson, $30 each. To son Sylvester Robinson, $50. To son James Robinson, $100. To son John Robinson, $50, a silver porringer, silver spoon and bed. To daughter Mary Dockray, $400, wearing apparel and bed, &c. To all granddaughters named Abigail (being eight of them), £100 divided. To granddaughter Hannah Brown, my easy chair. To children Christopher, Sylvester, James and John Robinson and Mary Dockray, rest of estate equally divided. To negro man Morocco, his freedom. To negro man Mingo, his freedom at thirty years of age and till then his services to be given to executors.

He was buried in the Robinson Burial Ground (near Narragansett Pier).

RODMAN.

THOMAS[2], (John[1]). * — b. 1640, Dec. 26. d. 1728, Jan. 11.
m. (1) 1682, Jun. 7. [Rob't.
PATIENCE MALINS, (w. of — b. 1655, Nov. 20. d. 1690, Nov. 21.
of Peter & Ann (Coggeshall) Easton.
m. (2) 1691, Nov. 26.
HANNAH CLARKE, — b. 1667, Oct. 28. d. 1732, Oct. 22.
of Walter & Hannah (Scott) Clarke.

Barbadoes, W. I., Newport, R. I.

He came from Barbadoes with his younger brother John, both being physicians. (His brother removed to Flushing, L. I.)

He was a Quaker, and clerk of their meetings for many years.

It is said he had a still earlier wife named Sarah, before coming to Newport, but no children by her.

1677. Newport. Freeman.

1680. Taxed £1, 7*s.*

1691, Apr. 1. He was witness to will of John Johnson.

1707, Apr. 28. He exchanged certain land with his niece Mary Brandiff of Flushing, Long Island. She describes herself as granddaughter to John Rodman of Christ Church Parish, Barbadoes, deceased, and mentions a bequest made by her grandfather to her mother. (She deeds her uncle Thomas all right in lands in Christ Church Parish, Barbadoes.)

1709, Apr. 7. He sold to William Ticol of Barbadoes, 4 acres, house, &c., in Christ Church Parish, Barbadoes.

1709, Apr. 20. He of Newport, and brother John Rodman of Flushing, sold to Francis Adams of Barbadoes, a messuage or tenement and 5 acres.

He was buried in Clifton Burying Ground.

1728, Feb. His widow Hannah deeded to dutiful and well beloved son-in-law Jonathan Easton of Newport, and daughter Patience his wife, for love, &c., a lot of land or garden.

* See: American Genealogist, v. 20, p. 57.

I. THOMAS, — b. 1683, Nov. 11. d. 1775. — Newport, South Kingstown, R. I.
m. 1706, Sep. 20.
CATHARINE FRY, — b. 1683, Dec. 23. d. 1740, May 4. — of Thomas & Mary (Griffin) Fry.

1. Thomas, 1708, Mar. 9.
2. Patience, 1710, Mar. 22.
3. John, 1711, Dec. 26.
4. Joseph, 1713, Oct. 1.
5. Samuel, 1716, Mar. 22.
6. Ann, 1718, Apr. 20.
7. Robert, 1720, Jun. 11.
8. William, 1723, May 3.
9. Benjamin, 1726, Jul. 22.

He was a physician.

1705. Kings Town. He had ear mark granted for sheep.

1762, Jan. 4. Will—codicil 1767, Dec. 4.—proved 1775, May 8. Exs. sons Samuel and Benjamin. To son Thomas, 140 acres at west end of homestead, and if he die without issue then to my son Joseph, and if he die without issue, to go to my sons living, they giving value in money to children of son Joseph. To son Thomas also, £60, and my riding horse. To son Joseph, £100, and next best suit of clothes, he having had portion. To son Robert, 85 acres of homestead, and my house and shop in Newport where Thomas Leach formerly lived. To son Samuel, remaining half of homestead, dwelling house, orchards, &c. To son Benjamin, meadow lot and house he lives in with land equal to Samuel, and one third of fruit in north end of orchard for ten years, and my clock and silver tankard. To grandson William, son of Joseph, riding horse at twenty-one, and if he die then to his brother Thomas. To daughter Patience, house room till otherwise provided for. To grandsons Thomas and James, sons of my son John, deceased, each £100, at twenty-one. To daughter-in-law Mary Greene, £20. To children of daughter Patience Bull, £250. To four daughters of my daughter Ann Greene, deceased, £600, at eighteen. To granddaughters Katharine Bull and Katharine Greene, each a silver spoon. Negro man John to have liberty to choose which son he lives with, and such son to treat him kindly. In codicil he states that being informed son Joseph is dead, he wishes land given him to go to son Thomas, and if he die without issue, land to go to brothers of Thomas, they paying to each son of Joseph, £200, and to each daughter of Joseph, £100.

Inventory, £779, 14*s.* 6¼*d.*, viz: 4 ivory headed walking sticks, pewter, wearing apparel, 2 silver porringers, 4 spoons, silver buttons, &c., notes £525, 16*s.* 7½*d.*, negroes, Cuff £0, Ely £0, Kate £0, Jack £51, Abraham £51, Israel £40, 2 mares, 3 colts, cow, calf, turkeys, hens, bible, Sewall's History, desk, old small case with five bottles, bell metal mortar, &c.

II. ANN, — b. 1686, Nov. 16. d. 1714, Jun. 25.
m. 1704, Feb. 20.
JOHN RICHARDSON, — b. 1683, Feb. 1. d. 1706, Sep. 26. — of William & Amey (Borden) Richardson.

1. Joseph, 1707, Mar. 9.

(2d WIFE.)

III. HANNAH, — b. 1694, Nov. 29. d. 1753, Jul. 10.
m. 1711, Oct. 31.
PHILIP WANTON, — b. 1686, May 9. d. 1735. — of Edward & Elizabeth (   ) Wanton.

1. Walter, 1712, Nov. 27.
2. Hannah, 1715, Jul. 15.
3. Philip, 1719, May 31.
4. Thomas, 1722, Mar. 14.
5. Mary, 1725, Mar. 29.
6. Elizabeth, 1727 ±

IV. CLARKE, — b. 1698, Mar. 10. d. 1752, Aug. 30. — Newport, R. I.
m. 1717, Jan. 3.
ANN COGGESHALL, — b. 1701, Apr. 14. d. 1758 + — of Daniel & Mary (Mowry) Coggeshall.

1. Walter, 1719, Aug. 13.
2. Mary, 1722, May 18.
3. Joseph, 1724, Feb. 2.
4. Thomas, 1726, Jun. 5.
5. Hannah, 1728, Jan. 9.
6. Daniel, 1731, Sep. 4.
7. Ann, 1733, Jul. 7.
8. Peleg, 1736, Jan. 27.
9. Samuel, 1738, Apr. 16.
10. Peleg, 1740, Feb. 20.

He was a physician and two of his sons (Walter and Thomas) were members of same profession.

1745, Aug. 26. He and wife Ann sold Daniel Bateman 230 acres in Jamestown.

1747. He was a member of Redwood Library at its incorporation.

1758, Mar. 20. His widow Ann deeded 14 acres in Jamestown to Hannah Wanton, widow, of Newport, for £30, paid her yearly for life by said Hannah.

He was buried in Clifton Burying Ground.

V. JOHN, — b. 1701, Sep. 29. d. 1702, Jan. 9.

VI. SAMUEL, — b. 1703, Jul. 23. d. 1748, Feb. 27. — Newport, R. I.
m. 1723, May 16.
MARY WILLETT, — b. d. — of Thomas Willett.

1. Thomas, 1724, Feb. 29.
2. Hannah, 1725, Sep. 22.
3. Charity, 1728, Jan. 15.
4. Samuel, 1730, Mar. 31.
5. William, 1732, Mar. 18.
6. Elizabeth, 1736, May 28.
7. Ann,

1728. Freeman.

1736, Jun. He was ordered by Assembly to have paid to him £30, towards finishing the bridge commonly called the Point Bridge in Newport.

1745, May 1. He was appointed on committee with two others by Assembly to view the pier at Block Island and see if the same be completely finished, and they reported soon after that it was completed.

1747. He was a member of Redwood Library at its incorporation.

He was buried in Clifton Burying Ground.

VII. PATIENCE, — b. 1706, Jun. 5. d. 1739, May 9.
m.
JONATHAN EASTON, — b. 1699. d. 1783, Mar. 4. — of Nicholas & Mary (Holmes) Easton.

1. Sarah,
2. Amey,
3. Mary,
4. Hannah,
5. Nicholas, 1733, Mar. 16.

VIII. WILLIAM, — b. 1707, Nov. 2. d. 1709, Jan. 26.

ROGERS (John).

John[2], (John[1]). { b. { d. 1732.
m. (1) 1666, Nov. 16.
Elizabeth Pabodie, { b. 1647, Apr. 24. { d.
of William & Elizabeth (Alden) Pabodie.
m. (2)
Marah ———, (widow). { b. { d. 1739.

Duxbury, Boston, Mass., Barrington, R. I.

He was a merchant.

1701, May 29. Boston. He sold certain land in Little Compton to son-in-law Sylvester Richmond, for £83.

1732, Sep. 5. Administration to three grandsons, Perez Bradford of Milton, William Richmond and Nathaniel Searle of Little Compton; the widow and two daughters refusing to administer.

Inventory, £977, 18s. 8d., viz: wearing apparel £5, 12s., cane 10s., silver tankard £30, 3 silver spoons £3, silver cup £2. 10s, silver dram cup 16s., small silver tankard £10, 2 gold rings £2, 10s., pair of silver shoe buckles, two dozen and nine silver buttons, table, beds, pewter, brass, wooden ware, 2 cows, old horse, 13 sheep, 2 lambs, notes and bonds £807, &c.

1733, Sep. 25. His widow Marah Rogers declared that she had a table cloth, five napkins and twenty pounds of feathers about, which said husband gave her in his life time, and £60, that she always kept to herself from her former widowhood and in her husband Rogers' lifetime to trade with, and was no part of estate he had with her. She made oath that she had not concealed or conveyed away or embezzled any of his estate since his sickness or death.

1739, Feb. 19. Administration on estate of widow Marah Rogers of Rehoboth, was given to John and Moses Newell of Brookline, sons of Marah Newell, who is nearest akin to Marah Rogers, at the request of their mother, she being advanced in years.

I. { Hannah, { b. 1668, Nov. 16. { d.
m 1689, Jul.
Samuel Bradford, { b. 1668. { d. 1714, Apr. 11. of William & Alice (Richards) Bradford.

1. Hannah, 1690, Feb. 14.
2. Gershom, 1691, Dec. 21.
3. Perez, 1694, Dec. 28.
4. Elizabeth, 1696, Dec. 15.
5. Jerusha, 1699, Mar. 10.
6. Welthea, 1702, May 15.
7. Gamaliel, 1704, May 18.

II. { John, { b. 1670, Sep. 22. { d.

III. { Ruth, { b. 1675, Apr. 18. { d.

IV. { Sarah, { b. 1677, May 4. { d. 1770, Jan. 19.
m.
Nathaniel Searle, { b. 1662, Jun. 9. { d. 1750, Feb. 5. of Searle.

1. Deborah, 1695, Nov. 17.
2. John, 1698, Mar. 12.
3. Sarah, 1700, Apr. 2.
4. Nathaniel, 1703, Apr. 26.

V. { Elizabeth, { b. { d. 1724, Oct. 23.
m.
Sylvester Richmond, { b. 1672. { d. 1754, Nov. 20. of Edward & Abigail (Davis) Richmond.

1. William, 1694, Oct. 10.
2. Elizabeth, 1696, May 10.
3. Sylvester, 1698, Jun. 30.
4. Peleg, 1700, Oct. 25.
5. Perez, 1702, Oct. 5.
6. Ichabod, 1704, Feb. 27.
7. Ruth, 1705, Mar. 7.
8. Hannah, 1709, Jul. 9.
9. Sarah, 1711, Oct. 31.
10. Mary, 1713, Nov. 29.
11. Rogers, 1716, May 25.

(2d Wife, no issue.)

ROOME.

John, { b. { d. 1663,
m.
Anna, { b. { b. 1663 +

Portsmouth, R. I.

He was a house carpenter.

1638. He was admitted an inhabitant of the island of Aquidneck, having submitted himself to the government that is or shall be established.

1641, Mar. 16. Freeman.

1639, Apr. 30. He and twenty-eight others signed the following compact: "We whose names are underwritten do acknowledge ourselves the legal subjects of his Majesty King Charles, and in his name do hereby bind ourselves into a civil body politicke, unto his laws according to matters of justice."

1644, May 27. He was granted an addition of land to his lot.

1645, Oct. 23. He sold to Nathaniel Browning, a dwelling house and two lots of 8 acres in Warwick for £3, in wampum.

1653, May 18. He and seven others were a committee for re-hearing matters that concern Long Island and in the case concerning the Dutch.

1654-55-56-59-61. Commissioner.

1655. Freeman.

1655-56. Assistant.

1663, Feb. 2. Administration to widow Anna, testimony being given that immediately before his death he made his wife executrix to all his estate.

The widow sold to William Cory, house, orchard and 85 acres for £83, 10s.

ROSE.

See: American Genealogist, v20, p. 58

Tourmet, { b. { d. 1684.
m.
Hannah George, { b. 1648, Sep. 7. { d. 1692 ±

of Peter & Mary ( ) George.

(She m. (2) 1685, Mar. 11, James Danielson.)

New Shoreham, R. I.

1660. He was one of the sixteen purchasers of Block Island, which was bought of John Endicott, Richard Bellingham, Daniel Dennison and William Hawthorne, for £400.

1661, Apr. He went with the first settlers to the island, and soon after received lot 3, in a division of lands in north part of the island and lot 3, in west part of island, having as partner in ownership of both lots, Nathaniel Wingley.

I. { John, { b. 1678, Oct. 10. { d. 1720. New Shoreham, R. I.
m. 1698, Dec. 28.
Mary Dodge, { b. 1682, Apr. 18. { d. 1720. + of John & Mary ( ) Dodge.

1720, Dec. 17. Will—proved 1720, Dec. Exs. wife Mary and Captain Simon Ray. To son Tormet, house where I live, and west part of farm, &c.; twelve cows, a yoke of oxen, two heifers, a bull, a pair of steers, a calf, twenty sheep, and wood from 5 acre piece of land given son Daniel. Legacies to be paid by son Tormet, as follows: To son John, £100, at age; to daughter Ann, £30 at age; and to son James, £20 at age. To son Daniel, east half of land and two meadow lots at age, he paying legacies as follows: to daughter Mary, £20 at age, to daughter Catharine, £15, at age, and to son Ezekiel, £80 at age. To wife, rest of goods and chattels to bring up younger children, and while she remained widow she was to have use of house, except Tormet have occasion of some part of the kitchen.

Inventory, £522, 1s., 9d., viz: wearing apparel and cash £52, 12s., 7d., 6 horses, 8 yearling cattle, 18 cows, 3 heifers, 5 calves, a yoke of oxen, a pair of steers, 6 swine, 52 sheep, 7 silver spoons, barley, corn, beans, loom, 9 beds, 2 flock beds, 600lb. cheese, 3 spinning wheels, 30 loads of hay, bonds £72, &c.

1. Tourmet, 1699, Nov. 3.
2. Daniel, 1701, Oct. 6.
3. John, 1703, Jun. 29.
4. Ezekiel, 1705, Jul. 17.
5. James,
6. Ann,
7. Mary,
8. Catherine,

1664. Freeman.

1676. Assistant Warden.

1684, Aug. 26. Inventory, £152, 15*s*., 8*d*., personal, viz: silver money £7, 14*s*., Indian man £12, sheep, and swine £47, 9*s*., 4 oxen, 2 steers, young cattle £15, 13 cows, a bull, horse, mare, pewter, gun, apparel, &c. Real estate, 243 acres with house £263, 8 acres Indian corn, English corn blasted.

1684, Oct. 1. Will—made by Town Council for orphans of Tormet Rose, who died intestate. Exs. Hannah Rose, widow, and Robert Guttredge, to be guardian for John Rose, only son of deceased, till John is of age, at which time he to be sole executor. To son John, all lands at age. To daughter Hannah Rose, £50 at twenty-one or marriage. To daughter Mary Rose, £50, at twenty-one or marriage. To widow Hannah Rose, her thirds while widow.

II. HANNAH, b. 1679, Oct 24. d.
m. 1705, Nov. 11.
ALEXANDER YOUNG, b. d. of Young.

III. MARY, b. d.

ROSS.

WILLIAM, b. d. 1712.
m.
HANNAH, b. d. 1712 +

Westerly, R. I.

1712, Apr. 27. Will—proved 1712, Jun. 12. Exx. wife Hannah. To eldest son William, half my land on east side of farm and if he sell it shall only be to brothers of name of Ross. To second son John, the other half of farm at wife's decease on same conditions. To wife, for life the use of all lands, house and movables. To son Thomas, one ewe sheep. To daughter Ann, a pot and kettle at wife's decease. To daughter Mary Ross, a pot and kettle. Son John to maintain his mother, and if he neglect to do so power is given her to sell the part of farm given John, to maintain herself in her old age. To John Babcock, two cows, a three year old heifer, two calves and a yearling, being for my son Thomas's joint debt.

Inventory, £37, 8*s*., 2*d*., viz: 2 beds, wearing clothes £3, 4 sheep, 11 lambs, mare, colt, cow, calf, steer, yearling, &c.

I. WILLIAM, b. d. Westerly, R. I.
m. 1711, Apr. 18.
ANN LEWIS, b. 1691, Jan. 6. d. of John & Ann ( ) Lewis.

1. Jemima, 1712, Mar. 14.
2. William, 1715, Aug. 3.
3. Thomas, 1719, Sep. 11.
4. Isaac, 1722, Apr. 5.
5. Ann, 1726, Jan. 21.
6. Hannah, 1727, Oct. 14.
7. Peleg, 1733, Sep. 9.

II. JOHN, b. d.

III. THOMAS, b. d. 1719. New London, Ct.
m.
PATIENCE, b. d. 1716 + of

1716, Nov. 10. Will—proved 1719, Aug. 15. Exx. wife Patience. To her all estate real and personal.

IV. ANN, b. 1694, Jan. 3. d.

V. MARY, b. 1700, May 21. d.
m. 1720, Feb. 11.
DANIEL PECKHAM, b. d. of Thomas & Hannah (Weeden) Peckham.

1. Hannah, 1720, Oct. 23.
2. Mary, 1722, Feb. 22.
3. Daniel, 1726, Sep. 25.
4. Sarah, 1729, Aug. 31.
5. Abel, 1733, Feb. 17.

RUTENBURG.

JOHN, b. d. 1723,
m. (1)
MARY SHIPPEE, b. d.
of David & Margaret (Scranton) Shippee.
m. (2)
SARAH, b. d. 1723 +

Warwick, R. I.

He was a ropemaker.

1697, Dec. 13. His wife Mary, had deed of 60 acres in East Greenwich, from her father David Shippee.

1701, Mar. 24. He and wife Mary, sold for £10 to William Underwood, of East Greenwich, 60 acres that came to wife as gift from her father David Shippee.

1701, Oct. 22. He received a deed from David Sweet, of 10 acres and was called therein "John Rutenburg, of Potowomut, ropemaker."

1712, Jan. 5. He received a deed from John Heath, of East Greenwich, of mansion house where latter dwelt and 10 acres, provided he should be suffered to dwell in it for life and have £6 paid him by John Rutenburg, yearly, house kept in repair, servant girl Betty allowed to live there, and at his death servant still to be allowed to live there by paying £2 per year rent to John Rutenburg.

1723, Nov. 10. Will—proved 1723, Dec. 9. Exs. sons Thomas and Solomon. To wife Sarah, all movables in house and she to dwell in same during widowhood. To son John, 5*s*. To daughter Mary, 20*s*. To son David, 5*s*. To son Peter, 5*s*. To daughters Margaret, Susannah and Katherine, 20*s*. each. To daughter Ruth, 5*s*. To daughter Mercy, £50. All legacies to be paid within five years of decease. To youngest sons Thomas and Solomon, all lands, houses and estate real and personal.

Inventory, £294, 4*s*., 4*d*., viz: feather beds, 2 woolen wheels, 5 guns, saddle, bridle and pillion, table, chairs, carpenter's tools, stilyards, 2 pair woolen cards, 2 razors, 23 books, ink horn, pen knife, shoemaker tools, rope making tools, 16 sheep, 2 oxen, 2 mares, 2 cows, cider mill, &c.

I. JOHN, b. d. Warwick, R. I.
m. 1719, Apr. 14.
SARAH COLLINS, b. 1698, Oct. 31. d. of Thomas & Abigail (House) Collins.

(She m. (2) 1743, Mar. 31, Thomas Harris.)

1. William, 1720, Sep. 22.
2. Mary, 1723, Aug. 22.
3. Peter, 1725, Jun. 9.

II. MARY, b. d.

III. DAVID, b. d. 1754, May 16. Providence, R. I.
m. 1727, Mar. 5.
HANNAH JENCKS, b. 1704, Feb. 15. d. of Daniel & Catharine (Balcom) Jencks.

1. John,
2. Daniel,
3. Ruth,
4. Anne,
5. Amey,

He was a carpenter.

1723, Mar. 7. He sold to Stephen Harding for £56, 10*s*., two parcels of land, 36½ acres, and also a 10 acre piece.

1754, Feb. 11. Will—proved 1754, May 27. Ex. son Daniel. To son Daniel, all lands (except 10 acres) and all personal, after payment of debts and legacies. To eldest daughter Ruth Brown, £200. To second daughter Anne Rutenburge, £200 and feather bed. To third daughter Amey Rutenburge, £200 and feather bed. To grandson Joseph Rutenburge, 10 acres, and he to be brought up to common learning, to learn to read, write and cipher, and to learn trade of a joiner or some other trade that he and executor may agree on. To granddaughter Hannah Rutenburge, £200 and feather bed at eighteen. To daughter-in-law Martha Rutenburge, as long as she remains widow of testator's son, the privilege of a room in my house, and two unmarried daughters of testator to have privilege of house till marriage.

Inventory £1,425, 8*s*., 2*d*., viz: bonds and notes £334, 12*s*., 6*d*., book debts £92, 15*s*., 8*d*., 3 feather beds, warming pan, 14 chairs, pewter, weaver's loom, spinning wheel, carpenter and joiner's tools, cider mill, hog, mare, pair of steers, 2 cows, 2 heifers, 2 calves, &c.

IV. PETER, b. d. 1723, Nov. 22. Warwick, R. I.

1723, Dec. 7. Inventory, £27, 9*s*., 8*d*., shown by Jerusha Westgate and Sarah Rutenburge. Silver shoe buckles £1, pot 18*s*., due from Solomon and Thomas Rutenburge, 9*s*., mariner's compass, pair of dividers, money due £3, 5*s*., &c.

V. MARGARET, b. d.
m. 1726, Dec. 11.
JOHN TREDWEN, b. d. of Tredwen.

VI. SUSANNAH, b. d.
m. 1717, Jun. 13.
ELISHA HEARNDEN, b. d. of William & Esther ( ) Hearnden.

1. William, 1718, May 15.
2. Mercy, 1721, Dec. 12.
3. Amey, 1723, Jan. 20.
4. Peter, 1727, Feb. 24.
5. Thomas, 1729, Feb. 25
6. Freelove, 1732, May 23.
7. John, 1734, Sep. 18.
8. Deliverance 1734, Sep. 18.
9. Rachel, 1736, Sep. 3.
10. Stephen, 1740, Feb. 27.
11. Penelope, 1742, Jul. 22.

VII. KATHERINE, b. d.

VIII. RUTH, m. 1726, Mar. 10. JEREMIAH HATHAWAY, b. d. b. d. of John Hathaway.

1. Elizabeth, 1727, May 7.
2. Jeremiah, 1730, May 30.
3. Caleb, 1732, May 20.

IX. MERCY, b. d.

X. THOMAS, m. 1726, Jul. 3. ANN DAVIS, b. d. 1727, Oct. 10. b. d. of Robert Davis. Warwick, R. I.

1. Mary, 1726, Dec. 10.
2. Thomas, 1728, Feb. 10.

1727. Inventory. 2 mares, old cow, goods in partnership with brother Solomon, due from brother John, &c.

Real estate in partnership with brother Solomon, viz: the half of homestead left by deceased father £145.

XI. SOLOMON, m. 1726, Oct. 13. MERCY FENNER, b. d. b. d. of Arthur & Mary (Smith) Fenner. Providence, Cranston, R. I.

1. Thomas,
2. Daughter,
3. Daughter,

1737, Jun. 7. He sold to Joseph Stafford, of Warwick, a certain meadow there that his father John Rutenburge had owned.

1755, Mar. 3. Cranston. He and others were warned out of town.

(2d WIFE, no issue.)

SABEERE.

STEPHEN, m. 1668, Nov. 14. DEBORAH ANGELL, b. d. b. d. of Thomas & Alice ( ) Angell.

Newport, R. I.

1671. Freeman.

1672, Feb. 27. The arbitrators (viz: John Easton and James Barker), made the following report as to a quarrel between him and Henry Palmer. "We do award that Stephen Sabeere, shall acknowledge unto Henry Palmer, that he hath done wrong unto him and his wife in saying that his wife is a witch and would have her so. We do award that Henry Palmer shall acknowledge unto Stephen Sabeere, that he hath done him wrong in calling of him the said Stephen, 'French dog, French rogue.'"

1672, Oct. 13. He confessed to having wronged the General Solicitor and promised more civil deportment for the future.

1676, Oct. 20. He bought of John Smith, of Providence, brother and heir of Leonard Smith, late resident in Newport, a house lot in Newport measuring 40 feet square, and the frame of a dwelling house.

1677, Apr. 1. He bought of John Hicks a house lot for 25s.

1680. Taxed 6s.

1688. He had a license granted.

I. DANIEL, m. SARAH BAILEY, b. d. b. 1681, Feb. 27. d. 1725, Apr. 19. of John & Sutton ( ) Bailey. Newport, R. I.

1702, Mar. 4. He was a proprietor in common lands.

1706, Feb. 8. He was called brother-in-law in the will of James Wilson, who gave him 200 acres to be laid out.

1709, Oct. 12. He was appointed one of the executors of Hugh Mosher's will.

1714, Oct. 13. He was one of the witnesses to Thomas Weeden's will.

II. JOHN, m. ANN, b. d. 1727 ± b. d. of Newport, R. I.

He was a merchant.

1702, Mar. 4. He was a proprietor in common lands.

1708. Freeman.

1727, Mar. His widow and executrix Ann Sabeere and his executor Daniel Sabeere, brewer, were sued by Edward Boss for £200 for molasses sold.

III. ALICE, m. JAMES WILSON, b. d. 1706 + b. 1673. d. 1706, Feb. of Samuel & —— (Tefft) Wilson.

1. Samuel,

SALMON.

JOHN, m. KATHARINE, b. d. 1676. b. d. 1680 +

Newport, R. I.

1667, Jun. 18. He wrote from Boston to Samuel Hubbard at Newport: "Dear and well beloved brother Hubbard, methinks it would be matter of joy unto me if I could hear that there were a comfortable end of those troubles or differences that have been of so long continuance; oh that if it were the good will of God, he would be pleased to give wisdom and direction unto all of his servants how to act in time of difficulty; and that myself and everyone would be endeavouring in the strength and fear of the Lord to be very careful that we do not give occasion to any to speak evil of the way of truth. And to have a special care to see that nothing of self be set up under the denomination of exalting the name of God," &c. "How long I may stay at Boston I know not. Let me hear from you as you have opportunity, your unfeigned friend and brother in gospel relations.
JOHN SALMON."

1671. Freeman.

1671, Oct. 18. Grand Jury.

1676, Apr. 20. His wife Katharine had a legacy of a ewe sheep by the will of Rev. John Clarke.

1676, Nov. 29. His death is alluded to in a letter of this date written by Samuel Hubbard of Newport to Dr. Edward Stennett of London.

1680, Aug. 12. Will. Widow Katharine. Witnesses Obadiah Holmes and another. Reference to this will is found in a list of seventeen wills (between the dates of 1676 and 1695), that were presented to the court in 1700 by parties interested, the law requiring three witnesses and these wills having but two.

SAMSON,
m.
JOANNA,

b.
d.
b.
d. 1684 +

Caversham, Oxford Co., Eng., Newport, R. I.

He was a fisherman.

1635. He came to America in ship "James," from Southampton.

1638, May 20. Newport. His name was recorded as one of the inhabitants admitted since the above date.

I. WILLIAM,
b.
d. 1684, Dec. 24.
Jamestown, R. I.

1684, Dec. 29. Inventory, £25, 4*s.*, viz: 45 sheep, mare, colt, 2 mares at Narragansett, heifer, gun, &c.

The record states that he left his aged mother Jane Salter not capable of managing his estate, and all said estate was given Peter Wells, to maintain William Salter's mother for life, and the said Peter Wells was constituted executor.

SANDS.

JAMES,
m.
SARAH WALKER,

b. 1622.
d. 1695, Mar. 13.
b.
d. 1709.

of John & Katharine ( ) Walker.

Portsmouth, New Shoreham, R. I.

He was born according to one account in Reading, Berks County, England.

1643, Oct. 5. Portsmouth. He had a grant of land next the round meadow.

1654, Apr. 2. He bought of William Earle and wife Mary their interest in 14 acres that came to them by right of late widow Walker, whose daughter Mary the said William Earle had married.

1655. Freeman.

1657. Commissioner. He was chosen to this office, but being sick and not able to attend, his fine was remitted by the court.

1659, Mar. 13. He bought of Robert Hazard and wife Mary, 8 acres.

1661. New Shoreham. He received lot 12 in the north part of the island, and with John Glover had lots 14 and 15 in south-east part of island, this being the first division of lands. The island had been purchased the year previous by sixteen persons, for £400.

1664, Mar. 1. He was ordered to come before the Governor or Deputy Governor to take his engagement as Constable or Conservator of the Peace at Block Island; and the Assembly desired the Governor or Deputy Governor to send to Block Island to declare unto our friends the inhabitants thereof, that they are under our care, and that they admit not of any other to bear rule over them but the power of this colony.

1665. Deputy.

1670, Oct. 26. He and four others were appointed to make a rate for Block Island.

1671, Feb. 2. He and wife Sarah sold Gideon Freeborn of Portsmouth, 54 acres there, with housing, orchards, &c., for £220.

1674, Nov. 7. He deeded Tourmet Rose a meadow lot, he paying £9, to my son John, now going to Boston.

1676. Assistant Warden. A large store house was garrisoned by him in King Philip's War, and the women and children gathered there.

1689, Jul. 3. Three French privateers landed a force on the island, and plundered the inhabitants, killing their cattle, &c. They made their headquarters at the house of James Sands, "which was large and accomadable for their purpose and not far from the harbor," as Samuel Niles (grandson of Mr. Sands) narrates.

1694, Jun. 18. Will—codicil 1695, Feb. 24.—proved 1695, May 6. Exx. wife Sarah. To her, all real and personal estate in Block Island for life. To son James, land in south-east part of island called the high land, half the orchard in the great swamp, &c. To son Samuel, land in south-east common. To youngest son Edward, all the homestead, half the orchard, the mill, &c. To other children, married some years since, viz: son John and daughters Sarah Niles, wife of Nathaniel, and Mercy Raymond, wife of Joshua, confirmation of what they have had. To wife Sarah, all stock and household goods at her disposal, and rest of estate to her.

Inventory, 400 acres, 56 head of cattle, 300 sheep, horses, mares, colts, 30 swine, negro woman, household goods, house, barn, mill, &c.

1699, Mar. 9. His widow Sarah gave negro Hannah to granddaughter Sarah Sands, daughter of Edward, also negro Sarah, to granddaughter Catharine Niles, and a negro boy to grandson Sands Raymond, and negro girl Rose to granddaughter Elizabeth Raymond. The negro girls were to be free at thirty and the boy at thirty-three.

1703, Oct. 17. Will—proved 1709, Jun. 13. Widow Sarah. Ex. youngest son Edward. To him, all estate, except what hereafter named. To five children, five cows, and one hundred sheep equally divided, viz: to John, James, Samuel, Sarah Niles and Mercy Raymond. To grand-daughter Sarah Niles, a feather bed, &c. To daughter Mercy Raymond, a chest, &c.,

I. JOHN,
m.
SYBIL RAY,

b. 1652.
d. 1712, Mar. 15.
b. 1665, Mar. 19.
d. 1733, Dec. 23.
of Simon & Mary (Thomas) Ray.
New Shoreham, R. I., Cow Neck, N. Y.

1678-80-90. Deputy.

1680. Captain.

1684. Freeman.

1696. Cow Neck. He moved thence this year.

1700, May 28. He, calling himself late of New Shoreham now of Cow Neck, Long Island, aged forty-eight years, testified as to will of Robert Guttredge.

He and his wife were buried in a parcel of ground (half an acre) that he had reserved for a burial place for his family.

1. John, 1684,
2. Nathaniel, 1687,
3. Edward, 1691,
4. George, 1694,
5. Mary, 1697,
6. Catharine, 1700,
7. Dorothy, 1703,
8. Abigail, 1708,

II. SARAH,
m. 1671, Feb. 14.
NATHANIEL NILES,

b.
d. 1726 (—)
b. 1642, Aug. 16.
d. 1727, Dec. 22.
of John & Jane ( ) Niles.

1. Samuel, 1674, May 1.
2. Nathaniel, 1677, Mar. 21.
3. Katharine, 1680, Mar. 13.
4. Ebenezer, 1683, Dec. 3.
5. Tabitha, 1685, Jan. 25.
6. Sarah,

III. MERCY,
m. 1683, Apr. 29.
JOSHUA RAYMOND,

b.
d. 1704 +
b. 1660, Sep. 18.
d. 1704.
of Joshua & Elizabeth (Smith) Raymond.

1. Sands,
2. Elizabeth,
3. Mercy,
4. Ann,
5. Caleb,
6. Joshua,

IV. JAMES,
m.
MARY CORNELL,

b.
d. 1733.
b.
d.
of John & Mary (Russell) Cornell.
Cow Neck, N. Y.

1684. Freeman.

1730, Sep. 21. Will—proved 1733, Jan. 19. Exs. Caleb Cornell and Samuel Underhill. To son Othniel, certain land, besides what he had by deed, he paying my sons Abijah and John, £13, each. To son James, all my farm and buildings at Matinecock, that is my home farm, &c., two young oxen, three cows, three horses and mares, ten sheep, six swine, cart, carpenter's and cooper's tools, he paying debts, and also paying £20, each to Abijah and John. To sons Abijah and John, half a share of land in Goshen, Orange County, New York, in partnership with Richard Cornell, except 100 acres. To sons Abijah and John, also half my right in Oyster Bay, and to them, £10, paid by son James if testator dies by next spring. To sons Abijah and John, bed, two cows, two heifers, four steers, and ten sheep. The rest of personal to be inventoried after my decease, and son James to have profits for four years, and then division to be made to four daughters, Mary, Zerviah, Jerusha and Sarah, only James to have half of Sarah's part till Sarah hath a child, and if that never be, then to remain to James. To granddaughter Sarah Everett, £10.

1. Othneil, 1699,
2. James, 1702,
3. Abijah,
4. John, 1710,
5. Mary,
6. Zerviah,
7. Bathsheba,
8. Jerusha,
9. Sarah, 1728,

V. SAMUEL, *
m. (1)
DOROTHY RAY,
m. (2)
ELIZABETH,

b.
d. 1716.
b. 1669, Oct. 16.
d.
of Simon & Mary (Thomas) Ray.
b.
d.
Cow Neck, N. Y.

SANDS. 2d column. V. Samuel. He m. (2) 1704, Nov. 9, Elizabeth Lessitt.

SANDS. 2d column V. Samuel. He m. (2) 1704, Nov. 9, Elizabeth Sessitt of

1713, Dec. 11. Will—proved 1716, Sep. 20. Exs. wife Elizabeth and Richbell Mott. To daughter Sybil, wife of Jonathan Rogers of New London, 1*s.*, she having had. To daughter Mercy, wife of Richard Stillwell of New York, two bonds for £50, each, a silver tankard and £10. To daughter Ann Sands, silver spoons, silver tumbler, ten sheep, a cow, Dutch wheel, &c., all at marriage, except £100. To daughter Sarah, wife of Nathan Selleck of Stamford, £5. To daughter Mary Sands, £100, bed, two silver spoons, silver tumbler, Dutch wheel and an Indian boy. To unmarried daughters, their living upon the farm till married. To wife Elizabeth, £40, per year, paid quarterly for life, and the furniture of new room (except the guns and sword), her choice of beds, books, plate made of silver since our marriage except silver tankard, her linen, pewter, all her rings, jewels, gold chains, &c., and the time of Indian girls' servitude, a bond for £50, cow and horse. To son Samuel, all the rest of whole estate, lands, messuages and tenements, household goods, debts, &c. If son Samuel die without issue, his wife to have the use for life, and then estate to go to Samuel's sisters. The will was dated at Cow Neck, and was proved at New Shoreham (and doubtless also in New York).

1. Sybil,
2. Mercy,
3. Ann,
4. Sarah,
5. Mary,
6. Samuel,
(2d wife no issue.)

VI. EDWARD,
m. 1693, May 7.
MARY WILLIAMS,

b. 1672.
d. 1708, Jun. 14.
b.
d. 1708 +
of John & Anna (Alcock) Williams.
New Shoreham, R. I.

1692, Jan. 10. Freeman.

1703. Deputy.

He held the office of Captain.

1708, Jun. 13. Will—proved 1708, Jul. 20. Exx. wife Mary. Overseers, brother John Sands and Nathaniel Mott. To wife, all estate for life and then to daughter Sarah, but if she marry with Samuel Dennison she is disinherited and all estate then to go to cousin Edward, son of brother John Sands.

He was buried in the Town Burial Ground.

1. Sarah, 1694, Jan. 30.

* See: American Genealogist, v. 27, p. 221-2.

and the goods in the chest equally to her and daughter-in-law Mary Sands, wife of Edward. To two daughters, a pewter platter apiece.

Inventory, £708, 12*s.* 9*d.*

An interesting account of his grandparents is given in the writings of Rev. Samuel Niles.

Of James Sands he says: "He was a benefactor to the poor; for as his house was garrisoned in the time of their fears of the Indians, many poor people resorted to it, and were supported mostly from his liberality. He was also a promoter of religion in his benefactions to the minister they had there in his day, though not altogether so agreeable to him as might be desired, as being inclined to the Anabaptist persuasion. He devoted his house for the worship of God, where it was attended being Lord's day or Sabbath." "Mr Sands had a plentiful estate, and gave free entertainment to all gentlemen that came to the Island."

Sarah Sands is thus described by her grandson. "His wife was a gentlewoman of remarkable sobriety and piety, given also to hospitality. She was the only midwife and doctress on the island, or rather a doctor, all her days, with very little, and with some and mostly no reward at all." She performed some wonderful cures in her vocation of doctress it appears.

He was buried in the Town Burial Ground.

SANFORD. 1st column. His 2d wife was daughter of William and Ann (Marbury) Hutchinson.

SANFORD. See: American Genealogist. v.20, p.58; v.26, p.54

JOHN, b. ; d. 1653.
m. (1)
ELIZABETH WEBB, b. ; d.
of Webb.
m. (2)
BRIDGET HUTCHINSON, b. ; d. 1698.
of —— & Susanna ( ) Hutchinson.

(She m. (2) Wm. Phillips.)

Boston, Mass., Portsmouth, R. I.

1631. He was a member of the church this year.

1632, Apr. 3. Freeman.

1633, Aug. 6. He with others was chosen to oversee the building of a sufficient cart bridge over Muddy river, and another over Stony river.

1634, May 14. He and another person were appointed to take notice of the ordnance, powder and shot and report to next court what condition they are in.

1634, Sep. 3. He was chosen cannoneer for the fort at Boston, and for two years service he hath already done at said fort and one year more he shall do, he was allowed £20.

1636, Sep. 8. He was allowed £10, for service year past.

1636, Oct. 28. He was chosen cannoneer and Surveyor of the arms and amunition and was to have £30, for his own and his man's pains.

1637, Nov. 2. He was granted £13, 6*s.* 8*d.*, for year past and so he is discharged upon delivery of an inventory to another which shall be appointed.

1637, Nov. 20. He and others were ordered to deliver up all guns, pistols, swords, powder, shot, &c., because "the opinions and revelations of Mr. Wheelwright and Mrs. Hutchinson have seduced and led into dangerous errors many of the people here in New England."

1638, Mar. 7. Portsmouth. He and eighteen others signed the following compact: "We whose names are underwritten do here solemnly in the presence of Jehovah, incorporate ourselves into a Bodie Politick, and as he shall help will submit our persons, lives, and estates unto our Lord Jesus Christ the King of Kings and Lord of Lords, and to all those perfect and most absolute laws of his given us in his holy word of truth, to be guided and judged thereby."

1638, May 13. He was present at a General Meeting of inhabitants. It was ordered that the meeting house shall be set on the neck of land that goes over to the main of island, where he and John Coggeshall shall lay it out.

1638, May 20. He had 6 acres allotted him on the north side of the Great Cove.

1638, Jun. 27. He and four others were appointed to repair highways.

1640. Constable.

1641, Mar. 16. Freeman.

1644. Lieutenant.

1647–49. Assistant.

1653. President of Portsmouth and Newport.

1653, Jun. 22. Will—proved 1653. Exx. wife Bridget. Overseers, brother-in-law Edward Hutchinson, of Boston, and friends, Richard Tew, of Newport, Richard Borden, Philip Sherman and Edward Fisher, of Portsmouth, and son John Sanford. To wife, my new dwelling house in which I live, with all and every chamber or room therein and half the cook room and all the houses on the north side of the aforesaid cook room, all my right in the

I. JOHN, b. 1633, Jun. 4; d. 1687. Portsmouth, R. I.
m. (1) 1654, Aug. 8.
ELIZABETH SPATCHURST, b. ; d. 1661, Dec. 6. of Henry Spatchurst.
m. (2) 1663, Apr. 17 [Peter
MARY GREENE, (w. of. b. ; d. 1688 + of Samuel & Elizabeth ( ) Gorton.

1. Elizabeth, 1655, Jul. 11.
2. Mary, 1656, Aug. 18.
3. Susanna, 1658, Jul. 31.
4. Rebecca, 1660, Jun. 23.
(2d wife.)
5. Mary, 1664, Mar. 30.
6. Eliphalet, 1666, Feb. 20.
7. John, 1672, Jun. 18.
8. Samuel, 1677, Oct. 5.

His first wife's father was of Bermuda.

1653, May 17. Freeman.

1655-56-57-58-59-60-61-62-63-64. General Treasurer.

1656-57-58-59-60-62-63. Commissioner.

1656-57-58-59-60-61-66-67-68-69-71-72-73-74-75-76. General Recorder.

1660, Apr. 5. He and his brother Samuel had legacies from their uncle Henry Webb, of Boston, by the terms of his will of this date: "To my late sister Elizabeth Sanford's sons, John and Samuel Sanford, each £80, apiece, they to be heirs each to other; to be paid in good English goods or other good pay, within two years after my decease, provided I give not so much or part of it to one or other of them before."

1663-64-70-71. Attorney General.

1664-65-66-68-69-70-71-72-73-74-77-78-81-82-83-86. Deputy.

1664-65-80. Assistant.

1667, Aug. 10. He enlisted in a troop of horse.

1673, May 7. He was appointed on committee to treat with the Indian Sachems "and with them seriously to consult and agree of some way to prevent the extreme excess of the Indians' drunkenness." The sachems were: Mawsup and Ninecraft, of Narragansett, Philip, of Mount Hope, Wetamo, of Pocasset, and Awashunks, of Seaconnett.

1676, Apr. 4. He and three others were appointed to take an exact account of all inhabitants in this island, English, negro and Indians, and make a list thereof, and also to take account how all persons are provided with corn, guns, powder, shot and lead. He was also on a committee to have the care of a barrel of powder for Portsmouth, and to see that the two great guns now in the yard of deceased Mr. William Brenton, be placed in Portsmouth, one on Ferry Neck and the other near house of John Borden.

1677, Oct. 31. He and forty-seven others were granted 5,000 acres to be called East Greenwich.

1686, Dec. 22. He and others were apprized by letter from Sir Edmund Andros, of their appointment as members of his council, and of a meeting to be held at Boston, 30th instant.

1688. His widow Mary, had a license granted her.

II. SAMUEL, b. 1635, Jul. 14; d. 1713, Mar. 18. Portsmouth, R. I.
m. (1) 1662, Oct.
SARAH WODELL, b. 1644, Oct.; d. 1680. Dec. 15. of William & Mary ( ) Wodell.
m. (2) 1686, Apr. 13.
SUSANNA SPATCHURST, b. ; d. 1723, Nov. 13. of William & Elizabeth ( ) Spatchurst.

1. Elizabeth, 1663, Oct. 2.
2. John, 1668, Jun. 10.
3. Bridget, 1671, Jun. 27.
4. Mary, 1674, Apr. 27.
5. William, 1676, May 21.
6. Samuel, 1678, Jul. 14.
(2d wife.)
7. Restcome, 1687, Feb. 26.
8. Peleg, 1688, Aug. 16.
9. Elisha, 1690, Feb. 24.
10. Endcome, 1691, Nov. 29.
11. Esbon, 1693, Oct. 20.
12. Francis, 1695, Oct. 24.
13. Joseph, 1698, Aug. 13.
14. Benjamin, 1700, Jun. 4.
15. Joshua, 1702, Apr. 18.
16. Elizabeth, 1706, Dec 7.

His second wife's parents were of Bermuda.

1658, May 18. Freeman.

1671, Jun. 7. Juryman.

1709, Apr. 30. Will—proved 1713, Apr. 13. Exx. wife Susanna. To daughter Elizabeth Allen, son John, daughter Mary Arnold, sons William and Samuel, each 1*s.* To sons Restcome, Peleg, Elisha, Endcome, Esbon, Francis, Joseph, Benjamin and Joshua, and daughter Elizabeth Sanford, each 5*s.* To wife Susanna, rest of estate within doors and without.

(2d WIFE.)

III. ELIPHALET, b. 1637, Dec. 9; d. 1724, Jan. 18.
m.
BARTHO STRATTON, b. ; d. of Stratton.

1. William
2. Anne,
3. Bridget,
4. Katharine,

IV. PELEG, b. 1639, May 10; d. 1701. Newport, R. I.
m. (1)
MARY BRENTON, b. ; d. 1674 (—) of William & Martha (Burton) Brenton.
m. (2) 1674, Dec. 1.
MARY CODDINGTON, b. 1654, May 16; d. 1693, Mar. of William & Ann (Brinley) Coddington.

(2d wife.)
1. Ann,
2. Bridget,
3. Elizabeth,
4. Daughter,
5. Son,
6. Peleg,
7. William,

1663, Oct. 19. He gave receipt to his father-in-law (*i. e.* stepfather) William Phillips, for his share of estate of deceased father John Sanford.

1667, Apr. 7. He had a legacy from will of his uncle Samuel Hutchinson, of orchard, &c., in Portsmouth.

1667, Jul. 24. He was appointed Captain of a troop of horse.

1667-68-69-70-77-78-79. Assistant.

1670–77. Deputy.

1675, May 8. He had from Thomas Gould, of Aquidneset, a confirmation of 1-300 of Canonicut and Dutch Islands, which had been given by said Gould, to William Brenton's daughter Mary, the wife of Peleg Sanford, by writing dated 1666, Jun. 9.

great orchard, land on north side of new dwelling house, meadow and a third of all cattle and movables, for life. To son John, certain land and the ferry, the old house, half the cook room, and two houses on south side of a certain path, all to him and his heirs male, failing of which, testator's son Samuel shall have and so on. To John, also great roan mare besides one which is his own, a negro man and wife, four oxen, two cows, the great ferry boat, five ewes, five ewe lambs, a breeding sow, feather bed, cutlass, great fowling piece, &c. To son Samuel, 40 acres at Black Point, four oxen, two cows, brown mare, five ewes, five ewe lambs, a sow, Spanish gun, sword, belt, best cloak and hat, feather bed and great bible. To son Peleg, at age, 20 acres at Black Point, second roan mare, five ewes, five ewe lambs, two cows, breeding sow, French gun, sword, &c. To son Restcome, at age, 40 acres at Black Point and a mare, and like legacies to sons William, Ezbon and Elisha. To daughter Eliphal Sanford, £100, of which £60 to be hers at marriage and £40 at her mother's marriage or death. To daughter Anne, £60 at marriage. To sons Samuel, Peleg, Restcome, William, Ezbon and Elisha, rest of estate. The hay and corn on ground for cattle and family. "And I do bequeath my children unto my wife, next unto God, entreating that they may be carefully provided for and tenderly brought up as hitherto they have been, and that they may be well educated and brought up in the fear of the Lord," &c. To overseers, a ewe lamb.

Inventory, £824, 11*s.*, 1*d.*, viz: 60 pounds gunpowder £94, 10*s.*, 84 pounds shot £1. 1*s.*, 8 pair men's shoes and a pair of woman's shoes £1, 16*s.*, 18 trading hatchets, peage £58, 10*s.* (8 per penny), carpet, cupboard cloth, stuff cloak, long cushion, corslet wanting the gorget, 7 chairs, table, form, cradle, parcel of books £2, 5 pewter platters and flagon, 2 silver spoons, 6 old scythes, warming pan, 3 fowling pieces, cutlass, 3 old swords, flock bed for the negroes, 80 ewe sheep £120, 36 wethers, 9 of them rams £27, 4 old oxen £30, 8 young oxen £56, 6 steers, 2 bulls, 4 calves, 12 milch cows, 4 heifers, 7 yearlings, 5 calves, bay horse, foal, 4 breeding mares, 5 breeding sows, 5 hogs, 5 sows, 2 negroes and negro boy £62, 10*s.*, great ferry boat and tackling £20, canoe £10, hay and corn £40.

1653, Nov. 20. His widow took receipts from sons John and Samuel for legacies.

1663, Oct. 17. His widow, now the wife of William Phillips, of Boston, took receipt from Bartho Stratton, husband of her daughter Eliphal, for the legacy apportioned by overseers of her husband's will.

1670, Jun. 17. His widow took receipt from son Ezbon, for his share of his father's estate.

1696, Sep. 29. Will—proved 1698, Aug. 18. Widow Bridget Phillips, of Boston. Exs. daughter Eliphal Stratton and sons, Samuel and William Phillips. To children of my two sons Samuel and William Phillips, certain lands in Saco and Cape Porpus, and her part of Cow Island and Boniton Island in said river. To two sons Samuel and William Phillips, land at Kennebunk, purchased by husband William Phillips, of Moghegen, an Indian, also tract of 2,000 acres, all said estate being given her by said husband in consideration of a considerable estate, which I brought him. To my four children, Peleg Sanford, Samuel Phillips, William Phillips and Eliphal Stratton, certain land bought of Indians. To grandson William Stratton, 1,000 acres that was made over to my son Elisha Sanford, by my said husband. To son Peleg Sanford, my Book of Martyrs. To my three children Samuel and William Phillips and Eliphal Stratton, all other books equally. To three daughters, Eliphal Stratton, Sarah and Deborah Phillips, all my wearing clothes and household stuff equally. To granddaughter in England, my son Ezbon Sanford's daughter, a gold ring. To Elizabeth, wife of my grandson William Stratton, a gold ring. To other grandchildren, the children of my said three sons and my said daughter, a gold ring apiece. To granddaughter Ann Atkins, and her daughter Ann, a silver bodkin, and to her daughter Eliphal, a bodkin. To granddaughter Bridget Ladd and her daughter Bridget, a silver bodkin. To grandson William Stratton's daughter Bridget, a silver dram cup, and to his other two daughters, a silver bodkin, each. To sons Samuel and William Phillips and unto my daughter Eliphal Stratton, all other my estate, goods and chattels. To daughter Eliphal, the best bed, she paying to my son Samuel, 8*s.*, and to son William, 20*s.* To great-grandsons William Stratton and Edward Ladd, each a set of silver buttons.

A deposition of a great-grandson of John Sanford, stated that Restcome, William, Ezbon and Elisha, sons of the first John Sanford, all died without issue. It appears however that Ezbon certainly had one child (mentioned in her grandmother's will).

1676, Aug. 11. He and Captain Goulding, informed Captain Church of King Philip's hiding place, and the next day that warrior was killed.

1677, May 24. He and Richard Bailey, were chosen agents to go to England about incursions made by Connecticut.

1678–79–80–81. General Treasurer.

1679. Major.

1680–81–82–83. Governor.

1683, Sep. 10. He was chosen agent to go to England with Captain Arthur Fenner, in regard to Governor Cranfield of New Hampshire, and the company who had lately been in Kings Town, but who would show no commission from the King for holding court.

1687. Lieutenant Colonel.

1687. Member of Sir Edmund Andros' council.

1698, Jan. 31. He wrote to the Board of Trade acknowledging receipt of His Majesty's commission to hold the office of Judge of the Court of Admiralty and complaining that upon presenting said commission to Governor Walter Clarke, he detained said commission from Sanford, though several times demanded, and Walter Clarke claimed the commission an infringement of charter.

1699, Nov. 8. He wrote Lord Bellomont commencing: "My Lord: Let a man's intentions be never so resolved faithfully to discharge His Majesty's commands, it's not to be effected so long as the government remains as now constituted." He complains of the countenance given pirates and that commissions immediate from His Majesty are yet regarded as infringement of the charter, &c.

1701, Feb. 28. Will—proved 1701, Sep. 1. Exs. Francis Brinley, Nathaniel Coddington and Andrew Willett (and they to be guardians to children Peleg, William, Bridget and Elizabeth). To wife Mary, a third of all the plate, household goods, negro woman Hull, and negro men Diruke and George. To eldest son Peleg, two houses and land in Newport, tract called Winnequot of 450 acres, another piece of 160 acres, all my lands upon Merrimack River, lands at Saco, all land given me by my mother, 573 acres on Elizabeth Island, several tracts in Portsmouth, &c., &c., and an eighth of all my plate. To son William, a tract of 290 acres, one of 256 acres, other land, and an eighth of the plate. To sons Peleg and William, jointly, land in Newport, half of Rose Island, and another tract of 1,020 acres. To eldest daughter Ann Sanford, 50 acres, house, &c., a third of plate not bequeathed and £8 in money. To daughter Bridget Sanford, 60 acres, &c., and a third of plate. To daughter Elizabeth, 90 acres, &c., a third of plate, and £8. To sister Eliphalet Stratton, £14 of money I lent her. To niece Mary Brinley, 40*s.* To niece Mary Cole, 40*s.* To niece Katherine Vernon, 40*s.* If all my children die without heirs, all estate to go to daughter of brother Esbon, deceased, and children of William Stratton, deceased. To executors, 40*s.* each.

1740, Mar. 17. Deposition of Ann Willett, of North Kingstown, aged about seventy-eight years. She well remembered that Mary Sanford, the first wife of Colonel Peleg Sanford and daughter of William Brenton, departed this life sometime before the said William Brenton, without issue, for that her last child dying some few days before her and was buried with her. After death of said Mary, the said Colonel Sanford, married this deponent's sister Mary Coddington, by whom he had four daughters and three sons, William Sanford, late of Newport, being the youngest, who married Mrs. Grissel Sylvester, by whom he had three daughters, Mary, Margaret and Grissel.

V. ENDCOME, { b 1640. Feb. 23. / d. young.

VI. RESTCOME, { b. 1642, Jan. 29. / d. 1667. — Portsmouth, R. I.
Unmarried,

1667, Apr. 7. He had a legacy of 20*s.*, from will of his uncle Samuel Hutchinson.

1667, Aug. 12. Will—Ex. brother Samuel Sanford. To brother Samuel, mare, silver cup, and bed. To sister Eliphal Stratton and her three children, a ewe sheep, each, and Eliphal to have also a silver spoon. To sister Sarah, wife of aforesaid brother Samuel Sanford, a mare, colt, and 5*s.* piece of gold, and to each of her children a ewe lamb. If brother Esbon is not heard of for a year, the four sheep assigned to him to be divided between brother Samuel and sister Eliphal, provided that if afterwards Esbon shall come again the sheep shall be returned to him. To brother Samuel and sister Eliphal, rest of estate equally. Any legacy due by gift of uncle Samuel Hutchinson, to be equally divided betwixt my five brothers and my sister, viz: Samuel, Peleg, William, Ezbon and Elisha Sanford and sister Eliphal Stratton.

1667, Sep. 24. Inventory, £35, 3*s.*, 1*d.*, viz: 16 ewe sheep, 4 lambs, apparel, 3 hats, 3 books, pair of shoes, gloves, mittens, silver cup, silver spoon, mare, colt, piece of gold 5*s.*, &c.

VII. WILLIAM, { b. 1644, Mar. 4. / d.

1667, Apr. 7. He had a legacy of 20*s.*, from will of his uncle Samuel Hutchinson.

VIII. ESBON, { b. 1646, Jan. 25. / d. — 1. Daughter,
m. { b. / d.
——— of

1667, Apr. 7. He had a legacy of 20*s.*, from will of his uncle Samuel Hutchinson.

IX. FRANCES, { b. 1648, Jan. 9. / d. young.

X. ELISHA, { b. 1650, Dec. 28. / d.

1667, Apr. 7. He had a legacy of 20*s.*, from will of his uncle Samuel Hutchinson.

1676. He had a deed from his stepfather of 1,000 acres being part of a tract eight miles square purchased of the Indians by William Phillips (lying in the now town of Wells, Maine).

XI. ANN, { b. 1652, Mar. 12. / d. 1654, Aug. 26.

TOBIAS, b. d. 1695.
m.
MARY CLARKE, b. d 1695 +
of Joseph Clarke.

Taunton, Mass., Newport, Westerly, R. I.

1643. He was thus early of Taunton.

1655. Newport. Freeman.

1661, Sep. 9. He had a quarter of a share in a division of Misquamicut (Westerly) lands.

1661, Nov. 1, He and Robert Burdick were arrested by Walter Palmer, Constable, and soon after were brought before Governor John Endicott, charged with forcible entry and intrusion into the bounds of Southertown (Stonington) in the Pequot Country. He answered that they looked upon the lands to be their right, and both of them were committed, refusing to give security for their appearance at the General Court.

1662, May 22. A letter from Rhode Island to Massachusetts authorities mentions the imprisonment of Tobias Saunders and Robert Burdick for not producing their deeds of lands in the Narragansett Country.

1666, May 20. Westerly. He, now living in Pawcatuck, sold to Benedict Arnold, for £48, all right in Conanicut.

1669, May 18. His name was in a list of inhabitants.

1669–71–72–80–81–83–90. Deputy.

1669–78–95. Conservator of the Peace.

1670, Mar. 11. He and John Crandall on behalf of the town of Westerly, answered a letter from the Governor and Assistants of Connecticut, wherein complaint had been made of encroachments by Westerly men upon Stonington lands. This they denied, closing as follows; "as for your advice to agree with those our neighbors of Stonington and the other gentlemen, we hope that your colony and ours will in the first place lovingly agree, and then we question not but there will be an agreement between us and our neighbors of Stonington and the rest of the gentlemen."

1670, Jun. 18. He and James Babcock were warned by warrant from the Connecticut Commissioners to appear before them at Mr. Stanton's house, or Captain Gookin's, to make answer for the seizure of three Connecticut men, by warrant granted from Tobias Saunders to James Babcock. Both desired to be released on bail.

1671, May 16. A warrant was issued by Rhode Island authorities to require the constables of Westerly to warn the inhabitants to appear at the house of Mr. Tobias Saunders, to-morrow morning at eight of the clock to attend the Court of justice.

1679, Sep. 17. He took oath of allegiance.

1688, Aug. 9. Will—proved 1695, Sep. 2. Exx. wife Mary. Overseers, John Maxson, Sr., and cousin (*i. e.* wife's nephew) Joseph Clarke. To son John, dwelling house and land and also a piece of land upon account of about £4, given my son John by my wife's uncle John Clarke of Rhode Island, deceased. To son Edward, farm and housing at Mouse Hill, but neither son to enter upon housing during the life of their mother except she see cause. If either son die before twenty-one, then son Stephen to receive such son's part, and if all of sons die, wife to dispose of estate to surviving children. When sons John and Edward enter into possession they to pay within three years to sons Stephen and Benjamin, £10, each. To wife, all movable estate at her disposal. To Israel Lewis, a heifer, to keep her and her increase till his time is out, and if he prove faithful the increase to be his and also a gun and young sow.

Inventory, £147, 12*s.*, viz: 100 acres and housing £40, Mouse Hill land, housing, &c., £40, pair of oxen, 3 cows, steer, 4 yearlings, calf, 30 sheep, 10 swine, pair of stags, mare, 4 beds, pewter, &c.

I. JOHN, b. d. 1746. Westerly, R. I.
m. (1)
SILENCE, Belcher b. d. of
m. (2)
SARAH, b. d. 1746 + of

1. Mary, 1700, Jan. 6.
2. Hannah, 1701, Dec. 17.
3. Elizabeth, 1703, Oct. 27.
4. John, 1705, Oct. 13.
5. Susannah, 1707, Dec. 4.
6. Samuel, 1710, Feb. 28.
7. Prudence, 1712, Jan. 19.
8. Joseph, 1721, Jul. 5.
(2d wife, no issue.)

1700. Freeman.

1707–13. Deputy.

1709. Justice of the Peace.

1744, Feb. 24. Will—proved 1746, Apr. 30. Exs. wife Sarah and son Joseph. To wife, profit of a third of real estate for life, and half of movables. To daughter Mary Haley, 6*s.* To daughter Hannah Potter, £20. To daughter Elizabeth Brown, 5*s.* To son John, gun, wearing apparel, and what he has had. To grandson Wait, son of John, £5, for executors to lay out in learning him to read and write, and to him also a small gun. To daughter Susanna Berry, £20. To son Samuel, 5*s.* To grandson Lemuel Vorse, son of daughter Prudence, 5*s.* To son Joseph, rest of land on condition he do not pass it by deed till thirty years of age, and if he die without issue before thirty, then to son John's son Wait. To son Joseph, also a bed, chest, and pewter that was his mother's, and half of movables. To wife and son Joseph, the rest of estate.

Inventory, wearing apparel and gun £15, 5*s.*, old wheel, loom, pewter, churn, 2 cows, 3 heifers, calf, pair of oxen, 2 swine, 8 lambs, &c.

II. EDWARD, b. d. 1732. Westerly. R. I.
m. (1)
SARAH, b. d. of
m. (2)
HANNAH, b. d. of

1. Edward, 1703, Jan. 10.
2. Sarah,
3. Abigail,
4. William,
5. Mary,
6. James,
7. Isaac,
8. Hannah,

1716. Freeman.

1731, Aug. 6. Will—proved 1732, Feb. 28. Exx. wife Hannah. To wife, profits of certain land till son James is of age, and to her all movables forever for bringing up children, &c. To son Edward, 15 acres, he paying my daughter Sarah Cross, £10, and £5, to my daughter Abigail Saunders, and said Abigail to have £5, more from executrix. To son William, 30 acres, he paying my daughter Mary Saunders, £5, when she is eighteen, and she to have £5, more from executrix. To son James, at age, land that wife has till then, he paying £20, to my son Isaac. To daughter Hannah, £5, at eighteen. Son Isaac to be bred to a trade. If son James dies, his brothers William and Isaac are to have the farm.

III. STEPHEN, b. d. 1746. Westerly, R. I.
m. (1)
———— b. d. of
m. (2) 1721, Nov. 19,
RACHEL BLIVEN, b. 1697, Mar. 19. d. 1746 + of Edward & Isabel (Macoone) Bliven.

1. Thankful,
(2d wife.)
2. Stephen, 1722, Aug. 3.
3. Rachel, 1724, Sep. 18.
4. Isabel, 1726, Oct. 14.
5. Ruth, 1729, Jul. 1.
6. Tobias, 1732, Mar. 28.
7. Mary, 1734, Jul. 9.
8. Peleg, 1737, Mar. 4.
9. Martha, 1740, Nov. 27.

1723. Freeman.

1746, Oct. 28. Will—proved 1746, Nov. 24. Exx. wife Rachel. To wife, profits of all land of my homestead while widow, and she to sell my salt marsh if she cannot pay for it. To her, all personal to dispose of to my daughters as she thinks fit. To son Stephen, all the rest of homestead farm (after 40 acres is taken out for my son Tobias) at the death or marriage of wife. To son Tobias, 40 acres southern side of the farm at death or marriage of wife, and when he possesses the land he to pay my daughter Thankful Stetson, £10, and to my son Peleg Saunders, £50. To daughters Rachel, Isabel, Ruth, Mary and Martha, £10, each to be paid by my son Stephen when he possesses the land.

Inventory, £394, 10*s.* 1*d.*, viz: wearing apparel £16, great bed £29, other beds, books £4, 6*s.*, pair of stillyards, pair of combs, pewter, loom, 2 swine, 16 sheep, calf, pair of steers, 2 heifers, 2 cows, 3 two years, old mare, &c.

IV. BENJAMIN, b. d. 1733. Westerly, R. I.
m.
ANN, b. d. 1767. of

1. Mary, 1714, Jan. 29.
2. Joshua, 1716, Mar. 6.
3. Daniel, 1717, Nov. 1.
4. Lucy, 1719, Nov. 13.
5. Tacy, 1722, Feb. 4.
6. Nathan, 1724, Mar. 17.
7. Ann, 1726, Dec. 15.

1721. Freeman.

1733, Aug 21. Will—proved 1733, Nov. 26. Exx. wife Ann. To her whole estate while widow, and she to give each of her daughters a feather bed. To son Joshua, shop and tools. To sons Daniel and Nathaniel, all land equally.

Inventory, £176, 18*s.* 6*d.*, viz: wearing apparel, feather beds, loom, 2 guns, pewter, 2 canoes, 2 cows, calf, yearling, heifer, hog, 2 mares, &c.

1767, Mar. 20. Will—proved 1767, Jun. 1. Widow Ann of Charlestown, R. I. Ex. son Daniel. To daughter Mary Clarke, a feather bed, &c., for life and then to her daughter Ann. To grandson Nathan Clarke, son of Mary, a calf. To granddaughters Freelove Remson and Ann Saunders, daughters of son Joshua, late of Newport, deceased, each a Spanish milled dollar. To son Daniel, two notes. To daughter Lucy Kenyon, a pair of sheets and to her three children Sarah Potter, Joshua Kenyon and Roger Kenyon, a note. To daughter Tacy Allen, £20. To daughter Ann Saunders, wearing apparel, three silver spoons, &c. To grandson Benjamin Saunders, a case of bottles, &c. To granddaughter Anne Saunders, daughter of Daniel, three silver spoons, &c. To four grandsons the children of Daniel, viz: Joshua, Nathan, Augustus and Daniel, £80, equally divided. To granddaughter Eliphal Littlefield, daughter of son Daniel, a silk crape gown, &c. To grandson Lyman, son to daughter Ann Saunders, a bed, &c. To four daughters Mary Clarke, Lucy Kenyon, Tacy Allen and Ann Saunders, the rest of wearing apparel. To son Daniel and four daughters, the rest of estate equally.

Inventory, £54, 7*s.* 2½*d.*

V. SUSANNA, b. d. 1725 +
m.
PETER BARKER, b. d. 1725. of James & Barbara (Dungan) Barker.

SAUNDERS. 2d column. V. Susannah, m. (2) Peter Wells. He d. 1752. She d. 1733 +. Children by 1st husband, 1. Joseph, 2. John, 3. Daughter, 4. Sarah, 5. Barbara, 6. Susannah, 7. Patience.

SCRANTON.

THOMAS, b. d.
m.
————, b. d.

Warwick, R. I.

1657, Nov. 26. He bought a house and lot of Henry Knowles.

1664, Aug. 15. At the time of his daughter Margaret's marriage to David Shippee, it was recorded on the town book that there were "present of the maid's kindred her brother and brother-in-law, her two sisters and other neighbors."

Margaret at this time was called of Prudence, late of Warwick. Who her sisters were has not been disclosed.

I. THOMAS, b. 1641. d. 1724. Portsmouth (Prudence Island), Warwick, R. I.
m.
MARY, b. d. 1742. of

1. Stephen,
2. Daniel,
3. Thomas,
4. John,

1680. Taxed 2*s.*

1691, Apr. 18. He bought 14½ acres of James Greene in Warwick.

1698, Mar. 29. He and others of Prudence Island had a suit brought against them.

1713, Aug. 6. He deeded to son Stephen of Warwick, 50 acres in Potowomut Neck.

1718, Sep. 3. Warwick. He, calling himself seventy-seven years of age or thereabout, deposed that John Gereardy, father-in-law to Jeremiah Smith, had quiet possession of certain land for upwards of fifty years.

1720, Apr. 16. He assigned to son Stephen, for love, &c., the deed of 1691.

1724, Aug. 29. Inventory, £10, 12*s.* 6*d.*, shown by son Stephen, administrator. (The appraisers met at Stephen's house.) Paper money, copper pennies 11*s.* 9*d.*, a New England shilling 2*s.*, wearing apparel 6s., 200 small nails, old gimlet, saw, compass, augur, square, hammer, 4 gouges, 2 new wheels, old reel, &c.

1742. Administration on widow Mary's estate to son Stephen.

II. MARGARET, m. 1664, Aug. 15. DAVID SHIPPEE, — b. d. — b. d. 1718 + — of Shippee.

1. Elizabeth,
2. Martha,
3. Mary,
4. Samuel,
5. David,
6. Thomas,
7. Solomon,

III. DAUGHTER, — b. d.

IV. DAUGHTER, — b. d.

SEARLE (RICHARD).

RICHARD, — b. d.

Portsmouth, R. I.

1638. He was admitted an inhabitant of the island of Aquidneck, having submitted himself to the government that is or shall be established.

1640. He had 4 acres granted for a house lot, and a 6 acre lot also.

1666, Dec. 8. Whereas Mary Tripp, wife of John Tripp, some twenty-five years ago bought of Richard Searle, for a pint of wine, 3 acres, the said Searle living then in Portsmouth, she being then unmarried, about which time Searle removed but left no deed to Mary, now therefore the commissioners confirm the land to Mary Tripp.

No relationship has been traced between him and Nathaniel Searle, of Little Compton (who was born 1662, Jun. 9, and died 1750, Feb. 5).

SEGAR.

JOHN, m. ——— — b. d. 1737. — b. d.

Newport, South Kingstown, R. I.

He was probably identical with John Segar, son of Richard, of Hartford, Conn., whose wife Elizabeth was indicted in 1663, for familiarity with Satan and practicing witchcraft. Mr. Savage thinks the family may have removed to Rhode Island where as he presumes (and rightly) "the Devil had less power or impudence."

1680. Taxed 5s.
1701. Freeman.
1708, Jun. 8. Kings Town. Ear mark.
1737, May 25. Administration to son John.

I. JOHN, m. 1708, Mar. 1. ALICE HULL, — b. 1684, May 3. d. 1753, Oct. — b. d. — Newport, South Kingstown, R. I. — of Joseph & Experience (Harper) Hull.

1704. Freeman.

1751, Dec. 2. Will—proved 1753, Nov. 19. Ex. son Joseph. To daughters Alice and Susanna Segar, 40 acres equally from land that was my father's. To son John, the rest of farm that was my father's. To son Joseph, the farm I bought of William Champlin, and other land. To son Samuel, land bought of Jeremiah Clarke's heirs, &c. To daughter Abigail Segar, house and land I bought of Experience Sheffield. To son Samuel, three cows, twenty sheep, negro boy Prince, a feather bed, and gun. To daughters Alice, Susanna and Abigail, a feather bed each. To son Joseph, a feather bed. To daughters Elizabeth and Bathsheba Segar, each £600, and rest of household goods equally divided, a riding beast and saddle. To daughter Mary Gould, negro woman Jenny and £500. To daughter Experience Sheffield, £100. To five grandchildren Jonathan, Benjamin, Sarah, John and Ichabod Babcock, each £20, at age. To grandchildren Elisha and Robert Clarke, each £20, at age. To grandchildren Ichabod James and Samuel Sheffield, £20, each at age. To son Joseph, time in mulatto girl Peg, and farming and other tools.

Inventory, wearing apparel £92, 16s. 8d., riding horse, bonds £3778, 15s. 3d., money due by book £203, 15s., cash £45, 14s. 8d., quilting frame, pair of worsted combs, some old wheels, carpenter's tools, bellows, 2 churns, coffee mill, pair of stillyards, 4 swine, 28 geese, 3 turkeys, 6 fowls, a sheep, 6 horses, pair of oxen, pair of steers, 3 two year cattle, 8 cows, 10 yearlings, 7 calves, negro boy £200, time in mulatto girl Peg £70, gun, mare, 4 colts, &c.

1. Elizabeth, 1709, Jan. 28.
2. Sarah, 1710, Aug. 17.
3. John, 1712, Nov. 29.
4. Mary, 1715, Feb. 12.
5. Alice, 1717, Jan. 28.
6. Judith, 1719, Mar. 17.
7. Susanna, 1720, Aug. 4.
8. Experience, 1722, Apr. 26.
9. Joseph, 1723, Sep. 6.
10. Hannah, 1725, Feb. 13.
11. Abigail, 1726, May 29.
12. Samuel, 1728, Jan. 25.
13. Elizabeth, 1729, Aug. 27.
14. Bathsheba, 1732, Jan. 31.

SEGAR. 2d column. Add comma after Ichabod, tenth line after 1751, Dec. 2.

SEGAR. 2d column. II. Judith, m. 1717, Oct. 3, John Taylor, b. 1687, Sep. 26, of Robert and Deborah (Peckham) Taylor. Children, 1. Robert, 1719, Jul. 13. 2. Judith, 1720, Feb. 13.

SHAW.

ANTHONY, m. 1653, Apr. 8. ALICE STONARD, — b. d. 1705, Aug. 21. — b. d. — of John Stonard.

Boston, Mass., Portsmouth, Little Compton, R. I.

His first three children were born at Boston.

1665, Apr. 20. Portsmouth. He bought of Philip Taber a house and ten acres, for £40, and three hundred good boards.

1675, May 10. He was bound over for good behavior.

1677, Oct. 24. He recovered 5s. in a suit against Edward Marshall of Warwick.

1680. Taxed 9s. 6d.

1688, Dec. 12. He was fined 3s. 4d., for breaking peace, &c.

1705, Oct. 1. Inventory, £213, 12s. 2d., shown by Israel Shaw. A cow, grindstone, silver money £9, bills due £165, 11s. 8d., negro man £30, pewter, brass, old horse very lame 10s., &c.

I. WILLIAM, — b 1654, Jan. 21. d. 1654, Mar.

II. WILLIAM, — b. 1655, Feb. 24. d.

III. ELIZABETH, — b. 1656, May 21. d.

IV. ISRAEL, m. 1689. ——— TALLMAN, — b. 1660. d. — b. d. — Little Compton, R. I. — of Peter Tallman.

1707, Feb. 11. He sold to brother-in-law John Cook of Tiverton, two parcels of land in Portsmouth, a right on Hog Island, buildings, orchards, &c., for £202, 10s.

1. William, 1690, Nov. 7.
2. Mary, 1692, Feb. 17.
3. Anthony, 1694, Jan 29.
4. Alice, 1695, Nov. 17.
5. Israel, 1697, Aug. 28.
6. Hannah, 1699, Mar. 7.
7. Jeremiah, 1700, Jun. 6.
8. Ruth, 1701, Feb. 10.
9. Peter, 1704, Oct. 6.
10. Elizabeth, 1706, Feb. 7.
11. Grace, 1707, Oct. 20.
12. Comfort, 1709, Aug. 9.
13. Deborah, 1711, Jul. 15.

V. RUTH, m. JOHN COOK, — b. d. — b. 1656. d. — of John & Mary (Borden) Cook.

1. Ruth,
2. John, 1685, Nov. 5.

VI. GRACE, m. JOSEPH CHURCH, — b. d. 1737, Mar. 1 — b. d. 1715, Dec. 19. — of Joseph & Mary (Tucker) Church.

1. Joseph, 1689, Jun. 17.
2. Sarah, 1691, Mar. 31.
3. Nathaniel, 1693, Feb. 8.
4. Alice, 1695, Feb. 8.
5. Deborah, 1697, Jan.
6. Elizabeth, 1699, Feb.
7. Caleb, 1701, Oct. 11.
8. Richard, 1703, Nov. 21.
9. Israel, 1707, Apr. 22.

See: American Genealogist, v. 20, p. 114. v. 30, no. 2, p. 125

ICHABOD, b. 1626.
m. 1660, d. 1712, Feb. 4.
MARY PARKER, b.
d.

of George & Frances ( ) Parker.

Portsmouth, Newport, R. I.

1655. Freeman. (The entry in Colonial records of "Fred." Sheffield as freeman, probably refers to him.)

1660. Publishment of his marriage was made this year.

1680. Taxed 5*s.*, 6*d.*

1690. Deputy.

He was buried in the Clifton Burying Ground.

I. JOSEPH, b. 1661, Aug. 22. Newport, R. I.
m. 1685, Feb. 12. d. 1706.
MARY SHERIFF. b.
d. 1706 + of Thomas & Martha ( ) Sheriff.

1684. Freeman.

1696. Deputy.

1696-98-99-1700-1-2-3-4-5. Assistant.

1699, Oct. 25. He and six others were appointed to inspect into the transcription of all laws of the Colony and make returns Nov. 21st, in performance of his Excellency the Earl of Bellomont's request made at a General Council sitting at Newport the 20th of September.

1700, Feb. 14. He was appointed agent for the Colony to England, with an allowance of £80, per annum, and reasonable expenses of transportation and accommodation.

1700, May 4. He was allowed £40, for his disbursements and charges in pursuance of his intended voyage for England as agent of the Colony, the Assembly having decided to keep but one agent there, viz: Johleel Brenton, who was already there.

1702, May 6. He and John Holmes, were empowered by Assembly to lease and settle the ferries in this Colony, that are not by law already settled.

1702, Sep. 17. He was appointed on a committee to draw up an address to her Majesty, relating to the militia, &c., a demand having been made on Rhode Island, by Colonel Dudley, Governor of Massachusetts, for the whole militia of Rhode Island.

1703, Feb. 2. He was appointed sole agent to England, to appear for the upholding and continuing the Letters Patent, granted us by his Majesty Charles II, as well as for any other differences. He was to have for the first year all necessary expenses, charges for passage, &c., and for his reasonable accommodation until his arrival in England. For his own use, besides the aforesaid charges, he was to have £100, and £60 per annum, each year thereafter. If he should be taken in going or coming from England, the charge and cost of his redemption was to be paid by the colony.

1703, Apr. The Assembly finding no occasion for the present to send an agent to England, the matter was referred to the meeting in May.

1703, May 12. He and other commissioners signed an agreement with the Connecticut commissioners for the settlement of boundaries between the two Colonies. (The question had caused in the words of the Assembly "a long, tedious and extensive debate.")

1703, Jun. 22. He and two others were appointed to draw up the methods and proceedings of Court of Common Pleas.

1704-5-6. Attorney General.

1705, Jun. 19. He was appointed on a committee with three others to transcribe and print the laws of the Colony.

1706, Feb. 3. Will—proved 1706, Feb 18. Exs. wife Mary and brother Nathaniel. He directs 12 acres to be sold to pay debts. To son Joseph, all lands in Portsmouth, he allowing his mother half of same for life, and to him also a gun, saddle, chest, and a sixth of a score of sheep in William Brownell's custody. To daughter Mary Sheffield, a feather bed, chest, and a sixth of above sheep. To sons Benjamin, Edmund and William, all my land in Kings Town, equally. To son Benjamin, a mare, box and a sixth of above sheep. To son Edmund, a heifer, chest and a sixth of above sheep, and like legacy to son William. To daughter Elizabeth Sheffield, a bed, &c., and a sixth of above sheep. To son Joseph, a gold ring. To son Benjamin, silver shoe buckles. To son Edmund, my speckled cane. To son William, my ivory headed staff. To wife, half of rest of movables, and the other half to six children.

Inventory, £120, 13*s.*, viz: wearing clothes, 2 beds, pewter, 2 guns, 3 weapons, books 40*s.*, 3 old spinning wheels, 6 old chairs, a churn, silver money and plate £12, corn, tallow, oats, meat, rum, cider, 12 neat cattle, 110 sheep and lambs, mare, 2 shoats, &c.

1. Joseph, 1685, Nov. 2.
2. Mary, 1687, Nov. 8.
3. Elizabeth, 1688, Feb. 15.
4. Benjamin, 1691, Jun. 18.
5. Edmund, 1694, Apr. 5.
6. William, 1696, Mar. 30.
7. Elizabeth, 1698, Jun. 1.

II. MARY, b. 1664, Apr. 30.
d.

III. NATHANIEL, b. 1667, Apr. 18. Newport, R. I.
m. (1) d. 1729, Nov. 12.
MARY, b. 1672.
m. (2) d. 1707, Oct. 3. of
CATHARINE GOULD (w. of [James. b. 1671, Sep. 6.
d. 1752, Jan. 25. of Walter & Hannah (Scott) Clarke.

1699, Oct. 25. He was appointed on same committee as his brother Joseph.

1699-1701-2-9-10-11-13-18. Deputy.

1702. Captain.

1704, Jan. 4. He and three others were given authority to see the laws printed.

1705-6-7-8. General Treasurer.

1706, May 1. He was appointed, with pay of 4*s.*, per day, for managing the repairing and further building, &c., of the fort at Goat Island *alias* Fort Island.

1706-8. Justice of the Peace.

1710-12-14-15-16. Major for the Island.

1712, Mar. 16. His daughter Ruth died, the young wife of Daniel Gould.

1713-14. Assistant.

1714, Jun. 15. He recorded his protest against the vote of the Assembly whereby they had granted the petition of Thomas Castleton, of London, for a special Court of Trials, in a case between him and Francis Brinley, of Newport, merchant.

1722, Jun. He had his petition granted for the restoration to him of his negro Ben, as also the latter's earnings since the constable has had him.

1732, May. In the case of James Sheffield, shipwright, against Samuel Sheffield, mariner, a paragraph from the will of Nathaniel Sheffield was brought in as evidence. To son Samuel, he gave conditionally a lot of land in Newport, with house, &c., and half of 1,000 acres in Narragansett, a gun with my name engraved on it, a carbine and sword, all on condition that he pay my wife £6, yearly for life if she demand it, and £50, to my daughter Sarah Fitch, and £60 to grandaughter Ruth Gould, daughter of Daniel Gould and Ruth, his wife. Samuel was also to pay Paul Richards, of New York, £424, before 1731, Nov. 30, said sum being due from said son Samuel, the testator being jointly bound to pay it.

The deposition of Paul Richards, declared that Samuel Sheffield, now of New York, told him that he had sold his brother James, that part of land that his father bequeathed him.

The executors of Nathaniel Sheffield's will were his widow Catharine and son James.

He and his two wives and children Ruth, James and Mary, were buried in the Clifton Burial Ground.

1. Ruth, 1692.
2. James, 1694.
3. Mary, 1699.
4. Samuel,
5. Sarah,

IV. ICHABOD, b. 1670, Mar. 6. South Kingstown, R. I.
m. 1694, Dec. 27. d. 1736.
ELIZABETH MANCHESTER b.
d. 1729 (—) of William & Mary (Cook) Manchester.

See: American Genealogist. Apr., 1954, v. 30, no. 2, p. 125

1729, Sep. 17. Will—proved 1736, Jun. 4. Ex. son Jeremiah. To son Isaac, £80. To son Ichabod, £80, at age. To daughter Deborah, £50, mare, and feather bed. To daughter and four sons, rest of household stuff equally. To sons Jeremiah and Nathaniel, rest of personal estate. To son Jeremiah, my house and 40 acres, he paying legacies and half the mortgage. To son Nathaniel, rest of South Kingstown lands, he paying rest of mortgage. To daughter Deborah, use of north-east room and privilege of room at one fire while widow. To son Ichabod, a colt.

Inventory, £368, 15*s.*, 4*d.*, viz: wearing apparel, beds, carpenter's tools, warming pan, linen wheel, pewter, cards, cider, 3 cows, yoke of oxen, swine, yearling bull, 4 mares, colt, &c.

1. Isaac, 1695, Sep. 30.
2. Jeremiah, 1697, Mar. 23.
3. William,
4. Deborah,
5. Nathaniel,
6. Ichabod,

V. AMOS, m. (1) 1696, Mar. 5. ANNE PEARCE, m. (2) 1708, Dec. 22. SARAH DAVIS, — b. 1673, Jun. 25. d. 1710. — b. 1674, Feb. 14. d. 1706, Nov. 27. of John & Mary (Tallman) Pearce. — b. d. of Aaron & Mary ( ) Davis. — Tiverton, R. I.

1. Susanna, 1697, Oct. 11.
2. John, 1699, Feb. 8.
3. Mary, 1701, Apr. 2.
4. Ruth, 1704, Jan. 10.
(2d wife.)
5. Aaron, 1709, Dec. 8.

He was a blacksmith.

1692, Mar. 2. He was an inhabitant at the organization of the town.

1703–9. Assessor.

1705–7. Selectman.

1709. Town Treasurer.

He held the office of Town Clerk, for sometime, and was a deputy and captain, &c.

1707, Apr. 17. Will—proved 1710, Jun. 7. Exs. father-in-law John Pearce and his wife Mary Pearce. To son John, at age my dwelling house and land, mare, colt, and book called "Josephus's Antiquities of the Jews." To daughters Susannah, Mary and Ruth Sheffield, certain land at eighteen and a feather bed, each. To son John, a bed of silk grass, one of deer's hair, and one of flocks, and a little gun. The housing and the smith's shop to be rented till son John is of age, and then he to have the shop and smith's tools if he learn the art or mystery of blacksmith, and if not he to have a third and the other children two-thirds of proceeds of sale of the shop and tools. Son John, to be bound out to what trade he likes best, at sixteen, and the three daughters to be bound out to tailor's trade at sixteen. After children are brought up the rest of estate to be equally divided to four children.

Inventory, £474, 4s. 1d., viz; wearing clothes, books, 2 guns, 2 swords, 2 canes, 4 feather beds, 3 other beds, 3 spinning wheels, 3 cows, 4 horses, 7 swine, housing, shop, &c., £247.

SHELDON (JOHN, OF KINGS TOWN). * American Genealogist, v. 27, p. 222.

JOHN, m. ——— — b. d. 1706. — b. d.

Kings Town, R. I.

1679, Jul. 29. He and forty-one others of Narragansett, petitioned the King, praying that he "would put an end to these differences about the government thereof which hath been so fatal to the prosperity of the place; animosities still arising in peoples minds as they stand affected to this or that government."

1683, Oct. 20. He bought 230 acres near Pettacomscott, for £7, of Benjamin Congdon.

1687, Sep. 6. Taxed 7s.

1704, Aug. 15. Will—proved 1706, Jan. 16. Ex. son John. To eldest son John, dwelling house I now live in and land belonging to it. To son Isaac, half of a tract of land in Kings Town (except 20 acres formerly given my son-in-law Daniel Sunderland), the western part with dwelling house. To son Joseph, eastern part of said tract. To daughter Elizabeth Sunderland, £4. To daughters Abigail, Mary and Dinah Sheldon, each £4. To son Joseph, two steers, two heifers and a saddle. To son John, rest of estate and he to take care of my honoured mother Sarah Sheldon, and pay children as they come of age, said legacies.

Inventory, £125, 7s. 6d., viz: a feather bed, 3 wool beds, pewter, warming pan, books 10s., gun, cutlass, bandolins, stillyards, carpenter's tools, 4 cows, 2 steers, 2 two year old, a yearling, 2 calves, 4 geldings, 4 mares, 31 sheep and lambs, 15 swine, 2 pair wool cards, 4 chairs, 2 tables, shoemaking tools, 20 loads hay, &c.

I. JOHN, m. 1706, Apr. 11. HERODIAS WATSON, — b. d. — b. d. of John & Dorcas (Gardiner) Watson. — Kings Town, R. I.

1. John, 1707, Feb. 10.
2. Dorcas, 1708, Jan. 4.
3. George, 1709, May 25.
4. Samuel, 1714, Jan. 15.
5. William, 1715, Mar. 27.
6. Elizabeth, 1720, Mar. 31.
7. Sarah, 1722, Mar. 26.

1712. Freeman.

SHELDON, (JOHN, OF KINGSTOWN). 2d column. II. Isaac. Perhaps 8th child was Palmer. VII. Dinah, m. 1716. Nov.. Jabez Gifford, b. 1686, Feb. 2, of William.

II. ISAAC, * m. (1) SUSANNA, m. (2) SARAH, — b. d. 1752. — b. d. — b. d. 1751 + of — South Kingstown, R. I.

SHELDON (JOHN, OF KINGS TOWN). 2d column. II. Isaac. He m. (1) Susanna Potter, b. 1688, Jun. 28, of Thomas & Susanna (Tripp) Potter.

1. Thomas, 1709, Feb. 18.
2. Roger, 1710, Dec. 15.
3. Elizabeth, 1713, Nov. 8.
4. Isaac, 1716, Mar. 4.
5. John, 1718, Aug. 21.
6. Susanna, 1720, Oct. 23.
7. Joseph, 1721, Mar. 17.
8. Palmer, 1724, May 16.
9. Benjamin, 1727, Mar. 4.
(2d wife.)
10. Sarah, 1735, Jan. 3.

1712. Freeman.

1751, May 31. Will—proved 1752, Aug. 25. Ex. son Isaac. To wife Sarah, £150, and household goods she brought when I married her. To son Thomas, 5s., he having had already. To son Roger, 5s. To daughter Elizabeth Tanner, a silver spoon. To son Isaac, all my homestead farm, 166 acres, where I live, and buildings, he paying debts, &c. To sons John, Joseph and Benjamin, £100, each. To son Benjamin, wearing apparel. To daughter Sarah, a feather bed, £150, and use of store bed room while single. To granddaughter Deliverance Reynolds, £5. To granddaughter Susanna Reynolds, a silver spoon. To grandson James Sheldon, son of Isaac, £50. To son Isaac, rest of real and personal.

III. JOSEPH, — b. d.

IV. ELIZABETH, m. DANIEL SUNDERLAND, — b. d. — b. d. 1733, of Sunderland.

1. Daniel,
2. John,
3. Son,
4. Elizabeth,
5. Margaret,
6. Sarah,
7. Mercy,
8. Joseph,
9. Samuel,

V. ABIGAIL, — b. d.

VI. MARY, — b. d.

VII. DINAH, — b. d.

SHELDON (JOHN, OF PROVIDENCE).

SHELDON (JOHN, OF PROVIDENCE). 2d column. I. Timothy, d. 1759 or later, in Johnston.

JOHN, * m. 1660. JOAN VINCENT, — b. 1630. d. 1708 + — b. d. 1708.

of ——— & Fridgswith (Carpenter) Vincent.

Providence, R. I.

He was a tanner.

1675, Feb. 23. He testified as to the corn mill at Pawtuxet in controversy between Stephen Arnold and Samuel Reape, calling his age forty-five years or thereabouts.

1683, Feb. 14. He desired to exchange 10 acres of swamp for 5 acres of meadow.

1685, May 18. He deeded eldest son Timothy, for love, &c., 60 acres of upland, &c., and on same date deeded to sons John and Nicholas, each one half of several parcels of land aggregating 85 acres, besides rights in common.

1687, Sep. 1. Taxed 4s.

1702. Deputy.

* See: American Genealogist, v. 20, p. 114.

I. TIMOTHY, m. SARAH BALCOM, — b. 1661, Mar. 29. d. 1744 + — b. d. of Alexander & Jane (Holbrook) Balcom. — Providence, R. I.

1. Martha, 1687, May 5.
2. Timothy, 1689, Mar. 1.
3. Daniel, 1691, Jan. 29.
4. Mary, 1693, Aug. 1.

He was a cooper.

1688. Ratable estate: 2 cows, 1 steer, 1 heifer, 1 horse, 1 mare, 1 acre planting, 4 acres pasture, 1 sow.

1714, Jan. 23. He deeded son Timothy, for love, &c., tract of land north side of homestead, &c.

1716, Dec. 6. He deeded brother John, for love, &c., a third of that land which honored father John Sheldon, deceased, formerly obtained of William Arnold.

1724, Apr. 20. He deeded to son-in-law Thomas Mathewson and Martha his wife, for love, &c., a sixteenth of a full purchase right west side of Seven Mile Line, for love, &c.

1725, Nov. 27. He and John, and Nicholas Sheldon sold to Jabez Bowen, practitioner of physic, half of a forty foot lot and privilege of wharf for £15.

1729, Oct. 6. He and John and Joseph Sheldon, sold Samuel Kilton half a lot of land, for £10.

1738, Jan. 20. He deeded to son Daniel, for love, &c., all my homestead farm whereon I now dwell, containing 80 acres, and certain fractional rights in land.

1744, Mar. 31. He was living at this date, his grandson Timothy (son of Timothy, deceased) still calling himself Timothy, Jr.

1708, Mar. 20. He deeded to son Nehemiah, for love, &c., all personal estate, goods, chattels and movables, and on same date his son signed an obligation "to do utmost of my ability to keep and maintain my ancient father John Sheldon as a dutiful son ought to do by a father."

II. JOHN, m. ——
b. / d. 1741, Aug. 16.
b. / d. 1732 (—) of
Providence, R. I.

1. Roger,
2. John,
3. William,
4. Edward,
5. Patience,
6. Deliverance,
7. Ezekiel,
8. Sarah,

He was a cordwainer, and also was called a tanner.

1687, Sep. 1. Taxed 4*d*.

1727, May 6. He deeded son John, Jr., 18 acres and subsequently deeded other sons.

1732, Apr. 27. Will—proved 1741, Aug. 29. Ex. son Roger. To him, homestead, dwelling house, &c. To son Ezekiel, meadow and all undivided lands east of Seven Mile Line. To son William, all land west of Seven Mile Line, now situated in town of Glocester, and part of a small lot in Providence. To son John, 10*s*. To son Edward, 10*s*. To son Ezekiel, £6, at age and a gun. To daughter Patience Thornton, £10. To daughter Deliverance Thornton, £6. To daughter Sarah Sheldon, a feather bed, a chest of drawers and £6. To son William, 10*s*. All the rest of estate to son Roger, viz: sheep, cattle, household goods, &c., and he to take care of testator, if he live to old age and be helpless and unable to provide for myself. (As Roger died before his father, administration was taken by eldest son John, the father being deemed to have died intestate.)

III. MARY, m. 1688, Jan. 12. STEPHEN ARNOLD,
b. / d. 1735, Apr. 28.
b. 1654, Nov. 27. / d. 1720, Mar. 1. of Stephen & Sarah (Smith) Arnold.

1. Stephen,
2. Philip, 1693, Feb. 12.
3. Edward,
4. Phebe, 1695, Mar. 5.
5. Mary, 1696, Dec. 12.
6. Sarah,
7. Penelope, 1701,
8. Larana, 1703,

IV. NICHOLAS, m. ABIGAIL TILLINGHAST,
b. / d. 1747, Nov. 23.
b. 1674, Mar. / d. 1744 (—) of Pardon & Lydia (Taber) Tillinghast.
Providence, R. I.

1. Mary,
2. Nicholas,
3. Joseph,
4. Abigail,
5. Lydia,
6. Hannah,
7. Pardon,
8. Jeremiah

1687, Sep. 1. Taxed 2*d*.

1741, Apr. 8. He deeded to son Jeremiah, for £1,000, all my homestead lands where I dwell, with house, &c.

1744, Jan. 16. Will—proved, 1748, Jan. 11. Ex. son Jeremiah. To daughter Mary, a riding horse, best feather bed, &c. To each grandchild, 20*s*. All the rest of estate to be divided into eight parts, the first choice being for daughter Mary; a share to son Nicholas; one to son Joseph; daughter Abigail Fenner, wife of Richard; daughter Lydia Arnold, wife of Elisha; daughter Hannah Arnold, wife of Edward; children of son Pardon, deceased (viz: Job, John, Pardon, and Mary), and to son Jeremiah the other eighth.

Inventory, £1717, 1*s*. 17*d*., viz: large bible and other books £10, gold necklace £16, cash £74, 12*s*., plate, 12 oz. £33, wearing apparel £88, 12*s*., bonds and notes £671, 13*s*., old musket, small gun, warming pan, desk, feather bed, yarn, flax, hemp, cooper's, carpenter's and shoemaker's tools, 7 loads hay, rye, 16 chairs, a settle, physick, 19 barrels cider, mare, saddle, &c.

V. NEHEMIAH, * m. RACHEL MANN,
b. 1672. / d. 1754 +
b. 1679, Apr. 15. / d. of Thomas & Mary (Wheaton) Mann.
Providence, R. I.

1. Abraham,
2. Philip,
3. Mary, 1705,
4. Rachel,
5. Welthian,

1699. He killed a wolf this year and received 10*s*. bounty.

1710, Aug. 14. Licensed to keep public house.

1712, Aug. 2. In a deposition at this date he calls himself aged forty years or thereabouts.

1735, Apr. 4. He and wife Rachel sold Anthony Sprague, of Smithfield, 80 acres in Scituate, for £800.

1753, Apr. 12. He deeded son Abraham, as a gift, 60 rods of salt meadow, situated at landing place cove in the lands of Pawtuxet.

1754, Jan. 14. He deeded son Philip, mansion house farm, &c., where I now dwell, the son having three days before signed an obligation "to keep and maintain my ancient father Nehemiah Sheldon as a dutiful son ought to do by a father during the term of his natural life." (Both papers were recorded 1754, Feb. 22.)

It is assumed that Mary Sheldon (who married 1721, Dec. 18, William Rhodes), Rachel Sheldon (who married 1728, Mar. 6, Fearnot Packer), and Welthian Sheldon (who married, 1731, Jun. 6, John Williams), must have been daughters of Nehemiah Sheldon.

* American Genealogist, v. 27, p. 222.

SHERIFF.

THOMAS, m. MARTHA,
b. / d. 1675.
b. / d. 1691 +

(She m. (2) Thomas Hazard and (3) Lewis Hues.)

Plymouth, Mass., Portsmouth, R. I

1641, Dec. 7. He and William Brown complained against James Laxford in an action of trespass. They attached four goats and a lamb in the hands of Samuel Eddy and Joshua Pratt, amounting to 33*s*., and several other sums in other persons' hands.

1666, Dec. 10. Portsmouth. He deeded Thomas Hazard a quarter of a share in Misquamicut and also paid him £20, receiving in exchange therefor 30 acres in Portsmouth, and house, orchard, &c., all to belong to Thomas Hazard for life, and at decease of Thomas Hazard to be for Thomas Sheriff and wife Martha for their lives, and at death of both of them to go to 2d son John Sheriff and heirs, and for want of issue of John to go to 3d son Caleb Sheriff, &c.

1675, Jun. 11. Inventory, £218, 12*s*., viz: house and land £15, a horse and mare £7, 2 cows, 3 calves, 5 ewes, 5 lambs, 8 shoats, a feather bed, 6 pillows, 2 bolsters, 6 blankets, ring, flock bed, 56 pounds pewter, warming pan, silver dram cup, looking glass, &c.

Her 2d husband, Thomas Hazard made a declaration (just after her first husband's death 1675, May 29): "This is to satisfy all men, whom it may anyway concern, whereas there is a promise of matrimony betwixt Thomas Hazard and Martha Sheriff, yet I the foresaid Thomas Hazard do take the said Martha Sheriff for her own person, without having anything to do with her estate or with anything that is hers," &c.

1691, Mar. 22. Martha Hues, wife of Lewis Hues, made agreement with her son John Shrieff, which she had by former husband. Whereas

I. THOMAS,
b. 1649, Sep. 2. / d.

II. JOHN, m. 1686, Aug. JANE HAVENS,
b. / d. 1739, Oct. 14.
b. / d. 1739 (—) of John & Ann ( ) Havens.
Portsmouth, R. I.

1. John, 1687, Jun. 10.
2. Thomas, 1692, Dec. 24.
3. Elizabeth, 1693, Nov. 16.
4. Mary, 1696, Jun. 10.
5. Caleb, 1699, Apr. 12.
6. Daniel, 1702, Jan. 16.
7. William, 1705, May 3.

1680. Taxed 2*s*.

1739, Sep. 27. Will—proved 1739, Nov. 12. Ex. son John. To son John, my andirons, iron crow, spit, and grindstone. To son Caleb, 5*s*. To son Daniel, £30, and two pewter platters. To son William, £30, and two pewter platters and all my bedding. To daughter Elizabeth Burrington, 5*s*. To daughter Mary Fish, 5*s*. To daughter-in-law Mary Sheriff, wife of son John, £5, and a pewter platter. To grandson John, son of Caleb, £5. To son John, rest of personal.

Inventory, £193, 8*s*., viz: wearing apparel, silver buttons and cane £20, money due by bond £115, 5*s*., pewter, grindstone, &c.

III. CALEB,
b. / d.

IV. MARY, m. 1685, Feb. 12. JOSEPH SHEFFIELD,
b. / d. 1706 +
b. 1661, Aug. 22. / d. 1706. of Ichabod & Mary (Parker) Sheffield.

1. Joseph, 1685, Nov. 2.
2. Mary, 1687, Nov. 8.
3. Elizabeth, 1688, Feb. 15.
4. Benjamin, 1691, Jun. 18.
5. Edmund, 1694, Apr. 5.
6. William, 1696, Mar. 30.
7. Elizabeth, 1698, Jun. 1.

V. SUSANNAH, m. —— THOMAS,
b. / d. 1714 +
b. / d. 1728. of Thomas.

VI. DANIEL, m. 1688 ± JANE,
b. / d. 1737.
b. / d. 1737 + of
Little Compton, R. I.

1. Martha, 1690, Jan. 2.
2. Sutton, 1692, Dec. 3.
3. John, 1694, Dec. 15.
4. Daniel, 1696, Oct. 15.
5. Elizabeth, 1698, May 20.
6. Thomas, 1699, Sep. 20.
7. William, 1701, Mar. 26.
8. Caleb, 1707, Mar. 3.
9. Benjamin, 1709,

1737, Jun. 8. Will—proved 1737, Dec. 20. Ex. son Daniel. To wife Jane, a third of real and personal estate in Little Compton. To sons Thomas, William and Caleb, and daughters Martha Linckin and Elizabeth Dyer, 10*s*. each. To grandson Benjamin Sheriff, 10*s*.

Inventory, £78, 17*s*. 6*d*., viz: wearing apparel, 4 cows, swine, woolen wheel, linen wheel, old mare, 2 old guns, pewter, &c.

said Lewis Hues was lawfully married to his above named wife Martha, took an occasion privately to go away within six or seven weeks after he was married, taking away great part of her estate that was hers in her former husband's time. She now surrenders all her estate real and personal to her son John, excepting provisions, bedding, &c., and such things as she formerly gave her daughter Susanna Sheriff, John Sheriff to pay his mother £6, on Dec. 25th yearly for life, and thirty pounds good butter, and thirty pounds good cheese, and two barrels cider, two barrels apples, firewood, room at north-east end of house she now lives in, east part of garden, and keep of a horse or mare, &c.

1719, Mar. 17. The will of his daughter Elizabeth Carter, widow (proved 1719, Jul. 13), mentions her brothers John and Daniel Sheriff, sisters Mary Sheffield, Sarah Moon and Susanna Thomas, besides nephews and nieces, &c.

VII. ELIZABETH,* { b. { d. 1719, Jun. 5.
m.
EDWARD CARTER, { b. { d. 1719 (—) of Carter.

No issue.

VIII. SARAH, { b. { d. 1732, Jun. 24.
m.
JOHN MOON, { b. { d. 1723 (—) of Moon.

1. John, 1685, May 16.
2. Sarah,
3. Abigail,
4. Martha,
5. Elizabeth,

* See: American Genealogist v. 20, p. 114-115.

SHERMAN.

PHILIP[4] (Samuel[3], Henry[2], Henry[1]). { b. 1610, Feb. 5. { d. 1687.
m.
SARAH ODDING, { b. { d. 1681 +
of —— & Margaret ( ) Odding.
Dedham, Essex Co., Eng., Portsmouth, R. I.

His wife was a daughter of John Porter's wife by her former husband.

1633. He came to Massachusetts this year, and made settlement soon at Roxbury.

1634, May 14. Freeman.

1637, Nov. 20. He and others were warned to deliver up all guns, pistols, swords, powder, shot, &c., because "the opinions and revelations of Mr. Wheelwright and Mrs. Hutchinson have seduced and led into dangerous errors many of the people here in New England."

1638, Mar. 7. Portsmouth. He and eighteen others signed the following compact: "We whose names are underwritten do here solemnly in the presence of Jehovah incorporate ourselves into a Bodie Politick, and as he shall help will submit our persons, lives and estates unto our Lord Jesus Christ, the King of Kings and Lords of Lords, and to all those perfect and most absolute laws of his given us in his holy word of truth, to be guided and judged thereby."

1638, Mar. 12. He and others having had license to depart from Massachusetts, summons was ordered to go out for them to appear, if they be not gone before, at the next court, to answer such things as shall be objected.

1638, May 13. He was present at a General Meeting held at Portsmouth upon public notice.

1639. Secretary.

1640. He and four others were chosen to lay out lands.

1641, Mar. 16. Freeman.

1648–49–50–51. General Recorder.

1655. Freeman.

1665–67. Deputy.

1676, Apr. 4. It was "voted that in these troublesome times and straits in this Colony, this Assembly desiring to have the advice and concurrence of the most judicious inhabitants, if it may be had for the good of the whole, do desire at their next sitting the company and counsel" of sixteen persons, among them Philip Sherman.

1681, Jul. 30. Will—proved 1687, Mar. 22. Ex. son Samuel. To wife Sarah, use of fire room in west end of dwelling house, a bed, and maintenance by son Samuel, in raiment and necessaries, and to her ten good ewe sheep, kept by executor. To eldest son Eber, 10 acres in Portsmouth, and what he has had and my horseflesh in Narragansett, except one mare, the second best, which I give to Thomas and Peleg Mumford, my grandchildren. To son Peleg, 5 ewe sheep. To son Edmund, a quarter share of meadow and a sixth share of upland in Ponegansett, in Dartmouth, and also a whole purchase right in Westerly. To son Samson, at death of wife, the west half of farm I dwell on. To son Samuel, rest of farm and my now dwelling house and other buildings, and to have two parts of the grass and hay during life of wife, and all neat cattle, horsekind, sheep and swine, except two oxen, and a fatting cow, and all movable goods except two great chests with lock and key each, which are for wife Sarah. To son Samson, a white faced mare with her foal and those four Indians which we jointly bought. To sons Samson and Samuel, my draught horse, and two draught steers, equally. To son John, my bay mare and her foal. To son Benjamin, all the remaining part of my land at Briggs' Swamp where said Benjamin's house now stands, about 20 acres. To daughter Sarah, ten ewe sheep. To daughter Mary, ten ewe sheep. To daughter Hannah, £5, for herself and children and five ewe sheep. To daughter Phillip, ten ewe sheep. To son Edmund, is given Benjamin Chase's son till of age, and he is to be found in food and clothes till then.

I. EBER, { b. 1634. { d. 1706. Kings Town, R. I.
m.
MARY, { b. { d. of

1670, Oct. 26. He and four others were appointed to make a rate for Pettaquamscutt.

1687, Sep. 6. Taxed 4*s.*, 5*d.*

1706, Nov. 13. Will—proved. To son Eber, 100 acres. To sons Samuel, Stephen, Elisha, William and Peleg, land.

Inventory. Oxen, 5 cows, 2 three years, calf, &c.

1. Eber,
2. Samuel,
3. Stephen,
4. Elisha,
5. William,
6. Peleg,
7. Abigail,

II. SARAH, { b. 1636. { d.
m.
THOMAS MUMFORD, { b. { d. 1692 (—) of Mumford.

1. Thomas, 1656.
2. Peleg, 1659.
3. Abigail,
4. Sarah, 1668.

III. PELEG, { b. 1638. { d. 1719. Portsmouth, R. I., Dartmouth, Swanzey, Mass., Kings [Town, R. I.
m. 1657, Jul. 25.
ELIZABETH LAWTON, { b. { d. 1711 + of Thomas Lawton.

1670, Jun. 6. Dartmouth, Mass. Grand Jury.

1701, Jul. 11. Portsmouth. He took a bond from his son Peleg, for £1,000, the latter paying to his mother Elizabeth, £18, per year for life, and £100, to brother Samuel, within a year of his father and mother's death, to brother Benjamin, £100, within two years, and to brother George, £100, within three years of parents' death.

1711, Sep. 19. Swanzey. The old bond being declared void a new one was given for £1,000, by Peleg Sherman, Jr., of Portsmouth, to Peleg, Sr., of Shawamett, the former agreeing to pay his mother, £18 yearly.

1719. Will—proved. To son Thomas, 20 acres. To son Peleg, loom, &c. To son Samuel, a bed. To son Eber, 10 acres and dwelling house west side of Taunton river. To son Benjamin, confirmation of lands already given. To brother Edmund, of Dartmouth, a sum of money. To six cousins (*i. e.* nephews), children of brother Eber, £5, each. Some other legacies illegible.

Inventory. 2 gallons rum, 14 sheep, 3 lambs, bonds, pewter, bible, &c.

1. Thomas, 1658, Aug. 8.
2. William, 1659, Oct. 3.
3. Daniel, 1662, Jun. 15.
4. Mary, 1664, Dec. 11.
5. Peleg, 1666, Oct. 8.
6. Ann, 1668, Apr. 30.
7. Elizabeth, 1670, Nov. 25.
8. Samuel, 1672, Jul. 15.
9. Eber, 1674, Oct. 20.
10. John, 1676, Oct. 28.
11. Benjamin, 1677, Jul. 15.
12. Sarah, 1680, Jan. 25.
13. Isabel, 1683, Jun. 3.
14. George, 1687, Dec. 18.

IV. MARY, { b. 1639. { d. young.

V. EDMUND, { b. 1641. { d. 1719. Portsmouth, R. I., Dartmouth, Mass.
m.
DORCAS, { b. { d. of

1677. Freeman.

1694, Nov. 13. Dartmouth. He was one of those who received a confirmatory deed of Dartmouth, from William Bradford.

1712, Oct. 20. Will—proved 1719, Jul. 6. Exx. wife Dorcas. To son Samuel, 5*s.*, he having had already. To sons David, Nathan and Nathaniel, each certain parts of homestead. To wife, rest of homestead lot on the farm with all housing, orchards, &c., for life, and at her death said housing and lands to go to sons Elkanah and Joseph, equally. To son Elnathan, 12 acres. To daughter Lydia Maxfield, 7 acres. To sons David, Nathan, Nathaniel, Elkanah and Joseph, certain land. To sons Samuel, David, Nathan, Nathaniel, Elkanah, Joseph and Elnathan, salt marsh and meadow. To sons David, Nathan, Nathaniel, Elkanah, Joseph and Elnathan, rest of estate.

Inventory. Housing and lands £490, 6 cows, 3 calves, 18 sheep, 4 two years, a yearling, horsekind, 6 swine, 4 beds, warming pan, pewter, &c.

1. Elkanah, 1674, May 7.
2. Nathaniel, 1676, May 1.
3. Nathan, 1678, Feb. 1.
4. David, 1680, Jan. 1.
5. Lydia, 1682, Feb. 1.
6. Samuel, 1686, Jul. 27.
7. Elnathan, 1694, Oct. 1.
8. Joseph, 1698.

VI. SAMSON, { b. 1642. { d. 1718, Jun. 27. Portsmouth, R. I.
m. 1675, Mar 4.
ISABEL TRIPP, { b. 1651 ± { d. 1716 (—) of John & Mary (Paine) Tripp.

1688. Grand Jury.

1716, Nov. 5. Will—proved 1718, Jul. 4. Ex. son Job. To daughter Sarah Chace, a great brass kettle and £10, to be paid by my son Philip. To son Philip, all land in Westerly and Dartmouth. To daughter Alice Tibbitts, a great iron pot, and £10, paid by son Abiel. To son Abiel, land in Kings Town which he is now in possession of, a gun or musket as he chooses, silver spoon, great bible, whip-saw and negro boy Tommy. To daughter Isabel Baker, great iron kettle and £10, paid by son Job. To son Job, all my housing and land in Portsmouth, where I dwell, a gun or musket and pair of andirons. To granddaughter Mary, daughter of son Philip, a feather bed, pewter, &c., and five sheep. To three daughters, equally divided, a riding horse, two good cows, twenty sheep and rest of household goods. To son Job, all the rest of estate.

Inventory, £216, 4*s.*, 9*d.*, viz: wearing apparel, armour £2, 10*s.*, 2 gold rings £1, 8*s.*, silver money £1, 2*s.*, 6*d.*, plate £1, 7*s.*, 4*d.*, books £1, 7*s.*, pewter, 3 feather beds, loom, 2 wheels, neat cattle £49, horsekind £27, sheep and lambs £14, 12*s.*, swine £4, 5*s.*, hay £8, warming pan, &c.

1. Philip, 1676, Jan. 16.
2. Sarah, 1677, Sep. 24.
3. Alice, 1680, Jan. 12.
4. Samson, 1682, Jan. 28.
5. Abiel, 1684, Oct. 15.
6. Isabel, 1686 ±
7. Job, 1687, Nov. 8.

VII. WILLIAM, { b. 1643. { d. young.

VIII. JOHN, { b. 1644. { d. 1734, Apr. 16. Portsmouth, R. I., Dartmouth, Mass.
m.
SARAH SPOONER, { b. 1653, Oct. 5. { d. 1720 + of William & Hannah (Pratt) Spooner.

1694, Nov. 13. Dartmouth. He was one of those who received a confirmatory deed of Dartmouth, from William Bradford.

1720, Jun. 19. Will—proved 1734, May 21. Exs. sons Philip and Timothy. To wife Sarah, dwelling house for life, and half of orchard, use of all household goods and a cow, with keep of cow by son

1. Philip,
2. Joshua, 1678, Sep.
3. Abigail, 1680, Sep.
4. Hannah, 1682, Jul.
5. Isaac, 1684, Oct.
6. Ephraim, 1689, Jan.
7. Timothy, 1691, Jul.
8. John,

Timothy, who is also to provide her with firewood and necessaries, said son already having a deed of homestead. To son Philip, 40*s*. To son Isaac, 40*s*. To son Ephraim, £8. To son Timothy, shop and smith's tools. To daughter Abigail Chase, £3. To daughter Hannah Akin, 20*s*. To grandson John Sherman, 20*s*. To grandchildren Jonathan and Phebe Sherman, 20*s*., each. To four sons Philip, Isaac, Ephraim and Timothy, rest of personal equally. At the death of wife, two-thirds of household goods to daughter Abigail Chase, and one-third to daughter Hannah Akin. Whereas, brother Peleg Chase gave me £20 payable in two years of death, I give it to my four sons equally.

Inventory, £735, 7*s*., 6*d*., viz: homestead, £594, heifer, mare, 2 swine, 6 cows, ox, 2 steers, bull, cash £5, wearing apparel, £4, 2*s*., 6*d*., books, &c.

IX. { MARY, — { b. 1645, May. / d.
m.
{ SAMUEL WILBUR, — { b. 1663, Apr. 1. / d. 1696 (—) of Shadrach Wilbur.

1. Child,

X. { HANNAH, — { b. 1647. / d.
m.
{ WILLIAM CHASE, — { b. / d. 1737. of William Chase.

1. William,
2. Nathaniel, 1680.
3. Isaac,
4. Eber,
5. Joseph,
6. Hezekiah,

XI. { SAMUEL, — { b. 1648. / d. 1717, Oct. 9. Portsmouth, R. I.
m. 1681, Feb. 23.
{ MARTHA TRIPP, — { b. 1658 ± / d. 1717 + of John & Mary (Paine) Tripp.

1. Sarah, 1682, Apr. 10.
2. Mary, 1683, Dec. 1.
3. Mehitable, 1685, May 8.
4. Samuel, 1687, Jan. 12.
5. Othniel, 1689, Jan. 29.
6. John, 1696, Mar. 28.
7. Ebenezer, 1701, Oct. 10.
8. Martha,
9. Rebecca,

1717, Sep. 30. Will—proved 1717, Oct. 14. Exs. sons John and Ebenezer. To wife Martha, in lieu of thirds a good riding horse, cow and ten sheep, and keep of same, privilege to keep fowls, feather bed, two chests, box, a third of rest of household goods, her choice of rooms in the house, privilege in cellar, choice of four apple trees, a good pear tree, use of garden and meat, drink and firewood for life. To daughter Sarah Chase, £10. To daughter Mary Baker, £5. To daughter Mehitable Baker, £5. These legacies to be paid by son Samuel. To son Samuel, 18 acres in Swanzey. To daughters Martha and Rebecca Sherman, two-thirds of household goods equally, and to each, £20. To sons John and Ebenezer, equally, all my housing and land in Portsmouth, and right at Dartmouth, containing a quarter of one share, they paying certain legacies. If either son die the other to enjoy his part. To sons John and Ebenezer, the rest of live stock, cattle, horses, sheep, swine and husbandry gear, equally.

Inventory, £139, 12*s*., 8*d*., viz: wearing apparel, gloves, cane, girdle, pocket knife, razor, cash £1, 4*s*., 10*d*., bills of credit £12, 13*s*., 6*d*., plate £4, 8*s*., books £1, 15*s*., 17 chairs, 2 tables, table linen, pair of stillyards, 3 feather beds, flock bed, linen wheel, pair of worsted combs.

XII. { BENJAMIN, — { b. 1650. / d. 1719, Sep. 24. Portsmouth, R. I.
m. 1674, Dec. 3.
{ HANNAH MOWRY, — { b. 1656, Sep. 28. / d. 1718 (—) of Roger & Mary (   ) Mowry.

1. Benjamin, 1675, Dec. 26.
2. Jonathan, 1677, Mar. 7.
3. Joseph, 1679, Feb. 11.
4. Hannah, 1680, Mar. 20.
5. Amey, 1681, Oct. 25.
6. Sarah, 1684.
7. Isaac, 1686, Apr. 22.
8. Mehitable, 1688, Mar. 4.
9. Deborah, 1691, Sep. 3.
10. Abigail, 1694, Mar. 13.
11. Freelove, 1696, Sep. 14.
12. Bethiah, 1699.

1677. Freeman.
1688. Constable.
1707. Deputy.

1718, Dec. 8. Will—proved 1719, Oct. 12. Ex. son Joseph. To son Benjamin, all lands in Portsmouth, south and westerly of a certain line. To son Joseph, land north of said line with the exception of dwelling house, orchard, garden, well, and yard around house. To unmarried daughters income and profit of dwelling house, &c., and to each the keep of a cow. To son Jonathan, 5*s*. To daughter Amey, wife of Stephen Gardiner, a cow. To daughter Sarah, wife of Francis Brayton, 5*s*. To daughter Mehitable, wife of Job Carr, a pair of steers. To daughter Deborah, wife of Elisha Johnson, five sheep. If either of daughters Abigail, Freelove or Bethiah, die or marry, the others to enjoy the profit of house, &c., and at death or marriage of all three daughters, the house to go to grandson Benjamin, son of Isaac, at age. To daughters Abigail, Freelove and Bethiah Sherman, each a cow and feather bed, and to them the rest of household stuff. To son Joseph, rest of stock and movables.

Inventory, £299, 2*s*., viz: wearing apparel, cane, books £2 10*s*., chairs, settle, money scales, cooper's tools, cider mill, 4 feather beds, warming pan, neat kind £72, horsekind £13, sheep and lambs £14, swine £13, pewter, &c.

XIII. { PHILLIP, — { b. 1652, Oct. 1. / d.
m.
{ BENJAMIN CHASE, — { b. 1639. / d. 1731. of William & Mary (   ) Chase.

1. Phillip, 1679, Jul. 5.
2. Benjamin, 1682, Jul. 15.
3. Walter, 1684, Oct. 23.
4. Bethiah, 1686, Dec. 3.
5. Mary,
6. Sarah,

SHIPPEE.

{ DAVID, — { b. / d. 1718 +
m. 1664, Aug. 15.
{ MARGARET SCRANTON, — { b. / d.

of Thomas Scranton.

Kings Town, East Greenwich, Providence, R. I.

1664, Aug. 15. His marriage was performed in Warwick, R. I. by Walter Todd. He was called of Maidfields, and his wife Margaret late of Warwick, now of Prudence. "There being present of the maid's kindred her brother and brother-in-law, her two sisters and other neighbors."

1682, Mar. 17. East Greenwich. He bought of Henry Matteson and wife Hannah of East Greenwich, a dwelling house and 10 acres.

1684, Nov. 22. He had certain cattle let to him by Clement Weaver, of East Greenwich, viz: two yearling heifers for seven years, and at end of the time to deliver back two heifers of three years old, two steers of two years old, and two yearlings. He received a calf for seven years, he to return a heifer of two years, and a yearling. He also received seven calves for three years, and was to return half the increase [illegible] four of the old stock.

1685, Mar. 24. Kings Town. He and wife Margaret sold 10 acres, housing, &c., in East Greenwich, to William Allen, of Prudence Island.

1688, Oct. 13. He deeded to daughter Elizabeth Cooper, wife of James Cooper, for love, &c., rights in Potowomut by reason of a deed of sale had of John Gereardy now living in Prudence Island.

SHIPPEE. 2d column. 1. Elizabeth. Her husband, d. 1716. Children, James, Stephen, Samuel, Matthew, Mary, Elizabeth.

I. { ELIZABETH, — { b. / d.
m.
{ JAMES COOPER, — { b. / d. of Cooper.

1. Matthew,
2. Samuel,

II. { MARTHA, — { b. / d.
m. 1695, Nov. 14.
{ THOMAS MATTESON, — { b. / d. 1740, Jan. 19. of Henry & Hannah (Parsons) Matteson.

1. Deliverance, 1696, Aug. 20.
2. Elizabeth, 1700, Oct. 9.
3. Thomas, 1703,
4. Joseph, 1705, Jul. 1.
5. Henry, 1707, Apr. 28.
6. Mercy,

III. { MARY, — { b. / d.
m.
{ JOHN RUTENBURG, — { b. / d. 1723. of Rutenburg.

1. John,
2. Mary,
3. David,
4. Peter,
5. Margaret,
6. Susanna,
7. Katherine,
8. Ruth,
9. Mercy,
10. Thomas,
11. Solomon,

IV. { SAMUEL, — { b. / d. 1740. East Greenwich, R. I.
m. 1702, Dec. 29.
{ ANN LEITHFIELD, — { b. / d. 1740 + of Leithfield.

1. Samuel, 1703, Feb. 8.
2. Stephen,
3. Thomas,
4. Elizabeth,
5. Ann,
6. Mary,
7. Margaret,
8. Sarah,
9. Deliverance,

1740, Jul. 15. Will—proved 1740, Sep. 27. Ex. son Stephen. To wife Ann, the house for life and maintenance by son Stephen. To son Stephen, homestead and half of farming tools. To daughters Elizabeth and Ann, £35, each. To grandson Palmer Shippey, £10. To four daughters, Mary Briggs, Margaret Tarbox, Sarah Bently and Deliverance Briggs, all personal not given, and daughter Mary to have 20*s*. more than the rest.

Inventory, £232, 13*s*. 4*d*., viz: money scales, pair of wool cards, yearling bull, heifer, 2 cows, 6 sheep, 3 lambs, &c.

1697, Feb. 21. East Greenwich. He deeded daughter Martha Matteson, for love, &c., 12 acres north side of the river running through my farm where I now live in East Greenwich.

1697, Dec. 13. He deeded daughter Mary Rutenburg, wife of John, 60 acres in East Greenwich, for love, &c.

1697, Dec. 18. He deeded son Samuel, for love, &c., 90 acres in East Greenwich, and if Samuel die without issue then to go to next son begotten of wife that now is, Margaret, and to his heirs forever.

1699, Mar. 25. He and wife Margaret sold Pardon Tillinghast, Jr., 70 acres, house and orchard in East Greenwich, for £107, 10s. and 72 acres, two houses and orchard in Providence.

1705, Mar. 27. Providence. He deeded son David, for love, &c., part of farm, and on same date deeded to son Thomas, being in perfect memory, my now dwelling house, orchard and all land thereto belonging, being same I now live upon.

1711, Sep. 5. He deeded son Solomon, for love, &c., 20 acres, being part of my homestead.

1718, Nov. 8. He deeded son David, for love, &c., part of homestead where I now dwell in the northern part of township of Providence, 41½ acres, bounded partly by son Solomon, and partly by son Thomas.

V. DAVID, { b. ; d. 1741, Jul. 28. } Providence, Smithfield, R. I.
m.
HANNAH, { b. ; d. 1758 + } of

1. David,
2. Hannah,
3. Zerviah,
4. Mary,

1713, Jun. 16. Taxed 3*s*. 9*d*.

1741, Sep. 21. Administration to widow Hannah. Inventory, wearing apparel £25, 9*s*., yoke of steers, 6 cows, 6 hogs, horse, carpenter's tools, pewter, block tin spoon, old testament, old warming pan, gun, shoemaker's tools, 2 old woolen wheels, worsted cards, wool cards, old loom, books 4*s*., &c.

On the same day administration was given her on estate of son David Shippee.

1742, Sep. 30. Widow Hannah took receipts for £66, 5*s*. 2*d*., each, from William Havens in right of his wife Hannah, Jacob Mowry of Gloucester in right of wife Zerviah, both of whom called her mother-in-law, and from Mary Shippee, daughter.

1758, Aug. 22. She took receipt from Martha Shippee, widow of Jonathan, for £620, (who called her honoured grandmother, administrator to her son David).

VI. THOMAS, { b. ; d. 1765, Aug. 5. } Providence, Smithfield, R. I.
m. 1711, Sep. 27.
SARAH PLACE, { b. 1686, Nov. 12. ; d. 1765, Nov. 29. } of Peter & Sarah (Steere) Place.

1. Rose, 1712, Mar. 8.
2. Nathan, 1714, Sep. 5.
3. Joseph, 1717, Feb. 8.
4. Henry, 1720, Feb. 15.
5. Margaret, 1722, Oct. 15.
6. Peter, 1725, Sep. 20.
7. Sarah, 1728, Dec. 22.

1713, Jun. 16. Taxed 3*s*.

1724, Nov. 24. He sold to David Shippee 4½ acres, being part of homestead where he dwells.

1765, Jul. 27. Will—proved 1765, Sep. 16. Exs. sons Nathan and Joseph. He calls himself an ancient man and under infirmity. To wife Sarah, profit of half my house and other real estate whereon I now dwell in Smithfield, for life, and a third of personal free and clear. To son Nathan, at death of wife the whole of above real estate. To four sons Nathan, Joseph, Henry and Peter, the cedar swamp called Littleworth in Glocester. To daughter Rose's three children, Sarah, Job and Solomon Shippee, each £50. To son Peter, £100. To son Nathan, one-eleventh of rest of personal. To other five children, viz: Joseph, Henry and Peter Shippee, Margaret Enches and Sarah Sayles, the rest of personal.

Inventory, £177, 12*s*. 11*d*., viz: wearing apparel £11, 18*s*., books £1, 1*s*., pewter, 2 guns, household goods £6, 13*s*., cooper's tools, 6 sides of leather, 4 skins, neat kind £36, 11*s*., horsekind £14, 10*s*., sheep £11, 8*s*., swine £3, 10*s*., &c.

1765, Dec. 3. Inventory, £44, 16*s*. 11*d*., widow Sarah. Shown by son Nathan.

VII. SOLOMON, { b. ; d. 1734, Mar. 13. } Providence, Smithfield, R. I.
m.
ELIZABETH, { b. ; d. 1733 + } of

1. Thomas,
2. Solomon,
3. Job,
4. Elizabeth,
5. Mehitable,
6. Christopher,
7. Samuel,
8. Mary,

1713, Jun. 16. Taxed 3*s*. 9*d*.

1733, Dec. 15. Will—proved 1734, Mar. 27. Exs. wife Elizabeth and son Thomas. To son Thomas, farm and dwelling house but wife Elizabeth to have a room and half of farm for life while widow, or if she marry again only £10. To son Solomon, a maintenance by brother Thomas, he being somewhat impaired in his senses. To son Thomas, other land. To son Job, £35. To son Christopher, £35, at age. To son Samuel, £35, at age. To daughter Elizabeth Hearndon, 10*s*. she having had. To daughter Mehitable Bishop, 10*s*. To daughter Mary Shippee, cow and calf, five ewe sheep, and 10*s*. at age of twenty-one or marriage. To executors, rest of movable estate, equally.

Inventory, £216, 9*s*. 2*d*., viz: wearing apparel £4, 5*s*., books 10*s*., 4 cows, 9 swine, yoke of oxen, bull, 2 steers, heifer, 7 sheep, 2 yearlings, cider and barrel £2, &c.

SHOTTEN.

SAMSON, { b. ; d. 1643, Sep. }
m.
ALICE, { b. ; d. 1666, Aug. }

(She m. (2) Ralph Cowland.)

Portsmouth, Warwick, R. I.

1638. He was admitted as an inhabitant of the island of Aquidneck having submitted himself to the government that is or shall be established.

1639, Apr. 30. He and twenty-eight others signed the following compact: "We whose names are underwritten, do acknowledge ourselves the legal subjects of his Majesty King Charles, and in his name do hereby bind ourselves into a civil body politicke, unto his laws according to matters of justice."

1641, Mar. 16. He and three others were disfranchised, and names struck from the roll of freemen.

1643, Jan. 12. Warwick. He and ten others bought of Miantonomi, for 144 fathoms of wampum the tract of land called Shawomet (Warwick).

1643, Sep. 19. He and the rest of Warwick settlers received notice from Massachusetts authorities informing them that commissioners were to be sent from that colony to Warwick, accompanied by a guard of soldiers.

1664, Nov. Will of Alice Cowland, wife of Ralph. She gave her daughter Rachel Shotten, land, &c., her first husband having died without making a will.

1667, Oct. 7. Upon motion of Robert Hodgson, husband of Rachel, only child of Samson Shotten, of Portsmouth, some years since deceased, in regard to lands of Shotten, the Council examined and made diligent search and cannot find Shotten made any will but died intestate, and find Rachel sole heir to deceased, and administration was given to Robert Hodgson and wife Rachel therefore.

I. RACHEL, { b. ; d. 1696 + }
m. 1665, Aug. 3.
ROBERT HODGSON, { b. 1626. ; d. 1696, May 10. } of Hodgson.

1. Mary, 1666, Aug. 6.
2. Alice, 1668, Apr.
3. Robert,

SISSON.

RICHARD, b. 1608. d. 1684.
m.
MARY, b. d. 1692.

Portsmouth, R. I., Dartmouth, Mass.

1653, May 17. Freeman.

1653, Aug. 2. He was on a jury that found in the case of Thomas Bradley (discovered dead on the highway), "that by extremity of heat the said Thomas was overcome and so perished by himself in the wilderness."

1658, Jul. 6. He bought of William Hall 1-300 part of Conanicut and Dutch Islands, and two years later he sold same to Peleg Sanford together with 1-300 part additional that he had bought of Thomas Manchester.

1667, Jun. 5. Dartmouth. Grand Jury.

1668, May 27. He gave testimony, calling himself sixty years of age or thereabouts: "John Archer being at my house did speak as followeth, and said the deed of gift made by Namumpam to John Sanford and himself was a cheat, and the intent thereof was to deceive Namumpam, squaw Sachem, of her land; and they were to have both corn and peage to secure her land, from Wamsutta or Peter Tallman, and was to resign up the deed at her demand." "And I, Mary Sisson, do testify that I heard the same words at the same time, and further, when my husband was gone out of the house, I heard them both say they were troubled in conscience they had concealed it so long, and did refuse to take part of the gratification."

1671, Jun. 5. Surveyor of Highways.

1683, Oct. 18. Will—proved 1684, Feb. 26. Ex. son James. To wife Mary, my dwelling house and movables during her life, and £12, yearly rent, with firewood, orchard, fruit, land for garden, liberty to keep poultry for her own use, a horse to be maintained and kept at her command to ride on, two oxen, and two cows that I bought with my money, all money due me and a milch cow maintained for her use with winter shelter and summer pasture for life, and two parts of all my swine. He further provided that her corn should be carried to the mill and the meal be brought home again sufficient for her use, and ten bushels of new Indian corn, three bushels of rye and half my wheat and barley. To son James, all my housing and land in Dartmouth, excepting land near Pogansett Pond, and the reservation aforesaid for wife. To daughter Ann Tripp and her husband Peleg, a tract of land near Pogansett Pond, and to daughter Tripp and her husband Peleg Tripp's children, all those sheep he is keeping. To son John, all my house and land in Portsmouth. To son George, £5, in money. To daughter Elizabeth Allen, wife of Caleb Allen, £5, in money. To Indian servant Samuel, a two year old mare. To grandchild Mary Sisson, three cows and a bed, &c., on the day of her marriage, and one pewter flagon and brass kettle, which was her aunt Mary's.

Inventory, £600, 19*s.*, viz: house and lands at Dartmouth £240, house and lands at Rhode Island £60, cattle and horsekind £113, 15*s.*, swine £30, sheep £14, 10*s.*, beds, &c. £50, new cloth, wool yarn, hemp and flax £13, negro servant £28, one Indian servant £10, money £12.

1690, Apr. 15. Will—proved 1692, Dec. 1. Widow Mary. Ex. son James. To son George, £35, in silver money of New England and a bible. To grandchildren John and Mary, children of son John, £35, to be divided equally. All beds, brass, pewter, iron, linen and woolen cloth, milk vessels, &c., to be divided into three parts. To daughter Elizabeth, wife of Caleb Allen, one of said parts, and a chest, wheel, and £6, 5*s.* To daughter Ann, wife of Peleg Tripp, one part and a chest, wheel, and £6, 5*s.* To granddaughter Mary, daughter of George Sisson, the other part and £5, 5*s.*

Inventory, £190, including £120, in silver money, twenty-nine cheeses, &c.

I. GEORGE, b. 1644. d. 1718, Sep. 7. Dartmouth, Mass., Portsmouth, R. I.
m. 1667, Aug. 1.
SARAH LAWTON, b. d. 1718, Jul. 5. of Thomas Lawton.

1671, Jun. 5. Grand Jury. At same date he and others were appointed to view the damage done to the Indians by horses and hogs.

1677, Apr. 7. Portsmouth. He sold Peleg Tripp 32 acres in Portsmouth with houses, orchards, fencing, &c., for ⅜ of a share in Dartmouth.

1683, May 19. He sold Isaac Lawton, for £100, a quarter share in Dartmouth.

1684, Aug. 16. He was on jury whose verdict was that an Indian "murdered himself."

1687. Constable.

1688. Grand Jury.

1690-1702-5-7. Deputy.

1703. Justice of the Peace.

1718, Aug. 20. Will—proved 1718, Sep. 20. Ex. son Richard. To eldest son Richard, about 80 acres in northerly part of farm where I dwell, also 17 acres near "Solentary Hole," and all lands owned in Warwick. To son George, farm now possessed by him at Touisset Neck, Swansey. To son Thomas, land at Newport, now possessed by him. To son John, land and housing in Tiverton, he paying £70 as follows: To daughters Elizabeth Clarke, Anne Weeden, Hope Sanford, Ruth Tew and Abigail Tew, £10, each, and £20 to granddaughter Jane Sisson, daughter of John, when she is eighteen. To son James, remainder of lands in Portsmouth, with all buildings, fencing and orchards, &c., "only excepting the burial place, to be kept well fenced by my son James Sisson, his heirs and assigns forever, which is hereby preserved for my posterity and any other of my relatives for a burying place," &c. To son James, also old negro man Abraham and Lucy his wife, twenty sheep, two great tables, two great forms, cupboard, yoke, chains, &c. "My grindstone I give equally between my sons Richard Sisson and James Sisson, for the improvement of them and theirs:" To five daughters, equally, silver money and plate, and to each a feather bed, &c. To granddaughter Sarah Clarke, a feather bed and £10. Rest of movables to daughters.

Inventory, 441, 18*s.*, 8*d.* (with subsequent additions of £10, 5*s.*). Wearing apparel £8, 11*s.*, armour £2, plate at 8*s.* per oz. £8, 12*s.*, 2*d.*, silver money £13, 12*s.*, 6*d.*, Bills of Public Credit £69, 8*s.*, 6*d.*, books, 4 cows, half of 5 steers, 3 yearlings, and 2 calves, 2 mares, colt, 93 sheep and lambs, half of 4 swine and 4 shoats, geese, turkeys and fowls, small table, 12 chairs, woolen wheel, cradle, churn, cheese motes, pewter, iron and brass ware, &c.

1. Elizabeth, 1669, Aug. 18.
2. Mary, 1670, Oct. 18.
3. Ann, 1672, Dec. 17.
4. Hope, 1674, Dec. 24.
5. Richard, 1676, Sep. 10.
6. Ruth, 1680, May 5.
7. George, 1683, Mar. 23.
8. Abigail, 1685, Mar. 23.
9. Thomas, 1686, Sep. 10.
10. John, 1688, Jun. 26.
11. James, 1690, Jul. 26.

II. ELIAZBETH, b. d.
m. 1670, Apr. 8.
CALEB ALLEN, b. 1648, Jun. 24. d. of George & Hannah ( ) Allen.

1. Richard, 1673, Oct. 8.
2. Mary, 1676, Feb. 29.
3. George, 1678, May 19.
4. Hannah, 1680, Nov. 5.
5. Caleb, 1683, Mar. 20.
6. Elizabeth, 1685, Dec. 3.
7. James, 1689, Jun. 17.

III JAMES, b. d. 1734. Dartmouth, Mass.
m.
LYDIA HATHAWAY, b. 1662. d. 1714, Jun. 23. of Arthur & Sarah (Cook) Hathaway.

1685. Surveyor of highways.

1686. Constable.

1686, Mar. 24. He took oath of fidelity.

1689. Selectman.

1694, Nov. 13. He was one of those who had a confirmatory deed of Dartmouth, from William Bradford.

1710, Feb. 9. His wife had a legacy of 5*s.*, from will of her father Arthur Hathaway.

1730. His son Philip, died this year, without issue, leaving his estate by will to his brother Thomas Sisson.

1734, Jun. 15. Will—proved 1734, Dec. 17. Ex. son Jonathan. To son Richard, all wearing apparel, he having had his part. To sons James, Jonathan and Thomas, 5*s.*, each. To daughter Sarah Davol, a feather bed. To daughter Rebecca West, warming pan and iron kettle. To granddaughter Susannah Sisson, a bed. To five daughters or representatives of deceased daughter Content's child, each one-fifth part of rest, viz: to daughters Mary, Sarah, Hannah and Rebecca, and to Content's child.

Inventory, £172, 18*s.*, 1*d.*, viz: wearing apparel £17, 13*s.*, 7*d.*, cash £30, 7*d.*, 3 silver spoons, pewter, 2 combs, stillyards, 3 cows, yearling, calf, 4 swine, 12 geese, &c.

1. Richard, 1682, Feb. 19.
2. Mary, 1685, Feb. 26.
3. James,
4. Jonathan,
5. Philip,
6. Thomas,
7. Content,
8. Sarah,
9. Hannah,
10. Rebecca,

IV. JOHN, b. d. 1687 ± Newport, R. I.
m.
MARY, b. d. 1687. of

1680. Taxed 18*s.*

1680, May 10. Juryman.

1682, Mar. 28. Grand Jury.

1687, Jun. 24. Administration on estate of widow Mary, was given to George Sisson.

Inventory, £187, 11*s.*, 6*d.*, including estate of both John Sisson and Mary his wife.

1. John,
2. Mary,

V. ANNE, b. d. 1713 +.
m.
PELEG TRIPP, b. 1642 ± d. 1714, Jan. 13. of John & Mary (Paine) Tripp.

1. John,
2. Priscilla,
3. Sarah,
4. Job,
5. Peleg,
6. Mary,
7. Anne,
8. Mehitable,
9. Richard,

VI. MARY, b. d. 1674 (—)
m.
ISAAC LAWTON, b. 1650, Dec. 11. d. 1732, Jan. 25. of Thomas Lawton.

No issue.

SLOCUM.

See: American Genealogist v. 20, p. 115.

GILES,[2] (Anthony[1]). b. d. 1683.
m.
JOAN, b. d. 1679, Aug. 31.

Portsmouth, R. I.

1648, Sep 4. He had a grant of 30 acres on payment of £3.

1650, Jan. 24. He bought land of John Cranston.

1655. Freeman.

1667, May 20. He bought land in Navesink, N. J., of Robert Carr, of Newport.

I. JOANNA, b. 1642, May 16. d. 1727, Jan. 6.
m.
JACOB MOTT, b. 1633. d. 1711, Nov. 15. of Adam & Sarah ( ) Mott.

1. Jacob, 1661, Dec. 13.
2. Hannah, 1663, Nov.
3. Mercy, 1666, Jan. 8.
4. Sarah, 1670, Feb. 3.
5. Elizabeth, 1672, Sep. 12.
6. Samuel, 1678, Sep. 4.

II. JOHN, b. 1645, May 26. d. 1702. Portsmouth, R. I., New Jersey.
m. 1674 (—)
MERIBAH PARKER, b. d. 1698 + of George & Frances ( ) Parker.

No issue

1668, Apr. 25. He had ear mark for his live stock granted.

He had deeds at different times of land in New Jersey, Dartmouth, Mass. and Portsmouth, R. I. He and his wife were Quakers.

1679, Aug. 31. "Joan Slocum the wife of old Giles she Dyed at Portsmouth the 31st 6mo. 1679," as Friends' Records state.

1681, Oct. 10. Will—proved 1683, Mar. 12. Exx. daughter Joanna Mott. Overseers, John Easton, Walter Clark and Arthur Cook.

To son Samuel, 5*s*. To son John, 5*s*. To son Giles, all lands and housing in Portsmouth, except 4 acres and small tenement in occupation of William Rickinson, house carpenter. To son Giles, also a great chest, table, bedstead and great chair. To son Ebenezer, 5*s*. To son Nathaniel, two shares of land near town of Shrewsbury, New Jersey. To son Peleg, half a share in Dartmouth. To son Eliezer, quarter of a share in Dartmouth. To daughter Johannah Mott, three-quarters of a share of land near Shrewsbury, N. J. To daughter Mary Tucker, 4 acres and small tenement in Portsmouth and 16 acres on Conanicut Island. To son Eliezer, two oxen, four cows and a horse. To daughter Johannah Mott, £5 and a riding horse. To "my loving friends the people of God called Quakers," £4, to be paid into the men's meeting on Rhode Island. To three children Nathaniel and Eliezer Slocum and Johannah Mott, all bedding equally. To each grandchild, five sheep. To five children Nathaniel, Peleg and Eliezer Slocum, Johannah Mott and Mary Tucker, rest of estate undisposed of.

1668, May. Navesink, N. J. Freeman.

1677, Jan. 2. He had deed from his father of land in Shrewsbury and Navesink, N. J.

1692, Jan. 14. He was appointed to assist in laying out lands in Shrewsbury.

1698, Apr. 6. Will—proved 1702, Feb. 2. Exx. wife Meribah. He gave estate to cousin (*i. e.* nephew), John Slocum, son of brother Nathaniel, cousin Peter Parker, son of Joseph, deceased, and cousin Patience Tucker.

III. GILES, b. 1647, Mar. 25. Portsmouth, Newport, R. I.
m. 1669, May 26. d.
ANN LAWTON, b. ; d. of Thomas Lawton.

1. Elizabeth, 1671, Apr. 8.
2. Joanna, 1672, Oct. 9.
3. Ann, 1674, Sep. 15.
4. Mary, 1676, Jan. 30.
5. Sarah, 1679, Mar. 1.
6. Giles, 1680, Dec. 8.
7. John, 1682, Sep. 22.

1669. He moved to Dartmouth, Mass., but returned before many years to Portsmouth.

1678. Portsmouth. Freeman.

1681. In this and other years he was appointed on committees of Quakers.

1682–85. He was chosen to serve on Grand Inquest.

1685–86–87–88–89–90–1701. Deputy.

1696–98–99–1700–3–4–5–8–10–12. Assistant.

He was often Moderator of Town meetings, and served as Councilman.

1705. He and his brother Ebenezer were on a committee in regard to boundary line between Rhode Island and Connecticut.

1720. Newport. Freeman.

He died at Newport, as one of his sons-in-law, Joseph Earle, mentions him in his will as late of Newport, deceased.

IV. EBENEZER, b. 1650, Mar. 25. Portsmouth, Jamestown, R. I.
m. d. 1715, Apr. 13.
MARY THURSTON. b. 1657, Feb. ; d. 1732, Nov. 16. of Edward & Elizabeth (Mott) Thurston.

1. Elizabeth, 1678, Jan. 1.
2. Mary, 1679, Jun. 21.
3. Joanna, 1680, Dec. 30.
4. Rebecca, 1682, Nov. 13.
5. Samuel, 1684, Mar. 2.
6. Ebenezer, 1686, Jan. 20.
7. Desire, 1688, Mar. 12.
8. Deliverance 1691, Aug. 15.
9. Mercy, 1693, Sep. 14.
10. Giles, 1696, Feb. 19.
11. Joseph, 1697, Apr. 21.
12. Abigail, 1697, Apr. 21.

1678, Oct. 25. Jamestown. He received land by deed from his father at this date and soon settled there.

1679–81–82–83–84–85–96–1701–5–7–8–9–11–12–13–14. Deputy.

1700. He gave £1, toward building the Quaker meeting house at Mashapaug.

1707, May 28. He had the privilege granted him by Assembly to keep a ferry on the west side of Conanicut Island, he finding sufficient boats, wharves, &c.

1710, Sep. 27. He gave a deed for a Friends' meeting house at Jamestown.

1712–13. Speaker of House of Deputies.

He often served as Moderator, Councilman and Head Warden.

He was "a valuable minister," of the Quakers as their records declare.

1714, Dec. 10. Will—proved 1715, Apr. 20. Exs. son Ebenezer & wife Mary. Overseers, friends John Hull and Joseph Mowry, and cousin Jacob Mott of Portsmouth. To wife, feather bed, negro woman "Kate," and all plate. To eldest son Samuel, all land on north side of farm. To second son Ebenezer, rest of farm, new buildings, orchards, &c., but wife to have equal privilege with son while widow, and Ebenezer to pay her £6 per year. To son Giles, farm in Warwick, bought of my son-in-law Peter Greene, and rights in Warwick and East Greenwich, at age, and two oxen, two cows, a a horse and negro Sam. To son Joseph, 4 acres in Jamestown, right in Dutch Island and £150 at age. To daughters Elizabeth, widow of Peter Greene, Rebecca, wife of William Burling and Desire, wife of Samuel Dyer, 5*s*., each, they having already had from their grandfather Thurston. To daughters Mercy and Abigail Slocum, each £50, at eighteen. To son Ebenezer, rest of stock and movables.

Inventory, £625, 8*s*., 6*d*., viz: 12 spoons £8, 2 cups £5, 4 porringers £11, tankard £15, feather beds, negro woman Kate £42, white horse, concordance, great bible, parcel of old books 6*s*., clock £20, money, seals, &c.

He was buried in Friends' Burying Ground in Jamestown.

1729, Nov. 5. Will—codicil 1732, Nov. 7,—proved 1732, Nov. 22. Widow Mary. Ex. son-in-law Samuel Dyer. To son Samuel, 5*s*. To daughter Desire Dyer, silver tankard, three silver porringers, and a silver cordial cup. To son Giles, two silver spoons. To son Joseph, two silver spoons, silk grass bed, two cows, twenty sheep, mare, sow, all husbandry tools, negro called Fortune, &c. To daughter Abigail Thomas, £20, two silver spoons, wheel, &c. To daughters Desire Dyer and Abigail Thomas, wearing apparel. She gave legacies also to granddaughter Patience Carr, daughter of Caleb, and to grandsons Caleb, Joseph and William Carr, grandson David Greene, grandson Ebenezer Slocum, granddaughters Mary and Ruth Slocum, grandson Thomas Rogers, grandchildren William, Rebecca, Benjamin, Hannah, Sarah, Ebenezer and Amey Burling, granddaughters Mary Carr, Mercy Thomas, Elizabeth Thomas and Susanna Greene. To Susanna Thurston, daughter of my brother Jonathan, £5. The codicil alludes to death of son Joseph and divides his legacy among certain others.

V. NATHANIEL, b. 1652, Dec. 25. Portsmouth, R. I., Shrewsbury, N. J.
m. d. 1703.
HANNAH TUCKER, b. ; d. 1702 + of Henry & Martha ( ) Tucker.

1. Samuel, 1682, Dec. 11.
2. Sarah, 1684, Mar. 15.
3. Meribah, 1686, Nov. 7.
4. Elizabeth, 1690, Jan. 15.
5. Naomi, 1692, Jul. 12.
6. John, 1694, Nov. 14.
7. Mary, 1697, Mar.

1679. Shrewsbury, N. J. He had a grant of 240 acres and others later.

1694, Mar. 1. In will of Henry Tucker, he mentions son-in-law Nathaniel Slocum.

1702, Jul. 28. Will—proved 1703, Mar. 29.

VI. PELEG, b. 1654, Aug. 17. Portsmouth, R. I., Dartmouth, Mass.
m. 1680 ± d. 1733.
MARY HOLDER, b. 1661, Sep. 16. ; d. 1737, Sep. 20. of Christopher & Mary (Scott) Holder.

1. Mary, 1681, Oct. 29.
2. Deliverance 1685, Feb. 10.
3. Content, 1687, Jul. 3.
4. Elizabeth, 1690, Feb. 12.
5. Peleg, 1692, Mar. 24.
6. Giles, 1695, Feb. 21.
7. Holder, 1697, Jun. 14.
8. Giles, 1699.
9. Joseph, 1701, May 13.
10. Silvester, 1704, Nov. 1.

1684. Dartmouth. He moved there this year or a little earlier.

1694, Nov. 13. He was named as one of the proprietors in confirmatory deed of Gov. Bradford.

1699, Jan. 6. He and Jacob Mott and two others, at a man's meeting held at John Lapham's in Dartmouth, "undertook to build a meeting house, for the people of God in scorn called Quakers, 35 foot long, 30 foot wide, and 14 foot stud." He gave £15, toward the expense. The house was built the same year, and was the first one erected for worship in that town.

He was a minister of that religious society.

1731, Jan. 13. Will—proved 1733, Feb. 7. Exs. sons Holder and Joseph. To wife Mary, while widow, best room in house, three cows, mare, firewood and £40 a year. If she marry, £20 a year. To son Holder, 429 acres, southerly part of homestead, half a right in Cuttyhunk Island, &c. To male issue of son Peleg, deceased, 669 acres, northerly part of homestead, &c. The mansion house that Peleg dwelt in to go to my grandson Peleg, and grandson Giles to have this my mansion house, and grandson Jonathan, house Nathaniel Tallman lives in, &c. To son Joseph, my land in Newport and Patience Island, and wharf and house at Newport and land in Dartmouth, &c. To sons and grandsons, live stock. To daughter-in-law Rebecca, widow of Peleg, the lands given grandchildren for her support while widow. To granddaughter Katharine Slocum, daughter of Peleg, £250. To granddaughters Content, Easton and Elizabeth Barker, land in Dartmouth. To grandson John Hedley, 5*s*. To grandsons Henry Hedley and John Chapman, land. To daughter-in-law, widow of son Giles, a mare. To Monthly Meeting of Friends, £10. To son Holder, rest of estate.

VII. SAMUEL, b. 1657 ± ; d.

1. Giles,
2. Joseph,

He is believed to have married and to have had children as given.

VIII. MARY, m. 1679, Oct. 30. ABRAHAM TUCKER, — b. 1660, Jul. 8. d. 1689, Sep. 25. — b. 1653, Dec. 13. d. 1725. of Henry & Martha ( ) Tucker.

1. Henry, 1680, Oct. 30.
2. Mary, 1684, Feb. 1.
3. Martha, 1686, Nov. 28.
4. Patience, 1686, Nov. 28.
5. Abigail, 1688, Dec. 21.

IX. ELIEZER, m. ELEPHEL FITZGERALD, — b. 1664, Dec. 25. d. 1727. — b. d. 1748. of Fitzgerald. Portsmouth, R. I., Dartmouth, Mass.

1. Meribah, 1689, Apr. 28.
2. Mary, 1691, Aug. 22.
3. Eliezer, 1694, Jan. 20.
4. John, 1697, Jan. 20.
5. Benjamin, 1699, Dec. 14.
6. Joanna, 1702, Jul. 15.
7. Ebenezer,

1684. Dartmouth. He moved there this year or a little earlier.

1699. He gave £3, toward building the Quaker meeting house.

1727, Mar. 11. Will—proved 1727, Jul. 30. Exs. sons Eliezer and Ebenezer. To wife Elephel, £20, per year for life, Indian girl Dorcas, during indenture, great low room, two bedrooms, &c., and she to have firewood for life, &c. To son Eliezer, northerly part of homestead farm, 100 acres, with houses, barns, orchard, &c. To son Ebenezer, southerly part of homestead farm on which my dwelling house stands, &c. To sons Eliezer and Ebenezer, other land. To son Ebenezer, 1 pair oxen, pair steers, eight cows, two heifers and £12. To sons Eliezer and Ebenezer, rest of stock, horses, cattle, cows, sheep and hogs. If son Ebenezer die without issue, his brother Eliezer to have his part. To grandson Benjamin Slocum, son of Benjamin, deceased, £100, and certain land when of age; and certain land to the child that son Benjamin's widow Meribah is now with, provided it be a boy. If the child should be a female the land to go to her brother Benjamin, he paying her £50. For the bringing up of son Benjamin's two children, he gives £200, to be in two payments. To daughter Meribah Ricketson, wife of William, £50. To daughter Joanna Weeden, wife of Daniel Weeden, £50. Rest of estate to executors.

Inventory, £5,790, 18*s.* 11*d.*, real estate. Personal £665, 18*s.*, 11*d.*

1746, Mar. 19. Will—proved 1748, Oct. 4. Widow Elephel. Ex. son-in-law William Ricketson. To eldest daughter Meribah Ricketson, a bed, and to son-in-law William Ricketson, a horse, and six spoons. To daughter Joanna Weeden, a brass kettle. To son Eliezer Slocum's granddaughter Mary Howland, hand irons. To son Ebenezer, hand irons. To grandsons Benjamin and John Slocum (sons of Benjamin), £3, each. To daughter Meribah Ricketson, rest of estate.

Inventory, £378, 1*s.*

SMITH (JOHN, OF NEWPORT).

JOHN, m. SUSANNAH, — b. d. 1699 (—) — b. d. 1712 +

Newport, R. I.

He was a surveyor, and much occupied in that calling.

1678, Nov. 15. He was appointed to join with Captain Peleg Sanford and assist him in survey of Narragansett lands.

1684, Apr. 5. He and wife Susanna, sold James Greene, of Potowomut, 17 acres there for £14.

1686, Aug. 14. Bristol. His three last children were born in this place.

1695, Jul. 2. Newport. He with others was chosen to run the eastern line of the Colony.

1695, Nov. 6. He was witness to will of Thomas Emmons.

1699, Jul. 20. Susanna Smith, widow of John, inhabitant of Newport, sold land to James Carder and Richard Greene.

1712, Mar. 17. Susannah Smith, widow of John Smith, of Newport, Gent., and Thomas Smith, son to said John Smith, sold for £200 to Joshua Davis, of East Greenwich, 55 or 60 acres there with sawmill, house, &c.

I. REBECCA, — b. 1678, Oct. 14. d.

II. MARGARET, — b. 1684, Feb. 29. d.

III. MARY, — b. 1686, Aug. 14. d.

IV. JOHN, — b. 1689, Oct. 28. d.

V. THOMAS, m. MARY, — b. 1692, Oct. 19. d. — b. d. of Newport, R. I.

1713. Freeman.

1715, Apr. 18. He and wife Mary sold Peter Mawney, of East Greenwich, 105 acres there for £120.

SMITH (JOHN, OF PRUDENCE ISLAND).

JOHN, m. MARGARET, — b. d. 1677 (—) — b. d.

(She m. (2) John Snook.)

Portsmouth (Prudence Island), R. I.

1664, May 5. His wife Margaret having been fined £5, by last Court of Trials, presented a petition to Assembly for the Court's favor and mercy in remitting fine, and said fine was thereupon remitted. (He was at this time called of Conanicut.)

1673, Aug. 19. He, and William Allen and John Snook, were witnesses to a deed from John Paine, of Boston, of certain land on Prudence Island, bounded partly by lands let unto John Smith, &c.

1677, Oct. 24. His widow and executrix Margaret Smith, recovered £25, in money and £37, 10*s.*, in country pay, in a suit against John Paine.

1678, Jun. 12. Margaret Smith's former sentence of being incapable of giving in evidence in any case, and thereby stands as a perjured person, is remitted, null and void.

I. JOHN, m. PHILLIS GEREARDY, — b. d. 1730. — b. d. 1729 + of John & Renewed (Sweet) Gereardy. Portsmouth (Prudence Island), South Kingstown, R. I.

1. John,
2. Daniel,
3. Son,
4. Hopestill,

1694, Jul. 23. He of Prudence Island, sold Philip Sweet, of Coweset, 13½ acres, bought of Eleazer Collins, for £8.

1696. He and Jeremiah Smith, made an agreement (dated at Prudence Island), relative to the ferry at Boston Neck, in Kings Town.

1703, Jul. 12. Kings Town. He and others were appointed to lay out highways.

1709, Aug. He and Jeremiah Smith, were granted the privilege of ferry at Boston Neck, by the Assembly, for term of seven years at £4, per year. All general officers, Justices, Deputies and Jurymen, and the post when on public concern, to be carried free.

1716, Jun. 19. He and Jeremiah Smith, owners of a tract of land lying between Pettaquamscutt river and Narragansett bay, having freely laid out and given a highway of four rods wide to the King and country, across Boston Neck, from the said river down to the ferry on said bay; the Assembly accept the gift, approving of said highway as very commodious and convenient for travelers passing from ferry to ferry, and enact that hereafter it shall be a public road.

1717, Oct. He and Jeremiah Smith, proprietors of a tract of land reaching from Pettaquamscutt river to the ferry at Westquage, having given to the country a highway from said river to said ferry, the Assembly orders them to make convenient gates and keep them well hung for the passing of carts, horses and foot.

1729, Sep. 1. Will—proved 1730, Feb. 8. Ex. son John. To wife Phillis, £20 yearly while widow, a third income of my part of ferry, half of lower room and bedroom, &c., use of apple trees, wood provided by son John, milk of one cow, household goods needful and negro girl Judah. To son John, farm at Boston Neck and building for life and then to his two sons John and William, and right in the ferry to be for son John, for life (and then to his two sons John and William). To son Daniel, farm in Coweset, where he dwells, 120 acres, for life, and then to his son Daniel. To daughter Hopestill Northup, £150, and 200 acres at Coweset. To grandson Ebenezer Smith, the rest of land in Coweset, to him and male heirs. To granddaughter Ruth Whipple, £5. To granddaughter Mary Card, £10. To granddaughter Margaret Smith, negro girl Flora. To daughter-in-law Mary Smith, negro girl Maria. To grandson John Smith, negro boy Cæsar. To granddaughter Celinda Smith, negro girl Hagar. To five granddaughters, children of my son John Smith, a gold ring each. To five children of my daughter Hopestill Northup, each a bible. To sons John and Daniel, certain rights in land.

II. JEREMIAH, m. 1672, Jan. 2. MARY GEREARDY, — b. d. 1720. Portsmouth (Prudence Island), R. I. — b. d. 1722 + of John & Renewed (Sweet) Gereardy.

1. John,
2. Ephraim,
3. Ebenezer,
4. Sarah, 1678, Apr.
5. Mary,
6. Deliverance,

1675. Warwick. Freeman. (He was married at Warwick.)
1680. Portsmouth. Taxed 4s.
1688. Constable.
1696. He and John Smith signed agreement about ferry at Boston Neck, in Kings Town (dated at Prudence Island).
1709. Justice of the Peace.
1710, Jan. 9. He bought 300 acres at Pettaconsett, of James Sweet, of Prudence Island, for £500, the said Sweet reserving certain land already given to his son-in-law Samuel Boone.
1716, Mar. 19. Will—proved 1720, Apr. 11. Exs. wife Mary and sons Ephraim and Ebenezer. To wife whole income of all lands for life, and negro woman Rachel and a negro girl at her disposal. To eldest son John, 300 acres in Kings Town, to him and his male heirs forever and in default thereof to female heirs, and he not to sell nor let without consent of his brothers, and John to give his eldest daughter Mary, £100. To two sons Ephraim and Ebenezer, all right in Boston Neck, the north part with house where he lives to be for son Ephraim, for life, and to heirs, &c., and the south part to son Ebenezer, and the ferry to be equally for two sons, with the ferry house. To eldest daughter Sarah Hazard, £50, and a silver cup. To second daughter Mary Congdall (*i. e.* Congdon), £50 and a negro girl Maria, and a silver cup. To daughter Deliverance Reynolds, £100 and a silver cup. To oldest son John, £4, per year for life, paid by my two sons Ephraim and Ebenezer, equally, and to said John, two cows and forty sheep. To son Ebenezer, £100, to build a house. Executors to build an addition to son John's house of £25, price.
Inventory, 10 oxen, 25 cows, 2 mares, old horse, colt, 3 steers, a three year old, a bull, a heifer, 11 yearlings, 672 sheep and lambs, 5 hogs, 22 shoats, negro man Will £60, negro boy Primus (two years old), £15, negro boy Pero (three and a half years old) £25, negro girl Violet (two months old) £5, negro woman Rachel £40, negro girl Maria £50, negro girl Demmis £30, feather bed, 4 flock beds, 3 wheels, loom, pewter, cider mill, his part of ferry house £25, &c.
1722. His widow Mary made a deed to her son Ephraim's children.

III. MERCY, m. BENJAMIN CLARKE, — b. d. — b. d. of Clarke.

SMITH (JOHN, OF PRUDENCE ISLAND). 2d column. III. Mercy, had a son Emanuel, b. 1697, Apr. 4.

IV. HANNAH, m. JOSEPH CASE, — b. d. 1712. — b. 1654. d. 1741. of William & Mary ( ) Case.

1. Joseph, 1678, Jul. 16.
2. William, 1681, May 27.
3. Mary, 1682, Dec. 2.
4. Hannah, 1687, Jul. 6.
5. Margaret, 1690, Aug. 20.
6. John, 1692, Nov. 20.
7. Emanuel, 1699, Nov. 2.

V. DANIEL, — b. d. 1707. Kings Town, R. I.

He was a mariner.
1698, Jun. 18. He bought of James Sweet, of Kings Town, a third of a right in Mashantatack. This was a renewal of an ancient deed now lost and not in being.
1695, May 13. Will—proved 1707, Jul. 15. Exx. sister Hannah Case. Overseer, Thomas Mumford. (The will was signed at Newport, proved at East Greenwich, and he calls himself of Kings Town. To sister Mercy Clarke, wife of Benjamin Clarke, of Kings Town, half of what was bequeathed me by my father-in-law (*i. e.* stepfather), John Snook, after my mother's decease. To sister Hannah Case, wife of Joseph Case, of Kings Town, all interest in Mashantatack lands, and all other estate real and personal.

SMITH (JOHN, OF WARWICK).

JOHN, m. ANN COLLINS (widow). — b. d. 1663, Jul. — b. d. 1678, Nov. 2.

Boston, Mass., Warwick, R. I.
He was a merchant.
1648, Jun. 5. Warwick. He was recorded as an inhabitant.
1648. Assistant.
1649, May 26. In a letter of this date written from Narragansett by Roger Williams to John Winthrop, Jr., he says that he "came hither late last night, and wet, from Warwick, where this colony met, and upon discharge of my service we chose Mr. John Smith, of Warwick, the merchant or shopkeeper that lived at Boston, for this year President."
1649–50. President of the four towns, comprising the colony.
1652–53. President of Providence and Warwick.
1655. Freeman.
1655, May 7. He and Stukely Westcott, were ordered "to cast up what damage is due to the Indians, and place every man's share according to his proportion and gather it up; and in case any one refuse to pay upon demand, then it shall be taken by distress, by a warrant from the Town Deputy."
1657, Dec. 17. He brought an action of debt against John Smith, mason, of same town.
1658–59–60–61–62–63. Commissioner.
1663, Aug. 11. Inventory, £439, 18*s*., 8*d*., viz: plate, beaker £4, 10*s*., 2 feather beds £10, 16 pieces of pewter, 21 yards oxenbridge, 16 yards cotton, 10 yards dowles, pair of wheels, 3 breeding mares, 5 colts, 12 cows, 4 steers, 6 yearlings, 4 calves, 26 ewes, a ram, 15 lambs, 25 swine, 4 hives of bees, half of 2 yearlings and 3 calves, &c. Dwelling house, stone house, orchards, corn land, 3 purchase shares, &c. £200.
1663, Sep. 14. The Town Council appointed his widow Ann, sole executrix, giving her all estates in Warwick or elsewhere; and it appearing that her son Elizur Collins, hath due him £200, as a legacy given him and his sister Ann Collins, which sister being dead the whole sum is due Elizur, therefore the executrix is ordered to make over all the housing and lands in Warwick, of John Smith, to her son Elizur for security of his portion, but she, Anne, to enjoy said housing and lands for life. If any of John Smith's kin appear they are to have 5*s*.

(No issue.)

RICHARD, b. 1596. d. 1666.
m.
——— b. d. 1664 (—)

Gloucester Co., Eng., Taunton, Mass., Kings Town, R. I.

1637 ± Kings Town. At about this time he came to the Narragansett country from Taunton (where he had tarried a while), and established a trading house, giving free entertainment to travelers passing through that section. He became a very large proprietor in lands in that region. Testimony as to him was given by Roger Williams years later (1679, Jul. 24) as follows: "Being now near to four score years of age, yet (by God's mercy) of sound understanding and memory, do humbly and faithfully declare that Richard Smith, Sen., deceased, who for his conscience toward God, left a fair possession in Gloucestershire and adventured with his relatives and estates to New England, and was a most acceptable and prime leading man in Taunton in Plymouth Colony, for his conscience sake (many differences arising) he left Taunton and came to the Nanhigansick country, where (by the mercy of God and the favor of the Nanhigansick sachems) he broke the ice (at his great charge and hazard) and put up, in the thickest of the barbarians, the first English house amongst them." Mr. Williams further says: "I humbly testify that about forty-two years from this date he kept possession, coming and going, himself, children and servants; and he had quiet possession of his housing, land and meadows, and there in his own house, with much serenity of of soul and comfort, he yielded up his spirit to God (the Father of spirits) in peace."

A petition of the inhabitants of Narragansett to the King (dated 1679, Jul. 29) states very much the same matter as the testimony of Mr. Williams.

"About forty-two years since, the father of one of your petitioners, namely Richard Smith, deceased, who sold his possessions in Gloucestershire, and came into New England, began the first settlement of the Narragansett country (then living at Taunton, in the colony of New Plymouth) and erected a trading house in the same tract of land where now his son Richard Smith inhabits, not only at his cost and charge, but great hazard, not without the consent and approbation of the natives, who then were very numerous, and gave him land to set his house on, being well satisfied in his coming thither, that they might be supplied with such necessaries as aforetime they wanted, and that at their own homes, without much travel for the same. The said Richard Smith, being as well pleased in his new settlement in a double respect, first that he might be instrumental under God in the propagating the gospel among the natives, who knew not God as they ought to know him, and took great pains therein to his dying day; secondly, that that place might afford him a refuge and shelter in time to come for the future subsistence of him and his." The petitioners state that there were no English living nearer to him than Pawtuxet, near twenty miles from his house.

1662, Oct. 15. He testified in relation to an Indian deed, calling himself about the age of sixty-six years.

1663, Jul. 3. He and his son Richard and others of Narragansett desired the protection of Connecticut.

1664, May 5. He was desired by the authorities of Rhode Island to come before the court in regard to his seeming estrangement from the Rhode Island government, as established over Narragansett.

1664, May 14. He wrote Captain Hutchinson, at Boston, enclosing the above letter, and requesting it be made known to the Connecticut government. He complains of John Greene, Sr., being taken from his house at Aquidneset by warrant from Rhode Island, and adds: "Sir, it will be necessary for you to give Connecticut intimation of their proceedings [for] we may be easily overturned by them, if they stick not by us."

1664, Jul. 14. Will—recorded 1666, Aug. 22. Exs. sons Richard Smith and John Viall. To son Richard, dwelling house and lands thereto belonging in Wickford, and all right to my propriety of lands in Conanicut and Dutch Islands. To daughter Elizabeth, wife of John Viall, of Boston, Vintner, certain lands. All cattle, horses, mares, sheep, swine, goods and debts, with certain lands, to be divided into four equal parts, and after debts, &c., are paid, to be divided as follows: To son Richard and his heirs, one quarter part; to daughter Elizabeth, wife of John Viall, and her issue, one quarter; to the children of my deceased daughter Katharine, sometime wife to Gilbert Updike, one quarter; and to children of deceased daughter Joan, sometime wife to Thomas Newton, the other quarter. The said grandchildren to have their parts at age (the grandsons at twenty-one and granddaughters at eighteen or marriage), and any one dying the survivors to have such portion.

I. RICHARD, b. 1630. d. 1692.
m.
ESTHER, b. d. 1692. of
Kings Town, R. I. — No issue.

He was a merchant, as he styles himself in a deed.

He served in Cromwell's army as Major it is said.

1659, Aug. 23. The Assembly declared that if Richard Smith, Jr., arrested any member of this colony for lawfully obstructing him in his pretended taking possession by building on Hog Island, &c., he should be liable for damages.

1662, Oct. 8. He testified in relation to an Indian deed, calling himself aged about thirty-two years.

1664, May 14. He wrote Captain Hutchinson and Captain Hudson: "I have lately been to Rhode Island, where I have seen men working wonders in their own conceits." He mentions that they were threatened with prison, (for not giving allegiance to Rhode Island). "They are resolved to drive all before them, if they cannot prevent them, not else."

1669, May 21. Conservator of the Peace.

1671, Sep. 26. Newport. He bought of John Porter and wife Horod, 240 acres in Portsmouth, for £40. He did not long dwell at Newport.

1672, May 14. He was appointed on a commission to meet the Connecticut commissioners to put a final end and issue of all differences between the two colonies.

1672, Jun. 25. He was empowered by the Assembly to take the best course he can to put the inhabitants of King's Province in the Narragansett country into a posture of defence.

1672–73. Assistant.

1673, May 7. He was appointed on a committee to treat with the Indian sachems; "and with them seriously to consult and agree of some way to prevent the extreme excess of the Indians' drunkenness." The sachems to be treated with were Mawsup and Ninecraft, of Narragansett, Philip, of Mount Hope, Wetamo, of Pocasset, and Awashunks, of Seaconnet.

1675, Jun. 25. In a letter dated from Mr. Smith's house at Narragansett, Roger Williams wrote to Governor Winthrop as follows: Mr. Smith is now absent at Long Island. Mrs. Smith though too much favoring the Foxians (called Quakers) yet she is a notable spirit for courtesy towards strangers, and prays me to present her great thanks for your constant remembrance of her, and of late, by Captain Atherton."

1678. He, on behalf of himself and other inhabitants of Narragansett, petitioned the King, asking that the government of Rhode Island might forbear to exercise any authority over them, but that the inhabitants there, and of the islands of Conanicut, Hope, Patience and Dutch Islands may be settled and restored to the government and jurisdiction of Connecticut, the petitioners claiming that the grant of Connecticut had precedence of Rhode Island, and that it took all lands east of Narragansett Bay.

1679, Jul. 19. A warrant was issued by Assembly for his apprehension, and ordered to be brought before Assembly at Newport, to answer such charges as shall be exhibited. (The arrest was on account of the above petition.)

1679, Jul. 24. Testimony of Roger Williams was given, that since the death of Richard Smith, Sr. "his honoured son Captain Richard Smith hath kept possession (with much acceptation with English and Pagans) of his father's housing, lands and meadows, with great improvement also (by his great cost and industry). And in the late bloody pagan war, I knowingly testify and declare that it pleased the Most High to make use of himself in person, his housing, his goods, corn, provisions and cattle, for a garrison and supply to the whole army of New England, under the command of the ever to be honoured General Winslow, for the service of his Majesty's honour and country of New England."

1683, Aug. 22. His house was the place of meeting of Governor Cranfield of New Hampshire, &c., and the said Governor, &c., were there prohibited by Governor Coddington, &c., from keeping court in any part of this jurisdiction.

1685, Jun. 2. He and wife Esther sold Joseph Mowry, of Jamestown, 24 acres there and a right in Dutch Island, for £50.

1686, May 28. He was appointed Justice of the Peace, also Sergeant Major and Chief Commander of his Majesty's militia, both horse and foot, within Narragansett country. This appointment was from the President and Council governing New England.

1687. Member of Sir Edmund Andros' Council.

1687, Sep. 6. Taxed £2, 10*d*. (Heaviest tax paid in Kings Town.)

1687–88. Justice of General Quarter Sessions and Inferior Court of Common Pleas.

1691, Mar. 16. Will—proved 1692, Jul. 12. Exs. wife Esther and Lodowick Updike. To wife, housing and lands for life, and at her death, the housing and land where I live, to a certain line, to go to Lodowick Updike, as also certain other land. To Daniel and James Updike certain land south of Wickford. To Israel and James Newton, land at Wasquque Farm. To Thomas Newton, of London, house and land at Bristol and Hog Island. To Elizabeth Vial, alias Newman, farm on Boston Neck. To Aquilla Ketch, a house and land. To negro man Caesar and wife Sarah, their freedom and 100 acres, and to Caesar's children their freedom at thirty years old. To negro Ebedmelik, freedom at wife's death. To Francis Brenley, all my right in housing and lands on Rhode Island, for life, and then to his son Thomas and heirs. To all my sisters' children and their children's children, certain land. To Richard Updike, Lodowick's son, £20. To Smith Newton, Thomas Newton's son, £10. To wife, the liberty to dispose of part of my goods to my relatives as she shall see cause and for their necessity. To Captain Fones 10*s*., to buy him a ring.

Inventory, £1159, 15*s*., contained in warehouse, shop, kitchen in the great house, store house chamber, hall, dairy room, kitchen chamber, porch chamber, hall chamber, leanto chamber, &c., &c. Shop goods £20, 12 guns and other small arms £15, map of the world, plat of Boston, sundry books, &c. £5, plate £25, linen and woolen wearing apparel £20, linen old and new and old watch £31, gold and rings £40, English money £15, New England and Spanish money £65, 5*s*., broken piece of plate £1, 10*s*., 2 negro men £40, 5 negro children and old woman £40, 3 horses £20, 30 sheep £9, 20 swine, carts, plows, &c., 135 cattle young and old £250, debt of Henry Bull £42, other debts £240, sloop Primrose £100, clock at Boston £20, &c.

II. JAMES, b. d. 1664 (—)
UNMARRIED,
Kings Town, R. I.

1659, Dec. 1. He signed as witness to a deed of Indians to the proprietors of Providence and Pawtuxet. (Other witnesses were Richard Smith, Sr., and Richard Smith, Jr., &c.)

III. ELIZABETH, ★ b. d. 1686 +
m. (1)
——— NEWMAN, b. d. of Newman.
m. (2)
JOHN VIALL, b. 1619. d. 1686, Feb. 26. of Viall.

(By 2d husband.)
1. James, 1664,
2. Samuel, 1667, Nov. 25.
3. Elizabeth, 1670, Apr. 6.
4. Benjamin, 1672,
5. Jonathan,

IV. JOAN, b. d. 1664 (—)
m.
THOMAS NEWTON, b. d. of Newton.

SMITH, (RICHARD.) 2d column. IV. Joan. Had also son Thomas.

1. Abigail,
2. Israel,
3. James,
4. Smith,

V. KATHARINE, b. d. 1664 (—)
m. 1643, Sep. 24.
GILBERT UPDIKE, b. d. of Updike.

1. Elizabeth, 1644,
2. Lodowick, 1646,
3. Sarah, 1650,
4. Daniel,
5. James,
6. Richard,

★ American Genealogist, v. 27, p. 222-3

SMITH (RICHARD). 3d column. IV. Joan, m. 1648, Apr. 16, Thomas Newton. V. Katharine, had 7. John. Her husband was son of Lodowick & Gertrude Op Ten Dyck.

WILLIAM, b.
m. d. 1671.
SARAH, b.
d. 1709.

Portsmouth, R. I.

1667, Aug. 10. He enlisted in a troop of horse.

1671. Deputy.

1671, Jun. 13. Will—proved 1671, Jul. 6. Exx. wife Sarah. Overseers, William Baulston, of Portsmouth, and Francis Brinley, of Newport. To wife Sarah, for life all estate, and at her death to children as wife shall see cause.

1671, Oct. 18. His widow had suit brought against her by John Gereardy, for £400. Non-suited.

1680. The Smiton land was taxed 4*s.*

I. SARAH, b.
m. d. 1715 +
WILLIAM BROWNELL, b.
d. 1715. of Thomas & Ann ( ) Brownell.

1. Thomas, 1674, May 25.
2. Sarah, 1675, Nov. 25.
3. Martha, 1678, May 24.
4. Anna, 1680, Jun. 4.
5. William, 1682, Aug. 11.
6. Benjamin, 1684, Oct. 20.
7. Robert, 1688, Apr. 11.
8. Mary, 1691, Feb. 13.
9. Smiton, 1691, Feb. 13.
10. George, 1693, Apr. 13.
11. Alice, 1695, Dec. 3.

II. BENJAMIN, b. Wapping, Eng.
m. 1693, Dec. 7. d. 1709 (—)
ELIZABETH BONHAM, b.
d. of Bonham.

1693, Dec. 7. He was married in the minories of the parish church of Trinity, he being called of St. Paul's, Shadwell, and his wife of Wapping.

1705, Nov. 18. He had his son Benjamin baptized at Stepney. He was now called of Wapping, parish of St. Dunstan's.

1723, Mar. Benjamin Smyton, infant, and grandson of William Smyton, brought suit by his guardian Nathaniel Byfield, of Bristol, against Thomas Borden for trespass, &c., on Hog Island.

It was declared that William Smiton, died in 1671, possessed of a dwelling house and land in Portsmouth, and Sarah his widow died about April, 1709, and the land came to Benjamin, grandson, who was son of Benjamin Smiton, then deceased, who was eldest son of said William Smiton. Testimony was given showing that after the death of William Smiton, his son Benjamin came over from England and desired deponent, Weston Clarke, recorder, to hear some discourse between him and his sister Brownell, wife of William Brownell, concerning said father's estate, and Benjamin left the farm to her to improve, he being bound to sea, but on what terms deponent cannot remember. The record of marriage of Benjamin, and his children's births were put in evidence.

Captain Samuel Bonham, deposed that Benjamin Smiton, departed from Barbadoes for Rhode Island, 1722, Jul. 8, on Brigantine Greyhound, and he was eldest son of Benjamin Smiton, deceased, late of parish of St. Dunstan's, Stepney, County Middlesex. The deponent's father was brother of the wife of Benjamin Smiton, the elder.

The deposition of Patrick Smiton, of Barbadoes, forty-eight years of age, declares that his father and William Smiton were brothers.

1728, Apr. 16. Benjamin Smiton, mariner, sometime of Barbadoes, but now of Bristol, Mass., son of Benjamin Smiton, late of Stepney, in Wapping, old England, deceased, and grandson and heir of William Smiton, of Portsmouth, deceased, sold to Thomas Borden for £30, two parcels of land in Portsmouth, 12 acres in the whole.

1. Mary, 1698, Dec. 3.
2. Sarah, 1700, Mar. 8.
3. Elizabeth, 1703, Jan. 20.
4. Benjamin, 1705, Nov. 12.
5. Samuel, 1707, Nov. 5.

SNOOK.

JOHN, b.
m. [John. d.
MARGARET SMITH, (w. of b.
d.

Portsmouth (Prudence Island), Kings Town, R. I.

1673, Aug. 19. He was witness to a deed from John Paine, of Boston, of certain land on Prudence Island, bounded partly by land let unto John Smith.

1680. Taxed 6*s.* 6*d.*

1687, Sep. 6. Kings Town. Taxed 9*s.* 10½*d.*

1695, May 13. In the will of Daniel Smith of Kings Town, he mentions a bequest from father-in-law (*i. e.* stepfather), John Snook, which was to be for said Daniel Smith, at decease of his mother.

SPENCER.

JOHN, b.
m. d. 1684.
SUSANNAH, b.
d. 1719, Apr. 12.

Newport, East Greenwich, R. I.

He may have been son of Michael Spencer who was of Cambridge, Mass., 1634, and later of Lynn; and may also have been identical with that John Spencer who was made the heir of his uncle John Spencer. (The latter made his will in 1637, at Newbury, returned to England, and his will was proved at Salem, Mass., 1648.)

1661, Sep. 15. He had lot 22 in a division of the Misquamicut (Westerly) lands. He did not settle there however.

1668. Freeman.

1671. Juryman.

1677, Oct. 31. He and forty-seven others were granted 5,000 acres to be called East Greenwich.

1677–78–79–80–81–82–83. East Greenwich. Town Clerk.

1678, Jun. 12. Conservator of the Peace.

1680. Deputy.

1684, Oct. 16. Inventory, £197, 3*s.* 6*d.*, viz: 4 oxen, 3 cows, 2 four years, 2 three years, 2 yearlings, 5 calves, 4 sheep, horse, mare, colt, 2 sows, 12 shoats, musket, cutlass, warming pan, &c.

As he died intestate the Town Council made his will. Exx. widow Susannah. To her, dwelling house and 10 acres, and half the farm of 90 acres for life, and one-third of the profit of house and land at Newport, for life. To eldest son John, the Newport house and land and certain

I. JOHN, b. 1666, Apr. 20. East Greenwich, R. I.
m. d. 1743.
AUDRY GREENE, b. 1667, Dec. 27.
d. 1733, Apr. 17. of John & Ann (Almy) Greene.

He was a cordwainer.

1699–1700–4–5–9–14–24–26–29. Deputy.

1704. Justice of the Peace.

1712–29. Speaker of House of Deputies.

1733, Jul. 2. Will—proved 1743, Dec. 31. Exs. son John and William. To son John, homestead, tanning utensils, bark and half the untanned leather. To son William, a farm in East Greenwich and half the untanned leather. To grandson John, son of William, a house lot. To grandson John, son of John, a house lot. To granddaughter Audrey Spencer, daughter of John, a house lot. To granddaughter Audry Spencer, daughter of William, a house lot. To sons John and William, the rest of personal equally.

Inventory, £238, 4*s.* 3*d.*, viz: old books, pewter, woolen wheel, linen wheel, joint stool, small desk, 5 chairs, candle stick, 2½ barrels of cider, barrel of beer, debts due estate £10, 6*s.*, 6 fowls, shoat, calf and sheep skins, &c.

1. John, 1693, Jun. 10.
2. William, 1695, May 6.

II. MICHAEL, b. 1668, May 28. East Greenwich, R. I.
m. 1692, Nov. 16. d. 1748, Oct. 10.
ELIZABETH, b.
d. 1748, Oct. 13. of

1700. He contributed 10*s.*, toward building the meeting house for Quakers at Mashapaug.

1706–7–15. Deputy.

1748, Sep. 28. Will—proved 1748, Nov. 26. Ex. son John. To wife Elizabeth, use of all household articles, all bonds, liberty of dwelling house, negro man Pero and keep of a cow and firewood. To son Samuel, a gun, canoe, &c., he already having had by deed. To son-in-law Joseph Bailey and my daughter Elizabeth Bailey, certain land during their lives, and then to go to Robert Bailey. To son Abner, certain land for life, and then to grandson Michael. To daughters Susannah Briggs, Mary Johnson and Ruth Winslow, £90, each. To four daughters, all household goods, bonds, money, sheep, and negro Pero at decease of wife. To son John, all homestead farming tools, &c.

Inventory, £2150, 18*s.*, viz: 4 bonds £347, money £121, silver tankard and spoons, old books, pewter, cider mill and press, loom, negro Pero £90, a bull, pair of oxen, 3 cows, mare, 17 sheep, 7 lambs, colt, &c.

1. Elizabeth, 1694, Sep. 10.
2. Samuel, 1696, Mar. 2.
3. Susanna, 1699, Mar. 13.
4. John, 1700, Jan. 5.
5. Abner, 1703, Jan. 8.
6. Isabel, 1705, Jun. 6.
7. Joanna, 1709, Jan. 1.
8. Mary, 1710, Jan. 31.
9. Ruth, 1711, Apr. 24.
10. Orpha, 1713, Oct. 31.
11. Michael, 1718, Apr. 27.

land at East Greenwich, he choosing as guardians for himself, Thomas Nichols and Richard Dunn of Newport. To Michael Spencer, at decease of his mother, all the housing and lands she now lives in, and he to have half of these at twenty-one. To sons Benjamin, William, Robert and Peleg, £9, apiece at age. To daughter Susannah, £6, at eighteen or marriage.

1684, Oct. 27. Testimony was given by Henry Matteson (aged thirty-eight years or thereabouts) that at the house of John Spencer, deceased, some time this last summer, did hear him say that he intended to give unto his son Michael, the house and land he, the said Spencer, lived upon.

The relationship between him and Michael Spencer, of East Greenwich, who died 1723, Mar. 16, has not been ascertained.

The latter made his will 1723, Mar. 23.—proved 1723, Mar. 30, and names wife Rebecca as executrix, and friend and kinsman Major Thomas Fry and Thomas Spencer, overseers. He mentions his sons Thomas and Amminuhamah, and daughter Susannah Odin. (His daughter Susannah was married 1708, Oct. 4, to John Odin.)

III. BENJAMIN, b. 1670, Jun. 22; d. 1723. East Greenwich, R. I.
m. (1) MARTHA, b. ; d. of
m. (2) 1718, Aug. 4. PATIENCE HAWKINS, b. ; d. 1748, Jul. 30. of Hawkins.

1703. He contributed 18s. toward building the meeting house for Quakers at Mashapaug.

1709–18. Deputy.

1723, Dec. 11. Administration to John Spencer. Inventory, £577, 4s. 6d., viz: wearing apparel and purse £11, 5s. 1d., pair of working cattle, £10, 4 cows, heifer, 2 two years, 3 yearlings, 42 sheep, horse, 3 swine, 2 shoats, geese, fowls, ducks, carpenter's tools, 2 wheels, pewter, gun, pair of cards, &c.

1732, May 27. His son Walter, now being administrator took a receipt from his brother Henry, and at later dates from other brothers and sisters, viz: Benjamin, Thomas, Peleg, Susannah, David, &c.

1744, Sep. 18. Will—proved 1748, Aug. 4. Widow Patience, of Providence. Ex. son David Spencer. To daughter Susanna Beers, a silver cup marked P. H., a brass mortar, and all wearing apparel. To son David, now of Providence, a lot of land and dwelling house. To daughter Susanna and son David, all movables equally.

Inventory, £151, 8s.

1. Amey, 1699, Mar. 14.
2. Walter, 1701, Feb. 13.
3. Benjamin,
4. Henry, 1704, Oct. 19.
5. Son,
6. Thomas, 1708, Feb. 13.
7. Peleg,
8. Martha, 1711, Jun. 22.
9. William, 1713, Aug. 17.

(2d wife.)

10. Stephen, 1719, Jul. 28.
11. Susanna, 1721, Jul. 1.
12. David, 1723, Oct. 12.

IV. WILLIAM, b. 1672, Jul. 1; d. 1748. East Greenwich, North Kingstown, R. I.
m. (1) ELIZABETH, b. ; d. of
m. (2) 1734, Apr. 11. [Thos. ELIZABETH ARNOLD (w. of, b. 1684, Jan. 9; d. 1752, May 5. of Roger & Mary ( ) Burlingame.

1696. Freeman.

1703. He contributed 3s. toward building the meeting house for Quakers at Mashapaug.

1709, May 27. He and twelve others bought 1824 acres of the vacant lands in Narragansett near Devil's Foot.

1714–24–26–27–29. Deputy.

1734–35. Justice of Inferior Court of Common Pleas for Kings County.

1748, Oct. 25. Will—proved. Exs. son Thomas and brother Thomas. To son John, £20, best suit of clothes and cane. To sons Christopher, Thomas and Henry, certain land equally. To wife Elizabeth, household goods and stock she brought, a mare, privilege of garden, keep of a cow, beef, corn and cider yearly, and a third of dwelling house for life. To daughter Elizabeth Herrington's children, 40s., each. To grandson William Nichols, £10. To grandson William Spencer, son of Thomas, £5, and rest of his children, 40s., each. To son Christopher's three children, 40s. each. To grandson William, son of Henry, £5, and other children of Henry, 40s. each. Son Henry to keep a cow for his mother-in law (*i. e.* stepmother). To daughter Mary Coggeshall, a feather bed, 40s., &c. To daughter Elizabeth Herrington, a feather bed, &c. He also mentions grandchildren Sarah, Job and Samuel Tripp, &c.

Inventory, 4 hogs, 4 shoats, 6 sheep, mare, bull, 5 cows, 2 heifers, 2 yearlings, &c.

1. John, 1698, Apr. 16.
2. Mary, 1700, Mar. 29.
3. Elizabeth, 1702, May 11.
4. Jonathan, 1705, Jan. 21.
5. William, 1706, Jun. 30.
6. Daughter, 1708, Jun. 20.
7. Daniel,
8. Christopher,
9. Thomas,
10. Henry,

V. ROBERT, b. 1674, Nov. 6; d. 1748. East Greenwich, North Kingstown, Exeter, R. I.
m. (1) 1697, Jul. 15. THEODOSIA WHALEY, b. ; d. of Theophilus & Elizabeth (Mills) Whaley.
m. (2) 1723, Nov. 7. [Jos. SUSANNA REYNOLDS (w. of, b. ; d. of James & Deborah ( ) Reynolds.
m. (3) [Jos. MARTHA HOPKINS (w. of, b. 1680; d. 1773. of Theophilus & Elizabeth (Mills) Whaley.

1696. Freeman.

1721. Deputy.

1723. North Kingstown. He became an inhabitant about this time or a little later.

1736, Aug. 3. He took administration on estate of his son Robert of East Greenwich. He was called Captain at this time and later.

1748, Jul. 29. Inventory, £1140, 9s., viz: wearing apparel £53, cash and pocket book £12, 12s. 6d., bonds £337, 10s., £112, 10s., &c., pewter, spice mortar, cheese tub, warming pan, rope making tackling, sow, 3 pigs, 2 shoats, 3 cows, &c.

1749, Jul. 26. The administrator George Reynolds (who had married Joanna) brought in account. He took receipts from John Spencer, Michael Spencer, Philip Greene and Benjamin Sweet for £84, each, from Jeremiah Boss, for £85, 2s., and from Thomas Place, Jr., for £234. (Ruth Spencer married her cousin John Spencer, son of William.)

His widow died at house of her son-in law, Othniel Gorton.

1. Susanna, 1698, Mar. 4.
2. Anna, 1699, Jun. 7.
3. Martha, 1700, Sep. 8.
4. Ruth, 1702, May 20
5. Robert, 1704, Mar. 5.
6. Theodosia, 1705, Dec. 8.
7. Theophilus, 1707, Sep. 16.
8. Michael, 1709, Dec. 27.
9. Joanna, 1711, Sep. 30
10. Caleb, 1713, Jul. 20.
11. Nathaniel, 1715, Sep. 4.
12. James, 1717, Feb. 6.
13. Samuel, 1718, Feb. 3.

(2d and 3d wives, no issue.)

VI. ABNER, b. 1676, Dec. 4; d. 1759, May 11. East Greenwich, R. I.
m. 1708, Dec. 9. SUSANNAH WELLS, b. 1684, Nov. 2; d. 1782, Jul. 25. of Peter Wells.

He was a weaver.

1703. He contributed £1, 9s. toward building the meeting house for Quakers at Mashapaug.

1759, Aug. 25. Administration to widow Susannah. Inventory, £599, 15s., viz: wearing apparel £52, oval table, 3 square tables, 11 chairs, case of bottles, pewter, warming pan, stillyards, scales, 4 old books, pair of worsted combs, 2 weaver's looms, quilt wheel, 3 old wheels, cow, shoat, &c.

1. Peter, 1709, Nov. 18.
2. Susanna, 1712, Aug. 30.
3. Ruth, 1714, May 8.
4. Alice, 1719, Oct. 8.
5. James, 1722, Apr. 10.
6. Abner, 1725, Feb. 11.
7. Thomas,

VII. THOMAS, b. 1679, Jul. 22; d. 1752, Apr. 25. East Greenwich, R. I.
m. (1) 1703, Dec. 30. ELIZABETH PEARCE, b. 1682, May 27; d. 1742, Sep. 30. of Giles & Elizabeth (Hall) Pearce.
m. (2) ELIZABETH, b. 1688, Sep.; d. 1747, May 13. of
m. (3) [Benjamin. SARAH HOWLAND (w. of, b. 1696, Apr. 27; d. of Joseph & Sarah (Freeborn) Wanton.

He was a physician.

The records call him the first English child born in East Greenwich.

Perhaps a portion of the offices accredited to him were held by a contemporary, viz: Thomas[3], (Michael[2]).

1703. Freeman.

1704–7–10–14–15–19–21–27–29–30–31–33–35–36–37–38–41–48–49–50–51. Deputy.

1720–21–27. Clerk of Assembly.

1734–35. He was one of the Justices of the Inferior Court of Common Pleas for county of Providence.

1738. Speaker of the House of Deputies.

1741, Dec. 2. He was appointed on committee to represent and manage the affairs of this colony before the Commissioners to hear and determine boundaries between Rhode Island and Massachusetts.

1741, Aug. He and two others were appointed by Assembly to set off part of Warwick into a township to be called Coventry.

1752, May 20. Administration to son-in-law Thomas Aldrich. Inventory £2055, 3s. 10d., viz: wearing apparel £156, plate £85, 4s., watch £25, bonds £409, 2s, 8d., bonds supposed to be desperate debts £33, 1s. 10d., notes £80, 1s. 10d., books £24, 10s., 3 framed maps or plans £3, 2 spinning wheels, pewter, oval table, the whole of his medicines with the vessels and utensils belonging to his practice £50, 4 feather beds £140, negro man and woman £400, 2 horses, 3 cows, 3 swine, &c.

1. Thomas,
2. Elizabeth, 1714, Feb. 19.
3. William, 1716, Sep. 6.
4. Susanna, 1720, Aug. 18

VIII. SUSANNA, b. 1681, Dec. 1. d.
m. 1700, Dec. 23.
RICHARD BRIGGS, b. 1675, Feb. 1. d. 1733. of John & Frances ( ) Briggs.

1. Richard, 1701, Oct. 17.
2. Frances, 1703, Oct. 27.
3. Audry, 1705, Aug. 10.
4. Susanna, 1707, Dec. 31.
5. John, 1709, Feb. 8.
6. Sarah, 1710, Feb. 27.
7. Caleb, 1713, Feb. 17.
8. Anne, 1715, Oct. 25.

IX. PELEG, b. 1683, Dec. 4. d. 1763, Sep. 13. East Greenwich, R. I.
m. 1708, Jul.
ELIZABETH COGGESHALL, b. 1686, Mar. 9. d. of Joshua & Sarah ( ) Coggeshall.

He was a weaver.

1709-11-16-28. Deputy.

1755, Mar. 15. Will—proved 1763, Sep. 24. Exs. sons William and Jeremiah. To daughter Sarah Pierce, large sealskin trunk and half of pewter and other metal. To son John, 20*s*., and what he has had already by deed, and half my right of watering places along shore. To daughter Mary Coggeshall, a chest, bed, and half pewter and other metal. To grandson Joshua Spencer, son of Joseph, 20*s*. To son Peleg, all wearing apparel (except plate buttons), my riding horse and £160. To son William, feather bed, flock bed, and half my grist mill for life, provided he allow my son Jeremiah privilege of half the store belonging to house lately built in Newtown; and also to William, profit of Indian apprentice, large history book, colonial law book and half of other books, and writing desk. To wife Elizabeth, half profits of homestead while widow, except grist mill, and use of all household goods for life, and at her disposal goods not given away and money. To her, use of best room, kitchen and kitchen chamber and profits of mulatto apprentice Samson. To son Jeremiah, all homestead place, and housing and cattle not given, farming tools, sealskin trunk, large bible, half other books, half watering place, &c.

Inventory. Horse, 3 heifers, churn, pewter, stillyards, money scales, gun, desk, linen wheel, beds, trunks, books, coffee mill, 6 silver spoons, &c.

1. Sarah, 1709, May 11.
2. John, 1710, Aug. 30.
3. Mary, 1713, May 9.
4. Benjamin, 1715, Feb. 20.
5. Peleg, 1717, Feb. 23.
6. Joseph, 1719, Jun. 11.
7. William, 1721, Dec. 25.
8. Elizabeth, 1724, Feb. 29.
9. Jeremiah, 1727, May 8.

SPINK.

ROBERT, b. 1615. d. 1695.
m.
ALICE, b. d. 1695 +

Newport, Kings Town, R. I.

1635, May 28. He embarked at London, in ship Speedwell, bound for Virginia, his age being given as twenty years. He and others were previous to sailing "examined by the minister of Gravesend of their conformity to the orders and discipline of the Church of England, and have taken the oath of allegiance."

1648. He was thus early of Newport.

1655. Freeman.

1662, Nov. 22. He bought of John Tefft and wife Mary, 7 acres.

1665, May 13. Kings Town. He and others petitioned the Assembly for accommodation of lands, &c., in Kings Province.

1671, May 20. He took oath of allegiance, and in the same year purchased land in Quidneset, of the Atherton Company.

1679, Jul. 29. He and forty-one others of Narragansett petitioned the King praying that he "would put an end to these differences about the government thereof which hath been so fatal to the prosperity of the place; animosities still arising in peoples minds as they stand affected to this or that government."

1687, Sep. 6. Taxed 10*s*., 2*d*.

1688, Mar. 6. He and others made complaint that several highways in Kings Town are stopped up, to the great damage of inhabitants.

1685, Dec. 2. Will—proved 1695, Mar. Exs. wife Alice and son Robert. Overseers, friends, Captain Wait Winthrop, Captain John Brown and Mr. Joseph Clarke.

To eldest son Robert and his heirs, my now dwelling house at Narragansett, and 100 acres, &c., and if he die without issue then son John to have. To Robert, also two oxen, five cows, ten sheep, and a bed. To son John, a fifth of remaining land at Narragansett, and if he die then son Shebna to have. To John, also two cows and four young cattle and ten sheep at age. To son Shebna, a fifth of land in Narragansett, and if he die son Nicholas to have. To son Nicholas, a fifth of Narragansett land, and if he die son Samuel to have. To son Samuel, a fifth of said land and if he die son Ishmael to have. To son Ishmael, a fifth of said land and if he die son Benjamin to have. To son Benjamin, my house and land in Portsmouth, and if he die then son Ishmael to have. To sons Shebna, Nicholas, Samuel, Ishmael and Benjamin, at age, the same legacy in cattle and sheep as that given son John. To eldest daughter Margaret Vaughan, wife of George Vaughan, 1*s*., she having formerly had at her marriage. To daughter Sarah Spink, two cows, four young cattle and ten sheep, five ewes and five lambs, at twenty-one or marriage. To daughter Elizabeth Spink, a like legacy. To wife Alice, half the profits of housing and 100 acres given son Robert, said income to be hers for life while widow. To executors rest of estate real and personal.

I. ROBERT, b. d. 1709 ± Kings Town, R. I.
m.
——— b. d. of

1679, Jul. 29. He signed the petition to the King.

1687, Sep. 6. Taxed 1*s*.

His children's names are disclosed by a suit brought against Nicholas Spink as seen below.

1. Robert,
2. Margaret,
3. Hannah,
4. Elizabeth,
5. Abigail,

II. JOHN b. d. 1697, Mar. Kings Town, R. I.

1687, Sep. 6. Taxed 1*s*.

III. MARGARET, b. d. 1704 +
m. 1680, Jul. 26.
GEORGE VAUGHAN, b. 1650, Oct. 20. d. 1704, May 7. of John & Gillian ( ) Vaughan.

1. George, 1682, Apr. 19.
2. David, 1683, Apr. 29.
3. Mary, 1685, Feb. 28.
4. Christopher 1686, Apr. 29.
5. Abigail, 1689, Feb. 24.
6. Robert, 1691, Mar. 7.

IV. SHEBNA, b. d. Kings Town, R. I.

1687, Sep. 6. Taxed 1*s*.

V. NICHOLAS, b. d. 1733. North Kingstown, R. I.
m. (1)
ABIGAIL, b. d. of
m. (2)
SARAH, b. d. 1733 + of

1702, Mar. 23. He and wife Abigail, sold Thomas Durfee, Jr., of Portsmouth, 11 acres for £50, said land having been purchased of brother Ishmael.

1730, Mar. A suit was brought against him by the children of his brother Robert, to recover certain lands in North Kingstown. The land had been left by grandfather of plaintiff Robert Spink (who they said died about 1686), to eldest son Robert, father of plaintiffs, said father dying about 1709, and leaving one son Robert, who died unmarried about 1728. In answer to this suit, Nicholas showed a deed from his nephew Robert, dated 1724, Apr. 17, duly witnessed. The deposition of James Braynor, declared that while a sailor on his Majesty's ship belonging to fleet in the Baltic Sea he saw Robert Spink, of North Kingstown, carpenter of his Majesty's ship Revenge, then alive and well, and that was three years ago come July. The plaintiffs in this suit were: Samuel Tarbox of East Greenwich, and wife Margaret, Thomas Jacques and wife Hannah, Alexander Huling and wife Elizabeth, of North Kingstown, and John Fry and wife Abigail, of Newport.

1733, Mar. 5. Inventory £473, 6*s*., 8*d*., shown by widow Sarah, the administratrix. An additional inventory was rendered amounting to £369, 2*s*., 4*d*. Among the items were pewter, old wheel, notes £190, 1*s*., negro slaves Sambo and Obadiah *alias* Fortune and Quash £150, cider mill and press, 9 cheeses, yoke of oxen, 8 cows, 8 young cattle, bull, 8 horses, one horse said to be Josiah's, 87 sheep, sow and pigs, 8 shoats, hay £24, &c.

1. John, 1700, Sep. 6.
2. Nicholas,
3. Josiah,
4. Abigail, 1704.

VI. SAMUEL, b. d.

VII. ISHMAEL, b. 1680, Sep. 1. d. 1759. Kings Town, East Greenwich, West Greenwich, R. I.
m. 1702, Jun. 9.
DELIVERANCE HALL, b. 1683, Jan. 8. d. of William & Alice (Tripp) Hall.

1700, May 4. He was summoned with others by the Assembly to appear in court and answer the charge of being engaged in a riot.

1720. East Greenwich. Freeman.

1725, Jan. 14. He took administration on estate of his son Robert.

1728. Captain.

1728-29. Deputy.

1736, Feb. He was to have £20 paid him by order of the Assembly, on completion of a bridge over the Pawtuxet river in the road from East Greenwich to Plainfield.

1740, Jan. 8. He was voted £9, by the Assembly for time and expense, in revising and renewing the boundary line between this Colony and Connecticut, he attending the committee at their request.

1741, Jan. 27. He was appointed on the committee to examine whether the boundary marks between Rhode Island and Connecticut at or near south-west corner of Warwick Purchase be removed.

1. Robert, 1703, Jan. 21.
2. Alice, 1705, Nov. 7.
3. Dinah, 1707, Nov. 27.
4. Mary, 1710, Apr. 11.
5. Benjamin, 1712, Feb. 14.
6. Elizabeth, 1714, Jan. 1.
7. Sarah, 1715, Feb. 2.
8. William, 1716, Jun. 8.
9. Ann, 1718, Jan. 22.
10. Samuel, 1720, Apr. 1.
11. John, 1722, Jul. 21.
12. Shebna, 1724, Apr. 20.

1743, Mar. He was allowed £6, for services on committee that revised boundaries at Warwick.

1743. West Greenwich. Deputy.

1759, May 28. Will—proved 1759, Jul. 14. Ex. son Shebna. To son Benjamin, land and a silver Spanish milled dollar, he having had already by deed. To son Samuel, 5*s*. To daughter Alice Reynolds, a bond for £38, 10*s*., 8*d*., signed by her husband James Reynolds. To grandson Benjamin Cahoone, son of daughter Dinah, deceased, 5*s*. To granddaughter Mary Wait, daughter of Mary, deceased, 5*s*. To daughter Elizabeth Spencer, 5*s*. To daughter Ann Comstock, 5*s*. To grandchildren Sarah, Abigail, Martha, Deliverance and John Spink, children of son Samuel, land near William Comstock, &c., the father Samuel, having profit till children are of age, and kinsman John Spink, of North Kingstown, to be guardian of said grandchildren. To negro man Cæsar, freedom. To son Shebna, rest of estate real and personal.

Inventory, £381, 11*s*., 6*d*., viz: riding horse, mare, colt, cow, calf, &c.

VIII. BENJAMIN, { b. / d.

IX. SARAH, { b. / d.

X. ELIZABETH, { b. / d.

SPRAGUE (JONATHAN).

JONATHAN[3] (Wm.[2], Edw[1].). { b. 1648, May 28. / d. 1741, Sep.
m.
MEHITABLE HOLBROOK, { b. / d.
of William & Elizabeth ( ) Holbrook.

Hingham Mass., Providence, Smithfield, R. I.

1672. Mendon, Mass. He came thence from Hingham, and in this year was living near his brother John Sprague and father-in-law William Holbrook.

1675. His father died this year and left a legacy to his son Jonathan, of 60 acres in Providence.

1680, Jul. 16. Providence. Taxed 1*s*., 7*d*.

1687. Ratable estate, 2 oxen, 6 cows, 2 mares, horse, 18 sheep, 8 acres planting ground, 6 acres meadow.

1687, Dec. 13. He was fined 6*s*., 8*d*., for refusing to take oath as juryman.

1695, Jul. 2. He was appointed by Assembly on a committee to propose a method for making a rate. He was also appointed with others to run the eastern line of the Colony.

1695-96-98-1700-2-3-4-5-6-7-8-9-10-11-12-14. Deputy.

1702. Justice of the Peace.

1703. Speaker of House of Deputies.

1703, Jun. 22. He and two others were appointed to draw up the method and proceedings of the Court of Common Pleas.

1705-6-7-8-9-10-11-12. Town Council.

1707. Clerk of Assembly.

1713, Jun. 16. Taxed 18*s*., 6*d*.

1719, May 23. He made an agreement with sons-in-law William Jencks, John Tefft and Daniel Brown, deeding them his house and all his lands, they maintaining him for life, and he to have choice of which son-in-law he would dwell with. They were to maintain his horse also, and pay him £6, a year, and £25, to such persons as he directed at his decease.

1719, Nov. 9. He deeded son-in-law Ebenezer Cook, certain land.

1722, Feb. 23 He wrote a long letter to three prominent Presbyterian ministers in Massachusetts (viz: John Danforth, Peter Thatcher and Joseph Belcher), in answer to one they had addressed to him and other citizens concerning the establishment of a church in Providence. Mr. Sprague and his fellow Baptists, failed to see the necessity of a Presbyterian establishment however, and in his letter he gave his views in very vigorous and unmistakable terms.

He preached as an exhorter, but was not ordained (as Morgan Edwards declares in his account of the Baptists).

I. JONATHAN, { b. / d. 1764, Apr. 22. — Providence, Smithfield, R. I.
m. (1) 1699, Nov. 28.
BETHIAH MANN, { b. 1683, Mar. 12. / d. 1712, Apr. 6. — of Thomas & Mary (Wheaton) Mann.
m. (2) 1713, Sep. 17 [Steph.
HANNAH HAWKINS (w. of { b. / d. — of Coggeshall.

1. Jonathan, 1701, Jul. 25.
2. Hezekiah, 1704, Jan. 13.
3. Bethiah, 1707, May 24.
4. Anne, 1709, Mar. 9.
5. Mehitable, 1711, Mar. 24.
(2d wife.)
6. William, 1714, Jun. 9.
7. Rachel, 1716, Nov. 20.
8. Stephen, 1722, Jun. 9.
9. John, 1727, Apr. 2.
10. Susanna, 1731, Jun. 20.

1718-20-21-24-25-26-30. Deputy.

1757, May 11. Will—proved 1764, May. Ex. son Hezekiah. To grandson Eleazer, son of William, deceased, £1,000 at age. To grandson Stephen, son of Stephen, deceased, £400 at age. To the male children of two sons and two daughters the rest of estate.

Inventory, £3,605, 15*s*., viz: notes, bonds, bible, pewter, bed, &c.

II. WILLIAM, { b. / d. 1768 + — Smithfield, R. I.
m.
——— { b. / d. — of

1. Sarah,
2. Joshua,

He bore the title of Captain.

1738, Aug. 31. He deeded the land whereon Baptist meeting house stands to certain persons, for and in consideration of a meeting house by my leave and consent already erected and built for the worship of God, by my honored father Jonathan Sprague, James Ballou, James Walling and Richard Sprague, with the help of self and some others.

1740, Dec. 15. He deeded to daughter Sarah Sly and her husband William, for love, &c., 11½ acres.

1750, Dec. 20. He deeded for love, &c., to dutiful and obedient son Joshua, half of lands in Smithfield and Cumberland, 300 acres and dwelling house on easterly part of homestead on the intervale on west side of Pawtucket river, also half the barn.

1754, Feb. 9. He and his son made a division of lands above deeded, and there being an orchard of which Joshua was to have the apples, the said William Sprague agrees not to put in any creature from the first of August, to last day of October, with liberty at other times to put in such creatures as will not hurt the trees.

1762, May 21. He bought of his son Joshua and latter's wife Abigail, for $1,250, certain land, &c.

1768, Apr. 15. He deeded for love, &c., to dutiful grandsons Elias and Nehemiah Sprague, and for my honorable maintenance, all my homestead farm where I dwell.

III. PATIENCE, { b. / d.
m.
WILLIAM JENCKES, { b. 1675. / d. 1765, Oct. 2. — of Joseph & Esther (Ballard) Jencks.

1. Joseph,
2. Susanna,
3. Mercy,
4. William,
5. Patience,
6. Margaret, 1704.
7. Jonathan, 1707, Jul.
8. John, 1710.
9. Esther,
10. Mehitable,

IV. JOANNA, { b. / d. 1757.
m.
JOHN TEFFT, { b. / d. 1762. — of Samuel & Elizabeth (Jenckes) Tefft.

1. John, 1699, Dec. 4.
2. Joseph,
3. Samuel,
4. James,
5. Nathan,
6. Daughter,
7. Mary,
8. Mercy,
9. Mehitable,
10. Tabitha,
11. Sarah,

V. MARY, { b. / d.
m.
DANIEL BROWN, { b. / d. — of Daniel & Alice (Hearnden) Brown.

1. Susanna, 1715, Oct. 2.
2. Daniel, 1717, May 20.
3. Phineas, 1719, Aug. 26.
4. Penelope, 1721, Feb. 11.
5. John, 1723, Dec. 19.
6. Phebe, 1725, May 7.

VI. ——— { b. / d.
m.
EBENEZER COOK, { b. / d. — of Cook.

WILLIAM[3] (Wm.[2] Edward[1]) b. 1650, May 7. d. 1723, Sep. 26.
m. (1) 1674, Dec. 30. DEBORAH LANE, b. 1652. d.
of Andrew & Tryphenia ( ) Lane.
m. (2) MARY TOWERS, b. d. 1731 +
of Towers.

Hingham, Mass., Providence, R. I.

He was Selectman several years at Hingham, before coming to Providence.

He took conveyance by his father of estate in Hingham, on conditions.

1712. Providence. Freeman.

1716, Mar. 12. He deeded to son Benjamin, for love, &c., half the easterly end of farm at Rocky Hill and at same date the other half to son John.

1721, Apr. 7. Will—proved 1723, Nov. 11. Exx. wife Mary. To eldest son William, 5s. and what he had already received. To second son David, 50 acres, without the 7 mile line. To third son Jonathan, 2s. and what he had already received. To fourth son John, land where he now dwells. To fifth son Benjamin, land where he now dwells. To eldest daughter Deborah Beale, £30, in cattle or movables, or if she be dead to her children. To grandchildren Deborah West, William West, John West, Abiah West, £5, each, to be paid when twenty-one. To wife Mary, whole use and improvement of all my homestead where I dwell, while she remains a widow, viz: till my son Rowland comes to age. All the movables to be for her maintenance, and for bringing up the children by her, viz: Rowland, Mary, Peter and Judah. If she married she was to lose the above provision and have best feather bed and one-half the movables in the house and two cows. As long as she remained a widow after Rowland came of age she was to have best end of the dwelling house and a third of the income of lands. To sons Rowland and Peter, at age, all the homestead where I now dwell except the provision he had made for his wife, and excepting half of certain rights in lands without the 7 mile line. To daughters Mary and Judah, 100 acres and a quarter of movables equally divided when eighteen. To three sons David, John and Benjamin, half of rights without the 7 mile line, equally divided.

Inventory, £181, 14s., 5d., viz: a bull, 2 steers, 8 cows, 1 heifer, a two year old, 5 yearlings, 3 calves, horse, 6 swine, cider mill and 4 barrels cider, 17 loads of hay, rye, oats, 6 platters, undressed cotton, flax, &c., &c.

1723, Nov. 11. Mrs. Mary Sprague, widow, had administration on estate of her mother Mrs. Elizabeth Towers (who died 1723, Aug. 9. Inventory £53, 17s., 11d.).

Possibly his daughter Mary was identical with that Mary who married Nathaniel Arnold, 1737, Sep. 27 (instead of having married Amos Keech as stated.)

SPRAGUE (WILLIAM.) 1st column. His 1st wife d. 1707, Feb. 4. He m. (2) 1709 Mary Tower, b. 1672, Nov. 3, of Jeremiah and Elizabeth.

I. WILLIAM, b. 1675, Dec. 24. d. — Weymouth, Mass.

1712. Providence. Freeman.

1715, Jan. 18. He sold land to Richard Aldrich.

1728, Oct. 21. Weymouth, Mass. He confirmed to his brother David a legacy of 50 acres made to him by father William, of Providence, deceased.

1731, Jun. 14. He, for £20, received of mother-in-law (*i. e.* step-mother) Mary Sprague, of Providence, widow, releases to brothers and sisters-in-law, viz: Rowland, Peter, Mary and Judah, all real estate given them by last will of father.

II. DEBORAH, b. 1678, May 24. d.
m. —— BEALE, b. d. of Beale.

III. JOANNA, b. 1680, Feb. 15. d.

SPRAGUE (WILLIAM). 2d column. IV. David, m. Jemima Ballou, of Peter and Barbara ( ) Ballou. VIII. Benjamin, d. 1788, Apr.

IV. DAVID, b. d. 1773, Dec. 6. — Providence, Scituate, R. I.
m. ——, b. d. of

1. David,
2. Deborah,
3. Millicent,

1733, May 31. Scituate. He deeded son-in-law Daniel Whitaker, for love, &c., 30 acres.

1738, Feb. 16. He sold son David, 35 acres adjoining my homestead for £60.

1772, Apr. 28. Will—proved 1774, Sep. 17. Exs. daughters Deborah Whitaker and Millicent Bickford, and granddaughter Miriam Potter, to whom all personal, equally. The reason why nothing was given other children was, he explains, because they had already received.

Inventory, £4, 14s, viz: bed, hetchell, coffee pot, pewter platter, basin, &c., plate, churn, chest, &c.

V. JONATHAN, b. 1686, Jul. 24. d. 1748. — Hingham, Bridgwater, Mass.
m. LYDIA LEAVITT, b. d. of Leavitt.

1. Lydia, 1715.
2. Hannah, 1717.
3. Jonathan, 1720.
4. Mary, 1722.
5. Sarah, 1725.
6. John, 1727.
7. Content, 1729.
8. Betty, 1731.
9. Benjamin, 1736.

He was a housewright.

1744, Oct. 29. He deeded to his son Jonathan, Jr., for love, &c., all rights in the estate left him by will of his brother John, of Providence, deceased. Two years later Jonathan, Jr., deeded back to his father the same property for £30. (At date of first deed both were of Bridgwater, but at the second Stafford, Ct.)

VI. ABIAH, b. 1689, Jan. 27. d.
m. —— WEST, b. d. of West.

1. Deborah,
2. William,
3. John,
4. Abiah,

VII. JOHN, b. 1692, Sep. 13. d. 1725, May 11. — Hingham, Mass., Providence, R. I.
m. BETHIAH WATERMAN, b. 1693, Feb. 27. d. 1753, Nov. 25. of Nathaniel & Mary (Olney) Waterman.

No issue.

1724, Dec. 20. Will—proved 1725, Jul. 3. Exx. wife Bethiah. To wife, dwelling house and land for life, and at her decease to my own brothers and sisters. To wife all movable estate.

Inventory, £145, 11s., 6d., viz: 2 oxen, a cow and heifer, mare, 2 swine, bible, spelling book, silver money £4, 8s., 8d., gold £1, 1s., &c.

1754, Jan. 15. Administration on widow's estate to brother Nathaniel Waterman.

Inventory, £615, 17s., 11d.

VIII. BENJAMIN, b. 1695, Jan. 3. d. — Providence, R. I.
m. 1716, May 11 ALICE BUCKLIN, b. d. of Bucklin.

1732, Dec. 25. He sold David Sprague, of Scituate, for £25, 3 acres.

The will of a "Benjamin Sprague, Jr.," was made in Cranston, 1776, Aug. 2 (proved 1776, Oct. 12) He mentions wife Elizabeth, son Amos and daughter Alice Hawkins, wife of Edward Hawkins.

(2d WIFE.)

IX. MARY, b. 1712, Aug. 10. d.
m. 1740, Jan. 17. AMOS KEECH, b. d. of Keech.

X. PETER, b. 1714, Oct. 1. d. 1790, May 4. — Cranston, R. I.
m. HANNAH, b. d. 1790 + of

1. William,
2. Amey,

1790, Apr. 28. Will—proved 1790, May 29. Ex. son William. To wife Hannah, use of west half of mansion house for life and west end of crib, and improvement of all household goods for life. To daughter Amey Sprague and grandson Abner, son of William, household goods at decease of wife. To wife, use of two cows and a horse and the keep of same, and at her death a cow to Amey, and the other cow and horse to grandson Abner. To wife, a swine and keep of same and firewood sufficient, and grandson Abner to live with her and take care of her business, cut and draw wood and be one of the family. If provision for wife be insufficient then son William to provide for her. To grandson Abner, twenty Spanish milled dollars at age. To son William, rest of estate both real and personal.

Inventory, £314, 4d., viz: wearing apparel £5, 14s., pair of oxen £12, 2 cows, calf, horse, 9 sheep, 4 lambs, pair of steers, 3 heifers, yearling bull, sow, 3 pigs, 6 geese, 4 barrels cider, tobacco, flax, cheese, beef, pork, linen wheel, woolen wheel, coffee mill, 2 guns, stillyards, pocket compass, money, £31, 6s., 7d., silver £1, 11s., 7d., securities £41, 3s., 6d., &c.

XI. ROWLAND, b. 1716, Oct. 21. d. — Providence, Warwick, R. I.
m. 1745, Jan. 14. LYDIA HEARNDEN, b. d. of Hearnden.

1. William, 1748, Oct. 9.

1745, Jan. 10. He sold brother Peter Sprague, for £300, half the homestead of father William, deceased, &c.

1752, Mar. 17. Warwick. He and wife Lydia, sold Martin Salisbury, of Warwick, certain land and mansion house 6½ miles west of the harbor in Providence, for £2,600.

XII. JUDITH, b. d.
m. 1742, Jan. 3. NATHANIEL WATERMAN, b. d. of Nathaniel & Hannah (Carpenter) Waterman.

2d column. I. William m. 1707, Apr. 23, Silence Tower, b. 1684, Aug. 27, of Samuel and Silence (Damon) Tower. Children, 1, Silence, 1708, Sep. 7. 2, William, 1711, Jan. 29. 3, Jedediah, 1713, Mar. 18. V. Jonathan m. 1712, May 23, Lydia Leavitt, of Israel and Lydia (Jackson) Leavitt. VI. Abiah m. 1709 William West. XI. Rowland. Children, 1, Mary, 1746, Oct. 28. 2, William, 1748, Oct. 9.

SAMUEL, m. 1678, Mar. 7. { b. 1640. d. 1717, Mar. 22.
MARY WHITE, { b. 1636. d. 1725, Nov. 1.

London, Eng., Newport, R. I.

His wife was of Newport Pagnel, County Bucks, England.

1680. Taxed £1, 7*s*.

1684. Freeman.

1687, Dec. 14. He and Christopher Hargill, both of Newport, being sent for, appeared in court. The reason being demanded of them why they kept not their shops shut on the first day of December, being a day set apart by His Excellency the Governor and Council, for thanksgiving and praise to God; the answer given by Samuel Stapleton was "that he was above the observation of days and times."

I. MARY, { b. 1679, Feb. 7. d. young.

II. ANN, { b. 1680, Jan. 4. d.

III. MARY, { b. 1681, Jun. 7. d.

IV. ELIZABETH, { b. 1681, Jun. 7. d.

V. SAMUEL, { b. 1682, Sep. 28. d.

STEERE. See: American Genealogist, v.39, p3

JOHN, m. 1660. { b. 1634. d. 1724, Aug. 27.
HANNAH WICKENDEN, { b. d. 1705 +
of William Wickenden.

Providence, R. I.

1660, Mar. 9. He was granted a parcel of land for a house lot on the west side of Moshosit river, near land of Thomas Olney, Jr., "on the condition that it be no damage unto the highway and also that it be no precedent for the future for any to take up land on that side of the river, within the bounds of habitation."

1660, Oct 27. His intention of marriage was published.

1661, Feb. 18. He was accepted as a townsman.

1662, Jun. He was appointed with others to get out the timber and frame a bridge that was to be built over the Mosshassuck River.

1662, Oct. 27. He bought 2½ acres of George Palmer.

1663. Town Sergeant.

1667, Apr. 1. He had a lot laid out at Weapasachuck "where his house stands" on the east side, said lot measuring 160 poles by 67 poles.

1667, May 24. He sold Pardon Tillinghast for full and valuable satisfaction, dwelling house, land and fencing, near Thomas Olney, Jr's, on the other side of the river.

1670, Sep. 6. He sold Pardon Tillinghast 20 acres bequeathed by William Wickenden.

1672, May 1. Freeman.

1680, Jul. 16. Taxed 1*s*. 7*d*.

1687, Sep. 1. Taxed 5*s*.

1694, Jun. 5. He deeded son William for good consideration, half his land west of Seven Mile Line.

1695, May 28. He deeded son-in-law Peter Place and Sarah my daughter, for love, &c., 6½ acres.

1696, Nov. 7. He deeded son Thomas, for fatherly love and natural affection, 40 acres.

1702, Oct. 19. He deeded son Samuel, for love, &c., a half of right on west side of Seven Mile Line. The William Blanchard who witnessed above deed it is assumed was the son-in-law of John Steere and father of Timothy Blanchard. (He certainly was father of Moses, Theophilus and William Blanchard.)

1704, Dec. 16. He made a lease for thirty years of 6 acres to "Indian known by the name of Sam Noforce, who hath for some years lived by me and hath well behaved himself towards me and mine." The Indian was to have sole management of the land to plant corn or fruit trees for thirty years and then the land was to go to the lessor's grandson Timothy Blanchard and for Blanchard's future benefit. Sam was to leave the land smooth and not in hills, and he was not to fence the spring, but leave it open for cattle to drink.

1705, Sep. 26. He deeded son Samuel, for love and natural affection, and to prevent controversies, mansion house, orchard and meadow, comprising 40 acres, together with other lands, all being deeded without limitation, except that it was to take effect at decease of said John Steere and wife Hannah.

1711, Jan. In a deposition made this month concerning certain land, he calls himself aged about seventy-seven years.

1713, Jun. 13. Taxed 6*s*.

1720, Sep. 3. He signed, as consenting, a deed from his son Samuel to Joseph Mowry of Ridge Hill meadow.

1724, Dec. 21. Administration to son Thomas. Inventory, £44, 6*s*., viz: 40 acres £12, cedar swamp of 4 acres £1, 12*s*., other land £8, bond £10, rent of farm £8, wearing apparel £4, 14*s*.

I. JOHN, m. { b. d. 1727, Jan. 5. Providence, R. I.
ESTHER WHITMAN, { b. d. 1748, Aug. 21. of Valentine & Mary ( ) Whitman.

1697, Apr. 9. He deeded to his brother William 40 acres in exchange for lot of same size and 20*s*.

1713, Jun. 16. Taxed 6*s*.

1724. Lieutenant.

1724, Aug. 31. He and his son Hosea were witnesses to a deed from Edward Hawkins to Joseph Mowry.

1726, Jan. 3. He was appointed administrator on estate of his sister Ann Lewis.

1726, Jan. 27. He gave receipt to his brother Samuel, for £60, making void a deed.

1727, Feb. 25. Inventory. Real estate £749, (including house and land where he last dwelt £540). Personal estate £211, 11*s*. 10*d*., viz: 6 books, 4 beds, warming pan, cooper's and carpenter's tools, gun, tobacco, 9 barrels cider, 3 barrels beer, 3 cows, a two year, yearling, yoke of oxen, cattle in partnership £11, horse £3, 3 swine, 2 spinning wheels, 4 pairs of cards, money scales, purse and apparel £13, 11*d*., &c.

1748, May 23. His widow was given a legacy of £10, a year, by will of her sister Hannah Whitman, of Warwick (proved 1752, Oct. 9).

1748, Aug. 28. Widow Esther Steere's estate, of Smithfield, administered upon by son Hosea of Glocester, the eldest son John, of Glocester, declining to administer. The administrator presented receipts two years later from his brothers John and Hezekiah for legacies of £222, 3½*d*., each, and from the guardians of brother Wickenden Steere, (viz: John Aldrich and Thomas Steere) for a like legacy, and also for £72, 15*s*., from his father's estate. Wickenden Steere was *non compos mentis*, as the town records state.

Inventory of widow Esther Steere, £1038, 10*s*., viz: bills of credit £289, 1*s*. 4*d*., silver, 15 oz. 18 pwt. £42, 18*s*. 7*d*., brass scales and weights, bible, spectacles, churn, table linen, 4½ loads of hay in barn, stack of hay, 3 swine, 3 pigs, 4 cows, heifer, calf, 2 tables, 8 chairs, pewter, &c.

1. John,
2. Hosea,
3. Hezekiah,
4. Wickenden,

II. SARAH, m. 1685, Dec. 24. { b. d.
PETER PLACE, { b. d. 1735, Jul. 6. of Enoch & Sarah ( ) Place.

1. Sarah, 1686, Nov. 12.
2. Nathan, 1688, Nov. 4.
3. Joseph, 1691, May 18.
4. Hannah, 1693, Aug. 6.
5. Aminette, 1695, Sep. 16.
6. Dinah, 1697, Feb. 10.
7. Ruth, 1700, Oct. 7.
8. Penelope, 1706, Jun. 27.

III. DINAH, m. { b. d. 1716 (—)
JOHN THORNTON, { b. d. 1716, Jan. 9. of John & Sarah ( ) Thornton.

1. John,
2. Josiah,
3. Dinah,
4. Stephen,
5. Ruth,
6. Daniel,
7. Elihu,
8. Ebenezer,

STEERE. 2d column. IV. Thomas. His 2d wife b. 1692, Jun. 1.

IV. THOMAS, { b. d. 1735, Aug. 27. Providence, Smithfield, R. I.
m. (1)
MARY ARNOLD, { b. d. of Richard & Mary (Angell) Arnold.
m. (2)
MEHITABLE PLUMMER (w. [of Samuel.] { b. d. 1742, Jan. 28. of Richard & Mary ( ) Evans.

1702, Dec. 10. He bought 30 acres for £8, of Richard Arnold, Sr.

1713, Jun. 16. Taxed 12*s*.

1715. Deputy.

1731, Jul. 19. His son Elisha died, administration being given to Thomas Steere, brother of deceased.

1731–34. Smithfield. Town Council.

1732, Jun. 5. He deeded son Richard, for love, &c., 160 acres in easternmost part of Glocester, where sons' house is.

1735, Aug. 23. Will—proved 1735, Sep. 15. Ex. son Thomas. To wife Mehitable, all real and personal estate was her former husband's that she had when testator married her, and £70, provided she quit herself of my estate, and she to have liberty to dwell in my house with her family till they are of age. To her also, £40, to pay a bond she owed when I married her. To daughter Phebe Mathewson and her children, £120. To daughter Mary Mowry, 25 acres, and £80. To sons Thomas and Richard, all my lands and tenements, &c.; the lands on easterly side of the great bridge to be for Thomas, provided that his mother-in-law (*i. e.* stepmother) have liberty in housing, &c., for comfortable maintenance while widow. To sons Thomas and Richard, all movable estate equally, except silver and gold which is for four children equally.

Inventory, £923, 11*s*. 6*d*., viz: carpenter's tools, gun, sheep £10, ox, 9 cows, 3 heifers, bull, 5 calves, mare, 5 swine, hay, pease, cider mill, 3 wheels, 4 beds, 18 chairs, bonds £211, 1*s*. 6*d*., books of divers sorts £4, 8*s*., 30¼ oz. silver £36, 6*s*., 5 pistoles £15, movable estate brought by widow £71, 8*s*.

1737, Jan. 4. Will—proved 1742, Apr. 20. Widow Mehitable of Glocester. Ex. son Samuel Plummer. To three sons Joseph, Samuel and Richard Plummer, all lands, tenements, &c., provided Joseph agrees to divide equally the land which deceased husband Samuel Plummer had. To daughter Hannah Plummer, £50. To grandson Zephaniah Eddy, £6, at age. To three sons, rest of estate. Inventory, £233, 2*d*.

Thomas Steere's son of same name resided in Smithfield, where he was Councilman, &c., and Deputy several years. Richard Steere lived in Glocester where he died in 1797, having been Town Clerk sixty years it is stated.

1. Phebe,
2. Mary, 1702,
3. Thomas,
4. Richard, 1707, Jun. 3.
5. Elisha,
(2d wife, no issue.)

V. JANE, b. d.
m.
WILLIAM BLANCHARD, b. d. of Blanchard.
1. Timothy,
2. Moses,
3. Theophilus,
4. William,

VI. RUTH, b. d. 1680.
UNMARRIED,

VII. WILLIAM, b. 1671, Nov. 25. d. 1737, Jan. 29. Providence, Glocester, R. I.
m.
SUSANNA, b. d. of
1. William,
2. Ruth,
3. Amey,
4. Samuel,

(She m. (2) 1739, Jul. 20, Isaac Fox.)

1708. Freeman.
1713, Jun. 16. Taxed 3*s.* 4*d.*
1733, Feb. 19. He deded to son William, for love, &c., 27½ acres.
1737, Jan. 21. Will—proved 1737, Feb. 28. Exx. wife Susannah, who being in weak condition asked that William Coman might assist her. To son Samuel, homestead place of 85 acres, and if he die before coming of age, then to two youngest daughters Ruth and Amey. To wife Susannah, all household goods and movables.

Inventory, £75, 14*s.* 4*d.*, viz: linen wheel, woolen wheel, 2 beds, wearing apparel, 4 chairs, cradle, gun, 13 sheep, 5 swine, 2 cows, mare, &c.

In view of the fact that he does not mention his son William in his will and the additional fact that the children whom he does mention were young, it is more than possible that he may have had an earlier wife than Susannah.

VIII. ANN, b. d. 1725, Oct. 28. See American Genealogist, v. 39, p. 3
m. 1706, Jan. 14.
RICHARD LEWIS, b. d. 1717, Oct. 4. of Lewis.
1. Edward, 1706, Oct. 22.
2. Nehemiah, 1708, Dec. 12.
3. Jane, 1711, Jun. 26.
4. Richard,

IX. SAMUEL, b. d. 1745, Oct. 18. Providence, Glocester, R. I.
m.
HANNAH FIELD, b. d. 1746 + of John & Elizabeth (Everden) Field.
1. Urania,
2. Son,
3. Anthony,
4. Jonah,
5. Jeremiah, 1722, Feb. 22.
6. Samuel, 1731, Nov. 12.

1713, Jun. 16. Taxed 6*s.*
1720, Sep. 3. He sold Joseph Mowry, for £36, Ridge Hill meadow.
1723. A son of his died this year, but the records do not give his name.
1725, Dec. 6. He and wife Hannah sold Joseph Mowry, 80 acres.
1746, Feb. 3. Administration to widow Hannah, but she refusing, it was given to son Anthony. Inventory, £723, 17*s.* 5*d.*, viz: gun, warming pan, 2 saddles, 2 linen wheels, woolen wheel, card, large loom, combs, hetchel, looking glass, spectacles, pewter, lignum vitae mortar, tobacco, 6 barrels cider, 2 barrels beer, bull, 4 oxen, 2 steers, 6 cows, 2 heifers, 4 calves, 10 sheep, 4 hogs, 4 shoats, &c. The account of administrator showed payments of £122, 1*s.* to Joseph Mowry, to William Coman £150, 12*s.*, to honored mother £150, 12*s.*, and £50, 4*s.* each to Jonah and Jeremiah Steere, with a like share to the administrator himself.
1754, Jun. 26. His children had legacies of £10, each from will of their uncle John Field, who names them as follows: nephews Anthony, Jonah, Jeremiah and Samuel Steere, and niece Urania Coman.

STEVENS.

HENRY, b. d.
m.
ELIZABETH, b. d.

Newport, R. I.

He was a blacksmith.

1648, May 16. He and Daniel Gould were charged by George Wright with having raised a scandalous report.
1652, Oct. 13. He bought of Peter Easton, certain land and agreed to keep it fenced, &c.
1656, Oct. 12. Elizabeth Stevens' fine of 6*s.*, 8*d.*, was remitted by the court, and on same date Henry Stevens was ordered to make his appearance before the court Friday next.
1667, May 13. He and certain others skilled therein, were to repair all arms brought to them by order of the Captain or Lieutenant of Train Band of Newport.
1669, May 6. His wife Elizabeth's petition for divorce was not granted.
1676, Feb. 20. He confirmed a deed made eighteen years before to Matthew Boomer, said deed having been lost when said Boomer's house was burned.

STONE.

HUGH, b. 1638. d. 1732.
m.
ABIGAIL BUSECOT, b. d. 1723 ±

of Peter & Mary ( ) Busecot.

Boston, Mass., Warwick, Providence, R. I.

He was a blacksmith.

1666, May 14. "I Hugh Stone, late servant to Mr. John Paine, of Boston, Merchant, by and with the consent of my aforesaid master, do covenant and agree with Mr. Randall Holden, of Warwick," &c., "to serve the said Randall Holden, from the day of the date hereof three years true and faithful service. Not absent without leave," &c.; "and I Randall Holden, agree to furnish meat, drink, clothes and all other necessaries all the time of his aforesaid service, and I do promise to give him double apparel," &c.
1678. Freeman.

I. HUGH, b. 1669. d. Providence, R. I.
m.
MARY POTTER, b. d. of Abel & Rachel (Warner) Potter.
1. Hugh, 1692.
2. Thomas, 1695.
3. Oliver, 1701.

He was a cordwainer.

1720, Mar. 10. He signed receipt for legacy paid his wife by her brother Abel Potter from estate of their father Abel Potter, deceased.
1720, Nov. 10. He sold for £40, to Nathaniel Waterman, house and 20 acres where I dwell.

He was buried in the family burial ground.

II. PETER, b. 1672, Mar. 14. d. 1725, Dec. 26. Providence, R. I.
m. 1696, Jun. 25.
ELIZABETH SHAW, b. d. of John Shaw.
1. Elizabeth, 1697, Mar. 25.
2. Peter, 1698, Oct. 22.
3. Sarah, 1700, Feb. 17.
4. Abigail, 1701, Sep. 15.
5. Priscilla, 1703, Feb. 2.
6. John, 1704, Sep. 29.

1696, Jun. 24. He bought 25 acres in Mashantatack.
1726, Feb. 21. Administration to son Peter. Inventory, £63, 13*s.*, 2*d.*, viz: wearing apparel £7, feather bed, 2 flock beds, 2 cows, calf, mare, 5 sheep, swine, pewter, sword, shoemaker's tools, Indian corn, linen wheel, woolen wheel, &c.

He was buried in the family burying ground.

STONE. 1st column. 1726, Feb. 24, agreement with son John, by which after his and wife's death, legacies were to be paid by said son, viz.: to son Hugh, £20 and a gun; grandsons Peter and John (sons of Peter), £20 each; daughter Mary Ralph, £40 10s.; daughter Catherine Spicer 40s.; daughter Abigail West, feather bed, etc.; daughter Alice Fisk, 40s., warming pan and iron kettle; daughter Ann Utter, £3; grandchildren Thomas Barnes and Ann Stone, 5s. each; son John the rest.

1680, Aug. 22. He and wife Abigail, gave to Edward Carter and Elizabeth his wife, the keeping and custody of our daughter Catharine, aged six years in this instant month of August, till seventeen years of age, to deal kindly with her, &c.

1692, Dec. 10. He and wife Abigail, exchanged land with Job Greene, giving him land deeded from father-in-law, Peter Busecot, deceased.

1704, Mar. 12. He made an agreement with son John, by which the latter was to have his father's house, orchard, meadow, &c., in Warwick, he paying to his brother Hugh Stone, Jr., fifty shillings, and like amount to brother George Stone, and if either Hugh Stone, Sr., or his wife should be disabled by the providence of God "or by old age or non ability to get our living and sustenance, and if our said John shall do his utmost to see and provide for us during time of our natural lives, sufficient maintenance, and behave himself as a dutiful son ought to do to his parents in all respects," &c., then agreement to be binding. If John did not fulfil the contract, the deed to be void. The deed never took effect, but was revoked and land sold subsequently to another person.

1706, Oct. 16. He deeded son John, for love, &c., 2 acres where son had set his house in Warwick.

1723. He sold Barlo Greene, homestead in Warwick; the same lands his son John was to have had by agreement of nineteen years previous.

1723, Jun. 29. Providence. He bought of Sarah Lawrence, widow, executrix of William Lawrence, deceased, for £265, mansion house and farm where she dwelt, bounded partly on the south and east by Pawtuxet river and partly on the north by land of John Stone, 60 acres area.

1726, Feb. 24. He sold his new homestead to son John, for goodwill, &c.

His last residence is marked by the monument erected to his memory in recent years in the old Stone Burial Ground.

III. CATHARINE. b. 1674, Aug. 22. d.

IV. JOHN, b. 1675. d. 1759. Providence, Cranston, R. I.
m. (1) HANNAH BARNES, b. 1689, Dec. 21. d. of Thomas & Prudence ( ) Barnes.
m. (2) ABIGAIL FOSTER, b. d. 1759 + of Foster.

1725, Jun. 28. He bought 127 acres, &c., of Tristram Derby for £125.

1738, Mar. 3. He deeded to son Jonathan, for love, &c., 50 acres of upland and meadow west side of Pauchassett River, a little eastwardly of my dwelling house.

1759, Sep. 29. Will—proved. Exx. wife Abigail. To wife all indoor movables. To son Joseph, all my outdoor movables, viz: all my cattle, horses, sheep, hogs, fowls, carts, ploughs, &c., and to him also wearing apparel. To rest of children, 5s., each, viz: to Hannah, George, John, William, Jonathan, Ruth, Benjamin, Abigail, Lydia, Anne and Prudence. These had received some estate before. To granddaughter Abigail Fisk, £50, at eighteen or marriage.

He was buried in the family burial ground.

1. John, 1705.
2. George, 1709.
3. William, 1711.
(2d wife.)
4. Anne, 1716.
5. Abigail, 1718.
6. Jonathan, 1720.
7. Alice, 1723.
8. Benjamin, 1725.
9. Joseph, 1727.
10. Lydia, 1730.
11. Prudence, 1732.
12. Hannah,
13. Ruth,

V. SARAH, b. d.
m. 1697, Mar. 25.
THOMAS BARNES, b. 1670, Nov. 13. d. 1706, Sep. 24. of Thomas & Prudence ( ) Barnes.

1. Mary, 1698, Apr. 13.
2. Thomas, 1699, Dec. 8.

VI. ABIGAIL, b. d.

VII. ANNE, b. 1682. d. 1762.
m. 1705, Sep. 27.
WILLIAM UTTER, b. 1679. d. 1761, Jun. of Nicholas Utter.

1. Sarah, 1707, Aug. 1.
2. William, 1709.
3. Alice, 1711, Sep. 27.
4. Ruth,
5. Zebulon, 1724.
6. Anne, 1725, Oct. 28.

VIII. GEORGE, b. d.
m.
———, b. d. of

1. George,
2. Obadiah,

2d column. III. Catherine m. ——— Spicer of Peter and Mary (Busecut) Spicer. IV. John. His 1st wife d. 1752. (Her mother was Prudence Albee.) His 2d wife b. 1677; d. 1760. His daughter Alice was perhaps Mercy. V. Sarah. Her husband's mother was Prudence Albee. VI. Abigail m. ——— West. IX. Mary d. 1726+; m. Samuel Ralph, d. 1723, Oct. 8, of Thomas and Elizabeth (Desborough) Ralph. Children, 1, Mary. 2, Deliverance. 3, Samuel. 4, Thomas. 5, Hugh. X. Alice m.——— Fisk.

STRAIGHT.

HENRY, b. 1652. d. 1728, Jun. 4.
m.
MARY LONG, b. d. 1757. of Joseph & Mary ( ) Long.

Portsmouth, East Greenwich, R. I.

1667, Dec. 24. He was apprenticed to Gershom Wodell, of Portsmouth, for six years.

1673. He was employed by Thomas Cornell, and testified at the trial of the latter for the murder of his mother Rebecca Cornell.

1679, Nov. 10. East Greenwich. He having received from Henry Brightman, of Portsmouth, his right in East Greenwich, and having built on the land; now petitioned to the Assembly, that he might be accepted to the privileges procured of said Brightman, and the Assembly granted the petition.

1684, Sep. 13. Constable.

1697, Nov. 26. He and wife Mary, were complained of by William Weaver, for slanderous words from said Mary against the wife of Weaver. The plaintiff and defendant were given liberty to withdraw themselves and try if they could agree, which they did and immediately returned and said they were agreed, and "the action fell with our consent."

1699. Deputy.

1728, May 15. Will—proved 1728, Jun. 29. Exx. wife Mary To son Henry, 5s. To son John, half of farm and other half at death of wife. To wife Mary, all movables and house and orchard, while widow. Inventory, £144, 13s., purse and wearing apparel £17, 19s., gun, sword, books £1, pair of oxen, 2 cows, 2 yearlings, 2 calves, a mare, colt, 20 sheep, 7 lambs, 8 swine.

1750, Sep. 15. Will—proved 1757, Jul. 30. Widow Mary. Ex. cousin John Tarbox. To grandson John Straight, residing in Coventry, feather bed, pewter, &c. To cousin Thomas Shippey, iron pot. To cousin Sarah Bentley, pewter basin. To cousin Anne Spink, pewter basin. To sister Shippey, clothes box. Executor to sell my cow and pay my grandson John Straight's seven children, 10s., apiece, viz: to Thomas, Phebe, William, Hannah, Henry, John and Job. To cousin John Tarbox, rest of estate.

I. HENRY, b. d. 1732. East Greenwich, R. I.
m. 1697, Feb. 13.
HANNAH, b. d. of

He was a blacksmith.

1732, Oct. 21. Will—proved 1732, Nov. 4. Ex. son Thomas. To eldest son Samuel, double portion; viz: a third of real and personal estate. To four sons John, Thomas, Joseph and Henry, the rest of estate, viz: a sixth each, after debts and legacies. The portions of John and Joseph, to be paid within two years, and son Henry to be brought up and educated. To daughter Rebecca, 5s. To daughter Elizabeth, 5s. To daughter Hannah Westcott, £5, in a year. To daughters Mary and Sarah Straight, £5, in two years. To daughter Abigail Straight, £5, at eighteen. To daughter Mercy Straight, £35, at eighteen. Son Thomas to be guardian to son Henry and daughter Mercy. To son Thomas, all lands, tenements, &c., he being impowered to sell all estate, and to pay legacies.

Inventory, £172, 19s., 6d.

1. Henry, 1698, Jan. 8.
2. Rebecca, 1700, Jan. 27.
3. Samuel,
4. John,
5. Thomas,
6. Joseph,
7. Elizabeth,
8. Hannah,
9. Mary,
10. Sarah,
11. Abigail,
12. Mercy,
13. Henry,

II. JOHN, b. 1678, Mar. 1. d. 1759. East Greenwich, R. I.
m. (1) 1705, May 30.
ROSE SMITH (w. of Dan'l). b. d. of
m. (2)
ELIZABETH, b. d. 1757 + of

1683, May 14. He was apprenticed by his father to John Watson, tailor, of Kings Town, for sixteen years from the first of March last past.

He lived for a time at Exeter, and dated his will there, but it was proved at East Greenwich.

1757, Jul. 16. Will—proved 1759, Mar 31. Ex. son Henry. To wife Elizabeth, all household goods remaining that she brought. To daughter Elizabeth Greene, £5. To daughter Rebecca Straight, £5. To daughter Mary Straight, £5. To granddaughter Rose Wightman, cupboard table. To son Henry, rest of indoor movables and all outdoor movables. To four children of son Samuel, deceased, £100, of which £50, to Samuel at age, and rest to three sisters at eighteen. To son Matthew or his heirs, if ever he or they return, £5. To son John, half of a 60 foot lot in East Greenwich and £5, he having already had portion. To son Thomas, £5, he having had portion.

Inventory, £597, 15s., 3d., viz: carpentering and farming tools, churn, warming pan, pewter, 5 chairs, 2 cows, 5 sheep, &c.

1. Elizabeth, 1705, Oct. 8.
2. John, 1707, Sep. 27.
3. Henry, 1709, Aug. 16.
4. Rebecca, 1711, Aug. 22.
5. Thomas, 1713, Apr. 5.
6. Samuel, 1715, Jan. 21.
7. Mary, 1718, Jun. 4.
8. Mary, 1720, Mar. 25.
9. Matthew, 1722, Mar. 22.
(2d wife, no issue.)

{ Lot, { b.
m. { d. 1683, Jul. 30.
{ Alice Paine, { b.
{ d. 1690.

of Anthony ( ) Paine.

Portsmouth, R. I.

1649, Oct. 27. He and wife Alice gave receipt to Rose Paine (exx. of Anthony Paine's will) for legacy.

1657. He was to be General Solicitor if James Rogers could not serve.

1664-65-66-69-70-74. Deputy.

1671, May 8. He was indicted for fencing in highway, but jury found him not guilty.

1675, Apr. 17. He deeded 8 acres "to thee John Keese and thine."

1683, Aug. 10. Administration to widow Alice.

1688, May 18. Will—proved 1690, Oct. 23. Widow Alice. Overseers, kinsmen John Albro and John Anthony and neighbor John Borden. Ex. kinsman John Keese. To kinsman John Keese, all my housing and lands. To cousin John Tripp, £35, and unto his son Lot, 10*s*. To cousin John Tripp's daughter Susannah Potter, my biggest silver cup. To cousin John Tripp's daughter Mary Tripp, a feather bed, &c. To cousin Peleg Tripp, £4, and a third of horsekind. To cousin Joseph Tripp, 40*s*., and a third of horsekind and to his daughter Alice Tripp, a silver cup. To cousin James Tripp, 40*s*. and a third of horsekind. To cousin Abiel Tripp's son Abiel, two ewe sheep and silver cup. To cousin Mary Gatchell, £3, and to three of her daughters, viz: Sarah Wodell and Priscilla and Isabel Gatchell, each, 20*s*. To cousin Elizabeth Hall, £5, &c., and to her daughter Joanna, two pewter platters. To cousin Alice Hall, £6, and to her daughter Abigail, best bed, silver porringer, gold ring, a cow, ten sheep, £5, &c. To cousin Alice Hall's daughter Alice, four ewe sheep and a silver spoon. To cousin Isabel Sherman, £5, and to her daughter Alice, a gold ring. To cousin Martha Sherman, £5, and to her daughter Sarah, my silver bodkin. To kinsman John Keese's daughter Alice Keese, my best gold ring, silver cup £10, &c., at eighteen. To kinsman John Keese's son William, a piece of gold and £5. To John Keese's second daughter Elizabeth Keese, a silver spoon and £5, &c., at eighteen or marriage. To cousin Peleg Tripp's son Peleg, a silver cup. To cousin James Tripp's son John, a silver spoon. To cousin Alice Hall's daughter Mary Hall, a pair of sheets, and to her daughter Deliverance Hall, tankard, &c., and to her daughter Abigail Hall, a red purse and what is in it. To kinswoman Frances Anthony, a lute string scarf. To uncle John Albro and his wife my aunt, silk cloth, for him a neck cloth and her a hood. To cousin John Tripp's wife Susanna, and to cousin Alice Hall and her daughter Abigail, all my wearing clothes. To overseers, 10*s*., each.

No issue.

SUCKLING.

{ Thomas, { b.
m. { d. 1680.
{ ——— { b.
{ d.

Providence, R. I.

1646. He was thus early at Providence.

1658, May 18. Freeman.

1668, Jun. He took the oath of allegiance.

1674, Mar. 23. He was granted liberty to exchange a 60 acre lot in the new division.

1674, Jul. 13. He sold 50 acres to Thomas Hopkins.

1680, May 22. Administration to Walter Clarke of Newport. It was testified by John Lapham, of Newport, that about the year 1674, Thomas Suckling and his wife, both of Providence, did give and bequeath what estate they should have left at time of death of the longest liver of them, unto the people called Quakers living in Rhode Island; on condition that the Quakers should provide for them during their lives. It was further testified that the Quakers did supply them, and board and shingle their house.

SWEET.

{ John, { b.
m. { d. 1637.
{ Mary, { b.
{ d. 1681.

(She m. (2) 1638 ± Ezekiel Holliman.)

Salem, Mass., Providence, R. I.

1632, Jul. 3. His land is referred to as bounding Mr. Skelton's land on the north, and near to Captain Endicott's.

I. { John, { b.
m. { d. 1677.
{ Elizabeth, { b. 1629.
{ d. 1684 + of

Warwick, R. I.

(She m. (2) Samuel Wilson.)

1648, Jun. 5. He was recorded as an inhabitant.

1655. Freeman.

1660. Commissioner.

1662. He was paid £5, in peage at eight per penny, for killing a wolf.

1. John,
2. Daniel, 1657.
3. James,
4. Henry,
5. Richard,
6. Benjamin,
7. William,
8. Jeremiah,
9. Daughter,

SWEET. 2d column. I. John. Eleventh line. Elizabeth Wilson, aged fifty-five not forty-five.

SWEET. 2d column. I. John. 1684, Sep. 18, deposition of Elizabeth Wilson calls herself aged fifty-five years, etc., (not forty-five).

1637, Jun. 6. He was presented by the Grand Jury for shooting a wolf dog of Colonel Endicott's in the yard of the latter, and was fined £5, for the offence, but subsequently the fine was remitted. The name of "Sweet's Cove" was given to an inlet near his residence.

1637. Providence. This year he had a grant of land here, and after his death his widow received a grant. She returned to Salem and had a grant this same year of land in that place also.

After the marriage of Mrs. Sweet to Ezekiel Holliman, he changed the name of her daughter Meribah to Renewed, and the daughter married under this latter name.

1639, Jul. 1. His widow, now the wife of Ezekiel Holliman, is alluded to in a letter of this date from Rev. Hugh Peters, of Salem, to the church at Dorchester.

He says that she and certain others had "the great censure passed upon them in this our church," and that "they wholly refused to hear the church, denying it and all the churches in the Bay to be true churches," &c.

1681, Jul. 31. Will—proved 1681. Widow Mary Holliman. To son-in-law John Gereardy and daughter Renewed, his wife, both formerly of Warwick, now of Prudence, all interest in house, lot, meadow and upland in Warwick.

1663, Apr. 17. He sold Francis Darby, of Warwick, my dwelling house, lot, &c., that I bought of Henry Townsend, for £45.

1671, May 20. He took oath of allegiance.

1675. His grist mill, &c., at Potowomut, were burned by the Indians.

1676, Mar. 7. The Council at Hartford, voted that he and Samuel Eldred "have liberty to transport ten bushels of Indian corn apiece for their distressed families."

1677, Jun. 27. He, of Warwick, now living in Newport, sold meadow in Warwick, to Randall Holden.

1677. Will—made at Newport. He named his wife Elizabeth, and children, John, Daniel, James, Henry, Richard, Benjamin, William, Jeremiah, and a daughter.

1684, Sep. 18. Elizabeth Wilson, widow, aged forty-five years or thereabouts, deposed that her first husband John Sweet, being a Warwick man, first built his dwelling house on Potowomut Neck and procured leave of the Narragansett Sachems to set down his mill and dam in Potowomut River. Her husband and herself kept possession peaceably of said house and land and mill for several years until forced off by the late Indian war, and after the war was over she and her children returned and kept possession of same place.

SWEET. 2d column. II. James, d. 1698. Jun. 18.

II. JAMES, b. 1622, d. 1695 +. Warwick, Kings Town, R. I.
m.
MARY GREENE, b. 1633, d. — of John & Joan (Tattersall) Greene.

1. Philip, 1655, Jul. 15.
2. James, 1657, May 28.
3. Mary, 1660, Feb. 2.
4. Benoni, 1663, Mar. 28.
5. Valentine, 1665, Feb. 14.
6. Samuel, 1667, Nov. 1.
7. Jeremiah, 1669, Jan. 6.
8. Renewed, 1671, Jul. 16.
9. Sylvester, 1674, Mar. 1.

1648, Jun. 5. He was recorded as an inhabitant.

1653-58-59. Commissioner.

1655. Freeman.

1656. Juryman.

1660, Sep. 30. He sold to Thomas Greene, lot granted me by town of Warwick, and housing thereon, by consent of William Ward, and also a share of meadow. Both Sweet and Ward signed the deed.

1682, Mar. 7. Portsmouth (Prudence Island). He and son Philip sold certain land in Warwick to Thomas Greene.

1686, Nov. 8. Kings Town. He deeded to eldest son Philip, of Prudence Island, all right of lands in Providence "as my father John Sweet, deceased, was one of the first purchasers thereof."

1686, Nov. 8. He and now wife Mary, deeded to son Benoni, certain land in Mashantatack, at death of said James and wife. On the same date he deeded to son James, of Prudence Island, and Valentine of Kings Town, land in Mashantatack. He deeded also to his son Samuel and daughter Mary Sweet, "both remaining with me."

1695, Apr. 4. He testified as to certain land, calling his age about seventy-three years.

III. RENEWED, b. —, d. 1681 +
m.
JOHN GEREARDY, b. —, d. 1681 + of — Gereardy.

1. Mary,
2. John,
3. Phillis,

TABER.

PHILIP, b. 1605, d. 1672 +
m. (1)
LYDIA MASTERS, b. —, d. — of John & Jane ( ) Masters.
m. (2)
JANE, b. 1605, d. 1669 +

Watertown, Mass., Portsmouth, Providence, R. I.

1634, Apr. 1. He promised 200 feet of 4 inch plank toward the sea fort. He bound himself in 40s. to appear to give testimony against a person for selling commodities contrary to order.

1634, May 14. Freeman.

1639, Mar. 5. Yarmouth. He was appointed on committee to make equal division of the planting land in first allotment.

1639, Jun. 4. Freeman.

1639, Dec. 21. John Masters of Cambridge, Mass., died, and in his will mentions his daughter Lydia Taber.

1639-40. Deputy.

1640, Nov. 8. He had his son John baptized at Barnstable, and six years later (1646, Feb.) his children Joseph, Philip and Thomas were baptized.

1651, Mar. New London. He came here at this time from Martha's Vineyard where he had been for quite a period.

1656. Portsmouth. Freeman.

1660-61-63. Commissioner.

1663. He was on a committee in relation to raising money to be paid John Clarke by the colony for his services as Agent to England.

1664, Jan. 31. He (calling himself of Newport at this date) sold a certain house in Portsmouth now or lately in occupation of Alexander Balcom.

1665, Apr. 20 He sold his house and 10 acres in Portsmouth to Anthony Shaw of same town for £40, and three hundred good boards.

1669, Jun. 10. Providence. He, aged sixty-four years, testified that being in his own house he heard a noise of holloaing, &c., and went down to the river which runneth by his house and saw William Wickenden, who told him there was a child drowned, and arriving at the river side saw a lad lie dead in the bottom of the river, who William Wickenden took out, and Wickenden's wife came down, and taking an apron off the widow Ballou who came down and stood a pretty way off the child, laid the apron on the lad, &c.; and on Taber's asking whose lad it was, Wickenden made answer it was the widow Ballou's lad. Testimony was also given by Jane Taber aged sixty-four years.

1672, Feb. 24. His testimony against William Harris of Providence was read before the Assembly.

By one account he settled finally at Tiverton, and there died.

I. JOHN, b. 1640, d. young.

TABER. 2d column. II. Lydia, m., 2d, 1718, Nov. 4, Samuel Mason.

II. LYDIA, b. —, d. 1718 +
m. 1664, Apr. 16.
PARDON TILLINGHAST, b. 1622, d. 1718, Jan. 29. of — Tillinghast.

1. Lydia, 1666, Apr. 18.
2. Pardon, 1668, Feb. 16.
3. Philip, 1669, Oct.
4. Benjamin, 1672, Feb. 3.
5. Abigail, 1674, Mar.
6. Joseph, 1677, Aug. 11.
7. Mercy, 1680,
8. Hannah,
9. Elizabeth,

III. JOSEPH, b. —, d. —

TABER. 2d column. IV. Philip m. Mary Cook of John and Sarah (Warren) Cook.

IV. PHILIP, * b. —, d. 1693 ±. Dartmouth, Mass.
m.
MARY, b. —, d. 1694 + of —
(She m. (2) —— Davis.)

1. Mary, 1668, Jan. 28.
2. Sarah, 1671, Mar. 26.
3. Lydia, 1673, Sep. 28.
4. Philip, 1675, Feb. 29.
5. Abigail, 1678, Oct. 27.
6. Esther, 1680, Feb. 23.
7. John, 1684, Jul. 18.
8. Bethiah, 1689, Apr. 18.

1678, Mar. 5. There was due him from the town £3, 10s.

1693, Mar. 4. Inventory, £231, 14s. 6d., sworn to (1693, Aug. 31) by Thomas Taber, Mary Davis and Philip Taber. Housing and land £120, 4 oxen, 10 cows, 6 two years, 8 yearlings, 5 calves, 3 mares, 2 horses, colt, 4 swine, 3 feather beds, 3 silk grass beds, 3 dozen napkins, 3 spinning wheels, carpenter's tools, 3 bibles, &c. Administration was given to widow Mary.

1694, Sep. 13. Division was made. To widow, a third of the real and personal, she having the lower room in new house and the cellar. To eldest son Philip, certain land and the other two-thirds of housing, amounting in all to £50, he paying sister Hester £14, 7s. 4d., at eighteen or marriage. To son John, land amounting to £30, he paying his sister Bethiah, £12, 3s. 8d. To five daughters Sarah, Lydia, Abigail, Esther and Bethiah, each £17, 16s. 4d. To daughter Mary Earle, £7, 16s. 4d.

V. THOMAS, b. —, d. 1730, Nov. 11. Dartmouth, Mass.
m. (1)
ESTHER COOK, b. 1650, Aug. 16, d. 1671. of John & Sarah (Warren) Cook.
m. (2) 1672, Jun.
MARY THOMPSON, b. —, d. 1734, May 3. of — Thompson.

1. Thomas, 1668, Oct. 21.
2. Esther, 1671, Apr. 17.
(2d wife.)
3. Lydia, 1673, Aug. 8.
4. Sarah, 1674, Jan.
5. Mary, 1677, Mar. 18.
6. Joseph, 1679, Mar. 7.
7. John, 1681, Feb. 22.
8. Jacob, 1683, Jul. 26.
9. Jonathan, 1685, Sep. 22.
10. Bethiah, 1687, Sep. 3.
11. Philip, 1689, Feb. 7.
12. Abigail, 1693, May 2.

1673. Surveyor of Highways.

1675. Fence viewer.

1678, Mar. 5. There was due him from the town £2, 10s.

1679. Town Clerk.

1679. Constable.

1684. Freeman.

1685-92-94-96-99-1700-1-2. Selectman.

1686. Ratemaker.

1689. Captain.

1693. Deputy.

1723, Jun. 15. Will—proved 1733, Mar. 20. Exs. four sons Joseph, John, Jacob and Philip. To wife Mary, south half of homestead, with all housing, orchard, &c., while widow, and to her, all personal. To six daughters, whatever personal is left at wife's death. To son Thomas, an eighth of a share of upland, swamp, &c., he paying £10, to his sisters. To sons Joseph and John, farm where they dwell, &c., they paying £10, to sisters. To son Jacob, north half of homestead, &c., he paying £14, to sisters. To son Philip, south half of homestead with housing, orchard, &c., except privilege to wife as above. To daughter Esther Perry and her husband, certain land and £6. To daughter Lydia Kinney, certain land and £6. To daughter Sarah Hart and husband, land and £6. To daughter Mary Morton, land and £20. To daughter Bethiah Blackwell, land and £6. To daughter Abigail Taber, £20. To former man servant, Simeon Spooner, 20 acres.

Inventory, £228, 2s. 3d., viz: money and apparel £3, 7s., pewter, 2 spinning wheels, 3 cows, heifer, mare, colt, 9 ewes and lambs, 11 sheep, 67 acres unimproved land £67, 10s., &c.

* See American Genealogist
V. 20, p. 115.
V. 30, no. 2, p. 125

 See: American Genealogist, v. 20, p. 115-116.

TALLMAN. 1651, Jun. 27. He, called Peter Taelman, had clearance of a vessel from Manhattan to South (Delaware) River. 1656, Jan. 25. He, of Middleburgh (Newtown), N. Y., was complained of by the magistrates of Middleburgh for removing tobacco attached by the court at Flushing.

PETER, { b. { d. 1708.
m. (1)
ANN, { b. { d.
m. (2) 1665.
JOAN BRIGGS, { b. { d. 1685 ± of Briggs.
m. (3) 1686 ±
ESTHER, { b. { d. 1708 (—)

Newport, Portsmouth, R. I.

1655. Freeman.

1658, Dec. 18. He bought 9 acres in Portsmouth, for 35*s.*, an acre, of Richard Morris and wife, and two days later bought 6 acres of William Wilbur next to the first purchase.

1661. Portsmouth. General Solicitor for the Colony of Rhode Island.

1661–62. Commissioner.

1662–65. Deputy.

1665. The Assembly granted him a divorce from his wife Ann.

1665, Jul. 24. An ante-nuptial agreement was made between him and Joan Briggs, of Taunton. He agreed to give her land he had bought of Richard Morris, Daniel Wilcox and William Wilbur, and also a house, all to be hers and her heirs born of this marriage. He gave her beside a bed and half the household goods, but if she die without issue the estate given her was to revert to Peter Tallman's eldest son, viz: Peter, Jr., and if the latter die without issue then to Peter Tallman Senior's eldest daughter, viz: Mary and her heirs. To Joan, absolutely as a "free gift of donation" he gave three good cows and a good breeding mare.

1674, Jun. 7. Having broken a law of Massachusetts prohibiting the receipt of land from Indians by deeds of gift, he was imprisoned, but on giving up the deeds he was at this date released.

1675, Oct. 20. He brought suit against Rebecca Sadler, wife of Thomas, for breach of peace and threatening his family.

1680. Taxed 8*s.*, 6*d.*

1683, Sep. 18. He was on a jury at Portsmouth, in the case of a man found dead and hanging by the head by a neckcloth fastened to the bough of a cherry tree. Verdict: "That we do not find but that the said man said to be named John Crags, was absolutely the only actor of his own death."

1708. Inventory, was presented by son James.

1709, May 3. Administration having been given to Jonathan Tallman, he took acquittances at this date from his brothers and sisters, the signers of the instrument being as follows: William Wilbur, Israel Shaw, Jonathan Tallman, James Tallman, Benjamin Tallman, Mary Pearce, Susanna Beckett, Peter Tallman, Isaac Lawton, William Potter, John Tallman, Joseph Tallman, Samuel Tallman.

I. { MARY, { b. { d. 1720.
m.
JOHN PEARCE, { b. 1647, Sep. 8. { d. 1707, Dec. 5. of Richard & Susanna (Wright) Pearce.

1. John,
2. Mary,
3. Susanna, 1672 ±
4. Anne, 1674, Feb. 14.
5. Sarah,
6. Elizabeth,
7. Rachel,
8. Alice,

II. { ELIZABETH, { b. { d. 1701, May 20.
m. 1674, Mar. 3.
ISAAC LAWTON, { b. 1650, Dec. 11. { d. 1732, Jan. 25. of Thomas Lawton.

1. Elizabeth, 1675, Feb. 16.
2. Sarah, 1676, Oct. 25.
3. Ann, 1678, Apr. 25.
4. Isaac, 1681, May 25.
5. Mary, 1683, Apr. 3.
6. Isabel, 1685, Mar. 12.
7. Thomas, 1687, Apr. 25.
8. Susanna, 1689, Apr. 3.
9. Job, 1691, Apr. 28.
10. Ruth, 1694, Apr. 9.
11. John, 1696, Sep. 2.

III. { PETER, { b. 1658, Mar. 23. { d. 1726, Jul. 6. Portsmouth, R. I., Guilford, Ct.
m. 1683, Nov. 7. [of John.
ANN WALSTONE, (w. { b. { d. 1731. of Benjamin & Jane ( ) Wright.

1. Elizabeth, 1687, Jun. 22.
2. Ebenezer, 1692, Sep. 1.
3. Peter, 1694, Nov. 13.

He was a physician, and also pursued the occupation of a shoemaker.

1683, Sep. 4. Guilford. In some notes of a journey to Rye, Samuel Hubbard of Newport, relates that when at Guilford, a little earlier than this date, he went to see Peter Tallman.

1685, May 14. He was propounded for a freeman.

1715. Deputy.

1722, Jul. 27. Will—proved 1726, Jul 27. Exx. wife Anna. To her all household goods, and for her use and disposal stock of cattle, horses, sheep and swine (except one black horse to son Ebenezer), but if any remain at her decease to be divided equally to son Ebenezer and granddaughter Elizabeth Davis. The land near Leets Island, to be sold, as bargained for, to Andrew Ward, for £77, and of proceeds £30, to be given granddaughter Elizabeth Davis and remainder to my wife. To wife all provisions for family use and the corn in the barn and on the ground, and all my drugs and books concerning physick, during her life, and then to son Ebenezer. To son Ebenezer, all my tools and implements of husbandry (except a hoe and an axe to wife), surgeon's tools, cane, belt and gold ring and confirmation of all gifts I have made him heretofore. To wife all personal not disposed of.

Inventory, £117, 6*s.*, 3*d.*, viz: oxen £9, calf £4, 2 cows £6, 16*s.*, &c.

1730, Feb. 25. Will—proved 1731. Widow Ann. Ex. John Collins. She names sons Thomas Walstone and Ebenezer Tallman, and granddaughter Elizabeth Morrison.

IV. { ANN, { b. { d.
m. 1679, Mar. 8.
STEPHEN BRAYTON, { b. { d. 1692 ± of Francis & Mary ( ) Brayton.

1. Mary, 1680, Feb. 12.
2. Elizabeth, 1681, Dec. 8.
3. Ann, 1683, Jul. 6.
4. Preserved, 1685, Mar. 8.
5. Stephen, 1686, Aug. 2.

V. { JOSEPH, { b. { d.

VI. { SUSANNA, { b. { d.
m.
——— BECKITT, { b. { d. of Beckitt.

VII. { ———, { b. { d. 1732 (—)
m.
WILLIAM WILBUR, { b. { d. 1738. of William Wilbur.

1. Mary, 1685.
2. William, 1687, Aug. 8.
3. Hannah, 1689, Jun. 17.
4. Samuel, 1691, Feb. 17.
5. John, 1693, May 1.
6. Joseph, 1695, May 26.
7. Abigail, 1697, Apr. 1.
8. Joan, 1698, Nov. 7.
9. Jedediah, 1700, Nov. 5.
10. Sarah, 1702, Sep. 10.
11. Phebe, 1704, Oct. 1.
12. Jeremiah, 1706, Dec. 17.

VIII. { JONATHAN, { b. { d. 1762. Dartmouth, Mass.
m.
SARAH, { b. { d. 1748 + of

1. Darius, 1690, Feb. 3.
2. Mary, 1695, May 3.
3. Nathaniel, 1696, Jan. 14.
4. James, 1698, Feb. 7.
5. Cyrus, 1702, Nov. 26.
6. Timothy, 1704, Feb. 24.
7. Jonathan,
8. Jedediah,

1748, Nov. 26. Will—proved 1762, Jul. 6. Ex. son James. Overseers, Benjamin Wing and Captain William Wood. To wife Sarah, best room and use of furniture while widow. To son Nathaniel, land in Dartmouth. To son Jonathan, southerly part of homestead where I live. To son James, rest of homestead, housing and orchard. To sons Darius, Cyrus and Jedediah, 5*s.*, each. To daughter Mary Briggs, 5*s.* To granddaughter Hannah Tallman, daughter of Timothy, deceased, a feather bed. To grandsons William, Weston and Timothy, sons of Timothy, deceased, £10, each at age. To son James, £15, per year during life of his mother Sarah, while she is widow, he maintaining her, said sum being paid by son Jonathan. To sons James and Jedediah, rest of estate.

IX. { JAMES, { b. { d. 1724. Portsmouth, R. I.
m. (1) 1689, Mar. 18.
MARY DAVOL, { b. { d. of Joseph & Mary (Brayton) Davol.
m. (2) 1701, Sep. 14.
HANNAH SWAIN, { b. 1679 ± { d. 1765. of John & Mary (Wyer) Swain.

1. John, 1692, Sep. 19.
2. Joseph, 1694, Jul. 13.
3. Elizabeth, 1699, Jun. 13.
(2d wife.)
4. Stephen, 1702, Jun. 30.
5. Mary, 1704, Jun. 26.
6. Peter, 1706, Jun. 17.
7. Jemima, 1708, Sep. 11.
8. James, 1710, Apr. 10.
9. Jeremiah, 1712, Sep. 25.
10. Silas, 1717, Sep. 10.
11. Joseph, 1720, Jun. 1.
12. Hannah, 1723, Sep. 14.

He was a physician.

1698, Jun. 3. He deeded to Mary Timberlake, of Tiverton, wife of Joseph, for many kindnesses formerly to me shown and given by her, certain land and buildings, in Portsmouth, for life and then to her daughters, Joan Cory and Sarah Timberlake.

1700. He had a lot assigned him, paying therefor £1.

1705, May 14. He deeded brothers Benjamin, Samuel and Joseph, for love, &c., 12 acres.

1706, Sep. 24. The will of Thomas Barnes, of Providence, directed that his debts be paid "especially to my careful and kind doctor, Mr. James Tallman," &c.

1724, Jan. 11. Will—proved 1724, Feb. Exx. wife Hannah. Overseer, John Earle. To son John, 100 acres in Tiverton, he paying brother Jeremiah, £500. To son Peter, 50 acres in Tiverton. To son Silas, land in Tiverton. To son Joseph, land in Portsmouth. To son Stephen, rest of homestead he paying sister Jemima, £200, and sister Hannah, £100. To wife Hannah, use of land given Joseph, till he is of age, and use of half of land given Stephen, with privilege of half the housing to live in. To wife rest of estate, she paying daughter Mary, £200. If Silas die before twenty-one, his share to go to Peter, and if Joseph die, his share to Stephen.

Inventory, £1,373, 16*s.*, 6*d.*, viz: neat cattle £138, 100 sheep £40, little boat £5, horsekind £35, 4 swine, poultry, bills due £287, 2 guns, sword, cider mill, 2 cheese presses, negro woman £40, bell metal mortar, 2 other mortars, still, physick and syrup £5.

1734, Dec. 9. His widow was allowed 20*s.*, "for keeping Job Bennett ten days and doctoring his foot."

1764, Jul. 18. Will—proved 1765, Sep. 9. Widow Hannah. Exs. sons-in-law David Fish and Matthew Slocum. To sons Stephen, Peter and Silas, 5s., each. To daughter Mary Freeborn, £700. To daughter Jemima Fish and son-in-law David Fish, £600. To son Jeremiah, £600. To daughter Hannah Slocum, household goods. To son-in-law Matthew Slocum, £500. To three daughters, land in Tiverton.

Inventory, £3,868, 18s.

X. ——, b. d.
m.
William Potter, b. d. of Potter.

Children: 1. Benjamin, 2. Mary, 3. Patience,

XI. John, b. d. 1709. Flushing, N. Y.
m.
Mary, b. d. 1707 + of

1707, Sep. 8. Will—proved 1709, Mar. 15. Exs. son John and friend Samuel Haight. To wife Mary, house for life. To son John, certain land, a bed, and cattle. To son Benjamin, land and £70, at age. To son James, land and cattle. To son Joseph, land and £95. To son Peter, the house at death of wife. He also mentions daughters Mary, Elizabeth and Sarah, and child that wife goes with.

Children: 1. John, 2. Benjamin, 3. James, 4. Joseph, 5. Peter, 6. Mary, 7. Elizabeth, 8. Sarah, 9. Child,

XII. ——, b. d.
m. 1689.
Israel Shaw, b. 1660. d. of Anthony & Alice (Stonard) Shaw.

Children:
1. William, 1690, Nov. 7.
2. Mary, 1692, Feb. 17.
3. Anthony, 1694, Jan. 29.
4. Alice, 1695, Nov. 17.
5. Israel, 1697, Aug. 28.
6. Hannah, 1699, Mar. 7.
7. Jeremiah, 1700, Jun. 6.
8. Ruth, 1701, Feb. 10.
9. Peter, 1704, Oct. 6.
10. Elizabeth, 1706, Feb. 7.
11. Grace, 1707, Oct. 20.
12. Comfort, 1709, Aug. 9.
13. Deborah, 1711, Jul. 15.

XIII. Benjamin, b. 1684, Jan. 28. d. 1759, May 20. Warwick, R. I.
m. (1) 1708, Sep. 23.
Patience Durfee, b. d. 1723 ± of Thomas & Deliverance (Hall) Durfee.
m. (2) 1724, Jun. 7.
Deborah Cook, b. d. 1759 + of John & Mary ( ) Cook.

1755, Jul. 5. Will—proved 1759, Aug. 13. Exx. wife Deborah. To son Benjamin, land in Portsmouth, with buildings. To daughter Mary Fish, £5. To daughter Deliverance Sisson, £50. To daughter Patience Tallman, £45, and new chest. To sons William and James, 20s., each. To daughter Sarah Godfrey, a feather bed. To granddaughters Bethaniah and Freelove Tallman, each a half of the bounty money that was their father's on account of the expedition against Cape Breton. To wife the homestead in Warwick, 2 acres for life, and then equally to grandsons William and Samuel, sons of James (with further provision if they die). To wife also the whole of movable estate.

Inventory, £498, 15s., 11d., viz: wearing apparel £26, shoemaker's tools £20, 16s., bond £90, 2 old wheels, 8 swine, 2 hens, &c.

Children:
1. Benjamin, 1710, Jun. 19.
2. Mary, 1712, Aug. 2.
3. Deliverance 1715, Feb. 4.
4. William,
5. Patience, 1721, Apr. 6.
(2d wife.)
6. James,
7. Sarah,
8. John,

(3d Wife.)

XIV. Samuel, b. 1688, Jan. 14. d.

TAYER.

Benjamin, b. d. 1716, Jun. 5.
m. [Wm.
Susanna James (w. of b. d. 1726, Mar. 4.

of Joseph Martin.

Newport, R. I.

He was a cordwainer.

1713, Feb. 16. Will—proved 1716, Aug. 6. Ex. son John. To daughter Mary, wife of John Holmes, he gives a legacy, as also to grandchildren Benjamin, Elizabeth, John, Charity and William Tayer. To wife Susanna, household goods she had before I married her, and half the cloth which we have made since we were married.

He was buried in Clifton Burial Ground.

His widow died at her son John James' house, and was buried in the Coddington Burial Ground by the side of her first husband.

I. John, b. d. Newport, R. I.
m. 1700, Jan. 16.
Charity Foster, b. d. of Foster.

He was a cordwainer.

Children: 1. Benjamin, 2. Elizabeth, 3. John, 4. Charity, 5. William,

II. Mary, b. d.
m.
John Holmes, b. 1672. d. 1748, Nov. 22. of John & Frances (Holden) Holmes.

No issue.

III. Mercy, b. 1683 ± d. 1683 ±

TAYER. 1st column. He had an earlier wife, mother of the children.

TAYLOR.

Robert, b. d. 1688, Jan. 13.
m. 1646, Nov.
Mary Hodges, b. d.

of Hodges.

Scituate, Mass., Newport, R. I.

He was a ropemaker.

1655. Freeman.

1673, Oct. 22. Juryman.

1673, Oct. 29. Prison-keeper, appointed by the Assembly.

1680. Taxed £1, 7s. 6d.

Though the birth of James[2] is not recorded he is yet believed to have been one of the children of Robert[1].

I. Mary, b. 1647, Nov. d.
m. 1664.
George Hulate, b. d. of Hulate.

II. Ann, b. 1650, Feb. 12. d.

III. Margaret, b. 1652, Jan. 30. d.

IV. Robert, b. 1653, Oct. d. 1707, Jun. 12. Newport, R. I.
m.
Deborah Peckham, b. d. 1707 + of John Peckham.

1706, Apr. 22. Will—proved 1707, Jul. 7. Exs. wife Deborah and son John. Overseers, brother John Taylor and William Barker. He provides for the care of son Thomas for his natural life. To son Robert, certain land, he paying £50, to his brother —— at age. To four daughters, Margaret, Elizabeth, Deborah and Mary Taylor, a feather bed, two cows and ten sheep, each at twenty years old or marriage.

Children:
1. John, 1687, Sep. 26.
2. Margaret, 1689, Jul. 5.
3. Elizabeth, 1691, Jul. 26.
4. Robert, 1694, Nov. 2.
5. Deborah, 1698, Jan. 13.
6. Thomas, 1699, Nov. 1.
7. Peleg, 1701, Mar. 8.
8. Mary, 1703, Nov. 23.

TAYLOR. 2d column. IV. Robert. His seventh child should be Peter, (not Peleg).

TAYLOR. 2d column. VI. Peter. His 2d wife b. 1701, Oct. 7, of John and Mary ( ) Wood. His daughter Mercy, b. 1717, Feb. 24

V. JOHN, b. 1657, Jun. d. 1747, Jun. 9. Little Compton, R. I.
m. (1)
ABIGAIL, b. d. 1720, Sep. 16. of
m. (2)
SARAH, b. d. 1764. of

1745, Apr. 24. Will—proved 1747. Exs. sons John and Robert. To wife Sarah, all goods that were hers before marriage, a mare, cow, half of all household goods that I have got since I married her and use and improvement of dwelling house, all the fruit of old orchard, half the garden, £6, per year, seven cords of wood at door yearly, as also six bushels Indian corn, three bushels English grain, and one hundred pounds of beef; also to her, a swine, six fowls, and the keep of mare and cow till my two grandsons Philip and Joseph are of age. To son John, 35 acres with buildings (part of homestead) and other land. To son Robert, 30 acres of homestead and other land. To grandsons Joseph and Philip, sons of Philip, deceased, 35 acres of homestead and other land at age, they keeping the cow, mare, &c., for testator's widow, while she remains unmarried. To daughter Margaret Woodman, £50. To daughter Lydia Cook, £50. To grandson Job Taylor, £20. To grandson Samuel Irish, £50. To granddaughter Comfort Taylor, remaining part of household goods. To grandson Jesse Irish, 10*s*. To three granddaughters Mary Davis, Hannah Viners and Ann Irish, 10*s*. apiece. To three granddaughters Susanna Palmer, Abigail Taylor and Deborah Taylor, each 10*s*. To three great-grandsons, viz: George, Jonathan and Joseph Wilbur, each 10*s*. To three great-grandchildren (children to granddaughter Priscilla Wilbur, deceased) viz: Job, Abner and Ann Wilbur, 10*s*. each. To son John, half of farming tools. To grandsons Joseph and Philip Taylor, other half of farming tools. To the two executors, all cattle, horses, hogs, money, bills, bonds, &c., and to them, two-thirds of rest of real and personal equally, and the other third to grandsons Joseph and Philip Taylor.

Inventory, £876, 2*s*., viz: wearing apparel £61, 10*s*., books £3, pewter, carpenter's tools, 2 mares, a pair of oxen, 5 cows, heifers, paper bills £65, 14*s*., &c.

1756, Oct. 27. Will—proved 1764, Aug. 7. Widow Sarah. She named friend and kinsman Simeon Palmer, kinswoman Sarah Soll, &c.

1. Mary, 1682, Oct. 25.
2. Anna, 1686, Sep.
3. Margaret, 1688, Jul.
4. Lydia, 1691, Apr.
5. John, 1694, Jan. 7.
6. Robert, 1695, Dec.
7. Philip, 1697, May 13.
(2d wife, no issue.)

VI. PETER, b. 1661, Jul. d. 1736. Newport, Little Compton, R. I.
m. (1)
ELIZABETH PECKHAM, b. d. 1714, May 24. of John Peckham.
m. (2) 1715, Nov.
HANNAH WOOD, b. d. of Wood.

1688, Dec. 26. He bought of Benjamin Church and wife Alice 100 acres in Little Compton.

1730, May 13. Will—proved 1736, Oct. 13. Ex. son Peter. To wife Hannah, half of stock of brute creatures and while widow improvement of dwelling house, and profits of half of all my lands and use of all household stuff, &c. To son Peter, house he lives in, half of orchard, and two-thirds of rest of lands, and improvement of whole till my son William is of age, and half of creatures and all my tools. To son William, dwelling house I now live in, half of orchard, and a third of rest of lands, and he to learn a trade at fifteen. To daughter Elizabeth, wife of John Davenport, £50. To daughter Mary, £80, and a bed. To daughters Mercy, Hannah and Ann, £50, each, at eighteen. To five youngest children, viz: those I had by present wife, rest of estate.

Inventory. Bonds £393, 16*s*., 4 silver spoons, 3 pairs of silver buttons and silver buckles £8, 15*s*., 26 oz. silver money £35, 14*s*., 3 yearling cattle, 3 calves, 9 cows, 2 oxen, a steer, heifer, 20 lambs, 11 swine, beds, apparel, 2 woolen wheels, 2 linen wheels, warming pan, &c.

1. Peter, 1697, Oct. 20
2. Elizabeth, 1701, Jan. 4.
3. Mary, 1703, Dec. 20
(2d wife.)
4. Mercy,
5. Hannah,
6. Anne,
7. William,
8. Daughter,

VII. JAMES, b. d. 1690, Oct. 7. Newport, R. I.
m.
CATHARINE, b. 1666. d. 1690, Sep. 15. of

1. Robert, 1689,

TENNANT.

ALEXANDER, b. d.
m.
———, b. d.

Kings Town, Jamestown, R. I.

1687, Sep. 6. Taxed 3*s*.

1696. Jamestown. Freeman.

I. HANNAH, b. 1680, Jan. 27. d.

II. DANIEL, b. d. Kings Town, R. I.
m.
ANN GREENE, b. d. of Benjamin & Humility ( ) Greene.

1709, Jun. 28. He and twenty-six others bought tract called Shannock Purchase, being part of the vacant lands in Narragansett.

1719, Jan. 7. His wife Ann had a legacy of 20*s*. from will of her father Benjamin Greene.

III. JOHN, b. 1689, Sep. 26. d. Newport, Jamestown, R. I.
m. 17—, Oct. 18.
MARTHA REMINGTON, b. d. of Remington.

1713, Jul 28. He and wife Martha sold for £65, to William Wanton, 90 acres in East Greenwich.

1724, Mar. Jamestown. He had a suit brought against him by Thomas Peckham, of Newport, house carpenter.

IV. ABIGAIL, b. 169-. d. 1758 +
m.
SAMUEL TEFFT, b. d. 1760. of Samuel & Elizabeth (Jenckes) Tefft.

1. Samuel, 1712, Jan. 19
2. Daniel, 1714, Jun. 14
3. Stephen, 1718, Oct. 5.
4. Tennant, 1720, Sep. 29
5. Abigail, 1724, Feb. 14

THOMAS.

JOHN, b. d. 1728.
m.
———, b. d.

Jamestown, North Kingstown, R. I.

1688. Grand Jury.

1700, Apr. 30. Freeman.

1701, Mar. 26. He bought of Benoni Gardiner and wife Mary, 80 acres in Pettaquamscott Purchase, for £48, and on same date bought of Nicholas Gardiner and wife Hannah, for £48, another tract in same region.

1707, Jan. 28. Kings Town. He bought of John Watson, Sr., and wife Rebecca, of Kings Town, 80 acres there for £30.

1713, Mar. 6. He deeded son John, for love, &c., 100 acre tract, and 80 acre tract, he allowing driftway to his brother George and £2, if demanded by wife or self, for life.

I. GEORGE, b. 1681, Aug. 20. d. 1740. Jamestown, North Kingstown, R. I.
m. (1) 1704, Jan. 20.
ALICE GORTON, b. d. of Benjamin & Sarah (Carder) Gorton.
m. (2) [of John.
ELIZABETH PHILLIPS (w. b. d. 1748. of

1703. Freemen.

1706, Dec. 20. He bought 36 acres in Kings Town of James Kenyon, Sr., and wife Ruth, for £25, 10*s*.

1733. Deputy.

1735. His son George, Jr., died this year. (Administration to widow Elizabeth.)

He (George, Sr.), held the title of Colonel at the time of his death.

1740, Jun. 26. Will—proved. Ex. son Samuel. To son John, land, a negro and twenty sheep. To son Benjamin, land and a boat. To wife Elizabeth, £200, a negro man and woman, all household goods she brought with her when she came to dwell with me, use of great room, bed room, &c., two cows, riding beast, corn, &c. To three daughters ———, Alice Tillinghast and Elizabeth Free——. To son Samuel, house and land not disposed of, and rest of real and personal.

1748, Jul. 4. Will—proved. Widow Elizabeth. Ex. son Thomas Phillips. She mentions son Christopher Phillips, daughter Mary Dickinson, sons Samuel and Thomas Phillips and grandchildren.

1. Sarah,
2. Mary,
3. George, 1708, Feb. 7.
4. John,
5. Benjamin,
6. Peleg,
7. Samuel,
8. Daughter,
9. Alice,
10. Elizabeth,
(2d wife, no issue.)

1714, Mar. 6. He deeded son George, for love, certain tracts of land with all the housing, orchard, &c., he allowing to wife and myself sufficient maintenance, and to allow his brother John poles or rails out of his part of cedar swamp, and a driftway to be maintained.

1715, Aug. 23. He testified as to land in Jamestown, that he had known about thirty-six years before.

1728, Oct. 8. Will—proved. Ex. son George. To son John, all wearing apparel, and a money legacy left in son George's hands for him. To granddaughter Mary Thomas, a legacy. (The rest of will illegible or destroyed.)

II. { JOHN, { b. 169–. Kings Town, R. I.
m. { d.
ABIGAIL, { b.
{ d. of

1718, Jul. 12. He and wife Abigail sold to George Thomas for £200, two tracts, one of 80 acres, and the other 100 acres.

III. { EBENEZER, { b. Kings Town, R. I.
{ d.

1721, Mar. 29. He deposed as to land formerly hired by his father John Thomas.

THORNTON.

{ JOHN, { b.
m. { d. 1695 +
SARAH, { b.
{ d. 1692 +

Newport, Providence. R. I.

1639. He had 10 acres granted, being in the employ of John Coggeshall at this time.

1648, Oct. 12. He was one of the twelve members of the First Baptist Church, in full communion.

1655. Freeman.

1679, Jan. 10. Providence. He wrote to Samuel Hubbard, at Newport, this being his first letter since his removal from that place. Mr. Hubbard replied saying, "Pray remember my respect unto Mr. Roger Williams," &c.

1679, Jul. 1. Taxed 2*s*., 6*d*.

1680. Deputy.

1683, May 10. He wrote Samuel Hubbard, as follows: "Dear brother, thee gavest me an account of the death of divers of our ancient friends; since that time the Lord hath arrested by death our ancient and approved friend Mr. Roger Williams, with divers others here. The good Lord grant these may be a means to alarm us that we may be stirred up with the wise virgins to be trimming our lamps and getting of them full of the spiritual oil," &c.

1683, May 22. He sold to son Solomon, for £33, 6*s*., 8*d*., 100 acres and commonage.

1686, Apr. 22. He and wife Sarah, deeded son John 60 acres at Neutaconconut Hill, three miles from Providence.

1686, Dec. 19. He had a letter from Samuel Hubbard who says: "My old brother who was before me, you and brother Joseph Clarke (only alive) in that ordinance of baptism, I next and my wife in New England, although we stept before you in other ordinances, Oh, let us strive still to be first in the things of God," &c.

1687, Sep. 1. Taxed 8*s*.

1688. Ratable estate, 2 oxen, a cow, 3 young cattle, 3 acres tillage, 50 acres woodland, &c.

1692, Mar. 7. He deeded son Thomas, "for and in consideration of his care and diligence in providing for myself and his aged mother," all right of land appertaining to homestead, together with my house, housing, fencing, meadow ground, orchard, stones and timber, with all appurtenances whatsoever, &c.—provided said Thomas "shall provide sufficient maintenance for myself and my wife during our natural life." The land was bounded partly by James Thornton's and partly by John Thornton, Jr.'s, land. The grantor put his son Thomas into actual possession, together with all cattle and movable estate whatsoever, with the obligation to pay each of my children, 2*s*., 6*d*., after my decease, and to each grandchild, 1*s*., and if wife should outlive grantor, son Thomas was to maintain her at any other child's house if she wished to move.

1692, Mar. 7. He deeded son James, for love, &c., 62 acres.

1695, Aug. 13. He made complaint with his son John, to the Town Council on behalf of his grandchildren, Zachariah Field's children, that they might be bound out to good places and educated.

I. { JOHN, { b. Providence, R. I.
m. { d. 1716, Jan. 9.
DINAH STEERE, { b.
{ d. 1716 (—) of John & Hannah (Wickenden) Steere.

1. John,
2. Josiah,
3. Dinah,
4. Stephen,
5. Ruth,
6. Daniel,
7. Elihu,
8. Ebenezer,

1684, Oct. 28. He gave acquittance to Nathaniel Mowry.

1687, Sep. 1. Taxed 2*s*., 1*d*.

1715, Dec. 29. Will—proved 1716, Jan. 18. Exs. sons John and Josiah. He empowers executors to sell and dispose of all his lands and tenements in Providence and bring it all to movable estate, and after payment of debts and also after son Josiah has had £40, then the remainder to be equally divided amongst all my children, sons and daughters-in-law.

Inventory, £37, 2*s*., viz: working tools, 3 cows, 4 yearlings, 2 calves, 5 loads of hay, pewter, fire slice, tongs, spoons, &c.

II. { THOMAS, { b. Providence, R. I.
m. { d. 1712, Mar. 27.
MARGARET, { b.
{ d. 1712 + of

1. Thomas,
2. William,
3. Patience,
4. Elizabeth,

1684, Oct. 28. He witnessed acquittance from his brother John to Nathaniel Mowry.

1712, Mar. 24. Will—proved 1712, Apr. 20. Exx. wife Margaret. Overseers, brother Solomon and friend John Sheldon. To wife, all movable estate and use of house while widow, and she to bring up children at her discretion. To son Thomas, at age, the part of homestead farm on east side of river that runs through the farm, he paying his sisters Patience and Elizabeth Thornton, each £10. To son William, the part of farm on west side of river, and rights in other land.

Inventory, £150, viz: money in bills £23, neat cattle £41, horse £4, swine, wool, flax, tobacco, cider, bible, &c.

III. { SOLOMON, { b. Providence, R. I.
m. { d. 1713, Sep. 18.
——— { b.
{ d. of

1. Child,

1687, Sep. 1. Taxed 2*s*.

1713, Oct. 18. Administration to Thomas Harris and Mercy Borden, and they took wardship of children and guardianship of the heir.

IV. { ELIZABETH, { b.
m. 1680, Dec. 9. { d. 1723 +
EDWARD MANTON, { b. 1658, Dec. 11.
{ d. 1723, Aug. 14. of Shadrach & Elizabeth (Smith) Manton.

1. Shadrach,
2. Edward,
3. John,
4. Ann,
5. Katharine,
6. Mary,
7. Elizabeth,
8. Sarah,

V. { SARAH, { b.
m. (1) { d. 1714, Apr. 16.
ZACHARIAH FIELD, { b.
m. (2) { d. 1693, Aug. 12. of John Field.
JOHN GURNEY, { b.
{ d. 1723. of Gurney.

1. Zachariah, 1685, Jan. 30.
2. John,
3. James,
4. Daniel, 1690, Aug. 7.
5. Joseph,
6. Sarah,
(By 2d husband, no issue.)

VI. { JAMES, { b. Providence, R. I.
m. { d.
SARAH, { b.
{ d. of

1692, Mar. 7. He had a deed of gift from his father of 62 acres.

1705, Nov. 30. He sold his brother Thomas 25 acres for £75.

1706, Mar. 23. He and wife Sarah, sold Ebenezer Eddy, of Swanzey, dwelling house and 25 acres, being part of lands formerly owned by John Thornton, deceased, four miles west of salt water.

1713, Jul. 13. He sold Nicholas Sheldon, 49 acres for £26.

1719, Aug. 10. He sold land and buildings where he dwelt, 150 acres, to Joshua Turner, of East Greenwich, for £88.

VII. { BENJAMIN, { b. Providence, Glocester, R. I.
m. { d. 1742 +
——— { b.
{ d. of

1. Benjamin,
2. Joseph,
3. Titus,
4. John,
5. David,
6. Mary,
7. Sarah.

1699, Feb. 23. He had 28¼ acres laid out.

1707, Dec. 30. He sold Mrs. Freelove Crawford, 28 acres for £20, 10*s*.

1713, Jun. 16. Taxed 2*s*.

1715, Feb. 28. He sold Experience Mitchell, 60 acres for £30.

1742, Jan. 12. Glocester. He sold son David, 23 acres where said Benjamin now dwells, for £500, excepting four rods for a burying place.

The will of his son David (who died 1772), besides mentioning wife Alice and only daughter Rhoda, &c., gives the names of his brothers and sisters as follows: Benjamin, Joseph and Titus, deceased, John, Mary Vallet and Sarah Paine, deceased. To each living he bequeathed 1*s*.

VIII. { WILLIAM, { b. Providence, R. I.
{ d.

1688, Aug. His name was in a list of one hundred and seventy-two persons in Providence, who were over the age of sixteen and taxable.

JOHN, b. d. 1687.
m.
——— b. d.

Salem, Mass., Providence, R. I.

1630, Dec. 1. He embarked at Bristol, Eng., in ship Lion.

1631, Feb. 5. He arrived at Boston, and soon went to Salem.

1631, May 18. Freeman.

1638, Oct. 8. Providence. He was one of the twelve persons to whom Roger Williams deeded land that he had bought of Canonicus and Miantonomi.

1639, Apr. 22. He bought of Roger Williams his interest in Chibachuwest, now called Prudence Island.

1639, Jul. 1. He and his wife are alluded to in a letter from Rev. Hugh Peters of Salem, to the church at Dorchester, as having had "the great censure passed upon them in this our church." He says that they and certain others "wholly refused to hear the church, denying it and all the churches in the Bay to be true churches."

1640, Jul. 27. He and thirty-eight others signed an agreement for a form of government.

1643, Jul. 6. He obtained a grant of land for himself and thirty-five associates, of Governor Kieft in New York. It was situated at what is now called Throgg's Neck (an abbreviation for Throckmorton). His settlement here was but brief, for Mr. Winthrop records in September of this year, that the Indians set upon the English who dwelt under the Dutch, and killed "such of Mr. Throckmorton's and Mr. Cornhill's families as were at home." He further says of the English settlers "these people had cast off ordinances and churches, and now at last their own people, and for larger accomodation had subjected themselves to the Dutch, and dwelt scatteringly near a mile asunder." Some that escaped from the Indian attack, he says, went back to Rhode Island.

1647, Feb. 27. He (now again of Providence) was granted the house and land that was Edward Cope's, and that he shall either bring a discharge for the town from the creditors of said Edward Cope, or else pay into the hands of deputies of Providence £15, in wampum at or before May 15th.

1650, Sep. 2. Taxed £1, 13*s.* 4*d.*

1651, Jan. 27. He sold John Sayles a house and lot.

1652. Moderator.

1654, Jun. 26. He sold Richard Parker of Boston, merchant, half of island called Chibachuwest or Prudence Island.

1655. Freeman.

1659, Apr. 24. He sold William Carpenter 60 acres bounded partly by Benedict Pond.

1659, Jun. 20. He entered three ankers of strong waters.

1664-65-66-67-68-70-71-72-73-75. Deputy.

1666, May 31. He swore allegiance.

1667. Town Council.

1667, Oct. 30. His letter to the Assembly concerning estate of his daughter Taylor, was referred to Town Council.

1672, Jul. 18. He wrote a letter to Roger Williams upbraiding him for his letter to George Fox, in which Mr. Williams had proposed a joint discussion touching Quakerism. He addressed two other sharp letters to Roger Williams, in one of which he warned him to provide an armor of proof as Goliath did for "G. Fox is furnished with that armour that thou hast no skill to make use of; having also the sword of the spirit to cut down thy airy imaginations."

1675, Jun. 15. He sold 140 acres to Daniel Abbott.

1677. Town Treasurer.

1679, Sep. 1. Taxed 7*s.* 6*d.*

1687. Ratable estate, 2 house lots, 4 shares of meadow.

1687, Sep. 1. Taxed 3*s.* Estate of deceased John Throckmorton.

He died and was buried at Middletown, N. J. where he had gone probably on a visit to his children. He early took up lands in New Jersey, but never permanently settled there, though all his sons removed thence.

Vital information touching this family has been received through the courtesy of J. E. Stillwell, M. D., of New York.

I. FREEGIFT, b. d. 1669 ±
UNMARRIED.

II. PATIENCE, b. 1640. d. 1676, Sep. 7.
m. 1655, Dec.
JOHN COGGESHALL, b. 1618. d. 1708, Oct. 1. of John & Mary ( ) Coggeshall.

1. Freegift, 1657, Mar. 1.
2. James, 1660, Feb. 18.
3. Mary, 1662, Mar. 10.
4. Joseph, 1665, May 31.
5. Rebecca, 1667, Jun. 20.
6. Patience, 1669, Aug. 13.
7. Benjamin, 1672, Jul. 27.
8. Content, 1674, Mar. 28.
9. Content, 1676, May 10.

III. JOHN, b. d. 1690. Providence, R. I., Middletown, N. J.
m. 1670, Dec. 12.
ALICE STOUT, b. d. 1690 + of John & Penelope ( ) Stout.

1. Joseph,
2. Rebecca,
3. Sarah,
4. Patience,
5. Alice,
6. Deliverance,

1668, Jun. He swore allegiance.

1669, Nov. 6. Middletown (Monmouth Co.), N. J. He gave a power of attorney at this date to his father John Throckmorton, of Providence, and calls himself lawful heir of his late deceased brother Freegift.

1675. Representative in this and later years. He held the office also of Justice, &c.

1690, Jul. 17. Will—proved 1690, Aug 22. Exx. wife Alice. To wife, dwelling house and orchard at Garrett's Hill, 100 acres adjoining and 20 acres meadow. To son Joseph and daughter Rebecca, the above house and lands at death of wife, and also certain other land. To daughters Sarah, Patience, Alice and Deliverance, the rest of land equally. He reserved ¼ acre for a burial plot where my father is buried in Middletown.

IV. JOB, b. 1650, Sep. 30. d. 1709, Aug. 20. Middletown, N. J.
m. 1685.
SARAH LEONARD, b. 1660, May 27. d. 1744, Feb. 5. of Henry & Mary ( ) Leonard.

1. John, 1688,
2. Joseph, 1693, Aug. 15.
3. Job,

He probably had sons James and Samuel also.

He was buried at Middletown and his widow at Shrewsbury.

V. DELIVERANCE, b. d.

VI. JOSEPH, b. d. 1690. Middletown, N. J.
UNMARRIED,

He was a mariner and owned two vessels.

He probably died at the Barbadoes.

1689, Dec. 2. Will—proved 1690. Ex. brother John Throckmorton. He being about to go to sea devises all real estate anywhere in the world to the heir male of John Throckmorton, of East Jersey, named Joseph Throckmorton and his heirs forever. The personal estate to be disposed of as laws of respective places where it lies shall order. He desires that his brother John Throckmorton shall be guardian for said Joseph.

1690, Oct. 13. Administration on his estate was given to his brother John's widow Alice.

EDWARD, b. 1617. d. 1707, Mar. 1.
m. 1647, Jun.
ELIZABETH MOTT, b. 1629. d. 1694, Sep. 2.
of Adam Mott.

Newport, R. I.

He was a Quaker.

1655. Freeman.

1663. Commissioner.

1667-71-72-73-74-80-81-82-83-84-85-86. Deputy.

1675-86-90-91. Assistant.

1686, Aug. 26. He signed an address with other Quakers to the King in regard to the writ of *Quo Warranto*. They desired to be excused from bearing arms, being a peaceable people and "willing to pay all just rates and duties for carrying on the commonwealth's affairs," &c.

1690, Jan. 30. He with five other assistants and Deputy Governor Greene wrote a letter to William and Mary, congratulating them on their accession to the crown and informing them that since the deposition of Sir Edmund Andros, the former government under the charter had been re-assumed, mentioning also the seizure of Andros, in Rhode Island, on his flight from confinement in Massachusetts, and his return to Massachusetts on demand of that Colony.

1705, Apr. 4. He confirmed a deed from his son Daniel to John Cory, declaring that he had given the land (90 acres in East Greenwich), to his son Daniel in his will.

1704, Jan. 11. Will—proved 1707, Mar. 12. Only fragmentary parts remain of this will. He names grandson Edward (son of his son Edward) and four surviving sons, Jonathan, Daniel, Samuel and Thomas. He also mentions granddaughter Elizabeth (daughter of son Jonathan) and sons-in-law Weston Clarke and Ebenezer Slocum and two granddaughters Slocum.

His wife was buried in the Coddington Burial Ground.

I. SARAH, b. 1648, Mar. 10. d.

II. ELIZABETH, b. 1650, Feb. d.

III. EDWARD, b. 1652, Apr. 1. d. 1690, Dec. 7. Newport, R. I.
m.
SUSANNA JEFFERAY, b. d. of William & Mary (Gould) Jefferay.

1679, May 6. Freeman.
1690. Deputy.

1. Edward, 1678.
2. William, 1680.
3. Abigail, 1686, Apr. 3.
4. Priscilla,
5. Jonathan,

THURSTON. 2d column. IV. Eleanor. Her 1st husband b. 1653; d. 1706, Feb. 25. Children, 1, George. 2, Jonathan, 1681, Feb. 2. 3, John. 4, William. 5, Ruth. 6, Content. 7, Patience. 8. Desire. 9, Abigail. She m. (2) 1708, Thomas Terry.

IV. ELEANOR, b. 1655, Mar. d. 1724 +
m. (1) 1674,
GEORGE HAVENS, b. d. 1702 + of William & Dionis ( ) Havens.
m. (2)
—— TERRY, b. d. of Terry.

1. George,
2. Jonathan, 1681, Feb. 2.

V. MARY, b. 1657, Feb. d. 1732, Nov. 16.
m.
EBENEZER SLOCUM, b. 1650, Mar. 25. d. 1715, Apr. 13. of Giles & Joan ( ) Slocum.

1. Elizabeth, 1678, Jan. 1.
2. Mary, 1679, Jun. 21.
3. Joanna, 1680, Dec. 30.
4. Rebecca, 1682, Nov. 13.
5. Samuel, 1684, Mar. 2.
6. Ebenezer, 1686, Jan. 20.
7. Desire, 1688, Mar. 12.
8. Deliverance 1691, Aug. 15.
9. Mercy, 1693, Sep. 14.
10. Giles, 1696, Feb. 19.
11. Joseph, 1697, Apr. 21.
12. Abigail, 1697, Apr. 21.

See: American Genealogist, v. 20, p. 118.

VI. JONATHAN, b. 1659, Jan. 4. d. 1740. Newport, Little Compton, R. I., Dartmouth, Mass.
m.
SARAH, b. d. of

1684, Jun. 3. Little Compton. Grand Jury.

The length of time from the birth of his first child to the last, suggests the idea that he had two wives named Sarah.

1735, Aug. 22. Will—proved 1740, Apr. 15. Ex. son Jonathan. He calls himself late of Little Compton, now of Dartmouth. To son Edward, 10*s*., he having had. To son Jonathan, £40. To son Joseph, £150. To son Job, £150. To daughters Mary Brownell, Constant Wood, Susanna Carr and Abigail Wait, £30, each. To grandson Lovet Peters, £30, and the bed that did belong to my daughter Eleanor, his mother. To granddaughter Rebecca Southworth, £30, and all household stuff that belonged to her mother Patience. To daughter Elizabeth Wood's children, each 10*s*. To daughter Sarah Sawdey's children, 10*s*., each. To youngest sons Joseph and Job, rest of household stuff.

Inventory, £1,357, 11*s*., viz: wearing apparel £33, 19*s*., trunk, bonds, money due, &c.

1. Edward, 1679, Oct. 18.
2. Elizabeth, 1682, Nov. 29.
3. Mary, 1685, Mar. 20.
4. Jonathan, 1687, Jul. 5.
5. Rebecca, 1689, Nov. 28.
6. Content, 1691, Aug. 18.
7. Sarah, 1693, Nov. 9.
8. John, 1695, Jul. 12.
9. Eleanor, 1696, Nov 26.
10. Hope, 1698, Nov. 26.
11. Abigail, 1700, May 7.
12. Patience, 1702, Feb. 16.
13. Amey, 1705, Jan. 29.
14. Peleg, 1706, Jul. 8.
15. Jeremiah, 1710, May 8.
16. Susanna, 1712, Aug. 20.
17. Joseph, 1714, Apr. 25.
18. Job, 1717, Jul. 1.

VII. DANIEL, b. 1661, Apr. d. 1712. Newport, R. I.
m.
MARY EASTON, b. 1668, Jun. 16. d. of John & Mehitable (Gaunt) Easton.

He was a butcher.

1702, Jan. 12. Proprietor in common lands.

1705, Apr. 4. He and wife Mary, sold John Cory, of Portsmouth, 90 acres, in East Greenwich for £40.

1712, Jul. 18. Will.

He was buried in the Coddington Burial Ground.

1. Daniel, 1687, Sep. 25.
2. Elizabeth, 1689, Jan. 14.
3. Mary, 1690, Mar. 9.
4. John, 1692, Jun. 10.
5. Edward, 1693, Sep. 1.
6. Eleanor, 1695, Jan. 18.
7. Benjamin, 1697, Mar. 25.
8. James, 1698, Jul. 15.
9. Peter, 1704, Jul. 3.

VIII. REBECCA, b. 1662, Apr. d. 1737, Sep. 16.
m. (1)
PETER EASTON, b. 1659, Jan. 11. d. 1690, Dec. 17. of Peter & Ann (Coggeshall) Easton.
m. (2) 1691, Nov. 21.
WESTON CLARKE, b. 1648, Apr. 5. d. 1728 + of Jeremiah & Frances (Latham) Clarke.

1. Rebecca, 1684, Jul. 5.
2. Peter, 1685, Nov. 18.
3. Ann, 1687, Sep. 3.
4. Joshua, 1689, Apr. 27.
(By 2d husband.)
5. Jeremiah, 1692, Jul. 27.
6. Mary, 1694, Feb. 8.
7. Elizabeth, 1695, Nov. 5.
8. Weston, 1697, Aug. 25.

IX. JOHN, b. 1664, Dec. d. 1690, Oct. 22. Newport, R. I.
m.
ELIZABETH, b. 1669. d. 1690, Oct. 7. of

1690, May 6. Freeman.

1690, Oct. 20. Will—Witnesses Mical Daniel, Benjamin Towe. This is referred to in a list of wills that were presented to the court in 1700, by parties interested, the law requiring three witnesses and these wills having but two.

He and his wife were buried in Clifton Burial Ground.

X. CONTENT, b. 1667, Jun. d.

XI. SAMUEL, b. 1669, Aug. 24. d. 1747, Oct. 27. Newport, R. I.
m.
ABIGAIL CLARKE, b. 1674. d. 1731, Nov. 30. of Latham & Hannah (Wilbur) Clarke.

1696, May 5. Freeman.

1740, May 13. Will—proved 1747, Nov. 2.

He was buried in the Coddington Burial Ground.

1. Edward, 1696, May 26.
2. Son, 1698, Jul. 18.
3. Samuel, 1699, Oct. 16.
4. Hannah, 1701, Dec. 11.
5. Latham, 1704, Jun. 3.
6. Joseph, 1706, Sep. 24.
7. Elizabeth, 1708, Dec. 22.
8. Mary, 1711, Feb. 11.
9. John, 1713, Apr. 10.
10. Phebe, 1715, Nov. 20.
11. Abigail, 1718, Jan. 6.
12. Sarah, 1720, May 16.

XII. THOMAS, b. 1671, Oct. 8. d. 1730, Mar. 22. Freetown, Mass.
m.
MEHITABLE TRIPP, b. d. 1730 + of Peleg & Anne (Sisson) Tripp.

1706. Grand Jury.

1708-9. Selectman.

1712-13. Surveyor of Highways.

1718-22. Assessor.

1730, Mar. 20. Will—proved 1730, Apr. 21. Exs. brother-in-law Peleg Tripp, of Rhode Island, and wife Mehitable. To wife Mehitable, all movables within and without doors except great bible. The house and land to be sold for debts, &c., and surplus remaining to be for wife and eleven children, divided as follows: To wife and sons Edward, Thomas, Peleg, Jonathan, Samuel and John, equally in seven shares, only £20 advance to wife and £20 to son Thomas. To daughters Ruth Eddy, Elizabeth Thurston, Anne Sprague, Mehitable Joslin and Mary Thurston, £100, the four eldest daughters having £60 and what they have already had, and daughter Mary receiving £40.

Inventory. Real estate, house and lands £185. Personal, £175, 13*s*., viz: purse and apparel £13, 6*s*., books, &c., £5, 10*s*., plate and pewter £3, 15*s*., earthen, glass and brass £3, 9*s*., bark and leather £1, 15*s*., 16 cord of wood at the landing £8, 16*s*., mare £8, mare and colt, old horse, 6 swine, cow, calf, 2 yearling cattle, 10 hens, 4 geese, stack of bees, a sheep, &c.

1. Edward, 1696.
2. Thomas,
3. Peleg,
4. Jonathan,
5. Samuel,
6. John,
7. Ruth,
8. Elizabeth,
9. Anne,
10. Mehitable,
11. Mary,
12. Nathaniel,

HENRY, m. 1661, Dec. — b. ; d. 1713.
SARAH STANTON, — b. ; d. 1708 +
of Robert & Avis ( ) Stanton.

Kings Town, R. I.

1663, Jul. 3. He and others of Narragansett desired to be under protection of Connecticut.
1665, May 13. He and others petitioned the Assembly of Rhode Island for accomodation of land, &c., in Kings Province.
1670, Jun. 22. Constable. He was appointed by Connecticut, and the inhabitants were desired to yield obedience to Connecticut rule.
1671, May 20. He took oath of allegiance to Rhode Island.
1672, Jan. 1. He with five others bought a tract of land of Awashuwett, Chief Sachem of Quohesett in Narragansett (the two brothers and three sons of the sachem joining in deed).
1677, May 2. He and others having been imprisoned by Connecticut authorities, the Rhode Island Assembly sent a letter of this date complaining thereof and asserting that if they persisted in "disturbing the inhabitants with your illegal and forcible intrusions, we shall be necessitated without further delay to represent the state of the difference between us unto His Sacred Majesty, in whose determination we shall acquiesce and to whose royal command we shall yield obedience," &c.
1678, Jun. 12. Constable; receiving his appointment this time from Rhode Island authorities.
1679, Jul. 29. He and forty-one others of Narragansett signed a petition to the King praying that he "would put an end to these differences about the government thereof, which hath been so fatal to the prosperity of the place; animosities still arising in people's minds as they stand affected to this or that government."
1687, Sep. 6. Taxed 8*s*. 4*d*.
1687–88. Grand Jury.
1688, Mar. 6. He and Daniel Vernon were empowered to take care that a certain highway in Kings Town be forthwith laid open for the use and benefit of the inhabitants.
1690. Conservator of the Peace.
1702. He gave 6*s*. toward building Quaker meeting house at Mashapaug.
1702, Oct. 26. He bought 150 acres in Coweset of George Havens of Shelter Island, for £80.
1703, Jul. 12. He was chosen with others to lay out highways.
1705. Deputy.
1710, Jan. 9. He deeded son John of East Greenwich, 90 acres there.
1708, Nov. 27. Will—proved 1713, Jul. 13. Exs. wife Sarah and son George. To wife, half of certain land while widow, as also half of orchard and housing. To son George and heirs male, the other half, and at wife's death he to have her part. To son John, land in East Greenwich where he lives. To eldest daughter Mary Greene, wife of Edward Greene of Aquidneset, £20, 4*s*. To daughter Sarah, wife of William Hall, £20, 4*s*. To daughter Martha Stanton, wife of Benjamin, £20. To grandsons, equally, (except sons of Edward Greene, they being provided for) certain land bought of Indians. To three grandsons, Thomas, Henry and William, sons of son Henry, deceased, daughter-in-law Rebecca Tibbitts, widow of Henry, and granddaughters Rebecca, Avis and Dinah, daughters of son Henry, each £5. To granddaughter Anne Fones, daughter of Samuel Fones, £10. To grandson William Tanner, land purchased of Thomas Stanton of Stonington, and five loads of hay. Son George to take care of his mother, &c.
Inventory, £64, 11*s*.

I. HENRY, m. — b. ; d. 1702, Dec. 27.
REBECCA, — b. ; d. 1752, Jun. 10. of
Kings Town, R. I.
Children: 1. Thomas, 2. Henry, 3. William, 4. Rebecca, 5. Avis, 6. Dinah,

1687, Sep. 6. Taxed 1*s*.
1696. Freeman.
1700, May 1. Fined 25*s*. for taking part in rescue of prisoner from Deputy Sheriff.
1703, Apr. 12. Administration to widow Rebecca. Inventory, £274, 8*s*. 2*d*.
1738, Jan. 26. Will—proved 1752, Aug. 10. Widow Rebecca of Warwick. Ex. son William. To grandson Thomas, son of Thomas, deceased, my mansion house and land where I dwell, housing, orchards, fencing, &c., with liberty for my two sons Henry and William to pass and repass through land. To daughters Avis Rice and Rebecca Greene, £10, each. To grandson Thomas, a right in a small lot at Apponaug, and a bed. To three daughters Avis Rice, Rebecca Greene and Dinah Tibbitts, rest of estate equally and daughter Dinah to live in house while single. To son Henry, 5*s*. To son William, 20*s*. both having had by deed.
Inventory, £530, 1*s*.

II. ANN, m. — b. ; d. 1702 (—)
SAMUEL FONES, — b. 1666. ; d. 1757, Dec. of John & Margaret ( ) Fones.
Children: 1. Ann, 1689, Oct. 16.

III. GEORGE, m. (1) — b. ; d. 1746.
MARY, m. (2) — b. ; d. of
ALICE SHERMAN, m. (3) 1725, Dec. 30. — b. 1680, Jan. 12. ; d. of Samson & Isabel (Tripp) Sherman.
SARAH BLIVEN, — b. ; d. 1759. of John Bliven.
North Kingstown, R. I.
Children: 1. Ann, 1702, Oct. 12. 2. Sarah, 1704, Mar. 29. 3. George, 1706, Mar. 1. 4. Martha, 5. Henry, (2d wife.) 6. Alice, 1720, Jul. 27.

1700. East Greenwich. He took oath of allegiance.
1721, May 4. His daughter Ann married Immanuel Northup. (She died 1727, Aug. 28.)
1723, Jun. 15. He and wife Alice gave receipt to Job Sherman, executor to our deceased father Samson Sherman, for legacy.
1736, Nov. 4. Will—proved 1746, Mar. 15. To wife Sarah, two cows, movables, &c., and forty pounds of sheep's wool annually. To son George, the homestead received of father. To daughter Martha Reynolds, £20. To son Henry, farm where he lives. To daughter Alice, £50, and two beds, when of age, and also two cows and twenty sheep. To grandson George Northup, £20, at age.
1759, Jul. 7. Will—proved 1759, Sep. 10. Widow Sarah. Exx. cousin Priscilla Bliven. To Mary Baker, wife of —— Baker, a bed. To Elce Pearce and her son John Pearce, a legacy. To loving cousin Priscilla Bliven, rest of estate.

IV. JOHN, m. 1705, Jun. 7. — b. ; d.
ELIZABETH HALL, — b. 1687, Oct. 2. ; d. of William & Alice (Tripp) Hall.
Kings Town, East Greenwich, R. I.
Children: 1. Mary, 1707, Mar. 25. 2. Anne, 1710, May 17. 3. Anne, 1712, Jul. 27.

See: AMERICAN GENEALOGIST, V.36, p.54

1700. He took oath of allegiance.
1700, May 1. He was fined 25*s*. for taking part in rescue of a prisoner from Deputy Sheriff.
1710. East Greenwich. Freeman.
1714, Mar. 9. He sold Joshua Davis a boggy meadow in East Greenwich, which came to me by my honored father Henry Tibbitts, deceased.
1715, Nov. 13. He and wife Elizabeth mortgaged for £60, to the colony, 87 acres and buildings.
1733, Dec. 26. He mortgaged 100 acres, house, &c., for £400.

V. MARY, m. — b. ; d.
EDWARD GREENE, — b. ; d. of John & Joan ( ) Greene.
Children: 1. Robert,

VI. SARAH, m. — b. ; d.
WILLIAM HALL, — b. 1672, Dec. 2. ; d. of William & Alice (Tripp) Hall.
Children: 1. Abiel, 1698, Jun. 20. 2. William, 1700, Jan. 7. 3. Abigail, 1702, Aug. 7. 4. Sarah, 1704, Feb. 7. 5. Alice, 1707, Aug. 16. 6. Benoni, 1710, 7. Henry, 1712, 8. Abel, 1714, 9. John, 1717, 10. Mary, 1719.

TILLINGHAST. 2d column. VII. Benjamin. His widow d. 1743, Jan. 5. XI. Hannah. Her husband, b. 1678, d. 1718, Feb. 19.

VII. MARTHA, m. — b. ; d. 1752, Jul. 11.
BENJAMIN STANTON, — b. 1684, Mar. 13. ; d. 1760, Sep. 18. of John & Mary (Harndel) Stanton.
Children: 1. Benjamin, 2. Avis, 3. Martha, 1712, 4. Sarah,

VIII. ——, m. — b. ; d.
WILLIAM TANNER, — b. ; d. of Tanner.
Children: 1. William,

TIBBITTS. 2d column. VIII. Hannah m. William Tanner. Children, 1, William, 1712, Sep. 22. 2, Benjamin, 1714, June 16. 3, Honor, 1716, Dec. 15. 4, H——ah, 1723, Oct. 16. 5, ——, ——, Jan. 19.

TILLINGHAST.

TILLINGHAST. 1st column. His widow did m., 2d, 1718, Nov. 4, Samuel Mason.

PARDON, m. (1) — b. 1622. ; d. 1718, Jan. 29.
—— BUTTERWORTH, of — b. ; d. Butterworth.
m. (2) 1664, Apr. 16.
LYDIA TABER, — b. ; d. 1718 +
of Philip & Lydia (Masters) Taber.

Seven Cliffs, Sussex Co., Eng., Providence, R. I.

He was a shop keeper, with other avocations, as cooper, &c.
1646, Jan. 19. Providence. He was received as a quarter shares man at this date, as a descendant (Moses Brown) declared, who further says that by tradition he had served in Cromwell's army.

See: American Genealogist. V.34, p.3.

I. SARAH, — b. 1654, Nov. 17. ; d. young.

II. JOHN, m. — b. 1657, Sep. ; d. 1690, Dec.
ISABEL SAYLES, — b. ; d. 1716 + of John & Mary (Williams) Sayles.
Providence, Newport, R. I.
Children: 1. Pardon, 2. Charles, 3. Hannah, 4. Mary, 1689.

(She m. (2) Robert Hicks.)

He was a cooper.
1677. Freeman.
1680, Mar. 12. He petitioned the Assembly that his fine of 20*s*., for not attending on the jury of General Court of Trials, might be remitted, and it was so ordered.
1684. Newport. Freeman.
1690. Deputy.

1649, May 9. He was granted a lot called Mrs. Lea's, paying her presently 30*s*.

1650, Sep. 2. Taxed 3*s*., 4*d*.

1658, May 18. Freeman.

1659, Nov. 19. Newport. He had a deed of certain land from Benedict Arnold.

1665, Feb. 19. Providence. He had lot 60, in a division of lands.

1671, Jan. 30. He was allowed 10*s*., for the use of his boat.

1672–80–90–94–97–1700. Deputy.

1680, Jan. 27. He was granted, on his petition, 20 feet square "for building him a storehouse with privilege of a wharf, over against his dwelling house."

1681. Pastor of the First Baptist Church, and so continued many years. Morgan Edwards declares that he was remarkable for his plainness and piety.

1684, Nov. 2. He and wife Lydia, deeded to son John, of Newport, certain land there, with houses, brew-house, warehouse, &c.

1687. Overseer of the Poor.

1687, Sep. 1. Taxed 14*s*.

1688, Aug. Ratable estate, shop goods £40, enclosed land 4 acres, vacant land 80 acres, 2 shares of meadow, 4 cows, 3 heifers, 24 sheep, 5 horsekind, 2 swine, part of 2 boats, a little sorry housing.

1688–91–93–94–95–96–97–98–99–1700–1–2–3–4–5–6–7. Town Council.

1700, May 7. He deeded a share of meadow to son-in-law Nicholas Sheldon.

1711, Apr. 14. He deeded his house called the Baptist meeting house, situated between the Town street and salt water, together with the lot whereon said meeting house standeth, to the church and their successors for "the christian love, good will and affection which I bear to the church of Christ in said Providence, the which I am in fellowship with and have the care of as being elder of the said church." "Memorandum, before the ensealing hereof I do declare that whereas it is above mentioned, to wit: to the church and their successors in the same faith and order, I do intend by the words same faith and order, such as do truly believe and practice the six principles of the doctrine of Christ mentioned Heb. 6 : 2, such as after their manifestation of repentance and faith are baptized in water, and have hands laid on them."

1714, Jun. 20. He, having formerly given son Joseph part of lot on which I dwell, now grants him all my right and interest, after my own and my wife's decease, in said 6 acre lot, with buildings, privileges, &c., bounded north by son Philip's land, west by the street, &c.

1715, Dec. 15. Will—proved 1718, Feb. 11. Exx. wife Lydia, with sons Philip and Benjamin, to help her. "I do bequeath my life and spirit into the hands of the Fountain of life and Father of spirits, from whom I have received it, and my body to the dust from whence it came, in hope of a resurrection to eternal life." To sons Pardon, Philip and Benjamin, £50, each. To son Joseph, my present dwelling house and house lot after his mother's decease. To five daughters Mary Carpenter, Abigail Sheldon, Mercy Power, Hannah Hale and Elizabeth Taber £10, each. To each grandchild, 5*s*.

Inventory, £1,542, 4*s*., 3*d*., viz: silver money £88, 18*s*., due by bonds £1,133, 18*s*., due by book £91, bills of credit £155, 4*s*., books, silver spoon, earthen ware, iron and pewter ware, 2 guns, wearing apparel, &c.

He was buried in his own lot at the south end of the town.

1718, Nov. 4. Under this date the marriage of Mrs. Lydia Tillinghast to Samuel Mason, of Swanzey, is recorded at Providence. Possibly this was Pardon Tillinghast's widow, though she was then aged.

No relationship has been traced between Pardon Tillinghast and that Charles Tillinghast who was on the grand jury 1687 and General Sergeant 1692.

1690, Dec. 4. Will—proved 1691, Mar. 7. Exx. wife Isabel, with assistance of father of testator. To wife, all estate for life. To son Pardon, certain land and part of house and warehouse. To second son Charles, the rest of land and housing at death of mother. To daughters Hannah and Mary, £10 each, at eighteen or marriage.

1716, Sep. 29. His widow Isabel, now the widow of Robert Hicks, deeded to her son Charles Tillinghast (her son Pardon, being deceased), certain land, he paying her a third of profits yearly.

III. MARY, { b. 1661, Oct. / d. 1711 +
m.
BENJAMIN CARPENTER, { b. / d. 1711, Mar. 3. of William & Elizabeth (Arnold) Carpenter.

1. Benjamin,
2. Joseph,
3. William,

(2d WIFE.)

IV. LYDIA, { b. 1666, Apr. 18. / d. 1707, Jun. 30.
m.
JOHN AUDLEY, { b. 1666. / d. 1738, Jun. 29. of John & Martha (   ) Audley.

1. John, 1689, Mar.
2. Elisha, 1690, Nov.
3. Martha, 1692.
4. Mary, 1694.
5. Son, 1700, Jul. 8.
6. Lydia, 1702, Jan. 29.
7. Abigail, 1703, Sep. 30.
8. Elizabeth, 1706, Oct.

V. PARDON, { b 1668, Feb. 16. / d. 1743. Providence, East Greenwich, R. I.
m.
—— KEECH, { b. / d. 1726, Feb. 7. of Keech.

1. Mary, 1694.
2. Philip,
3. John,
4. Joseph,
5. Mercy, 1706.

1688, Aug. His name was in a list of one hundred and seventy-two taxable persons over sixteen.

1699, Mar. 25. He bought of David Shippee and wife Margaret, 70 acres, house and orchard in East Greenwich, paying therefor £107, 10*s*., and two houses, 72 acres and orchard in Providence.

1699, Oct. 11. East Greenwich. Freeman.

1702–4–5–6–8–14–16–19–20–22–25. Deputy.

1705–10. Justice of the Peace.

1743, Oct. 3. Will—proved 1743, Nov. 5. Exs. son-in-law Peter Mawney and son Philip Tillinghast. To son John, £100. To son Joseph, £250, a pair of oxen, cow, certain land, and negro Jack to serve him six years and then to have his freedom. To daughter Mercy Mawney, £250, two cows, and two silver spoons. To grandson Pardon, son of John, the farm where he dwelleth of 260 acres, a pair of oxen, black mare, and negro Cæsar for six years and then to have his freedom. To grandson John, son of John, £300, a pair of oxen, cow, ten sheep and a horse. To grandson John Mawney, £150, a cow, and ten sheep. To grandson Pardon Mawney, £100, and certain land. To granddaughter Welthian Tillinghast, daughter of John, £200, a feather bed, two cows and silver spoons. To granddaughters Elizabeth Olney, Lydia Mawney, Mercy Fry and Mary Mawney, £50, each. To granddaughters Mary Spencer, Ann, Lydia and Amey Tillinghast, daughters of son John, £30, each. To grandsons Benjamin, Charles, Thomas and Joseph, sons of John, £30, each. To granddaughters Elizabeth Bentley, daughter of son Joseph, Sarah and Amey Mawney, daughters of Peter Mawney and Mary Tillinghast, daughter of son Philip, each a feather bed. To each great-grandchild, £5. To well beloved brethren of Baptist Church under care of Timothy Peckham, my silver cup, for their use forever, and £25, "towards defraying their necessary charges in spreading the gospel." To the poor of Baptist Church under care of Richard Sweet, £25. To son Philip, all the homestead, he paying legacies as follows: To his sons Pardon and Thomas, £30, each, and £500, for other legacies. To son-in-law Peter Mawney, £50. To Sarah Atherton, £5. To granddaughters Elizabeth Olney, Lydia Mawney, Mercy Fry, Mary Mawney and Welthian Tillinghast, rest of estate.

Inventory, £3,089, 8*s*., 11*d*., viz: wearing apparel £49, 5*s*., bonds £1,586, 19*s*., plate £22, 10*s*., linen wheel, tables, chairs, desk, pewter, coffee mill, cooper and carpenter tools, gun, 4 hogsheads of beer, cider, &c., 2 bulls, 10 cows, 3 heifers, 2 oxen, 2 steers, 6 calves, swine, 24 sheep, horse, 2 mares, geese, fowls, 2 negro men £120, &c.

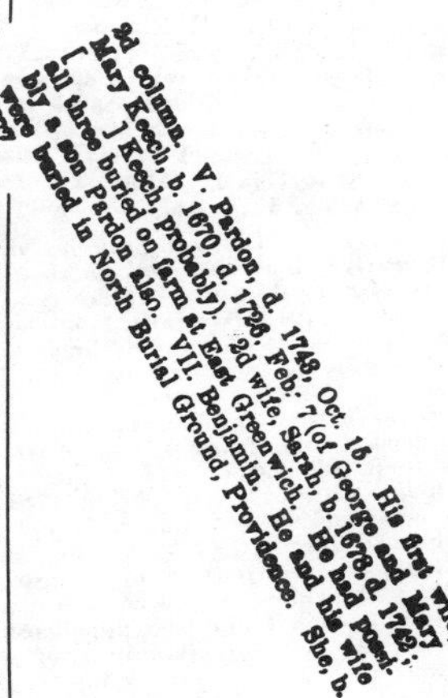
2d column. V. Pardon, d. 1743, Oct. 15. His first wife, Mary Keech, b. 1670, d. 1726, Feb. 7 (of George and Mary [ ] Keech, probably). 2d wife, Sarah, b. 1678, d. 1742; all three buried on farm at East Greenwich. He had possibly a son Pardon also. VII. Benjamin. He and his wife were buried in North Burial Ground, Providence. She, b. 1677

VI. PHILIP, { b. 1669, Oct. / d. 1732, Mar. 14. Providence, R. I.
m. 1692, May 3.
MARTHA HOLMES, { b. 1675. / d. 1729, Mar. 10. of Jonathan & Sarah (Borden) Holmes.

1. Charles, 1693, Mar. 5.
2. Philip, 1694, Aug. 9.
3. John, 1696, Apr. 14.
4. Jonathan, 1698, Sep. 18.
5. Martha, 1699, Dec. 20.
6. Pardon, 1701, Dec. 15.
7. Obadiah, 1703, Dec. 2.
8. Joseph, 1706, May 18.
9. Lydia, 1708, Oct. 16.
10. Sarah, 1710, Mar. 5.
11. Samuel, 1711, Nov. 5.
12. Anne, 1713, Apr. 13.
13. William, 1714, Jan. 12.
14. Elisha, 1716, Aug. 29.
15. Mary, 1718, Feb. 16.

He was a merchant.

1690. His name was in the list of those who were in Captain Samuel Gallup's Company in expedition against Canada.

1696, Jan. 25. He and others were granted a lot forty feet square to build a school house on, if they would build it in some considerable time.

1705. Justice of the Peace.

1707–8–9–10–12–13–15–22–23–26–27–31. Deputy.

1708, Oct. 27. He was appointed on a committee to agree with Ninegret, what may be a sufficient competence of land for him and his men to live upon, and to view the state of the country in Narragansett, in order for the settling of a new town.

1713, May 6. He was appointed on a committee by the Assembly for making the public road leading through this Colony from Pawtucket river to Pawcatuck river more straight, fair and passable.

1714. Assistant.

1719–20–21–24–25–26–27–28–29–30–31. Town Council.

1732, Feb 12. Will—proved 1732, Mar. 27. Exs. sons Charles, Philip and John. To son Charles, the dwelling house where he lives and land adjoining (the lands between my house and his to lay open for convenience of both), also four rods square where Charles' lime pits are, so as to take in the brook where he hath used to soak his hides, and other land. To sons Philip, John, Jonathan and Pardon, lands in New Purchase, west of East Greenwich. To son Samuel, half a lot, at Cold Spring, in Providence Neck. To son William, land at Providence Neck, To son Elisha, land at Tuncowotten. To son Philip, land on west side of Town street, and £250. To son Charles, £100. To sons John, Jonathan, and Pardon, £250, each. To sons William, Samuel and Elisha, £300, each at age. To daughter Martha Potter, £150. To daughters Lydia, Sarah, Anne and Mary £150, each, and £50, each in household goods. To daughter Sarah, negro women Nimfo. To son Elisha, negro boy Primus. To all the children, silver money and plate. To son Charles, half of my dwelling house, warehouse, &c., and half of land on west side of Town street. To sons Samuel and William the other half, with liberty to daughters Sarah, Anne and Mary, to dwell there while single. After some other bequests of land, &c., the rest of estate was given to children equally.

Inventory, £4,964, 10*s*., viz: negro boy £100, woman £100, horse £20, cow £8, shop goods, viz: silk, mohair, camblet, buckram, brimstone, shoe buckles, &c., bills of public credit £626, 19*s*., 6*d*., bonds and notes £2,991, 18*s*., book debts £346, 7*s*., 9*d*., silver money £96, 1*s*., 1*d*., watch £10, 10*s*., silver tankard, 8 spoons, and shoe buckles £41, 15*s*., 6*d*., gold doubloon and moider £16, 18*s*., 29 chairs 3 oval tables, 2 looking glasses, 2 pair of old cards, wheel, 4 feather beds, 2 flock beds.

He and his wife were buried in the family ground.

VII. BENJAMIN, { b. 1672, Feb. 3. / d. 1726, Sep. 14. Providence, R. I.
m.
SARAH RHODES, { b. / d. 1735 + of Malachi & Mary (Carder) Rhodes.

1. Benjamin,
2. James,
3. Sarah, 1702, May 20.
4. Mary,
5. Abigail,
6. Mercy,
7. Lydia,
8. Elisha,

He was a merchant.

1701. Freeman.

1726, Sep. 13. Will—proved 1726, Oct. 17. Exx. wife Sarah. To son Benjamin, land south end of Providence Neck formerly belonging to honoured father Pardon, deceased, &c. To son James, land at Fox Hill, and Thatch Cove, except what will yield a load of thatch per year. To wife a lot of land. To five daughters Sarah, Mary, Abigail, Mercy and Lydia Tillinghast, £200, each, the two eldest having in one year, and the rest at twenty-one. To each daughter a feather bed. To son Benjamin, a third part of sloop building at Weybossett Neck and £100, within a year. To son James, £100, at age. To wife Sarah, the whole use of dwelling house, shop, warehouse, and of all land till son Elisha is of age. To son Elisha, two lots on Town street (bounded partly by my brother Philip), at age, and my now dwelling house, shop, warehouse and land on Town street at decease of wife. To wife Sarah, all the rest of personal. To son Elisha, enough of Thatch Cove to yield a load per year.

Inventory, £4,887, 1*s.*, viz: bonds for paper money £2,077, 14*s.*, 6*d.*, shop goods £434, 6*s.*, paper money £404, 14*s.*, silver money £121, 18*s.*, 7 silver spoons and silver cup £6, 10*s.*, book debts £922, 6*s.*, 9*d.*, 4 bibles and other books £2, 4*s.*, 3 wheels, 3 guns, warming pan, 2 pairs of cards, rum and other spirits £58, 10*s.*, sugar £66, sheep £14, 4 cows, heifer, 2 mares, colt, 3 swine, 3 hens and duck, ¼ sloop Lyon £75, ¼ negro wench £12, 10*s.*, due for cider £55. Rooms named, great room, bed room, great chamber, shop chamber, leanto, leanto chamber, garret, cellar, new and old warehouse.

1735, Oct. 29. His widow Sarah, sold to son Benjamin for £350, certain land, dwelling house, stables, &c.

VIII. ABIGAIL, { b. 1674, Mar. { d. 1744 (—)
m.
NICHOLAS SHELDON, { b. { d. 1747, Nov. 23. of John & Joan (Vincent) Sheldon.

1. Mary, 2. Nicholas, 3. Joseph, 4. Abigail, 5. Lydia, 6. Hannah, 7. Pardon, 8. Jeremiah,

IX. JOSEPH, { b. 1677, Aug. 11. { d. 1763, Dec. 1. Providence, Newport, R. I.
m. (1)
FREELOVE STAFFORD, { b. { d. of Samuel & Mercy (Westcott) Stafford.
m. (2) [ow.
MARY HENDRON, (wid- { b. 1700. { d. 1765. of Paris.

1. Joseph, 2. Freelove, 3. Anna, 1709, Jun. 25. 4. Samuel, 1711, Oct. 8. (2d wife.) 5. Elizabeth, 6. Samuel, 7. Nicholas, 1726, May 26. 8. Daniel, 9. Mary, 10. Henry,

He was a merchant.

1701. Freeman.

1702, Dec. 22. He bought of Samuel and Daniel Brown, of Kings Town, for £30, a lot of 90 acres in East Greenwich.

1704, Jul. 22. He deeded above to his brother Pardon "in presence of our father and mother Pardon and Lydia Tillinghast."

1722, Aug. 6. His son Joseph Tillinghast, Jr., of Tiverton, recorded his intention of marriage to Mercy Howland (at Bristol).

1726, Jun. 16. Newport. He and wife Mary, sold to Pardon Tillinghast, of Providence, for £250, a six acre lot there with house, &c., and a 40 foot lot which also belonged to our father Pardon Tillinghast, deceased.

There was a Joseph Tillinghast, who married Lydia Simmons, at Tiverton (1723, Apr. 4), but he has not been clearly shown as being identical with this Joseph.

X. MERCY, { b. 1680. { d. 1769, Nov. 13.
m.
NICHOLAS POWER, { b. 1673. { d. 1734, May 18. of Nicholas & Rebecca (Rhodes) Power.

1. Hope, 1701, Jan. 4. 2. John. 1703, Apr. 3. Joseph, 4. Anne, 1707, Dec. 12. 5. Sarah, 6. Nicholas, 7. Lydia, 8. Mercy,

XI. HANNAH, { b. { d.
m.
JOHN HALE, { b. { d. of Hale.

1. Barnard, 1709, Sep. 15. 2. Freelove, 1712, Apr. 3. 3. Lillis, 1714, Oct. 2. 4. Hannah, 1716, Sep. 17.

XII. ELIZABETH, { b. { d. 1750 +
m.
PHILIP TABER, { b. 1689 Feb. 7. { d. 1750, Dec. 27. of Thomas & Mary (Thompson) Taber.

1. Pardon, 1710. 2. Jeremiah, 3. Samuel, 4. Lydia, 5. Hannah, 6. Daughter,

TILLINGHAST. 2d column. IX. Joseph. His 2d wife d. 1765, May 16. Children by 1st wife, 1, Lydia. 2, Joseph, 1703. 3, Freelove. 4, Anna, 1709, June 25. 5, Samuel, 1711, Oct. 8. 6, Stukeley, 1716. Perhaps all the rest by 2d wife. 7. Elizabeth. 8, Mary, 1725, Mar. 9, Nicholas, 1726, May 26. 10, Henry, 1727, Aug. 11, Sarah, 1728, Feb. 26. 12, Daniel, 1732, June 2. 13, Henry. 14, Amey. (Of these children Sarah is not recorded as his child, but the evidence is strong that she was. She m. 1747, Oct. 2, Lemuel Wyatt); Elizabeth m. Matthew Cozzens, 1754, Oct. 17; Anna m. Robert Gardiner; Lydia m. Job Almy, 1717, July 18; Amey m. Thomas Eyres, [illegible], July 12. His son Stukeley d. at 24 and Herny at 12 nearly. The other sons married. 1722, Aug. 6. Add at end of line—but m. (1) at Tiverton, 1723, Apr. 4, Lydia Simmons; m. (2) at Newport, 1760, Oct. 9, Mary Cranston. 1726, June 16. Add at end of line.—He and his last wife (and son Joseph and first wife) are buried in Newport Cemetery. The last wife of Joseph, Sr., may have been daughter of that Abraham Paris, of Barbadoes, mariner, who deeded land at Newport for £200 to William Wanton, 1700, Sep. 13; and mother of that Paris Hendron, who with her witnessed a paper in 1740. Erase two lines commencing "There was a Joseph," etc., 1766, Mar. Nicholas Tillinghast of Providence, and Nicholas Paris Tillinghast of Newport, administrators of estate of Mary Tillinghast, widow, who was executrix of last will of her husband Joseph Tillinghast, appellees, and Ann Gardner, widow, of Newport, daughter of Joseph, appellant. Parties left differences to referees, who decided that appellees pay appellant £1,424 4s. 7d., being her proportion of residuary part of personal estate (the seventh part of the £9,000 ordered to be paid by Joseph Tillinghast included in the above sum) of Joseph Tillinghast, on and after decease of widow—exclusive of yearly legacy left by Joseph to said Ann Gardiner. The Nicholas Paris Tillinghast above was son of Samuel,[4] (Joseph,[2] Pardon[3]), of Warwick, R. I., as appears by a letter. To still farther clear the record of the family of Joseph,[2] (Pardon[1]), it may be said that his son Joseph made his will 1776, Feb. 19—proved 1780, Apr. 3. Exs. wife Mary and Nicholas Paris Tillinghast. He was a merchant, like his father. He mentions daughter Lydia, son Stukeley, and grandson John Bryer. XI. Hannah m. John Hale, b. 1678, d. 1718, Feb. 19, of Richard and Mary (Bullock) Hale.

TIMBERLAKE.

TIMBERLAKE. 2d column. I. William. Daughter Mary, b. 1672.

HENRY, { b. { d.
m.
MARY, { b. { d. 1705, Sep. 10.

Newport, R. I.

1644. Corporal.

1663. Commissioner.

1671, Jan. 30. Mary Timberlake was allowed 15*s.* for a horse hired to New London for Richard Bailey.

1680. His widow Mary was taxed 16*s.*

1697, Feb. 12. His widow Mary sold for 1*s.* to her son-in-law John Coggeshall, and my daughter Elizabeth his wife, 112 acres in Newport.

1706, Jul. 3. Inventory, £92, 1*s.* 3*d.* Widow Mary of Little Compton. Administrator, her son-in law John Woodman. Division of £74, 13*s.* 7*d.*, balance remaining, in following manner: To children of Henry Timberlake, a quarter; to Joseph Timberlake, a quarter; to children of John Timberlake, a quarter and to Hannah, wife of John Woodman, a quarter. Oath was made by John Woodman to following effect: Mary Timberlake had four sons and two daughters, viz: William, Henry, Joseph, John, Elizabeth and Hannah. William hath a daughter now Mrs. Mumford, who had the greater part of her father's estate. Henry is dead, left a son Henry and two daughters. Joseph remains alive. John is dead, left three daughters, Elizabeth, Mary and Hannah. Elizabeth Coggeshall is living, hath had of her mother's estate before the making of the will, land unto about £60, in Newport. Hannah Woodman is yet alive.

I. WILLIAM, { b. { d. 1678. Newport, R. I., Boston, Mass.
m.
MARY. { b. { d. of

1. Daughter, 2. ——

1668. Freeman.

1685, Aug. 25. Administration to widow Mary. Inventory, £6, 6*s.*, viz: table, 6 chairs, pewter, warming pan, feather bed, &c. The inventory was settled on widow in consideration of seven years education of two children since her husband's departure.

II. HENRY, { b. { d. 1687. Newport, R. I.
m.
SARAH, { b. { d. 1687 + of

1. Henry, 2. Daughter, 3. Daughter,

1676. Ensign. He served with Captain William Turner in King Philip's War.

1678. Freeman.

1680. Taxed £4, 8*s.*

1688, Jan. 4. Administration to widow Sarah.

Inventory, £31, 6*s.* 10*d.*

III. JOSEPH, { b. { d. Portsmouth, Little Compton, R. I.
m. 1683 ±
MARY CORY (w. of Wm.) { b. { d. 1718, Mar. 22. of Ralph & Joan ( ) Earle.

1. Sarah,

He was a cordwainer.

1688. Licensed.

1691, Jun. 23. Little Compton. Agreement (recorded at this date) before marriage between him and Mary Cory, widow of William of Portsmouth, carpenter, to whom she was sole executrix. It was agreed that said Mary should after marriage have full liberty to improve and dispose of all her former husband's estate, and said Joseph Timberlake to confirm above, delivers an instrument to Edward Moss and to George Bunnell, giving them full power of her estate while widow and for bringing up of her children, &c., reserving only to myself a mare, four neat cattle, four hogs, four sheep. He gave up all his own estate also, house, land, &c., he being free of all debts, &c.

IV. JOHN, { b. { d. 1706 (—)
m.
——— { b. { d. of

1. Elizabeth, 2. Mary, 3. Hannah,

V. ELIZABETH, m. 1670, Dec. 24. JOHN COGGESHALL, — b. / d. / b. 1650, Feb. 12. / d. 1706, Nov. 9. of John & Elizabeth (Baulstone) Coggeshall.

1. Elizabeth, 1671, Nov. 27.
2. Baulstone, 1672, Sep. 29.
3. John, 1673, Sep. 23.
4. Mary, 1675, Sep. 18.
5. William, 1677, Sep. 7.
6. Patience, 1680, Jan. 1.
7. Constant, 1682, Mar. 14.
8. Peter, 1684, Jun. 18.
9. James, 1686, May 29.
10. Rebecca, 1688, Oct. 9.
11. Baulstone, 1690, Oct. 8.
12. Daniel, 1693, Oct. 25.
13. Job, 1694, Nov. 10.
14. Abigail,

VI. HANNAH, m. JOHN WOODMAN, — b. / d. 1718, May 3. / b. / d. 1713, Apr. 24. of Woodman.

1. Robert, 1677, Sep. 8.
2. Hannah, 1679, Jun. 27.
3. John, 1682, Feb. 25.
4. Edith, 1685, Sep. 7.
5. Edward, 1688, Mar. 17.
6. Rebecca, 1690, Jan. 10.
7. Elizabeth, 1694, May 31.
8. Sylvia, 1698, Sep. 17.

TODD.

WALTER, m. MARGARET BARTON (w. of [Rufus. — b. / d. 1673 + / b. / d.

Warwick, R. I.

1648, Jun. 5. He was recorded as an inhabitant.

1651, Feb. 3. He with three others made an agreement with the town of Warwick to build a mill at their own cost and to grind the town's corn for two quarts in a bushel, the town granting them for their encouragement the lot that was formerly Mr. Gorton's.

1652–53–56–57–58–63. Commissioner.

1655. Freeman.

1657, Apr. 4. He and three others were to take bonds of William Harris and his son Andrew in £500, concerning the charge of high treason against said William Harris.

1664–65–73–74. Assistant.

1664–71–72–78. Deputy.

1665, Feb. 22. He was desired by the town to agree with some workmen to make a pair of stocks for the use of said town.

1665. Treasurer for the town.

1673, May 7. He was appointed on a commission to treat with the Indian Sachems: "and with them seriously to consult and agree of some way to prevent the extreme excess of the Indians' drunkenness. The sachems therein intended to be treated withal, are Mawsup and Ninecraft of the Narragansetts, Philip of Mt. Hope, Weetamo of Pocasset, Awashunk of Seaconnett; or so many of them as do appear."

No issue.

TOMPKINS.

NATHANIEL, m. 1671, Jan. 15. ELIZABETH ALLEN, — b. / d. 1724. / b. 1651, Jul. / d. 1714, Mar. 24.

of John & Elizabeth (Bacon) Allen.

Newport, Little Compton, R. I.

1675. He was at Newport thus early.

1680. Taxed 7*s*.

1719, May 30. Will—proved 1724, May 19. Ex. son Samuel. To son Nathaniel, £15. To son Samuel, all lands not already given him by deed. To daughter Elizabeth, wife of William Ladd, a cow. To daughter Mary Tompkins, 30*s*., a bed, and £4, borrowed of her. To daughter Mercy, wife of William Bowditch, a ewe sheep. To daughter Priscilla, wife of Samuel Lyndon, a cow. To daughter Sarah, wife of Benjamin Gifford, a cow. To daughter Rebecca Tompkins, a cow and a bed. To daughter Hannah, wife of Timothy Gifford, a cow. To son Samuel's three sons, Joseph, John and Christopher, any estate remaining.

Inventory, £87, 10*s*. 6*d*., viz: wearing apparel £3, 10*s*., bed, pewter, linen wheel, 15 sheep, yoke of oxen, 5 cows, mare, &c.

TOMPKINS. 1st column. His wife's mother was Elizabeth Bull.

I. ELIZABETH, m. 1696, Feb. 17. WILLIAM LADD, — b. / d. 1729 + / b. / d. 1729. of Joseph & Joanna ( ) Ladd.

1. Sarah, 1696, Mar. 22.
2. William, 1697, Nov. 18.
3. Mary, 1699, Mar. 5.
4. Priscilla, 1700, Jun. 22.
5. Joseph, 1701, Oct. 19.
6. Samuel, 1703, Feb. 26.
7. Elizabeth, 1704, Oct. 12.
8. John, 1706, Jan. 15.
9. Katharine, 1707, Sep. 14.
10. Jeremiah, 1710, Aug. 31.
11. Lydia, 1711, Mar. 1.
12. Hannah, 1712, Aug. 12.
13. Ruth, 1714, Jan. 19.

II. NATHANIEL, — b. 1676, Dec. 31. / d. 1748. Tiverton, R. I.

1748, Jul. 31. Will—proved 1748, Aug. 15. Ex. brother-in-law Timothy Gifford, of Dartmouth. To kinsman Timothy Gifford, Jr., of Dartmouth, all my lands and buildings, but if he die, then to his two brothers Daniel and Robert Gifford. To sister Hannah Gifford, a brass kettle. To Mary King, a piece of gold and right in a black cow. To kinsman Robert Gifford, largest gun. To Timothy Gifford, Jr., all personal estate not disposed of, and if he die without issue, then to my kinswomen Constant and Hannah Gifford, daughters of my executor, £100, each.

Inventory, £751, 15*s*. 11*d*., viz: wearing apparel £242, 11*s*. 8*d*., bed £59, 6*s*., 2 guns, pair of stillyards, half of 2 mares, half of 2 cows, 3 barrows, a shoat, 9 pigs, neat cattle £105, mill and press, &c.

III. MARY, — b. 1677, Sep. 16. / d.

IV. PRISCILLA, m. 1703, Jul. SAMUEL LYNDON, — b. 1679, May 24. / d. 1732, Dec. 11. / b. 1676. / d. 1750, Dec. 10. of Josias Lyndon.

1. Josias, 1704, Mar. 10.
2. Samuel,

V. SAMUEL, m. SARAH COE, — b. 1681, May 24. / d. 1760, May. / b. / d. 1747, Jan. 2. of John & Sarah (Pabodie) Coe. Little Compton, R. I.

1. Joseph, 1712, Oct. 26.
2. John, 1714, Sep. 14.
3. Christopher, 1715, Dec. 8.
4. Elizabeth, 1716,
5. Abigail, 1717, Jan. 28.
6. Nathaniel, 1719, Nov. 9.
7. Gideon, 1720, Nov. 19.
8. Micah, 1722, Jan. 20.
9. Benjamin, 1723, Jan. 26.
10. Augustus, 1725, Mar. 19.
11. Priscilla, 1726, Jun. 6.
12. William, 1730, Oct. 17.

1758, Jul. 4. Will—proved 1760, Jun. 3. Exs. sons Gideon and Micah. To son Joseph, £40, a cow, and half of apparel. To son Christopher, £40, and half of apparel. To sons Gideon and Micah, all real estate, land and buildings in Little Compton. To son Gideon, a bed. To son Benjamin, £5. To son William, £50, and privilege to live in the house while single, if the house is not sold. To daughters Elizabeth and Abigail Tompkins, £30, each, all the rest of household goods, privilege of living in the house while single, use of garden, &c., while the house and land are unsold, and yearly to each, ten pounds of flax, six bushels of winter apples and a barrel of cider, while they are single. To four grandchildren, the children of son John, deceased, £5, each, at ages of twenty-one and eighteen. To sons Gideon and Micah, husbandry tools and rest of personal.

Inventery, £1837, 10*s*., viz: wearing apparel £180, books £10, cider mill and press £30, 4 wheels, old gun, warming pan, 5 cows, 4 yearling cattle, 3 yearlings, 5 swine, 4 geese, mare, &c.

see: American Genealogist, Apr., 1954, v. 30, no. 2, p. 125.

VI. { MERCY, { b. 1685, Oct. 20.
m. { d.
WILLIAM BOWDITCH, { b.
{ d. of Bowditch.

VII. { SARAH, { b.
m. { d.
BENJAMIN GIFFORD, { b.
{ d. of Robert & Sarah (Wing) Gifford.

VIII. { REBECCA, { b.
{ d.

IX. { HANNAH, { b.
m. { d.
TIMOTHY GIFFORD, { b.
{ d. of Robert & Sarah (Wing) Gifford.

1. Timothy,
2. Daniel,
3. Robert,
4. Constant,
5. Hannah,

TORREY.

TORREY. 1st column. Joseph[5] (Philip[4], William[3], Philip[2], William[1]). He was born at Combe, St. Nicholas, Somerset Co. 1621, Jun. 21. His father's will of this date mentions three daughters, Anne, Mary and Sarah, and four sons, William, James, Philip and Joseph. 1634, his mother Alice's will mentions the same children. 1640, he and his brother came to America. He settled first at Weymouth.

{ JOSEPH, { b.
m. { d. 1676.
———— { b.
{ d.

Rehoboth, Mass., Newport, R. I.

1644, Jul. 3. He and twenty-nine others signed a compact for good government.

1647, Mar. 2. He and Obadiah Holmes were released from paying fees of their bonds for good behavior, but not of attending court.

1647–48. Juryman.

1648, Jun. 7. Freeman.

1650, Jun. 5. He and Obadiah Holmes were bound one for the other in the sum of £10, apiece.

1650, Oct. 2. He and wife were presented by Grand Jury for continuing of meeting upon the Lord's day from house to house contrary to the order of this court.

1652, Oct. Newport. Samuel Hubbard writes: "I and my wife had hands laid on us by brother Joseph Torrey."

1653, May 17. Freeman.

1654. General Recorder for Providence and Warwick.

1655. Freeman.

1656–58–59–60–61–62–63. Commissioner.

1661–62–63–64–65–66–69–70–71. General Recorder for the colony.

1664, May 26. He wrote to Samuel Hubbard at Misquamicut (Westerly). "Dear and much respected brother Hubbard and brother Robert and sister Ruth; though your condition be at present a lonesome condition with respect to that fellowship and communion that sometimes you have enjoyed, yet I hope you are under such fruitful seasons with respect to the drops of heaven, that your actions that you are necessitated to be labouring about will put you in mind of that building that shall never decay. The objects your eyes behold are good; it is the spring time, the earth is putting forth its strength, the trees blossom and bud and that which hath long been kept down by the winter cold doth now receive life and vigour; a new form from the shinings of the sun. I hope it is so with your hearts. I rest and remain yours in any service of love in the best relation.
JOSEPH TORREY."

1664–65–66–67–68–69–70–71–72–74. Deputy.

1667, May 13. He and three others were ordered to go forth from house to house throughout Newport and the villages and precincts thereof, to take a precise and exact account of all the arms and ammunition and weapons of war each person is furnished with. At the same date he was on a committee with two others required with all possible speed to mount the great guns on carriages.

He held the office of Lieutenant some years.

1670, Jun. 29. He and two others were allowed the sum of £10, 10*s*., for services as commissioners to Connecticut.

1671, Jan 30. He was allowed £6, 8*s*. 8*d*., for several services.

1671, Dec. 16. A letter from Samuel Hubbard to his children in Westerly, alludes to the differences between those who held Seventh Day views and the rest of the congregation. Mr. Hubbard gave his views in favor, "Brother Torrey said they required not my faith." "They replied fiercely, it was a tumult, J. Torrey stopped them at last."

1671–72. Attorney General.

1676, Nov. 29. In a letter from Samuel Hubbard of Newport, to Dr. Edward Stennett of London, he says: "In the beginning of these troubles of the wars Lieut. Joseph Torrey, elder of Mr. Clarke's church, having but one daughter, living at Squamicut, Misquamicut, and his wife being there, he said unto me—come let us send a boat to Squamicut, my all is there and part of yours. We sent a boat so as his wife, his daughter, and his son-in-law and all their children and my two daughters and their children (one had eight the other three) with an apprentice boy, all came, and brother John Crandall and his family, with as many others as could possibly come," &c.

He alludes to the death of Mr. Torrey as having occurred this year.

I. { DAUGHTER, { b.
m. { d.
———— { b.
{ d. of

TOSH.

WILLLIAM, b. d. 1685.
m.
——— b. d.

New Shoreham, R. I.

1660. He was one of the 16 purchasers of Block Island, the price paid therefor being £400, to John Endicott, Richard Bellingham, Daniel Dennison and William Hawthorne. His name does not appear with those who had lots in first division of lands the subsequent year when the island was settled, but he early came to the island.

1664. Freeman.

1676. Constable.

1684, Aug. 25. Will—proved 1685. Overseers, Robert Guttredge, Simon Ray, Sr., Nathaniel Niles and my son Daniel Tosh. To son Daniel, house I now live in and a double portion of land, with all stock, cattle, swine, horses, &c., till my son William and my son James are of age, and then they equal portions of stock and certain land. To son Daniel, an Indian girl called Abigail, he paying his two sisters Sarah and Catharine, £40. To John Mott and Simon Pulling, 6 acres.

Inventory. 263 acres and house £288, 13 cows, a bull, 4 oxen, 4 two years, a heifer, 14 calves, mare, colt, 30 swine, 50 sheep, gun, Indian servant for life £7, wearing apparel, &c.

I. MERCY, b. d.
m. 1683, Oct. 16.
JOHN MOTT, b. d. of Nathaniel & Hannah ( ) Mott.

1. Anna, 1684, Jan. 9.
2. Anna, 1685, Jan. 8.
3. Sarah, 1688, Jan. 19.

II. SARAH, b. d. 1717 +
m. 1694, Jan. 23.
NATHANIEL MOTT, b. 1657, Dec. 28. d. 1717. of Nathaniel & Hannah ( ) Mott.

1. Sarah, 1694, Dec. 24.
2. Lydia, 1697, Mar. 18.
3. John, 1700, Jan. 1.
4. Bathsheba, 1702, Apr. 24.
5. Experience, 1705, Oct. 27.
6. Nathaniel, 1706, Nov. 25.
7. Edward, 1710, Mar. 19.
8. Miriam, 1712, Jul. 20.

III. ———, b. d.
m.
SIMON PULLING, b. d. of Pulling.

IV. DANIEL, b. 1663, Feb. 13. d. New Shoreham, R. I.
m. 1685, Oct. 19.
MARGERY ACRES, b. 1665, May 24. d. of John & Margery ( ) Acres.

1. Acres, 1687, Apr. 5.
2. Margery, 1689, Apr. 26.
3. Jane, 1691, May 5.
4. Sarah, 1693, Aug. 26.
5. William, 1695, Aug. 26.
6. Elizabeth, 1697, Feb. 19.
7. Martha, 1700, Sep. 8.
8. Mercy, 1703, Jan. 19.

1696. Freeman.

1717, Apr. 28. Testimony was given as to the seizure of his son William Tosh and two others from a boat by the crew of a sloop of which Paulsgrave Williams was commander, she being then in the harbor's bay. In a letter written May 31st by Governor Samuel Cranston to Colonel Shute, he says: "in case the pirate Williams should fall into your Excellency's hands, that the poor men therein mentioned may receive such favour as justice will allow."

V. WILLIAM, b. 1665, Jul 8. d. 1691, Dec. 3. New Shoreham, R. I.
m.
PENELOPE, Niles * b. d. of

1. Daniel.
2. William,
3. Penelope,

(She m. (2) 1695, Dec. 3, Edward Mott.)

He started from Rhode Island in a small sloop for Block Island on a stormy day, and was never heard of—as records tell us.

1691. Administration to widow Penelope. Inventory, £17, 14s. 4d., viz: 8 swine, 50 sheep, gun, cutlass, 1 mare, 1 colt, &c. Real estate £16, dwelling house and 6 acres.

1701, Jan. 21. Agreement between James Tosh of one part and James Danielson and Daniel Tosh, guardians of Penelope Tosh, daughter of William, deceased, an exchange of land being effected.

VI. MARY, b. 1669, May 8. d. young.

VII. CATHARINE, b. 1672, Jan. 10. d.
m. 1704, Jul. 9.
JAMES MOSHER, b. 1675. d. of Hugh & Rebecca (Harndel) Mosher.

1. Daniel, 1705, Oct. 13.

VIII. JOHN, b. 1674, Aug. 12. d. young.

IX. BETHIAH, b. 1676, Sep. d. young.

X. JAMES, b. 1679, Dec. 16. d.

* Deposition of Chisa Billington, R.I.H.S.

TOURTELLOT.

ABRAHAM, b. d.
m.
MARY BERNON, b. d.

of Gabriel & Esther (Le Roy) Bernon.

Bordeaux, France, Roxbury, Mass, Newport, R. I.

He was a merchant and mariner.

1687. He arrived in Boston in ship Friendship, John Ware, commander, from London.

1688, Feb. 23. He was appointed administrator of the estate of his brother Benjamin who died 1687, Sep. 25, on the voyage from London. (He was called a French merchant, and his inventory amounted to £643, 10s. 10d.)

1697. Newport. He went there with his father-in-law.

His two first children were born at Roxbury, and his third probably at Newport.

1699, Jun. 1. He and wife Mary joined in a deed with Gabriel Bernon and wife Esther, and Andrew Faneuil, of Boston, attorney of his brother Benjamin Faneuil, conveying their mansion house at Roxbury and 2½ acres (meadow and orchard), for £110, to Prudence Thompson, now wife of Benjamin Thompson, late of Braintree, now of Roxbury, physician, of her own proper and separate money.

Both he and his son Gabriel were lost at sea while on the way to Newport on a vessel of which he was master.

His widow died at her son Abraham's in Glocester.

There are some indications that he may have made an earlier marriage and had children by a first wife, but if so they evidently did not come with their father to this country.

I. GABRIEL, b. 1694, Sep. 24. d. Newport, R. I.
UNMARRIED,

He was lost at sea with his father, as already noted.

TOURTELLOT. 2d column. II. Esther. **Her husband was son of John and Sarah (Butcher) Harding. Children. 1. Sarah. 2. Esther, 1725, Mar. 8. 3. John.** 4. Stephen. **5. Israel. 6. Benjamin. 7. Henry. 8. Mary.**

II. ESTHER, b. 1696, Jun. 12. d.
m. 1716, Jan. 19.
ISRAEL HARDING, b. d. of John Harding.

III. ABRAHAM, b. d. 1762, Nov. 23. Newport, Glocester, R. I.
m. (1)
LYDIA BALLARD, b. 1700, Mar. 29. d. of Isaac & Dorothy (Hearnden) Ballard.
m. (2) 1743, Jan. 29. [emiah.
HANNAH CORPE (w. of Jer- b. 1713, Nov. 6. d. of William & Elizabeth (Stafford) Case,
m. (3) [of John.
WELTHIAN WILLIAMS (w. b. d. 1770 + of Nehemiah & Rachel (Mann) Sheldon.

1. Mary, 1721, Mar. 20.
2. Lydia, 1723, Jan. 24.
3. Esther, 1723, Jan. 24.
4. Abraham, 1725, Feb. 27.
5. Jonathan, 1728, Sep. 15.
6. Benjamin, 1730, Nov. 30.
7. Sarah, 1735, Apr. 22.
(2d wife.)
8. Stephen,
9. William,
10. Jesse,
11. Daniel,
12. Anne,
(3d wife, no issue.)

(She m. (3) 1770, May 27, Samuel Thurber.)

He was a joiner.

1722. Providence. Freeman.

1722, Mar. 23. He bought of Joseph Hopkins 67 acres, dwelling house, &c., in Providence, for £300.

1724, Jan. 29. He bought of Samuel and Elizabeth Inman a house and 20 acres, for £60.

1724, Jan. 29. He and wife Lydia sold to William Bates 20 acres, where Samuel Inman dwelleth, with house, &c., for £40.

1743, Mar. 14. His wife brought in account of charges and disbursements on account of her administration on estate of Stephen Arnold, Jr., deceased, her former husband, £237, 16s, 8d., including seven years board of Sarah Arnold, daughter of said Stephen, at 8s. per week, £145, 12s.

1744, Aug. 28. Glocester. He was granted a license to keep tavern in house where he dwelleth, for one year, paying 40s. for privilege.

1744, Sep. 18. He and wife Hannah brought in account of her administration on estate of former husband Jeremiah Corpe. (He was an Innholder, and was drowned by falling out of a sloop on the 22d of April, 1741, as the records declare.)

1747. Deputy.

1757, Nov. 19. Will—proved 1763, Apr. 13. Exs. wife Welthian and John Smith, Jr. (son of Solomon). To son Abraham, 10s., he having had his portion. To son Jonathan, 10s. To son Benjamin, half a right in 170 acres. To granddaughter Mary Mitchell, £60, at age or marriage. To daughter Lydia Knowlton, £50. To daughter Esther Dunn, £5. To daughter Sarah Inman, 10s. To daughter Anne Tourtellot, two best beds, silver porringer, all her mother's clothes and her grandmother Tourtellot's clothes, at eighteen or marriage. To son William, 50 acres at age To son Jesse, 50 acres at age. To youngest son Daniel, 50 acres at age. To son Stephen, all the rest of homestead with dwelling house, &c., at age. To wife Welthian, feather bed, all pewter marked W. T., the wearing apparel she brought, £100, and use of east room and north-east bed room while widow, as also use of well, oven and kitchen, table and chairs. At her death or marriage these things and the rooms to be returned to estate. She to be maintained by Stephen when he comes of age. The rest of estate to be sold (both real and personal) and debts paid, &c. Old Tenor money given away to be valued at the passing currency of our Old Tenor now is, or to be valued at the rate of £6, for an ounce of silver. The five youngest children to be brought up at discretion of executors. The witnesses to will testified in a contradictory manner. One declared he was not well and apt to be vapory and another that he was in perfect mind. His sons Abraham and Benjamin prayed an appeal to Governor and Council, and the executors named refusing to take administration it was given to son Abraham.

Inventory, £1385, 18s., viz: books, bed, great table, desk, scales, worsted comb, linen wheel, woolen wheel, loom, warming pan, coffee mill, 5 silver spoons, tankard, gun, joiners' tools, churn, &c.

JOHN, b. 1610. d. 1678.
m.
MARY PAINE, b. d. 1687, Feb. 12.

of Anthony Paine.

(She m. (2) 1682, Apr. 4, Benjamin Engell.)

Portsmouth, R. I.

He was a carpenter.

1638. He was admitted an inhabitant of the island of Aquidneck.

1639, Apr. 30. He signed a compact with twenty-eight others as follows: "We whose names are underwritten do acknowledge ourselves the legal subjects of his Majesty King Charles, and in his name do hereby bind ourselves into a civil body politic, unto his laws according to matters of justice."

1643, Mar. 1. He was granted 3 acres of land next to Thomas Gorton.

1648-54-55-58-61-62-63-64-66-67-68-69-72. Deputy.

1649, Oct. 27. He and wife Mary gave receipt to Rose Weeden, widow of Anthony Paine, for legacy from the will of the latter.

1655. Commissioner.

1655. Freeman.

1657, Nov. 30. He had a grant of land on Hog Island for term of seven years.

1660, Feb. 6. He, calling himself about forty-nine years old, gave testimony that he had heard his uncle Robert Potter say he had sold a certain house and land to John Anthony.

1665, Sep. 8. He deeded son Peleg, one-quarter of a section of land in Dartmouth, formerly bought of John Alden.

1666, Dec. 8. Whereas, Mary Tripp, wife of John Tripp, Sr., some twenty-five years ago bought of Richard Searle for a pint of wine 3 acres of land, the said Richard Searle living then in Portsmouth, she being then unmarried, about which time Searle removed but left no deed to Mary — now therefore said sale is confirmed by commissioners.

1670-73-74-75. Assistant.

1671, May 3. He deeded son Joseph, one-quarter of a section of land in Dartmouth, formerly bought of John Alden.

He was a member of Town Council many years, and held other town offices.

1677, Dec. 6. Will—proved 1678, Oct. 28. Exx. wife Mary. To her all estate, lands, goods and chattels, movable and immovable, during her natural life, "only my old house excepted, or north end of my building which I have given to my son John Tripp formerly." To son John, house and lot, and 10 acres in the Clay Pit field, meadows at Hog Island, all fencing, houses, orchard, &c., "excepting my new house or south end of my building," &c. To son Abiel, south end of building last mentioned with lot adjoining and other land. To son Peleg, £5. To son Joseph, £10. To son James, one-eighth of a share of land at Dartmouth and rights in Narragansett and Westerly. To daughter Martha, £20. To granddaughter Elizabeth Wodell, £10.

1685, Jan. 15. Stephen Manchester and Elizabeth gave receipt for £10, legacy from will of John Tripp to his granddaughter Elizabeth Wodell, who Stephen had married; the said John Tripp's widow and executrix Mary, having married Benjamin Engell and these two last named having delivered the £10, to Peleg Tripp, uncle to Elizabeth, for her use. Receipt was now given for same by Elizabeth, to both her uncle Peleg and Benjamin Engell and Mary.

I. JOHN, b. 1640 ± d. 1719, Nov. 20. Portsmouth, R. I.
m. 1665, Sep. 7.
SUSANNA ANTHONY, b. d. 1716 + of John & Susanna ( ) Anthony.

1716, Sep. 7. Will—proved 1719, Dec. 14. Ex. son John. To son John, all housing and land in Portsmouth, whereon I now dwell, and all lands at Hog Island, he paying his mother Susanna, £4, yearly for life, and paying his brother Lot, £5. To son Benjamin, a bible which he hath already. To son Othniel, biggest pewter basin at death of wife. To son Lot, biggest pewter platter at death of wife. To daughter Susanna Potter, wife of Thomas, my bell metal skillet. To daughter Mary Potter, my brass kettle. To son John, great chest, spit, and dripping pan. To wife Susanna, rest of movables.

Inventory, £9, 14s., viz: apparel, £5, chest, table, 3 chairs, 3 bedsteads, &c.

1. Susanna, 1667, Oct. 31.
2. Mary, 1670, Dec. 9.
3. John, 1673, Jul. 19.
4. Othniel, 1676, Jun. 5.
5. Benjamin, 1678, Feb. 21.
6. Lot, 1684, Dec. 26.

II. PELEG, b. 1642 ± d. 1714 Jan. 13. Dartmouth, Mass., Portsmouth, R. I.
m.
ANNE SISSON, b. d. 1713 + of Richard & Mary ( ) Sisson.

1667. Constable.

1672-73. Surveyor of Highways.

1677-78-79-83. Portsmouth. Town Council.

1680-81-86. Deputy.

1713, Nov. 6. Will—proved 1714, Feb. 8. Exx. wife Anne. Overseer, kinsman William Sanford. To wife, dwelling house and a third of great orchard for life and my garden and £18 yearly for life paid by son Job. To daughter Priscilla Tripp, £15. To daughter Sarah Rogers, £15. To son Job, rest of land where I dwell, he paying rents and legacies and at death of wife he to have other land, great scales, weights and bed. To son Peleg, 5s. To daughter-in-law Sarah Tripp, 1s. To daughter Mary Smith, 10s. To daughter Anne Rogers, 10s., and land in Portsmouth. To daughter Mehitable Thurston, 10s. To daughter Priscilla Tripp, feather bed, &c. To wife Anne, 14 acres. To son Richard land, in Dartmouth, he paying his mother £5, yearly. To wife Anne, rest of movable estate, money, cattle, sheep, swine, household goods, &c. To overseer, 20s.

1. John,
2. Priscilla,
3. Sarah,
4. Job,
5. Peleg,
6. Mary,
7. Ann,
8. Mehitable,
9. Richard,

III. JOSEPH, b. 1644 ± d. 1718, Nov. 27. Portsmouth, R. I., Dartmouth, Mass.
m. 1667, Aug. 6.
MEHITABLE FISH, b. d. of Thomas & Mary ( ) Fish.

1668. Freeman.

1677, Oct. 2. Member of Court of Trials.

1685. Dartmouth. Deputy.

1686-90. Selectman.

1713, Dec. 29. Will—proved 1719, Jan. 6. Ex. son Joseph. To wife Mehitable, £5, per year and her diet and house room for life, with most of the movables in dwelling house. To son Peleg, 3s. To son Ebenezer, £5. To son Abiel, £5. To son Daniel, £20. To daughter Alice Sherman, brass chafing dish. To daughter Mehitable Sherman, a Dutch pewter pot or flagon. To daughter Mary Wait, 10s. To grandson Joseph Tripp, son of Jonathan, £5. To son Joseph, all my homestead, &c.

1. John, 1668, Jul. 6.
2. Thomas, 1670, Mar. 28.
3. Jonathan, 1671, Oct. 5.
4. Peleg, 1673, Nov. 5.
5. Ebenezer, 1675, Dec. 17.
6. James, 1677, Jan. 12.
7. Alice, 1679, Feb. 1.
8. Abiel, 1681, Jan. 8.
9. Mehitable, 1683, Oct. 9.
10. Joseph, 1685, Aug. 24.
11. Jabez, 1687, Nov. 3.
12. Mary, 1689, Aug. 22.
13. Daniel, 1691, Nov. 3.

IV. MARY, b. 1646 ± d. 1716 +
m. (1)
GERSHOM WODELL, b. 1642, Jul. 14. d. of William & Mary ( ) Wodell.
m. (2) 1683, Mar. 5.
JONATHAN GATCHELL, b. d. of Gatchell.

1. William, 1663.
2. Mary,
3. Elizabeth,
4. Richard,
5. Return,
6. Gershom,
7. Sarah,
8. Innocent,

(By 2d husband.)

9. Priscilla, 1683, Nov. 10.
10. Isabel, 1685, Oct. 22.

V. ELIZABETH, b. 1648 ± d. 1701 +
m.
ZURIEL HALL, b. d. 1691 Sep. 5. of William & Mary ( ) Hall.

1. Mary,
2. Zuriel, 1677.
3. Joanna,
4. Benjamin, 1692, Apr. 13.

VI. ALICE, b. 1650 ± d.
m. 1671, Jan. 26.
WILLIAM HALL, b. d. 1698. of William & Mary ( ) Hall.

1. William, 1672, Dec. 2.
2. Preserved, 1675, Aug. 29.
3. Abigail, 1677, Dec. 20.
4. Mary, 1679, Sep. 24.
5. John, 1681, Jul. 2.
6. Deliverance 1683, Jan. 8.
7. Alice, 1685, Jan. 14.
8. Elizabeth, 1687, Oct. 2.
9. Robert, 1690, Feb. 16.

VII. ISABEL, b. 1651 ± d. 1716 (—)
m. 1675, Mar. 4.
SAMSON SHERMAN, b. 1642. d. 1718, Jun. 27. of Philip & Sarah (Odding) Sherman.

1. Philip, 1676, Jan. 16.
2. Sarah, 1677, Sep. 24.
3. Alice, 1680, Jan. 12.
4. Samson, 1682, Jan. 28.
5. Abiel, 1684, Oct. 15.
6. Isabel, 1686 ±
7. Job, 1687, Nov. 8.

VIII. ABIEL, b. 1653 ± d. 1684, Sep. 10. Portsmouth, R. I.
m. 1679 Jan. 30.
DELIVERANCE HALL, b. d. 1721. of William & Mary ( ) Hall.

(She m. (2) Thomas Durfee.)

1678. Freeman.

1678, May 27. He had ear mark for sheep recorded.

1684, Sep. 9. Will—proved 1684, Oct. 1. Exx. wife Deliverance. To son Abiel, all real and personal estate, at death of testator's wife, and at age of sixteen, he to have a cow, and ten sheep, which are to be improved till he is of age. To son, at age, a silver cup, set of silver buttons, pair of silver buttons for breeches, chest marked with brass nails with letters I. T., and a feather bed.

1. Abiel, 1684, Jun. 22.

IX. JAMES, b. 1656 ± d. 1730, May 30. Portsmouth, R. I., Dartmouth, Mass.
m. (1) 1682, Jan. 19.
MERCY LAWTON, b. d. 1685 (—) of George & Elizabeth (Hazard) Lawton.
m. (2)
LYDIA, b. d. of
m. (3) 1702, Aug. 12.
ELIZABETH CUDWORTH, b. d. 1729 + of Cudworth.

1678, Jun. 3. He had ear mark for sheep recorded.

1689. Dartmouth. Ensign.

1702, Aug. 12. His marriage to his third wife took place at his house, though the bride's residence was Scituate.

(2d wife.)

1. John, 1685, Nov. 3.
2. Elizabeth, 1687, Nov. 21.
3. Robert, 1691, May 15.
4. James, 1694, Jul. 17.
5. Mary, 1700, Jan. 9.

(3d wife.)

6. Francis, 1705, Jun. 3.
7. Lydia, 1707, Apr. 30.
8. Thankful, 1709, Mar. 8.
9. Stephen, 1710, Sep. 30.
10. Isabel, 1713, Dec. 31.
11. Israel, 1716, Mar. 22.

1717, Nov. 22. His daughter Mary was married to Daniel Goddard, and her mother Lydia Tripp is mentioned as deceased.

1729, May 10. Will—proved 1730, Jul. 21. Ex. son John. To wife Elizabeth, feather bed, use of five cows and horse, use of housing, profit of half orchard, negro boy Toby, firewood, £5, yearly, and use of all household goods, while widow. To son John, great bible, ivory headed cane and great silver spoon. To daughter Elizabeth Mitchell, son Robert and son James, 5*s.*, each. To son Francis, certain land, he paying to sister Lydia, £10, and to sisters Thankful Taylor and Isabel Tripp, each a like amount. To son Stephen, £100, paid by brother John, and negro boy Toby, when his mother dies and a feather bed. To son Israel, half of 100 acre lot. To daughter Isabel Tripp, a feather bed, good cow, and £10. To four daughters Mary Goddard, Lydia Tripp, Thankful Taylor and Isabel Tripp, household goods at death or marriage of wife. To eldest son John, south half of 100 acre lot, other land and rest of movables.

Inventory, £860, viz: apparel £11, 2 canes, bible, negro boy £100, 5 swine, poultry £4, 18*s.*, 8 cows, heifer, pair of oxen, pair of steers, 3 yearlings, 2 calves, real estate £500, &c.

X. MARTHA, b. 1658 ±, d. 1717 +
m. 1681, Feb. 23.
SAMUEL SHERMAN, b. 1648. d. 1717, Oct. 9. of Philip & Sarah (Odding) Sherman.

1. Sarah, 1682, Apr. 10.
2. Mary, 1683, Dec. 1.
3. Mehitable, 1685, May 8
4. Samuel, 1687, Jan. 12.
5. Othniel, 1689, Jan. 29.
6. John, 1696, Mar. 28.
7. Ebenezer, 1701, Oct. 10.
8. Martha,
9. Rebecca,

TURNER.

LAWRENCE, b. d.
m.
——— b. d.

Newport, R. I.

1656. Freeman.
1664. General Solicitor.
1680. Taxed £1, 13*s.* 10*d.*
1687. Overseer of the Poor.
1688. Grand Jury.
1691. Deputy.
1702, Mar. 4. He was a proprietor in common lands.

See: American Genealogist. V. 20, p. 118.

I. LAWRENCE, b. d. Newport, R. I.
m.
——— b. d. of

1690. Freeman.
1723, Nov. 24. His daughter Phebe married James Coggeshall[4] (Joshua[3], Joshua[2], John[1]).

1. Phebe.

TURPIN.

TURPIN. 1st column. I. William. His daughter Catharine b. 1719, Oct. 25.

WILLIAM, b. d. 1709, Jul. 18.
m. (1)
——— b. d.
m. (2)
ANN, b. d. 1716 +

Providence, R. I.

He was a schoolmaster and also kept a public house.

1684, Jun. 11. He made a contract with William Hawkins for the schooling of Peregrine Gardiner (the stepson of Hawkins).

1685, Jan. 27. He petitioned the town for a parcel of land formerly granted for the use and benefit of a schoolmaster "which said order or grant was read to me in the presence of several gentlemen that were the occasion of my settling at this town, who promised to be instrumental in the performance thereof," &c.

He desired that the land should be conferred on him and his heirs "so long as he or any of them shall maintain that worthy art of learning."

1687, Sep. 14. He was forbidden to sell any strong drink by retail till bond was given according to law.

1687, Dec. 14. Not appearing to take license, it was ordered that he be suspended from keeping a victualling house or selling ale, beer, liquor or other strong drink by retail, on penalty by law provided.

1695. Constable.

1696, Jan. 27. He and others having requested of the town to be accommodated with a small spot of land for a school house, they were granted a lot forty feet square if they would build a school house in some considerable time.

1709, Jul. 29. Administration was refused by widow Ann, who presented inventory of his estate, and one of the council, viz: Jonathan Sprague, took administration the next month.

1710, Dec. 11. His widow Ann was licensed to keep a public house and sell liquors, she paying 20*s.* for the privilege.

1711, Aug. 9. His son having arrived at age and entered into possession of house and lands, and he and the widow, and the two daughters Anne and Persis, calling for their part of the movables the which each one has now received, and said son William having given bonds for debts that may appear, the following division was recorded: To widow, £102, 4*s.* 4*d.*, and to each child, £68, 2*s.* 11*d.*, making a total of £306, 13*s.* 1*d.*

1711, Aug. 19. An agreement was made between the widow Ann, and the heir William Turpin. She made over the house, land, cattle, &c. to him, and he agreed with his mother-in-law (*i. e.* stepmother), his deceased father's widow,

I. WILLIAM, b. 1690. d. 1744, Mar. 15. Providence, R. I.
m.
CATHARINE JENCKES, b. 1694. d. 1782. of Joseph & Martha (Brown) Jenckes.

He was an innkeeper.

1711, Aug. 9. He was licensed to keep a house of entertainment at his residence.
1712, May 6. Freeman.
1717, Jul. 15. He sold two-thirds of a right of common to William Brooks, for £11, 6*s.* 8*d.*
1722–23–29. Deputy.
1727. Town Council.
1727, Jul. 27. He was appointed by the town to repair the pound, stocks and whipping post.
1736. His son William died this year.
1737–38–39–40–41–42–43–44. Town Treasurer.

1744, Mar. 12. Will—proved 1744, Apr. 2. Exx. wife Catharine. To son John, lands on westerly side of the Seven Mile Line and rights in certain land held in partnership with brother Captain Nathaniel Jenckes, &c. To wife, full benefit of homestead and dwelling house till son Joseph is of age, and then she to release half to him, retaining the other half while widow, and she also to have £500. To son Joseph, half of homestead at age and the other half at marriage or death of his mother, and to him also other lands. To daughters Elizabeth Smith, Martha Metcalf and Catharine Hopkins, each £5. To daughters Anne, Esther, Lydia and Mary, £105, each, at age. To seven daughters rest of movables.

Inventory, £3255, 18*s.* 8*d.*, viz: negro boy £60, negro woman and child £40, 3 horsekind, 15 head of cattle, 5 swine, carpenter's tools, 3 feather beds, spoons and other plate £30, 2*s.*, books £3, 5*s.*, piece of gold £2, 17*s.*, copper money £4, 19*s.* 6*d.*, bonds £10, 17*s.* 11*d.*, 4 punch bowls, 2 warming pans, pewter, stock of shop goods, as buckram, broad cloth, garlic, spice, indigo, mohair, 8500 shoe nails, 1500 clap board nails, &c. Mention was made of the slaughter house and salt house.

1782, Jul. 18. Administration on estate of widow Catharine Turpin was given to widow Elizabeth Allen.

1. John,
2. Elizabeth, 1715,
3. William, 1716,
4. Martha,
5. Catharine,
6. Joseph,
7. Anne,
8. Esther,
9. Lydia,
10. Mary,

II. ANNE, b. d.

III. PERSIS, b. d.
m. (1)
WILLIAM BROOKS, b. d. 1727, Oct. 19. of Brooks.
m. (2) 1734, Oct. 31.
JAMES KING, b. d. 1756, Nov. 19. of Clement & Elizabeth ( ) King.

to give her the use and command of a room on the north side of the house for life, together with a good bedstead, feather bed, bolster, two pairs of sheets, pair of blankets, two good pillows, two pillow beeres, and a good coverlid, and to keep and maintain her in good and sufficient meat, drink and washing, with benefit of the fire to go to and from it and abide by it, and make use of it. He was also to pay her £40, within four years, in silver, £10, each year till paid. If she had a physician it was to be at her own charge.

1715, Sep. 10. The widow (calling herself formerly Anna Pratt) deeded land to her grandson Job Beers, to be his when he came of age.

1716, Jan. 9. She gave rceeipt to stepson for the bed and £40.

TYLER.

JOHN, b. d. 1700.
m.
SARAH HAVENS, b. d. 1718 +

of William & Dionis ( ) Havens.

Portsmouth, R. I.

1655, Jul. 8. He bought of Matthew Grinnell, a dwelling house and 13 acres.

1672, May 1. Freeman.

1697, Feb. 17. Will—proved 1700, Apr. 10. Exs. friends Benjamin Hall and George Brownell. To son Lazarus and male heirs all right of lands at Misquamicut, and also 1*s.*, to said son Lazarus. To grandson William Tyler, all land in Portsmouth, to him and male heirs, so to remain in name of Tylers, (except 5 acres in possession of Benjamin Potter), but wife Sarah, to have benefit of house and land whereon I dwell, for life, and at her decease to the said William Tyler. To daughter Miriam Tyler, use of about 5 acres for life, and then to grandson William, and to Miriam also a feather bed, mare, &c. To daughter Tamar, wife of Robert Cook, 10*s.*, and what sheep her husband hath in possession. To daughter Question, wife of John Inion, 10*s.*, per year, and to daughter Friendship Tyler, 10*s.*, per year, for their lives, to be paid by those who possess land where I dwell. To executors, rest of movables for the comfortable maintenance of my wife.

1718, Aug. 2. His widow Sarah Tyler, of Preston, Conn., deeded to grandson John Tyler, of East Greenwich, R. I., for love, &c., all her interest in housing and lands in Portsmouth, of late husband.

I. LAZARUS, b. d. — Preston, Conn.
m.
———, b. d. of

1718, Mar. 15. The will of William Tyler, of Bristol, (evidently son of Lazarus), which was proved 1718, Apr. 14, names his brother John, of Warwick, wife Rebecca, sister Rebecca Havens, wife of Robert Havens, and grandmother Sarah Havens.

1718, Aug. 2. He (Lazarus of Preston), deeded to son John Tyler, of East Greenwich, all right in housing and lands that my honoured father John Tyler, of Portsmouth, deceased, died possessed of.

1719, Mar. 4. He, of Preston, and John Tyler, of East Greenwich, sold to Nathaniel Hall, 3 acres in Portsmouth, for £220.

1723, Mar. 14. John Tyler, of Voluntown, Ct. (evidently son of Lazarus) sold to Joseph Dennis, of Portsmouth, 6 acres in Portsmouth, for £60. At same date Miriam Tyler *alias* Bettys, of Portsmouth, daughter of late deceased John Tyler, of Portsmouth, deeded all her interest in above land for the payment of £13, by said John Tyler, of Voluntown.

Children (of Lazarus): 1. William, 2. John, 3. Rebecca,

II. MIRIAM, b. d.
m.
——— BETTYS, b. d. of Bettys.

III. TAMAR, b. d.
m. 1678, Dec. 5.
ROBERT COOK, b. d. of Cook

IV. QUESTION, b. d.
m.
JOHN INION, b. d. of Inion.

V. FRIENDSHIP, b. d.

UNDERWOOD.

HENRY, b. d.
m.
JANE, b. d. 1710 +

Newport, R. I.

His three first children were born at Newport.

1673. Jamestown. Freeman.

He probably returned to Newport, sometime before his death.

1710, Jul. 19. His widow Jane, had a maintenance for life given her by the will of her son-in-law John Weeden, who calls her his "loving mother-in-law."

I. HENRY, b. 1667, Nov. 31. d. 1733. — Newport, R. I.
UNMARRIED,

1733, Nov. 23. He bought of Teddeman Hull and wife Sarah, 40 acres at Jamestown, for £750.

II. JANE, b. 1669, Mar. 17. d. 1736.
m.
JOHN WEEDEN, b. d. 1710, Aug. 26. of William Weeden.

1. John,	1687, Nov. 9.
2. Sarah,	1690, Apr. 25.
3. Jane,	1693, Mar. 1.
4. Daniel,	1696.
5. Hannah,	1699, Apr. 14.

III. WILLIAM, b. 1671, May 24. d. 1744 (—) — Jamestown, Newport, R. I.
m.
SARAH, b. d. of

1. William,	1694, Mar. 14.
2. Sarah,	1698, Sep. 7.
3. Thomas,	
4. Daughter,	1703, Oct. 27.
5. Tamsen,	
6. Henry,	1707, Nov. 29.

He was an Innholder.

1705, Apr. 17. First Constable.

1705–14. Town Sergeant.

1716, May 16. He and wife Sarah, had a deed of an acre of land from Mercy Paine, of Jamestown, widow of Thomas Paine, for consideration "best known to self." The land was to be William Underwood's for life, and to his wife Sarah, for life, if she survived him, and while she remained his widow, and then to return to grantor.

1734, Jan. 6. Newport. He, calling himself Innholder, sold Teddeman Hull, of Jamestown, practitioner of physic, 40 acres there, being land that came to William, as heir at law of Henry Underwood, who died intestate and who had made an indenture of said land (between Teddeman Hull and wife Sarah and Henry Underwood), the land having been sold to Henry, for £750, but money never paid.

IV. JOHN, b. 1673, Aug. 3. d. 1737. — Jamestown, R. I.
m.
SARAH PECKHAM, b. d. 1737 (—) of Thomas Peckham.

1. John,	1699, Feb. 28.
2. Joseph,	1701, Sep. 8.
3. Daniel,	1703, Feb. 27.
4. Philip,	
5. George,	
6. Mary,	
7. Tamsen,	

1698, Apr. 19. First Constable.

1703. Freeman.

1714, Apr. 20. Viewer of highways.

1715–17–20–26. Deputy.

1737, Apr. 7. Administration to oldest surviving son Joseph.

Inventory, £1,464, 15*s.*, 6*d.*, viz: wearing apparel, old books, feather beds, warming pan, 4 cheese fats, silver money and plate 17½ oz. £23, 7*s.*, 6*d.*, mare, colt, 6 cows, 112 sheep, 5 hogs, 2 turkeys, 3 geese, negro Peter £120, bonds due from Joseph and Daniel Underwood, &c.

1739, Oct. 11. The will of his son George (proved 1739, Nov. 7), mentions brothers Joseph, Philip, and Daniel, sister Mary, deceased, and nephew John, son of brother Philip and niece Tamsen Pugh. He directs graves to be put for himself, his father and sister Mary.

UNTHANK.

CHRISTOPHER, b. d. 1680 +
m.
SUSANNA, b. d. 1680 +

Providence, Warwick, R. I.

1640, Jul. 27. He and thirty-eight others signed an agreement for a form of government.

1646, Sep. 21. He bought a house and lot of William Wickenden.

1648, Jun. 5. Warwick. His name was recorded as an inhabitant.

1655. Freeman.

1671, Jul. 13. He sold to Joshua Winsor, of Providence, certain land there for a valuable sum.

1677, Sep. 1. He and wife Susanna, for love, &c., sold son-in-law Job Almy, certain land. (He calls himself of Portsmouth, but soon returned to Warwick.)

1680, Feb. 8. He and wife Susanna, sold to Joseph Carder, two 6 acre lots for £29, with improvements, only reserving land where some relations are buried with liberty to entomb therein.

I. MARY, b. d. 1724 +
m. (1)
JOB ALMY, b. d. 1684. of William & Audry ( ) Almy.
m. (2)
THOMAS TOWNSEND, b. d. of John & Elizabeth ( ) Townsend.

1. William, 1664, Jan. 20.
2. Christopher 1664, Jan. 20.
3. William, 1665, Sep. 5.
4. Susanna, 1667, Jan. 29.
5. Audrey, 1669, Apr. 5.
6. Deborah, 1671, Aug. 5.
7. Catharine, 1674, Jan. 22.
8. John, 1676, Jan. 25.
9. Mary, 1678, Sep. 6.
10. Job, 1681, Mar. 3.
11. Anthony, 1683, Mar. 24

UTTER.

NICHOLAS, b. d. 1722.
m. (1)
———— b. d.
m. (2)
ELIZABETH, (widow) b. d. 1722 +

Kings Town, Westerly, R. I., Stonington, Ct.

1687, Sep. 6. Taxed 3s., 2½d.

1709, Jun. 28. He, with his sons Nicholas, Thomas and William, were concerned with others in the purchase of a tract called Shannock Purchase.

1711, Feb. 28. He bought of Samuel Tefft and twenty-one others two tracts of land in Westerly, one containing 286 acres and the other 156 acres.

1711, May 29. Westerly. He sold for £200, to his son Nicholas 286 acres on Pawcatuck river.

1722, May 5. Will—proved 1722, Aug. 17. Exs. Peter Crandall, John Maxson and John Richmond. To wife Elizabeth, a bed, small iron kettle, two small iron pots, three pewter platters, two cows and £10, per year; all in lieu of dower. To "my brethren the First Day Baptists at Groton or belonging to that meeting, £20, for the use of that meeting." To daughter-in-law Eleanor Randall, wife of Matthew, £10. To well beloved friend John Richmond, £5. To oldest son Jabez Utter, one-seventh of rest of estate both real and personal. To second son Thomas, two-sevenths. To sons Nicholas and William and daughter Millicent Yeomans, one-seventh, each. To children of daughter Sarah Forman, the other seventh. The double share to son Thomas was given because of his care in looking after his father in his old age.

He desired that his daughter Millicent would give her share to one of her children as she might choose.

I. JABEZ, b. d. Canterbury, Ct.
m.
MARY, b. d. of

1717, Mar. He had a suit brought against him by Samuel Rogers of New London, the damage being set at £6.

II. THOMAS, b. d. 1726. Stonington, Ct.
m.
———— b. d. of

UTTER. 2d column. II. Thomas. His wife's mother was Bethiah Wilcox.

1726. Administration on his estate was given to his son John Utter, of Preston, Ct.

1. John, 1703, Jun. 29.
2. Thomas, 1705, Sep. 1.
3. Desire, 1707, Nov. 13.
4. Benjamin, 1709, Nov. 24.
5. Thankful, 1717, May 9.
6. William, 1719, Nov. 8.

III. NICHOLAS, b. d. Kings Town. R. I.

1704. He had ear mark granted.

UTTER. 2d column. II. Thomas. His wife was daughter of Gershom & Bethiah ( ) Cottrell. 1719, Aug. 3. He appeared on behalf of his wife in regard to administration on estate of her brother Gershom Cottrell.

IV. MILLICENT, b. d.
m. 1693 ±
JOHN YEOMANS, b. d. of Yeomans.

1. Thomas, 1695, Mar. 28.
2. John, 1696 ±
3. Mabel, 1698, Feb. 25.
4. Sarah, 1700, Mar. 21.
5. Elisha, 1702, Apr. 23.
6. Elizabeth, 1704, Aug. 21.
7. Millicent, 1707, Apr. 1.
8. Elijah, 1710, Sep. 25.
9. Mary, 1711, Sep. 26.
10. Ebenezer, 1714, Jun. 2.
11. Mabel, 1719 ±

V. SARAH, b. d. 1722 (—)
m.
———— FORMAN, b. d. of Forman.

VI. WILLIAM, b. 1679. d. 1761, Jun. Kings Town, Warwick, R. I.
m. 1705, Sep. 27.
ANNE STONE, b. 1682. d. 1762. of Hugh & Abigail (Busecot) Stone.

1. Sarah, 1707, Aug. 1.
2. William, 1709.
3. Alice, 1711, Sep. 27.
4. Ruth,
5. Zebulon, 1724.
6. Anne, 1725, Oct. 28.

1709, Jun. 28. He was concerned in the Shannock Purchase.

1711, Feb. 26. He bought 100 acres in Warwick, for £60, of Thomas Greene.

1716. Freeman.

1722, Jul 28. He bought of William and Patience Smith, of Kings Town, 25 acres in Warwick, for £12.

1723. Warwick. He went thence about this time.

1731, Aug. 17. He bought of Amos Stafford, 19 acres and 152 rods for £60.

1733, Nov. 27. He bought of Josiah Arnold and Elizabeth, 56 acres with all the buildings, &c., for £350.

1735, Oct. 27. He deeded son William, for love, &c., three lots of land in lower division south of place called "Jenk's wading place."

1746. He took administration on his son William Utter, Jr.'s, estate.

1750, Jun. 5. Will—proved 1761, Jun. 15. Exx. wife Ann. To wife all personal estate absolutely, and half the real estate for life. To son Zebulon, half the real estate and other half at death of wife, he paying legacies. To daughters Sarah, Ruth and Anne, £10, each. To Barbara and Sarah, daughters of son William, deceased, 20s., each.

1761, Jun. 17. Will—proved 1763, Jun. 14. Widow Anna. Ex. son-in-law Amos Lockwood. To grandson William Reynolds, son of daughter Anne, £50. To wife of Zebulon Utter, £20. To daughter Ruth, £20. To granddaughter Ann Reynolds, £30. To granddaughters Barbara and Sarah Utter, 20s., each. To son Zebulon, cash and farm tackling. To daughters Sarah Lockwood and Ann Reynolds, rest of estate equally.

He and his wife, and others of his family, were buried in the family burial ground, one and a half miles south of Pawtuxet Bridge.

VAUGHAN (WILLIAM).

WILLIAM, b. d. 1677.
m. [of Jeremiah
FRANCES CLARKE (w. b. d. 1677, Sep.
of Lewis Latham.

Newport, R. I.

1648, Oct. 12. He was one of the twelve members of First Baptist Church in full communion. He was ordained this year it is said.

1655. Freeman.

1656. He and Thomas Baker and others separated from the First Baptist Church and organized a new society, known as the Second

No issue.

Baptist Church. The reasons therefor are thus stated. "Said persons conceived a prejudice against psalmody and against the restraints that the liberty of prophesying was laid under and also against the doctrine of particular redemption, and against the rite of laying on of hands as a matter of indifference."

1656, Jan. 18. His wife entered into an agreement with her son Walter Clarke, through his guardians John Cranston and James Barker. Her son was to have dwelling house where Mrs. Vaughan lived, garden, orchard, &c., which was his inheritance, but possession to be had by his mother till September 29th or till tobacco was cured. The house where Captain John Cranston lived was to be his, as appeared by deed. Mrs. Vaughan was to pay all debts, and for that purpose had half of a house which she was to sell, and she also had certain land, the household goods, &c., for herself and the rest of the children of Jeremiah Clarke, other than Walter.

1673, Nov. 8. Samuel Hubbard notes under this date: "This week two of Christ Church called Mr. Vahan departed: to wit John Turner and Jeremy Osborne, schoolmaster. Lord prepare all."

1676, Apr. 4. It was voted by Assembly: "That in these troublesome times and straits in this Colony, this Assembly desiring to have the advice and concurrence of the most judicious inhabitants if it may be had for the good of the whole, do desire at their next sitting the company and counsel of"—sixteen persons, among them, William Vaughan.

1677, Sep. 2. In a letter of this date from Samuel Hubbard, of Newport, to his children at Westerly, he says: "For news, Mr. Vahan is gone to his long home and his wife is like to follow him if not dead."

His widow was buried in Newport Cemetery, the stone bearing the following inscription. "Here Lyeth ye Body of Mrs. Frances Vaughan, Alius Clarke, ye mother of ye only children of Capt'n Jeremiah Clarke. She died ye 1 week in Sept., 1677, in ye 67th year of her age."

VERIN.

JOSHUA[2], (Philip[1]),	b. d 1695.
m. (1) JANE,	b. d.
m. (2) AGNES,	b. d.1719 +

(She m. (2) Thomas King.)

Salisbury, Wilts Co., Eng., Providence, R. I. Barbadoes, W. I.

He was a roper.

1635. Salem. He came in ship James, from Southampton. He was granted a house lot of 2 acres this year.

1636. Providence. He came with Roger Williams and four others, and made settlement earlier than July of this year, having spent the preceding winter at Seekonk.

1638, May 21. "It was agreed that Joshua Verin upon the breach of a covenant for restraining of the liberty of conscience shall be withheld from the liberty of voting till he shall declare the contrary." He had refused to let his wife attend meeting for worship as often as she wished, and after much discussion and controversy among the settlers, the foregoing vote was passed.

1638, May 22. The above matter is alluded to in a letter from Roger Williams to Governor John Winthrop. "Sir: we have been long afflicted by a young man boisterous and desperate, Philip Verin's son of Salem, who as he hath refused to hear the word with us (which we molested him not for), this twelve month, so because he could not draw his wife, a gracious and modest woman, to the same ungodliness with him, he hath trodden her under foot tyrannically and brutishly; which she and we long bearing, though with his furious blows she went in danger of life, at the last the major vote of us discard him from our civil freedom, or disfranchise him," &c.

1638. Salem. He was granted 10 acres.

1640, Jan. 21. He was granted 40 acres.

1640, Jun. 21. His wife Jane, joined the church.

1640, Sep. 30. He obtained judgment against Richard Ingersoll.

1650, Nov. 21. He wrote to the town of Providence. "Gentlemen and countrymen of the whole town of Providence. This is to certify you that I look upon my purchase of the town of Providence to be my lawful right. In my travel I have inquired and find it recoverable according to law, for my coming away could not disinherit me. Some of you cannot but recollect that we six which came first should have the first convenience," &c. He closes thus: "Therefore deal not worse with me than

No issue.

VERIN. 1st column. His widow Agnes, m. 2d, John Drake, m., 3d, Thomas King. 1724, Aug. 13 Recorded at Boston. "Agnes, widow of Thomas King of the Parish of St. James, in the island of Barbadoes, planter who was heretofore the wife of Joshua Verin, planter, deceased, and after his decease became the wife of John Drake, planter, deceased, and after the death of said Drake married said King; appointed Edward Oxnard, of St. Michael, in Barbadoes, merchant, who was about to sail for North America, her attorney, &c., to enter upon all lands belonging to the said Agnes in the Colony of Rhode Island and Providence Plantations."

we dealt with the Indians, for we made answer by purchasing it of them, and hazarded our lives. So hoping you will take it into your serious consideration and to give me reasonable satisfaction, I rest yours in the way of right and equity. Joshua Verin."

1651, Apr. 27. The town answered him that if he came into court and proved his right they should do him justice.

1663, Sep. 28. Barbadoes. He having sent unto William Harris to demand in his behalf a right of land, the answer of the town was that they do own he has a right, and what he can make appear to be yet in his hands, not being passed away by sale unto any other, he may have it laid out unto him, &c.

1675, Jan. 28. "Laid out to John Whipple, Jr., attorney unto Joshua Verin, in the right of the said Verin, now of Barbadoes," &c., 94 acres, being part of his purchase right in the first division, "the other part being his house lot and one share of salt meadow which he sold unto Mr. Richard Scott," &c.

1688, May 3. He, of Parish of St. James, freed a negro slave, named John Ansepa "born in my house at Barbadoes and by me sent for New England unto my brother Hilliard Verin." (His brother Hilliard died 1683, Dec. 20, aged sixty-three, and the slave had returned to Barbadoes.)

1695, May 15. Will—proved 1695, Dec. Exx. wife Agnes. Trustees, William Holder, Francis McKennie. To wife half of all estate, real and personal, and to each child she shall go with, the remaining half. In default of a child the said half to go to children of my cousin (*i. e.* nephew) Timothy Lindall, and children of my cousin (*i. e.* niece) Mary Williams, widow. Out of the above the sum of £5, was to be paid to the children of John Balch, £5, to Verin Parkman, and £25, to cousin Dorcas Verin. To each trustee a guinea for a ring.

Timothy Lindall, who is mentioned in the will, married 1673, Feb. 7, Mary Verin, daughter of Nathaniel Verin, and Samuel Williams married 1662, Apr. 2, Mary Verin, daughter of Hilliard. Both Nathaniel and Hilliard were brothers of Joshua Verin.

1704, May 17. Samuel Williams, of Salem, sold to John Whipple, of Providence, for £12, all right of land there which formerly belonged to Joshua Verin, excepting only the house lot or home share of 5 acres, and 3 acres of salt marsh.

1715, Apr. 29. Joshua Rainer and wife Sarah, Joshua Williams and Mary Hole, widow, all of Boston, children of Mary Williams, late of Salem, widow, deceased, who was niece to Joshua Verin, of Barbadoes, deceased, sold for £6, to Timothy Lindall, of Boston, all their interest in Providence lands to which they were heirs.

1719, Mar. 25. His widow and executrix Agnes King, of Barbadoes, with her husband Thomas King, gave a power of attorney to William Brown, of Boston, to sell certain land in Providence, and two years later (1721, Jun. 26), the said William Brown sold half of two lots of 94 acres and 70 acres respectively, to William Antram, for £75.

See: American Genealogist, v. 20, p. 118.

VINCENT.

WILLIAM, { b. d. 1695.
m. (1) 1670, May 31.
PRISCILLA CARPENTER, { b. d. 1690 +
of William & Elizabeth (Arnold) Carpenter.
m. (2)
JEMIMA, { b. d.

Providence, R. I.

He was a cooper.

His mother was Fridgswith, sister of William Carpenter, of Providence, and perhaps she sent over her children William and Joan to the care of their uncle in America.

1660. His sister Joan married John Sheldon.

1661, Feb. 5. He had a deed of 64 acres from his uncle William Carpenter, who calls him cousin (*i. e.* nephew).

1666, May. He took oath of allegiance.

1671, Dec. 14. His mother Fridgswith Vincent, of Amesbury (Wiltshire, Eng.), had a deed from her brother William Carpenter of Providence, of a house in Frog Lane, Amesbury, the same being a free gift to her from her brother.

1679, Jul. 1. Taxed 4*s.*, 4½*d.*

1687, Sep. 1. Taxed 6*s.*, 1*d.*

1688. Ratable estate, 6 cows, 2 oxen, 3 yearling heifers, 3 horses, 2 colts, 4 hogs, 4 acres planting, 8 acres meadow, 10 acres wild pasture, 1 lot of land thrown out.

1690, Nov. 15. He and wife Priscilla, sold Timothy Carpenter, a parcel of meadow on

I. THOMAS, { b. d. — Providence, R. I.

1713, Sep. 18. He sold to Thomas Olney, half a warehouse lot for £4, 15*s.*

1722. Freeman.

VINCENT. 2d column. II. Nicholas, m. (according to family account) Elizabeth Reynolds, daughter of John Reynolds, of North Kingstown. III William. He married and settled in Gloucester, R. I., it is said

II. NICHOLAS, { b. d. 1749.
m.
ELIZABETH, { b. d. 1749 +
of — Westerly R. I.

He was a cordwainer.

1724, Sep. 6. Westerly. He and wife Elizabeth, sold to brother William of Providence, for £21, certain land there.

1725, Jun. 8. He, of Westerly, and William Vincent, of Providence, for £4, sold Robert Currie, of Providence, half a thatch right in Providence.

1749, Feb. 25. Will—proved 1749, Apr. 24. Exx. wife Elizabeth. To son Nicholas, lands and buildings, two cows and a riding horse (reserving to wife Elizabeth, profits of same for life). To son Nicholas, also all husbandry tools, he doing for our lives all husbandry work needful and we to have profits. To wife Elizabeth, all household goods. To daughter Jemima, son William, daughters Mary, Mercy, son Joseph, daughters Elizabeth, Deborah, Hannah and son Joshua, each, 5*s.*

Inventory, £485, 9*s.*, viz: apparel £31, 5*s.*, stillyards, 3 swine, horses, 2 cows, money due £34, &c.

1. Nicholas,
2. Jemima,
3. William,
4. Mary,
5. Mercy,
6. Joseph,
7. Elizabeth,
8. Deborah,
9. Hannah,
10. Joshua,

III. WILLIAM, { b. d.
m. 1724, Oct. 22.
ELIZABETH BENNETT, { b. d.
of — Bennett. — Providence, R. I.

He was a cordwainer.

1726, Mar. 8. He and wife Elizabeth, sold to Richard Sayles, 67 acres at Locosqusset, in northerly part of Providence, dwelling house, &c., for £70, paid, and £150, to be paid.

1729. Warwick. Freeman.

Mashapauge Brook which was by father-in-law William Carpenter deeded to Priscilla.

1695, Dec. 21. Will—proved 1696, Mar. 3. Exx. wife Jemima. To her 98 acres at Sichotonconett Hill, a half right of commons and 5 acres of meadow east of now dwelling, all of which with house and movables at her decease to go to three sons, Thomas, Nicholas and the youngest, and son William to dwell with wife till of age. To son William, a bed, a heifer calf, 5 sheep, and shortest gun. To sons Thomas and William, all tools divided equally.

Inventory, £63, 2*s.*, viz: wearing apparel of his own £4, 6*s.*, wearing apparel of William Vincent, Jr., £2, 13*s.*, 3 beds, pewter, 2 guns, sword, books, 2 wheels, sheep £7, cowkind £14, horsekind £3, swine, £3, cider, &c.

WALKER.

JOHN, b. d. 1647 ±
m.
KATHARINE, b. d. 1654 ±

Boston, Mass., Portsmouth, R. I.

1634, May 14. Freeman.

1637, Nov. 20. He and others were warned to deliver up all guns, pistols, swords, powder, shot, &c., because "the opinions and revelations of Mr. Wheelwright and Mrs. Hutchinson have seduced and led into dangerous error many of the people here in New England."

1638, Mar. 7. Portsmouth. He and eighteen others signed the following compact: "We whose names are underwritten do here solemnly in the presence of Jehovah incorporate ourselves into a Bodie Politicke, and as he shall help will submit our persons, lives and estates unto our Lord Jesus Christ, the King of Kings and Lord of Lords, and to all those perfect and most absolute laws of his given us in his holy word of truth, to be guided and judged thereby."

1638, May 13. He was present at a General Meeting held upon public notice.

1647, Mar. 18. Will—(recorded 1671, Dec. 16). Exx. wife Katharine. To daughter Mary, 20 acres at marriage or twenty years of age. To daughter Sands, 20 acres, and if she die childless her husband James Sands to have it. To wife, house for life and then to two daughters equally.

1671, Dec. 16. Will—recorded. Widow Katharine. Exs. two daughters. Overseers, William Freeborn and Adam Mott. To daughter Sarah Sands, feather bed, warming pan, brass kettle, &c., red cow, brown heifer, this summer's calf and ½ the new out-house (and Mary to give her 30*s.* for her part). To James Sands, 3 wedges. To daughter Mary, rest of bedding, pewter, brass kettle, chafing dish, &c., sow and barrow. Sarah also to have a sow and barrow. To goodman Freeborn, a green jacket. To daughter Mary, also, a black cow, red heifer, &c. The things to be divided within three days or a week.

1654, Apr. 2. At this date William and Mary Earle deeded James Sands, all right in 14 acres of land that had come to Mary in right of her mother the late widow Walker.

I. SARAH, b. d. 1709.
m.
JAMES SANDS, b. 1622. d. 1695, Mar. 13. of Sands.

1. John, 1652,
2. Sarah,
3. Mercy,
4. James,
5. Samuel,
6. Edward, 1672,

II. MARY, b. d.
m.
WILLIAM EARLE, b. d. 1715, Jan. 15. of Ralph & Joan ( ) Earle.

1. Mary, 1655,
2. William,
3. Thomas,
4. Ralph, 1660,
5. Caleb,

WALLING.

THOMAS, b. d. 1674, Jul. 19.
m. (1)
MARY ABBOTT, b. d. 1669.
of Daniel & Mary ( ) Abbott.
m. (2) 1669, Jun. 19. [Rob't.
MARGARET COLWELL (div. b. d. 1717 +
of White.

(She m. (3) 1678, Dec. 25. Daniel Abbott.)

Providence, R. I.

1651, Jan. 22. He is alluded to probably in a letter of this date from Roger Williams at Narragansett to the town of Providence. "I understand that one of the orphans of our dead friend Daniel Abbott is likely (as she herself told me) to be disposed of in marriage. 'Tis true she is now come to some years, but who knows not what need the poor maid hath of your fatherly care, counsel and direction. I would not disparage the young man (for I hear he hath been laborious)," &c. He desires the town however to have some assurance that the young man will "forsake his former courses."

1651, Jul 28. He was received as a townsman.

1655. Freeman.

1657. Commissioner.

1657, Jan. 25. He sold to Richard Pray a home share of land.

I. THOMAS, b. d. Providence, R. I., Cohansey, N. J.
m. 1695, May 20.
SARAH ELWELL, b. d. of Elwell.

1676, Aug. 14. He was one of those "who staid and went not away" in King Philip's War, and so had a share in the disposition of Indian captives whose services were sold for a term of years.

1687, Sep. 1. Taxed 1*s.* 10*d.*

1687. Ratable estate, 3 cows, a steer, 4 acres enclosed land, 1½ acres tillable, ⅓ share of meadow.

1718, Jan. 7. He brought in account as administrator of brother John, showing that he had paid his brother James £13, 16*s.*, as legacy, and that he had remaining £9, 8*s.* 10*d.*, whereupon it was voted that Thomas keep it for his part.

1718, Feb. 17. Cohansey (county of Salem, West New Jersey). He sold Thomas Olney of Providence a share in thatch bed there, for £4, 5*s.*

1719, Jun. 26. He deeded to eldest son Thomas of Cohansey, for love, &c., certain land and tenements in Providence, viz: farm of 140 acres three or four miles north-west from Providence, and dwelling house, and 69 acres, and a small lot west side of river near Weybossett Hill, &c., all given me as eldest son and heir of Thomas Walling, deceased.

1. Abigail, 1698, Mar. 5.
2. Thomas, 1699, Feb. 8.
3. John, 1700, Jun. 20.
4. William, 1701, Nov. 21.
5. Mary, 1703, Sep. 8.
6. James, 1705, Apr. 2.
7. Samuel, 1707, Mar. 14.
8. Elisha, 1708, Jul. 26.
9. Joseph, 1709, Apr. 30.
10. Rebecca, 1717, Jun. 22.

II. GERSHOM, b. d. Providence, R. I.

1667, Jan. 27. He was to be apprenticed to Nathaniel Mowry till of age.

III. ABIGAIL, b. d. 1677.
UNMARRIED.

1660. Surveyor of Highways.

1665, Feb. 19. He had lot 72 in a division of lands.

1670, Jul. 27. He was complained of by Thomas Olney, Jr., for debarring him from going over certain land to said Olney's meadow, by which means he cannot get home his hay by reason of Walling's blocking up the way. The town appointed a committee to debate the matter with Walling.

1674, Jul. 19. Will—proved 1675, Nov. 22. Exx. wife Margaret. To sons Thomas, John and William, farm which I now dwell upon, equally, as each arrives at age, the dwelling house to be for son William, and his share of land to be adjoining house with orchard included. The farm not to be sold except among brethren, that is to say Thomas, John, James, William and Cornelius. To son James, land at age. To son Cornelius, land on west side of Seven Mile Line, and if James and Cornelius die without issue, their part to brothers. If there be more divisions than one of land west of Seven Mile line, then my right in second division to son Gershom, and to him 10*s*. To daughter Abigail Walling, 5*s*. To wife Margaret, all movable goods and cattle and benefit of all the land to bring up children. To her also the disposing of the dwelling house, &c., till William comes of age, at which time he to take half the land and housing, and other half to be for wife Margaret till her marriage or death, and then to William.

Inventory, £171, 7*s*., viz: 3 cows, 2 young bulls, 3 calves, 10 swine, 2 bibles, 2 spinning wheels, 2 guns, ironware, earthen ware, bedding, wearing clothes, a pair of boots without tops, a pair of shoes, 2 home-made blankets, sheep's wool, cotton wool, Indian corn, cheese, butter, churn, tallow candles, his working tools, &c. The dwelling house with lands and meadows adjoining, &c. £100. The rooms mentioned were outer room, inner room, leanto, chamber, cellar, and cellar chamber.

1675, Dec. 13. His widow Margaret confirmed 50 acres, &c., to Daniel Abbott, her husband having sold the same to him in his lifetime.

IV. JAMES, { b. / d. 1753, Apr. 4. — Providence, Smithfield, R. I.
m. (1) { b. / d. — of
m. (2) 1751, Mar. 24.
ELIZABETH NOX, { b. / d. 1752 + — of — Nox.

1. James,
2. Cornelius,
3. Daniel,
4. William,
5. Abigail,
6. Mercy,
7. Mary,
8. Elizabeth,
9. Daughter,

1687, Sep. 1. Taxed 6*d*.

1721, Aug. 5. He deeded son James, for love, &c., 75 acres.

1738, Jan. 1. Smithfield. He deeded son Cornelius of Glocester, 60 acres, for £120.

1743, Nov. 28. His son Daniel Walling and Priscilla his wife, deeded to brother Cornelius of Glocester, 60 acres for £740.

1752, Mar. 7. Will—proved 1753, Apr. 13. Ex. son-in-law William Sprague. To wife Elizabeth, £250, and provisions in house, and what estate she brought before I had her. To son William, wearing apparel and gun. To grandson Hezekiah Herenden, 20*s*. To daughter Abigail Blackmar's two eldest daughters, 20*s*. each. To son-in-law William Sprague, 15*s*. Rest equally to daughters' children, and to my daughter Mercy Sprague, viz: daughter Mary's children (Hannah Phillips, Joseph Cook, Abigail Cutler and Samuel Cook) a third part, to daughter Elizabeth's children (Elizabeth Tourtellot and Rebecca Williams) a third, and to daughter Mercy Sprague, a third part.

Inventory, £839, 16*s*. 9*d*., viz: books, old linen wheel, linen and woolen yarn, gun, pewter, warming pan, bonds, 3 cows, 2 calves, &c.

He may have had a son John also (who lived in Glocester in 1731).

(2d WIFE.)

V. WILLIAM, { b. 1670, May 20. / d.

VI. JOHN, { b. 1670, May 20. / d. 1694, Nov. 11. — Providence, R. I.
UNMARRIED.

1687, Sep. 1. Taxed 1*s*. 10*d*.

1687. Ratable estate, 2 cows, heifer, steer, 3 acres enclosed land, ½ acre tillable, ⅓ share of meadow.

1694, Nov. 20. Administration to eldest brother Thomas.

Inventory, £41, 11*s*., viz: mare, bridle, saddle, 2 cows, 2 two years, 3 yearlings, 3 calves, hay, rye, Indian corn, tobacco, pewter, working tools, &c.

VII. CORNELIUS, { b. 1672, Oct. 25. / d.

WANTON.

{See: PEMBROKE QUAKER RECORDS-BIRTHS, DEATHS & MARRIAGES
{See: American Genealogist, v. 20, p. 119

EDWARD, { b. 1629. / d. 1716, Dec. 16.
m. (1)
MARGARET, { b. / d. 1661.
m. (2) 1663,
ELIZABETH, { b. / d. 1716 (—)

Scituate, Mass.

He was a ship builder.

After witnessing the persecution of the Quakers, he became a convert to their doctrines and a preacher of that sect.

1658. Boston.

1661. Scituate. Freeman.

1664. May 4. The constable was ordered "forthwith to repair to Edward Wanton's house," where a stranger and a Quaker was "endeavoring to seduce his Majesty's good subjects and people to his cursed opinions by his preaching amongst them," &c. When the constable got there the meeting was ended "and the stranger was gone."

1716, Jul. 14. Will—proved 1717, Jan. 7. Ex. son Michael. Overseers, John Wing of Sandwich, Matthew Eustes, of Lynn, and Matthew Eustes, Jr., of Pembroke. To daughter Elizabeth Scott, mulatto boy Daniel and £5. To sons Joseph, William and John, all lands in Pennsylvania, and what money shall be in hands of Edward Shipin. To grandson William Wanton, son of William, a third of a sloop. To son John, what money of testator's he has in his hands at testator's decease and two young oxen. To son Philip, £5. To daughter Hannah Barker, £5. To granddaughter Mary Wanton, £450. To granddaughter Lydia Wanton, £450. To Nathaniel Chamberlain, of Pembroke, wearing apparel. To Abigail and Johannah Chamberlain, daughters of said Nathaniel, each £5. To son Michael, residue of estate.

He was buried on his farm.

WANTON. 1st column. His 2d wife d. 1674, Sep. 30. He m. (3) 1676, Sep. 25. Mary Phillips. She d. 1706. Dec. 4. At time of his 3d marriage, it is stated that his wife Mary Phillips had "come lately out of Old England." 2d column. I. Edward, d. 1695, Mar. VIII. Sarah, d. 1675, Oct. IX. Margaret, d. 1676, Apr. 19. X. Hannah m. 1697, Apr. 1, Robert Barker, b. 1650, Dec. 27; d. 1729, July 25, of Robert and Lucy (Williams) Barker. XI. Michael, d. 1741, June 13. XII. Stephen, d. 1709, Aug. 5. Both his daughters born on last day of respective months.

I. EDWARD, { b. 1658, Sep. 13. / d. young.

II. MARGARET, { b. 1661, Aug. 13. / d. young.

(2d WIFE.)

III. JOSEPH, { b. 1664, May 1. / d. 1754, Mar. 3. — Scituate, Mass., Tiverton, R. I.
m. 1690, Jan. 29.
SARAH FREEBORN, { b. 1667, Jan. 14. / d. 1737, Jul. 10. — of Gideon & Sarah (Brownell) Freeborn.

1. Elizabeth, 1691, Jan. 5.
2. Edward, 1692, Apr. 20
3. Gideon, 1693, Oct. 20.
4. Sarah, 1696, Apr. 27
5. Joseph, 1698, Jun. 9.
6. Mary, 1700, Jun. 10

He was a shipbuilder.

Both himself and wife were public speakers of the Quaker denomination.

1692, Mar. 2. Tiverton. He was an inhabitant at organization of town.

1749, Aug. 14. Will—proved 1754, Apr. 1. Exs. sons Gideon and Edward. To son Gideon, land in Tiverton and a cow. To daughter Elizabeth Borden, of Newport, widow, a cow and £800. To daughter Mary Richardson, wife of Thomas, of Newport, a feather bed, cow and £800. To daughter Sarah Spencer, wife of Thomas, of East Greenwich (practitioner of physic), use of house and lot in Tiverton, where she formerly lived, and after her death to go to my grandsons Benjamin and Wanton Howland, sons of said daughter Sarah. To daughter Sarah Spencer, also £300. To son Edward, homestead farm where I live and buildings, &c. (except house lot given above), to be for him and his heirs, and if no heirs, then to go to my son Gideon and daughters Elizabeth Borden, Mary Richardson and Sarah Spencer, equally. To son Edward, other land, and to him for life use of all my stock of cattle, horses, sheep, hogs, household goods and negroes, and if he have no heirs to go to Gideon and three daughters of testator equally (except a silver tankard). If son Edward die without issue, the silver tankard to go to grandson Joseph, son of Gideon. If grandson Joseph die before son Edward, the tankard to go to wife that now is of Joseph and if she die then to grandson, Joseph's daughter Sarah.

Inventory, £5,078, 2*s*., 7*d*., viz: 226 sheep, 10 cows, 2 four years, 6 three years, 8 two years, 10 yearlings, 9 swine, 6 geese, cider mill and press, cider in cellar £18, beds, 2 wheels, pewter, bonds £823, 14*s*., 7*d*., 523¼ oz. wrought plate £168, 16*s*., 6 negroes, Domine, Rose, Peter, Jenny, Hagar and Solomon £1,165, 10*s*., &c. The rooms named were east great room, west great room, bedroom, store bedroom, kitchen, shop, kitchen chamber, porch chamber, east chamber, west chamber and garret.

His son Gideon became Governor.

IV. GEORGE, { b. 1666, Aug. 25. / d. 1684, Jan. — Scituate, Mass.
UNMARRIED.

He was buried at Scituate.

V. ELIZABETH, { b. 1668, Sep. 16. / d.
m.
JOHN SCOTT, { b. 1664, Mar. 14. / d 1725 + — of John & Rebecca ( ) Scott.

1. Mary,
2. Elizabeth,
3. Catharine,
4. Edward, 1703, Jun. 13.
5. George, 1706, May 25.
6. Joseph, 1709, Mar. 14.

VI. WILLIAM, { b. 1670, Sep. 15. / d. 1733, Dec. — Scituate, Mass., Newport, R. I.
m. (1) 1691, Jun. 1.
RUTH BRYANT, { b. / d. — of John & Mary (Hiland) Bryant.
m. (2) 1717, Apr. 10.
MARY GODFREY, { b. 1702, Mar. 23. / d. — of John & Elizabeth (Carr) Godfrey.

1. Margaret, 1692, Oct. 24.
2. George, 1694 Aug. 24.
3. William, 1696, Oct. 26.
4. Peter, 1698, Mar. 22.
5. Ruth, 1701, Jun. 12.
6. Edward, 1702, Apr. 11.
7. Joseph, 1705 Aug. 15.
8. Benjamin, 1707 Jun. 9.
9. Elizabeth, 1709, Oct. 4.

(She m. (2) 1745, Mar. 14, Daniel Updike.)

He was a merchant.

1698. Newport. Freeman.

1703, Feb. 2. The Assembly enacted that the charges of entertaining the prisoner taken by Captain William Wanton, should be paid out of Her Majesty's tenths of said prizes, and if not allowed by her to be paid by the Colony.

1705-6-8-9-10-11-13-15-16-17-18-19-20-21-22-23-24. Deputy.

1705-6-8-9-10-11-15-16-17-18-19-20-21-22-23-24. Speaker of the House of Deputies.

1705-7-8-9. Major for the Island.

1706-7-13-25-26-27-28-29-30-31-32. Assistant.

1708, Sep. 8. He had command of a sloop that made chase for a privateer.

1709, May 4. The Assembly voted to buy his new sloop Diamond for £400, and the quarter of sloop Endeavour belonging to him and Henry Beere, for £112, 10s.

1719-20. He was Colonel of the regiment of militia on the island.

1726, Jan. 10. He was appointed one of the four commissioners to meet the commissioners from Connecticut to settle line of partition between Colonies.

1732-33. Governor.

He was buried in his family burial ground.

His son Joseph held the office of Governor.

VII. JOHN, m. MARY STAFFORD, — b. 1672, Dec. 24. d. 1740, Jul. 5. Scituate, Mass., Newport, R. I. — b. d. of Stafford.

1. John, 1697, Dec. 22.
2. Elizabeth, 1700, Jun. 9.
3. Susanna, 1704, Oct. 21.
4. Mary, 1707, Jun. 16.
5. James, 1717, Sep. 16.

He was a merchant.

He belonged to the same religious denomination as his father, and the Friends' records declare that "for many years he was a valuable public friend."

1706-7-8-9-10-13. Newport. Deputy.

1707-10-13. Speaker.

1707. He took prizes this year, as shown by petition of John Dublin, who was wounded with Colonel John Wanton, in taking the French privateers.

1721-22-29-30-31-32-33-34. Deputy governor.

1734-35-36-37-38-39-40. Governor.

He was buried in the Coddington Burial Ground.

VIII. SARAH, — b. 1674, Sep. 22. d.

IX. MARGARET, — b. 1674, Sep. 22. d.

X. HANNAH, m. ROBERT BARKER, — b. 1677, Jul. 25. d. 1726, Aug. 16. — b. d. 1726. of Robert Barker.

1. Isaac, 1699, Mar. 15.
2. Mary, 1701, Mar. 15.
3. Margaret, 1704, Apr. 18.

XI. MICHAEL, m. (1) 1705, Jan. 15. MARY MEW, m. (2) 1717, Jan. 2. [Wm. ABIGAIL CARR, (w. of — b. 1679, Apr. 9. d. 1741 ±. Scituate, Mass. — b. 1689, Aug. 15. d. 1711, Jul. 22. of Noel & Mary ( ) Mew. — b. 1682, Aug. 24. d. 1726 ± of Robert & Alice ( ) Barker.

1. Ruth, 1705, Oct. 30.
2. Mary, 1707, Oct. 4.
3. Stephen, 1709, Nov. 18.
(2d wife.)
4. Susanna, 1717, Nov. 11.
5. Hannah, 1721, Jan. 17.
6. Michael, 1724, Aug. 14.

He was a shipbuilder. His religious faith was that of the Quakers and he was a preacher of that sect.

XII. STEPHEN, m. 1706, Sep. 10. HANNAH ALLEN, — b. 1682, Mar. 5. d. Scituate, Sandwich, Mass. — b. d. of Allen.

1. Mary, 1707, May.
2. Lydia, 1708, Oct.

He was married at Sandwich and his children were born there.

XIII. PHILIP, m. 1711, Oct. 31. HANNAH RODMAN, — b. 1686, May 9. d. 1735. Scituate, Mass., Newport, R. I. — b. 1694, Nov. 29. d. 1753, Jul. 10. of Thomas & Hannah (Clarke) Rodman.

1. Walter, 1712, Nov. 27.
2. Hannah, 1715, Jul. 15.
3. Philip, 1719, May 31.
4. Thomas, 1722, Mar. 14.
5. Mary, 1725, Mar. 29.
6. Elizabeth, 1727 ±

He was a merchant and apothecary.

He was buried in the Clifton Burial Ground.

WARD (JOHN, OF PORTSMOUTH).

JOHN, m. SARAH NICHOLSON, — b. d. 1705. — b. 1653, Mar. 1. d. 1705 + of Joseph & Jane ( ) Nicholson.

Portsmouth, R. I.

1699-1701-3. Deputy.

1705, Jan. 6. Will—proved 1705, Feb. 12. Exx. wife Sarah. Overseers, brother-in-law Joseph Nicholson and Robert Taylor. To daughter Elizabeth Gould, 20 acres, four oxen, six cows, two steers, a bull, mare, colt, 40 sheep, two feather beds, flock bed, five pairs of blankets, four pairs of sheets, two coverlids, two bolsters, four pillows, an iron pot, brass kettle, table, three joint stools, six chairs and three silver spoons. To son Joseph, all lands in Portsmouth except 20 acres. To wife Sarah, the enjoyment of half of land given son Joseph, while she remains widow. To son Joseph and wife Sarah, rest of movables equally.

He may have been a son of Marmaduke Ward whose name appears in a list of inhabitants admitted to Newport after 1638, May 20.

(It is noticeable that John had a grandson named Marmaduke.)

I. ELIZABETH, m. JEREMIAH GOULD, — b. d. — b. 1683, Apr. 22. d. of Daniel & Mary ( ) Gould.

1. Sarah,
2. Mary,
3. Catharine,
4. Elizabeth,
5. Waite,
6. Daniel,
7. Ruth,
8. Hannah,

II. JOSEPH, m. 1724, Jul. 26. SARAH WEEDEN, — b. 1688, Aug. 18. d. 1750, Mar. 23. Portsmouth, R. I. — b. d. 1750 + of Philip & Ann (Sisson) Weeden.

1. Elizabeth, 1725, Jun. 29.
2. John, 1727, Dec. 1.
3. Joseph, 1729, Nov. 26.
4. Richard, 1731, Aug. 7.
5. Sarah, 1734, Mar. 19.
6. Philip, 1735, Aug. 13.
7. Marmaduke, 1737, Jun. 6.

1748, Jun. 6. Will—proved 1750, Apr. 9. Exx. wife Sarah. Overseers, William Wood and John Allen of Middletown, To son John, £5, best gun, sword, silver buttons on coat and my shirt buttons of silver. To son Joseph, £120, two sets of silver buttons and a silver tankard. To son Richard, £120, and two sets of silver buttons. To son Philip, £120, a set of silver buttons and silver shoe buckles. To daughter Elizabeth Ward, £60, 2s., and oldest mare. To daughter Sarah Ward, £60, 2s. To son Marmaduke Ward, £120, rest of silver money and a piece of gold. To seven children, a silver spoon each. To wife Sarah and son John all stock of cattle, sheep and swine, after debts are paid, and all husbandry gear, for the support and to bring up younger children. To wife Sarah, rest of personal while widow, and at her death equally to children. He gives permission to wife to sell all land not given me by honored father John Ward in his will.

Inventory, £1,628, 16s. 11d., viz: wearing apparel and silver buckles £80, 15s., armour £9, pewter, silver tankard and 9 silver spoons £108, warming pan, pair of wool combs, neat cattle £230, horsekind £250, sheep £101, 15s., swine £14, poultry £3, 10s., &c.

JOHN,	b.	
	d. 1728.	
m. (1)		
DORCAS GARDINER,	b.	
	d.	
of George & Herodias (Long)		Gardiner.
m. (2)		
REBECCA GARDINER,	b.	
	d.	
of George & Herodias (Long)		Gardiner.

North Kingstown, R. I.

He was a tailor.

It is assumed that his first wife was a sister of his last.

1673, Nov. 7. He and Dorcas were witnesses to deed from George and Tabitha Gardiner to Nicholas Gardiner.

1683, May 14. He took John Straight for an apprentice to serve sixteen years from the first of March last past, to learn his master's trade of tailoring.

1687. Constable.

1687, Sep. 6. Taxed 8*s.* 8½*d.*

1688. Grand Jury.

1690. Conservator of the Peace.

1690. Deputy.

1702, Aug. 4. He and wife Rebecca deeded to son John all my farm, 90 acres, orchard, housing, &c.

1705, Nov. 17. He and wife Rebecca signed a deed with her brothers Benoni, Henry, George, William and Nicholas Gardiner.

1707, Jan. 28. He and wife Rebecca sold John Thomas, 30 acres for £30.

1728. Will—proved. Ex. son Samuel. To daughter Frances Brown, £20. To daughter Herodias Sheldon, £15. To sons-in-law John Sheldon and Daniel Brown, equally, a share in cedar swamp in South Kingstown. To son John Watson, —*s.* To son William Watson, 2*s.* To granddaughter Ann Wells, a kettle, brass warming pan, &c. To son Samuel, rest of estate.

WATSON. 2d column. I. John, b. 1676, July 22; d. 1772, Nov. 8; m. (1) 1703, Apr. 8, Hannah Champlin, d. 1720, Oct. 31, of Jeffrey; m. (2) 1722, Abigail Eldred, (widow of Samuel), d. 1737, Aug. 22, of Stephen and Mary (Thomas) Northup. Children by her, 8, Freelove, 1722. 9, Mary, 1725. 10, Margaret. He m. (3) 1738, Sarah Money. She d. 1769, Mar. 12. He is said to have been the first child born in Narragansett after the Indian war. II. Samuel, b. 1686; d. 1779, Nov. 24; m. (1) Mercy Helme, of Rouse and Mary. Children, 1, Samuel. 2, Dorcas. 3, Mary. 4, Frances. 5, Freelove. 6, Ann. 7, Benjamin. 8, Stephen. 9, Nicholas. Erase the ten children previously given him. He m. (2) Hannah Slocum (widow of Samuel), b. 1691, Oct. 13, of Edward and Hannah (Stanton) Carr. Perhaps part of his children were by her. 1713, he gave receipt to his brother-in-law Rouse Helme, for share in father Rouse Helme's estate. Erase 1762, Apr. 2, etc., (two last lines). III. William. Erase wife's name and also first line. 1711, Mar. 14, etc. He m. Mary. Children, 1, William. 2, Simeon, 1726, Feb. 21. 3, Abigail, 1729, June 5. 4, Elizabeth, 1732, June 6. 5, John, 1735, Jan. 20.

I. JOHN,	b.		South Kingstown, R. I.
	d.		
m.			
HANNAH,	b.		
	d.	of	

1708, Apr. 12. He and wife Hannah, for £7, sold Alice Wilson, widow, 1½ acres in the division of land that fell to the Gardiners.

1712. Kings Town. Freeman.

1718–21–22–23–24–25–26. Deputy.

1726, Dec. 6. South Kingstown. He became surety for his sister Frances Brown of Westerly, who took administration on estate of her husband Daniel.

1731, Mar. 29. He was appointed guardian to Desire Brown, daughter of Daniel Brown, deceased.

1731, Aug. 18. He deeded to son John, 40 acres, for love, &c.

1733, Sep. 10. He deeded to son Jeffrey, 30 acres.

1. Hannah, 1704, Mar. 1.
2. Ann, 1709, Mar. 27.
3. John, 1710, Mar. 13.
4. Jeffrey, 1712, Aug. 3.
5. Elisha, 1714, Sep. 14.
6. Dorcas, 1716, Oct. 25.
7. Amey, 1719, Oct. 18.

II. SAMUEL,	b.		North Kingstown, R. I.
	d. 1762 +		
m. (1)			
ABIGAIL NORTHUP,	b.		
	d.	of Stephen & Mary (Thomas)	Northup.
m. (2)			
HANNAH HAZARD,	b. 1714, Apr.		
	d. 1801, Dec. 17.	of Jeremiah & Sarah (Smith)	Hazard.

1712. Freeman.

1748, Apr. 10. He deeded to son Nicholas, for love, &c., a dwelling house and 40 acres in South Kingstown, where son lives. His wife Hannah signed.

1751, Jun. 2. He deeded to son Benjamin, 20 acres in South Kingstown.

1762, Apr. 29. Will of his son Hazard (proved 1762, Dec. 14), names father and mother (Samuel and Hannah Watson), and brothers and sister, Robert, Silas, Nicholas, Mary, Samuel, Freeborn.

1. Benjamin,
2. Margaret,
3. Freeborn,
4. Robert,
5. Silas,
6. Nicholas,
7. Mary,
8. Samuel,
9. Freeborn,
10. Hazard,

III. WILLIAM,	b.		Kings Town, Charlestown, R. I.
	d. 1740 +		
m.			
MERCY HELME,	b.		
	d.	of Rouse & Mary ( )	Helme.

1711, Mar. 14. His wife had a legacy from will of her father Rouse Helme, of a heifer.

1717, Mar. 9. He was sued for £8, debt by John Gibson, and not appearing, judgment was given against him for £4.

1740, Aug. 1. Charlestown. He and William Watson, Jr., gave deposition.

1. William,

IV. FRANCES,	b.		
	d. 1726 +		
m.			
DANIEL BROWN,	b.		
	d. 1726.	of	Brown.

1. Elizabeth, 1705, Mar. 13.
2. Mary, 1706, Aug. 3.
3. Benjamin, 1708, Mar. 16.
4. Daniel, 1709, Nov. 15.
5. Elisha, 1711, Jan. 26.
6. Dorcas, 1713, May 22.
7. John, 1714, Feb. 18.
8. Desire, 1723, Jan. 8.

V. ANN,	b.		
	d.		
m.			
PETER WELLS,	b. 1681.		
	d. 1732.	of Peter	Wells.

1. James, 1706, Sep. 30.
2. Ann, 1708, Oct. 20.
3. Rebecca, 1710, Dec. 30.
4. Peter, 1713, May 4.
5. John, 1716, Apr. 14.
6. Samuel, 1725, Feb. 2.
7. Mary,
8. Dorcas,

VI. HERODIAS,	b.		
	d.		
m. 1706, Apr. 11.			
JOHN SHELDON,	b.		
	d.	of John	Sheldon.

1. John, 1707, Feb. 10.
2. Dorcas, 1708, Jan. 4.
3. George, 1709, May 25.
4. Samuel, 1714, Jan. 15.
5. William, 1715, Mar. 27.
6. Elizabeth, 1720, Mar. 31.
7. Sarah, 1722, Mar. 26.

WATSON. 2d column. II. Samuel. He may not have had either of the wives given him, for in 1748 the wife of Samuel Watson, of South Kingstown, was Hannah Carr, b. 1691, Oct. 13, of Edward and Hannah (Stanton) Carr. IV. Frances. Her husband was son of Jeremiah and Mary (   ) Brown.

WELLS (PETER).

PETER,	b.	
	d. 1715 +	
m.		
——	b.	
	d.	

Jamestown, Kings Town, R. I.

1679. Freeman.

1680. Taxed 5*s.* 10*d.*

1684, Dec. 29. He was given all the estate of William Salter (deceased 1684, Dec. 24), by Town Council, on condition of his maintaining the aged mother of William Salter, viz: Jone Salter. (The inventory of Salter showed £25, 4*s.*, viz: 3 mares and colts, heifer, 45 sheep, gun, &c.)

1687, Sep. 6. Kings Town. Taxed 4*s.* 3*d.*

1702, Sep. 11. He deeded that farm I now live on, 100 acres, housing, orchard, &c., to son Peter for love to him, he having behaved himself dutifully to his said father in this my aged and feeble condition.

1715, Aug. 23. He testified as to knowledge of land in Jamestown forty-two years before and many years after that time.

I. DAUGHTER,	b. 1667, May.	
	d.	

II. THOMAS,	b. 1669, Sep.		East Greenwich, R. I.
	d. 1727, Oct. 16.		
m.			
SARAH ROGERS,	b.		
	d.	of Thomas & Sarah ( )	Rogers.

1716, Nov. 28. His wife had a legacy of £5, from will of her father Thomas Rogers of Newport.

1729, Apr. 26. Administration to eldest son Peter. Inventory, £163, 7*s.* 6*d.*

1. Peter.

III. DAUGHTER,	b. 1672, Dec.	
	d.	

IV. DAUGHTER,	b. 1673, Jul. 20.	
	d.	

V. JOHN,	b. 1676, May		North Kingstown, R. I.
	d. 1732.		
m.			
ELIZABETH CONGDON,	b.		
	d. 1732 +	of Benjamin & Elizabeth (Albro)	Congdon.

1732, Jul. 11. Will—proved. Exs. sons John and Benjamin. To wife Elizabeth, a third of personal, and privilege of house while widow. To eldest son John, half of homestead, &c., and the other half to younger son Benjamin. To two sons, wearing apparel and farming tackling. To daughters Mercy Whitford, Elizabeth Sweet, —— Wells and Susanna Wells, rest of personal estate.

Inventory, mare, colt, cattle £31, woolen wheel, wearing apparel, &c.

1. John,
2. Benjamin,
3. Mercy,
4. Elizabeth,
5. Daughter,
6. Susanna,

VI. DAUGHTER,	b. 1678, Jan. 21.	
	d.	

VII. DAUGHTER,	b. 1680, Jun.	
	d.	

VIII. PETER, m. (1) ANN WATSON, m. (2) SUSANNA BARKER (w. of [Peter. | b. 1681. d. 1732. b. d. b. d. | South Kingstown, R. I. of John & Dorcas (Gardiner) Watson. of Tobias & Mary (Clarke) Saunders.

1712. Kings Town. Freeman. He was called junior at this date.

1732, Nov. 13. Will—proved 1732, Dec. 11. Ex. son James. To son James, a quarter of a farm in South Kingstown. To sons Peter and John, rest of farm equally; except 8 acres I gave to son Samuel and firewood off the rest. To daughter Ann Wells, best bed and privilege to live in the house with son James while single, £28, &c. To daughter Rebecca Clarke, £8. To daughter Mary Wells, land and £8, at twenty years of age. To daughter Dorcas, a bed and £8, at twenty. Son Samuel to live with James till of age, and James to keep a horse for his brother Peter till latter is of age. To son James, rest of movables.

Inventory, £372, 10s. 6d., viz: riding horse, 9 cows, heifer, 5 yearlings, mare, 37 sheep, 10 books £1, 5s., 3 beds, gun, money 17s., fowl, loom, &c.

1733, Feb. 1. His widow Susanna gave a receipt to her stepson James Wells.

1. James, 1706, Sep. 30.
2. Ann, 1708, Oct. 20.
3. Rebecca, 1710, Dec. 30.
4. Peter, 1713, May 4.
5. John, 1716, Apr. 14.
6. Mary,
7. Dorcas, 1720, Sep. 17.
8. Samuel, 1725, Feb. 2.
(2d wife no issue.)

IX. SUSANNA, m. 1708, Dec. 9. ABNER SPENCER, | b. 1684, Nov. 2. d. 1782, Jul. 25. b. 1676, Dec. 4. d. 1759, May 11. | of John & Susanna ( ) Spencer.

1. Peter, 1709, Nov. 18.
2. Susanna, 1712, Aug. 30.
3. Ruth, 1714, May 8.
4. Alice, 1719, Oct. 8.
5. James, 1722, Apr. 10.
6. Abner, 1725, Feb. 11.
7. Thomas,

WELLS (THOMAS).

THOMAS, m. NAOMI, | b. d. 1700. b. d. 1700 +

Ipswich, Mass., Westerly, R. I.

He was a shipbuilder.

1656, Jun. 7. The birth of his oldest son was recorded at Boston.

1677, Jul. He bought 180 acres of Amos Richardson, of Stonington, agreeing to pay him therefor by building one or more vessels of fifty tons in all. The land purchased was on the east side of the Pawcatuck River and was thus in the territory long in dispute between Connecticut and Rhode Island.

1679. Westerly. He came in this or previous year but was warned off by the Rhode Island authorities as an intruder, and refused therefore to fulfill his contract with Mr. Richardson, till the latter should make good the title to land.

1679, Sep. 17. He took oath of allegiance in Rhode Island.

1680, Mar. He was arrested and imprisoned on the suit of Mr. Richardson, who laid damages at £300. The constable was Stephen Richardson (son of plaintiff), and the Rhode Island authorities soon retaliated on behalf of Wells by arresting the Connecticut constable and imprisoning him from July to October, for exercising his office by arresting Wells within the jurisdiction of Rhode Island.

1699, Dec. 27. Will—proved 1700, Feb. 12. Exx. wife Naomi. To eldest son Joseph, 5s., he having had double portion already. Son Thomas had already received his portion also in a horse and neat cattle valued at £7. Eldest daughter Mary Wells, daughters Ruth and Sarah Wells and sons John and Nathaniel, had all had their portions. To wife Naomi, rest of estate for life, and sons Thomas, John and Nathaniel to "take best care you can of her," and what is left at her decease to go to these three sons.

Inventory, £8, 16s., viz: a cow, mare, swine, bedding, wearing clothes and spinning wheel.

I. JOSEPH, m. 1681, Dec. 28. HANNAH REYNOLDS, | b. 1656, Jun. 7. d. 1711, Oct. 26. b. d. 1711 + | Westerly, R. I., Groton, Ct. of John Reynolds.

He was a shipbuilder.

1680. He testified in his father's law suit, calling himself aged twenty-two years.

He early moved to Groton, and became the first ship builder on the Mystic river.

1711, Oct. 21. Will—proved 1712, Feb. 12. Ex. son Joseph. To wife Hannah, house and land where I dwell, with orchard, &c., for life for her maintenance. To son Joseph, all lands, &c., aforesaid at death of wife, he taking care of his mother for life. To sons John and Thomas, certain land. To daughter Anne Wells, all my cattle at her marriage, except one cow for wife's use. To wife household stuff for life and then to daughter.

1. Joseph,
2. John,
3. Thomas,
4. Ann,

II. THOMAS, m. SARAH, | b. 1663. d. 1716, Jun. 29. b. d. 1716 + | Westerly R. I. of

1680. He testified in his father's law suit, calling himself aged seventeen years.

1716, Apr. 11. Will—proved 1716, Jul. 9. Exx. wife Sarah. Overseers, brother Nathaniel Wells and Joseph Maxson. To wife, while widow, use of best room; a cow, young mare and best bed, and she to have a third of homestead while widow, viz: the part that belongs to my son Edward. To sons Thomas and Edward, land where I dwell (divided). Certain articles at eldest son Thomas's as parcel of sheep, gun, &c., not to be counted in inventory. To son Edward, two heifers, a gun, bed, &c. To two sons, cattle, carpenter tools, silver money and wearing apparel, &c. To daughter Sarah, a parcel of sheep, cow, and household stuff.

Inventory, £165, 19s., viz: 6 oxen, 6 cows, 4 calves, 3 horsekind, 14 sheep, 2 lambs, 3 hogs, 9 pigs, wearing clothes, 3 beds, silver money, cards, &c.

1. Thomas,
2. Edward,
3. Sarah,

III. MARY, | b. d.

IV. RUTH. | b. d.

V. SARAH, | b. d.

VI. JOHN, | b. d. | Westerly, R. I.

1688, Jun. 12. He was presented at court for killing sundry swine of George Denison's, but the jury found him not guilty.

VII. NATHANIEL, m. MARY CRANDALL, | b. d. 1769. b. d. 1763 (—) | Westerly, Hopkinton, R. I. of Joseph & Deborah (Burdick) Crandall.

1763, Jul. 5. Will—proved 1769, May 1. Ex. son Jonathan. To daughter Naomi Kenyon, £5. To daughter Tacy Burdick, a bed, &c. To son Jonathan, rest of estate.

Inventory, £16, 1s., 3d., viz: mare, saddle, household goods, &c.

1. Naomi, 1707, May 11.
2. Elizabeth, 1710, Jan. 9.
3. Jonathan, 1712, Jun. 22.
4. Tacy, 1715, Jan. 4.
5. Ruth, 1717, Sep. 6.

WEST.

MATTHEW, m. —— | b. d. b. d.

Lynn, Mass., Newport, R. I.

He was a tailor.

1636. He was of Lynn thus early.

1637, Mar. 9. Freeman.

1646. Newport.

1655. Freeman.

1677, Jan. 16. He deeded grandson Nathaniel West, for love, &c., son of my eldest son Nathaniel West, who departed this life many years ago—and forasmuch as he hath for many years past and now does live with me, and is the comfort of me in my old age—dwelling house I now live in (bounded partly by land of John Cran-

I. NATHANIEL, m. —— | b. d. 1659. b. d. | Newport, R. I. of

1648, Oct. 12. He and his wife were among the twelve members of the First Baptist Church in full communion at this date.

1659, Mar. 1. The jury in Plymouth Colony rendered verdict that "Nathaniel West, a stranger to us, belonging to Rhode Island, being by God's providence amongst us, and being under care of an infirmity of his body, it appears that he fell in and was drowned. When his body was taken up it appeared to us that his death was no way violent nor wilful, but accidental, as far as we apprehend."

1. Nathaniel,

II. JOHN, | b. d. | Newport, R. I.

1655. Freeman.

III. ROBERT, m. ELIZABETH, | b. d. 1697 (—) b. d. | Providence, Portsmouth, R. I., Monmouth, N. J. of

1. Joseph,
2. John,
3. Robert,

WEST. 2d column. III. Robert, d. 1688(—). He had also a daughter Ann. IV. Bartholomew. He had also a daughter Audry. His widow m. —— Brown. 1684, Nicholas Brown, of New Jersey testified that he was the deceased Bartholomew West's nearest relation; in a suit where Catherine Brown, sister of Christopher Almy, also testified. Perhaps Catherine was his wife.

dall and John Thornton) immediately after my decease.

It is assumed that John, Robert, Bartholomew and Francis were sons of Matthew.

Perhaps he was also father of Joan West who married Joshua Coggeshall, 1652, Dec. 22.

Son of Francis West of Duxbury, proved in Mayflower Descendant v. 24.

1640, Jul. 27. He and thirty-eight others signed an agreement for civil government.

1641, Nov. 17. He and twelve others complained in a letter to Massachusetts of the "insolent and riotous carriages of Samuel Gorton and his company," and therefore petitioned Massachusetts to "lend us a neighborlike helping hand," &c.

1650, Sep. 2. Taxed 13*s.* 4*d.*

1655. Freeman.

1657, Aug. 27. He had 2½ acres laid out.

1663, Oct. 18. Portsmouth. He and wife Elizabeth sold to John Nixon, of Newport, 28 acres in Portsmouth.

1667. Monmouth. He was among the original purchasers.

1697, May 10. He died earlier than this date, as is seen by a deed from his son Joseph West, wherein he reserves land where his "loving father Robert West lies interred."

IV. BARTHOLOMEW, { b. { d. 1703, (—) — Portsmouth, R. I., Monmouth, N. J.
m.
CATHARINE ALMY, { b. { d. — of William & Audry ( ) Almy.

1. Bartholomew,
2. William,
3. John,
4. Stephen, 1654,

1651, Feb. 23. He bought of William Baulstone, 70 acres, for £7.

1667. Monmouth. He was among the original purchasers.

1667. Deputy.

1703, Oct. 30. He died earlier than this date, as is seen by a deed from his son John West, of Shrewsbury, wherein he reserves ½ acre where his father lies interred. (It is noticeable that this son John named one of his children Matthew.)

V. FRANCIS, { b. { d. — Kings Town, R. I.
m.
——— { b. { d. — of

1. Francis,
2. Richard,

1687, Sep. 6. Taxed 3*s.* 1*d.* (and Francis, Jr. and Richard, each 1*s.*)

There was a Francis West of Duxbury, Mass., who married Margery Reeves, 1639, Feb. 27, and had children Samuel, Peter, Pelatiah and Richard. He died 1692, Jan. 2, and could not have been identical with Francis of Kings Town, though he may have been related to the Rhode Island Wests.

WESTGATE.

ROBERT, { b. { d. 1717, Dec. 23.
m.
SARAH, { b. { d. 1723, Sep. 23.

Warwick, R. I.

1687. Constable (for Newport).

1700, Apr. 8. He contributed 12*s.*, toward a meeting house to be set up at or near Mashapaug (Quaker).

1716, Sep. 1. Will—proved 1718, Jan. 10. Exx. wife Sarah. To her all movables, and for life half of house, and half income of land adjoining and orchard. To eldest son George, half of house, orchard, &c., at testator's decease, and other half at decease of wife and all other land to George (except a small lot to son Silvanus) and legacies to be paid by George. To sons Silvanus, Robert, John and James, each, £5, as they come of age. To daughters Catharine, Sarah, Rebecca and Mary, each 40*s.*, at age. Son George to have whole management of orchard, paying widow half income of same, and supplying her also with firewood.

Inventory, £131, 18*s.*, 3*d.*, viz: wearing apparel £10, 16*s.*, plate £2., 10*s.*, money and books £11, 2*s.*, feather beds £34, 15*s.*, 8*d.*, flock bed £3, 14*s.*, 6*d.*, pewter, a cane, 2 drinking glasses, 4 spinning wheels, pair of worsted combs, 3 pair scales, a cow, 5 swine, &c.

1723, May 15. Will—proved 1723, Oct. 19. Widow Sarah. Ex. son Robert. To grandchildren, children of son Silvanus, 20*s.* To son George, a pair of buckles and coverlid. To sons Robert, John, and James, 20*s.*, each. To daughter Catharine Northup, £5. To daughters Sarah, Rebecca, and Mary, rest of goods equally.

Inventory, £239, 17*s*, 4*d.*, viz: 11 oz. plate and silver money £6, 12*s.*, stillyards, scales, &c.

I. CATHARINE, { b. 1684, Dec. 23. { d.
m.
——— NORTHUP, { b. { d. — of Northup.

II. JOHN, { b. 1686, Apr. { d. 1687, Jul. 24.

III. GEORGE, { b. 1688, Apr. 24. { d. — Warwick, R. I.
m. 1727, Oct. 5.
ELIZABETH EARL, { b. 1699, Sep. 6. { d. — of John & Mary (Wilcox) Earl.

(She m. (2) 1757, Nov. 14, John Adams.)

1. George, 1728, Sep. 16.
2. John, 1731, Feb. 1.
3. Priscilla, 1732, Sep. 8.
4. Mary, 1735, Jan. 7.
5. Earl, 1736, Feb. 26.

1716. Freeman.

1757, Nov. 14. Elizabeth Westgate, widow, of Warwick, married Captain John Adams, of Warren.

IV. SILVANUS, { b. 1691, Feb. 19. { d. 1719, Sep. 27. — Warwick, R. I.
m. 1711, Dec. 13.
JERUSHA DAVIS, { b. 1690, Jan. 17. { d. — of Robert Davis.

(She m. (2) 1726, Jul. 22, John Stafford.)

1. Sarah, 1713, Jan. 10.
2. Robert, 1716, Mar. 19.
3. Silvanus, 1719, Jul. 16.

He was lost at sea.

1749, Nov. 2. His son Robert (called "Robert, Jr."), made his will (proved 1750, Feb. 4). He mentions his sisters Sarah Rhodes, Jerusha Stafford, brother Silvanus, sister Amey Stafford, besides his mother and wife.

V. PRISCILLA, { b. 1693, Feb. 23. { d.

VI. SARAH, { b. 1695, Jan. 15. { d.

VII. REBECCA, { b. 1697, Jan. 8. { d.
m. 1726, May 28.
BENJAMIN EARLE, { b. 1691, May 25. { d. — of John & Mary (Wilcox) Earle.

1. William, 1727, Feb. 12.
2. John, 1729, Jan. 27.
3. Sarah, 1731, Feb. 8.
4. Benjamin, 1733, Nov. 25.

VIII. ROBERT, { b. 1698, Sep. 18. { d. 1759. — Warwick, R. I.
m. (1) 1723, Jul. 9.
PATIENCE CARR, { b. 1701, Feb. { d. 1753, Mar. 27. — of Edward & Hannah (Stanton) Carr.
m. (2)
MARY HAWKINS (widow) { b. { d. — of

1. Edward, 1724, Apr. 23.
2. Avis, 1725, Nov. 9.
3. Patience, 1728, Dec. 16.
4. Sarah, 1732, Mar. 11.
5. Hannah, 1735, Jun. 1.
6. Mary, 1740, Jun. 30.
(2d wife, no issue.)

He was a carpenter.

1757, Mar. 26. Will—codicil, 1759, Apr. 4. proved 1759, Apr. 23. Ex. son-in-law Peleg Arnold, of Cranston. To wife Mary, household goods she brought, half of sheeting made since marriage, half provisions, &c., and privilege to live in east end of house, and a sixth of what house and land may be sold for after legacies of £110 have been paid. To grandson William Smith, son of daughter Avis, a gun. To daughter Patience Arnold, wife of Peleg, a bible and small trunk. To daughter Sarah Watson, wife of Benjamin, a large kettle. To daughter Hannah Aborn, wife of James, a cabinet, silver spoon and £60. To daughter Mary Westgate, household goods and £50. The executor to sell house and land, and after legacies are paid to divide rest to grandson William Smith, and daughters Patience Arnold, Sarah Watson, Hannah Aborn, and Mary Westgate, equally.

IX. JOHN, { b. 1700, May 19. { d.

X. JAMES, { b. 1703, Sep. 19. { d.

XI. MARY, { b. 1706, Sep. 7. { d.
m. 1732, Nov. 30.
JOHN CARDER, { b. { d. — of John Carder.

1. Joseph, 1738, Aug. 11.
2. Richard, 1739, Sep. 26.
3. John, 1744, Feb. 15.
4. William, 1746, Dec. 26.
5. Robert, 1750, May 5.

 See: American Genealogist, v. 21, p. 208.

FRANCIS, m. MARGARET,	b. d. 1645 ± / b. d. 1651 +

Salem, Mass., Providence, Warwick, R. I.

1633, Nov. 5. Freeman.

1634. Deputy.

1635, May 6. He was chosen on a committee "to consider of the act of Mr. Endicott, in defacing the colours, and to report to the court how far they judge it censurable."

1635, Nov. 3. It was ordered that John Pease "shall be whipped and bound to his good behaviour for striking his mother Mrs. Weston," &c.

1637. He gave his grounds of withdrawal from the church, one of his reasons being "that which is now called damnable was once called lawful."

His wife had signed the church covenant this year, but afterwards taxed the minister with hypocrisy, &c., and her case was referred to the next meeting.

1638, Mar. 12. He and others of Salem, having had license to depart from Massachusetts, they were ordered to appear (if they be not gone before) at the next court, to answer such things as shall be objected.

1638, Jun. 5. His wife was "censured to be set two hours in the billboes here (Boston) and two hours at Salem upon a lecture day."

1638, Oct. 8. Providence. He was one of the twelve persons to whom Roger Williams deeded land that he had bought of Canonicus and Miantonomi.

1639. He was one of the twelve original members of First Baptist church.

1641, Nov. 17. He and others of Pawtuxet were complained of by a portion of their neighbors who wrote to the Massachusetts authorities asking their aid: The letter charges that Weston had refused to satisfy a debt of £15, found due by arbitrators, whereupon "we went to attach some of his cattle to impound." Weston "came furiously running with a flail in his hand, and cried out 'Help Sirs! Help Sirs! They are going to steal my cattle.'" Weston's friends then came running to his assistance, crying "Thieves! Thieves! Stealing cattle! Stealing cattle!" The Weston party were successful and carried away the cattle "and then presumptuously answered they had made a rescue."

1643, Jan. 12. Warwick. He and ten others bought of Miantonomi the tract of land called Shawomet (Warwick) for 144 fathoms of wampum.

1643, Sep. 12. He, with others of Warwick, was notified to appear at General Court at Boston to hear complaint of two Indian sachems Pomham and Socconocco, as to "some unjust and injurious dealing toward them by yourselves." The Warwick men declined to obey the summons, declaring that they were legal subjects of the King of England and beyond the limits of Massachusetts territory, to whom they would acknowledge no subjection Soldiers were soon sent who besieged the settlers in a fortified house. In a parley it was now said "that they held blasphemous errors which they must repent of" or go to Boston for trial, and they were soon carried thence.

1643, Nov. 3. He was brought with others before the court, charged with heresy and sedition, and they were sentenced to be confined during the pleasure of the court, and should they break jail or preach their heresies or speak against church or state, on conviction they should die. He was sent to prison at Dorchester, and not released till the following March, being then banished from both Massachusetts and Warwick.

1645, Jun. 4. He died before this date, from the trials that had attended his imprisonment, for he "through cold and hardship fell into a consumption, and in a short time after died of it."

1651, Jan. 22. His widow's distemper is alluded to by Roger Williams in a letter to the town, for he says he is confident; "that although not in all things, yet in a great measure, she is a distracted woman. My request is that you would be pleased to take what is left of hers into your hands, and appoint some to order it for her supply."

1652, Jun. 24. In a deed of this date from Ralph Earle to William Arnold, of certain land formerly owned by Richard Harcut, the latter is called the heir or assignee of Francis Weston and Margaret his wife. (Another deed mentions Harcut as cousin (*i. e.* nephew) of Weston, and that he had inherited land from him.)

No issue.

THEOPHILUS, { b. 1616. d. 1720 ±
m. 1670 ±
ELIZABETH MILLS, { b 1645 ± d. 1715 ±

of Mills.

Virginia, Kings Town, R. I.

He is said to have been of wealthy parents and to have had a collegiate education; in support of which he is quoted as saying that "till he was eighteen years old, he knew not what it was to want a servant to attend him with a silver ewer and napkin whenever he wanted to wash his hands."

He came to Virginia before he had reached his majority and served there in a military capacity, but soon returned to England and was an officer in the Parliamentary army.

1649. His regiment took part in the execution of King Charles I.

1660. Virginia. He came again from England and married while in Virginia, where part of his children were born.

1680. Kings Town. He came thence about this time, his departure from Virginia, being occasioned by a difference in religious views from his neighbors, he being a Baptist. His residence was near the head of Pettaquamscut Pond in what is now South Kingstown.

He lived by fishing, weaving and teaching, being conversant with Hebrew, Greek and Latin, and his services as a penman were brought into requisition in executing the deeds and papers of his neighbors.

The visits of distinguished men from Boston and other places, and his silence in regard to his previous history, perhaps account for the persistently held tradition that he was one of the regicide judges and had signed the death warrant of King Charles.

Much of mystery still clings to his history notwithstanding the great service done by Rev. Dr. Stiles, in his account of this interesting personage. The town record gives but sparse items concerning him, and he seemed to shrink from public office, though he occasionally appears as witness to a will or deed.

It has been conjectured that Theophilus Whaley may have been identical with Robert Whaley, a brother of Edward, the Regicide, and that he may have changed his name for some reasons connected with the execution of King Charles.

1687, Sep. 6. Taxed 3s., 11d.

1710, Jan. 30. He had 120 acres in East Greenwich, conveyed to him from the proprietors of the tract of land now comprising West Greenwich.

1711, Feb. 20. He and wife Elizabeth, deeded son Samuel for love, &c., 120 acres in East Greenwich.

He moved in the latter part of his life to the house of his son-in-law Joseph Hopkins, situated in what is now West Greenwich.

He was buried with military honors on Hopkins Hill.

He left a will, as Francis Willett mentioned to Dr. Stiles that he wrote one for him.

I. JOAN, { b. d.

II. ANN, { b. d
UNMARRIED.

III. THEODOSIA, { b. d.
m. 1697, Jul. 15.
ROBERT SPENCER, { b. 1674, Nov. 6. d. 1748. of John & Susannah ( ) Spencer.

1. Susanna, 1698, Mar. 4.
2. Anna, 1699, Jun. 7.
3. Martha, 1700, Sep. 18.
4. Ruth, 1702, May 20.
5. Robert, 1704, Mar. 5.
6. Theodosia, 1705, Dec. 8.
7. Theophilus, 1707, Sep. 16.
8. Michael, 1709, Dec. 27.
9. Joanna, 1711, Sep. 30.
10. Caleb, 1713, Jul. 20.
11. Nathaniel, 1715, Sep. 4.
12. James, 1717, Feb. 6.
13. Samuel, 1718, Feb. 3.

IV. ELIZABETH, { b. d. 1752.
m.
CHARLES HAZLETON, { b. d. 1712, Mar. 28. of Charles Hazleton.

1. James, 1694, Feb. 1.
2. Samuel, 1696, Mar. 25.
3. Catherine, 1697, Oct. 25.
4. Elizabeth, 1699, Oct. 2.
5. William, 1701, Apr. 24.
6. Ann, 1704, Apr. 27.
7. Mary, 1706, Feb. 6.
8. Ellen, 1707, Nov. 15.
9. Martha, 1711, Apr. 10.

V. MARTHA, { b. 1680. d. 1773.
m. (1)
JOSEPH HOPKINS, { b. d. 1735, May 15. of Thomas & Sarah ( ) Hopkins.
m. (2)
ROBERT SPENCER, { b. 1674, Nov. 6. d. 1748. of John & Susannah ( ) Spencer.

1. William,
2. Samuel, 1704, Jan. 6.
3. John, 1712, Apr. 2.
4. Robert 1713, Jun. 2.
5. Thomas,
6. Hannah,
7. Theodosius, 1718, Apr. 13.
8. Francis,
(By 2d husband, no issue.)

VI. LYDIA, { b. d.
m.
JOHN SWEET, { b. d. of Sweet.

WHALEY. 2d column. VII. Samuel. Fourth line. Samuel Whaley was at Voluntown, not Samuel Hopkins.

VII. SAMUEL, { b. d. North Kingstown, R. I.
m. (1)
——— HOPKINS, { b. d. of Samuel & Susanna ( ) Hopkins.
m. (2)
PATIENCE HEARNDEN, { b. d. of Isaac & Sarah ( ) Hearnden.

1. Thomas,
2. Samuel,
(2d wife.)
3. Theophilus,
4. Jeremiah,
5. John,
6. Ann,
7. Sarah, 1729, Aug. 11.

1713, Jul. 1. He and wife ———, signed a deed.

The accounts about him are rather conflicting. A descendant gave his death to Dr. Stiles, as having occurred at about 1782, at the age of seventy-seven, but this would apply better, it would seem, to a Samuel of the next generation. (It is noticeable too, that a Samuel Hopkins was at Voluntown, Ct., as early as 1721, when he held the office of Selectman, and was on a committee in regard to a tax for support of a minister, &c.

WHALEY. 2d column. VII. Samuel. He had children born at Voluntown, Ct., by his 2d wife, as follows: 3, Patience, 1713, Dec. 24. 4, Ann, 1716, Jan. 24. 5, Theophilus, 1718, Aug. 10. 6, James, 1721, Nov. 16. 7, John, 1724, May 28. 8. Timothy, 1727, Mar. 14. 9. Sarah, 1729, Aug. 11.

WHIPPLE.

JOHN, { b. 1617 ± d. 1685, May 16.
m. 1639 ±
SARAH, { b. 1624 ± d. 1666.

Dorchester, Mass., Providence, R. I.

1632, Oct. 3. He was ordered to give 3s. 4d. to his master Israel Stoughton for wasteful expenditure of powder and shot.

1637. He received a grant of land.

1640, Mar. 9. He had his son John baptized, and other children as follows: Sarah (1642, Feb. 6), Samuel (1644, Mar. 17), Eleazer (1646, Mar. 8), Mary (1648, Apr. 9), William (1652, May 16), Benjamin (1654, Jun. 4) and David (1656, Sep. 28).

1641. He and wife united with the church.

1658. He sold his homestead and lands to James Minot.

1659, Jul. 27. Providence. He was received as a purchaser.

1665, Feb. 19. He had lot 45 in a division of lands.

1666. He took oath of allegiance.

1666-69-70-72-74-76-77. Deputy.

1674. He had a license granted to keep an ordinary.

1676, Aug. 14. He was one of those "who staid and went not away" in King Philip's War, and so had a share in the disposition of Indian captives, whose services were sold for a term of years.

I. JOHN, { b. 1640. d. 1700, Dec. 15. Providence, R. I.
m. (1) 1663, Dec. 4.
MARY OLNEY, { b. d. 1676 ±. of Thomas & Mary (Small) Olney.
m. (2) 1678, Apr. 15. [John.
REBECCA SCOTT (w. of { b. d. 1701 + of

1. Mary, 1665, Mar. 4.
2. John, 1666, Oct. 2.
3. Elnathan, 1675, Jan. 2.
(2d wife.)
4. Deliverance, 1679, Feb. 11.
5. Dorothy,

1668-83. Town Treasurer.

1670-71-72-78-81. Town Clerk.

1670-81-82-84-86-90. Deputy.

1672, Apr. 2. Fine of 20s. for not serving on jury remitted, he being Town Clerk.

1674-81-82-87. Town Council.

1676, Aug. 14. He was one of the committee who advised as to disposition of Indian captives.

1677-78-79-80. Assistant.

1679, Jul. 1. Taxed 7s. with orphans of John Scott.

1687, Sep. 14. He was forbidden to sell any strong drink by retail, till bond was given.

1688. Ratable estate, 2 oxen, 6 cows, 4 young cattle, 4 horses, old mare, rights in land.

1701, Apr. 8. Testimony was taken as to his will, which had been presented by widow for probate, but was now declared void by Town Council. John Hart testified that John Whipple being questioned by him as to a will he had made disinheriting his only son, answered "he could not help the doing as he had done for he was now blind and he must do as others would have him do," but he added that it was not his desire to disinherit his son, "for I would willingly help him if I could."

1701, Apr. 22. Differences having happened among relatives of deceased—now all considering that to bring it to law would be greatly troublesome to all parties, and great charge, and would cause animosities of spirit and alienation of affection—an agreement was made. To John Whipple, the homestall, dwelling house, barn, and certain land. To Mary Carder, Elnathan Rice, Deliverance Whipple and Dorothy Rhodes, certain land. Movable estate to go one-third to widow, and the rest in five parts to five children. John Whipple to allow his mother-in-law (i. e. stepmother) £10, in surrender of her third.

1705, Jul. 21. His daughters Deliverance Arnold (and husband William Arnold), and Dorothy Rhodes (and husband Malachi Rhodes), sold certain land, and allude to an agreement made by children of John Whipple to divide real estate in 1701.

1682, May 8. Will—proved 1685, May 27. Ex. son Joseph. He premises by saying that having many children, and having formerly given to three of his sons all his lands and meadows at Loquassuck, viz: to Samuel, Eleazer and William, equally, (except 30 acres given John), he now therefore gives to those three sons each one-quarter of a right of commonage. To sons Benjamin and David, rights in land. To son Jonathan, 25 acres where he now dwells, and rights. To son Joseph, my dwelling house, three home lots, garden next the river, &c. To sons John, Samuel, Eleazer, William, Benjamin, David and Jonathan, 12*d.* each. To daughters Sarah, Mary and Abigail, 10*s.* each. To son Joseph, all rights of land in Narragansett country and all movables whatsoever, and he to see the testator decently buried.
Inventory, £41, 11*s.* 10*d.*, viz: yoke of oxen, 2 cows, 2 yearlings, 2 two years, 2 calves, steer, 3 swine, feather bed, 7 pewter platters, 5 pewter porringers, 3 old spoons, chisel, guage, augurs, &c.

He and his wife were first buried on his own land, and subsequently were removed to the North Burial Ground.

WHIPPLE. 2d column. IV. Eleazer. He had also probably daughters Deborah, 1670, Aug 1, and Hannah, 1695, Mar. 25.

II. SARAH, b. 1642. d. 1687 +
m.
JOHN SMITH, b. d. 1682. of John & Alice (   ) Smith.

1. John,
2. Sarah,
3. Alice, 1665.
4. Mary,
5. Joseph,
6. Benjamin, 1672 ±
7. Israel,
8. Daniel,
9. Elisha, 1680, Apr. 14.
10. William, 1682.

WHIPPLE. 2d column. III. Samuel. His wife b. 1639
Her mother's name was Elizabeth.

III. SAMUEL, b. 1644. d. 1711, Mar. 12. Providence, R. I.
m.
MARY HARRIS, b. d. 1722, Dec. 14. of Thomas Harris.

1. Noah,
2. Samuel, 1669.
3. Thomas,
4. Abigail, 1683.
5. Hope,

1679, Jul. 1. Taxed 6*s.* 3*d.*

1681, Apr. 27. He was granted a forty foot lot with consent of his father-in-law Thomas Harris.

1684, Aug, 21. He agreed with the town to provide a pair of stocks of stout oak plank.

1688. Constable. He gave in his ratable estate this year: 2 oxen, 8 cows, 8 young cattle, 5 swine, 1 horse, meadow, 11 acres corn land, 7 acres mowing, 22 acres pasture, 300 acres wood.

1691. Deputy.

1695, May 8. He deeded son Noah for well being and settlement 169 acres, &c.

1711, Mar. 9. Will—proved 1711, Mar. 20. Exs. sons Samuel and Thomas. To them, 150 acres equally, and other land to Thomas, including house where he dwells. To grandsons Noah, Enoch and Daniel, land; the two latter having testator's dwelling house for life, and then to daughters Abigail and Hope. To wife, movable estate for life and then to sons Samuel and Thomas.
Inventory, £149, ± viz: 5 cows, 2 heifers, 2 steers, 2 oxen, 2 yearlings, 2 horses, mare, 2 sows, 2 hogs, 26 sheep, hay, rye, Indian corn, tobacco, cider, flax, wearing apparel, 3 feather beds, warming pan, woolen wheel, linen wheel, &c.

He and his wife were buried in North Burial Ground, (his being the first interment there).

IV. ELEAZER, b. 1646. d. 1719, Aug. 25. Providence, R. I.
m. 1669, Jan. 26.
ALICE ANGELL, b. 1649. d. 1743, Aug. 13. of Thomas & Alice (   ) Angell.

1. Eleazer,
2. Alice, 1675, Jun. 3.
3. Margaret,
4. Elizabeth, 1680.
5. Job, 1684.
6. James, 1686.
7. Daniel,

He was a housewright.

1676, Mar. 11. He gave receipt for £6, for what the town paid for his curing, he having been wounded.

1679, Jul. Taxed 2*s.* 6*d.*

1688. Ratable estate, 2 oxen, 6 cows, 7 young cattle, horse, mare, 2 acres meadow, 6 acres pasture, 3½ acre lot, 70 acres woodland.

1693, 1701. Deputy.

1710, Apr. 27. He deeded land to son Job, and a few years later to son Eleazer.

1714, Jan. 1. He deeded son James, for love, &c., homestead farm, he paying his brother Daniel £50, and sister Elizabeth £50, and wife Alice to have for life a residence in house.

1719, Nov. 9. Administration to widow Alice and son James.
Inventory, £495, 4*s.* 5*d.*, viz: wearing apparel, linen wheel, wool cards, 2 beds, warming pan, table linen, silver money, £11, 3*s.*, silver cup, spoons, &c., egg turner, bills and bonds £333, 3*s.* 6*d.*, cow, calf, carpenter's tools, &c.

1722, Feb. 24. His sons Eleazer, James and Job, of Providence, deeded their brother Daniel of Wrentham, certain lands.

1733, Jan. 22. His widow being very ancient (she now living in Smithfield), and not willing further to act as administratrix on husband's estate, administration was given to John Rhodes, of Warwick, who had married the widow of James Whipple.

V. MARY, b. 1648. d. 1698 +
m. 1666, Mar. 9.
EPENETUS OLNEY, b. 1634. d. 1698, Jun. 3. of Thomas & Mary (Small) Olney.

1. Mary, 1668, Jan. 13.
2. James, 1670, Nov. 9.
3. Sarah, 1672, Sep. 10.
4. Epenetus, 1675, Jan. 18.
5. John, 1678 ±
6. Thomas, 1686, May 18.
7. Lydia, 1688, Jan. 26.

VI. WILLIAM, b. 1652. d. 1712, Mar. 9. Providence, R. I.
m.
MARY, b. d. 1712 + of

1. Mary,
2. William,
3. Seth,

1687, Sep. 1. Taxed 2*s.* 3*d.*

1712, Feb. 27. Will—proved 1712, Mar. 27. Ex. son William. To him, all lands, housing, &c., he paying legacies. To son Seth, £30 at age. To daughter Mary Sprague, £10 and what she has already had (viz: cow, calf, 8 sheep and household stuff). To wife Mary, her maintenance by son William, and if she choose to change her abode to live with another child, he to allow her what she needs, &c.
Inventory, £110, 14*s.* 2*d*, viz: beds, pewter, 2 wheels, woolen yarn, 2 oxen, 5 cows, 2 heifers, 2 yearlings, 3 mares, 4 swine, 27 sheep, &c.

VII. BENJAMIN, b. 1654. d. 1704, Mar. 11. Providence, R. I.
m. 1686, Apr. 1.
RUTH MATHEWSON, b. d. 1704 + of James & Hannah (Field) Mathewson.

1. Benjamin, 1688, Nov. 11.
2. Ruth, 1691, May 12.
3. Mary, 1694, Mar. 3.
4. Josiah, 1697, Jul. 29.
5. John, 1700, Feb. 25.
6. Abigail, 1703, Jun. 12.

1683, Apr. He brought in a wolf's head

1687, Sep. 1. Taxed 2*s.* 6*d.* Ratable estate same year: 2 acres planting, 2 acres meadow, 3 cows, 2 heifers, steer, mare, swine, 3 sheep.

1704, Mar. 9. Will—proved 1704, Apr. 12. Exx. wife Ruth. To sons Benajmin and John, home farm equally. To son John, the dwelling house by salt water in Providence. To wife Ruth, all movables, she paying sons Benjamin and John each three cows when sons are of age. To daughters Ruth, Mary and Abigail Whipple, £10 each at marriage or twenty-one. To wife, use of land till sons are of age, and then one-third of profits for life paid by sons equally. To son Benjamin, house in which I now dwell, at age, he living in western part and wife in eastern part, while widow.
Inventory, £99, 5*s.* 11*d.*, viz: silver money £1, 6*s.*, augers, chisels, 2 guns, 3 feather beds, 2 spinning wheels, yarn, flax, horse, 18 head cattle, 30 sheep, &c.

VIII. DAVID, b. 1656. d. 1710. Dec. Providence, R. I., Rehoboth, Mass.
m. (1) 1675, May 15.
SARAH HEARNDEN, b. d. 1677, Apr. 2. of Benjamin & Elizabeth (White) Hearnden.
m. (2) 1677, Nov. 11.
HANNAH TOWER, b. d. 1722, Nov. of John & Margaret (   ) Tower.

1. David,
(2d wife.)
2. Israel, 1678, Aug. 16.
3. Deborah, 1681, Sep. 12.
4. Jeremiah, 1683, Jun. 26.
5. William, 1685, May 27.
6. Sarah, 1687, Nov. 18.
7. Hannah, 1690, Jan. 9.
8. Abigail, 1692, Oct. 20.

1679, Jul. 1. Taxed 7½*d.*

1681, Feb. 2. He and another "lately killed a wolf, by their going a hunting after deer."

1687, Sep. 1. Taxed 8*s.*

1692. Rehoboth. He bought land of John Blackstone (son of Rev. William Blackstone.)

He was Ensign at time of his death.

1709, Mar. 24. Will—proved 1711, Jan. 8. Exx. wife Hannah. To son David, £10, he having had. To sons Israel, Jeremiah and William, 1*s.*, each. To daughters Sarah and Abigail, land bought of John Blackstone, &c. To daughter Deborah Tower, 1*s.* To wife Hannah, certain land for life, best bed, rest of household stuff, all money, cattle and rest of personal.

Inventory. Purse, plate and bills, £9, 1*s.*, 11*d.*, wearing apparel, books, 5 beds, 2 great wheels, linen wheel, 2 churns, 28 barrels cider, half a cider press, horses, cattle, goats, &c.

1720, May 28. Will—proved 1722, Dec. 8. Widow Hannah, of Attleboro, Mass. Ex. son Israel. To son Joseph Cowell, £10. To son Jeremiah Whipple, 20*s.* To daughter Deborah Tower, a feather bed, chest and half apparel. To daughter Sarah Razee, feather bed and half apparel. To four children, Israel and William Whipple, Deborah Tower and Sarah Razee, rest.

Inventory, £198, 10*s.*

IX. ABIGAIL, b. ; d. 1725, Aug. 19.
m. (1)
STEPHEN DEXTER, b. 1647, Nov. 1; d. 1679. of Gregory & Abigail (Fullerton) Dexter.
m. (2) 1682, Jan.
WILLIAM HOPKINS, b. 1647; d. 1723, Jul. 8. of Thomas Hopkins.

1. John, 1673.
2. Abigail,
(By 2d husband.)
3. William,

X. JOSEPH, b. 1662; d. 1746, Apr. 28. Providence, R. I.
m. 1684, May 20.
ALICE SMITH, b. 1664; d. 1739, Jul. 20. of Edward & Anphillis (Angell) Smith.

1. John, 1685, May 18.
2. Jeremiah, 1686, Sep. 3.
3. Joseph, 1687, Dec. 30.
4. Anphillis, 1689, Oct. 6.
5. Sarah, 1691, Mar. 29.
6. Susannah, 1693, Apr. 14.
7. Freelove, 1694, Mar. 18.
8. Alice, 1696, Feb. 6.
9. Amey, 1699, Jun. 16.
10. Christopher, 1701, Sep. 14.
11. Mary, 1704, Apr. 9.
12. Christopher, 1707, Mar. 6.

He was a merchant.

1687, Sep. 1. Taxed 5*s.*, 7*d.*

1688. Ratable estate, 100 acres, meadow right, 3 home lots (3 acres of which is planting ground and orchard), other lots and rights, 9 cows, 2 oxen, 2 young cattle, 2 horses and swine.

1696, Jan. 27. He and others were granted lot to build a school house on.

1698-99-1702-3-4-5-6-7-8-10-11-12-13-14-16-17-22-23-25-28. Deputy.

1703-4-15-16-17-18-19-20-21-22-23-25-26-27-28-29. Town Council.

1710, Dec. 11. Licensed to keep a public house, paying 20*s.*, for privilege.

1714. Assistant.

1719-20. Colonel of the regiment of militia on the mainland.

1744, Jan. 20. Will—proved 1746, May 19. Exs. sons John and Joseph. To son Joseph, farm on Chapatset Hill, in Glocester; also 100 acres in Glocester, near Wolf Hill, &c. To grandson Joseph, son of John, land toward southern end of Providence, and dwelling house west side of Town street, land on Weybosset Plains, &c. To daughter Alice Young, land. To son John, my homestead and all other farms in Providence, Smithfield and Glocester, undisposed of, reserving half acre at the burying place in my homestead "for the generations that shall proceed from my line forever." To daughter Sarah Crawford, £300, reserved by executors for her support, and at her death half of sum to her surviving children. To daughter Alice Young, negro girl Sarah, a cow, and £300. To daughters Ann Lippitt, Susannah Dexter, and Amy Gibbs, £300 each. To grandson Jonathan Bardin, son of daughter Mary, deceased, £300. To grandson Joseph Dexter, son of daughter Susannah, £100, at age.

Inventory, £5,292, 18*s.*, 2*d.*, viz: books £5, sword, pistols, cutlass, canes, bonds £3,640, 16*s.*, 2*d.*, 62 oz. plate £108, 10*s.*, 5 feather beds, 5 flock beds, clock, 24 chairs, 10 cushions, tables, warming pan, shoe buckles, 3 links gold buttons, gold buckle, 20 cows and calves £300, pair oxen, horse, 30 sheep and lambs, 6 negroes £600, viz: Cæsar, Aaron, Jeffrey, Betty, Jenny and Phebe.

He was buried in North Burial Ground.

XI. JONATHAN, b. 1664; d. 1721, Sept. 8. Providence, R. I.
m. (1)
MARGARET ANGELL, b. ; d. of Thomas & Alice ( ) Angell.
m. (2)
ANNE, b. ; d. 1725, Mar. 5. of

1. Sarah,
2. Margaret,
3. Jonathan, 1692, Feb. 22.
4. Thomas, 1694, Feb. 26.
5. Paratine,
6. Mary,
7. Alice,
(2d wife, no issue.)

1680, Oct. He brought in a wolf's head "that he had killed not far of the town."

1687, Sep. 1. Taxed 2*s.*, 8*d.*

1688. Ratable estate, 2 oxen, 4 cows, steer, mare and colt, 4½ acres planting, 3 acres mowing, 20 acres in woods.

1720, Dec. 23. He deeded son Jonathan, for love, &c., 65 acres, dwelling house and orchard.

1721, Sep. 5. Will—proved 1721, Sep. 27. Exs. sons Jonathan and Thomas. To son Jonathan, £5. To sons Jonathan and Thomas, lands undisposed of and wearing apparel. To son Jonathan, cane. To wife Ann, a third of housing and homestead lands, and movable goods while widow, and her third of movables to go to executors for their care of her (at her decease remainder of her movables going to children equally) To daughter Alice Whipple, £20. To Paratine White, £5. To grandson Jonathan Haman, a gun. To children equally, all silver money. To daughter Alice, privilege to live in house while single. To five daughters, rest of movable estate, viz: To Sarah Irons, Margery Barnes, Paratine White, Mary Haman and Alice Whipple.

Inventory, £221, 3*s.*, 7*d.*, viz: wearing apparel, cane, sword, gun, linen wheel, warming pan, pewter, flax, hay, barley, horse, ox, cows, young cattle, sheep, pigs, &c., and some estate brought by widow.

1723, Jul. 11. Will—proved 1725, Mar. 15. Widow Anne. Exs. William Haman and his wife. To William and Jonathan Haman, sons of William, 40*s.* each, at age. To Thomas Haman, youngest son of William, all money due, and paper money by me. To Mary Haman, my daughter-in-law (*i. e.* stepdaughter), wife of William Haman, a bible and bracelets for her, and her daughter after her, also wearing apparel and all other goods and estate.

Inventory, £105, 12*s.* 11*d.*

WHITFORD.

PASCO, b. ; d.
m.
——— b. ; d.

Newport, East Greenwich, Kings Town, R. I.

1680. Taxed 2*s.*

1689. East Greenwich. Freeman.

1697, Apr. 13. Kings Town. He was witness to a deed from Samuel Eldred, Sr., to his son John.

It is assumed that he was the progenitor of all of the name in Rhode Island, and that he was father of Nicholas and Pasco.

I. NICHOLAS, b. ; d. 1748. Portsmouth, East Greenwich, West Greenwich, R. I.
m.
MARY, b. ; d. 1743 (—) of

1. Pasco,
2. Robert,
3. David,
4. Ezekiel,
5. Catharine,
6. Dinah,
7. Mary,
8. Ruth,
9. Daughter,
10. Daughter,

He was a weaver.

1683, Mar. 13. He had a legacy of a loom, &c., from the will of Orpheus Pomeroy of Portsmouth.

1697, Jan. 21 East Greenwich. He bought land for £6, of David Shippee.

1703, Nov. 29. He sold to William Underwood for £15, a house and 30 acres.

1710, Feb. 3. He had a quarter of a right of land in a tract of 30,000 acres that afterwards became West Greenwich.

1721, Aug. 14. He and wife Mary mortgaged 25¼ acres, house, buildings, &c., for £30, to the colony.

1733, Mar. 12. He deeded son Pasco 20 acres in said son's occupation.

1733, Nov. 7. The mortgage (of 1721) was discharged.

1743, Dec. 3. Will—proved 1748, Mar. 28. Ex. son Ezekiel. To eldest son Pasco, 5*s.*, he having had land already. To second son Robert, two swamp lots and £5. To son David, £10. To eldest daughter Catharine Peckham, £5, and like legacies to daughters Dinah Weaver, Mary Greene and Ruth Summers. To grandson Jonathan Hill, 5*s.* To grandson Thomas Jackwaise, 5*s.* To great-grandson Henry Jackwaise, son to my granddaughter Elizabeth Jackwaise, 40*s.* To youngest son Ezekiel Whitford, all my homestead farm, buildings, &c., and all movables after debts and legacies are paid.

Inventory. Wearing apparel £20, bed, loom, quilt wheel, woolen wheel, pair of cards, 3 linen wheels, warming pan, cow, &c.

II. PASCO, b. ; d. East Greenwich, Kings Town, R. I.
m.
MARY STAFFORD, b. ; d. of Joseph & Sarah (Holden) Stafford.

1. Pasco,
2. Joseph,
3. John,
4. Ezekiel,
5. Nicholas,

1709, May 28. Kings Town. He and three others bought 275 acres of the vacant lands in Narragansett, ordered sold by the Assembly.

1713, Sep. A suit was brought against him for breach of covenant and damage to amount of £50, by Samuel Boone, and £10, was awarded by jury.

1723, Jul. 5. His son Pasco Whitford, Jr., married Deborah Fowler.

1734, Jun. 13. He brought suit against Jonathan Nichols, for £6, book account.

VALENTINE, b. d. 1701, Jan. 26.
m.
MARY, b. d. 1718, May 31.

Providence, R. I.

He was probably a brother of George Wightman of Kings Town, R. I.

His descendants have more generally adopted Whitman as the spelling of surname.

1656, Jun. Surveyor of highways.
1657–61. Juryman.
1658, May 18. Commissioner. (The General Court of Commissioners met at Warwick at this date.)
1660, Oct. 13. He signed his name as witness and interpreter to a deed of mortgage from Ninegret and other Indians to Humphrey Atherton, &c.
1665, Feb. 19. He had lot 39 in a division of lands.
1666, May 31. He took oath of allegiance.
1675–79–82–85–86. Deputy.
1676, Aug. 14. He was one of those "who staid and went not away" in King Philip's War, and so had a share in the disposition of the Indian captives whose services were sold for a term of years.
1677, Mar. 9. He and wife Mary sold to Ephraim Pierce, 60 acres, for £15.
1679, Jul. 1. Taxed 6*s*. 2*d*.
1680, Dec. 14. He addressed the authorities in these words: "I pray the town to consider that there is a great many strangers come in to this town, and others may come quickly, therefore I pray the town to make an order that no person shall come to this town to inhabit in the town but what may be accepted by the Town Council, and the Town Council to have power to send any out of this town that come from other colonies, so I rest yours,
VALENTINE WHITMAN."
1682. He and wife Mary deeded land in Kings Town to George Wightman.
1688. He gave in his ratable estate as follows: 11 cows, 2 oxen, 2 steers, 6 yearlings, 2 horses, mare, 6 acres tillage, 4½ acres meadow, 4 acres pasture, 60 acres woodland, and rights in other lands.
1695, Sep. 11. He deeded to son Valentine, for love, &c., 50 acres in place called by Indians Loakquisset, about eight miles north of said town (reserving 2 acres).
1701, Jan. 13. Will—proved 1701, Mar. 11. Exx. wife Mary. Overseers, son Valentine Whitman, son-in-law James Ballou and friend Richard Arnold. To eight daughters, 40*s*. each, viz: to Mary, Elizabeth, Susanna, Deborah, Alice, Hannah, Esther and Grace. To daughter Elizabeth, 60 acres "in consideration that she is weakly of body and may not be capable to provide for herself as other of my daughters." To son Valentine, 40*s*., and after decease of mother he is to have all my farm on which I now live, and other lands, and at his death all to go to his male issue, but if he have no male issue, then one-ninth to go to said son's female issue, and eight-ninths to the eight sisters of Valentine. To three grandsons, all rights in land west of Seven Mile Line, viz: to John and Mary Inman's eldest son, to James and Susannah Ballou's eldest son, and to Joseph and Deborah Smith's eldest son. To wife, all profits of farm, goods, chattels and cattle for life, and at her death she to have disposal among my and her children, "desiring her to consider specially such children as stay longest with her and help her in her age."
Inventory, £180, ± viz: old horse, 8 cows, 5 young cattle, 15 sheep, 3 young swine, cash in New England coin £38, 6*s*., cash in Spanish money £42, 8*s*., wheat, rye, Indian corn, pork, butter, cheese, cider, hay, tobacco, iron, glass and wooden ware, linen yarn, homespun cloth, 8 pewter platters, testament, part of a bible, &c.
1713, Jun. 16. His widow was taxed 13*s*. 6*d*.
1718, Jun. 9. Administration on estate of Mary Whitman, widow, was given to son Valentine. Inventory, £296, 10*s*.

I. MARY, b. 1652, Nov. 16. d. 1720, Apr. 27.
m.
JOHN INMAN, b. 1648, Jul. 18. d. 1712, Aug. 6. of Edward Inman.
1. Mary,
2. Deborah,
3. Sarah,
4. Anne,
5. John, 1684.
6. Valentine,
7. Naomi,
8. Joanna,
9. Talitha,

II. ELIZABETH, b. 1653, Jul. 3. d. 1727, Nov. 19.
UNMARRIED.

III. SUSANNA, b. 1658, Feb. 28. d. 1754.
m.
JAMES BALLOU, b. 1652. d. 1741 ± of Maturin & Hannah (Pike) Ballou.
1. James, 1684, Nov. 1.
2. Nathaniel, 1687, Apr. 9.
3. Obadiah, 1689, Sep. 6.
4. Samuel, 1692, Jan. 23.
5. Susanna, 1695, Jan. 3.
6. Bathsheba, 1698, Feb. 15.
7. Nehemiah, 1702, Jan. 20.

IV. DEBORAH, b. d.
m.
JOSEPH SMITH, b. d. 1735 + of John & Elizabeth ( ) Smith.
1. Joseph,
2. John,
3. Deborah,

V. ALICE, b. d.

VI. HANNAH, b. d. 1752, Aug. 7.
UNMARRIED.

VII. ESTHER, b. d. 1748, Aug. 21.
m.
JOHN STEERE, b. d. 1727, Jan. 5. of John & Hannah (Wickenden) Steere.
1. John,
2. Hosea,
3. Hezekiah,
4. Wickenden,

VIII. GRACE, b. d. 1748 +
m. 1716, May 23.
JABEZ GREENE, b. 1673, May 17. d. 1741, Oct. 1. of James & Elizabeth (Anthony) Greene.
1. Mary. 1718, Dec. 18.

IX. VALENTINE, b. 1668, Aug. 25. d. 1750, Aug. 26. Providence, Smithfield, R. I.
m. 1694, Dec. 12.
SARAH BARTLETT, b. d. of Bartlett.
1. Sarah, 1696, Jan. 26.
2. John, 1698, Feb. 20.
3. Henry, 1700, Jan. 16.
4. Abijah, 1708, Jan. 4.
5. Robert, 1712, May 2.
6. Benjamin, 1715, Jul. 22.
7. Noah, 1717, Dec. 31.

WHITMAN. 2d column, IX. Valentine. His wife was daughter of John & Sarah (Aldrich) Bartlett.

1713, Jun. 16. Taxed 17*s*.
1719. Deputy.
1731, Mar. 17. Smithfield. The first meeting of Town Council was held at his house.
1732, Jan. 10. He signed a letter on behalf of the church at Smithfield in answer to one from Elder Brown of Providence, in which they inform the Providence church that they hold to the faith as anciently held.
1733, Sep. 10. He deeded son Robert, for love, &c., half of lands in Scituate.
1750, Aug. 4. Will—proved 1750, Sep. 15. Ex. son Noah. To him, all my homestead farm on which I dwell, 60 acres, with house, &c., also 16 acres in another piece, and all household goods and movables. To son Robert, £60. To son Henry, 20*s*.
Inventory, £1,262, 12*s*. 6*d*., viz: swine £17, old horse, bull, 6 cows, 2 steers, 2 yearlings, 2 calves, 27 sheep, 13 lambs, woolen wheel, pair of worsted combs, cheese press, 5 tables, warming pan, 4 beds, 8 silver spoons £40, books £8, pewter, money scales, sword, cane, &c.

WICKENDEN.

WILLIAM, b. d. 1670, Feb. 23.
m. (1)
——— b. d.
m. (2) 1663
ELEANOR SHERRINGHAM, b. d.
of Sherringham.

Salem, Mass., Providence, R. I.

1637, Aug. 20 (or a little later.) Providence. He and twelve others signed the following compact: "We whose names are hereunder, desirous to inhabit in the town of Providence, do promise to subject ourselves in active and passive obedience to all such orders or agreements as shall be made for public good of the body in an orderly way, by the major consent of the present inhabitants, masters of families incorporated together in a Town fellowship, and

I. RUTH, b. d. 1670, Jan. 16.
m. 1659,
THOMAS SMITH, b. d. 1670, Jan. 16. of Christopher & Alice ( ) Smith.
1. John, 1661, Aug. 4.
2. Thomas, 1664, Aug. 9.
3. William, 1667, Jan. 10.
4. Joseph, 1669, Feb. 18.

II. HANNAH, b. d. 1705 +
m. 1660.
JOHN STEERE, b. 1634. d. 1724, Aug. 27. of Steere.
1. John,
2. Sarah,
3. Dinah,
4. Thomas,
5. Jane,
6. Ruth,
7. William, 1671, Nov. 25.
8. Ann,
9. Samuel,

III. PLAIN, b. d.
m.
SAMUEL WILKINSON, b. d. 1727, Aug. 27. of Lawrence & Susannah (Smith) Wilkinson.
1. Samuel, 1674, Sep. 18.
2. John, 1678, Jan. 25.
3. William, 1680, Aug. 1.
4. Joseph, 1683, Jan. 22.
5. Ruth, 1686, Jan. 31.
6. Susannah, 1688, Apr. 27.

(2d WIFE, no issue.)

William Wickenden. See also The Providence Oath of Allegiance, by Bowen. p.58-61.

others whom they shall admit unto them, only in civil things."

1640, Jul. 27. He and thirty-eight others signed an agreement for a form of government.

1641, Nov. 17. He and twelve others complained in a letter to Massachusetts of the "insolent and riotous carriages of Samuel Gorton and his company;" and therefore petitioned Massachusetts to "lend us a neighborlike, helping hand."

1645, Jan. 27. He bought of William Field, 6 acres lying upon Fox Hill.

1646, Sep. 21. He sold to Christopher Unthank, a house and house lot.

1647. Ordained as pastor of First Baptist Church.

1650, Sep. 2. Taxed 10*s*.

1651-52-53-54-55. Commissioner.

1655. Freeman.

1663, Dec. 23. He declared his intention of marriage with Eleanor Sherringham, of Newport.

1664-66. Deputy.

1665, Feb. 19. He had lot 66 in a division of lands.

1666, Jul. 9. He deeded son-in-law Thomas Smith and my daughter Ruth, his wife, certain land on south side of Pawtuxet river bounded partly by Benjamin Smith.

1670, Feb. 20. Will — proved 1670. Overseers, Gregory Dexter, Daniel Brown, John Hawkins. (This will is found at Warwick, though he was still called of Providence). To wife Eleanor, all goods she brought, yet remaining, and to have this my house to dwell in while she liveth, and half fruit trees in orchard and half the planting land for life, as well as the cow and calf called old and young "Bouncer," with meadow and a young colt and pied steer. To daughter Plain, certain land, a cow, heifer, yearling, share of meadow, &c. To daughter Hannah Steere, 10 acres upland and share of meadow, the said 10 acres adjoining son John Steere's 10 acres I formerly gave to him. To grandchildren Thomas and John Smith, 50 acres on both sides Moshassuck river and meadow on both sides Woonasquatucket river, desiring that none of my neighbors would defraud the fatherless. To son John Steere, 5 acres lying adjoining his 15 which lyeth by Pawtucket river, and the black steer. The debt to Stephen Paine and any other debts if any appear, to be paid from sale of oxen, the said oxen and debts to be at the ordering of wife, Gregory Dexter and daughter Plain. To daughter Plain, half of fruit trees, and half of meadow to her and half to daughter Hannah Steere. To wife a new piece of red cloth. Any contention between children to be settled by overseers. To grandsons William and Joseph Smith my two other yearlings. To wife, corn, grain and provisions at her dispose. His body he desired should be interred by his former wife. Finally he closes—"I cease from this world & yet hope for a better," adding that at decease of wife the house and 8 acres to be for use of grandchildren Smith.

WICKHAM.

SAMUEL, { b. 1664, Jun. 16. d. 1712 ±
m. (1) 1688, Aug. 2.
ANN, { b. d.
m. (2) 1691, Jun. 4.
BARBARA HOLDEN, { b. 1668, Jul. 2. d. 1707.
of Randall & Frances (Dungan) Holden.
m. (3) 1707, May 23.
MARY PLACE (w. of Enoch) { b. 1660, Feb. 2. d. 1746.
of James & Mary (Greene) Sweet.

Warwick, Kings Town, R. I.

1697, Feb. 6. He gave testimony calling himself aged thirty-two years or thereabout.

1700, May 27. Commander of Train Band. He was ordered to review all persons who had neglected to perform duty.

1701-3-4-7. Deputy.

1702. He gave 2*s*., toward building the Quaker meeting house at Mashapaug.

1703-9-10. Clerk of Assembly.

1708, Mar. 23. Kings Town. He sold to Israel Arnold, of Pawtuxet, for £113, homestead, mansion house and farm at Warwick.

1709-10. Deputy.

1710, May 17. He and seventeen others bought 7,000 acres of the vacant lands ordered sold by Assembly.

1712 ± Inventory. Feather bed, 3 flock beds, 30 oz. plate, pewter, warming pan, negro woman, yearling cattle, hour glass, goods at Newport, &c.

1738, Jun. 17. Will — proved 1746, Jan. 15. Widow Mary, of South Kingstown. Ex. son-

I. ANN, { b. 1689, Sep. 4. d. 1689, Dec. 14.

II. DAUGHTER, { b. 1690, Oct. 4. d. 1691, Jan. 4.

(2d WIFE.)

III. SARAH, { b. 1692, Mar. 9. d.

IV. SAMUEL, { b. 1693, Sep. 2. d. 1753, Feb. 23. Newport, R. I.
m. 1723, Mar. 17.
ELIZABETH COLLINS, { b. 1695, Jun. 28. d. of Arnold & Amy (Billings) Collins.

1. Samuel,
2. Henry, 1725.
3. Gideon, 1735.
4. Elizabeth, 1737.
5. Deborah, 1740.

1730. He was a member of a literary society that later developed into Redwood Library.

1734. Freeman.

1742. He was one of the original members of Newport Artillery Company.

1744-45-46-47 Deputy.

1744, Feb. 14. He and three other members of Assembly dissented from the vote of their associates, on an act for emitting £40,000 in Bills of Public Credit; "believing that posterity will never be able to discharge them, but must unavoidably end in the utter ruin of a vast number of families."

1747. Speaker of House of Deputies. This same year Redwood Library was incorporated, and he and two others were appointed on building committee.

V. JOHN, { b. 1695, Jun. 26. d. 1729, Jun. 20. Newport, R. I.

He was buried in Newport Cemetery.

VI. GIDEON, { b. 1697, Jan. 22. d.

in-law George Hazard. She mentions her daughter Mary Hazard, grandchildren Benjamin, Simeon, Enoch, Mary and Susannah Hazard, former husband Enoch Place, brother Samuel Sweet and son-in-law (*i. e.* stepson) Samuel Wickham, of Newport. She also mentions grandson George Place Hazard.

Inventory, £622, 13*s*.

VII. MARY, — b. 1698, Jul. 15. d.

VIII. THOMAS, — b. 1700, Jul. 30. d. 1777, Sep. 19. — Newport, R. I.
m. 1725, Mar. 23.
HANNAH BREWER, — b. 1700, Jun. 9. d. 1778, Nov. 12. — of — Brewer.

He was a shopkeeper.

1735. Freeman.

1742. He was one of the orginal members of Newport Artillery Company.

1747. He was a member of Redwood Library at its incorporation.

1748. Deputy. He bore the title of Captain at this time.

1755, May. He and two others were appointed a committee to treat with Josiah Arnold, about land at Beaver tail on which the light house stands, in order to purchase same of him.

1772, Nov. 18. Will—proved 1783, Aug. 5. Exs. wife Hannah, brother Charles and my three sons. All real estate at Newport, to be disposed of, and proceeds after payment of debts, to be divided equally to sons Thomas, Samuel and Charles. To wife Hannah, negro woman Bell. To daughter Sarah Wickham, negro Nancy. To daughter Rebecca Deblois, negro Bet. To wife and two daughters, rest of personal equally, except deduction from Rebecca's portion for what had.

Inventory, £86, 5*s*., 2*d*., viz: household goods, clock, £7, 10*s*., 2 silver tankards, silver cup, salver, soup spoon, 4 porringers, spoons and tongs, making 78½ oz. plate £32, 16*s*., 8*d*.

He and his wife were buried in Trinity Church yard.

1. John, 1728.
2. Thomas, 1730.
3. Samuel, 1734.
4. Thomas, 1736.
5. Sarah, 1737.
6. Mary, 1739.
7. Samuel, 1742.
8. Rebecca, 1743.
9. Rebecca, 1744.
10. Charles, 1745.
11 Hannah, 1746.
12. Amey,

IX. BENJAMIN, — b. 1701, Nov. 17. d. 1779, Sep. 10. — Newport, R. I.
m. (1) 1733, Sep. 11.
REBECCA WATMOUGH, — b. 1714, Aug. 1. d. 1741, Oct. 3. — of George — Watmough.
m. (2) 1743, Dec. 25.
MARY GARDINER, — b. d. 1788, May 8. — of John & Frances (Sanford) — Gardiner.

His first wife was an English lady to whom he was married at St. Paul's, London.

1747. He was a member of Redwood Library at its incorporation.

1756–57–58. Deputy.

1756, Oct. 14. He was chosen Lieutenant Colonel of the regiment ordered to be raised by the Assembly under "an act for raising, subsisting and paying four hundred men, to be sent to Albany as a re-inforcement to the army gone upon the expedition against Crown Point."

1757. Speaker of House of Deputies.

1774, Aug. He having represented to the Assembly that the lottery granted him by act of that body for the disposing of his real estate to enable him to pay his debts, hath met with discouragement so that there was little prospect of its being filled or drawn; now therefore the Assembly having a debt against him of £60, voted that to recover said sum, and encourage the lottery, they would take as many tickets as his debt amounted to.

1. Elizabeth, 1736, Sep. 10.
2. Deborah, 1739, Feb. 3.
(2d wife.)
3. John, 1745, Aug. 3.
4. Benjamin, 1747, Jan. 18.
5. John, 1748, Jun. 9.
6. Samuel, 1750, Oct. 27.
7. Frances, 1754, Jun. 5.
8. Mary, 1756, Jun. 17.
9, Katharine, 1757, Oct. 18.
10. Samuel, 175-, Oct. 3.
11. Sarah, 1760, Sep. 26.

X. CHARLES, — b. 1703, Dec. 6. d. 1787, Sep. 6. — Newport, R. I.
m.
REBECCA BREWER, — b. 1710. d. 1770, Mar. 18. — of — Brewer.

1741. Freeman.

1747. He was a member of Redwood Library at its incorporation.

1786, Apr. 19. Will—proved 1791, Jan. 3. Exs. son-in-law Robert Crooke, friend John Bourse and grandson William Crooke. To daughter Anne Crooke, use of mansion house where I now dwell for her life, and certain other land, stables and Rocky Farm with buildings, &c., also for her life. To grandchildren Charles, John and Rebecca Wickham Crooke, 816 acres in Foster with buildings. To granddaughter Catharine Dudley, certain land and house in Newport. To grandson John Crooke, land. At death of daughter Anne, the estate given her to go to grandchildren Catharine Dudley and Charles, John, William and Rebecca Wickham Crooke. To five grandchildren rest of estate.

Inventory, £33, 9*s*. (besides notes), wearing apparel, mahogany table, clock £4, old bay mare £6, very old roan horse, £2, &c.

1. Anne, 1731.

XI. WILLIAM, — b. d. — Newport, R. I.
m.
ANNA, — b. 1715. d. 1743, Aug. 31. — of

1739. Freeman.

XII. BARBARA, — b. d.
m. 1736, Jan. 28.
JOHN COTTRELL, — b. d. — of — Cottrell.

See: American Genealogist, v. 20, p. 119.

WIGHTMAN.

GEORGE, — b. 1632, Jun. d. 1722, Jan.
m.
ELIZABETH UPDIKE, — b. 1644. d. 1722 (—) — of Gilbert & Katharine (Smith) — Updike.

Kings Town, R. I.

Tradition makes him a descendant of Edward Wightman burned for heresy at Litchfield in England, 1612, Apr. 11 (being the last to suffer death for religious liberty, as is stated).

He was a relative (perhaps brother) of Valentine Whitman, who early settled in Providence. The descendants of George have more generally preserved the spelling of the name as Wightman, though occasionally using the other form — Whitman.

1669. He and others were arrested by Connecticut authorities and taken to Hartford, because they owned allegiance to Rhode Island. They were kept in jail some time.

1671, May 20. He took oath of allegiance.

1673, May 6. Freeman.

1679, Jul. 29. He and forty-one others of Narragansett petitioned the King praying that he "would put an end to these differences about the government thereof, which hath been so fatal to the prosperity of the place; animosities still arising in people's minds as they stand affected to this or that government."

1686. Constable.

I. ELIZABETH, — b. 1664, Jul. 26. d. 1756.
m.
ALEXANDER HULING, — b. 1665. d. 1725, Jul. 29. — of James & Margaret ( ) — Huling.

1. James,
2. Alexander,
3. Honour,
4. Margaret,
5. Elizabeth,
6. Catharine,
7. Mary,

II. ALICE, — b. 1666, Dec. 29. d. 1747 +
m.
SAMUEL WAIT, — b. d. 1752. — of Samuel & Hannah ( ) — Wait.

1. Joseph, 1697, Apr. 27.
2. George, 1699, Aug. 14.
3. Samuel, 1701, Oct. 13.
4. Benjamin, 1703.
5. Martha,
6. John, 1709, Feb. 22.

III. DANIEL, — b. 1668, Jan. 2. d. 1750, Aug. 31. — Kings Town, Newport, R. I.
m. (1)
CATHARINE HOLMES, — b. 1671. d. 1699, Sep. 8. — of Jonathan & Sarah (Borden) — Holmes.
m. (2)
MARY, — b. 1669. d. 1732, Nov. 4. — of
m. (3) [of Joseph.
CATHARINE GARDINER(w. — b. 1673. d. 1758, Oct. 28. — of John & Frances (Holden) — Holmes.

He was a house carpenter.

1687, Sep. 6. Taxed 1*s*.

1704. Newport. He was ordained as minister of Second Baptist Church, having joint care with Rev. James Clarke. His pastorate extended over nearly fifty years, his colleague dying 1736, Dec. 1, after which Nicholas Eayres was associated with him, and the latter succeeded him in the pastorate.

1718, Sep. He brought suit against John Langford, damage of £65, 2*s*.

1743, Mar. 21. He deeded son George Wightman of North Kingstown, 250 acres in Exeter, for £300.

He was buried in the Newport Cemetery, as were his three wives.

1. Daughter,
2. Daughter,
(2d wife.)
3. George, 1703 ±
4. Elizabeth, 1705 ±
5. Daniel, 1707.

1687, Sep. 6. Taxed 11*s*.

1687. Grand Jury.

He was for some years member of the Town Council.

1710, May 17. He and seventeen others bought 7,000 acres in Narragansett of the vacant lands ordered sold by the Assembly.

1712, Feb. 19. He and wife Elizabeth sold William Gardiner 27½ acres in Boston Neck, for £103.

1722. Will—codicil—proved 1722, Feb. 12. Exs. sons Daniel and Valentine. Overseer, friend John Jones. To son Valentine, all the lands bought of Joseph Dolover. To son Daniel, part of land on Great Plain. To son George, the farm on which said George now dwells, with houses, &c. To son John, the 300 acres where he dwells, with houses, &c. To son Samuel, a money legacy. To daughter Elizabeth Huling, £20. To daughter Aylie (*i. e.* Alice) Wait, £30. To daughter Sarah Peterson, £20. To grandson George, son of Daniel, £10, gun, wearing clothes, linen, chest brought from England and great bible. To two children of his son Daniel, viz: Daniel and another, a legacy of 50*s*. a year. He desires "that all my dear children named to be contented for what I have given," and that they would live in the fear of God and at peace among themselves, "the God of peace be with you." He gives 20*s*. to the congregation to buy wine to celebrate the Lord's Supper. In the codicil he gives further property to son Daniel.

Inventory, fowling piece, 3 swords, books, yoke of oxen, bull, 8 cows, 19 young cattle, 57 sheep, several horsekind, 10 swine, &c.

IV. SARAH, b. 1671, Feb. 25. d.
m. (1) 1697, Apr.
WILLIAM COLLINS, b. d. 1712. of Collins.
m. (2)
——— PETERSON, b. d. of Peterson.

1. Anna, 1698, Jan. 29.
2. Sarah, 1700, Feb. 27.
3. William, 1701, —— 16.
4. Elizabeth, 1709, Dec. 28.

V. GEORGE, b. 1673, Jan. 8. d. 1761. Warwick, R. I.
m. (1)
ELIZABETH, b. d. of
m. (2) 1738, Aug. 13.
SARAH LADD, b. d. 1759 + of Ladd.

1. George,
2. John, 1701 ±
3. Samuel,
4. Elizabeth,
5. Phebe,
6. Deborah,

1716. Freeman.

1719, Dec. 22. He bought 150 acres in East Greenwich.

1724. Deputy.

1759, Sep. 1. Will—codicil 1760, Mar. 1.—proved 1761, Jan. 15. Exs. son John and grandson Elisha. To son George, 50 acres south end of farm where I live for life, and then to his three sons Reuben, Stephen and David. To son John, half of land not disposed of. To son George, for life, rest of lands undisposed of, and then to his sons Reuben, Stephen and David. To wife Sarah, best room in house and improvement of land two rods south of house while widow, and one cow with keep of same by sons John and George, who are to provide her with sufficient firewood, five bushels corn, a bushel of rye, two barrels cider, two barrels cider beer and two bushels good winter apples yearly, while widow. To her also, two spinning wheels, silver spoon and half the bedding she has spun since she hath been my wife, side saddle, and £250, all in lieu of dower (or else 5*s*.) To daughter Elizabeth Havens, £200. To daughter Phebe Weaver, £200. To daughter Deborah Rhodes, £200. To son John, iron kettle and coat with plate buttons. To son George, iron pot and andirons. To grandson Elisha Wightman, jacket and plate buttons. To grandson Philip Wightman, a pair of plush breeches. To grandson Reuben Wightman, a duray coat. To Barbara Colvin, daughter of Benjamin Colvin, a cupboard. To three daughters, all indoor movables. To four grandsons, sons of Samuel, £50 (viz: £20 to Samuel and £10 each to Benjamin, George and Asa), and all wearing apparel not disposed of. To Margaret Wightman, widow of son Samuel, £50. To three daughters, £50, equally. To executors, the rest of estate. The codicil gives to three daughters, £100, each.

VI. JOHN, b. 1674, Apr. 16. d. 1750. Kings Town, Exeter, R. I.
m. (1) 1700, Jan. 6.
JANE BENTLEY, b. d. of William & Sarah ( ) Bentley.
m. (2)
VIRTUE, b. d. 1746 + of

1. Alice, 1702, Oct. 16.
2. Sarah, 1704, Jan. 23.
3. John,
4. James,
5. Valentine,
6. Jane,
7. Mary,
8. Deborah,

1700, May 4. He was summoned by the Assembly to answer charge in court of being engaged in a riot.

1746, Dec. 3. Will—proved 1750, May 8. Exs. sons John and James. To wife Virtue, all the goods, &c., she brought, £30, and great bible. To sons John, James and Valentine, and daughters Sarah Whitford, wife of Joseph, Jane Spink, wife of Benjamin, Mary Boone, wife of Samuel Boone, Jr., and Deborah Records, wife of John Records, Jr., each, one silver spoon. To son Valentine, an additional spoon that was his grandfather's. To seven children, equally, rest of silver except silver buttons. To four daughters, rest of household goods. To granddaughter Lydia Wilcox, wife of Abraham Wilcox, £5. To son James, an iron chain. To son Valentine, rest of estate.

Inventory, £1,264, viz: cash £82, 20 oz. silver £45, 10*s*., 9 chairs, bed, warming pan, linen wheel, books £7, 10*s*., stillyards, pair of cards, farming utensils, mare, 4 cows, yoke of oxen, 2 two years, 5 swine, 41 sheep, &c.

He was buried on his own farm.

VII. SAMUEL, b. 1676, Jan. 9. d. Kings Town, R. I.

VIII. VALENTINE, b. 1681, Apr. 16. d. 1747, Jun. 9. Kings Town, R. I., Groton, Conn.
m. 1703, Feb. 17.
SUSANNAH HOLMES, b. d. of Holmes.

1. Daniel,
2. Valentine,
3. Abraham,
4. Timothy, 1718.
5. Sarah,
6. John,
7. Susanna,
8. Elizabeth,
9. Mary,

1700, May 4. He was summoned by Assembly to answer charge in court of being engaged in a riot.

1705. Groton. He organized the First Baptist Church, of which he became pastor, and was presented with a house and twenty acres on his arrival at that place. He remained pastor of the Groton church till his death.

1712. He organized a church in New York this year.

His son Timothy was ordained as pastor of the Groton Church a few years after his father's death, and continued his pastorate till his own death in 1796, and his son John Gano Wightman became pastor in 1800.

WILBUR (SAMUEL)

SAMUEL, b. d. 1656, Sep. 29.
m. (1)
ANN, b. d. [of Thomas.
m. (2)
ELIZABETH LECHFORD (w. b. d.

Boston, Mass., Portsmouth, R. I., Taunton, Mass.

His first wife has been called daughter of Thomas Bradford, of Doncaster, York Co., Eng., but if the latter's will was of date 1607, Mar. 1, and mentions a daughter Ann, as wife of Samuel Wilbur, that Samuel could hardly be this one.

1633, Mar. 4. Fceeman.

1633, Dec. 1. Admitted to church, as also his wife Ann.

1634, Nov. 10. Assessor of taxes.

1637, Nov. 20. He was one of those disarmed "in consequence of having been seduced and led into dangerous error by the opinions and revelations of Mr. Wheelwright and Mrs. Hutchinson," and therefore "having license to depart," he went soon to Rhode Island.

1638, Mar. 7. Portsmouth. He and eighteen others signed the following compact: "We whose names are underwritten do here solemnly in the presence of Jehovah incorporate ourselves into a Bodie Politick, and as he shall help, will submit our persons, lives and estates, unto our Lord Jesus Christ, the King of Kings and Lord of Lords, and to all those perfect and most absolute laws of his given us in

I. SAMUEL, b. d. 1679 ± Portsmouth, R. I.
m.
HANNAH PORTER, b. d. 1722, Apr. 6. of John & Margaret ( ) Porter.

1. Abigail,
2. Hannah,
3. John,
4. Elizabeth, 1665.
5. Mary,
6. Rebecca,

1646, Feb. 4. He was ordered to run his fence straight at the upper end of his lot.

1655. Freeman.

1656. Juryman.

1656-58-59-60-62-63. Commissioner.

1657, Jan. 20. He and others bought a large tract in Narragansett of the Indian sachems, called Pettaquamscott Purchase.

1662, Sep. 29. He and others of his company were complained of by Ninecraft and other Indians, for pretending title to Point Judith and other lands adjoining, and have endeavored to possess themselves, both by building and bringing cattle.

1664-65-69-70. Deputy.

1665-66-67-68-69-77-78. Assistant.

1667, Aug. 10. He enlisted in the troop of horse.

1671, Oct. 14. He deeded his daughter Hannah Clarke, wife of Latham Clarke, 500 acres, and mentions son-in-law Caleb Arnold, who had a deed of land previously from him.

1676. Captain.

1676, Aug. 24. He was a member of the Court Martial held at Newport for the trial of certain Indians charged with being engaged in King Philip's design. Several of the Indians were sentenced to be executed.

1678, Aug. 21. Will—proved 1710, Nov. 7. Exs. wife Hannah and son John. Overseers, son-in-law Latham Clarke and cousin William Wilbur, Sr. To wife, all personal estate on Rhode Island, as houses, lands, cattle or chattels, for life, and then to go to son John, and if he die without issue then to his three younger sisters. To daughter Elizabeth Wilbur, all land in Point Judith, except 100 acres to youngest daughter Rebecca Wilbur. To daughter Mary Wilbur, my whole share in the 1,000 acres of land in Narragansett country. To daughter Rebecca Wilbur, 250 acres in Narragansett. To son John Wilbur, 250 acres in Narragansett and all my share of house lots between Jirah Bull and John Tefft, &c. To grandson Latham Clarke, 100 acres in Narragansett. To grandson Samuel

his holy word of truth, to be guided and judged thereby."

1638, May 13. He was present at a General Meeting, upon public notice.

1638, Jun. 27. Clerk of Train Band.

1639, Jan. 24. Constable.

1639, Feb. 21. He was allotted a neck of land lying in Great Cove, containing about 2 acres.

1640, Jan. 7. He and his co-partner Ralph Earle were ordered to serve the town of Newport with good sufficient stuff, viz: with sawn board at 8*s*., the hundred, and half inch board at 7*s*., to be delivered at the pit by the water-side.

1641, Mar. 16. Freeman.

1644. Sergeant.

1645, Nov. 29. Boston. He having returned here, his wife Elizabeth was received into the church at this date.

1648, May 2. He deposed that when he married the widow of Thomas Lechford, he never received anything of his estate, "no not so much as his said wife's wearing apparel."

1655. Portsmouth. Freeman.

At the time of making his will he was living in Taunton, having a house also at Boston, and his will was placed on record in both Massachusetts and Plymouth colony.

1656, Apr. 30. Will—proved 1656, Nov. 1. Exs. wife Elizabeth and son Shadrach. To wife, all movables in house, all sheep and lambs, a mare and a colt. To eldest son Samuel, lands at Rhode Island, debts due from Richard Smith the eldest, sheep due from Henry Bull, cow in hands of James Babcock, &c., with rent for said cattle, also five hundred pounds of iron, &c. To son Joseph, house and land in Taunton, where said Joseph lives, share in iron works, &c. To youngest son Shadrach, my house and land at Taunton wherein I dwell, and all movables, cattle, &c., with exceptions to wife, and a white horse. To wife, half the house, two best cows, &c., if she continue to live there, but if she marry another man and move, then my son Shadrach to have same, and allow wife £10. The rest of cattle and goods undisposed of to go to executors equally. To Robert Blatt, of Boston, 20*s*. To goodman Blasko, 20*s*. To son Shadrach, the time of my man John Muskalett. To son Joseph, ten yards of cloth among the goods in house at Boston and £10, to be paid him by Shadrach.

Inventory, £282, 19*s*., 6*d*., viz: books, 16*s*., bedding, wearing apparel, pewter, ammunition, still, horse, 10 head of cattle, yearling heifer, 3 calves, 2 swine, dwelling house and land £40, house and land given son Joseph, £10, 12*s*., debts due deceased £51, 10*s*., 8*d*., interest in iron works at Taunton £25, 10*s*., money £1, 6*d*.

Arnold, 100 acres in Narragansett, To cousin (*i. e.* niece) Ann Wilbur, daughter of Joseph, 100 acres in Narragansett. To cousin Samuel Wilbur, son of Shadrach, 100 acres in Narragansett. To sister, Sarah Sherman (meaning his wife's half sister), 200 acres in Narragansett. To cousin William Wilbur, Sr., 250 acres in Narragansett. To Francis Gisborne, 100 acres in Narragansett. To wife, rest of Narragansett lands, Indian man and three squaws for full term they have to serve, and what horses, mares or colts shall be found to be mine in Narragansett country. The land given three youngest daughters to be theirs at sixteen or marriage. Son-in-law Latham Clarke and my cousin William Wilbur, Sr., to take care of my deeds in Narragansett country.

His daughters married as follows: Abigail to Caleb Arnold (1666, Jun. 10), Hannah to Latham Clarke, Elizabeth to Morris Freelove (1681, Feb. 9), Mary to Samuel Forman, and Rebecca to William Browning.

1680. Hannah Wilbur, taxed 10*s*. This was evidently his widow.

1712, Feb. 13. Widow Hannah confirmed husband's will in regard to three youngest daughters, sisters of John, who were to have his part if he died without issue, and she now therefore confirmed "to survivors of my said three youngest daughters and their heirs."

1722, Apr. 9. Administration on estate of widow Hannah Wilbur to Josiah Arnold. Inventory £143, 14*s*., 9*d*.

1738, Mar. His daughter Elizabeth Freelove called herself aged seventy-three years.

II. { JOSEPH, { b. / d. 1691. Taunton, Mass.
m.
{ ELIZABETH DEANE, { b. / d. 1670, Nov. 9. of John & Alice ( ) Deane.

1. Anna,

1660-67-69-75-81. Grand Jury.

1665-71-84. Constable.

1673-80. Surveyor of Highways.

1678. He was on a jury which found that Mary Gould aged four years, "came to its death by some accident, as falling in or adventuring to wade through."

1690, Apr. 1. Will—proved 1691, Nov. 18. Exx. daughter Anna. To daughter Anna Wilbur, movables and my share in iron works in Taunton, called Old Iron Works, and house where I dwell, barn, warehouse, other land, &c. To cousin (*i. e.* nephew), John Wilbur, son of brother Shadrach, 40 acres, &c. To cousin Eleazer Wilbur, son of Shadrach, 30 acres, &c. To cousins Samuel, Joseph, Shadrach and Benjamin, sons of brother Shadrach, a share in North Purchase. To cousin Sarah, wife of Nathan Hoar, two ewe sheep. To cousin Rebecca, wife of Abraham Hathaway, a neat beast a year old. To Hannah Briggs, daughter of William Briggs, a neat beast half a year old. To daughter Ann, all the rest of estate.

His daughter's birth is recorded as 1672, May 7, and if this date is correct she must have been by a later wife, or else the date of death of Joseph's wife Elizabeth, is recorded erroneously.

III. { SHADRACH, { b. / d. 1698. Taunton, Mass.
m. (1)
———— { b. / d. of
m. (2)
HANNAH (widow). { b. / d. 1696 + of

1. Sarah,
2. Mary, 1662, Mar. 8.
3. Samuel, 1663, Apr. 1.
4. Rebecca, 1665, Jan. 13.
5. Hannah, 1668, Feb. 24.
6. Joseph, 1670, Jul. 27.
7. Shadrach, 1672, Dec. 5.
8. John, 1675, Mar. 2.
9. Eleazer, 1677, Jul. 1.
10. Benjamin, 1683, Jul. 23.
(2d wife, no issue.)

He was Town Clerk for more than thirty-five years.

1672, Aug. 14. He was on a jury to view the body of Peter Treby, son of Peter of Newport, being at Taunton, with his mother Bethiah. Verdict, that the child of three years "being near the riverside, by some accident fell into the river," &c.

1674. Grand Jury.

1685, Oct. 27. He was granted liberty to sell strong liquor by the gallon, if "careful not to sell to such as will abuse same."

1687, Aug. 30. A warrant was issued for his arrest on the charge that he "hath lately in the name and with the consent of the said town, written and published a certain scandalous, factious and seditious writing, therein very much reflecting upon and contemning the laws, authority and government of this his Majesty's territory and dominion of New England," &c. He suffered imprisonment for a time under the government (then in force) of Sir Edmund Andros.

1696, Sep. 12. Will—proved 1698, Mar. 1. Exs. sons Joseph and Shadrach. To wife Hannah, £30, two good cows and all estate that was hers that she brought from Braintree, that is if she desires to return to her children at Braintree, but if she choose to stay with my children and be a mother to them, then she is to have use of best room in house while widow and be maintained out of my estate as my wife. To wife and child of son Samuel, deceased, confirmation of what land he had. To son Joseph, land and house, he paying his brother John, £5, toward building him a house. To son Shadrach, land, he paying brother Eleazer, £10. To son John, land adjoining that which his uncle Joseph gave him. To son Eleazer, land. To son Benjamin, all house where I dwell with barn, and lots they stand on, meadow swamp and little orchard. To daughter Sarah, wife of Nathaniel Hoar, £10. To daughter Rebecca, wife of Abraham Hathaway, £10. To sons Joseph, Shadrach, Eleazer and Benjamin, and to my grandson Samuel Wilbur, all purchaser's rights in township of Taunton. To executor, £5. To five sons, lands undisposed of. Son Joseph to take care of all writings, books of accounts, &c.

Inventory, £7,720, 9*d*., viz: 3 feather beds, arms and ammunition, books £2, pewter, carpenter's tools, silver money, spoon, bauble and thimble £5, 3*s*., 8*d*., bull, 4 oxen, 4 cows, 3 heifers, steer, 3 calves, 50 sheep, 3 mares, horse, colt, swine, dwelling house, barn and lot with Benjamin £163, house and land with Joseph, £80, trading goods £21, 8*d*., &c.

(2d WIFE, no issue.)

WILBUR (WILLIAM)

* { WILLIAM, { b. / d. 1710.
m.
———— { b. / d. 1710 (—)

Portsmouth, R. I.

He was a weaver.

1654, Jun. 10. He received a deed of 10 acres from Samuel Wilbur, Sr , of Taunton.

1657, Dec. 10. He was granted 8 acres.

1658, Dec. 21. He sold 6 acres to Peter Tallman.

1671, Jun. 7. Juryman.

1678, Aug. 21. He was appointed one of the overseers of his cousin Samuel Wilbur's will of this date.

1678. Deputy.

1687, Dec. 27. He deeded to son Joseph, for love, &c., 30 acres in Little Compton.

1705, Feb. 23. He deeded son Benjamin, for love, &c., all my dwelling house, orchard and lands in Portsmouth, and 70 acres in Swanzey.

1705, May 7. He deeded grandson Samuel, son of Thomas, 250 acres in Kings Town, bounded partly by land of John Wilbur. The income of said land was to be for granddaughters Mary

I. { MARY, { b. / d. 1720, Apr. 17.
m.
{ JOSEPH MOWRY, { b. 1647. / d. 1716, May 27. of Roger & Mary ( ) Mowry.

1. Mary, 1672, Oct. 17.

II. { JOHN, { b. / d. Portsmouth, R. I.
m.
{ HANNAH, { b. / d. of

1. John,
2. Mary,

1694, Mar. 13. He and wife Hannah, sold John Sweet of Narragansett, 450 acres there for £90.

III. { JOSEPH, { b. / d. 1729, May 4. Little Compton, R. I.
m.
{ ANN BROWNELL, { b. / d. 1747, Apr. 2. of Thomas & Ann ( ) Brownell.

1. Martha, 1684, Aug. 20.
2. Anna, 1686, May 8.
3. William, 1688, Mar. 25.
4. Joseph, 1689, Dec. 30.
5. John, 1691, Dec. 15.
6. Thomas, 1694, Jan. 14.
7. Mary, 1696, Jan. 4.
8. Benjamin, 1699, Jun. 20.
9. Stephen, 1701, Mar. 22.
10. Abigail, 1703, Aug. 21.

1728, Jan. 11. Will—proved 1729, Jun. 5. Ex. son Joseph. To wife Anna, all household stuff, money, debts, &c., improvement of biggest room for life, £10, per annum paid by son Thomas, victuals and drink provided by said son, and ten cords of firewood yearly provided by son Joseph. To son William, certain land and buildings, he paying legacies of £150. To son Joseph, certain land and buildings, he paying legacies of £80. To son John, 25 acres. To son Thomas, land and my dwelling house, &c., also benefit of certain stock of creatures while wife lives, which then go equally to children. To son Benjamin, 5*s*. To son Stephen, 5*s*. To daughter Anna Wood, £50. To daughters Mary Eldridge and Abigail Wilbur, £50, each. To grandson Joseph Closson, 15 acres, £40, and a cow. To grandson Timothy Closson, 20 acres, £40 and a cow. To son-in-law Thomas Burge, 5*s*. To nine children the rest of estate.

Inventory, £643, 5*s*., 3*d*., viz: wearing apparel, books, 30*s*., beds, pewter, pair of cards, 70 sheep, 24 lambs, 3 mares, 2 colts, 10 cows, 2 oxen, 2 heifers, 3 two years, 3 yearlings, 5 hogs, 3 hives of bees, cider mill, &c.

* See. N.E.H.G. Reg. V. 112, p. 108, et seq. for English ancestry

and Martha Wilbur, daughters of Thomas, until their brother Samuel was twenty-one years of age.

1710, Mar. 1. Will—proved 1710, Aug. 15. Ex. son Joseph. Overseers, John and William Wilbur. To son John Wilbur's two children, John Wilbur and Mary Records, £30, equally, due by bond from said John Wilbur. To son Daniel, land at Shawamoke Great Neck. To son Samuel, £43, for his children equally. To daughter Mary Mowry's grandchildren, £20, due from her. To son William, £50. To son Joseph, £100. To son John, £20. To son Benjamin, the money due me by bond from Daniel Wilcox, deceased. To daughter Martha Sherman, £10. To daughter Jone, £10, and great kettle of iron. To four sons John, William, Joseph and Samuel, all my land in Little Compton equally. To all grandchildren, equally, the rest of estate.

1711, Jul. 13. A receipt was given for legacy by William Sherman of Little Compton and wife Martha.

1712, Oct. 1. A receipt was given by Nathaniel Potter of Little Compton and wife Jone.

1739, Dec. 12. Will—proved 1747, Apr. 7. Widow Ann. Ex. son Joseph. To six sons, William, Joseph, John, Thomas, Benjamin, and Stephen, 5*s*., each. To daughter Ann, wife of George Wood, £50, feather bed and pair of blankets. To daughter Mary Eldridge, widow of William, bond for £51. To daughter Abigail, wife of Joseph Rathbone, £60. To grandsons Joseph and Timothy Closson, 10*s*., each. To five grandchildren Joseph, John, Thomas and Jacob Burgess and Mary Wood, wife of John, 5*s*., each. The rest of estate to go to grandchildren, but none to great-grandchildren.

Inventory, £271, 11*s*. 8*d*.

IV. THOMAS, b. / d.
m.
——, b. / d. of

1. Samuel,
2. Mary,
3. Martha,

V. WILLIAM, b. / d. 1738. Portsmouth, Little Compton, R. I.
m.
—— TALLMAN, b. / d. 1732 (—) of Peter Tallman.

1. Mary, 1685.
2. William, 1687, Aug. 8.
3. Hannah, 1689, Jun. 17.
4. Samuel, 1691, Feb. 17.
5. John, 1693, May 1.
6. Joseph, 1695, May 26.
7. Abigail, 1697, Apr. 1.
8. Joan, 1698, Nov. 7.
9. Jedediah, 1700, Nov. 5.
10. Sarah, 1702, Sep. 10.
11. Phebe, 1704, Oct. 1.
12. Jeremiah, 1706, Dec. 17.

1677, Oct. 31. He and forty-seven others were granted 5,000 acres, to be called East Greenwich.

1678. Freeman.

1683, Nov. 5. He sold Ezekiel Hunt, of Newport, 100 acres in East Greenwich.

1732, Dec. 30. Will—proved 1738, Jun. 20. Ex. son Joseph. To son William, 10*s*., he having had. To son Joseph, all housing and lands in Little Compton and all household goods, bonds and rest of estate, not otherwise given, he paying debts and legacies. To son Jeremiah, 10*s*. To daughters Hannah Lippincott, Abigail Hilliard, Jane Dennis, Sarah Tallman and Phebe Shaw, each, 5*s*. To heirs of son Samuel, deceased, 10*s*.

Inventory, £213, 7*s*., 6*d*., viz: wearing apparel £12, beds, mare, colt, 5 cows, 3 yearlings, 5 year and vantage cattle, 3 calves, warming pan, looking glass, &c.

VI. MARTHA, b. / d.
m. 1681, May 12.
WILLIAM SHERMAN, b. 1659, Oct. 3. / d. of Peleg & Elizabeth (Lawton) Sherman

1. William.
2. Thomas,
3. Eleanor,
4. Mary,
5. Elizabeth,
6. Peleg,
7. Benjamin,
8. Sarah,
9. Hannah,

VII. SAMUEL, b. / d. 1740. Little Compton, R. I.
m.
MARY POTTER, b. / d. of Nathaniel & Elizabeth ( ) Potter.

1. Martha, 1690, Oct. 22.
2. Samuel, 1692, Nov. 7.
3. William, 1695, Jan. 6.
4. Mary, 1697, Oct. 9.
5. Joanna, 1700, Jun. 8.
6. Thankful, 1700, Jun. 8.
7. Elizabeth, 1702, Dec. 23.
8. Thomas, 1704, Dec. 2.
9. Abial. 1707, May 27.
10. Hannah, 1709, Feb. 9.
11. Isaac, 1712, Aug. 24.

1730, Jan. 14. Will—proved 1740, Jun. 17. Ex. son William. To son Samuel, his now dwelling house, certain land and £100. To son William, my now dwelling house, west half of land where house is, old gray mare and andirons. To son Isaac, at age, east half of homestead, gun, chest, bible, stock of cattle, sheep and swine and £100. To daughter Martha Pearce, £40, and like amount to daughters Mary Brownell, Joanna Taylor, Thankful Irish and Elizabeth Peckham. To daughter Abial Wilbur, a bed, cow, two calves and £50. To daughter Hannah Wilbur, a bed, cow, two calves, and £50. To sons William and Isaac, working tools. To children, the rest of household stuff equally. He directed that four rods square be laid out for a burying place.

Inventory, £5,344, 13*s*., 3*d*., viz: wearing apparel £25, 6*s*., pair of cards, 2 woolen wheels, linen wheel, 15 cows, 4 yearlings, 3 calves, mare, bonds £217, 5*s*., 3*d*., homestead £2,000, other lands and housing £800, &c.

WILBUR (WILLIAM). 2d column. VIII. Daniel, m. Ann Barney, possibly daughter of Jacob and Ann (Witt) Barney.

VIII. DANIEL, b. / d. 1741. Swanzey, Mass.
m.
ANN, b. / d. 1740 + of

1. William,
2. Peleg,
3. Daniel,
4. Ann,
5. Martha,
6. Lydia,
7. Elizabeth,
8. Thomas,

1740, May 4. Will—proved 1741, Dec. 15. Ex. son Daniel. To wife Ann, east half of certain land, Indian slave Jane (who was to be freed when my son Thomas is thirty-five), and her thirds. To son William, south part of homestead and my dwelling house thereon, except burying place four rods square, other land and certain stock. To son Peleg, my house and land at Narragansett for life and then to my grandson John, son of Peleg. To son Daniel, north part of homestead, dwelling house, certain stock, mulatto slaves Jacob and Rose and household furniture. To son Thomas, farm and buildings bought of William Chase, stock thereon and mulatto slave Jeptha. To daughters Martha, Lydia and Elizabeth £60, each. To daughter Ann Carpenter, west part of certain land. To grandson William Carpenter, land.

Inventory, £10,860, 11*s*., 6*d*., viz: purse and apparel £74, 14*s*., 16 cows, 5 heifers, 4 oxen, 10 yearlings, 13 calves, 82 sheep and lambs, mulatto girl Dinah £55, mulatto slave £100, mare, colt, 5 hogs, 10 shoats, homestead farm £6,500, other land £2,719.

IX. JOAN, b. / d. 1759.
m.
NATHANIEL POTTER, b. / d. 1736. of Nathaniel & Elizabeth ( ) Potter.

1. William, 1689, Nov. 12.
2. Mary, 1702, Mar. 25.

X. BENJAMIN, b. / d. 1729. Portsmouth, R. I., Dartmouth, Mass.
m. (1) 1700, Jun. 22.
MARY KINNECUT, b. / d. 1708, Feb. 14. of Roger Kinnecut.
m. (2) 1710, Nov. 2.
ELIZABETH HEAD, b. / d. 1734 + of Henry & Elizabeth ( ) Head.

1. Daniel, 1701, Mar. 8.
2. William, 1703, Oct. 6.
3. Benjamin, 1705, Dec. 6.
4. Samuel, 1708, Feb. 7.

(2d wife.)

5. Abigail, 1711, Sep. 9.
6. Henry, 1716, Aug. 29.
7. George, 1718, Sep. 23.
8. Joseph,
9. Walter,
10. Barsheba,
11. Elizabeth,
12. Mary,
13. Child,

1719, Dec. 2. He and wife Elizabeth, sold to John Burrington, 20½ acres for £205.

1729, Apr. 21. Will—proved 1729, Dec. 13. Exs. wife Elizabeth and son Henry. To wife, half the income of homestead farm, half of household furniture, and half of profit of live stock, and if she marry to surrender her executorship to son Henry. To her, also, £10, a year, feather bed, cow, riding mare and £15. To son Daniel, £60. To son William, land in Dartmouth. To son Benjamin, land in Tiverton, 120 acres. To son Samuel, land in Newport. To son Henry, all my homestead, dwelling house, orchards, &c., 160 acres and all my live stock. To son George, £140. To son Joseph, £150. To son Walter, £150. To daughter Abigail Wilbur, £50, feather bed and cow, at age, and like legacy to daughters Barsheba, Elizabeth and Mary, at age. To child wife is with £150, if a male, and a feather bed, cow and £50, if a female. The younger children to be brought up, and apprenticed at thirteen. To wife and son Henry rest of estate.

Inventory, £596, 7*s*., 2*d*., viz: purse and apparel £20, 3*s*., 6*d*., arms £1, 3*s*., 6*d*., negro £90, 6 silver spoons, 4 spinning wheels, quilting wheel, cheese press, 15 cows, pair of oxen, 15 young cattle, 8 calves, 6 horsekind, 84 sheep, 30 lambs, 7 swine, &c.

1734, Mar. 19. His widow brought in account of legacy given daughter Abigail Wilbur (£60) now Abigail Lapham, daughter Barsheba Richeson, &c.

SAMUEL, b. 1622. d. 1682 ±
m. (1)
MARY TEFFT, b. d.
of John & Mary ( ) Tefft.
m. (2)
ELIZABETH SWEET (w. of John. b. 1629. d. 1684 +

Portsmouth, Kings Town, R. I.

1644, May 27. He had an addition to his lot granted.

1653, Aug. 2. He was on a jury who found in the case of Thomas Bradley, discovered dead on the highway, "that by extremity of heat the said Thomas was overcome, and so perished by himself in the wilderness."

1655. Freeman.

1657, Jan. 20. Kings Town. He and others bought of certain Indian Sachems, a large tract called Pettaquamscut Purchase.

1669–70–78. Conservator of the Peace.

1669, Aug. 19. He and two others were empowered to require Suckquash and Ninecraft to appear before Council Wednesday next at Newport, to give satisfaction touching the alarm of the country upon the suspicion of the Indians plotting to cut off the English.

1670, Jun. 21. He had a letter sent him by the Commissioners of Connecticut sitting at Wickford, requesting the delivery of two of their men detained by Thomas Mumford, they being messengers of Connecticut inoffensively riding on the King's highway. He complied and released the men.

1670, Jul. 13. He and Jireh Bull having informed the Governor and Council of the murder of Walter House, who was illegally and disorderly buried, they were ordered to repair forthwith to the place where the body was buried and cause it to be taken up and a jury inquest to pass thereon. (The Connecticut authorities who claimed jurisdiction over the country had already held an inquest with their own jury.)

1670, Oct. 26. He and four others were appointed to make a rate for Pettaquamscutt.

1678, Jun. 26. He sold James Sands, of Block Island, half of my share of land at Point Judith, except the little neck adjoining harbor, the consideration being for favors, &c.

1679, Jul. 29. He and forty-one other inhabitants of Narragansett, petitioned the King that he "would put an end to these differences about the government thereof, which hath been so fatal to the prosperity of the place, animosities still arising in people's minds as they stand affected to this or that government."

1684, Sep. 18. Elizabeth Wilson, widow, aged fifty-five years or thereabouts, deposed as to her first husband John Sweet's settlement at Potowomut Neck, &c.

1684, Jun. 30. An agreement was made by the orphans of Samuel Wilson with consent of Jireh Bull, executor. The eldest brother Samuel Wilson was to have three lots adjoining the housing, with said housing, &c., part had of his father-in-law Tefft. The rest of the land was to go equally to the children, including Samuel, and so all of them a share. The agreement was signed by Samuel Wilson and Robert and Mary Hannah.

1694, Mar. 15. A partition of estate was made at this date signed by Thomas Mumford, as guardian of James Wilson, Robert Hannah and wife Mary, John Potter and wife Sarah, and by Hannah and Potter in behalf of the orphan Jeremiah, brother of James.

No relationship has been discovered between him and John Wilson, who married Rose Knowles, and who was taxed as early as 1687, at Kings Town (living subsequently at East Greenwich and Jamestown, where he died in 1752).

I. SAMUEL, b. d 1690 ± Kings Town, R. I.

1687, Sep. 6. Taxed 2*s.* 8*d.*

1688. He had a license granted.

1690, Sep. 4. Will—witnesses Thomas Fry and Ephraim Turner. A reference to this is found in a list of wills presented to the court in 1700 as having but two witnesses, whereas the law required three.

II. MARY, b. 1663. d. 1737.
m. (1)
ROBERT HANNAH, b. d. 1706.
m. (2)
GEORGE WEBB, b. d. 1735. of Webb.

WILSON. 2d column. II. Mary m (2) 1708, Apr. 21, George Webb.

1. Robert,
2. Mary,
(By 2d husband no issue.)

III. SARAH, b. 1666. d. 1739 +
m.
JOHN POTTER, b. 1665 ± d. 1715. of Ichabod & Martha (Hazard) Potter.

1. Martha, 1692, Dec. 20.
2. John, 1695, May 20.
3. Samuel, 1699, Sep. 2.
4. Sarah, 1702, Apr. 15.
5. Susanna, 1704, Sep. 17.
6. Mary, 1707, Mar. 2.
7. Samuel, 1715, Jul. 28.

IV. JAMES, b. 1673. d. 1706, Feb. Kings Town, R. I.
m.
ALICE SABEERE, b d. 1706 + of Stephen & Deborah (Angell) Sabeere.

1. Samuel,

1706, Feb. 8. Will—proved 1706, Feb. 23. Exs. wife Alice and Joseph Smith. To wife and her son Samuel Wilson and his heirs, my now dwelling house and lot, half of farm, and all movables, and if her son Samuel die without issue, then the land to go to my brother Jeremiah Wilson or his heirs. To brother-in-law Daniel Sabeere of Newport, 200 acres to be laid out. To brother Jeremiah Wilson's children, at age, the rest of lands.

Inventory. Money £20, 17*s.*, wearing apparel and arms £30, 12 swine, 200 sheep, 14 yearlings, 16 two years, 6 oxen, 11 steers, 31 cows, 31 horsekind, stillyards, feather bed, pewter, &c.

1706, Jun. 27. Daniel Sabeere, of Newport, for £300, paid by sister Alice Wilson, of Kings Town, widow of James, sold her 200 acres, given me by my brother-in-law in his will, &c.

1722, Oct. 29. He would have been forty-nine years of age if he had lived till the fall of this year, according to the depositions of Elizabeth Teft and Tabitha Gardiner.

V. JEREMIAH, b. 1674. d. 1740, Jun. 2. New Shoreham, Newport, South Kingstown, R. I.
m. (1) 1700, Dec. 8.
ANN MANOXON, b. d. of Manoxon.
m. (2)
MARY, b. d. 1740 + of

1. Mary, 1701, Sep. 13.
2. Ann, 1702, Dec. 7.
3. Sarah, 1707, Mar. 5.
(2d wife.)
4. Elizabeth,
5. Judith,
6. Mary, 1721, Nov. 13.
7. Samuel, 1723, Mar. 23.
8. Jeremiah, 1726, May 11.
9. John, 1726, May 11.
10. James, 1728, Sep. 2.
11. George, 1730, Feb. 7.
12. Alice, 1733, Jun. 15.

His marriage and the births of his three first children were recorded at New Shoreham. Possibly his daughters Elizabeth and Judith were also by his first wife.

1706, Mar. 12. He, calling himself now of Block Island, for future maintaining of love and good will between myself and near relatives, confirms 448 acres that Robert and Mary Hannah had by deed of partition in 1694, being part of portion that fell to said sister Mary, and of which a deed of gift had been given to Robert Hannah and Mary by Samuel Wilson, elder brother of Jeremiah. Now therefore Jeremiah conveys all right which he has either from his father Samuel or brother Samuel or brother James which are deceased, and privilege of fishing, fowling, hawking and hunting, &c., "so long as wood groweth and water runneth."

1722. Newport. Freeman.

1740, May 19. Will—proved 1740, Jun. 9. Exs. wife Mary and son Samuel. To daughter Mary Robinson, wife of Edward of New London, Ct., merchant, £50. To daughter Ann Mumford, wife of William, £50. To daughter Sarah Fanning, wife of William, 20*s.*, and confirmation of house and lot in Newport given by deed, and release of mortgage, but if she die without issue, then house and land to my sons Jeremiah and John, equally. To son-in-law Rev. Joseph Torrey, land in South Kingstown, and £100. To daughter Judith Wilson, £300. To son Samuel, east half of my farm where my dwelling house stands, south part of dwelling house, blacksmith shop, two yoke of oxen, six cows and two breeding mares, at age. To sons Jeremiah and John, all lands in Providence, purchased of Daniel Abbott, when they are of age. To sons James and George, west half of homestead farm at age, they paying my daughter Alice Wilson, £300. To dear and loving wife, north part of dwelling house, garden, liberty of cutting firewood for life, negro man Virgie and woman Phillis, and six cows. To sons Jeremiah and John, certain land at death of wife. To sons James and George, at death of wife, the part of dwelling house she has and the garden. To sons Jeremiah and John, one hundred sheep, a riding beast to each, and negro Cæsar to be sold and money put at interest for use of said Jeremiah and John, at age. To wife Mary, power to sell certain land. To daughter Elizabeth Torrey, wife of Rev. Mr. Torrey, 20*s.* To Mary Pollock, wife of William, 20*s.* To sons Samuel, Jeremiah, John and James, and daughters Judith and Alice, rest of estate equally.

Inventory, £1,778, 19*s.* 11*d.*, viz: wearing apparel £17, plate £4, firelock £4, books £1, 10*s.*, stillyards, lime kiln £7, 22 cows, 8 calves, 8 oxen, 4 three years, 11 two years, 10 yearlings, 10 horsekind, 14 swine, 5 sucking pigs, 280 sheep, 152 lambs, 2 negro men and women £240, 6 years' time in mulatto servant Jacob £35, worsted comb, &c.

WOOD.

See: American Geneologist, v. 20, p. 119; v. 26, p. 236

JOHN, b. d. 1655.
m. (1)
———, b. d.
m. (2)
———, b. d. 1655 +

Portsmouth, R. I.

1655, Mar. 17. Town Council chose appraisers on his estate (he having died intestate), viz: John Coggeshall, Thomas Cornell, Jr., James Babcock, and William Hall. Inventory, £130, viz: Land £45. In widow's hands £50. In Thomas Wood's hands £20. Goods and cattle £15. The council disposed of estate as follows: To John Wood, land in his present possession, he paying his sister Manchester £8. To Thomas Wood, the land that was his father's

I. GEORGE, b. d.

II. JOHN, b. d. Newport, R. I.
m.
MARY, b. d. of

1. Thomas,

1655. Freeman.

1671, Jun. 7. Juryman.

1673–74–75. Deputy.

1695, Nov. 14. He and wife Mary, deeded to son Thomas Wood, of Little Compton, two lots there of 50 acres each, with housing, &c.

He may have been father of Henry (freeman at Newport, 1673), and of Walter (who was married as early as 1675).

WOOD. 2d column. II. John. He had probably a son John, b. 1664 (lived at Little Compton)—certainly. Thomas, b. 1666 (lived at Little Compton), and perhaps Jonathan of Little Compton.

in Newport (40 acres about, near William Weeden's farm). To William Wood, 10 acres where widow lives (the present crop of corn growing upon part of the land excepted, and that to go to widow). To widow, rest of land in her possession to improve for life, she paying George Wood (eldest son of deceased), the sum of £4, and to two younger children of deceased, Susanna and Elizabeth, £3, apiece, at age of sixteen. At decease of widow, William Wood to have all the land in his mother-in-law's (*i. e.* stepmother's) possession, he paying the £8, to the two youngest children if he has possession before they arrive at ages of sixteen. The widow to have cattle and goods to bring up young children.

III. THOMAS, b. d. Portsmouth, R. I., Swanzey, Mass.
m.
REBECCA, b. d. of

1657, Jan. 1. He sold to Richard Tew of Newport, 40 acres granted by freemen of Newport to John Wood of Portsmouth, who died intestate, said land being given to Thomas by Town Council of Portsmouth.
1680. Taxed 3*s*.
1680, May 7. Swanzey. He and wife Rebecca, for £34, sold Benjamin Hall 12 acres in Portsmouth.
1681, Sep. 7. He took oath of fidelity.
1686-87. Surveyor of Highways (for Bristol).
1690. Deputy.

1. Thomas, 1664.
2. Abigail,
3. George, 1679, Jul. 30.
4. Jonathan, 1681, Nov. 20.
5. Hannah, 1685, Feb. 18.
6. Margaret, 1687, Mar. 1.
7. Sarah, 1687, Mar. 1.

IV. WILLIAM, b. d. 1697. Portsmouth, R. I., Dartmouth, Mass.
m.
MARTHA EARLE, b. d. of Ralph & Joan ( ) Earle.

1686, Mar. 24. Dartmouth. He took oath of fidelity.
1697, Jul. Inventory, £422, 6*s*. 8*d*., less debts of £52, 2*s*. 4*d*. Lands £166, house £60. Division was made to ten children, each having £33, 13*s*. To William Wood, eldest son, housing, 100 acres, meadow, a quarter of a half share (after 300 acres laid out to George Wood), two guns and £2, 10*s*., which made £168, 10*s*. He being eldest son had two shares, £67, 6*s*.; and was to pay Josiah, Daniel and John Wood, £33, 13*s*. each. To George Wood, 300 acres, three-quarters of undivided lands, £60, and a loom and bed; and was to pay Joseph, £33, 13*s*. To Mr. Mallett's wife, a bed, two oxen, two yearlings, horse, eight goats, seven sheep, &c. To Sarah Wood, a feather bed, two cows, 8 goats, horse, seven sheep, swine, pewter, &c. To Margaret Wood, a feather bed, 2 cows, two yearlings, white mare, 8 goats, seven sheep, &c. To Rebecca Wood, a feather bed, cow, two yearling steers, a two year horse, eight goats, sheep, &c.
1701, Apr. 14. Division was made of lands of deceased William Wood.

1. William,
2. George,
3. Josiah,
4. Daniel,
5. John,
6. Joseph,
7. Daughter, Mary
8. Sarah,
9. Margaret,
10. Rebecca,

V. MARGARET, b. d.
m.
THOMAS MANCHESTER, b. d. of Manchester.

1. Thomas,
2. William,
3. John,
4. George,
5. Stephen,
6. Job,
7. Mary,
8. Elizabeth,

VI. SUSANNA, b. d.

VII. ELIZABETH, b. d.

WOODMAN.

JOHN, b. d. 1713, Apr. 24.
m.
HANNAH TIMBERLAKE, b. d. 1713, May 3.

of Henry & Mary ( ) Timberlake.

Newport, Little Compton, R. I.

He was a cordwainer.

1675. Freeman.
1680. Taxed 14*s*.
1682-84-86. Deputy.
1682, Jun. 28. Deputy clerk of the Assembly, the clerk, John Sanford, being by lameness disenabled.
1685-86. General Treasurer.
1687. Overseer of the Poor.
1691, Jan. 7. He and John Irish bought a piece of salt marsh of Joseph Wait, for £34.
1709, Jun. 14. Will—proved 1713, Jun. 2. Exx. wife Hannah. To eldest son Robert, housing where I dwell in Little Compton, and land east of highway, he quitting all claim to my house and land at Newport. To son John, land west of aforesaid highway, salt marsh in Puncatest, &c. To son Edward, half share in Pocasset purchase, in Tiverton, and my house and land at Newport. To daughter Hannah, wife of Nicholas Howland £30. To four daughters Edith, Rebecca, Elizabeth and Sylvia Woodman, £100, at 8*s*. per oz. To wife Hannah, for life, house, orchard and garden, and she authorized to sell certain small parcels of land.
Inventory, £1,905, 10*s*. 2*d*., viz: house and land and barn in Little Compton £1,200, upland and salt marsh in Tiverton £200, wearing apparel £8, cash at 8*s*. per oz. £314, 2 silver cups and other plate 19¾ oz. £7, 18*s*., gold ring 12*s*., gun, 2 swords, 5 feather beds, silk grass bed, 20 pewter platters, 4 basins, 6 porringers, sundry books £1, 3 spinning wheels, pair of cards, 2 barrels cider, warming pan, livestock £121, 8*s*.
1713, Jun. 16. Articles of agreement were signed by Robert, John and Edward Woodman, Nicholas Howland and Hannah his wife, Thomas Church and Edith his wife, and Rebecca and Elizabeth Woodman, by which they made certain division of estate, conforming as near as could be to their father's wishes in his will. Robert and John Woodman administered upon the estate, and were guardians to their sister Sylvia.

I. ROBERT, b. 1677, Sep. 8. d. 1757. Little Compton, R. I.
m.
———, b. d. of

1754, Dec. 23. Will—proved, 1757, Sep. 5. Ex. son Constant. To eldest son John, half of farm. To son Thomas, 26 acres. To daughter Hannah Sanford, household stuff, negro girl Peg, and £30. To daughter Priscilla Woodman, negro girl Prue and £100. To son Constant, house and buildings, and land not before given, negro boy Tobey, plate, buttons, gun, a third of household goods and all money due.
Inventory, £4,033, 4*s*. 8*d*.

1. John,
2. Thomas,
3. Hannah,
4. Priscilla,
5. Constant,

II. HANNAH, b. 1679, Jun. 27. d.
m.
NICHOLAS HOWLAND, b. d. of Howland.

WOODMAN. 2d column. II. Hannah. Children, 1. Abigail, 1698, Nov. 3. 2. Mary, 1700, Sep. 21.

III. JOHN, b. 1682, Feb. 25. d. 1733. Little Compton, R. I.
m.
ELIZABETH BRIGGS, b. 1689, Dec. 27. d. 1733 + of William & Elizabeth (Cook) Briggs.

1733, May 3. Will—proved 1733, May 15. Ex. son Sylvester. To wife Elizabeth, use of new room south end of new house, bed room and chamber, a quarter profit of orchard, use of garden, £100, in bills of credit, all the silver money, horse to ride, cow, heifer, swine, thirty pounds of wool, twenty pounds of flax, wood cut, &c., at her door, all while widow. To son Sylvester, all my farm where I now live, about 120 acres, with other land, housing, barn, cattle, horses, sheep, silver seal, spoons, bonds, negro Daniel and wearing apparel. To son Enoch, £200, my own silver spoon and his silver spoon, a horse, and half of lands in Pocasset at age. To son William, £200, horse, silver spoon and half of lands at Pocasset. To daughter Patience, £100, a bed and silver spoon. To daughter Elizabeth, £100, bed, silver spoon and chest. To daughter Edith, same legacy at twenty-one, and a new riding hood at eighteen. To daughter Deborah, same legacy (except a bed). The executrix to maintain three youngest children till of age to learn a trade, in case of William, and Edith and Deborah till eighteen.
Inventory, £3,956, 3*s*. 5*d*., viz: house and lands £2,520, salt meadow in Tiverton £240, wearing apparel £42, 10*s*., 17 chairs, cheese fats, churns, worsted combs, linen and woolen wheel, sword, gun, cider press, silver spoons £120, 2 pair oxen, 10 cows, bull, 6 three years, 6 two years, 3 yearlings, 4 horsekind, 128 sheep, 39 lambs, 7 swine, &c.

1. Sylvester,
2. Enoch,
3. Patience,
4. Elizabeth,
5. William,
6. Edith,
7. Deborah,

IV. EDITH, b. 1685, Sep. 7. d. 1718, Jun. 3.
m. 1712, Apr. 16.
THOMAS CHURCH, b. 1674. d. 1746, Mar. 12. of Benjamin & Alice (Southworth) Church.

1. Elizabeth, 1713, Jan. 10.
2. Hannah, 1714, Sep. 23.
3. Priscilla, 1717, Jan. 6.
4. Thomas, 1718, May.

V. EDWARD, b. 1688, Mar. 17. d.

He may have married Margaret Taylor, born 1688, Jul., daughter of John and Abigail.

VI. REBECCA, b. 1690, Jan. 10. d.

VII. ELIZABETH, b. 1694, May 31. d.

VIII. SYLVIA, b. 1698, Sep. 17. d.

WOODMAN. 2d column. I Robert, m. 1706, Nov. 11, Deborah Paddock, of John and Ann (Jones) Paddock. Children, 1, John, 1708, May 2. 2, Constant, 1710, Aug. 28. 3, Hannah, 1713, Apr. 22. 4, Joseph, 1716, May 4. 5, Thomas, 1718, Sep. 19. 6, Priscilla. 1721, July 1. II. Hannah m. 1697, Oct. 26. III. John m. 1708, Oct. 21. Children, 1, Sylvester, 1709, Jan. 25. 2, Mary, 1710, Sep. 3. 3, Sarah, 1712, Apr. 3. 4, Elizabeth, 1713, Sep. 10. 5, Enoch, 1715, Jan. 28. 6, Edith, 1719, Dec. 20. 7, William, 1721, May 27. 8, Patience. 9, Deborah, 1726, Oct. 21. V. Edward m. 1708, Oct., Margaret Taylor, b. 1688, July, of John and Abigail. Children, 1, John, 1711, Jan. 25. 2. Abigail, 1714, Aug. 23. VII. Elizabeth m. Joshua Easton.

JOSEPH, b. — d. 1726, Feb. 26.
m. (1) 1677, Jan. 15.
MARY PRAY, b. — d. — of Richard & Mary ( ) Pray.
m. (2)
RUTH, b. 1658. d. 1728, Dec. 19.

Providence, R. I.

1676, Aug. 14. He was one of those "who staid and went not away" in King Philip's war, and so had a share in the disposition of the Indian captives whose services were sold for a term of years.

1679, Jul. 1. Taxed 7*s.*, 12*d.*

1680, May 16. He had lands laid out.

1682. Freeman.

1687, Sep. 1. Taxed 2*s.*, 10*d.*

1688. Grand Jury.

1703, May 26. He had laid out to him at his request, a highway from the common road to land where he dwells in Loquasquesuck.

1713, Jun. 16. Taxed 12*s.*

1718, Aug. 29. His wife Ruth, in a deposition calls herself aged about sixty years.

1724, Sep. 16. Will—proved 1726, Mar. 21. Ex. not named. To wife Ruth, 50 acres in Attleboro, &c., and household goods and movables. To grandsons Woodward Arnold and Woodward Lovett, homestead farm at decease of wife, and meadow in Attleboro.

Inventory, £263, 10*s.*, 6*d.*, viz: cash £33, 7*s.*, 6*d.*, books 12*s.*, bonds £79, 8*s.*, pewter, cider mill, woolen wheel, linen wheel, pair of cards, yoke oxen, 6 cows, yearling, 2 horsekind, 3 swine, &c.

1729, Jan. 7. Administration on widow Ruth's estate to Joseph Arnold, Jr.

Inventory, £132, 7*s.*

1730, Feb. 9. Administrator brought in account on estate of his grandmother-in-law Ruth Woodward, widow. Among bills paid were to James Lovett and Woodward Arnold (for tending cattle, &c.), John Lovett, Jr., &c. An appeal was taken to account by Robert Currie, one of attorneys to heirs of said Ruth.

1731, Aug. 4. Joseph Arnold, Jr., being discharged by act of General Assembly, and still some estate remaining, William Turpin and Robert Currie, attorneys to Jonathan Butler and others of the heirs, gave bond and took administration.

I. MARY, b. — d. —
m.
RICHARD ARNOLD, b. — d. 1745, Jun. of Richard & Mary (Angell) Arnold.

1. Thomas, 2. Richard, 3. Joseph, 4. Woodward, 5. Edmund, 6. Mary.

II. DAUGHTER, b. — d. —
m.
—— LOVETT, b. — d. — of Lovett.

1. Woodward.

(2d WIFE, no issue.)

WOOLEY.

EMANUEL, b. — d. —
m.
ELIZABETH, b. — d. —

Newport, R. I.

1653, May 17. Freeman.

1667, May 13. He and others skilled therein, were ordered to repair all arms brought to them by the Captain or Lieutenant of the Train Band of Newport.

1680. Taxed £1, 7*s.*, 11*d.*

1681, May 4. The Assembly remitted his forfeiture of a bond of recognizance for good behavior and appearance at last General Court of Trials, he not appearing.

Part of his children settled in New Jersey.

WOOLEY. 2d column. II. Edward. Children, 1, Elizabeth, 1685, May 28. 2, Hannah, ——, July 8. 3, Adam, 169–, Feb. 4. 4, Edward, 1693, Jan. 16. 5, Content, 1694, Nov. 9. 6, George, 1697, Dec. 14. 7, William, 1699, Feb. 22. 8, Ruth, 1701, June 8. 9, Lydia, 1703, Mar. 23. V. John, Shrewsbury, N. J. Children, 1, Thomas. 2, Ruth, ——, Aug. 22. 3, William, ——, Aug. 17. 4, John, 1690, Dec. 31. 5, Eliab, 1690, Dec. 31. 6, Benjamin, 1693, Feb. 25. 7, James, 1695, Aug. 6. 8, Elizabeth, 1697, Apr. ? 9, Sarah 1699, Feb. 15. 10, Elizabeth, 1700, Apr. 11, Ann, 1703, Feb. 20. 12, Mary.

I. ADAM, b. 1653, Mar. d. 1676, Jun. 13. Newport, R. I.
m.
MARY, b. — d. — of

1675. Freeman.

1. John, 1674, Sep. 18.

II. EDWARD, b. 1655, Dec. d. — Monmouth, N. J.
m.
LIELIA, b. — d. — of

1691. He sold land to his brother William, and at this time was called of Manasquam (Monmouth county).

1. Elizabeth, 1685, May 28.

III. ELIZABETH, b. 1657, Nov. d. —

IV. MARY, b. 1657, Nov. d. —

V. JOHN, b. 1659, Oct. d. 1714 + Monmouth, N. J.
m.
MERCY POTTER, b. — d. — of Thomas & Sarah ( ) Potter.

1690. His name appears upon Freehold records and continued there till 1714.

1691. Juryman.

1702, Nov. 2. His wife had a legacy from will of her father.

1705. County road commissioner.

1. John, 2. Thomas, 3. William.

VI. WILLIAM, b. 1662, Sep. 15. d. — Monmouth, N. J.

1691. He bought land of Nicholas Brown, and at this time was living at Shark river (Monmouth county).

1691. Juryman.

VII. RUTH, b. 1664, Oct. 12. d. —
m. 1688,
JOHN TUCKER, b. — d. — of Tucker.

WOOLEY. 2d column. VII Ruth, m. 1688, Apr. 25, John Tucker, of Henry & Martha ( ) Tucker. She d. 1750, Dec. 23. He b. 1655, Aug. 28, d. 1751, Sep. 3. Children, 1. James, 1691, Aug. 27. 2. John, 1693, Oct. 25. 3. Joseph, 1696, Nov. 7.

VIII. GRACE, b. 1666, Apr. d. —

IX. JOSEPH, b. 1668, May. d. 1691, Feb. 4.

PUBLISHER'S NOTICE

Page 233 of the original 1887 edition of Austin's GENEALOGICAL DICTIONARY was blank and, hence, page 233 of our reprint is blank.

-Genealogical Publishing Company
Baltimore, 1969

Daniel, m. **Mary,**	b. d. 1647. b. d. 1643.	Cambridge, Mass., Providence, R. I.

1630, Oct. 19. He requested admission as freeman.

1631, May 18. Fined 5*s.* for refusing to watch, and for other ill behavior showed toward Captain Pattrick.

1638, May 18. Fined 5*s.* but remitted.

1639, Jun. 4. Providence. "Daniel Abbott is departed to New Providence."

1644, May 20. He sold Robert Morris 20 acres upland and a share of meadow, bounded partly by Spectacle Pond, also a tract of 60 acres, and another share of land.

1650, Jul. 27. His estate was ordered into the hands of Nicholas Power and Gregory Dexter, who were to take charge of the goods of the children of deceased.

1651, Jul. 28. Administration on his estate was given to Thomas Harris and Nicholas Power, and they were to "equally divide the goats and goods and what else belongeth unto the two orphans of Daniel Abbott, deceased, and possess Thomas Walling, husband of Mary Abbott, the daughter of the said deceased, with one-half of the said goats, goods, &c., and the other half to order for Daniel Abbott, the son of the said deceased's, best advantage."

I. **Mary,** m. **Thomas Walling,**	b. d. 1669. b. d. 1674, Jul. 19.	of	Walling.

II. **Daniel,** m. 1678, Dec. 25. [of Thos. **Margaret Walling** (w.	b. d. 1709. b. d. 1717 +	of	Providence, R. I. White.

1665, Feb. 19. He had lot 20 granted him in a division of lands.

1665, Oct. 1. He received a deed of a 5 acre house lot in Providence from Robert Williams of Newport, formerly of Providence, who declares that Daniel Abbott was formerly his servant, and that the house lot was one which did in the original belong to Daniel Abbott, Senior, father to above said Daniel, it being by him sold to Mr. Williams.

1672, Apr. 30. Freeman.

1673, May 24. He and Thomas Walling had lots laid out together not far from John Steere's dwelling house, said lots measuring 160 poles by 120.

1675, Mar. 12. He had two 50 acre shares laid out to him.

1675, Mar. 13. He was appointed overseer of Thomas Walling's will by terms of that instrument.

1676. Surveyor and Hay-ward.

1676, Aug. 14. He was one of the men "who staid and went not away" in King Philip's War and so had a share in the disposal of the Indians about to be sold. The services of these Indian captives were sold for certain terms of years. Those above thirty years old were sold for seven years, &c.

1677-78-79-80-81. Town Clerk.

1679, Dec. 22. He wrote to the town desiring that a town house be built "now without much further delay before the boards and timber be most all sent out of the town," &c.

1681, Jan. 15. He had a letter sent him under this date from Roger Williams, regarding taxes levied upon the town. "Loving remembrance to you. It hath pleased the Most High, and Only Wise, to stir up your spirit to be one of the chiefest stakes in our poor hedge."

1687, Sep. 1. Taxed 5*s.* 11*d.*

1694. Deputy.

1707, Feb. 7. He made an agreement about bounds of lands between himself and William Hopkins, trustee of John Lapham.

1709, Mar. 19. He being deceased, his son Daniel gave to sister Mary Abbott, single woman, certain land, and £150, to be paid in ten annual installments in consideration of all dower, &c.

1717, Dec. 28. His widow Margaret made complaint that she needed relief, her husband having left a competent estate and his son Daniel having had administration. The Council ordered the administrator to pay to relief of his mother Margaret, 8*s.* per week into the hands of the Overseer of the Poor.

ALBRO.

John, m. [Nathaniel. **Dorothy Potter** (w. of	b. 1617. d. 1712, Dec. 14. b. 1617. d. 1696, Feb. 19.	Portsmouth, R. I.

1634, Apr. 30 He embarked in ship Francis, from Ipswich for New England, under the care of William Freeborn. His age was called fourteen, which was not exact but as near as was often the case in making returns to the officials.

1638. He accompanied William Freeborn to Rhode Island.

1639. He was granted a lot if he would build within one year.

1644. Corporal, rising successively in after years to the office of Lieutenant, Captain and Major.

1649. Chosen to view cattle and also Clerk of weights and measures. He was soon after a member of Town Council, and served frequently as Moderator of town meetings, even into old age.

1655. Freeman.

1660-61. Commissioner.

1661. He was on committee to receive contributions for agents in England.

1666. He, with two others, was appointed to take area of all highways and driftways not set off.

1670. He with three others, lent the colony sum of £7, on account of town of Portsmouth.

1671-72-77-78-79-80-81-82-83-84-85-86. Assistant.

1676, Apr. 4. He and three others had the care and disposal of a barrel of powder for supply of Portsmouth, and it was also ordered that the two great guns now in the yard of late deceased William Brenton, be pressed for country's service, and carried to Portsmouth, and placed one on the Ferry Neck, and one near John Borden's.

1676. He was appointed commissioner with others to order watch and ward of the island. This vigilance was rendered necessary by the war with King Philip, and it was voted the same year "that in these troublesome times and straits in this colony, the Assembly desiring to have the advice and concurrence of the most judicious inhabitants, if it may be had for the good of the whole, do desire at their sitting the company and counsel" of sixteen individuals, among them Captain John Albro.

1676, Aug. 24. He was a member of the Court Martial held at Newport for the trial of certain Indians.

1677. He was on a committee in the matter of injurious and illegal acts of Connecticut.

1679. He was on a committee to draw up a letter to the King, giving a true account of the territory of Mount Hope and of the late war with the Indians.

1679. He with another was appointed to lay out the western line of the colony.

1685, Jan. 14. Major John Albro, Assistant and Coroner, summoned a jury in case of an Indian found dead upon Clay Pit lands. Verdict "That the said Indian being much distempered with drink was bewildered, and by the extremity of the cold lost his life," &c.

1686, Dec. 30. Member of Sir Edmund Andros' Council and present at their first meeting in Boston at this date. The members were sworn to allegiance, and due administration of justice.

I. **Samuel,** m. **Isabel Lawton,**	b. 1644. d. 1739, Apr. b. d. 1730, Apr. 1.	of George & Elizabeth (Hazard)	Portsmouth, North Kingstown, R. I. Lawton.

1667, Aug. 10. He enlisted in a troop of horse for protection of Aquidneck.

1671. Kings Town. He took oath of allegiance.

1677, Oct. 31. He and forty-seven others had a grant of 5,000 acres to be called East Greenwich.

1679, Jul. 29. He and forty-one others of Narragansett petitioned the King, praying that he "would put an end to these differences about the government thereof, which hath been so fatal to the prosperity of this place, animosities still arising in people's minds as they stand affected to this or that government."

1679, Dec. 5 He and twenty-four others had 7,630 acres in Narragansett laid out to them.

1683. Treasurer.

1687, Sep. 6. Taxed 9*s.* 7½*d.*

1687. Overseer of the Poor. He held other offices in the town as selectman, &c.

1688. He had license granted.

1690, Sep. 10. He was chosen with two others to apportion a tax for Kings Town.

1709. He and wife Isabel were baptized at Trinity Church, Newport, prior to this year.

1715, Oct. 20. He and seven others signed a letter to The Society for the Propagation of the Gospel in Foreign parts, earnestly requesting that there might be a regular minister settled at Narragansett.

1718, Apr. 14. Warden of the Episcopal Church at Narragansett.

1725, Jan. 8. His daughter Ruth Sweet had a legacy of £5, from will of her aunt Ruth Wodell.

1739, Apr 17. He was buried at this date, being in his ninety-fifth year, as the records of Narragansett Church state.

II. **Elizabeth,** m. **Benjamin Congdon,**	b. d. 1720, Nov. 15. b. 1650 ± d. 1718, Jun. 19.	of	Congdon.

III. **Mary,** m. **Thomas Hicks,**	b. d. 1710 + b. d. 1698.	of Samuel & Lydia (Doane)	Hicks.

IV. **John,** m. 1693, Apr. 27. **Mary Stokes,**	b. d. 1724, Dec. 4. b. d. 1729 (—)	of	Portsmouth, R. I. Stokes.

1677, Oct. 31. He was among those who were granted 5,000 acres to be called East Greenwich.

1687, Dec. 13. He was fined 6*s.* 8*d.*, for refusing to take oath as Grand Juryman.

1720. Will—proved 1724, Dec. 14. Exs. son Samuel and daughter Sarah. He directs that a straight line be drawn from south-west corner of circuit wall to a white thorn bush, and all lands and housing in Portsmouth north of said line to go to son Samuel, to whom is given other land also. To son John, rest of land in Portsmouth and an acre on Hog Island. To brother Samuel Albro, all interest in lands in Narragansett country. To daughter Mary Martin, a good ewe sheep. To daughter Sarah Albro, two-thirds of movables. To son Samuel, one third of movables.

1. Thomas,
2. Gershom,
3. Abigail,
4. James,

I. MARY, b. 1679, Dec. 18. d.
m.
THOMAS FENNER, b. d. of Thomas & Dinah (Borden) Fenner.

1. Thomas,
2. Daniel,
3. William,
4. Mary,

II. DANIEL, b. 1682, Apr. 25. d. 1760, Nov. 7. Providence, R. I.
m.
MARY FENNER, b. 1692. d. 1759, Jan. 7. of Thomas & Dinah (Borden) Fenner.

No issue.

1708, May 4. Freeman (called Daniel Abbott, Jr.).

1713. Town Council.

1713-16-17-18-20-21-23-24-28-29-30-33-34-35-36-37-40-42-47-48-49-50-53-54-55-57-59-60. Deputy.

1720. Clerk of Assembly.

1723, Jul. 18. He and wife Mary, for £30, and of his own free bounty for the setting up of the worship of God in the Presbyterian or Congregational way in the town of Providence, deeded to Rev. Joseph Baxter, of Medford, Rev. Nathaniel Cotton, of Bristol, Rev. John Greenwood of Rehoboth, and the eldest deacon in each of their churches, twenty-seven rods, about twelve poles eastward from said Town Street, to them and their successors, for the erecting and building a meeting house.

1727. Curritor. (One of the offices for docking of estates.)

1733, Jan. 23. He and two others were appointed by Assembly to build a new jail in Providence of same bigness of that in Kings County.

1737-38. Speaker of House of Deputies.

1738-39-40. Deputy Governor.

1740, Jan. 8. He was voted £20, 13*s.* 10*d.*, for time and expense in revising and renewing the boundary line between this colony and Connecticut.

1740, Dec. 2. He was appointed on committee to represent and manage the affairs of this colony before the commissioners to hear and determine the boundaries between Rhode Island and Massachusetts.

1741, Aug. He and two others were appointed to set off part of Warwick into a township to be called Coventry, and the committee proceeded the same month to run the line.

1760, Jul. 2, Will—codicil 1760, Sep. 15—proved 1760, Nov. 17. Exs Jabez Bowen, Jr. and Darius Sissons. To nephew Thomas Fenner, rent of farm occupied by James Hoyle, for life. To Abbott and Antram Fenner, sons of nephew Thomas, to Samuel, Daniel and Thomas Fenner, sons of nephew Daniel, to William and Stephen Fenner, sons of nephew William, and to Jabez and Oliver Bowen, sons of niece Mary Bowen, all my house, lands and real estate whatever, under certain conditions, payments, &c. The codicil provides that debts be paid out of income first.

Inventory, £3,928, 10*s.*, viz: notes £323, 5*s.*, cash £23, bonds £600, clock £180, sword, belt, cane, writing desk, gold, 1 oz. 5pwt. 21 gr. £116, 10*s.*, silver, 8 oz. 4 pwt. £49, 6*s.*, pair of studded buttons, surveying instruments (not come to hand), horse, cow, pair of oxen, hog, coat and vest of scarlet, 4 pairs breeches, 3 jackets, coat, and other apparel, baize gown, 2 hats, light wig, money scales, decanters, 2 wine glasses, sundry books, bolster, &c.

ALBRO.

I. JOHN, b. d. 1747. North Kingstown, R. I.
m. (1)
MARGARET, b. d. 1727, Nov. 2. of
m. (2)
BARBARA, b. d. of

1. Samuel. 1716.
2. John,
3. James,
4. Benoni,
5. Elizabeth,
6. Isabel,

(2d wife.)

7. Stephen,
8. Margaret,
9. Elizabeth, 1731, Apr. 17.
10. Lawton,
11. Isabella,
12. Barbara, 1737, Oct. 27.
13. William,

1712. Kings Town. Freeman.

1718, Apr. 14. Vestryman of Episcopal Church at Narragansett.

1724, Oct. 21. He (Lieutenant) with Lieutenant Colonel Christopher Allen and Ensign James Eldred, met at the house of George Thomas, they being a commission appointed by the Assembly, and divided the inhabitants of North Kingstown into three companies of militia, separating the town into three districts therefor.

He held the title of Major at time of his death, having successively filled the subordinate military offices.

1747. Administration on his estate was given to his son Samuel.

II. DOROTHY, b. d.
m.
JAMES BENTLEY, b. d. of William & Sarah ( ) Bentley.

1. Hannah, 1703, Mar. 25.

III. RUTH, b. d.
m.
—— SWEET, b. d. of Sweet.

IV. SARAH, b. d.
m. 1706,
SAMUEL DAVIS, b. d. of Aaron & Mary ( ) Davis.

1. William,
2. Benjamin,
3. John,
4. James, 1686, Apr. 19.
5. Elizabeth,
6. Susanna,

1. Sarah,
2. Thomas,
3. Samuel,
4. Ephraim,
5. Susanna,
6. Abigail,
7. Elizabeth,

I. JOHN, b. 1694, Aug. 23. d. Portsmouth, North Kingstown, R. I.
m. 1713, Jun. 7.
ABIGAIL BALLOU, b. d. of John & Hannah (Garret) Ballou.

1. John, 1714, Jun. 7.
2. Samuel, 1716, Oct. 10.
3. Mary, 1718, Feb. 2.
4. Maturin, 1721, Jun. 4.
5. Sarah, 1723, Feb. 24.
6. Peter, 1728, Mar. 19.

1717. Freeman.

1739. North Kingstown. He moved there at about this time, some of his children subsequently going to town of Exeter, &c. There were at one time four John Albros in North Kingstown, viz: John[3] (Samuel[2], John[1]), who was then called Captain John Albro; his son John, Jr.; John[3] (John[2], John[1]), who was called John Albro, yeoman; and his son called John Albro 4th.

II. MARY, b. d.
m.
—— MARTIN, b. d. of Martin.

1697. He was allowed 20s. for going to Boston.

1710, Dec. 28. Will—proved 1718. Exs. son-in-law John Anthony and latter's wife Susannah. Overseers, William Sanford and Giles Slocum. To son John, all land south-easterly of a line "beginning at a white thorn bush standing at the circuit corner," &c., and running to Henry Brightman's fence. To grandsons John and Albro Anthony, all land north-westerly of said line, about 30 acres and housing, orchard, &c., they paying legacies. If either desired to sell they were to sell one to the other. To granddaughter Sarah Anthony, £80. If daughter Susannah outlive her husband, she to have equal privilege with her sons in house and land for life. To grandson Albro Anthony, bed, chest, &c. To grandson John Anthony, bed, chest, five sheep and great bible. To granddaughter Sarah Anthony, looking glass, chest, two pewter platters and five sheep. To son John Albro, a cow and two napkins, and to John's children, 40s. equally divided. To children of son Samuel, 50s. equally divided. To daughter Mary Hicks, a cow and two napkins. To daughter Elizabeth Congdon, 50s. in silver money (at 17 pwt.), a bolster case, pair of sheets and two pewter platters. To daughter Susannah Anthony, two cows, a heifer, feather bed, warming pan, stillyards, spice mortar, brass kettle, lanthorn, old brass kettle, little brass kettle, little iron pot, and skillet. To granddaughter Dorothy Bentley, daughter of my son Samuel, 16s. To sons John and Samuel, all rights in Misquamicut purchase, equally. To daughter Susannah, rest of movables.

He "was buried in his own orchard" as the Friends' records state.

Inventory, £246, 18s. 7d., viz: wearing apparel £11, silver money £6, money scales, 3 feather beds, pewter, linen and woolen wheels, table linen, hay £41, 5s., neat cattle £35, sheep and lambs £20, swine £3, 8s., &c.

V. { SUSANNA, — { b. / d. 1715 +
m. 1694, Jan. 3.
JOHN ANTHONY, — { b. 1642. / d. 1715, Oct. 20. of John & Susanna ( ) Anthony.

ALMY. See: American Genealogist, v. 20, p. 119-120.

{ WILLIAM, — { b. 1601, Lynn, Sandwich, Ms., Portsmouth, R. I. / d. 1676.
m.
AUDRY, — { b. 1603. / d. 1676 +

1631, Jun. 14. He was fined 11s., for taking away Mr. Glover's canoe without leave.

1634, Jul. 1. He was fined 10s., for not appearing at last court, being summoned, and was enjoined to bring to next court an inventory of goods he had received of Edward Johnson, duly prized by disinterested parties.

1635. Having been home to England he came the second time to New England this year in ship Abigail. His age was given as thirty-four years, wife Audry, thirty-two, daughter Ann, eight, and son Christopher, three.

1636, Mar. 1. He gained a suit and judgment against David Johnson, but upon some consideration execution was respited and now by consent of all parties it was agreed that widow Johnson pay 5 nobles, and James Ludham 5 nobles, and said William Almy to lose the rest.

At same date Robert Way was ordered to serve William Almy till he hath satisfied the sum of £111.

1637, Apr. 3. Sandwich. He and nine others were given liberty to view a place to set down and have sufficient land for three score families.

1638, Dec. 4. He was fined 11s., for keeping swine unringed.

1640, Apr. 16. He had a grant of 8½ acres.

1641, Dec. 7. An attachment was made on a calf of his, in the hands of Robert Bodfish, to answer charges to the clerk of a suit said Almy left unpaid when he left Sandwich.

1642, Jun. 22. He sold Sandwich land to Edmund Freeman.

1644, Nov. 14. Portsmouth. He had land granted at Wading River.

1655. Freeman.

1656, Jan. 5. He sold 8 acres to Richard Bulgar.

1656. Juryman.

1656–57–63. Commissioner.

1668. Foreman of Jury.

1676, Feb. 28. Will—proved 1677, Apr. 23. Exs. sons Christopher and Job. He first requests that his body be buried beside his son John. If testator's wife outlive him she to have all estate for life. To son Christopher, at death of wife, the half of farm next the land which I gave to son John. To son Job, the other half of farm, with dwelling house, two orchards, &c. The malt house not to be divided but held in equal shares and kept for a malt house every season. To daughters Anna and Catharine, each two parts of cattle and movables, and to sons Christopher and Job, each one part. To grandchild Bartholomew West, £20, at twenty-one years of age paid equally by executors.

I. { ANN, — { b. 1627. / d. 1709, May 17.
m.
JOHN GREENE, — { b. 1620. / d. 1708, Nov. 27. of John & Joan (Tattersall) Greene.

II. { CHRISTOPHER, — { b. 1632. / d. 1713, Jan. 30. Portsmouth, R. I.
m. 1661, Jul. 9,
ELIZABETH CORNELL, — { b. / d. 1708 + of Thomas & Rebecca ( ) Cornell.

1656, Mar. 17. He was ordered to be recompensed in part for a vessel that he had bought of William Dyer and which had been seized in Massachusetts, his father engaging for himself and son to make no further claim.

1658. Freeman.

1667. He and others bought lands of the Indians at Monmouth, New Jersey, and he lived there some years, returning to Rhode Island before 1680, however.

1679, Dec. 2. He having brought suit against John Pococke, at the General Court of Trials, in October last, and jury having brought in for plaintiff and court suspended judgment for present, and being referred to the Assembly, the latter returned it to the Court of Trials, with the opinion that judgment be barred forever.

1680, Mar. 5. He and seven others bought Pocasset (Tiverton) lands for £1,100, he having 3¾ shares out of 30 shares in the whole. The purchase was made of Gov. Josiah Winslow, &c.

1690. Deputy.

1690. Assistant.

1690, Feb. 27. He was elected Governor but refused to serve for reasons satisfactory to Assembly. (This was the first election for Governor since the deposition of Andros.)

1693, Aug. 24. He, being in England as messenger from Rhode Island, delivered the address from Rhode Island, and his own petition to Queen Mary, stating that he was sent over to represent their grievances and that he had come above four thousand miles to lay these matters before her, and prays she may grant such encouragement therein as she see fit, &c. The address showed that some presumed to affirm that the persons commissioned by Governor Andros ought to contiuue till some immediate order from the crown of England.

1696, Oct. 28. The Assembly allowed him £135, 10s., 8d., for his charge and expense in England for the colony's use.

1708, Sep. 4. Will—codicil 1711, Sep. 17—proved 1713, Feb. 9. Ex. son Job. He calls himself in his seventy-seventh year. To eldest son William, all my housing and lands in Puncatest Neck, Tiverton, other land, and negro Arthur. To son Christopher, land in Pocasset Purchase, Tiverton, land in Sapowet Neck and all lands in East New Jersey if not deeded before decease. To son Job, all lands in Rhode Island, half at my death and half at death of my wife Elizabeth, also land in Tiverton, and negro Ned. To daughter Elizabeth, wife of John Leonard, £40. To children of deceased daughter Sarah, formerly wife of Richard Cadman and latterly wife of Jonathan Merihew; that is to her first born son William Cadman, 10s., for a bible. To her second son Christopher Cadman, £10. To two sons she had by Merihew, viz: John and Thomas, each £10. To grandson Richard Durfee, £60. To grandson Thomas Durfee, £10, at twenty-one. To granddaughter Mary Wodell, £20. To granddaughter Amey Durfee, £20, at twenty-one. To wife Elizabeth, negro man Cumbo and woman Margaret for life, and one year after wife's death said negroes to be free and to then have a bed, cow and use of 20 acres in Pocasset, for their lives. To wife, two cows, horses and best feather bed, and to her for life half the housing and lands in Rhode Island, half the fruit of orchard and all household goods. To three sons, the rest of livestock. To three children of deceased daughter Rebecca Townsend, £40, divided equally at age. To son Job, rest of Pocasset land. The codicil provides that children not accepting, will lose their shares.

III. SARAH, b. / d.

IV. SAMUEL, b. 1701, Jun. 16. d. 1766, Oct. 5. Portsmouth, R. I.
m. 1725, Nov. 25.
RUTH LAWTON, b. / d. 1766 + of Lawton.

1722. Freeman.

1766, Sep. 10. Will—proved 1766, Nov. 10. Ex. son James. To son James, dwelling house and certain land, he keeping a cow for his mother and allowing her to live in the house for life. To son Jonathan, northerly half of old meadow, he paying my daughter Ruth £60, and my daughter Elizabeth £50. To sons David and Josias, southerly half of old meadow, David paying my daughter Mary £50, and Josias paying my daughter Sarah £50. To son Samuel, a cow. To grandson John, son of Daniel, deceased, 2½ acres. To wife Ruth, rest of personal, and privilege of living in house with son James.

Inventory, £3,455, 9*s.*, viz: wearing apparel £270, money £32, 17 silver buttons, 24 books £5, gun, 2 foot wheels, worsted comb, warming pan, churn, 2 cows, heifer, 2 yearlings, ½ a beef cow, ½ swine, turkeys, fowls, geese, mare, &c.

1. Samuel,	1727,	Feb. 10.
2. Mary,	1728,	Aug. 31.
3. John,	1730,	Jan. 30.
4. Daniel,	1731,	Jan. 17.
5. Jonathan,	1734,	Jan. 2.
6. David,	1736,	Apr. 1.
7. James,		
8. Ruth,		
9. Elizabeth,		
10. Josias,		
11. Sarah,		

1. Albro,	1694, Sep. 25.
2. Sarah,	1697, Aug. 1.
3. John,	1699, Feb. 16.

ALMY.

1. Deborah,	1649, Aug. 10.
2. John,	1651, Nov. 6.
3. William,	1653, Mar. 1.
4. Peter,	1655, Feb. 7.
5. Job,	1656, Aug. 24.
6. Phillip,	1658, Oct. 7.
7. Richard,	1660, Feb. 8.
8. Anne,	1663, Mar. 19.
9. Catharine,	1665, Aug. 15.
10. Audry,	1667, Dec. 27.
11. Samuel,	1671, Jan. 30.

I. SARAH, b. 1662, Apr. 17. d. 1708 (—)
m. (1)
RICHARD CADMAN, b. / d. 1695 (—) of William & Elizabeth ( ) Cadman.
m. (2)
JONATHAN MERIHEW, b. / d. of Merihew.

1. William,
2. Christopher 1686.
3. Elizabeth,
4. Rebecca,
(By 2d husband.)
5. John, 1695, Mar. 4.
6. Thomas, 1697, Mar. 1.
7. Timothy, 1702, Aug. 11.
8. Elias, 1704, Sep. 6.

II. ELIZABETH, b. 1663, Sep. 29. d. 1712 +
m. (1)
JOHN MORRIS, b. / d. of Morris.
m. (2)
JOHN LEONARD, b. / d. 1712. of Henry & Mary ( ) Leonard.

(By 2d husband.)
1. John,
2. Henry,
3. Samuel,
4. Christopher,
5. Sarah,
6. Ann,

III. WILLIAM, b. 1665, Oct. 27. d. 1747, Jul. 6. Tiverton, R. I.
m. (1)
DEBORAH COOK, b. / d. of John & Mary (Borden) Cook.
m. (2)
HOPE BORDEN, b. 1685, Mar. 3. d. 1762. of John & Mary ( ) Borden.

1692, Mar. 2. He was an inhabitant at organization of the town.

1747, Apr. 29. Will—proved 1747, Aug. 3. Ex. son William. To son Job, lands in Dartmouth, housing and wearing apparel. To two children of my grandson John Almy, deceased, who was son of my son John, deceased, £600, viz: to Elisha, £400, and to Anstice, £200, at age. To grandson Benjamin Almy, son of John, deceased, £500. To granddaughter Anstice Sayer, daughter of son John, deceased, £300. To granddaughter Mary Greene, daughter of son John, deceased, £300. To son Samuel, a certain part of homestead farm in Tiverton, housing, &c. To son William, the rest of homestead farm in Puncatest, Tiverton, dwelling house, orchard, &c. (north part), and negroes Cuff, Peter, Sherpo and Sambo. To grandson William, son of Samuel, land in Dartmouth, thirteen cows, three heifers, pair of oxen, mare, saddle horse, four young cattle, breeding sow, barrow hog, ram, twenty sheep, gun, certain farming tools, silver cup with a foot to it, and negro Pero, all at age. To wife Hope, all household goods she brought at marriage, also a bed, riding horse, £400, improvement of great room and bedroom, &c., fruit of orchard, milk of a cow, two spring pigs, one hundred pounds of beef, firewood, &c., and negro Peg. To granddaughter Amey Ellet, £300. To grandson Job Almy, son of daughter Elizabeth, deceased, £200. To daughter Rebecca Slocum, £500, bed, chairs, negro woman Hagar, &c. To son William and daughter Rebecca Slocum, all my silver spoons. To sons Job and Samuel, rest of live stock. To cousin Deborah Cook, £1000 and privilege of house room, victuals and drink for six years after my death. To son William, great silver tankard, money and rest of estate.

Inventory, £7,560, 19*s.*, 6*d.*, viz: books, apparel and cane £146, 10*s.*, 7 beds, pewter, wheel, loom, cheese press, 2 negro men £200, negro woman and girl and 3 boys £460, 14 swine, 30 geese, 4 oxen, 2 steers, 10 cows, 7 fatting cattle, calf, 320 sheep, 21 cattle at Brightman Farm, 23 cattle at Swanset Farm, 21 head horsekind and 14 cattle at Cadman's Neck, &c.

1752, Aug. 25. Will—proved 1762, Oct. 4. Widow Hope. Exs. kinsman Nathan Chase and friend Jonathan Freeborn. To Gideon Almy, son of William, a brass kettle, feather bed, &c., that I brought with me when I married his grandfather. To Ann Almy, daughter of William, a clothes press. To Job Almy's daughter Hope Almy, a small trunk and silver spoon. To Amey Durfee, wife of Benjamin, and Peace Borden, wife of Samuel, my best doctor book. To Elizabeth Chase, wife of Nathan, gown and hood. To Amey Slocum, and Ann, Content and Hannah Chase, £50, each, and to the last three (all being daughters of Nathan Chase), the rest of wearing apparel and household goods. To cousin Nathan Chase, the rest of money, bonds, &c.

Inventory, £2,386, 4*s.*, 9*d.*

1. Mary,	1689,	Aug. 7.
2. John,	1692,	Oct. 10.
3. Job,	1696,	Apr. 28.
4. Elizabeth,	1697,	Nov. 14.
5. Samuel,	1701,	Apr. 15.
6. Deborah,	1703,	Jul. 27.
7. Rebecca,	1704,	Oct. 14.
8. Joseph,	1707,	Oct. 3.
9. William,	1707,	Oct. 3.

(2d wife, no issue.)

IV. ANN, b. 1667, Nov. 29. d.
m. (1)
RICHARD DURFEE, b. / d. 1700. of Thomas Durfee.
m. (2)
BENJAMIN JEFFERSON, b. / d. of Jefferson.

1. Richard,
2. Mary,
3. Thomas,
4. Ann,
5. Hope,
6. Amey,

ALMY. 3d column. V. Christopher. He m. (2) 1705. Mary Bryer (w. of Joseph), dau. of——Palmer. He d. 1746. He was a merchant.

1745, Sep. 3. Will-proved 1746, Jul. 21. Exs. Mary Almy, William Almy, Walter Chaloner. He mentions wife Mary; grandsons, William, Benjamin and Job, sons of son William, deceased; granddaughter, Ann Chaloner, wife of Walter Chaloner, and daughter of my son William; daughter Elizabeth, widow of son William Almy; granddaughter, Mary Sylvester, wife of Joseph Sylvester, of Newport; Mary Wanton, wife of Gideon Wanton; grandsons, Samuel, and Christopher.

V. CHRISTOPHER, b. 1669, Dec. 26. d. Newport, R. I.
m. (1) 1690, Apr. 16.
JOANNA SLOCUM, b. 1672, Oct. 9. d. of Giles & Ann (Lawton) Slocum.
m. (2)
MARY, b. 1670, Mar. d. 1759, Sep. 15. of

His widow Mary, was buried in Clifton Burial Ground.

1. Ann,	1695,	Sep. 29.
2. William,	1699,	Jun. 22.
(2d wife.)		
3. Sarah,	1707,	Jan. 26.
4. Christopher	1711,	Jun. 10.

VI. REBECCA, b. 1671, Jan. 26 d. 1708 (—)
m. 1692, Apr. 28.
JOHN TOWNSEND, b. / d. of Thomas Townsend.

1. Thomas,	1693,	Oct. 16.
2. Silvanus,	1696,	Apr. 9.
3. Sarah,	1698,	Apr. 9.
4. Philena,	1699,	Nov. 13.

VII. JOHN, b. 1673, Apr. d. 1678.

III. JOHN, m. MARY COLE, — John: b. ; d. 1676, Oct. 1. Mary: b. ; d. — Portsmouth, R. I. — of James & Mary ( ) Cole.

(She m. (2) 1677, John Pococke.)

He was a merchant.

1658. Commissioner.

1667, Jul. 24. Lieutenant of a troop of horse.

1671, Jan. 30. He was allowed £9, 10*s.*, for his horse, and his own and his man's time in going to Plymouth.

1675, Jan. 27. He and wife Mary, sold Thomas Ward, of Newport, half a share of land at Seaconnet for £7.

1676. He served as Captain in King Philip's War.

1676, Oct. 20. Will—made by Town Council. Exx. widow Mary. To her the use of all personal estate after payment of debts.

1676, Nov. 1. The court of Plymouth Colony gave his widow administration on his estate in that colony and his real estate there for life.

1677, Jun. 28. Mary Pococke, formerly wife of John Almy, acknowledged a deed made 1675, Jan. 27, as above.

1679, Nov. 10. The Assembly desired of Town Council of Portsmouth, that they would request Mary Pococke the executrix of late deceased John Almy, to give account of the estate left in her custody, it being reported that she hath disbursed far more for payment of his debts than the estate left in her possession.

IV. JOB, m. MARY UNTHANK, — Job: b. ; d. 1684. Mary: b. ; d. 1724 + — Portsmouth, Warwick, Portsmouth, R. I. — of Christopher & Susanna ( ) Unthank.

(She m. (2) Thomas Townsend.)

1660, Jul. 15. He was on a jury in Plymouth Colony, in case of James Pierce, of Boston, who "died by an immediate hand of God, by thunder and lightning," &c.

1670–72. Warwick. Deputy.

1673, May 7. He was appointed on a committee to treat with the Indian Sachems, "and with them seriously to consult and agree of some way to prevent the extreme excess of the Indians' drunkenness," &c. The sachems to be treated with, were: Mawsup and Ninecraft, of Narragansett, Philip, of Mount Hope, Wetamo, of Pocasset and Awashunks, of Seaconnet.

1673–74–75. Assistant.

1680, Mar. 5. He and seven others bought Pocasset lands for £1,100, he having 3¼ shares out of 30 shares in all.

1684, Jan. 19. Will—proved 1684, Mar. 1. Exx. wife Mary. To her all visible estate while widow to bring up children till of age. To eldest son John, all land and buildings in Portsmouth, only reserving best room for wife while widow, and to son John, also lands at Pocasset. To son Job, all lands in Punketest, except a meadow. To son Anthony, land at Sepowit Neck, &c. To four eldest daughters, Susanna, Audry, Deborah and Catharine Almy, a share at Pocasset, at eighteen years of age, divided equally. To youngest daughter Mary, £10, at eighteen or marriage. To wife Mary, half a share at Pocasset.

Inventory, £287, 16*s.*, viz: 30 head of cattle £50, 9 horsekind, 17 swine, 70 bushels Indian corn, 2 negro servants £42, Indian servants £35, cider, tobacco, 2 guns, 2 silver cups, &c.

1724, Aug. 28. Mary Townsend, widow, deposed that while wife of Job Almy, she had certain children born.

ALMY. 2d column. IV. Job. 1721 Sep. 9. Mary Townsend, widow, of Newport, quitclaimed certain land in Portsmouth, R. I., to daughter Susanna Almy, four grandchildren, John, Robert, Mary and Elizabeth Hicks, grandchild Samuel Snell, grandchildren Christopher and Solomon Townsend, Deborah Hicks, Anne Townsend, Hannah Townsend. Same date, Jacob Townsend of Oyster Bay, Long Island, deeded to Abraham Anthony, 2 acres obtained of Capt. Job Almy by heirs-at-law. V. Catherine m. 2), —— Brown. 3d column. V. Audry m. James Townsend. Children, 1. Jacob. 2, Mary. 3, Deborah. VI. Deborah m. John Hicks. Children. 1, John. 2, Robert. 3, Mary. 4, Elizabeth. 5. Deborah. VII. Catherine m. Solomon Townsend. Children. 1, Job. 2, Christopher. 3, Solomon. 4, Anne. 5, Hannah.

V. CATHARINE, m. BARTHOLOMEW WEST, — Catharine: b. ; d. Bartholomew: b. ; d. 1703 (—) — of Matthew West.

VIII. JOB, m. (1) 1696, Mar. ANN LAWTON, m. (2) [of Wm. ABIGAIL GARDINER (w. — b. 1675, Oct. 10. d. 1743, Dec. 2. — b. 1678, Apr. 25. d. 1739, Feb. 12. of Isaac & Elizabeth (Tallman) Lawton — b. 1681. d. 1763, Mar. 6. of John & Abigail (Richmond) Remington. — Newport, R. I.

1. Child,
2. Christopher 1698, May 5.
3. Elizabeth, 1703, Aug. 1.
4. Ann,
(2d wife, no issue.)

1708. Freeman.

1709, May 4. He was appointed on a special Council to assist the Governor for advice to manage affairs for the more speedy expediting of the great design now intended against Canada.

1709-16-17-18-19-20-25-26. Deputy.

1715, Oct. 20. He petitioned the Assembly for charges and expense his father Christopher Almy was at during his agency in England.

1726. Captain.

IX. CHILD, — b. 1676. d. young.

No issue.

I. WILLIAM, — b. 1664, Jan. 20. d. 1664, Mar. 10.

II. CHRISTOPHER, — b. 1664, Jan. 20. d. 1664, Mar. 10.

III. WILLIAM, — b. 1665, Sep. 5. d. 1666, Jan. 3.

IV. SUSANNA, — b. 1667, Jan. 29. d. 1710 +

V. AUDRY, — b. 1669, Apr. 5. d.

VI. DEBORAH, — b. 1671, Aug. 5. d.

VII. CATHARINE, — b. 1674, Jan. 22. d.

VIII. JOHN, — b. 1676, Jan. 25. d.

IX. MARY, m. 1705, Dec. 13. SAMUEL SNELL, — b. 1678, Sep. 6. d. — b. d. of Thomas Snell.

1. Samuel,

X. JOB, m. 1705, Dec, 6. BRIDGET SANFORD, — b. 1681, Mar. 3. d. 1767, Jan. 25. — b. d. 1766 (—) of Peleg & Mary (Coddington) Sanford. — Tiverton, R. I.

1. Job, 1707, Mar. 4.
2. Peleg, 1709, Oct. 25.
3. Mary, 1711, Jun. 20.
4. Eliphal, 1713, Aug. 3.
5. Bridget, 1716, May 16.
6. Ann, 1718, Jan. 28.
7. John, 1720, Apr. 18.
8. Job, 1722, May 16.
9. Deborah, 1724, Mar. 21.

1766, Jan. 14. Will—proved 1767, Feb. 2. Exs. son John and friend Thomas Cory. To son John, all land in Portsmouth, Tiverton and Little Compton and all land and housing in Massachusetts (with some exceptions) and two houses in Newport, reserving burial place in Tiverton and also in Portsmouth where my father and mother and one of my sons lie buried. To my undutiful son Job, one Spanish milled dollar only, having expended upon him upwards of £2,000, for which he gives me no thanks, &c. To daughter Mary Almy, relict to Samuel Almy, 1,500 Spanish milled dollars and a horse, chair, and privilege in wood lot. To grandson Sanford Thompson, $500. To grandson William Thompson, $500. To granddaughter Catharine Thompson, $20. To granddaughter Eliphal Thompson, $200. To granddaughter Ann Thompson, $200 and feather bed. To grandson Henry Thompson, what I allotted for him when last in America. To granddaughter Deborah Cory, wife of Thomas, 100 Spanish milled dollars. To granddaughter Bridget Cook, a like legacy, as also to great-granddaughter Eliphal Cory. To great-granddaughter Ann Cory, $50. The great-granddaughters' legacies to be deposited with their father Thomas Cory till they are of age. To friend Constant Bailey, 100 Spanish milled dollars. To Ann and Deborah Bailey, daughters of Constant Bailey, of Newport, each $50. To kinsman John Hicks, of Groton, $50, and to kinswomen Deborah and Elizabeth Hicks, each $50. To pastor of Baptist Church in Tiverton, and his successors, the interest of sale of my right in the ministry land. To slaves Jack and Isaac, their freedom Jan. 1st, 1770, if they behave well. To Thomas Cory, 100 dollars.

Inventory, £2,377, 19*s*., 9*d*., viz: wearing apparel £10, 16*s*., wrought plate £34, 7*s*., 4 gold rings, pair of gold sleeve buttons, 2 silver mounted swords, gun, 2 porringers, churn, cheese fat, pewter, old canoe, 6 working cattle, 13 cows, 4 three year, 4 two year, 7 yearlings, 8 hogs, 2 horses, 178 sheep, warming pan, negro boy and girl £67, silver watch, &c.

XI. ANTHONY, — b. 1683, Mar. 24. d. 1711. — Portsmouth, R. I.

1710, May 18. Will—proved 1711. May 7. He calls himself of Portsmouth, but the will was made and proved in Newport. He mentions his mother Mary Townsend, brother Job, sister Susanna Almy, four cousins (*i. e.* nephews), John, Robert, Mary and Elizabeth Hix, cousin Samuel Snell, son of Samuel and Mary Snell, cousin Christopher and Solomon Townsend, cousins Deborah Hix, Ann Townsend and Hannah Townsend.

1. Bartholomew,
2. William,
3. John,
4. Stephen, 1654.

See: American Genealogist v. 20, p. 120-121.

THOMAS[6], (Thos.[5], Rich'd[4], Rich.[3], Thos.[2], Rog.[1]) — b. 1599. Cheselbourne, Dorset Co., Eng.; d. 1674, Sep. Providence, R. I.
m. (1) —— — b. d.
m. (2) PHEBE PARKHURST, — b. d. 1688 +
of George & Susanna (   ) Parkhurst.

1635, May. He came to America in ship Plain Joan, and soon settled at Watertown, Mass.

1640, May 13. Freeman.

1648, Dec. 20. He bought 30 acres of George Parkhurst.

1651, Oct. He was fined 20s. for offence against law concerning baptism.

1654, Apr. 2. He was fined £5, for neglecting public worship twenty days.

1655, Mar. 30. He sold brother-in-law George Parkhurst, 30 acres which he had bought in 1648, "of our father George Parkhurst and his wife Susanna."

1655, Apr. 2. He was fined £10, for neglecting public worship forty days.

1661, Oct. 17. Providence. He sold land in Watertown to John Whitney.

1662, Oct. 20. He and wife Phebe sold John Wincoll, house, barn, and 16 acres in Watertown.

1665, Feb. 19. He had lot 83 granted in a division of lands.

1666-67-70-71-72. Deputy.

1672. Town Council.

1685, Jun. 29. Agreement of heirs. He having died in September, 1674, as was declared, leaving an estate of lands, goods and cattle behind him not disposed of by will but only by word of mouth, leaving his mind with his wife and children how they should settle his estate: It was therefore agreed between his widow Phebe, and Richard the eldest son, Thomas, John and Eleazer, also sons of deceased, and Elizabeth Comstock, his daughter, that there should be five instruments of covenant prepared and signed by all of them, Samuel Comstock signing as husband of Elizabeth. "Whereas the said deceased, Thomas Arnold, did by word of mouth leave his mind with his wife and children how they should divide his estate of lands, goods and cattle amongst them after his decease; the aforementioned persons all and every of them, the same do hereby endeavour to propagate and perform to the best of their understanding and abilities," &c. To Phebe, the widow, the lot bought of William Fenner, with orchard, and at her decease the same to revert to son Thomas. To Phebe also, land east of Moshassuck river, said home lot at her decease going to son John. To Phebe also, all household goods, two cows and nine swine at her own disposal. To Elizabeth Comstock, £20. To Thomas Arnold, a house lot in town, two other lots, a meadow, a tract of 50 acres, and rights of common. To John Arnold, three lots, an orchard, a piece of land of 17½ acres, share of meadow, &c. To Eleazer Arnold, 50 acres near place called "World's End," a fifteen acre lot, 3 shares of meadow, &c. To John and Eleazer, an equal share in certain land. To Thomas and John equally, the tackling and tools of deceased. To Richard the eldest son, all the rest of lands.

1687, Sep, 1. His widow was taxed 6d.

ARNOLD (THOMAS). 1st column. 1655, Apr. 6. He of Providence, bought land of William Burrows of same place. 2d column. V. Richard. Published 1687, Nov. 1. for marriage to Sarah Smith; probably widow of John[2]. (John[1]). The Miller. 3d column. I. Richard. Children, 1. Joseph, 1700, Apr. 20. 2, Richard, 1702, Apr. 10. 3, Thomas, 1705, Feb. 19. 4, Woodward, 1707, Oct. 8. 5, Mary, 1712, June 30. 6, Edmund, 1714, Dec. 1. 7, Josiah, 1716, Oct. 8. 8, Naomi, 1717, Nov. 8. 9, Dinah, 1719, Sep. 4. 10, Hannah, 1721, Aug. 29. IV. Mary, b. 1668, Sep. 9, d. 1725, Jan. 20. Her husband b. 1674, Sep. I. Jonathan m. 1724, Aug. 27, Elizabeth Mathews. Children, 1, John. 2, Eleazer. 3, David, 1736. 4, William. 5, James. 6, Alice. 7, Jonathan, 1743. 8, Thomas. V. John d. 1752, Feb. 22, m. 1st ——, m. 2d, Sarah. Children, 1, Enoch. 2, Mary. 3, Zebedee. 4. Christopher. 5, Comfort. VI. Jeremiah. Children, 1, Freelove. 1722, Jan. 10. 2, Lavina. 1727, Nov. 11. 3, Oliver, 1730. Apr. 21. 4, James, 1733, Aug. 4. 5, Jeremiah, 1735. Mar. 12. 6, Sarah, 1736, Feb. 1. 7, Eleazer, 1739, July 10. 8, Charles, 1743.

I. THOMAS, — b. 1625, May 3. d. young.

II. NICHOLAS, — b. 1627. d. young.

III. SUSANNA, m. 1654, Apr. 7. JOHN FARNUM, — b. d. — b. d. of Farnum.

ARNOLD (THOMAS). 2d column. III. Susanna. Children, 1. John, 1655, May 20. 2. Jonathan, 1659, Nov. 18. 3. Elizabeth. 4. David.

(2d WIFE.)

IV. ICHABOD, — b. 1641, Mar. 1. d. young.

V. RICHARD, — b. 1642, Mar. 22. Providence, R. I.; d. 1710, Apr. 22.
m. (1) MARY ANGELL, — b. d. 1695 (—) of Thomas & Alice (   ) Angell.
m. (2) SARAH, — b. d. 1712. of

1671-76-79-80-81-96-98-1700-1-2-5-7-8. Deputy.

1679, Jul. 1. Taxed 6s. 3d.

1681-82-83-84-85-86-90-98-99. Assistant.

1685, May 6. He was on a committee to draw up address of congratulation to King James II, on his peaceable succession to the crown.

1686, Dec. 22. He with others were apprized by letter from Sir Edmund Andros, of their appointment as members of his Council, and that a meeting would be held at Boston, on the thirtieth of December.

1695, Jul. 2. He and two others were chosen to run the northern line of the colony.

1700-1. Town Council.

1707-8. Speaker of house of Deputies.

1708, Apr. He was appointed on the committee in relation to vacant lands in Narragansett.

1708, Jun. 8. Will—proved 1710, May 10. Exs. sons Richard, John and Thomas. The will was not witnessed and the Town Council offered administration to widow Sarah, but she refusing, the three sons of testator were appointed, viz: Richard, John and Thomas. To wife Sarah for life, two lots in town, with house and orchard upon them, and a meadow, and at her decease the estate to go to his three sons. To wife also, two cows, and a third of household as a free gift, and all estate that was hers before I married her. To son Richard, land where he dwells at Wansoket, east side of river. To son John, land where he dwells, with testator's interest in saw mill at the Falls, and meadow called the Island, &c. To sons Richard and John, rest of Wansoket lands, equally. To son Thomas, land where he dwelt on both sides of highway leading from town to Loquasquuck with house, &c., he paying his brother Richard, £15, and brother John, £10, and sister Mary Steere, £25. To son Thomas, other land and half the mill at Napatuckett, and service of negro Tobey till twenty-five years of age, at which time said Tobey to be freed and given two suits of apparel, a good narrow axe, broad hoe and sickle.

Inventory, £134, 5s. 10d., viz: 9 cattle, horse, carpenter's tools, cash £15, 9s. 10d., &c.

1710, May 12. His widow gave up all right in house, two lots, and orchard, on condition of payment to her of £8, per year for life, from the three sons of Richard Arnold, deceased.

VI. THOMAS, — b. d. Providence, R. I.

1672. Freeman.

1676, Aug. 14. He was one of those "who staid and went not away" in King Philip's War, and so was entitled to a share in the disposition of the Indian captives whose services were sold for a term of years.

1676-80-83-84-85. Town Council.

1678-82-83-84-91. Deputy.

1679, Jul. 1. Taxed 5s. 7½d.

1688. Ratable estate, 2 acres orchard, 5 acres meadow, 2 acres tillage, 23 acres English pasture, 75 acres vacant lands, 14 sheep, a swine. He adds: "It is to be understood that I give an account of what lands I have in my hands of my mother's."

1693, Jan. 5. He sold William Turpin, 5 acres, mansion house, &c., for £61.

VII. JOHN, — b. 1648, Feb. 19. Providence, R. I.; d. 1723, Jan. 5.
m. HANNAH, — b. d. 1723 + of

1679, Jul. 1. Taxed 3s. 9d., "John Arnold and his mother."

1687, Sep. 1. Taxed 2s. 6d. The same year his ratable estate was as follows: 4 cows, a two year old, horse, a swine, 80 acres, of which 18 acres was within fences, some of it orchard — "as one year with another beareth about thirty bushels of fruit."

1716. Deputy.

1723. Administration to widow Hannah and son Jonathan. Inventory, £428, viz: cow, 2 heifers, calf, sow and shoats, barley, oats, &c.

VIII. ELEAZER, — b. 1651, Jun. 17. Providence, R. I.; d. 1722, Aug. 29.
m. ELEANOR SMITH, — b. d. 1722 (—) of John & Elizabeth (   ) Smith.

1679, Jul. 1. Taxed 3s. 1½d.

1684-85-86. Town Council.

1686-1700-1-3-6-7-11-15. Deputy.

1687. Ratable estate, 2 oxen, 9 cows, 3 steers, 2 two year olds, 3 yearlings, horse, 3 mares, colt, 5 swine, 12 acres planting land, 3 acres meadow, 2 acres pasture, 6 acres wild pasture.

1705. Justice of the Peace.

I. Richard, m. (1) Mary Woodward, m. (2) 1715, Nov. 14. Dinah Thornton,
{ b. { d. 1745, Jun. — Providence, Smithfield, R. I.
{ b. { d. — of Joseph & Mary (Pray) — Woodward.
{ b. { d. — of John & Dinah (Steere) — Thornton.

1. Thomas, 2. Richard, 3. Joseph, 4. Woodward, 5. Edmund, 6. Mary, (2d wife.) 7. Josiah, 8. Naomi, 9. Dinah, 10. Hannah,

1711, Mar. 26. He and his brothers John Arnold, Jr. and Thomas Arnold, Jr., sold Thomas Steere half of certain land both sides Woonasquatucket river, near the corn mill and saw mill formerly belonging to honored father Richard Arnold, deceased.

1711, May 14. He and his brothers John and Thomas, confirmed to an Indian, 7 acres that he had bought of father Richard, deceased.

1713, Jun. 16. Taxed 18s.

1729, Dec. 8. He deeded son Thomas, for love, &c., 60 acres where dwelling house of son stands, bounded partly by meeting house land.

1731, May 11. Smithfield. He deeded son Richard, for love, &c., 60 acres. At subsequent dates he deeded sons Joseph, Woodward, Edmund and Josiah.

1744, Nov. 8. He deeded son Joseph, for love, &c., all the homestead farm where I dwell, containing 60 acres.

1746, Jan. 15. Administration to son Thomas.

II. John, m. (1) Mary Mowry, m. (2) 1742, Oct. 31. Hannah Hayward,
{ b. 1670, Nov. 1. { d. 1756, Oct. 27. — Providence, Smithfield, R. I.
{ b. 1675. { d. 1742, Jan. 27. — of Nathaniel & Joanna (Inman) — Mowry.
{ b. { d. — of — Hayward.

1. William,	1695, Dec. 9.
2. John,	1697, Jul. 27.
3. Daniel,	1699, May 1.
4. Mercy,	1701, Dec. 22.
5. Anthony,	1704, Mar. 12.
6. Seth,	1706, Sep. 6.
7. Israel,	
8. Anna,	
9. Susanna,	
10. Abigail,	
(2d wife, no issue.)	

He was a miller.

1706, May 21. He had 12s. worth of pewter taken from him for not training, he being a Quaker.

1712. At about this date he built his corn and fulling mill on the island near Woonsocket Falls.

1719, Dec. 9. He was appointed to build the Quaker meeting house, to be twenty foot square, and the height thereof left to him.

1719, Dec. 17. He sold for 10s. to Samuel Aldrich, Samuel Wilkinson, Jr. and Samuel Comstock, Jr., and their survivors forever, an acre of ground on northerly side of highway near the place formerly called the dugway, whereon is a burying place of people called Quakers.

1731–32. Smithfield. Town Council.

1753, May 5. Will—proved 1756, Nov. 1. Ex. son William. To wife Hannah, half of homestead and dwelling house for life, and £700. To son William, £30. To sons Daniel, Anthony and Israel, each £5. To daughters Mercy Lapham, Abigail Bartlett and Susanna Malavery, each £100. To grandson Moses Arnold, £5. To grandson Noah Arnold, £40. To grandson David Arnold, £10. To grandson Arnold Paine, the other half of homestead and reversion of half that wife has, and £200. To grandson Arnold Paine and to wife Hannah Arnold, equally, all swine and provisions. To grandson Nicholas Lapham, a gun called French gun. To son Seth, my part of saw mill standing at the Falls situated in Cumberland. To eight children, rest of estate equally, viz: to William, Daniel, Anthony, Seth, Israel, Mercy Lapham, Abigail Bartlett and Susanna Malavery.

Inventory, £9,453, 19s., viz: bible with book of Apocrypha £12, wearing apparel £192, silver money £227, 5s., books of several kinds £7, 10s., silver plate, porringer, cup and 9 spoons £140, 10s., paper money £594, 18s. 8d., best feather bed £150, 6 other beds, 2 leather chairs, 2 churns, woolen wheel, foot wheel, clock real, warming pan, pewter, 4 turkeys, swine, 5 cows, young creatures, yoke of oxen, 18 sheep, horse, carpenter's tools, 3 pairs of nippers to draw teeth, book debts, cane and 2 other walking sticks, &c.

III. Thomas, m. 1706, Dec. 5. Elizabeth Burlingame.
{ b. 1675, Mar. 24. { d. 1727, Feb. 3. — Providence, R. I.
{ b. 1684, Jan. 9. { d. 1752, May 5. — of Roger & Mary (   ) — Burlingame.

1. Job,	1707, Nov. 16.
2. Jonathan,	1708, Nov. 18.
3. Mary,	1710, Oct. 28.
4. Thomas,	1713, Nov. 4.
5. Elizabeth,	1717.
6. Sarah,	1722, Apr. 10.

(She m. (2) 1734, Apr. 11, William Spencer.)

1711. Distraint was made on his estate for refusing to go in Her Majesty's service in late intended expedition against Canada.

1711–23. Deputy.

1725, Apr. 8. Will—codicil, 1727, Jan. 29—proved, 1727, Mar. 6. Exs. wife Elizabeth and son Job. To wife, half the movables to bring up the children to read and write. To six children, the other half equally. To wife, half the homestead, and son Job the other half, and he to have wife's half at her death.

Inventory, £845, 1s. 10d., viz: 26 neat cattle, 3 horses, 2 colts, 42 sheep, 10 goats, 6 swine, guns, gold, silver, &c.

1750, Jan. 22. Will—proved 1752, May 20. Widow Elizabeth Spencer. Ex. son Job Arnold. To son Job Arnold, great bible. To son Jonathan Arnold, book called Barclay's Apology. To daughters Mary Newell and Sarah Turpin, £50, each, and all wearing apparel, &c. The rest of estate to go one-fifth to son Job's daughters Lydia, Sarah and Keziah, one-fifth to son Jonathan's daughters Mercy and Elizabeth, one-fifth to deceased son Thomas' daughters Amey, Huldah, Phebe and Alice, one-fifth to daughter Mary Newell's daughters Sylvia and Elizabeth, and one-fifth to granddaughter Elizabeth Turpin. Inventory, £557. 5s.

IV. Mary, m. Thomas Steere,
{ b. { d.
{ b. { d. 1735, Aug. 27. — of John & Hannah (Wickenden) — Steere.

1. Phebe,	
2. Mary,	1702.
3. Thomas,	
4. Richard,	1707, Jun. 3.
5. Elisha,	

(2d Wife, no issue.)

I. Jonathan, m. 1727. Elizabeth Mathewson,
{ b. { d. 1770 ± — Providence, Johnston, R. I.
{ b. { d. — of — Mathewson.

1. John, 2. David, 3. William, 4. James, 5. Alice, 6. Jonathan, 7. Thomas,

I. Phebe, m. Thomas Smith,
{ b. 1672, Nov. 5. { d. 1741 +
{ b. 1671, Feb. 19. { d. 1741, Sep. 2. — of Edward & Anphillis (Angell) — Smith.

1. Thomas,	1697, Dec. 5.
2. John,	1700, Oct. 7.
3. Phebe,	1703, Mar. 28.
4. Mary,	1705, Apr. 22.
5. Hannah,	1707, Apr. 10.
6. Daniel,	1709, Jun. 29.
7. Ruth,	1712, Jun. 13.

II. Elizabeth m. —— Smith,
{ b. { d.
{ b. { d. — of — Smith.

1. Deborah,

1706, Jan. 7. He and Thomas Hopkins, sons-in-law of Elizabeth Smith, widow of John Smith, agreed to support and take care of her provided they had all the personal estate left her by will of her husband.

1708, Oct. 2. He deeded Thomas Smith, Joseph Smith, Jr., Samuel Wilkinson, Jr., Samuel Comstock, Jr., Thomas Arnold, Jr., Eleazer Arnold, Jr. and Joseph Arnold, half an acre (near his house) on which stands a meeting house of people called Quakers.

1713, Jun. 16. He and son Joseph were taxed £1, 9*s*.

1716, Jun. 4. He deeded to son Joseph, for love, &c., 60 acres on which Joseph's dwelling house standeth.

1722, Aug. 25. Will—proved 1723, Jan. 14. Exs. sons Joseph, John and Jeremiah. To son Joseph, a 6 acre lot, and 3 acres near land formerly given him. To son John, land bounding partly on testator's brother John's land. To son Jeremiah, dwelling house and all homestead lands lying north side of Moshassuck river. To daughter-in-law Sarah Arnold, half the profit of dwelling house that was settled on son Eleazer during his life, to be for said Sarah while she remains widow. To grandson Eleazer, 20 acres that his father had. To grandson David, half the above house and other half at death of his mother. To three sons and two grandsons, other land. To three sons, rest of land and all movables except legacies. To daughter Phebe Smith, £20. To daughter Elizabeth Smith, £10. To daughter Eleanor Arnold, £30, and what else she needs by reason of weakness. To daughter Mary Thomas, £30. To daughter Abigail Mann, £10. To granddaughter Deborah Smith, 40*s*.

Inventory, £441, 17*s*. 1*d*., viz: horse, 2 colts, 19 head of cattle, 19 sheep, 11 swine, barley, rye, 2 guns, silver money £14, 5*s*. 4*d*., &c.

IX. { ELIZABETH, m. 1678, Nov. 22. SAMUEL COMSTOCK, { b. { d. 1747, Oct. 20. { b. 1654. { d. 1727, May 27. of Samuel & Ann (   ) Comstock.

ARNOLD (WILLIAM).

See: N.E. Hist. & Gen. Reg. v. 69, p. 64

{ WILLIAM[6] (Thos.[5], Rich.[4], m. [Rich.[3], Thos.[2], Roger[1] CHRISTIAN PEAK, { b. 1587, Jun. 24. Cheselbourne, Dorset Co., Eng., { d. 1676 ± [Providence, R. I. { b. 1583. { d.

of Thomas Peak.

1616, Nov. 23. He was appointed administrator of his brother John's estate.

1635, May 1. He sailed from Dartmouth, England, with his family.

1635, Jun. 24. He arrived in New England and was for a time at Hingham, Mass.

1636, Apr. 20. Providence. He came at this date (as his son Benedict records.)

1638, Oct. 8. He and eleven others had a deed from Roger Williams of lands the latter had bought of Canonicus and Miantonomi. In this year he moved to Pawtuxet.

1639. He was one of the twelve first members of Baptist church.

1640, Jan. 27. He signed an agreement with thirty-eight others of Providence for civil government.

1641, Apr. 2. He had land laid out in north part of Providence where he had set a wolf trap. (A few years later the town ordered a tax of ½*d* a head on all cattle, payable to any one who killed a wolf in Providence.)

1641, Nov. 17. The Pawtuxet settlers sent a letter to Massachusetts authorities complaining of the Gortonists, and closed by asking aid of Massachusetts. The latter Colony replied refusing assistance unless they came under their jurisdiction.

1642, Sep. 8. He and others of Pawtuxet subjected themselves to the government of Massachusetts, and he was appointed to keep the peace. This separation from Rhode Island lasted sixteen years, and meanwhile Mr. Arnold kept Massachusetts well apprized of doings in Rhode Island.

1643, May 10. It was ordered by Massachusetts authorities that he should have payment of £7, 2*s*., which he disbursed for thirty-one bushels and a half of corn for Pomham, &c.; to be paid him in wampum or such commodities as he desires; and "the Court is thankful to him for his care and pains herein."

1648, Aug. 15. He wrote a long letter to the Governor of Massachusetts complaining of the injustice shown the Indians by the Warwick settlers, who are going on "with a high hand."

1650, Sep. 2. Taxed £3, 6*s*., 8*d*.

1651, Sep. 1. He wrote again to Massachusetts, protesting against Roger Williams' proposed errand to England seeking a charter, and he says of the Rhode Island settlers generally, "under the pretence of liberty of conscience, about these parts there come to live all the scum, the runaways of the country, which in time for want of better order may bring a heavy burden on the land."

1652, May 27. He was allowed 26*s*., together with the sachems Pomham and Wotapunkum, he having acted as interpreter for these sachems in the case brought against them by Ninecraft.

1658. The Pawtuxet settlers expressed a desire this year to be re-united to Providence, and upon their own motion it was done.

I. { ELIZABETH, m. WILLIAM CARPENTER, { b. 1611, Nov. 23. { d. 1683 + { b. { d. 1685, Sep. 7. of Richard Carpenter.

II. { BENEDICT, m. 1640, Dec. 17. DAMARIS WESTCOTT, { b. 1615, Dec. 21. Providence, Newport, R. I. { d. 1678, Jun. 19. { b. { d. 1678 + of Stukeley Westcott.

1637, Aug. 20. At this date (or a little later) he and twelve others signed the following compact: "We whose names are hereunder desirous to inhabit in the town of Providence, do promise to subject ourselves in active and passive obedience to all such orders or agreements as shall be made for public good of the body in an orderly way, by the major consent of the present inhabitants, masters of families incorporated together in a Town fellowship, and others whom they shall admit unto them, only in civil things."

1640, Jul. 27. He signed an agreement with thirty-eight others for a form of government.

1650, Sep. 2. Taxed £5. (The highest in the list.)

1651, Nov. 19. Newport. He moved here from Providence at this date as he records.

1653, May 17. Freeman.

1654-55-56-57-58-59-60-61-62-63. Commissioner.

1655-56-60-61. Assistant.

1657-58-59-60-62-63. President of the four towns.

1661, Sep. 3. He and others were complained of for their intrusion into the bounds of Southertown on east side of the Pawquatuck River. He and others answered that they owned themselves to be the men that claimed the lands, and said they would keep possession and that they would not try their title anywhere but in Rhode Island or in England, and Arnold said if any should attach him at Boston he would lie in prison seven years before he would try the title there.

1663-64-65-66-69-70-71-72-77-78. Governor.

1676, Apr. 4. It was voted: "that in these troublesome times and straits in this colony, this Assembly desiring to have the advice and concurrence of the most judicious inhabitants, if it may be had for the good of the whole, do desire at their next sitting the company and counsel of Mr. Benedict Arnold," and fifteen others.

1677, Nov. 3. He, eldest son and heir of William Arnold, late of Pawtuxet, deceased, sold to brother Stephen Arnold all the land of our said father lying and being within the bounds of Pawtuxet, that is to say between Pawtuxet River and Providence bounds, for £100. The land consisted of upland, meadow, pasture, marsh, wood grounds, gardens, orchards, &c, and included buildings, materials for buildings, fences, &c.

1677, Dec. 24. Will—codicil, 1678, Feb. 10, proved 1678. Exs. wife Damaris, sons Benedict and Josiah and Mr. James Barker, Sr. "By the permission of God Almighty, I, Benedict Arnold, of Newport," &c.—"aged sixty and two years, finding myself subject to weakness and infirmities, the usual attendants on aged persons," &c. He desired that his body should be buried at north-east corner of parcel of ground containing three rods square in or near the line or path from dwelling house to my stone built wind mill in the town of Newport. The centre of the three rods square was the tomb already erected over the grave of his grandchild Damaris Goulding—there buried fourteenth of August 1677. He ordered—that he and his wife should be interred in this ground and that the lot should be forever reserved for his kindred. To wife, for life, the house and 2 acres bought of

III. ELEAZER, m. SARAH HAWKINS,
b.
d. 1712, Dec. 18.
b.
d. 1722 + of William & Lydia (Ballou) Hawkins.
Providence, R. I.

1. Eleazer,
2. David,
3. Susanna,
4. Lydia,
5. Patience,

IV. JOSEPH, m. 1716, Jun. 20. MERCY STAFFORD,
b.
d. 1746, Nov. 4.
b. 1694, Sep. 21.
d. 1753 + of Amos & Mary (Burlingame) Stafford.
Providence, Smithfield, R. I.

1745, Oct. 26. His son Eleazer died at Cape Breton, administration being given to brother Amos. (Eleazer may have been son of an earlier wife.)

1746, May 13. Will—proved—1746, Dec. 1. Exs. wife Mercy and son Benjamin. To sons Benjamin and Caleb, certain land. To sons Joshua, Nathan, Stukely and Samuel, homestead farm in Smithfield where I now dwell, to be equally theirs when of age. He mentions also sons Joseph and Amos. To wife, privilege of half homestead for life, and half personal.

1. Eleazer,
2. Joseph, 1717, Apr. 30.
3. Benjamin, 1719, Mar. 16.
4. Amos, 1721, Mar. 29.
5. Elizabeth, 1723, Apr. 10.
6. Caleb, 1725, May 26.
7. Deborah, 1727, May 15.
8. Joshua, 1729, Jul. 14.
9. Nathan,
10. Stukely,
11. Mercy, 1735, Apr. 22.
12. Samuel, 1736, Jul. 12.

V. JOHN,
b.
d.

VI. JEREMIAH, m. FREELOVE,
b.
d.
b.
d. of
Providence, Smithfield, R. I.

1728, Jul. 20. He and wife Freelove sold to his brother Joseph, 21 acres for £73.

1736, Dec. 7. Smithfield. He and wife Freelove sold Job Arnold, land for £24.

VII. ELEANOR, UNMARRIED,
b.
d.

VIII. MARY, m. 1717, Nov. 29. GEORGE THOMAS,
b.
d.
b.
d. of Thomas.

IX. ABIGAIL, m. 1720, Jun. 29. JOHN MANN,
b.
d. 1775 (—)
b. 1695.
d. 1782, Dec. 17. of Thomas & Mary (Wheaton) Mann.

1. Abigail, 1720, Dec. 11.
2. Sarah, 1723, Nov. 13.
3. Mary, 1726, Sep. 6.
4 Dorcas, 1731, Jun. 27.
5. John, 1734, Dec. 13.

X. DEBORAH,
b.
d.

1. Samuel. 1679, Apr. 16.
2. Hazadiah, 1682, Apr. 16.
3. Thomas, 1684, Nov. 7.
4. Daniel, 1686, Jul. 19.
5. Elizabeth, 1690, Dec. 18.
6. John, 1693, Mar. 26.
7. Ichabod, 1696, Jun. 9.
8. Job, 1699, Apr. 4.

ARNOLD (WILLIAM).

1. Joseph,
2. Lydia,
3. Ephraim,
4. Timothy,
5. William,
6. Priscilla,
7. Benjamin,
8. Silas, 1650.

I. BENEDICT, m. (1) 1671, Mar. 9. MARY TURNER, m. (2) SARAH MUMFORD,
b. 1642, Feb. 10.
d. 1727, Jul. 4.
b.
d. 1690, Dec. 16. of John Turner.
b. 1668.
d. 1746, Oct. 14. of Thomas & Sarah (Sherman) Mumford.
Newport, R. I.

1686, Oct. 22. He and wife Mary, with his brother Josiah and wife Sarah, sold to Francis Brinley, 71½ acres in Jamestown, for £71, 10*s*.

1686-90-99-1701-2-6-8-9-12. Deputy.

1687. Overseer of the Poor.

1690-91-96. Assistant.

1691, Jun. 27. He was ordered by the Assembly to go with all speed to Boston, to take an address to their Majesties, and was allowed 12*s*., pay.

1693, May 26. He made an agreement with the Taunton Iron Works by which the latter were to have the iron ore on his land in Taunton at 3*s*., 6*d*., per ton, paid in iron at 22*s*., a hundred. He was to dig and cart the ore and deliver it at the works. He owned two shares in the work and took his dividends in iron.

1706-7. Speaker of House of Deputies.

1727. Will—proved. Exx. wife Sarah. To wife Sarah, house for life and stone wharf, &c. To her forever 200 acres and buildings in Narragansett at Point Judith, and a third of movable estate and negro woman Peggy. To her also for life, 201 sheep and 14 head of neat cattle. To son Sion, farm at Beaver Tail, in Jamestown, with housing, &c. To daughter Godsgift Martindale, £100. To daughter Mary Clarke, £150. To son-in-law William Coddington, £150. To daughter Ann Chase, certain land at decease of mother. To son Benedict, 140 acres in Newport, formerly called Earl's wigwam now called Springfield, with buildings, &c., and other land, &c.

1746, May 7. Will—proved 1746, Nov. 5. Widow Sarah. Ex. grandson Samuel Chase. To daughter Ann Scott, £1,000. To grandson William Chase, £1,000. To grandchildren Samuel Chase, Sarah Griffith and Elizabeth Chase, £2,000 equally divided. To grandson Samuel Chase, silver tankard. To two granddaughters, household goods. To grandson William Chase, my servant boy Cæsar.

1. Godsgift, 1672, May 19.
2. Sion, 1674, Sep. 12.
3. Mary, 1678.
4. Content, 1681, Feb. 26.
5. Benedict, 1683, Aug. 28.
6. Caleb,
(2d wife.)
7. Comfort, 1695, May 21.
8. Ann, 1696, Jul. 14.
9. Sarah, 1698, Nov. 3.

II. CALEB, m. 1666, Jun. 10. ABIGAIL WILBUR,
b. 1644, Dec. 19.
d. 1719, Feb. 9.
b.
d. 1730, Nov. 17. of Samuel & Hannah (Porter) Wilbur.
Portsmouth, R. I.

He was a "practicioner of physic," as he styles himself.

1671-80-84-1706-7. Deputy. He bore the title of Captain, part of this time.

1676, Aug. 24. He was member of a Court Martial held at Newport, for the trial of certain Indians charged with being engaged in King Philip's designs.

1716, Jul. 7. Will—proved 1719, Mar. 9. Exs. wife Abigail and sons Oliver and Josiah. To wife, half of house, orchard and land in Portsmouth, for life. To her for her use and to dispose of to children, half of all living stock and half of household stuff. To son William, 10*s*. To son Samuel, 10*s*., he having had 200 acres by deed. To son Josiah, my now dwelling house and lands in Portsmouth, half at my decease, and if he die without issue, then to my son Samuel, and if latter die, &c., then to son Oliver. To daughter Sarah Arnold, a feather bed, good cow and £5, having already had £80. To daughter Penelope Hazard, 10*s*., and silver tankard. To son Josiah, half of personal estate, he keeping fenced the three rods square that I ordered for a burying place in upper part of my orchard where my son Peleg was buried. To Elizabeth Carter, £6. A tract of 90 acres in Kings Town, to be sold to pay debts and legacies. The executors are empowered to act in the estate in partnership between me and my relatives that belonged to brother-in-law John Wilbur, late deceased.

Inventory. Wearing apparel, silver money and plate £8, 10*s*., books £17, gallipots, vials, 3 cases of bottles, 10 chairs, 2 tables, mortar, pestle, lancets, 2 canes, cider mill, 3 hives of bees, sheep £25, horse, 2 mares, hogs, geese, hens, guns, woolen wheel, loom, &c.

1. William, 1667, May 31.
2. Penelope, 1669, Aug. 3.
3. Josiah, 1671, Dec. 26.
4. Caleb,
5. Peleg,
6. Samuel,
7. Oliver,
8. Josiah,
9. Sarah,

1658, Mar. 9. He complained that he was lately robbed of property by the Indians.

1658, Aug. 31. He deeded land to his grandson Jeremiah Rhodes.

1661. Commissioner.

1663, Apr. 4. He deeded son Stephen, a lot north-west from Pawtuxet Falls.

He received deeds at sundry times from Thomas Olney, Henry Fowler, William Harris, Ralph Earl, &c., the last of which indicates that he was then living (in 1652), near Pawtuxet Falls on the north side of the river.

1665, Feb. 19. He had lot 75 in a division of lands.

1673, Jan. 9. He sold John Sheldon, all rights of common, &c., that he had as one of the proprietors of Providence.

1675, Mar. 15. He owned his signature to a deed of his rights in new purchase of land at Wayunkeek, to Abraham Mann.

1677, Nov. 3. He had died previous to this date as seen by a deed of his son Benedict.

1678, Oct. 16. Testimony was given by William Hopkins, that at the beginning of the Indian war they heard at Providence that William Arnold, of Pawtuxet, would not leave his own house, and some neighbors desired deponent to go to him and persuade him to go to some garrison or down to Rhode Island to his son Benedict. The deponent went and told him of his danger and he said he would not go down to Rhode Island, "but if he must leave his own house he would go to Providence"—but he would rather be nearer home. He was finally prevailed on by his son Stephen to go to the latter's garrison house.

William Haviland, and the 90 acres bought of William Vaughan, and at wife's death to go to daughter Godsgift Arnold. To wife, for life, certain land with mansion house and stone built wind mill, and a tract of 130 acres called Lemmington Farm, and at her death to go to daughter Freelove Arnold. To wife, for life, all cattle, horsekind, sheep and swine, and at her death the same to go to daughters Godsgift and Freelove Arnold. To wife, all servants of what sorts soever and all household stuff and utensils for life, and a third of same to be at her disposal to give away, the other two-thirds being for daughters Godsgift and Freelove, at her death. To eldest son Benedict Arnold, north half of a neck of land, being southernmost part of Conanicut Island, by me named Beaver Neck, containing 1,000 acres, surrounded by the sea, except by a narrow beach called Parting Beach. To Benedict, also a third interest in Dutch Island. To son Josiah, 4 acres in Newport, &c., and the other half of Beaver Neck, viz: 500 acres, and a third interest in Dutch Island. To youngest son Oliver, quarter of an acre in Newport, 300 acres on Conanicut Island called Cajaset land, bounded partly by land of the assignees of William Weeden, deceased, a triangular piece of 60 acres on Conanicut, an interest in 260 acres on same island called the Township, and a third interest in Dutch Island, &c. The three sons named to have also equally, all cattle, horses and sheep found on said island of Conanicut, south of Caleb Carr's. To son Caleb, in addition to considerable sums already given as book accounts show amounting to £200, he gives ¼ acre in Newport, and 160 acres on Conanicut, to be held by Caleb, till his eldest son is of age, when the latter shall possess it. To daughter Damaris Bliss, wife of John Bliss, 27 acres in Newport. To daughter Penelope Goulding, wife of Roger Goulding, 22½ acres purchased of William Dyer, late deceased. To two youngest daughters Godsgift and Freelove Arnold, each £50, at twenty years of age or marriage, they to be advised by their mother in their marriages, and if either is refractory both the amounts of £50, to go to the obedient daughter. "What silver spoons, cups, bowls, beakers and porringers are now mine, I leave them to the use of my said wife during her natural life or until in her lifetime she shall please to give any of it to either of our sons, daughters or grandchildren." To sons Benedict, Josiah, and Oliver, one-seventh interest in Pettaquamscott, in Narragansett country, with all cattle found there—excepting a tract five miles north and westward of Pettaquamscott Rock, may be set apart for accommodating one or two townships to be ordered and erected by General Assembly, wherein shall be accommodated not only four sons, but also Major John Cranston, Captain Peleg Sanford, Captain Roger Goulding, Mr. James Barker, Ensign John Bliss, Mr. John Coggeshall, Sr., with other deserving persons that may be proposed by the rest of the partners; and if a town or two be not settled, yet the four sons and aforesaid persons are each to have 250 acres, and what remains to be disposed of by executors towards erecting and maintaining a free school in Newport, and towards relief of the poor people in said town, and to be ordered and disposed of to the ends promised, by Town Council of said town and their successors forever. The codicil changes his son Benedict's 500 acres to south part and son Josiah's 500 acres to north part of Beaver Neck, and son Oliver's part of land which contains house, &c., to be made up to 500 acres to equal the others.

1678, Jun. 29. In a letter of this date from Samuel Hubbard, of Newport, to Dr. Edward Stennett, of London, he says: "Our Governor died the 19th day of June, 1678, buried 20th day, all this island was invited, many others was there, judged near a thousand people, brother Hiscox spoke there excellently led forth, I praise God."

III. { JOANNA, m. (1) 1646 ± ZACHARIAH RHODES, m. (2) 1667, Jan. 11. SAMUEL REAPE, } { b. 1617, Feb. 27. d. 1692 + } { b. 1603 ± d. 1665. } of Rhodes. { b. d. } of Reape.

IV. { STEPHEN, m. 1646, Nov. 24. SARAH SMITH, } { b. 1622, Dec. 22. d. 1699, Nov. 15. } Providence, R. I. { b. 1629. d. 1713, Apr. 15. } of Edward Smith.

1650, Sep. 2. Taxed £1.

1658, Aug. 6. He gave notice of receiving two ankers of strong liquor. (He received 17 ankers of liquor from 1660 to 1664.)

1659, Aug. 14. He bought 125 acres at Pawtuxet, of John Sayles.

1663, Oct. 27. At Quarter Court Sessions it was ordered that he should have notice to take the barrel of pork which he left at William Field's towards the last rate, again into his custody, it not being merchantable when he brought it in. The other provisions that people had brought in toward the last rate were also ordered to be searched to see what condition they were in.

1664–65–67–70–71–72–74–75–76–77–84–85–90. Deputy.

1672–77–78–79–80–90–91–96–98. Assistant.

1674, Jul. 30. He bought of Quononthott "eldest son now living of Miantonomi" lands south of Pawtuxet River.

1678. He having delivered six or eight sheep to the forces sometime lodged at Pawtuxet, he was in this year allowed 50*s*., to be paid by the several New England Colonies in proportion.

1681. He bought 750 acres of Randall Holden, and made other purchases the same year.

1725, May 4. Will—proved 1730, Dec. 14. Widow Abigail. Exx. daughter Sarah. To son Samuel, feather bed. To son Oliver, a cow. To son William, 20*s.*, for his children. To son Joseph, 5*s.* To daughter Penelope Hazard, 5*s.* To daughter Sarah Arnold, rest of movables.

Inventory, £352, 7*s.*, 3*d.*

III. JOSIAH, { b. 1646, Dec. 22. { d. 1725. Jamestown, R. I.
m. (1) 1683, Sep. 4.
SARAH MILLS, { b. 1665. { d. 1704, Sep. 1. of —— & Elizabeth ( ) Mills.
m. (2) 1704, Feb. 12. [Wm.
MARY BRINLEY, (w. of { b. 1674, Apr. 27. { d. 1721, Jul. 15. of Samuel & Sarah (Wodell) Sanford.

1. Damaris, 1684, May 19.
2. Elizabeth, 1684, May 19.
3. Abigail, 1685, Dec. 14.
4. Ann, 1687, Oct. 31.
5. Frances, 1689, Sep. 30.
6. Benedict, 1691, Jul. 18.
7. Josiah, 1693, Apr. 13.
8. Sarah, 1695, Oct. 3.
9. Edward, 1697, May 27.
10. Penelope, 1698, Jun. 16.
11. William,
12. Freelove, 1704, Aug. 22.
(2d wife.)
13. Abigail, 1706, Mar. 28.
14. Josiah, 1707, Aug. 25.
15. Mary, 1709, Apr. 19.
16. Content, 1711, Jul. 14.
17. Katharine, 1713, Feb. 7.
18. Comfort, 1715, Jul. 17.

1686–1709–16. Deputy. He was called Captain during many years.

1700, Mar. 25. He was granted privilege of running a ferry between Jamestown and Narragansett for seven years at £2, 10*s.*, per year.

1709. He had privilege of the west ferry for seven years at £4, per year.

1721, Sep. 23. Will—proved 1725, Feb. 23. Exs. sons Benedict and Josiah and friend Colonel William Coddington. Overseers, son-in-law John Odlin, of Newport and brother-in-law William Sanford, of Portsmouth. He appointed the south-west corner of his orchard where two wives Sarah and Mary Arnold, and three sons by first wife, Joseph, Edward and William, are buried—to be a perpetual burying place, and he to be buried between two wives. To six daughters, Elizabeth Odlin, Ann Tibbalds, Frances Allen, Sarah Sanford, Penelope and Freelove Arnold, all household goods that he had before marrying last wife Mary, except a bed to Penelope and bed and silver tankard to Freelove. To five youngest daughters Abigail, Mary, Content, Catharine and Comfort, the profits of 4 acres in Jamestown and profits of new ferry boat and pier on west side of Jamestown, all to be for their bringing up, and to them all household goods that their mother Mary brought me, distributed equally according to their mother's desire with her rings, jewelry, necklace, &c. To these five daughters, proceeds of sale of Indian woman Dinah. To eldest son Benedict, north part of farm where I dwell called "Beaver Head," and negroes Lancaster and Hagar, he supporting his sister Penelope five years, &c. To youngest son Josiah, south part of above farm, when of age, and negro man Bristol, and Indian slave George, till thirty-four years of age and then freed. To Benedict and Josiah, equally, certain land in Jamestown and rights in Dutch Island, with ferry boat, pier, housing, &c., in Jamestown, when my youngest daughter is eighteen, they paying to my daughter, £300, equally divided. To two sons, husbandry tools, wearing apparel, pistols, swords, canes, &c. To daughter Sarah Odlin, £90, besides what she has had. To daughter Ann Tibbalds, £50. To daughter Frances Allen, £10. To daughter Sarah Sanford, £20. To daughter Penelope Arnold, £100, and like amount to daughters Freelove, Abigail, Mary, Content, Katharine and Comfort. To granddaughter Sarah Piggott, 20*s.*, her mother having had her portion in her lifetime. To granddaughter Damaris Whitman, £10. To grandson Jonathan Law, £10. All stock to be sold to pay legacies. To friend Colonel William Coddington, £10. To each overseer, £5.

Inventory, £1,252, 15*s.*, viz: wearing apparel £30, a box and 46 bound books £4, 16*s.*, fire lock, negroes Lancaster £40, Bristol £50, Hagar £20, Indians, Dinah £40, George (10 years' service) £30, 83 oz. plate, viz: tankard, 2 porringers, 6 spoons, 6 forks, 3 sweetmeat spoons and a candlestick £68, 16*s.*, a wheel, silver hilted sword, 2 canes, stillyards, 12 cheese fats, 9 cows, pair of oxen, pair of steers, 8 young cattle, 2 mares, 3 colts, 5 hogs, 693 sheep, ferry boat £75, worsted comb, warming pan, 4 brass candlesticks, 3 pair of snuffers, &c.

IV. DAMARIS, { b. 1648, Feb. 23. { d. 1717 +
m. 1666, Jan. 24.
JOHN BLISS, { b. 1645 ± { d. 1717. of George Bliss.

1. Son, 1668, Sep. 29.
2. Damaris, 1670, May 25.
3. Freelove, 1672, Nov. 16.
4. John, 1674, Oct. 22.
5. Henry,
6. Josiah,
7. George,
8. Mercy,

ARNOLD (William). 3d column. IV. Damaris, d. 1720. VI. Penelope. Her 2d husband was probably Thomas Cutler.

V. WILLIAM, { b. 1651, Oct. 21. { d. 1651, Oct. 23.

ARNOLD (William). 3d column. III. Josiah. Change Sarah Odlin to Elizabeth Odlin—twelfth line after 1721, Sep. 23.

VI. PENELOPE, { b. 1653, Feb. 10. { d. 1702 +
m. (1) 1673, Jan. 1.
ROGER GOULDING, { b. { d. of Goulding.
m. (2)
—— CUTLER, { b. { d. of Cutler.

1. Damaris, 1676, Mar. 17.
2. Thomas,
3. George 1685, Jul. 30.
(By 2d husband, no issue.)

VII. OLIVER, { b. 1655, Jul. 25. { d. 1697, Nov. 6. Jamestown, R. I.
m.
PHEBE COOK, { b. 1665. { d. 1732. of Thomas & Mary (Havens) Cook.

(She m. (2) Jonathan Marsh, and (3) 1705, Oct. 7, Robert Barker.)

1. Damaris, 1680, Dec. 30.
2. Phebe, 1682, Dec. 30.
3. Patience, 1684.
4. Mary, 1687.
5. Sarah, 1689.
6. Oliver, 1694.
7. Freelove,

1680, Mar. 31. He and wife Phebe, gave receipt for legacy from will of her grandfather Thomas Cook.

1682. Deputy.

1687. Overseer of the Poor.

1688. Grand Jury.

1697, Sep. 10. Will—proved 1697, Nov. 20. Exs. wife Phebe, brother Caleb, of Rhode Island, and brother Josiah, of Conanicut. To son Oliver, dwelling house and farm where I live he paying legacies. To child wife goes with if a male, 100 acres and if a daughter £100. To daughters Damaris, Phebe, Patience, Mary and Sarah, £100, each at age. To wife's kinswoman Abigail Remington (daughter of Daniel Remington, of Jamestown), £10. The lands in Kings Town to be sold. To cousin Oliver, son of brother Caleb, £10. To brothers Caleb and Josias Arnold, £10, each. To wife, all personal, and a third of real estate for life.

Inventory, £1,725, 3*s.*, viz: farm and dwelling house at Cajassett £900, farm and housing at Eel Pond £300, feather beds, warming pan, leather chairs, wearing apparel, books 10*s.*, 8*d.*, silver tankard, spoons, 2 porringers, dram cup, wine cup, &c. £33, 10*s.*, 6 oxen, 12 cows, 4 two years, 9 yearlings, 10 calves, 350 sheep and lambs, 5 horsekind, 16 swine, old negro woman, £10, 2 Indian prentice boys £20, 2 stacks of bees.

VIII. GODSGIFT, { b. 1658, Aug. 27. { d. 1691, Apr. 23.
m.
JIREH BULL, { b. 1659. { d. 1709, Jul. 16. of Jireh Bull.

1. Jireh, 1682, Oct. 18.
2. Benjamin, 1685, Sep. 5.
3. Benedict, 1687, May 1.

IX. FREELOVE, { b. 1661, Jul. 20. { d. 1711, Sep. 8.
m. 1682, Apr. 18.
EDWARD PELHAM, { b. { d. 1730, Sep. 20. of Herbert & Elizabeth (Bosvile) Pelham.

1. Edward,
2. Thomas,
3. Elizabeth,
4. Penelope,

1. Jeremiah, 1647, Jun. 24.
2. Malachi,
3. Zachariah,
4. Elizabeth,
5. Mary,
6. Rebecca,
7. John,
8. Peleg.

I. ESTHER, { b. 1647, Sep. 22. { d. 1688 ±
m. (1) 1671 ±
JAMES DEXTER, { b. 1650, May 6. { d. 1676, of Gregory & Abigail (Fullerton, Dexter.
m. (2) 1680, Oct. 30.
WILLIAM ANDREWS, { b. { d. of Edward & Bridget ( ) Andrews.
m. (3)
EDWARD HAWKINS, { b. { d. 1726, May 24. of William & Margaret ( ) Hawkins.

1. Peleg,
2. Isabel,
3. James,
(By 2d husband.)
4. Mary,
(By 3d husband.)
5. Esther, 1685, Jul. 19.

II. ISRAEL, { b. 1649, Oct. 30. { d. 1716, Sep. 15. Warwick, R. I.
m. 1677, Apr. 16. [Elisha.
MARY SMITH, (w. of { b. { d. 1723, Sep. 19. of James & Barbara (Dungan) Barker.

1. Israel, 1678, Jan. 18.
2. Mary,
3. William,
4. Stephen,
5. Elisha,
6. James, 1689.
7. Sarah,
8. Josiah,
9. Joseph,
10. Barbara,

1681. Freeman.

1683–90–91–99–1702–3–5–6. Deputy.

1690. He was empowered with others to apportion tax in respective towns.

1703. He protested against the act for raising money to send agents to England.

1716, Mar. 23. Will—proved 1717, Sep. 23. Exs. wife Mary and son Joseph. To son Israel, house and land where he lives in Pawtuxet, &c. To sons William and Elisha, £5, each, both having had already. To son Stephen, 50 acres, he paying £5, to brother James. To son James, 350 acres at Wonsoacit, &c., and £10. To son Joseph, mansion house where I now dwell with land, &c., but wife Mary, to have half of house and lands for life. If Joseph have no heirs then to sons James and Josiah, and if they have none to go to son Israel. To daughters Mary Low, Sarah Carpenter

1688, Aug. 10. Ratable estate: "This is an account as near as I can according to order—of my estate within the Town of Providence,"—152 acres of land and rights in other land, 16 cows, and of dry cattle, 6 yearlings, 6 two year old, 5 three year old, 2 four year old; a bull, 4 oxen, 2 horses, 4 mares, a young horse, 87 sheep, 5 swine.

1699, Mar. 24. He deeded land to grandson James Dexter.

1698, Jun. 2. Will—proved 1699, Dec. 12. Exs. sons Elisha and Stephen. To son Israel, land south of Pawtuxet River bought of Zachary Rhodes, in 1658, and lands bought of Kokootanako, Sachem of Pawtuxet, in 1660. To sons Elisha and Stephen, land. To daughters Sarah Carpenter and Elizabeth Greene, land. To wife Sarah, a third of household stuff for life, and the executors are to see their mother buried "comely and decently." He closes thus: "And so now I do humbly pray and desire the Almighty and Eternal God of Heaven and earth to bless, prosper and keep all my friends and children, that they may live so worthily and righteously in this world, that they may live with our blessed Saviour Jesus Christ to all Eternity."

Inventory, £495, 11*s.*, 1*d.*, viz: wearing apparel £12, gold and silver £130, homemade cloth £10, books £6, plate £17, pewter and glass £1, 5*s.*, case of bottles £1, 1*s.*, 100 sheep £20, 4 oxen and 22 cows £56, 5 two year, 7 yearlings, 8 calves, 2 stacks of bees, money and bills £146, 5*s.*, 3*d.*

1708, Apr. 26. Will—proved 1713, May 2. Widow Sarah. Ex. son-in-law Benjamin Smith. To grandson James Dexter, £3, of the £20, owing from him. To Isabel Dexter, 50*s.* To granddaughter Esther Hawkins, 50*s.* To eldest son Israel, £6. To youngest son Elisha, £6. To daughter Elizabeth Greene, £10 and a new coverlid. To daughter Sarah Carpenter, £10. To granddaughter Mary Smith, 50*s.* To granddaughters Elizabeth, Hannah, Mary and Phebe Smith, £5, each. To granddaughters Phebe, Mary, Sarah and Penelope Arnold, daughters of son Stephen, 40*s.*, each. To son Stephen, great case of bottles. To granddaughters Elizabeth, Hannah and Phebe Smith, each a great pewter platter. To granddaughter Sarah Smith, rest of pewter (except bed pan), and my silver dram cup. To granddaughter Sarah, daughter of Sarah Carpenter, a silver spoon and great chest. To daughter Sarah Carpenter, a gown and petticoat. To granddaughter Sarah Arnold, daughter of son Stephen, a bed and three blankets. To daughter Phebe Smith, wife of Benjamin Smith, the rest of estate.

Inventory, £145, including silver plate £15, silver money £60, silk hood and fine head lining, 7 petticoats, 2 gowns, 8 napkins, &c.

Both Stephen Arnold and his wife were buried at Pawtuxet; the stones marking their graves have in recent years however been carried to Swan Point Cemetery, in Providence, and the inscriptions are still legible.

AUSTIN (Robert).

Robert, m. —— | b. d. 1687 (—) | b. d. | Kings Town, R. I.

1661, Sep. 15. His name appears in a list of sixty-five persons (residents of Newport, Portsmouth and Kings Town mostly) who were to have lots at the new settlement of Misquamicut (Westerly). The lots measured 12 rods by 80, and every man was to pay £7, or forfeit his right. Lot number twelve fell to Robert Austin, but he never made settlement there so far as is known, and comparatively few of those who drew lots ever went to Westerly.

1687, Sep. 6. In the tax list of inhabitants of Kings Town his name does not appear, though the names of two Austins of a generation later than Robert, are found upon the list.

The name of Robert was revived in two instances in the third generation. The positive proofs that Robert Austin was the ancestor of this family, are not found, but the belief is thought to be well founded.

I. Jeremiah, m. Elizabeth, | b. d. 1754. | b. d. 1752 + of | Kings Town, Exeter, R. I.

1687, Sep. 6. Taxed 1*s.* under Governor Andros' levy. One hundred and thirty-eight inhabitants were taxed, the largest amount being paid by Major Richard Smith, £1, 19*s.* 10*d.*

1720 ± He and his son Jeremiah, Jr., had ear marks for sheep granted.

1722. He and Jeremiah, Jr., attended town meeting. This year the town was divided into North and South Kingstown, the records of the old town remaining in North Kingstown. Twenty years later Exeter was set off from North Kingstown, and Jeremiah Austin though found successively in the three towns, may yet have lived on one piece of land.

1752, Mar. 6. Will—proved 1754. Exx. wife Elizabeth. He signed by mark, perhaps through infirmity of age, for he calls himself "weak in body and well stricken in years." To wife Elizabeth, two feather beds, iron pot, all the pewter, two iron kettles and all movable estate. He mentions no real estate, which had perhaps been already deeded to his children.

At the time of his decease there were seven Austins bearing the name of Jeremiah, viz: Jeremiah, Jeremiah, Jr. and Jeremiah 3d, Jeremiah son of Robert[3], Jeremiah son of Pasko[3], Jeremiah son of Ezekiel[3], and Jeremiah son of Robert[3] (Joseph[2]).

and Barbara Carpenter, 100 acres of land bought of Robert Potter. To son Josiah, privilege to cut four loads of hay on farm where I now dwell for seven years after my decease, and privilege of making six barrels of cider from orchard for seven years. To wife, all household goods, and half of stock, tools and tackling. To son Joseph, the other half.

Inventory, £257, 4s., viz: cattle £47, sheep £20, swine £6, 20s., books £1, plate £3, 10s., &c.

1721, Jul. 29. Will—proved 1723, Oct. 19. Widow Mary. Ex. son James. To son Israel, biggest silver cup, case of bottles £5, &c. To daughter Mary Low, £5, biggest platter, silver spoon, &c. To sons William and Elisha, £5, each. To son Stephen, a bed, &c. To son Josiah, a platter, &c. To daughter Sarah Carpenter, £10, a great platter and silver spoon. To daughter Barbara Carpenter, £5, great platter, silver spoon, gold ring and maid Sarah, till of age.

III. STEPHEN, b. 1654, Nov. 27. d. 1720, Mar. 1. — Providence, R. I.
m. 1688, Jan. 12.
MARY SHELDON, b. d. 1735, Apr. 28. of John & Joan (Vincent) Sheldon.

1. Stephen,
2. Philip, 1693, Feb. 12.
3. Edward,
4. Phebe, 1695, Mar. 5.
5. Mary, 1696, Dec. 12.
6. Sarah,
7. Penelope, 1701.
8. Larana, 1703.

1704-6-19. Deputy.

1716, Nov. 24. His son Stephen died (administration to widow Christian), and his grandson Stephen died 1736, Mar. 16.

1717, Apr. 18. Will—proved 1720, Mar. 26. Exs. wife Mary and son Edward. To son Philip, land. To son Edward, land including the dwelling house. To grandson Stephen Arnold, 5s., he having had by deed. To daughter Phebe, 12d. To four youngest daughters Mary, Sarah, Penelope and Larana, £30, each, at age or marriage. To wife Mary, third of house and half household goods for life.

Inventory, £608, 1s., viz: bonds £102, 14s., silver money £51, 13s., case of bottles and rum, 5 horsekind, 4 oxen, 11 cows, 4 two year, 4 calves, 72 sheep, hogs, bees, &c.

1726, Mar. 31. Will—proved 1735, Jun. 2. Widow Mary. Exs. daughters Penelope and Larana. To son Philip, 10s. To daughter Penelope, £10. To daughter Larana, £15. To son Edward, a piece of eight. To grandson Stephen Arnold, silver buttons, which were his grandfather Stephen Arnold's. To granddaughter Christian Arnold, £5, 5s. To five daughters Phebe Potter, Mary Rhodes, Sarah Carpenter, Penelope and Larana Arnold, the rest of estate, equally.

IV. ELIZABETH, b. 1659, Nov. 2. d. 1728, Jun. 5.
m. 1680, Dec. 16.
PETER GREENE, b. 1655, Feb. 7. d. 1723, Aug. 12. of John & Ann (Almy) Greene.

1. Peter, 1682, Jan. 20.
2. Sarah, 1685, Oct. 27.
3. John, 1687, Mar. 1.
4. Stephen, 1688, Sep. 19.
5. William, 1690, Jul. 29.
6. Elisha, 1692, Feb. 13.
7. Barlow, 1695, Dec. 24.

V. ELISHA, b. 1662, Feb. 18. d. 1710, Mar. 24. — Providence, R. I.
m.
SUSANNAH CARPENTER, b. d. 1753, Sep. 6. of Ephraim & Susannah (Harris) Carpenter.

1. Katharine, 1690, Feb. 28.
2. Susannah, 1692, Apr. 14.
3. Elisha, 1694, Apr. 9.
4. Ephraim, 1695, Nov. 30.
5. Elizabeth, 1699, Jul. 23.
6. Esther, 1701, Dec. 14.

1694, Jul. 3. He bought land of Ephraim Carpenter, for £5.

1700-6 Deputy.

1710, Mar. 22. Will—proved 1711, Apr. 20. Exx. wife Susannah. To son Elisha, homestead farm at Pawtuxet, and a farm at Rocky Hill. To son Ephraim, land at Coweset, &c., in Warwick, and other land. To each daughter, £10, and when sons come of age they are to give to each sister then living, £5. To wife, all movable estate.

Inventory, £250±, viz: 21 cattle, 2 tables, 9 chairs, 3 small guns, sword, &c.

VI. SARAH, b. 1665, Jun. 26. d. 1701 +
m.
SILAS CARPENTER, b. 1650. d. 1695, Dec. 25. of William & Elizabeth (Arnold) Carpenter.

1. Silas,
2. William,
3. Phebe,
4. Sarah,

VII. PHEBE, b. 1670, Nov. 9. d. 1730 +
m. 1691, Dec. 25.
BENJAMIN SMITH, b. 1661. d. 1730, Apr. 27. of Benjamin & Lydia (Carpenter) Smith.

1. Elizabeth, 1693, Jan. 11.
2. Hannah, 1694, Oct. 7.
3. Sarah, 1695, May 30.
4. Benjamin, 1697, Jun. 21.
5. Phebe, 1699, Dec. 5.
6. Philip, 1700, Nov. 30.
7. Almy, 1703, Jun. 17.
8. Lydia, 1705, Jun. 11.
9. Alice, 1707, Feb. 3.
10. Katharine, 1708, Jan. 23.
11. Giffe, 1710, Apr. 20.
12. Stephen, 1713, Feb. 20.

AUSTIN (ROBERT).

I. ROBERT, b. d. 1752. — Westerly, Charlestown, R. I.
m.
HANNAH CRANDALL, b. d. 1752 (—) of Jeremiah & Priscilla (Warner) Crandall.

1. Robert,
2. Jeremiah, 1730, Mar. 24.

He was a cordwainer.

1716, Jun. 4. It was voted that he and two others be allowed 3s. apiece "for conveying of a distracted to the authority of Stonington."

1721, Sep. 29. He bought of William and Ellen Davol, for £15, a lot of 3 acres more or less, bounded on the east by a fresh pond, "and also a small island which is part of said three acres."

1727. Freeman.

1745, Jan. 16. Charlestown. He bought 130 acres for £270, from George Ninegret, "Chief Sachem of the Narragansett Country in New England, Indian." This Indian sachem was crowned 1735, and died 1746. He was son of King Ninegret[2], who died 1722, and grandson of Ninegret[1], of whom a portrait has been preserved. George Ninegret[3] (Ninegret[2], Ninegret[1]), was succeeded by his son Thomas[4], who died after the year 1765, and the latter's sister Esther[4] was then crowned with great pomp and ceremony according to the account given, some twenty Indians escorting her to Coronation Rock in Charlestown. She was succeeded by her son George[5], who reigned during the Revolutionary War, and who was accidentally killed by the fall of a tree when he was twenty-two years of age.

1745, Mar. 12. Robert Austin sold Joseph Dodge 3 acres more or less with all buildings and improvements, for £278. This was the same piece of ground that he bought of William Davol.

1752, Apr. 13. Administration to son Robert. (The administrator did not take up his bond till 1768, Dec. 1.)

1752, May 30. Inventory, £258, 17s., viz: wearing clothes £5, cash £7, 12s., pair of steers, cow, heifer, 9 goats, 2 hogs, 3 sheep, 6 chair frames, table, chest and box, 2 spinning wheels, wash tub, lamp, warming pan, ironware, 2 axes, sickle, cart, shoemaker's tools, &c.

II. PASKO, b. d. 1774. — Exeter, R. I.
m. 1725, Oct. 25.
MARGARET SUNDERLAND, b. d. 1773 (—) of Daniel & Elizabeth (Sheldon) Sunderland.

1. Sarah, 1727, Jul. 26.
2. Margaret, 1729, Jun. 9.
3. Gideon, 1731, Jul. 16.
4. Daniel, 1733, Jul. 6.
5. Pasko, 1735, Mar. 30.
6. Isaac, 1737, Mar. 10.
7. Hannah, 1739, Apr. 1.
8. Jeremiah, 1741, Mar. 16.
9. Elizabeth, 1743, Oct. 27.
10. David, 1745, May 12.
11. Jonathan, 1747, Jun. 29.
12. Stephen, 1751, May 30.

1773, Sep. 6. Will—proved 1774. Ex. son David. To son Gideon, three silver dollars, and like amount to sons Daniel, Pasqua, Jeremiah, Jonathan and Stephen, and daughter Hannah Whaley To son Isaac, three and a half dollars. To son David, household goods, farming tools and stock. In giving certain of his sons, he says: "The reason I don't give him no more is I have done for him before."

Inventory, £205, 11s. 5½d.

His children scattered very widely, as is seen by settlement of his son David's estate (1792) at which time Gideon was of Scituate, R. I., Daniel, of Newport, R. I., and Pasko, Isaac, Jeremiah, Jonathan and Stephen in different parts of New York.

III. JEREMIAH, b. d. 1778. — North Kingstown, Exeter, R. I.
m. 1729, Nov. 2.
SARAH AUSTIN, b. d. 1776 (—) of John & Mary (Austin.

1. Jeremiah, 1730, Sep. 9.
2. Elizabeth, 1733, Jun. 29.
3. Sarah, 1738, Aug. 15.
4. Thomas, 1741, Aug. 8.
5. Daniel, 1743, Mar. 17.
6. Katharine, 1746, Jun. 14.
7. John, 1750, Jul. 4.

1722. He attended Town Meeting with his father.

1729. Freeman.

1741-42. Surveyor of Highways.

1743-45. Exeter. Juryman.

1744-45-46-47-48. Surveyor of Highways.

1776, Jul. 3. Will—proved 1778. Ex. son Thomas. He mentions sons Thomas, John, Daniel, Jeremiah. To daughter Catharine, two beds, £3, 15s., and pots and kettles.

Inventory, £114, 4s. 4d.

II. EDWARD, m. ——— | b. d. 1731 + | b. d. of | Kings Town, R. I.

1687, Sep. 6. Taxed 2*s.* 6½*d.*

Possibly he had only one son, viz[t]: Edward, Jr., in which case John[3] instead of being ascribed to him, should be given as a son of Jeremiah[2].

III. JOSEPH, m. MARY, | b. d. 1743 ± | b. d. 1752 + of | Kings Town, R. I.

He was a blacksmith.

1706. He had earmark for sheep granted.
1709, May 27. He and twelve others purchased "Devil's Foot," 1,824 acres.
1713, Dec. 8. He and wife Mary sold 60 acres to George Thomas.
1722. Surveyor of Highways.

IV. JOHN, m. MARY, | b. d. 1752, Apr. 17. | b. d. of | Kings Town, East Greenwich, West Greenwich, R. I.

1709. He and eleven others bought "Swamptown," 1,608 acres.
1716, Nov. 21. He and wife Mary sold 105 acres to James Hyams.
1728. North Kingstown. He was a witness to John Watson's will.
1737. East Greenwich. Freeman.
1748, May 30. West Greenwich. He deeded land to son John.
1752, Jun. 27. Inventory shown by son John.

IV. DAVID, b. d. — Charlestown, R. I.
m.
DINAH, b. d. of

1. Joseph, 1731, Feb. 1.
2. Martha, 1733, Dec. 7.
3. Mary, 1735, Sep. 5.
4. Dinah, 1738, Jan. 8.
5. David, 1740, Jul. 21.
6. Mercy, 1743, Jan. 16.

V. STEPHEN, b. d. 1752. — North Kingstown, Exeter, R. I.
m. 1729, Apr. 25.
MARY FISH, b. d. 1752 + of Daniel & Abigail (Mumford) Fish.

1. Abigail, 1733, Aug. 25.
2. Keziah, 1739, Aug. 19.
3. Rufus, 1742, Apr. 11.
4. Eunice, 1745, Mar. 31.
5. Lucy, 1747, Jul. 8.

1730. He had ear mark for sheep granted.
1732. Freeman.
1742, Mar. 22. Exeter. The first town meeting at organization of town was held at his house.
1743-44-45-46-47-48. Constable.
1747-48-50-51. Surveyor of Highways.
1753, May 18. Will—proved 1752. Exs. wife Mary and brother Jeremiah Austin, till son Rufus is of age. To wife, bedding, old mare, cow, and half real estate, while widow. To daughter Abigail Lewis, £5. To daughter Kezia, £30, and same amounts to daughters Eunice and Lucy.
Inventory, £907, 17*s.* (debts £361, 1*s.* 6*d.*)

VI. MERCY, b. d.
m. 1729, Aug.
BENONI AUSTIN, b. d. of John & Mary ( ) Austin.

VII. DANIEL, b. d. 1737. — North Kingstown, R. I.
m. 1732, Apr. 9.
ANN BAKER, b. d. 1743 + of Thomas & Mary ( ) Baker.

(She m. (2) Stephen Sweet)

1737, Feb. Inventory shown by widow Ann.

VIII. EZEKIEL, b. d. — North Kingstown, R. I.
m.
—— CHAMPLIN, b. d. of Champlin.

AUSTIN (ROBERT). 3d column. VIII. Ezekiel. His son Ezekiel, b. 1757.

1. Jeremiah, 1749.
2. Ezekiel,
3. Stephen,
4. William,
5. Elizabeth,
6. Joanna,

By another account he is given for his wife, Elizabeth, daughter of John Eldred, and the list of children includes son Eldridge and daughter Mary.

I. EDWARD, b. d. 1749 (—) — Westerly, R. I.
m.
ISABEL HARDY, b. d. 1749 + of William & Priscilla ( ) Hardy.

1. Thomas,
2. Jedediah,

1730, Dec. 28. He was complained of by his mother-in-law, who said she could not live peaceably with him.
1742, Apr. 20. He and wife Isabel sold land.
1749, Apr. 24. The widow Isabel Austin and her two sons Thomas and Jedediah were ordered to appear before the Town Council, as these sons were to be bound out apprentices.

II. JOHN, b. d. — North Kingstown, R. I.
m.
PRISCILLA WEATHERS, b. d. of Weathers

1. John, 1717 ±

His son John gave some most remarkable names to his children, viz: Parvis, Picas, Ierasmus, Phineas, Percius, Pollipas, Lois, Lettice, Annice, Anstice, Eunice, Mary, John, Elizabeth, Freelove, Ruth.

I. JOSEPH, b. d. 1736 (—) — North Kingstown, R. I.
m.
——, b. d. of

1. Elizabeth,

II. JOHN, b. d. — Westerly, R. I.

1751, May 21. He deeded brother Robert Austin of West Greenwich, 40 acres in Exeter, for love, &c. (dated at Westerly).

III. ROBERT, b. d. 1783. — North Kingstown, Exeter, West Greenwich, R. I.
m.
JUDITH, b. d. of

1. Benjamin,
2. Jeremiah,
3. Ellis,
4. Rufus,
5. Joseph,
6. George,
7. Lois,
8. Sarah,
9. Phebe,

1734. Freeman.
1743. Exeter. Juryman.
1746. West Greenwich. Juryman. He was called "Robert Austin, son of Joseph," to distinguish him from cousin of same name.
1752. Surveyor of Highways.
1752, Feb. 17. He and wife Judith, and Mary Austin, widow of Joseph, sold 40 acres.
1765, Mar. 14. He and wife Judith deeded land to son Jeremiah.
1783, Apr. 9. Inventory shown by administrator's son Benjamin.
The brothers and sisters of the administrator made deeds of their share of the estate to him.

I. JOHN, b. d. 1757. — East Greenwich, West Greenwich, R. I.
m.
ALICE, b. d. 1757 + of

AUSTIN (ROBERT). 3d column. I. John m. 1731, May 31, Alice Wood, b. 1702, Apr. 23, of John and Alice.

1. John, 1731, Sep. 23.
2. Sarah, 1734, Mar. 27.
3. Mary, 1736, Aug. 24.
4. Benoni, 1739, Aug. 31.

1737. Freeman.
1753, Jun. 7. West Greenwich. He deeded to son John same land that he (the grantor) had received from his father.
1754, Dec. 3. He and wife Alice sold land to Pardon Tillinghast.
1757, Mar. 4. Inventory shown by widow Alice.
1757, Apr. 2. Administration to son John.
He was killed in the expedition against Crown Point.

II. BENONI, b. d. — East Greenwich, R. I.
m. 1729, Aug.
MERCY AUSTIN, b. d. of Jeremiah & Elizabeth ( ) Austin.

III. SARAH, b. d. 1776 (—)
m. 1729, Nov. 2.
JEREMIAH AUSTIN, b. d. 1778. of Jeremiah & Elizabeth ( ) Austin.

1. Jeremiah, 1730, Sep. 9.
2. Elizabeth, 1733, Jun. 29.
3. Sarah, 1738, Aug. 15.
4. Thomas, 1741, Aug 8.
5. Daniel, 1743, Mar. 17.
6. Katharine, 1746, Jun. 14.
7. John, 1750, Jul. 4.

{ RUFUS, { b. New York, Portsmouth, Warwick, R. I.
{ m. { d. 1648.
{ MARGARET, { b.
{ d.

(She m. (2) Walter Todd.)

1640. Portsmouth. He came here about this time, having fled from the persecution of the Dutch at New York.

1641, Feb. 4. He had a grant of land.

1647, Aug. 8. Warwick. Town Council.

1647. Town Magistrate.

1648, May 22. Having been sent with another messenger to petition the General Court of Massachusetts (in matters then in difference between Warwick and Massachusetts), he learned at Dedham that the Court had adjourned, and hence wrote the following letter under above date, from the inn of Michael Powell, at Dedham.

"To the right worshipful Mr. John Winthrop, Governor of the Massachusetts: Humbly presented to your worship's consideration. That whereas I, with another, was chosen by the General Court held at Providence the eighteenth of this month, and sent with an humble request to this honourable state concerning Shaomet business but when we came to Dedham hearing that the General Court was adjourned, I, your suppliant (being an inhabitant of Shaomet), seriously weighing my present condition there, I made bold to advise with Mr. Powell concerning the same, who advised me to repair to your worship, which (on consideration) I could not, till I had some knowledge of your worship's favourable acceptation. My humble request therefore is, that your worship would be pleased to send me your mind in a few lines concerning the premises. So, craving your worship's favourable construction, I remain yours, most humbly,

RUFUS BARTON,

Dedham, May 22, 1648."

1648. He died in this year intestate, and the Town Council made an inventory and distribution of estate.

1666, Aug. 20. At this date, on complaint of Benjamin Barton (son and heir of Rufus and yet in his nonage) to overseers appointed for children of deceased during their nonage, and the heir finding himself much grieved for violence already done unto him, and insufferable wrongs for the future, &c., therefore the will made by Town Council was now confirmed and recorded as follows: To three children of Rufus Barton, £90, viz: to Benjamin, £30, at age, to Elizabeth, £30 at eighteen or marriage and to Phebe, £30, at eighteen or marriage. To Benjamin, the house, outhousing, lands, &c., at age. To Margaret, late wife of Rufus Barton, a third of house and lands, &c., while widow, and use of whole to bring up children, &c. The guardians John Smith, Samuel Gorton and Randall Holden, to take bond of widow, for due performance, &c.

I. { ELIZABETH, { b.
{ m. 1659, Jun. 30. { d. 1693, Aug. 20.
{ THOMAS GREENE, { b. 1628.
{ d. 1717, Jun. 5. of John & Joan (Tattersall) Greene.

II. { PHEBE, { b
{ m. 1671, May 23. { d.
{ RICHARD CODNER, { b.
{ d. of Codner.

III. { BENJAMIN, { b. 1645. Warwick, R. I.
{ m. 1672, Jun. 18. { d. 1720.
{ SUSANNAH GORTON, { b.
{ d. 1734, May 28. of Samuel & Elizabeth ( ) Gorton.

1674–75–83–84–99–1700–1–2–3. Assistant.

1679–81–85–90–96–1704–5–6–7–9–13–14–15–17. Deputy.

1698, Aug. 29. He calls himself aged sixty years or thereabouts, in giving testimony concerning will of James Greene.

1699, Oct. 25. He and five others were given power to agree as to boundaries between Connecticut and Rhode Island.

1700, Jul. He contributed a hog (£1, 8s., 6d.), toward a meeting house for Quakers, to be set up at or near Mashapaug "which is to be a free house for the worship of the Lord God of Heaven and Earth (that is) for all true worshippers who worship him in spirit and truth." Contributions continued to be taken up for some three years, and among the charges for constructing were 9s., for rum for raising frame, and 10s., 6d., paid for beer.

1703–4. Speaker of House of Deputies.

1720, Oct. 22. Will—proved 1720, Nov. 9. Exx. wife Susannah. To three grandchildren, Benjamin Greene, son of Jabez, Benjamin Tucker, son of Henry and Ruth Slocum, daughter of Ebenezer, all my right of land in Cowesct, equally. To son Andrew, all my right in land and buildings called Nachuck, lands being on both sides the north-west branch of Pawtuxet River, and also my right of lands in Mashantatack and land in Toseunk, &c. To daughters Phebe and Naomi, land in East Greenwich. To eldest son Rufus, all the rest of lands, buildings and orchards, with use, however, to wife Susannah, of great dwelling house, half of homestead and half of land in Warwick Neck, for life, and also to Rufus, £5. To son Andrew, £5. To two daughters Phebe and Naomi, £10. To wife Susannah, all rest of estate.

Inventory, £503, 17s., 11d., viz: 14 oz. of silver money £8, 8s., 68 oz. plate at 12s. per oz., £40, 16s., bonds, books 15s., pewter, 14 cows, 1 steer, ½ a yoke of oxen, 4 calves, negro woman Cate £60, Indian boy John £20, Indian woman Betty £25, Betty's son Daniel £10, swine, young draught mare, bald face pacing mare, the old draught mare and her colt, roan pacing mare and her colt, 38 sheep and lambs, 29 loads of hay, 11 barrels cider, 9 geese, 8 turkeys, 4 ducks, 14 fowls. Receipts were given for legacies by Phebe Tucker and Henry, and by Naomi Carr and Edward.

1727, May 3. Will—proved 1735, Dec. 8. Widow Susannah. Ex. son-in-law Henry Tucker, of Dartmouth. To son Rufus, feather bed, silver cup or bowl, marked S. S. A. and R. B. M., and after him to his son Rufus, because it hath his name on it. To granddaughter Susanna Chelsey, wife of William Chelsey, £25. To six grandsons, sons of daughter Mary Greene, deceased, each a bible of 10s., price. To grandson Benjamin Barton, son of Andrew, a feather bed, &c. To granddaughter Susanna Barton, daughter of Andrew, a black suit of clothes and a bible of 10s., price. To three grandchildren, the children of daughter Naomi Carr, deceased, late of Jamestown, viz: Ruth Slocum, Edward Carr and Benjamin Carr, each a bible at age. To granddaughter Ruth Slocum, £50, at eighteen, and another sum of £50, due her by will of her father Ebenezer Slocum, she is to have if she can secure it from her father-in-law (i. e. stepfather) Edward Carr, it being a matter in controversy. To daughter Phebe Tucker, all household goods of all sorts, and rest of estate, as money, cattle, &c.

Inventory, £152, 10s., 11d., viz: feather bed, silver cup and 5 spoons, bond, 2 cows, pewter, &c.

BRAYTON.

{ FRANCIS, { b. 1612. Portsmouth, R. I.
{ m. { d. 1692.
{ MARY, { b.
{ d. 1692 +

1643. He was received as an inhabitant, gave his engagement unto the government and propounded for a lot of land.

1655. Freeman.

1662–63. Commissioner.

1667, Aug. 10. He enlisted in a troop of horse.

1669–70–71–79–84. Deputy.

1671, Jan. 6. He made an agreement with his son-in-law Joseph Davol, by which the latter in behalf of his daughter Mary Davol, was to pay her £5, at fifteen years of age, and said sum to be paid into hands of his father-in-law Francis Brayton, if then living, and if Mary Davol died before fifteen the sum of £5, was to be set apart for use of Joseph Davol's son Joseph. The daughter Mary Davol was freely given and commended by her father to the care of Francis Brayton, during life of Mary's grandmother or till Mary is married, and said Francis Brayton engages that at time of his decease he will pay Mary £5.

1674, Jan. 30. In a deposition he is called sixty-two years of age.

1688, Sep. 1. He was summoned to appear for selling drink to Indians on the first day of the week, and confessed in court the fact and referred himself to the judgment of the court, and was fined 10s.

1688. Grand Jury.

1690, Oct. 17. Will—proved 1692, Sep. 5. Exx. wife Mary. Overseers, friends George Brownell, John Borden and John Anthony. To wife, use and profit of all land I bought of Stephen Burton and housing thereon in Portsmouth, and she to have use of all movables and real estate, goods, cattle, chattels, &c. and if needful she may dispose of any part for comfortable maintenance. To eldest son Francis, all wearing apparel and confirmation of lands already given. To 2d son Stephen, confirmation of lands already given, and 5s. At death of wife the land bought of Stephen Burton, about 4 acres, and housing, to go to eldest son Francis, he paying legacies. To eldest daughter Martha Pearce, 5s. To daughter Elizabeth Bourne, £2. To daughter Sarah Gatchel, £2. To grandson Francis, son of Francis, £2. To grandson Preserved, son of Stephen, £2. To grandson Francis Pearce, £2. To granddaughter Mary, wife of James Tallman, £2. At death of wife, movables (with some exceptions) to be divided to children and grandchildren, viz: sons Francis and Stephen, daughters Elizabeth Bourne and Sarah Gatchell, and my grandson Francis Pearce, and granddaughter Mary, wife of James Tallman.

I. { FRANCIS, { b. Portsmouth, R. I.
{ m. 1671, Mar. 18. { d. 1718, Jan. 30.
{ MARY FISH, { b.
{ d. 1747, Apr. 4. of Thomas & Mary ( ) Fish.

1672, Apr. 30. Freeman.

1715, Jan. 6. Will—proved 1718, Feb. 10. Exs. wife Mary and son Francis. Overseers, Jacob Mott, William Anthony and Preserved Fish. To wife, use of all housing and lands in Portsmouth while widow. To son Thomas and male heirs, land where son lives, &c., he allowing my son Benjamin liberty to cut two loads of hay yearly for ten years after death of my wife. To son Francis Brayton, all my homestead where I dwell, he paying to my son Benjamin, sum of £50. To son Benjamin, several pieces of land, 120 acres, 100 acres, 50 acres, 40 acres, &c., all in Tiverton. To daughter Mary Brayton, house lot of 9 acres in Tiverton, feather bed, &c., and £60. To daughter Mehitable Brayton, a feather bed and £100. To sons Thomas, Francis and Benjamin, a feather bed each. To wife Mary, rest of movables. To two daughters, one cow between them while unmarried.

Inventory, £817, 16s. 10d., viz: wearing apparel, cane, gloves, pocket knife and razor £22, silver money £151, 16s., plate £1, 9s., pewter, warming pan, books £1, gun, 4 spinning wheels, beds, apples and cider £5, 10s., cider mill, 2 pair oxen, 7 cows, a bull, 2 calves, 3 horsekind, 50 sheep, service in an Indian boy and girl £25, &c.

1742, Apr. 28. Will—proved 1747, May 11. Widow Mary. Exx. daughter Mary. Overseers, grandsons William and David Earle. To son Benjamin, a cow, half of sheep and increase, bed, &c. To four children of son Thomas, late deceased, viz: Mary, Hannah, Gideon and Francis, each £5. To five children of my son Benjamin, viz: David, Benjamin, Francis, Rebecca and Sarah, each £5. To two sons of my daughter Mehitable Earle, late deceased, viz: William and David, each £5, and other half of sheep and increase. To granddaughter Mary Earle, daughter of Mehitable, £5, great pewter platter, pewter basin, great brass skillet and frame. To daughter Mary Brayton, rest of personal estate.

Inventory, £545, 15s.

* See: American Genealogist, v. 28, no. 4, Oct., 1952, p. 210.

1. Elizabeth, 1660, Jul. 12.
2. Thomas, 1662, Aug. 14.
3. Benjamin, 1666, Jan. 10.
4. Richard, 1667, Mar. 5.
5. Welthian, 1670, Jan. 28.
6. Rufus, 1673, Jan. 6.
7. Nathaniel, 1679, Apr. 10.

1. Richard, 1676, Aug. 11.
2. Elizabeth, 1678.
3. Savory, 1679.

* **I.** RUFUS, b. 1673. d. 1752. — Warwick, R. I.
m. 1705, Jan. 4.
SARAH ROBINSON, b. d. 1760. of Rowland & Mary (Allen) Robinson.

Children: 1. Rufus, 2. Rowland, 3. Margaret, 4. Sarah, 5. William,

1750, Mar. 27. Will—proved 1752, Nov. 6. Ex. son Rufus. To wife Sarah, use of ½ largest dwelling house, and all of small house adjoining and of small house called store house, with use also of garden, half income of all land in Warwick Neck (except three 5 acre lots) for life, also old mare and two cows and keep of same. To son Rowland, farm at Coweset where he dwells and other land. To daughter Margaret Wicks, negro girl Jane and £10. To daughter Sarah Barton, negro girl Flora, two feather beds and privilege to live in great house while single, and the sum of £160. To son William, three 5 acre lots in Warwick, rights in Coweset and £160, and feather bed and negro boy Cæsar. To son Rufus, all land where I dwell, and all land in Warwick Neck undisposed of and feather bed, all live stock and outdoor tools. To wife Sarah, all indoor household goods and negroes Tony, Peg, Pero, Hagar and Phillis, and liberty to keep two swine and fowls and to have ten pounds of wool yearly.

Inventory, £4,061, 19s., viz: weaver's loom, old negro man and woman £350, negro boy Cæsar £325, boy Pero £200, girl Flora £300, girl Hagar £150, and Phillis £125, 9 cows, 3 heifers, 3 calves, 1 yoke of oxen, 6 yearlings, 11 swine, mare, colt, 73 sheep and lambs, &c. Rooms named were: great chamber, bedroom chamber, kitchen chamber, low chamber, garret, great room, bedroom below, kitchen.

II. ANDREW, b. d. 1723, Apr. 19. — Warwick, R. I.
m.
REBECCA LOW, b. d. 1723 + of John & Mary (Rhodes) Low.

Children: 1. Benjamin, 1703. 2. Samuel, 3. Andrew, 4. Rufus, 5. Anthony, 6. Phebe, 7. Susanna,

1704. Freeman.

1723, Mar. 17. Will—proved 1723, May 30. Exx. wife Rebecca. Overseers, brother Rufus and brother-in-law Anthony Low. To eldest son Benjamin, all lands in Warwick Neck at age, but wife to enjoy a third income of same during her widowhood. To son Samuel, part of my homestead at Natick (near former dwelling house) with a dwelling house and half saw mill, meadow, &c., at age. To son Andrew, all remaining part of homestead at Natick, orchards, &c., with former dwelling house at age if his mother marries before that time, but if she remains widow she to enjoy half of profits during her widowhood. To son Rufus, the farm Nathaniel Williams now dwells on at Mashantatack, 110 acres with housing, orchard, &c. To son Anthony, at age, half a farm in Natick, and rights in Warwick, but wife to enjoy a third of profits while widow. To daughters Phebe and Susanna, land at Natick, in fork of two rivers, and to each £20, at marriage. To son Benjamin, £10, at age, and to each of the other sons, £5, at age. To wife Rebecca, all remaining part of estate, real and personal.

Inventory, £354, 11s., 10d., viz: paper money 11s., silver spoons 18s., a pair worsted combs, 2 feather beds, a flock bed, pewter, a bible, 2 small books, a pair of oxen, 3 cows, 2 three year old steers, 2 two year old steers, 5 mares, 1 colt, 3 yearling horses, 80 sheep, 20 lambs, 20 goats, 5 kids, 1 hog. Also let to Jeremiah Westcott the following stock: a pair oxen, 8 cows, 2 heifers, a bull, 20 sheep and a mare.

III. MARY, b. 1678, May 1. d. 1713, Mar. 6.
m. 1698, Mar. 17.
JABEZ GREENE, b. 1673, May 17. d. 1741, Oct. 1. of James & Elizabeth (Anthony) Greene.

Children: 1. Susannah, 1699, Jun. 30. 2. James, 1701, Apr. 24. 3. Benjamin, 1704, Feb. 16. 4. Jabez, 1705, Jul. 26. 5. Nathaniel, 1707, Nov. 4. 6. John, 1710, Feb. 14. 7. Rufus, 1712, Jun. 2.

IV. PHEBE, b. d.
m. 1704, Oct. 5.
HENRY TUCKER, b. 1680, Oct. 30. d. of Abraham & Mary (Slocum) Tucker.

Children: 1. Susan, 1706, Jan. 8. 2. Mary, 1708, Jul. 12. 3. Patience, 1710, Oct. 31. 4. Henry, 1713, Apr. 8. 5. Benjamin, 1716, Oct. 24. 6. Abraham, 1719, Feb. 16.

V. NAOMI, b. d.
m. (1)
EBENEZER SLOCUM, b. 1686, Jan. 20. d. 1715, Oct. of Ebenezer & Mary (Thurston) Slocum.
m. (2) 1721, Jul. 13.
EDWARD CARR, b. 1689, Sep. 14. d. of Edward & Hannah (Stanton) Carr.

Children: 1. Ruth, (By 2d husband.) 2. Edward, 3. Benjamin,

BRAYTON.

I. MARY, b. 1676, Jan. 1. d. 1742 +
UNMARRIED.

II. THOMAS, b. 1681, Jun. 14. d. 1728. — Portsmouth, East Greenwich, R. I.
m. 1704, Aug. 23.
MARY FREEBORN, b. 1679, Aug. 24. d. 1761. of Gideon & Mary (Boomer) Freeborn.

Children: 1. Mary, 1708, Jul. 1. 2. Hannah, 1711, Mar. 28. 3. Thomas, 1713, Jul. 21. 4. Francis, 1715, Sep. 21. 5. Gideon, 1718, Jan. 27. 6. Francis, 1721, Mar. 30.

1719–21. Deputy.

1725–27. East Greenwich. Deputy.

1728, Mar. 11. Will—proved 1728, Apr. 19. Exs. wife Mary and son Thomas. To son Thomas, all lands and housing in Portsmouth (with exception of right in Hunting Swamp), he paying my wife Mary £20, per year when he is of age, during her widowhood. If Thomas die, his part to go to my sons Gideon and Francis, but till Thomas is 21 the profits of Portsmouth estate to go toward finishing house in East Greenwich where I now live. To son Gideon at 21, farm where I dwell, with housing, &c. To son Francis, a farm. To daughters Mary and Hannah Brayton, land in Coweset, which father-in-law Gideon Freeborn gave wife Mary in his will. To wife, the best room in house allowed for her use by son Gideon, and suitable attendance while widow, and firewood furnished. To son Thomas, negro boy Pero. To daughter Mary, negro girl Jude. To wife, negro woman Betty, and to her all the rest of lands, and right in sloop "Elizabeth & Mary," &c. Rest of personal to wife and children.

Inventory, £934, 5s. 6d., viz: wearing apparel £15, 1s., books £2, 5 silver spoons, 4 silver cups, pewter, money scales, warming pan, negroes, Cuffe £76, Betty £60, Jude £40, Pompo £10, 1 pair oxen, 1 cow, 1 heifer, 2 steers, 1 horse, 1 mare, 20 gallons rum, 97 lbs. logwood, ¼ sloop "Mary & Elizabeth" £118, 6s.

1756, Jul. 27. Will—proved 1761, Jun. 27. Widow Mary Brayton. Ex. son Francis. To son Thomas, £3. To son Gideon, 40s. and a pewter platter, and weaving loom. To son Francis, 40s. To daughter Mary Gifford, £30. To daughter Hannah Straight, a pewter platter and 30s. To grandsons (sons of Thomas), 10s. each, except David and to him silver cup marked T. B. To four grandsons (sons of Gideon), viz: Thomas, Gideon, Joseph, John, each, 10s. To four grandsons (sons of Francis), viz: Francis, Daniel, Benjamin and George, each 10s. To grandson Freeborn Brayton, my piece of silver money. To grandson David Gifford, 20s. To grandsons Thomas, William Henry, John and Job Straight, each 30s., and to grandson William Straight, 1 ewe sheep also. To daughters Mary Gifford and Hannah Straight, feather bed, equally, and all wearing apparel. To granddaughter Elizabeth Gifford, 1 feather pillow. To each granddaughter a pewter platter and a pewter spoon, except granddaughter Mary Gifford, and to her a pewter platter. To children Thomas, Gideon and Francis Brayton, and Mary Gifford and Hannah Straight, the rest of estate.

III. FRANCIS, b. 1684, Mar. 17. d. 1740, Apr. 22. — Portsmouth, R. I.
m. 1717, Apr. 25.
SARAH SHERMAN, b. 1684. d. 1740 + of Benjamin & Hannah (Mowry) Sherman.

Children: 1. Francis, 1718, Oct. 5.

1709. Freeman.

1740, Mar. 18. Will—proved 1740, May 12. Exs. wife Sarah and son Francis. To wife Sarah, right in wind mill, &c., standing upon the Watch Hill and the little house thereby, and £400, in bills, half the silver money, silver tankard, five silver spoons, all household goods (except what son Francis has), a cow, a fire room, fruit in orchard, privilege in cellar, &c. To sister-in-law Abigail Sherman, the privilege to reside in house and a horse. To son Francis, all my lands in Portsmouth and buildings, received by will of my father Francis, he giving privilege to mother and aunt Abigail, and also to his grandmother Mary Brayton. To him, also, husbandry tools, negro man Peter, a bed, silver dram cup, four silver spoons, bills of credit, arms, cattle, swine, sheep, &c., and rest of personal.

II. { MARY, m. JOSEPH DAVOL, { b. d. b. d. 1716. of William Davol.

III. { STEPHEN, m. 1679, Mar. 8. ANN TALLMAN, { b. d. 1692 ± b. d. Portsmouth, Newport, R. I. of Peter & Ann ( ) Tallman.

1678. Freeman.
1687. Grand Jury.

IV. { MARTHA, m. JOHN PEARCE, { b. d. b. d. 1715 + of John & Mary ( ) Pearce.

V. { ELIZABETH, m. JARED BOURNE, { b. d. 1718 + b. 1651 ± d. 1718. of Jared & Francis ( ) Bourne.

VI. { SARAH, m. THOMAS GATCHELL, { b. d. b. d. of Gatchell.

BRENTON.

{ WILLIAM, m. MARTHA BURTON, { b. Hammersmith, Middlesex Co., Eng., d. 1674. [Newport, R. I. b. d.

of Thomas Burton.

1634, May 15. Boston. Freeman.

1634, Sep. 25. He was appointed to oversee the building of the house of correction.

1634-35-36-37. Selectman.

1635, May 6. He was appointed on a committee to consider of the act of Mr. Endicott in defacing the colors, and to report to the court how far they judge it censurable.

I. { MARY, m. PELEG SANFORD, { b. d. 1674 (—) b. 1639, May 10. d. 1701. of John & Bridget (Hutchinson) Sanford.

II. { MARTHA,* m. JOHN CARD, { b. d. 1667 (—) b. d. 1705. of Richard Card.

III. { ELIZABETH, m. 1672, Mar. 28. JOHN POOLE, { b. 1650. d. 1694, Oct. 17. b. d. of William & Mary ( ) Poole.

* See: American Genealogist, v. 20, p. 121; v. 32, Jan., 1956, p. 38

Inventory, £2,225, 13s. 11d., viz: gun, 2 swords, silver money and wrought plate £86, 17s. 6d., bonds and notes £1,217, 16s., spinning wheels, building and mill utensils, horsekind, &c. £40, oxen, cows and calves £180, 3 yearlings, swine, &c.

Portsmouth, R. I.

IV. DAVID, b. 1686, Oct. 23. d.
UNMARRIED.

1709. Freeman.

V. MEHITABLE, b. 1693, Jan. 12. d. 1742 +
m. 1718, Jun. 25.
WILLIAM EARLE, b. d. 1744. of Thomas & Mary (Taber) Earle.

1. William, 1721, Mar. 6.
2. David, 1722, Jul. 11.
3. Mary, 1725, Aug. 11.

Portsmouth, Newport, R. I.

VI. BENJAMIN, b. 1695, Sep. 8. d. 1749, Apr. 2.
m. 1719, Nov. 12.
MARY BUTTS, b. d. of Zaccheus & Sarah ( ) Butts.

1. David, 1720, Aug. 5.
2. Benjamin,
3. Francis,
4. Rebecca,
5. Sarah,

1717. Freeman.

1. Mary,
2. William,
3. Joseph,

I. MARY, b. 1680, Feb. 12. d.

II. ELIZABETH, b. 1681, Dec. 8. d. 1749, Sep. 6.
UNMARRIED.

1. John,

III. ANN, b. 1683, Jul. 6. d. 1747, Aug. 28.
m.
JOHN DENNIS, b. 1682, Aug. 15. d. 1732, Aug. 4. of Robert & Sarah (Howland) Dennis.

Portsmouth, R. I., Swanzey, Mass.

IV. PRESERVED, b. 1685, Mar. 8. d. 1761, May 21.
m.
CONTENT, b. d. 1759 (—) of

BRAYTON. 3d column. IV. Preserved, had also son David, b 1716, Feb. 14.

1. John, 1712, Feb. 14.
2. Stephen, 1713, Dec. 24.
3. Baulstone, 1717, May 11.
4. Content, 1724, Apr. 3
5. Israel, 1727, Oct. 13.

1706. Freeman.

1759, Dec. 7. Will—proved 1761, Jun. 3. Exs. sons Baulstone and Israel. To granddaughter Elizabeth Robinson, daughter of son John Brayton, deceased, £1,000, and 50 acres in Freetown. To grandson Preserved Brayton, son of Stephen, deceased, the Rock River Farm in Rehoboth, where my son Stephen did dwell, with buildings, &c. To grandson Stephen, son of Stephen, certain land. To four grandchildren, children of son Stephen, certain land. To son Baulstone, farm in Smithfield, R. I., where he dwells and £4,000, he paying my grandson Stephen, son of Stephen, £2,400, at age. To son Israel all this my homestead farm, all livestock, farming tools, negroes Cuff, Ned, Flora, boy Moses, another farm in Swanzey, and movable estate in house, &c. To daughter Content Gardiner, a silver tankard, six silver porringers, twelve silver spoons, and £800. To several grandchildren, £10, at age. To sons Baulstone and Israel, apparel. To children Baulstone, Israel and Content, residue of estate.

Portsmouth, R. I.

V. STEPHEN, b. 1686, Aug. 2. d. 1753, May 25.
m. 1709, Apr. 14.
PATIENCE NASON, b. d. 1749 (—) of Joseph & Mary (Swain) Nason.

1. Charity, 1710, Jun. 24.
2. Isaac, 1713, Sep. 19.
3. Charity, 1716, May 8.
4. Martha, 1718, Sep. 10.
5. Patience, 1721, Aug. 30.
6. Ann, 1724, Aug. 24.
7. Mary, 1727, Jan. 18.

1710. Freeman.

1728, Mar. 27. He and wife Patience sold to Edward Wing and John Wing, Jr., of Sandwich, land where said Brayton lives, &c., for £888, 14s. 6d.

1749, Aug. 19. Will—proved 1753, Jun. 14. Exx. daughter Patience. Overseer, nephew Baulstone Brayton, of Smithfield. To daughters Martha and Patience Brayton, certain land and housing at Newport, &c. To daughter Ann Smith, £2,500. To three granddaughters, children of daughter Charity Rogers, deceased, viz: Sarah, Abigail and Charity, £100, each at eighteen. To grandson John Rogers, certain land in Newport. To granddaughters Patience and Mary, children of son Isaac, deceased, a feather bed each and £500. To grandson Stephen, son of Isaac, all farm where I dwell, at age, all wearing apparel, silver buttons, buckles, walking cane, great bible and husbandry tools, he making payments to sisters. To daughters Martha, Patience and Ann, rest of estate. The overseer to see that grandson Stephen and the latter's sister Patience, are educated.

Inventory, £7,849, 12s. 2d., viz: wearing apparel, 96 silver buttons, silver shoe and knee buckles £186, 19s., bible, desk, gun, can, notes, woolen wheel, 2 linen wheels, 6 oxen, 2 bulls, 2 horses, 136 sheep, 52 lambs, 2 mares, colt, 9 cows, 6 calves, 4 two years, 5 yearlings, 11 swine, 5 geese, 12 goslings, turkeys, hens, negro man Fortune £450, boy Tony £450, woman Violet £100, &c.

Newport, R. I.

VI. ISRAEL, b. d. 1756 +
m. 1721, Aug. 24.
ELIPHAL SANFORD, b. d. of Sanford.

1. Bathsheba, 1722, Sep. 7.
2. Son, 1724, Mar. 11.

1721 Freeman.

1756, May 8. He and certain others of Newport preferred a petition to Assembly, setting forth that whereas there is great danger of approaching war, and this government is repairing the fort and putting the colony in a posture of defence, and as the greater part of petitioners have been used to the exercise of cannon; that therefore an act may be passed that masters of vessels in town of Newport may instead of being obliged to bear arms in trained bands of said town, be obliged by an order from the Captain of said fort to exercise cannon there, thus gaining further knowledge of that exercise and better enabled to defend in case of an attack on said fort. The prayer was granted, and the Captain of Fort George was to enlist fifty men for purposes of petition.

1. John,
2. Francis,
3. Preserved,

1. Mary,
2. Elizabeth,
3. Francis,
4. Patience,
5. Martha,
6. Son,

BRENTON.

No issue.

1. John,

1. John,
2. Elizabeth,
3. Courtney,
4. William, 1680.
5. Jane, 1682.

1635, Sep. 3. He was ordered to finish at the public charge all that which is necessary to be done at the prison at Boston.

1635–36–37. Deputy.

1638, Aug. 23. Portsmouth. He was given the oversight of work on the prison, which was ordered to be twelve feet in length, ten feet in breadth and ten feet stud, and to be built forthwith of sufficient strength.

1639, Apr. 29. He signed a compact with eight others preparatory to the settlement of Newport.

1640, Mar. 10. He had land to the amount of 399 acres recorded.

1640–41–42–43–44–45–46–47. Deputy Governor of Portsmouth and Newport.

1643, Apr. 10. The town of Portsmouth chose him to order the days of training.

1650, Sep. 25. Boston. He and wife Martha, sold Francis Brayton, of Rhode Island, a house and 12 acres for £49, said sum being receivable by a bill payable at Saint Michael, 1652.

1652–53–54–55–56–57. Selectman.

1655. Freeman (at Newport).

1658. He had grant of a large tract of land on Merrimack River.

1660–61–62. Newport. President.

1660–61–62–63. Commissioner.

1663–64–65–66. Deputy Governor.

1666–67–68–69. Governor.

1667, Aug. 10. He enlisted in a troop of horse.

1667, Dec. 16. He deeded to son-in-law John Card, certain estate that latter's wife Martha, deceased, would have had.

1670, Mar. 25. Taunton, Mass. He deeded son-in-law Peleg Sanford, for love, &c., and for service done by him, land in Newport.

1671, Jul. 24. A deed from Stephen Burton to Francis Brayton, shows that said Stephen was son of Stephen Burton, merchant of London, and grandson of Thomas Burton, deceased, late of Portsmouth, R. I. The said Stephen Burton, Jr., afterwards married William Brenton's daughter Abigail.

1674, Aug. 18. He, William Brenton, still residing at Taunton, deeded to son Joseph Brown, of Charlestown, Mass., and daughter Mehitable his wife, a farm in Rhode Island, formerly in possession of John Gard, deceased, called Middleford, being about 250 acres, and another piece of land at Newport of 120 acres, also 1-16 of lands on Merrimack River, two breeding mares and one hundred breeding sheep.

1673, Feb. 9. Will—proved 1674, Nov. 13, at Newport where he died. Ex. son Jahleel. Overseers, Peleg Sanford, John Cranston, George Shove. To son Jahleel, two farms at Hammersmith, now in possession of John Rathbone, with houses, &c., and marshes and upland at Newport Neck, and ⅛ of lands at Natticot on Merrimack River (being by estimation 10,000 acres in all); also 4 oxen and working steers, 2 breeding mares, 100 breeding sheep. To son William Brenton, a farm in possession of William Casey, with house, &c., ⅛ of Merrimack lands, 2 mares and 100 sheep. To son Ebenezer, a neck of land called Mattapoisett, in possession of Jared Bourne, Sr., with houses, &c., 1-16 of Merrimack lands, £150, a pair oxen, 2 mares, 8 cows and heifers and a bull. To daughter Sarah Brenton, a farm on Conanicut, in possession of Michael Kaly with houses, &c., 1-16 of Merrimack lands, 2 mares and 100 sheep. To daughter Mehitable Brenton, farm formerly in possession of Mr. John Gard, deceased (now to be called by the name of Middleford), with house, &c., and a piece of land in Conanicut 120 acres, and 1-16 Merrimack lands, 2 mares and 100 sheep. To daughter Abigail Brenton, farm bought of Elisha Hutchinson, of Boston, and the Baker farm, 1-16 Merrimack lands, 2 mares, and a hundred sheep. The daughters to have their share at twenty-one or within three months of marriage. To son-in-law Peleg Sanford, ⅛ Merrimack land, all rights in Elizabeth Islands, and Gay Head lands and debts due in Island of Barbadoes. To son-in-law John Poole, ⅛ Merrimack land. To much honoured friend Major General John Leveret, Esq., 1-16 Merrimack land. To respected friend Captain John Crandall, 1-16 Merrimack land. To respected friend Mr. George Shove, pastor of church at Taunton, 1-16 Merrimack land. To cousin Philip Sandy, 100 acres on Merrimack. To Michael Kaly, 100 acres on Merrimack. To John Winchrombe, 200 acres at Merrimack. The overplus of land at Merrimack River to be disposed of toward a stock for any children that may decay in their estate by Providence of God, whether by fire or any other casualty. Son-in-law Peleg Sanford to be guardian over sons Jahleel, William and Ebenezer Brenton and daughter Abigail Brenton, to maintain and educate them till 21. To son-in-law Peleg Sanford, ⅜ and to Captain John Cranston, ⅜ of debts and damages due from estate of George Bliss, of Newport, deceased. To sister Catharine Cook's children, £20. To sister Christian Sandy's children, £10. To Mr. George Shove, £5. To grandchild John Poole, £10. To Seth Shove, 20*s*. To Elizabeth Shove, 20*s*. To James Bell, of Taunton, 40*s*. To John Winchrombe, £5. To Michael Kaly, ⅔ and to his wife, ⅓ of £15, due from land granted him at Pettacomscott. To Rachel Wilkinson, a young cow at Mettapoisett and £5. To negro Abraham, £4, negro Antonia, 40*s*., negro Rose, 30*s*., negro Zipporah, 20*s*., negro Samson, 20*s*., Indian named Edom, 20*s*., at end of his time. All the rest of estate, equally to all children. To negroes, Abraham and Antonia, their freedom at end of five years if dutiful, &c., and to have £5, paid them. Sons-in-law Peleg Sanford and John Poole, already had received portions with their wives as testator declares. For prevention of differences testator annexes inventory drawn up by himself. To Mr. Roger Williams of Providence, 12 ewes and a wether.

Inventory, £10,768, 13*s*., 4*d*., viz: Farm at Hammersmith and stock £2,600. Farm in possession of William Case and stock £1,100. Farm at Mettapoisett £1,150. Farm in possession of Michael Kaly and stock £650. Farm formerly in possession of John Gard, deceased, and piece of land at Conanicut and stock £650. Farm bought of Elisha Hutchinson and Baker's Farm and stock £600. To house, land and wharf at Newport £1,200. Land at Naticott on Merrimack River £800. Land north part of Conanicut (260 acres) £300. House and land in Taunton £300. Interest in land at Narragansett and Pettacomscott £300. My part in Elizabeth Islands £40. 70 horses and mares, young and old £210 (in sundry places besides what is disposed of by will). 34 head of cattle in custody of tenants besides what is disposed of by will £102. 1,100 sheep in hands of tenants besides what is disposed of by will £366, 13*s*., 4*d*., ¼ part of ketch Dove £150, ⅓ part of ketch Industry £50. Household goods £200.

IV. { **Sarah**, { b.
m. { d.
Joseph Eliot, { b. 1638, Dec. 20.
{ d. of John & Ann (Mountfort) Eliot.

V. { **Mehitable**, { b. 1652, Nov. 28.
m. { d. 1676, Sep. 14.
Joseph Brown, { b.
{ d. of Brown.

VI. { **Jahleel**, { b. 1655, Nov. 14. Newport, R. I.
{ d. 1732, Nov. 8.
Unmarried.

1677. Freeman.

He was Collector of Customs some years.

1698, Mar. 8. In a letter to the Board of Trade, he mentions his arrival from England and his delivery to the Governor and Council the letters your Lordships were pleased to entrust me with. He recommends that the colony be commanded to print all such laws as have been there made and are in force, "for they are so meanly kept and in such blotted and defaced books (having never yet any of them been printed) that few of his Majesty's subjects there are at present able to know what they are."

1699, May 27. He was commended to the Board of Trade in a letter from Governor Samuel Cranston, who calls him late Collector of Customs in these parts, but now agent of the Colony to England to answer charges of Rhode Island favoring the pirates, &c.

1720, May. His appeal from the decision of the Assembly to her Majesty in Council in England, was denied by said Assembly. He had recovered £500, in an action of debt against Edward Mott, of Kings Town, in the General Court of Trials, but the Assembly chancerized the debt down to £15, and costs, on the appeal of Mott.

1731, Jul. 2. Will—codicil 1731, Jul. 3—proved 1732, Nov. 13. Ex. nephew Jahleel Brenton. To nephew Jahleel, mansion house and farm at Newport Neck called Hammersmith and Rocky Farm. To cousin (*i. e.* niece) Martha Church, land and house on Thames St., Newport, for life, and then to cousins Benjamin Church and Abigail Wanton. The lands on Merrimack River given by father's will to be sold to pay debts and legacies. To nephew Jahleel Brenton, farm of 500 acres in South Kingstown, and privilege of cutting 50 cords of wood annually from other farm in Point Judith. To cousin Martha Wanton, daughter of cousin Abigail Wanton, six-sevenths of Mumford's Island in Point Judith Pond. To nephew Benjamin Brenton, one-seventh of Little Point Judith Neck, 26 acres, and a farm of 300 acres in South Kingstown. To cousins Martha Church and Benjamin Church, and nephews Ebenezer and Benjamin Brenton, 1,000 acres, part in North and part in South Kingstown. To cousin Martha Church, 200 acres in South Kingstown. To cousin Benjamin Church, Ram Island in South Kingstown. To nephew Ebenezer Brenton, 18 acres west side of Pettaquamscutt River. To cousin Martha Church, 600 acre farm at Point Judith. To cousin Martha Smith, wife of John Smith, half the proceeds of sale of 800 acres in Kingstown, she having interest on said sum, and at her death distribution to children. To nephew Ebenezer Brenton and cousin Benjamin Church, the proceeds of sale of other half of above 800 acres. To Rev. Nathaniel Clapp, minister of the church to which I belong, £20, yearly for twenty years, to him or his successors in office if he die. To Augustus Lucas, Jr., £100, and to his sister Barsheba, like legacy. To the poor of Newport, £10, yearly for ten years. To Mary Bun, negroes Betty and Dungalo and Indian Elizabeth, servants in the house, each 20*s*. To cousin Martha Church, negro Lucy and her child, and table, chest of drawers and looking glass. To nephew Jahleel, rest of estate both real and personal. The codicil gives interest in Warwick land to nephew Jahleel Brenton and cousin Benjamin Church. The dwelling house in Boston to be sold and money divided equally to cousins Martha Church, Benjamin Church, Abigail Wanton, Jeremiah Wheeler, Benjamin Brenton, Martha Smith, Ebenezer Brenton, Augustus Lucas, Jr., Barsheba Lucas and Martha Wanton.

VII. { **Abigail**, { b.
m. { d. 1684, Mar.
Stephen Burton, { b.
{ d. 1693, Jul. 22. of Stephen Burton.

VIII. { **William**, { b. Boston, Mass, Bristol, R. I.
m. 1680 ± { d. 1697.
Hannah Davis, { b. 1661.
{ d. 1697, Jul. 17. of Nicholas & Sarah ( ) Davis.

He was a mariner.

1680, May 19. He appointed his wife Hannah attorney to collect debts, &c.

1685, Nov. 18. Bristol. He and wife Hannah sold John Wally, of Bristol, for £620, farm of 240 acres in Newport, with housing, &c., willed by father William Brenton.

1691. Boston. Collector.

1692, Mar. 9. His wife Hannah, formerly Hannah Davis, gave receipt, her husband William Brenton, being absent, for legacy from will of her father-in-law (*i. e.* stepfather), John Clarke, deceased of Newport, to the surviving executor Philip Smith.

1696, Sep. 1. The administrator of his estate, viz: his brother Ebenezer Brenton, gives an account of charges under this date (and extending to 1697), for goods delivered children, viz: to William, Jr., £19, 7*s*. To Samuel, £22, 16*s*., 1*d*. To Benjamin, £13, 3*s*., 5*d*., and to Jahleel, £5, 16*s*. (Part of disbursements had probably been made while William Brenton was absent but before he died.)

1698, Feb. 19. Inventory, £288, 4*s*., 7*d*., sworn to by administrator Ebenezer Brenton. Dwelling house at Bristol and land £90, ⅛ of bark Sea-flower, whereof William Brenton was late master, as she came home from Barbadoes, the said ⅛ and other things belonging to said William Brenton, deceased, and it is declared worth £75. 188½ gallons rum £32, 19*s*., 9*d*., 241 gallons molasses £20, 1*s*., 8*d*., feather bed, chairs, clothes, 2 books, quadrant, 4 silver spoons £1, 19*s*., 8*d*., compasses, cash for wages on Sea-flower, £40, &c.

1709, Jan. 30. It being represented that the house and land of William Brenton, deceased, cannot be divided among children without great prejudice and despoiling the whole, and being estimated at £120, said house and land are assigned to Benjamin Brenton, eldest son of deceased, saving to the executor of Major Ebenezer Brenton, deceased, who administered the estate of said William, the sum of £54, 9*d*., due from estate, and to Benjamin's brother Jahleel Brenton, his part of remaining sum said house and land is appraised at, being a third part.

IX. { **Ebenezer**, { b. Swanzey, Mass., Bristol, R. I.
m. { d. 1708.
Priscilla Byfield, { b.
{ d. 1705, May 4. of Byfield.

1. Mehitable, 1676, Oct. 6.
2. Ann, 1677, Dec. 12.
3. Jemima, 1680.
4. Bashua, 1682.

No issue.

I. WILLIAM, b. ; d. young

II. SAMUEL, b. ; d. young.

III. MARTHA, b. 1678. d. 1750, Apr. 14.
m.
EDWARD CHURCH, b. ; d. 1707. of Benjamin & Alice (Southworth) Church.

1. Abigail, 1703, Mar. 4.
2. Benjamin, 1704, Oct. 8.

IV. BENJAMIN, b. 1686, Dec. 23. d. 1740 (—) Newport, R. I.
m. 1708.
SARAH COLLINS, b. ; d. of Collins.

1. Benjamin, 1710, Oct. 16.

1740, Mar. In a suit brought by his son Benjamin, to recover certain land, he is described as Benjamin Brenton only son and heir of Benjamin Brenton, eldest son of William Brenton, one of the sons of William Brenton, Sr.

V. JAHLEEL, b. 1691, Aug. 15. d. 1767, Mar. 12. Newport, R. I.
m. (1) 1715, May 30.
FRANCES CRANSTON, b. 1698. d. 1740, Feb. 2. of Samuel & Mary (Hart) Cranston.
m. (2) 1744, Apr. 25.
MARY SCOTT, (w. of Geo.) b. 1726. d. 1760, May 1. of Edward Neargrass.

1716. Freeman.

1721-23-25-26-27-28-29-30-32. Sheriff.

1727. Custus Brevium.

1737. Deputy.

1740, May. He and George Goulding were appointed by the Assembly to go to Ipswich court in Massachusetts, to attend the trial and give evidence against persons to be tried there for uttering counterfeit bills in imitation of the bills of this colony, and likewise to attend court in New Hampshire.

1742. Newport Artillery. One of the original members.

1746, Sep. 29. He was appointed on the committee to finish the new battery and make alteration in the old battery at Goat Island.

1750, Sep. 4. He and others signed a petition to the King, praying that the Assembly might be restrained from making or emitting any more Bills of Public Credit upon loan, without royal permission, the sum on loan already amounting to £390,000, worth at time of issue £78,111 sterling, but at present only £35,445. Amongst those whose estates were involved in the loan were numbers of widows and orphans, who were grieviously injured, oppressed and almost ruined.

He and both his wives were buried in Newport Cemetery.

His son Jahleel Brenton[4], died 1802, Jan., having become a Rear Admiral of the British navy, and was father of Sir Jahleel Brenton born at Newport, 1770, Aug. 22.

1. William, 1716, Apr. 3.
2. Samuel, 1717, Feb. 4.
3. Thomas, 1719, Nov. 4.
4. Mary, 1721, Jul. 10.
5. Hart, 1723, Feb. 26.
6. Martha, 1726, Jan. 12.
7. Elizabeth, 1727, Feb. 3.
8. Jahleel, 1729, Oct. 22.
9. Frances, 1730, Dec. 31.
10. Hannah, 1732, Mar. 19.
11. Samuel, 1733, Nov. 10.
12. Abigail, 1735, Apr. 18.
13. James, 1736, Nov. 2.
14. Benjamin, 1738, Feb. 7.
15. John, 1739, Oct. 21.

(2d wife.)

16. Thomas, 1745, Jun. 5.
17. Susanna, 1747, Apr. 2.
18. Edward, 1748, Mar. 29.
19. William, 1750, Jan. 4.
20. Sarah, 1751, Aug. 27.
21. John, 1754, Apr. 28.
22. Mehitable, 1756, Feb. 15.

I. EBENEZER, b. 1687, Dec. 7. d. 1706. South Kingstown, R. I.
m.
———, b. ; d. of

1. Ann,
2. Elizabeth,

He was a merchant.

His two first children were born in Swanzey.

1693, Dec. 13. Bristol. He and wife Priscilla deeded land.

He held the title of Major at the time of his death.

1706, Jan. 8. Will—proved 1709, Apr. 26. Exs. brothers Jahleel Brenton, of Newport, and Colonel Nathaniel Byfield, of Bristol. To son Ebenezer, half of estate real and personal at age. To daughters Martha and Sarah, a part for support in their minority and rest of the other half at marriage or on coming of age.

Inventory, £882, 8s., 10d. (taken 1708, Oct. 25), viz: silver hilted sword, musket, pistols, parcel of old books, farm in Bristol £280, house, outhouse and grounds in town £150, goods in warehouse, 74½ oz. plate at 8s., £29, 16s., apparel £30, &c.

BRINLEY. 2d column. I. Thomas. His wife was dau. of John and Catharine Page. II. William. Possibly he was brother instead of son of Francis. 1704, Will-proved. 1704, Jun. 4, Exs. Nathaniel Sylvester and Robert Gardner, of Newport. He mentions son William, wife Mary, and son's grandmother.

BRINLEY.

FRANCIS[2] (Thomas[1]), b. 1632, Nov. 15. Datchet, Bucks Co., Eng.; d. 1719. Newport, R. I., Boston, Mass.
m.
HANNAH CARR, b. ; d. 1719 +
of Carr.

1651. Newport. He returned in three or four years to England.

1656, Jul. 27. He came in the ship Speedwell to Boston, and soon made settlement at Newport.

1657, Apr. 15. He was a witness to deed of Conanicut Island, and was one of the original proprietors.

1663, May 22. He was one of those appointed to make a rate for the share of money that Conanicut Island should pay towards John Clarke's expenses as agent of the Colony to England.

1670, Oct. 26. He and five others were appointed to make a rate for Conanicut.

1672, May 14. He was appointed on a committee to meet the Connecticut commissioners to put a final end and issue of all differences between the two colonies.

1672–73. Assistant.

1674, Feb. 19. He and wife Hannah sold William Mays, of Newport, ¼ acre of land and a house in Newport bounded north by land of my sister Ann Coddington, west by land given to my cousin (*i. e.* nephew) William Coddington, &c.

1680, May 5. He was appointed on a committee to put the laws and acts of the Colony into such a method that they may be put in print.

1685, Sep. 25. He bought of Joseph Clarke, 89 acres in Jamestown and rights there and at Dutch Island for £101.

1686. Justice of the Peace.

1686, Jul. 16. He and others signed a petition to the King in regard to writ of *Quo Warranto*, presenting their full and free submission, and resignation of power given in the charter, and desiring to be relieved from all levies and contributions which the Assembly would expose them to in sending an Agent to England, to which the petitioners do not consent.

1686, Oct. 22. He bought of Benedict Arnold and Mary, of Newport, and Josiah Arnold and Sarah, of Jamestown, 71½ acres at Jamestown, for £71, 10s.

1687. Member of Sir Edmund Andros' council.

1687–88. Chairman and Judge of the General Quarter Sessions and Inferior Court of Common Pleas, holding said office under the government of Sir Edmund Andros.

1687, Dec. 15. He and Peleg Sanford addressed a letter to Governor Andros concerning a court house, having no convenient one, and compute the cost of two small houses for that use at £140, judging it convenient that one be erected in Newport and the other in Rochester (*i. e.* Kings Town).

1690, Feb. 22. He wrote to his son Thomas Brinley, merchant, in London. "At New York Jacob Liesler rules at his will and pleasure, puts in prison whom he pleases, and there keeps them. We are here in great confusion: John Coggeshall styles himself Deputy Governor, and John Greene, of Warwick, calls himself Assistant (both being of the Governor's Council) intend next week to call a General Assembly, and to rule by the sword. It is high time that his Majesty would settle a government over New England. We can never govern ourselves with justice nor impartiality unless there be a good government established here, as in the other plantations. I must remove." He adds (dated on the 27th). "Three days since we heard that a town above Albany was cut off by the French and Indians where seventy persons were killed; the rest carried captives." He alludes to Henry Bull having been chosen Governor.

1691, Mar. 16. He had a legacy from the will of Richard Smith, of Kings Town, of certain housing for life, which was to be for his son Thomas at death of Francis.

1702, Jan. 12. He was a proprietor of common lands.

1713, Mar. 27. He signed "an account taken of my books," which shows a large library (for those times) divided under the heads of Law books, Books of Divinity, Books of several sorts, viz: Philosophy, &c.

1714, Sep. 9. He made a deposition, calling himself aged eighty years and upwards, and testifying that he had been an inhabitant of Rhode Island for upwards of sixty-three years and he never knew or heard of any privilege or liberty for one neighbour to go over another man's land at his will and pleasure to hunt deer, kill fowls, &c., but on the contrary Mr. William Coddington, deceased, would not permit or suffer any person to hunt deer in the neck where he dwelt at New Lodge, without leave from himself.

1715, Aug. 6. He signed a paper giving an account of the purchasing and settlement of Conanicut Island; he being as he says the "only original Proprietor living that is now concerned. To remain in *perpetuam rei memoriam*." He declares that in 1656, a company of one hundred persons and upwards agreed to purchase the island and drew up a writing under thirteen heads or articles. Richard Smith, Jr., was employed to purchase the land, and he agreed with Cajanaquant, a chief sachem, for £100, to be paid in wampum and peage, and the deed was signed at Mr. William Coddington's house, at New Lodge, said Brinley being a witness. Possession

I. THOMAS, b. ; d. 1693. Boston, Mass., London, Eng.
m.
CATHARINE PAGE, b. 1663; d. 1755. of Page.

(She m. (2) Edward Lyde.)

1681. Member of Artillery Company.

1686. He was one of the founders of Kings Chapel.

He went to London, before 1690, and established himself as a merchant and there was married. He and his youngest son died of small pox, whereupon his widow and the two surviving children came to America to live with the grandfather of said children.

His widow died at her son's house in Roxbury and was buried in the family tomb in Kings Chapel Burial Ground, Boston.

II. WILLIAM, b. ; d. 1704. Newport, R. I.
m. (1)
——— REAPE, b. ; d. of William & Sarah ( ) Reape.
m. (2)
MARY SANFORD, b. 1674, Apr. 27; d. 1721, Jul. 15. of Samuel & Sarah (Wodell) Sanford.

(She m. (2) 1704, Feb. 12, Josiah Arnold.)

1676. Juryman.

1677. Freeman.

1677, Oct. 31. Commissary. He having powder in his custody was directed to pay over one barrel to Captain Arthur Fenner in part pay for the charge of the garrison called Kings Garrison, at Providence, and if lead, bullets, or shot be in the Colony's store, Captain Fenner was to have not exceeding a hundred weight.

1678, Aug. 31. He petitioned the Assembly to take out of his custody the remaining part of powder belonging to the Colony, and the Deputy Governor and Captain Peleg Sanford were accordingly given power to receive the powder and audit the Commissary's account.

1680. Taxed 19s.

1685, Sep. 25. He was witness to a deed from Joseph Clarke to Francis Brinley.

1699. He was one of the founders of Trinity Church.

1703, Oct. 21. He took acknowledgement of William Wilson and Mehitable his wife, at Newport, they belonging to the town of Saybrook, Ct.

1703–4. Justice of the Peace.

He bore the title of Captain for sometime.

1735. Major.

1765, Mar. 16. Will—proved 1766, Apr. 13. Ex. son-in-law Martin Howard. To son-in-law Martin Howard, Jr., of Newport, a farm in South Kingstown of 214 acres, in occupation of Jeremiah Hoxie and John Hoxie, with house, &c., for life and to him all stock of creatures, &c., on said farm. To daughter Elizabeth Perkins, widow of Edward, £70, yearly. To granddaughter Ann Howard, daughter of Martin, all aforesaid farm at death of her father, she paying her aunt Elizabeth Perkins, £70.

II. MARTHA, b. 1689, Jan. 4. d.
m.
JOHN SMITH, b. d. 1707. of Smith.

III. WILLIAM, b. 1694, Nov. 28. d. young.

IV. SARAH, b. 1697, May 6. d.

BRINLEY.

I. ELIZABETH, b. d.
m.
WILLIAM HUTCHINSON, b. 1680 ± d. of Eliakim & Sarah (Shrimpton) Hutchinson.

1. Eliakim,
2. Shrimpton,
3. Francis,

London, Eng., Roxbury, Mass.

II. FRANCIS, b. 1690. d. 1766.
m. 1718, Apr. 13.
DEBORAH LYDE, b. d. of Edward & Deborah (Byfield) Lyde

1. Deborah,
2. Catharine, 1724.
3. Thomas, 1726.
4. Francis, 1729.
5. Edward, 1730, Aug. 7.
6. Nathaniel, 1733.
7. George,

He was educated at Eton, in England.

1730, Apr. 10. Roxbury. He sold John Paine, of Jamestown, R. I., 28 acres there and buildings for £500.

1742, Apr. 29. He sold Godfrey Malbone, of Newport, merchant, a farm of 366 acres with buildings, &c., in Jamestown, for £10,248.

The house that he erected at Roxbury it is said was modelled after the family mansion at Datchet, England, though on a smaller scale.

1766, May 7. Administration to sons Thomas Brinley, of Boston, distiller, Edward Brinley, of Roxbury, grocer, and Nathaniel Brinley of Framingham, yeoman. Inventory. Pewter, silver spoons, spinning wheel, 12 barrels cider, 2 beakers, 15 wine glasses, 3 wheel barrows, books, reading glass, watch, pair of oxen, 4 cows, horse, mare, chaise, negro man £8, another man £12, woman £12, man £60, another negro at Newport, supposed value 66s., &c. The real estate aggregated over 6,690 acres valued at about £9,600, and included the homestead at Roxbury (98 acres, house and barn worth £3,000,) and tracts of land in Watertown, Needham, Brookline, Framingham, Hopkinton, Leicester, Blanford, and county of Worcester.

He built a family tomb in Kings Chapel Burial Ground, Boston, and was buried therein.

III. WILLIAM, b. d. 1693.

Shrewsbury, N. J.

I. WILLIAM, b. d.
m.
ELIZABETH, b. d. of

1. Francis,
2. William,
3. Thomas,
4. Reape,
5. Sarah,

1713. He and wife Elizabeth deeded land to George Rogers.

1715, Apr. 12. He and his children were mentioned in the will of his grandmother Sarah Reape, of Shrewsbury, widow of William Reape, of Newport, R. I.

was given by turf and twig. The island was computed to be 6,000 acres in extent, and 4,800 acres were allotted to the proprietors for farms, 260 acres for a township, &c., provision being made for an artillery garden, place of burial for the dead, prison house, highways, &c.

He moved to Boston shortly before his death.

1719, Oct. 19. Will—codicil 1719, Oct. 21—proved 1719, Nov. 16. Exs. grandsons Francis Brinley and William Hutchinson. Overseer, Captain Timothy Clark. To wife Hannah, £20, her dower in the estate being sufficient for her years and my degree. To daughter-in-law Catherine Lyde, £20, and an annuity of £60, yearly for life in lieu of her jointure. To granddaughter Elizabeth Hutchinson, £20, and having given her £800, at sundry times by delivery to William Hutchinson, her husband, a further sum of £2,200, is now added to make up a complete sum of £3,000, the said William Hutchinson settling an equivalent jointure on her. To her also certain land in Kings Town, R. I., and £200 sterling, owing in England. To Eliakim Hutchinson, eldest son of my granddaughter Elizabeth, certain land in Norton, Mass. To Edward Lyde, of Boston, £10. To Mrs. Mary Cole, daughter of John Cole, of Kings Town, £5. To Mr. Mahoe, of Roxbury, 40*s*. To my kinswoman Mary Viall, of Barrington, 40*s*. To negro man Guy, 40*s*. To Alice Wait, wife of Samuel Wait, of Kings Town, a new hammock. To Samuel Wakeham, of Newport, eleven books. To Mr. Timothy Clarke, of Boston, my plat of the world and a law book. To grandchildren Francis Brinley and Elizabeth Hutchinson, all my printed books not bequeathed. To kinsman Mr. Francis Willett, £5. To Thomas Brandon, Esq., of the Inner Temple, London, ten guineas. To grandson Francis Brinley, £500 sterling, due in England. To Deborah, wife of grandson Francis Brinley, £20. To grandson Francis Brinley, all my lands in Horton and Stanwell, in counties of Middlesex and Bucks, England, as in my father's will is more largely expressed. To grandson Francis, also land and tenement at south end of Boston Neck, he paying annuity, and a messuage at north end of Conanicut Island, and if he die without issue all to go to my granddaughter his sister, Elizabeth Hutchinson. To children of my two granchildren, each £15. To grandson Francis, all the rest real and personal. To executors, £10, each. The codicil makes void the annuity of £60, to daughter-in-law Catharine Lyde, from income of land at Boston Neck, and directs that the annuity be paid sixty days after Lady Michaelmas Day.

Among his writings was "A brief account of the several settlements and governments in and about the lands of the Narragansett Bay in New England." The narrative is brought down to 1689.

See: American Genealogist, v. 20, p. 121

BROWN (Chad).

CHAD, { b. / d. 1650 (—) } Providence, R. I.
m.
ELIZABETH, { b. / d. 1650 + }

He was a surveyor, with other avocations, and the first settled pastor of the First Baptist Church.

1638, Jul. He landed in Boston from ship Martin, and in a deposition made a short time after, mentions that he and wife Elizabeth and son John came in said ship.

He came to Providence the same year and there signed with twelve others the following compact: "We whose names are hereunder, desirous to inhabit in the town of Providence, do promise to subject ourselves in active or passive obedience to all such orders or agreements as shall be made for public good of the body, in an orderly way, by the major assent of the present inhabitants, masters of families incorporated together into a town fellowship, and such others whom they shall admit unto them, only in civil things."

He was soon after chosen on a committee to compile a list of the first lots situated on the Town street. His service in such directions is mentioned by Roger Williams years after in a letter to John Whipple, Jr. (1669, Jul. 8), wherein he says: "the third sort of bounds were of favor and grace, invented, as I think, and prosecuted by that noble spirit, now with God, Chad Brown."

1640. He was appointed on a committee with three others in all matters of difference between Providence and Pawtuxet, regarding the division line, and they reported in July that they had seriously and carefully considered all those differences. "We have gone the fairest and equallest way to produce our peace."

1640, Jul. 27. He and thirty-eight others signed an agreement for a form of government, and he was on the committee that drew up this paper.

1642. Ordained as pastor of First Baptist Church.

1643. He and three others were employed in making peace between the people of Warwick and Massachusetts.

1650, Sep. 2. Widow Brown taxed 6*s*. 8*d*.

He was buried in his original home lot, where the Court House now stands, and from here his body was removed in 1792 to the North Burial Ground, where a monument was erected to his memory by the town of Providence.

A descendant, Moses Brown, wrote Dr. Wayland under date of 1833, May 25, "Chad and his wife were buried on their own lot, near the north-west corner of the now town house, and had a large square monument of granite over them. I saw their remains when taken up."

He left a will, as shown by allusions in deeds of his sons.

I. JOHN, { b. 1630. / d. 1706 ± } Providence, R. I.
m.
MARY HOLMES, { b. / d. 1690 + } of Obadiah & Catharine ( ) Holmes.

1649, Nov. 3. He and five others drew lots for the home share of Mr. Lea, deceased, whose widow was to have 30*s*.

1650, Sep. 2. Taxed 3*s*. 4*d*.

1651. He was on a jury concerning death of Margaret Goodwin, the verdict being that "the terribleness of the crack of thunder on the second of the third month, 1651, or the coldness of the night, being she was naked did kill her."

1652–55–59–60–64. Juryman.

1655. Freeman.

1659, Jun. 6. Surveyor of Highways.

1661, Mar. 25. He was on a committee to levy a rate of £35, for a colony prison.

1661, May 10. He and two others received a deed on behalf of Providence from Wuttiashant of tract called Wayunckeke.

1662, Mar. 14. Moderator of town meeting. In the same year he was on a committee to build a bridge over the Moshassuck River, and also on a committee to levy a rate of £76, 2*s*. 6*d*., to send Mr. Clarke to England.

1662–64–65. Town Council.

1663–64. Deputy.

1665–66. Assistant.

1666, May 31. He took oath of allegiance.

1669, Feb. 27. He and wife Mary sold James Matteson 5 acres given him by his father Chad Brown in last will.

1672, Dec. 21. He sold a lot to his brother Jeremiah, of Newport, which his father Chad had bought of George Rickard.

1672, Dec. 31. He sold to his brother James of Newport, the home lot of their father Chad Brown, deceased, which had come to said John, by reversion from his mother Elizabeth "according as my father Chad Brown by his will disposed" &c. A reservation was made of 20 feet square, within the orchard where my father and mother are buried, with free egress. This land was sold the same day to Daniel Abbott, and part of it subsequently repurchased by John and Moses Brown, and presented to Brown University, and built upon by that corporation.

1679, Jul. 1. Taxed 5*s*.

1687, Sep. 1. Taxed with son John 9*s*.

1687. Ratable estate, 4 oxen, 5 cows, 4 two years, 2 three years, 45 sheep, 3 horses, 3 hogs, 7 acres planting land, 7 acres pasture, 7 acres swamp meadow, 5 acres bog meadow.

1690, Jul. 6. He deeded to son James "for his well being and settlement, and also in consideration of his good obedience and pains, care and diligence, which he constantly hath taken in providing for my family, my three house lots or home shares of land lying all together, with my dwelling house," &c., and other land. Reservation was made to his wife and himself for life, of dwelling in the house, and comfortable maintenance.

1701. He and Pardon Tillinghast, as elders of the church, ordained James Clarke, of Newport, as Pastor of the Second Baptist Church there.

1703, Mar. 13. He recorded the ear mark of his cattle, "in each ear a hole."

John Brown. See also: Bowen, The Providence Oath of Allegiance, p. 61-63.

BROWN (Chad).

I. Sarah, m. 1678, Nov. 14. John Pray,
b. — d. 1733 +
b. — d. 1730, Oct. 9. of Richard & Mary ( ) Pray.

1. John,
2. Hugh,
3. Richard,
4. Mary,
5. Catharine,
6. Sarah,
7. Penelope,
8. Martha, 1689.

II. John, m. 1696, Jun. 9. Isabel Mathewson,
b. 1662, Mar. 18. d. 1719, Sep. 19. Providence, R. I.
b. — d. 1719 + of James & Hannah (Field) Mathewson.

1. John, 1697, Mar. 26.
2. Mary, 1699, Jul. 30.
3. Lydia, 1701, Dec. 21.
4. Isabel, 1705, Apr. 17.
5. Nathan, 1707, Aug. 24.
6. Obadiah, 1710, Aug. 17.

He held the title of Ensign.

1706, May 20. He deeded his brother Obadiah for his well being and settlement, certain lands heired from his father.

1719, Nov. 23. Administration to widow Isabel and son John. Inventory, £253, 1*s.* 8*d.*, viz: 2 woolen wheels, linen wheel, pewter, brass, earthenware, books, carpenter's tools, warming pan, bills of credit, silver money, hay, rye, oats, barley, tobacco, flax, cider, 13 swine, 46 sheep, 2 oxen, 7 cows, 2 steers, 4 two years, 3 yearlings, 2 heifers, mare, &c. Real estate; homestead farm, &c. £500, lands and meadows at Wanscott £100, land west of Seven Mile line, &c.

III. James, m. 1691, Dec. 17. Mary Harris,
b. 1666. d. 1732, Oct. 28. Providence, R. I.
b. 1671, Dec. 17. d. 1736, Aug. 18. of Andrew & Mary (Tew) Harris.

BROWN (Chad). 3d column. II. James, m. (2) Catharine, b. 1702, Mar. 19, of Job & Phebe (Sayles) Greene. Possibly his 1st wife was a daughter of James & Hope (Power) Clarke.

1. John, 1695, Oct. 8.
2. James, 1698, Mar. 22.
3. Joseph, 1701, May 15.
4. Martha, 1703, Oct. 12.
5. Andrew, 1706, Sep. 20.
6. Mary, 1708, Apr. 29.
7. Anna,
8. Obadiah, 1712, Oct. 2.
9. Jeremiah, 1715, Nov. 25.
10. Elisha, 1717, May 25.

1705-6-7-8-9-10-11-12-13-19-20-25. Town Council.

1714-18. Town Treasurer.

1726. Pastor of First Baptist Church, succeeding Ebenezer Jenckes in the ministry. He continued as pastor till his death.

1729, Mar. 3. Will—proved 1732, Dec. 4. Exs. sons James and Joseph. To wife Mary, house for life, and then to sons Jeremiah and Elisha. To wife also, household goods, £280, and to be provided in victuals, drink, firewood, &c. To son James, land at Wansocut; great bible, book called Robert's Key, and a gun which was my father's. To son Joseph, land. To son Andrew, house at Chapatsett, and half the land there. To son Obadiah, the other half of Chapatsett land, except 6 acres, a lot in town, &c. To grandson James Greene, 150 acres. To daughters Mary and Ann, £200, each, paid partly with a negro woman at £80. To sons Jeremiah and Elisha, the homestead, all lands between Town street and highway, &c., they taking care of their mother.

Inventory, £915, 6*d.*, viz: books, bonds £178, 5*s.*, 6 silver spoons, 24 chairs, 2 canes, shoemaker's tools, loom, spinning wheel, negro woman Quassi, and boy Cuffy £100, 4 hogsheads of apple beer, 2 hogsheads cider, 2 horses, mare, 2 swine, 30 sheep, 4 oxen, 6 cows, 5 calves, cider press, cheese press, hay, oats, flax, &c. The rooms named were kitchen, great kitchen chamber, little kitchen chamber, east lower bed room, great chamber, north-east little chamber, and south-east little chamber.

1736, Jul. 20. Will—proved 1736, Nov. 29. Widow Mary. Exs. sons Jeremiah and Elisha. To sons Jeremiah and Elisha, 33½ acres in Smithfield given her by brother Andrew Harris. To son Joseph, £40. To daughter Ann Brown, wearing apparel, £100, due from brother Toleration Harris, &c. She mentions her daughters Martha Greene and Mary Brown as deceased. To son Jeremiah, apprentice boy Othniel Hearnden. To son Elisha, negro boy Cuffey, &c.

He and his wife were buried in North Burial Ground.

IV. Obadiah, m. ——
b. — d. 1716, Aug. 24. Providence, R. I.
b. — d. — of

1. John,
2. Chad, 1705, Oct. 13.

1688, Aug. His name was in the list of taxable persons over the age of sixteen. (One hundred and seventy-two in all.)

1716, Sep. 12. Administration to brothers John and James. Inventory, £377, 1*d.*, viz: 17 cows, yoke of oxen, 2 yokes of steers, yearling bull, two year bull, two year steer, 5 yearling steers, 11 calves, red roan mare, two year mare, 5 swine, 7 pigs, 30 loads English hay, 16 loads meadow hay, gun, musket, rapier, belt, small pistol, 2 books, pewter, pair of silver buckles, cooper's stuff, wife's wearing apparel, &c.

1724, Feb. 23. His son "John Brown, Jr., son of Obadiah, deceased," deeded to brother Chad 200 acres.

V. Martha, m. Joseph Jenckes,
b. — d.
b. 1656. d. 1740, Jun. 15. of Joseph & Esther (Ballard) Jenckes.

1. Joseph,
2. Obadiah,
3. Catharine, 1694.
4. Nathaniel,
5. Martha,
6. Lydia,
7. John,
8. Mary,
9. Esther,

① See: American Genealogist, v. 28, no. 4, Oct., 1952, p. 210-211.

II. JAMES, b. d. 1683 (—) Newport, R. I.
m.
ELIZABETH CARR, b. d. 1697 + of Robert Carr.

(She m. (2) Samuel Gardiner.)

He was a cooper.

1671, Jan. 30. He was allowed 2*s.* for four day's service.

1671. Freeman.

1672, Dec. 31. He and wife Elizabeth sold the home lot of his father Chad Brown, deceased, to Daniel Abbott, of Providence, excepting the land where his father Chad and mother Elizabeth were buried.

1679, Feb. 15. He bought of Daniel Stanton, of Newport, land in Coeset, for 40*s.*

1680. Taxed 12*s.*

1683, May 5. Elizabeth Brown of Newport, widow and executrix of James Brown, sold land in East Greenwich to Clement Weaver for £12.

BROWN (CHAD). 2d column. III. Jeremiah. He had also sons Daniel, Samuel, and probably William. 3d column. II. Daniel, d. 1726, Westerly, R. I. He m. Frances Watson, of John and Dorcas (Gardiner) Watson. She d. 1726+. Children, 1. Elizabeth, 1705, Mar. 13. 2. Mary, 1706, Aug. 3. 3. Benjamin, 1708, Mar. 16. 4. Daniel, 1709, Nov. 15. 5. Elisha, 1711, Jan. 26. 6. Dorcas, 1713, May 22. 7. John, 1714, Feb. 18. 8. Desire, 1723, Jan. 8. He sold to his brother Samuel land that had been given by father Jeremiah. III. William, b. 1676, d. 1753, S. Kingstown, R. I. m. 1707, Nov. 2, Elizabeth Robinson, of Rowland and Mary (Allen) Robinson. Children, 1. John, 1708, Aug. 6. 2. Mary, 1710, Jun. 4. 3. Thomas, 1711, Aug. 23. 4. Elizabeth, 1713, Feb. 28. 5. Ruth, 1715, Sep. 25. 6. Robert, 1718, Jul. 26. 7. George, 1721, Sep. 30. IV. Samuel, b. 1680, Mar., d. 1762, Jul., S. Kingstown, R. I. m. 1702, Oct. 22, Mary ——. Children, 1. Sarah, 1703, Dec. 12. 2. Mary, 1705, Jul. 17. 3. Jeremiah, 1707, Oct. 29. 4. Penelope, 1709, Oct. 27. 5. Samuel, 1711, Nov. 5. 6. Elizabeth, 1713, Oct. 28. 7. John, 1715, Nov. 14. 8. Freelove, 1718, Jan. 29. 9. Zephaniah, 1721, Dec. 23 Perhaps he m. (2) Mercy Carr, b. 1696, Feb. 24, of Edward and Hannah (Stanton) Carr.

①
III. JEREMIAH, b. d. 1690. Newport, R. I.
m. (1)
MARY, b. d. of
m. (2) 1680 ±
MARY COOK (w. of Thos.) b. d. of

1671. Freeman.

1671, Jan. 30. He was allowed £2, for hire of his boat to bring down about twenty persons from Providence, and also for his boat to go to Narragansett with Mr. John Crandall, Sr.

1672, Dec. 31. He and wife Mary sold Daniel Abbott of Providence, a lot there that Chad Brown, father of grantor, had owned.

1674, Aug. 25. He bought land of Sarah Reape, widow of William Reape, of Newport, for £13, being commonage in Providence.

1674, Oct. 28. He was released from payment of a fine for not serving on jury, on his petition for said release.

1680. Taxed £1, 8*s.*

1686. Grand Jury.

1687, Sep. 6. Kings Town. Taxed 2*s.* 2*d.* He probably returned to Newport.

1690, Sep. 16. He and two others were appointed by Assembly to proportion rate of tax for Kings Town's part of money for French and Indian War.

1690, Oct. 30. Whereas Mr. Jeremiah Brown is dead, the Assembly ordered two others in his stead to assist in making rate for Kings Town.

1688, Apr. 11. Will—proved 1690. Witnesses. Samuel Carr and Ephraim Turner. A reference to this is found in a list of wills (between the dates of 1676 and 1695), that were presented to the Court in 1700, by parties interested, the law requiring three witnesses and these wills having but two.

1691, Oct. 9. Mary Brown, widow of Jeremiah, had 90 acres laid out at East Greenwich.

(Possibly Samuel, Daniel and William Brown, of Kings Town, were his sons, but there is no direct evidence to show it.)

IV. JUDAH, b. d. 1663, May 10. Newport, R. I.
UNMARRIED.

He was buried in the Clifton Burial Ground.

V. DANIEL, b. d. 1710, Sep. 29. Providence, R. I.
m. 1669, Dec. 25.
ALICE HEARNDEN, b. 1652. d. 1718 + of Benjamin & Elizabeth (White) Hearnden.

1656. Hay-ward.

1665, Feb. 19. He had lot 9 in a division of lands.

1679, Jul. 1. Taxed 2*s.* 6*d.*

1687, Sep. 1. Taxed 3*s.*

1706, Dec. 10. He deeded to two eldest sons Judah and Jabesh, for well being, &c., 50 acres in the neck, being farm we live upon, only wife Alice to have maintenance, and if grantor decease before five years, then three youngest sons to have for the five years.

1710, Feb. 18. He deeded son Daniel, for love, &c., a forty foot lot, a little north of Great Bridge from the town over to Weybosset.

1710, Nov. 10. Administration to widow Alice, and later at her request, to herself and son Daniel. Inventory, £78 ±, viz: wearing apparel, pewter, 3 spinning wheels, 2 pairs of cards, hetchel, old books, cider mill, pair of small oxen, 3 cows, pair of yearling steers, 20 sheep and lambs, 7 swine, 34 marking irons. a barrel of peach juice, and 13 old barrels and cider which he left at Newport. (He died while temporarily at Newport.)

1718, Aug. 4. His widow called herself aged about sixty-six years in a deposition at this date.

VI. MARY, m. ARTHUR AYLSWORTH, b. | d. | b. 1653. | d. 1726. of Aylsworth.

1. Robert,
2. Arthur, 1685.
3. John,
4. Philip, 1692.
5. Chad, 1696.
6. Mary,
7. Elizabeth,
8. Catherine,
9. Martha,

VII. DEBORAH, b. | d.

Newport, R. I.

I. JOHN, m. ELIZABETH CRANSTON, b. 1671. | d. 1731, Oct. 20. | b. 1671. | d. 1736, Jun. 3. of John & Mary (Clarke) Cranston.

1706-9-21-22-23-24-25-26. Deputy.
1709. Captain.
1709, May 4. He was appointed on a Special Council to assist the Governor at this juncture of time for advice to manage the affairs for the more speedy expedition of the great design now intended against Canada.
1721, Jun. 13. He was appointed on a committee to rebuild or repair Fort Ann.
1730, Jun. It was voted by the Assembly to deliver Captain John Brown at the fort, the great guns and appurtenances now on board the brigantine Two Brothers.

1. John, 1696, Dec. 26.
2. Jeremiah,
3. James,
4. William,
5. Robert,
6. Peleg,
7. Elizabeth,

Newport, Scituate, R. I.

II. JAMES, m. (1) ANN, m. (2) CATHARINE, b. | d. 1756. | b. | d. of | b. | d. 1754 + of

BROWN (CHAD). 3d column. II. James. Date of 2d marriage, 1740, April 27. IV. Samuel m. (2) Mercy Weeden, (widow of John), b. 1696, Feb. 24, of Edward and Hannah (Stanton) Carr. II. Jabez. Children, 3, Jabez 4, Mary. 5, Jerusha.

1706-7-8-9-10-11-12-13-15. Deputy.
1708, Jul. 14. He and wife Ann sold John Spencer, of East Greenwich, 30 acres there for £60.
1708. Justice of the Peace.
1711, Jun. 2. He and two others were appointed to buy a vessel for the Colony's service for intended expedition against Canada.
1711-13. Major for the Island.
1712, Feb. 27. He and the Governor were empowered to employ workmen to enlarge the Colony House.
1715-16-17-18-19-20-21-22-23. Assistant.
1754, Dec. 19. Will—proved 1756, Nov. 27. Ex. son Thomas. To wife Catharine, 500 oz. silver, all plate and household goods that she brought with her, my negro boy, a cow, horse, and half of dwelling house and ground for a garden, while widow, and sufficient summer and winter feed for cow and horse, all in lieu of dower. To son James, land in South Amboy, N. J., and a third of land in Northfield, Mass., and £500, for use of son John and family to be employed by James. To son John, 20*s*. To son Clarke Brown, a third of Northfield lands, and a bond against him for £1,200, large bible, silver tankard marked J. B., and all my household goods I left with him in my house at Newport when I moved from there, and £100. To daughter Hope Coddington, £500. To son Thomas, all land and tenements in Scituate, except use to wife as aforesaid, and a third of land in Northfield. To each grandchild, £3. To son Thomas, rest of estate.

1. James, 1700.
2. John,
3. Clarke,
4. Hope,
5. Thomas,

Newport, R. I., Swanzey, Mass.

III. ESEK, m. 1705, Nov. 29. MERCY CARR, b. 1679, Mar. 8. | d. 1772, Dec. 10. | b. 1683, Oct. 7. | d. 1776, Dec. of Caleb & Deborah ( ) Carr.

1715, Mar. 10. Swanzey. His daughter Roby and perhaps the rest of his children were born there.

1. Mary, 1707, Mar. 28.
2. Elizabeth, 1708, Oct. 10.
3. Deborah, 1711, Jun. 11.
4. Esek, 1712, Aug. 13.
5. Roby, 1715, Mar. 10.
6. Deborah, 1716, Oct. 13.
7. Mary, 1718, Jan. 15.
8. James, 1719, Nov. 12.
9. Benjamin, 1721, Jul. 17.
10. Jeremiah, 1723, Aug. 22.
11. Daniel, 1723, Aug. 22.

Newport, R. I.

I. JAMES, b. | d.

He was a cooper.
1693, Feb. 13. He sold to William Gibson, of Kings Town, for £12, certain land in Providence given by last will of his father Jeremiah.
1693, Oct. 10. He and John Brown, of Newport, sold Joseph Latham of Providence, 30 acres there for £9.

Providence, Scituate, R. I.

I. JUDAH, m. HANNAH, b. | d. 1734, Jan. 18. | b. | d. 1745 + of

BROWN (CHAD). 3d column. I. Judah. His first child should be Judah, not Joseph.

1688, Aug. His name was in the list of taxable persons.
1712, Jan. 9. He and wife Hannah deeded to his brother Daniel, half of a farm of 55 acres given said Judah by deed of gift from his father Daniel, also dwelling house, and his interest in two other houses on said farm where his father formerly dwelt.
1734, Jan. 31. Administration to eldest son Judah, the widow Hannah refusing. Inventory, £124, 18*s*. 6*d*., viz: wearing apparel, old books, pewter, turning tools, linen wheel, pair of spectacles, 3 cows, yearling, 3 calves, 2 horses, 4 swine, &c.
1738, Apr. 16. His son Elisha died at Scituate, and in his will mentions his mother Hannah, brothers Judah and David, and sisters Hannah Burlingame and Phebe Brown.
1745, Dec. 5. Hannah Brown, widow, being adjudged *non compos mentis*, her son Captain Judah Brown was appointed guardian. She was now aged.

1. Joseph,
2. Deborah,
3. Abigail,
4. David,
5. Hannah,
6. Elisha,
7. Phebe,

Providence, R. I.

II. JABEZ, m. ANNE, b. | d. 1724, Sep. 9. | b. | d. 1727, Feb. 25. of

He was a dishturner, as he calls himself in deeds.
1714, Jul. 24. He and wife Ann sold John Jenckes, for £80, dwelling house, shop, and 10 acres.
1715, Oct. 31. He sold his brother Daniel, for £110, my part of dwelling house, and 17½ acres.

1. William,
2. Jeremiah,

BROWNING. See: American Genealogist, v. 20, p. 182.

{ NATHANIEL, { b. Portsmouth, R. I.
{ m. { d.
{ SARAH FREEBORN, { b. 1632.
{ d. 1670, Apr. 23.

of William & Mary (   ) Freeborn.

1645, Oct. 23. He bought of John Roome, a dwelling house and two lots of 8 acres in Warwick, for £3, in wampum.

1652, Jan. 2. His wife had a deed of gift from her father of a small parcel of land adjoining James Weeden's and eight years later she had a further gift of 20 acres from her father.

1652, Jan. 11. He assigned his deed from John Roome to Henry Lake.

1655. Freeman.

1690, Mar. 5. James Sweet and Jane his wife, of Prudence Island, for £12, paid by our uncle Gideon Freeborn, sold him a quarter of 20 acres in Portsmouth, given by my grandfather William Freeborn, unto the said Jane's mother, deceased.

I. { WILLIAM, { b. Portsmouth, South Kingstown, R. I.
m. (1) { d. 1730.
REBECCA WILBUR, { b.
{ d. of Samuel & Hannah (Porter) Wilbur.
m. (2)
SARAH, { b.
{ d. 1730 + of

1684. Freeman

1685, Mar. 19. He exchanged certain land with Thomas Manchester, Jr.

1688, Feb. 25. He sold Robert Fish 20 acres, for £70, being land given by deed of grandfather William Freeborn. His wife Rebecca, and uncle Gideon Freeborn signed also.

1730, Jan. 12. Will—proved 1730, Feb. 8. Ex. son Samuel. To wife Sarah, £30, yearly for life. To eldest son Samuel, 250 acres in South Kingstown, £100, and to have also £100, paid him by his brother William, and £50, by his brother John. To son William, 250 acres in South Kingstown, on which he now dwelleth. To son John, 100 acres at Point Judith, where he dwelleth. To daughter Sarah, £200. To deceased daughter Hannah Knowles' two children Rebecca and Hannah, £100, at eighteen, equally divided. To three sons, rest of estate, equally.

Inventory, £1,199, 16*s.*, 7*d.*, viz: 61 oz. silver £24, 8*s.*, wearing apparel, cane, gloves and belt £19, 2*s.*, bond £61, 17*s.* 5*d.*, riding horse, negro woman £80, pair of oxen, 57 sheep, 9 cows, 5 horsekind, 7 swine.

II. { JANE, { b.
{ m { d. 1719 +
{ JAMES SWEET, { b.
{ d. 1719, Jun. 26. of John & Elizabeth (   ) Sweet.

1725, May 17. Administration to widow Ann. Inventory, £198, 17*s.* 8*d.*, viz: bible, silver money 9*s.* 11*d.*, sword, feather bed, 3 spinning wheels, shoemaker's and cooper's tools, carpenter's tools, yoke of oxen, 8 cows, 4 young cattle, 5 calves, horse, 8 swine, &c. Real estate £485, including homestead of 80 acres £350.

1727, Sep. 18. Ann Brown, widow of Jabez; administration on her estate to son William. Inventory, £141, 3*d.* On the same date Jeremiah Brown took administration on his father's estate, the widow and administratrix Hannah being dead.

III. SARAH, b. 1677, Oct. 10. d. 1744 +
m. 1700, Apr. 4.
THOMAS ANGELL, b. 1672, Mar. 25. d. 1744, Sep. 14. of John & Ruth (Field) Angell.

1. Martha, 1703, Mar. 24.
2. Isaiah, 1704, Nov. 17.
3. Jeremiah, 1707, Jan. 29.
4. Jonathan, 1709, Feb. 14.
5. Sarah, 1710.
6. Nehemiah,
7. Thomas,

IV. JEREMIAH, b. d. Providence, Smithfield, R. I.
m. 1715, Dec. 8.
SARAH TUCKER, b. d. of Tucker.

He was a brickmaker, and was also called innkeeper.

1715, Dec. 16. He sold Joseph Dalie 50 acres for £10, in the right of honoured father Daniel, deceased.

1736, Feb. 14. Smithfield. He and wife Sarah, for £900, sold David Hearnden 121½ acres.

V. HALLELUJAH, b. d. 1771.
m. 1702, Aug. 31.
JAMES OLNEY, b. 1670, Nov. 9. d. 1744, Oct. 6. of Epenetus & Mary (Whipple) Olney.

1. James, 1703, Sep. 18.
2. Mary, 1704, Sep. 30.
3. Joseph, 1706, Jun. 7.
4. James, 1708, Dec. 28.
5. Jonathan, 1710, Mar. 9.
6. Jeremiah, 1711, Mar. 20.
7. Lydia, 1716, Nov. 1.
8. Mercy,

VI. HOSANNA, b. d. Providence, Glocester, R. I.
m.
MARY HAWKINS, b. d. of John & Sarah ( ) Hawkins.

1. Mary,
2. Othniel,

1708. Freeman.

1713, Jun. 16. Taxed 6*s.* 6*d.*

1725, Feb. 1. He sold to William Hawkins, for £5, a lot of 10 acres in original right of father Daniel, deceased.

1730, Jun. 3. He deeded son-in-law David Burlingame and Mary his wife, half of homestead where I dwell east side of Chapatset river, 100 acres, and half of dwelling house and corn mill, and quarter of saw mill.

1732, Apr. 10. Glocester. He bought of Isaiah Inman, for £80, land and part of a saw mill.

VII. JONATHAN, b. d. Providence, R. I.

1713, May 21. He sold Nicholas Sheldon 75 acres, but not having so full a power as he ought to have had from his brothers Judah and Daniel, they confirmed the deed three years later.

VIII. DANIEL, b. d. Providence, R. I.
m.
MARY SPRAGUE, b. d. of Jonathan & Mehitable (Holbrook) Sprague.

He was a cooper.

1. Susanna, 1715, Oct. 2.
2. Daniel, 1717, May 20.
3. Phineas, 1719, Aug. 26.
4. Penelope, 1721, Feb. 11.
5. John, 1722, Dec. 19.
6. Phebe, 1725, May 7.

BROWNING.

I. SAMUEL, b. 1688, Feb. 9. d. South Kingstown, Exeter, R. I.
m.
MERCY, b. d. of

1. Samuel.

1718, Sep. He and wife Mercy, for £1,600, sold to father William Browning, three tracts of land measuring 100, 250 and 500 acres, respectively.

1751, Apr. 19. At this date a mortgage was given by Samuel Browning, Jr., for £150, to the Colony, on 10 acres.

II. HANNAH, b. 1691, Jul. 16. d. 1726 (—)
m.
WILLIAM KNOWLES, b. d. 1727. of William & Alice (Fish) Knowles.

1. Rebecca,
2. Hannah,

III. WILLIAM, b. 1693, Sep. 29. d. 1773, Feb. 11. South Kingstown, R. I.
m. (1) 1721, Dec. 7.
MARY FREELOVE, b. 1700, Aug. 10. d. of Morris & Elizabeth (Wilbur) Freelove.
m. (2) 1728, Aug. 5.
MARY WILKINSON, b. d. of William & Dinah ( ) Wilkinson.

1. William, 1724, Nov. 28.
(2d wife.)
2. Wilkinson, 1731, Jul. 14.
3. John, 1735, Jul. 26.
4. Mary, 1735, Jun. 10.
5. Dinah, 1736, Sep. 10.
6. Joseph,
7. Ruth,
8. Tabitha,

1770, Jun. 19. Will—proved 1773, Mar. 8. Ex. son William. To wife Mary, use of house and 3 acres where I live, and of household goods and two of my negroes, while widow, also one-fifth of rest of personal, except farming tools, and yearly provided with thirty bushels Indian corn, four bushels wheat, two hundred pounds of beef, one hundred and fifty pounds of pork, forty pounds of wool, twenty pounds of flax and fifteen cords firewood. She was to have three cows kept for her, and a gentle beast to ride whenever she have occasion. To son William, the homestead, except 100 acres, and to him half the farming tools. To son Wilkinson, 7 acres meadow and negro boy Abraham. To five grandchildren, viz: William, John, Ephraim, Anne and Ruth, children of son John, deceased, land in Richmond, equally. To son Joseph, 100 acres of homestead, 148 acres in Charlestown, and half of farming tools. To daughter Dinah Champlin, a fifth of personal, except farming utensils and household goods, and a quarter of household after wife is done. To daughters Ruth Browning and Tabitha Gardiner, like legacies. To five children of daughter Mary Browning, deceased, viz: Robert, Thomas, William, Mary and Anne, like legacy.

Inventory, £1,279, 15*s.*, 2¾*d.*, viz: wearing apparel. £15, 12*s.*, 9*d.*, old gun, keg of wine, cash £598, 4*s.*, 4¾*d.*, 89 sheep, swine 7*s.*, 4*d.*, sorrel horse, 14 cows, 2 pair oxen, 2 pair steers, heifer, 8 young cattle, old mare, colt, negro Bristol £30, Abram £30, boy Cæsar £37, farming and carpenterng tools, &c.

IV. SARAH, b. 1694, Apr. d.
m. 1721, Oct. 6.
ELEAZER KELLY, b. d. of Kelly.

V. JOHN, b. 1696, Mar. 4. d. 1777. South Kingstown, R. I.
m. 1721, Apr. 21.
ANN HAZARD, b. 1701, Feb. 28. d. 1770 (—) of Jeremiah & Sarah (Smith) Hazard.

1. Thomas,
2. Jeremiah,
3. Hannah,
4. Sarah,
5. John,
6. Ephraim,
7. Martha,
8. Ann,
9. Mary,
10. Eunice,

1770, Aug. 23. Will—proved 1777, Apr. 14. Ex. son Jeremiah. To grandsons Thomas and William, sons of Thomas, deceased, all my lands in South Kingstown, being part of my homestead farm, about 100 acres, they paying as hereafter expressed, and to them 14 acres of salt marsh in Charlestown. To son Jeremiah, daughter Hannah Frink, daughter Sarah Stanton, son John, and son Ephraim, 6*s.*, each. To granddaughters Temperance and Abigail Frink, a bed. To six children, rest of estate, viz: to Jeremiah, a whole share, Sarah Stanton, a quarter share, Martha Powers, Ann Browning, Mary Champlin and Eunice Clark, a whole share each, and so divide the whole.

Inventory, £106, 6*s.*, 4*d.*, viz: wearing apparel £7, 10*s.*, loom, bible, &c.

1. Daniel,
2. William,
3. Nathaniel,
4. Mary,
5. Sarah,
6. Elizabeth,
7. Renewed,
8. Susanna,

{ FRANCIS, { b. Warwick, R. I.
m. 1669, Mar. 19. [Joseph. { d. 1675, Nov.
REBECCA HOWARD, (w. of { b.
{ d. 1675, Nov.
of John Lippitt.

1672, Apr. 30. Freeman. (The name given in Colonial Records as Thomas, refers doubtless to him.)

1672, Jun. 15. He was one of townsmen pledged to stand together against the intrusions of Connecticut and to send an agent to England praying relief therefrom.

1674 Juryman.

1675, Nov. He was killed by the Indians, with all his family except his son John.

I. { JOHN, { b. 1672. Warwick, R. I.
m. { d. 1744, Oct. 4.
ISABEL POTTER, { b. 1674, Oct. 17.
{ d. 1731 (—) of John & Ruth (Fisher) Potter.

1675, Nov. He was taken captive by the Indians, at the same time his father and the rest of the family were killed, but was afterwards returned by his captors, and was placed in the care of his uncle Moses Lippitt.

1693, May 20. He deeded to his uncle Moses Lippitt, 12 acres in Warwick, calling himself twenty-one years of age and upwards.

1696, Apr. 28. He was propounded for freeman.

1715, Nov. 11. He bought of Ephraim and Hannah Pierce for £30, a parcel of 6 acres in Warwick.

1720, Oct. 18. He, and Isabel Budlong, his wife, witnessed will of Mary Greene (widow of James).

1722, Jan. 26. He and his wife were given legacy of 14*s*., by will of Isabel Burton of this date. (She was widow of William Burton and daughter of Robert and Isabel Potter.)

1731, Oct. 4. Will—proved 1744, Dec. 17. Ex. son John. To eldest daughter Rebecca Pearce, £5, and what she had. To second daughter Mary Pearce, £60. To youngest daughter Isabel Budlong, a feather bed, &c., to value of £35, also £15 cash and £50, at end of two years. To son Moses, 70 acres and £300. To son Daniel, 2 lots of land and £300, at age. To eldest son John, all the rest both real and personal, housing, goods, &c.

Inventory, £760, 18*s*., 6*d*., viz: notes, bonds, &c.

He was buried on his farm.

See: American Genealogist Apr., 1954, v. 30, no. 2, p. 122

BULL (HENRY).

{ HENRY, { b. 1610. Boston, Mass., Newport, R. I.
m. (1) { d. 1694, Jan. 22.
ELIZABETH, { b.
m. (2) 1666 ± { d. 1665, Oct. 1.
ESTHER ALLEN, { b. 1648, Dec. 8.
{ d. 1676, Mar. 26.
of Ralph & Esther (Swift) Allen.
m. (3) 1677, Mar. 28. [Nich. { b. 1628.
ANN EASTON (w. of { d. 1708, Jan. 30.
of Clayton.

1635, Jul. 17. He sailed in ship James from London, his age being entered as twenty-five years.

1636. He and his wife Elizabeth joined the church at Roxbury.

1637, May 17. Freeman. The Roxbury church record says of him: "Being weak and affectionate was taken and transported with the opinion of familism." &c.

1637, Nov. 20. He, and others, were warned to deliver up all guns, pistols, swords, powder, shot, &c., because "the opinions and revelations of Mr. Wheelwright and Mrs. Hutchinson have seduced and led into dangerous error many of the people here in New England."

1638, Mar. 7. Portsmouth. He and eighteen others signed the following compact. "We whose names are underwritten do here solemnly in the presence of Jehovah incorporate ourselves into a Bodie Politick, and as he shall help will submit our persons, lives and estates unto our Lord Jesus Christ,

I. { JIREH, { b. 1638, Sep. Newport, Kings Town, R. I.
m. { d. 1684 ±
——— { b.
{ d. of

1661, Mar. 22. He signed certain articles relative to Misquamicut (Westerly) lands.

1668, Jun. 4. He bought 500 acres in Pettaquamscutt for £28, from the purchasers of said tract.

1669, Aug. 19. Kings Town. He and two others were desired by the Governor and Council to require Suckquansh and Ninecraft to appear before the Council Wednesday next touching the alarm of the country upon suspicion of the Indians plotting to cut off the English.

1669-70-78-83. Conservator of the Peace.

1670, Jul. 13. He and Samuel Wilson (Conservators of the Peace) informed the Governor, &c., of the murder of Walter House, and of his being illegally and disorderly buried without coroner and inquest; and Henry Palmer was constituted High Constable in the matter to go to Narragansett and give notice to Samuel Wilson and Jireh Bull to repair to the place where Walter House is buried and cause the body to be taken up and jury's inquest to pass thereon, &c.

1670, Oct. 26. He and four others were appointed to make a rate for Pettaquamscut.

1671, May 19. Lieutenant.

1672, May 14. He was appointed on a committee to meet the Connecticut Commissioners to put a final end and issue of all differences between the two Colonies.

1675, Jun. 27. In a letter from Roger Williams to John Winthrop (written from Richard Smith's at Narragansett), he says: "Sir, just now comes in Sam Dier in a catch from Newport, to fetch over Jireh Bull's wife and children and others of Pettaquamscutt."

I. JOHN, b. 1698. d. 1763, Jan. 24. Warwick, R. I.
m. (1) 1730, Jan 8,
TABITHA PIERCE, b. 1717, Aug. 27. d. of Azrikim & Elizabeth (Esten) Pierce.
m. (2)
RENEW MOON (widow.) b. d. 1779. of

1. Isabel, 1731, Apr. 10.
2. John, 1733, Aug. 25.
3. Sarah, 1736, Jan. 10.
4. Nathan, 1739, Apr. 12.
5. Pearce,
6. Tabitha,
(2d wife.)
7. William, 1748, Aug. 30.
8. James, 1750.
9. Joseph, 1756.
10. Benjamin, 1758.
11. Stephen, 1760.

1724. Freeman.

1763, Jan. 16. Will—proved 1763, Mar. 14. Ex. son John. To son John, all lands at Brush Neck, Warwick. To son Nathan, house and land where my son John lives. To son Pearce Budlong, land at Rocky Hill, Warwick. To sons William and James, three lots of land adjoining homestead, and rights at Otter Creek. To wife Renew, quarter of house and homestead while widow, and at her decease said quarter to be to sons Joseph, Benjamin and Stephen and the other three-quarters of homestead to these three sons at decease of testator. To sons John, Pearce, William and James, £500, each. To daughter Isabel Greene, wife of Elisha Greene, Jr., £500. To daughters Sarah and Tabitha Budlong, £500, each. To granddaughter Tabitha Greene, £50. To wife Renew, all household goods. His sons John, Nathan, Pearce, William, James, Benjamin and Stephen, to each help maintain their brother Joseph, who hath had the misfortune to lose his sight. To son John, daughter Isabel Greene, son Nathan, daughter Sarah Budlong, sons Pearce, William, James, daughter Tabitha and sons Joseph, Benjamin and Stephen, all the rest of personal estate.

Inventory, £14,269, 11*s.*, 6*d.*, viz: 15 Spanish milled dollars, 3½ pistareens, and 1 English shilling (in Old Tenor) £108, 12*s.*, wearing apparel £213, cash in Old Tenor and lawful money computed in Old Tenor (at the rate of 18⅓ for 1), £251, 6*s.*, bonds and notes £6,447, 17*s.*, 6*d.*, pewter, 6 large silver spoons, linen wheel, 2 churns, cider barrels, eel spear, 1,100lb. tobacco, large bible, &c., a black mare, bull, pair of oxen, pair of steers, 3 heifers, 2 yearlings, 3 calves, 9 cows, 47 sheep, 9 shoats, 18 fowls, &c.

1779, Feb. 4. Will—proved 1779, Sep. 13. Widow Renew. Exs., sons James and Stephen Budlong. To son William silver spoon marked I B R. To 2d son James, a feather bed and silver spoon and hetchel. To 3d son Benjamin, feather bed and silver spoon. To 4th son Stephen, great bible, feather bed, silver shoe buckles I now wear, three large silver spoons marked like others, gold buttons which I now wear in my sleeves, great hetchel, cow, colt, writing desk and other household furniture and a quarter of homestead farm given to my son Joseph by his father, which I recovered by law. To sons James, Benjamin and Stephen, rest of beds. To sons Benjamin and Stephen, all my stock of cows, a mare, sheep, a pair of oxen and young cattle. To Ruth Pearce, daughter of Pardon Pearce, gold necklace and feather bed and three silver tea spoons. To granddaughter Renew Moon, daughter to my son John Moon, note against her father. To granddaughter Tabitha Budlong, daughter of eldest son William, gold necklace and locket and three silver spoons. To granddaughter Phebe, daughter of William, gold ring. To granddaughters Ruth Pearce, Tabitha and Phebe Budlong, wearing apparel.

Inventory, £2,541, 9*s.*, 8*d.*, viz: 5 sheep, 2 fat sows, 2 heifers 2 cows, 2 oxen, 1 mare, &c.

II. REBECCA, b. 1700. d.
m. 1721, Nov. 26.
SAMUEL PIERCE, b. d. of Azrikim & Sarah (Hayward) Pierce.

1. Azrikim, 1723, May 27.
2. Sarah, 1725, Oct. 12.
3. Samuel, 1728, Mar. 16.
4. Rebecca, 1734, Jun. 17.
5. Freelove, 1736, Jan. 14.

III. MARY, b. 1706. d.
m. 1730, Jan. 8.
BENJAMIN PIERCE b. d of Azrikim & Sarah (Hayward) Pierce.

1. Benjamin, 1732, Jun. 1.
2. Pardon, 1735, Aug. 1.
3 Mary, 1737, Oct. 29.

IV. MOSES, b. 1708. d. 1789. Warwick, R. I.
m. (1) 1734, Jul. 4.
HANNAH STAPLES, b. d. of Samuel & Hannah ( ) Staples.
m. (2) 1780.
MARY DAVIS, b. d. 1789 + of Davis.

1. Samuel, 1736.
2. Moses, 1738.
3. Susannah, 1744.
4. Mary, 1750.
(3d wife.)
5. George, 1780.

1784, Sep. 10. Will—(not proved). Exs. wife Mary and friend Samuel Tillinghast. To son Samuel, a Spanish milled dollar. To son Moses, a Spanish milled dollar. To daughter Susannah Carder, a Spanish milled dollar. To granddaughter Waitstill Wood, two Spanish milled dollars. To eldest son of daughter Mary Wood, deceased, who should be living at his decease, a Spanish milled dollar. To wife Mary, all the rest of personal at her disposal, and use of all real till son George is of age. To son George, two-thirds of real estate in Warwick, he paying his mother my now wife, 200 Spanish milled dollars of which sum 100 was to be paid after he was of age, and other 100 in two years after he was of age. To wife Mary, the use of other third of real estate for life, and if son George died without issue she to have all real estate in Warwick.

1789, May 4. On presentment of will for probate it was objected to by sons Samuel and Moses who declared that when their father signed he was old and childish. The Council finally concluded not to approve will and the widow praying an appeal to Governor, the Council granted her appeal if she would give bond.

1781, Apr. 10. Will—proved 1789, Oct. 5, Exs. wife Mary and friend Benjamin Arnold. To wife Mary, use of real estate for life and then to such children as shall be born of her, and if none, then at her decease to my six grandchildren, viz: Moses, son of my son Samuel, Hannah, daughter of my son Samuel, Joseph, son of my son Moses, Hannah, daughter of my son Moses, William Wood, son of my daughter Mary Wood, deceased, and Welthian Webb, now wife of Jeremiah Webb, and daughter of my said daughter Mary, deceased. To wife Mary, all movables except wearing apparel. To sons Samuel and Moses, all wearing apparel, equally. To daughter Susannah Carder, five Spanish milled dollars. The two sons and daughter Susannah Carder, had no more because they had already received sufficient.

Inventory, £13, 15*s.*, 11*d.*, viz: cow, heifer, old linen wheel, wearing apparel 6*s.*

He was buried on his farm.

V. DANIEL, b. d. 1795. Warwick, R. I., Voluntown, Ct.
m.
REBECCA DAVIS, b. 1722. d. 1802, Mar. 1. of Davis.

1. Daniel, 1741.
2. Rosanna, 1742.
3. Joseph, 1750.
4. Benjamin, 1758.
5. John, 1760.
6. David, 1763.
7. Aaron, 1766.

He was an Elder in the Baptist church.

He lived in Warwick and Coventry, R. I., Preston and Voluntown, Ct., and perhaps moved finally to New York state.

His widow died at Oneida, N. Y., and was buried in her sons' lot there.

VI. ISABEL, b. d.

BULL (HENRY).

I. JIREH, b. 1659. d. 1709, Jul. 16. Newport, R. I.
m. (1)
GODSGIFT ARNOLD, b. 1658, Aug. 27. d. 1691, Apr. 23. of Benedict & Damaris (Westcott) Arnold.
m. (2)
SARAH, b. d. of

1. Jireh, 1682, Oct. 18
2. Benjamin, 1685, Sep. 5.
3. Benedict, 1687, May 1.

See: American Genealogist, Apr., 1954, v. 30, no. 2, p. 124.

He was a cordwainer.

1682. Freeman.

1685, Dec. 5. He, calling himself eldest son of Jireth Bull, of Kings Town, deceased, made an agreement with his brothers Henry, Ephraim and Ezekiel Bull. He disposes of all his interest in housing and 92 acres in Kings Town, where their father had lived, together with 500 acres westward from aforesaid housing commonly called Jireth Bull's farm, to said three brothers, always provided that I for my heirs enjoy my grandfather Bull's farm after his decease, adjoining to my farm in Newport, but if in case said Jireth or heirs shall not enjoy said farm nor it should be bequeathed me or my heirs, then (notwithstanding a bond of £1,000 which he binds himself for to his three brothers) he and aforesaid brothers are to equally divide amongst us all the land of our deceased father in Kings Province, Narragansett, but if my grandfather bequeaths his said farm unto me or my heirs then the above said bond to be of full force.

1687. Constable.

1698. Sheriff.

1699, Sep. 26. He was forty years old at this date.

1702, Jan. 12. He was a proprietor in the common lands.

1703, Nov. 13. He and wife Sarah and Jireh, Jr., son and heir of Godsgift Arnold, late wife of said Jireh, Sr., sold certain land to Stephen Hookey, for £105.

1704, Aug. 18. He deeded his son Jireh Bull, blockmaker, certain land in Newport, for love, &c,

the King of Kings and Lord of Lords and to all those perfect and most absolute laws of his given us in his holy word of truth, to be guided and judged thereby."

1638, Mar. 12. He and others, having had license to depart from Massachusetts were ordered by that government to appear (if they had not gone before) at the next court to answer such things as shall be objected.

1638, Jun. 27. He was present at a General Meeting held at Portsmouth, upon public notice.

1638. Corporal of the Train Band.

1639, Jan. 24. Sergeant. The duties of the office at this time included the keeping of the prison. At the same date it was ordered that the prison should be finished and that it be set near or joined unto the house of Henry Bull.

1639, Apr. 28. He and eight others signed the following compact preparatory to the settlement of Newport. "It is agreed by us whose hands are underwritten, to propagate a plantation in the midst of the island or elsewhere, and to engage ourselves to bear equal charge, answerable to our strength and estates in common; and that our determination shall be by major voices of Judge and Elders, the Judge to have a double voice." He signed as Elder, the Judge being William Coddington.

1640–41–42. Newport. Sergeant.

1641, Mar. 16. Freeman.

1655. Freeman.

1655–57. Commissioner.

1663, Dec. 12. He and son Jireh sold Caleb Carr 43 acres in Conanicut and rights there and at Dutch Island.

1665, Oct. 1. The Friends' records of Portsmouth give the death of his first wife as occurring at this date, while the Friends' records of Sandwich give the date of his marriage to his second wife Esther Allen as 1665, Feb. 14. One of these dates was evidently erroneously recorded (unless the possibility be admitted that Henry Bull had a son Henry who married Esther Allen and died without issue).

1666–72–73–74–79–80–81–90. Deputy.

1671. Juryman.

1674–75. Assistant.

1685–86–90. Governor.

1688, Nov. 27. He deeded for love, &c., to grandchildren Christopher and Elizabeth Allen, of Little Compton, 26 acres there and 7 negroes (two men, a woman and four children).

1692, Feb. 16. He bought of Edward Richmond, of Little Compton, for £80, a tract of 120 acres there, for the use and behoof of Henry and Ann Richmond the two youngest children of said Edward, together with housing, garden, &c., reserving to Edward Richmond and wife Amey; the whole profits for life. In this deed Edward Richmond calls him father-in-law, grandfather of my two youngest children.

1694, Jan. 22. The Friends' records make the following mention of his death. "Henry Bull aged about eighty-four years, he departed this life at his own house in Newport (he being the last man of the first settlers of this Rhode Island) ye 22d 11mo. 1693–4."

1703, Jan. 29. His widow deeded to her kinswoman Sarah Borden, wife of Matthew, of Portsmouth, all household stuff, goods, chattels, &c., in my house at Newport, formerly dwelling place of deceased husband Henry Bull. She calls herself of Newport, now residing in Portsmouth.

1709, Mar. 2. The executors of his will, viz: Daniel Gould, Thomas Cornell and Benjamin Newbury, rendered an account, from which it appears that the inventory was £968, 1s., consisting of money, plate, cattle, sheep, household goods and accounts. The payments were to widow, &c., as follows. To widow Ann, a legacy and what was owing her for milk, her choice of six cows, fifty sheep, mare, colt, three feather beds, a quarter of the pewter, roan horse given her by children, allowance for a family of four persons for one year according to husband's will, and sundry things challenged by her as her own by agreement before marriage. The funeral charges were £10, 7s., 8d. The legacy to overseers, £10. Mary Coggeshall's legacy (wife of James), £50. Henry and Ann Richmond's legacy, £60, Jireh, Ephraim and Ezekiel Bull and Mary Coggeshall, £124. The children of Henry Bull, in Narragansett, their fifth of money in overseer's hands. Elizabeth Allen's legacy four young cattle and forty sheep. The three grandsons had the wearing apparel.

He was buried in the Coddington burial ground.

1675, Dec. 16. Hubbard in his account of the Indian wars, says: "Captain Prentice with his troop being sent to Pettaquamscut, returned with the sad news of burning of Jerry Bull's Garrison house and killing ten English men and five women and children, but two escaping in all."

1676. Lieutenant.

1676, Apr. 4. Newport. He was on a committee with three others to take exact account of the inhabitants on the island, English, negroes and Indians, and also to take account how all persons are provided with corn, guns, powder shot and lead.

1676, Aug. 24. He was a member of the Court Martial held at Newport for the trial of certain Indians charged with being engaged in King Philip's designs.

1679, Jul. 29. Kings Town. He and forty-one other inhabitants of Narragansett sent a petition to the King praying "that he would put an end to these differences about the government thereof which hath been so fatal to the prosperity of the place, animosities still arising in people's minds as they stand affected to this or that government."

1683. He had services held at his house on Pettaquamscutt Hill, by Rev. Mr. Spear, minister of the Church of England (as deposed by Henry Gardiner in 1738).

1713, Aug. 16. Administration on estate of Katharine Bull was granted Peleg Mumford. Inventory, £30, 16s., 5d. (She may have been the widow of Jireh Bull.)

BULL (HENRY). 2d column. Perhaps II. Elizabeth, m. (1), —— Bacon; m. (2), 1650, Oct. 14, John Allen. He d. 1708 Oct. 30. Children, 1. Elizabeth, 1651, Jul. 2. Mary, 1653, Feb. 4. 3. John, 1654, Nov. 4. Mercy, 1656, Dec. 5. Priscilla, 1659, Dec. 6. Samuel, 1661, Apr. 7. Christopher, 1664. If II. Elizabeth made these two marriages she must have been earlier born than her brother Jireh, and changes should be made in Allen, Robinson, and Tompkins pages. 3d column. IV. Ephraim. His widow m. 1724, Aug. 27, Job Card.

II. { DAUGHTER, { b.
m. { d.
—— ALLEN, { b.
{ d. of Allen.

III. { AMEY, { b.
m. { d.
EDWARD RICHMOND, { b. 1632.
{ d. 1696. of John Richmond.

(2D and 3D WIVES, no issue.)

BURTON.

{ WILLIAM, { b. Providence, R. I.
m. (1) { d. 1714, Feb. 20.
HANNAH WICKES, { b. 1634.
{ d.
of John & Mary ( ) Wickes.
m. (2) 1701 ± { b.
ISABEL MOSS (widow), { d. 1724, Aug. 26.
of Robert & Isabel ( ) Potter.

He lived at "Mashantatack" (north side of Pawtuxet River).

1668, Feb. 1. He and wife Hannah of Mashantatack, sold for £35, to John Gorton, a house, orchard, &c., now in my possession in Warwick.

1680, May 17. He and wife Hannah had a deed from John Wickes of certain land for life, and then to go to grantor's cousin (*i. e.* nephew) John Burton, son to said William and Hannah. The grantor calls William Burton his brother-in-law.

1687, Sep. 1. Taxed 4s.

1688. Grand Jury.

1701, Dec. 15. He being about to be married to Isabel Moss, now of Warwick, made an agreement with her as to their estates.

1703, Mar. 20. Will—codicil 1713, Jul. 8.—proved 1714, Jun. 25. Ex. son John. Overseers, Captain James Greene and Lieutenant James Carder. To wife Isabella, house, and all lands during widowhood and half the stock of cattle, sheep and swine, and all household goods, &c., for life, while widow. To only son John, at decease of mother, all housing and lands and all household goods; and to him, half the stock of cattle, &c., and all real and personal estate not otherwise disposed of. To son-in-law Samuel Gorton and wife Susannah, £10. To granddaughter Mary Curbit, £10, at

I. { ELIZABETH, { b.
m. 1674, Oct. 30. { d.
THOMAS HEDGER, { b.
{ d. of Hedger.

II. { DAUGHTER, { b.
m. { d.
—— CURBIT, { b.
{ d. of Curbit.

III. { HANNAH, { b.
m. { d. 1726 (—)
TIMOTHY CARPENTER, { b.
{ d. 1726, Aug. 19. of William & Elizabeth (Arnold) Carpenter.

IV. { ROSE, { b.
m. { d.
—— FOWLER, { b.
{ d. of Fowler.

V. { ETHALANNAH, { b.
m. { d.
—— CLARKE, { b.
{ d. of Clarke.

VI. { SUSANNAH, { b. 1665.
m. (1) 1684, Dec. 11. { d. 1737, Jun. 25.
SAMUEL GORTON, { b. 1630.
m. (2) { d. 1724, Sep. 6. of Samuel & Elizabeth ( ) Gorton.
RICHARD HARRIS, { b. 1668, Oct. 14.
{ d. 1750. of Thomas & Elnathan (Tew) Harris.

1709, Aug. 1. His son Jireh Bull, Jr., mariner, having lately deceased at the Cape de Verde Islands, administration was granted to Benjamin and Benedict Bull, brothers of deceased.

1709, Sep. 15. The account of funeral charges of Jireh Bull (who deceased at Newport, 1709, Jul. 16), was presented by Benjamin Bull. Among the items were ten gallons of wine, two gallons of rum, twelve pounds of sugar, four ounces of clove, one ounce of cinnamon, &c.

II. MARY, m. JAMES COGGESHALL, — b. 1663. d. 1754, Jun. 13. — b. 1660. Feb. 18. d. 1712, Apr. 2. of John & Patience (Throckmorton) Coggeshall.

No issue.

III. HENRY, m. ANN COLE, — b. d. 1691 ± — b. 1661, Mar. 7. d. 1704, May 31. of John & Susanna (Hutchinson) Cole. Kings Town, R. I.

1. Henry, 1687, Nov. 23.
2. Ephraim, 1690, Jan. 23.
3. Ann, 1690, Jan. 23.

He was called Henry Bull, Jr., to distinguish him from his grandfather.

1687. Grand Jury.

1690, Mar 3. Conservator of the Peace.

1704. Inventory of Ann Bull, widow, was filed at Kings Town, 7 cows, 7 two year old, a bull, yearlings, sheep. 2 sows, chest, trunk, brass kettle, pillion, old warming pan, &c.

His widow was buried in Newport Cemetery.

BULL (HENRY). 3d column. IV. Ephraim. In will change son John to Ephraim, and have will read "to wife and her four abovesaid daughters the east end," &c. Children by 2d wife. 4. Ephraim, 1702, Apr. 18. 5. Hannah, 1702, Apr. 18. 6. Amey, 1706.

IV. EPHRAIM, m. (1) 1692, Oct. 27. MARY COGGESHALL, m. (2) 1700, Jun. 20. HANNAH HOLWAY, — b. 1669. d. 1721. — b. 1662, Mar. 10. d. 1699, Dec. 2. of John & Patience (Throckmorton) Coggeshall. — b. 1667, Mar. 1. d. 1721 + of Holway. Kings Town, R. I.

1. Mary, 1693, Jul. 30.
2. Rebecca, 1697, Jul. 27.
3. Content, 1699, Nov. 24.
4. Amey, 1699, Nov. 24.
(2d wife.)
5. Ephraim, 1702, Apr. 18.
6. Hannah, 1702, Apr. 18.
7. Daughter,
8. Daughter,
9. Daughter,

1687, Sep. 6. Taxed 5*s*., 7*d*.

1694, Mar. 12. He had a deed from his brother Jireh Bull, of Newport, of all that tract of land in Narragansett formerly part of the land of our deceased father Jireh Bull, Sr., bounded partly by land of Ezekiel Bull.

1701. Town Clerk.

1718, Sep. 4. He called himself aged about forty-nine years in a deposition at this date.

1721, Feb. 14. Will—proved 1721, Jun. 12. Ex. son Ephraim. Overseers, friends, Rouse Helme and Abiel Sherman, and they to be executors till son John is of age. To wife Hannah, her choice of two houses on west part of farm (one the house I now dwell in and the other near it) while widow, and then to return to my son Ephraim. To wife and son Ephraim and my four daughters, Mary, Rebecca, Content and Amey, the movable estate, equally divided. To wife and her four daughters, the east end of farm during their lives but not to their heirs. When wife and all said daughters die, the land to go to son Ephraim or his heirs. To son Ephraim, the upper western part of farm with housing, orchard, &c.

Inventory, £355, 5*s*, 9*d*., viz: 25 grains of gold, 26 ounces silver money, gun, pewter, warming pan, silver cup, bible and 8 other books, silver spoon, bonds, 8 cows, 3 yearlings, 4 calves, a two year old, 2 mares, 2 colts, a swine, 72 sheep, 42 lambs, &c.

V. EZEKIEL, m. ELIZABETH, — b. 1671. d. 1727, Sep. 7. — b. 1669. d. 1726, Feb. 19. of Kings Town, Newport, R. I.

1. Elizabeth, 1708, Jul. 1.
2. Nathan, 1711, Nov. 30.

1687, Sep. 6. Taxed 1*s*.

1693, Nov. 21. He sold Joseph Case for £90, all my farm in Pettaconsett, containing 260 acres, buildings, orchard, &c., bounded partly by land of brother Ephraim, the which land I had of brother Jireh Bull (as appeareth by bill of sale bearing date 1693, Jan. 23).

1704. Newport. Freeman.

1713, Oct. 21. He and Mary Coggeshall made declaration as to wishes of Rouse Helme, deceased.

He and his wife were buried in Newport Cemetery.

1. Christopher,
2. Elizabeth,

1. Henry,
2. Ann,

BURTON.

1. Mary,

1. Ethalannah,
2. Elizabeth,
3. Hannah,
4. Timothy,
5. William,

1. Samuel, 1690, Jun. 1.
2. Hezekiah, 1692, Jun. 11.
3. Susannah, 1694, Jun. 4.
(By 2d husband, no issue.)

eighteen. To eldest daughter Elizabeth Hedger, £5. To daughter Hannah Carpenter, £5. To daughter Rose Fowler, £5. To daughter Ethalannah Clarke, £5. The codicil explains that the half of cattle to wife were intended for her life only and then to son John, and augments legacies as follows: To Susannah, £12. To Mary Curbit, £12. To Hannah, Elizabeth, Ethalannah and Rose, £8, each.

Inventory, £111, 8s, viz: 1 pair oxen, 5 cows, 3 calves, ½ interest in 6 other cattle, 24 sheep, 7 swine, 1 old mare, pewter, brass, flax, feather bed, flock bed, warming pan, books, 3 pair of cards, linen wheel, &c.

1722, Jan. 26. Will—proved 1724, Sep. 15. Widow Isabel of Warwick. Ex. Fones Greene. To sons of Captain James Greene, viz: Elisha, John, and Jeremiah, 20s. each and to Samuel, 30s. To Deliverance Holden, daughter of above said Captain James Greene, my biggest silver beer cup, a silver spoon, 3 pewter platters, tankard and feather bed. To Mary, daughter of Captain James Greene, 3 platters, biggest silver dram cup and silver spoon. To John Budlong and his wife, 14s. To mulatto woman Jane, a feather bed, worsted combs, a spinning wheel and her freedom. To Fones Greene, eldest son of Captain James Greene, all the rest.

Inventory, £243, 1s.

VII. JOHN, m. MARY, — b. 1667, May 2. d. 1749, Jul. 15. — b. d. 1768, Dec. 29. of — Providence, R. I.

(She m. (2) Benjamin Searle.)

1702. He gave 3s. toward building Quaker meeting house at Mashapaug.

1716. Deputy.

1749, Jan. 23. Will—proved 1749, Sep. 2. Exs. wife Mary and son William. To wife, use of dwelling house at Chestnut Hill while widow, with small orchard, meadow, &c., and ½ of cattle, sheep and swine, and my mare and all household goods, all while widow for her use. If she marry to have a feather bed and 1 chest and £10, per year paid her by sons William and John, each £5. To son John, all the above homestead at death or marriage of widow. To son William, the homestead farm where my honored father William, late of said Providence, deceased, dwelt at Mashantatack, and also a piece of land between Quaker Meeting House and Mashantatack meadow, &c., and 50 acres in another place. To each son, a bed. The stock to be equally divided between sons William and John, as also other movable estate at death of wife. To grandson John, son of John, £100, at age.

Inventory, £2,512, 9s. 1d., viz: a horse, mare, colt, 5 cows, 3 two year, 3 yearlings, a calf, 5 shoats, a negro man and his apparel £300, carpenter's tools, books, silver money £5, 10s., plate £12. Bonds £735, 14s. 10d., 3 feather beds, a flock bed, yarn, silver bowed spectacles, screw press, apple mill, &c.

His widow married Benjamin Searle, of Edward & Ann ( ) Searle.

1759, Nov. 29. Will—proved 1768, Dec. 31. Widow Mary Searle, of Cranston. Exs. sons William and John Burton. To son William, part of estate and equal portion to daughter Persis Burton, granddaughter Mary Baker, grandson Benjamin Burton, grandson William Burton, Jr., son John Burton, daughter Mary Burton, grandson John Burton, Jr., granddaughter Dinah Harris, granddaughter Mary Burton, grandson Benjamin Burton, grandson David Burton, granddaughter Elizabeth Burton, grandson George Burton and grandson Rufus Burton.

(2D WIFE, no issue.)

CADMAN. See: American Genealogist, v. 20, p. 182-183.

WILLIAM, m. ELIZABETH, — b. d. 1684 ± — b. d. 1688 + — Portsmouth, R. I.

1659, Aug. 23. He complained to Assembly for want of money due from one Quissuckquoanch, his men, by judgment of the General Court at Providence in March last, which is not yet paid. The Court do request the President to cause demand of satisfaction from Quissuckquoanch according to justice in both the former cases, and further to signify him that if he do it not the court will take a speedy course to force him to do it, which will prove troublesome to him.

1667. Juryman.

1670–72–72–74–79–82. Deputy.

1671. He was on a committee of four persons to go to Governor Nicholas Easton and demand and receive the charter and other writings, and give a receipt.

1672–76–82–83. Assistant.

1673, Aug. 13. He and four others were appointed a committee to prepare matters for the Assembly concerning the Indians' drunkenness, encouragement of the militia, the danger we are in by the late enterprize of the Dutch taking New York, &c.

1674, May 18. He was on a committee to receive charter from the late Governor Nicholas Easton.

1674. Town Council.

1674. Overseer of the Poor.

1676, Apr. 11. He was one of the commissioners appointed "to take care and order the several watches and wards on this island and appoint the places."

1676, Aug. 24. He was a member of the Court Martial held at Newport for the trial of certain Indians charged with being engaged in King Philip's designs.

He held the office of Lieutenant several years.

1682, Jun. 28. He deeded son George of Dartmouth, half a share there, for love, &c.

1684, Jan. 11. He was appointed one of the overseers of the will of Hugh Parsons.

1688, Sep. 22. His widow Elizabeth joined in the deed made by her son Richard at this date.

I. GEORGE, m. HANNAH HATHAWAY, — b. d. 1718, Nov. 24. — b. d. 1718 + of Arthur & Sarah (Cook) Hathaway. — Portsmouth, R. I., Dartmouth, Mass.

1676. Juryman.

1684, Sep. 24. Dartmouth. He was on a committee to lay out a way through the town.

1686, May 24. His name is in a list of inhabitants of this date.

1686. Surveyor of Highways.

1688. He was named in the suit of Wood et al *versus* the Proprietors.

1692. Grand Jury.

1692–94–96. Selectman.

1694, Nov. 13. He and others had a confirmatory deed made to them of Dartmouth, by William Bradford.

1698–1709–11. Treasurer.

1710, Feb. 9. His wife Hannah had a legacy of 5s. from her father Arthur Hathaway's will of this date.

1712, Jun. 2. He had surveyed to him 512 acres.

1712. Overseer of the Poor.

1718, Nov. 24. Will—proved 1719, Jan 6. Exx. wife Hannah. To wife, all homestead farm and housing till grandson George is twenty-one, and then to said grandson half of the farm on north side, and wife to have south half and housing for life, and at her death that also to go to grandson George. To daughter Elizabeth White and her husband William White, land where they live, &c., for life, and at their death the part where William White lives to go to grandson William White, another part to grandson Roger White, and the rest to grandson Christopher White. To four grandsons William, George, Roger and Christopher, other lands, half at my death and the other half at death of their father and mother. To granddaughter Sarah White, £20. To Alice Anthony, daughter of John Anthony, of Rhode Island. £5, bed, &c. To negro man James, his freedom at thirty-three years. To daughter Elizabeth White, £30. To wife Hannah, the rest of personal.

Inventory, £2,282, 5s. 4d., viz: homestead £1,700, silver money and books £22, 17s. 2d., 7 horsekind, 24 neat cattle, 35 sheep, 5 swine, rum, cider, case of bottles £4, 16s., &c.

II. RICHARD, m. SARAH ALMY, — b. d. 1695 (—) — b. 1662, Apr. 17. d. 1708 (—) of Christopher & Elizabeth (Cornell) Almy. — Portsmouth, R. I.

(She m. (2) Jonathan Merihew.)

1684. Freeman.

1688, Sep. 22. He and wife Sarah sold to Robert Fish for £140, a piece of land containing 28 acres, with house, barn, orchards, &c.

CADMAN. 2d column I. George. His widow Hannah, d. 1749. 1749. Feb. 13. Will—proved 1749, May 2. Ex. grandson William White. She mentions her daughter Elizabeth White, wife of William White, and grandchildren, William, George, Roger, Christopher, Oliver, Thomas and Susanna White, Sarah Brown (wife of John, of Tiverton) and Hannah Taber (wife of William, of Dartmouth). She also mentions great-grandchildren Hannah and Mary Slocum, children of granddaughter Elizabeth Slocum.

I. { WILLIAM, m. 1722, Feb. 8. PERSIS BURLINGAME, { b. d. 1773, Jan. 8. b. 1703, Aug. 14. d. 1772, Jun. 22. of Providence, Cranston, R. I. Burlingame.

1. George, 1722, Nov. 3.
2. Mary, 1724, Dec. 24.
3. Anne, 1726, Nov. 11.
4. Elizabeth, 1728, Jan. 24.
5. William, 1731, Feb. 1.
6. Patience, 1733, Jan. 12.
7. George, 1735, Jul. 20.
8. Tabitha, 1737, Jan. 26.
9. Benjamin, 1739, Nov. 4.
10. William, 1743, May 16.
11. James, 1745, Sep. 7.
12. Son, 1748, Nov. 7.

1735–42. Deputy.

1740, Mar. 11. He and wife Persis sold Joseph Jenckes, Jr., 28 acres and 20 rods with house, &c., for £300.

1743–44–48–49–50. Assistant.

1758. Cranston. Deputy.

1772, Sep. 10. Will—proved 1773, Jan. 23. Ex. son William. To son Benjamin, wearing apparel (with exceptions). To sons Benjamin and William, farming tackling and yoke of oxen equally. To grandson John Anthony Burton, a bed. To three children, viz: Benjamin and William Burton and Mary Baker, all rest of movables. To son Benjamin, house in which he lives. To son William, use of my dwelling house, and at his decease equally to the male heirs of my son Benjamin, viz: John Anthony, Benoni, Edmond and Gideon; but if son William have male issue then said son William and his heirs to have it. To sons Benjamin and William, use and profits of rest of real estate, for life, and at the decease of Benjamin his half to go to his heirs male, and the half of son William also to go at his decease to male heirs of Benjamin unless William have issue.

Inventory, £139, 18*s.* 8*d.*, viz: wearing apparel £12, 10*s.* 6*d.*, pewter, 123 silver buttons, 1 pair silver shoe buckles, 2 large silver spoons, notes £49, 18*s.* 9*d.*, books 6*s.*, gun, sword, stillyards, 2 woolen wheels, 2 foot wheels, cheese tub, churn, yoke of oxen, 2 cows, 10 sheep, 4 case bottles, punch bowl, &c.

II. { JOHN, m. MARY, { b. d. 1799. b. d. 1768, Sep. 9. of Providence, Cranston, R. I.

1. John, 1733, Sep. 8.
2. Joseph, 1735, Sep. 19.
3. Dinah, 1737, Sep. 30.
4. Mary, 1740, Jan. 12.
5. Hannah, 1742, Jun. 18.
6. David, 1744, Aug. 30.
7. Caleb, 1746, Oct. 15.
8. Elizabeth, 1749, Jan. 24.
9. George, 1751, Sep. 11.
10. Rufus, 1753, Nov. 29.
11. Hannah,

1744. Deputy.

1762. Cranston. Deputy.

1766. Assistant.

1799, Feb. 20. Will—proved 1799, Mar. 9. Exs. son Rufus and grandson George. To son John, £100, and privilege of cutting two tons hay in a certain meadow, as long as he lives on same farm. To two grandsons (sons of John), viz: Joseph and John, £50, each. To four grandsons (sons of David, deceased), viz: Amos, John T., Charles and Nathan, £600, equally divided. To great grandson (son of grandson Caleb Burton, deceased), viz: George Burton, £150, at age, and if he die to go to his surviving sisters. To daughter-in-law Rosannah Burton, widow of son George, deceased, use of homestead farm where I live with buildings, &c., while widow of George, and a cow. To grandson George Burton (son of George), my homestead farm, &c., when his mother Rosannah ceases to be widow. To grandson George, also, a large chest, flock bed, all wearing apparel, cow and pair of stags. To five granddaughters (daughters of Thomas Baker), viz: Sarah Searle, Lydia Ellis, Amey Dexter, Mary and Elizabeth Baker, £300, equally. To son Rufus and grandson George, all farming tools, &c. To Phebe Clemmens, wife of John Clemmens, feather bed, case drawers, table, and £100. To daughter Dinah Harris, rest of household goods and £300. To Benoni Burton, of Pownal, Vt., £50. To sons John and Rufus and grandson George, all books equally. To great grandson William Brayton, son of Lodowick, £50. To son Rufus, rest of cattle, horses and sheep. To son Rufus and grandson George, rest of estate both real and personal.

CADMAN.

I. { ELIZABETH, m. WILLIAM WHITE, { b. d. b. d. of White.

1. William,
2. George,
3. Roger,
4. Christopher,
5. Sarah,

I. { WILLIAM, m. AMEY, { b. d. 1760. b. d. 1764 + of Dartmouth, Mass.

1. Sarah, 1707, Feb. 21.
2. Richard, 1712, Jun. 3.
3. William, 1715, Oct. 26.
4. Christopher, 1717, Sep. 4.
5. George, 1722, Jul. 6.
6. Edward, 1725, May 28.

1748, Apr. 21. Will—proved 1760, May 6. Ex. son George. To wife Amey, bed, side saddle, worsted comb, use of a third of homestead farm, so much of dwelling house as she needs, and household goods and money, a good cow and a riding beast. To son Richard, all land in Tiverton and £200. To son Christopher, farm where he lives with housing. To son George, a farm, he making certain payments. To son Edward, all my homestead where I live. To daughter Sarah Davol, £80. To five children Richard, Christopher, George, Edward and Sarah, rest of personal estate.

Inventory, £102, 3*s.* 17*d.*, viz: apparel £6, 2*s.*, money £21, 11*s.* 7*d.*, cow, mare, horse, pewter, spinning wheel, worsted comb, real estate £30, &c.

1765, Apr. 20. His son George, schoolmaster, died at Portsmouth, administration being given to Christopher, brother to said George.

1765, Oct. 30. His son Christopher's will was proved (made 1764, Feb. 16) at Portsmouth. He mentions honored mother Amey, who is to be maintained by wife Hannah. He also mentions sons William, Alpheus, Gideon, daughters Mary, Amey, Deborah, Ruth and wife Hannah.

II. { CHRISTOPHER, m. MARY, { b. 1686. d. 1716, Jul. 12. b. 1693. d. 1780, Sep. 3. of Newport, R. I.

CADMAN. 3d column. II. Christopher. He was a mariner. 1712, Mar. 19. Will-proved 1716. Exx., wife Mary. He mentions two youngest brothers and sister, John and Thomas Merithew, and Rebecca Cadman, who were to have £10 each if executrix have no living issue.

(She m. (2) 1718, Feb. 6, Gideon Wanton.)

He was buried in Clifton Burying Ground at Newport.

III. { ELIZABETH, { b. d.

IV. { REBECCA, { b. d.

 See: American Genealogist, v. 20, p. 183-184. v. 32, p. 33. Jan. 1956

CARD.

RICHARD, m. —— | b. d. | b. d. 1674 + | Newport, R. I.

1655. Freeman.

It is assumed that he was the father of John, Joseph, Job and James.

CARD. 2d column. II. Joseph d. 1729. Children, I. Ann. II. Elisha. III. Joseph. IV. Edward. V. Mary. VI. Elizabeth. 1717, Jun. 19. Will-proved, 1729, Nov. 3. He mentions sons Elisha and Joseph, daughters, Ann Sweet, Mary Phillips and Elizabeth Arnold; grandchildren, Edward Card and Jane Sisson. III. Job. Put Job (3d column in this place. He m. (2) 1724, Aug. 27, Hannah Bull (w. of Ephraim), b. 1667, Mar. 1, of —— Holway.

There is a more accurate Card gen. in the N.E. Hist. & Gen. Reg. Volume 83 pp 89 ff.

I. JOHN, [garde] m. (1) ~~MARTHA BRENTON,~~ m. (2) MARTHA, | b. d. 1705. | b. d. 1667 (—) of William & Martha (Burton) Brenton. | b. d. 1705 + of | Portsmouth, Kings Town, R. I.

~~1664-65-66-67.~~ Deputy.

~~1664, Mar.~~ 1. He was fined 12*d*., for not appearing at eight of the clock as Deputy, but upon consideration as he and certain others were employed as a commission on the court's business and thereby have broken the laws, the court sees fit to remit the fine.

~~1664, May 4.~~ He was named as next to William Brenton, Deputy Governor, and next to three Assistants first named in case of inability of any of them to serve.

~~1665-66.~~ Assistant.

1687, Sep. 6. Kings Town. Taxed 1*s*., 9*d*.

1705. Administration to widow Martha.

CARD. 2d column. II. Joseph, b. 1648, d. 1729, Oct.

II. JOSEPH, m. JANE, | b. d. 1708 + | b. d. of | Newport, R. I.

1671, May 2. Freeman.

1674, Jul. 1. He had the bounds of 60 acres recorded, being near land given Job Card and now owned by his mother.

1680. Taxed £1, 2*s*., 9*d*.

1680, Mar. 16. He petitioned Assembly for remission of fine of 20*s*., for not attending court on a jury two years before: "and he pleading illness and sickness at that time, this Assembly do remit the said Joseph Card's fine."

1702, Mar. 4. He was one of the shareholders in Proprietors' lands.

1707, Jan. 23. He and other members of the Second Baptist Church received a deed from their pastor James Clarke of land and church building, which had been paid for by Mr. Clarke from contributions of members of the church.

III. JOB, | b. d.

IV. JAMES, | b. d. | Newport, R. I.

1675. Freeman.

1680. Taxed 5*s*.

CARDER.

RICHARD, m. (1) —— m. (2) MARY, | b. d. 1676 ± | b. d. | b. d. 1691. | Boston, Mass., Portsmouth, Warwick, R. I.

1636, May 25. Freeman.

1637, Nov. 20. He with others was ordered to deliver up all guns, pistols, swords, powder, shot, &c., the court declaring that "the opinions and revelations of Mr. Wheelwright and Mrs. Hutchinson have seduced and led into dangerous errors many of the people here in New England."

1638, Mar. 7. Portsmouth. He was one of the nineteen signers of following compact: "We whose names are underwritten do here solemnly in the presence of Jehovah incorporate ourselves into a Bodie Politick, and as he shall help will submit our persons, lives and estates unto our Lord Jesus Christ, the King of Kings, and Lord of Lords, and to all those perfect and most absolute laws of his, given us in his holy word of truth to be guided and judged thereby."

1638, Jun. 27. He was present at a general meeting of inhabitants.

1640, Feb. 18. He had 30 acres confirmed.

1641, Mar. 16. He and three others were disfranchised and their names cancelled from the roll of freeman.

1642, Mar. 17. It was ordered that if he and four others came upon the island armed, they should be disarmed and give surety for good behavior. The same year he and others desiring to be re-united "are readily embraced by us."

1643, Jan. 12. Warwick. He and ten others bought of Miantonomi, for 144 fathoms of wampum, tract of land called Shawomet (Warwick).

1643, Sep. 12. He with others of Warwick was notified to appear at General Court at Boston to hear complaint of two Indian sachems, Pomham and Socconocco, as to "some unjust and injurious dealing toward them by yourselves." The Warwick men declined to obey the summons, declaring that they were legal subjects of the King of England and beyond the limits of Massachusetts territory, to whom they would acknowledge no subjection. Soldiers were soon sent who besieged the settlers in a fortified house. In

I. SUSANNA, m. 1663, Mar. 14. NATHANIEL WATERMAN, | b. d. | b. 1637. d. 1712, Mar. 23. of Richard & Bethiah ( ) Waterman.

(2D WIFE.)

II. JOHN, m. (1) 1671, Dec. 1. MARY HOLDEN, m. (2) HANNAH, | b. d. 1700, Oct. ~~26.~~ 27 | b. 1654, Aug. d. Feb. 9, 1689/90 of Randall & Frances (Dungan) Holden. | b. d. 1700 + of [m. Mar. 31, 1607] | Warwick, R. I.

1678-96. Deputy.

1700, Sep. 13. Will—proved 1700, Nov. 23. Ex. son John. Overseers, friend Benjamin Barton and brother James Carder. To wife Hannah, one-third of movables, use of lower rooms of dwelling house, buttery, cellar privilege, &c., and a third of meadows, pasture, and orchard, while widow. She to bring up two youngest children Sarah and Joseph. To son John, housing, homestead, &c., half of right at Mashantatack and use of all lands in Warwick, till my son William is twenty-one. To son William, land near Rocky Point and half right at Mashantatack. To sons Richard and Joseph, land at Natick and meadow at Toseunk, &c. To four sons, equal privilege in common lands for wood, &c. To daughter Mary Greene, land and £5. To son Richard, £5. To son William, £5, at age. To daughter Sarah, £10, at eighteen. To son Joseph, £5, at twenty-one.

CARD.

I. JOHN, b. d. — Kings Town, R. I.

1687, Sep. 6. Taxed 1*s*.

CARD. 3d column. I. Job, m. (2) 1724, Aug. 27, Hannah Bull, of Ephraim and Hannah (Holway) Bull, b. 1702, April 18.

I. JOB, b. d. 1739. — New Shoreham, Charlestown, R. I.
m. (1) 1689, Nov.
MARTHA ACRES, b. 1668, Feb. 26. d. of John & Margery ( ) Acres.
m. (2)
HANNAH, b. d. 1731 + of

1. Job, 1690, Sep. 2.
2. Rebecca, 1694, May 4.
3. Martha, 1699, Apr. 6.
4. Margery, 1701, Feb. 19.
5. Jane, 1703, Sep. 18.
6. Sarah, 1705, Aug. 9.
(2d wife, no issue.)

1688. New Shoreham. Licensed
1706. Town Clerk.
1708–9. Deputy.
1731. Will—proved 1739. Ex. son Job. He mentions wife Hannah, and alludes to agreement made with her before marriage. The children named were son Job, daughters Rebecca Tosh, Margery Foster, Sarah Sheffield, Martha Rathbone and Jane Sheffield, wife of Isaac. His daughter Sarah had previously been married to a Rathbone. He mentions several grandchildren.

II. ANN, b. d.
m. 1701, Jul. 17.
RICHARD SISSON, b. 1676, Sep. 10. d. 1752. of George & Sarah (Lawton) Sisson.

1. George, 1702, Mar. 30.
2. Sarah, 1703, Oct. 1.
3. Joseph, 1705, Jan. 27.
4. Jane, 1706, Jul. 5.
5. Richard, 1708, Feb. 25.
6. Job, 1711, Oct. 28.
7. Ann, 1714, Mar. 26.
8. John, 1716, Jan. 5.
9. Mary, 1717, Sep. 10.
10. Isaac, 1719, Oct. 25.
11. Elizabeth, 1723, Feb. 19.

III. JOSEPH, b. d. — Newport, R. I.
m. 1710, Jul. 13.
HOPE, b. d. of

1. Joseph, 1712, Oct. 5.
2. Phebe, 1714, May 6.
3. Richard, 1717, Jan. 11.

1708, May 4. He, called "Joseph Card, Jr.," was admitted freeman.

IV. EDWARD, b. d. — Newport, R. I.
m. 1709, Jul. 24.
—— CORY, b. d. of Cory.

1713. Freeman.

V. ELIZABETH, b. d.
m. 1715, Jun. 15.
OLIVER ARNOLD, b. d. of Caleb & Abigail (Wilbur) Arnold.

1. Oliver, 1719, May 26.
2. Abigail, 1721, Dec 21.
3. William, 1723, Feb. 4.
4. Elizabeth,

VI. ELISHA, b. d.
m.
REBECCA, b. d. of

1. John,
2. Mary,
3. Elizabeth,
4. Jane,

CARDER.

1. Bethiah, 1664 ±
2. Nathaniel,
3. Richard,
4. Benjamin,
5. Anne,

CARDER. 3d column. I. John m. 1701, Dec. 25, Elizabeth Paine, of William (of Boston). Children. 1. Elizabeth, 1703, May 2. 2, Mary, 1704, Apr. 16. 3. Katherine 1705, Aug. 4. 4, John, 1707, June 15. 5, Frances, 1708 Dec. 15. 6, Susanna, 1710, Apr. 11. 7. James, 1712, Nov. 11. 8, Ede, 1715, Feb. 15. 9, William, 1716, Jan. 19. 10, Joseph.

I. JOHN, b. 1673, Mar. 19. d. 1749. — Warwick, R. I.
m.
ELIZABETH, b. d. 1751. of

1. Elizabeth,
2. Mary,
3. Katharine,
4. John,

1706, Feb. 11. He and wife Elizabeth, and his brother William Carder, sold certain land for £55, to John Colvin, of Dartmouth.
1712, Jan. 31. He and wife Elizabeth sold John Wickes, 15 acres for £56.
1749, Aug. 9. Inventory, £395, 7*s*. Administration by John Carder.
1751, Dec. 2. Inventory of Elizabeth Carder, widow of John, £344, 17*s*., 6*d*., set forth by John Carder.

II. MARY, b. d.
m.
RICHARD GREENE, b. 1667, Mar. 5. d. of Thomas & Elizabeth (Barton) Greene.

1. Mary,
2. Richard,
3. Thomas,
4. Elizabeth,
5. Welthian,

III. WILLIAM, b. d. 1707 ± — New London, Ct.
UNMARRIED.

He was lost at sea.
1707, Aug. 2. Will—proved 1714, Aug. 28. Ex. brother Richard. He mentions that he was now residing at New London. To sister Mary Greene, of Warwick, £50. To brother Joseph, £5. To sister Sarah Carder, £5. To brother John Carder's children, viz: Elizabeth, Mary, Katharine and John, £5, each. To children of sister Mary Greene, viz: Mary and Richard, 30*s*., and a ring to each. To children of brother Richard Carder, of New London, rest of estate, both real and personal.
1714, Sep. 21. Inventory, £21, 7*s*., 6*d*., including £17, 1*s*., 6*d*., due from Mary Carder, widow of James.
1718, Jan. 12. Administration on his estate was given to brother-in-law Richard Greene, it being declared that William Carder had gone to sea some ten or eleven years since, and had not been heard from nor had the executor appointed in William Carder's will been heard from in some time, and Captain James Carder who had been appointed administrator of William's estate having also died.

a parley it was now said, "that they held blasphemous errors which they must repent of,"—or go to Boston for trial, and they were soon carried thence.

1643, Nov. 3. Having been brought with others before the court, charged with heresy and sedition, they were sentenced to be confined during the pleasure of the court, and should they break jail or preach their heresies, or speak against church or state, on conviction they should die. He was sent to prison at Roxbury.

1644, Mar. He was released from prison but banished from both Warwick and Massachusetts.

1644, Apr. 19. He was one of the witnesses to the "voluntary and free submission of the Chief Sachem and the rest of the Princes, with the whole of the Nanhigansetts, unto the government and protection of That Honorable State of Old England." The paper was signed by Pessicus, Chief Sachem, and successor to late deceased Miantonomi, "that ancient Canonicus" protector of late deceased Miantonomi during his nonage, Mixan, son and heir of Canonicus and two of the chief counsellors of Pessicus.

1655. Freeman.

1659-60-63. Commissioner.

1664-65-66. Deputy.

1666. Assistant, but refused engagement.

1675, Nov. 29. Will—It was probably proved at Newport, where he died, having sought a refuge there during King Philip's war.

1683, Jul. Will—proved 1691, Apr. 3. Widow Mary, of Warwick. Ex. son James. She alludes to having considerable estate from will of deceased husband Richard Carder (bearing the date of 1675, Nov. 29). To son James, dwelling house and land belonging thereto, purchased in my name since date of will of husband, and all her interest in saw mill, all household goods not otherwise bequeathed, all working cattle, and half of other chattels. To son Joseph, feather bed, iron pot, formerly promised him and half of stock of chattels. To daughter Mary Rhodes, widow, all wearing apparel and 20*s*. To son John, 40*s*. To daughter Sarah Gorton, 40*s*. To daughter-in-law (*i. e.* stepdaughter) Susanna Waterman, 40*s*. To Charles Holden, a year old beast at twenty-one.

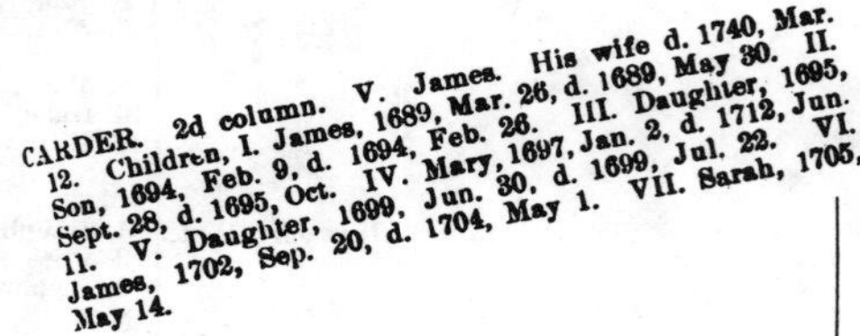
CARDER. 2d column. V. James. His wife d. 1740, Mar. 12. Children, I. James, 1689, Mar. 26, d. 1689, May 30. II. Son, 1694, Feb. 9, d. 1694, Feb. 26. III. Daughter, 1695, Sept. 28, d. 1695, Oct. IV. Mary, 1697, Jan. 2, d. 1712, Jun. 11. V. Daughter, 1699, Jun. 30, d. 1699, Jul. 22. VI. James, 1702, Sep. 20, d. 1704, May 1. VII. Sarah, 1705, May 14.

III. MARY, b. — d. 1698, Jan. 22.
m. 1675, May 27.
MALACHI RHODES, b. — d. 1682. of Zachariah & Joanna (Arnold) Rhodes.

IV. SARAH, b. — d. 1724, Aug. 1.
m. 1672, Dec. 5.
BENJAMIN GORTON, b. — d. 1699, Dec. 25. of Samuel & Elizabeth (   ) Gorton.

V. JAMES, b. 1655, May 2. d. 1714, Apr. 25. Warwick, R. I.
m.
MARY WHIPPLE, b. 1665, Mar. 4. d. 1721 + of John & Mary (Olney) Whipple.

1678. Freeman.

1688. Constable.

1698-1701-7-8. Deputy.

1703, Oct. 27. He and two others were appointed by Assembly to run the line between Rhode Island and Connecticut.

1707, Oct. 29. He was appointed one of the commissioners to settle with Massachusetts regarding northern boundary of Rhode Island.

He was appointed at same date (with John Mumford) to survey vacant lands in Narragansett.

1714. He was appointed administrator on estate of his nephew William Carder, but died before distribution of the property could be made. His death was caused by drowning.

1719. His widow had £3, 16*s*., allowed for her husband's trouble in administering on estate of William Carder, which sum was to be deducted from £17, 1*s*., 6*d*., due from her to estate of William Carder.

1721, Dec. 9. His widow made agreement with George Hazard, Jr., of Kings Town and his wife Sarah, daughter of said widow Mary, by which certain real estate of Captain James Carder, deceased, viz: the house where the widow lived, meadow, orchard, &c., should be hers for life in lieu of dower, and all other real estate should belong to George and Sarah.

VI. JOSEPH, b. 1659. d. 1694, Mar. 14. Warwick, R. I.
m.
BETHIAH, b. — d. of

CASE.

WILLIAM, b. — d. 1676 (—) Newport, R. I.
m.
MARY, b. — d. 1680 +

1655. Freeman.

1658, Jun. 22. He, calling himself William Case, Sr., sold Caleb Carr of Newport all his interest in Conanicut and Dutch Island.

1667-73-74-75. Deputy.

1671. Juryman.

1676, Oct. 18. His widow and executrix Mary Case, brought suit against Lawrence Turner for non-performance of a bargain, and obtained a judgment of £4.

1680. His widow Mary was taxed 5*s*.

I. WILLIAM, b. — d. 1713. East Greenwich, R. I.
m. (1) b. — d. of
m. (2)
ABIGAIL, b. — d. 1736. of

1713, Sep. 26. Will made by Town Council, he having died intestate. Exs. widow Abigail and son John. To son William, half of movable goods, cattle, &c., when of age. To son John, the other half of movables, both sons paying debts equally. To son William, the house and half of 61½ acres south of highway, and half of undivided lands in East Greenwich. The widow relinquished all rights of thirds to her son-in-law (*i. e.* stepson) John Case, in consideration that he had given up his right in above lands to her son William.

Inventory, £68, 19*s*. 2*d*., viz: loom, 2 pair cards, 2 spinning wheels, pewter, parcel of old books, money £2, 2 pair of oxen, 3 cows, 2 steers, heifer, horse, colt, 5 sheep, lamb, 15 swine, &c.

1729, Oct. 22. Will—proved 1736, Nov. 6. Widow Abigail. Ex. friend John Manchester. To three grandchildren Mary, Abigail and Margaret Case, children of son William, all estate equally, except to Margaret who had 20*s*. more than others.

Inventory, £236, 2*s*. 6*d*., including a bond for £190.

II. JOSEPH, b. 1654. d. 1741. Portsmouth, South Kingstown, R. I.
m.
HANNAH SMITH, b. — d. 1712. of John & Margaret (   ) Smith.

1680. Taxed 2*s*.

1687, Sep. 6. Kings Town. Taxed 8*s*. 6*d*.

1703, Jul. 12. He and others of Kings Town were appointed to lay out highway.

1722, Mar. 17. In a deposition he calls himself aged sixty-eight years.

1734, Feb. 21. Will—codicil 1738, Jul. 24.—proved 1741, Jun. 8. Exs. sons Joseph and Emanuel. To son Joseph, 5*s*. he having had already his part. To grandson William Case, eldest son of William, deceased, one-quarter of my whole farm I bought of Ezekiel Bull, and the housing, he paying his brothers and sisters, viz: to Edward Case, Elizabeth York, Hannah Arnold, Sarah, Mary and Margaret Case, 40*s*. yearly for five years. He directs that a burying place three rods square, where wife was buried, shall be fenced and the same maintained by three sons and grandson William. To son John, 5*s*. To son Imanuel, rest of farm, and housing and orchard. To three sons, wearing

IV. { RICHARD, m. 1700, Jun. MARY RICHARDSON, { b. Jan. 8, 1679/80 d. 1707 ± { b. d. of — New London, Ct. — Richardson.

1. Mary, 1700, Sep. 29.
2. Lydia, 1702, Aug. 2.
3. Rachel, 1704, Sep. 4.

He was lost at sea.

1707, Aug. 2. He was appointed executor of his brother William Carder's will, but like him went a voyage to sea, and in 1718 neither of them had been heard from for ten or eleven years.

V. { SARAH, { b. March 27, 1698 d.

VI. { JOSEPH, m. ANN, { b. ~~March 27, 1698~~ Feb. 14, 1699/00 d. 1728, Jan. 24. { b. d. 1728 + of — Warwick, R. I.

1728, Feb. 2. Inventory, £193, 12s., 11d., set forth by widow Ann. Among the items were shoemaker's tools, wheel, cards, books, cow, calf, 2 pigs, geese, hens, turkeys, &c.

Real estate inventory included house and land £280, land at Natick £480, land at Tuscaunk, £12, &c.

1. Malachi,
2. Sarah,
3. Mary.

1. Mary, 1673, Oct. 31.
2. Sarah,
3. Benjamin
4. Samuel,
5. Alice.
6. Maplet.

I. { SARAH, m. GEORGE HAZARD, { b. d. 1738 + { b. 1700, Oct. 9. d. 1738. of George & Penelope (Arnold) — Hazard.

1. Mary,
2. George,
3. Abigail,
4. Sarah,
5. Penelope,
6. Carder,
7. Arnold.

I. { HANNAH, { b. 1693, Apr. 16. d.

II. { MARY, { b. 1693, Apr. 17. d.

3d column. II. Mary. Her husband d. 1724, Sep. 25 Children, 1. Mary, 1700, Sep. 23. 2. Richard, 1702, Apr. 17. 3. Elizabeth, 1710, Aug. 22. 4. Thomas, 1713, Apr. 14. 5. Welthian, 1715, Feb. 19. I. Sarah. Children born: 1. Mary, 1722, Jul. 16. 2. George, 1724, Jun. 15. 3. Abigail, 1726, Mar. 12. 4. Sarah, 1729, Sep. 15. 5 Penelope, 1732, May 7. 6. Carder, 1734, Aug. 11. 7. Arnold, 1738, May 15.

This is Mary Carder who m. Richard Greene p. 271 see p. 271.

I. { JOHN, m. ABIGAIL FISH, { b. d. { b. d. of John & Joanna ( ) — East Greenwich, R. I. — Fish.

1. Mary, 1720, Apr. 7.
2. Martha, 1720, Apr. 7
3. Jemima, 1721, Sep. 29.
4. John, 1723, Apr. 23.
5. Sarah, 1726, Feb. 19,

1737, Apr. 4. His wife had a legacy of £50, from will of her father John Fish, of Dartmouth.

(2D WIFE.)

II. { WILLIAM, m. (1) MARGARET, m. (2) 1725, Jun. 17. FRANCES DAVIS, { b. d. { b. d. of { b. d. of William & Frances ( ) — East Greenwich, R. I. — Davis.

1. Mary, 1715, Feb. 22.
2. Abigail, 1717, May 19.
3. Margaret, 1720, Feb. 20.
(2d wife.)
4. Frances, 1727, Jul. 17
5. William, 1730, Feb. 14.

I. { JOSEPH, m. ELIZABETH MITCHELL, { b. 1678, Jul. 16. d. 1739, Jan. 13. { b. 1686, Nov. 10. d. 1739 + of Elisha & Hannah ( ) — South Kingstown, R. I. — Mitchell.

1. Ann, 1704, Jan. 18.
2. Joseph, 1706, Dec. 17.
3. Mary, 1710, Aug. 29.
4. Elisha, 1712, Jun. 28.
5. Hannah,
6. Elizabeth,
7. Mitchell, 1722, May 29.
8. Sanford,
9. Alexander,

1712. Kings Town. Freeman.

1732, Mar. 9. He brought suit against Robert Case, who also sued him.

1739, Jan. 11. Will—proved, 1739, Feb. 11. Ex. son Joseph. To wife Elizabeth, one-third of estate, real and personal, while widow, and Indian girl Moll till eighteen (the use of dwelling house to be in wife's third). To son Joseph, £100, and silver cup. To seven children Ann Milleman, Mary Sheffield, wife of Jeremiah, Hannah Crandall, wife of John, Elizabeth Herrick, wife of Timothy, Mitchell, Sanford and Alexander Case, two-thirds of personal. The seventh given Ann Milleman to remain in hands of executors for her three children, and the three-sevenths given three sons to be theirs at age. To said three sons, my homestead farm, and the house and lot of Aaron Milleman, and these three sons to be put to a trade. To daughter Ann, the household goods in house she dwells in.

Inventory. Wearing apparel £23, 6s. 6d., purse, pocket book and cash £5, 6s., 6 silver spoons £10, 10s., bonds £258, 15s., negro man Pero £120, Dinah £110, man Roger and boy James £40, yoke of oxen, 10 cows, 3 heifers, 2 calves, 6 two years, 3 yearlings, 4 horsekind, 65 sheep, 11 swine, 6 fowls, 13 geese, gun, stillyards, Dutch wheel, old wheel, old lime kiln, book, book debts £110, &c.

apparel. To son-in-law Henry Knowles, 3*s*., his former wife having received her portion. To daughter Hannah Brooks, 10*s*., a cow, half of pewter and a spinning wheel. To daughter Margaret Perkins, a cow, half of pewter and a linen wheel. To son Imanuel, a bèd. To each grandchild, a Boston shilling. To negro woman Arabella, her choice of master among my children. To son John, a parcel of sheep. To children, rest of estate and negro girl Sarah. Hannah Brooks' part of estate to be taken by son John Case and son-in-law Abraham Perkins and delivered to her as necessity require. The codicil gives Hannah Brooks' legacy to Margaret Perkins, for her to give Hannah as she see cause, by reason Hannah's husband is a very extravagant man, &c. Negro Arabella to be maintained if she grow impotent.

Inventory, £305, 13*s*. 9*d*., viz: wearing apparel £10, 17*s*., 2 bonds £72, 12*s*., 28¼ oz. silver £37, 16*s*., 3 pwt. 19 grains gold £3, 16*s*., 2 sheep, 3 cows, heifer, old spinning wheel, 2 old small books £3, &c.

III. { JAMES, * { b. Portsmouth, Little Compton, R. I.
m. { d.
{ ANNA, { b.
{ d. of

1677, May 7. He brought into Court a negro and was released from bonds.

1680. Taxed 10*s*.

1682, Oct. 31. Little Compton. He and Thomas Butts were to be sent for to the next Court to give reason of their living and continuing at Puncatest without liberty first obtained to do so from the government of Plymouth Colony.

1689, Jan. 10. He and wife Anna sold 12 acres in Newport to Joseph Card for £40.

1689, Jan. 24. He and wife Ann bought of Benjamin Church 40 acres at Little Compton.

*See: American Genealogist, v. 20, p. 184.

CHAMPLIN. See: American Genealogist, v. 20, p. 184-185. v. 32, p. 38

{ JEFFERY, { b. Newport, Westerly, R. I.
m. { d. 1695 (—)
{ ——— { b.
{ d.

1638. He and others were admitted inhabitants of the island of Aquidneck, having submitted themselves to the government that is or shall be established.

1639, Apr. 28. He having complained of a debt due to William Cowley and himself from Mr. Aspinwall, warrant was granted forth for attachment of the latter's shallop till both that debt and other actions of the case be satisfied and discharged by him.

1640, Sep. 7. Freeman.

1640. He was granted 10 acres.

1655. Freeman.

1661. Westerly. He moved thence about this time.

1669, May 18. Freeman.

1671, May 17. He took oath of allegiance to Rhode Island.

1671, May 20. Fined 20*s*., for not attending jury.

1679, Sep. 17. He took oath of allegiance.

The same year he was appointed with others to levy a rate of tax.

1680. Town Council.

1680-81-82-83-84. Moderator of Town Meeting.

1681-82-83-84-85-86. Deputy.

1685, Dec. 4. He and others were appointed to survey highways.

I. { JEFFERY, { b. 1652 ± Westerly, Kings Town, R. I.
m. { d. 1715 ±
{ ——— { b.
{ d. of

1671, May 17. He was called to take oath of allegiance to Rhode Island but did not appear.

1679, Sep. 17. He took oath of allegiance.

1685. He bought 600 acres in Kings Town of Anthony Low.

1687, Sep. 6. Kings Town. Taxed 14*s*., 10*d*.

1690. Captain.

1690, Sep. 16. He and three others were appointed by Assembly to proportion a tax for Kings Town.

1695, Dec. 6. He acknowledged that his brothers William and Christopher had full power to dispose of that house and 100 acres which was my deceased father's, which lies in Westerly.

1696-98-99-1700-1-3-4-5-6-7-8-9-10-11-12-13-14-15. Assistant.

CHAMPLIN. 2d column. I. Jeffrey. He had a daughter Hannah, d. 1720, Oct. 31; m. 1703, Apr. 8, John Watson, b. 1676, July 22, d. 1772, Nov. 8, of John and Dorcas (Gardiner) Watson. Children, 1. Hannah, 1704, Mar. 1. 2, Ann, 1709, Mar. 27. 3, John, 1710, Mar. 13. 4. Jeffrey, 1712, Aug. 3. 5, Elisha, 1714, Sep. 14. 6, Dorcas, 1716, Oct. 25. 7, Amey, 1719, Oct. 18.

II. { WILLIAM, { b. 1654. Westerly, R. I.
m. { d. 1715, Dec. 1.
{ MARY BABCOCK, { b.
{ d. 1747. of James & Sarah ( ) Babcock.

1679. His name was in a list of inhabitants of Westerly.

1679, Sep. 22. He was appointed with others to levy a tax.

1681. Freeman.

1681. Town meeting was held at his house.

1684. Juryman.

1684-85. Town Council.

1687. He and another were chosen to present a petition to Sir Edmund Andros for a town charter.

He and another were chosen to have charge of branding cattle and horses.

1690. Captain.

1690-91-96-98-99-1700-3-5-6-7-8-10-12. Deputy.

1693, Feb. 23. He bought of Gershom Cottrell, a quarter share of land, 100 acres housing, &c., for £95.

1694, May 14. He sold 50 acres and housing to John Davis.

II. { William, m. Elizabeth Stafford,	{ b. 1681, May 27. d. 1728. { b. d. 1756, Aug. 21.	South Kingstown, R. I. of Joseph & Sarah (Holden) Stafford.	1. William, 1705, Sep. 8. 2. Elizabeth, 1706, Dec. 7. 3. Edward, 1708, Feb. 17. 4. Hannah, 1713, Nov. 6. 5. Sarah, 1715, May 3. 6. Mary, 1718, Jan. 5. 7. Margaret, 1721, Dec. 19.

(She m. (2) 1730, Jun. 27, Israel Arnold.)

1712. Kings Town. Freeman.

1728, Aug. 29. Inventory, £171, 11s. 8d. Administration to widow Elizabeth. Wearing apparel and sword £7, 5s., woolen wheel, linen wheel, pewter, silver cup, riding horse, 2 mares, colt, cows and other cattle, 30 sheep, 12 lambs, 7 swine, &c.

1754, Jun. 14. Will—proved 1756, Sep. 29. Widow Elizabeth Arnold, of Providence. Ex. son Edward Case. To eldest son William Case, 5s. To son Edward Case, an equal share in estate with all my daughters, viz: Elizabeth York, Hannah Tourtellot, Sarah Moss, Mary Case, Margaret Field and Bathsheba Davis. Inventory, £808, 9s. 11d.

III. { Mary, m. Henry Knowles,	{ b. 1682, Dec. 2. d. 1709, Nov. 16. { b. 1675, Sep. 29. d. 1740, May 1.	of William & Alice (Fish) Knowles.	1. Mary, 1702, Sep. 25. 2. Margaret, 1705, Nov. 9. 3. Sybil, 1707, Feb. 11. 4. Henry, 1708, Nov. 20.
IV. { Hannah, m. ——— Brooks,	{ b. 1687, Jul. 6. d. { b. d.	of Brooks.	No issue.
V. { Margaret, m. 1718, Jun. 29. Abraham Perkins,	{ b. 1690, Aug. 20. d. 1752. { b. d. 1746.	of Perkins.	
VI. { John, m. Elizabeth Sunderland,	{ b. 1692, Nov. 20. d. 1763. { b. d. 1787.	West Greenwich, R. I. of Daniel & Elizabeth (Sheldon) Sunderland.	1. John, 2. Daniel, 1721, May 18. 3. Elizabeth, 1727, Dec. 5. 4. Joseph, 1730, Apr. 22. 5. James, 1732, Nov. 23. 6. Hannah, 7. Margaret,

1752, Sep. 8. He and his brother Imanuel had legacies from the will of their sister Margaret Perkins.

1762, Dec. 29. Will—proved 1763, Apr. 30. Ex. son Joseph. To son Joseph, all real estate. To wife Elizabeth, a third of movable estate. To sons John, Daniel and Joseph, and daughters Hannah Case and Margaret Case, the other two-thirds of movable estate. To son Daniel, £800, old tenor. To grandson Nathaniel Case, one Spanish milled dollar.

1787, Jun. 15. Will—proved 1788, Oct. 27. Widow Elizabeth. Ex. son John Case, Jr. She mentions sons Joseph and John Case, heirs of son Daniel, deceased, daughter Margaret Godfrey, and heirs of daughter Hannah Case, and granddaughter Deborah Boss. To son John, she gives all movables indoor and out.

VII. { Emanuel, m. Hannah,	{ b. 1699, Nov. 2. d. 1770. { b. d.	South Kingstown, R. I. of	1. Amey, 1725, Dec. 4. 2. Hannah, 1727, Nov. 12. 3. Mary, 1730, Aug. 19. 4. Joseph, 1732, Jan. 27. 5. Penelope, 1736, Jul. 27. 6. Emanuel, 1739, Nov. 8.

1770, Feb. 11. Administration to son Emanuel. Inventory, £4,896, viz: negro Peter £1,200, Prince £1,100, Lucy £800, 2 pair of oxen, cow, mare, 2 woolen wheels, churn, linen wheel, &c.

I. { Susanna,*	{ b. 1686, May 18. d.
II. { Isaac,	{ b. 1688, Aug. 19. d.

*See: American Genealogist, v. 20, p. 184.

CHAMPLIN.

I. { Jeffery, m. (1) Susanna Eldred, m. (2) Hannah Hazard, m. (3) Susanna,	{ b. d. 1718. { b. d. { b. d. { b. d.	Kings Town, R. I. of Thomas & Susanna (Cole) Eldred. of Robert & Mary (Brownell) Hazard. of	1. Emblem, 1702, Jan. 30. 2. Jeffery, 1703, Feb. 2. (2d wife.) 3. Thomas, 1708, Sep. 3. 4. Stephen, 1710, Feb. 16. 5. William, 1713, Mar. 3. (3d wife.) 6. Hannah, 1714, Jun. 11. 7. John, 1717, Feb. 12.

1717, Feb. 14. Will—proved 1718, Mar. 10. Exs. son Jeffery and kinsman Thomas Hazard. To sons Thomas and Stephen, all farm and housing in Point Judith, equally, the north part and half of housing being for Thomas, and the other half to Stephen. To son Jeffery, half of farm on border of Great Plain, viz: the farm and house that my honoured father last possessed before his death, but the north half and all the housing except a fireroom reserved for wife till son John is of age. To son John, south half of said farm. To sons Jeffery and John, land in Westerly. To son William, land west side of Point Judith Pond. To daughter Emblem Champlin, £100, at eighteen and a feather bed, and to daughter Hannah like legacy. To wife Susanna, £100, and a feather bed. To sons Jeffery, Thomas, Stephen, William and John, rest of estate.

Inventory, £1,457, 7s., 1d., viz: wearing apparel £35, riding horse, 5 beds, 2 warming pans, 4 flock beds, pair of worsted combs, 3 woolen wheels, linen wheel, 2 guns, 10 silver spoons £7, 16s., pair of silver clasps and other old silver 15s., piece of gold £1, 1s., silver money 5s. 5d., 6 horses, 4 mares, colt, bull, 42 cows, 6 working cattle, 16 steers, 9 heifers, 21 two years, 29 yearlings, 23 horsekind young and old, 312 sheep, 18 swine, negro £50, negro woman £40, &c.

I. { William, m. 1700, Jan. 18. Mary Clarke,	{ b. d. 1747. { b. 1680, Dec. 27. d. 1760 +	Westerly, R. I. of Joseph & Bethiah (Hubbard) Clarke.	1. William, 1702, May 31. 2. Jeffery, 1704, Mar. 6. 3. Joseph, 4. Samuel, 5. Joshua, 6. James, 7. Susanna,

1700. Freeman.

1731–32. Deputy.

1746, Aug. 3. Will—proved 1747, Dec. 29. Ex. son William. To son William, all estate real and personal, he paying legacies. To wife Mary, bed, mare, two colts, negro girl Dinah, two milch cows and £200. To son Joseph, £1,000. To son Samuel, 10s., he having had. To son Joshua, £200. To son James, £100, and a feather bed. To daughter Susanna Stanton, £400. Executor to take care of my ancient mother if she outlives me.

Inventory, £821, 4s., 9d., viz: wearing apparel £27, 17s., silver tankard £36, pewter £10, 16s., warming pan, woolen wheel, linen wheel, mare, two years and vantage £25, negro girl Dinah £150, pair of oxen, 6 cows, 8 yearlings, 4 calves, Indian girl, twelve years old, if she belongs to the estate £40, &c.

II. { Mary, m. John Babcock,	{ b. d. 1746 + { b. d. 1746, Mar. 28.	of John & Mary (Lawton) Babcock.	1. John, 1701, May 4. 2. Ichabod, 1703, Dec. 21. 3. Stephen, 1706, May 2. 4. William, 1708, Apr. 15. 5. Amey, 1713, Feb. 8. 6. Mary, 1716, Jul. 23. 7. Ann, 1721, Sep. 14.

1695. Conservator of the Peace.

1698, Jan. 30. He bought land between Quonacontaug and Pawcatuck Rivers for £35, of Thomas Stanton, Sr., Joseph Stanton, Sr., Robert Stanton, Sr., and Samuel Stanton, Sr., who are four brothers, Joseph living at Quonacontaug, and all the rest at Stonington.

1699, Oct. 25. He and five others were given power to agree about boundaries between Connecticut and Rhode Island.

1708. Justice of the Peace.

1712, May 7. His petition to Assembly for a bridge over the Pawcatuck River, by contribution, was allowed, if built in the highway.

1716, Jan. 18. Agreement between William Champlin, only son and heir of deceased Captain William Champlin, and Mary Champlin, his mother, Captain John Babcock and Samuel Clarke and their wives. It was agreed that William should pay his mother £200, and also £10, annually for life, and she to have two beds, four dozen napkins, &c., and he to maintain his mother so long as she see cause to live with him—all in lieu of dower. To brother-in-law John Babcock and wife Mary, £100. To brother-in-law Samuel Clarke and wife Ann, £100.

1747, Sep. 8. Inventory, £508, 13*s*. Widow Mary. Sworn to by William Champlin.

III. CHRISTOPHER, { b. 1656 ± { d. 1732, Apr. 2. Westerly, R. I
m. (1) { b. { d. of
m (2) [of Wm. ELIZABETH DAVOL (w. { b. { d. 1722 + of

1693. Town Council.

1698. Constable.

1706–7. Deputy.

1711, Feb. 11. He deeded son Christopher for love, &c., and £300, and a further sum of £200 to my order or will in nine or ten years, my farm, house, &c., which I bought of Sachem Ninecroft; the farm containing 150 acres.

1732, Apr. 24. Administration to son Christopher. Inventory, £189, 4*s*., 10*d*., viz: mare, horse, pewter, old negro woman worth nothing, desperate debt £106, &c.

See: American Genealogist, v. 20, p. 186.

CODDINGTON.

WILLIAM, { b. 1601. { d. 1678, Nov. 1. Boston, Lincoln Co., Eng., [Newport, R. I.
m. (1)
MARY MOSELY, { b. { d. 1630.
of Richard Mosely.
m. (2) 1631 ±
MARY, { b. { d. 1647, Sep. 30
m. (3)
ANNE BRINLEY, { b. 1628. { d. 1708, May 9.
of Thomas & Anna (Wase) Brinley.

1627, Mar. 8. He had his son Michael baptized, followed by his son Samuel (1628, Apr. 17).

1630. Boston, Mass. He came here this year, having arrived first at Salem in a vessel from Southampton.

1630–31–32–33–34–35–36–37. Assistant.

1631, Apr. 1. He went to England and returned in a year or two.

1633, Aug. 6. He was chosen with others to oversee the building of a sufficient cart bridge over Muddy River, and another over Stony River.

1634, Mar. 2. He had his daughter Mary baptized (and son Benajah 1636, May 31).

1634–35–36. Treasurer.

1635, Mar. 4. He was appointed on committee on military affairs.

1636, May 5. He was appointed to keep particular courts.

1636, Oct. 26. His account as Treasurer for two years past was allowed, the country owing him £25, 14*s*. 6*d*.

1636–37. Deputy.

1637, Mar. 24. He and his friends had a deed from Cononicus and Miantonomi, Chief Sachems of Narragansett, of the island of Aquidneck, &c., for forty fathom of white beads. Item, that by giving by Miantonomi of ten coats and twenty hoes to present inhabitants, they shall remove themselves from off the island before next winter.

I. MICHAEL, { b. 1627. { d. 1627,

II. SAMUEL, { b. 1628. { d. 1629, Aug.

(2D WIFE.)

III. CHILD, { b. 1632. { d.

IV. MARY, { b. 1634. { d. young

V. BENAJAH, { b. 1636. { d.

(3D WIFE.)

VI. WILLIAM, { b. 1651, Jan. 18. { d. 1689, Feb. 5. Newport, R. I.
UNMARRIED.

1675, May 4. Freeman.

1679–80. Deputy.

1681–82–83. Assistant.

1683–84–85. Governor.

III. { ANN, m. 1699, Jan. 19. SAMUEL CLARKE, { b. d. { b. 1672, Sep. 29. d. 1719 ± of Joseph & Bethiah (Hubbard) Clarke.

1. Samuel, 1700, Jan. 19.
2. Mary, 1701, Nov. 27.
3. Bethiah, 1703, Jul. 18.
4. Joseph, 1705, Aug. 29.
5. Ann, 1707, Sep. 3.
6. William, 1709, May 21.
7. James, 1711, Jan. 20.
8. Joshua, 1712, Sep. 22.
9. Amos, 1714, Nov. 14.
10. Simeon, 1716, Apr. 7.
11. Christopher 1717, Oct. 26.
12. Samuel, 1719, May 6.

Westerly, R. I.

I. { CHRISTOPHER, m. 1705, Dec. 5. ELIZABETH DENISON, { b. 1684, Sep. 26. d. 1734, Oct. 23. { b. 1689, Sep. 11. d. 1749, Nov. 22. of George & Mercy (Gorham) Denison.

1723–26. Deputy.

1734. Oct. 12. Will—proved 1734. Ex. son Christopher. To son Christopher, all estate real and personal, he paying debts and legacies. To son Joseph, £500. To sons George, Jabez, and Oliver, £500, each at twenty-three years of age. To daughters Ann and Elizabeth Champlin £300, each at twenty-five. To daughter Mary Champlin, £400, at twenty-five. To wife Elizabeth, £400, her choice of personal estate for a like amount of £400, a negro, and profits of the portions of Jabez, Oliver and Mary, till they are fourteen, at rate of £6, on the hundred, for bringing up those children.

Inventory, £3,703, 11*s.*, 6*d.*, viz: cash £62, wearing apparel £131, 13*s.*, sword £12, case of pistols, &c., £14, tables, silver tankard £31, 10*s.*, 2 silver cups, pepper mill, quilting frame, 3 woolen wheels, 2 linen wheels, 7 pair of cards, 6 silver spoons £19, 10*s.*, window curtains, feather beds, stillyards, 4 negro slaves £410, 3 bound servants £45, carpenter's tools, 123 loads of hay at 30*s.* £184, 10*s.*, 40 loads salt hay at 20*s.* £40, bull, 20 cows, 14 working cattle, 6 fat cattle, 28 yearlings, 7 calves, 12 mares, 8 three year horses and mares, 5 two year horses and mares, colt, 202 sheep, 18 fat swine, 14 lean swine, 12 turkeys, &c.

1749, Nov. 19. Will—proved 1749, Dec. 4. Widow Elizabeth, of Charlestown, R. I. Ex. son Christopher. To son Joseph, negro boy Pero. To daughter Ann Gardiner, £150, a third of wearing apparel, &c. To daughter Elizabeth Belcher, £150, and a third of wearing apparel, &c. To sons Jabez and Oliver, £150, each To daughter Mary, £150, a third of wearing apparel, silver cup, two silver spoons, and rest of household goods. To son Christopher, negro woman Dinah.

1. Christopher 1707, Nov. 30.
2. Joseph, 1709, Aug. 4.
3. Elijah, 1711, Jul. 20.
4. Ann, 1714, Mar. 29.
5. George, 1716, Feb. 15.
6. Elizabeth, 1719, Jan. 10.
7. Thankful, 1721, Mar. 27.
8. Lydia, 1723, Nov. 19.
9 Elijah, 1726, May 23.
10. Jabez, 1728, Aug. 31.
11. Oliver, 1730, May 12.
12. Mary, 1731, Jun. 29.

Westerly, R. I.

II. { JEFFERY, m. SARAH, { b. d. 1751. { b. d. 1751 + of

1751, Jul. 28 Inventory, shown by widow Sarah. Bond £97, 19*s.*, 9*d.*, wearing apparel £73, 14*s.*, steer, 2 hogs, mare, cow, pair of calves, half of a cow and steer, &c.

Westerly, R. I., New London, Ct.

III. { WILLIAM, m. JOANNA, { b. d. { b. d. of

1723. Freeman (called William Champlin, son to Christopher).

1758. New London. He made a deed to son William.

A John Champlin of New London is mentioned as son of William, of same place.

1. William,
2. John,

Westerly, R. I.

IV. { JOSEPH, m. SARAH BROWN, { b. d. 1727. { b. d. 1763 + of George & Charity (Crandall) Brown.

1727, Nov. 13. Administration to widow Sarah. Inventory, £107, 5*s.*, 3*d.*, viz: mares, 2 cows, heifer, hog, 3 sheep, 6 shotes, smith's tools, 4 beds, &c.

1763, Mar. Will—widow Sarah, of Stonington.

1. Andrew, 1723, Feb. 25.
2. Joseph, 1725, Jul. 20.

Lyme, Ct.

V. { JOHN, m. ELIZABETH, { b. d. 1763, Dec. 15. { b. d. of

(2D WIFE, no issue.)

1. Silas,
2. Edward,

CODDINGTON.

1638, Mar. 7. Portsmouth, R. I. He and eighteen others signed the following compact. "We whose names are underwritten do here solemnly in the presence of Jehovah incorporate ourselves into a Body Politicke, and as he shall help, will submit our persons, lives and estates unto our Lord Jesus Christ, the King of Kings and Lord of Lords, and to all those perfect and most absolute laws of his given us in his holy word of truth, to be guided and judged thereby."

On the same day he was chosen Judge, the rest covenanting to yield all due honour unto him according to the laws of God, &c. He in turn covenanted "to do justice and judgment impartially according to the laws of God and to maintain the fundamental rights and privileges of this Bodie Politick, which shall hereafter be ratified according unto God, the Lord helping us so to do."

1638, Mar. 12. The Massachusetts authorities having given him and others license to depart, summons was now ordered to go out for them to appear (if they be not gone before) at the next court to answer such things as shall be objected.

1638, May 20. He was granted a house lot of 6 acres.

1639, Apr. 28 He and eight others signed the following compact preparatory to the settlement of Newport. "It is agreed by us whose hands are underwritten to propagate a plantation in the midst of the island, or elsewheres, and to engage ourselves to bear equal charge answerable to our strength and estates in common; and that our determination shall be by major voices of Judge and elders, the Judge to have a double voice." He signed as Judge.

1639–40. Newport. Judge.

1640, Mar. 6. He had 750 acres recorded.

1640–41–42–43–44–45–46–47. Governor of Portsmouth and Newport.

1644, Aug. 5. He wrote a long letter to Governor Winthrop, touching on a variety of topics. He alludes to the loss of a large corn barn the last winter that cost £150, besides farm house, twelve oxen, eight cows, and six other beasts, "the fire breaking forth in the night, neither bedding nor household stuff nor so much as my servants' wearing cloth, nothing but the shirts of their back was saved," &c. He congratulates himself however that he still has a considerable surplus, so that he has enough. He declares that Gorton shall not be protected by him.

1647. Assistant.

1648–49. President of the four united towns of the Colony.

1649, Jan. He went to England, sailing this month, and there procured a commission as Governor of the island, which in effect would vacate the charter. The colonists denied his authority and dispatched John Clarke as agent to secure a new charter.

1652, Aug. 14. He made acknowledgement that he had no more right in the purchase of Rhode Island, &c., than his associates, but only his proportion, and the sale of said purchase from the Indians having ever since lain in his hands, being a great trouble to aforesaid purchasers, he now promises to deliver said deeds of purchase, with records, into the hands of such as the major part of the freemen and purchasers shall appoint to receive them.

1653, May 18. He refused to lay down his commission.

1656, Mar. 11. "I William Coddington, do freely submit to the authority of his Highness in this colony as it is now united, and that with all my heart." This he publicly professed in the General Assembly of Commisioners.

1656–63. Commissioner.

1663, Jul. 28. He was named in the Charter.

1666. Deputy.

1666–67. Assistant.

1672, Jun. 17. He and wife Ann sold Nicholas Easton 32 acres.

1673–74. Deputy Governor.

1674–75–76–78. Governor.

1677, Sep. 27. He made a deposition relative to the purchase of the Island, calling himself aged about seventy-six years.

1708, Jun. 7. Will—proved. Widow Ann. She mentions son Nathaniel, daughter Sanford and daughter Ann Willett. She makes bequests of silver salt cellar, rug, two Dutch blankets, silver tankard, &c. The "people whom the world calls Quakers" are mentioned.

VII. { NATHANIEL, m. SUSANNA HUTCHINSON, } { b. 1653, May 23. d. 1724, Jan. } Newport, R. I. { b. d. } of Edward & Catharine (Hamby) Hutchinson.

1675, May 4. Freeman.

1683–85–86–1703–19. Deputy.

1686, Apr. 13. He and wife Susanna sold 300 acres called Rocky Farm for £400, to Noel Mew.

1688. Constable.

1698, Aug. 2. He was appointed with five others, by the Assembly, to meet the Connecticut gentlemen to treat before Lord Bellomont about the west bounds of the colony.

1698–1703–4–5–6–7–15–16–17. Assistant.

1703. Major for the Island.

1703. Clerk of Assembly.

1703, Jun. 22. He and two others were appointed to draw up the method and proceedings of Courts of Common Pleas.

1704, Jan. 4. He and two others were chosen to draw out the colony laws and fit them for the press.

1706, May 1. He was appointed on a committee to direct as to further building and repairing of the fort on Goat Island.

1708, Oct. 27. He, as one of the attorneys for Captain Stephen Remington, appealed from the decision of the Assembly in the suit of Jahleel Brenton, Exr. *versus* Captain Stephen Remington. The Assembly had granted leave to Brenton to redeem a mortgage of 256 acres, and the appellant produced several laws which plainly hold forth that upon extraordinary occasion the mortgagee shall have liberty to redeem a mortgage notwithstanding twenty years being passed (being the time limited for mortgages), and this case appeared to Assembly to be extraordinary.

VIII. { MARY, m. 1674, Dec. 1. PELEG SANFORD, } { b. 1654, May 16. d. 1693, Mar. b. 1639, May 10. d. 1701. } of John & Bridget (Hutchinson) Sanford.

IX. { THOMAS, m. (1) PRISCILLA JEFFERAY, m. (2) 1690, Jan. 22. MARY HOWARD, } { b. 1655, Nov. 5. d. 1694, Mar. 4. } Newport, R. I. { b. 1654. d. 1688, Aug. 7. } of William & Mary (Gould) Jefferay. { b. d. } of Howard.

(She m. (2) 1695, Jan. 18, Anthony Morris.)

1686, Jul. 16. He and others signed a petition to the King in regard to the writ of *Quo warranto*, presenting their full and free submission, and resignation of power given in the charter, and desiring to be discharged from all levies and contributions which the Assembly would expose them to in sending an agent to England, to which the petitioners do not consent.

1708, Aug. 2. Notification was sent from Newport to Edward Shippin of Philadelphia, that he render account of executorship of estate of Thomas Coddington, late of Newport, deceased. The father-in-law (*i. e.* stepfather) of the heir of Thomas Coddington, viz: Anthony Morris, was also notified, he being husband of executrix. It was the opinion of the court that the heir be kept here in this colony in her minority, where the estate lieth.

X. { JOHN, } { b. 1656, Nov. 24. d. 1680, Jun. 1. } Newport, R. I.

1679, Dec. 27. Will. Witnesses Francis Brinley and another. A reference is found to this in a list of seventeen wills (between dates of 1676 and 1695) that were presented to the court in 1700 by parties interested, the law requiring three witnesses and these having but two.

XI. { NOAH, } { b. d. 1658, Dec. 12. }

XII. { ANNE. } { b. d. 1660, Jun. 26. }

XIII. { ANNE, m. 1682, May 30. ANDREW WILLETT, } { b. 1663, Jul. 20. d. 1751, Dec. 4. b. 1655, Oct. 5. d. 1712, Apr. 6. } of Thomas & Mary (Brown) Willett.

I. Anne, b. 1677, Dec. 26. d. 1752.
m. 1716, Nov. 22.
Samuel Niles, b. 1674, May 1. d. 1762, May 1. of Nathaniel & Sarah (Sands) Niles.

1. Susanna,
2. Elisha,

II. Catharine, b. 1679, Feb. 8. d.

III. William, b. 1680, Jul. 15. d. 1755. Newport, R. I.
m. (1) 1700, Nov. 12.
Content Arnold, b. 1681, Feb. 26. d. 1721, May 27. of Benedict & Mary (Turner) Arnold.
m. (2) 1722, Oct. 11.
Jane Bernon, b. 1696, May 15. d. 1752, Jun. 18. of Gabriel & Esther (Le Roy) Bernon.

1705-6-15-16-18-19-20. Sheriff.
1707-15-21-22-23-24-25-26-27-34-35-36. Deputy.
1711, Jun. 28. Commissary. He was to have £5, per month for his care of the stores of the colony for the intended expedition against Canada.
1717-18. Major for the Island.
1719-20. Lieutenant Colonel of the regiment of militia on the Island.
1722-23-24-25-26. Speaker of House of Deputies.
1727. Master of the Alienation office.
1727-28-29. Assistant.
1733, Jul. He was appointed on a committee to go over to Block Island to consider of a convenient place to build a pier, or harbor, and of the charge, &c. On the same date he was appointed on a committee to procure £4,000, worth of cannon, carriages, and other necessaries for Fort George.
1734-35. He was one of the four Justices of Inferior Court of Common Pleas for Newport County.
1738. Mr. Callender dedicated his Historical Discourse to The Honorable William Coddington, Esq.
1750, Sep. 4. He and others signed a petition to the King, praying that the Assembly might be restrained from making or emitting any more Bills of Public Credit upon loan, without royal permission, the sum on loan already amounting to £390,000, worth at time of issue £78,111, sterling, but at present only £35,445. Amongst those whose estates were involved in the loan were numbers of widows and orphans, who were grievously injured, oppressed and almost ruined.

1. Susanna,	1708, May 30.
2. William,	1710, Oct. 8.
3. Edward,	1712, Jul. 30.
4. Thomas,	1715, Dec. 4.
5. Nathaniel,	1717, Jun. 22.
6. Arnold,	1718, Jul. 4.
(2d wife.)	
7. Content,	1724, Apr. 12.
8. Esther,	1727, Jan. 21.
9. John,	1728, Oct. 23.
10. Jane,	1730, Mar. 29.
11. Francis,	1732, Feb. 2.
12. Anne,	1734, May 30.

IV. Edward, b. 1687, Jul. 28. d. 1727 ± Newport, R. I.
m. 1724, Jun. 4.
Elizabeth King, b. d. 1727 + of King.
Coddington. 3d column. IV. Edward. His widow d. 1730, Feb. 19.

1714. Freeman.
1727, Jun. 13. It being deemed probable that he had died at sea, a petition was laid before Assembly by his widow Elizabeth, his brothers William, John and Nathaniel, and Catharine, one of his sisters, for leave to sell land to pay debts, &c., they having had a view of his will. The petition was granted, and after the incumbrances had been paid, the remaining part was to be kept at interest for Elizabeth, wife of said Edward, and her child Susanna, till the said Edward be deemed deceased, and finally what remains to go as the will of Edward directs.

1. Susanna,

V. John, b. 1690, Mar. 23. d. 1743. Newport, R. I.
m. 1726, Aug. 25.
Elizabeth Rogers, b. 1705. d. 1745, Sep. 23. of Rogers.

He was a silversmith.
1721-22-23-26-27-28-29. Deputy.
1723-27-28. Clerk of Assembly.
1726. Colonel.
1727. Prothonotary.
1733-34-35. Sheriff.

1. Elizabeth,

VI. Nathaniel, b. 1692, Jan. 18. d. Newport, R. I.
m. 1719, Mar. 20.
Hope Brown, b. d. of James & Ann ( ) Brown.

1714. Freeman.

1. Ann,	1721, Feb. 19.
2. John,	1724, Dec. 28.
3. Catharine,	1726, Aug. 27.
4. Mary,	1728, Dec. 21.
5. Nathaniel	1730.
6. Hope,	1733, Jun. 18.
7. James,	1736, Jan. 19.
8. Susanna,	1737, Jan. 19.
9. Edward,	1738, Apr. 11.
10. Elizabeth,	1739, Apr. 23.

1. Ann,
2. Bridget,
3. Elizabeth,
4. Daughter,
5. Son,
6. Peleg,
7. William,

I. William, b. 1684. d. 1689, Feb. 19.

II. Thomas, b. 1687, Apr. 17. d. young.

(2d Wife.)

III. William, b. 1691, Mar. 1. d. young.

IV. Mary, b. 1694, Jan. 15. d.

1. Anne,	1689, Sep. 26.
2. Mary,	1690, Sep. 21.
3. Francis,	1693, Jun. 25.
4. Thomas,	1696, May 13.
5. Martha,	1698, Mar. 6.

SAMUEL[2] (William[1]). b. Wethersfield, Ct., Providence, R. I.
m. d. 1660 (—)
ANN, b.
d. 1661 +

(She m. (2) John Smith, the Mason.)

He was son doubtless of William Comstock, of Wethersfield, who came from England with wife Elizabeth, and subsequently removed to New London. Other sons of William were William, Jr., and Daniel (who died at New London, in 1683, aged about fifty-three), and apparently Christopher, of Fairfield in 1661.

1648, Mar. He gave a bond (as seen by Court records of Hartford), for his good behaviour for ten days, and for satisfying "what damage Mr. Robins shall sustain for want of his servant."

1649, Apr. 24. He was freed from his recognizances.

1654, Mar. 1. Providence. He bought of John Smith (Mason), his house and lot bounded east by common and west by highway.

1655, May 25. Ordered by General Assembly "that John Parker is freed from his bonds of prosecuting of Samuel Comstock, and hath liberty either to compose or prosecute."

1660, Mar. 9. It was ordered that three men, viz: Arthur Fenner, John Brown and Henry Brown, should be added unto the Town Council to order about estate of Samuel Comstock and John Smith, deceased, and that what the major part of them shall order shall stand in force.

1661, May 4. Anne Smith, of Providence, widow of John Smith, and formerly wife of Samuel Comstock, deceased, for a valuable sum of money, bargained and sold to Roger Mowry the house and home share formerly belonging to John Smith, Mason, and purchased of John Smith by aforesaid husband Samuel Comstock, and since my said husband Samuel Comstock his decease, it was by a will made by the Town Council of Providence disposed of to me. The land comprised 4 acres in a row of houses in north part of Providence.

1665, Feb. 19. At this date a Daniel Comstock drew lot 40, in a division of lands. He was probably a brother of Samuel, but did not long continue a resident of Providence after this date it would seem, though for some years before he had been there.

I. SAMUEL, b. 1654. Providence, R. I.
m. 1678, Nov. 22. d. 1727, May 27.
ELIZABETH ARNOLD, b.
d. 1747, Oct. 20. of Thomas & Phebe (Parkhurst) Arnold.

1679, Jul. 1. Taxed 8*d.*

1680, Mar. 16. His sentence to pay sum of 40*s.* (imposed by General Court of Trial held in October, 1678), was remitted by the Assembly, on his petition.

1687. Ratable estate, 4 cows, a horse, a mare, a swine, 2 acres planting and an acre of pasture.

1687, Sep. 1. Taxed 3*s.*

1695, Jun. 10. He sold Jonathan Whipple, 60 acres for £25.

1699–1702–7–8–11. Deputy.

1702, May 6. He was appointed on a committee by Assembly, to audit the General Treasurer's accounts and other colony debts.

1708, Apr. He was appointed on a committee empowered to proportion and affix the rates of grain and other specie brought to the treasury on account of a tax. The committee ordered that Indian corn be accepted at 2*s.* per bushel, barley at 1*s.*, 8*d.*, rye at 2*s.*, 6*d.*, oats 14*d.*, wool 9*d.*, wheat 3*d.*

1713, Jun. 16. Taxed 12*s.*

1717, Mar. 22. He gave testimony about certain land, calling his age sixty-three years.

He was called Captain at time of his death.

1727, Mar. 15. He received back from his sons Samuel Comstock, Jr., Hazadiah, Daniel, Thomas, John and Ichabod Comstock and John Sayles, Jr., by quit claim deed, all that land whereon he dwelt (and which he had deeded them the 16th of December previous), except 40 acres only, which they kept. The former deed, however, had effect it would seem at his death.

1726, Dec. 21. Will—proved 1727, Sep. 18. Exx. wife Elizabeth. To wife, he gave negro woman Effie, and all the rest of movable estate for life, and at her death to be disposed of to children. To sons Samuel, Hazadiah, Thomas, Daniel, John, Ichabod and Job, 2*s.* each, and to daughter Elizabeth Sayles, a like amount.

Inventory, £296, 6*s.*, 1*d.*, viz: books £2, 12*s.*, old sword and staff £1. negro woman Effie £60, a mare, yoke of oxen, 6 cows, 2 steers, 2 heifers, 12 calves, 18 sheep, 5 swine, cider in 2 hogsheads, butter, cheese, beef, pork, rye, corn, beans, 4 pewter platters, 2 silver spoons, 2 feather beds, flock bed, table linen, &c.

1745, Apr. 10. Will—proved 1747, Dec. 8. Widow Elizabeth, of Smithfield. Ex. son Thomas. To grandson David Comstock, 20*s.* To granddaughter Sarah Aldrich, 10*s.* To great-granddaughter Anne Steere, 10*s.* To son John, 20*s.* To son Job, 20*s.* To son Hazadiah, 40*s.* To son Thomas, £20. To son Daniel, £10. To son Ichabod, £5. To daughter Elizabeth Sayles, 40*s.* To six sons' rest.

Inventory, £415, 13*s.*, 8*d.*, viz: testament, bible, and other books, 3 silver spoons, 3 chairs, table, 2 beds, pewter, remnant of garlic, &c.

II. DANIEL, b. 1655, May. Providence, R. I.
d.

1662. He, having been for sometime resident with Thomas Walling, but latter having departed the town, his wife Mary desired the authorities would bring him up, she not being able. The town therefore apprenticed him to William Carpenter.

1667, Feb. 10 "This we certainly affirm, that to our knowledge, Daniel Comstock, Ann Comstock's son, now dwelling with William Carpenter, is the next May twelve years old, the beginning of the month: this by Mary Pray, and Samuel Bennett, was declared in the face of a Town Meeting, from one by word of mouth, the other in writing on the 10th of February, 1667."

I. SAMUEL, b. 1679, Apr. 16. d. 1727, Apr. 1. — Providence, R. I.
m.
ANNE INMAN, b. d. 1727 + of John & Mary (Whitman) — Inman.

1. David,
2. Sarah, 1706, May 24.
3. Anne,

1707, May 14. He had 14*s.*, and chattels taken from him to satisfy a fine of 12*s.*, for not training, he being a Quaker.

1713, Jun. 16. Taxed 8*s.*, 4*d.*

1727, Apr. 1. Will—proved 1727, Apr. 13. Ex. son David. To wife Anne, a third of lands and half of house for life. To son David, all lands and tenements, two-thirds of land and half of house at death of testator and the rest at death of testator's wife, mother of said David. To daughter Anne, £40, at eighteen or marriage. The rest to three children, equally, viz: Sarah Aldrich, David and Anne Comstock.

Inventory, £319, 19*s.*, 3*d.*, viz: 3 horses, yoke of oxen, 10 cows, 4 heifers, 4 steers, 3 yearlings, 4 swine, hay, 3 barrels cider, &c.

II. HAZADIAH, b. 1682, Apr. 16. d. 1764, Feb. 21. — Providence, Smithfield, R. I.
m. (1)
CATHARINE PRAY, b d. 1728, Nov. 27. of John & Sarah (Brown) — Pray.
m. (2) 1730, Aug. 10.
MARTHA BALCOM, b. 1714, May 21. d 1794, May 6. of Joseph & Phebe ( ) — Balcom.

COMSTOCK. 3d column. II. Hazadiah. In the third item, instead of wife Catherine, read Martha. VI. John. His sons James b. 1734, Feb. 15. Nathan, 1735, Dec. 6. He had also a daughter Esther.

1. Susanna, 1707, Apr. 7.
2. William, 1708, May 3.
3. Gideon, 1709, Nov. 4.
4. Rachel, 1711, Sep. 9.
5. Catharine, 1713, Sep. 19.
6. Hazadiah, 1715, Jan. 9.
7. Penelope, 1717, Feb. 11.
8. Anthony, 1719, Nov. 7.
9. Andrew, 1721, Jan. 22.
10. John, 1724, Apr. 16

(2d wife.)

11. Anne, 1731, Apr. 7.
12. Ezekiel, 1733, May 1.
13. Phebe, 1735, Jun. 5.
14. Rufus, 1738, Oct. 26.
15. Martha, 1742, Jan. 3.

1708, May 5. He had a mare worth £2, taken from him for not training, he being a Quaker. The mare was afterwards returned.

1713, Jun. 16. Taxed 8*s.*

1730, Nov. 19. He deeded sons William and Gideon, 100 acres for love, &c. (his wife Catharine also signing): said land having been received by deed from brother Job Comstock.

1734, Jun. Smithfield. The Assembly voted that he be taken up by Sheriff of Court of Providence and safely conveyed to the authority of Massachusetts Bay, so that he have a trial on complaint of Jonathan Draper, pursuant to request of the Great and General Court of Massachusetts Bay.

1763, Mar. 10. Will—proved 1764, Mar. 5. Ex. son John. To son Ezekiel, all my homestead and 3 acres near Branch Bridge, he paying legacies. To son Gideon, twenty Spanish milled dollars. To daughter Rachel Steere, $80. To son Hazadiah, $100. To son John, $100. To children of daughter Catharine Steere, deceased, viz: Elisha, Nathan, David and Rachel, $100, divided. To grandchildren Penelope and Andrew Comstock, $50, divided. To four sons, Gideon, Hazadiah, John and Ezekiel, wearing apparel. To son John, the carpenter and husbandry tools. To wife Martha, provisions, warming pan, mare and a third of personal. To grandchildren Mary Aldrich, Thomas Arnold and Catharine Arnold, $300, divided. To grandchildren Susanna and Anthony Comstock, children of son Anthony, deceased, $25, each at age. To daughter Rachel Steere, £500. To daughter Anne Comstock, £500. To daughter Martha Staples, £200. To seven children, rest of estate, viz: to Gideon, Rachel, Hazadiah, John, Anne, Ezekiel and Martha.

Inventory, £10,421, 12*s.*, 10*d.*, viz: wearing apparel, spectacles and razor £500, 6*s.*, bible, "Barclay's Apology," 4 feather beds, flock bed, pewter, block tin quart pot, 2 silver spoons, warming pan, mare, 4 cows, heifer, 2 sheep, hog, &c.

1784, May 30. Will—proved 1794, May 14. Widow Martha. Exs. Joseph Comstock and Caleb Greene, of Providence. To grandson Laban, son of Joseph Comstock, my horse. To grandson Anthony, son of Anthony, deceased, a cow. To grandson Henry, son of Ezekiel, deceased, £1. To three children of son Ezekiel, viz: Henry, Wait and Hannah, half of rest of personal. To daughter Anne, wife of Joseph Comstock, and three children of daughter Martha Staples, deceased, viz: Sylvania Whipple, wife of Asa, Martha Randall, wife of Eleazer, and Diana Staples, the other half of personal.

Inventory, £307, 16*s.*

III. THOMAS, b. 1684, Nov. 7. d. 1761. — Providence, West Greenwich, R. I.
m. 1713, Jul. 9.
MERCY JENCKES, b. d. 1761 + of William & Patience (Sprague) — Jenckes.

1. William,
2. Job,
3. Thomas,
4. Patience,
5. Susanna,
6. Esther,
7. Sarah,
8. Lydia.

1708, Jan. 21. He had a horse worth 24*s.*, taken from him for not training, he being a Quaker.

1713, Jun. 16. Taxed 2*s.*, 6*d.*

1735. East Greenwich. Freeman. He subsequently moved to West Greenwich.

1761, Jun. 10. Will—proved 1761, Oct. 3. Ex. son Thomas. He calls himself old and full of days. To son Job, certain land, &c., at death of wife. To son Thomas, land north of that last given and house, buildings, &c., at death of wife, and a suit of clothes with plate buttons. To sons William and Job, rest of apparel and silver shoe buckles. To son William, one Spanish milled dollar, he having had already. To daughters Patience and Susanna Comstock, $1, each. To daughter Esther, $20. To grandson Charles, eldest son of my daughter Sarah, deceased, $1. To daughter Lydia Scott, $20. To wife Mercy, rents and profits of house and land for life, and the rest of personal.

IV. DANIEL, b. 1686, Jul. 19. d. 1768, Dec. 22. — Providence, Smithfield, R. I.
m. (1)
——— b. d. of
m. (2) 1750, Aug. 2.
ELIZABETH BUFFUM, b. 1709, Apr. 26. d. 1768 + of Benjamin & Elizabeth ( ) — Buffum.

1. Azariah,
2. Daniel,

1708, Dec. 20. The Monthly Meeting of Friends denied him "to be of our profession till he repent and amend his ways," for beating and abusing a man "with other disorderly walking."

1713, Jun. 16. Taxed 5*s.*

1735, Dec. 21. Smithfield. He deeded son Azariah, for love, &c., part of homestead.

1738, Apr. 8. He deeded son Daniel, for love, &c., 30 acres.

1768. Administration to widow Elizabeth. Inventory, £114, 12*s.*, 3*d.*, viz: cash £10, 4*s.*, bible and other books, 5 silver spoons, 4 beds, woolen wheel, linen wheel, 12 chairs, pewter, cider, 8½ tons of hay, horse, 4 cows, 4 heifers, 3 calves, 22 sheep, 2 store swine, 2 fat swine, &c.

V. ELIZABETH, b. 1690, Dec. 18. d.
m. 1717, Dec. 1.
JOHN SAYLES, b. 1692, Jan. 13. d. 1777, Sep. 16. of John & Elizabeth ( ) — Sayles.

1. Mercy, 1718, Jul. 19.
2. Elizabeth, 1720, Apr. 14.
3. Mary, 1721, Apr. 22.
4. Phebe, 1723, Feb. 26.
5. Anne, 1724, Dec. 9.
6. Ezekiel, 1726, Jul. 11.
7. John, 1728, Jun. 24.
8. Caleb, 1730, May 4.
9. David, 1731, Jul. 24.
10. Lydia, 1735, Oct. 26.

VI. JOHN, b. 1693, Mar. 26, d. 1750, Jan. 12. — Providence, R. I.
m. (1)
ESTHER JENCKES, b. d. of William & Patience (Sprague) — Jenckes.
m. (2)
SARAH DEXTER, b. 1698, Jun. 27. d. 1773. of John & Alice (Smith) — Dexter.

1. Samuel, 1715.
2. Joseph,
3. Jeremiah,
4. John,
5. Jonathan,
6. James,
7. Nathan,
8. Ichabod,

He was a blacksmith.

1736, Jan. 16. He deeded son Samuel, for love, &c., 30 acres, dwelling house and barn.

1745, Mar. 24. He deeded son Joseph, 17 acres and dwelling house.

1746. Assistant.

1747, Jul. 7. He deeded son Jeremiah, for love, &c., 150 acres.

1749, Aug. 15. He deeded son John, a quarter of forge adjoining to corn mill, &c.

1749, Aug. 16. He deeded sons John, Jonathan, James, Nathan and Ichabod, my homestead farm and dwelling house in which I now dwell, about 170 acres, and also land in the neck I bought of Sam, an Indian, and other lots

1750, Feb. 12. Administration to sons Samuel and John. Inventory, £1,968, 2*s.*, viz: wearing apparel £120, silver money £10, 5*s.*, bonds and notes £901, 8*s.*, books £5, 9 silver spoons £36, pewter, spinning wheel, 2 yoke of oxen, 4 cows, horse, 20 sheep, sea coal £3, old anvil, stillyards, a barrel cider, &c.

He was buried in North Burial Ground.

VII. ICHABOD, b. 1696, Jun. 9. d. 1775, Jan. 26. — Smithfield, R. I.
m. (1) 1722, Sep. 13.
ZIBIAH WILKINSON, b. 1702, Oct. 2. d. of Samuel & Huldah (Aldrich) — Wilkinson.
m. (2) 1747, Mar. 26.
ELIZABETH BOYCE, b. d. 1770 + of — Boyce.

1. Ruth, 1724, Jan. 30.
2. Elizabeth, 1726, Dec. 18.
3. Ichabod, 1728, Mar. 17.
4. Zibiah, 1730, Mar. 19.
5. Abraham, 1734, Dec. 30.
6. Jonathan, 1737, Sep. 7.

(2d wife, no issue.)

See: American Genealogist v. 34, p. 169

COOK (THOMAS). See: American Genealogist, v. 20, p. 185-186.

THOMAS, m. (1)	b. d. 1674, Feb. 6.	Portsmouth, R. I.
——	b. d.	
m. (2) MARY,	b. d.	

(She m. (2) 1680 ±, Jeremiah Brown.)

He was a butcher.

1643. He was received an inhabitant, gave his engagement to government and propounded for a lot.

1649, Oct. 25. He bought of William Brenton, a parcel of land where said Cook hath built his house, &c.

1655. Freeman.

1657, Feb. 6. He was granted 8 acres.

1660, May 14. He, called Thomas Cook, Sr. *alias* butcher, deeded son John Cook, *alias* butcher, 80 acres bounded partly by land of Captain Thomas Cook.

1664. Deputy.

1674, Feb. 6. Will—proved 1677, Jun. 20. Exx. wife Mary. Overseers, Obadiah Holmes and Joseph Torrey. To wife, mansion house and land belonging thereto, for life, and she to enjoy whole estate of movables, cattle, &c., and all household stuff. To son John, a cow, and to all his children, 1*s*., each. To deceased son Thomas's two youngest daughters, £15, apiece at eighteen or marriage, viz: to Phebe and Martha. To grandson John, son of Thomas, deceased, my house and land adjoining, orchard, &c., at death of my wife, being bounded partly by brother Giles Slocum, and said grandson when in possession to pay his brothers, viz: George Stephen and Ebenezer, 40*s*., apiece, when they are twenty-one. If grandson should die, then Ebenezer, the youngest son of deceased son Thomas, to have said estate, and if he die then George, and if he die then Stephen. To Sarah Parker, wife of Peter Parker, 5*s*., and to Sarah's three children Penelope, Peter and Sarah, each, 5*s*., at eighteen. If my son George Cook come to demand it, 5*s*.

1678. His widow Mary, took receipt from John Cook, for his legacy from his father's estate, he calling her mother-in-law (*i. e.* stepmother).

1680, Mar. 31. Jeremiah Brown and Mary, his wife, took receipt from Oliver and Phebe Arnold, of Newport, for legacy, said Phebe being granddaughter of Thomas Cook, who deceased 1674, Feb. 6.

1683, Dec. 24. Jeremiah Brown and wife Mary, took receipt from John Woodcock and wife Martha, of Newport; Thomas Cook, having been the grandfather of said Martha.

No relationship has been traced between Thomas Cook and Robert Cook, of Portsmouth (who married 1678, Dec. 5, Tamar Tyler) and Arthur Cook, who had wife Margaret, and was living in Portsmouth, in 1683, but later moved to Philadelphia.

I. JOHN, m.	b. 1631. d. 1691.		Portsmouth, R. I.
MARY BORDEN,	b. d. 1691 (—)	of Richard & Joan ( )	Borden.

He was a butcher.

1655. Freeman.

1668, Jun. 3. He and Daniel Wilcox were given the privilege of running the ferry at Pocasset.

1670. Deputy.

1676, Aug. 25. He, aged about forty-five years, testified before a court martial held at Newport (on certain Indians) that being at Puncatest in the middle of July or thereabout, did ask of several Indians, whom they were that killed Low Howland, the aforesaid Indians' answer was that there was six of them in company, and Manasses was the Indian that fetched him out of the water.

1688. Licensed.

1691, May 15. Will—proved 1691, May 25. Ex. son Joseph. Overseers, George Sisson and Isaac Lawton. He calls himself aged, and "considering the sore visitation of the small-pox wherewith many are now visited, and many have been taken away," &c. To son John, 150 acres at Punketest with all housing, &c., and 4 acres at Sapowet, in Little Compton, half the upland there, and eight head of neat cattle and feather bed at Punketest where he liveth and twenty sheep; reserving the right to my son Joseph, of getting hay at Punketest, for fifteen head of cattle. To son Joseph, housing and land where I dwell at Portsmouth and 4 acres at Sapowet of marsh, and half upland there, but if Joseph die without heirs male then to go to my son Thomas. Son Joseph to pay his sisters Mary Manchester, wife of William, Elizabeth Briggs, wife of William, Sarah Wait, wife of Thomas, Hannah Wilcox, wife of Daniel, and Martha Cory, wife of William, each, £10; to Deborah Almy, wife of William, 1*s*., to Amey Clayton, wife of David, £10, and to each other sister, being six of them, a cow. To daughter Mary Manchester, ten sheep also, and to daughter Elizabeth Briggs, a feather bed. To son Joseph Cook, negro man Jack, for life, and Indian woman Maria, to be his servant for ten years and then freed, and Indian boy Joan Francisco, to serve with him till twenty-four years of age, at which time son Joseph was to give him a suit of good apparel, a cow, and a horse. To son Thomas, a share of land at Pocasset, twenty sheep, &c. To son Samuel, a share of land at Pocasset, &c. To son John, negro woman Betty and child. To granddaughter Sarah Manchester, a cow.

COOK (THOMAS.) 2d column. I. John. d. 1691, May 16. His wife. b. 1633. d. 1690. 3d column. IV. John. d. 1737. Will-proved 1737, Aug. 7. To wife. Ruth, slave Phillis and other personal estate. To sons John and Thomas 5 s. each, both having had lands. To daughter Mary Howland, £100. To daughter Deborah Howland, £100. To daughters Ruth Fish, Mary Howland, Deborah Howland, and Anne Tripp, rest of movable estate.

1770, Oct. 5. Will—proved 1775, Feb. 6. Ex. son Jonathan. To sons Ichabod and Jonathan, all lands, equally. To wife Elizabeth, half the profits of real estate for life, and one-third personal estate. To daughters Ruth Comstock and Elizabeth Malvery, rest of personal, equally.
Inventory, £153, 15*s.*, 8*d.*, viz: bible, "Barclay's Apology," notes, silver spoon, 4 pewter platters, weaver's loom, old gun, cider barrel, sundry bee hives, chairs, table, settle, woolen wheel, linen wheel, horse, 3 cows, yearling, 5 loads of hay, &c.

VIII. Job, m. (1) Phebe Jenckes, m. (2) 1735, Nov. 22. Phebe Balcom,
Job: b. 1699, Apr. 4. d. — Providence, Glocester, R. I., Dutchess Co., N. Y.
Phebe Jenckes: b. 1703, Jan. 16. d. — of Ebenezer & Mary (Butterworth) Jenckes.
Phebe Balcom: b. d. — of Joseph & Phebe (   ) Balcom.

1. Mercy,
2. Job,

1727, Oct. 17. He and wife Phebe, sold James Musey, of Mendon, homestead of 100 acres in Providence, for £850.
1729, Jan. 2. He and wife Phebe, sold Ebenezer Jencks, for £35, all their interest in estate of honoured father, Ebenezer Jenckes, deceased.
1732. Glocester. Deputy.
1758, Aug. 14. Buteman Precinct, Dutchess Co., N. Y. He deeded son-in-law Amos Sprague and daughter Mercy, his wife, all right in land in Glocester.

COOK (Thomas).

I. Mary, m. William Manchester,
Mary: b. d. 1716 +
William Manchester: b. 1654. d. 1718. — of Thomas & Margaret (Wood) Manchester.

1. John,
2. William,
3. Mary,
4. Sarah,
5. Deborah,
6. Elizabeth,
7. Margaret,
8. Amey,
9. Susanna,
10. Rebecca,
11. Thomas,

II. Elizabeth, m. 1680, William Briggs,
Elizabeth: b. 1653. d. 1716 +
William Briggs: b. 1650. d. 1716, May 12. — of John Briggs.

1. Susanna, 1681, Apr. 9.
2. John, 1685, Nov. 13.
3. William, 1688, Jan. 11.
4. Elizabeth, 1689, Dec. 27.
5. Thomas, 1693, Sep. 5.
6. Deborah, 1693, Sep. 6.
7. Job, 1696, Aug. 3.

III. Sarah, m. Thomas Wait,
Sarah: b. d. 1733 +
Thomas Wait: b. d. 1733, Jun. — of Thomas Wait.

1. Mary,
2. Thomas, 1681, Dec. 21.
3. Benjamin,

See American Genealogist, Oct., 1951, p. 216.

IV. John, m. Ruth Shaw,
John: b. 1656. d. — Tiverton, R. I.
Ruth Shaw: b. d. — of Anthony & Alice (Stonard) Shaw.

1. Ruth,
2. John, 1685, Nov. 5.

1707, Feb. 11. He bought of Israel Shaw, of Little Compton (who calls him brother-in-law), two parcels of land in Portsmouth, a right on Hog Island, and buildings, orchards, &c., for £202, 10*s.*

V. Hannah, m. (1) Daniel Wilcox, m. (2) Enoch Briggs,
Hannah: b. d. 1736.
Daniel Wilcox: b. d. — of Daniel & Elizabeth (Cook) Wilcox.
Enoch Briggs: b. d. 1734. — of John & Sarah (   ) Briggs.

1. Daniel,
2. Mary, 1682, Feb. 25.
3. Hannah, 1684, Apr. 11.
4. Joseph, 1687, Oct. 28.
5. Eliphal,
(By 2d husband.)
6. Abigail,
7. Sarah,
8. Susanna, 1697, Sep. 21.

VI. Joseph, m. 1692, Apr. 19. Susanna Briggs,
Joseph: b. d. 1746, Mar. 21. — Portsmouth, R. I.
Susanna Briggs: b. d. — of John & Hannah (Fisher) Briggs.

1. Deborah, 1692, May 5.
2. John, 1694, Feb. 27.
3. Joseph, 1695, Apr. 20.
4. Thomas, 1697, Mar. 31.
5. William, 1701, Sep 11.

1704-7-8-9. Deputy.
1742, Apr. 25. Will—proved 1746, Mar. 27. Ex. son Thomas. To son William, land in Portsmouth. To daughter Deborah Sisson, land in Portsmouth. To son William and grandson Constant, son of Joseph, deceased, certain land in Tiverton, Constant paying his sister Mary, £20, and sister Rachel, £25. To son Thomas—already had by deed. To grandson John, son of John, deceased, all my housing and lands in Portsmouth, given me by my honoured father John Cook's last will, and certain other land, he paying mortgage. To grandson John, the chest which was his great-grandfather's, &c. To daughter Deborah Sisson, iron pot and two silver spoons, &c. To granddaughter Mary, daughter of Deborah Sisson, a brass skillet. To son Thomas, all my neat cattle, feather bed, negro man Abraham, two sets of plate buttons, &c. To son William, a cow, old mare, long table, three silver spoons, least silver cup and set of plate buttons. To each grandson named Joseph, in the first line, 2*s.*, and rest of grandchildren, 1*s.*, each. To sons Thomas and William and daughter Deborah, rest of silver money. To grandson David Cook, great silver buttons for breeches. To each child of son John, deceased, £10, except grandson John, at age. To granddaughter Susanna, daughter of William, a silver spoon. To sons Thomas and William, wearing apparel, except plate buttons. To sister-in-law Mary Briggs, £30, and a cow. To cousin Sarah Durfee, daughter of Thomas Durfee, now of Bristol, £5, at eighteen. To son Thomas, biggest silver cup. To daughter Deborah, next biggest silver cup. Rest of real estate sold and balance after debts, &c., to go to children Thomas, William and Deborah.
Inventory, £1,117, 15*s.*, 2*d.*, viz: wearing apparel £27, plate buttons £32, 5*s.*, wrought plate 23¼ oz. £42, 7*s.*, 6*d.*, silver money £28, 10*s.*, piece of gold, £3, books £6, armour £4, bonds, flagon, cheese press, carpenter tools, negro man Abraham £30, old mare £5, sheep £30, 3 cows, calf, 2 shotes, limbeck or still £3, &c.

VII. Martha, m. William Cory,
Martha: b. d. 1704 (—)
William Cory: b. d. 1704. — of William & Mary (Earle) Cory.

1. Michael, 1688, Apr. 21.
2. William,
3. Thomas,
4. Patience,
5. Mary,
6. Amey,
7. Sarah,

VIII. Deborah, m. William Almy,
Deborah: b. d.
William Almy: b. 1665, Oct. 27. d. 1747, Jul. 6. — of Christopher & Elizabeth (Cornell) Almy.

1. Mary, 1689, Aug. 7.
2. John, 1692, Oct. 10.
3. Job, 1696, Apr. 28.
4. Elizabeth, 1697, Nov. 14.
5. Samuel, 1701, Apr. 15.
6. Deborah, 1703, Jul. 27.
7. Rebecca, 1704, Oct. 14.
8. Joseph, 1707, Oct. 3.
9. William, 1707, Oct. 3.

IX. Thomas, m. Mary Cory,
Thomas: b. d. 1726. — Tiverton, R. I.
Mary Cory: b. d. 1726 + — of William & Mary (Earle) Cory.

1. Stephen,
2. Joseph,
3. Chaplin,
4. Deborah,
5. Mary,
6. Amey,

1726, Apr. 25. Will—proved 1726, Jun. 11. Exs. wife Mary and son Chaplin. To wife, feather bed, all indoor movables, with exceptions, cow, mare, yearling horse, colt, ten sheep, two swine and all geese and fowls. To youngest son Chaplin Cook, south half of homestead and other land

II. { THOMAS, m. MARY HAVENS, } { b. d. 1670 (—) b. d. } Portsmouth, R. I. of William & Dionis ( ) Havens.

He bore the title of Captain, and was thus distinguished from his father Thomas Cook, Sr.

1655. Freeman.

1658, Mar. 10. A fine of 10*s.*, was remitted to him

III. { GEORGE, } { b. d. }

IV. { SARAH, m. PETER PARKER, } { b. d. b. d. } of George & Frances ( ) Parker.

Craw, Robert (omitted by Austin) See: American Genealogist, v. 27, Oct., 1951, p. 216

DAVOL.

{ WILLIAM, m. ——— } { b. d. 1680 + b. d. } Duxbury, Rehoboth, Mass., Newport, R. I.

1640, Aug. 3. Duxbury. He desired a parcel of land lying between Edmund Chandler and John Rouse and Abraham Sampson, such a portion as the Court shall be pleased to allow him.

1643, Jun. 24. Braintree. His son John was born here.

1645, Dec. 26. Rehoboth. He was granted the house lot, &c., that was laid out to John Sutton, "forasmuch as he hath not come to live among us."

1646, Jan. 7. He bought of John Hazell the house which William Davol now dwelleth in and the lot.

1647, Feb. 9. Certain persons were granted leave to set up a weir upon the cove before William Davol's house, and one upon Pawtucket River; "provided they hinder not either English nor Indians from fishing at the falls in either place, and they shall sell alewives at 2*s.* a thousand, and other fish at reasonable rates."

1649. Constable.

1650, Oct. 2. At this date he and his wife were presented by Grand Jury with others, for continuing of meeting upon the Lord's day from house to house contrary to order of this Court enacted June 12, 1650.

1653, May 17. Newport. Freeman.

1672. He deeded to son Benjamin certain land at Monmouth, N. J. previously purchased of Mark Lucar, of Newport.

1673, Oct. 22. Juryman.

1679, Feb. 18. He witnessed the deed of his son Joseph.

1680. Taxed £1, 1*s.* 2*d.*, William and Joseph Davol (his son).

I. { JOHN, } { b. 1643, Jun. 24. d. 1643, Jul. }

II. { JOSEPH, m. (1) MARY BRAYTON, m. (2) ELIZABETH, } { b. d. 1716, Feb. b. d. b. d. 1716 + } Newport, Westerly, R. I. of Francis & Mary ( ) Brayton. of

He was a surveyor and much employed in that calling.

1666, Jun. 5. Dartmouth. Freeman. He remained there but a short time.

1670. Newport. Freeman.

1671, Jan. 6. He engaged himself to his father-in-law Francis Brayton for and in behalf my daughter Mary Davol, to pay her £5, at fifteen years of age, said sum to be paid Francis Brayton if then living or to whom he shall assign it, and if she die before fifteen then the £5, to be set apart for use of son Joseph. Mary is freely given and commended by her father to the care of Francis Brayton during life of said Mary's grandmother or until Mary is married, and said Francis Brayton engages that at time of his decease he will pay Mary £5.

1672, Jan. 20. He bought of Daniel Wilcox, of Dartmouth, a share at Puncatest, for £5.

1679, Feb. 11. He sold Thomas Ward, of Newport, a share in Puncatest, for £9.

1687. He and another were chosen to have charge of branding horses and cattle.

1692, Mar. 28. Westerly. Surveyor. He laid out 100 acres.

1695. Town Council. He had the title of Captain for some years.

1702, Mar. 27. He and wife Elizabeth deeded land in Narragansett to son William.

To son Stephen, north half of homestead. To son Joseph, rest of lands. To daughter Deborah Cook, feather bed, silver spoon, &c. To daughter Mary Cook, feather bed, silver cup and silver spoon. To daughter Amey Cook, feather bed and silver spoon. To three sons, a silver spoon each. To son Stephen, the biggest gun, newest set of silver buttons, ten sheep and two yearling steers. To son Chaplin, least gun, chest, table, twenty sheep, old set of silver buttons, &c. To three daughters, the rest of household goods and a cow, each. To son Joseph ten sheep and a heifer and a swine. To son Chaplin, working oxen, cow, mare, two swine, and farming tools, he paying his three sisters £10, each, Amey being under eighteen. To wife, house room for life, with one of her daughters if she see fit, and use of ten apple trees, and son Chaplin, to keep for her a cow, mare, two swine, five geese, six fowls, &c.

Inventory, £301, 15s., 5d., viz: 2 sets of silver buttons, buckles, &c. £30, stillyards, scales, 7 silver spoons, silver cup, 5 feather beds, pewter, 2 guns, barrel of cider, worsted comb, wool cards, 3 woolen wheels, linen wheel, cider mill, 2 mares, colt, 2 oxen, 4 cows, heifer, 2 yearlings, 3 calves, 45 sheep, 21 lambs, 12 swine, 8 geese, fowls, &c.

X. AMEY, b. d. 1729 +
m.
DAVID CLAYTON, b. d. 1730. of Clayton.

1. Ann, 1689, May.
2. Abraham,
3. David,
4. John,
5. Margaret,

XI. SAMUEL, b. d.

I. THOMAS, b. d. 1699. Portsmouth, R. I., Monmouth, N. J.
m.
ELIZABETH, b. d. 1699 + of

1. Thomas,
2. William,
3. Elizabeth,

He was called Thomas Cook, Jr., to distinguish him from his grandfather Thomas Cook, Sr.

1670, Oct. 14. He sold to John Cook, 6 acres for £30, said land being bounded north by land of Thomas Cook, Sr., and he agreed that the land conveyed should be free from any manner of molestation from me or any of the children of my deceased father Thomas Cook.

1696. Monmouth. He and wife Elizabeth were living here at this period.

1698, Dec. 12. Will—proved 1699, Oct. 3. Exx. wife Elizabeth. He mentions sons Thomas and William and daughter Elizabeth.

II. JOHN, b. d. 1727. Portsmouth, Tiverton, R. I.
m.
MARY, b. d. 1754. of

1. Thomas,
2. John,
3. Peleg,
4. George,
5. Joseph,
6. Sarah,
7. Phebe,
8. Mary,
9. Deborah,
10. Martha,
11. Patience,

1678. Freeman.

1683, Mar. 12. He and wife Mary, testified to having witnessed will of Giles Slocum, in 1681. He was called "son of the deceased Cap'n Cooke."

1694, May 26. He and wife Mary sold Abraham Anthony 12 acres.

1727, Sep. 15. Will—proved 1727, Oct. 17. Exx. wife Mary. To her the movable estate. To eldest son Thomas, land where he liveth already deeded. To son John, land deeded, &c. To son Peleg, land deeded, &c. To son George, land. To youngest son Joseph, 5s. To daughters Sarah Witman, Phebe Allen, and Mary Pierce, each, £15, &c. To daughters Deborah Tallman, Martha Sherman, and Patience Church, each, £30, &c.

1751, Mar. 27. Will—proved 1754, Jul. 29. Mary Cook, widow of Captain John Cook. Ex. son Joseph. She calls herself "very ancient and full of pains." To son Joseph, all estate.

III. GEORGE, b. d. Monmouth, N. J.

1699 He was living in Monmouth at this date.

IV. STEPHEN, b. d. Monmouth, N. J.

1689. He was named as of Monmouth.

V. EBENEZER, b. d. Monmouth, N. J.
m.
MARY, b. d. of

1695. He and wife Mary, were of Monmouth.

VI. PHEBE, b. 1665. d. 1732.
m. (1)
OLIVER ARNOLD, b. 1655, Jul. 25. d. 1697, Nov. 6. of Benedict & Damaris (Westcott) Arnold.
m. (2)
JONATHAN MARSH, b. d. 1704, Jun. 10. of Marsh.
m. (3) 1705, Oct. 7.
ROBERT BARKER, b. d. of Barker.

1. Damaris, 1680, Dec. 30.
2. Phebe, 1682, Dec. 30.
3. Patience, 1684.
4. Mary, 1687.
5. Sarah, 1689.
6. Oliver, 1694.
7. Freelove,
(By 2d husband.)
8. Jonathan, 1702, Jan. 27.

VII. MARTHA, b. d.
m.
JOHN WOODCOCK, b. d. of Woodcock.

1. Penelope,
2. Peter,
3. Sarah.

DAVOL.

I. MARY, b. d.
m. 1689, Mar. 18.
JAMES TALLMAN, b. d. 1724. of Peter & Joan (Briggs) Tallman.

1. John, 1692, Sep. 19.
2. Joseph, 1694, Jul. 13.
3. Elizabeth, 1699, Jun. 13.

II. WILLIAM, b. d. 1719. Westerly, R. I.
m.
ELIZABETH, b. d. 1722 + of

1. William, 1698, Aug. 2.

(She m. (2) Christopher Champlin.)

1702, Jun. 29. He was chosen as constable, but refused the office.

1719, Jan. 6. Will—proved 1719, Mar. 2. Ex. son William. To wife Elizabeth, half of household stuff, three cows, riding horse, and the dwelling house now rented to Philip Griffin; all to be for her life. To son William, all lands and housing and rest of movables, and Indian boy Jeffrey. To wife, Indian girl Mercy, and she to have the keep of the cow and horse by her son William, who shall also pay his mother £30, every year, and twenty loads of firewood supplied to her yearly by him.

1722, Aug. 21. Elizabeth Champlin gave receipt to her son William Davol, for legacy from her late husband William Davol's estate.

III. JOSEPH, b. d.
m. 1705, Jun. 29. [widow.
ELIZABETH YEOMANS b. d. of

1711, Jul. 31. He was living in Stonington at this date as shown by a deposition, but returned to Westerly before his death.

1716, Feb. 24. He was buried.

1716, Feb. 27. Inventory, £28, 14s. Administration to son and heir William. The Town Council ordered a third part to widow, and the other two-thirds as by law directed. Among the items of inventory, were: 2 feather beds, 12 silver spoons, silver cup, pewter, bible, pair of stillyards, churn, cow, mare, &c.

DAVOL. 2d column. III. Jonathan m. Hannah Audley, b. 1643. Oct. of John and Margaret Audley of Boston. 3d column. VI. William. His son William b. 1716, Sep. 18.

III.	JONATHAN,	b.	Newport, R. I., Dartmouth, Mass.
	m.	d. 1709 +	
	HANNAH ADLEY,	b.	
		d.	of Adley.

1677, Oct. 31. He and forty-seven others were granted 5,000 acres to be called East Greenwich. He never settled there.

1698, Aug. 19. Dartmouth. He sold Nathaniel Potter, Sr., of Dartmouth, 50 acres there for £14.

IV.	BENJAMIN,	b.	Newport, R. I., Monmouth, N. J.
	m.	d.	
	ELIZABETH PEABODY,	b.	
		d.	of John Peabody.

1682, Mar. 28. Grand Jury.

I. JONATHAN, b. ; d. 1709. Dartmouth, Mass.
m.
HANNAH, b. ; d. 1709 + of

1709, Aug. 8. Will—proved 1709, Sep. 7. Exx. wife Hannah. To son William, my homestead farm which my father Jonathan Davol gave me by deed of gift, 50 acres, with housing, orchard, &c.; he allowing my wife her thirds during life. To son Jonathan 50 acres. To two sons, privilege in lands in Dartmouth. To daughter Hannah, £6, paid by son William when she is twenty. To daughter Abiah, £6, when eighteen, and like legacy to daughter Meribah. To wife, rest of personal.
Inventory, £176, 7*s.* 8*d.*, viz: house and land £100, 4 cows, 2 two years, 2 oxen, 5 yearlings, 5 calves, 3 mares, 18 sheep, 5 swine, fowls, 3 beds, pewter, gun, stillyards, 2 wheels, pair of cards, carpenter's tools, warming pan, &c.

1. William, 1698, Apr. 16.
2. Hannah, 1699, Jan. 29.
3. Jonathan, 1702, May 1.
4. Abiah,
5. Meribah, 1707, Oct. 21.
6. Mary, 1710, Feb. 26.

II. JOSEPH, b. ; d. 1726. Dartmouth, Mass.
m.
MARY SOULE, b. ; d. 1726 + of George & Deborah ( ) Soule.

1706. He and his wife gave a receipt to her brother William Soule as executor of his father George Soule's will.
1726, Nov. 14. Inventory, £190, 14*s.* 10*d.* Administratrix Widow Mary. Books and apparel £8, bed, pair of worsted combs, pewter, warming pan, cow, lamb, hogshead of cider, &c.

1. Christopher, 1700, Jan. 27.
2. Lydia, 1701, Apr. 3.
3. Joseph, 1703, Jan. 15.
4. Mary, 1705, Jul. 14.
5. Hannah, 1707, Apr. 4.
6. Benjamin, 1709, Jan. 26.
7. Jonathan,

III. BENJAMIN, b. ; d. 1735. Dartmouth, Mass.
m.
ANN BROWNELL, b. 1680, Jun. 4. ; d. 1735 + of William & Sarah (Smiton) Brownell.

1734, Dec. 16. Will—proved 1735, Feb. 10. Exx. wife Ann. To wife, use of all my homestead farm, &c., till son John is twenty-one, and she to bring up children. To son Peter, £5, paid by son John when the latter inherits gift. To son John, at age, homestead farm, housing and orchard, and all personal, and rights in undivided lands, he paying £125, in legacies to brothers and sisters when he arrives at age. To sons Peter and John, right in a cedar swamp. To daughter Sarah Mosher, £20, and like legacy to daughters Elizabeth Davol (in two years), Rebecca Brownell (in three years), Freelove Davol (in four years), Ann Davol (in five years) and Mary Davol (in six years). If son John die before twenty-one without issue, then Peter to have his legacy, he paying £30, to sisters, and if Peter dies, half of the property to go to Peter's children and half to mine.
Inventory, £1,340, 4*s.*, viz: pewter, books, cattle, hay, 44 sheep, 3 horsekind, 9 swine, homestead £900, &c.

1. Peter,
2. Sarah,
3. Elizabeth,
4. Rebecca,
5. Freelove,
6. Ann,
7. Mary,
8. John,

IV. JEREMIAH, b. ; d. 1753, Nov. 29. Dartmouth, Mass.
m. (1) 1711, May 24.
SARAH ALLEN b. ; d. of Joseph & Sarah ( ) Allen.
m. (2)
SARAH WHITRIDGE, b. ; d. 1753 + of Whitridge.

1753, Oct. 24. Will—proved 1754, Jan. 29. Ex. son Abraham. Overseers for children under age, Thomas Hathaway, Bartholomew Taber and Jethro Hathaway. To wife Sarah, feather bed which she brought me at marriage and £13, 6*s.* 8*d.*, provided she marries, and use of personal (with exceptions) while widow. To her also, use of all real estate while widow till son Joseph is twenty-one, and then use of best room, keep of a cow, and swine, and firewood, while widow. To son Reuben, 6*s.*, he having had. To son Timothy, 6*s.* To son Tristram, 6*s.* To son Silas, wearing apparel, &c. To son Abraham, £3. To son Ephraim, £3. To son Joseph, all my housing, &c., at age, but if he die before then, to go to all children; and he to keep a cow for his mother, furnish her with firewood, &c., and pay his two sisters Priscilla and Mary Davol, 30*s.* each. To daughter Ruth How land, 6*s.* To daughter Sarah Davol, all pewter which I had by me at first wife's decease, and a feather bed, &c.
Inventory, £84, 6*s.* 1*d.*, viz: books, wearing apparel, gun, pewter, loom, cheese press, 20 sheep, 4 cows, mare, 4 geese, &c. Among the books was "Barclay's Apology."

1. Reuben, 1712, Jul.
2. Timothy, 1714, Jan. 1.
3. Tristram, 1716, Mar. 20.
4. Silas, 1717, Aug. 9.
5. Ruth, 1719, Mar. 14.
6. Jeremiah, 1721, May 8.
7. Abraham,
8. Ephraim,
9. Sarah,
(2d wife.)
10. Joseph,
11. Priscilla,
12. Mary,

V. MARY, b. ; d.
m. 1714 May 22.
JAMES MOSHER, b. 1675. ; d. of Hugh & Rebecca (Harndel) Mosher.

1. William, 1715, Jun. 4.
2. Timothy, 1716, Oct. 27.
3. Jonathan, 1718, May 9.
4. David, 1720, Mar. 29.
5 Jeremiah, 1722, Jun. 16.
6. James,
7. Phebe, 1725.

VI. WILLIAM, b. ; d. 1772. Dartmouth, Mass.
m.
SARAH SISSON, b. ; d. of James & Lydia (Hathaway) Sisson.

1753, Sep. 6. Will—proved 1772, Feb. 14. Ex. son David. He calls himself in declining years. To son David, half of husbandry tools, and north part of homestead with buildings. To son Joshua, the south half and housing, with other land and half husbandry tools, a gun, cow, &c. If Joshua die, David to have his part, he paying my five children, viz: William, Lydia Stafford, Hannah Mosher, Sarah Wood and Phebe Merihew, £45, each. To son William, £22, a gun, and what he has had. To four daughters Lydia Stafford, Hannah Mosher, Sarah Wood and Phebe Merihew, £1, equally divided, and wearing apparel and household goods. To sons, other privileges. To son David, rest of estate.

1. Lydia,
2. Hannah, 1712, Jan. 13.
3. Sarah,
4. Phebe,
5. Joshua,
6. David,
7. William,

VII. ANNE, b. ; d.
m.
BENJAMIN SWEAT, b. ; d. of Sweat.

1. Jonathan,

VIII. HANNAH, b. ; d. 1744 +
m.
JOSEPH WEEDEN, b. ; d. 1745. of William Weeden.

1. Joseph,
1. Jonathan,
3. William,
4. Phebe,
5. Sarah,
6. Hannah,
7. Hope,
8. Daughter,

IX. ABIGAIL, b. ; d.
m.
JOB MILK, b. ; d. of Milk.

1. David,
2. Job,
3. Jonathan,
4. Abigail,
5. Elizabeth,
6. Mary,

X. SARAH, b. ; d.
m. 1717, Jul. 25.
HUGH MOSHER, b. 1690, Nov. 16. ; d. of Nicholas & Elizabeth ( ) Mosher.

1. Hugh,
2. Nicholas,
3. Abner,
4. Ephraim, 1726 Sep. 21.
5. Adley,
6. Sarah,
7. Mary,
8. Hannah,
9. Barbara,
10. Phebe,

XI. ELIZABETH, b. ; d. 1742 +
m. 1716, Jun. 22.
GEORGE BROWNELL, b. 1693, Apr. 13. ; d. 1742. of William & Sarah (Smiton) Brownell.

1. William,
2. Jonathan,
3. George,
4. Benjamin,
5. Timothy,
6. Elijah,
7. Hannah,
8. Sarah,
9. Elizabeth,
10. Phebe,

Dexter, Gregory. See also: Bowen's PROVIDENCE OATH OF ALLEGIANCE, p. 75-77.

{ GREGORY, { b. 1610. Olney, Northampton Co., Eng., [Providence, R. I.
m. d. 1700.
ABIGAIL FULLERTON, { b.
d. 1706 +
of Fullerton.

He was a stationer in England and in New England was a minister, &c.

1638 ± Providence. He had a lot assigned him.

1640, Jul. 27. He and thirty-eight others signed an agreement for a form of government.

1643. The "Key to the Indian Language" (by Roger Williams), was printed at his establishment in London, and possibly he had returned to England, coming again to Providence with Roger Williams the next year.

He joined the Baptist Church at Providence, having been a preacher before his arrival.

1646. About this time (as Morgan Edwards relates) he "was sent for to Boston to set in order the printing office there, for which he desired no other reward than that one of their almanacks should be sent him every year."

1650, Feb. 4. He bought of Joshua Winsor, a share of meadow west side of Moshassuck River.

1650, Sep. 2. Taxed £1.

1651-52-53-54. Commissioner.

1653-54. Town Clerk.

1653-54. President of Providence and Warwick.

1654. Ordained as pastor of First Baptist Church. He was colleague with Chad Brown, and also with William Wickenden.

1655. Freeman.

1664-66. Deputy.

1665, Feb. 19. He had lot 15, in a division of land.

1669, Jul 8. He is alluded to in a letter of Roger Williams to John Whipple, wherein Mr. Williams allows that he had said that Gregory Dexter made a "fool of his conscience," but continues "yet it is commendable and admirable in him that being a man of education, and of a noble calling, and versed in militaires, that his conscience forced him to be such a child in his own house."

1673, Jan. 27. He deeded to eldest son Stephen, 80 acres and a meadow share, except the privilege to inhabitants of Providence to fetch for their own use as much lime rock from rock commonly called Hackston's Rock, as they please, provided also that equal allowance be made for a way to the said rock through the said 80 acres.

1676, Apr. 4. It was voted "that in these troublesome time and straits in this Colony, this Assembly desiring to have the advice and concurrence of the most judicious inhabitants, if it may be had for the good of the whole, desire at their next sitting the company and counsel of" sixteen persons, among whom was Gregory Dexter.

He was absent at Long Island during part of King Philip's war.

1680, Jul. 16. He and son John were taxed together 4*s*., 1*d*.

1684, Oct. 29. He and son John were taxed together 12*s*., 6*d*.

1685, Oct. 7. His son John had land laid out in the father's right, bounded partly in land "whereon the said Gregory Dexter and John Dexter now dwelleth."

1695, Jan. 28. He signed a paper in which he declared that he had "provided for two children of my son James Dexter, deceased, about nineteen years, namely Peleg and Isabel Dexter; and whereas my said son James Dexter died when I was gone to Long Island, and signified that his desires were that the said Peleg and Isabel might have each of them one of these two lots where he dwelt," &c., now, therefore, Gregory Dexter confirms these lots to the children in accordance with his son's wishes, and gave the lot where the house stood to Peleg, and the other lot to Isabel. He provided that it should not be lawful for Peleg or Isabel to sell, change or let, or give away the lands without the advice of their uncles Elisha Arnold and John Dexter, Sr. A reservation was made as to Isabel's lot that if Gregory or his wife died in Providence "we may have room to be buried by her father."

Morgan Edwards writes of him: "Mr. Dexter was not only a well bred man, but remarkably pious. He was never observed to laugh, seldom to smile. So earnest was he in his ministry that he could hardly forbear preaching when he came into a house or met with a concourse of people out of doors. His religious sentiments were those of the Particular Baptists."

I. { STEPHEN, { b. 1647, Nov. 1. Providence, R. I.
m. d. 1679.
ABIGAIL WHIPPLE, { b.
d. 1725, Aug. 19. of John & Sarah ( ) Whipple.

(She m. (2) 1682, Jan., William Hopkins.)

1679, Jul. 1. Widow Abigail Dexter, taxed 1*s*., 3*d*.

1679, Dec. 22. Inventory, £23, 10*s*., viz: cow, steer, calf 2 young swine, gun, sheets, linen, wearing apparel, pewter, &c.

1680, Jan. 5. Administration to widow Abigail.

1680, Jul. 16. Widow Abigail Dexter, taxed 7*d*.

1681, Jun. 6. His widow petitioned the town not to be taxed for house rent, &c, having no vote, &c. Her petition was granted.

1725, Aug. 16. Will—proved 1725, Sep. 20. Widow Abigail Hopkins. Ex. grandson William Hopkins. To three children, John Dexter, William Hopkins and Abigail Field, 40*s*., each. To daughter Abigail Field, biggest brass kettle, pewter, six napkins, tablecloth, bed curtains, pillows, bolster cases, trunk, box, chairs, linen and flannel sheets, and wearing apparel. To granddaughter Abigail Dexter, an iron kettle, three pewter plates, pair of sheets and pair of pillow cases. To grandson Stephen Dexter, a great chest. To son William Hopkins and his children, William, Hope, and Abigail Hopkins, she made further bequests.

II. { JAMES, { b. 1650, May 6. Providence, R. I.
m. 1671 ± d. 1676.
ESTHER ARNOLD, { b. 1647, Sep. 22.
d. 1688 ± of Stephen & Sarah (Smith) Arnold.

(She m. (2) 1680, Oct. 30, Wm. Andrews and (3) Edward Hawkins.)

1680, Jul. 16. His estate was taxed 6*d*.

1684, Oct. 29. Orphans of James Dexter, taxed 10*d*.

III. { JOHN, { b. 1652, Nov. 6. Providence, R. I.
m. 1688, Feb. 16. d. 1706, Apr. 28.
ALICE SMITH, { b. 1665.
d. 1736, Feb. 19. of John & Sarah (Whipple) Smith.

(She m. (2) 1727, Feb. 3, Joseph Jenckes.)

1677. Freeman.

1680, Mar. 16. His fine of 10*s*., for not attending jury was remitted by Assembly on his petition.

1680-84-85-86-90-94-96-97-98-1700-1-2-3-4-5. Deputy.

1687. Ratable estate, 6 acres planting, 2 shares of meadow, 6 acres of other mowable land, 2 oxen, 12 cows, 4 heifers, 4 steers, 5 two years, 12 yearlings, bull, horse, 20 sheep, 6 hogs, &c.

1688-99-1700-1. Town Council.

1690-91. Assistant.

1696, Jan. 27. He and others were granted a lot, measuring forty feet square, for a school house if they would build in some considerable time.

1699-1700-1-2-3-4-5. Major for the main land.

1704-5. Speaker of the House of Deputies.

1706, Apr. 15. Will—proved 1706, May 20. Exx. wife Alice. Overseers, brother-in-law John Smith, Captain Thomas Fenner, Captain Samuel Wilkinson and Lieutenant Joseph Jencks. To wife, the profit and benefit of house, barn, orchard, land, cattle, &c., "to be wholly at her dispose for the looking after and maintenance of my honored mother and also for the maintenance and bringing up my own dear children," &c. She to retain the estate till son Stephen is of age, and then she to have half while widow. To son Stephen, at age, one-half of homestead, &c., and at marriage or death of his mother the other half. To sons James and John, certain land. To wife, the 40 acres given her by her father, and also £50. To daughters, £20 each, at twenty-one. To children, equally, all money due. To Hannah Sprague, ten pieces of eight above her wages if she tarries with wife and is helpful to my honoured mother during her life. To wife, household goods for her use and disposal. Inventory, £757, 19*s*., 6*d*., viz: horse, 36 head of cattle, 86 sheep and lambs, 32 goats and kids, 5 swine, bills £343, 8*s*., 6*d*., cash £168, pewter tankard, 2 silver dram cups, 7 pewter platters, carpenter's tools, &c.

1735, Dec. 22. Will—proved 1736, Apr. 17. Widow Alice, now wife of Joseph Jenckes. Ex. son-in-law Elisha Greene. To son Stephen Dexter and grandson John Dexter, son of James, deceased, all her books, sword, rapier and cane, equally. To son Stephen, a gun. To daughter Mary Angell, a cow. To five daughters Abigail Greene, Phebe Kilton, Anne Brown, Alice Olney, and Sarah Dexter, £3, each. To son Stephen, the rest of money remaining in his hands after above sums are paid. To six daughters, equally, the £75, that is in hands of John Angell, and they to have the silver money, wearing apparel and household goods, equally. To grandsons John and James Dexter, sons of James, deceased, 50 acres in Smithfield, equally, they paying their brother David, £4.

Inventory, £201, 2*s*.

I. JOHN, b. 1673. d. 1734, Apr. 22. — Providence, R. I.
m. (1)
MARY FIELD, b. 1673, Jun. 1. d. 1727, Jun. of Thomas & Martha (Harris) — Field.
m. (2)
MARY MASON, b. 1682, Dec. 12. d. 1754, Feb. 4. of Noah & Sarah (Fitch) — Mason.

1. Naomi, 1698.
2. Mary, 1699.
3. John, 1701.
4. Stephen, 1703.
5. Jeremiah, 1705.
6. Sarah, 1707.
7. Lydia, 1709.
8. William, 1711.
9. Jonathan, 1713.
10. Abigail, 1715.
(2d wife, no issue.)

1713, Jun. 16. Taxed 17*s*.

1734, May 20. Administration to widow Mary. Inventory, £340, 11*s*., viz: cow, calf, old gun, books, cider, molasses, cooper's tools, bonds £233, &c.

1753, Dec. 28. Will—proved 1754. Widow Mary. Ex. kinsman Amaziah Waterman. To John Mason, son of brother Noah Mason, deceased, £5. To niece Mary Baristo, £5. To cousin Hannah Mason, £5. To nephew James Mason, joint stool. To Mary Mason, daughter of my brother Daniel Mason, deceased, best silver spoon and looking glass. To nephews John and Benjamin Mason and to Sybil Mason, children of brother Timothy Mason, deceased, the bond which my sister Sybil Mason, gave me for a sum of money and now due to me from said Timothy's estate, that is, half equally to John and Benjamin Mason, and half to Sybil Mason. To cousin Hannah Mason, such wearing apparel as I usually wear every day. To niece Sarah Waterman, oval table. To niece Hannah Brown, a chest. To cousins Sarah Waterman and Hannah Brown, rest of apparel. To nephews, John and George Baristo, 24*s*., each. To daughter-in-law (*i. e.* stepdaughter) Mary Whipple, fire tongs, &c. To Mary Whipple, daughter of Noah Whipple, kettle, &c., and to her sister Anphillis, my gold ring. To daughter-in-law Abigail Smith, a silver spoon. To granddaughter-in-law Naomi Dexter, one Spanish milled dollar. To cousins Sarah Waterman, Hannah Brown and Martha Hunt, rest of estate.

Inventory, £522.

He and both wives were buried in North Burial Ground.

II. ABIGAIL, b. d.
m.
THOMAS FIELD, b. 1670, Jan. 3. d. 1752, Jul. 17. of Thomas & Martha (Harris) — Field. Providence, R. I.

1. Thomas, 1696 ±
2. Stephen,
3. Jeremiah,
4. Nathaniel,
5. Anthony,
6. Joseph,

I. PELEG, b. d. 1708 (—)
UNMARRIED,

1708, Apr. 26. He died before this date, and probably much earlier. His grandmother Sarah Arnold, in her will mentions only three children of her deceased daughter Esther, viz: James and Isabel Dexter, and Esther Hawkins (the latter being a child of Esther Arnold's third marriage).

II. ISABEL, b. d.

III. JAMES, b. d. 1732, Jan. 23. — Providence, R. I.
m.
SARAH, b. d. 1732 + of

1. James,
2. Peleg,
3. Esther,
4. Philip,
5. Paul,
6. Thomas,
7. Sarah,
8. Priscilla,
9. Mary,

He was a cordwainer and also styled merchant.

1699, Mar. 24. He had a deed of a piece of 70 acres from his grandfather Stephen Arnold.

1706. Town Sergeant.

1708, Apr. 26. His grandmother Sarah Arnold, in will of this date gave him £3, of the £20, he owed her.

1711. Town Treasurer.

1711-13-17. Deputy.

1724-25-26. Town Council.

1732, Jan. 19. Will—proved 1732, Feb. 28. Exx. wife Sarah. To her use of whole estate till son Philip is of age, and then if not married she to have use of half estate for life. To son Philip, half the homestead at age and other half at death or marriage of his mother. To son James, land near Bennett's Hollow. To son Paul, 100 acres at Huckleberry Hill, at age, he providing a maintenance for life to brother Thomas, with help of mother. To son Peleg, £100. To daughter Esther, £40, and like legacy to daughters Sarah, Priscilla, and Mary, when each is eighteen. To wife, if she marry again a feather bed and £30, only.

Inventory, £751, 17*s*., viz: store goods, law books, 18 cattle, 2 horses, bonds £431, 2*s*., 4*d*., &c.

I. STEPHEN, b. 1689, Apr. 15. d. 1758, Dec. 27. — Providence, R. I.
m.
SUSANNA WHIPPLE, b. 1693, Apr. 14. d. 1776, Dec. 15. of Joseph & Alice (Smith) — Whipple.

1. John,
2. Joseph,
3. Christopher,
4. Jeremiah,
5. Edward,
6. Susan, 1713, Oct. 28.
7. Freelove, 1719.
8. Waitstill, 1721, Sep. 10.

1712. Freeman.

1727. Deputy.

1727-29-31-32-33-34-35-36. Town Council.

1738, Sep. 13. He deeded his cousin (*i. e.* nephew) John Dexter, son of brother James, deceased, all lands west of Seven Mile Line which honored father John Dexter, deceased, by last will gave to his son James, my brother, except 33 acres.

1759, Feb. 26. Administration to widow Susannah. Inventory, £2,053, 16*s*., 8*d*., viz: old mare, 6 cows, yoke of oxen, 3 two years, 3 yearlings, 2 three years, 4 hogsheads cider, 50 oz. plate £333, 6*s*., 8*d*., large oval table, small table, 18 chairs, looking glass, 50 pounds pewter, quarto bible, wearing apparel £271, &c.

1765, Oct. 28. Susannah Dexter, widow, being represented to Town Council of North Providence, as being discomposed in mind, by her son Jeremiah, he was appointed guardian.

II. JAMES, b. 1691, Feb. 22. d. 1731, Nov. 7. — Providence, Smithfield, R. I.
m.
HANNAH WILKINSON, b. d. of Josias & Hannah (Tyler) — Wilkinson.

1. John, 1717, Feb. 1.
2. Anne, 1718, Oct. 22.
3. James, 1721, Feb. 24.
4. David, 1723, Feb. 24.
5. Hopestill, 1726, Jul. 5.
6. Mercy, 1730, Oct. 10.

He was called James Dexter, Jr., joiner, to distinguish him from his older cousin.

1732. Inventory, £76, 19*s*., 2*d*., viz: wearing apparel, £6, 6*s*., 6*d*. pair of pistols, pewter, warming pan, books £1, 2*s*., table, chest, joiner's and carpenter's tools, turning wheel, 3 swine, &c.

III. JOHN, b. 1692, Oct. 24. d. 1716, Jun. 29. — Providence, R. I.
UNMARRIED.

He was a mariner and called Captain.

1716, Jun. 26. Will—proved 1716, Aug. 4. Ex. William Crawford. To honoured mother Alice, a jenney. To sisters Mary, Abigail, Sarah, Phebe, Anne and Alice, £20, each. To brothers Stephen and James, wearing apparel, books and instruments. To brother James' eldest son, rest of estate.

Inventory, negro woman and boy £60, silver money, quadrant, nocturnal, pair of pistols, silver buckles, 1,599 gallons molasses, 10 books, 2 wigs, &c.

A deposition was given at Saybrook, Ct. (1716, Jul. 9), by James Readfield, Thomas Anderson and Charles Guyllam, that they had received above will of John Dexter, from Captain Joseph Southworth, who was ill it is supposed of small-pox and dangerous for any but those that have had it to speak to him. Also Robert Burnett, mate of the sloop where Captain Dexter died.

IV. MARY, b. 1694, Apr. 30. d. 1760, Sep. 22.
m. 1713, Dec. 10
JOHN ANGELL, b. 1691, Oct. 4. d. 1785, Feb. 11. of James & Abigail (Dexter) — Angell.

1. John, 1720, Aug. 30.
2. James, 1723, Jan. 28.
3. Abigail, 1729, Jun. 29.

V. ABIGAIL, b. 1696, Apr. 26. d.
m. (1)
ARTHUR FENNER, b. d. 1723 (—) of Arthur & Mary (Smith) — Fenner.
m. (2)
ELISHA GREENE, b. 1698, Aug. 5. d. of James & Mary (Fones) — Greene

DEXTER. 3d column. V. Abigail. Her 2d husband d. 1780, at Glocester, R I. She d. before 1780. She had a 4th child, viz: James Greene.

1. Sarah,
(By 2d husband.)
2. Elisha,
3. Abigail,

VI. SARAH, b. 1698, Jun. 27. d. 1773.
m.
JOHN COMSTOCK, b. 1693, Mar. 26. d. 1750, Jan. 12. of Samuel & Elizabeth (Arnold) — Comstock.

IV. { ABIGAIL, { b. 1655, Sep. 24.
m. 1678, Sep. 3. { d. 1711 +
JAMES ANGELL, { b.
{ d. 1711, Mar. 3. of Thomas & Alice ( ) Angell.

See: American Genealogist, v. 20, p. 186. v. 26, p. 229. v. 27, p. 216

DYER.

WILLIAM, { b. London, Eng., Boston, Mass.
m. (1) { d. 1677 ± [Newport, R. I.
MARY, { b.
m. (2) { d. 1660, Jun. 1.
CATHARINE, { b.
{ d. 1687 +

He was a milliner while in England.

1635, Dec. Boston. He and wife Mary joined the church whereof Mr. Wilson was pastor.

1635, Dec. 20. He had his son Samuel baptized.

1637, Mar. 15. He and others signed a remonstrance, affirming the innocence of Mr. Wheelwright, and that the court had condemned the truth of Christ.

1637, Nov. 15. He was disfranchised for signing the above remonstrance.

1637, Nov. 20. He and others were warned to deliver up all guns, pistols, swords, powder, shot, &c., because "the opinions and revelations of Mr. Wheelwright and Mrs. Hutchinson have seduced and led into dangerous errors many of the people here in New England."

1638. Mr. Winthrop thus alludes to him and his wife. "The wife of one William Dyer a milliner in the New Exchange, a very proper and fair woman, and both of them notoriously infected with Mrs. Hutchinson's errors, and very censorious and troublesome."

1638, Mar. 7. Portsmouth. He and eighteen others signed the following compact: "We whose names are underwritten do here solemnly in the presence of Jehovah incorporate ourselves into a Bodie Politick, and as he shall help will submit our persons, lives and estates unto our Lord Jesus Christ, the King of Kings and Lord of Lords, and to all those perfect and most absolute laws of his given us in his holy word of truth, to be guided and judged thereby."

He was elected clerk this same day.

1639, Apr. 28. He and eight others signed the following compact preparatory to the settlement of Newport: "It is agreed by us whose hands are underwritten, to propagate a plantation in the midst of the island or elsewheres, and to engage ourselves to bear equal charge, answerable to our strength and estates in common; and that our determination shall be by major voices of Judge and elders, the Judge to have a double voice." He signed as clerk, the judge being William Coddington.

1639, Jun. 5. He and three others were to proportion land.

1640, Mar. 10. Newport. He had 87 acres of land recorded.

1640-41-42-43-44-45-46-47. Secretary for the towns of Portsmouth and Newport.

1648. General Recorder.

1650-51-52-53. Attorney General.

1653. He returned from England early in this year, having gone there with John Clarke and Roger Williams to obtain a revocation of Governor Coddington's power.

He left his wife abroad.

1653, May 18. He received a commission from the Assembly to act against the Dutch. The officers were to be "Captain John Underhill, Commander in Chief upon the land and Captain William Dyer, Commander in Chief upon sea."

1654, Feb. 15. In describing the bounds of certain highways laid out by himself and two others, he complains of encroachments upon the highway by Mr. Coddington and Richard Tew, closing with the following language: "Let them therefore that know any injury in this kind put it down under their hands, as I now have done, and be ready to make it good as I am, so shall we avoid hypocrisy, dissimulation, backbiting and secret wolvish devourings, one of another, and declare ourselves men, which, how unmanlike the practice of some sycophants are, is and may safely be demonstrated Therefore let us all that love the light come forth to the light and show their deeds."

1655. Freeman.

1657. His wife returned from England after five years' stay there, where she had become a Quaker and was a minister of that denomination. On disembarking at Boston she was soon put into prison by the authorities, but was released at the intercession of her husband and leave granted him to take her home to Rhode Island — "bound in a great penalty not to lodge her in any town of the colony, nor to permit any to have speech with her in the journey." She spent some time at Newport after this.

1659. She returned to Boston and was tried and condemned to death with Marmaduke Stephenson and William Robinson, but was reprived on the very scaffold with the rope already about her neck.

1659, Oct. 31. She wrote (the next day after her reprieve): "Once more to the General Court assembled in Boston, speaks Mary Dyer, even as before: My

I. { SAMUEL, { b. 1635. Newport, Kings Town, R. I.
m. { d. 1678 ±
ANN HUTCHINSON, { b. 1643, Nov. 17.
{ d. 1717, Jan. 10. of Edward & Catharine (Hamby) Hutchinson.

(She m. (2) 1679, Sep. 22, Daniel Vernon.)

1661, Mar. 22. He signed certain articles relative to Misquamicut (Westerly) lands.

1669, May 21. Kings Town. Conservator of the Peace.

1671, May 20. He took oath of allegiance to Rhode Island.

1675. His wife had a legacy of lands in Narragansett from will of her father.

1680. Estate of Samuel Dyer taxed 15*s.* 6*d.*

1687, Oct. 18. His widow, now wife of Daniel Vernon, confirmed a deed of her son Samuel Dyer.

1717, Jan. 1. Will—proved 1717. Widow Ann Vernon, of Newport. Ex. son Samuel Vernon. To son Samuel Dyer, 5*s.* To sons Elisha, Henry and Barrett Dyer, £30, each. To son Samuel Vernon, £45. To daughter Catharine Vernon, £65. To sons Henry and Barrett Dyer and Samuel Vernon, all rents due me from Edward Dyer of Kings Town, being due from 1710, Nov. 20, at £6, per annum, and all hereafter found due which should have been for my yearly support and maintenance.

II. { MARY, { b.
{ d.

III. { WILLIAM, { b. Newport, R. I., New York, Delaware.
{ d.

1659, Oct. 18. His petition on behalf of his mother to Massachusetts authorities, was thus answered: "Whereas Mary Dyer is condemned by the General Court to be executed for her offence; on the petition of William Dyer, her son, it is ordered the said Mary Dyer shall have liberty for forty-eight hours after this day to depart out of this jurisdiction, after which time being found therein she is to be executed."

1674. New York. Collector of Customs for America, receiving his appointment from the Duke of York.

1675-76. Member of Governor's Council.

1681. He was indicted for high treason, on the charge of collecting unlawful duties, and was sent to England for trial.

1682. He returned to New York with more ample powers, no one having appeared to prosecute him.

He went to Delaware from New York.

IV. { MAHERSHALLALHASHBAZ, { b. Newport, R. I.
m. { d. 1670 (—)
MARTHA PEARCE, { b. 1645, Sep. 13.
{ d. 1744, Feb. 24. of Richard & Susanna (Wright) Pearce.

1661, Mar. 22. He signed certain articles relative to Misquamicut (Westerly) lands.

1670, Jul. 7. His father in deed of this date to son Henry mentions part of farm where my son Maher's tobacco house stood.

V. { HENRY, { b. 1647. Newport, R. I.
m. { d. 1690, Feb.
ELIZABETH SANFORD, { b. 1655, Jul. 11.
{ d. 1718, Aug. 27. of John & Elizabeth (Spatchurst) Sanford.

(She m. (2) —— Remington, and (3) —— Simpson.

1667, Aug. 10. He enlisted in a troop of horse.

1668. Freeman.

1677, Oct. 31. He and forty-seven others were granted 5,000 acres to be called East Greenwich.

1680. Taxed 4*s.* 6*d.*

1688, Sep. 8. He made an agreement with his brother Charles about a fence.

He was buried in Newport Cemetery

VI. { CHARLES, { b. 1650. Newport, R. I.
m. (1) { d. 1709, May 15.
MARY, { b.
m. (2) [Jeremiah. { d. of
MARTHA WAIT (w. of { b. 1643, May.
{ d. 1744, Feb. 15. of Thomas & Ann ( ) Brownell.

DYER. 2d column. VI. Charles. 1709, May 9. Will—proved 1709. Exx. wife Martha. Overseers brother George Brownell, Thomas Cornell and Benjamin Thayer. To son James, all land and tenements in Little Compton, which he now liveth on, part of which I had with my wife Martha Dyer. To son Samuel, all my land and homestead that I now live on, with the old end of the dwelling house, barns, stables, &c., to be for him and his heirs unto the third generation, he paying legacies. To him also commonage in Newport and great bible. To son William, £100. To son Charles, £100. To daughter Elizabeth, the now wife of Tristram Hull, £30. "My earnest will and desire is (that) piece of ground that is now called the Burying Ground, shall be continued for the same use unto all my after generations that shall see cause to make use of it, and I order that it shall be well kept fenced in by my son Samuel Dyre and his heirs forever." To wife Martha, the new end of Newport house for life, and then to son Samuel. To her also, all my household stuff, plate, cash, bills, bonds, six of best cows of her choice, twenty ewe sheep, best of flock, and two cows and six sheep to be kept for her winter and summer by Samuel, who is to take a reasonable care of her, as food, firing, &c., "without any grudging or grumbling." To four sons James, William, Samuel and Charles, rest of stock. To son Samuel, carts, plows, &c. To overseers, £3 each.

3d column. V. Samuel. 1765, Feb. 19. Will—proved 1768, Nov. 15. Ex. kinsman Samuel Dyer, son of William Dyer, of South Kingstown. To Captain Samuel Dyer,

VII. PHEBE, m. 1716, Sep. 13. THOMAS KILTON, — b. 1700, Aug. 4. d. 1766. — b. 1690, Jan. 17. d. 1749, May 11. of Robert & Bethiah (Fenner) Kilton.

1. Freelove, 1717, Sep. 14.
2. Joseph, 1723, Jun. 2.
3. Thomas, 1725, Sep. 17.
4. William, 1727, Nov. 12.
5. Stephen, 1730, Feb. 16.
6. James,
7. Phebe,

VIII. ANNE, m. 1725, Jan. 18. JOHN BROWN, — b. 1702, Nov. 6. d. — b. d. of Brown.

IX. ALICE, m. 1725, Feb. 10. WILLIAM OLNEY, — b. 1705, Oct. 14. d. — b. 1706, Feb. 22. d. of John & Rachel (Coggeshall) Olney.

1. John, 1725, Jul. 13.

DEXTER. 3d column. **IX.** Alice. Children, 1, John, 1725, July 13. 2. Abraham. 3. Eliezer. 4. Asa. 5, Coggeshall, 1743, Dec. 28.

1. Abigail, 1679, Feb. 2.
2, Mary, 1680, Mar. 7.
3. James, 1682, Nov. 22.
4. Alice, 1684, Feb. 29.
5. Joseph, 1687, Oct. 5.
6. John, 1691, Oct. 5.
7. Deborah, 1695, Apr. 4.
8. Phebe, 1697, Oct. 10.

I. SAMUEL, — b. d. Boston, Mass.

He was a carpenter.

1687, Oct. 5. He, of Boston, sold Charles Dyer of Newport, for £200, certain land in Newport, with house, orchard, &c., excepting a third part thereof laid out unto Mrs. Katharine Dyer, by order of Town Council of Newport in 1681, as right of dower. All the aforesaid land is now or was lately in occupation of Charles Dyer, and is bounded partly by land now or lately in possession of Henry Dyer.

II. NATHANIEL, m. 1688, Aug. 9. ELIZABETH PARROTT, — b. d. — b. d. of Simon & Elizabeth (   ) Parrott. Newport, R. I.

1. Elizabeth, 1689, Sep. 15.
2 Mary, 1691, Dec. 1.
3. Phebe, 169–, Dec. 6.
4. Ann, 1700, Jan. 10.

He was a butcher.

1702–3–4. Attorney General.

1718, Mar. He brought suit against Thomas Pelham, for £17, 5*s*. 7*d*., the bill being for butcher s meat sold and delivered at sundry times.

III. EDWARD, m. MARY GREENE, — b. 1670. d. — b. 1677, Jan. 8. d. of William & Mary (Sayles) Greene. Kings Town, R. I.

1. Edward, 1701, Jan. 6.
2. Samuel,
3. William, 1705,

He was a house carpenter.

1691, Feb. 9. He and his brother Elisha were complained of by Daniel Vernon, of Kings Town, for taking possession of his farm at Aquidneset, forcing open the door of the cellar, &c., they both being non residents.

1698, Sep. 22. He and wife Mary signed an obligation at Newport, binding themselves in sum of £200, to stand by arbitration of Thomas Olney and Weston Clarke, regarding a house and lot in Warwick for which an action had been commenced by Edward Dyer for his wife, daughter of William Greene, deceased, against said Samuel Greene, to whom the bond was given.

1699, Mar. 17. He and wife Mary gave a receipt to uncle Samuel Greene, for £15, and also £10, already had, according to the award.

IV. ELISHA, — b. d. Kings Town, R. I.

V. HENRY, — b. d.

VI. BARRETT, — b. d.

VII. ANN, m. 1693, Feb. 4. CAREW CLARKE, — b. d. — b. d. of Joseph Clarke.

1. Carew, 1696, Sep. 20
2. Ann, 1698, Sep. 8.
3. Joseph, 1699, Oct. 20.
4. Mary, 1700, Aug 8.
5. Caleb, 1703, May 22.
6. Jonathan, 1705, Aug. 12.
7. William, 1707, Jan. 15.
8. Elisha, 1709, May 6.
9. Samuel, 1711, Oct. 1.
10. Margaret, 1713, Oct. 24.
11. Hutchinson,
12. James,

DYER. 2d column. **I.** Samuel. He had also son William, born 1663, Mar. 7. **III.** William, d. 1690, m. Mary, d. 1690+. 1688, Feb. 20 Will-proved 1690, Sep. 4, at London, England, on oath of William Dyer, his son.—power reserved for relict Mary Dyer when she should come to ask for probate. Exs. son William and wife Mary. Overseers friends John Hill and Samuel Gray for Pennsylvania, and Sir Edmund Andros, Governor, for New-England. Will registered also in county of Sussex, Pennsylvania. To dear and well beloved wife Mary about 2600 acres in Pennsylvania, and two lots in Lewes begun to be built upon and improved, with personal estate for life and then to children, or as she sees fit, also land and debts in New York, land and horses in Narragansett, rights inherited from father, William Dyer, deceased, upon Rhode Island, including Dyer Island, 20 acres at Reading, in New England and the islands called Clabboard Islands in Casco Bay, for life, and then to children as she sees fit. Also £150 in silver money of New England in hands of Sir Edmund Andros. To eldest son William, now of Boston, 2000 acres in the Broad Kill, Sussex county, Pennsylvania, 10 cows and 10 young cattle. To 2d son Edmund, about 1000 acres in Pennsylvania, 6 cows and 2 young cattle. To youngest son James about 1000 acres and 6 cows. To eldest daughter Sarah 500 acres and 6 cows. To youngest daughter Mary 555 acres and 6 cows.

I. WILLIAM, m. ABIGAIL THURSTON, — b. d. — b. 1686, Apr. 3. d. 1761, Oct. 16. of Edward & Susanna (Jefferay) Thurston. Newport, R. I.

1. William, 1712.
2. Abigail, 1714.
3. Edward, 1716.
4. Priscilla, 1718.
5. John, 1720.
6. Daughter,

(She m. (2) Job Bennett.)

1709, Dec. 21. He sold to Thomas Cornell, for £110, certain land, and Elizabeth Remington joined in the deed.

II. MARY, m. 1702, Dec. 17. JOSEPH COGGESHALL, — b. d. — b. 1679. d. of John & Mary (   ) Coggeshall.

DYER. 3d column. **II.** Mary, d. 1768, Oct. 20. Her husband d. 1740, Nov. 21.

1. Elizabeth, 1706, —— 23.
2. Samuel, 1709, Feb. 23.
3. Mary, ——, Jun. 23.
4. Eliphal, ——, —— 19.
5. Henry, ——, May 7.
6. Catharine, ——, Sep. 26.
7. Susanna, ——, Sep. 17.
8. Abigail, ——, Nov. 10.
9. Rebecca, ——, May 26

I. JAMES, m. ——— — b. d. — b. d. of Little Compton, R. I.

1. Charles, 1697, Mar. 22.
2. Freelove, 1699, Jun. 21.

£88, a good cow kept for him five years, and ten bushels of Indian meal a year for him five years if he needs it. To Captain Samuel Dyer's daughter Mary Dyer, a feather bed at marriage, and to his daughter Desire, the same. To four sons of my brother Charles Dyer, deceased, viz. Charles, Samuel, John and William, £17 each, and to their sister Mary Barton, twenty Spanish milled dollars. To Desire Bull, widow of Nathan Bull, negro Peggy, her child Sarah, and a good cow. To Silence Arnold, £50, feather bed, &c. To my kinsman Samuel Dyer, son of William Dyer of South Kingstown, all my lands and housing in Newport, four negroes and all my stock and personal estate. To John Dyer son of Captain Samuel Dyer, of Newport, £50.

life is not accepted neither availeth me in comparison of the lives and liberty of the truth," &c. She was sent by the magistrates to Rhode Island and thence went to Long Island, &c.

1660, May 31. Having returned to Boston, ten days before, she was now brought before Governor Endicott. He said, "Are you the same Mary that was here before?" She replied, "I am the same Mary Dyer," &c. He then said "You will own yourself a Quaker will you not?" She answered "I own myself to be reproachfully so called." He sentenced her to be hung the day following.

1660, Jun. 1. On the gallows she was abjured to repent by her early pastor Mr. Wilson and not to be "so deluded and carried away by the deceit of the devil." She was accused of having said she had been in Paradise, to which she replied, "Yea I have been in Paradise these several days," and added: "No ear can hear, no tongue can utter, no heart can understand the sweet incomes and the refreshings of the spirit of the Lord which I now feel." She was accompanied from the prison to the gallows by a band of soldiers and drums were beaten before and behind her that none might hear her speak. She is described as "a person of no mean extract or parentage, of an estate pretty plentiful, of a comely stature and countenance, of a piercing knowledge in many things, of a wonderful sweet and pleasant discourse." The Friends' records of Portsmouth thus note her death: "Mary Dyer the wife of William Dyer of Newport in Rhode Island: She was put to death at the town of Boston with the like cruel hand as the Martyrs were in Queen Mary's time upon the 31 day of the 3d mo 1660." (The execution was a day later as given in other accounts.)

1661-62. Commissioner.

1664-66. Deputy.

1665-66-68. General Solicitor.

1666, Mar. 27. Execution was ordered by Assembly to proceed in case brought against him by William Coddington for killing a mare.

1669. Secretary to the Council.

1669, Oct. 18. Testimony was given in his behalf by Governor Coddington: "I do affirm that we the purchasers of Rhode Island (myself being the chief), William Dyer desiring a spot of land of us, as we passed by it, after we had purchased the said island, did grant him our right in the said island, and named it Dyer's Island." Others so testified also.

1670, Jul. 7. He deeded son Henry northerly end of farm, but if he only had female issue then the land was to go to son Samuel at decease of Henry, said Samuel giving to daughter or daughters of Henry, £150 (the oldest having a double portion).

1670, Jul. 25. He received an obligation from sons Samuel and Henry in the sum of £300, they binding themselves to pay their sister Mary Dyer, the eldest daughter of William, a portion of £100, within three years after death of said William; provided that whatever goods said William Dyer shall order or appoint his daughter Mary to have, shall be deducted from the £100. The sons also agreed to pay Elizabeth Dyer, second daughter of William, £40, at eighteen years of age, and to be careful of her maintenance in case of her mother's death. The proportion of payment was to be three parts by Samuel and one part by Henry, and the agreement being carried out the obligation was void.

1670, Aug. 5. He deeded as a free gift to son William, all that my island commonly called Dyer's Island.

1677, Dec. 24. Governor Benedict Arnold in his will of this date mentions William Dyer, Sr., now late deceased.

1681. His widow Catharine had her dower set off by order of Town Council, and she was alive six years later.

1680. Taxed 4*s*.

1687, Oct. 15. He bought for £200, of his nephew Samuel Dyer, of Boston, certain land in Newport with housing and orchard.

1702, Jan. 12. He was proprietor in common lands and also held as guardian for William Dyer.

1709, May 9. Will—proved 1709. He devised to his eldest son James, certain estate. The eldest son of said James was Charles, and said Charles had a son James and two other sons who died before their father. These items appear on the court records, no copy of the will in full, appearing however.

1734, Jan. 29. Will—proved 1744, Mar. 12. Widow Martha of Portsmouth. Exs. cousins (*i. e.* nephews) Joseph and Stephen Brownell. Overseers, cousin John Read and William Hall. To cousin George Borden, son to cousin Sarah Read, £20. To three sisters Mary Hazard, Anne Wilbur and Susanna Brownell, all wearing apparel. To cousins John Read of Freetown, and William Hall of Portsmouth, each £3. To cousins Joseph and Stephen Brownell, sons of brother George Brownell, late deceased, £3. To all my cousins, children of my brothers and sisters, rest of estate, bonds, debts, &c.

He was buried on the Dyer Farm at Newport.

(2D WIFE.)

VII. ELIZABETH, b. / d.

EASTON.

NICHOLAS, b. 1593. Lymington, Herts Co., Eng., d. 1675, Aug. 15. [Newport, R. I.
m. (1) ———, b. / d.
m. (2) 1638. CHRISTIAN BEECHER, (w. of Thomas. b. / d. 1665, Feb. 20. of James Barker.
m. (3) 1671, Mar. 2. ANN CLAYTON, b. 1628. d. 1708, Jan. 30. of Clayton.

(She m. (2) 1677, Mar. 28, Henry Bull.)

He was a tanner.

1616, Jun. 6. He made an agreement with Henry Button, with bond of £200.

1634, Mar. 25. He embarked at Southampton for New England, with his sons Peter and John.

His first tarrying place was at Ipswich, Mass.

1634, Sep. 3. He was chosen overseer of the powder, shot, &c., in plantation where he lived.

1635. Newbury, Mass.

1637, Nov. 20. He and others were warned to deliver up all guns, pistols, swords, shot, &c., because, "the opinions and revelations of Mr. Wheelwright and Mrs. Hutchinson have seduced and led into dangerous errors many of the people here in New England."

1638. Hampton, N. H.

1638, Mar. 12. He and others having had license to depart, they were ordered by Massachusetts authorities to appear (if they be not gone before) at the next court to answer such things as shall be objected.

1638. Portsmouth, R. I. He was among the inhabitants admitted to the island of Aquidneck this year.

1638, May 20. He was allotted 6 acres north side of Great Cove.

Mr. Winthrop writes in this same year: "Those who were gone with Mrs. Hutchinson to Aquiday fell into new errors daily. One Nicholas Easton, a tanner, taught that gifts and graces were that antichrist mentioned Thes., and that which withheld, &c., was the preaching of the law, and that every of the elect had the Holy Ghost and also the devil in dwelling."

1639, Apr. 28. He and eight others signed the following compact preparatory to the settlement of Newport. "It is agreed by us whose hands are underwritten, to propagate a plantation in the midst of the island, or elsewhere,

I. PETER, b. 1622. Newport, R. I. d. 1694, Feb. 12.
m. 1643, Nov. 15.
ANN COGGESHALL, b. 1626. d. 1687, Mar. 6. of John & Mary ( ) Coggeshall.

He left quite a record of the movements of his father's family in their first journeyings.

He notes their removals from Ipswich to Newbury, Hampton, and finally to Rhode Island.

1638. He notes their arrival this year at Pocasset (Portsmouth).

1639, May 1. Having embarked at Portsmouth for Newport, he says that at this date "in the morning" they gave the name of Coasters Harbour Island to the piece of ground still known by that name.

1644. Sergeant.

1645. His record states that in this year they came to live at the east end of beach.

1655. Freeman.

1660-61. Commissioner.

1663. He records that they built the first wind mill this year.

1666-71-72-73-74-75-80-81. Deputy.

1667. Assistant.

1672-73-74-75-76-77. General Treasurer.

1674-75-76. Attorney General.

1680, May 17. He was on a committee that reported to the Assembly that four hundred and fifty-five persons had died in the Colony for the time of seven years last past.

1687. Overseer of the Poor.

1691, Apr. 28. Will—proved 1694, May 1. Ex. grandson Nicholas Easton. Overseers, sons-in-law John Carr and Thomas Rodman. He mentions son-in-law William Barker and Elizabeth his wife, son John Easton, daughter Waite Carr, grandson Nicholas Easton, brother's children James, John and Mary Easton, sons-in-law Weston Clarke, Thomas Rodman and John Carr, granddaughters Ann and Patience Clarke, grandsons Joshua, son of John, and Joshua, son of Peter. The Point and house lots at Newport, were to go to son John, grandson Nicholas, Thomas Rodman and Weston Clarke, at death of testator's mother Ann Bull. The two Joshuas above mentioned were to have the £10, which was old Joshua's gift to them (*i. e.* Joshua Coggeshall's gift probably) when of age.

He was buried in the Coddington Burial Ground.

II. WILLIAM,
m.
HANNAH BRIGGS,

b.
d. 1719, Apr. 21.
b. 1676, May 1.
d. 1719, Feb. 13. of Thomas & Mary (Fisher) Briggs.

Newport, R. I.

1. William, 1705, May 15.
2. Charles, 1707, Mar. 2.
3. Mary, 1709, Nov. 5.
4. Samuel, 1712, May 4.

He was a house carpenter.

He was indicted for murder of his wife Hannah, and executed on that charge.

1719, Jun. 16. Whereas Samuel Dyer of Newport, yeoman, has petitioned Assembly to release the forfeiture of the estate of his brother William Dyer (who was lately executed in the town of Newport, which was forfeited to this colony) for the subsistence of his children; ordered that after charges of imprisonment, trial and execution of William Dyer are satisfied, real and personal shall be discharged.

III. ELIZABETH,
m. 1699, Feb. 9.
TRISTRAM HULL,

b.
d. 1719.
b. 1670, Oct. 8.
d. 1718. of Joseph & Experience (Harper) Hull.

1. Mary,
2. Samuel,
3. Joseph, 1706, Oct. 1.
4. Hannah,
5. Bathsheba,
6. Charles,
7. Stephen,
8. Elizabeth,
9. Sarah,

IV. CHARLES,
m. 1709, Aug. 26.
MARY LAPHAM,

b.
d. 1727, Jan. 7.
b. 1686, Oct. 5.
d. of John & Mary (Mann) Lapham.

Newport, R. I., Dartmouth, Mass., Providence, R. I.

1. Mary,
2. Elizabeth,
3. Charles,
4. Samuel,
5. John,
6. William,
7. Thomas,

She m. (2) 1734, Nov. 21, John Colvin.

He was a blacksmith.

1712, Jul. 25. Dartmouth. He bought of John Scott and Elizabeth his wife, of Newport, for £600, a house and 113 acres in Providence, three miles west of salt water, and several other parcels of land in Providence.

1713, Apr. 30. Providence. He sold Nathaniel Brown, of Rehoboth, certain land in Providence formerly belonging to Richard Scott, now deceased, and which grantor had bought of John Scott of Newport.

1727, Jan. 5. Will—proved 1727, Feb. 6. Exx. wife Mary. Overseers, brother Samuel Dyer and friend Silas Carpenter. To wife, whole command of all estate both real and personal, for support and bringing up of children. To daughters Mary and Elizabeth, £30, each at age of twenty-one. To wife, movable estate to dispose of to children and one-third of real for life. The rest of estate to be divided to sons Charles, Samuel, John, William and Thomas, and to Charles, £20, more than rest.

Inventory, £533, 1*s.* 1*d.*, viz: 4 feather beds, flock bed, spinning wheel, cards, pair of looms, woolen and linen yarn, 9 chairs, 110 bushels corn, flax, rye, buckwheat, beans, butter, cheese, 15 loads of hay, canoe, cider mill, 2 yoke of oxen, 2 steers, 6 cows, 4 yearlings, 5 calves, 2 mares, 5 swine, 8 small pigs, book debts £29, 9*s.* 10*d.*, books £1, bonds and notes £31, plate £4, 17*s.* 6*d.* (6½ oz.), &c.

1735, Jun. 30. His widow Mary, wife of John Colvin, deeded for love, &c., to son John Dyer, 60 acres and dwelling house in Mashantatack, where her husband Charles Dyer had lived.

V. SAMUEL,
m. 1710, Jan. 19.
DESIRE SLOCUM,

b. 1686.
d. 1767, Sep. 15.
b. 1688, Mar. 12.
d. 1760, Sep. 3. of Ebenezer & Mary (Thurston) Slocum.

Newport, R. I.

1710. Freeman.

1713, Mar. 28. He and wife Desire joined in a deed with Charles Dyer of Dartmouth, to Jonathan Nichols of Newport, selling him 33½ acres there for £220.

1714, Jun. 15. He, being gunner at Fort Ann, was allowed by Assembly £20, per year provided he take care of the guns, ammunition, and all other stores lodged in said fort belonging to this colony.

1720, Jun. 14. He was allowed £10, for wharf and causeway by him built on Fort Island including his charges on the old boat.

1724, Jun. 23. It was voted by Assembly that Samuel Dyer, gunner of Fort Ann, shall have £90, upon his delivery of all the buildings and fences which he hath erected on Fort Island, *alias* Goat Island, with all other utensils belonging to colony, and the said Samuel Dyer is dismissed from his service.

He was buried on the Dyer farm.

(2D WIFE, no issue.)

EASTON.

I. NICHOLAS,
m. 1666, Nov. 30.
ELIZABETH BARKER,

b. 1644, Nov. 12.
d. 1677, Feb. 1.
b.
d. 1676, Jul. 5. of James & Barbara (Dungan) Barker.

Newport, R. I.

1. Nicholas, 1668, Feb. 24.
2. Elizabeth, 1669, Dec. 6.
3. Freelove, 1671, Mar. 12.
4. Patience, 1675, Apr. 22.

1676, Jun. 14. Constable. He was ordered to see safely to the water-side, where he had landed, an Indian sent to the island by Awasuncke (sachem squaw of Seaconnet), with a message from her to the Governor and Council.

1676, Jan. 15. Will—proved 1677, Mar. 5. Ex. brother John. Overseers, Christopher Holder, Daniel Gould and John Easton. To son Nicholas, household lands and half of plate. To daughter Elizabeth, a house and lot. To Christopher Holder, best hat. To uncle Daniel, a piece of cloth. To uncle John Easton, an old horse. To mother, a gray pacing horse. To brother John, wearing apparel. To sisters Mary and Patience, a barrel of pork each. To Christopher Holder and uncle John Easton, a small lot and house for people called Quakers. To Christopher Holder, a barrel of pork to be disposed of to help fence the place where wife was buried. To brother John, £30, to help build a town house. To poor Quakers, £20, as men's meeting see cause. To poor of town, £20, as Town Council see cause. He leaves his son to the tuition of brother John, till of age, and his daughter to tuition of Amey Borden, till married or twenty. To son, two-thirds and to daughter one-third of rest. To brothers Peter and Joshua, 20*s*, each. To sisters Elizabeth and Waite, 10*s*., each. To Indian squaw her freedom and Indian child and negro to be freed at age of twenty-five. To Joseph Bryer, a saddle.

II. JOHN,
m. 1679, Aug. 23.
DORCAS PERRY,

b. 1647, Feb. 6.
d.
b. 1661.
d. 1746, Jan. 16. of Edward & Mary (Freeman) Perry.

Newport, R. I.

1. Ann, 1681, Jan. 25.
2. Hannah, 1682, Aug. 9.
3. Samuel, 1684, Sep. 13.
4. Mary, 1687, Feb. 19.
5. Joshua, 1689, Aug. 22.
6. Peter, 1691, Aug. 5.
7. John, 1694, Apr. 3.
8. Patience, 1696, Aug. 6.
9. James, 1698, Dec. 22.
10. Edward, 1701, Feb. 23.
11. Benjamin, 1706, Jan. 12.
12. Dorcas, 1706, Jan. 12.

1667, Aug. 10. He enlisted in a troop of horse.

1746, Feb. 6. Will—proved 1746, Mar. 16. Widow Dorcas of Middletown, R. I. Ex. son Samuel. To son Samuel, £10 and a silver spoon. To son Peter, £10. To son John, a feather bed. To son James, £10. To son Edward, a clock, concordance, and biggest brass kettle. To daughter Mary Mott, £10, case of drawers, high cupboard and Dutch table. To daughters Hannah and Patience Easton, two cows. To daughters Ann, Hannah and Patience Easton, the rest of estate both real and personal.

Inventory, £312, 13*s*.

III. MARY,
m. 1668, Dec. 25.
WESTON CLARKE,

b. 1648, Sep. 25.
d. 1690, Nov. 16.
b. 1648, Apr. 5.
d. 1728 + of Jeremiah & Frances (Latham) Clarke.

1. Mary, 1670, Jan. 11.
2. John, 1672, Sep. 15.
3. Weston, 1674, Feb. 18.
4. Weston, 1677, Apr. 15.
5. Walter,
6. Ann,
7. Jeremiah, 1685, Nov. 29.
8. Patience,

IV. PETER,

b. 1651, Feb. 1.
d. 1653, Sep. 10.

V. ANN,
UNMARRIED,

b. 1653, Feb. 9.
d. 1676, Aug. 25.

and to engage ourselves to bear equal charge, answerable to our strength and estates in common; and that our determination shall be by major voices of Judge and Elders, the Judge to have a double voice."

The Judge was William Coddington, and Mr. Easton signed as one of the Elders.

1639, Nov. 25. Newport. He and John Clarke, were appointed to inform Mr Vane by writing of the state of things here, and desire him to treat about obtaining a Patent of the Island from his Majesty, and likewise to write to Mr. Thomas Burwood, brother to Mr. Easton, concerning the same thing.

1639, Dec. 17. He was fined 5s., for coming to public meeting without his weapon.

1640, Mar. 1. He had land to the amount of 389 acres recorded, with bounds, &c.

1641, Mar. 16. Freeman.

1640–42–43–44–53. Assistant.

1650–51–54. President.

1653, May 18. He and seven others were appointed a committee for ripening matters that concern Long Island, and in the case concerning the Dutch.

1655. Freeman.

1660. Commissioner.

1665–66. Deputy.

1666–67–68–69–70–71. Deputy Governor.

1672–73–74. Governor.

1674, Jan. 2. Will—proved 1675, Aug. 30. Exx. wife Ann. Overseers William Coddington, Christopher Holder and William Wodell. To wife Ann, 60 acres, the house in which I now live with two house lots adjoining, garden, orchard, barn, stables, &c., also a house now or lately in possession of Zachariah Gaunt. To eldest son Peter, part of the farm on which he now lives except 20 acres. To grandson Nicholas Easton, Jr., 20 acres where his dwelling house is. To son John, remainder of the farm on which he now lives. To grandson John Easton, son of Peter, 20 acres, and to the rest of Peter's children, certain land. To the children of son John Easton, certain land. To son John half of all the sheep, cattle, horsekind and cowkind. To wife Ann, the rest of real and personal, and a deed to her made before marriage is to remain in full force, power and strength.

He and his wife Christian were buried in the Friends' Burial Ground.

EASTON. 2d column. II. John. His 1st wife was daughter of Peter and Lydia ( ) Gaunt.

II. JOHN, m. (1) 1661, Jan. 4. MEHITABLE GAUNT, m. (2) ALICE,
- b. 1624. d. 1705, Dec. 12.
- b. d. 1673, Nov. 11. of Peter Gaunt
- b. 1621. d. 1689, Mar. 24. of

1653–54. Attorney General for Portsmouth and Newport.

1654–55–56–57–58–59–60–63. Commissioner.

1655. Freeman.

1656–57–60–61–62–63–64–65–66–67–68–69–70–72–73–74. Attorney General for the Colony.

1665–66–71–72. Deputy.

1666–67–68–69–70–71–72–73–74–76–81–82–83–84–85–86–89–90. Assistant.

1674–75–76. Deputy Governor.

1675. He wrote this year an account of the Indian war, entitled: "A True Relation of what I know & of Reports & my Understanding concerning the Beginning & Progress of the War now between the English and the Indians."

1676, Aug. 24. He was a member of a Court Martial held at Newport for the trial of certain Indians charged with being engaged in King Philip's designs.

1680, May 18. He calling himself aged fifty-five or thereabouts, testified that about the year 1674 Thomas Suckling and wife bequeathed to people called Quakers what estate they should have left at their death, on condition that they should be provided for during their lives, and further testified that the Quakers did supply them with board and shingle their house.

1690, Jan. 30. He with five other Assistants and the Deputy-Governor, wrote a letter to their majesties William and Mary congratulating them on their accession to the throne, and informing them that since the deposition of Sir Edmund Andros the former government under the charter had been re-assumed, mentioning also that Andros was seized in Rhode Island on his flight from confinement in Massachusetts, and that he had been returned to the latter Colony on their demand.

1690–91–92–93–94–95. Governor.

He was buried in the Coddington Burial Ground.

ESTEN.

THOMAS, m. 1640, Apr. 23. ANN,
- b. 1612, Jul. d. 1691 + Hertford Co., Eng., [Providence, R. I.
- b. d. 1686 +

1665, Oct. 2. He came to America, from Hertford County, England, according to the family account.

1668, Apr. 27. He is called "Astin Thomas the Welchman," in the description of the bounds of a grant made to Walter Rhodes by the town. The land of said Astin Thomas, is described as "by the highway that goeth to Pawtucket."

1668, Dec. 23. He sold John Pitt, for 20s., lot of 2 acres, calling himself husbandman. He signed "Estance Thomas," and Ann Thomas, also signs with him. The changes that his name has undergone are peculiar. He generally signed Eustance Thomas, but sometimes Thomas Eustance, and when he and his son deeded together he calls himself Eustance Thomas and his son Thomas Eustance. In the next generation the name Eustance was kept as a surname being called Eustance, Estance (which form was

I. JOANNA, m. 1671, Apr. 26. JOHN MARTIN,
- b. 1645, Jun. 1. d. 1733, Mar. 23.
- b. 1632. d. 1713, Mar. 21. of Martin.

II. THOMAS, m. PRISCILLA HARDING,
- b. 1647, Feb. 17. d. 1708, Nov. 5.
- b. d. 1708 (—) of Stephen & Bridget ( ) Harding.

1707, Nov. 25. He deeded Josiah Owen, half of 150 acre tract of land.

1708, Sep. 26. Inventory, £34, 7s., 10d., shown by Mary Owen and Mercy Esten, daughters of deceased and Josiah Owen, Jr., husband of Mary. Henry Esten, brother of deceased, also declares the inventory. Among items were 7 head of cattle, and hay £15, 5s., money £52, 7s., 4d., apples, 3½ barrels of beer, &c.

VI. PATIENCE, b. 1655, Nov. 20. d. 1690, Nov. 21.
m. (1) 1675, Jan. 1.
ROBERT MALINS, b. 1649. d. 1679, Aug. 26. of — Malins.
m. (2) 1682, Jun. 7.
THOMAS RODMAN, b. 1640, Dec. 26. d. 1728, Jan. 11. of John — Rodman.

1. Mary, 1675, Oct. 21.
2. Robert, 1677, Jan. 22.
(By 2d husband.)
3. Thomas, 1683, Nov. 11.
4. Ann, 1686, Nov. 16.

VII. WAIT, b. 1657, Jul. 25. d. 1658, Jan. 6.

VIII. PETER, b. 1659, Jan. 11. d. 1690, Dec. 17. — Newport, R. I.
m.
REBECCA THURSTON, b. 1662, Apr. d. 1737, Sep. 16. of Edward & Elizabeth (Mott) — Thurston.

1. Rebecca, 1684, Jul. 5.
2. Peter, 1685, Nov. 18.
3. Ann, 1687, Sep. 3.
4. Joshua, 1689, Apr. 27.

(She m. (2) 1691, Nov. 21, Weston Clarke.)

1691, Mar. 4. Will recorded. Exs. father Peter, and Edward Thurston, till son Peter is of age. To son Joshua, all his land. To eldest son Peter, all the land that my father Peter has willed me, but in case father disannuls it, then the land given Joshua to be equally shared with Peter. To daughter Rebecca, at marriage half of movables. To wife Rebecca, the other half of movables. He gives his son Peter to his grandfather Easton.

He was buried in the Coddington Burial Ground.

IX. JOSHUA, b. 1662, Jul. 30. d. 1690, Apr. 22. — Newport, R. I., Jamaica, W. I.
m.
ROSE, b. 1665. d. 1690, Sep. 24. of

He died of small-pox at Jamaica.

X. JAMES, b. 1664, Jan. 29. d. 1664, Oct. 30.

XI. ELIZABETH, b. 1666, Feb. 18. d. 1715, Mar. 24.
m.
WILLIAM BARKER, b. 1662. d. 1741, Nov. 3. of James & Barbara (Dungan) — Barker.

1. Ann, 1688, Nov. 29.
2. Elizabeth, 1690, May 24.
3. James, 1692, Jan. 26.
4. Patience, 1694, Apr. 27.
5. Peter, 1696, Jan. 28.
6. Mary, 1698, Jan. 10.
7. William, 1700, Apr. 9.
8. Frances, 1702, Mar. 10.
9. Wait, 1705, Jun. 20.
10. Joshua, 1707, Nov. 1.
11. Abigail, 1707, Nov. 10.

XII. WAITE, b. 1668, Nov. 5. d. 1725, Aug.
m.
JOHN CARR, b. d. 1714. of Caleb & Mercy ( ) — Carr.

1. Samuel,
2. Caleb,
3. Ann,
4. John, 1691, Nov. 23.
5. Francis,
6. Patience,

XIII. JAMES, b. 1671, Oct. 7. d. 1676, Aug. 22.

I. JAMES, b. 1662, Feb. 23. d. 1697, Mar. 23. — Newport, R. I.
m.
MIRIAM ALLEN, b. 1661, Jun. d. 1732 ± of Matthew & Sarah (Kirby) — Allen.

1. Stephen, 1682, Apr. 5.
2. Nicholas, 1683, Dec. 27.
3. Mary, 1685, Nov. 10.
4. Mehitable, 1687, Nov. 19.
5. Sarah, 1689, Sep. 29.
6. Peter, 1691, Nov. 4.
7. Alice, 1695, Nov. 4.
8. Ruth, 1697, Oct. 31.

II. PETER, b. 1665, Sep. 10. d. 1690, Jun. 4. — Newport, R. I.
UNMARRIED,

He died at his father's house, as Friends' records declare.

III. MARY, b. 1668, Jun. 16. d.
m.
DANIEL THURSTON, b. 1661, Apr. d. of Edward & Elizabeth (Mott) — Thurston.

1. Daniel, 1687, Sep. 25.
2. Elizabeth, 1689, Jan. 14.
3. Mary, 1690, Mar. 9.
4. John, 1692, Jun. 10.
5. Edward, 1693, Sep. 1.
6. Eleanor, 1695, Jan. 18.
7. Benjamin, 1697, Mar. 25.
8. James, 1698, Jul. 15.
9. Peter, 1704, Jul. 3.

IV. JOHN, b. 1670, Sep. 7. d. 1720, Jul. 14. — Newport, R. I.

V. PAUL, b. 1673, Feb. 2. d.

(2D WIFE, no issue.)

ESTEN.

1. Jemima, 1672, May 29.
2. Melatiah, 1673, Apr. 30.
3. John, 1674, Mar. 15.
4. Ephraim, 1676, Feb. 7.
5. Ann, —, Nov. 14.
6. Manasseh, 1681, Feb. 2.
7. Joanna, 1683, Feb. 15.
8. Ebenezer, 1684, Feb. 16.
9. Judith, 1686, Nov. 13.

I. MARY, b. d.
m.
JOSIAH OWEN, b. d. of Josiah — Owen.

ESTEN. 3d column. I. Mary, Her husband, b. 1661, d. 1741, Apr. 27, of Samuel and Priscilla (Belcher) Owen. Children, 1. Thomas, 1707, Jul. 2. 2. Joseph. 3. John.

II. MERCY, b. d.

used sometimes by first ancestor) and Esten. Other corruptions of the name have been Easton and Asten occasionally (the former being an utterly different family name, and the latter a common form of Austin).

1674, Jun. 13. Eustance Thomas and Thomas Eustance, purchased of John and Catharine Rice, of Providence, for £12, a parcel of land, and a 6 acre lot and dwelling house for £12.

The same year they bought land of Stephen Paine, jointly.

1679, Jul. 1. He and two sons taxed together 6*s.*, 3*d.*

1686, Feb. 12. He deeds son Henry for his "well being and settlement," the dwelling house where the father lives, a mile and a half north of Town, which "lieth upon a small brook called 3d Lake." On same date his son Henry deeds father and mother half of south end of house and part of the orchard, with 3 acres of planting ground and enough meadow to make a load of hay. This deed from son Henry, was a life deed to parents. Besides the homestead which the father deeded to his son he gave him a right of common that he purchased jointly with his son Thomas (alluding to purchase of Paine).

1688. He gave in the joint estate of himself and 2 sons, £33, 4*s.*, 3*d.*, viz: 2 oxen £18, 6 cows £3, 10*s.*, 2 three year old, 6 two year old, a horse and 2 sows. He also returned 4 acres planting ground, 4 acres orchard, 2 acres meadow and 5 acres more of enclosed lands.

1691, Dec. 21. He deeded son Henry, half of a 60 acre piece of land.

1708, Dec. 7. Testimony by Joseph Jenckes, that he married Thomas Esten and Priscilla Harden, and by Esther Jenckes, that Mary Owen was born after the marriage.

III. HENRY, — b. 1651, Jan. 11; d. 1711, Mar. 23. Providence, R. I.
m. (1) ELIZABETH MANTON, — b. ; d. of Shadrach & Elizabeth (Smith) Manton.
m. (2) SARAH HARDING, — b. ; d. 1731, Aug. 20. of Stephen & Bridget ( ) Harding.

1685, Nov. 18. He and Elizabeth, his wife, had 11¾ acres laid out to them in right of deceased Edward Manton.

1689, Feb. 20. He bought 60 acres of Josias Wilkinson.

1708, Dec. 20. He accepted the custody of his niece Mercy's half share of her father's estate, she being under age.

1711, Mar. 17. Will—proved 1711, Apr. 20. Exx. wife Sarah. To his two sons Henry and Cornelius, lands and house in Providence, when they are of age, and he says Henry would be fourteen on Aug. 29, and Cornelius, thirteen on Mar. 9, next. His son Henry is to have the first choice of half above real estate. To three daughters Elizabeth, Amey, and Rebecca, £5, each, to be paid by sons when of age, and they are to have 20*s.*, each paid immediately by executrix. The daughters are to have also a cow each when sons are of age. All estate that is left that belonged to first wife is to go to daughters Elizabeth and Amey. Wife Sarah, to have rest of movables and privilege of house.

Inventory, £172, 12*s.*, 4*d.*, viz: 8 cows, 2 steers, 3 heifers, 3 yearlings, 20 sheep, 1 mare, swine, cash £13, 4*s.*, gun, 3 spinning wheels, 15 barrels cider, cider mill and press, warming pan, &c.

1731. Administration on widow Sarah Esten's estate by son Cornelius.

Inventory, £2, 12*s.* "As widow Jemima Estance saith," including 2 tables and other small things 10*s.* Sheeps wool 8*s.* and 2 sheep £1, 14*s.*

FREEBORN.

WILLIAM, — b 1594; d. 1670, Apr. 28. Boston, Mass., Portsmouth, R. I.
m. MARY, — b. 1601; d. 1670, May 3.

1634, Apr. 30. He embarked in ship Francis, from Ipswich for New England, his age being called forty years, wife Mary, thirty-three, daughter Mary, seven, and daughter Sarah, two years. (The Quaker records call him and his wife aged about eighty years at time of their death.)

1637, Nov. 20. He and others were warned to deliver up all guns, pistols, swords, powder, shot, &c., because "the opinions and revelations of Mr. Wheelwright and Mrs. Hutchinson have seduced and led into dangerous errors many of the people here in New England."

1638, Mar. 7. Portsmouth. He and eighteen others signed the following compact. "We whose names are underwritten do here solemnly in the presence of Jehovah incorporate ourselves into a Bodie Politick, and as he shall help, will submit our persons, lives and estates unto our Lord Jesus Christ, the King of Kings and Lord of Lords, and to all those perfect and most absolute laws of his given us in his holy word of truth to be guided and judged thereby."

1638, Mar. 12. He and others having had license to depart from Massachusetts, summons was ordered to go out for them to appear (if they be not gone before) at the next court in that Colony, to answer such things as shall be objected.

1638, May 13. He was present at a General Meeting in Portsmouth, upon public notice.

1639. He was granted a lot on condition he built within a year.

1641, Mar. 16. Freeman.

1642. Constable.

1655. Freeman.

1657. Commissioner.

I. MARY, — b. 1627; d.
m. CLEMENT WEAVER, — b. ; d. 1683. of Weaver.

See: American Genealogist, v. 20, p. 186.

II. SARAH, — b. 1632; d. 1670, Apr. 23.
m. NATHANIEL BROWNING, — b. ; d. of Browning.

III. GIDEON, — b. ; d. 1720, Feb. 28. Portsmouth, R. I.
m. (1) 1658, Jun. 1. SARAH BROWNELL, — b. ; d. 1676, Sep. 6. of Thomas & Ann ( ) Brownell.
m. (2) 1678, Jun. 3. [John. MARY LAWTON, (w. of — b. ; d. 1715 + of Matthew & Eleanor ( ) Boomer.

1675-90-1703-4-13. Deputy.

1687. Overseer of the Poor.

1690, Mar. 5. He bought of James Sweet and Jane his wife, of Prudence Island, for £12, a quarter of 20 acres in Portsmouth, given by Jane's grandfather William Freeborn to the mother deceased of said Jane.

1697, Sep. 27. He deeded son-in-law (*i. e.* stepson) George Lawton, of Portsmouth, a quarter share in Misquamicut, for love, &c.

1708, May. He and wife Mary, deeded daughter Mercy Coggeshall, wife of Thomas, of Newport, and her child or children, a half share in East Greenwich.

1709, Aug. 1. He and wife Mary, deeded daughter Mary Brayton, wife of Thomas, of Portsmouth, a half share in East Greenwich, for love, &c., the whole of said tract being 180 acres.

1712, Jul. 26. He deeded kinsman William Manchester, son of Thomas, of Portsmouth, for love, &c., 10 acres in Potowomut.

1715, Jan. 27. Will—proved 1720, Mar. 14. Ex. son Gideon. Overseers, sons-in-law Joseph Wanton, and Thomas Cornell. To son Gideon, all homestead farm for life and at his death half to male heir and other half to rest of sons' children (at disposal of said son Gideon), and whoever enjoys farm at death of son Gideon, shall pay their mother £30, a year while widow. If son Gideon die without male issue, then next male heir to have, and to pay each female issue of son Gideon, £50, and to granddaughter Sarah, daughter of my son William, deceased, £50. To wife Mary, £15, yearly while widow, use of great lower room in my new house, and lodging room adjoining, firewood, fruit of orchard, use of riding horse, feather bed, &c., and to her a good bed at her disposal. If she marries, only £10 a year. To grandson Gideon Wanton, 120 acres in Tiverton. To daughters

I. ELIZABETH, m. 1713, May 29. AZRIKIM PIERCE,
b. 1683, Apr. 8. d. 1718, Aug. 18.
b. 1672, Jan. 4. d.
of Ephraim & Hannah (Holbrook) Pierce.

1. Joseph, 1714, Apr. 7.
2. Hopestill, 1716, Aug. 14.
3. Elizabeth, 1716, Aug. 14.
4. Tabitha, 1717, Aug. 27.

II. AMEY, m. 1716, Jul. 26. JOSEPH RANDALL,
b. 1685, Jun. 1. d. 1764, Feb. 8.
b. 1684. d. 1760, Mar. 30.
of William & Rebecca (Fowler) Randall.

1. Amey, 1717, May 27.
2. Joseph, 1718, Aug. 25.
3. Henry, 1720, Mar. 2.
4. Peter, 1723, Jun. 12.

(2D WIFE.)

III. REBECCA, m. 1714, May 13. PETER BALLOU,
b. 1695, May 9. d. 1787, Feb. 13.
b. 1689, Aug. 1. d. 1784, May 9.
of John & Hannah (Garret) Ballou.

1. Rebecca, 1715, Aug. 26.
2. Sarah, 1717, Aug. 30.
3. Mary, 1720, Aug. 19.
4. Hannah, 1720, Aug. 19.
5. Maturin, 1722, Oct. 30.
6. Abigail, 1725, Mar. 20.
7. Amey, 1727, Sep. 5.
8. Elizabeth, 1730, Jul. 15.
9. Hopestill,
10. Mercy,
11. Peter, 1737.

IV. HENRY, m. JEMIMA,
b. 1697, Aug. 29. d. 1730, Apr. 30.
b. d. 1754 +
of

ESTEN. 3d column. IV. Henry m. 1724, Feb. 6, Jemima Salisbury, b. 1700, Sep. 23, of Samuel and Jemima (Martin) Salisbury.

Providence, R. I.

1. Henry, 1726, Jan. 25.
2. John, 1727, Oct. 29.
3. Jemima, 1729, Aug. 21.

(She m. (2) 1735, Nov. 13, Elijah Hawkins.)

1716, May 17. He had 60 acres laid out.

1718, Dec. 11. He made his choice of half the real estate left by his father's will, taking land on east side of the highway, and leaving land on west side of highway with the house, to his brother Cornelius.

1727, Oct. 29. Following the entry of birth of his son John, the records say: "about an hour after the great earthquake, which was on the first day of the week at about ten o'clock in the evening."

1730. Inventory, £225±, viz: 16 head of cattle, mare, 23 sheep and lambs, 9 swine and pigs, pewter platters, plates, porringers, tankard, &c., wearing apparel, books, cheese press, old clock, loom, sheep's wool, rye, barley, beans, &c. Administration on his estate was taken by widow Jemima.

His sons Henry and John both married, and the latter died 1805, Jun. 21, leaving a large family.

V. CORNELIUS, m. (1) 1726, Dec. 7. SARAH JENCKES, m. (2) 1736, Nov. 17. RACHEL JENCKES,
b. 1699, Mar. 9. d. 1776, Jan. 11.
b. 1695, Dec. 26. d. 1735, May 3. of Ebenezer & Mary (Butterworth) Jenckes.
b. 1706, Dec. 1. d. 1777, Jan. 17. of Ebenezer & Mary (Butterworth) Jenckes.

Providence, North Providence, R. I.

1. Mary, 1728, Feb. 23.
2. Freelove, 1729, Aug. 17.
3. Cornelius, 1732, Mar. 18.
4. Thomas, 1733, May 23.
5. Son, 1735, Apr. 16.
6. Son, 1735, Apr. 16.

(2d wife.)

7. Sarah, 1737, Nov. 18.
8. James, 1739, Sep. 14.
9. Anne, 1742, Mar. 28.
10. Rachel, 1743, Jun. 9.
11. Daniel, 1745, Mar. 24.
12. Phebe, 1745, Mar. 24.
13. Son, 1746, Dec.
14. Esek, 1748, Jun. 18.

He was a tanner.

1729, Apr. 8. He had land laid out.

1730, Dec. 24. He and wife Sarah, for £60, sold Ebenezer Jenckes, all interest in real estate, &c., of honoured father Ebenezer Jenckes, deceased.

1749, Apr. 11. He received deed of land from Joseph Randall.

1751, Apr. 2. He and his brother Henry, deceased, having purchased lands together, he makes an agreement with nephew Henry, son of deceased.

1763, Dec. 17. He had land laid out to him in north-east part of Glocester, 37½ acres.

1767, Aug. 17. North Providence. He deeded son-in-law Thomas Mann and Anne his wife, of North Providence, 34 acres in Johnston — for love, &c.

1767, Dec. 31. He deeded son Esek, cordwainer, homestead and lands, bounded westerly by Moshassuck River, also a 12 acre piece, all for love, &c.

1769. He deeded land in Glocester, to daughters Rachel, Phebe and Sarah.

1787, Sep. 29. Administration to son Esek, who three years later exhibited receipts from all the heirs and declared that previous to taking administration he had settled said estate; and his prayer that inventory might be dispensed with was granted.

The only son of Cornelius who left issue was Esek.

FREEBORN.

1. Elizabeth,
2. Clement,
3. William,
4. John,
5. Thomas,

1. William,
2. Jane,

I. MARY,
b. 1664, Feb. 12. d. 1676, Oct. 25.

II. SARAH, m. 1690, Jan. 29. JOSEPH WANTON,
b. 1667, Jan. 14. d. 1737, Jul. 10.
b. 1664, May 1. d. 1754, Mar. 3.
of Edward Wanton.

1. Elizabeth, 1691, Jan. 5.
2. Edward, 1692, Apr. 20.
3. Gideon, 1693, Oct. 20.
4. Sarah, 1696, Apr. 27.
5. Joseph, 1698, Jun. 9.
6. Mary, 1700, Jun. 10.

III. ANN, m. THOMAS DURFEE,
b. 1669, Mar. 28. d. 1729 (—)
b. d. 1729, Feb. 11.
of Thomas Durfee.

1. Ann, 1691, Aug. 25.
2. Sarah, 1693, Mar. 1.
3. Freeborn, 1695, Dec. 15.
4. Patience, 1697, Jun. 12.
5. Mary, 1701, Jan. 22.
6. Martha, 1702, Feb. 20.
7. Gideon, 1704, Jan. 15.
8. Thomas, 1706, Jun. 6.
9. Susanna,
10. Job,
11. Elizabeth,

IV. MARTHA, m. 1696, Mar. 26. THOMAS CORNELL,
b. 1671, Aug. 8. d. 1748, Nov. 15.
b. 1674, Nov. 30. d. 1728, Jun. 18.
of Thomas & Susannah (Lawton) Cornell.

1. Thomas, 1698, Feb. 3.
2. Susanna, 1702, Jul. 22.
3. Gideon, 1704, Mar. 12.
4. William, 1705, Jul. 26.
5. George, 1707, Dec. 11.
6. Gideon, 1710, Jul. 11.
7. Sarah, 1713, Feb. 20.

V. SUSANNA, UNMARRIED,
b. 1674, Mar. 24. d. 1723, Jan. 21.

Sarah Wanton, Anne Durfee, Martha Cornell, Susanna Freeborn and Patience Anthony, 500 acres in Pennsylvania, equally. To daughter Comfort Freeborn, 100 acres in Freehold, East New Jersey. To grandson John Freeborn and his children, farm in Coweset, Warwick, of 200 acres, and negro boy Samson—when grandson is of age. To grandson Gideon Durfee, 100 acres in Coweset. To daughters Mary Brayton, Mercy Coggeshall and Comfort Freeborn, each 3 acres in Coweset, &c. To granddaughter Sarah Freeborn, 100 acres in Coweset. To granddaughters Elizabeth Borden, Sarah Wanton, Mary Wanton, Ann, Sarah, Patience, Mary, Martha, Susanna and Elizabeth Durfee, Susannah and Sarah Cornell, Abigail and Susanna Anthony, Mary and Hannah Brayton and Elizabeth and Comfort Coggeshall, 40*s.* each, at eighteen. To grandsons William, George and Gideon Cornell, 50 acres each in Coweset. To grandsons Gideon and David Anthony, each 50 acres in Tiverton, and to grandson William Anthony, 45 acres in Tiverton. To grandsons Thomas and Job Durfee, each 50 acres in Coweset. To grandson Edward Wanton, 25 acres in Tiverton. To grandsons Gideon and Thomas Freeborn, each 50 acres in Tiverton. To grandson William Freeborn, land in Portsmouth, at decease of said William's father, and if he die before his father, then to brother Thomas. To granddaughter Susanna Freeborn, 50 acres in Coweset. To wife's two granddaughters, the daughters of George Lawton, each 20*s.*, at age. To wife's grandson John Lawton, 40*s.* To my daughter Comfort Freeborn, £20. To daughters Mary Brayton and Mercy Coggeshall, each £15. To daughter Susanna Freeborn, £25. To daughter Ann Durfee, £25. Son Gideon to care for negro woman Betty, for life. To son Gideon, negro man Eben. To grandson Thomas Freeborn, 100 acres in Coweset. To daughter Susannah Freeborn, 20*s.*, per year while unmarried paid her by son Gideon. To daughter Patience Anthony, £10. To daughters Sarah Wanton and Martha Cornell, each £10. To wife Mary, two cows and keep of same by son Gideon, who is to maintain his mother while widow. To Quakers, ten cords of wood delivered at Meeting house, a cord each year for ten years. To grandson Gideon Freeborn, silver spoon and silver cup. To grandson William Freeborn, a silver spoon. To son-in-law Joseph Wanton, land in Tiverton. To son Gideon, rest of real estate, two cows, a pair oxen, black mare, fifty sheep, two swine, husbandry gear, bed, silver tankard, &c. To daughters Susanna Freeborn, Comfort Freeborn and Mercy Coggeshall, each a certain share of personal. To son Gideon, and daughters Sarah Wanton, Ann Durfee, Martha Cornell, Patience Anthony, and Mary Brayton, rest of movables.

Inventory, £676, 12*s.*, 2*d.*, viz: wearing apparel, bible and spectacles £25, 10*s.*, 1 gun, silver money £35, 4*s.*, 4*d.*, plate £11, 12*s.*, 8*d.*, warming pan, feather bed, pewter, cider £2, 14*s.*, 1 pair oxen, 8 cows, 5 yearlings, a bull, 4 horsekind, sheep and lambs £78, swine £2, 5*s.*, 3 negroes, (man, woman and boy) £102, &c.

He was buried in his own burying ground, the Friends' records declare.

1723, Nov. 16. His daughter Susanna in will of this date (proved 1724, Feb. 10), mentions brother Gideon and wife, sisters Patience Anthony, Mary Brayton, Mercy Coggeshall, Comfort Coggeshall, Sarah Wanton and Martha Cornell; also sister Sarah Wanton's three daughters (viz: Elizabeth Borden, Sarah Wanton, Mary Wanton), sister Ann Durfee's seven daughters (viz: Ann Estes, Sarah Dennis, Patience, Mary, Martha, Susannah and Elizabeth Durfee); sister Martha Cornell's daughter (viz: Susannah Bennett), sister Patience Anthony's two daughters (viz: Abigail and Susannah Anthony). She further mentions cousin (*i. e.* nephew) David Anthony, and cousins (nieces) Susannah and Elizabeth Freeborn and Sarah Freeborn. To Susannah Dow, named for my sake, a silver spoon. To the woman's Meeting of Friends, called Quakers, £6, &c.

FRY.

THOMAS, m. **MARY GRIFFIN**, — Newport, R. I.
b. 1632. d. 1704, Jun. 11.
b. 1649. d. 1717, Mar. 12.
of Griffin.

1669. Freeman.

1671, Jan. 30. He was allowed 2*s.* 6*d.*, for provisions for John Galliardy who was pressed to go to Narragansett to fetch Mr. Crandall.

1676-77-78-81-90-91. General Sergeant. (He succeeded James Rogers who had held the office continuously since 1659.)

1677, Oct. 31. He and forty-seven others were granted 5,000 acres to be called East Greenwich.

1684-90. Deputy. (He represented East Greenwich in these years but his residence was only temporarily there if at all.)

1687. Grand Jury.

1689, Mar. 11. He deeded eldest son Thomas, glazier, living in East Greenwich, all rights in lands there, reserving profits of 100 acres for life.

He was buried in Newport Cemetery.

I. **THOMAS**, m. 1688, Feb. 1. **WELTHIAN GREENE**, — East Greenwich, R. I.
b. 1666. d. 1748, Sep. 3.
b. 1670, Jan. 23. d. 1746 (—) of Thomas & Elizabeth (Barton) Greene.

He was a glazier.

1690. Freeman.

1696-1701-2-3-5-6-7-8-9-10-13-14-15-17-18-19-20-23-24-25-26-27-29-30-31-32. Deputy.

1698-1704. Justice of the Peace.

1701, Mar. 29. He was appointed by the Assembly on a committee for General Audit of the Colony.

1707, Oct. 29. He was appointed one of the commissioners to treat and settle with Massachusetts about the northern bounds of Rhode Island.

1708-9-10-11-18. Clerk of Assembly.

1709, Oct. He was appointed on a committee to run lines between Rhode Island and Massachusetts.

1710, Jul. 14. He deeded cousin John Spencer, 13½ rods, for love, &c., for a burial place.

1713, May 6. He was appointed on a committee to make the public road leading through this colony from Pawtucket River to Pawcatuck River, more straight, fair and passable.

1713-14-17-18-22-24-25-26-27-29-30. Speaker of House of Deputies.

1714. Major for the Main.

1715, Jul. 5. He and Andrew Harris were appointed by Assembly to transcribe, fit and prepare for the press all the laws of the colony.

1719, May. He was allowed £10, for his trouble and pains in getting the laws of the colony printed.

1726, Jan. 10. He was appointed one of the four commissioners to meet the Connecticut commissioners to settle line between two colonies.

1727-28-29. Deputy Governor.

VI. PATIENCE, m. 1698, Sep. 7. WILLIAM ANTHONY,
b. 1676, Mar. 4. d. 1757, Apr. 27.
b. 1676, Jul. 18. d. 1757, Nov. 9. of John & Frances (Wodell) **Anthony.**

1. William, 1702, Mar. 13.
2. Abigail, 1704, Jun. 23.
3. Gideon, 1706, Aug. 14.
4. David, 1709, Sep. 19.
5. Susanna, 1712, Sep. 26.
6. Joseph, 1715, Sep. 4.

(2D WIFE.)

VII. MARY, m. 1704, Aug. 23. THOMAS BRAYTON,
b. 1679, Aug. 24. d. 1761.
b. 1681, Jun. 14. d. 1728. of Francis & Mary (Fish) **Brayton.**

1. Mary, 1708, Jul. 1.
2. Hannah, 1711, Mar. 28.
3. Thomas, 1713, Jul. 21.
4. Francis, 1715, Sep. 21.
5. Gideon, 1718, Jan. 27.
6. Francis, 1721, Mar. 30.

VIII. WILLIAM, m 1698, Dec. 21. MARY HALL,
b. 1682, Feb. 3. d. 1705. **Portsmouth, R. I.**
b. 1678, Apr. 3. d. 1711, Nov. 14. of Benjamin & Frances (Parker) **Hall.**

(She m. (2) Clement Weaver.)

1. Sarah,
2. John, 1702, Mar. 18.

1703. Freeman.

1705, Apr. 9. Administration to widow Mary.

1725, Mar. 8. John Freeborn made his appearance before Town Council of Portsmouth, and complained that he had not received his part of personal estate left him by his father William Freeborn, who died intestate, and that his grandfather Benjamin Hall became bond with the administratrix, viz: his daughter Mary, for performance of administration. It was ordered that Benjamin Hall be notified by Town Sergeant to make his appearance the 12th day of 2d month next to render a just account.

1725, Jul. 12. John Freeborn and his grandfather Benjamin Hall, consented to arbitration.

IX. GIDEON, m. (1) 1706, Feb. 1. ELIZABETH NICHOLS, m. (2) 1733, Aug. 9. BETHIAH SHERMAN,
b. 1684, Apr. 29. d. 1753, Feb. 21.
b. 1688, Jun. 14. d. of Thomas & Hannah ( ) **Nichols.**
b. 1699. d. 1749. of Benjamin & Hannah (Mowry) **Sherman.**

1. William, 1706, Nov. 19.
2. Gideon, 1708, Oct. 26.
3. Susanna, 1710, Jan. 7.
4. Thomas, 1711, Oct. 11.
5. William, 1713, Mar. 1.
6. Elizabeth, 1714, Jul. 22.
7. Joseph, 1717, Feb. 25.
8. Jonathan, 1719, Mar. 4.
9. Benjamin, 1722, Jan. 9.
10. Hannah, 1726, May 10.

(2d wife.)

11. Robert, 1735, Jan. 11.

1716-19-20-21-23-27-28-29-31-32-33-40-41. Deputy.

1717. Assistant.

1734-35. Justice of Inferior Court of Common Pleas of Newport County, with three others.

1749, Aug. 20. Will—proved 1753, Mar. 12. Ex. son Gideon. To son Gideon, certain land in Portsmouth, north side of a line, with buildings, being a gift from will of his grandfather Gideon, also other land. To son Jonathan, rest of my farm lands in Portsmouth and buildings. To son Robert, a farm in Coventry, &c., confirmed. Sons Thomas and Joseph, already had by deed. To son Gideon, also lands in Warwick. To three daughters Susanna Hicks, Elizabeth Coggeshall and Hannah Brayton, £100, each, and to Susanna, negro girl Dinah and two children. To wife Bethiah, service of negro man Dominie, for seven years, and negro girl Jenny, and she to take care of two younger children for my son, to whom they are given. To son Gideon, negro man Prince, and service of Indian lad. To son Jonathan, negro boy Eben. To son Benjamin, certain land, feather bed, and negro boy Samson. To son Robert, a bed. To wife, while widow, sole improvement of great lower room, the room adjoining, privilege in cellar and garden, and my sister Freelove Sherman to have liberty to cohabit with my wife, her sister. To wife, all household goods, &c., two cows, riding beast, and firewood, while widow, and to have yearly twenty bushels corn, four barrels cider, fruit of orchard sufficient, two hundred pounds of pork and same of beef. To four sons Gideon, Jonathan, Benjamin and Robert, rest of personal.

Inventory, £3,324, 15*s.*, viz: books £8, wearing apparel, 90 silver buttons and pair of silver shoe buckles £88, desk, 43 oz., 16 pwt. silver in a tankard and 12 spoons £140, 3*s.*, pewter, gun, loom, 3 woolen wheels, linen wheel, 8 turkeys, 23 sheep, 4 swine, 5 geese, 3 cows, 2 mares, negro Domine £200, Jane, £350, Eben £400, George £330, Samson £300, child Prince £50, &c. Rooms named were great room, middle room, bedroom, great chamber, kitchen, cheese room, &c.

X. THOMAS,
b. 1688, Feb. 5. d. 1688, Oct. 1.

XI. COMFORT, m. 1715, Feb. 4. JOSIAH COGGESHALL,
b. 1691. d. 1725, Nov. 1.
b. 1690, Dec. 12. d. 1725 + of Joshua & Sarah ( ) **Coggeshall.**

XII. MERCY, m. 1708, Mar. 11. THOMAS COGGESHALL,
b. 1692. d. 1776, May 26.
b 1688, Apr. 25. d. 1771, Jan. 26. of Joshua & Sarah ( ) **Coggeshall.**

1. Elizabeth, 1710, Aug. 20.
2. Comfort, 1712, Sep. 17.
3. Mercy, 1714, Jun. 30.
4. Sarah, 1715, Aug. 20.
5. Waite, 1718, Jan. 4.
6. Mary, 1720, Mar. 27.
7. Joshua, 1722, May 11.
8. Mercy, 1724, Feb. 23.
9. Gideon, 1726, Apr. 13.
10. Thomas, 1728, Aug. 26.
11. Hannah, 1731, Mar.

FRY.

I. THOMAS, m. (1) 1719, Dec. 31. MARY GREENE, m. (2) 1740, Nov. 16. ELEANOR GREENE,
b. 1691, Feb. 16. d. 1782. **East Greenwich, R. I.**
b. 1698, Aug. 25. d. 1739, Oct. 28. of Samuel & Mary (Gorton) **Greene.**
b. 1702, Feb. 19. d. 1764, Aug. 19. of Richard & Eleanor (Sayles) **Greene.**

1. Welthian, 1720, Oct. 19.
2. Mary, 1722, Jul. 15.
3. Thomas, 1723, Dec. 29.
4. Anne, 1725, May 14.
5. Sarah, 1726, Dec. 21.
6. John, 1728, Jan. 22.
7. Samuel, 1729, Mar. 22.
8. Hannah, 1730, Apr. 16.
9. Elizabeth, 1732, Nov. 18.
10. Ruth, 1734, May 20.
11. Joseph, 1736, Mar. 3.

(2d wife.)

12. Amey, 1741, Nov. 23.
13. Richard, 1743, Mar. 19.

1726-40-46. Deputy.

1740, Sep. He and Colonel Peter Mawney in behalf of the town, petitioned the Assembly for a highway in North Kingstown, that the Council of that town had refused to make, which was to meet one built in East Greenwich. The Assembly ordered it made.

1773, Dec. 27. Will—proved 1782, Dec. 9. Exs. sons Samuel and Richard. To son Thomas, land in West Greenwich, ten sheep, a cow, debt he oweth me, and all wearing apparel, he having had his portion before. To son John, a Spanish milled dollar. To son Samuel, several lots of land, a farm in Exeter, and half of Still House, water lot and wharf. To son Joseph, rest of farm where Joseph lives, given by deed, half of another farm, &c., and negro man Winsor. To son Richard, homestead where I dwell, between the country road and the sea, &c., half of a certain farm, and the rest of Still House, water lot, and wharf, &c., two feather beds, and all silver and plate marked with the letters of his mother, grandfather and grandmother's names, a clock, desk, looking glass and silver watch. To grandson Thomas Fry, 327 acres in West Greenwich. To grandson Joseph Fry, 200 acres. To grandson Rhodes Fry, 160 acres. To grandson Benjamin Fry, 100 acres. To grandson Peleg Fry, 80 acres. Al of these farms were in West Greenwich. To daughters Mary Greene and Sarah Greene, each an eighth of all personal not already given sons Thomas, John, Joseph and Richard. To daughters Anne Gardiner and Ruth Tillinghast, five-eighths of personal not already given. To grandson Thomas Sherman, the other eighth of personal.

Inventory, £382, 2*s.* 2¾*d.*, viz: linen and woolen wheel, cane, bible with silver clasp, desk, pair of seals, warming pan, pair of gold buttons, 32 silver spoons, silver tankard, 3 silver porringers, notes £136, 9*s.* ½*d.*, 22 pewter plates, coffee mill, wearing apparel £3, 12*s.*, &c.

II. MARY, m. 1716, Sep. 13. JOHN SPENCER,
b. 1693, Jun. 24. d. 1746 (—)
b. 1693, Jun. 10. d. 1774. of John & Audry (Greene) **Spencer.**

1. Thomas, 1717, Jul. 18.
2. Welthian, 1719, Feb. 16.
3. Audry, 1720, Dec. 1.
4. John, 1722, Nov. 10.
5. Rufus, 1724, Aug. 21.
6. Charles, 1726, Jan. 31.
7. Susanna, 1729, Sep. 10.
8. Mary, 1731, Mar. 14.

1746, Jun. 9. Will—proved 1748, Sep. 24. Exs. sons Thomas and John. To eldest son Thomas, the land I bought of the two Samuel Bennetts, adjoining south side of son's now dwelling place, also a farm bought of Richard Codner of 140 acres. To son John, land east side of his dwelling place, and all of testator's homestead, the house and land both sides of roadway, also other land. To grandchildren (children of my daughter Mary Spencer, deceased), each £150. To granddaughter Welthian Gorton, one silver porringer which I intended for her mother. To son-in-law John Spencer, £650. To daughter Hannah Holden, negro named Mary and all her children, and negro named Jack, and a silver porringer, and £1,700. To daughter Elizabeth Fry, negro named Cuff, a feather bed, silver porringer, £3,000, and privilege to dwell in house while unmarried. To daughter Ruth Fry, a negro woman named Juda, and her children, a feather bed, silver porringer and £3,000, and privilege to dwell in house while unmarried. To each grandchild, an English bible "and to write in each bible at the end of the Prophets, the gift of my grandfather Thomas Fry of East Greenwich, deceased." To each grandchild, a silver spoon. To sons Thomas and John, all the rest both real and personal equally.

Inventory, £22,309, 8s. 5d., viz: silver and plate £228, 12s. 4d. Bonds for £450, £562, £378, &c. Goods in shop including apothecary ware, syrups, indigo, Spanish flys, silk, wafers, &c. Books £20, stillyards, gun, tobacco, 23 barrels of cider, cider mill, 4 negro boys £850, negro woman Juda and her 3 children £450, 1 horse, 1 mare, 40 sheep, 21 lambs, 11 swine, &c.

II. JOSEPH, m. 1700, Dec. 12. MARY CLARKE, — b. d. b. d. — Newport, R. I. — of Latham & Hannah (Wilbur) Clarke.

He was a glazier.

1701. Freeman.

1703, Jan. 15. He bought a small lot for £10, of Thomas Mallett.

1714. Deputy.

1714. Captain.

1714, Jun. 15. He and two others were appointed by the Assembly to ascertain what was due from the colony to Colonel William Wanton.

1715, Mar. 21. He bought land of Charles Whitefield and wife Sarah, for £60.

III. RUTH, UNMARRIED. — b. 1674. d. 1733, Nov. 24.

IV. KATHARINE, m. 1706, Sep. 20. THOMAS RODMAN, — b. 1683, Dec. 23. d. 1740, May 4. b. 1683, Nov. 11. d. 1775. — of Thomas & Patience (Easton) Rodman.

V. SARAH, m. 1708, Jul. 5. THOMAS LEACH. — b. d. 1733. b. 1682. d. 1733, Sep. 13. — of Leach.

VI. ELIZABETH, m. 1711, Sep. 18. JOSEPH ANTHONY, — b. d. b. 1682, May 19. d. — of Joseph & Mary (Wait) Anthony.

GEREARDY.

GEREARDY. 2d column. I. Mary, d. 1722, +. Her husband d. 1720.

JOHN, m. RENEWED SWEET, — b. d. 1681 + b. d. 1681 + — Warwick, R. I. — of John & Mary ( ) Sweet.

He was of Dutch parentage.

1648, Jun. 5. He was recorded as an inhabitant.

1652, Mar. 1. He sold to Stukely Westcott, certain lands of late John Warner, taken by execution by Harmanus Harforth, of New York.

1654, May 16. He had lately bought some deer skins in trade with the Dutch, as appears by the testimony of Giles Glover before the Assembly.

1655. Freeman.

I. MARY, m. 1672, Jan. 2. JEREMIAH SMITH, — b. d. 1720 + b. d. 1722 + — of John & Margaret ( ) Smith.

II. JOHN, m. (1) — m. (2) DELIVERANCE CORP, (w. [of John. — b. d. b. d. b. d. — Warwick, R. I. — of — of

III. John, m. Elizabeth, — b. 1695, Oct. 31. d. 1753, Sep. 6. — b. d. 1753 + of — East Greenwich, R. I.

1. John, 1724, May 18.
2. Elizabeth, 1726, Dec. 28.
3. Benjamin, 1728, Feb. 11.
4. Susanna, 1730, Nov. 27.
5. Welthian, 1735, Mar. 23.
6. Elizabeth, 1739, Dec. 2.
7. Mary, 1743, Feb. 26.
8. Ruth, 1745, May 14.

1742-43-44-52-53. Deputy.

1742, Jun. 21. He was chosen one of the Trustees by the Indian Sachems, in the room of his father Thomas Fry, Esq., who wished to resign.

1743, Mar. He was allowed £7, 10s. 9d. by the Assembly for his services on the committee that revised the boundaries at Warwick south-west corner.

1753, Aug. 17. Will—proved 1753, Sep. 27. Exs. wife Elizabeth and son Benjamin. To wife, best bed, bay mare, £1,000, negroes Yallow and Phillis, five cows and whole profits of dwelling house and lands both sides of highway for her comfort and to bring up children. To son Benjamin, my now dwelling house and homestead, and also the farm and house where I lately dwelt, 200 acres, meadow, &c. To daughter Susanna, £1,000, a feather bed and negro Grace. To daughter Welthian, £1,000, a feather bed, and negro Dinah. To daughters Elizabeth, Mary and Ruth, a feather bed; and £300, or a negro boy or girl, to each at eighteen. To son Benjamin, negro Solomon. To daughters Susanna, Welthian, Elizabeth, Mary and Ruth, 50 acres in Warwick, and lands in partnership with brother Thomas Fry, given me by last will of father. To daughters, rest of estate.

Inventory, £14,867, 7d., viz: wearing apparel £123, plate £131, 4s., 25 chairs, desk, pewter, coffee mill, 4 candle sticks, linen wheel, woolen wheel, feather beds, flock beds, bonds £4,603, 2s. 9d., notes £300, 5 hogsheads molasses £500, 1-16 sloop Humbird £80, ⅛ brigantine Victory and cargo, now at sea £1,500, 15 cows, 6 working cattle, 4 two years, 5 yearlings, pair of fat cattle, 2 fat cows, 2 bulls, calf, 106 sheep and lambs, sow, 6 pigs, 8 other swine, 4 mares, 6 colts, hay £800, oats £75, cider mill, negro man Yallow £300, Phillis £300, Solomon £400, Grace £300, Dinah £300, Watt £350, Peter £350, Cæsar £200, Primus £100, sucking child Ellen £20, &c.

IV. Elizabeth, — b. 1697, Dec. 7. d.

V. Welthian, — b. 1700, Jul. 27. d.

VI. Hannah, m. —— Holden, — b. 1702, Mar. 31. d. — b. d. of — Holden.

FRY. 3d column. VI. Hannah m. 1732, Jan. 6, John Holden of Charles and Catherine (Greene) Holden. Children, 1, Welthian, 1733, Dec. 24. 2, Charles, 1737, June 2. 3, Deliverance, 1738, Sep. 28, 4, Thomas, 1741, June 27.

VII. Ruth, Unmarried. — b. 1704, Jun. 5. d. 1755, Feb. 4.

I. Joseph, m. 1729, Nov. 13. Mary Coggeshall, — b. d. — b. 1712, Jan. 31. d. of Abraham & Elizabeth ( ) — Newport, R. I. Coggeshall.

II. John, m. 1724, Mar. 26. Abigail Spink, — b. d. — b. d. of Robert — Newport, R. I. Spink.

III. Ruth, Unmarried. — b. d. 1716, Dec. 17.

IV. Mary, — b. 1705. d. 1711, Dec. 11.

V. Elizabeth, m. 1729, Jan. 1. Edmund Casey, — b. d. — b. d. of Thomas & Rebecca ( ) — Casey.

VI. Thomas, m. 1741, Mar. 12. Abigail Scranton, — b. d. — b. d. of — Scranton.

VII. Hannah, m. 1739, Jan. 7. Thomas Cranston, — b. d. — b. d. of John & Penelope (Godfrey) — Cranston.

VIII. Freelove, m. 1740, Dec. 18. Randolph Eldredge, — b. d. — b. d. of — Eldredge.

1. Thomas, 1708, Mar. 9.
2. Patience, 1710, Mar. 22.
3. John, 1711, Dec. 26.
4. Joseph, 1713, Oct. 1.
5. Samuel, 1716, Mar. 22.
6. Ann, 1718, Apr. 20.
7. Robert, 1720, Jun. 11.
8. William, 1723, May 3.
9. Benjamin, 1726, Jul. 22.

1. Ann, 1710, Jun. 29.
2. Thomas, 1712, Jul. 25.
3. Mary, 1714, Feb. 16.
4. John, 1715, Oct. 10.
5. Joseph, 1717, Jul. 29.
6. Sarah, 1719, Jun. 24.
7. Elizabeth, 1720, Oct. 31.
8. Ruth, 1722, Feb. 22.
9. Benjamin, 1723, Oct. 22.
10. James, 1725, Sep. 30.
11. Son,
12. Child,

GEREARDY.

1. John,
2. Ephraim,
3. Ebenezer,
4. Sarah, 1678.
5. Mary,
6. Deliverance.

(2d Wife.)

I. John, m. 1720, Nov. 3. Mary Draper, — b. 1696, Dec. 22. d. — b. d. of — Warwick, R. I. Draper.

1. John, 1722, Feb. 12.
2. Mary, 1724, Mar. 5.
3. Ephraim, 1727, Mar. 6.
4. Phebe, 1730, Mar. 8.
5. Sarah, 1733, Aug. 9.
6. Elizabeth, 1737, Aug. 24

1662, Oct. 1. He sold Francis Derby, for £4, a right in two shares meadow, &c.

1663, Apr. 13. He sold all his right to a certain house and lands to Mrs. Mary Holiman.

1664, May 5. He and two others were allowed £3, 2s., 6d., by Assembly for bringing an Indian to prison, from Warwick to Newport, they having spent five days in the service.

1669, Mar. 19. He and wife Renewed, sold John Read for £42, all interest in Mashantatack.

1681, Jul. 13. He, and wife Renewed, had a deed for love, &c., from his wife's mother Mary Holiman, widow of Ezekiel, of her house, lot, orchard, &c.

1719, Feb. 24 It was deposed by Samuel Gorton, that John Gereardy, late of Warwick, deceased, did marry a daughter of Mary Holiman formerly wife to Ezekiel Holiman, named Renewed, and that the wives of Jeremiah Smith, of Prudence, and John Smith, now of Kings Town, were reputed to be daughters of John Gereardy by Renewed, their names being Mary and Phillis.

III. { PHILLIS, { b.
m. { d. 1729 +
{ JOHN SMITH, { b.
{ d. 1730 of John & Margaret ( ) Smith.

Thomas Gorton (omitted by Austin)

GORTON. See: American Genealogist, v. 20, p. 186-187.

{ SAMUEL, { b. 1592. Gorton, Lancaster Co., Eng.,
m. { d. 1677. [Warwick, R. I.
{ ELIZABETH, { b.
{ d. 1677 +

His occupation in England had been that of a clothier.

His family, he says, had been for many generations at Gorton (a chapelry within the parish of Manchester, in Lancaster County).

1635, Jun. 18. He (called Samuel Gorton, of London, clothier) had release from John Dukenfield, of Dukenfield, Chester County, England, of all sorts and causes of action from the beginning of the world.

1637, Mar. He arrived at Boston from London, having with him wife Elizabeth, eldest son Samuel and other children.

1637 Plymouth. He hired part of a house of Ralph Smith with whom he soon had a difference on religious topics.

1638, Dec. 4. He was summoned to court to answer complaint of Ralph Smith (Elder of the church at Plymouth), and there he carried himself so mutinously and seditiously as that he was for the same and for his turbulent carriages towards both magistrates and ministers in the presence of the Court, sentenced to find sureties for his good behavior during the time he should stay in the jurisdiction, which was to be only fourteen days.

1639, Apr. 30. Portsmouth. He and twenty-eight others signed the following compact: "We whose names are underwritten do acknowledge ourselves the legal subjects of his Majesty King Charles, and in his name do hereby bind ourselves into a civil body politick, unto his laws according to matters of justice."

1640. His servant maid assaulted a woman whose cow had trespassed on his land, and the servant was ordered before the court, but he appeared in her behalf refusing to allow her to come to court. He was indicted on fourteen counts, among the charges brought against being the following: That he had said "that the government was such as was not to be subjected unto." He called the magistrates "Just Asses"—He called a freeman in open court "saucy boy and Jack-an-Apes"—He charged the court with acting the second part of Plymouth magistrates, who, as he said, "condemned him in the chimney corner ere they heard him speak"—When the Governor said "all you that own the King take away Gorton and carry him to prison," he replied "all you that own the King take away Coddington and carry him to prison," &c. Having already suffered imprisonment, he was now sentenced to be whipped, and went soon to Providence.

1640, Mar. 8. Providence. His democratic ideas for church and state, &c., soon led to division of sentiment here, and Roger Williams wrote to Winthrop under this date as follows: "Master Gorton having abused high and low at Aquidneck, is now bewitching and bemadding poor Providence, both with his unclean and foul censures of all the ministers of this country (for which myself have in Christ's name withstood him), and also denying all visible and external ordinances in depth of Familism," &c.

1641, Nov. 17. He had taken up his residence with the Pawtuxet settlers before this time, and here too there was a division into parties, the majority adhering to his views. A letter was sent to Massachusetts at this date signed by thirteen persons, who complained of the "insolent and riotous carriage of Samuel Gorton and his company" and therefore petitioned Massachusetts to "lend us a neighborlike helping hand."

1643, Jan. 12. Warwick. He and ten others bought of Miantonomi for 144 fathoms of wampum, tract of land that was called Shawomet (Warwick).

1643, Sep. 12. He with others of Warwick, was notified to appear at General Court at Boston, to hear complaint of two Indian Sachems Pomham and Socconocco, as to "some unjust and injurious dealing toward them by yourselves." The Warwick men declined to obey the summons, declaring that they were legal subjects of the King of England and beyond the limits of Massachusetts authority, to whom they would acknowledge no subjection. Soldiers were soon sent, who besieged the settlers in a fortified house. In a parley it was now said "that they held blasphemous errors which they must repent of" or go to Boston for trial, and they were soon carried thence.

1643, Oct. 17. He was brought with others before the court, and the following charge preferred against him. "Upon much examination and serious consideration of your writing, with your answers about them, we do charge you to be a blasphemous enemy of the true religion of our Lord Jesus Christ and his Holy Ordinances, and also of all civil authority among the people of God and particularly in this jurisdiction."

1643, Nov. 3. He was sentenced as follows: "Ordered to be confined to Charlestown, there to be kept at work and to wear such bolt or irons as might hinder his escape; and if he broke his confinement or by speech or writing published or maintained any of the blasphemies or abominable heresies wherewith he hath been charged by the General Court, or should reproach or reprove the churches of our Lord Jesus Christ in these United Colonies, or the civil government, &c., that upon conviction thereof by a trial by jury he should suffer death." All but three of the magistrates condemned him to death at the trial.

1644, Mar. He was released from prison (but banished from both Massachusetts and Warwick), and same year went to England with Randall Holden and John Greene, to obtain redress for their wrongs. They were obliged to take ship at New York.

I. { SAMUEL, { b. 1630. Warwick, R. I.
{ m. 1684, Dec. 11. { d. 1724, Sep. 6.
{ SUSANNA BURTON, { b. 1665.
{ d. 1737, Jun. 25. of William & Hannah (Wickes) Burton.

(She m. (2) Richard Harris.)

1655. Freeman.

1670, Jun. 29. He had his fine remitted for not attending Court of Trials, at Newport, having been several times employed as interpreter between the English and Indians, and so was allowed for his satisfaction the fine of 20s.

1676, Aug. 24. He was a member of the Court Martial held at Newport for the trial of certain Indians charged with being engaged in King Philip's designs.

1676-77-78-79-80-81-82-83. Assistant. He had the title of Captain during much of this time.

1680, May 17. He was on a committee who reported to Assembly that 455 persons had died in the Colony for the space of seven years last past.

1684-91. Deputy.

1685. He was elected Assistant, but refused to serve.

1687. Grand Jury.

1721, Dec. 21. Will—proved 1724, Sep. 28. Exx. wife Susannah. He calls himself in his ninety-second year. To wife, all housing and lands where I dwell and all lands in Warwick Neck, &c., to be at her disposal for life, and at her decease son Samuel to have land joining his house, and certain other land. The rest of lands and housing given wife to be for son Hezekiah, he paying his sister Susannah Stafford, £30. To wife, all out lands at Cowesct, and all other lands undisposed of, and the back room both above and below in house where son Samuel now dwells if she have occasion for it, and at her death to go to Samuel. To son Hezekiah, one-half cart and tackling. To wife, rest of goods and chattels with my negro man and girl. To Hezekiah, at decease of wife, the negro girl.

Inventory, 5 cows, 2 two year old in the woods, 3 yearlings, 3 calves, a pair of oxen, 3 swine, 6 pigs, 80 sheep and 20 lambs in the woods, 4 mares, 2 colts, one-half of a two year old horse, 3 guns, warming pan, tables, form, silver seal, silver money and plate £2, 16s., 31 books £24, 65 small books, £6, &c.

1733, Jul. 15. Will—proved 1739, Sep. 15. Susannah Harris, wife of Richard, of Smithfield. Ex. son-in-law Joseph Stafford and Susannah, his wife. She calls herself sixty-eight years of age. To loving husband Richard Harris, all my sheep in his custody and young horse and mare. To son Samuel Gorton, one mare and twenty sheep, and my silver cup to his wife Freelove, to his son Samuel, the long gun that was his grandfather's, to his son Benjamin, £5, to his son William, £5, and to his daughters Freelove, Ann, and Lydia Gorton, each a pair of sheets. To son Hezekiah Gorton, all the rest of horse and cowkind and sheep, that I let him, with my house, land, &c., tools, debts due from him, &c. To daughter Susannah and husband Joseph Stafford, the £10, due from them, and a cow. To granddaughters Mercy and Susannah Stafford, feather bed, &c. To grandson Joseph Stafford, all my part of lands at Coweset. To negro girl, feather bed, &c.

II. { JOHN, { b. Warwick, R. I.
{ m. 1668, Jun. 28. { d. 1714, Feb. 3.
{ MARGARET WHEATON, { b.
{ d. of Wheaton.

Possibly the reading of his wife's name should be Weeden.

1668, Feb. 1. He bought a house, orchard, &c., for £35, of William and Hannah Burton.

1677, Oct. 31. He and forty-seven others were granted 5,000 acres to be called East Greenwich.

GORTON. 1st column. The mother of most of his children, and perhaps his only wife, was Mary Maplett, of John and Mary. If he had an earlier wife Elizabeth, she was mother of his eldest son Samuel, (who was considerably older than the other children, apparently) and possibly of one or two more. In 1638 Mr. Gorton wrote (of his Plymouth, Mass. residence,) concerning his wife, that she was "as tenderly brought up as any man's wife then in that town." This might well have applied to his wife Mary Maplett. Her brother Doctor John Maplett was one of the physicians extraordinary to King Charles II., as seen on his tombstone in Bath Abbey Church, Bath, England, where he latterly lived, though called of Middlesex County, England. 1646, Dec. 7, Mrs. Mary Maplett in will of this date gives to "daughter Mary Gorton, wife of Samuel Gorton, living in New England, all the money which her said husband, Samuel Gorton, doth owe me, and a herd of cattle which he hath of mine." Also £10 to buy her mourning. 1662, Apr. 9, he and wife Mary deeded land. 1670, Apr. 13, in will of Dr. John Maplett, of Bath, England, he gives to "my dear sister, Mrs. Mary Gorton of New England"—20 s., and to each of her children 10 s. apiece. 2d column. II. John. At end of first line add—or Weston. 3d column. I. Samuel d. 1784, Jan. (Buried Jan. 23.) His wife's mother was Lydia Bowen. Son Benjamin b. 1725, July 2, and add 8, Susanna, 1734, June 6. 9, Hezekiah, 1736, July 9. I. Othniel m. Mercy Burlingame of Roger and Mary. He may not have had a 2d wife Mercy. III. John m. (2) 1717, Nov. 17, Elizabeth Peirce, at Nantucket, Mass.; unless this be a John of different ancestry, for his first wife Patience m. (2) 1711, Oct. 18, John Corp. Evidently her first husband must have been either dead, or supposed so from long absence, unless possibly divorced. IV. Benjamin. First Nov 1765, etc., belongs to III. Benjamin

II. { SWEET, { b. 1699, May 15. d.

1 John,
2 Daniel,
3. Son,
4. Hopestill,

GORTON.

I. { SAMUEL, m. 1715, Jun. 1. FREELOVE MASON, { b. 1690, Jun. 1. d. 1784, Apr. b. 1695, Jun. 5. d. of Joseph & Lydia ( ) Warwick, R. I. Mason.

1714. Warwick. Freeman.

1784, Mar. 8. Inventory, shown by administrator Benjamin Gorton, 25 silver coat buttons, and 18 jacket buttons £2, 3s., wearing apparel 30s., warming pan, 2 pair of old cards, a poor old sheep, 2 cows, one of them very poor and distempered, 2 notes of hand £50, 9s., 3d., cash in gold £6, 16s., 2 continental bills, one of £80, and one of £40, out of circulation, &c.

1. Samuel, 1717, Mar. 7.
2. Freelove, 1718, Aug. 27.
3. Ann, 1721, Sep. 7.
4. Lydia, 1723, Feb. 1.
5. Benjamin,
6. William,
7. Joseph,

II. { HEZEKIAH, m. 1719, Aug. 20. AVIS CARR, { b. 1692, Jun. 11. d. 1748. b. 1698, May 29. d. of Edward & Hannah (Stanton) Warwick, R. I. Carr.

1716. Freeman.

1720, Jan. 14. He and wife Avis gave receipt to Edward Carr, Jr., for legacy from her father's will.

1724, Jun. 23. He was granted liberty to keep a ferry from Warwick Neck to north end of Prudence Island.

1748, May 24 (and 1749, Apr. 10). Inventory, £683, 14s., 2d. Administration to Samuel Gorton. Among items was a sorrel horse, a pair of stags, desk, 4 links sleeve buttons, silver spoon, linen wheel, &c.

1. Samuel, 1720, May 21.

III. { SUSANNAH, m. JOSEPH STAFFORD, { b. 1694, Jun. 4. d. 1734, Aug. 29. b. d. of Joseph & Sarah (Holden) Stafford.

1. Mercy, 1717, Jun. 2.
2. Joseph, 1719, Jan. 6.
3. Susanna, 1721, Aug. 15.
4. Susanna, 1723, Mar. 10.

GORTON. 31 column. I. Othniel, m. (2) Mercy Burlingame, of Thomas or John.

I. { OTHNIEL, m. (1) MERCY, m. (2) MERCY, { b. 1669, Sep. 22. d. 1733, Jun. 13. b. d. of b. d. 1733 + of Warwick, R. I

He was an Innholder, with other occupations.

1726, Nov. 17. He sold to sons Israel and John Gorton, of Providence, 12½ acres each for £20, paid by each.

1726-30-31-32-33. Deputy. He held the title of Captain also.

1733, Jun. 5. Will—proved 1733, Jun. 29. Exx. wife Mercy. To son Israel, east end of house at Mashantatack, where son lives, and west end to son John, wherein he lives. To them equally old orchard and rest of lands at Mashantatack. To youngest son Othniel, all my now dwelling house and lot at age, and wife Mercy to have privilege of house till then, and after that to have kitchen and bedroom while widow. To son Othniel, at age, all lands in Scituate, Warwick, or elsewhere, and a feather bed, but wife to have use of lands till he is of age. To daughter Frances, if she marry with Jeremiah Pearce "which is against my will," 5s., otherwise she to have £40. To wife, all movables whatsoever.

Inventory, £1,046, 3s., 9d., viz: book debts £307, 14s., 4d., silver money £19, 2s., 10d., silver cup, pair of shoe buckles, 5 links shirt buttons, a silver hook, gold ring, punch bowl, 60 gallons rum, 3½ barrels of cider, law book, &c., £2, 16s., Indian girl eight years to serve £9, black horse, 3 cows, heifer, 2 calves, 34 sheep, 8 lambs, 10 goats.

1. Israel,
2. John,
3. Frances, 1707, Mar. 15.
(2d wife.)
4. Othniel, 1718, Oct. 1.

II. { SAMUEL, m. 1695, May 9. ELIZABETH COLLINS, { b. 1672, Jul. 22. d. 1721, Jun. 5. b. 1672, Nov. 1. d. 1724, Sep. 9. of Elizur & Sarah (Wright) Warwick, R. I. Collins.

1696. Freeman.

1714-18. Deputy.

1721, Jun. 2. Will—proved 1721, Aug. 10. Exx. wife Elizabeth. To eldest son Edward, the old place so called, which honoured father John Gorton formerly dwelt on, and lot at Horse Neck with timber, nails, &c., ready to build a house thereon. To 2d son Samuel, all my homestead farm with dwelling house, orchard, &c., one-half at age and other half at death of his mother. To youngest son William, lot at Cowesct, &c. To eldest daughter Ann Gorton, £26, in household stuff. To 2d daughter Margaret Gorton, £24. To 3d daughter Sarah, £24, at eighteen or marriage. To youngest daughter Elizabeth, £24, at eighteen or marriage. To wife, use of homestead till son Samuel is of age, and then one-half for life and she to have all movables.

Inventory, £221, 12s., 7d., viz: pewter, wearing apparel, old cider mill, 10 cows, 4 oxen, 2 steers, 3 heifers, 4 yearlings, 3 calves, 41 sheep, 15 lambs, 17 swine, fowls, &c.

1724. Administration on widow Elizabeth's estate to son Edward. Inventory, £191, 6s., 6d.

1. Ann, 1696, Feb. 19.
2. Edward, 1698, May 18.
3. Margaret, 1701, May 12.
4. Samuel, 1706, Jan. 2.
5. William,
6. Sarah,
7. Elizabeth,

III. { JOHN, m. 1700, Feb. 2. PATIENCE HOPKINS, { b. d. b. d. of Thomas & Sarah ( ) Warwick, R. I. Hopkins.

1696. Freeman.

1. Patience, 1700, Dec. 12.
2. Samuel,
3. Hopkins, 1704, Apr.

1646. This year he published while abroad, a book entitled "Simplicity's Defence Against Seven Headed Policy," in which he details the wrongs put upon the settlers of Warwick. The same year an order was issued from the Commissioners of Plantations, to Massachusetts to suffer the petitioners, &c., "freely and quietly to live and plant upon Shawomet and all other the lands included in the patent lately granted to them, without extending your jurisdiction to any part thereof or otherwise disquieting their consciences or civil peace," &c.

1647. He published the "Incorruptible Key, composed of the 110th Psalm."

1648, May 10. He landed in Boston on his return, and his arrest was ordered, but he had a letter of protection from the Earl of Warwick, securing his safety.

1649. Assistant.

1651-56-57-58-59-60-62-63. Commissioner.

1651-52. President of Providence and Warwick.

1655. Freeman.

1655. He published "Saltmarsh returned from the Dead."

1656. He published "Antidote against the Common Plague of the World" and another work entitled—"Antidote against Pharisaical Teachers."

1656, Mar. 17. He and three others were appointed by Assembly to treat with Pomham, upon complaint of the town of Warwick, of oppressions by the Indians.

1664-65-66-70. Deputy.

1666, Jan. 3. He with four others on behalf of themselves and rest of purchasers of Warwick, delivered Pomham £10, in peage at eight a penny. This was a gratuity conditioned on Pomham and rest of his company departing from Warwick. They were to report to Mr. Gorton when ready to remove.

Besides the works already mentioned he left a manuscript of several hundred pages, entitled "Exposition upon the Lord's Prayer."

1677, Nov. 27. He, "professor of the mysteries of Christ," deeded to son Samuel, Jr., for goodwill and by reason of his being instrumentally a great support unto me to help me bring up my family when my children were young and when I was absent from my family, &c., all interest in house, house lot, &c., and all goods, movables and chattels "as also my library, together with all my deeds and writings." He makes mention of land already given to sons John and Benjamin. To son Samuel, he commits the care of my beloved wife during widowhood if she live to be a widow, and she to be maintained with convenient housing and necessaries; and provision is also made for her "recreation in case she desires to visit her friends."

On same date he deeded to son John, all lands west of Warwick, the other two-thirds being betwixt sons Samuel and Benjamin.

He further deeded for love, &c., to sons-in-law and daughters, certain land in Narragansett, viz: to Daniel Cole and wife Maher, John Sanford and Mary, William Mace and Sarah, John Warner and Ann, John Crandall and Elizabeth, and Benjamin Barton and Susanna.

He died before December 10th, of this year. No relationship has been traced between him and Thomas Gorton, who was early of Portsmouth.

III. BENJAMIN, — b. — d. 1699, Dec. 25. — Warwick, R. I.
m. 1672, Dec. 5.
SARAH CARDER, — b. — d. 1724, Aug. 1. — of Richard & Mary ( ) Carder.

1672. Freeman.

1677, Oct. 31. He was among those to whom was granted 5,000 acres to be called East Greenwich.

1680, Nov. 3. The Assembly remitted his fine and returned him 5*s*.

1686. Deputy.

1687, Grand Jury.

1688. Licensed.

He was called Captain at the time of his death.

1721, Aug. 25. Will—proved 1724, Aug. 7. Widow Sarah. Exs. son Benjamin and son-in-law George Thomas. To daughter Mary Greene, £25. To daughter Sarah Wickes, £25. To sons Benjamin and Samuel, four pewter platters, nine plates and two brass candlesticks, equally. To daughter Alice Thomas, £25. To daughter Maplet Remington, £25. To grandson Benjamin Gorton, son of Benjamin, a feather bed, silver tankard, &c., and if he die before twenty-one then to grandson Lancaster Gorton. To aforenamed daughters, eight pewter platters and seven plates, equally. To son Benjamin, spectacles. To grandson Benjamin Greene, biggest silver spoon. To six children aforenamed, twelve silver spoons, equally. To grandson Samuel Gorton, my great silver cup. To granddaughter Mary Fry, a painted box. To granddaughter Sarah Wickes, red chest. To granddaughter Sarah Thomas, a trunk. To four daughters, little silver cup and silver porringer. To granddaughter Maplet Remington, little yellow trunk. To granddaughter Alice Gorton, black trunk. To son Benjamin, warming pan, &c. To granddaughter Sarah Gorton, dark colored silk crape suit. To son Benjamin Gorton's children, £25 each, except Benjamin, who had as above. To children of Samuel Gorton, £15. To four daughters, all wearing apparel. To six children, rest of estate.

Inventory, £258, 13*s*., viz: pewter, silk hood, muslin neck-cloth and lace, silver tankard £30, silver cup £5, money scales, 2 bibles, 14 silver spoons, small silver cup, 2 silver porringers, 4 coats, gown, pair of stays, £100, in hands of Mary Greene, widow of Samuel, suit of crape cloth, black suit, books, loose gown, camblet hood, &c.

IV. MAHERSHALLALHASHBAZ, — b. — d.
m.
DANIEL COLE, — b. — d. 1692, Nov. 29. — of Robert & Mary ( ) Cole.

V. MARY, — b. — d. 1688 +
m. (1)
PETER GREENE, — b. 1622. — d. 1659. — of John & Joan (Tattersall) Greene.
m. (2) 1663, Apr. 17.
JOHN SANFORD, — b. 1633, Jun. 4. — d. 1687. — of John & Elizabeth (Webb) Sanford.

VI. SARAH, — b. — d.
m.
WILLIAM MACE, — b. — d. — of Mace.

VII. ANN, — b. — d.
m. 1670, Aug. 4.
JOHN WARNER, — b. 1645, Aug. 1. — d. 1712, Apr. 22. — of John & Priscilla (Holliman) Warner.

VIII. ELIZABETH, — b. — d. 1704 +
m. 1672, Jun. 18.
JOHN CRANDALL, — b. — d. 1704 — of John & Hannah ( ) Crandall.

IX. SUSANNA, — b. — d. 1734, May 28.
m. 1672, Jun. 18.
BENJAMIN BARTON, — b. 1645. — d. 1720. — of Rufus & Margaret ( ) Barton.

GOULD.

JEREMIAH[6], (Rich.[5], Rich.[4], — b. — Bovingdon, Hertford Co., Eng.,
m. [Thos.[3], Rich.[2], Thos.[1]) — d. — [Newport, R. I.
PRISCILLA GROVER, — b. — d. — of Grover.

1637. He came to New England this year, and perhaps tarried for a short time with his brother Zaccheus at Weymouth, Mass.

1638, Nov. 20. He was among those admitted as inhabitants at Newport after this date.

1641, Mar. 16. Freeman.

1649. He was on a committee (composed of one person from each town) appointed "to examine some votes brought into court."

1655. Freeman.

I. MARY, — b. — d. 1675 +
m. 1640 ±
WILLIAM JEFFERAY, — b. 1591. — d. 1675, Jan. 2. — of William & Audry (Harvey) Jefferay.

II. THOMAS, — b. — d. 1693, Aug. 20. — Newport, Kings Town, R. I.
m. 1655. [divorcée of John.
ELIZABETH COGGESHALL, — b. — d. 1696 + — of William & Elizabeth ( ) Baulstone.

1644. Corporal.

1654-60. Commissioner.

1655. Freeman.

1657, Mar. 28. He bought of Koshtosh, Indian sachem, the island called by the English, Gould Island.

1705. Deputy.
In the Burial Ground at Hartford, Ct., there is a stone with following inscription: "Here lieth the body of Hopkins Gorton, who died Mar. 27, 1725, about 20 years and 11 months of age. Born at Warwick, in Rod Island."

IV. { BENJAMIN, { b. 1682. { d. 1745, Apr. 15. Warwick, R. I.
UNMARRIED.

1705. Apr. 17. An agreement was made between him (son of Captain Benjamin Gorton, deceased), and Samuel Gorton, Sr., as to lands.
1713. Deputy.
1745, Apr. 13. Will—proved 1745, Apr. 22 Ex. cousin (*i. e.* nephew) Samuel Gorton. "I give and bequeath twenty pounds towards the printing a book now lying in my grandfather Gorton's writing, entitled 'Exposition upon the Lord's Prayer.'" To cousin Benjamin Gorton, son to my cousin Samuel Gorton, £1,000. To cousin Samuel Wightman, son to Samuel, deceased, £10, at twenty-one. To cousin Samuel Gorton, all lands and tenements in Warwick and Coventry and all the rest of estate.
Inventory, £1,034, 13*s.*, 6*d.*, viz: notes and bonds £386, 4*s.*, 9*d.*, cash £507, 17*s.*, 3*d.*, sundry old books, &c.

I. { MARY, { b. 1673, Oct. 31. { d. 1732, Jan. 7.
m. 1695, Jan. 24.
SAMUEL GREENE, { b. 1671, Jan. 30. { d. 1720, Sep. 18. of John & Ann (Almy) Greene.

1. William, 1696, Mar. 16.
2. Mary, 1698, Aug. 25.
3. Samuel, 1700, Oct. 22.
4. Benjamin, 1703, Jan. 5.
5. Anne, 1706, Apr. 5.

II. { SARAH, { b. { d. 1753, Jan. 31.
m. 1698, Dec. 15.
JOHN WICKES, { b. 1677, Aug. 8. { d. 1741, Dec. 27, of John & Rose (Townsend) Wickes.

1. John, 1699, Feb. 26.
2. Sarah, 1700, Sep. 21.
3. Rose, 1702, Aug. 12.
4. Robert, 1704, Dec. 22.
5. Elizabeth, 1707, Feb. 5.
6. William, 1710, Aug. 26.
7. Richard, 1712, Oct. 23.
8. Thomas, 1715, Sep. 8.
9. Mary, 1717, Dec. 11.

III. { BENJAMIN, { b. { d. 1737. Warwick, R. I., Norwich, Ct.
m.
ANN, { b. { d. 1737 + of

1737, Aug. 9. Administration to widow Ann and son Lancaster. Inventory, warming pan, mare, colt, two yearlings, sermon book, testament, woolen wheel, chest, table, chairs, &c.

1. Benjamin,
2. Lancaster,
3. Stephen, 1704, Mar. 21.
4. Sarah,

IV. { SAMUEL, { b. { d. 1723, Aug. 21. Warwick, Providence, R. I.
m. 1706, Jul. 25.
ELIZABETH GREENE, { b. { d. 1723 + of Thomas & Ann (Greene) Greene.

GORTON. 3d column. IV. Samuel. His wife b. 1687, May 3.

1708. Warwick. Deputy.
1723, Oct. 21. Administration to widow Elizabeth. Inventory, £174, 6*s.*, 13*d.*, viz: books 12*s.*, linen and cotton yarn, 3 cows, 3 yearlings, a sheep, 6 hogs, 2 pigs, Indian servant girl two years and ten months to serve £5, 10*s.*, hens, chickens, &c. Real estate £470. (Including house and 60 acres £400.)

1. Alice, 1707, Aug. 5.
2. Elizabeth, 1709, Sep. 26.
3. Samuel, 1711, Jul. 14.
4. Thomas, 1713, Nov. 2.
5. Benjamin, 1715, Dec. 11.
6. Ann, 1718, May 22.
7. Richard, 1720, Jun. 15.
8. John, 1723, Apr. 22.

V. { ALICE, { b. { d.
m. 1704, Jan. 20.
GEORGE THOMAS, { b. 1681, Aug. 20. { d. 1740. of John Thomas.

1. Sarah,
2. Mary,
3. George, 1708, Feb. 7.
4. John,
5. Benjamin,
6. Peleg,
7. Samuel,
8. Daughter,
9. Alice,
10. Elizabeth.

VI. { MAPLET, { b. { d. 1723 +
m. 1710, Dec. 28.
THOMAS REMINGTON, { b. { d. 1723, Sep. 25. of Thomas & Mary (Allen) Remington.

1. Maplet, 1712, Jul. 11.
2. Mary, 1715, May 17.
3. Stephen, 1720, Jun. 26.
4. Thomas, 1723, Aug. 19.

1. Samuel,
2. Benjamin,
3. Joseph,
4. Susanna,
5. Sarah,
6. Dinah,
7. Mary,
8. Ann.

(By 2d husband.)
1. Mary, 1664, Mar. 30.
2. Eliphalet, 1666, Feb. 20.
3. John, 1672, Jun. 18.
4. Samuel, 1677, Oct. 5.

1. John, 1673, Jun. 5.
2. Priscilla,
3. Ann,
4. Ezekiel.

1. John,
2. Peter,
3. Samuel,
4. Elizabeth,
5. Mary,

1. Rufus, 1673.
2. Andrew,
3. Mary, 1678, May 1.
4. Phebe,
5. Naomi.

GOULD.

1. Mary, 1642, Mar. 20.
2. Thomas,
3. Susanna,
4. Priscilla, 1654.
5. Sarah, 1656.

No issue.

His wife died after 1655 it is said, and he buried her on a farm (now in Middletown, R. I.), which he had given his son John. He returned to England and died there, as is further stated.

1670. Kings Town. Constable.

1670, Jun. 20. He was sent as constable, to seize any persons pretending to exercise jurisdiction in Narragansett on behalf of Connecticut.

1671, May 20. Conservator of the Peace at Acquidneset. He was also chosen Lieutenant of the military company.

1673, May 20. He sold John Cranston of Newport, for £20, Gould Island, half now and other half at death.

1674, May 12. He sold John Cranston the whole of Gould Island for full satisfaction.

1677, May 2. He and others petitioned Assembly for instruction, assistance and advice as to oppressions they suffer under from the colony of Connecticut. He and others suffered imprisonment by Connecticut this year.

1678, Jun. 12. He was again appointed Conservator of the Peace.

1679, Jul. 29. He and forty-one others of Narragansett petitioned the King, praying that he "would put an end to these differences about the government thereof, which hath been so fatal to the prosperity of the place, animosities still arising in people's minds as they stand affected to this or that government."

1689, Dec. 6. He made an agreement with his nephew Daniel Gould, by which the latter was to pay Thomas Gould's wife Elizabeth, £10, a year for life, in lieu of all her claims of land in Narragansett.

1690. Deputy.

1693, Sep. 15. The widow being desirous of being with her children, her husband's nephew Daniel Gould engages to pay her £10, a year for life, as agreed with his uncle Thomas Gould, who he says had deceased on the twentieth of August.

III. JOHN, | b. | Newport, R. I.
m. | d. 1680 +
MARGARET HART (w. of [Edward. | b.
| d. 1671 + | of

1653, May 17. Freeman.

1655-57-61-62. Commissioner.

1664-65-70-72-73. Deputy.

1667, May 13. He was on a committee to make a rate for a levy of £150, for defence of the place against the common enemy, and for supplying defects in prison, stock and pound, and mounting of great guns.

1671, Apr. 20. He received a letter of this date from Barbadoes, signed your cousin (*i. e.* nephew) Peleg Witherington.

1672, May 14. He with the Governor, Deputy Governor, and Walter Clarke, were appointed to draw up instructions for the Rhode Island Commissioners who were to meet a committee from Connecticut.

1674, Dec. 8. He and his brother Daniel were appointed overseers of their brother-in-law William Jefferay's will. The family account states that he lived about four miles from Newport, and that having no children he gave his estate to his brother Daniel's son John.

1680. Taxed £2, 6*s*. 11*d*.

IV. ——— | b.
m. | d.
WILLIAM WITHERINGTON | b.
| b. | of | Witherington.

V. DANIEL, | b. 1625. | Newport, R. I.
m. 1651, Dec. 18. | d. 1716, Mar. 26.
WAIT COGGESHALL, | b. 1636, Sep. 11.
| d. 1718, May 9. | of John & Mary ( ) | Coggeshall.

1656. Commissioner.

He joined the Quakers, embracing their views among the earliest of those who united with that sect.

1659. In a pamphlet of his, relating to sufferings of Marmaduke Stevenson and William Robinson in Boston (they belonging to the same sect as Daniel Gould), he mentions that after coming from Salem to Charlestown Ferry; "there meets us a constable and a rude company of people with him, and takes us all up (about ten in number, besides the two banished Friends), and after much scoffing and mocking examinations, all of us were led to prison, and God doth know, who is a just rewarder of all, how harmless, peaceable and innocent we came into the town, behaving ourselves in much fear and humility of mind, yet, notwithstanding, being Quakers, to prison we must go, where we remained some days," &c. Being criticised as a "Dumb Devil" when he refused to be led into speech, and they saying he was simple and ignorant, beguiled and led by others more subtle, he answered: "If you think I am simply beguiled and not willfully in error how have you showed kindness to me or where has your love appeared to help me out of the ignorance and delusion you suppose I have fallen into" — "Do you think your prison whip and base usage are the way to do it? Is that the way to begin with to restore any one from the error of his ways. Then some one cried out 'he is more knave than fool.' Then I answered again and said if I hold my tongue I am a Dumb Devil, a fool and ignorant; If I speak I am a knave. After this Richard Bellingham, the Deputy Governor, being full of envy, said to me: 'Well, Gould you shall be severely whipped,' which was afterwards done with thirty stripes upon my naked back, being tied to the carriage of a great gun." He and others who had been whipped were then led back to prison, "where we remained till after the execution."

1669. He traveled as a minister this year, and in his Journal gives an account of his first voyage to Maryland. He says: "It pleased the Lord to make me find good favor, and my travels and labour was very successful wherever I went, and my return home was in the end of 1669."

1671, May. He went on a second voyage to Maryland.

1672-73. Deputy.

1673-74-75. Assistant.

1680. Taxed £2, 11*s*. 9*d*.

1683, Apr. 1. He arrived in Newport on his return from his fifth voyage, which included travel in Maryland, New Jersey, Delaware and Pennsylvania, the distance aggregating nineteen hundred and eighty-seven miles.

1687, Nov. 1. He started on his sixth voyage to Maryland.

1693, Oct. 1. He was returning from his last voyage and dated his letter at Narragansett: "I went over the water in a canoe with Old Place to Canonicut, and lodged that night at Joseph Mowry's."

1716, Apr. 9. Inventory, £96. 17*s*., appraised by Jonathan Nichols and Samuel Rogers.

He was buried in the Friends' Burying Ground near the meeting house.

No issue.

1. Peleg,

I. MARY, b. 1653, Mar. 2. d. 1691, Jan. 9.
m. 1672, Jun. 22.
JOSEPH BRYER, b. 1645. d. 1704, May 31. of Bryer.
1. Elizabeth, 1682, Jun. 18.

II. THOMAS, b. 1655, Feb. 20. d. 1734, May 11. Newport, R. I.
m. 1691, Jan. 13.
ELIZABETH MOTT, b. 1672, Sep. 12. d. 1749, Mar. 22. of Jacob & Joanna (Slocum) Mott.
1677. Freeman.
1696–1702–4–7. Deputy.
1. Priscilla, 1693, Feb. 3.
2. Mercy, 1694, Dec. 13.
3. Daniel, 1696, Dec. 18.
4. Thomas, 1698, Dec. 1.
5. Joanna, 1700, Oct. 24.
6. Jacob, 1704, Nov. 21.
7. Elizabeth, 1707, May 4.
8. John, 1709, Feb. 15.
9. James, 1711, Jul. 5.

See: American Genealogist, v. 20, p. 187.

III. DANIEL, b. 1656, Oct. 24. d. Newport, Kings Town, R. I.
m.
MARY CLARKE, b. 1661, Jan. 11. d. 1711, Aug. 10. of Walter & Content (Greenman) Clarke.
(She m. (2) Ralph Chapman.)
1684. Freeman.
1. Mary, 1681, Mar. 22.
2. Jeremiah, 1683, Apr. 22.
3. Daniel, 1686, Dec. 22.
4. Thomas, 1693, Mar. 23.

IV. JOHN, b. 1659, May 4. d. 1704, Mar. 5. Newport, R. I.
m. 1686, Aug. 30.
SARAH PRIOR, b. 1664, Oct. d. 1714 + of Matthew & Mary ( ) Prior
(She m. (2) 1711, Aug. 31, Walter Clarke.)
He was buried in Clifton Burying Ground.
1. Mary, 1688, Nov. 29.
2. Wait, 1691, May 28.
3. Sarah, 1694, Mar. 12.
4. Content, 1695, Apr. 25.
5. John, 1698, Aug. 19.

V. PRISCILLA, b. 1661, Jun. 20. d. 1689, Jan. 23.
m.
JOHN HART, b. d. of Thomas & Freeborn (Williams) Hart.
No issue.

VI. JEREMIAH, b. 1664, May 5. d. 1666, Apr. 27.
He was drowned.

VII. JAMES, b. 1666, Oct. 13. d. Newport, R. I.
m.
CATHARINE CLARKE, b. 1671, Sep. 6. d. 1752, Jan. 25. of Walter & Hannah (Scott) Clarke.
(She m. (2) Nathaniel Sheffield.)
1. James, 1696, Jun. 14.
2. Walter, 1698, Apr. 2.

VIII. JEREMIAH, b. 1669, Feb. 2. d. 1670, Aug.

IX. CONTENT, b. 1671, Apr. 28. d. 1720, Sep. 3.
m. 1692.
JOHN WHITPIN, b d. of Whitpin.

X. WAIT, b. 1676, May 8. d.
m.
JOSEPH PECKHAM, b. 1679, Mar. 8. d. 1726, Jan. 14. of John & Sarah ( ) Peckham.
1. Peleg, 1710, May 1.
2. Daniel, 1711, Nov. 4.
3. Wait, 1713, Dec. 29.
4. Mary, 1716, Jun. 29
5. Sarah.

 See: American Genealogist, v.21, p. 208

JOHN, m. ——— | b. d. | b. d. | Newport, R. I.

1638, May 20. His name was in a list of inhabitants admitted to Newport, since this date.

He is assumed to have been the father of David, Edward and Content, but may possibly have been an elder brother.

I. DAVID, | b. d. | Newport, R. I.

1655. Freeman.

II. EDWARD, m. MARY, | b. d. 1688 + | b. d. of | Newport, R. I.

He was a wheelwright.

1647, Feb. 20. He and David Greenman (wheelwrights), sold John Greene 22 acres of land near endship or village called Green End, on the highway leading from Newport unto Portsmouth.

1655. Freeman.

1657. Commissioner.

1661, Sep. 9. He had a quarter share in Misquamicut (Westerly) lands assigned him.

1668-69-70-82. Deputy.

1671. Juryman.

1678, Jun. 12. He petitioned the Assembly concerning estate of George Brown, praying that commissioners be appointed to order the estate bankrupt.

1680. Taxed £1, 10*s*., 8*d*.

1688. Foreman of Grand Jury.

III. CONTENT, m. 1660 ± WALTER CLARKE, | b. 1636. d. 1666, Mar. 27. | b. 1640. d. 1714, May 23. of Jeremiah & Frances (Latham) Clarke.

GRINNELL.

MATTHEW, m. ROSE, | b. d. 1643 (—) | b. d. 1673 + | Newport, R. I.

(She m. (2) 1643, Anthony Paine, (3) 1650, James Weeden.

1638, May 20. His name was in a list of inhabitants of Newport admitted since this date.

1643, Nov. 10. His widow made a pre-nuptial agreement with Anthony Paine. She deeded to her three sons Matthew, Thomas and Daniel Grinnell, "two sheeder goats apiece" and to her son Matthew, a cow also, which animals were to abide in the hands of Anthony Paine for three years, and the milk to be his, but the increase was to belong to her three sons. It was also agreed between Anthony and Rose that after their marriage, upon the death of either, the property of the one deceased should go to the children of such person, Rose having four children and Anthony Paine having three children.

1649, May 5. She was made executrix of her husband Anthony Paine's will of this date. He alludes to their former covenant.

1649, Oct. 27. She took receipt from Lot Strange and wife Alice for legacy.

1650, Mar. 18. She took receipt from John and Mary Tripp for legacy.

1673, Dec. 17. Rose Weeden, of Portsmouth, for maintenance for life and £30, sold Matthew Grinnell 53 acres in Portsmouth.

I. MATTHEW, m. ——— | b. d. 1705 + | b. d. 1705 + of | Portsmouth, East Greenwich, R. I.

He was a maltster.

1649, Oct. 29. He and his mother Rose Paine deeded Lot Strange 8 acres.

1655. Freeman.

1655, Jul. 8. He sold John Tyler a dwelling house and 13 acres.

1657, Dec. 10. He had a grant of 8 acres.

1676-81-82. Constable.

1679, May 5. Testimony of John Anthony and wife Frances was given; they stating that on the 27th of November, 1678, Matthew Grinnell and Lot Strange and wife came to house of John Anthony, and brought a deed which said Lot Strange had from Matthew Grinnell and his mother, formerly, and Alice Strange desired that her name be put in the deed.

1680. Taxed 10*s*.

1682, Oct. 6. He and William Manchester sold Thomas Ward of Newport, half a share of land at Pocasset, for £30, bounded partly by Dartmouth.

1696, Jun. 4. East Greenwich. He deeded son Daniel, for love, &c., 90 acres now in his possession.

1699, Oct. 11. Moderator.

1705, Nov. 28. He deeded son-in-law John Carpenter, for love, &c., 10 acres,

1705, Nov. 29. He deeded son Matthew, for love, &c., mansion house, with all my lands to me belonging, and all goods, chattels and cattle, with all other estate both real and personal, always provided said son Matthew do always maintain and provide for me and my wife during our lives.

II. THOMAS, | b. d.

I. { EDWARD, m. MARGARET, } b. 1663. d. 1749. b. d. 1739 + of — Kings Town, Charlestown, R. I.

1. Abigail,
2. Silas,
3. Phebe, 1692, Jan. 29.
4. Edward,
5. Nathan,

1700-4-5-9-10. Deputy.
1701-2. Assistant.
1704. Speaker of House of Deputies.
1708, Apr. 5. He bought 250 acres for £215, of Samuel and Isaac Worden and their wives Hopestill and Rebecca.
1709, Feb. 11. He and wife Margaret sold George Hazard 120 acres.
1719, Mar. 31. He deposed as to land, calling himself fifty-six years old or thereabouts.
1739, Jul. 13. Will—proved 1749, Sep. 11. Ex. son Edward. He calls himself ancient. To daughter Abigail Greenman, 10s, after my and wife's death. To son Silas, 10s., on same conditions. To daughter Phebe Whiting, 10s. To son Edward, all the rest of estate, real and personal, at death of wife and self.
1769, Dec. 7. His sons Silas, Edward and Nathan Greenman, for good will to negro named Southwick, formerly belonging to our father Edward deceased, and for £26, 5s., paid by said negro, give him his freedom.

II. { WILLIAM, m. ANN CLARKE, } b. d. b. 1675. d. of Jeremiah & Ann (Audley) Clarke. — Kings Town, Westerly, Newport, R. I.

GREENMAN. 3d column. II. William, b. 1671, d. 1732, Jul. 30. His widow d. 1732, Oct. 29.

1. Ann,
2. William,
3. Jeremiah,
4. James,
5. Elisha,
6. Mary,
7. Elizabeth,
8. Amey,

1703, Mar. 14. He and wife Ann, sold Benjamin Perry 100 acres for £55.
1706, Mar. 2. Westerly. He and wife Ann, sold David Lewis, 88 acres housing, &c., for £103.
1707, Jan. 23. Newport. He and other members of the Second Baptist Church received a deed of the church and land therewith from the pastor Rev. James Clarke.

III. { JOHN, m. ELIZABETH, } b. 1666. d. 1727, Sep. 30. b. d. of — Newport, R. I.

1. Eunice, 1698.
2. Jerusha, 1709.
3. Leah,

1702, Mar. 4. He was one of the proprietors of common lands.
1707, Jan. 23. He was one of those who received the deed from Rev. James Clarke.
1724, Jun. 17. He and wife Elizabeth, were sued by Stephen Bailey.
He was buried in the Newport Cemetery.

IV. { THOMAS, m. MARY WEEDEN, } b. 1669. d. 1728. b. d. 1728 + of William & Sarah (Peckham) Weeden. — South Kingstown, R. I.

1. Sylvanus,
2. Son,
3. Daughter,
4. Daughter,

He was a tailor.
1700, Oct. 17. He had ear mark granted.
1706, Oct. 4. He sold to George Babcock, of Westerly, 13 acres of homestead farm for £6.
1719, Aug. 31. He deposed as to land, calling himself fifty years old and upwards.
1728, Sep. 30. Will—proved 1728, Oct. 14. Exs. wife Mary and Captain William Clarke, of Westerly. To wife, a third of movable estate, and a third of what house and lands may be sold for. As for rest of estate my two sons to have twice as much as each of my daughters.
Inventory, a yoke of oxen, 6 cows, 3 yearlings, 2 calves, mare, colt, horse, 32 sheep, 8 lambs, 5 hogs, 4 shoats, 15 geese, wearing apparel £6, 12s., tailor's goose and shears, gun, 2 spinning wheels, old bible, worsted comb, &c.

V. { MARY, m. 1706, Mar. 8. ADAM CASEY, } b. d. 1747 ± b. 1667 ± d. 1765, Apr. of Thomas & Sarah ( ) Casey.

1. Thomas, 1706, Nov. 18.
2. Silas, 1708, Oct. 20.
3. Mary, 1710, Sep. 10.
4. Sarah, 1715, Sep. 22.
5. Edward, 1718, Feb. 14.

1. Mary, 1661, Jan. 11.
2. Content,
3. Son.

GRINNELL.

I. { DANIEL, m. SARAH CHASE, } b. d. b. d. of Benjamin & Phillip (Sherman) Chase. — Freetown, Mass.

1. Benjamin, 1696, Jan. 12.
2. Daniel,

1696, Jan. 12. His son Benjamin's birth is recorded at Freetown and the statement is made that said Benjamin was son of Daniel, son of Matthew of Rhode Island. The name of Daniel's wife is not given upon the town record.
1730, Sep. 6. Benjamin Chase of Freetown, in will of this date mentions grandchildren Benjamin and Daniel Grinnell.

II. { MATTHEW, m. MARY, } b. d. 1718, Jun. 17. b. d. of — East Greenwich, R. I.

1. Thomas, 1711, May 2.
2. Matthew, 1713, Sep. 2.
3. John, 1716, Jan. 23.

(She m. (2) 1719, Jul. 16, John Manchester.)

1718, Aug. 30. Administration to widow Mary. Inventory, £151, 8s. 6d., viz: 4 oxen, 4 steers, 5 cows, heifer, yearling, horse, mare, colt, 8 sheep, 5 lambs, 4 swine, purse and apparel £8, 2 beds, 2 guns, &c.
1719, Nov. 28. His widow and her husband John Manchester were appointed guardians of her children, and the Town Council ordered said children to be provided with victuals, clothing and learning, and to be brought up by guardians, and at age each child to have as follows: To eldest son Thomas, £4, 18s To second son Matthew, £36. To third son John £36.

III. { THOMAS, UNMARRIED. } b. d. 1705. — East Greenwich, R. I.

1696. Freeman.
1701. He gave 11s. 4d., toward building Quaker meeting house at Mashapaug.
1705, Sep. 23. Will—proved 1705, Nov. 5. Ex. brother Matthew. To brother Matthew, all estate both real and personal.
Inventory, £12, 17s. 6d., viz: pair of oxen, 2 horses, saddle, bridle, musket, chest, &c.

IV. { ——— m. JOHN CARPENTER, } b. d. b. d. 1753. of Abiah Carpenter.

1. Mary,
2. Sarah,
3. Diademe,
4. Dinah,
5. Cornel,
6. Joseph,

III. DANIEL, m. MARY WODELL, b. 1636 ± d. 1703 + ; b. 1640, Nov. d. — Portsmouth, Little Compton, R. I. of William & Mary ( ) Wodell.

He was a maltster.

1656, Nov. 24. He bought land of Ralph Earle.

1657. Freeman.

1658, Mar. 31. He had a deed from James Weeden (his stepfather) of 6 acres.

1667-69-73. Juryman.

1674. Constable.

1676. Grand Jury.

1679, Apr. 5. He sold 6 acres to Francis Brayton.

1681, Nov. 9. He sold 13 acres to Abraham Anthony.

1683, Dec. 31. He and wife Mary sold Henry Brightman 23 acres for £124.

1687. Little Compton. He was there thus early.

1688, Jan. 20. He deeded his son Daniel, Jr., south half of thirteenth lot in grand division.

1694, Jan. 5. He deeded son Richard, for love, &c., the other half of above lot, containing 45 acres.

1703, Jul. 6. He deeded land, &c., to son Richard (being same that his son had deeded him the year before).

IV. DAUGHTER, b. d.

Thomas Harris: See also: Bowen, The Providence Oath of Allegiance, p. 53-58.

HARRIS (THOMAS).

THOMAS, m. ELIZABETH, b. d. 1686, Jun. 7. ; b. d. 1687 + — Providence, R. I.

1630, Dec. 1. He came with his brother William, and Roger Williams, in ship Lyon, from Bristol, England.

1637, Aug. 20. At this date (or a little later) he and twelve others signed following compact: "We whose names are hereunder, desirous to inhabit in the town of Providence, do promise to subject ourselves in active or passive obedience, to all such orders or agreements as shall be made for public good of the body in an orderly way, by the major assent of the present inhabitants, members of families incorporated together into a town fellowship, and such others whom they shall admit unto themselves, only in civil things."

1640, Jul. 27. He and thirty-eight others signed an agreement for a form of government.

1650, Sep. 2. Taxed £1.

1652-53-54-55-56-57-61-62-63. Commissioner.

1654, Lieutenant.

1655. Freeman.

1656. Juryman.

1658, Jul. 19. He received fifteen stripes with a three fold corded whip while in jail at Boston, because he would not work for the jailor and let him have 8*d*., in 12*d*., of what he should earn. He had before this had twenty-two blows following an eleven days' imprisonment, "five of which he was kept without bread." The occasion of this persecution is thus given in Bishop's "New England Judged."—"After these came Thomas Harris from Rhode Island into your Colony, who declaring against your pride and oppression as he could have liberty to speak in your meeting place at Boston, after the priest had ended, warning the people of the dreadful terrible day of the Lord God, which was coming upon that town and country, him much unlike to Ninevah, you pulled down and hall'd him by the hair of his head out of your meeting, and a hand was put on his mouth to keep him from speaking forth, and then had before your Governor and Deputy, with other Magistrates, and committed to prison without warrant or mittimus that he saw," &c.

1664-66-67-70-72-73. Deputy.

1664-65-66-69. Town Council.

1665, Feb. 19. He drew lot 7, in a divison of lands.

1666-67-68-69-71-72-73-74-75. Assistant.

1667, May. He as surveyor, laid out lands, &c.

1676, Aug. 14. He was on a committee that recommended certain conditions under which the Indian captives should be disposed of by the town. They were to be in servitude for terms of years.

1679, Jul. 1. Taxed 5*s*., 7½*d*.

1683, Apr. 27. He made the statement that about 1661, being then a surveyor, he laid out a three score acre lot for my son Thomas, at Paugachauge Hill, and a 25 acre lot on the south side, &c.

1686, Jun. 3. Will—proved 1686, Jul. 22. Ex. son Thomas. Overseers, sons-in-law Thomas Field and Samuel Whipple. To wife, use of two home lots, orchards, dwelling house, household stuff, &c., for life; and a horse, three cows, three calves, half the swine, and two hives of bees at her dis-

HARRIS (THOMAS). 1st column. 1639, Oct. 29, Richard Iles of Charlestown, Mass., who died at this date, left 20 s. each to cousins Thomas and William Harris. 2d colnmn. I. Thomas. His widow d. 1718, Jan. 11. 3d column. II. Richard. His son Jonathan b. 1710, July 12.

I. THOMAS, m. 1664, Nov. 3. ELNATHAN TEW, b. d. 1711, Feb. 27. ; b. 1644, Oct. 15. d. 1711 + — Providence, R. I. of Richard & Mary (Clark) Tew.

1665, Feb. 19. He had lot 49 in a division of lands.

1679, Jul. 1. Taxed 8*s*. 9*d*.

1671-79-80-81-82-85-91-94-97-1702-6-7-8-10. Deputy.

1684-85-86. Town Council.

1687, Sep. 1. Taxed 14*s*., 5*d*.

1688. Ratable estate, 10 cows, 4 oxen, 6 steers, 3 yearlings, 4 two year old, 3 horses, mare, 10 sheep, 4 swine.

1708, Jun. 21. Will—proved 1711, Apr. 16. Exs. wife Elnathan and son Henry. To eldest son Thomas, 140 acres where he dwells (except 6 acres that Henry is to have, and a small orchard to Henry), and other land. To son Richard, 60 acres where he dwells, and right of common, &c., and a third of orchard. To son Nicholas, land where he dwells, 150 acres, &c., and a third of orchard. To son William, land where he dwells, 12 acres, &c. To son Henry, 130 acres and a third of an acre, being part of his father's orchard, also half the land and housing where I dwell containing 120 acres. To wife Elnathan, the other half of homestead for life in lieu of dower and at her decease to son Henry. To daughter Amity Morse, £20. To daughter Elnathan Harris, a feather bed, and weaver's loom and £20. To daughter Mary Harris, a feather bed, weaver's loom and £20. To wife and son Henry, all stock and neat cattle, horse, sheep and swine, husbandry tools, negro man, household goods, &c., they to have the profits of same, and at death of wife, Henry to have the stock and negro man, &c., but the household goods to be for three daughters of testator. Inventory, £146± viz: 3 guns, cash £3, 6*s*., 7*d*., bible, warming pan, settle, pair of stillyards, wheat, rye, Indian corn, barley, 20 barrels cider, negro man £10, a bull, 5 cows, 2 oxen, 4 three year old, 6 yearlings, swine, 33 sheep, &c.

GRINNELL. 3d column. I. Daniel. (Page 311.) His wife d. 1748, July 13. Add another child Priscilla, b. 1689. 1703 he bought land in Pochauge, Saybrook, Ct. (The part now called Westbrook, was his home.) 1724 he was chosen deacon of Congregationalist Church at Westbrook, but declined. His wife was a member. Perhaps the William Grinnell who married 1703, June 4, Mary Sanford, at Tiverton, R. I., was a brother.

I. { DANIEL, { b. Little Compton, R. I., Saybrook, Conn.
m. { d.
LYDIA PABODIE, { b. 1667, Apr. 3.
{ d. of William & Elizabeth (Alden) Pabodie.

1. Peabody,
2. George,
3. Jemima, 1704.
4. Daniel, 1707.

1694, Jul. 31. He and wife Lydia sold land to Samuel Crandall.
1695, Jan. 25. He and wife Lydia exchanged land with Daniel Grinnell, Sr.
1703, Sep. 6. He and wife Lydia sold 50 acres to his brother Richard.

II. { JONATHAN, { b. 1670. Little Compton, R. I.
m. (1) { d.
REBECCA IRISH, { b.
m. (2) 1698, Dec. 8. { d. of Elias & Dorothy (Witherell) Irish.
ABIGAIL FORD, { b.
{ d. of Ford.

(2d wife.)
1. Hope, 1699, Jul. 18.
2. Sarah, 1703, Apr. 11.
3. Daniel, 1705, Nov. 18.
4. Mary, 1709, Mar. 12.
5. Jonathan, 1711, Feb. 7.
6. Stephen, 1715, Jul. 18.
7. Rebecca, 1718, Apr. 22.

1704, Apr. 17. He had a deed from John Irish, of Little Compton, for love, &c., of half a lot on the east side of Cold Brook, about 10 acres. The grantor calls Jonathan my kinsman, who sometime was the husband of my brother Elias Irish his daughter Rebecca Irish, my cousin (*i. e.* niece).

III. { RICHARD, { b. 1675. Little Compton, R. I.
m. 1704, May 25. { d. 1725, Jul. 1.
PATIENCE EMERY, { b. 1681.
{ d. 1749, Mar. 10. of James Emery.

1. George, 1705, Jan. 25.
2. William, 1707, Mar. 19.
3. Rebecca, 1710, Dec. 16.
4. Elizabeth, 1713, May 21.
5. Patience, 1715, Apr. 24.
6. Richard, 1717, Mar. 8.
7. Ruth, 1719, Apr. 3.
8. Daniel, 1721, Apr. 20.
9. Sarah, 1723, May 6.

1701, Jul. 15. He bought of William Palmer for £500, the fourteenth great lot containing 100 acres.
1702, Feb. 13. He sold to his father for £700, the above 100 acres with house on it and half of thirteenth lot.
1719, Jan. 23. He bought of Daniel Emery, his wife's brother, certain land for £105.
1721, May 4. He bought of Daniel Irish two 10 acre lots and housing and other land, in all 60 acres, for £600.

He was entrusted by the town to keep the ordinary.

1723, Dec. 9. Will—proved 1725, Jul. 20. Exs. wife and my kinsman Edward Thurston. To wife Patience, a third of movables, and a third of income of real estate for life. To son George, 100 acres in little Compton, &c., and two cows, 40 sheep, and old mare; he paying my daughter Rebecca Grinnell, £50, at age, and £50, to daughter Elizabeth, at age. To son William, the house and land that was formerly my grandfather-in-law's Daniel Eaton's, also other land, two cows, forty sheep and a mare. To son Richard, house and land where I now dwell, &c., forty sheep, he paying to my daughter Patience £50, and to daughter Ruth £50, and to daughter Sarah £50. To son Daniel, the house and land I bought of David Irish, and other land and forty sheep.

Inventory, £816, 5*s.* 6*d.*, viz: wearing apparel, feather beds, stillyards, loom, 5 old spinning wheels, case of bottles, gun, pewter, 2 churns, 2 cheese presses, 2 silver tankards £42, 3*s.*, money scales, 2 pair oxen, 4 steers, 10 cows, 2 heifers, 6 yearlings, a bull, 9 mares, 8 colts, a horse, negro called Toby £60, negress, Phillis £55, 240 sheep, 60 lambs, &c.

1747, Jul. 23. Will—proved 1749, Mar. 18. Widow Patience. Ex. son Richard. To son George, 20*s.* To son William, all interest in farm where he lives and 20*s.* To son Richard, 20*s.* To son Daniel, 20*s.* To four daughters, rest of estate (except £10,) viz: to Rebecca White, Elizabeth Grinnell, Patience Woodman, and Sarah Woodman. To granddaughter Ruth Paddock, £10, to be at interest till eighteen years of age.

Inventory, £1,105, 2*s.* 6*d.*, including negro woman and boy, plate £217, 6*s.*, gold, £22, 10*s.*, cash £137, 10*s.*, &c.

HARRIS (THOMAS).

I. { THOMAS, { b. 1665, Oct. 19. Providence, R. I.
m. { d. 1741, Nov. 1.
PHEBE BROWN, { b.
{ d. 1723, Aug. 20. of Henry & Wait (Waterman) Brown.

1. Wait, 1694, Apr. 21.
2. Phebe, 1698, Dec. 16.
3. John, 1700, Sep. 17.
4. Henry, 1702, Oct. 5.
5. Thomas, 1704, Oct. 21.
6. Charles, 1709.
7. Gideon, 1714, Mar. 15.
8. Lydia, 1715, Jun. 9.

1718. Deputy.
1716-17-18-19-20-21-22-23-24. Town Council.

He was called Captain at his death.

1740, Jan. 31. Will—proved 1742, Jan. 18. Exs. sons Henry and Thomas. To son Henry, the homestead, &c. To son Thomas, land where he dwells, with house, &c., and a right of thatch land that was in original right of testator's "honoured grandfather Thomas Harris," &c. To son Charles, land in Scituate, with house, and in Glocester. To son Gideon, 100 acres near Alum Pond, Glocester, and land in Scituate with a small dwelling. To daughter Wait Fenner, a weaver's loom, pair of worsted combs and £10. To sons Henry, Charles and Gideon, the cattle, sheep and swine. To sons Henry, Thomas, Charles and Gideon, rest of movables.

Inventory, £839, 4*s.*, 6*d.*, viz: wearing apparel, cane, and walking staff with silver ferrule and ivory head, 4 swords, warming pan, cooper's and carpenter's tools, pewter, 4 pieces of gold £18, 1*s.*, 6*d.*, silver money £35, 1*s.*, 3*d.*, large pair silver shoe buckles, 4 feather beds, 2 pair oxen, pair of steers, bull, 6 cows, 2 heifers, 4 yearlings, 3 calves, 31 sheep, great bible, other books, &c.

II. { RICHARD, { b. 1668, Oct. 14. Providence, Smithfield, R. I.
m. (1) { d. 1750.
—— KING, { b.
m. (2) [of Samuel. { d. of Clement & Elizabeth ( ) King.
SUSANNAH GORTON, (w. { b. 1665.
{ d. 1737, Jun. 25. of William & Hannah (Wickes) Burton.

1. Uriah,
2. Richard,
3. Amaziah,
4. Jonathan,
5. David,
6. Preserved,
7. Amity,
8. Dinah,
9. Elnathan,
(2d wife, no issue.)

1724, Jan. 27. He deeded to son Richard, Jr., 100 acres for £150.
1729, May 14. He deeded to son-in-law Christopher Smith, Jr., 10 acres west of Seven Mile Line, adjoining his father Christopher Smith.
1729, Jul. 7. He was administrator on estate of his son Uriah, who died 1729, Apr. 14.
1739, Mar. 6. Will—proved 1750, Sep. 15. Ex. son Preserved. To son Richard, 7 acres. To son Amaziah, 5*s.* To son Jonathan, 5*s.* To son David, 5*s.* To daughter Amity Smith, 1*s.* To daughter Dinah Smith, a cow. To daughter Elnathan Gile, 1*s.* To son Preserved, all my homestead farm whereon I dwell, with housing, &c., subject to privilege of passing through said farm by sons David and Richard, from their own farms to a driftway. To son Preserved, all the rest of estate both real and personal.

Provision was also made for Elnathan by appointment of Amaziah Harris and Jacob Smith, as Trustees, to have £100, for use of Elnathan, at interest.

1733, Jul 15. Will—proved 1739, Sep. 15. Wife Susannah. Exs. son-in-law Joseph Stafford, and wife Susanna. She names son Samuel Gorton and his wife Freelove and their sons Samuel, Benjamin and William. Also names her son Samuel's daughters, Freelove, Ann and Lydia. She mentions her son Hezekiah, and her daughter Susannah Stafford, and children of latter, viz: Mercy and Joseph. Inventory, £128, 12*s.*

III. { NICHOLAS, { b. 1671, Apr. 1. Providence, R. I.
m. { d. 1746, Mar. 27.
ANN, { b.
{ d. of

1. Thomas,
2. Joseph,
3. Nicholas,
4. Jedediah,
5. Christopher,
6. Anne,
7. Zerviah,
8. Mary,
9. Sarah,
10. Amity,

1724, Jan. 27. He and wife Ann, deeded land.
1725, Jul 16. Will—Codicil 1739, Apr. 22—proved 1746, Apr. 27. Exs. wife Ann and son Thomas. To sons Thomas and Joseph, homestead, lands and tenements when of age, with equal privilege to wife Ann and son Thomas, till Joseph is of age. After Joseph is of age, wife Ann to have a convenient room, and son Thomas to provide for her and also to provide for daughter Amity. To sons Nicholas and Jedediah, land west of Seven Mile line. To son Christopher, 2 acres with two rows of apple trees and convenience of water for setting up a smith's shop. To daughter Ann Kilton, 5*s.* To daughter Zerviah Waterman, £10. To daughters Mary and Sarah Harris £25 each, at age of twenty-one or marriage. Rest to wife and son Thomas. Codicil gives the homestead to Thomas and Christopher. To Joseph, some land before given Nicholas, and to Nicholas, £100, &c.

Inventory, £383, 6*s.*, viz: large bible and other books £5, warming pan, spinning wheels, Bills of Credit £67, 14*s.*, stillyards, pewter, 3 steers, 3 cows, heifer, ox, 31 sheep and lambs, mare, &c.

IV. { WILLIAM, { b. 1673, May 11. Providence, R. I.
m. { d. 1726, Jan. 14.
ABIGAIL, { b. 1679.
{ d. 1724, Nov. 4. of

1. Job, 1700, Aug. 10.
2. Sarah, 1702, Jul. 4.
3. Dorcas, 1704, May 16.
4. Alice, 1714, Jun. 28.

1713-14-15-16-17-18. Town Council.

posal. To son Thomas and heirs at death of testator's wife, the part of the lot that my shop now standeth on and appurtenances so high as the cherry hedge. To daughter Martha Field and heirs, at death of wife, the dwelling house, lot, &c., and if she have no surviving child then son Thomas to have the same. To daughter Mary Whipple and her heirs, born of my son-in-law Samuel Whipple, land on north side Moshasset River and 60 acres upland. To son Thomas, rest of land. To son Samuel Whipple and his wife Mary, for use of their children, a cow and yearling at his house. To son Thomas Field and his wife Martha, for use of children, two cows. To son Thomas Harris, two oxen and rest of horsekind. To three children Thomas Harris, Mary Whipple and Martha Field, the household stuff for use of their children.

Inventory, £45, 10*s*., viz: 3 pair of cards, linen wheel, woolen wheel, warming pan, earthen and pewter ware, old bible, 6 chairs, small table, grindstone, gun, pair of scales, compass and dial, 4 cheese fats, butter, candles, 2 horses, mare, colt, 7 cows, 2 oxen, 2 two years, a yearling, 8 calves, 8 swine, 6 pigs, 7 hives of bees, &c.

1687, Sep. 1. Widow Elizabeth Harris, taxed 1*s*.

II. MARY, b. 1639. d. 1722, Dec. 14.
m.
SAMUEL WHIPPLE, b. 1644. d. 1711, Mar. 12. of John & Sarah ( ) Whipple.

III. MARTHA, b. d. 1717 (—)
m.
THOMAS FIELD, b. d. 1717, Aug. 10. of Field.

HARRIS (THOMAS). 2d column. III. Martha. Erase her 5th child.

See: American Genealogist, v. 20, p. 187.

HARRIS (WILLIAM).

WILLIAM, b. 1610. d. 1681. Salem, Mass., Providence, R. I.
m.
SUSANNAH, b. d. 1682 +

1630, Dec. 1. He came in ship Lyon from Bristol, England, to Boston, in company with his brother Thomas, and Roger Williams.

1636. Providence. He was one of the six persons who arrived as first settlers here before July of this year, having spent the preceding winter at Seekonk.

1638, Oct. 8. He was one of the twelve persons to whom Roger Williams deeded land that he had bought of Canonicus and Miantonomi.

1639. He was one of the twelve original members of First Baptist Church.

1640, Jul. 27. He and thirty-eight others signed a compact for good government.

1640. He was appointed with three others on a committee to consider all matters of difference between Providence and Pawtuxet as to the dividing line. They reported in July that they had seriously and carefully endeavoured to weigh all these differences to bring them to amity and peace. "We have gone the fairest and equallest way to produce our peace."

1650, Sep. 2. Taxed £1, 6*s*. 8*d*.

1655. Freeman.

1657, Mar. 12. A warrant was issued for his arrest on the charge of High Treason, signed by Roger Williams as President. This was the culmination of a quarrel between them of some years duration, in which neither had spared invective. Williams believed that Harris's views went beyond legal liberty, to the dangerous ground of unbounded license for individuals. The warrant charges him with having published "dangerous writings containing his notorious defiance to the authority of his highness the Lord Protector," &c., and with having inciting the people "into a traitorous renouncing of their allegiance," &c. He "now openly in the face of the court declareth himself resolved to maintain the said writings with his blood."

1657, Jul. 4. "Concerning William Harris his book and speeches upon it; we find therein delivered as for doctrine, having much bowd the scripture to maintain, that he that can say it is his conscience, ought not to yield subjection to any human order amongst men. Whereas the said Harris hath been charged for the said book and words with High Treason," &c. The Assembly decided that being so remote from England as not to be well acquainted with the laws touching this matter—"though we cannot but conclude his behaviour therein to be both contemptuous and seditious"—that it was best to send over his writings, &c., to Mr. John Clarke, desiring him to commend the matter in our and the Commonwealth's behalf for further judgment, &c., and in mean time to bind said Harris in good bonds to good behaviour till sentence be known.

I. ANDREW, b. 1635. d. 1686, May 1. Providence, R. I.
m. 1670, Dec. 8.
MARY TEW, b. 1647, Aug. 12. d. 1688 + of Richard & Mary (Clarke) Tew.

1661, Sep. 25. He had land laid out to him, viz: a 5 acre house lot, 60 acres, 20 acres, 6 acres, 5 acres, all joined together, and a spot of meadow and swamp.

1669-70-76. Deputy.

1679, Jul. 1. Taxed 3*s*. 1½*d*.

1686, Jul. 22. Administration to widow Mary. Inventory, £98, 9*s*., viz: a chest wherein were his writings, wearing apparel, 2 old bibles, Pilgrim's Progress, Arithmetic, pewter, 2 guns, shoemaking tools, carpenter's tools, horse, 3 mares, 2 oxen, 9 cows, 7 steers, 5 heifers, 7 yearlings, bull, 3 calves, 2 young pigs, &c. The rooms named were lower room, chamber over fire room, and cellar.

1687, Sep. 1. His widow was taxed 9*s*.

1688. His widow gave in her ratable estate as follows: 2 oxen, 2 steers, 5 cows, 4 heifers, 6 two year, 2 yearlings, 3 mares, 2 colts, 3 acres corn land. (The next year she added 500 acres upland, 2 shares of meadow, &c. to her account.)

1714-17-18-19-20. Deputy.

1717-20. Town Treasurer.

He was called Lieutenant at his death.

1726, Apr. 16. Administration to son Job. Inventory, £635, 12*s.*, 6*d.*, viz: 26 pewter plates, 6 small ditto, 8 pewter platters, &c., 33 chairs, books £1, 18*s.*, settle, 2 long tables and an old table, 3 joint stools, spinning wheel, 2 horsekind, yoke of oxen, 2 yoke steers, 10 cows, 9 two year, 5 calves, 36 poor sheep, 1 silver tankard, 2 silver cups, 10 silver spoons, pair of money scales, &c. (His son Job, died 1729, Dec. 17, leaving widow Mary and children Sarah, Abigail and Mary.) He and his wife and children were buried in North Burial Ground.

V. HENRY, m. LYDIA OLNEY,
- b. 1675, Nov. 10. — Providence, R. I.
- d. 1727, Mar. 29.
- b. 1688, Jan. 26.
- d. 1727 (—) of Epenetus & Mary (Whipple) — Olney.

1. Thomas,
2. Henry,
3. Lydia,

1723. Deputy.

1727, Mar. 26. Will—proved 1727, Apr. 13. Exs. brother Thomas and brother-in-law Thomas Olney. To two sons Thomas and Henry, all real estate in Providence. To daughter Lydia, £150, at twenty-one or marriage, and £50, in household goods. All rest of estate to two sons. To Ann Blake, single woman, living with me, £100, a feather bed and black mare.

Inventory, £1,241, 16*s.*, 9*d.*, viz: money due £609, 13*s.*, 9*d.*, silver plate, 3 hogsheads cider, 2 old mares, 2 young horses, 2 yearling horses, pair of small oxen, 3 steers, 12 cows, 6 heifers, 7 yearlings, 8 calves, 40 sheep, 5 swine, books £1. (His son Thomas died at Surinam, 1736, Apr. 23, and his estate was administered by Henry the brother.)

VI. AMITY, m. ——— MORSE,
- b. 1677, Dec. 10.
- d.
- b.
- d. of — Morse.

VII. JOB,
- b. 1682, Jan. 11.
- d. 1689, Jan.

VIII. ELNATHAN, m. NATHANIEL BROWN,
- b.
- d. 1749 +
- b. 1689, Sep. 24.
- d. 1749 + of Nathaniel & Sarah (Jenckes) — Brown.

1. William,
2. Sarah,
3. Elnathan,

IX. MARY, m. (1) 1712, GABRIEL BERNON, m. (2) 1737, Dec. 23, NATHANIEL BROWN,
- b.
- d.
- b. 1644, Apr. 6
- d. 1736, Feb. 1. of Andre & Suzanne (Guillemard) — Bernon.
- b.
- d. of — Brown.

1. Gabriel,
2. Susannah, 1716.
3. Mary, 1719, Apr. 1.
4. Eve,

(By 2d husband, no issue.)

1. Noah,
2. Samuel, 1669.
3. Thomas,
4. Abigail, 1683.
5. Hope,

1. Thomas, 1670, Jan. 3.
2. Mary, 1673, Jun. 1.
3. Amos, 1677.
4. William, 1682, Jun. 8.
5. Martha,
6. Elizabeth.

HARRIS (WILLIAM).

I. MARY, m. 1691, Dec. 17. JAMES BROWN,
- b. 1671, Dec. 17.
- d. 1736, Aug. 18.
- b. 1666.
- d. 1732, Oct. 28. of John & Mary (Holmes) — Brown.

1. John, 1695, Oct. 8.
2. James, 1698, Mar. 22.
3. Joseph, 1701, May 15.
4. Martha, 1703, Oct. 12.
5. Andrew, 1706, Sep. 20.
6. Mary, 1708, Apr. 29.
7. Anna,
8. Obadiah, 1712, Oct. 2.
9. Jeremiah, 1715, Nov. 25.
10. Elisha, 1717, May 25.

II. ANNE, m. RESOLVED WATERMAN,
- b. 1673, Nov. 22.
- d.
- b. 1667 ±
- d. 1719, Jan. 13. of Resolved & Mercy (Williams) — Waterman.

1. Resolved,
2. Mary,
3. Joseph,

III. ANDREW, UNMARRIED.
- b. 1677, Feb. 4. — Providence, R. I.
- d. 1725, Dec. 20.

1705-7-10-15-21. Deputy.

1715, Jul. 5. He and Thomas Fry were appointed by Assembly to transcribe, fit and prepare for the press, all the laws of the colony.

1721-22-23-24. Assistant.

1722, Apr. 27. He deeded to his sister Mary Brown, for love, &c., 33½ acres.

1726, Mar. 21. Administration on his estate to brother Toleration. Inventory, £927, 9*s.* 6*d.*, viz: Bonds for money due £756, 8*s.* Money due on book £82. Surveying tackling £2, 10*s.* Watch £4. A horse, bridle, saddle and old portmanteau £15. Ink horn and case, two razors, 2 walking staves, &c.

Inventory of real estate later in the year showed £4,220, including the homestead farm and house (320 acres—£1,300,) and many other parcels of land.

IV. HOPE,
- b. 1679, Dec. 14.
- d. young.

V. PATIENCE, m. 1709, Mar. 15. WILLIAM SMITH,
- b. 1682, Jun. 21.
- d. 1759, Nov. 20.
- b. 1664, Dec. 27.
- d. 1745, Dec. 18. of Benjamin & Lydia (Carpenter) — Smith.

1. William, 1715, Feb. 21.
2. Lydia, 1721, Aug.

VI. TOLERATION, m. SARAH FOSTER,
- b. 1685, Jun. 10. — Providence, Warwick, R. I.
- d. 1767.
- b.
- d. 1766 + of — Foster.

1. Anne, 1709, Dec. 31.
2. William, 1711, Jul. 22.
3. Joseph, 1713, Jun. 15.
4. Andrew, 1715, Nov. 18.
5. Mary, 1718, Dec. 18.
6. Sarah, 1722, Jun. 9.
7. John, 1724, Aug. 19.
8. John, 1726, Sep. 7.
9. Phebe, 1726, Sep. 7.
10. Lydia,

1727, Jun. 23. He and Sarah, for valuable sum of money from Rev. Mr. Henry Harris, of Boston, clerk, sold full right of undivided land west side of Seven Mile Line, being upon original right of William Harris, deceased.

1730, Apr. 18. He deeded to the heirs of Rev. Henry Harris, late of Boston, for sum of money that had been paid by Henry, a small lot lately laid out in right of honored grandfather William Harris.

1660–62–63. Commissioner.

1663, Jun. 13. He entered ten ankers of liquor. He went to England this year on business concerning the Pawtuxet lands.

1665, Feb. 19. He had lot 37 in a division of lands.

1665–66–72–73. Deputy.

1666–67–68–69–70–73–74–75–76. Assistant.

1667, Jul. 2. He was discharged from his office of assistant, there being many grievous complaints against him, he being apt to take advantages against the members of this corporation, &c. He was fined £50, having unjustly occasioned the presenting of four deputies more to sit in the Assembly for Providence than by law ought to be received, through wilfully calling together part of the townsmen of Providence without warrant of General Sergeant. Protests against this action of the Assembly were made by William Carpenter and Benjamin Smith, Assistants.

1668, Oct. 29. The fine was remitted.

1670, Nov. 10. He deeded to eldest son Andrew for his welfare and comfort, 150 acres on both sides Pochasset River "with all that I have laid out on a house," &c. If Andrew should die without heirs then youngest son Toleration was to have, or finally to three daughters, viz: Mary, wife of Thomas Borden, Susanna, wife of Ephraim Carpenter, and Howlong Harris, and their heirs female.

1670–77. Town Council.

1671. General Solicitor.

1672, Feb. 24. He was brought by the constable before the Assembly at Newport, and did disown matters testified to by Roger Williams and Philip Taber. He was ordered to be committed to prison "for speaking and writing against his Majesties gracious Charter," &c.

1675. He went to England as agent for the proprietors of Pawtuxet to lay their case before the King.

1679, Jul. 1. Taxed 15*s.* 7½*d.* He went this year to England for the third time.

1679, Dec. 25. He again set sail for England to support the cause of Pawtuxet proprietors; and embarked at Boston on the ship Unity, Captain Condy. He was appointed by Connecticut as their agent to support their claims to the Narragansett country as against Rhode Island.

1680, Jan. 6. A verdict in favor of himself and partners against the Town of Providence, by a special court of Commissioners, is alluded to by Governor Cranston in a letter to King Charles II, at this date. The Governor presents "our proceedings in these affairs, which we would have sent in the ship that William Harris went lately to England in; but William Harris was so secret and private in his voyage that he never came to us to know what we had done by way of return to your Majesty, neither did he let us know of his going." The question of jurisdiction and title to Pawtuxet lands was not finally settled till many years after his death.

1680, Jan. 24. The vessel in which he had embarked was taken by an Algerine corsair, and he was sold in Barbary, and after more than a year's slavery was ransomed at a high figure, of which sum the colony of Connecticut paid £289, 9*s.* 7*d.* He traveled through Spain and France and finally, arrived in London in 1680, where he died three days afterward at the house of his friend John Stokes. He wrote several letters while in captivity. (One to his wife was dated at Algiers 1680, Apr. 6.)

1678, Dec. 4. Will—proved 1682, Feb. 20. Exs. wife Susanna, son Andrew and daughter Howlong. He calls himself 68 years old. He premises his will with remarks upon the "great sickness and mortality that is among our neighbors (not far off), many being sick of small pox and fevers, and many being dying thereby." He further says that he intends "if God please, to sail over the great and wide sea to England." To wife, he gives half of all lands, goods and cattle for life, and a third of farm, &c., of 750 acres, and a third of meadow, the said third at her decease going to son Andrew. To son Andrew, a third of 750 acres, meadow, &c., and another third at death of wife of testator as provided. To daughter Howlong, a third of 750 acres, meadow, &c.

All the rest of lands except 50 acres, to be in four equal parts, one to son Andrew, one to daughter Howlong, one in trust to son Andrew with private instructions, and one part in trust to daughter Howlong with private instructions. To daughter Mary Borden, 50 acres that I obtained of Thomas Borden, husband that was of said daughter, and to Mary, other land also. He desired that Andrew's part should be to him for life, and that then it should go to heirs of fourth generation, by entail, giving long reasons therefor. He makes mention of son Toleration, deceased.

Inventory (appraised by Thomas Harris, Sr., and Thomas Field), £145, 0*s.* 8*d.*, viz: bay mare, 3 cows, 4 steers, 2 two years, 3 calves, 2 barrels summer cider, 2 barrels winter cider, firelock musket, 2 pistols, pinchers, nippers, two bibles and other books, some of the titles being London Dispensatory, The Chirurgeon's Mate, Norwood's Triangles, Contemplations Moral and Divine, The Competent Clerk, The Touchstone of wills, Coke's Commentary on Littleton, &c. The articles enumerated in the inventory were scattered in different parts of the colony.

There was an Anne Harris taxed at Providence for 4*s.* 4½*d.*, in 1679, and again for 1*s* 8*d.* in 1687, but no relationship has been traced between her and this family.

II. { MARY, { b.
m. 1664, Jan. 20. { d. 1718, Mar. 22.
THOMAS BORDEN, { b.
{ d. 1676, Nov. 25. of Richard & Joan ( ) Borden.

III. { SUSANNAH, { b.
m. { d.
EPHRAIM CARPENTER, { b.
{ d. 1703 ± of William & Elizabeth (Arnold) Carpenter.

IV. { HOWLONG, { b.
m. 1684, Dec. 16. { d. 1708, Nov. 19.
ARTHUR FENNER, { b. 1622.
{ d. 1703. Oct. 10. of Thomas Fenner.

V. { TOLERATION, { b. 1645.
{ d. 1675.
UNMARRIED.

1673–75. Deputy.

1675. He was killed in the Indian war.

1682, Mar. 6. Inventory, £7, 1*s.* Administration by sister Howlong. Among the items were 6 pewter platters, 2 basins, 5 porringers, a quart pot, pint pot, half pint pot, gill pot, half gill pot.

HART (Edward).

{ EDWARD, { b. Providence, R. I.
m. { d.
MARGARET, { b.
{ d. 1671 +

(She m. (2) John Gould.)

1638 ± He had a lot apportioned to him.

1640, Jul. 27. He and thirty-eight others signed an agreement for a form of government.

1646, Jan. 19. He and others signed the following agreement: "We whose names are hereafter subscribed having obtained a free grant of 25 acres of land apiece, with right of commoning according to the said proportion of land, from the free inhabitants of this town of Providence, do thankfully accept of the same and hereby promise to yield active or passive obedience to the authority of King and Parliament, the estate of England established in this Colony according to our charter, and to all such wholesome laws and orders that are or shall be made by the major consent of this town of Providence; as also not to claim any right to the purchase of the said plantation, nor any privilege to vote in Town affairs until we shall be received as free men of the said town of Providence." (All did not sign this so early as the above date.)

I. { THOMAS, { b. Newport, R. I.
m. { d. 1671.
FREEBORN WILLIAMS, { b. 1635, Oct.
{ d. 1710, Jan. 10. of Roger & Mary ( ) Williams.

(She m. (2) 1683, Mar. 6, Walter Clarke.)

1666. Deputy.

1666, Sep. 4. Voted that a boat be forthwith procured and sent to Warwick, to signify to the Magistrates and Deputies of that town—the Court desire of their advice and assistance. Thomas Hart is ordered to procure a boat and hands to go to Warwick.

1670, Mar. 22. Will—proved 1671, Aug. 7. Overseers, friends Jireh Bull and Walter Clarke. He mentions wife Freeborne, eldest son John, daughter Mary Hart, son James, son Thomas, father-in-law (*i. e.* stepfather) John Gould, mother Margaret Gould.

1672, Apr. 2. John Sanford, Recorder of Colony, presents that forasmuch as there was an action commenced by Mr. Thomas Hart, late deceased, against one Mark Ridley, defendant, who was no free inhabitant of this country—Court orders if Mark cannot be found then execution be given forth by Recorder against bondsman of Mark Ridley.

1750, May 8. Warwick. He deeded three sons William, Joseph and John, all of Providence, for love, &c., 230 acres in two parcels, situated west side of Pauchasset River.

1766, Sep. 30. Will—proved 1767, Feb. 9 Ex. son William Harris, of Cranston, for personal estate in Providence County, and for the rest Jabez Reynolds, Jr., of North Kingstown. To grandsons James and John, sons of John, all my mansion house and farm in Cranston east side Pauchasset River, 500 acres, on condition that they procure of their father John Harris, if ever he return home again, a quit claim to my two sons William and Joseph to the farm William dwells on in Cranston, but if John die before he return, then the two grandsons at age to make the deed to two sons as above. To son William, house and 160 acres at Cranston, and all profits since I removed from there, in consideration of his care of his mother for many years last past. To sons William and Joseph, remaining part of farm in Cranston, 160 acres, and so divided that William may have his half adjoining other land. Also to two sons, a farm in Cranston which Thomas Wales lives on, upon certain conditions. To wife Sarah, use of all household goods that I left with her at my son William's, when I removed from there, and she to be supported by sons William and Joseph for life. To daughter Ann, wife of Colonel Christopher Harris, 5*s*., she having already received her portion. To daughter Mary, widow of Obadiah Brown, 5*s*. To grandsons John and Sarah Kilton, children of daughter Sarah, deceased, 5*s*. each. To daughter Phebe Arnold, wife of Philip Arnold, 5*s*. To daughter Lydia, wife of Captain George Jackson, 5*s*. To son John, provided he be living, 5*s*., "he having behaved himself undutifully to me, and I have given his two sons James and John Harris, his proportion of my estate." To grandson John Arnold, for service done and to be done (he having lived with testator some time), half part of my mansion house and farm where I dwell, half of grist mill and half of sheep and stock of cattle and horses and hogs, at age. To Susanna Reynolds, wife of Jabez Reynolds, Jr., of North Kingstown, half part of mansion house which is given by deed to Susanna Latham for life, and half grist mill, all at decease of Susanna Latham, and Susanna Reynolds is also to have half money and securities. To Susanna Latham, for living with me and keeping my house for about thirty years last past, all household goods, and half cattle, horses, sheep and hogs, money and securities, and negro man Cuff and negro wench Jane and her child Jeffrey. To grandson John Arnold and to Jabez Reynolds, tools, wearing apparel, &c. To sons William and Joseph, all real estate not given already.

Inventory, £538, 10*s*., 1¼*d*., viz: a riding horse, 5 cows, yearling bull, pair of oxen, 28 sheep, 6 hogs, negro man Cuff £45, negro girl Jane £45, and child Jeffrey £7, 10*s*., silver seal £1, 9*s*., 38 silver buttons £1,8*s*. 6*d*., money and securities £250, 14*s*. 8*d*., old desk, pair of pistols, old sword, walking staff with silver ferule, compass, linen wheel, 3 pocket books, &c. Buildings and rooms were named as follows: mill, crib, barn, shop, great room, south-west bedroom, great chamber, north-west chamber, north-east chamber, kitchen, cellar, garret.

1. Mary, 1664, Oct.
2. Dinah, 1665, Oct.
3. Richard,
4. William, 1668, Jan. 10.
5. Joseph, 1669, Nov. 25.
6. Mercy, 1672, Nov. 3.
7. Experience, 1675, Jun. 8.
8. Meribah, 1676, Dec. 19.

1. Ephraim,
2. Susanna,

No issue.

HART (Edward).

I. John, m. Priscilla Gould,
- John: b. ; d. — Newport, R. I. — No issue.
- Priscilla Gould: b. 1661, Jun. 20.; d. 1689, Jan. 23. — of Daniel & Wait (Coggeshall) — Gould.

He was a Quaker.

1685, Jun. 12. He and wife Priscilla, sold Joseph Mowry, of Jamestown, 4 acres at Jamestown, for £5.

II. Mary, m. Samuel Cranston,
- Mary: b. 1663.; d. 1710, Sep. 17.
- Samuel Cranston: b. 1659, Aug.; d. 1727, Apr. 26. — of John & Mary (Clark) — Cranston.

HART (Edward). 3d column. II. Mary. Her 6th child was Frances, not Thomas

1. Mary,
2. John, 1684, Aug. 4.
3. James,
4. Samuel,
5. Thomas,
6. Thomas, 1698.
7. Hart, 1699.

III. James, m. (1) Mary Clarke, m. (2) Frances Clarke,
- James: b. 1666.; d. 1693, Jul. 20. — Newport, R. I. — No issue.
- Mary Clarke: b. 1670, Jan. 11.; d. 1690, Nov. 11. — of Weston & Mary (Easton) — Clarke.
- Frances Clarke: b. 1673, Jan. 17.; d. 1693, Jun. 25. — of Walter & Hannah (Scott) — Clarke.

HART (Nicholas).

Nicholas, — b. — d. 1654 ± — Taunton, Mass., Warwick, Portsmouth, R. I.
m.
Joan Rossiter, — b. — d. 1685 +

of Edward Rossiter.

He was a merchant.

1643. He was thus early of Taunton, and was later of Boston, for a short time.

1648, Jun. 5. Warwick. He was recorded as an inhabitant of this town.

1651, May 21. Portsmouth. He and wife Joan, bought of Ralph Earle, 8 acres and message, for a valuable consideration.

1683, Jul. 18. Joan Hart sold 8 acres with orchards, fencing, &c., to Richard Hart, for £25.

1685, Jun. 4. Mrs. Joan Hart, youngest surviving child of the late Mr. Edward Rossiter, one of the adventurers, was granted 500 acres by Massachusetts authorities, in full of all claims of any heirs of said Mr. Edward Rossiter. The widow's petition was made through John Cotton.

I. Richard, — b. — d. 1696 (—) — Portsmouth, R. I.
m.
Hannah, — b. — d. 1696 + — of

1657, Dec. 10. He had a grant of 8 acres.

1662, Nov. 16. He sold Thomas Butts 4 acres.

HAWKINS (William).

William, — b. — d. 1699 + — Providence, R. I.
m.
Margaret, — b. — d.

1638, Dec. 20. He received land.

1640, Jul. 27. He and thirty-eight others signed an agreement for a form of government.

1645, Jan. 27. He bought of Hugh Bewitt, his home share of land.

1650, Sep. 2. Taxed 13*s.*, 4*d.*

1655. Freeman.

1672, Apr. 30. Freeman.

1673, Feb. 2. He deeded to his son William, two house lots, and the housing thereon, bounded west by Town street, also a 6 acre lot, some shares of meadow, &c.

1676, Aug. 14. He was one of those "who staid and went not away" in King Philip's War, and so had a share in the disposition of the Indian captives whose services were sold for a term of years.

1679, Jul. 1. Taxed 7½*d.*

1683, Jun. 25. He deeded to his son Edward certain rights in lands between Pawtucket and Pawtuxet Rivers that he had bought twenty years before of John Sayles.

I. John, — b. — d. 1726. — Providence, R. I.
m.
Sarah, — b. — d. — of

1679, Jul. 1. Taxed 3*s.*, 1½*d.*

1683, Apr. He brought in a wolf's head.

1687, Dec. 13. Fined 6*s.*, 8*d.*, for refusing to take oath as juryman.

1710, Dec. 29. He deeded 40 acres to Richard Evans, Jr., and Sarah his wife, for love, &c.

1711, Mar. 28. He deeded 40 acres to Elizabeth Smith, his daughter, wife of Joseph.

1711, Jul. 27. He confirmed a deed made by his brother Edward in 1692, to John Aldrich, and calls himself "John Hawkins eldest son of William Hawkins, deceased, and of Margaret his wife, also deceased."

1713, Aug. 12. He deeded 93 acres for love, &c., to son-in-law Elisha Knowlton and Lydia, his wife.

1713, Jun. 16. Taxed with son Edward, £1.

1714, Jun. 5. He deeded 52 acres for love, &c., to son-in-law Hosannah Brown and Mary his wife.

1715, Oct. 19. He gave free consent to sons William Hawkins, Hosannah Brown and Elisha Knowlton to sell all their lands which they had of him.

1717, Nov. 30. He deeded 50 acres of land to Jonathan Salisbury and Abigail his wife, for love, &c., and same date deeded to Joseph Smith (son of Joseph Smith, joiner), and Patience his wife, 50 acres, for love, &c. (also deeding certain rights to each).

He was a Quaker.
His first wife died at her father Weston Clarke's.
His second wife died with still born son.
He died on ship Elizabeth, coming from Barbadoes.

IV. THOMAS, b. / d.

HART (NICHOLAS).

I. ALICE, m. 1687, Apr. 7. GEORGE PEARCE, — b. 1664, Mar 8. d. 1718, Mar. 11. b. 1662, Jul. 10. d. 1752, Aug. 30. of Richard & Susanna (Wright) Pearce.

1. Susanna, 1688, Aug. 21.
2. James, 1691, Sep. 4.
3. Samuel, 1695, Feb. 3.
4. George, 1697, Mar. 2.
5. Mary, 1700, May 16.

II. RICHARD, m. (1) 1693, HANNAH, m. (2) 1708, Oct. 31. AMEY GIBBS, — b. 1667. d. 1745. b. d. of — b. d. of Gibbs. Portsmouth, Little Compton, R. I.

1. Alice, 1694, Oct. 16.
2. Mary, 1697, Jan. 16.
3. Sarah, 1703, Jan. 7.
4. Richard, 1704, Dec. 22.
(2d wife).
5. Comfort, 1710, Apr. 4.
6. Stephen, 1712, Aug. 2.

1696, May 4. He sold John Keese two parcels of land containing 8 acres, with buildings, &c., for £80. Hannah Hart, widow, mother of said Richard, and Hannah Hart wife of said Richard, also signed, giving full consent.

1696, Jul. 4. He bought of his brother-in-law George Pearce, 100 acres in Little Compton, with buildings, &c., for £108.

1745, Apr. 19. Will—proved 1745, Jun. 10. Ex. son Stephen. To wife Amey, table linen, sheets, feather bed, &c., and for life the rest of household goods and improvement of a cow. To son Richard, my beetle, rings, wedges and 5*s*. To son Stephen, all my lands and housing, orchards, &c., where I live, with husbandry utensils, cider tubs, barrels and hogsheads, stillyards, mare, &c., he maintaining his mother in victuals, drink, clothes, &c., and keeping for her a cow, the increase of said cow to be his at his mother's death for his trouble. To four daughters Alice Closson, Mary Peckham, Sarah Wilcox and Comfort Gifford, 20*s*., divided among them. To three daughters Alice, Mary and Sarah, household goods at death of wife. To daughter Comfort, a warming pan, churn, &c., at death of wife. To granddaughter Hannah, daughter of my son Richard, a trammel. To daughters Alice and Sarah, all my wearing apparel. Son Stephen to sell all livestock except sheep, and after debts are paid the balance to go equally to four daughters. To grandson Richard, son of Richard, fire tongs, at death of wife. To son Stephen, my box of writings.

Inventory, £297, 6*s*., viz: purse and apparel £5, 6*s*., books £8, 9*s*., houses and land £250, steer, cow, heifer, calf, colt, 2 beds, pewter, &c.

III. MARY, m. 1693, Sep. 6. JOHN TRIPP, — b. d. b. 1673, Jul. 19. d. of John & Susanna (Anthony) Tripp.

1. John, 1694, Nov. 3.
2. Sarah, 1696, Apr. 23.
3. Richard, 1698, Jan. 24.
4. Susanna, 1699, Nov. 26.
5. Isabel, 1702, Jan. 14.
6. Mary, 1703, Dec. 11.
7. Othniel, 1705, Jul. 6
8. Anna, 1707, Jun. 16.
9. Abiel, 1709, Dec. 1.
10. Abigail, 1711, Nov. 12.
11. Richard, 1716, Feb. 16.

IV. NICHOLAS, m. 1699. ——— — b. 1673. d. b. d. of. Tiverton, R. I.

1. Robert, 1700, Feb. 28.
2. Martha, 1701, Sep. 18.
3. Edith, 1706, Nov. 26.

Possibly his wife was Alice Pearce, daughter of John & Mary (Tallman) Pearce, for the said Alice married to a Hart.

V. SAMUEL, m. 1705, Mar. 29. [Jon'th. MARTHA TRIPP, (w. of — b. d. b. 1678, May 24. d. of William & Sarah (Smiton) Brownell. Tiverton, R. I.

1. Jonathan, 1706, Jan. 6.
2. Samuel, 1708, Dec. 10.
3. Smiton, 1712, Jan. 24.

1706, Dec. 4. His wife refused administration on estate of her first husband Jonathan Tripp, and she with her present husband desired that her father, William Brownell, of Dartmouth, might have administration.

VI. WILLIAM, m. SARAH, — b. d. 1735. b. d. 1735 + of. Dartmouth, Mass.

1. Archippus,
2. Luke,
3. William,
4. Hannah, 1713, Jun. 9.
5. Mary, 1715, Nov. 7.

He was a house carpenter.

1734, Feb. 1. Will—proved 1735, Aug. 19. Exs. wife Sarah and sons Luke and William. To wife, half of household goods and half dwelling house for life, use of two cows and ten sheep and keep of same, privilege of ten apple trees, and to have yearly ten bushels of corn, two hundred pounds of pork, one hundred pounds of beef, firewood cut at her door, and £6, also, paid yearly. To son Archippus, 10 acres of homestead and other land. To sons Luke and William, the rest of homestead, all the housing, orchard, &c., and other land, they paying their sisters Hannah and Mary Hart, £5 a year to each, till £50, are paid. To daughters Hannah and Mary, half of household goods and £50. Sons Luke and William, to allow their mother, the firewood, &c., and to find her a jade to ride as often as she shall have occasion.

Inventory, £229, 11*s*., 6*d*., viz: apparel £12, 10*s*., books £14, 4*s*., 6*d*., 7 beds £177, 12*s*., 6*d*., silver spoons and other silver £11, 4*s*., 3 wheels, quilting wheel, pewter, 4 oxen, 5 cows, heifer, 3 calves, 2 two years, 25 sheep, 15 lambs, 6 swine, &c.

Possibly his wife was Sarah Taber, daughter of Thomas & Mary (Thompson) Taber, for the said Sarah married to a Hart.

HAWKINS (WILLIAM).

I. WILLIAM, m. MARY, — b. d. b. d. of. Providence, R. I.

1. Job,

1716, Dec. 14. He (calling himself "Wm. Hawkins, Jr., son of John"), sold 5 acres to Joshua Winsor.

1721, Mar. 6. He and wife Mary for £60, sold Elisha Knowlton, land.

1744, Jan. 7. He deeded son Job, for love, &c., rights in land west of Seven Mile Line.

HAWKINS (WILLIAM). 3d column. II. Edward. Children, 1, Jemima, 1708, Feb. 21. 2, Stephen.

II. EDWARD, m. LYDIA, — b. d. 1741, Aug. 19. b. d. 1641 + of. Providence, R. I.

HAWKINS (WILLIAM). 3d column. II. Edward. His widow d. 1741 +.

1726, Apr. 13. He (calling himself "Edward Hawkins, Jr., son of Mr. John Hawkins, deceased") and wife Lydia, sold for £840, to Joseph Smith (son of Edward Smith, deceased), 194 acres, the homestead farm of honoured father John Hawkins, deceased, dwelling, orchard, &c.

1741, Sep. 18. Administration to widow Lydia. Inventory, £52, 18*s*.

III. Sarah b. 1685, Apr. 15; m. 1708. June 5. Child, 1, Sarah, 1709, May 2.

III. SARAH, m. RICHARD EVANS, — b. d. 1727 + b. 1681, Aug. 10. d. 1726, Nov. 28. of Richard & Mary ( ) Evans.

1. Sarah,

1687, Sep. 1. He and his son John, were taxed together 5*s.*

1688. His ratable estate was returned as follows: 2 oxen, 4 steers, 6 cows, 3 heifers, a horse, 2 mares, 6 acres Indian corn, 3 acres rye, 10 acres meadow, 10 acres pasture.

1699, Jun. 17. He freed his negro Jack, to take effect in twenty-six years from date, "having a respect for him." The negro was twenty years old about, when he bought him in 1695, of William Mackcollin of Barbadoes.

It seems by a deed of his son William, that he made a will, which however, is not found upon the records.

1719, Feb. 11. He confirmed a deed made seventeen years before to youngest son Edward, and now gave him half the homestead, house and lands, and the other half at his decease.

1723, Aug. 24. He and son Edward sold Joseph Mowry 30 acres on south part of farm on which they dwelt.

II. WILLIAM, { b. / d. 1723, Jul. 6. } Providence, R. I.
m. 1678, Jun. 14. [of Geo.
LYDIA GARDINER, (w. { b. / d. 1722 (—) } of Robert & Susanna ( ) Ballou.

1677, Jan. 23. He gave notice that he had found a strange mare of a dark bay color, with four white streaks of saddle gall, &c.

1678. Deputy.

1685, Dec. 3. He had 30 acres laid out in the right of his father William Hawkins, Sr.

1687, Sep. 1. Taxed 7*s.*

1687. Ratable estate, 2 oxen, 6 cows, 4 three year and 2 two year cattle, a horse, 2 mares, 13 acres meadow, 5 acres corn land, 12 acres pasture.

1688, Nov. 30. He took receipt from Mary Gardiner, who calls him father-in-law (*i. e.* stepfather), for £13, balance of legacy of £20, bequeathed by last will of her father George Gardiner of Newport, deceased.

1691, Jan. 9. He received a deed of 12 acres of land in Newport from Joseph Gardiner of that place—said land having been owned by George Gardiner of Newport, father of Joseph Gardiner and Peregrine.

1703–5–6. Deputy.

1704, Jul. 25. He deeded son Stephen, for love, &c., 50 acres and a dwelling house on north-east side of West River mostly, being part of land whereon I dwell.

1708, Sep. 27. He deeded land to son Stephen, for goodwill and affection, and also at same date deeded son John, but John's lands were to be in care of his brother Stephen, till John was of age, and if he died before that, then William and Stephen were to have it.

1713, Jun. 16. Taxed 6*s.*

1721, Jan. 28. He sold William Hopkins a salt cove called Hawkins's Cove, formerly Dirty Cove, which my father William Hawkins, deceased, gave me by his last will. (Consideration £3, 7*s.*, 6*d.*)

1722, Mar. 17. Will—proved 1723, Oct. 22. To his two grandsons Elijah and Joseph (sons of son William, deceased), all the remaining part of homestead farm which had not before been disposed of by deed, being situated north side of West River, and including two houses, barn, orchard, &c. To these grandsons he also gives other land, and if either died without issue other was to have his share. Mem. "That I had before given my children such a portion as I thought convenient, excepting my son William, and this estate I have given to my aforenamed grandsons is that which I intended for their father, my son William Hawkins, deceased." If the grandsons could not agree the Town Council was to make division to them when of age.

Inventory, £40, 13*s.*, of personal property undisposed of, and his son John was appointed administrator of the personal estate, consisting of bed, wearing apparel, pewter, warming pan, money due on bond £20, &c.

III. EDWARD, { b. / d. 1726, May 24. } Providence, R. I.
m. (1) [of Wm.
ESTHER ANDREWS, (w. { b. 1647, Sep. 22. / d. 1688 ± } of Stephen & Sarah (Smith) Arnold.
m. (2)
ANNE, { b. / d. 1745, Sep. 25. } of

1686, Mar. 10. He had 60 acres laid out in his father's right, situated three-quarters of a mile from William Hawkins' now dwelling house.

His first wife had been twice married before; 1st to James Dexter, about 1671, and 2d to Wm. Andrews, 1680, Oct. 30. She had three children by her first husband, viz: Peleg, Isabel, James.

1687, Sep. 1. Taxed 6*s.*

1687. Ratable estate, 2 oxen, 4 cows, 2 steers, 5 heifers, 2 yearlings, 2 horses, 4 mares, 5 acres fenced land of which 1½ acres were planted.

1692, Jun. 25. He and wife Anne sold 50 acres (received from father William Hawkins), to John Aldrich.

1713, Apr. 18. He deeded David Evans and wife, for love and goodwill, &c., 40 acres.

1713, Jun. 16. Taxed 15*s.*

1726, Apr. 16. Will—proved 1726, Jul. 7. Ex. son-in-law Edmond Hawes. To wife Anne, £20, per year for life. To grandson Edward Evans, half a meadow and half a 70 acre lot. To daughter Esther Evans, half of household goods at death of wife and half other movables. To daughter Mary Hawes and son-in-law Edmond Hawes, the homestead farm east side of Seven mile line; and at death of wife, they were to have half of movable estate and household goods. Inventory, £101, 7*s.*, viz: a yoke of oxen, 8 cows, a heifer, calf, 3 swine, 2 spinning wheels, 2 beer barrels, pewter, adze, square, chisel, handsaw, auger, &c.

1734, Dec. 22. Will—proved 1745, Nov. 25. Widow Anne Hawkins, of Smithfield. Ex. friend David Rutenburg. To granddaughter Anne Hawes, all household goods and movables at eighteen or marriage, and if she die before then son-in-law Edmund Hawes to have, and if both die then equally to David Evans's children.

Inventory, £86, 15*s.* 6*d.*

IV. MARY, { b. / d. 1724, Feb. }
m.
JAMES BLACKMAR, { b. / d. 1709, Aug. 14. } of Blackmar.

V. MADELINE, { b. / d. }
m.
JEREMIAH RHODES, { b. 1647, Jun. 24. / d. } of Zachariah & Joanna (Arnold) Rhodes.

IV. ELIZABETH, m. 1699, Apr. 4. JOSEPH SMITH, b. d. b. 1669, Feb. 18. d. 1739, Nov. 8. of Thomas & Ruth (Wickenden) Smith.
1. Sarah, 2. Joseph, 3. Waite,

V. MARY, m. HOSANNAH BROWN, b. d. b. d. of Daniel & Alice (Hearnden) Brown.
1. Mary, 2. Othniel,

VI. LYDIA, m. ELISHA KNOWLTON, b. d. b. d. of Knowlton.

VI. Lydia. Her husband d. 1757, Oct. 20. Children, 1, Thomas. 2, Keziah. 3, Lydia.

VII. ABIGAIL, m. JONATHAN SALISBURY, b. d. b. d. of Cornelius & Mercy ( ) Salisbury.
1. Elizabeth, 1721, Apr. 23. 2. Abigail, 1726, Jul. 18. 3. Jonathan, 1727, Dec. 31. 4. Sarah, 1729, Dec. 12. 5. Bethiah, 1731, Aug. 29. 6. Edward, 1733, Sep. 6. 7. Rhoda, 1735, Oct. 20. 8. Anne, 1737, Nov. 27.

VIII. PATIENCE, m. JOSEPH SMITH, b. d. b. d. of Joseph & Deborah (Whitman) Smith.

I. WILLIAM, m. 1704, Dec. 14. ELIZABETH ARNOLD, b. d. 1712, Oct. 8. b. d. 1758, Jul. 11. of Arnold. Providence, R. I.
1. Elijah, 1705, Sep. 12. 2. Uriah, 1707, Jul. 30. 3. Joseph, 1709, Mar. 29. 4. Ruth, 1711, Mar. 14. 5. Deborah, 1713, May 15.

(She m. (2) 1718, Jun. 3, Israel Smith.)

1712, Dec. 9. Administration on his estate was given his widow Elizabeth. Inventory, £110, 10*d.*, viz: 4 cows, 2 steers, mare, 2 colts, swine, 200lbs. tobacco, cider mill, gun, 2 spinning wheels, 6 barrels of cider, meat in cellar, soap, warming pan, books, &c.

1758, Jul. 1. Will—proved 1758, Jul. 17. Widow Elizabeth Smith, of Glocester. Exs. son Stephen Smith and grandson William Hawkins. To son Stephen Smith, all cooper's tools that did belong to my husband. To daughters Ruth Hopkins and Deborah Wai, best feather bed, equally. To daughter Elizabeth Mann, a chest of drawers. To daughter Naomi Angell, a table and £5. The rest of estate to children, equally, viz: Stephen Smith, Ruth Hopkins, Deborah Wai, Elizabeth Mann and Naomi Angell. To son Elijah Hawkins' children, nothing, he having had his part. To granddaughter Elizabeth Hopkins, silver sleeve buttons. To granddaughter Martha Smith, sleeve buttons, &c.

II. STEPHEN, m. 1706, Feb. 6. HANNAH COGGESHALL, b. d. 1711, Mar. 10. b. d. 1711 + of Coggeshall. Providence, R. I.
1. Jemima, 1708, Sep. 30. 2. Keziah, 1710, Jan. 30.

(She m. (2) 1713, Sep. 17, Jonathan Sprague, Jr.)

1705, May 29. He had land laid out.

1711, Apr. 9. Administration to widow Hannah. Inventory, bible and other small books, silver cup, warming pan, wearing apparel, money 17*s.*, yoke of small cattle, 2 cows, 2 yearlings, mare, 17 sheep, 2 lambs, 4 small swine, Indian girl servant £1, 10*s.*, &c.

1730, Oct. 20. Partition was made of land of deceased by his only heirs, viz: Jemima, who had married Zephaniah Peck, and Keziah, who had married Job Arnold, these being the two daughters of deceased.

III. JOHN, m. MARY, b. d. 1755, Mar. 25. b. d. 1755 + of Providence, R. I.
1. Stephen, 2. Isaiah, 3. Jeremiah, 4. Zephaniah, 5. Lydia, 6. Abigail, 7. Martha, 8. Sarah, 9. Mary,

1725, Dec. 17. He sold James Dexter, 29¼ acres for £31, 10*s.*, calling himself John Hawkins, Jr., (to avoid confusion with his uncle John probably.)

1755, Mar. 22. Will—proved 1755, May 31. Exs. sons Isaiah and Zephaniah. To wife Mary, use of biggest room in house and bedroom adjoining below stairs, with privilege of cellar and three cows and keep of same by son Zephaniah, who was to provide his mother with firewood, all while widow only. To son Zephaniah, all that part of homestead where I dwell being north-east of a certain line, with buildings, &c. To sons Isaiah and Jeremiah and grandson Ezekiel, son of my son Stephen, deceased, all rest of homestead farm, but whereas it is doubtful grandson Ezekiel will be capable to support himself by reason of incapacity, if he so prove then sons Isaiah and Jeremiah to be obliged to look after him for his life, and his lands to be to Isaiah and Jeremiah. To sons Isaiah, Jeremiah and Zephaniah, other lands. To wife Mary, a feather bed and other household stuff sufficient to keep house with. To three daughters Lydia Olney, Abigail Sayles and Martha Olney, £50, each. To daughters Sarah and Mary Hawkins, £120, each. Rest of personal, except legacies, to wife and five daughters. To son Zephaniah, cider mill and press (with use of press to other two sons), carpenter and husbandry tools, &c.

Inventory, £1,535, 12*s.*, viz: bible and other books £3, flax hetchel, 3 spinning wheels, tobacco, apple mill and press £30, cheese tub, 12 sheep, mare, 6 cows, 2 steers, bull, heifer, 2 yearlings, swine, pigs, &c.

IV. SARAH, m. ELEAZER ARNOLD, b. d. 1722 + b. d. 1712, Dec. 18. of Eleazer & Eleanor (Smith) Arnold.
1. Eleazer, 2. David, 3. Susanna, 4. Lydia, 5. Patience.

I. ESTHER, m. DAVID EVANS, b. 1685, Jul. 19. d. b. d. 1754 + of Richard & Mary ( ) Evans.
1. Edward, 1710, Nov. 27. 2. Anne, 1712, Sep. 2. 3. Esther, 1714, Dec. 17. 4. Thankful, 1718, Feb. 17. 5. David, 1721, May 16. 6. Zerviah, 1724, Nov. 17.

HAWKINS (WILLIAM). 3d column. I. Esther. Her husband b. 1684, Mar. 9.

(2D WIFE.)

II. MARY, m. 1722, May 8. EDMOND HAWES, b. 1690, Dec. 11. d. b. d. of John & Mary ( ) Hawes.
1. John, 1725, Aug. 30. 2. Mary, 1727, Aug. 31. 3. Anne,

III. ANNE, b. 1697, Sep. 22. d. young.

1. John,
2. Mary.
3. Elizabeth, 1682.

1. Zachariah.
2. John,
3. Daughter.

 See: American Genealogist, v. 20. p. 187.

THOMAS,	b. 1610.	Boston, Mass., Portsmouth, R. I.
m. (1)	d. 1680 +	
MARTHA,	b.	
m (2) 1675. [Thomas.	d. 1669 +	
MARTHA SHERIFF (w. of	b.	
	d. 1691 +	

He was a ship carpenter.

1635, He was at Boston thus early.

1636, Mar. 25. Freeman.

1638. Portsmouth. He was among those admitted as inhabitants of Aquidneck.

1639, Apr. 28. He and eight others signed the following compact preparatory to the settlement of Newport. "It is agreed by us whose hands are underwritten to propagate a plantation in the midst of the island, or elsewheres, and to engage ourselves to bear equal charge, answerable to our strength and estates in common; and that our determination shall be by major voices of judge and elders, the judge to have a double voice."

1639, Jun. 5. Newport. He was named as one of four proportioners of land, any three of whom might proportion it, the company laying it forth to have 4*d.* an acre for every acre laid out.

1639, Sep. 2. Freeman.

1640, Mar. 12. Member of General Court of Elections.

1641, Mar. 16. Freeman.

1655. Portsmouth. Freeman.

1656. Newtown (Long Island), N. Y. He remained here but a short time.

1658, Jan. 30. Portsmouth. He deeded as dower, with his daughter Hannah Hazard, unto Stephen Wilcox, of Portsmouth, 34 acres adjoining farm of said Hazard.

1666, Dec. 10. He deeded Thomas Sheriff, house, 30 acres, orchard, &c., in Portsmouth, for £20, and a quarter of a share in Misquamicut. Possession was not to be had till death of said Thomas Hazard, and then to be for Thomas Sheriff and his wife Martha for life, and at death of both to go to second son John Sheriff, and he failing of issue to go to third son, Caleb Sheriff, &c.

1669, Nov. 30. Will. Ex. son Robert. He mentions wife Martha, daughters Elizabeth, wife of George Lawton, Hannah, wife of Stephen Wilcox of Misquamicut, and Martha, wife of Ichabod Potter, son Robert Hazard, and grandson Thomas Hazard. (This will was rendered void by later ones.)

1674, Oct. 16. He testified as to the corn mill at Pawtuxet in controversy between Stephen Arnold and Samuel Reape, calling his age sixty-four years.

1675, May 29. He recorded a declaration previous to making his marriage with Martha Sheriff, widow of Thomas Sheriff. "This is to notify all men whom it may anyway concern, whereas there is promise of matrimony betwixt Thomas Hazard and Martha Sheriff, yet I, the aforesaid Thomas Hazard, do take the same Martha Sheriff for her own person, without having anything to do with her estate, or anything that is hers' for matter of goods," &c.

1677, Aug. 6. He had his declaration recorded: that whereas son Robert claims right to my lands by virtue of a writing as he saith by me formerly passed and given him, &c.—this is denied. I, Thomas Hazard, do by these presents solemnly protest and affirm that I never made any writing, only in a will drawn by John Porter at John Lawton's house about thirty years past, wherein if I had then deceased, being sick and weak, my said son was to have had my lands and my other children my movables; nor made any writing to said son only in a will 1669, Nov. 30, in which I appointed him executor, since which time have seen cause to make null and void, and do absolutely abolish the two wills and have made another will dated 1676, Nov. 6.

1676, Nov. 13. Will. Exx. wife Martha. To her, 30 acres in Portsmouth for life, as declared in deed to Thomas Sheriff, dated 1666, Dec. 10, by which said Thomas Hazard was to have for life and then to my beloved yoke fellow Martha Hazard. To wife also all movable and immovable estate, as housing, goods, cattle and chattels. To son Robert, 1*s.* To daughters Hannah Wilcox and Martha Potter, wife of Ichabod Potter, 1*s.*

1680. Taxed 9*s.* 6*d.*

I. ROBERT,	b. 1635.		Portsmouth, Kings Town, R. I.
m.	d. 1710 +		
MARY BROWNELL,	b. 1639.		
	d. 1739, Jan. 12.	of Thomas & Anne ( )	Brownell.

1655. Freeman.

1658, Jan. 2. He sold John Roome, of Portsmouth, all his interest in Conanicut and Dutch Islands (1-300 part).

1659, Mar. 13. He and wife Mary sold James Sands 8 acres.

1662-70. Commissioner.

1663, Mar. 1. He bought 25 acres of Abel Potter.

1664-65-67-70-71. Deputy.

1667, Oct. 31. The Court at Plymouth ordered in reference to a controversy between the English and Indians about bounds in Dartmouth, that in case Robert Hazard of Rhode Island may be procured, he should run the line, &c.

1670-71. Juryman.

1671. He bought 500 acres in Kings Town of the Pettaquamscott purchasers.

1671, Nov. 24. He sold Gideon Freeborn, for £18, two-thirds of 10 acres in Narragansett, having sold the other third to George Brownell.

1676, Mar. 13. He, and three others of Portsmouth, were a committee who were ordered by Assembly to appoint their own men as keepers of Indians above twelve years of age (in custody of several inhabitants), that the Indians should be so secured as that they may be hindered from doing damage to the inhabitants in this juncture of time, &c. The Indians were to have a sufficient keeper in company with them by day, and locked up at night in a sufficient place of security. Any master offending was to pay a fine of £5.

1676, Apr. 4. He was on a committee to procure boats for the colony's defence for the present, and there were to be four boats with five or six men in each. At the same date he and three others were empowered to take the exact account of all inhabitants on the island, English, negroes and Indians, and make a list of same, and also to take account how all persons are provided with corn, guns, powder, shot and lead. A barrel of powder was put in charge of himself and three others, and two great guns in the yard of late deceased William Brenton were to be pressed for country's service and carried to Portsmouth, and placed one in the Ferry Neck and one near the house of John Borden. Robert Hazard and three others were to cause said guns to be set on carriages and fitted for service.

1676, Apr. 11. He and others were appointed as commissioners "to take care and order the several watches and wards on this island and appoint the places."

1680. Taxed £1, 5*s.*

1686, Jan. 6. He signed in full consent of a deed given by his nephew Edward Wilcox, of Westerly, to Isaac Lawton, of Portsmouth, of 60 acres, buildings, &c., in Portsmouth.

1687, Sep. 6. Kings Town. Taxed 11*s.* 7*d.*

1693, Jan. 14. He deeded son Stephen, for love, &c., certain land at Point Judith Neck. (He calls himself late of Portsmouth, now of Kings Town.)

1698, May 2. He deeded son Jeremiah, for love, &c., right in 200 acres in Tiverton.

1710, Dec. 9. He deeded to son Robert for £300, land where I now dwell, 100 acres, with housing, orchard, &c.

1734, Jan. 29. His widow had a legacy from will of her sister Martha Dyer, of a third of her wearing apparel.

1739. His widow's estate was divided by agreement of her heirs, as appears by deposition of Stephen Hull. The deponent stated that sometime in January or February he was at the house where Robert Hazard, son of Robert, now lives, and there were several people gathered, it being after the death of Mrs. Mary Hazard, widow, and they were about dividing her estate. The persons concerned in the division were Thomas Hazard, George Hazard, Sarah Watson, Stephen Hazard and Stephen Champlin, all of South Kingstown; Jeremiah Hazard, Martha Wilcox and Jeffrey Hazard, all of North Kingstown, and Stephen Wilcox, of Charlestown. It was debated whether they should divide the estate without proving the will of said Mary, and Thomas Hazard said he was very free to do it either way, and they all agreed the estate should be divided without proving the will. Robert Wilcox deposed that in said will, which was read, half of said Mary's estate within doors was given Martha Wilcox, and that the executor of the will was Thomas Hazard. Robert Hazard deposed that he read the will to Martha Wilcox, widow, daughter of Mary Hazard. (The above depositions were brought in as evidence in a suit by Martha Wilcox against Thomas Hazard for concealing the will, and the court of Common Pleas having decided against her, she appealed the case to Supreme Court.)

II. Thomas of Newtown, Long Island, abt. 1652-3.

III. Jonathan of Newtown in 1664

IV Nathaniel of Newtown in 1659

HAZARD. 3d column. I. Thomas. His wife was probably Susanna Nichols, b. 1669, Oct. 15, of Thomas and Hannah ( ) Nichols.

I. THOMAS, b. 1660. d. 1746.
m.
SUSANNA, b. d. 1746 (—) of

Portsmouth, South Kingstown, R. I.

1. Mary, 1683, Oct. 3.
2. Hannah, 1685, Apr. 14.
3. Sarah, 1687, Jul. 15.
4. Robert, 1689, May 23.
5. Thomas, 1691, May 11.
6. Stephen, 1693, Jun. 13.
7. Jeremiah, 1697, Jun. 5.
8. George, 1699, Jan. 18.
9. Benjamin, 1702, Nov. 2.
10. Jonathan, 1704, Oct. 1.

1684. Freeman.

1738, Mar. 23. He testified, calling himself aged seventy-eight years and upwards, that his father was formerly a surveyor and was employed by the purchasers of Pettaquamscott, &c.

1746, Nov. 12. Will—proved 1746, Nov. 27. Ex. son Robert. To sons Jeremiah, George, Benjamin and Jonathan, 5*s*. each, all having had their portions. To grandson Fones Hazard, 260 acres, and 116 acres, and if he die, then to my four sons Robert, George, Benjamin and Jonathan. To daughter Hannah Easton, 5*s*. To granddaughters Miriam Hazard and Hannah Easton, children of daughter Mary Easton, of Newport, deceased, £100, each, in ten years after my decease. To granddaughter Mary Hazard, £50, in ten years. To granddaughter Susannah Gardiner, £50, in ten years. To children of my granddaughter Ruth Underwood, deceased, £50, equally. To my daughter Easton, £200, in ten years, but if she needs it before, executors to pay her, and if she die then to go to her sons James and John Easton. To children of my granddaughter Sarah Gardiner, which she had by Ichabod Potter, deceased, £50, equally. To son Robert, 5*s*. and all remaining part of estate of all kinds.

Inventory, £3,745, 1*s*. 9*d*, viz: wearing apparel £40, 15*s*, beds, large bible and other books £2, 15*s*., money scales, silver buttons 5*s*. 1*d*., silver spoon, bond £1,367, 17*s*., bond £2,116, desk, looking glass, warming pan, 2 cows, &c.

II. GEORGE, b. d. 1743.
m.
PENELOPE ARNOLD, b. 1669, Aug. 3. d. 1742 + of Caleb & Abigail (Wilbur) Arnold.

South Kingstown, R. I.

1. Abigail 1690, Mar. 19.
2. Robert, 1694, Nov. 3.
3. Caleb, 1697, Nov. 24.
4. George, 1700, Oct. 9.
5. Thomas, 1704, Mar. 30.
6. Oliver, 1710, Sep. 13.

1696. Kings Town. Freeman.

1701-2-6-7-8-9-12-13. Deputy.

1702-3. Assistant.

1713, May 6. He was appointed by the Assembly on a committee to make the public road leading through this colony from Pawtucket River to Pawcatuck River, more straight, fair and passable.

1719-20. Lieutenant Colonel of militia for the main land.

1742, Nov. 3. Will—proved 1743, Nov. 14. Ex. son Thomas. To wife Penelope, half my house for life, two negroes Jack and Jane, three cows kept for her, by son Thomas in summer, and son Oliver in winter, a riding beast kept by son Thomas, and £20, per year paid by said son, he also providing for her forty pounds of wool, one fat beeve, two fat hogs, firewood cut for her on his land, and son Thomas further to allow her 2 acres of good corn. To wife, also, two good beds, and what household stuff necessary. To son Thomas, homestead where I live, housing, &c., and all goods, chattels and credit, and he to have the profits till 1747, of northern part of the Back Side Farm, and profits of land given grandsons Robert and Caleb, till said Caleb is twenty-one. To son Oliver, 300 acres, other land, negroes Cæsar, Mingo and Prish, 2 cows and money he oweth the colony. To grandson William, 10*s*., and to grandsons Robert and Caleb, certain land; their father Caleb having had before his death 170 acres deeded to him. To grandson Ebenezer Niles, 5*s*. he having had his portion. To granddaughter Penelope Niles, negro girl Betty, and £100. To granddaughter Sarah Niles, 5*s*. having had. To granddaughter Abigail, negro Jenny and £100. To grandchildren Mary, George, Abigail, Sarah, Penelope and Carder, each 10*s*. To son Thomas, all estate real and personal remaining.

Inventory, £3,321, 17*s*. 8*d*., viz: wearing apparel £71, 16*s*., silver tankard £35, 11 silver spoons £22, 10*s*., beds, pewter, 2 pair stillyards, linen wheel, gun, negro Joe £150, Jack £150, Paro £140, Harry £120, Will £110, Jacob £70, John £55, Dinah £40, Janey £130, Betty £100, Cuff and infant £20, Moll £120, 31 cows, pair of oxen, 2 pair of steers, 6 yearlings, 165 sheep, 5 fat pigs, 5 store pigs, 7 pigs, mare, 4 colts, 20 calves, 60 loads of hay £240, &c.

III. STEPHEN, b. d. 1727, Sep. 29.
m.
ELIZABETH HELME, b. d. 1727 (—) of Rouse & Mary ( ) Helme.

South Kingstown, R. I.

1. Mary, 1695, Jul. 20.
2. Hannah, 1697, Apr. 20.
3. Susanna, 1699, Apr. 23.
4. Stephen, 1700, Nov. 29.
5. Robert, 1702, Sep. 12.
6. Samuel, 1705, Jun. 29.
7. Thomas, 1707, Jul. 28.
8. Elizabeth,
9. Sarah,

1687, Sep. 6. Kings Town. Taxed 1*s*.

1696. Freeman.

1702 6-8-9-15. Deputy.

1708-18-19-20-21-22. Assistant.

1715, Jun. 13. He was allowed 18*s*. by Assembly for running the line between Eldred's Purchase and Hall's Purchase.

1727, Sep. 19. Will—proved 1727, Oct. 9. Exs. sons Stephen and Robert. To son Stephen, land where I live in Point Judith Neck, 150 acres, housing, &c., he paying to my son Samuel, £50, and to my daughter Hannah Mumford, £50. To son Stephen also, 50 acres in north-west corner of said homestead. To son Robert, remaining part of homestead, he paying Samuel, £150. To son Robert, also, negro called Long Joe. To son Samuel, land in North Kingstown, 200 acres called Middleport Neck, part of Mumford Island, &c. To son Thomas, 300 acres in North Kingstown, and rest of Mumford Island in Point Judith Pond. To son Samuel, negro Short Joe and negro woman Megg. To son Thomas, negro boy Jefferay. To daughter Hannah Mumford, £250. To daughter Susanna Perry, £250. To daughter Elizabeth Hazard, £600. To daughter Sarah Hazard, £600, at eighteen.

Inventory, £2,760, 15*s*., viz: suit of wearing apparel with silver buttons, and a new beaver hat £19, 15*s*. 6*d*., rest of apparel £10, 16*s*. 6*d*., bond £522, and other bonds, book debts £126, 19*s*. 1*d*., silver tankard £24, 18*s*. 8*d*., 4 silver spoons £5, 8*s*. 2*d*., pair of silver shoe buckles, &c., case of bottles with some metheglin £1, 10*s*., pewter, 7 feather beds, stillyards, warming pan, woolen and linen wheel, canoe, 4 apprentices £40, negro Long Joe £100, Megg £80, boy slave Jefferay £85, books £21, 7 horses, 4 fat oxen, fat cow, 36 milch cows and heifers, 4 working oxen, 22 fat cattle, and a fat bull, all on the Great Island; a three year, 31 two year, 29 yearlings, 24 calves, 4 working neat cattle, cow, 15 horsekind, 21 swine, 5 shoats, 24 geese, turkeys and other fowls, 4 hives of bees, &c.

IV. MARTHA, b. d. 1753.
m.
THOMAS WILCOX, b. d. 17? of Stephen & Hannah (Hazard) Wilcox.

1. Robert,
2. Stephen,
3. Jeffrey,
4. Thomas, 1693, Oct. 24.
5. Abraham,
6. George,
7. Edward,
8. Hannah,

V. ——— b. d.
m.
EDWARD WILCOX, b. 1662 + d. 1715, Nov. 5. of Stephen & Hannah (Hazard) Wilcox.

1. Mary,
2. Hannah,
3. Stephen,
4. Edward,

× See: American Genealogist v. 32, no. 1, Jan., 1956, p. 39.

VI. ROBERT, b. d. 1718.
m.
AMEY, × b. d. 1718 + of

Kings Town, R. I.

1. Jeffrey, 1698, Sep. 29.
2. Susanna, 1701, Jan. 16.
3. Hannah, 1703, Feb. 26.
4. Robert, 1709, Jan. 19.
5. Thomas, 1713, Jun. 18.
6. Amey, 1715, Sep. 20.
7. Mary, 1718, May 14.

1696. Freeman.

1718, Sep. 30. Will—proved 1718, Nov. 10. Ex. son Jeffrey. Overseer, brother Thomas. To wife Amey, great room of dwelling house where I live, £20, a year while widow, cow, riding beast, bed, keep of cow, and what household stuff is convenient. To son Jeffrey, farm where I now live of 300 acres. To son Robert, land in Kings Town where my mother liveth, 100 acres, with housing, &c., after death of his grandmother. To son Thomas, 200 acres in Kings Town and 165 acres at Westerly, at eighteen. To daughter Susanna Hazard, £100, and like amount each, to daughters Amey and Mary, at seventeen. To son Jeffrey, rest of real and personal, he bringing up children, &c.

Inventory, £748, 9*s*. 8*d*., viz: wearing apparel, 2 bibles and other books £3, 15*s*., beds, loom, spinning wheel, churn, 2 guns, warming pan, 3 Indian children servants £23, 5 swine, 4 shoats, 11 pigs, 30 geese and turkeys, 219 sheep and lambs, 6 working oxen, 9 steers, 26 cows, 8 yearlings, riding beast, bull, 8 calves, horse, 6 mares, 5 colts, 4 yearling jades, &c.

VII. JEREMIAH, b. 1675, Mar. 25. d. 1768, Feb. 2.
m.
SARAH SMITH, b. 1678, Apr. d. 1765, Mar. 12. of Jeremiah & Mary (Gereardy) Smith.

North Kingstown, R. I.

1. Mary, 1699, Mar. 16.
2. Ann, 1701, Feb. 28.
3. Robert, 1703, Apr. 11.
4. Sarah, 1706, Jan. 11.
5. Martha, 1708, Oct. 8.
6. Hannah, 1714, Apr.
7. Susanna, 1716, May 21.

1707, Apr 18. Kings Town. He and wife Sarah sold land to William Browning.

1710, May 17. He and seventeen others bought 2,000 acres of the vacant lands ordered sold by Assembly.

VIII. MARY, b. 1676. d. 1722.
m. 1704, Oct. 19.
JOHN ROBINSON, b. 1680. d. 1712, Apr. 6. of Rowland & Mary (Allen) Robinson.

1. Mary, 1705, Sep. 30.
2. Sarah, 1707, Jan. 22.
3. Ruth, 1709, Mar. 12.
4. Susannah, 1712, Feb. 9.

HAZARD. 3d column. VIII. Mary. Erase her and children. It was Mary,[4] (Thomas,[3] Robert,[2] Thomas,[1]) who married John Robinson. She m. (2) Peter Easton.

II. ELIZABETH, m. GEORGE LAWTON, { b. d. } { b. d. 1693, Oct. 5. } of Lawton.

III. HANNAH, m. 1658. STEPHEN WILCOX, { b. d. } { b. 1633 ± d. 1690 ± } of Edward Wilcox

IV. MARTHA, m. (1) ICHABOD POTTER, m. (2) BENJAMIN MOWRY, { b. d. } { b. d. 1676. } of Nathaniel & Dorothy ( ) Potter. { b. 1649, May 8. d. 1719 + } of Roger & Mary ( ) Mowry.

(2D WIFE, no issue.)

HELME.

CHRISTOPHER, m. MARGARET, { b. d. 1650. } { b. d. 1650 + } Warwick, R. I.

1647, Aug. 8. Sergeant.

1648. Member of Court of Trials.

1648, Jan. 23. He bound himself for any damage by occasion of receiving into my custody Robert Andrews, after the town had sent him back to master and he escaped from messenger.

1649, Jan. 23. He was disfranchised "for going about to undermine the liberty of the town," but subsequently the censure was removed.

He had died before December of 1650.

See: American Genealogist, v. 20, p. 223-4.

I. WILLIAM, { b. d. } Warwick, Kings Town, R. I.

1661, Jan. 13. He, eldest son and heir of Christopher Helme and Margaret, late of Warwick, now deceased, confirmed a purchase made by Richard Carder from my loving mother Margaret (late of Warwick) some eight years since. He also ratified a deed from Margaret and her attorney Ralph Earle, of Portsmouth, bearing date 1650, Dec. 19. He acknowledges himself satisfied for 6 acres of land and house, sold Richard Carder.

1671, May 20. Kings Town. He took oath of fidelity.

II. CHRISTOPHER, { b. d. } Kings Town, R. I.

1671, May 19. He took oath of fidelity.

1673. Freeman.

III. SAMUEL, { b. d. } Kings Town, R. I.

1673. Freeman.

IV. ROUSE, m. MARY, { b. d. 1712, May 17. } { b. d. 1712, May 9. } of Kings Town, R. I.

1671, May 19. He took oath of fidelity.

1671, May 28. He took as apprentice Thomas Marshall, with the consent of the boy's father and mother, Edward and Mary Marshall of Warwick.

1679, Jul. 29. He and forty-one other inhabitants of Narragansett petitioned the King, praying that he "would put an end to these differences about the government thereof, which hath been so fatal to the prosperity of the place, animosities still arising in people's minds as they stand affected to this or that government."

1684, Oct. 27. He took a receipt from Thomas Marshall, whose term of apprenticeship had ended.

1687, Sep. 6. Taxed 9*s.*, 11*d.*

1687. Grand Jury.

1692, Jan. 30. He sold James Carder, of Warwick, 26 acres, 12 acres, a whole right of undivided land, and a right in commons, and all other interests there, for £50.

1711, Mar. 14. Will—proved 1712, Jun. 9. Exs. wife Mary and son Rouse. Overseers, Thomas Eldred, John Eldred, William Knowles and Ephraim Bull. To son Samuel, east part of a farm (reserving 30 acres to be for wife's maintenance for life and then to son Rouse), so long as my son William liveth and then to return to son Samuel. To son Rouse, rest of above land and housing, and orchards and other land and negro Jack. To wife, half of the use of house, barn and orchard for life. To daughter Elizabeth Hazard, £5, paid by her brother Rouse, and to her a negro girl. To son Samuel, youngest negro boy. To daughter Margaret Potter, negro Moll. To daughter Mercy Watson, a heifer. To wife Mary, half of movables to dispose of to children, and the other half equally, to son Samuel and daughters Margaret Potter and Mercy Watson, and sons Rouse and William, but son Rouse to have William's part to keep him and if Rouse dies before William, the part given for care of William, to go to those who take care of him and to find him in meat, drink, apparel, lodging, &c. All the children are charged to have a tender care of William.

Inventory, £284, 17*s.*, 1*d.*, viz: 77 sheep, 37 lambs, 4 oxen, 5 cows and calves, 2 three years, 5 two years, 4 yearlings, horse, 5 mares, 4 colts, negro Jack £30, Nan £15, stillyards, money scales, gun, 4 swine, &c.

1713, Oct. 21. A declaration signed by Mary Coggeshall and Ezekiel Bull that Rouse Helme's wife died before him and that he considering his wife's care of son William, that she would have taken, &c., desired her part given to his son Rouse.

IX. HANNAH, b. d.
m.
JEFFREY CHAMPLIN, b. d. 1718 + of Jeffrey Champlin.

1. Thomas, 1708, Sep. 3.
2. Stephen, 1710, Feb. 16.
3. William, 1713, Mar. 3.

1. Isabel,
2. John,
3. Mary,
4. George,
5. Robert,
6. Susanna,
7. Ruth,
8. Mercy,
9. Job,
10. Elizabeth.

1. Edward, 1662 ±
2. Thomas,
3. Daniel,
4. William,
5. Stephen,
6. Hannah,
7. Jeremiah.

1. Thomas,
2. John,
3. Robert,
4. Ichabod,
(By 2d husband.)
5. Roger,
6. Joseph,
7. Benjamin,
8. John.

HELME.

South Kingstown, R. I.

I. SAMUEL, b. d. 1728.
m.
DORCAS, b. d. 1727 (—) of

1727, Sep. 3. Will—proved 1728, Feb. 12. Ex. son Christopher. To son Christopher, my homestead farm, house, &c., he paying legacies, and to him all movable estate in doors and out. To son John. £100. To son Samuel, £100. To son William, £70, at age To son Thomas, £70, at age. To daughter Mary Perry, 10s., she having had. To daughter Dorcas Helme, £40, at eighteen and a feather bed To daughter Mercy Helme, £40, feather bed, riding beast and side saddle. The Town Council to be guardian to young children and William and Thomas to learn to read, write, and cipher, and to be put out to a trade, and Mercy to learn to read the bible.

1. Mary, 1700, Jun. 14.
2. Christopher 1702, Mar. 30.
3. John, 1704, Feb. 11.
4. Samuel, 1706, Oct. 21.
5. Dorcas, 1710, Jun. 14.
6. William, 1714, Mar. 12.
7. Thomas, 1718, Jan. 3.
8. Mercy,

II. ELIZABETH, b. d. 1727 (—)
m.
STEPHEN HAZARD. b. d. 1727, Sep. 29. of Robert & Mary (Brownell) Hazard.

1. Mary, 1695, Jul. 20.
2. Hannah, 1697, Apr. 20.
3. Susanna, 1699, Apr. 20.
4. Stephen, 1700, Nov. 29.
5. Robert, 1702, Sep. 12.
6. Samuel, 1705, Jun. 29.
7. Thomas, 1707, Jul. 28.
8. Elizabeth,
9. Sarah,

III. MARGARET, b. 1679. d. 1727 (—)
m.
ICHABOD POTTER, b. d. 1730. of Ichabod & Martha (Hazard) Potter.

1. Ichabod,
2. Rouse, 1703, Feb. 13.
3. Thomas,
4. William, 1709, Mar. 4.
5. Margaret, 1714, Oct. 11.

IV. MERCY, b. d.
m.
WILLIAM WATSON, b. d. 1740 + of John & Dorcas (Gardiner) Watson.

HELME. 3d column. IV. Mercy m. Samuel Watson, (not William).

1. William,

South Kingstown, R. I.

V. ROUSE, b. d. 1751, Aug. 28.
m. 1709, Jul, 21.
SARAH NILES, b. d. 1748 + of Nathaniel & Sarah (Sands) Niles.

1714-17-20-22. Deputy.
1717-23-24-25-26-27-28-29-30-31-32-33-34-35-36-37-38-39-40-41-42-43-44. Assistant.
1720. Clerk of Assembly.
The Town records state that he was Judge of the Superior Court over twenty years successively.
1723, Feb. He and Francis Willett were appointed by Assembly to draw a copy of all records belonging to South Kingstown, from the records of the late Kings Town, and then to be delivered to the clerk of South Kingstown. (The two towns of North and South Kingstown had been lately formed from Kings Town.)
1723, Nov. 26. He and Francis Willett petitioned for their pay for transcribing 1,230 pages, £66; being willing in consideration of prompt payment to take £60, the towns of North and South Kingstown having refused. The Assembly ordered North Kingstown to pay £30, to Willett, and South Kingstown, £30 to Helme, and if the towns refused, the General Treasurer to pay same, and withhold certain interest money from town.
1748, Apr. 15. Will—proved 1751, Sep. 9. Exs. sons James and Rouse. To wife Sarah, half of dwelling house and a third of whole estate real and personal for life. To daughter Sarah Helme, £150. To six sons James, Rouse, Nathaniel, Silas, Oliver and Samuel, rest of estate. At death of wife all the sons, except James and Rouse who have had their parts, to have the house and land. The two youngest sons Oliver and Samuel to have opportunity of learning a trade, being bound out, and they to have my tools, equally. All sons and daughters to be kind to your mother, and dutiful to her in all respects.

1. James, 1710, May 7.
2. Sands, 1711, Aug. 21.
3. Rouse, 1713, Feb. 11.
4. Nathaniel, 1714, Dec. 17.
5. Benedict, 1717, Feb. 17.
6. Simeon, 1718, Dec. 15.
7. Benedict, 1720, Oct. 3.
8. Silas, 1724, May 20.
9. Sarah, 1727, May 16.
10. Jonathan, 1729, Oct. 14.
11. Oliver, 1731, Jun. 17.
12. Samuel, 1734, Jun. 3.

VI. WILLIAM, b. d.

Thomas Hopkins. See also: Bowen's PROVIDENCE OATH OF ALLEGIANCE, p. 67-69.

THOMAS[2] (William[1]). b. 1616. Providence, R. I., Oyster Bay, N. Y.
m. d. 1684.
——— b.
d.

1640, Jul. 27. He and thirty-eight others signed an agreement for a form of government.

1650, Sep. 2. Taxed 13s., 4d.

1652-59-60 Commissioner.

1655. Freeman.

1665, Feb. 19. He had lot 93, in a division of lands.

1665-66-67-72. Deputy.

1667-72. Town Council.

1675. Oyster Bay. He removed here at the outbreak of King Philip's war or a little earlier, with a son who died before his father.

1684, Sep. 17. It was ordered by the authorities of Oyster Bay, on the application of William and Thomas Hopkins, of Providence, sons of deceased Thomas Hopkins, that an inventory should be taken on the estate of said Thomas Hopkins, Sr., who had deceased at the house of Richard Kirby, of Oyster Bay.

1684, Nov. 10. On receipt of a letter from Richard Kirby in regard to the death of Thomas Hopkins, the two sons in Providence to whom the letter was addressed, wrote to the Selectmen of Oyster Bay, of plantation called Littleworth, asking them to appoint Ephraim Carpenter and William Thornicraft to look after the matter of the estate for them: "For we do conclude them to be men knowing as to our father's affairs," &c.

1685, Oct. 29. Administration on the estate having been given to the oldest son, William Hopkins, he wrote at this date to the authorities at Oyster Bay, that with consent of younger brother Thomas he desired the estate movable of his father divided as follows: To our sister Elizabeth Kirby, wife of Richard Kirby, 10s., and to each of her children by him, 5s., and all the rest of estate not before disposed of to the two children Anne and Ichabod of our said sister Elizabeth which she had before she married Richard Kirby. The administrator appointed as overseers, Ephraim Carpenter and William Thornicraft of Musketo Cove, and Richard Kirby of Littleworth, to look after the interests of the two children.

See: American Genealogist, v. 20, p. 224-225.

I. WILLIAM, b. 1647. Providence, R. I.
m. 1682, Jan. d. 1723, Jul. 8.
ABIGAIL DEXTER, (w. of Stephen) b.
d. 1725, Aug. 19. of John & Sarah ( ) Whipple.

He was a surveyor, besides having other occupations.

1672, Apr. 30. Freeman.

1674-77-80-82-93-95-97-99-1710-12-13-14-15-16. Deputy.

1676, Aug. 14. He was one of those "who staid and went not away" in King Philip's War, and so had a share in the disposition of the Indian captives whose services were sold for a term of years.

1679, Jul. 1. Taxed 5s., "Captain Hopkins and his father's right."

1679, Dec. 5. In a deposition of this date he calls himself aged thirty-two years.

1681-82-83-87-91-93-94-95-96-97-98-99-1707-8-9-10-11-12-13-14-15. Town Council.

1682. Town Treasurer.

1687, Sep. 1. Taxed 7s., 7d.

1688. Ratable estate, 2 oxen, 5 cows, 3 heifers, 5 yearlings, bull, 9 sheep, 3 swine, 2 horses, mare, 2 colts, 2 shares of meadow, 6 acres of planting land, 20 acres pasture, 40 acres vacant lands, a right in land.

1692, Dec. 22. He deeded his beloved brother Thomas for natural affection, &c., 20 acres where said Thomas dwelleth, with half of right in common belonging to my father Thomas Hopkins, deceased, and a forty foot lot.

1696, Jan. 27. He and others were granted by the town a lot 40 by 40 feet to set a school house on if they would build in some considerable time.

1698. Major for the main land.

1700-1-2-3-4-5-6-7. Assistant.

1703, Oct. 27. He and two others were appointed by the Assembly to run the line between Rhode Island and Connecticut according to agreement of the Commissioners of two colonies.

1715-16. Speaker of the House of Deputies.

1723, Jul. 1. Will—proved 1723, Sep. 30. Exx. wife Abigail. To grandson William, all that my homestead, meadows and tenements, where I now dwell near place called Massapauge, 200 acres in all, on condition that wife Abigail shall have a convenient room and be provided for in sickness and health for life, if she remain a widow. If she is not contented to dwell with grandson, he to maintain her at another place of her choosing. The said grandson shall not dispose of any part of estate during his grandmother's life, and he is to give his brother Rufus, when twenty-one, privilege of cutting two loads of hay yearly. To grandson Rufus, a house lot upon Stamper's Hill. To son William, the farm where he dwells and all other lands not disposed of either in Providence or elsewhere. To grandson William, a feather bed and cow, having before given him a heifer. To wife Abigail, rest of movables to dispose of to my children and grandchildren, and what estate she brought with her to do with as she will.

Inventory, £111, 1s., 6d., viz: rapier, cane, bible, law book, 5 pewter platters, feather bed, 2 spinning wheels, 4 cows, 3 swine, 4 shoats, silver money £2, 7s., 4d., &c. The rooms named were the great room, bedroom, chamber bedroom, leanto chamber.

1725, Aug. 16. Will—proved 1725, Sep. 20. Widow Abigail. Ex. grandson William Hopkins. To three children John Dexter, William Hopkins and Abigail Field, 40s. each, to be taken from money due me from Proprietors of Providence for services done by my husband, and the rest of money so due, about £3, to go to grandson William Hopkins. To grandson William Hopkins, also two cows, certain pewter, brass and ironware, case of bottles, and his grandfather's silver buttons for a shirt. To granddaughters Hope and Abigail Hopkins, certain pewter, equally, and to each of them a pair of linen sheets, &c. To granddaughter Abigail Field, granddaughter Abigail Dexter and grandson Stephen Dexter, legacies. To executor all the rest of estate.

II. THOMAS, b. Providence, R. I.
m. 1678. d. 1718, Apr. 21.
MARY SMITH, b.
d. 1718 + of John & Elizabeth ( ) Smith.

1672, May 1. Freeman.

1672, May 14. He and Nicholas Power were voted 10s., each, for apprehending an Indian

1679, Jul. 1. Taxed 1s., 3d.

1687, Sep. 1. Taxed 4s., 1d.

1688. Ratable estate, 2 oxen, 2 mares, 4 cows, steer, heifer, 162 acres, of which 10 acres improved lands, 5 acres being in tillage and 5 acres English pasture, 2 swine.

1706, Jan. 7. He and Eleazer Arnold, sons-in-law of Elizabeth Smith, widow of John Smith, agreed to support their mother-in-law provided they had the whole personal estate left her by will of her husband John Smith, deceased.

1711, Apr. 26. Will—proved 1718, May 19. Exs. wife and son William. To eldest son Thomas, a third of all land adjoining house, being part that said son's house was on, and to him certain other land. To son William, a third part of same tract, being the part testator lives on, and it was to go to William at his mother's decease. To son Joseph, all upland at Shenegachoconet. To son Zebedee, a third of land already alluded to, being the north part, also other land, he paying his sister Anne, a legacy when she is eighteen or married. To son Elisha, 64 acres a mile and a half west of house. To son Ezekiel, all land west of Seven Mile Line that had been laid out. To two sons Amos and Jeremiah, all undivided lands west of Seven Mile Line, &c. To three daughters Elizabeth, Mary and Rachel Hopkins, £10, each, payable three years after his decease. To four sons Thomas, William and Zebedee and Elisha, all right of commonage, equally, on east side of Seven Mile Line. To son William, a further gift was made of a forty foot lot on the Town Street and a share of Thatch Cove.

Inventory, £109, 15s., viz: testament and part of another, feather bed, linen yarn, warming pan, 2 wool beds, pewter, iron, 2 spinning wheels, gun, sword, cooper's tools, yoke of oxen, horse, 3 cows, 14 sheep, 3 lambs, 9 swine, tobacco, oats, rye, &c.

I. WILLIAM, b. ; d. 1738. Providence, Scituate, R. I.
m.
RUTH WILKINSON, b. 1686, Jan. 31; d. 1738 (—) of Samuel & Plain (Wickenden) Wilkinson.

1738, Jun. 11. Will—proved 1738, Oct. 29. Ex. son-in-law Henry Harris. To sons William, Stephen and John, each 5s., having already given them sufficient. To my two youngest sons Esek and Samuel, a gun, log chain, horse and all my working tools, to be divided equally between them, and they also to have all my wearing apparel. To the two younger daughters Abigail and Susanna Hopkins, my two trunks and all in them except my papers. To daughter Susanna, bed, &c. To daughters Hope Harris, Abigail and Susanna Hopkins, £40, each, to be paid them one year after testator's decease. To sons Esek and Samuel, all the rest of money and goods, equally.

1. William,
2. Stephen, 1707, Mar. 7.
3. Rufus,
4. John,
5. Hope, 1717, Mar. 3.
6. Esek. 1718, Apr. 26.
7. Samuel,
8. Abigail,
9. Susanna,

I. THOMAS, b. ; d. 1746 + Scituate, R. I.
m.
ELIZABETH, b. ; d. 1751, Feb. 1. of

1. Susanna, 1708, Oct. 8.
2. Sarah, 1710, May 27.
3. Bethiah, 1713, Feb. 24.
4. Thomas, 1715, Sep. 9.
5. Reuben, 1717, Jul. 1.
6. Hanan, 1719, Jul. 17.
7. Mercy, 1721, Feb. 5.
8. Jonathan, 1722, Sep. 25.
9. Mary, 1724, Feb. 17.
10. Timothy, 1725, Jul. 25.
11. Elizabeth, 1726, Aug. 9.
12. Anne, 1729, Jan. 24.

II. WILLIAM, b. ; d. Scituate, R. I.
m.
DEBORAH ALLEN, b. 1691, May 7; d. 1781, Apr. 11. of Isaac Allen.

1. Jabesh, 1713, Jul. 15.

III. JOSEPH, b. ; d. 1740, Jul. 19. Scituate, R. I.
m. (1)
BETHIAH ALLEN, b. ; d. of Isaac Allen.
m. (2)
MARTHA, b. ; d. 1740 + of

1740, Jul. 4. Will—proved 1740, Sep. 1. Exs. wife Martha and son Jonah. To son Jeremiah, at age, 60 acres, &c. To son Jonah, rest of homestead, he paying Abner at age, £200. To daughter-in-law Desire Tucker, a bed, cow, &c. To daughter Dorcas, at eighteen, £100. To wife Martha, the income of half of homestead till Jonah is of age, and then an eighth while widow. In case of death of sons, provision was made as to how the others should have. Jonah appeared before Town Council, aged about sixteen, and chose his brother Joseph as guardian.

1. Joseph,
2. Oziel,
3. Jeremiah,
4. Abner,
5. Jonah, 1724,
6. Dorcas,

IV. ELIZABETH, b. ; d. 1731, Feb. 26.
UNMARRIED,

V. MARY, b. ; d.
m. 1716, Mar. 8.
ROBERT DAVIS, b. ; d. of Davis.

VI. RACHEL, b. ; d.

VII. ZEBEDEE, b. 1697, Feb. 22; d. 1789, Mar. 4. Scituate, R. I.
m.
SUSANNA JENCKES, b. 1700, May 24; d. 1755, Mar. 18. of Daniel & Catharine (Balcom) Jenckes.

1731, Oct. 25. He took administration on his sister Elizabeth's estate.

1. Rachel, 1725, Dec.
2. Susanna, 1728, Oct. 5.
3. Deborah, 1730.
4. Zebedee, 1737. Nov. 5

VIII. ELISHA, b. ; d. Scituate, R. I.
m. 1722, Jul. 13.
MERCY WAIDE, b. ; d. of Waide.

1738. Town Council.

1. Elisha,

IX. EZEKIEL, b. ; d. 1762. Scituate, R. I.
m.
ELIZABETH, b. ; d.

1731. Town Council.
1745. Deputy.
1761, Sep. 16. Will—proved 1762, Aug. 16. Exs. wife Elizabeth and sons Daniel and Nicholas. He gave legacies to wife Elizabeth, sons Daniel, Ezekiel, Charles and Nicholas, and daughters Abigail and Patience, and to children of daughter Catharine, viz: Ruth, Catharine and Sarah.

1. Daniel,
2. Ezekiel,
3. Charles,
4. Nicholas,
5. Abigail,
6. Patience,
7. Mary,
8. Catharine,

III. —— m. ELIZABETH, { b. d. 1685 (—) } { b. d. } of — Oyster Bay, N. Y.

(She m. (2) Richard Kirby.)

1688, Oct. 27. The will of Richard Kirby, of this date (proved 1689, Jan. 10), gave legacies to his wife Elizabeth and her two children Ichabod and Ann Hopkins, as well as to his own children, William, Thomas, Elizabeth and Mary Kirby.

Inman, Edward. See also: Bowen's THE PROVIDENCE OATH OF ALLEGIANCE, p.31-36.

EDWARD, m. (1) —— m. (2) BARBARA PHILLIPS (w. of [Michael. { b. d. 1706. } { b. d. } { b. d. 1706 + } Warwick, Providence, R. I.

He was a glover.

1648, Jun. 5. He was recorded as an inhabitant of Warwick.

1651, Oct. 27. Providence. He was recorded as a townsman, and was granted a small piece of ground by the place where his house is, if no damage to highway, provided he alloweth 6 acres of ground for it elsewhere.

1652, Dec. 13. He bought an acre of Thomas Harris.

1653, Jan. 3. He was not liable to forfeit his home lot for not building, "because he hath built in another more convenient place for his trade of dressing fox gloves."

1656, Jan. 27. He was granted 5 acres between the bridge that goeth to Mr. Scott's meadow and Mr. Dexter's bridge.

1657, Jun. 10. He entered two ankers of rum.

1658. Commissioner.

1661, Feb. 18. Grand Jury.

1663, Jul. 27. He entered two ankers liquor.

1663, Dec. 7. He and Thomas Hopkins gave bond to the town for any money to be used for the relief of Joanna Hazard.

1664, Feb. 27. He had permission to exchange land.

1665, Feb. 19. He had lot 73 in a division of lands.

1666, May 14. He and John Mowry bought of William Minnion, of Punskepage, Massachusetts, for good consideration, 2,000 acres, lying from Loquesit northward, bounding partly on Pawtucket River: "To have and to hold without any trouble or molestation by any Indians."

1666-67-68-72-74-76-77-78. Deputy.

1667, Sep. 2. He sold his dwelling house, &c., to Stephen Paine, Sr., of Rehoboth.

1669, May 13. He, calling himself late of Providence, received a deed of 500 acres on Pawtucket River from William Manannion for £20, said deed being confirmed by King Philip and others.

1679, Jul. 1. Taxed 1*s.* 10½*d.*

1682, Apr. 26. He and his associates had a grant from town of Providence of 3,500 acres in north part of town, having already settled their families there. This grant was in settlement of some differences, the town "inclining to part with some of their right that so a neighborly amity might be settled, rather than to use extremity by which animosities might arise."

1684, Oct. 29. Taxed 2*s.*

1686, Aug. 17. He deeded Joshua Clark, for good respect, and for that said Clarke married with the daughter of my now wife, and for the propagation of a neighborhood, 66 acres.

1688. Ratable estate, 4 cows, a two year, 2 mares, 2 swine, 16 acres within fence. He adds to the account: "I pray consider our condition, for you have formerly." Passed to be heard.

1689, May 22. He and wife Barbara for well being and settlement of John, James and Richard Phillips, sons of aforesaid Barbara, deeded them certain lands situate on Pawtucket River, ten miles north of Providence.

1695, May 26. He sold son-in-law (*i. e.* stepson) Richard Phillips, 20 acres.

1698, Dec. 7. He had 28 acres laid out that he had exchanged with the town.

1702, Nov. 14. He and wife Barbara sold John Sayles, for £60, silver money, mansion house, home lands, orchard, meadow, and mowing, in all 180 acres, situated both sides of highway in northern part of township at a place called Westquodonesset. The farm was bounded partly by land of John Inman, and Edward Inman, Jr.

1706, Aug. 17. Inventory of his estate was presented by his son John, and the Town Council summoned the widow Barbara and son Edward to appear.

1706, Aug. 26. Edward Inman, son of deceased, appeared and made oath to inventory of movable estate of his father, exhibited by brother John Inman, and the widow Barbara declining to come to make oath and rejecting administration, and Edward and John Inman refusing also, the Council appointed one of their number, viz: Jonathan Sprague.

INMAN. See: American Genealogist, v. 21, p. 208.

I. JOANNA, m. 1666. NATHANIEL MOWRY, { b. d. 1718 + } { b. 1644. d. 1718, Mar. 24. } of Roger & Mary ( ) Mowry.

II. JOHN, m. MARY WHITMAN, { b. 1648, Jul. 18. d. 1712, Aug. 6. } { b. 1652, Nov. 16. d. 1720, Apr. 27. } of Valentine & Mary ( ) Whitman. — Providence, R. I.

1669, Jan. 20. His intentions of marriage with Sarah Hearnden were published, but they were not married. (She subsequently married David Whipple, 1675, May 15.)

1672, May 1. Freeman.

1673, Apr. 6. He made proclamation that he had taken up a stray horse, light bay color, small star in forehead, and branded on near shoulder with letter P.

1679, Jul. 1. Taxed 1*s.* 10½*d.*

1684, Oct. 27. Taxed 2*s.*

1687. Ratable estate, 2 oxen, 5 cows, heifer, horse, mare, colt, 4 acres tilled land, 6 acres pasture, 70 acres not enclosed.

1693, Feb. 8. He exchanged land with John Whipple, lying in Loquassuck woods near the dwelling of John Inman.

1706, Jul. 27. He sold certain rights in land to John Gully, for £17, and alludes to his father Edward Inman, deceased.

1702, Mar. 30. Will—proved 1712. Exx. wife Mary. Overseers, Samuel Wilkinson, Richard Arnold. To eldest daughter Mary Bartlett, 10*s*, and what she had already received. To six daughters Deborah, Sarah, Anne, Naomi, Joanna and Tabitha, 20*s.*, each, when twenty-one. To eldest son John, certain lands adjoining river, "where my mill formerly stood," comprising 80 acres, and also other land, all at age. To son Valentine, 30 acres, and at decease of his mother he to have all the homestead, house, orchard, &c. To wife, the homestead, orchard and enclosed lands for life, and certain other lands till sons are of age. He alludes to land had from his father Edward Inman. To wife, all movable estate.

Inventory, £224, 18*s.*, 7*d.*, viz: 2 oxen, 7 cows, 2 heifers, 4 young cattle, 5 swine and some pigs, old mare, hay, rye, oats, barley, flax, butter, cheese, tobacco, carpenter's tools, cash £53, 6*s.* 6*d.*, bible, psalter, &c.

1720, Jun. 24. Administration on widow Mary Inman's estate to son John. Inventory, £128, 8*s.* 8*d.*

1723, Nov. 2. The following children of John Inman signed an instrument concerning the estate of their sister Tabitha Inman, deceased, to the end, "that peace and tranquility may be preserved;" Samuel Bartlett, of Attleboro, John Inman, Valentine Inman, Deborah Inman, Daniel Mathewson, John Ballou and Samuel Comstock, Jr. It was agreed that Deborah should have a double share, and the rest equally.

An agreement was also made concerning their sister Joanna Inman's estate, that all should share equally.

X. Amos, m. 1727, Oct. 29. Sarah Smith, — b. d. 1769. b. d. of Joseph & Elizabeth (Hawkins) Smith. — Scituate, Providence, R. I.
He was a member of Town Council seven years.
1753. Providence. He settled in what later became North Providence.

1. Amos,
2. Jeremiah,
3. Uriah, 1738, Dec. 26.

XI. Jeremiah, Unmarried. — b. d. 1733, Apr. 26. — Scituate, R. I.
1733, Sep. 19. Administration to brother Thomas. Inventory, £25, 4s., 6d., viz: wearing apparel, chest, gun, mare, colt, &c.

XII. Ann, — b. d.

I. Ann, — b. d.

II. Ichabod, m. Sarah Cole, — b. d. 1730. b. d. 1726 (—) of Daniel & Mahershallalhashbaz (Gorton) Cole. — Oyster Bay, N. Y.
1726, Mar. 17. Will—proved 1730, Feb. 25. Exs. son Daniel, brother Thomas Kirby, and Thomas Carpenter. To son Thomas, my long gun. To son Daniel, my small gun. To grandson William, cooper's tools. To four daughters Elizabeth, Sarah, Dinah and Ann, legacies.

1. Thomas,
2. Daniel.
3. Elizabeth,
4. Sarah,
5. Dinah,
6. Ann,

INMAN.

1. Nathaniel,
2. John,
3. Henry,
4. Joseph,
5. Sarah,
6. Mary, 1675.
7. Joanna,
8. Patience,
9. Mercy,
10. Experience,
11. Martha,

I. Mary, m. 1695, Dec. 19. Samuel Bartlett, — b. d. 1743 (—) b. d. 1743. of John & Sarah (Aldrich) Bartlett.

1. Samuel, 1696, Oct. 9.
2. Jerusha, 1698, May 3.
3. Noah, 1700, Apr. 22.
4. Mary, 1709, Jan. 5.

II. Deborah, m. 1725, Jul. 6. Joseph Baster, — b. d. 1762, Dec. 29. b. d. 1744 (—) of Baster.

No issue.

III. Sarah, m. 1704, Feb. 10. Daniel Mathewson, — b. d. b. 1683, Jan. 28. d. 1751, Jun. 13. of James & Hannah (Field) Mathewson.

1. Othniel, 1705, Feb. 2.
2. Peregrine, 1707, Sep. 12.
3. Mary, 1710, Nov. 7.
4. Nero, 1713, Jun. 27.
5. Daniel, 1716, Mar. 7.
6. Sylvanus, 1719. Jul. 25.
7. Winchester,

IV. Anne, m. Samuel Comstock, — b. d. 1727 + b. 1679, Apr. 16. d. 1727, Apr. 1. of Samuel & Elizabeth (Arnold) Comstock.

1. David,
2. Sarah, 1706, May 24.
3. Anne,

V. John, m. 1716, Jun. 28. Susanna Ballou, — b. 1684. d. 1741, Aug. 3. b. 1695, Jan. 3. d. of James & Susanna (Whitman) Ballou. — Providence, Glocester, R. I.
(She m. (2) 1742, Jan. 10, Richard Sayles.)
1708. Freeman.
1712, Mar. 17. He made an agreement with his uncle Edward, already alluded to.
1713, Jun. 16. Taxed with his mother 18s. 6d.
1717, Jan. 19. He made an agreement as heir of his father John, and grandfather Edward Inman, with his uncle Nathaniel Mowry, &c., about the division of 3,500 acres.
1723. He took administration on estates of his sisters Joanna and Tabitha.
1741, Jul. 28. Will—proved 1741, Nov. 21. Exs. daughter Rachel, and son John when of age. To wife Susanna, privilege of dwelling house while widow, and she to be provided for by executors. To son John, all the homestead, at age, except 40 acres. To son David, 40 acres. Daughter Rachel to sell certain land, and with the money together with the £50, raised from sale of stock, and money and notes due, to make division of £40, first to Ruth, and the rest to go to daughters Ruth, Sarah, Martha and Susanna. The children under age to have learning, &c. To son John, at age, ten cows and a yoke of oxen. To son David, at age, five cows, and half the value of yoke of oxen. To sons John and David, 100 acres. To son David, right in Inman's saw mill, two miles from house.
Inventory, £1,426, 7s. 7d., viz: books £2, 19s., 52 oz. silver £70, 4s., a dozen silver spoons £20, 5s., stillyards, 2 guns, warming pan, worsted comb, 8 spinning wheels, several pair of cards, loom, yoke of oxen, 19 cows, bull, 6 heifers, 2 steers, 5 calves, 2 mares, colt, 6 large swine, 6 small swine, 36 sheep, 5 barrels cider, 6 barrels beer, &c.

1. Rachel, 1720, Jun. 11.
2. Ruth,
3. Sarah, 1726, Mar. 9.
4. Martha, 1729, Oct. 16.
5. John, 1733, Aug. 5.
6. David, 1736, May 5.
7. Susanna,

VI. Valentine, m. (1) Barbara Ballou, m. (2) Ruth, — b. d. 1770. b. d. of Peter & Barbara ( ) Ballou. b. d. 1770 + of — Providence, Glocester, R. I.
1713, Jun. 16. Taxed 4s.
1720, Dec. 9. He bought 3½ acres of Joseph Hopkins for £3, 10s.
1754, Mar. 7. Will—proved 1770, Apr. 21. Exs. sons John and Oziel. To son John, homestead farm, house, orchard, &c. To son Oziel, all laid out lands except 20 acres. To wife Ruth, £100, and feather bed, while widow, and then to testator's sons. To daughter Tabitha Eddy, £10. To two sons, all stock in creatures, and farming tools. To Sarah Eddy and Mary Eddy, my other feather bed. To sons, wearing apparel, and common lands to them. To daughter Jemima Eddy, proceeds of sale of 20 acres where Thomas Eddy did live, to bring up her child.
Inventory. Note £188, 17s. 6d., wearing apparel, warming pan, foot wheel, 16 sheep, pair of oxen, 2 cows, heifer, mare, 3 shoats, &c.

1. John,
2. Oziel,
3. Tabitha,
4. Jemima,
(2d wife, no issue.)

VII. Naomi, m. 1714, Feb. 5. John Ballou, — b. d. b. 1683, Aug. 26. d. 1765, Dec. 7. of John & Hannah (Garret) Ballou.

1. John,
2. Abraham,
3. David,
4. Mary,
5. Sarah,
6. Tabitha,
7. Peter,

III. { **Edward**, { b. 1654. **Providence, Smithfield, R. I.**
m. { d. 1735, Jun.
{ **Elizabeth Bennett**, { b.
{ d. 1721 + of Samuel & Anne ( ) Bennett.

He was a carpenter.

1679, Jul. 1. Taxed 1*s.* 10½*d.*

1684, Oct. 27. Taxed 1*s.*

1687. Ratable estate, 3 cows, heifer, horse, 3 acres planting, 2 acres pasture, share of meadow, 70 acres laid out lands.

1704, Aug. He and wife Elizabeth sold Isaac Bull quarter of an acre for 10*s.*

1712, Mar. 17. An agreement was made between Edward Inman, son of Edward, Sr., deceased, glover, and John Inman, son of John, deceased, which deceased was also son of Edward, Sr.—for a division of lands which were originally in the right of Edward Inman, Sr., deceased. Deeds were made and signed interchangeably.

1713, Jun. 16. Taxed 14*s.* 2*d.*

1717, Feb. 18. He testified, calling himself aged about sixty-three years, that John Inman, aged about thirty-three years, was eldest son of John Inman, deceased, who was eldest son of Edward Inman, deceased.

1721, Oct. 30. He deeded to son Joseph, for love, &c., "together with the regard which I have to the future subsistence and support of myself and my wife during the time of our continuance in the land of the living" — the house where grantor dwells, with improved lands, &c., half to be Joseph's immediately and the other half so managed that Edward and his wife may have full half the produce, and if not sufficient then they to have what further was needed. At decease of parents all to go to Joseph.

1724, Jan 7. He deeded son Edward land in Glocester, for love, &c.

1736, May 24. Administration on estate of Edward Inman of Smithfield, to his son Edward, of Glocester.

(2d Wife, no issue.)

VIII. JOANNA, b. / d. 1728, Jul. 26.
UNMARRIED.

IX. TABITHA, b. 1693. / d. 1728, Jul. 30.
UNMARRIED.

I. EDWARD, b. / d. 1755, Jun. 11. — Providence, Glocester, Smithfield, R. I.
m. (1)
MARY MALAVERY, b. / d. 1744, Nov. 20. of John & Elizabeth ( ) Malavery.
m. (2) 1745, Jan. 5.
LYDIA WHIPPLE, b. / d. 1764, Jul. 14. of Whipple.

Children: 1. Michael, 2. Elisha, 3. Israel, 4. Abraham, 5. Edward, 6. Elijah, 7. Susanna, 8. Priscilla, 9. Penelope, 10. Mary, (2d wife, no issue.)

1713, Jun. 16. Taxed 6s.
1718, Sep. 18. His wife's brother John Malavery died, leaving a legacy to nephew Michael Inman, if his own two sons died under age.
1728, Feb. 2. He deeded son Michael 40 acres.
1734. Glocester. Surveyor.
1755, May 28. Will—proved 1755, Jun. 30. Ex. son Edward. (The testator is called late of Glocester, now Smithfield.) To grandson Daniel Inman, £3, his father Michael having had his portion by deed. To son Elisha, 5 acres. To son Israel, 32 acres, and privilege of fruit from orchard till he can raise fruit. To son Abraham, all my interest in farm where he dwells, to him and male heirs. To son Edward, land adjoining Branch River, and where Tarkill River meets Branch River, with grist mill, saw mill, dwelling house, and all other lands undisposed of. To son Elijah, £15. To daughter Susannah Walling, £6. To daughter Priscilla Walling, 10s. To daughter Penelope Mowry, 10s. To daughter Mary Walling's children, viz: Mary and Hannah, 10s. each. To wife Lydia, a third of movables, and best room in house while widow, but she not to sell or rent privilege except to sons Elisha or Israel.
Inventory. Bond £563, 13s. 6d., pewter, anvil, &c., in shop, horse, yoke of oxen, 3 cows, 2 heifers, bull, 2 steers, yearling, 2 hogs, &c.

II. SAMUEL, b. / d. — Providence, Glocester, R. I.
m. (1)
ELIZABETH, b. / d. of
m. (2) 1737, Dec. 24.
MEHIPSABETH MACKINTINE, b. / d. of Mackintine.

Children: 1 Isaiah,

1708. Freeman.
1711, Aug. 14. He sold Joseph Whipple 20 acres for £10, 5s.
1713, Jun. 16. Taxed 3s.
1724, Jan. 29. He and wife Elizabeth sold Abraham Tourtellot, 20 acres where I dwell, with house, &c., for £60.
1737, Dec. 10. Glocester. He deeded son Isaiah, for love, &c., 26 acres. (This son was called Isaiah, Jr., to distinguish him from his uncle.)

III. FRANCIS, b. / d. 1776, Feb. 11. — Providence, R. I., Bellingham, Mass., Cumberland, R. I.
m. (1)
ROSE BULL, b. / d. of Isaac Bull.
m. (2)
SUSANNA BARTLETT, b. / d. of Bartlett.

INMAN. 3d column. III. Francis. His 2d wife was daughter of Jacob Bartlett.

Children: 1. Aaron, 1709, Nov. 29. 2. Abiah, 1712, Nov. 4. (2d wife.) 3. Jeremiah, 1720, Feb. 7. 4. Susanna, 1722, May 23. 5. Francis, 1724, Jan. 11. 6. Joanna, 1729, Jun. 7. 7. John, 1734, Nov. 22.

1708. Freeman.
1716, Apr. 5. His wife had a legacy from will of her father Isaac Bull, who also gave to his grandson Aaron Inman.
1775, Apr. 19. He being much impaired in understanding by reason of extreme old age, had guardians appointed, viz: Nathaniel Jillson and Philip Capron.
1776, Feb. 26. Administration to Philip Capron. Inventory, £139, 6s. 5¼d., viz: old bible, testament, and another very old book 7s. 4d., woolen and linen wheels, 2 pair of cards, gun gone into the American service £1, 10s., gold chain £1, 10s., piece of gold, pair of ear buttons, pair of shoe buckles, 2 cows, 12 sheep, 2 fowls, &c.

IV. BENJAMIN, b. / d. — Providence, Smithfield, R. I.
m.
———, b. / d. of

He was a blacksmith.
1722, Feb. 13. He bought 28 acres of John Pierce.
1733, Sep. 10. Smithfield. He was licensed to sell strong liquors.
1738, Jan. 20. He sold William Gully homestead I purchased of brother Joseph Irons, deceased, 6 acres, dwelling house, &c., for £120.

V. JOSEPH, b. / d. 1734, May 9. — Providence, Smithfield, R. I.
m. 1717, Dec. 8.
DEBORAH SMITH, b. / d. 1734 + of Joseph & Deborah (Whitman) Smith.

Children: 1. Stephen, 2. Joseph, 3. Deborah,

(She m. (2) John Knox.)

1720. Freeman.
1726, Apr. 20. He sold William Gully for £600, land in north part of Providence, 160 acres.
1734, Sep. 9. Inventory, £247, 14s. 6d. Administration to widow Deborah. Wearing apparel £28, books 4s., 4 beds, pewter, gun, sword, black horse, mare, yoke of oxen, 6 cows, 3 heifers, 10 goats, 5 kids, 5 swine, &c.
1739, Dec. 8. His son Stephen chose his uncle John Smith for guardian, and at this date Deborah had married John Knox. His sons Stephen and Joseph lived in Cumberland, where the latter died 1750, Feb. 13, administration being given to his brother Stephen, who died 1750, May 19.

VI. ISAIAH, b. / d. 1755, Feb. 2. — Providence, Glocester, R. I.
m. (1)
———, b. / d. of
m. (2) 1744, Oct. 14.
SARAH CUTLER, b. / d. of Cutler.

Children: 1. Mary, 2. Lydia, (2d wife.) 3. Isaiah, 1755, Oct. 1.

1724, May 23. He sold Edward Inman, Jr., 60 acres.
1730, Jun. 12. He made an agreement with Hosannah Brown about a saw mill on Chapatset River owned between them, concerning flowage.
1734. Glocester. Surveyor.
1753, Apr. 8. Will—proved 1755, Feb. 15. Ex. brother-in-law John Smith, of Smithfield, and friend Elisha Eddy. To wife Sarah, use of a third of dwelling house and sufficient income of real estate for comfortable maintenance while widow, and use of sufficient household goods, but if she marry only to have goods she brought with her and £100, according to agreement before marriage. To grandson Stephen Aldrich, and my two daughters Mary and Lydia, and child my said wife is like to have if it be a female, all real estate equally. If the child be a male, to have land bought of Abraham Ballou, and my house where I now dwell, &c., and wearing apparel. If the child be a female, wearing apparel to go to grandson Isaiah Aldrich.
Inventory. Wearing apparel £126, 12s., 4 beds, sword, carpenter's tools, 2 spinning wheels, stillyards, notes and bonds £386, 12s., sheep £15, 3 cows, 2 yearlings, bull, 2 horses, &c.

ROBERT, { b. 1605. d. } Charlestown, Mass., Newport, R. I.
m.
MARY, { b. 1608. d. }

1635. He came from London in ship Elizabeth & Ann; his age being given as 30, wife Mary, 27, son Thomas, 7, daughter Elizabeth, 6, Mary, 3, maid servant Susannah Brown, 21, and Hannah Day, 20.

1636, Apr. His wife united with the church.

1638. Newport. His name was in the list of inhabitants this year.

1639, Jun. 5. He and three others were chosen to proportion lands, and those laying it forth to have 4*d.*, per acre.

1639, Nov. 25. He was appointed to train the band for the present.

1640–41–42. Treasurer for Portsmouth and Newport.

1641–42–43–44. Treasurer for Newport.

1642. Captain.

I. THOMAS, { b. 1628. d. }

II. ELIZABETH, { b. 1629. d. }

III. MARY, { b. 1632. d. }

IV. JETHRO, { b. 1638. d. 1739, Apr. 6. } Newport, R. I.
m.
MEHITABLE, { b. d. } of

KNIGHT.

RICHARD, { b. d. 1680. } Newport, R. I.
m. 1648 ±
SARAH ROGERS, { b. d. 1685 + }

of James & Mary ( ) Rogers.

He was a carpenter.

1648, Jan. 16. He had a deed from James Rogers, for valuable consideration, of two parcels of land, one of 40 acres and one of 2 acres.

1648, Feb. 18. He deeded land lately bought of James Rogers and Robert Griffin to wife "Sarah Rogers" and her heirs forever, especially to eldest son at twenty-one, and in failure of such issue to eldest daughter at sixteen. Should he decease, wife Sarah to have a third during life.

1648–49. Keeper of the prison.

1648–49–50–53–54–57–58. General Sergeant.

1655. Freeman.

1656, Mar. 17. He and two others were sent by warrant for the sachem Pomham, to require him to come before the court.

1656, Dec. 22. He sold George Kenrick of Providence, 12 acres at 20*s.*, per acre in merchantable peage at rate of eight to a penny of white or four of black, or equivalent.

1658, Dec. 5. He sold Lawrence Turner 4 acres.

1658. Water Bailey.

1663. He bought lands in Narragansett with Henry Hall.

1677, Oct. 31. He and forty-seven others were granted 100 acres each in a plantation to be called East Greenwich.

1679, Dec. 11. He and wife Sarah and eldest son John sold certain land to Francis Brinley and Richard Smith.

1680. Taxed 7*s.*

1680, Oct. 27. His widow, of Newport, petitioned the Assembly for confirmation of a share of lands settled by her deceased husband without court order, at East Greenwich, and she was ordered to be possessed of aforesaid share upon same terms as rest of East Greenwich inhabitants, she paying 40*s.*, to General Treasurer within six months.

1683, Oct. 12. His widow, now of East Greenwich, deeded to eldest son John, a 10 acre lot, house, &c., and also farm in first division containing 90 acres, reserving privilege of egress and regress of lower room to live and lodge in.

1685, Feb. 24. Sarah Knight, with other widows and matrons, served as a jury in case of a young woman supposed to be with child.

No relationship has been ascertained as existing between Richard Knight and Toby Knight (Clerk of Military Company at Newport 1642–43).

See: American Genealogist, v. 20, p. 225-226.

I. JOHN, { b. d. 1710 ± } East Greenwich, R. I., Norwich, Ct.
m.
ANNE, { b. d. } of

1682, May 2. Freeman.

1685, Mar. 18. He and wife Anne sold David Shippee 90 acres.

1685, Apr. 8. Town Sergeant.

1688, Nov. 8. He sold Gideon Freeborn, of Portsmouth, a house and 100 acres in East Greenwich for £40, being the same property he had received from his mother by deed five years before.

1692, Jun. 21. Norwich. He and David Knight made friend Henry Hall their agent for Chippachoog lands.

1693. In this year he, of Canterbury near Norwich, Henry Hall of Westerly and David Knight, of Woodstock, employed Joseph Davol to lay out and survey lands called Hall's and Knight's Purchase. This was deposed to later (1711, Jul. 31), by Joseph Davol, who says further that John Knight approved his work and that two highways were laid out for the convenience of the purchasers.

1711, Mar. 27. Testimony of James Fitch, of Canterbury, Ct., was given, that in the year 1694, John Knight, late of Norwich, deceased, with David Knight, his brother, came to my house in Norwich and declared an agreement, whereby John sold his whole right to brother David, and a tract of land purchased by his deceased father and Henry Hall, of the Indians.

II. JONATHAN, { b. d. 1717, Jun. 25. } Warwick, Providence, R. I.
m.
HANNAH, { b. d. } of

1678, Apr. 30 Freeman.

1678, May 28. He bought certain land in Warwick of Elizur Collins and his mother Mrs. Anne Smith.

1679, May 12. He was fined 20*s.*, for not attending jury.

1693. He had 200 acres laid out to him in Narragansett, of the Hall and Knight Purchase.

1694, Mar. 15. He and wife Hannah, sold to Thomas Greene, Sr., the house "in which I now dwell," orchard, meadow, &c., being all his interest in Warwick.

1695, Mar. 19. He bought of Enoch Place, for £65, a certain tract of land, meadow, &c., in Mashantatack, 200 acres of which were divided off and bounded.

1695. Providence. He moved thence about this time.

1704. Deputy.

1704. Lieutenant and subsequently Captain.

1717, Aug. 19. Administration to son and heir Jonathan. Inventory, £198, 7*s*, 8*d.*, viz: gun, sword, 2 working cattle, 12 cows, steer, 7 two years, 8 yearlings, 8 calves, mare, colt, 31 sheep, 15 lambs, 10 swine, 7 shoats, 3 stacks of bees, 2 spinning wheels, &c.

He may have had another daughter besides Hannah, viz: Rebecca Knight, who gave 2*s.*, 6*d.*, toward building the Quaker Meeting house at Mashapaug, in 1702.

I. { THOMAS, m. 1699, Dec. 13. SARAH TIMBERLAKE, { b. 1679, Apr. 11. d. 1761, Sep. 2. { b. d. 1769, Oct. 7. of Joseph & Mary (Earle) — Newport, R. I. — Timberlake.

1. Thomas, 1701, Jun. 10.
2. Henry, 1703, Oct. 30.
3. Caleb, 1707, Feb. 2.
4. Jethro, 1709, Feb. 23.
5. Mehitable, 1711, Jul. 4.
6. Mary, 1711, Jul. 4.
7. Sarah, 1714, Dec. 19.
8. Rebecca, 1717.

He and his wife were buried in the Coddington Burial Ground.

II. { JOHN, { b. d.

KNIGHT.

I. { JOHN, m. ELEANOR, { b. d. 1775. { b. d. 1771 + of — Providence, Cranston, R. I.

KNIGHT. 2d column. I, John. 1702, Jan. 11, Knight d. at Providence. Perhaps his wife.

Elizabeth - See: American Genealogist v.36, p.54.

1710, Mar. 20. He bought of Josiah Westcott, 45½ acres.

1710, Sep. He, eldest son of John Knight, of Norwich, deceased, and grandson and heir of Richard Knight, of Newport, deceased, brought suit against Job Babcock and others for partition of certain lands.

1712, Feb. 27. He petitioned the Assembly through his attorney Samuel Greene, requesting an appeal from the decision of Court of Trials, in a case between said Knight and Job Babcock concerning lands in Narragansett. The appeal to Great Britain was allowed.

1718, Jul. 30. He bought of Josiah Westcott, 12 acres for £14.

1758, Jan. 12. Cranston. He and wife Eleanor, sold John King, 10 acres for £650.

1764, Jan. 30. He sold 10 acres to Josiah Potter, for £700, and by indenture of same date received a lease for life of same to himself and wife Eleanor, for sum of one farthing per year rental.

1771, Jan. 5. He sold Nathaniel Potter farm whereon I live of 20 acres, and by indenture of same date, in consideration of reasonable sum for which he had sold his homestead, he had an agreement from Potter to pay said Knight and Eleanor his wife, for their natural lives, half the rents of another piece of land adjoining the farm, and if this proved insufficient for support, then additions for a comfortable living.

1771, Jan. 7. He sold Nathaniel Potter for £7, 10s., a cow, 2 swine, 2 beds, 3 tables, desk, brass kettle, 2 chests, chest of drawers, 3 iron kettles, large trunk, 2 bedsteads, narrow axe, beetle, 2 iron wedges, 6 case knives and forks, 6 pewter plates, fire tongs, fire shovel, 2 stacks of hay and all goods and chattels, except wearing apparel, mare, saddle and bridle.

II. { RICHARD, m. DELIVERANCE RALPH, { b. d. 1754, May 15. { b. d. 1758 May 8. of Samuel & Mary ( ) — Providence, R. I. — Ralph.

1. John,
2. Richard,
3. David,
4. Thomas,
5. Daughter,
6. Anne,
7. Daughter,
8. Deliverance,

He was a house carpenter.

1717, Feb. 15. He (called Richard Knight, son of John, deceased), bought of John Blackmar, son and heir of James Blackmar, certain land.

1719, Oct. He ("son of Ann Knight") was complained of to Assembly with others for abusing Captain Thomas Harris on training day in execution of his office. Authority was given to the Deputy Governor and Colonel and Major of Regiment on Main land to examine into affairs, &c.

1724, Mar. 11. He and wife Deliverance sold Moses Bowditch 15 acres for £10.

1744, Jul. 6. He deeded his eldest son John, 30 acres for £250. (This son was called John, Jr., to distinguish him from his uncle John.)

He held the title of Captain some years.

1754. Administration to son John Knight, Jr., the estate being resigned to him by his brother Richard Knight, 3d, who had been guardian of their father, the deceased Captain Richard Knight, he having been delirious sometime before his departure. The amount due from the guardian to administrator was £414, 10s.

1756, Oct. 3. Will—proved 1758, Jun. 5. Widow Deliverance Knight, of Cranston. Ex. son Richard Knight, Jr. To son John, 10s. To son David, a kettle and pot. To son Thomas, a bed, &c. To granddaughter Elizabeth Dyer, my red cloak. To three daughters Anne Edwards, —— Taylor and Deliverance Mason, rest of wearing apparel, equally. To son Richard, rest of estate.

Inventory £457, 12s.

III. { ANN, UNMARRIED. { b. d. 1685.

I. { HANNAH, m. 1700, Apr. 15. WILLIAM CLARKE, { b. 1680, Apr. 3. d. 1743 + { b. 1673, May 27. d. 1746. of Latham & Hannah (Wilbur) — Clarke.

1. William, 1701, Aug. 26.
2. Jonathan, 1703, Oct. 18.
3. Hannah, 1704, Sep. 8.
4. Thomas, 1706, Mar. 13.
5. Ruth, 1708, Jul. 15.
6. Robert, 1710, Oct. 28.
7. Judith, 1712, Aug. 8.
8. Elisha, 1714, Jul. 10.
9. Caleb, 1716, Jul. 20.

II. { JONATHAN, m. 1718, Apr. 3. MARTHA ANGELL, { b. d. 1762. { b 1703, Mar. 24. d. of Thomas & Sarah (Brown) — Providence, Cranston, R. I. — Angell.

1. Jonathan,
2. Benjamin,
3. Ezra,
4. Philip,
5. Dorcas,
6. Elizabeth,
7. Andrew,

1717, Jul. 12. He deeded to brothers Richard and Robert, 100 acres each, where they dwell, and to each a share of meadow, stating that their father Jonathan died intestate, without having made these deeds. On same date he deeded to brother Joseph of Kings Town, 240 acres there.

1750, Oct. 4. He deeded eldest son Jonathan, for love, &c., 57 acres and dwelling house where son lives. A few years later he deeded his homestead to son Benjamin and land to son Philip also.

1756, Oct. 4. Will—proved 1762, Sep. 29. Ex. son Benjamin. To wife Martha, the best room, negro girl Phillis, bed, chest, two cows and keep of same by executor, a riding horse, and all things suitable provided for her by executor while widow. If she marries again only the bed and chest to her, the rest returning to executor, except the negro girl, who was to go to daughters Dorcas and Elizabeth, equally. If the negro girl had children, the oldest boy was to be given son Benjamin and any other children of said negro girl were to go to children of testator. To son Jonathan, £5, he having already had. To son Ezra, £100, in movables. To son Philip, 53 acres, dwelling house and feather bed. To son Andrew, £300, and he to be brought up to learning till fifteen and then put to such trade as he choose. To daughter Dorcas Knight, £5. To daughter Elizabeth Knight, two feather beds, case of drawers, oval table, and cow. To son Benjamin, the rest both real and personal.

III. { RICHARD, m. —— { b. d. 1754, Oct. 24. { b. d. of — Providence, Cranston, R. I.

1. Christopher,
2. William,
3. Richard,
4 Jeremiah, 1719, Dec. 23.

He was sometimes called "Richard Knight, Jr., yeoman," to distinguish him from his cousin Richard.

III. { DAVID, m. 1691, Mar. 17. SARAH BACKUS, } { b. d. 1744, Nov. 24. } East Greenwich, R. I., Norwich, Ct.
{ b. 1668, Apr. d. } of Stephen & Sarah ( ) Backus.

1691, Sep. 8. He was one of the appraisers of estate of Captain Clement Weaver.

1693. Woodstock, Ct. He was associated with his brother John as already seen, concerning the surveying and laying out of lands in Narragansett.

His marriage and children's births were recorded at Norwich, which was his residence for most of his life.

Perhaps he had another daughter, viz: Sarah, who married 1708, Feb. 21, at Norwich, to Enos Randall and had children, Elizabeth, b. 1709, Dec. 10; Sarah, b. 1711, Nov. 2, and Abigail, b. 1713, Dec. 27.

KNOWLES. See: American Geneologist, v. 20, p. 226-227.

{ HENRY, m. —— } { b. 1609. d. 1670, Jan. } Portsmouth, Warwick, R. I.
{ b. d. 1670 + }

1644, May 27. It was ordered that he cut his lot shorter at discretion of Lieutenant Sanford and Goodman Borden, and Goodman Mott.

1654, Jan. 21. He sold Thomas Lawton for valuable consideration, "my now dwelling house" with 9 acres of land, fruit trees, privilege, &c.

1655. Warwick. Freeman.

1657, Jan. 4. Action of trespass was brought against him by Randall Holden.

1657, Nov. 20. He sold a house and lot to Thomas Scranton.

1660. He had a 6 acre lot laid out to him, on land adjoining his own.

1663. Grand Jury.

1664, Mar. 23. He and three others were authorized by the town to keep Ordinaries for the entertainment of strangers during the time the King's Commissioners keep their court in Warwick.

1666, Mar. 8. He was on a jury which found the following verdict: "We who are engaged to see this dead Indian, do find by diligent search that he was beaten, which was the cause of his death."

He was apparently living in Kings Town when he made his will, though it was proved at Warwick.

I. { JOHN, UNMARRIED. } { b. d. 1716, Sep. 16. } Warwick, R. I.

1670, Oct. 26. He, having commenced a suit against Wawenockshott, an Indian, for burning his hay, the Assembly stopped proceedings in the way of law, because the Indians could not understand the way of proceedings, and the matter was left to the determination of three Assistants of Providence, and two of Warwick.

1672. Freeman.

1677, Oct. 31. He and forty-seven others were granted 5,000 acres to be called East Greenwich.

1687. Grand Jury.

1702. He gave 6*s.* toward building the Quaker meeting house at Mashapaug.

1714, Dec. 14. Will—proved 1716, Oct. 15. Exs. brother William Knowles and cousin (*i. e.* nephew) John Knowles. Overseers, cousin Moses Lippitt and friend Randall Holden. To cousin John Knowles, son of my brother William Knowles, of Kings Town, all my whole estate both real and personal not otherwise disposed of. To cousin Moses Lippitt, a right of land in Warwick, he paying my cousin Mary Burlingame, wife of John, and cousin Martha Burlingame, wife of Thomas, £5, apiece. To cousin John Lippitt, and his wife Rebecca, a share of meadow north of Mashapoge Brook. To cousin John Wilson and wife Rose, a share of salt meadow in Potowomut Neck. To sister Martha Eldred, wife of Samuel, £20. To aforesaid cousin Mary Burlingame, bed called my mother's bed.

Inventory, £162, 2*s.* 5*d.*, viz: wearing apparel, bible, spectacles, bonds £101, pewter, pair of silver buttons, 2 small pieces of garlic, apple mill and press, 3 horsekind, 3 cattle, &c.

1723, Aug. 28. He (called Richard Knight, son of Jonathan, deceased) bought of Andrew Harris, for £120, land west side of Pauchasset River, consisting of 60 acres, bounded partly by land of Richard Knight, son of John, deceased.

1733, Jul. 8. He deeded son Christopher, for love, &c., 288 acres in Warwick, where Christopher dwells.

1738, Apr. 25. He deeded son Richard, 60 acres, and son William, 74 acres and dwelling house, for love, &c.

1752, May 9. He deeded son Jeremiah, for love, &c., 53 acres and buildings with reservation of best room for life.

1752, May 22. Will—proved 1754, Nov. 7. Ex. son Richard. To son Christopher, £40, and a cross cut saw and a gun. To son William, half a meadow, &c. To sons Richard and Jeremiah, a lot of land equally, and to each separately, land. To grandson Richard Knight, my dwelling house and lot of land. To son William, a third of profits of orchard, north side of highway, for seven years. To sons Richard and Jeremiah, all remaining part of homestead lot, equally. To sons William, Richard and Jeremiah, all the rest of personal, equally.

Inventory, £4,521, 5*s.*, 5*d.*, viz: wearing apparel £109, 10*s.*, bonds and notes £2,580, 18*s.*, 11*d.*, silver money £6, books £2, 10*s.*, pewter, warming pan, 4 feather beds, old worsted combs, cooper's tools, gun, cider mill, 23 loads of hay, old horse, old mare, colt, pair of oxen, 7 cows, 3 young cattle, 16 sheep, 9 swine, &c.

IV. ROBERT, b. —, d. 1771. Providence, Cranston, R. I.
m. 1721, Jul. 21.
MARY POTTER, b. —, d. 1767 + of John & Jane (Burlingame) Potter.

Children: 1. Edward, 2. William, 3. Robert, 4. Charles, 5. Joseph, 6. Mary, 7. Esther, 8. Ruth, 9. Patience,

1720. Freeman.

1729, Mar. 6. He sold John Potter a bog meadow, 5 acres, 73 rods, for £11.

1736. Deputy. He was called Captain at this date.

1767, Dec. 21. Will—proved 1771, Aug. 24. Ex. son Edward. To wife Mary, all indoor movables, cow, riding beast, side saddle, and keep of said creatures, and use of best room while widow. To grandsons, Joseph and William Knight, at twenty-one, sons of William, deceased, 4 acres. To sons Robert and Charles, each a Spanish milled dollar and like amount to daughters Mary Hudson, Esther Miller, Ruth Knight, and Patience Brayton. To grandson Thomas Knight, son of Joseph, deceased, feather bed, cow, and £2,000, at age, but if he die then £500, to his sister Alice, and rest to go equally to my sons Charles and Edward, and daughters Mary Hudson, Ruth Knight and Patience Brayton. To son Edward, rest of estate, real and personal.

V. JOSEPH, b. —, d. 1750, Jul. 17. Kings Town, Scituate, R. I.
m.
MARY, b. —, d. 1750 + of

Children: 1. Jonathan, 2. Mary, 3. Susanna,

1721, Feb. 7. He and wife Mary, sold Thomas Potter, 240 acres in Kings Town for £260.

1741, Jun. 1. Scituate. He deeded son Jonathan, for love, &c., south part of my homestead, 80 acres.

1743. Deputy.

1750, Jul. 11. Will—proved 1750, Aug. 13. Ex. son Jonathan. To wife Mary, dark bay mare and colt, two side saddles, a third of rest of personal and a third of real, and east end of house for life. To daughter Mary Ralph, £100, and equal part of movables. To daughter Susanna Knight, £300, and equal part of movables after debts and wife's thirds. To son Jonathan, rest of personal, equal with sisters, and two-thirds of real at my death and the rest at death of wife.

Inventory, £1,492, 6*s.*, viz: wearing apparel £100, old bible 10*s.*, 4 feather beds, flock bed, pewter, brass, iron, glass, pewter, razor, spectacles, worsted combs, 2 oxen, 5 cows, 13 swine, 10 shoats.

I. RACHEL, b. 1691, Nov. 14. d.

II. JONATHAN, b. 1698, Jul. 2. d. 1770, Mar. 7. Norwich, Ct.
m. 1726, May 3.
ABIGAIL LONGBOTTOM, b. 1705, Oct. 21. d. of Daniel & Elizabeth (Lamb) Longbottom.

III. MARY, b. 1700, Apr. 2. d.

IV. HANNAH, b. 1702, Jan. 30. d.

V. LURANA, b. 1704, Feb. 1. d.

VI. JOSEPH, b. 1705, Nov. 7. d. 1739, May 25. Norwich, Ct.
m. 1732, Dec. 7.
SARAH READ, b. d. of Read.

Children: 1. Sarah, 1733, Dec. 2. Anna, 1735, Nov. 15. 3. Temperance 1738, Mar. 24.

1739, Jul. 2. Inventory, £664, in land, and also some personal.

VII. BENJAMIN, b. 1707, Aug. 14. d. Norwich, Ct.
m. 1729, Nov. 5.
HANNAH JEWETT, b. d. of Jewett.

Children: 1. Benjamin, 1730, Aug. 17. 2. Elizabeth, 1733, Aug. 27. 3. Mary, 1734, Dec. 12. 4. Lydia, 1737, May 10. 5. Joseph, 1739, May 12. 6. Priscilla, 1742, Mar. 12. 7. Sarah, 1744, Jun. 4. 8. Caleb, 1745, Oct. 7.

KNOWLES.

1670, Jan. 2. Will—proved 1670, Jan. 20. Ex. son William. To wife, north-east half of house that is in Warwick, well fitted for her use, and son John to conveniently fit said house for his mother. To wife, the meadow in front of the house, and John to mow and make the grass annually and put it in a convenient place for foddering. To wife also, certain other land for life. To daughter Mary, £15, of which she is to receive £5, from her brother John three years after testator's death, and £5, annually afterward. To daughter Martha, £20, of which £5, is to be paid by John in two years, and £5, annually afterward. To son John, half the house and rest of lands and meadows, at Warwick and Potowomut, &c., and at decease of wife, her part of house and meadows to go to John. To son Henry, the house and half the lands "of my now dwelling." To son William, the other half of these lands. To sons William and Henry, the rest of all lands equally, "as Robert Hazard and John Albro shall divide it for their convenience." The stock was divided as follows: To wife, two cows and a hog. To son Henry, a calf. The rest of the cattle and hogs, and a mare, to remain to the farm but eventually to be divided between William and Henry, a sum of 40*s.*, annually being paid to wife. The household goods to be divided as wife shall see cause; the best bed at Warwick to be for wife, and the other one for John; and of "those which are here" the best to Henry and the other to Martha. He charges William to be careful over Henry till latter is of age, and then to give him full and quiet possession of the house and half the land, only Henry shall allow William the liberty of the house and half of all appertaining, for two years after Henry comes of age, and William also to have half the nursery to plant if he see fit.

It was testified by witnesses that they heard deceased say after he had signed the will, that if his son John did not take what he gave him he was to have his brother William's right, while William was to take John's share except the executorship, and whoever shall enjoy the Warwick estate was to provide sufficient wood for their mother during her life. The 40*s.* was to be paid by son William to his mother till Henry came of age and then he to pay 20*s.*

II. WILLIAM,	b. 1645.		Warwick, South Kingstown, R. I.
m.	d. 1727.		
ALICE FISH,	b.		
	d. 1734.	of Thomas & Mary ( )	Fish.

1661, Oct. 22. He was apprenticed, with consent of his father, to Thomas Smith, tailor, of Pawtuxet, for five years.

1671, Sep. 25. Kings Town. He was appointed on committee to make a rate and levy an assessment on inhabitants of Pettacomscott.

1679, Jul. 29. He and forty-one other inhabitants of Narragansett signed petition to the King, praying that he "would put an end to these differences about the government thereof which hath been so fatal to the prosperity of the place; animosities still arising in people's minds as they stand affected to this or that government."

1687, Sep. 6. Taxed 5*s.* 11½*d.*.

1688, Mar. 6. Grand Jury.

1690, Oct. 30. He was appointed on a committee to make a rate of tax for Kings Town.

1701. He gave 12*s.* toward building Quaker Meeting house at Mashapaug.

1703, Jul. 12. He was chosen with others to lay out highways.

1706–7. Deputy.

1721, Oct. 6. Will—proved 1727, Apr. 21. Ex. son Robert. Overseers, friends Stephen and George Hazard. To son Henry, part of homestead and half of land on the plain. To son William, 5*s.* he having had his portion. To son Daniel, 5*s.* To son Robert, rest of homestead, with all the housing, &c., and 149 acres in East Greenwich, &c. To son John, rest of land in East Greenwich and 5*s.* To wife Alice, all movable estate belonging to dwelling house, as household stuff, &c., and half of cattle, sheep, horsekind, and swine, at her disposal, and one-half use of home lands given Robert, while widow. To her also, great room and bedroom in the house, and half the orchard where William liveth. To daughters Rose Wilson, Martha Sherman and Mary Chase, £5, each, paid by son William. To daughter Margaret Knowles, £40, a fire room, firewood, &c.. while unmarried, and a riding horse. To daughter Alice Screven, £5.

Inventory. Feather bed, stillyards, pewter, worsted comb, cheese press, riding mare, yearling horse, 9 cows, 5 heifers, 2 yearlings, steer, yoke of oxen, shoat, &c.

1732, Oct. 7. Will—proved 1734, Jul. 20. Widow Alice. Ex. son Robert. To daughter Margaret Knowles, all wearing apparel. To three grandsons Isaac, Thomas and William Screven, sons of daughter Alice Screven, deceased, each a bible of 10*s.* value at twenty-one. To granddaughters Mary and Susanna Screven, daughters of Alice, a fifth of rest of estate, to be at interest till they are eighteen. To daughters Rose Wilson, Margaret Knowles, Mary Chase and Martha Sherman, rest of estate.

Inventory, £167, 5*s.* 5*d.*

III. MARY,	b.		
m. 1668, Nov. 19.	d. 1719, Dec. 28.		
MOSES LIPPITT,	b.		
	d. 1703, Jan. 6.	of John	Lippitt.

IV. MARTHA,	b.		
m.	d. 1728.		
SAMUEL ELDRED,	b. 1644, Oct. 26.		
	d. 1720 ±	of Samuel & Elizabeth ( )	Eldred.

V. HENRY,	b. 1654.	Warwick, South Kingstown, R. I.
	d. 1726.	
UNMARRIED.		

1678. Freeman.

1687, Sep. 6. Kings Town. Taxed 3*s.* 5*d.*

1721, Mar. 20. In a deposition he calls himself aged sixty-seven years.

1726, May 10. Will—proved 1726, Jul. 13. Ex. cousin (*i. e.* nephew) Henry. To sister Martha Eldredge, £12. To cousin Margaret Knowles, daughter of William, £30. To cousin Moses Lippitt, £20. To cousin William Knowles, £3. To cousins John, Robert and Daniel Knowles, £3, each. To cousin Mary Greene, £6. To cousin Margaret Knowles, daughter of cousin Henry, £5. To cousin Sybil Knowles, £5. To cousin Henry Knowles, all my homestead and land, 140 acres, and rest of personal estate.

KNOWLES. **3d column. I. Henry. Children by 2d wife 5, Thomas. 6, Susanna. 7, Martha. III. Daniel. Children, 1, Robert. 2, Amey. 3, Mary. 4, Deliverance. 5 Daniel. 6, Reynolds. 7, Hazard, 1736.**

I. HENRY, b. 1675, Sep. 29. d. 1740, May 1. South Kingstown, R. I
m. (1) MARY CASE, b. 1682, Dec. 2. d. 1709, Nov. 16. of Joseph & Hannah (Smith) Case.
m. (2) 1712, May 28. SUSANNA BOSS, b. 1687, Jul. 21. d. of Edward & Susanna (Wilkinson) Boss.

1. Mary, 1702, Sep. 25.
2. Margaret, 1705, Nov. 9.
3. Sybil, 1707, Feb. 11.
4. Henry, 1708, Nov. 20.

1740, May 16. Inventory, £625, 19*s.* 2*d.*, presented by Robert Knowles, of Charlestown, administrator. 5 cows, 5 pigs, hog, 23 other swine, old horse, 3 mares, 2 colts, negro Harry £10, Indian woman £8, 10 sides of sole leather, 17 sides in bark, 35 sides, 2 kips, and a horse hide, 19 calf skins, 15 goat skins, and much more leather, 7½ cords bark, 3 suits wearing apparel, 4 turkeys, 15 geese, warming pan, gun, quilting frame, 6 cheese moulds.

II. WILLIAM, b. d. 1727. South Kingstown, R. I.
m. HANNAH BROWNING, b. 1691, Jul. 16. d. 1726 (—) of William & Rebecca (Wilbur) Browning.

1. Rebecca,
2. Hannah,

1726, Apr. 26. Will—proved 1727, Aug. 19. Exs. brother Henry Knowles, and brother-in-law John Browning. To daughters Rebecca and Hannah Knowles, all my worldly estate equally, at eighteen. All estate to be turned into money and let out till daughters are of age.

Inventory, £769, 17*s.*, viz: 5 bonds £534, 6*s.*, wearing apparel £24, warming pan, linen wheel, 2 horses, 2 mares, cow, store hog, &c.

III. DANIEL, b. d. 1759. South Kingstown, R. I.
m. 1721 May 5. HANNAH, b. d. of

1737, Jun. 3. He bought of John Tibbitts and Sarah, of Providence, 260 acres there, &c., for £2,400.

1759, Sep. 5. Inventory, £1, 352, 10*s.* Administrator Robert Potter. Among items were wearing apparel, 4 old sheep, 6 hogs, old horse, yearling mare, linen wheel, pair worsted combs, mulatto boy £200, negro wench and bedding £12, 4 geese, &c.

IV. ROBERT, b. d. 1759. South Kingstown, R. I.
m. 1721, Apr. 27. ANN HULL, b. 1702, Oct. 26. d. 1758 + of Joseph & Ann (Gardiner) Hull.

1. Sarah, 1722, May 9.
2. William, 1725, Oct. 13.
3 Robert, 1728, Feb. 27.
4. Joseph, 1730, Mar. 16.
5. Ann, 1737, Oct. 20.

1758, Nov. 29. Will—proved 1759, Jan. 8. Exs. sons William & Joseph. To wife, for life, use of lower largest room, bedroom adjoining, privilege to bake in oven, cellar room, &c., negro woman Tent and her children, four cows, horse (and keep of same for life), and £40, annually. To wife also, corn and meat, and to be provided with firewood, and she to have all household goods. To father-in-law Joseph Hull, a maintenance by executors. To grandson Benjamin Hoxie, at age, a silver tankard value of £180, old tenor, equivalent to Spanish milled dollars at £6, old tenor, each. To granddaughters Barsheba and Ann Hoxie, a silver tankard each at age, and to each £1,000. To daughter Ann Reynolds, £2,800. To granddaughters Hannah and Ann Reynolds, each a silver tankard at eighteen. To sons William and Joseph, rest of estate equally.

Inventory, £7, 279, 12*s.* 6*d.*, viz: wearing apparel, riding horse, cash £18, 3*s.*, silver spoon, pewter, warming pan, pair of worsted combs, negro man £1,000, woman £800, boy £150, boy £50, horse, mare, 64 sheep, 10 cows, 2 oxen, heifer, 5 yearlings, 12 calves, &c.

V. JOHN, b. d. 1772. Richmond, R. I.
m. 1718, May 22. ELIZABETH WARNER, b. 1697, Apr. 19. d. 1771 + of John & Elizabeth (Coggeshall) Warner.

1. John,
2. Daniel,
3. Robert,
4. Samuel,
5. Daughter,

1771, Apr. 4. Will—proved 1772, Nov. 13. Ex. son John Knowles, of South Kingstown. To wife Elizabeth, best room, two beds and other household goods necessary, and use of heifer till grandson John Sherman is twenty-one. To son John, homestead farm where I dwell. To son Daniel, feather bed. To son Robert, ten silver dollars. To son Samuel, one dollar. To grandson William Sherman, five dollars at twenty-one. To grandson John Sherman, a cow. To son John, rest of estate.

Inventory, £54, 3*s.*, viz: wearing apparel £5, 2*s.*, pied cow, black cow, red cow, yearling, 2 calves, 14 sheep, 10 lambs, old mare, cider, pewter, side saddle, stillyards, 4 beds, &c.

VI. ALICE, b. d.
m. ——— SCREVEN, b. d. of Screven.

1. Isaac,
2. Thomas,
3. William,
4. Mary,
5. Susanna,

VII. ROSE, b. d. 1749 (—)
m. JOHN WILSON, b. d. 1752. of Wilson.

1. Jemima,
2. Ann, 1709, Apr 26.
3. Alice,
4. Mary,
5. Sarah,
6. Daughter,

VIII. MARTHA, b. d.
m. 1711, May 7. SAMUEL SHERMAN, b. d. of Sherman.

IX. MARY, b. d.
m. 1706, Oct. 22. EBER CHASE, b. d. 1740 of William & Hannah (Sherman) Chase.

1. Daniel,
2. William,
3. Eber,
4. Patience,
5. Hannah,
6. Alice,
7. Mary,

X. MARGARET, b. d.

1. Mary,
2. Martha,
3. Rebecca,
4. Moses,

1. Penelope,
2. Margaret,
3. Mary,

LANGFORD. See: American Geneologist, v.20, p.227.

{ THOMAS, { b. Newport, R. I.
m. { d.
——— { b. { d.

1670, Jun. 20. He and Jacob Pender were employed to carry a delegation of Deputies from Newport to Narragansett in Robert Carr's boat. (The order of the General Assembly being dated as above.)

I. { THOMAS, { b. Newport, East Greenwich, R. I.
m. (1) { d. 1709, Jun.
COMFORT, { b.
m. (2) 1701, { d. 1699 ± of
SARAH, { b. { d. 1756 ± of

(She m. (2) 1711, Sep. 13, Immanuel Rouse.)

He was a carpenter.

1694, Sep. 4 He had legacy of a pied horse by will of John Greene, of Newport.

1698, Jul. 13. East Greenwich. He owned land there at this date.

1699, Apr. 12. Freeman.

1708, Feb. 13. He and wife Sarah, sold Zachariah Jenkins, of Sandwich, Mass., for £330, a farm of 90 acres in East Greenwich, bounded partly by land belonging to heirs of John Smith, surveyor, of Newport, deceased.

1709, Jun. 11. As he had died intestate the Town Council now made his will, appointing his widow Sarah, exx. To Thomas Langford his oldest son was given £100, silver whistle, chain, box and 2 bodkins, all of silver, 3 gold rings, 3 gold jewels, silk mantle, silk gown and petticoat, a sash, christening cloth, &c., amounting to £26, 3*d*. To John Langford, eldest son of widow, £60. To son Jonathan, £60. These sums to be paid forthwith to guardians of children to be improved to best advantage. To daughters Ruth and Comfort, £60, each at 18 or marriage. The widow to have residue of estate after legacies and debts were paid and children brought up.

Inventory, £482, 7*s*., 11*d*., viz: wearing apparel £4. Bills and bonds £284, 15*s*. Mortgage £26, 17*s*. Silver whistle, currel and bells (3 oz) and scissors and chain £1, 10*s*., 10*d*., silver box, 2 bodkins, and small silver spoon 16*s*, 8*d*., 4 gold rings £4, 5*s*., 3 gold jewels 16*s*., 6 silver spoons £3, 18*s*., 24 napkins, 1 silk gown and petticoat (his former wife's) £10, sash and christening cloth £1, 10*s*., 2 spinning wheels, 6 cows, 1 heifer, 3 mares, 58 sheep, 18 lambs, 1 ram, 2 oxen, 4 swine, 1 negro man £35, &c.

II. { JOHN, { b. Newport, R. I.
m. { d.
ALIDA, { b. { d. of

He was a merchant.

1710, Jul. 30. His son Richard was baptized at Trinity Church, and other children later.

1713, Oct. His suit against Evan Henry was heard in the Assembly. Voted that he should pay £30, and all costs of court.

1714, Sep. He brought suit against Edward Pelham, Jr., for £200 debt.

1717, Apr. 30. Freeman.

1720, May 3. He sued John Russell and Aaron Williams, tailors.

LIPPITT.

{ JOHN, { b. Providence, Warwick, R. I.
m. { d. 1669 +
——— { b. { d.

1638. Providence. He was one of those who had a house lot and 6 acre lot.

1640, Jul. 27. He and thirty-eight others signed an agreement for a form of government.

1647, May 16. He and nine other "well betrusted friends and neighbors" were chosen by the town of Providence as commissioners to meet with commissioners from the other three towns at Portsmouth, there to form a government under the charter. Having given this committee full power to act they close: "Thus betrusting you with the premises, we commit you unto the protection and direction of the Almighty, wishing you a comfortable voyage, a happy success, and a safe return to us again."

1648, Jun. 5. Warwick. His name was recorded as an inhabitant.

1652, Apr. 27. He sold to Arthur Fenner, of Providence, all lands and meadows in Providence, only reserving a 5 acre lot and 3 acres of meadow. (Enrolled 1680, Apr. 1, with the town's consent.)

1655. Freeman.

1662, Feb. 10. He bought 6 acres of John Gereardy.

1665, Feb. 19. He had lot 53 in a division of lands in Providence.

1669, May 22. He deeded to son Moses, for love, &c., and 10*s*., in peage, sixteen per penny, my late dwelling house standing near the brook that runneth between said house and land of James Greene, also lands and meadows.

I. { JOHN, { b. Warwick, R. I.
m 1665, Feb. 9. { d. 1670 ±
ANN GROVE, { b. { d. of Grove.

(She m. (2) 1671, Feb. 21, Edward Searle.)

1652, May 4. He was fined £5, for selling a gun to Indians.

1668, Apr. 27. He, with consent of his father, sold Thomas Greene, a third of a 30 acre lot for 20*s*.

II. { MOSES, { b. Warwick, R. I.
m. 1668, Nov. 19. { d. 1703, Jan. 6.
MARY KNOWLES, { b. { d. 1719, Dec. 28. of Henry Knowles.

He was a tanner.

1672, Apr. 30. Freeman.

1681-84-90-98-99. Deputy.

1687. Overseer of the Poor.

1700, Jan. 6. Will—proved 1703. Exx. wife Mary. Overseers, brother-in-law John Knowles, and Randall Holden. To wife, 20 acre lot at Warwick Great Neck and all housing and lands till son Moses is of age. His son Moses, at age, to have the house where Edward Carter now dwelleth and land adjoining and certain other lands, a bed, three cows, half of tanning instruments and half profits of tanning trade, he being at half the charge. To grandson Moses Burlingame, all rights in Potowomet purchase. To wife, all lands and housing undisposed of for life and then to son Moses. To three daughters Mary Burlingame, Martha Burlingame and Rebecca Lippett, 20*s*. each, paid in plate. To wife Mary, all movable estate.

Inventory, £456, 4*s*., viz: silver money £15, 2 silver cups and 6 spoons £7, 19*s*., gun, sword, 4 feather beds, flock bed, warming pan, 4 spinning wheels, 3 tables, 15 chairs, 4 benches, 4 stools, a horse, 2 oxen, 7 cows, 5 two years old, 2 yearlings, a bull, 12 swine, stock of leather, green hides and bark £140, book debts £100, &c.

East Greenwich, R. I., Dutchess Co., N. Y.

I. THOMAS, b. 1695, Mar. 22. d.
m. 1723, Dec.
HANNAH, b. d. of

1. Holden, 1724, Sep. 24.
2. Joseph, 1726, Dec. 22.
3. Stephen, 1728, Mar. 16.
4. Thomas, 1731, Jan. 19.

1731, Jan. 22. He received a deed of 10 acres in North Kingstown from his stepfather Immanuel Rouse, and for a time he lived in North Kingstown.
1756, Jan. 5. Dutchess Co., N. Y. (as appears by allusion in E. Greenwich records).

(2D WIFE.)

II. RUTH, b. 1702, Feb. 19. d.
m. 1720, Oct. 20.
THOMAS NICHOLS, b. 1691, Dec. 13. d. of John & Hannah (Forman) Nichols.

1. Thomas, 1722, Jan. 4.
2. Hannah, 1723, Mar. 20.
3. Ruth, 1729, Oct. 27.
4. Benjamin, 1731, Dec. 6.

III. COMFORT, b. 1704, Jan. 1. d. 1784, Apr. 2.
m. 1728, Nov. 22.
THOMAS CASEY, b. 1706, Nov. 18. d. 1797, Apr. 20. of Adam & Mary (Greenman) Casey.

1. Sarah, 1729, Oct. 20.
2. Ruth, 1730, Nov. 28.
3. Silas, 1734, Jun. 5.
4. Barbara, 1737, Mar. 24.
5. Elizabeth, 1744, Oct. 24.

East Greenwich, R. I.

IV. JOHN, b. 1705, Oct. 10. d. 1785, May.
m. 1727, May 11.
BARBARA RICE, b. 1706, Apr. 24. d. of John & Elnathan (Whipple) Rice.

1. Thomas, 1729, Sep. 9.
2. Sarah, 1731, Oct. 6.
3. Phebe, 1734, Apr. 26.
4. Ellen, 1737, May 12.
5. John, 1740, May 15.
6. Barbara, 1745, Mar. 20.

1727, May 2. Freeman. He was member of Town Council many years, Justice of Peace, &c.
1785, May 25. Inventory, £121, 0*s*., 9½*d*. Administration to son John. Wearing apparel, money and plate £45, 7*s*., 3½*d*., desk, pewter, coffee mill, case and bottles, 2 cows, 2 calves, 10 sheep, woolen wheel, &c.

East Greenwich, Warwick, R. I.

V. JONATHAN, b. 1708, Feb. 20. d. 1739.
m. 1727, Nov. 15.
ANN CLAPP, b. d. of Clapp.

1. Jonathan, 1731, Jan. 4.
2. Mary, 1733, Aug. 1.

1734, Feb. 4. Warwick. Freeman.
1738, Nov. 5. Will—proved 1739, Jan. 1. Exs. wife Ann, and Thomas Casey To son Jonathan, all lands and housing at 21. To daughter Mary Langford, £40, at 18. To wife Ann, rest of movable estate.
Inventory, £391, 5*s*., 6*d*., viz: plate £11, 9*s*., linen wheel, barrel of beer, worsted card, cooper's stuff, 2 cows, 1 shoat, 12 fowls, &c.

I. RICHARD, b. 1710. d.

II. CATHARINE, b. 1712. d.

III. GEORGE, b. 1714. d.

IV. ALIDA, b. 1717. d.

V. JOHN, b. 1719. d.

LIPPITT.

Warwick, R. I.

I. JOHN, b. 1665, Nov. 16. d. 1723, Oct. 31.
m.
REBECCA LIPPITT, b. d. 1723 + of Moses & Mary (Knowles) Lippitt.

1. John,
2. Mary,
3. Moses,
4. Ann,

1696. Freeman.
1723, Oct. 27. Will—proved 1723, Dec. 7. Exx. wife Rebecca. To eldest son John, homestead, housing and all other lands in Warwick, except my right in division, he paying annually to wife Rebecca, 40*s*., and to find her in firewood. To wife while widow, best room in house. To son Moses, £5, at twenty-one years of age paid by John. To daughter Mary Colvin, 5*s*. To daughter Ann Lippitt, £25, at eighteen. To son Moses, £25, in a year after decease of testator, and he to have right in first and second division of lands. To wife, all the rest of estate.
Inventory, £245, 13*s*., 8*d*., viz: plate and money £3, 12*s*., 9*d*., scales, stillyards, 3 feather beds, 1 flock bed, brass, pewter, gun, pair of oxen, 2 cows, mare, carpenter's tools, barrel of cider, spinning wheel and cards, books 8*s*., 2 looking glasses, &c. His son Moses died intestate 1727, Mar. 26, administration being given to his brother John.

Warwick, R. I., Middletown, N. J.

II. MOSES, b. 1668, Feb. 17. d.
m. 1697, Dec. 8.
SARAH THROCKMORTON, b. d. of John & Alice (Stout) Throckmorton.

1. Sarah, 1705, Dec. 11.
2. John,

1674, Jul. 3. He, with full consent of his father-in-law (*i. e.* stepfather) Edward Searle, and Anna Searle his mother, resident at Mashantatack, put himself apprentice to William Austin, of Providence, for fifteen years and a half and two months from date, to learn the trade and occupation of a weaver—to give faithful service, not to frequent taverns nor ale houses, &c., and he to have sufficient meat, drink and apparel and be instructed in art and trade of a weaver, and at end of time to have two sufficient suits of apparel. If William Austin should die, Moses was to serve his mistress, or with whom his master should assign him.
1697, Dec. 7. His marriage license was issued at New York but he soon took up his residence in Middletown. His son John married Catharine ——, and was alive as late as 1750, but the family is now extinct in Monmouth county

I. MARY, b. d.
m.
JOHN BURLINGAME, b. 1664, Aug. 1. d. of Roger & Mary (   ) Burlingame.

1. John,
2. Roger,
3. James,
4. David,
5. Barlingstone 1698, Jun. 25
6. Benjamin,
7. Elisha,

II. MARTHA, b. d. 1723.
m.
THOMAS BURLINGAME, b. 1667, Feb. 6. d. 1758, Jul. 9. of Roger & Mary (   ) Burlingame.

1. Thomas, 1688, May 29
2. Moses,
3. Samuel,
4. Peter,
5. Joshua,
6. Daughter,
7. Mary,
8. Margaret,
9. Sarah,
10. Freelove,
11. Alice,
12. Patience,
13. Stephen,

1719, Mar. 6. Will—proved 1720, Feb. 3. Widow Mary. Ex. son Moses. To son-in-law Thomas Burlingame and Martha his wife, £20. To son-in-law John Lippitt and Rebecca his wife, £20, and debt of £32, due from John, remitted. To granddaughter Mercy Gorton, wife of Othniel, £20. To grandson David Burlingame, son of John, £10. To granddaughter Mary Colvin, daughter of John Lippitt, £20. To grandson Moses Lippitt, son of John, £20. To granddaughter Margaret Remington, daughter of Thomas Burlingame, £20. To sister Martha Eldridge, £10. To cousin John Budlong, 40*s*. To son Moses, all the rest of estate.

Inventory, £452, 5*s*., 4*d*., viz: hides in the tan, raw hides, bark and leather £140, 5 cows, 2 oxen, 2 heifers, 2 calves, 6 swine, book debts £150, 2 table cloths, a dozen napkins, pewter, warming pan, plate £12, 18*s*., &c.

III. NATHANIEL, { b. / d. } Monmouth, N. J.

1676. He was plaintiff in a suit this year.

Possibly he may have had a son Moses, who married Sarah Throckmorton (instead of that marriage having been made by Moses, son of John[2]).

IV. JOSEPH, { b. / d. }

V. REBECCA, { b. / d. 1675, Nov.
m. (1) 1664, Feb. 2.
JOSEPH HOWARD, { b. / d. } of Howard.
m. (2) 1669, Mar. 19.
FRANCIS BUDLONG, { b. / d. 1675, Nov. } of Budlong.

LOW.

ANTHONY[2], (John[1]). { b. / d. 1692. } Boston, Mass., Warwick, R. I., [Swanzey, Mass.
m.
FRANCES, { b. 1632. / d. 1702, Jun. }

He was son of John & Elizabeth ( ) Low, his father being a wheelwright in Boston, where he died 1653, Dec. 1.

1666, Mar. 29. Warwick. He bought of Christopher Hauxhurst, his dwelling house and land in Pawtuxet.

1670, Feb. 1. Swanzey. He deeded to son John, for love, &c., 20 acres and dwelling house in Warwick and other land.

1675, Jun. 27. The burning of his house is alluded to in a letter from Roger Williams to John Winthrop. He mentions a report that the Indians "had burnt about twelve houses, one new great one (Anthonie Loes)." This house was in Swanzey.

1676. He bought the terms of service of five Indians "great and small," for £8. They had been taken captive by Providence men, and were to serve out a certain term of years and then be free.

1676, Jun. Captain Benjamin Church was negotiating with the Seaconnet Indians and much needed a vessel, but met with disappointment owing to false and faint hearted men, &c., "until at last Mr. Anthony Low put into the harbor with a loaden vessel bound to the westward, and being made acquainted with Mr. Church's case told him that he had so much kindness for him and was so pleased with the business that he was engaged in, that he would run the venture of his vessel and cargo to wait upon him." He brought him to Newport where Mr. Church disembarked.

1682, Oct. 31. His Indian servant James now living with him at Swanzey, having often solicited the court for his freedom, (he having been out in the rebellion) it was now ordered by the court that he should be free the Tuesday after March Court unless Mr. Low appears to give satisfying reason to contrary; and when he goes away his master shall give him a good suit of clothes.

1692, Aug. 6. Will. "The last will and testament of Anthony Low, this sixth day of August 1692; first I do will and bequeath to my loving wife the house she now lives in, during her life, and after her decease to my son Samuel Low & his heirs forever. And to my eldest son John Low, all in right and title at Warwick to him and his heirs forever. And to my son Samuel, my sloop Dolphin which now I am in, my wife and my son Samuel taking care to maintain my daughter Elizabeth during her life; so resting with dear love to all my friends, this I leave as my last will and testament this sixth day of August, 1692. I also bequeath my plantation at Swanzey to my son Simon Davis, and all the rest that is mine to my wife and my son Samuel as aforesaid."

His wife's gravestone is still to be seen in the burial ground at New Meadow Neck Warren, R. I.

I. JOHN, { b. / d. } Warwick, R. I.
m. 1675, Mar. 3.
MARY RHODES, { b. / d. } of Zachariah & Joanna (Arnold) Rhodes.

1675. Freeman.

1678, May 6. He was fined 20*s*. for not serving on jury.

1682. Deputy.

1688. Grand Jury.

1692, Nov. 10. He quit-claimed to his brother Samuel all his interest in lands and housing at Swanzey.

1695, Oct. 30. The Assembly met at his house.

LOW, 2d column. I. John. He had also a daughter Mary m. Ephraim Pierce. He b. 1674+; d. 17[illegible] of Ephraim and Hannah (Holbrook) Pierce. Children. 1. Mial, 1693, Apr. 24. 2. Mary, 1697, Nov. 16. 3. [illegible] 1701, July 26. 4. Elizabeth, 1703, May 30. 5. [illegible] 1708. 6, Ephraim. 3d column. I. Samuel. Marriage intentions, 1736, Jan. 31.

II. SAMUEL, { b. / d. 1718. } Swanzey, Barrington, Mass.
m. (1)
ANN, { b. / d. } of
m. (2)
RACHEL, { b. / d. 1718 + } of

1718, Aug. 4. Administration to relict Rachel and brother-in-law Simon Davis, of Bristol. Inventory, £3,925, viz: house and 300 acres £1,800, homestead £1,100, 100 acres £600. Riding horse, 5 horses in woods, 300 sheep and lambs, 15 cows, 3 yoke of oxen, 5 steers, a heifer, 5 two year old, 10 yearlings, 7 calves, 4 negroes £130, linen wheel, household articles in following rooms; great lower room, kitchen, leanto, leanto chamber, kitchen chamber, great chamber, north-western chamber, garret.

Division of estate was made to widow Rachel, son Samuel, eldest daughter Anne Low, and youngest daughter Rachel Low.

III. ELIZABETH, { b. / d. }

IV. ANN, { b. / d.
m, 1685, Sep. 24.
SIMON DAVIS, { b. 1660. / d. 1736, Sep. 11. } of Nicholas & Sarah ( ) Davis.

LOW. 2d column. Add V. Francis, d. 1685, Jul. 15, unmarried.

III. REBECCA, b. ; d. 1723 +
m.
JOHN LIPPITT, b. 1665, Nov. 16. ; d. 1723, Oct. 31. of John & Ann (Grove) — Lippitt.

1. John,
2. Mary,
3. Moses,
4. Ann,

Warwick, R. I.

IV. MOSES, b. ; d. 1745, Dec. 12.
m. 1707, Nov. 20.
ANPHILLIS WHIPPLE, b. 1689, Oct. 6. ; d. 1744 + of Joseph & Alice (Smith) — Whipple.

1704. Freeman.
1708, Jun. 14. He bought of Robert Westcott the lot that the latter had bought of his brother Zorobabel, being the same where Robert's grandfather Stukley Westcott, had lived.
1714, May 5. He bought of Benjamin Carpenter, of Pawtuxet, for £52, 40s., a whole purchase right of land.
1715-16-21-22-27-30. Deputy.
1741, Jun. 20. Will—proved 1745, Jan. 24. Exx. wife Anphillis. To son Moses, a 14 acre lot in Warwick, land in Providence and 100 acres joining Pascouge Cedar Swamp. To son Jeremiah, a lot in Horse Neck and half of warehouse and lot in Warwick near the wharf. To son Christopher, 110 acres in Natick. To son Joseph, lots of land and slaughter house and half of warehouse, as also a feather bed, cow and twenty sheep. To son John, land in Warwick and half of homestead and buildings, half of stock and half appurtenances belonging to tannery, as also £100, a feather bed, silver tankard and great bible, all at age, besides other land 180 acres. To daughter Ann Francis, £50, and negro woman Wango. To daughter Freelove, £50, and negro girl Violet. To daughter Mary, £1 00, and negro girl Cynthia, a great square bed, 100 acre lot and £200. To wife Anphillis, rest of real and personal estate.
Inventory, £2,090, viz: silver tankard, porringer, salt and pepper box and 10 spoons £120, 5 negro slaves £350, 2 Indian servants' time £30, wearing apparel £100, books £10, bond £100, warming pan, coffee mill, foot wheel, woolen wheel, mahogany tea table, 2000lbs. tobacco, pair of oxen, pair of stags, 8 cows, bull, 2 heifers, 2 steers, 4 yearlings, 5 calves, 88 sheep and lambs, 5 barrels of cider, &c. The rooms named, were: garret, 2 little bedrooms, great chamber, kitchen chamber, great room, kitchen, cellar, new bedroom, old bedroom, cheese room, slaughter house, shop.

1. Moses, 1709, Jan. 17
2. Jeremiah, 1711, Jan. 27.
3. Christopher 1712, Nov. 29.
4. Joseph, 1715, Sep. 4.
5. Anphillis, 1717, Aug. 29.
6. Freelove, 1720, Mar. 31.
7. Mary, 1723, Dec. 2.
8. John, 1731, Dec. 24.

(By 2d husband.)
1. John, 1672.

LOW.

Warwick, R. I.

I. ANTHONY, b. ; d. 1752.
m.
MARY ARNOLD, b. ; d. 1746 + of Israel & Mary (Barker) — Arnold.

1. John, 1702, Oct. 8.
2. Stephen,
3. Anne,
4. Christian,

1704. Freeman.
1704. Constable.
1710, Nov. 27. He deeded his brother John, for love, &c., land in Warwick.
1713-15-16-18-20-22-25-26-28-32. Deputy.
1718. Lieutenant.
1719, Apr. 27. He and wife Mary sold for £144, certain land in Warwick to Anthony Holden.
1726. Major.
1746, Feb. 10. Will—proved 1752, Jun. 8. Exs. sons John and Stephen. To wife Mary, mansion house, that is old part where I now dwell, for life, and all household goods at her disposal except silver tankard, and use of all negroes for life, and an acre of land for a garden, three cows and a mare, and keep of same by sons John and Stephen, who were to find her in firewood, as also three barrels of cider every year, and what apples she needs for eating, and £5, annually from each son. To son John, use of all land in Horse Neck bought of my brother John Low, and at decease of son John, said land to go to his son Anthony. To son John, at decease of wife, negro man Newport, and negro woman Peg. To son Stephen, use of house where he lives and all my homestead lands west of highway, and all the land and housing given wife, at her decease; all the foregoing at the death of Stephen to go to his son John, grandson of testator. To son Stephen, all lands undisposed of and at decease of wife he to have negro boy named Bristol. To sons John and Stephen my silver tankard and at wife's decease, two negro boys, Fortune and Prince. To daughter Anne Rice, £5, and what she has had. To daughter Christian Carpenter, £90, and negro Patience at decease of wife. To grandchildren Edmund, Anne, Mary and Francis Haynes, £15, each. To grandson Anthony Carpenter, a horse of £20 value at twenty-one years of age.
Inventory, £2,549, 4s., viz: silver tankard, cup and 7 spoons £153, 12s., silver hilted sword £15, pewter, woolen wheel, linen wheel. Negro Peg £220, Newport £440, Bristol £400, Fortune £350, Prince £200. 3 cows £90, 2 calves, mare and colt £60, a two year horse, 26 sheep, 6 lambs, 3 shoats, warming pan, &c.

Warwick, R. I.

II. JOHN, b. ; d. 1757.
m.
ANN HOLDEN, b. ; d. of Charles & Catharine (Greene) — Holden.

1. Anthony,
2. John,
3. Ann,

1712. Freeman.
1719, Mar. 22. He and wife Ann sold to his brother Anthony Low, certain land in Warwick, for £55.
1731, Sep. 15. He deeded to cousin (*i. e.* nephew) John Low, Jr., certain land, for £13.
1736. Deputy.
1757, Jan. 4. Inventory, £5,803, 16s. 8d. Administrator, son Captain Anthony Low. Notes £434, 12s., book accounts £1,468, 16s. 2d., 25 chairs, 1 great chair, linen wheel, woolen wheel, coffee mill, old small arm, warming pan, pewter, 4 barrels cider, some cider beer, 5 shoats, 5 turkeys, 6 fowls, sundry old books £2, old razor, ink stand, negro boy £350, mare £50, yoke of oxen, 7 cows, 5 two year old, 10 yearlings, 5 calves, 30 sheep, 30 lambs, 13 loads of hay, 500 lbs. tobacco, &c.

III. REBECCA, b. ; d. 1723 +
m.
ANDREW BARTON, b. ; d. 1723, Apr. 19. of Benjamin & Susanna (Gorton) — Barton.

1. Benjamin, 1703
2. Samuel,
3. Andrew
4. Rufus,
5. Anthony,
6. Phebe,
7. Susannah,

Warren, R. I.

I. SAMUEL, b. 1701, Mar. 29. ; d. 1749.
m.
ISABEL GREENE, b. 1698, Sep. 3. ; d. 1750 + of Richard & Eleanor (Sayles) — Greene.

1. Ann,
2. Hooker,
3. John Wilson,
4. Samuel,

1748, Jun. 25. Will—proved 1749, Oct. 2. Exx. wife Isabel. To wife, a third of movables, and a third of income of real estate. To three sons Hooker Low, John Wilson Low, and Samuel Low, the other two-thirds of movables. To wife, the use of two south lower rooms, in the house where I dwell and privilege in kitchen for brewing, baking, washing, &c., and yard room, for life. To three sons, all real estate, a third to each, and if either die without issue, the others to have his part, and to said sons the privilege in house and income of a third of real estate after decease of wife. The two eldest sons to have improvement of Samuel's part till he is of age. To grandchildren Samuel, Lewis and Joseph Bosworth, children of my daughter Ann, late deceased, £500, a third to each at age, which with what already done for daughter I value at £1,000.
Inventory. Wearing clothes and apparel £89, 5s., books £50, riding beast, saddle, and saddle bags £179, Bills of Credit, note and bond £184, guns, sword, &c. £22, 15s., 2 razors and hone, silver tankard and 2 silver porringers £126, 10 silver spoons £26, silver pepper box £4, 7s., 5 pictures in lower south room £26, warming pan, lignum vitae mortar, 2 woolen wheels, 2 linen wheels, pair of cards, negro man £200, negro woman £200, boy Pero £300, Chloe £250, Phillis £210, Rit £190, Sip £150, Effe £100, 8 large swine, 5 shoats, 3 fatted steers, 3 fatted cows, 14 milch cows, 2 pair oxen, pair of steers, 5 heifers, 6 yearlings, 8 calves, 95 sheep, 45 lambs, mare and colt, corn, rye, barley, cider mill and screw press £30, &c.
1750, Oct. 3. Receipt was taken by Isabel Low from Hooker Low, for £1,029, 13s. 4d., in full for his part of personal, and also a receipt from John Wilson Low, for same amount.

II. ANNE, b. ; d.

III. RACHEL, b. ; d.

1. Nicholas, 1686, Oct. 9.
2. Sarah, 1689, Jun. 15.
3. Ann, 1694, Sep. 23.
4. Hannah, 1696, Jan. 12.
5. Samuel, 1698, Jun. 30.
6. Elizabeth, 1699, Aug. 8.
7. Simon, 1701, Oct. 11.
8. Frances, 1703, Sep. 23.

* American Genealogist, v. 28, no. 4, Oct., 1952, p. 212

JOSIAS, b. 1647. d. 1709, Aug. 8. Newport, R. I.
m.
——— b. d.

1677, May 1. Freeman.
1680. Taxed 6s.
He was buried in Newport Cemetery.

LYNDON. 1st column. Josias,[2] (Augustin[1]). 1699. Apr. 10—proved 1699, Aug. 29, will of his father. Augustin Lyndon, shipwright, late of Boston in New England, now of parish of St. Paul's, Shotwell, Middlesex, England. To son Josias estate in Boston, and also mentions grandson Samuel.

I. SAMUEL, b. 1676. d. 1750, Dec. 10. Newport, R. I.
m. (1) 1703, Jul.
PRISCILLA TOMPKINS, b. 1679, May 24. d. 1732, Dec. 11. of Nathaniel & Elizabeth (Allen) Tompkins.
m. (2) 1735, Dec. 25.
SARAH MINOT, b. 1693. d. 1762, Mar. 24. of Minot.

1710. Freeman.
He was buried in Newport Cemetery.

II. JOSIAS, b. d. Newport, R. I.
m.
ABIGAIL, b. d. of

MALAVERY.

JOHN, b. d. 1712. Providence, R. I.
m.
ELIZABETH, b. d. 1718 +

1687, Sep. 1. Taxed 3s.
1688. Ratable estate, 7 cows, 5 yearlings, horse, mare, colt, 12 sheep. 56 acres of land.
1704, Sep. 11. He had 12 acres laid out in exchange with the town
He died the records say either in September or October.
1712, Jul. 24. Will—proved 1712, Dec. 12. Ex. son John. To him all lands and housing and all movables except 40s. each, to daughters Elizabeth Phillips, Deliverance Mathewson and Mary Inman. Wife Elizabeth, to be maintained by son John, suitably.
Inventory, £127, 17s., 6d., viz: 9 cows, 2 heifers, 3 yearlings, calf, two year bull, horse, 18 loads of hay, 14 barrels cider, brass, pewter, iron glass, wearing apparel, gun, sword, &c.

I. JOHN, b. d. 1718, Sep. 18. Providence, R. I.
m.
EXPERIENCE MOWRY, b. d. 1718 + of Nathaniel & Joanna (Inman) Mowry.

(She m. (2) William Bates.)
1713, Mar. 21. He had 130 poles of land laid out adjoining lot where he dwells.
1713, Jun. 16. Taxed with mother £1, 13s.
1718, Sep. 15. Will—proved 1718, Oct. 13. Exx. wife Experience. He desires his wife to provide things fit and comfortable for my mother, in her old age, and authorizes his wife to raise £30, which shall be levied out of his estate. The rest of movable estate to wife and income of land and use of dwelling house for life while his widow. To sons John and Nathaniel, all lands, equally, but if they die before of age then the land was to go to Michael Inman, David Phillips and Daniel Mathewson, my three sisters' three sons.
Inventory, £245, 9s., 4d., viz: wearing apparel and money £29, 1s., horse and 6 young cattle £30, yoke of oxen and 10 cows £48, 4 calves, 2 beds, 4 guns, 2 swords, pewter, another horse, 7 swine, &c.

II. ELIZABETH, b. d. 1719 +
m.
JOSEPH PHILLIPS, b. d. 1719, Sep. 3. of Michael & Barbara ( ) Phillips.

III. DELIVERANCE, b. d. 1716 +
m. 1698, Nov. 17.
JOHN MATHEWSON, b. d. 1716, Sep. 18. of James & Hannah (Field) Mathewson.

IV. MARY, b. d. 1744, Nov. 20.
m.
EDWARD INMAN, b. d. 1755, Jun. 11. of Edward & Elizabeth (Bennett) Inman.

LYNDON. 3d column. I. Josias. His wife was daughter of Robert and Hannah (Hale) Carr; b. 1710, d. 1790, Mar. 14.

I. JOSIAS, m. 1727, Oct. 5. MARY CARR, | b. 1704, Mar. 10. d. 1778, Mar. 30. b. 1693, Oct. 26. d. 1790. | Newport, Warren, R. I. of Edward & Hannah (Stanton) Carr. | No issue.

1728. Freeman.
1728, to 1767 and 1770 to 1777 (inclusive) Clerk of Assembly.
1729, Feb. He (called Josias Lynden the Scrivener), was employed by the committee appointed to revise and print the laws, and was allowed £10, for his services.
1730. He was one of the founders of the literary and philosophical society subsequently known as Redwood Library.
1740, Sep. He was appointed on a committee to audit the accounts of billeting out soldiers lately raised in this colony to go against Spain, &c.
1764. He was among the incorporators of Brown University.
1768–69. Governor.
1778, Mar. 19. Will—proved 1778, May 24. Exx. wife Mary. He calls himself of Newport, now residing in Warren. To descendants of Mr. John Boydle. late of Boston, deceased, £300. To wife, all the rest of personal at her disposal, excepting negroes, Great Cæsar and Little Cæsar, who are to be freed at death of wife. To wife, use of all real estate for life, and our 2 acre lot in town of Warren, adjoining land of sister Wheaton, will be hers at my decease, as we hold same as joint tenants. If the personal estate is not enough for wife's support she is empowered to sell what real estate is necessary, as she being in poor, helpless condition, may not be able to act for herself, the Town Council is empowered to assist and direct her in disposing of real estate. Any real estate left undisposed of at death of wife to go to William Peckham, of Middletown, and Henry Peckham, house carpenter, of Newport, and to such other persons as shall be chosen in my room, and as our assigns of executors of last will of Mr. John Clarke, late of Newport, deceased, who gave the farm, now in Middletown known by name of Charity Farm, for charitable uses; that is to say all for same uses as said Charity Farm was given, and the income to be used in same manner as by John Clarke's will
Inventory, £388, 14*s*., 2½*d*., as shown by widow (1779, Nov. 2), viz: clock £21, mahogany desk £9, mahogany desk not of best kind £7, 10*s*., ½ dozen mahogany chairs, leather bottoms, £3, 12*s*., ½ dozen black walnut chairs, leather bottoms, £2, 8*s*., silver watch £6, warming pan, large bible with silver clasps 30*s*., old horse and chaise £9, negro Sarah £24, Great Cæsar and Little Cæsar £30, pair of pistols and silver hilted sword £7, 10., pair of gold sleeve buttons 18*s*., 104 oz., 11 pwt. 12 gr. plate, such as tankard, spoons, &c. £34, 17*s*. 4*d*., table, old chest full of papers, case with 11 bottles, library of 400 or thereabout, books and pamphlets, bound and unbound £45, &c.
He was buried at Warren, and the inscription on his tombstone declares that he received a good education in early life, was chosen clerk of the lower House of the Assembly and of the Inferior Court of the County of Newport, in 1730, and continued so with great applause with the intermission of only two years until his death. "In the year 1768, to put an end to the violence of party rage, he was prevailed on to accept the place of Governor, which he filled with reputation."
1787, Aug. 30. Will—proved 1790, Apr. 6. Widow Mary, of Newport. Ex. brother Jonathan Wilson. To sister Hannah Wheaton, a bed, six silver spoons, &c. To nephew Robert Carr, mahogany table, six leather bottom chairs, mahogany desk, and silver tankard formerly belonging to his grandfather, &c. To nephew Josias Lyndon Wilson, books. To brother Jonathan Wilson, rest of estate.
Inventory, £64, 6*s*. 8*d*.

II. SAMUEL, m. 1734, Dec. 22. ELIZABETH GARDINER, | b. 1706. d. 1786, Jun. 16. b. d. | Newport, R. I. of Gardiner. | 1. Priscilla, 1742. 2. John, 1751, Sep. 14. 3. John, 1752, Sep. 1. 4. Mary, 1752, Sep. 1. 5. Peter, 1754, Apr. 30. 6. Abigail 1758, Aug. 14.

He held the title of Colonel.

III. MARY, | b. 1713, Jul. d. 1713, Sep. 23.

IV. JOHN, | b. 1714, Feb. 9. d. 1714, Jun. 14.

V. ELIZABETH, | b. 1718, Apr. 20. d. 1719, Apr. 23.

VI. PRISCILLA, | b. 1720, Mar. 4. d. 1731, Aug. 26.

VII. AUGUSTUS, | b. 1722, Sep. 28. d. 1723, Aug. 31.

I. JOSIAS, | b. 1713, Aug. 17. d.

II. DAUGHTER, | b. 1718, Apr. 2. d.

MALAVERY.

I. JOHN, m. (1) 1736, Dec. 26. SUSANNAH ARNOLD, m. (2) 1753, Jan. 9. ELIZABETH COMSTOCK, | b. d. b. d. b. 1726, Dec. 18. d. | Providence, Smithfield, R. I. of John & Mary (Mowry) Arnold. of Ichabod & Zibiah (Wilkinson) Comstock. | 1. Amey, 1740, Dec. 18. 2. Mary, 1745, Jun. 6. (2d wife.) 3. Iscah, 1754, Oct. 2. 4. Michael, 1756, Jun. 10. 5. Orpah, 1758, Jul. 28.

1737, Nov. 21. Smithfield. He gave receipt to father-in-law (*i. e.* stepfather) William Bates and mother Experience Bates, for legacy from father John Malavery's will, late of Providence, deceased.

II. NATHANIEL, | b. d.

1. John,
2. Joseph,
3. David,
4. Daniel,
5. Elizabeth,
6. Phebe,
7. Jeremiah,

1. John, 1699, Oct. 6.
2. Lydia, 1701, Jun. 7.
3. Daniel, 1704, Mar. 5.
4. Elizabeth, 1706, Dec. 21.
5. Israel, 1708, Jan. 3.
6. Ann, 1712, Jan. 21.
7. Jemima, 1715, Jul. 10.

1. Michael,
2. Elisha,
3. Israel,
4. Abraham,
5. Edward,
6. Elijah,
7. Susannah,
8. Priscilla,
9. Penelope,
10. Mary.

EDWARD, b. d. 1682 (—) Providence, R. I.
m. ——— b. d.

1640, Jul. 27. He and thirty-eight others signed an agreement for a form of government. (Some signed later than this date.)

1643, May 2. He was called of Seekonk at this date, and having challenged his house lot upon the neck there to be 12 acres (as he saith the rest of the lots were at the first division), if it be so he was to have 12 acres, but if the lots were to be 6 acres he was to have no more, or else valuable consideration for his labors according to Mr. Winslow's agreement with him, &c.

1645, Jan. 27. He bought of Robert Morris a share of meadow, bounding on a half share already owned by said Edward Manton.

1650, Sep. 2. Taxed £1.

1655. Freeman.

1659, Oct. 8. Juryman.

1660, Mar. 6. He sent a request to town, by his son Shadrach, that the authorities would take course for settling of Town bounds of lands near Neutaconkonett Hill, and the Town ordered a committee to view and report.

1661, Mar. 7. He having been warned by the town to speedily pluck up the fence with which he had enclosed a piece of ground, returned the message that he "was not minded to give them an answer at that time."

1665, Feb. 19. In a division of lands he drew lot No. 31. (Some signed later than this date.)

1682, May 13. He was mentioned in a deed, as deceased before this date.

I. SHADRACH, b. d. 1714, Jan. 27. Providence, R. I.
m.
ELIZABETH SMITH, b. d. of John & Alice ( ) Smith.

He was a cooper.

1658, Apr. 27. He received from the town a house share next Epenetus Olney, and meadow above Wanskuck.

1658, May 18. Freeman.

1661, Feb. 4. The town gave him a house lot and a 6 acre lot in one parcel on the Neck, with meadow right.

1661-65-69-75. Juryman.

1664. Constable.

1665, Feb. 19. In a division of lands he drew lot No. 48.

1667, May 30. He took oath of allegiance.

1667-68-69-70. Town Clerk.

1667-68-69-70-71. Deputy.

1669, Apr. 3. He bought of Henry Brown and Waite, a house lot with dwelling house and other housing except a barn already sold to Shadrach's father Edward.

1669, Jul. 8. He is alluded to in a letter from Roger Williams to John Whipple, wherein Mr. Williams says: "Shadrach deals more ingenuously than yourself," &c.

1677, Apr. 9. He sold William Hawkins, Jr., land that was in the original laid out unto John Smith, his father-in-law, and which appertained to said John Smith, as he was admitted equal purchaser in Providence. The meadow being inherited by John Smith, Jr., miller, was by him sold Shadrach Manton who sold it as above.

1679, Jul. 1. He and his son Edward taxed together 1*s*., 3*d*.

1683. Surveyor of Highways.

1687. Overseer of the Poor.

1687, Sep. 1. Taxed 1*s*., 1*d*.

1688. Ratable estate. A lot and house upon it wherein James Wakely dwells and the little island opposite thereto, also a piece of meadow adjoining of 1½ acres, and 4 acres more joining on to it, a cow, 1 yearling, ¼ right of common.

1703, May 31. He bought of Nicholas Power, land four or five miles west of Providence.

1712 ± He deeded certain land to his grandchildren, the daughters of Henry Esten; the said deed being alluded to by Joseph Randall (who married one of the grandchildren referred to), in a deed that he made in 1717.

1714, Jan. 27. He was found dead upon the road—the verdict of the jury being; "that his time being come he died a natural death."

By one account he had two other sons who died young.

MAXSON.

RICHARD, b. d. Boston, Mass., Portsmouth, R. I.
m. ——— b. d.

He was a blacksmith.

1634, Oct. 2. He was admitted to the church; being at this time in the employ of James Everill.

1638. Portsmouth. He and others were admitted as inhabitants of the island of Aquidneck, having submitted themselves to the government that is or shall be established.

1639, Feb. 7. "Richard Maxson, blacksmith, upon complaints made against him, was accordingly detected for his oppression in the way of his trade, who being convinced thereof, promised amendment and satisfaction."

1639, Apr. 30. He and twenty-eight others signed the following compact: "We whose names are underwritten, do acknowledge ourselves the legal subjects of his majesty King Charles, and in his name do hereby bind ourselves into a civil body politicke, unto his laws according to matters of justice."

1640, Mar. 6. He had 36 acres recorded.

MAXSON. 1st column. Family tradition says that he and his son Richard were killed by Indians at Throgg's Neck, afterwards Maxson's Point. 3d column. V. Jonathan. His widow b. 1678; d. 1777; m. (2) 1739, Dec. 4: Richard Dake, m. (3) 1756, June 24, Timothy Peckham.

I. JOHN, b. 1639. d. 1720, Dec. 17. Newport, Westerly, R. I.
m.
MARY MOSHER, b. 1641. d. 1718, Feb. 2. of Hugh Mosher.

1661, Mar. 22. He signed certain articles in regard to Misquamicut (Westerly) lands.

1668, Oct. 29. Westerly. Freeman.

1669, May 18. His name was in a list of inhabitants.

1670-86-90-1705. Deputy.

1677, Oct. 24. He was excused from serving on jury because his mother-in-law and wife were both sick.

1687. Overseer of the Poor. He was chosen this year with another to present a petition to Sir Edmund Andros for a town charter.

1687-88. Grand Jury.

1690, Sep. 16. He and two others were appointed by the Assembly to proportion a rate for Westerly.

1692, Mar. 28. He had a grant of 50 acres near Captain Joseph Davol's.

1694, Mar. 11. He sold the above land to Edward Larkin.

1702, Mar. 4. He was one of the proprietors in common lands at Newport.

1707, Jun. 25. He deeded son Jonathan, for love, &c., 22 acres.

1708, Sep. 20. Elder of Seventh Day Baptist Church. "Our beloved brother John Maxson, Sr., was ordained to the office of an elder to the congregation in and about Westerly."

1716, Jan. 22. Will—proved 1721, Feb. 16. Exs. three sons John, Joseph and Jonathan. To wife, £40, two cows, with keep of same, and the house we now live in to be her abode for life. To son John, £5, an iron kettle, and great bible which was my father's. To son Joseph, husbandry tools, riding mare and £5. To son Jonathan, 20*s*. To daughter Hannah Maxson, a feather bed. To grandsons John, son of John, John, son of Joseph, and John, son of Jonathan, 20*s*. each. To son Joseph's five daughters, viz: Tacy, Judith, Mary, Ruth and Elizabeth Maxson, each 10*s*. To daughter Mary Lewis, £12. To children of deceased daughter Dorothy Clarke, each 40*s*., viz: to Freegift, Dorothy, Experience and Joseph.

Inventory. Mare, colt, bonds, wearing apparel, bible, books, including "Doolittle on Sacrament," feather beds, warming pan, pewter, &c.

MANTON.

I. EDWARD, m. 1680, Dec. 9. ELIZABETH THORNTON,
b. 1658, Dec. 11.
d. 1723, Aug. 14.
b.
d. 1723 + of John & Sarah ( ) Thornton.
Providence, R. I.

1. Shadrach,
2. Edward,
3. John,
4. Ann,
5. Katharine,
6. Mary,
7. Elizabeth,
8. Sarah,

1682, May 13. He exchanged lands with the town, describing the land he conveyed as having been formerly in possession of his father Shadrach, and grandfather Edward deceased.

1687, Sep. 1. Taxed 7*s.*, 11*d.*

1688. Ratable estate. House where he dwelleth, 5½ acres tillage whereon 11 loads of hay may be cut, other land where about 5 loads of rubbish may be cut, 6 acres of wild pasture, 2 lots in town and a house thereon, 275 acres woodland and rights in other land, 7 cows, 2 oxen, a three year old, 3 two year old, 4 yearlings, 2 horses, 3 swine.

1723, Aug. 7. Will—proved 1723, Oct. 22. Exs. three sons Shadrach, Edward and John. To three sons Shadrach, Edward and John and two daughters Katharine and Mary, all the homestead lands where dwelling house standeth, on both sides of Woonasquatucket River; to be theirs equally on condition "that they take care and provide attendance and things necessary for their two poor helpless sisters, my daughters Elizabeth Manton and Sarah Manton," for life, and any neglecting care to be cut off and excluded from their part, &c. If all neglected such care then the Town Council were authorized to seize the homestead, and lease, rent or improve it for relief of two daughters till seven years after the longest liver, if the charge be not answered for seven years. To wife, a third part of homestead and lands, and till death or marriage the two daughters Katharine and Mary were to have liberty to dwell in a convenient room, and a half acre of land to use. To daughter Katharine, 60 acres, and to daughter Mary, 60 acres, without conditions. To three sons Shadrach, Edward and John, all the rest of lands and commons. To wife Elizabeth, a third of movables. To daughter Ann Tripp, 10*s.*, and each of her children, 5*s.* All the rest of movable estate, equally to Shadrach, Edward, John, Katharine and Mary.

Inventory, £373, 13*s.*, 8*d.*, viz: a horse, mare, bull, 2 yoke of oxen, 6 cows, 5 heifers, 2 two year old, 3 calves, 27 sheep, 6 small swine, 23 loads of hay, 90 bushels Indian corn, 9 bushels rye, 25 bushels oats, 3 guns, hand mill, pewter, brass, spun yarn, surveyor's compass and 2 small compasses, pair of dividers, 2 maps of the world, 100 books, silver money £7, 7*s.*, 11*d.* Pennies 11*s.*, 3*d.*

II. ANN, m. 1682, Sep. 18. JOHN KEESE,
b.
d. 1728.
b.
d. 1700, Dec. 10. of Keese.

1. Alice, 1683, Aug.
2. William, 1685, Oct. 26.
3. Patience, 1690, Jun. 27.
4. John, 1693, Mar. 14.
5. Shadrach, 1695, Oct. 5.
6. Ann, 1698, Oct. 26.

III. ELIZABETH, m. HENRY ESTEN,
b.
d.
b. 1651, Jan. 11.
d. 1711, Mar. 23. of Thomas & Ann ( ) Esten.

1. Elizabeth, 1683, Apr. 8.
2. Amey, 1685, Jun. 1.

MAXSON.

I. JOHN, m. 1688, Jan. 19. JUDITH CLARKE,
b. 1667.
d. 1748, Jul.
b. 1667, Oct. 12.
d. of Joseph & Bethiah (Hubbard) Clarke.
Westerly, R. I.

1. Judith, 1689, Sep. 23.
2. Mary, 1691, Oct. 26.
3. Bethiah, 1693, Jul. 31.
4. Elizabeth, 1695, Nov. 7.
5. Hannah, 1698, Jun. 13.
6. John, 1701, Apr. 21.
7. Dorothy, 1703, Oct. 20.
8. Susanna, 1706, Oct. 19.
9. Joseph, 1709, Dec.
10. Avis, 1712, Dec. 27.

1712, Aug. 21. Ordained as Deacon of Seventh Day Baptist Church.

1716. Freeman.

1719, Jul. 5. Ordained as Elder.

1748, Jul. 25. Inventory, £277, 5*s.* 4*d.*, viz: pocket book, money and wearing apparel £34, 1*s.* 4*d.*, books and gloves £1, 7*s.*, cow, heifer, parts of bible, Josephus' History, part of a warming pan, part of a spinning wheel, 7 sheep, old mare, calf, 2 wether sheep, £20 due next Christmas for a sheep, &c. Administration to son Captain John Maxson, who took receipts in the next year from his sisters' husbands, and from his nephew Joseph.

II. DOROTHY, m. 1692, Jan. 5. JOSEPH CLARKE,
b.
d.
b. 1670, Apr. 4.
d. 1718. of Joseph & Bethiah (Hubbard) Clarke.

1. Freegift, 1694, Jul. 4.
2. Dorothy, 1696, May 28.
3. Experience, 1699, Jul. 6.
4. Joseph,

III. JOSEPH, m. TACY BURDICK,
b. 1672.
d. 1750, Sep.
b.
d. 1747 + of Robert & Ruth (Hubbard) Burdick.
Westerly, R. I.

1. Joseph, 1692, Mar. 10.
2. John,
3. Tacy,
4. Mary,
5. Judith,
6. Ruth,
7. Elizabeth.

1705. Deputy.

1732. He was ordained "an evangelist or traveling minister."

1739. He was appointed an Elder, to assist his brother.

1747, Apr. 24. Will—proved 1750, Oct. 29. Exx. wife Tacy. To wife, profits of all movables for maintenance, while widow, and if she marry, £10. To five daughters, the rest of estate, except legacies, viz: to Tacy Burdick, Mary Champlin's representatives, Judith Randall, Ruth Babcock and Elizabeth Wells. To four daughters living, 20*s.* each, the reason why daughter Mary's representatives have no 20*s.* is because Jeffrey Champlin had part of lands. To sons Joseph and John, 20*s.* each, they having had land.

Inventory, £562, 3*s.*, viz: wearing apparel £10, 5*s.*, 2 cows, bull, old mare, pewter, notes, &c.

IV. MARY, m. DANIEL LEWIS,
b.
d. 1721 +
b.
d. 1718. of John Lewis.

1. John,
2. Jonathan,
3. Mary,
4. Dorcas,
5. Daniel,
6. Hannah,

V. JONATHAN, m. 1707, May 1. CONTENT ROGERS,
b. 1680.
d. 1732, Nov. 20.
b.
d. 1732 + of Jonathan & Naomi (Burdick) Rogers.
Westerly, R. I.

1. Jonathan, 1708, Jan. 16.
2. Content, 1710, Jan. 28.
3. Joseph, 1712, Jan. 4.
4. John, 1714, Mar. 2.
5. Naomi, 1716, May 6.
6. Samuel, 1718, Jul. 20.
7. Caleb, 1721, Nov. 1.
8. Mary, 1723, Nov. 20.

1732, Jun. 8. Will—proved 1732, Dec. 25. Exs. wife Content and son John. To wife, a third of real estate for life, and a third of movables forever, the west end of dwelling house while widow, and profits of sons' part till they are of age. To son Jonathan, a quarter of a certain tract of land and £100. To son Caleb, a quarter of same land. To son Joseph, the other half of said land. To son John, half of the homestead where the house stands. To son Samuel, other half of homestead. To daughter Content Babcock, a feather bed, two cows, and if she outlive her husband, the same to go to her daughter Anne. To daughter Naomi Maxson, £10, bed, &c. To two youngest sons and three daughters equally, the rest of movable estate left at death of wife.

Inventory, £713, 1*s.* 5*d.*, viz: bonds, warming pan, 4 oxen, pair of steers, 7 cows, 6 two years, yearling, 7 calves, 7 shoats, 47 sheep, two year horse, mare, 14 turkeys, 13 geese, 43 fowls, feather beds, bee hives, &c.

VI. HANNAH, m. HUBBARD BURDICK,
b.
d. 1752 (—)
b.
d. 1758. of Robert & Ruth (Hubbard) Burdick.

1. Hubbard,
2. Nathan,
3. John,
4. Ezekiel.

ADAM, m. (1) — m. (2) SARAH LOTT (widow) — b. 1596. Cambridge, Cambridge Co., Eng., d. 1661. [Portsmouth, R. I. — b. — d. — b. 1604. — d. 1661 +

He was a tailor.

1635, Jul. 2. He was a passenger in ship Defence, his age being thirty-nine, his wife Sarah thirty-one, children, John, fourteen, Adam, twelve, Jonathan, nine, Elizabeth, six, and Mary, four. These children were four of them by his first wife, while the other child, Mary Lott, was by his second wife's former husband. Before embarking he "brought testimony from the Justices of Peace, and minister in Cambridge, of his conformity to the orders and discipline of the Church of England. He hath taken the oath of allegiance and supremacy."

1636, May 25. Roxbury, Mass. Freeman.

He and his wife were members of the First Church at Roxbury.

He moved soon to Hingham where he had a grant of land.

1638. Portsmouth. He and others were admitted inhabitants of the island of Aquidneck, having submitted themselves to the government that is or shall be established.

1638, Jun. 23. He had a grant of land on the west side of the spring.

1638, Sep. 6. The Massachusetts authorities directed the constable of Hingham to attach him and bring him before the Governor or some one of the Council. The order seems to have been too late to take any effect.

1640, Jan. 12. He and others were chosen to lay out lands at Portsmouth.

1641, Mar. 16. Freeman.

1642. Clerk of the Military Company.

1644, May 27. He was granted an addition to his lot.

1652, Sep. 20. He deeded son Adam 12 acres.

1655. Freeman.

1661, Apr. 2. Will—proved 1661, Aug 31. Exx. wife Sarah, she being appointed by Town Council, the will being somewhat dubious. Overseers, friends Edward Thurston and Richard Tew. To wife Sarah, housing and lands in Portsmouth, and all goods, cattle, and other movables for her needs for life. At her death estate to be divided into three shares, to sons Jacob, Eleazer and Gershom. Son Jacob is to have if he be contented, what I gave him at upper corner of my farm, and if not, then other land. If either of these three brothers die before my wife then whoever of them live are to have the others' part. Those who enjoy the land are to pay son John, 20s., and to Adam, an ewe lamb, within three months of their mother's decease. To Elizabeth Thurston, wife of Edward, an ewe lamb. To Edward Thurston and Richard Tew, an ewe lamb each. The overseers were empowered to give all the children some gift of movables.

Inventory, £372, 6s., viz: house and land £150, 4 oxen, 5 cows, bull, horse, mare, colt, 2 calves, 30 ewe sheep, 2 rams, 6 swine, wampum peage £3, wearing clothes, books, 2 feather beds, 2 flock beds, 6 pewter platters, wine pot, warming pan, 7 pair of sheets, 6 napkins, 2 tables, joint stool, 1½ acres wheat, 2 acres oats, 2 acres peas, 3 acres Indian corn.

see American Genealogist v. 35, p. 107.

I. JOHN, — b. 1621. — d. — Portsmouth, R. I.

1638. He was admitted an inhabitant.

1644, Aug. 29. It was ordered by Assembly that Mr. Baulstone shall have £9 a year for John Mott's washing and diet, and what bedding he shall want to be furnished by the town.

1655. Freeman.

II. ADAM, m. 1647, Oct. MARY LOTT, — b. 1623. d. 1673 + — b. 1630. d. 1712. of —— & Sarah ( ) Lott. — Portsmouth, R. I.

1655. Freeman.

1673. Deputy.

1711, Feb. 24. Will—proved 1712, Sep. 8. Widow Mary. Exx. daughter Sarah Tripp. To daughters Sarah Tripp, widow, and Bethiah Abbott, widow, 12 acres laid out to me by townsmen of Portsmouth. To daughter Elizabeth Wing, new cotton and linen sheets, and like legacy to daughter Abigail Hefferland. To my maid Dinah Stephens, bed, and a good ewe sheep. To daughters Sarah Tripp and Bethiah Abbott, rest of movables.

III. JONATHAN, — b. 1626. — d. — Portsmouth, R. I.

1652, Sep. 20. He was witness to a deed from Adam Mott, Sr., to Adam Mott, Jr.

1653, May 17. Freeman.

IV. ELIZABETH, m. 1647, Jun. EDWARD THURSTON, — b. 1629. d. 1694, Sep. 2. — b. 1617. d. 1707, Mar. 1. of Thurston.

(2d WIFE.)

V. JACOB, m. JOANNA SLOCUM, — b. 1633. d. 1711, Nov. 15. — b. 1642, May 16. d. 1727, Jan. 6. of Giles & Joan ( ) Slocum. — Portsmouth, R. I.

1674. Deputy.

1687. Constable.

1699, Jan. 6. He and three others at a meeting held at John Lapham's in Dartmouth, undertook "to build a meeting house, for the people of God in scorn called Quakers; 35 foot long, 30 foot wide, and 14 foot stud." He gave £3 toward expenses. The house was built the same year, being the first one erected for worship in the town of Dartmouth.

1705, Aug. 28. He deeded son Jacob, for love, &c., southernmost half of my farm, bounded partly by land formerly belonging to my brother Adam Mott, deceased, with all buildings, orchards, &c.

1711, Jan. 31 Will—proved 1712, Jan. 11. Exs. wife Joanna, kinsman Giles Slocum, Jr., and John Coggeshall. To son Jacob, confirmation of half the farm as per deed. To wife Joanna, the other half of farm for life, and all household goods, and if son Jacob outlives her, he to have what part of farm she leaves undisposed of for his maintenance. If Jacob dies before his mother, then testator's son Samuel to have his mother's part. Legacies to be paid by son Jacob. To son Samuel, £40. To daughter Hannah Tucker, £20. To daughter Elizabeth Gould, £10. To daughter Mary Cook, £10. To daughter Sarah Wodell, £5.

VI. ELEAZER, — b. — d. — Portsmouth, R. I.

I. Rebecca, b. 1649, Sep. d.

II. Adam, Unmarried. b. 1650, Sep. d. 1676, Dec. 19. Portsmouth, R. I.
1673. Freeman.

III. Mary, b. 1656, Jan. 1. d.

No issue.

IV. Sarah, m. John Tripp, b. 1657, Oct. 11. d. — b. d. 1687, Mar. 9. of Peleg & Anne (Sisson) Tripp.
1. Rebecca, 1681, May 4.
2. John, 1683, Feb. 11.
3. Elizabeth, 1684, Sep. 17.
4. William, 1686, Feb. 20.
5. Jonathan, 1688, Apr. 7.
6. Timothy, 1690, Jan. 22.
(By 2d husband.)
7. Joseph, 1697, Feb. 20.
8. Benjamin, 1698, Feb. 1.
9 Abigail, 1702, Feb. 1.

V. Elizabeth, m. (1) 1679, May 14. William Ricketson, m. (2) 1696, Sep. 4. Matthew Wing, b. 1659, Aug. 6. d. 1723 + — b. d. 1691, Mar. 1. of Ricketson. — b. 1674, Mar. 1. d. 1724. of Stephen & Sarah (Briggs) Wing.

VI. Phebe, Unmarried. b. 1661, Aug. 20. d.

VII. Bethiah, m. —— Abbott, b. 1664, Apr. 1. d. — b. d. of Abbott.
1. Abigail,

MOTT (Adam). 3d column. VII. Bethiah m. Josiah Abbott. Children. 1. Abigail.

VIII. Abigail, m. John Hefferland, b. 1666, May 3. d. 1720 (—) — b. d. 1721. of Hefferland.

IX. John, Unmarried. b. 1671, Jan. 1. d.

1. Sarah, 1648, Mar. 10.
2. Elizabeth, 1650, Feb.
3. Edward, 1652, Apr. 1.
4. Eleanor, 1655, Mar. 1.
5. Mary, 1657, Feb.
6. Jonathan, 1659, Jan. 4.
7. Daniel, 1661, Apr.
8. Rebecca, 1662, Apr.
9. John, 1664, Dec.
10. Content, 1667, Jun.
11. Samuel, 1669, Aug. 24.
12. Thomas, 1671, Oct. 8.

I. Jacob, m. (1) 1689. Cassandra Southwick, m. (2) 1705, Nov. 20. Rest Perry, b. 1661, Dec. 13. d. 1737, Mar. 14. Portsmouth, R. I. — b. 1666. d. of Josiah & Mary (Boyce) Southwick. — b. 1675. d. 1709, Nov. 29. of Edward & Mary (Freeman) Perry.
1. Jacob, 1690, Oct. 8.
2. Adam, 1692, Jun. 12.
3. Joseph, 1695, Jan. 5.
4. Elizabeth, 1698, Jun. 29.
5. Joanna, 1700, Dec. 9.
(2d wife.)
6. Mary, 1708, Apr. 25.
7. Rest. 1709, Nov. 22.

1684. Freeman.
1705 9. Deputy.
1730, Mar. 5. Will—proved 1737, Mar. 14. Ex. son Jacob. To son Jacob, all my lands and housing in Portsmouth, he paying legacies, &c. To son Adam, £100. To son Joseph, £50. To daughters Elizabeth, Joanna, and Mary Mott, £100, each. To daughter Mary, two feather beds, pewter platter and tankard, four silver spoons, and a silver cup. To daughter Rest Rider, £80. To daughter Elizabeth Mott, rest of household goods, except books. To daughters Elizabeth, Joanna and Mary, equally, a good cow, ten sheep, and a horse to ride, to be theirs while unmarried, and the keep of the same by son Jacob, who is to allow to daughters who remain unmarried, three cords of firewood, ten bushels of apples, and a barrel of cider, and they to have use of great lower room, southernmost bedroom, and porch chamber while unmarried. To granddaughter Cassandra Mott, £10. To grandson Jacob, son of Adam, a good cow at age. To son Jacob, rest of movables.
Inventory, £672, 8s. 6d., viz: wearing apparel, canes, spectacles, books £6, 10s., plate £14, money scales, feather beds, warming pan, pewter, loom, spinning wheel, hogshead of cider, 2 mares, ½ a mare, 9 cows, heifer, 5 two years, 4 yearlings, 2 steers, bull, 73 sheep and lambs, 10 shoats, geese, turkeys, his part of cider mill £2, &c.

II. Hannah, m. 1690, Nov. 26. Abraham Tucker, b. 1663, Nov. d. 1730. — b. 1653, Dec. 13. d. 1725, Apr. 26. of Henry & Martha ( ) Tucker.
1. Elizabeth, 1691, Aug. 24.
2. Sarah, 1693, Apr. 23.
3. Constant, 1695, Mar. 12.
4. Abraham, 1697, Mar. 1.
5. Joanna, 1699, Oct. 14.
6. Ruth, 1701, Jan. 16.
7. Hannah, 1704, Apr. 22.

III. Mary, m. —— Cook, b. 1666, Jan. 8. d. — b. d. of Cook.
1. William, 1702, Jun. 13.

IV. Sarah, m. Gershom Wodell, b. 1670, Feb. 3. d. 1738 + — b. d. 1741, Sep. 4. of Gershom & Mary (Tripp) Wodell.
2 Gershom,
3. Elizabeth,
4. Ruth,
5. Patience,
6. Alice,
7. Innocent,

V. Elizabeth, m. 1691, Jan. 13. Thomas Gould, b. 1672, Sep. 12. d. 1749, Mar. 22 — b. 1655, Feb. 20. d. 1734, May 11. of Daniel & Wait (Coggeshall) Gould.
1. Priscilla, 1693, Feb. 3.
2. Mercy, 1694, Dec. 13.
3. Daniel, 1696, Dec. 18.
4. Thomas, 1698, Dec. 1.
5. Joanna, 1700, Oct. 24.
6. Jacob, 1704, Nov. 21.
7. Elizabeth, 1707, May 4.
8. John, 1709, Feb. 15.
9. James, 1711, Jul. 5.

VI. Samuel, m. Mary, b. 1678, Sep. 4. d. 1727, Jan. 25. Newport, R. I. — b. d. 1729 + of
1. Jacob,

He was a butcher.
1713. Freeman.
1729, Mar. His widow Mary, administratrix of his estate, brought suit against Giles Slocum surviving executor of will of Jacob Mott, father of her late husband Samuel Mott, for a legacy of £40, due from will of said Jacob Mott to his son Samuel.

VII. GERSHOM, m. ——— | b. d. 1698. | b. d. of | Portsmouth, R. I.

1691, Aug. 22. He sold William Wodell, Jr., of Pocasset, for £71, 8*s.* a certain part of a ferry lot lying over against Sanford's Ferry at Pocasset, with buildings, &c. (He called himself of Little Compton but did not stay long.)

1698, Jan. 12. He made over to his brother Jacob all his interest in land given by his father's will, except house, orchard, meadow, and homestead land of 4 acres, reserving privilege to get firewood. A lease was made by him to brother Jacob for the term of Gershom's life, by which he was to receive £7, 10*s.* a year from Jacob.

MOWRY. See: American Genealogist, v. 20, p. 228.

ROGER, m. MARY, | b. d. 1666, Jan. 5. | b. d. 1679, Jan. | Plymouth, Salem, Mass., [Providence, R. I.

(She m. (2) 1674, Mar. 16, John Kingsley.)

1631, May 18. Freeman.

1636. Salem. He was a member of the church this year.

1637, Jan. 20. It was agreed with Roger Mowry, neat herd, by the town of Salem, that he should begin the keeping of all the town's cattle the fifth of the next second month and to so continue eight months, with the help of another sufficient man. He was to be ready at the pen gate an hour after sunrise each day to take them. Those who did not have their cattle ready, were to bring them after the herd. He was to have 7*s.*, per head of all except bulls, to be paid in four equal payments and always one-quarter before hand.

1637, Feb. 20. He had 50 acres laid out.

1637, Apr. 2. He had his son Jonathan baptized, and other children as follows: Bethiah (1638, Jun. 17), Mary (1640, Jan. 16), Elizabeth (1643, Jan. 20), Benjamin (1649, May 20).

1637, Dec. 25. His name was in a list of inhabitants, and five persons formed his family.

1638, Jun. 25. He was granted a strip of meadow containing 2½ acres, and 1½ acres upland.

1642, Mar. 25. He and Lawrence Southwick agreed to keep the cows in all things according to agreement of last year, except wages, which were to be 5*s.*, per head.

1643. Providence. He came probably about this year to Providence, as the deposition of Nathaniel Felton, of Salem (made 1700, Sep. 18), declares that Roger Mowry removed from Salem "before the year 1644;" having sold his land in the woods unto Emanuel Downing.

1655. Freeman.

1655, May 25. He was appointed by the Court of Commissioners to keep a house of entertainment. A convenient sign was to be set out at the most perspicuous place of said house to give notice to strangers.

1656, Jul. 29. He entered ten ankers of liquors, and same year three ankers of rum and two barrels of sack.

1656, Aug. 27. He had a house lot laid out to him "upon the hill over against Roger Williams, his meadow."

1657, Jan. 27. He was allowed 6*d.*, for this day's firing and houseroom.

1658, Jan. 15. He bought a house and 4 acres of Robert Colwell.

1658, Aug. 6. He testified as to the births of his children Benjamin, Thomas and Hannah.

1658. Commissioner.

1661, Jan. 21. Isaac Heath, of Roxbury, died at this date and in his will gives 20*s.*, to his kinswoman Mary Mowry.

1661, Feb. 18. Juryman.

1661, May 4. He bought of Anne Smith, widow of John, a house and lot.

1664, Jan. 1. Elizabeth Heath, of Roxbury, widow of Isaac, left a legacy of 10*s.*, to Mary Mowry and like sum to her son Thomas Mowry.

1669, May 6. Administration on his estate was refused by his widow Mary, though he had left a will and made her executrix, because the property would not discharge just debts and pay legacies. The Town Council gave her somewhat above £20, of the estate at her request, to help relieve her old age and for good reasons to them appearing. This action of the council was opposed by the Assembly at the above given date, and the council was further given full power to settle the estate.

1671, Sep. 5. His widow sold to Stephen Paine, of Rehoboth, the dwelling house, outhousing and three house lots and commoning.

1679, Jan. 29. His widow (now the widow of John Kingsley), was buried at Rehoboth at this date. Possibly part of Roger Mowry's children were by an earlier wife. There was a Hannah Mowry who was a member of the church at Salem in early times, and an Elizabeth Mowry, member of the church in 1641 (with the mark of removed subsequently placed against her name).

One tradition of the family may be alluded to, viz: that Roger Williams and Roger Mowry were cousins or kinsmen in some degree. The fact that they lived successively in the same towns (Plymouth, Salem and Providence) is cited, with the coincidence of christian names, as corroborative of this tradition.

MOWRY. 1st column. Under date 1669, May 6. read approved by Assembly, not opposed.

MOWRY. 1st column. His wife was Mary Johnson, of John and Margery (   ) Johnson. 1659, Oct. 12. Roger Mowry, of Providence, and Mary, his wife, "being the eldest daughter of John Johnson, late of Roxbury, in Suffolk, in the Massachusetts Colony of New England, deceased," for £60 deeded to William Parkes, of Roxbury, that one-sixth part of the estate of said Johnson, devised to them by his will, dated 1659. Sep. 30.

I. ROGER, | b. d. young.

II. JONATHAN, m. (1) 1659, Jul. 8 [Rich'd. MARY FOSTER, (w. of m. (2) HANNAH | b. 1637. d. 1708. | b. d. of Robert & Mary (Warren) | b. d. of | Plymouth, Mass. Bartlett.

1668, Jun. 3. Surveyor of highways.

1680, Jun. 1. He was licensed to sell wine, liquor, beer and cider, and provide lodging for refreshing of travelers.

1688, Jul. 16. He, calling himself son and heir of Roger Mowry, confirmed an agreement made three years before between his sister Mehitable Brooks and Henry Esten, wherein she sold 12 acres, after declaring that she had received in her father Roger Mowry's lifetime, a marriage portion of land from him on her marriage to Eldad Kingsley. (Her present husband signed.)

1699, Feb. 24. Will—proved 1708, Jun. 16. Exx. wife Hannah. To oldest son what was promised by a deed. To wife Hannah, her wearing clothes, two oxen, three cows, two beds, a horse and household stuff she brought with her. To wife, son John and daughter Hannah Bumpus, rest of estate in equal parts.

Inventory, £166, 8*s.*, viz: apparel £18, 10*s.*, money £17, 15*s*, 3*d.*, arms and ammunition £2, 5*s.*, 2 cows, bull, 2 yearlings, swine, &c.

III. BETHIAH, m. 1662, Sep. 30. GEORGE PALMER, | b. 1638. d. | b. d. of | Palmer.

IV. MARY, | b. 1640. d.

V. ELIZABETH, | b. 1643. d.

VI. NATHANIEL, m. 1666. JOANNA INMAN, | b. 1644. d. 1718, Mar. 24. | b. d. 1718 + of Edward | Providence, R. I. Inman.

1672, May 1. Freeman.

1680, Jul. 16. Taxed 7*d.*

1686, Jul. 14. He and wife Joanna, and his brother John Mowry and wife Mary, deeded to John Reed of Norwalk, Ct., for £20, certain rights to land in Providence, being a confirmation of a deed made some years before.

1695, Dec. 22. He deeded son Joseph, 56½ acres for well being and settlement.

1710, Apr. 3. He having formerly given land to son Henry, now bounds the same.

1711, Jan. 6. He calls himself sixty-six years of age in a deposition of this date.

1713, Jun. 16. Taxed 15*s.*

1718, Mar. 18. Will—proved 1718, Apr. 4. Ex. son Joseph. To son Nathaniel, 100 acres at Wanescutt Hill. To son John, 40 acres. To son Henry, 50 acres north side of testator's homestead at Wesquatomskit Hill. To son Joseph, the homestead, including dwelling house, orchard and 110 acres, this bequest being larger than others he says, because he had received money from Joseph. To wife Joanna, use of the house for life and of all household goods. To daughter Martha Mowry, land. To six daughters, viz: Sarah Phillips, Mary Arnold, Joanna Phetteplace, Patience Smith, Mercy Smith and Experience Malavery, all household goods at death of wife, and all cattle to them, equally.

Inventory, £166, 8*s*, 2*d.*, viz: mare, 6 cows, 2 heifers, 5 yearlings, 4 swine, 2 barrels cider, gun, spinning wheel, 4 old books, bible, &c.

1718, May 5. Receipts were given for legacies by Sarah Phillips, Mary Arnold, Mercy Smith, Patience Smith, (Jo) Hannah Phetteplace, Experience Malavery and Martha Mowry. The husbands signed as follows: Richard Phillips, John Arnold, Edward Smith, Joseph Smith, Walter Phetteplace and John Malavery.

I. { GERSHOM, { b. { d. 1720 ± Kings Town, R. I.
m.
MARY, { b. { d. 1720 + of

1698, Apr. 8. He, of Kings Town, sold his uncle Jacob Mott of Portsmouth, for £30, all his right in farm where uncle Jacob lives 92 acres, orchards, buildings, &c., the estate conveyed having been left by my father Gershom Mott, of Portsmouth, who died intestate, and who had received said estate from his father Adam Mott, deceased.

1720 ± Administration on his estate was taken, and legacies paid to widow Mary, and to Gershom, Jacob, William, Abigail, Rebecca and David Mott, Joseph Eggleston, John and Patience Mott.

1. Gershom,
2. Jacob,
3. William,
4. Abigail,
5. Rebecca,
6. David,
7. Daughter,
8. John,
9. Patience,

II. { JOHN, { b. { d. Kings Town, R. I.
m.
ELIZABETH, { b. { d. of

1. John,	1694, Aug. 9.
2. Mary,	1696, Sep. 15.
3. Elizabeth,	1700, Apr. 17.
4. Jonathan,	1703, Nov. 12.
5. Hannah,	1705, Aug.
6. Samuel,	1708, Mar
7. Sarah,	1713, Oct. 16.

MOWRY.

I. { JONATHAN, { b. { d. 1733. Plymouth, Mass.
m.
HANNAH BOURNE, { b. { d. of Bourne.

1732, Sep. 1. Will—proved 1733, Apr. 26. Exx. wife Hannah. To eldest son Benjamin, certain land. To son Jonathan, land. To daughters Mariah Swift and Thankful Swift, 20s., each. To daughter Reliance, £20. To wife, son Joseph and daughter Reliance, all movable estate. To the two children of Maria Trowbridge, viz: Mary and Maria, £10. To son Joseph, rest of real estate in Plymouth. To sons Benjamin, Jonathan and Joseph, all of estate in Providence.

Inventory, £354, 10s., viz: cattle and swine £31, 10s., furniture £30, 1s., 6d., real estate £278.

1. Benjamin,	1690.
2. Maria,	1692.
3. Mary,	1694.
4. Thankful,	1696.
5. Jonathan,	1699.
6. Reliance,	1702.
7. Cornelius,	1706.
8. Silas,	
9. Joseph,	

II. { JOHN, { b. { d.

III. { HANNAH, { b. { d.
m.
—— BUMPAS, { b. { d. of Bumpas.

I. { NATHANIEL, { b. { d.
UNMARRIED.

II. { JOHN, { b. { d. 1730 + Providence, R. I.
m. 1699, Mar. 29.
ELIZABETH CLARKE, { b. { d. of Clarke.

1. Jacob,

1713, Jun. 16. Taxed 5s.

1719, Feb. 27. He and wife Elizabeth, sold John Mowry, Sr., for £305, messuage where I dwell of 64 acres, twelve miles north-westerly from Providence.

1730, Nov. 2. He deeded to son Jacob, for £55, homestead where I dwell of 37 acres, with house, &c.

III. { HENRY, { b. { d. 1759, Sep. 23. Providence, Smithfield, R. I.
m. (1) 1701, Nov. 27.
MARY BULL, { b. { d. of Isaac Bull
m. (2) 1734, Jan. 4. [John.
HANNAH MOWRY, (w. of { b. { d. 1754 (—) of Nathaniel Packard.

1. Mary,	1702, Sep. 28.
2. Uriah,	1705, Aug. 15.
3. Jonathan,	1708, Jun. 1.
4. Jeremiah,	1711, Apr. 7.
5. Sarah,	1717, Apr. 5.
6. Elisha,	
7. Phebe,	

1713, Jun. 16. Taxed 8s., 6d.

1754, Dec. 17. Will—proved 1759, Nov. 12. Exs. sons Jonathan and Elisha. To grandson Israel Mowry, a chest. To granddaughter Wait Mowry, a trunk and pewter basin. To grandson Esek Mowry, 20s. To granddaughter Sarah Mowry, 20s. To son Elisha Mowry, all the homestead farm in Smithfield, except four rods square, for a burial place, also a cart, cooper's tools, great table, &c. To grandchildren Stephen and Anne Wilkinson, 5s. each. To sons Uriah, Jonathan, Jeremiah and Elisha, all wearing apparel. To six children Uriah, Jonathan, Jeremiah, Elisha, Mary Sprague and Phebe Arnold, all money, bills, bonds, book debts, pewter, brass, &c., and any child dissatisfied to lose his or her part. The reason that Elisha has more is because he is youngest son and has lived with me and taken care in old age, and the other children had a great deal before.

Inventory, £1,323, 3s., 8d., viz: notes, bills, accounts, &c., bond £360, 5s., pewter, silver money £31, 4s., 4d., half dozen old chairs, cooper's tools, money scales, 2 cows, heifers, &c.

IV. { JOSEPH, { b. { d. 1755, Jun. Providence, Smithfield, R. I.
m. 1695, Jun. 3.
ALICE WHIPPLE, { b. 1675, Jun. 3. { d. 1746 + of Eleazer & Alice (Angell) Whipple.

1. Daniel,	1697, Sep. 6.
2. Joseph,	1699, Feb. 26.
3. Oliver,	1700, Sep. 26.
4 Alice,	1712, Jan. 6.
5. Waite,	1716, Jun. 6.

1713, Jun. 16. Taxed £1, 8s.

1714–25–29. Deputy.

1731. Smithfield. Town Council.

1734. Deputy.

1746, May 19. Will—proved 1755, Aug. 18. Ex. son Joseph. To sons Daniel and Oliver, all land at Pascoag, equally, &c. To son Oliver, land in Smithfield. To son Joseph, homestead in Smithfield, and a farm adjoining dwelling place of John Sayles, being farm on which my honored father Nathaniel, deceased, last dwelt, containing 110 acres, land in Glocester, Woodstock and Killingly, &c. To son Daniel, £1,338. To son Oliver, £1,486. To daughter Alice Mowry, £1,500. To daughter Wait Arnold, £1,500. To five children, silver money. To son Joseph, two negroes, all household goods, movables, money due, &c., he taking care of his mother, my wife Alice, for life, providing her with all things necessary for her old age. If wife removes from Joseph, he to pay her £300, and the other four children to be helpful to their brother in gathering debts, &c.

V. { SARAH, { b. { d.
m.
RICHARD PHILLIPS, { b. 1667. { d. 1747, Dec. 13. of Michael & Barbara ( ) Phillips.

1. John,
2. William,
3. Richard,
4. Mercy,
5. Ruth,

VII. JOHN, m. MARY, | b. d. 1690, Jul. 7. | b. d. 1690 ± of | Providence, R. I.

1666, May 14. He and Edward Inman bought of William Minnion, of Punskepage, Massachusetts, for good consideration, 2,000 acres lying from Loquesit northward, bounding partly on Pawtucket River: "To have and to hold without any trouble or molestation by any Indians."

1672, May 1. Freeman.

1676, Aug. 14. He was one of the men "who staid and went not away," in King Philip's War, and so had a share in the disposition of the Indian captives whose services were sold for a term of years.

1680, Jul. 16. Taxed 8*d*.

1688. Ratable estate, 8 cows, 2 oxen, bull, 5 young cattle, mare, horse, 8 acres tillage, 8 acres pasture, 5 acres meadow.

1690, Oct. 3. Administration to brother Nathaniel. Inventory, £36, 3*s*., 4*d*., viz: yoke of oxen, 6 cows, 2 heifers, bull, steer, horse, mare, colt, 6 small swine, 3 old cow bells, pewter, iron, 6 loads of hay, fruit in orchard, corn in field, gun, sword, wearing apparel, old bible, some small books, 2 spinning wheels, 3 pair of cards, money £4, 8*s*., 8*d*., boards at saw mill, &c. The administrator soon rendered a partial account, and among his payments were 12*s*., "paid to my brother Joseph Mowry of Conanicot," and 8*s*., each, for carrying Experience and Sarah to Conanicut.

1695, Apr. 16. The administrator's account showed £18, 10*s*., remaining after payment of debts, &c. What estate James Phillips and his wife had before the death of John Mowry, was to be considered divided with the rest, and John Mowry heir of the deceased John, being now of full age, was to receive his part.

He and his wife were buried at Sayles Hill.

VIII. MEHITABLE, m. (1) 1662, ELDAD KINGSLEY, m. (2) TIMOTHY BROOKS. | b. d. | b. 1638. d. 1679, Aug. 28. of John Kingsley. | b. d. of Brooks.

IX. JOSEPH, m. MARY WILBUR, | b. 1647. d. 1716, May 27. | b. d. 1720, Apr. 17. of William Wilbur. | Kings Town, Jamestown, R. I.

1673, May 6. Freeman.

1677, Oct. 31. He and forty-seven others were granted 5,000 acres to be called East Greenwich.

1679. He had 50 acres laid out.

1686-98-99-1701-3-4-5-8-11. Jamestown. Deputy.

1687. Constable.

1693, Dec. 20. He bought of executors of Joseph Nicholson, 100 acres in Portsmouth R. I., with buildings, orchards, &c., for £447.

1716, May 22. Will—proved 1716, May 31. Exx. wife Mary. To her the farm called by me Strawberry Plain Farm for life, and then to grandson Joseph Coggeshall, and if he die without issue to

VI. MARY, — b. 1675. d. 1742, Jan. 27.
m.
JOHN ARNOLD, — b. 1670, Nov. 1. d. 1756, Oct. 27. of Richard & Mary (Angell) — Arnold.

1. William, 1695, Dec. 9.
2. John, 1697, Jul. 27.
3. Daniel, 1699, May 1.
4. Mercy, 1701, Dec. 22.
5. Anthony, 1704, Mar. 12.
6. Seth, 1706, Sep. 6.
7. Israel,
8. Anna,
9. Susanna,
10. Abigail,

VII. JOANNA, — b. d. 1750 (—)
m. 1709, Aug. 4.
WALTER PHETTEPLACE, — b. d. 1753, Dec. 29. of Philip — Phetteplace.

1. Jonathan,
2. Job,
3. Philip,
4. Benjamin,
5. Sarah,
6. Mercy,

VIII. PATIENCE, — b. d. 1734 +
m.
JOSEPH SMITH, — b. 1680, Oct. 12. d. 1734, Feb. 17. of Edward & Anphillis (Angell) — Smith.

1. Jacob, 1706, May 3.
2. Susanna, 1708, May 26.
3. Joseph, 1710, Feb. 4.
4. Abigail, 1712, Mar.
5. Samuel, 1718, Dec.
6. Jethro,
7. Rebecca,
8. Bathsheba,
9. Dinah,
10. Elnathan,

IX. MERCY, — b. d.
m. (1)
EDWARD SMITH, — b. d. 1726, Nov. 9. of Edward & Anphillis (Angell) — Smith.
m. (2) 1741, Nov. 26.
WILLIAM HALL, — b. d. of — Hall.

1. Edward,
2. Alice,
3. Martha,
4. Mercy,
5. Sarah,
6. Rachel,
7. Amey,
8. Mary,
9. Freelove,
10. Anne,
11. Abraham,

X. EXPERIENCE, — b. d. 1718 +
m.
JOHN MALAVERY, — b. d. 1718, Sep. 18. of John & Elizabeth ( ) — Malavery.

1. John,
2. Nathaniel.

XI. MARTHA, — b. d. 1775 +
m. 1718, May 8.
JOHN SMITH, — b. 1694, Dec. 8. d. 1778, Mar. 28. of Benjamin & Mercy (Angell) — Smith.

3d column. XI. Martha. Children. 1, Benjamin, 1719, Sep. 8. 2. Elias, 1722, Sep. 21. 3, Mary, 1724, July 9. 4. Esther, 172[illegible], Dec. 23. 5, Rufus, 1730, May 11. 6, Anne, 1732, Jan. 21. 7, Martha, 1735, Mar. 1.

1. John,
2. Rufus,
3. Esther,
4. Anna,
5. Martha,

I. MARY, — b. d.
m.
JAMES PHILLIPS, — b. d. 1746, Dec. 12. of Michael & Barbara ( ) — Phillips.

1. Michael,
2. John,
3. Jeremiah,
4. Joshua,
5. Samuel,
6. Mary,
7. Phebe,
8. Elizabeth,

II. JOHN, — b. d. 1732, Sep. 19. — Providence, Smithfield, R. I.
m. (1) 1701, Apr. 18
MARGERY WHIPPLE, — b. d. of Eleazer & Alice (Angell) — Whipple.
m. (2) 1722, Aug. 23.
HANNAH PACKARD, — b. d. 1754 (—) of Nathaniel — Packard.

(She m. (2) 1734, Jan. 4, Henry Mowry.)

He was called John Mowry, Sr., to distinguish him from his cousin John, who was called John Mowry, Jr.

1713, Jun. 16. Taxed 14*s*.

1719, Mar. 16. He and wife Margery sold John Mowry, Jr., 65 acres. &c., for £100.

1731–32. Smithfield. Town Council.

1732, Oct. 9. Administration to widow Hannah. Inventory, bonds £51, 1*s*., silver money £5, 11*s*., 7*d*., books £5, 7*s*., pewter, woolen yarn, 4 spinning wheels, linen wheel, warming pan, silver cup and spoon £11, 8*s*., carpenter's tools, 4 horses, bull, 16 cows, 2 oxen, young cattle, goats, 10 swine, 2 guns, cider, &c.

1732, Oct. 16. Administration was now given to eldest son Ananias. It was declared that Ananias and Abigail Mowry had detained part of the estate in their custody, and an officer was sent to take same.

1733, Oct. 2. Ananias Mowry deeded to brother John Mowry, all right in 64 acres that honored father had bought of John Mowry, Jr., and other land, and dwelling house, orchard, &c.

1. Mary, 1702, May 2.
2. Ananias, 1705, May.
3. Philip,
4. John,
5. Abigail,
6. Margery,
7. Amey,
8. Meribah,

(2d wife.)

9. Ezekiel, 1723, Sep. 15.

III. EXPERIENCE, — b. d.
m.
ELISHA SMITH, — b. 1680, Apr. 14. d. 1766 + of John & Sarah (Whipple) — Smith.

1. Penelope, 1701, Dec. 5.
2. Philip, 1703, Jan. 6.
3. Noah, 1705, May 7.
4. Sarah, 1707, Apr. 28.
5. Jonathan, 1710.
6. Abraham, 1712.
7. Richard, 1714, Apr. 12.
8. Mary, 1716, Oct. 29.
9. Stephen, 1718, Oct. 28.
10. Daniel, 1723, Mar. 1.

IV. SARAH, — b. d.

1. Elizabeth, 1663, Jan. 29.
2. John, 1665, May 6.
3. Samuel, 1669, Jun. 1.
4. Jonathan, 1671, Feb. 21.
5. Mary, 1675, Oct. 7.
6. Nathaniel, 1679, Feb. 5.

I. MARY, — b. 1672, Oct. 17. d.
m. 1689, Aug. 23.
DANIEL COGGESHALL, — b. 1665, Apr. d. 1717, May 17. of Joshua & Joan (West) — Coggeshall.

1. Joshua, 1691, Jan. 3.
2. Wait, 1692, Dec. 14.
3. Mary, 1694, Sep. 6.
4. Anna, 1701, Jun. 14.
5. Daniel, 1704, Aug. 20.
6. Phebe, 1706, Nov. 11.
7. Joseph, 1709, Jun. 3.
8. Peleg, 1712, Apr. 20.

granddaughter Ann Coggeshall. To wife, other land for life and then to granddaughter Phebe Coggeshall, and if she die without issue to granddaughter Ann Coggeshall. To wife, the choice of a room in the house and keep of a horse and cow for life. To daughter Mary Coggeshall, £5, besides deed of gift of land already. To granddaughter Mary Clarke, land and buildings. To granddaughter Mary Clarke and grandson Joseph Coggeshall and granddaughter Phebe Coggeshall, land at Dutch Island, and if granddaughter Mary Clarke die without issue then to grandson Peleg Coggeshall. To grandson Joshua Coggeshall, £20. To granddaughter Ann Coggeshall, land. To grandson Peleg Coggeshall, £20. To brother Benjamin Mowry, £5, per annum in wearing apparel for life. To cousin (*i. e.* nephew) Joseph Mowry, son of Benjamin, £10. To cousin Mary Mowry, wife of John, of Kings Town, £10. To cousin Joseph Sherman, son of Benjamin, of Portsmouth, £5. To wife Mary, all the rest of real and personal estate.

Inventory, £1,216, 12*s.*, 2*d.*, viz: silver tankard and cup £32, 7 porringers and 2 cups of silver £24, 10*s.*, 24 silver spoons £18, silver money £2, bonds £148, 2*s.*, 8*d.*, clock £10, feather bed, negro man £40, boy £40, woman £40, Indian girl £40, 2 spinning wheels, wool cards, 3 boats £70, 2 oxen, 2 stags, 12 cows, 8 yearlings, 5 calves, 2 mares, 2 colts, 600 sheep and their lambs, swine, &c. The rooms named were: kitchen, cellar, garret, buttery, buttery chamber, hall, bedroom, parlor, hall chamber, parlor chamber.

1717, Aug. 26. Will—proved 1720, Dec. 15. Widow Mary. Exx. daughter Mary Coggeshall. To her all movables, and four negro servants, while widow, and if she marry she must previously give estate to children that are not provided for by their grandfather Joseph Mowry's will.

Inventory, £583, 10*s.*, 6*d.*

The Friends' records, in commenting on her death, state that she was a valuable minister and celebrated doctress and in great repute in the Society and with people generally, and that her maiden name was Wilbur.

X. { BENJAMIN, | b. 1649, May 8. | Roxbury, Mass., Kings Town, R. I.
m. [Ichabod. | d. 1719 +
MARTHA POTTER, (w. of | b. | d. | of Thomas & Martha ( ) Hazard.

1661, Jan. 19. He is mentioned in will of Isaac Heath, of Roxbury: "If Benjamin Mowry, duly serves out his time my will is that at the end of his time he shall receive £5."

1677, Oct. 31. Kings Town. He was one of those to whom were granted 500 acres to be called East Greenwich.

1687, Sep. 6. Taxed 3*s.*, 2*d.*

XI. { THOMAS, | b. 1652, Jul. 19. | Roxbury, Mass.
m. 1673, Sep. 6. | d. 1717, Dec. 25.
SUSANNA NEWELL, | b. 1656, Mar. 30. | d. | of Abraham & Susanna (Rand) Newell

XII. { HANNAH, | b. 1656, Sep. 28.
m. 1674, Dec. 3. | d. 1718 (—)
BENJAMIN SHERMAN, | b. 1650. | d. 1719, Sep 24. | of Philip & Sarah (Odding) Sherman.

I. { Roger, { b. d. 1719 (—) Kings Town, R. I.
Unmarried.

1698, Apr. 16. He and his brothers Joseph and Benjamin, all of Point Judith, had deed from Ichabod Potter, of same place, for love, &c., of a right of land in Narragansett which grantor bought of his grandfather (*i. e.* step-grandfather), John Albro, of Portsmouth. The grantor calls the grantees his brothers (*i. e.* half-brothers).

1719, Jan. 12. Administration to brother Benjamin, Jr., he not having been heard of for five years. Inventory, £83, 18*s*., viz: wearing apparel £8, 14*s*., bed, books, old papers 3*s*., bond £25, &c.

II. { Joseph, { b. d. 1718. m. Sarah, { b. d. 1718 + of Kings Town, R. I.

3d column. II. Joseph. Will, 1718, Oct. 2; proved, 1718, Dec. 11. III. Benjamin, m. Mary 1728, Jan. 12. A deed from them recorded.

1. Mary, 1704, Oct. 18.
2. Robert, 1706, Aug. 31.
3. Joseph, 1708, Aug. 24.
4. Benjamin, 1710, May 2.
5. Roger, 1712, Jul. 2.
6. Martha, 1714, Dec. 5.
7. Sarah, 1717, Aug. 31.

1718. Will—proved. Exs. wife Sarah and son Robert. To four sons Robert, Joseph, Benjamin and Roger lands, equally. To daughter Mary, £50, at eighteen or marriage. To wife, profit of movables while widow.

1718, Nov. 6. Inventory, 19 calves at Seaside Farm, 19 yearlings, 11 cows, heifer, 6 mares, 8 colts, other cattle and horses, 5 swine, 2 spinning wheels, &c.

III. { Benjamin, { b. d. 1719 + Kings Town, R. I.

IV. { John, { b. d. 1718. m. Mary, { b. d. 1724. of Kings Town, R. I.

1. John,
2. Jonathan,
3. Abigail,
4. Daughter,
5. Daughter,
6. Daughter,

1709, Jun. 30. He and eleven others bought a tract of 1,618 acres in Narragansett called Swamptown.

1718. Will—proved. (Inventory, Mar. 6.) Exx. wife Mary. He mentions eldest son John, daughter Abigail, and rest of children to have when of age.

1724, Sep. Will—proved 1724 Oct. Widow Mary. Ex. son Jonathan. To daughter Abigail, a bed. To four daughters, legacies. To son Jonathan, rest of real and personal.

I. { Thomas, { b. 1678, May 15. d.

II. { Abigail, { b. 1680, Apr. 4. d.

III. { Abigail, { b. 1681, Mar. 30. d.

IV. { Mary, { b. 1682, Aug. 11. d.

V. { Susanna, { b. 1685, Apr. 27. d.

VI. { John, { b. 1687, Jul. 13. d.

VII. { Elizabeth, { b. 1689, Dec. 11. d.

VIII. { Nathaniel, { b. 1694, May 28. d.

1. Benjamin, 1675, Dec. 26.
2. Jonathan, 1677, Mar. 7.
3. Joseph, 1679, Feb. 11.
4. Hannah, 1680, Mar. 20.
5. Amey, 1681, Oct. 25.
6. Sarah, 1684.
7. Isaac, 1686, Apr. 22.
8. Mehitable, 1688, Mar. 4.
9. Deborah, 1691, Sep. 3.
10. Abigail, 1694, Mar. 13.
11. Freelove, 1696, Sep. 14.
12. Bethiah, 1699.

 See: American Genealogist, v.20, p.228.

THOMAS, m. **MARY SMALL**, — b. 1600. d. 1682. St. Albans, Hertford Co., Eng. [Providence, R. I. — (Mary) b. 1605. d. 1679 (—) of Small.

He was a shoemaker.

1635, Apr. 2. He embarked in ship Planter from London for New England. His age was called thirty five, wife Mary thirty, son Thomas, three, and son Epenetus, one. He had a certificate from the minister of St. Albans to show before taking his departure.

1637, May 17. Salem. Freeman. He had a grant of land this same year.

1637, Aug. 27. He had his son Nedabiah baptized.

1637, Dec. 25. His name was in a list of inhabitants, and five persons formed his family.

1638, Mar. 12. He and others having had license to depart from Massachusetts, they were ordered to appear at the next court (if they, be not gone before) to answer such things as shall be objected.

1638, Oct. 8. Providence. He was one of the twelve persons to whom Roger Williams deeded land that he had bought of Canonicus and Miantonomi.

1638. Treasurer for the town.

1639. He was one of the twelve original members of First Baptist Church.

1639, Jul. 1. He and his wife are alluded to in a letter from Rev. Hugh Peters, of Salem, to the church at Dorchester, as having had "the great censure passed upon them in this our church." He says that they and certain others "wholly refused to hear the church, denying it and all the churches in the Bay to be true churches," &c.

1640, Jul. 27. He and thirty-eight others signed an agreement for a form of government.

1649-53-54-55-56-64-65-66-67. Assistant.

1650, Sep. 2. Taxed £1, 13*s*. 4*d*.

1656-58-59-61-62-63. Commissioner.

1665, Feb. 19. He had lot 23 in a division of lands.

1665-67-70-71. Deputy.

1665-66-69-70-71-74-77-81. Town Council.

1669. Town Treasurer.

1679, Jul. 1. Taxed 9*s*. 4½*d*.

1679, Mar. 21. Will—proved 1682, Oct. 17. Ex. son Thomas. Overseers, Thomas Harris, Sr. and Joseph Jenckes, Sr. To son Epenetus, 60 acres and other lands, a cow, my smith's vice, and my bible. To son-in-law John Whipple, for natural life, my right in house lot where he now dwelleth, &c., and at his death to his son John, and if John Whipple, Jr., die before coming of age, then to eldest daughter surviving of daughter Mary formerly wife of said son-in-law John Whipple. To son Thomas, my dwelling house with all other buildings, and all lands whatsoever not otherwise disposed of, whether upon Wonasquatucket or Moshassuck Rivers, &c., and to have all my books and writings except bible. To son-in-law Joseph Williams, all my part of yoke of oxen which is now between us. All cattle and movable goods undisposed of to be divided into three parts, one for Thomas, one for Epenetus and one for daughter Lydia Williams.

Inventory, £78, 9*s*. 5*d*., viz: wearing apparel, 2 hats, two feather beds, one being of English ticking, a flock bed, warming pan, bellows, shoemaker's tools, pewter, 3 brass candlesticks, 3 books, viz: Ainsworth's Annotations, Concordance, Fisher's Ashford Dispute. Money £2, 14*s*., 4 cows, gun, &c. The rooms mentioned were parlor, old bedroom, hall chamber, cellar, kitchen. In the shop there was a smith's vice, 2 currier's shears, shoemaker's last.

I. **THOMAS**, m. 1660, Jul. 3. **ELIZABETH MARSH**, — b. 1632. d. 1722, Jun. 11. Providence, R. I. — (Elizabeth) b. d. 1722 (—) of Marsh.

1655. Freeman.

1664-65-66-67-83-84-85-86-87-88-89-90-91-92-93-94-95-96-97-98-99-1700-1-2-3-4-5-6-7-8-9-10-11—12-13-14-15. Town Clerk.

1665, Feb. 19. He had lot 41 in a division of lands.

1668. Ordained pastor of First Baptist Church.

1669-70-71-77-78-79. Assistant.

1671-73-74-82-83-84-85-86-91-93-94-96-97-98-99-1700-1-2-3-4-5-6-7-8-9-10-11-12-13-14. Town Council.

1672-76-77-80-82-83-85-86-92-96-1706-7-8-11. Deputy.

1679, Jul. 1. Taxed 7*s*. 6*d*.

1683, Mar. 13. At his request a Town Council meeting considered matter of a cow and her increase, which deceased Thomas Olney left in care of Town Council, the said cattle being in custody of Epenetus Olney, the said cow formerly being of estate of deceased James Olney, and being left in care of Town Council by Thomas Olney, deceased, for three children of John Whipple, &c.

1687, Sep. 1. Taxed 12*s*. 7*d*.

1688. Ratable estate, 9 cows, 3 heifers, 3 steers, 2 oxen, 5 two years, 3 yearlings, 4 swine, 3 horses, mare, 2 acres salt marsh, 3 acres mongrel meadow, 7 acres fresh meadow, 3 acres mowing, 10 acres tillage, 6 acres wild pasture.

1695, Jul. 2. He and two others were chosen by Assembly to run the northern line of colony.

1698, Aug. 2. He was appointed on a committee to meet the Connecticut gentlemen to treat before Lord Bellomont about the western bounds of Colony.

1699, Oct. 25. He was chosen agent for the colony to go to England for maintaining of liberties granted in our charter. He refused the appointment.

1722, Feb. 20. Will—proved 1722, Jul. 9. Ex. son William. To son William, two home lots (6½ acres each), one of which was my father Thomas Olney's homestead, also 40 foot lots by water side on west side of Town street, &c., with a reservation of burying place in father's homestead lot, where my father and mother and some of my children and relatives are buried, and where testator himself desired to be laid. This reservation was to be 5 poles square and to be fenced, &c. To son William he also gave all homestead lands and tenements where I now dwell on both sides the river at place called the Stampers, with dwelling house and appurtenances. To son William, half of southern end of farm at Wenscott, the other half of southern end being already confirmed by deed to grandson William. To son William, other land, meadow by the Woonasquatucket River, farm at Westquadnaig, &c. To grandson Thomas, son of son Thomas, deceased, half of farm at Wenscott, being the northern end, with buildings, &c., and if he died without issue his brother Obadiah was to have it, but his mother Lydia was to have whole rule of what my son Thomas left her in possession of during life while his widow, and Obadiah to have a living in the house with his brother Thomas till he could get a settlement of his own. To grandson Thomas, also, 196 acres in a farm west of Seven Mile Line, near colony line on Killingly road, &c. To grandson Obadiah, land at "Observation" east side of Seven Mile Line, and 150 acre farm west side of Seven Mile Line near Round Hill, &c. To grandson Thomas, son of William, land near Edward Hawkins. All other lands to grandsons Obadiah and Richard. To son-in-law John Waterman, law book called "Coke upon Littleton," and to daughter Anne Waterman, a piece of eight. To son William, all rest of estate.

Inventory, £115, 5*s*. 6*d*., viz: feather bed, flock bed, 55 bound books, 23 small unbound books, pewter, 2 combs, great table, 6 chairs, silver money £30, leaden standard to hold ink, 5 wooden trenchers, shoemaker's tools, warming pan, &c.

II. **EPENETUS**, m. 1666, Mar. 9. **MARY WHIPPLE**, — b. 1634. d. 1698, Jun. 3. Providence, R. I. — (Mary) b. 1648. d. 1698 + of John & Sarah (   ) Whipple.

He kept a tavern.

1662, Jun. He was appointed with others to get the timber out and frame a bridge, that was to be built over the Moshassuck River.

1665, Feb. 19. He had lot 87 in a division of lands.

1666-76-84-86. Deputy.

1671, Oct. 23. His bill of 8*s*. for charges about a horse committed to his custody by the town, was allowed.

1679, Jul. 1. Taxed 6*s*. 3*d*.

1687, Sep. 1. Taxed 8*s*.

1688. Ratable estate, 270 acres, 3½ shares of meadow, house and lot, 3 acres within fence, 5 acres tillage, 2 horses, 1 mare, 4 cows, 4 oxen, 2 yearlings, 5 swine, 23 sheep.

1695-96-97. Town Council.

1696, Jan. 27. He and others were granted a lot measuring 40 feet square, for a school house if they would build in some considerable time.

1698, Jul. 12. Inventory, £145, 13*s*. 7*d*, exhibited by widow Mary. 2 oxen, a steer, 5 cows, 2 three year old, a two year steer, yearling, heifer, 2 calves, 50 sheep and lambs, 3 swine, 4 shoats, 2 horses, 5 stacks of bees, 2 tables, 6 chairs, bible and other books, 1 gun, 1 warming pan, a barrel of cider 3 sides of leather, augers, chisels, gauge, &c.

Administration was given to widow Mary and son James.

III. **NEDABIAH**, — b. 1637, Aug. d. young.

IV. **STEPHEN**, **UNMARRIED**. — b. d. 1658 ±. Providence, R. I.

V. **JAMES**, **UNMARRIED**. — b. d. 1676, Oct. Providence, R. I.

1676, Aug. 14. He was one of those "who staid and went not away" in King Philip's War, and so had a share in the disposition of the Indian captives whose services were sold for a term of years.

1676, Oct. 20. He was buried at this date as town records declare.

1677, Apr. His will is alluded to as in custody of Town Clerk.

I. THOMAS, | b. 1661, May 4. | d. 1718, Mar. 1. | Providence, R. I.
m. 1687, Jul. 13.
LYDIA BARNES, | b. | d. 1722 + | of Thomas & Prudence ( ) | Barnes.

1. Lydia, 1688, Apr. 30.
2. Phebe, 1689, Oct. 29.
3. Sarah, 1693, Aug. 26.
4. Thomas, 1696, Jan. 18.
5. Elizabeth, 1698, Jan. 29.
6. Anne, 1700, Mar. 26.
7. Mary, 1702, Feb. 25.
8. Obadiah, 1710, Feb. 14.

He was a carpenter.

1690–1707. Deputy.,

1707, Feb. 25. He and two others were appointed to audit the colony's accounts.

He was called Captain at his death.

1718, Aug. 4. Administration to widow Lydia and son Thomas. Inventory £141, 7*s.* 5*d.*, viz: an ox, 2 cows, 5 steers, 2 heifers, a bull, 7 shoats, carpenter's tools, surveyor's compass, &c., cider mill, 3 barrels cider, part of a corn mill £4, 7*d.*, part of a saw mill £5, flax, corn, hay, gun, 5 spinning wheels, warming pan, &c.

II. WILLIAM, | b. 1663, Jun. 25. | d. | Providence, R. I.
m. 1692, Dec. 28.
CATHARINE SAYLES, | b. 1671. | d. 1751, Feb. 21. | of John & Mary (Williams) | Sayles.

1. William, 1694, Oct. 6.
2. John, 1699, May 9.
3. Catharine, 1701, Aug. 11.
4. Thomas, 1706, Apr. 26.
5. Deborah, 1708, Jul. 30.
6. Richard, 1711, Nov. 4.

III. ELIZABETH, | b. 1666, Jan. 31. | d.
UNMARRIED.

IV. ANNE, | b. 1668, Jan. 13. | d. 1745, Oct. 26.
m.
JOHN WATERMAN, | b. 1666. | d. 1728, Aug. 26. | of Resolved & Mercy (Williams) | Waterman.

1. Elizabeth, 1692, Apr. 18.
2. Mercy, 1694, Jun. 27.
3. Anne, 1696, May 20
4. John, 1698, Feb. 5.
5. Benoni, 1701, May 25.
6. Resolved, 1703, Oct. 13.
7. Phebe,
8. Patience,

V. PHEBE, | b. 1675, Sep. 15. | d.
UNMARRIED.

OLNEY. 3d column. II. William. 1722, Dec. 24. "Whereas my honored father, Thomas Olney, deceased, did some considerable time before his death freely give unto Major William Smith, of Providence, aforesaid, his grandson-in-law, who married his granddaughter, Mary Sayles," 10 acres; the same was now confirmed. 1725, Sep. 23. He deeded land to "cousin," John Whitman. III. Elizabeth, d. 1699, Nov. 2, m. John Sayles, b. 1654, Aug. 17, d. 1727, Aug. , of John and Mary (Williams) Sayles. Children, 1. Mary, 1689, May 20. 2. John, 1692, Jan. 13. 3. Richard, 1695, Oct. 24. 4. Daniel, 1697, Dec. 13. 5. Thomas, 1699, Feb. 2.

I. MARY, | b. 1668, Jan. 13. | d. 1725 (—)
m. 1692, May 9.
NATHANIEL WATERMAN, | b. | d. 1725, Jun. 14. | of Nathaniel & Susanna (Carder) | Waterman.

1. Bethiah, 1693, Feb. 27.
2. Nathaniel, 1695, Sep. 9.
3. Joseph, 1697, Jan. 17.
4. Zuriel, 1701, Mar. 19.
5. Sarah, 1702, Nov. 6.
6. Mary, 1705, Mar. 23.
7. John, 1709, Oct. 6.

II. JAMES, | b. 1670, Nov. 9. | d. 1744, Oct. 6. | Providence, R. I.
m. 1702, Aug. 31.
HALLELUJAH BROWN, | b. | d. 1771. | of Daniel & Alice (Hearnden) | Brown.

1. James, 1703, Sep. 18.
2. Mary, 1704, Sep. 30.
3. Joseph, 1706, Jun. 7.
4. James, 1708, Dec. 28.
5. Jonathan, 1710, Mar. 9.
6. Jeremiah, 1711, Mar. 20.
7. Lydia, 1716, Nov. 1.
8. Mercy,

He held the title of Captain.

1740, Feb. 26. He and other Baptists were given permission by the Assembly to meet on the first day of the week in the County House in Providence, to worship during the pleasure of the Assembly, upon security being given to the Sheriff, for repairing and making good all damages.

1744, Sep. 2. Will—proved 1744, Nov. 19. Exx. wife Hallelujah. To son Joseph, homestead, &c., half at my decease and half at death or marriage of wife. To son Jonathan, £10, and privilege to cut thatch, he having already had his portion. To daughter Mary, wife of Arthur Fenner, and daughter Lydia, wife of Robert Sterry, £40, each. To daughter Mercy Olney, £300. To wife, the use of the homestead, and all estate not disposed of to be hers for life and then disposed of to children. (She to keep negro woman Amey and negro boy Billy for life, and have £100, paid her by son Joseph if she married, in lieu of dower.)

Inventory, £987, 15*s.*, viz: feather bed, flock bed, warming pan, rum and wine £8, a yoke of oxen, 3 cows, 3 small cattle, horsekind £15, 6 swine, negro man and woman £220, 7 silver spoons, &c.

1766, Feb. 5. Will—proved—1771, Sep. 30. Widow Hallelujah. Ex. son Joseph. To son Joseph, all estate acquired in widowhood and negro man Billy, in consideration of son's great care and kindness to me in my widowed state. To only surviving daughter Lydia Sterry, best suit of apparel and silver shoe buckles. To son Jonathan, £5, he having already received husband's wearing apparel. Rest of estate to son Joseph.

III. SARAH, | b. 1672, Sep. 10. | d.

IV. EPENETUS | b. 1675, Jan. 18. | d. 1740, Sep. 18. | Providence, R. I.
m.
MARY WILLIAMS, | b. | d. 1740 + | of Daniel & Rebecca (Rhodes) | Williams.

1. James,
2. Charles,
3. Joseph,
4. Anthony,
5. Mary,
6. Amey,
7. Anne,
8. Martha,
9. Freeborn,

1716, Mar. 26. He had deed from Peleg Williams, for love, &c., that latter bore to my brother-in-law, Ensign Epenetus Olney of Providence, and to my sister Mary, his now wife, &c.

1735, Dec. 16. Will—codicil 1740, Jan. 18—proved 1740, Oct. 20. Exx. wife Mary. To son James, land where he dwelleth near Woonasquatucket River, &c. To son Charles, my dwelling house, &c., but wife Mary to have till Charles is of age, then to him half till death of mother, and other half at her death, &c. To son Joseph, 122 acres at Sweet Fern Plain, near Paskhoge, Glocester. To son Anthony, land. To sons Joseph and Anthony, rest of land west of Seven Mile Line. To sons James and Charles, undivided lands east of Seven Mile Line, my part of saw mill at Wenscott, &c. To three daughters Mary, Amey and Anne Olney, £100, each. To wife Mary, £150. To daughters Martha Angell and Freeborn Winsor, 20*s.* each. Rest to wife. Codicil gives son-in-law William Colwell and wife Anne, 10 acres, and to daughters Martha Angell, Freeborn Winsor, Amey Hawkins and Anne Colwell, each, £5, &c. Inventory, £1,010, 19*s.* 3*d.*, viz: 15 cattle, 62 sheep, 5 swine a horse, cider mill, books, 3 feather beds, cane, silver 10¾ oz. Bills Public Credit £441, 11*s.* 6*d.*, &c.

V. JOHN, | b. 1678, Oct. 24. | d. 1754 Nov. 9. | Providence, R. I.
m. 1699, Aug. 11.
RACHEL COGGESHALL, | b. | d. 1760, Jun. 24. | of | Coggeshall.

1. John, 1701, May 27.
2. William, 1706, Feb. 22.
3. Jeremiah, 1708, Nov. 4.
4. Freelove, 1711, Nov. 29.
5. Nedabiah, 1715, Feb. 10.
6. Stephen, 1717.
7. Abigail,
8. Tabitha, 1723.
9. Jabez,

He was a blacksmith.

1760, Sep. 29. Administration was taken at this date on estates of both John Olney and his widow Rachel by their son William Olney.

Inventory of the widow Rachel amounted to £787, 7*s.* 6*d.*

VI. Mary, m. 1663, Dec. 4. John Whipple, | b. | d. 1676 ± | b. 1640. | d. 1700, Dec. 15. of John & Sarah ( ) Whipple.

VII. Lydia, m. 1669, Dec. 17. Joseph Williams, | b. 1645, | d. 1724, Sep. 9. | b. 1643, Dec. 12 | d. 1724, Aug. 17. of Roger & Mary ( ) Williams.

POTTER (Nathaniel).

Nathaniel, m. Dorothy, | b. | d. 1644 (—) | b. 1617. | d. 1696, Feb. 19. Portsmouth, R. I.

(She m. (2) John Albro.)

1638. He was admitted an inhabitant of island of Aquidneck.

1639, Apr. 30. He and twenty-eight others signed the following compact: "We whose names are underwritten do acknowledge ourselves the legal subjects of his Majesty King Charles, and in his name do hereby bind ourselves into a civil body politicke, unto his laws according to matters of justice."

No relationship is known to exist between him and Thomas Potter, who had wife Ann, and a daughter Mary, born at Newport, 1664, July.

I. Nathaniel, m. Elizabeth, | b. 1637. | d. 1704, Oct. 20. | b. | d. 1704 + of Portsmouth, R. I., Dartmouth, Mass.

1664, Sep. 5. He and Abel Potter confirmed a deed of 8 acres that was once in their fathers' possession, said deed having been made 1663, May 7, by Samuel Wilbur to John Tripp, shaft carpenter.

1677. Freeman

1680. Taxed 5*s*.

1704, Oct. 18. Will—proved 1704, Nov. 20. Exs. wife Elizabeth and son Stokes. Overseers, James Tripp and Hugh Mosher. To wife, all movables, her living in the house for life and a third of estate. To son Stokes, half my land on south side of highway. To son John, half my land on north side of highway, with orchard. To son Nathaniel, 1*s*. To son William, £4. To son Benjamin, £3. To son Samuel, 1*s*. To daughter Mary Wilbur, £2, and a cow. To daughter Rebecca Kirby, £2 and a cow. To daughter Elizabeth Potter, £3. To daughter Katharine Potter, £4, at age. To son Ichabod Potter, 2 acres.

Inventory, £198, 12*s*., 6*d*, viz: house and land £120, 2 beds, brass, glass, iron and pewter ware, loom, cheese press, 2 oxen, 5 cows, 3 yearlings, calf, 19 sheep, 10 swine, time of prentice girl £2, 10*s*., 4 spinning wheels, 3 chests, 6 chairs, &c.

His children were not born in the exact order he names them probably.

VI. THOMAS, m. 1710, Jun. 15. PATIENCE BURLINGAME,
b. 1686, May 18. d. 1752, Jul. 28. — Providence, R. I.
b. 1685. d. 1746, Aug. 8. of Roger & Mary ( ) — Burlingame.

1. Lydia, 1711, Jun. 2.
2. Esther, 1714, Jul. 7.

1708. Freeman.
1722-23-25-28-30-32-34. Deputy.
1722. Town Treasurer.
1725-26. Town Council.
1752, Sep. 26. Administration to son-in-law Daniel Eddy and daughter Esther Olney.

Inventory, £534, 1*s.*, viz: silver money £8, wearing apparel £91, gun, woolen wheel, linen wheel, 2 books, &c.

He and his wife were buried in North Burial Ground.

VII. LYDIA, m. HENRY HARRIS,
b. 1688, Jan. 26. d. 1727 (—)
b. 1675, Nov. 10. d. 1727, Mar. 29. of Thomas & Elnathan (Tew) — Harris.

1. Thomas,
2. Henry,
3. Lydia,

1. Mary, 1665, Mar. 4.
2. John, 1666, Oct. 2.
3. Elnathan, 1675, Jan. 2.

1. Joseph, 1670, Sep. 26.
2. Thomas, 1672, Feb. 16.
3. Joseph, 1673, Nov. 10.
4. Mary, 1676, Jun.
5. James, 1680, Sep. 20.
6. Lydia, 1683, Apr. 26.

POTTER (NATHANIEL).

I. STOKES, m. ELIZABETH,
b. d. 1718. — Dartmouth, Mass.
b. d. 1718 + of

1. Isabel, 1703, Oct. 19.
2. Margaret, 1705, Jun. 30.
3. Hannah, 1707, May 3.
4. Nathaniel, 1709, Jan. 7.
5. Benjamin, 1711, Jun. 21.
6. Dorothy, 1714, Feb. 2.
7. Sarah,

1718, Jan. 25. Will—proved 1718, Feb. 3. Exx. wife Elizabeth. To son Nathaniel, all lands in Dartmouth. To son Benjamin, £5, paid by Nathaniel, when twenty-one. To daughter Isabel Potter, 5*s.*, paid by Nathaniel. To daughter Margaret Potter, 5*s.*, and like amount to daughters Hannah, Dorothy and Sarah Potter. To wife, rest of estate.

Inventory, £384, 4*s.*, viz: house and land £200, money £10, 11*s.*, 6*d.*, 5 cows, pair of oxen, 4 two years, 2 yearlings, mare, colt, 9 sheep, 6 swine, 4 geese, 4 wheels, warming pan, 2 barrels cider, pewter, &c.

II. JOHN, m. MARY,
b. d. 1769. — Dartmouth, Mass.
b. d. of

1. Job, 1708, Apr. 8.
2. Nathaniel, 1710, Jan. 8.
3. Hannah, 1712, Mar. 22.
4. Margaret, 1716, Apr. 22.
5. John, 1720, Sep. 16.
6. Amey,

1760, Sep. 11. Will—proved 1769, Dec. 25. Ex. son Nathaniel. To wife, bed, warming pan, and use of indoor movables, best room in house, ten bushels apples, cow, two geese and use of garden. To son Nathaniel, all my homestead and house, he keeping wife's cow, &c. To son John, rest of lands not before deeded and buildings, he paying my granddaughter Comfort Potter, 12*s.*, and allowing use of room in house where he dwells to my wife, his mother, and providing firewood. To daughter Hannah Brightman, 6*s.*, and a third of indoor movables, and like legacy to daughters Margaret Macomber and Amey Cass. To son John, £20, all wearing apparel, weaver's loom, &c. To sons Nathaniel and John, all stock and hay, equally.

III. NATHANIEL, m. JOAN WILBUR,
b. d. 1736. — Dartmouth, Mass.
b. d. 1759. of William — Wilbur.

1. William, 1689, Nov. 12.
2. Mary, 1702, Mar. 25.

1732, Nov. 15. Will—proved 1736, Nov. 16. Exs. wife Joan and son William. To wife, dwelling house and part of homestead and negro Cæsar, for life, and all money and movables forever. To son William, south-easterly part of my homestead wherein his dwelling house stands. To son-in-law Isaac Wood and daughter Mary his wife, land whereon she dwells, and Cæsar, at death of wife. To son William, the part of homestead where I dwell, at death of wife, during his life, and then equally to my two grandsons Nathaniel and Daniel.

Inventory, £424, 12*s.*, 10*d.*, viz: wearing clothes £40, cash in paper £174, 6*s.*, 11*d.*, 27 oz. silver, bed, pewter, warming pan, pair of worsted combs, carpenter's tools, 2 cows, 2 swine, sheep, fowls, negro lad £70, sword, &c.

1743, Jul. 3. Will—proved 1759, May 1. Widow Joan. Ex. friend John Sanford, of Little Compton. To son William, 5*s.* To daughter Mary Brownell, 5*s.*, and negro Cæsar. To grandson Nathaniel Potter, bible and a pair of silver buttons. To granddaughters Mary and Rachel Wood, each a feather bed. To grandchildren Benjamin, William, Jane Soule, Nathaniel, David, Sarah, Mary, Robert and Martha Potter, children of son William, one-half of rest of estate. To grandchildren Rachel and Gideon Wood, children of daughther Mary Brownell, other half.

IV. WILLIAM, m. ANN DURFEE,
b. d. 1720 + — Portsmouth, R. I.
b. d. 1710 + of Thomas — Durfee.

1. Nathaniel,
2. William, 1696, Nov. 11.

1696. Freeman.
1697, Jun. 14. He and wife Ann, sold William Burrington, 10 acres for £50.
1720, May 9. He deeded for love, &c., to son William Potter, Jr., all lands and housing in Portsmouth.

V. BENJAMIN, m. MARY,
b. d. 1709. — Portsmouth, R. I., Dartmouth, Mass.
b. d. 1709 + of

1696. Freeman.
1709, Dec. 7. Inventory, £140, 17*s.*, 11*d.*, shown by widow Mary, administratrix. Among items were house and lands £100, 2 cows, calf, mare, 2 pigs, 13 geese, fowls, loom, 2 wheels, gun, pair of cards, hive of bees, &c.

VI. SAMUEL, m. MARY,
b. 1675. d. 1748. — Dartmouth, Mass.
b. d. 1748 + of

1. Aaron, 1701, Sep. 26.
2. Nathaniel, 1703, Sep. 9.
3. Fear, 1705, May 11.
4. Mary, 1709, Feb. 1.
5. Elizabeth, 1711, Aug. 10.
6. Benjamin, 1714, Sep. 23.
7. Samuel, 1714, Sep. 23.
8. Job, 1717, Nov. 29.

1738, Mar. 5. Will—proved 1748, Aug. 17. Exx. wife Mary. Overseers, son Aaron and brother Ichabod. To her, improvement of all estate real and personal for life. To sons Aaron and Nathaniel, 5*s.*, each. To son Benjamin, 10 acres at death of wife and like legacy to son Samuel. To son Job, 20 acres at death of wife. To daughters Fear Holladay, wife of William, Mary Tripp, wife of Othniel, and Elizabeth Day, wife of Richard, all household goods at death of wife, and half of stock and outdoor movables. To sons Benjamin, Samuel and Job, the other half of stock and outdoor movables.

VII. MARY, m. SAMUEL WILBUR,
b. d.
b. d. 1740. of William — Wilbur

1. Martha, 1690, Oct. 22.
2. Samuel, 1692, Nov. 7.
3. William, 1695, Jan. 6
4. Mary, 1697, Oct. 9.
5. Joanna, 1700, Jun. 8.
6. Thankful, 1700, Jun. 8.
7. Elizabeth, 1702, Dec. 23.
8. Thomas, 1704, Dec. 2.
9. Abial, 1707, May 22.
10. Hannah, 1709, Feb. 9.
11. Isaac, 1712, Aug. 24.

II. { ICHABOD, { b. Portsmouth, R. I.
m. { d. 1676.
MARTHA HAZARD, { b.
{ d. of Thomas & Martha ( ) Hazard.

(She m. (2) Benjamin Mowry.)

1661, Mar. 22. He signed certain articles relative to Misquamicut (Westerly) lands.

1671. Oct 18. Grand Jury.

1680. His widow Martha was taxed 4*s*, 2*d*., at Portsmouth. She moved to Kings Town not many years after this (where her brother Robert Hazard went about 1687).

1683, Dec. 31. The land of Ichabod Potter, deceased, is alluded to in a deed from Daniel Grinnell and wife Mary to Henry Brightman, of 23 acres in Portsmouth.

By one account he had daughters Susannah and Sarah.

POWER.

{ NICHOLAS, { b. Providence, R. I.
m. { d. 1657, Aug. 25.
JANE, { b.
{ d. 1667 +

1640, Jul. 27. He and thirty-eight others signed a compact for good government.

1643, Oct. 17. He was among the band of Gortonists arraigned at Boston at this date, though his residence was very brief at Warwick, if indeed he ever lived there. He was dismissed with an admonition but his companions suffered imprisonment.

1648, Dec. 25. He bought of William Burrows a 5 acre lot that had been William Wickenden's, adjoining Nicholas Power's own lot.

1649 Constable.

1650, Sep. 2. Taxed £1.

I. { NICHOLAS, { b. Providence, R. I.
m. 1672, Feb. 3. { d. 1675, Dec. 19.
REBECCA RHODES, { b.
{ d. 1727. of Zachariah & Joanna (Arnold) Rhodes.

(She m. (2) 1676, Dec. 2, Daniel Williams.)

1665, Feb. 19 He had lot 85 in a division of lands.

1670, Jul. 27. It was voted that Nicholas Power, son of Nicholas, deceased, "be entered in our Town book a purchaser as by his father's purchase right," &c.

1672, May 14. He and Thomas Hopkins, Jr., were voted 10*s*., each, for apprehending an Indian.

1675, Jan. 27. He was granted right to exchange 60 acres.

1675, Dec. 19. He was killed in the Great Swamp Fight in Narragansett, by a shot from the command with which he was serving, being in an advanced position himself. In this battle over a thousand Indians and more than two hundred Englishmen were killed and wounded. There were thirty-five hundred Indians and fifteen hundred colonists engaged in the fight.

VIII. Rebecca, b. d.
m.
Robert Kirby, b. 1674, Mar. 10. d. of Richard & Patience (Gifford) Kirby

1. Remembrance,
2. Nathaniel,
3. Ichabod,
4. Recompense,
5. Silas,
6. Robert,

IX. Elizabeth, b. d.
m. 1707, Jul. 31.
Benjamin Tripp, b. 1678, Feb. 21. d. of John & Susanna (Anthony) Tripp.

1. Katharine, 1708, May 17.
2. Benjamin, 1709, Nov. 15.
3. Nathaniel, 1712, Feb. 27.
4. Lydia, 1714, Oct. 31.
5. Rebecca, 1717, May 1.
6. Elizabeth, 1722, May 6.
7. Stokes, 1725, May 13.

X. Katharine, b. d.
m.
Thomas Cornell, b. d. 1763. of Samuel Cornell.

1. Rebecca, 1717, Aug. 3.
2. Peleg, 1719, Dec. 9.
3. Susanna, 1722, May 13.
4. Joshua, 1724, Jun. 22.
5. Catharine, 1724, Jun. 22.
6. Elizabeth, 1729, Jul. 17.

XI. Ichabod, b. d. 1755. Dartmouth, Mass.
m.
Eleanor, b. d. 1754 + of

1. Rebecca, 1710, Mar. 29.
2. George, 1714, Jan. 3.
3. Jonathan, 1716, Nov. 14.
4. Elizabeth, 1718, Dec. 16.
5. Stokes, 1720, Dec. 16.
6. Ichabod, 1722, Feb. 9.
7. Sarah, 1725, Mar. 13.

1754, Mar. 15. Will—proved 1755, Nov. 4. Ex. son Jonathan. To son Jonathan, part of homestead. To son Ichabod, the part of homestead farm where I live, he paying certain legacies. To grandson Thomas Potter, son of George, deceased, land. To son Stokes Potter, certain land. To daughter Rebecca, a bed and privilege to live in house with her mother while unmarried, and at marriage, £10, by son Jonathan, said son maintaining her if she never marries. To daughter Sarah Wood, £4. To granddaughter Elizabeth Potter, daughter of George, deceased, £2. To wife Eleanor, all household goods, all money in the house, a cow, privilege in dwelling house while widow and maintenance by sons Jonathan and Ichabod. To sons Jonathan, Stokes and Ichabod, rest of live stock and husbandry tools. To daughters Rebecca Potter and Sarah Wood, all household goods left at death of wife. To son Jonathan, all wearing apparel.

Inventory, 13 geese, an ox, 2 heifers, 3 cows, &c.

I. Thomas, b. d. 1728. South Kingstown, R. I.
m. (1) 1687, Jan. 20.
Susanna Tripp, b. 1667, Oct. 31. d. of John & Susanna (Anthony) Tripp.
m. (2) 1720, Dec. 8 [Thos.
Lydia Sherman, (w. of b. d. 1727 + of Daniel & Elizabeth (Cook) Wilcox.

1. Susannah, 1688, Jun. 28.
2. Sarah, 1690, Jul. 25.
3. Ichabod, 1692, Sep. 23.
4. Thomas, 1696, Feb. 8.
5. John, 1697, Oct. 2.
6. Nathaniel, 1700, Apr. 15.
7. Benjamin, 1703, Jan. 19.
8. Joseph, 1706, Jan. 30.
9. Mary, 1708, Aug. 16.
10. Martha,
(2d wife, no issue.)

1727, Jun. 3. Will—codicil, 1727, Jun. 4—proved 1728, Jun. 3. Ex. son Thomas. To wife Lydia, £100. To daughter Susan Sheldon, £70. To daughter Sarah Earle, £70. To granddaughter Mary Sherman, £100. To sons Ichabod and Nathaniel, all that farm I bought of Joseph Knight, Nathaniel having the dwelling house in his share. To sons John and Benjamin, east end of farm where I live. To son Joseph, rest of farm, and also the farm bought of Thomas Hazard. To son Thomas, £300. In codicil he gives to wife a riding beast and feather bed. To daughter Martha Potter, £100, and a feather bed.

Inventory, £4,092, 8*s.*, 7*d.*, viz: wearing apparel £22, 16*s.*, books, cane, 5 oz., 17 pwt. silver money, warming pan, pewter, spinning wheel, linen wheel, gun, 18 horses, mares and colts, bull, 14 oxen, 4 steers, 12 cows, 3 calves, other cattle £19, 72 ewes, 72 lambs, 62 dry sheep, 36 year old sheep, negroes, Harry £20, Scipio, £45, Simon £85, Pero £55, apprentice and an Indian boy £16, &c.

II. John, b. 1665 ± d. 1715. Kings Town, R. I.
m.
Sarah Wilson, b. 1666. d. 1739 + of Samuel & ——— (Tefft) Wilson.

1. Martha, 1692, Dec. 20.
2. John, 1695, May 20.
3. Samuel, 1699, Sep. 2.
4. Sarah, 1702, Apr. 15.
5. Susanna, 1704, Sep. 17.
6. Mary, 1707, Mar. 2.
7. Samuel, 1715, Jul. 28

1715, Jun. 25. Will—proved 1715, Jul. 12. Ex. son John. To wife Sarah, house in Point Judith, half acre of land, £500, ten cows, a good riding horse, three beds, a man servant, two women servants, the wintering of two cows by son John, and privilege of firewood for one fire. To daughter Martha Allen, £400. To daughter Susannah Potter, £500, at eighteen, a bed, two cows, mare, horse, &c. To daughter Mary Potter, £500, bed, two cows, horse, &c. The rest of household stuff to be divided among my own daughters at wife's death as she may see cause. To son John, all housing and land in Matunock Neck, 450 acres, and 400 acres of other land, all movables, money, bills, bonds, chattels, horsekind, farming utensils, &c. If child wife is with be a son he to have house and land at Point Judith, 160 acres, at age and other land. If child prove to be a girl said lands to go to John, he paying said girl £500.

1739, Mar. His widow Sarah Potter, called herself aged seventy-three years in testimony given this month.

POTTER (Nathaniel.) 3d column. III. Robert. His first child was Marbury, (not Barbara).

III. Robert, b. d. 1745. South Kingstown, R. I.
m.
Elizabeth, b. d. 1744 (—) of

POTTER (Nathaniel). 3d column. III. Robert. His wife was Elizabeth Cole, of John and Susannah (Hutchinson) Cole. 1720±. His daughter Susanna had a legacy from the will of her aunt Mary Cole, of Newport.

1. Barbara, 1688, Feb. 2.
2. Martha, 1699, Aug. 10.
3. Robert, 1702, Jul. 26.
4. Ichabod, 1703, Nov. 30.
5. Susanna 1705, Feb. 14.

1744, Apr. 23. Will—proved 1745, Jul. 14. Ex. son Robert. To son Robert, 10 acres and my dwelling house thereon, also 80 acres bounded partly by land of son Ichabod, deceased, and half the cedar swamp, and all personal estate. To daughter Susanna Reynolds, £5. To grandson Robert, son of Ichabod, 54 acres and half the cedar swamp, he paying his brothers and sisters as they come of age as follows: to sisters Elizabeth and Deborah, £50, each, brothers Ichabod, Thomas and William, £100, each, and sister Margaret, £50. Said grandson Robert, to pay his mother-in-law (*i. e.* step-mother) Margaret Potter, widow of his father Ichabod, £10 yearly while widow, at the expiration of five years.

IV. Ichabod, b. d. 1730. South Kingstown, R. I
m.
Margaret Helme, b. 1679. d. 1727 (—) of Rouse & Mary ( ) Helme.

1. Ichabod,
2. Rouse, 1703, Feb. 13
3. Thomas,
4. William, 1709, Mar. 4.
5. Margaret, 1714, Oct. 11

1698, Apr. 16. He, of Point Judith, bought of John Albro, of Portsmouth, for £45, a right that latter purchased of Josiah Arnold, lying in Pettaquamscott purchase, in Narragansett.

1698, Apr. 16. He deeded to brothers Roger, Joseph and Benjamin Mowry, for love, &c., land in Narragansett, being a right which I bought of my grandfather (*i. e.* step-grandfather) John Albro, of Portsmouth.

1716, Mar. 24. His wife Margaret, in testimony at this date calls herself aged thirty-seven years or thereabouts.

1727, Nov. 19. Will—codicil 1729, Sep. 28—proved 1730, Mar. 9. Exs. sons Rouse and Thomas. To son Ichabod, £30, to be paid him by my sons Rouse, Thomas and William, said Ichabod having already received his part To only daughter Margaret Potter, feather bed, oval table, iron pot and £100, at eighteen. To sons Rouse, Thomas and William, rest of estate, real and personal. To daughter Margaret, negro woman Moll. To above three sons, three negro boys. In codicil he gives daughter Margaret, £80, instead of £100, and liberty to live with either brother till eighteen. To son Ichabod, negro or mustee boy Dick. To son William, a chest.

Inventory, £712, 18*s.*, 6*d.*, viz: wearing apparel £14, 10*s.*, loom, pair of worsted combs, pair of cards, spinning wheel, linen wheel, negro, books, swarm of bees, 6 cows, calf, 4 yearlings, pair of oxen, 5 horsekind, bull, 44 sheep, sow, 3 pigs, 11 shoats, &c.

POWER.

I. Hope, b. d. young.

II. Nicholas, b. 1673. d. 1734, May 18. Providence, R. I.
m. (1)
Mary Haile, b. d. of Haile.
m. (2)
Mercy Tillinghast, b. 1680. d. 1769, Nov. 13. of Pardon & Lydia (Taber) Tillinghast.

1. Mary,
(2d wife.)
2. Hope, 1701, Jan. 4.
3. John, 1703, Apr.
4. Joseph,
5. Anne, 1707, Dec. 12.
6. Sarah,
7. Nicholas
8. Lydia,
9. Mercy

1684, Oct. 29. Heirs of Nicholas Power taxed 4*s.*, 2*d.* (in a levy of £25).

1685, Dec. 12. Laid out to heirs of Nicholas Power, in right of predecessors, the deceased Nicholas Power both the elder and the younger; 50 acres of land.

1701, Mar. 4. He bought of Daniel Williams for good satisfaction, a house lot in lower end of the town

1651, Jul. 28. He and Thomas Harris were ordered to "equally divide the goats and goods and what else belongeth unto the two orphans of Daniel Abbott, deceased," &c.

1655. Freeman.

1655. Juryman.

1656. Surveyor of Highways.

1667, May 27. Will for Nicholas Power (who died Aug. 25, 1657), was made at this date by Town Council. He "by reason of extreme sickness and sudden death made no will," and now application being made by the widow, and the children coming near the age of possessing and to prevent differences, the Town Council took action. To widow Jane, was given dwelling house and half the cellar which she built, with the house lot and other lands, and at her death her son Nicholas was to have house and lot, and her daughter Hope, other land. Certain land was given to the widow at her own disposal, "and considering what she the said widow hath added to the stock of cattle, that is to say of mares and colts, and built the cellar by her industry, to her sixty pound charge," &c., she was given all the household goods in her possession, and cattle not otherwise disposed of to children. Besides certain lands which Nicholas was to have at age (and the house, &c., at decease of mother) he was also given when of age, two working steers, a yearling steer, mare and foal, his father's working tools, a bed, &c. Hope, besides certain lands at death of mother, was to have when twenty-one, a cow, two young cattle, a mare and a yearling foal. If either Nicholas or Hope die without issue the share is to go to the one surviving, except that right of dower of wife of Nicholas, should he have one, and husband's courtesy, if Hope should have a husband, were to be preserved.

II. { HOPE, m. JAMES CLARKE, } b. 1650. d. 1713, Feb. 27. b. 1649. d. 1736, Dec. 1. of Jeremiah & Frances (Latham) Clarke.

PRAY.

{ RICHARD, m. (1) MARY, m. (2) 1688 ± [w. of Benj. ELIZABETH HEARNDEN, of William White. } b. 1630. d. 1693. b. d. 1686. b. d. 1701 + Providence, R. I.

He was a collier; so calling himself in deeds.

1653, Jan. 3. He and wife Mary bought of Robert Coles, his house and home lot next Thomas Olney's house lot and near the Pound.

1655, May 25. He was appointed by the Court of Commissioners to keep a house of entertainment. A convenient sign was to be set out at the most perspicuous place of said house to give notice to strangers.

1656, Apr. 15. His wife Mary gave notice of landing six ankers of sack and later in same year gave notice of nine ankers of sack.

1657, May 29. He gave notice of three ankers sack.

1659, Sep. 13. He gave notice of three-quarter casks wine, and an anker liquor, and next year 66 gallons wine and two ankers liquor.

1665, Feb. 19. In a division of lands he drew lot No. 27.

1666, Dec. 26. He made over part of his estate to Town Council for use of wife Mary and her children.

1667, May 1. He and wife Mary having petitioned Assembly for a divorce and final parting, it was not granted so far as to allow either to marry again, though they may live apart.

1672, Nov. 6. Information having been presented to Assembly showing that Captain John Greene had given a bill of divorce to Mary Pray and Richard Pray, the act was discountenanced there being no authority for any Assistant to grant a divorce.

1675, May 21. He deeded son John, my dwelling house standing at Loquassuck with half purchase right of land and meadow.

1676, Aug. 14. He was one of those "who staid and went not away" in King Philip's War, and so had a share in the disposition of the Indian captives whose services were sold for a number of years.

1678, Apr. 15. He deeded son Ephraim half a tract of meadow and upland.

1679, Jul. 1. Taxed 6*s.* 3*d.*, with wife Mary and son Ephraim.

1680, Mar. 16. He petitioned Assembly to remit sentence of General Court of Trials (in October, 1678) against him for £10, by him forfeited, being bound and not attending said Court. He pleading God's hand upon him by sickness, and considering poverty of petitioner, his request was granted.

1681, Apr. 27. His wife Mary was licensed by Town Council to keep a public house of entertainment for the relieving of travelers and strangers, providing both for horse and man, as also by retail to sell unto the inhabitants beer, wine, or strong liquor for one whole year, she not to suffer any unlawful game in the house nor any evil rule there.

She was to pay 20*s.* for license, but being willing to give liberty to Town for Town meetings to be kept there, the Council accepted in lieu of 20*s.*

1685, Jan. 27. He, "aged 55 or thereabouts," testified that he had heard Robert Cole say that he had sold Valentine Whitman his share of meadow at Mashapog.

1686, Jan. 20. He deeded son William a house and lot formerly belonging to Robert Cole, bounded partly by lot of Thomas Olney, Jr., also upland and meadow on a small brook.

1687, Sep. 1. Taxed 9*d.*

1688, Oct. 20. He and wife Elizabeth, late wife to Benjamin Hearnden, deceased (and executrix of will dated 1686, Feb. 1), deeded to her son Isaac Hearnden, the homestead farm, orchard, &c., given her by late husband's will for her life.

1688, Oct. 20. His wife Elizabeth quitclaimed all her right to thirds of husband's lands, and obliged herself to sign a more ample instrument when thereunto legally required.

I. { EPHRAIM, m. SARAH, } b. d. 1727, Mar. 22. b. d. 1726 + of Providence, R. I.

1676, Aug. 14. He was one of those "who staid and went not away" in King Philip's War.

1684, Feb. 4. He took the license that his mother had received three years before.

1687, Sep. 1. Taxed 2*s.*

1687. Ratable estate, 2 acres tillage, ½ share meadow, 4 acres meadow, 8 acres wild pasture, 2 cows, a mare, and a yearling horse.

1696. Freeman.

1700, Jul. 2. He and wife Sarah sold John Keese of Portsmouth, a right of land.

1713, Jun. 16. Taxed 13*s.*

1726, Apr. 19. He deeded to grandson Job Whipple, Jr., for good will and affection "as also for the good service he my grandson hath already done for me," my homestead farm and dwelling house, &c. Wife Sarah joined in deed.

1726, Aug. 3. Will—proved 1727, May 15. Ex. son Job Whipple. To wife Sarah, all movables for life, and at her decease to go as follows: To brother John Pray, £5. To cousin (*i. e.* nephew) John Pray, £5, and two lots of land. To cousin Hugh Pray, £5. To cousin Richard Pray, £5. Rest of estate to all my grandchildren, the children of son Job Whipple.

Inventory, £220, 4*s.* 7*d.*, viz: carpenter's tools, 2 bulls, 2 oxen, a steer, 7 cows, 3 calves, mare and colt, sheep, old book, silver money £1, 8*s.* 4*d.*

II. { JOHN, m. 1678, Nov. 14. SARAH BROWN. } b. d. 1733, Oct. 9. b. d. 1733 + of John & Mary (Holmes) Brown. Providence, Smithfield, R. I.

1676, Aug. 14. He was one of those "who staid and went not away" in King Philip's War.

1679, Jul. 1. Taxed 1*s.* 10½*d.*

1682. Freeman.

1687, Sep. 1. Taxed 3*s.*

1694, Mar. 6. He made an exchange of 6 acres land with John Whipple, said land having been given him by father Richard Pray, now deceased.

1708, Sep. 20. He sold William Crawford half a 40 foot lot for £2, 5*s.*

1713, Jun. 16. Taxed 11*s.*

1714, Apr. 7. He sold Joseph Davis 89 acres for £40.

1717, Jul. 23. He deeded son Richard, for love, &c., all that my farm where I dwell, with dwelling house, that is half the said farm at signing and half at my decease and decease of his mother.

1721, May 20. He sold John Inman 16 acres in original right of Richard Pray.

1724, May 27. He sold David Shippee, 10 acres for £3, 10*s.*, in original right of honoured father Richard Pray.

1733, Mar. 29. He deeded son Richard, for love, &c., house and lands where he (John) lived.

1726, Apr. 29. Will—proved 1734, Feb. 1. Ex. son Richard. To wife Sarah, half homestead farm, with dwelling house, all cattle and household goods for life, while widow, but if she married said half to son Richard. To son John, 5*s.* To son Hugh, 5*s.* To son Richard, all homestead, cattle, &c., half at my decease, and half at decease or marriage of wife. The homestead is described as situated in north part of Providence. To daughter Mary Brown, 5*s.* To daughter Catharine Comstock, 5*s.* To daughter Sarah Brown, 5*s.* To daughter Penelope Aldrich, 5*s.* To daughter Martha Wilkinson, 5*s.*

Inventory, £61, 4*s.*, viz: wearing apparel £6, books 6*s.*, copper pennies 8*d.*, feather bed £12, wool bed £5, flock bed £6, pewter, warming pan, 2 razors, yarn, 2 cows, calf, 15 sheep.

PRAY. 2d column. I. Ephraim b. 1657; m. (2) 1691, Sarah Claghorne, of Barnstable, b. 1662; d. 1726, Sep. 8. He and his wife buried near Lime Rock. 3d column. II. Hugh. Children, 1, Patience, 1718, July 8. 2, Abigail, 1719, June 1. 3, Sarah, 1721, Mar. 29. 4, John, 1722, Dec. 3. 5, Jonathan, 1724, Sep. 9. 6, Hugh, 1726, Aug. 9. 7, Mary, 1728, Oct. 14. 8, Martha, 1731, May 28. 9, Jeremiah, 1733, Apr. 1. 10, Ann, 1735, Mar. 4. 11, David, 1739, Mar. 18. 12, Mercy, 1741, Oct. 7. 13, Susan.

1704-8-22-23-30. Deputy.

1705, Jan. 12. He gave £3, toward a new bridge. "Whereas there is a great need for the building and erecting a bridge over Providence River, and there hath been by the town many debates concerning the great benefit as will ensue," &c., measures were therefore taken to get subscriptions, and "it was concluded that said bridge is to be erected and set up where the bridge formerly was."

1711, May 2. He was appointed with William Crawford to build a bridge at Weybossett.

1713-21-29-30. Town Council.

1720-21-24-25-26-27-28-29-31-32-33. Assistant.

1721, Oct. 27. A letter addressed to Capt. Nicholas Power and others of Providence, was signed by three Presbyterian ministers of prominence in Massachusetts, viz: John Danforth, Peter Thatcher and Joseph Belcher, who sought to establish a Presbyterian foothold in Baptist Rhode Island.

1726, Jan. 10. He was appointed by the Assembly for the town of Providence, in room of Andrew Harris, deceased, to let out Colony's bills of credit for said town, and to do and act in all other things, as the laws of colony require.

1733, Jan. 23. He was appointed on committee with two others by the Assembly, to build a new jail and jail house in Providence of the same bigness of that in Kings County.

1732, Mar. 18. Will—proved 1734, Jul. 3. Exs. wife Mercy and son Nicholas. To son John, land where he was raising a house, and £50, toward finishing it, the location being on west side of the Town street. He gave him also land which was bounded partly by land before given to testator's daughter Anne and her husband John Stewart. To son John, he gave also a third part of an orchard, a yoke of oxen, 4 yearling heifers, 50 sheep and negro Toney. To son Joseph, a dwelling house and land on east side of Town street, 120 acres in another place, a lot of land bounded partly by land before given testator's daughter Sarah and her husband William Burrough, and a third of orchard and a small sloop. To son Nicholas, "my dwelling house wherein I now dwell, and all my housing, building and land adjoining on west side of Town street;" and other lands when of age, including 200 acres in Glocester, also a third of the orchard and stills. To daughter Mary and her husband Daniel Cooke, certain lands, as also to daughter Hope and her husband James Brown, Jr. To daughters Lydia and Mercy, lands and £100, each, when eighteen. To each grandchild a crown apiece. Of the movables remaining half to children equally, and half to wife. He provides for burying place in home lot where some of his relatives are buried, to be for that use "for my children and grandchildren from generation to generation."

Inventory, £1,751, 13*s.*, 3*d.*, of Colonel Nicholas Power, merchant—3 horses, a bull, a steer, 5 cows, a heifer, 81 sheep, 33 lambs, 10 swine, sloop Sparrow £100, "Cuffey a negro man being now sick" £0, Tony £90, Cæsar £100, Peg, negro woman £70, 3 hogsheads molasses, 646 pounds tobacco, 385 pounds bacon, apothecary drugs, 3 stills with worm tubs, &c., hops, cheese press, 3 guns, silver hilted sword and belt £7, ivory headed cane, books and Colony law book, wearing apparel £21, 15*s.*, glass decanters and wine glasses, plate and silver money £175, 13*s.*, 9*d.*, cider mill, furniture, &c. The rooms named were: great lower room, dining room, bedroom, little bedroom, kitchen, S. E. chamber, N. E. chamber, N. W. chamber, and little south chamber and garret, besides warehouse, cooper's shop, &c.

He was buried in North Burial Ground.

1. Hope, 1673, Dec. 29.
2. Jonathan, 1681.

PRAY.

I. SILENCE, m. JOB WHIPPLE,
b. 1682. d. 1767, Jan. 1.
b. 1684. d. 1750, Apr. 19. of Eleazer & Alice (Angell) Whipple.

1. Job, 1704.
2. Sarah,
3. Dorcas,
4. Hannah,
5. Abigail, 1711.
6. Simon, 1713.
7. Alice, 1715.
8. Mary,
9. Anna, 1722.
10. Amey, 1724.
11. Stephen, 1726.

I. JOHN, m. 1713, Jul. 14. SARAH DOWNING,
b. d.
b. d. of Downing.

1. Job,

1708. Freeman.

1728, Oct. 12. He ("John Pray, Jr."), sold Joseph Whipple, for £1, 10*s.*, ¼ of a lot.

II. HUGH, m. ABIGAIL,
b. d. 1761, Apr. 13. Providence, Scituate, R. I.
b. d. of

1. Jonathan,
2. Susan,
3. Hugh,
4. Patience, 1718, Jul. 8.
5. Abigail, 1719, Jun. 1.
6. Sarah, 1721, Mar. 29.
7. John, 1722, Dec. 3.
8. Mary,

1708. Freeman.

1713, Jun 16. Taxed 2*s.* 6*d.*

1726, Sep. 20. He sold John Pray, Jr., 30 acres for £14, 10*s.*

1744, Jul. 18. Scituate. He deeded son John, for love, &c., 62 acres, and 55 acres next year to son Jonathan.

1750, Dec. 31. His son Jonathan rendered account of administration on estate of deceased brother John Pray, and took receipts for £18, 13*s.* 2*d.* each from following brothers and sisters: Elijah Blake and wife Susan, Hugh Pray, Jr., John Greabeak and wife Patience, Abner Hopkins and wife Mary, and sister Abigail Pray.

1761, Apr. 25. Administration to eldest son Jonathan. Inventory, £156, 1*s.*, viz: pocket book and money £33, 2*s.*, pewter, a cow, heifer, calf, pair of oxen, 2 sheep, lamb, hog, riding beast, &c.

III. RICHARD, m. RACHEL,
b. d. 1755, Jul. 10. Providence, Smithfield, Scituate, R. I.
b. d. 1755, (—) of

1. Rachel
2. Mary,
3. Sarah,

1741, Apr. 18. Scituate. His wife and children having lately come from Smithfield, procured a certificate from latter town as desired by Scituate.

1755, Mar. 15. Will—proved 1755, Nov. 10. Ex. son-in-law Ezekiel Hopkins, Jr. To daughter Sarah Pray, all household goods and all movables. To daughter Rachel Hinds, 5*s.* After disposal of all lands the executor is ordered to make division as follows: To daughter Sarah Pray, half, to daughter Mary Hopkins, wife of Ezekiel, Jr., a quarter, and to daughter Rachel Hinds' children, a quarter. Inventory, £91, 9*s.* 11*d.*, viz: wearing apparel, bed, warming pan, looking glass, old table, &c.

IV. MARY, m. —— BROWN.
b. d. 1765 (—)
b. d. of Brown.

1691, Dec. 17. He deeded son John for affection, &c., "as also considering how his said son in care towards him from time to time hath still been manifesting of his duty unto him"—60 acres.

1692, May 7. He sold Nathaniel Mowry half a purchase right, the deed being confirmed by Elizabeth, wife of Richard Pray.

1693, Mar. 11. He deeded son Ephraim, for love, &c., a 25 acre right in town of Providence.

1693, Sep. 10. Testimony of John Whipple concerning an instrument made some years since by Richard Pray, wherein was made a disposition of his estate (witnessed by John Greene and Edmund Calverly), but sometime after Richard Pray and Mary his wife, considering the weakness of the instrument in itself—it being in itself annulled, &c., they declared it null and void, and declared it should be burned, and he did give further instruments for his sons to hold land by and made deeds to sons John and Ephraim, said deeds being written by John Whipple. The deposition further says that when Mary Pray lay on her death bed she did desire of her husband Richard Pray, that he would give unto their son William Pray the house and lot in town wherein and whereon they dwelt, and also the upland and meadow at a small brook.

1701, Dec. 13. His widow sold for £55, to Joseph Whipple, dwelling house and 10 acres, being part of it land that formerly belonged to my father, one William White (now deceased but formerly of Providence), and bought of him by Benjamin Hearnden, and given to her by last will of the latter for her life and then to son Isaac, and having been bought of Isaac Hearnden by his mother.

III. { WILLIAM, { b. / d. — Providence, R. I.

1686, Jan. 26. He received a deed from his father of house and lot in town, next Thomas Olney, with a piece of upland and meadow on a small brook.

1687, Sep. 1. Taxed 1*s*. 6*d*.

1687. Ratable estate, 1½ acres English pasture, 1½ acres meadow, 2 shares meadow, 2 acres wild pasture, a cow, a horse.

1692, Jul. 9. He sold Thomas Olney the house and lot given him by his father Richard Pray, six years before, concerning which the deposition was taken (already given).

IV. { MARY, { b. / d.
m. 1677, Jan. 15.
JOSEPH WOODWARD, { b. / d. 1726, Feb. 26. — of Woodward.

(2D WIFE, no issue.)

RALPH.

{ THOMAS, { b. / d. 1682. — Guilford, Ct., Warwick, R. I.
m. (1)
ELIZABETH DESBOROUGH, { b. / d.
of Desborough.
m. (2) 1656,
MARY COOK, (w. of [John. { b. / d. 1682 +

1651, Oct. 1. His first wife, from whom he had been divorced, married John Johnson.

1671, Sep. 25. Warwick. He and two others were appointed to make a rate and levy assessment upon the inhabitants of Mashantatack.

1682. Will—proved 1682, Jun. 15. Ex. son Thomas. Overseers, John Potter and cousin Samuel Stafford. He dated his will at Prudence Island but it was proved at Warwick. To son Samuel, 50 acres in Mashantack and two shares of meadow in Tuckaunk. To son Thomas, all the rest of lands and chattels in Mashantatack and elsewhere, except such cattle as are his mother's, and he to give her sufficient maintenance for life. To daughter Deliverance Ralph, £20, paid by her brother Thomas, of which £10, to be paid her at eighteen and £10. at twenty-one, with a feather bed. To daughter Sarah Benjamin, £7, paid her by Thomas in seven years. To grandchild William Fenner, £5, when of age, paid by testator's son Thomas

See: American Genealogist, v. 20, p. 228-229.

I. { SAMUEL, { b. / d. 1723, Oct. 8. — Providence, R. I.
m.
MARY, { b. / d. 1723 + — of

1687, Sep. 1. Taxed 1*s*.

1719, Apr. 4. He and wife Mary, deeded to son Thomas, 18 acres where son liveth.

1720, Jan. 16. He deeded to son Hugh, 12 acres adjoining my homestead in Mashantatack.

1719, Apr. 18. Will—proved 1723, Dec. 9. Exx. wife Mary. Overseers, Joseph Jenckes and James Brown. To eldest son Samuel, the homestead, house, land, orchard, &c. To son Thomas, confirmation of a deed already made him of a house and 18 acres. To youngest son Hugh, 18 acres. To wife, best feather bed, chest she puts her clothes in, use of best room while widow, half income of land I now improve, and son Samuel to improve said land to best advantage. To eldest daughter Mary Ralph, a good feather bed and £3. To daughter Deliverance Knight, £1. To wife, half the movable estate, she paying half the debts and half the daughters' portions. To son Samuel, half the movables, he paying half the debts and half of the legacies to daughters.

Inventory, £140, 5*s*., 4*d*., viz: money £2, 10*d*., pewter, glass, earthen ware, books, yarn, wool, tobacco, hay £7, 10*s*., corn and leather £7, 6*s*., horses £9, cattle £28, 15*s*., hogs and hens £5, 13*s*., &c.

RALPH. 2d column. I. Samuel m. Mary Stone (d. 1726+), of Hugh and Abigail (Busecot) Stone. 3d column. III. Samuel d. 1777±; m. (1) 1711, Mar. 15, Joan Spicer, m. (2) Elizabeth. Children, 1, Samuel. 2, Edward. 3, Silvanus. He was of Providence and Cranston, R. I. Give him all the text in place of Samuel[3], (Thomas,[2] Thomas[1]). I. Samuel. Erase everything concerning him, for it appears that his father left but two daughters; a son born after his father's death, having died young.

(2D WIFE)

II. { ALICE, { b. 1657, Jan. 13. / d. 1682 (—)
m.
THOMAS FENNER, { b. 1652, Sep. / d. 1718, Feb. 27. — of Arthur & Mehitable (Waterman) Fenner.

V. CATHARINE, b. d. 1728, Nov. 27.
m.
HAZADIAH COMSTOCK, b. 1682, Apr. 16. d. 1764, Feb. 21. of Samuel & Elizabeth (Arnold) — Comstock.

1. Susanna, 1707, Apr. 7.
2. William, 1708, May 3.
3. Gideon, 1709, Nov. 4.
4. Rachel, 1711, Sep. 9.
5. Catharine, 1713, Sep. 19.
6. Hazadiah, 1715, Jan. 9.
7. Penelope, 1717, Feb. 11.
8. Anthony, 1719, Nov. 7.
9. Andrew, 1721, Jan. 22.
10. John, 1724, Apr. 16.

VI. SARAH, b. d.
m.
JOSEPH BROWN, b. d. 1742, Jul. 20. of Henry & Waite (Waterman) — Brown.

1. Abigail, 1704, Oct. 14.
2. Deborah, 1706, Feb. 10.
3. Sarah, 1709, Mar. 19.
4. Anne, 1713, Jan.
5. Stephen, 1715, Mar. 3.
6. Benjamin, 1717, Jan. 28.
7. Mary, 1718, Feb. 12.
8. Martha, 1721, Oct. 23.
9. Amey, 1723, Aug. 21.
10. Joseph, 1727, Feb. 19.

VII. PENELOPE, b. d. 1752, Dec. 25.
m.
JOHN ALDRICH, b. 1688, Nov. 27. d. 1750, Mar. 25. of Jacob & Huldah (Thayer) — Aldrich.

1. Jeremiah, 1711, Oct. 26.
2. Rachel, 1713, Jun. 28.
3. Rachel, 1714, Aug. 12.
4. Ruth, 1716, Sep. 16.
5. Joseph, 1718, Sep. 29
6. John, 1720, Oct. 21.
7. Isaac, 1722, Nov. 20.
8. Stephen, 1726, Nov. 29.
9. Desire, 1729, Dec. 2.
10. Solomon, 1731, Mar. 28.

VIII. MARTHA, b. 1689. d. 1786.
m.
JOSEPH WILKINSON, b. 1683, Jan. 22. d. 1740, Apr. 24. of Samuel & Plain (Wickenden) — Wilkinson.

1. Mary,
2. Daughter.

1. Susannah, 1708, Jun. 10.
2. Prudence,
3. Ishmael, 1712, Nov. 13.
4. Benjamin, 1713, Oct. 9.
5. Christopher, 1715, Sep. 9.
6. Martha, 1718, Jan. 11.
7. Mary, 1720, Apr. 21.
8. Joseph, 1721.
9. John, 1723, Jul. 29.
10. William,
11. Samuel, 1726, Feb. 8.
12. Susannah,
13. Sarah,
14. Ruth,
15. William, 1734.

RALPH.

I. MARY, b. d.

II. DELIVERANCE, b. d. 1758, May 8.
m.
RICHARD KNIGHT, b. d. 1754, May 15. of John & Anne ( ) — Knight. Providence, R. I.

1. John,
2. Richard,
3. David,
4. Thomas,
5. Daughter,
6. Anne,
7. Daughter,
8. Deliverance,

III. SAMUEL, b. d.

1720. Freeman. — Providence, Scituate, R. I.

IV. THOMAS, b. d. 1780, May 8.
m.
PATIENCE, b. d. of

1. Thomas,
2. Christopher,
3. David,
4. Daughter,
5. Deliverance,
6. Mary,
7. Patience,
8. Sarah,

1719, Apr. 4. He and wife Patience sold John King, for £115, house and 18 acres at Mashantatack.
1720. Freeman.
1731, Feb. 15. He sold to Hugh Ralph, 150 acres in Westquadnaig, in Providence, for £225.
1737–42–49–53. Scituate. Deputy.
1741, Jun. 5. He deeded son Thomas for love, &c., 130 acres.
1743, Nov. 14. He deeded son-in-law Ebenezer King and daughter Deliverance, his wife, for love, &c., 50 acres.
1745, Apr. 17. He deeded son Christopher, for love, &c , 150 acres, and on same date deeded to daughter Patience Collins and her husband Eleazer, Jr., and daughter Mary Whitman and her husband George Whitman, Jr., of Warwick.
1753. Captain.
1777, Jul. 8. Will—proved 1780, Sep. 6. Ex. grandson Samuel Fenner. To daughter-in-law Freelove. Ralph, use of a third of homestead where I dwell, while widow. To grandsons Thomas and David Ralph, all homestead farm, equally, and six small lots in Cranston. To granddaughter Lydia Fenner, three lots in Cranston. To granddaughter Zilpha Ralph, a lot in Cranston. To son Christopher, a Spanish milled dollar. To granddaughter Patience Knight, a third of one half of movables. To three granddaughters Ruth Burlingame, Elizabeth Burlingame and Saintony Priest, a third of one-half of movables. To three granddaughters Patience and Mary Arnold and Robe Whitman, a third of one-half of movables. To four grandchildren Thomas and David Ralph, Lydia Fenner and Zilpha Ralph, all the rest of estate. (These four were David's children.)
Inventory, £1,136, 11*s.*, viz: Continental money £63, 15*s.*, notes, feather bed, &c.

Providence, Scituate, R. I.

V. HUGH, b. d. 1789, May 27.
m.
SARAH, b. d. 1755 + of

1. Alice,
2. Jabez,
3. Mary,
4. Sarah,

1720. Freeman.
1731, Feb. 3. He and wife Sarah sold Jonathan King, 22 acres for £330.
1748, Apr. 30. Scituate. He bought of Jeremiah Lippitt, of Warwick, 209 acres in Coventry at a place called Seven Men's land, for £567.
1761, Jan. 21. He and wife Sarah, for love, &c., deeded son Jabez, of Coventry, certain land there in part called Seven Men's land.
1755, Mar. 19. Will—proved 1789, Sep. 21. Ex. son Jabez. To wife Sarah, best bed, rent of half of homestead, west end of house, &c., for life. To wife and three daughters, viz: Else Ralph, Mary Utter and Sarah Potter, the indoor movables and outdoor movables, with some exceptions. To son Jabez, all real estate and the outdoor tackling, as plows, cooper's tools, &c., and gun, and wearing apparel. To wife and three daughters, money, bonds and notes.
Inventory, £19, 12*s.*, 4*d.*, viz: testament, spelling book, drinking glass, cheese tub, cooper's tools, 2 beds, warming pan, stillyards, &c.

1. William, 1677, Mar. 11.

III. { **Thomas**, m. **Eleanor**, } { b. 1658, Jul. 12. d. 1696 ± } { b. d. 1696 + } of — Providence, R. I.

1687, Sep. 1. Taxed 4*s*.

1696, Jun. 24. Eleanor Ralph, widow and administratrix of Thomas, sold Peter Stone, for £6, 10*s*., northerly half of a 50 acre lot laid out near dwelling house of Samuel Ralph, given me since decease of my husband Thomas Ralph.

1708, Jun. 4. The guardians (viz: Richard Searle and Roger Burlingame). of two daughters of deceased Thomas Ralph, proceeded to divide the real estate. To eldest daughter Alice Searle, wife of Richard Searle, 50 acres which Richard Searle's house stands on, and two shares of meadow adjoining on each side of Mashantatack Brook, and a piece of land lying by Samuel Ralph, son of deceased. To the other daughter, Eleanor Ralph, her father's home lot and other land.

IV. { **Sarah**, m. ——— **Benjamin**, } { b. 1661, Dec. 4. d. } { b. d. } of Benjamin.

V. { **Deliverance**, } { b. 1666, Aug. 20. d. }

REYNOLDS.

{ **William**, m. ——— } { b. d. } { b. d. } Providence, R. I.

1637. He and certain others were to pay in consideration of ground at present granted unto them, 2*s*., 6*d*., apiece.

1637, Aug. 20 (or a little later.) He and twelve others signed the following compact: "We whose names are hereunder, desirous to inhabit in the town of Providence, do promise to subject ourselves in active and passive obedience to all such orders or agreements as shall be made for public good of the body in an orderly way, by the major consent of the present inhabitants, masters of families, incorporated together in Town fellowship, and others whom they shall admit unto them only in civil things."

1640, Jul. 27. He and thirty-eight others signed an agreement for a form of government.

1641, Nov. 17. He and twelve others complained in a letter to Massachusetts of the "insolent and riotous carriage of Samuel Gorton and his company;" and therefore the petitioners desire Massachusetts to "lend us a neighbor-like helping hand," &c.

1644, Jan. 30. He and others of Providence, testified as to the outrage on Warwick settlers by Massachusetts.

1645, Jan. 27. He sold Robert Williams all his houses and home share and three small pieces of meadow. On the same date he sold to William Field a share of 6 acres on Fox's Hill.

1646, Apr. 27. He sold to Thomas Lawton his valley containing 80 acres, and 3 acres meadow, "provided that if in case hereafter the town shall be put to any charge about Indians, that he or they that doth possess the land shall pay their share."

I. { **James**, m. **Deborah**, } { b. d. 1700. } { b. d. } of — Kings Town, R. I.

1665, May 13 He and others petitioned the Assembly for accommodation of land in Kings Province.

1671, May 20. He took oath of allegiance.

1671. Constable.

1673, Dec. 26. He and wife Deborah, deeded to son John, 50 acres.

1677, May 2. He and others petitioned the Assembly for instruction, assistance and advice, as to the oppressions they suffer under from the colony of Connecticut.

1677, May 24. He and the others who had been carried away prisoners to Hartford, had a letter written to them by the Rhode Island authorities: "that you might receive all suitable encouragement that as you continue true to your engagement to this colony and upon that account are kept prisoners, we shall equally bear your charges of imprisonment, and with all expedition address ourselves to his Majesty for relief."

1679, Jul. 29. He and forty-one other inhabitants of Narragansett petitioned the King that he "would put an end to these differences about the government thereof, which hath been so fatal to the prosperity of the place; animosities still arising in peoples minds as they stand affected to this or that government."

1684, Apr. 29. He and wife Deborah deeded 100 acres in East Greenwich to son James.

1687. Overseer of the Poor.

1688. Grand Jury.

1690. Conservator of the Peace.

1692, Apr. 3. He deeded a slave named Elizabeth to son-in-law Thomas Nichols and Mercy his wife, if said slave be alive at decease of the grantor.

1699, Jan. 21. He deeded a negro boy named John to son Francis, to be his at death of grantor.

1699, Mar. 22. He deeded 50 acres to son Henry.

1699, Jun. 5. He ratified a deed to granddaughter Sarah Aires and her male heirs, having previously omitted to use the word heirs when deeding to son John.

1700, Sep. 21. A declaration was made by John Sweet, that James Reynolds, Sr., made a deed of gift to daughter Deborah and her husband John Sweet, of a negro girl Betty, but that afterwards he gave Betty freedom when she should arrive at thirty years of age, and to this John Sweet and his wife consented. Allusion was also made to the will of James Reynolds.

1703, Mar. 14. The executor of his will, viz: his son James, took a receipt from his brother Henry for £5, legacy, and receipts also from brothers Joseph and Francis.

Providence, Cranston, R. I.

I. SAMUEL, b. / d. 1777 ±
m.
ELIZABETH, b. / d.

Children: 1. Samuel, 2. Edward, 3. Silvanus,

He was a cooper.

1738, Jan. 16. He sold Benjamin Westcott (son of Benjamin), 24 rods at Mashantatack for 16*s*.

1744, Dec. 29. He and wife Elizabeth sold to Ezekiel Warner, for £750, homestead farm of 46 acres where I dwell in Mashantatack, reserving 4 rods square for a burying place where my honoured father and mother and some other of my friends and relations are already buried.

1770, Nov. 12. Cranston. He deeded son Samuel, for love, &c., 6 acres and dwelling house, and three years later had same deeded back.

1776, Apr. 23. He, being incapable of caring for his estate by reason of old age, Caleb Potter was appointed guardian, but in September following his rights were restored.

1777, Dec. 25. Mr. Knight was appointed to settle with Caleb Potter, concerning Samuel Ralph's estate.

1781, Nov. 24. Caleb Potter, former guardian unto Samuel Ralph, deceased, was called upon for an account.

II. ALICE, b. / d.
m.
RICARD SEARLE, b. / d. 1771, Dec. 22. of Edward & Ann (Grove) Searle.

Children: 1. Thomas, 2. Edward, 3. Richard, 4. Alice,

III. ELEANOR, b. / d. 1766 +
m.
THOMAS BURLINGAME, b. 1688, May 29. / d. 1770, Jan. 7. of Thomas & Martha (Lippitt) Burlingame.

Children: 1. Thomas, 2. Peter, 3. Barbara, 4. Esther, 5. Eleanor, 6. Susanna, 7. Ann, 8. Wait,

REYNOLDS.

Kings Town, R. I.

I. JOHN, b. 1648, Oct. 12. / d. 1675.
m.
——— b. / d. of

Children: 1. Sarah,

1675. He was killed by the Indians in this year.

Kings Town, R. I

II. JAMES, b. 1650, Oct. 28. / d.
m. (1) 1685, Feb. 19.
MARY GREENE, b. 1660, Sep. 8 / d. of James & Deliverance (Potter) Greene.
m. (2)
JOANNA, b. / d. of

Children: 1. James, 1686, Feb. 20

1679, Jul. 29. He signed the petition to the King.

1687, Sep. 6. Taxed 7*s*., 5½*d*.

1699, Mar. 2. He and Joanna, were witnesses to a deed from James Reynolds, Sr., to his son Henry.

1714, Sep. 23. He sold his brother Benjamin, half of a farm for £22.

North Kingstown, R. I.

III. JOSEPH, b. 1652, Nov. 27. / d. 1722.
m.
SUSANNA, b. / d. of

(She m. (2) 1723, Nov. 7, Robert Spencer.)

REYNOLDS. 3d column. III. Joseph d. 1739; m. (1) ——— ———; m. (2) Mercy. Children, 1, Joseph. 2, John. 3, Robert. 4, Benjamin. Erase previous record of Joseph who d. 1722 and had wife Sarah and 9 children. (This latter was Joseph Jr., son of Joseph above), 1713. He and wife Mary deeded land to son John, who gave bond to support father and mother-in-law (i. e. step-mother). 1739 will-proved. Exx. wife Mercy. He mentions sons John and Robert. Rest of will much burned.

Susanna
Mercy

Children: 1. Joseph, 2. Benjamin, 3. George, 4. Samuel, 5. Elizabeth, 6. John, 7. Susanna, 8. Deborah, 9. Mary,

1679, Jul. 29. Kings Town. He signed the petition to the King.

1687, Sep. 6. Taxed 5*s*., 10*d*.

1714, Sep. 14. He deeded son Benjamin, for love, &c., half of a tract of land in East Greenwich, bought of brother Henry.

1722, Apr. Will—proved. Exs. wife Susanna and brother Job Babcock. To eldest son Joseph, half of farm where he lives. To son John, the other half of said farm. To wife Susanna, homestead farm for life. To sons George and Samuel, certain land, equally. To son John, a yoke of oxen and two cows, at age. To daughter Elizabeth Rogers, £20. To daughters Susanna, Deborah and Mary, a feather bed each and sum of money at age.

Perhaps he had an earlier wife than Susanna.

Kings Town, East Greenwich, R. I.

IV. HENRY, b. 1656, Jan. 1. / d. 1716.
m.
SARAH GREENE, b. 1664, Mar. 27. / d. 1716 + of James & Deliverance (Potter) Greene.

Children: 1. Henry, 1686, Jul. 3; 2. John, 1688, Jun. 1[illegible]; 3. Sarah, 1690, Jan. 5; 4. Deliverance 1692, Dec. 2; 5. Mary, 6. James, 7. Thomas, 8. Deborah, 9. Elisha, 1706.

1679, Jul. 29. He signed the petition to the King.

1696, Jun. 15. He and wife Sarah sold John Knowlman, certain land at Coweset, for £10.

1699, Apr. 1. He sold Richard Mitchell, one-ninth of a 90 acre farm in East Greenwich, for £4.

1716, Apr. 28. Agreement between Sarah Reynolds, widow of Henry, lately deceased intestate, and her son Henry, &c. Henry to give brother John, £20, and deed of what land his father had in Westerly. To sister Sarah Briggs, £10. To sister Deliverance Reynolds, £12, 10*s*., within two years, and a feather bed. To sister Mary Reynolds, £12, 10*s*., and a feather bed. To brother James, £50, at age. To brother Thomas, £50, at age. To sister Deborah Reynolds, £15, at eighteen or marriage and a chest. To brother Elisha, £50, at age and a deed of certain land at Aquidneset. To widow Sarah, in lieu of dower, the new house that was her husband's to live in, half the cellar, half what is raised on the land, half the profits of stock and other movables, so long as either of sons James, Thomas or Elisha, dwell with her, &c., also six bushels of Indian corn, firewood, &c., while widow, the keep of two cows and of a beast to ride, &c.

Inventory, £126, 11*s*., 6*d*., viz: 2 oxen, 14 cows, 4 two years, 2 yearlings, 5 calves, mare, colt, 22 sheep, swine, gun, pewter (and £8, that is to be for the children, given them by their grandfather Greene not inventoried).

V. DEBORAH, b. 1658. / d. 1716 (—)
m.
JOHN SWEET, b. / d. 1716. of John & Elizabeth (   ) Sweet.

Children: 1. John, 2. Benjamin, 3. James, 4. Deborah, 5. Mary,

North Kingstown, R. I.

VI. FRANCIS, b. 1662, Oct. 12. / d. 1722.
m.
ELIZABETH GREENE, b. 1668, Oct. 17. / d. 1722 + of James & Elizabeth (Anthony) Greene.

Children: 1. Francis, 2. Peter, 3. James, 4. Jabez, 5. Elizabeth, 6. Deborah, 7. Mary, 8. Susanna,

1687, Sep. 6. Kings Town. Taxed 2*s*., 5*d*.

1707, Sep. 26. He bought of Sarah Barney, widow, of Newport, 37 acres in Kings Town, for £22.

1722, Apr. 14. Will—proved. Ex. son Jabez. To son Francis, half of farm where he dwells. To son Peter, the other half of farm where he dwells. To son James, two 50 acre lots. To son Jabez, land. To wife, a support by sons while she is a widow, corn being provided by James and meat and firewood by Jabez. To four daughters Elizabeth, Deborah, Mary and Susanna, £22, 10*s*., each. To son Jabez, rest of estate.

Inventory, £684, 7*s*., 3*d*., viz: pair of worsted combs, 2 spinning wheels, 2 linen wheels, &c.

RHODES.

{ ZACHARIAH, { b. 1603 ± Rehoboth, Mass., Providence, R. I.
{ m. 1646 ± { d. 1665.
{ JOANNA ARNOLD, { b. 1617, Feb. 27.
{ d. 1692+

of William & Christian (Peake) Arnold.

(She m. (2) 1667, Jan. 11, Samuel Reape.)

1643. His estate was given as £50, in a list of fifty-eight inhabitants of Rehoboth.

1644, Jun. 30. He drew a share of woodland in a division at this date.

1644, Jul. 3. He and twenty-nine others signed a compact: "We whose names are underwritten, being by the Providence of God inhabitants of Seacunk, intending there to settle, do covenant and bind ourselves one to another," &c. The government was to rest in nine persons chosen from the inhabitants, and it was agreed "to assist them according to our ability and estate, and to give timely notice unto them of any such thing as in our conscience may prove dangerous unto the plantation, and this combination to continue until we shall subject ourselves jointly to some other government."

1645, Jun. 4. He was propounded for a freeman.

1645, Jun. 9. He drew a lot on the great plain.

1647, Feb. 18. He drew a lot in the new meadow.

1648, Aug. 21. He was on a commission sent by Massachusetts to ascertain the damage done to Pomham, of Warwick, and to demand redress for him, &c.

1650, Sep. 2. Providence. Taxed £1.

1655, Nov. 15. He is mentioned by Roger Williams in a letter to General Court of Massachusetts. He, "being in the way of dipping, is (potentially) banished by you."

1657, Mar. 6. In a deposition of this date he is called aged about fifty-four.

1658, May 18. Freeman.

1658, Jun. 1. He and others of Pawtuxet desired to be dismissed from the government of Massachusetts (under whose rule Pawtuxet had been since 1642), and the petition was granted in the following October.

1659–61–62–63. Commissioner.

1660. Constable.

1661. He was on a committee concerning letter from Massachusetts authorities.

1661–63. Juryman.

1663. He was on a committee to agree with the Indians on amount to be paid for confirmation of lands previously purchased.

1664. He was on a commission to run the boundary between Rhode Island and Plymouth Colony.

1664–65. Deputy.

1665. Town Treasurer.

1665. Town Council.

1665, Oct. 11. He was committed in Charlestown or Boston by the General Court, for saying "the Court has not to do in matters of religion."

He was drowned "off Pawtuxet shoare," before April 10, 1666.

1662, Apr. 28. Will—recorded 1666, May 29. Exx. wife Joan. Overseers, William Carpenter, Sr. and John Brown. To wife for life, my dwelling house on north side Pawtuxet River, with meadow, uplands and commonage. To youngest son Peleg, said house and land at decease of his mother, but if it so fall out that my eldest son now living with his grandfather Arnold, be not comfortably provided for and settled upon his grandfather's land after the latter's decease, then my eldest son to have equal share with youngest in house and land, at decease of their mother. To eldest and youngest son, all lands within precincts of Providence, equally divided. To son Malachi, at twenty-one, privileges and rights of land in Rehoboth. To sons Zachariah, Malachi and John, the lands south of Pawtuxet River, at age of twenty-one respectively, and until then the land to be for their mother's use, and she to divide it. To eldest daughter Elizabeth, at twenty-one or marriage, £80. To daughters Mary and Rebecca each, £60 at twenty-one or marriage. If any daughter marry or match themselves with any contrary to the mind of their mother, or of my two friends the overseers, they shall have anything or not according as their mother says. To wife Joanna, for life and to dispose of to children as she chooses, all household goods, debts, and chattels. To each overseer, £5.

1666, Nov. 9. Will—enrolled 1668, Jan. 28. Joanna Reape. Exs. and overseers, William Carpenter, John Brown and Thomas Olney, Sr. To son Malachi, £20, at my death, or when he is twenty-one, which cometh first, and like legacies to sons Zachariah, John and Peleg at twenty-one, and to daughters Elizabeth, Mary and Rebecca, at twenty-one or marriage. If she

I. { JEREMIAH, { b. 1647, Jun. 24. Providence, R. I.
{ m. { d.
{ MADELINE HAWKINS, { b.
{ d. of William & Margaret ( ) Hawkins.

1672, May 1. Freeman.

1676. He was at Oyster Bay, N. Y., during King Philip's War, but soon returned to Providence.

1679, Jul. 1. Taxed 1*s*. 3*d*. (at Providence).

1680, Mar. 4. He deeded to brothers Malachi and John, half my right in certain land south of Pawtuxet River, for love, &c.

1681, Apr. 19. He, calling himself eldest son and heir of Zachariah Rhodes, deceased, sold Daniel Abbott a right of common disposed of to said Jeremiah by last will of his father.

1681, Apr. 27. He desired to change a piece of land that was laid out to his father Zachariah Rhodes, deceased, by Thomas Harris, Surveyor, in the year 1667, the which lieth on the right hand of the way going up to his father William Hawkins'. He and wife Maudlin signed a deed this month.

1687, Sep. 1. Taxed 9*d*.

1687. Ratable estate, 12 acres of English pasture.

II. { MALACHI, { b. Warwick, R. I.
{ m. 1675, May 27. { d. 1682.
{ MARY CARDER, { b.
{ d. 1693, Jan. 22. of Richard & Mary ( ) Carder.

1678. Freeman.

1682, Oct. 11. Will—proved 1682, Dec. 11. Exs. wife Mary and son Malachi. Overseers, brothers-in-law John Low and Daniel Williams, and brother John Rhodes. To eldest son Malachi, all housing and lands and half of movables and chattels. To daughters Mary and Sarah Rhodes, £10, each, in two years after son is of age. To wife Mary, all the rest of movables, and the land also till son is of age, and after that half the house and lands for life.

III. { ZACHARIAH, { b.
{ d.

IV. { ELIZABETH, { b.
{ d.

V. { MARY, { b.
{ m. 1675, Mar. 3. { d.
{ JOHN LOW, { b.
{ d. of Anthony & Frances ( ) Low.

VI. { REBECCA, { b.
{ m. (1) 1672, Feb. 3. { d. 1727.
{ NICHOLAS POWER, { b.
{ d. 1675, Dec. 19. of Nicholas & Jane ( ) Power.
{ m. (2) 1676, Dec. 2.
{ DANIEL WILLIAMS, { b. 1642, Feb.
{ d. 1712, May 14. of Roger & Mary ( ) Williams.

VII. { JOHN, { b. 1658. Warwick, R. I.
{ m. (1) 1685, Feb. 12. { d. 1716, Aug. 14.
{ WAITE WATERMAN, { b. 1668 ±
{ d. 1711 + of Resolved & Mercy (Williams) Waterman.
{ m. (2)
{ SARAH, { b. 1653.
{ d. 1730, Mar. 30. of

VII. MERCY, b. 1664. d.
m.
THOMAS NICHOLS, b. 1660, Aug. 6. d. 1745. of Thomas & Hannah ( ) Nichols.

1. Hannah, 1684, Mar. 9.
2. Mercy, 1686, Oct. 26.
3. Deborah, 1688, Feb. 17.
4. Susanna, 1690, May 9.
5. Mary, 1693, Mar. 19.
6. James, 1693, Mar. 19.
7. Elizabeth, 1695, Mar. 16.
8. Frances, 1697, Nov. 29.
9. Comfort, 1701, Mar. 7.
10. Thomas, 1702, Apr. 27.
11. Benjamin, 1703, Jun. 28.

VIII. ROBERT, b. d. 1715. Kings Town, R. I.
m.
DELIVERANCE SMITH, b. d. 1715 + of Jeremiah & Mary (Gereardy) Smith.

1. Robert,
2. Mary,
3. Deborah,
4. John,

1713, Aug. 22. Will—proved 1715, Dec. 14. Exx. wife Deliverance. To wife, all estate, real and personal, while widow, and at her decease the house and land where I dwell to go to son Robert, he paying £40, to my daughter Mary Reynolds and £10, to daughter Deborah Reynolds. To wife, authority was given to sell certain land and buy a farm for son John, which he was to have at her decease. To daughter Deborah, £30, to make her equal to her sister Mary.

Inventory, £290, viz: 2 hives of bees, horse, mare, shoemaker's tools, sword, loom, pewter, beds, 3 gold rings, silver, &c.

IX. BENJAMIN, b. d. Kings Town, R. I.

See: American Genealogist v.34, p.169-170 v.35, p.108.

RHODES.

I. ZACHARIAH, b. 1676. d. 1761, May 13. Warwick, Smithfield, R. I.
m.
———, b. d. of

1. Elizabeth,
2. Patience,
3. Daughter,

1698, May 9. He sold Stephen Arnold, Jr., all his right in lands at Ponagansett, in Pawtuxet, in any way belonging to him by virtue of his father Jeremiah Rhodes.

1707, Apr. 15. He deeded to brother-in-law Hope Corp, certain land north side of Pawtuxet River, given by my honoured grandfather William Arnold to my honoured father Jeremiah Rhodes (in deed bearing date 1658, Aug. 31).

1708. Freeman.

1712, Aug. 21. In a deposition at this date he calls himself aged thirty-six years.

1751, Mar. 15. Smithfield. He deeded son-in-law John Carpenter of Providence, and wife Elizabeth, 97 acres in Smithfield.

1755, Jul. 5. Will—proved 1762, Aug. 17. Exs. friend Resolved Waterman and Captain Enoch Barnes. To daughter Patience Knapp, £750. To grandson Zachariah Tucker, £400. To grandson Rhodes Tucker, £400. To granddaughter Tryphenia Aldrich, £?00. To granddaughter Penelope Tucker, £200, and a cow. To grandson John Carpenter, £100. To three granddaughters, Tryphenia Aldrich, Penelope Tucker and Lydia Carpenter, bed, pewter, &c. To daughter-in-law Rachel Carpenter, £10, and a cow.

II. JOHN, b. d. 1744, Jun. 19. Providence, Scituate, R. I.
m. (1)
ELIZABETH DAILEY, b. d. of John Dailey.
m. (2)
MARTHA, b. d. 1744 + of

1718, Jan. 30. He was to have 12*s.* 6*d.*, paid him by Joseph Dailey, and 11*s.* 6*d.*, by Morris Brook, for keeping their father John Dailey the last six months.

1719, Oct. 5. He engaged with the Town Council to keep his father-in-law John Dailey till the twenty-seventh of the month for £3, 12*s.*, with term already since June 10.

1728, Apr. 15. His wife Elizabeth took Deborah Moss's child to nurse for three months, at 7*s.* per week.

1744. Administration to widow Martha.

III. ———, b. d. 1762 (—)
m.
HOPE CORP, b. 1681, Nov. 8. d. 1765. of John & Deliverance ( ) Corp.

1. John,
2. Jeremiah,
3. William,
4. Joseph,
5. Daughter,
6. Phebe,

I. MALACHI, b. d. 1714, Aug. 17. Warwick, R. I.
m. 1700, Mar. 8.
DOROTHY WHIPPLE, b. d. 1728, Sep. 10. of John & Rebecca ( ) Whipple.

1. Malachi, 1701, Apr. 15.
2. Mary, 1703, Sep. 15.
3. Dorothy, 1705, Nov. 15.
4. Malachi, 1707, Apr. 15.
5. Dorothy, 1709, Aug. 16.
6. James, 1711, Dec. 15.
7. Rebecca, 1714, Apr. 5.

(She m. (2) 1719, Dec. 24, Israel Arnold.)

1704. Freeman.

1707-8-9. Deputy.

1713, May 6. He was appointed by Assembly on committee for making the public road from Pawtucket River to Pawcatuck River, more straight and passable.

1714, Jul. 22. Will—proved 1714, Sep. 20. Exx. wife Dorothy. To eldest son Malachi, my mansion house, homestead and all lands south of Pawtuxet, except 2 acres adjoining on river against the Falls, and a reservation of 50 acres at Boggy meadow. To son James, all that right bought of my uncle Peleg, west of Pauchasset River, and the 2 acres and 50 acres already mentioned. To son Malachi, and three daughters Mary, Dorothy and Rebecca, all rights of land in jurisdiction of Providence called Westquidnet. To sons and daughters, £10, each, at age or marriage. To wife Dorothy, the income of all lands and house till children are of age and then the income of half the homestead while widow, and she to bring up the children and give them suitable learning. If she marry to have a third of income. To her, the rest of estate real and personal.

Inventory, £317, 10*s.* 6*d.*, viz: bonds £37, 2*s.* 6*d.*, plate £4, 16*s.*, 2 tables, 18 chairs, 4 beds, linen wheel, books 15*s.*, warming pan, 2 guns, rum, molasses, sugar, 8 cows, pair of oxen, 3 two year, 5 swine, 2 mares, colt, 28 sheep, ½ saw mill, &c.

II. MARY, b. d. 1765 (—)
m.
RICHARD BROWN, b. 1676. d. 1774, Feb. 20. of Henry & Waite (Waterman) Brown.

1. Malachi, 1698, Feb. 1.
2. Mercy, 1703, Dec. 12.
3. William, 1705, Jun. 3.
4. Richard, 1712, Feb. 28

III. SARAH, b. d. 1743, Jan. 5. **RHODES. 3d column. III. Sarah, b. 1677.**
m.
BENJAMIN TILLINGHAST, b. 1672, Feb. 3. d. 1726, Sep. 14. of Pardon & Lydia (Taber) Tillinghast.

1. Benjamin,
2. James,
3. Sarah, 1702, May 20.
4. Mary,
5. Abigail,
6. Mercy,
7. Lydia,
8. Elisha,

1. Anthony,
2. John,
3. Rebecca,

1. Hope,
2. Nicholas, 1673.
(By 2d husband.)
3. Mary,
4. Peleg,
5. Roger, 1680, May.
6. Daniel,
7. Patience,
8. Providence, 1690.
9. Joseph,

I. ZACHARIAH, b. 1687, Nov. 5. d. 1740, Jan. 10. Warwick, Scituate, R. I.
m. (1) 1712, Jan. 24.
MARY RANDALL, b. d. of William & Rebecca (Fowler) Randall.
m. (2) 1735, Jan. 5.
MARY SHELDON, b. d. 1740 + of Sheldon.

1. William, 1712, Nov. 18.
2. Mercy, 1714, Apr. 11.
3. Rebecca, 1716, Jun. 29.
4. Mary, 1720.
(2d wife, no issue.)

die before children are twenty-one, the amounts are to go into the hands of the overseers. As husband Zachariah Rhodes did not dispose clearly to daughters, she provides that any daughter dying, the others shall possess their sisters' part of her or her husband's legacies, and if any son die the others shall have his portion.

1681, Oct. 26. On petition of Joanna Reape, wife of Samuel Reape, of Pawtuxet, the Assembly considering "the deplorable estate of said Joanna, being left destitute by her said husband Samuel Reape," &c., order that all estate of Samuel Reape be sequestered for use of Joanna for her life, and appointed her son-in-law Daniel Williams, and son John Rhodes, feofees in trust to take possession in her behalf and receive rents for her use.

1687, Sep. 1. Joanna Reape taxed 7*s*.

1687. Her ratable estate: 2 acres orchard, 6 acres planting land, 20 acres pasture, 13 acres meadow.

1693, Feb. 11. Joanna Reape and her son Peleg Rhodes sold John Fowler, of Providence, an eighth of a thirteenth right in land west side of Pauchasset River, for a valuable sum.

No relationship is known to exist between Zachariah Rhodes and Walter Rhodes who was early of Providence for a period.

1676, Aug. 14. He was one of those "who staid and went not away" in King Philip's War, and so had a share in the disposition of the Indian captives whose services were sold for a term of years.

1688. Constable.

1700–1. Attorney General.

1702–3–4–7. Deputy.

1707. Clerk of Assembly.

1712, Feb. 21. Will—proved 1716, Aug. 23. Exx. wife Waite. To eldest son Zachariah, all my meadows, land and rights on north side Pawtuxet River, and half a right at Westquadnaick. To son John, a right of land at Westquadnaick. To son Joseph, a right of land at Westquadniack. To son William, two lots south side of Pawtuxet and privilege to make use of boggy meadow at the Pond, for twenty-five years after he is of age, and then to revert to my son Resolved, also privilege to cut five loads of hay, half swamp and half upland, for fifteen years after he is of age off this farm where I now dwell, and a quarter right at Westquadnaick. To son Resolved, at age, all my homestead where I now dwell, &c. To daughter Phebe Rhodes, £30, at eighteen or marriage, and like legacy to daughter, Wait Rhodes. To five sons, Zachariah, John, Joseph, William and Resolved, all right in lands of Quiniphoge. To wife Wait, all movable estate to bring up children, and all income of farm till son Resolved is of age, and then a third income and privilege of half the house at her choice for life.

Inventory, £532, 10*s*. 8*d*., viz: brass, iron, pewter, rum, cider, furs, ¼ saw mill, shop goods £139, 17*s*. 15*d*., yoke of oxen, 9 cows, 2 horses, 3 guns, book debts £113, 10*s*. 5*d*., beds, wearing apparel, &c.

VIII. PELEG, b. d. 1724, Oct. 6. Providence, R. I.
m.
SARAH, b. d. 1731, Jan. 29. of

1710, May 2. He was appointed to build the bridge at Pawtuxet Falls, and in regard to that one and also the one at Weybossett, and at Pawtucket Falls, he was to "appoint the bridges in the most convenient places."

1710–11. Deputy.

1718, May 2. He petitioned the Assembly on behalf of Providence, to consider the great damage that hath by them been sustained in having Weybossett bridge destroyed by an unusual and violent flood. The Assembly allowed £30, to enable them to repair same.

1724. Town Council.

1720, Jun. 15. Will—proved 1724, Dec. 7. Exx. daughter Mary. To wife Sarah, best room, a third of household goods, and income of £500, for life, all in lieu of dower. To daughter Elizabeth Arnold, wife of James, rights in land west side of Pauchasset River, two lots in Pawtuxet Neck, and £200, at death of wife. To daughter Lydia, all homestead lands eastward of road leading to Providence on north side of the Pawtuxet River near the Falls (with some exception), and £300. To daughter Mary, my mansion house, a third of household goods, all my mills adjoining on said Pawtuxet River, all lands on west side of road leading to Providence, and all other lands, goods and chattels.

Inventory, £938, 3*d*., viz: silver money £9, 14*s*. 4*d*., plate £11, 16*s*., pewter, tin, 2 cases bottles, cider, 2 cows, horse, heifer calf, his part of saw mill, 3 old guns, wool cards, worsted combs, 13 fowls, 4 feather beds, books, bonds £551, 18*s*. 4*d*., &c.

1731, Feb. 9. Administration on estate of widow Sarah to son-in-law James Arnold. Inventory, £193, 3*s*. 6*d*.

(BY 2D HUSBAND, no issue.)

1712. Freeman.
1713, Jul. 3. His son William died at Providence.
1731. Scituate. Town Council.
1738, Apr. 4. He deeded daughter Rebecca and her husband William Sheldon, for love, &c., northerly part of homestead in Westquanaid.
1740, Mar. 5. Administration to eldest daughter Mercy Sheldon, his widow Mary refusing. Inventory, £887, 19*s.* 8*d.*, viz: books £2, wearing apparel £60, 10*s.* 6*d.*, money £7, 8*s.* 6*d.*, 3 feather beds, flock bed, churn, woolen wheel, 2 Irish wheels, 2 tables, pewter, carpenter's tools, worsted combs, beer 30*s.*, cider £8, 5*s.*, mare, horse, yoke of oxen, pair of steers, 7 cows, 3 yearlings, 2 calves, 26 sheep, 4 swine, &c.

II. MERCY, b. 1689, Nov. 20. d. young.

III. JOHN, b. 1691, Nov. 20. d. 1776. — Warwick, R. I.
m. (1) 1714, Apr. 29.
CATHARINE HOLDEN, b. d. 1731, Jul. 25. of Charles & Catharine (Greene) Holden.
m. (2)
MARY WHIPPLE (w. of James. b. d. of

1. Wait, 1714, Dec. 29
2. John, 1716, May 5.
3. Catherine, 1717, Aug. 1.
4. Charles, 1719, Sep. 29.
5. Mercy, 1721, Mar. 29.
6. Anthony, 1722, May 29.
7. Joseph, 1723, Aug. 22.
8. Zachariah, 1727, Sep. 8.
9. Holden, 1731, May 20.
(2d wife)
10. James, 1734, Mar. 31.

17.6. Freeman.
1731-35-42-43-44-51-53-54. Deputy.
He held the office of Major for many years.
1774, Jul. 16. Will—proved 1776, Jun. 21. Ex. son Charles. To daughter Wait Lippitt's children, two Spanish milled dollars. To son John Rhodes' children, two dollars. To daughter Catherine Barton, house where she dwells and 2 acres, and a third of household goods. To son Joseph, a third of household goods and half of stock and tackling. To grandson Holden Rhodes, £18. To children and grandchildren of son Anthony Rhodes, £18, that is to Mary Billings, £6, and to my grandson William Rhodes' children, £12. To son Charles, rest of estate.
Inventory, £94, 18*s.* 3½*d.*, viz: 6 silver spoons £3, 15*s.*, 6 best silver spoons £5, 8*s.*, old coat and jacket buttons, 7½ oz. £20, 8*s.* 4*d.*, silver porringer and 2 spoons £3, 8*s.* 4*d.*, silver tankard £9, 6 tea spoons 18*s.*, pair of gold buttons £1, 4*s.*, 4 wine glasses, warming pan, staff, scales, 5 old chairs, 3 books, 2 shoats, 2 heifers, 2 cows, 15 sheep, linen wheel, woolen wheel, &c.

IV. JOSEPH, b. 1693, Sep. 25. d. 1738, Sep. 17. — Providence, R. I.
m. 1723, Sep. 10.
MARY ARNOLD, b. 1696, Dec. 12. d. 1745, May 22. of Stephen & Mary (Sheldon) Arnold.

1. Joseph,
2. Penelope,
3. Phebe,

1738. Aug. 15. Will—proved 1738, Sep. 27. Exx. wife Mary. To son Joseph, dwelling house, slaughter house, my half part of wharf and warehouse, 700 acres lately bought of brother Resolved, deceased, and other land. To daughter Penelope, 300 acres and £220, at eighteen. To daughter Phebe, 280 acres and £200, at eighteen. To three children Joseph, Penelope and Phebe, my third part of still and still house, and rest of personal. To brother Resolved's three youngest children, viz: Resolved, Deliverance and Mary, £690, to be divided equally. To wife Mary, a third of income of house and lands for life and a third of movables.
Inventory, £3,488, 13*s.* 8*d.*, viz: pair of oxen, 3 cows, 2 heifers, horse, negro man £100, store goods, cider mill, silver tankard £46, books £4, 12*s.*, 21 oz. plate £27, 6*s.*, bonds £1,388, 2*s.* 6*d.*, 13 barrels cider, 4 barrels beer, spinning wheel, scale, dividers, ink horn, &c.
1745, May 15. Will—proved 1745, Jun. 10. Widow Mary. Exs. daughter Penelope and brother John Potter. To son Joseph, bed, mare, silver tankard, &c. To daughters Penelope and Phebe Rhodes, all household goods. To Phebe, £100. To three children, rest of estate.
Inventory, £3,636, 9*s.* 11*d.*

V. WILLIAM, b. 1695, Jul. 14. d. 1772, Nov. 11. — Providence, Cranston, R. I.
m. 1721, Dec. 18.
MARY SHELDON, b. 1705. d. 1767, Nov. 24. of Nehemiah & Rachel (Mann) Sheldon.

1. Waitstill, 1722, Feb. 18.
2. William, 1725, Aug. 26.
3. Joseph, 1728, Mar. 15.
4. Nehemiah, 1731, Aug. 9.
5. Eunice. 1741, Dec. 13.

1724, Dec. 29. The sum of £20, was allowed by Assembly for repairing Pawtuxet bridge, on the prayer of James Arnold and William Rhodes.
1731-35-37. Deputy.
1745-46-47. Assistant.
He held the title of Captain at his death.
1772, Jul. 13. Will—proved 1772, Nov. 25. Exs. sons William, Joseph and Nehemiah. To son William, half my farm in Scituate, where Thomas Hazard dwells, 7 acres with buildings. To son Joseph, 60 acres in Scituate. To son Nehemiah, farm and buildings east of highway, and 140 acres, &c. To grandson William, son of Nehemiah, land at twenty-one. To daughter Waitstill Corliss, certain land. To son Joseph, a farm, dwelling house, &c., bounding south on Pawtuxet River, two dwelling houses, cooper's shop, still house, &c., but privilege reserved for Nehemiah of use of old wharf. To daughter Waitstill, four hundred Spanish milled dollars. To daughter Eunice Hazard, half of a farm in Scituate, and two hundred dollars, and another farm till her son Thomas Hazard is of age. To daughter Waitstill Corliss, half of a farm in Scituate. To grandson Joseph Rhodes, half the house my son William dwells in. To granddaughter Mary Howell, £10. To sons William and Nehemiah, 200 acres in Cumberland County, New York. To three sons and my daughter, rest of estate.

VI. PHEBE, b. 1698, Nov. 30. d. 1761 +
m. (1)
ANTHONY HOLDEN, b. d. 1720, May 13. of Charles & Catharine (Greene) Holden.
m. (2)
SAMUEL ABORN, b. 1697. d. 1761, Mar. 16. of Aborn.

1. Catherine, 1717, Oct. 13.
(By 2d husband.)
2. Mary, 1724, Feb. 26.
3. Samuel, 1726, Mar. 3.
4. John, 1728, Apr. 9.
5. Phebe, 1730, Jul. 11.
6. Wait, 1732, Sep. 23.
7. James, 1734, Sep. 28.
8. Anthony, 1736, Aug. 20.
9. Mercy, 1739, Feb. 17.

VII. RESOLVED, b. 1702, May 22. d. 1738, Aug. 8. — Providence, R. I.
m. 1724, Jan. 23.
MARY GREENE, b. 1703, Sep. 25. d. of James & Mary (Fones) Greene.

1. Resolved,
2. Deliverance,
3. Mary,

The recorded marriage is to Phebe Greene upon town book, but the clerk seems to have made an error in the name, and the family account is sustained by the fact that Resolved and wife Mary signed receipt for legacy from her great aunt Isabel Burton's will.
1738, Sep. 5. Inventory, spinning wheel, apples on trees £2, 1*s.*, case of bottles, cane, 2 silver cups, 4 silver spoons, 2 books, warming pan, pewter, table, settle, chairs, punch bowl and glasses, bond £38, &c.

VIII. WAITE, b. 1703, Dec. 16. d.
m. 1730, Jul. 13.
ABRAHAM SHELDON, b. d. of Nehemiah & Rachel (Mann) Sheldon.

VIII. Waite. Her husband d. 1783, +, at Killingly, Ct. Children, 1. Abraham, 1731, Oct. 25. 2. Wait, 1736, Dec. 29. 3. Caleb, 1741, May 14.

(2d WIFE, no issue.)

I. ELIZABETH, b. d. 1767, Jul. 30.
m. 1711, Oct. 25.
JAMES ARNOLD, b. 1689. d. 1777, Feb. 1. of Israel & Mary (Barker) Arnold.

1. Sarah, 1713, Aug. 31.
2. Barbara, 1715, Dec. 31.
3. Anna, 1718, Mar. 2.
4. Elizabeth, 1721, Jun. 9.
5. James, 1724, Jul. 11.
6. Sion, 1726, Jun. 19.
7. Rhodes, 1733, Mar. 19.

II. LYDIA, b. d.

III. MARY, b. d.
m. 1725, Jan. 14.
ISRAEL ARNOLD, b. 1701, Jul. 19. d. of Israel & Elizabeth (Smith) Arnold.

1. Israel, 1727, Jan. 13.
2. Peleg, 1728, Oct. 18.
3. Mary, 1730, Dec. 27.
4. Rosanna, 1737, Dec. 27.

{ JAMES, { b. Newport, R. I.
{ m. { d. 1676.
{ MARY, { b.
{ d. 1678 +

(She m. (2) 1677 ± John Peabody.)

He was a miller.

He may have been son of Thomas Rogers, who came in the May Flower in 1620, with son Joseph, and died next year. Bradford says: "the rest of his children came over, are married, and have (1650) many children." John Rogers of Duxbury was probably a son of Thomas, and perhaps James should be added.

1638, May 20. His name was in the list of inhabitants admitted since this date.

1640, Sep. 14. Freeman.

1643-59-60-61-62-63-64-65-66-67-68-69-70-71-72-73-74-75-76. General Sergeant.

1648, Jan. 16. He deeded Richard Knight for a valuable consideration 40 acres in one parcel and a 2 acre lot. (The next month Richard Knight deeded this and other land to wife Sarah and her heirs forever, especially to eldest son at twenty-one, and in failure of such issue to eldest daughter at sixteen. Should he decease, wife Sarah to have a third for life.)

1655. Freeman.

1657-58-59. General Solicitor.

1659, Aug. 23. He complained that being both General Sergeant and Town Sergeant and also being infirm in body, &c., therefore desireth the court to allow him to constitute a deputy upon occasion for executing some writs belonging to his office of General Sergeant, he being responsible for the deputy. The application was granted by Assembly.

1669, May 13. His bill for paying Grand Jurymen's dinners four times, which comes to £2, 7s., was approved and ordered paid, as also another bill for £8, 18s.

1669, Jul. 20. He was ordered to apprehend the Indian sachem Ninecraft and bring him before the Governor and Council on Thursday next at eight o'clock in the morning, to answer the charge of a plot among the Indians to cut off the English. He was empowered to take assistance of a boat and two men for transportation, and also two men and three horses in the King's Province.

1671, Jan. 30. He was allowed £1, 10s., for disbursements about Thomas Flounders (who had been executed for the murder of Walter House).

1673, Oct. 29. It was voted that "forasmuch as the debts of the colony are very much by reason of the Sergeant's great wages, and thereby the inhabitants greatly oppressed and grieved, and his the said Sergeant's sums amount very high," &c., he having great fees at the Court of Trials, and 4s., a day also, &c.; therefore it was enacted by the Assembly that said Sergeant for attending the Assembly shall have 3s., per day, and for Court of Trials no day wages but only such fees as set by law.

1676, May 3. It was voted for the future that "the General Sergeant's fee for the attending the jury is doubled."

1676, Aug. 24. He attended at the trial of certain Indians before a court martial held at Newport. The Indians were charged with being engaged in King Philip's designs and several were executed.

1676, Sep. 1. An Indian servant of his was examined before a court martial, and it was voted that Sergeant Rogers shall have his Indian home with him provided that said Indian shall be brought forth if required, which Rogers engages to do.

1676. He bought the terms of service of two Indian captives for twenty-two bushels of Indian corn, said Indians having been taken by Providence men.

1676, Oct. 25. A petition having been made by Mary Rogers, executrix of late deceased James Rogers, General Sergeant, for moneys due said sergeant in his lifetime; a committee was appointed by Assembly to audit the petitioner's account.

1678, Jun. 12. A petition having been presented to Assembly by John Peabody, and Mary Peabody, late wife to the deceased James Rogers, General Sergeant, concerning accounts between the colony and deceased, and said accounts having been diligently examined by the late General Audit, they were found so imperfect that they could neither allow or disallow same. By agreement it was settled there is a clear balance of all accounts between James Rogers and the colony and to be a final issue of all differences, &c.

I. { SARAH, { b.
{ m. 1648 ± { d. 1685 +
{ RICHARD KNIGHT, { b.
{ d. 1680. of Knight.

II. { THOMAS, { b. 1639. Newport, R. I.
{ m. { d. 1719, Nov. 23.
{ SARAH, { b.
{ d. 1716 + of

1668. Freeman.

1680. Taxed 19s., 4d

1696, Sep. 8. He bought of Thomas Earle, for £110, land in Dartmouth. He is called of Portsmouth at this date, but he was not there long probably, his residence being chiefly at Newport.

1702, Feb. 4. He was a proprietor in common lands at Newport.

1716, Nov. 28. Will—proved 1719, Dec. 17. Ex. son Samuel. He calls himself aged seventy seven years. To wife Sarah, half of dwelling house and land. To son Samuel, half of dwelling house and land. To son James, 5s. To son Thomas, £7. To daughter Sarah, wife of Thomas Wells, £5. To son John Rogers, 5s. To daughter Elizabeth, wife of Samuel Bailey, £5. To son Jeremiah, £3. To son Joseph, £6. To son Daniel, £6. To daughter Abigail Rogers, unmarried, £12. To grandson Edward Rogers, 10s.

III. { JOHN, { b. 1641, Oct. 5. Newport, R. I.
{ m. { d. 1716, Mar. 27
{ ELIZABETH, { b.
{ d. 1676, Oct. 24. of

1668. Freeman.

1678-1701-3-4-5. Deputy

1680. Taxed £1, 5s., 4d.

1701. Captain.

1701-2-3-4. Justice of the Peace

1702, Mar. 4. He was a proprietor in the common lands.

1703, Jun. 22. He was on a committee to audit the debt of the colony.

1. John,
2. Jonathan,
3. David,

I. James, b. d. m. Elizabeth, b. d. — Newport, R. I.

1704, Mar. 10. He and wife Elizabeth, sold for £100, to Joseph Weatherhead, of Newport, 20 acres given me out of his farm at Newport by father Thomas Rogers.

He may have gone to Westerly (like his brother Thomas) and have been identical with that James Rogers who died intestate at Providence, 1719, Apr. 4, being then called late of Westerly. (This latter James left a widow Elizabeth, and a son James of Westerly, who took administration on his father's estate with consent of his mother.)

II. Thomas, b. d. 1736, Aug. 22. m. Ann Tripp, b. d. 1736. of Peleg & Anne (Sisson) Tripp. — Newport, Westerly, R. I.

1. Peleg,
2. Job,
3. Anna,
4. Mary,
5. Elizabeth,
6. Sarah,
7. Ruth,
8. Leah,
9. Priscilla,
10. Rebecca,
11. Penelope,

1706, Dec. 30. He bought of Peleg Tripp, 12 acres in Portsmouth. (He was of Dartmouth at this date, but was at Newport in 1709.)

1709, Jan. 29. He bought of Samuel Bailey, of Newport, 16 acres for £80. (He was called Thomas Rogers, Jr.)

1713, Jan. 1. He sold Job Sherman, for £140, the 12 acres, "which I purchased of my father-in-law Peleg Tripp, of Portsmouth." His wife Anne, released her dower.

1716, Feb. 16. He, still calling himself Thomas Rogers, Jr., sold Captain James Clarke, of Portsmouth, 30 acres in Newport, bounded northerly on land of Thomas Rogers, for £394.

1725, Feb. 1. Westerly. He and wife Anne, for love to son Peleg of Newport, cordwainer, deeded him all their right of lands in Portsmouth.

1736, Feb. 20. Will—codicil—1736, Aug. 3, proved 1736, Aug. 30. Exx. daughter Leah. Overseer, friend John Hoxie. To wife Anna, all estate, real and personal, while widow. To son Peleg, 5s., he having had. To son Job, 5s. To daughters Anna George and Mary Richmond, £5, each. To daughter Elizabeth Wheeler, 30 acres. To grandson John Mason, son to daughter Sarah Mason, deceased, 10 acres, he paying 20s., each to brothers and sisters, viz: Robert, Simeon, Margaret, Elizabeth and Sarah. To grandchildren, children of daughter Ruth Wilcox, viz: Thomas, Stephen, John and Anne, 5s., each. To daughter Leah Rogers, 30 acres. To daughters Priscilla Hill, Rebecca Rogers and Penelope Macknear, rest of land equally. The codicil gives daughter Elizabeth Wheeler, £20, daughter Ann George, £15, granddaughter Mary George, £5, and to daughter Leah, rest of movables. Leah was now made sole executrix, her mother who had been named with her as executrix at first having evidently died.

Inventory, £254, 9s., 9d., viz: wearing apparel £10, bible and other books 10s., cash and a bond £43, 10s., gun £3, 10s., 2 spinning wheels, , warming pan, silver spoon, 4 young oxen, 3 cows, 2 yearlings, 8 hogs, mare, &c.

III. Jonathan, b. d. 1716 (—) m. 1701, Jun. 18. Mary Sawdey, b. d. of Sawdey. — Newport, R. I.

At the time of his marriage he was called son of Thomas.

IV. Sarah, b. d. m. Thomas Wells, b. 1669, Sep. d. 1727, Oct. 16. of Peter Wells.

1. Peter,

V. John, b. 1677. d. 1761, Apr. 28. m. Jane Brown, b. 1677. d. 1769, Sep. 2[illegible]. of William Brown. — Newport, R. I.

ROGERS. 3d column. V. John. He had also a son William, who d. 1747, and devised estate to his father.

1. Sarah,
2. Martha, 1703.
3. Elizabeth,
4. John,
5. Thomas,
6. James,
7. Jonathan,

1701, Oct. 29. He and his wife gave receipt for legacy to her of £10, from will of her grandfather Nicholas Brown.

He held the title of Major at the time of his death.

1747, Jun. 25. Will—proved 1761. Ex. son Jonathan. He orders a highway fifteen feet wide to be laid through land where he lives. To son James Rogers, part of the home lot. To son Thomas, part of the home lot. The rest of home lot which lies west of aforesaid highway with three dwelling houses thereon, &c. (excepting two lower rooms in westward of house I now dwell in) to be let out, and profits arising therefrom to be for wife Jane, for her life, as also two rooms aforesaid and use of all household goods. To grandson John Rogers, son of John, deceased, part of home lot with two dwelling houses thereon, at decease of wife Jane, he paying his brother Thomas, £100. To son Jonathan, part of home lot with the dwelling house thereon, at decease of wife Jane, he paying his brother Thomas and three sisters each £100. To daughters Sarah Gardiner, wife of Benoni, Martha Reynolds, widow, and Elizabeth Pike, each £100, as above. To grandson Thomas, £100, paid as above. To daughters Sarah Gardiner, Martha Reynolds, and Elizabeth Pike, all household goods, equally, at her mother's decease. To sons Thomas and James, all my working tools, equally. To sons Thomas, James and Jonathan, all wearing apparel, equally. To granddaughter Mary Russell, my maple desk. To three sons, two-thirds of rest of estate, and to three daughters, the other third.

He and his wife were buried in the Newport Cemetery.

VI. Elizabeth, b. d. m. Samuel Bailey, b. d. of William & Grace (Parsons) Bailey.

VII. Jeremiah, b. d. — Newport, R. I.

VIII. Joseph, b. d. — Newport, R. I.

IX. Daniel, b. d. — Newport, R. I.

X. Samuel, b. d. — Newport, R. I.

ROGERS (James). 3d column. X. Samuel. His wife was Alice.

1713. Freeman. He was called "Samuel Rogers, Jr.", to distinguish him from his cousin of same name.

XI. Abigail, b d.

I. John, b. 1668, Aug. 26. d. 1727, Aug. 11. m. 1698, Nov. 4. Sarah Lawton, b. 1676, Oct. 25. d. 1731, Feb. 20. of Isaac & Elizabeth (Tallman) Lawton. — Newport, R. I.

1. William, 1709, Jul. 14.
2. James, 1714.
3. Isaac, 1716, Apr. 4.

1702, Mar. 4. He was a proprietor in common lands.

1709–14. Deputy.

1714. Ensign.

1727, Jan. 20. His wife had a legacy of 5s., from will of her father.

He was a Deacon in the First Baptist Church, under Rev. William Peckham's pastorate.

He and his wife were buried in Newport Cemetery.

1705. Speaker of the House of Deputies.

1705-7-8-9-10-11-12. Assistant.

1708, Apr. He and three others were chosen and empowered to proportion and affix rates of grain and other specie for a tax. They appointed Indian corn to be accepted at 2*s.*, per bushel, barley 1*s.*, 8*d.*, rye 2*s.*, 6*d.*, oats 14*d.*, wool 9*d.*, per pound and wheat 3*d.*, per bushel.

He was buried on the homestead farm. The Holy Cross Chapel in Middletown, R. I., occupies part of this homestead, and his gravestone may still be seen in the churchyard, to which place this and several other stones were moved a few years since from another part of the farm not far distant.

SAYLES. See: American Genealogist, v. 20, p. 229.

JOHN, b. 1633. d. 1681. Providence, R. I.
m. 1650 ±
MARY WILLIAMS, b. 1638, Aug. d. 1681.
of Roger & Mary ( ) Williams.

1651, Jan. 27. He bought a house and lot of John Throckmorton.

1652, May 12. He bought land of Ralph Earle, near West River.

1653-55-57-58-59. Assistant.

1655. Freeman.

1655-59. Commissioner.

1655-57. Town Clerk.

1656, May 10. He entered an anker of liquor.

1657, Mar. 4. He wrote a letter on behalf of Providence to town of Warwick, in regard to the illegal arrest of Richard Chasmore, by Massachusetts authorities.

1658. Warden.

1659-60. Town Treasurer.

1660, May 26. He sold William Hawkins, for a valuable sum of money, all rights in land lying between Pawtucket and Pawtuxet Rivers, "beginning at the end of seven miles upon a west line from the hill called Foxe's Hill (the Town of Providence having the same for a boundary), and so to go up the streams of those rivers unto the end of twenty miles from the said Foxes' Hill."

1665, Feb. 19. He had lot 24 in a division of lands.

1666, May 31. He took oath of allegiance.

1669-71. Grand Jury.

1669-70-71-74-76-77-78. Deputy.

1670, May 4. He and three others were appointed to audit the colony's accounts.

1670, Jun 24. He sold to Stephen Arnold, a thirteenth of the island called the vineyard, at Pawtuxet "which my father-in-law Mr. Roger Williams gave me."

1670-71. Town Council.

1671, Aug. 21. He and Thomas Roberts were appointed to prize and transport the horse belonging to the town to Rhode Island, and deliver to Joseph Torrey for payment of debt due from this town.

1675, May 24. He drew lot 18 in division of lands.

1677, May 7. He (called John Sayles, Sr.), was fined 20*s.*, for not attending Grand Jury.

1679, Jul. 1. Taxed 1*s.*, 3*d.* (his "right").

He may have had a daughter Deborah, identical with that Deborah ——, who married Caleb Carr[2] (Caleb[1]), and who had a son named Sayles Carr. Perhaps one or two of the children accredited to his daughter Mary by her second husband, were born by said husband's earlier wife (Frances Holden).

He and his wife, and their son-in-law William Greene, are buried in the Easton Burial Ground, Middletown, R. I., near Sachuest Beach.

SAYLES. 1st column. I. John. His wife's birth was 1633, not 1638.

I. MARY, b. 1652, Jul. 11. d. 1717.
m. (1) 1674, Dec. 17.
WILLIAM GREENE, b. 1652, Dec. 6. d. 1679. of John & Ann (Almy) Greene.
m. (2) 1680, Oct. 12.
JOHN HOLMES, b. 1649. d. 1712, Oct. 2. of Obadiah & Catharine ( ) Holmes.

II. JOHN, b. 1654, Aug. 17. d. 1727, Aug. 2. Providence, R. I.
m.
ELIZABETH, b. d. 1699, Nov. 2. of

1681, May 3. Freeman.

1687, Sep. 1. Taxed 8*s.*, 7*d.*

1688. Ratable estate, 4 oxen, 7 cows, 7 steers, 6 heifers, 3 yearlings, a horse, mare, 2 swine, 4 acres of planting, 16 acres pasture, share of meadow.

1688. Grand Jury.

1694, Jan. 23. He had laid out to him 35 acres, "which said land he had of his grandfather Mr. Roger Williams."

1694-1706. Deputy.

1703, Jan. 23. He sold to Richard Phillip, dwelling house, barn, and all lands and meadows at Mashapauge in Providence, for £100, reserving forever two poles square where several graves are contained about thirty rods west of house, &c.

1710, Aug. 14. Licensed to keep a publick house and sell liquor.

1713, Jun. 16. Taxed 16*s.*, 8*d.*

1722, Jan. 29. He deeded to his daughter Mary Smith and son-in-law William Smith, for love and goodwill, a 40 foot lot on west side of Town street extending to the channel, and also another small lot.

1726, Sep. 14. Will—proved 1727, Aug. 21. Ex. son John. To son Thomas, 10 acres and £10. To son Richard, £10. To daughter Mary Smith, 40*s.* To son John, my homestead farm bought of Richard Phillips, with dwelling house, &c., 250 acres in all, and also to John, all movable goods. The other lands, equally to three sons and to them money and bills of credit. Inventory, £114 ±, viz: a horse, 2 cows, carpenter's tools, wearing apparel, books, money, warming pan, pewter, &c.

The gravestones to the memory of John Sayles' wife Elizabeth and son Daniel, are still to be seen, being located west of railroad track, nearly opposite foot of Earl St.

SAYLES. 2d column. II. John. His wife was Elizabeth Olney, b. 1666, Jan. 31, of Thomas and Elizabeth (Marsh) Olney.

II. JOSEPH, m. (1) ELIZABETH SMITH, m. (2) MARY JENKINS, (w. of [Rich'd.
b. 1670. d. 1710, Oct. 2. — Newport, R. I.
b. d. 1704, May 24. of Philip & Mary ( ) Smith.
b. d. of John & Anstis (Gold) Wilkins.

1. Mary, 1699, Aug. 24.
2. Elizabeth, 1701, Jan. 23.
3. Smith, 1702, Dec. 13.
4. Joseph, 1704, May 14.
(2d wife.)
5. John, 1708, Jul.
6. Child, 1710 ±

(She m. (4) 1716, Jul. 26, Stephen Mumford.)

1710, Sep. 10. Will—proved 1710, Nov. 6. Exs. brother John Rogers, brother-in-law Edward Smith, and wife Mary Rogers. To wife £300. To son Joseph, £700, provided child wife now goes with be a daughter, but if a son then £500, to said Joseph. If child wife is with be a son, such son to have £500. To daughter Mary, £300. To daughter Elizabeth, £300. If child wife is with be a daughter, £300. To wife, all estate while widow, till children are of age. To daughter-in-law (*i. e.* stepdaugther), Anstis Jenkins, £10.

He was buried in Newport Cemetery. His first wife was buried at Tiverton, where the births of his first four children were recorded.

III. SAMUEL, m. 1706, Jan. 31. LYDIA HOLMES,
b. 1673, Apr. 25. d. 1752, Nov. 14. — Newport, Middletown, R. I.
b. 1683, Jan. 4. d. 1750, May 19. of Jonathan & Sarah (Borden) Holmes.

1. Elizabeth,
2. John, 1708.
3. Joseph,
4. Jonathan,
5. Samuel,

1704. Freeman.

At the time of his marriage he was called "son of John Rogers."

1706, Aug. 28. He bought 15½ acres of Peleg Smith, for £91.

1750, Jun. 2. Will—codicil 1751, Oct. 8—proved 1752, Nov. 20. Ex. son John. To daughter Elizabeth Smith, use of lower great room, bedroom and closet while widow, and her two sons Elisha and Edward, my grandsons, to live there till fourteen. To said Elizabeth also a cow, all household stuff and a support from estate. To son John, land. To sons Joseph and Jonathan, certain land, but if Joseph do not live to return home again, then his son Samuel to have, and if he die then the latter's brother Peleg. If son Joseph should come home and wish to sell land, I recommend him to his father Brown, for his advice. To son Samuel, rest of land and buildings, he giving his sister Elizabeth, firewood, &c., while she is a widow. To sons John and Samuel, husbandry tools. To son John, rest of personal estate.

Inventory, £1,925, 12*s.*, 1*d.*, viz: wearing apparel £200, 4 silver spoons, books £1, 2 guns, horse, 2 cows, hog, 20 geese, &c.

He and his wife are buried in the Holy Cross Chapel.

SAYLES.

1. Mary, 1677, Jan. 8.
(By 2d husband.)
2. William,
3. Frances,
4. Ann,
5. Susanna,
6. Deborah,
7. Phebe,

I. MARY, m. WILLIAM SMITH,
b. 1689, May 30. d. 1754 +
b. 1682. d. 1753, Dec. 11. of John & Sarah (Whipple) Smith.

1. Daniel,
2. Richard,
3. Elizabeth,
4. Sarah,
5. Abigail,

II. JOHN, m. (1) 1717, Dec. 1. ELIZABETH COMSTOCK, m. (2) SARAH,
b. 1692, Jan. 13. d. 1777, Sep. 16. — Smithfield, R. I.
b. 1690, Dec. 18. d. of Samuel & Elizabeth (Arnold) Comstock.
b. d. 1777 + of

1. Mercy, 1718, Jul. 19.
2. Elizabeth, 1720, Apr. 14.
3. Mary, 1721, Apr. 22.
4. Phebe, 1723, Feb. 26.
5 Anne, 1724, Dec. 9.
6. Ezekiel, 1726, Jul. 11.
7. John, 1728, Jun. 24
8. Caleb, 1730, May 4
9. David, 1731, Jul. 24.
10. Lydia, 1735, Oct. 26.
(2d wife, no issue.)

1731 to 1751. Town Treasurer.

1741–42–45. Deputy.

1756–57–58–59. Town Clerk.

1768. Town Council.

1774, May 10. Will—proved 1777, Nov. 19. Exx. wife Sarah. To her a lot of land and dwelling house in Providence, a cow, a riding horse, great bible and all personal estate which she brought when she came to live with him (except moneys), and half profits of my homestead whereon I dwell, with best room and kitchen for life. To grandson Stukeley Sayles and his heirs, all my homestead farm. To granddaughter Leah Sayles, 50 Spanish milled dollars. To son Ezekiel, 6*s.* To daughter Mercy Ballard, 7*s.* To daughters Mary Ballou, Anne Sayles and Lydia Wheelock, a fifth each of rest of personal, and a fifth to children of daughter Elizabeth Mowry, and a fifth to children of daughter Phebe Sayles. The executrix by reason of her age asked that Silvanus Sayles might assist her in administration and he was appointed with her.

Ezekiel Sayles was granted an appeal from the probate of will by Town Council, provided he filed bond, his claim being that the will was made by unlawful solicitation.

Inventory, a horse, 8 cows, a pair of young oxen, a yearling bull, 2 yearling heifers, calf, colt, 3 hogs, 2 shoats, 9 geese, pewter, china, bible, testament, spelling book, spinning wheel, linen wheel, weaver's loom, quilting wheel, hetchel, cheese tub, churn, 1 small silver grater, 6 silver spoons, 3 large silver spoons, warming pan, &c.

III. RICHARD, m. (1) 1720, Nov. 24. MERCY PHILLIPS, m. (2) 1738, May 14. ALICE ARNOLD (w. of Da- [vid m. (3) 1742, Jan. 10. SUSANNAH INMAN (w. of [John
b. 1695, Oct. 24. d. 1775 ± — Smithfield, R. I.
b. d. of Richard & Sarah (Mowry) Phillips.
b. d. 1741 ± of Maturin & Sarah ( ) Ballou.
b. 1695, Jan. 3. d. of James & Susannah (Whitman) Ballou.

1. Daniel, 1722, Feb. 7.
2. Richard, 1723, Aug. 5.
3. Israel, 1726, Mar. 17.
4. Elisha, 1728, Apr. 15.
5. Jonathan, 1730, May 12.
6. Gideon, 1732, May 30.
(2d & 3d wives no issue.)

1731. Town Clerk.

1741, Sep. 25. He delivered up the two children of his wife Elce, by her former husband David Arnold (viz: William and Lydia Arnold), to their grandfather Maturin Ballou, their mother being deceased and their grandfather having been appointed guardian.

1750, Feb. 21. He deeded son Richard, for love, &c., and £3, a lot of 2¾ acres.

1757, Jul 5. He deeded to sons Jonathan and Gideon, all of homestead farm not disposed of.

1772, May 27. He sold Caleb Aldrich, 3 acres for one dollar and one pistareen.

1775, May 24. He was alive at this date, as his son Richard calls himself "Jr.," in a deed to his son John.

IV. DANIEL,
b. 1697, Dec. 13. d. 1698, Feb. 3.

V. THOMAS, m. 1721, Dec. 14. ESTHER SCOTT,
b. 1699, Feb. 9. d. 1754, Nov. 9. — Smithfield, R. I.
b. 1700, Dec. 5. d. 1788. of Silvanus & Joanna (Jenckes) Scott.

1. John, 1723, Jan. 6.
2. Silvanus, 1724, Mar. 29.
3. Stephen, 1727, Jul. 16.
4. Joseph, 1730, Sep. 9.
5. Thomas, 1733, Jun. 21.
6. Martha, 1735, Aug. 5.
7. Esther, 1738, Jan. 7.
8. Elizabeth, 1740, Oct. 15.
9. Jeremiah, 1743, Dec. 17.

1732–37. Town Council.

1736–37–38. Deputy.

1736–38–42–43–44–45. Moderator of Town meeting.

1739, Feb. He and William Arnold having petitioned the Assembly that £53, yet due and unpaid toward bridge at Wansokit Falls, might be paid, it was so voted.

1744, Jul. 6. He deeded son John, for love, &c., 100 acres where John dwelleth.

1745–46–47–48–49–50–51–52–53. Town Clerk.

1754, Dec. 2. Administration to Captain John Sayles.

III. { ISABEL, { b.
m. (1) d. 1716 +
JOHN TILLINGHAST, { b. 1657, Sep.
m. (2) d. 1690, Dec. of Pardon & —— (Butterworth) Tillinghast.
ROBERT HICKS, { b.
d. of Hicks.

IV. { PHEBE, { b
m. 1685, Jan. 22. d. 1744 (—)
JOB GREENE, { b. 1656, Aug. 27.
d. 1745, Jul. 6. of John & Ann (Almy) Greene

V. { ELEANOR, { b. 1671.
m. 1693, Feb. 16. d. 1714, Mar. 11.
RICHARD GREENE, { b. 1660, Feb. 8.
d. 1711, May 24. of John & Ann (Almy) Greene.

VI. { CATHARINE, { b. 1671.
m. 1692, Dec. 28. d. 1751, Feb. 21.
WILLIAM OLNEY, { b. 1663, Jun. 25.
d. of Thomas & Elizabeth (Marsh) Olney.

SAYLES. 2d column. ~~[illegible]~~. He probably had also VII. Deborah who m. Caleb Carr,[2] (Caleb[1]). See Carr. 3d column. I. Mary. See Smith Ad. and Cor.—Concluded.

SCOTT. 1st column. He drew bills on his brother Joseph Scott, in London, upholsterer.

SCOTT. *See: American Genealogist, v. 20, p. 229-231.*

{ RICHARD, { b. 1607. Ipswich, Mass., Providence, R. I.
m. d. 1680 ±
{ CATHARINE MARBURY, { b. 1617.
d. 1687, May 2.

of Francis & Bridget (Dryden) Marbury.

He was a shoemaker.

His wife's mother, Bridget Dryden, was sister of Sir Erasmus Dryden, Bart. (grandfather to the poet Dryden). Bridget Dryden's husband was Rev. Francis Marbury, of London.

1634. He came in ship Griffin this year.

1634, Aug. 28. He joined the church at Boston.

1634, Nov. 24. Gov. Winthrop, notes that "one Scott and Eliot, of Ipswich were lost in their way homewards and wandered up and down six days and eat nothing. At length they were found by an Indian, being almost senseless for want of rest."

1637, Aug. 20 (or a little later). Providence. He with twelve others signed the following compact: "We whose names are hereunder, desirous to inhabit in the town of Providence, do promise to subject ourselves in active and passive obedience to all such orders or agreements as shall be made for the public good of the body in an orderly way, by the major consent of the present inhabitants, masters of families incorporated together in a Town fellowship and others whom they shall admit unto them, only in civil things."

He was one of the fifty-four persons who had home lots assigned them.

1639, Jan. 16. Gov. Winthrop says, "At Providence things grew still worse, for a sister of Mrs. Hutchinson, the wife of one Scott, being affected with Anabaptistry and going to live at Providence, Mr. Williams was taken (or rather emboldened) by her to make open profession thereof and accordingly was re-baptized by one Holyman, a poor man late of Salem. Then Mr. Williams re-baptized him and some ten more. They also denied the baptising of infants and would have no Magistrates."

1640, Jul. 27. He and thirty-eight others signed compact providing for arbitration, &c.

1650, Sep. 2. Taxed £3, 6s., 8d. (The heaviest tax was £5, paid by Benedict Arnold.)

1655. Freeman.

1658, Sep. 16. At this date his future son-in-law, Christopher Holder, had his right ear cut off at Boston, for the crime of being a Quaker (he having come from England two years before bringing the obnoxious views of that sect along with him). Richard Scott's wife was present. "A mother of many children, one that had lived with her husband, of an unblameable conversation, and a grave, sober, ancient woman, and of good breeding as to the outward, as men account." She protested in these words: "That it was evident they were going to act the works of darkness, or else they would have brought them forth publicly and have declared their offences that all may hear and fear." For this utterance she was committed to prison and they gave her "ten cruel stripes with a three fold corded knotted whip," shortly after—"though ye confessed when ye had her before you, that for ought ye knew, she had been of an unblameable character; and though some of you knew her father and called him Mr. Marbery and that she had been well bred (as among men, and had so lived), and that she was the mother of many children; yet ye whipped her for all that, and moreover told her; that ye were likely to have a law to hang her if she came thither again." To which she answered: "If God calls us woe be to us if we come not, and I question not but he whom we love, will make us not to count our lives dear unto ourselves for the sake of his name. To which your Governor John Endicott replied: And we shall be as ready to take away your lives as ye shall be to lay them down."

1659, Jun. His daughter Patience "a girl of about eleven years old," having gone to Boston as a witness against persecutions of Quakers, was sent to prison, others older being banished, "and some of ye confest that ye had many children, and that they had been well educated, and that it were well if they could say half so much for God as she could for the Devil."

SCOTT. 1st column. Richard,[2] (Edward[1]), 1640, Sep. 9. Will-proved 1642, Apr. 22, of George Scott, merchant, London. He mentions loving father Edward Scott, the elder, of Glemsford, County Suffolk, clothier; also brothers Frederick, Matthew, Edward; and Richard, "now resident in New England." He also mentions Richard Scott, deceased, brother of said Edward, etc.

I. { JOHN, { b. Providence, R. I.
m. d. 1677.
REBECCA, { b.
d. 1701 + of

(She m. (2) 1678, Apr. 15, John Whipple.)

1662, Sep. 30. He bought a house and 4 acres of George Palmer.

1665, Feb. 8. He bought of Robert Williams, of Newport, schoolmaster, a dwelling house in Providence, and a home share, orchard and other land.

1668, Oct. 27. He complained of Thomas Clemence entering upon 20 acres which he had bought of Clemence and Robert Williams.

1668, Nov. 23. He bought 20 acres of Thomas Clemence.

He took oath of allegiance this year.

1671, Jan. 1. He bought of Thomas Wilmot of Rehoboth, and Elizabeth, his wife, 41½ acres in Providence, being half of tract called Reynold's valley.

1671, Jul. 27. He petitioned the Town; "that they would lay out a highway to Mr. Blackstone's river, where it may be most convenient." It was so ordered.

1671, Oct. 13. He and wife Rebecca, sold Leonard Smith, a house and 4 acres.

1675, Jun. 27. He is referred to in a letter from Roger Williams to John Winthrop, Jr., "Some say John Scot at Pawtucket Ferry is slain." (By the Indians.)

1676, Aug. 25. Testimony was given at a Court Martial held at Newport, on certain Indians, by Wenanquabin of Pawtuxet, that he was not at the wounding of John Scott, but was at that time living with Abiah Carpenter.

1677, Feb. 2. He had lands laid out (confirmation of grant of 1668, now bounded).

1677, Nov. 8. Rebecca Scott, widow, bought by John Fitch, of Rehoboth, 41½ acres in Providence, for £10.

1678, Jan. 7. The heirs of John Scott had 60 acres laid out to them, bounded partly by 83 acres in possession of executrix of John Scott. (The above land had been laid out in 1668, to John Scott, but not bounded.)

1678, Feb. 19. The heirs of John Scott received a confirmatory deed from Walter Clarke, of Newport, who calls himself brother-in-law of John Scott, to whom he had formerly sold 60 acres of land with former dwelling house of said Scott. Consideration £20. The confirmation to executrix and heirs was in accordance with the will of John Scott.

1680. "The Orphans of John Scott," were taxed 4s., 1d.

The tradition is well established that John Scott met his death by being shot by an Indian in the door way of his own house. He made a will, however, as is seen by references made to it in deeds, though a copy of it has not been found. Perhaps therefore the effect of the shooting was not instantaneous death.

II. { SON, { b.
d.

Inventory, £3,654, 3s., 8d., viz: bonds, books £23, 16s., 4 feather beds, 2 flock beds, desk, 4 tables, 18 chairs, 3 wheels, clock £25, silver watch £70, 2 looking glasses, 7 silver spoons, pewter, linen yarn, carpenter's and cooper's tools, gun, pair of cards, hetchell, cider press, mare and colt, 4 oxen, 6 cows, 4 yearlings, 3 calves, heifer, 10 fowls, 2 shoats, 7 sheep, flax, rye, hay, blacksmith tools, &c.

1788, Jan. 7. Inventory of widow Esther Sayles' estate £37, 16s., 9d. Administration being refused by sons, it was taken by James Appleby.

1. Pardon,
2. Charles,
3. Hannah,
4. Mary, 1689.

1. Anne, 1686, Feb. 23.
2. Mary, 1687, Dec. 3.
3. Deborah, 1690, Feb. 28.
4. Job, 1692, Jul 5.
5. Phebe, 1694, Oct. 12.
6. Christopher 1697, Mar. 9.
7. Daniel, 1699, Feb. 20.
8. Richard, 1701, Feb. 12.
9. Catharine, 1702, Mar. 19.
10. Philip, 1705, Mar. 15.

1. Audry, 1694, Jan. 8.
2. John, 1695 Nov. 7.
3. Amey, 1696, Oct. 4.
4. Isabel, 1698, Sep. 3.
5. Eleanor, 1702, Feb. 19.
6. Mercy, 1704, Apr. 9.
7. Mary, 1707, Feb. 16.
8. John, 1709, Dec. 23.

1. William, 1694, Oct. 6.
2. John, 1699, May 9.
3. Catharine, 1701, Aug. 11.
4. Thomas, 1706, Apr. 26.
5. Deborah, 1708, Jul. 30.
6. Richard, 1711, Nov. 4.

SCOTT.

I. SARAH, b. 1662, Sep. 29. d.

II. JOHN, b. 1664, Mar. 14. d. 1725 +
m.
ELIZABETH WANTON, b. 1668, Sep. 16. d. of Edward & Elizabeth ( ) Wanton.

Newport, R. I.

1. Mary,
2. Elizabeth,
3. Catharine,
4. Edward, 1703, Jun. 13.
5. George, 1706, May 25.
6. Joseph, 1709, Mar. 14.

He was a merchant and house carpenter.

1696, Jun. 1. He bought land at Newport, of Nathaniel Coddington.

1701. Freeman.

1702, Mar. 4. He was a proprietor in common lands.

1704–5. Deputy.

1705, Feb. 14. He and Joseph Latham stood bound to build a jail in the town of Providence, in as good manner as that which was burnt. It was agreed that if Assembly did not allow they should build the jail, then Latham and Scott were to pay £33. The Assembly enacted now that they should not build the jail but should pay the £33, into the General Treasury.

1712, Jul. 25. He and wife Elizabeth sold Charles Dyer, of Dartmouth, for £600, mansion house in Providence and 113 acres, three miles west of salt water, and several other parcels. (These latter parcels were deeded by Dyer the next year, and described as formerly belonging to Richard Scott, deceased).

1715, Oct. 20. He appealed to the Assembly from a judgment of the General Court of Trials in the suit against him brought by Thomas Peckham, wherein damage was £27. The Assembly ordered Peckham's account chancerized down from £13, 19s., 6d., to £11, 8s., 6d., by reason of sundry errors.

1725, Aug. 31. He took a mortgage on the homestead of Joshua Davis, of East Greenwich, for £480, 11s.

1734, Jan. 14. He is spoken of as lately deceased in a deed of this date from Edward Scott, schoolmaster of Newport, to Joshua Davis, of East Greenwich.

III. MARY, b. 1666, Feb. 1. d. 1734 +
m.
JOSHUA DAVIS, b. d. 1736, Jan. 8. of Aaron & Mary ( ) Davis.

1. William,
2. Aaron,
3. John,
4. Rebecca,
5. Katharine,
6. Samuel, 1706.
7. Jeffrey, 1708.

IV. CATHARINE, b. 1668, May 20. d.

V. DEBORAH, b. 1669, Dec. 20. d.

VI. SILVANUS, b. 1672, Nov. 10. d. 1742, Jan. 13.
m. 1692 ±
JOANNA JENCKES, b. 1672. d. 1756, Mar. 12. of Joseph & Esther (Ballard) Jenckes.

Providence, Smithfield, R. I.

1. John, 1694, Sep. 30.
2. Catharine, 1696, Mar. 31.
3. Joseph, 1697, Aug. 15.
4. Rebecca, 1699, Feb. 11.
5. Esther, 1700, Dec. 5.
6. Silvanus, 1702, Jun. 20.
7. Joanna, 1703, Dec. 11.
8. Charles, 1705, Aug. 23.
9. Sarah, 1707, Jun. 15.
10. Jeremiah, 1709, Mar. 11.
11. Nathaniel, 1711, Apr 19

1695, Nov. 25. He bought land in Rehoboth, of John Whipple, of Providence.

1697, Jul. 1. He took a mortgage for £32, 5s., on 50 acres in Attleboro, owned by Henry Stacey, to be repaid before the 27th of next June.

1709–17. Deputy.

1710, Jun. 8. He had an allowance of land for a highway.

1713, Jun. 16. Taxed £1, 4s.

1713-14-15-16-17-18. Town Council

1716, Jun. 1. He and two others were granted liberty by the Assembly to use and improve so much of Starve Goat Island as shall be needful for their making, drying and securing of fish on said island during their following the trade of fishing.

1721, Dec. 9. He bought of John Wilkinson, for £160, all the farm and homestead of 80 acres which John's father John Wilkinson had bought of John Blackstone, &c.

1742, Mar. 1. Administration on his estate to widow Joanna.

Inventory, £3,664, 10s., 6d., viz: apparel £34, warming pan, bible and other small books £2, 5s., pewter, 6 silver spoons £11, 10s., clock £6, 10s., 4 cows, yearling, 1 mare, negro man £60, money £122, bonds £523, &c.

1744, Mar. 15. Will—proved 1756, Apr. 21. Widow Joanna. Ex. son John. To grandson Jeremiah, £5. To children of deceased son Joseph, a ninth of estate. To grandson Sylvanus, son of deceased son Nathaniel, a ninth. To daughters Catharine Jenckes, Rebecca Wilkinson, Esther Sayles, Joanna Jenckes and Sarah Hopkins, all apparel, equally. To all of children, rest equally.

Inventory, £2,214, 5s., viz: bonds, notes, &c. £1,700 ±, 6 silver spoons, 3 pewter platters, 5 porringers, negro man worth nothing, feather bed, warming pan, &c.

A short time after, his daughter Mary went to visit Christopher Holder in prison, and was herself, apprehended and put in prison and kept there a month.

Richard Scott it is claimed was the first Quaker resident at Providence.

1660, Sep. 8. His wife is alluded to in a letter from Roger Williams to Governor John Winthrop, of Connecticut, "Sir, my neighbor Mrs. Scott is come from England, and what the whip at Boston could not do, converse with friends in England, and their arguments, have in a great measure drawn her from the Quakers, and wholly from their meetings."

1665, Feb. 19. He had lot 88, in a division of lands.

1666. Deputy.

1668, Nov. 23. He had 20 acres laid out to him by Arthur Fenner, surveyor.

1671, Dec. 25. He sold Leonard Smith, a parcel of meadow, "being part of my meadow which lieth upon Moshoosick River."

1676, Feb. 26. He confirmed a deed made many years before, of Patience Island to Christopher Holder and wife Mary.

1678. A letter from him was published this year in the book "A New England Fire Brand Quenched," &c. (being the answer of George Fox to Roger Williams's book, "George Fox digged out of his Burrow," &c.): "Friends, concerning the conversation and carriage of this man Roger Williams, I have been his neighbor these 38 years: I have only been absent in the time of the wars with the Indians, till this present I walked with him in the Baptists' way about 3 or 4 months, but in that short time of his standing I discovered he must have the ordering of all their affairs or else there would be no quiet agreement amongst them." * * *. "That which took most with him and was his life was to get honor amongst men especially amongst the great ones." His letter alludes to Roger Williams being met by his neighbors (when he returned with the Charter), at Seaconck, they coming in fourteen canoes; "And the man being hemmed in in the middle of the canoes, was so elevated and transported out of himself that I was condemned in myself that amongst the rest I had been an instrument to set him up in his pride and folly. And he that before could reprove my wife for asking her two sons why they did not pull off their hats to him, and told her she might as well bid them pull off their shoes as their hats. (Though afterward she took him in the same act, and turned his reproof upon his own head.) And he that could not put off his cap at prayer in his worship, can now put it off to every man or boy that pulls off his hat to him." He further charges Roger Williams with inconsistency in professing liberty of conscience, and yet persecuting those who did not join in his views. The book alluded to, as also Bishop's "New England Judged," also quoted from, contain a good deal of interest about Richard Scott and his family.

1679, Jul. 1. "Richard Scott's land" was taxed 6*s*, 3*d*. (He died this year or next.)

1680, Jul. 16. "Richard Scott's estate," was taxed 2*s*., 6*d*.

1681, Mar. There was laid out and bounded some 70 acres of land to Sarah, Catharine and Mary Scott, granddaughters to Richard Scott, of Providence, deceased.

1682, Aug. 1. His heirs had confirmatory deed from Roger Williams, of Patience Island (which he had deeded to Richard Scott about the year 1651).

1686, Apr. 27. Deposition of Epenetus Olney and John Whipple, of Providence. "That nine years since or thereabout, being on board of the vessel that then Henry Beere was master of, there being also aboard Richard Scott," &c., he desired deponents to come to him into the cabin, and declared that he "by the great desire of his wife, had freely given and granted unto his three grandchildren, Sarah Scott, Mary Scott, and Catharine Scott, his 50 acre division of upland," &c.

1705, May 28. Testimony was given by Samuel Whipple that he had once asked Richard Scott as to his purchase of land from Joshua Verin: "the said Scott said that he thought he had bought all said Verin's right in Providence, but upon search of his deed he found he had bought no more than his house lot and his meadow, and claimed no more than his deed mentioned."

III. { MARY, m. 1660, Aug. 12. CHRISTOPHER HOLDER, } { b. d. 1665, Oct. 17. } { b. 1631. d. 1688, Jun. 13. } of Holder.

IV. { HANNAH, m. 1667, Feb. WALTER CLARKE, } { b. 1642. d. 1681, Jul. 24. } { b. 1640. d. 1714, May 23. } of Jeremiah & Frances (Latham) Clarke.

V. { PATIENCE, m. 1668, Sep. 28. HENRY BEERE, } { b. 1648. d. } { b. d. 1691, Jun. 11. } of Edward Beere.

VI. { DELIVERANCE, m. 1670, Aug. 30. WILLIAM RICHARDSON, } { b. d. 1676, Feb. 10. } { b. d. 1684 + } of Richardson.

SEARLE (EDWARD).

{ EDWARD, m. JOAN WHITE (widow). } { b. d. 1679 + } { b. d. } Warwick, Providence, R. I.

of Calverly.

1671, Jul. 20. He had a deed from Edmund Calverly, of Warwick, R. I.—"for love and affection unto my brother-in-law Edward Searle, late of Warwick, but now of Mashantatack, as also for love and affection I have to his wife Joan Searle, now in Old England at present. To said Edward Searle and Joan his wife, 50 acres of land in Mashantatack, which right and property of mine said Edward Searle is now at this present set down upon and hath a house builded thereon of his own." He then provides that Edward Searle and his wife shall jointly enjoy the estate for their lives if they please to accept thereof, and at their death it shall descend to Edward Searle, the younger son of the said Edward Searle the elder, and to John White, son of the said Joan Searle, now in England with his mother, but in case Joan Searle and her son by her first husband shall either refuse to accept of this free gift (which should be known by their not coming to live on the land after they had knowledge of same), then after decease of Edward Searle the elder, his son Edward and Ann, his wife late the wife of John Lippitt, and their heirs, were to inherit. The privilege of commonage, as timber for building, feed for cattle, &c., was also conveyed, provided that those who took this deed of gift were to conform at all times to wholesome orders of proprietors, &c. (This deed was recorded 1727, Aug. 4.)

I. { SON, } { b. d. }

II. { EDWARD, m. 1671, Feb. 21. ANN LIPPITT (w. of John) } { b. d. 1727, Apr. 23. } { b. d. } of Grove. Providence, R. I.

1674, Jul. 3. He apprenticed his stepson Moses Lippitt to William Austin of Providence, for a term of fifteen years, to learn the weaver's trade.

1687, Sep. 1. Taxed 4*s*. (Total levy £33, 9*s*. 6*d*.)

1699. He killed a wolf this year and received 10*s*. bounty.

1727, Feb. 2. He deeded to son Benjamin, for love and good will, the 50 acres that originally derived from Edmund Calverly (with a share of meadow originally derived from Walter Todd), and my now dwelling house, without limitation.

1727, Feb. 2. He deeded to son Benjamin, for love and affection, 40 acres that was bought of Thomas Hopkins, and a 30 acre lot bought of Robert Potter, and a half right of common.

1727. Inventory, £267, 9*s*. 4*d*. Administration to son Benjamin. Among items were 6 cows, 3 two year olds, 3 yearlings, 4 calves, a mare, 5 swine, 4 small pigs, feather bed, 2 flock beds, a woolen wheel, linen wheel, books, pewter, warming pan. Bonds £104, 5*s*., &c.

1730, Mar. 16. His son Benjamin's account as administrator of his father's estate was examined by Town Council. Due from administrator £43, 19*s*. To eldest son, £14, 13*s*., to each other child or legal representative, £7, 6*s*.

1. Mary, 1661, Sep. 16.
2. Elizabeth, 1665, Jan. 4.

1. Hannah, 1667, Oct. 28.
2. Catharine, 1671, Sep. 6.
3. Frances, 1673, Jan. 17.
4. Jeremiah, 1675, Feb. 21.
5. Deliverance 1678, Jul. 4.

1. Henry, 1673, Sep. 7.
2. Catharine, 1675, Oct. 22.
3. John, 1678 Dec. 29.
4. Catharine, 1681, Feb. 25.
5. Charles, 1683, Sep. 4.
6. Mary, 1684, Sep. 15.

No issue.

SEARLE (Edward).

I. { **Benjamin**, m. **Mary Burton** (w. of [John. } b. 1671. d. 1756, Sep. 22. b. d. 1768, Dec. 29. of — Providence, Cranston. R. I. — No issue.

1699, Sep. 15. He gave testimony, calling himself about twenty-eight years old.

1741, Apr. 17. He was given a legacy in his nephew Thomas's will of this date, consisting of 4 cows, 2 four year old steers, and 2 two year old heifers.

1742, Feb. 27. He sold Richard Searle the homestead farm whereon Richard lived, consisting of 98 acres, 29 rods, and also farm whereon Fearnot King lived, 143 acres, with buildings, for £3,200, for the whole.

1756, May 1. Will—proved 1756, Sep. 29. Ex. brother Richard Searle, and brother's son, Richard, Jr. To wife Mary, £100, and dower, which "is as much as my present circumstances can well afford." To Anne Gorton and Roby Searle, daughters of my cousin (*i. e.* nephew) Thomas Searle, deceased, £100, each, and all my household goods and furniture, except what my wife brought to me. To Thomas Searle, son of aforesaid cousin Thomas, deceased, all my real estate whatsoever and wheresoever, at age or marriage, but if he die before of age without issue, then equally to Ann Gorton, Roby Searle, and my brother Richard.

Inventory, old mare, 6 cows, two yearlings, 46 sheep and lambs, 6 swine, cooper's tools, books £22, bonds £588, 7*s.*, 3 feather beds, a flock bed, brass, pewter, warming pan, &c.

1759, Nov. 29. Will—proved 1768, Dec. 31. Widow Mary Searle. Exs. sons William and John Burton. She leaves her estate to two sons, and grandchildren.

II. { **Richard**, m. (1) **Alice Ralph**, m. (2) **Hannah Holden** (w. of [John. } b. d. 1771, Dec. 22. b. d. of Thomas & Eleanor ( ) Ralph. b. d. 1770 + of — Providence, Cranston, R. I. — 1. Thomas, 2. Edward, 3. Richard, 4. Alice, (2d wife, no issue.)

1708, Jun. 4. He and Roger Burlingame (both of Mashantatack) having been appointed guardians of Thomas Ralph's (deceased) two daughters, proceeded to divide the real estate. The eldest daughter Alice Searle, wife of Richard Searle, was given 50 acres which Richard's house stood on, and

SMITH (Christopher).

{ Christopher, { b. Providence, R. I.
m. { d. 1676, Jun.
{ Alice, { b.
{ d. 1681 +

1650, Sep. 2. Taxed 3*s.* 4*d.*
1655. Freeman.
1655, Apr. 27. Juryman.
1656, Mar. 16. He was granted a share of meadow to be laid out beyond the meadow called World's End, in lieu of a share formerly laid out to him beyond Great Meadow and Pawtuxet Path.
1658, Jul. 27. He took up 60 acres and a share of meadow.
1665, Feb. 19. He drew lot 25 in a division of lands.
1667, Jun. 1. He took the oath of allegiance.
1668, Aug. 21. He and wife Alice sold Asten Thomas, 20 acres.
1672, Nov. 28. He and wife Alice sold Shadrach Manton a parcel of lowland.

He went to Newport at the time of King Philip's War when so many took refuge there; and died at that place as declared by Friends' records, which call him an ancient Friend of Providence

It is assumed that Benjamin Smith was his son, but the evidence is not as yet conclusive. It is noticeable that Benjamin Smith's land was adjoining to Thomas Smith's, and that Benjamin had two grandchildren named Christopher. Edward Smith (son of Christopher) was witness to the will of Benjamin Smith, and Edward was as careful to name a son Benjamin as he had been to give others the family names of Christopher and Thomas. In the Providence tax list of 1650, there were but two Smiths old enough to be enrolled, viz: the widow of John Smith (miller) and Christopher Smith. The descendants of John Smith (miller), and John Smith (mason) a later comer, are accounted for; leaving Benjamin Smith alone of his generation, and there is little probability of his having been himself an emigrant.

I. { Susanna, { b.
m. { d. 1692 (—)
{ Lawrence Wilkinson, { b.
{ d. 1692, Aug. 9. of William Wilkinson.

II. { Thomas, { b. Warwick, R. I.
m. 1659. { d. 1670, Jan. 16.
{ Ruth Wickenden, { b.
{ d. 1670, Jan. 16. of William Wickenden.

He was a tailor

1661, Dec. 20. He was a witness to the confirmatory deed of Roger Williams to his associates.
1666, Jul. 9. He and his wife Ruth received a deed from her father William Wickenden of certain land on south side of Pawtuxet River, bounded partly by Benjamin Smith's land.
1670, Jan. 18 The jury called to consider the death of himself and wife, found that they "were both drowned in the river of Pawtuxet the 16th inst. at night." Testimony was given of his son John, aged eight years, who said that last Sabbath day within the night his father Thomas Smith came to the river side over against his house and hallooed, whereupon his mother Ruth Smith went out, and his father asked his mother if he might row over, and his mother answered that no one but children had come over and cautioned him not to row. But his father would not stay but went to row over and fell into the water, and his mother went and caught up a stick and he said to her "give me hold of the stick" and he took hold thereof and presently the stick broke and they both fell into the water together. The boy then went to a neighbor for help, saying his father and mother were in the river by the house a drowning; "the child having with him his brother Joseph in his arms and his brother William by him."
1670, Feb. 20. The will of his father-in-law mentions the fatherless children of Thomas Smith
1670, Mar. 14. The ages of his four sons were testified to by their aunt Plain Wickenden, who then received an order for her taking the youngest child, Joseph.
1670, Jun. 4. He and his wife having died intestate, leaving four orphans, John, Thomas, William and Joseph, to be provided for, the Town Council being instead of a father, appointed the house and land to be sold by Mr. Edmund Calverly the administrator, and he disposed of same to Abiah Carpenter for £40.

III. { Benjamin, { b. 1631 ± Providence, Warwick, R. I
m. { d. 1713, Dec. 23.
{ Lydia Carpenter, { b.
{ d. 1711, Oct. 1. of William & Elizabeth (Arnold) Carpenter.

1654. Sergeant of military company.
1658, Jun. 1. He and others of Pawtuxet asked to be dismissed from the government of Massachusetts (under whose jurisdiction Pawtuxet had been since 1642), and the petition was granted in October of same year.
1666-67-68-69-70-71-72-73-75-86-89-90-96-98-1700-1-2 3-4. Warwick. Assistant.
1670-71-73-74-80-82-84-85. Deputy.
1675, Mar. 17. He testified as to the corn mill at Pawtuxet in controversy between Stephen Arnold and Samuel Reape, calling his age about forty-three years.
1690, Jan. 30. He and five other Assistants, and the Deputy Governor, sent a letter to their Majesties William and Mary, congratulating them on their accession to the throne, and informing them that since the deposition of Sir Edmund Andros, the former government under the charter had been re-assumed. It was also mentioned that Andros had been seized in Rhode Island on his flight from confinement in Massachusetts, and that he had been returned to that colony on their demand.
1692, Aug. 13. Will—proved 1714, Jan 23. Exx wife Lydia. To four sons, all undivided lands south side of Pawtuxet River. To eldest son Benjamin, all lands in Passounkit Neck. To second son Joseph, land at Cowad. To third son William, parcel of land near Cowad where dwelling house stands and piece of meadow. To fourth son Simon, at decease of his mother, my dwelling house and home stall, orchards, &c., fenced in; he having half of house during life of his mother. To eldest daughter Lydia Foues, £5. To second daughter Elizabeth Smith, £5. To wife, rest of estate, goods and chattels. His wife after the signing of above will by her husband confirmed the disposition he made of lands south of Pawtuxet River to four sons, stating that said land was received by deed of gift from her father William Carpenter with the understanding that at her husband's decease it should go to such as she might make heir of them. (The deed referred to from her father was dated 1666, Feb. 21, and her confirmation was dated 1706, Feb. 7.)

Inventory, £102, 4*s.*, viz: silver money £14, 1*s.* 6*d.*, pewter, brass, wearing apparel, 2 guns, table, settle, chairs, books £4, cattle and horses £18, razor, looking glass, &c.

two shares of meadow adjoining, each side of Mashantatack Brook, and a piece of land lying by Samuel Ralph, son of deceased. The other daughter Eleanor Ralph, had her father's home lot, and other land.

1713, Feb. 16. He and wife Alice and Thomas Burlingame and wife Eleanor, exchanged 16 acres in Mashantatack (taken from right called Thomas Ralph's) for two meadow shares in Warwick on Pawtuxet River. The exchange was made between them and Thomas Stafford.

1741, Apr. 17. He was appointed one of executors of his son Thomas's will of this date. (This son died 1741, May 1, leaving widow Penelope, son Thomas, daughters Anne and Roby.)

1746, Apr. 1. He sold his son Edward, for love and good will, a dwelling house and 30 acres at Mashantatack.

1770, Apr. 5. Will—proved 1772, Mar. 28. Exs. son Edward and Richard. To wife Hannah, all household goods, and all the money we sold a certain privilege my said wife had in a house and land left her by will of first husband John Holden, late of Warwick, &c. To wife also, a negro girl named Duchess, and interest of £1,000, and a cow, all in lieu of dower. To son Edward, farm in Coventry, meadow in Cranston, and negro fellows Jeffrey and Keler. To son Richard, my farm in Cranston called Forman's Farm, and a lot of 2 acres. To grandson Thomas Searle, 2 pieces of land adjoining homestead formerly belonging to my brother Benjamin, deceased. To grandson Ezekiel Searle, at age, negro boy Cuffy, and should Ezekiel die, then to grandson William Searle. To daughter Alice Philbrook, 25 Spanish milled dollars. To granddaughter Alice Searle, daughter of son Richard, negro girl Violet. To son Edward, negro boy Toby. To sons Edward and Richard, rest of estate.

Inventory, £603, 11*s.* 11*d.*, viz: wearing apparel, feather bed, linen yarn, 3 large and several small silver spoons, note £167, 13*s*, old cow, 10 sheep, negro Jeffrey £40, Keler £40, Toby £40, Primus £40, Cæsar £40, Cuffy £40, Aaron £40, negro girl Violet £30, negro woman Duchess £30, negro boy Sharper £15.

SMITH (Christopher).

1. Samuel,
2. Susanna, 1652, Mar. 9.
3. John, 1654, Mar. 2.
4. Joanna, 1657, Mar. 2.
5. Josias,
6. Susanna, 1662, Feb.

I. John, b. 1661, Aug. 4. d. 1683, May 16. — Providence, R. I.
Unmarried.

He was drowned.

He left an estate of £1, 17*s.* 2*d.*, debts £13, 2*s.* 4*d.*, and his goods were given creditors in settlement. He was called son of Thomas Smith, Tailor, formerly of Warwick, and a letter was written from Providence to Warwick authorities as to whether any estate was there.

II. Thomas, b. 1664, Aug. 9. d.

1672, Jan. 15. He was apprenticed to Edmund Calverly and was to have at age two suits of apparel and a set of tools for a shoemaker (and he to be instructed in that art).

III. William, b. 1667, Jan. 10. d. — Kings Town, R. I.

He was a cordwainer.

1715, Mar. 10. He made a deed of gift to his brother Joseph of Providence of his right in all lands in Providence that descended to him from his grandfather William Wickenden, deceased.

IV. Joseph, b. 1669, Feb. 18. d. 1739, Nov. 8. — Providence, Glocester, R. I.
m. (1) 1699, Apr. 4.
Elizabeth Hawkins, b. d. of John & Sarah ( ) Hawkins,
m. (2)
Mary, b. d. of

1. Sarah,
2. Joseph,
3. Waite,

He was a carpenter.

1697, Mar. 24. He had a deed of gift from kinsman Samuel Wilkinson and wife Plain, and John Steere, Jr., of 18 acres formerly belonging to William Wickenden, deceased.

1713, Jun. 16. Taxed 6*d.*

1716, Mar. 28. He, calling himself Joseph Smith, carpenter, son of Thomas, deceased, deeded to Joseph Smith, yeoman, son of Edward, deceased, a third of a right of common, and a forty foot lot.

1730, Feb. 11. He bought of his son Joseph all interest that said son had in land deeded his mother Elizabeth, deceased, by John Hawkins, grandfather of said Joseph Smith, Jr.

1731, Apr. 27. Glocester. He deeded son Waite, for love, &c., 45 acres. (He and wife Mary signed a deed in Glocester.)

1739, Nov. 7. Administration to son Joseph, of Smithfield. Inventory, £130, 15*s.* 11*d.*, viz: 2 beds, carpenter's tools, hetchel, pair of cards, 2 spinning wheels, gun, testament, psalter, swine, horse, mare, 2 cows, fowls, &c.

I. Benjamin, b. 1661, d. 1730, Apr. 27. — Warwick, R. I.
m. 1691, Dec. 25.
Phebe Arnold, b. 1670, Nov. 9. d. 1730 + of Stephen & Sarah (Smith) Arnold.

1. Elizabeth, 1693, Jan. 11.
2. Hannah, 1694, Oct. 7.
3. Sarah, 1695, May 30.
4. Benjamin, 1697, Jun. 21.
5. Phebe, 1699, Dec. 5.
6. Philip, 1700, Nov. 30.
7. Almy, 1703, Jun. 17.
8. Lydia, 1705, Jun. 11.
9. Alice, 1707, Feb. 3.
10. Katharine, 1708, Jan. 23.
11. Giffe, 1710, Apr. 20.
12. Stephen, 1713, Feb. 20.

1729, Nov. 7. Will—proved 1730, Jun. 8. Ex. son Benjamin. He calls himself in sixty-ninth year. To wife Phebe, a bed, best room, sufficient firewood, a good cow, with keep of same, use of half household goods, and £8, per year for life while widow. To grandson Benjamin Sheffield, son of daughter Elizabeth, 5*s.*, she having had before. To daughter Sarah Westcott, wife of Jeremiah, 5*s.* To daughter Phebe Gargil, wife of James, 5*s.* To daughters Almy, Lydia, Catharine and Giffe Smith, each £50. To son Philip, 5*s.*, he having had. To son Stephen, all land west side of road from Warwick to Pawtuxet Falls (except what Philip had received by deed of gift) and liberty in the clay for making bricks, and in orchard for two barrels of cider and ten bushels of apples, for ten years. To son Benjamin, all the rest of housing, lands, goods and chattels.

Inventory, £392, 16*s.*, viz: warming pan, pewter, 2 guns, loom, carpenter's tools, old white mare, yoke of oxen, 10 cows, 2 heifers, 7 calves, 22 sheep, 12 geese, 12 fowls, 2 large books, &c.

II. Joseph, b. d. — Warwick, Kings Town, R. I.
m.
Sarah Stafford, b. d. of Joseph & Sarah (Holden) Stafford.

1. Sarah,
2. Mercy,
3. Elizabeth,

1705, Nov. 2. Kings Town. He and wife Sarah, late of Warwick, sold Gideon Crawford land in Providence.

III. William, b. 1664, Dec. 27. d. 1745, Dec. 18. — North Kingstown, R. I.
m. 1709, Mar. 15.
Patience Harris, b. 1682, Jun. 21. d. 1759, Nov. 20. of Andrew & Mary (Tew) Harris.

1. William, 1715, Feb. 21.
2. Lydia, 1721, Aug.

He and his wife were buried in the Smith Burial Ground, North Kingstown.

IV. Simon, b. d. 1712, Mar. 4. — Warwick, R. I.
m. 1699, Jan. 5.
Mary Andrews, b. d. 1714 + of William & Esther (Arnold) Andrews.

1. Esther, 1699, Oct. 9.
2. Mary, 1701, Apr. 4.
3. Christopher, 1703, Oct. 14.
4. Phebe, 1705, Dec. 13.
5. Simon, 1710, Jul. 1.

1704-5-7-8-9-10-11. Deputy.

1705, Jun. 19. He was chosen on a committee with three others to transcribe and perfect the laws of the colony.

1705-7-8-11. Clerk of Assembly.

1706-7-8-9-10-11-12. Attorney General.

1709. Speaker of House of Deputies. He held the offices of Lieutenant and Captain some years.

IV. (EDWARD, { b. Providence, R. I.
m. 1663. { d. 1693, Nov. 8.
(ANPHILLIS ANGELL, { b.
{ b. 1694 + of Thomas & Alice ( ) Angell.

1656, Aug. 27. He was granted common equal to other townsmen, and was to have a vote with inhabitants.

1656. Hayward.

1658, May 18. Freeman.

1659. Juryman.

1662. Town Sergeant. He was to have 20*s*., for his year's service, paid in peage at eight per penny.

1663, May 9. Intentions of marriage recorded.

1665, Feb. 19. He had lot 22 in a division of lands.

1665–68–75–76–80–82–83. Deputy.

1667, Jun. 1. He took the oath of allegiance.

1672, Jan. 27. He sold Richard Everden, 3½ acres meadow.

1673, Jan. 27. His bill for the accomodation of difficulties was recorded. "A reasonable, seasonable and ready way of encouragement to planters in their labors in this our plantation of Providence presented to the town met. Neighbors, whereas there hath been and yet is uncomfortable differences in this town about a new division of lands which you all sufficiently know." He therefore provides a way for settlement and division, and closes; "so much of the forest be suddenly subdued by the laborious and become a fruitful field which is the desire of your neighbor, Edward Smith."

1678–79–81–82–83–84–85–86–88. Town Council.

1679, Jul 1. Taxed 6*s*., 3*d*.

1681, Oct. 3. He sold to Eleazer Whipple, for £5, a right of commoning "which did in the original belong to my father Christopher Smith, now deceased, and was by my said father freely given to me, taking the care of my mother during her said natural life." He agrees to hold Eleazer Whipple harmless of all claims by me or father Christopher, deceased, or said mother

1687, Sep. 1. Taxed 7*s*.

1688. Ratable estate, 5 cows, 4 three years, 2 two years, 4 yearlings, 2 oxen, 2 horses, 1½ shares of meadow, 6 acres tillage, 4 acres pasture, 5 acres wild pasture, 140 acres of woods, &c.

1691. Assistant.

1692, Aug. 13. He was one of the witnesses to will of Benjamin Smith.

1694, Jan. 9. Administration to widow Anphillis and son Edward.

By one account he had also daughters Mary and Susannah.

1712, Mar. 3. Will—proved 1712, Apr. 19. Ex. not named. To son Christopher, all right in land at Westquadnaid. To son Simon, all right in land at Mashantatack. To daughters Hester, Mary and Phebe Smith, all land at Narragansett.
Inventory, £193, 4*s.*, viz: wearing apparel, plate £5, 4*s.*, cash £10. 4*s.*, 4*d.*, money scales, books £7, 5 beds, &c. £48, 18*s.*, sword, gun, cane, case of bottles, pewter, linen, woolen and worsted, leather, shoemaker's tools, cask and cider, 5 cows, ox, bull, yearling, steer, horse, mare, 3 swine, &c.
1714, Jan. 22. His widow received a deed from her husband's brother Benjamin, of all that quarter of undivided lands which it had been the intention of Benjamin Smith, Sr., to have confirmed to children of Simon, but which he had neglected to do, being very aged and memory much decayed. A deed was now made to Mary Smith, widow of Simon, in trust for Christopher, the eldest son.

V. LYDIA, m. JOHN FONES,
b. 1668. d. 1741, Jan. 24.
b. 1663, Sep. d. 1738, Feb. 17. of John & Margaret ( ) Fones.

1. Margaret,
2. Lydia, 1698.
3. Mary,

VI. ELIZABETH, m. 1698, Feb. 28. ISRAEL ARNOLD,
b. 1672. d 1718, Feb. 7.
b 1678, Jan. 18. d. 1753. of Israel & Mary (Barker) Arnold.

1. Elizabeth, 1699, Jan. 19.
2. Israel, 1701, Jul. 19.
3. Lydia, 1702, Jan. 8.
4. Benjamin, 1707, Jan. 18.
5. Christopher 1710, Nov. 7.
6. Stephen, 1710, Nov. 7.
7. Sion, 1713, Oct. 31.
8. Mary, 1714, Feb. 25.
9. Simon, 1717, Dec. 25.

I. ALICE, m. 1684, May 20. JOSEPH WHIPPLE,
b. 1664. d. 1739, Jul. 20.
b. 1662. d 1746, Apr. 28. of John & Sarah ( ) Whipple.

1. John, 1685, May 18.
2. Jeremiah, 1686, Sep. 3.
3. Joseph, 1687, Dec. 30.
4. Anphillis, 1689, Oct. 6.
5. Sarah, 1691, Mar. 29.
6. Susanna, 1693, Apr. 14.
7. Freelove, 1694, Mar. 18.
8. Alice, 1696, Feb. 6.
9. Amey, 1699, Jun. 16.
10. Christopher 1701, Sep. 14.
11. Mary, 1704. Apr. 9.
12. Christopher 1707, Mar. 6.

II. EDWARD, m. MERCY MOWRY,
Providence, R. I.
b. d. 1726, Nov. 9.
b. d. of Nathaniel & Joanna (Inman) Mowry.

(She m. (2) 1741, Nov. 26, William Hall.)

1703, Jan. 5. He, as eldest son of Edward Smith (who had died intestate), having heired his lands, now deeds to brother Joseph, 62 acres, knowing it to be the mind of his father, &c. The same year he deeded his brother Christopher, 50 acres.
1706, May 8. He had 11*s.* worth of pewter taken from him, to pay his fine for not training, he being a Quaker.
1712, Sep. 10. He deeded his brother Benjamin two pieces of land, 150 acres, with house, &c., knowing that it was his father's mind, &c.
1713, Jun. 16. Taxed 18*s.*
1714-15-16-17-18 19-20. Town Council.
1716-17. Deputy.
1727, Mar. 6. Administration to widow Mercy and son Edward. Inventory, £396, 11*s.*, viz: 3 feather beds, 4 pewter platters, tankard, &c., cheese press, weaving loom, cooper's and carpenter's tools, negro man £60, 2 oxen, 4 steers, 8 cows, 2 heifers, 8 young cattle, 2 horses, 16 poor sheep, &c.
1728, Jul. 26. His son Edward took receipt from his sister Alice and her husband Thomas Harding, for their share of father Edward Smith's estate, and subsequently he took receipts also from Martha Gully and husband William, Mercy Scott and husband Nathaniel, Amey Arnold and husband Thomas, Mary Hawkins and husband Joseph, Freelove Angell and husband Abiah, Rachel Smith and husband Hezekiah.
1734, Jan. 8. His son Edward (of Smithfield), deeded to brother Abraham, 140 acres, a portion of estate of honoured father Edward Smith, deceased, the land to be held in trust till Abraham is of age by brother-in-law Hezekiah Smith. (Besides the children mentioned as giving receipts, there was Anne, who married Jonathan Whipple, and Sarah who married Hezekiah Sprague.

1. Edward,
2. Alice,
3. Martha,
4. Mercy,
5. Sarah,
6. Rachel,
7. Amey,
8. Mary,
9. Freelove,
10. Anne,
11. Abraham,

III. ANPHILLIS. m. NOAH WHIPPLE,
b. d. 1703 +
b. d. 1703, Nov. 10. of Samuel & Mary (Harris) Whipple.

IV. THOMAS, m. PHEBE ARNOLD,
Providence, Smithfield, R. I.
b. 1671, Feb. 19. d. 1741, Sep. 2.
b. 1672, Nov. 5. d. 1741 + of Eleazer & Eleanor (Smith) Arnold.

1706, May 21. He had a hand saw and bell taken from him worth 10*s.*, to pay his fine for not training, he being a Quaker.
1713, Jun. 16. Taxed 9*s.*
1727, Feb. 3. He sold son Thomas, blacksmith, for £50, a house and 70 acres where I dwell, but the grantor to possess for life.
1741, Sep. 1. Will—proved 1741, Dec. 7. Exs. wife Phebe and son Thomas. To sons Thomas and John, 5*s.* each, and like amount to daughters, viz: to Phebe Smith, wife of Jonathan, of Dartmouth, Mary Hawkins, wife of John, of Smithfield, and Ruth Thornton, wife of Ebenezer. To granddaughter Phebe Appleby, 5*s.* To wife Phebe, rest of movables to dispose of to children, but if she marries again only a third of movables. To son Daniel, a small piece of cedar swamp.
Inventory, £158, 3*s.*, 6*d.*, viz: books, 2 spinning wheels, gun, pewter, flax, horse, 2 cows, 6 sheep, hog, 3 fowls, &c.

1. Thomas, 1697. Dec. 5.
2. John, 1700, Oct. 7.
3. Phebe, 1703, Mar. 28.
4. Mary, 1705, Apr. 22.
5. Hannah, 1707, Apr. 10.
6. Daniel, 1709, Jun. 29.
7. Ruth, 1712, Jun. 13.

V. CHRISTOPHER, m. MARY,
Providence, Scituate, R. I.
b. d. 1755 +
b. d. 1726 + of

SMITH (CHRISTOPHER). 3d column. V. Christopher, d. 1758, (—). His widow d. 1758, +. 1758, Oct. 21, she joined in a deed with her son Benjamin and latter's wife Molly.

He was a blacksmith.
1696. Freeman.
1713, Jun. 16. Taxed 9*s.*
1725, Dec. 2. He deeded son Christopher, for love, &c., half of land on Corke Brook, 118 acres.
1726, Dec. 5. He and wife Mary, sold William Jenckes, Jr., 50 acres formerly belonging to honored father Edward Smith, deceased, for £600.
1750, Apr. 3. Scituate. He deeded all of homestead farm to son Benjamin. (He also deeded other land to him in 1755, recorded in 1761.)

1. Christopher
2. Benjamin,
3. Elizabeth,
4. Abigail,
5. Anphillis,

VI. BENJAMIN, m. (1) SARAH BURLINGAME, m. (2) 1742, Jun. 24. ANN SMITH,
Smithfield, R. I.
b. d. 1749, Dec. 26.
b. d. of Burlingame.
b. 1717, Oct. 5. d. of Benjamin & Mercy (Angell) Smith.

(She m. (2) 1755, Jan. 2, Stephen Hopkins.)

1719, Jul. 3. He and Christopher and Joseph, sons of Edward, deceased, made division of certain land in original right of grandfather Christopher.
1749, Oct. 22 Will—proved 1750, Jan. 22. Exs. wife Anne and Jonathan Arnold. To wife, benefit of all lands in Smithfield and Providence, till son Benjamin is of age, for her use while widow. A tract of land near brother Christopher Smith's to be sold by executors. To son Benjamin, rest of real estate. To wife, £400. To daughters Sarah, Ruth and Amey, £400, each. To wife, one-fifth of rest of personal after children are brought up, and to said children the other four-fifths.
Inventory, £4,673, 15*s.*, 5*d.*

1. Sarah, 1743. Apr. 19.
2. Benjamin, 1744, Oct. 4.
3. Ruth, 1746, Sep. 7
4. Amey, 1748, Sep. 7.

VII. JOSEPH, m. PATIENCE MOWRY,
Providence, Smithfield, R. I.
b. 1680, Oct. 12. d. 1734, Feb. 17.
b. d. 1734 + of Nathaniel & Joanna (Inman) Mowry.

1708, May 11. He had property worth 13*s.*, taken from him to pay a fine for not training, he being a Quaker.
1733, Jun. 19. Will—proved 1734, Apr. 1. Ex. son Joseph. To sons Samuel and Jethro, 400 acres both sides of Branch River at Trout Brook, &c. To daughters Susanna Aldrich, Abigail Hains, Rebecca and Barsheba Smith, certain land (150 acres) about a mile south of son Jacob's house. To daughters Dinah and Elnathan Smith, £50 each, at twenty-one. To son Joseph, homestead farm where I dwell, 257 acres, and other land and all household goods and movables, he taking good care of his mother for life.
Inventory, 2 horses, 15 sheep, 4 young cattle, 9 cows, 3 heifers, bull, 10 loads of hay, 2 spinning wheels, books, pewter, gun, 20¼ oz. plate, cider, &c.
1734, Apr. 1. As his wife was not mentioned in will, except as left to care of her son Joseph, an agreement was made between her and said son. He was to provide for her, and she to have best room in the house for life, feather bed, flock bed, horse and £5, a year, and to relinquish her dower.

1. Jacob, 1706, May 3
2. Susanna, 1708, May 26
3. Joseph, 1710, Feb. 4.
4. Abigail, 1712, Mar.
5. Samuel, 1713, Dec.
6. Jethro,
7. Rebecca,
8. Bathsheba,
9. Dinah,
10. Elnathan,

EDWARD,	b.	Weymouth, Rehoboth, Mass.,
m.	d. 1675 +	[Newport, R. I.
———	b.	
	d.	

1642, Jul. 15. "Thomas Rock, servant to Edward Smith," died. Before this Edward Smith had received several grants of land in Weymouth. At a period a little later (the date is lacking) he sold 5½ acres, dwelling house, barn, and cellar, together with 3 acres of fresh marsh, to Thomas Dyer.

1643. Rehoboth. Estate valued at £252. He had an allotment of land this year.

1644, Jul. 3. He was one of the thirty signers of compact for good government. In the same year he received another lot in division of lands.

1644, Oct. 10. He and eight others were chosen to hear causes of contention, make levies, &c.

1645. Town Clerk.

1645, Apr. 9. He and six others were chosen to order the prudential affairs of the town for half a year, and the same year he with others ordered a levy of 12*d*., on each £100 estate, said tax to be paid either in butter at 6*d*. per pound, or in wampum.

1646. He was on a committee to lay out a five rail fence.

1650. He was appointed to make a convenient way four rods wide for use of town of Rehoboth, or any that shall have occasion to pass from town to Providence or to Mr. Blackstone.

1650, Oct. 2. He and his wife, with others, were presented by Grand Jury for continuing of meeting upon the Lord's Day from house to house, contrary to the order of this court.

1653, May 17. Newport. Freeman.

1654, May 18. He with two others were appointed to examine Captain Partridge's estate, "and what the said three shall doe therein shall be authenticque."

1654-55-58-59-65-66. Assistant.

1655. Freeman.

1655-59. Commissioner.

1659, Aug. 23. He was on a committee to receive contributions to amount of £50, to be sent to John Clarke in England, the agent for the colony.

1661, Mar. 22. He with others signed an agreement in relation to the settlement of Westerly, and four months later he was allotted half a share there, but never went there to settle.

1665-66-69. Deputy.

1667. He was on a committee to make a rate for a levy of £150 for prison, pound and stocks at Newport.

1671. His fine for non-attendance as juror was remitted for good excuse.

1675, Oct. 16. He was alluded to at this date as "old Mr. Smith," in an agreement between his son Elisha and James Barker.

1681, May 14. In a letter from Samuel Hubbard, of Newport, to Isaac Wells, of Jamaica, he alludes to the death of Mr. Smith and others. Most of those he mentioned died in 1676.

A stone to his memory has been placed in the family burial ground in Middletown, R. I.

I. SARAH,	b. 1629.	
m. 1646, Nov. 24.	d. 1713, Apr. 15.	
STEPHEN ARNOLD,	b. 1622, Dec. 22.	
	d. 1699, Nov. 15.	of William & Christian (Peak) Arnold.

II. PHILIP,	b. 1634.	Newport, R. I.
m.	d. 1700, Dec. 6.	
MARY,	b. 1644.	
	d. 1700, Dec. 3.	of

1671. Freeman.

1676, Apr. 20. He was appointed one of the trustees of Dr. John Clarke's will. He this year bought the terms of service of two Indians (captured by Providence men) for £4, 10*s*.

1680. Taxed £5, 5*s*., 6*d*., Philip Smith and others.

1681, Jun. 8. He and wife Mary sold Nicholas Cottrell, of Westerly, for £30, a tract of 200 acres laid out to my father Edward Smith, deceased, being not yet divided from the other half of same share laid out to John Crandall, deceased, and now in possession of John Cottrell, of Kings Town.

1681-83-84-90-91. Deputy.

1687. Foreman of Grand Jury.

1701, Jan. 6. Will—and codicil, proved. Exs. sons Edward and Peleg.

1701, Jan. 13. Agreement of Peleg Chase, William Slade, of Swanzey, and William Hiscox, of Newport, guardians of Peleg Smith — with Edward Smith. The will was confirmed by this agreement. Edward Smith was to take benefit of all lands and goods of Philip Smith, deceased, and to pay all legacies (except the household goods bequeathed three youngest children). Legacies to be paid as per will, as follows: To Mary Gray, £30. To Elizabeth Rogers, £50. To Phebe Smith, £100. To Hannah Smith, £100. To William Hiscox, £5. The said Peleg Smith to abide with Edward, who was to find him covenient meat, drink, washing and lodging, &c., and to keep him a horse, and Peleg to be helpful in managing the farm, having four month's time in schooling. Edward chose that part of farm on which his father did dwell, with buildings, &c. Peleg was to enjoy the other division, and two years from date was to possess same, and was then to receive from Edward sixty ewe sheep, forty lambs, five cows, a yearling heifer, two calves, two oxen, a sow, and hay sufficient for wintering stock, &c.

He and his wife were buried in the family burial ground.

III. PHEBE,	b. 1642, Aug. 15.
	d.

IV. ELISHA,	b.	Newport, R. I.
m.	d. 1676 ±	
MARY BARKER,	b.	
	d. 1723, Sep. 19.	of James & Barbara (Dungan) Barker.

(She m. (2) 1677, Apr. 16, Israel Arnold.)

1675, Oct. 16. He made an agreement with James Barker, Sr., wherein said Elisha Smith binds himself to maintain a fence between his land and Mr. Barker's on the line of the old fence near "old Mr. Smith's house."

1676. He this year bought the terms of service of two Indian captives (captured by Providence men) paying for one a hundred pounds of wool, and for the other three fat sheep.

V. EDWARD,	b.	Middletown, N. J.
UNMARRIED.	d. 1704.	

1669, Nov. 6. He signed as witness to a power of attorney (given by John Throckmorton, Jr., to his father John, of Providence), and calls himself "Edward Smith, son of Edward Smith, of Rhode Island."

1703, Apr. 1. Will—proved 1704, Apr. 14. Exs. James Cox and Richard Mount. He made bequests to friends and to the poor of Middletown. He named no relatives.

SMITH (JOHN, THE MASON).

JOHN,	b.	Providence, R. I.
m. (1)	d. 1660.	
———	b.	
	d.	
m. (2)	b.	
ANNE COMSTOCK (w. of [Samuel.	d. 1661 +	

He was a mason, and so called to distinguish him from his contemporary, John Smith the Miller.

(There was still another John Smith, of Providence, called "Jamaica John," who died before 1685, in which year his son John was living at Medfield, Mass.)

1654, Mar. 1. He sold Samuel Comstock his house and home lot, bounded on the east with common and on the west by highway.

1657, Dec. 17. Warwick. Action of debt was brought by John Smith, of Warwick, against John Smith, Mason, of same town.

1659, Sep. 10. He sold Walter Todd dwelling house and lot and 6 acres adjoining, two shares of meadow and all rights in Warwick.

1660, Mar. 9. Providence. It was ordered that three men, viz: Arthur Fenner, John Brown and Henry Brown, should be added unto the Town

I. JOHN,	b.	Providence, R. I.
m.	d. 1687.	
ELIZABETH,	b.	
	d. 1706 +	of

He was a mason.

1665, Feb. 19. He had lot 43 assigned him in a division of lands.

1670. Freeman.

1679, Jul. 1. Taxed 1*s*. 10½*d*. with son Joseph.

1687, Mar. 16. Will—presented 1688, Apr. 4. Ex. son Joseph. (This will is alluded to in court records.)

1687, Sep. 1. Taxed 3*s*. Estate of deceased John Smith, Mason, and Joseph his son.

1706, Jan. 7. His widow Elizabeth being likely to become a charge upon the town, it was agreed by her two sons-in-law Eleazer Arnold and Thomas Hopkins, that they would care for their mother-in-law, provided they had all the personal estate left her by will of her husband.

1706, Jan. 19. Whereas, John Smith, Mason, by last will dated 1687, Mar. 16, gave to wife Elizabeth certain land (two house lots of 5 acres each) for life and for her disposal, expecting his son Benjamin to be maintained by said lands, and he also giving to wife all movables and cattle, &c., and whereas said son Benjamin is in such a condition as not to be capable of providing for his own maintenance by

1. Esther, 1647, Sep. 22.
2. Israel, 1649, Oct. 30.
3. Stephen, 1654, Nov. 27.
4. Elizabeth, 1659, Nov. 2.
5. Elisha, 1662, Feb. 18.
6. Sarah, 1665, Jun. 26.
7. Phebe, 1670, Nov. 9.

SMITH, (EDWARD). 3d column. I. Edward d. 1730, Sep. 18. V. Hannah b. 1688, Dec. 20; d. 1768, Nov. 16; m. 1707, Dec. 6, Samuel Gardiner, b. 1685, Oct. 28, d. 1773, Feb. 10, of Samuel and Elizabeth (Carr) Gardiner. Children, 1, Elizabeth, 1708, Nov. 11. 2, Mary, 1710, Oct. 26. 3, Samuel, 1712, Oct. 30. 4, Samuel, 1717, Feb. 17. 5, Peleg, 1719, Feb. 22. 6, Patience, 1721, Feb. 17. 7, Hannah, 1724±. 8, Sarah, 1726±. 9, Edward, 1731, Apr. 22. 10, Martha.

I. EDWARD, { b. / d. 1730 ± — Newport, R. I.
m. (1)
ELIZABETH LAWTON, { b. 1675, Feb. 16. / d. 1711, Dec. 17. of Isaac & Elizabeth (Tallman) Lawton.
m. (2) 1712, Sep. 17.
ELIZABETH TEW, { b. / d. 1769. of Henry & Dorcas ( ) Tew.

1. Isaac, 1699.
2. Elisha, 1700, Jul.
3. Mary, 1702, Apr. 27.
4. Elizabeth, 1703, Sep. 9.
5. Sarah, 1705, Jun. 7.
6. Phebe, 1707, Jul. 10.
7. Edward, 1709, Oct. 4.
8. Hannah, 1711, Jun. 21.
(2d wife.)
9. Dorcas, 1714, Jul. 20.
10. Henry, 1716, Feb. 10.
11. William, 1718, Apr. 7.
12. Ann, 1720, Mar. 2.
13. Elizabeth,

1703-4-6-7-10-19. Deputy. He had the title of Lieutenant part of this time.
1705. Justice of the Peace.
1700, Jul. 13. Will—Ex. son Elisha. (The receipts given by Henry and William Smith allude to date of will.)
1737, May 9. Receipt for legacy of £300, was given by Henry Smith, to his brother Elisha.
1739, Apr. 28. Receipt for legacy of £300, was given by William Smith.
1757, May 6. Will—proved 1769, Jun. 19. Widow Elizabeth, of Middletown, R. I. She names daughters Dorcas, Anne and Elizabeth, and her son William, deceased, and granddaughter Sarah Church.
His first wife was buried in the Smith Family Burial Ground.

II. MARY, { b. / d.
m.
EDWARD GRAY, { b. 1667, Jan. 31. / d. 1726. of Edward & Dorothy (Lettice) Gray.

1. Mary, 1691, May 16.
2. Edward, 1693, Jan. 10.
3. Elizabeth, 1695, Jan. 3.
4. Sarah, 1697, Apr. 25.
5. Phebe, 1699, Sep. 6.
6. Philip, 1702, Feb. 11.
7. Thomas, 1704, Feb. 4.
8. Hannah, 1707, Nov. 3.

III. ELIZABETH, { b. / d. 1704, May 24.
m.
JOSEPH ROGERS, { b. 1670. / d. 1710, Oct. 2. of John & Elizabeth (Rogers.

1. Mary, 1699, Aug. 24.
2. Elizabeth, 1701, Jan. 23.
3. Smith, 1702, Dec. 13.
4. Joseph, 1704, May 14.

IV. PHEBE, { b. / d.

V. HANNAH, { b. / d.

VI. PELEG, { b. 1681. / d. 1760. — Newport, Middletown, R. I.
m. 1711, Nov. 8.
JEMIMA LORD, { b. / d. 1760. of Lord.

1. Mary,
2. Sarah,
3. Benjamin, 1723.

1725, May. The Assembly declared that if he satisfied judgment of £200 damages, recovered in Court of Trials by John Davis, for an assault of Smith's Indian slave Dick on said Davis, that then he may take the slave again, he selling him out of the colony. If this was not done then said Davis had power to sell the Indian, he paying prison fees, &c.
1730. Deputy. At this time he bore the title of Captain.
1760, Mar. 17. Inventory rendered. Administration to son Benjamin.
1760, Apr. 19. Will—proved 1760, Nov. 3. Widow Jemima. She mentions son Benjamin, daughters Mary Little and Sarah Turner, grandchildren Peleg, Ellery, Jemima and Abigail Turner and granddaughter Jemima Little.
1769, Dec. 5. His death is alluded to in a letter of this date from Mary Taylor, of Middletown, R. I., to John Boune, of Monmouth, N. J. She says "I am sorry to acquaint you with the death of Peleg Smith. He has been dead between nine and ten years. His wife was buried a few months after. He left but one son, who has now living thirteen children."

No issue.

SMITH (JOHN, THE MASON).

I. LEONARD, { b. / d. 1676. — Providence, Newport, R. I.
UNMARRIED.

1665, Feb. 24. He was witness to a deed from Roger Williams to Richard Arnold.
1670. Freeman.
1672, Feb. 24. Constable. He was ordered to bring William Harris before the Council sitting at Newport.
1674. Deputy.
He was living at Newport at the time of his death.
1676, Sep. 23. Will—proved 1676, Oct. 16. Ex brother John Smith. Advisers, Pardon Tillinghast, Gregory Dexter. To brother John, all estate, he paying debts.

II. JOHN, { b. / d. 1676, Nov. — Providence, R. I.
UNMARRIED.

1676, Oct. 20. He, calling himself brother and heir to Leonard Smith, late resident in Newport, sold Stephen Sabeere, of Newport, a house lot measuring 40 by 40 feet, and a frame for a dwelling house, at Newport, for £17.

Council, to order about the estate of Samuel Comstock and John Smith, deceased, and that what the major part of them shall order shall stand in force.

1661, May 4. Anne Smith, of Providence, widow of John Smith, and formerly wife of Samuel Comstock, deceased, sold Roger Mowry for a valuable sum of money, a house and home share formerly belonging to John Smith, Mason, and purchased of him by Samuel Comstock, and since my husband Samuel Comstock, his decease, it was by order by a will made by the Town Council of Providence, disposed of to me. There were about four acres of land, in a row of houses in the north part of Providence.

reason of weakness of mind and insanity, and his mother Elizabeth being very aged and unable to care for him; she now therefore puts into the hands of Major William Hopkins and Mr. Joseph Williams, Assistants, and all the rest of the Justices of Providence, all lands and other estate bequeathed her; for the support and maintenance of herself and Benjamin.

SMITH (John, the Miller).

JOHN,	b. 1595.	Dorchester, Mass., Providence, R. I.
m.	d. 1648 ±	
ALICE,	b.	
	d. 1650 +	

It was declared by Roger Williams (1677, Nov. 17,) as follows: "I consented to John Smith, Miller, at Dorchester (banished also) to go with me."

1635, Sep. 3. It was ordered by the General Court of Massachusetts "that John Smith shall be sent within these six weeks out of this jurisdiction, for divers dangerous opinions which he holdeth and hath divulged, if in the meantime he removes not himself out of this plantation."

1636. Providence. He came with Roger Williams and four others in the spring or summer of this year, and made the first settlement of white persons in this territory.

1641. Town Clerk.

1646, Mar. 1. It was agreed at a monthly court meeting that he should have the valley wherein his house stands in case he set up a mill, as also excepting sufficient highways. The town agreed to permit no other mill to be erected.

1647. He had laid out to him about this time ten acres where mill now standeth, six acres of meadow at upper end of the great meadow south-west side of Mashausick River, and six acres at Wainscote. Part of the land was granted him as purchaser and part for building a mill.

1649. Articles of agreement were made between inhabitants of town of Providence on one part, and Alice Smith widow and John Smith her son, administrators on estate of John Smith, Miller, late deceased, on the other part: Whereas deceased of late in his livlihood at his own proper cost and charge with the free grant and liberty of said town, built a water mill in the said plantation upon the river commonly called Moshausick, for grinding the said inhabitants' corn, now therefore the said town and administrators agree: First: Alice and John Smith shall hold mill for their profit and benefit. Second: that the water course shall not be stopped. Third: one sixteenth (the part) to be allowed for grinding. Fourth: no other mill allowed so long as this is maintained. Fifth: the town grants them for maintaining mill that quantity of land formerly granted unto the aforesaid John Smith, viz., 150 acres, whereof 15 acres are meadow grounds, with common proportionable. Sixth: on consideration of these premises said Alice and John agree to maintain and uphold said mill serviceable and useful sufficiently and truly to grind the corn of the inhabitants according to the custom of other mills.

1650, May 6. It was ordered that Hugh Bewit shall issue the matter touching the Indians demand for corn, and to capitulate with widow Smith about

I. JOHN,	b.		Providence, R. I
m.	d. 1682.		
SARAH WHIPPLE,	b. 1642.		
	d. 1687 +	of John & Sarah ( )	Whipple.

He was a miller.

1654, Nov. 6. Ensign.

1655, Apr. 27. He bought of Hugh Bewit two shares of land.

1661, Feb. 18. He was chosen on jury.

1665, Feb. 19. He drew lot 21 in a division of lands (in his father's right).

1666–72. Deputy.

1672–73–74–75–76. Town Clerk.

1673, May 24. He had sundry lots of land confirmed to him as in the lawful right of his father.

1676, Mar. 30. His house was burned by the Indians as were many others in the town. The town records in his custody were saved by being thrown into the mill pond it is said, and from there subsequently rescued. Roger Williams in noting their return from Newport in April of the next year, says they were "saved by God's merciful Providence from fire and water."

1679, Jul. 1. Taxed 6*s.* 3*d.*

1682, Feb. 22. Will—proved 1682, Jun. 2. Exs. wife Sarah and son John. To wife, one-half the mill, and ten acres near upon the hill and valley where the house standeth, and one-half of all lands at West River and Great Meadow, also one-half his part of saw mill and meadow at Wenscott and of six acres at Neck, besides half of house, goods and cattle. The provision for wife to be for her life, and son John to have other half of above. At death of wife the meadow at Wenscott to be divided between son John and his brethren into seven parts. To daughter Sarah, forty acres. To daughter Alice, forty acres. To daughter Mary, 10*s.* To son John, sixty acres at Wenscott, the remainder of lands there being given to six brothers of John. The provision made for son John is upon condition that he be helpful to his mother to bring up his brothers and sisters, some of them being very young.

Inventory, £90, 1*s.* 9*d.*, viz: old mare, a two years and a yearling mare, a two years and a yearling horse, a two year bull, yearling bull, heifer, steer, 16 swine, corn in the mill, 2 guns, 2 spinning wheels, old bible (some leaves torn out), &c. The corn mill and house over it £40, and 1-7 part of saw mill adjoining corn mill £3, 10*s.*

1709, May 21. Whereas John Smith, Miller, now deceased, by last will dated 1682, Feb. 22, disposed of lands to sons John, Joseph, Benjamin, William and Elisha, as also to Israel and Daniel who both died not long after their father, &c.; therefore partition was now made of said lands, amongst the brothers living.

1676, Nov. 9. He was buried at this date as town records declare.
1677, Mar. 24. Administration to brother Joseph.

III. BENJAMIN, { b. / d. 1706 + } Providence R. I.
UNMARRIED.

He was insane.

IV. ELEANOR, { b. / d. 1722 (—) }
m.
ELEAZER ARNOLD, { b. 1651, Jun. 17. / d. 1722, Aug. 29. } of Thomas & Phebe (Parkhurst) Arnold.

1. Phebe, 1672, Nov. 5.
2. Elizabeth,
3. Eleazer,
4. Joseph,
5. John,
6. Jeremiah,
7. Eleanor,
8. Mary,
9. Abigail,
10. Deborah,

V. JOSEPH, { b. / d. 1735 + } Providence, Smithfield, R. I.
m.
DEBORAH WHITMAN, { b. / d. } of Valentine & Mary (   ) Whitman.

1. Joseph,
2. John,
3. Deborah,

He was a mason, and was also called joiner.

1677, Jun. 15. He sold Ralph Paine, of Newport, land in Providence for £35, calling himself administrator to estate of brother John Smith, deceased, who was heir and executor to brother Leonard Smith, deceased.

1681. Freeman.

1687. He gave in an account of the estate of "Joseph Smith and my mother."

1688. Ratable estate, 2 oxen, 2 cows, 3 three year, a mare, 1½ acres planting land, 9 acres English pasture, 1½ acres bog meadow, 44 acres in the woods.

1690, Mar. 3. He sold John Keese, of Portsmouth, 56½ acres in Providence, two miles north-west from Wanskuck Meadow, inherited by said Joseph Smith, as administrator of estate of brother John Smith, deceased, heir unto my brother Leonard Smith, deceased.

1706, Mar. 11. He deeded to the Magistrates, and to the Justices of the Peace of Providence, his interest as heir of his father John Smith, Mason, to lands which were left by will of said John Smith for support of imbecile son Benjamin, said Benjamin being now taken care of by the town. He reserved the right to move off a house from one of the lots.

1714, Apr. 19. His son Joseph sold to John Inman, land given by will of honored grandfather Valentine Whitman.

1732, Jan. 31. Smithfield. He deeded son Joseph, for love, &c., 65 acres, and also a quarter right of common in the original right of honored father John Smith, deceased. At the same date he deeded son John, for love, &c., 100 acres, and a quarter right of common.

1735, Mar. 31. His sons Joseph and John deeded John Aldrich, 20 acres in first division and 20 acres in second division, calling themselves sons of Joseph Smith, the Mason, of Smithfield, and describing the land as in the original right of our honored grandfather, John Smith, deceased.

1748, May 23. His son John had a legacy of £10, from his aunt Hannah Whitman, who calls him "John Smith, son of Joseph, called Smith, Mason."

VI. MARY, { b. / d. 1718 + }
m. 1678.
THOMAS HOPKINS, { b. / d. 1718, Apr. 21. } of Thomas Hopkins.

1. Thomas,
2. William,
3. Joseph,
4. Elizabeth,
5. Mary,
6. Rachel,
7. Zebedee, 1697, Feb. 22.
8. Elisha,
9. Ezekiel,
10. Amos,
11. Jeremiah,
12. Anne,

SMITH (JOHN, THE MILLER).

I. JOHN, { b. / d. 1737, Apr. 20. } Providence, R. I.
m.
HANNAH, { b. / d. 1756, Sep. 5. } of

1. John,
2. Mercy,
3. Sarah,
4. William,
5. Philip,
6. Prince,
7. Hannah,

He was a miller, the last of that title, his son John Smith, Fuller, dying before him (1719, May 24) and leaving but one child Martha.

1687, Sep. 1. Taxed with his mother Sarah, 11*s*.

1688. Ratable estate, 2 oxen, 4 cows, ½ a steer, 2 three year steers, a heifer, 2 yearlings, 2 horses, 2 mares, 9 sheep, 3 swine, and half the mill, lands and meadows.

1731, Aug. 6. He deeded son Philip Smith, Miller, all my homestead lot, dwelling houses, corn mill, fulling mill, &c. (except eighty foot square of homestead) also half of farm at Wenscott, &c.

1737, Mar. 15. He sold John Whipple, son of Colonel Joseph Whipple, certain land at Wenscott, for £200, that formerly belonged to my son Philip in partnership with his brother William, and was conveyed to me by my daughter-in-law Sarah Smith, widow of Philip, &c.

1724, Feb. 10. Will—codicil 1734, Aug. 2.—proved 1737, May 21. Ex. son Philip. (Guardians brother William Smith, and friend John Warner, of Warwick, till Philip is of age.) To son Philip, homestead. To son William, lands at West River, and two-thirds of farm at Wenscot. To son Prince, 100 acres west of Seven Mile Line. To three sons, rest of land. To wife, suitable maintenance and comfortable room while widow. To daughters Mercy Burlingame and Sarah Field, £5, each. To daughter Hannah Smith, £30, at eighteen or marriage. To granddaughter Martha Smith, £20, at eighteen. Wife Hannah to have care of two small children Hannah and Prince. The codicil mentions death of son Philip and makes son William executor, giving him movable estate, cattle, &c.

Inventory, £180, 7*s*. 9*d*., viz: a sow, 2 pigs, young mare, colt, bull, 3 cows, a yoke of stags, pair of worsted combs, warming pan, pewter, beds, &c.

1737, Oct 12. Will—proved 1757, Sep. 29. Widow Hannah. Exx. daughter Hannah. To daughter Hannah, best bed, iron pot, brass skillet and all pewter. To son Prince and daughter Hannah, the rest equally. (She may have been second wife to John Smith).

II. SARAH, { b. / d. 1725, Oct. 14. }
m.
RICHARD CLEMENCE, { b. / d. 1723, Oct. 11. } of Thomas & Elizabeth (   ) Clemence.

1. Sarah, 1688, Nov. 11
2. Mary, 1689, May 24.
3. Anne, 1690, Dec. 11
4. Thomas, 1693, Aug. 6.
5. Abigail, 1695, Dec. 4.
6. Richard, 1698, Jul. 19.

III. ALICE, { b. 1665. / d. 1736, Feb. 19. }
m. (1) 1788, Feb. 16.
JOHN DEXTER, { b. 1652, Nov. 6. / d. 1706, Apr. 23. } of Gregory & Abigail (Fullerton) Dexter.
m. (2) 1727, Feb. 3.
JOSEPH JENCKES, { b. 1656. / d. 1740, Jun. 15. } of Joseph & Esther (Ballard) Jenckes.

1. Stephen, 1689, Apr. 15.
2. James, 1691, Feb. 22.
3. John, 1692, Oct. 24.
4. Mary, 1694, Apr. 30.
5. Abigail, 1696, Apr. 26.
6. Sarah, 1698, Jun. 27.
7. Phebe, 1700, Aug. 4.
8. Anne, 1702, Nov. 6.
9. Alice, 1705, Oct. 14.

IV. MARY, { b. / d. 1737, Dec. 13. }
m.
ARTHUR FENNER, { b. / d. 1725, Apr. 24. } of Arthur & Mehitable (Waterman) Fenner.

1. Arthur,
2. John,
3. Edward,
4. Mary,
5. Mercy,

it, and see what she will give for her part, and what he pays to the said Indians, the town will pay it to him. The Indians require two bushels of corn and five shillings in wampumpeage, and the town agrees thereto.

1650, Sep. 2. Widow Smith taxed £2, 10*s*.

II. ELIZABETH, m. SHADRACH MANTON, { b. d. } { b. d. 1714, Jan. 27. } of Edward Manton.

STAFFORD.

THOMAS, m. ELIZABETH, { b. 1605. d. 1677. } { b. d. 1677 + } Warwickshire, Eng., Newport, R. I., [Warwick, R. I.

He was a miller.

1626. Plymouth, Mass. He is said to have been there thus early, and it is claimed built the first mill in the country for grinding corn by water.

1638, May 20. His name was in the list of inhabitants admitted to Newport after this date, and he soon received a grant of 17 acres there, being spoken of at this time as in the employ of Nicholas Easton.

1647, Mar. 18. He was a witness to will of John Walker, of Portsmouth.

1652, Jun. 7. Warwick. It was ordered by Town Council "that whereas Thomas Stafford hath bought a house of Christopher Unthank, which was formerly given to Mr. Walter Todd, by the town, and hath subscribed, the town hath likewise received him into vote, and so he is become a townsman."

1653, Mar. 1. He bought of Christopher Unthank, a house that the latter had bought of George Baldwin, and the house lot therewith, also a 6 acre lot, for satisfaction in hand received.

1655. Freeman.

1657, Apr. 16. He bought a house, &c., in Warwick, of Thomas Lawton of Portsmouth.

I. THOMAS, m (1) 1671 Dec. 28, JANE DODGE, m. (2) SARAH. { b. d. 1723, Jan. 26. } { b. d. } of Dodge. { b. d. } of Warwick, R. I.

1675. Freeman.

1719, Feb. 4. Will—proved 1723, Feb. 11. Ex. son Thomas. To wife Sarah, all movables in doors and out for life. To son William, 5*s*. To daughters Eleanor, Amey and Elizabeth, 20*s*., each. To granddaughter Mary King, 20*s*. To son Thomas, all land in Warwick or elsewhere and my mansion house after decease of his mother, he paying her annually £3, 10*s*.

Inventory, £26, 6*s*., 9*d*., viz: warming pan, 2 spinning wheels, ladle, 6 old spoons, 2 cows, calf, 10 sheep, hog, &c.

V. JOSEPH, m. 1689, Apr. 4. LYDIA GARDINER, — b. ; d. 1750, Jan. 13. — b. ; d. 1723. of George & Lydia (Ballou) Gardiner. — Providence, R. I.

1. Israel, 1690, Jan. 13.
2. Lydia, 1692, May 25.
3. Sarah, 1694, May 24.
4. Joseph, 1695, Dec. 18.
5. Robert, 1698, Mar. 3.
6. Alice, 1700, Jan. 25.
7. William, 1703, Mar. 15.
8. David, 1705, Dec. 10.
9. Jeremiah,

He was a weaver.

1700, Dec. 16. He (called Joseph Smith, Weaver, son of John Smith, Miller, deceased) had land laid out at Wanskuck.

1742, Oct. 26. Will—proved 1750, Mar. 17. Ex. son Jeremiah. To son Jeremiah, rights in land east of Seven Mile Line, (including 50 acres that my son Joseph had deed of from William Edmonds, but paid for by testator since Joseph died). To grandson Stephen, all the farm and house, &c., which was homestead of my son Israel, deceased, but his mother, my daughter-in-law, Elizabeth Smith, widow of Israel, to have use and profits of one-half of homestead, &c., while widow. To sons Robert and David, he gives nothing because they have already had their portion of lands. To daughter Alice Sayles, he had already given, therefore gives no more now. To daughter Sarah Olney, 40*s*. To son Jeremiah, rest of movables, he providing for my daughter Lydia Smith. To Jeremiah also, rest of land.

Inventory, £592, 13*s*. 9*d*., viz: money scales, wearing apparel £68, bed, 3 books £5, woolen wheel, loom, warming pan, silver £2, 5*s*., 4 pewter platters, 4 pewter porringers, 4 cows, 5 young cattle, old saddle, &c.

VI. BENJAMIN, m. (1) 1693, Apr. 12. MERCY ANGELL, m. (2) 1730, Jun. 11. [Res'd MERCY WATERMAN (w. of — b. 1672 ±; d. 1751, Apr. 23. — b. 1675; d. 1721, Sep. 3. of John & Ruth (Field) Angell. — b. ; d. 1750 (—) of — Providence, R. I.

1. John, 1694, Dec. 8.
2. Daniel, 1697, Jun. 27.
3. Mercy, 1699, Apr. 18.
4. Solomon, 1702, Mar. 4.
5. Mary, 1704, Aug. 3.
6. Hezekiah, 1706, Aug. 18.
7. Jonathan, 1708, Mar. 3.
8. Nehemiah, 1710, May 2.
9. Sarah, 1712, Apr. 26.
10. Abigail, 1714, Jun. 10.
11. Ann, 1717, Oct. 5.
12. Ruth, 1719, Apr. 9.

(2d wife.)

13. Freelove, 1733, Mar. 25.
14. William, 1736, Apr. 15

1700, Dec. 18. He had land laid out at Wanskuck meadow in the right of his father John Smith, deceased.

1724, Mar. 7. He deeded son John, for love, &c., 160 acres (bounded partly by son Solomon's land) at place called Tar Kill.

1750, Jan. 20. Will—proved 1751, May 25. Ex. son Hezekiah. To son Hezekiah, homestead at Wanskuck. To sons John, Daniel and Solomon, £5, each. To daughter Mercy Brown, £300. To daughter Mary Whipple, £200. To daughter Abigail Arnold £300. To daughters Anne and Freelove Smith, £300, each.

Inventory, £1,820, 4*s*. 6*d*., viz: wearing apparel £63, silver money £11, bonds and notes £1,458, 14*s*. 6*d*., 4 silver spoons, pewter, warming pan, cooper's tools, gun, 2 spinning wheels, 2 bibles and other old books £18, steel trap, sword, 2 bells, churn, &c.

VII. ISRAEL, — b. ; d. 1683 ±

VIII. DANIEL, — b. ; d. 1683 ±

SMITH (JOHN, THE MILLER). 3d column. IX. Elisha. His last child b. 1723 not 1733. X. William. He had also a daughter Mary, who was 1st wife of Abraham Winsor.

IX. ELISHA, m. EXPERIENCE MOWRY, — b. 1680, Apr. 14; d. 1766 +. — b. ; d. of John & Mary ( ) Mowry. — Providence, Smithfield, R. I.

1. Penelope, 1701, Dec. 5.
2. Philip, 1703, Jan. 6.
3. Noah, 1705, May 7.
4. Sarah, 1707, Apr. 28.
5. Jonathan, 1710.
6. Abraham, 1712.
7. Richard, 1714, Apr. 12.
8. Mary, 1716, Oct. 29.
9. Stephen, 1718, Oct. 28.
10. Daniel, 1733, Mar. 1.

1713, Jun. 16. Taxed 13*s*. 6*d*.

1732. Smithfield. Town Council.

1733, Jun. 29. He deeded son Philip, for love, &c., my homestead farm on which I dwell, containing 140 acres.

1735, Feb. 21. He and wife Experience sold 100 acres, dwelling house, &c., for £825, to Robert Staples, of Bellingham.

1744, Jan. 5. He (of Smithfield) and Joseph and Benjamin Smith (of Providence) joint tenants in certain land released to them by Lieut. William Smith, of Providence, Gent., being part of original right of John Smith, Sr., and John Smith, Jr.—agreed to a division of said land, &c.

1744, Apr. 18. He deeded to son Jonathan, for love, &c., 40 acres where son dwells, bounded partly by sons Noah and Daniel.

1758, May. 2. He sold to grandson Noah, 6 acres, bounded partly by son Stephen's land, for £3.

1766, Nov. 25. He deeded grandson Ezekiel, for love, &c., half of 120 acres where son Richard dwells.

X. WILLIAM, m. MARY SAYLES, — b. 1682; d. 1753, Dec. 11. — b. 1689, May 30; d. 1754 + of John & Elizabeth ( ) Sayles. — Providence, Smithfield, R. I.

1. Daniel,
2. Richard,
3. Elizabeth,
4. Sarah,
5. Abigail,

1714–16–20–21–24–27–29. Deputy. He held the title of Major many years.

1723. The "burning ague," raged in the town this year, and forty-three persons died from July to October. "All died except two, one was Major Smith that had it. Eighteen men, sixteen women, nine children."

1729–30–31. Assistant.

1731, Jun. Smithfield. It was ordered by Assembly that the balance of his account (£364, 9*s*.), for building County Court house and jail in Providence, be paid. The whole charge was £664, 9*s*.

1733–34–35–40. Moderator of Town Meeting.

1735–44. Deputy.

1753, Dec. 5. Will—proved 1754, Jan. 14. Exs. wife Mary and son Daniel. To wife, profits of half homestead and other real estate, and all personal estate (except wearing apparel) while widow. To son Daniel, the homestead except one acre for burial place, where already are buried some of my children and grandchildren. To son Richard, certain land and wearing apparel. To daughters Elizabeth Winsor and Sarah Winsor, £30 each. To daughter Abigail Smith, £100.

Inventory, £547, 6*s*., viz: wearing apparel £96, bible £3, coined silver £4, a silver spoon, coffee mill, warming pan, loom, quilting wheel, woolen wheel, linen wheel, cheese press, cow, &c.

1. Edward, 1658, Dec. 11.
2. Ann,
3. Elizabeth.

SMITH (JOHN, THE MILLER). 3d column. X. William. Children, 1. Daniel, 1712, Sep. 2. Richard. 3. Elizabeth, 1717, Jan. 5. 4. Sarah, 1725, Jun. 21. 5. Abigail, 1725, Jun. 21. 6. Mary.

STAFFORD.

I. WILLIAM, — b. ; d.

1714. Warwick. Freeman.

II. THOMAS, — b ; d.

III. ELEANOR, — b. ; d.

IV. AMEY, — b. ; d.

V. ELIZABETH, — b. ; d.

1657. He had action of trespass brought against him by James Greene and Randall Holden.

1658. The Warwick settlers were subject to more serious trespassers at this period: "Ordered that if any one kill the great gray wolf that hath done so much mischief in the town, he shall have £5, for his pains; and for any other wolf £4; and if any Indian kill a wolf within the confines of the town he shall have 40s., for his pains," &c. (The reward of £5, was paid four years later to John Sweet, for killing a wolf, the sum being settled in peage at eight per penny.)

1659, Mar. 2. He sold the estate that he had bought six years before of Christopher Unthank, to Henry Knowles, including in addition some meadow land. At the same date he sold his interest in Potawomut meadow being half a share, to Anthony Low.

1662. He was granted a lot in division of Potawomut, and also one in division of Toseunk.

1673. Deputy.

1677, Nov. 4 Will—proved 1678, Apr. 27. Executor not named. To well beloved wife Elizabeth, half of dwelling house for life, half of orchard, meadow and other land and two cows. To son Thomas, the other half of land, and at wife's death her part also, and the two cows, besides a cow which he was to have at testator's death. To wife for life, the bedding and household stuff, and at her death to go to son Thomas and daughter Deborah Westcott. To daughter Deborah Westcott, a cow. To son Samuel, a calf. To son Joseph, a calf. To Hannah Bromley, a calf.

II. { SAMUEL, m. MERCY WESTCOTT, } b. 1636. d. 1718, Mar. 20. b. d. 1700, Mar. 25. of Stukeley Westcott. Warwick, R. I.

1670-72-74-79-82-86-90-1705. Deputy.

1671, Feb. 24. He and wife Mercy sold Richard Carder certain land for £20.

1674-86. Elected Assistant, but refused to serve.

1687. Overseer of the Poor.

1700, Sep. 1. He gave 6*s*., toward building Quaker Meeting house at Mashapaug.

1711, Mar. 16. Will—proved 1718, Apr. 16. Ex. son Thomas. To eldest son Amos, all right in land south side of Potawomut River in Kings Town. To eldest daughter Sarah Scranton, 40*s*., and any debts due from her, and like legacy to daughters Patience Howland, Freelove Tillinghast and Elizabeth Devotion. To granddaughter Mary Thurber, 20*s*. To granddaughter Mary Stafford, 20*s*. To youngest son Thomas, all lands in purchase of Potawomut, and all movable estate, he paying legacies and debts.

Inventory, £101, 4*s*., 6*d*., viz: money £3, 16*s*., 6*d*., cane 14*s*., pewter, looking glass, wheel, 4 stools, 8 chairs, 2 tables, 9 head of cattle, 4 horsekind, &c.

III. { HANNAH, m. LUKE BROMLEY, } b. d. 1692 (—) b. d. 1697. of Bromley

IV. { SARAH, m. 1667, Jul. 13. AMOS WESTCOTT, } b. d. 1669. b. 1631. d. 1685. of Stukeley Westcott.

V. { JOSEPH, m. SARAH HOLDEN, } b. 1648, Mar. 21. d. 1697 + b. 1658, Feb. d. 1731. of Randall & Frances (Dungan) Holden. Warwick, R. I.

1661, Apr. 11. He was apprenticed to Thomas Smith, Tailor, of Pawtuxet, from 21st of March, last past.

1678. Freeman.

1727, Jan. 5. Will—proved 1731, Jun. 28. Widow Sarah. Ex. son Joseph. To eldest son Stukeley, 10*s*., he having had his part by will of husband. To second son Joseph, a bond of his for land she sold. To third son John, his bond for land sold. To four daughters now living and my daughter Sarah Smith's three daughters, the rest of estate; that is to say to Frances Congdon, Elizabeth Case, Mary Whitford and Margaret Place, and to Sarah, Mercy and Elizabeth Smith.

Inventory, £157, 6*s*., 8*d*., including wearing apparel, small cow and calf, bond from son Joseph for £43, 6*s*., 4*d*., bond from son John, £43, 6*s*., 8*d*., due from son Stukeley £6, 8*s*., woolen wheel, &c.

I. Stukeley, — b. 1661, Nov. 7. d. young.

II. Amos, — b. 1665, Nov. 8. d. 1760. — Warwick, R. I.
m. 1689, Dec. 19.
Mary Burlingame, — b. d. 1760. of Roger & Mary ( ) — Burlingame.

1702. He gave 6s., toward building Quaker Meeting house at Mashapaug.

1708–21. Deputy.

1753, Mar. 24. Will—proved 1760, Oct. 20. Exs. wife Mary and son Amos. To wife, half of house and lands, all household goods, 5 cows, all young cattle and sheep, half of horsekind, and negro boy called London. To son Amos, farm number nine in Coventry and land in Warwick. To daughter Mary Bennett, a farm in Coventry, &c. To daughter Mercy Arnold, lot number thirty-four in Coventry. To daughter Freelove Barton, lot number twenty-four in Warwick. To grandsons Amos and Stukeley Stafford and Stukeley Arnold, three lots in Warwick. To grandson Amos Arnold, a house lot. To grandson Thomas Stafford, son of Samuel, deceased, the rest and residue of real estate. To grandchildren Thomas Stafford, Mary Greene, Hannah Tillinghast, Patience, Mercy and Sarah Stafford, all children of son Samuel, deceased, the residue of personal estate.

Inventory, £2,547, 7s., viz: cash in silver £1, bonds £277, 15s., gun £20, warming pan, 10 silver spoons £92, woolen and linen wheels, vice, anvil and smith's tools, 13 store sheep, 3 cows, 2 yearlings, half of 7 hogs and 8 shoats, &c.

1760, Dec. 8. Inventory, £1,704, 2s. Widow Mary. The inventory was set forth by Captain Amos Stafford, of West Greenwich.

1. Mary, 1690, Sep. 16.
2. Samuel, 1692, Sep. 24.
3. Mercy, 1694, Sep. 21.
4. Amos, 1702, Apr. 24.
5. Stukeley, 1704, Nov. 7.
6. Patience, 1707, Apr. 21.
7. Freelove, 1709, Oct. 14.

III. Mercy, — b. 1668, Jul. 8. d.
m.
——— Thurber, — b. d. of — Thurber.

1. Mary,

IV. Sarah, — b. 1671, Apr. 18. d.
m.
John Scranton, — b. d. of Thomas & Mary ( ) — Scranton.

1. Stukeley,

V. Samuel, — b. 1673, Nov. 19. d. young.

VI. Patience, — b. d. 1721, Oct. 23.
m.
Jabez Howland, — b. 1669, Nov. 15. d. 1732, Oct. 7. of Jabez & Bethiah (Thatcher) — Howland.

1. Patience,
2. Bethiah, 1702, Dec. 5.
3. Mercy, 1704, Jan. 27.
4. Elizabeth, 1707, May 15.
5. Elizabeth, 1709, Jul. 17.
6. Sarah, 1711, Apr. 10.
7. Jabez, 1713, Jul. 20.
8. Patience, 1717, Mar. 23.
9. Thomas, 1719, Feb. 5.

VII. Freelove, — b. d.
m.
Joseph Tillinghast, — b. 1677, Aug. 11. d. 1763, Dec. 1. of Pardon & Lydia (Taber) — Tillinghast.

1. Joseph,
2. Freelove,
3. Anna, 1709, Jun. 25.
4. Samuel, 1711, Oct. 8.

VIII. Elizabeth, — b. d.
m.
——— Devotion, — b. d. of — Devotion.

IX. Thomas, — b. 1682. d. 1765, Nov. 18. — Warwick, Coventry, R. I.
m. (1) 1707, Dec. 25.
Anne Greene, — b. 1686, Feb. 23. d. 1718, Aug. 24. of Job & Phebe (Sayles) — Greene.
m. (2) 1719, Jul. 16.
Audry Greene, — b. 1694, Jan. 8. d. 1763, Apr. 7. of Richard & Eleanor (Sayles) — Greene.

1708. Freeman.

1720–22–25–26–28. Deputy.

1747. Coventry. Deputy. He bore the title of Captain at this time.

1. Phebe, 1710, Apr. 10.
2. Anne, 1712, Jan. 4.
3. Mercy, 1715, Mar 12.
4. Job, 1716, Apr. 11.
5. Samuel, 1717, Feb 8.
6. Deborah, 1718, Apr 9.
(2d wife.)
7. Eleanor, 1720, Apr 25.
8. Richard, 1721, Sep 24.
9. Thomas, 1723, Apr. 20.
10. Samuel, 1724, Dec. 6.
11. Almy, 1728, Apr. 19.
12. Job, 1729, Nov. 14.
13. Audry, 1731, Feb. 8.
14. John, 1735, May 5.

1. Amos, 1668.

I. Stukeley, — b. d. 1740, Jun. 4. — Warwick, R. I.
m.
Elizabeth Waterman, — b. 1692, Apr. 18. d. 1764, Jun. 14. of John & Anne (Olney) — Waterman.

1714. Freeman.

1725–26–28–29. Deputy.

1727, Jan. 24. He and Elizabeth were witnesses to will of Martha Eldred, widow of Samuel.

1740, Feb. 24. Will—proved 1740, Jun. 23. Exx. wife Elizabeth. To daughter Anne, £200. To daughters Sarah and Mercy, £200, each, at eighteen or marriage. To son Stukeley, £200, at age and all my houses and lands, reserving the best room with profit of half farm for use of wife while widow. To wife, all goods and chattels undisposed of and the negro named Keller, to serve her till son Stukeley is of age.

Inventory, £2,121, 10s., 4d., viz: wearing apparel £60, bonds and notes £964, 17s., 1d., warming pan, worsted combs, spinning wheel, 700 pounds tobacco, leather and hides in the tan, 80 sheep, 40 lambs, 17 cows, 2 riding mares, pair of oxen, parcel of young cattle, 12 swine, geese, fowls, negro man £120, &c.

1763, Apr. 14. Will—proved 1764, Jul. 2. Widow Elizabeth. Ex. son Stukeley. To son Stukeley, use of farm I bought of Captain John Crawford, till his two sons John and Stukeley, are of age. To son Stukeley, also a stock of creatures (except two cows) a feather bed and £100, he paying his sister Ann Rice 16⅔ Spanish milled dollars for ten years and my funeral expenses. To son Stukeley, she further gives negroes Keeler and Rose. To daughter Ann Rice, a silver cup, riding beast and cow, &c., for life, and then to her issue if she have any, and if not to daughter Mercy Hill. To daughter Mercy Hill, negroes Cæsar and Flora, feather bed, cow, &c. To two daughters, wearing apparel. To three children, books. She mentions her sons-in-law Nathan Rice, and Caleb Hill, cousins Phebe and Elizabeth Tibbitts and grandchildren John, Stukeley, Elizabeth, Sarah, Ann, and Edward Stafford, Stukeley, Caleb and Ann Hill.

Inventory, £11,660, 3s., 7d., viz: old negro Rose £450, Reuben £800, Tamar £700, Cæzar £800, Flora £700, 10 cows £1,200, 4 heifers, 2 calves, 12 sheep, 2 pigs, pewter, warming pan, &c.

1. Stukeley,
2. Ann,
3. Sarah,
4. Mercy,

II. Joseph, — b. d. — Warwick, R. I.
m. (1)
Susanna Gorton, — b. 1694, Jun. 4. d. 1734, Aug. 29. of Samuel & Susanna (Burton) — Gorton.
m. (2) [of Wm.
Margaret Havens, (w. — b. d. of Alexander & Elizabeth (Wightman) — Huling.

STAFFORD. 3d column. II. Joseph, d. 1770, +.

He was a blacksmith.

1730–31–32–33–35–37–39–41–42–43–44–46. Deputy.

1739. Major and later Colonel.

1. Mercy, 1717, Jun. 2.
2. Joseph, 1719, Jan. 6.
3. Susanna, 1721, Aug. 15.
4. Susanna, 1723, Mar. 10.

VI. { DEBORAH, { b. 1651.
m. 1670, Jun. 9. { d. 1706.
AMOS WESTCOTT, { b. 1631. { d. 1685. of Stukeley Westcott.

STANTON.

{ ROBERT, { b. 1599. Newport, R. I.
m. { d. 1672, Aug. 29.
AVIS, { b. { d.

1638. He and others were admitted inhabitants of island of Aquidneck, having submitted themselves to the government thereof as it shall be established.

1638, Sep. 15. He was fined 5s., for having been engaged in a riot of drunkenness on the 13th.

1639, Apr. 30. He and twenty-eight others signed the following compact: "We whose names are underwritten do acknowledge ourselves the legal subjects of his Majesty King Charles, and in his name do hereby bind ourselves into a civil body politicke, unto his laws according to matters of justice."

1640, Mar. 12. He was present at a General Court of Elections.

1641, Mar. 16. Freeman.

1642. Sergeant Junior.

1644. Sergeant.

1652, Sep. 29. He sold Benedict Arnold, dwelling house and 8 acres.

1655. Freeman.

1670. Deputy.

1671. Juryman.

1698, Jan. 30. A deed of this date from the sons of Thomas Stanton, of Stonington (probably brother of Robert[1], of Newport), is valuable as grouping part of the children of said Thomas[1], who are sometimes confounded with children of Robert.[1] The deed was made by Thomas Stanton, Sr., Joseph Stanton, Sr., Robert Stanton, Sr., and Samuel Stanton, Sr., "who are four brothers," the said Joseph living at Quonocontaug, all the rest in Stonington: they selling to Captain William Champlin, Sr., for £35, land between Quonocontaug and Pawcatuck Rivers.

Earlier than this (viz: 1682, Oct. 16), Anne Stanton, of Stonington, widow of Thomas, sold 200 acres of land for £24, to George Denison, said land having been given by will of Thomas Stanton to his son Daniel, who had empowered his mother to sell it. (Daniel was in Barbadoes, in 1682.) The Joseph Stanton mentioned in the first deed as of Quonocontaug, was doubtless the same Joseph who was constable in Westerly, 1688, and whose son Joseph, Jr., was deputy from Westerly, in 1708, &c., and who later was deputy from Charlestown (after that was set off from Westerly). This son Joseph died at Charlestown, in 1752 (inventory, £10,008, 5s., 8d.), and was a Colonel at time of his decease.

I. { SARAH, { b.
m. 1661, Dec. { d. 1708 +
HENRY TIBBITS, { b. { d. 1713. of Tibbitts.

II. { JOHN, { b. 1645, Aug. Newport, R. I.
m. (1) { d. 1713. Oct. 3.
MARY HARNDEL, { b. 1647, Jul. 6.
m. (2) [of John. { d. of John Harndel.
MARY CRANSTON, (w. { b. 1641. { d. 1711, Apr. 7. of Jeremiah & Frances (Latham) Clarke.

1666. Freeman.

1680. Taxed £1, 2s, 9d.

1694, Jun. 21. He and Joseph Gardiner, of Newport, for £10, sold Joseph Clarke, of Westerly, 200 acres in Narraganset, being part of a neck of land formerly owned in partnership of Robert Stanton, father of said John, and George Gardiner, father of said Joseph.

1696. Deputy.

Possibly his last child was by his second wife.

STANTON. 2d column. II. John. His son Henry was by his 2d wife. 1708, Nov. 1. Will-proved, 1711, Jun. 10. Mary Stanton. She mentions children, Samuel, John and Benjamin Cranston, Elizabeth Brown and Henry Stanton, and certain grandchildren. 3d column. 1. Mary, d. 1747, May 11. She m. John Coggeshall, b. 1659, Dec., d. 1737, May 1, of Joshua and Joan (West) Coggeshall. Children. 1. John. 2. Caleb. 3. Joshua. 4. Joseph. 5. Mary. 6. Hannah. 7. Mercy. 8. Daughter. 9. Avis. 10. Humility. II. Hannah, d. 1752.

See: American Genealogist, Apr., 1954, v. 30, no. 2, p. 124-125.

STANTON. 3d column. John, d. 1763, Jan. 23, at Richmond, R. I. He m. (2) Susanna Lanphere, of Theodosius & Rachel (Covey) Lanphere. She b. 1716, Dec. 14, d. 1807, Sep. 25. She m. (3) Peter Boss. John Stanton, had by 2d wife, 13. Robert, 1735, Aug. 18. 14. Job, 1737, Feb. 15. 15. Susannah, 1738, Aug. 17. 16. Benjamin, 1740, Jul. 4. 17. Hannah, 1743, Mar. 28. 18. Elizabeth, 1743, Jan. 2. 19. Samuel, 1745, Dec. 3. 20. John, 1748, May 4. 21. Mercy, 1750, Jan. 11. 22. Sebra, 1752, Dec. 4. 23. Mary, 1754, Nov. 23. 24. Joseph, 1757, Mar. 26. 25. Hannah, 1759. The first three children were born in Westerly, the next five in Charlestown, and the last five in Richmond. 1733. He purchased a large tract in Westerly and moved thence from Newport. Erase the sentence beginning "By one account, &c."

III. JOHN, m. ELIZABETH, — b. / d. 1753. / b. / d. 1755 + — of — Warwick, R. I.

He was called Captain at the time of his death.

1753, Dec. 14. Inventory, £2,833, 15*s*., 8*d*., also additional inventory (1755, Apr. 12), £954, 5*s*., both shown by widow Elizabeth. Bonds and notes £480, 16*s*., 8*d*., gun, pistol, negro boy and girl £600, horse, pair of oxen, 4 cows, calf, hog, 16 barrels of cider, sea instruments, sea chest, books, fountain pen, ⅛ of brig £187, 10*s*., molasses came in the brig £636, &c.

IV. FRANCES, m. 1701, Dec. 1. BENJAMIN CONGDON, — b. / d. / b. / d. 1756. — of Benjamin & Elizabeth (Albro) — Congdon.

1. Benjamin, 2. Joseph, 3. William, 4. James, 5. John, 6. Frances, 7. Mary, 8. Elizabeth.

V. ELIZABETH, m. (1) WILLIAM CASE, m. (2) 1730, Jun. 27. ISRAEL ARNOLD, — b. / d. 1756, Aug. 21. / b. 1681, May 27. / d. 1728. — of Joseph & Hannah (Smith) — Case. / b. 1678, Jan. 18. / d. 1753. — of Israel & Mary (Barker) — Arnold.

1. William, 1705, Sep. 8.
2. Elizabeth, 1706, Dec. 7.
3. Edward, 1708, Feb. 17.
4. Hannah, 1713, Nov. 6.
5. Sarah, 1716, May 3.
6. Mary, 1718, Jan. 5.
7. Margaret, 1721, Dec. 19.
(By 2d husband.)
8. Bathsheba, 1732, Oct. 2.

VI. MARY, m. PASCO WHITFORD, — b. / d. / b. / d. — of Pasco — Whitford.

1. Pasco, 2. Joseph, 3. John, 4. Ezekiel, 5. Nicholas,

III. John, d. 1767. Erase name and date of his wife, and all the text concerning him. He m., 1st, Marbury Place, b. 169–, May 5, of Thomas and Hannah (Cole) Place. He m., 2d, 1726, Jul. 22, Jerusha Westgate (wid. of Silvanus), b. 1690, Jan. 17, of Robert Davis. Children, 1. John, 1727. 2. Jerusha, 1728, Aug. 24. 3. Anne, 1731, May 8. 4. Amey. IV. Frances. Children, 1. Benjamin, 1702, Oct. 20. 2 Frances, 1703, Dec. 6. 3. Joseph, 1705, Feb. 15. 4. John, 1706, Sep. 23. 5. Sarah, 1708, Jun. 26. 6. William, 1711, Nov. 6. 7. James, 1713, May 15. 8. Elizabeth, 1715, Apr. 8. 9. Mary, 1718, Mar. 10. 10. Susannah, 1720 Feb. 7. 11. Stukeley, 1722, Dec. 11. VIII. Margaret, m. 1730, Mar. 16, Thomas Place, b. 1697, Nov. 2, of Thomas and Hannah (Cole) Place.

VII. SARAH, m. JOSEPH SMITH, — b. / d. / b. / d. — of Benjamin & Lydia (Carpenter — Smith.

1. Sarah, 2. Mercy, 3. Elizabeth,

VIII. MARGARET, m. —— PLACE, — b. / d. / b. / d. — of — Place.

1. Solomon, 2. Sarah, 1673. 3. Penelope, 4. Mercy, 5. Luranah.

STANTON.

1. Henry, 2. Ann, 3. George, 4. John, 5. Mary, 6. Sarah, 7. Martha, 8. Daughter,

I. MARY * — b. 1668, Jun. 4. / d.

II. HANNAH, m. 1686, Oct. 6. EDWARD CARR, — b. 1670, Nov. 7. / d. 1712 + / b. 1667. / d. 1711 Oct. 14. — of Caleb & Mercy ( ) — Carr.

1. Edward, 1689, Sep. 14
2. Hannah, 1691, Oct. 13.
3. Mary, 1693, Oct. 26.
4. Mercy, 1696, Feb. 24.
5. Avis, 1698, May 29.
6. Patience, 1701, Feb. 14.
7. James, 1703, Oct. 21.
8. Phebe, 1706 Sep. 6
9. Sarah, 1708, Dec. 28.

III. PATIENCE, — b. 1672, Sep. 10. / d.

IV. JOHN, m. 1698, Feb. 9. ELIZABETH CLARKE, — b. 1674, Apr. 22. / d. / b. 1680. / d. 1730, Sep. 10. — of Latham & Hannah (Wilbur) — Newport, R. I. — Clarke.

1696. Freeman.

1699, Jun. 20. He deeded his brother Robert all interest in 10 acres in Newport, bequeathed by my grandfather John Harndell to my brother Robert.

By one account he is given a second wife, viz: Susanna Lanphere, to whom it is claimed he was married in 1734 (she being nineteen), and he is given thirteen more children by this wife, the last born in 1759, when the father would have been eighty-five years old.

1. Hannah, 1698, Dec. 4.
2. John, 1700, Sep. 21.
3. Robert, 1702, Feb. 27.
4. Mary, 1703, Dec. 12.
5. Joseph, 1705, Dec. 12.
6. Samuel, 1708, Mar. 25.
7. Daniel, 1710, May 5.
8. Latham, 1712, Aug. 12.
9. Elizabeth, 1714, Sep. 18.
10. Joseph, 1717, Jun. 6.
11. Jonathan, 1719, May 5.
12. David, 1721, Dec. 23

V. CONTENT, — b. 1675, Dec. 20. / d.

VI. ROBERT, m. PENELOPE, — b. 1677, May 4. / d. 1712, Feb. 18. / b. / d. 1712 + — of — Newport, R. I.

No issue.

He was a mariner.

1711, Dec. 11. Will—proved 1712, Mar. 10. Exx. wife Penelope. To nephew Benjamin Norton and niece Elizabeth Norton, 50*s*., apiece. To Church of England in this town, £5. To beloved wife Penelope, all the rest of estate.

VII. BENJAMIN, m. MARTHA TIBBITS, — b. 1684, Mar. 13. / d. 1760, Sep. 18. / b. / d. 1752, Jul. 11. — of Henry & Sarah (Stanton) — Newport, R. I. — Tibbits.

1. Benjamin, 2. Avis, 3. Martha, 1713. 4. Sarah,

He was a physician.

1708. Freeman.

1712, May 7. He and wife Martha sold Jeremiah Weeden, for £50, a parcel of land.

* See: American Genealogist. v. 25, p. 251-252.

III. Daniel, m. Elizabeth, — b. 1648. d. 1690 ±. b. d. 1690 + of — Newport, R. I.

1679, Feb. 15. He sold James Brown, cooper, of Newport, land in Coeset, for 40*s*.

1680. Taxed 12*s*.

1688. Grand Jury.

STRANGE (John).

John, m. Alice, — b. d. 1687 +. b. d. 1687 + — Portsmouth, R. I.

He was a hatter.

1669, Aug. 31. He bought 20 acres in Portsmouth, of Joseph Parker, of Shrewsbury, N. J., for £34.

1677, Oct. 31. He and forty-seven others were granted 5,000 acres to be called East Greenwich. He never went there to settle.

1680. Taxed 8*s*., 3*d*.

1681, Oct. 21. He bought of Increase Robinson and Sarah, for £13, a parcel of land down Taunton River, 60 acres, &c., possession being given of said land "both of turf and twig."

1683, Oct. 27. He, brother of Lot Strange, who died leaving no child to inherit his land and houses, and being his only brother and so next of blood, for divers considerations and sum of money paid by sister-in-law Alice Strange, widow of Lot, confirms to her all said lands and houses, &c., and Alice Strange, wife of John, joins in deed to Alice Strange, widow of Lot and sister-in-law of John Strange.

1684, Dec. 15. He deeded son Lot Strange, for love, &c., land bought of Increase Robinson.

1687, Oct. 15. He "John Strange, Sen.," for sufficient maintenance of me and his beloved mother, in meat and drink during our natural lives, "fit for such ancient people as we are to have, and he is able to give"—freely and absolutely confirms to son John, 20 acres, with now dwelling house and all movables.

I. John, — b. d.

II. Lot, m. Mary Sherman, — b. d. 1699. b. 1664, Dec. 11. d. 1699 + of Peleg & Elizabeth (Lawton) Sherman. — Portsmouth, R. I.

1698, Nov. 16. Will—proved 1699, Jun. 12. Exx. wife Mary. Overseers, brother-in-law Thomas Sherman and neighbor James Tallman. To wife, land in Providence. To son John, land in Taunton, deeded by Increase Robinson. To son James, 20*s*. at age. To three daughters Comfort, Grozigon and Alice Strange, each 5*s*., at 18 or marriage. To the child wife is now with, 1*s*. To wife Mary, all the rest of estate.

III. Grizzel, m. 1668, Dec. 10. Thomas Fish, — b. d. b. d. 1684. of Thomas & Mary (   ) Fish.

VIII. HENRY, m. 1707, May 22. MARY HULL, — b. 1688, May 22. d. — b. 1685, Sep. d. — of John & Alice (Teddeman) Hull. — Newport, R. I.

1. Mary, 1708, May 30.
2. Alice, 1709, Oct. 17.
3. Mary, 1712, May 6.
4. Katharine, 1713, Oct. 28.
5. Hannah, 1716, Sep. 25.
6. Henry, 1719, May 22.
7. Joseph, 1724, Mar. 30.

1710. Freeman.

He is said to have gone to Beaufort in Carteret County, North Carolina, and to have had another son named John, after whose birth his wife died, and he married for a second wife Lydia Allison. The children ascribed to this second wife are Benjamin, Sarah, Avis and John.

I. ELIZABETH, — b. 1676, Jun. 20. d.

II. MARTHA, — b. 1678, Jun. 3. d.

III. SARAH, — b. 1680, Feb. 27. d.

IV. DANIEL, m. 1707 ± ABIGAIL SPICER, — b. 1682, Apr. 19. d. 1708. — b. d. 1714. — of Spicer. — Newport, R. I.

1 Daniel, 1708.

He was a mariner, and made voyages for some years between Barbadoes and Philadelphia, and he died at sea on his way from Barbadoes to that city. His child was born after his death and after the mother (who had accompanied her husband from Barbadoes) had arrived in Philadelphia.

1714, May 10. Will—proved 1714, May 31. Widow Abigail, of Philadelphia. To son Daniel she gave her estate, but if he died before twenty-one her brother Thomas Spicer was to have it. The son's death did not occur till 1770, Jun. 29. He was a distinguished Quaker preacher.

V. RUTH. — b. 1687, Apr. 8. d.

VI. BENJAMIN, — b. d. 1690, Oct. 20.

STRANGE (John).

1. Alice, 1671, Sep. 15.
2. Grizzel, 1673, Apr. 12.
3. Hope, 1676, Mar. 5.
4. Preserved, 1679, Aug. 12.
5. Mehitable, 1684, Jul. 22.

I. JOHN, — b. d.

II. COMFORT, — b. 1689, Jun. 4. d.

III. GRIZZEL, — b. d.

IV. ALICE, — b. 1694, Oct. 15. d.

V. JAMES, m. 1718, Mar. 26. SARAH CORY, — b. 1696, Sep. 18. d. 1745, Oct. 21. — b. d. 1745 + — of Cory. — Portsmouth, R. I.

1. John, 1718, Dec. 30.
2. Mary, 1720, Dec. 3.
3. Caleb, 1723, Feb. 1.
4. Sarah, 1725, Mar. 29.
5. Alice, 1727, Feb. 8.
6. James, 1728, Feb. 8.
7. Ruth, 1731, Nov. 2.
8. Lot, 1733, Feb. 7.
9. Elizabeth, 1736, May 4.
10. Benjamin, 1740, Apr. 27.

1717. Freeman.

He died in his Majesty's service at Cape Breton.

1746, Apr. 14. Inventory, £28, 15s., basket hilted rapier, &c. Administration was given to widow Sarah.

VI. LOT, m. HANNAH, — b. 1699, Mar. 4. d. — b. 1701, Feb. 24. d. — of — Freetown Mass

1. Lot, 1720, May 10.
2. Phillip, 1722, Oct. 4
3. John, 1724, Feb. 25
4. Mary, 1725, Nov. 14.
5. Abigail, 1727, Sep. 24.
6. Jacob, 1729, Jan. 3.
7. Joseph, 1729, Jan. 3.
8. Meletiah, 1732, Sep. 24.
9. Sylvanus, 1734, Aug. 10.

JOHN, { b. Portsmouth, Kings Town, R. I.
m. { d. 1676.
MARY, { b.
{ d. 1679 +

1648. William Tefft of Boston died this year, and in his will (1646, May 1) gave to eldest child of my brother Tefft, least steer calf. Perhaps William Tefft was a brother of John.

1655. Freeman.

1662, Nov. 22. He and wife Mary sold 7 acres to Robert Shink of Newport.

1671, May. Kings Town. His name was recorded as an inhabitant of Pettaquamscott.

1674, Nov. 30. Will—Ex. son-in-law Samuel Wilson. To son-in-law Samuel Wilson, my now dwelling house and 20 acres in Pettaquamscott. To wife Mary, all cattle, viz: two oxen, two cows, two yearling steers, eight swine kind, a ewe and a lamb, and all other movables. To son Samuel Tift, 2*s.* To son Joshua, 1*s.* To daughter Tabitha Tift, 1*s.*, and an iron pot after wife's decease. Debts to the sum of £1, 3*s.*, to be paid equally by son-in-law Samuel Wilson, and son Joshua Tift.

1676, Jan. 26. His death is alluded to in a letter from Captain James Oliver (written at the house of Richard Smith in Narragansett). He first mentions that Joshua Tefft had married a Wamponag, that he shot twenty times at the English in the Narragansett fight, was captured and executed at Providence; and then declares he was "a sad wretch, he never heard a sermon but once these fourteen years. His father, going to recall him, lost his head and lies unburied."

1679, Nov. 19. His widow signed in satisfaction of her thirds, her signature being witnessed by Tabitha Gardiner.

TEFFT. 1st column. In fifth line change Shink to Spink.

I. —————, { b.
m. { d.
SAMUEL WILSON. { b. 1622.
{ d. 1682 ± of Wilson.

II. SAMUEL, { b. 1644. Providence, South Kingstown, R. I.
m. { d. 1725.
ELIZABETH JENCKES, { b. 1658.
{ d. 1740. of Joseph & Esther (Ballard) Jenckes.

1677. Freeman.

1679, May 12. He was fined 20*s.*, for not attending jury.

1679, Jul. 1. Taxed 3*s.*, 1½*d.*

1680, Mar. 12. His fine of 20*s.*, for not attending Jury of General Court of Trials, was remitted by the Assembly, he having had no warning by the General Sergeant.

1687, Sep. 6. Kings Town. Taxed 9*s.*, 4½*d.*

1709, Jun. 28. He and twenty-six others bought the tract called Swamptown, being part of the vacant lands in Narragansett, ordered sold by the Assembly.

1721, Mar. 20. In a deposition at this date he calls his age about seventy-seven years.

1722, Oct. 29. His wife Elizabeth, in testifying as to what age James Wilson would have been had he lived, calls her own age seventy years, but other evidence makes her not quite so old.

1725, Mar. 16. Will—proved 1725, Dec. 20. Exx. wife Elizabeth. To son John, 100 acres in South Kingstown. To son Samuel, south half of homestead. To sons John and Samuel, 135 acres in Westerly. To son Joseph, land in Shannock Purchase, Westerly. To wife Elizabeth, dwelling house, barn, orchards, &c., and north half of homestead, for life, and then to sons John and Samuel equally, and these two sons to be at equal charge in maintaining daughter Tabitha Tift, supporting her for life. To daughters Elizabeth Carpenter, Esther Mumford and Mary Newton, each £20, paid by son John. To daughters Mercy Tift and Susanna Crandall, £20 each. To children of Sarah Witter, deceased, £20. To daughter Mercy Teft a further sum of £30. To granddaughter Sarah Witter, £10 at eighteen. To grandson Daniel Tift, son of Peter, deceased, £20, if he lives in my family till of age. To wife Elizabeth, all movables not given away, at her disposal to children.

Inventory, £1,010, 2*s.*, 8*d.*, viz: wearing apparel £27, 19*s.*, sword, 11 cows, 4 oxen, 2 pairs of steers, 4 yearlings, 5 calves, 121 sheep, 5 mares, 3 horses, 15 swine, hay £40, pewter, 2 linen wheels, 2 spinning wheels, pair of worsted combs, 6 beds, 2 warming pans, pair of wool cards, carpenter's tools, bonds £155, &c., silver £5, 12*s.*, cider £12, cider mill, 22 geese, &c.

1738, Jul. 4. Will—proved 1740, May 12. Widow Elizabeth. Ex. son John. To son John, 20*s.* To son Samuel, 20*s.* To granddaughter Sarah Witter, £5. To daughters Elizabeth Carpenter, Mary Newton, Esther Mumford, Tabitha Teft, Susanna Crandall, and children of daughter Sarah Witter, deceased, rest of estate.

Inventory, £401, 12*s.*

III. JOSHUA, { b. Kings Town, R. I.
m. { d. 1676, Jan. 18.
SARAH, { b.
{ d. of

1672, Mar. 14. The birth of his son Peter was recorded at Warwick.

1676, Jan. 14. He was brought in captive to Providence as related in a letter of same date written by Roger Williams to Governor Leveret of Massachusetts: "This night I was requested by Captain Fenner and other officers of our town, to take the examination and confession of an Englishman who hath been with the Indians before and since the fight; his name is Joshua Tift, and he was taken by Captain Fenner this day at an Indian house, half a mile from where Captain Fenner's house (now burned) did stand." He was asked how long he had been with the Narragansetts, and answered twenty-seven days more or less. In answer to the question how he came amongst them, he said he was at his farm a mile and a-half from Puttuckquamscot where he hired an Indian to keep his cattle, himself proposing to go to Rhode Island, but the day he prepared to go a party of Indians came and told him he must die. He begged for his life and promised he would be servant to the Sachem for life, and his life was given him as such slave. He was carried to the fort where were eight hundred fighting men. His eight cattle were killed. He said he was in the fort and waited on his master the Sachem till he was wounded, of which wound the Sachem died nine days afterward.

1676, Jan. 18. He was executed, his answers obviously not being satisfactory to the examiners, but it may still be doubted whether much that is related of him by the old chroniclers is more than fable. It was asserted by these that he was of Providence, which was not the fact, though he was captured there, and that he turned Indian and married a squaw, renounced his religion and nation, and fought against the whites. Probably the closing sentence of one of these narrators was considered excellent religion by some of his readers. "As to his religion he was found as ignorant as a heathen, which no doubt caused the fewer tears to be shed at his funeral."

IV. TABITHA, { b. 1653.
m. { d. 1722 +
GEORGE GARDINER, { b.
{ d. 1724. of George & Herodias (Long) Gardiner.

1. Samuel,
2. Mary, 1663.
3. Sarah, 1666.
4. James, 1673.
5. Jeremiah, 1674.

South Kingstown, R. I.

I. JOHN, b. d. 1762.
m.
JOANNA SPRAGUE, b. d. 1757. of Jonathan & Mehitable (Holbrook) Sprague.

1709, Jun. 28. He was one of those engaged in Shannock Purchase.

1754, Jan. 5. Will—Codicil, 1757, Dec. 22—proved 1762, Jan. 21. Exs. wife Joanna and son Joseph. To wife, £500. To son John, 120 acres "near about north from place where the old house stood that did belong to my honored father Samuel Teft, deceased," having already given to John a tract in Richmond and house on said land. To son Joseph, £300, and a shot gun, having already given him a house and land in Richmond. To son Samuel, a gun, having given him already two tracts of land in Richmond. To sons James and Nathan 5*s.*, each. To six grandchildren, viz: George Webb, John Webb, Margaret Rogers, Elizabeth Sheblin, Mehitable James and Mary Teft, £150 divided among them. To five daughters Mary Barber, Mercy Rogers, Mehitable Rogers, Tabitha Teft and Sarah Brown, £750 equally divided. The rest of estate to children, the six grandchildren having an equal part with them. Codicil mentions decease of wife, and the £500 given her he now gives to five daughters. To granddaughters Margaret Rogers, Elizabeth Shilbe, Mehitable James and Mary Teft, £5 each.

Inventory, £6,148, 16*s.*, 7*d.*, viz: wearing apparel £55, bonds £3,137, 9*s.*, 7*d.*, coffee mill, warming pan, 19 sheep, gun, horse, 2 cows, swine, 2 pair of cards, &c.

1. John, 1699, Dec. 4.
2. Joseph,
3. Samuel,
4. James, 1715, Apr. 21.
5. Nathan,
6. Daughter,
7. Mary,
8. Mercy,
9. Mehitable,
10. Tabitha,
11. Sarah,

South Kingstown, R. I.

II. SAMUEL, b. d. 1760.
m.
ABIGAIL TENNANT, b. 169– d. 1758 + of Alexander Tennant.

1758, Feb. 20. Will—proved 1760, Jul. 14. Ex. son Daniel. To wife Abigail half of indoor movables, a cow, bay mare, use of best room, &c., while widow. To son Samuel, £10, he having had. To son Stephen, £30. To son Tennant, £30. To son Ebenezer, certain land. To son Daniel, all the rest both real and personal, and the apprentice boy's time.

1. Samuel, 1712, Jan. 19.
2. Daniel, 1714, Jun. 14.
3. Stephen, 1718, Oct. 5.
4. Tennant, 1720, Sep. 26.
5. Ebenezer, 1724, Feb. 14.

Westerly, R. I., Stonington, Ct.

III. PETER, b. d. 1725 (—)
m.
MARY, b. d. of

The births of six of his children were recorded at Westerly.

1718. Stonington. His seventh child's birth was recorded here.

1. Peter, 1699, Dec. 19.
2. Samuel, 1705, Feb. 24
3. John, 1706, Dec. 27.
4. Joseph, 1710, Jan. 8.
5. Daniel, 1712, Apr. 10.
6. Sarah, 1715 Feb. 14.
7. Jonathan, 1718, Oct. 18.

TEFFT. 3d column. IV. Sarah m. John Witter, b. 1677, Mar. 11, of Josiah and Sarah (Crandall) Witter. Children, 1, Sarah. 2, John. 3, Joseph. 4, Martha.

IV. SARAH, b. d.
m.
EBENEZER WITTER, b. 1668, Mar. 25. d. of Josiah & Elizabeth (Wheeler) Witter.

1. Sarah,
2. Mary, 1696.
3. Josiah, 1698.
4. Joseph, 1698.

V. ELIZABETH, b. d. 1750 (—)
m.
SOLOMON CARPENTER, b. 1678, d. 1750. of Abiah Carpenter.

1. Elizabeth, 1703, Jan. 4.
2. Solomon, 17—, Feb. 26.
3. Daniel, 1712, Dec. 28.
4. Sarah, 1716, Aug. 24.

VI. ESTHER, b. d. 1726 +
m. 1708, Nov. 25,
THOMAS MUMFORD, b. 1656, d. 1726, Apr. of Thomas & Sarah (Sherman) Mumford.

1. John,
2. Sarah,
3. Tabitha,
4. Esther,

VII. MARY, b. d.
m.
——— NEWTON. b. d. of Newton.

VIII. TABITHA, b. d.
UNMARRIED.

IX. MERCY, b. d.
UNMARRIED.

X. SUSANNA, b d.
m.
PETER CRANDALL, b. d. of John & Elizabeth (Gorton) Crandall.

1. James, 1709, Apr. 17.
2. Mary, 1711, Feb. 17.
3. Peter, 1713, Jul. 4.
4. John, 1716, Jun. 18.
5. Elizabeth, 1719, Feb. 1.

I. PETER, b. 1672, Mar. 14. d.

1. Joseph,
2. Nicholas,
3. Samuel,
4. Robert,
5. John,
6. George,
7 Hannah,
8. Tabitha,
9. Joanna.

RICHARD[2], (Henry[1]). { b. } Maidford, Northampton Co., Eng., [Newport, R. I.
m. { d. 1673 ±
MARY CLARKE, { b. { d. 1687 +

of William Clarke.

1633, Oct. 18. The following instrument was placed upon record in Rhode Island at a date later than the instrument itself. "This Indenture made the 18th day of October, in the 9th year of the reign of our Sovereign Lord Charles, of England and Ireland, King, Defender of the Faith, &c. Between Henry Tew, of Maidford, &c., yeoman, and William Clarke, of Prior Hardwick, &c., yeoman, witnesseth: That for and in consideration of a marriage by the grace of God shortly to be had and solemnized between Richard Tew son and heir apparent of said Henry, and Mary Clarke one of the daughters of said William Clarke, and for the sum of £20, of lawful money of England, by bond secured to be paid by said William Clarke, unto the said Henry Tew, upon last day of May next, and for the sum of £120, by bond secured to be paid by him the said William Clarke to him the said Richard Tew, upon 29th day of September, 1640, and for divers other good causes," &c. Then follows an engagement entered into by Henry Tew to make over on his part to his son Richard, houses, barns, tenements, hereditaments, fields, &c.

1640. He came to New England this year, his daughter Seaborn receiving her name because born on the ocean. In subsequent years he became a Quaker, and had recorded upon the French Records his children's births.

1642. Newport. He bought 59½ acres of John Anthony, of Portsmouth.

1643. He bought 30 acres of John Layton, bounded within the situate land of John Peckham, on north side of Maidford River.

1653. He was on a committee for ripening matters that concern Long Island and in the case concerning the Dutch. He was called at this time of Portsmouth, but he abode there only a short time.

1654-56-57-58-60-63. Commissioner.

1655. Freeman.

1657. He bought 40 acres of Thomas Wood.

1657-62-63-66-67. Assistant.

1659, Jun. 19. He bought of John Fones, servant to William Coddington, 3-900 part of Conanicut, for a good ewe and six ewe lambs, or a mare colt.

1661. He was on a committee to receive contributions for the agents in England (Roger Williams and John Clarke).

1663. He is named in the Royal charter granted Rhode Island by Charles II. The same year he was on a committee for setting bounds between Portsmouth and Newport.

1663-64-65. Deputy.

1664, Mar. 11. He bought of Thomas Painter his now dwelling house with half acre land originally granted by town to Edward Andrews, bounded westerly by Maidford River, together with a marsh near Sachuest River—for a "certain sum."

1667. He was on a committee appointed in the matter of Prison and Pound.

1671. He was nominated with twenty-seven others as persons from whom a Special Court should appoint a jury in case of two Indians, who were imprisoned on a criminal charge.

A tradition of the family relates that he died in London, where he had gone to look after some property.

1687. His widow Mary signed as a witness in settlement of estate of John Peabody, Sr., of Newport.

TEW. 1st column. 1673, Jan. 19. Will-proved 1674, Mar. 27. Ex. son Henry Tew of Newport, and brother John Tew. Overseers Edward Wharton of Salem, and Joseph Nicholson of Rhode Island. He calls himself of Newport, in Rhode Island, in New England, yeoman, and now of St. Leonards, Shoreditch, Middlesex. "Being desirous to settle my affairs and concerns which I have in Old England, my native country, according as I have already done in New England." To brother John Tew of Towcester, County of Northampton, doctor of physick, 20s. to buy him a ring to wear for my sake. Rest of goods in Old England to son Henry, of Newport in Rhode Island, yeoman. 2d column. II. Elnathan d. 1718, Jan. 11. 3d column. XVIII. Paul d. 1784, Aug. 3, Woodstock, Ct.; m. (2) 1770, Sep. 27, Mary Child. Children, 1, Paraclete. 2, Zerviah, 1773. 1776, and previously Sheriff of Providence county, 1777±, Woodstock, Ct. His gravestone in Woodstock Cemetery says: "In memory of Capt. Paul Tew, who departed this life Aug. 3, 1784, in ye 69th year of his age. This is the place where I repose my head, and here to rest till Christ shall raise the dead." Also a grave to Zerviah Tew, d. 1779, Jan. 16, aged 6 years and month.

TEW. 1st column. Under date of 1640 French Records should be changed to Friends' Records.

I. SEABORN, { b. 1640, Jun. 4. { d.
m. (1) 1658, Jan. 5.
SAMUEL BILLINGS, { b. { d. of Billings.
m. (2)
OWEN HIGGINS, { b. { d. of Higgins.

II. ELNATHAN, { b. 1644, Oct. 15. { d. 1711 +
m. 1664, Nov. 3.
THOMAS HARRIS, { b. { d. 1711, Feb. 27. of Thomas & Elizabeth ( ) Harris.

III. MARY, { b. 1647, Aug. 12. { d. 1688 +
m. 1670, Dec. 8.
ANDREW HARRIS, { b. 1635. { d. 1686, May 1. of William & Susannah ( ) Harris.

IV. HENRY, { b. 1654. { d. 1718, Apr. 26. Newport, R. I.
m. (1)
DORCAS, { b. { d. 1694 ± of
m. (2)
SARAH, Paul { b. 1668, July 5 { d. 1718 + of see p. 16 The ancestry of Katharine Choate Paul " Milwaukee

1674, Nov. 15. He had bounds of two lots recorded that his father, late deceased, had bought of John Anthony and John Layton. The two lots contained 89 acres and included dwelling house, barn, orchard, &c.

1680-98. Deputy.

1698. He was on a committee to inspect into our body of laws, &c. He now had the title of Captain.

1699. He was chosen Agent to go to England, but declined. He signed a letter this year with others, concerning matters of controversy between Connecticut and Rhode Island.

1699-1700-1-4-6. Major for the Island.

1702, Feb. 4. He was on a committee of fourteen persons appointed to attend to matter of proprietors' lands and continued to serve many years.

1702, Mar. 17. He and son Henry sold Edward Smith 44½ acres, part of Sachuest farm, &c., in exchange for 36 acres and £40, silver money of New England paid by said Smith.

1702, Nov. 4. He had permission to hang a gate athwart the way from his land near Sachuest Beach. The gate was to hang seven years or "till judged prejudicial to the neighbors."

1703-4-5-8-9-10-11-12. Assistant.

1706. He was on committee to superintend work at the fort on Goat Island.

1707. He was with others given power to impress a vessel into commission "to beat up for volunteers."

1708. He was on a committee that met at Captain John Eldred's house in Kings Town to act in regard to the vacant lands in Narragansett.

1709. He was on a special committee for advising Governor Cranston concerning the expedition against Canada.

1714. Deputy Governor, taking the place of Walter Clarke, deceased. He was now Lieutenant Colonel.

1717, Jun. 18. He deeded son Henry, for love, &c, certain land in Newport with mansion house, barns, orchards, garden, &c., and sundry other parcels, reserving six rods where mother and wife of grantor were buried, to be laid out twelve rods wide and three in length for use as a burial place forever.

He also deeds one hundred sheep, two oxen, six cows, five young cattle and a mare, already in son's possession. (The son agreed to keep one hundred sheep for his father for life and to make certain payments to his five sisters.)

He and both of his wives were buried in the family burial ground, half a mile north of Sachuest Beach.

1718, Apr. 20. Will—proved 1718, May 18. Exs. wife Sarah and son Edward. Overseers, Captain William Weeden, of Newport, and William Sanford, of Portsmouth. To son Henry, a great bible besides what he had already invested him with by instrument dated 1717, Jun. 18. To son Richard, all lands in Jamestown, he paying to his five sisters £20, each, viz: to Mary Peckham, Elizabeth Smith, Sarah Sweet and Abigail and Elnathan Tew. To son John Tew, all housing and lands in township of Dighton, but if he die without issue then son Paul to have at age, on condition that he pay his three brothers George, Thomas and James Tew, £200, equally divided. If both John and Paul die without issue then the same to be divided "amongst all my youngest sons of the whole blood," viz: Edward, George, Thomas and James Tew. To sons George and Thomas, certain housing and land. To daughters Mary Peckham, Elizabeth Smith, Sarah Sweet, Abigail and Elnathan Tew, £40, each, to be paid by son Henry according to the instrument of Jun. 18th. To son James Tew, a shop and dwelling house in Newport, and a right in the town wharf. To son Paul, a lot and housing in Newport and my other right in town wharf. Having already given to son William Tew "I omit to give my bequest to his children." To daughter Mary Peckham, £60. To daughter Elizabeth Smith, £70, and a silver cup. To daughter Sarah Sweet, £50. To daughters Abigail and Elnathan Tew, £6, each, feather bed, &c. To wife Sarah, great bible and concordance, and all the rest of the books to be divided equally, to children. To son Edward, my now dwelling house, mill, &c., and all lands in Newport not included in above written articles. To wife Sarah and son Edward, the income of housing and lands in Newport bequeathed to younger children during minority, also profits of dwelling house, mill, &c., and movable estate, they bringing up children, &c. When children are of age wife to have two-thirds of all household goods and a third of cattle, horse, sheep, swine, and one-third of negroes. To son Edward, the remaining third of household goods and two-thirds of negroes, with housing, mill, lands, &c. In codicil of same date he provides that wife shall have half profits of will during widowhood, and if Edward dies without issue his inheritance to go to George, &c.

Inventory, £637, 14*s*, 9*d*., viz: wearing apparel £30, cane, armour. 62 oz. plate at 8*s*., per oz., clock, books £18, 3 negroes £130, utensils in the mill (showing his possession of a fulling mill), oxen, cows, &c. £94, sheep and lambs £56, swine, 2 horses, 2 mares, bees, leathern chairs, drinking glasses, warming pan, &c.

There was a Thomas Tew, who was perhaps brother of Henry. He received a privateer's commission from the Governor of Bermuda and sailed in an armed sloop for the African coast, going around the Cape of Good Hope and finally to the Red Sea. He made many captures and after some years of cruising settled down quietly in Newport again, having, as is said, repaid the value of the vessel fourteen times over to his employers. After a few years of inaction at Newport, he was again induced to start on a venture by some of his old companions, though against his inclination, and in an attack on a ship of the Great Mogul, in the Red Sea, he was desperately wounded in the bowels, which he supported with his hands for a brief period in order to still lead the attack, but his men lost heart at his downfall, and the enemy triumphed. The foregoing is an abstract of the story as told in a little book which purports to give the "History of the Pirates" (including Captains Kidd, Tew, &c., in its narration.)

1. Amey, 1658, Oct. 20.
(2. Mary, 1662, Apr. 5.
By 2d husband.)
3. Richard,

1. Thomas, 1665, Oct. 19.
2. Richard, 1668, Oct. 14.
3. Nicholas, 1671, Apr. 1.
4. William, 1673, May 11.
5. Henry, 1675, Nov. 10.
6. Amity, 1677, Dec. 10.
7. Job, 1682, Jan. 11.
8. Elnathan,
9. Mary,

1. Mary, 1671, Dec. 17
2. Anne, 1673, Nov. 22.
3. Andrew, 1677, Feb. 4.
4. Hope, 1679, Dec. 14.
5. Patience, 1682, Jun. 21.
6. Toleration, 1685, Jun. 10.

I. MARY, b. 1680, Oct. 12. d. 1752, May 3.
m. 1703, Jun. 10.
WILLIAM PECKHAM, b. 1675, Aug. 30. d. 1764, Jan. 18. of William & —— (Clarke) Peckham.

1. Mary, 1704, Sep. 7.
2. William, 1706, Sep. 3.
3. Dorcas, 1709, Jul. 3.
4. Henry, 1711, Feb. 26.
5. Elisha, 1716, May 8.

II. HENRY, b. 1681 ± d. 1731. Newport, R. I.
m. (1) 1704, Apr. 6.
ANN RICHMOND, b. d. of Edward & Amey (Bull) Richmond.
m. (2) 1728, Oct. 2.
MARGARET EASTON, b. 1701. d. 1779, May 29. of Easton.

1717. Ensign.
1718–24. Deputy.
1731, Dec. 31. Inventory, watch £10, plate 59 oz., sword, belt, and arms £4, wearing apparel, &c.
1732, Mar. 6. Testimony as to his will was taken, and on account of interlinings, erasures, &c., the will was not probated.
1732, Apr. 6. His widow Margaret was granted guardianship of her two children John and Elizabeth Tew.
1778, May 15. Will—proved 1781, Apr. 2. Widow Margaret. Exs. James and Elizabeth Drew. To son-in-law James Drew and daughter Elizabeth Drew, my dwelling house and lot for life and then to my grandson John Drew, son of James and Elizabeth, and to his heirs. To granddaughters Margaret and Elizabeth Drew, privilege to live in house while unmarried. To grandson John Drew, silver tankard and small silver porringer. To Margaret and Elizabeth Drew, the silver marked with their names. To daughter Elizabeth Drew and her three children, 600 Spanish milled dollars each, and certain silver to the two granddaughters. To son-in-law and daughter, rest of worldly goods.
Inventory, £788, 14*s*.

1. Henry, 1705, Jan. 23.
2. Amey, 1707, May 18.
3. Ann, 1709, Nov. 2.
4. Elizabeth, 1711, May 13.
5. Edward, 1712, Aug. 8.
6. Amey, 1714, Jun. 1.
7. James, 1715, Sep. 2.
8. Edward, 1717, Sep. 4.
9. Dorcas, 1719, Sep. 21.
(2d wife.)
10. John, 1730.
11. Elizabeth,

III. WILLIAM, b. 1683. d. 1718, Apr. 5. Tiverton, R. I.
m. 1708, Mar. 16.
ABIGAIL SISSON, b. 1685, Mar. 23. d. 1723, Aug. 30. of George & Sarah (Lawton) Sisson.

1718, Apr. 1. Will—proved 1718, May 6. Exs. three brothers, Richard Tew, of Jamestown, George Sisson, of Swanzey, and William Sanford, of Portsmouth. To wife Abigail, all household goods, in lieu of her dower, and she and daughter Dorcas Tew, to have maintenance. If daughter Dorcas be restored to reason she to have equal part with testator's sons. To son William, £300. To son Edward, £300. To daughters Sarah and Abigail Tew, £200, each. One-half of legacies to Sarah and Abigail, to be paid them when twenty-one and the rest to remain for maintenance of wife and daughter Dorcas, and for the bringing up of children. The executors were empowered to sell all real estate.
Inventory £1,501, 11*d*., viz: farm at Dighton with buildings £575, homestead farm and buildings at Tiverton, £500, sheep £3, swine £2, pair of oxen, 2 cows, mare, carpenter's tools, punch bowl, drinking glasses, case of bottles, stillyards, plate £9, 12*s*., arms and ammunitions £4, 10*s*., purse and apparel £28, 15*s*., 11*d*., books £3, &c.

1. Dorcas, 1709, Dec. 9.
2. Sarah, 1711, Dec. 18.
3. William, 1713, Sep. 8.
4. Abigail, 1715, Nov. 10.
5. Edward, 1717, Oct. 18.

IV. RICHARD, b. 1684 ± d. Jamestown, R. I.
m. 1709, Dec. 1.
RUTH SISSON, b. 1680, May 5. d. of George & Sarah (Lawton) Sisson.

1718–24–27–36. Deputy.

1. Richard, 1710, Aug. 25.
2. Child, 1712, Mar. 5.
3. Henry, 1713, Jun. 21.
4. Elisha, 1715, Mar 23.
5. Child, 1716, Aug. 9.
6. George, 1717, Nov. 9.
7. William, 1720, Apr. 18.
8. John, 1721, Dec. 24.
9. Azariah, 1723, May 26.

V. JOHN, b. d. 1718 + Newport, R. I.

VI. ELIZABETH, b. d. 1769.
m. 1712, Sep. 17.
EDWARD SMITH, b. d. 1730 ± of Philip & Mary ( ) Smith.

1. Dorcas, 1714, Jul. 20.
2. Henry, 1716, Feb. 10.
3. William, 1718, Apr. 7.
4. Ann, 1720, Mar. 2.
5. Elizabeth,

VII. SARAH, b. d.
m.
SYLVESTER SWEET, b. 1674, Mar. 1. d. of James & Mary (Greene) Sweet.

1. Sylvester, 1719.

VIII. ELISHA, b. 1691. d. 1714, Feb. 23.

IX. EDWARD, b. d. 1702, Jan. 18.

(2D WIFE)

X. DORCAS, b. 1696, Sep. 26. d. 1715, Feb. 5.

XI. PAUL, b. 1699, Sep. d. 1711, May 24.

XII. EDWARD, b. 1703, Nov. 1. d. 1749, Nov. 4. Newport, Middletown, R. I.
m. 1744, Jan. 3.
MARY HOAR, b. 1723 d. 1800, Sep. 18. of Hezekiah & Sarah (Brightman) Hoar.

1725. Freeman.
1749. Middletown. Town Clerk.

1. Edward, 1746, Mar. 13.
2. Mary. 1748, Jan. 21.

A deposition of John Easton, Sen., made in 1698, shows that in 1694, while he was Governor, there came to him Captain Thomas Tew and proffered him £500, if he would give him a commission as Privateer. The Governor answered that "he knew not his design, and the said Tew replied, he should go where perhaps the commission might never be seen or heard of. The which he wholly refused to give." It may have been this refusal of Governor Easton which induced Captain Tew to seek a commission abroad.

There was a Henry Tew, of Boston, mariner, who died in 1712, at least his widow Mary took administration that year on his estate (viz: 1712, Jan. 29). His inventory amounted to £1,050, 3*s.*, including house and land £300, silver £193, 2*s.*, 6*d.*, gold £136, 10*s.*, books, silver tankard, &c. The widow in 1719, was appointed guardian of daughter Mary, aged seventeen, and daughter Elizabeth, aged twelve. It becomes a matter of conjecture whether this Henry Tew was not a son of Thomas the pirate, and a nephew of Deputy Governor Henry Tew, of Newport.

UPDIKE.

GILBERT[2] (Lodowick[1]). { b. Wesel, Germany, Lloyds Neck, N. Y.
m. 1643, Sep. 24. { d. [Kings Town, R. I.
KATHARINE SMITH, { b.
{ d. 1664 (—)

of Richard Smith.

He was a physician, according to traditions of the family.

He bore the name of Gysbert op Dyck, the surname in the next generation becoming Updike. He was the son of Lodowick & Gertrude Op Ten Dyck.

1605. Baptized at Wesel in the church of St. Willitrode.

1635. New York. He came this year from Germany, establishing himself on Long Island at Lloyds Neck.

1638–39–40. Commissary at Fort Good Hope.

1641. He returned to Germany this year, it is thought, but if so he emigrated again in the next year.

1642. Commisary of provisions for the colony.

He signed a contract with Governor William Kieft and others, in this year, for building a church.

He was a member of the council for trial of Hendrick Jansen.

1643, Sep. 24. His marriage took place at New Amsterdam (*i. e.*, New York).

1644, May 24. He was granted a patent for Coney Island.

1644, Jul. 27. He had his daughter Elizabeth baptized (and other children as follows, Lodowick, 1646, Jun. 10. Sarah, 1650, Oct. 23. John and James, 1658, Jan. 16).

1645, Aug. 30. He and others signed a treaty of peace with the sachems of the Mohicans, Hackensacks, &c.

1645. Member of Council of War.

He with seven others was chosen this year to deliberate on Indian affairs and safety.

1647. Commander of Fort Good Hope.

1656, Jul. 6. Assessor, to commute for a tenth of crops or quit rents due by farmers on Long Island.

1658. Court Messenger.

1664. By one account he came to Rhode Island in this year, New York having surrendered to the English under Colonel Nichols. It is somewhat uncertain, however, whether he came; but it is certain that most of his children lived in Rhode Island. The best authority gives his death as occurring on Long Island.

I. { ELIZABETH, { b. 1644.
m. { d. 1722 (—)
GEORGE WIGHTMAN, { b. 1632, Jun.
{ d. 1722, Jan. of Wightman.

II. { LODOWICK, { b. 1646. North Kingstown, R. I.
m. { d. 1736 ±
ABIGAIL NEWTON, { b.
{ d. 1745. of Thomas & Joan (Smith) Newton.

He and his descendants bore the name of Updike.

1646, Jun. 10. He was baptized at New Amsterdam, with the following sponsors: Mochiel ten Oycken Jean de la Montague, Richard Smith and Margaret Kalden.

1668, May 4. Kings Town. He and others of Wickford, petitioned Connecticut for protection of their government, or else that they might look for government elsewhere.

1670, Jul. 15. He was present in the shop at the time of the difference between Thomas Flounders and Walter House (resulting in the death of the latter); and Flounders testified that said Updike could inform as touching the matter.

1671, May 20. He took oath of allegiance to Rhode Island.

1679, Mar. 3. He petitioned concerning land of Richard Smith.

1679, Jul. 29. He and forty-one others of Narragansett, petitioned the King, that he "would put an end to these differences about the government thereof; which hath been so fatal to the prosperity of the place; animosities still arising in people's minds, as they stand affected to this or that government."

1687. Lieutenant.

1687, Sep. 6. Taxed 7*s.*, 9*d.*

1687–88 Grand Jury.

1692. He took oath as to inventory of his uncle Richard Smith, as sole surviving executor.

1696. Deputy.

1702, Feb. 25. He, only surviving executor to will of his uncle Richard Smith, deeded land to Israel Newton, declaring that said uncle Richard Smith, gave to Israel Newton and James Newton all his right of land on a farm in Boston Neck, now in possession of James Newton and myself, having formerly had three full shares bequeathed by my grandfather Richard Smith (father to my said uncle), one to myself, and one that I bought of my kinsman James Newton many years since.

1703, Jul. 12. He was chosen with others to lay out highways.

1713, Apr. 28. He and wife Abigail sold to Henry Lloyd, of Boston, a quarter acre for £4.

1734, Aug. 16. He sold to son Daniel Updike, of Newport, two tracts of land in North Kingstown, 300 acres, for £3000.

1742, May 10. Will—proved 1745, May 8. Widow Abigail. Exx. daughter Catharine. To son Daniel, £5. To grandchildren, John, Richard, Smith, Daniel, James, Mary and Elizabeth, all children of Richard Updike, deceased, £200, equally divided at age; £100 being in hands of son Daniel, £50 in hands of son-in-law Thomas Fosdick, and £50 in hands of son-in-law Giles Goddard. To daughter Abigail Cooper, wife of Matthew Cooper, a feather bed and all my wearing apparel. To five daughters, the remainder of estate, viz: to Esther, Catharine, Abigail, Sarah and Martha.

UPDIKE. 2d column. II. Lodowick, d. 1737. 1734, will; proved, 1737. He directs his son Daniel to provide for the "six children of my son Richard Updike."

1749, Nov. 20. Administration to widow Mary. Inventory, £1,775, 3s. (and later a supplementary inventory of £48, 7s.). Negro Rose and her child, £200, pair of oxen £105, 6 cows, 3 yearlings, calf, 2 mares, colt, 8½ loads of hay, &c.

1751, Apr. 15. His widow brought in an account with the estate, which was allowed at this date.

She charged seventy-three weeks board for the children at 50s. per week, each of them.

XIII. ABIGAIL, { b. / d.
m. 1723, Mar. 9.
ROBERT WRIGHTINGTON, { b. / d. of Robert & Margaret (Ward) Wrightington.

1. Robert, 1725.
2. Elnathan, 1737.

XIV. ELNATHAN, { b. / d.

XV. GEORGE, { b. 1706, Mar. 11. / d. 1733. Newport, R. I.

He was a mariner.

1733, Nov. 8. Inventory presented by his eldest brother.

XVI. THOMAS, { b. 1709, Feb. / d. Newport, R. I.

1731. Freeman.

XVII. JAMES, { b. 1711, Oct. 26. / d. 1784, Feb. 6. Newport, R. I.
m. 1734, Sep. 15.
ANN ARNOLD, { b. 1715. / d. 1805, Oct. 17. of Benedict & Patience (Coggeshall) Arnold.

1. James, 1735.
2. Thomas, 1738,
3. William, 1745, Apr. 5.
4. Benedict,
5. Patience,
6. Sarah,
7. Anne,
8. Bathsheba.

1732. Freeman.

1762, Jan. 22. Will—proved 1784, Apr. 8. Exs. wife Ann and sons James and Thomas. To four sons, James, Thomas, William and Benedict, equally divided, dwelling house where I now live, &c., but wife to have the house till youngest son is of age, and after that such a part of the house as she chooses for life. To wife, all household goods. To four daughters, Patience, Sarah, Ann and Bathsheba, £100 each, paid by their brothers. To sons James and Benedict, all my working tools. If the two youngest sons or the four daughters die before twenty-one their estate to go to rest.

Inventory, £115, 15s., 6d., viz: wearing apparel, carpenter's tools, warming pan, 3 tables, desk, 6¾ oz. silver plate £2, 4s., 6d., &c.,

XVIII. PAUL, { b. 1715, Mar. 27. / d. Newport, Providence, R. I.
m. 1734, May 3.
PATIENCE LILLIBRIDGE, { b. 1716. / d. 1736, Aug. 10. of Thomas & Sarah ( ) Lillibridge.

He was a merchant.

1736. Freeman.

1754, Nov. 11. Providence. He bought of John Brown certain land, with dwelling house, &c., for £1,753, 16s.

UPDIKE.

1. Elizabeth, 1664, Jul. 26.
2. Alice, 1666, Dec. 29.
3. Daniel, 1668, Jan. 2.
4. Sarah, 1671, Feb. 25.
5. George, 1673, Jan. 8.
6. John, 1674, Apr. 16.
7. Samuel, 1676, Jan. 9.
8. Valentine, 1681, Apr. 16.

3d column. I. Richard, m. 1726, Feb. 24, Hannah Eldred, b. 1708, Mar. 20. Erase son Richard and Smith, and insert son, Richard Smith. IV. Catharine, b. 1696. d 1782, Sep. V. Abigail. Children, 1. Thomas. 2. Gilbert. 3. James 4. Abigail. 5. Christiana. 6. Catharine. 7. Elizabeth.

I. RICHARD, { b / d 1734 North Kingstown, R. I
m.
——— ELDRED, { b. / d. of Daniel and Mary Eldred.

1. John,
2. Richard,
3. Smith,
4. Daniel,
5. James,
6. Mary,
7. Elizabeth.

1712. Kings Town. Freeman.

1720, Jun. 9. He was executor of the will of his cousin Israel Newton (proved at this date), and by the terms of said will was given a farm at Boston Neck.

1730, Sep 21. He bought 102 acres of Stephen Cooper for £400.

1734, Jun. 12. Inventory £296.

His sons John and Richard were sea captains.

II. DANIEL, { b. / d. 1757, May 15. Kings Town, Newport, North Kingstown, R. I.
m. (1) 1716, Dec. 20.
SARAH ARNOLD, { b. 1698, Nov. 3. / d. 1718, Jan. 26. of Benedict & Sarah (Mumford) Arnold.
m. (2) 1722, Dec. 21.
ANSTIS JENKINS, { b. 1702, Oct. 28. / d. of Richard & Mary (Wilkins) Jenkins.
m. (3) 1745, Mar. 14. [Wm.
MARY WANTON (w. of { b. 1702, Mar. 23. / d. of John & Elizabeth (Carr) Godfrey.

See: American Genealogist v. 34, p. 170

UPDIKE. 3d column. II. Daniel. Where the word McSharron occurs change it to McSparran.

(2d wife,)
1. Lodowick, 1725, Jul. 12.
2. Mary, 1727, Apr. 11.
3. Gilbert, 1729, May 9.
4. Wilkins, 1729, May 9.

He received a careful education at his father's house, including in his studies the Greek, Latin and French languages; and after the completion of his education he went to Barbadoes. Upon his return he studied law and changed his residence soon to Newport.

1719, Jun. 16. He signed a petition with his uncle James regarding the fencing up of a highway.

1722-23-24-25-26-27-28-29-30-31-32-43-44-45-46-47-48-49-50-51-52-53-54-55-56-57. Attorney General.

1723. Newport. Freeman. He was appointed counsel for the colony to attend the trial of thirty-six pirates captured by Captain Solgar, commander of his Majesty's ship Greyhound. Twenty-six of the pirates were executed in July of this year.

1729, Feb. He and three others were members of a committee appointed to revise and print laws, and they were allowed £15 each by the Assembly.

1730. Lieutenant Colonel.

1730, May 2. He was baptized in Pettaquamscutt river by Rev. James McSharron.

1730, He was one of the founders of the literary institution later known as Redwood Library, at Newport. His fellow members were Scott, Callender, Honeyman, &c., and Dean Berkeley was sometimes present. The latter on his departure for England presented Mr. Updike with a coffee pot of wrought silver, and after his arrival in England sent a copy of his book, "The Minute Philosopher."

1732. Nominated for Governor in opposition to William Wanton.

1740, Dec. 2. He was appointed on a committee to manage the affairs of this colony before the commissioners to hear and determine the boundaries between Rhode Island and Massachusetts.

1741-42-43. North Kingstown. Attorney for Kings County.

1742, Nov. He was appointed on a committee to revise the laws.

1755, Oct. He and Governor Stephen Hopkins were appointed as commissioners to appear and represent the colony at any meeting of commissioners of the other British northern colonies, with his Excellency Major General Shirly, Commander-in-Chief of all his Majesty's forces in North America, with them to concert proper measures for quartering, subsisting, furloughing and discharging provincial troops now in the field; to concert proper measures that the campaigns may be rendered successful this year.

The records of St. Paul's Church (under the rectorship of Dr. McSharron) thus note his decease: "Colonel Updike of North Kingstown, Attorney General of the Colony, died on Saturday the 15th of May, 1757, about noon, and after a funeral discourse was preached by Dr. McSharron, was interred in the burial ground of the family, beside the remains of his father and second wife Anstis Jenkins, mother of Lodowick and Mary Updike his surviving children."

1757, May 30. Administration to son Lodowick. Inventory: Wearing apparel, silver hilted sword, 8 gold rings, 119 oz. plate, books, 2 desks, book case, pair of pistols, clock, oval table, tea table, pair of andirons, 2 linen wheels, woolen wheel, coffee mill, warming pan, cooper's tools, negroes

III. SARAH, b. 1650. d.
m.
—— WHITEHEAD, b. d. of Whitehead.

IV. DANIEL, b. d. 1704. Kings Town, R. I., London, Eng.
m.
MARTHA, b. d. 1704 + of

He was a mariner.

1675, Dec. 19. He was wounded in the Narragansett Swamp Fight, at which time over a thousand Indians and more than two hundred Englishmen were killed and wounded. There were thirty-five hundred Indians and fifteen hundred colonists engaged in the fight.

1680, Apr. 4. He was captured by Algerine pirates and at this date was still held for a ransom, as a letter from William Harris (also a captive) to Mr. Brinley at Newport, shows. He says "pray tell Mr. Smith, Daniel Updike is well. He may do well to redeem him."

1680, Apr. 6. He is again alluded to in a letter written by William Harris at Algiers to the wife of the latter. "Since I came I saw Daniel Updike, and he says he had a plague sore and that this sickness is here every summer and begins in May, and that the last summer here died nine or ten of the English captives, but some say not so many. Speak to Mr. Smith to redeem him, and tell Lodowick his brother, Mr. Smith, Mr. Brinley, and others." He was finally ransomed by his uncle Major Richard Smith, for 1500 gun locks.

1704, Feb. 9. Will—proved 1704, Sep. He calls himself of St. Dunstans, Stepney, county Middlesex. To sister Sarah Whitehead, the cattle in hands of brother Lodowick. To nephew Richard Whitehead, land in Boston Neck. To nephew Daniel Updike, half of land in New Rochester and to brother James, the other half. As to property in old England or at sea, &c., he devises as follows; To brothers Lodowick and James and sister Elizabeth Whiteman, each a ring. To poor of parish of St. John Baptist at Margate in the Isle of Thanet, £20. To niece Sarah Whitehead, £200. To Stephen Smith (son of Matthew Smith the younger), testator's part of ketch Loving Brothers. To Elizabeth, daughter of Moses Moyle, his part of ship Generous Adventure. To wife Martha, rest of estate, and if she happen to have a son or daughter by him, all legacies to be revoked and half of estate go to wife and half to child.

See: American Genealogist v. 34, p. 170 →

V. JAMES, b. d. 1729. North Kingstown, R. I.

1675, Dec. 19. He was wounded in the Narragansett fight.

1719, Jun. 16. He and two others petitioned the Assembly for liberty to fence up a highway lately run through Daniel Updike's land, for that it is of very little good to the inhabitants thereabout. Leave was granted to hang gates and bars across the highway till a further necessity appear to the Assembly for opening the same.

1727, Oct. 12. Will—proved 1729, Jul. 8. To nephew Richard Updike, a money legacy. To Richard Whitehead and —— Dunham, sister of the latter, £25 each. To kinsman Daniel Updike of Newport, his interest in a farm in Kings Town. To Rev. James Mason, a legacy. To Daniel Updike, the rest of estate.

VI. RICHARD, b. d. 1675, Dec. 19. Kings Town, R. I.
UNMARRIED.

1671, May 20. He took oath of allegiance.

1675, Dec. 19. He was killed in the Narragansett Swamp Fight.

VII. JOHN, b. d. 1729. Hopewell, N. J.
m.
—— b. d. of

He and his son Albert bore the name of Opdyck, but his son Lawrence and descendants used the form of Updike in spelling the surname.

1728. Will—proved 1729, Mar. 26. Exs. son Lawrence Opdyck, and Eliaskin Anderson. He left his property equally to his eight living children.

UPDIKE. 2d column. VII. John. Erase his marriage, death, residence and all else about him, and erase his children.

Nathaniel, Charo, Moses, Joseph, Dimas, Newport, Dublin, Mingo, Clara, James, Caesar, Domine, Paul (two years old), Prince, Sue, Lillie and child, Bridget and Noble, 10 mares, 3 colts, stallion, 6 oxen, 3 steers, 8 cows, 3 heifers, bull, 270 sheep, &c.

The family burial ground where he was laid is at Cocumscusset (Cawcawmsqussick) or Smith's Castle, near Wickford, for nearly two hundred years the seat of this family.

His two last children died in infancy.

III. { ESTHER, m. 1720, Jun. 29, THOMAS FOSDICK, { b. d. 1755 (—) { b. 1696, Aug. 20. d. 1774, Jul. 17. of Samuel & Mercy (Picket) Fosdick.

1. Esther, 1722, Apr. 30
2. Thomas, 1725, Apr. 30.
3. Katharine, 1727, Feb. 7.
4. Sarah, 1730, Apr. 9.

IV. { CATHARINE, UNMARRIED. { b. d.

V. { ABIGAIL, m. MATTHEW COOPER, { b. d. { b. d. of James & Elizabeth (Shippee) Cooper.

VI. { SARAH, m 1735, Dec. 11, GILES GODDARD, { b. d. 1770, Jan. 5. { b. 1705. d. 1757, Jan. 31 of Joseph Goddard.

1. Mary Catharine, 1736.
2. William, 1740, Oct. 20

VII. { MARTHA, UNMARRIED. { b. d.

1. Sarah,
2 Richard.

I. { LAWRENCE, m. AGNES, { b. d. 1748 { b. d. 1748 + of Lawrenceville, N. J.

1748. Will—proved. Ex. son William. He mentions wife Agnes, sons William, John and Tunis, and daughters Catharine Johnson, Rachel Price and Atholiah Updike.

1. William,
2. John,
3. Tunis,
4. Catharine,
5. Rachel,
6. Atholiah.

II. { ALBERT, m. ELIZABETH, { b. d. 1752. { b. d. 1752 + of Hopewell, N. J.

1718. He and Lawrence Updike and Joshua and Enoch Anderson, all of Maidenhead (town ship of Hopewell), joined with others in buying a lot in Maidenhead for the Presbyterian church.
1715. He was a member of Baptist church.
1728. He gained his case in a lawsuit.
1752. Will—proved 1752, Aug. To wife Elizabeth, one-third of estate, and the rest to following children, viz: John, Joshua, Benjamin, William, Sarah, Catharine, Franck and Hannah.

Inventory of personal estate £165.

1. John,
2. Joshua,
3. Benjamin,
4. William,
5. Sarah,
6. Catharine,
7. Franck,
8. Hannah.

III. { TRYNTJE, m. ENOCH ANDERSON, { b. d. { b. d. of Anderson.

1. Francina,
2. Jochem,
3. Enoch.

IV. { ENGELTJE, m. JOSHUA ANDERSON, { b. d. 1731 + { b. d. 1731 of Anderson.

1. Joshua,
2. John,
3. Benjamin,
4. Isaac,
5. Jacob,
6. Abraham,
7. Catharine,
8. Hannah.

V. { CHILD, { b. d.

VI. { CHILD, { b. d.

VAUGHAN (John).

John, b. d. 1687 + Newport, R. I.
m.
Gillian, b. d.

1634, Mar. 4. He and others dwelling in Massachusetts were fined for mis-spending their time, drinking strong waters, &c., and selling others contrary to law. His fine was 20*s*.

1638, May 20. His name was in a list of inhabitants admitted at Newport since this date.

1639. He was granted a lot this year on condition that he built within a year. He was to have 42 acres at place called the Hermitage.

1655. Freeman.

1662, May 22. He had 79¾ acres laid out.

1673, Apr. 16. He deeded 8 acres for love, &c., to son John.

1680. Taxed £2, 2*s*., 8*d*.

1687, Jul. 23. He deeded son Daniel of Newport, for love, &c., farm and mansion house where I dwell, 50 acres, with orchard, &c.

I. John, b. 1644, Apr. 19. d. Newport, R. I.

1668. Freeman.

II. David, b. 1646, Jul. 19. d. 1678, Newport, Portsmouth, R. I.
m.
Mary, b. d. 1681 + of

(She m. (2) Thomas Joslin.)

1666, Nov. 7. He bought of John Anthony of Portsmouth, a house and 35 acres there for £80.

1671. Portsmouth. Freeman.

1678, Mar. 1. Will—proved 1678, May 25. Exs. father John Vaughan, and brother John. Overseers Richard Dunn and Daniel Gould, of Newport. To father John Vaughan, Indian boy called Sam. To wife Mary, all household stuff, and all stock of cattle, sheep and horses, provided she gives my son John at age, ten ewe sheep. To wife, also all land and housing till son John is of age. If wife die without more children, what she has to go to John, and if he be under age at her death the executors to have profits for maintenance and bringing up of John with suitable learning, as to read and write.

1680. Widow Vaughan taxed 12*s*.

1681, Dec. 14. Thomas Joslin of Portsmouth, and Mary his wife, late widow of David Vaughan, released to John Vaughan, of Newport, all right in will of said David, house, lands, &c., for £37, 2*s*.

III. George, b. 1650, Oct. 20. d. 1704, May 7. Newport, East Greenwich, R. I.
m. 1680, Jul. 26.
Margaret Spink, b. d. 1704 + of Robert & Alice ( ) Spink.

1677, Oct. 31. He and forty-seven others were granted 5000 acres to be called East Greenwich.

1680. Taxed 5*s*., 2*d*.

1684–98–99–1704. East Greenwich. Deputy.

1687. He was a member of cavalry company.

1688. Grand Jury.

1699, Apr. 11. Will—proved 1704, May 25. Exs. wife Margaret and son George. To eldest son George, dwelling house and lands thereto, and all other land in township undisposed of, he allowing his mother a room with a chimney in it during her life. To son David, two cows, a horse, half my smith tools, &c., and his cattle, sheep and increase to be kept on home lot or otherwise by executors till David is of age. To son Christopher, two cows, a horse, cattle, sheep, &c., to be kept till of age. To son Robert, two cows, a horse, and twenty sheep at age. To eldest daughter Mary Vaughan, two cows and £10 at eighteen or marriage. To daughter Abigail Vaughan, two cows and £10 at eighteen or marriage. Rest of personal to wife Margaret and eldest son George The half part of smith's tools he left undisposed of were ordered to be given to son Christopher, upon a statement of the circumstances by executors.

Inventory, £124, 10*s*., viz: 5 cows, 4 three year heifers, 4 oxen, 5 calves, 20 sheep, 20 lambs, a mare, 2 horses, colt, 6 two year cattle, 2 yearlings, 3 swine, 1 pair stillyards, cordwainer's working gear, smith's tools, bellows, anvil, vice, &c., pair of cards, 3 spinning wheels, 7 tar barrels, tanned and curried leather, pewter, &c.

IV. Daniel, b. 1653, Apr. 27 d. 1715 (—) Newport, R. I.
m. 1678, Mar, 27,
Susanna Grimes, b. 1657, Nov. 22. d. 1715 + of Samuel & Ann (Grimes.

See V. F. (Vertical File) Jennings V. F. J-441

1677, Oct. 31. He and forty-seven others were granted 5000 acres to be called East Greenwich. He never went there to settle.

1680. Taxed 4*s*.

1686, Mar. 19. He exchanged land in East Greenwich for land in Newport, with his brother George now of East Greenwich.

1715, Jun. 13. His widow Susanna of Newport, petitioned the Assembly that her negro man Job might be permitted to return to this colony, he having been sometime since banished this government by Court of Trials. The petition was granted.

VII. Child,
b.
d.

VIII. Child,
b.
d.

VAUGHAN (John).

I. John,
m. 1698, Nov. 24.
Elizabeth Bull,
b.
d.
b.
d. of Isaac Bull.
Portsmouth, R. I.

1. Elizabeth, 1701, Dec. 18.
2. David, 1704, Oct. 25.
3. Isaac, 1707, Mar. 31.
4. George, 1709, Jul. 24.
5. Mary, 1713, Jul. 19.
6. Charity, 1716, Jun. 20.
7. John, 1721, Jul. 8.

I. George,
m. 1708, Apr. 8.
Jane Nichols,
b. 1682, Apr. 19.
d. 1729.
b.
d. of Richard & Phebe ( ) Nichols.
East Greenwich, R. I.

1729, Nov. 17. Will—proved 1729, Nov. 29. Exs. brother Christopher and son George. To son George, homestead. To son David, a farm. To both sons, a feather bed. To daughter Elizabeth Vaughan, £60 and half household goods. To daughter Jane, £60 and half household goods at eighteen. To son David, £20, a pair oxen, three cows and twenty sheep at age. To son George, all rest of real and personal. Son David to be put out to learn trade of a tailor in case he be a cripple. (As his son George was a minor he chose his uncle John Hall of North Kingstown guardian to act as executor till he should be of age.)

Inventory, £61, 19*s.*, 4*d.*, viz: silver money 15*s.*, 5*d.*, paper money £22, 7*s.*, 6*d.*, bonds and notes £127, 18*s.*, 5 guns, carpenter's tools, shoemaker's tools, cider, beer, tobacco, corn, &c., 33 sheep, [illegible] lambs, 1 pair oxen, 5 cows, 2 two year, 1 yearling, 1 calf, 1 horse, 1 mare, 12 geese, 36 fowls, 2 woolen wheels, 1 linen wheel, 4 pair cards, &c.

VAUGHAN (John). 3d column. 1. George. Change amount of inventory to £611, 19*s.*, 4*d.*

1. Elizabeth, 1709, Oct. 14.
2. Jane, 1712, Mar. 1.
3. George, 1714, Jan. 18.
4. David, 1717, Jan. 27.

II. David,
m. 1709, Mar. 10.
Mary Pearce,
b. 1683, Apr. 29.
d. 1728, Dec. 19.
b. 1690, Feb. 7.
d. 1728 + of Giles & Elizabeth (Hall) Pearce.
East Greenwich, R. I.

1728, Dec. 28. Administration to widow Mary.

Inventory, £2,138, 17*s.*, 4*d.*, viz: wearing apparel £8, 18*s.*, cash £14, 13*s.*, 7 silver spoons, 5 feather beds, warming pan, pewter, 2 linen wheels, negro boy Jack £80, 4 cows, a heifer, calf, mare, 40 sheep, 8 geese, half of a set of smith's tools, a quarter of sloop "Elizabeth and Mary," third of twenty barrels of fish, dwelling house £60, farm, orchard, &c., £700, &c.

1. Elizabeth, 1710, Nov. 3.
2. Margaret, 1713, Apr. 12.
3. Mary, 1717, Dec. 1.
4. Rebecca, 1720, Apr. 3.
5. Waity, 1722, May 10.
6. Susanna, 1724, May 13.

III. Mary,
b. 1685, Feb. 28.
d.

IV. Christopher,
m. 1709, Jun. 26.
Deborah Nichols,
b. 1686, Apr. 29.
d. 1752, Aug. 18.
b. 1688, Feb. 17.
d. of Thomas & Mercy (Reynolds) Nichols.
East Greenwich, R. I.

1707. Freeman.

1751, Oct. 11. Will—proved 1752, Aug. 29. Ex. son Christopher. To three daughters Mary Nichols, Deborah Weaver and Ruth Spencer, all money left at decease and all due by bond, notes, &c., and to each two silver spoons. To son Christopher, two silver spoons, loom, all my corn and all provisions. To three daughters, rest of household goods. To son Christopher, house and homestead farm for life and then to his son Christopher. To son Christopher, rest of estate.

Inventory, £2,648, 7*s.*, 9*d.*, viz: wearing apparel £60. 8 silver spoons £40, 2 old tables, a joint stool, 14 chairs, 2 looking glasses, 5 pewter platters, pewter tankard, 9 plates and 6 porringers of pewter, warming pan, 2 candle sticks, pair stillyards, pair worsted cards, 2 woolen wheels, linen wheel, loom, old books 10*s.*, cider mill, cooper's tools, anvil and smith's tools, 3 cows, 3 yearlings, 26 sheep and lambs, gun, small gilded trunk, bonds and notes £1,890, 13*s.*, 9*d.*, &c.

1. Christopher 1710, Jul. 6.
2. Benjamin, 1713, Jul. 2.
3. Mary, 1715, May 8.
4. Deborah, 1719, Jul. 13.
5. Ruth, 1729, Aug. 12.

V. Abigail,
m.
John Hall,
b. 1689, Feb. 24.
d.
b. 1681, Jul 2.
d. 1760, Mar. 4. of William & Alice (Tripp) Hall.

1. George,
2. Preserved,
3. Mary,
4. William, 1723, Aug. 3.
5. Christopher,
6. Abigail.

VI. Robert,
m. 1719, Feb. 18.
Joanna Sweet,
b. 1691, Mar. 7.
d.
b. 1695, Feb. 13.
d. of Henry & Mary ( ) Sweet.
East Greenwich, R. I.

1. Caleb, 1720, Jun. 7.
2. David, 1722, Apr. 14.
3. Daniel, 1722, Apr. 14.
4. Susanna, 1726, May 24.
5. Benjamin, 1730, Nov. 4.
6. Robert, 1732, Nov. 11.
7. Margaret, 1734, Jul. 13.

I. John,
m.
Mary Lawton,
b. 1679, Sep. 14.
d.
b. 1683, Apr. 3.
d. of Isaac & Elizabeth (Tallman) Lawton.
Newport, R. I.

1713. Freeman.

1734, Mar. 21. He and wife Mary of Newport, sold 60 acres in Smithfield to Henry Laughton of Boston, for £100.

1. Daniel.

II. Ann,
b. 1683, Ap. 6.
d.

III. Daniel,
m.
Rebecca,
b. 1685, Mar. 17.
d.
b.
d. of
Newport, R. I.

1. Rebecca, 1715, Nov. 30.

V. MARY, b. 1658, Jul. 3.
d.

VERNON.

DANIEL[2], (Samuel[1]). b. 1643, Sep, 1. London, Eng.,
m. 1679, Sep. 22. [Sam'l. d. 1715, Oct. 28. Kings Town, R. I.
ANN DYER, (w. of b. 1643, Nov. 17.
d. 1717, Jan. 10.

of Edward & Catharine (Hamby) Hutchinson.

1666. He came to America at about this time, and was at Newport for a short period, thence moving to Kings Town, where he married, and where his son Samuel was born.

1683. Kings Town. Town Clerk.

1683-84. Constable.

1686. Marshal of Kings Province and keeper of the prison.

1687, Sep. 6. Taxed 1*s*., 11*d*.

1687. He was appointed with another to lay out highways

1688, Mar. 6 He and Henry Tibbitts were empowered to take care that a certain highway in Kings Town, be forthwith laid open for use and benefit of inhabitants.

1691, Feb. 9. He makes complaint that Edward Dyer and Elisha Dyer his brother, both non-residents, did contrary to all law upon the third of this instant, February, enter and take possession of my farm at Aquidneset, &c., and in a most flagrant manner put themselves in possession of my cellar (my house of late being burned by casualty), and that in forcing open my door, it being at that time locked and the key in my pocket, and that notwithstanding my prohibition which they take no notice of; and do therefore by these presents protest against the said Edward and Elisha Dyer, for all damages that may accrue thereby. He further protested and warned them that they would have to answer for it when the law should take place.

In his family bible he recorded the death of his father Samuel (1681, Apr. 25), his brother John (1682, Apr.—42 years), his mother (1701, Apr. 24—"aged four score years the time Queen was crowned") and his brother Samuel (1703, Jul. 17—42 years, "drowned at ye New River a fishing"). He also gives the date of his own birth in London, and his marriage and births of his children.

1717, Jan. 1. Will—proved 1717. Widow Ann Vernon, of Newport. Ex. son Samuel Vernon. To son Samuel Dyer, 5*s*. To sons Elisha, Henry and Barret Dyer, £30, each. To son Samuel Vernon, £45. To daughter Catharine Vernon, £55. To sons Henry and Barrett Dyer and Samuel Vernon, all rents due me from Edward Dyer, of Kings Town, being due from 1710, Nov. 20, at £6, per annum, and all hereafter found due which should have been for my yearly support and maintenance.

She was buried in Newport, where the gravestone may still be seen.

1736, May 15. A deposition was made by Elisha Dyer, of North Kingstown, that when he was in London, the widow of Samuel Vernon, desired him to bring her husband's legacy of a gold ring to his brother Daniel Vernon, but he refused it by reason he was not coming directly to New England and she sent it by John Scott to the said Daniel Vernon and he received it according to this deponent's knowledge.

1736, May 28. Deposition of Daniel Updike, of Newport, aged about 42 years, who saith that about the year 1715, one Daniel Vernon died at the deponent's father's house in North Kingstown after having lived for many years preceding said time at said place as a Tutor to the deponent's and to his father's other children, &c. He further testifies that Daniel Vernon showed him a seal ring, being a cornelian stone cut with three wheat sheaves, the arms borne by the family of Vernon, which was (as he said) his said brother Samuel's. Also testifies that a French bible by him produced printed at Rochelle 1616, was the bible of the said Daniel Vernon, and that the handwriting on the back side of a leaf in said bible (giving an account of Daniel Vernon's father, &c.), was handwriting of said Daniel Vernon. He also testified that he knew Samuel Vernon, of Newport, to be lawful son and heir of Daniel, &c.

At same date Katharine Updike testified that Daniel Updike died at her father's house in 1715, &c.

These depositions were made in order that Samuel Vernon, of Newport, son of Daniel, deceased, might get title to warehouse property in London on the Thames, &c., which had been injured by fire, and which he possessed himself of on the death of his father and his father's sister, by going to London, where he disposed of the estate.

I. DANIEL, b. 1682, Apr. 6.
d. young.

II. SAMUEL, b. 1683, Dec. 6. Newport, R. I.
m. (1) 1707, Apr. 10. d. 1737, Dec. 5.
ELIZABETH FLEET, b. 1685.
m. (2) 1725, Jan. 12. d. 1722, Mar. 5. of Fleet.
ELIZ'TH PRINCE (widow). b. 1680.
d. 1759, Mar. 15. of Nathaniel & Dorothy ( ) Paine.

He was a merchant.

1714. Freeman.

1729-30-31-32-33-34-35-36-37. Assistant.

1730, Jun. He was appointed by the Assembly with two others as a committee to treat with the proprietors of the Great Purchase (granted out of the vacant lands in Narragansett), and consider of some way and means whereby the differences relating to the gore of land in controversy may be settled. The committee were subsequently voted £9, for their time and trouble in the affair.

The same year he and the Governor were appointed a committee to have care and oversight of the people and goods that should be suspected to have come from Boston, where the small pox prevailed.

1754, Aug. 29. Will—proved 1759, May 7. Widow Elizabeth, of Bristol. Ex. brother-in-law Joseph Russell. She mentions her aged and honoured mother Dorothy Paine; the Presbyterian Society in Bristol; sisters Dorothy Huntington and Sarah Russell; Sarah and Anne Russell, daughters of Joseph; Mrs. Abigail Godfrey, wife of Caleb; children of brother Stephen Paine, deceased (viz: Stephen, Royal, Hannah and Mary); Sarah Paine, daughter of Edward; Sarah Paine, daughter of kinsman Nathaniel Paine; Sarah Drowne, wife of Thomas, of Boston; Irene Drowne; kinsman Jonathan Fales and his sister Deborah; kinswoman Mary Bosworth, wife of William; Mary Church, daughter of Constant, deceased; Hannah Church, daughter of Nathaniel, deceased; Mary Price, wife of Thomas, of Dorchester; children of Dorothy Huntington (viz: John and Elizabeth Williams); kinsman Charles Church, son of Constant, and his brother Peter; Jonathan Russell, one of my brother Joseph Russell's sons, and Nathaniel Russell, another son.

III. CATHERINE, b. 1686, Oct. 3.
d. 1769, Mar.
UNMARRIED.

IV. { DAVID, { b. 1688, Feb. 13. d.

V. { SAMUEL, m. MARY, { b. 1690, Jun. 17. d. 1717, Mar. 16. { b. 1696. d. 1724, Nov. 22. of — Newport, R. I.

He and his wife were buried in Newport Cemetery.

VERNON.

I. { ANN, m. ——— SANFORD, { b. 1708, Jan. 23. d. 1782, Sep. 23. { b. d. of — Sanford.
1. Samuel,

II. { ELIZABETH, m. (1) ——— COX, m. (2) 1750, Sep. 5. ELNATHAN HAMMOND, { b. 1709, Aug. 4. d. 1775, May 11. { b. d. of — Cox. { b. 1703, Mar. 7. d. 1793, May 24. of John & Mary (Arnold) — Hammond.

III. { SAMUEL, m. AMEY WARD, { b. 1711, Sep. 6. d. 1792, Jul. 6. { b. 1717, Feb. 21. d. 1792, Jan. 17. of Richard & Mary (Tillinghast) — Newport, R. I. — Ward.

VERNON. 3d column. III. Samuel, m. 1736, Dec. 29.

1. Elizabeth, 1738, Apr. 24.
2. William, 1739, Aug. 3.
3. Samuel, 1740, Jul. 12.
4. Amey, 1741, Sep. 12.
5. Mary, 1743, Feb. 17.
6. Samuel, 1745, Feb. 17.
7. Amey, 1746, Jul. 19.
8. Amey, 1747, Nov. 19.
9. William, 1749, Jul. 21.
10. Wm. Ward, 1752, Mar. 7.
11. Thomas, 1753, Jun. 6.
12. Ann, 1754, Sep. 29.

He was a merchant.

1733. Freeman.

1747, Aug. He was one of the applicants for charter of Redwood Library.

1750, Sep. 4. He and others petitioned the King to restrain the Assembly from issuing bills of credit upon loan without royal permission, the sum on loan already amounting to £390,000, worth at time of issue £78,111 sterling, but at present only £35,445. Amongst those whose estates were involved in the loan were numbers of widows and orphans, who were grieviously injured, oppressed and almost ruined.

1785, Nov. 24. Will—proved 1792, Aug. 8. Exx. wife Amey. To her all estate real and personal.

Inventory, £265, 13s., 1d., viz: household goods, 108½ oz. plate (including punch ladle, waiter, 3 porringers, tea pot, tea tongs, spoons, &c.), knee buckles, old seal, pair of stone sleeve buttons, gold £195, 16s., old negroes Lot and Hannah nothing, &c.

He and his wife were buried at Newport.

IV. { ESTHER, UNMARRIED. { b. 1713, Aug. 20. d.

V. { DANIEL, UNMARRIED. { b. 1716, Aug. 20. d. — Newport, R. I.

1738. Freeman.

VI. { THOMAS, m. (1) 1741, Sep. 9. JANE BROWN, m. (2) 1766, May 20. MARY MEARS, { b. 1718, May 31. d. 1784, May 1. { b. 1724, Jan. 23. d. 1765, Apr. 28. of John & Jane (Lucas) — Brown. { b. d. 1737, Aug. of — Mears — Newport, R. I.

No issue.

He was a merchant.

1745 to 1775. Postmaster.

1753 to 1771. Secretary of Redwood Library.

He was Register of the Court of Vice-admirality twenty years. Secretary of the Redwood Library and Senior Warden of Trinity Church. He was imprisoned for four months for being a Tory in sentiment, and wrote a journal of his captivity.

1784, Apr. 21. Will—proved 1784, May 31. Exs. brother William and his son Samuel. To wife Mary, house and lot of land in Newport where I now live, for her life, and to her all personal. To brother William Vernon and his son Samuel, my house and lot at death of wife, equally, as "some return for the great kindness and attention to me in my difficulties and sickness." To wife Mary, negro Cato, and his wife Sylvia, and the boy Richard, seven years old. At her death the three negroes to be freed.

Inventory £95, 12s., 11d., viz: household goods, 62 oz. plate. £18, 1s., 8d., 47 volumes printed books and a parcel of pamphlets £2, notes, negro Cato £9, Sylvia £6, Richard £3, silver watch £3, mahogany and black walnut furniture, &c.

VII. { WILLIAM, m. JUDITH HARWOOD, { b. 1719, Jan. 17. d. 1806, Dec. 22. { b. 1724. d. 1762, Aug. 29. of Philip & Mary (Cranston) — Newport, R. I. — Harwood.

1. Samuel, 1757, May 29.
2. William, 1759, Mar. 6.
3. Philip H., 1761, Apr. 3.

He was a merchant.

1742. He was one of the founders of Newport Artillery Company.

1747. He was a member of Redwood Library at time of its being chartered.

1758. At about this time he had eight of his vessels captured.

1773. He was appointed by the Assembly on a committee to prepare a letter to his Majesty's Secretary of State, in regard to a bill then pending in the House of Commons, affecting the fishing interests of Rhode Island merchants in the Gulf of St. Lawrence, &c.

He strongly espoused the cause of the Americans in the Revolutionary period, and advanced sums to the government.

1777, May 6. He was elected by Congress one of the Continental Navy Board, and was President of that board during its existence.

1778, Oct. 21. In a letter of this date written to Josiah Hewes, he estimates his losses at £12,000 sterling besides his real estate at Newport. Nevertheless he expressed himself as content "if we establish our rights and privileges upon a firm and lasting basis," &c.

He was one of the founders of the Newport Bank.

1791-92-93-94-95-96-97-98-99-1800-1. President of Redwood Library.

1809, May 10. Administration to son Samuel, Jr. (who had asked for same two years earlier).

He and his wife were buried at Newport.

VIII. { MARY, UNMARRIED. { b. 1721, Dec. 23. d. 1770, May 17.

(2D WIFE, no issue.)

 See: American Genealogist, v. 20, p. 230-232.

{ **Thomas**, { b. Portsmouth, R. I.
{ m. { d. 1677 (—)
{ —— { b.
{ d.

1639, Jul. 1. He was granted a house lot next Mr. Wickes'.
1641, Mar. 16. Freeman.
1649, May 6. He was a witness to the will of Anthony Paine.
1655. Freeman.
1661, Apr. 30. He bought land in Acushnet and Cohasset.

His will was made by Town Council, as seen by a reference made by his son Samuel.

I. { Samuel, { b. Kings Town, Portsmouth, Kings Town, R. I.
{ m. { d. 1694 +
{ Hannah, { b.
{ d. of

1663, Jul. 3. He and others of Narragansett desired to be under protection of Connecticut colony.
1668, May 4. He and others of Wickford petitioned the Connecticut authorities to re-assume protection of their settlement, or that they might look for government and protection elsewhere.
1671, May 20. He took oath of allegiance to Rhode Island.
1673, May 6. Freeman.
1677, Feb. 11 Portsmouth. He and wife Hannah deeded Thomas Wait the house and all the land in Portsmouth, given and appointed by will made by Town Council, being 30 acres which had been owned by the father of said Samuel and Thomas.
1685, Feb. 2. Freeman.
1693, Mar. 30. He sold William Burrington for £50, two pieces of land in Portsmouth with houses, &c., one piece of land containing 16 acres and the other being 2 acres.
1694, May 7. Kings Town. He sold James Reynolds, Sr., 50 acres in Kings Town for £12.

WAIT. 2d column. I. Samuel. He had probably a daughter Elizabeth, m. George Wightman. He b. 1673, Jan. 8; d. 1761, of George and Elizabeth (Updike) Wightman. Children, 1, George. 2, John, 1701+. 3, Samuel. 4, Elizabeth. 5, Phebe. 6, Deborah.

WAIT. 2d column. I. Samuel, b 1649.

II. { Joseph, { b. Portsmouth, R. I.
{ m. { d. 1665, Aug. 25.
{ Sarah, { b.
{ d. 1665 + of

It is assumed that William Wait of Rochester was his son.

1665, Sep. 16. Administration to widow Sarah. The Town Council determined that as she was with child, if it was a son and lived to twenty-one he should have £40, and if a daughter same sum at marriage, and if it do not live said sum to said widow.

Inventory, £89, 15*s.*, 10*d.*, viz: pewter, wearing apparel, spinning wheel, working tools, 2 guns, pair of bandoliers, 2 cows, 2 yearlings, calf, 7 swine, 4 shoats, 6 pigs, lamb, 10 pounds of butter, cow in hands of Samuel Wait, &c.

III. { Jeremiah, { b. Portsmouth, R. I.
{ m. { d. 1677 (—)
{ Martha Brownell, { b 1643, May.
{ d. 1744, Feb. 15. of Thomas & Ann ( ) Brownell.

(She m. (2) Charles Dyer.)

1673, May 6. Freeman.
1677, May 10. His widow Martha bought for £16, of Daniel Wilcox and wife Elizabeth of Dartmouth, an eighth of a share there.
1690, Mar. 8. Martha Wait, widow of Jeremiah, bought for £20 of Robert and Mary Brownell 30 acres in Little Compton, they calling her sister.
1734, Jan. 29. Will—proved 1744, Mar. 12. Widow Martha Dyer. Exs. cousins (*i. e.* nephews) Joseph and Stephen Brownell. She gave legacies to various nephews and nieces, and to her three sisters Mary Hazard, Anne Wilbur and Susanna Brownell.

IV. { Thomas, { b. Portsmouth, Tiverton, R. I., Dartmouth, Mass.
{ m. { d. 1733, Jun.
{ Sarah Cook, { b.
{ d. 1733 + of John & Mary (Borden) Cook.

He was a tailor.

1673, May 6. Freeman.
1680, Mar. 25. He and seven others bought Pocasset lands for £1,100 of Gov. Josiah Winslow, &c. There were 30 shares, he having one.
1680, Aug. 28. He and wife Sarah sold Thomas Ward of Newport for £12, 10*s.*, land in Dartmouth.
1684, Feb. 9 He and wife Sarah sold Abraham Anthony 27 acres, garden, buildings, &c., for £159.
1687, Aug. 18. Little Compton. He petitioned for 300 acres at Pocasset, "having made improvements there and was one of the purchasers."
1691, Jan. 7. He sold John Woodman, cordwainer, and John Irish, house carpenter, salt marsh for £34.
1692, Mar. 2. Tiverton. He was an inhabitant at organization of the town.
1727. Dartmouth.
1733, Jun. 16. Inventory, £245, 15*s.*, shown by widow Sarah, administratrix. Wearing apparel £16, 16*s.*, 2 old bibles, 8 siver spoons, and 2 silver cups £13, 4*s.*, 3 linen wheels, 2 woolen wheels, 2 cows, heifer, 2 yearlings, 2 calves, 4 swine, 2 stacks of bees, &c.

V. { Mary, { b.
{ m. 1676, Apr. 5. { d. 1713 +
{ Joseph Anthony, { b.
{ d. 1728. of John & Susanna ( ) Anthony.

VI. { Reuben, { b. Dartmouth, Mass.
{ m. { d. 1707, Oct. 7.
{ Tabitha Lounders, { b.
{ d 1707 + of —— & Jane (Kirby) Lounders

1685. He and others appeared at Plymouth Court as proprietors of Dartmouth.
1707, Oct. 11. Will—proved 1707, Nov. 5. Exx. wife Tabitha. To son Thomas, half of farm, &c. To wife, 20 acres, dwelling house, and orchard for life, and movables forever. To four sons, Benjamin, Joseph, Reuben and Jeremiah, rest of lands in Dartmouth, and at death of wife the house and land that she occupies to go to them. To daughters, Eleanor, Abigail and Tabitha Wait, each £3.

Inventory, £271, 10*s.*, 4*d.*, viz: lands £150, 7 cows, 2 oxen, 2 steers, 4 yearlings, 20 sheep, 24 lambs, horse, half a yearling mare, 14 swine, 4 calves, 9 geese, 2 stacks of bees, 7 barrels of cider, 4 beds, warming pan, gun, pair of cards, books, &c.

Kings Town, Exeter, R. I.

I. { SAMUEL, { b. { d. 1752.
m.
ALICE WIGHTMAN, { b. 1666, Dec. 29. { d. 1747 + of George & Elizabeth (Updike) Wightman.

1705, Apr. 21. He quitclaimed certain land to his uncle Reuben, and is called grandson of Thomas, of Portsmouth.
1706, Sep. 2. Grand Juryman.
1709, May 27. He and five others bought 792 acres of the vacant lands in Narragansett.
1747, Dec. 13. Will—proved 1752, Apr. 15. Ex. son John. To son Joseph, all of farm whereon his house stands, containing 200 acres, with buildings, and £50, and my riding beast and bridle. To son Samuel, west half of my homestead farm, he having a house thereon. To children of my deceased son Benjamin, viz: Virtue, Abigail, and John Wait, £250 divided at age. To son John, east half of my homestead and old part of my house, with new part at wife's decease, he paying the £250 above. To wife Alice, use of west half of house while widow, all indoor movables and £18, per year while widow, paid by son John.
Inventory, £208, 2*s.*, viz: wearing apparel £55, cash £5, 6*s.*, pewter, bible and other books £6, linen wheel, stillyards, warming pan, spice mortar, &c.

1. Joseph, 1697, Apr. 27.
2. George, 1699, Aug. 14.
3. Samuel, 1701, Oct. 13.
4. Benjamin, 1703.
5. Martha,
6. John, 1709, Feb. 22.

Kings Town, R. I.

II. { JOSEPH, { b. { d.

1702, Oct. 7. He sold Daniel Briggs of Patience Island, 90 acres at East Greenwich for £40.

III. { SUSANNA, { b. { d. 1758.
m. 1692, Mar. 24.
MOSES BARBER, { b. 1652. { d. 1733. of Barber.

1. Dinah, 1693, Jan. 5.
2. Lydia, 1694, Feb. 24.
3. Samuel, 1695, Nov. 8.
4. Susanna, 1697, Oct. 23.
5. Thomas, 1699, Oct. 19.
6. Joseph, 1701, Oct. 16.
7. Martha, 1703, Nov. 30.
8. Ruth. 1705, Jun. 23.
9. Benjamin, 1707, Mar. 10.
10. Mercy, 1709, Mar. 13.
11. Ezekiel, 1710, Mar. 6.
12. Abigail, 1713, Jan. 6.
13. Daniel, 1715, Apr. 22.
14. Ann, 1717, Oct. 8.

Rochester, Mass.

I. { WILLIAM, { b. { d.
m.
ELIZABETH, { b. { d. of

1. Elizabeth, 1696, Feb. 4.
2. Ruth, 1699, Sep. 29.
3. William, 1701, Jul. 29.
4. Samuel, 1704. Apr. 15
5. Abigail, 1707, Sep. 26.

No issue.

I. { MARY, { b. { d. 1759 +
m. 1700, Feb. 27.
JOHN EARLE, { b. { d. 1759, Aug. 12. of William & Prudence Earle

1. Prudence, 1701, Nov. 18.
2. Mary, 1703, Feb. 19.
3. Oliver, 1705, Feb. 24.
4. Martha, 1708, Sep. 29.
5. William, 1710, Mar. 28.
6. John, 1717, Nov. 10.

Tiverton, R. I.

II. { THOMAS, { b. 1681, Dec. 21. { d. 1757.
m.
ELIZABETH, { b. { d. 1746 (—) of

1708, Mar. 16. He bought land.
1710, Feb. 16. He and Job Briggs bought land.
1720. He sold land.
1746, Aug. 7. Will—proved 1757, Feb. 7. Ex. brother-in-law John Earle and cousin William Earle, of Dartmouth. To daughter Elizabeth, a feather bed. To daughters Sarah and Mary, rest of household stuff. To sons Thomas and John, certain land, they giving their sister Elizabeth a maintenance. To son John, rest of personal estate.

1. Sarah, 1713, Sep. 23.
2. Joseph, 1715, Jan. 10.
3. Thomas, 1716, Sep. 6.
4. Elizabeth, 1718, Dec. 21.
5. John, 1720, Nov. 6.
6. Mary, 1722, Apr. 11.

Portsmouth, R. I.

III. { BENJAMIN, { b. { d. 1734, Aug. 4.
m.
MARY, { b. { d. 1739. of

He was a mariner.
1734, Sep. 9. Administration to widow Mary. Inventory £196, 2*s.*, 8*d.*, viz: wearing apparel, pocket book with £17, 10*s.*, in it, 4 beds £69, 13*s.*, plate £6, 14*s.*, pewter, quadrant £2, 10*s.*, books 5*s.*, ship carpenter's tools, 3 old spinning wheels, warming pan, &c.
1739, Sep. 6. Will—proved 1739, Nov. 12. Widow Mary. Exs. daughters Sarah and Elizabeth. Overseers, brother-in-law John Earle and friend Daniel Howland. To daughter Amey Wait, a spinning wheel, pewter platter, &c. To daughter Sarah Wait, feather bed, spinning wheel, &c. To daughter Deborah Wait, two feather beds, black silk hood, pewter platter, &c. To daughter Judith Wait, spinning wheel, &c. To daughter Elizabeth Wait, spinning wheel, &c, To executors, swine and fowls. To daughters Judith and Elizabeth, the use of wearing apparel and movables.
Inventory £106, 15*s.*

1. Amey,
2. Sarah,
3. Deborah,
4. Judith,
5. Elizabeth,

1. John, 1678, Sep. 16.
2. Joseph, 1682, May 19.
3. Susanna, 1684, Oct. 24.
4. Thomas.

Dartmouth, Mass.

I. { THOMAS, { b. 1683, Apr. 23. { d.
m. 1711, Jan. 25.
MARY TRIPP, { b. 1689, Aug. 22. { d. of Joseph & Mehitable (Fish) Tripp.

1721. He sold his right in his father's homestead to his brother Benjamin.

1. John, 1711, Nov. 30.
2. Reuben, 1714, Feb. 7.
3. Thomas, 1716, Feb. 29.
4. Mary, 1718, Apr. 5.
5. Meribah. 1720, Jul. 20.
6. Mehitable, 1722, Nov. 18.
7. Martha, 1725, Apr. 5.
8. Alice, 1729, Apr. 23.

II. { ELEANOR, { b. 1688, Jan. 4. { d.
m, 1704, Jan. 5.
ABIEL TRIPP, { b. 1684, Jun. 22. { d. of Abiel & Deliverance (Hall) Tripp.

1. Wait, 1705, Apr. 19.
2. Abiel, 1707, May 21.
3. Mary, 1711, Mar. 9.
4. Sarah, 1712, Sep. 3.
5. Eleanor, 1715, Dec. 26.
6. Joseph. 1717, May 25.
7. Thomas, 1719, Dec. 3.
8. Rebecca. 1722, Aug. 28.
9. Elizabeth, 1725, Apr. 16.
10. Amey, 1728, Jan. 19.

See American Genealogist, v. 26, p. 229-30

WARD (John, of Newport).

John,	b. 1619.	Gloucester, Eng., Newport, R. I.
m.	d. 1698, Apr.	
——	b.	
	d.	

He served as an officer in one of Cromwell's regiments, and came to this country on the accession of Charles II.

1666, Mar. 9. He and his son Thomas witnessed a deed from Thomas Waterman to Caleb Carr.

1673. Freeman.

1680. Taxed 13*s*.

He was buried in Newport Cemetery.

His wife may possibly have been that Phebe Ward mentioned in the will of William Fenner (1680) as his sister. This will gives 20*s*., each to children of sister Phebe Ward.

I.	Thomas,	b. 1641.		Newport, R. I.
	m. (1)	d. 1689, Sep. 25.		
	Mary,	b.		
	m. (2)	d.	of	
	Amey Billings.	b. 1658, Oct. 20.		
		d. 1732, Jan. 11.	of Samuel & Seaborn (Tew)	Billings.

(She m. (2) 1692, Mar. 16, Arnold Collins.)

He was a merchant.

1671. Freeman.

1671, Jul. 29. He bought land in Dartmouth, of Thomas and Lydia Burgess, of Newport, for £26, 10*s*.

1672, Feb. 24. Constable. He was ordered to give notice to the constable of Providence to bring William Harris before the council at Newport.

1677, Jun. 11. He and three others were chosen by the Assembly to go to such persons in Newport as they see cause, to know who will advance money for the colony's use in sending Agents to England.

1677–78. General Treasurer.

1678–79–83–84–85–86. Deputy.

1679–80–81. Assistant.

1680, May 5. He was appointed on a committee to put the laws and acts of the colony into such a method that they may be put in print.

1680, May 17. He was on a committee who reported that four hundred and fifty-five persons had deceased in the colony for the space of seven years last past.

1683, Jun. 9. Will—proved 1690, Jun. 2. The will is alluded to but no copy found.

He was buried in Newport Cemetery.

1690, Nov. 25. Amey Ward, widow, and Mary Billings, both of Newport, daughters and co-heirs of Samuel Billings, deceased, of Newport, ratified and confirmed to Henry Tew, a sale that was made by Samuel Billings, deceased, to Richard Tew, deceased, of 1-300 of Conanicut Island.

III. BENJAMIN, b. 1690, Jan. 12. d. 1772. — Dartmouth, Mass.

He was a carpenter.
1714 to 1759. He bought and sold land.
1758, Feb. 1. Will—proved 1772, Feb. 24. Ex. cousin Thomas Anthony. To cousins Mary and Elizabeth Anthony, daughters of Joseph Anthony, of Tiverton, all my real and personal estate.

IV. JOSEPH, b. 1693, Jun. 24. d. — Dartmouth, Mass.
m. 1715, Nov. 30.
ELIZABETH WOLF, b. d. of — Wolf.

He was a blacksmith.
1714. He sold his right in his father's estate to his brother Benjamin.

V. ABIGAIL, b. 1693, Jun. 24. d.

VI. TABITHA, b. 1695, Jan. 15. d.

VII. REUBEN, b. 1695, Jan. 15. d. 1757. — Dartmouth, Mass.
m 1720, Aug. 2.
ELIZABETH, b. d. 1757 + of

1. Jeremiah.

1757, Nov. 1. Administration to widow Elizabeth. Inventory, apparel, 2 cows, heifer, swine, calf, wool cards, bee hives, &c.

VIII. JEREMIAH, b. 1698, Jan. 16. d. 1754. — Dartmouth, Mass.

1727. He sold his interest in his father's estate to his brother Benjamin.
1754, May 20. Will—proved 1754, Nov. 5. Ex. Richard Cornell of Dartmouth. To Reuben Wait and his son Jeremiah, all my lands and buildings. To brother Thomas Wait's wife Mary, certain rooms for life. To cousin Phebe Wait, a red heifer To cousin Jeremiah, rest of live stock and half of farming tools. To cousin Reuben, rest of farming tools. To cousin Meribah Soule, a bed. To cousin Jeremiah, rest of indoor movables. To cousins Reuben and Jeremiah, all my money. To brother Thomas, appparel.
Inventory, apparel, cash, £3, 4*s.*, 10*d.*, mare and colt, 4 cows, pair of oxen, pair of steers, 3 yearlings, 43 sheep, 3 calves, &c.

WARD (JOHN, OF NEWPORT).

x See: American Genealogist, v. 32, no. 1, Jan. 1956, p. 39

I. MARGARET, x b. 1671. d. 1728, Sep. 26.
m.
ROBERT WRIGHTINGTON, b. d. of — Wrightington.

WARD (JOHN, OF NEWPORT). 3d column. I. Margaret. Children, 1. Robert. 2. Thomas. 3. Margaret. 4. Ann.

1 Robert
2 Thomas
3 Margaret
4 Ann

(2D WIFE.)

II. MARY, b. 1679, Nov. 8. d. 1754, Jun. 1.
m. 1700, Feb. 7.
SION ARNOLD, b. 1674, Sep. 12. d. 1753, Aug. 6. of Benedict & Mary (Turner) — Arnold.

III. THOMAS, b. 1683, May 20. d. 1695, Dec. 22.

IV. RICHARD, b. 1689, Apr. 15. d. 1763, Aug. 21. — Newport, R. I.
m. 1709, Nov. 2.
MARY TILLINGHAST, b. 1689. d. 1767, Oct. 19. of John & Isabel (Sayles) — Tillinghast.

1. Amey, 1710, Sep. 4.
2. Thomas, 1711, Oct. 24.
3. Mary, 1713, Dec. 16.
4. Elizabeth, 1715, Feb. 19.
5. Amey, 1717, Feb. 21.
6 Isabel, 1719, Sep. 19.
7. Hannah, 1721, Sep. 4.
8. John, 1723, Aug. 4.
9. Samuel, 1725, May 27. (Gov.)
10. Mercy, 1727, Jun. 3.
11. Margaret, 1729, Apr. 14.
12. Richard, 1731, Jan. 22.
13. Henry, 1732, Dec. 27.
14. Elizabeth, 1735, Jun. 6.

1710. Freeman.
1712–13. Attorney General.
1714. Deputy and Clerk of Assembly.
1714–15–16–17–18–19–20–21–22–23–24–25–26–27–28–29–30. General Recorder.
1719, Mar. He brought suit of trespass to recover land, testimony showing that the will of Thomas Ward was made in June, 1683, and that he died in 1689; and the dates of birth of the three children of Thomas Ward by his wife Amey, with the date of marriage of Mary Ward to Sion Arnold, were also given.
1723, Sep. He was allowed £6, by the Assembly for service in attending the trial of the pirates. Two piratical crafts, the Ranger and Fortune, were engaged by the British ship Greyhound, of twenty guns, Captain Solgar commanding; and one of them was taken into Newport, with her crew of thirty-six men. The pirates were tried and twenty-six of their number were sentenced to be hung. The execution took place at Newport (1723, Jul. 19), on Gravelly Point "within the flux and reflux of the sea."
1726, Jan. 10. He was appointed one of the four commissioners to meet the Connecticut commissioners to settle the line of partition between the two colonies.
1730–31–32–33. Secretary of State.
1740, Sep. He and Samuel Perry were appointed trustees to the Sachem Ninegret.
1740. Deputy Governor.
1741–42. Governor.
1741, Jan. 9. He wrote a letter to the Board of Trade in England in regard to the emission of paper money, &c., in answer to a letter of inquiry. He gave a history of the paper currency issues from 1710 to 1740 and the causes of expenditure, which included the expedition against the French and Indians in 1710 and 1711; a public jail and repairs to the fort at Newport "the metropolis of the colony," in 1715; further repairs to the fort in 1721; a bounty of 9*d.*, per pound in 1731, on all good water rotted, well manufactured hemp, to be paid farmers for their encouragement, the soil being found very suitable for its production; and a bounty of 5*s.* per barrel on whale oil, 1*d.* on whale bone per pound, and 5*s.* per quintal on good merchantable codfish taken in any vessels belonging to this colony, a scheme for a harbor at Block Island for the encouragement of the fishing interest in 1733; and in the same year (just finished) a very handsome regular fort of stone and mortar much larger than the former one, with a large battery on the west side and a purchase of cannons and other military stores being made for it. He says that in 1738 there was issued £100,000, for building a large brick State House for colony use, and to erect a light house; in 1740 a fine sloop was bought of one hundred and fifteen tons, mounted with twelve carriages and twelve swivel guns, for defence against Spain if we should be attacked. He declares that we have now (1741) above one hundred and twenty sail of vessels belonging to the inhabitants of this colony, all constantly employed in trade, some on the coast of Africa, others in neighboring colonies, many in the West Indies, and a few in Europe. Besides two hundred soldiers raised for his Majesty's immediate service, the merchants of the town of Newport have equipped five privateers with near four hundred men who are now cruising against the Spaniards. Our fort is supplied with thirty-six cannon well mounted and furnished with a suitable quantity of military stores, by which, and our privateer, able to fight a hundred men on her deck, we are become the barrier and the best security of the New England trade. Within six or seven years several Newport merchants have contracted a correspondence in London and procured goods to be sent them, and thereby so well supplied our shop keepers that our dependance on Boston hath been in some measure taken off, and in return our merchants have remitted their correspondents ships of our own building, logwood fetched from Honduras, and bills of exchange purchased of planters in the West Indies. Bills for six years past had been equal to silver at 27*s.*, per oz. In regard to the easiest method of sinking the Bills of Credit now outstanding, after our utmost efforts to do our money justice and save the inhabitants from inevitable ruin, we have not been able to find out a better way than to sink the several banks in ten annual payments. We have learnt from experience that this is a safe course and therefore pursue it. He closes finally by saying that considering the good foundation on which our bills have been emitted and substantial security taken (according to the several acts) for paying same, no possible damage can accrue, notwithstanding revilings of that Province (Massachusetts), for loss of their trade. The whole amount of bills outstanding at the time he wrote was £340,000, or reduced to sterling money £88,074, 16*s.*, 10¾*d.*
1755, Jul. 17. Will—proved 1763, Sep. 7. Exx. wife Mary. Overseer son Samuel. To son Thomas, all my law books and largest silver tankard. To son Samuel, lot of land in Little Compton and a farm there of 130 acres, and land in Newport. To son Henry, land in Newport where he dwells. To grandson Richard Ward, son of Thomas, all interest in Nashawana Island (one of the Elizabeth Islands). To daughters Mary Flagg, Amey Vernon, Isabel Merchant, Hannah Ward, Margaret Ward and Elizabeth Ward, land in Dartmouth, equally. To wife Mary, all my plate and all other household goods, negro man Scipio, negro woman Mercy, negro boy Cæsar, horse, riding chaise and three pews in Sabbatarian Meeting House. To five daughters Isabel, Mary, Hannah, Margaret and Elizabeth, the sum of £1,600. To Sabbatarian Church in Newport, commonly called Seventh Day Baptist, £500 toward support and maintenance of minister. To Joseph Maxon, of Newport, 50 Spanish milled dollars. To wife Mary, and six daughters Mary, Amey, Isabel, Hannah, Margaret and Elizabeth, the rest of personal estate. To son Samuel, £400.
He and his wife were buried in Newport Cemetery.

JOHN, m. PRISCILLA HOLLIMAN, | b. 1615. d. 1654 ± | b. d. 1652 + | London, Eng., [Providence, Warwick, R. I.

of Ezekiel & Susanna (Oxston) Holliman.

1635, Apr. 15. He embarked at London, in the ship Increase, for New England, "having taken the oaths of allegiance and supremacy." He was called twenty years of age at this time.

1637, Aug. 20. Providence. At this date (or a little later), he with twelve others signed the following compact: "We whose names are hereunder desirous to inhabit in the town of Providence, do promise to subject ourselves in active or passive obedience, to all such orders or agreements as shall be made for public good of the body in an orderly way, by the major assent of the present inhabitants, members of families incorporated together into a town fellowship, and such others as they shall admit unto themselves, only in civil things."

1640. He and three others were appointed a committee in all matters of difference between inhabitants of Providence and Pawtuxet as to dividing line. They reported in July of this year that they had seriously and carefully endeavored to weigh and consider all these differences to bring them to amity and peace: "We have gone the fairest and equallest way to produce our peace."

1640, Jul. 27. He and thirty-eight others signed an agreement for a form of government.

1643, Jan. 12. Warwick. He and ten others bought of Miantonomi for 144 fathoms of wampum, a tract of land called Shawomet (Warwick).

1643, Sep. 12. He with others of Warwick were notified to appear at General Court at Boston to hear complaint of two Indian Sachems, Pomham and Socconenocco, as to "some unjust and injurious dealing toward them by yourselves." The Warwick men declined to obey the summons, declaring that they were legal subjects of the King of England and beyond the limits of Massachusetts territory, to whom they would acknowledge no subjection. Soldiers were soon sent who besieged the settlers in a fortified house. In a parley it was now said "that they held blasphemous errors which they must repent of"—or go to Boston for trial, and they were soon carried thence.

1643, Oct. 17. He was brought with others before the court charged with heresy and sedition.

1643, Nov. 3. They were sentenced to imprisonment during the pleasure of the court, and should they break jail or speak against church or state, on conviction they should die. He was imprisoned till March of following year in Boston, his companions being sent to other places in Massachusetts. On release they were expelled from both Massachusetts and Warwick.

1644, Jun. 20. He, as secretary for the proprietors of Warwick, signed a letter to Massachusetts authorities informing them that "since you expelled us out of your coast" the Narragansett Indians had subjected themselves and their lands unto King Charles of England, &c.

1647. Town Clerk.

1648. Clerk of Assembly.

1652, Apr. 24. It was ordered at a town meeting that he for his misdemeanors under annexed, should be disenabled from bearing any office in the town until he give satisfaction, and denied a vote in the town concerning its affairs. The charges against him were First; for calling the officers of the town rogues and thieves with respect to their office. Second; for calling the whole town rogues and thieves. Third; for theatening the lives of men, &c.

1652, May 19. It was agreed by Assembly that the case of Priscilla Warner now depending in the General Court of Trials, shall there be issued.

1652, May 27. He, desiring liberty to ship himself and family to England from some port in Massachusetts, the request was granted "provided he take up his abode in the ship, and thence not to come forth until his departure, except upon urgent occasion, for his voyage, by order of two magistrates." He took with him his family except his daughter Rachel. He died abroad, and his daughters Susanna and Mary remained in England, his son John returning to inherit his grandfather Ezekiel Holliman's estate, at the request of the latter, who sent for him.

I. JOHN, m. 1670, Aug. 4. ANN GORTON, | b. 1645, Aug. 1. d. 1712, Apr. 22. | b. d. | Warwick. R. I. | of Samuel & Elizabeth ( ) Gorton.

1655, Jun. 4. It was ordered by Town Council of Providence that the care of John Warner, his child, be transferred to Mr. Holliman, with his house at Warwick, and all other rights belonging to said Warner.

1659, Feb. 2. He was "by consent of overseers or fathers" bound apprentice unto William Field, of Providence, for seven years from August 1st next ensuing; he agreeing to keep his master's secrets, not to frequent taverns or alehouses, &c., and to be found by William Field with convenient apparel, meat, drink and lodging. It was stipulated that he was not to be assigned by his master to anyone without consent of overseers, nor was he to be removed out of the colony, and when set free he was to have one new suit of apparel.

1665, Feb. 19. He drew lot 14, in a division of lands at Providence.

1665, May 31. He had a legacy of a young mare from will of William Field.

1668, Feb. 22. He agreed with Mrs. Mary Holliman, widow of Ezekiel, to mow the grass in her meadow yearly for her use, and give her liberty to be buried by her husband Ezekiel Holliman, she surrendering to said Warner the house she now dwells in, &c.

1672-74-79-83-85-90. Deputy.

1682, May 19. He sold to Stephen Arnold, of Pawtuxet, a thirteenth part of a little neck east of Pawtuxet Falls, bounded with water, called the vineyard, for £2, 5*s*., said land having in the original belonged to Ezekiel Holliman, grandfather of the grantor.

1688 Grand Jury.

1696, Mar. 26. He had a power of attorney given him by Elizabeth Gould (widow of Thomas), to collect rents due from land bequeathed by her father William Baulstone, she being blind.

1702. He gave 6*s*., toward building the meeting house for Quakers at Mashapaug.

1708, Jan. 6. He deeded youngest son Ezekiel, for love, &c., all my right in purchase of Mashantatack, and also certain land in Warwick.

1710, Aug. 19. He deeded eldest son John, for love, &c., land in Coweset.

1712, May 26. Administration to son John. Inventory, £84, 10*s*., 2*d*., viz: wearing apparel £6, 2*s*., 8*d*., household goods £17, 17*s*., 8*d*., beds, &c. £15, 17*s*., 6*d*., neat cattle £22, 10*s*., 7 swine, 17 sheep, 7 lambs, a horse, Indian boy £4, &c. Sworn to by son John Warner.

1712, Jul. 18. A receipt was given by Jeremiah Crandall and wife Priscilla, of Westerly, for £10, a legacy ordered to be paid us by deceased father John Warner, said legacy being received from brother John Warner.

II. SUSANNA, | b. d.

III. MARY, | b. d.

IV. RACHEL, m. 1669, Nov. 16. ABEL POTTER, | b. d. 1724, Nov. 8. | b. d. 1692. | of George Potter.

WATERMAN.

RICHARD, m. BETHIAH, | b. 1590 ± d. 1673, Oct. 26. | b. d. 1680, Dec. 3. | Salem, Mass., Providence, R. I.

1629. He came from England this year, and was alluded to in a letter from the "Company of Massachusetts Bay," (dated at Gravesend, April 17), to Mr. Endicott. The letter says that Richard Waterman's "chief employment will be to get you good venison."

1632, Sep. 4. He was allowed 40*s*., for killing a wolf at Salem about two months since.

1637, Aug. 20. He had his son Nathaniel baptized.

1637, Dec. 25. His name was in a list of inhabitants, and seven persons formed his family.

1638, Mar. 12. He and others having had license to depart from Massachusetts, summons was to go out for them to appear (if they be not gone before) at the next court to answer such things as shall be objected.

1638, Oct. 8. Providence. He was one of the twelve persons to whom Roger Williams deeded land that he had bought of Canonicus and Miantonomi.

1639. He was one of the twelve original members of First Baptist Church.

1640, Jul. 27. He and thirty-eight others signed an agreement for a form of government.

1643, Jan. 12. Warwick. He and ten others bought of Miantonomi for one hundred and forty-four fathoms of wampum, the tract called Shawomet (*i. e.* Warwick).

1643, Oct. 17. He was among the band of Gortonites arraigned at Boston at this date; he and the other Warwick men having surrendered to the armed expedition sent against them by Massachusetts. They were assured that

I. MEHITABLE, m. ARTHUR FENNER, | b. d. 1684 (—) | b. 1622. d. 1703, Oct. 10. | of Thomas Fenner.

II. WAIT, m. HENRY BROWN, | b. d. | b. 1625. d. 1703, Feb. 20. | of Brown.

III. NATHANIEL, m. 1663, Mar. 14. SUSANNA CARDER, | b. 1637. d. 1712, Mar. 23. | b. d. | Providence, R. I. | of Richard Carder.

1666, May 31. He took the oath of allegiance to the King.

1668-78-80-81-82-83-85-90-97-99-1702. Deputy.

1676, Aug. 14. He was one of those to whom a whole share in the Indian captives was voted. He had been one of those who "staid and went not away" in King Philip's war.

1676-81-82-83-86-87-89-91-93-94-95-96-97-1700-1-2-3-4-5-6-7. Town Council.

1879, Jul. 1. Taxed 18*s*., 9*d*., "Nathaniel Waterman and his mother."

1687, Sep. 1. Taxed 19*s*., 9*d*.

1688. Ratable estate, 16 cows, 3 heifers, 4 oxen, 9 two years, 3 three years, 11 yearlings, 6 horses, 5 colts, 8 acres tillage, 8 acres pasture, 6 acres meadow, 1½ acres salt marsh, 8 acres mowing pasture, 300 acres woodland, swine, 20 sheep, rights in land.

1711, Feb. He deeded his homestead lot with all real and personal estate to his son Richard, half at date and half at death of himself and wife.

I. JOHN, | b. 1673, Jun. 5. d. 1732, Nov. 18. | Warwick, R. I.
m. (1) 1694, Nov. 27.
ELIZABETH COGGESHALL, | b. 1671, Nov. 27. d. 1711, Mar. 13. | of John & Elizabeth (Timberlake) | Coggeshall.
m. (2) 1713, Aug. 6.
SUSANNAH PEARCE, | b. 1679, May 7. d. 1727, Aug. 4. | of Giles & Elizabeth (Hall) | Pearce.
m. (3) 1730, Sep. 24.
ELIZABETH COWELL, | b. d. 1732 + | of | Cowell.

1. John, 1695, Aug. 8.
2. Elizabeth, 1697, Apr. 19.
3. Anne, 1699, Apr. 29.
4. Susanna, 1701, Sep. 4.
5. Rachel, 1704, Feb. 8.
6. William, 1706, Aug. 31.
7. Samuel, 1708, Dec. 13.
(2d wife.)
8. Mary, 1714, Sep. 5.
9. Priscilla, 1716, Jan. 10.
10. William, 1718, Mar. 4.
(3d wife, no issue.)

1702-9-23-25-26-27-29-31. Deputy.

1712, Dec. 9. He made a confirmatory deed to his brother Ezekiel, of one-half certain land in Coweset, which his honoured father John Warner on his death bed gave to his youngest son Ezekiel.

1728, May 2. Will—proved 1732, Dec. 23. Ex. son John. To daughter Elizabeth Knowles, £10. To daughters Anne, Susannah, Rachel and Mary Warner, £50, each. To son Samuel, bed, &c., and £5 in tools for husbandry work at age of twenty-one. To son William, feather bed, &c., that was his mother's and £5, in husbandry tools at age. To son Samuel, dwelling house and twelve acres bought of Stukeley Westcott and other land. To son William, lot at Brush Neck and land in Coweset. To eldest son John, all other housing, lands and rights, and residue of movable estate.

Inventory, £445, 1*s.*, 6*d.*, viz: books £7, 16*s.*, 6*d.*, surveyor's instruments £3, money scales, ink horn, spectacles, razors, spinning wheel and cards, 3 drinking glasses, warming pan, lignum vitæ mortar, stillyards, carpenter's tools, pair of oxen, mare, 4 cows, 6 yearlings, calf, 52 sheep and lambs, 5 swine, 5 barrels of cider, 3 barrels of apple beer, 47½ oz. plate £38, pewter, 4 candle sticks.

1732, Dec. 23. Agreement was made by three sons John, Samuel and William Warner, concerning certain lands of deceased. It was declared by them that knowing in what manner their father intended to give land unto his three sons, and although he left a written will made some years ago, yet having greatly altered the property after execution of the will—they therefore quitclaim to each other, thus making division.

At the same date an agreement was made between the widow Elizabeth Warner and her son-in-law (*i. e.* stepson) John Warner. He engaged to deliver to her all goods she brought from Boston to my deceased father, and to be at expense of transportation to Boston again to same place where they were, and to pay her £50, she agreeing to discharge and acquit the estate.

WARNER. 3d column. II. Priscilla. Births of part of children, 1, Jeremiah, 1702, June 25. 3. John, 1704. Oct. 1. 5. James, 1706, Sep. 4. 7. Experience, 1709. Dec. 28. 9, Susanna, 1715, Mar. 11. 10. Mary, 1717. May 13.

II. PRISCILLA, | b. d. 1750, Feb. 24.
m. (1)
JEREMIAH CRANDALL, | b. d. 1718. | of John & Hannah ( ) | Crandall.
m. (2)
ABRAHAM LOCKWOOD, | b. 1670 ± d. 1747, Jun. | of | Lockwood.

1. Jeremiah,
2. Ann,
3. John,
4. Hannah,
5. James,
6. Sarah,
7. Experience,
8. Patience,
9. Susanna,
10. Mary,
(By 2d husband, no issue.)

III. ANN, | b. d.

IV. EZEKIEL, | b. d. 1761, Sep. 16. | Warwick, Providence, Cranston, R. I.
m. 1717, May 30.
SARAH BENNETT, | b. 1693, Jan. 31. d. 1761 + | of Samuel & Sarah (Forman) | Bennett.

1. John,
2. Martha,
3. Sarah,
4. Anne.

1714. Freeman.

1728-29-30-33-34-45-47. Providence. Deputy.

1734-35-36-37-38-39-40-41-42. Assistant.

1741, Jan. 27. He was appointed by Assembly on committee to examine whether boundary marks between Rhode Island and Connecticut had been removed (near south-west corner of Warwick purchase).

1743. He was elected Assistant but refused to serve.

1750, Aug. His daughter Sarah married Thomas Fenner, Jr.

1755, Jan. 23. Will—proved 1761, Sep. 29. No executor named and widow Sarah was appointed by Town Council to administer. To wife Sarah, all indoor household goods, sorrel white face mare, two side saddles, bridle, what cow she pleases, ten sheep and two swine, provided that when she is done with goods and chattels what remains be divided among my two daughters and granddaughters, viz: to Martha Searle and Anne Fenner, and granddaughter Penelope Warner, the division to be at discretion of widow. To wife, use of all the dwelling house and of one-half the barn and twenty acres of homestead farm, with privilege of pasturage, cutting firewood, &c., while widow. To son John, all wearing apparel and 48½ acres at Coventry, which was my father-in-law Captain Samuel Bennett's, late of said Coventry, deceased. To grandson Ezekiel Warner, a gun. To daughter Martha Searle, a cow, ten sheep and £100. To daughter Anne Fenner, a cow, ten sheep and £100. To son John, use for life of all my land in plantation of Mashantatack, except farm purchased of Samuel Ralph and that which wife has use of, but at decease of wife that to be for his use. At decease of son John, the land he has use of to be divided to my three grandsons Ezekiel, Samuel and John Warner. The homestead where I dwell, 170 acres, buildings, &c., to go to grandson Ezekiel. The farm bought of Samuel Ralph, to be grandson Samuel's part. The land where son John now dwelleth to be grandson John's part, and he to have also other land. To son John, negro Toney and all movable estate not given away, as stock, tools, &c.

Inventory, £7,472, 15*s.*, viz: books of account and other books £12, cash and securities £2,158, gun, 4 beds, round table, 21 chairs, a pair worsted combs, 2 woolen wheels, desk, negro Toney and his clothes and bedding £600, black mare, white face, £90, 4 oxen £500, 8 cows £480, 3 steers, 2 heifers, 3 calves, 60 sheep, 5 hogs, 3 pigs, &c.

1. George,
2. John,
3. Abel,
4. Benjamin,
5. Stephen,
6. Mary,
7. Ichabod,
8. Job,

WARNER. 3d column. Add V Mary m. Jeremiah Westcott, b. 1666, Oct. 7, d. 1757, Oct. 7 of Jeremiah and Eleanor (England) Westcott. Children, 1. Zephaniah. 2. Thomas 1707, May 5. 3. Jabez. 4. Eleanor.

WATERMAN.

1. Thomas, 1652, Sep.
2. Arthur,
3. Sarah,
4. Freelove, 1656.
5. Bethiah,
6. Phebe,
7. Samuel,

1. Henry,
2. Phebe,
3. Richard,
4. Joseph.

I. BETHIAH, | b. 1664 ± d. 1742, Jul. 23.
m. 1687, Jan. 27.
RANDALL HOLDEN, | b. 1660, Apr. d. 1726, Sep. 13. | of Randall & Frances (Dungan) | Holden.

1. John, 1687, Oct. 26.
2. Wait, 1690, Feb. 26.
3. Susanna, 1692, Jan. 21.
4. Randall, 1694, Feb. 2.
5. Wait, 1696, Sep. 2.
6. Mary, 1699, Mar. 15.
7. Frances, 1701, Sep. 29.

II. NATHANIEL, | b. d. 1725, Jun. 14. | Providence, R. I.
m. 1692, May 9.
MARY OLNEY | b. 1668, Jan. 13. d. 1725 (—) | of Epenetus & Mary (Whipple) | Olney.

1. Bethiah, 1693, Feb. 27.
2. Nathaniel, 1695, Sep. 9.
3. Joseph, 1697, Jan. 17.
4. Zuriel, 1701, Mar. 19.
5. Sarah, 1702, Nov. 6.
6. Mary, 1705, Mar. 23.
7. John, 1709, Oct. 6.

1725, Jun. 10. Will—proved 1725, Jul. 3. Ex. son Zuriel. To son Nathaniel, westward part of my homestead at Mashipauge, &c. To son Zuriel, rest of homestead, dwelling house, &c. To son Joseph, 80 acres where he dwelleth, a 70 acre piece, &c. To son John, 150 acres. To sons Nathaniel,

they should go "as free men and neighbors" when captured, but notwithstanding this they were committed to jail and their captors took "eighty head of cattle besides swine and goats." The sentence of the court was imprisonment for most of the offenders, but Waterman was released on payment of a fine, only to be again arrested later and then imprisoned. The sentence declared that "Richard Waterman being found erroneous, heretical and obstinate" it was agreed he should be detained prisoner till September, unless five magistrates do see cause to send him away. When released, the penalty of a return to Massachusetts was to be death.

1650, Sep. 2. Providence. Taxed £2, 10*s*.

1651, Jan. 27. He bought of Hugh Bewit a house and lot next where the former dwells.

1655. Freeman.

1655–56–58. Commissioner.

1656. Juryman.

1658. Warden.

1665, Feb. 19. He had lot 79 in a division of land.

1670, Sep. 5. He came before the Town Council and presented a deed of gift (signed by himself and wife Bethiah under date of September 1st) of certain lands which he gave to his three grandchildren, the sons of Resolved Waterman, deceased. It was ordered that the deed be recorded. To Richard the eldest grandson and Resolved the youngest, 80 acres between Providence and Pawtuxet divided between them, and also a share of meadow, all to be theirs at age. To grandson John, half of all grantor's lands in Warwick, meadow, upland and commoning. To the mother Mercy Waterman, use of land while the children are under age, and if any die before coming of age all the rest of the children, including Wait and Mercy, to have equal share of estate of such deceased brother.

The children of his deceased son as named in the deed of September 1st (recorded at Warwick), were Richard, John, Resolved, Wait and Mercy.

The Friends' records state that he lived till he was old, and died and was buried at Providence upon the 26th day of the 8th mo., 1673.

1712, Mar. 22. Will—proved 1712, Apr. 22. Administration by son Richard. To grandsons the two Zuriel Watermans, all lands at Westquenock equally, viz: to Zuriel, son of Richard, and to Zuriel, son of Nathaniel. To son Richard, 20 acres. To son Benjamin, the rest of land that is to be taken up in my right according to agreement of men of Pawtuxet and men of Providence. To son Nathaniel, lands in Pawtuxet, but if he enjoys them without much trouble then he is to allow his brother Benjamin a quantity as he may see fit.

Inventory, £1,019, 3*s*., 7*d*., viz: mortgage bond, &c. £688, 12*s*., 4*d*., neat cattle £63, 14*s*., 100 sheep £30, horsekind £30, 15*s*., money £103, 1*s*., 6*d*., 3 barrels cider, books £1, 18*s*., musket, pewter, oats, rye, flax, hemp, Indian corn, &c.

IV. RESOLVED, b. 1638, d. 1670. Providence, R. I.
m. 1659 ±
MERCY WILLIAMS, b. 1640, Jul., d. 1705 + of Roger & Mary ( ) Williams.

(She m. (2) 1677, Jan. 3, Samuel Winsor.)

1667. Deputy.

1670, Aug. 29. Inventory, £72, 13*s*., viz: house and home shares £30, other parcels of land aggregating about 100 acres, besides shares and rights in undivided lands, 4 cows, 2 oxen, 6 two years, 2 yearlings, 2 calves, horse, mare, colt, foal, sow, 4 shoats, 3 spring pigs, gun, sword, working tools, spinning wheels, 3 beds, warming pan, table, 4 chairs, pewter, iron, brassware, 5 acres, lying at Gotham Valley, house standing in the woods, &c.

1671, Jan. 23. The widow Mercy positively refused to receive any power of administration from the Town Council or to give any bond, and the council found she had already administered without order from them. They therefore concluded that "they have proceeded as far in the matter as is for them to do, and that the said Mercy Waterman is liable to respond for the said estate when legally called thereunto as administrator of her own wrong."

There was some jangling after Mercy's second marriage, between her new husband and her son by her first marriage, concerning property.

1679, Jul. 1. Taxed, 6*s*., 3*d*. Samuel Winsor and orphans of Resolved Waterman.

A grandson of Resolved Waterman (viz: Benoni), recorded in his family bible that his grandfather the said Resolved, had five children, viz: Richard, Resolved, John, Mercy and Wait.

WATERMAN. 3d column. IV. Resolved. His daughter Mercy change to Mary.

Joseph and John, rest of land equally, and sons Nathaniel and Zuriel to help John when the latter builds his house. To daughter Mary Waterman, a feather bed, &c., and £94. To daughter Bethiah Sprague, £13. To son Zuriel, a feather bed. To sons Nathaniel, Joseph, Zuriel and John, the rest of movables.

Inventory, £566. 5s., 9d., viz: silver 255 oz. £204, feather bed, linen yarn, blanketing yarn, flax, pewter, 2 wheels, 6 chairs, 8 swine, 6 cows, 2 calves, a bull, 47 sheep and lambs, mare, &c.

III. RICHARD, m. 1697, Apr. 1. ABIGAIL ANGELL, — b. / d. 1744, Aug. 3. — b. 1679, Feb. 2. / d. 1742 (—) of James & Abigail (Dexter) — Providence, R. I. — Angell.

1. Richard,
2. Neriah,
3. Nathan,
4. Zuriel,
5. Abigail,
6. Amaziah, 1713, Aug. 27.

1708. Justice of the Peace.

1712–18–19–23–24–25–26–27–32 33. Deputy.

1713–19–27–28–29–30. Assistant.

1715 to 1755. Town Clerk.

1718–24–25–26–27. Clerk of Assembly.

1731–34. Town Council.

1736, Oct. He was authorized by the Assembly to draw £80, toward rebuilding Weybosset Bridge.

He bore the title of Captain, and was thus distinguished from his cousin of same name.

1742, Aug. 16 Will—proved 1744, Aug. 20. Exs. sons Richard and Amaziah. To son Amaziah, homestead where I dwell, and lands in Neck, at Masipauge, at Weybosset Plain, &c. To son Richard, privilege for life of dwelling house where testator formerly lived and brought up his family, also 7 acres east side of Town street, 11 acres on the Plains and 242 acres in Warwick, &c. To son Neriah, lands both sides of Woonasquatucket River, and meadows on Moshassuck River, &c. To grandson William Field, 100 acres in Warwick. To three sons of my son Zuriel, deceased, viz: Thomas, Jonathan and James, land in Warwick. To son Amaziah, land in Attleboro. To granddaughter Susanna Waterman, an acre. To daughter Abigail Field, £100. To four children Richard, Neriah, Amaziah and Abigail, silver money equally. To three sons, beds, &c. To son Richard, a cow and cooper's tools. To son Neriah, a log chain, half the sheep, cow and heifer. To son Amaziah, the rest of cattle, half of the sheep, mare, saddle, and husbandry tools. To three sons, rest of movables.

Inventory, £2,229, 4s., 7d., viz: silver 67¾ oz., £101, 12s., 6d., piece of gold £4, 10s., 2 razors, 2 pairs of spectacles, 2 mortars, warming pan, pocket compass, 4 feather beds, books £18, cooper's tools, 30 old barrels, gun, pistol, sword, pewter, cider mill, 30 loads of hay, 8 swine, 26 sheep, 6 lambs, bull, 7 cows, 4 oxen, heifer, 4 calves, mare, &c.

IV. BENJAMIN, m. ——— — b. / d. 1762, May 11. — b. / d. of — Providence, Johnston, R. I.

1. Benjamin,
2. Job,
3. Charles, 1705, Mar. 12.
4. Mary,
5. Martha.

1700, Dec. 20. He had 17 acres laid out.

1738, Mar. 14. He deeded son Job, for love, &c., 50¼ acres and 30 poles near Abbott's Pond on east side of road to Killingly, also another acre, &c., and orchard and fencing.

1760, Oct. 9. Will—proved 1762, May 29. Exs. son Job and grandson Gideon. To grandson Gideon Waterman, northerly part of farm where I dwell. To gandson Benjamin, 175 acres on westerly side of farm. To grandson Charles, my mansion house, land, &c. To grandson Jeremiah, land. To granddaughter Susannah Angell, wife of Christopher, Amey Brown, wife of Obadiah, Lydia, Martha, Prudence, Wait and Freelove Waterman, land in Glocester. The widows of testator's sons to be supported by grandsons Charles and Benjamin respectively. To grandsons Abraham and James, land in Glocester. To daughters Mary Sheldon and Martha Brown, £300 each. To three granddaughters, children of son Charles, £50, each. If any grandchild die, their share to go equally to surviving grandsons (viz: sons of testator's sons Charles and Benjamin), and to Job, son of testator.

Inventory, £3,214, 17s., viz: 14 sheep, 2 cows, 3 heifers, 3 bulls, 3 yearlings, pewter, sword and belt, cash £97, money scales, &c.

V. ANNE, m. RICHARD WATERMAN, — b. / d. — b. 1660, Jan. / d. 1748, Sep. 28. of Resolved & Mercy (Williams) — Waterman.

1. Mercy, 1702, May 11.
2. Richard, 1706, Apr. 30.
3. Resolved, 1711, Aug. 20.

I. RICHARD, m. ANNE WATERMAN, — b. 1660, Jan. / d. 1748, Sep. 28. — b. / d. of Nathaniel & Susanna (Carder) — Providence, R. I. — Waterman.

1. Mercy, 1702, May 11.
2. Richard, 1706, Apr. 30.
3. Resolved, 1711, Aug. 20.

1681, Feb 21. His age was declared to be twenty-one last January, by Samuel Winsor, who calls him his son-in-law (*i. e.* stepson).

1687, Sep. 1. Taxed 3s., 7d.

1688. Ratable estate, 2 cows, steer, horse, mare, yearling, 3 swine, 3 acres planting, 2 shares of meadow, 8 acres pasture, lot in town, 60 acres by my house, 90 acres at Sockanosett, 66½ acres unlaid out, 20 acres, 2½ acres, &c.

1742, Feb. 24. Will—proved 1749, Feb. 11. Ex. son Richard. To son Resolved, 2 cows, and wearing apparel. To son Richard, all household goods, husbandry tackling, &c., and all other movable goods, cattle, sheep and horses.

Inventory, £187, 10s., viz: 2 cows, cooper's tools, great chair, feather bed, loom, wearing apparel, pewter, gun, warming pan, &c

II. MERCY, — b. 1663 ± / d.

III. JOHN, m. ANNE OLNEY, — b. 1666. / d. 1728, Aug. 26. — b. 1668, Jan. 13. / d. 1745, Oct. 26. of Thomas & Elizabeth (Marsh) — Warwick, R. I. — Olney.

1. Elizabeth, 1692, Apr. 18.
2. Mercy, 1694, Jun. 27.
3. Anne, 1696, May 20.
4. John, 1698, Feb. 5.
5 Benoni, 1701, May 25.
6. Resolved, 1703, Oct. 13.
7. Phebe,
8. Patience,

1680, Feb. 1. He chose guardians, being of sufficient age.

1706–7–8–11–16–18–20–23–24–25–26. Deputy.

1718, Sep. 1 He called himself aged about fifty-two years in testimony at this date.

1721–22–26–27–28. Assistant.

1728, Oct. 2. Inventory, £1,239, 14s., 11d. (Administration to widow Ann.) Gun, sword, belt and bandoliers, 5 feather beds, 2 flock beds, warming pan, tankard, beer cup, porringer, silver cup 12½ oz. £10, silver money 43 oz. £34, 8s., gold ring £1, 5s., bonds £133, 13s., 10d., negro man Will £75, girl Raney £75, 2 steers, 17 cows, 5 heifers, 5 two years, 16 yearlings, 4 calves, 5 swine, riding mare, 16 horse kind, 3 colts, 130 sheep, 30 lambs, 12 fowls, 20 geese, turkey, 14 barrels cider, 1,000 lbs. tobacco.

1745. Inventory £389, 10s. Widow Ann. Administration to son Captain Resolved.

IV. RESOLVED, m. (1) ANNE HARRIS, m. (2) MERCY, — b. 1667 ± / d. 1719, Jan. 13. — b. 1673, Nov. 12. / d. of Andrew & Mary (Tew) — b. / d. 1750 (—) of — Providence, R. I. — Harris.

1. Resolved, b. 1703
2. Mercy,
3. Joseph,
(2d wife.)
4. Wait,
5. John,
6. Hannah, 1719, Jan. 13.

(She m. (2) 1730, Jun. 11, Benjamin Smith.)

1687, Sep 1. Taxed 5d.

1688. Constable.

1715. Deputy.

He held the office of Ensign.

1719, Oct. 5. Administration to widow Mercy. Inventory, £445, 16s., 1d., viz: silver and bills of credit £3, 10s., great bible, little bible, and several small books, a bible and testament which were by his first wife, 10 pewter platters, 6 plates, 7 basins, 12 porringers, 20 spoons, dividers, box rule, carpenter's tools, 2 flock beds, 3 feather beds, 2 pairs of oxen, 8 cows, 10 heifers, bull, 2 steers, 9 yearlings, 2 horses, 4 mares, 6 swine, 12 loads of hay, apple mill, cider press, cider, beer, 2 spinning wheels, pair of cards, &c. Real estate £1,479.

1721, Dec. 2. His widow having complained that there was no way from her dwelling house to the town, it was voted by the Town Council to summon a jury to lay a convenient way from the house to highway. Resolved Waterman, son-in-law (*i. e.* stepson) appeared on behalf of Mercy, and hearing the vote read, refused to accept, "and so it fell."

WEAVER.

CLEMENT, b. d. 1683. Newport, R. I.
m.
MARY FREEBORN, b. 1627. d.

of William & Mary ( ) Freeborn.

He was called Sergeant Clement Weaver, Sr., to distinguish him from his son Clement, Jr.

1655. Freeman.

1664, Mar. 6. His wife Mary, having had a piece of land given me by my father William Freeborn, to me and my children (being 20 acres in Portsmouth), exchanged said land with her brother Gideon Freeborn, and signed with consent of husband, and children along with me. Mary Weaver, Clement Weaver, Sr., Clement Weaver, Jr., William Weaver, John Weaver. (Perhaps her son Thomas was too young to sign.)

1671, Jun. 7. Juryman.

1678. Deputy.

1680. Taxed £4, 4*s*., 3*d*.

1680, Aug. 28. He deeded to son Clement Weaver, of East Greenwich, 90 acres there, and at his decease to go to William Weaver, son of aforesaid son Clement.

1682, Feb. 13. He sold George Vaughan, of Newport, 10 acres in East Greenwich.

1683, Oct. 20. Under this date Samuel Hubbard, of Newport, wrote William Gibson, of New London: "Old Weaver is dead, near an hundred years old."

1680, Nov. 4 Will—proved 1683. Witnesses, William Hitchcock and Thomas Ward.

A reference to this will is found in a list of seventeen wills (between the dates of 1676 and 1695), that were presented to the court in 1700, by parties interested, the law requiring three witnesses, and these wills having but two.

I. ELIZABETH, b. d.
m.
THOMAS DUNGAN, b. d. 1688. of William & Frances (Latham) Dungan.

II. CLEMENT, b. d. 1691. Newport, East Greenwich, R. I.
m. (1) b. d. of
m. (2) 1677, Sep. 26.
RACHEL ANDREW, b. d. of Andrew.

(She m. (2) William Bennett.)

1676, Jan. 15. He and John Weaver, sons to Sergeant Clement Weaver and Mary his wife, daughter to deceased William Freeborn, of Portsmouth, sold for £30, to Gideon Freeborn, 20 acres in Portsmouth.

1677, Oct. 24. He was indicted for having declared himself married to Rachel Andrew at the house of Joseph Clarke.

1677, Oct. 31. He and forty-seven others were granted 5,000 acres to be called East Greenwich.

1680, Sep. 14. East Greenwich. He and John Wood exchanged 90 acres each, to be to Clement for life and then to his son William.

1683–90. Deputy.

1684, Nov. 22. He let out certain cattle to David Shippee, for seven years, and three years, and then to have return made of certain cattle and part of increase of same.

1687. Overseer of the Poor.

1688. Grand Jury.

1691, Sep. 8. Inventory, £151, 2*s*., 6*d*., shown by widow Rachel. 2 oxen, 5 cows, 9 heifers, 2 yearlings, 3 calves, 38 sheep, 8 lambs, 2 horses, 3 mares, 2 colts, 10 lean swine, 6 pigs, 3 shoats, 59 cheeses, pair of stillyards, 2 spinning wheels, loom, 2 ploughs, 6 hives of bees, carpenter's tools, pewter, &c.

1692, Mar. 14 His widow Rachel made an indenture with Clement Weaver, son of deceased. She was to have all housing, orchard, &c., and half of 10 acres, for seven years, she keeping house in repair and paying to Clement, 20*s*., each year on March 1st, and if she married before the term was out to deliver peaceably said property. She was not to suffer the hay from 5 acres to be carried from the lot but it was to be foddered upon the said 5 acres. Clement was to allow her £3, per year upon her changing her condition, till the seven years are out.

Possibly he had another son, viz: Richard Weaver, who died at East Greenwich, 1752, Oct. 11, aged 70 years, 10 months and 26 days.

III. WILLIAM, b. d. Newport, R. I.

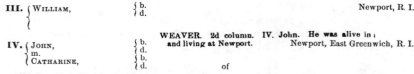

WEAVER. 2d column. IV. John. He was alive in
and living at Newport.

IV. JOHN, b. d. Newport, East Greenwich, R. I.
m.
CATHARINE, b. d. of

1676, Jan. 15. He joined with his brother Clement and mother Mary in a deed to Gideon Freeborn.

1677, Oct. 31. He was one of the grantees of 5,000 acres to be called East Greenwich.

1685, Feb. 24. Catharine Weaver, with other matrons and widows, composed a jury of women in case of a young woman with child. It would seem that this Catherine could have been none other than wife or widow of John Weaver.

WEAVER. 2d column. IV. John. Erase wife's name and the item 1685. (It was his brother Clement's wife Rachel who served on the jury.) He died before 1702, at Newport, and probably never lived at East Greenwich. Probably he had 1 Thomas who was father of the first eight children now given Thomas 3 (Thomas 2); and probably he had also II John, who was father of five children, now given John 3, (Thomas 2). 3d column. I. Thomas. Middletown, not Newport. His wife in 1740, was Mary Coggeshall, of John and Mary (Stanton) Coggeshall. Erase first eight children. IV. Benjamin. His wife was Hannah Coggeshall of John and Mary (Stanton) Coggeshall. VII. John. Erase marriage and children. He lived at Middletown, R. I., where he had a wife and children.

WEAVER. 2d column. IV. John. 1703, Feb. 11.—**Thomas Weaver, Jr., of Newport,** (son of John Weaver, and **grandson of Clement Weaver** the elder), with wife Mary, **deeded his interest** (1-2 of 1-15) in Westquadnoid, in **Narragansett country** (15 miles square) to **Thomas Lillibridge of Newport. 3d column.** I. Thomas, d. 1760. 1760, **Aug. 20. Will-proved** 1760, **Dec. 15. He** mentions **daughters Patience Rogers, wife of John,** and **Mary Dyer.**

1725, May 17. The movable estate of Resolved Waterman was proportioned as follows: To widow, £86, 12*s.*, 8*d.* To son Resolved, £49, 10*s.*, 1*d.* To other five children, £24, 15½*d.* each, viz: Mary, Joseph, Wait, John, Hannah.

1726, Oct. 17. His son Resolved laid claim as legatee of his uncle Andrew Harris' estate, as legal representative of his deceased mother.

1734, Feb. 25. Agreement as to division of real estate was made by following persons: Benjamin Smith and Mercy his wife, of Providence, late widow of Resolved Waterman, Resolved Waterman of Smithfield, eldest son of deceased, Alexander Lovell and Mary his wife, eldest daughter of deceased (now both of Scituate), Joseph Waterman, second son of deceased, Wait Waterman, second daughter of deceased, John Waterman, youngest son of deceased, Hannah Waterman, youngest daughter of deceased, and Samuel and Joshua Winsor, guardians of John and Hannah Waterman. The widow was to have her thirds as laid out till daughter Hannah is twenty-one, and after that to have a third of the old homestead farm, and choice of dwelling houses thereon, and to resign up to her son John the other two-thirds of old homestead, but she hold her part in the mill thereon standing. To Alexander Lovell and wife Mary, 50 acres, &c. To Joseph Waterman, land. To Wait Waterman, £130, paid by brother John. To Hannah Waterman, £130 paid by John. To Wait and Hannah, land also.

V. WAIT, b. 1668 ±, d. 1711 +
m. 1685, Feb. 12.
JOHN RHODES, b. 1658, d. 1716, Aug. 14. of Zachariah & Joan (Arnold) Rhodes.

1. Zachariah, 1687, Nov. 5.
2. Mary, 1689, Nov. 20.
3. John, 1691, Nov. 20.
4. Joseph, 1693, Sep. 25.
5. William, 1695, Jul. 14.
6. Phebe, 1698, Nov. 30.
7. Resolved, 1702, May 22.
8. Wait, 1703, Dec. 16.

WEAVER.

1. William,
2. Clement,
3. Thomas,
4. Jeremiah,
5. Elizabeth,
6. Mary,
7. John,
8. Rebecca,
9. Sarah,

I. CLEMENT, b. 1669, Feb. 19, d. 1738, Feb. 19. East Greenwich, R. I.
m. 1691, Jan. 1.
HANNAH LONG, b. , d. 1759. of Philip & Hannah (   ) Long.

1. Clement, 1695, Oct. 27.
2. Alice, 1698, Oct. 22.
3. Jonathan, 1704, Sep.
4. Clement, 1707, Jul. 7.
5. Mary, 1710, Mar. 19.
6. Gideon, 1714, Feb. 22.

1690. Freeman.

1691, Dec. 19. He deeded certain land to his brothers Joseph and Benjamin.

1697, Nov. 2. He gave a receipt to William Bennett upon the account of his wife that now is, my mother-in-law (*i. e.* stepmother), for full satisfaction of all that is or was or may be due by reason of a lease or covenant made between me and my mother-in-law Rachel Weaver, bearing date 1692, Mar. 17.

1702. He gave 6*s.*, toward building the Quaker Meeting house at Mashapaug.

1705. Deputy.

1713, Mar. 19. He deeded to cousins (*i. e.* nieces) daughters of brother-in-law Philip Long, deceased, viz: Elizabeth, Hannah, Susannah and Mary, certain land.

1736, Oct. 16. Will—proved 1738, Mar. 25. Exs. wife Hannah and son Jonathan. Overseers, Town Council. To eldest son Jonathan, homestead of 137 acres, house, orchard, &c, and other land. To son Clement, 15 acres, house, &c. (reserving place where my honoured father was buried), land in Coweset, a cow, feather bed, &c.; but if Clement die without issue or is unable to manage same, then the Coweset land to go to Jonathan, and a house lot in East Greenwich to go to grandson Philip Weaver, and the above said goods and chattels to daughter Mary's children. To daughter Mary Weaver, £80. (She had married her cousin John, son of William Weaver.) To son Gideon, certain land bought of Henry Matteson, with house, orchard, &c., other land, a cow, feather bed, &c.; but if he die without issue, to go to son Jonathan's children. To wife Hannah, all household goods to dispose of to children and grandchildren, and while widow to have equal privilege with son Jonathan in the house and to movable estate, also chief power over the negro man, who at her decease was to go to son Jonathan. Son Jonathan to provide for my son Gideon, and daughter Mary to provide for my son Clement, during their natural lives, if they prove incapable to manage their affairs.

Inventory, £797, 15*s.*, viz: purse and wearing apparel £29, 10*s.*, pewter, stillyards, woolen wheel, loom, negro man and his bedding £120, bonds £151, 7*s.*, a hogshead and 2 barrels of cider, 2 mares, 4 oxen, 4 cows, steer, 3 two year, 3 yearlings, 42 sheep, sow, 4 shoats, fowls, geese, &c.

1757, Dec. 5. Will—proved 1759, Mar. 31. Widow Hannah. Exs. son Jonathan Weaver and kinsman Thomas Casey. To son Jonathan, a loom, quilt wheel and 20*s.* To grandchildren, children of son Jonathan viz: Sarah Andrews, George, Peleg, Philip and Hannah Weaver, each £3. To great-grandchild Hannah Greene, £10, at interest till eighteen. To grandson John Weaver, a feather bed, &c., at age and £20, at interest. To grandson Clement Weaver, great arm chair. To granddaughter Mary Weaver, feather bed, warming pan, linen wheel, table, &c. To granddaughter Comfort Weaver, feather bed, chest, &c. To great-grandson Philip Weaver, £3, at interest till of age. To grandson John Weaver, handiron. To son Clement, £10. To son Gideon, 20*s.* To granddaughters Mary and Comfort Weaver, all indoor movables undisposed of. To grandsons Clement and John Weaver, cattle, sheep, &c.

Inventory, £957, 10*s.*

II. WILLIAM, b. , d. 1718, May 22. East Greenwich, R. I.
m. 1693, Dec. 17.
ELIZABETH HARRIS, b. , d. 1748. of Harris.

1. William, 1695, Sep. 19.
2. Clement, 1696, Oct. 29.
3. Joseph, 1698, Apr. 2.
4. Thomas, 1700, Apr. 11.
5. John, 1701, Nov. 24.
6. Alice, 1703, Nov. 7
7. Thomas, 1708, Jan. 12.
8. Benjamin, 1710, Jun. 16.
9. Harris, 1712, Nov. 3.

1718, Jul. 14. Administration to widow Elizabeth. Inventory, £127, 17*s.*, 8*d.*, viz: cider mill, pewter, pair of oxen, 4 steers, 4 cows, 2 two years, 3 calves, horse, mare, colt, 12 sheep, 10 hogs.

1745, Apr. 8. Will—proved 1748, Sep. 24. Widow Elizabeth. Ex. son-in-law Samuel Bassett. To daughter Alice Bassett, a feather bed, wearing clothes, &c. To son Harris Weaver, chest, &c. To son Benjamin, flock bed, &c. To rest of children, 5*s.*, each, viz: to William, Thomas, Joseph, John, and grandson David, son of Clement, deceased.

Inventory, £230, 6*s.*

III. JUDITH, b. , d. 1751 +
m. 1694.
HENRY MATTESON, b. , d. 1752, Apr. 13. of Henry & Hannah (Parsons) Matteson.

1. Judith, 1694, Oct. 16.
2. Henry, 1696, Apr. 22.
3. Jonathan, 1701, Jun. 6.
4. Mary, 1704, Feb. 13.
5. John, 1706, Oct. 27.
6. Sarah 1709, Apr. 13.
7. James, 1712, Mar. 20.
8. Elizabeth, 1714, Dec. 15.
9. Ebenezer, 1718, Mar. 15.
10. Hezekiah,

(2D WIFE.)

IV. JOSEPH, b. 1679, Dec. 4, d. 1751, Jul 11. East Greenwich, R. I.
m. 1706, Feb. 21.
ELIZABETH SWEET, b. , d. of Daniel & Eleanor (   ) Sweet.

1. Benjamin, 1706, Nov. 29.
2. Mary, 1708, Apr. 21.
3. Elizabeth, 1709, Sep. 20.
4. Rachel, 1711, Jan. 26.

1702. Freeman.

1716–20. Deputy.

1751, Jul. 23. Inventory, £1,125, 16*s.*, 6*d.* Administration to widow Elizabeth. Wearing apparel, 2 tables, 9 chairs, walking cane, bonds £655, cheese press, woolen wheel, linen wheel, pewter, court book, 2 bibles, hat case, old horse, mare, 3 milch cows, sow, 5 shoats, 3 yearling barrows, &c.

V. BENJAMIN, b. , d. East Greenwich, R. I.
m.
MERCY, b. , d.

1702, Mar. 15. He having been defamed by William Case, the latter was admonished and owned that what he said was but what he heard others say and desireth William Bennett and others to pass by the offence. Benjamin Weaver was called William Bennett's son-in-law (*i. e.* stepson) in the above proceedings.

V. Thomas. He was probably not son of Clement, but son of John[2] (Clement[1]). 1703, Feb. 11 Thomas Weaver, of Newport, son of John Weaver, of Newport, deeded land in East Greenwich, which "I received from my honored grandfather, Clement Weaver, the elder late of said Newport," which he bequeathed, etc., in will of said Clement Weaver, the elder, bearing date Nov. 21, 1680. The term "cousin" used in the fourth line by Thomas Dungan would thus have the more usual meaning of nephew.

V. THOMAS, — b. ; d. 1753. — Newport, Middletown, R. I.
m.
MARY, — b. ; d. ; of

1680, Aug. 28. He was witness to a deed from his father to Clement Weaver, Jr.

1682, Feb. 13. He was witness to a deed from his father to George Vaughan.

1682, Jun. 28. He had a deed from Thomas Dungan, of Newport, of 100 acres in East Greenwich, for love, &c. The grantor calls him cousin meaning evidently brother-in-law.

1684, Dec. 3. He had 10 acres laid out at East Greenwich.

1696–1710–15–21–22–23. Deputy.

1699, May 11. He deeded to friend George Foster, of Newport, for love, &c., 100 acres at East Greenwich, house, orchard, &c. His wife Mary joined him in this deed.

1702, Feb. 18. He was one of the proprietors of common lands.

1750, Jan. 6. His daughter Elizabeth made her will (proved 1751, Feb. 18), leaving all personal to her sister Comfort.

1752, Mar. 9. His daughter Comfort made her will (proved 1752, Jul. 20). She mentions brothers Thomas, Clement, Benjamin and John, and sister Mary Foster.

1752, Jul. 17. Will—proved 1753, Jun. 18. Ex. son Thomas. To son Thomas, all my homestead farm and buildings, where I dwell. To son Clement, certain land and buildings where he liveth. To son Benjamin, certain land in Middletown and buildings where he liveth. To son John, 50s. To daughter Mary Foster £5.

Inventory, £401, viz; wearing apparel £100, cupboard, great chair, churn, 7 chests, &c.

If V. Thomas be proved identical with the Thomas, son of John, several changes should be made in several generations.

WEEDEN.

See: American Genealogist, v. 20, p. 232-233

JAMES, — b. ; d. 1673 (—) — Boston, Mass., Newport, R. I.
m. (1)
——— — b. ; d.
m. (2) 1650.
ROSE PAINE [Anthony (w. of] — b. ; d. 1673 +

1638, Jul. 13. He and Chad Brown testified regarding the will of Sylvester Baldwin, a fellow passenger in ship Martin, which had arrived same year.

1648. Newport. Member of Court of Trials.

1655. Freeman.

1657, Dec. 10. He had a grant of 8 acres.

1658, Mar. 31. He sold Daniel Grinnell, 6 acres. (He was living at Portsmouth at this time.)

1673, Dec. 17. He probably died before this time, for at this date Rose Weeden, of Portsmouth, for maintenance for life and £30, sold Matthew Grinnell 53 acres in Portsmouth.

(His wife had been twice married before, first to Matthew Grinnell, and second to Anthony Paine in 1643.)

I. WILLIAM, — b. ; d. 1676. — Newport, R. I.
m.
——— — b. ; d. ; of

1648, Oct. 12. He was one of the members of First Baptist Church, in full communion.

1655. Freeman.

1659–62. Commissioner.

1661, Mar. 20. He was one of those associated in purchase of Misquamicut (Westerly).

1665–69–71–72–74. Deputy.

1670. He "laid down 3s. for the present," to accommodate a committee going to Connecticut. The same year he with three others lent the colony £30, on behalf of Newport, and it was ordered that he should be paid 5s., 6d., that he had previously loaned.

1670–72. Sergeant.

1674, Jun. 30. He had recorded his ownership of 60 acres, bounded partly by Joseph Card and James Rogers and partly by mill pond, together with house, barn and orchards.

1676, Apr. 20. He was appointed one of the three trustees under will of Rev. John Clarke, of this date. These trustees were directed at death of Mr. Clarke's widow to devote the profits of certain land to the relief of the poor of Newport, and bringing up of children unto learning.

1676, Nov. 29. Under this date Samuel Hubbard writes from Newport to Mr. Edward Stennitt in England, and after mentioning the devastation caused by King Philip's war, he recounts the recent deaths in the First Baptist Church. He says "of the old church first Mr. Joseph Torrey, then my dear brother John Crandall, then Mr. John Clarke, then William Weeden, a deacon, then John Salmon; a sad stroke in very deed, young men and maids, to this day I never knew or heard the like in New England."

1677, Dec. 24. Benedict Arnold's will of this date mentions land on Conanicut Island, bounded partly by land of assignees of William Weeden, deceased. It was this ownership in land there that led his son John Weeden to settle at Jamestown.

Possibly one or two of those assumed to be his sons may have been grandsons (and sons of William[3]).

II. JAMES, — b. ; d. 1702. — Newport, R. I.

1655. Freeman.

1682. Juryman. (He was called James Weeden Sr., at this time, to distinguish him from his nephew James.)

1702, Sep. 7. Will—proved. Exs. William Weeden, Sr., and William Weeden, son of James Weeden, brother to said William Weeden. He first makes provision for his cousin (*i. e.* nephew) James Weeden, but if he does not come "to his right senses and understanding," then all said houses and lands to go to my cousin William Weeden, son of said James Weeden, he paying legacies to his brothers and sisters, viz: To my cousin James Weeden, son of above said James Weeden, 5s., and like amount to cousin Robert Weeden. To cousins Jonathan, Job and Philip Weeden, £5 each. To cousin Mary Greenman, wife of Thomas Greenman, £3. To cousin Mary Weeden, £3, and like amounts to cousins Rebecca, Sarah and Elizabeth Weeden. If the testator's cousin (*i. e.* nephew) James Weeden comes to his senses he was to pay above legacies, otherwise the aforesaid William Weeden was to pay them at death of his father James Weeden, and as the children come of age. If said cousin James Weeden's wife Mary survived him she was to be maintained out of the land during widowhood. He bequeathed the rest of his estate equally to cousin William Weeden and ——— Weeden.

VI. RACHEL, b. 1684, Dec. 24. d.

I. THOMAS, b. d. — Newport, R. I.
m.
——, b. d. of

1713. Freeman.

His last three children (and perhaps the others) were by wife Mary.

1. John, 1694, Aug. 5.
2. Mary, 1697, Jul. 7.
3. Hannah, 1700.
4. Benjamin, 1702.
5. Martha, 1704.
6. Peleg, 1706.
7. Joseph, 1708.
8. Jonathan, 1711.
9. Patience, 1716, Aug. 4.
10. Mary, 1721, Feb. 23.
11. Thomas, 1723, Jul. 6.

II. CLEMENT, b. d. 1711 + — Newport, R. I.
m.
MARY FREEBORN, [Wm. (w. of b. 1678, Apr. 3. d. 1711, Nov. 14. of Benjamin & Frances (Parker) Hall.

III. MARY, b. d.
m.
GEORGE FOSTER, b. d. of Foster.

1. Hannah, 1700, Nov. 29.

IV. BENJAMIN, b. d. 1754. — Middletown, R. I.
m.
HANNAH, b. d. 1763. of

1752, Aug. 17. Will—proved 1754, Sep. 16. Ex. son Thomas. He calls himself "somewhat advanced in years." To son Benjamin, part of my farm, and a third of cattle, horses, sheep and swine, after wife has had her two cows and horse. To wife Hannah, all household goods, two cows, horse, negro woman Sylvia (or if latter is deceased then Phebe), use of biggest lower room and bedroom and privilege in cheese house. To her also seven cords of wood, cut at the door, two hundred pounds of pork, and beef, apples, cider and £50 yearly, paid half by son Benjamin and half by son Thomas. To daughters Hannah Mott, Avis Carr, Mary and Rebecca Weaver, £50 each, the latter having privilege with mother while unmarried till death of mother. To son Thomas, rest of real and personal estate.

Inventory, wearing apparel £180, pewter, warming pan, 2 woolen wheels, pair of cards, 34 cheeses, 3 oxen, a yearling, pair of steers, 3 calves, 7 cows, a heifer, 60 swine, 54 sheep and lambs, 3 mares, horse, colt, negro Sylvia £150, Peter £400, Phebe £350, Kate £350, &c.

1763, Jan. 10. Will—proved 1763, Feb. 21. Widow Hannah. Ex. son-in-law Jacob Mott, Jr. She mentions son Benjamin, daughter Avis Carr, wife of Benjamin, daughter Mary, wife of Thomas Weaver, and daughter Rebecca, wife of Charles Dyer.

1. Benjamin, 1717, Jan. 18.
2. Thomas, 1718, May 1.
3. Hannah, 1720, Mar. 18.
4. Avis, 1725, May 26
5. Mary, 1726, Oct. 10.
6. Rebecca, 1734, Jul. 7.

V. ELIZABETH, b. d. 1751.
UNMARRIED.

VI. COMFORT, b. d. 1752.
UNMARRIED.

VII. JOHN, b. d. — Newport, R. I.
m. 1710, Mar. 15.
ALICE BERRY, b. d. of Elisha & Eleanor ( ) Berry.

1. Elizabeth, 1712, Mar. 1.
2. Thomas, 1713, Oct. 3.
3. Julia, 1616, Mar. 1.
4. Mary, 1718, May 9.
5. Ruth, 1719, Mar. 11.

WEEDEN.

I. JAMES, b. d. 1711 + — Newport, R. I.
m.
MARY, b. d. 1725 ± of

1674, Jan. 7. The birth of his son James was placed in the Quaker records, but he became a member of the First Baptist Church afterwards.

He was for some years bereft of his reason, as is seen in the church records and by the will of his uncle James Weeden. This will (which was proved 1702, Sep. 7) made provision for him if he came "to his right senses and understanding," but if not his son William was to have certain houses and land, after paying legacies to his brothers and sisters, all of whom are named. Provision was also made for the wife if she outlived her husband. One daughter was married at the time the will was made (viz: Mary wife of Thomas Greenman), but some of the children were not yet of age.

1711, Nov. 15. He was living, at this date, but unable to act at the ordination of William Peckham, "owing to distraction."

1725. Will—Mary Weeden, widow. She mentions son William and his daughter Mary, daughter Elizabeth Peckham, and sons James, Robert, Jonathan, Job and Philip.

1. William,
2. Mary,
3. James, 1674, Jan. 7.
4. Robert,
5. Jonathan, 1687, Jan. 16.
6. Job,
7. Philip,
8. Rebecca,
9. Sarah,
10. Elizabeth.

II. WILLIAM, b. d. 1722 + — Newport, R. I.
m.
SARAH PECKHAM, b. d. of John Peckham.

1680. Taxed £1, 9s., 10½d.

1698. Clerk of House of Deputies.

1698-1703-4-14. Deputy.

1702-3-4-5-6-7-8-9-10-11-12-13-14-15. Treasurer of the proprietors' land association, and member of the committee of fourteen persons, who were appointed to attend to proprietors' land. He had a share allotted him of 18 acres at Green End.

1703. Captain.

1703, Jan. 17. He was one of the eighty-four shareholders in Coaster's Harbor and Goat islands. "Tenements built in Goat Island shall be built low, not to hinder the guns of the fort to shoot over them."

1708, May 21. He was witness to the will of Thomas Peckham.

1710. He was one of the appraisers of inventory of John Weeden of Jamestown.

1718. A difficulty and division occurred in the First Baptist Church, of which he was a member, occasioned by his alleged maladministration in the office of Trustee under the will of Dr. John Clarke. There was a difference of opinion in the church and four years later the case was still unsettled.

1718, Apr. 20. He was appointed one of the overseers of Henry Tew's will.

1. Mary.

III. PHILIP, b. d. 1727 + — Newport, R. I.
m.
ANN SISSON, b. 1672, Dec. 17. d. of George & Sarah (Lawton) Sisson.

He was a shoemaker.

1698. He and wife Ann sold land.

1714. Freeman.

1724, Jul. 26. His daughter Sarah was married to Joseph Ward.

1727. He was a member of First Baptist Church.

1. Sarah.

IV. JOHN, b. d. 1710, Aug. 26. — Jamestown, R. I.
m.
JANE UNDERWOOD, b. 1669, Mar. 17. d. 1736 of Henry & Jane ( ) Underwood.

1694, Aug. 5. He sold to John Fones of Narragansett, certain land at Jamestown for £10.

1705-7-10. Deputy.

He was drowned.

1710, Jul. 19. Will—proved 1710, Sep. 16. Exx. wife Jane. To son John, two cows and twenty sheep. To son Daniel, two cows and twenty sheep. To daughter Sarah Weeden, £20 and a bed, and like legacies to daughters Jane and Hannah Weeden. To son John, a house and land, and a right at Dutch Island. To sons John and Daniel, all working tools. To son Daniel, house and land which was given me by my father. To loving mother-

1. John, 1687, Nov. 9.
2. Sarah, 1690, Apr. 25.
3. Jane, 1693, Mar. 1.
4. Daniel, 1696.
5. Hannah, 1699, Apr. 14.

WESTCOTT. See: American Genealogist, v. 20, p. 233.

STUKELEY,	b. 1592.	Salem, Mass., Providence,
m.	d. 1677, Jan. 12.	[Warwick, R. I.
———	b.	
	d.	

1636. Freeman, and received as an inhabitant.

1637, Dec. 25. He had a house lot of 1 acre allotted to him, his family consisting of eight persons.

1638, Mar. 12. He with others of Salem, &c., having had license to depart, it was ordered by General Court of Massachusetts that summons should go out for them to appear at the next court in May if they be not gone before, to answer such things as shall be objected.

1638, Oct. 8. Providence. He and eleven others had a deed from Roger Williams of land the latter had bought of Canonicus and Miantonomi.

He had a lot granted him soon after.

1639, Jul. 1. He and his wife are alluded to in a letter from Rev. Hugh Peters of Salem to the church at Dorchester, as having had "the great censure passed upon them in this our church." He says that they and certain others "wholly refused to hear the church, denying it and all the churches in the Bay to be true churches," &c

He was one of the twelve original members of First Baptist Church, organized at Providence this year.

1640, Jul. 27. He signed an agreement with thirty-eight others of Providence for their civil government.

1648, Jun. 5. Warwick. He was recorded as one of the inhabitants.

1650, Sep. 2. Taxed 13*s*., 4*d*. (at Providence, where he still owned real estate.)

1651, May 6. It was ordered "that the ditch which Stukeley Westcott made upon the street way, shall stand; being about three or four pole, having paid his fine to the town which he was fined."

1651-52-53-55-60 Commissioner.

1652, Mar. 1. He bought 36 acres of John Gereardy.

1652, Jun. 7. John Cooke was granted liberty to make a highway between his uncle Stukeley Westcott and himself. At the same date Stukeley Westcott and two others were appointed to lay out the meadows about the town on Thursday next, "for the inhabitants which are yet not provided for, and so it is to be cast lot for."

1652-53-54-55-56, &c. Surveyor of Highways. He was often on juries, the pay of a juryman then being 6*d*. for each case.

1653. Assistant. He was on a committee this year to confer with the Indians about fencing, &c.

1654. The Town Council met at his house.

I. DAMARIS,	b.		
m. 1640, Dec. 17.	d. 1678 +		
BENEDICT ARNOLD,	b. 1615, Dec. 21.		
	d. 1678, Jun. 19.	of William & Christian (Peak)	Arnold.

II. ROBERT,	b.	Warwick, Kings Town, R. I.
m.	d. 1676.	
CATHARINE,	b.	
	d.	of

(She m. (2) 1678, Apr. 10, James Hazleton.)

1648, Jun. 5. He was recorded as an inhabitant.

1654, May 16. He had lately been at the Dutch settlements, where he went about to buy beavers and liquors, according to the testimony of Giles Glover before the Assembly.

1655. Freeman.

1659. Commissioner.

1659, Aug. 3. He was accused by the General Attorney of endeavoring by profession and likewise by progression to action—to subvert part of the jurisdiction to Plymouth Colony, and he was suspended from acting as a commissioner at this court.

1671. Lieutenant.

1671, May 20. Kings Town. He took oath of allegiance.

1676. He was "killed by the Indians in the late war," as the records state.

in-law, her maintenance for life. To wife Jane, all cash, bills, bonds, household goods and rest of movables, and Indian servant Toby, she paying legacies to daughters Sarah and Jane, and wife to enjoy house and land given son Daniel till he is of age, while she remain widow.

Inventory, £271, 14*d.*, viz: cash £41, 17*s.*, 6*d.*, beds, warming pan, pewter, 8 silver spoons, silver cup, 2 hives of bees, stillyards, money scales, looms, 3 spinning wheels, carpenter's tools, 10 cows, pair of oxen, 3 two year old, 3 yearlings, 3 calves, 2 mares, 80 sheep, 30 lambs, 12 swine, Indian boy Toby £6, &c.

1725, Dec. 31. Will—proved 1736, Apr. 16. Widow Jane. Ex. brother John Underwood. To son John, £15 and a silver spoon. To daughter Jane Cook, £20. To daughter Hannah Carr, £60. To three grandchildren, John, Sarah and Jane Cook, £10 divided. To children John and Daniel Weeden, Jane Cook and Hannah Carr, silver money equally. To daughter Hannah Carr, a silver spoon and silver cup. To granddaughters Sarah and Jane Carr, each a silver spoon. To daughters Jane Cook and Hannah Carr, all my wearing apparel. To son John, what I have there. To son Daniel, what he has there. To daughter Hannah Carr, all household goods I have there.

Newport, R. I.

V. JEREMIAH, { b. ; d. 1756. **WEEDEN. 3d column. V. Jeremiah. He had also a daughter Frances.**
m. (1)
MARY CLARKE, { b. ; d. of Jeremiah & Ann (Audley) Clarke.
m. (2)
SARAH CLARKE, { b. ; d. 1729. of Jeremiah & Ann (Audley) Clarke.

1. Jeremiah,
2. William,
3. Ann,
4. Mary,
5. Margaret, 1701.
6. James,
7. Caleb,
8. Francis.
(2d wife, no issue.)

1707. Member of Second Baptist Church.
1708. He was a witness to will of Thomas Peckham.
1714, Oct. 13. His son Jeremiah, Jr., was an adult as early as this date (witness to will of Thomas Weeden).
1719. He had a deed from his father-in-law of certain land in Providence, providing for certain annual payments to said Jeremiah Clarke or his wife Ann during their lives.

Newport, R. I.

VI. JOSEPH, { b. ; d. 1745.
m.
HANNAH DAVOL, { b. ; d. 1744 + of Jonathan & Hannah (Adley) Davol.

1. Joseph,
2. Jonathan,
3. William,
4. Phebe,
5. Sarah,
6. Hannah,
7. Hope,
8. Daughter.

1707. Member of Second Baptist Church.
1708. Freeman.
1744, Mar. 17. Will—proved 1745. Exs. sons Joseph and William. He mentions wife but not her name. To son Joseph, land, &c. To son Jonathan, land, &c. To son William, £50 at death of wife. To daughters Phebe Phillips and Sarah Tripp, £30 each. To daughters Hannah and Hope, dwelling house and £10 each at death of wife. To grandson Joseph Sweet, £10.

Newport, R. I.

VII. THOMAS, { b. ; d. 1714, Dec. 28.
m.
GRACE, { b. ; d. 1714 + of

1. Mary,
2. Samuel,
3. Thomas,

He was a weaver.
1700. Constable.
1714, Oct. 13. Will—proved 1715, Jan. 11. Exx. wife Grace. To sons Samuel and Thomas, a gun, sword and cow each at sixteen. To them also the dwelling house and land at death or marriage of wife Grace, they supporting her for life or widowhood. To daughter Mary Weeden, £5 at twenty years of age. To wife, all movable estate for life or widowhood, she paying £20, to daughter Mary at twenty years of age, and to bring up children to learn to read and write English, and two sons to be apprenticed to useful trades. He appoints his brother William guardian for daughter Mary.

VIII. PHEBE, { b. 1660 ± ; d. 1745.
m.
WILLIAM PECKHAM, { b. 1647 ± ; d. 1734, Jun. 2. of John & Mary (Clarke) Peckham.

1. Samuel,
2. Mary,
3. Phebe,
4. Deborah,

IX. HANNAH, { b. ; d. 1722 +
m. (1)
WILLIAM CLARKE, { b. ; d. 1683, Sep. 30. of Joseph Clarke.
m. (2)
THOMAS PECKHAM, { b. ; d. 1709. of John Peckham.
m. (3)
JOSEPH CLARKE { b. 1643, Apr. 2. ; d. 1727, Jan. 11. of Joseph Clarke.

1. William,
2. Thomas, 1682, Feb. 15.
3. Hannah, 1683, Mar. 25.
(By 2d husband.)
4. Daniel,
5. James,

WESTCOTT.

1. Benedict, 1642, Feb. 10.
2. Caleb, 1644, Dec. 19.
3. Josiah, 1646, Dec. 22.
4. Damaris, 1648, Feb. 23.
5. William, 1651, Oct. 21.
6. Penelope, 1653, Feb. 10.
7. Oliver, 1655, Jul. 25.
8. Godsgift, 1658, Aug. 27.
9. Freelove, 1661, Jul. 20.

I. CATHARINE, { b. 1664, May 16. ; d. 1692 ±
m. 1688, Mar. 25.
CHARLES HAZLETON, { b. ; d. 1712, Mar. 28. of Charles Hazleton.

1. Charles, 1689, Apr. 11.

North Kingstown, R. I.

II. ZOROBABEL, { b. 1666, Apr. 15. ; d. 1745.
m. (1)
JANE, { b. ; d. of
m. (2)
MARY DAVIS, { b. ; d. 1743 + of Davis.

1. Philip,
2. Freelove,
3. Robert, 1700, Dec. 5.
4. Margaret, 1702, Mar. 8.
5. Zorobabel, 1703, Nov. 8.
6. Catharine, 1705, Apr. 17.

1687, Sep. 6. Kings Town. Taxed 2*s.*, 10*d.*
1700, May 1. Fined 20*s.* for taking part in a riot.
1743, Nov. 15. Will—proved 1745, Oct. 9. Exs. wife Mary and son Robert. To daughters Margaret Matteson, Freelove Wilkie, and Catharine Whitman, legacies. To grandchildren Valentine Whitman, Thomas Wilkie and Abraham Matteson, 50 acres each. To grandsons Zorobabel and Stukeley, all homestead at death of wife. To four children Robert, Margaret, Catharine and Freelove, all personal at death of wife. To granddaughter Jeane Westcott, daughter of Philip, a house and lot at Warwick.

Warwick, New Shoreham, R. I.

III. ROBERT, { b. 1668, Apr. 2. ; d. 1723.
m. 1713, Jan. 5.
MERCY WILLIAMS, { b. ; d. of John & Anna (Alcock) Williams.

No issue.

1708, Jun. 14. He sold to Moses Lippitt a lot of land deeded to me by brother Zorobabel, and where my grandfather Stukeley formerly lived.
1719–20. New Shoreham. Deputy.
1723, Mar. 30. Inventory, 20 cows, 15 cattle above a year, 11 yearlings, 4 oxen, 200 sheep, 5 mares, 5 colts, 10 hogs, 13 geese, 3 turkeys, 3 slaves £165, books, &c.

Receipts were given by Zorobabel and Samuel Westcott to Teddeman Hull for all goods and chattels, real and personal, delivered into hands of Teddeman Hull by Town Council of New Shoreham (except £24 paper money).

IV. DINAH, { b. 1670, Feb. 12. ; d. 1711 +
m.
JEREMIAH WILKIE, { b. ; d. 1711. of Wilkie.

No issue.

★ See: American Genealogist, v. 24, p. 75.

1655. Freeman.

1655, May 7. He and Mr. Smith were ordered "to cast up what damage is due to the Indians, and place every man's share acccording to his proportion and gather it up; and in case any one refuse to pay upon demand, then it shall be taken by distress, by a warrant from the Town Deputy."

1655, May 25. He was appointed to keep a house of entertainment. A sign was to be set out at the most perspicuous place.

1657, Jun. 14. He received from John Bennett of Warwick, eight cattle, nine pound of peage at eight a penny, and a house and land, and goods, engaging on behalf of himself and heirs to maintain the said John Bennett during his life in meat, drink and apparel. The only reservation was £5, to be at John Bennett's disposal during life.

1660, Mar. 3. He was foreman of Grand Inquest, his sons Amos and Jeremiah being also on the jury. Verdict: "We who are engaged to see the dead Indian, do find by diligent search that he was beaten, which was the cause of his death."

1664. He was authorized to keep an ordinary for entertainment of strangers during the time the King's Commissioners held court in Warwick.

1671. Deputy.

1677, Jan. 12. Will—Ex. son Amos He died the same day will was made, while temporarily at Portsmouth. He calls himself aged about eighty-five. To eldest son Amos, all movable estate, as cattle, goods and chattels, and land at Potawomut Neck, meadow at Toseunk, and three-fourths of land at Coweset with privileges, &c. To grandson Amos, a town lot in Warwick, where I formerly lived, with orchard fencing, &c., 60 acre lot at Shawomet, 6 acre lot there, a share of land south of Pawtuxet River and a quarter of Coweset lands. He died before he could sign the will, but on petition of his sons Amos and Jeremiah, the Town Council approved it in effect as follows: To Amos "the now eldest son," all goods, chattels, movables and lands, not otherwise disposed of, he being made sole executor. A deed of gift from the deceased to his son Jeremiah, was now confirmed by the Town Council and other lands were given Jeremiah, but he was to pay £7, to the executor. To daughter Damaris Arnold, 20*s*. To daughter Mercy Stafford, bed, &c. To grandson Zorobabel Westcott, eldest son of Robert, certain land. To grandson Amos Stafford, son of Samuel, land. To grandson Amos Westcott, son of Amos, land.

1695, Nov. 1. Testimony as to his will was given by Joseph Stafford, Mercy Stafford, and her son Amos, before John Greene, Deputy Governor. It was shown that testator would have signed it but was requested by Caleb Arnold to wait while his (the testator's) sons were sent for from Prudence Island, but by the time they came he was unable to sign.

1697, Feb. 18. The will was finally ordered recorded, by the Town Council.

III. AMOS, b. 1631, d. 1685. — Warwick, R. I.
m. (1) 1667, Jul. 13.
SARAH STAFFORD, b. d. 1669. — of Thomas & Elizabeth (   ) Stafford.
m. (2) 1670, Jun. 9.
DEBORAH STAFFORD, b. 1651. d. 1706. — of Thomas & Elizabeth (   ) Stafford.

1648, Jun. 5. He was recorded as an inhabitant.

1651-55-56, &c. Town Sergeant. He also held the office of Water Bailey, and was often Juryman.

1655. Freeman. He was appointed this year to go to each inhabitant for the votes for General Court of Elections.

1656. He was sent with two others to bring Pomham, the Indian sachem, before the court.

1661, Aug. 26. He bought of his brother Robert, land, orchard, &c., for half a mare, colt, two steers, and ten pounds peage, at eight a penny.

1662. He had a lot in division of Potawomut lands, and also in division of Toseunk lands.

1665, Feb. 18. He was on a jury in case of Mary Samon (daughter of John and Ann) found drowned in the brook by Mr. Anthony Low.

1666-70-71-72. Deputy.

1671. He was authorized to make assessments for arrears of taxes due colony.

1682, Feb. 2. He sold Joseph Stafford his interest in land rights of father Stukeley and brother Robert Westcott, deceased.

1685, Apr. 12. He testified as to certain lands, and called his age fifty-four years.

1685. He being very sick, &c., appointed his loving brother-in-law Samuel Stafford to "make up such reckonings" as are needful, and after debts are paid to dispose of lands as he thinks best, to members of his family most needing it.

1697, Feb. 15. His widow Deborah proved by testimony before Town Council (Samuel Stafford and Abraham Lockwood appearing on her behalf) that she had been in peaceable possession of the estate which her deceased husband Amos and his son Amos had heired, for many years.

1699, Mar. 23. His widow wrote Town Council as follows: "Gentlemen: These are to inform you of my inability in many respects, and altogether unable to take care for the maintenance of myself and my son Solomon; therefore I humbly petition and request that you will please to consider my condition with my son aforesaid, and I should and do freely submit myself to the dispose of the town, with surrender of what small estate is yet left, to be ordered and disposed at their discretion for my relief; and since it is so that my said son Solomon is very much void of common sense and understanding, I do resign up to the town council and their successors in that office, whatever is my present possession, either lands, goods or chattels, to be at their dispose forever."

1706. Deborah Westcott, deceased, having surrendered all her lands, &c., to the town, for the support of herself and idiot son Solomon, it was now decided by the authorities to offer what estate remained to four daughters of deceased, on condition they support son Solomon.

IV. MERCY, b. d. 1700, Mar. 25.
m.
SAMUEL STAFFORD, b. 1636. d. 1718, Mar. 20. — of Thomas & Elizabeth (   ) Stafford.

V. JEREMIAH, b. d. 1686. — Warwick, R. I.
m. 1665, Jul. 27.
ELEANOR ENGLAND, b. d. 1686. — of William & Elizabeth (   ) England.

1670, Nov. 22. He had a deed of certain land from his father as a free gift.

1672. Freeman.

1686, Dec. 13. Will was made by Town Council, as he died intestate. To Eleanor Westcott and son Jeremiah, who was appointed assistant unto her, the whole of movable estate, for her to bring up the children and pay debts. To children, male and female each 12*d*., at age, viz.: to Jeremiah, Stukeley, Josiah, Samuel, William, Benjamin and Eleanor.

V. Mary, — b. 1672, Jul. 2. d.

VI. Samuel, m. 1712, May 20. Naomi Goff, — b. 1674, Sep. 15. d. 1747 (—) — b. d. — of — Kings Town, R. I., New London, Conn. — Goff.

1. Phebe, 1717, Apr. 18.
2. Robert, 1719, Mar. 11.
3. Samuel, 1721, Apr. 8.
4. Dinah, 1723, Sep 19.
5. Benedict, 1726, Mar. 19.
6. Naomi, 1728, Aug. 20.

1730. New London. He was a trustee of the Baptist Church.

I. Amos, Unmarried. — b. 1668. d. 1692. — Warwick, R. I., Oyster Bay, N. Y.

1688, May 28. He gave receipt for £3, to mother-in-law (*i. e.* stepmother) Deborah Westcott, that she lent him. He gave her all right in home lot for life with fruit of the ground and trees, and if he should not pay her in three years, the property to be absolutely hers.

1693, Feb. 18. A receipt was given Deborah Westcott by William Carpenter of Mosqueto Cove, Long Island, for all his charge for expenses of sickness and burial of her son-in-law Amos Westcott, who died at said William Carpenter's house.

(2d Wife.)

II. Solomon, Unmarried. — b. d. 1711. — Warwick, R. I.

1711, Mar. 13. The children of Amos Westcott, deceased, viz: Luranah Westcott, daughter, and James Baker and John Smith, Jr., sons-in-law living in Kings Town, and Abraham Lockwood, son-in-law of Warwick—gave a full receipt to the town of Warwick "considering the great care and diligence the Town Council have been at these many years in bringing up Solomon Westcott, son of our father Amos," &c. The town gave the surplus remaining at Solomon's death (of lands sold for his support) to his four sisters, first taking above receipt.

III. Sarah, m. Abraham Lockwood, — b. 1673. d. — b. 1670 ± d. 1747, Jun. — of — Lockwood.

1. Abraham,
2. Amos, 1695 ±
3. Adam,
4. Deborah,
5. Sarah, 1708, Oct. 20.

IV. Penelope, m. James Baker, — b. d. — b. d. — of Thomas & Sarah ( ) — Baker.

1. Daughter,
2. Daniel,
3. Abel,
4. George,
5. Alice,

V. Mercy, m. 1708, Jan. 8. John Smith, — b. d. — b. d. — of John & Phillis (Gereardy) — Smith.

1. Margaret, 1708, Oct. 3.
2. Bathsheba, 1710, Apr. 7.
3. John, 1712, Jul. 26.
4. Mary, 1715, Jul. 17.
5. Mercy, 1717, Aug. 5.
6. William, 1719, Oct. 9.
7. Phillis, 1723, Sep. 29.

VI. Luranah, — b. d.

1. Stukeley, 1661, Nov. 7.
2. Amos, 1665, Nov. 8.
3. Mercy, 1668, Jul. 8.
4. Sarah, 1671, Apr. 18.
5. Samuel, 1673, Nov. 19.
6. Patience,
7. Freelove,
8. Elizabeth,
9. Thomas, 1682.

ESTCOTT. 3d column. I. Jeremiah. His wife was daughter of John and Ann (Gorton) Warner 1712, Jun. 6 he gave receipt to brother-in-law, John Warner, for a piece of drugget which was inventoried at 31*s*., 6*d* in brother-in-law John Warner's estate.

I. Jeremiah, m. Mary, — b. 1666, Oct. 7. d. 1757, Oct. 7. — b. d. — of — Warwick, R. I.

1. Zephaniah,
2. Thomas, 1707, May 5.
3. Jabez,
4. Eleanor.

1717, Apr. 22. He testified as to certain land, calling himself aged fifty years and upwards.

II. Eleanor. — b. 1669, Oct. 20. d.

III. Persis, — b. 1670. d. 1673, Aug.

IV. Stukeley, m. 1693, Dec. 21. Priscilla Bennett, — b. 1672, Oct. d. 1750, May 25. — b. d. 1754, Apr. 9. — of Samuel & Anna ( ) — Providence, R. I. — Bennett.

1. Josiah, 1694, Dec. 2.
2. Stukeley, 1698, May 2.
3. Freelove, 1702, Jul. 5.
4. Benjamin, 1709, Dec. 31.

1702. He gave 4*s*. toward building the Quaker Meeting house at Mashapaug.

1737, Nov. 12. Will—codicil 1738, Apr. 21, proved 1750, Jun. 8. Exx. wife Priscilla. To son Josiah, house where he lives and 35 acres. To male heir of son Stukeley, deceased, 35 acres. To son Benjamin, rest of land and housing at death or marriage of wife. To daughter Freelove Turner, £5. To wife, house for life and all movables in lieu of dower.

Inventory, £867, 8*s*., viz: books £3, 10*s*., wearing apparel £89, 19*s*., bills of public credit £76, 6*s*., pewter, 2 wheels, gun, 2 oxen, 3 cows, yearling, 9 sheep, 5 lambs, swine, &c.

1751, Aug. 10. Will—proved 1754, Apr. 29. Widow Priscilla. Exs. son Josiah and son-in-law Joshua Turner. To grandson Stukeley Westcott, £52. To daughter Freelove Turner, all indoor household goods. To eleven grandchildren, £5 each, viz: to Priscilla Battey, Ethalannah Lockwood, Joshua Turner, Jr., Freelove and William Turner, Stukeley, Joseph, Dorcas, Freelove, Almey and Lydia Westcott. To sons Joseph and Benjamin Westcott and son-in-law Joshua Turner, rest of estate equally.

Inventory, £817, 8*s*., 11*d*.

V. Josiah, m. 1701, Jan. 1. Hannah Gardiner, — b. 1675. d. 1721, Nov. 11. — b. d. 1756 + — of George & Tabitha (Tefft) — Providence, R. I. — Gardiner.

1. Nicholas, 1702, Aug. 27.
2. Hannah, 1704, Aug. 11.
3. Tabitha, 1706, Dec. 7.
4. Josiah, 1709, Mar. 6.
5. Nathan, 1711, Mar. 23.
6. Damaris, 1713, Jun 12.
7. Caleb, 1716, Dec. 6.
8. Oliver, 1720, Sep. 5.

(She m. (2.) Thomas Burlingame.)

1698, Jul. He called his age twenty-three years at this date.

1721, Dec. 16. Administration to widow Hannah. Inventory, £450, 9*s*, 6*d*., viz: sword, surveyor's instruments, debts due estate £133, 11*s*., rum, cider, molasses, cash £23, 4*s*, bonds £56, 2*s*, 6*d*., 4 cows, 8 swine, mare, negro woman £40, &c. Inventory of real estate £336, 17*s*., 10*d*., viz: dwelling house, saw mill, upland and meadow £300, 17*s*., 10*d*., and 90 acres at Pawtuxet £36.

1726, Feb. 21. Hannah Burlingame, that was relict and administratrix to Captain Josiah Westcott, having rendered account of the estate, the town council declared same imperfect, and that estate owed £58, 1*s*. She desired therefore to sell part of real estate.

1728, Apr. 24. Hannah Burlingame, late widow of Captain Josiah Westcott, accepted 56 acres and meadow and saw mill as her thirds.

WICKES.

JOHN, m. MARY, — b. 1609. Staines, Middlesex Co., Eng., d. 1675, Nov. [Warwick, R. I. — Mary: b. 1607. d.

He was a tanner.

1635, Sep. He embarked at London in ship Hopewell, his age being given as twenty-six, wife Mary twenty-eight, and daughter Ann one year old. (This daughter was perhaps identical with his daughter Hannah.)

1637. Plymouth.

1639, Apr. 30. Portsmouth. He and twenty-eight others signed the following compact: "We whose names are underwritten do acknowledge ourselves the legal subjects of his Majesty King Charles, and in his name do hereby bind ourselves into a civil body politicke, unto his laws according to matters of justice."

1643, Jan 12. Warwick. He and ten others purchased of Miantonomi the tract of land called Shawomet (Warwick) for 144 fathoms of wampum.

1643, Sep. 12. He, with others of Warwick, was notified to appear at General Court at Boston, to hear complaint of two Indian sachems, Pomham and Socconocco, as to "some unjust and injurious dealing toward them by yourselves" The Warwick men declined to obey the summons, declaring that they were legal subjects of the King of England and beyond the limits of Massachusetts territory, to whom they would acknowledge no subjection. Soldiers were soon sent who besieged the settlers in a fortified house. In a parley it was now said "that they held blasphemous errors which they must repent of," or go to Boston for trial, and they were soon carried thence.

1643, Nov. 3. He was brought with others before the court, charged with heresy and sedition, and they were sentenced to be confined during the pleasure of the court, and should they break jail or preach their heresies or speak against church or state, on conviction they should die. He was sent to prison at Ipswich, and not released till the following March, being then banished from both Massachusetts and Warwick.

1647. Town Council.

1647, Aug. 8. Town Magistrate.

1650-65-66. Assistant.

1651, Feb. 3. He and three others made an agreement with the town of Warwick to build a mill at their own cost, and to grind the town's corn for two quarts in a bushel. The town granted them for their encouragement a lot that was formerly Mr. Gorton's.

1651-56-57-58-60-61-62-63. Commissioner.

1655. Freeman.

1656. Juryman.

1664-65-66-67-68-69-70-71-72-73-75. Deputy.

1666, Oct. 10. He bought two shares of meadow of Richard Townsend of Pawtuxet, for £7, the latter calling him his father-in-law.

1675, Nov. "He was slain by the Indians 1675, a very ancient man;" as Callender declares.

I. HANNAH, — b. 1634. d.
m.
WILLIAM BURTON, — b. d. 1714, Feb. 20. of Burton.

II. MARY, — b. d.
m. 1671, Jun. 8.
FRANCIS GISBORNE, — b. d. of Gisborne.

III. ELIZABETH, — b. d.
m. (1)
RICHARD TOWNSEND, — b. d. 1671 (—) of John & Elizabeth ( ) Townsend.
m. (2)
JOHN SMITH, — b. d. of Smith.

IV. JOHN, — b. d. 1689. Warwick, R. I., Oyster Bay, N. Y., Warwick, R. I.
m.
ROSE TOWNSEND, — b. d. 1689 + of John & Elizabeth (Cole) Townsend.

He lived some years at Musketo Cove (Oyster Bay) L. I., where his father-in-law resided.

1671, Apr. 8. He was appointed overseer of his sister Elizabeth Townsend's will, on condition that he would come to Oyster Bay (where she was) to live.

1675. Freeman.

1680, May 17. He deeded to brother-in-law William Burton and Hannah his wife, for love, &c., certain land for life and then to go to cousin John Burton, son to said William and Hannah.

1689, Mar. 2. Will—proved 1689, Apr. 18. Exx. wife Rose. Overseers, Randall Holden, Jr., John Carder, James Carder, Moses Lippitt and John Knowles. To her, all movables, cattle, household goods, &c., for bringing up and civil education of our children in their nonage. To eldest son John, all rights in Warwick, land, housing, orchard, &c., at age, but until then wife to have benefit, and after coming of age John to pay her half income. To daughter Sarah, share in undivided lands. To son Thomas, right in Coweset, parcel of 30 acres, and farm of 200 acres at age. To youngest son Robert, right at Mashantatack, at age. To wife, the profits of all foregoing lands till children are of age.

VI. SAMUEL, m. FREELOVE FENNER,
b. d. 1716, Mar. 17.
b. d. 1716 + of Thomas & Dinah (Borden)
Providence, R. I.
Fenner.

(She m. (2) ——— Stone.)

1716, Feb. 21. Will—proved 1716, Apr. 17. Exs. brothers Josiah Westcott and Joseph Fenner. To wife Freelove, all movables, and executors to dispose of lands when they see meet. To daughter Freelove, £20, at eighteen. To child that wife is with, £20, if it be a daughter. To sons Samuel, Joseph and Thomas, lands. To child wife is with if it be a son, equal share with brothers.

Inventory, £79, 9*s.*, 6*d.*, viz: mare and colt, yoke of oxen, 3 cows, 5 yearlings, swine, pewter, ironware, &c.

1. Samuel,
2. Jabez,
3. Freelove,
4. Thomas,
5. Benjamin,
6. Jeremiah.

VII. WILLIAM, m. ABIGAIL,
b. d.
b. d. of
Providence, R. I.

1723, May 9. He and wife Abigail sold Benjamin Greene of Warwick 250 acres in Mashantatack for £30.

1733, Jul. 17. He deeded son Ezekiel for love, &c., 60 acres.

1. William,
2. Ezekiel,

VIII. BENJAMIN, m. BETHIA GARDINER,
b. 1684, Jul. 4. d. 1765.
b. 1687, Feb. 2. d. 1760. of
Providence, Cranston, R. I.
Gardiner.

1720. Freeman.

1738, Nov. 28. Will—(no probate). To wife Bethiah, a third of whole estate. To eldest son Benjamin, 1*s.* To son Stukeley, 1*s.* To eldest daughter Bethiah Westcott, 1*s.* To daughter Dorcas Congdon's three children, 40*s.* apiece. To daughter Hannah Westcott, 1*s.* To youngest daughter Phebe, £30. To youngest son Josiah, southernmost part of farm. To son Samuel, rest of lands, housing, orchard, &c., and rest of movables.

1748, May 21. He deeded son Samuel, for love, &c., house and 20 acres. He deeded at other times to several of his sons.

1760, May 2. Will—(no probate). Ex. son Samuel. "And as to the small personal estate God hath bestowed on me in this life, I give and dispose of as follows." To son Samuel, all personal estate after payment of debts.

1. Bethiah,
2. Dorcas,
3. Benjamin,
4. Stukeley,
5. Samuel, 1719, Aug. 28
6. Josiah,
7. Hannah,
8. Phebe,

WICKES.

1. Elizabeth,
2. Daughter,
3. Hannah,
4. Rose,
5. Ethalannah,
6. Susannah, 1665.
7. John, 1667, May 2.

(By 1st husband.)
1. Hannah,
2. Deliverance,
3. Mary,
4. John,
5. Richard.

I. JOHN, m. 1698, Dec. 15. SARAH GORTON,
b. 1677, Aug. 8. d. 1742, Dec. 27.
b. d. 1753, Jan. 31. of Benjamin & Sarah (Carder)
Warwick, R. I.
Gorton.

1704. Constable.

1706-7-9-10-11-12-13-14-15. Deputy.

1712 to 1741. Town Clerk (except in 1720.)

1715 to 1738 and 1740-41. Assistant.

1741, Dec. 26. Will—proved 1742, Jan. 21. Ex. son Thomas. To wife, half house and all household goods, two cows, riding horse, and keep of same, and executor to provide her firewood, fence her a garden of half an acre, and she also to have two barrels of cider a year, what fruit she needs and £10 per year while widow. If she marry, £5 a year, and household goods only. To son Robert, all land at Salt Box and harbours mouth, and other land. To son William, all lands at Mashantatack, 180 acres, and ten other lots, &c. To three daughters Sarah, Rose and Elizabeth, £50, each. To daughter Mary, girl Peg in two years or marriage and £100. To granddaughter Sarah, daughter of son Richard, £130, at age or marriage. To wife, two negro wenches. To son William, three cows, a mare and colt, and 50 sheep. To son Thomas, all the rest of lands and housing. To sons Robert and Thomas, equally all the rest of stock and tackling. To son Thomas, negro Samuel. To Robert, Indian Tom.

Inventory, £1,947, 11*s.*, 13*d.*, viz: books £13, bonds and book debts £345, 14*s.*, 9*d.*, 2 silver cups, 2 spoons, &c. £12, 10*s.*, 16 barrels cider, 9 barrels apple beer, wheels and hetchel, 16 geese, 12 turkeys, 20 fowls, 2 pair of oxen, 10 cows, 2 heifers, 6 yearlings, 2 calves, 6 horses and mares, 180 sheep, 47½ loads of hay, negro woman and child £120, girl Phillis £110, boy Samuel £100, girl Peggy £70, Indian boy Tom's time £30, &c.

1749, Mar. 13. Will—proved 1753, Feb. 12. Widow Sarah. Ex. son Thomas. To three daughters Sarah Waterman, Rose Holden and Elizabeth Greene, all apparel, &c., eight of best pewter platters, and all plate, money and bonds. To son Thomas, negro woman called Juda, he paying £80 amongst his sisters equally. To son Robert, feather bed, small bible, &c. To three granddaughters Mary Holden, Mary Waterman and Phebe Greene, a note for £23, due from son Thomas. To granddaughter Sarah, daughter of son Richard, deceased, £50 at eighteen. To grandson William Wickes, £10, at age. To son Thomas, clock, desk, great bible, suit of worsted curtains, &c., and all remainder of estate.

Inventory, £1,557, 18*s.*, 6*d.*, viz: 2 cows, negro woman Juda £90, warming pan, woolen wheel, bonds &c. £317, large bible and other books £34, china punch bowl, pewter tankard, looking glass, 2 silver cups and 3 silver spoons £36.

1. John, 1699, Feb. 26.
2. Sarah, 1700, Sep. 21.
3. Rose, 1702, Aug. 12.
4. Robert, 1704, Dec. 22.
5. Elizabeth, 1707, Feb. 5
6. William, 1710, Aug 26.
7. Richard, 1712, Oct. 23.
8. Thomas, 171[illegible], Sep. 8.
9. Mary, 1717, Dec. 11.

II. SARAH,
b d.

III. THOMAS, m. 1702, Feb. 20. ANN COLE,
b. d.
b. d. of Daniel & Mahershallalhashbaz (Gorton)
Warwick, R. I., Oyster Bay, N. Y.
Cole.

His first two children were twins who died soon as born, and his last two were twins and died soon.

1708. Freeman.

1. Athaliah, 1704, Oct. 10.
2. ———, 1704, Oct. 10.
3. Mary, 1706, Aug. 15.
4. Sarah, 1708, May 8.
5. Thomas, 1710, Jan. 28.
6. John, 1712, Feb. 6.
7. Daniel, 1714, May 10.
8. Benjamin, 1716, Aug. 18.
9. Joseph, 1719, May 31.
10. Samuel, 1722, Feb. 22.
11. Robert, 1722, Feb. 22.

IV. ROBERT,
b. d.

 See: American Genealogist, v. 20, p. 233-234.

{ EDWARD, { b. Portsmouth, King Town, R. I.
{ m. { d.
{ —— { b.
{ d.

1638. His name was in a list of inhabitants admitted to the island of Aquidneck—having submitted themselves to the government that is or shall be established.

1638 ± Kings Town. A declaration was made by Randall Holden and John Greene (in 1680), that prior to Richard Smith's coming to Narragansett a Mr. Wilcox was there. "But in process of time Mr. Roger Williams and one Mr. Wilcockes, for the advantage of trade, set up trading houses, and afterwards Mr. Richard Smith, Senr., came there, having joined in partnership with said Wilcockes, whereby he much augmented his estate, and had no occasion to expend anything, for the Indians would not let them have any land to improve nor suffer them to keep a beast there."

Edward is assumed to have been the father of Stephen and Daniel Wilcox.

WILCOX. Add at end of 1st column; but perhaps John Wilcox was their father, for the records of Manhattan mention John Wilcox as a partner of Richard Smith.

I. { STEPHEN, { b. 1633 ± Portsmouth, Westerly, R. I.
{ m. 1658. { d. 1690 ±
{ HANNAH HAZARD, { b.
{ d. of Thomas & Martha ( ) Hazard.

1657, Dec. 10. He and Thomas Kent had a grant of 16 acres at 2*s*., per acre, each paying therefor 16*s*.

1658, Jan. 30. He had a deed of 34 acres from Thomas Hazard as dower with the latter's daughter, Hannah Hazard.

1658, May 18. Freeman.

1669, May 18. Westerly. His name was in the list of inhabitants.

1670, Jun. 21. He was complained of, with his partakers, by John Richards, Treasurer of Harvard College, for unjustly possessing 500 acres in Pequot country, east side of Pawcatuck River, within bounds of Stonington.

1670–72 Deputy.

1690, Feb. 6. He was mentioned at this date as lately deceased.

II. { DANIEL, { b. Portsmouth, R. I., Dartmouth, Mass., Tiverton, R. I.
{ m. 1661, Nov. 28, { d. 1702, Jul. 2.
{ ELIZABETH COOK. { b.
{ d. 1715, Dec. 6. of John & Sarah (Warren) Cook.

1656, Dec. 10. He had a grant of 15 acres.

1658, Mar. 15. He sold Thomas Lawton, 30 acres.

1664, Jan. 31. Dartmouth. He bought of Philip Taber a house in Portsmouth, for £45.

1665. Constable.

1668, Jun. 3. He and John Cook were granted privilege to keep the ferry at Pocasset.

1669. Grand Jury.

1672, Jan. 20. He sold Joseph Davol, of Newport, a share at Puncatest for £5.

1676, Sep. 1. Testimony was given at Newport by his Indian servant Suckats Squa, that she heard Manasses say that he had killed an Englishman at Pocasset. In Benjamin Church's account of the Indian wars it is mentioned that Daniel Wilcox was "a man that well understood the Indian Language."

1677, May 10. He and wife Elizabeth sold Martha Wait, widow of Jeremiah, of Portsmouth, one-eighth of a share of land in Dartmouth for £16.

1678, Jun. 5. He was granted £10, in consideration of a considerable charge by him sustained in answer of a suit against him in Rhode Island, and verdict of £20 obtained against him, to make good the charge of a man lately cured who was wounded in the late war.

1680, Mar. 5. He, of Puncatest, and seven others, bought of Gov. Josiah Winslow, &c., land at Pocasset for £1,100. He had two of the 30 shares.

1692, Mar. 2. Tiverton. He was an inhabitant at the organization of the town.

1699, Sep. 26. Lord Bellomont in his journal, under this date mentions that he had received a petition from the sheriff of Bristol County, complaining that one Daniel Wilcox, of Little Compton, having been convicted of high misdemeanor and sentenced to pay a fine of £150, &c., had made his escape and fled unto the government of Rhode Island, notwithstanding a demand made on the Governor of Rhode Island by Lieutenant Governor of Massachusetts.

I. EDWARD, b. 1662 ±, d. 1715, Nov. 5. — Westerly, R. I.
m. (1)
——— HAZARD, b. d. of Robert & Mary (Brownell) Hazard.
m. (2) 1698, May 1.
THOMASIN STEVENS, b. 1677 Jul. 3. d. of Richard Stevens.

1. Mary,
2. Hannah,
3. Stephen,
4. Edward,
(2d wife.)
5. Sarah, 1700, May 30.
6. Thomas, 1702, Feb. 18.
7. Hezekiah, 1704, Apr. 4.
8. Elisha, 1706, Jul. 9.
9. Amey, 1709, Oct. 18.
10. Susanna, 1712, Apr. 4.

1686, Jan. 6. He, of Misquamicut *alias* Westerly, sold Isaac Lawton, 60 acres in Portsmouth, for £135, said land being bounded partly by land of grandfather Thomas Hazard, and including buildings, orchard, &c. His uncle Robert Hazard signed the deed also in full consent.

1708, Feb. 28. He sold Joseph Johnson 100 acres.

1714, Dec. 29. Grand Jury.

1715, Nov. 15. Administration on personal estate to widow Tamsen, said Wilcox leaving ten children, some young and incapable of taking care for themselves. The Town Council authorized the widow after paying debts to draw forth £50, for her trouble in bringing up children that are under age. She was to have her choice of best room in the house and a third income of real estate. The eldest son Stephen, to enter forthwith into possession of rest of house, and the orphans to have rest of movables according to law.

Inventory, £283, 3*s*., viz: 4 beds, 4 cots, bible and 2 small books given Tamsen by her father and brother, other books, pewter, gun, 2 oxen, 2 steers, 12 cows, 6 two years, 8 calves, bull, 4 mares, horse, 4 colts, sow, 12 shoats, 9 hogs, &c.

1716, Dec. 17. His widow asked for division to be made of £83, 2*s*., left of estate, and it was made as follows: To widow, £7, 14*s*. To each child, £5, 10*s*., viz: Mary Lewis, wife of Joseph, Hannah Garrett, wife of Ezekiel, Stephen, Edward, Sarah, Thomas, Hezekiah, Elisha, Amey and Susanna Wilcox.

II. THOMAS, b. d. 1728. — North Kingstown, R. I.
m.
MARTHA HAZARD, b. d. 1753. of Robert & Mary (Brownell) Hazard.

1. Robert,
2. Stephen,
3. Jeffrey,
4. Thomas, 1693, Oct. 24.
5. Abraham,
6. George,
7. Edward,
8. Hannah,

1710, May 17. Kings Town. He and seventeen others bought 2,000 acres of the vacant lands ordered sold by Assembly.

1728, Apr. 9. Will—proved. Exx. wife Martha. Overseer, brother-in-law Stephen Hazard. To seven sons, certain land, equally, viz: eldest son Robert, and Stephen, Jeffrey, Thomas, Abraham, George and Edward. To sons George and Edward, the part of land where house stands, the north side being Edward's part, and neither to sell except to the other. To wife, the stock and household goods and negro man, and also the housing till youngest son Edward is of age, and after that she to have the best room. The young children to be brought up by wife.

1743, Oct. 18. Will—proved 1753, Jan. 9. Widow Martha, of Exeter. Ex. Thomas Sweet, of North Kingstown. To daughter Hannah Place, interest of £200, for life, and to said daughter's heirs at death. To eldest daughter of Hannah, if she ever happen to have any, a bed, chest, &c., and to second daughter of Hannah, a brass kettle. To sons Robert, Stephen, Jeffrey, Thomas, George, Edward and Abraham, 5*s*., each. To daughter Hannah Place, rest of estate. (Enoch Place receipted for legacy).

Inventory, £259, 7*s*.

III. DANIEL, b. d. — Kings Town, R. I., Stonington, Ct.
m. 1697.
MARY WORDELL, b. d. of Wordell.

1. Stephen,

1697, Mar. 28. His marriage with Mary Wordell, of Kings Town, was declared illegal by Assembly because not published, though the ceremony was performed by William Gibson, Assistant.

1709, Jun. 28. He and twenty-six others bought 1,824 acres of the vacant lands in Narragansett, near Devil's Foot.

1717. Stonington. He and wife Mary were residents there at this date.

IV. WILLIAM, b. d. — Stonington, Ct.
m. 1698, Jan. 25.
DOROTHY PALMER, b. d. of Palmer.

1. Dorothy, 1698, Oct. 28.
2. Anna, 1701, Jun. 14.
3. William, 1703, Jun. 3.
4. Jemima, 1705, Jul. 21.
5. Mary, 1709, Dec. 1.
6. Amey, 1711, Jul. 7.
7. Sarah, 1713, Aug. 29.
8. Nathan, 1716, Dec. 3.

1699. He had cattle mark granted.

V. STEPHEN, b. d. — Kings Town, Westerly, R. I.
m. 1704, (—)
ELIZABETH CRANDALL, b. d. of John & Elizabeth (Gorton) Crandall.

1. Stephen,
2. Robert,
3. John,

1713, May 7. He had ear mark granted.

1715, Jan. 7. He and wife Elizabeth, sold 186 acres in Westerly for £150.

1715, Nov. 14. He deeded sons Stephen and Robert, certain lands.

1720, Feb. 8. Westerly. He deeded land to his son Robert, of South Kingstown.

1720, Apr. 8. He deeded son John, one-third of land where he dwells, being the middle part.

VI. HANNAH, b. d.
m.
SAMUEL CLARKE, b. d. of Jeremiah & Ann (Audley) Clarke.

1. John,
2. Audley,
3. Samuel,
4. Daniel,

VII. JEREMIAH, b. d. — Newport, R. I.
m.
MARY MALLETT, b. d. of Thomas & Mary ( ) Mallett.

1704, Dec. 8. He was mentioned in will of Thomas Mallett, of Newport, as his son-in-law.

1708. Freeman.

I. DANIEL, b. d. — Portsmouth, R. I.
m.
HANNAH COOK, b. d. 1736. of John & Mary (Borden) Cook.

1. Daniel,
2. Mary, 1682, Feb. 25.
3. Hannah, 1684, Apr. 11.
4. Joseph, 1687, Oct. 28.
5. Eliphal,

(She m. (2) Enoch Briggs.)

1734, Jun. 14. Will—proved 1736, Nov. 8. Widow Hannah Briggs. To daughter Abigail Butts, sundry household articles. To granddaughter Hannah Wilcox, daughter of son Daniel, lately deceased, a white chest. To daughters Sarah Briggs and Susannah Cook, rest of estate. (Her second husband in his will had directed her to devise to her three youngest daughters.)

II. SAMUEL, b. d. 1702 (—) — See American Genealogist, v. 26, p. 230. Dartmouth, Mass.
m.
———, b. d. of

1. Jeremiah, 1683, Sep. 24.
2. William, 1685, Feb. 2.
3. Jeremiah, 1688, Feb. 14.

1686, Mar. 24. He took the oath of fidelity.

III. MARY, b. d. 1735.
m.
JOHN EARLE, b. d. 1728. of Ralph & Dorcas (Sprague) Earle.

1. John, 1687, Aug. 7.
2. Daniel, 1688, Oct. 8.
3. Benjamin, 1691, May 25.
4. Mary, 1693, Jun. 1.
5. Rebecca, 1695, Dec. 17.
6. Elizabeth, 1699, Sep. 6.

IV. SARAH, b. d. 1751.
m.
EDWARD BRIGGS, b. d. 1718, May 11. of John & Hannah (Fisher) Briggs.

1. Deborah, 1693, Mar. 11.
2. Hannah, 1698, Dec. 19.
3. Walter, 1701, Feb. 19.
4. Josiah, 1703, Mar. 4.
5. Charles, 1711, Feb. 20.

V. STEPHEN, b. d. 1736, Nov. 13. — Little Compton, R. I., Dartmouth, Mass.
m. (1) 169–, Feb. 9.
SUSANNA BRIGGS, b. 1672, Mar. 14. d. 1719, Oct. 6. of Thomas & Mary (Fisher) Briggs.
m. (2)
JUDITH, b. d. of

1. Susannah, 169–, Feb. 14.
2. Daniel, 1699, Dec. 29.
3. Thomas, 1701, Oct. 12.
4. Elizabeth, 1704, Jan. 18.
5. Stephen, 1708, Jan. 10.
(2d wife.)
6. John,

1702, Jun. 9. Will—proved 1702, Aug. 25. Exs. wife Elizabeth and sons John and Edward. Overseers, Thomas Cornell, of Newport, Joseph Wanton, of Tiverton and John Coggeshall, Newport. To eldest son Daniel, 200 acres of land and meadows in Dartmouth where said son formerly lived, and after his decease to his eldest son Daniel and his male heirs successively. To children of son Samuel, deceased, nothing, because already provided for by deed of gift. To son Stephen, 200 acres in Dartmouth where I formerly lived. To son John, 100 acres where he liveth at Capolowest, and if he be removed from there by course of law by persons justly claiming, he then to have my house, lands, orchards, &c., at Rhode Island in Portsmouth, and until John has removed from land where he lives, my wife to have yearly rent of house, &c., on Rhode Island for life; and if John is not removed then my daughter Susannah Wilcox to have Rhode Island lands at decease of wife. To son Edward and heirs, the house, buildings, &c., on southwest side of highway, only reserving to my own and wife Elizabeth's use during our natural lives the great house and half the orchard, all in Tiverton at place called Namaquid, he paying yearly 40*s.*, to me and wife if we demand it, &c. To son Thomas and heirs, if he have any, all land and buildings in Tiverton at place called Namaquid on north side of highway going down to Puncatest Neck, he paying 40*s.*, to me or my wife, if either need. If Edward or Thomas die without issue the survivor to have his brother's part. To daughter Mary, wife of John Earle, certain land. To daughter Lydia, land. To son-in-law Edward Briggs and Sarah his wife, 120 acres. For all lands that are in difference four sons to be at equal charge in recovering, and to have equally lands so recovered. To Joseph Wilcox, 2*s.* To children, rest of estate both real and personal.

Inventory, £1,290, 7*s.*, viz: bedstead, chairs, pewter, &c., at Rhode Island. At Tiverton, wearing clothes, cane, pewter, warming pan, stillyards, gun, churn, 41 sheep, 13 lambs, pair of oxen, 5 cows, 2 heifers, pair of steers, 4 two years, 6 yearlings, 3 calves, bull, 18 old goats, 10 kids, swine, horseflesh, £30, &c.

WILKINSON.

Lawrence[1] (Wm.,[2] Lawrence.[1]) { b. Lancaster, Durham Co., Eng. d. 1692, Aug. 9. [Providence, R. I.
m.
Susannah Smith, { b. d. 1692 (—)

of Christopher & Alice ( ) Smith.

He early took service as Lieutenant in the Royal army, fighting on the side of Charles I. and was taken prisoner at the fall of Newcastle, his estates being sequestered by Parliament.

1645–47. Sequestrations in Durham. "Lawrence Wilkinson of Lanchester, officer in arms, went to New England."

1657, Jan. 27. Providence. He had 3 acres of land granted him, lying by the Newfield, beyond the great swamp.

1659, Jan. 27. Juryman.

1659. Commissioner.

1661, Mar. 9. He was granted a 5 acre lot, that Christopher Smith laid down.

1665, Feb. 19. He had lot 50 in a division of lands.

1667. Commissioner.

1667–73. Deputy.

1675, Jun. He had land laid out to him near World's End Meadow, on both sides of the Moshassuck River.

1679, Jul. 1. Taxed 3*s.*, 9*d.*, "Lawrence Wilkinson and his two sons."

1684, Mar. 17. He drew lot 32 in a division of lands west of 7 mile line.

1687, Sep. 1. Taxed 5*s.*, 6*d.*

1691, Aug. 31. He deeded son Josias for love and affection, &c., a house and lot of 60 acres where said Lawrence lately dwelt, also 12 acres of swamp, and three-quarters right in common.

1692, Aug. 31. Administration to sons Samuel and John, with bond for £60.

I. **Samuel**, { b. Providence, R. I. d. 1727, Aug. 27.
m.
Plain Wickenden, { b. d. of William Wickenden.

1679, Jul. 1. Taxed 3*s.*, 1½*d.*

1687, Sep. 1. Taxed 4*s.*, 1*d.*

1688. Ratable estate: 2 oxen, 6 cows, 2 yearlings, a horse, 5 acres planting, share of meadow, 4 acres pasture, 60 acres wood land.

1693–97–98–99–1701–4–5–6–7–12–16–23. Deputy.

1702. Town Council.

1707, May 14. He had edge tools worth £1, 1*s.*, taken from him to pay a fine of 12*s.*, for not training, he being a Quaker.

1710, Mar. He was voted £5, by Assembly, for his service in treaties with Colonel Joseph Dudley about north bounds of this colony.

1713, Jun. 16. Taxed £1, 10*s.*

1715, Nov. 26. He deeded son Samuel for love, goodwill, &c., 50 acres with a house, &c., lying about ten miles northwest of Providence, on southeastern side of Westquattersett Brook and near Pawtucket River.

1727, Sep. 26. Inventory, £1,403, 14*s.*, 10*d.* (of which £952, 1*s.*, 5*d.*, was real estate, including homestead farm £880). Administration to son Joseph. Among items were: wearing apparel, books, £9, 14*s.*, 6*d.*; bullion and plate £49, 3*d.*, a pistole of gold, &c. £3, 15*s.*, bills of credit £178, feather beds, yarn, woolen wheel, money scales, warming pan, pocket book, compass, razor, pewter, 2 great chairs, 5 small chairs, saddle and pillion, 1 horse, 2 bulls, a yoke of oxen, 8 cows, 2 heifers, 4 yearlings, &c.

II. **Susannah**, { b. 1652, Mar. 9. d. young.

1729, Jun. 17. He being *non compos mentis* had guardian appointed, viz: James Tripp, who took inventory the next month amounting to £12, 14*s*., viz: old mare, grindstone, &c.

1736, Jul. 20. His son Stephen took the guardianship.

1737, Apr. 6. Administration to son Stephen, the widow Judith refusing. Inventory, £2,565, viz: homestead farm £2,100, land in fork of river 122 acres, £366, &c.

1737, Apr. 16. Edward Cornell, of Dartmouth, was appointed guardian to John Wilcox, son of Stephen, under fourteen years of age.

VI. JOHN, b. ; d. 1718. Little Compton, R. I.
m.
REBECCA, b. ; d. 1725 + of

1. Jacob, 1699, Oct. 14.
2. Daniel, 1701, Feb. 25.
3. Elizabeth, 1702, Dec. 13.
4. John, 1704, Sep. 22.
5. Jabez, 1707, Mar. 21.
6. Peramus, 1708, Nov. 23.
7. Rebecca, 1711, Aug. 14.
8. Thomas,

1718, Feb. 21. Inventory, £750, 15*s*., sworn to by widow Rebecca, 3 beds, pewter, gun, pair of oxen, 5 cows, 11 young cattle, 2 mares, colt, 28 sheep, swine, fowls, money 12*s*., &c. House and land £600.

1725, Nov. 16. Division of his estate was ordered, viz: to widow for life, the north part of farm, 64 acres and old dwelling house. The rest of farm, 88 acres, to be divided into nine parts. To eldest son Jacob, two parts, and one part each to sons Daniel, John, Jabez, Peramus and Thomas, and daughters Elizabeth, wife of Joseph Tripp, and Rebecca Wilcox.

VII. EDWARD, b. ; d. 1718. Tiverton, R. I.
m.
SARAH MANCHESTER, b. ; d. 1718 + of William & Mary (Cook) Manchester.

1. Josiah, 1701, Sep. 22.
2. Ephraim, 1704, Aug. 9.
3. William, 1706, Dec. 26.
4. Freelove, 1709, Dec. 18.

1718, May 19. Will—proved 1718, Jun. 2. Exx. wife Sarah. To her, all personal for support and to bring up children. To son Josiah, land at Puncatest, Dartmouth, &c. To son Ephraim, 5*s*., and land he had from his grandfather's will, at age. To William, 5*s*., and land from his grandfather's will. To daughter Freelove, 5*s*., at marriage or at her mother's decease. To children, the rest of personal at death of wife. Sons Josiah, Ephraim and William, to provide for their mother.

Inventory, £1,859, 16*s*., viz: purse and apparel £20, land and buildings £1,500, books £1, 5 beds, brass, pewter, 4 spinning wheels, pair of cards, 2 guns, sword, 9 cows, 5 calves, 5 two years, a three year, 48 sheep, 30 lambs, horsekind £9, 16*s*., swine, geese, turkeys, &c.

VIII. THOMAS, b. ; d. 1712. Tiverton, R. I.
UNMARRIED.

1712, Aug. 9. Will—proved 1712, Sep. 2. Ex. brother Edward. To brother Edward, all movables and land at Namaquid. To rest of brothers and sisters the rest of land.

Inventory, £47, 2*s*., 4*d*., viz: land £18, 15*s*., horsekind £15, neatkind £5, 12*s*., swine £1, 15*s*., smith's tools, &c. Additional inventory £5, 4*s*., 3*d*.

IX. LYDIA, b. ; d. 1727 +
m. (1) 1702, May 26.
THOMAS SHERMAN, b. 1658, Aug. 8; d. 1719. of Peleg & Elizabeth (Lawton) Sherman.
m. (2) 1720, Dec. 8.
THOMAS POTTER, b. ; d. 1728. of Ichabod & Martha (Hazard) Potter.

1. Josiah, 1703, Mar. 2.
2. Daniel, 1706, Nov. 26
3. Ruth,
4. Benjamin,
(By 2d husband, no issue.)

X. SUSANNA, b. ; d.

WILCOX. 3d column. X. Susanna, m. 1704, Dec. 7, Jonathan Head, d. 1748, of Henry and Elizabeth, Child, 1, Joseph, 1705, Sep. 1.

WILKINSON.

I. SAMUEL, b. 1674, Sep. 18; d. 1727, Jan. 18. Providence, R. I.
m. 1697, Apr. 13.
HULDAH ALDRICH, b. 1680, Nov. 6; d. 1727 + of Jacob & Huldah (Thayer) Aldrich.

1. Huldah, 1697, Dec. 16.
2. Josiah, 1699, Aug. 29.
3. Samuel, 1701, Feb. 9.
4. Zebiah, 1702, Oct. 2.
5. Patience, 1704, Jun. 9.
6. Mercy, 1705, Dec. 12.
7. David, 1707, Oct. 16.
8. Jacob, 1709.
9. Israel, 1711, Mar. 21.
10. William, 1713.
11. Ruth, 1715.
12. Caleb, 1716.
13. Plain, 1717, Feb. 28.
14. Peleg, 1718.
15. Ichabod, 1720.

He was a tanner.

1707, Mar. 14. He had edge tools worth £1, 1*s*, taken from him to pay a fine of 12*s*., for not training, he being a Quaker.

1727, Jan. 13. Will—proved 1727, Mar. 6. Exs. wife Huldah and son David. To daughter Zebiah Comstock, £5. To daughter Patience Arnold, £10. To daughters Huldah and Mercy Wilkinson, £20 each. To daughters Ruth and Plain Wilkinson, £20 each. The rest of estate equally to sons Josiah, Samuel, David, Israel, Ichabod. Inventory, £399, 18*s*., 10*d*., viz: 2 swarms of bees, geese, hens, 5 fat swine, 10 lean swine, 22 goats, 15 sheep, 3 horses, 4 oxen, 9 cows, 3 two years, 3 yearlings, 6 calves, carpenter's tools, shoemaker's tools, 1 hogshead of beer, 9 barrels cider, books, &c.

II. JOHN, b. 1678, Jan. 25; d. 1751. Providence, R. I., Wrightstown, Pa.
m.
MARY, b. ; d. of

1. Mary, 1708, Jul. 17.
2. Kezia,
3. Plain,
4. Ruth,
5. John,
6. Joseph,

1700. He left Rhode Island at about this time and tarried awhile in Hunterdon county, New Jersey, where he married, and where his first child was born.

1713, May 27. He bought 307 acres at Wrightstown.

1728, Jul. 8. He gave receipt for £71 to his brother Joseph for part of legacy of father's estate.

1751, Apr. 31. Will—proved at this date. He was buried on his farm at Wrightstown.

III. WILLIAM, b. 1680, Aug. 1; d. 1721 + Providence, R. I., London, Eng.
m.
MARY, b. ; d. of

1. Hannah Maria.

He early became a Quaker, and was a preacher of that sect.

1708, Apr. 20. He wrote a letter from Barbadoes (where he had gone with a cargo of horses, &c.), to his father and mother, describing graphically the long and tempestuous passage of thirty-three days, mentioning that being driven on St. George's Banks "where the waves shined like fire in the night," they were obliged to throw overboard some of the honey, and feared they might have to throw over some of the horses also. He "was very seasick almost all the way." He went to England later, and married in Yorkshire and settled in London, never returning to America.

1721. He wrote a letter to his parents this year. He published one or two controversial works.

IV. JOSEPH, b. 1683, Jan. 22; d. 1740, Apr. 24. Providence, Scituate, R. I.
m.
MARTHA PRAY, b. 1689; d. 1786. of John & Sarah (Brown) Pray.

1. Susannah, 1708, Jun. 10.
2. Prudence,
3. Ishmael, 1712, Nov. 13.
4. Benjamin, 1713, Oct. 9.
5. Christopher, 1715, Sep. 9.
6. Martha, 1718, Jan. 11.
7. Mary, 1720, Apr. 21.
8. Joseph, 1721.
9. John, 1722, Jul. 29.
10. William,
11. Samuel, 1726, Feb. 8.
12. Susannah,
13. Sarah,
14. Ruth,
15. William, 1734.

1728, Jul. 6. He bought of the other heirs the homestead of his father Samuel, deceased, 120 acres at Locosquisset, with dwelling houses, &c., for £770.

He was a surveyor, and held offices of Town Treasurer, Justice of the Peace, &c.

1731. Deputy.

1740, Apr. 7. Will—proved 1740, May 21. Ex. sons Ishmael and Benjamin. To son Joseph, part of homestead south of highway, &c., he paying my son William, £200 at age. To son John, 117 acres in Glocester and meadow there. To son Samuel, 100 acres, being part of homestead, he paying to son John, £50. To son Ishmael, two lots in Scituate and a lot in Glocester, &c. To son Benjamin, land including a quarter of original right of Lawrence Wilkinson. To sons Ishmael and John, each a third of original right of William Wickenden. To son William, all residue of rights and land. To two youngest daughters Sarah and Ruth, £50, each. To son Joseph, cart, plow, &c., and use of ten cows, a yoke of oxen, a bull and all sheep for five years after decease of testator, towards looking after and maintaining two youngest children Ruth and William. To daughter Martha, best feather bed. To daughter Susanna, next best bed. To four children Martha, John, Susanna, and William (after wife has her third, &c.), all the rest of cattle, horses, goats, and money due, and household goods equally. To son Ishmael, log chain, carpenter's tools. To sons Joseph, John and Samuel, after five years, the stock given Joseph as above. To sons Ishmael and Benjamin, residue of personal estate.

III. JOHN, m. 1689, Apr. 16. DEBORAH WHIPPLE, { b. 1654, Mar. 2. d. 1708, Apr. 10. } { b. 1670, Aug. 1. d 1748, Jun. 24. } of Eleazer Whipple. — Providence, R. I.

1681, May 3. Freeman.

1682, Oct. 25. He was voted £10; having been wounded in the late war with the Indians.

1687, Sep. 1. Taxed 4s.

1700–6. Deputy.

1708, Apr. 30. Administration to widow Deborah. Inventory, £273, viz: wearing apparel and canes, joiner's, cooper's and carpenter's tools and husbandry tools, a horse, 29 head of neat cattle, 12 calves, swine, negro youth £30, a piece of drugget at the fullers, and a piece at the weavers, corn in crib, rye in barn, cider, flax, tobacco, pork, beds, bedding, table linen, pewter, brass, &c. The rooms mentioned were, north room, north chamber, east chamber, lower east room, west chamber, corner west room, pantry, garret and cellar.

1713, June 16. Widow Deborah taxed £1, 10s.

1748, Nov. 8. Administration on estate of Deborah Wilkinson, widow, of Smithfield, to son John. Inventory, £227, 3s.

IV. JOANNA, { b. 1657, Mar. 2. }

V. JOSIAS, m. HANNAH TYLER, { b. d. 1692, Aug. 10. } { b d. 1707 + } of Tyler. — Providence, R. I.

1682, May 9. He took oath of allegiance.

1692, Aug. 31. Administration to Edward Smith and John Wilkinson.

1699, Dec. 26. Petition of Joseph Tucker and Hannah his wife concerning estate of Josias Wilkinson. (Joseph Tucker had married the widow of Josias.)

1707, Jul. 7. Hannah Tucker presented inventory of her second husband's estate. It was ordered also that she should have use and profits of former husband's (Josias Wilkinson) farm for a period.

VI. SUSANNAH, m. EDWARD BOSS, { b. 1662, Feb. d. } { b d. 1724, Aug. } of Boss.

WILLETT.

THOMAS[3] (Andrew[2] Thos[1]) m. 1636, Jul. 6. MARY BROWN, { b. 1610. d. 1674, Aug. 4. } { b. d. 1669, Jan. 8. } of John & Dorothy ( ) Brown. — Plymouth, Swanzey, Mass.

He was a merchant.

Both his father and grandfather were ministers; the latter having been Rector of Barley (Wiltshire), and Prebend of Ely Cathedral.

1629. He was associated with the Leyden congregation.

1632. He came in ship Lion this year.

1633, Jan. 1. Freeman.

1637, Jun. 6. He was appointed on a committee to consider and act as to the trade of beaver "now likely to go to decay."

1638. Grand Jury.

1639, Feb. 11. He was granted 100 acres near Jones River.

1642, Jan. 24. He gave a sixteenth part for the building of a bark of forty or fifty tons, estimated to cost £200.

I. MARY, m. (1) 1658, Sep. 22. SAMUEL HOOKER, m. (2) 1703, Aug. 10. THOMAS BUCKINGHAM, { b. 1637, Nov. 10. d. } { b. d. 1697, Nov. } of Thomas & Susanna ( ) Hooker. { b. 1646. d. } of Buckingham.

II. MARTHA, m. 1658, Dec. 2. JOHN SAFFIN, { b. 1639, Aug. 6. d. 1678, Dec. 11. } { b. d. 1710, Jul. 28. } of Simon & Grace (Garrett) Saffin.

WILLETT. 1st column. He was born 1605; m.(2) 1671, Sep. 19, Joanna Pruden (widow of Peter), née Boyse. She m. (3) John Bishop. In 3d line read Hertford, instead of Wiltshire. He was baptized 1605, Aug. 29. 2d column. VIII. James. His first wife, b. 1654, Mar. 1, of Peter and Elizabeth (Smith) Hunt.

Inventory, £1,289, 7s., 2d., viz: books £3, 5s., 6d., sword, cutlass, surveying tackling, portmanteau, bonds and notes £378, 5s., 2 feather beds, 4 flock beds, warming pan, worsted comb, 5 spinning wheels, 2 pair cards, great and small table, 11 chairs, cider mill, a horse, 2 mares and colt, 2 bulls, 18 cows, yoke oxen, 2 steers, 6 two year old, 13 yearlings, 10 calves, 7 swine, 2 pigs, 12½ loads of hay, carpenter's tools, &c.

V. RUTH, b. 1686, Jan. 31. d. 1738 (—)
m.
WILLIAM HOPKINS, b. d. 1738. of William & Abigail (Whipple) — Hopkins.

1. William,
2. Stephen, 1707, Mar. 7.
3. Rufus,
4. John,
5. Hope, 1717, Mar. 3.
6. Esek, 1718, Apr. 26.
7. Samuel,
8. Abigail,
9. Susannah,

VI. SUSANNAH, b. 1688, Apr. 27. d.
m.
JAMES ANGELL, b. 1684. d. 1742. of John & Ruth (Field) — Angell.

1. Ruth,
2. William,
3. Amey
4. James,
5. John,
6. Martha, 1718.
7. Samuel.

Providence, Smithfield, R. I.

I. JOHN, b. 1690, Mar. 16. d. 1756, Sep. 25.
m. 1718, Mar. 20.
REBECCA SCOTT, b. 1699, Feb. 11. d. 1756 + of Silvanus & Joanna (Jenckes) — Scott.

1. Amey, 1719, Jan. 23.
2. Anne, 1721, May 19.
3. John, 1724, Mar. 20.
4. Sarah, 1727, Jun. 27.
5. Susanna, 1729, Sep. 20.
6. Ruth, 1731, Mar. 5.
7. Joanna, 1732, Sep. 12.
8. Ahab, 1734, Dec. 16.

1753, Jun. 11. Will—proved 1756, Nov. 22. Exx. wife Rebecca. To wife, improvement of a third of homestead, and best room in the house for life, while widow, and to her the indoor movables. To son John, £5, he having already had. To daughters Anne Bucklin, Sarah Arnold, Susannah, Ruth, and Joanna Wilkinson, each £100. To son Ahab, all lands and buildings in Smithfield, and all outdoor movables, cattle, &c., and reversion of lands of Donas, a negro man. The legacies to be paid by Ahab at certain intervals after he comes of age.

Inventory, £1,991, 13s., 4d., viz: wearing apparel £104, 7 French crowns £35, 8 Spanish milled dollars £36, gold shirt buckles £5, 7 silver spoons, stillyards, pewter, foot wheel, carpenter's and cooper's tools, 8 barrels cider, 3 cows, heifer, 2 yokes of oxen, yoke of steers, 25 sheep, old mare, 2 swine, 8 pigs, &c.

II. MERCY, b. 1694, Jun. 30. d.
m. 1718, Mar. 12.
JOHN SCOTT, b. 1694, Sep. 30. d. of Silvanus & Joanna (Jenckes) — Scott.

III. SARAH, b. 1696, Jun. 22. d.
m.
DAVID HOGG, b. d. of — Hogg.

1. Hannah,
2. Sarah.

IV. FREELOVE, b. 1701, Jun. 25. d.
m.
MICHAEL PHILLIPS, b. d. of James & Mary (Mowry) — Phillips.

Providence, Cumberland, R. I.

V. DANIEL, b. 1703, Jun. 8. d. 1777 +
m. 1740, Sep. 22.
ABIGAIL INMAN, b. d. of — Inman.

1. Joab, 1741, Jul. 30.
2. Daniel, 1743, Jul. 7.
3. Nedabiah, 1745, Sep. 24.
4. Lydia, 1747, Oct. 14.
5. Abigail, 1749, Feb. 9.
6. Son, 1751, Aug 6.
7. John, 1758, Nov. 13.
8. Olive, 1761, Mar. 28.

1747, Feb. 23. Cumberland. Town Council. He held the office some years.
1759. Overseer of the Poor.
1762. Deputy this and several years.

Providence, Cumberland, R. I.

VI. JEREMIAH, b. 1707, Jun. 4. d.
m.
AMY WHIPPLE, b. 1718, May 21. d. of Jeremiah & Deborah (Bucklin) — Whipple

1. William, 1739, Jul. 31.
2. Jeremiah, 1741, Jul. 6.
3. Simon. 1743, Sep. 24.
4. Benjamin, 1745, Nov. 1.
5. Patience. 1747, Mar. 20
6. Amey. 1747, Mar. 20.
7. Mercy 1750, Aug. 14
8. Jemima, 1752, Nov. 29
9. Stephen, 1755, Jan. 29
10. Jeptha, 1757, Apr. 3.
11. Elizabeth, 1760, Dec. 6.
12. Deborah, 1764, Aug. 28

His eighth child Jemima, was the celebrated prophetess.

I. HANNAH, b. d.
m.
JAMES DEXTER, b. 1691, Feb. 22. d. 1731, Nov. 7. of John & Alice (Smith) — Dexter.

1. John, 1717, Feb. 11
2. Anne, 1718, Oct. 29
3. James, 1721, Feb. 24
4. David, 1723, Feb. 24
5. Hopestill, 1726, Jul. 5.
6. Mercy, 1730, Oct. 10

1. Edward, 1685, Jan. 20.
2. Susanna, 1687, Jul. 21.
3. Peter, 1695, Sep. 15.
4. Jeremiah.

WILLETT.

1. Thomas, 1659, Jun. 10.
2. Samuel, 1661, May 29.
3. William, 1663, May 11.
4. John, 1665, Feb. 20.
5. James, 1666, Oct. 27.
6. Roger, 1668, Sep. 14.
7. Nathaniel, 1671, Sep. 28.
8. Mary, 1673, Jul. 3.
9. Hezekiah, 1675, Nov. 7.
10. Daniel, 1679, Mar. 25.
11. Sarah, 1681.

1. John, 1659, Sep. 13.
2. John, 1662, Apr. 14
3. Thomas, 1664, Mar. 18.
4. Simon, 1666, Apr. 4.
5. Josiah, 1668, Jan. 30
6. Joseph, 1670, Feb. 2.
7. Benjamin, 1672, Jun. 15.
8. Joseph, 1676, Jan. 24.

1648, Mar. 7. Captain of military company.

1649, Jun. 6. Surveyor of highways.

1649, Jul. 4. He and four others leased the trade of the Kennebec for three years, on same term as formerly had.

1651-52-53-54-55-56-57-58-59-60-61-62-63-64. Assistant.

1653, Apr. 6. He was appointed with eight others on the Council of War, and part of the powder and shot was to be kept by him.

1654, Jun. 20. He was directed to repair to the Commander-in-chief in Massachusetts to accompany them to Manhattan and to be assistant unto them in advice and counsel.

1656, Mar. 5. He and two others were leased the trade of the Kennebec for seven years at £35, per annum in money, moose or beaver, payable half in April and half in November, and if they are able £5 more for such of the seven years as they can. At the end of seven years their debts of beaver among the Indians shall not be above the number of five hundred skins, half of them valued at 8*s.*, per skin and the rest at 4*s.*

1661, Mar. 4. He was deputed to speak to Wamsutta about exchanging lands &c., and bought land of him the same year.

1665, Mar. 5. Rehoboth. He had a grant of 400 or 500 acres on the north side of the town.

1665, Jun. New York. Mayor. He was the first Englishman to hold the office, having received his appointment from Colonel Nicolls, to whom the Dutch had surrendered the previous year.

1668, Mar. 5. Swanzey. The court ordered that the township granted unto Captain Willett and others at Wawnamoisett and places adjacent, shall henceforth be called and known by the name of Swanzey. At the same date he was given liberty to purchase lands he can there, so as he do not too much straiten the Indians.

1670, Oct. 29. He and four others were impowered to dispose of lands, and for admission of inhabitants.

1672. Member of General Council.

1671, Apr. 26. Will—proved 1674, Nov. 25. Exs. sons James, Hezekiah, Andrew and Samuel. Overseers, son-in-law John Saffin, friend Robert Holmes, brother-in-law James Brown, son-in-law Samuel Hooker and Rev. Mr. John Myles. He mentions the fact that he is blessed with several children, and a liberal estate, consisting in goods, cattle, lands, houses, vessels for the sea, debts due, &c. To his four sons (the executors), all my dwelling house, warehouse, gardens and various large parcels of lands, 400 acres, rights in Rehoboth, &c. If any son sells he is first to proffer to one of his brothers, to the end that the said house and lands might be inherited by those of posterity that bear the name of Willett. To four sons was also given his library of books equally, and all commonage in Rehoboth and Swanzey to them, except what was given Samuel Hooker. When sons marry they to have consent of major part of overseers surviving, on penalty of being disinherited, and such son's part given to other sons by the overseers. To grandson Samuel Hooker, 80 acres upland and £50 worth of commonage in Rehoboth. To grandsons hereafter named, land in Narragansett country, viz: to grandson Thomas Saffin a double portion, and each grandchild surviving to have his benefit of Narragansett lands. To son Hooker's six sons already born and all those that shall be born by his wife, my daughter Mary; and to my son Saffin's four sons, and to all sons born of his wife, my daughter Martha; and to all such sons born to my daughter Esther (before division takes place in regard to all); to all these aforesaid grandchildren, the Narragansett lands to be equally divided. To son James Willett, £50, to be paid him by three other sons. To daughter Esther Willett, £50 paid by above three sons; and to her £100, already provided for her marriage portion. To four sons James, Hezekiah, Andrew and Samuel, all right to all lands not already mentioned. To three sons Hezekiah, Andrew and Samuel, £50 each, towards maintenance in books and other attainments of learning. To granddaughter Sarah Eliot, £50. To old servant John Paddock, £10. To overseers, each 10*s.* To the church of Plymouth, £10. To church at Swanzey, £10. To church at Rehoboth, £5. To Rev. John Myles, £10 To sons and daughters, rest of estate; goods, horses, cattle, household stuff, money, plate, negroes, &c., as follows: To four sons each a seventh and to three daughters each a seventh.

Inventory, £2,798, 14*s.*, 7*d.*, viz: books, silver tankard, porringer, large wrought fruit dish, snuffers, spoons, tobacco box, wine bowl, mustard pot, &c. (amounting to 14 pounds, 2 ounces in weight) £67, 16*s.*, 4 cabinets, chairs, castor hats, household goods, store goods, &c. The titles of some of books were, "Pilgrimage in Holland," "General Practice of Physic," "Luther's Table talk," "Allen's Doctrine of the Gospel," "Holy War," "Smith's Voyages," "Heber's Episcopal Policy," "Heber's Cosmography," "History of New England," "Wilson's Dictionary," "Calvin's Harmony," &c.; snuffers, candlesticks, warming pan, 13 feather beds, carpenter's tools, 149 sheep, 22 oxen, 27 cows, 27 steers, 20 heifers, 25 yearlings, 24 calves, a bull, 10 riding horses, 18 mares, 18 colts, swine, leather, dwelling house, orchard and land adjoining £720, land at Rehoboth, &c.

He and his wife were buried at the head of Bullock's Cove, in what is now the town of East Providence, R. I.

1676, Nov. 1. In reference to the negro Jeptha taken prisoner by the Indians and re-taken by an army, which said negro appertaineth to estate of Captain Willett, deceased; the General Court agreed with John Saffin, as representing the estate, that the negro forthwith betake himself to his former service for two years' time, and to be provided with meat, drink and apparel, and at the end of the time to go forth completely provided for in reference to apparel.

III. John, — b. 1641, Aug. 21.; d. young.

IV. Sarah, — b. 1643, May 4.; d. 1665, Jun. 13.
m.
John Eliot, — b. 1636, Aug. 31.; d. 1668, Oct. 13. — of John & Ann (Mumford) Eliot.

V. Rebecca, — b. 1644, Dec. 2.; d. 1649.

VI. Thomas, — b. 1646, Oct. 1.; d. young.

VII. Esther, — b. 1648, Jul. 10.; d. 1737, Jul. 26.
m. 1672, Jan 24.
Josiah Flint, — b. 1645, Aug. 24.; d. 1680, Sep. 15. — of Henry & Margery (Hoar) Flint.

VIII. James, — b. 1649, Nov. 23.; d. — Rehoboth, Mass., New London, Ct.
m. (1) 1673, Apr. 17.
Elizabeth Hunt, — b.; d. — of Peter Hunt.
m. (2) 1677, Jun.
Grace Frink, — b.; d. — of Frink.

1681. New London. He was admitted inhabitant.

IX. Hezekiah, — b. 1651.; d. 1651, Jul. 26.

X. Hezekiah, — b. 1653, Nov. 17.; d. 1676, Jul. 1. — Swanzey, Mass.
m. 1676, Jan. 7.
Ann Brown, — b.; d. — of John & Lydia (Bucklin) Brown.

He was killed by the Indians.

XI. David, — b. 1654, Nov. 1.; d. young.

XII. Andrew, — b. 1655, Oct. 5.; d. 1712, Apr. 6. — Newport, Kings Town, R. I.
m. 1682, May 30.
Ann Coddington, — b. 1663, Jul. 20.; d. 1751, Dec. 4. — of William & Ann (Brinley) Coddington.

He was a merchant.

1684. Freeman.

1687. Grand Jury.

1691, Jun. 27. His due was found to be 44*s.*, for fifteen hundred clapboards of his, used by order, on the Court House in Newport.

1696-98-1703-4. Kings Town. Deputy.

1700-3. Town Clerk.

1703, Jul. 12. He and others were appointed to lay out highways.

1712, Mar. 16. Will—proved 1712, Apr. Exs. wife Ann and son Francis. To sons Francis and Thomas, land where I dwell, when Thomas is of age, and meanwhile to be for wife, and she to bring up children Francis, Thomas, and Martha Willett. The son who has dwelling house in division of farm to pay other son £20. To sons also, other land. To son Francis, a pair of pistols. To son Thomas, an embroidered belt, &c. To daughter Martha, a certain amount in household goods at eighteen. To daughter Mary Carpenter, £5, she having had her portion. To wife Ann, half of all stock and the other half to two sons. To wife, all household goods, plate, and negro man Joseph, and she to be very kind to him for the good service he has done. To wife, also use of great room and bedroom adjoining and little cellar and half of garret, and to her all debts due, and to have a sum paid her yearly by two sons.

Inventory, £515, 15*s.*, viz: 2 oxen, 16 cows, 10 heifers, 2 steers, 6 yearlings, bull, 180 sheep, 13 hogs, 2 silver tankards, 2 porringers, 2 cups, 9 spoons £26, silver buckle and waist girdle, 2 guns, 2 pair of pistols, 2 silver hilted swords, square oak table, oval oak table, 7 leather chairs, 6 chairs wooden bottoms, 3 chairs flag bottoms, 6 Turkey work chairs, 6 chairs covered with serge, turkey work carpet, clock, andirons, bellows, 94 books, history, &c. £15, brass, pewter, wearing apparel £30, silver headed cane, negro man £35, woman £45, country bills, £20, &c. Among the rooms named were: kitchen, garret, hall, room adjoining below stairs, hall chamber, kitchen chamber, long room, &c.

1740, Mar. 12. His widow Ann made a deposition regarding Peleg Sanford's two marriages, &c., she calling herself aged about seventy-eight years.

He and his wife were buried on the homestead farm.

1. Sarah, 1662.

1. Mary, 1672, Nov.
2. Henry, 1674, Feb. 9.
3. Henry, 1675.
4. Dorothy,

I. MARY, b. 1678, Jun. 16. d.

II. MARTHA, b. 1680. d.

III. THOMAS, b. 1681. d.

IV. SARAH, b. 1683. d.

No issue.

I. ANNE, b. 1689, Sep. 26. d. 1709, Feb. 9.
m. 1707,
JOSEPH CARPENTER, b. 1685, Oct. 16. d. 1776, May 3. of Joseph & Ann (Simpkins) Carpenter.

No issue.

II. MARY, b. 1690, Sep. 21. d.
m. 1710.
JOSEPH CARPENTER, b. 1685, Oct. 16. d. 1776, May 3. of Joseph & Ann (Simpkins) Carpenter.

1. Willett, 1714, Jun. 8.
2. Ann, 1716, Sep. 24.
3. Phebe, 1718, Aug. 28.
4. Joseph. 1720, Jul. 15.
5. Andrew, 1722, Dec. 1.
6. Thomas, 1726, Apr. 15.
7. Francis, 1728, Nov. 8.
8. James, 1731, Mar. 5.
9. Willett 1736, Jan. 5.

III. FRANCIS, b. 1693, Jun. 25. d. 1776, Oct. 6. North Kingstown, R. I.
m.
MARY TAYLOR, b. 1678. d. 1769, Apr. 17. of Taylor

No issue,

1715-16-17-18-19-20-21-22. Kings Town. Town Clerk.
1722-23-24-25-26-27-28-29-30-31-32-33-34-35-36. North Kingstown. Town Clerk.
1723-24-26-30-32-34-36-37-39. Deputy.
1724-26. Clerk of Assembly.
1726-27-28-29-59-60-61. Assistant.
1736, Feb. He was voted £20, by the Assembly, toward building a bridge across Queens River, to be paid him on completion.
1736-37-39. Speaker of House of Deputies.
1740, Dec. 2. He was appointed on a committee to represent and manage the affairs of the colony, before the commissioners who were to hear and determine the boundaries between Rhode Island and Massachusetts.
1747. He was a member of Redwood Library, which was incorporated in this year.
1776, Feb. 12. Will—proved 1776. Ex. kinsman Francis Carpenter. He gave his homestead farm to Francis Carpenter, making him his residuary legatee.
He and his wife were buried in the family burial place on his own farm.

IV. THOMAS, b. 1696, May 13. d. 1725, Sep. 24. North Kingstown, R. I.
UNMARRIED.

1724, Jan. 28. Will—proved 1725, Oct. 15. Ex. brother Francis Willett. To brother Francis, farm on Boston Neck, and all my lands, messuages and tenements, but if he have no issue then to my two cousins (*i. e.* nephews), viz: Willett Carpenter, son of my sister Mary Carpenter and William Pease, son of my sister Martha Pease, equally divided. To mother, £20, for life, paid by my brother from profits of estate. To sisters Mary Carpenter and Martha Pease, £10, each. To brother Francis, rest of personal estate, money, goods and chattels, movables or immovables.

V. MARTHA, b. 1698, Mar. 6. d.
m.
SIMON PEASE, b. d. of William Pease.

WILLETT. 3d column. V. Martha, d. 1780, at Newport

1. William
2. Francis,
3. Ann,
4. Judith,
5. Martha,
6. Simon,
7. Mary,

Williams, Robert (omitted by Austin) See: American Genealogist, v. 20, p. 235.
Williams, John (omitted by Austin) See: American Genealogist, v. 24, p. 72-73-74.

WILLIAMS. 1st column. He was son of James and Alice (Pemberton) Williams. His father was a merchant tailor of London, and died there in 1621, mentioning in his will, wife Alice, sons Sidrach, Roger and Robert, daughter Katharine Wightman, and her husband, James Wightman, brother-in-law Roger Pemberton, &c.

1629, May 2. High Laver, Essex County, England. Roger Williams wrote at this date, and previously, to Lady Joan Barrington, (widow of Sir Francis Barrington), regarding his affection for her niece. He was then Chaplain to Sir William Masham, of Otes (in parish of High Laver), who had married a daughter of Lady Barrington. 1634. His mother died in this year, and in her will mentioned son Sidrach, son Roger, "now beyond the seas," (£10 yearly for twenty years, or in case of his death to his wife and daughter); son Robert, daughter Katharine, the now wife of John Davis, grandchildren, &c. She was baptized in 1564, and was daughter of Robert and Catharine Pemberton, of St. Albans, Hertfordshire. Perhaps Roger's father had come to London from St. Albans, for it is noticeable that he there found his wife, Alice Pemberton, and two Williams's of his generation lived there, viz.: Rev. Roger Williams, Rector of St. Albans in 1583; and Lewis Williams, who had a son Roger born there in 1607.

(The above concerning Williams is the result of special work of Mr. Henry F. Waters, communicated to the New Eng. His. and Gen. Register.)

ROGER, — b. 1599 ± — d. 1683 — Plymouth, Salem, Mass [Providence, R I.
m.
MARY, Barnes — b. — d. 1676 +

1621, Jun. 25. London. He was elected scholar in Sutton's Hospital, and three years after took an exhibition there. Years later Mrs. Sadleir (daughter of Sir Edward Coke) appended the following note to one of Roger Williams' letters to herself. "This Roger Williams, when he was a youth, would in a short hand take sermons and speeches in the Star Chamber, and presented them to my dear father. He, seeing so hopeful a youth, took such liking to him that he sent him into Sutton's Hospital," &c.

1625, Jul. 7. He entered Pembroke College, Cambridge.

1627, Jan. He took the degree of Bachelor of Arts.

1630, Dec. 1. He embarked at Bristol in ship Lion.

1631, Feb. 5. He arrived in Boston. Winthrop in noting the event calls him "a godly minister."

1631, Apr. 12. Salem, He was settled as minister.

1631. Plymouth. He went there in the summer, and became assistant to the pastor Mr. Ralph Smith.

1633. Salem. He returned in the autumn to this place, and became assistant to Rev. Mr. Skelton, and on the death of the latter (the next year) became pastor.

1635, Apr. He was summoned before the court at Boston, his offence being that he had taught publicly that a magistrate ought not to tender an oath to an unregenerate man, &c., and "he was heard before all the ministers and very clearly confuted," as Gov. Winthrop relates.

1635, Oct. 9. The General Court sentenced him to banishment. "Whereas Mr. Roger Williams, one of the Elders of the church of Salem, hath broached and divulged new and dangerous opinions against the authority of magistrates, as also written letters of defamation, both of the magistrates and churches here, and that before any conviction, and yet maintaineth the same without any retraction; it is, therefore, ordered that the said Mr. Williams shall depart out of this jurisdiction within six weeks now next ensuing," &c. He received permission to remain till spring, but the Court hearing that he would not refrain from uttering his opinions and that many people went to his house, "taken with an apprehension of his Godliness," and that he was preparing to form a plantation about Narragansett Bay; resolved to send him to England.

1636, Jan. A messenger was sent to Salem to apprehend him, but when the officers "came to his house, they found he had gone three days before, but whither they could not learn." He wrote, thirty-five years after his banishment, "I was sorely tossed for one fourteen weeks in a bitter winter season, not knowing what bed or bread did mean." He obtained from Massasoit a grant of land on the east bank of the Seekonk River, and commenced to plant, when he was advised by Governor Winslow that he was within the limits of Plymouth colony. He accordingly embarked in the spring or early summer, with five companions, landed at Slate Rock (as since called) to exchange greetings with the Indians, and then pursued his way again by boat to the site of his new settlement on the Moshassuck River, which for the many "Providences of the Most Holy and Only Wise, I called Providence." This same year his mediation, at the request of Massachusetts, prevented a coalition of the Pequots with the Narragansetts and Mohegans. He wrote of this service in later years: "Three days and nights my business forced me to lodge and mix with the bloody Pequot ambassadors, whose hands and arms methought reeked with the blood of my countrymen murdered and massacred by them on Connecticut river."

1638, Mar. 24. He took a deed from Canonicus and Miantonomi of the lands already purchased and settled upon, being "the lands and meadows upon the two fresh rivers called Moashausick and Wanaskatuckett," &c. He says of this purchase, "I spared no cost towards them in tokens and presents to Canonicus and all his, many years before I came in person to the Narragansett; and when I came I was welcome to the old prince Canonicus, who was most shy of all English to his last breath." "Here, all over the colony, a great number of weak and distressed souls, scattered and flying hither from Old England and New England, the Most High and Only Wise hath, in his infinite wisdom, provided this country and this corner as a shelter for the poor and persecuted according to their several persuasions." (These words were written years after his coming, when the settlement was an assured one.)

1638, Oct. 8. He deeded to his loving friends and neighbors an equal privilege with himself in his recent purchase, the consideration named being £30.

1639. He was baptized by Ezekiel Holliman, and then baptized him and others. For a few years he acted as pastor of First Baptist church.

XIII. SAMUEL, — b. 1658, Oct. 27. — d. — Queens County, N. Y.
m.
——— — b. — d. — of

He held the office of Sheriff of Queens County, Long Island, it is said, but there is little found on the records as to him, and the possibility is admitted that the children usually ascribed to him may have been descendants instead of Thomas Willett, of Flushing, who married 1643, Sep. 1, Sarah Cornell. Certainly Thomas Willett, of Flushing, had a grandson named Elbert, who married in 1701, Joanna Varick and had a son Edward.

WILLIAMS. See: American Genealogist, v. 20, p. 234-235.

I. MARY, — b. 1633, Aug. — d. 1681.
m. 1650 ±
JOHN SAYLES, — b. 1633. — d. 1681. — of Sayles.

II. FREEBORN, — b. 1635, Oct. — d. 1710, Jan. 10.
m. (1)
THOMAS HART, — b. — d. 1671. — of Edward & Margaret ( ) Hart.
m. (2) 1683, Mar. 6.
WALTER CLARKE. — b. 1640. — d. 1714, May 23. — of Jeremiah & Frances (Latham) Clarke.

III. PROVIDENCE, — b. 1638, Sep. — d. 1686, Mar. — Newport, R. I.
UNMARRIED.

1676, Aug. Under this date the town records of Providence state "By God's Providence it seasonably came to pass that Providence Williams brought up his mother from Newport in his sloop, and cleared the town by his vessel of all the Indians, to the great peace and contentment of all the inhabitants"

1680. Taxed 16*s*.

1686, May 14. Inventory, taken by Pardon Tillinghast and Daniel Williams, £22, 12*s*., 3*d*., viz: 3 pairs of stillyards, 2 pairs of brass scales and a nest of weights, small gun, pistol, 25 gallons rum £1, 17*s*., 6*d*., small money, silver spoon and cup £3, 14*s*., 20 pipes, broken parcel of silk, beads of glass, jews-harps, buttons, about 4000 pins, 5 Bermuda baskets, knives, scissors, knitting needles, silk crape, bible, lex mercatory, sun dial, half hour glass, razor, old pewter and tin vessels, &c.

1687, Sep. 1. Taxed 2*s*., 9*d*. "Estate of deceased Providence Williams." (Taxed at Providence.)

IV. MERCY, — b. 1640, Jul. — d. 1705 +
m. (1) 1659 ±
RESOLVED WATERMAN, — b. 1638. — d. 1670. — of Richard & Bethiah ( ) Waterman.
m. (2) 1677, Jan. 2.
SAMUEL WINSOR, — b. 1644. — d. 1705, Sep. 19. — of Joshua Winsor.

V. DANIEL, — b. 1642, Feb. — d. 1712, May 14. — Providence, R. I.
m. 1676, Dec. 7. [Nich.
REBECCA POWER (w. of — b. — d. 1727. — of Zachariah & Joan (Arnold) Rhodes.

1661, Feb. 24. He and his brother Joseph were each granted a full purchase right on the same terms as the original purchasers, on account "of some courtesies" received from their father by the proprietors of Providence. None others were to be so accommodated."

1665, Feb. 19. He had lot 11 in a division of lands.

1668, Jun. 1. He took oath of allegiance to Charles II.

1675–79–85–1709. Juryman.

1676, Dec. 2. His marriage was recorded by his father (then Town Clerk) as "the first marriage since God mercifully restored the town of Providence."

1679, Jul. 1. Taxed 12*s*., 6*d*. In the same year he was on a committee to levy a rate

1680, Jun. 7. Surveyor of Highways.

1685, Mar. 6. He bought of Valentine Whitman a house and lot.

1687, Sep. 1. Taxed 13*s*., 6*d*. "Daniel Wiliams, with estate of deceased Nicholas Power."

1695–98. Hay Warden.

1700, Dec. 24. He having had a controversy with William Hawkins concerning a Fulling Mill, which they had built in partnership on Hawkins' land, the matter was left to arbitrators. It was awarded that he should pay William Hawkins £8, and said mill and appurtenances should remain in hands of Daniel Williams for thirty years and then to revert to William Hawkins or heirs. If mill was not kept suitable for service or was idle two years, it reverted to Hawkins.

1710, Aug. 24 He wrote a letter to town of Providence, saying of his father that he "gave away his lands and other estate to them that he thought were most in want, until he gave away all." "I do not desire to say what I have done for both father and mother. I judged they wanted for nothing that was convenient for ancient people," &c. In a postcript he adds: "If a covetous man had that opportunity as he had, most of this town would have been his tenants I believe."

1712, May 9. He deeded son Providence for his settlement, land at Wescotomsett, the words being taken from his own mouth at his request and put in writing by Mr. Richard Waterman, and his senses being taken from him soon after, he had not opportunity to finish it, as was testified by Richard Waterman. On the same date he made deeds to his son Roger of 5 acres and dwelling house, and other land, provided he disturb not his mother Rebecca of her reasonable privileges, &c. Another deed was made to son Joseph of land on Woonasquatucket River, &c., and also dwelling house and 50 acres, always provided he doth his part toward relief of his brother Daniel as need requireth. To daughter Patience, he deeded 5 acres, negro girl Ann, 4 cows, and goods she hath in chests and trunks. These deeds were confirmed the next month by his son Peleg, who then ratified to his brothers and sister.

I. { EDWARD, { b. 1701. { d. 1794. Queens County, N. Y.
m.
ARLETTA CLOWES, { b. { d. of Clowes.

His son Marinus was a Colonel in the Revolutionary War, and became Mayor of New York

1. Edward, 1724.
2. Marinus, 1740, Jul. 31.
3. Son,
4. Son
5. Son,
6. Son,
7. Daughter,
8. Daughter,
9. Daughter,
10. Daughter,
11. Daughter.
12. Daughter,
13. Daughter,

II. { ELBERT, { b. 1703. { d. 1793. Albany, N. Y.

III. { ISAAC, { b. { d. 1758.
m.
———— { b. { d.

He was lost at sea.

1. Son,
2. Son,
3. Mary,
4. Anne.

WILLIAMS.

1. Mary, 1652, Jul. 11.
2. John, 1654, Aug. 17.
3. Isabel,
4. Phebe,
5. Eleanor, 1671.
6. Catharine, 1671.

1. John,
2. Mary, 1663.
3. James, 1666.
4. Thomas.
(No issue by 2d husband.)

1. Richard, 1660, Jan.
2. Mercy, 1663 ±
3. John, 1666.
4. Resolved, 1667 ±
5. Wait, 1668 ±
(2d husband.)
6. Samuel, 1677, Nov. 18.
7. Hannah,
8. Joshua, 1682, May 25.

I. { MARY, { b. { d. 1740 +
m.
EPENETUS OLNEY, { b. 1675, Jan. 18. { d. 1740, Sep. 18. of Epenetus & Mary (Whipple) Olney

1. James,
2. Charles,
3. Joseph,
4. Anthony,
5. Mary,
6. Amey,
7. Anne,
8. Martha,
9. Freeborn

II. { PELEG, { b. { d. 1766, Feb. Providence, Johnston, R. I.
m.
ELIZABETH CARPENTER, { b. { d. of Timothy & Hannah (Burton) Carpenter

1740, Apr. 14. He deeded son Peleg for love, &c., two parcels of land, 118 acres.
1740, Dec. 11. He deeded son Silas for love, &c., 150 acres, part in Glocester and part in Scituate.
1741, Jun. 13. He deeded son Robert for love, &c., half of 496 acres, &c.
1744, Jul. 4. He deeded son Timothy for love, &c., 192 acres in Scituate.
1751, Oct. 31. He deeded son Daniel for love, &c., half of 520 acres, and other half to son Robert
1779, Jun. 12. Inventory, £684, viz: an ox, 3 cows, a heifer, a two year, 3 pigs, 12 sheep. Administration to son Robert. (Reference is made to an agreement made in 1751, Apr. 8, in writing.)

1. Daniel,
2. Robert,
3. Silas,
4. Peleg,
5. Timothy,
6. Freelove,
7. Elizabeth.

III. { ROGER, { b. 1680, May. { d. 1763, Jan. 30. Providence, Scituate, R. I.
m. 1729, May 1.
ELIZABETH WALLING, { b. { d. of James Walling.

1728, May 30. He sold for £15 to Nathan Wade, 50 acres in original right of honored father Daniel Williams.
1734, Nov. 8. Scituate. He sold for £80 to Christopher Arnold of Warwick, a forty foot lot west side of Town St., in Providence.
1742, Sep. 20. He sold for £8 to Jabez Bowen, part of house lot that was my honored grandfather Roger Williams'.
1748, Jul. 25. He and wife Elizabeth sold for £300 to Nehemiah Sprague, lot on east side Town St., in Providence.
1752, Mar. 14. He sold for £120 to son-in-law Jonathan Tourtellot of Glocester, and Elizabeth his wife, a forty foot lot.
1752, Apr. 14. He deeded for love, &c., to son-in-law David Thayer of Mendon, and Rebecca his wife, 2 acres in Providence.
1760, Jan. 12. He, being deprived of his reason in the latter part of his life, was placed under guardian, and having but two children, viz: Elizabeth, wife of Jonathan Tourtellot and Rebecca wife of David Thayer, they divided the estate by quit claim deeds at the above date.

1. Elizabeth,
2. Rebecca, 1735, Apr. 20.

1642. He was appointed Agent to England to secure a charter, proceeding by way of New York.

1643, Jun. He embarked, and on the voyage wrote his "Key to the Indian Languages." In his dedication he says, "A little key may open a box where lies a bunch of keys."

1644, Sep. 17. He landed at Boston on his return, having secured the charter as well as a safe conduct through Massachusetts. He was met by his neighbors on his way to Providence, they coming in fourteen canoes on the Seekonk.

1647-48-64-65-70-71-72. Assistant.

1649, May 25. He was granted leave to sell a little wine or strong water to natives in their sickness.

He was also given leave to suffer a native, his hired household servant, to kill fowl for him on his hill at Narragansett about his house.

1650, Sep. 2. Taxed £1, 1*s.*, 4*d.*

1651, Nov. He went again to England, with John Clarke.

1652. He published in London, "Experiments of Spiritual Life, and Health and their Preservation," which he dedicated: "To the truly honorable the Lady Vane." He says of this work that he wrote it "in the thickest of the naked Indians of America, in their very wild houses and by their barbarous fires."

He wrote to his wife while abroad, "My dearest love and companion in this vale of tears," congratulating himself and her upon her recovery from recent illness: "I send thee, though in winter, a handful of flowers made up in a little posy, for thy dear self and our dear children to look and smell on, when I, as grass of the field, shall be gone and withered."

1653, Apr. 1. He wrote a letter to his friends and neighbors in Providence and Warwick, from Sir Henry Vane's at Belleau in Lincolnshire, relative to the confirmation of the charter secured by Vane's mediation, charging them to dwell in peace, &c., and in a postscript adds: "My love to all my Indian friends."

1654. He returned from England early in the summer.

1654, Jul. 12. In a letter to John Winthrop written from Providence, he says: "Sir, I have desires of keeping home, I have long had scruples of selling the natives aught but what may bring or tend to civilizing. It pleased the Lord to call me for some time, and with some persons, to practice the Hebrew, the Greek, Latin, French and Dutch. The Secretary of the Council, Mr. Milton, for my Dutch I read him, read me many more languages. Grammar rules begin to be esteemed a tyranny," &c.

1654-55-56-57. President of the colony.

1655. Freeman.

1658-59-61. Commissioner.

1667. Deputy.

1670-78-79-80. Town Council.

1675-76. Town Clerk.

1676, Aug. 14. As he was one of those "who staid and went not away" in King Philip's war, he had a share in the disposition of the Indian captives whose services were sold for a term of years.

1679, Jul. 2. He calls himself "near to four score years."

1682, May 6. He wrote Gov. Bradstreet, calling himself "old and weak and bruised (with rupture and colic) and lameness on both my feet." He proceeds: "By my fireside I have recollected the discourses, which (by many tedious journeys) I have had with the scattered English at Narragansett before the war and since. I have reduced them unto these twenty-two heads (enclosed) which is near thirty sheets of my writing. I would send them to the Narragansetts and others; there is no controversy in them, only an endeavour of a particular match of each poor sinner to his maker." He asks advice as to printing it, and alludes to news of Shaftsbury and Howard's beheading and contrary news of their reprieve, &c. "But these are but sublunaries, temporaries and trivials. Eternity, O Eternity, is our business."

1683, Jan. 16. He signed a deed.

1683, Apr. 25. He died previous to this date, as shown by deed of William Carpenter, wherein he calls himself last survivor of the thirteen proprietors of Pawtuxet lands (Roger Williams having been one of them).

1687, Sep. 1. Taxed 1*s.*, 6*d.*, estate of Roger Williams, deceased.

He was buried on his own land (north east of the junction of Benefit and Bowen streets).

1712, Jun. 23. Administration to widow Rebecca. Inventory £248, 16*s.*, viz: wearing apparel, money and bills £44, 10*s.*, pewter, table, chairs, books, warming pan, still, rye, Indian corn, tobacco, pork, beef, 2 negro children £40, sheep, young cattle, 4 oxen, 10 cows, a horse, &c.

1725, Jun. 12. Will—proved 1728, Jan. 1. Widow Rebecca. Ex. son Peleg. To son Providence, command of negroes Jack and Hope, but to be employed partly toward relief of my son Daniel, and if Providence die before Daniel, then son Peleg to have command of negroes for same use. At decease of sons Providence and Daniel, negroes to be freed if they prove good and profitable servants. To daughter Patience Ashton, negro Jenny, but not to be a servant for life except she commit some fault that may give just cause, or some other like reason, "so I leave it with my daughter Patience to deal Christian like by her." To sons Roger and Daniel, rest of estate equally.

VI. { JOSEPH, { b. 1643, Dec. 12. { d. 1724, Aug. 17. Providence, R. I.
m. 1669, Dec. 17.
{ LYDIA OLNEY, { b. 1645. { d. 1724, Sep. 9. of Thomas & Mary ~~(Small)~~ Ashton Olney.

1665, Feb. 19. He had lot 43 in a division of lands.

1676. He served in King Philip's war, as his gravestone testifies.

1679, Jul. 1. Taxed 6*s.*, 3*d.*

1683-84-93-96-97-98-1713. Deputy.

1684-85-86-87-88-91-93-94-1713-14-15. Town Council.

1687, Sep. 1. Taxed 7*s.*, 10*d.*

1687. Ratable estate, 2 oxen, a horse, a steer, 6 cows, 4 three years, 4 two years, 3 yearlings, a colt, 10 acres pasture, 3½ shares meadow.

1698-99-1700-1-2-3-4-5-6-7. Assistant.

1699, Oct. 25. He was appointed on committee, by Assembly, to inspect into the transcription of all laws of the colony, in performance of His Excellency the Earl of Bellomont's request.

1717, Oct. 26. Will—proved 1724, Oct. 12. Exx. wife Lydia. To son Thomas, 330 acres at Rocky Hill where he dwelleth, and other land. To son Joseph, 130 acres at Mashapauge adjoining house where he dwelleth, &c. To son James, 200 acres at Rocky Hill, and 130 acres at Mashapauge, adjoining my house, with dwelling house, orchard, &c., but wife Lydia to have use of outward room, wherein I now dwell, for life. To wife, bed and bedding. To son James, all the rest of movable estate and cattle, he providing for his mother all things she needs and that are necessary for an ancient woman.

Inventory, £55, 4*s.*, 2*d.*, viz: wearing apparel, cane, pewter, books, warming pan, churn, 2 bedsteads, 6 cows, a calf, a case of bottles. His son James took administration on his father's estate.

1724, Sep. 3. Will—proved 1724, Oct. 12. Widow Lydia. Ex. son James. To him, all estate.

Inventory, £16, 10*s.*, 6*d.*

He and his wife, and many descendants, were buried on his homestead farm; the graveyard being now within the limits of Roger Williams Park, Providence.

IV. DANIEL, b. / d. 1738 + — Providence, R. I.

V. PATIENCE, b. / d. 1764 (—)
m.
WILLIAM ASHTON, b. 1680. / d. 1765, Apr. 19. of James Ashton.

1. Joshua, 1716, Mar.
2. William,
3. Thomas,
4. Rebecca.

VI. PROVIDENCE, b. 1690. / d. 1769 + — Providence, Smithfield, R. I.
m.
ELIZABETH, b. / d. 1769 + of

1. Elizabeth.

1725, Dec. 24. He sold John Smith (son of Benjamin), for £6, 7*s*., 6*d*., lot of 15 acres in original right of honored uncle Providence Williams.

1740, May 9. Smithfield. He and wife Elizabeth sold for £150 to Daniel Mowry, 60 acres southwest corner of homestead farm.

1749, Mar. 10. He sold Richard Steere for £22 one-quarter right in the original right of uncle Providence Williams.

1750, May 14. Glocester. He sold land to Thomas Arnold.

1763, Oct. Smithfield. Dr. Stiles relates that he saw Providence Williams at Squire Aldrich's. He says, "Providence Williams, now superannuated, has one child, a poor daughter. He himself was once rich in land, until about seven years ago he sold all and is satisfied by the town." He mentions that his age was seventy-three years.

1769. Elizabeth, wife to Providence Williams, executed a release of certain land that had been sold by Providence Williams in 1744.

VII. JOSEPH, b. / d. 1739, Mar. 4. — Providence, Scituate, R. I.
m. 1716, Feb. 19.
SARAH WHITMAN, b. 1696, Jan. 26. / d. 1749, Oct. 27. of Valentine & Sarah (Bartlett) Whitman.

1. Benoni, 1716, Nov. 15.
2. Goliah, 1724, Sep. 17.

He "was killed by the Spaniards near the bay of Campeachy," as is stated on Town records of Scituate.

1738, Sep. 26. Will—proved 1739, Jun. 2. Exs. Joseph Wilkinson and Charles Tillinghast. To son Benoni, £100. To wife Sarah, £100. To sons Benoni and Goliah, all the rest both real and personal.

Inventory, £1,721, 7*s*., viz: a bull, yoke of oxen, 7 cows, 2 steers, 2 heifers, 5 yearlings, 6 calves, 14 sheep, 2 lambs, 6 hogs, a mare, bonds £1,218, 9*s*., 8*d*., loom, &c.

1749, Oct. 13. Will—proved 1749, Nov. 6. Widow Sarah. Exs. sons Benoni and Goliah. To son Benoni, gun, kettle, &c. To son Goliah, 2 cows, bible, 2 spoons, &c. To Goliah's wife Susannah, a mare, gold beads, &c. To granddaughter Sarah Williams, wearing apparel, but if she die then two daughters-in law to have, viz: Abigail and Susannah Williams. To grandson Joseph, son of Benoni, land. To grandson Roger, son of Goliah, rest of land and house.

I. JOSEPH, b. 1670, Sep. 26. / d. young.

II. THOMAS, b. 1672, Feb. 16. / d. 1724, Aug. 27. — Providence, R. I.
m.
MARY BLACKMAR, b. / d. 1717, Jul. 1. of James & Mary (Hawkins) Blackmar.

1. Joseph,
2. Thomas,
3. Stephen,
4. John,
5. Abigail,
6. Jonathan,
7. Mary.

1722, Apr. 16. He deeded son Joseph for love, &c., 100 acres near Rocky Hill adjoining my homestead farm.

1723, Jul. 12. He deeded son Thomas for love, &c., 99 acres, being part of homestead farm.

1724, Oct 19. Administration to son Joseph, he bringing up young children.

Inventory, £166, 1*s*., viz: tables, chairs, weaver's shuttle, shoemaker's seat and tools, flax, rye, Indian corn, cheese press, a pair of oxen, 7 cows, 2 heifers, 30 sheep, an old mare, 9 swine, &c. Real estate, £865, 9*s*., 8*d*., viz: homestead of 100 acres £455, and other land.

1727, Nov. 20. His sons Joseph and Stephen were to have their part of land of deceased father set off, by order of Town Council.

1729, Oct. 18. His son John was to have his part of land of deceased father, set off.

1738, Jul. 19. Receipts were given by Jonathan and Mary Williams for £144 each to brother Joseph Williams, Jr., administrator of estate of honored father Thomas, deceased. (Four years earlier Abigail had given receipt for £148.)

III. JOSEPH, b. 1673, Nov. 10. / d. 1752, Aug. 15. — Providence, R. I.
m.
LYDIA HEARNDEN, b. / d. 1763. of Benjamin & Lydia ( ) Hearnden.

1. Mercy,
2. Jeremiah,
3. Mary,
4. Lydia,
5. Martha,
6. Barbara,
7. Freelove,
8. Jemima,
9. Meribah,
10. Patience.

1748, Aug. 24 Will—proved 1752, Sep. 24. Exx. wife Lydia. To her all personal, and use of homestead for life; and at her decease to go to grandson Jeremiah Williams, he paying to daughters of testator, £100 each, viz: to Mercy Randall, Mary Atwood, Lydia Randall, Martha Randall, Barbara Congdon, Freelove Dyer, Jemima Potter, Meribah Brown and Patience Dyer. To son Jeremiah, rest of land.

Inventory, £246, 19*s*, viz: bills of credit £39, feather bed £42, linen wheel, 5 old chairs, pewter, testament, mare £60, &c.

1763, Jul 26. Will—proved 1763, Sep. 29. Widow Lydia (of Cranston). Ex. son-in-law John Dyer. To daughter Mercy Randall, feather bed, &c. To son Jeremiah, 5*s*. To eight daughters Mercy Randall, Mary Atwood, Lydia Randall, Martha Randall, Barbara Congdon, Patience Dyer, Jemima Potter and Freelove Dyer, all the rest of estate. Inventory £797, 13*s*.

IV. MARY, b. 1676, Jun. / d.

WILLIAMS. 3d column. V James. In his will change Elizabeth Harris to Elizabeth Hines.

V. JAMES, b. 1680, Sep. 20 / d. 1757, Jun. 25. — Providence, Cranston, R. I.
m.
ELIZABETH BLACKMAR, b. 1682. / d. 1761, Mar. of James & Mary (Hawkins) Blackmar.

1. James, 1704, Feb. 20.
2. Anne, 1706, Mar. 17.
3. Sarah, 1707, Dec. 4.
4. Joseph, 1709, Oct. 24.
5. Mary, 1711, Oct. 1.
6. Nathaniel, 1714, Oct. 11.
7. Elizabeth, 1717, Oct. 21.
8. Hannah, 1719, Jun. 22.
9. Lydia, 1724, Oct. 20.
10. Nathan, 1728, Jun. 15.

1741, Dec. 4. Will—proved 1757, Jul. 16. Ex. son Nathaniel. To son Nathaniel, confirmation of deeds of part of homestead, and to him rest of homestead, buildings, &c., reserving to wife use of ell part of house for life, half of orchard, &c., but if she marry, only £40. To son James, certain land. To son Joseph, land near Benedict Pond. To son Nathan, 119 acres at Pascoag, &c., and a feather bed. To wife Elizabeth, all household goods for life while widow. To daughters Anne Potter, Mary Potter and Elizabeth Harris, each £10. To daughter Lydia Williams, £35. To son Nathaniel, rest of estate.

Inventory, £810, 13*s*., viz: wearing apparel £89, 5*s*., bed, 2 bibles and other books £13, pewter, 2 spinning wheels, a pair oxen, a pair of steers, 3 cows, 2 two years, 2 yearlings, 5 swine, 20 sheep, &c.

VI. LYDIA, b. 1683, Apr. 26. / d. 1725, Aug. 17.
UNMARRIED.

{ JOSHUA, { b. Providence, R. I.
m. { d. 1679.
{ ——— { b.
{ d. 1655, Feb.

1637, Aug. 20 (or a little later). He and twelve others signed the following compact: "We whose names are hereunder, desirous to inhabit in the town of Providence, do promise to subject ourselves in active and passive obedience to all such orders or agreements as shall be made for public good of the body in an orderly way, by the major consent of the present inhabitants, masters of families, incorporated together in a Town fellowship, and others whom they shall admit unto them, only in civil things."

1637, Nov. 20. He is thus alluded to in a letter from Roger Williams to Governor John Winthrop. "Sir, I have often called upon your debtor Joshua, but his ill advisidness of refusing my service and spending of his time upon a house and ground, hath disabled him," &c.

1640, Jul. 27. He and thirty-eight others signed an agreement for a form of government

1641, Nov. 17. He and twelve others complained in a letter to Massachusetts of the "insolent and riotous carriages of Samuel Gorton and his company," and therefore petitioned Massachusetts to "lend us a neighborlike, helping hand," &c.

1650, Feb. 4. He sold Gregory Dexter a share of meadow west side of Moshasuck River.

1650, May 27. He had certain land on condition of paying town £30, 15*s*., for Matthew Weston's use, whose land it formerly was.

1660, Sep. 2. Taxed 3*s*, 4*d*.

1655. Freeman.

1655, Feb. 15. His wife's death is alluded to in a letter from Roger Williams to John Winthrop, Jr., "It hath pleased God, Sir, to take away (some few days since) the wife of Mr. Joshua Windsor, once a servant to your dear father." An unborn child died with the mother it seems.

1660, Sep. 8. He is mentioned in a letter from Roger Williams to Governor Winthrop, of Connecticut. "I promised to a neighbour, a former servant of your father (Joshua Windsor) to write a line on his behalf and at his desire, unto you. His prayer is that when you travel toward Boston you would please to come by Providence, and spare an hour to heal an old sore — a controversy between him and most of his neighbors, in which, I am apt to think, he hath suffered some wrong. He hath promised to submit your sentence." The dispute was about a few poles of ground.

1663, Oct. 29. He and James Ashton signed a bond consenting to arbitration in all matters of difference between them, occasioned by a certain lot in Providence, called Matthew Weston's lot.

1665, Feb. 19. He had lot 36 in a division of lands.

1671, Dec. 1. He deeded to his son and heir Samuel, for valuable consideration, all right and interest in all lands within liberties of Town of Providence, divided or undivided, without limitation, "the dwelling house in which I now dwell in only excepted, it being to remain for my use during the life of me the said Joshua Winsor, but after my decease it also to come into the possession of my aforesaid son Samuel."

1679, Jul. 8. The above deed was recorded with the town's consent.

I. { SAMUEL, { b. 1644. Providence, R. I.
{ m. 1677, Jan. 2. [Resolved. { d. 1705, Sep. 19.
{ MERCY WATERMAN [w. of { b. 1640, Jul.
{ d. 1705 + of Roger & Mary ( ) Williams.

1674. Deputy.

1676, Aug. 14. He was one of those "who staid and went not away" in King Philip's war, and so had a share in the disposition of the Indian captives, whose services were sold for a term of years.

1677, Jan. 2. His marriage was entered as of this date by Roger Williams (then Town Clerk), though the town book of births gives it erroneously as of a later date (viz: 1677, Apr. 10).

1679, Jul. 1. He and the orphans of Resolved Waterman, deceased, were taxed together 6*s*., 3*d*.

1679, Dec. 4. In a deposition of this date he calls himself aged thirty-five years.

1680, Apr. 19. His brother-in-law, Stephen Harding, in will of this date, gave him a legacy of "my wife's best suit of apparel."

1680, May 22. He petitioned Town Council about the better settling of the estate belonging to the widow Mercy, whom he married with, and also for the assistance of the Town to correct the irregular courses of Richard Waterman, his son-in-law (stepson), concerning with Nathaniel Waterman and Daniel Williams, who he says had dealt maliciously by him. There had been trouble about the settlement of estate of his wife's first husband long before this, as in 1671, Jan. 23, the Town Council found she had already administered on her husband's estate, having refused to take administration from the Town Council, and also refusing to give bonds. The Town Council accordingly decided that she was liable to respond for said estate when legally called. The inventory of her first husband's estate (1670, Aug. 29), was £172, 13*s*.

1687. Grand Jury.

1687. Ratable estate, 2 oxen, 3 cows, heifer, 4 two year cattle, 3 yearlings, horse, mare, two year horse, 18 sheep, 5 small swine, 2 house lots, 87 acres in the wilderness, a share of land beyond the Seven Mile Line, a swamp of five or six acres called Joshua's swamp, a share of meadow called Shepherd's meadow, about 30 acres at the house, 3 ploughed, and 5 or 6 of the 30 rough pasture. "This is the best account that I can give." He adds "one horse more belonging to Resolved Waterman, who is with me upon wages," and 7 acres of land in the Neck.

1691, May 7. He sold to Gideon Crawford a lot of 5 acres, which "in the original was my father Joshua Winsor's, but since in consideration of keeping the ancient man it became mine."

1705, Nov. 28. Administration on his estate to widow Mercy and eldest son Samuel. Inventory, £250 ±. At his old dwelling house, 3 horses, ½ a mare and colt, 5 yearling cattle, 33 sheep and lambs, a swine, 18 loads of hay, apples, standing corn, and various tools in the shop, viz: vice, handsaw, joiner's tools, planes, saws, gouge, beetles, wedges, &c. Other articles at this old dwelling house were: tobacco, yarn, hops, books, spectacles, gun, 3 silver spoons, a silver dram cup, &c.

At his farm in the woods there were 3 pair of oxen, 8 cows, a bull, 4 heifers, a steer, a bible and other books, &c.

II. { SARAH, { b.
{ m. { d.
{ ——— TYLER, { b.
{ d. of Tyler.

III. { SUSANNA, { b.
{ m. { d.
{ ——— TURNER, { b.
{ d. of Turner.

IV. { MERCY, { b.
{ m. 1672, Jan. 28. { d. 1680,
{ STEPHEN HARDING, { b.
{ d. 1680, May 31. of Stephen & Bridget ( ) Harding.

V. { HANNAH, { b.
{ m. 1675, Sep. 30. { d. 1715, Dec. 14.
{ JONATHAN CARY, { b. 1647, Jan. 15.
{ d. 1737. of James & Eleanor ( ) Cary.

WODELL.

{ WILLIAM, { b. Boston, Mass., Portsmouth,
{ m. { d. 1693. [Tiverton, R. I.
{ MARY, { b.
{ d. 1676, Mar. 23.

1637, Nov. 20. He and others of Boston, &c., were ordered to deliver up all guns, pistols, swords, powder, shot, &c., because "the opinions and revelations of Mr. Wheelwright and Mrs. Hutchinson have seduced and led into dangerous errors many of the people here in New England."

1643, Jan. 12. He and ten others bought of Miantonomi for 144 fathoms of wampum, tract of land called Shawomet (Warwick).

1643, Sep. 12. He with others of Warwick, was notified to appear at General Court at Boston to hear complaint of two Indian sachems Pomham and Soconocco, as to "some unjust and injurious dealing toward them by yourselves" The Warwick men declined to obey the summons, declaring that they were legal subjects of the king of England, and beyond the limits of Massachusetts terriory, to whom they would acknowledge no subjection. Soldiers were soon sent who besieged the settlers in a fortified house. In a parley it was now said "that they held blasphemous errors which they must repent of," or go to Boston for trial.

1643, Oct. 5. Portsmouth. He had a grant of 10 acres.

1643, Nov. 3. Having been brought with others before the court at Boston charged with heresy and sedition, they were sentenced to be confined during the pleasure of the court, and should they break jail or preach their heresies or speak against church or state, on conviction they should die. He was sent to Watertown but not to prison, and remained at large till the following March, and was then banished from both Massachusetts and Warwick. He thereupon returned to Portsmouth. Most of his companions in the trial suffered close imprisonment for several months.

1655. Freeman.

1656-63. Commissioner.

1664-65-66-67-69-70-72-73-74-75-80-81-82-83-84-86. Deputy.

1676, Apr. 4. It was "voted that in these troublesome times and straits in this colony, this Assembly desiring to have the advice and concurrence of the most judicious inhabitants if it may be had for the good of the whole, do desire at their next sitting the company and counsel of Mr. Benedict Arnold," and fifteen others, among whom was William Wodell.

1680, May 5. He was appointed as a committee to put the laws and acts of the colony into such a method that they may be put in print.

1684. Assistant. He was chosen but positively denied to engage.

I. { MARY, { b. 1640, Nov.
{ m. { d.
{ DANIEL GRINNELL, { b. 1636 ±
{ d. 1703 + of Matthew & Rose ( ) Grinnell.

II. { GERSHOM { b. 1642, Jul. 14. Portsmouth, R. I.
{ m. { d.
{ MARY TRIPP, { b. 1646 ±
{ d. 1716 + of John & Mary (Paine) Tripp.

(She m. (2) 1683, Mar. 5, Jonathan Gatchell.)

1667, Dec. 24. He took Henry Straight for apprentice for six years.

1672, Jun. 21. He took a receipt from Richard Cornell of Cow Bay, N. Y., for all demands.

1716, Nov. 29. Mary Gatchell gave receipt to her daughter-in-law Ruth Wodell for £12, being all that was due her from will of son William Wodell up to 13th of December next on account of legacy from said son.

WINSOR. 3d column. I. Samuel. His wife b. 1685, d. 1771, Dec. 21.

I. SAMUEL, b. 1677, Nov. 18. d. 1758, Nov. 17. Providence, R. I.
m. 1703, Jan. 7.
MERCY HARDING, b. d. 1749 + of Abraham & Deborah ( ) Harding.

1. Martha, 1703, Dec. 10.
2. Mary, 1707, Aug. 5
3. Lydia, 1709, Aug. 5.
4. Hannah, 1711, Aug. 26.
5. Joseph, 1713, Oct. 4.
6. Deborah, 1715, Oct. 12.
7. Mercy,
8. Freelove, 1720, Sep. 15.
9. Samuel, 1722, Nov. 1.

1706, Apr. 21. He deeded his brother Joshua for goodwill and affection, a mansion house and 52 acres, stating in the deed that as his father died intestate he became heir, but that whereas his brother Joshua was "destitute of any house, the which if his father had made disposal of his estate he might have supplied and provided, but it otherwise falls out," now therefore he Samuel, the eldest son, deeds to brother Joshua, as above.

1713, Feb. 16. He testified that he had seen William Turpin and Edward Hawkins, Jr., play cards at said Turpin's house.

1733. He was ordained pastor of First Baptist Church and preached till his death. Morgan Edwards says that he was "a man remarkable for preaching against paying ministers, and for refusing invitations to Sunday dinners for fear they should be considerations for Sunday sermons." (His son Samuel succeeded his father as pastor, being ordained 1759.)

1749, Dec. 20. Will—proved 1758, Nov. 29. Exs. wife Mercy and son Joseph. To son Joseph, land where he dwells (except 60 acres) and other land. To son Samuel, land where he lives, &c. To daughter Martha Colwell, £40. To sons Joseph and Samuel, my homestead farm where I dwell, equally, they paying £600 apiece to six sisters, that is £200, to each sister, viz: Mary Potter, Lydia Angell, Hannah O'ney, Deborah Olney, Mercy Angell, Freelove Winsor. To grandchildren Mary, Fisher, Jeremiah, Phebe and Christopher Potter, land. To grandson John Potter, £20. To grandsons Philip and Samuel Potter, land. To daughter Lydia Angell, land near Seekonk Ferry. To daughters Hannah Olney and Mercy Angell, land. To daughter Deborah Olney, land and £50. To grandson John Power, son of daughter Lydia, land. To daughter Freelove Winsor, £100. To sons Joseph and Samuel, working tools, &c. To wife Mercy, a third of movables not disposed of, £150, and privilege of the house in town and garden. Rest of movables to nine children.

Inventory, £3,347, 6s., 9d., viz: a linen and woolen wheel, 15 chairs, 2 tables, silver cash £29, 1s., silver cup, 2 large spoons, 3 links of buttons, shoe buckles, &c., £52, cider press, 17 barrels cider £35, 5 barrels cider beer £12, 10s., 6 stacks of hay and stacks of oats and thatch, 4 hogs, 10 sheep, 6 cows, &c. (Only his son Joseph took administration.)

II. HANNAH, b. d. 1742 +
m. 1702, May 2.
DANIEL ANGELL, b. 1680, May 2. d. 1750, Jan. 16 of John & Ruth (Field) Angell.

1. Samuel, 1707, Dec. 12.
2. John, 1709, Oct. 18.
3. Nedabiah, 1712, Apr. 19.
4. Joshua, 1714, Feb. 26.
5. Mercy, 1716, Jan. 4.
6. Job, 1718, Jan. 1.
7. Daniel, 1720, Oct. 27.
8. Ezekiel, 1722.
9. Wait,

III. JOSHUA, b. 1682, May 25. d. 1752, Oct. 10. Providence, Smithfield, R. I.
m. (1) 1706, Oct. 18.
MARY BARKER, b. 1678, Mar 13. d. 1718, Dec. 30. of James & Sarah (Jefferay) Barker.
m. (2) 1719, Dec. 3.
DEBORAH HARDING, b. d. 1752 + of Abraham & Deborah ( ) Harding.

1. Sarah, 1707, Aug. 27.
2. Joshua, 1709, Sep. 17.
3. Samuel, 1712, Nov. 7.
4. Susannah, 1715, Jun. 19.
5. Mary, 1718, Dec. 18.
(2d wife.)
6. Abraham, 1720, Oct, 4.
7. John, 1723, Mar. 2.

1706, May 27. He had 17 acres laid out upon exchange with the town.

1713, Jun. 16. Taxed 16s.

He was pastor of First Baptist Church, Smithfield, for some time.

1749, Aug. 4. Will—proved 1752, Oct. 28. Exs. wife Deborah and son Joshua. To wife Deborah, a feather bed, £300, and east end of dwelling house while widow, but if she marry, half of sum to four sons, equally, viz: Joshua, Samuel, Abraham and John. To three daughters, Sarah Mathewson, Susanna Smith and Mary Smith, £300 each. To son Joshua, half a certain tract of land, piece of meadow, half a lot on Town street, &c. To son Samuel, right of cutting timber from a 6 acre lot for eighteen years, and then resigned to son Abraham, with rest of farm on which Abraham dwells. To sons John and Abraham, land, the former receiving the homestead farm, house, barn, &c. Sons Abraham and John to take care "of their affectionate mother both in sickness and in health." Movable estate to four sons, Joshua, Samuel, Abraham and John.

Inventory, £3,559, 4s., 10d., viz: books new and old £18, 14s., 37 milled dollars £103, 12s., bonds, notes and book debts, pewter, 6 silver spoons £40, hour glass, 3 looms, double and twisted stocking yarn, linen yarn, cooper's and carpenter's tools, old sword, fat cow, warming pan, &c.

No issue.

1. Hannah,
2. Eleanor,
3. James,
4. Abigail,
5. Samuel, 1683, Apr. 1.
6. Ebenezer, 1684, Aug. 17.
7. James,
8. Freelove, 1688, Feb. 26.

WODELL.

1. Daniel,
2. Jonathan, 1670.
3. Richard, 1675.

I. WILLIAM, b. 1663. d. 1699, Jan. 6. Portsmouth, R. I.
m. 1681, Feb. 10.
RUTH LAWTON, b. d. 1726, Apr. 15. of George & Elizabeth (Hazard) Lawton.

No issue.

He was a mariner.

1686. Freeman.

1697, Dec. 6. Will—proved 1699, Jun. 8. Exx. wife Ruth. To her all housing and lands in Portsmouth for life, and if she have a child within 200 days of his death then to that child all said lands and housing. If she have no child then half to go to Robert Lawton, son of my brother-in-law Robert Lawton, and half to Ruth Manchester, daughter of my brother-in-law Stephen Manchester, which he had by my sister Elizabeth, deceased. If either of these heirs die without issue then survivor to have, and if both die then to my brother Richard Wodell, and if he die without issue then to my brother Return, and if he die to next heir and so forever heir to heir to world's end. To wife Ruth, all lands in Tiverton. If wife marry, the negro "Jo" to be free, but if she remain widow, Jo to be for her ten years and then to be free. To mother Mary Gatchell, £6 yearly for life. To brother Richard, £12. To brother Return, £12. To brother Gershom, 1s. To sister Mary, wife of Robert Lawton, 1s. To sister Sarah, wife of John Humery, 1s. To sisters Priscilla and Isabel Gatchell, 20s. each. To wife Ruth, all movables, cattle, chattels, household goods, money, interest in shipping, &c.

1725, Jan. 8. Will—proved 1726, Apr. 21. Widow Ruth. Exs. cousins (nephew and niece) Jonathan Nichols and Elizabeth his wife. She desires that legacy given her by her brother Robert Lawton be returned to Captain George Lawton, executor of said Robert. To Captain George Lawton, also my silver seal and an English crown. To cousin Mary Sherman, wife of Benjamin, £20. To cousin Elizabeth Curtis, widow, £5. To cousin Ruth Sweet, daughter to my sister Isabel Albro, £5. To cousin Elizabeth Sherman, daughter of Benjamin, my bed, &c. To negro woman Cate, all my woolen wearing clothes (excepting stockings), black trunk, side saddle, pillion, twelve sheep, to be for her and her children equally divided, together with my reading books. To executors, my four negroes Cate, Scipio, Betty and Jo, and all other estate real and personal.

II. MARY, b. d. 1732, Jan. 14.
m. 1681, Feb. 16.
ROBERT LAWTON, b. d. 1706, Jan. 25. of George & Elizabeth (Hazard) Lawton.

1. Mary, 1682, Feb. 20.
2. George, 1685, Sep. 1.
3. Elizabeth, 1688, Sep. 12.
4. Robert, 1690, Jan. 5.

III. ELIZABETH, b. d. 1697 (—)
m. 1684, Sep. 13.
STEPHEN MANCHESTER, b. d. 1719. of Thomas & Margaret (Wood) Manchester.

1. Gershom,
2. Ruth, 1690, May.

IV. RICHARD, b. d. 1710 (—) Tiverton, R. I.
m.
SUSANNA PEARCE, b. 1672 ± d. 1710 (—) of John & Mary (Tallman) Pearce.

1. Mary, 1691, Oct. 14.
2. Susan, 1693, May 7.
3. Sarah, 1693, May 7.

1692, Sep. 8. Will—proved 1693, May 2. Exs. grandson Gershom Wodell and latter's mother Mary. Overseers Samson and Samuel Sherman. To granddaughter Sarah Wodell, £15. To Priscilla and Isabel Gatchell, each £10 at sixteen years of age. They are called sisters of Sarah Wodell (*i. e.* half sisters) To daughter Mary Grinnell, wife of Daniel, £5. To grandson Richard Grinnell, £5. To grandsons William and Samuel Sanford, each £5. To grandson John Anthony, son of daughter Frances, 40*s*. To grandsons Joseph and William Anthony, each £5. To granddaughters Susanna, Elizabeth, and Alice Anthony, each 50*s*., at fifteen years of age. To grandson William Wodell, 1*s*. To daughter Alice Anthony, 1*s*. To loving friend John Greene of Warwick, 20*s*. To grandson Richard Wodell, £5. To grandson Return Wodell, £5. To grandson Gershom Wodell, northernmost share of land to pay above legacies, and to Gershom also southernmost share of land where my house stands, his mother having equal share with him in this share during life. To granddaughter Sarah Wodell, best feather bed. To Priscilla and Isabel Gatchell, a feather bed each. To grandson-in-law Robert Lawton, two books "Gadberry" and "Wing." To John Potter of Warwick, and rest of free inhabitants, for an enlargement of the commons of said town, half of all my right as purchaser, and other half to friend John Greene. "And whereas it hath been said by several persons that I with some others did go about to wrong the town of Portsmouth in purchasing of Hog Island of an Indian Sachem called Mososup, I am so far from doing any wrong therein that I do give unto the free inhabitants of the said town of Portsmouth" Hog Island, &c. He makes same statement in regard to some land bought on Rhode Island.

His will was recorded at both Portsmouth and Taunton.

Inventory, £324, 17*s*.

III.	SARAH,	b. 1644, Oct. d. 1680, Dec. 15.		
	m. 1662, Oct. SAMUEL SANFORD,	b. 1635, Jul. 14. d. 1713, Mar. 18.	of John & Elizabeth (Webb)	Sanford.
IV.	ALICE,	b. 1650, Feb. 10. d. 1734.		
	m. 1671, Dec. 26. ABRAHAM ANTHONY,	b. d. 1727, Oct. 10.	of John & Susanna ( )	Anthony.
V.	FRANCES,	b. 1652, Jul. 6. d.		
	m. 1669, Nov. 23. JOHN ANTHONY,	b. 1642. d. 1715, Oct. 20.	of John & Susanna (	Anthony.

1697, Apr. 24. He, owner of sloop Friends Adventure, fifty tons burden, now riding at anchor in Tiverton harbor, sold for £63, 10*s.*, to William Paine of Boston, an eighth part of said sloop. On the same date he sold nine-sixteenths of the sloop to Read Elding and Anthony Paine of New Providence, Bahamas for £272, 5*s.*

1710, Apr. 5. He and his wife being dead, the children were to receive their part of their grandfather John Pearce's estate through their guardian Amos Sheffield.

V. RETURN, b. / d.

VI. GERSHOM, b. / d. 1741, Sep. 4. — Tiverton, R. I.
m.
SARAH MOTT, b. 1670, Feb. 3. / d. 1738 + — of Jacob & Joanna (Slocum) — Mott.

1. William, 1702, Jun. 13.
2. Gershom,
3. Elizabeth,
4. Ruth,
5. Patience,
6. Alice,
7. Innocent.

1692, Mar. 2. Tiverton. He was an inhabitant at formation of town.

1699, Mar. 16. He and wife Sarah sold to Robert Lawton of Portsmouth, half a share in Tiverton for £72.

1738, Dec. 30. Will—proved 1741, Oct. 20. Exs. sons William and Gershom. To wife Sarah, a third of income of all real estate while widow, and all movables. To daughter Elizabeth Wodell, a feather bed. To daughter Ruth Phineas, 5*s.*, she having had, and like legacies to daughters Patience Crandall, Alice Butts and Innocent Sherman. To son William, south half of homestead where I dwell. To son Gershom, north half of homestead. To daughter Elizabeth, £12. To sons William and Gershom, a six score acre lot and all other lands in Tiverton.

Inventory, £1,894, 8*s.*, 6*d.*, viz: wearing apparel £5, 2*s.*, half of homestead farm £1,200, 6 score acre lot, £650, pewter, 2 tables, chairs, &c.

VII. SARAH, b. / d.
m.
JOHN HUMERY, b. / d. — of — Humery.

VIII. INNOCENT, b. / d.

WODELL. 3d column. VIII. Innocent, m Richard Borden b. 1671, Oct 25, of John and Mary (Earle) Borden. Children, 1. Sarah, 1694, Jul. 31. 2. John, 1695, Dec. 10. 3 Thomas, 1697, Dec. 8. 4. Mary, 1701, Jan. 29. 5. Joseph, 1702, Nov. 4. 6. Samuel, 1705 Oc[illegible] 7. Rebecca, 1712, Jul. 18.

WODELL. 3d column. VIII. Innocent. She did not marry Richard Borden. It was Innocent Cornell,[3] (Thomas,[2] Thomas[1]), who married him.

1. Elizabeth, 1663, Oct. 2.
2. John, 1668, Jun. 10.
3. Bridget, 1671, Jun. 27.
4. Mary, 1674, Apr. 27.
5. William, 1676, May 21.
6. Samuel, 1678, Jul. 14.

1. John, 1672, Nov. 17.
2. Susanna, 1674, Aug. 29.
3. Mary, 1674, Aug. 29.
4. William, 1675, Oct. 31.
5. Susanna, 1677, Oct. 14.
6. Mary, 1680, Jan. 2.
7. Abraham, 1682, Apr. 21.
8. Thomas, 1684, Jun. 30.
9. Alice, 1686, Jan. 22.
10. James, 1686, Jan 22.
11. Amy, 1688, Jun. 30.
12. Isaac, 1690, Apr. 10.
13. Jacob, 1693, Nov. 15.

1. John, 1671, Jun. 28.
2. Joseph, 1673, Oct. 28.
3. William, 1676, Jul. 18.
4. Susanna, 1679, Jan. 1.
5. Mary, 1681, Jun. 16.
6. Sarah, 1683, Oct. 1.
7. Elizabeth, 1686, Sep. 14.
8. Alice, 1689, Apr. 26.
9. Samuel, 1691, Oct. 8.

ADDITIONS AND CORRECTIONS.

ALDRICH. 2d column. II. Samuel, had daughters: 5 Mary, 6 Ruth, 7 Abigail. IV. John. He and his brother Samuel were appointed (1725, Apr 20) overseers of will of Joseph Hide, of Providence, R. I., who calls them his brothers-in-law. VI. Mercy, m. Joseph Hide. He d. 1725, Apr. 30. She d. 1725 +. Children, 1. Phebe, 2. Hannah, 3. Patience.

ALLEN (John). 1st column. Erase Kings Town. Erase Possibly, &c. Add 1706, Sep. 30. Will—proved 1709, Mar. 16 Ex. son Samuel. He mentions son Samuel, son John Allen's children, (viz: John, Sarah, Elizabeth, Mercy and Mary), son Christopher, daughters Elizabeth Tompkins, Mary Robinson, Mercy Dunkin, and granddaughter Mary Tompkins. He gave a legacy to mens' meeting of Friends. As his son Samuel was insane the executorship was given to latter's wife Elizabeth.

2d column. VI. Samuel, Newport, R. I., m. Elizabeth Sanford, of Samuel & Sarah (Wodell) Sanford. She b. 1663, Oct. 2, d. 1743, Apr. 4. He was a cordwainer. 1717 ± Will. He mentions wife Elizabeth, daughter Sarah wife of Joseph Peabody, daughter Mary Allen, sons Samuel and Rowland under age. To son John, land in Newport. VII. Christopher, Little Compton, South Kingstown, R. I. He m. 1687, Elizabeth Seyouche, of Little Compton. Children, 1. James, 1688, Jun. 15. 1693, Sep. 29. He sold to Joseph Allen, of Dartmouth, 50 acres in Narragansett for £140. 1703-11-14-15-16-20. Kings Town. Deputy. 1714. Captain. 1715. Clerk of Assembly. 1739, Sep. 17. Administration to William Robinson. Inventory, £1,823, 7*s.*, 10*d.*, viz: wearing apparel, cane, pair of silver buttons, pair of gold buttons, pocket book and money therein £20, 18*s.*, 11*d.*, 141 sheep, 60 lambs, 2 horses, 5 mares, 15 colts, 2 bulls, 4 oxen, 4 steers, 47 cows, 16 calves, 6 yearlings, bible, law book, 19 silver buttons, bee hive, negroes Moll, Phillis, young Moll, Andrew, Jeffrey, mulatto Jacob, 6 silver spoons, 2 silver porringers, &c, He b. 1664, d. 1739, Sep. 13. His wife, b. 1668, Jul. 7, d. 1737, Mar. 17.

ALLEN (William). 2d column. II. William, had children, 1. William, 2. John, 3. Ebenezer. V. Matthew. His wife was daughter of John & Mary (   ) Cook.

ANGELL. 2d column. V. Alice, b. 1649, d. 1743, Aug. 13. Children, 1. Eleazer, 2. Alice, 1675, Jun. 3, 3. Margaret, 4. Elizabeth, 1680, 5. Job, 1684, 6. James, 1686, 7. Daniel. VI. James, m. 1678, Sep. 30. His widow, d. 1718 +.

ARNOLD (William). 3d column. III. Josiah. Change Sarah Odlin to Elizabeth Odlin—twelfth line after 1721, Sep. 23.

AUDLEY. 1st column, John[2] (John[1]), b. 1642, Feb. 3. Boston, Mass., Newport, R. I. He was a blacksmith. 1685, Mar. 6. He had a legacy of certain land in Roxbury, Mass; from will of his father. 1687, Jul. 17. He and wife Martha, deeded to his brother Elisha, of Boston, tailor, certain land in south part of Boston, devised by father John Odlin, armorer, deceased.

2d column. 1. John, m. (2) Elizabeth Arnold, b. 1684, May 19, of Josiah & Sarah (Mills) Arnold.

AYRAULT. 1st. column. Sort for sect, second line after 1692.

BAILEY (William). 1st column. Add the name of Samuel after Stephen, next to last line.

2d column. VI. Samuel, Newport, R. I., m. Elizabeth Rogers, of Thomas & Sarah (   ) Rogers.

BAKER (Thomas). 1st column. He m. Sarah. He was a tailor. 1685, Dec. 24, Newport. He bought of Ralph Paine, of Newport, 25 acres in Providence, for £4. 1689, Feb. 25, Kings Town. He tailor, and wife Sarah, sold to Joseph Smith, of Providence, for full satisfaction, right of common in Providence, bought of Ralph Paine.

BALCOM. 2d column. IV. John. His wife, b. 1690, Oct. 21, of John & Alice (   ) Bartlett. Add at end of will: The Arnold cousins were children of his niece Martha Jenckes, she having married Daniel Arnold. IX. Deborah. Erase marriage and children.

BALLOU (Maturin). 2d column. 1. John, m. (2) 1679, Jan. 4.

BALLOU (Robert). 2d column. 1. Lydia, m. (2) 1678, Jun. 14.

BARBER. 2d column. Add another child, viz: Sarah, b. 1682, Mar. 25, d. 1779, Jun. 29, m. 1706, Jun. 24, David Greene, of James & Elizabeth (Anthony) Greene, b. 1677, Jun. 24, d. 1761, Jan. 29. Children, 1. Mary, 1707, Jun. 5. 2. Sarah, 1709, Jan. 20. 3. Elizabeth, 1711, Mar. 25. 4. Susanna, 1713, May 1. 5. Abigail, 1715, Mar. 25. 6. Waite, 1716, Dec. 2. 7. Bathsheba, 1720, Jul. 30. 8. Jonathan, 1722, Aug. 2. 9. Joseph, 1724, May 30. 10. Patience, 1726, Feb. 15.

BARKER. 2d column. II. James, d. 1722, Dec. 1. 1722, Nov. 3. Will—proved 1723, Jan. 7. Ex. son James. To son James, housing and lands whereon I now dwell, 120 acres, bounded westerly on a highway, northerly on land of widow Sarah Tew, &c., southerly on land of brother William Barker, &c.; together with houses, orchard, &c., on condition that he confirms by deed of gift to my son Jeremiah, 20 acres where said James dwells, &c. To son William, 500 acres in Narragansett and £100. To daughters Abigail Wright, Jane Lawton and Priscilla Lawton, £50, each. To son Nicholas, £50. To son Jeremiah, 20 acres, negro man Jack and a third of live stock. To granddaughter Sarah Winsor, £10. To son James, two-thirds of live stock. To daughters Abigail, Priscilla and Jane, all plate and pewter. To sons James and Jeremiah, rest of personal. Son James to provide well beloved wife Sarah, his mother, an "honorable, decent and comfortable maintenance." If son Jeremiah, by reason of a long sickness he has had should be weakened in understanding, his brother James to be guardian. Inventory, wearing apparel with plate buttons thereon £22, plate £4, 12*s.*, books, spectacles, razor, &c. Rooms named were new room, out room, leanto out chamber, new chamber, cellar, cheese room. His daughter Mary, was b. 1678, Mar. 13.

VI. Peter. His widow Susanna, d 1733 +. Children by her were 6. Joseph, 7. John, 8. Daughter, 9. Sarah, 10. Barbara, 11. Susanna, 12. Patience His widow m. Peter Wells. 1733, Feb. 1, Susanna Wells, of South Kingstown gave receipt to son in-law (*i. e.* stepson) James Wells, executor of Peter Wells, for £8, due from deceased Peter Wells to "my daughter Sarah Barker." Other receipts showed names of additional children of Peter Barker.

BASTER. 1st column. Roger, b. 1621, d. 1687, Apr. 23. Unmarried. He was a blockmaker. Buried in Newport Cemetery. Erase sentence between 1680 and 1687, Apr. 27. Erase 2d and 3d columns.

BENNETT (Robert). 2d column. IV. Jonathan, m. Anne. She d. 1708 +. 1708, Jul. 5. Will—proved 1708, Sep. 6. Exx. wife Anne. Overseers, Thomas Cornell, and brother Robert Bennett. To first born son John, west half of housing and lands, at age. To son Jonathan, eastern half, and silver tankard at decease of his mother. To daughters Rebecca and Anne Bennett, £50 each, at twenty-one. To wife Anne, rest of personal, and profits of land till eldest son is of age, and her thirds for life. To her also a lot of land to set a windmill on. Inventory, silver spoon, tankard, cup, porringer, &c.. 48 oz., at 6*s.*, per oz.; goods in shop, &c.

BERNON. 1st column. McSparran for McSparrow, fifth line after 1724.

BILLINGS. 2d column. I. Amey. Her 2d husband d. 1735.

BLACKSTONE. 2d column. I. John. His son John, b. 1699, Jan. 19. Change last sentence thus—His son John d. 1785, Jan. 3, at Branford, Conn., and was buried in the center of the graveyard. He left two sons and two daughters, and descendants of the name are still (or were recently) living.

BLISS. 2d column. 1. John, d. 1717. His widow d. 1717 +. 1717, Feb. 3. Will—proved 1717, Mar. 4. Ex. son Josiah. To wife Damaris, all household goods and use for life of land in town. To son Josiah, a lot in Newport. To son George, the rest of lands undisposed of, my windmill, twenty ewe sheep, and a cow. To grandchild Jemima Meacham, £5, at eighteen. To grandchild John Meacham, £5, at age. To grandchild John Jersey, £5, at age.

BOOMER. 2d column. II. Matthew, d. 1744, Freetown, Mass. 1732, Oct. 8. Will—proved 1744, Mar. 20. He mentions wife Hannah, eldest son Matthew, sons Caleb and Joshua, five surviving daughters, Lydia, Mercy Luther, Deborah Mason, Ruth Salisbury, Mary; and children of deceased daughter Hannah Jenckes, &c.

BRAYTON. 3d column. IV. Preserved, had also son David, b 1716, Feb. 14.

BRIGGS (John, of Kings Town). He d. 1708. He was a Quaker, and meetings were held at his house.

BROWN (Chad). 3d column. II. James, m. (2) Catharine, b. 1702, Mar. 19, of Job & Phebe (Sayles) Greene. Possibly his 1st wife was a daughter of James & Hope (Power) Clarke.

BROWN (Henry). 2d column. III. Richard. Erase marriage. He m. Mary Rhodes, of Malachi & Mary (Carder) Rhodes. IV. Joseph. The surname of his 1st wife's mother was Brown.

BURDICK. 2d column. IV. Thomas, had a son Thomas, who m. 1723, May 1, Abigail Richmond. (At this time Thomas, Sr., lived in Stonington, Ct.). V. Naomi, m. 1678, Mar. 2.

BURGESS. 2d column. I. Thomas. His 2d wife was widow of Timothy Closson.

BURLINGAME. 2d column. II. Thomas. His wife Martha, d. 1723. IX. Elizabeth. Her husband Thomas Arnold, d. 1727, Feb. 3.

BUSECOT. 1st column. Erase under date of 1638, the two lines after Salem. 1643, Hartford. He had a trial to make nails with less loss and at as cheap a rate as Thomas Hurlbut. 1647, Sep. 2. Fined 20*s.* for resisting the watch. 1648, Oct. 17. The court (at Hartford) sentenced him to be committed to prison "there to be kept in safe custody till the sermon, and then to stand in the time thereof in the pillory, and after the sermon to be severely whipped." (He had spoken profanely of the members of the church.)

CADMAN. 2d column. I. George. His widow Hannah, d. 1749. 1749. Feb. 13. Will—proved 1749, May 2. Ex. grandson William White. She mentions her daughter Elizabeth White, wife of William White, and grandchildren, William, George, Roger, Christopher, Oliver, Thomas and Susanna White, Sarah Brown (wife of John, of Tiverton) and Hannah Taber (wife of William, of Dartmouth). She also mentions great-grandchildren Hannah and Mary Slocum, children of granddaughter Elizabeth Slocum.

CARPENTER (William). 2d column. III. Ephraim, m. (1) Susannah Harris, of William & Susannah (   ) Harris. Erase her death.

CARR (Caleb). 2d column. III. Caleb. His wife may have been daughter of John & Mary (Williams) Sayles, as he named a child Sayles Carr.

CARR (Robert). 2d column. I. Caleb. His widow Phillip, d. 1706 (—). II. Elizabeth, m. (2) Samuel Gardiner, of George & Herodias (Long) Gardiner. He d. 1696. Dec. 8. She d. 1697 +. Children, 1. Elizabeth, 1684. 2. Samuel, 1685, Oct. 28. 3. Martha, 1686, Nov. 16. 4. Patience.

CHAPMAN (Ralph). 1st column. Ralph, d. 1711 (—). He had a daughter Mary by 2d wife, and daughter Catharine by 3d wife. 1711, Sep. It appeared by evidence that he had been absent about six years and not heard of, and was by presumption therefore deemed dead. 1704, Nov. 4. Will—proved 1711, Sep. Exx. wife Mary. To son Ralph, 2*s.*, having done much for him. To sons John and Isaac, a house lot, each. To son-in-law (*i. e.* stepson) Jeremiah Gould, a lot already sold him—to be laid out. To four daughters Abigail, Mary, Lydia and Catharine Chapman, each a lot. (The lots given children adjoined each other and were each fifty-three feet in breadth). To wife Mary, all houses and lands not mentioned, and she to give what she thinks fit to son Walter, to whom I have not given any part of my estate.

1711, Jun. 27. Will—proved 1711, Sep. 3. Widow Mary. Exs. brother Nathaniel Sheffield and sons Jeremiah and Daniel Gould. She directs that stock and personal estate at Mattapoisett given by late husband be sold. To Isaac Chapman, Abigail Prince, Mary, Catharine and Walter Chapman, children of late husband, £52, divided, and a further amount after debts are paid. To executors, a legacy, and also to sisters Hannah Rodman, Catharine Sheffield and Deliverance Cornell. To grandchildren William and John Chapman, sons of Ralph, each £3. To Sarah, Mary, Catharine and Elizabeth Gould, daughters of son Jeremiah Gould, each £3. To Mary and Ruth Gould, daughters of son Daniel Gould, each £3. To Elizabeth Hix, daughter of my daughter Mary Hix, deceased, £3. Negro Pegg to be set free and certain provision made for her. As to estate real and personal left by husband in Newport; she gives to daughter Catharine Chapman a lot of land, to son Walter, a house and certain land, bed, six chairs, &c., to husband's daughter Mary Chapman, a bed, and to daughter Catharine, the rest of personal estate with certain exceptions. Son Walter to be put to a useful trade, and estate delivered him at age. The debts due to estate of former husband Daniel Gould to go equally to sons Jeremiah and Daniel Gould.

2d column. I. Ralph He was a shipwright. By 1st wife he had a son William, and by 2d wife a son John. 1728, Inventory. £3,135. II. John, d. 1710. 1710, Apr. 28. Inventory, £37, 19*s.*, 2*d.* Also sundry goods on board the sloop at New York and since returned, 4 firkins nails, 2 cribs of glass, green diamond glass, &c. Administration to widow Patience. V. Abigail. Her husband d. 1719. Children, 1. Abigail.

CLARKE (Jeremiah). 2d column. I. Walter. Philip for Phillip, eighth line after 1714, Jun. 13. II. Mary, erase all after her 10th child. She may have had one child, Henry, by her 2d husband. III. Jeremiah, 1728, Jun. 13. Will—codicil, 1729, Jan. 9, proved 1729, Feb. 3. He mentions wife Anne, sons Jeremiah, James, Henry and Weston, daughters Anne Greenman, and Sarah Weeden. He mentions also children of deceased daughter Mary Weeden, viz: Jeremiah, William, Caleb and Francis Weeden, Ann Sanford, Mary ———— and Margaret Weeden; children of deceased daughter Frances Sanford, viz: Samuel, William and John Sanford, Frances Gardner and Sarah Paul; four sons of deceased son Samuel Clarke, viz: John, Audley, Samuel and Daniel Clarke. He mentions son-in-law Jeremiah Weeden. In codicil he alludes to death of daughter Sarah Weeden.

CLEMENCE. 1st column. 1676, Oct. 16. He is alluded to in a letter of Roger Williams. "Two Indian children were brought to me by one Thomas Clements, who had his house burnt on the other side of the river. He was in his orchard, and two Indian children came boldly to him the boy being about seven or eight, and the girl (his sister) three or four years old. The boy tells me that a youth, one Mittonan, brought them to the sight of Thomas Clements, and bid them go to that man, and he would give them bread," &c.

COLE (JOHN). 1st column. Change to John[2] (Samuel[1]). Change Sandwich, Kent Co., Eng., to Boston, Mass. Erase sentence 1634, &c.

1666, Dec. 21. He and his eldest son Samuel were mentioned in the will of his father Samuel Cole of Boston.

COLE (ROBERT). 1st column. 1638, Oct 8. He was one of the twelve persons to whom Roger Williams deeded land he had bought of Canonicus and Miantonomi.

2d column. I. John, Warwick, R. I., Oyster Bay, N. Y. He had a son Solomon. Erase all the text and add—1683. Jan. 1. His widow being about to marry William Lynes, deeded to her son Solomon, half of her land and estate, she having a life estate in the whole by will of her late husband. IV. Daniel, 1677, Sep. 27. He and his brothers Robert and Nathaniel and two other persons, had confirmation by patent from Governor Andros of lands at Oyster Bay. 1692, Nov. 10, Will. VI. Nathaniel. His wife Martha d. 1668, Dec. 17. He m. (2) Deborah. Children, by 1st wife: 1. Nathaniel, 1668, Aug. 24. Children by 2d wife: 2. Caleb. 3. Harvey. 4. Deborah, 1694, Dec. 16. He deeded to sons Caleb and Harvey, land at Duck Pond. (They deeded same to their half brother Nathaniel Jr., 1703, Mar. 29.)

COLLINS (ARNOLD). 1st column. Arnold, d. 1735. 1735, Aug. 4. Will—proved. The name of an heir is obliterated but must have been his son Henry. He mentions daughter Mary, wife of Jeremiah Wilcox, daughter Sarah, wife of Josiah Bliss, daughter Elizabeth Wickham and grandson Arnold Belcher. 2d column. II. Sarah, m. (1) ——— Belcher, m. (2) Josiah Bliss, of John & Damaris (Arnold) Bliss. Her 2d husband d. 1748. Her children were: 1. Arnold, and by 2d husband: 2. Elizabeth, 3. Henry, 1722. 4. Sarah 5. Amey. 6. William, 1728, Feb. 5. 7. Martha. IV. Elizabeth, m. 1723, Mar. 17. Samuel Wickham, of Samuel & Barbara (Holden) Wickham. He b. 1693, Sep. 2, d. 1753, Feb. 23. Children: 1. Samuel 2. Henry, 1725. 3. Gideon, 1735. 4. Elizabeth, 1737. 5. Deborah, 1740.

COLVIN. 2d column. VIII. James, m. (1) Mary Lippitt, of John & Rebecca (Lippitt) Lippitt.

CONGDON. 2d column. I. William, m. (1) 1693, Mar. 3. Mary Brownell, of Robert & Mary (   ) Brownell. She d. 1718 (—). 1718, Jan. 29. In Robert Brownell's will of this date he gives legacies of £5 each to "daughter Mary's three children," she evidently having died. II. Benjamin. 1721, Town Council. 1723, Town Sergeant. 1756, Jan. 15. Will—proved 1756, Oct. 11. To son John, land in Boston Neck where testator now dwells, he paying £500 to my son Benjamin, and £400 to second son Joseph. To nine daughters of son William, deceased, £40. To grandson John Congdon, son of James, deceased, land in Exeter. To grandson Stukeley Congdon, land. To daughters Frances Gardiner and Mary Brown, and to eight children of daughter Mary Brown, certain legacies. To daughter Elizabeth Sweet, for life, certain land. Change list of children. 1. Benjamin. 2. Joseph. 3. William. 4. James. 5. John. 6. Frances. 7. Mary. 8. Elizabeth.

CORNELL. 2d column. IX. Samuel. 1686, Mar. 24. He took oath of fidelity. 1694, Nov. 13. He and others received a confirmatory deed of Dartmouth from William Bradford.

CRANDALL. 2d column. VI. Joseph. His daughter Mary was baptized in 1709, and she was his 3d child. He also had a daughter Jane who m. 1718, Dec. 8, Cyrus Richmond. VII. Samuel. His wife's surname is called Celly upon the records.

DAILEY. 2d column. Brook for Rrook.

DAVIS (NICHOLAS). 2d column. III. Sarah. Her husband b. 1666, Nov. 19, son of John & Mary (   ) Miles.

DENNIS. 1st column. Parents of Sarah Howland were Henry & Mary (Newland) Howland.

DEXTER. 3d column. V. Abigail. Her 2d husband d. 1780, at Glocester, R. I. She d. before 1780. She had a 4th child, viz: James Greene.

DURFEE. 2d column. VI. Benjamin, b. 1680, d. 1754, Jan. 6. His wife Prudence, b. 1681. Children: 1. James, 1701, Aug. 28. 2. Ann, 1703, Jan. 11. 3. Pope, 1705, Jan. 7. 4. William, 1707, Dec. 5. 5. Benjamin, 1709, Jan. 5. 6. Mary, 1711, Jan. 30. 7. Susannah, 1713, Jan. 28. 8. Martha, 1719, Jul. 15. 9. Thomas, 1721, Nov. 5. VIII. Deliverance, m. 1724, Apr. 23, William Cory, of William & Martha (Cook) Cory. Children: 1. Patience, 1725, Mar. 25. 2. Caleb, 1729, Jul. 13. 3. John, 1731, Sep. 7.

DYER. 2d column. VI. Charles. 1709, May 9. Will—proved 1709. Exx. wife Martha. Overseers brother George Brownell, Thomas Cornell and Benjamin Thayer. To son James, all land and tenements in Little Compton, which he now liveth on, part of which I had with my wife Martha Dyer. To son Samuel, all my land and homestead that I now live on, with the old end of the dwelling house, barns, stables, &c., to be for him and his heirs unto the third generation, he paying legacies. To him also commonage in Newport and great bible. To son William, £100. To son Charles, £100. To daughter Elizabeth, the now wife of Tristram Hull, £30. "My earnest will and desire is (that) piece of ground that is now called the Burying Ground, shall be continued for the same use unto all my after generations that shall see cause to make use of it, and I order that it shall be well kept fenced in by my son Samuel Dyre and his heirs forever." To wife Martha, the new end of Newport house for life, and then to son Samuel. To her also, all my household stuff, plate, cash, bills, bonds, six of best cows of her choice, twenty ewe sheep, best of flock, and two cows and six sheep to be kept for her winter and summer by Samuel, who is to take a reasonable care of her, as food, firing, &c., "without any grudging or grumbling." To four sons James, William, Samuel and Charles, rest of stock. To son Samuel, carts, plows, &c. To overseers, £3 each.

3d column. V. Samuel. 1765, Feb. 19. Will—proved 1768, Nov. 15. Ex. kinsman Samuel Dyer, son of William Dyer, of South Kingstown. To Captain Samuel Dyer, £83, a good cow kept for him five years, and ten bushels of Indian meal a year for him five years if he needs it. To Captain Samuel Dyer's daughter Mary Dyer, a feather bed at marriage, and to his daughter Desire, the same. To four sons of my brother Charles Dyer, deceased, viz: Charles, Samuel, John and William, £17 each, and to their sister Mary Barton, twenty Spanish milled dollars. To Desire Bull, widow of Nathan Bull, negro Peggy, her child Sarah, and a good cow. To Silence Arnold, £50, feather bed, &c. To my kinsman Samuel Dyer, son of William Dyer of South Kingstown, all my lands and housing in Newport, four negroes and all my stock and personal estate. To John Dyer son of Captain Samuel Dyer, of Newport, £50.

EARLE. 2d column. II. William. His daughter Prudence, b. 1681.

EVANS (RICHARD, OF PROVIDENCE). Children b. as follows: 1. Martha, 1679, Jan. 19. 2. Richard, 1681, Aug. 10. 3. David, 1684, Mar. 9. 4. Mary, 1686, Apr. 23. 5. Elizabeth, 1688, Apr. 23. 6. Mehitable, 1692, Jun. 1.

EVERDEN. 2d column. I. Richard. Providence, R. I.

FENNER (ARTHUR). 2d column. VII. Samuel, d. 1680 +

FENNER (WILLIAM). 1680, Aug. 30. Will—proved 1680, Sep. 6 (at Newport). Exs. brothers Arthur and John Fenner. To late sister Lay's two children she left, and to sister Phebe Ward's children, 20s. each. To brother Arthur Fenner's children Samuel and Phebe, £10 apiece, in addition to an equal share in whole estate. To children of brothers Arthur and John Fenner, all estate equally.

FIELD (THOMAS). 1st column. Erase last sentence: "Perhaps," &c.

2d column. II. Mary, d. 1727, Jun., m. John Dexter. He b. 1673, d. 1734, Apr. 22, of Stephen & Abigail (Whipple) Dexter. Children: 1. Naomi, 1698. 2. Mary, 1699. 3. John, 1701. 4. Stephen, 1703. 5. Jeremiah, 1705. 6. Sarah, 1707. 7. Lydia, 1709. 8. William, 1711. 9. Jonathan, 1713. 10. Abigail, 1715.

FONES. 2d column. II. Jeremiah, m. (2) Martha Card (w. of James) daughter of Francis West.

GARDINER. 2d column. VIII. Samuel. Freetown. Swanzey, Mass. His wife was widow of James Brown and daughter of Robert Carr. He d. 1696, Dec. 8. His widow Elizabeth d. 1697 +. Children: 1. Elizabeth, 1684. 2. Samuel, 1685, Oct. 28. 3. Martha 1686, Nov. 16. 4. Patience. 1687, Oct. 31. He bought of George Lawton, 400 acres in Freetown for £250. 1688–90–92. Freetown. Selectman. 1688–90–92, Town Clerk. 1690–92, Deputy. 1693, Dec. 30, Swanzey. He and Ralph Chapman bought land of Ebenezer Brenton for £700 (having already sold his Freetown land). 1696, Selectman. 1697, Feb. 15. Inventory, £1,046, 5s., sworn to by widow Elizabeth. IX. Joseph, b. 1659, d. 1726, Aug. 22. He and his wife were buried in Newport Cemetery. Children: 10. William, 1712. 11. Mary, 1718. X. Lydia, d. 1723.

GEORGE. 2d column. V. Samuel. His wife was Sarah Rathbone, of John & Margaret (   ) Rathbone.

GIFFORD. 2d column. IV. Enos. Children: 1. Deborah, 1725, Apr. 2. 2. Rachel, 1727, Mar. 3. 3. Elijah, 1729, Jul. 22. 4. Canaan, 1731, May 15. 5. Phillis, 1734, May 14. 6. Dorcas, 1736, Aug. 18. 7. Enos, 1740, Mar. 22. 8. Joseph, 1742, Jan. 2. VI Christopher. Dartmouth, Mass. Children: 1. William, 1722, Jun. 29. 2. Richard, 1725, Dec. 31. 3. Susannah, 1730, Aug. 23. 4. Christopher, 1737, Aug. 8. VIII. John. Possibly his name should be erased.

GORTON. 3d column. I. Othniel, m. (2) Mercy Burlingame, of Thomas or John.

GRAY. 2d column. V. John. Plymouth. Mass., m. Joanna Morton. Children: 1. Edward, 1687. 2. Mary, 1688. 3. Ann, 1691. 4. Desire, 1693. 5. Joanna, 1696. 6. Samuel, 1702. 7. Mercy, 1704. VII. Susannah, m. John Cole, of Hugh & Mary (Foxwell) Cole. Children: 1. John. 2. Edward. 3. Thomas. 4. Joseph, 1706. 5. Benjamin, 1708. 6. Elizabeth, 1710. 7. Samuel. 8. Mary. 9. Susanna. VIII. Thomas, m. (2) Phebe Peckham, of John Peckham. XI. Rebecca, m. Ephraim Cole, of James Cole. Children: 1. Ephraim, 1691. 2. Samuel, 1694. 3. Rebecca, 1696. 4. Mary, 1698. 5. Dorothy, 1701. 6. James, 1705. 7. Samuel, 1709.

HARNDEL. 1st column. 1698, Apr. 22. Will—proved. Exx. daughter Mary Stanton, wife of John. Overseers Robert Hodgson and John Coggeshall. To kinsman Robert Stanton, son to John Stanton, house and 10 acres at age, but if he die without issue then to kinsman Benjamin Stanton, son of John Stanton. To son-in-law John Stanton, a mare, and to kinsman Robert Stanton, a mare. To daughter Rebecca, wife of Hugh Mosher, of Portsmouth, a good ewe sheep. To Mary and Hannah Stanton, daughters of John, two good ewe sheep each.

2d column. III. Mary. Erase her death, and add to her children: 7. Benjamin, 1684, Mar. 13. 8. Henry, 1688, May 22 (Henry may possibly have been by 2d wife of John Stanton).

HICKS. 2d column. VII. Elizabeth, m. 1719, Apr. 17, John Casey, b. 1695, of Thomas & Rebecca (   ) Casey. Children: 1. Mary, 1720, Feb. 1. 2. Elizabeth, 1722, Jun. 3.

HILLIARD. 2d column. VII. Jonathan m. Abigail Wilbur b. 1697, Apr. 1, of William & ——— (Tallman) Wilbur.

HOLDEN. 2d column. VIII. Charles. His widow, d. 1756.

HOLDER. 1st column. Change England to Newport, second line after 1680.

HOLMES (OBADIAH). 2d column. VII. John. Erase daughter Mary. His widow Mary, d. 1717.

1713, Sep. 21. Will—proved 1717, May 6. Widow Mary. Ex son-in-law Nicholas Carr. To three daughters Mary Dyer, Frances Carr and Ann Peckham, certain legacies.

HOPKINS (THOMAS, OF MASHANTATACK). Instead of his being the father of Joseph and Samuel, possibly the latter were sons of William & Susannah (Goff) Hopkins, of Roxbury, Mass. This William Hopkins, d. 1688, Nov. 8. He had a son Samuel, baptized 1663, Nov. 15, and Joseph, 1667, Mar. 8.

HUBBARD. 2d column. IV. Rachel. Her 2d child was James, not Andrew.

HULL (JOHN). 2d column. I. Mary. Her husband's mother was Mary Harndel perhaps, instead of Mary Clarke.

IRISH. 2d column. III Jonathan. His wife was Mary Taylor, b. 1682, Oct. 25, of John & Abigail (   ) Taylor. His 5th child was named Ann.

JEFFERAY. 2d column. V. Sarah. Her husband d. 1722, Dec. 1.

JENCKES. 1st column. Esther Ballard, b. 1633.

2d column. IV. Nathaniel. His wife Hannah, b. 1663, Nov. 5, of Jonathan & Hannah (Howland) Bosworth. VI Ebenezer. His wife Mary, b. 1677, Oct. 20, of John & Hannah (Wheaton) Butterworth.

LANGWORTHY. 2d column. II. Andrew. Erase all about him and his children. Insert instead II. James, Newport, R. I. Children, 1. Abigail, 1707, Sep. 20. 2. Mary, 1709, Feb. 27. 3. James, 1711, Apr. 11. 4. Andrew, 1713, Feb. 14. 5. Stephen, 1715, Aug. 6. 6. Jonathan, 1717, Dec. 9. 7. Benjamin, 1720, Sep. 11.

MANN (THOMAS). 1st column. His 2d wife, b. 1656, Nov. 4. She m. (2) 1698, Mar 3, Ebenezer Darling.

2d column. II. Rachel, m. Nehemiah Sheldon, of John & Joan (Vincent) Sheldon. He b. 1672, d. 1754 +. Children, 1. Abraham, 2. Philip, 3. Mary, 4. Rachel, 5. Welthian. VI. Mehitable, d. 1725 ± unmarried. VIII. Daniel, d. 1744, Mar. 31.

MATTESON. 2d column. VI. Hezekiah. His wife, b. 1702, Mar. 8.

MITCHELL. 2d column. II. Thomas. New Shoreham R. I.

NILES. 2d column. V. Tabitha. She had 4. Tabitha. 1715, Jun. 17. IV. Ebenezer, m. Abigail Hazard, b. 1680, Mar. 19, of George & Penelope (Arnold) Hazard. Children, 1. Ebenezer, 1710, Mar. 4. 2. Penelope. 3. Sarah.

PABODIE. 2d column. XII. Lydia. Erase son Benjamin.

PEABODY. 1st column. 1687 for 1087.

PECKHAM. 2d column. VII. Sarah, had 1. Mary. IX. Deborah. Her son John, b. 1694, not 1684.

PELHAM. 2d column. VI. Penelope, should be IV.

PERRY. 2d column. 1. James. His wife Alice's father was James not John. III. Samuel. His wife d. 1756, Jun. 27. Additional births of children: 6. Edward, 1730, Jun. 15. 7. John, 1732, May 15. 8. Alice, 1734, Feb. 25. 9. Stephen, 1736, Jan. 6. 10. Sarah, 1738, Feb. 16. 11. Ruth, 1740, Jan. 17. 12. Susanna, 1742, Mar. 25. 13. Meribah, 1744, Aug. 18.

PIERCE. 2d column. VI. Michael, m. (1) Judith. Children, 1. Ephraim, 1712, Nov. 9. 2. Wheeler, 1714, Jul. 11; m. (2) 1719, Oct. 15, Mary Wood. Children, 3. Sarah, 1720, Sep. 13. 4. Mary, 1721, Oct. 26. 5. Phebe, 1723, Feb. 16. 6. Elizabeth, 1725, Apr. 7. 7. Michael, 1728, Sep. 25. 8. Freelove, 1730, Feb. 5. 9. Bethiah. VII. John, of Swanzey, Mass., d. 1750. 1738, Jun. 28. Will—proved 1750, Nov. 6. He mentions wife Patience, sons Miall, John, Jonathan, Clother, Samuel, daughters Ruth Cornell, Jael Chase, Mary Norton.

RAY. 2d column. IV. Simon, m. (2) 1725, Nov. 22. His 2d wife, b. 1690, Feb. 28, d. 1763, Dec. 11, at Warwick, R. I. 1762, Jan. 14. Will—proved 1764, Mar. 12. She mentions daughter Judith Hubbard, father Job Greene, deceased, daughters Ann Ward and Catharine Greene, grandchildren Simon Ray Littlefield, William, Catharine, Phebe and Ann Littlefield, son-in-law William Greene, Jr.

RICHMOND. 2d column. II. John, d. 1740. Children, 7. Rebecca, 8. Esther, 9. Content, 10. Priscilla.

1740, Feb. 24. Will—proved 1740, Jul. 28. Ex. son Stephen. To wife Elizabeth, for life, bed, linen, chests, six best chairs, pewter, profits of orchard, riding beast, two cows, &c. To son Cyrus, of Stonington, half of wearing apparel. To son Stephen, the other half. To daughter Rebecca Worden, a brass kettle, bed, &c. To daughters Sarah Lawton, Esther Tracy, of Preston, Ct., Ann Hoxsie, and Content Davis, household utensils, &c. To granddaughter Ruth Reynolds, daughter of my daughter Priscilla, two pewter plates, and to grandsons Richmond Reynolds and Joseph Reynolds, 5*s.* each at age. To daughter Abigail Burdick's five children, Simeon, Abigail, Edmond, Jonathan and Elizabeth, 5*s.*, each. To daughter Elizabeth Hull's three children, Sarah, Tristram and Hannah, 5*s.*, each. The executor was impowered to sell farm and all stock.

Inventory, £295, 2*s.*, 11*d.*, viz: wearing apparel £28, 17*s.*, 6*d.*, 12 plate buttons £2, 8*s.*, sundry reading books £4, 5*s.*, spectacles, seal, wax, and studs 9*s.*, 2 warming pans, 11 chairs, 1 great chair, 4 pewter platters, 4 porringers, 13 plates, 16 wooden trenchers, mare, 2½ hives of bees, 2 ewes, 2 lambs, case of bottles, cards, wool wheel, old lancet, &c.

SAUNDERS. 2d column. V. Susannah, m. (2) Peter Wells. He d. 1752. She d. 1733 +. Children by 1st husband, 1. Joseph, 2, John, 3. Daughter, 4. Sarah, 5. Barbara, 6. Susannah, 7. Patience.

SAYLES. 1st column. I. John. His wife's birth was 1633, not 1638.

SEGAR. 2d column. Add comma after Ichabod, tenth line after 1751, Dec. 2.

SHELDON (John, of Kings Town). 2d column. II. Isaac. He m. (1) Susanna Potter, b. 1688, Jun. 28, of Thomas & Susanna (Tripp) Potter.

SHIPPEE. 2d column. 1. Elizabeth. Her husband, d. 1716. Children, James, Stephen, Samuel, Matthew, Mary, Elizabeth.

SMITH (Richard). 2d column. IV. Joan, m. 1648, Apr. 16, Thomas Newton. V. Katharine, had 7. John. Her husband was son of Lodowick & Gertrude Op Ten Dyck.

STANTON. 3d column. John, d. 1762, Jan. 22, at Richmond, R. I. He m. (2) Susanna Lanphere, of Theodosius & Rachel (Covey) Lanphere. She b. 1716, Dec. 14, d. 1807, Sep. 25. She m. (2) Peter Boss. John Stanton, had by 2d wife, 13. Robert, 1735, Aug. 18. 14. Job, 1737, Feb. 15. 15. Susannah, 1738, Aug. 17. 16. Benjamin, 1740, Jul. 4. 17. Hannah, 1742, Mar. 28. 18. Elizabeth, 1743, Jan. 2. 19. Samuel, 1745, Dec. 2. 20. John, 1748, May 4. 21. Mercy, 1750, Jan. 11. 22. Sebra, 1752, Dec. 4. 23. Mary, 1754, Nov. 23. 24. Joseph, 1757, Mar. 26. 25. Hannah, 1759. The first three children were born in Westerly, the next five in Charlestown, and the last five in Richmond.

1733. He purchased a large tract in Westerly and removed thence from Newport. Erase the sentence beginning "By one account, &c."

SWEET. 2d column. I. John. Eleventh line. Elizabeth Wilson, aged fifty-five not forty-five.

TILLINGHAST. 2d column. VII. Benjamin. His widow d. 1743, Jan. 5. XI. Hannah. Her husband, b. 1678, d. 1718, Feb. 19.

UPDIKE. 3d column. II. Daniel. Where the word McSharron occurs change it to McSparran.

UTTER. 2d column. II. Thomas. His wife was daughter of Gershom & Bethiah (   ) Cottrell. 1719, Aug. 3. He appeared on behalf of his wife in regard to administration on estate of her brother Gershom Cottrell.

VAUGHAN (John). 3d column. 1. George. Change amount of inventory to £611, 19*s.*, 4*d.*

WHALEY. 2d column. VII. Samuel. Fourth lin Samuel Whaley was at Voluntown, not Samuel Hopkins

WHIPPLE. 2d column. III. Samuel. His wife b. 1639 Her mother's name was Elizabeth.

WHITMAN. 2d column, IX. Valentine. His wife was daughter of John & Sarah (Aldrich) Bartlett.

WOODMAN. 2d column. II. Hannah. Children, 1 Abigail, 1698, Nov. 3. 2. Mary, 1700, Sep. 21.

WOOLEY. 2d column. VII. Ruth, m. 1688, Apr. 25, John Tucker, of Henry & Martha (   ) Tucker. She d. 1759, Dec. 23. He b. 1656, Aug. 28, d. 1751, Sep. 2. Children, 1. James, 1691, Aug. 27. 2. John, 1693, Oct. 25. 3. Joseph, 1696, Nov. 7.

PAGE 363 is by error numbered 263.

GENERAL INDEX.

(1) Family names on other pages at later dates than on their own.

GENERAL INDEX.

(2) Surnames of other Families.

The American Genealogist

Whole Number 75 Volume XIX, No. 3

January, 1943

ADDITIONS AND CORRECTIONS TO AUSTIN'S GENEALOGICAL DICTIONARY OF RHODE ISLAND

By G. Andrews Moriarty, A.M., LL.B., F.S.A.

The following additions and corrections to Austin are by no means exhaustive, but are certain matters which the compiler has come across in the course of his searches into Rhode Island family history. Some of these are already in print, others are here presented for the first time. In connection with New Shoreham families it should be noted that some of the earlier dates given by both Austin and Arnold are at fault, owing to the peculiar way in which the first town clerk made his 7, easily misread as a 9; the result is that a number of persons born between 1670 and 1680 are listed as being born between 1690 and 1700.

ACRES (p. 1, 1st col.). Deed dated 16 Oct. 1674, of John Acres of New Shoreham of land in that town to "my loving brother, John Rathbone now of Hammersmith on Rhode Island" (New Shoreham Deeds). Hammersmith was the Brenton estate in the Southwesterly part of Newport.

AUDLEY (p. 5, 1st col.). John of Newport. Undoubtedly identical with John, born at Boston 3:12 mo.:1641, the son of John Odlin or Audley, the Boston armourer and his wife Margaret (*cf.* Pope's Pioneers p. 334).

BAILEY (p. 9, 2nd col.). Edward of Newport and Tiverton. On 16 May 1717, Edward and John Bailey of Tiverton discharged Joel Lake and Sarah his wife of their obligation to support "Frances, wife of Edward Bailey of Tiverton late deceased," and the same day Joel Lake and wife Sarah of Tiverton sold 17 acres, "which did formerly belong to our father Edward Bailey at his decease" (Bristol Co. Deeds, Bk. X, pp. 644, 646).

BALL. Edward (p. 11, 1st col.). He is perhaps the Edward Ball who was a fisherman on the Maine coast 1660-1667 (*cf.* Libby's Gen. Dic. Maine and N. H., Pt. 2, p. 73).

Mary (2nd col.) married Edward Hall (Henry[1]) of Westerly, R. I. Elizabeth married John Hall (Henry[1]) of Westerly (*cf.* N. E. Hist. & Gen. Reg., Vol. 87, pp. 354, 356; Austin, p. 90).

BORDEN. Richard (p. 23, 1st col.) was of Headcorn and Cranbrook, co. Kent, son of Matthew and Joan (———) Borden, bapt. at Headcorn 22 Feb. 1595/6, married at Headcorn 28 Sept. 1625 Joan dau. of Richard Fowle of Frittenden and Headcorn.

Richard (2nd col.), bapt. Headcorn 9 July 1626; died young; Thomas, bapt. Headcorn 3 Oct. 1627; Francis, bapt. Cranbrook 23 Dec. 1628; Mary, bapt. Cranbrook 13 Jan. 1632/3; Elizabeth, bapt. Cranbrook 25 May 1634, died young. (The remaining children born in Rhode Island.) (N. E. Hist. & Gen. Reg., Vol. 84, pp. 226-229.)

BUTTS. Thomas (p. 34, 1st col.) married Elizabeth daughter of Henry Lake of Dorchester, Mass., and Portsmouth, R. I.

Zaccheus (2nd col.) married about 1693 Sarah, daughter of Thomas and Sarah (Earle) Cornell. Zaccheus died before 21 Aug. 1712 and his widow married 2ndly, 25 Aug. 1712, John Cole of Swansea. She died 16 Jan. 1748/9.

Moses (2nd col.) married about 1695 Alice, daughter of Thomas Lake of Dartmouth, who was born 6 Dec. 1677 (Am. Gen. July 1935, pp. 19, 24, 20).

CARR. Mercy (p. 37, 2nd col.) married Capt. Thomas Paine of Jamestown. Capt. Thomas Paine, a quasi privateer, arrived in Newport in 1689 with a forged commission from the Lieut. Gov. of Jamaica. Prior to this he had been engaged in piratical activities on the Florida coast ("Pirates' Who's Who"). He was commissioned 1689 by the Gov. of Rhode Island to go out against the French, who under a privateer captain named "Peckar" had captured New Shoreham (Block Island). He defeated the French whose captain was an old friend of Paine and had sailed with him on some common enterprises on the Spanish Main (Niles' "Hist. of the Ind. Wars"). Esquemelling mentions a Capt. Picquart, who was with Lolonois at the sack of Maracaibo. It is suggested that Capt. Picquart equals Capt. Peckar and that Paine was with Lolonois at Maracaibo. After his victory off Block Island, Paine settled at Jamestown. He was one of the founders of Trinity Church at Newport. Just before he was apprehended, Capt. Kidd visited his old friend, Capt. Paine, at Jamestown and left certain monies with Mrs. Paine (Cal. of State Papers Am. & West Indies). Paine died *s.p.* in 1714. His will, dated 8 June 1714, left his property successively to John, Thomas and Samuel, sons of his brother, Andrew Paine. John came to Jamestown where he is described as a "marriner" in 1717. He married and left issue (Jamestown Probate and Deeds).

Caleb (2nd col.). His wife, Deborah, was undoubtedly the daughter of John and Mary (Williams) Sayles of Providence or else of Richard Sayles of that town, probably a brother of John (Am. Gen., April 1939).

CLARKE (p. 43, 1st col.). Carew (Thomas[3], John[2], John[1], ? John) came from Westhorpe, co. Suffolk, and was baptized there on 17 Feb. 1602/3, the son of Thomas and Rose (Kerrich) Clarke of Westhorpe. He derived his given name from the family of his grandmother, Katherine Cooke alias Carew (N. E. Hist. & Gen. Reg., Vol. 75, pp. 278-279).

Jeremiah (William, James, George, John, &c) (p. 44, 1st col.) was a citizen and merchant from London. Bapt. at East Farleigh, co. Kent, on 1 Dec. 1605, the son of William, gent., of East Farleigh and St. Botolph Aldgate, London, by his wife Mary, daughter of Sir Jerome Weston, Baron of the Exchequer and sister of Richard Weston, 1st Earl of Portland, Lord High Treasurer of England (Clarke Genealogy by Justice).

Dr. John (p. 45, 1st col.), brother of Carew, bapt. at Westhorpe 8 Oct. 1609. Married 1st, Elizabeth, daughter of John Harris, lord of the manor of Westlingworth, co. Beds. (*cf.* V. C. H. Beds. "Wrestlingworth"). The will of Dr. John names his cousin Fiske (not Fish) and her children. Margaret Clarke, sister of Dr. John, married, as his 1st wife, Nicholas Wyeth of Cambridge, Mass., and had Sarah, who married on 11 Dec. 1651 John Fiske of Watertown and had issue (*cf.* Bond's Watertown and N. E. Hist. & Gen. Reg., Vol. 75, p. 279).

Joseph (p. 47, 1st col.), brother of Dr. John, bapt. at Westhorpe 16 Dec. 1618.

Thomas (p. 47, 1st col.), brother of Carew, Dr. John and Joseph, bapt. at Westhorpe 31 March 1605.

COGGESHALL. John (p. 49, 1st col.), gent., bapt. at Halstead, co. Essex, 9 Dec. 1601, son of John, gent., of Halstead, and Anne, his wife, daughter of Pierce Butter, clothier of Dedham and Colchester, co. Essex. His gravestone at Newport, R. I., erected many years after his death, overstates his age by ten years. He was a merchant at Sibel Headingham prior to his emigration. Taxed at Sibel Headingham 17 Dec. 1628. On 1 June 1629 he, together with his wife Mary and John Warman and wife Sarah, sold land by fine in Halstead and Sibel Headingham, probably the inheritance of the wives. There is a brass in Halstead Church to his aunt, Elizabeth Coggeshall, wife of

the Rev. John Watson, vicar of Halstead. His grandfather, John Coggeshall, gent., had been a merchant at London and was a clothier at Halstead, where he owned and lived in "Monchensies House" (later called "Blue Bridge House"), a capital messuage on the Halstead-Colchester Road. His arms appear in the architrave of an alms house in Halstead built by him in 1563, viz. "Silver a cross between 4 escollops sable." The ancestry of this first John for a number of generations will be made public by this compiler at a later date.

John (2nd col.), born about 1620. Married 3rdly, Mary, widow of Samuel Sturgis of Yarmouth, Mass., and daughter of Capt. William Hedge, Sr. She was born at Yarmouth in 1648.

Anne, bapt. Castle Headingham 7 May 1626. Add Mary, bapt. 22 June 1628, and James bapt. there 14 March 1629/30. Died young. Both were alive 16 April 1645. (N. E. Hist. & Gen. Reg., Vol. 73, pp. 19-32.)

CORNELL (pp. 54-55, 1st col.). Will of Rebecca, widow of Thomas, dated 2 Sept. 1664, proved 1673. Gave her Portsmouth lands to son Thomas and his eldest son Thomas and his wife Elizabeth. To son Richard, land at Acushnet and Accoxet in Dartmouth (now New Bedford and Westport, Mass.). Bequest to son William. To sons John, Samuel and Joshua, lands at Accoxet. To daughter Sarah, lands in the Bronx (New York). To daughter Anne and her husband Thomas (i.e. Thomas Kent). ten acres in Portsmouth. To daughter Rebecca, land in the Bronx. Bequests to daughters Elizabeth and Mary. The will disposes of a considerable amount of plate. (Original will among unrecorded papers at the Portsmouth Town House.)

Thomas (2nd col.). His wife was probably daughter of Edward Fiscock of New Amsterdam, formerly of Plymouth, England.

Samuel. Will of Samuel of Dartmouth, 15 May 1699, proved 7 Feb. 1714/5. Dartmouth lands to sons Thomas and Samuel. To daughter Comfort, 40/ at 18 years of age. Overseers, executors and guardians of his children "cousin Thomas Cornell of Portsmouth" (Thomas[2], Thomas[1]) "and cousin George Cadman of Dartmouth" (Bristol County Probate). Agreement 17 May 1688 between Samuel Cornell and his "cousin" (nephew) Thomas Cornell of Rhode Island for the division of the estate of his mother Rebecca (Bristol County Deeds). Thomas son of Samuel Cornell born 22 Sept. 1685; Samuel son of Samuel Cornell born 11 Jan. 1687/8; Comfort daughter of Samuel Cornell born 4 Dec. 1691 (Dartmouth Vital Records). On 13 Feb. 1716/7, Samuel Cornell and wife Deborah mortgaged the land of their father Samuel of Dartmouth (Bristol County Deeds).

Add William and Mary (2nd col.).

CRANSTON. Gov. John (p. 60, 1st col.). Son of the Rev. James Cranstoun, M.A., parson of St. Mary Over's Church, Southwark, London, near the Bridge. He was chaplain of Charles I. He placed his son (Gov. John) with Capt. Jeremiah Clarke, citizen and merchant of London, who brought him to Rhode Island. The Governor's two brothers Samuel and Caleb were of the King's Life Guards at Edinburgh (Letter of Gov. Samuel to his cousin Elizabeth Cranstoun of Edinburgh, dated 26 Dec. 1724). Rev. James was son of John Cranstoun of Bold by Christian, his wife, daughter of Sir Robert Stewart. This John was undoubtedly the son of James Cranstoun, the portioner of Bold, the son of Sir William Cranstoun of that Ilk, who died in May 1569.

Gov. Samuel (2nd col.) obtained a confirmation of the Cranstoun arms, "Gules 3 cranes silver within a bordure embattled silver," in 1724 from the Lord Lyon King at Arms (*cf.* N. E. Hist. & Gen. Reg., Vol. 79, pp. 57-66). This confirmation is now in the Rhode Island Historical Society.

DICKENS. Nathaniel (p. 66, 1st col.) was undoubtedly identical with Nathaniel, son of Thomas and Joan Dickens, bapt. at Chesham, co. Bucks., on 1 Feb. 1614/5. He was a land owner at Providence on 21 Sept. 1646 (The Home Lots of Providence, p. 48). He witnessed a deed of John Greene, the surgeon, on 16 July 1647. On 27 June 1648 he had a share of meadow and 60 acres of land at Providence. On 24:6:1648 he, together with "Goody Dickens" his wife, testified (Providence Town Rec., Vol. 15, p. 16). On 10:3 mo.:1649 he was present at a Court of Trials and on 2 June 1649 was on a Providence jury. On 20 June 1650 he was summoned to Boston by Edward Rawson, the Secretary, in a letter addressed to "his loving friend, Nathaniel Dickens," to answer the complaints of William Arnold and William Carpenter (*ib.*, Vol. 15, p. 32). In 1651 he was occupying the house of Alexander Partridge in Newport and was ejected under a writ issued by the Coddington Government. A riot ensued by Coddington's opponents and Partridge's son killed a man, for which he was tried, convicted and executed by a Court convened by the opposition. On 28:1:1655 "Nathaniel Dickens of Newport" bought a lot in that town of Marmaduke Ward (R. I. Colony Deeds) and the same day he bought land there from James Richardson (*ib.*). He was town treasurer of Newport on 13:1:1659/60. He was one of the purchasers of Misquamicut (Westerly, R. I.) on 15 Sept. 1661. On 7 May 1679 he exchanged his house and lot in Newport for a large tract in the southwesterly part of New Shoreham (Block Island) with John Williams of that town. On 3 Sept. 1680, he, together with his wife, Sarah, of New Shoreham, sold 60 acres in that town to Richard Cozzens (New Shoreham Records). On 3 Oct. 1692, Sarah, widow of Nathaniel Dickens, bought 8 acres in Newport of Thomas Partridge of Flushing, Long Island (R. I. Colony Deeds). He probably had three wives: 1st, Joan Tyler, who was a widow at Providence as early as 1640; 2ndly, ———; 3rdly, Sarah ———, who remarried Thomas Brown. Sarah was undoubtedly the mother of his sons John and Roger.

Thomas (2nd col.). On 27 Dec. 1692, his step-mother, Sarah, deeded to him 80 acres on the west side of New Shoreham, and that same year he was on a jury. On 9 April 1706, he was Constable at New Shoreham and a Freeman there in 1708. On 18 Feb. 1711/2 he sold land in the west part of the town inherited from his father. On 22 March 1711/2, he sold land in Westerly inherited from his father to Capt. John Babcock (Westerly Deeds, Bk. II, p. 102). His wife Sarah was undoubtedly identical with Sarah, daughter of William and Sarah (George) Dodge of New Shoreham, born 24 Jan. 1674/5.

John (2nd col.). Married prior to 17 Aug. 1705, when his wife Joanna Dickens witnessed the Quaker marriage of John Rodman (New Shoreham Records). She signed a deed with him on 1 Dec. 1728 (*ib.*). Joanna was baptized as "Hannah Dickens, an aged woman," together with Anstiss Dickens her granddaughter on 7 April 1742 in the Stonington (Conn.) Church. John was a Freeman at New Shoreham on 11 April 1699, and in 1705 and 1708 (New Shoreham Town Records). In March 1729/30, "John Dickens of New Shoreham yeoman" sued Thomas Staples of Newport in the Newport Court (Superior Court Files, Newport County, Bk. B, p. 369). On 11 April 1732 he was town sergeant at New Shoreham and in April 1734 and 1735 a member of the Town Council (New Shoreham Town Records). His son, John Esq., was of New Shoreham, Stonington, South Kingstown and Newport (N. E. Hist. & Gen. Reg., Vol. 86, pp. 174-182).

(2nd col.) Add Mercy. In 1690 Nathaniel Dickens deeded land at New Shoreham to his daughter Mercy and her husband Gregory Mark of Oyster Bay, Long Island (New Shoreham Deeds). They were living at New Shoreham on 3 Sept. 1696 (New Shoreham Records, Bk. I, p. 230).

DODGE. Tristram (p. 66, 1st col.). On 26 Sept. 1647 he witnessed a deed at Ferryland, Newfoundland and on 24:3:1648 Valentine Hill gave a power of attorney to Joseph Grafton to recover from Tristram Dodge et als. in Newfoundland (Aspinwall, pp. 126, 127-8). His house appears upon the oldest map of Block Island. He was a foreman of a jury at New Shoreham on 23 Feb. 1681/2 (New Shoreham Records, Bk. I, p. 542). On 6 Dec. 1683, John Williams of Newport agreed with John, Tris-

447

tram, William and Israel Dodge as to the land bought of "their late father, Tristram Dodge deceased" to deliver it to them after the decease of their mother Anne Dodge (New Shoreham Records, Bk. I). She was probably alive on 27 Feb. 1685/6 (*ib.*, p. 450).

John (2nd col.). His wife Mary was probably a daughter of Alexander Enos (Innis), one of the Scotch prisoners, who settled on Block Island.

William (2nd col.) was deeded land on 10 Jan. 1680/1 (New Shoreham Deeds). On a Coroner's jury 8 June 1702. Deposed 6 Jan. 1706/7 aged 57 years (New Shoreham Records, Bk. I, p. 386). Freeman at New Shoreham 1678. William was alive on 16 Dec. 1731, when his son William made his will. He married on 24 April 1674 Sarah George and had: Sarah, born 24 Jan. 1674/5; William, born 8 March 1679/80; Samuel, born 9 Sept. 1681; Elizabeth, born 1 May 1683.

EARLE. Ralph (p. 69, 1st col.). Son of Ralph and Margaret (Brown) Earle of Bishop's Stortford, co. Herts, bapt. there on 9 Feb. 1606/7. Married there on 29 June 1631 Joan Savage, probably daughter of Richard Savage of Widford, co. Herts, whose daughter Joan was baptized on 18 Feb. 1609/10. In 1699 Samuel Sewell records in his diary that at Portsmouth he saw the aged Joan Earle, "Savage that was," aged, by repute, 105 years. Her age was evidently overestimated. Ralph was of Newport in 1638. In 1646 "Ralph Earle of Portsmouth, formerly of Newport," sold land in the latter town (R. I. Colony Deeds). In August 1653 he testified in the case of Capt. Kempo Sybada vs. Edward Hull concerning the latter's depredations upon the plaintiff's property, while in command of the bark "Swallow," commissioned as a privateer by Rhode Island in the Dutch War (Essex County, Mass., Quarterly Court Files). In 1667 he had a suit in Connecticut claiming to have bought "The Dutch House of Good Hope" at Hartford from Capt. John Underhill in 1653.

[To be continued]

The American Genealogist

Whole Number 76 Volume XIX, No. 4

April, 1943

ADDITIONS AND CORRECTIONS TO AUSTIN'S GENEALOGICAL DICTIONARY OF RHODE ISLAND

By G. Andrews Moriarty, A.M., LL.B., F.S.A.

[Continued from Vol. 19, p. 135]

ACRES (p. 1, 2nd col.). Martha, birth date may be 28 Feb. 1675/6 (R. I. Hist. Soc. Coll., Vol. 31, p. 81).

BENNET (p. 18, 2nd col.). Jonathan. Married Anna (born in Boston 4 Nov. 1674), daughter of John and Anna (Alcock) Williams (The Genealogical Magazine, ed. Putnam, Vol. 3, p. 10).

CRANSTON. Samuel (p. 60, 2nd col.) married Judith Parret who was, at the time of their marriage, the widow of Capt. William Pease of Newport, mariner (N. E. Hist. & Gen. Reg., Vol. 87, p. 74).

DODGE. John (p. 66, 2nd col.) married 24 Oct. 1676.

Add Mary (p. 66, 3rd col.), dau. of John, born 29 Dec. 1677, probably died young (R. I. Hist. Soc. Coll., Vol. 31, p. 81).

GARDINER. George (p. 81, 1st col.) probably came from England as a young man with William Coddington. He witnessed Coddington's deed of his Braintree farm in 1639 (Suffolk Deeds). Went with Coddington from Portsmouth to Newport in 1639. At the end of 8th month 1639 the Portsmouth records mention the "land which was George Gardiner's." Freeman at Newport 17 Dec. 1639 and a landowner there on 29 Jan. 1639/40. Sergeant of the Newport company on 17 Mar. 1641. On 1 Dec. 1641 and 3 Dec. 1643 on the Grand Jury. On 22 Aug. 1662 he, together with Robert Stanton of Newport, purchased a large tract lying to the west of the Pettyquamscot Purchase at Narragansett. His wife Herodias was already being divorced from her first husband John Hicks 7:1 mo.:1644, and a letter from Hicks to John Coggeshall dated at Flushing 12 Dec. (?1643) was filed in the Quarter Sessions Court 7:1 mo.:1644. Hicks also obtained a divorce from her in New York for adultery (*cf.* Chapin's Doc. Hist., Vol. 2).

Nicholas (2nd col.). His wife was undoubtedly Hannah, born 10 Oct. 1662?, daughter of George and Bethia (Mowry) Palmer of Warwick, and Kingstown. Married about 1681 and had, besides the three sons recorded by Austin, seven daughters, whose births are recorded in Nicholas' bible now in private hands. One of them, Sarah, born 18 March 1698/9, married 5 April 1719 Edmund Sheffield of Kingstown (*cf.* AMERICAN GENEALOGIST, Vol. 17, pp. 50-52).

Dorcas (2nd col.). Undoubtedly a daughter of George and Herodias.

Rebecca (2nd col.). Undoubtedly a daughter of George and Herodias.

Samuel (2nd col.). Delete. He belonged to another family.

Robert (2nd col.). His will, which names his brothers Peregrine and Joseph and his "father-in-law" (i.e. step-father) William Hawkins was proved at Providence on 28 April 1690. Austin has confused him with another Robert Gardiner, not of this family.

Jeremiah (2nd col.). Delete; he was not of this family. (*cf.* "The Gardiners of Narragansett" by Caroline Robinson).

GEORGE. Peter (p. 83, 1st col.). On 19:9:1647 Peter George of Braintree, oatmeal maker, and Mary his wife gave a power of attorney to Peter Bracket of Braintree (Mass.) to collect a legacy from the executors of the estate of John Rowning of Hundon, co. Suffolk, father of the said Mary, due upon the decease of her former husband Simon Ray (Aspinwall, p. 105). Mary, daughter of John Rowning (Thomas, John, William, John) of Hundon, bapt. at Hundon 12 Aug. 1613, married at Wratting Parva 1635 Simon Ray of Hundon (Hutchinson MSS. at Soc. of Genealogists, London), and secondly 1641-42 Peter George. For her ancestry see N. E. Hist. & Gen. Reg., Vol. 69, pp. 24-28.

Samuel (2nd col.) married Sarah, daughter of John and Margaret Rathbone of New Shoreham, on 20 Dec. 1678.

GOULDING. Major Roger (p. 84, 1st col.). Will of Roger Goulding of Rhode Island, "now resident in Barbados," 22 Dec. 1694, proved 1 March 1694/5. Executors, John Bates and Benjamin Rawlins. His ship, the *Thomas and George*, now lying in Carlisle Road (i.e. Bridgetown) to be sent home to Rhode Island. Confirms his will made in R. I. before his departure (Probate Records in Colonial Sec. Office, Bridgetown; *cf.* N. E. Hist. & Gen. Reg., Vol. 67, p. 363).

GUTTREDGE. Robert (p. 89, 1st col.) was, apparently, one of the Scottish prisoners taken at Dunbar or Worcester and sold to Bex & Co. of London and sent by them to work the iron works at Braintree, Mass. In a letter to Alexander Enos (Innis) he calls him "my countryman" (New Shoreham Records). Married first, at Braintree, Mass., on 25:10:1656, Margaret Ireland (N. E. Hist. & Gen. Reg., Vol. 37, p. 286).

HALL. Henry (p. 90, 1st col.) was undoubtedly a nephew of William Hall of Portsmouth (see p. 91) and the son of John Hall who was of Newport 1:3:1638. John had land in Portsmouth 23 Dec. 1644 and 25 Jan. 1648/9, and was a Freeman at Newport in 1655. John had also, in all probability, another son James, who was of New London in 1662, when he was a tenant of John Winthrop, Jr., at Fisher's Island (Savage, Gen. Dict., Vol. 2, p. 333). This James had a wife Margaret and was of Westerly in 1669 (R. I. Colonial Deeds, Vol. 1, p. 276).

On 19 Jan. 1663/4 Henry Hall and Richard Knight, both of Newport bought a large tract in the Narragansett Country (in Westerly) of Coginaquant, Chief Sachem, which purchase was later known as "the Hall and Knight Purchase." On 17 Sept. 1679 he took the oath of allegiance. In 1675 Thomas Staunton sold 50 acres in Stonington to Henry Hall. In 1692 he had 100 acres laid out to him. On 2 June 1692 he bought of John Knight of Norwich 1200 acres in the Hall and Knight Purchase (Westerly Deeds, Vol. 2, p. 68). Constable at Westerly and a Member of the Town Council. On 24 May 1703 he bought land in Westerly of Ninicraft, Sachem of Niantic. On 13 Aug. 1703 he deeded land in Westerly to son James and son-in-law Thomas Stephens (*ib.*, Vol. 1, p. 96).

Edward (2nd col.) married Mary daughter of Edward and Mary (George) Ball of New Shoreham. Freeman at Westerly 29 June 1702.

John (2nd col.) of Westerly and Charlestown, married Elizabeth, dau. of Edward and Mary (George) Ball of New Shoreham. Constable, Westerly, 12 July 1703. Ear mark recorded 20 Oct. 1703. On 1 Jan. 1703/4 owned lot 15 at Westerly. On 28 Sept. 1709 he bought 127 acres in Westerly of the Colony (Westerly Deeds, Vol. 2, p. 37). On 27 Feb. 1710/11 he bought land of brother Edward. On 27 Feb. 1735/6 he deeded land (80 acres) to his son John, Jr. On 17 Jan. 1738/9 he, of Charlestown, deeded 100 acres to son Peter. On 23 April 1750 he and wife Elizabeth sold land in Charlestown (Deeds, Vol. 1, p. 287). His will of 25 March 17—, proved 4 July 1764, gave land to son Peter and his homestead farm to son John. Land in Charlestown to sons George, Nathan and Thomas. Goods to daughters Mary Harvey, Jennie Adams, Patience Adams, Margaret Hall, Freelove Hall, Dinah Hall, Elizabeth Hall, and Sarah Tucker (N. E. Hist. & Gen. Reg., Vol. 87, pp. 352-358).

HANNAH. Robert (p. 91, 1st col.) was of Portsmouth prior to his settlement in Kingstown.

HOLMES. Obadiah^3 (Robert^2, Robert^1) (p. 103, 1st col.). Son of Robert Holme of Reddish, co. Lancs., husbandman, whose will, dated 20 Aug. 1640, was proved 24 Nov. 1649. Bapt. at Didsbury 18 March 1609/10. Married Manchester, 20 Nov. 1630, Katherine Hyde. His brothers John and Samuel were of Brasenose College, Oxford, where Samuel took his B.A. on 17 May 1636.

Add John (2nd col.), buried Stockport 27 June 1633. (N. E. Hist. & Gen. Reg., Vol. 64, p. 238; Vol. 67, p. 21).

JEFFREY. William (p. 111, 1st col.). According to the late J. Gardner Bartlett, he was not the Cambridge graduate.

KENYON. Roger (p. 116, 2nd col.). Delete. He was not a brother, but may have been a kinsman, of John and James.

LAKE. David (p. 118, 1st col.). Son of Henry and nephew of Deacon Thomas of Dorchester, Mass. Henry and Thomas were probably members of the Lake family of Chidwell, co. Lancs., near Liverpool, in which family the names of David and Thomas predominate. They evidently emigrated to Dorchester, Mass., in the Lancashire group, which came with the Rev. Richard Mather. Henry was of Dorchester, Mass., Portsmouth, R. I., Dartmouth, Mass., and Warwick, R. I. About 1650 his wife, Alice, was executed as a witch and he soon after removed to Portsmouth, where he was admitted as an inhabitant in 1652, having previously witnessed a deed there on 23 April 1651. In 1652 he sold a lot at Warwick, R. I. In 1661 he was on a Coroner's Jury at Portsmouth and his ear mark was recorded in that town in July 1666. On 21 Feb. 1672/3 he was "of Dartmouth." By Alice his wife he had issue: Elizabeth, wife of Thomas Butts of Portsmouth; Thomas of Dartmouth; David of Portsmouth, Little Compton and Tiverton, and two other children, who died young.

Thomas Lake, son of Henry above, brother of David. He was of Dartmouth and served in Philip's War. On 19 (12) 1659 he is styled "kinsman and servant" of Deacon Thomas Lake in the Dorchester records. On 1 Nov. 1676 was granted, together with his brother David, 100 acres at Puncatest (Tiverton) for his services in Philip's War. One of these Lakes was with Benjamin Church in the Peasefield Fight. Died after 29 May 1687. Wife's name unknown. Children, all born at Dartmouth: Alice, born 6 Dec. 1677, married about 1695 her cousin, Moses Butts, son of Thomas and Elizabeth (Lake) Butts of Little Compton; Thomas, born 13 Nov. 1680; John, born 23 Aug. 1683; Joseph, born 17 July 1686; Mary, born 19 Sept. 1689, married at Tiverton, 14 Sept. 1720, Richard Borden; Benjamin, born 29 May 1697, probably *non compos* and died single after 6 Mar. 1718/19.

David Lake, son of Henry, was a Freeman at Portsmouth 27 Feb. 1668/9 and his ear mark was recorded 29 Mar. 1669 (Portsmouth Town Records, pp. 144, 278). On 22 Sept. 1679 he bought land on the Taunton River (in Dighton, Somerset and Freetown) and also at Sippican (Rochester) and Acushnet (New Bedford). In 1689 he was a proprietor at Dartmouth and a Selectman at Tiverton on 28 July 1694 and in 1698. On 16 March 1695/6 and in 1698 he was Town Clerk of Tiverton. On 11 March 1701/2 he was Moderator of the Tiverton Town Meeting. On 15 June 1709 he, "of Little Compton," deeded to Zaccheus Butts his rights in the lands in Dorchester and Stoughton, Mass. (inherited from his uncle Thomas) (Bristol Co. Deeds at Taunton, Book 10, p. 649).

Sarah (2nd col.) married about 1698 Josiah Stafford.

Joel (2nd col.) married Sarah, daughter of Edward and Frances Bailey of Newport and Tiverton. (THE AMERICAN GENEALOGIST, Vol. 12, pp. 17-24.)

MALLET. Thomas (p. 127, 1st col.) came from Great Marlow, co. Bucks, England, and married Mary, widow of Samuel Wilcox of Dartmouth, and daughter of William Wood of Dartmouth. Jeremiah Wilcox was her child by her first husband. Thomas Mallet, aged 55 years, died 16 Jan. 1704/5 (buried in Trinity Church Yard at Newport), without issue. His widow married 3rdly, John Sanford of Newport. She died 15 Dec. 1721, aged 56 years. She is buried in the Common Burying Ground at Newport under a flat slate stone with the Sanford arms thereon. (N. E. Hist. & Gen. Reg., Vol. 60, p. 400.)

MANCHESTER. Thomas (p. 127, 1st col.) He was first of New Haven, Conn., the servant of Mr. Perry on 4 Dec. 1639 and 5 March 1639/40. Bought land in Portsmouth on 3 Dec. 1654. Town Sergeant at Portsmouth, 7 June 1675, 5 June 1676, 2 July 1679, and thereafter in 1680, 1681, 1683, 1684, 1685 and 1690. Ear mark recorded 29 March 1669/70.

Thomas, Jr. (2nd col.) was Freeman at Portsmouth, 29 April 1673. Juryman at Portsmouth 1681, 1687 and 1695. Married Mary, daughter of Nathaniel and Sarah (Freeborn) Browning of Portsmouth and had issue at least Thomas, John and William, to the last of whom his "kinsman," Gideon Freeborn, deeded 10 acres at Potowomut (Warwick) on 26 July 1712 (unrecorded papers at Portsmouth Town House; Warwick Deeds). Administration on the estate of Thomas, Jr., 13:6:1722 (unrecorded Portsmouth papers, *op. cit.*)

William (2nd col.). Delete deed from Gideon Freeborn 26 July 1712. (R. I. Hist. Soc. Coll., Vol. 21, p. 128.)

MITCHELL. Thomas (p. 133, 1st col.) was a hatter and died before 6 May 1687 (Inventory of John Williams of Newport, Suffolk Co. Mass. Probate). He was undoubtedly the son of Experience Mitchell and Jane, his wife, daughter Francis Cooke of the *Mayflower*. His parents were of Bridgewater, Mass. (THE AMERICAN GENEALOGIST, Vol. 12, pp. 193-199.) Sued Joseph Billington on a note at New Shoreham 15:9:1677. Occurs at a town meeting at New Shoreham 5 Jan. 1677/8. Found guilty of causing the death of Ochokomah, an Indian, 9 March 1679/80. Juryman, 23 Feb. 1681/2. Freeman, 1684. Bought of Capt. Thomas Terry 1/4 of 1/16 of New Shoreham on 20 Oct. 1677 (New Shoreham Deeds, Vol. 1, p. 463). On 8 April 1679 leased of John Williams 1/16 of the Island, i.e. Mr. Bellingham's share

(*ib.*, p. 97). On 1 Jan. 1679/80 he sold land at New Shoreham to Josias Helling (*ib.*, p. 229) and on 6 March 1683/4 he bought land there of Robert Guttridge (*ib.*, p. 465). He is undoubtedly the Thomas Mitchell who, prior to his arrival at Block Island, was of Dartmouth in 1669 and of Duxbury in 1672. In 1673 he is described as "of Rhode Island" (Am. Gen., *op. cit.*). He had issue: Capt. Thomas, John, Joseph, and probably daughters.

Capt. Thomas (2nd col.), born about 1660, died about 1740. Married before 1682 Margaret, probably the daughter of John and Margaret Rathbone. Ear mark recorded 1688. Freeman, 7 April 1690. Constable, 12 April 1692. Town Sergeant, 10 April 1705. Mortgaged land, together with wife Margaret, to the Colony, 28 Feb. 1715/6. Deputy, 1725, 1736. Justice, 1726. Moderator, 1726, 1727 and "Townsman," 1706, 1737. On 8 Sept. 1723 he, and wife Margaret, deeded to his brother Joseph his rights in 20 acres held by them in common, which had belonged to their father (New Shoreham Deeds, Vol. 2, p. 167). On 23 Sept. 1728 he, styled "Capt. Thomas," deeded to his son Thomas Mitchell of Boston, cheesemonger, 232 acres at New Shoreham (*ib.*, Vol. 2, p. 172). On 17 Feb. 1734/5 he and wife Margaret deeded 140 acres to their son George (*ib.*, p. 245). On 14 June he and Caleb Littlefield bought 500 acres in North Kingstown (now in Exeter, R. I.) (North Kingstown Deeds Bk. 5A, p. 79), and in 1727 he deeded part of it to son Joseph of North Kingstown (*ib.*, Bk. 5B, p. 106). On 19 July 1736 Capt. Thomas and wife Margaret made an indenture with Thomas Mitchell, Jr., of New Shoreham (New Shoreham Deeds, Vol. 2, p. 263). He last occurs 19 April 1738. Children: Capt. Thomas, Jr., George, Joseph, Margaret (m. 16 June 1726 Nathaniel Littlefield), Benjamin of Newport, hatter, 1736 (North Kingstown Deeds, Bk. 7B, p. 211). Capt. Thomas, Jr., while living at Boston, married 11 April 1726 Margaret, widow of Capt. John Peck of Boston, the ancestor of the eminent Boston merchant, Thomas Handasyde Perkins.

John (2nd col.) probably removed to Newport. Married before 6 Jan. 1692/3 Sarah, probably widow of Samuel George and daughter of John Rathbone. The will of Sarah Mitchell of Newport, widow, proved 22 April 1718, names her son John and her daughter Mehitable (Newport Town Council, Vol. 3, pp. 157, 196). He occurs with his brother Thomas April 1686 (New Shoreham Town Rec., Vol. 1, p. 138). Freeman, 10 Jan. 1692/3 (*ib.*, Vol. 1, p. 202). Coroner's Jury, Nov. 1693. On 3 Nov. 1699, he, with wife Sarah, both of New Shoreham, sold land there formerly belonging to his father Thomas (*ib.*, Vol. 1, p. 375). Witnessed a New Shoreham deed, 20 March 1706/7 (New Shoreham Deeds, Vol. 1, p. 385). Probably removed soon after to Newport, and died before 1708, when Sarah Mitchell of Newport, widow, bought land in that town (Newport Court Files, March 1742, case of Mitchell vs. Hammett). Children: (1) John, married at Newport as "John Mitchell of New Shoreham," on 19 June 1729, Lois Greenman; in March 1742 John Mitchell of New Providence, Bahamas, mariner, brought suit in the Newport Court for the land of his mother Sarah late of Newport deceased, bought in 1708 (*ib.*); (2) Mehitable.

Joseph (2nd col.). Signed petition 30 Sept. 1691. Occurs 3 Sept. 1696; at a Town Meeting on 10 April 1705 with his brothers John and Sergt. Thomas. Married 1st, 5 July 1703, Mary, daughter of Samuel and Sarah (Rathbone) George, who died prior to 8 May 1740 (New Shoreham Deeds, Vol. 2, p. 254), and 2ndly, ———. Will 7 Feb. 1757, proved 28 Apr. 1764, names sons Jonathan, Thomas and Jeremiah and daughters Mary, wife of Nehemiah Dodge, and grandson John, son of son Thomas, under 21 (*ib.*, Vol. 4, p. 60). Children: Jonathan, born 25 May 1704; John, born 19 Aug. 1707; Jeremiah, born abt. 1710; Thomas, born 30 May 1712; Mary, born 5 Feb. 1714/5 (New Eng. Hist. & Gen. Reg., vol. 82, p. 456).

MOSHER. Hugh (p. 135, 1st col.). It seems probable, although absolute proof is lacking, that he was a son of Hugh Mosher, the early settler of Casco Bay and Saco, Maine. Two of the latter's sons, James and John, removed from Maine to Brookhaven, Long Island, and it seems likely that a son Hugh went to Newport (*cf.*, Libby-Noyes-Davis, Gen. Dict. of Me. & N. H., pt. 4, p. 496).

MOTT. Nathaniel (p. 135, 1st col.). In 1645 he was one of the Scituate men who went in the Plymouth Colony quota in the expedition against the Narragansetts. On 22 Dec. 1663 he was living on Mr. Parker's farm (Middlesex Co. Court Files). This may refer to Richard Parker, the early merchant of Boston. He was killed by the Indians during Philip's War at Braintree on 23 Feb. 1675/6.

Nathaniel (2nd col.), born 28 Dec. 1657, died 13 March 1660/1, and a second Nathaniel, the man listed by Austin, was born on 30 Aug. 1661.

John (2nd col.), the eldest surviving son, was born at Braintree on 19 Aug. 1659. Freeman at New Shoreham 1684. Sold land there on 19 Dec. 1689; and on 27 March 1693 he, "formerly of Block Island but now of Lyme, Conn.," sold land at New Shoreham. Besides the children listed by Austin, he had Mary, born at Lyme 5 Jan. 1692/3 (perhaps an error for Marcy), and Marcy, born about 1695, wife of Caleb Littlefield, Jr., of New Shoreham.

Edward (2nd col.), born 11 May 1673, of New Shoreham, Kingstown and Westerly, R. I. Freeman, New Shoreham 1696. Of Kingstown in March 1713, when he sued Capt. John Greenman of Kingstown for trespass (Newport Co. Ct. Files). Freeman at Westerly, 1 May 1730. His widow Penelope was living at Westerly 29 April 1751. Children: John of Stonington and Westerly; Hannah m. 5 Oct. 1732 John Mott of Lyme, her cousin; Sarah, m. 16 July 1738 William Thorne of Westerly; Samuel of Westerly (father of Gen. Samuel Mott of Preston, Conn.); a daughter, m. before 27 Jan. 1751/2 John Lewis; ? Abigail, m. 27 Jan. 1722/3 Samuel Worden of Kingstown; ? Patience, m. 8 May 1726 Nicholas Holway of Kingstown.

Add Mary (2nd col.), born 15 Dec. 1664.

Add Lydia (2nd col.), born 12 July 1666. Probably married Caleb Littlefield, Sr.

Add Samuel (2nd. col.) born 25 Jan. 1668/9. Died 1753. Of Lyme, Conn., 6 April 1692. Lived in the section of Lyme called Joshuatown. Will dated 20 Aug. 1751, proved 16 April 1753. Married 1st, at Lyme 6 April 1692, Mary ———, and 2ndly, Margaret, who survived him. Children, all born at Lyme: Mary, born 10 March 1692/3; Samuel, born 1 Feb. 1693/4, died before 12 June 1735; Hannah, born 11 March 1696/7; John, born 25 Dec. 1698, m. 5 Oct. 1732 his cousin Hannah Mott of Westerly; Experience, born 8 March 1703/4; Lydia, born 22 March 1706; Nathaniel, born 16 July 1707; Deborah born 1 June 1710.

Add Elizabeth (2nd col.), born 17 May 1671, m. at Braintree 30 Dec. 1690 Edmund Littlefield of Wells, Me., and Braintree, Mass.

Add Experience (2nd col.), died 24 Dec. 1672 at Braintree.

Add Ebenezer (2nd col.), born 16 Sept. 1675, of Scituate, Mass. Married 19 Feb. 1699/1700 Grace Vinall. Died 1 June 1736. Children, all born at Scituate: Ebenezer, born 26 Sept. 1700; Grace, born 17 Aug. 1702; John, born 11 June 1707; Mary, born 24 March 1713; Elizabeth, born 17 July 1716; Nathaniel, born 23 June 1720. (See New Eng. Hist. & Gen. Reg., Vol. 67, pp. 23-27.)

Note. Care must be taken not to confuse members of this family with the descendants of Adam Mott of Portsmouth, R. I., who also settled in Kingstown and Westerly, R. I.

[*To be continued*]

The American Genealogist

Whole Number 77 Volume XX, No. 1

July, 1943

ADDITIONS AND CORRECTIONS TO AUSTIN'S GENEALOGICAL DICTIONARY OF RHODE ISLAND

By G. Andrews Moriarty, A.M., LL.B., F.S.A.

[Continued from Vol. 19, p. 229]

MANN. William (p. 129, 1st col.) appears to have been a Somersetshire or Wiltshire man (R. I. Hist. Soc. Coll. Vol. 14, p. 83).

PALMER. George (omitted by Austin, add on page 143) was of Warwick, Providence and Kingstown. Perhaps a kinsman of George Palmer of Ipswich, Boston and Kittery, wine cooper (*cf.* Noyes-Libby-Davis, Gen. Dic. Me. & N. H., Pt. IV, p. 525). Grantee at Warwick 19 Sept. 1654. Freeman there 18 June 1654. Mentioned in a letter of Roger Williams 6:6:1656 (*N. E. Hist. & Gen. Reg.* Vol. 36, p. 78). Grantee at Providence 27 April 1659. Bought land at Aquednesset (in North Kingston) 27 Jan. 1660/1. Styled "of Providence" in a deed of 27:7:1662. Took oath of allegiance at Kingstown 19 May 1671. Signed a petition, as an inhabitant of Narragansett, in favor of Conn. jurisdiction, on 3 July 1663 (Fones Rec. p. 25). Petition to the King 29 July 1679. He operated the grist mill

on the Mattatuxet, and on 30 Nov. 1686 this land was in the possession of his widow Bethia. Married 30 Sept. 1662 Bethia, daughter of Roger Mowry of Providence (*q. v.*). They undoubtedly had issue at least two daughters: 1. Hannah, born 10 Oct. 1663, married 1680-82 Nicholas Gardiner of Kingstown, son of George and Herodias (Long) Gardiner (for their issue see Gardiner; *cf.* also article by Dr. Sheridan E. Gardiner in Am. Genealogist, Vol. 17, pp. 50-52; they had a great-grandson and a great-great-grandson named Palmer Gardiner); 2. Deliverence, born about 1664/5, married Edward Cleveland of Kingstown, and Exeter, R. I. (born 20 May 1663, died 1746), son of Moses and Anne (Winn) Cleveland of Woburn, Mass., and had issue: Deliverence of North Kingstown, R. I., and Killingworth, Conn.; Edward of Canterbury, Conn., born about 1686, married 17 Apr. 1716 Rebecca Payne, died 1770; Palmer of Exeter, R. I., died 1768, married Deborah Northop; Isaac of Canterbury, Conn.; Samuel of Pomfret, Conn.; Mary, married Richard Adams of Canterbury, Conn.; George of Walpole, Mass.; Elizabeth, married Jonathan Shepard of Canterbury, Conn.; Abigail.

PARKER. George (p. 143, 1st col.) may be the George Parker bapt. at Margate, co. Kent, in March 1612, son of George. Water Bailiff and Town Sergeant at Portsmouth, R. I., 3 June 1651.

PARROTT. Judith (p. 144, 2nd col.) also married Capt. William Pease of Newport, mariner (came from England) and was his widow when she married Gov. Samuel Cranston. Capt. Pease died prior to 1 Dec. 1712 at which date she was the wife of Gov. Cranston (*N. E. Hist. & Gen. Reg.*, Vol. 87, p. 74).

Add III Hester (2nd col.) married 1st, Capt. Thomas Fleet, at Huntington, Long Island, on 1 Nov. 1681, and had issue Simon and Parrott; married 2nd, before 1725, Samuel Burke of Southold, L. I. (Mrs. Josephine Frost of Brooklyn, N. Y.)

PECKHAM. John (p. 147, 1st col.). His wife is said by some to have been Mary, sister of Dr. John Clarke, who was bapt. at Westhorpe, co. Suffolk, on 26 July 1607, the daughter of Thomas and Rose (Kerrich) Clarke.

PELHAM (p. 149, 1st col.). Edward (Herbert[3], Herbert[2], Herbert[1]) was son of Herbert of Boston, co. Lincs., Cambridge, Mass., and Bures, co. Essex, 1st Treas. of Harvard, by his second wife Elizabeth (Bosvile) Harlarkenden, widow of Roger. This Herbert was M. P. for the County of Essex in 1654. Edward's grandmother, Penelope West, was sister of Thomas, Lord De la

Warr, Gov. of Va., and a descendant of Mary Boleyn, sister of Queen Anne. Edward was A.B., Harvard 1673 (Sibley). In 1693 Harvard held a mortgage on his lands in and about Cambridge. On 28 May 1684 he sold land in Cambridge inherited from his father to Harvard College. He was one of the addressors of the King on 16 July 1686 in re the Quo Warranto against the Rhode Island Charter. Besides his lands in Newport, he had a large estate in Cambridge, Watertown and Sudbury, Mass., and a life estate in Smeeth Hall in Chapel Hall, co. Lincs. In 1711 he, together with his sons, Edward and Thomas, sold Pelham's Island, Sudbury, Mass. (For a very full account of this family, *cf.* AM. GENEALOGIST, Vol. 18, pp. 137-146, article by Meredith B. Colket, Jr.)

PENDLETON. Capt. James (p. 149, 1st col.) was a Freeman at Watertown 10 May 1648, and a few years after 1651 he removed from Sudbury to Portsmouth, N. H. Was a witness at Portsmouth 20 Jan. 1656/7. Constable 1661; Town Clerk 1663-4; Selectman 1663-4, 1667-8. Captain of the militia Oct. 1666. At Saco or Scarborough, Me., Aug. 1671. Deposed July 1672 aged 44 years. Removed by 1675 to Stonington, Conn., and Westerly, R. I. Married 1st, at Sudbury 22 Oct. 1647, Mary Palmer.

James (2nd col.) alive Aug. 1677, died s. p. by 1698.

Mary (2nd col.) unmarried 16 Apr. 1680. Married 1st, Joseph Cross; and 2nd, Nicholas Morey.

Hannah (2nd col.) m. in Sudbury 13 Jan. 1678/9 John Bush. Lived in Sudbury and Maynard. She is apparently the Hannah Bush who married John Rutter at Sudbury 12 March 1690.

Brian (2nd col.) died s. p. before 1703.

Edmund (2nd col.) born 24 June 1665 not 1664. Living with John Kettle at Great Island when a boy. Blinded by a stone thrown by Walter Westcott while there. Of Westerly in 1734 when he sued John Downing and Thomas Trickey for about 70 acres in Newington.

Caleb (2nd col.). His wife's name was Elizabeth.

Sarah (2nd col.) bapt. at Stonington 18 Apr. 1675, probably died young.

Eleanor (2nd col.) bapt. Stonington 20 July 1679.

Dorothy (2nd col.) bapt. Stonington 3 Oct. 1686. She was alive in 1734.

(See Noyes-Libby-Davis, Gen. Dic. Me. & N. H., Pt. IV, pp. 537-38.)

RATHBONE. John (p. 159, 1st col.) of Newport, R. I., as well as of New Shoreham, was undoubtedly first at Dorchester, Mass., and came from Lancs., where the name belongs, in the

Lancashire group, with the Rev. Richard Mather. He was closely associated at New Shoreham with Edward Vose of Dorchester and Milton, Mass., a known Lancashire man. John Acres of Dorchester and New Shoreham calls him "brother-in-law." Freeman at Newport 25 July 1683 and sold land there 10 Oct. 1687. He had land at "Hammersmith" in the Southern part of Newport and a house and shop in the town proper. In 1701 he had a share in the common lands at Newport. On 30 July 1707 his widow, Margaret, had a lot in Newport (Newport Town Records). He returned to New Shoreham in 1701 or 02 and died there.

Thomas (2nd col.) owned land at Newport in 1701. On 31 May 1699 John Rodman and William Huddlestone of New York City sold to Thomas Rathbone of New Shoreham land at Poughkeepsie, bought of Henry Ten Eyck.

John (2nd col.). He or perhaps his father on 16 March 1702/3 was a proprietor of the Town Wharf at Newport (Newport Town Records).

RAY (p. 160, 1st col.). Simon[9] (Simon[8], Simon[7], Robert[6], Robert[5], John[4], John[3], Robert[2], John[1]) descended from an ancient family of Suffolk yeomanry, settled at Wickhambrook in that county at the beginning of the 15th century. His ancestors also lived in the neighboring parishes of Denston, Hunden and Cowling. Bapt. at Hunden 20 Dec. 1638, the son of Simon and Mary (Rowning) Ray of Hunden, co. Suffolk, and Braintree, Mass. Married 2nd, before 18 Oct. 1690, Elizabeth, widow of "Squire" Humphrey Tiffany of Rehoboth, Mass. (Full information upon the Ray family in *N. E. H. and G. Register*, Vol. 64, pp. 51-61; Vol. 69, pp. 27-28; Vol. 86, pp. 324-330; The Cullum Family, London 1928, pp. 223-286.)

Mary (2nd col.). Her husband, Roger Kenyon, Esq., was eldest son and heir of Roger Kenyon, Esq., M. P., of Peele Hall, near Manchester, co. Lancs. The father was M. P. for Clitheroe and Governor of the Isle of Man, and his mother was Anne Rigby. Roger, Jr., emigrated to Barbados, going thence to New York and eventually to Block Island, where he married. He returned to England and back to Rhode Island again. Died in Ireland, a young man leaving an only son Roger of Westchester, N. Y., who later settled, apparently, as a merchant at Perth Amboy, N. J., and went subsequently to Newburn, N. C. Mary (Ray) Kenyon was, according to her niece, Mrs. Gov. William Greene, the first native-born American lady to be presented at Court. (Trans. Colonial Soc. of Mass., Vol. 28, pp. 295-301; Trans. Lancs. & Cheshire Antiq. Soc., Vol. 43, pp. 14-20.) Mary m. 2nd, as it would seem, Samuel Sands of Cow Neck, L. I., and Westchester Co., N. Y., son of James and Sarah (Walker) Sands of New Shoreham. The Lord Chief Justice of England, Lloyd Kenyon, created Baron Gredlington, descended from William, third son of Roger the M. P. and Anne Rigby.

Dorothy (2nd col.) married John Clapp of Rye, N. Y., Clerk of the Writs for the County of Westchester.

Simon (2nd col.) was for some time a merchant at Newport and Westerly. On 18 Oct. 1706 he bought a house and lot, apparently on Spring St. in Newport, and in 1725 he was of Newport and bought land there on 20 Oct. 1726. In the latter year he removed to Westerly, where he was a landowner, but he subsequently returned to New Shoreham (Newport & Westerly Town Records). In 1742 he, styled "Simon Ray of Westerly, gent.," sued Samuel Champlin in the Newport County Court (Newport County Court Files). On 27 June 1743 he, "of Westerly," bought land in Middleborough, Mass., which he sold 20 Feb. 1745/6 (Plymouth Co., Mass., Deeds).

RICHMOND. Edward (p. 163, 1st col.). His father John Richmond, of Taunton in 1638, may be identical with the John Richmond, who was at Saco in 1636-37 (*cf.* Noyes-Davis-Libby, Gen. Dic. Me. & N. H., Pt. IV, p. 586). He removed from Taunton to Newport, where he was a juror in 1642 and a householder in 1643, Commissioner 1656. He was perhaps of Brinkworth, co. Wilts., and the son of Henry Richmond (for a very exhaustive account of the probable English ancestry of the family, see R. I. Hist. Soc. Coll., Vol. 21, pp. 17-32).

ROBERTS. Thomas (p. 165, 1st col.). His wife Pernel was a Harris from Kent, the sister of William and Thomas Harris of Providence. On 4 March 1634/5, Pernel Harris of Bow Parish, London, embarked for New England on the *Hercules* of Sandwich, John Witherly, master (Am. Colonists in the English Records, 1st series, by George Sherwood, London, 1932).

RODMAN. Thomas (p. 166, 1st col.) was son of John of Barbados, who was buried at Christ Church Parish, 15 Oct. 1686. Will of John Rodman of Christ Church Parish, Barbados, dated 16 Sept. 1686, proved 4 Nov. 1686. To be buried in Christ Church churchyard, near deceased wife. To wife Elizabeth, the plantation in Christ Church. To sons Thomas and John Rodman. To daughters Anne Wayt and Katherine Brandroth. Thomas married at Christ Church, Barbados, as his first wife, on 9 March 1671/2, Sarah Pead; second, Patience (Easton) Malins; third, Hannah Clarke. Elizabeth, wife of John Rodman, Sr., was buried at Christ Church, Barbados, on 5 Nov. 1691. (*N. E. H. and G. Register*, Vol. 67, pp. 367-68.)

ROSE. Tormet (p. 167, 1st col.). His name was Dermot Rose or Ross, corrupted into Tormet. He was one of the Scots taken at Dunbar and sold as an indentured servant to Bex & Co. of London, who sent him to work in the Iron Works at Braintree, Mass. He went to New Shoreham, in the first settlement, as a tenant of Thomas Faxon of Braintree, one of the original purchasers of Block Island. On 17 Sept. 1662, Faxon sold land at New Shoreham to John Williams of Boston "now in the possession of William Toys (*i.e.* Tosh or McIntosh) and Dormat (*i.e.* Rose) Scotsmen," tenants of the said Faxon, reserving 5 acres of upland for the said Scotsmen. (Suffolk Deeds, Bk. IV, fo. 54-55.) Married at New Shoreham 22 July 1676.

Add Daniel (2nd col.) born 1 May 1677, died young (R. I. Hist. Soc. Coll., Vol. 31, p. 81).

SANFORD. John (p. 171, 1st col.) probably came from Essex County, Eng., and had probably served in the English forces in the Low Countries. Edward Howes, writing from England to John Winthrop, Jr., in 1632, desired to be remembered to "my loving friend John Samford and his true loue," and in a letter from the Inner Temple dated 23 Sept. 1632 promises to send instruments to John Samford (Mass. Hist. Soc. Coll. 4th Ser., Vol. VI, pp. 479, 482). He had land early at Pullen Point (Winthrop, Mass.). His first wife, who came from Titherly in Hants., was a sister of Henry Webb, the early Boston merchant, who came from Salisbury in Wilts., which Henry was an early benefactor of Harvard. His second wife was Bridget, daughter of William and Anne (Marbury) Hutchinson, born Jan. 1618/9, bapt. Alford, co. Lincs., 15 Jan. 1618/9; her second husband was of Boston and Saco. (*N. E. H. and G. Register*, Vol. 20, p. 363; Diary & Letters of Thomas Hutchinson, Vol. II, p. 462.)

John (2nd col.). His 1st wife's father, Henry Spatchurst, was of Somerset, Bermuda, on 25 Oct. 1622; in 1658 he went to Jamaica. The Inventory of John Sanford, Jr., dated 1687, is in the Archives of the Sec. of State at Boston.

Peleg (2nd col.) was at Barbados in 1663-4 as a merchant. In 1668 he was in Boston goal for debt in a commercial matter.

William (2nd col.) was a merchant at Barbados in 1666.

Ezbon (2nd col.) was alive in New England on 27 June 1666.

Elisha (2nd col.) was a merchant residing in Barbados, 10 March 1671/2.

(Sanford Papers, ed. R. I. Hist. Soc., 1928.)

Peleg (3rd col.), son of Gov. Peleg and Mary (Coddington) Sanford, died young in Boston and was buried in King's Chapel Burying Ground 1701-02.

[*To be continued*]

The American Genealogist

Whole Number 78 Volume XX, No. 2

October, 1943

ADDITIONS AND CORRECTIONS TO AUSTIN'S GENEALOGICAL DICTIONARY OF RHODE ISLAND

By G. Andrews Moriarty, A.M., LL.B., F.S.A.

[Continued from Vol. 20, p. 58.]

COWLAND. Ralph (p. 58, 1st col.) married secondly about 1668 Eleanor widow of Thomas Wait of Portsmouth, R. I., and thirdly on 25 June 1677 Joan Hide.

HOOMERY or Hoomeryhoo. Omitted by Austin. John was propounded for a freeman at Portsmouth, 28 Nov. 1673 (Rec. of Town of Portsmouth, p. 179). 28 Dec. 1674, Mary, wife of John Hoomeyhoo confessed she had slandered William Brownell but, being poor, her fine was remitted (*ib.* p. 427). John Hoomery died soon after this date. Married Mary, daughter of Thomas and Anne Jennings of Portsmouth. She married 2ndly, Elias Williams of Portsmouth. Deed of Mary Williams of Portsmouth dated 13 Feb. 1678/9, recorded 3: 1 mo: 1678/9. Names father and mother Thomas and Anne Jennings of Portsmouth, son Samuel Hoomery, daughter Mary Hoomery and daughter Deliverence Hoomery, and Elias Williams renounced any claim to her estate (*ib.* p. 435).

Mary was apparently alive as late as 1700. Children:

1. Samuel living 13 Feb. 1678/9.
2. Mary living 13 Feb. 1678/9.
3. Deliverance living 13 Feb. 1678/9.
4. William. Undoubtedly another son. He was a mariner. His will in the form of a letter apparently written abroad was addressed to "Loving brother and sister Gershom and Sarah Wodell" (*cf.* Austin, p. 437) to take care of his business. He had paid in Barbados for William Wanton £3/16/0 and there was due him from William Wanton for coming from Barbados 45/ per month, from Ebenezer Laurence due 13/6, from John Homry 14/4 and he owed An Clark and ——— Woofford. He had a gun at Thomas Cook's to be sold and the money given to his mother. The residue to be disposed of by Gershom Wodell. Proved 13 Aug. 1700. Bond by Gershom Wodell and John Fry of Bristol, executors, 19 Aug. 1700.
5. John, undoubtedly son of John and Mary. Married Sarah, daughter of William and Mary Wodell of Portsmouth (*cf.* Austin, p. 437). Sarah was alive on 6 Dec. 1697 and John in 1700. (*R. I. Hist. Soc. Coll.*, Vol. 21, p. 130.)

JAMES. Thomas (p. 111, 1st col.), bapt. 5 Oct. 1595 at Boston, Lincs., son of John James, rector of Skirbeck, Lincs. Matriculated at Emmanuel College, Cambridge, as a Pensioner, Easter term 1611. B.A. 1614/5; M.A. 1618. Ordained in 1616/17. Emigrated to New England 1632, on the *William & Francis,* with wife Elizabeth and son Thomas; first pastor of the church at Charlestown. Quarrelled with his church and was expelled or resigned 1636. Went to Providence and joined Roger Williams in 1637 and was an original proprietor there in 1638. While in Charlestown, another son John was baptized. He moved to New Haven, Conn., in 1640. In 1642 one of three ministers sent in a special mission to Va. Was at Nansemond until ejected by Gov. Berkeley. Returned to New Haven, June 1643. Returned to England before 1648 and was pastor at Needham Market, co. Suffolk. Ejected 1662. Died in Feb. 1682/3. Described by William Harris of Providence as "a man of learning and wisdom." (*R. I. Hist. Soc. Coll.*, Vol. 23, p. 120; Morison's "The Founding of Harvard College," p. 384. Prof. Morison was evidently unaware of his Rhode Island sojourn, for he makes no mention of it.) He had married (1) at Fishtoft, Lincs., 20 Apr. 1620, Olive Ingoldsby, niece of Rev. Peter Bulkeley, and (2) Elizabeth ———. For the genealogy of this family, see "James, Mellowes and Ingoldsby Family Connections," by Donald Lines Jacobus and Clarence Almon Torrey in THE AMERICAN GENEALOGIST, Vol. 11, pp. 26-30, 98-101, 143-145, 208-216.

JENNINGS (p. 114, 1st col.), Thomas. Add to his children in 2nd col. one of his daughters, named Mary, married 1st, John Humery of Portsmouth, who died soon after 28 Dec. 1674, and 2ndly, before 13 Feb. 1678/9, Elias Williams of Portsmouth. She was living in 1700.

SHEFFIELD. Ichabod (p. 175, 1st col.), son of Edmund and Thomazin Sheffield of Sudbury, co. Suffolk, Eng., bapt. at St. Peter's, Sudbury, on 23 Dec. 1630. His brother Edmund settled at Braintree, Mass., and his brother William was of Dover, N. H. (1658), Braintree (1660), Holliston (1673) and Sherborn (1686), Mass. Ichabod was a Freeman at Portsmouth on 10 July 1648 (Portsmouth Town Records). In 1658 he was at Dover, N. H., with his brother William, and was taxed there but returned soon to Rhode Island. (*New Eng. Hist. & Gen. Reg.*, Vol. 77, pp. 190-94.)

Nathaniel (2nd col.). His first wife was Mary Chamberlain, daughter of William of Hull, Mass. They sold land there inherited from her father (Suffolk Co. Deeds).

Ichabod, Jr. (2nd col.), of Portsmouth and South Kingstown. He was Lieut. of the Kingstown Co., Feb. 1714, and J. P., June 1717. Town Treasurer of South Kingstown.

SHELDON. John of Providence (p. 176, 1st col.). His wife was the daughter of Thomas and Fridiswide (Carpenter) Vincent of Amesbury, Wilts. (*R. I. Hist. Soc. Coll.*, Vol. 14, pp. 81-82.)

SHERIFF (p. 178, 2nd col.). Elizabeth. Will of Elizabeth Carter of Portsmouth, widow, dated 17 March 1718/9, proved 13: 5 mo. 1719. Brother Daniel Shrieve. Sister Mary Sheffield (wife of Joseph). Sister Sarah Moone (wife of John). Sister Susanna Thomas. Cousin Elizabeth Shrieve (daughter of brother John Shrieve). Cousin Ruth Shrieve (daughter or granddaughter of brother John Shrieve). Cousin Caleb Shrieve (son of brother John Shrieve). Cousin Daniel Shrieve (son of brother John Shrieve). Cousin William Shrieve (son of brother John Shrieve). Cousin Mary Shrieve (daughter of brother John Shrieve). Cousin Abigail Vaughan (daughter of sister Sarah Moon). Cousin Elizabeth Moon (daughter of sister Sarah Moon). Cousin Elizabeth Wait (daughter of sister Mary Sheffield and wife of Joseph Wait of Kingston, R. I.). Cousin Martha Cory, daughter of sister Sarah. Four cousins Mary, Caleb, Daniel, and William Shrieve. Executor, brother John Shrieve. Overseer, friend and neighbor George Cornell. (Portsmouth Town Council, Bk. II.)

SLOCUM. Giles (p. 181, 1st col.) was undoubtedly the Giles Slocum bapt. at Old Cleeve, co. Somerset, 28 Sept. 1623, son of Philip and Charity (Bickham) Slocombe, who were married there on 20 Nov. 1621. Giles was first mentioned at Portsmouth 4 Sept. 1648. He had lands in Taunton which he sold to Nicholas White, and he was undoubtedly a near relative of Anthony Slocum of Taunton, who removed about 1670 to Albemarle County, N. C., where he was a member of the Palatine Court in 1679 and died in 1689 testate. Anthony was the ancestor of the Southern Slocums. Joan, wife of Giles, was excommunicated by the Baptist Church at Newport 16: 8: 1673, and Giles on 23: 8: 1673. They joined the Quakers. In 1667 he was granted land at Navesink, N. J., by Robert Carr, and on 3 April 1670 he bought two shares of land at Shrewsbury, N. J.

TABER. Philip (p. 195, 2nd col.). His wife Mary was a daughter of John and Sarah (Warren) Cooke of Plymouth and Dartmouth. John Cooke came in the *Mayflower*, as did his wife's father, Richard Warren. (*ex inform.* George E. Bowman.)

TALLMAN. Peter (p. 196, 1st col.) came from Hamburg, Germany, of a burgher family, which probably originated in Schleswig-Holstein. He was born about 1623, probably the son of Heinrich and Anna Taelmon of Hamburg and was made a burgher of that City 14 Aug. 1646. Soon after he emigrated to Barbados, where on 2 Jan. 1649 (?1648/9) he married in Christ Church Parish, Anne, daughter of Philip and Anne Hill of that parish. Soon after, he came to Rhode Island. On 2 June 1648 he contracted with Nathaniel Maverick to transport him, with his goods, in the ship *Golden Dolphin* to New England. He occurs on 5: 12: 1650 as "Peter Talmon of Newport on Rhode Island apothecary" (Aspinwall, pp. 259, 370). He was at New Amsterdam in 1651 and was trading with Delaware. He was at Hartford and on 20 May 1652 he was styled "Dutchman" in the Conn. records. He was residing at Flushing and New Amsterdam 1655-1658, but was a Freeman at Newport, R. I.,

457

in 1655. On 4 Oct. 1655, he bought a house and lot in New Amsterdam, and on 25 May 1658, "Pieter Taelman burgher and inhabitant of New Amsterdam," sold the same to Dirck Jansen van Daventer (N. Y. City Rec., Dutch Deeds, Bk. A, pp. 95, 135). He returned to Rhode Island and settled at Portsmouth in 1658. Bought lands on the Taunton River in Plymouth Colony (now Dighton, Mass.) and at Dartmouth, as well as a considerable tract on Martha's Vineyard. He was Commissioner in 1661 at Warwick, R. I. In 1665 his wife Anne was sentenced to be whipped for adultery. He deposed at Portsmouth on 13 March 1702/3, aged 80 years or thereabouts, that he was born in Hamburg and went to Barbados, where he married at Christ Church Parish, Anne, daughter of Philip and Anne Hill, and thereafter removed to R. I. with his wife's mother, who remarried Mr. John Elton and removed to Flushing and later to Staten Island and eventually went with her son Robert Hill to Virginia, where, as he had heard, she married once more, a Capt. Hudson. Dr. Peter Tallman of Guilford, Conn., was his son (Portsmouth Town Records).

Peter of Guilford (2nd col.) on 5 Nov. 1703 sold land at Dragon Swamp in Farnham Parish, Rappahannock Co., Va., as heir of Robert Hill (his uncle) of Rappahannock Co., Va. (Essex Co., Va., Deeds, Bk. 11, p. 115).

Anne (2nd col.) married 2ndly, William Potter.

Susanna (2nd col.) married Joseph Beckett [Beckwith] of New London.

Delete the nameless daughter, "——— married William Potter."

(*New Eng. Hist. & Gen. Reg.*, Vol. 69, p. 90; Vol. 85, pp. 69-74.)

THROCKMORTON. John (p. 200, 1st col.) was undoubtedly the son of Bassingburn Throckmorton, grocer and Alderman of Norwich, bapt. there 9 May 1601, who on 20 March 1621 was apprenticed to a scrivener. In 1638 this John's whereabouts was unknown to his father and, in 1640, to the latter's executors. Roger Williams says that the Providence John had been the officer of a corporation in England and had some knowledge of the law. Bassingburn belonged to the cadet branch of the Throckmortons of Coughton, co. Warwick, settled at South Elmham and Bungay, co. Suffolk. Winthrop records the arrival in the *Lion* on 5 Jan. 1630/1 of "Mr. Throckmorton" and on 18 May 1631 "Mr. George Throckmorton" was made a Freeman (*New Eng. Hist. & Gen. Register*, Vol. 3, p. 90). This may be an error for John, as George occurs no more. John was a merchant at Salem and had a landing place on the south side of Salem harbor at "Tagmutton's Cove," now in Marblehead. He

was at Salem 23:9mo:1635 (Essex Quarterly Court Files IV, 102). He had a case in Plymouth Court in 1641. He carried mail for Roger Williams and John Winthrop (Winthrop Papers, Mass. Hist. Soc.), and occurs in the New Netherlands records trading with "South River" (Delaware) and Virginia. Went with the Hutchinsons and Thomas Cornell to New Netherlands in 1642 and on 6 July 1643 had a grant of land at Vreeland (now Throggs Neck, Westchester Co., N. Y.) from Gov. Kieft. Returned to Rhode Island. Was a "Townsman" at Warwick 2 June 1651. On 26 June 1654 sold his half of Prudence Island to Mr. Richard Parker of Boston, which Mr. John Winthrop and Mr. Roger Williams had purchased of the Narragansett sachems. In 1656 he was at Barbados (Warwick Town Records, Book A, p. 67). Died between 17 March 1683/4 and 25 April 1684. Married Rebecca (?Colvill), who occurs in the Providence town records 13 March 1656/7 and the Middlesex Co., Mass., Records on 4:8mo:1660.

Freegift (2nd col.) born about 1636, died unmarried at Jamaica before 17 June 1669 (Middlesex, Mass., Probate, Misc. Docket Index, p. 405; Throckmorton Family, by C. Wickliffe Throckmorton, p. 211).

John (2nd col.) in 1675 was granted 240 acres in East Jersey "in right of his father." He had a legacy by the will of Edward Colvill, gent., of Bradwell, co. Essex, England, dated 1 Aug. 1679, proved 9 Feb. 1679/80, and the latter calls him kinsman (*New Eng. Hist. & Gen. Reg.*, Vol. 59, p. 327). J. P., Monmouth Co., N. J., 1682/3. Judge, 1683 until his death. His wife was daughter of Richard and Penelope (van Princess) Stout of Gravesend, N. Y.

Deliverance (*ib.*) married Rev. James Ashton of Middletown, N. J., Deputy to N. J. General Assembly 25 May 1669, Constable at Portland Point Court, N. J., 26 Nov. 1669. Adm. to widow Deliverance 19 May 1705.

Children (3rd col.) (named Ashton):

- i. Rev. James, of age 1693. Baptist minister at Crosswicks in Upper Freehold, N. J.
- ii. John, will proved 1 June 1744.
- iii. Mary, died unmarried 1739.
- iv. Alice, born 1671; died 27 April 1716; married 1693 Obadiah Holmes.
- v. Rebecca, married 1688 David, son of Richard and Penelope (van Princess) Stout.
- vi. Deliverance, died before 1715, married Jonathan, son of Jonathan and Sarah (Borden) Holmes.
- vii. Joseph, married Sarah ———.

Job (2nd col.) married on 2 Feb. 1683/4. Deputy from Middletown, N. J., 1693. Deposed 22 May 1708 aged 57 years. Administration to widow Sarah, 3 June 1711.

Children (3rd col.):

i. Sarah, born 2: 2mo.: 1684/5.
ii. John, born 10 Aug. 1688.
iii. Rebecca, born 10 Feb. 1690/1.
iv. Joseph, born 14 Aug. 1693.
v. Mary, born 1695.
vi. Job, born about 1699.
vii. Samuel, born 4 July 1706.
viii. Patience, born about 1708.

Joseph (2nd col.). Mariner. Landowner in East and West Jersey, New York and Pennsylvania. On 25 Dec. 1685 had license to purchase 1200 acres of Indian lands at Crosswick, N. J. On 20 Jan. 1687/8 bought 474 acres in East Jersey of his brother John. Will dated at Philadelphia, 2 Dec. 1689, proved 3 Oct. 1690. Unmarried.

(2nd col.) A daughter married ——Taylor and died before 30 Oct. 1666. ("Throckmorton Family History" by F. G. Sitherwood, 1929.)

THURSTON. Jonathan (p. 201, 2nd col.), in his will change "daughter Abigail Wait" to "daughter Abigail White." William White, Jr., of Dartmouth married, 2 Oct. 1729, Abigail Thurston, dau. of Jonathan and Sarah (*American Genealogist*, Vol. 17, p. 194; Arnold's Vital Rec. of R. I., Vol. 4, pp. 66, 64.)

TOSH. William (p. 207, 1st col.) is evidently identical with the William Mackontoss, who was one of the Scotch prisoners taken at Worcester and shipped to New England in the *Sarah and John* to work at their iron works at Braintree, Mass. (*New Eng. Hist. & Gen. Reg.*, Vol. 1, p. 379). He went from Braintree to Block Island in the first settlement as a tenant of Thomas Faxon of Braintree and occurs there on 17 Sept. 1662, as "William Toys Scotsman" (*cf.* Tormet Rose, *ante*). Married at Braintree on 7: 6mo.: 1660, Jael Swilvan (?Sullivan).

Mercy (2nd col.). To her children add Mary, born at Lyme, Conn., on 5 Jan. 1692/3, and Mercy, born about 1695.

TURNER. Lawrence (p. 209, 1st col.) is evidently the Lawrence Turner who figures as an unsavory character in the early Essex Co., Mass., Court Records as of Lynn, Mass. His Rhode Island career shows him as a reformed character.

VINCENT. William (p. 213, 1st col.) was the son of Thomas and Fridiswide (Carpenter) Vincent of Amesbury, Wilts., bapt. 17 June 1638 (*cf. R. I. Hist. Soc. Coll.*, Vol. 14, p. 81). His mother was a sister of William Carpenter of Providence.

WANTON. Edward (p. 215, 1st col.) was first of York, Me., where in Nov. 1651 he bought land at Cape Neddick, which he sold in Nov. 1657 to his brother-in-law, John Smith. By tradition he came, aged 19 years, with his mother from London. He was a shipwright at Boston in 1658 and a resident of Scituate, Mass., in 1661. Deposed in April 1716 aged 84 years that about 64 years before he had lived in Wells, Me. Married 1st, Elizabeth ———, and 2ndly, Mary ———. The first three children were by the first wife.

John (2nd col.) of Scituate and Newport. Delete "married Mary Stafford" and replace with "married Mary, daughter of Sylvester and Elizabeth (Norton) Stover of Cape Neddick, York, Me. (their intention in Boston was forbid 15 Nov. 1695, but they were married nevertheless) (Libby's *Gen. Dic. Me. & N. H.*, Pt. V, pp. 718, 667).

Edward (3rd col.), son of William & Ruth, died in Barbados on 21 Feb. 1720/1 and was buried in the Cathedral churchyard at Bridgetown (*N. E. Hist. & Gen. Reg.*, Vol. 67, p. 371).

WHALLEY. Theophilus (p. 221, 1st col.) was of Farnham Parish, Rappahannock Co., Va., prior to his coming to Rhode Island (Essex Co., Va., Records).

WIGHTMAN. George (p. 226, 1st col.) was probably the son of George Wightman, whose brother, Ralph Wightman, citizen and merchant tailor of St. Mary-le-Bow parish, London, married Katherine, sister of Roger Williams, and whose will was dated 27 Dec. 1628 and proved 9 Feb. 1628/9 (*N. E. Hist. & Gen. Reg.*, Vol. 43, p. 293).

WOOD. John (p. 230, 1st col.) was also of Newport. He, "of Newport," was defendant in a suit in the Newport Quarter Sessions Court on 7 June 1643 and was a surety in that Court in March 1645; in Dec. 1646 he was sued in the Newport Court by William Withington (Chapin's *Doc. Hist. of R. I.*, Vol. 2). He was granted 40 acres, "near William Weeden's farm." Freeman at Portsmouth 10 July 1648. Juryman at a Trial Court at Warwick 26 May 1649. On 1 March 1649/50 "John Wood Sr." of Portsmouth bought 45 acres in that town near the Newport line. He was recorded as a Freeman of Newport in 1655, the year of his death.

ALMY. William (p. 236, 1st col.) of Saugus, Sandwich, Mass., and Portsmouth, R. I. Probably born at Dunton Basset or South Kilworth, co. Leics., about 1600 (deposed 20 (4) 1654 aged about 53; Pope). Was son of Christopher, gent., of South Kilworth (Thomas[2], John[1]). The Almey pedigree appears in Vis. Northants. 1619, Metcalf. Married at Lutterworth, co. Leics., 1626, by license, as William, gent., of South Kilworth, to Audrey Barlow of Lutterworth. Exec. of father's will 29 Oct. 1624. Defendant in a suit in Ct. Requests concerning tithes of Lutterworth parsonage, commenced against his father, in 1625 and styled "William, yeoman." Settled at Saugus, with other Leicestershire men, 1631. Returned and brought back wife and children, 1635. Removed to Sandwich 1637 and to Portsmouth 1641.

Anne or Annis (2nd col.) bapt. So. Kilworth 26 Feb. 1626/7.

Christopher (2nd col.). His wife Elizabeth died 12 Jan. 1714/5 in her 72nd, 73rd or 78th year. Of Shrewsbury, N. J., 22 June 1676 (*R. I. Hist. Soc. Coll.*, Vol. 21, p. 131).

Peleg (4th col.), son of Job and Bridget, died 18 Feb. 1734/5 at Barbados, buried in St. Michael's churchyard at Bridgetown, Barbados (*New Eng. Hist. & Gen. Reg.*, Vol. 67, p. 370; see *ib.*, Vol. 71, pp. 310-322).

ARNOLD. Thomas (p. 240, 1st col.). Delete Cheselbourne, co. Dorset, and his ancestry as given by Austin. He was probably the Thomas Arnold of Hollesley, co. Suffolk, named in the will of his father William Arnold of Hollesley, husbandman, dated 22 Nov. 1616, when Thomas was under age. Richard Arnold of London, goldsmith, who came apparently, from Gillingham, co. Kent, in his will, dated 8 Nov. 1644, left a legacy to Richard Arnold of Kelshall, co. Suffolk (13 miles from Hollesley), son of the testator's uncle William Arnold, and to Richard Arnold of Killingworth, co. Warwick, son of his uncle Richard, and they were to pay to their brothers and sisters "except Thomas Arnold who is now supposed to be in New England or some other part beyond the seas." Richard Arnold of Offchurch, near Kenilworth, husbandman, in his will dated 2 July 1604, proved 3 Aug. 1604, names a son Thomas, then under age. Of these two Thomases the Suffolk man is undoubtedly our man for two reasons. First: Thomas of Providence married, probably in England, the daughter of George Parkhurst, who came to Watertown from Ipswich, co. Suffolk (12 miles from Hollesley). Second: Watertown, where Thomas Arnold first settled, on coming to New England, was almost entirely an East Anglian settlement, made up of persons from Essex and Suffolk. (*Cf. New Eng. Hist. & Gen. Reg.*, Vol. 69, pp. 68-69; *ib.*, Vol. 48, pp. 374-75.)

William (p. 243, 1st col.). Delete Cheselbourne, co. Dorset, and ancestry as given by Austin. The pedigree compiled by Somerby is entirely erroneous. Born at Ilchester, co. Somerset,

24 June 1587, son of Nicholas of Ilchester, tailor, and his wife, Alice, dau. of John and Alice Gully.

Stephen (2nd col.), bapt. at Ilchester, 22 Dec. 1622. (*R. I. Hist. Soc. Coll.*, Vol. 14, pp. 46-49.)

BRENTON. Martha (p. 252, 2nd col.) married, probably, John Garde not Card.

BROWN. Chad (p. 258, 1st col.) married at High Wycombe, co. Bucks., 11 Sept. 1626, Elizabeth Sharparowe (*New Eng. Hist. & Gen. Reg.*, Vol. 65, p. 84). On 10 June 12 Eliz. (1570) Chad Brown, son of Arthur of Melcheborne, co. Beds., was apprenticed for 8 years to Leonard Omston of Northampton, currier (*New Eng. Hist. & Gen. Reg.*, Vol. 47, p. 266). This may refer to the grandfather of the emigrant.

[*To be continued*]

THE AMERICAN GENEALOGIST
Whole No. 79 Jan., 1944 Vol. XX, No. 3

ADDITIONS AND CORRECTIONS TO AUSTIN'S GENEALOGICAL DICTIONARY OF RHODE ISLAND

By G. Andrews Moriarty, AM., LL.B., F.S.A.

[Continued from Vol. 20, p. 121]

BULGAR. Richard (p. 30, 1st col.) was dismissed to church at Exeter, N. H., from Boston church, 6 Jan. 1638/9. Lived at Exeter but was a planter at Dover, N. H., 1640. Lieutenant, 1641. In 1642 witnessed a deed of Ralph Blaisdell of Salisbury to Robert Knight of York. In 1646/7 was of Boston and acting for Henry Walton, gent., of Portsmouth, R. I., formerly of Lynn, Mass. Admitted inhabitant and freeman at Portsmouth, R. I., 29 April 1650. Licensed to sell beer 5 June 1654. One of town auditors 3 June 1656. Town Sargeant, 4 Oct. 1656, 29 May 1657, 7 June 1658, and 6 June 1659. Solicitor General, R. I., 1656. Town Clerk, Portsmouth, 4 June 1660, 3 June 1661, 1 June 1663, 5 June 1665. Town Recorder 9 July 1660. On Coroner's Inquest on body of Richard Elles, 3 June 1661. Granted land at Portsmouth, 12 Oct. 1664. Occurs frequently in Portsmouth records up to 1679. Dead before 29 5 mo., 1687.

Married Lettice, daughter of John and Leonora (Pawley) Underhill, and step-daughter of Capt. Richard Morris.

Add (2nd col.) John, bapt. Boston, 20 April 1634. Probably died young.

(Libby's *Gen. Dic. Me. & N. H.*, Pt. II, p. 118; Records of the Town of Portsmouth [printed], to which reference is made for further information about him.)

FIELD. John (p. 75, 1st. col.). His brother James Field of St. Alban's, Herts, bequeathed £100 by his will to his brother, John Field, and if he be dead to his children. (Note in the handwriting of Thomas Olney, the Providence town clerk, made after the death of John Field in 1686. In the original paper the words "dwelling in Providence in New England" are crossed out; *cf. New Eng. Hist. & Gen. Reg.*, Vol. 51, p. 359.) Field belonged to the small group of Hertfordshire men of whom Thomas Olney was an outstanding figure, who were among the earliest adherents of Roger Williams at Providence. It may be suggested that the fact that Roger's mother belonged to the prominent St. Alban's family of Pemberton may have influenced these Hertfordshire men to join him in the settlement of Providence.

MORRIS. Richard (Thomas) (p. 134, 1st col.). Joined Boston Church with 2nd wife and step-son, Capt. John Underhill, on 27 Aug. 1630. Called 'an experienced soldier.' Signed the Exeter

(N. H.) Combination 1639 and was a 'Ruler' in that settlement. Dismissed with wife from the Boston to the Exeter Church. Dealing in pipestaves at Dover, 1639/40. Called Lt. in July and Capt. in Nov. 1639. Went to Portsmouth, R. I., and admitted an inhabitant there 1: 8 mo.: 1640. In charge of arms there, 15 Oct. 1643. Juryman, 21 Nov. 1649. Had suit with John Sanford, 8 July 1650. On Com. to treat with the Narragansett Sachems 8 April 1656. Sold land at Portsmouth to Thomas Brownell on 15 Jan. 1657/8.

Married 2ndly, at The Hague, Holland on 28 Nov. 1628, as "Dirck Thomas (i.e. Richard son of Thomas) swordcutler and widower from England" Leonora (Pawley), widow of John Underhill of Warwickshire, who was related through her mother to Capt. Richard Boynthon, the early Cornish settler at Saco; and 3rdly in Rhode Island, before 18 Dec. 1658, Mary ——. His 2nd wife was the mother of the famous Capt. John Underhill and of Lettice wife of Richard Bulger.

(Libby's *Gen. Dic. Me. & N. H.*, Pt. IV, p. 494; Records of Town of Portsmouth, R. I. [printed]; Underhill Genealogy by Frost [1932] I, 14-27.)

BROWNING. Nathaniel (p. 262, 1st col.). Will of Nathaniel Browning, made by the Portsmouth Town Council on 4 April 1673. His five children, Mary, Sarah, William, Rebecca and Jane, all under age and unmarried but Mary the eldest soon to come of age. Land given by William Freeborne to the deceased Nathaniel Browning and Sarah his wife by deed of 2 Jan. 1652/3 mentioned. Estate given to the children by their grandfather William Freeborne. Executors: Gideon Freeborne and Clement Weaver of Newport, "both nearly related to the said children."

(2nd col.) *Add* Mary born after 1652. Married Thomas Manchester Jr. (son of Thomas Sr.) prior to 6 Jan. 1677/8 and had at least William and Thomas.

(2nd col.) *Add*: Sarah born after 1652, died s.p. before 6 Jan. 1677/8. On the latter date the estate of "Sarah Browning, single woman, late of Portsmouth" was divided by the Portsmouth Town Council among her brothers and sisters, namely: Mary, wife of Thomas Manchester Jr. 1/4; William Browning at 21 years 1/4; sisters Rebecca and Jane at 16 or marriage 1/4 each. Administration to Gideon Freeborne uncle of the deceased.

(2nd col.) William. Add born after 1657.

(2nd col.) Add: Rebecca born after 1662.

(2nd col.) Jane. Add born after 1662.

(*R. I. Hist. Soc. Coll.*, Vol. 21, p. 128.)

CADMAN. Add to George (p. 268, 2nd col.): The will of Samuel Cornell (Thomas[1]) of Dartmouth, dated 5: 3 mo: 1699,

proved 7 Feb. 1714/5, named "cousins" George Cadman and Thomas Cornell (Thomas[2], Thomas[1]).

Elizabeth (3rd col.), dau. of George. Her husband William White was undoubtedly the son of Sylvanus[3] of Scituate, Mass. (Peregrine[2], William[1]). They had, besides the children listed by Austin, Hannah, Elizabeth, Susanna, Abner, Oliver and Thomas. William was both blacksmith and gentleman. He was on a petit jury at Dartmouth on 5 July 1705. Agent at Dartmouth for Thomas Coleman of Scituate in 1713. Deputy from Dartmouth in 1724. Constable 29 March 1715/6. Proprietor at Dartmouth 1714. His house near Hix's Bridge is still standing. Will dated 6 Jan. 1768, proved 3 Oct. 1780. "Very aged." Names his son, William; his deceased son, George's ten children, i.e. Israel, Peleg, William, Silvanus, Obed, Ruth, Sarah, Hannah, Mary and Eunice; daughter Sarah Brown; daughter Hannah Taber; sons Roger, Christopher and Thomas; children of daughter Elizabeth Slocum deceased; sons Abner and Oliver; and grandchild, Phoebe Smith. Residue to daughter Susanna. Executors, daughter Susanna, and grandson Peleg, son of his son George deceased. (*Am. Genealogist*, Vol. 17, pp. 197-206.)

CARD. Richard (p. 270, 1st col.) Probably came from the Southwest of England. Juryman at Newport, 29 Aug. 1653, in the case of Kempo Sybada vs. Edward Hull (Essex Co., Mass., Court Files, I, 314). One of the original grantees of Conanicut Island (Jamestown, R. I.) in 1656. Juryman 1654 and 1658. Married Rebecca ——, who married 2ndly, George Hassall of Newport and Westerly. Richard died before 1 July 1674.

Delete (2nd col.) John.

Joseph (2nd col.), born 1649, died 13 Oct. 1729, "aged 80 years." Married Jane ——, who died before 19 June 1717. On 1 July 1674 Newport confirmed to him 60 acres bounded "partly on Job Card land, now in the possession of his mother" (R. I. Col. Deeds, I, 56). Taxed Newport 1680. On 20 Nov. 1692 he bought of George Hassall and wife Rebecca of Newport and Job Card of New Shoreham 10 acres in Newport bounding in part on sd. Joseph (*ib.*, I, pt. 1, 73). On 8 May 1701, he bought land in Newport of James Card (*ib.*, II, 134). Constable at Newport 3 June 1702. Grand Juryman on 5 July 1711 and on 23 Jan. 1706/7 a member of the Second Baptist Church. Will 19 June 1717, proved 4 Nov. 1729; names children Elisha, Joseph, Anne Sisson, Mary Phillips and Elizabeth Arnold and grandchildren Edward Card and Jane Sisson.

James (2nd col.) of Newport and Kingstown. On 8 May 1701, he, "of Kingstown," sold land in Newport to Joseph Card. Married 1st, —— (perhaps Ruth Havens); 2ndly, Martha West on 24 March 1703. She married 2ndly, 9 Nov. 1710 Jeremiah Fones. Adm. on his estate to widow Martha 1705. Children: Jonathan, born 1684; Peleg, born about 1686; by 2nd wife: James, born Kingstown Sept. 1703; Martha born Kingstown 24 Aug. 1706. (He had probably also a dau. Ruth, who married Samuel Whipple at Groton, Conn., on 15 Nov. 1720.)

Job (2nd col.). Transfer to this Job the Job in 3rd col. He was also of South Kingstown and Westerly. Add 2nd wife Margery, widow of Daniel Tosh and daughter of John Acres, married at New Shoreham 28 May 1716 (New Shoreham Rec. I, 164); married 3rdly, Hannah Bull at South Kingstown 27 Aug. 1724. Owned 10 acres at Newport on 1 July 1674, then in possession of his mother. Freeman, New Shoreham, April 1686 (*ib.*, I, 138) and on 10 Jan. 1692/3 (*ib.*, I, 201). Constable 1691. At Pettyquamscott (South Kingstown) in 1695. On New Shoreham Town Council, 9 April 1700. Rate-maker there, 6 June 1701. On 15 Dec. 1698, owned land at Matunock (in South Kingstown) in partnership with William Champlin. On 14 April 1703 he was Second Townsman at New Shoreham; 17 Aug. 1705, Deputy Warden (*ib.*, I, 338). On this date he, and wife Martha, witnessed the Quaker marriage of Dr. John Rodman at New Shoreham (*ib.*). Town Clerk and Deputy 1708. Removed to Westerly and on 24 July 1713 as "of Westerly" sold land at New Shoreham (*ib.*, I, 437). Justice at Westerly, 1714, and Moderator of Westerly town meeting on 2: 1 mo.: 1714/5 (Westerly Town Meeting-Rec.). At time of his second marriage, 28 May 1716, called "of New Shoreham," but resided in that part of Westerly later set off as Charlestown. He made his will 5 Jan. 1730/1, proved at Charlestown 7 Sept. 1739, as "of South Kingstown." His daughter Jane married before 21 Sept. 1721 Capt. Isaac Sheffield and had Mary and Martha. His daughter Sarah had a son Joshua Rathbone, and married on 20 April 1727 Capt. Isaac Sheffield, her sister's widower (*New Eng. Hist. & Gen. Reg.*, Vol. 83, pp. 89-93.)

CASE. James[2] (William[1]) (p. 274, 2nd col.) died before 1 May 1719. His daughter Susanna married John, son of Thomas Lake of Dartmouth; he also had daughters, Penelope (married Joseph, son of the said Thomas Lake), Mary (m. ——— Howard); Elizabeth (m. ——— Springer) and Sarah (m. ——— Huddlestone).

CHAMPLIN. Jeffrey (p. 274, 1st col.) was undoubtedly a near kinsman of the John Champlin "late of Fayal but now of Newport merchant," who, as "heir of John Garde deceased," freed the latter's negro on 30 March 1673 (*Mag. of N. E. Hist.* III, 232 *et seq.*). This was probably the John Garde, who married Martha, daughter of William Brenton (Austin calls him Card), who was dead when Brenton made his will on 9 Feb. 1673/4. This John Garde was probably the son or nephew of John Garde, merchant of Fayal in May 1643 (Aspinwall, p. 109), who was later of Newport, R. I., where he died on 7 Aug. 1665 aged 61 years. The elder John Garde was probably a brother of Roger Garde of Biddeford, co. Devon, and York, Maine, whose daughter, Rebecca (bapt. at Biddeford 9 May 1616) married there on 25 Nov. 1641 William Champlin. (Libby's *Gen. Dic. Me. & N. H.*, Pt. III, p. 252). As Jeffrey Champlin lived in Newport next to John Champlin, it seems likely that John Champlin was his nephew and the child of William and Rebecca (Garde) Champlin, in which case Jeffrey evidently came from in or around Biddeford.

Jeffrey (2nd col.). He undoubtedly had other children besides Jeffrey 3rd, among them a daughter Amy, who married Robert[3] Hazard (Robert[2], Thomas[1]) of South Kingstown, who by his wife Amy, had a son "Stout" Jeffrey Hazard.

CODDINGTON. William (p. 276, 1st col.). Son of Robert Coddington of Marston, co. Lincs., a prosperous yeoman, by his wife Margaret, who m. 2ndly, Richard Wylles, and 3rdly, Richard Smyth. William son of Robert Coddington born about 1602-3 ("William Coddington A Sketch," by Emily Coddington Williams, Boston 1941). William of Newport had a seal marked "R. C.", doubtless his father's (Chapin's Doc. Hist. R. I., II, 23). Burgess of Boston, Lincs. 1625. His sons Michael and Samuel were bapt. and buried at St. Botolph's Church, Boston, Lincs. Married 1st, probably Mary Burt of Alford about 1626; 2ndly, Mary, daughter of Richard Moseley of Owsden, Bury St. Edmund's, Suffolk (Vis. of London, Harl. Soc.)

COOKE. Thomas (p. 282, 1st col.). Called "brother" by Giles Slocum, so undoubtedly from Somersetshire. Bond on his estate given by widow Mary 6 Feb. 1673/4. Mary the second wife of Thomas was probably Mary, daughter of William and Dionis Havens.

Sarah (2nd col.) delete.

Capt. Thomas, Jr. (2nd col.). Oral will. Division of estate of Capt. Thomas Cooke, Jr., 12 Oct. 1670. Wife Thamasin, then deceased, eldest son Thomas executor, sons John, George, Stephen and Ebenezer under age and daus. Sarah, wife of Peter Parker, Mary, wife of Thomas Langford, Elizabeth, Phoebe and Martha. Bond 14 Oct. 1670.

Add to his children (in 3rd col.) Sarah (from 2nd col.); Mary, married Thomas Langford; Elizabeth. (Ebenezer was his youngest son.)

(3rd col.) Thomas[3] (Capt. Thomas[2], Thomas[1]). Will dated

29 Jan. 1670/1. To brother John at 21. To brothers George, Stephen and youngest brother Ebenezer at 21. Sister Sarah, wife of Peter Parker. Overseers and executors, grandfather Thomas Cooke, uncle John Cooke, and Joseph Torrey Sen. (The settlers at Monmouth, N. J., were a later generation.)
(*R. I. Hist. Soc. Coll.*, Vol. 21, p. 129; Vol. 26, pp. 59-61).

DYER. William (p. 290, 1st col.), son of William Dyer, yeoman, of Kirkby Laythorpe, Lincs., bapt. 19 Sept. 1609. The father was churchwarden and also had children Nicholas and Margaret. The father may have been a younger son of John Dyer of Bratton Seymour, co. Somerset and Jane Ernley (Byfleet) (cf. Vis. Somerset 1623). He was apprenticed as the son of William Dyer, yeoman, of Kirkby, Lincs., on 20:6: 1625 to Walter Blackborne, fishmonger, and on 19 Aug. 1641 William Dyer, "millyner", "now in New England" was taxed as a member of the Fishmonger's Company (Lay Sub. London Livery Companies, 1641, at P.R.O.). On 14 Dec. 1635 and 16 Jan. 1637/8 he was granted land at Rumney Marsh (Chelsea, Mass.). (*R. I. Hist. Soc. Coll.*, Vol. 30, pp. 9-26.)

FREEBORN. Sarah (p. 296, 2nd col.) married Nathaniel Browning; add to their children Mary b. after 1652, m. Thomas Manchester, Jr.; Sarah, died single bef. 6 Jan. 1677/8; Jane, born after 1662; and Rebecca, born after 1662.

GORTON. Samuel (p. 302, 1st col.). Bapt. at Manchester, Lancs., 12 Feb. 1692/3, son of Thomas, husbandman, and Anne, of Gorton. Thomas was probably son of Thomas, who was taxed at Gorton 1543, and he was the probable son of Thomas of Gorton taxed 1524. They were members of an ancient family settled at Gorton in Manchester, which occurs there in 1332 and 1421. On 10 Feb. 1634/5 he was complainant in the chancery case of Gorton vs. Foster and Lambe, where he is described as "Samuel Gorton of London, clothier." On 27 Jan. 1647/8, while in England, he brought suit in the Chancery against one Walker touching his dealings with John Dukinfield, the member of a gentle Lancashire family. Married prior to 11 Jan. 1629/30 Mary, daughter of John Mayplet, haberdasher, of St. Lawrence Jewry, London, and Mary his wife. She was granddaughter of the Rev. John Mayplet, B.A. (Queen's Coll., Camb.) 1564, M.A. 1567, Rector of Great Leighs, co. Essex, and Vicar of Northolt, co. Middlesex, a writer upon natural history and astrology. Mary Gorton's brother, Dr. John Mayplet (Christ Church, Oxon), B.A. 1634, M.A. 1638, M.D. 1647, was Principal of Gloucester Hall (now Worcester College, Oxon.) and Physician to Charles II. He later resided at Bath, co. Somerset, and is

buried in the Abbey Church there with a tablet to his memory. (*New Eng. Hist. & Gen. Reg.*, Vol. 82, pp. 185-93, 333-42; Vol. 70, p. 115.) Samuel was a volunteer for the Pequot War from Plymouth.

Othniel (3rd col.) married 1st, Mercy dau. of Roger and Mary (1st wife) Burlingame and 2ndly, Mercy, granddau. of Moses and Mary (Knowles) Lippett. (*R. I. Hist. Soc. Coll.*, Vol. 19, p. 16).

Add Thomas, omitted by Austin. Brother of Samuel. Bapt. Manchester 17 Nov. 1588, died, probably *s.p.*, at Portsmouth, R. I., between 16 July and 21 Nov. 1649. Married at Manchester, 14 Sept. 1612, Anne Grimshaw. Volunteer to the Pequot War from Plymouth, Mass., 1637, with his brother Samuel. Ferryman at Portsmouth, R. I., 7 Sept. 1640. On a jury at Portsmouth, 1 Dec. 1641. Freeman and General Sergeant, 16 March 1641/2; Ensign for Portsmouth 13:1: 1644; sued by Richard Morris in 1646 for the "extravagancie of his wife's tongue" in abusing Richard (Chapin's Doc. Hist. R. I., Vol. II, pp. 108, 120, 128, 161). Present at a Portsmouth town meeting, 29 Aug. 1644. Had land laid out to him at Wading River on 25 Jan. 1648/9. Town Sergeant and Water Bailiff at Portsmouth on 16 July 1649. Successor appointed 21 Nov. 1649. Died without issue or removed.

GOULD. (p. 307, 3rd col.). Daniel^3 (Daniel^2, Jeremiah^1) of Newport and Kingstown. Died at Barbados. The will of Daniel Gould of Rhode Island, mariner, at present in Barbados, dated 5 March, proved 30 March 1694. To wife Mary and sons Jeremiah and Thomas, his lands at Quidincitt in Narragansett. To son Daniel, house in Newport. To daughter Mary, under 18, 70 acres at Hope Island. Executors in Barbados, friends Joseph Grove, John Grove and William Chearmely of Barbados, and in Rhode Island, father Daniel Gould and father-in-law Walter Clarke (*New Eng. Hist. & Gen. Reg.*, Vol. 67, p. 362).

HARRIS. William (p. 312, 1st col.) had been a morris dancer in Kent before he came to New England (Roger Williams).

HAZARD. Thomas (p. 320, 1st col.) probably came from Dorsetshire and probably had, besides Robert, sons Thomas of Newtown, Long Island, abt. 1652-3; Jonathan of Newtown in 1664; and Nathaniel occurs there is 1659 (Cal. of N. Y. Hist. Manuscripts, Dutch, p. 190).

Robert (3rd col.). His wife Amie was probably a daughter of Jeffrey^2 Champlin (Jeffrey^1).

[To be continued]

The American Genealogist

Whole Number 80 Volume XX, No. 4

April, 1944

ADDITIONS AND CORRECTIONS TO AUSTIN'S GENEALOGICAL DICTIONARY OF RHODE ISLAND

By G. Andrews Moriarty, A.M., LL.B., F.S.A.

HELME. Christopher (p. 322, 1st col.) was son of William Helme of Long Sutton (Sutton St. Mary), co. Lincs., gent., probably by his third wife, Priscilla, daughter of Christopher Went-

worth, gent., of Waltham; grandson of William Elmes or Helmes of Long Sutton and Elizabeth, daughter of John Payne or Baynes of Southwell, co. Notts; great-grandson of John Elmes or Helmes of Northants, living at Long Sutton, and of Mary, daughter of William Cookson of Long Sutton. Arms: Ermine 2 bars sable each charged with 3 elm leaves gold. [Ms. c 23, College of Arms; Dodsworth Mss. Lib. 22, fo. 55; Add. Mss. 5822 (Cole); Maddison's Lincs. Ped. Harl. Soc.].

Christopher Wentworth's wife was Catherine Marbury, sister of the Rev. Francis Marbury, father of Anne Hutchinson and Katherine Scott. Christopher Helme evidently came to New England with his cousin William Wentworth and went with him to Exeter, N. H., in 1639. He was sued at Piscataqua (Portsmouth, N. H.) in 1642 and in 1644 the Court ordered certain moneys sent to him (at this date he was probably at Warwick, R. I., where he lived henceforth). That same year he witnessed the submission of the Narragansett sachems. In November 1649 Valentine Hill (the prominent merchant of Boston and Dover, N. H.) sold 500 acres near Oyster River (Dover, N. H.), which he had purchased of Christopher Helme, then in possession of Darby Field (the Irishman, who was of Dover and the first white man to climb Mount Washington) (*cf.* Libby's *Gen. Dict. of Me. & N. H.*, Pt. 3, p. 324).

He was received an inhabitant of Warwick and was granted land 1 May 16— (Early Rec. Town of Warwick, pp. 321, 322). Chosen Town Sergeant, 8 Aug. (?1647) (*ib.*, p. 77). One of those to lay out lots and highways, 13 Aug. 1647 (*ib.*, p. 78). Signed a list of Warwick inhabitants, 10 Nov. 1648 (*ib.*, p. 73). Disenfranchised by the town for seditious speeches, 23 Jan. 1647/8 (*ib.*, p. 307). Mrs. Helmes accepted as an inhabitant, 8 Aug. 1648 (*ib.*, p. 1).

On 19 Dec. 16— his widow Margaret gave a deed of land in Warwick to Richard Carder (*ib.*, p. 331), and on 13 Jan. 1661/2 his son and heir William gave Carder a quitclaim deed of the same. (In the printed copy of Mrs. Helmes' deed the date is given as "19 Dec. —56." This is wrong, it is "19 Dec. 16—," the rest being worn away.—*Richard LeBaron Bowen.*)

HOPKINS. Thomas (p. 324, 1st col.) was the son of William Hopkins of Yeovilton, co. Somerset, by his wife Joan (bp. at Ilchester, co. Somerset, 30 Nov. 1577), daughter of Nicholas Arnold of Ilchester and his first wife Alice Gulley. Joan was sister of William Arnold, the early settler of Providence. Thomas Hopkins was bapt. at Yeovilton 7 April 1616. He came to New England in 1635 with his uncle, William Arnold. He was the great-grandfather of Gov. Stephen Hopkins, signer of the Declaration of Independence, and of Esek Hopkins, the first Commander-in-Chief of the American Navy (*R. I. Hist. Soc. Coll.*, Vol. 14, p. 47).

KNIGHT. Richard (p. 330, 1st col.) was first of Hampton, N. H., a carpenter. He may perhaps have come from co. Norfolk, England, whence most of the Hampton settlers came. On 4 Aug. 1640 he agreed with the town of Hampton to build and keep a mill at the landing and was granted 100 acres. On 14 Sept. 1640 he contracted to build the meeting house. On 29 Jan. 1640/1 he was to make a gate for the pound. In Dec. 1641 he was defendant in a suit brought by Stephen Kent. In 1644 he was suspected of theft and was then "of Salisbury," Mass. In 1645 a warrant was issued for the arrest of Richard Knight of Hampton and in Feb. 1646 he sold his house and mill in Hampton to Christopher Lawson of Boston and left for Rhode Island. On 9 Sept. 1645 Joseph Armetage was ordered by the Court to hold all the goods in his hands of "Richard Knight late of Hampton, now of Rhode Island" (Essex Quarterly Court Files, Vol. 1, p. 88; *cf.* History of Hampton). In Dec. 1646 he had a suit in the Newport, R. I., Court against William Jaffray (Aquidneck Quarterly Court Files). Married first, ———, by whom he had a son living in England on 8 Feb. 1648/9, and secondly, Sarah, daughter of James Rogers (*cf.* R. I. Colony Deeds, ed. Chapin, I, 6).

To his children (2nd col.) add Richard, probably; of Newport and Little Compton, weaver, who on 7:4 mo.:1680 had leave to sojourn at Portsmouth. Summoned before the Newport Court for contempt, 6 Sept. 1681 (Newport Co. Court Files, Bk. A, p. 58). Named on 7 Dec. 1692 by Idido Butts as among the rioters at Daniel Wilcox's house in Little Compton, resisting the Massachusetts authorities (Supreme Jud. Ct. Files, Suffolk Co., Mass., No. 2787). He had a daughter Mary married at Little Compton on 19 June 1713 to Joseph Springer.

Add Priscilla (2nd col.), probably; before the Newport Court 25 March 1684/5 for fornication (Newport Co. Ct. Files, Bk. A, p. 70).

Rebecca (2nd col.), probably; gave 6/ towards building the Quaker Meeting House at Mashapaug in 1702.

John (2nd col.), eldest son. Before the Newport Court 11 May 1674 for stealing a bridle and summoned to the Rochester (Kingstown, R. I.) Court on 14 June 1687 (Newport Co. Ct. Files, Bk. A, pp. 20, 82). About 1678 granted lots at East Greenwich. On 10 Oct. 1683 " Sarah Knight widow, now residing in East Greenwich" deeded land there to eldest son John (East Greenwich Deeds, I, 9). He "of Dept ford" (i.e. East Greenwich) sold the same land on 8 Nov. 1688 to Gideon Freeborn of Portsmouth (*ib.* II, 236). On 24 Oct. 1687, Capt. James Fitch of Norwich, Conn., leased his farm at Peagscomsuch (Plainfield and Canterbury) to James Sweet et als., including John Knight, "all living in the Narragansett Country" (New London Co. Ct. Files, Bundle 1705). On 16 Sept. 1690 he sued James Sweet for his portion of the rent due to Fitch (New London Co. Ct. Rec., Bk. 7, p. 32). On 27 Oct. 1701 his wife was aided by the town of Providence, and on 11 Jan. 1701/2 her inventory was allowed by the Providence Town Council.

To the children of John (3rd col.), add perhaps Sarah married at Norwich 2 Feb. 1707/8 Enos Randall of Colchester, Conn.

Jonathan (2nd col.). On 30 Jan. 1681/2, Jonathan Knight of Warwick sold land on the north side of the Patuxet River (Warwick Deeds, A2, p. 265). He bought land in Warwick on 19 April 1684 (*ib.*, I, 39) and on 7 Nov. 1684 (*ib.*, p. 43). Taxed at Providence, 3 April 1698, with his son Jonathan, Jr.

David (2nd col.). To his children add David, born at Woodstock 10:12:1693, and Sarah, born there on 9 Dec. 1695, married Elisha Lilly. (*cf. New Eng. Hist. & Gen. Reg.*, Vol. 87, pp. 264-70.)

KNOWLES. Henry (p. 332, 1st col.). He, aged 25, came to New England in 1635 in the *Susan & Ellen*, as servant of Ralph Hudson, who came from in or about Hull, co. York. The name Knowles occurs in Hull in the preceding century, where William Knowles was Mayor of Hull 1525-34. Henry was on a grand jury at Newport, R. I., 3 Dec. 1643, and at Portsmouth, R. I., 7:1 mo.:1644. In 1648 he attested his submission to Cromwell's government. He was a juryman in 1650. In January 1661/2, he was sued for trespass by Randall Holden.

William (2nd col.). A proprietor of East Greenwich lands 6 June 1700 and had lands in West Greenwich in 1709.

Henry (3rd col.). In 1663/4 he bought of Jan Gerardy a meadow in Warwick. In 1700 he was apparently living in East Greenwich. On 8 March 1721/2 his ear mark was recorded. In 1731 he occupied 260 acres in South Kingstown belonging to Jahleel Brenton. A Quaker.

To his children (4th col.), by first wife, add Joan and Stephen; and by second wife, Susanna and Martha.

Daniel (3rd col.). Freeman at Kingstown 1 May 1722. Apparently of Providence 1732. Married Hannah Hazard. Although not named in his will, she was probably Hannah (born 26 Feb. 1703), daughter of Robert and Amey Hazard of Kingstown, R. I.

Add children (4th col.): 1. Amey (m. 19 June 1740 Amos Greene of Charlestown, R. I.); 2. Daniel of Charlestown, R. I.;

3. Robert, born 27 Feb. 1727/8; 4. Mary, bapt. 1730 (m. David Larkin of Richmond, R. I.); 5. Hazard, b. 2 Oct. 1736 or 7; 6. Deliverance (m. 18 July 1782 John Babcock); 7. Reynolds of South Kingstown, R. I. (a Revolutionary soldier); 8. Deborah possibly (m. 2 Dec. 1761 Col. Oliver Babcock of Hopkinton, R. I.).

Robert (3rd col.) was also of Charlestown, R. I. Freeman at South Kingstown on 1 May 1722. Ear mark recorded 8 March 1721/2. A Quaker.

John (3rd col.) was first of Warwick. Freeman, Warwick 3 May 1720. Proprietor at Warwick 1748. He and his son John admitted Freemen at Richmond, R. I., 1 May 1750. Gave land at Richmond to the Quakers, 1753. To his children (4th col.) replace "daughter" with Mary (or Margaret) and add Ezekiel (a Revolutionary soldier).

Alice (3rd col.) died between 6 Oct. 1721 and 7 Oct. 1732. Her husband may have been Thomas Screven, possibly of Dover, N. H.

Margaret (3rd col.) died unmarried after 7 Oct. 1732. (*New Eng. Hist. & Gen. Reg.*, Vol. 87, pp. 359-366; 88, pp. 33-37.)

LANGFORD. Thomas (p. 336, 1st col.) married, apparently, Mary, daughter of Capt. Thomas Cooke, Jr., of Portsmouth. His will, dated 30 Oct. 1670, names his son Thomas and makes his wife Mary the executrix. Her will, 7:11 mo.:1670/1, names sister Sarah Parker and brother Thomas Cooke. Executors were "uncle" John Cooke and Obadiah Holmes. Note that John is not mentioned, so John Langford (2nd col.) of Newport, merchant, may not be his son. (*cf. R. I. Hist. Soc. Coll.*, Vol. 21, p. 129.)

MANN. William (p. 129, 1st col.). He was from Yeovilton and Ilchester, co. Somerset. His wife, Frances, was bapt. at Yeovilton 28 May 1614, the daughter of William and Joan (Arnold) Hopkins of Yeovilton. They came to New England in 1635 with his wife's uncle, William Arnold, the early settler of Providence (*R. I. Hist. Soc. Coll.*, Vol. 14, p. 47).

MOTT. Adam (p. 344, 1st col.) was the son of "oulde John Mott," who was admitted a freeman at Aquidneck in 1638. In 8 mo.: 1639 John Mott's land is mentioned. On 29 Aug. 1644, 25 Jan. 1648/9, 2 June 1650, 19 Jan. 1651/2, 9 June 1652, 2 June 1653, 20 June 1653 and 17 June 1654, the town of Portsmouth, R. I., provided for his care (Records of the Town of Portsmouth). On 23 Jan. 1654/5, the town agreed to pay the passage of "ould John Mott to Barbados Iland and back again if he cannot be

received there, if he live to it, if the shipp owners will carrie him" (*ib.*, p. 66). On 3 July 1656 further provision was made for his keep and "the oulde mans son Adam" engaged to give a cow and a supply of corn towards it (*ib.*, p. 72). The ould man was evidently held in high esteem, for the order of 9 June 1652 provided "that there shallbe a stone house built for the more comfortabl beinge of ould John Mott in the winter" (*ib.*, p. 58).

John (2nd col.), son of Adam. The entries attributed to him by Austin refer to the above "ould John Mott," his grandfather. John, son of Adam, is named in his father's will dated 2:2 mo.: 1661, which provides that his brothers shall pay him 20/ "if he demand it in such pay as in ye place passeth for pay here amonge us." This would seem to indicate that at this time he had removed from Rhode Island.

MOWRY. Roger (p. 346, 1st col.) perhaps came from Barnstable, co. Devon, where, at this period, there was a Mowry family, in which the name of Roger frequently occurs. He probably had a first wife Elizabeth, who was a member of the First Church at Salem in 1641. His second wife, Mary, was the daughter of John Johnson of Roxbury, Mass. (*cf.* Pope's *Pioneers*, p. 260).

Bethia (2nd col.) married George Palmer. They evidently had two daughters: Hannah, wife of Nicholas Gardiner of Kingstown, and Deliverance, wife of Edward Cleveland of the same town.

OLNEY. Thomas (p. 352, 1st col.). His wife was not Mary Small but Mary Ashton; their marriage is recorded in the register of St. Alban's Abbey, Herts, on 16 Sept. 1629. She was bapt. there on 25 Aug. 1605, the daughter of James Ashton, who was buried on 27 May 1651.

Thomas (2nd col.), bapt. 6 Jan. 1631/2.

Epenetus (2nd col.), bapt. 14 Feb. 1633/4.

The name is derived from Olney in the neighboring county of Bucks; there was a knightly family of the name settled at Weston Underwood in that county in the 14th and 15th centuries.

(Clarence A. Torrey in *The American Genealogist*, Vol. 10, pp. 88-90.)

RALPH. Thomas (p. 360, 1st col.). His first wife, from whom he was divorced, was Elizabeth daughter of Isaac Desborough or Disborough of Elseworth, co. Cambridge, gent., whose will dated 6 Dec. 1660 was proved 21 Dec. 1660 (P. C. C. Nabbs 264). After her divorce from Ralph she married John Johnson of Guilford, Conn., and is named as "Elizabeth Johnson" in her father's will. Isaac Disborough was evidently a close relative of John Disborough, Oliver's Major General, and of Samuel Disborough the early settler of Guilford, Conn., who returned to England and was M. P. for Edinburgh (1656) and Mid Lothian in Oliver's Parliaments, and Chancellor of Scotland under Oliver and Richard Cromwell. Samuel died on 10 Dec. 1690 at the family manor of Elseworth, Cambs., which he purchased in 1656. It eventually descended to his granddaughter, who married Matthew Holworthy, Esq. (*New Eng. Hist. & Gen. Reg.*, Vol. 41, pp. 353-364).

ROGERS. James (p. 368, 1st col.) was born about 1609. Joined the First Baptist Church at Newport on 16 Nov. 1652. One of the purchasers of Conanicut (Jamestown, R. I.), 19 Nov. 1659. Town Sergeant of Newport, 1659. Deposed 3 May 1673 aged about 64 years (Suffolk Co. Mass. Supreme Jud. Ct. Files, No. 1245, at Boston).

Sarah (2nd col.) wife of Richard Knight. Add to their children: Richard probably; Priscilla probably; Rebecca probably.

SAYLES. John (p. 370, 1st col.). He was undoubtedly the son of John Sayles, who joined the Charlestown Church in 1630. On 1 April 1633 this John was whipped for stealing and bound to Mr. John Coggeshall for 14 years. On 4 March 1633/4 he was to be severely whipped for running away from his master, Mr. Coggeshall. On 7 April 1635, Mr. Treasurer and Mr. Pyncheon were to examine and prepare "the business between Mr. Coxall, Sayles his daughter and John Levens" (i.e. of Roxbury) (Mass. Col. Rec. I, p. 144). The elder man is evidently the John Sayles, who occurs in Providence 19:11 mo.:1645 (Providence Town Rec. II, p. 30). The late Col. Banks claimed that he came from Lavenham, co. Suffolk, but upon what evidence is not clear. He probably had, besides John of Providence and Phoebe, a son Richard, who on 1 Oct. 1663 witnessed a deed of the younger John Sayles. This Richard was taxed at Providence in 1688 (Prov. Town Rec. Vol. I, p. 6; Vol. 17, pp. 127-28). It may here be noted that the Deborah ———, who married Caleb Carr of Jamestown and had a son, Sayles Carr, born 24 Nov. 1692, was probably a daughter of John, Jr., or of this Richard. (*The American Genealogist*, Vol. 15, pp. 228-230.)

SCOTT. Richard (p. 372, 1st col.) was bapt. at Glemsford, co. Suffolk, in 1605, the son of Edward Scott, clothier, of Glemsford, by Sarah, his wife, sister of Richard Carter of Brook Hall, co. Essex. Edward was son of Edward, son of Edward of Glemsford, who is stated in the pedigree to have been the third

son of Richard Scott, third son of Sir John Scott of Scotts' Hale, co. Kent. The above is taken from the ancient illuminated pedigree on vellum, drawn up between 1608 and 1612 for Edward, father of the emigrant, with many carefully painted coats of arms. This pedigree eventually came into the possession of Richard Scott of Providence and passed down in the family of his descendants, the Scotts of Newport. It is now owned by a descendant, Mrs. Frank B. Fox of Rehoboth, Mass.

John (2nd col.), add born 1640.

II. Son (2nd col.), delete and replace with Richard.

Patience (2nd col.), add died after 1707.

(R. LeBaron Bowen in *New Eng. Hist. & Gen. Reg.*, Vol. 96, pp. 1-27.)

WAIT. Thomas (p. 404, 1st col.) may have belonged to the Wait family of Weathersfield, co. Essex. He was a husbandman. Died before 13 Sept. 1665. Married Eleanor ———, who married secondly as his second wife, Ralph Cowland of Portsmouth, about 1669, and died before 25 June 1677. Thomas was granted land in Portsmouth in 1644 and 1646. Juryman 8 July 1650. Constable 7 June 1658 and 1663. One of the purchasers of Conanicut Island, 1656. Owned land at Narragansett and Misquamicut (Westerly). Estate divided by Portsmouth Town Council, 4 Dec. 1669. Inventory 13 Sept. 1665 (*R. I. Hist. Soc. Coll.*, Vol. 21, p. 131). Division of estate between widow Eleanor and children Samuel, Thomas, Benjamin, Reuben, Jeremiah, and Mary. Son Joseph had died *s.p.* 25 Aug. 1665 and sons Thomas and Jeremiah were under age. (Portsmouth Misc. Papers.)

Samuel (2nd col.). Born about 1640, died Feb. 1676/7. His widow, Hannah, m. secondly, before 12 Oct. 1694, James Sampson of Dartmouth, Mass. (son of Henry of the *Mayflower*). He witnessed, as interpreter, an Indian deed at Narragansett on 8 March 1656/7. He testified, "aged about 22 years," concerning the above deed on 23 June 1662. Deposed 26 Feb. 1667/8, aged about 27 years. Adm. on his estate granted to his widow Hannah in Feb. 1676/7. The last three items in Austin's account of him belong to his son Samuel. To his children (3rd col.), add probably Hannah, who occurs in the Bristol Co., Mass., Court Files, 12 April 1698.

Joseph (2nd col.) died *s.p.* 25 Aug. 1665. Delete his son (3rd col.), William of Rochester, Mass. This man was William Wiett or Wyatt and misread by Austin as William Wait.

Add Benjamin (2nd col.) of Hadley, Hatfield and Deerfield, Mass. Slain at the taking of Deerfield 29 Feb. 1703/4. Married at Hatfield on 8 June 1670, Martha, dau. of John Leonard of Springfield, Mass. In the division of his father's estate he received lands at Misquamicut (Westerly, R. I.). One of the guides of Capt. William Turner at the Falls Fight, May 1676. On 3 Feb. 1703/4 William Rooker assigned 40 acres in Brookfield to Thomas Wait of Sakonnet (Little Compton, R. I.) and to Benjamin Wait of Hadley, Mass. On 24 May 1717, Jeremiah, John and Joseph Wait of Hatfield and John Belden, Joseph Smith and Ebenezer Wells, husbands of the daughters of Benjamin Wait, deceased, sold the above land to Capt. Thomas Baker of Northampton and warranted against their uncle Thomas Wait, brother of the said Benjamin (Hampshire Co., Mass., Deeds).

Children of Benjamin and Martha, add (3rd col.): 1. Mary, b. at Hatfield 25 Feb. 1672/3, m. 4 Dec. 1690 Ebenezer Wells; 2. Martha, b. 23 Jan. 1673/4; 3. Sarah, b. abt. 1676, m. John Belden; 4. Canada, b. in Canada 22 Jan. 1678/9, where her mother was an Indian captive, died 5 May 1749; m. 5 Dec. 1696 Joseph Smith; 5. John of Hatfield, b. 17 Jan. 1680/1, m. 12 Feb. 1702/3 Mary Belding; 6. Joseph, b. 17 July 1682, died 21 Jan. 1686/7; 7. Jeremiah, b. 24 Sept. 1684, died at Hatfield Dec. 1733, m. 4 April 1706 Mary Graves; 8. Lieut. Joseph, b. 11 Nov. 1688, died about 1780, m. first, 19 Nov. 1713 Hannah Billings and secondly, 22 Sept. 1720 Mary Warner.

Reuben (2nd col.). His house built in 1669, in Dartmouth, was recently standing, an interesting example of early Rhode Island architecture. It was erected between Accoxet (Westport) and Appomagansett (South Dartmouth).

Thomas (2nd col.) born soon after 1648. One of the original purchasers of Pocasset (Tiverton) from Gov. Josiah Winslow on 25 March 1680. Sold land in Dartmouth 28 Aug. 1680. Sold land in Punketest Neck (in Tiverton), 13 March 1683/4, and again as "of Little Compton" on 7 Jan. 1691/2, and also on 31 Jan. 1721/2, being then styled "of Dartmouth." Bought land in Brookfield, Mass., on 3 Feb. 1703/4 with brother Benjamin.

Jeremiah (2nd col.) was born soon after 1648. His widow m. secondly after 8 March 1690/1.

(3rd col.) Samuel³ (Samuel², Thomas¹) of Kingstown sold land in Portsmouth at "Little Silver" on 30 March 1693 to William Burrington and James Sampson and wife Hannah released her thirds on 12 Oct. 1694 (Portsmouth Deeds).

(3rd col.) Thomas³ (Reuben², Thomas¹) removed from Dartmouth to East Greenwich, R. I., and was a Freeman there 2 May 1732. His lands were in that part of East Greenwich afterwards set off as West Greenwich. On 6 June 1741 he, "of West Greenwich" deeded land there to son Thomas. On 31 Dec. 1743 he "of Dartmouth" deeded land in West Greenwich to said son, Thomas. His youngest child, Alice, was born in East Greenwich, the rest in Dartmouth.

(3rd col.) Benjamin³ (Reuben², Thomas¹) was *non compos* 14 June 1749, and William Davol and Edward Cornell were his guardians.

(3rd col.) Joseph³ (Reuben², Thomas¹). On 4 Nov. 1763 Joseph Wait of Dartmouth, yeoman, recalled a power of attorney given to his son Samuel Wait of Dartmouth, "labourer alias sea faring man." Will dated 15 Sept. 1761, proved 15 Aug. 1774. Names sons Samuel and Stephen, daughter Keziah, granddaughter Roba, dau. of his dau. Marcy Wrightington and daughters Mary Wait, Alice Sherman, Elizabeth Wilcox, Hannah Tripp and Marcy Wrightington.

To children (4th col.) add: 1. Samuel, b. Aug. 1716; 2. Mary, b. 24 May 1718; 3. Stephen; 4. Keziah; 5. Alice, m. Robert Sherman (int. 26 Nov. 1742); 6. Elizabeth, m. 29 March 1744 Barjonas Wilcox of Little Compton; 7. Hannah, m. David Tripp (int. 23 Aug. 1744); 8. Marcy, m. George Wrightington (int. 31 Dec. 1757).

(3rd col.) Reuben³ (Reuben², Thomas¹) m. Elizabeth Hathaway 2 Aug. 1720. Add children: 1. Joseph, b. 17 Sept. 1722; 2. (?) Jeremiah, m. 7 Dec. 1754 Patience Kirby; 3. (?) Elizabeth, m. 1 Nov. 1746 Joseph Hicks.

(3rd col.) Jeremiah³ (Reuben², Thomas¹) died *s.p.* 16 Sept. 1754.

(3rd col.) Thomas³ (Thomas², Thomas¹). Admitted Freeman of R. I. 10 Feb. 1746/7, when Tiverton was set off from Mass. to R. I. On 19 Feb. 1750/1 was *non compos* and son-in-law Benjamin Macomber was his guardian.

Children: 1. Joseph, b. 10 Jan. 1714/5, d. y.; 2. Thomas, b. 6 Sept. 1716; 3. Sarah, b. 23 Sept. 1717, m. Benjamin Macomber at Portsmouth, 9 May 1735; 4. Elizabeth, b. 21 Dec. 1718, feeble-minded in care of William Sanford of Tiverton on 8 April 1747; 5. John, b. 6 Nov. 1720, m. Mary Soule (int. 25 Jan. 1755); 6. Mary, b. 11 April 1722, m. abt. 1745 William Sanford, gent., of Tiverton. (*New Eng. Hist. & Gen. Reg.*, Vol. 73, pp. 291-304.)

WEEDEN. James³ (p. 414, 1st col.), bapt. 30 July 1585 at Chesham, co. Bucks., son of Richard² and Joan Weeden of Chesham (James¹, of Chesham). Undoubtedly a descendant of a cadet branch of the ancient feudal family of the name, who held Chesham as early as 1333. Married first at Chesham, 11 Sept. 1615, Philippa (bapt. Chesham 14 Jan. 1587/8), dau. of William and Joan Cocke of Bilenden in Chesham, who was the mother of his children. On 16 May 1651 he was on a Committee at Portsmouth. Juryman 2 June 1653, 4 June 1655, and 4 Oct. 1656. Rate-maker 17 June 1654. Agreed *re* land with William Freeborne on 31 Aug. 1657.

Children all bapt. at Chesham: 1. John, bapt. 15 Sept. 1616, alive 9 Jan. 1636/7; 2. Deacon William, bapt. 30 May 1619; 3. Alice, bapt. 26 Sept. 1621 (probably child of James buried 2 March 1628/9); 4. James, bapt. 10 Feb. 1624/5; 5. Anna, bapt. 1627, alive 9 Jan. 1636/7; 6. Martha, bapt. 1 June 1632, alive 9 Jan. 1636/7.

(*New Eng. Hist. & Gen. Reg.*, Vol. 76, pp. 115-129.)

WESTCOTT. Steukeley (p. 416, 1st col.) m. at Yeovil, co. Somerset, 5 Oct. 1619, Julian Marchante.

To his children add: Samuel, bapt. Yeovil 31 March 1622, probably died young. The dau. Damaris was bapt. at Yeovil, 27 Jan. 1620/1. (*Cf. R. I. Hist. Soc. Coll.*, Vol. 14, p. 77; R. L. Whitman, The Stukeley Westcott Family, Vol. 2, 1929.)

WILCOX. Edward was father of Daniel and undoubtedly of Stephen. On 13:2 mo.:1660 Daniel Wilcox sold land in Portsmouth to John Briggs, "which was my fathers, Edward Wilcox" (Portsmouth Deeds; *cf. R. I. Hist. Soc. Coll.*, Vol. 25, p. 109). He was probably a kinsman of Mr. John Wilcox, a merchant of Narragansett and New Amsterdam, who had a trading house at Cocumscussuc (Wickford, R. I.) very early.

Daniel (2nd col.) married first ———, who died before 1 Aug. 1661, when he conveyed land in Portsmouth to Edward Lay, reserving "the land where the grave of my deceased wife" is situated (Portsmouth Deeds, I, p. 16). His eldest son, Daniel, undoubtedly, and probably his second son, Samuel, were the children of his first wife.

(3rd col.) Jeremiah^3 (Stephen^2, Edward^1), delete.

(3rd col.) Daniel^3 (Daniel^2, Edward^1) died before 9 June 1702.

(3rd col.) Samuel^3 (Daniel^2, Edward^1) married Mary (born 1664), daughter of William and Martha (Earle) Wood of Dartmouth. Samuel died before 9 June 1702. His widow Mary married secondly Thomas Mallet, merchant of Newport from Great Marlow, co. Bucks., who died *s.p.* 16 Jan. 1703/4 in his 56th year (M. S. Trinity Church Yard, Newport). She m. thirdly, John Sanford of Newport, and died on 15 Dec. 1721 in her 57th year (M. S. with Sanford coat of arms in Island Cemetery, Newport).

Children of Samuel and Mary: 1. Jeremiah, b. 24 Sept. 1683; 2. William, b. 2 Feb. 1684/5; 3. Mary, b. 14 Feb. 1688/9, of Newport (*cf. New Eng. Hist. & Gen. Reg.*, Vol. 60, p. 400).

(3rd col.) Stephen^3 (Daniel^2, Edward^1). His second wife was Judith, dau. of Stephen and Mary (Bunker) Coffin of Nantucket. She m. first, Peter Folger (d. 1707) of Nantucket, and secondly, Nathaniel Barnard of Nantucket (d. 28 Feb. 1717/8). Stephen

Wilcox was her third husband. She died 2 Dec. 1760 (*New Eng. Hist. & Gen. Reg.*, Vol. 24, p. 152).

(See for Wilcox family, the present writer's account in *The American Genealogist*, Vol. 19, pp. 23-31.)

WILLIAMS. Roger (p. 430, 1st col.), son of James Williams, Citizen and Merchant Tailor of London. His mother, Alice Pemberton, bapt. St. Albans, co. Herts, 18 Feb. 1564/5, was the dau. of Robert and Catherine (Stokes) Pemberton of St. Albans. Alice was sister of Roger Pemberton, Esq., of St. Albans, Lord of the Manor of Wotton, co. Beds., and High Sheriff of Herts., 1620; his son was Ralf Pemberton, Esq., Mayor of St. Albans, and his son, Sir Francis, was Lord Chief Justice of England under Charles II and senior counsel for the Seven Bishops in their trial.

Roger was still a minor on 16 March 1622/3, so certainly born after 1602 (Orphan's Recognizances, 1590-1633) and about 1603-05. Married at High Lever, co. Essex, while Chaplain to Sir William Masham, Mary Barnard, maid to Sir William's step-daughter, Joan Altham, on 15 Dec. 1629. She was undoubtedly Mary, daughter of the noted Puritan divine, the Rev. Richard Barnard, rector of Worksop, co. Notts., and Batcombe, co. Somerset, who was bapt. at Worksop in 1609. Her brother, Musachiel Barnard, a tailor from Batcombe, sailed from Weymouth to New England on 20 March 1634/5 and settled at Weymouth, Mass. He is undoubtedly the "Mr. Barnard, Mr. Williams' wife's brother," mentioned by William Harris, in a letter dated 14 Nov. 1666, as residing in or near Boston, Mass. Prior to his marriage to Mary, Roger had wished to marry Joan Whalley, granddaughter of Lady Joan Barrington (born Cromwell), aunt of Oliver Cromwell, to whom he addressed several letters at this time, which greatly offended her. On 15 Aug. 1644, while on his first visit to England, Roger Williams, clerk, and Sidrach Williams, merchant, both of London, brought suit in chancery to recover certain real estate, which had belonged to their mother Alice Williams, which their brother Robert Williams, "then beyond seas," had improperly alienated. The bill states that Sidrach had been absent for seven years in Italy and that Roger had also been beyond seas. Sidrach was a member of the Merchant Tailors Company, in whose records he is described as a merchant to Italy and the Levant. Roger Williams speaks of his brother, a "Turkey Merchant." Robert, their other brother, came to Providence and was later schoolmaster at Newport; he, apparently, had no issue. James Williams, their father, citizen and merchant tailor of London, was made free of the Merchant Tailors Company on 7 April 1587. His will, dated 7 Sept. 1620, was proved 19 Nov. 1621. He resided in Cow Lane in the parish of St. Sepulcher's without Newgate in London. In his reply to the chancery bill of Roger and Sidrach, dated 28 Aug. 1644, the respondent states that Roger "stands in contempt." This is evidently the Chancery case referred to by Roger, as the one where he lost great sums for refusing to take an oath. (*New Eng. Hist. & Gen. Reg.*, Vol. 43, pp. 290-303, 427; Vol. 97, pp. 176-181; Ryder's Book Notes, 25 May 1912.) He died between 15 March 1682/3 and 25 April 1683.

WILLIAMS. Robert. (Omitted by Austin. Of London, Providence and Newport. Born about 1610. Died about 1680-1). Brother of Roger Williams. Legatee under the will of his father. James Williams, citizen and Merchant Taylor of the parish of St. Sepulchres without Newgate, London, on 7 Sept. 1620. (*New Eng. Hist. & Gen. Reg.*, Vol. 43, p. 291.) Under age 16 March 1622/3 (Orphan's Recognizances, 1590-1633). Apprenticed to his brother Sydrach Williams in the Merchant Taylors Company, 6 March 1626/7 (*Register*, Vol. 43, p. 427). Executor and residuary legatee under the will of his mother Alice Williams of St. Sepulchres, 1 Aug. 1634 (*ib.*, p. 292). His maladministration of her estate was the cause of the chancery suit brought by his brothers, Sydrach and Roger, on 15 Aug. 1644 against Walter Chauncy, citizen and Goldsmith of London and the overseers of the will. Met with financial reverses and emigrated to New England shortly before this date (*Register*, Vol. 97, p. 178).

Settled in Providence about 1643-44 and signed the Providence Combination (Chapin's *Doc. Hist.*, Vol. 1, pp. 114, 120). Purchased on or before 27 Jan. 1644/5 a house lot in Providence of William Reynolds (*ib.*, p. 234). On 10:7 mo.:1646 he and others signed a declaration regarding their purchase of lands from Ousamequin (Massasoit) on behalf of the town of Providence (*ib.*, p. 240). Write to John Winthrop, Jr., 18 April 1647 (*ib.*, Vol. 2, p. 180). Chosen on 16 May 1647 one of ten men to represent Providence in a General Court held at Portsmouth 18 May 1647 (*ib.*, Vol. 1, p. 243). Signed an agreement at Providence Dec. 1647 (*ib.*, p. 249). Moderator of Providence Town Meeting 25:10 mo.:1647 (*ib.*, p. 236) and frequently thereafter. Commissioner from Providence 16 May 1648, 4 Nov. 1651, 18 May 1652 and 28 Oct. 1652 (*ib.*, p. 250; R. I. Col. Rec. I: 235, 241, 245). On Providence Roll of Freemen 1655 (R. I. Col. Rec., I: 299). Appointed 8 April 1665 Magistrate for the King's Province (Narragansett) by the Royal Commissioners (*ib.*, II: 94). Removed to Newport, where he was the schoolmaster in 1672 (G. Fox Digged out of his Burrows). General Solicitor of the Colony, 7 May 1673, 6 May 1674, 2 May 1676 and 5 May 1680 (R. I. Col. Rec. II, III).

The American Genealogist

Whole Number 83 Volume XXI, No. 3

January, 1945

ADDITIONS AND CORRECTIONS TO AUSTIN'S GENEALOGICAL DICTIONARY OF RHODE ISLAND

By G. Andrews Moriarty, A.M., LL.B., F.S.A.

A few additional items are presented herewith.

ANGELL. Thomas (p. 4, 1st col.) was undoubtedly a near relative, but of a younger generation, of William Angell, Citizen and Baker of London, whose daughter Catherine married John Pemberton, Esq., of St. Alban's, first cousin of Roger Williams (cf. *New Eng. Hist. & Gen. Reg.* 43:295), which would account for his presence in Williams' family in New England. His wife Alice is said to have been Alice Ashton, daughter of John and sister of Mary Ashton, wife of Thomas Olney. Alice was baptized in the Abbey Church at St. Alban's, Herts, 1 Feb. 1617/18 (*The American Genealogist*, 10:89; Stilwell's *Hist. Gen. Misc.*, III; *ex inform.* Richard LeBaron Bowen, Esq.).

ASHTON. James (p. 5, 1st col.) was probably a son of James Ashton of St. Alban's, Herts, and a brother of Mary, wife of Thomas Olney and of Alice wife of Thomas Angell (*vide* Angell above).

He witnessed a memo. of William Arnold to Thomas Olney on 11 Feb. 1642 (Prov. Town Rec. I, 64). Commissioner, 1650 (*ib.* II, 52).

Add James (2nd col.), who settled in Monmouth Co., N. J., and was a Baptist lay preacher and magistrate. Married about 1670 Deliverance, daughter of John Throckmorton of Providence (cf. *Throckmorton Genealogy*).

BENNET. Samuel (p. 18, 1st col.) received 19 Feb. 1645 a grant of 25 acres in Providence and took an oath of allegiance to the Parliament of England (Prov. Town Rec. II, 29). On

1 Dec. 1651 he was one of five commissioners to be paid 2/12/4 for going to Warwick (*ib.*, XV, 48).

COWLAND. Ralph (p. 58, 1st col.) had land in Portsmouth mentioned 10 mo.: 1639 (Portsmouth Town Rec., First Bk., printed, p. 5). Twenty-five acres were laid out 10 Dec. 1656 to Ralph Cowland "for himself and in lieu of a former grant to John Greenman belonging to Sarah Greenman" (Portsmouth Deed Bk. I, 534). Mrs. Cowland was mentioned 23 Aug. 1659 (R. I. Col. Rec. I, 426). On 1 Oct. 1661 land "laid out to Ralph Cowland for the use of Sarah Greenman" was mentioned (Portsmouth Town Rec. I, 108). Will of Alice Cowland 9 mo. 1664 mentioned Sarah Greenman but did not call her daughter. On 21 Nov. 1670, Ralph Cowland for love and affection to "my daughter in law Sarah Green" granted her 20 acres next "Aspinwall's Farm" and adjoining 5 acres not otherwise specified (R. I. Col. Deeds, III, 344). John Green conveyed 20 Feb. 1721/2 to Giles Slocum land "that Ralph Cowland gave to Sarah Green on 21 Nov. 1670" (Portsmouth Deeds, II, 402).

Ralph Cowland married 1st, prior to 23 Aug. 1659, Alice Shotten; 2nd, widow Ellen Wait shortly after 14 Dec. 1669 (on which date she was made administratrix of her husband Thomas Wait's estate as "Elen Wait"—Portsmouth Scrap Bk.) and before 13 June 1671 when "Elen Cowland and Thomas Wait" [Jr.] were taxed (Portsmouth Tax List). Ellen died before 21 Jan. 1675/6, when Samuel Wait was made administrator of his father's estate in her place (Portsmouth Scrap Bk.). Cowland married, 3rd, Joan Hide, who died 15 Nov. 1679 (Portsmouth Quaker Records).

The above suggests that Ralph may have had still another wife before Alice Shotten, namely, the widow of John Greenman, whose daughter, Sarah Greenman, was "daugther-in-law" of Ralph Cowland and who married, prior to 21 Nov. 1670, John Green (cf. Austin, p. 87; *ex inform.* Edward H. West, Esq.).

GREEN. John of Newport (p. 87, 2nd col.). The John Green on whose estate administration was granted to his son John, the widow Mary refusing, 3 Oct. 1753, was probably another and younger man. This John married prior to 21 Nov. 1670 Sarah Greenman, apparently a daughter of John Greenman and step-daughter to Ralph Cowland (*vide* Cowland, above).

MOSHER. John (p. 135, 2nd col.). Delete from his children in the 4th col. 6. Hannah born 13 March 1712. She was Hannah Davol wife of John Mosher, Jr. (born 12 March 1703). (*Ex inform.* Mr. Robert R. Phillips of Nassau, N. Y.)

PENDLETON. James (p. 149, 1st col.). His father, Bryan Pendleton (born about 1599) married at Birmingham, co. Warwick, 22 Apr. 1619, Eleanor Price (Par. Reg. St. Martin's, Birmingham, 1554-1653, p. 108; *The American Genealogist,* 10:15).

PLACE. Enoch (p. 154, 1st col.) may have been a near relative of Peter Place of Boston and of Thomas Place of Cambridge (cf. Pope's Pioneers, p. 364). The Dinah Place who died at Dorchester on 28 : 5 : 1657 may have been a first wife. He married at Dorchester on 5 : 9 : 1657 Sarah ———, and the following children's births are recorded there: Enoch, born 18 : 7 : 1658; and Peter, born 16 : 12 : 1660.

WESTON. Francis (p. 220). His wife Frances probably married 2nd, Adam Goodwin. John Pease, of Salem, who went to Warwick to warn the Gortonists of the intended attack by the Massachusetts soldiers, was called a son-in-law of Francis Weston (*ex inform.* Bradford Swan, Esq., of Providence).

GREENMAN. John (p. 308, 1st col.) was more likely a brother than the father of David and Edward. He may have had a wife who remarried, as his first wife, Ralph Cowland, and a daughter Sarah Greenman, called "daughter in law" by Ralph, who married, prior to 21 Nov. 1670, John Green of Newport. On 15 Oct. 1643 the five acres of John Greene[man] in Portsmouth were mentioned (Portsmouth Town Rec., Bk. I, printed, p. 23). (*Ex inform.* Edward H. West, Esq.)

INMAN. Edward (p. 326, 1st col.) received 25 acres in Providence and swore allegiance to the Parliament 19 Feb. 1645 (Providence Rec. II, 30).

THE AMERICAN GENEALOGIST

Whole No. 94 April, 1948 Vol. XXIV, No. 2

ADDITIONS AND CORRECTIONS TO AUSTIN'S GENEALOGICAL DICTIONARY OF RHODE ISLAND

By G. Andrews Moriarty, A.M., LL.B., F.S.A.

(Previous instalments have appeared in Vols. 19, 20 and 21.)

BENNET. (Robert, p. 18). Jonathan (2nd col.) married Anna (born 4 Nov. 1674), daughter of John and Anna (Alcock) Williams. Children: John; Rebecca, married Peleg (born 24 Mar. 1691/2), son of Peleg and Mary (Holder) Slocum of Dartmouth. (Crapo's Certain Comeoverers, 1:342.)

CLARKE. (Joseph, p. 47, 2nd col.). Mary, delete "married Tobias Saunders." (See Saunders.)

GARDINER. (Page 82, col. 2). Mary, daughter of George Gardiner of Newport by his second wife, Lydia Ballou, married at Providence, R. I., 18 July 1690, Archibald Walker of Providence and had issue:

- i. Charles, b. 6 May 1691.
- ii. Susanna, b. 28 Sept. 1695.
- iii. Abigail, b. 15 Jan. 1698/9.
- iv. Hezekiah, b. 14 Mar. 1701/2.
- v. Nathaniel, b. 26 June 1704; it seems probable that he is identical with Nathan Walker, ensign in a detachment of the English forces on the island of Ratan, commanded by Major John Cauldfield, which belonged to the late American Regiment, commanded by Col. Gooch. This Nathan Walker made his will at Augusta, 25 Nov. 1744, proved in the P. C. C., 15 Oct. 1746. He left his arrears of pay to his "cousin John Gardiner merchant in Rhode Island in New England" (i.e., Dep.-Gov. John Gardiner of Newport, son of Joseph of Newport and grandson of George and Lydia Gardiner of Newport); other bequests to brother officers.(P.C.C. 314 Edmunds)
- vi. Ann, b. 14 Feb. 1708/9.

(Rhode Island History, R. I. Hist. Soc., 4:61-63.)

GUTTREDGE. (Page 90.) Will of Ann Guttredge (1st col.). Change daughter "Mercy" Westcott to daughter "Mary" Westcott.

PAINE. John Paine of Newport, saddler [family omitted by Austin]. Born about 1642, died 17 May 1704 "aged 62 years" (gravestones, Common Burying Ground at Newport). Freeman, Newport, July 1686 (Newport Town Meetings, 1:20). 25 May 1698, Isaac Martindale of Newport to John Paine of Newport, saddler, 90 acres at Jamestown, bounded east on salt water, north on Capt. Thomas Paine, west on highway, south on John Weeden, together with Dyer's Island; on 30 May 1698 John Paine and wife, Mary, reconveyed the same to Martindale (R. I. Colony Deeds, 2:72, 73). 21 Nov. 1700, he purchased of Latham Clarke of Newport, merchant, 30 acres in the Pettyquamscot Purchase bounded south on highway and undivided land, north on William Gibson, survivor [?successor] to Jeremiah Brown of Newport, deceased; wit. by William Brown (son of Jeremiah) and Daniel Vernon (R. I. Colony Deeds, 2:141). Jan. 1701/2, John Paine made a Kingstown man his attorney touching these lands, ackn. 2 Jan. same year (North Kingstown Deeds, 1:5), and that same day John Paine of Newport, saddler, sold same land, "interim of Jeremiah Browne, late of Newport," to Samuel Brown of Pettyquamscott (ib. 2:195). In May 1697 Isabel Morse of Warwick quitclaimed land in Kingstown to John Paine (ib., 2:129). On 5 Jan. 1702/3, John and Thomas Paine each received a share in Newport common lands adjoining each other (Newport Misc. Rec. p. 6).

Will 15 May 1704, proved 4 June 1704. House in Newport to wife Mary for life, remainder to son John Paine in fee tail, remainder to his three daughters or the survivors of them and their heirs. To eldest son Thomas, 20/. To son John, 40/. To three daughters Elizabeth, Mary and Mercy, £40 at 21. Wife Mary executrix and guardian of his three children, John, Elizabeth and Mercy, until 21. Inventory 31 May 1704. (Newport Town Council, 1:43.) On 20 April 1715, Jonathan Turner and wife Elizabeth, Mercy Hazelton, widow of William of Kingstown, deceased, and Benjamin Peckham, with the consent of their mother, Mary Paine, all of Kingstown, sold a house and land in Newport, which their father John Paine, deceased, purchased of the freemen of Newport and of Thomas Weedon, to Oliver Arnold of Portsmouth, practitioner of physick (Newport Deeds, 1:105).

Married Mary, perhaps second wife and perhaps daughter of Jeremiah Browne of Newport (Register, 80:77); she was alive 20 April 1715.

Children:

- i. Thomas (possibly by a first wife), of Newport 5 Jan. 1701/2. Undoubtedly identical with Thomas Paine of

New Shoreham. Died before 27 Jan. 1766. Married before 12 Dec. 1718, Elizabeth, widow of Timothy McCarthy, mariner, of New Shoreham, and daughter of John and Anna (Alcock) Williams of Boston, New Shoreham and Newport. Married (2) in 1723, Susanna, widow of Samuel Arnold, trader, of New Shoreham, and of Stamford, Conn., daughter of Samuel and Sarah (Rathbone) George of New Shoreham.

On 18 Apr. 1717, he deposed as to the kidnaping of three New Shoreham men by Palgrave Williams. The will of his mother-in-law, Ann Guthrie, dated 12 Dec. 1718, gave two cows to her grandson Thomas McCarthy to remain in the possession of her son Thomas Paine until her said grandson come of age, and bequeathed to her daughter Elizabeth Paine. He occurs frequently in New Shoreham land transactions. On 8 May 1740 he is described as tenant by the courtesy of George land in a deed to Capt. Simon Ray from Silas Clapp (New Shoreham Records, 2:264). On 31 Dec. 1747, Benjamin Potter of New Shoreham and wife, Margaret, sold to Thomas Paine their share of the land of Samuel George and recited that Samuel George left two daughters, Mary, wife of Thomas Mitchell, and Susanna, late wife of Thomas Paine; that said Susanna left five daughters, of whom Margaret was one (New Shoreham Records, 3:552). (By her first husband, Samuel Arnold, Susanna had Mary, Sarah, Elizabeth and Rebecca, as per New Shoreham Vital Records.) On 26 March 1755, he conveyed the said land for love to his son, John Payne, yeoman, of New Shoreham (ib., 3:552). Freeman, New Shoreham, May 1736. Taxed New Shoreham up to 1764.

Child by first wife: John, b. about 1718. Child by second wife: Margaret, b. about 1724-5; m. 13 Feb. 1746/7, Benjamin Potter of Kingstown and New Shoreham.

ii. John (by second wife), b. after 1683; d. without issue before 20 Apr. 1715.

iii. Elizabeth (by second wife), b. after 1683; m. at South Kingstown, 9 June 1709, Jonathan Turner of Kingston. Children: Mary, b. 1711; Paine, b. 1713; Hannah, b. 1715.

iv. Mercy (by second wife), b. after 1683; m. at Kingstown, 27 Sept. 1710, William Hazelton of Kingstown, who d. prior to 20 Apr. 1715. Child: Jarvis, b. 11 Oct.1711.

v. Mary (by second wife), b. after 1683; m. before 20 Apr. 1715, Benjamin Peckham of South Kingstown. Known children: Peleg, b. 28 June 1723; Joseph, b. 14 Jan. 1725/6; Isaac, b. 23 Dec. 1728; Mary, b. 28 May 1730; Timothy, b. 19 July 1737.

(See Register, 83:84-88.)

By tradition, the New Shoreham Paines were related to Capt. Thomas Paine of Jamestown, the privateer, who came from Jamaica to Newport in 1689 and married Mercy, daughter of Gov. Caleb Carr of Newport; but proof of this is lacking.

PECKHAM. John (p. 147, col. 1) married first, Mary, baptized at Westhorpe, co. Suffolk, 26 July 1607, daughter of Thomas and Rose (Kerrich) Clarke of Westhorpe (cf. Register, 75:279). (Add in col. 2) Mary, married Tobias Saunders of Newport and Westerly. (See Saunders.)

SAUNDERS. Tobias (p. 173, col. 1) married, not Mary Clarke but Mary daughter of John and Mary (Clarke) Peckham. Mrs. Andrew Wallace of Cranston, R. I., furnishes new evidence on this marriage, supplied by Miss Peckham, daughter of the author of the Peckham Genealogy. Mr. Austin points out that Mary Clarke, the first wife of John Peckham, who died prior to 30 May 1651, may have been a sister of Dr. John and Joseph Clarke. This is now proved to have been so.

Tobias and Mary Saunders had a daughter Susanna who married, as his second wife, prior to 1712, Peter Barker, son of James and Barbara (Dungan) Barker. (Austin, pp. 14, 173.) John Peckham had a son James who died s. p. 26 Feb. 1711/12. On 25 Dec. 1712, a power of attorney was given by his heirs to Philip and William Peckham and John Taylor to sell the realty of the said James on behalf of the heirs, among whom appear Peter Barker and his wife Susanna. (Austin, p. 148.) Elizabeth Babcock, wife of James Babcock of Westerly, with her husband, appointed her brother-in-law, Peter Barker of Newport, to "receive in charge, all legacies which may fall to them of that estate which their honored uncle James Peckham left at his death." On 19 May 1712, Edward, John, Stephen and Benjamin Saunders, all of Westerly, [sons of Tobias and Mary, cf. Austin, p. 173], appointed their "brother-in-law, Peter Barker of Newport, to transact business for them and their sister Elizabeth. (Bristol County Deeds, 8:70.) From the foregoing it would appear that Mary, wife of Tobias Saunders, was the daughter of John Peckham by Mary sister of Dr. John and Joseph Clarke, rather than a daughter of Joseph.

(Col. 2) Add Elizabeth, married prior to 1712, James Babcock of Westerly.

WILLIAMS (omitted by Austin). John Williams, merchant, of Boston, New Shoreham and Newport, son of the Boston merchant and selectman, Nathaniel Williams. Baptized at Boston, 18 Aug. 1644 "aged 3 days." Died at Newport, R. I., 1687. Married 1670, marriage contract dated 25 Jan. 1669/70, Anne, daughter of Dr. John and Sarah (Palgrave) Alcock of Roxbury, Mass. She married second, 5 June 1689, as his second wife, Robert Guthery of New Shoreham, and died 1723. Her will, 12 Dec. 1718, proved 27 June 1723 (cf. Austin, p. 90). In her will she names grandsons Palgrave and John Williams, Robert Sands, and Joseph and Thomas McCarthy.

John Williams was executor, 21 Oct. 1674, of the will of Hugh Williams, merchant, of Boston and New Shoreham.

Attorney for Capt. John Williams, felt-maker, of Barnaby Street, London, brother of Hugh Williams of Boston, felt-maker, for the sale of his New Shoreham lands, and was living at New Shoreham, 16 Apr. 1666 (R. I. Colonial Deeds). Received Dr. John Alcock's New Shoreham lands and part of the latter's lands on the Assobet River, Stow, Mass. Deputy for New Shoreham, May, 1679. Purchased of Nathaniel Dickens, 20 acres in Newport, 10 May 1679. On 3 Dec. 1679, John Williams of Boston, merchant, attorney to Capt. John Williams of Barnaby St., Camberwell, London, sold land at New Shoreham to Tormut Rose and William Tosh (New Shoreham Deeds). Freeman of Newport, 23 July 1683. Deputy from Newport, 1 Oct. 1684. Signed the petition against the Rhode Island charter, 1686, and the same year was Attorney General of Rhode Island.

Will 18 Apr. 1687, proved 25 Oct. 1687. Devised lands at New Shoreham, Boston, Stow, and Newport. Devised lands to Mr. Hiscox's Baptist congregation at Newport. Named wife and children, Nathaniel, Palgrave, Anna, Mary, Elizabeth, Arabella, and unborn child. Executor for his son Nathaniel, until he come of age, Robert Guthery. Overseers, brother, Mr. Nathaniel Williams of Boston, and Mr. Thomas Ward of Newport (Suffolk County, Mass., Probate, 10:335).

Children:

i. Nathaniel, b. at Boston, 11 Nov. 1672. Inherited lands at Boston and New Shoreham. On 10 Nov. 1788, John Whitman Williams, late of Newport, mariner, sold his right in Fort Island, New Shoreham, which John Williams of Boston and wife Anna left to their son Nathaniel Williams, to whom John Williams of Newport, father of the said John Whitman Williams, was heir (New Shoreham Deeds).

ii. Palgrave. Freeman of Newport, 31 Jan. 1704. Went to the Spanish Main and became a pirate. Quartermaster of the pirate, Bellamy. On 18 Apr. 1717, he came to New Shoreham and kidnaped three men, George Mitchell, William Tosh and Dr. James Sweet (Livermore's History of Block Island, pp. 85-86). He escaped Bellamy's shipwreck at Wellfleet and later conducted a supply base for pirates in the Bahamas. On 5 Oct. 1741, Elizabeth Williams, mother of Paul (Palgrave) Williams, desired that Stephen Hookey of Newport be made guardian to the children of Paul (Palgrave) Williams "who is gone and left his children, to wit Paulgrave and John Williams" (Newport Town Council Records).

Note: In 1760 Palgrave Williams of Jamaica, peruke maker, aged 56 years, who was born at Newport, R. I., deposed regarding John de Courcy, Lord Kingsale, who was born at Newport, son of Miles or Michael de Courcy, mariner, of Newport, and Abigail Williams of Newport, his wife. This Palgrave was undoubtedly the son of Palgrave Williams the pirate and is evidently the "Paul" Williams who in 1741 had left his children, Palgrave and John, at Newport. Abigail wife of Miles or Michael de Courcy of Newport was probably another child of Palgrave the pirate (cf. New Complete Peerage, 7:290-291 and notes).

iii. Mary, b. 2 Oct. 1670 in Boston; m. (1) 7 May 1693, Edward Sands of New Shoreham, who d. 14 June 1708; m. (2) 5 Jan. 1712/13, Robert Westcott of New Shoreham. No issue by second husband. Child by first husband: Sarah Sands, m. 28 May 1711, Teddeman Hull of Jamestown, R. I. (cf. Austin, p. 108).

iv. Anna, b. 4 Nov. 1674; m. Jonathan Bennett of Newport. 11 Sept. 1714, Ann Guttery of Block Island, relict of Robert Guttery, deceased, and administratrix of her former husband, John Williams of Boston, deeded Newport land to her daughter, Anna Bennett of Newport, widow of Jonathan Bennett of Newport (Newport Deeds). Children: John; Anna.

v. Elizabeth, b. at Boston, 5 Dec. 1679; m. (1) at New Shoreham, 21 Nov. 1700, Timothy McCarthy, mariner, of Newport; m. (2) before 12 Dec. 1718, Thomas Paine of New Shoreham; d. before 1723. Children by first husband: Joseph; ?Daniel; ?Catherine; Thomas. Child by second husband: John.

vi. Arabella, m. 14 Mar. 1717/18, Edward Pelham, Esq., of Newport, son of Edward and Freelove (Arnold) Pelham. His will, 21 May 1741, was proved that year; to daughter Hermione wife of John Bannister. Children: Hermione, b. 3 Dec. 1718; Elizabeth, b. 20 Oct. 1721; Penelope, b. 23 May 1724.

(See Putnam's Genealogical Magazine, Dec. 1915, pp. 4-12.)

WILSON. (p.230) Samuel (col. 1) married Mary Tefft, according to his great-granddaughter, Jane Wilson.

To the children of the first Samuel Wilson, add (col. 2) John, who died without issue.

James (col. 2) married a Hubbard, according to his grand-niece Jane Wilson.

Jeremiah (col. 2) married first, a New London Mainwaring, according to his granddaughter, Jane Wilson. This is undoubtedly correct—Mr. Austin apparently misread the New Shoreham entry of his marriage as "Manoxon." Miss Wilson stated that by his first wife, he had issue, nine daughters: Mary, m. a Robinson of New London [Edward of New London, merchant]; Anna, m. (1) a Ray and (2) William Mumford [Nathaniel Ray of New Shoreham and Lieut. William Mumford of South Kingston]; Alice, m. a Shaw; Sarah, m. (1) a Banning [Mr. Austin read the name in Jeremiah's will as Fanning] and (2) a Gould, she had no issue; Elizabeth, m. Dr. [Rev.] Joseph Torrey. The remaining four daughters, among whom evidently was Judith, died without issue. Jeremiah married second, a widow, Mary Gutridge, whose maiden name apparently was

Smith. She had by her first husband a daughter who married a Woodbridge of Groton, Conn. Jeremiah had by his second wife, five sons and two daughters: *Samuel*; *Jeremiah*; *John*; *James*; *George*; *Mary*, m. (1) Robert Pollock, (2) John Wills; and *Alice*, m. Zephiniah Brow.

Of these, Samuel married a Case and had four sons and a daughter; Jeremiah married a widow Dye [*quaere*, Dyer] and had three sons and a daughter; John married Hannah Hazard and had three sons; and James married Jane, daughter of Capt. John Rouse of the parish of St. Pierre Port, Guernsey, and Newport, R. I., and had two daughters, Jane and Mary.

(Much data regarding this family will be found in the account written by Jane Wilson (died at Newport, R. I., 23 Aug. 1834 aged 83 years), daughter of the above James and Jane (Rouse) Wilson; cf. *Register*, 69:380-382.)

WESTCOTT. (p. 417) Robert married 5 Jan. 1712/13, *Mary*, daughter of John and Anna (Alcock) Williams, and widow of Edward Sands.

THE AMERICAN GENEALOGIST

Whole No. 99 July, 1948 Vol. XXV, No. 3

NOTES AND ERRATA

HOOMERY-WODELL. In my "Additions and Corrections to Austin's *Genealogical Dictionary of Rhode Island*," in *The American Genealogist*, 20:113, under Hoomery I stated by a slip of the pen that John Hoomery, the probable son of John and Mary (Jennings) Hoomery, married Sarah, daughter of William and Mary Wodell. This is wrong. Sarah, daughter of William and Mary Wodell, married, as stated by Austin, Samuel Sanford of Portsmouth. The Sarah who married John Hoomery was her niece, the daughter of her brother Gershom and Mary (Tripp) Wodell, as stated by Austin (p. 437).

-G. Andrews Moriarty, Ogunquit, Maine

TAG W. No. 100 Oct., 1949 V. XXV, No. 4 249

ADDITIONS AND CORRECTIONS TO AUSTIN'S GENEALOGICAL DICTIONARY OF RHODE ISLAND

By G. Andrews Moriarty, A.M., LL.B., F.S.A.

(Previous instalments have appeared in Vols. 19, 20, 21 and 24)

BROWN. (Henry, p. 28.) He came from Rusper, co. Sussex, where he was baptized 28 Dec. 1626, the son of William and Jane (Burgis) Brown. William and Jane were married at Rusper on 20 June 1611. William was perhaps the son of Joseph Brown of Rusper. William Brown also came to New England and settled at Saybrook, Conn., after 1645, and died on Long Island in 1650.

Phoebe Brown, daughter of William and Jane, was baptized at Rusper on 12 July 1601 and married Thomas Lee of Rusper. Their son Thomas, baptized at Rusper 29 Sept. 1644, settled at Lyme, Conn., and was the ancestor of the Lees of Lyme. His sister, Jane Lee, baptized at Rusper, 12 Sept. 1640, married 1st, Samuel Hyde of Norwich, Conn., and 2nd, John Birchard. She was the aunt of Joshua Hempstead of New London. [New England Hist. and Gen. Register, 61:116-118.]

Note: Attention should also be called to the article of Mary Lovering Holman in The American Genealogist, 15: 84-86, which shows that William Browne (father of Henry and Phoebe) was baptized at Horley, co. Surrey, (son of Rev. Joseph and Margery (Patching) Browne of Horley and Rusper), on 5 Dec. 1585; and that this William Browne's sister, Sarah, baptized at Rusper, 22 Oct. 1592, married Arthur Fenner and became mother of the Rhode Island Fenners.—D.L.J.

CRANSTON. (John, p. 60, 1st col.) He was the son of the Rev. James Cranston, chaplain of Charles I and rector of St. Marys Overie or St. Saviour's Church, in Southwark. Rev. James was son of John Cranston of Bold, co. Peebles, Scotland, by his wife Christian, daughter of Sir Robert Stewart, uncle of John Stewart, Lord of Traquair. John was the eldest son and heir of James Cranston, portioner of Bold, probably by his first wife Jane Dewar, and James was undoubtedly a younger son of Sir William Cranston of that ilk by his wife Elizabeth, daughter of Andrew Johnston of Elphiston, the ancestors of Lord Cranston. The descent has been traced to Andrew de Cranston of that ilk, who died before 1338.

Gov. John Cranston was brought over as a lad to New England about 1637 by Jeremiah Clarke, whose daughter he married. His wife's will, dated 1 Nov. 1708, was proved 10 June 1711. She names her children Samuel, John and Benjamin, Elizabeth Brown and Henry Stanton, son-in-law John Brown, grandsons John and Robert Brown, John Cranston (son of Gov. Samuel), and granddaughter Mary Cranston.

A full account of the Cranstons, by William Jones, A.B., of Mount Vernon, N.Y., will be found in the New England Hist. and Gen. Register, 79:57-66, 247-268.

(William, p. 61, 2nd col.) This William should go in the third column. He was the grandson and not the son of Gov. John Cranston. He was the son of William[2] Cranston, son of Gov. John[1] [ibid., 79:254, 258]. He was a shipwright, and was born 9 Dec. 1692. He deposed, aged 80 years, on 23 Aug. 1773, in the Chancery Case of Pope vs. Smith, and described himself as "nephew of Henry Stanton, shipwright" and of "John Cranston, who married a daughter of Walter Newbury" [Sr.] [Chancery Proc. 1758-1800, No. 932, preserved in the Public Record Office, London; cf. Register, op. cit., 100:219]. He was bequeathed by James[3] Cranston (Gov. Samuel[2], Gov. John[1]), in his will, dated 2 Nov. 1731, a silver snuff box, with the name of his father, William, engraved upon it, which Gov. Samuel, by his will, dated 17 Mar. 1726/7, had bequeathed to the said James, his son [Register, op. cit., 79:254].

In place of this William substitute William[2] (Gov. John[1]), born about 1670, died, probably at Newport, before 1697. Married Mary or Marcy, born 4 June 1668, daughter of John and Mary (Harndel) Stanton of Newport [ibid., 100:219]. She married 2nd, about 1696, Samuel Gibbs of Jamestown, R.I., and had issue. She died probably in 1732 [ibid., 79:254].

FENNER. (Arthur and William, pp. 74, 75.) They were not sons of Thomas of Branford, Conn., as suggested by Austin, but his brothers. Arthur Fenner of Horley, co. Surrey, son of Thomas Fenner, of Horne, co. Surrey, married Sarah Browne, baptized at Rusper, co. Sussex (see Brown, above), 22 Oct. 1592. Their children include the following, all baptized at Horley: Sarah, bapt. 26 Nov. 1615, married 1st, at Horley, 17 Oct. 1637, John Tully, with whom she settled in Saybrook, Conn., and 2nd, at Saybrook, Dec. 1647, Robert Lay; Thomas, bapt. 20 July 1617, died at Branford, Conn., 15 May 1647; Arthur, bapt. 17 Oct. 1619, settled in Providence, R.I.; William, bapt. 11 Sept. 1625, settled in Newport, R.I.; John, bapt. 13 Feb. 1630/1, settled in Saybrook, Conn.; and Phoebe, bapt. 5 Jan. 1633/4, married a Ward, probably William Ward of Middletown, Conn. See the article of Mary Lovering Holman in The American Genealogist, 15:80-84. —D.L.J.

STANTON. (Mary[3], John[2], Robert[1], p. 389, 3rd col.) She married 1st, about 1690, William[2] Cranston (John[1]) and had issue: ? Benjamin of Marcus Hook (Chichester), Penn.; William of Newport, born 9 Dec. 1692 (cf. above). She married 2nd, about 1696, Samuel Gibbs of Jamestown, R.I., and died probably in 1732. [Register, op. cit., 79:254; 100:219.] By Gibbs she had issue: Siles, born

31 Oct. 1697; Amey, born 19 June 1699; Samuel, born 11 Feb. 1701/2; Hannah, born 31 Dec. 1702; and Phebe, born 13 Aug. 1704 [Arnold's Vital Record of R.I., Jamestown, p. 22, which requires verification].

THE AMERICAN GENEALOGIST

Whole No. 101 Jan., 1950 Vol. XXVI, No. 1

ADDITIONS AND CORRECTIONS TO AUSTIN'S GENEALOGICAL DICTIONARY

By G. Andrews Moriarty, A.M., LL.B., F.S.A.

(Previous instalments have appeared in Vol. 25 and earlier volumes.)

CLARKE. Jeremiah, p. 44, and Joseph, p. 47. After William, son of Latham, son of Jeremiah (p. 44, 3rd col.), delete date of birth, 27 May 1673, and place it after William, son of William, son of Joseph (p. 47, 3rd col.). Austin confused the two Williams. William3 (William2, Joseph1) was of Westerly and lived in that part which was set off as Richmond and later as Charlestown, R. I. When he entered the births of his children on the Charlestown records, he gave his own birth date as 27 May 1673 and that of his wife Hannah or Anna Knight as 3 April 1680, as well as the date of their marriage on 15 April 1700. They were married at Newport and their marriage took place, according to Arnold, on 11 April 1700, in that town [Arnold, Vital Record of R. I., IV, Newport, p. 18]. See New England Hist. and Gen. Register, 85:417-423.

SANFORD. John, p. 171. Esbon (p. 172, 2nd col.) had a wife Sarah. On 27 June 1666, he was at Portsmouth [Sanford Papers, R. I. Hist. Soc., p. 10], but soon went to England with Capt. Zachery Gillam of Boston, who married his step-sister, Phoebe Phillips, daughter of Major William Phillips of Boston and Saco [Gen. Dict. of Maine and N.H., p. 548]. He entered the service of The Hudson's Bay Company, and in 1672-3 he was at Hudson's Bay as mate of the dogger Messenger, and spent the winter there. In 1674-5 he was mate of the Company's Prince Rupert, Capt. Zachery Gillam commander. In 1682 he was sent to Port Nelson as Deputy Governor in command of the Albemarle. He died there on 6 Oct. 1682, evidently in the troubles with the French under Radisson, who was sent from Quebec to break up the Company's post. On 5 Dec. 1683, the Company voted to pay his salary to his widow Sarah, and on 6 Feb. 1683/4 she had a further allowance as he "had lost his life in the Company's service" [Minutes of the Hudson's Bay Company, 1679-84, Second Series 1682-84, Champlain Society, Toronto, 1947, pp. 333-4].

ADDITIONS AND CORRECTIONS TO AUSTIN'S GENEALOGICAL DICTIONARY OF RHODE ISLAND

By G. Andrews Moriarty, A.M., LL.B., F.S.A.

(For previous instalments see vols. 19, 20, 21, 24, 25, 26)

AUDLEY. (John, p. 5, 1st col.) John was born at Boston 3:12mo.:1641, son of John Odlin, the armorer [Boston Births, Baptisms, Marriages and Deaths, 1630-1699, p. 11].

ACRES. (John, p. 1, 2nd col. Martha.) According to Mr. George R. Burgess, who made a very careful study of the New Shoreham vital records [R. I. Hist. Soc. Coll., vol. 31, p. 79-82], Martha was born 28 Feb. 1675/6, but the date of her marriage to Job Card, November 1689, would indicate that Mr. Austin was probably correct as to the date of her birth.

CLARKE. (Jeremiah, p. 44, 2nd col.) Jeremiah Clarke Jr. married Ann Audley. She was undoubtedly the sister of John Audley of Newport and one of the daughters of John Odlin, the armorer or cutler of Boston, whose will, dated 6 March 1685, mentions daughters but does not name them. She was born about 1645. The name Audley was long preserved as a given name in this branch of the Clarke family. It may be suggested that the reason John Audley or Odlin Jr. settled in Newport was because of his sister's marriage with Jeremiah Clarke, Jr. (cf. New Eng. Register, vol. 41, p. 266).

COLLINS. (Arnold, p. 51, col. 2.) Add to the children of Arnold Collins a daughter Mary, probably by 1st wife. On 8 Dec. 1703, Gov. Samuel Cranston certified to the marriage of Jeremiah Wilcox and Mary Collins, daughter of Arnold Collins, all of Newport [Original certificate advertised for sale in The Collector].

DODGE. (Tristram, p. 66, col. 1.) On 14 Apr. 1665, he had license from the Government of New York to purchase the island of No Man's Land (500 acres), southwest of Martha's Vineyard [Tristram Dodge and his Descendants, Robert Dodge, 1886, p. 34], then under New York. On 13 Dec. 1681 and 31 Aug. 1682 he, together with Nathaniel Briggs, was before the Warden's Court at New Shoreham charged with sheep stealing. He declared he was of a very brittle memory. The case was settled. [New Shoreham Records, Bk. I, p. 90-93.]

(2nd col.) Israel was a Freeman at New Shoreham, July 1670. In 1694 he was living in North Parish (Montville), New London, Conn. In 1705 it was reported to the Court that he was living on the Indian Fields there. In 1707 he bought land there of Samuel Rogers. In 1719 he and wife Hannah deeded part of his land to son John. In 1722 he deeded land to his son Thomas near son John's portion. In 1725 John sold land to his brother Israel. He deeded land to his son William and Samuel, and in 1725 they sold 16 acres of it to their brother Israel. Israel, Sr., died after 1724 and, apparently, before 1730. Married Hannah ———. Children:

i. John, b. in 1689; bapt. an adult, 16 Dec. 1722; d. 16 Nov. 1776.
ii. Israel, bapt. as adult, 16 Dec. 1722; d. 1745.
iii. Thomas, bapt. an adult, 16 Dec. 1722.
iv. William, bapt. an adult, 16 Dec. 1722.
v. Samuel, bapt. an adult, 16 Dec. 1722.
(Possibly daughters.)

[Dodge Genealogy, Woodward, 1904, p. 7.]

DYER. (William, p. 290, 1st col.) William married first, 27 Oct. 1633, at St. Martin-in-the-Fields, London, England, Mary Barret. She was the famous Quaker martyr. Their son Samuel named his sixth son Barret for his mother's family.

(2nd col.) Samuel was baptized at Boston, 20:10:1635 [Boston Births, op. cit., p. 3].

FENNER. (p. 74) The Fenners of co. Sussex bore as arms: Vert a cross silver charged with a cross formée gules between 4 eagles displayed silver [Burke's Gen. Arm, ed. 1884, p. 345; cf. New England Register, vol.62, p. 199-200; vol. 63, p. 99-100; and in particular, The American Genealogist, vol. 15, p. 80-84; vol. 25, p. 250].

MITCHELL. (p. 133, 2nd col.) George seems to have had an older child, Samuel, who must have been born at an earlier date than George's marriage to Sarah Mott. Samuel married at New Shoreham, 4 Aug. 1727, Sarah, daughter of Tristram Dodge, Jr., and had Desire, born 2 May 1729, Mary, born 6 Aug. 1731, and perhaps others. On 14 Jan. 1745, Samuel Mitchell was ordered to pay towards the support of his sister Rebecca Mitchell. Rebecca daughter of George was born 20 July 1714. [New England Register, vol. 82, p. 463.]

WARD. (John of Newport, p. 406, col. 1) Austin suggests that John Ward's wife was possibly the Phoebe Fenner who was called Phebe Ward in the will of her brother William Fenner of Providence, 1680/1. However, consideration should be given to the following facts. Ensign

William Ward (d. 28 Mar. 1690) of Middletown, Conn., married 28 Mar. 1660 a Phebe (d. 1 Sept. 1691) whose surname is not stated. Their eldest son, Capt. Thomas Ward (b. 7 Feb. 1660/1, d. 1728) married 6 Dec. 1683 Hannah Tappin (d. 30 Nov. 1712). Their eldest son, Thomas Ward, Jr. (b. 17 Oct. 1684, d. 1730), had a son Tappin born 19 Mar. 1717/18, and a son Fenner born 15 Nov. 1725. Clearly Thomas Jr. named the son Tappin for his mother, and it seems likely that he named the son Fenner for his grandmother. No other Fenner descent has been located in the ancestry unless Phebe wife of Ensign William Ward was the Phebe Ward named in the will of her brother William Fenner.

This was the view of Mrs. Mary Lovering Holman in her article on the Fenner family [ante, vol. 15, p. 84]. —D.L.J.

WILCOX. (Samuel, p. 423, col. 3) His son Jeremiah, in 4th col., born 14 Feb. 1688, should probably read "Mary" as stated by James B. Congdon in New England Register, vol. 22, p. 67.

Jeremiah, son of Samuel Wilcox, married, shortly before 8 Dec. 1703 or upon that date, Mary, daughter of Arnold Collins of Newport [vide Collins note above].

WOOD. (John, p. 230-231) William Wood, 2nd col. (p. 231). His seventh child, 3rd col., was named Mary. She was born in 1664 or 1665. Died 15 Dec. 1721 or 15 Jan. 1721/2, and is buried in the Newport burying ground. She married first, about 1682, Samuel Wilcox of Dartmouth, Mass., and had three children, to wit: Jeremiah, born 24 Sept. 1683; William, born 2 Feb. 1685; and Mary, born 14 Feb. 1688 [New England Register, vol. 22, p.67]. Married second, Thomas Mallett of Newport, who died 8 Dec. 1704—5 Feb. 1704/5; no issue; and third, before 29 Nov. 1715, John Sanford of Newport, son of Samuel of Portsmouth and grandson of President John Sanford of Portsmouth [cf. New England Register, vol. 60, p. 400].

ADDITIONS AND CORRECTIONS TO AUSTIN'S GENEALOGICAL DICTIONARY OF RHODE ISLAND

By G. Andrews Moriarty, A.M., LL.B., F.S.A.

(Previous instalments in vols. 19, 20, 21, 24, 25, 26)

COOK. (Page 283.) John[3] Cook, son of John[2] (Thomas[1]) and Mary (Borden) Cook, b. 1656, d. 1737. His will, 23 Jan. 1736/7, prob. 1 Aug. 1737, mentioned wife Ruth; children: John, Thomas, Ruth Fish, Mary Howland, Deborah Howland, Ann Tripp; sons-in-law: Preserved Fish, James Howland, James Tripp, John Howland. Administrators: four sons-in-law. Witnesses: Peleg Sherman, Richard Sisson, Giles Slocum. Inventory taken 25 July 1737.

[Mary Cook m. 2 Oct. 1712, John Howland of Dartmouth.] (Information from Helen M. Cook, Brookline, Mass.)

CRAW. Robert Craw, not in Austin, but according to Savage, a resident of Newport in 1651. The name is distinctly Scotch, and it is not unlikely that Robert may have come from Berwickshire. Nothing more is known of him, but it is quite likely that Richard Craw of Little Compton and Tiverton was a near relative.

Richard Craw, born about 1670?, died before 16 Jan. 1736. Of Little Compton and Tiverton. Married Mercy. In October, 1698, he, of Little Compton, was deeded 120 acres in Tiverton by William Manchester [Bristol County Deeds]. On 28 Dec. 1702, he witnessed the will of Thomas Butts of Little Compton. On 21 Jan. 1712, he, of Tiverton, deeded land to his son John [ibid.]. Administration on his estate to his widow Mercy, 16 Jan. 1736 [Bristol County Probate].

Children:

- i. John, of Tiverton.
- ii. Ellen, b. 1709; m. 1726, William Springer.
- iii. Sarah, b. ca. 1710; m. 18 Nov. 1729, David Lake.
- iv. Abigail, m. Oct. 1731, Jonathan Lake.
- v. ?Joseph, probably removed to Southeast, Dutchess Co., N.Y.
- vi. Anne, b. 1717. On 12 Mar. 1738/9, Anne Craw of Tiverton released her rights in the estate of her father Richard Craw late of Tiverton deceased to David Lake of the same (Bristol County Deeds). Married in 1739, John Russell of Dartmouth, Mass.

(Information from Ralph Phillips, Esq., New York, N.Y.)

DYER and SCOTT. William Dyer (p. 290, 2nd column). Many years ago G. D. Scull in Dorothea Scott published matter which not only relates to Capt. William Dyer

(Jr.) but sheds interesting light on the career of the adventurer, Capt. John Scott, who left descendants on Long Island. The page references for these items are to the Scull volume, published in 1883.

For the preservation of the few epistolary relics of Dorothea Gotherson contained herein, we are indebted to the careful, business-like habits of Samuel Pepys, the author of the well-known Diary, and Secretary to the Admiralty for the Duke of York. Mrs. Gotherson, Pepys, and Sir Anthony Deane (the Naval Constructor to Charles II.), were the unfortunate victims of that most unscrupulous and plotting adventurer, the (so called) Colonel John Scott; and Pepys was long put to the greatest trouble, expense, and vexation, before he could effectually clear himself from the malicious aspersions thus cast upon him. Upon going through the voluminous papers thus collected by Pepys [now in the Bodleian Library] for his and Sir Anthony's defence, the name of Dorothea Gotherson was frequently met with, and she was only identified as one and the same with Dorothea Hogben by the note which Secretary Pett wrote, January 17, 1679-80, when he sent to the Secretary of the Admiralty Mrs. Hogben's written answers to his thirteen queries. [Preface, pages iv, v.]

Pepys had an interview, September 19, 1679, with Captain William Dyre, and engaged him to collect information in New York and elsewhere, concerning Scott's antecedents in America. Captain Dyre wrote to Pepys "from on board ye Ship Bever, in ye Downes ye 2^d of 8ber, 1679," and incidentally mentions that Mr. Randolph, who was a passenger with him, "sends his service." This was Edward Randolph, Charles II.'s Commissioner to New England, who made eight voyages across the Atlantic in nine years. Thomas Lovelace, an important witness for Pepys, was making a visit to England in 1680, and on his return in that year to New York, he gave him letters of introduction to Captain Dyre, Mathias Nicolls, Mr. Lewin, and Sir Edmund Andross. This Captain Dyre was the son of the Mary Dyre who was executed in 1660, in Boston, for her professions of Quakerism. [Pages 59-60.]

"S. Pepys to Capt. Wm. Dyre.

"September 20th, 1679.

"Sir, - Were it not y^t ye Honour of his Majestie's and his service is more concerned in it then any interest of my owne, I should not hold it so excusable in me to offer ye trouble I am now designing you, but knowing how acceptable any thing is to you wherein His Honour and ye Justice due to His Ministers is concerned, I take ye liberty of putting into your hands an Extract

of a letter wrote by Coll. Nicoll to Mr Secretary Maurice, dated from Fort James (N. York) ye 24 of October, 1666, relating to severall practises by him therein charged upon one Captain John Scott, concerning which I am to desire y^t so soon as you shall be arrived where you are now going (and towards wch I wish you a happy voyage) you will use ye speediest and most effectuall means you can of informing yo^rselfe and inabling me to report to his Majesty what evidences you can collect of ye truth of ye particulars menc'oned in ye said Extract, and of whatever other undue behaviours you shall (upon inquiry into ye legend of Scott's life in New England, Long Island, and parts adjacent) obtaine ye certaine knowledge of wch takeing ye liberty of recommending to you, I beg you to favour me wth any commands of yours wherein I may in some measure answer yor respect to me in this particular, assuring you of my being with all faithfulness,

"y^r most humble servant,

"S.P.

"Since I wrote this, it comes into my head to desire y^t (in case it has not been already said to you by my friend Mr Blaithwaite, to whom I this morning menc'oned it) you will communicate to Sir J. Berry, at yor meeting to-morrow, what you can help to for inabling me to prove Scott's haveing been married in New England, & his wife being (& perhaps children) at this very day, or lately, alive there, as I think you told me last night, it being a point wch may afford very good matter in reference to ye buinesse he is now driving in Kent about a second wife. Pray give my humble service to Sir John Berry."

"Capt. Dyre to Saml. Pepys.

"Sir, - Yours of ye 20th ult. I received, but had not y^t conveniancie of discoursing Sr John Berry in ye premises as desired, however, in answer to ye postcript of yo^{rs}, can assure you that Capt John Scott's wife (whose maiden name was Reyner) was living at Southampton on Long Island in our Government in April last, and was sed lately married again to another man, not receiving of many years from her former husband Scott any supplyes to maintain hirself and children wch shee had by him, the eldest whereof is a son of his own name (who, as I have been credibly informed, is socn intended for England). Capt Scott's mother I also know to be a very poor widow (and lives on ye charity of ye people of Cornbury, near New York), hir name now is Smith, commonly call'd Goodwife Smith, of all wch shall give you a more lengthened and particular account at my arrival there, that ye truth in all things may appeare. I am now in ye Downes wayting only a ffair winde, wch pray God grant in order to a prosperous voyage, which with Mr Randolph's and my h'arty service to you and Mr Blaithwaite is all at present from, &c., &c.,

"Wm. Dyre.

"From on Board ye Ship 'Bever' in ye Downes, ye 2d of 8ber, 1679."

"Worthy Sir, - Yours of the 24 Augt, by Mr Lovelace, I have received, for which great favour of correspondence I own myselfe much obliged, and am unexpressibly rejoiced that Sir Anthony and yourselfe are out of ye pernitious power of that villain Scott, whome doubtlesse the hands of Justice one day will reach for all his horrid contrivances and practices wth condign punishment. You may please to know hee has a son now gone from here to England to seek out his ffather, hearing that hee was famous in yt Kingdome, but I doubt ye young man will be disappointed in his Expedition; hee can certainly informe you that his mother is alive in ye province, and yett as wee heare old Scott had the Impudence to make his addresses to ye Lady Vane, and that in a very splendid manner, and had not Death (which some say hee occasioned) put a period to her days hee had most miserably deluded, deceived, and abused her Ladyshipp. Sir, you will (by the occasion of some like Coll Scott) have the advantage of seeing my Governor, Sir Edmund Andross, in England, who doubtless is a person of that great worth and honour as not to have his name or reputation blemished by anything but what is false, envious, and malicious, which has caused the Duke's desires of seeing him at home with all speed, and soe hath given his Excellency the trouble and danger of a severe winter's voyage, but I hope ye sunshine of his happy returne to us in the Spring will dispell all those malevolent clouds and render the people of this country (under his Majtie's and Royall Highness' dominion) as fortunate as formerly by his prudence and noble government, the continuance of which together with your health and prosperity is the hearty desire of yours, &c., &c.,

"Wm. Dyre.

"New York, 4 January, 1680."

[Note on Scott Family. Capt. John Scott of Southampton, L.I., married Deborah, daughter of Thurston Raynor. After a troublesome career, he left his family and returned to England. His wife seems to have divorced him, and she certainly married second, Charles Sturmy. There were two sons, John and Jeckamiah. It was John who according to the Dyre letters was going to his father in England. He seems to have returned, as a John Scott sold land in Southampton in 1690, but his later history has not been learned. Jeckamiah had a wife Mary and numerous children. The elder John wrote

a letter from London, 6 May 1681, to his son, not called by name, but doubtless Jeckomiah; mentioned (an older) son who was soon to go on his first voyage; urged his son to study hard and to be dutiful to his mother, from whom the father was separated; "my service to your uncle Joseph" (i.e., Joseph Raynor). This letter may be found in Southampton Town Records, 6:189. Those interested in the family will find other items, ibid., 1: 117, 118, 159; 2:29, 33, 122, 204, 274; 5:217, 243, 268; 6:8, 148; and the will of Jeckomiah Scott in New York Wills, 4:220-1. Capt. Jeckamiah Scott died 9 Mar. 1749, aged 86 (gravestone). His wife was daughter of Col. John Jackson of Hempstead. Although properly this note has no place in connection with Rhode Island families, the Dyer-Pepys correspondence tells us more about the Scott family than it does about the Dyer family, and Captain Scott is a figure of sufficient importance and interest to justify the foregoing brief assembling of facts and references. The full title of the Scull volume, if Scott descendants wish to consult it, is Dorothea Scott, otherwise Gotherson and Hogben, of Egerton House, Kent (1611-1680). —D.L.J.]

LAKE. David (page 118, 2nd column). Sarah (Bailey) widow [of Joel Lake] of Tiverton deeded land there bought of William Cornell to son Joseph, mentioning son Joel, 10 Aug. 1750 [Tiverton Deeds, 1:183].

(Column 3.) David, son of Joel and Sarah Lake, born 17:3:1705, died before 9 Feb. 1776; married 18 Nov. 1729, Sarah Craw, daughter of Richard [cf. Pierce MSS, ex penes New Bedford Public Library]; six children. On 22 Mar. 1762, David Lake and Sarah his wife of Tiverton deeded to son Job of Tiverton, in consideration of his agreement to contribute to the support of their aged mother Marcy, widow of their father Richard Craw, late of Tiverton deceased, land of said Richard [Tiverton Deeds, 3:26]. The inventory of the estate of David Lake, late of Tiverton, was presented 9 Feb. 1776 by the administratrix, Sarah Lake [Tiverton Probate].

(Column 3.) Jonathan son of Joel and Sarah Lake, married October, 1731, Abigail daughter of Richard Craw and had five children [Pierce MSS, op. cit.].

(Column 3.) Joel son of Joel and Sarah Lake on 4 June 1756 deeded land there to his sister Sarah, widow of William Tripp, late of Tiverton [Tiverton Deeds].

(Information from Ralph Phillips, Esq., New York, N. Y.)

MANN. Thomas (page 129) married secondly, at Rehoboth, on 3 July 1676, not 9 April 1678, Mary Wheaton [original Rehoboth Vital Rec. 1:46]. She was born at Rehoboth, 4 Nov. 1656. Thomas Mann was son of Richard Mann of Scituate, Mass., who was there in 1648 and was drowned 16 Feb. 1655/6. His inventory was taken 14 Apr. 1656. His widow Rebecca married John Carwin. Thomas Mann was born 15 Aug. 1650.

(Deane's Scituate; Pope's Pioneers, p. 298; information from Richard LeBaron Bowen, Esq., of Rehoboth.)

RAY. Simon (page 160). Mary (2nd column) married first, Roger Kenyon, son of Roger Kenyon, Esq., of Peele Hall, co. Lancaster, England, and had issue, Roger, b. 25 Jan. 1684/5. Her husband Roger died in Ireland before 1688, and Mary married secondly, about 1688-9, Samuel Sands of New Shoreham and Cow Neck, Long Island, son of Capt. James and Sarah (Walker) Sands of Portsmouth and New Shoreham, R.I., who died in 1716. Mary died in or before 1698. She had issue by Sands: Sibel, Marcy (b. ca. 1693), Anne, Sarah, Mary and Samuel, but the order of births is not known.

Dorothy (2nd column), delete the statement of marriage to Samuel Sands and the children assigned. She married, about 1689, as his third wife, Capt. John Clapp, gent., of Charleston, S.C. (1680-87), Flushing, L.I. (1687-92), New York (1692-1708/9), and Rye, Westchester Co., N.Y. (1709). He died before 18 Feb.1725/6. Capt. Clapp was Clerk of the New York Provincial Assembly, 9 Apr. 1691 to 22 Apr. 1697, and Clerk of Westchester County, 14 Oct. 1707 to 1711. He was given by Royal Patent two tracts of land in Rye in 1705 and another in 1708. Capt. Clapp married first, ———, and secondly, Sibilla, perhaps daughter of Daniel Axtell, Landgrave of South Carolina. By Dorothy Ray he had: John, b. at Flushing, 12:7mo.:1690; Elias; Benjamin (d. 1727), and Cornbury. A son by a former marriage, named Gilson, lived in Charleston, S.C. Silas Clapp of New Shoreham, named as "kinsman" in the will of Simon Ray II, was son of John Clapp Jr. and Dorcas Quinby, and a grandson of Capt. John and Dorothy. [cf. Ring-Mailler Genealogy, by Josephine C. Frost, pp. 121-5.]

SANDS. James (page 170). Samuel (2nd column) married first, about 1688-9, Mary, widow of Roger Kenyon, Jr., of Peele Hall, Lancs., and daughter of Simon and Mary (Thomas) Ray. They had issue: Sybil, m. Jonathan Rogers of New London, Conn.; Marcy, b. about 1693, died 1746 "aged 53 years," m. Richard Stilwell of New York City; Anna, single in 1713; Sarah, m. at Hempstead, L. I., 1 Jan., prob. 1712/13, Nathan Selleck of Stamford, Conn.; Mary, single in 1713; and Samuel, ancestor of the Sands family of Westchester County, N.Y.

Samuel married secondly, license 9 Nov. 1704, Elizabeth Lessitt [N. Y. Record, 2:27].

On 10 June 1691 John Clapp, merchant, of Flushing, gave a power of attorney to "brother Mr. Samuel Sands

of New Shoreham alias Block Island." [Court of Ordinary, 1672-1692; Grants, vol. 7, p. 312; State Hist. Comm., Columbia, S.C.]

By his will, dated 11 Dec. 1713, proved 3 Sept.1716, Samuel Sands gave his daughter Anne two silver spoons marked S^S^M and to his daughter Mary a silver cup marked in like manner [New York Wills, 11:16-17]. There can be little doubt that these letters stood for Samuel and Mary Sands. [Ring-Mailler Genealogy, by Josephine C. Frost, pp. 123, 271-2.]

SHELDON (John of Kings Town, page 176). Isaac (column 2) married first, Susanna, who was probably a granddaughter of George and Bethia (Mowry) Palmer of Warwick and Kingstown. "Valmer" (column 3), son of Isaac and Susanna, born 16 May 1724, should read Palmer.

SHELDON (John of Providence, pages 176-7). Nehemiah (column 2, p. 177) is here hypotheitically assigned three daughters, one being Welthian Sheldon who married 6 June 1731 John Williams. She was not daughter of Nehemiah, but of his nephew, Timothy Sheldon, Jr., born 1 March 1689, son of Nehemiah's brother Timothy (p. 176).

The will of Timothy Sheldon, Jr., of Providence, who died in vita patris on 3 Dec. 1741, dated 27 March 1741, names his wife, Rebecca, his six sons, Timothy, Jonathan, Benijah, Benjamin, Daniel and James Sheldon, and his loving daughter Welthian Williams. Son Timothy executor. [Providence Probate.]

(Information from Miss M. Sarah Sutherland of Washington, D.C.)

SMITH. Richard (page 185). Elizabeth (2nd column) married first, as his second wife, John Viall, vintner and gentleman, of Boston and Swansea, Mass.; and secondly, Deacon Samuel Newman of Rehoboth, Mass., son of the Rev. Samuel Newman of Rehoboth. John Viall kept the Old Ship Tavern in Boston in 1662, and in 1679 removed to Swansea [Winsor's Boston, I:551]. John and Elizabeth had issue:

James, bapt. at Boston, 12 June 1664.
Samuel, b. at Boston, 25 Nov. 1667.
Elizabeth, b. at Boston, 6 Apr. 1670.
Benjamin.
Jonathan, b. after 1673.

On 4 May 1668, John Viall was living at Wickford, R. I., where he signed a petition [R. I. Col. Rec., 2:226-227]. On 25 Aug. 1679, John Viall, vintner, and Mr. Eliakim Hutchinson, both of Boston, purchased 600 acres in Swansea. On 6 Aug. 1680, John Viall, gent., of Swansea, and Elizabeth his wife sold land in Bristol,

Mass. (now R. I.) to Nathaniel Bosworth of Bristol [Bristol County, Mass., Deeds, IV:125]. John Viall died 26 Feb. 1685/6. The will of John Viall, dated 3 Jan. 1681, proved 31 Aug. 1686, names his wife Elizabeth and their children [Suffolk County Probate, Boston, II:34-36].

By his will 15 March 1690/1, proved 12 July 1692, Major Richard Smith devised to "Elizabeth Vial alias Newman" a farm at Boston Neck in Narragansett. On 4 Feb. 1692/3, Elizabeth Newman of Swansea deeded this farm to her eldest son Samuel Viall, except three acres which she gave to her children Benjamin and Jonathan Viall and Elizabeth Thomas [Bristol County Deeds, I: 316]. On 21 Dec. 1723, Samuel Viall of Bristol sold the same. The husband of Elizabeth Thomas was John Thomas, cordwainer, of Swansea [ibid., I:319].

Deed of Daniel Allen of Swansea, dated 30 Oct. 1693, recites the difference between himself and Noah Floyd, late of London, draper, now resident of Rhode Island, and Samuel and Benjamin Viall and Samuel Newman, guardian of Jonathan Viall, all of Swansea, yeomen, and quitclaims to them [Bristol County Deeds, I:318].

(Information from Richard LeBaron Bowen, Esq., of Rehoboth, Mass.)

210 TAG W. No. 112 Oct., 1952 V. XXVIII, No. 4

ADDITIONS AND CORRECTIONS TO AUSTIN'S GENEALOGICAL DICTIONARY OF RHODE ISLAND

By G. Andrews Moriarty, A.M., LL.B., F.S.A.

(Previous instalments in vols. 19 to 21, 24 to 28)

BARTON. (Pages 250-1, 3rd column.) Rufus: had issue by his wife Sarah (Robinson):

i. Mary, b. 2 Dec. 1705, 1st day of the week.
ii. Benjamin, b. 21 July 1707, 2nd day of the week.
iii. Rowland, b. 7 April 1709, 5th day of the week.
iv. Margaret, b. 13 Sept. 1711, 5th day of the week.
v. John, b. 7 March 1714, 3rd day of the week.
vi. Ebenezer, b. 28 May 1717, 2nd day of the week.
vii. Rufus, b. 9 Jan. 1719, 7th day of the week.
viii. Sarah, b. 28 April 1722, 5th day of the week.
ix. William, b. 12 Sept. 1726, 2nd day of the week.

(From a family document, see New Eng. Hist. & Gen. Register, 65: 380-1, where some additional information is given.)

BROWN (Chad, page 258). (Page 260, 2nd column.) Jeremiah of Newport. Add to his children in 3rd column (page 261):

ii. John, of age 1693 when James and John Brown of Newport sold to Joseph Latham land in Providence adjoining lands which in later deeds are described as adjacent to the land which Latham "purchased of the sons of Jeremiah Browne" (Providence Deeds). Children not traced.

iii. (perhaps) William, b. about 1676; will dated 1 June 1752, proved 12 Feb. 1753; m. at Kingstown, R.I., 2 Nov. 1707, Elizabeth, dau. of Rowland and Mary (Allen) Robinson. Seven children. In 1711, called "of Jamestown," he purchased land in the Pettyquamscot Purchase. Removed to Kingstown. Communicant of Church of England.

iv. Samuel, b. Mar. 1680; d. at South Kingstown in 1762 (will dated 22 June 1757, proved 16 Aug. 1762); m. (1) at Kingstown, 22 Oct. 1702, Mary ——; m. (2) Marcy (b. 24 Feb. 1698/9), dau. of Edward and Hannah Carr of Jamestown, and widow of John Weeden. Ten children.

v. Daniel, b. probably at Newport; d. probably 1726 (inventory taken 16 Nov. 1726); m. Frances, dau. of John and Dorcas (Gardiner) Watson. His farm of 429 acres was in the Shanack Purchase, with 447 acres adjoining in Wood River Purchase (in old Westerly). On 26 Apr. 1712, Daniel Browne and wife Frances conveyed to "brother Samuel Browne" his rights in the farm where Samuel lived in Pettyquamscot Purchase bequeathed to Daniel by the will of his father, Jeremiah Browne (So. Kingston Deeds, 2:209). Eight children.

vi. Joseph, b. probably at Newport; d. at Glocester, R.I., 13 Mar. 1764; will dated 2 Feb. 1764, proved 21 Mar. 1764; m. (1) about 1703, Sarah, dau. of John and Sarah (Brown) Pray; ten children, b. at Attleborough; m. (2) at Glocester, 27 Apr. 1751, Hannah, dau. of John and Mary (Russell) Lapham; four children, b. at Glocester. Joseph lived at Newport, Westerly and Kingstown, R.I., Attleborough, Mass., and Glocester, R.I. In 1714 Joseph Browne of Attleborough, "son of Mr. Jeremiah Browne, late of Newport, deceased," sold land in Swansea (Taunton Deeds, 8:720).

vii. (possibly) Mary, m. John Paine of Newport, saddler, whose will, dated 15 May 1704, was proved 4 June 1704 (New Eng. Hist. and Gen. Register, 83:85). In the article referred to below, Mr. Browne suggests that Mary may have been a daughter of Jeremiah because John Paine and his wife Mary in 1701/2 sold to Samuel Browne of Kingstown land in the Pettyquamscot Purchase, 30 acres "interim of Jeremiah Browne late of Newport" (So. Kingston Deeds). However, as John Paine bought this land of Lathom Clarke on 25 Nov. 1700 (R.I. Colony Deeds), this conclusion seems to be very uncertain.

viii. Hannah, b. 1688/9; d. 4 Aug. 1754; m. Jonathan Haven of Shelter Island, N.Y.

Perhaps other children.

(Most of the above data are from "Chad Browne and His Descendants" by William Bradford Browne of North Adams, Mass., in New Eng. Hist. and Gen. Register, 80:73-86, 170-185), q. v. for the children of the next two generations.)

HULL (Joseph). Page 108, 1st column. Joseph was apparently alive in October, 1720.

Page 110, 2nd column. To the children of Joseph add Reuben, who was executed for murder, 23 June 1720. In Oct. 1719, the General Assembly of Rhode Island ordered the sheriff to sell the personal estate of Reuben Hull, "now in His Majesty's jail, convicted of murder" [R.I. Col. Rec., 1:262]. In May 1720, Reuben Hull, who was convicted of murder in October 1719, and who was in jail, was granted a stay of execution until 23 June next, but on 14 June 1720 the Assembly ordered that he be no longer reprieved and that he be executed 23 June [ibid., 1:269, 272].

In Oct. 1720 the General Assembly granted the petition of John Segar of Kingstown, touching an estate of 150 acres in Westerly, late of Reuben Hull, lately executed for murder. The petition set forth that Reuben Hull had received the land by deed of gift from his father Joseph, with remainders, if he died without issue, to Joseph Hoxie and John Segar, sons of John Hoxie and John Segar, "the brothers-in-law of the said Reuben Hull." It appeared that after the arrest of Reuben,

John Hoxie had given the deed to Reuben's father Joseph, "who has since concealed the same, whereby the aforesaid Joseph Hoxie and John Segar, sons of John Hoxie and John Segar, are like to be defrauded." The Assembly ordered that the land be given to the said John Segar and John Hoxie as feofees in trust for their sons. (Document in the possession of Mr. Charles J. Clark of Perryville, R.I., transcribed by W. Louis Frost, Esq., of Perryville.) Reuben died without issue. The murder was referred to by "Shepard" Tom Hazard in his "Johnnycake Papers."

LOW. (Page 339, 3rd column.) Samuel of Warren, R. I., married first, about 1722, Elizabeth (b. Medfield, Mass., 31 Oct. 1689), daughter of Dr. John Wilson of Braintree, Mass., and granddaughter of the famous John Wilson, M.A. (Cambridge, 1609) of Boston, Mass. They had issue three children: Anne (m. 10 Dec. 1743, Joseph Bosworth, Jr., of Rehoboth, Mass.), John Wilson, and Hooker. Samuel married second, intention 31 Jan.1735/6 Isabel, daughter of Richard and Eleanor (Sayles) Greene of Warwick, R.I., and had: Samuel. [New Eng. Hist. and Gen. Register, 61:129.]

ROBINSON. (Rowland), page 165, 2nd column. Elizabeth. Her husband was probably a son of Jeremiah Brown of Newport, R.I., and a grandson of Chad of Providence [New Eng. Hist. and Gen. Register, 80:80.]

SAUNDERS, Tobias. Page 173, 1st column. Tobias Saunders appears to have been an iron worker and in 1649 he was at the Saugus iron works and was living in the house of Lawrence Turner. On 11: 7mo.: 1649 he was a witness in the Salem Court for Nicholas Pinion in the case of Pray vs. Pinion. On 24: 7mo.: 1650 John Chackswell testified in the Ipswich Court in the case of Lawrence Turner vs. Henry Lenord et ux. Mary regarding the unseemly doings of Saunders and Sarah wife of said Turner. [Essex Quarterly Court Records, 1:173-4, 198.] At this same Court, Saunders was surety for John Bond in the case of Bond vs. Hardman for slander concerning the brisk attempts of Bond on Dorothy Pray, aged 16 years. Saunders, Pinion and Bond, workers at the Iron Works, were clearly close friends.

TOSH. Page 207, 2nd column. (William.) A statement by Simon Ray, Jr., in 1734, in the case of Penelope Holway (daughter of William Tosh and wife of Benjamin Holway of South Kingstown) against Acres Tosh (son of Daniel, brother of William) for certain land on Block Island, shows that William Tosh's wife, Penelope, was born Penelope Niles and at that date she had a sister living in Connecticut, named Abigail. Penelope and Abigail were probably the children of John Niles of Block Island (son of John[1] of Braintree) who died there 7 Sept. 1683. [Statement in possession of Bradford F. Swan, Esq., of Providence, R.I.; New Eng. Hist. and Gen. Register, 85:140.]

SANFORD. The following will, sent me by the well-known genealogist, Mr. Francis Richmond Sears of Swansea, Mass., adds somewhat to our knowledge of the Tiverton Sanfords and is an unusually valuable genealogical document.

The will of "Samuel Sanford of Tiverton....weaver," dated 26 Aug. 1773, and, possibly, proved 4 Oct. 1773, mentioned:

"to my brother in Law Smiton Hart, my blue Duroy Coat....

"to my Couzen William Sanford, son of my brother Restcome Sanford, Deceas[d], my blue broad Cloth strait body coat, also two Silver Dollars that he hath now in his hands....

"unto my beloved sister Eliphal Hart wife of Smiton Hart the Sum of Twenty Silver Dollars twelve of which Twenty she hath now in her possession & the other Eight to be paid her in three months after my Decease by my Executor herein after named....

"to my Couzen Joseph Hart son of Smiton Hart aforesaid two Silver Dollars to be paid to him in three months after my Decease by my Executor....

"to my Couzen Deborah Hart Daughter of Smiton Hart aforesaid two Silver Dollars & to be paid as above said by my Executor....

"to my Couzen Isaac Sanford son of my brother Peleg Sanford Deceas[d] three Silver Dollars to be paid in three months after my Decease by my Executor....

"unto my Couzen Sarah Davis wife of Jonathan Davis of Dartmouth my three Quart puter bason also four silver Dollars to be Delivered to her in three months after my Deceas by my Executor....

"unto Peleg Sanford son of my Couzen William Sanford son of my brother Restcome Sanford Deceas[d] & unto his Heires & assigns forever Fifty Silver Milled Dollars to be paid in three months after my Decease as aforesaid..

"to my thirteen Couzens Namely Restcome Sanford, Geor Sanford, Ephraim Sanford, Mary Borden wife of Samuel Borden, Deborah Hart wife of Constant Hart, Sarah Taber wife of George Taber, Elizabeth Willingstone wife of Ichabud Willingstone children of my brother Restcome Sanford Deceas[d] — also John Sanford, Philip Sanford, Peleg Sanford, Samuel Sanford, Prissiller Sanford, children of my brother Peleg Sanford Deceas[d] & Deborah Taber Daughter of Philip Taber of Dartmouth & Mary his

wife the sum of one shilling to Each of them my sd thirteen Couzens & to be paid in three months after my Decease by my Executor....

"to the Reverend Mr Othniel Campbell two Silver Dollars to be paid in three months after my Decease [etc.]

"to my Couzen Samuel Sanford son of my brother Restcome Sanford Deceas[d] & to Peleg Sanford son to my Couzen William Sanford aforesaid all the Rest of my Estate ....Equally to be Divided between them

"I Do Hereby nominate, Constitute & appoint my trusty & well beloved Couzen Samuel Sanford son of my brother Restcome aforesaid & Peleg Sanford son of William sanford aforesaid Joint Executors....

Water Taber Samuel Sanford"
Hanner Taber
Walter Cook

The above is recorded in Probate Records of Tiverton No. 2, 1747-1768, pages 138-9. At the end of this will is inscribed "Turn Over" and in the middle of the following page (140) is found, "In Town Councill on the fourth Day of October." One would have expected to find this will in the next volume of probate records, as it is preceded and followed by Town Council meetings in 1759, but there are some records found following this will in the 1770's.

THE AMERICAN GENEALOGIST

Whole No. 118 April, 1954 Vol. XXX, No. 2

ADDITIONS AND CORRECTIONS TO AUSTIN'S GENEALOGICAL DICTIONARY OF RHODE ISLAND

By G. Andrews Moriarty, A.M., LL.B., F.S.A.

(Continued from Vol. 28, p. 210)

ALLEN (John, page 2, column 1). Of Newport, but died in 1708 at South Kingstown, where his son-in-law, the first Rowland Robinson, was then living. His will (see Austin's Additions, p. 438) in 1706 named children of his son John; son Christopher; daughters Elizabeth Tompkins, Mary Robinson, and Mercy Dunkin; thus confirming the guess (on p. 2) that Christopher was son of John. John Allen married, says Mr. Austin, on 14 Oct. 1650, Elizabeth Bacon. Christopher Allen married in 1687 Elizabeth Seyouche of Little Compton and settled there, but later moved to South Kingstown and

died there in 1739.

Gov. Henry Bull of Newport on 27 Nov. 1688 deeded for love 28 acres in Little Compton to his grandchildren Christopher and Elizabeth Allen of that town (Austin, p. 266). From this it might appear that John Allen's wife (Elizabeth Bacon, married 14 Oct. 1650) may have been a daughter of Gov. Henry Bull and the young widow of a Bacon.

[Note by Editor. It should, however, be noted that the only Allen named in the account of Gov. Henry Bull's estate (Austin, p. 266) was Elizabeth Allen, who had a legacy of some livestock. Also that John Allen's daughter Elizabeth was already Mrs. Tompkins at the date of Bull's deed (1688) to Christopher and Elizabeth Allen, but that Christopher had married Elizabeth Seyouche in 1687, the previous year; and that Christopher and his wife were specifically the Allens who were living in Little Compton at that date. An alternate theory may therefore be suggested, that Elizabeth Seyouche was a granddaughter of Gov. Henry Bull, and that Christopher Allen as her husband was included in the term "grandchildren" used in the deed in the sense of grandson-in-law.]

ALLEN (William, page 2). John of North Kingstown (2nd column), born 26 Oct. 1670, died 30 Mar. 1747, had a wife Sarah, entered as born at New Haven, 14 June 1677; they had four daughters, the eldest being Mercy, born 17 Aug. 1701. The date and place of birth identify the wife as Sarah Mansfield, born at New Haven 14 June 1677, daughter of Major Moses and Mercy (Glover) Mansfield, who married at New Haven, 1 June 1698, William Rhodes. He could not long have survived, since Sarah would seem to have married Allen by 1700. Sarah Mansfield's younger sister, Bathshua, born 1 Jan.1682/3, married at New Haven, 22 Jan. 1705, Joseph Chapman of Newport. [Contributed by Donald L. Jacobus.]

BOWDISH or BOWDITCH (William) [omitted by Austin].

1. William Bowdish or Bowditch of Salem, Mass., and Newport, R.I., was admitted an inhabitant at Salem 20:9:1639. Granted 10 acres, 23:11:1642. Married Sarah ——, who was admitted a member of the First Church at Salem 10:3mo.:1640. They became Baptists. On 4:6mo.:1646 she was admonished "for offensive withdrawing from ye ordinance of Baptizing Infants" [Essex County Quarterly Court Files, 1:101]. He was granted 30 acres in the Salem Common Lands on 13:8:1649. This is his last appearance in the Salem records. Rev. Obadiah Holmes records that he baptized "Goodwife Bowditch." In 1651 Hugh Peter, writing from England to John Win-

throp, Jr., at Pequot asks him "to entertain Goodwife Bowditch and her husband if they go thither." They undoubtedly lived in Newport after leaving Salem.

Children:

2 i. Nathaniel^2, bapt. Salem, 12:12:1642/3.
ii. (undoubtedly) a daughter, m. Richard Dunn, Sr., of Newport, R.I., and had: 1. Richard. 2. Samuel. 3. Nathaniel, ancestor of the Block Island Dunn family. (Austin, p. 68.)

2. Nathaniel^2 Bowdish (William^1), of Newport, R.I., weaver, baptized at Salem, 12:12:1642/3, died before 12 Apr. 1706 (date of inventory). On 9 Dec. 1673, layers out of common lands at Salem were ordered to lay out land formerly granted to William Bowdish and on 12 Oct. 1674 Nathaniel Bowdish of Newport, R.I., sold to John Pudney 30 acres at Salem Commons [Essex County Deeds; New England Hist. and Gen. Register, 72:224]. He was granted land in the Commons at Newport, 12 Mar. 1701/2 [Newport Town Records]. His will dated 5 — [1706?] names sons William and Nathaniel; daughters Sarah Bull, Hannah and Katherine, and cousin Richard Dunn. Administration granted to son William on 2 May 1706. [Newport Town Council Records.] His wife's name has not been learned.

Children:

3 i. William^3.
ii. Nathaniel, occurs in Newport County Court Records in 1705. Probably the ancestor of the Bowdish family of East and West Greenwich, 1750.
iii. Sarah, m. after 23 Apr. 1691, as second wife, Jireh Bull, Jr. (d. 1709), of Newport.
iv. Hannah, bapt. as an adult at Trinity Church, Newport, before and about 1709.
v. Katherine.
vi. (?) Mary, m. at Trinity Church, Newport, 8 Oct. 1720, John Davis.

3. William^3 Bowdish (Nathaniel^2, William^1) of Dartmouth, Mass., tailor; married Mercy Tompkins, born 20 Oct. 1685, daughter of Nathaniel and Elizabeth (Allen) Tompkins of Little Compton, R.I. He sold his father's house in Newport on 22 Apr. 1712 to Capt. Richard Dunn [Newport Town Deeds]. His will, dated 5 Apr. 1750, proved 6 May 1755 [Bristol County, Mass., Probate].

Children:

i. Nathaniel^4, b. 22 — 1709.
ii. William, b. Sept. 1712.
iii. Katherine, b. 6 Aug. 17--.
iv. Hannah, b. Apr. 1717; m. Joseph Brownell.

v. Elizabeth, m. Paul Russell of Dartmouth.
vi. Freegift, b. 31 Mar. 1726(?); of Tiverton, R.I.

Note: There is no known connection between the above family and the distinguished Bowditch family of Salem, descended from William Bowditch of Salem in 1671. But it is probable that, like them, they came from Devon or Dorset, where the Bowditches are numerous.

BROWN (Nicholas, page 28). William (2nd column) had daughters Martha and Jane and a son Tobias. Evidently Martha married John Sims and Jane married John Rogers. The will of John Bailey of Newport, dated 8 May 1733, proved 2 Feb. 1735/6, mentions "daughter-in-law Martha Sims and daughter-in-law Jane Rogers [Newport Town Council, Probate Records]. In Jan. 1714/15, Tobias Brown of Portsmouth (son of William) sold land in Newport to John Bayley. From this it would appear that the widow of William Brown married secondly, John Bailey of Newport, as his second wife. [Information furnished by Edward H. West, Esq., of Laurel, Maryland.]

BULL (Henry, page 264). For Allen connection, see Allen, ante. Jireh, Jr. (page 265, 3rd column), married secondly, Sarah. She was the daughter of Nathaniel Bowdish of Newport [ante, Bowdish, and Essex Institute Hist. Coll., 48:335-7].

CRANSTON and STANTON. This is to revise statements made in The American Genealogist, 25:250, specifically the conclusion that William^2 Cranston (Gov. John^1) married Mary Stanton. That was based upon the statement of William's son William^3 in the chancery case of Pope vs. Smith (cf. New England Hist. and Gen. Register, 100:219) to the effect that he was nephew of John Cranston (i.e., Col. John^2, son of Gov. John^1) and also of Henry Stanton.

Gov. John Cranston married Mary Clarke, who married secondly, Capt. John Stanton of Newport, and had a son Henry by him. Thus William^3 Cranston, the deponent of 1773, was a nephew of Col. John Cranston on his father's side, and of Henry Stanton on his grandmother's side, through her second marriage. The maiden name of Mary, wife of William^2 Cranston, is still unknown.

The will of Capt. John Stanton of Newport, dated 16 — 1712, proved 5 July 1725(?), names daughters Mary Coggeshall, Hannah Carr, and Avis Norton [Newport Town Council Records]. Accordingly, in Austin's account of Capt. John Stanton's children (page 389), add daughters Mary (married ——— Coggeshall) and Avis. The will of Mary Coggeshall, dated 4 Mar. 1740, proved 1 June 1747 [Newport Town Council Records] names sons John, Joshua, and Joseph, daughters Mary wife of Thomas Weaver, Hannah wife of Benjamin Weaver, Marcy Fish, Avis and Humility, also son-in-law Peleg Wood, and brother Benjamin Stanton.

I am indebted to Miss Bertha W. Clarke of Boston for valuable assistance upon this matter.

DUNN (page 68). Richard (1st column) undoubtedly married a daughter of William Bowdish or Bowditch of Salem, Mass., and Newport, R.I. See Bowdish herein and Essex Institute Hist. Coll., 48:335-7.

HOLLIMAN (Ezekiel, page 102). Ezekiel Holliman, who came from Tring, co. Herts, to New England in 1634, was undoubtedly the Ezekiel Holyman named in the will of John Holyman, weaver, of Cholesbury, co. Bucks, dated 12 Jan. 1597/8, proved 6 Mar. 1597/8, together with Priscilla Holyman. Tring is near Cholesbury, and John's father, Leonard Holyman of Cholesbury, owned land in Tring. Ezekiel's daughter, Priscilla, was evidently named for the Priscilla mentioned in John Holyman's will.

SHEFFIELD (Ichabod, page 175). Joseph (2nd column), delete Newport and replace with Portsmouth; Capt. Joseph Sheffield never lived in Newport. [Cf. New England Hist. and Gen. Register, 104:5.]
Mary (3rd column), daughter of Joseph, married Samuel Arnold of North Kingstown. [Rhode Island History, 12 (1953):75-81.]

STANTON: see Cranston herein.

TABOR (Philip, page 195). The wife of Philip, Jr. (2nd column) was Mary, daughter of John and Sarah (Warren) Cooke of Plymouth and Dartmouth. John Cooke was the Mayflower passenger, and Sarah was daughter of Richard Warren of the Mayflower. [Information of the late George Ernest Bowman.]

TOMPKINS (Nathaniel, page 205). Mercy (page 206, 2nd column) married William[3] Bowdish (Nathaniel[2], William[1]) [see Bowdish herein and Essex Institute Hist. Coll., 48:335-7].

THE AMERICAN GENEALOGIST

Whole No. 125 Jan., 1956 Vol. XXXII, No. 1

ADDITIONS AND CORRECTIONS TO AUSTIN'S GENEALOGICAL DICTIONARY OF RHODE ISLAND

By G. Andrews Moriarty, A.M., LL.B., F.S.A.

(Continued from Vol. 30, p. 125)

BRENTON (Page 252, column 2). Martha. She was the wife of John Garde, not Card, the son of Roger Garde of Biddeford, co. Devon, England, and York, Maine, bapt. at Biddeford 8 Nov. 1618, died 1668-1673. John was a merchant at Boston in 1662, when he quitclaimed his rights in his father's land at York [cf. Noyes-Libby-Davis, Gen. Dict. of Me. and N.H., p. 252]. He was at Portsmouth, R.I., 1664 and 1668, and died prior to 9 Feb. 1673/4. His heir was John Champlin of Newport, merchant, in 1673 and 1674. He evidently died s.p., and Martha was probably a second wife.

CARD (Page 270, column 2). John. Delete first wife Martha Brenton and, from the account, all before "1687 Sept. 6. Taxed at Kings Town 1/9."

CHAMPLIN (Page 274, column 1). Jeffrey. He probably came from Biddeford, co. Devon, and was probably the brother of William Champlin, who married at Biddeford, 25 Nov. 1641, Mary (bapt. 1 Feb. 1626/7) daughter of Roger Garde. Their son, John Champlin, was a merchant at Fayal and later at Newport, R.I., who lived in Newport next to Jeffrey Champlin and in 1673 and 1675 was heir of John Garde [Cf. Aspinwall and R.I. Colonial Deeds].

(column 2). Jeffrey[2] (Jeffrey[1]) of Westerly and Kingstown, R.I., undoubtedly had other issue besides Jeffrey 3rd, among whom was Amey, wife of Robert[3] (Robert[2], Thomas[1]) Hazard of Kingstown. Robert and Amey had a son Jeffrey ("Stout Jeffrey") Hazard of Kingstown, born 29 Sept. 1698. The rare name of Jeffrey occurs, at this period in Narragansett, only in the Champlin family.

HAZARD (page 321, column 3). Robert[3] (Robert[2], Thomas[1]) Hazard; his wife Amey was undoubtedly a daughter of Jeffrey[2] (Jeffrey[1]) Champlin of Westerly and Kingstown.

WARD (page 406). John (column 1) and granddaughter Margaret (column 3). The will of George Bradley was in the lost Newport records, but a certified copy was filed in the records of the Norfolk County Court, Virginia, 15 July 1695 (Book V, fo. 247; published in vol. 1, p. 156 of McIntosh's Lower Norfolk and Norfolk Wills). The will of George Bradley of Newport on Rhode Island, merchant, 24 Aug. 1694, being bound on a voyage to sea. To grandfather John Ward for a ring. To friends Mr. Weston Clarke and Mr. Robert Kittle, both of Newport, for rings. If my wife Margaret be now with child and should it be a son, he to be called George, £300, if a daughter £200, to be managed by wife Margaret until the child is of age. If she remarry, then feoffees or executors in trust as guardians. Residue to wife Margaret, the executrix. Witnessed by Samuel Cranston and William Wilson.

Unless John Ward had an otherwise unknown daughter who married an unknown Bradley and was mother of George Bradley, then it seems likely that George Bradley was the first husband of Margaret[3] Ward (Thomas[2], John[1]) before her marriage to Robert Wrightington. This would have given Bradley the right to call John Ward his grandfather.

TAG W. No. 135 July, 1958 V. XXXIV, No. 3 169

ADDITIONS AND CORRECTIONS TO AUSTIN'S GENEALOGICAL DICTIONARY OF RHODE ISLAND

By G. Andrews Moriarty, A.M., LL.B., F.S.A.

COGGESHALL. Page 49, 1st column. John. He was not born in 1591 but was baptized at Halstead, co. Essex, 9 Dec. 1601. The date in Austin was taken from his gravestone, which was not erected until many years after his death, at the close of the seventeenth century. The Friends' record of his death in 1647 gives his age as 48 years, which is nearer the mark.

COOK. Page 282, 1st column. Thomas. He is evidently the Thomas Cook who occurs at Taunton, Mass., in an undated list prior to 1640. In 1640 he was a Freeman at Taunton. (Bailies' New Plymouth.)

JEFFERAY. Page 111, 1st column. William. Delete the following:

"1603 July 7. He matriculated as sizar of Caius College, Cambridge.
1606. He took degree of B.A. at graduation.
1610. He took degree of M.A."

The William Jefferay at Caius was a different man and came from Norfolk. He was a cleric and preacher at Nantwich 1616-19. [Venn's Alumni Cantabrigienses, vol. II, Pt. 1, p. 466.]

RHODES. Page 365. Through the courtesy of Mr. Charles W. Farnham of Providence, R.I., I am enabled to add the following to Austin's account of this family.

Zachariah[3] (Jeremiah[2], Zachariah[1]), change date of his death from 13 May 1761 to 3 May 1760. In the last column, children of said Zachariah: 1. Elizabeth, m. Joseph Carpenter of Smithfield, R.I. (Smithfield Land Evidence); 2. Patience, m. David Knapp (Warwick, R.I., Land Evidence); 3. The "daughter" was Ruth, who m. John Tucker (Cranston, R.I., Land Evidence).

Action in trespass and ejectment in R.I. Court of Common Pleas, December Term 1796, brought by Joseph Carpenter, grandson of Joseph and Elizabeth Carpenter, against Benjamin Aldrich of Gloucester, R.I., and Daniel Mowry and Daniel Mowry Jr. of Smithfield, R.I. Zachariah Rhodes of Smithfield died 3 May 1760 and a third of his undivided land descended to Joseph Carpenter, eldest son of Elizabeth Carpenter, now deceased. Patience Knapp and Ruth Tucker were the other children of said Zachariah. Joseph Carpenter, son of Elizabeth, died 10 Nov. 1784 in Newburgh, N.Y., and an undivided third descended to the plaintiff, Joseph Carpenter, grandson of Elizabeth, and to his sisters, i.e., Elizabeth, Margaret, Mary, Sarah, Charity, and Lydia Carpenter. Reviewed by R.I. Supreme Court, September Term 1799 (vol. 4, p. 209).

SANFORD. [Not an Austin correction; see The American Genealogist, 26:202.] Restcome Sanford married secondly, not Content Cornell, but Content Manchester, widow of Eber Crandall of Tiverton and Little Compton. Restcome Sanford by his will left legacies to Content's three children by her first husband, viz., Elizabeth Mosher, Mary Hart, and Eber Crandall.

Elizabeth, daughter of Eber and Content Crandall, born 20 June 1731, married 23 June 1748 Nicholas Mosher. Mary, her sister, was born 23 Sept. 1735, and their brother Eber Crandall was born 14 March 1740.

I am indebted for the above data to Mr. Edwin G. Sanford of Belmont, Mass.

UPDIKE. Page 397. Under Daniel[3] (Lodowick[2], Gilbert[1]), for McSharron read Rev. Dr. James MacSparran.

Page 398. James[2] Updike (2nd column). In 1675 he was a shipwright at Boston and on 27 Apr. 1675 he, together with other shipwrights, was found guilty of riding John Langworthy on a pole from the North End of Boston to the Town House as an interloper, who had never served his time to the trade of shipwright. He was fined 5/. On 21 Apr. 1679 he took the oath of allegiance as of Boston. [Records of Suffolk County Court, 1671-1680, Colonial Soc. of Mass., 2:602, 968.]

TAG W. No. 138 April, 1959 V. XXXV, No. 2

ADDITIONS AND CORRECTIONS TO AUSTIN'S GENEALOGICAL DICTIONARY OF RHODE ISLAND

By G. Andrews Moriarty, A.M., LL.B., F.S.A.

In the summer of 1958, Mr. Waldo C. Sprague of Wollaston, Mass., visited England and made searches in Essex County relating to the families of Thomas Cornell and Adam Mott of Portsmouth, R.I., and he has kindly given me the results to present to The American Genealogist.

CORNELL. Page 54.

The Saffron Walden, co. Essex, parish register contains the following entries:

Baptized

Sarah dau. of Thomas and Rebecca Cornell,	30 Mar.1623
William son of " " " "	4 Apr. 1625
Thomas son of " " " "	21 Oct. 1627
Rebecca dau. of " " " "	31 Jan.1629/30
Elizabeth dau.of " " " "	1 May 1631
William son of Mr." " " "	9 Dec. 1632
John son of Thomas " " "	6 June 1634
Elizabeth dau.of Mr.Thomas & Rebecca "	15 Jan.1636/7

Buried

William son of Thomas and Rebecca Cornell	7 Jan.1627/8
Kelame[?] son of " " " "	19 Oct. 1632

The above refer to the family of Thomas of Portsmouth, R.I. According to the Briggs Genealogy, Thomas Cornell married Rebecca, daughter of Henry Briggs of St. James Clerkenwell parish, London, where she was baptized 25 Oct. 1600. John and Joyce, children of Henry Briggs, were baptized 8 Apr. 1618; Joyce was buried 3 Dec. 1620 and Henry on 14 Aug. 1625 [cf. Austin, p. 55, col. 1].

The Thomas Cornell who married Elizabeth Fiscock at New Amsterdam in 1642 [p. 54, col. 2] was not the son of Thomas of Portsmouth, but another man.

MOTT. Page 344, 1st column.

The printed Portsmouth Town Records [p. 72] show that Adam Mott was son of "ould John Mott" when the Town provided for the latter's support, 3 July 1656. The first two items given by Austin in col. 2 under John son of Adam Mott actually refer to Adam's father John, who probably died not long after the 1656 entry.

In the shipping list, Adam is stated to have come from Cambridge. He evidently belonged in the nearby

Essex parish of Saffron Walden, where the surname occurs as far back as 1570 in the parish register. The following entries pertain to Adam of Portsmouth: Married 28 Oct. 1616, Adam Mott and Elizabeth Creel; Buried 18 June 1617, a man child of Adam Mott; and Baptized 6 Sept. 1618, John son of Adam Mott. At the neighboring parish of Horseheath, co. Cambridge, Adam Mott and Sarah Lott were married 11 May 1635.

The following entries from Saffron Walden may pertain to Adam Mott's father, John Mott: Buried 2 Jan. 1610/11, Elizabeth wife of John Mott; Buried 4 May 1619, Catherine wife of John Mott; Buried 2 Jan. 1616/17, Ann daughter of John Mott; and Baptized 29 Sept. 1625, Elizabeth daughter of John and Mary Mott.

Another Adam Mott came to Newbury, Mass., and later migrated to Long Island. In the shipping list in 1638 he was aged 19 years, and in his will in 1681 he called himself aged about 60. At his marriage to his first wife, Jane Hallet, in 1647, the Dutch Church records of New Amsterdam enter him as from Essex County. This Adam Mott had children by his first wife named James, Grace, Henry, John, Joseph, and Gershom. The Saffron Walden Parish Registers contain the following baptisms of children of James and Grace Mott:

Adam, 21 Jan. 1620/1;
Henry, 31 May 1623;
George, 20 Nov. 1625.

It will be noted that the Adam baptized 1620/1 was of the proper age to be the Long Island settler, and that the names James, Grace and Henry correspond. James Mott, father of the above Adam, may possibly have been son of a Mr. George Mott who was buried at Saffron Walden 7 Feb. 1614/15.

Probably the two Adams were closely related. Further research in Essex and Cambridgeshire is indicated.

RHODES. Page 365. (Courtesy of Charles W. Farnham)

Austin states that John Rhodes of Providence and Scituate (Jeremiah[2], Zachariah[1]) died 19 June 1744; married first, Elizabeth Dailey, of John, and second, Martha —— who died after 1744.

John[3] Rhodes had but the one wife, Elizabeth Dailey, and never resided in Scituate but lived in Providence in the section which later became Johnston. His will was made 22 Oct. 1748 and, after providing for his wife Elizabeth and sons Peleg and Jeremiah, gives 10 shillings to daughter Ann Stephens (wife of Henry, she having had her portion before, and "To two grandsons, the children of my son John, deceased, 5 shillings each, my son John having had his share of the estate."

On 8 Feb. 1749, John Rhodes made a deed of gift to his daughter, Ann Stevens, and son-in-law, Henry Stevens (the name frequently appears in Johnston records as Strivens). A deed of gift of 41 acres, part of his homestead, was made by John to his son Peleg, 23 Feb. 1749/50. On 15 Dec. 1754, John conveyed 30 acres to his son Jeremiah. In the two latter deeds John's wife Elizabeth yielded her dower rights.

Although John made his will in 1748, he was still living on 25 May 1756, when he sold his homestead farm to David Thayer, with his wife Elizabeth yielding her dower rights. He may have died not long after, for no further mention of him is found in Johnston deeds, and no reference to the probate of his will, either in Johnston or Providence.

Johnston Town Council records, 17 Mar. 1770, refer to Elizabeth Roades, widow of John, having a small dwelling house nearly opposite David Brown's dwelling. Johnston Town Council, 10 July 1773: "Thomas Angell, Esq., exhibited an account for winding sheet, and cap, and digging a grave for Elizabeth Rhodes." After her death a town council minute mentions "Ann Strivens... mother Elizabeth Rhodes."

The John Rhodes whose death in Scituate is placed by Austin on 19 June 1744 died intestate and his widow Martha was administrator. Since I know of no other unidentified John Rhodes who would have been of the right period, I am convinced that this John of Scituate who died in 1744 was the son of John of Johnston whose will four years later described him as deceased leaving two sons, and as having received his portion. Although no deed of gift from the elder to the younger John has been found, the latter may have received a cash settlement. With two small children on her hands, John Jr.'s widow Martha married soon after (27 Dec. 1744, Scituate V.R.) Oziel Hopkins of Scituate.

Apparently Mr. Austin was not aware of the will of John Rhodes of Providence (Johnston) or he would not have fallen into this error.

LANGWORTHY. Page 119.

Andrew (col. 1). Owing to the destruction of the Newport records, Austin's account of the family is meagre. He undoubtedly came from Devonshire where the name is widely spread. An Andrew Langworthy, son of Richard, was baptized at Widecombe, Devon, on 30 Nov. 1610. He may be a near kinsman of the Newport man. According to his father-in-law, Samuel Hubbard, Andrew had ten children, of whom three were dead and seven living in 1688. Andrew was still living, according to Hubbard, on 28 Mar. 1686. On 10 Mar. 1655/6 he was one of the purchasers of Canonicut Island (completed 1666) and on 29 June 1660 one of the purchasers of Misquomicutt (Westerly, R.I.). On 7 May 1666 he was a member of the Grand Jury at Newport, and in Feb. 1676 he joined the Seventh Day Baptist Church in Newport. On 4 July 1690 he deeded 50 acres in Westerly, bought of Hugh Moshier, to the heirs of William Reap. As for the children (2nd col.) and grandchildren (3rd col.):

1. Samuel, of Newport. Born about 1659. Died about or before 28 Nov. 1711. Married probably on 21 July 1680 Rachel ——, who died before 23 Nov. 1716. She is probably the Rachel who joined the Seventh Day Baptist Church of Westerly on 21 July 1708, but this Rachel may be a daughter. On 23 Nov. 1716 John Phillips and wife Ruth testified that Samuel was the eldest son of Andrew, that he lived in Newport and died at Pettyquamscott. Children:

i. Ann, whose will was proved 29 Nov. 1773.
ii. Samuel, d. 1 Aug. 1763.
iii. Rachel, d. after 19 Feb. 1745/6.

2. John. Born about 1661, died before 30 Sept. 1700. He was of Newport and a member of the Seventh Day Baptist Church there in 1692. He may have removed to Little Compton. He may be the John Langworthy who was serving in the garrison at Westfield, Mass., 24 July 1676 [Bodge, Soldiers in King Philip's War]. Married Elizabeth -----, who died after 30 Sept. 1700. Child (probably):

i. John, m. Mary Lewis before 4 Aug. 1721.

3. Andrew. Died at the fort at Newport in 1739.

4. Robert (probably). Born about 1675, died about 1720. He lived in Little Compton near Saconnet Point. He does not occur in the records, but the family tradition makes him probably a son of Andrew. The Langworthy Genealogy states that he married Mary daughter of Robert Brownell of Little Compton, but as this Mary married William Congdon on 3 Mar. 1693, this is evidently an error, and Robert clearly married her sister Patience Brownell, who married secondly, as his second wife, John[3] Sanford of Little Compton (John[2], Pres. John[1]) on 9 Oct. 1722 [cf. New England Hist. and Gen. Register, 103:215]. Children:

i. Robert, a house carpenter, d. young of colic.
ii. Thomas, b. 1704, d. 25 Aug. 1777. Born in Little Compton, but about 1724 removed with his stepfather and mother to North Stonington, Conn. On 11 Oct. 1726 married his stepsister, Content, daughter of John Sanford and his first wife, Content Howland. His wife died at the age of 105 yrs. 1 mo. and 5 days. They had issue six children: Thomas, b. 12 Feb. 1727; Mary, b. 20 July 1731; Amos, b. 12 Nov. 1733; Anna, b. 7 Mar. 1736; Sanford, b. 30 Oct. 1738; John, b. 22 Nov. 1742.

iii. Joseph, of Stonington, Conn. Married before 1729, Elizabeth, dau. of Robert and Rebecca Burdick of Westerly. On 27 Nov. 1742 he deeded to John Brownell of Little Compton land there which descended to his brother Thomas and himself from their grandfather, Robert Brownell of Little Compton [Bristol Co., Mass., Land Evidence, 31:283]. Children: Comfort, b. 28 Feb. 1729; Robert, b. 28 July 1731; Elizabeth, b. 12 Apr. 1733; Joseph, b. 7 Mar. 1735/6; Andrew, b. 7 Jan. 1741/2.
iv. Mary, d. young.

5. James. Born about 1680, died 1720.

Other children not known.

No relationship has beenestablished with Lawrence Langworthy of Newport, pewterer, from Ashburton, co. Devon, who died at Newport 19 Oct. 1739 in his 47th year and is buried there with an armigerous tombstone. For an account of him, see supra, 15:1-8, the article by Mr. Meredith B. Colket, Jr.

(See the Langworthy Genealogy (1940, by Prof. W. F. Langworthy.)

THE AMERICAN GENEALOGIST

Whole No. 141 Jan., 1960 Vol. XXXVI, No. 1

ADDITIONS AND CORRECTIONS TO AUSTIN'S GENEALOGICAL DICTIONARY OF RHODE ISLAND

Communicated by G. Andrews Moriarty, F.S.A.

CARPENTER, FIELD, KNIGHT (pp. 37, 76, 331). Through the kindness of Mrs. Winifred Lovering Holman, F.A.S.G., of Lexington, Mass., and her client, Mrs. Folwell Welles Coan of Minneapolis, Minn., I am enabled to present the following note, the result of Mrs. Holman's researches. --G.A.M.

In connection with exhaustive research on one branch of the William Carpenter of Providence family, made in behalf of my client, Mrs. Folwell Welles Coan (née Olivia Carpenter), of Minneapolis, Minn., I have reached the conclusions given below. The full evidence and proofs of my statements will appear in the "Carpenter Lineage" now in preparation.

William3 Carpenter (Silas2, William1), born in Pawtuxet in Providence about 1694 (in my opinion, William was the youngest child of Silas and born a decade later than is generally attributed to him), died there 20 Apr. 1728, intestate. He married there, by 11 Jan. 1724/5, Elizabeth, who was undoubtedly the daughter of John and Eleanor (——) Knight, and born about 1705. (See G. Andrews Moriarty, "The Early Knights of Rhode Island," N.E.H.G. Register, 1933.) Elizabeth was living in Cranston with her husband, Edward Potter, as late as 25 Jan. 1756; she had married secondly, as his second wife, by 25 Jan. 1730/1, the said Potter, by whom she had Nathaniel, Robert, Josiah and Thomas Potter. I have reason to think that the Potters, Edward and Elizabeth, died in Cranston about 1768.

Austin credits this William3 Carpenter with three children, which is not correct; there was but the son, William4, born 5 Apr. 1727, who inherited, as shown by the records of the elder William's estate.

Elizabeth (Knight) Carpenter's sister was evidently Abigail (her surname hitherto unknown), wife of Thomas Field, which explains why the latter is called uncle of William4 Carpenter in the 1745 guardianship record. In 1757, William conveyed to John Knight in Cranston; in 1770, William sold to Nathaniel Potter, and in 1771 John and Eleanor Knight, of Cranston, made a [recorded] agreement there with Nathaniel Potter, for life care and maintenance. Nathaniel Potter, their grandson, as he was Elizabeth's eldest son by her second husband, died unmarried leaving a will drawn in 1775, in which he remembered his half-brother, William4 Carpenter.

By his wife, Comfort, the daughter of John and Deliverance (Corp) King, William4 Carpenter had children of these names: John, William, Elizabeth, Ellen [Eleanor], Mercy, Comfort [a son], Phebe, Joseph, Knight (b. 1769), Jesse and William, born between 1750 and 1773, of which I have the full dates of birth from an old family record. (This record was published in 1882 in a Scranton, Pa., newspaper, of which I have a certified photostatic copy, and I am grateful to Mrs. Ruth Adair of Wollaston, Mass., for calling my attention to it.)

As John and Eleanor Knight had no heirs male, we are not surprised that the name of Knight was accorded to a son of the only Carpenter child of their daughter Elizabeth. This was a common practice. Samuel Sewall Jr., writing about the birth of his son in 1703, states that he "Was named Hull for my grandfather Hull's sake, to bear up his name, that it might not be forgotten" [see Mass. Hist. Soc. Coll., 5th ser., 5:xxvi, also 7:246, these being vols. I and III of Sewall's "Diary"].

TIBBITS, BORDEN. These two items relate to the considerable Quaker migration from Rhode Island to Carteret County, North Carolina, in the fourth decade of the eighteenth century. I am indebted to Waldo Sprague, Esq., of Wollaston, Mass., for the information.

TIBBITS (p. 202, 2nd col.). John married secondly, as "John Tibbits of East Greenwich", 19:2:1726 (Dartmouth, Mass., V.R.) Sarah, youngest daughter of George and Deborah Soule. She was born about 1688 and was still single in 1719 in the estate papers of her parents [cf. Mayflower Descendant, 7:210]. Add to his children sons Henry and George, daughter Alse (?Alice), and change one of the daughters, Anne, to Avis. Mary Tibbits married William Hopkins 2 March 1726/7, and Avis (wrongly printed by Arnold as Alice) Tibbits married George Soule 3 Dec. 1730 (East Greenwich V.R., Arnold). The children of Henry and Hannah Tibbits appear in East Greenwich Vital Records from 1735.

John and Sarah Tibbits removed in the Quaker migration to North Carolina. The will of John Tibbits of Carteret Co., N.C., dated 4 April 1755, proved at the June Court 1755, names his wife Sarah, sons Henry and George, daughters Mary Hopkins, Aves Soule, Anne Bala (?Bailey) and Alse Hill [N. C. Hist. & Gen. Register, 1:496]. Witnessed by Ephraim Bull, who was probably son of Henry2 or Ephraim2 (cf. Austin under Bull, p. 267). The same will in Grimes' N. C. Wills, 1910,

493

omits the son Henry and dates it 9 April 1755. On 3: 8mo:1756 the Core Sound Monthly Quaker Meeting granted a certificate to Sarah Tibbits to go to New England [N.C. Quaker Records, W.W. Hinshaw, 1:277]. The will of her nephew John (son of Nathan) Soule of Dartmouth, Mass., dated 9 Nov. 1768, gave Sarah Tibbits the use of the best chamber in his house for life.

BORDEN (p. 23, 3rd col.). William[3] (John[2], Richard[1]) Borden, born 15 Aug. 1689, removed to Carteret Co., N. C. The will of William Borden of Carteret County, dated 10 Feb. 1748/9, proved Aug. 1749, names his wife Susanna, son William, children of daughter Alice Stanton, daughters Catherine and Hannah Borden, son-in-law Henry Stanton, daughter Sarah wife of William Pratt, nephew William Borden son of Joseph in Rhode Island, brother Thomas Borden's children, sister Amy Chase's children; witnessed by Sarah Newby, Joseph Robinson and Joseph Newby; executors, brother Benjamin and Henry Stanton [N.C. Hist. & Gen. Register, vol. 1]. Grimes omits nephew William, son of Joseph of Rhode Island.

PIERCE (p. 153, col. 2). Hannah Pierce (Ephraim[1]) married William Martin. Azrikam Pierce of Warwick sold land in Warwick to his "mother Hannah, widow of Ephraim Pierce, formerly of Rehoboth," which his father bought of Anthony Low, dated 20 Sept. 1720 [Warwick, R.I., Deeds, 3:33-34]. On 1 Sept. 1721, Hannah Pierce, "formerly of Swansea," deeded the same to her son-in-law William Martin [Warwick Deeds]. I am indebted for the above to H. Minot Pitman, Esq., of Bronxville, N. Y.

MEW (p. 133, 1st col.). Noel[2] (Richard[1]). Walter Lee Sheppard, Jr., Esq., of Havertown, Pa., has called attention to a series of deed [New Jersey Archives, 1st ser., pp. 49, 56, 65, 414, 461, etc.) in which the Mews figure. Lady Carteret et al. deeded 1 and 2 Feb.1681/2 to Richard Mew and others a large tract in New Jersey. The Duke of York gave a patent 15 Mar. 1682/3 to several including Richard Mew of Stepney, merchant. Richard and Noel Mew of Stepney sold 1/48th of East New Jersey, 2 Jan. 1684/5. Richard Mew of Ratcliff, co. Middlesex, merchant, gave a deed 7 July 1677 for 1/6 of West Jersey to William Snowden of Edwinsboro, co. Notts, yeoman, and John Hooton of Skegly, co. Notts. (Snowden and Hooton settled in South Jersey.) John Roberts of Pimsawquin, West Jersey, conveyed 10 Aug. 1685 to Noel Mew of Newport, R.I. On 12:2m.(Apr.):1686, Noell Mew, of Newport, R.I., mariner, and wife Mary, conveyed to William Allen of the same, land in New Jersey.

TAG W. No. 147 July, 1961 V. XXXVII, No. 3

ADDITIONS AND CORRECTIONS TO AUSTIN'S GENEALOGICAL DICTIONARY OF RHODE ISLAND

By G. Andrews Moriarty, A.M., LL.B., F.S.A., F.A.S.G.

CLARKE. Families of Jeremiah Clarke, p. 44, 3rd column, and of Joseph Clarke, p. 47, 3rd column. William Clarke, born 27 May 1673, was not the son of Latham[2] Clarke (Jeremiah[1]) but the son of William[2] Clarke (Joseph[1]) of Jamestown, R.I., and his wife Hannah Weeden. William[3] married 15 Apr. 1700 Hannah Knight. They later removed to Westerly, R.I., in that part later set off as Charlestown and still later as Richmond, R.I. (See the evidence in New England Hist. & Gen. Register, 85: 418.)

LOW. Page 339, Samuel, 3rd column. Samuel Low, of Warren, R.I., married first, about 1722, Elizabeth, daughter of Dr. John Wilson of Braintree, Mass., born in Medfield 31 Oct. 1689. They had:

- i. Anne, m. 10 Dec. 1743 Joseph Bosworth, Jr., of Rehoboth, Mass.
- ii. John.
- iii. Hooker.

Elizabeth was great-granddaughter of the famous Rev. John Wilson of Boston [J. Gardner Bartlett in New England Hist. & Gen. Register, 61:129]. Samuel Wilson married second, Isabel Greene, and had:

- iv. Samuel

SMITH. John Smith the Miller, p. 385, 4th column. Philip[4] Smith (Elisha[3], John[2], John[1]), born 6 Jan. 1703. He married Wait Waterman, daughter of Resolved Waterman [Austin, p. 411, 4th column]. Arnold in his Vital Record of Rhode Island, and the Waterman Family (1954), 3: 21, following Arnold, wrongly married Wait to Philip Smith Field on 16 Feb. 1734/5. [Cf. Smithfield Deeds, 2:436; I owe this correction to Charles W. Farnham of Providence, R.I.]

THE AMERICAN GENEALOGIST

Whole Number 153 Volume 39, No. 1

January 1963

ADDITIONS AND CORRECTIONS TO AUSTIN'S GENEALOGICAL DICTIONARY OF RHODE ISLAND

By G. Andrews Moriarty, A.M., LL.B., F.S.A., F.A.S.G.

Editor's Note: G. Andrews Moriarty, Esq., has been a Contributing Editor of The American Genealogist since the quarterly was first published under that title (vol. 9) in July 1932. In addition to many other articles, since Volume 19 he has been contributing from time to time a series of "Additions and Corrections to Austin's Genealogical Dictionary of Rhode Island." Previous instalments of this series appeared in the following volumes, starting at the pages indicated: 19:129, 221; 20:53, 112, 181, 223; 21:206; 24:69; 25:168, 249; 26:54, 157, 228; 27:216; 28:210; 30:121; 32:38; 34:169; 35:107; 36:54; and 37:185. Librarians and private owners of the Dictionary who have frequent occasion to refer to it may find it useful to draw up a list of surnames with references to Mr. Moriarty's notes and paste it inside their copies of the book.

Page 15, 1st col. John Audley was the son of John Audley of Boston, bapt. 13 Feb. 1641/2 [Savage and Pope under Odlin]. 2nd col. John married (2) Elizabeth, b. 19 May 1684, dau. of Josiah and Sarah (Mills) Arnold of Jamestown, R.I.

BENNET. Page 18, 2nd col. Jonathan Bennet married Anne, dau. of John and Anna (Alcock) Williams of Boston, Block Island and Newport. She was b. 4 Nov. 1674 [Boston Births]. On 11 Sept. 1714, Anna Guthrie, adm'x of her former husband, John Williams, deeded land in Newport to her daughter Anna Bennet of Newport, widow of Jonathan [Newport Deeds]. Jonathan and Anna had: John, who m. 1722 [Portsmouth Friends Records] Susanna Cornell, b. 22 July 1702; Rebecca, who m. Peleg Sherman, b. 24 Mar. 1691/2; and also probably Anna, who m. 15 Nov. 1733 James Perry of So. Kingstown, R.I. [Friends Records]. [Information of Miss Helen M. Cook of Brookline, Mass.]

BROWN. For Henry's English connections see New England H. & G. Reg., 61:116-118; 62:199-200; 63:99-100;

and TAG, supra, 15:84-86, and 37:34-38.

CORNELL. For the English origin, the discovery of the late Waldo C. Sprague, see TAG, supra, 35:107, and comment, supra, 35:16-18. Thomas (Austin, page 54, 1st col.) was probably the Thomas son of William Cornell bapt. at Saffron Walden 11 Mar. 1592/3. Abstracts of the wills of Rebecca widow of Thomas[1] and of their son, Samuel[2] of Dartmouth, were given supra, 19:132. That of Samuel names his cousin George Cadman of Dartmouth. George was son of William and Elizabeth Cadman, and if nephew is meant, it is not known how such a relationship came about. Thomas[1] Cornell had two daughters named Elizabeth bapt. in England; one certainly married Christopher Almy of Portsmouth, and the will of Rebecca Cornell indicates that she had only one surviving daughter named Elizabeth. Perhaps George Cadman was a cousin in the usual modern sense.

GARDINER. Page 81, 1st col. Discussions of the alleged English origin of George Gardiner will be found TAG, supra, 14:243-246, and 21:191-200. His common-law wife, Herodias Long, married (1) at St. Faith's (crypt of St. Paul's), John Hicks, marriage licence 14 March 1636/7 [London Marriage Licences, p. 153, British Rec. Soc.]. Hicks obtained a divorce in New Netherland 1 June 1655 [O'Callaghan, Hist. MSS. Office of Sec. of State, Albany, p. 149]. By Hicks she had Hannah, b. ca. 1638-9, and Thomas, b. ca. 1642. She was divorced from Hicks in Rhode Island 2 Dec. 1643 [information of Dr. Herbert F. Seversmith]. For an account of the career of Herodias, see paper by G. Andrews Moriarty in Rhode Island History, published by R. I. Hist. Society.

HILLIARD. Page 98, col. 2. Jonathan; his wife Abigail was a dau. of William Wilbour, Jr., of Portsmouth and Little Compton, b. 1 Apr. 1697, d. 5 Oct. 1741 [cf. Austin, p. 229].

LEWIS, see STEERE.

MANN. Page 128, 1st col. Thomas Mann, b. in Scituate, Mass., 15 Aug. 1650, son of Richard and Rebecca. His first wife, Rachel, slain in 1675 with her infant child by the Indians at Rehoboth, Mass. [Richard LeBaron Bowen, Early Rehoboth, 3:47].

MORRIS. Page 134, 1st col. Richard Morris's first wife, Leonora (Pauley) Underhill was mother of the redoubtable Capt. John Underhill [Gen. Dict. of Maine and New Hampshire].

MOTT. For English data, see TAG, supra, 35:107-108. Page 135, 1st col. Nathaniel Mott of Scituate, Mass. On 21 June 1664 he was in jail for selling liquor to the Indians and petitioned the Cambridge Court for release as he was poor and had a wife and four small children [Original Petition, ex penes Richard LeBaron Bowen]. He was slain at Braintree, Mass., 23 Feb. 1675/6 by the Indians in King Philip's War.

NEWBURY. Page 137, 2nd col. Walter Newbury. Add XI Ann Mercy m. as his first wife Col. John Cranston of Newport, R.I. She d. 8 Apr. 1728 [New Eng. H. & G. Reg. 79:254].

STEERE. Page 191, 1st col. John Steere was probably the one of the name bapt. 1634 at Ockley, Surrey, near Rusper, Sussex, where the Steers were numerous at that period. [Cf. John G. Hunt in TAG, supra, 37:141].

STEERE-LEWIS. Page 192, 2nd col. Ann Steere married Richard Lewis. To their children add a son Thomas abd a daughter, name unknown. On 30 Dec. 1728, John Steere, adm'r of his sister Ann Lewis being deceased, Ezra Bartlett, "who married one of Ann's daughters," was appointed in his place [Providence Town Council, Bk. 3, p. 24]. Ezra Bartlett and wife Jane appear in Glocester, R.I., vital records. "Thomas Lewis, son of Richard Lewis," chose his uncle, Thomas Steere, as his guardian 18 Oct. 1729 [ibid. p. 39]. Thomas Lewis is apparently the Thomas Lewis of Smithfield, R.I. [Courtesy of Charles W. Farnham, Providence, R.I.]

TILLINGHAST. Page 202, col. 1. It has frequently been stated that Pardon Tillinghast was the son of Pardon Tillinghast and his wife Elizabeth Tichborne, the latter of royal descent [cf. F. L. Weis, Ancestral Roots, Line 5]. Recent research indicates that he was son of Pardon Tillinghast, b. ca. 1593, a cooper of Ilfield, Sussex, by his wife Sarah Browne, and grandson of Rev. John and Alice (Pardon) Tillinghast of Street, Sussex, and of Rev. Benjamin Browne of Ilfield. [John G. Hunt in TAG, supra, 37:34-38.]

WILBOUR. Page 228, 1st col. William Wilbour came from Braintree, Co. Essex, England, the family having originated in Yorkshire, and his line of descent being through John[a], Joseph[b], Nicholas[c], and Thomas[d]. His wife was named Martha. 2nd col. William, Jr., b. Dec. 1660, married (2) Joan Briggs. A fully documented account of the family and English ancestry, by Benjamin F. Wilbour, is in New Eng. H. & G. Reg., vols. 112 and 113, passim.